(Genoese)
Orvieto
Spoleto
Viterbo
STATES
Civitavecchia
Rome
Ostia
Tiber
Velletri
Aquila
Pescara
ADRIATIC SEA
Sora
KINGDOM
Venafre
Cajazzo
Capua
Aversa
Nola
Benevento
(Papal)
OF
Pozzuoli
Naples
Ischia
Gravina
Atella
Altamura
NAPLES
Taranto
SARDINIA
(Spanish)
TYRRHENIAN SEA
Cosenza
Palermo
Squillace
Reggio
SICILY
(Spanish)
Molly Marsh

THE NEW CENTURY

ITALIAN RENAISSANCE ENCYCLOPEDIA

APPLETON-CENTURY-CROFTS
Educational Division
MEREDITH CORPORATION
New York

THE NEW CENTURY

ITALIAN RENAISSANCE ENCYCLOPEDIA

Edited by Catherine B. Avery

EDITORIAL CONSULTANTS

MARVIN B. BECKER

Professor, Department of History
University of Rochester

LUDOVICO BORGO

Associate Professor, Department of Fine Arts
Brandeis University

7101-1

Library of Congress Catalog Card Number: 76-181735

PRINTED IN THE UNITED STATES OF AMERICA
390-66950-X

Preface

In the following pages appear many great and/or flamboyant figures of a brilliant and exhilarating period in western culture. Historians disagree on the limits of that period, which is generally called the Renaissance. There are those who deny its existence on the grounds that there are no sharp breaks between different ages: one develops gradually from another, characteristics of one age persist deep into the following ones, and the heralds of what become characteristic of one age may have appeared generations earlier. A notable characteristic of the Renaissance, however, is that the men of the time were exuberantly conscious that theirs was a special age. Petrarch (1304–1374), who, it is true, did not exult in his perception, was among the earliest to voice the concept of a new age—a modern, and dark, age, as distinct from the resplendent era of the Romans, whose passing he mourned and for whose return he longed. Boccaccio (1313–1375) credited Dante with restoring the Muses to Italy and Giotto with the restoration of the art of painting. Giovanni Gherardi (1367–1446?) in his *Il Paradiso degli Alberti*, discusses the glorious culture of the past and its rediscovery in his own age. Lorenzo Ghiberti (c1378–1455) attributed to Cimabue and Giotto the revival of the art of painting according to nature. Flavio Biondo (1392–1463) marks Petrarch as he who awakened, or reawakened, or brought again to light, poetry and eloquence. Much later, Vasari (1511–1574) articulated the concept of art as one of birth, youth, maturity, and decline and was the first to use the term *La Rinascita*—the rebirth—to describe the development of art in Italy beginning with Cimabue. He considered that art had reached perfection in his own time in such a master as Michelangelo and worried that henceforth, according to his concept, it could only decline. These few examples reveal the awareness of the men of the age that theirs marked, at first, a revival of what they considered their own glorious past, and later, a rebirth of culture in its many aspects. For the purposes of this book, the ebullient era known as the Renaissance runs from the time of Dante (1265–1321) and Giotto (c1267–1337) to about the death of Michelangelo (1564). The approximately 300 years that intervened witnessed a marvelous upsurge of interest, energy, and development in the arts and literature and a boiling activity in political life such as the west had not known for over a thousand years.

The emphasis in *The New Century Italian Renaissance Encyclopedia* is on men and events in Italy, where there was a formidable concentration of political, intellectual, and artistic energy. However, articles are included on many figures from outside Italy who had important consequences for the peninsula, short identifying articles are included on a great number of non-Italians who were active in the period, and there are a few entries of figures of an earlier era who influenced Renaissance thought. Hundreds of books by great and lesser scholars have been written on various aspects of the Renaissance, including broad surveys or, at the other end of the scale, concentrated analyses of particular aspects or areas of interest. *The New Century Italian Renaissance Encyclopedia* is unique in its presentation of detailed articles that cover so many facets of the sparkling prism that was the Italian Renaissance. The aim of the book is to supply immediate information on a wide variety of subjects. The entries, arranged in alphabetical order, provide biographical material on painters, popes, and poets, writers, soldiers, rulers, sculptors, architects, and engravers, prominent families, remarkable ladies, and others. There are résumés of literary works and identifications of characters in them, subject articles on such topics as *Astrology and Magic, Humanism,* and *Painting,* and definitions of some political as well as of some art and other terms with which a reader may be unfamiliar. Information is provided on some of the great Italian museums. The master drawings, reproductions of which are scattered throughout the text, include quick sketches, studies for paintings or frescoes, and finished drawings as independent works of art. Photographs located at the back of the book are arranged in groups to give a chronological survey of the arts of painting, sculpture, and architecture in the period covered.

In compiling a book of such scope and detail, the work of many great scholars has been consulted. The debt to them cannot be sufficiently acknowledged. The resulting material has been reviewed by Marvin B. Becker, Professor of History, University of Rochester, Ludovico Borgo, Associate Professor of Fine Arts, Brandeis University, and Charles E. Trinkaus, Professor of History, University of Michigan. The editor is as appreciative of their generous encouragement as of their careful study of the material for accuracy and the valuable comments and suggestions they made to increase the usefulness of the book to the student and to the general reader. Articles signed by the initials P. K. were prepared by Pearl Kibre, Professor of History, Hunter College of the City University of New York; those signed L.B. were prepared by Professor Borgo.

Without the resources available through the Research Division of the New York Public Library, this book would have been impossible. The editor wishes to express, however inadequately, her deep appreciation for such resources and her gratitude for the interest and courtesy of the staff. The lively interest shown in the work in progress and the cheerfulness and trust with which their priceless treasures were made available by the librarians of the Biblioteca Ambrosiana, Milan, Biblioteca Civica, Bergamo, and Biblioteca Palatina, Parma, were a great spur to the completion of the task and a source of delighted amazement. In these libraries especially there was not the slightest hesitation in pulling out manuscripts and drawings and confiding them to the editor's reverent hands. Besides those mentioned, other libraries contributed to the fulfillment of the work, as the Thomas J. Watson Library in The Metropolitan Museum of Art, the Library of the New York University Institute of the Fine Arts, and the Frick Art Reference Library. The editor wishes to thank the Trustees of Smith College for permission to quote *passim* from Leona C. Gabel's *The Commentaries of Pius II, Smith College Studies in History,* Vols. 22, 25, 30, 35 and 43 (hard cover reprint by Octagon Press), and the following museums for permission to reproduce drawings and paintings: Musée Bonnat, Bayonne; Biblioteca Civica, Bergamo; Kupferstichkabinett, Berlin; Isabella Stewart Gardner Museum, Boston; Fogg Art Museum, Cambridge; Art Institute of Chicago; Cleveland Museum of Art; Gabinetto Disegni e Stampe degli Uffizi, Florence; British Museum, London; National Gallery, London; Biblioteca Ambrosiana, Milan; The Frick Collection, New York; The Metropolitan Museum of Art, New York; The Pierpont Morgan Library, New York; Bibliothèque Nationale, Paris; Cabinet des Dessins, Musée du Louvre, Paris; Biblioteca Palatina, Parma; Pennsylvania Academy of the Fine Arts, Philadelphia; Biblioteca Reale, Turin; National Gallery of Art, Washington, D.C.; Royal Library, Windsor Castle.

Others have contributed in immeasurable ways to the completion of the work.

In a more personal vein, I should like to express my appreciation to my sister, Mary Gray Dey, who, over the course of years, enthusiastically accompanied me on my rounds of museums and libraries in Europe and in the United States; to Gertrude Schafer, who out of sheer interest read a great deal of the manuscript and picked up a number of peculiarities that were subsequently eliminated; and to Joan Donovan of Appleton-Century-Crofts for her unfailing cheerfulness, expertise, and help in seeing the book through its tortuous way from manuscript to finished book.

September, 1971 CATHERINE B. AVERY

List of Photographs

ANTONIO POLLAIUOLO. *Martyrdom of St. Sebastian.* Reproduced by courtesy of the Trustees, The National Gallery, London.
ANTONIO POLLAIUOLO. *Hercules and Antaeus.* Bargello, Florence. Alinari-Scala.
ANTONIO ROSSELLINO. *Bust of Matteo Palmieri.* Bargello, Florence. Alinari-Scala.
ANTONIO ROSSELLINO. *Monument of the Cardinal of Portugal.* San Miniato al Monte, Florence. Alinari-Scala.
DESIDERIO DA SETTIGNANO. *Bust of a Little Boy.* National Gallery of Art, Washington, D.C. (Andrew Mellon Collection 1937).
DESIDERIO DA SETTIGNANO. *St. Jerome in the Desert* (relief). National Gallery of Art, Washington, D.C. (Widener Collection 1942).
DESIDERIO DA SETTIGNANO. *Marsuppini Monument.* S. Croce, Florence. Alinari-Scala.
PIETRO LOMBARDO. *Tomb of Dante.* Ravenna. Alinari-Scala.
ANTONELLO DA MESSINA. *St. Sebastian.* Dresden. Alinari-Scala.
ANTONELLO DA MESSINA. *Crucifixion.* Antwerp. Alinari-Scala.
ANTONELLO DA MESSINA. *St. Jerome in His Study.* Reproduced by courtesy of the Trustees, The National Gallery, London.
GENTILE BELLINI. *Mohammed II.* Reproduced by courtesy of the Trustees, The National Gallery, London.
CARLO CRIVELLI. *Annunciation.* Reproduced by courtesy of the Trustees, The National Gallery, London.
GIOVANNI BELLINI. *Agony in the Garden.* Reproduced by courtesy of the Trustees, The National Gallery, London.
GIOVANNI BELLINI. *St. Francis in Ecstasy.* The Frick Collection, New York. Copyright The Frick Collection.
ANDREA MANTEGNA. *Agony in the Garden.* Reproduced by courtesy of the Trustees, The National Gallery, London.
ANDREA MANTEGNA. *Family of Ludovico III.* Camera degli Sposi, Ducal Palace, Mantua. Alinari-Scala.
ANDREA MANTEGNA. *Dead Christ.* Brera, Milan. Alinari-Scala.
CIMA DA CONEGLIANO. *St. Jerome in the Wilderness.* National Gallery of Art, Washington, D.C. (Samuel H. Kress Collection 1939).
VITTORE CARPACCIO. *The Dream of St. Ursula.* Accademia, Venice. Alinari-Scala.
VITTORE CARPACCIO. *Meditation on the Passion.* The Metropolitan Museum of Art (Kennedy Fund 1911).
ANDREA VERROCCHIO. *Christ and St. Thomas.* Orsanmichele, Florence. Alinari-Scala.
ANDREA VERROCCHIO. *Putto with a Fish.* Palazzo Vecchio, Florence. Alinari-Scala.
DOMENICO VENEZIANO. *St. John in the Desert.* National Gallery of Art, Washington, D.C. (Samuel H. Kress Collection 1943).
SANDRO BOTTICELLI. *The Birth of Venus.* Uffizi, Florence. Alinari-Scala.
SANDRO BOTTICELLI. *Madonna of the Eucharist.* Isabella Stewart Gardner Museum, Boston.
GIULIANO DA SANGALLO. *S. Maria della Carceri.* Prato. Alinari-Scala.
GIOVANNI ANTONIO AMADEO. *Colleoni Chapel.* Bergamo. Alinari-Scala.
ANDREA BRIOSCO. *Pascal Candlestick.* Basilica of St. Anthony, Padua. Alinari-Scala.
DOMENICO GHIRLANDAIO. *Pope Honorius III Giving the Rule to St. Francis.* Sassetti Chapel, S. Trinita, Florence. Alinari-Scala.
PERUGINO. *The Crucifixion with the Virgin, SS. John, Jerome, and Mary Magdalen.* National Gallery of Art, Washington, D.C. (Andrew Mellon Collection 1937).
LEONARDO DA VINCI. *Baptism of Christ* (with Verrocchio). Uffizi, Florence. Alinari-Scala.
LEONARDO DA VINCI. *Ginevra de' Benci.* National Gallery of Art, Washington, D.C. (Ailsa Mellon Bruce Fund).
LEONARDO DA VINCI. *The Virgin of the Rocks.* Louvre, Paris. Alinari-Scala.
LEONARDO DA VINCI. *The Virgin and St. Anne* (cartoon). Reproduced by courtesy of the Trustees, The National Gallery, London.
GIOVANNI BOLTRAFFIO. *Casio Madonna.* Louvre, Paris. Alinari-Scala.
FILIPPINO LIPPI. *Apparition of the Virgin to St. Bernard.* Badia, Florence. Alinari-Scala.

A

Abano (dä′bä-nō), **Pietro d'.** See **Pietro d'Abano.**

Abate (del-lä-bä′tā), **Niccolò dell'.** See **Dell' Abate, Niccolò.**

Abraham Cresques (ā′bra̤-ham kres′ke̤s). [Called **Cresques lo Juheu,** meaning "Cresques the Jew"; **Lo Jueu buscolor,** meaning "the map Jew"; **El Judio de las brujulas,** meaning "the compass Jew."] Cartographer; fl. at Palma de Mallorca on the Island of Majorca; d. 1387. Believed to have been a member of a Jewish family from Catalonia, he was one of the greatest cartographers of his age, and is recognized as the founder of the Jewish cartographical school at Palma de Mallorca. He was probably the author of *Atlas Catalan,* made in 1375 for Charles V of France and now considered one of the outstanding cartographical achievements of the Middle Ages.

Abramo di Balmes (äb′rä-mō dē bäl′mēs), **Ben Meir.** Hebrew grammarian; b. at Lecce; d. at Venice, 1523. He was educated at the University of Padua. Using medieval Hebrew versions, he translated Arab philosophical and scientific works, especially those of Averroës, into Latin. He also compiled a Hebrew grammar that was published posthumously in 1523.

Abravanel (ä-brä-vä-nel′), **Isaac.** [Also, **Abrabanel, Abarbanel.**] Jewish scholar, theologian, and statesman; b. at Lisbon, 1437; d. at Venice, 1508. The most notable member of a Sephardic family which claimed descent from the royal house of David and which produced a number of scholars and scientists during the 15th and 16th centuries, Abravanel is now perhaps best known for his commentaries on the Old Testament, particularly those on the books of Kings and Samuel. Convinced that such scholarship was most productive if it dealt with the meaning of a book in its entirety, rather than with the mere interpretation of isolated words and sentences, he sought also to have his commentaries reflect an understanding of the social, political, and economic conditions of the period within which a particular book of the Old Testament was actually prepared. The result was a body of theological writing widely used by both Christian and Jewish religious scholars for centuries after his death. In his own lifetime, Abravanel was treasurer to Alfonso V of Portugal until that ruler died in 1481. Thereafter he was for eight years in the service of King Ferdinand and Queen Isabella at Madrid. Forced to quit Spain after the expulsion of the Jews (1492), he lived successively at Naples, Sicily, Corfu, and Venice, being employed by the Venetian republic as a member of its diplomatic corps.

Academies. Academies flourished particularly in humanist circles from the 15th century on in Italy. They were voluntary groupings or free associations of persons who came together primarily to further their literary, philosophical, and scientific interests, following the example of the academies of ancient Athens. More individualistic and aristocratic

fat, fāte, fär, fâll, ȧsk, fãre; net, mē, hėr; pin, pīne; not, nōte, möve, nôr; up, lūte, pu̇ll; oi, oil; ou, out; (lightened) e̤lect, agǫny, ṳnite; (obscured) erra̤nt, arde̤nt, acto̤r; ch, chip; g, go; th, thin; ᴛʜ, then; y, you; (variable) d̤ as d or j, s̤ as s or sh, t̤ as t or ch, z̤ as z or zh; *o,* F. cloche; ü, F. menu; ċh, Sc. loch; ṅ, F. bonbon; ʙ, Sp. Córdoba (sounded almost like v).

than the university associations and lacking the primary function of the latter to transmit the learning of the past to the young and uninitiated, the academies had less formal organization and continuity.

Among the most famous of the academies founded in the 15th century was the Accademia Platonica of Florence. It was founded by Cosimo de' Medici in 1439, but had its most flourishing period under the direction of Marsilio Ficino, who became its leading light in 1459. The avowed purpose of the Platonic Academy was to reassemble and to make known to the members the entire corpus of Platonic writings, of which the Middle Ages had known only the *Timaeus* and the two famous dialogues the *Phaedo* and the *Meno*. Under the direction of Ficino, the Platonic Academy held regular meetings in the quarters provided for it by the Medici. This building had as a central motif a bust of Plato before which a candle was kept burning day and night.

Another famous academy with perhaps more varied interests, but primarily literary, was the Accademia Pontaniana in Naples. This academy had earlier been preceded by the Accademia Panormita, so called after its chief guide during the years 1468–1471, or until his death. It comprised the persons gathered around the library of Alfonso I of Aragon in Naples to discuss literary and philosophical questions. The members of this circle read Livy and other Latin and Greek classical authors and engaged in discourse relating not only to the literary points of the work in hand but also to its moral and scientific content. From 1471 to 1503 this academy came successively under the direction of the humanist Giovanni Pontano (d. 1503) and, following Pontano's death, under that of Sannazzaro (d. 1530), author of the *Arcadia*. A roster of the members of this academy comprised the names of the most famous literary men of Italy, among whom might be noted the learned Greek and Latin scholars and translators Johannes Argyropoulos, Giovanni Aurispa, Cardinal Bessarion, Manuel Chrysoloras, Theodorus Gaza, Constantine Lascaris; Filelfo, Poggio, Piccolomini, Valla, and many others in addition to Pontano.

Still other 15th century and early 16th century academies are worthy of noting. Among these are the Accademia di Santo Spirito, founded in 1421 in Florence; also the Orti Oricellari in which leading writers and statesmen, including Machiavelli, participated from 1502 to 1522. The Accademia Liviana-Pordenone was originally founded at the end of the 15th century by General Alviana (d. 1515), who wished to establish a scientific society. One of the luminaries of this academy was the noted physician Fracastoro. Following Alviana's death in 1515, the name of the academy was changed to Accademia dei Perseravanti. Another academy, the Accademia Pomponiana di Roma, was made up largely of the companions of Pomponio Leto who shared his antiquarian and archaeological interests.

The great ages of the academies were in fact the 16th and following centuries. In addition to those already named in the early 16th century were the Accademia degli Intronati of Siena and the Accademia dei Rozzi, founded about 1520 by a group of artisans and merchants chiefly for the purpose of reading poetry and comedies. Perhaps one of the most famous 16th century academies in Florence was the Accademia della Crusca, founded in 1582 or possibly earlier. This academy included the leading Florentine men of letters and science, among them Michelangelo Buonarroti the Younger and Galileo Galilei. Founded for a somewhat different purpose was the Accademia Fiorentino. This academy was established (1540) under the protection of the Medici Grand Duke to fulfill a specific function—namely, to serve with the University of Florence as a tribunal for all civil cases relating to the book trade in Florence. However, most of the academies in the 16th century were primarily literary societies, although they generally acknowledged "an obligation to the universal knowledge of the sciences and the liberal arts." Their members were expected periodically to deliver oral discourses or lectures before the assembled members. Most of the academies had a princely protector or patron. P.K.

Acciaiuoli (ät-chä-ywô′lē), **Angelo.** Italian cardinal; b. at Florence, April 15, 1340; d. at Pisa, 1408 or 1409. He was named (1375) bishop of Rapolla, in the kingdom of Naples, by Gregory XI, archbishop of Florence (1383) by Urban VI, and cardinal in either 1384 or 1385. In the era of the Great Schism he supported Urban VI and Boniface IX. He also supported Ladislaus in his claim to the throne of Hungary and assisted at his coronation,

1403. Although he helped elect Gregory XII, he later took part in the Council of Pisa, which tried to limit the authority of the popes.

Acciaiuoli, Donato. Scholar, orator, humanist, and government official; b. at Florence, 1429; d. at Milan, 1478. Highly respected as an orator, he held a number of governorships and embassies and was gonfaloniere of Florence (1474). He was one of a group of ardent scholars who surrounded Lorenzo de' Medici. A student of philosophy and rhetoric, he was a follower of Johannes Argyropoulos and became an exponent of the new humanist interpretation of the philosophy of Aristotle, on whose *Ethics* and *Politics* he wrote commentaries. He also wrote lives of Hannibal, Scipio, and Charlemagne, and translated part of Plutarch's *Lives*. Charged to do so by the commune, he made an official translation into Italian of Leonardo Bruni's *History of Florence*. To his fascination with the writers and ideas of antiquity was joined a sincere piety. His writings and translations were influential in promoting classical culture.

Acciaiuoli, Niccolò. Soldier and statesman; b. at Monte Gufoni, September 12, 1310; d. at Naples, November 8, 1365. Of an old and powerful Florentine family, in 1331 he was sent to Naples to look after family commercial and financial interests there. In 1335 he became attached to the court of Robert of Naples and ever after served the kingdom. His services in securing the kingdom to the Angevins, after several years of bitter warfare, were praised by Boccaccio, who was in Naples at the same time. Niccolò was given immense rewards and fiefs in recognition of his services. He was instrumental in securing the marriage of Queen Joanna I, King Robert's successor, to Louis of Taranto (1346). (Joanna was recently widowed, having arranged the murder of her first husband.) Niccolò took an increasingly conspicuous part in the government of the kingdom, and was ultimately named Grand Seneschal, in which position he exercised almost royal power. He fought in Sicily, where he conquered Messina (1356), against the Turks in Greece (1358), and, as the result of a visit to the pope at Avignon (1360), at the side of Cardinal Albornoz in the wars against the Visconti. He made a treaty with Bernabò Visconti at Milan (where he met Petrarch, one of his admirers) from which he emerged as governor of Bologna and the Romagna, under the nominal authority of the pope. Rebellions, and raids by the companies of adventure, in Naples, recalled him to the kingdom, where he put down the disorders (1364). He had become the most powerful man in the kingdom of Naples, and possessed one of the largest fortunes of his age, having been richly rewarded by the sovereigns of Naples whom he served. A faithful, energetic, and honest counselor to his chosen land, Niccolò did not forget his native republic, and sought to strengthen commercial and economic ties between Naples and Florence, to the advantage in general of Florence. He used some of his vast wealth to found the Certosa (Carthusian monastery) just outside the gates of Florence, in which, as he had wished, he was buried. A letter he wrote to a Florentine relative, in which he detailed the events of his life and justified his actions, constitutes a valuable 14th century political document.

Acciaiuoli, Zanobi. Prefect of the Vatican Library; b. at Florence, May 25, 1461; d. at Rome, 1519 or 1520. His family, which had been exiled from Florence, returned to that city in 1478 and he took up his studies there. He was the student and friend of the most illustrious men of the age, including Poliziano and Marsilio Ficino. In 1495 he entered the Dominican order and turned to ecclesiastical studies. Leo X appointed him (1518) prefect of the Vatican Library and charged him with making a new catalogue. He also made an index of the secret archives of the Castel Sant' Angelo. He wrote original works in Latin and made translations from the Greek.

Accolti (äk-kôl′tē), **Benedetto.** Jurist, classical scholar, and historian; b. at Arezzo, 1415; d. at Florence, 1466. He was of an ancient family that had gone to Arezzo (c1300) due to civil strife in Florence, but took up Florentine citizenship later during an amnesty. He studied at Bologna and then studied civil and canon law at Florence, where his father taught at the university. In his turn, he lectured on law to large and appreciative audiences, and became one of the most celebrated jurists in Italy. His official positions at Florence dated from 1448. In 1458 he succeeded Poggio Bracciolini as chancellor and was an ornament to the office. Vespasiano writes that in addition to his profound knowledge of law, the humanities, and sacred literature he had "a pleasant trick of repeating popular songs and verse," had a magnificent memory and a genial disposition. Besides countless official documents and legal opinions he wrote passable verse, a dialogue in which he defended the superiority of the men of his own age, as opposed to the then current idolatry of men of antiquity, and (with his brother Leonardo) a history of the wars of the Christians to regain the Holy Sepulchre at Jerusalem, up to 1187. This last was based on older chroniclers, notably William of Tyre, and included their defects; it is said to have been used by Tasso as a source for *Jerusalem Delivered*.

Accolti, Benedetto. Cardinal and poet; b. at Florence, October 29, 1497; d. there, September 21, 1549. He was the grandson of Benedetto, the chancellor (1415–1466), and the nephew of Pietro, the cardinal of Ancona (1455–1532), and Bernardo, the poet (1458–1534). He entered upon an ecclesiastical career at an early age, and as a protégé of Leo X was named apostolic abbreviator. His rise in the Church was rapid. He was named bishop, archbishop, and (1527) cardinal. It is said of the last that he bought the position from Clement VII. As papal legate he governed Ancona for two years, at the end of this period being removed for misgovernment. Paul III imprisoned him (1535) in Castel Sant' Angelo and instituted proceedings against him. He was condemned but secured his freedom with a payment of 59,000 scudi. Thenceforth he led a retired life, at Ravenna, Ferrara, Venice, and Florence. He died under mysterious circumstances in the latter city; poison was suspected. He was the author of prose and Latin poems.

Accolti, Bernardo. Poet; b. at Arezzo, September 11, 1458; d. at Rome, March 1, 1534. He was the son of Benedetto (1415–1466) and the brother of Pietro, the cardinal of Ancona (1455–1532), and passed his youth at Florence. He enjoyed great renown at the end of the 15th and the beginning of the 16th century for his extemporaneous verse, and was given the epithet "L'Unico Aretino." In his wanderings he visited, and was warmly received at, the courts of Urbino, Mantua, Naples, and Rome, where he was a protégé of Leo X. His works, including the comedy *Virginia* in the manner of Boccaccio, first appeared at Florence (1513), were reprinted at Venice (1519) and several times thereafter. He is known (partly through Castiglione's *The Courtier*) to many modern readers of Italian literature.

Accolti, Francesco. Jurist and humanist; b. at Arezzo, 1416; d. at Siena, 1488. He was the brother of Benedetto Accolti (1415–1466), and like him studied under his father at Florence. He studied letters under Filelfo and law at Siena, and became a celebrated jurist. He taught law at Ferrara, Siena, and Pisa, remaining a number of years in each place. He also served as secretary to Francesco Sforza at Milan for the five years preceding the duke's death (1461–1466). He is noted primarily for his legal writings and commentaries, but also wrote verse and translated Leonardo Bruni's history of the Gothic wars into Italian.

Accolti, Leonardo. Historian and writer; fl. 15th century. He shared the authorship, with his brother, Benedetto Accolti (1415–1466), of a history of the First Crusade used by Tasso as a source for *Jerusalem Delivered.*

Accolti, Pietro. Cardinal; b. at Florence, 1455; d. at Rome, December 12, 1532. He was the son of Benedetto (1415–1466) and the brother of Bernardo the poet (1458–1534). He studied canon law at Pisa and then entered the Church, where he rose rapidly. Julius II made him bishop (1505) and cardinal (1511) of Ancona, where he served as papal legate. Clement VII made him archbishop of Ravenna, but he was usually known as the "Cardinal of Ancona." He was influential in the curia and is noted for having drafted the bull *Exsurge, Domine* by which (July 15, 1520) Leo X condemned Luther.

Accoramboni (äk-kō-räm-bō'nē), **Vittoria.** Mentioned as a poetess, but known more for her dramatic life and horrible death; b. at Gubbio, February 15, 1557; murdered at Padua, December 22, 1585. Of an impoverished family, her father and ambitious mother took their children to Rome to improve their fortunes. Vittoria was immediately courted for her beauty and supposed talents. At 16 she was married to Francesco Perretti, the nephew of the future pope, Sixtus V. He was deeply in love with her, and overlooked her wanderings from the path of virtue. But Vittoria, under her brother Marcello's influence, was dissatisfied, and soon yielded to the importunities of Paolo Giordano Orsini, duke of Bracciano and head of the powerful Orsini family. He, who had already killed his wife,

Isabella de' Medici, on the grounds of infidelity, arranged with Vittoria's brother Marcello to murder Francesco Perretti. The murder was carried out April 16, 1581, and the duke of Bracciano secretly married Vittoria. The pope, Gregory XIII, had necessarily to investigate these events. Vittoria was brought to trial for the murder of her husband but made such a winning picture before her judges that she was freed. The duke of Bracciano overcame the pope's opposition, and publicly married Vittoria again (1583). However, Gregory XIII died shortly thereafter, and his successor was Francesco Perretti's uncle, Sixtus V. Before his elevation to the papacy he had not insisted on prosecuting Vittoria, but once he was pope he made it clear that it was dangerous for the lovers to remain in Rome. They fled to the shores of Lake Garda, and there Paolo Orsini died, November 10, 1585, poisoned, it was said, at the instigation of Francesco de' Medici. Vittoria's attachment to the duke was purely practical. He was much older than she, and so grossly fat that he had been excused from genuflecting. She was already considering her next marriage when Ludovico Orsini, the duke's brother, invaded her house with a band of his men and murdered Vittoria and her young brother. It is said that as the poniard was plunged into her heart the assassin twisted it and sneeringly asked to know how it felt. Ludovico Orsini was brought to trial by the Republic of Venice after he had been besieged in his castle. He was condemned and strangled in prison. Seventeen of his followers were executed, and others were condemned to the galleys. Sixtus had Marcello, Vittoria's evil genius, apprehended and beheaded for his earlier crimes. The horrors of a Senecan tragedy could not match those of Vittoria's life. John Webster made her story the subject of his tragedy, *The White Devil, or Vittoria Corombona* (1612).

Accorso (äk-kōr′sō), **Buono.** See **Bonaccursius Pisanus.**

Accorso, Francesco. See **Accursius, Franciscus.**

Accorso, Francesco. [Latinized, **Franciscus Accursius.**] Italian jurist; b. at Bologna, 1225; d. there, 1293. He was the son of Franciscus Accursius (c1182–c1260), was professor of law at Bologna, entered the service of Edward I of England, and lectured on law at Oxford (c1275). He is mentioned in Dante's *Divina Commedia* (*Inferno*, xv) in company with other jurists, clerics, and men of letters.

Accursio or **Accorsi** (äk-kör′syō; -kōr′sē), **Mariangelo.** Critic and philologist; b. at Aquila, c1490; d. there, 1546. He studied Greek at Rome, and there was one of the earliest to begin collecting Roman epigraphs. His studies in philology and his knowledge of modern languages won him a reputation. He traveled in Germany and Poland, consulting codices and collecting epigraphs. The epigrams he wrote in inelegant and muddied Latin were less esteemed by later critics than they were in his own day. His most valuable work was in the collating of Greek and Latin texts and in his editions of Latin texts.

Accursius (a̤-kėr′s̤i-us; -shus), **Franciscus.** [Original name, **Francesco Accorso.**] Jurist; b. at Bagnolo, Tuscany, or in Florence, c1182; d. at Bologna, c1260. He taught law at Bologna and was the author of various works. His most celebrated work was a methodical compilation of all the commentaries on Roman law, called, in English, *The Great Gloss*. This work remained the final authority until the time of Bartolo (late 14th century).

Accursius Pisanus (pī-sā′nus). See **Bonaccursius Pisanus.**

Achillini (ä-kēl-lē′nē), **Alessandro.** [Called the **Second Aristotle.**] Anatomist and philosopher; b. at Bologna, October 29, 1463; d. there, August 2, 1512. He studied medicine and philosophy at Bologna, and subsequently taught these two subjects at the universities of Bologna and Padua. He was one of the first European medical scholars to dissect cadavers. Noted in his own day for his many works on philosophy and medicine, he is now best known for his anatomical studies, *Humani corporis anatomia* (published 1516) and *Annotationes anatomiae* (published 1520), among others.

Achillini, Gian Filoteo. Poet and scholar; b. at Bologna, 1466; d. 1538. He studied classical letters, philosophy, music, and numismatics, wrote verse and prose in the vernacular, and was noted for his vast learning. He founded a literary academy at Bologna (1511) called the Accademia del Viridario, and wrote a poem (1513) on various men of letters. His erudition, and lack of a poetic gift, is displayed in another poem, *Fedele* (Bologna, 1523), in five books of twenty cantos each. It draws its material from Greek and Latin writers, as well as from such Italian works as the *Dittamondo* of Fazio degli Uberti and the *Divina Commedia.* Achillini also published a collection of Greek, Latin, and Italian verse, and a treatise on the vernacular (to justify his use of the Bolognese idiom) which he dedicated to Ercole II, Duke of Ferrara.

Ackermann (äk′ėr-män), **Alexander.** Original name of **Agricola, Alexander.**

Acuto (ä-kö′tō), **Giovanni.** Italian name for the English mercenary captain Sir John Hawkwood. See **Hawkwood,** Sir **John.**

Adam of Genoa (ad′ạm, jen′ọ̄-ạ). Carmelite monk. d. 1494. He preached at Rome against simony. He was found murdered in his bed.

Adolf of Nassau (ad′olf, ā′dolf; German, ä′dolf). [Latinized, **Adolphus.**] King of Germany and Holy Roman emperor (never crowned) (1292–1298); b. c1255; d. in battle at Gölheim, in the Rhine Palatinate, 1298. He was the son of Walfram, count of Nassau, and was elected king of the Germans in 1292 to succeed Rudolf I of Hapsburg, over the opposition of the supporters of Albert, son of Rudolf I. His position in relation to the nominally subordinate German princes who elected him was always unsure. It was not improved by his seizure (1294–1296) of Meissen and Thuringia. The princes deposed him (1298). Albert marched against him, and Adolf was killed in the battle.

Adrian V (ā′dri-ạn). [Original name, **Ottoboni Fiesco.**] Pope in 1276. A native of Genoa, he succeeded Innocent V, but lived only five weeks after his accession. He was succeeded by John XXI.

Adrian VI. [Also, **Hadrian;** original name, **Adrian Florensz.**] Pope (1522–1523); b. at Utrecht, 1459; d. 1523. He studied at the University of Louvain, of which he later became vice-chancellor, and was chosen by the Emperor Maximilian I to tutor his grandson, the archduke Charles (who was later to be the emperor Charles V). Bishop of Tortosa and grand inquisitor of Aragon (1516), he was created a cardinal by Leo X (1517), and was for a short time regent of Spain (1520). Largely through the influence of Charles V, he succeeded Pope Leo X in 1522, and the Italians were enraged with the cardinals for having chosen a non-Italian pope and, furthermore, a man they had scarcely heard of. Adrian went to Rome for the first time after he had been elected pope, and was shocked by what he found there. A pious and traditionally devout man, he at once sought to clear the papal court of the humanists, poets, men of letters, and charming hangers-on, not unduly celebrated for their sterling spiritual qualities, who had surrounded Leo X. He reduced the great staff kept by Leo and lived a frugal life, cared for by a few Flemish servants. He left the works that had been interrupted by Raphael's death unfinished, had no use for ancient statues and was even thought to be considering burning them for lime. He regarded the recently found, and greatly admired, *Laocoön,* as a pagan idol, and walled up the Belvedere in the Vatican, with its great collection of statues. He was regarded as a barbarian by the cultivated and prodigal humanists, and became the butt of cruel satires. Francesco Berni, whom he particularly disliked and whom he threatened to have thrown into the Tiber, lampooned him without mercy. Adrian's desire and aim were to refurbish the moral tone of the clergy, to check the Reformation, and to stem the Turkish tide. He was completely outnumbered and outflanked at Rome by extravagant and high-living members of the clergy, and could not, in the twenty months that he was pope, make the least impression on the luxury and sensuality that prevailed in the Rome of his time. In his efforts to check the Reformation and the Turks he was equally unsuccessful, but he had not much time at his disposal. The Italians celebrated when he died, and placed an inscription on the door of his physician's house, naming him the liberator of Rome. He was succeeded by Clement VII and was the last non-Italian to become pope to this date.

Adriani (ä-drē-ä′nē), **Francesco.** Musician and composer; b. at San Severino (in the Marches), c1539; d. at Rome, August 16, 1575. He was choirmaster in St. John Lateran at Rome from 1573 until his death. Noted in his own time as an expert contrapuntist, he composed motets, hymns, and psalms.

Adriani, Giovanni Battista. Florentine historian and statesman; b. at Florence, 1511; d. there, 1579. He played an honorable part in the defense of Florence (1530) against the armies of the pope and of Charles V. Afterward he went to Padua to complete his studies. On his return to Florence he was admitted (1540) to the Florentine Academy and met the leading literary men of Florence. He held the chair of eloquence at the university from 1549 until his death. On the death of Benedetto Varchi (1565), Duke Cosimo I de' Medici, having assured himself of Adriani's loyalty in various posts, commissioned him to go on with the history of Florence that Varchi had begun. Adriani covered the years 1536 to 1574, which were, in effect, the years of the duke's reign. Energetic and exact, Adriani had an intuitive understanding of his own times that is revealed in his work. He also understood the connection of the history of Florence with events in the rest of Italy and in Europe. His work was published in 1583.

Adriani, Marcello. Florentine humanist and statesman; b. at Florence, 1464; d. there, December 1, 1521. He was a student of Cristoforo Landino and of Poliziano, and was highly gifted in classical languages. He taught at the university from 1497 to 1502. His greatest activity was as chancellor of the restored republic, to which he succeeded in 1498, and a position that he held until 1521. Machiavelli served the chancellery under him. In his office Adriani carried on the literary and humanist tradition of some of his predecessors. His official correspondence was noted for its clarity, style, and effectiveness. He wrote accomplished Latin orations, and translated and commented upon the *De materia medica* of the Greek physician Dioscorides, who wrote in the first or second century A.D.

Adriano di Corneto (ä-drē-ä′nō dē kôr-nā′tō). [Real name, **Adriano Castellesi.**] Cardinal and scholar; b. at Corneto, 1458 or 1459; d. c1521. He was nuncio of Pope Innocent VIII in Scotland in 1488, agent at Rome of Henry VII of England, collector of Peter's pence in England, and papal protonotary. He obtained (1492) the prebend of Ealdland in Saint Paul's Cathedral, and the rectory of Saint Dunstan-in-the-East, but returned to Rome on the death of Innocent VIII. He was made bishop of Hereford in 1502, bishop of Bath and Wells in 1504, and cardinal in 1503. Pope Julius II, who succeeded in 1503, was hostile to him, and the cardinal, amidst plots and intrigues, several times fled Rome in fear of the pope, but was present at the conclave that elected Leo X (1513), and took part in the sessions of the Lateran Council. In 1517 he was implicated in the conspiracy of Cardinals Petrucci, De Sauli, and Riario to poison Pope Leo X. The plot was discovered; Adriano was condemned but pardoned and fined, and again fled Rome. He was deprived of his cardinalate (1518), and his enemies, of whom Wolsey of England was foremost, seized his dignities in England. He disappears from history and it is thought that he was slain. A cultivated and active man, he left many written works, some enlivened by a glint of mockery. His works include the poem *Venatio* (1505), *De Vera Philosophia* (1507), *De Sermone Latino et modo Latine loquendi* (1513), and others. Many of his letters are preserved in the Vatican.

Aegidius (ē̦-jid′i-us). Dialogue by Giovanni Pontano, in which he exalted free will as opposed to astrology. This was a reversal of his earlier stand in his *De fortuna* and his *De rebus caelestibus,* which had attributed power over man's fate to the stars.

Aeken (ä′ke̦n), **van.** See **Bosch, Hieronymus.**

Africa. Epic poem by Petrarch, recalling the high-water mark of Roman greatness at the time of the Second Punic War, and glorifying Scipio Africanus the Elder, the hero of the war and the epitome, as Petrarch and many others thought, of all the noble qualities of the ancient Romans. It was written in Latin hexameters. Petrarch, who intended it to be his masterpiece, worked on it for years, but was never satisfied with it. Those who had seen the manuscript spread word of its greatness, and it was partly on account of this work, still incomplete, that Petrarch was crowned poet laureate at Rome in 1341.

Agazzari (ä-gäd-dzä′rē), Fra **Filippo.** Sienese religious and writer; b. at Siena, c1339; d. 1422. Of a noble Sienese family, he entered the Augustinian order of hermits in 1353, and after a time became noted for the ascetic life he led at the hermitage at Lecceto, near Siena. He became prior of his convent and favored the strictest adherence to the rules. Noted for his asceticism, he was called Blessed. He was also known as a writer. Many of his works have been lost. Extant are his *Assempri* (*Ensamples*), which are equally remarkable for the purity of the Sienese idiom, for the clarity and felicity of style, and for the vivid picture they present of 14th century Sienese life. The episodes they present are drawn from daily life, and portray the beliefs, superstitions, and customs of the age. He was a contemporary of Boccaccio and Franco Sacchetti, and wrote his *Assempri,* a collection of sixty-two didactic and moralistic tales begun in 1397, with the express aim of rooting out evil, an aim that he tried to fulfill by making it terrifying. The horrendous visions that fill his stories, the unutterable wickedness of Satan, are often balanced in his tales by the tenderness of the Madonna. The stories, rife with the superstitions of the age, illuminate the good and evil of his times, for St. Catherine of Siena was also a contemporary, as was the "very wicked English knight," Sir John Hawkwood.

Agli (ä′lyē), **Antonio degli.** Florentine humanist; b. 1400; d. 1477. A member of an ancient Florentine family, he was a cathedral canon, archbishop of Ragusa (1465), bishop of Fiesole (1467), and bishop of Volterra (1470). He was a friend of Marsilio Ficino, had an excellent knowledge of Latin and Greek, and wrote verse, theological treatises, and a book on the lives of the saints.

Agnolo (dä′nyō-lō), **Baccio d'.** See **Baccio d'Agnolo.**

Agnolo di Domenico di Donnino (ä′nyō-lō dē dō-men′i-kō dē dôn-nē′nō). Florentine painter; b. 1466; d. after 1513. He was a follower of Cosimo Rosselli and was a skillful draftsman. To him are attributed the portraits of Rosselli and Benedetto da Rovezzano on which the engravings in the 1568 edition of Vasari's *Lives* were based, and perhaps others as well. According to Vasari, he spent all his time drawing, and never got down to work. Little of his work survives, but according to documents he painted frescoes in the loggia of a hospital and in a church at Florence, as well as in the Palace of the Podesta and other buildings. He also executed frescoes at Pistoia. All have been lost, destroyed, or whitewashed over. About 1508 he went to Rome with other artists to consult with Michelangelo, who was about to begin the frescoing of the Sistine ceiling, on the art of fresco. His *Virgin and Angel Adoring the Infant Christ* is in the Museum of Fine Arts, Boston.

Agnolo, Giuliano d'. Florentine sculptor and architect; b. 1491; d. 1555. He was the son of Baccio d'Agnolo (1464–1543), and learned his art as his father's pupil. In his architectural style, as in the palaces he designed at Colle Val d'Elsa and S. Miniato al Tedesco, he adapted the style of his father and Cronaca. About the middle of the century he worked with Bandinelli on the marble rail that encloses the choir in the cathedral at Florence.

Agnolo da Siena (dä sye′nä). Architect and sculptor. See **Agostino and Agnolo da Siena.**

Agostini (ä-gō-stē′nē), **Lodovico.** Musician; b. at Ferrara, 1534; d. there, September 20, 1590. He was an apostolic protonotary and was chaplain and musician to Duke Alfonso II at Ferrara. He was also in friendly contact with the Mantuan court and especially with the music-loving Duke Guglielmo, to whom he dedicated (1586) a book of madrigals, *Le lagrime del peccatore*. His known compositions were all madrigals, and in his work he sought to complement the texts of poems with his music and new ways of giving color and expression, as well as emphasis, to the words.

Agostini, Niccolò degli. Venetian poet; active in the first half of the 16th century. He composed a continuation of Boiardo's *Orlando Innamorato,* in three books, in which he attempted to fuse classical and romantic material with allegory and philosophy. He translated the *Metamorphoses* of Ovid and wrote poems, in Italian, on the love of Lancelot and Guinevere. Twenty cantos on the love of Tristan and Isolde are also attributed to him.

Agostino (ä-gō-stē′nō) and **Agnolo da Siena** (ä′nyō-lō dä sye′ nä). Architects and sculptors; active in the first half of the 14th century. Often mistakenly treated as brothers, which they were not, they were together influenced by Giovanni Pisano, under whom they both worked. Together they designed the Sienese church and convent of San Francesco and the Porta Romana of Siena. Their best sculptural work is usually considered to have been Bishop Tarlatti's tomb at Arezzo, which was destroyed by the French during the Napoleonic period.

Agostino di Duccio (dē döt′chō). Florentine sculptor; b. at Florence, 1418; d. at Perugia, after 1481. He had two brothers, Cosimo and Ottaviano, who were goldsmiths and also sculptors. His father died while he was still a boy, and in 1433 he enlisted under Niccolò da Tolentino as a mercenary soldier and left Florence. Little is known of his education and training, but as his name does not occur at Florence again until 1446, most of it must have taken place outside his native city. Prior to the 19th century most of his work was attributed to other artists. In that century documents were discovered that have made it possible to distinguish the body of his work, and that show him to have been an individual and gifted artist. His work in relief and his drawing suggest that his early contacts were with goldsmiths and workers in bronze. To say that the influence of Donatello is ever present in his work does not imply dependence or imitation, since Agostino's vision is fundamentally pictorial; his swirling draperies are decorative in their rhythms rather than naturalistic in their modeling. The energy of his line animates his figures and scenes. Evidently, but superficially, he was influenced by classical sculpture. His independent imagination, lyric and emotional sense, and delicate technique make him one of the most interesting sculptors of his age. However, at a time when Florence boasted such artists as Desiderio da Settignano, Antonio Pollaiuolo, and Verrocchio, Agostino may have found himself overshadowed and left his native city to seek his fortune elsewhere. Thus we find his greatest work in the cycles he executed in the Tempio Malatestiano at Rimini and at Perugia.

His first known work is the tomb of S. Gemignano, now dismantled, made for the cathedral at Modena. The bas-reliefs (signed *Agostinus de Florentia F. 1442*), with scenes from the life of the saint, have since been built into the outside walls of the apse; other fragments are in the sacristy. In 1446 he was working, perhaps as a goldsmith, on the Church of SS. Annunziata at Florence. He and his brother Cosimo were accused of stealing some silver and both fled to Venice. Little is known of his work in Venice. In 1449 he undertook, perhaps under Matteo de' Pasti, master of the works, to furnish the sculptural decoration of the Church of S. Francesco at Rimini for which, at the order of Sigismondo Malatesta, Leon Battista Alberti designed a new façade and redesigned some of the interior to create six new chapels. Agostino worked there at least until 1454, carving with his own hand and directing the work of many assistants, including his brother Ottaviano. Guided by the suggestions of Sigismondo Malatesta himself, the advice of Matteo de' Pasti, and the ideas of various humanists at Sigismondo's court, he decorated with spirit and grace a number of the chapels in what came to be called the Tempio Malatestiano. The figures of the Liberal Arts, of Sibyls, Shield-bearers, Planets, dancing and frolicking putti, worked as they are in variegated marbles, painted stuccos, and picked out in gold and bronze, make of the Tempio one of the most richly decorated and carved of Renaissance buildings. Agostino also executed there the celebrated tomb of the Malatesta ancestors, with the *Triumph of Sigismondo* shown on one panel, and the tomb of Isotta degli Atti, Sigismondo's mistress. Other works executed for Sigismondo included a bas-relief of Isotta, now lost but known through an engraving, and a scene from the legend of St. Sigismund, originally in the saint's chapel in the Tempio and now at Milan. In July, 1457, Agostino was called to Perugia to decorate the façade of the Oratory of S. Bernardino. He ornamented it with statues, bas-reliefs, and painted figures. The work, completed in 1462, is an outstanding example of polychrome architectural adornment. At Bologna (1462) he made a model for the façade of S. Petronio, and then went back to Florence (1463) and made a gigantic statue, probably in terra-cotta, for one of the buttresses of the cathedral. This work has been destroyed. In the same year, a block was ordered for which he sketched a design for Piero da Settignano, called Baccellino. The block was spoiled and abandoned. It was from this block that forty years later Michelangelo carved his *David*. By 1473 Agostino was again at Perugia, and worked on the altar for a chapel of the Pietà in the cathedral (destroyed in 1625) to which belonged the great relief on a blue ground that is now in the cathedral. From May of 1473 he was working on the decoration for the *Porta S. Pietro*, still unfinished in 1481. Some works in the National Gallery of Umbria at Perugia are attributed to him, as well as some bas-reliefs and other works in the Church of S. Domenico. In 1477, with assistants, he carved two tombs for the Geraldini family in Amelia. After 1481 no further notices are recorded of him, and it is presumed that he died in that year. Other works include a *Madonna* in the Church of SS. Annunziata, two *Angels* in the Ognissanti, a *Madonna* of painted stucco in the Bargello, all at Florence; and works in the Louvre at Paris, the Victoria and Albert Museum at London, and The Metropolitan Museum of Art at New York.

Agostino de' Musi (dā mö′sē). Engraver; active in the first quarter of the 16th century. He was of the school of Marcantonio Raimondi, and copied the work of Iacopo de' Barbari and Dürer, but was most influenced by Giulio Campagnola, whom he copied and imitated at Rome (1517).

Agoust (dȧ-göst), **Bertrand d'.** Original name of Pope **Clement V.**

Agramante (ä-grä-män'tā). In Matteo Maria Boiardo's *Orlando Innamorato* and Lodovico Ariosto's *Orlando Furioso*, an African king who claims to be a descendant of Alexander the Great. He decides to invade France, is at first dangerously successful, but is finally slain by Orlando.

Agricane (ä-grē-kä'nā). In Matteo Maria Boiardo's *Orlando Innamorato*, a king of Tartary who besieges Albracca to win Angelica. She is the daughter of Galafrone, king of Cathay, and Albracca is his capital. Angelica calls on Orlando for help, and Agricane can make no headway against him in the press of battle. To draw Orlando off so that he can engage him in single combat, Agricane pretends to flee. Orlando follows him and they fight from noon to dark. As night falls they agree to interrupt their duel and resume it at daybreak. They lie down near each other, in perfect confidence, but before going to sleep engage in conversation. Orlando speaks of the wonders of God's world. Agricane replies that he knows nothing of science or religion. If Orlando must talk, let the subject be of arms or love. He asks Orlando who he is and what his history is. Orlando gives his name, which is what Agricane suspected, and begins to tell of his love for Angelica. At the mention of her name Agricane starts up. He asks Orlando to give up his love for Angelica, as he also loves her. Orlando replies that even if he promised to do so he could not. In the darkness they resume their fight. It is of epic proportions and valor on both sides, but at last Orlando delivers a mortal wound. Before he dies, Agricane asks Orlando to take care of his faithful horse, and asks Orlando to baptize him so that he may die a Christian. Orlando baptizes him, and Agricane, a noble warrior, expires.

Agricola (ạ-grik'ọ-lạ), **Alexander.** [Original surname, **Ackermann.**] Composer of religious music; b. probably in the Netherlands, c1446; d. at Valladolid, Spain, c1506. He was employed at the court of France, and by Lorenzo de' Medici. His works include motets, songs, and several masses.

Agrippa von Nettesheim (ä-grip'ä fọn net'ẹs-hīm), **Heinrich Cornelius.** German physician, philosopher and student of alchemy; b. at Cologne, Germany, September 14, 1486; d. at Grenoble, France, February 18, 1535. He was the author of *De incertitudine et vanitate scientiarum* (1527), *De occulta philosophia* (1510), and others. He advised an Italian prince to put down those who were the opponents of tyranny.

Aimo (ī'mō), **Domenico.** See **Varignana.**

Aladine (ä-lä-dē'nā). In Torquato Tasso's *Gerusalemme Liberata* (*Jerusalem Delivered*), the pagan tyrant of Jerusalem. He is overcome and slain by the Crusaders under Godfrey of Bouillon.

Alagna (dä-lä'nyä), **Lucrezia d'.** A beautiful lady of poor but noble parents. It was said that she was the mistress of King Alfonso I of Naples in his old age. She proclaimed her piety and her unsullied honor, but some of her contemporaries were dubious. Pius II wrote of Alfonso's attachment to her that the "great king, . . . was finally conquered by love and like any captive of war was a slave to a weak woman."

Alamanni (ä-lä-män'nē), **Antonio.** Florentine poet and writer; active at the end of the 15th century and the beginning of the 16th. In his verse he was a follower of Burchiello. He also wrote carnival songs and a play on the conversion of St. Mary Magdalen. His sonnets were published with those of Burchiello (Florence, 1552); other works appeared in various collections.

Alamanni or **Alemanni** (-lā-), **Luigi.** Poet and diplomat; b. at Florence, 1495; d. at Amboise, France, 1556. He studied Latin and Greek letters at the University of Florence. At Florence he was on terms of warm friendship with the outstanding literary figures of the time; Machiavelli was his great friend. As a literary figure, he attended the gatherings of literary men that took place frequently in Florence. An opponent of the Medici, he took part in the abortive conspiracy against Cardinal Giulio de' Medici (later Pope Clement VII), and was forced to flee when the conspiracy failed. He went first to Venice, then to France, and returned to Florence when the Medici were expelled (1527). On the restoration of the Medici, he was again forced into exile and ultimately was declared a rebel by the Florentines. Francis I of France welcomed him to his court, and often employed him on diplomatic missions. Under Francis I's benevolent patronage, Alamanni wrote quantities of poems. His works include eclogues, hymns, satires, elegies, an epic poem *Girone il cortese*, and others. His lyrics, following classical models and written in Italian, are notable for sincere expression of love and patriotism. Those on moral and religious subjects ring less true. Politics and the corruption of the clergy are the main themes of his satires. Pindar, Ovid, Vergil, and others are among the models for his lyrics. As a playwright, he wrote *Flora*, a comedy along classical lines, and *Antigone*, a tragedy adapted from Sophocles. His epic *Avarchide* is a transmutation of the *Iliad* to a romance and epic of Brittany. His didactic poem *Coltivazione*, in six books, is modeled on Vergil and Columella. It describes rustic life in all its manifestations and maintains its pace and interest by the inclusion of many episodes. His many letters reflect his spirited temperament and love of country.

Alaminos (ä-lä-mē′nōs), **Antón** or **Antonio.** Spanish navigator; fl. 1499–1520. He accompanied Columbus in 1499 and 1502, and was chief pilot of successive expeditions (1517–1520) made by Córdoba, Grijalva, and Cortés to Mexico. He discovered the Bahama channel in 1520.

Alatri (ä-lä′trē), **Antonio da.** See **Antonio da Alatri.**

Albani (äl-bä′nē), **Giovanni Girolamo.** Italian soldier, cardinal, and diplomat; b. at Bergamo, Italy, 1504; d. 1591.

Alberegno (äl-bā-rā′nyō), **Jacobello.** Venetian painter; d. 1397. The only signed work extant, a *Crucifixion*, in the Accademia, Venice, shows the Byzantine influence in the elongation of the figures of the saints in the side panels. The work, somewhat primitive, also shows the influence of Lorenzo Veneziano in the more Gothic central panel of the *Crucifixion*. Other works attributed to this painter are at Ferrara and Venice.

Albergati (äl-ber-gä′tē), **Niccolò.** Italian cardinal; b. at Bologna, 1375; d. at Siena, May 9, 1443. Of a noble Bolognese family, he entered on a religious life in 1395 and was ordained in 1404. On being named bishop of Bologna (1417) he energetically set about reform of the clergy, calming the turbulent Bolognese, and trying to reconcile the differences between Bologna and the Holy See. In 1426 he was elevated to the purple. In the service of the Church he was charged with many missions. Three times he went to France to try to bring about peace between that country and England. As ambassador to Lombardy an equal number of times, he attempted to resolve the conflicts between Milan, Venice, and Florence. In 1433 he took the presidency of the Council of Basel in the name of the Holy See and there upheld the authority of the pope. When Eugenius was compelled to flee from Rome, Cardinal Albergati joined him in Florence, continued to support him in the struggle with the Council, and contributed largely to the ultimate victory of the papacy in that struggle. The learned cardinal, noted for his sanctity, did what he could to further humanistic studies. Filelfo, Poggio, Enea Silvio Piccolomini, and Tommaso Parentucelli were among his protégés. The last named was his constant companion for more than twenty years and acknowledged his debt to his beloved mentor by taking the name Nicholas V when he became pope.

Alberico da Barbiano (äl-bā′rē-kō dä bär-byä′nō). [Called **Alberico il Grande.**] Count of Cunio and condottiere; b. c1344; d. at Castello della Pieve, April 26, 1409. He was an outstanding member of an ancient and noble family that claimed descent from the Carolingians. In the course of years the family had extended its sway over large areas in the Romagna, and had walled and fortified the towns and castles it controlled. Alberico had engaged in the study and practice of warfare since his youth, and had served under the English mercenary Sir John Hawkwood (Giovanni Acuto, as the Italians called him) in the bloody battles at Faenza (1376) and Cesena (1377), among others. Alberico was an apt pupil and an able soldier. He was not willing to be subject to a foreign captain and undertook to build up an Italian force. He founded the Company of St. George, a disciplined band of 7,000 men. Bernabò Visconti engaged him to fight in his cause. Urban VI, to whose pleas for aid St. Catherine of Siena joined her prayers, called him to Rome to fend off the Gascon and Breton soldiers of the antipope Clement VII. Alberico won a great victory over the foreigners (1380) and was welcomed to Rome as a savior. The victory was decisive in preventing the Avignon popes from winning control of Rome. Urban created him a Knight of Christ and gave him a white standard with a red cross; on the standard were the words "Italia liberata dai barbari" (Italy liberated from the Barbarians). On several occasions he fought against Louis of Anjou on behalf of Charles II of Durazzo, who claimed the throne of Naples. In general successful, he was once taken prisoner but ransomed by Gian Galeazzo Visconti on his promise to enter the latter's service. Alberico's example as a nobleman and a military man led other Italian princes or captains to build their own forces and thus win control of states, dukedoms, and principalities, as did Braccio da Montone at Perugia and Pandolfo Malatesta at Rimini, though his influence should not be exaggerated. Machiavelli, in *The Prince*, cites Alberico as the originator of Italian companies used by nobles or captains to win and control states for their own benefit and to the ruin of Italy. The historian Flavio Biondo praised him because he was more humane in his treatment of the Italian people than foreign condottieri.

Albert I (of *Germany*). [German, **Albrecht.**] Duke of Austria (1282 *et seq.*) and king of Germany (1298 *et seq.*); b. c1250; murdered at Windisch, Switzerland, 1308. He was the son of Rudolf I of Hapsburg. He defeated and killed Adolf of Nassau, his predecessor, at Göllheim, and became king of Germany. The Ghibellines of Italy, ever looking to the German king for help against the Guelphs, turned to Albert without success. Dante, in the *Divina Commedia* (*Purgatorio*, vi), describes Italy:

Ah servile Italy, woe's hostelry,
Ship without steersman in a mighty storm,

and then, changing the metaphor, attacks Albert for neglecting the riderless horse:

O German Albert, for neglecting her,
Now wild and past the reach of discipline,
Whose saddle 'twas your duty to bestride,
May a just judgment from the stars descend
Upon your blood, fearful and manifest,
So your successor may be terror-struck.
You and your father, yonder held in thrall
By your own avarice, you have allowed
The garden of the empire to be ruined.

Albert had all he could manage in Germany and never went to Italy. He obtained Bohemia (1306) for his son, but failed in his campaign (1307) against Thuringia. His abolition of tolls on the Rhine, in existence since 1250, united the archbishops and the leading nobility of the Rhine against him, and he was murdered by his nephew John. Albert was succeeded by Henry VII.

Albert II (of *Germany*). [Also, **Albert V** (of *Austria*).] German king, king of Bohemia and Hungary; b. 1397; d. 1439. He succeeded his father as duke of Austria (1404) and, as son-in-law of the emperor Sigismund, succeeded him as king of the Germans (1438). His rule of Hungary, Austria, and Bohemia was marked by revolts. He died of dysentery during an unsuccessful war against the Turks.

Albert of Westphalia. See **Aldegrever, Heinrich.**

Alberti (äl-ber′tē). Distinguished merchant and banking family (of many branches) of Florence, and one of the great landholding families of Tuscany. They were known in the city from the beginning of the 13th century. They were Guelphs, and were exiled after the Ghibelline victory at Montaperti (1260) but returned to Florence soon after and held a prominent place in its affairs. Alberto was prior in 1298; his brother Neri served with Dante as prior in 1300. In the rivalry between the Neri and the Bianchi at the beginning of the 14th century, the Alberti were Neri. After the middle of the century they espoused the cause of the Ricci (and the Medici) as representing the popular faction, against the Albizzi, as representing the oligarchical elements, and finally were proscribed and banished. Benedetto Alberti, called by Machiavelli the wisest man in Florence, died (1388) at Rhodes after a year of exile. Others of the family returned to Florence when the Medici party removed the sentence of banishment (1423). Thereafter, the Alberti were ardent supporters of the Medici. In the years after 1282, when the government of the priors was established, the Alberti contributed forty-eight priors and nine gonfalonieri to the republic. They were prominent merchants and bankers in the 14th and 15th centuries; their house had branches in Spain, France,

Flanders, England, Germany, Hungary, Greece, Syria, and Rhodes, as well as in the chief cities of Italy. Their banking house did not suffer as much as some others at Florence in the financial disaster of the mid-14th century. It was said of the Alberti that no matter how poor they were, they were among the richest of Florentine families. In addition to their palace at Florence, they owned the Villa del Paradiso, in the surrounding countryside, whose beauty is celebrated in the *Il Paradiso degli Alberti* of Giovanni Gherardi. They were traditionally generous to the poor and supporters of religious establishments. Agnolo Gaddi painted for them in Santa Croce and Spinello Aretino in S. Miniato al Monte. The most celebrated member of the family was Leon Battista Alberti.

Alberti, Antonio. Painter; b. at Ferrara, between 1390 and 1400; d. at Urbino, 1449. His few surviving works show him to have been a forerunner of the Ferrarese school of painting of the 15th century. These works include signed frescoes in the Talamello chapel near Pesaro (1437); a gonfalon (banner or standard); fragments of frescoes in the campanile of the Church of S. Francesco and an *Annunciate* in the same church; and thirteen panels from a polyptych, signed and dated 1439 in the National Gallery of the Marches, all at Urbino. He was the grandfather of the painter Timoteo Viti.

Alberti, Antonio degli. Florentine poet; born at Florence, July, 1363; d. at Bologna, September 1, 1415. A wealthy and liberal member of the powerful Alberti family, he was a patron of men of letters and shared in their interests and activities. In 1401, with other members of his house, he was forced into exile by a hostile government. While he was in Bologna, where it is thought that he studied mathematics and astrology, he was condemned to death (1412) by the Florentine government, but as he did not return to Florence the sentence was ineffective. He wrote sonnets and canzoni in the vernacular.

Alberti, Francesco d'Altobianco. Florentine poet; b. at Florence, June 14, 1401; d. there, June 6, 1479. Son of a wealthy father who was exiled, he lived for a long time at Rome but returned to Florence about 1450. He was a productive poet, took part in the poetry contest of 1441, the *Certame Coronario*, wrote Petrarchan sonnets, satiric verse in the manner of Burchiello and, above all, ballate in the popular Florentine manner that were among the best Tuscan verses of the period.

Alberti, Leandro. Dominican and writer on history and geography; b. at Bologna, 1479; d. after 1553. He completed his early studies at Bologna, entered the Dominican order (1495), and began his studies in philosophy and theology. On church business, he traveled widely in Italy, and also went to France. Through his Italian journeys he acquired a broad knowledge of Italy and a lively interest in its history and geography. His work on Italy, *Descrittione di tutta Italia* (Bologna, 1550), was widely read. He used Biondo's *Italia illustrata* as a model, and in fact used Biondo's material in some instances. However, he was more careful in his use of ancient sources. In addition, there was available to him, as a result of the great activity in the 15th century, much information that had not been available in Biondo's time. Alberti included economic and demographic data as well as descriptions of monuments and historical and epigraphical information. His history was among the best of the age. Among his many other writings is a collection on outstanding preachers (his earliest work, 1517), a volume on lives of the saints, a history of Bologna, and a work on prominent families of Bologna.

Alberti, Leon Battista. Florentine architect, painter, art theorist, mathematician, humanist, musician, and athlete; b. probably at Genoa, 1404; d. at Rome, April 25, 1472. Alberti was the prototype of the "universal man" of the Renaissance—the many-sided man who investigated, was active in, and excelled in all fields of knowledge. He was the natural son of an old and powerful Florentine family that had been forced into exile. His father carefully supervised the education of his sons, providing an education designed to develop their bodies as well as their minds and, above all, deliberately planned to keep them from idleness. For two years Alberti studied Greek, Latin, Italian, and mathematics in the house of Gasparino Barzizza, a distinguished master whose pupils had included Filelfo, Guarino da Verona, and Vittorino da Feltre. At the age of 17 he went to Bologna to study law. In the same year (1421) his father died; and his relatives, who wanted Alberti to go into the family business, refused him financial aid for the continuation of his studies when he declined to follow their wishes. Determined to pursue his studies, Alberti earned his way by day and studied at night, a routine that presently affected his health. In 1428 he entered the service of Cardinal Albergati and traveled with him on missions to France and Germany. In 1431 he went to Rome, where he was attached to the court of Eugenius IV. He held the position of apostolic abbreviator from 1432 to 1464. For one steeped in classical literature, as he was, the sight of Rome and its ancient monuments was, as it has been for succeeding generations of students and travelers, a dream become reality. What had become familiar to him through his studies now stood before his ravished eyes in stone and concrete. He studied the ruins, analyzed them, and later adapted architectural elements and what he could learn of ancient structural techniques in the buildings he designed. Eugenius was compelled to flee from Rome (1434), and went to Florence. Alberti joined him and there came into close and friendly contact with the leading artistic and literary figures of the day: Donatello, Brunelleschi, Luca della Robbia, Gianozzo Manetti, Niccolò Niccoli, and that enlightened prince in all but name, Cosimo de' Medici. In this period he occupied himself with, among other things, a study and analysis of the fundamentals of sculpture and painting, and set down basic rules in a short work, *De Statua*, in which he advised sculptors to study living models and anatomy for proportion, and *Della Pittura* (1436), which was the earliest treatise on the theory of painting. In the latter he gives methods and describes techniques, and adds that painting should be not merely a representation of nature, but should involve a knowledge and awareness of nature that can be expressed by the new rules of perspective. He further adds, on the uses of painting, that it translates one age for another, thus prolonging our existence (in this he exemplifies the intense interest of the humanists in securing their future fame), that it completes the image given by writers and poets, and that by its spiritual and ethical qualities it turns our thoughts to God. When Eugenius returned to Rome (1443), Alberti went with him; and on the elevation of his friend Tommaso Parentucelli as Nicholas V he had a patron who ardently desired his assistance in his grandiose plans for the reconstruction of Rome. His advice was sought in the restoration of the papal palace, Santa Maria Maggiore, and the fountain of Aqua Vergine. In 1446 he accepted the commission of Sigismondo Malatesta to transform the outside of the Church of S. Francesco at Rimini. With Pope Pius II, he went to Mantua (1459), and met there Ludovico Gonzaga, who commissioned him to design the Church of S. Sebastiano in Mantua (begun 1460) and, later, the Church of Sant' Andrea (begun 1472). In neither case was Alberti's plan followed to completion. For the Gonzaga family he also designed the choir of the Church of the Annunziata at Florence. Giovanni Rucellai, a rich Florentine banker, commissioned him to design the Rucellai Palace and the Rucellai Chapel with the shrine of the S. Sepolcro, and paid for the façade of Santa Maria Novella, all at Florence. In his architectural works, Alberti was profoundly influenced by the monuments he had seen and studied in Rome and elsewhere. His principle was to adapt elements of the classical style and ancient techniques to the needs of his age. He was not supinely dependent on antiquity. The façade of the Church of S. Francesco (called the Tempio Malatestiano) at Rimini has three great arches, modeled after the triumphal arch of Augustus that still stands at Rimini, and a shallow pediment. On the flank, deep niches set behind round arches, to hold the sarcophagi of eminent men, are patterned after Roman aqueducts. The church was to have been surmounted by a domelike cupola, but this was never completed. Alberti's design was immediately accepted and widely praised by his contemporaries and ever since. The Rucellai Palace at Florence, begun in 1446, makes use of pilasters, which are essentially modified columns, and rows of round-headed double windows set in round arches to provide symmetry and balance vertically as well as horizontally, and to transform a fortresslike palace front into one of grace and elegance. The arch and superposed orders of columns or pilasters, as those of the Rucellai Palace, were characteristic of Alberti's designs and became characteristics of much Renaissance architecture. He employed such elements from classical architecture more to achieve symmetry and harmony and to provide decorative elements than to fulfill structural needs. Alberti set down his theories on architecture in *De re aedificatoria*. His treatise, in ten books, was the first one printed (1485) on architecture. In it he gives his interpretation, adapted to the circumstances of his age, of the work *De architectura* by the 1st century architect and military engineer Vitruvius. The work embodies Alberti's ideals of simplicity, order, proportion, and elegance, contains plans for a town and buildings for different classes, reveals his enormous culture, and states his esthetic creed.

In his writings Alberti expresses the conviction—one that came to exemplify the individualists of the Renaissance—that what a man is is the result of his own will and effort; that it is only if man lacks self-discipline that he becomes the prey of Fortune. He held the conviction despite the many assaults of chance in his own life, beginning with the one that made him, as an illegitimate son, of, but not in, a prominent and powerful family. A treatise from his early years on the rewards and difficulties of the pursuit of learning, *De commodis literarum atque incommodis*, describes the hardships of his student life and concludes that the rewards far outweigh them. From this period also are some Latin eclogues, a number of dinner speeches, sometimes humorous in tone but with a serious purpose, and a number of dialogues on love and women. These last were written in Italian. Alberti deplored the tendency of the humanists to despise the vernacular, and wrote in Italian as well as in Latin, sometimes producing the same work in the two languages. His Latin style, however, was of such excellence that at the age of 20 he wrote a Latin comedy, *Philodoxeos*, pretending he had transcribed it from an ancient codex. In this he was believed, and it was published as the work of a Latin comic poet called Lepidus. Between 1432 and 1434 he wrote the dialogue *Della Famiglia* in, eventually, four books (published in 1443). For Alberti, the family was the center of an individual's life and the primary sphere in which he could reach fulfillment. In the first book he discusses the education of children and concludes that the purpose is to prepare for an active and independent life—one that not only will satisfy the individual's needs but will contribute to the satisfaction of the needs of others. A recurrent theme in Alberti's writings is that the aim of learning and life is action and execution, not speculation and contemplation. He valued learning for its practical applications in leading to further knowledge and in attaining a full and happy life. The second book expresses his ideas on marriage; the third, his ideas on the management of the household and on the family as an interdependent and self-contained unit; and the fourth, added later, his thoughts on friendship. His other writings include a description of Rome, *Descriptio urbis Romae*, and *Ludi mathematici*, in which he posed problems and presented solutions, and in which he described several of his inventions, as the odometer, the *bolide albertiana* for sounding the depth of the sea, and others. In his last work, *De iciarchia*, he sums up for future generations the principles and values that had inspired him throughout his life as an artist and a writer. Noted as a man of great learning, as an architect, inventor, and artist, Alberti was almost a legend in his own day. Burckhardt (*The Civilization of the Renaissance in Italy*) tells us that as an athlete he could, with his feet together, jump over the head of a man and that he could tame any horse; that he composed music, having learned how to do so by himself. Witnesses of his own day testify to his brilliance as a man of energy and of action. By his own testimony he was also a thoughtful man who occupied himself with questions of beauty and with the problems of this life and how a man could most enjoy it and at the same time contribute to the advancement of mankind in general.

Albertinelli (äl-ber-tē-nel′lē), **Mariotto.** Florentine painter; b. at Florence, October 13, 1474; d. there, November 5, 1515. In the workshop of Cosimo Rosselli he was a pupil of Piero di Cosimo. He lived and worked most of his life at Florence. In the 1490's he set up a workshop with Fra Bartolommeo, and his earlier work is hardly distinguishable in style from that of his colleague. An *Annunciation* (1497), however, painted in collaboration with Fra Bartolommeo in the cathedral at Volterra, shows some influence of Ghirlandaio and of Leonardo in its softened outlines. In 1500 Fra Bartolommeo abandoned painting for a time to devote himself to the religious life. Albertinelli completed the *Last Judgment* Fra Bartolommeo had begun in the cloister of S. Maria Nuova. His masterpiece, *The Visitation* (1503), in the Uffizi, is notable for its spacious, balanced composition, and was greatly influenced by the oil technique of Perugino. The predella panels, representing *The Annunciation*, *The Nativity*, and *The Presentation in the Temple*, are slightly archaic and expressive of a poetic serenity. By 1505 he had fully developed his own style. From 1506 dates a *Crucifixion*, in the Certosa del Galluzzo, near Florence. Other works are in the Accademia, Pitti and S. Marco at Florence, the Accademia Carrara at Bergamo, the Poldi Pezzoli Museum at Milan, and a *Madonna and Child with the Infant St. John the Baptist*, in The Metropolitan Museum of Art at New York. Besides those mentioned, paintings closely connected with Fra Bartolommeo are *Holy Family with the Infant St. John*, Sarasota, Florida, and another on the same subject (1511), Borghese Gallery, Rome. Other paintings are at Genoa, Siena, Berlin, Munich, Cambridge (Massachusetts), Columbia (South Carolina), Detroit, and elsewhere.

Albertini (äl-ber-tē′nē), **Francesco.** Canon who, between 1506 and 1509, wrote *Opusculum de mirabilibus novae et veteris urbis Romae*, on the marvels of ancient and modern Rome. The first edition was published in 1510. In the third and final section of his work he describes the monuments of the new city of Rome: churches, chapels, pontifical palaces, the Belvedere, hospitals, libraries, new streets, squares, fountains, and bridges. He mentions frescoes of Fra Angelico, Botticelli, Perugino, Pinturicchio, and the ancient statues that have been recovered. His work is a guidebook (incomplete) to the structures erected in Rome in the 15th century. He also wrote a work on the statues and pictures of Florence (1510) and a little work on music.

Albertino da Lodi (äl-ber-tē′nō dä lō′dē). See **Piazza, Albertino.**

Alberto dalla Piacentina (äl-ber′tō däl′lä pyä-chen-tē′nä). Translator; d. at Venice, c1332. He was a notary at Florence in 1323. Some time after that date he was imprisoned at Venice and remained there the rest of his life. He occupied himself in prison by translating, in prose and terza rima, the *On the Consolation of Philosophy* of Boethius.

Alberto di Sarteano (dē sär-tyä′nō). [**Albertus Sarthianensis.**] Observantist preacher and ecclesiastical diplomat; b. 1385; d. at Milan, August 15, 1450. He joined the Observantists in 1415, having been a member of the Friars Minor earlier. He studied at Verona under the famous humanist, Guarino da Verona, and became one of the most learned members of his order. To combat the pagan influence of some humanists he became a preacher, first at Modena and then in Tuscany. In the period 1434–1439, Pope Eugenius IV took advantage of his talents and knowledge of the Greek language in his attempts to reconcile the Eastern and Western churches. Alberto went to Jerusalem and, later (1438–1439), acted as interpreter for the members of the Greek Church at Florence. When the accord that briefly united the Eastern and Western churches was adopted at the Council of Florence (1439), Alberto was sent on missions to secure the ratification of the Syrian Jacobites, the Ethiopians, and the Copts. His writings were printed at Rome (1688).

Albertus Magnus (al-bėr′tus mag′nus), Saint. [Called **Albert the Great, Doctor Universalis**; hereditary title, Count **von Bollstädt.**] German scholastic philosopher; b. at Lauingen, Swabia, c1193 (or 1205); d. at Cologne, Prussia, 1280. He was a Dominican, and taught at Paris, Cologne, Strasbourg, and elsewhere. He was noted as one of the foremost scholars of his time by Roger Bacon, his contemporary, and was named by later writers the most powerful expositor of the intellectual efforts of the 13th century. He was chiefly known for his interest in Aristotle, whose works he endeavored to free from Arabic interpolations. His pioneering efforts to reconcile the study of Aristotelian logic and philosophy with Catholic theology were excelled only by his favorite pupil, Thomas Aquinas. He was, however, without a rival in his day, preeminently successful as a teacher in interpreting and making comprehensible to his contemporaries the Aristotelian works in natural philosophy. Raised in 1260 to the bishopric of Ratisbon, he retired two years later in order to continue his teaching at Cologne. His scientific studies based on the Aristotelian method and plan were supplemented by his own observations of the animal and plant life around him, and by his visits to the mines, mineral deposits, and the laboratories of alchemists in the vicinity of his residence at Cologne. He was canonized (1932) by Pope Pius XI.

Albizzi (äl'bēt-tsē). Old, powerful, and distinguished Florentine family, originally from Arezzo, members of which played a conspicuous part in Florentine affairs from the middle of the 14th century to 1434. The Albizzi were Guelphs; one of the earliest documented members of the family was Albizo di Piero, who in 1199 swore allegiance to the Guelph League of Tuscany. After the creation of a government of the guilds (1282), the Albizzi (who had become rich in the wool trade) contributed ninety-three priors and fifteen gonfalonieri to the government of Florence. A large family, with many branches, their members held many other offices in the republic and included distinguished men of letters. As Neri, the Albizzi opposed the overweening ambition of Corso Donati early in the 14th century, and later played a part in ridding Florence of the duke of Athens (1343). In the same century they overcame their rivals, the Ricci, and became the leading faction in the government. In 1378, in the revolt of the Ciompi (woolworkers), their houses were burned by the rebellious woolworkers, who wished to end the control the Albizzi had exercised for thirty years and to win a share in the government. The Albizzi fled, but conspired to return and regain power. Piero degli Albizzi was seized near Florence and beheaded (1379). The popular government fell (1382), and the Albizzi returned from exile. Maso degli Albizzi (d. 1417), nephew of Piero, became head of the dominant party, and in 1393, by means of a *parlamento* and a *balìa*, reformed the government and banished many notable citizens, including the Alberti. Under Maso, and his son and successor Rinaldo, Florence knew its greatest power as a republic. But the power of the Albizzi party was not undisputed, despite the fact that Maso had tried to keep peace between the factions by admitting outstanding men of other parties to share in the government. Giovanni di Bicci de' Medici, noted for his moderation and generosity, had a large following among the people. His son Cosimo the Elder used this base of support, and his wealth, to overcome the Albizzi; he was exiled in 1433, but on his triumphant return the following year, banished the Albizzi and their party, thereby establishing his own party and, more importantly, his family, in power in Florence. The Albizzi, though they continued to be a prominent family (restored to Florence by Cosimo's grandson, Lorenzo il Magnifico), never regained their political influence in Florentine affairs.

Albizzi, Bartolommeo. [Latinized, **Bartholomaeus Albicius Pisanus.**] Franciscan monk and religious writer; b. at Rivano, in Tuscany; d. at Pisa, December 10, 1401. He was the author of a work comparing St. Francis with Christ, *Liber conformitatum sancti Francisci cum Christo*.

Albizzi, Rinaldo degli. Florentine statesman; b. at Florence, 1370; d. at Ancona, February 2, 1442. Of an ancient and aristocratic Florentine family, he was the son of Maso degli Albizzi, a political moderate who furnished direction and leadership to the Florentine government. The family traditionally belonged to the Guelph party. Under his father's guidance, Rinaldo was active in affairs of state from young manhood, being charged with missions and embassies of great importance to the state. When Maso died (1417), Rinaldo succeeded him as the most influential man in Florence. To secure his power, which Maso had kept by unobtrusive manipulation, Rinaldo sought to reduce the number of the lesser guilds who had civil rights. Thus he alienated a large part of the populace and turned them toward the Medici, upon whom he looked as rivals, because Giovanni di Bicci de' Medici opposed his plan. But Rinaldo, capable but arrogant and headstrong, pursued his plans. He waged war on Lucca, a war that at first had the full and enthusiastic support of the Florentines, but the war ended in failure and the capricious Florentines turned against him. He was able to cling to his control of the city by manipulation of the process by which members of the Signory were chosen. Since these members were all of the Albizzi party, he was able to secure the exile of his most prominent rival, Cosimo de' Medici (1433). His success was short-lived. His rashness, arrogance, overt scorn for the people, but principally his unsuccessful and expensive foreign policy cost him the support the Albizzi party had enjoyed under his father. A Signory favorable to the Medici was elected. Rinaldo sought to rally his supporters for a demonstration in his favor—an ancient and often-used device for overawing enemies in Florence—but Pope Eugenius IV, at that time an exile residing in Florence, offered to mediate. While negotiations dragged on, Rinaldo's supporters melted away. Cosimo de' Medici returned in triumph (1434), and Rinaldo, in his turn, was exiled. His continual attempts and intrigues, while in exile, to return to power in Florence were completely thwarted. When the Florentines, under the Medici, defeated the Milanese at Anghiari (1440), Rinaldo seemed to realize his hopes of overthrowing the Medici were dead. He went to Ancona and there, after a journey to the Holy Land, died.

Albornoz (äl-bôr′nōth), **Gil Alvarez Carillo de.** Spanish soldier and cardinal; b. at Cuenca, Spain, c1300; d. at Viterbo, August 24, 1367. He was a general in the service of Castile, was made archbishop of Toledo (1337), and cardinal (1350). A successful soldier, at the request of Pope Innocent VI he accompanied (1354) Cola di Rienzi to Rome, with the aim of restoring order in the Papal States. Rienzi was murdered at Rome in the same year, and Albornoz used force and any other means at his command to pacify the Papal States and reestablish papal authority. He was successful in securing the pope's authority in parts of the Papal States, but after his death his work was undone. He went to Bologna as papal legate and died soon after. Cardinal Albornoz commissioned the Chapel of St. Catherine of Alexandria in the Lower Church of the Basilica of San Francesco at Assisi. It was added in 1367 and decorated by Andrea da Bologna with scenes from the life of the saint, including one that has a representation of the cardinal. He was buried in the chapel, but his bones were later removed to the Cathedral of Toledo.

Albrecht von Eyb (or **Eybe**) (äl′brec̈ht fon īp′; ī′bẹ). German cleric and author, b. in Franconia, Germany, 1420; d. at Eichstätt, Germany, 1475. His witty *Ehestandsbuch* (1472) debates whether a man should marry or tarry and contains among other things the translations of two Italian stories. Likewise his posthumous *Spiegel der Sitten* (1511) was accompanied by translations of Ugolini's *Philogenia* and Plautus' *Menaechmi* and *Bacchides.* He published an anthology of Latin classics in the original called *Margarita poetica* (1472).

Albrecht von Halberstadt (fon häl′bėr-shtät). Middle High German poet; fl. c1210. He translated Ovid's *Metamorphoses* directly from the Latin.

Albuquerque (äl-bö-ker′kẹ), **Affonso de.** Portuguese navigator and colonial administrator; b. at Alhandra, Portugal, 1453; d. at sea near Goa, India, 1515. He was the founder of the Portuguese empire in the East. He made his first expedition to India in 1503–1504; his second with Tristão da Cunha in 1508. He conquered Goa (1510); Malacca and the Malabar coast (1512); Ceylon, the Sunda Islands, and Ormuz (1515). An able and beneficent colonial administrator, he gained the respect of both Hindus and Moslems.

Alcaforado (äl-kạ-fö-rä′dö), **Francisco.** Portuguese navigator. He took part in the expedition of João Gonzales Zarco to Madeira (1420), of which he wrote an account.

Alcazava Sotomayor (äl-kạ-zä′vạ sō-tö-mạ-yōr′), **Simão de.** [Also, **Alcazaba, Alcazova, Alcaçoba.**] Portuguese explorer; b. c1490; d. on the coast of Patagonia early in 1536. He was in the service of Spain as a naval officer from 1522. In 1534, at his own expense, he led an expedition to try to reach Peru via the Straits of Magellan but was driven back by a storm at the Straits. He led an expedition by land which crossed to the Andes and was the first to explore the Patagonian plateau. Obliged by sickness to return to the ship he was murdered in a mutiny.

Alciati (äl-chä′tē), **Andrea.** Legal scholar and humanist; b. at Alzate, near Como, May 8, 1492; d. at Pavia, January 11/12, 1550. He studied Greek under Andreas Lascaris and attended lectures at the University of Milan. At the age of 15 he began the study of law at Pavia, continued it at Bologna, and received his doctorate at the age of 22. Returned to Milan, he practiced law and continued the humanistic studies he loved. He won renown with his *Adnotationes,* his *Paradoxa,* and others, and was honored with an invitation to Avignon. Later, he lectured at Bourges, Pavia, Bologna, Ferrara, and Padua. He produced several literary works as a result of his classical studies but is best known for the pioneer study he made of civil law, in which he introduced humanist principles and which was based on original classical sources and was not merely a reworking of contemporary glosses. His *Emblems,* a collection of aphorisms in Latin, was later published at Padua (1661) with commentaries.

Alcina (äl-chē′nä). In Matteo Maria Boiardo's *Orlando Innamorato* and Lodovico Ariosto's *Orlando Furioso*, a fairy. She is the embodiment of carnal delights. She is described as the sister of Logistilla (Reason) and Morgana (Lasciviousness). When tired of her lovers she changes them into trees, beasts, and other objects. She is finally, by means of a magic ring, displayed in her real senility and ugliness, and her lovers regain their original shapes.

Alcionio (äl-chō′nyō), **Pietro.** [Latinized, **Petrus Alcyonius.**] Humanist and teacher; b. at Venice, 1487; d. at Rome, 1527. He was a pupil of the Cretan scholar Marcus Musurus, taught Greek at Venice, where he worked as corrector for the press of Aldus Manutius, and taught Greek at Florence under the patronage of Cardinal Giulio de' Medici. In 1524 he went to Rome, but his expectations of success there vanished when the city was sacked (1527). Alcionio took refuge in the Castel Sant' Angelo, was wounded, and died shortly thereafter. His works include Latin orations and verses, a tragedy on the death of Christ, and translations into elegant, if inexact, Latin verse, of Aristotle, Galen, and Demosthenes, among others. He also wrote *Medicis legatus, sive de exilio*, in which he attempted to prove that exile, though an evil, can be endured.

Aldegrever (äl′dẹ-grā-vėr), **Heinrich.** [Also, **Aldegraf**; original name, **Heinrich Trippenmeker**; sometimes called **Albert of Westphalia.**] German engraver and painter; b. at Paderborn, Prussia, 1502; d. at Soest, Prussia, c1562. One of a group known as the "Little Masters," he is noted for his expert and delicate engravings, influenced by the Italian Renaissance masters and by Albrecht Dürer.

Alderotti (äl-dā-rôt′tē) or **Alderotto** (-tō), **Taddeo.** Physician; b. at Florence, 1223; d. after 1270. He was one of the earliest and most reliable translators of Aristotle, and wrote one of the earliest medical works in the vernacular, *Sulla conservazione della salute*. He was also noted as a teacher. Dante cites him in the *Divina Commedia* (*Paradiso*, xii).

Aldine (âl′dēn) **Academy.** Name given to a group that began meeting in Venice (1500) for the purpose of promoting Greek studies and furthering the publication of Greek authors. The rules of the association were in Greek; members spoke Greek; and their titles within the group were Greek. Most of the members were associated in one way or another with Aldus Manutius and his project of publishing Greek texts.

Aldobrandini (äl-dō-brän-dē′nē), **Aldobrandino.** Florentine official; b. at Florence, 1388; d. there, 1453. A member of a celebrated Florentine family, he held several offices at Florence, including that of gonfaloniere; was a member of the Medicean party; and was instrumental in recalling Cosimo de' Medici from exile, 1434.

Aldobrandini, Giovanni. Florentine official; b. at Florence, 1422; d. at Sarzana, 1481. He was the son of Aldobrandino Aldobrandini and, like his father, held the office of gonfaloniere. When he turned against the Medicean party he withdrew to Sarzana, where he died.

Aldobrandini, Salvestro. Florentine jurist; b. at Florence, November 23, 1499; d. at Rome, January 6, 1558. He studied law at Pisa, took part in the rebellion against the Medici that broke out in 1527, and served briefly at that time as gonfaloniere. When the revolt was crushed he was taken prisoner but escaped. At Naples he was one of a group of Florentine exiles who addressed themselves to Charles V with a plea to free Florence. The plea was fruitless. Paul III called him to Rome (1549), where he became a consistorial advocate.

Aldobrandini, Tommaso. Man of letters; b. c1530; d. 1572. He was the son of Salvestro Aldobrandini. Scholar and writer, he made a Latin translation of Diogenes Laërtius.

Aldrovandi (äl-drō-vän′dē), **Ulisse.** [Latin, **Ulysses Aldrovandus.**] Naturalist and encyclopedist; b. at Bologna, September 11, 1522; d. there, May 4, 1605. Like Aristotle, with whom he was compared, he seemed to embrace all the knowledge that was available in his time. In addition to his work as professor of natural history at Bologna, he was deeply involved in study, research, expeditions, and the collection of a library on all subjects pertaining to natural history. With equal passion, he collected specimens of herbs, animals, minerals, fossils, etc. He was also the founder (1568) of the Bologna botanical gardens. As inspector of drugs, he published *Antidotarii Bononiensis Epitome* (1574). His chief work was an encyclopedic work on natural history. Some of the volumes, printed after his death, included those on birds, insects, and mollusks. These are profusely illustrated with his own drawings. Aldrovandi was a pioneer in his interest and approach to the study of natural history. In his enthusiasm he was not critical, and later natural historians have sometimes depreciated him on that ground. Nevertheless, he was a trailblazer in his method, which was founded on observation and experiment, to the end that the special character, properties, origin, and purpose of the creatures of the natural world should be discovered and catalogued.

Aldus Manutius (âl′dus mạ-nū′shi-us). See **Manutius, Aldus.**

Aleandro (ä-lā-än′drō), **Girolamo.** [Also, **Hieronymus Aleander.**] Humanist and ecclesiastic; b. at Motta in the March of Treviso, February 13, 1480; d. February 1, 1542. He studied theology, philosophy, science, Hebrew, Greek, and Latin; became professor of Hebrew and the humanities at the University of Paris, of which he was ultimately rector; and furthered the findings of and enthusiasm for humanistic studies in France. He arrived in Rome (1516) in the suite of a German bishop, and made a great impression on Pope Leo X. Leo appointed him (1519) librarian of the Vatican Library. As a noted man of letters he was on familiar terms with the great publisher Aldus Manutius, as well as with Erasmus of Rotterdam. From the time of his arrival in Rome he was engaged in the service of the Church. He made several journeys to Germany in an attempt to suppress Lutheranism. Failing that, he was one of the principal architects of the political phases of the Counter-Reformation and active in persecution of the Protestants. As a diplomat for the Church he succeeded in having Luther condemned at the Diet of Worms (1521). As papal nuncio to the court of France he was with Francis I at the battle of Pavia (1525) and was taken prisoner with him. On his release he returned to Rome and was there when it was sacked (1527). Paul III created him cardinal in 1538. Some manuscripts of his own Latin and Greek writings are preserved in the Vatican. His rich personal library, left to San Giorgio in Alga, at Venice, was destroyed by fire (1716).

Alençon (då-läṅ-sôṅ′), **Charles IV,** Duc **d'.** Prince of the blood and constable of France; b. 1489; d. April 11, 1525. He was the husband of Margaret of Valois, sister of Francis I. His cowardice is said to have caused the loss of the battle of Pavia (1525) and the capture of Francis I.

Aleni (ä-lā′nē), **Tommaso.** [Also, **De Alenis, Tomaso;** called **il Fadino.**] Painter of Cremona; active between 1500 and 1515. He was a very dear friend of the Cremonese painter Galeazzo Campi, and painted so much like him, according to Galeazzo's son, that the works of one could not be distinguished from those of the other. In 1505 he signed a contract for the decoration of a chapel in the Church of S. Domenico at Cremona, and in 1509 took part in the contest for decoration in the cathedral. Three works can be definitely ascribed to Aleni: *Madonna and Child with SS. Anthony of Padua and Francis,* signed and dated (1500), Museo Civico, Cremona; *Nativity,* signed and dated (1515), Cremona; and a *Madonna,* London. These works reveal Aleni as a modest provincial painter, trained in the local Cremonese school, who was a follower of Boccaccino, although he failed to attain that master's elegance and delicacy. He was also deeply impressed, as were other Cremonese painters, by the grace and spirit of Perugino.

Alessandri (ä-les-sän′drē), **Alessandro.** Humanist and jurist; b. at Naples, c1461; d. 1523. He studied under Francesco Filelfo at Rome, where he was introduced to humanistic methods and objectives. His chief interest was the law. His work, *Genialium dierum,* is an early effort to restore the Twelve Tables of Roman law to their original meaning and language, shorn of medieval interpretations and glosses.

Alessandri, Alessandro degli. Florentine humanist and statesman; b. 1391; d. 1460. He was a student of the humanities under Roberto de' Rossi, Cosimo de' Medici's teacher, and was noted for his humanistic culture. Matteo Palmieri dedicated his dialogue *Della vita civile* (1439) to him because of his interest in the liberal arts. Alessandri served Florence in the Signory and as gonfaloniere of justice, and on many missions and councils. Prominent and able in public life, he was knighted by the emperor in 1452 when Frederick III made his progress through Italy to Rome to be crowned, selling all sorts of benefits and titles as he passed.

Alessandri, Antonio. Jurisconsult; b. at Naples, c1420; d. October 26, 1498 or 1499. He was a professor in the university at Naples, a noted lawyer, and the king's agent on political missions. His writings include those on Neopolitan practices, commentaries, and a treatise on inheritance when there is no will.

Alessi (ä-les'sē), **Galeazzo.** Architect; b. at Perugia, c1512; d. 1572. He was the builder of the Church of Santa Maria di Carignano at Genoa, and of churches and palaces at Genoa and elsewhere.

Alexander IV (al-eg-zan'dėr). [Original name, **Rinaldo,** Conte **di Segni.**] Pope (1254–1261); b. at Anagni; d. at Viterbo, 1261. He was the successor of Innocent IV and was the nephew of Gregory IX. He established the Inquisition in France and encouraged mendicant friars, especially the Franciscans. He engaged in a long struggle with the Hohenstaufen family, especially Manfred, Ghibelline leader and king (1258) of Naples and Sicily, whose influence in Rome gave rise to factional struggles. The disturbances in Rome were so violent that Alexander withdrew to the fortified city of Viterbo, where he spent the last years of his pontificate. He was succeeded by Urban IV.

Alexander V. [Original name, **Petros Philargos;** called **Pietro di Candia.**] Antipope (1409–1410); b. at Candia, Crete, c1339; d. at Bologna, 1410. He was elected by the Council of Pisa (1409) on a basis of his efforts, as cardinal (1405–1410) under Innocent VII, to reconcile the Great Schism. The Council deposed Pope Gregory XII and the antipope Benedict XIII, but since neither recognized its authority, with the elevation of Alexander there were three who claimed to be pope. Alexander was prevented from reaching Rome and died at the castle of Baldassare Cossa, who succeeded him as John XXIII and who was accused, though without proof, of having poisoned him.

Alexander VI. [Original name, **Rodrigo Lanzol y Borja** (Italianized to **Borgia**).] Pope (1492–1503; b. at Játiva (Xátiva), Valencia, Spain, c1431; d. at Rome, August 18, 1503. Licentious, accused in his own and later days of the most depraved crimes, to say nothing of the genial crimes of murder by the dagger and what was thought to be a mysterious and slow-acting poison (arsenic); excessively devoted to his children, whom he recognized by papal bulls, and apparently completely under the influence of his sinister son Cesare; abstemious, yet surrounded by the most ostentatious splendor Rome had yet seen; a munificent patron of the arts and letters and, at the same time, frankly delighted by the most vulgar and lewd entertainments, Alexander has come to symbolize the depths of corruption and degradation to which the papacy sank as the Renaissance neared its peak. Of a noble family of Valencia, his mother was the sister of Alonso de Borja. Rodrigo went to Italy, probably about 1449, where his ecclesiastical career was greatly advanced by his uncle. On the latter's elevation as Pope Calixtus III (1455), Rodrigo's rise in the Church accelerated. He studied canon law at Bologna, was made apostolic protonotary (May, 1455), cardinal (February, 1456), and given the lucrative and powerful office of vice-chancellor of the Church (May, 1457), a position he continued to hold until he was elected pope. He survived the outbursts against the "Catalans" following the death of Calixtus (August 6, 1458), continued to heap up rich benefices, and became one of the wealthiest princes of the Church. He served Sixtus IV as legate in Spain to promote a crusade (1472–1473), and while there was influential in promoting the union of the kingdoms of Castile and Aragon. His experience as vice-chancellor and legate gave him a wide knowledge of political negotiations, diplomacy, and the business of the Church. Further, it was said that he "thoroughly understood money matters." On the death of Innocent VIII he was elected pope (August 10, 1492) through the influence of Cardinal Ascanio Sforza (whose vote he bought), through simony, bribery, and promises of more to come to other cardinals.

In the pontificate of the weak and indolent Innocent VIII, not law, justice, nor order prevailed; Rome was a prey to robbery in the streets, assassinations, and the incessant warfare of rival Roman barons. The condition of the States of the Church was chaotic. The election of the experienced and vigorous Cardinal Rodrigo Borgia as Alexander VI was hailed with extraordinary enthusiasm at Rome. (King Ferrante of Naples, however, was pessimistic. According to Guicciardini, he "told his wife with tears—which he was unaccustomed to shed even at the death of his children—that a pope had been elected who would be fatal to Italy and the whole Christian world: truly a prophecy not unworthy of the wisdom of Ferdinand.") Cardinal Borgia was accounted by some a handsome man, serene, wonderfully agreeable, "of a joyful countenance and of cheerful aspect, of beautiful and mellifluous speech." He was also a passionate and sensuous man and made no attempt to conceal his licentious life. His virile sensuality attracted women to him at once. At the time he became pope he flaunted as his mistress one of the most beautiful young women of Rome: Giulia Farnese, "la bella," of whose marriage contract to the Roman noble Orsino Orsini, as Cardinal Rodrigo Borgia he had been a witness. At the same time, he was maintaining his former mistress of long standing, Vannozza Cattanei, who was the mother of four of his children: Giovanni (Juan) (b. 1474 or 1476), assassinated 1498; Cesare (b. 1475 or 1476); Lucrezia (b. 1480); and Goffredo (Jofré) (b. 1481). There was an older son, Pedro Luis, the first duke of Gandia, and two other children by an unknown mistress; and Giulia Farnese bore him a daughter, Laura, soon after he became pope. (Subsequently, there were two other children: Giovanni and Rodrigo.) These facts were known of the man whose election as pope was so deliriously welcomed. Regardless of his personal life, it was hoped that his shrewd intelligence, diplomatic experience, and personal vigor would bring justice to the city of Rome, zeal for war against the Turks, and perhaps even reform to the Church. (As to the war against the Turks, one of the most cynical maneuvers of his reign concerned Prince Djem, brother of Bajazet II, sultan of Turkey. This prince, inherited from Innocent VIII, was held in custody by the pope in return for a payment of 40,000 ducats annually from the sultan. The latter, against whom Djem had rebelled, was willing to pay to keep Djem in captivity but would have preferred to pay a ransom for his corpse, and entered into negotiations with Alexander on the matter, offering to pay the pope 300,000 ducats for the delivery of Djem's body. In the French invasion of 1494 Alexander released Djem to Charles VIII for a large payment and a guarantee of his return at the end of six months. Djem, in the custody of Charles, died near Naples in 1495. The French were not accused of causing his death. It was thought to have been caused by the famous slow-acting poison the pope was accused of administering on a number of occasions. A contemporary witness, however, Johann Burchard, attributed his death to the prince's unbridled appetite.)

The new pope's first acts were encouraging. Order was restored in Rome and salaries were paid on time. Thereafter, his pontificate was shaped to a large degree by his love for his children (nor did he hesitate to use them in pursuit of his policy). He loaded them with honors and gave them vast sums of money, at the expense of the Church and through seizure of estates and property. His nepotism was unrestrained. Swarms of Borgias came to Rome and were given ecclesiastical and secular posts of great honor and importance; in the course of his pontificate he created a number of Borgia cardinals. In political affairs he was uncertain and equivocal. Indebted for his election to Cardinal Ascanio Sforza; suspicious of Cardinal Giuliano della Rovere, the chief opponent of his election; annoyed with Ferrante of Naples and Piero de' Medici because they had supported Franceschetto Cibo (Innocent VIII's son) in his wish to sell some minor castles in Cervetri and Anguillara (castles Alexander planned to give to his son Giovanni) to Virginio Orsini, a supporter of Ferrante and Cardinal Giuliano della Rovere; he negotiated with Milan, and in April, 1493, concluded a league with Milan and Venice. To cement his friendship with Milan he married his daughter Lucrezia (June, 1493) to Giovanni Sforza, lord of Pesaro, having annulled her previous marriage by proxy to a Spanish nobleman. But by August of the same year he had patched up his differences with Ferrante, the Orsini, and Della Rovere, and married his son Goffredo to Sancia, the granddaughter of Ferrante. In September of the same year he swung back to the Sforza, as he needed the assistance of Cardinal Ascanio to create new cardinals (September 20, 1493), among whom were his son Cesare, Ippolito d'Este, and Alessandro Farnese (the future Paul III, brother of Giulia). He tried to win both Ferrante and Ludovico Sforza by proposing that the Italian states combine to oppose the French (with whom Ludovico had already been secretly negotiating), but this proposal came to nothing. When Charles VIII actually invaded Italy, Alexander allied himself with Alfonso II of Naples, Ferrante's son and successor, but was ineffective in action. He neither defended nor aided Giovanni Bentivoglio, lord of Bologna, who dominated one of the invasion routes, nor Piero de' Medici of Florence, who had changed the traditional Florentine friendship for France to win an alliance with Naples. With Ostia occupied by his enemies the Colonnesi, with the Orsini rising against him at Rome, Alexander opened the gates of the city to the French army (December 27, 1494), having himself sought refuge in Castel Sant' Angelo, and was thereafter compelled to yield to the terms set by Charles. The latter went on to conquer Naples. The Spanish, the emperor Maximilian I, and the Italian states were thoroughly alarmed by the ease with which Charles had marched through Italy, and now formed a league to prevent him from escaping with his army from Italy. At the battle of Fornovo (July 6, 1495) the troops of the league, under the command of Francesco, marquess of Mantua, claimed a victory, but it was a hollow one, since the French army escaped almost intact. Following the temporary disappearance of French power in Italy, Alexander decided to crush the Roman barons. He seized some of their castles but was forced to restore them following the defeat of the papal armies, commanded by his son Goffredo, near Soriano (January 25, 1497). The pontificate itself was in danger. On the night of June 14, 1497, his adored son Giovanni disappeared. A few days later his body, pierced by nine dagger thrusts, was hauled from the Tiber. Alexander was frantic with grief; an intensive investigation was begun, and then abruptly halted. Cesare was held responsible for the murder of his brother and for so frightening his father that the investigation was called off. In the same year, Alexander decided it was no longer profitable to be allied to Milan and the Sforza family. He wished instead to strengthen his ties with the Aragonese of Naples. To this end he unblushingly annulled Lucrezia's marriage to Giovanni Sforza, on the grounds of Giovanni's impotence, and married her (July, 1498) to Alfonso, duke of Bisceglie, an illegitimate son of Alfonso II of Naples. Gossip about his own licentious behavior and that of the cardinals provoked cynicism and unrest in Rome. The prevalence of Spaniards about him and the power they wielded infuriated the people. The Colonnesi and the Orsini, traditional enemies, temporarily buried their differences to unite against him. At Florence, Girolamo Savonarola thundered against the iniquities of Italy and especially against Rome, the fountainhead of all corruption, and called for a General Council. Alexander could not silence him, but the pope's desire to muzzle Savonarola led the latter's Florentine enemies to seize him and burn him at the stake at Florence (May 23, 1498).

The next five years of Alexander's reign are chiefly marked by the deeds of his son Cesare, a man of iron will and utter ruthlessness who seemed to hold his father in the hollow of his hand. Cesare requested (August, 1498) to be relieved of the dignity of the cardinalate. This freed him for the political and military role he envisioned for himself. His aim, which became that of his father, was to win a state for himself in the Romagna and the Marches. The pretext on which he proposed to wage war was that princelings in those areas had not fulfilled their duties to the Church, of which they were vassals. (His subsequent conquests did prepare the way for the inclusion of these areas in the territories of the Church.) Alexander thought he had an ally in Louis XII, the new king of France, because Louis wanted to divorce his wife and marry his predecessor's widow, Anne of Brittany (for her lands), and needed a dispensation from the pope to do so. Louis promised to forward Cesare's plans, named him duke of Valentinois, and promised him a French bride. Cesare himself carried the papal dispensation to France (October, 1498) and was married there the next year. Papal negotiations with the French aroused fear and suspicion among the Spaniards, who did not wish to see Spanish interests (as the kingdom of Naples) subordinated to the ambitions of the French king. Alexander himself, by tradition and inclination, would have been more comfortable with friendly relations with the Spanish. Any hope he may have had of attaining these was shattered by the assassination of Lucrezia's handsome young husband, the Neapolitan Alfonso, duke of Bisceglie (August 18, 1500). Cesare was responsible for the murder, and his motive was apparently to sever the alliance with Naples in order to strengthen that with France. Already named vicar of the Romagna by his father, he was made duke of Romagna (May, 1501), and began his sweep over the area. The vast amounts of money he needed were supplied by the pope. Alexander created new offices and sold them. He sold other offices as they became vacant, a process he frequently hastened by preferring charges against wealthy prelates, nobles, or officials, imprisoning them, and confiscating their estates. The unfortunates so charged usually died in prison. He created new cardinals who bought their dignities for huge sums, then seized the goods (money, plate, furnishings) of churchmen who died. So many wealthy cardinals died that many Romans believed they were poisoned for their money, and perhaps two or three were. The French again invaded Naples (1501), and Alexander took advantage of the confusion to march against the Colonnesi. He left his daughter in charge of the Holy See during his absence, nor was this the first time the world had been treated to the spectacle of the bastard daughter of the pope in charge of the affairs of the Church. The estates of the Colonna and Savelli were confiscated and given to various members of the Borgia family. Lucrezia was married, for the third time, to Alfonso d'Este, heir to the duchy of Ferrara (January, 1502) to assure Ferrarese acquiescence in Cesare's conquest of the Romagna. In the meantime, Cesare had taken Imola (November, 1499) and Forlì (January, 1500). He went on to take the duchy of Urbino (1502), the fiefs of Camerino (1502), and other states. There seemed no limit to his ambitions, but despite Machiavelli's portrayal, it is doubtful that they extended to creation of an Italian monarchy. In July, 1503, Cesare was preparing another expedition into central Italy, when suddenly the pope died. Cesare was ill at the same time, and poison was rumored, but the death of the pope was later ascribed to malaria and apoplexy, and Cesare's illness to malaria, which was particularly virulent at Rome that summer.

To his contemporaries Alexander was a somewhat inept politician, dangerous because he was endowed with enormous spiritual and temporal power. Machiavelli wrote of him, "More than any other pontiff . . . , he showed the extent to which a pope's power could prevail through money and force." His activities as a spiritual leader included protection of the religious orders and missions, defense of the privileges of the Church, war against heretics, and the establishment of ecclesiastical censorship. On May 4, 1493, he settled the dispute between the Spanish and the Portuguese by publishing a bull that divided the New World between them. (The next year the line was moved, so that Brazil fell into the Portuguese sector.) A secular ruler, his most urgent motivation was aggrandizement of his family. Rome was treated to spectacles of unparalleled splendor in the form of processions and festivals, and at the same time to the spectacle of the pope's own immoral life, his predilection for hunting, the dance, and orgies in the Vatican. A man of the Renaissance, he was a lover of culture, and favored such famous humanists as Julius Pomponius Laetus, Johannes Lascaris, Adriano di Corneto, and others. A great patron of the arts and architecture, under him the building of the Via Alessandrina (Borgo Nuovo) was completed; Antonio da Sangallo strengthened Castel Sant' Angelo; Giuliano da Sangallo rebuilt the roof of S. Maria Maggiore (adorned, it was said, with gold from America); the loggia for the papal blessing was completed. Bramante, Michelangelo, and Perugino worked at Rome in his reign. An outstanding artistic contribution was the decoration of the Borgia apartments in the Vatican. The frescoes Pinturicchio painted there were on sacred and pagan subjects. Of the latter one is the worship of the bull Apis (the Borgia arms included a bull on a red shield; the Borgia bull appeared in so many decorations about the Vatican and Rome that it became the subject of some wicked epigrams); others in the series of frescoes include what are presumed to be portraits of members of the Borgia family, as in the *Dispute of St. Catherine*, in which the saint is supposedly represented by a portrait of Lucrezia. A *Resurrection* shows Alexander kneeling before the risen Christ.

The facts of Alexander's private life were scandalous enough, but rumors about it combined licentiousness with criminality and depravity. He and his family came to be intensely hated. Many Europeans who came to the jubilee of 1500 (by which he garnered much revenue) went away with a shocked awareness of what was going on at Rome.

The history of his reign and of his family is crisscrossed with streaks of infamy. He has been accounted an able administrator, which seems a puzzling estimate, since he left the finances of the Church in complete disorder, the States of the Church in disarray, the spiritual influence of the papacy appallingly weakened, and the papacy itself in dishonor. Although he was not the first pope, nor yet the last, to degrade his great office, in his reign so many evils were combined that he has come to represent the epitome of corruption and wickedness. He was succeeded by Pius III.

Alfani (äl-fä′nē), **Domenico.** Painter; b. at Perugia, c1480; d. after 1553. He was the son of Paride di Pandaro, a goldsmith of Perugia, and was enrolled in the Painters' Guild at Perugia in 1510. From 1508, when he performed various services for Raphael at Perugia, he was the follower, collaborator, and friend of the master from Urbino. Raphael had the greatest influence on his development as a painter, and to his influence was added that of the Florentines, to whom he was closer in spirit than to the school of Perugino in his native city. At Perugia he was active in civic affairs and was twice chamberlain of his guild. His early association with Raphael as a painter began when he painted *The Eternal Father* in the finial of the *Deposition* that Raphael painted for Atalanta Baglioni (now in the Borghese Gallery, Rome). He left a number of works in Perugia and the neighboring towns. A *Holy Family* and a *Madonna* (1518), in the National Gallery of Umbria at Perugia, were painted to designs by Raphael or were inspired by him, as was another *Madonna* (1521) in the Cathedral of Città della Pieve. His masterpiece is an altarpiece, *Madonna and Child, with Angels and Saints* (1524) in the National Gallery at Perugia. It is notable for its rich tones and spacious composition. From 1527, when Rosso Fiorentino came to Perugia, he was closely associated with that painter, and executed some paintings to his designs. Domenico had two sons, Orazio and Cesare, whom he legitimized in 1520. (He married their mother in 1536.) Orazio was his pupil and assistant, and worked with him on frescoes for the churches of S. Pietro (1547) and S. Francesco (1553) at Perugia. In his later years, Domenico's style changed somewhat; his palette lost some of its warmth and his draftsmanship took on some of the exaggerations of Michelangelo.

Alfani, Gianni. Florentine lyric poet; b. at Florence between 1272 and 1283; d. c1320. He was a younger contemporary of Dante, held public office in Florence, and was declared a rebel by Henry VII. Alfani was a follower of Dante and, especially, of Guido Cavalcanti, to whom he dedicated a sonnet. He wrote in the manner that Dante characterized (*Purgatorio*, XXIV) as *il dolce stil nuovo*. A few of his ballate are extant.

Alfani, Giovanni Battista. Perugian jurisconsult and professor of law in the university, who wrote (1446) a treatise, in thirteen books, on legal decisions and agreements, *De arbitris et compromissis*.

Alfani, Orazio. Painter, worker in stucco, and architect; b. at Perugia, c1510; d. at Rome, December, 1583. He was an illegitimate son of Domenico Alfani and, with his brother Cesare, was legitimized in 1520. He worked in Sicily (1539–1544), where he agreed to paint a tabernacle and a marble tomb for the Church of the Annunziata at Trapani, executed decorations in stucco for the cathedral at Palermo, and carried out other commissions. In 1545 he returned to Perugia, where he took an active part in the civic life of the city, served his guild in various positions, and founded (1573) an academy. He was for a time public architect of Perugia. With other artists he painted a number of frescoes, now lost, for various churches at Perugia. The pupil and collaborator of his father, he was later influenced by Raffaellino del Colle and Parmigianino. Several of his works, including a *Deposition, Madonna and Child, Rest on the Flight into Egypt*, and *Holy Family*, are in the National Gallery of Umbria at Perugia.

Alfonso (äl-fôn′sō). Duke of Bisceglie; b. c1481; slain at Rome, August 18, 1500. He was the natural son of Alfonso II of Naples. Called by some "the most beautiful youth in Italy," at the age of 17 he was married to Lucrezia Borgia (July 21, 1498). The marriage, to affirm the friendship between Alexander VI, Lucrezia's father, and the Aragonese house of Naples, became a liability two years later, when the pope's policy changed to suit the ambitions of his son Cesare. Alfonso fled from Rome for his life as the new policy began to take shape. On Alexander's order, Lucrezia persuaded her young husband, whom she seems to have loved, to join her and the pope at Nepi, from which they all returned to Rome in the autumn of 1499. The following year (July 15, 1500) the young duke was set upon by bravoes at the gate of St. Peter at Rome. Gravely wounded, he managed to reach the Vatican, where he was tenderly cared for by his wife. On August 18, 1500, ruffians invaded his room in the Vatican and strangled him in his bed. Cesare was generally held responsible for the murder, and no investigation was made. It was said by some that Cesare murdered the duke because the latter had first tried to kill him: as Cesare was walking in the courtyard the duke, so it was said, shot at him from the window of his room in the Vatican—but this was after the first attack on the duke had taken place.

Alfonso I (of *Sicily* and *Sardinia* and of *Naples*). [Called **Alfonso the Magnanimous;** also, **Alfonso V** (of *Aragon*).] King of Sicily and Sardinia and of Naples, and as Alfonso V, king of Aragon; b. 1396; d. at Naples, June 27, 1458. He was the son of Ferdinand I of Aragon (Ferdinand the Just), whom he succeeded in 1416 as king of Aragon and of Sicily and Sardinia. In 1420 Joanna II of Naples adopted him as her heir and eventual successor to the throne of Naples. He quarreled with her, was compelled to leave Naples, and Joanna disinherited him (1423) and named Louis III of Anjou as her heir. When Louis died she named his brother René as her successor. On the death of Joanna (1435), Alfonso attempted to claim the throne of Naples. Hostilities broke out with the Italian states and the papacy, which favored the Angevin claim. Later in the same year, Alfonso was taken prisoner by the Genoese acting for Filippo Maria Visconti of Milan. Alfonso persuaded Filippo Maria that it was more to the interest of Milan to have the Aragonese in control of Naples rather than the French. Filippo Maria treated him well, released him without ransom, and made a treaty with him. It was not until 1442 that Alfonso defeated René and his allies and took possession of Naples. He marched into the city in February, 1443, with all the splendor of an ancient triumphal procession, having caused a breach to be made in the walls so that his gilded chariot could pass through. Scenes of the procession were sculptured on the triumphal arch that was erected at the Castel Nuovo in Naples. In the struggle between Pope Eugenius IV and the Council of Basel, Alfonso favored now one side, now the other, in an attempt to force the pope to recognize him as the rightful king of Naples. He reached (1443) an agreement with the pope by which Eugenius invested him with the kingdom of Naples and later (1444) recognized Alfonso's illegitimate son, the capable but cruel Ferrante, as heir to the throne. In return, Alfonso supported Eugenius against the Council. Having turned over his Spanish domains to his brother, Alfonso devoted himself to Italy, and played an active and devious role in its affairs. Fearless himself, he never hesitated to send his armies where he thought they would do him the most good. He was an uncertain ally of the popes, one of whom, Calixtus III, his former friend and counselor, was elected through his influence. Alfonso refused to sign the Peace of Lodi (1454), reserving the right to war on Sigismondo Malatesta, who had betrayed him. In 1447, on the death of Filippo Maria Visconti, Alfonso claimed Milan under a will that had allegedly been executed by Filippo Maria. In pursuit of his claim he became involved in war, and frightened Pope Nicholas V lest he win control of northern Italy as he had won control of the south. Francesco Sforza was victorious in the war, however, and ended Alfonso's pretensions in that area.

Alfonso was an ardent lover of antiquity, and a generous patron of the arts, artists and scholars; Poggio received 500 gold pieces for his translation of Xenophon's *Cyropædia*. Gianozzo Manetti, who had been ambassador from Florence, was invited to his court, received a large competence, and was made a member of Alfonso's council. Alfonso did not require him to attend the court, however, saying it was enough just to know such a learned man was attached to it. Antonio Panormita, Alfonso's biographer, and Lorenzo Valla also enjoyed his patronage. It is said that he set aside 20,000 florins a year for the support of the scholars and artists at his court. In testimony of his love of the classics, he carried them with him everywhere, even on his campaigns, and had some passages from Livy, his favorite, or Seneca read to him every day. The readings at the court were attended by the gentlemen of his brilliant court, and those in the field by the gentlemen of the army. He was deeply religious, heard Mass three times a day and had passages from the Bible read to him daily, so that by the time of his death he knew much of it by heart. He was a great collector of relics. Like many of his day, he delighted in pageantry, and produced magnificent spectacles whenever the occasion provided an excuse. When Frederick III visited Naples (1452), Alfonso spent 150,000 florins on the entertainment. Fountains spouting wine were set up everywhere, and as Vespasiano notes, "the Germans took their due share." Such extravagance kept Alfonso in continual need of money, and he resorted to any and all means to raise it. Thus, though he had removed some burdens from his harried subjects he was compelled to levy others. Despot though he was, Alfonso was mild and magnanimous to his enemies, courteous and modest, affable, and one who delighted to puncture any inflated egos that might be about him, especially if they happened to be Sienese egos, for he considered that the Sienese had betrayed him by making a separate peace in one of his many wars. Vespasiano cites many incidents to illustrate his piety, his boundless generosity, and his mercy and kindness to the poor and unfortunate. Such incidents, however, affected a very small percentage of the totality of his subjects. He left the kingdom of Naples to his illegitimate son Ferrante and his Spanish possessions and Sicily and Sardinia to his brother John. It is said that when he was on his deathbed Alfonso advised Ferrante never to go back to Spain, where he was detested, to make friends with the Italians and put them in high positions (his own custom of elevating the Catalans had kept the Italian barons in a constant state of rebellion), and to keep on friendly terms with the papacy, for he realized that all his wars had crushed his subjects and accomplished little.

Alfonso II (of *Aragon*). King of Naples (1494–January 23, 1495); b. at Naples, November 4, 1448; d. at Messina, December 18, 1495. He was the son of Ferrante of Aragon and Isabella di Chiaramonte, and as the eldest son became duke of Calabria when his father ascended the throne of Naples (1458). He began his military career at the age of 14 and fought in all his father's wars, beginning with that in which Ferrante secured his throne by the suppression of his own rebellious barons and the expulsion from Italy of the Angevin claimants to the throne. As gonfaloniere of the Church he waged war on Florence following the Pazzi conspiracy. He drove the Turks from Otranto (1481), or was given credit for so doing (the Turks withdrew as a consequence of the death of the Sultan Mohammed II rather than as a consequence of Italian military expertise), next taking part in the war against Venice and the pope in defense of Ferrara (1482–1484). In military matters he had a great reputation. His activities in the political arena, which he shared with his father after 1484, were disastrous. He made an enemy of Innocent VIII, and on his return to Naples caused the smoldering resentment of the barons to burst into flame by his arrogance and gratuitous cruelty. The famous conspiracy of the barons erupted (1485) into war. They were crushed without mercy; many of them, promised amnesty, were betrayed, seized, and murdered. The hatred universally felt for Alfonso was among the reasons that the kingdom eventually fell to the French. For reasons of state he had married (1465) Ippolita Sforza, the cultivated daughter of Francesco Sforza, duke of Milan. Their daughter, Isabella, was married to Gian Galeazzo Sforza, duke of Milan, but he was under the domination of his uncle, Ludovico il Moro. Isabella, an energetic and intelligent young woman, constantly complained to her father of the humiliation she and her husband, rightful rulers of Milan, suffered at the court of Ludovico. Alfonso, in his turn, as constantly urged his father to restore his son-in-law to his rightful place. Fear on the part of Ludovico il Moro that Ferrante might make an attempt to do so led Ludovico to open negotiations with the French, with the suggestion that they take up their old claim to the kingdom of Naples and conquer it. Ferrante died (January 25, 1494) and Alfonso became king. To win cooperation in opposing Charles VIII, now preparing his descent into Italy, Alfonso approached the Orsini, Pope Alexander VI (who in a show of defiance of the French had crowned him at Rome), and the Florentines. The general agreement they reached was not supported by any action. Alfonso sent his son, Ferrantino, and his brother, Federigo, against Charles VIII, but they were defeated and forced to fall back on Naples. Alfonso, aware of the hatred of him on the part of his subjects, abdicated in favor of his son Ferrantino (Ferdinando II) (January 23, 1495) in the hope that the affection the Neapolitans felt for Ferrantino would inspire them to resist the French. Alfonso withdrew to Mazzara in Sicily, entered a monastic order, and died the same year at Messina, haunted, it was said, by the ghosts of those he had murdered or starved to death.

Alfonso III (of *Aragon*). [Also, **Alphonso** and **Alonzo.**] King of Aragon (1285–1291); b. 1265; d. June 18, 1291. He was succeeded by his brother James II.

Alfonso IV (of *Aragon*). [Also, **Alphonso** and **Alonzo.**] King of Aragon (1327–1336); b. 1299; d. 1336. He succeeded his father, James II, on the throne of Aragon, and passed his reign in war with the Genoese over possession of Corsica and Sardinia. The islands had been given to his father by the pope in return for surrendering a claim to Sicily. He was succeeded by his son Pedro IV.

Alfonso V. Hereditary king of Aragon and of Sicily and Sardinia; king by conquest of Naples. See **Alfonso I** of *Sicily* and *Sardinia* and of *Naples*.

Alfonso V (of *Portugal*). [Also, **Affonso, Alphonso;** called **Alfonso the African.**] King of Portugal (1438–1481); b. at Cintra (now Sintra), Portugal, January 15, 1432; d. there, August 28, 1481. He was the son of King Duarte of Portugal. His father died while he was still an infant. His uncle, Dom Pedro, assumed the regency while Alfonso was still under age, and was made to relinquish it only as a result of civil war; Dom Pedro was killed in the war (1449). Alfonso defeated the Moors in Africa in 1458 and 1471, whence his epithet "the African." His marriage to Juana la Beltraneja of Castile led Alfonso to attempt the annexation of Castile to his throne. In pursuit of such an annexation, he engaged in a war with Ferdinand the Catholic in which he was disastrously defeated at Toro, and Castile submitted to Ferdinand (1479).

Alfonso y Castro (ē käs′trō). See **Castro, Alfonso y.**

Alghisi (äl-gē′sē), **Galasso.** Military engineer and architect; b. at Carpi; d. at Ferrara, 1573. From 1549 to 1558 he was working at Rome, perhaps on the Farnese Palace and then, with others, on the fortifications of the city for Pope Paul III. In 1549 he worked on the Sanctuary at Loreto, and in 1550 was at Macerata, where he began the Church of S. Maria delle Vergini, a great building on a central plan, with an octagonal dome, that shows the influence of Bramante. It was completed in 1587. After 1558 he was most often at Ferrara, where he carried out commissions for Alfonso II d'Este, including the campanile of the Certosa, the Loggiato dei Camerino for the ducal palace, and a theater. He left a work, *Delle Fortificationi* (Venice, 1570), in which he speaks, among other things, of his work at Rome on what is presumed to be the Farnese Palace.

Alibrandi (ä-lē-brän′dē), **Girolamo.** Painter; b. at Messina, between 1470 and 1480; d. c1524. He is thought to have traveled to northern Italy where he fell under the influence of Giorgione at Venice, of Leonardo and Cesare da Sesto at Milan, and of Raphael, as well as the Ferrarese school. His *Purification* in the museum at Messina betrays the Venetian influence, while his best work, *The Presentation in the Temple* (1519), also in the museum, clearly shows the influence of Leonardo and Raphael. It is because of the elements reminiscent of Raphael in his work that he was called "the Raphael of Messina" by local writers. In general an eclectic, pervasive in his work is also the influence of Antonello da Messina.

Alidosi (ä-lē-dō′sē), **Francesco.** Cardinal; b. at Castel del Rio, between 1450 and 1460; d. at Ravenna, May 24, 1511. While still a youth he was sent to Rome, where he was received in the household of Pope Sixtus IV. The handsome, gentle, and gifted youth became secretary and warm friend of Cardinal Giuliano della Rovere. The intimacy between the youth and the cardinal, possibly based on their common enthusiasm for the arts and letters, gave rise to much gossip. Alidosi remained at Rome when Rodrigo Borgia became Pope Alexander VI, but on being solicited by Alexander to poison Cardinal Giuliano, Alidosi warned the cardinal. The latter fled to France. Alidosi joined him there and remained with him in his exile. When Cardinal Giuliano succeeded as Pope Julius II (1503) he showered his younger friend and protégé with benefices, named him bishop of Miletus and treasurer general and, over the opposition of the cardinals, elevated him to the Sacred College on the death of Cardinal Ascanio Sforza (1505). In May, 1508, Julius named him legate of Bologna, which the papal armies had won back for the Church. The cardinal was met by the deep hostility of the partisans of the Bentivoglio, the ruling family that had been expelled by Julius. Julius provided him with arms and provisions, and named him legate of the Romagna and the Marches. After the defeat of the Venetians at Agnadello (May, 1509), other cities, including Ravenna, fell under his control. But the situation of Alidosi vis-à-vis the Bolognese worsened. He was hated for the cruelty with which he suppressed the friends of the Bentivoglio, and for the crushing tribute that he levied to support papal policy. In the military strategy that he developed for the papal forces Francesco Maria della Rovere, duke of Urbino and nephew of Julius, suspected him of treating with the enemy. He took Alidosi prisoner at Modena (October, 1510) and sent him under guard to Bologna. Julius freed him immediately. In July, 1511, Bologna threw off the papal yoke. The duke of Urbino, whose forces had been unable to defend the city, possibly because of his excessive caution, blamed the loss of the city on Alidosi. The pope was loyal to Alidosi and when the duke sought an interview with his uncle he was coldly received. On leaving the pope's presence he met Alidosi, pulled him from his mule, and mortally wounded him. Alidosi, known as the Cardinal of Pavia, was a highly cultivated man, well versed in the humanistic studies of the time, a friend and patron of men of letters and artists. A friend of Michelangelo, he sometimes acted as intermediary between the sculptor and the often choleric pope. He was an admirer of Bramante, and entertained Erasmus when he visited Italy. A portrait of the cardinal, attributed to Raphael, is in the Prado at Madrid. A beautifully worked bronze medal, by a medalist of the school of Francia, is in the Brera at Milan.

Alighieri (ä-lē-gyā′rē), **Dante.** Full name of **Dante.**

Alighieri, Jacopo. Son of Dante; b. at Florence; d. there, 1348? He held a benefice at Verona, but returned to Florence after his father's death released him from the ban of exile, and continued to live at Florence. He wrote a superficial commentary on his father's *Divina Commedia.*

Alighieri, Pietro. Son of Dante; b. at Florence; d. at Treviso, April 21, 1364. He returned to Florence briefly, after his father's death removed the ban of exile, then studied civil law at Bologna and acted as a judge at Verona, Vicenza, and Treviso. He wrote canzoni and several commentaries, in Latin, on his father's *Divina Commedia.*

Alladio (äl-lä′dyō), **Gian Giacomo de.** See **Macrino d'Alba.**

Allegri (äl-lā′grē), **Antonio.** See **Correggio.**

Allegri, Pomponio. Painter; b. at Correggio, September 3, 1522; d. at Parma, 1593. He was the son of Antonio Allegri (Correggio), and began painting seriously when he settled at Parma. Through his father's fame he secured many commissions, but he never truly understood his masterly father's work; he imitated it as best he could. He executed a number of works at Parma, including a fresco of *Moses on Sinai* in the cathedral and a *Madonna* for the Church of S. Trinità. A *Madonna and Child and Angels* and a *Madonna and Child with the Young St. John,* both originally painted for churches, are in the National Gallery of Parma. His best work, *Plenty,* in the mannerist style of Parmigianino, is at Ravenna.

Allori (äl-lō′rē), **Alessandro.** Painter; b. at Florence, May 3, 1535; d. September 22, 1607. He was orphaned at the age of five and was taken in and brought up by the painter Agnolo Bronzino, who may have been a relative. (Bronzino's name was originally Allori, and Alessandro, in gratitude, often signed himself Alessandro Bronzino, which later led to some confusion as to the authorship of paintings.) He became one of Bronzino's assistants and was imbued with his master's style, which he often reproduced, sometimes in a superficial and pedestrian manner, but often with his own additions of imagination and taste. At the age of 19 he went to Rome, where he studied Michelangelo's *Last Judgment* in the Sistine Chapel. He became an ardent admirer of Michelangelo and adapted and imitated some of that master's elements of the grand style in his own work. (A *Descent into Limbo,* in the Colonna Gallery at Rome, is markedly imitative of the *Last*

Judgment.) Throughout his painting life he remained faithful to Bronzino and Michelangelo. He was the possessor of a fine and delicate technique, and was one of the most prolific of the mannerist painters working at Florence. A group of frescoes, already detached from their original site in the 19th century, was formerly attributed to Vasari. Stored in the Refectory of the Church of Ognissanti, they were inundated by the flood of November, 1966. Subsequently detached from the wall that formed part of the original detachment, they have been restored and are now attributed to Allori on the basis of the fine technique with which they were executed. The group, including a number of prophets, *Creation of Eve* and *Original Sin,* is in the museum of the Church of Ognissanti. Other important frescoes are to be found in the Gaddi Chapel and the Refectory in S. Maria Novella, in the Salviati Chapel in S. Marco, and in the Uffizi, all at Florence. Other works are the beautiful paintings in the *studiolo* in the Palazzo Vecchio, panel paintings in the Accademia, in the Uffizi, and at Pisa and Rome. A portrait in the Uffizi is thought to be of Bianca Capello. In the same gallery is his *Sacrifice of Isaac,* notable for its deep feeling and its vast landscape.

Aloisi (ä-lō-ē′zē), **Andrea.** See **Ingegno.**

Altarpiece. In churches of the Renaissance and earlier periods, usually a painting on a sacred subject placed behind an altar as a decoration. The altarpiece may be a single panel, as Piero della Francesca's *Montefeltro Altarpiece,* at Milan, or may be composed of several panels, as his *Madonna della Misericordia,* at San Sepolcro.

Altdorfer (ält′dôr-fėr), **Albrecht.** German engraver, landscape painter and architect; b. probably at Regensburg, Bavaria, c1480; d. there, 1538. He was one of the "Little Masters." His painting *The Battle of Arbela* (1529) is in the Pinakothek at Munich; a collection of his etchings and engravings is at Regensburg. His style was close to that of Dürer, with whom he may have studied.

Altercazione (äl-ter-kä-tsyō′nā). Youthful poem by Lorenzo de' Medici; it is a dialogue between Lorenzo and a shepherd on the merits of city life and country life. Lorenzo holds that country life is superior. The shepherd, whose life is hard, argues for the city. Neither has the better of the argument. Ficino appears and is appealed to for his opinion. After much discourse, he rules that true happiness is found only in the spiritual life, thus turning the dialogue into a treatise on happiness that follows Neoplatonic doctrine.

Altichieri (äl-tē-kye′rē), **Altichiero.** [Also called **Altichiero da Zevio.**] Veronese painter; b. at Zevio, near Verona, c1320; d. c1385. He was the founder of the Veronese school of painting and brought to it the influence of Giotto, whose work at Padua he must have known well. His greatest works are at Padua and include a *Crucifixion* in the Chapel of St. Felix (formerly dedicated to St. James), in the Basilica of St. Anthony, and frescoes, executed (c1380–1384) on the walls of the Oratory of St. George. The frescoes in the Oratory: a *Crucifixion,* with a Giottesque monumentality and vigor; *Coronation of the Virgin; Annunciation; Nativity; Adoration of the Magi;* scenes from the life of St. George and from the lives of St. Catherine of Alexandria and St. Lucy, are called by some his masterpiece. They are notable, among other things, for his interest in portraying huge and detailed architectural backgrounds, experiments in perspective, and lovely color. Other critics question the attribution of these frescoes to Altichieri, and the authorship of the frescoes remains a subject of great scholarly debate. A *Madonna* (S. Anastasia, Verona) is generally attributed to him.

Altieri (äl-tye′rē), **Marcantonio.** Humanist; b. at Rome, 1450; d. 1532. Of an ancient and prominent Roman family, he was of the humanist school of Julius Pomponius Laetus, a lover of antiquity, and of all its customs and manner of life (idealized as they were by Laetus). The ancient Roman society seemed much purer, and preferable to the society of his own day. He expressed his ideas and his longing for the restoration of the greatness of his beloved Rome in his *Li nuptiali.*

Altilio (äl-tē′lyō), **Gabriele.** [**Gabriel Altilius.**] Humanist; b. at Caggiano (Salerno), 1440; d. 1501. He was a friend of Pontano, who mentions him in several of his writings, of Sannazzaro, Cariteo, and other humanists and writers, and a member of the so-called Neopolitan Academy. He was active in the service of Alfonso, duke of Calabria (later, Alfonso II of Naples), and of his successor, Ferrandino (Ferdinando II). His nomination as bishop of Policastro (1493) did not interfere with his services to the Aragonese court. He remained with Ferrandino when the French invaded Italy and Naples, but retired to his see of Policastro when Ferrandino was forced by the capture of Naples to flee (1495). From that time he devoted himself to the study of theology. His most famous poem is a marriage hymn in Latin, in the style of Catullus, celebrating the nuptials of Isabella of Aragon and Gian Galeazzo Sforza (1489). It was published after his death, was often reprinted, and was translated into Italian. Other Latin poems and elegies have remained largely unpublished.

Altobello Melone (äl-tō-bel′lō mā-lō′nā). See **Melone, Altobello.**

Alunno (ä-lön′nō), **Niccolò.** [Real name, **Niccolò di Liberatore.**] Umbrian painter; b. c1430; d. in August, 1502. His name "Alunno" came from a mistaken reading by Vasari of a signature on a predella now in the Louvre. The signature, "Alumnus Fulginie," referred to the fact that he was a native of Foligno. He may have received his first training from one Mazzaforte, whose daughter Caterina he married about 1452, but a more important early influence on his development was the frescoes painted by Benozzo Gozzoli at Montefalco, near Perugia, between 1450 and 1452. The frescoes Alunno painted (1456) in the chapel under the campanile of S. Maria in Campi, near Foligno, show a strong influence of Benozzo, as well as Alunno's own youthful ardor and originality. Only parts of these frescoes survive. Other early works are in the museum at Deruta, and a polyptych, now in the Brera at Milan, that he painted in collaboration with his father-in-law. From about 1466 he lived in the Marches and there came into contact with the Venetians Antonio Vivarini and Carlo Crivelli, whose influence in the way of more exact draftsmanship, stronger modeling, and richer color appeared in his work. Polyptychs he painted at Montelparo (now in the Vatican), Sanseverino, and Assisi reflect these influences. One of his finest works, in its technical mastery, vigorous color, and naturalism of expression and gesture, is the polyptych at Gualdo Tadino (1472). Others are in the Vatican, at Nocera Umbra, Foligno, and London. Besides a large number of panels, standards, and gonfalons, Alunno left frescoes at Spello and Foligno. Sincere and original, his artistic temperament was at times agitated and passionate, and at others verged on the mystical. In his later years his style became somewhat mannered, with thin, elongated figures and exaggerated expressions and gestures. He had great influence on his contemporaries, and through him the influence of Benozzo Gozzoli was transmitted to the school of Foligno; but when he returned to Umbria after his long stay in the Marches he found his reputation overshadowed by those of Perugino and Pinturicchio, who were painting at Perugia. In addition to those mentioned above, there are paintings at Bologna, Perugia, Ravenna, Spoleto, Budapest, Karlsruhe, Paris, Vienna; in the Walters Art Gallery, Baltimore; the Museum of Fine Arts, Boston; the Fogg Museum, Cambridge; and elsewhere.

Alva (äl′bä), Duke of. [Birth name, **Fernando Álvarez de Toledo**]. Spanish general and governor of the Netherlands (1567–1573); b. 1508; d. c1582. He served as an officer under Charles V from the siege of Tunis (1535) through the victory at Mühlberg (1547) over the Elector of Saxony, and as commander in chief (from 1553) in Italy. After the abdication of Charles V, he was appointed by Philip II of Spain to suppress the revolt in the Netherlands, which he put down with ruthlessness until checked (1572) by the prince of Orange, William I of Nassau ("William the Silent"). His Council of Troubles (known popularly as the Council of Blood) imposed death sentences on leading patriots of the Netherlands and others, and reached a total of 18,000 persons by the end of his regime. He fell from favor on his return to Spain, but was recalled (1580) to head the attack on Portugal which resulted in the collapse of the Portuguese government and a massacre of the Lisbon populace.

Alviano (däl-vyä′nō), **Bartolomeo d'.** Condottiere; b. at Rocca d'Alviano, in Umbria, 1455; d. at Bergamo, October 7, 1515. He was a member of a family in which the practice of the military arts was hereditary. Early in his career he fought in the pay of the pope and of the king of Naples, but soon after 1478 he linked his fortunes and his achievements to those of the Orsini. He became one of their most loyal adherents. A brilliant and brave fighter, he gave of his best to his employers without concerning himself with the political causes of their actions. He fought against Pope Alexander VI and the Colonnesi, against Florence in the attempt to restore Piero de' Medici, against the French in Naples and for the Spanish, and was largely responsible for the Spanish victory at the Garigliano (1503) and the expulsion of the French from the kingdom. In 1507, with Niccolò Orsini, he went into the pay of Venice. After some brilliant successes for Venice, he was taken prisoner by the French in the disastrous defeat of the Venetians at the battle of Agnadello (May, 1509). On his release (1513), he regained his command for Venice. His last great battle was in the victory of the French over the Milanese at Marignano, a month before his death. For a time, Alviano had Friuli as his base, where the so-called Academy of Pordenone was part of his court.

Amadeo (ä-mä-dā'ō), **Giovanni Antonio.** [Also, **Omodeo.**] Lombard sculptor and architect; b. near Pavia, in Lombardy, c1447; d. August 27, 1522. From the age of 19, when he worked with his brother on the Certosa at Pavia, he carried out innumerable commissions as architect and sculptor, and became one of the most famous Lombard architects and sculptors of his time. His many works included those at Pavia (on the Certosa and the cathedral, and the tomb of S. Lanfranco in a church near Pavia), at Cremona (*St. Imerio Giving Alms,* and other reliefs now in the cathedral there are among the best preserved examples of his mature manner), at Castiglione d'Olona, Isola Bella (two monuments for the Borromeo family), and at Milan. In the latter city he worked on the cathedral and the Ospedale Maggiore (now the university). Also at Milan he collaborated with Bramante and knew Leonardo da Vinci, with whom he was associated (1490) in planning the cathedral at Pavia. Many of his architectural works and sculptural designs were carried to completion, often with changes, by assistants and followers. Illustrative of his brilliantly decorative style, in which he combined, without perfectly fusing, classical styles, motifs, and themes with a Lombard love of ornamentation, are the Colleoni Chapel at Bergamo and the façade of the Certosa at Pavia. The Colleoni Chapel was begun early in the 1470's to hold the tomb of the condottiere Bartolomeo Colleoni, at that time still living. With its high, octagonal drum, dome, and lantern, the building recalls the Brunelleschi dome at Florence. Colleoni wished to insure that his chapel could be viewed uninterruptedly from the length of the Piazza Vecchia. To this end, the old sacristy of S. Maria Maggiore was torn down and his chapel was built in its place, with the result that the chapel is jammed up against the Gothic porch of S. Maria Maggiore. The façade of the chapel is covered with ornamentation and broken by pilasters, a deeply recessed window over the central doorway, lateral windows, and niches filled with classical busts. Any surface that is not ornamented with carving or statues is decorated with a geometric design of red and white marble. Black marble is used to separate reliefs and for columns. The overriding effect, in comparison with the classic severity and simplicity of Tuscan architecture, is of an indiscriminately decorated cake, but this suited the taste of Amadeo's Lombard clients. The interior is richly decorated with low reliefs on classical and Biblical themes, friezes, statues and medallions, and holds the tombs of Bartolomeo and of his daughter Medea (d. 1470). Her tomb, with its virginal effigy, was designed for another church, and was placed in the chapel in 1842. Signed by Amadeo, it is considered to be completely by his hand. Opposite the doorway of the chapel is the tomb of Bartolomeo, surmounted by a gilded wooden equestrian statue of the condottiere. In 1490 Ludovico il Moro called him to Pavia to work on the Certosa as chief architect. He had worked there at various times since his youth. From his early days is a terra-cotta *Virgin Annunciate,* in the lunette over the doorway leading from the church to the small cloister. Even though he was ultimately chief architect, so many architects and sculptors worked on the Certosa in the course of the next 150 years that Amadeo's share in the total design is obscure. He is credited with at least the lower part of the polychrome marble façade. Here again his exuberant creativity resulted in such a profusion of sculpture and ornamentation that the fundamentally simple lines are overwhelmed. The ornamentation includes a frieze of marble medallions with emperors and rulers of antiquity, reliefs, statuettes, foliage. Individual carvings and statues are beautiful in themselves. In addition to working as sculptor and architect, Amadeo was also employed as engineer. One of his projects, never carried out, was a plan to divert the Adda River. Amadeo is an outstanding example of the difference between the austerity and simplicity of Tuscan taste and training, and the exuberance of the Lombards. He had many pupils and followers.

Amadeus VIII (am-ạ-dē′us). Count (later duke) of Savoy, and antipope (1439–1449); b. at Chambéry, Savoy, September 4, 1383; d. at Ripaille, near Geneva, Switzerland, January 7, 1451. He succeeded to the title of count in 1391, was created duke in 1416, and developed the country into a small kingdom. According to Enea Silvio (later Pope Pius II), "They say that witches, who are very numerous in Savoy, and predict the future by tricks and the art of demons, went to Amadeo and prophesied that he would be pope because Eugenius would be deposed by the Council and Amadeo would be elected in his place." Whatever the reason, in 1434 he turned over his duchy to his eldest son, though he continued to take a hand in its affairs, and retired to the shores of the Lake of Geneva. There, with six elderly companions, he established a hermitage and lived the life of a religious and a hermit. He was related to many of the ruling families of Europe, and was reputed to be rich and wise, although as to the latter, it was said he was less wise than others were foolish. In 1439 the Council sitting at Basel deposed Eugenius IV and elected Amadeus pope, under the name Felix V. He may have been influenced to accept the office because of his desire to control the bishop of Geneva. The expected support from his highly placed relatives did not materialize. He carried out some of the functions of a pope, but his influence was small, and the power of the Council of Basel was eroded by the successes of Eugenius, although it continued to cause difficulties. In 1449 Amadeus recognized Nicholas V as the true pope and resigned. Nicholas made him a cardinal and apostolic legate to Savoy. Amadeus retired to Ripaille, where he died (1451). He was the last antipope in Roman Catholic history.

Amalteo (ä-mäl-tā′ō), **Cornelio.** Humanist; b. at Oderzo, 1530; d. at Rome, 1603? He was the son of Francesco Amalteo, and the brother of Giambattista and Girolamo Amalteo, but his achievements were less notable than those of his brothers. Like his brother Giambattista, he was secretary of the Republic of Ragusa. At Rome he worked on the Latin catechism with Aldus Manutius, grandson of the famed printer and publisher of Venice.

Amalteo, Francesco. Humanist; active early in the 16th century. He was the father of Girolamo, Giambattista, and Cornelio Amalteo, all humanists, poets, and teachers, whose poems and letters and other works in manuscript are in many collections. A collection of the works of the three brothers was published at Venice (1627), and examples of their works appear in many collections of humanist poetry.

Amalteo, Giambattista. Humanist, statesman, and poet; b. at Oderzo, 1525; d. at Rome, February, 1573. He was learned in law, philosophy, and theology, knew the classical languages, and wrote in Greek and in Latin. In addition, he held many public offices, was secretary of the Republic of Ragusa, and worked at Rome in the service of the Counter-Reformation. He left interesting Italian and Latin letters and Italian poetry, and is notable above all for his Latin elegies and eclogues. These last, expressive of his own spirit and that of his times, are among the best of his age.

Amalteo, Girolamo. Humanist, poet, and physician; b. 1507; d. 1574. Learned in the classical languages, and among the best and most noted Latin poets of his age, he had been a professor of medicine at Padua, then a physician at various places. He was above all noted for his Latin epigrams. He was the brother of Giambattista and Cornelio Amalteo.

Amalteo, Marcantonio. Humanist and teacher; b. at Pordenone, 1475; d. 1558. He was the brother of Paolo Amalteo (1460–1517), and taught in Austria, Hungary, and many places in northeast Italy in the area about Venice. He left Latin poetry and a great many letters.

Amalteo, Paolo. Humanist and poet; b. at Pordenone, 1460; d. at Vienna, 1517. He was a professor of humane letters at Vienna, and court poet of the Holy Roman Emperor Maximilian I.

Amalteo, Pomponio. Painter; b. at Motta di Livenza (Friuli), 1505; d. at S. Vito al Tagliamento, March 9, 1588. He was a pupil of Pordenone, whose daughter Graziosa he married, and followed closely in his master's

POMPONIO AMALTEO
Flight into Egypt
Courtesy of The Pierpont Morgan Library, New York

footsteps. In his frescoes as in his canvases he shows his dependence on Pordenone, without approaching him in originality and quality. A number of his altarpieces and frescoes remain in churches in the Friuli, as at Udine, S. Vito, Treviso, Pordenone, and elsewhere. He completed *The Story of the True Cross*, Church of S. Croce, Casarsa della Delizia (Udine), which had been begun by Pordenone.

AMASEO (ä-mä-sā′ō), **GEROLAMO.** Humanist and teacher; d. 1517. Of an old family of Udine, he was the brother of Leonardo (1452–1510) and Gregorio Amaseo (1464–1541), and was superintendent of the public schools of Udine.

AMASEO, GREGORIO. Humanist, teacher, and chronicler; b. March 13, 1464; d. July 21, 1541. He taught humane letters at Udine, Venice, and again at Udine, succeeding his brother Gerolamo (d. 1517) as superintendent of schools there, a position he held until 1532. With his brother Leonardo (1452–1510), he wrote a chronicle of Udine, *Diari Udinesi dal 1508 al 1541*. Leonardo wrote on the years 1508–1510; Giovanni Azio covered the years 1510–1517; and Gregorio wrote on the years 1517–1541. The chronicle, written in the Venetian dialect, is rich in the history of Friuli, details the customs and manners, describes the struggles of the classes and parties, the catastrophes, and the violent political and military ups and downs of a turbulent era. Gregorio was the father of Romolo Amaseo (1481–1552), who was the most celebrated member of the family.

Amaseo, Leonardo. Humanist and chronicler; b. 1452; d. 1510. With his brother Gregorio (1464–1541), he wrote *Diari Udinesi dal 1508 al 1541.* Leonardo's contribution covered the years 1508 to 1510. The chronicle was continued to 1541 by Azio and Gregorio. The *Diari Udinesi,* written in the Venetian dialect, is a rich record of a stormy period.

Amaseo, Romolo. Humanist and teacher; b. at Udine, June 24, 1481; d. at Rome, July 4, 1552. He was a noted professor of Latin and Greek, greatly honored at Padua, where he taught, and at Bologna, where he served the Senate in addition to his teaching. He was on friendly terms with the leading scholars and literary figures of his day, and was universally admired; Bembo called him the leading humanist lecturer of Italy, although as an advocate of Latin over Italian as a literary language he was in opposition to Bembo. He went to Rome on the invitation of the pope, and lectured in the university there. Foreign students flocked to his lectures.

Amati (ä-mä′tē), **Andrea.** Italian violinmaker; b. at Cremona, c1520; d. there, 1611. He was the first of his family to become internationally famous for the quality of his work. Few of his instruments are now known to exist, but those that do support the claim that he was the first craftsman to produce a modern violin. He was the father of Antonio and Geronimo Amati, also famous violinmakers.

Amatus Lusitanus (ạ-mā′tus lō-si-tā′nus). Portuguese physician; b. 1511; d. 1568. He is said to have been the second author to describe the valves in the veins.

Amboise (däṅ-bwȧz), **Georges d'.** French cardinal; b. at Chaumont-sur-Loire, France, 1460; d. at Lyons, France, 1510. He was the archbishop of Narbonne and of Rouen (1493–1498) and was a member of Louis' party before his accession. When the latter became king (1498), Amboise became his chief minister and director of his foreign policy. Directing his efforts toward the increase of French power in Italy and toward a papacy for himself, he organized the campaign of 1500 for the conquest of Milan but, preferring diplomacy, let slip the opportunity to force himself on the papal conclave as the successor of Pope Alexander VI. He was an eminent patron of the artists and writers of his time.

Ambra (äm′brä). A pastoral by Lorenzo de' Medici that celebrates his love for his Tuscan villa at Poggio a Caiano. It sings the love of the shepherd Lauro for the nymph Ambra. The nymph is pursued by the river god Ombrone. To save her from his embraces, Diana transforms the nymph into a rock in the river's embrace. The story is a thread Lorenzo uses to describe the Tuscan countryside, the harsh winter landscape and the onrush of spring, with its destructive as well as life-giving force.

Ambrogio da Rosate (äm-brō′jō dä rō-sä′tā). Physician and astrologer to Ludovico il Moro, whose life he was said to have saved (1488). No journey, ceremony, or movement, even in time of war, was undertaken before Messer Ambrogio had consulted the stars. Ludovico, who believed implicitly in the influence of the stars, was completely dependent on him, and at Milan "without him, nothing can be done here."

Ambrogio Camaldolese (kä-mäl-dō-lā′sā). See **Traversari, Ambrogio.**

Ambrogio da Fossano (dä fôs-sä′nō). See **Bergognone, Ambrogio.**

Ambrogio de' Predis (dā prā′dēs). See **Predis, Giovanni Ambrogio de'.**

Ambrose of Camaldoli (am′brōz, kä-mäl-dō′lē). See **Traversari, Ambrogio.**

Ambrosiana (äm-brō-zyä′nä). Library and art gallery at Milan, founded by Cardinal Federico Borromeo. The library was inaugurated in 1609; the art gallery in 1621. To the original gift of the cardinal's large collection of manuscripts and books, many thousands have been added and the library now contains over 500,000 printed volumes and more than 30,000 manuscripts. It is particularly rich in ancient literary works, including Greek and Latin verse and prose, Greek and Latin texts on rhetoric, grammar, and commentaries, and has a large collection of illuminated manuscripts. Among the famous works is Petrarch's copy of Vergil, with a frontispiece by Simone Martini. Among the treasures of the Ambrosiana are a number of drawings by Renaissance painters, the famous *Codice Atlantico,* with the largest single collection of notes and sketches from the notebooks of Leonardo da Vinci (given to the library in 1637 by a relative and admirer of the founder), paintings attributed to Leonardo, works by other Renaissance masters, and Raphael's enormous (over 9 feet by 25½ feet) cartoon for *The School of Athens*. The cartoon had been cut in two but was repaired after Cardinal Federico acquired it. He gave it to the Ambrosiana, where it now occupies an entire wall of a special room.

Ameto (ä-mā'tō). Prose idyll in Italian by Giovanni Boccaccio (1341–1342), with poetical interludes. Seven nymphs over whom Ameto, a young hunter, presides recount the story of their lives and loves. Each story concludes with eclogues, which were among the first in Italian literature. The collecting of separate stories about a unifying situation is a device that Boccaccio expanded in the *Decameron*. In descriptions of the pastoral setting the romance has Vergilian echoes.

Aminta (ä-mēn'tä). A pastoral play, in five short acts, by Torquato Tasso. It has been called a perfect example of the Arcadian play. It was first produced (1573) for the delight of the court at Ferrara by a group of players called the Gelosi, under Tasso's direction, and was immediately successful. In elegant and graceful verse it tells the simple story of the love of the shepherd Aminta for the nymph Silvia. It is an idyll of the pastoral life, the beauty of nature, and the joys of love to which even the proudest spirit must ultimately yield. With their lyrical choruses of shepherds and melodic laments, the Arcadian dramas of *Aminta*, and later Battista Guarini's *Pastor fido*, were the forerunners of opera.

Ammannati (äm-män-nä'tē), **Bartolomeo.** Florentine sculptor and architect; b. at Settignano, 1511; d. at Florence, April 22, 1592. He worked under Baccio Bandinelli at Florence, and as a boy saw Michelangelo working on the Medici tombs in San Lorenzo. The effect of Michelangelo's work on the youthful sculptor was profound and one of the greatest influences in the development of his own style. From his early period is a lunette for an altar in the Duomo at Pisa (1536). From about the same period are three statues he carved for the Sannazzaro monument at Naples. In 1540 he filled a commission at Florence, but he felt that the pieces he carved for this monument (a *Victory* from it is in the Bargello) were not shown to good advantage. In disappointment with the results, he left for Venice, where he worked with Jacopo Sansovino on the Library of St. Mark's. The elegance and refinement of Sansovino's style had great influence on the development of his own. In this period he was often at Padua, and produced there a colossal *Hercules* and statues of *Jupiter* and *Apollo*, as well as the Benavides monument in the Church of the Eremitani (finished 1546). In 1550 he married the poetess Laura Battiferri at Loreto; their union was noted for the happiness it brought both partners. Shortly after this date he went to Rome, where he made the monument of Antonio del Monte in S. Pietro in Montorio, of which Vasari was the architect, and carved some statues for Pope Julius III. Between 1551 and 1553 he worked with Vasari and Vignola on the elegant Villa Giulia at Rome, its austere façade broken only by a *loggetta* in the center. After the death of Julius III he returned (1555) to Florence, and remained there, with brief exceptions, until his death. There he worked, often with Vasari, for Cosimo I. Among his works at Florence were a fountain for the Hall of the Five Hundred in the Palazzo Vecchio, the bronze group of *Hercules and Antaeus* for a fountain designed by Tribolo at the Villa Castello, and the Neptune Fountain in the Piazza della Signoria in front of the Palazzo Vecchio (Palazzo della Signoria). Benvenuto Cellini had wanted to do the fountain, and had prepared a model, but in the contest for the commission (Giambologna and a sculptor of Perugia were two other contestants), Ammannati won. The fountain, with its elongated figures and delicately modeled, slightly exaggerated heads, is a fine example of his mannerist style. One of the most distinguished of his architectural works at Florence was his enlargement of the Pitti Palace, carried out for Cosimo I between 1558 and 1570. Also at Florence, he built the Ponte S. Trinita, with its flattened arches (1567–1570). (The bridge was destroyed in World War II and rebuilt to Ammannati's design.) Toward the end of his life he came under the influence of the Jesuits and the Counter-Reformation. His attitude toward art changed. He desired Grand Duke Ferdinand I, as he wrote in a letter of 1590, to prohibit the carving or painting of nude figures. Furthermore, he recommended that those already made, including his own, be covered up "so that Florence shall cease to be regarded as a nest of idols, or of lustful provocative things that are displeasing to God." In addition to buildings in Florence and Lucca (Palazzo della Prefettura, begun 1578 and finished 150 years later, and others), he designed a number at Rome, including the Ruspoli Palace (1586) and the façade of the Palazzo di Firenze.

Ammannati, Jacopo. Italian cardinal; b. at Villa Basilica, near Lucca, 1422; d. at Siena, 1479. He was the son of an obscure and impoverished family, who managed to study at Florence and Siena, became the humanist protégé and friend of Pius II, and rose to a high position in the Church. In Florence he had been the tutor of the sons of a prominent family, and there he laid the foundations for his humanist studies. He went to Rome in the time of Nicholas V, became a secretary of Cardinal Capranica, an apostolic secretary of Calixtus III, and was named bishop of Pavia (1460) and then cardinal (1461) by Pius II. In gratitude to Pius for his friendship he added the name Piccolomini to his own. On the accession of Paul II, Ammannati was ignored at the papal court, as were most of the cardinals elevated by Pius II. He performed some services for Sixtus IV and spent his last years in Siena. He wrote a life of Pius II, since lost, and *Commentaries* that were intended as a continuation of those written by Pius himself.

Ammirato (äm-mē-rä′tō), **Scipione.** Historian; b. at Lecce, September 27, 1531; d. at Florence, 1601. A descendant of a noble family, he traveled widely as a youth, studied law at Naples, Rome, and Padua, and went at last to Venice, where he became secretary to the cultivated Venetian Alessandro Contarini. At Venice he was profoundly impressed by the literary atmosphere and became acquainted with such leading writers as Sperone Speroni and Pietro Aretino. Vittoria Colonna is said to have been numbered among his friends. He became involved with one of the ladies of the Contarini family and was forced to flee to Bari. He later went to Lecce and devoted himself to his studies and founded an academy of letters. Because of the wide variety of his writings—poems, orations, hymns, dialogues in the manner of Plato, canzoni—he was given the name "Proteo." He had hopes of becoming the historiographer of Naples. These hopes were thwarted and he went to Florence, where Grand Duke Cosimo welcomed him and commissioned him to write a history of Florence. This work, *Istorie Fiorentine*, ending at the year 1574, was widely acclaimed in its day. Later critics have been less generous in their evaluation, recognizing the uncritical use Ammirato made of earlier sources, and deploring his inclusion of fables and legends. His lack of historical perception is a further fault of the work. Other historical writings of Ammirato include biographies of Ladislaus and Joanna II of Naples, as well as works on the Medici.

Amone (ä-mō′nā). In Lodovico Ariosto's *Orlando Furioso*, the father of Rinaldo and Bradamante. He has arranged a marriage between Bradamante and Leone, the son of the emperor Constantine. Rinaldo quarrels with his father over the proposed match, since he knows of the love of Bradamante for Ruggiero. Amone is reconciled with Rinaldo and consents to Bradamante's marriage to Ruggiero.

Amorosa visione (äm-ō-rō′sä vē-zyō′nā). Allegory in terza rima by Giovanni Boccaccio (1342–1343). The incomplete poem was intended to show how love elevates man from the sensual to the spiritual life. Only the first half, depicting the sensual life, is complete. In this section the poet, having chosen the wide hall of the senses, enters and beholds a series of frescoes. By the device of describing the frescoes Boccaccio permits himself to take up a wide range of subjects—myths of all ages, heroes and heroines of legend and history, philosophers, poets, etc.—revealing his knowledge of ancient literature and enabling him to tell a wide variety of stories.

Anagni (ä-nä′nyē), **Giovanni da.** See **Giovanni da Anagni.**

Ancarano (dän-kä-rä′nō), **Pietro d'.** See **Pietro d'Ancarano.**

Ancina (än-chē′nä), **Giovenale.** Ecclesiastic, composer, and musicologist; b. at Fossano (Piedmont), October 19, 1545; d. at Saluzzo, August, 1604. He was a physician and theologian, taught medicine, and rose to be a bishop. Encouraged by St. Philip Neri to pursue the musical studies that interested him, he wrote several studies on the theory and practice of music, and collected the polyphonic music of the best composers of the time in *Tempio armonico della Beata Vergine* (Rome, 1599), in which some of his own compositions were included.

Andrea (än-drā′ä), **Monte.** Florentine poet;

active in the middle and latter part of the 13th century. Little is known of his life. He lived in Bologna before 1259, and is mentioned in Florentine documents of 1259 and 1280. Some love lyrics and political verse favoring the Guelphs are extant.

Andrea, Zoan. See **Zoan Andrea.**

Andrea dell' Aquila (del-lä′kwē-lä). Painter and sculptor of the Abruzzi; active in the middle of the 15th century. According to documents, he was paid in 1456 as one of the sculptors who worked with Isaia da Pisa on the Triumphal Arch of Alfonso I at Naples.

Andrea d'Assisi (däs-sē′zē). See **Ingegno.**

Andrea da Barberino (dä bär-bā-rē′nō). Writer; b. at Barberino in Val d'Elsa, c1370; d. after 1431. Andrea's Italian prose narratives, *Guerrino il meschino* and *I reali di Francia,* have given pleasure to generations of Italians. They are still in print. *Guerrino il meschino* is the story of the thousand and one adventures of the upright and imperturbable Guerrino. Perilous journeys, miraculous escapes, deeds of heroism flash by in succession. Guerrino, supposedly the child of slavery, at last finds and frees his mother and father from prison, and learns he is of noble blood. *I reali di Francia,* a tale of chivalry and heroics, relates the fabulous history of the French royal house from Fiovo, son of the emperor Constantine, to Charlemagne. It is based on the Carolingian legends.

Andrea di Bartolo (dē bär′tō-lō). Sienese painter; d. at Siena, June 3, 1428. He was the son of Bartolo di Fredi, had a house and a workshop at Siena, and several times held municipal office in the commune. He worked with his father and Luca di Tommè, and was a follower of his father and Taddeo di Bartolo. Most of his work was that of a diligent craftsman, lacking in individual inspiration. Perhaps for this reason he was able to produce so much, for he left many works. Among them are a signed *Annunciation, with Mary Magdalen and St. Anthony Abbot,* at Buonconvento (near Siena); eight panels of saints, from a signed and dated (1413) polyptych, in the Church of the Osservanza, Siena; other works at Siena in the Palazzo Pubblico, Pinacoteca, and S. Pietro Ovile; two panels in the National Gallery of Umbria at Perugia; a *Madonna* at Brooklyn; *Birth of the Virgin* with the homely details of a genre painting, National Gallery, Washington; and two companion panels, *St. Thomas Aquinas* and *St. Anthony Abbot,* in the Johnson Collection, Philadelphia. Besides paintings in the Pinacoteca and in churches and museums in and about Siena, there are paintings, many of which are panels from dismembered polyptychs, at Bologna, Milan, Pisa, in the cathedral at Tuscania, at Berlin, Budapest, Dublin, London (Victoria and Albert Museum), Oxford, Stockholm; in the Walters Art Gallery, Baltimore; Fogg Museum, Cambridge, Massachusetts; Detroit; Greenville, South Carolina; Yale University, New Haven; the Metropolitan Museum, New York; Princeton; Toledo; Worcester; and elsewhere.

Andrea da Bologna (dä bō-lō′nyä). Painter; active from 1340 to c1385. He painted scenes from the life of the saint in the Chapel of St. Catherine of Alexandria, in the Lower Church of the Basilica of San Francesco at Assisi (1368). Also from his hand are a polyptych, *St. Catherine,* with episodes from the lives of several saints, signed and dated (1369), Palazzo Comunale, Fermo; a fresco, now mounted on canvas, *Virgin and Child and St. John the Evangelist,* Pinacoteca, Bologna; and a *Madonna del Latte* (1372), Corridonia.

Andrea di Bonaiuto (dē bō-nä-yö′tō). [Also, **Andrea da Firenze.**] Florentine painter of the 14th century. He was listed in the rolls of the Guild of Physicians and Apothecaries in 1343 and later (1374) became a member of the Company of St. Luke, an artists' guild. In 1366 and 1367 he was one among several artists and architects who gave advice on the plans for the building of the Florentine cathedral, begun in 1298. This is testimony of his reputation at that time. Frescoes on the west wall of the Camposanto at Pisa on three episodes from the life of St. Ranieri (formerly attributed to Simone Martini because of a story in Vasari) are credited to him. His great work is the decoration of the Spanish Chapel in the cloister of Santa Maria Novella at Florence. This chapel (called the Spanish Chapel because it was given to the Spanish residents of Florence in 1566), is completely frescoed, including the vault and the arches. The frescoes were painted probably between 1366 and 1368, with the aid of assistants. They present a trend away from the humanizing that Giotto brought to religious painting and the mysticism and lyricism of the Sienese, and reflect a preoccupation with the correct interpretation of Church doctrine and creed as well as an enhancement of Church authority. The subjects of the frescoes include a *Navicella* (the ship symbolizing the Church), *Way to Calvary, Crucifixion, Resurrection, Ascension, Descent to Limbo, Descent of the Holy Spirit, The Church Militant, The Church Triumphant, The Apotheosis of the Dominican Order, The Triumph of St. Thomas Aquinas,* and episodes from the life of St. Peter the Martyr. In his narrative and decorative qualities Andrea shows the influence of the Sienese school. Other works are attributed to him on stylistic grounds, as an *Annunciation* and two panels in the Accademia, Florence.

Andrea del Castagno (del käs-tä′nyō). See **Castagno, Andrea del.**

Andrea di Cione (dē chō′nā). See **Orcagna, Andrea.**

Andrea Corsini (kôr-sē′nē), Saint. Carmelite; b. at Florence. November 30, 1302; d. January 6, 1373. Of a distinguished Florentine family, he entered the Carmelites while young, studied at Paris and Avignon, and on his return to Italy devoted himself to preaching. He won such fame in his calling that he came to be considered the apostle of Tuscany. He was made bishop of Fiesole (1360). Pope Eugenius IV permitted the worship of his relics, but he was not canonized until 1629, under Urban VIII.

Andrea da Firenze (dä fē-ren′dzā). See **Andrea di Bonaiuto.**

Andrea di Giovanni (dē jō-vän′nē). Umbrian painter; active 1378–1412. In 1378 and 1380 he assisted Ugolino di Prete Ilario at Orvieto. A fresco, *Madonna and Child* (1412), in the lunette over one of the side doors of the cathedral at Orvieto shows the influence of Simone Martini in its grace and somewhat mystical quality.

Andrea di Giusto (dē jös′tō). Florentine painter; d. 1455. He worked with Bicci di Lorenzo (1424) and with Masaccio at Pisa (1426) and adopted such of their forms as suited his talent, later adding to these the elongated figures and arabesques of Lorenzo Monaco. Other painters by whom he was influenced were Fra Angelico and Piero della Francesca. From the latter he began to give serious heed to the problems of perspective and space. The central panel of a polyptych, *Virgin and Child* (1435), Galleria Comunale, Prato, is highly imitative of Lorenzo Monaco, as is a *Madonna,* Accademia, Florence. Frescoes in the cathedral at Prato reveal his awareness of the developments that were taking place in Florentine painting and that revolutionized the interest in and treatment of space, depth, and movement. Several of his works are in the Johnson Collection at Philadelphia, including two predella panels—*Presentation in the Temple* and *Christ Among the Doctors*—and *Virgin and Child with SS. Rose, Bartholomew, Lucy and Baptist.* In addition to those mentioned and works in the Laurentian Library and S. Marco at Florence, there are paintings at Fiesole, Figline, Poggio di Loro, Turin; at Altenberg, Berlin, Copenhagen, Edinburgh, Helsinki, Leningrad, Paris (Musées Nationaux, Montauban), Vienna; at Allentown (Pennsylvania), the Walters Art Gallery, Baltimore, Cambridge (Massachusetts), Tulsa, and elsewhere.

Andrea de Litio (dā lē′tyō). See **Delitio, Andrea.**

Andrea da Murano (dä mö-rä′nō). Venetian painter; notices from 1462 to 1507. In the latter year he received payment for an altarpiece for the Church of Trebaseleghe that he had begun in 1484. This altarpiece, with echoes of his teacher and collaborator, Bartolomeo Vivarini, is his finest work, notable for its composition and for its naturalistic atmosphere and landscape. Other works are a triptych, with St. Vincent Ferrer, St. Roch, and other saints, in the Accademia, Venice; a *Madonna with the Sleeping Child,* Cannon Collection, Princeton; and paintings in the cathedral at Asolo; Church of SS. Giovanni e Antonio, Camposampiero; at Faenza; Church of S. Niccolò, Treviso; at Budapest, London, and elsewhere.

Andrea Pannonio (pän-nō′nyō). Miniaturist, writer, and humanist; active in the second half of the 15th century. He was a Carthusian and vicar of the Certosa near Ferrara. For Ercole I d'Este he wrote and illuminated a book on the origin of the house of Este. For Matthias Corvinus of Hungary, whose wife Beatrice was the sister of Ercole's wife Leonora of Aragon, he wrote and illuminated *De regiis virtutibus* (1467).

Andrea del Sarto (del sär′tō). [Original name, **Andrea d'Angelo di Francesco.**] Florentine painter; b. at Florence, July 17, 1486; d. there of the plague, late September, 1530. His father was a tailor, whence the name by which he was known (Andrea the

ANDREA DEL SARTO
Saddled Ass Grazing
Study for *The Sacrifice of Isaac,* Dresden
British Museum, London
Alinari-Art Reference Bureau

Tailor's Son). At the age of seven he was apprenticed to a goldsmith, but as he was forever drawing he was placed with a painter (one Gian Barile, a mediocre craftsman of whom nothing further is known) to learn that art. His new master soon recognized his marvelous aptitude for drawing and after a few years placed him with Piero di Cosimo. While he was with Piero he took every opportunity to study the cartoons, on exhibition at Florence, that had been prepared by Leonardo da Vinci and Michelangelo for frescoes in the Palazzo della Signoria. In the same period he struck up a friendship with Franciabigio, and about 1508 left Piero di Cosimo and opened a workshop with him. According to Vasari, they executed a number of works together, but almost nothing survives to prove their collaboration. The association of Andrea del Sarto and Franciabigio seems to have ended about 1511, and they became rivals. In the meantime, Andrea had become a warm friend of the young Jacopo Sansovino, and the two frequently exchanged designs, drawings, and models. Andrea's style was formed while Leonardo was in Florence on one of his visits, and all the artists fell more or less under his influence. He succeeded to perfection in achieving the misty sfumato of Leonardo and the utmost softness of modeling and delicacy of atmosphere. Later, in admiration and imitation of Michelangelo, he undertook a somewhat more monumental manner, but his native delicacy and taste, as well as the limitations of his inspiration, prevented him from falling into the exaggerated mannerisms that some of his contemporaries adopted as a result of Michelangelo's influence. Because of his excellent and correct draftsmanship he was called "Faultless Andrea," and as a colorist he was among the greatest Florentines of his age. Vasari, who was for a time his pupil, remarked that if he had not lacked a spark of genius to fire his timid and conventional creative spirit, he would be counted among the greatest of artists. The warmth of his color, the infinitely refined gradations of light and shade to produce form, the youthful beauty of his faces with their intent expressions, create tenderness rather than ardor. A few strong faces give the impression of power, but sometimes his sweetness verges on sentimentality. But nothing obscures, and few equaled, his marvelous draftsmanship.

In 1508 he matriculated in the Guild of Physicians and Apothecaries; and soon afterward, beguiled, according to Vasari, by a sacristan in the monastery of the Servites, he painted a series of scenes on the life of S. Filippo Benizzi in the cloister of the monastery (Cloister of the Church of the SS. Annunziata), in which it is possible to observe the continual evolution and softening of his coloristic style, beginning with a *Resurrection of a Boy,* still in the manner of the 15th century, to a *Procession of the Magi* (1511) in which appear elements of the High Renaissance. In this series he showed himself a master of color. (In the Oratory of the Annunziata is a *Head of the Redeemer,* done at a later date, and in another cloister, on the tympanum of a door that leads to the church, is one of his masterpieces, *Madonna of the Sack,* a fresco executed in 1525.) However, in the execution of a commission he had accepted before completing this series he sacrificed his gift for sumptuous color to paint a series in monochrome in the Cloister of the Scalzo (Compagnia di San Giovanni Battista allo Scalzo). In a more monumental style than his previous compositions, this work most brilliantly shows his mastery of drawing and design. The series of sixteen frescoes (two of which were painted by Franciabigio while Andrea was in France) depict scenes from the life of John the Baptist. Because of the long period over which the work was carried on (begun in 1509 or 1510, interrupted by a presumed visit to Rome, 1514–1515, and a trip to France, 1518–1519, and completed perhaps as late as 1526) the frescoes record the development of his style. Damaged in their lower parts by dampness infiltrating from the ground, and threatened by infiltrations from the roof, the frescoes have been detached and mounted on masonite to protect and preserve them. *The Birth of the Virgin* (1514), SS. Annunziata, is a masterpiece in which he harmoniously united exquisite tone and a noble and serene composition. For the triumphal entry of Leo X into Florence (1515) he painted, in monochrome, the false façade that his friend Sansovino had constructed to decorate the cathedral. In 1517 he completed his *Madonna of the Harpies*, so called from the harpies that appear on the pedestal on which the Madonna stands. (The harpies, looking up at the Madonna, perhaps signify pagan submission to her.) The work, one of his most grandiose compositions, is in the Uffizi. It has been greatly admired for its design and the resolution of the colors by toning them down almost to the point of chiaroscuro. Vasari especially admired the draperies; the art historian Bernard Berenson criticized it on the ground that they are excessive. In the same year (1517) Andrea married Lucrezia del Fede. She was a beautiful and capricious widow, to whom Andrea had become deeply attached even before the death of her husband. Vasari writes disgustedly of her influence on Andrea, and the trouble he claims she brought on him. He was critical because Andrea had become involved with her before she was a widow, and equally so because after he married her Andrea was so uxorious. Vasari wrote that her features were engraved on Andrea's heart, and that there was something of her in all the women Andrea painted. He left a number of portraits of her, one of the loveliest being that in the Prado, Madrid. A sidelight on the life of the Florentine artists is that Andrea belonged to two clubs: the *Paiuolo* (Kettle), limited to twelve members, and the *Cazzuola* (Trowel), of a somewhat larger membership. Members of the Paiuolo met for dinners which they joined the chef in designing and preparing. A famous dinner of Andrea's concoction was a temple, the floor of which was of varicolored aspic to simulate mosaic, the columns of sausages with bases and capitals of cheese, the cornices of pastry, and the balconies of marzipan. Within the temple was a choir desk made of veal; on it rested a book made of lasagne, in which the script was composed of grains of pepper, and around it was a choir of cooked birds. Members of the Cazzuola entertained themselves with fantastic costumes, settings, and food, and sometimes presented plays.

In 1518 Andrea was invited to France, where he subsequently made a portrait of the infant dauphin and others, and a *Charity* (1518), now in the Louvre. He was graciously received by Francis I and was highly successful, but Lucrezia wrote letters entreating him to return to her in Florence, and the following year he did so. (This is another of Vasari's grievances against her—he considered

ANDREA DEL SARTO
Head of a Youth in Profile
Uffizi, Florence   Alinari-Art Reference Bureau

that her effect on his career was highly adverse.) He promised Francis that he would return and would bring with him works of art. He never did so and, again according to Vasari, spent the money the king had paid him for work he had not completed as well as that he had received to buy ancient and contemporary artworks for the king. Perhaps he used some of it to build (1520) the handsome house that still stands at Florence. In 1521 he was invited, with others, to decorate the Medici villa at Poggio a Caiano. He began the fresco *Tribute to Caesar*, a composition filled with figures, animals, and an architectural background, but he did not complete it. Alessandro Allori finished it at a later date. Plague broke out in Florence (1523) and he withdrew with his family to the Mugello and executed several works while out of Florence, among them a *Pietà* (1524), now in the Pitti Palace. During the siege of Florence (1530) the buildings outside the walls on the right bank of the Arno were razed to prevent the enemy from finding shelter as they attacked the city. However, the people could not find it in their hearts to destroy a beautiful *Last Supper* (one that Berenson says is the only one that can be looked at with pleasure after seeing Leonardo's) he had frescoed (1527) in the Church of S. Salvi. The church was spared and the fresco can be seen there to this day, in a very good state of preservation. During the same siege he is thought to have painted, on the walls of the Palace of the Podesta, the likenesses of the captains who had been hanged in effigy as traitors to Florence. Marvelous preparatory drawings of them are in the Uffizi. He left many frescoes and panel paintings, in general marked by his personal gentleness and sweetness and by his technical excellence of draftsmanship, strong composition, exquisite color, and softness of modeling. Most of his works are at Florence where, in addition to the frescoes just cited, the greatest number of his paintings are in the Pitti Palace. These include a *Dispute over the Trinity* (1517) notable for mood, strength of characterization, and warmth of color; two *Assumptions* (1519, 1529); works on the *Story of Joseph*, the *Holy Family*, *Madonna in Glory with Saints*, and a youthful *St. John the Baptist*. Among the several works in the Uffizi are the aforementioned *Madonna of the Harpies*, a beautiful *Portrait of a Young Woman*, a moving *St. James*, showing the saint caressing children, and a self-portrait. At Naples is his copy of Raphael's *Leo X*, so close to the original that, according to Vasari, it could be distinguished from Raphael's only by a benchmark he inscribed on the back. Five *Saints*, including the celebrated *St. Agnes*, are in the cathedral at Pisa. His paintings are to be found in museums at Paris, Rome (Borghese, Doria Pamphili, and National galleries), Vienna, Dresden, Leningrad, Madrid, Venice, Berlin, in private collections in England and elsewhere, and at London (a magnificent portrait, *The Sculptor*). In the Cleveland Museum of Art is the first, and most spontaneous, of three very similar paintings, *Sacrifice of Isaac* (the others are at Dresden and Madrid). There is a *Charity*, National Gallery, Washington, and *The Holy Family*, The Metropolitan Museum of Art, New York. In addition to those and other paintings in the museums already mentioned, there are paintings at Lisbon; Munich; Coral Gables, Florida; Johnson Collection, Philadelphia; Raleigh, North Carolina; and elsewhere.

For some, the most perfect expression of Andrea's genius and his artistic personality lies in his drawings. These, lyrics of line and form, have an immediacy of flow and spontaneity that bespeak a miraculous control and an observation free of concern with composition or symbolic significance. His absolute mastery in drawing is such that his work seems effortless. His drawings were left to his pupil, Domenico Conti, but soon found their way into the hands of other artists. Vasari owned a number of them. The largest collections are now in the Uffizi and the Louvre. Other important examples are in the British Museum, the Albertina (Vienna), the Fogg Museum (Cambridge, Massachusetts), and the Morgan Library (New York), as well as in other museums and private collections.

Andrea Schiavone (skyä-vō′nā). [**Andrea Meldolla**, called **Schiavone.**] Painter and engraver; b. at Zara, 1522; d. at Venice, December 1, 1563. Active at Venice before 1541, he was a pupil of Bonifacio de' Pitati and was later strongly influenced by Parmigianino. Frescoes that he painted on the façades of a number of Venetian palaces have disappeared, but many paintings from his hand are to be found in churches and collections at Venice. A facile adapter, he exaggerated Tintoretto's dramatic style and elongated his figures in the mannerist style of Parmigianino. His temperament turned him to the romantic subjects Giorgione and his followers had made popular, and his paintings on these themes were sometimes attributed to Giorgione himself. Among his works is *Deucalion and Pyrrha,* National Gallery of Parma, that in its elongations shows the mannerist influence of Parmigianino. Another painting on the same subject is in the Accademia Venice, along with *The Judgment of Midas, Christ Before Pilate,* and *Circumcision,* the last being a work of his maturity. Subjects drawn from mythology gave scope for his romantic fantasy, and several of them are in the Carrara Academy at Bergamo. Other examples of his work are in the Pitti Palace and other collections at Florence, in the principal museums at Milan, Naples, Padua, Turin, Dresden, Hampton Court, London (National Gallery), Moscow, Munich, Paris, Split (Spalato), Stockholm, Vienna, Princeton, Tulsa, Oklahoma, and elsewhere.

Andrea di Vanni (dē vän′nē). See **Vanni, Andrea.**

Andrea da Velletri (dä vel-lā′trē). Painter; active in the 14th century. A triptych by him is in the Chapel of Leo X in Castel Sant' Angelo, Rome.

Andrelini (än-drā-lē′nē), **Publio Fausto.** Poet and teacher of humanistic letters; b. at Forlì, c1462; d. at Paris, February 25, 1518. Under Charles VIII, who became his patron and named him "Poet of the King," he went to Paris (1489) and lectured on poetry, rhetoric, and history at the university, to universal acclaim. He was among the earliest of the humanists to inspire the French with an interest in and love for humanistic studies. Louis XII and Francis I continued the benefits bestowed on him by Charles VIII. He must have been a very winning personality to have gained such renown, for the foundations of his own culture were shaky, and his Latin style far from impeccable. He wrote eclogues, bucolics, other lyrics and poems that indicate facility rather than profound feeling or inspiration.

Andronicus III Palaeologus (an-dron′i-kus, an-drǫ-nī′kus; pā-lē-ol′ǫ-gus). Byzantine emperor (1328–1341); b. c1296; d. June 15, 1341. He was the grandson of Andronicus II, whose throne he usurped. He carried on war with the Ottoman Turks, who detached (1326–1338) nearly the whole of Asia Minor from the Empire.

Andronicus IV. Name sometimes given to the son of John V Palaeologus who usurped the Byzantine throne and held it from 1376 to 1379.

Androuet du Cerceau (äṅ-drö-e dü ser-sō), **Jacques.** [Original surname, **Androuet.**] French architect; b. c1510; d. 1584. He was the founder of a line of architects, and was better known from his writings and etched drawings than from actual buildings. He was a pioneer of the Italian Renaissance in France. The family name derived from the trademark of a circle (*cerceau*) which marked his place of work.

Anelida and Arcite (ạ-nel′i-dạ, är′sīt). Unfinished poem by Geoffrey Chaucer. It was among those printed by Caxton, and is mentioned in both Lydgate's and Thynne's lists of Chaucer's works. In the latter it is mentioned as "Of Queen Anelida and False Arcite." There are passages in it from Boccaccio's *Teseide,* and the *Thebaid* of Statius was also drawn upon. Chaucer himself tells us that he took it from the Latin. Anelida was the Queen of Armenia. In the poem is included "The Complaint of Fair Anelida upon False Arcite," occasioned by the fact that the Theban knight (who is not the true Arcite of the *Knight's Tale*) deserted her for another. The poem breaks off at the end of her complaint (which is considered to be, by itself, one of the most polished and charming examples of perfect balance of strophe and antistrophe in medieval literature).

Angela Merici (än′jā-lä mā-rē′chē), Saint. Franciscan nun; b. at Desenzano, on Lake Garda, probably March 21, 1474; d. at Brescia, January 27, 1540. She became a Franciscan tertiary at an early age, fasted, and mortified the flesh, made many pilgrimages to shrines in Italy, and went to the Holy Land (1524). In 1525 she was received by Pope Clement VII. She maintained that God appeared to her in a vision and commanded her to establish a company to promote the welfare of souls; as a result, she founded (1535) the teaching order of the Ursulines at Brescia. The aim of the order was the reestablishment and exaltation of the Christian virtues through the education of future wives and mothers. The members of her company lived at home and attempted to exert their influence over members of their own families and over the people in their neighborhoods. The members combined a monastic way of life—practicing poverty, chastity, and obedience—with the task of educating young girls.

Angeli (än′jā-lē), **Pietro degli.** [Also called **Il Bargeo**, from his birthplace.] Poet; b. at Barga, near Lucca, April 22, 1517; d. at Pisa, February 26, 1596. He studied law at Bologna under Ugo Buoncompagni (the future Pope Gregory XIII) and letters under Romolo Amaseo, and was for a time in the service of the king of France, through his ambassadors, and of various eminent Italians. He taught Greek and Latin at Reggio, the humanities at Pisa, where he upheld the value of Latin, and held the chair of ethics and politics at Rome. Henry III, king of France, honored him and gave him a pension; Tasso was influenced by his Latin epic, *Siriade*. Angeli wrote Catullan lyrics of great delicacy. Among his other works is one on hunting, *Cynegeticon*, in twelve books, which was widely praised and often reprinted.

Angelica (an-jel′i-kä). In Matteo Maria Boiardo's *Orlando Innamorato*, a princess of Cathay, the most beautiful of women, "a lily of the field, a rose of the garden, and a morning star." Orlando, and all the other knights at Charlemagne's court, and pagan princes as well, fall in love with her. Orlando pursues her and performs all sorts of glorious and perilous deeds for her sake. She uses him whenever necessary but never returns his love. Having drunk at the magic spring of Cupid that causes all who drink of it to fall in love, she sees Rinaldo, Orlando's cousin, and is instantly smitten with a passion for him. She pursues him with all her arts. He, however, having drunk of Merlin's fountain, despises and repulses her. In Lodovico Ariosto's *Orlando Furioso*, Angelica, who possesses a magic ring that makes her invisible and which she often uses to get out of tight places, decides that she has no need of man and can do without a champion. Cupid is offended by her arrogance and her scorn of love, and decides to punish her. As she is gazing on wounded Medoro, a brave soldier of humble birth, Cupid shoots one of his arrows into her heart, and the princess, who had been wooed by the most renowned princes of Christendom and Heathendom, falls desperately in love with the humbly born soldier. He returns her love and they enjoy many happy hours in cottage and bower. It is the sight of their entwined names, *Angelica and Medoro*, carved in every available tree and wall where they have been, that causes Orlando to go mad with jealousy.

Angelico (än-jel′i-kō), Fra. [**Guido** or **Guidolino, di Pietro;** called **Beato Angelico** and **Fra Giovanni da Fiesole.**] Florentine painter; b. at Vicchio in the Mugello, between 1400 and 1402; d. at Rome, February 17, 1455. Little is known of his early life and training. Modern scholarship has revealed that the date (c1387) traditionally given as that of his birth and continued by Vasari, was derived from an erroneous inscription giving 1407 as the year when he entered the Dominican convent at Fiesole as a novice. Some time before 1423, when he had taken the name Giovanni and was known as Fra Giovanni da Fiesole, he entered the convent (of which he became prior in 1449). Just when he took his vows is not known, but by this time he was already a painter. Throughout his life he remained attached to the house at Fiesole and its daughter house of San Marco at Florence, to which the Dominicans moved in 1436 under the patronage of Cosimo de' Medici. Vasari says he might have gained great wealth as a painter but that he preferred to spend his life in the service of God. The dates of his earliest paintings are not known. From the early period is an *Annunciation*, now in the Diocesan Museum at Cortona, painted when he was already master of his art. His copies or repetitions of this masterpiece are in the monastery at Montecarlo, near Arezzo, and at Madrid. Also at Cortona is a *Virgin and Saints*. Five panels, *Christ in Glory*, with a multitude of saints, Apostles, Doctors of the Church, Evangelists, and Beati of the Dominican Order, in the National Gallery at London, are of the period before 1435. The panels formed the predella of the altarpiece he painted for the Church of S. Domenico near Fiesole. The main panel of the altarpiece, *Virgin and Child Enthroned with Eight Angels between SS. Thomas Aquinas, Barnabas, Dominic, and Peter Martyr*, now in a chapel of the church, was repainted and radically changed by Lorenzo di Credi in 1501. Another painting of the early period is a *Virgin and Child Enthroned*, now in the Museum of San Marco at Florence. It was commissioned by the guild of the linen drapers and is known as the Linaiuoli triptych. It is the only secular commission Fra Angelico is known to have executed. Around the central panel of the triptych is a wooden frame, on which he painted twelve music-making angels. These, singing or playing various instruments, are among the widest known of Fra Angelico's paintings. The angels have been reproduced, together or singly, over and over again. In their delicate colors, their winsome, winning reverence and joy, they touch some universal chord.

In 1436, as noted above, the Dominicans of Fiesole moved to San Marco. Cosimo de' Medici commissioned the architect Michelozzo to rebuild the convent there. The reconstructed convent, with its lovely cloister, is in the simple, austere style of mid-15th century Florentine architecture. Fra Angelico, of whom Cosimo was ever the devoted patron, decorated the convent, and it is now the repository of the greatest single collection of his paintings and frescoes. With his assistants he frescoed all the cells on the upper floor, including that of Cosimo and that later occupied by Savonarola. The frescoes, with religious themes, were intended as aids and inspiration to meditation, not as decorations. On the same floor is what some consider to be his masterpiece, an *Annunciation.* In the Chapter Room another superb work is a *Crucifixion,* one of the most beautiful examples of Italian painting. His *Coronation of the Virgin* in San Marco portrays the Court of Heaven in his characteristic clarity of color. (Other paintings on this theme are in the Louvre and in the Uffizi.) A *Deposition,* in the museum of San Marco, shows him to have reached his full powers and is a complete expression of his style. It also reveals that he had made his own such developments of Florentine painting as variety of expression and gesture and the naturalistic approach to landscape, with which he replaced the Gothic gold backgrounds of his earlier paintings. Other works in the museum include some lovely panels he painted to decorate the doors of a silver chest for the Annunziata. At the end of 1445 he went to Rome on the invitation of Pope Eugenius IV, who had spent a number of years in Florence and knew his work. Eugenius died (February 23, 1447) and the work Fra Angelico did at Rome was carried on under the patronage of Nicholas V. Most of this work has perished. Paul III built a staircase (1540) through the Chapel of the Holy Sacrament that he had frescoed. Surviving, in a damaged and repainted state, are scenes from the lives of St. Stephen and St. Lawrence that he frescoed in the Chapel of Nicholas V in the Vatican. Perhaps by arrangement, he spent several months or about two years at Orvieto where, with his assistants, particularly Benozzo Gozzoli, he painted *Christ in Majesty* and *Sixteen Prophets,* in the Chapel of S. Brizio in the cathedral. The work he began there was ultimately carried to completion by Luca Signorelli and includes a portrait of Fra Angelico. Signorelli's style was conditioned by all the advances in technique that had taken place in Renaissance painting, with particular emphasis and interest in the human figure, as well as by his own dramatic temperament. Fra Angelico's style is at least partially derived from Lorenzo Monaco and conditioned by his own serene religiosity. The contrast is striking. Back in San Marco by 1449, he returned to Rome about 1452 and died there in 1455. He was buried in S. Maria sopra Minerva. The celebrated humanist Lorenzo Valla wrote the inscription for his tomb.

Fundamental to Fra Angelico's painting was his unblemished and unquestioning faith. It is impossible to look at his work without being aware of the joyously religious spirit that animates it. Vasari writes that he never began a painting without praying, that he wept when he painted a *Crucifixion,* and that he never retouched or repainted, leaving his work as it had been sent to him by God. Artistically influenced by Lorenzo Monaco and Ghiberti, he was also aware—perhaps from observation of Masaccio's frescoes in the Brancacci Chapel in the Church of the Carmine at Florence, as well as from the work of other innovators—of developments that were taking place in Florence. There is evidence of an interest in perspective and of the fascination of the Florentines with the human figure in some of his work (as in the lovely *Adoration of the Magi,* National Gallery, Washington, although these factors may be owing to Fra Filippo Lippi, who painted part of it). On the other hand, his beautiful *Coronation of the Virgin* in San Marco, with its lovely harmonies and arrangement of color, betrays no interest in perspective as a tool for providing space for the great crowd worshipping the Queen of Heaven. His awareness of technical developments, and his use of them when it suited his purpose, combined with a painting tradition that looked back to Giotto and his followers, plus a medieval religious orientation, make him a painter of the transition between the Middle Ages and the full Renaissance. The atmosphere he creates with the clarity of his beautiful color (his translucent blue is almost a hallmark) and a sharpness of outline that bespeaks the miniaturist is one of joy in the love of God. His output was prodigious and, perhaps because of the esteem and affection in which he was held, has been unusually well preserved, although heavily repainted in many cases. Well over two hundred of his paintings in tempera and fresco have survived. These were done with the assistance of his pupils and collaborators, chief of whom were Benozzo Gozzoli and Zanobi Strozzi. The greatest collection of his works is at Florence, primarily in San Marco and its museum, with others in various churches and galleries. Among the various cities of Italy where his paintings may be seen are Rome, Perugia, and Bergamo. Outside of Italy they appear in museums at Paris, London, Munich, Frankfurt, Leningrad, Dublin, and elsewhere. In the United States there are paintings in the National Gallery, Washington; the Museum of Fine Arts and the Isabella Stewart Gardner Museum, Boston; the Fogg Museum, Cambridge; the Johnson Collection, Philadelphia; The Metropolitan Museum of Art, New York; Detroit, Hartford, Houston, and elsewhere. Loved and admired for his goodness and piety in his own time, by as early as 1481 he was spoken of as *Beato*, although it is not certain that he was ever formally beatified. Vasari writes lovingly of this kind, gentle, and deeply religious man. And indeed his dedication, devotion, and simplicity glow through all his works. For him, to paint the choirs of heaven was to worship God with his whole soul.

Angelo da Castro (än′jā-lō dä käs′trō). Jurisconsult; d. at Padua 1485. He was the son of the jurisconsult Paolo da Castro. He was especially notable in his time for his knowledge of canon law, taught at Padua, served in Rome as a consistorial advocate, and returned (1458) to Padua to resume the teaching of law at the university.

Angelo di Taddeo Gaddi (dē täd-dā′ō gäd′dē). See **Gaddi, Agnolo.**

Angelo da Tivoli (dä tē′vō-lē). Sculptor; active in the 15th century. Works attributed to him are in the Church of S. Maria Maggiore at Tivoli.

Anghiera (däng-gyā′rä), **Pietro Martire d'.** Historian and geographer; b. at Arona, 1459; d. at Granada, Spain, 1526. Little is known of his early life. He apparently had a solid humanist education, for in 1478 he was at Rome, first as secretary to the governor and then in the service of the cardinals Ascanio Sforza and Giovanni Arcimboldi. He next entered the service of the count of Tendilla, Spanish ambassador to the Holy See, and, in August, 1487, left Italy with the count for Spain. He remained in Spain for the rest of his life, and it was there that he made his greatest contributions. He took part in the Spanish wars against the Moors. After the fall of Granada (1491) he remained in that city, gave up his military career, and became a priest. From this time he was the protégé and confidant of Queen Isabella. He was an observer of the great undertakings of Columbus and a participant in the triumphal welcome accorded the navigator on his return from his first voyage. In 1492 he had opened a school for young nobles at Madrid; later he was tutor of the Spanish princes, and in 1501 he was sent as ambassador to Venice and Egypt. The careful description of what he had observed in Egypt served to dispel many curious notions that were entertained about that country even as late as the 15th century. An industrious letter-writer, he had described the wars of the Moors in his letters, and began to write of the numerous expeditions, discoveries, and explorations of the New World that were taking place. His letters are among the most important of contemporary sources of the events of those stirring days. His contacts with Vasco da Gama, Amerigo Vespucci, Hernando Cortés, and Magellan gave him a central position from which to view and record the discoveries of the earth that were taking place. He continued as the trusted adviser of Isabella and after her death (1504) maintained his exalted position at the Spanish court. In 1524 he became a member of the Council of the Indies, and he held other public offices. His great work is *De Orbe Novo Decades Octo*, the first complete edition of which was published after his death (Alcalá, 1530). The eight books cover more than thirty years of exploration and discovery, beginning with Columbus. His work, the most complete contemporary account, is recorded with the utmost care and industry, and with scrupulous impartiality.

Angiolieri (än-jō-lyā′rē), **Cecco.** Sienese poet; b. at Siena, c1260; d. 1312. He was a contemporary of Dante, with whom he corresponded and with whom he may have fought at the battle of Campaldino (1289). He led a highly irregular life, which is reflected in some of his 150 extant lyrics; hated his father and mother for their avarice, which he memorialized in his often bitter poems on the penniless state in which they kept him; often chose as his subjects little dramas, frustrations, or amusing incidents of daily life; and was one of the earliest masters of humorous verse. His style was impetuous and headlong, usually sardonic in its approach to the accepted ideas and tenets of his day, and an expression of his own temperament, as distinguished from the conventional approach of many of his contemporaries. His disappointment and defiance are indicated in the following selection (Rossetti's translation):

If I were fire, I'd burn the world away;
If I were wind, I'd turn my storms thereon;
If I were water, I'd soon let it drown;
If I were God, I'd sink it from the day.

Anglerius (ang-glā′ri-us), **Petrus Martyr.** See **Anghiera, Pietro Martire d'.**

Anguillara (äng-gwēl-lä′rä). Ancient noble family that, as counts of Anguillara, about fourteen miles from Rome, played a prominent role in the medieval history of Rome and of Tuscia Romana. The family, perhaps of Lombard origin, began to emerge from obscurity and to be important with Pandolfo I (1186). As enemies of their Ghibelline neighbors of Vico, the counts of Anguillara were Guelphs. In the 14th century they confirmed their power in the patrimony and held high offices in Rome. Supporters of the Angevin party in Naples, Francesco and Pandolfo III were vicars of King Robert. Orso was a senator many times, and it was he who, for King Robert, crowned Petrarch on the Capitoline, at Easter, 1341. Petrarch had been his guest in his castle at Capranica, and dedicated a sonnet to him. In the 15th century, Count Everso dell' Anguillara was a swashbuckling Renaissance lord. Under him the power of the family reached its height. At the same time, the seeds of its decline were sown. He supported Pope Eugenius IV and destroyed the prefects of Vico, neighbors of Anguillara, but did so at a time when the popes were expanding their temporal power and could no longer permit independent princedoms within the Papal States. He allied himself with the Colonna family to resist the pope's attempts to bring Anguillara under the Church. Pius II, who battled with him, wrote that he was always hostile to the pope. "He was tenacious of his own possessions and greedy for those of others, cared nothing for religion or God, and said repeatedly that the world was governed by chance and that the souls of men and beasts alike were mortal. He was blasphemous and cruel and it was as easy for him to kill a man as a sheep." Pius wrote that Everso planned to kill him by attaching poison to his chair. Everso was intermittently subdued by the pope. Paul II excommunicated Everso's sons, Francesco and Deifobo, for breaking their sworn oath to the Church, banished them, and destroyed their power. Francesco languished in prison until 1471. Deifobo entered the service of the Venetians, and the family power in the affairs of Rome and the patrimony became negligible. The red tower of the Anguillara family at Rome still stands.

Anguissola (än-gwē-sō′lä), **Sofonisba.** Painter; b. at Cremona, c1528; d. at Palermo, c1624. At Cremona she studied painting under Bernardino Campi (1546–1550) and then under Soiaro (Bernardino Gatti). By the middle of the century she had achieved such renown that she was invited (1559) to Spain. She went there the following year, was received with honor at the court of Philip II, and painted portraits of the royal family. In 1580, as the wife of the Spaniard Don Fabrizio Moncada, she was at Palermo. Five years later, with her second husband, Orazio Lomellino, she was at Genoa and it is said that by this time (1585) she was blind. Later she returned to Palermo, and there Anton Van Dyck saw her (July 12, 1624) and drew a picture of the 96-year-old artist. Through her training under Campi she was exposed to the influence of the school of Raphael and of Parmigianino. To this were added, under

Soiaro, the sweetness and languor of Correggio, which appear in her rare religious paintings, as the *Holy Family* in the Accademia Carrara at Bergamo and the *Pietà* in the Brera at Milan. But in her special field of portrait painting the influences were rather from the Venetians. Among her self-portraits are those in the Uffizi, in the Brera, at Naples, and at Vienna. Other works are at Brescia, Siena, Berlin, Poznań, Baltimore (Walters Art Gallery), Oberlin, Ohio, and elsewhere.

Animuccia (ä-nē-möt′chä), **Giovanni.** [Called **Father of the Oratorio.**] Italian composer of sacred music; b. at Florence, c1500; d. at Rome, 1571. He was the predecessor (1555 *et seq.*) of Palestrina as maestro di cappella at Saint Peter's and the source of some of his ideas. He has been called "The Father of the Oratorio" for his dramatic laude, considered predecessors of the later form.

Anne of Brittany (an, brit′a̤-ni). [**Anne de Bretagne.**] Queen of France; b. at Nantes, France, 1476; d. at Blois, France, 1514. She was the daughter and heiress of Francis II, duke of Brittany. She married (1491) Charles VIII of France and, after his death, became (1499) the wife of his successor, Louis XII. Through her, Brittany, the last of the great fiefs of France, was permanently united to the French crown.

Anne de France (ȧn de̤ fräṅs). [Also, **Anne de Beaujeu.**] Regent of France (1483–1490); b. c1460; d. 1522. A daughter of Louis XI, she served as regent for her brother, Charles VIII.

Annio (än′nyō) or **Nanni** (nän′nē), **Giovanni.** [Also called **Annius of Viterbo.**] Dominican monk and scholar; b. at Viterbo, 1432; d. November 13, 1502. He was noted in his day for his knowledge of Oriental languages, for his theology, and as a preacher and archeologist. Popes Sixtus IV and Alexander VI honored him during his lifetime, and gave him church posts. After his death he was sharply attacked for his *Antiquitatum variarum volumina XVII*, which was a collection of fragments supposedly from ancient authors, many of whom were unknown and most of whose quotes were of doubtful authenticity.

Anselmi (än-sel′mē), **Giorgio.** Music theorist; b. at Parma; d. before 1443. Little is known of his life. He was one of the 15th century scholars and theorists who linked music and mathematics. His *De musica*, highly regarded in his own day, was misplaced and considered as lost, but was found in 1824 by the prefect of the Ambrosian Library at Milan. It is written in dialogue form, and its three parts (on celestial, instrumental, and vocal harmony) came to be called *De harmonia dialoghi*. Interesting as an example of the theoretical work of his time, it does not actually contribute new elements to musical theory nor a new system of musical notation.

Anselmi, Michelangelo. Painter of the school of Parma; b. at Lucca, 1491 or 1492; d. at Parma, between 1554 and 1556. He went to Siena, where he studied the works of Sodoma, but by c1520 was at Parma, and thereafter became one of the most ardent, and also one of the best, disciples of Correggio. Henceforth the vigor of Sodoma was replaced by the melting sweetness of Correggio. He painted frescoes in the principal church of Busseto, near Parma (1538–1539), and executed many frescoes in churches at Parma. Works in the National Gallery of Parma include *Madonna and Child with the Young St. John* and *Holy Family with St. Barbara and an Angel*. Other paintings are at Naples, Milan, and Paris.

Antico (län-tē′kō), **L'.** [Real name, **Pier Iacopo Alari Bonacolsi.**] Mantuan goldsmith, sculptor, and medalist; b. c1460; d. at Gazzuolo, July, 1528. He worked for Federigo I Gonzaga and for his brother Gianfrancesco, lord of Bozzolo. After the death of the latter he returned to Mantua and then went to Rome, where he studied the remains of ancient statues with great industry. The Gonzaga were his lifelong patrons. Isabella d'Este, wife of Francesco II, gave him ancient statues to restore. His own sculpture was manifestly derived from the antique (whence his name, L'Antico), and includes an *Apollo* at Venice, a *Cupid* and a *Cupid Drawing His Bow* in the Bargello at Florence, his masterpiece, *Hercules and Antaeus*, at Vienna, where there are other examples of his work, and works at Modena, London, and Berlin. He designed medals of several members of the Gonzaga family, and made a bronze vase, richly ornamented with a scene of Neptune and his court in a ship drawn by seahorses; it is at Modena.

Antiquarj (än-tē-kwä′rē), **Jacopo.** [**Jacobus Antiquarius.**] Humanist; b. at Perugia,

MICHELANGELO ANSELMI
Young David Playing the Harp
Study for a monochrome fresco painted in S. Maria della Steccata, Parma
Courtesy of The Metropolitan Museum of Art, New York, Rogers Fund, 1961

c1444; d. at Milan, 1512. Of a noble Perugian family, he studied humane letters in his native city, entered (1468) the service of Giovanni Battista Savelli, governor of Perugia, as a secretary, and later went with him to Bologna. He was later at the court of Galeazzo Maria Sforza at Milan, first in an ecclesiastical capacity. His marked gifts won him the respect and admiration of the court and he became secretary to Galeazzo Maria. His services and talents, the many missions he skillfully fulfilled, preserved his place at the court during the reign of the Sforzas and their successors. Admired for his learning and taste and loved for his generous spirit, he enjoyed friendly contacts with many of the men of letters of his day. He had an excellent knowledge of Latin, and wrote many essays and studies, of which few remain. Among his extant works are an oration on King Louis of France, a collection of letters, and some verses, *Carmina*.

Antonello da Messina (än-tō-nel′lō dä mes-sē′nä). Painter; b. at Messina, c1430; d. there, between February 14, when he made his will, and February 25, 1479. Although some documents exist concerning his life, there are long gaps in his painting life when nothing is known of his activities. The first notices of him date from 1457, when he was commissioned to paint a gonfalon for Reggio Calabria similar to one he had previously painted at Messina. In the same year he took a pupil. Thus he was by this time already a painter of local note. His first teacher is thought to have been Colantonio, with whom he worked at Naples. At Naples he would have seen a triptych of the *Annunciation* in the king's palace, painted by Jan van Eyck, as well as the work of other painters who worked in the Flemish tradition. This would perhaps account for the strong Flemish influence in some of his work, as in the *St. Jerome in His Study*, in the National Gallery, London, which abounds in the meticulously worked details and individual still lifes so dear to the Flemish painters of interiors, as well as for the minutely executed landscapes and walled towns of his *Crucifixions* (as at Sibiu and Antwerp). It would also account for his knowledge of the technique of painting in oils, which he adopted, introduced at Venice, and applied in an Italian spirit with warmth and intensity. (Vasari writes that he discovered the method of oil painting, but the technique was in fact known before his time.) Shortly after 1457 he left Messina, for he is known to have returned there in 1460 and to have remained at least until 1465. From this year (1465) is the earliest known painting that has survived, the *Salvator Mundi* or *Christ Blessing*, in the National Gallery, London. This signed and dated work, compelling in its majesty and mysticism, is the work of a fully developed painter, yet one whose development continued as he selected and modified elements from the works of painters of genius to suit his own genius and style. In 1475 he went to Venice, where he painted the altarpiece of S. Cassiano that a certain Pietro Bono had commissioned. Even before it was completed, his delighted patron wrote of it (March, 1476) that it was "one of the most excellent works of the brush in Italy, or outside of Italy." The good Bono was overenthusiastic, for in this work, the largest that Antonello ever attempted, judging by the fragments of it that remain (at Vienna) he was less successful than was ordinarily the case in his painting at infusing it with charm and life. But the Venetians were enchanted, especially by the geometry of its composition. In 1475, probably at Venice, he also painted one of his most exquisite and dramatic works, a *Crucifixion* now at Antwerp. In the three nude figures on the crosses he achieved the perfection of modeling by the use of light and shadow, which is one of his greatest gifts. The arched body of the thief on the cross to the right, echoing and exaggerating as it does the curved main stem of the cross, is instinct with drama and superb artistic knowledge and control. In the violence of the reality, Antonello presents idealized abstractions of figures. The painting combines the chief elements of Antonello's art: the creation of form and substance by light and shadow, a carefully detailed landscape, intensity of color, and spiritual drama. His *St. Sebastian*, at Dresden, is also a superb example of these characteristics. The substance and form of the saint's idealized figure is realized by an exquisite play of light and shadow. The figure is further given volume by an architectural background that recedes through judiciously spotted figures to a minutely detailed balustrade against which carefully executed miniscule figures lean.

While he was still at Venice, Galeazzo Maria Sforza invited him to Milan to paint portraits, for which he was already known. Of 1475 is a portrait called, from the impression it gives, *The Condottiere*, now in the Louvre, Paris. Antonello may have gone to Milan, but probably by the end of the year 1476 he was back at Messina, and in 1478 he was there carrying out a commission for another gonfalon. As far as is known, he spent most of his painting life in and about Messina, except for the brief visits to Venice and Milan, carrying out commissions for churches in little towns of Sicily and Calabria and painting portraits. (Vasari says he went to Flanders, and though some scholars think he must have done so, in order to account for his knowledge of Flemish painting and his contemporary fame, no evidence exists of such a journey.) He painted a number of highly individualized and naturalistic portraits, so psychologically penetrating that though the sitters are in most cases unknown, the impressions of their characters are so strong that they have been given names, as *The Condottiere*, cited above, and *The Pirate* (*Portrait of a Man*), at Cefalù. Other portraits are at Berlin, London (National Gallery), Milan (Castello Sforzesco), Pavia, Rome (Borghese Gallery), Turin, and in the Metropolitan Museum (New York), the National Gallery (Washington), and the Johnson Collection (Philadelphia). Other works include a *Virgin Annunciate*, at Palermo, a lovely painting of the bust of the Virgin, a shawl over her head and shoulders of the intense blue that is characteristic of Antonello, her right hand, beautifully foreshortened, slightly raised as if to bless, and a tender expression of expectancy and acceptance on her youthful but not childlike face. Another *Virgin Annunciate* is at Munich. In the Museo Nazionale, Reggio Calabria, is *St. Jerome Penitent*; at Messina is a damaged polyptych of St. Gregory (1473). Besides a damaged *Annunciation* (1474) at Syracuse, there are three panels of saints at Palermo, an *Ecco Homo* at Genoa and another at Piacenza, a *Pietà* at Venice, a *Madonna and Child*, National Gallery (Washington), and another in the Metropolitan (New York). A *Madonna Reading* (the subject has been identified as St. Rosalia), Baltimore, is also attributed to him. A painting recently (1965) acquired by the Prado in Madrid, *Dead*

Christ Supported by an Angel, has his characteristic intense blue sky.

Antonello has been called the greatest Italian painter of his period. His beautiful paintings are intensely personal yet possess universality; they abound in charm and life and are executed with consummate technique. He is an intriguing painter for the influences that worked on him and for those he exerted on others, especially on the Venetians and through them on the painters of Lombardy and Emilia. In spite of the fact that he appears to have spent most of his painting life in and about Messina, not noted as an outstanding art center in his time, he was not a provincial painter but one who made developments that had taken place in Flanders and in northern Italy his own—one, in fact, who blended these elements to form a personal, Italian style that influenced Italian painters well into the 16th century. The Venetians had lagged behind the Tuscans in developing their own school. Through Mantegna they had adopted Florentine interest in form and structure, and perhaps from this Venetian element Antonello profited in his brief stay in Venice. In turn he had a profound impact on Venetian painting and stimulated it to leap ahead into what amounted to the leading school, with his oil technique, his nonlinear modeling, his intense color, and his naturalistic portraits. Giovanni Bellini, a leading Venetian at the time of Antonello's visit and for many years thereafter, was one of those who felt his influence. Whether Antonello was a painter of the Venetian school, as is sometimes said, or whether many Venetians were Antonellians is a question argued by scholars. What is a fact is that he was one of the great painters of the 15th century.

Antonello da Saliba (dä sä-lē′bä). See **Saliba, Antonello da.**

Antoniano (än-tō-nyä′nō), **Silvio.** Humanist and ecclesiastic; b. at Rome, December 31, 1540; d. August 16, 1603. At the age of 11 he showed such skill at improvising that he was given the epithet "Il poetino." He had a full and varied career: as a teacher of eloquence and letters at Ferrara (at the age of 16), Venice, Florence, and Rome; and in various capacities in the service of Cardinals Borromeo at Milan and Morone in Germany, and at the Vatican. As a humanist, he favored Cicero as the model for style. He wrote a great deal himself—Latin verses and orations—but he is best remembered for his treatise on education, *De l'educazione cristiana e politica dei figliuoli* (Verona, 1584), written as a guide to help parents give their children a sound Catholic upbringing and education. Cardinal Carlo Borromeo had suggested the treatise as part of his vigorous action to combat the Reformation. Influences of Plutarch, Cicero, and Quintilian appear in the work, but above all it reflects the moral and educational principles of the reforming Council of Trent, and presents some educational theories that have passed into modern pedagogy. The book was immensely popular, was widely used, and continued to be reprinted in succeeding centuries.

Antoniazzo Romano (än-to-nyät′tsō rō-mä′no). [Real name, **Antoniazzo Aquili.**] Umbrian painter; b. at Rome; active 1461–1508. Umbrian in his training, his earliest known work is an alterpiece in the Museo Civico at Rieti, painted 1464. It indicates, as do frescoes at Rome, that in his early period he was a follower of Benozzo Gozzoli. Later he was influenced by Piero della Francesca, as noted in a *Madonna* (1467) in the Church of S. Francesco near Subiaco, a *St. Anthony* at Tivoli, and a very beautiful *Madonna and Child*, and others. Later still he was influenced by Melozzo da Forlì. He collaborated (1475) with Domenico Ghirlandaio in the Vatican, and later worked there with Pietro Perugino. A vigorous and individual painter, he left many works. Besides those cited above, there are mural paintings in the Chapel of St. Catherine in S. Maria sopra Minerva and paintings in many other churches and galleries in or near Rome, frescoes in the castle of Bracciano and in the Church of S. Giovanni Evangelista, Tivoli; paintings of the Madonna in the Uffizi, Florence; *St. Jerome* in the Poldi Pezzoli Museum, Milan; Madonnas in the National Gallery of Umbria at Perugia, The Metropolitan Museum of Art, New York, and the Fogg Museum, Cambridge, Massachusetts. An *Annunciation* in the Isabella Stewart Gardner Museum, Boston, is attributed to him, and there are paintings at Baltimore (Walters Art Gallery), Detroit, Houston, Lewisburg, Pennsylvania, Los Angeles, Providence, Worcester, Massachusetts, and elsewhere.

Antonino de Ferraris (än-tō-nē′nō dā fer-rä′rēs). Lombard painter; active in the beginning of the 15th century. He executed frescoes of scenes from the life of St. John the Baptist in the Church of S. Luca at Cremona, fragments of which remain, and also worked on the castle at Pavia.

Antoninus (an-tō-nī′nus), Saint. [Original name, **Antonio Pierozzi**; called **Antonio de' Forciglioni.**] Archbishop of Florence; b. at Florence, March 1, 1389; d. at Montughi, May 2, 1459. He entered the Dominican order in 1405 and had a successful career. He was prior at Cortona (1420), Naples (1428), and Rome (1431). In 1439, after filling other offices in his order, he became prior of the convent of S. Marco at Florence. There he was overseer of the work of Fra Angelico and of the miniaturist Fra Benedetto, and, with the legacy of Niccolò Niccoli, opened the first public library in Europe. Pope Eugenius IV named him archbishop of Florence in 1445. He was assiduous in the care of his archdiocese, ministered to the poor and needy and, although retiring by nature, undertook missions for Florence to popes Calixtus III and Pius II. As a defender of Florentine liberty he opposed the Medici. Antoninus was a model prelate and an outstanding example of the dedicated ecclesiastic. Free of fanaticism, he understood men and their needs, and was activated by a profound and pure faith. Among his works, written in the vernacular and with the aim of giving practical as well as pious guidance and counsel, are his *Opera a ben vivere*, written for the edification of Lorenzo de' Medici's wife; *Regola di vita cristiana*, outlining a guide for the Christian life; and letters of principle and instruction. His *Summa theologica moralis* (Venice, 1477) is among the earliest to consider ethics in commerce and banking, and was printed in fifteen editions during the succeeding fifty years. The works of Antoninus are shining testimonials of his practical good sense, moderation, firm moral principles, and purity of soul. He was buried in S. Marco at Florence and was canonized by Pope Adrian VI (May 31, 1523).

Antonio da Alatri (än-tō′nyō dä ä-lä′trē). Painter; active in the first half of the 15th century. Only one painting signed by him is known. It is a *Virgin* in S. Maria Maggiore at Alatri, and shows, in simpler forms, the influence of Gentile da Fabriano. Other paintings in churches in the neighborhood are attributed to him on stylistic grounds. His works, with those of his followers, are forerunners of Renaissance developments in areas near Rome.

Antonio da Bitonto (dä bē-tôn′tō). Franciscan preacher; b. at Bitonto, c1380; d. 1459. He won renown for his interpretation of Holy Writ and for his preaching. He modeled himself, in the latter respect, on St. Bernardino of Siena. He preached in many parts of Italy and lectured on theology at Ferrara, Bologna, and Mantua. While preaching at Naples (1444), he engaged in a dispute with Lorenzo Valla, the philologist, on the origin of the Credo. Pope Nicholas V chose him as one of the Franciscans who were to preach a crusade against the Turks (1455). He left many collections of sermons.

Antonio della Corna (del′lä kôr′nä). Painter; active in the second half of the 15th century. He was a pupil of Mantegna and may have assisted him in painting the *Camera degli Sposi* in the palace at Mantua. The influence of Mantegna clearly appears in a polyptych, *Madonna of Mercy*, in the Church of S. Andrea at Asola (Mantua), among others. His painting also reflects the influence of the Ferrarese school. Other work attributed to him includes some detached frescoes in the Museo Civico at Cremona: *Tobias and the Archangel* and *Madonna Adoring the Child.*

Antonio da Ferrara (dä fer-rä′rä). [Also, **Antonio Beccari.**] Poet; b. at Ferrara, 1315; d. between 1371 and 1374. He was the son of a poor butcher, spent his youth in study, and then entered upon a wandering life during which he had many brushes with the law. From his autobiography, written in terza rima, it is apparent that in 1340 he vowed to reform his disorderly life, and made pilgrimages to Florence, Padua, and St. James of Campostella. The reform was not permanent; in 1343 he was exiled from Florence for his part in a brawl there. His wanderings took him to Ravenna, Forlì, Padua, Venice, back to Florence, and Siena. Petrarch knew him, and mentions his death. An early type of court poet and hanger-on of many despots, Beccari's songs are in the jongleur tradition, and include love lyrics, verses on political subjects, laments, and melancholy lays on world weariness.

Antonio Alberti da Ferrara (äl-ber′tē dä fer-rä′rä). Painter of the Marchigian school; b. at Ferrara, between 1390 and 1400; d. before 1449. He went to Urbino as a young man, and was principally influenced by the school of Gentile da Fabriano, of which he was a competent, if uninspired follower. The decorative curves with which he outlined the borders of drapery are exaggerations of the international Gothic style. In the National Gallery of the Marches at Urbino there is a polyptych, signed and dated 1439. Around the central panel, a *Madonna*, are fourteen additional panels, in two rows, with figures of saints, including St. Agatha carrying her breasts on a plate. Other works of this painter and fragments of frescoes by him are in the same gallery.

Antonio Lombardo (lôm-bär′dō). Sculptor; b. c1458; d. at Ferrara, 1516? He was the son of the sculptor Pietro Lombardo (c1435–1515), was trained in his father's shop, and with his brother Tullio (c1455–1532) worked on many commissions for the shop. These included the Pietro Mocenigo monument, SS. Giovanni e Paolo, Venice, completed in 1481, and the Vendramin and Giovanni Mocenigo monuments at Venice as well as others at Treviso. In 1503 he, with Alessandro Leopardi, received the commission to execute the Zen Chapel and monument in S. Marco. Cardinal Zen had left money in his will for the structures, and had laid down detailed specifications as to the monument and its gilded bronze figures, with emphasis on his wish to have it follow the antique as closely as possible where stated. Leopardi withdrew and in 1504 Antonio and his brother, with assistants, carried on the work. Antonio's model of the *Virgin and Child* for the altar is a lovely work that translates in bronze the humanity of the Madonna as Giovanni Bellini was expressing it in paint. A relief, *The Miracle of the Newborn Child*, in the chapel of the saint in the Basilica of St. Anthony at Padua, with its group of what appear to be Roman matrons, indicates his close study of the antique and lacks spontaneity or feeling. In 1506 Antonio went to Ferrara to work for Alfonso d'Este. For him he executed a series of reliefs in alabaster on mythological subjects; a number of these are now at Leningrad.

Antonio di Mario (dē mä′ryō). Florentine copyist and notary; active between 1417 and 1461. He practiced his profession as a notary and was an expert copyist of classical manuscripts, one of the most active of his time. He copied books for Cosimo and Piero de' Medici, Cardinal Albergati, and others. Over forty manuscript copies signed by him have been discovered.

Antonio da Negroponte (dä nā-grō-pōn′tā). Venetian painter of the second half of the 15th century. He was a follower of Jacopo Bellini. Only one certain work from his hand is known. It is a painting in tempera, *Madonna and Child and Angels* (1465–1470), Morosini Chapel, S. Francesco della Vigna, Venice, and is notable for its graceful ornamentation and decorative garland of fruit above the Virgin's throne. Such garlands became a hallmark in the work of Carlo Crivelli. Otherwise, the painting is a rather old-fashioned work that looks back to the Gothic tradition, of interest for its luminous color and elegant details.

Antonio Veneziano (ve-nā-tsyä′nō). See **Veneziano, Antonio.**

Antonio da Viterbo (dä vē-ter′bō). [Called **Il Pastura.**] Painter; active between 1478 and 1509. He entered the Corporation of St. Luke (Painters' Guild) at Rome in 1478. A provincial master whose main inspirations were, first, Pinturicchio, with whom he studied at Rome and with whom he may have worked in the Borgia apartments in the Vatican; and second, Perugino, who later in his life had great influence on him. He worked on several occasions at Orvieto, restoring frescoes in the cathedral painted over a century earlier by Ugolino di Prete Ilario, and executing some of his own. Several other works at Orvieto, in the cathedral and other churches, are attributed to him. Several works are at Viterbo, where he worked in 1504, including an *Adoration of the Shepherds* and a detached fresco. His most important work is a series of frescoes, some of which have been destroyed or damaged, at Tarquinia (1509). Of those surviving, that on the *Birth of the Virgin* shows familiarity with Ghirlandaio's painting on this subject in S. Maria Novella, Florence, and the *Marriage of the Virgin* is strongly influenced by Pinturicchio and Perugino. The frames he painted in grisaille for the frescoes at Tarquinia are fine examples of his love of decoration, being composed of garlands, medallions with coats-of-arms, putti, and mythological figures. Other works are a *Virgin and Child with the Youthful Baptist and St. Jerome*, Johnson Collection, Philadelphia; a *Madonna*, in the Morgan Library, and *Madonna and Child with St. Jerome and St. Francis*, the Metropolitan Museum, New York; a *Madonna and Saints*, in the Church of S. Cosimato, Rome, a youthful work with a typically Umbrian landscape; there is a triptych in the Vatican, and paintings at Assisi, Montefiascone, Berlin, and Atlanta, Georgia.

Antonius (an-tō′nyus). Dialogue by Giovanni Pontano in which, by the device of a trip through Italy, he comments, often maliciously, on customs, superstitions, and manners in various parts of Italy.

Apianus (ap-i-ā′nus), **Petrus.** [Also, **Peter Apian**; original name, **Peter Bienewitz** or **Bennewitz.**] German mathematician and cosmographer; b. at Leipzig, Saxony, 1501; d. April 21, 1552. He was the author of an astronomical work and of *Cosmographicus liber* (1524), a mathematical geography containing some of the earliest known maps of America.

Apostolius (ap-o̤s-tō′li-us), **Arsenius.** Greek scholar and ecclesiastic; b. in Crete, 1465; d. at Venice, 1535. He was the son and pupil of Michael Apostolius, Greek scholar who fled to Italy on the fall of Constantinople (1453). Arsenius Apostolius entered upon an ecclesiastical career, and was named metropolitan of Monemvasia but was forced to relinquish his office for a time when a conflict over orthodoxy arose. He was restored to his office ten years later. He spent a short time at Florence, then went to Venice, where he joined with other learned Greeks in the preparation of Greek texts for the press of Aldus Manutius. He was a noted calligrapher, and a number of manuscripts in his hand are extant.

Aquilano (ä-kwē-lä′nō), **Serafino.** See **Serafino dell' Aquila.**

Aquilante (ä-kwē-län′tā). In Lodovico Ariosto's *Orlando Furioso*, a knight called "the Black," and the brother of Grifone, who is called "the White." The brothers were brought up by two fairies. They meet Astolfo on the banks of the Nile. Aquilante accompanies Astolfo to Jerusalem and the land of the Amazons and, after many trials, to Paris.

Aquinas (a̤-kwī′na̤s), Saint **Thomas.** [Called **Doctor Angelicus, Father of Moral Philosophy,** and, in fun by his schoolmates, the **Dumb Ox.**] Dominican theologian; b. at Roccasecca, near Aquino, c1225; d. at Fossanuova, 1274. A leading scholastic philosopher, he is ranked with the fathers of the Latin Church. Founder of the philosophical system now called Thomism, and synthesizer of the theology that was pronounced (1879) as official for the Roman Catholic Church, he was a great medieval scholar in breadth of scope and brilliance of logic. His *Summa Theologica* (1267–1273) is a three-part work dealing with God, Man, and Christ. It is intended to summarize all learning and to demonstrate his fundamental belief in the compatibility of faith and reason. It is still studied as one of the greatest philosophical works of all time.

Aquino (dä-kwē′nō), **Maria d'.** See **Fiammetta.**

Aragona (dä-rä-gō′nä), **Tullia d'.** Poet; b. at Rome, 1508; d. there, 1556. She wrote lyrics, *Rime* (1547), that are rather rigidly patterned on Petrarch and, in their content, on Marsilio Ficino's Platonic philosophy of love. A few of these, written for her lover, evince genuine poetic feeling. She is an example of the beautiful and cultivated courtesans whose salons were frequented by the most eminent literary men of the day.

Araldi (är-äl′dē), **Alessandro.** Painter of the school of Parma; b. at Parma, c1460; d. there of the plague, 1528. Lacking in originality, he adopted elements from Francia, Raphael, Costa, Sodoma, Mantegna, and, above all, Pinturicchio. Some think that from 1507 to 1510 he was at Siena, working with Pinturicchio. The style he formed from this amalgamation of the styles of others was at first marked by a certain delicacy, but his lack of discipline and of originality prevented him from achieving any distinction as an artist. He is interesting as a local painter who attempted to unite in his work the best elements of the artists he admired. The frescoes he executed for the Convent of S. Paolo at Parma (1510–1514) remain, including the room decorated with allegories and grotesques. Those he painted in the cathedral (1522) at Parma have been destroyed. An *Annunciation*, signed and dated 1514, and an *Annunciation with Saints Catherine and Sebastian* are in the National Gallery at Parma; his *Portrait of Barbara Pallavicino* is in the Uffizi.

Araldi, Josaphat. Painter of the school of Parma; active in the first three decades of

ARCANGELO DI COLA DA CAMERINO
Annunciation
Biblioteca Ambrosiana, Milan

the 16th century. A rare surviving painting is his *St. Sebastian* in the National Gallery of Parma.

ARCADELT (är′kä-delt), **JACOB.** [Also, **ARCHADELT, ARCHADET, ARCADET, HARCADELT.**] Dutch composer, b. in the Netherlands, c1514; d. at Paris, c1570. He composed masses and other church music, but is best known for secular contrapuntal pieces, especially madrigals. Among the poems he set to music were two by Michelangelo.

ARCADIA (är-kä′dyä). Pastoral work, in Tuscan prose and verse, by Iacopo Sannazzaro, a description of an idealized rural world of shepherds and nymphs that was enormously popular in its day and influenced later poets.

ARCANGELO DI COLA DA CAMERINO (ärk-än′jā-lō dē kō′lä dä kä-mā-rē′nō). Painter; b. at Camerino in the Marches; active 1416–1429. He worked at Città di Castello, visited Florence, and went to Rome (1422) at the invitation of Pope Martin V. In 1425 he was back in Camerino, where he witnessed the will of the widow of the condottiere Braccio da Montone. In his earlier work the international Gothic style of Gentile da Fabriano is the dominant influence, but without Gentile's love of detail; Arcangelo's paintings are almost lacking in ornamentation. He was a contemporary of Masaccio, who was revolutionizing painting at Florence, and some awareness of the Florentine forms and solidity is evident in his later painting. Several panels of the Madonna are attributed to him, as those at Bergen, Bibbiena, Camerino, and New Haven, as well as a fresco, *Madonna and Child Enthroned*, Church of S. Marco, Osimo. A signed diptych, *Madonna and*

Child Enthroned and *Crucifixion*, is in the collection of Miss Helen C. Frick, New York. Four predella panels—*Visitation*, *Nativity*, *Adoration*, and *Flight into Egypt*—are in the Johnson Collection, Philadelphia; another, *Martyrdom of St. Lawrence*, is in the collection of Conte Vittorio Cini, Venice.

Archadelt (är′ċhȧ-delt) or **Archadet, Jacob.** See **Arcadelt, Jacob.**

Architecture. Those historians who maintain that the Renaissance of the Quattrocento constituted a new period of history, one clearly distinguishable from anything that had gone before, offer Brunelleschi and the Renaissance architecture of which he was the founder as solid grounds for their thesis. Before Brunelleschi, architecture in Italy had been largely influenced by the Gothic style of France and Germany. The Trecento buildings of S. Francesco at Assisi, S. Maria Novella and S. Croce at Florence, mark the transition from the Romanesque to the Gothic. The cathedrals of Siena, Orvieto, Florence, and Arezzo, all large architectural projects that remained under construction throughout the Trecento, reveal various adaptations of Gothic forms. In Italy, however, some of the most basic elements of Gothic architecture were rejected. One such rejected element was the flying buttress, which permitted the transformation of walls into opened areas that could be filled with stained glass windows. In Italian Gothic the wall remained an essential component of the structure. Instead of the great areas of stained glass of the northern churches, there were the great fresco series of the Italian churches, as those in the three Trecento churches mentioned above. Also, the extreme vertical quality of the northern Gothic was modified in most Italian examples by the introduction of horizontal members. Typical of this is S. Croce at Florence, believed to have been designed by Arnolfo di Cambio in 1294. Here the nave is covered with a wooden roof-truss whose horizontal beams balance the thin, vertical pilasters, forming with them rectangular patterns that reinforce the basic cubic shape of the plan. Despite the openness of the arches, the linear demarcation of the architectural members and the flat surfaces of the walls create a lucidity of geometric design that is particularly Florentine.

Brunelleschi turned to architecture after an initial experience in another art. He had been trained as a goldsmith, but after losing the competition for the North Doors of the Baptistery at Florence to Ghiberti he decided to become an architect. How he accomplished this, exactly what he did in order to master the techniques of building that resulted in his solution of the problem of how to erect a dome over the preexisting structure of the Cathedral of Florence, is one of the most fascinating mysteries in the history of architecture, since none of his drawings has survived. Evidently he had learned the technique of drawing to scale that enabled him not only to reproduce on paper plans and elevations of existing buildings drawn in perspective, but also to calculate, with mathematical precision and imaginative subtlety, projects for his own buildings. Although scale drawing may have been known previous to Brunelleschi, it had not been employed by medieval architects, who had followed completely different procedures. In the very first buildings that he designed—the Ospedale degli Innocenti and the Church of S. Lorenzo—there appeared a new architectural repertory. His arches are no longer pointed but rounded, and they come to rest on Corinthian columns. Architraves are supported by fluted pilasters, and the Gothic rib vaulting is eliminated in favor of simple domes. This vocabulary of forms was in part derived from classical antiquity, which he had studied and measured at Rome, and from the Romanesque. More important than the revival of these styles implicit in Brunelleschi's architecture, however, is his system of simple, mathematical relationships that give harmonious, clear proportions to his buildings. The materials he employed—white painted walls and the clear, gray stone known as *pietra serena*—not only indicate his economy of expressive means, but emphasize the lightness and grace of his structures as well. It was only at a more advanced phase of his career that he began to conceive of walls in massive, sculptural terms.

Other developments in Renaissance architecture are apparent in the Medici and Rucellai palaces, begun toward the middle of the 1440's. The commission for the Medici Palace went to Michelozzo, who had become the favorite architect of Cosimo the Elder. Its construction marks the beginning of a new era in the sociology of the merchant class that had far-reaching consequences upon urban development, as well as upon domestic architecture. It is built upon an imposing scale, even discounting the enlargements and alterations made to it in the 17th century. In its original plan the palace was square, with an open central courtyard, framed at ground level on all sides by an arcade of Brunelleschian derivation. The courtyard and the rough masonry of the lowest story are derived from previous Florentine architecture, such as the fortified city palace, the Bargello. The novelty and importance of the Medici Palace lie in its regular square plan and three-storied façades with their Brunelleschian regularity and symmetry of order. The Rucellai Palace, designed by Leon Battista Alberti, is more refined and gentler; it is less a symbol of power than one of an elegant, cultivated mode of existence. This palace is also three stories high, but here the three levels of the façade are divided in equal bays by thin pilasters supporting an entablature. The pilasters, in accordance with ancient Roman architecture, are each of a different order. Alberti's evocation of the antique is more a display of erudition than a true adaptation of ancient structural forms: the system of pilasters and entablature is but a screen that has no functional purpose but that gives the façade a harmonious appearance. Nevertheless, the Rucellai Palace is the first of the Renaissance palaces in which a system of mathematical proportions is fused with a vocabulary borrowed from the antique.

In Rome, after the middle of the century, cardinals from rich families began to erect imposing residences. The two stately palaces commissioned by Cardinal Barbo and Cardinal Riario—the Palazzo Venezia and the Cancelleria—echo the style of Alberti, though their actual design cannot be directly attributed to him. Florence and Tuscany, in the second half of the Quattrocento, were recognized as "the springhead of architecture," according to Federico da Montefeltro, duke of Urbino, in a famous document of 1468. Nevertheless, the duke must have felt that architects from other areas were beginning to master the language of Renaissance architecture, since in the same document he appointed Luciano Laurana, a native of Dalmatia, as chief architect of his ducal palace of Urbino. After the erection of the Medici Palace the central courtyard was a main feature of palace architecture. In some places the open space within the solid block of masonry was necessitated by practical, climatic reasons as well as by social and esthetic ones: it was a means to provide light and air in a structure insulated from its environment. Luciano Laurana's courtyard in the ducal palace at Urbino, with its open arcade framing the lower sides, is a descendant of the Michelozzo courtyard in the Medici Palace. It is superior in that it is completely unified, both in its design and in the elevation of its façades, and, consequently, more regular and harmonious. After Brunelleschi, Quattrocento architects strove to attain harmony, which they equated with beauty. For them a harmonious work, as Alberti defined it, was one having "a concord of all the parts, achieved in such a manner that nothing could be added, taken away, or altered." Laurana's courtyard unquestionably fulfills this esthetic prescription.

Leon Battista Alberti was second only to Brunelleschi in the field of church architecture. A great humanist, he was steeped in classical learning and profoundly influenced by it. His treatise on architecture shows how thoroughly he had read Vitruvius and how intensely he had researched ancient architecture. With Alberti a new concept emerged that draws a clear distinction between the experienced mason (the builder) and the architect (the man of scientific and humanistic learning who, with "marvelous reason," can plan buildings fit for the needs of humanity). In his own practice Alberti made the distinction; the construction of the buildings he designed was delegated to an assistant. Among his outstanding works was his project for transforming the old Church of S. Francesco at Rimini into a new building to serve as a memorial to the dubious glory of Sigismondo Malatesta and Isotta degli Atti. In the massive cubic shell that was to enclose the preexisting Gothic structure, Alberti made free use of Roman architecture. The lower story of the façade repeats the basic motif of a triumphal arch. A medal made of the original design shows that Alberti intended to complete the upper story with another arch over the central one below and with a gigantic hemispheric dome, somewhat similar to that of the Pantheon in Rome. (The reconstruction of the building, begun in 1450, was never completed.) The most complete statement of Alberti's religious architecture can be found in the Church of S. Andrea at Mantua, which was erected after his death in fairly close adherence to his design. The church is built upon the traditional basilican, or Latin cross, plan, as is Brunelleschi's Church of S. Lorenzo. Alberti, however, eliminated the side aisle and covered the nave with an enormous barrel vault comparable in monumentality to those of ancient Rome. The effect of impressive severity is produced by the unified central space of the nave and the massive piers. Alberti's influence on Italian architecture is almost incalculable. Through his Tempio Malatestiano (the Church of S. Francesco at Rimini) and Matteo de' Pasti, who was in charge of the actual construction, his influence reached northward and is seen in some of the buildings erected at Venice. His interior of S. Andrea inspired Bramante in his plan for St. Peter's at Rome; it was also significant in the planning of Latin cross churches for centuries thereafter.

Another leading architect of the later Quattrocento was Giuliano da Sangallo. A Florentine who was patronized by the Medici and by Pope Julius II, Sangallo remained anchored to Brunelleschian tradition, and eventually fell out of favor at the papal court when Bramante launched his new style at Rome. As is implied by Alberti in his architectural treatise, the simplest geometric shapes, such as the square and the circle, were considered the most fitting for religious architecture, since, in their perfection, they are the clearest symbols of the Divine. This explains in part the success enjoyed during the Renaissance by the centralized church, despite its unsuitability for liturgical ritual. Giuliano Sangallo's most famous church is S. Maria delle Carceri, at Prato. A centrally planned church, it is a pure Greek cross, two-story building. The crossing is a square to whose sides are attached four rectangular arms, thus creating a plan that fuses the symbolic design of the cross with one of the two most regular of geometric forms. The other, the circle, is added to the whole through the base of the dome above the crossing. The lucidity of shape and the lightness of structure make the church one of the most perfect expressions of the ideals of the Florentine Quattrocento.

As Brunelleschi's and Alberti's ideas spread throughout Italy, they were fused with local traditions to produce regional styles. In Milan and its surrounding territories a preference for elaborate ornamentation and coloristic effects was never relinquished. One example of the intermingling of Tuscan and Lombard vocabularies is the Portinari Chapel, which, though designed by Michelozzo upon a Brunelleschian scheme, displays four turrets that are derived from traditional Lombard architecture. Even more colorful examples are such buildings designed by Lombard architects as the Colleoni Chapel at Bergamo by Amadeo and the façade of the Certosa di Pavia, believed to be by the same architect. Milan, throughout the Quattrocento, was a center of patronage for central Italian architects. In 1451 Francesco Sforza brought the Florentine Filarete (Antonio Averlino) to the city, and put him in charge of the construction of a vast hospital complex. Later, under Francesco Sforza's successor, Ludovico il Moro, Leonardo da Vinci and Bramante came to Milan. This period marked the beginning of a new phase in Renaissance architecture. There is no evidence that Leonardo ever constructed a building of his own, but in the architectural drawings of his Milanese sojourn it is evident that he had a new approach to architectural form. In his plans and perspective views of domed, centralized churches, the elements of design are borrowed from solid geometry. Buildings are no longer conceived as additions of circles and squares, but as compounds of solid shapes in a reciprocal state of existence. Leonardo was as preoccupied with the mathematical relationships among the parts of his buildings as his Quattrocento predecessors had been. However, he dispensed with the planar geometry that had been essential to them.

Whereas Leonardo's drawings represent experiments with new concepts of architecture, Bramante succeeded in actual practice in opening a new phase in the history of architecture. Certainly he was influenced by Leonardo, and already his Milanese buildings, primarily the choir of S. Maria delle Grazie, demonstrated his concern with the interrelation of solid, massive shapes on a monumental scale. His style did not fully mature, however, until (1499) he moved to Rome

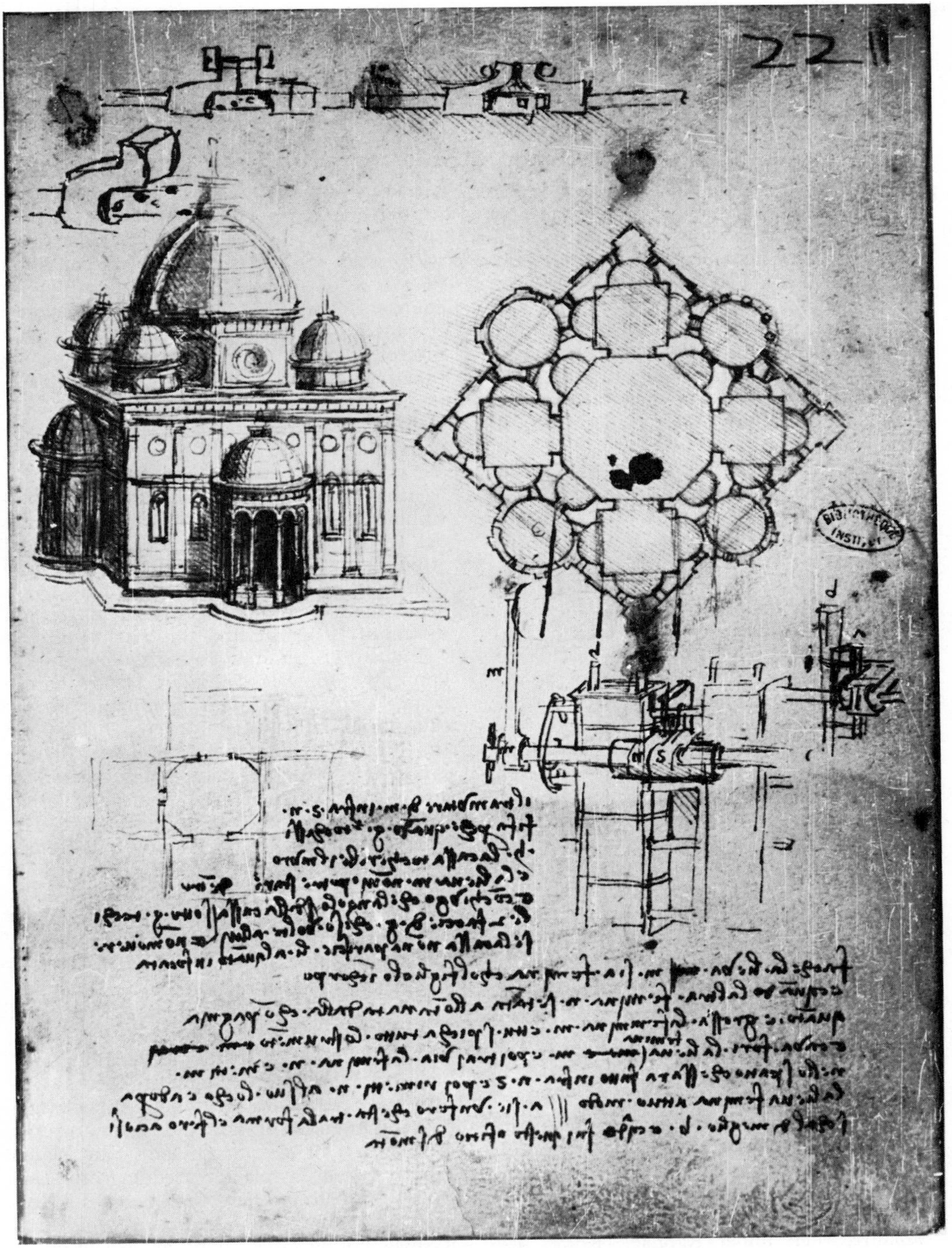

LEONARDO DA VINCI
View and plan of a church with a central dome and four cupolas
Photo Bibliothèque nationale, Paris

thin; ꟻH, then; y, you; (variable) ḏ as d or j, s̱ as s or sh, ṯ as t or ch, ẕ as z or zh; o, F. cloche; ü, F. menu; ċh, Sc. loch; ṅ, F. bonbon; ʙ, Sp. Córdoba (sounded almost like v).

and first experienced ancient architecture. Here he became the favorite architect of Julius II, who, shortly after his elevation to the papacy, put him in charge of his many projects in the Vatican, as the Belvedere court, and, of course, St. Peter's, the greatest architectural project of the Renaissance. The new St. Peter's was to be built on the plan of a Greek cross and was to be capped by a dome of unprecedented magnitude and grandeur. Bramante could not have planned as he did without appropriating the technique of building with concrete that had permitted ancient Roman architects to vault such gigantic structures as their baths and basilicas. Concrete, a more malleable material than the brick and stone used by his predecessors, allowed Bramante to mold the walls of St. Peter's as plastic, sculptural entities that seem to take shape in response to the space they enclose. The new St. Peter's, of which only part of the crossing was completed before Bramante's death, revealed to Cinquecento architects the possibility of handling architectural forms as fluid, rather than static, shapes. The Tempietto, a shrine built by Bramante as a memorial to St. Peter, proclaimed the birth of a new style known today as the High Renaissance. The basic form is a cylinder which is surrounded by a colonnade and capped by a hemispheric dome. The Doric order is employed throughout, and niches on the exterior of the cylindrical core show that Bramante conceived the walls as parts of a solid mass. The Tempietto was no longer a space defined by walls, but a piece of solid sculpture occupying a pivotal function in space. Also at Rome, Bramante influenced the style of palace façades, introducing motifs such as half columns and pedimented windows reaching to the floor, with low balustrades, all of which enriched, sculpturally, the planar surface of the wall. His scheme for a façade, however, was sober and severe in its use of classical motifs.

Among Bramante's followers at Rome, Raphael was the first to elaborate on his basic vocabulary in order to create palace façades that would be characterized by elegance and gracefulness, and would appear as more complicated, yet unified, structures. First under Bramante, then under Raphael, Rome became the training ground for a group of highly gifted and original architects. Their personal attitudes toward the new architecture, as formulated by Bramante on the basis of the antique, was by no means homogeneous. Peruzzi, active at both Rome and Siena, retained a preference for the planar surfaces that give his buildings a Quattrocento lightness. An innovational subtlety, however, can be found in the plans of some of his buildings. The famous Farnesina, a small palace composed as a rectangular block with projecting wings, is a clever adaptation of a type of structure used in antiquity for country houses. For the Massimo Palace he designed a curved façade, and in still other projects, known only through drawings, he experimented with an oval plan. Giulio Romano, who seems in his early Roman palaces to have had an aversion to the classical vocabulary of Bramante and Raphael, adopted it in an extravagant fashion when he went to Mantua. His buildings there are at once disturbing and amusing. In his famous Palazzo del Tè the visitor is confronted by a series of stunning surprises. Chaos and order, strangely combined, appear to be the principles on which Giulio manipulated the architectural motifs of Bramante and Raphael.

Bramante's tradition found more orthodox application in Venice under Jacopo Sansovino. From 1529, when Sansovino became the official architect of the city, he applied the principles of the Roman High Renaissance to his plans. Venice had developed an architecture based upon open arcades, rather than upon uninterrupted, solid walls. The white stone traditionally employed at Venice made it possible to erect edifices in which light and shade played a substantial role. In Sansovino's Library of San Marco, one of the greatest accomplishments of the Cinquecento, the sculptural vocabulary of High Renaissance architecture—columns, piers, arches, and balustrades—is used to create rich and impressive framings for the series of openings that line both levels of the two-storied building. A wall no longer can be said to exist. We experience the building as a varied textured interplay of light and shadow against the expanse of sky. Sansovino's San Marco Library is such a splendid wedding of classic motifs with atmosphere that one would expect the ensuing architecture in Venice and its neighboring cities to be an expansion of this approach. Such a development did not take place. Instead, architecture in the Venetian territories during the second half of the

Cinquecento was dominated by the personality of Andrea Palladio, an artist who converted Bramante's and Sansovino's impressionistic approach to a rational, intellectualized system. Whereas for Bramante and his close followers the planning did not rigidly follow a predetermined, fixed idea, but was a flexible process guided by the visual effectiveness of a structure as it took shape in space, Palladio believed that architectural forms should be first perfected in the mind. As a consequence, Palladio planned his buildings in accordance with a system of abstract proportions. He made use of the repertory of classical forms brought to Venice by Sansovino and to the surrounding area by Michele Sanmicheli, adapting it to his own schemes of proportional relationships and symmetries. For Palladio, a studied and calculated application of the principles of classical architecture to palaces and country residences was an expression of an erudite and cultivated approach to antiquity itself. His classicism was enthusiastically accepted by families of the cultured, aristocratic elite. For them he built a series of villas, the most famous of which is the so-called Villa Rotonda on the outskirts of Vicenza. Constructed on a square plan with a dome over its center and four equal temple porticoes projecting from the four façades, the Villa Rotonda is an imposing example of order and symmetry. Its clarity of shape and effect of dignity and elegance were particularly appreciated in the 18th century, when it became the prototype for country houses in England and North America. One of the many splendors of Venice is Palladio's Church of S. Giorgio Maggiore, built along the edge of the small island that faces the Doge's Palace and Sansovino's Library. The church reflects Palladio's study of Alberti's S. Andrea at Mantua, and its façade offers the most ingenious solution to a problem that vexed all Renaissance architects: how to impose a classical, templelike façade with columns, pediments, and pilasters, upon a basilican church whose nave is higher than the side aisles. In a brilliant display of virtuosity and inspiration, Palladio conceived the façade as a combination of two separate classical temple fronts: a tall, narrow one superposed on a shorter, wider one. The two create a whole that shows no discrepancy with the shape of the structure behind it.

In central Italy Michelangelo revolutionized architecture as he did sculpture and painting. In describing the architectural decoration for the Medici Chapel in S. Lorenzo at Florence, Vasari writes that the artist's inventions were absolutely different from what had been the common practice of the day and from what the ancients had done. In the Medici Chapel he combined the traditional Brunelleschian scheme of *pietra serena,* for the pilasters and moldings against white painted walls, with a second scheme of sculptured marble architecture, and produced dissonance and a sense of movement rather than harmony and tranquillity. The novelty of the Medici Chapel is surpassed by the entrance hall of the Laurentian Library. A visitor entering this interior space is confronted by a cascade of steps pouring toward him and forming one of the most sculptural, animated stairways in existence. In the combination of columns and walls, Michelangelo reversed the tradition sanctified by antiquity and Renaissance practice. The columns do not project from the walls, but are squeezed into tall, narrow niches. Michelangelo also violated accepted practice by designing the tabernacles with pilasters tapering downward and by attaching to the lower part of the wall volutes with no function whatsoever. Altogether, the architecture creates a movement in space that overwhelms the spectator passing through it. At Rome, where he spent the last thirty years of his life, his architectural projects assumed a majesty of scale and magnitude of force that had not been so obvious at Florence. His Roman architecture generally shows a marked degree of acceptance of the antique vocabulary. When he took over the construction of St. Peter's he retained the Greek cross plan of Bramante, but gave greater tautness and unity to the design. He conceived of the various parts of the building as being interlocked in dynamic, muscular tensions, all converging upward in support of the enormous dome. The unique quality of Michelangelo's architecture rests to a degree in his capacity for dramatizing architectural elements so that they affect the viewer physically and psychologically. He viewed architecture in terms of the human body. He was not interested, as his Quattrocento predecessors had been, in transposing ideal or abstract human proportions into architectural measurements. He believed that architecture should be humanized by making its structural forces metaphors of human, muscular tensions. Architecture was thus, for him, conceived from the same point of view as sculpture. Florentine architects of the second half of the Cinquecento, as Vasari and Ammannati, followed the example set by Michelangelo in his Florentine period. They accepted not only his arbitrary license toward classical architecture with its fantasy of invention, but also his early reliance upon hard, linear design. The influence of his Roman works was of greater consequence. Mostly through Guglielmo della Porta, who completed several of his buildings, his influence was transmitted to Roman architects and ultimately gave rise to the Baroque. An obvious legacy of Michelangelo's great work at St. Peter's is the number of stately domes that adorn churches and government buildings, as St. Paul's at London and the Capitol at Washington, D.C. L.B.

Arcimboldi (är-chēm-bōl′dē), **Giovanni.** Milanese jurisconsult; d. at Rome, 1491. He was the son of Niccolò Arcimboldi, also a jurisconsult, and became the confidential councillor of Duke Galeazzo Maria Sforza at Milan, for whom he served on embassies to the Medici at Florence, to Venice, France, the emperor, and the papal court at Rome. On the death of his wife he entered upon an ecclesiastical career, and in 1468 was made bishop of Novara. Sixtus IV raised him to the cardinalate (1473), and in 1484 he became archbishop of Milan. He continued to perform political services and sought to make ecclesiastical reforms, but the atmosphere of Milan was not conducive to the latter activities and he resigned as archbishop and retired to Rome. The writings he left, many of which are unpublished, include works on canon law, orations, homilies, letters, and a description of a magnificent spectacle presented at Rome by Cardinal Pietro Riario, in February, 1473.

Arco (där′kō), **Nicolò d'.** Humanist and poet; b. at Arco (in the Trentino), December 3, 1479; d. there, November or December, 1546. He was of a noble family that had held the territory of Arco for generations. He served as a page at the court of Emperor Frederick III (1415–1493), completed his classical studies, attended the university at Pavia, went to Bologna where he became a friend of Flaminio, to Padua, and to other cities of Italy. He also served the emperor Maximilian I (1459–1519). His personal life was saddened by domestic misfortunes, and was disrupted by rebellion of the people of Arco. A conspiracy caused him to flee to Germany to save himself and his family (1542). He was restored to his lands (1543), and died a few years later. Nicolò d'Arco had an excellent classical education, knew Latin, Greek, Italian, French, German, and Spanish, wrote lyrical Latin verses in the manner of Vergil and Catullus, and was in contact with the leading men of letters of his day. His Latin poems were first published at Mantua (1546).

Arderne (är′dėrn), **John.** English surgeon; fl. c1370. He performed an operation for fistula believed impossible by most European surgeons. He derived his surgical precepts largely from actual practice rather than from written sources, although his *Liber de fistulis* and *De arte medicinae* indicate an awareness of Galen's works.

Arditi (är-dē′tē), **Andrea.** [Also, **Andrea di Ardito.**] Florentine goldsmith and enamel worker; active in the first half of the 14th century. He was one of the first of the Italians to take advantage of the advances the French had made in enamel work. He made (1330) the silver reliquary bust of St. Zenobius and the mitre with figures of saints in enamel in the medallions that is now in the cathedral at Florence. In 1338 he made a silver cross for S. Miniato al Monte at Florence. A gilded silver chalice decorated with brilliant enamels is in the Victoria and Albert Museum at London.

Ardizone (är-dē-tsō′nā), **Simone di.** See **Simone di Ardizone.**

Arena Chapel. Chapel at Padua, so called because it is built on the site of a Roman amphitheater, erected in the first century A.D., a few parts of which remain. (See **Scrovegni Chapel.**)

Aretino (ä-rā-tē′nō), **Giovanni.** Florentine copyist; active in the first half of the 15th century. Little is known of his life or his background, except that he probably came from Arezzo. Gifted with an elegant, trained, exact hand, and with a sufficient knowledge of Greek to copy excerpts in that language correctly, he copied books for some of the leading families of Florence, as the Medici, Portinari, and Ricci.

Aretino, Leonardo. See **Bruni, Leonardo.**

Aretino, Pietro. [Called the **Scourge of**

Princes; original surname, **Bacci.**] Prose writer and playwright; b. at Arezzo, April 20, 1492; d. at Venice, October 21, 1556. Born of plebeian parents, he left home at 14 to become an art student and then a vagabond. In 1516 he took a menial position with the immensely wealthy Roman banker, Agostino Chigi. He attracted the attention of Pope Leo X with a mordant satire, and learned, as he progressed from the position of a lackey in Chigi's service to court wit of Leo, how to turn to his own account the corruption and decadence of princes. He had no particular education and lacked the style and elegance in writing that was generally not only admired but demanded at the time. But the knowledge he possessed of the weaknesses, crimes, and sensuality of some of the leading men of his time gave him an invincible weapon. He used it with reckless delight or destructive power as he wished. As a hired wit and literary bravo, he served Pope Leo, the marquess of Mantua, and Pope Clement VII. He was the intimate friend of the Medici warrior Giovanni delle Bande Nere (who died in his arms at Mantua in 1526). He made his living by his wits, by his arrangement of and participation in his patrons' pleasures, and by his pen. His extravagantly flattering sonnets were eagerly sought (and highly rewarded) by all fortunate or wealthy enough to be the subjects of them. He became known and admired, or feared, throughout Italy as a literary figure—feared because he had as much talent for ruining a man in verse as for praising him. The objects of his praise outdid each other in rewarding him. Those who feared him paid tribute to be spared his attentions. A scandal in 1524 caused him to leave Rome for a time. Shortly after his return, an attack on his life caused him to leave it again. In 1527 he went to Venice and remained there the rest of his life. Venice was indifferent to the contents of his writings so long as he refrained from roiling the political waters. This he was content to do. He had taken the measure of the society of his time and shrewdly manipulated it. What made him more dangerous and feared was the printing press, for he used it freely to print and circulate the mixture of calumnies, flatteries, and thinly disguised threats that constituted his thousands of letters. He lived in magnificent style at Venice, gaining the money to do so by his pen and by the pensions and presents he extorted or received as gifts from an enormous circle of friends and patrons. Emperor Charles V was but one of many who paid him tribute money. Aretino had learned that he need not be dependent on any one patron; the world was truly his oyster. His palace was filled with great art and an unknown number of rowdy hangers-on. The finest wines and choicest foods appeared on his table. His dress and furnishings were sumptuous. And he shared his magnificence with all and sundry; he had a great reputation for generosity. The great and near-great visited him. Titian was his warm friend and almost daily companion. (A splendid portrait of him by Titian hangs in the Frick Collection, New York. Tintoretto, on the other hand, threatened to cut him to pieces.) Another intimate friend was the sculptor and architect Jacopo Sansovino. Aretino boasted of the honors that were showered on him, the medals that were struck of his likeness, the portraits of him that appeared on items of household use and on the façades of palaces (with those of Titian and Sansovino, his head is sculptured in relief on the bronze door of the sacristy of St. Mark's), of certain kinds of glass that were named "Aretine" for him, and of the fact that the little canal by his house was renamed Rio Aretino. And it all came to him, he claimed, simply because he told the truth without fear or favor.

Aretino turned out reams of writing, and as fast as it was written it was sent off to the press. His works include a treatise "On the Humanity of Christ"; lives of the Virgin, St. Thomas Aquinas, and St. Catherine of Siena; prose dialogues; satires; lyrics; the *Giudizi*, which were annual prophecies in which he named names; a tragedy, *Orazia*, based on Livy's story of the combat between the Horatii and the Curiatii in which the patriotism of Horatius triumphs over the love of his sister for one of the Curiatii; five comedies, including *La cortigiana*, which presents a devastating picture of court life and betrays an intimate knowledge of the iniquities therein from bottom to top; and thousands of letters. He collected 3,000 of his own letters and published them. Two volumes of letters written to him by the leading literary and princely figures of his time, to say nothing of cardinals and popes, were also published. His religious works have little merit as either literature, theology, or biography. The letters, taken en masse, are tedious in their adulation and endless fulsomeness, but are marked by a reckless vigor of expression and a certain originality of attack, and are of interest for their variety of subject matter. His *Ragionamenti* now appear as a spread of rather dull pornography. Included in his letters are comments on pedantry in language and on art. His slashing attacks on the writers of his day constitute valid literary criticism of the exaggerated devotion to style, as opposed to content, that was a danger of the time. His remarks on art reveal a real appreciation. It was Ariosto who, in his *Orlando Furioso,* gave Aretino the epithet "Scourge of Princes," in admiration, and who also called him "Divine." A literary swashbuckler, Aretino combined in himself the vices and vitality of his age. It is doubtful that he could have operated so successfully in any other.

Aretino, L'Unico. See **Accolti, Bernardo.**

Aretusi (ä-rā-tö'zē), **Pellegrino.** See **Pellegrino da Modena.**

Argalia (är-gä-lē'ä). In Matteo Maria Boiardo's *Orlando Innamorato,* the brother of Angelica, princess of Cathay. He accompanies her to Charlemagne's court at Paris, under an assumed name, for the purpose of overcoming the king's paladins and carrying them off to Cathay. With this aim, he undertakes to fight against the paladins one by one in a tournament. If he unhorses them they are to become his captives. If one overcomes him, his sister Angelica will be the prize. What the paladins do not know is that Argalia is armed with an invincible lance, but since all have fallen in love at sight with Angelica, all are anxious to fight him. He overcomes Astolfo, the first to meet him, but when he unhorses the Saracen Ferraù, the latter refuses to give up, and startles Argalia and the entire court by unchivalrously continuing the fight on foot and with his sword. Argalia, dropping his lance, flees. Ferraù ultimately finds him and slays him. His ghost reappears in Lodovico Ariosto's *Orlando Furioso.*

Argyropoulos (är-ji-rǫ-pō'lǫs), **Johannes.** [Also, **Argyropulus** or **Argyropulo.**] Greek scholar; b. at Constantinople, c1410; d. at Rome, 1491 or 1492. In 1438 he journeyed to Italy with the Byzantine emperor to take part in the Council of Ferrara. The Council adjourned to Florence in 1438, and there he met many eminent Florentine men of letters. After a brief return to Constantinople he was back in Italy, visiting the Florentine patron of Greek studies Palla degli Strozzi, then in exile at Padua. In Padua, Argyropoulos gave private lessons. He went back and forth to Constantinople until the fall of the city (1453), when he moved to the Peloponnesus. In 1456 Cosimo de' Medici invited him to Florence as a public and private teacher of Greek language and literature. There he remained until 1471, when he was invited to Rome. He lived in Rome until his death. Although Argyropoulos wrote little, he made important and accurate translations of Aristotle and Plato. His contribution was both as a teacher of Greek language and literature and as the founder of a new humanistic interpretation of the philosophy of Aristotle. Among his pupils were Cristoforo Landino, Angelo Poliziano, Marsilio Ficino, and Donato Acciaiuoli.

Arias de Ávila (ä'ryäs dā ä'bē-lä), **Pedro.** See **Pedrarias.**

Aridano (ä-rē-dä'nō). In Matteo Maria Boiardo's *Orlando Innamorato,* a giant who guards a bridge. He captures Rinaldo and hangs up his armor, but is overcome by Orlando.

Arienti (ä-ryen'tē), **Giovanni Sabadino degli.** Bolognese writer and notary; d. 1510. He served for many years as secretary to Andrea Bentivoglio at Bologna. He had a lively but facile intelligence and a superficial culture. His principal work, *Porretane,* is a collection of tales within a Boccaccesque framework of a group of people gathered for a certain number of days who tell stories to amuse themselves. The sixty-one tales that make up the collection are largely drawn from earlier sources. His additions and modifications of the traditional stories adds to the picture of 15th century life. He also wrote a series in praise of thirty illustrious women of his time, and a version of Ovid's *Pyramus and Thisbe.*

Ariodante (ä-ryō-dän'tā). In Lodovico Ariosto's *Orlando Furioso,* an Italian at the Scottish court. He marries Ginevra, princess of Scotland, then goes to France to aid Charlemagne against the Infidels.

Ariosto (ä-rē-ôs'tō), **Lodovico.** [Called **Divino Lodovico.**] Poet; b. at Reggio, September 8, 1474; d. at Ferrara, July 6, 1533. His father, who held posts under the dukes of Ferrara, was of an ancient and honorable family. Lodovico received a good education. He acquired a thorough grounding in Latin, but always regretted that he had not had the opportunity to learn Greek. To carry out the wishes of his father he studied law for a time. However, that discipline was uncongenial to his tastes, and he persuaded his father to let him give it up and devote himself to his literary studies. When he was 26 his father died, leaving him, as the eldest, in charge of his four brothers and five sisters. The family property was not large, and Ariosto was compelled to turn his attention to affairs of business to provide for the children. In 1503 he entered the service of Cardinal Ippolito d'Este as a secretary, and remained in the post until 1517. His duties involved many difficult and dangerous journeys on confidential missions for the cardinal. In his *Satires*, Ariosto complained that the cardinal used him as a messenger and endangered his health and life. His great work, *Orlando Furioso*, on the other hand, has many passages of the highest praise and flattery of the cardinal, as was the custom of that age when writers depended on the generosity and good will of a patron. The cardinal paid him as an agent, not as a poet. The pay was good enough, but not always promptly rendered, and sometimes not forthcoming at all. The cardinal tried to persuade Ariosto to take orders so that he could present him with Church benefices that would have assured him a comfortable income, but Ariosto feared restraints on his liberty and refused to do so. He valued his personal freedom above all things. He said he would prefer eating a turnip at his own table to dining on pheasant with princes. (According to his son Virginio, his taste in food was simple, and he greatly enjoyed turnips.) In his writing there are many references to the advantages of a simple life and contented mind over wealth and the intrigues of court life. He loved Ferrara where, it appears, he carried on many love affairs and where he enjoyed the society of cultivated men and women. The Ferrarese court was noted for its interest in theatricals, and Ariosto was involved with these. In 1508 his *La Cassaria*, a comedy, was produced there, and in 1509 his *I Suppositi*, another comedy. The latter was given a spectacular production at the Vatican in 1519. Raphael painted the scenery, which represented Ferrara, and Pope Leo X himself stood at the door and admitted the spectators. The two comedies, each in five acts, were modeled after Plautus and Terence. Two other comedies, *Il Negromante* (1520) and *Lena* (1530), were completed. These, still on the classical model, contained much satiric comment on contemporary topics, particularly on the corruption of the clergy. Ariosto helped in the production of the plays, which at this time were produced in any room that was large enough for a temporary stage and an audience.

In 1516 Ariosto published the first edition of his masterpiece, the romantic epic *Orlando Furioso* (see entry), and dedicated it to Cardinal Ippolito. The cardinal thought it rather a waste of time but did buy a copy. In other quarters it was an instant success. Success, however, meant that it was popular, not that it brought Ariosto great financial gain. The following year Ariosto left the cardinal's employ rather than go to Hungary for him. And the year after, 1518, he entered the service of Duke Alfonso I d'Este, the cardinal's brother and Lucrezia Borgia's third husband. This prince, a great commander, was a cultivated man who understood and valued Ariosto. Ariosto was in charge of the court theatricals. (He later planned the first permanent stage to be erected at Ferrara for Duke Alfonso, in 1532. It burned the following year.) His duties were light, and he spent four tranquil years at Ferrara. He continually revised and polished his *Orlando*, and published a second edition in 1521. He was on friendly terms with the Medici at Florence and with the members of the Gonzaga court at Mantua and the Montefeltri at Urbino. He had no desire to travel, preferring to look at maps when he wanted to see the world, and was content with peace and the leisure to write. In 1513, at Florence, he had seen and fallen in love with Alessandra Benucci, the wife of Tito Strozzi. His love for her was lasting, and ultimately, when she was widowed, it is thought that he married her, but he was very discreet about his love life. On his inkstand was a Cupid with his finger to his lips in a command for silence. During these four years he continued to write comedies and to assist in producing them. His happy and peaceful life was interrupted in 1522 when Alfonso could no longer pay a salary for such services as Ariosto rendered. In order to provide for him, Alfonso named him governor of the district of Garfagnana. This was a remote region, infested with bandits and brigands, and consisting of a number of villages whose inhabitants passed their lives in flouting the law and resisting any attempts at control. Ariosto was miserable there, away from his friends, constantly occupied with brawls and trying to find and punish criminals, and so distracted by his uncongenial duties—which, however, he honorably and ably carried out—that he was unable to pursue his literary interests. With him was his illegitimate son Virginio, to whom he was devoted. (Another natural son was Giovanni Battista, who followed a military career.) In 1525 he was recalled to Ferrara and his exile ended. He built a small house, still standing in Ferrara, and enjoyed the remaining years of his life refining and polishing *Orlando Furioso*. He was as great a reviser and corrector of his work as Petrarch. It is said that, knowing his own propensity for correcting his work, he wrote on the right-hand side of the page only. There is a famous autograph copy of the *Orlando* in the university at Ferrara, heavily scored with his changes. The definitive, enlarged edition of the work, with forty-six cantos, appeared in 1532.

In addition to the *Orlando* and the comedies mentioned above, Ariosto wrote elegies, *capitoli*, canzoni, sonnets, and madrigals, but his genius lay rather in the broad but detailed sweep of the romantic narrative epic than in the melody of lyricism. He reveals himself most frankly in the so-called *Satires*, metrical letters in which he discussed many matters and presented his observations of contemporary life. There are seven of the *Satires*. Ariosto appears as a keen, somewhat mocking, broad-minded commentator on the society in which he lived. He was a bystander, watching the turbulent events of his day but not taking part in them if he could avoid it. It was during his lifetime that the French and Spanish invaded Italy and caused such misery, but what did it matter, Ariosto asked, whether it was a foreign or a native tyrant who held the tormented peninsula in thrall? Righteous indignation and the crusading spirit were absent from his nature. He jealously guarded his own freedom and tranquillity; as for the rest, he gave it level-eyed acceptance. The *Satires* are less critical and corrective in intent than vehicles to portray Ariosto's own views and interests. The seventh *Satire*, addressed to his friend Pietro Bembo, is concerned with the education of his son Virginio. Another deals with the qualities one should look for in a wife. One describes his trials in Garfagnana, and another states that a contented mind is more to be treasured than fame or wealth. In each, many matters are introduced that give us the picture of the man. But it is the poet of *Orlando Furioso* to whom Galileo gave the epithet "Divino."

Arlotto (är-lôt′tō). [Real name, **Arlotto Mainardi.**] Florentine parish priest; b. 1396; d. 1484. He was a parish priest for many years in a little church in Fiesole. A merry and kindly man, he was noted for his talent for coining witticisms, jokes, and witty stories. A collection of these, *Facezie*, was made by a friend after his death, and became enormously popular. It went through a number of editions and was translated into French and German. Some of the items included were from traditional popular sources, adapted and animated by Arlotto.

Armida (är-mē′dä). In Torquato Tasso's *Gerusalemme liberata* (*Jerusalem Delivered*), the niece of a wizard king of Damascus and herself an enchantress. She used her charms to seduce the Crusaders from their vows and duty. Her palace, surrounded by magnificent pleasure grounds, was so luxurious and splendid that "the gardens of Armida" became a synonym for gorgeous luxury. She also possessed a magic girdle which surpassed even the cestus of Venus in its power. Her voluptuous witchery was finally destroyed by a talisman brought from the Christian army; and Rinaldo, who had been enslaved by her, escaped. Coming up with her army to the aid of the pagans besieged in the city, she sees Rinaldo the first to mount the walls as the city falls to the Crusaders. She flees and resolves to kill herself. Rinaldo follows her and prevents her from plunging in the fatal shaft. Her magic had not protected her from falling in love with Rinaldo, and she succumbs as he persuades her to become a Christian.

Arnolfo di Cambio (är-nôl′fō dē käm′byō). [Also, **Arnolfo di Lapo.**] Tuscan sculptor and architect; b. at Colle Val d'Elsa near the middle of the 13th century; d. at Florence, in March, 1301 or 1302. He became a pupil of the sculptor Nicola Pisano and worked with him at Siena. He also worked with him at Perugia, where he went in 1277, in the creation of the famous fountain there. The work on the fountain specifically by Arnolfo is indistinguishable. His sculpture, originally much influenced by his teacher and the Pisan school, was modified after a visit to Rome, where he saw the remains of classical sculpture. Judging by the commissions he received, he was well known and enjoyed a high reputation. His sculptural works include the tomb of Cardinal Guglielmo de Braye (d. 1282) at Orvieto; a tabernacle and ciborium for the high altar of St. Paul's at Rome (1285), signed by him; a chapel of Boniface IV at Rome; monuments to Adrian V (d. 1276) at Viterbo, and Cardinal Annibale (d. 1276) at Rome; and statues of a *Madonna with Child*, *Santa Reparata*, and *Boniface VIII* in the Museo dell' Opera del Duomo, Florence. There is a *Censing Angel* in the Fogg Art Museum, Harvard University. It is thought to have been originally one of a pair at each side of the aforementioned *Madonna with Child*, and that the group ornamented the portal of the Duomo. As the "most famous master and the most expert in church construction in the vicinity," Arnolfo was called upon to build a new cathedral for Florence. The contract called for "the most beautiful and noteworthy temple in Tuscany." The foundation stone was laid, and blessed by the pope's legate, on September 8, 1296. Arnolfo died in 1301 or 1302, and his plans for the cathedral, which was consecrated in 1439, underwent many modifications. The same is true of the other buildings in Florence credited to him: the Palazzo della Signoria (also known as the Palazzo Vecchio), begun in 1298; the Church of Santa Croce; and the rebuilding and campanile of the Badia. In architecture, as in sculpture, Arnolfo's work is a modification of medieval and Gothic with, in sculpture, elements of the classical.

Arrigo Tedesco (är-rē′gō tā-des′kō). See **Isaac, Heinrich.**

Ars nova (ärs nō′vä). A Latin phrase, meaning "new art," applied to music in western Europe beginning with the 14th century to distinguish it from earlier music (*ars antiqua*). The term comes from a treatise written by Philippe de Vitry, bishop of Meaux, a poet and musician of the 14th century, but the meaning of the term was greatly extended from its original appearance in the treatise. Among the innovations in the *ars nova* is a new system of musical notation, systematization of measure, and new rhythms and harmonies. Francesco Landino was an outstanding composer in the *ars nova* manner.

Artevelde (är′tẹ-vel-dẹ), **Jacob van.** [Also, **Arteveld;** called the **Brewer of Ghent.**] Flemish popular leader, b. at Ghent, c1290; killed there, 1345. Supposedly a brewer, he was chosen (1337) to represent Ghent during hostilities between England and France (at the beginning of the Hundred Years' War) which threatened Flemish trade. He made a treaty (1338) with England establishing Flemish neutrality and assuring Flemish weavers of their supply of English wool. By bringing Bruges and Ypres to the support of Ghent, he began the federation of Netherlands towns of which he became head. In 1339 he recognized Edward III's claim to France (thus also to the Netherlands). He was instrumental in building up commerce and in reviving communal institutions. Suspected of supporting Edward the Black Prince to replace Louis as count of Flanders he was killed by a mob.

Artevelde, Philip van. [Also, **Arteveld.**] Flemish popular leader; b. c1340; killed at Roosebeke, in what is now Belgium, 1382. He was the son of Jacob van Artevelde. He led the workers, headed by the weavers, of Ghent in a revolution (1381) against Count Louis of Flanders (son of his father's enemy) and defeated him at Bruges. He was thereafter for a short time in control of all Flanders, but was conquered and slain by an army of Charles VI of France, who came to Louis' support.

Ascensius (ạ-sen′shus), **Jodocus Badius.** See **Badius Ascensius, Jodocus.**

Ascham (as′kạm), **Roger.** English classical scholar and author; b. at Kirby Wiske, Yorkshire, England, 1515; d. at London, 1568. He became an accomplished Greek scholar at St. John's College, Cambridge, then a center of humanism. As tutor (1548–1550) to Elizabeth Tudor (later to be Queen Elizabeth), he can probably be held responsible for her great interest in the classics. He was subsequently Latin secretary to both Mary and Elizabeth. His chief works are *Toxophilus* (1545), a treatise in dialogue form on archery, an early masterpiece of modern English prose, and *The Scholemaster* (1570),

AMICO ASPERTINI
Bacchanalia
Free and bizarre rendering of a Mantegna engraving, *The Bacchanal with a Wine Press*
Courtesy of The Metropolitan Museum of Art, New York, Rogers Fund, 1908

highly valued for its method of teaching Latin.

ASOLANI (ä-zō-lä′nē), **GLI.** Three prose dialogues on the nature of love, in Italian, by Pietro Bembo. The setting is Asolo, where the Queen of Cyprus has her garden, and the participants in the dialogue are six young newcomers to love. The six discuss the aspects and qualities of Platonic love, a concept that greatly attracted the minds of Italians of a certain class at that time. In bringing his *Il Cortegiano* to a close, Castiglione makes Bembo his last speaker with an eloquent exposition of the ideas expressed in *Gli Asolani*. Bembo's treatise was dedicated to Lucrezia Borgia.

ASPERTINI (äs-per-tē′nē), **AMICO.** Bolognese painter; b. at Bologna, 1474; d. there, 1552. His father, Giovanni Antonio, was a painter (of whose work nothing is now known), as were his brothers Leonello and Guido. He had his first lessons from his father and was later greatly influenced by Filippino Lippi. Perhaps with his brother Guido, he went to Ferrara, where he worked first in the shop of Ercole de' Roberti and then with Costa and Francia. He is thought to have made two visits to Rome, and produced some works in and about that city, including some of the decoration of the fortress of Civita Castellana (1503) and a *St. Christopher*, now in the Spada Gallery. He was at Lucca (1508–1509) and frescoed a chapel and painted a *Holy Family* in the Church of S. Frediano. At Bologna he frescoed two scenes on the lives of St. Valerian and St. Tiburtius in the Church of S. Cecilia, and a *Last Judgment*, now lost. He also carved some of the sculpture for the doors of S. Petronio, for he was a sculptor and miniaturist, as well as a decorator of cassone panels, as those at Bergamo, Madrid, and Vienna. He designed clocks and sham architecture for festivals. Vasari called him a capricious man of bizarre spirit. This estimate is justified by his works, which are often overwhelmed by accessories and decorative conceits, sometimes picked out in gold; faces may be round and squashed, with small eyes and pinched mouths. Among his works in the Pinacoteca and churches of Bologna are an *Adoration of the Magi* and a fresco transferred to canvas, *The Holy Family,* as well as the Tirocinio altarpiece. *The Adoration of the Child* is in the Uffizi; *Deathbed of St. Nicholas of Tolentino* is in the Johnson Collection, Philadelphia; and other works are at Hanover, London (British Museum), and the National Gallery, Washington. A number of his drawings after the antique are preserved in the British Museum.

Aspertini, Guido. Bolognese painter; b. at Bologna, c1467; d. 1502 or 1503. He was the older brother of Amico Aspertini (1474–1552), and like him had his first lessons from their father, Giovanni Antonio, also a painter. He is thought to have accompanied Amico to Ferrara and to have worked under Ercole de' Roberti, Costa, and Francia. Between 1486 and 1491 he frescoed a noteworthy *Crucifixion* under the portico of the cathedral at Bologna. It was destroyed in 1605 except for two heads that are now preserved, in a damaged state, in the sacristy.

Aspramonte (äs-prä-mōn′tā). Italian epic poem, by an unknown author, which appeared at Milan in 1516, in the same year as the first version of Lodovico Ariosto's *Orlando Furioso*. The subject is the defeat of the Saracens by the French when the former came over in large numbers under Garnier, king of Carthage, to sack Rome. This accomplished, they went across to France where Charlemagne and the great paladins under him defeated them near Aspramonte (Aspremont), a small place in France.

Astarotte (äs-tä-rôt′tā). In Luigi Pulci's *Morgante maggiore,* a courtly and intelligent fallen angel, the servant, as a result of his fall, of a magician. He believed that the earth was round, and that there were people on the other side of it. He also expressed the conviction that heaven loved all who believed sincerely, no matter what they believed in.

Astolfo (äs-tol′fō). In Matteo Maria Boiardo's *Orlando Innamorato,* the son of the king of England. He is a knight at Charlemagne's court, surpassingly handsome, brave, boastful, often overcome but always ready to try again. In a tournament at Charlemagne's court he is quickly unhorsed by Argalia, brother of Angelica, princess of Cathay, and blames it on his saddle. Argalia has a magic lance that, in a later combat, he lays aside. Astolfo, whose lance has been broken, picks up Argalia's, without being aware of its properties. From the moment the lance comes into his hands he is invincible, to his own and everyone else's amazement. In Lodovico Ariosto's continuation of Boiardo's epic, *Orlando Furioso,* Astolfo has many adventures, including a trip to the Inferno riding on a hippogriff, and another, in company with St. John the Evangelist, to the moon in Elijah's chariot. On the moon he sees a heap of rubbish. It is composed of broken promises, lovers' tears, days lost by idlers, flattery of princes, presents made in hope of reward, and vials filled nearly to the stopper with the lost wits of men. Astolfo finds Orlando's wits, lost through love and jealousy, and is permitted to take them and restore them to Orlando. He also finds his own.

Astrology and Magic. Astrology, "the supposed influence of the heavenly bodies on human affairs," was considered during the so-called Renaissance a subdivision of magic, and according to the late Professor Lynn Thorndike, was "the most widespread and most pseudo-scientific of any variety of magic." Like the other occult arts or sciences included among the magic arts and related to divination, astrology involved the need to know and to foretell the future in order to regulate one's life and activities. Unlike magic, however, astrology was an art which was based upon well-defined and apparently predictable results. It was not a manipulative art in which knowledge of its techniques would lead to a mastery of the forces of nature to meet man's needs or desires. Astrology, or the rule of the stars, was rather thought of as a universal law of nature, and astrologers based their confidence in divination of the future on the acceptance of this law. The resort to astrological divination appears to have been particularly prevalent in the past in societies undergoing stress and change, a fact that may account for its popularity in the 14th to the 17th century, as well as today.

The belief in astrology, which is of ancient origin, was widespread in the Hellenistic and Graeco-Roman world and in the last centuries of the Roman Empire in the west. It continued to be cultivated throughout the medieval period; and astrological prediction found high favor among many Christian scholars of note. Some of them held that the power of the stars is comparable to that of the winds that blow ships on their courses. They frequently sought also to distinguish between natural astrology and judicial astrology. The former they related to the study of the stars and their physical effects on tides, climate, and the like, the latter to divination or the forecasting of future events or of human character and actions, based on the position of the constellations at a given time or at birth. Judicial astrology, which thus held that man's actions and destiny are not wholly within his control but are determined by the stars, was contrary to the Christian doctrine of free will, and hence was opposed by a number of churchmen. Nevertheless, belief in both forms of astrology continued to be manifest among Christian writers. St. Augustine of Hippo (354–430) had in his early writings accepted astrology, but in his later works rejected it, and in so doing had drawn attention to the inherent conflict between the view, on the one hand, that man's destiny is determined by physical forces beyond his control, and on the other, that he has freedom of will and the ability to choose either the path of righteousness or of nonrighteousness. However, the fact that St. Augustine had shifted from an earlier acceptance to a later and more mature rejection of astrology did little to stem the tide of interest in and acceptance of the belief in astrology and in the predictability of the effects of the stars. As a natural law of the universe, astrology was defended on the premise that knowledge of the operation of that law would lead men to avoid the pitfalls that had been forecast, just as one who listens to a weather forecast is prepared for changes in the weather. Also to meet the objections occasioned by astrology's antipathy to free will, churchmen, like Albertus Magnus in the 13th century, fell back on the division of astrology into the two branches noted above, namely, natural and judicial. The first, involving a study of the shapes, sizes, and motions of the heavenly bodies, was fully condoned and encouraged since it led to more accurate charting of the stars, to weather prediction, and to developments needed in navigation. The second was perhaps more vulnerable to censure because it involved forecasts and prognostications of future human actions and relied upon the drawing up of horoscopes and their interpretation. The horoscope involved, of course, a careful study of natural astrology as well as of mathematics, since it was necessary to calculate the position of the constellations at the moment of birth of the individual whose horoscope was being cast. From this calculation the length of life and the fortune of the individual could presumably be determined. This was established according to the planet that appeared in the astrological house of one of the twelve signs of the zodiac.

Despite occasional ecclesiastical disapproval, the belief in astrology, both natural and judicial, continued among both the unlettered and the learned segments of the populace throughout the 14th to the 17th century. It was particularly stressed in the Italian universities. At Bologna, for example, professors of astrology in the 14th to the 16th century were required to make annual prognostications and also were expected to produce individual horoscopes on request. Moreover, as a university subject, astrology was supported by so-called authoritative literature transmitted from antiquity and by the writings of influential scholars throughout the Middle Ages. One of the latter, for example, was the *Liber astronomicus* by Guido Bonatti (d. c1300), a work on astrology based on Ptolemy, Hermes, and Arabic sources. Bonatti was the astrologer for Guido da Montefeltro, captain of the people of Forlì. Another early 14th century advocate of astrology, Arnald of Villanova, was particularly important in the field of astrological medicine.

In the epoch between the 14th and the 17th centuries there was indeed a great spurt of interest in judicial astrology—that is, in prognostications and the casting of horoscopes. But it is difficult to decide whether this was due to the revival and rediscovery of the astrological writings from the Hellenistic era or to the stresses of the time arising from the Black Death, the continued civil strife, and foreign invasions of French and Spanish, or the more imminent threat posed by the advance of the Turkish armies into eastern Europe after the fall of Constantinople in 1453. In any event, that there was a quickened interest in divination and in the desire to fathom the future through astrological prognostications seems clear. Yet the extent to which adherence to such a belief involved the necessity to be reassured as to the future or to be protected in the present is uncertain. Nevertheless, it is possible that such motives may very well have enhanced the importance of astrology and of astrologers. Honor and renown were indeed accorded to those who predicted the future through their increasingly elaborate and detailed knowledge of the positions, orbits, and motions of the heavenly bodies. Astrological predictions continued to hold a place high in public favor despite the attacks made on astrology by such prominent personages as Pico della Mirandola and his nephew Giovanni Francesco Mirandola, as well as by Savonarola. Their criticisms were in fact countered by the support and praise of astrology by professors in the universities. Orations lauding astrology were delivered in Padua and Ferrara in 1506 and 1507 by Bartolomeo Vespucci of Florence and by Luca Gaurico, a noted astrologer. Agostino Nifo (1473–1538) defended astrology and tried to find in the stars an explanation of the calamities of his own time. Another defense of astrology was composed (1508) by Gundisalvus of Toledo, physician to the queen of France, while further orations in praise of astrology were delivered at Bologna by Giovanni Garzoni, a noted professor of medicine. Annual astrological predictions appeared both before and after 1500 in considerable numbers. For example, Antonio Campanuzzo addressed predictions for the year 1507 to Pope Julius II; Giovanni di Rogerius addressed predictions from Rome to the French king, Francis I (1537). As the preceding instances suggest, prominent astrologers not only lauded astrology but also were themselves honored by the chief potentates of Europe. This may be demonstrated by illustrative examples in addition to those already mentioned. The Estense court at Ferrara was particularly hospitable to astrologers. Among the astrologers there, Pietro Buono Avogaro was the author of a number of astrological predictions, some of which he addressed to the duke of Ferrara and Modena; Pellegrino Prisciano, the librarian for Duke Ercole I, was noted as the court astrologer. Of the 16th century popes who were patrons of astrology, mention might be made, in addition to Julius II, of Leo X, Adrian VI, and Paul III. Moreover, as Lynn Thorndike and others have shown, astrology maintained its position as the most important of the occult sciences, on which others were dependent, until the close of the 17th century.

On the positive side, although astrology may be considered a magical art, since it tends to give objective form to man's desire for a better knowledge of his future, it has also in the past led him to a closer study and better understanding of nature and of the relationship of meteorological phenomena. In proof of these assertions there are the positive results in astronomical knowledge and techniques noted above, as well as the suggestive statements made by the eminent physician and historian Arturo Castiglioni. He has drawn attention to the modern studies on the constitution of the human body, traceable back to ancient Hippocratic doctrines, that affirm the relationships between meteorological facts and the normal and pathological life of the human organism. He has also noted that modern research in radiations emitted by substances contained in the stars and revealed by the spectrum, as well as hypotheses recently advanced regarding the relations between solar spots and extraordinary historical events, have led to a belief that intuitive human conceptions and man's immediate sensitivity to the action of the stars may have a vaster and deeper foundation of truth than has generally been acknowledged. P.K.

Atanagi (ä-tä-nä′jē), **Dionigi.** Humanist and writer; b. at Cagli, 1510; d. 1573. He earned a meager living editing and publishing the works of others. He wrote verse, a treatise on history, and a *Life of Irene da Spelimbergo* (1561).

Atlante (ät-län′tā). In Matteo Maria Boiardo's *Orlando Innamorato* and Lodovico Ariosto's *Orlando Furioso*, an enchanter. He lives on Mount Carena in a castle surrounded with a wall of glass, and here he educated young Ruggiero. Astolfo destroys his palace. His ghost appears and separates Ruggiero and Marfisa, engaged in a deadly duel, and reveals to them that they are twins.

Attavanti (ät-tä-vän′tē), **Paolo.** Preacher and humanist; b. at Florence, 1419; d. there, May, 1499. Of a patrician Florentine family, he was educated by the Servites and entered that order. He took his doctorate in law at Pisa, spent some time at Rome, and thereafter held various positions in his order. He preached in various cities of northern Italy and then (1496) was inscribed in the faculty of theology at Florence, where he had earlier been a member of the group of humanists and men of letters that surrounded Lorenzo de' Medici. In addition to his reputation as a preacher, he was known for the collections of sermons he left, for some lives of the saints, for histories of Mantua and of the Gonzaga family, for a dialogue on the origin of the Servite Order, and for his theological works.

Attendolo (ät-ten′dō-lō), **Muzio.** See **Sforza, Muzio Attendolo.**

Aubert (ō-ber), **Étienne.** Original name of Pope **Innocent VI.**

Aubry de Montdidier (ō-brē dẹ môṅ-dē-dyā). French courtier; d. c1371. A favorite of Charles V, he was murdered in the forest of Montargis by another courtier, named Richard de Macaire. It is said that Macaire would have escaped unpunished but for Aubry's dog, which followed him until, suspicion being aroused, the king ordered Macaire to fight the dog as his accuser. Though armed with a club, Macaire was knocked down, confessed, and was hanged. The story is the subject of many ballads and plays, including the French-Italian chanson *Macaire*.

Augurello (ou-gö-rel′lō), **Giovanni Aurelio.** Humanist and teacher; b. at Rimini, c1440; d. at Treviso, 1524. He went to Venice (1457), and then to Padua where he studied law. He became a friend of Bernardo Bembo, and greeted with pleasure the first attempts of Bernardo's son Pietro to write poetry. When Bernardo went to Florence on an embassy, Augurello accompanied him. At Florence he was welcomed by Poliziano and Ficino and taught and spread Petrarchan culture. In 1485 he went to Venice where he was associated with Aldus Manutius. Disappointed in his expectation of a chair at Venice, he went to Treviso and remained there the rest of his life. Augurello wrote Latin verse on the model of Horace, a didactic poem on alchemy, *Crisopeia*, and Italian verses in the manner of Petrarch.

Aurispa (ou-rē′spä), **Giovanni.** Humanist; b. 1376; d. at Ferrara, 1459. Aurispa's great contributions to humanism and Western culture arise from the fact that he was one of the first to realize the importance of Greek manuscripts, one of the earliest collectors of them on a large scale, and vigorous in his efforts to awaken contemporary interest in Greek classics. He was educated in Naples and remained there probably until about 1410. In 1413 he made a journey to the Byzantine Empire and is known to have been in Chios in that year. He made a second journey, to Constantinople, in 1421 and remained there until 1423. On both trips he was tireless in his search for manuscripts of the ancient Greeks. Among those he found and brought back to Italy were two copies of the *Greek Anthology*, two volumes of the *Iliad*, works by Aeschylus, Sophocles, Apollonius Rhodius, Plato, Pindar, Dionysius, and Empedocles, as well as some of the Homeric *Hymns* and the *Moralia* of Plutarch. Altogether he brought back over 250 manuscripts. He was a teacher, as at Savona, Bologna, and Florence, and went to Ferrara (c1428) where he was the tutor of the lord of Ferrara's son. In the course of his career he had joined Martin V at Florence and accompanied him to Rome. Later he was papal secretary to Eugenius IV and went to the Council of Basel. On this mission he found important Latin texts in Germany. He accompanied Eugenius back to Bologna, Ferrara, and Florence, and remained attached to his court until 1443. His time in his remaining years was divided between Ferrara, which he made his home, and Rome. In addition to teaching and his duties for the popes, Aurispa wrote and translated, but his great importance for his own and later times was in the finding and preserving of so many Greek texts, especially in view of the rapid advance of the Turks against the Byzantine Empire and their imminent conquest of Constantinople.

Avalos (dä′vä-lōs), **Fernando Francesco d'.** See **Pescara,** Marquis of.

Avanzi (ä-vän′tsē), **Iacopo degli.** [Also known as **Iacopo da Bologna.**] Bolognese painter; active in the last part of the 14th century. For long confused with Altichieri's collaborator at Padua, Jacopo Avanzo, he is now known to have been a separate artist. A vigorous and meritorious painter, a fresco attributed to him is in the Pinacoteca at Bologna, and there is a signed *Crucifixion* in the Colonna Gallery at Rome.

Avanzo (ä-vän′tsō), **Jacopo**(?). Veronese (or Paduan) painter; active in the second half of the 14th century. With Altichiero Altichieri he painted frescoes in the Oratory of St. George at Padua. The master hand was that of Altichieri. Avanzo is thought to have painted the scenes from the life of St. Lucy. These, strongly influenced by Giotto, are more crudely executed than the others. Both Avanzo and Altichieri were attracted by the details of the life of the people of their own time and inserted them freely into their religious works. The frescoes also reveal a preoccupation with architectural backgrounds, and are interesting for experiments in empirical perspective. Realistic details, rich costumes, and homely incidents frequently give the work the flavor of genre painting.

Avellino (ä-vel-lē′no), **Antonio di Pietro.** See **Filarete.**

Averroës or **Averrhoës** (a̤-ver′ō̤-ēz). [Arabic, **ibn-Roshd** or **ibn-Rushd.**] Spanish-Arab philosopher and physician; b. at Córdoba, Spain, 1126; d. at what is now Marrakech, Morocco, December 10, 1198. He is the most celebrated of the scholars produced by Spain's remarkable Moslem culture. In addition to treatises on astronomy, grammar, jurisprudence, and medicine, he produced the extensive commentaries on Aristotle upon which a great part of medieval Christian scholastic thought depended. In fact, Averroës' fame in history largely developed through use of his work by Christian (rather than Moslem) theologians, one group of whom became known as Averroists through their virtually complete acceptance of his metaphysics. One of his distinctions as a philosopher is that he worked from genuine Aristotelian writings that had become available in the Arab world, rather than from the Neoplatonic works that had been the basis of the work of generations of Moslem philosophers. In seeking to reconcile Aristotle's ideas with Moslem theology he was attacked for his allegedly dangerous lack of orthodoxy. Although his fame as a philosopher has eclipsed his fame as a physician, we know (from his medical encyclopedia) that he had a knowledge of medicine that alone would have secured him a place in the history of science. For example, he recognized that a person who has smallpox and recovers may be assured thereafter of immunity to the disease, and he also understood the function of the retina in the eye.

Avicenna (av-i-sen′a̤). [Also, **ibn-Sina;** called the **Prince of Physicians.**] Arab philosopher and physician; b. near Bukhara, 980; d. at Hamadan, Persia, 1037. He early displayed his medical proficiency, and became physician and adviser to rulers at Khiva (c1004) and Hamadan (until 1037). His *Canon of Medicine*, an encyclopedia of medical knowledge largely drawn from ancient writers, is the most important of his more than 100 works. It was studied in European universities (in a Latin translation) for about 500 years. His philosophy is rooted in Aristotelian thought, with a distinct element of Neoplatonism in its cosmology.

Ávila (ä′bē-lä), **Pedro Arias de.** See **Pedrarias.**

Avilés (ä-bē-lās′), **Pedro Menéndes de.** See **Menéndez de Avilés, Pedro.**

B

Babylonian Captivity. Period (1305–1376) in Roman Catholic history during which the popes lived at Avignon, France. The term derives from the original Babylonian Captivity of the Jews in the 6th century B.C., which is traditionally reckoned as having lasted for seventy years. Clement V, who had been elected pope through the influence of Philip IV of France, removed the papal court from Rome to Avignon to please him. The popes who succeeded him were all French and were subject, in greater or lesser degree, to direct political control by the French throne. Rome fell into ruin and anarchy in the absence of the popes. Many voices were raised to urge their return, among them, those of Dante and St. Catherine of Siena. Florence and others rebelled against the rule of the papal legates (1375); Italy was in a ferment of insurrection. Gregory XI (1370–1378) excommunicated Florence and declared war. St. Catherine of Siena wrote to both parties to plead for peace, unhesitatingly told both wherein they erred, and went to Avignon as an emissary of the Florentines to negotiate with the pope. Gregory, a Frenchman, reluctantly decided to return to Rome. He left in September, 1376, and entered Rome in January, 1377. With the return of Gregory to Rome the Babylonian Captivity came to an end. It had by no means been the only instance when the papacy had been absent from Rome but it was the longest continuous period. In the 11th, 12th, and 13th centuries the popes were often away from Rome, exiled for more than half the time by turbulent mobs, by unruly barons, and by political strife. The end of the Babylonian Captivity, however, did not bring peace to the Church; see **Great Schism.**

Bacchiacca (bä-kyäk′kä). [Real name, **Francesco Ubertini.**] Florentine mannerist painter; b. in the Mugello, near Florence, March 1, 1494; d. at Florence, October 5, 1557. He was the son of a goldsmith. With his older brother, also a painter, of whom nothing is known, he was a pupil of Perugino when the latter had a workshop at Florence between 1505 and 1515. (His younger brother Antonio was a highly skilled weaver.) The influence of Perugino is strong in his early work and was later modified by his interest in the work of the northern engravers. This interest was particularly apparent in the sharpness of his line, in the minute care with which he depicted small figures in his backgrounds, and in a greater concern with detailed landscape. In 1515, with Pontormo, Ghirlandaio, and Franciabigio, he decorated the residence Leo X was to occupy when he returned to his native city. In 1525 he went to Rome. There he was a friend to Benvenuto Cellini and took part with him in the activities of a club whose members were artists and men of letters, and who seem to have enjoyed a Bohemian life traditionally associated with artists. In Rome, too, he fell in love with a Roman courtesan who is thought to have been the model for his *La Maddalena*, now in the Pitti Palace, Florence. The slight distortions of the sharply outlined long head with its pointed chin and the elegant tapering hands are typically mannerist. Back in Florence before 1527, he was enrolled in the Physicians' and Apothecaries' Guild in 1529. Earlier (1516–1518), with his good friend Andrea del Sarto, with Granacci and Pontormo, he had decorated the bridal chamber of Giovan Francesco Borgherini in the Borgherini Palace at Florence. Bacchiacca had by this time a reputation for his skill at painting small figures, animals, plants, and birds. To decorate the panels and furniture of the bridal chamber he painted a series on the *Story of Joseph*, the separate panels of which are crowded with figures. Two of these are in the National Gallery, London; others are in the Borghese Gallery, Rome. In 1539 he painted some of the decorations for the marriage of Cosimo I de' Medici and Eleonora of Toledo, and from this time until his death he was frequently employed by Cosimo. Among the ornamental works he executed for Cosimo were designs for two series of tapestries—one on the months of the year, the other a series of *groteschi*—and decorations in and about the Pitti Palace. Many of his works were prepared for patrons in France and England, and of these many have been attributed to other artists at one time or another. The reason for the attributions is not difficult to understand. From the beginning Bacchiacca was not only strongly influenced by other painters, he borrowed freely from their works, often infusing with his own spirit the elements he borrowed. His *Adam and Eve with Two Children*, Johnson Collection, Philadelphia, has been cited as an adaptation and reworking of Perugino's painting of *Apollo and Marsyas*. A *Deposition from the Cross*, Uffizi, is derived from Perugino, with Bacchiacca's additions and coloring. A *Holy Family* is an outright copy of Michelangelo. Other works illustrate his narrative gift, diversity of composition, and a spirit of originality, as the *Three Scenes from the Life of St. Acacius* (1521), predella panels in the Uffizi. The *Gathering of the Manna*, National Gallery, Washington, abounds in the animals he loved to paint. He also painted portraits which have been admired for their individuality if not for deep insight. Works attributed to him are to be found in many European museums; others are at Boston (*Lady with a Nosegay*, Isabella Stewart Gardner Museum); at New York (*Charity*, the Metropolitan Museum); at Memphis, Tennessee (*Last Supper*, derived from an engraving); at Hartford, Connecticut (*Tobias and the Angel*, Atheneum); at Poughkeepsie, New York (*Baptism of Christ*, Vassar); and at Baltimore, Coral Gables, Florida, New Orleans, Rochester,

Springfield, Massachusetts, and elsewhere. Always an eclectic and mannerist, who in his later life was influenced toward monumentality by Michelangelo and by his friend Vasari, he was an excellent draftsman, an acute observer, and a painter who delighted in injecting a bizarre note into his work. While borrowing freely from others he borrowed from his own works, switching elements and details from one painting to another, and modifying the influences and borrowings from others to produce, at times, works of marked individuality.

Bacci (bät′chē), **Andrea.** Physician, philosopher, and naturalist; b. at S. Elpidio d'Ancona, about the middle of the 16th century; d. at Rome, 1600. He taught botany and pharmacology at Rome, was a friend of Cardinal Ascanio Colonna, and was the physician of Pope Sixtus V. Among his many works on the history and monuments of Rome is his *De thermis, lacubus, fluminibus, balneis totius orbis libri* VII (Venice, 1571), which contains and preserves much information and has as well a number of precious drawings. He wrote several medical works, including one on poisons and antidotes, and a history of wine.

Baccio d'Agnolo (bät′chō dä-nyō′lō). [Real name, **Bartolomeo d'Agnolo Baglioni.**] Woodcarver and architect; b. at Florence, May 15, 1462; d. there, May 6, 1543. He is thought to have learned his craft of woodcarving in his father's workshop, and to have perfected it by studying the works of his contemporaries. He attained such skill and artistry that his own workshop became a meeting place for some of the most celebrated artists of his time, including Michelangelo, Raphael, Cronaca, and the brothers Antonio and Giuliano da Sangallo. Three of his five sons—Giuliano, Filippo, and Domenico—became woodcarvers and architects also, and aided him in carrying out his commissions. Often called upon to construct and carve altars, dossals, armoires, and other ecclesiastical furniture, he became skilled at designing pieces of harmonious proportion and pleasing form, and was also the best carver of frames for altarpieces of his day. Among the more notable of his extant carvings (Vasari says he filled many commissions for objects that were lost or destroyed even in his time) are the choir stalls he carved (1491–1496) for S. Maria Novella at Florence, and the inlaid stalls he made (1502–1532) for the choir of the 13th-century Church of S. Agostino at Perugia. Almost without realizing it he became an architect, and spent the second half of his life working in that field. He worked with Cronaca and Antonio da Sangallo the Elder in the Palazzo della Signoria, and was one of the masters of the works in the continuing construction of the cathedral. One of his charges in the latter case was to complete the drum gallery around the dome, which had been left unfinished by Brunelleschi. It was opened in 1515 and then left incomplete because of the scathing criticism Michelangelo leveled against it. He called it a "cricket cage," with reference to its fragility in contrast to the powerful dome. Other examples of Baccio's work as an architect are the graceful campanile of S. Spirito (1511) and that of S. Miniato, both at Florence. He also designed several palaces characterized by the flat façade and elegant severity that fixed the type of noble Florentine dwelling for a number of years. The Bartolini Salimbeni Palace, perhaps inspired by a building designed by Raphael (and destroyed in 1660), is typical of Baccio's palace architecture in its simplicity and elegance. In his best work he united the solidity and strength of an earlier age to the spontaneity that developed in the beginning of the 16th century to form a harmonious new style.

Baccio da Montelupo (dä mōn-tā-lö′pō). [Real name, **Bartolomeo Sinibaldi.**] Florentine sculptor and architect; b. at Montelupo, 1469; d. at Lucca, 1535. Gay and dissolute in his youth, he was converted by the preaching of Savonarola and became one of his most ardent followers. His artistic creations reflect the religious spirit and mysticism with which he was imbued as a result of this experience. At Bologna, in a chapel of S. Domenico, four statues in terra-cotta from his hand have come to light. They once formed part of a *Pietà*. Grandiose in form, imaginatively posed, and exquisitely modeled, these project a sense of drama and intensity that indicate the influence of Antonio Rossellino and Benedetto da Maiano. In 1498 at Bologna he molded terra-cotta busts of the twelve Apostles, some of which are in the cathedral at Ferrara. When the persecution of Savonarola began (1498), Baccio was forced to flee Florence. He went to Venice, where he carved (1503) an uninspired statue, *Mars*, for the Pesaro monument in the Church of the Frari. On his return to Florence (1504) he carved a number of statues in wood, most of which have been lost. Of the sculptures he carved for S. Lorenzo, only the marble *Crucifix* on the high altar survives. The form and careful realism of the modeling reach back to the tradition of 15th-century Florentine sculpture. The *Crucifix* in the Museum of S. Marco is of a later date. His *St. John the Evangelist*, carved (1515) for Orsanmichele, derives its pose and drapery from Ghiberti's *St. Matthew*, also in Orsanmichele. Using the *St. John the Evangelist* as a standard of comparison, painted wooden statues of *St. Anthony Abbot* at Lucca and of *St. Peter* and *St. Paul* at Anghiari, near Arezzo, are attributed to him. From this period, or a little earlier, are the arms of Leo X, posted on a corner of the Pucci Palace at Florence. The work has suffered from weathering, but not enough to obscure the grace of the two putti holding the Medici arms surmounted by Leo's papal insignia.

Baccio spent the last years of his life at Lucca. There he began (1522) the Church of S. Paolino, patterned after a church designed by Cronaca, S. Salvatore al Monte, across the Arno from Florence. Baccio's church had the same plan—a Latin cross with a single nave and side chapels divided by pillars—but with a simplified façade and a minimum of external ornamentation. Vasari describes many works executed by him at Lucca. A tomb he began (1527) for Silvestro Gigli was completed by his son Raffaello. It was broken up and dispersed in the next century. Most of the other works mentioned by Vasari have disappeared. One of the best of the Florentine sculptors of his time, Baccio da Montelupo built on the traditions of the 15th century, adding such contemporary elements as suited his artistic temperament. His works are naturalistic in the manner of the 15th century, with a certain intense spirituality, and have something of the monumentality of the 16th century.

Bacon (bā′kǫn), **Roger.** [Called **Doctor Mirabilis,** Anglicized as the "Admirable Doctor."] English philosopher and scientist; b. at or near Ilchester, Somersetshire, England, c1214; d. probably at Oxford, England, in 1294. A Franciscan who had been educated at Oxford and Paris, and knew Hebrew and Greek, he incurred the resentment of his superiors by his openly expressed contempt for their knowledge, and was placed in confinement on more than one occasion as a consequence. His chief work, the *Opus majus*, a general treatise on the sciences, was completed before 1268. Other notable works are *Opus minus*, *Opus tertium*, and *Compendium philosophiae*. Bacon was essentially an encyclopedist; he constantly sought better to grasp and to explain the unity of knowledge. He denounced the narrowness of scholasticism and called on philosophers and theologians to enlarge their basis of knowledge. His greatest entitlement to fame, however, was that he saw better than anyone else in his time that without experimentation and without mathematics, natural philosophy is very soon reduced to verbiage. He also realized the utility of knowledge, and this was even more remarkable than to realize its unity, for the latter had been done instinctively by almost every philosopher. This double point of view, unity (to be discovered experimentally and proved with the help of mathematics) and utility, led him to entirely new conceptions of knowledge, of learning, and of education. His accomplishments fell considerably short of his visions. His thought was not systematic, as was the dogmatic Thomistic system, but on the whole it was more original. He was a harbinger of modern civilization, while St. Thomas Aquinas (not to speak of the other great scholastics of the Continent) was destined to become virtually a symbol of medievalism.

A very original thinker and a forerunner of modern science, Bacon was also very orthodox and, in many ways, a fundamentalist. For him, theology was still the crown of all knowledge, and the Bible its repository.

Badile (bä-dē′lā), **Giovanni.** Veronese painter; b. at Verona, 1379; d. before 1451. He was one of a family that produced painters in eight generations. His work shows the influence of Stefano da Verona and is interesting for its abundant portrayal of Gothic architecture. Frescoes in the Church of S. Maria della Scala at Verona are in a poor state of preservation. A polyptych, *Madonna and Child with Saints*, is in the art museum at Verona; a *Virgin and Child* is in the Cannon Collection at Princeton. Giovanni's son Bartolomeo was also a painter, and a descendant, Giovanni Antonio, is noted as the master of Paolo Veronese.

Badile, Giovanni Antonio. Painter; b. at Vicenza, c1516; d. there, 1560. He was a member of an ancient family that had produced painters in several generations, was a pupil of Torbido, and was influenced by Moretto da Brescia and, to a small extent, by Titian. But he was an artist of modest capacity, and his main claim to fame is that he was the director of the artistic education of Paolo Veronese, his nephew, and guided him beyond the circle of Veronese painting. Several of his works are extant at Verona, including a *Resurrection of Lazarus* that shows the influence of Titian, and a *Madonna Enthroned with Saints* inspired by one of Titian's most celebrated works. Portraits by him, sometimes attributed to other artists, are in several galleries; other works are at Turin and Venice, and an *Architectural View* is in the Johnson Collection, Philadelphia.

Badius Ascensius (bā′dḝ-ůs ạ-sen′shus), **Jodocus.** [Latin name of **Josse Bade.**] Parisian humanist, teacher, and printer; b. at Asche (the Roman Ascensius), near Brussels, 1462; d. 1535. He studied in Italy and taught Greek (1492–1499) at Lyons, where he published an edition of Terence. In 1499 he removed to Paris and by 1503 had his own printing establishment there, the "Praelum Ascensianum"; his printer's marks give early pictures of a printing press. Among his own writings was a life of Thomas à Kempis.

Badoer (bä-dō-är′), **Federico.** Venetian humanist; b. 1518; d. 1593. He served on embassies to the emperors Charles V and Philip II. In 1558 he founded the celebrated Accademia della Fama in his house at Venice. About one hundred of the most prominent men of letters of his day belonged. Its purpose was to spread knowledge of all kinds by means of printed books, and the books printed by the Aldine press for this purpose are beautiful models of bookmaking. In furtherance of his plans for spreading knowledge, Badoer ran into debt and was imprisoned.

Badoer, Sebastiano. Venetian statesman; b. 1424; d. 1489. He served the Republic of Venice many times as diplomat and ambassador, as to Matthias Corvinus, king of Hungary, to enlist his aid for a crusade against the Turks (1474), as Venetian legate to the emperor Frederick III (1484), and as an ambassador of Pope Innocent VIII to make peace with Austria (1487).

Baglioni (bä-lyō′nē). Ancient family of Perugia where, in early times, they linked their interests to those of the more popular faction against the nobles. They were skilled warriors and held important civil and military offices in various cities of Italy, including the chief offices at Florence. Baglioni Novello was podesta of Florence at the time of the Duke of Athens (1342) and was expelled with him for his alleged crimes (members of the Baglioni family were banished in perpetuity from Florence, but the banishment was revoked in 1377). The Baglioni turned their attention to Perugia, their own city, which was, nominally at least, part of the papal dominions. They won control, according to the chronicler, by arms and any crimes that occurred to them, and made Perugia one of the most internally embattled, bloodstained cities of Italy. Their struggle was at first one between the Baglioni and rival families, and later became a murderous struggle within the family itself. In 1331 they entered a conspiracy to assassinate Oddo degli Oddi, of a noble ruling house, and put themselves at the head of the popular party. In 1390 Pandolfo Baglioni betrayed the head of another rival party and hounded him from the city. In 1393 the Perugians rebelled against them, burned their houses, and made their crimes a matter of public record. The ascendancy of the people was short. Braccio da Montone restored the fortunes of the Baglioni. Malatesta I Baglioni, comrade in arms of Braccio da Montone, increased his domains as a result of papal grants. His son Braccio received absolution from the pope for the murder of his cousin Pandolfo and his nephew Niccolò (1460), by which double murder he had secured unquestioned control of Perugia. Under Braccio, a cultivated man and a generous patron, the fortunes of the family reached a peak; the dominions they controlled were increased by the addition of small states in Umbria. Rivals who dared to oppose them were suppressed without mercy. Members of the Oddi family were always suspect. In 1482 and again in 1488, members of that family were massacred wholesale. Communal forms of government persisted, but by 1488 the Baglioni controlled

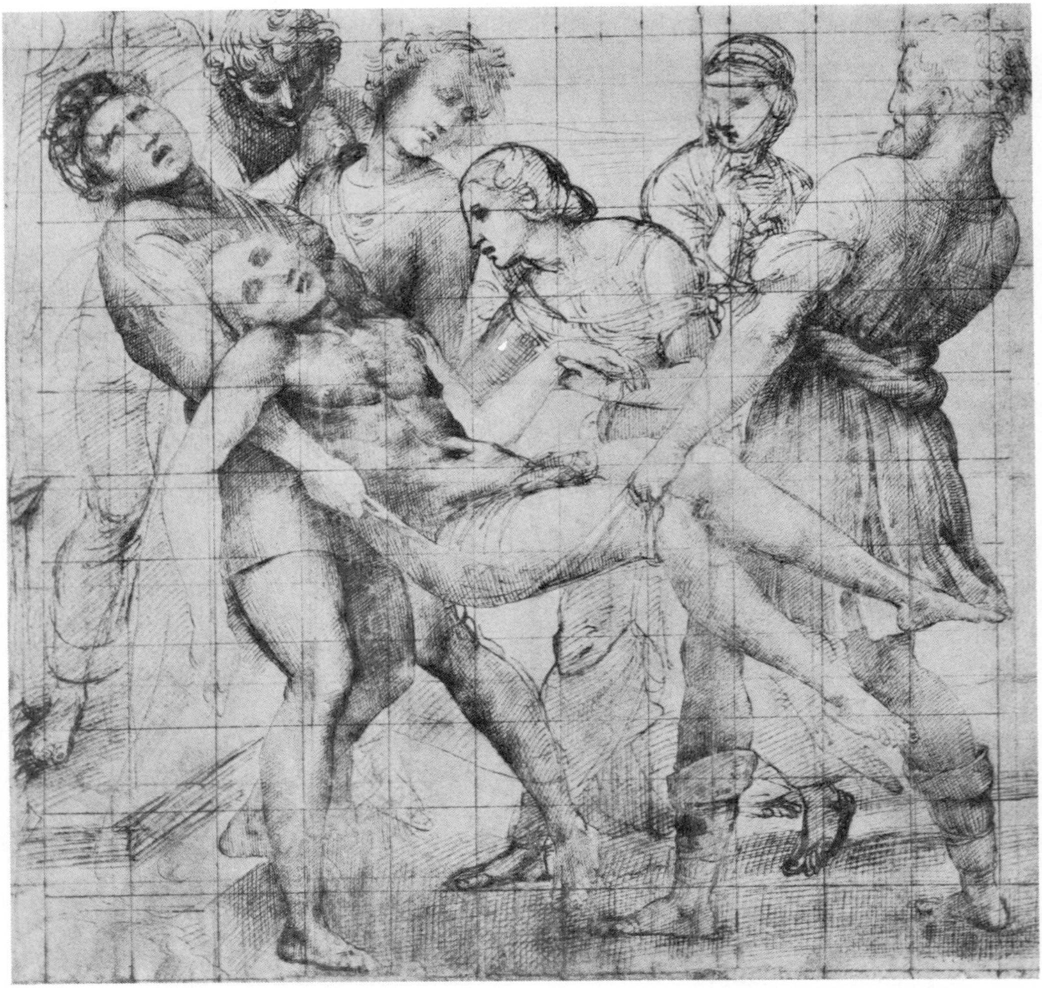

Raphael
Deposition
Study for a *Deposition*, Borghese Gallery, Rome, painted for Atalanta Baglioni
Uffizi, Florence Alinari-Art Reference Bureau

all the chief magistracies of the city and packed the regime with their adherents. The lust for power of the Baglioni was not limited to the slaying of rivals outside the family. The numerous kinsmen constantly intrigued against each other, and murder in the family was commonplace. The most shocking instance of familial strife occurred on July 14, 1500, when young Grifonetto Baglioni with a band of his bravos murdered four members of his own family who opposed him. Two days later, Giampaolo Baglioni, who had escaped that massacre, returned to Perugia and attacked Grifonetto in the piazza. As Grifonetto lay dying, his young mother, Atalanta, and his young wife, Zenobia, came to find him. His mother had beseeched him not to conspire against his relatives, and now came to urge him to forgive his slayer before he died. In commemoration of her grief over her dead son and the murders in the family, she commissioned Raphael to paint *The Deposition* (signed and dated 1507) for the family chapel in the Church of San Francesco al Prato at Perugia. (The painting is now in the Borghese Gallery at Rome.) Giampaolo, with the aid of Vitelozzo Vitelli, regained power in Perugia and kept it, after the short-lived triumph of Cesare Borgia in Umbria, but his crimes, especially that of refusing submission to the Church, brought on his death. Pope Leo X lured him to Rome. He was seized and beheaded in Castel Sant' Angelo (1520). (It was this Giampaolo that Machiavelli accused of incest and parricide, and whom he condemned because when he had Pope Julius II in his power he respected his freedom; Machiavelli thought Giampaolo would have won immortal glory if he had taken advantage of this opportunity to rid the world of the warlike Julius.) Giampaolo's son Malatesta, a captain in the pay of Florence, betrayed the Florentines in the siege of 1527–1530; he died (1531) full of remorse, it was said, for his treachery. Malatesta's son Ridolfo, a captain in the pay of Cosimo I, also proved disloyal to his employer. When Pope Paul III wore the tiara (1534–1549), he determined to bring Umbria back under papal domination. Malatesta IV Baglioni led in the heroic defense of Perugia against the pope's forces, but after a prolonged siege the city was forced to capitulate (1540). Thereafter, the influence of the Baglioni, except as military men in the pay of others, declined.

Bagnacavallo (bä-nyä-kä-väl′lō). [Real name, **Bartolomeo Ramenghi,** called **il Bagnacavallo** from the place of his birth.] Painter; b. at Bagnacavallo, 1484; d. at Bologna, August, 1542. He studied under Francia at Bologna. Drawn by the fame of Raphael, he went to Rome and studied under him, assisting him in the paintings in the Vatican. In 1520 he returned to Bologna, and worked there successfully the remainder of his life. Much of his work has been lost or destroyed, but some examples remain in the galleries and churches of Bologna. A signed and dated (1522) *Crucifixion with the Magdalen* is in the sacristy of the Church of S. Pietro, a badly damaged *Virgin Enthroned with Her Son* is in Santo Stefano, and a beautiful, but again badly damaged, *Visitation* is in S. Vitale. From what remains of his work, it appears that Bagnacavallo was an uneven artist of moderate talent. He was an eclectic who drew on Ferrarese, Bolognese, and Roman sources. His great admiration for Raphael sometimes led him to copy his master directly, with unfortunate results. The fortunate influences of Raphael are in his grace and color. Among his other surviving works are a *Madonna and Child with Saints Joseph and Jerome* (the National Gallery of Parma), works at Berlin and Paris, and a collection of drawings in the Uffizi.

Baiardo (bä-yär′dō). In the *Orlando* romances of Matteo Maria Boiardo and Lodovico Ariosto, Rinaldo's magic horse.

Baïf (bȧ-ēf), **Jean Antoine de.** French poet; b. at Venice, 1532; d. at Paris, September 9, 1589. He was the son of Lazare de Baïf (c1496–1547), was a friend of Pierre Ronsard, and was one of the most active members of his group, the Pléiade. He invented a fifteen-syllable line and a system of phonetic spelling. His *Le Brave* (1567) is an adaptation of the *Miles gloriosus* of Plautus.

Baïf, Lazare de. French humanist; b. at La Flèche, c1496; d. at Paris, 1547. He translated the *Electra* of Sophocles and some of Plutarch's *Lives* into French.

Bajazet I (baj-ạ-zet′). [Also, **Bajasid, Bayazid;** called **Ilderim** or **Yilderim,** meaning "Lightning."] Turkish sultan (1389–1403); b. 1347; d. 1403. He was the son of Murad I, whom he succeeded, and was given the name "Ilderim" because of his rapid movements. He conquered Bulgaria and a great part of Asia Minor, Macedonia, Serbia, and Thessaly, defeated the allied Hungarians, Poles, and French at Nicopolis in 1396, but was defeated (1402) by Tamerlane at Angora, and held prisoner by him until his death. He is said to have been carried about in an iron cage, but this is probably an invention of later writers. He was succeeded by his son Mohammed I.

Bajazet II. Turkish sultan (1481–1512). He was the son and successor of Mohammed II. On the death of his father, Bajazet's brother Djem rebelled and sought to seize power. Djem was forced to flee and finally fell into the hands of Pope Innocent VIII. Bajazet paid the pope 40,000 ducats annually to keep Djem a prisoner, and paid Innocent's successor the same amount, but would have preferred to pay a ransom for Djem's corpse, as the prospect of his return and a new rebellion was a constant threat to Bajazet. Bajazet was negotiating with Pope Alexander VI, and had suggested a ransom of 300,000 ducats for Djem's body, when the captive prince died while with the French army (1495) near Naples. Bajazet was engaged in almost uninterrupted warfare with Hungary, Poland, Venice, Egypt, and Persia. He was deposed by his son Selim and died soon after, probably by poison.

Balbi, Gasparo. Italian traveler; b. at Venice; fl. in the 16th century. He spent the years 1579–1588 in India. On his return to Venice he published *Viaggio all'Indie Orientali* (1590), which was inserted by the De Bry brothers into their collection of voyages (1606).

Balbi (bäl'bē), **Girolamo.** Humanist; b. at Venice, about the middle of the 15th century; d. c1535. He is thought to have studied at Rome under Julius Pomponius Laetus, and is known to have been in Paris, where he later held a professorship, in 1485. In that year he engaged in a bitter quarrel that involved religious as well as grammatical questions. After another great quarrel (1496) he was accused of the sins of pride and heresy, and fled to England. Restless and quarrelsome, he appeared in Vienna, Prague, and Hungary. In 1514 he altered his way of life and entered the Church, ultimately attaining to a bishopric, that of Pressburg. His main contribution was not in his literary work, which included poems, orations, dialogues, and letters, but in his presentation of Italian humanism to the cities across the Alps.

Balboa (bal-bō'ạ), **Vasco Núñez de.** Spanish conquistador and soldier of fortune; b. at Jerez de los Caballeros, or at Badajoz, Spain, c1475; d. at Acla, on the Isthmus of Panama (Darien), January 12, 1519. He discovered the "South Sea," later named the Pacific. He came to the Americas in 1500. In 1510 he led an expedition to the north coast of the Isthmus of Panama, and founded Santa Maria de la Antigua del Darien, the first Spanish settlement on continental America. Learning from the Indians that there was a large body of water south of the Isthmus, he set out to find it on September 1, 1513. Twenty-six days later he stood on the shore of the Pacific and took possession of it in the name of King Ferdinand.

Baldassare d'Este (bäl-däs-sä'rā des'tā). See **Este, Baldassare d'.**

Baldini (bäl-dē'nē), **Baccio.** Goldsmith and engraver; b. c1436; d. c1487. Nothing is known of his work as a goldsmith. Vasari mentions him as an engraver, and he worked in Florence between 1460 and 1480. Two of the three engravings in *Monte Santo di Dio* (Florence, 1477), the first book in which copper engravings appear, are by him. The nineteen engravings to designs by Botticelli that appear in Landino's commentary on the *Inferno* of Dante (Florence, 1481) are by Baldini. Also attributed to him is a series of twenty-four prophets and twelve sibyls, seven planets, and some miscellaneous prints with themes of love or allegory. The latter are circular in form and may have served as decorative lids for spice boxes. A copy of the 1481 edition of Landino's commentary on the *Inferno* with Baldini's engravings is in the Isabella Stewart Gardner Museum at Boston.

Baldo degli Ubaldi (bäl'dō de'lyē ö-bäl'dē). [Latinized, **Baldus de Ubaldis.**] Jurist; b. at Perugia, 1327 (or 1319?); d. at Pavia, April 28, 1400. Considered to be one of the greatest jurists of his time, he taught law at Bologna, Perugia, Pisa, Florence, Padua, and Pavia. He was consulted by Pope Urban VI with regard to action against the antipope Clement VII, and was also frequently consulted by the great merchants of Perugia. He was one of the first jurists to give legal opinions concerning bills of exchange.

Baldovinetti (bäl-dō-vē-net'tē), **Alessio** or **Alesso.** Florentine painter; b. at Florence, probably October 14, 1425; d. there, August 29, 1499. He was the illegitimate son of an old and prominent Florentine family, studied painting with masters whose names are not now known, was enrolled in the Company of St. Luke (Painters' Guild) in 1448, and was obviously influenced in his early work by Domenico Veneziano and Fra Angelico. He collaborated with the latter (1449) in the decoration of the doors of a silver chest for the SS. Annunziata. The three scenes he painted—*Marriage at Cana, Baptism of Christ,* and *Transfiguration*—are in the Museum of San Marco at Florence. He worked for Andrea del Castagno (1454) on a *Last Judgment*, now lost, and about the same time executed, as his own commission, an altarpiece for the Medici villa at Cafaggiolo, *Madonna and Child with Saints*, now in the Uffizi. From this period also are the *Madonna* (Musée Jaquemart-André, Paris), *Annuncia-*

Dante and Vergil, with the Vision of Beatrice
Engraving by Baccio Baldini, to a design by Botticelli, for Cristoforo Landino's *Commentary* on Dante's *Divine Comedy*, Florence, 1481
Courtesy of the Isabella Stewart Gardner Museum, Boston

tion (Uffizi), and the glazed terra-cotta cornice for Luca della Robbia's tomb of Bishop Federighi (S. Trinità, Florence). In 1460 and 1461 he finished the fresco cycle (now almost entirely lost) in S. Egidio that had been begun by Domenico Veneziano and Piero della Francesca (1439–1445) and continued by Andrea del Castagno. Between April, 1461, and September, 1462, he painted his most noted work, the fresco *Nativity*, in the little cloister of SS. Annunziata. The lovely work exemplifies his stylistic grace and his charming Tuscan landscapes. For the Chapel of the Cardinal of Portugal in S. Miniato, he painted (1467) an *Annunciation* and *Prophets, Evangelists, and Doctors of the Church*. (The beautiful Chapel of the Cardinal of Portugal is the result of collaboration among the architect Antonio Manetti, the sculptors Antonio and Bernardo Rossellino and Luca della Robbia, and, in addition to Baldovinetti, the painters Antonio and Piero Pollaiuolo.) From about this period are his *Madonna in Adoration* (Louvre, Paris) and *Portrait of a Lady in Yellow* (National Gallery, London). Two years later he received his most important commission, an altarpiece and the decoration of the main chapel of S. Trinità at Florence. The altarpiece, now in the Accademia, Florence, indicates a decline in his creative powers. The decorations of the chapel, except for the painting on the ceiling that is barely visible, have disappeared. A portrait in the Carrara Academy at Bergamo is thought to be a self-portrait.

In 1449 Baldovinetti began a journal, *Ricordi*, parts of which were published. In it he mentions the engraver Maso Finiguerra and speaks of sulfur engraving. The journal also revealed his association with various artists and artisans—engravers, glaziers, workers in intarsia, and mosaicists—and that throughout his life he maintained an interest in the other arts, and sometimes practiced them. Two early documented works (1453 and 1455) are of mosaics he designed for the arches over Ghiberti's doors in the Baptistery. In the 1460's he was concerned with the intarsia work being carried on in the north sacristy of the cathedral, and designed a mosaic, *St. John the Baptist*, for the cathe-

ALESSIO BALDOVINETTI
Three Young Men and a Young Woman Who Offers them a Wreath
Gabinetto Disegni e Stampe degli Uffizi Foto Soprintendenza

dral at Pisa. The first record in his journal of a design for a stained glass window is of 1466, but he had probably made and carried out such designs earlier, most of which have been lost. However, the two magnificent windows of the Pazzi Chapel—*The Eternal Father* and *St. Andrew*—are attributed to him. His knowledge of mosaic earned him the position, given in 1483, of conservator and restorer of the mosaics of the Baptistery and S. Miniato, and he spent the last years of his life fulfilling his duties in this respect.

A gifted and original artist, throughout his life Baldovinetti was preoccupied with the techniques of his art. He experimented with different methods of preparing the surfaces he was to paint and the media, including oils, with which to paint them. (In the case of his Annunziata *Nativity* his experiments were injurious to the work.) In his artistic approach he followed his own vision. He did not follow the general Florentine interest in obtaining a three-dimensional and naturalistic effect by means of perspective and modeling. He had an almost scientific interest in design and pattern. His figures are strongly outlined, rather than molded. His surfaces are flat; details are meticulously executed to give an almost one-dimensional structural appearance. His faces, lacking a play of light and shade to give depth and tone, have a characteristic pallor —and innocence. His delicate and winning compositions, executed with technical authority, are cool and unemotional. His tone is dispassionate. To some, he gives the impression of being more interested in how he expresses his artistic intention that in what he expresses.

Balducci (bäl-döt′chē), **Matteo.** Painter; b. at Fontignano, near Perugia, 1480; d. at Città della Pieve, after 1554. Little is known of the life of this painter of the Umbro-Sienese school whose artistic vision looked rather to an earlier day than to the developments that had taken place by the time he began his painting life. In 1509 he appeared as a witness in a suit concerning Pinturicchio; in 1517 he was known as a pupil of Sodoma; in 1523 he painted a panel for a church near Amiata; and in 1543 he was listed as the owner of land at Città della Pieve, where he was living in 1550 and 1554. Pinturicchio, with whom he worked at Siena decorating the Piccolomini Library, was one of the Umbrians who most influenced his development. Balducci's *Virgin in Glory,* in the Church of S. Spirito at Siena, reflects, in addition to traditional Sienese elements, Pinturicchio's influence especially in the rendering of landscape, the figures of the saints, and the pleasing color tones. Using this work as a standard, several other paintings have been attributed to Balducci. Among them are a number in the Pinacoteca and churches of Siena, and others at Bergamo, Florence, Gubbio, Rome (Spada Gallery), Princeton, Tulsa, and elsewhere.

Baldung (bäl′dủng), **Hans.** [Called **Hans Baldung Grien** or **Grün.**] German painter and engraver; b. at Gmünd, Swabia, c1480; d. at Strasbourg, 1545. He was a friend of Matthias Grunewald and probably a pupil of Albrecht Dürer, and showed in his work (which included book illustrations, stained glass, and portraits as well as religious paintings) some influence of these two painters, but also a distinctly individual treatment of figures, and a predilection for the color green, whence his surname. An altarpiece of *The Coronation of the Virgin* (1516), painted for the cathedral at Freiburg im Breisgau, is one of his best-known works.

Balhorn (bäl′hôrn), **Johann.** [Also **Ballhorn.**] German printer; b. at Lübeck, Germany, c1530; d. 1603. His name has been perpetuated in the German verb *balhornisieren* or *verbalhornen,* meaning to change for the worse.

Balìa (bä-lē′ä). An extraordinary commission resorted to more frequently after the 14th century in North Italy. The Balìa was especially important in dealing with financial and military affairs for the government, and thus provided regimes with a stable mechanism for handling the two most pressing of public concerns.

Ballata (bä-lä′tä). [Also, **canzone a ballo.**] A poem intended to be sung during the dance; a dance-song. Dante, Boccaccio, and Sacchetti, among many others, wrote ballate.

Ballhorn (bäl′hôrn), **Johann.** See **Balhorn, Johann.**

Balmes (bäl′mēs), **Abramo di.** See **Abramo di Balmes.**

Baltazarini (bäl-tä-tsä-rē′nē) or **Baltagerini** (-jä-). [French, **Balthasard de Beaujoyeulx.**] Italian musician; fl. c1550. He was the leading violinist of his time. He became intendant of music and first *valet de chambre* to Catherine de' Medici, and apparently introduced the Italian ballet into Paris.

Balue (bȧ-lü), **Jean de la.** French cardinal and politician; b. at Poitiers, France, 1422; d. at Ancona, Italy, October, 1491. Imprisoned (1469–1480) by Louis XI for treason, he was liberated through the influence of Pope Sixtus IV and went to Rome. He was sent back to France as legate *a latere.* On the death of the Pope he returned to Rome where he was made bishop of Orléans and of Praeneste.

Balzo (bäl′tsō), **Iacopo del.** See **Del Balzo, Iacopo.**

Bambaja (bäm-bä′yä). [Real name, **Agostino Busti.**] Milanese sculptor; b. at Busto Arsizio, 1483 (or 1480?); d. at Milan, June 11, 1548. He seems to have received his early training at the Certosa di Pavia under Benedetto Briosco. In 1512 he was working with his brother Polidoro in the pay of the overseers of the Cathedral of Milan and worked there at intervals later in his life. From 1513 is a signed work, the tomb of the poet Lancino Curzio (d. February 2, 1512), now in the Museo Civico at Milan. Three lithe Graces that ornament it recall the elegance of Gian Cristoforo Romano, who also worked at Pavia. About 1515 he began work on the tomb of Gaston de Foix (d. April 11, 1512). The tomb, finished years later, was broken up in 1629 and its parts were scattered. Bambaja's moving effigy of the young hero with his laurel-wreathed head also reflects the influence of Romano. The effigy is in the Museo Civico. The reliefs and statuettes he made for the Franchino Gaffurio monument were incorporated in the Bua monument at Treviso. After 1537 Bambaja carved the Caracciolo and Vimercati tombs in the cathedral at Milan and the Orsini tomb in S. Fedele. His statuettes, friezes, and richly carved pilasters are preserved in several collections. Two figures of Virtues, from the monument of Gaston de Foix, are in the Victoria and Albert Museum, London. Bambaja's intricately planned and skillfully executed works are often overcharged, as was the Lombard fashion, with ornamentation. His later works show a better sense of composition in the distribution of the figures than his early works.

Banco (bäng'kō), **Maso di.** See **Maso di Banco.**

Banco, Nanni d'Antonio di. See **Nanni d'Antonio di Banco.**

Bandello (bän-del'lō), **Matteo.** Writer of novelle (short stories); b. at Castelnuovo, in Tortona, 1485; d. at Bassens, France, 1561. About 1497 he went to study at the Convent of Santa Maria delle Grazie, at Milan, where his uncle Vincenzo was the prior. He next entered the university at Pavia, vastly enjoyed the gay university life, and formed many warm friendships. Following his university days, he entered upon the religious life, at Genoa, but his religious ardor soon burned out: life in the world called him. In 1501 his uncle was made general of the Dominican order. He took his young nephew with him as his companion on inspection visits throughout Italy. The youth fell in love in Florence, observed the secular life of the ecclesiastical court at Rome, was delighted with Naples, and other courts, and everywhere he went made friends, with men of letters and scholars, princes, and men of lesser positions. His travels, his natural zest for life, and his curiosity gave him a wide knowledge of the world. He had no illusions about the way the world wagged, yet was not disillusioned or cynical. He accepted society as it existed and enjoyed it as much as possible. Following the death of his uncle (1506), he returned to the convent at Milan briefly, continued to take part in court and literary life, as well as to taste the delights of the town. Since the contemplative life had no appeal for him, the convent did not long hold him. He entered the service of Alessandro Bentivoglio, visited the court of Louis XII, in France, and then went to Mantua. Here he was received with distinguished attention by Isabella d'Este, famed patroness of men of letters and of poets. Wherever he visited in his wanderings about Lombardy, he was warmly welcomed for his gay spirit and his literary talents.

In the first quarter of the 16th century Italy had become the helpless pawn in the struggle between the French and the Spanish. Bandello, who favored the French, made no secret of his hatred for Spanish avarice and haughtiness. When Francis I was defeated at the battle of Pavia (1525), the Spanish entered Milan and sacked the city. Bandello's house was destroyed, and with it the manuscripts of the novelle he had been writing since 1510. In response to this blow, he began rewriting his stories and continued his wandering from court to court. Among others, he served Francesco Gonzaga at Mantua, Giovanni delle Bande Nere, Ranuccio Farnese at Rome, Cesare Fregoso, with whom he went to France, and Francis I. He remained in France, in voluntary exile, from 1542 until his death. Henry II made him bishop of Agen; he turned over the duties of the see to a colleague and worked on the preparation of his stories for the press. His literary works include a verse translation of Euripides' *Hecuba* (dedicated to Marguerite of Navarre), and canzoni, sonnets, ballate, madrigals, and so on. His lyrics have a somewhat hollow Petrarchan ring. It is for his novelle that he is remembered. About 214 of these are known. In forming his collection, Bandello abandoned the overimitated device that Boccaccio employed in the *Decameron*, of setting the stories in a general framework. Instead he prefaced each tale with a dedication. The persons to whom the stories are dedicated come from all classes, but chiefly from the world of princes, of church and state. In the dedication Bandello set the stage for the tale that was to follow, often with delightful descriptions of the locale of the action. The stories present pictures of all sorts and conditions of men, their life and manners, in Italy and in lands beyond the Alps. The tales are drawn from Bandello's own adventurous life, from history and from legend, and from earlier writers. Some of them are licentious, others dramatic, rustic, broadly humorous, or of rollicking adventure. Many deal, in a tone of amused observation, with the corruption that was rampant in the clergy. Others paint vivid pictures of the luxurious court life at Milan, or concern the courtesans of Venice. Not all tell of the world of princes; some are marked with a poetic pathos, but all are joyously recorded. One of his stories is the foundation of Shakespeare's *Romeo and Juliet*. Bandello gave his story a different ending. In his, the hero rapturously embraces the heroine as she wakes from her drugged sleep, then chills as he remembers that he has taken poison and has but minutes to live. The stories were immensely popular. His work, which he himself considered light, unintellectual, and popular, was called a magic mirror that reflected the century. His writings were perhaps even more popular across the Alps than in Italy. The Italians criticized him on the ground that his language was not pure, was larded with dialect and regionalisms. It lacked the level of elegance that was demanded at the time. His work was not criticized on the grounds of immorality and licentiousness, conditions of life that were taken for granted by his world, or if it was, his retort was that what he wrote was true. In his chosen circle, it caused hardly a ripple that such tales should be published by a bishop.

Bandinelli (bän-dē-nel′lē), **Baccio.** Florentine sculptor; b. at Florence, October 7, 1488; d. there, February, 1560. A great deal is known about this sculptor from the writings of Giorgio Vasari, a contemporary and a hostile witness; from the writings of Cellini, also a contemporary, and one who had no use at all for Bandinelli; and from his own *Memoriale*, in which he traced the history of his family and described his own life. His father, Michelangelo Bandinelli di Vivano, was a noted goldsmith who had close contacts with the Medici family. It was through him that Baccio established the relationship with the Medici that meant so much in his career. Baccio's original intention had been to become a painter, and he studied with various masters, including Giovanfrancesco Rustici, who, it is believed, directed him toward sculpture. Andrea del Sarto, whose advice and assistance he sought, discouraged him from pursuing a career in painting. At the same time, by 1512 he had earned a considerable reputation as a draftsman. As noted earlier, the Medici were his protectors and patrons throughout his life. Giuliano de' Medici secured for him (1515) the commission to carve a statue of *St. Peter* for the cathedral, his first important commission. In the same year he made a *Giant* for the Piazza della Signoria as part of the decorations for the visit of Leo X to Florence. Cardinal Giulio de' Medici secured a contract for him to carve an *Orpheus*. The statue, on a base carved by Benedetto da Rovezzano, still stands in the Medici Palace. The statue is obviously modeled on the *Apollo Belvedere* at Rome, and shows the degree to which Bandinelli had studied and absorbed classical examples and techniques. Evidence of the classical exists in much of his work, but he never truly assimilated it and made it a part of an individual style. He had many commissions, many of which were never carried to conclusion. He went to Rome before the death of Leo X, and made a marble copy of the recently discovered *Laocoön* group. The work, begun in 1520 but not completed until 1525, was intended as a gift for Francis I of France, but was never sent there and is now in the Uffizi. Returned to Florence, Clement VII gave him a block of Carrara marble. The block had been set aside for a statue that would form a counterpart to Michelangelo's *David*. The Florentine Signory opposed giving the block to Bandinelli. They wanted Michelangelo to have it but were overruled. In opposing Bandinelli as the sculptor for the block, the Florentines showed their good taste and artistic sophistication. When the Medici were driven from Florence (1527) the block was given to Michelangelo, but the Florentine republic reestablished in 1527 was short-lived. The Medici were restored in 1530, and once again the block was given to Bandinelli. (He had spent the intervening three years at Lucca and then at Genoa where he began a statue of Andrea Doria as Neptune.) From the block he carved the *Hercules and Cacus* that stands on the terrace of the Palazzo della Signoria, a static group of no particular artistic value, although it is a technical solution to the shape and size of the original block. The Florentines were shrill in their criticism. Their scorn for Bandinelli's sculpture was perhaps also an expression of scorn for his Medici patrons, whom they could not openly criticize. Bandinelli's most important commission (1536) was the ornamentation of the tombs of Leo X and Clement VII in S. Maria sopra Minerva at Rome. The architect was Antonio da Sangallo the Younger. Bandinelli, however, did not complete the statues of the popes themselves that surmounted the tombs. He finished only the statues on the sides and some reliefs. Under Duke Cosimo de' Medici he pictured himself as arbiter of the artistic life of the court. In his later life he lost some of his influence with the duke. Younger and better artists appeared at Florence. Vasari began to work for Cosimo about 1555 and had great influence with him. Cellini, who detested Bandinelli no less as an artist than as a man, returned from France in 1540 and entered into immediate competition for the duke's favor. Bandinelli relied more and more on the support of the duchess, who was his friend and who did not like Cellini. Bartolomeo Ammannati was also a threat to Bandinelli, but the worst threat of all was the good taste of the Florentines. His art as a sculptor was a compound of many elements, most of which he borrowed, without ever modifying them into an individual style, from 15th-century Florentines. To these elements he attached a talent for copying from the antique, especially from the somewhat overwrought Hellenistic period. His small figures were more successful, as the bust of Cosimo in the Bargello, and the figures in half relief with which he decorated the enclosure rail for the high altar and the balustrade for the choir in the cathedral. These efforts are more individual and harmonious. His other works include a statue of Giovanni delle Bande Nere (1540) and one of his best works, *Dead Christ Supported by Nicodemus,* in his own memorial chapel in the Annunziata. A *Self-Portrait,* about his only surviving painting, is in the Isabella Stewart Gardner Museum, Boston. (Some critics attribute this to Jacopino del Conte.) He was an industrious worker and a good draftsman, and had many pupils, but he deluded only himself in thinking of himself as a rival of Michelangelo.

Barbarelli (bär-bä-rel′lē), **Giorgio da Castelfranco.** See **Giorgione.**

Barbari (bär′bä-rē), **Iacopo de'.** See **De' Barbari, Iacopo.**

Barbarigo (bär-bä-rē′gō), **Agostino.** Venetian doge; b. 1419; d. September 20, 1501. After a long and successful career in public affairs, he succeeded his brother Marco as doge of Venice (August 28, 1486), in the only known case where a member of the same family succeeded. The fact that he became doge was a victory for the new Venetian nobility over the old nobility. Marco, a man of gentle temper, had been chosen to conciliate the classes. Agostino, difficult, able, but avaricious and suspicious, was psychologically unfit for the task of conciliation. He made many enemies and after his death was one of very few doges in Venetian history whose acts as doge were reviewed with critical intent. Only minor irregularities were uncovered.

Barbaro (bär-bä′rō), **Daniele.** Ecclesiastic and humanist; b. at Venice, February 8, 1513; d. there, April 12, 1570. A learned man, he was commissioned by the Republic of Venice to continue Bembo's history of Venice. As an ecclesiastic he took an active part in the proceedings of the Council of Trent. Barbaro translated the work of the Roman architect and engineer Vitruvius (1st century B.C.), and left many works in Italian and Latin on general and scientific subjects. A portrait of him by Paolo Veronese is in the Pitti Palace at Florence. His villa was decorated by Paolo Veronese.

Barbaro, Ermolao. [Original name, **Almorò di Zaccaria Barbaro.**] Venetian nobleman and humanist; b. at Venice, 1453; d. at Rome, 1493. He studied at Verona, at Rome, where he mastered Latin and Greek, and at Padua, where he held the chair of philosophy. He was noted as an interpreter of the Aristotelian system, basing his views on the Greek texts rather than on the Arab commentators, and (1484) established a private school in Venice that became noted for its advocacy of that system. Venice honored him and entrusted him with many diplomatic missions. However, his gifts as a teacher were greater than those as a diplomat. He offended the republic and removed to Rome. He edited and translated a number of classical works, among them Aristotle's *Rhetoric,* and began to translate Themistius, a 4th century rhetorician and philosopher who taught at Constantinople and wrote *Paraphrases* of Aristotle. His letters are valuable for the topics he treated, and of interest for his ironic, personal style. Though he wrote well in Latin, he did not consider it beneath him to use the vernacular.

Barbaro, Francesco. [Full name, **Francesco di Candiano Barbaro.**] Venetian nobleman, humanist and administrator; b. at Venice, 1390; d. there, 1454. He studied under three of the most celebrated teachers of his time—Giovanni Malpaghini, Gasparino Barzizza, and Guarino da Verona—and became so proficient in Greek he translated some of Plutarch's *Lives*. In Florence he mingled with the leaders of the humanistic circle (1415) and then, having completed his studies, entered on an official career for the Republic of Venice. In addition to service on many embassies, he governed Treviso, Vicenza, Bergamo, Verona, and Brescia for Venice. He left a rich collection of letters which have been valuable as a source of literary, historical, and political information on the men and events of his time.

Barbaro, Giosaphat. Venetian merchant and traveler; b. at Venice, 1413; d. 1494. In pursuit of his commercial interests, he began his travels in the east in 1436, and spent the next sixteen years journeying in southern and central Russia, Caucasia, and nearby lands. At the end of 1451 he returned to Venice, held various public offices, as in Dalmatia and Albania, and distinguished himself in assisting Skanderberg to defend Scutari. In 1473 he was named ambassador to the Shah of Persia and sent there to encourage Persian resistance to the Turks. His journey, begun in February of that year, was filled with incident and peril. On Cyprus he found the island seething with rebellion, and warned Venice. Two of his companions were killed by Kurds but he, though wounded, continued his journey and arrived in Tabriz in August, 1474. The Shah welcomed him, showered him with honors, and took him along on many expeditions in Persia. He became thoroughly acquainted with all the regions of Persia and acquired a knowledge of Oriental languages. Recalled to Venice, he reached his native land in March, 1477. His account of his travels, both those he took in the early period (1436–1451) and those to Persia (1473–1477), include historical and ethnographical information and detailed descriptions of the many cities he visited. One of the most observant and objective of Italian travelers of his age, his work was invaluable for knowledge of the regions it discussed. It was first printed (1543) by Aldus Manutius, and won great popularity and aroused much interest when Ramusio included it in his *Delle Navigationi e Viaggi* (1559).

Barbarossa (bär-ba̤-ros′a̤), **Khair ed-Din.** [Also, **Barbarossa II;** original name, **Khizr.**] Mohammedan corsair; b. c1483; d. at Constantinople, 1546. He was the brother of Koruk Barbarossa, whom he succeeded (1518) as ruler of Algiers. Having surrendered the sovereignty of Algiers to the Turkish sultan Selim I in order to gain support against the Spaniards, he was appointed governor general, and received (1519) a reinforcement of 2,000 Janizaries. In July, 1534, he raided Fondi, above Naples, with the intention of kidnapping Giulia Gonzaga, noted for her beauty and chastity, and carrying her off as a gift for Suleiman the Magnificent, son and successor of Selim I. Cardinal Ippolito de' Medici, one of her admirers, rode to her rescue, and Barbarossa's attempt to make a magnificent gift to his magnificent sultan failed. In the same year, he made himself master of Tunis, but in 1535 forces of the emperor Charles V besieged and captured the city. Barbarossa had, however, in the meantime laid the foundations for Turkish rule in North Africa. He was appointed (1537) high admiral of the Ottoman fleets and twice defeated Andrea Doria. He preyed on the coasts of Greece, Spain, and Italy, and in conjunction with Francis I captured Nice in 1543.

Barbarossa, Koruk. [Also, **Barbarossa I;** his first name is also written **Arooj, Aruch, Horuc, Horuk,** and **Uruj.**] Mohammedan corsair; b. c1474; d. 1518. He was at one time in the service of the Mamelukes, at Cairo, Egypt, but turned to operations in the Mediterranean on his own behalf and (with his brother, Khair ed-Din Barbarossa) raided many coastal towns in Spain and North Africa. He was slain in a battle against the Spaniards. After 1515, the brothers were in effective control of Algiers, and their exploits against the various Christian rulers of the Mediterranean area made them heroic figures in contemporary Islamic history. They were probably of Albanian descent (although their father is known to have lived on the Greek island Mytilene, and for this reason they are given as Greeks by some sources), and the derivation of their surname "Barbarossa" has been the subject of considerable conjecture.

Some authorities follow the traditional etymology (i.e., that they had red beards), and others have seen in it a development of one of Koruk Barbarossa's names (Baba Arooj).

Barberino (bär-bā-rē′nō), **Andrea da.** See **Andrea da Barberino.**

Barberino, Francesco da. Florentine didactic poet and jurist; b. at Barberino in Val d'Elsa, in Tuscany, 1264; d. 1348. He traveled widely in Italy and France, and had visited the papal court as well as the courts of Philip the Fair and the king of Navarre. From his travels and his powers of observation he got the material for his two principal works, *Documenti d'Amore* and *Del Reggimento e Costume di Donna.* The latter takes up every phase of the life of women, from girlhood through marriage to old age, and prescribes the conduct suitable for women in all walks of life, including that applicable to nuns, weavers, bakers, nurses, servants, even beggars. The work provides beauty hints, discusses problems that arise in love and marriage, tells riddles, and recites anecdotes. Barberino was also an artist and made the drawings for his *Documenti d'Amore* himself. Designs he made for some miniatures are at the Vatican.

Barbiano (bär-byä′nō), **Alberico.** See **Alberico da Barbiano.**

Barbiere (bär-bye′rā), **Domenico del.** See **Del Barbiere, Domenico.**

Barbieri (bär-byā′rē), **Giovanni Maria.** Poet and scholar; b. at Modena, 1519; d. there, March 9, 1574. He gave up his early profession as a notary to tutor Count Claudio Rangoni's son, and accompanied the latter to Paris in 1538. He remained in France a number of years, perfected his French, and collected and studied ancient French and Provençal poetry. In 1560 he returned to Modena and became chancellor of his native city, a post he held until his death. He knew French, Provençal, and Spanish, collected chronicles and Roman and medieval inscriptions at Modena, and studied the ancient Italian, French, and Provençal poets. In his literary researches he applied the historical method and is considered by some to have been the founder of the study of Romance languages. He made a collection of Provençal poets, now lost, and translated widely from the older poets. His chief work, *Dell' arte del rimare* (published under the title *Dell' origine della poesia rimata,* 1790), is the first attempt at a history of Neo-Latin poetry based on authentic sources.

Barbo (bär′bō). Distinguished Venetian family that played an important part in the political life of Venice in the 14th and 15th centuries. Pantaleone di Marco, who lived in the 14th century, was one of the most conspicuous Venetian figures of his age. He helped suppress the Falieri Conspiracy of 1355 and the rebellion in Candia in 1365; he was also effective in securing treaties with neighbors of Venice in 1370, 1372, and 1386. In the 15th century Pietro Barbo became Pope Paul II and Marco Barbo was created cardinal of S. Marco and patriarch of Aquileia. Paolo Barbo helped to bring about the Peace of Lodi (1454) with Francesco Sforza.

Barbo, Pietro. [Original name of Pope **Paul II.**]

Barclay (bär′kli), **Alexander.** British poet; b. probably in Scotland, c1475; d. at Croydon, England, 1552. He was the author of *The Shyp of Folys* (*The Ship of Fools*), which was partly a translation and partly an adaptation to English customs and manners of the *Narrenschiff* of the German satiric poet Sebastian Brant. Barclay was also the author of *Egloges* (*Eclogues*) patterned after the Vergilian eclogues of Battista Mantovano. These were among the earliest eclogues in English. He was a monk of Ely and Canterbury, priest at the College of Ottery St. Mary, vicar of Much Badew in Essex, and rector of All Hallows, Lombard Street, London.

Bardi (bär′dē). Family of Florentine magnates, known to have been in Florence since the late 12th century. They had their houses near the Arno, on a street still called by their name. From 1282, when a government by priorate was established, they held the most important offices; a Bartolo di Bardi was one of the first priors. Wealthy bankers, in its heyday the house of Bardi had branches in all the chief cities of Italy, across the Alps, and beyond the seas. Enormous loans to Edward III of England for his war against the French, and to Florence for its war with Lucca, brought disaster to the house (1345) when Edward III defaulted. The banking house that had collected pontifical tithes throughout the world, been a center of exchange in all the chief cities, and held royal crowns and the taxes of kingdoms in pledge, failed.

Though it recovered, it never regained a place of first importance.

Bardi, Donato di Niccolò di Betto. See **Donatello.**

Bardi, Giovanni di Antonio Minelli de. See **De Bardi, Giovanni di Antonio Minelli.**

Bargagli (bär-gä′lyē), **Scipione.** Sienese writer; b. 1540; d. 1612. Of a noble Sienese family, he spent his life in study and writing. He wrote poems, letters, and a dialogue on the subject of language. His *Trattato delle imprese* is a compilation of items of curious information. His chief work is the collection of merry or dramatic tales of the *Trattenimenti*.

Bargello (bär-jel′lō). In medieval Italian communes, as Siena, Modena, Mantua, Genoa, and Florence, the officer in charge of public security. In Florence the official was usually a foreigner, and was responsible either to the podesta or to the Signory, and lived with his family in the palace of the podesta. The building came to be called, after the official who lived in it, Bargello. The Bargello at Florence is now a national museum (Museo Nazionale) and houses some of the great works of Donatello, Desiderio da Settignano, Luca della Robbia, Verrocchio, Cellini, and others.

Bargeo (bär-jā′ō), **Il,** or **Bargeo, Pier Angeli.** See **Angeli, Pietro degli.**

Barili (bä-rē′lē) or **Barile** (bä-rē′lā), **Antonio di Neri.** Architect, engraver, and master of inlay; b. August 12, 1453; d. at Siena, 1517. As an architect he restored the bridges of Buonconvento and Macerata, and made plans and models for fortifications. His first work of carving and inlay was for the choir of the Chapel of St. John in the cathedral at Siena (1483–1502). This work was removed from its place in the 18th century because of serious deterioration; fragments of it are in the Church of S. Quirico d'Orcia and the Museum of Art and Industry at Vienna. Fragments in the latter place include a self-portrait in wood inlay, signed and dated. Other works executed for the cathedral at Siena include the benches for the Piccolomini Library (1496), stalls for the choir (1506), intaglio work in the sacristy (1509–1510) and on the chantry. For a great hall in Pandolfo Petrucci's palace he worked (1511) magnificent carved decorations on the pilasters. These are now to be seen in the Accademia, Siena. He was assisted in much of his work at Siena by his nephew Giovanni and by other assistants. A splendid intaglio coffer is in the Palazzo Comunale at Siena. On the lid is the wolf suckling the twins, the symbol of Siena, a daughter of Rome, as it was of Rome. Barili added to the tradition of Sienese masters who carved in wood a grace of his own that makes his works among the most exquisite of the Renaissance. His pupils and followers continued his manner well into the 16th century.

Barili, Giovanni. Carver in wood and metal; b. in the second half of the 15th century. He was the nephew of Antonio di Neri Barili (1453–1517), whom he assisted in the carving in the choir (1506) and the chantry (1510) of the cathedral at Siena. At Rome he was master of the wooden models for St. Peter's, then in process of being rebuilt. Raphael, having completed the painting in the *Stanze* of the Vatican, put him in charge of carving the decorations in the woodwork of the rooms. He later returned to Siena where he lived, it is thought, to 1531.

Barlaam (bär′lä-ạm). [Also, **Bernardo of Seminara.**] Theologian, humanist, logician, and mathematician; b. at Seminara, in Calabria, toward the end of the 13th century; d. probably in 1350. He went to Constantinople soon after 1328, and won favor with that faction of the Byzantine court (including the empress) which sought a reconciliation of the Orthodox and Roman churches. In 1333 he began to negotiate with legates from Rome on this subject, and was sent (1339) to Avignon to negotiate, in the emperor's name, with Pope Benedict XII. One of the principal aims of the negotiations was to obtain the help of the Roman Church in the struggles against the Turks. The mission was a failure, and Barlaam returned to Constantinople where he continued to try to win over that faction in the Orthodox Church which opposed union with Rome. In 1341 he returned to Italy, where (at Naples) he met Boccaccio, and proceeded thence to Avignon, where he met Petrarch. A new attempt to reconcile the Eastern and Western churches failed (1346). He is known to have surrendered his bishopric in 1348, and died shortly thereafter (probably in 1350).

Barletta (bär-let′tä), **Gabriele.** Dominican friar of Naples; d. 1470. He was a noted preacher, who endeavored to correct by a ridicule that sometimes degenerated into vulgarity. His sermons were so famous that his name became proverbial. Those subsequently printed (from 1507 on) under his name have been tampered with by a later hand.

Barna da Siena (bär′nä dä sye′nä). Sienese painter; active in the second half of the 14th century. His exact identity is under question; he may have been the same as a Sienese mentioned as Barna Bertini. To him is attributed a series of frescoes on the New Testament in the Collegiata (Cathedral) at San Gimignano, near Siena. These are characterized by vigor and dramatic concentration, and an absence of typically Sienese decorative elements. They were nearly finished in 1381, at which time, according to Vasari, Barna fell off his painting scaffold and was killed. The frescoes were completed after his death by his nephew and pupil. His *The Marriage of St. Catherine* is in the Museum of Fine Arts, Boston, and several medallions from a predella are in the Johnson Collection, Philadelphia. Other works are at Asciano, Palermo, Rome (Vatican), Siena, Frankfurt, Baltimore (Walters Art Gallery), and elsewhere.

Barnaba da Modena (bär′nä-bä dä mō′de-nä). Modenese painter; active in the second half of the 14th century. The grace and good draftsmanship of his early work disappear from his later work. Byzantine influence is strong in the types of faces and in the conventional portrayal of eyes and the long straight line of the nose. Gold-threaded fabrics are among other elements of his strongly Byzantine style. Several of his half-length *Madonnas* are extant, as that in the Museum of Fine Arts, Boston, one at Frankfurt (1367), at Berlin (1369) (destroyed in 1945), a signed and dated (1370) one at Turin, and one at Pisa. In his *Madonna and Child* paintings he had a predilection for showing the Child scratching His left foot, as in the signed painting at Frankfurt, and in paintings at Milan (Crespi Morbio Collection), Rome (Schiff Collection), San Remo, and Turin. An artist of repute, Barnaba was invited to Genoa (1364) to help in the decoration of the Doge's Palace, and to Pisa (1380) to finish the panels of the S. Ranieri story in the Camposanto, a commission that he did not carry out. Surviving works include a *Crucifixion* and *Virgin with Child* (Palazzo dei Musei, Modena), *Ascension* (Capitoline, Rome), a polyptych painted for a Spanish chapel and showing Spanish figures (Murcia), *Pentecost* and a signed and dated (1374) *Coronation of the Virgin* and three other scenes, with a two-part predella (National Gallery, London), and paintings at Claremont, California, Indianapolis, Vaduz, Liechtenstein, and elsewhere.

Barnabas of Reggio (bär′nạ-bạs, red′jō). [Also, **Barnabas de Reatinis.**] Physician; b. at Reggio nell' Emilia; d. at Venice, c1365. He practiced first at Mantua (where he wrote, in 1331, a short treatise entitled *De conservanda sanitate*, based almost entirely on Arabic sources), but was called (c1334) to Venice by the medical college there, and spent the rest of his life in Venice. He was the author of *De naturis et qualitatibus alimentorum* (1338), a discussion, in alphabetical order, of the natures and qualities of various foods, and of *De conservanda sanitate oculorum* (1340), a collection of aphorisms and general statements on the care of the eyes, based on the works of Galen and others.

Barocci (bä-rôt′chē) or **Baroccio** (-rôt′chō), **Federico.** [Real name, **Federico Fiori.**] Painter; b. at Urbino, 1535; d. there, 1612. He studied at Urbino under a Venetian, then went to Pesaro to his uncle, Bartolomeo Genga, who was a painter and architect. After this his father sent him to Rome. There he was encouraged to pursue a career as a painter by Taddeo Zuccaro, Michelangelo, and Vasari. At first, drawn by the fame of his fellow townsman, he studied the works of Raphael. His own temperament, however, soon led him to follow a different direction. The dominant and all-important influence on his development was Correggio. It is thought he made a journey to Parma (1555–1557) and that there he became familiar with Correggio's painting and recognized his affinity with it. In any case, he made the glorious color, soft modeling, luminous atmosphere, and winning sweetness of Correggio his own. In 1560 he was again at Rome and, with other artists, frescoed the Casino that Pirro Ligorio had built for Pope Pius IV. Shortly thereafter he fell seriously ill. It was hinted that he had been poisoned by jealous colleagues (a not unusual accusation for the time). When he had recovered sufficiently he returned to Urbino, but ever after the state of his health was precarious. Even so, he lived to be 77 years old and worked industriously all his life. In addition to the work he had done at Rome, he worked a great deal at Perugia and especially at Urbino, as well as other cities in the vicinity. He left over a hundred paintings, hundreds of drawings, and other works. Among his paintings are a dramatic *Deposition from the Cross,* in the cathedral at Perugia; *Rest on the Flight into Egypt* and others, in the Vatican; and his masterpiece, *Madonna del Popolo,* painted for Arezzo and now in the Uffizi. Also in the Uffizi is a fresh and intense sketch, *The Stigmatization of St. Francis,* which was probably the forerunner of the panel in the National Gallery of the Marches at Urbino on the same subject, and a *Noli me tangere* (1590) that was a sketch for the panel now at Munich. Many of his works are to be found in his native Urbino, as a *Last Supper* in the cathedral and others in the Ducal Palace (National Gallery of the Marches). Other works include *Entombment of Christ* (1582) at Senigaglia; *Martyrdom of S. Vitale* (1593), Brera, Milan; *Visitation* and *Presentation in the Temple* (1594) Chiesa Nuova, Rome; *Crucifixion* (1595), Genoa; paintings at Ravenna, Bologna, Paris, Brussels, Madrid, and Dresden. Of a deeply religious spirit, except for one, *The Burning of Troy* (1598), painted for the Emperor Rudolf II and repeated for Cardinal della Rovere (Borghese Gallery, Rome), Barocci did not treat mythological or secular subjects. He left a few portraits. Among these is the magnificent *Francesco Maria II della Rovere,* Duke of Urbino, in the Uffizi. A *Self-Portrait* is in the Palazzo Venezia, Rome. Faithful to his own temperament and the source of his artistic style—Correggio—Barocci was unaffected by the mannerism that pervaded the second half of the 16th century. His glowing color, irradiated by light from a mysterious source, and his barely perceptible gradations of light and shade to give form and depth, were derived from Correggio; these elements are infused with his intense, and often even sensual, spirituality to create a style that was unmistakably his own.

Baroncelli (bä-rōn-chel′lē), **Niccolò.** [Called **Niccolò del Cavallo,** "of the Horse."] Florentine sculptor; d. at Ferrara, in October, 1453. According to Vasari, he was a pupil of Brunelleschi at Florence, but as a very young man went to Padua. There (1436) he began to carve ten statues, now lost, for a sepulchral monument. Almost all the work he did at Padua, where he was working at various times between 1436 and 1442, has been lost or scattered. In the museum there is a terracotta relief representing a miracle of a saint; also there, he carved the side door for the Church of the Eremitani and some busts of saints in the Basilica of St. Anthony. He left Padua for Ferrara, where he worked for Leonello d'Este. Among his works at Ferrara was an equestrian monument of Niccolò III d'Este (1451), of which Baroncelli made only the horse (whence his sobriquet), while Antonio Cristoforo made the figure. (The monument was destroyed in 1796.) Documents mention other sculptures he executed at Ferrara. In 1450 he was commissioned to execute five bronze statues for the cathedral and actually finished three, a *Crucifixion with Mary and St. John.* This work shows the strong influence of Donatello without, however, quite achieving the animated realism of that master. A bust of Ludovico III Gonzaga, at Berlin, is attributed to him on stylistic grounds. At Ferrara, Baroncelli set up a workshop which, after his death, was carried on by his son Giovanni, a sculptor and woodcarver, in partnership with Domenico di Paris. All the work of Giovanni has perished except that which he did in collaboration with his father, with whom he worked on the *Crucifixion.*

Baronio (bä-rō′nyō), **Cesare.** [Also, **Caesar Baronius.**] Cardinal and ecclesiastical historian; b. at Sora, October 30, 1538; d. at Rome, June 30, 1607. He took his doctorate in jurisprudence at Rome (1561), and a few years later was ordained as a priest (1564). He became a devoted follower of St. Philip Neri and was admitted to the Congregation of the Oratory, studied church history, preached, and carried out the humble tasks required by the Oratory in the communities where it operated. In the next years he held many positions in the Oratory and in 1593 succeeded St. Philip Neri as its superior. Under Pope Clement VIII, whose confessor he was, his influence was great, and he persuaded the pope to admit Henry IV of France into the Church. In 1595 he was named apostolic notary and in the following year was raised to the cardinalate. He was also librarian of the Vatican. His influence was great and good, and but for the opposition of Spain (because he questioned the claim of Spain to Sicily) he might have become pope. Along with his ecclesiastical activities he had devoted himself to the study, teaching, and writing of ecclesiastical history, begun as lectures under the encouragement of St. Philip Neri as a means of combatting Lutheranism. His great work, *Annales ecclesiastici a Cristo nato ad annum 1198*, on the history of the Church from the birth of Christ to 1198, although criticized by some on the grounds that he knew neither Greek nor Hebrew, is a work of formidable erudition and honest scholarship.

Baronzio (bä-rôn′tsyō), **Giovanni.** Riminese painter; active in the middle of the 14th century. He appears to have been a pupil of Giuliano da Rimini, and became the center of a school about Rimini in his own right. His work is characterized by vivacity and clear soft colors. Of the few works that can be assigned to him with assurance, one is a signed and dated (1345) polyptych in the National Gallery of the Marches at Urbino. The central panel is of the *Virgin Enthroned*. Above the side panels are six steep pinnacles, three on each side of a curious elaborately shaped central pinnacle, on which is painted a *Crucifixion*. Other works attributed to him include a polyptych, *Madonna and Child Enthroned with Saints and Angels* (Church of S. Francesco at Mercatello, near Pesaro), *Coronation of the Virgin* (New Haven), and works in the Vatican.

Barozzi (bä-rôt′tsē), **Francesco.** Venetian humanist and mathematician; d. after 1587. His great interest and work was in mathematics. Among others, he translated a commentary on Euclid into Italian and wrote a number of works on mathematical subjects, including one on the geometric proposition that parallel lines, though stretched to infinity, never meet. He studied the classical and later writers on mathematics, and invented mathematical devices. Accused of sorcery, he was fined and imprisoned, and compelled to perform pious works as a penance.

Barozzi, Pietro. Ecclesiastic and humanist; b. at Venice, 1441; d. at Padua, January 10, 1507. He became bishop of Belluno (1470) and of Padua (1487) and remained in the latter place until his death. Equally esteemed for his piety and his learning, he expounded his ascetic views in several Latin works that were published after his death, as his *De modo bene moriendi*, on life as a preparation for death, his *Consolatorii libri III*, and others. His skill in Latin verse appears in his *Vita Christi*. He also left sermons and hymns.

Barrel vault. In architecture, a semicylindrical ceiling. It may be plain, painted, or coffered. The barrel vault of the study of Francesco de' Medici, in the Palazzo Vecchio at Florence, is ornamented with allegorical frescos and stuccos of the 16th century.

Barros (bär′rōsh), **João de.** Portuguese writer; b. at Viseu, Portugal, 1496; d. near Pombal, Portugal, 1570. He is generally considered the most outstanding historian in Portugal in the 16th century. His chief work, *Ásia*, was divided into *Décadas*, of which only three were published in his lifetime (the first in 1552, the second in 1553, and the third in 1563). He also wrote *Gramática da língua portuguesa* (1540), the second Portuguese grammar ever published, and *O Imperador Clarimundo*, a romance of chivalry.

Barsegapé (bär-sā-gä-pā′), **Pietro da.** See **Pietro da Barsegapé.**

Bartholomew of Bologna (bär-thol′ǫ-mū, bō-lōn′yä). Dominican ecclesiastic; b. at Bologna, toward the end of the 13th century; d. probably at what is now called Erzurum, in Turkey, August 15, 1333. He is notable as the first scholar from western Europe to acquire an intimate knowledge of Armenian. He translated a considerable amount of religious literature into Armenian, and was for many years bishop of Maragha, in what is now Iran.

Bartholomew of Bruges (brözh). [Latinized, **Bartholomaeus de Brugis.**] Flemish physician, philosopher, and commentator on the works of Aristotle; d. c1354–1356. From c1330 to 1342 he was physician to the count of Blois. Of the many writings ascribed to him, the most interesting is *Remedium epydimie*, which may have been composed at the time of the Black Death, and which asserts that dying people are more infectious than others.

Bartholomew of Messina (me-sē′nä). Scholar; fl. 1258–1266. He is notable for his translations from Greek into Latin of various Aristotelian and pseudo-Aristotelian works, and also of a treatise by Hierocles on the veterinary art.

Bartholomew of Parma (pär′mä). Astrologer and geomancer; b. at Parma; fl. at Bologna, 1286–1297. His best-known work, *Ars geomantiae*, was the most elaborate treatise on geomancy written in that age.

Bartolo (bär′tō-lō), **Andrea di.** See **Andrea di Bartolo.**

Bartolo di Fredi (dē frā′dē). Sienese painter; b. at Siena, c1330; d. there, 1410. In 1353 he opened a workshop at Siena with Andrea Vanni. Documents show that he was active in civic affairs and several times held municipal office. A certain hardness and fixedness of line and composition that marked his early work was replaced later with a more rhythmical design. His works include frescoes on Old Testament stories in the Collegiata (Cathedral) at San Gimignano, completed in 1367; *Adoration of the Magi* and *Coronation of the Virgin,* Pinacoteca, Siena; a fine *Madonna and Child with Saints* and *The Mystic Marriage of St. Catherine,* National Gallery of Umbria, Perugia; *The Presentation of the Virgin,* National Gallery, Washington; *St. Lucy,* the Metropolitan Museum; *The Adoration of the Shepherds,* Cloisters, New York; and, with an assistant (of which he had many), *Death and Assumption of the Virgin,* Museum of Fine Arts, Boston. The work that best shows his creativity and individuality, and that is also his masterpiece, is a polyptych, originally painted for Montalcino and now divided between Montalcino and Siena. The central panel, *Coronation of the Virgin,* and a side panel, *Deposition,* are in the Palazzo Comunale at Montalcino. Scenes from the life of the Virgin from the polyptych are in the Pinacoteca at Siena. His frescoes on the life of the Virgin in Sant' Agostino at San Gimignano are fragmentary. At Pienza is a signed and dated (1364) *Madonna of Mercy,* Diocesan Museum; as in most of his surviving work, the color has remained clear and bright.

Bartolomeo degli Erri (bär-tō-lō-mā′ō dā-lyē er′rē). Painter; b. before 1430; d. after 1479. He was of the school of Modena. His *A Miracle of Saint Dominic* and *Saint Thomas Aquinas Aided by Saints Peter and Paul* are in the Metropolitan Museum, New York.

Bartolomeo di Giovanni (dē jō-vän′nē). Florentine painter; active at the end of the 15th century and the beginning of the 16th. He has been identified as the Alunno di Domenico (pupil of Domenico), which was the name given by Bernard Berenson to the artist who assisted (1488) Ghirlandaio in painting *The Adoration of the Magi* in the Foundling Hospital at Florence. Bartolomeo di Giovanni painted the seven predella panels. Using these as a standard of comparison it is thought that he collaborated with Ghirlandaio on the frescoes of S. Maria Novella (1488–1490), and that he collaborated with Pinturicchio in the decoration of the Borgia apartments in the Vatican (1493). Among the works in Italian and other galleries and collections attributed to him are a *St. Jerome* and three other panels, Accademia, Florence;

St. Jerome as a Cardinal
Attributed to Bartolomeo di Giovanni, or to a 15th-century painter of the Umbro-Florentine School
Fogg Art Museum, Harvard University
Gift of Paul J. Sachs

two small panels on miracles of St. Benedict, Uffizi; the *Archangel Raphael*, Dresden; *Flagellation*, Carrara Academy, Bergamo; *The Birth of St. John the Baptist*, Art Institute of Chicago; and *Communion of St. Jerome* and *John the Baptist Preaching*, Johnson Collection, Philadelphia. In addition, there are a number of cassone panels, as those in the Colonna Gallery, Rome; Walters Art Gallery, Baltimore; Cambridge, England; Capetown; and Paris. Other paintings are at Arezzo, Liverpool, London (Victoria and Albert Museum), Lucca, Madrid, Narni, New Haven, San Francisco, and elsewhere. An eclectic of moderate talent, Bartolomeo di Giovanni reflects preeminently the influence of Domenico Ghirlandaio and Sebastiano Mainardi, with echoes from time to time of Filippino Lippi and Botticelli, and with a rather conspicuous absence of a personal style.

Bartolomeo de' Grossi (dā grôs'sē). Painter of Emilia; active about the middle of the 15th century; d. 1464. He was at Parma before 1436, and executed some frescoes in the cathedral there. In Milan in 1448, he painted coats of arms for the newly established republic and decorations to celebrate the freedom of the city following the death of Filippo Maria Visconti (1447). He also worked on the Milan Cathedral.

Bartolomeo Pellerano da Camogli (pel-lā-rä'nō dä kä-mō'lyē). Ligurian painter; d. before 1349. He is known to have been at Genoa in 1346, but his only extant authentic work is in the museum at Palermo. It is a *Madonna of Humility*, signed and dated 1346. It shows him to have been a provincial painter who adapted the sweetness and mysticism of the art of Simone Martini to his own talents.

Bartolomeo da San Concordio (dä sän kōn-kôr'dyō). Dominican writer; b. at Pisa?, 1262; d. there, July 11, 1347. He entered the Dominican order as a youth, studied at Bologna and Paris, and lectured at Florence (1297, 1304). Thereafter he was at Pisa, where he founded the library of the Convent of Santa Caterina. His *De documentis antiquorum* is a Latin treatise in which he organized and commented upon fragments from over a hundred ancient writers. He later translated the work into energetic and lucid Italian. He also translated, occasionally epitomizing, the historical works of Sallust. His major work, written in 1338, is a summation of canon law, known variously as *Summa casuum conscientiae* and *Summa Bartolinae Pisanella*.

Bartolomeo di Tommaso (dē tôm-mä'sō). Painter of Foligno; d. after 1455. Although much of his working life was spent at Foligno, he also worked at Ancona and Fano, and was at Rome (1451–1453) at the invitation of Pope Nicholas V. At Rome he decorated several rooms in the Vatican. His elongated, Gothic forms and awkward figures reveal him as a provincial painter of no great inspiration or talent. Three unrelated frescoes from the Church of S. Caterina and now in the Pinacoteca at Foligno are signed and dated (1449). Two panels—*The Betrayal* and *The Entombment*—are in the Metropolitan Museum, New York, and there are examples of his painting, mostly panels from dismembered altarpieces, in the Brera (Milan), the Vatican (predella panels and an altarpiece), Terni (frescoes, Church of S. Francesco), the Walters Art Gallery (Baltimore), and elsewhere.

Bartolomeo Veneto (ve-nā'tō). See **Veneto, Bartolomeo.**

Bartolommeo (bär-tō-lôm-mā'ō), Fra. [Original name, **Bartolomeo di Pagholo del Fattorino;** called **Baccio della Porta** because he lived close to the old city gate, no longer in existence, Porta a San Piero Gattalini.] Florentine painter; b. at Florence, March 28, 1472; d. at Pian di Mugnone, near Florence, October 31, 1517. From 1485 he was a pupil of Cosimo Rosselli. He was early a follower of Ghirlandaio, softening the latter's style with the techniques he had observed in Perugino and Leonardo. He became an excellent draftsman, and was noted for his treatment of drapery and for his luminous landscapes. As early as 1494 he had a workshop with his fellow pupil, Mariotto Albertinelli. In the period 1496–1497 the preaching of Savonarola so deeply touched him that when he heard of the "Burning of the Vanities" he destroyed all his own drawings of nudes (although he later continued to make such drawings). The earliest extant work, an *Annunciation* (1497) in the cathedral at Volterra, was done in collaboration with Albertinelli. The strong portrait of Savonarola in the museum of S. Marco is of about this period. Two youthful works, *Nativity and Circumcision,* with an *Annuncia-*

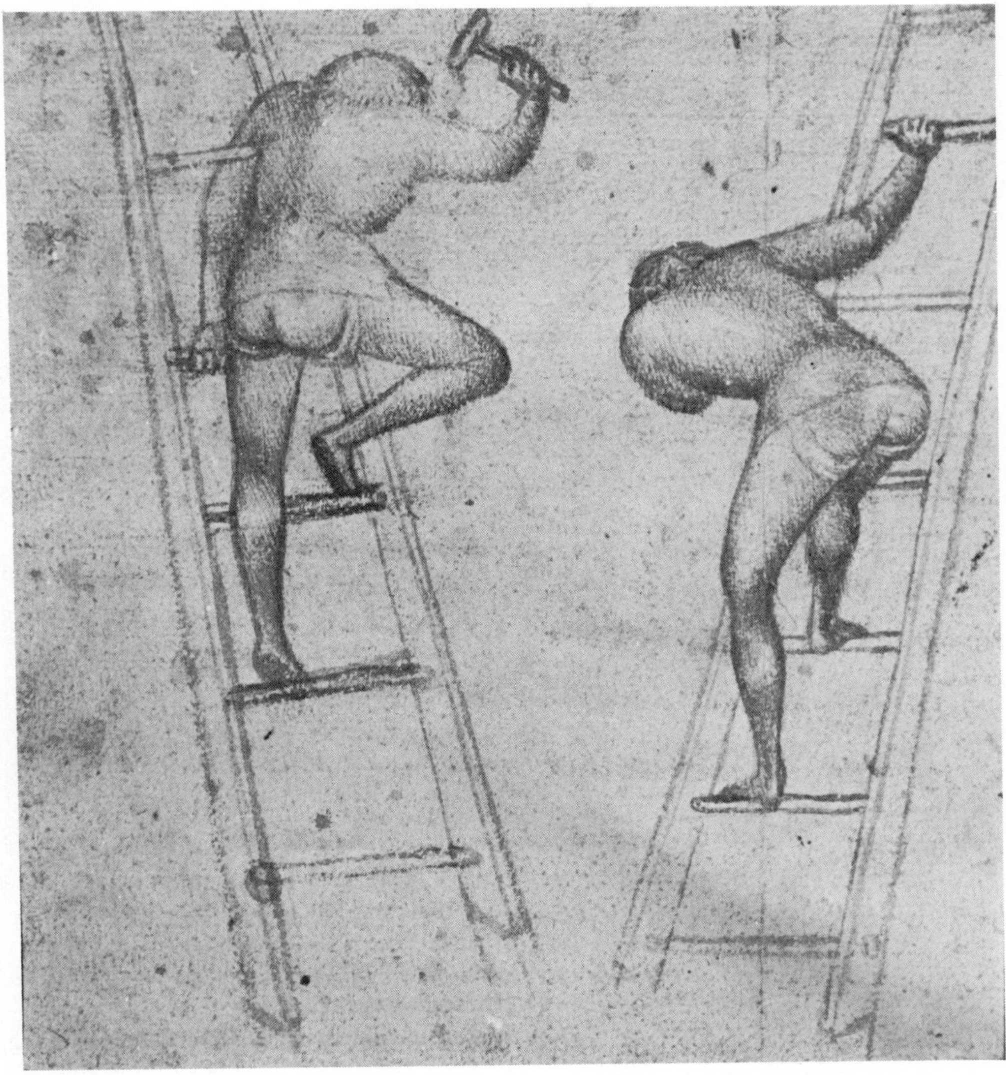

Bartolomeo de' Grossi
Two Men on Ladders
Biblioteca Ambrosiana, Milan

FRA BARTOLOMMEO
Assumption of the Virgin
Uffizi, Florence Alinari-Art Reference Bureau

tion on the back, are in the Uffizi. They are of the period 1498–1500 when he was painting in the Florentine tradition with some influence of the Umbrian school. He began to fresco a *Last Judgment* in the cemetery of S. Maria Nuova, in which he showed a new preoccupation with perspective and the use of light, but he decided to give up painting, and in July, 1500, he entered the Dominican order. His *Last Judgment* was completed by Albertinelli. Although he had abandoned painting, he continued to draw and produced lovely works in pencil and pen and ink. The increasing use of oils as a medium drew him

FRA BARTOLOMMEO
Farm on the Slope of a Hill
Courtesy of The Cleveland Museum of Art, Gift of Hanna Fund, Delia E. and L. E. Holden Funds, Dudley P. Allen Fund

thin; ᴛʜ, then; y, you; (variable) ḏ as d or j, ȿ as s or sh, ṯ as t or ch, ẕ as z or zh; *o*, F. cloche; ü, F. menu; ċh, Sc. loch; ṅ, F. bonbon; ʙ, Sp. Córdoba (sounded almost like v).

back to painting, for when he saw the results Albertinelli, Piero di Cosimo, and his young friend Raphael obtained with them he could no longer resist. In 1504 he accepted a commission for *The Apparition of the Virgin to St. Bernard* (originally painted for the Badia, it is now in the Accademia, Florence). In 1508 he went to Venice, where he may have been influenced by Giovanni Bellini and Giorgione, but on his return to Florence he once more was subject to the influence of Perugino, Leonardo, and his friend Raphael. He worked with Albertinelli again for a time, and founded a school at Florence (1509). In 1510 he began the large panel (never completed) for the Hall of the Five Hundred in the Palazzo della Signoria. Inspired by Raphael's unfinished *Baldaquin Madonna*, it was intended for the space between the great frescoes that Leonardo and Michelangelo were commissioned to paint for the hall (but never did). So that his work would not be overpowered by that of these giants, Fra Bartolommeo broadened his style and conception. His solemn, monumental figures, in majestic draperies, were grouped rhythmically about the Madonna's throne. This broadened, rather monumental and solemn style became characteristic of his work, as in the *Marriage of St. Catherine* (1511) in the Louvre, Paris. In 1514 he went to Rome. There he fell ill of a malarial fever. He left Rome soon after, and left behind him a *St. Paul* (Vatican) and a *St. Peter* (Vatican), the latter completed, according to Vasari, by Raphael. Deeply impressed by the grandiose manner of the Roman school, his work thereafter showed the effects of his Roman sojourn, as in the colossal *St. Mark* (Pitti Palace) and the *Madonna della Misericordia* (1515) at Lucca. His personal style, less monumental and grandiose and more serene and spiritual, reasserted itself soon after he returned to Florence, however, as in the *Savior between the Evangelists* at the Pitti Palace and the moving *Pietà* (completed by Giuliano Bugiardini) in the same gallery. Never fully restored to health, he died (1517) in the Convent of the Magdalen at Pian di Mugnone. His last work, *Noli me tangere* (1517), was among the frescoes he painted in a chapel outside the convent. Other works are three on the *Holy Family*, at Rome, London, and Leningrad, and a number of exquisite drawings. Among the latter are delicately drawn landscapes and studies for prospective paintings. In his characteristic pen style, the drawings are serene reflections of his own artistic personality. Examples of them are in many museums, as the Cleveland Museum of Art, the Metropolitan Museum and the Morgan Library (New York), the Johnson Collection (Philadelphia), the Uffizi, and others, as well as in private collections.

Bartolommeo da Pisa (dä pē′zä). Physician and member of the Franciscan order; d. 1401. He was the author of *Epitoma medicinae*, a summary of medical knowledge.

Bartolommeo da Varignana (vä-rē-nyä′nā). Physician; b. at Bologna; d. there, 1318. His practice of medicine at Bologna brought him fame and wealth at a comparatively young age, and he was employed by the city of Bologna to teach medicine. Assisted by another physician and three surgeons, he is said to have performed the earliest postmortem examination on record.

Bartolus (bär′tō-lus). [Italian, **Bartolo da Sassoferrato.**] Jurist; b. at Sassoferrato, 1314; d. at Perugia, July, 1357. Generally considered to have been one of the greatest jurists of the Middle Ages, he studied law at Perugia and Bologna and was a professor of law at Perugia from 1343 until his death. Among his many works was a commentary on the Justinian Code (*Corpus juris civilis*) and many treatises on legal questions. His followers were known as "Bartolists," and his influence continued to be felt until the 17th century wherever Roman law was cultivated.

Barzizza (bär-tzē′tzä), **Gasparino.** Teacher and humanist; b. at Barzizza, a village of Bergamo, c1360; d. at Milan, 1431. Noted as a teacher of many who became outstanding humanists, he earned his doctorate in grammar and rhetoric at Pavia and taught those two disciplines (1403–1407). He went to Venice (1407) and then to Padua, where he held the chair of rhetoric. After attending some sessions of the Council of Constance as an apostolic secretary, he was invited (1421) to Milan, and taught there until his death. Barzizza wrote model letters with their model replies, orations, treatises on rhetoric, letters, commentaries, and a manual of Latin orthography, in which he weeded out errors that had crept in during the medieval period. He also corrected and edited the rhetorical works of Cicero.

Barzizza, Guiniforte. Humanist; b. at Pavia, 1406; d. at Milan, 1463. He was the son of Gasparino Barzizza (c1360–1431), studied with his father at Padua, took his doctorate at Pavia (1422), and then studied law and moral philosophy there. After the death of his father he gave private lessons for a time and then went to Novara where he lectured on Terence and Cicero. He was in the service of Alfonso I at Naples and later went to Milan to teach. On the death of Filippo Maria Visconti (1447) he went to Monferrato and then to the court of the Estensi at Ferrara, but was recalled to Milan (1457) by Francesco Sforza to undertake the education of Galeazzo Maria Sforza. He left some orations, letters, and a commentary in the vernacular (because Filippo Maria, for whom he wrote it, preferred the vernacular) on Dante's *Inferno*.

Basaiti (bä-zī'tē), **Marco.** Venetian painter; b. at Venice or in the Friuli; active 1496–1530. He was of Greek origin but had his training and formed his style at Venice, where he worked much of his life. Fundamentally a painter in the 15th-century style, he sought in his later years to broaden his composition. Evidence of the influence of Alvise Vivarini, with whom he worked on an altarpiece in the Frari Church at Venice (1503), occurs in his work. Examples of his signed and dated work in the Accademia at Venice include *The Calling of the Sons of Zebedee* (1510), *Christ Praying in the Garden* (1516), and *St. George and the Dragon* (1520). Other works at Venice are in the Correr Museum, the Frari, and other churches. In addition, there are paintings in the Carrara Academy, Bergamo, at Milan (Ambrosiana and Brera), Padua, Palermo, Rome (Doria-Pamphili Gallery), Aix-en-Provence, Budapest, Cambridge (England), Liverpool, London, Madrid, Munich, and Vienna; three paintings at Berlin were destroyed in 1945. In the United States there are works in the Walters Art Gallery, Baltimore; Museum of Fine Arts, Boston (*Pietà*); Minneapolis; the Johnson Collection, Philadelphia (*Venetian Gentleman, Virgin and Child with St. Liberale*); Providence; the National Gallery, Washington.

Baschi (bäs'kē), **Matteo.** [Also, **Bassi.**] Italian friar and visionary; b. at Bascio, near Urbino, 1495; d. at Venice, 1552. He founded the order of the Capuchins, moved by a need for reform which was felt almost all through the Franciscan order. The reform was approved by Clement VII.

Basel (bä'zẹl), **Council of.** Council held at Basel from July 23, 1431, to May 7, 1449, the last of the three great reforming councils of the 15th century. It was called by Pope Martin V and by his successor Eugenius IV. Its main objects were the union of the Greek and Latin churches, the reconciliation of the Bohemians, and the reformation of the Church. It adopted certain decrees for financial reform, principally with the aim of limiting the power of the pope to collect revenues. Some of these remained to plague the papacy for years afterward, especially in France. Eugenius definitely broke with the Council (1438), after previous compromises with it on many matters, when he called a council to meet in Ferrara. The outstanding members of the Council of Basel joined him there. The Council of Basel deposed (June 25, 1439) Eugenius, who had refused to acknowledge its authority, and replaced him as pope with Amadeus VII, duke of Savoy, who took the name of Felix V. Eugenius excommunicated the members of the Council and retained the allegiance of most of Europe. In 1439 he achieved a union, albeit of brief duration, with the Greek Church, and the power of the Council was greatly weakened. In 1449 Felix V resigned, the Council acknowledged Nicholas V, successor of Eugenius, as the true pope, and the struggle to assert the supremacy of councils over the papacy ended in victory for the papacy.

Basinio da Parma (bä-zē'nyō dä pär'mä). [Also, **Basinius Parmensis.**] Humanist; b. at Vezzano (Parma), 1424; d. at Rimini, 1457. He studied Latin under Vittorino da Feltre at Mantua, and Greek under Theodorus Gaza. On the death of Vittorino (1446) he went to Ferrara with Gaza and spent the next five years in the rich humanistic atmosphere created by Guarino da Verona and his patron Leonello d'Este. At Ferrara he wrote his mythological poem *Meleagris* and some love poems. Following the death of Leonello, he went to the court of Sigismondo Malatesta at Rimini, and was well treated by his new patron. There he entered into lively debate with other humanists on the merits of studying Greek, which he upheld. (A poem addressed to Sigismondo Malatesta, now in the library at Parma, describes the debt of the Latin poets to the Greeks). Most of his works were completed at Rimini. He wrote his *Liber Isottaeus* on the love of Sigismondo Malatesta for Isotta. Sigismondo is the hero of his *Hesperis*, in which he adds to the episodes adapted from Homer's *Iliad* and *Odyssey* some adapted from Vergil's *Aeneid* to create a vivid and swift narrative that is one of the most original Latin poems of the century. In all his writings Basinio shows his ardent interest in the classical Greek authors, modeling his own epics on the ancient writers, as his *Astronomicon* is modeled on Aratus of Soli (Greek poet of the 3rd century B.C.), and his *Argonautica* on Apollonius Rhodius. A letter to Nicholas V, who had invited him to translate Homer, reveals his keen humanistic spirit; his writings in the classical languages reveal sensitivity and a refined appreciation of them.

Bassano (bäs-sä′nō), **Francesco.** [Real name, **Francesco da Ponte**; called **Francesco Bassano il Vecchio, the Elder.**] Painter; b. at Bassano del Grappa, between 1470 and 1475; d. there, 1541. He was the founder of a family of painters who took their name from his birthplace. He was an able painter whose art derived from Montagna and the Veronese school, and was relatively unaffected by Venetian developments. Among his extant works are *Madonna Enthroned between Saints*, formerly in the cathedral and now in the museum at Bassano; the signed and dated (1519) *Madonna Enthroned between Saints Peter and Paul*, in the same museum; and works in local churches in the neighborhood of Bassano. His son Jacopo (1510/1518–1592) was a highly successful painter, as was his grandson Leandro (1557–1622).

Bassano, Jacopo. [Real name, **Jacopo da Ponte.**] Venetian painter; b. at Bassano del Grappa, between 1510 and 1518; d. there, 1592. He was the son of Francesco Bassano il Vecchio (1470/1475–1541), an able painter who was his son's first teacher. Jacopo probably studied also at Venice, which he revisited at intervals, but he spent most of his life in his native place. He is mentioned in public documents as having been honored for his art on various occasions, and three times (1541, 1551, and 1566) was exempted from taxes because of it. Bonifacio Veronese, Pordenone, and Titian (who continued to inspire him in his later work) were among the early influences on his development, but the dominant influence came from Tintoretto, especially in the luminosity that glimmers in his scenes. In his paintings, intended as they were for local churches and patrons, he presented Biblical stories in the familiar accents of Bassano: they are filled with the homely details and contemporary costumes of his native place, and are set against landscapes truly observed from the countryside about Bassano. His several paintings on the *Adoration of the Shepherds* (Bologna; Florence; Hampton Court and Victoria and Albert Museum, London: the Metropolitan Museum, New York; Raleigh, North Carolina; Borghese and National Galleries, Rome; Accademia, Venice; Vienna) are tender evocations of the types of people and the life and animals of the peasants about his birthplace. In his preoccupation with genre detail he was influenced by the Flemish and in turn influenced them. But it was from the Venetians that he derived his deep, jewel-like color. His vivid, rustic presentations of Bible stories or religious themes make him one of the earliest of the Italian genre painters. Because of his representation of landscape as it is, rather than as a suitably composed background, he has been called (Bernard Berenson) "the first modern landscape painter." He had four sons, two of whom, Francesco il Giovane (1549–1592) and Leandro (1557–1622), became successful painters. All his sons, however, assisted and worked in his flourishing workshop, and because of their collaboration it is occasionally difficult to distinguish Jacopo's work. The greatest concentration of his painting is in the museum and churches in and around Bassano. Another large number of works are at Vienna. There are several in the Accademia at Venice, including *Rest on the Flight into Egypt* and *St. Jerome*, the latter a vigorous and mature work. Other paintings are in the cathedrals at Asolo and Belluno, in the Carrara Academy (Bergamo), in the Brera and Ambrosiana (Milan), at Mantua, Modena, Padua, Verona, Vicenza, and in many museums in Europe outside Italy. A charming genre work, *Hunting Dogs*, is in the Uffizi, along with one of his rare portraits, *Portrait of an Artist*. A well-known work is the *Expulsion of the Money Changers* in the National Gallery, London. His *Portrait of a Man of Letters* and an *Annunciation to the Shepherds* are in the National Gallery, Washington; *Lazarus and the Rich Man* is in the Cleveland Museum of Art; and *Portrait of a Bearded Man*, Art Institute of Chicago, is attributed to him. Other paintings in the United States are at Boston (Museum of Fine Arts), Detroit, Minneapolis, Princeton, Providence, and Springfield, Massachusetts.

Bassi (bäs′sē), **Matteo.** See **Baschi, Matteo.**

Bastard of Orléans (ôr-lēnz′). See **Dunois, Jean.**

Bastiani (bäs-tyä′nē), **Lazzaro.** Venetian painter; b. at Venice(?), c1430; d. there, c1512. He passed almost all of his long painting career at Venice, where he was a follower of the Bellini and Vivarini, and where, according to some scholars, he was the teacher of Vittore Carpaccio. His artistic individuality is expressed in his use of perspective and parallelism in composition, in his stylization of figures and his landscape. His works are to be found in churches and collections at Venice where, among a number of others, his *Funeral of St. Jerome* and *Communion of St. Jerome* are in the Accademia. Other works are at Asolo (cathedral), at Barletta (Church of S. Andrea), in the Carrara Academy, Bergamo (*Coronation of the Virgin*), Brera and Poldi Pezzoli museums (Milan), at Padua, Verona, Dublin, London, Paris (Musée Jacquemart-André), Stuttgart; works in the United States are at Boston (Museum of Fine Arts); Buffalo; Newark, New Jersey; New York (Frick Collection); Philadelphia (Johnson Collection); Portland, Oregon; and Toledo.

Battiferri (bät-tē-fer′rē), **Laura.** Poet; b. at Urbino, 1523; d. 1589. She married the architect and sculptor Bartolomeo Ammannati, and lived at Florence. In her own day she was praised as a second Sappho—praise that to a later age hardly seems justified. Her collection of lyrics, *Il primo libro delle opere toscane* (Florence, 1560) contains poems of praise, poems of lament, and poems on spiritual subjects. Benedetto Varchi, the historian, was her mentor and friend, and her correspondence with him is an interesting record of their affectionate relationship. The painter Agnolo Bronzino wrote poems celebrating her virtue (she was also celebrated for her beauty).

Battista da Crema (bät-tēs′tä dä krā′mä), Fra. Dominican ascetic; b. at Crema, c1460; d. January 2, 1534. He entered the Dominican order in 1519, and was the spiritual counselor of Gaetano Thiene, who founded the order of the Theatines at Rome (1523). He was known especially for his asceticism and for his ascetic works, in which he called for a renewal of the spiritual and religious life. His works in the vernacular circulated widely in manuscript and were eagerly read. They included *Via dell' aperta verita*, *Specchio interiore*, and *Vittoria di se stesso*, and all pointed the way to spiritual and moral regeneration. Fra Battista opposed Luther, but on grounds that did not stem entirely from accepted doctrine. His own harsh asceticism and practice of mortification, as well as that of his followers, were ridiculed as fantasy by some of the writers of his day, and his writings were placed on the Index. The Church frowned on fanaticism.

Battista da Vicenza (dä vē-chen′tsä). Painter, of Vicenza; active late in the 14th and early in the 15th century. He was a primitive of the Venetian school. Two signed and dated works of his are known: a polyptych of the *Virgin and Child with Saints*, now in the Museo Civico at Vicenza, signed and dated 1404; and a polyptych with the *Virgin, Saints and Donors*, originally in the Church of S. Giorgio at Velo d'Astico, signed and dated 1408, and now lost. Other works attributed to him are a *Madonna* and panels with scenes from the life of St. Sylvester, in the Museo Civico at Vicenza.

Baudo (bou′dō), **Luca.** Painter; b. at Novara, 1460/1465; d. at Genoa, 1510. A signed and dated (1501) *Crib* (*Il Presepe*) by him is in the Poldi Pezzoli Museum at Milan.

Bayard (bā′ąrd; French, bȧ-yȧr), Chevalier **de.** [Original name, **Pierre Terrail.**] French national hero; b. near Grenoble, France, c1475; killed at the river Sesia, Italy, April 30, 1524. Called *le Chevalier sans peur et sans reproche*, he distinguished himself in the Italian campaigns of Charles VIII, Louis XII, and Francis I.

Bazzi (bäd′dzē), **Giovanni Antonio.** See **Sodoma.**

Beato Angelico (bā-ä′tō än-jel′i-kō). See **Angelico, Fra.**

Beatrice Portinari (bā-ä-trē′chā pōr-tē-nä′rē). Italian lady immortalized by Dante; b. 1266; d. June 9, 1290. Dante's *Vita Nuova* tells of his love for Beatrice, whom he first saw in Florence when he (and she, too) was nine years old. This work, consisting of thirty-one sonnets and canzoni celebrating his love for Beatrice and connected by prose explanations and interpretations, describes how he feigned a "courtly" love to hide his real love, and how wounded he was when Beatrice and some of her ladies mocked him. It also describes an illness he had and a vision of Beatrice that came to him then and restored his love and his purpose. Beatrice married Simone de' Bardi, a Florentine, sometime before 1287, and Dante married Gemma Donati in 1290, shortly after the death of Beatrice; but Beatrice remained his love, idealized and purified, and his inspiration. In the *Vita Nuova* Dante expressed a desire to write of Beatrice as had never been written of any woman, and did so later in the *Divina Commedia,* in which Beatrice, his guide through Paradise, represents divine revelation and redemption.

Beatrice di Tenda (dē ten′dä). See **Tenda, Beatrice di.**

Beaufort (bō′fọrt), **Henry.** English cardinal and statesman; b. at Beaufort Castle, Anjou, France, c1377; d. at Winchester, England, April 11, 1447. He was a natural son of John of Gaunt by Catherine Swynford (but legitimized by an act of Richard II), and the half brother of King Henry IV. He became bishop of Lincoln, and later (1404) of Winchester, and a cardinal in 1427. At the Council of Constance (1414–1418) he was one of those who used his influence to elect Martin V. At the Council he met Poggio Bracciolini, and invited him to England (1418). Poggio visited him and was amazed at the English way of life. Beaufort was chancellor under Henry IV (1403–1405), under Henry V (1413–1417), and Henry VI (1424–1426). He served as papal legate in Germany, Hungary, and Bohemia, and crowned Henry VI (1431) at Paris.

Beaufort (bō-fôr), **Pierre Roger de.** Original name of Pope **Gregory XI.**

Bebel (bā′bel), **Heinrich.** German humanist; b. at Ingstetten, Germany, 1472; d. at Tübingen, Germany, 1518. He was a professor at Tübingen after 1497. One of the greatest Latinists of his time, he collected and translated German proverbs into Latin (1508), wrote a Latin history of the ancient Germans (1508), and in his collection of anecdotes, *Facetiae* (1506), turned his sharp wit on human follies, chiefly of the clergy. His lengthy poem *Triumphus Veneris* (1509) attacks immorality. He was crowned poet by the emperor Maximilian I in 1501.

Beca da Dicomano (be′kä dä dē-kō-mä′nō), **La.** Poem by Luigi Pulci that celebrates the love of a peasant for his sweetheart. It was patterned after Lorenzo de' Medici's *La Nencia da Barberino* but is more self-conscious and less sympathetic than its model.

Beccadelli (be-kä-del′lē), **Antonio.** See **Panormita, Antonio.**

Beccafumi (bek-kä-fö′mē), **Domenico.** [Called **il Meccherino.**] Painter; b. near Montaperti, near Siena, between 1482 and 1486; d. at Siena, in May, 1551. He was the son of Jacomo di Pace, who worked on the land of Lorenzo Beccafumi. Lorenzo observed the lad's aptitude for drawing, took him into his own household, had him taught to paint, and gave him his name. About 1510 Domenico went to Rome to study the works of Michelangelo and Raphael. Two years later he returned to Siena and worked with Sodoma. In 1516 he bought a house at Siena. In 1536 and 1541 he was painting at Pisa and in the latter year painted frescoes (now lost) in the Doria Palace at Genoa. Otherwise he led a lonely (Vasari wrote that he was "excessively solitary"), pious life at Siena almost uninterruptedly until his death. Influenced by Perugino, Sodoma, Michelangelo, and Fra Bartolommeo whose monumentality he affected, he became a mannerist painter, noted for his luminous color, fanciful conceptions, and lightstruck clouds. His early works include *St. Catherine Receiving the Stigmata,* a work Vasari praised for its harmonious color and excellent modeling, and for the spirit and vivacity of the three scenes from her life that form the predella. It was painted for the Olivetan Convent of St. Benedict, and is now in the Pinacoteca, Siena. He frescoed the ceiling of the Sala del Concistoro in the Palazzo Pubblico at Siena with scenes from Greek and Roman history and with allegorical figures of *Concord* and *Justice,* and frescoed the ceiling of the Bindi-Sergardi Palace. Some consider his frescoes, in which his bizarre fantasy is expressed with freedom and spontaneity, as his best works. His imaginative and disturbed *St. Michael Casting down the Rebellious Angels* is in the Church of S. Maria del Carmine at Siena. Perhaps his widest known work is the series of thirty-five designs he made for the pavement of the Cathedral of Siena. The designs,

Domenico Beccafumi
Gaius Mucius Scaevola Holding His Hand in the Fire
Courtesy of The Pierpont Morgan Library, New York

which he prepared over a period of years (1517–1546), are on such Old Testament themes as the story of Elijah, of Moses, Sacrifice of Abraham, and others, and are executed in different colored marbles, as well as graffiti, to give the effect of shading. Among a great number of other works at Siena are *Descent of Christ into Limbo, The Birth of the Virgin,* and paintings in the churches of S. Martino and S. Spirito, the Oratory of S. Bernardino, and civic buildings and palaces. Works at Rome are to be found in the Doria Pamphili Gallery, the Borghese Chapel of S. Maria Maggiore, and the National Gallery. A mannerist, stylized *Holy Family* is in the Uffizi; *A Fate,* a detached fresco, is in the Johnson Collection, Philadelphia; and there are two paintings in the Museum of Fine Arts, Boston. Other paintings are at Ancona (Church of S. Domenico), Pesaro, Pisa (cathedral), Dublin, Leningrad, London (National Gallery and Victoria and Albert Museum), Munich, Paris, Allentown (Pennsylvania), Greenville (Alabama), Sarasota (Florida), Washington, and elsewhere. After 1548 he tried his hand at sculpture, and produced eight bronze angels that are in the Cathedral of Siena. Among his other artistic productions was a celebrated series of ten engravings on *The Discovery of Metals.*

Beccari (bek-kä′rē), **Agostino de'.** Poet; b. at Ferrara; d. 1590. He is the author of one of the first pastoral plays, *Il Sacrificio* (1555). It was presented twice at Ferrara in 1554, once for Ercole II and once for Renée of France. Based on classical models, but adapted to the demands of 16th-century theaters and tastes, it tells the story of three shepherds and their love for three nymphs. A second pastoral play, *Dafne,* is now lost.

Beccari, Antonio. See **Antonio da Ferrara.**

Beccaruzzi (bek-kä-röt′tsē), **Francesco.** Painter; b. at Conegliano, c1492; d. at Treviso, 1562. A facile painter of moderate talent, he adopted elements from a number of masters—Pordenone, Bonifacio Veronese, Titian, Bassano, and others—for which reason his work is often confused with that of others. A number of portraits are attributed to him. These are generally correct, pleasingly colored, and lacking psychological insight. A *Portrait of a Young Lady* is in the Carrara Academy at Bergamo. Other works attributed to him are at Venice, Conegliano, Treviso, Castelfranco, Florence, Vienna, and elsewhere; often these attributions are disputed.

Beccuti (bek-kö′tē), **Francesco.** [Called **il Coppetta.**] Poet; b. at Perugia, 1509; d. 1553. Although he held many public offices, as governor of cities and ambassador to Urbino, he is best remembered for his poetry, especially for his love poetry. This, though Petrarchan in form, is highly individual and personal in his rendering of the joys and pangs of love. His other poetry is on many topics; thus, in the manner of Berni, he wrote a *capitolo, Noncovelle,* that is sharply satirical and did not endear him to the court at Rome, where he wrote it, and a canzone on the death of his cat. He also wrote on politics and patriotism. His *O dell' arbor di Giove* is an urgent plea to the Italian princes to rescue Italy from the foreign invaders. He translated Vergil, Horace, and Ovid, and began a poetical version of the myth of Psyche. In the last years of his life his poetry was on religious themes.

Becichemi (bā-chē-kā′mē), **Marino.** Humanist and teacher; b. at Scutari, c1468; d. 1526. He fled from Scutari before the Turks (1477) and went to Ragusa, where he later taught. In 1502 he was at Brescia and in 1514 went to Mantua at the invitation of Isabella d'Este. From 1519 until his death he held the chair of eloquence at Padua. He was highly esteemed for his humanistic culture, left orations and commentaries on the classics, and was the author of a poem, now lost, in praise of Isabella d'Este.

Beckington (bek′ing-tọn), **Thomas.** [Also, **Bekyinton.**] English prelate and statesman; b. in Somerset, England, c1390; d. 1465. After serving in diplomatic posts, he was appointed bishop of Bath and Wells, adorning the latter place with many fine buildings.

Bedoli Mazzola (be-dō′ lē mät-tsō′lä), **Gerolamo.** [Original name, **Gerolamo Bedoli.**] Painter; b. at Moile (S. Lazzaro), Parma, c1500; d. there, 1569. He was a pupil of Parmigianino, to whom he became related when he married (1529) Elena Mazzola. He added her family name to his own after 1540. His first datable work is of 1533, an altarpiece, the *Conception,* now in the National Gallery of Parma. The work is stamped with the mannerist style of his master, and is notable for the excellence of its coloring and composition, for the beauty of the heads, and for its grace. His mannerist affectation and grace also appear clearly in two *Annunciations*, one at Naples, the other in the Ambrosiana, Milan. Other works are a *St. Tecla*, in the cathedral at Mantua; *St. Clara*, at Naples; the altarpiece for the Church of St. John the Evangelist at Parma; and the *Marriage of St. Catherine* in the National Gallery at Parma (another on this subject is in the Carrara Academy, Bergamo). The two last again reflect Parmigianino. Other works are at Naples, Monaco, Budapest, and the churches and gallery at Parma. In his later life his style approached that of Correggio. He executed some frescoes in the Church of the Madonna della Steccata and in the cathedral at Parma, but these, though adequately executed, suffer from comparison with the imaginative inventiveness shown in those by Parmigianino nearby. He left a number of portraits, as at Parma and Naples.

Begarelli (bā-gä-rel′lē), **Antonio.** Sculptor in terra-cotta; b. at Modena, c1499; d. there, 1565. Little is known of his life. His father was a potter, and the son must early have worked in clay, shaping the vessels in his father's shop. Thereafter he developed the art of terra-cotta sculpture. From scattered remarks in chronicles he appears to have been solitary, deeply religious, and of a sensitive spirit. He lived near the Benedictines at Modena and always maintained close contact with the order, for which he ultimately filled many commissions. In his youth he made a vow of chastity and faithfully observed it throughout his life. The qualities of his personality appear in his work. In his search for an ideal of life and the spirit, he infused his statues and groups with a profound religious feeling, in contrast to the sensual beauty that came to mark much of 16th-century artistic endeavor. He was affected by artistic developments of his time, but drew the noble serenity and harmony of his forms from classical models, infusing them with his own religiosity. (His statues and groups were painted, sometimes to give them the appearance of marble and sometimes in color. Some of the colored ones have been so heavily repainted as to destroy Begarelli's original delicacy. In others the color has faded or crumbled away, as he frequently covered the statues with a thin layer of stucco on which the color was laid.) In 1524 he completed a *Pietà*, with eight figures, for the Church of S. Antonio at Modena, which his contemporaries considered a significant work. His reputation grew rapidly, and in a short time he had commissions from a number of churches and organizations at Modena. Many of his works are to be found in his native city, in the Estense Gallery, the churches, and museums. Among these is a *Deposition* (1531), comprising thirteen figures, in the Church of S. Francesco. Spontaneous and sincere, in its unity of composition, breadth of form, and delicacy of modeling it is one of his finest works. Another lovely group is a *Madonna and Child with the Young St. John*, in the Municipal Museum, that is notable for freshness of inspiration, modeling, and a sense of motion, as if a slight breeze were blowing. Having molded a number of *Madonnas* and other works at Modena, his reputation spread. He was called to fill commissions at Ferrara (1536), Parma (c1540, 1558, 1561, 1563), Naples (1548), and Mantua (1559). The work he did at Ferrara and Naples has been dispersed or broken up; some groups and fragments remain at Parma and Mantua. His nephew Ludovico accompanied him to Naples and assisted him in the execution of thirteen statues, and continued to work with him later. A *Madonna*, *Pietà*, and *Baptism of Christ*, all three in the Estense Gallery at Modena, are typical of the fresh inspiration, grace, spontaneity, and sincerity, united in a harmonious whole, that characterized Begarelli's best work.

Begarelli, Ludovico. Sculptor in terra-cotta; b. at Modena, between 1515 and 1524; d. before July, 1577. He was the nephew of Antonio Begarelli (c1499–1565), worked with him, and accompanied him to Naples (c1548) to assist in the execution of thirteen statues for the prior of the Convent of S. Lorenzo at Aversa. He had a number of modest commissions in his own right, and completed statues for the altar of S. Pietro, Modena, begun by his uncle, after the latter's death. His share in the work is not identifiable.

Behaim (bā′hīm), **Martin.** [Also, **Behem, Boeheim, Böheim.**] Navigator and cosmographer; b. at Nuremberg, about the middle of the 15th century; d. at Lisbon, July 29, 1506. He was in the service of Portugal, and took part in expeditions along the African coast. He was one of the inventors of the astrolabe and, in 1492, constructed the Nuremberg globe, which is interesting as showing how cosmographers viewed the world just before the discovery of America.

Beham (bā′häm), **Barthel.** German engraver and painter; b. at Nuremberg, Germany, 1502; d. at Venice, 1540. He was one of the "Little Masters," and a brother of Hans Sebald Beham.

Beham, Hans Sebald. German painter and engraver; b. at Nuremberg, Germany, c1500; d. at Frankfort on the Main, Germany, 1550. He was a brother of Barthel Beham, and one of the "Little Masters." Among his notable works are a series of *Village Weddings*, religious miniatures for prayer books, and scenes from the life of David (painted on a table top).

Behem (bā′hem), **Martin.** See **Behaim, Martin.**

Bekyinton (bek′ing-tọn), **Thomas.** See **Beckington, Thomas.**

Belcari (bel-kä′rē), **Feo.** Poet and public official; b. at Florence, February 4, 1410; d. 1484. A man of profound religious conviction, he expressed it in the writing of *laude* (songs or hymns, of praise, faith, commemoration, etc.) that limpidly reveal his serene and childlike faith. His life of Giovanni Colombini, the founder of the order of Gesuati, is based on Colombini's letters and contemporary notices and contains as well a number of legendary incidents. Belcari also wrote a number of *rappresentazioni sacre* (religious dramas). Among the earliest of these, and one of the best in Italian, is his *Abramo ed Isac,* in which the story is treated as a simple human incident, from which all mysticism has vanished. Devout as he was, Belcari never renounced the world and often held public office in Florence.

Beldomandi (bel-dō-män′dē) or **Beldemandis** (bel-dā-män′dēs), **Prosdocimo de'.** Mathematician, astronomer, and music theorist; b. at Padua, between 1370 and 1380; d. there, 1428. He was a pupil of Biagio Pelacani, took his doctorate in medicine at Padua (1399), and lectured on astrology at Padua from 1422 to 1428. His *Algorismi tractatus* gives a method for the extraction of cube root. He also wrote on musical theory.

Belfagor (bel′fā-gôr), **Story of.** [Italian, **Novella di Belfagor arcidiavolo.**] Satirical tale by Niccolò Machiavelli, published in 1549. An archdevil is chosen by lot to go up to earth and find out if there is any truth in the statement, made by the men who come flocking down to hell after death, that all their misfortunes and sins were due to the fact that they were married. Belfagor's mission is to go into the world, marry, and stay with his wife ten years; then report back. While on earth he is to be subject to all the evils and misfortunes of men unless he is clever enough to steer clear of them. He goes to Florence, marries, and the ensuing experiences with a demanding and nagging wife cause him to return to hell with relief. The tale has frequently been translated, and was remodeled by Jean de La Fontaine.

Bellano (bel-lä′nō), **Bartolomeo.** Sculptor and architect; b. at Padua, c1434; d. there, 1496/1497. He was the son of a goldsmith. A child when Donatello first came to Padua (1443), he followed him to Florence when Donatello returned there ten years later. Throughout his career he remained a follower in the tradition of Donatello, without possessing that master's skill in the understanding and use of perspective, or his dramatic realism. In his delicately executed reliefs he made great use of *rilievo schiacciato* (flattened relief), introduced into Italian sculpture by Donatello. Bellano, however, makes more use of incised line than Donatello; his figures lose something in modeling and sense of depth and, in some of the reliefs, appear to be in one flattened plane parallel to the background. In 1464 Pope Paul II called him to Rome to carry out several architectural and sculptural commissions. In 1466–1467 he made a bronze statue of Pope Paul (signed and dated 1467) that was attached to the façade of the cathedral at Perugia (it was melted down and minted in 1798). He returned to Padua in 1469 and there executed what is considered to be his masterpiece, the marble reliquary chest for the Basilica of St. Anthony. The central panel, *The Miracle of the Mule,* is Bellano at his exquisite best. The reliquary is adorned with beautiful decorative details, singing putti, and angelic musicians. A panel, *Lamentation over the Dead Christ,* in the Victoria and Albert Museum, London, is of about this same period. Also of this period is his monument of Giacomo dei Zocchi in the Church of S. Giustina at Padua. In 1479, having made peace with the Venetians, the Sultan Mohammed II asked the Venetian Signory to send a painter and one skilled in bronze casting to his court. The Venetians chose to send Gentile Bellini as the painter and Bellano as the sculptor. His sojourn at Constantinople must have been brief for, according to Vasari, he was commissioned to make the figure of the condottiere for the Colleoni monument, for which Verrocchio had been chosen to make the horse in 1479. In the end, Bellano had nothing to do with the Colleoni statue at Venice, and returned to Padua. In 1484 he was commissioned to make the bronze reliefs to decorate the outside of the new choir in the Basilica of St. Anthony. He completed the work by the middle of 1490. The ten reliefs represent stories from the Old Testament and, in the variety of subjects (*Cain and Abel, Sacrifice of Isaac, Joseph Sold by his Brethren, Crossing of the Red Sea, Worship of the Golden Calf, Samson Destroying the Temple, David and Goliath,* and *Story of Jonah,* among others), provide generous scope for Bellano's virtuosity. In 1491 he began work on a bronze monument for Pietro Roccabonella in the Church of S. Francesco. He died before it was completed and it was finished by Andrea Riccio (1498). Parts of this powerful work survive. Among the works credited to Bellano either by documents or on stylistic grounds, the earliest is the signed and dated (1461) marble *Madonna and Child* in flattened relief in the Musée Jacquemart-André at Paris. At Florence he worked on the panels in high relief that Donatello, in his old age, had undertaken to carve on the pulpits in S. Lorenzo. A bust of Pope Paul II from his hand is in the Palazzo Venezia at Rome. Other works attributed to Bellano include the monument to Erasmo Gattamelata in the Basilica of St. Anthony at Padua; a *Madonna and Child* in the Church of the Eremitani in the same city and another at Amsterdam; the bronze *Rape of Europa,* in the Bargello, Florence; some bronzes in the Louvre, and the statuette of *David,* at Philadelphia; a carving in wood in half relief, *Madonna between Two Angels,* in the museum at Padua; and a bronze candelabrum in the cathedral at Pistoia. Of the medals that Vasari says he cast, none remain.

Bellarmino (bel-lär-mē′nō), **Roberto.** [Full name, **Roberto Francesco Romolo Bellarmino.**] Cardinal, archbishop of Capua, Jesuit theologian and controversialist; b. at Montepulciano, October 4, 1542; d. at Rome, September 17, 1621. He entered the Society of Jesus (1560), studied philosophy at Rome, taught at Florence, and (1567) studied theology at Padua. He completed his theological studies at the University of Louvain, where he also preached and became famous for his sermons and the number of converts he made. He was ordained March, 1570, and remained at Louvain teaching theology until 1576, when he returned to Italy. In 1589 he was sent to France by Pope Sixtus V to defend Catholicism against the Huguenots. In 1590 he returned to Rome, and in the following year, at the request of Pope Gregory XIV, he began a revision of the Sistine Vulgate. His revision, completed in 1592, came to be known as the Sisto-Clementine Vulgate. (It was because of some of the changes Bellarmino made that his enemies later tried to prevent his beatification.) He held many important posts in his order and was a consultor of the Holy Office (Inquisition) during the trial of Giordano Bruno. Bellarmino was made cardinal (March, 1599) and archbishop of Capua (April, 1602), and left Rome to take charge of his archdiocese. A few years later he returned to Rome to take part in the conclave that elected Pope Paul V. The new pope, of whom Bellarmino became the trusted adviser and assistant, kept him in Rome; and thenceforth he took part in all the great religious questions of his time, including the controversies with the French, and especially with the English, over the pope's power in political (as opposed to religious) spheres. He also had a part in the first process brought against Galileo (1615–1616), but he was an admirer of Galileo and had nothing to do with the condemnation of his work.

Bellarmino was an outstanding figure and an ornament to his order and his Church. His contributions, besides those as administrator and preacher, were his writings. Of these the most important is his *Controversie,* or *Disputationes de controversiis christianae fidei adversus huius temporis haereticos.* This is a systematic arrangement, in one three-volume work (published 1586, 1588, 1593), of all the controversies and questions concerning the faith that had arisen and been dealt with in the course of centuries. These questions and controversies had been treated in single works and were scattered through many works. He organized and summarized and added new opinions and dicta in the twelve years that he devoted to his great work (1576–1588). Because of the view of the pope's temporal power that he expressed in one volume of his work, Pope Sixtus V had the volume placed on the Index (1590) until it should be corrected, but when the pope died later in the same year the volume was removed from the Index. The influence of his great *Controversie* was enormous. Catholics and Protestants alike agreed that it was a powerful defense of Catholicism. Among the more than thirty other works he left, including many on theology, are his *Dottrina cristiana breve* (Rome, 1597), and a catechism, in the form of a simple dialogue, that he composed at the request of Pope Clement VIII. This catechism, *Dichiarazione più copiosa della dottrina cristiana* (1598), has been used in many countries, has gone through many editions, and has been translated into more than sixty languages. He also left collections of letters. Bellarmino was beatified by Pope Pius XI (1923).

Bellay (be-le), **Guillaume du.** See **Langey,** Seigneur **de.**

Bellay, Jean du. French cardinal and diplomat; b. 1492; d. at Rome, February 16, 1560. He was the brother of Seigneur de Langey (Guillaume du Bellay). He became bishop of Bayonne in 1526, bishop of Paris in 1533, and cardinal in 1535. He was a friend of letters, and is noted as the patron of François Rabelais.

Bellay, Joachim du. [Called the **French Ovid** and **Prince of the Sonnet.**] French poet; b. at the Château de Liré, near Angers, France, c1524; d. at Paris, January 1, 1560. He was a fellow student of Pierre Ronsard, and became one of the most noted members of the group about Ronsard known as the Pléiade. He urged French writers, in his prose work *La Deffence et illustration de la langue françoise* (1549), to take Greek and Latin writers as their models, and thus make of French a glorious literary medium. The principles outlined in this notable work were adopted by the Pléiade. He wrote *L'Olive* (sonnets to his presumed mistress, Mademoiselle de Viole, of whose name Olive is an anagram) in the Petrarchan manner, and a collection of forty-seven sonnets, *Les Antiquités de Rome,* on the ruins of Rome. These latter derive from his stay in Rome as secretary to his relative, Cardinal Jean du Bellay. *Les Regrets,* also sonnets, deal further with his Roman experiences, which were not always happy. Edmund Spenser translated the collection under the title *Complaints* (1591). Other works include *Poemata* and *Jeux Rustiques.*

Bellenden (bel′e̩n-de̩n), **John.** [Also, **Ballantyne, Ballenden, Bannatyne.**] Scottish poet, scholar, clergyman, and translator; b. at Haddington (or Berwick), Scotland, c1490; d. perhaps at Rome, in 1550 or 1587. He was educated at the universities of St. Andrews and Paris, and received his doctor of divinity degree from the latter. He was attached to the court of King James V of Scotland, at whose suggestion he translated into Scots the Latin chronicle-history of Hector Boece, *Historia Gentis Scotorum* (1527), for which he received 78 pounds. In the course of his translation he added much new material. His translation (1530–1533) was published at Edinburgh in 1536. He also translated the first five books of Livy's Roman history, for which he received 36 pounds. This work, however, was not published until 1822. Bellenden was also the author of two poems, *Proem of the Cosmographie* and *Proem of the History,* and a prose *Epistle,* all of which were published in 1536. He was archdeacon of Moray and canon of Ross. Opposed to the Reformation, he is said to have fled to Rome and to have died there in 1550. The editor of his Livy, however, declared that he was living in 1587.

Belli (bel′lē), **Onorio.** Botanist; d. after 1597. He worked and collected specimens on the island of Crete and in Egypt. He described his findings in *Epistolae de rarioribus quibusdam plantis Creticis,* which was published in Clusio's famous book on plants, *Rariorum Historia plantarum.*

Belli, Valerio. [Also called **Valerio Vicentino.**] Gem-cutter, engraver on crystal, and medalist; b. at Vicenza, 1468; d. there, 1546. He lived for some time at Rome, returned to Vicenza in 1520, and then went to Venice, where he remained until 1530. Although he had enjoyed great favor at the courts of princes and rulers, he died in modest circumstances. In his early work he sought depth and modeling. Later, he tended more toward the manner of classical friezes. Some of his designs were provided by Renaissance artists; others were taken from antique gems. He worked for popes Leo X, Clement VII, and Paul III. A silver casket inlaid with twenty crystal panels on which he engraved scenes of the Passion was made for Clement VII. It is in the Pitti Palace, Florence. A rock-crystal cross, probably made for Paul III, is in the Vatican; another is in the Victoria and Albert Museum, London. Many of his carved stones and crystals have been lost, and are now known through impressions or bronze reproductions. Vasari speaks of crystal vases, but nothing remains of them, nor of his work as a goldsmith. Of several series of medals, as of men of letters, artists, and famous women of Greece and Rome, a medal representing Bembo is known, but that with the portrait of Clement VII has been lost. For his artistry of design and delicacy of execution he was known in his own time as "the prince of engravers."

Bellincioni (bel-lēn-chō′nē), **Bernardo.** Court poet; b. at Florence, 1452; d. at Milan, 1492. In his youth he was a member of Lorenzo de' Medici's circle and was befriended by him. After 1480 he left Florence for the court of the Gonzaga at Mantua, and later (1485) entered the service of Ludovico Il Moro at Milan. He remained at Milan until his death. There he turned his talent for facile versifying to producing sonnets, love poems, poems of praise or of politics, and satires for the court. He was also a contributor, in his poetry, to the spectacular scenic and choral representations so greatly enjoyed in his time. Among others, Leonardo da Vinci did not scorn to place his great gifts at the service of these entertainments.

Bellini (bel-lē′nē), **Gentile.** Venetian painter; b. c1429; d. at Venice, February, 1507. He was the elder son of Jacopo Bellini, who was his first teacher, and worked in his father's busy shop until about 1465. An altarpiece, now lost, was signed by all three members of the family and dated 1460. By about 1464 he was recognized as a painter in his own right, for from about that year is his earliest independent work, a commission to paint figures of saints on the organ shutters in S. Marco. In 1466 he was commissioned to paint two canvases for the Scuola Grande di S. Marco, and in 1469 he was created Count Palatine by Emperor Frederick III. The reasons for such recognition are unknown. (In general, Frederick preferred to sell titles.) In 1474 he was put in charge, for life, of repairing and keeping in repair the paintings deteriorating from dampness in the Hall of the Great Council at Venice. He began to replace them with a series of historical paintings. The Sultan Mohammed II, having made peace with Venice (1479), invited the doge to visit him and at the same time requested the services of an excellent Venetian painter and a skilled bronze caster. Gentile was selected as the painter and went to Constantinople, leaving his brother Giovanni to take his place on the work in the Hall of the Great Council. The sultan required him to paint portraits, erotic pictures in the apartment of the prince, a dervish, a self-portrait, and a view of Venice. From his stay in Constantinople are his portrait of Mohammed II (much repainted but long attributed to Gentile), in the National Gallery, London, *A Turkish Artist* (the Isabella Stewart Gardner Museum, Boston), and *Two Orientals* (the Art Institute of Chicago). A story is told that the sultan, dissatisfied with a rendering of the beheading of John the Baptist, had a slave beheaded before Gentile to illustrate how the severed neck should look. This so frightened the painter that he returned to Venice forthwith (November, 1480). In the meantime, however, he had greatly pleased the sultan with his work and his character. A contemporary described him as "frank, of an independent spirit, dignified and disinterested." The sultan gave him the title of bey, rich gifts, and a pension. On his return to Venice he again took up the work in the Hall of the Great Council. His plan was to execute a series of pictures that would exalt the role of Venice in the struggle between the pope and Emperor Frederick Barbarossa. The paintings, with others executed by various artists in the Hall, were destroyed by fire in 1577. In 1492 he offered to replace, with the help of his brother, the paintings they had executed with their father in the Scuola Grande di S. Marco; these had been destroyed by fire in 1485. His offer was accepted. The next year he had commissions from Francesco, Marquess of Mantua. From the time of his return to Venice notices of his activity as a citizen and as a painted appear regularly to the time of his death. Under his will he left most of his possessions to his second wife, but he left his precious album of his father's drawings to his brother, on condition that the latter finish the work

Gentile had begun for the Scuola di S. Marco. Because of this, Giovanni finished the painting, *The Preaching of St. Mark in Alexandria,* now in the Brera, Milan.

From his youth Gentile was deeply influenced by his father, by his brother, and by his brother-in-law Andrea Mantegna. In his early works all these influences are somewhat awkwardly represented. His natural talent was for portraiture, and in this area he was most successful and individual. Among the earliest of the portraits attributed to him is one of *Doge Francesco Foscari* (d. 1457), now in the Correr Museum, Venice. Here his gift for seizing the personality of the sitter is evident; the doge, with the air of giving a courteous ear to a speaker whose advice he has not the slightest intention of taking, appears as a strong personality untroubled by self-doubt. If this unsigned and undated portrait is indeed by Gentile, it is his earliest known work. Among the earliest of the dated (1465) portraits is that of *Blessed Lorenzo Giustiniani,* Accademia, Venice, notable for the drawing of the emaciated ecclesiastic's bony, pious face, and suggesting, in its lack of color, the holy man's purified spirit. A likeness of Cardinal Bessarion, painted on the cover of a reliquary, is at Vienna, and there are other portraits of doges, including that of *Doge Andrea Vendramin* in the Frick Collection, New York. The portrait of Mohammed II (1480), mentioned above, beautifully realizes the highly bred and cultivated sultan, whose secretive nature has abysses of cruelty. Other portraits include that of *Caterina Cornaro* (c1500), at Budapest, and a *Portrait of a Venetian Gentleman,* in the Carrara Academy at Bergamo. Of interest for the accuracy with which he represented them are his great canvases of ceremonial occasions. Famous is his *Procession in the Piazza S. Marco* (1496), now in the Accademia, Venice. Against a background of a marvelously detailed (even to the old mosaics on the façade) Basilica of S. Marco, Gentile has painted the procession that marched around the square. The architectural details are exact. This is the way the piazza looked. The figures in the foreground seem so varied and individual as to be portraits. Other works on the same scale are the *Miracle of the Cross Fallen into the Canal* (1500) and the *Miraculous Cure of Pietro dei Ludovici* (1501), both in the Accademia. These huge canvases, often with rigid rows of spectators, faithfully reproduce architectural details of Venice. The *Preaching of St. Mark in Alexandria,* begun in 1504 and finished by Giovanni, reflects Gentile's stay in Constantinople in the minarets, obelisk, and nearly windowless houses of its Oriental style. Among his other works is a *Virgin and Child Enthroned,* in the National Gallery, London. The religious works quite clearly show the influence on Gentile of his father and his gifted brother and brother-in-law. The huge canvases are historically interesting for the strict accuracy with which he represented the Venetian scene. But as a painter of portraits Gentile found his artistic personality, the freedom to exercise his psychological insight, and a technique, perhaps refined by his exposure to Islamic art, equal to the task of expressing his artistic design.

Bellini, Giovanni. Venetian painter; b. c1435; d. at Venice, November 19, 1516. He was one of the founders of Venetian Renaissance painting. He perfected a technique in oil that lends a glowing radiance to his paintings, studied the effects and expressive value of the light at all times of day, and combined light and color to produce form. He excelled at painting landscapes, full of accurately observed details of plant, animal, and bird life, that faithfully reflect the serene and gentle aspects of the typical Italian scene; and he infused his paintings on religious themes with a moving and loving sense of humanity that was one of his outstanding characteristics. He was the son of Jacopo Bellini. The facts that he lived apart from his father and his brother Gentile and that he was not mentioned in the will of his father's widow seem to indicate that he was an illegitimate son. Nevertheless, he was devoted to his father, who was his first teacher and whom he far surpassed, and to his brother. He collaborated on commissions with them in his father's workshop. To this family, to whom painting was as natural as breathing, was added another painter in the person of Andrea Mantegna, who married (1453) Jacopo's daughter Niccolosa. From his early days, when he was working at Padua and was strongly influenced by Mantegna's linearity and classicism, to the end of his life, Giovanni was constantly assimilating, and transmuting to a personal style, various influences and techniques in a continual development and enrichment of his art. His works are to be found in the principal galleries of Europe and the United States; the largest number of them is at Venice.

The first notice of Giovanni is in 1459, when he witnessed a will. The following year, with his father and brother, he signed the altarpiece for the Gattamelata Chapel in the basilica at Padua (now lost), on which all three had collaborated. He married and had a son, Alvise. He was quickly recognized at Venice as an accomplished artist and had a busy workshop and many pupils. Because of the number of assistants who helped on the many commissions he had in his long and successful career, works bearing his signature might frequently be the products of his shop rather than of his brush. Dates are scarce for his paintings, and not always easy to assign. The development of his style in the early period lacks sharp breaks that would aid materially in dating a specific work; paintings in tempera and oil, or those in oil alone, are of the second half of his life. Throughout his long career he painted the Madonna, giving to each one of the paintings its own individuality through his endlessly inventive presentation and imaginative touches. His earlier *Madonnas,* some, small panels with half-length figures, were frequently painted for the devotions of private patrons. They are expressive of sincere, personal, deep religious conviction. The later *Madonnas,* especially those of the large altarpieces, are lovely reflections of the humanity of this world. They are tranquil, radiant, or regal, as the case may be. His earliest dated work is *The Madonna of the Trees* (1487), Accademia, Venice. Others in the great series of *Madonnas* are an early one in the Correr Museum and a later one in the Church of the Madonna del Orto, Venice; three in the Carrara Academy, Bergamo; the *Greek Madonna* (so called because of a Greek inscription on the border of the Madonna's headdress), Fogg Museum, Cambridge; a lovely early example in tempera, the Davis Madonna, the Metropolitan Museum, New York, where there are also several later ones in oil; and several in the National Gallery, London, including the signed *Madonna of the Pomegranate* and the *Madonna of the Meadow*. In the United States, besides those mentioned, there are *Madonnas* attributed to Bellini in the National Gallery, Washington; the Isabella Stewart Gardner Museum, Boston; the Johnson Collection, Philadelphia; Detroit; Kansas City; Houston; and Muncie, Indiana. Between 1462 and 1464, with collaborators, he painted four triptychs with Madonnas for the Church of the Carità, now the Accademia, Venice, where they may still be seen. Several times he painted the *Pietà,* as in the Correr Museum, Venice, the Brera and the Poldi Pezzoli Museum, Milan, the National Gallery, London, and the Carrara Academy, Bergamo. Other works considered to be of the early period are *Crucifixion, Transfiguration* (a later one is at Naples), and *Dead Christ Supported by Angels* (others of a later date are at Rimini and Berlin) in the Correr Museum, Venice, and *Agony in the Garden,* National Gallery, London. The last was perhaps painted in friendly competition with his brother-in-law Mantegna, and was perhaps derived, as was Mantegna's, from a sketch in his father's album. The two paintings hang near each other in the National Gallery, and make possible a compari-

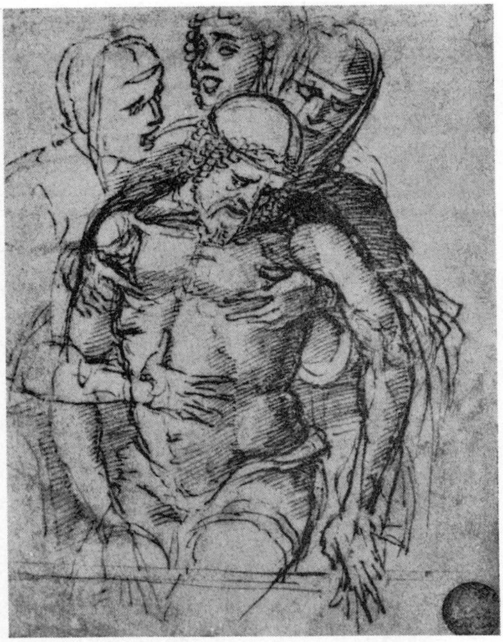

GIOVANNI BELLINI
Pietà
Accademia, Venice Alinari-Art Reference Bureau

GIOVANNI BELLINI
Miracle of St. Mark, the Healing of Ananias the Cobbler
Kupferstichkabinett, Berlin

son of the artists' styles—Mantegna's concern with line as a symbol of form, his harsher color, and his failure, in this case at least, to concentrate the drama on the central figure: his Christ is dimmed against one of the craggy hills full of blocky stones, cracks, and ravines so dear to Mantegna, and against an alabaster city lying partway down the hill. These elements contrast with Bellini's use of color to produce form, his glowing dawn, and the dramatic impact achieved by placing the figure of Christ against the sunrise. Even in the representation of a profoundly emotional moment, Bellini's world is benign; Mantegna's is harsh and foreboding (the cheerful effect of three rabbits playing in the road is cancelled by the presence of a vulture perched above them). Among the greatest of Bellini's early works is his *St. Francis* in the Frick Collection, New York. Painted probably between 1479 and 1485, it has been called "one of the most beautiful paintings of the Quattrocento" (Millard Meiss; Sir Osbert Sitwell, who shared this view, thought it was "probably" Bellini's masterpiece). The saint, face raised to the sun, stands before a trellis by his rocky cell, his arms outflung in ecstasy. His compelling figure is set in a beautifully composed and tender landscape. A castle crowns the distant hill; a town lies by a stream; a donkey, a rabbit peering from its hole, a flock of sheep, birds, plants so accurately painted they are identifiable, make up the saint's world. All are harmoniously united to create a serene, poetic, evocative atmosphere—a loving representation of the world and its creatures that the saint so deeply loved. Other works notable for their landscapes are four on *St. Jerome in the Wilderness* (Birmingham, England; S. Giovanni Crisostomo, Venice; National Gallery, Washington; Contini-Bonacossi Collection, Florence). To paint the altarpiece commissioned by Costanzo Sforza, Giovanni went to Pesaro, making one of his rare trips away from Venice. On the way he passed through Ferrara, where he must have seen the work of noted painters, including Piero della Francesca, through Rimini, and Ravenna. Afterward, the buildings that appeared in his paintings were no longer representations of classic architecture. Instead he often represented buildings he had actually seen. The scene painted on the back of the throne in the Pesaro altarpiece, for example, seems to represent a Pesaro stronghold, the fortress of Gradara; the buildings in the background of the *Pietà* in the Accademia at Venice recall those of Vicenza and Ravenna. In 1475 Antonello da Messina was at Venice. From him Bellini learned the technique of painting in oils. Prior to this he had painted, as did most artists, in tempera, which dried fast and produced bright, clear color surfaces. Bellini's Pesaro altarpiece, *The Coronation of the Virgin*, is from about this time (a *Pietà*, formerly the apex of the altarpiece, is in the Vatican). It was painted in tempera which was then covered with a glaze of slow-drying oil that lent a soft glow to the painting. Thereafter Bellini perfected his oil technique and ultimately abandoned tempera as a medium. The fusion of colors and tender gradations of tone that were possible with oil vastly increased the range, richness, and radiance of Bellini's paintings. Through him, his pupils, and assistants, the new technique spread to other Venetian painters. While at Venice Antonello painted the S. Cassiano altarpiece (fragments of which are at Vienna). From this may be derived a series of great altarpieces Bellini painted in various churches at Venice. Dating from perhaps late in the 1480's is the S. Giobbe altarpiece, *Madonna and Child Enthroned with St. Giobbe and Other Saints*, Accademia, Venice, which in its monumental grandeur reveals a new mastery. A radiant Madonna in a cloak of luminous blue is the central figure of the altarpiece of the Frari Church (1488). Other great altarpieces are the first one painted on canvas, *Madonna of Doge Barbarigo* (1488), S. Pietro Martire, Murano; *Baptism* (1500–1502), S. Corona, Vicenza; and *Madonna and Saints*, S. Zaccaria, Venice, one of his greatest paintings.

In 1497 Gentile Bellini went to Constantinople to paint for the sultan. Giovanni took over his work of painting the walls of the Hall of the Great Council for the Venetian Signory. According to Vasari, the great historical pictures that Gentile had begun were to "depict the glory and magnificence of Venice, her deeds in war, her most important undertakings, and all things worthy of being remembered, . . ." Vasari describes the pictures of the series, of which Giovanni was still the state painter at the time of his death. They were all destroyed by fire in 1577, and with them were destroyed the early examples of historical painting in Venice. A later work, *The Martyrdom of St. Mark*, for the Scuola Grande di S. Marco, was incomplete at the time of his death and was finished by Belliniano. Bellini was fundamentally a painter of religious pictures, and one who developed his own themes and attitudes. (Isabella d'Este was determined to have a painting by him. She ordered one, rigidly prescribing, as was her custom, the allegorical subject she desired and the manner of presenting it. After long delays that drove the impatient lady wild, Bellini delivered (1504) a picture that bore no relation to her specifications—*Madonna and Saints*. She ordered another, but it was never delivered.) About 1490 he painted the visionary *Sacred Allegory*, Uffizi, the interpretation of which remains a mystery, and later painted five smaller *Allegories* now in the Accademia, Venice. Toward the end of his life he made a few works on mythological themes. Two of these, *Feast of the Gods*, painted for Alfonso d'Este and signed and dated (1514) (Titian repainted the background), and *Orpheus*, are in the National Gallery, Washington. Another late one is the *Toilet of Venus*, at Vienna. In 1483 he became official state painter of Venice and was exempted from paying dues to the Painters' Guild. In his official capacity he painted portraits of the doges. That of *Doge Leonardo Loredano*, National Gallery, London, is one of the best known of any of his portraits; others are *Condottiere* and others in the National Gallery, Washington; the striking *Man with Long Black Hair*, Louvre; and those in the Palazzo Venezia, Rome; the Uffizi, Florence; Carrara Academy, Bergamo; the Metropolitan, New York; and elsewhere.

Bellini was born to a city that was ready for him. Venice was rich and powerful. The opalescent light of a city built on lagoons cast a glow on the many-colored marbles of its palaces. The population, enriched by commerce, was cosmopolitan and worldly. Men of many races, in brilliant and varied costume, filled the squares and rode the canals. The Adriatic was a Venetian lake. The city that tamed so many areas beyond its watery borders enjoyed an internal peace that was unparalleled in Italy, a peace that was imposed by a complete autocracy. A certain observance of religion was taken for granted, but the Church had little control and was not oppressive. A Venetian citizen enjoyed order, a chance to carry on his business and promote his prosperity as long as he did not roil the waters on which the ship of state purposefully pursued its course. Venetians did not tease their minds with theories of government. Everything had already been decided. Nor did they speculate uncomfortably about philosophy, science, the human condition. Florence, with its concern for intellectual matters and political theory, for order and form, was in an almost continual state of turmoil. Venice, eschewing speculation, was at peace within. Rich, worldly and tolerant, the Venetians saw the beauty of this world and intended to enjoy it. Among the things that gave them pleasure was the addition of splendor and beauty to their splendid and beautiful city. Bellini, less worldly, gently spiritual, inspired by a sympathy with mankind and a love of nature, supplied beauty in abundance. Through his many pupils, including Giorgione, Titian, Palma Vecchio, and Sebastiano del Piombo, he influenced a generation of Venetian painters, and his ideas were spread throughout Europe. Extraordinarily productive, many works known to have been executed have been lost, but about 150 survive. He was admired and respected throughout his life, and Albrecht Dürer, visiting Venice in 1505 and 1506, wrote of him that he was still the best in the art of painting. He died in November, 1516, and was buried beside his brother Gentile in the family vault in SS. Giovanni e Paolo.

Bellini, Jacopo. Venetian painter; d. 1470. He was the founder of a family of painters that included his two sons, Gentile and Giovanni, and his son-in-law Andrea Mantegna. Between them they infused new life into Venetian painting and made it a leading school of Italy. The earliest notice of Jacopo (his birth date is not known for certain) is of 1425. At that time Gentile da Fabriano was in Florence painting the *Adoration of the Magi*. Jacopo, his helper or apprentice, was haled before the magistrate for beating a boy who had thrown stones into the courtyard of his master's studio. Jacopo was devoted to Gentile, his first master and teacher, and named his eldest son for him. As a boy he probably worked with Gentile (1408–1414) on the decorations of the Ducal Palace at Venice. Afterward he followed him to Brescia and to Florence, as noted above, and perhaps accompanied him to Rome. In any event, he was back at Venice in 1429 and had acquired a great enthusiasm for antiquity and for some of the ideas about it that were being advanced by the Humanists. He was a busy master whose commissions took him to several cities on the mainland. In 1436 he was at Verona. A great *Crucifixion* with many figures that he painted there was destroyed in 1759. In 1441 he was at Ferrara. There, according to a sonnet extolling his art, in a competition with Pisanello he won the right to paint Leonello d'Este's portrait. Pages in his sketchbooks of the Estense eagles and designs for a monument for Niccolò III d'Este indicate a comparatively long stay at Ferrara. He also visited Padua, where he studied the antique and where he was friendly with young Andrea Mantegna. The latter eventually (1453) married his daughter Niccolosa and brought a new painting influence into the family. Meanwhile, Jacopo maintained a flourishing workshop at Venice. There, in collaboration with his sons, he carried out a number of commissions. His sons were by this time accomplished painters in their own right but, devoted as they were

JACOPO BELLINI
St. George Killing the Dragon
A page from Bellini's Sketchbook
Cabinet des Dessins Musée du Louvre Cliché Musée Nationaux

to their father and to each other, were content for some time to paint in the workshop over which he kept firm control. In 1460 the three Bellini painters signed an alterpiece (now lost) painted for the Gattamelata Chapel in the Basilica at Padua. In 1465 and 1466 they completed paintings for the Scuola Grande di S. Marco at Venice. These works were destroyed by fire in 1485. Few authentic works of Jacopo survive. Among these is a *Madonna* in the Uffizi, a beautifully preserved painting, rich in color and ornamentation. Though derived from the tradition of Gentile da Fabriano, the delicate gradations of color and more expressive forms foretell the richness and splendor of developed Venetian painting. Other *Madonnas* are in the Accademia, Venice; the Brera, Milan; the Tadini Gallery, Lovere; and the Carrara Academy, Bergamo. His *St. Jerome* and a poorly preserved *Crucifixion* are at Verona, and several other works attributed to him or to his workshop are to be found in other galleries, as at Padua, Paris, Brooklyn, San Diego, California, and Washington. Precious surviving works of Jacopo are two sketchbooks: one in the Louvre, Paris, and the other in the British Museum. Many of the sketches in both books are on the same subject, and it is thought one sketchbook is to some extent a copy of the other, made so that each of his two sons would have an album of his father's drawings. Drawings in both books have been retraced or worked over. The drawings are on a variety of themes and show Jacopo's interest in secular subjects. These include studies of mythological creatures and natural animals, architectural sketches, Roman ruins, landscapes. He was evidently fond of drawing the castles and courtyards of princes, the stairways and balconies of palaces. His architectural drawing reflects an interest in mass and symmetry, and the problems that could be solved by perspective, rather than possible architectural designs for real buildings. He loved to draw heavy, robust horses bearing nobles garbed for the tourney or for war, or engaged in combat with monsters. He made sketches representing cheetahs (sometimes used for hunting), lions, dogs, and other animals of the chase. He drew antique monuments and inscriptions, allegories (as *The Meeting of the Quick and the Dead,* Louvre), nudes, and scenes from peasant life. His drawings lack the vigor and incisiveness of Pisanello's but excel in animation and atmosphere. In them he gave free rein to his love of fantasy and expressed many interests that do not appear in the religious paintings that so thoroughly occupied the artists of the age. The albums were so esteemed by his sons that Gentile left his to Giovanni in his will. Through his works and his sketchbooks Jacopo's influence spread far beyond the confines of his workshop. A hardworking and intelligent man, he was not so much a great painter as a formative influence in sparking the splendor of Venetian painting.

Belliniano (bel-lē-nyä′nō), **Vittore.** [Original name, **Vittore di Matteo.**] Painter; b. at Venice, c1456; d. there, 1529. He took his name from his master, Giovanni Bellini, whom he assisted in the decoration of the Hall of the Great Council in the Ducal Palace. He lived in an age of great Venetian painters, worked with Giovanni Bellini and Carpaccio, and shows their influence in his own work. His works include *Youth Praying Before a Crucifix,* in the Carrara Academy at Bergamo; and a signed and dated (1524) *Coronation of Mary,* at Spinea, near Mestre. In 1526 he finished the *Martyrdom of St. Mark,* begun by Giovanni Bellini, for the Scuola di S. Marco.

Bello (bel′lō), **Francesco.** See **Cieco, Francesco.**

Bello or **Belli** (bel′lē), **Marco.** Painter; b. at Venice, c1470; d. c1523. He was a follower of Giovanni Bellini. Among his surviving works are *Madonna and Child,* Carrara Academy, and paintings at Rovigo, Venice (Accademia), Budapest, Leningrad, Ottawa, and elsewhere.

Bellunello (bel-lö-nel′lō), **Andrea.** [**Andrea di Bertolotto da S. Vito.**] Painter; b. at Belluno, c1430; d. at S. Vito al Tagliamento, 1494. Trained under local masters of the Friuli, he went to S. Vito al Tagliamento in 1455 and remained there until his death. Celebrated in his area in his own day, he left several works in and about Udine, as a rather Gothic *Crucifixion* (Museo Civico, Udine), a polyptych, *St. Florian and Saints* (Church of S. Floriano a Cella, Forni di Sopra, Udine), a *Madonna and Child* (S. Vito al Tagliamento), with draperies falling in the caligraphic curves and angles of the international Gothic style, and frescoes at Savorgnano and S. Vito al Tagliamento.

Bembo (bem′bō), **Benedetto.** Brescian painter of the 15th century. Little is known of his life. A polyptych, *The Virgin and Child, with Four Saints,* signed and dated 1462, is in the Davanzati Palace at Florence. Some frescoes and a *Flight into Egypt* are at Cremona. His preoccupation with detail and ornamentation show him to have been strongly attached to the Flowery Gothic tradition, while at the same time aware of Renaissance developments in painting.

Bembo, Bonifacio. Painter; probably born at Brescia, c1420; d. after 1477. He settled at Cremona and painted portraits for the Sforza at Milan, and many altarpieces for their castles at Pavia and Milan. Profile portraits of Francesco Sforza and Bianca Maria Visconti, kneeling, are in the Church of Sant' Agostino at Cremona; a *St. Francis* and some tarot cards are in the Accademia Carrara at Bergamo.

Bembo, Pietro. Man of letters, the foremost stylist of his age, and cardinal; b. at Venice, May 20, 1470; d. at Rome, January, 1547. His father, a cultivated Venetian nobleman and man of affairs, was an early influence in developing Bembo's studies. The son was educated in Venice, went to Messina to study Greek under the noted Hellenist Constantine Lascaris, and studied philosophy at Padua under Pomponazzi. He accompanied his father on a mission to Florence (1478–1480) where he met the Medici, and later to the court of the Estensi at Ferrara (1498). At that court he met Lucrezia Borgia, who arrived there as the bride of Alfonso d'Este. A great beauty, with powerful connections, she and Bembo became warm friends. He dedicated his *Gli Asolani,* three prose dialogues on Platonic love, to her, and she gave him a lock of her yellow hair. (The lock of hair is preserved in the Ambrosian

Library at Milan.) In 1506 Bembo went to the court of the Montefeltri at Urbino, and was an intimate of the circle described in Castiglione's *Il Cortegiano*. In 1512 he accompanied Giuliano de' Medici to Rome, where he became associated with Giuliano's brother, Pope Leo X, entered minor orders, and was named one of Leo's secretaries. He also formed a liaison with the beautiful Roman Morosina, who bore him three children. Some years later (1520), he retired to Padua. There he amassed a library, engaged in horticulture, attended to his wide correspondence (he was a notable letter-writer), and cultivated his style. His house at Padua was a rendezvous for the most brilliant men of the day. Paul III recalled him to Rome (1539) and made him a cardinal. He later invested him with the bishoprics of Gubbio and Bergamo.

Bembo was the foremost stylist of the so-called Golden Age of Renaissance Literature. Although neither profound nor original as a thinker, his word became law in matters of style. He was as interested in perfecting Italian as a literary language, as he was in perfecting the Latin style. One of his works, *Prose della volgar lingua* (1525), expresses his conviction that Tuscan should be the chosen Italian literary language. In this he put himself in opposition to those who wanted the Italian literary language to include elements from other dialects. In the same work he discusses style and presents rules of grammar. His other writings include a history of Venice, in Latin, from 1487 to 1513, *Rime*, passionless Italian lyrics that revived the manner of Petrarch's *Canzoniere*, and many polished, interesting and valuable letters in Latin and Italian. As an authority, he prepared the text for Aldus Manutius' edition of Petrarch's *Canzoniere* (1501) and Dante's *Divina Commedia* (1502). There is a handsome portrait of Bembo by Titian in the Museo Nazionale, at Naples. In three-quarter view, we see his high intellectual forehead, deep-set eyes, thin aquiline nose, and flowing beard—a man who would certainly make an impression. As the arbiter of Latin and Italian letters he won great fame, surprisingly few enemies, and had so many and such powerful friends that he was considered a possibility for the papacy.

Benaglio (bā-nä′lyō), **Francesco.** Painter; b. at Verona, c1432; d. before 1492. Of the generation that followed Pisanello, he had not fully grasped the Renaissance developments in painting that the Tuscans were spreading through North Italy. His *St. Bernardino* triptych at Verona was inspired by one Mantegna had painted three years earlier in the Church of S. Zeno. Benaglio's is an unimaginative and awkward composition in which the figures, clad in rigid drapery, stand in a row. His *Madonna and Child* in the Accademia, Venice, is more spacious. Other works are *Madonnas* in the National Gallery, Washington, at Rochester, New York, and in the Johnson Collection, Philadelphia. He was relatively untouched by the influence of his great contemporaries, Mantegna and Giovanni Bellini, but did pass on to the next generation of Veronese painters his understanding of chromatic values, as well as his rather hard and common types.

Bene (bā′nā), **Bartolomeo del.** See **Del Bene, Bartolomeo.**

Bene, Sennuccio del. See **Del Bene, Sennuccio.**

Benedetto da Maiano (or **Majano**) (bā-nā-det′tō dä mä-yä′nō). [Original name, **Benedetto di Leonardo.**] Sculptor, architect, and woodcarver; b. at Maiano, 1442; d. at Florence, May 24, 1497. He was born into a family that had been workers in stone for generations; his father was a stonemason, and Benedetto and his five brothers followed him in that craft. Benedetto's career was linked, more or less closely, with those of his elder brothers, the architect Giuliano (b. c1431) and the sculptor Giovanni (b. c1438). According to Vasari, the family was also noted for intarsia work, but no clear proof of this survives. His earliest surviving work is the monument of S. Savino in the cathedral at Faenza (1471–1472). The refined detail in the narrative scenes of its reliefs indicates the influence of Antonio Rossellino, who was one of the major sources of Benedetto's art. In 1473 he entered the Guild of Stonemasons and Woodcarvers. Works of this period reveal the mastery he had attained. Of 1474 is the signed and dated portrait bust in marble of Pietro Mellini (Bargello, Florence). The delicate pattern of the wealthy merchant's robe is as faithfully portrayed as his deeply lined, skeptical face. For the same patron he carved (1472–1475) the pulpit in S. Croce that many consider to be his masterpiece, and that some consider to be the supreme achievement of Italian sculpture in pictorial relief. The pulpit consists of five reliefs with scenes from the life of St. Francis, separated by pilasters and surmounted by a frieze. Beneath the panels are niches with seated figures. (He attached the pulpit partway up one of the huge supporting pillars of the church, and hollowed out the pillar to conceal a staircase to the pulpit.) Masterly is the carving of details, as the minute umbrella pines and houses on the distant hills in *The Stigmatization of St. Francis,* the intensity of the saint's figure, skillful perspective, and the complete finish and reach toward monumentality of all the reliefs. He had many commissions outside Florence. About this time he completed (1475) the beautiful altar of S. Fina, with three reliefs of scenes from the saint's life, in a chapel designed by Giuliano and frescoed by Domenico Ghirlandaio, in the Collegiata (Cathedral) at S. Gimignano. In the period 1475 he designed and executed the tabernacle with two angels in the Collegiata, and the richer and more harmonious one in S. Domenico at Siena. From 1480 is the tabernacle, designed by Giuliano, with Benedetto's terra-cotta *Madonna of the Olive,* in the cathedral at Prato. In 1480 and 1481 he was at Florence, working with Giuliano in the Palazzo Vecchio, where he completed the door of the Audience Chamber. (The carved ceiling of the Hall of the Two Hundred, of an earlier date, is also attributed to him.) In 1481 he was at Loreto, where he finished the lavabo in the sacristy and completed two terra-cotta *Evangelists.* He went next to Naples. There he finished (1485) the upper part of the tomb of Maria d'Aragona, begun by Rossellino in 1481, in the Church of Monte Oliveto (S. Anna dei Lombardi). In 1489 he completed an altar for the same church. The altar, with a marble relief of the *Annunciation* flanked by figures of SS. John the Baptist and Jerome, surmounted by medallions with Sibyls, and supported by a predella with seven scenes, rivals the S. Croce pulpit for the title of Benedetto's masterpiece. The perspective of the low relief of the background, as well as the higher relief of the two main figures, recalls Donatello. The medieval purity of the Virgin's head is movingly rendered with 15th-century knowledge, technique, and elegance. From 1490 is the medallion with the bust of Giotto in the cathedral at Florence. (The Latin inscription that begins "I am he by whom the extinct art of painting was revived," was composed by the poet Angelo Poliziano.) Probably before 1490 he began the Strozzi tomb (incomplete at the time of Filippo Strozzi's death in 1491) in S. Maria Novella, with the lovely *Madonna* in the tondo above the sarcophagus, and of about the same time is the marble bust of Filippo Strozzi now in the Louvre. He had earlier designed the palace for Filippo Strozzi, begun in 1489, that epitomizes the type of 15th century Florentine palace created by Brunelleschi and refined by Michelozzo. Close to the *Madonna* of the Strozzi tomb in spirit and execution are the *Madonnas* of Scarperia and of the altar of S. Bartolo in the saint's chapel in the Church of S. Agostino at S. Gimignano. *St. Sebastian* and *Virgin and Child,* in the Misericordia, Florence, were probably his last works. In their somewhat overblown drapery there are foretastes of the mannerism to come. Benedetto added intensity, drama, and monumentality to the elegance and grace that he had absorbed from the Rossellino brothers. An observant student of Ghiberti also, he became a master of composition in relief and achieved an exquisite accuracy. He sometimes prepared terra-cotta models for his large works of sculpture. Several of these were found in his workshop at the time of his death. The model of the Virgin for the Naples altar is in the Metropolitan Museum, New York. Models for three of the reliefs of the S. Croce pulpit are in the Victoria and Albert Museum, London. A terra-cotta *Madonna and Child* is in the Isabella Stewart Gardner Museum, Boston, and an *Angel* in the Carrara Academy, Bergamo.

Benedict XI. [Original name, **Niccolò Boccasini.**] Pope (1303–1304); b. at Treviso, 1240; d. at Perugia, July 7, 1304. He annulled the bulls of Boniface VIII against Philip IV (called Philip the Fair) of France. He succeeded Boniface VIII and was succeeded by Clement V.

Benedict XII. [Original name, **Jacques Fournier.**] Pope (1334–1342); b. at Saverdun, in Toulouse, France; d. at Avignon, April 24, 1342. Earlier a Cistercian monk and abbot of Montfroide, and named cardinal by his uncle John XXII in 1327, he was the third of the Avignon pontiffs, and the successor of John XXII. He was a severe ecclesiastical reformer, opposed nepotism, and reformed the monastic orders. Unsuccessful in his wish to restore the papal court to Rome, he began construction of the papal palace at Avignon. He was a friend of Petrarch, to whom he offered the post of apostolic secretary, but Petrarch declined lest it interfere with his work and his peace. Benedict was succeeded by Clement VI.

Benedict XIII. [Original name, **Pedro de Luna.**] Antipope (1394–1424); b. in Aragon; d. at Peñiscola, Valencia, Spain, in November, 1424. He was elected by the French cardinals to succeed Clement VII. The Council of Pisa, assembled to end the Great Schism and unite the Church, deposed him in 1409 but he refused to recognize its authority. The Council of Constance again deposed him, in 1415. He fled at that time but continued to claim to be pope until his death. Aragon, Castile, and Scotland supported his claim.

Benevento (ben-ẹ-ven′tō), **Battle of.** Victory gained (February, 1266) by Charles of Anjou over Manfred of Hohenstaufen, king of Sicily. Manfred was killed, and the kingdom of Sicily passed to Charles.

Benigno Salviati (bā-nē′nyō säl-vyä′tē), **Giorgio.** Theologian, philosopher, and writer; d. 1520. His family fled from their native Bosnia to Ragusa to escape the Turks. Giorgio entered the Franciscan order at an early age, and went to Italy to study. He also passed some time in France and England, studying philosophy, and then returned to Florence. There, for about thirty years, he taught theology. He was greatly loved by the Medici and, especially, by the Salviati family; the latter gave him their name. He was a member of the circle of learned men about Lorenzo the Magnificent, and highly regarded in his time as a philosopher. (Francesco Guicciardini, the historian and Benigno Salviati's younger contemporary, classed him with Marsilio Ficino and Pico della Mirandola.) Pope Julius II made him a bishop (1507) and Pope Leo X made him an archbishop (1513). He left a number of works on theology and moral philosophy.

Benivieni (bā-nē-vyā′nē), **Antonio.** Physician; b. at Florence; d. 1502. The minute observations he made of cadavers were published in his *De abditis morborum causis* (Florence, 1507); they constituted early objective studies of cadavers as a means of determining the causes of death. He made pioneering studies in teratology, in helminthology, and in the transmission of syphilis from the mother to the fetus.

Benivieni, Girolamo. Florentine poet; b. at Florence, 1453; d. there, 1542. He studied classics and Hebrew. With Ficino, Poliziano, and Pico della Mirandola he was a member of the circle of poets, writers, and philosophers that surrounded Lorenzo de' Medici, and was on terms of particular friendship with Pico della Mirandola (with whom he wished to be buried). He wrote a canzone in which he summarized Ficino's *Libro dello amore*, love lyrics, and other verse in which he expressed his deep love of nature. Under the influence of Savonarola he denounced his former carefree life, devoted to literature and pleasure, destroyed many of his poems, changed some to give them religious overtones, became the poet of Savonarola's reformation, and translated (1496) and published Savonarola's treatise on the Christian life. Later, he relented about his earlier vernacular works, collected what had not been destroyed, and published them.

Bennewitz (ben′ẹ-vits), **Peter.** See **Apianus, Petrus.**

Benozzo Gozzoli (bā-nôt′tsō gōt′tsō-lē). [Original name, **Benozzo di Lese.**] Painter; b. at Florence, 1420; d. at Pistoia, October 4, 1497. The name Gozzoli does not appear in contemporary documents or on his signed paintings. Vasari, who admired his industry as well as his inventiveness, ability to draw animals, skill in landscape, and richly varied decorative resources, added the name Gozzoli in his second edition of the *Vite*, and it is the name by which he has been known ever since. He received his training under the best of masters. The first of these was Fra Angelico, with whom he worked in S. Marco at Florence. His hand can be distinguished in the frescoes in some of the cells. His next master was Ghiberti. On January 25, 1444, he agreed to work for Lorenzo and Vittorio Ghiberti on the doors of the Baptistery for three years. His efforts in this work were largely those of an apprentice, and he seems thereafter to have abandoned sculpture. In March, 1447, he was working with Fra Angelico at Rome on the Chapel of the Holy Sacrament in the Vatican, and in June of the same year was with the Dominican painter at Orvieto, where at that time and

BENOZZO GOZZOLI
St. Augustine Suffering from a Toothache
Fogg Art Museum, Harvard University. Bequest of Charles A. Loeser

at intervals in following years he helped in decorating the vault of the Chapel of S. Brizio in the cathedral. During this early period he faithfully followed the instructions of his master, but he did not achieve the clarity of color that was a hallmark of Fra Angelico's painting, and in contrast to his spirituality, Benozzo was frankly secular in temperament. He was 30 when he began his independent career with a commission to paint a series of frescoes on the life of St. Francis of Assisi in the Church of S. Francesco at Montefalco. Though thoroughly grounded in the pure Tuscan style, he was still unsure and dependent. The great series on the life of St. Francis at Assisi was an accomplishment he could not hope to equal, much less rival. He yielded to his taste and talent for depicting pleasing episodes, cheerful landscapes, and all sorts of polychrome architecture in the execution of the series. With his undoubted gift for narrative, these elements remained constant in his painting. In 1453 he painted a series (now lost) of frescoes on the life of S. Rosa at Viterbo in which presumably his art reached maturity, for six years later (1459) he was commissioned by Piero de' Medici to paint *The Procession of the Magi* in the chapel of the Medici Palace (now the Riccardi Palace) at Florence. The well-preserved series, sparkling with gold and brilliant color against the young green of a springlike landscape, has all the appearance of a splendid and colorful tapestry. Over the altar in the chapel was a painting of *The Nativity*, by Filippo Lippi. (The painting now there is a copy; the original is at Berlin.) On the walls on each side of it he painted groups of angels, some in the clouds of heaven, some on the ground, and some in the gardens of the background. A town bristling with towers in the hilly landscape is thought to represent S. Gimignano; a castle resembles the Medici castle at Cafaggiolo. On each of the other three walls he painted one of the three Wise Men with his retinue. In 1439 the Byzantine emperor and emissaries of the Eastern Church had come to Florence to meet with Pope Eugenius IV in an attempt to resolve the differences between the Greek and Roman churches and to unite them in the face of the menacing Turk. The rich fabrics, threaded with gold and crimson, of the Greeks, their bizarre costumes and turbans, the magnificence of their equipment, left a great impression on the Florentines. Benozzo, who had seen it all as a young man, recaptured much of the splendor of the scene in his Medici frescoes. The young king with his train representing the first Wise Man is an idealized portrait of young Lorenzo, later called "the Magnificent." Many of the members of his suite are portraits of contemporary Florentines, including that of Piero. Other portraits in the series represent Galeazzo Maria Sforza, who was visiting Florence in 1459, Piero's three daughters, and Benozzo himself, with his name inscribed on the rim of his cap. The Byzantine emperor, John VII Paleologus, represents the second Wise Man. Clad in a robe of green and gold trimmed with fur, he rides a white horse caparisoned with gold and crimson. The patriarch of Constantinople appears as the third Wise Man. Against a landscape background crowded with trees, birds, animals, scenes of the hunt, castles, and towns, the *Procession* flows up and down high-arched hills around the walls to *The Nativity*. In a completely secular spirit, the sacred moment is presented as a gay and luxurious festival.

Between 1463 and 1465 he worked on a series of frescoes on the life of St. Augustine in S. Agostino at S. Gimignano, in which he continued to show his gift for invention and for popularizing religious subjects. A facile and able artist, he was industrious and modest, and was not above accepting commissions for panels and tabernacles in the neighborhood of Florence and Siena. In 1467 he received a commission to cover the greatest space that had been made available to any artist up to that time. This was to finish the series of frescoes on the walls of the Camposanto, the monumental cemetery at Pisa. His wife, his children, and his brothers joined him; and except for brief trips to Florence and the neighborhood to fill small commissions, to Volterra to escape the plague and to paint in the cathedral, and to Legoli, he worked at Pisa from 1467 to 1484. On the huge walls he painted the stories from Genesis, from the Creation to Noah and the Ark, and continued with a cycle of stories from the Old Testament. Such subjects as *The Drunkenness of Noah*, the *Curse of Cain*, *Building the Tower of Babel*, *Destruction of Sodom*, stories of Moses and Joseph, Jacob and Esau, and others, provided unlimited scope for his facile and colorful invention, his love of painting architecture and crowds in gay costumes, and his intense interest in presenting details. He painted peasants at work, fantastic buildings, broad reaches of landscape. He painted the 15th-century life of the city and of the country, the dances of women and the games of children, the freshness of the rustic landscape and the gaiety of festivals, all in presenting the Bible stories. The frescoes are testimonials of his enormous inventiveness, great narrative skill, and wondrous fantasy. The broadness of his conception, freedom of invention, and wealth of his fantasy more than compensate for his too great concern with cluttering detail. The Pisans were delighted, and gave him a place in the Camposanto for his own tomb, near his pictures and the tombs of the great men of the city (but he was buried at Pistoia). In the Camposanto, a place of the dead, he painted the joyousness of life in bright colors and with a spontaneity and verve that, despite damage, frequent repainting and clumsy restoring, was preserved almost to the present. In July, 1944, a bomb fell on the Camposanto, the wooden beams caught fire, the lead roof melted and crashed. Most of the frescoes were shattered, many were completely ruined. Those that could be saved were detached and remounted. Under them were revealed the numerous *sinopie* Benozzo and his assistants had drawn to guide the work. Some of these are rapid sketches, hints, or suggestions to the assistants or to himself; others are fully developed studies—of heads, limbs, or drapery (on which the Florentines set such store). The enormous drawings are free and vigorous. Joking remarks, sketches that have nothing to do with the finished frescoes, phrases of jests with which the painters rallied each other, directions for the execution of the work, have also been found on the plaster, making poignant and immediate a sense of the artist who painted there over 500 years ago. Having finished the vast series at Pisa, he painted banners, gonfalons, and tabernacles in the city and its environs until the beginning of 1497, when he was again at Florence. The *Procession of the Magi* in the Medici-Riccardi Palace is probably the best-known of Benozzo's works; it has been reproduced any number of times, in whole or in part, and is easily accessible to tourists to Florence. Next best known, and far more inventive, are the frescoes in the Camposanto: examples par excellence of his narrative gift and talent for illustration. Far outclassed in skill and composition, artistic genius, and intellectual or spiritual inspiration by other Florentine painters, he endears himself to all ages with his charming scenes of 15th-century Italian life, customs, interests, and gaiety, and with his own delightfully fanciful representations of other ages. Best at letting his imagination roam, at telling stories on large surfaces, his panel painting is fairly mediocre. In the panels the weakness of composition is more obvious, the drawing of figures less skilled, and the color somewhat opaque. His *Virgin and Child Enthroned Among Angels and Saints* (National Gallery, London) was the main panel of an altarpiece. Panels from its predella are in the Brera, Milan, at Berlin, Buckingham Palace, in the National Gallery, Washington, and in the Johnson Collection, Philadelphia. Other works are in the Uffizi, the National Gallery of Umbria, Perugia, the Vatican, and the Metropolitan Museum, New York, Cambridge, Massachusetts, and elsewhere.

Bentivoglio (ben-tē-vō′lyō). An ancient and powerful family of Bologna, members of which were prominent in the affairs of the city from the 12th to the 16th century. From the end of the 13th and the beginning of the 14th centuries they belonged to the Guelph, or popular, faction of the city. At the end of the 14th century, after the expulsion (1360) of Giovanni da Oleggio, the Bentivoglio became either actual lords of the city or its leading citizens. Giovanni I Bentivoglio was proclaimed signore (lord) in February, 1401. By treachery, conspiracy, and military defeat at the hands of Gian Galeazzo Visconti, he lost his place and was killed (June, 1402), and the Visconti claimed the city. His son Anton Galeazzo returned to Bologna from exile and took part (1416) in a rebellion against the pope (the popes always claimed Bologna, but their grip on it was often weak). He seized the castle and proclaimed himself signore (1420), but his enemies within the city allied against him and drove him out. He secured a reconciliation with the pope, by which Bologna again recognized the latter's overlordship (except for important concessions to the citizens), returned to Bologna (December, 1435), and was welcomed as a hero. He was so popular that the papal legate resolved to get rid of him. Anton Galeazzo was invited by the legate to hear mass, and afterward was seized by the legate's bravos in front of the cathedral and slain. His son Annibale fled, but returned in 1438. He wished to free Bologna from the Visconti yoke. He was captured and imprisoned in a fortress near Parma by Niccolò Piccinino, but escaped with the aid of friends, returned to Bologna in triumph, and drove out the Visconti governor. By other military successes he became lord of Bologna. As always, there were a great number who aspired to this position, and he fell a victim of their intrigues. Members of the rival Canetori family asked him to serve as godfather at the baptism of a Canetori infant. Aware of their enmity, he nevertheless accepted, in the hope of healing the breach between the families. He was stabbed as he came out of the church (June 24, 1445) after serving at the baptismal rite. The enraged Bolognese rose up against the Canetori, killed every one they could lay their hands on, and destroyed their houses. The Bolognese wished a member of the family to succeed Annibale who could control the factions, but Annibale's son, Giovanni, was a child. The city was in tumult. Word came that a natural son of Ercole, son of Giovanni I, was at Florence, where he was employed, under the name Cascese, by the wool guild. This youth was Sante, then twenty years old. Representatives from Bologna went to him, revealed his true lineage, and invited him to return to Bologna. He was reluctant to do so, but on the advice of Cosimo de' Medici the Elder and Neri Capponi, decided to accept. He entered Bologna in November, 1446, and was acclaimed by the people. Sante acted decisively. He made peace with Pope Nicholas V and drew up a pact with him. By it the overlordship of the Church was again recognized, and a new government was established. This consisted of a senate of sixteen members who acted for the city under the supervision of a papal legate. In their turn, the Bolognese had an ambassador, called an orator, at Rome. With great firmness, Sante suppressed the warring factions in the city, negotiating when that was possible, but never hesitating to use force when it was necessary. Wise and prudent, as unscrupulous as necessary, by the time he died (October, 1462) life was once again secure at Bologna. He began a great building program that was continued by his successors, and laid the foundations for the famous Bentivoglio Palace. Sante was succeeded by Annibale's son Giovanni II (b. at Bologna, February 13, 1443). He was admitted to the Senate of Sixteen Reformers in 1459, won over all who had admired his popular father, was made gonfaloniere, and won from the pope the right to bequeath his honors and offices to his descendants. In 1467 the Sixteen was increased to Twenty-one. Giovanni was the only one to have permanent tenure, and dominated Bologna through control of the constitutional machinery. He proved his friendship to Lorenzo de' Medici in the wars following the Pazzi Conspiracy (1478); defended the Estensi in the war with Venice (1482); and aided the Riario to reconquer Forlì. In turn he was supported by the Medici and the Sforza. He married Ginevra Sforza, natural daughter of Alessandro Sforza of Pesaro; married his daughter Francesca to Galeotto Manfredi of Faenza (1481; she murdered her husband), and his daughter Violante to Pandolfo Malatesta of Rimini (1489). Giovanni's sons, Alessandro, Annibale, and Ermes, served in the armies of the greatest princes. His firm policy of friendship with the larger states was rewarded with peace and with honors to him from other princes. At home he encouraged display, festivals, and the arts. He carried on construction of his magnificent palace, built churches, beautified the city with new streets and squares, promoted industry and commerce, and welcomed artists and men of letters at his court. The Bentivoglio Chapel, a Renaissance structure in the Church of S. Giacomo Maggiore at Bologna, is decorated with frescoes by Lorenzo Costa, an altarpiece by Il Francia, and has a bas-relief of Annibale Bentivoglio on horseback. But Bologna was a nest of envious vipers. Such prosperity and ease aroused the jealousy of the leading families. A conspiracy was hatched by the Malvezzi (1488). It was discovered and numbers of the Malvezzi were hanged, imprisoned, or exiled, and their goods confiscated. In 1501 over 200 members and friends of the Marescotti, another rival family, were massacred. This slaughter was carried out by Giovanni's sons, perhaps not at his instigation but with his knowledge, and it cost the family the good will they had built up. In the meantime, Charles VIII of France had invaded Italy (and departed), and the system of princely alliances so carefully constructed by Giovanni was destroyed. The Medici had been banished from Florence, and the Sforza from Milan. Giovanni had alienated the pope, and Julius II set out to bring Bologna back into the fold (1506). Giovanni and his large family fled before the forces of the pope (November 2, 1506) and never returned to Bologna. His wife Ginevra threw herself on the pope's mercy, begging to be allowed to remain, but he denied her and drove her into exile too, on the ground that she was largely responsible for her husband's misfortunes. (She died at Busseto, May 16, 1507). Giovanni II, hunted from city to city, was imprisoned at Milan, where he died of grief (1508). His sons tried to return to Bologna, but the people, enraged by their earlier crimes, drove them out and sacked the magnificent Bentivoglio Palace. The sons came back with French aid in 1511, but were again expelled. Subsequent attempts to regain power in Bologna were fruitless. Many members of the family went to Ferrara, where they were a distinguished family in succeeding centuries.

Bentivoglio, Ercole. Poet and playwright; b. at Modena, 1506; d. at Venice, November 6, 1573. He spent most of his life at Ferrara, where he was a friend of Ariosto. He wrote some satires in the manner of Ariosto, some *capitoli* in the manner of Berni, and two comedies, based on Latin models. His works, of no great literary or artistic merit, are of interest for the picture they provide of the taste, manners, culture, and inclinations of his own age at Ferrara.

Bentivoglio, Francesca. She was the daughter of Giovanni II of Bologna and died, 1504. In 1481 she married Galeotto Manfredi, lord of Faenza. He maintained his attachment for Cassandra Pavoni, and Francesca, a violent girl, perhaps out of jealousy and possibly in furtherance of her father's policy, conspired to have her husband murdered (May 31, 1488). She later married Guido Torelli (1494).

Bentivoglio, Ginevra. Virago of Bologna; d. at Busseto, May 16, 1507. She was the natural daughter of Alessandro Sforza, Lord of Pesaro, and married (1454) Sante Bentivoglio, who had been called from Florence to rule Bologna. When her husband died (1462), she married (1465) his successor, Giovanni II, in whom she had shown a lively interest even before the death of her husband. A vigorous, cultivated, spirited, and at the same time extremely superstitious woman, she had great influence on her husband, and her ambitions for him and her family were, according to some, the cause of his ruin. It was thought that she was in back of the ruthless suppression of the Malvezzi (1488) and the Marescotti (1501) families for having conspired against her husband. The murders and proscriptions that were carried out in this suppression, and the witches, sorcerers, and hermits with whom she surrounded herself, made her extremely unpopular. When Julius II marched against Bologna (1506), she sent her family away, but remained in Bologna herself to seek pardon from the pope and the restoration of her family. Julius refused to see her and accused her of being the cause of all the evils that had befallen her family. She fled to Busseto, where she continued to intrigue for the return of her family to Bologna. Her attempts to unseat the Marescotti failed and she died suddenly.

Benvenuti (ben-ve-nö′tē), **Giovanni Battista.** See **Ortolano l'.**

Benvenuti, Lorenzo. Florentine humanist; b. c1383; d. 1423. Little is known of his background. He wrote (c1420) an invective against Niccolò Niccoli in which he charged him with vanity, snobbishness, arrogance, and lack of patriotism for not playing an active role in civic life. Lorenzo himself, like many humanists of his day, several times served the Republic.

Benvenuto di Giovanni (ben-ve-nö′tō dē jō-vän′nē). [Full name, **Benvenuto di Giovanni di Meo del Guasta.**] Painter; b. at Siena, September 13, 1436; d. there, c1518. One of the last fine painters of the Sienese school, he was a pupil and follower of Vecchietta, was influenced by Matteo di Giovanni and, to a lesser extent, by Francesco di Giorgio, Gerolamo da Cremona, and Benozzo Gozzoli. In 1455 he frescoed some stories on the life of St. Anthony of Padua in the Baptistery at Siena. In 1466 he painted an *Annunciation* for the Church of S. Gerolamo at Volterra (the painting is now in the museum there), and in 1470 painted another *Annunciation* at Sinalunga. These works are original and characteristic of the artist in the elegance of the types and the refinement of the details. Of 1475 is a signed and dated triptych at Siena in which the influence of Matteo is evident, as it is also, in the composition, types, and drapery, of his *Virgin Enthroned and Saints* (1483) at Siena, while the fresco *Virgin of Mercy* (1481), Monte dei Paschi (Palazzo Salimbeni), Siena, reflects his teacher Vecchietta. In the period following this the idyllic quality so freshly presented in his earlier works disappears in a somewhat harsh aridity; his clear colors become opaque. His *Adoration of the Magi* (National Gallery, Washington), painted about 1470, sparkles with gold, lapis lazuli, and a clear vermilion; in it he represents with great charm a procession in contemporary Sienese dress. His *Madonna with St. Jerome and St. Bernardino* is also in the National Gallery, Washington. A late work, *The Assumption of the Virgin,* signed and dated (1498), is in the Metropolitan Museum, New York. Much of his painting is in the Pinacoteca, churches, and public buildings of Siena. Other works include *The Slaughter of the Innocents* (Aix); a triptych, *The Virgin and Child with SS. Peter and Nicholas,* signed and dated (1478), and *The Virgin and Child* (National Gallery, London); a predella panel (National Gallery of Umbria, Perugia), another at Bolsena (S. Cristina); a fresco at Asciano (SS. Fabiano e Sebastiano); and paintings at Baltimore (Walters Art Gallery); Boston; Cambridge, Massachusetts; Detroit; Kansas City, Missouri; Los Angeles; Minneapolis; New Haven; Raleigh, North Carolina; and elsewhere.

Benvenuto da Imola (dä ē′mō-lä). [Also **Benvenuto de' Rambaldi;** Latinized, **Beneventus de Rambaldis.**] Humanist; b. at Imola, c1336; d. at Ferrara, June 16, 1390. Now considered to have been the most important early commentator on Dante. In 1365 he was sent to Avignon as ambassador to Pope Urban V from Imola, and in 1367 he went to Bologna where he taught grammar until 1376. In the latter year he left Bologna, owing to some unpleasantness, and went to

Ferrara. There, under the protection of the lord of Ferrara, he continued teaching. He was acquainted with Petrarch and Boccaccio, who jointly served as the main guide to his thought for the rest of his life. Florence established a lectureship on Dante, and Boccaccio, who was the first to hold it, read and expounded on the *Divina Commedia* in the little Church of Santo Stefano del Populo near Florence, in 1373. Benvenuto heard some of the readings and took notes on the exposition. His interest in Dante was clearly evidenced by the completion, in 1373, of a first draft of his elaborate *Commentum* (*Commentary*). His was the most learned early commentary, and has remained important in all later discussions of Dante's work; moreover, such a piece of writing is bound to be as encyclopedic as Dante himself, and hence Benvenuto's commentary has come to be also an important source of information about 14th-century thought. Indeed it contains information of interest even to historians of science. Important and unexpected is a discussion of probabilities in connection with *Purgatorio*, vi, which constitutes the earliest mention of probabilities in world literature. It concerns the throwing of three dice: the lowest and highest throws (3 and 18) can occur in only one way, and this is true (according to Benvenuto) also of the next to the lowest and highest (4 and 17), which can occur only in the combinations (1-1-2) and (6-6-5). This latter is incorrect to the extent that it does not distinguish between permutations and combinations: there are actually three ways (1-1-2, 1-2-1, and 2-1-1) of throwing the next to the highest and lowest, and the permutations are what count here. However, the comment remains extremely interesting and important in its early recognition of what was later to develop as a point of major scientific importance. Moreover, his study of the ancient writers, his Latin commentaries on them, and his own works in Latin, including a history of Rome from its founding to the time of Diocletian, greatly contributed to the revival of interest in ancient literature, especially in Ferrara.

Benzi (ben′tsē), **Ugo.** Physician; b. at Siena, c1360; d. at Ferrara, 1439. Of a noble Sienese family, he studied philosophy and medicine at Siena, and taught medicine at Siena, Bologna, Parma, Pavia, and Paris, where he was physician to the king of France. He was physician to Niccolò III d'Este at Ferrara, and his best known work was probably dedicated to Niccolò. It was a book of instructions and advice on personal hygiene, *Tractato utilissimo circa la conservazione della sanitade*. It was one of the earliest medical texts in the vernacular, and after its first printing (Milan, 1481) was reprinted many times.

Benzo d'Alessandria (ben′tsō dä-les-sän′drē-ä). [Also, **Benzo Cona**; Latinized, **Bencius Alexandricus.**] Historian and humanist; b. at Alessandria, in Piedmont, in the second half of the 13th century; d. at Verona, c1335. He was a notary, studied in Milan, and became chancellor to the bishop of Como (1312–1322) and to the ruling family of Verona (1325–1335). He is considered by some scholars to have been, in the matter of humanism, the most genuine Italian forerunner of Petrarch. As chancellor he was one of the first to apply humanistic attitudes and thought to political affairs. He traveled widely in northern and central Italy, and in his travels collected facts of historical or literary interest. The great mass of material he thus gathered was assembled in his *Chronicon*, a kind of encyclopedia, in three volumes. This work, of which only the first part is still extant, was based upon a great variety of classical and medieval sources, and reveals the painstaking care of a researcher and archivist in some ways far ahead of his time. Benzo anticipated Petrarch, Aurispa, and Poggio in his search for ancient manuscripts.

Benzoni (ben-dzō′nē), **Gerolamo.** Traveler; b. at Milan, 1519; d. sometime after 1566. As a youth he went to France, Spain, and Germany on business for his father, and acquired a taste for travel. In 1541 he decided to travel to the New World, of which such marvellous tales were told. His journeys thither, with various Spanish expeditions, took him to Puerto Rico, Haiti, Cuba, across the Isthmus of Panama, and up the Pacific coast of Guatemala, and along the coasts and inland in Peru. He covered most of the area then known, and sometimes joined the Spaniards in their raids on the Indians. He is last heard of in Seville, in 1565, after which date no more is known of him. He wrote of his travels in *Historia del nuovo mundo*, which is of great interest as an autobiography and for the freedom with which he commented on Spanish colonization. The weakness of the work is that it is based in generous measure on reports by earlier travelers.

Beolco (bā-ōl'kō), **Angelo.** See **Ruzzante, Il.**

Beoni (bā-ō'nē), **I.** [English, **The Drinkers.**] Poem in terza rima by Lorenzo de' Medici. With ribald and original humor, joined to realistic details, it describes the broaching of a cask of wine and a paradise for drinkers in a parody of the *Divine Comedy*.

Bergamasco (ber-gä-mäs'kō), **Il.** See **Castello, Giambattista.**

Bergognone (ber-gō-nyō'nā), **Ambrogio.** [Original name **Ambrogio di Stefano da Fossano;** called **Bergognone** or **Borgognone.**] Lombard painter; b. probably between 1450 and 1460; d. 1523. A follower, rather than a pupil, of Vincenzo Foppa, he was called by Berenson the "most remarkable painter of the whole Milanese land." In any event, he was, with Foppa, the outstanding representative of Lombard painting until Leonardo introduced new forms and principles to it. The first notice of Bergognone is of 1481, when he matriculated in the Painters' Guild at Milan. From this time until his death certain dates exist for his artistic activity. Between 1488 and 1494 he was working in the Certosa at Pavia; in 1495 he was at Milan, where he painted frescoes, fragments of which are now in the Brera, in the Church of S. Satiro; from 1498 to 1500 he painted in the Church of the Incoronata at Lodi; in 1514 he was again at Pavia, and finally at Milan. The last date certainly known is 1522, in which year he signed and dated an altarpiece, now in the Brera. His manner of painting, although it did not develop greatly, may be divided into two periods. In the earlier period, to about 1495, he followed Foppa's use of ashy color for flesh tones. His heads, hair, and figures have a distinctly northern aspect, as *The Virgin with the Carthusian* and *The Virgin and Child with Angels*, both in the Brera, and *The Virgin Enthroned and Saints*, Ambrosiana, Milan. Other works in this manner are those in the Certosa at Pavia, a *Christ Carrying the Cross*, at Pavia, and a number of little paintings, now scattered in various collections, that he made for monastic cells, of which the aforementioned *Virgin with a Carthusian* is one and others are *Virgin of the Veil*, also in the Brera, and *Virgin and Child*, in the National Gallery, London. After about 1495 his flesh tones become warmer and the atmosphere seems less coldly ascetic. Examples from this period are a *Baptism* (1496) at Melegnano, and the altarpieces for the Church of the Incoronata at Lodi. The warmth of coloring and a sense of humanity appear also in his late works, as the frescoes in the apse of S. Simpliciano, Milan, with *The Coronation of the Virgin*. In the last years of his life Bergognone was strongly attracted by the work of Leonardo and made some attempts to adapt his own without fully understanding Leonardo's purposes and principles, and thus rather spoiled his own spontaneous and pleasing artistic approach without succeeding at all in attaining to Leonardo's. On the whole, however, there is little influence of Leonardo in his work. Other extant works, besides those mentioned, are several in the Poldi Pezzoli Museum at Milan; a number in the Carrara Academy at Bergamo, including some panels of saints—*St. John the Evangelist, St. Martha, St. Jerome*—that may be from the same polyptych as the panel of *Mary Magdalene* in the Johnson Collection at Philadelphia; several in the National Gallery, London; *The Assumption of the Virgin* and *The Twelve Apostles* in the Metropolitan Museum, New York, and paintings at Amsterdam; Basel; Budapest; Cologne; Paris; Athens, Georgia; Bridgeport, Connecticut; Philadelphia (Johnson Collection); Washington; Williamstown, Massachusetts; and elsewhere.

Bergognone, Bernardino. Lombard painter; active 1492–1523. He was a younger brother of Ambrogio Bergognone (1450/1460–1523), and assisted him in painting the mural decorations of the Certosa of Pavia. He also worked with him on the frescoes in the Church of the Incoronata at Lodi. The only work certainly known to be from his hand is a signed and dated (1523) *S. Rocco* in the Brera, Milan. Others of his works may be confused with those of Ambrogio.

Berlinghieri (ber-lēng-gyā'rē), **Francesco.** Humanist and geographer; b. at Florence, September 17, 1440; d. February 17, 1500. He was a pupil of Argyropoulos and Cristoforo Landino at Florence, was a friend of Lorenzo de' Medici, and a member of the group of men of letters and humanists called the Platonic Academy. Little else is known of his life. He wrote a version of Ptolemy's

Geography in terza rima that contained, among its maps, the earliest modern maps of Italy, Spain, and France. The oldest copy of this rare work is one on parchment in the Brera at Milan.

Bernabeo (ber-nä-bā′ō), **Tommaso di Arcangelo di.** See **Papacello, il.**

Bernard Délicieux (ber-nȧr dā-lē-syė). [Latinized **Bernardus Deliciosus.**] French ecclesiastic; b. at Montpellier, France, in the latter half of the 13th century; d. 1320. He was a Franciscan who became an opponent of the methods of the Inquisition. After the death of Pope Clement V, who tried vainly to repress the inquisitors, Bernard was imprisoned, tried, and twice tortured.

Bernardes (bėr-när′dēsh), **Diogo.** [Full name, **Diogo Bernardes Pimenta.**] Portuguese poet; b. at Ponte de Lima, Portugal, c1530; d. c1605. He became one of the most productive poets of the Renaissance in Portugal. His best known books are *Varias Rimas ao Bom Jesús*, 1594; *O Lima*, 1596, and *Rimas Varias; Flores do Lima*, 1596.

Bernard of Treviso (bėr-närd′, trā-vē′zō). [Assumed title, Count of the **March of Treviso.**] Italian alchemist; b. at Padua, 1406; d. 1490. After many years of study and experiment, he is said to have declared that the secret of the philosopher's stone lay in the adage "To make gold one must have gold." He was the author of many works on alchemy.

Bernardino de' Conti (ber-när-dē′nō dā kôn′tē). See **Conti, Bernardino de'.**

Bernardino da Feltre (dä fel′trā). [Original name, **Martino Tomitano;** called **il Piccolo,** because of his short stature.] Franciscan preacher; b. at Feltre, 1439; d. at Pavia, September 28, 1494. His mother was a cousin of the celebrated teacher Vittorino da Feltre. Martino studied at Padua and took the habit of the Friars Minor there (1456). It was at that time that he took the name Bernardino. Ordained at Mantua (1463), he afterward became a powerful preacher whose understanding of the needs of his congregations and clear appeals to their consciences gave him great power over his hearers. On this account he was respected and feared by those who disagreed with his ideas of reform. He preached throughout northern and central Italy. He was one of those who promoted the institution of the *Monte di pietà*, a means by which the poorest could borrow money, at low interest rates and on pledge of various goods, and thus escape falling into the hands of the ruinous usurers. The first *Monte* he established (1484) was at Mantua; altogether he set up about thirty of these establishments. For his influence on the masses, his power over them, and his good works, he was attacked and persecuted, especially by usurious bankers, and was compelled to flee Florence (1488), to which he returned in 1493 but only under strict conditions. A few of his sermons on the Christian life are extant. He is the patron of pawnbrokers.

Bernardino di Mariotto (dē mä-ryôt′tō). Umbrian painter; b. at Perugia, c1478; d. there, 1566. His work was marked by a certain hardness of drawing and by a highly polished finish, characteristics that he may have learned from his teacher, Ludovico di Angelo. His work reflects, but always with indifferent success, the influences successively of the Crivelli, Pinturicchio, Signorelli, and Raphael. Among his best works are *Madonna of Help* (1509), in the Cathedral of S. Severino; *Madonna and Saints* (1512), in the Church of S. Domenico; an *Annunciation* and two smaller paintings (1514) in the art gallery, all at S. Severino, where he worked from 1502 to 1521. Other works include a *Pietà* in the Carrara Academy at Bergamo and another in the Johnson Collection, Philadelphia; several paintings, including *The Mystic Marriage of St. Catherine* and *Coronation of the Virgin*, at the National Gallery of Umbria, Perugia; *St. Andrew and St. Lawrence*, at Palazzo Venezia, Rome; a *Virgin and Child* in the Vatican, another in the Museum of Fine Arts, Boston; and paintings at Foligno, Gualdo Tadino, Venice (Ca' d'Oro), Altenburg, Baltimore (Walters Art Gallery), Cambridge, Massachusetts, and elsewhere.

Bernardino of Siena (sye′nä), Saint. Franciscan monk, famous as a preacher; b. at Massa Maritima, September 8, 1380; d. at Aquila, in the Abruzzi, May 20, 1444. Orphaned by the age of 6, he was cared for by an aunt until the age of 11, when he was sent to relatives in Siena. There he pursued his studies in the humanities and philosophy, and there he continued his education with the study of canon law. He was an enthusiastic student of the classics, as well as of the Scriptures and theology. He also devoted himself to good works, and ministered to those ill of the plague (1400) in Siena until he himself was stricken. From youth he had a strong religious inclination, and after a severe illness and a prophetic dream, he gave away part of his possessions to religious organizations and the rest to the poor, and entered the Friars Minor (1402). He was ordained in 1404 and began to preach in 1405. He continued preaching until his death. He was an enormously successful preacher. Wherever he went such crowds gathered to hear him that they could not be accommodated in churches, and he preached in the open air, sometimes to crowds that were said to have numbered as great as 30,000. The aim of his sermons was to inspire a renewed spirit of religion in his audiences, rather than to criticize or point up the weakness in the clergy or the Church. The subjects of the sermons were those of most interest to his audiences. He spoke with perfect clarity, in language readily intelligible to the simple people who heard him, gave homely examples and down-to-earth illustrations of his points, was frequently gay, and always eloquent. The future Pope Pius II heard him as a youth and listened to him "as to another St. Paul." In the early years of his apostolate he preached to the peasants in the countryside about Siena. Later, his missions took him all over Italy, as he sought to reawaken a sense of the Christian life and virtue. Wherever he went he instituted reforms in the convents of his order, composed quarrels, sought to heal factions and to restore peace. His character, his formidable knowledge of the Church fathers, his humor, and his piety made him welcome in all areas, as a preacher and a teacher, and his influence extended to high places: Pope Eugenius IV and Emperor Sigismund were among those who consulted him. St. Bernardino revered and promoted devotion to the Holy Name. To replace what he considered superstitious symbols, he devised a symbol. It consisted of the lower-case Gothic letters "yhs" surrounded by a sunburst whose rays had a mystical significance. He is represented in many paintings holding the symbol in his right hand. His zeal in promoting devotion to the Holy Name was most effective and the cult spread rapidly. In fact, St. Bernardino was accused by some of raising a new superstition in place of an old one. He was criticized by some on the ground that his devotion to the Holy Name seemed to indicate a lack of respect for the Trinity and to place too much emphasis on the human aspect of Christ. Charges were brought against him, but his own saintly life, manifest piety, and orthodoxy of doctrine won for him vindication from two popes: Martin V and Eugenius IV. Most of his sermons were edited by St. Bernardino himself; the forty-five he preached to enormous crowds in the Campo at Siena (1427) were recorded by a Sienese clothcutter. (Two paintings by Sano di Pietro, 1406–1481, of the saint preaching, in the Campo and in front of S. Francesco at Siena, are in the Chapter Room of the Duomo at Siena. These are only two of the many representations of the saint.) In addition to the sermons, left for the help and guidance of others, he left treatises on theological matters. He was on his way to preach in the kingdom of Naples when he fell ill of a fever and died. He was given a magnificent funeral and was buried in the Church of S. Francesco at Aquila, but his body was later removed to a basilica especially erected for it. Many miracles were attributed to him after his death. He was canonized by Pope Nicholas V on May 24, 1450.

Bernardo Daddi (ber-när′dō däd′dē). See **Daddi, Bernardo.**

Bernardo Nello di Giovanni Falconi (nel′lō dē jō-vän′nē fäl-kō′nē). See **Nello, Bernardo, di Giovanni Falconi.**

Berni (ber′nē), **Francesco.** Poet; b. at Lamporecchio, in Valdinievole, 1497/1498; d. at Florence, May 26, 1535. Of a Florentine family, he passed his first twenty years in that city. His patrons included his relative, Cardinal Bibiena, and other Church notables, with one of whom he was in Rome when the city was sacked (1527). Cardinal Ippolito de' Medici, whose service he entered in 1532, gave him a canonry. Berni is thought to have died of poison, administered to him by Cardinal Cibo because he refused to sanction the poisoning of Cardinal Giovanni Salviati.

Berni moved in the highest circles, and enjoyed it. His blithesome spirit took accurate note of the weaknesses and defects of the society in which he moved, and recorded them with bright-eyed mockery. He wrote facile, swift, often keen Latin verse, a stage piece, *La Catrina* (one of the last imitations of Lorenzo de' Medici's rustic *La Nencia da Barberino*), a dialogue against poetasters, and some Italian verse. His fame rests on his witty verses—sonnets and *capitoli* (a form for burlesque verse that he perfected and made traditional)—and on his reworking of Boiardo's *Orlando Innamorato*. As regards this last, it is not thought that Berni meant to plagiarize (there was no effort to disguise the origin of his work) or to parody. His aims seem to have been to purify the language of its regionalisms and dialect, to render it in a pure and limpid Tuscan, to smooth out awkwardnesses of phrasing and diction, and to give a lighter touch to what he considered (as did others) Boiardo's too serious approach to honor, love, and courtesy in his vision of chivalry. That his changes erased the freshness and impact of Boiardo's language, and altered his tone and his sincere conception, does not seem to have occurred to Berni. The poem had been criticized for its inelegant language and eclipsed by Ariosto's continuation in the *Orlando Furioso*. Berni set out to polish it up and to raise it to the standard of elegance and style admired in his time. He also introduced interludes and prefaces to the cantos that were strictly his own, but did not tamper with the plot itself. In his jocose and witty verse, Berni was the spiritual heir of Luigi Pulci and Burchiello. His sonnets direct their fire against his enemies, especially against Aretino, and against the debauchery and gluttony of the clergy. He takes gleeful aim at the vacillations and defects of Clement VII, and caricatures poets who too ardently worship (and imitate) Petrarch. He delights to treat with grave and exaggerated dignity the most trivial subjects. He is merry, brutal, or sentimental, but the overriding effect is of gaiety—a joyous and clear-eyed look at the world and its manifest imperfections and follies. His tone of "light and elegant mockery" is the source of the descriptive adjective "bernesque."

Beroaldo (bā-rō-äl′dō), **Filippo.** [Called **the Elder.**] Humanist; b. at Bologna, November 7, 1453; d. there, July 17, 1505. He began teaching rhetoric and poetry at Bologna (1472), later taught at Parma and Paris, and returned to Bologna in 1478. There he resumed his teaching and held high office in the state. Among the great quantity of writings he produced the best are his commentaries on Latin authors—Pliny, Propertius, Apuleius, who was his favorite—in which he pointed out peculiarities of style and grammar, suggested corrections to the text and, in his comparisons and conclusions, cited scores of Greek and Latin writers. In his commentaries, Beroaldo, to rest the reader, inserted many comments and details of contemporary life, and items concerning personal matters. His manner of interpolating sections that were, properly speaking, irrelevant, gave rise to a somewhat florid style among his Bolognese followers.

Beroaldo, Filippo. [Called **the Younger**, to distinguish him from his older cousin.] Humanist; b. at Bologna, October, 1, 1472; d. August, 1518. He taught rhetoric at Bologna (1498–1502), then went to Rome where Leo X named him (1516) to the Roman Academy. He wrote Latin odes in the manner of Horace, and a book of epigrams, but he is best remembered for editing the *Annales* of Tacitus (Rome, 1515), from a manuscript discovered in an abbey.

Berto di Giovanni (ber′tō dē jō-vän′nē). Perugian painter; documented from 1488; d. in October, 1529. He was an assistant and pupil of Perugino and became one of the earliest followers of Raphael. He worked mainly at Perugia where, between 1497 and 1501, he painted banners and pennons and in 1499 became chamberlain of his guild. The predella panels he painted (1525) with stories of the Virgin, now in the National Gallery of Umbria at Perugia, were probably part of the altarpiece *Coronation of the Virgin*, in the Vatican. (Raphael was originally commissioned to execute the painting; it was executed after 1523 by Giulio Romano and Francesco Penni.) Other works in the National Gallery of Umbria at Perugia include his *St. John on Patmos* and a *Coronation of the Virgin*.

Bertoldo di Giovanni (ber-tōl′dō dē jō-vän′nē). Florentine sculptor and medalist; b. c1420; d. at the Medici villa at Poggio a Caiano, December 30, 1491. He made reliefs, statuettes, and medals in bronze, and was, according to Vasari, expert at casting his own and others' work. He was a pupil of Donatello, with whom he worked (1460–1470) on the bronze reliefs for the pulpits in S. Lorenzo, in which he was largely responsible for the friezes. This is his earliest known work. From the 1470's he was the friend and artistic adviser of Lorenzo the Magnificent, was in charge of the collections in the Medici villa near S. Marco, and was head of the school that Lorenzo established in his garden for young artists. Michelangelo, as a youth, was one of his pupils. In his naturalism and the realistic expressions of his *Pietà* and *Crucifixion* (both in the Bargello), as well as in several reliefs of the *Madonna*, Bertoldo was a follower of Donatello. Symmetry of composition and a balancing of the motion caused by gestures were personal additions to his style. His use of contrapposto (in which directions of different parts of the figure are in opposition) anticipated and influenced Michelangelo and the 16th-century mannerists, and was increasingly evident in his statuettes. In his reliefs he favored the flattened form derived from Donatello. An exception is his classical *Battle Relief* (Bargello), with its high relief and strongly modeled figures, whose movements are fluid, varied, and rich in contrast. The relief, made for the Medici and still in their palace in Vasari's time, is derived from a Roman sarcophagus in the Camposanto at Pisa, but was not a mere copy, as Bertoldo freely invented new motifs and rearranged and organized the movement in his work. His *Bellerophon and Pegasus,* now at Vienna, has been called "one of the most beautiful small bronzes ever produced" (Pope-Hennessy). To its generally classical style he added his own touch of contrapposto, showing Bellerophon's body twisted, with the shoulders back and the hips forward. The *Bellerophon and Pegasus* and *Crucifixion* are certainly works of Bertoldo. Using these as a standard, other works attributed to him include *Bacchanal of the Cupids* (Bargello); several *Madonnas* (Paris); the statuettes *Apollo* (Bargello), *Hercules on Horseback* (Modena), *Hercules with the Apples of the Hesperides* (Victoria and Albert Museum, London); and a bearded male figure (Frick Collection, New York). A third certain work left by Bertoldo is a signed medal of Mohammed II, with a *Triumph* on the reverse, probably executed about 1480.

Bertucci (ber-töt′chē), **Giacomo.** [Also called **Iacopone da Faenza.**] Painter; b. c1500; d. 1579. He was the son of Giovanni Battista Bertucci (d. 1516), and received his training from his father. According to Vasari, he was a teacher of Taddeo Zuccari. He painted decorations, now scattered, in the dome of S. Vitale at Ravenna. Other works include a *Birth of the Virgin* and a *Crucifixion,* at Faenza.

Bertucci, Giovanni Battista. [Also known as **Giovanni Battista da Faenza.**] Painter; b. at Faenza, probably between 1465 and 1470; d. there, between March 30 and April 6, 1516. He was a member of a family of painters at Faenza, which included his younger brother Gerolamo, whose work cannot be identified as distinct from Giovanni Battista's; two of his sons, Giacomo and Michele; and a grandson, Giovanni Battista the Younger. A painter of the school of the Romagna, he owed the delicate grace of his figures to such Umbrians as Perugino and Pinturicchio, the balance of his composition to Tuscan influence, and his sense of color to Lorenzo Costa; and he blended and adapted these influences to form his own style. Among his works is the signed and dated (1506) polyptych *Madonna and Child Enthroned and Saints,* in the Pinacoteca at Faenza; a lunette, *Coronation of the Virgin* (1508) now in a private collection; *The Virgin and Child in Glory,* the central panel of an altarpiece, and the *Incredulity of St. Thomas,* both in the National Gallery, London; *The Holy Family,* Museum of Fine Arts, Boston; and a *Pietà,* Johnson Collection, Philadelphia; and paintings at Rome (Spada Gallery and Palazzo Venezia), Budapest, Paris (Musée Jacquemart-André), Baltimore (Walters Art Gallery), New Haven, and elsewhere. An *Adoration of the Magi,* at Berlin, was destroyed in World War II.

Besozzo (bā-zôt′tsō), **Michelino Molinari da.** See **Michelino da Besozzo.**

Bessarion (be-sā′ri-ọn), **Basilius** or **Johannes.** Greek scholar, humanist, statesman, and Roman Catholic cardinal; b. at Trebizond, January 2, 1402; d. at Ravenna, November 18, 1472. He contributed largely to the preservation and dissemination of Greek literature, stimulated interest in the Greek language and Greek ideas, and energetically promoted the spread of learning and the study of Plato in 15th-century Italy. As a brilliant youth he had studied at Constantinople, and was at one time a fellow student of Francesco Filelfo. He entered the order of St. Basil in 1423, and in the same year went to the Peloponnesus to study under the Platonic scholar Georgius Gemistus Plethon, with whom he later enjoyed the most cordial relations. His rise in the Greek Church was rapid. By 1438, when he accompanied John VIII Palaeologus to Florence to effect a union of the Greek and Latin churches, he had already become noted for his oratory, his writings, and his ability to compose quarrels. He had become archbishop of Nicaea in 1437. In the Council of Florence, where Pope Eugenius IV met with representatives of the Greek Church, Bessarion was one of the principal speakers for the Greeks and was a supporter of the Latin Church. His persuasive powers, and the learning with which they were informed, were instrumental in securing the convention of union that was signed in 1439. (The union was of brief duration.) Eugenius IV, impressed by his ability, his scholarship, and his purity of spirit, invited him to remain with the Curia and offered him a pension. Bessarion returned to Constantinople briefly, then joined the papal court at Florence. While there he embarked on the study of Latin and Italian. He perfected his knowledge and style in both and became one of the luminaries of humanistic circles. Eugenius made him a cardinal (1439) and he was successively invested with the archbishopric of Sipinto and the bishoprics of Sabina and Tusculum. In 1450 he was sent to Bologna as papal legate. He calmed the turbulent Bolognese and governed them successfully until 1455. In that time he also restored the university, which had fallen into decay, and saw to it that the distinguished professors he secured were properly paid. Around him gathered a small intellectual court. When Nicholas V died (1455), some thought he would be the new pope. However, his opponents in the conclave cited his previous connection with the Greek Church and on this account called him a former heretic. Under Calixtus III he had fewer political and diplomatic missions and more time for his studies. At the same time, as a patriotic Greek and a dedicated ecclesiastic, he was an ardent supporter of Calixtus in his attempts to promote a crusade against the Turks. On the death of Calixtus (1458) it was again thought that he would surely become pope, but his candidacy was unsuccessful for the same reasons as in 1455. Pius II, who succeeded Calixtus, was an outstanding humanist and gave his friendship to the learned Greek. Pius named him protector of the Minorite Order and charged him with carrying out the processes for the canonization of St. Catherine of Siena. He came to enjoy the confidence of Paul II, and Sixtus IV sent him, though he was then old and ill, to France. His mission there (1471) was unsuccessful. He returned to Italy and died in Ravenna.

Cardinal Bessarion was a noted scholar and a friend and patron of scholars. He encouraged Valla to apply the new philological methods in his Biblical studies. Federico da Montefeltro was his good friend, and Bessarion was a frequent student of the Montefeltro library at Urbino. He was in particular the protector of learned Greeks who came to Italy after the fall of Constantinople (1453). His house was a meeting place for some of the most distinguished literary men of his day. He was a notable collector of books and manuscripts, especially of Greek manuscripts that he feared might be lost after the Turkish conquest. Nicholas V had named him visitor of the Greek monasteries in Italy, and it was thus, perhaps, that he found many valuable manuscripts, copied and kept by the monks, but long since neglected. He left his valuable collection of over 700 Greek and Latin manuscripts to the Republic of Venice, which agreed to build a library for them where scholars of all nations could consult them. A part of Bessarion's collection is still to be found in the Library of St. Mark's. He translated Greek works into Latin and wrote many of his own. Of these, the most important is *In Calumniatorem Platonis,* in four books, a defense of Plato. It was written to answer attacks on Plato's philosophy by George of Trebizond (a translator who did some poor work for Nicholas V). He dedicated to Cardinal Cesarini his edition of Xenophon's *Memorabilia,* and to his friend Alfonso of Naples his correction of the medieval version of Aristotle's *Metaphysics.* There is a representation of Cardinal Bessarion, showing him with deep-set, heavy-lidded eyes, lined face and patriarchal beard, in Piero di Cosimo's *The Passage of the Red Sea,* painted for Sixtus IV in the Sistine Chapel.

Béthencourt (bā-tän-kör), **Jean de.** French adventurer; d. c1425. He was the conqueror of the Canary Islands, and later was given the title of seigneur of the Canary Islands.

His exploits are recorded in *Histoire de la premiere descouverte et conqueste des Canaries, faite des l'an 1402 par messire Jean de Béthencourt, escrite du temps mesme par F. Pierre Bontier . . . et Jean le Verrier* (1630).

Betussi (bā-tös'sē), **Giuseppe.** Man of letters; b. at Bassano; d. c1573. He worked at the press of Giolito at Venice, was a friend of Aretino, Doni, and others, and served several noble lords. He left lyrics and letters that appear in various collections. He translated part of the *Aeneid* and some of the Latin works of Boccaccio, and wrote treatises and dialogues on beauty and love, which he equated. His major work was one on love and its effects, *Il Raverta,* which was reprinted many times and had a place of its own among the many treatises and works on love of the 16th century. The love of which Betussi wrote was ideal and philosophical.

Biagio di Antonio (byä'jō dē än-tō'nyō). [Also called **Biagio da Firenze** and **Utili.**] Painter; b. at Florence. He was a follower of Verrocchio and Domenico Ghirlandaio, and worked at Faenza at various times between 1476 and 1515. Though no documented work exists, a number of paintings are attributed to him on stylistic grounds. Among them are a *Madonna and Child* at the Poldi Pezzoli Museum, Milan, and *Pietà* and *Annunciation,* both in the Pinacoteca, Faenza, where there are other works attributed to him. Other paintings are at Fiesole, Ravenna, Rome (where he is thought to have assisted Cosimo Rosselli in the Sistine Chapel), Venice (Ca' d'Oro); and in a number of European museums outside Italy, at São Paulo, Brazil; Allentown, Pennsylvania; Baltimore; Birmingham, Alabama; Cambridge, Massachusetts; New Haven; New York; Johnson Collection in Philadelphia; Princeton; Tulsa; Washington; and elsewhere.

Bianchi (byäng'kē). Political faction that arose in Tuscany c1300 and split the Guelph party. The Guelph family of the Cancellieri at Pistoia having banished the Ghibelline family of the Panciatichi, a struggle for power arose between two distantly related branches of the Cancellieri, who were distinguished from each other by the names of Bianchi and Neri (the Whites and the Blacks). In the period 1296–1300, the two factions became so violent that Florence, in order to bring peace to Pistoia, required that city to banish the whole family of the Cancellieri, but at the same time opened its own gates to them. In Florence the Neri allied themselves with Corso Donati and other violent Guelphs, and the Bianchi with the de' Cerchi and the moderate Guelphs, and subsequently with the Ghibellines. Pope Boniface VIII espoused the party of the Neri, and sent, nominally to bring about a reconciliation, Charles de Valois to Florence in 1301. The Bianchi, who were then in power, supinely allowed Charles to enter the city. He sent the Bianchi, Dante among them, into exile. The Bianchi fled to Ghibelline towns and plotted their return to Florence, but with no effect.

Bianchi. Popular religious movement that sprang up spontaneously in many cities of Italy, in 1399. Its members were mostly from the people but some princes and ecclesiastics joined it. The members were flagellants, wore white robes tied with rope, hoods with two holes for eyes, and had a red cross on their breast. The chief expression of the movement consisted in processions, in which penitence was urged and the call for peace was intoned through the various cities where its membership had sprung up. Sometimes the procession was led by the lord of the city or state, as by Francesco Carrara at Padua, Carlo Malatesta at Rimini, and Niccolò d'Este at Ferrara. In September, 1399, about 120,000 Bianchi marched in solemn procession in Rome, singing songs and hymns, some of which were composed for the occasion. Late in 1399 an outbreak of plague killed many, and the movement waned as fast as it had waxed. It was similar to many fervent outbreaks of religious and penitential enthusiasm that occurred in the 13th, 14th, and 15th centuries in Italy. Chroniclers of the Bianchi were cautious in discussing the miracles allegedly performed at this time. Rather, they took a social view of the benefits brought to the populace by the movement, and showed a historical awareness of the social rather than the supernatural character of the movement.

Bianchi Ferrari (fer-rä'rē), **Francesco.** Modenese painter; b. c1460; d. at Modena, 1510. A careful and correct painter whose work is pervaded by a profound religious spirit, he had a facility for pleasing color and a gift for narrative; he is best known, however, as the teacher of Correggio. He worked often in the service of his native city and its various churches and organizations. His earliest known work is a *Crucifixion*, now in the Estense Gallery at Modena but originally painted for the Church of S. Francesco at Mirandola. It is a work of great dramatic force and indicates his familiarity with the Ferrarese school of painters, especially Ercole de' Roberti. Other works are a *Madonna Enthroned with Her Son and Saints*, at Berlin, and another on the same theme, of softer and more graceful form, in the Church of S. Pietro at Modena; *Christ in the Garden*, National Gallery, Rome; and several frescoes in the cathedral at Modena.

Bianchini (byän-kē'nē), **Giovanni.** [Latinized, **Blanchinius.**] Fifteenth century astronomer; b. either at Ferrara or Bologna and honored in both cities. He was professor of astronomy at Ferrara, and worked out astronomical tables.

Bianco or **Biancho** (byäng'kō), **Andrea.** Venetian cartographer; fl. early in the 15th century. He left a collection of hydrographical charts anterior to the discovery of the Cape of Good Hope and of America. In a chart dated 1436 he shows two islands west of the Azores, named "Antillia" and "De laman Satanaxio," which some scholars have claimed as evidence of a knowledge of the two Americas prior to the voyage of Christopher Columbus.

Bianco (di Santi) da Siena (dē sän'tē dä sye'nä). Religious poet and mystic; b. at Anciolina (Valdarno), c1350; d. at Venice(?). In his youth he was engaged in the wool trade in Siena. There, about 1367, he became a member of the Gesuati, a lay order founded by Giovanni Colombini, and became one of its outstanding members. He wrote many *laude* (hymns) and has been compared, in his mystic fervor and in his description of the physical pangs of his longing for God, to Jacopone da Todi. He wandered about central Italy, composing and singing his hymns, and toward the end of his life went to Venice, where he probably died.

Bibbiena (bēb-byā'nä) or **Bibiena** (bē-). See **Dovizi, Bernardo.**

Bicci di Lorenzo (bēt'chē dē lō-ren'tsō). Florentine painter; b. at Florence, 1373; d. at Arezzo, 1452. He was the son of Lorenzo di Bicci, also a painter, studied and worked with his father, and is often confused with him. Alone or with his many assistants, he painted on panels and in fresco at Florence and in neighboring places: in the Casentino, at Arezzo, Empoli, Pescia, and elsewhere. A *Madonna and Child*, part of an altarpiece from his hand in the National Gallery at Parma, shows strong influence of Gentile da Fabriano and Fra Angelico. Frescoes by him are to be found in the churches of S. Francesco and S. Antonio at Pescia. At Empoli is a triptych, *Crucifixion, Virgin and Saints;* a *Marriage of St. Catherine* (there is another at Perugia) and *St. Bernard with a Worshipper* are in the Accademia at Florence; a *Madonna and Child with St. Lawrence and St. John the Baptist* is in the Cannon Collection at Princeton; a *Madonna and Child with Saints* is in the Isabella Stewart Gardner Museum, Boston; and two panels on the story of St. Nicholas, from the predella of an altarpiece painted in 1433, are in the Metropolitan Museum, New York. Other paintings are at Baltimore (Walters Art Gallery), Cambridge, Greenville (South Carolina), Indianapolis, San Francisco, and in a number of museums in Europe. His work was relatively unaffected by the developments taking place in painting in the first half of the 15th century. He was influenced by Gentile da Fabriano and Lorenzo Monaco and the international Gothic style, with its interest in decorative detail, bright color, and sinuous line. His compositions were simple and varied but little, and his attainments were modest—he was an honest craftsman whose job it was to carry out commissions. Death interrupted his most important commission, the decorating of the choir and vault of the Church of S. Francesco at Arezzo. Piero della Francesca was called upon to finish the task, thus giving to Arezzo one of the glories of Renaissance painting.

Bienewitz (bē'ne̤-vits), **Peter.** See **Apianus, Petrus.**

Bigordi (bē-gôr'dē), **Domenico.** Original name of **Ghirlandaio, Domenico.**

Biondo (byōn'dō), **Flavio.** [Also called, **Biondo da Forlì.**] Historian, geographer, and humanist; b. at Forlì, 1392; d. at Rome, June 4, 1463. In their enthusiasm for classical literature and Latin, many humanists Latinized their names. Flavio is Italianized Latin of Flavus, which in its turn is Latin for Biondo. In his youth Biondo studied grammar, rhetoric, and poetry and early acquired a reputation for his learning and wisdom. He performed (1427) official duties for Cardinal Capranica, who was governing Forlì for the Church, and was on the best of terms with that learned ecclesiastic. In 1432 he served as chancellor of the March of Ancona, left for Rome the next year, and was attached to the court of Eugenius IV, to whom he became an apostolic secretary in 1434. When Eugenius was compelled to flee Rome in the same year, Biondo carried out several missions for him, as to Venice and to Francesco Sforza at Milan. Apart from his official duties for the pope, he then devoted himself to study and writing. His great interest was in the history and monuments of ancient Rome. He offended Nicholas V by criticizing the destruction of existing Roman buildings to make way for the new ones Nicholas planned, and had to give up his post. He was restored to papal favor when Pius II ascended the papal throne, accompanied him to Mantua (1459), shared Pius' enthusiasm for visiting historical and archaeological sites, and went with him on many such excursions. He was among those who, vainly, urged the Italian states to unite in the face of the Turkish menace. After the fall of Constantinople (1453) he joined in the call for a holy war against the Turks, again in vain. Although he wrote in Latin, he had great respect and love for the vernacular, and wrote *De verbis romanae locutionis* to expound his thesis that Italian is a direct and natural continuation of Latin. In his historical and geographical works he discarded myths and traditional tales, and studied ancient, medieval, and contemporary documents, inscriptions, and monuments as bases for his works. His *Decadi* is a universal history from the fall of Rome down to his own time. *Roma instaurata*, in three books, dedicated to Eugenius IV (1447, printed at Rome in 1474), is a systematic attempt to reconstruct the topography of Rome and to describe the ancient city. He gathered the material for *Italia illustrata* (1453) in wandering up and down Italy, searching out documents, histories, inscriptions, and so on, and produced a picture of Italy from the Gulf of Salerno to the Alps, with its outstanding monuments and men. *Roma triumphans* (1457–1459), in ten books, was dedicated to Pius II. It is an account of the religious, civil, and military institutions of ancient Rome and the possible links of institutions of his own time to those of the past. Biondo, recognized in his own time as a learned, modest, hardworking man of exemplary life, was a pioneer of the historical method, using documents and concrete witnesses as a basis for his historical works. His method and results had a profound influence on the rest of the Western world of learning.

Biondo, Michelangelo. Physician; b. at Venice, 1497; d. 1565. He practiced medicine at Naples. He advised the application of cold water to cuts and contusions as being more efficacious than some of the medicaments then commonly used which, he said, only retarded healing. He was an outstanding early practitioner of therapeutic surgery. Among his works was a translation into Italian of some of the work of the 4th century B.C. philosopher Theophrastus, medical works that included an epitome of Hippocrates, and a work on the origin of syphilis.

Biondo da Forlì (dä fôrlē′). See **Biondo, Flavio.**

Bird (bėrd), **William.** See **Byrd** or **Byrde** or **Bird, William.**

Bireno (bē-rā′nō). In Lodovico Ariosto's *Orlando Furioso*, the faithless duke of Zealand, lover of Olimpia, whom he abandons on a desert isle. He loses his dominions and is slain by Oberto.

Biringuccio (bē-rēn-göt′chō), **Vannoccio.** Engineer, metallurgist, and mineralogist; b. at Siena, October 20, 1480; d. before April 30, 1539. His father was an engineer and architect employed by the Petrucci family of Siena. The patronage of the Petrucci enabled the son to travel in Italy and Germany to inspect works and methods in those places. Vannoccio was employed by the Petrucci until 1515, when they were driven out of Siena. He visited Rome, Naples, and Sicily, and later became military engineer to the Estense family of Ferrara and then to the Farnese of Parma. In 1538 he became head of the pope's foundry. He had mastered all the practical knowledge of his day as a metallurgist and engineer, and set it all down in an important treatise, *De la pirotechnia* (published at Venice, 1540). The work, sponsored by the pope, the emperor, and the senate of Venice, was in ten books. The topics covered in the ten books included minerals, ores, steel, brass, assaying, smelting, casting, alloys, melting, alchemy, distillation, gold- and silversmithery, and fireworks.

Bissolo (bēs-sō′lō), **Francesco.** Painter; b.

Francesco Bissolo
St. Helena between SS. Lawrence and Dominic
Courtesy of The Pierpont Morgan Library, New York

probably at Treviso, c1470; d. at Venice, April 20, 1554. He was a rather pedestrian follower of Giovanni Bellini, whom he assisted (1492) in painting the walls of the Hall of the Great Council in the Ducal Palace at Venice. His paintings include *Madonna Enthroned and Saints* (1516) on the island of Lagosta; an altarpiece (1528), Church of S. Andrea, Treviso; *The Baptist and Two Saints*, Cathedral of Treviso; a triptych with *St. Martin, St. Andrew, and St. Jerome*, S. Giovanni in Bragora, Venice; *Circumcision*, Verona; *Virgin and Child*, National Gallery, London; and works at Cremona, Genoa (SS. Annunziata), Milan (Castello Sforzesco), Padua, Rovigo, Berlin, Düsseldorf, Leipzig, Toledo, Ohio, and elsewhere.

Bittino or **Bitino da Faenza** (bē-tē′nō dä fä-en′dzä). Painter; d. before 1427. Originally from Faenza, he spent most of his life at Rimini. In that city is to be found his one signed work. It is a panel of St. Julian (1409), in which the saint is surrounded by eleven scenes (arranged in three horizontal rows) depicting events in his legend. The little scenes are carefully and appealingly executed. The panel is now in the Church of S. Giuliano at Rimini.

Black Death. In European history, the name given to the epidemic that swept across the world in the middle of the 14th century, one of the most terrible calamities in the recorded annals of mankind. There had been earlier plagues (the earliest one of this nature was almost certainly not the one described by Thucydides as occurring at Athens in the period 430–425 B.C., but there were many outbreaks of disease in Europe during the ten centuries immediately preceding the 14th which were unquestionably of the same type as the Black Death), but the Black Death was enormously more disastrous than any of the others. There can be no doubt as to its nature; it was the true Oriental plague, whether bubonic or pulmonic (indeed, axillary, inguinal, and pulmonary lesions were witnessed and duly recorded). The Black Death, so far as we can ascertain, began in India in 1332; epidemics occurring in Russia in 1341 and in Styria in 1342 may have been its forerunners in Europe. By the latter part of 1347 it had progressed, via Constantinople, as far as Sicily, Naples, and Genoa. Venice was visited by the pestilence early in 1348, and from that great commercial center it spread rapidly. Boccaccio, who drew on earlier literary sources describing plague, gives a vivid description of the Black Death at Florence in the *Decameron*. It reached its climax in central Europe and England in 1349, and in Russia in 1352 (which was a recurrence, if the epidemic of 1341 had been, indeed, the Black Death). The climax in each region lasted from about four to six months. If it broke out during the winter, it assumed the pulmonic form, and kept it or became the bubonic type in the spring. We now know that the disease was spread by fleas and rats, but nobody suspected that at the time, and the prophylactic measures were therefore irrelevant (except insofar as cleanliness tended to keep down every sort of parasite, and segregation restricted contagion). It was called the Black Death or Black Plague because of the dark color of the body after death. It is impossible to estimate with any precision how many people were its victims, although some have thought that a quarter of the population of the civilized world was wiped out. In any case, it had enormous social, political, moral, and religious impact. For example, probably because they were more subject to the presence of rats than the wealthy and powerful, there was a very high incidence of deaths among the poor, and this led to a shortage of labor which, in turn, gave rise in all probability to an atmosphere more favorable to the laborer than had ever before been possible, and also led to some political demands. The impact on religion was two-edged. Some, appalled at the speed with which the plague could strike and cut short their lives, abandoned religion and morality, and gave themselves up to snatching what pleasure they could while life lasted. To others, the Black Death appeared as a punishment from heaven for the sins of mankind; these turned ever more devoutly to religion and an austere life, and called on their contemporaries to repent. Its effect on art and literature, while temporary, was nevertheless deeply felt.

Black Prince, The. See **Edward** (1330–1376).

Blanche of Bourbon (blanch, bör′bo̤n). French princess; b. c1338; d. at Medina Sidonia, Spain, 1361. She was the daughter of Pierre, Duc de Bourbon, and wife of Pedro of Castile (Pedro the Cruel), by whom she was abandoned shortly after the marriage on a charge of infidelity, and imprisoned. Her death was ascribed to poisoning. Her fate produced a profound impression, and has furnished the subject matter for a number of poems.

Blasius of Parma (blā'zhus, pär'mä). See **Pelacani, Biagio.**

Blondus (blon'dus) **of Forlì.** See **Biondo, Flavio.**

Blount (blunt), **William.** [Title, 4th Baron **Mountjoy.**] English nobleman and patron of learning; d. in Staffordshire, England, 1534. He studied (c1496) at Paris under Erasmus and brought (1498) the noted humanist to England. An intimate of Henry Tudor, later Henry VIII of England, he fought against Perkin Warbeck (pretender to the English crown) in 1497, was bailiff of Tournai (1514–1517), and served as an attendant of Henry VIII at the meeting of the Field of the Cloth of Gold (1520) and at a meeting with Charles V at Dover (1522). Erasmus lamented his patron's death in his dedications to *Ecclesiastes* (1535) and to *Adagia* (1536 edition).

Boateri (bō-ä-tā'rē), **Iacopo.** Bolognese painter; b. c1480; d. c1530. He was one of the many pupils of Francesco Francia and devoted himself to a mediocre imitation of his master. A signed painting, *The Holy Family*, in the Pitti Palace at Florence, serves as a point of reference by which other works are attributed to him. Among them are a *Madonna and Child and St. Jerome*, in the Vatican; *Holy Family*, at Vercelli; and another on the same subject in the Louvre, Paris.

Bobadilla (bō-ʙä-ᴛʜē'lyä), **Francisco de.** Spanish officer; d. probably at sea, July 1, 1502. In 1500, he was sent to Hispaniola, in the West Indies, to investigate the affairs of that colony, and especially to inquire into charges made against Christopher Columbus, whom he succeeded (1499) as viceroy of the Indies. On his arrival (August 23, 1500) at Santo Domingo, he summoned Columbus before him, imprisoned him and his brothers, and sent them to Spain. Bobadilla remained a governor of the colony until the arrival of Nicolás de Ovando, on April 15, 1502, when he was himself sent under arrest to Spain.

Boccaccino (bō-kä-chē'nō), **Boccaccio.** Painter; b. at Ferrara, c1467; d. at Cremona, between January 24, 1524, and December 26, 1525. He had rather a stormy life. His early artistic education probably began at Ferrara under Ercole Grandi and Ercole de' Roberti, but the lasting influence on his development occurred at Venice, where he was inspired by the Bellini, the Vivarini, Giorgione, and, especially, Cima da Conegliano. He worked at Genoa and Cremona and by 1497 was already noted as a painter. In that year he was at Milan and was imprisoned, but was freed through the good offices of the Ferrarese ambassador. The latter took him into his home and then sent him back to Ferrara with a letter of recommendation to Duke Ercole I. Ercole welcomed him and put him to work, with others, at decorating the cathedral. For some reason, perhaps because he was accused of killing an adulterous wife, his stay at Ferrara was brief. He left there soon after 1500. In 1505, his second wife having died, he was at Cremona decorating the apse of the cathedral. In 1510 he took a third wife and settled down at Cremona permanently. From 1515 to 1519 he was painting frescoes in the cathedral, along with a number of other artists. Boccaccino's work is deeply influenced by the Ferrarese school, to which was added the influence of the Venetian painters. From the time of his earliest work, as *The Road to Calvary* (National Gallery, London), the Ferrarese influence is apparent, and in successive works that of Venice appears. In his signed masterpiece, *The Marriage of St. Catherine* (Accademia, Venice), the influence of Cima da Conegliano is felt in the exquisite, glittering, enamel-like painting. Other works are *La Zingarella,* a delicate work with Venetian coloring (Uffizi); *Annunciation,* in a private collection (Rome); *Virgin and Child* (Museum of Fine Arts, Boston); *Madonna and Child* (the Metropolitan Museum, New York), as well as paintings at Milan (Brera), Modena, Naples, Padua, Rome (Doria-Pamphili Gallery), Vicenza, Hamburg, Leningrad, Munich, Paris, Vienna, Oneonta, New York (Hartwick College), and the series of frescoes at Cremona. This series in the cathedral at Cremona, portraying episodes from the lives of the Virgin and of Christ, with the series of frescoes executed in collaboration with Romanino and Pordenone, forms one of the more important pictorial cycles of the Italian Renaissance. Not gifted with unusual originality, Boccaccino yet had a significant influence on his contemporaries; he had an important role in the development of the Cremonese school of painters that began with Galeazzo Campi and that had its effects on Lombard, Venetian, and Ferrarese painting.

Boccaccino, Camillo. Painter; b. 1501; d. at Cremona, 1546. He was the son of Boccaccio Boccaccino (c1467–1524/1525) and worked for a time with his father. In 1522 he went to Parma to work with Correggio, whose influence on his development was lasting. Two years later he returned to Cremona, and in 1532 painted four pictures now in the Brera, Milan. They were originally painted for the Church of S. Bartolomeo at Cremona. At Cremona he painted in the cathedral and in the Church of S. Sigismondo.

Boccaccio (bōk-kät′chō), **Giovanni.** Author, humanist, and poet; b. at Paris, 1313; d. at Certaldo, near Florence, December 31, 1375. He was the natural son of a wealthy Florentine merchant and a French mother. Brought as a child to Florence by his father, he spent his childhood in or near Florence. About 1328, when he was 15, his father sent him to Naples to learn to become a merchant. Moved as he was by a great love for learning and literature, he worked desultorily and much against his will at the merchant business. His great desire was to devote his life to study and writing. His father finally yielded to his wishes, on the condition that he study canon law. The latter had no more attraction for young Boccaccio than had business. Naples, the center of King Robert's court, was a city of active life, rich, cheerful, and gay, and Boccaccio seems to have entered wholeheartedly into the pleasures offered by the city. Like many other poets, he had one great love, in his case for Maria d'Aquino, the natural daughter of King Robert, and wife of a Neapolitan nobleman. As did Dante and Petrarch, he first saw his love in church. To her he gave the name Fiammetta in his imaginative writing. For Boccaccio it was a real enough love affair, in which Fiammetta yielded to his desires fairly soon, but she proved inconstant and as unfaithful to her lover as she had been to her husband. This affair with Fiammetta is usually ascribed to the middle 1330's. From this Neapolitan period and that immediately following date all of his early work in Italian. They describe his love and his anguish, his jealousy, his disillusionment, and his bitterness. During the 1330's Boccaccio's father was evidently in fairly comfortable financial circumstances, but economic reverses at the end of the decade made it necessary for Boccaccio to return to Florence, and from 1340 onward his permanent base was at that city. Of the works having to do with his love for Fiammetta, *Il Filocolo,* his first long novel, was written to please her. His early lyrics as well as his two long poems in ottava rima (which he was the first to use)—the *Filostrato,* on the story of Troilus and Cressida, and the *Teseida,* modeled on the *Aeneid* (both of which were later to be used freely as sources by Geoffrey Chaucer)—make use of his early experience of love: "polite," "courtly," and otherwise. The same source is used for his *Elegy of Madonna Fiammetta,* the *Ameto,* and the *Amorosa Visione.* The last-named is an allegorical treatment of a series of lovers from history and legend. Some of these works were finished at Florence, shortly after his recall from Naples. All are intensely personal and concern, in one guise or another, his love for Fiammetta. The *Elegy of Madonna Fiammetta* differs from the others in that in this case she is supposedly telling the story, and here she is the one who has been abandoned and grieves.

Little is known of Boccaccio's life in the 1340's, and nearly all that can be said is that he lived in obscurity and apparently in considerable want and discomfort. He seems to have traveled at least somewhat in central Italy in this decade, and more in the 1350's. He became a fervent admirer of Petrarch, whose works he had read. When Petrarch passed through Florence in 1350 he stayed with Boccaccio, and they became good friends. Boccaccio became his humble but ardent disciple, engaged in correspondence with him, and copied out Dante's *Divina Commedia* with his own hand for the poet. (In his will, Petrarch left Boccaccio fifty gold florins for a warm gown to wear "when he is studying or meditating on winter nights.") Perhaps it was owing to Petrarch's influence that he abandoned his writings in the vernacular, his true creative efforts, and, with increasing study of the classics, began his Latin writings. In the 1350's Boccaccio began to emerge from obscurity, and was sent on several occasions as Florentine ambassador to Avignon and Ravenna. It is doubtful whether he was in Florence in 1348, when the Black Death reached that city, although he graphically describes its effects in the introduction to the *Decameron.* During this time, he was gradually turning away from his youthful dissipations to a more serious and ascetically inclined attitude. He became preoccupied with religion and the state of his soul. A prophecy made to him by a monk concerning his study of pagan writers frightened him, and he decided to sell his library. He offered it to Petrarch, explaining his reasons for wishing to sell. Petrarch reacted mildly, advised him that the study of the ancients was compatible with the Christian religion, thanked him for offering the library to him first, and added that since Boccaccio had put no price on it he could not conclude a purchase. Petrarch's letter calmed Boccaccio and lulled his doubts, and no more was heard of the matter of selling the library. Boccaccio never married; his youthful experiences had given him an antipathy toward marriage and toward the female sex in general, which found its expression especially in the *Corbaccio,* written 1354–1355, a scathing satire on women and their ways and an invective against love. In his mature years, Boccaccio devoted more and more time to the study of the Latin classics and of Dante. He wrote the first life of Dante, one of the earliest attempts to give a portrait of a man and not just an accumulation of facts about him. In his old age he took up the study of Greek, for which he succeeded in having a chair established at the University (Studio) of Florence. Because Petrarch had a copy of Homer in Greek that he could not read, Boccaccio had a translation into Latin made for him by Leonzio Pilato. Pilato was a Calabrian Greek of mediocre accomplishments and not a very good translator, and since he also occupied the chair of Greek at the university, Boccaccio's efforts in this direction were not completely successful.

Despite increasing recognition, Boccaccio's financial position remained precarious, and he apparently entertained hopes of returning to a happier situation at Naples. Finally, in 1362, he did return, hoping to find a home with a former friend who had risen to the position of grand seneschal to the king of Naples. However, Boccaccio was treated as a mere mendicant and hanger-on, and soon returned, in disgust, to Florence. In following years he took further trips, to visit Petrarch at Venice in 1367, and again to Naples in 1370–1371. His poor financial position eventually excited some degree of public sympathy and a willingness to help him, and he was granted a professorship at Florence in 1373 for the public reading and exposition of Dante. His poor health forced him to end his lectures in 1374, and he died in the following year.

After he returned to Florence from Naples (1340) and finished his works on the story of his love for Fiammetta, Boccaccio turned from that theme. He wrote *Il Ninfale Fiesolano,* a mythological poem concerning the love of two rivers that flow near Florence. The poem exhibits a delight in and love for the countryside near Fiesole (the scene of the garden where the 100 tales of the *Decameron* were told), a new objectivity and a freedom from autobiographical themes pointing to the full maturity of his narrative art that was realized in the *Decameron.* This very famous collection of tales was written, according to most authorities, between 1348 and 1353. His works of erudition in Latin, all compiled in the last years of his life, include *De casibus virorum illustrium,* in nine books, which discusses, through the lives of famous men from the beginning of time to his own age, the turns of fortune that bring great men down; *De claris mulieribus,* a work on a similar theme but applying to famous women; and *De genealogiis deorum gentilium,* a work on mythology, in an appendix to which he defends the study of ancient literature and poetry. His Latin works became widely popular in Europe long before the *Decameron* was known beyond the Alps.

Any estimate of Boccaccio's personality must depend entirely upon what can be deduced from his written works. He must obviously have been a man of considerable intellectual ability, both in the extent of his learning and in his observation of the life of his times. That he had a very keen understanding of human psychology is evident from the tales of the *Decameron.* His nature must have been intensely emotional, as we can tell both from the history of his youth and his earlier works, and from his later ascetic revulsion against his youthful excesses. The inclination on the part of some to regard the bulk of his stories, particularly those in the *Decameron*, as essentially lascivious, if not actually immoral, is surely an error. It was his intent simply to represent the world as it was and, in certain basic respects, as it still is, rather than to concern himself with what might be considered the world that should be. In later life Boccaccio himself seemed to look with regret on this greatest of his creative works. When he learned that a friend had given the *Decameron* to the ladies of his family to read, Boccaccio addressed an anguished letter to him, requesting him not to allow the ladies to sully their minds with that work, and expressing the fear that they would judge him a shameless and foul-mouthed old man. Pius II, the humanist pope and man of letters of the mid-15th century, in discussing illustrious Florentines, listed Boccaccio as one of the three most eminent writers, "though he was a little more frivolous (than Dante and Petrarch) and his style was not highly polished." The three–Dante, Petrarch, and Boccaccio–form a trinity of Italian letters known as "I tre coroni," each with a distinct personality and temperament, and each with distinct gifts that found expression in completely different approaches to life on this earth and beyond it. In his studies, as distinct from his creative work, Boccaccio was essentially a man of the Middle Ages, accepting and assimilating traditional knowledge without broadening its horizon or making new discoveries or interpretations. In his creative work he pictured the ebullient society of his own time, bringing to his tales of it an original, modern approach that set the pattern for many writers of the Renaissance. In bringing new content and new techniques to vernacular literature, he was a man thoroughly aware of his age and a stimulus to those who came after him. See also **Decameron.**

Boccanera (bōk-kä-nā′rä) or **Bocanegra** (bō-kä-nā′grä), **Simone.** The first doge of Genoa; b. c1300; poisoned at Genoa, 1363. He was elected in 1339, abdicated in 1344, and was reelected in 1356.

Boccasini (bō-kä-zē′nē), **Niccolò.** Original name of Pope **Benedict XI.**

Boccati (bō-kä′tē), **Giovanni.** [Original name, **Giovanni di Piermatteo.**] Umbrian painter; b. at Camerino, c1410; d. after 1480. He worked mainly at Perugia, where he obtained citizenship in 1445. His work shows the influence of the Sienese and Florentine schools. Among his several paintings in the National Gallery of Umbria at Perugia is the signed and dated (1447) altarpiece with predella, *Madonna of the Pergola,* which is his oldest surviving work. It shows the influence of the Sienese Domenico di Bartolo. Another altarpiece in the same gallery is his *Madonna of the Orchestra,* so called from the angelic musicians that surround the Virgin's throne. *The Madonna and Child with Angels and Serafim* is in the Uffizi, Florence. Other paintings are at Camerino, Nemi, Rome (Colonna Gallery and Vatican), Tolentino (S. Francesco), Turin (Sabauda Gallery), Venice (Ca' d'Oro), Ajaccio, Budapest, Oberlin, Ohio, Princeton, and elsewhere.

Bocchi (bôk′kē), **Achille.** Humanist; b. at Bologna, 1488; d. there, November 6, 1562. He taught Greek literature, rhetoric, and poetry at the university, and was organist at the cathedral in Bologna. About 1546 he founded the Accademia Bocchiana, one of many literary groups founded in the late 15th and beginning of the 16th century. In connection with his Accademia there was a printing press that issued some fine editions. Bocchi was the friend of Sadoleto, Flaminio, and other leading men of letters of his day. He left Latin verses and other Latin works, including *Apologia in Plautum,* . . . (Bologna, 1508), and *Symbolicarum quaestionum de universo genere* . . . (Bologna, 1555), and letters, dialogues, verses, and a history of Bologna to 1263 (commissioned by the senate of Bologna) that are preserved in manuscript.

Bocksberger (boks′ber-gėr) or **Bocksperger** (boks′per-gėr), **Hans** or **Heironymus.** German painter, b. at Salzburg, Austria, 1540; d. c1600. Noted especially for hunting scenes and battle pictures.

Boece (bō-ēs′) or **Boethius** (bō-ē′thi-us) or **Boetius** (bō-ē′shus), **Hector.** Scottish humanist and historian; b. at Dundee, Scotland, c1465; d. at Aberdeen, Scotland, c1536. His family name was *Boyce* (also spelled *Boys, Bois, Boyis*), *Boyis* being an adaptation of *Boetius*. He studied and later taught at Paris, where he attracted the interest and friendship of Erasmus, and subsequently served as a chief adviser to William Elphinstone, bishop of Aberdeen, in the founding of the University of Aberdeen. He was appointed (c1498) to be the first principal of the university, and is known to have been at the university when lectures were given for the first time in 1500. The work for which he is now best known is a history of Scotland (which had the full title *Scotorum Historiae a prima gentis origine cum aliarum et rerum et gentium illustratione non vulgari*), first published in seventeen books in 1527 (a later edition, published in 1574, contains an eighteenth book and part of a nineteenth). Boece's primary purpose in this work was not to prepare a chronicle of events, but to tell the story of the Scottish people as reflected in their legends (despite the obviousness of which, many historians on the Continent and England used it as a source of what they took to be actual facts. Holinshed took much from it, and thus, coincidentally, provided Shakespeare with the plot for *Macbeth*). During the 16th century the work was twice translated from its original Latin: first into Scottish verse, and later (between 1530 and 1533) by John Bellenden into Scottish prose. An edition of the latter of these versions was last published during the first quarter of the 19th century. Boece also wrote a Latin account of the lives of the Scottish bishop William Elphinstone, of Aberdeen, and the bishop of Mortlack.

Boeheim (bė′hīm), **Martin.** See **Behaim, Martin.**

Boethius (bō-ē′thi-us) or **Boetius** (bō-ē′shus), **Hector.** See **Boece** or **Boethius** or **Boetius, Hector.**

Böheim (bė′hīm), **Martin.** See **Behaim, Martin.**

Boiardo (bō-yär′dō), **Matteo Maria.** [Also, **Bojardo.**] Poet; b. at Scandiano, near Reggio, 1440 or 1441; d. there, in December, 1494. Matteo Maria Boiardo, Count of Scandiano and Lord of Arceto, of an ancient and noble family, nephew of the outstanding humanist Tito Vespasiano Strozzi, is one of the most original, inventive, masculine yet lyrical of the Italian poets of the Renaissance. He went to Ferrara with his mother as a child, and passed his youth and young manhood in court circles. He had a good humanist education, knew Latin and Greek, and studied law and philosophy at Ferrara. Much of his life was spent in the service of the dukes of Modena and Ferrara—Borso, Ercole, and Sigismondo d'Este—to whom he was unswervingly loyal. On behalf of his princes he was one of those who received Emperor Frederick III at Ferrara, 1469, and he later went to Naples to escort Leonora of Aragon, Ercole d'Este's affianced bride, to Ferrara. In 1481 he was named governor of Modena, and remained there until 1487, when he became governor of Reggio. As a governor, he was benevolent, even indulgent, too lenient, according to some of his critics, who said he was better at writing verses than at punishing criminals. His reputation for generosity and helping out his less fortunate neighbors was such that the saying, "May God send a Boiardo to your house," became proverbial in his jurisdiction. His early literary works include translations from the Greek and Latin classical writers; *Carmina*, verses in praise of Ercole d'Este; Latin eclogues in the Vergilian model; madrigals, and other verse. In 1469 he fell in love with Antonia Caprara, and celebrated his love in a series of Petrarchan lyrics, *Amorum libri tres.* (He married Taddea Gonzaga.) His masterpiece is his *Orlando Innamorato* (*Roland in Love*), a chivalric romance now generally recognized as one of the major achievements of Italian literature. It was begun about 1472, interrupted for service in the Venetian war (1482), and afterward worked on until his death. Himself a man of truly noble and knightly character, he grew to maturity in what was perhaps the best place in the Italy of that day for such a nature: the court of Ferrara, where the tradition of feudalism and the true spirit of chivalry had lingered longer than elsewhere in Italy. Both his character and the atmosphere of that court are reflected in the *Orlando Innamorato*, which comes closer, perhaps, to the spirit of medieval chivalry than any other Italian work. In its immediate sources, it is a Carolingian epic, but he reworked the material from these sources in the spirit of the Arthurian romances. The old unity of the Carolingian epic, its nationalistic and religious enthusiasm, has been replaced by a new unity based on the principles of chivalry and courtly love, and the portrayal of its effect on different natures. The work is in three books, of which the third remained unfinished at the time of Boiardo's death (he died just as the French were invading Italy, and the last lines of the poem, which are translated into English as follows, refer in pathetic and prophetic fashion to this: "While I sing, O God our Saviour, I see all Italy set on fire and in flames by these Gauls, who come with great fury, to devastate I know not what region"). As a narrator, Boiardo is extremely able and rich in invention. He developed, to a very high point of excellence, the technique of concurrent narration of several different threads of the action, with skillful use of cutting at high points of suspense and of the flashback to take up an action left off at some previous point. In this way, he keeps several narratives going at once, and maintains the reader's interest in all of them without letting the action flag or become dull. The various adventures and tales are further knit together by interlocking characters and actions, so that each episode has its beginning in previous events of the story, and eventually dissolves into new episodes. The *Orlando Innamorato* strikes an almost perfect balance between merit of narrative technique and interest of content, with good understanding of psychology (according to the conventions of romantic legend) and motivation of action. The one respect in which it is deficient (and to the readers and critics of 15th century Italy it was a most important respect) is that of polished language and style. Boiardo's versification is facile and his words flow easily, but his usage is far from that demanded by Tuscan purism. The modern reader, especially if he has not been brought up in the Italian puristic tradition, finds this unimportant, but Boiardo's 15th century Italian readers placed such great emphasis on it that as soon as Ariosto's *Orlando Furioso* (a continuation of *Orlando Innamorato* which had a diction and style which were acceptably Tuscan) appeared, the *Orlando Innamorato* fell into an undeserved oblivion. The disrepute of Boiardo's work was further increased by the unfortunate distortions it underwent at various times through the efforts of well-intentioned but inept editors to bring it up to the Tuscan purity of Ariosto. However, the discovery in the 19th century of the original manuscript by Boiardo enabled readers once more to evaluate his work without the impediment of intervening bowdlerization, and it may be safely said that Boiardo has now been restored to his proper position as a great poet and teller of stories. See also **Orlando Innamorato.**

Bokenham or **Bokenam** (bok′ẹn-ạm), **Osbern.** English dialect poet and member of the Augustinian order; b. possibly at Bokeham (or Bookham), Surrey, England, October 6, 1393; d. c1447. He was the author of a collection of thirteen poems dedicated to twelve holy women and the 11,000 virgins. He was familiar with Latin and Greek authors, and was influenced by Chaucer and John Lydgate. His work is important as an example of 15th century Suffolk dialect.

Bologna (bō-lō′nyä), **Andrea da.** See **Andrea da Bologna.**

Bologna, Giovanni da. See **Giambologna.**

Bologni (bō-lō′nyē), **Girolamo.** Poet, humanist, and jurisconsult; b. at Treviso, May 16, 1454; d. there, September 23, 1517. He practiced his professions as notary and lawyer in Treviso, and from 1477 to 1481 assisted at the press of Michele Manzolo in that same city. Frederick III crowned him poet for his Latin verses. Most of his work was not printed; it included many poems addressed to various people, *Promiscuorum poeticorum, Apologia pro Plinio,* and *Antiquarii Libri duo ad Julium filium,* which contained, among other matters, descriptions of the antiquities of Treviso.

Bolognini (bō-lō-nyē′nē), **Lodovico.** Jurist, diplomat, and humanist; b. at Bologna, 1446; d. at Florence, 1508. He was a pupil of Alessandro Tartagni, took his doctorate in civil law in 1569, and in the following year received his doctorate in canon law. He taught civil law at Bologna, Ferrara, and again at Bologna, and was known in and beyond Italy for his legal learning and his skill as a diplomat. The popes made use of this skill on more than one occasion. Pope Julius II made him senator and then gonfaloniere of Bologna. He had a valuable library, a treasury of books and codices on canon and civil law. He left his valuable collection to the library of the convent of S. Domenico at Bologna.

Boltraffio (bōl-träf′fyō) or **Beltraffio** (bel-), **Giovanni Antonio.** Painter; b. at Milan, 1467; d. there, 1516. He seems to have dedicated himself to art after the arrival (1482) of Leonardo da Vinci at Milan, and to have practiced it, according to the inscription on his tombstone (in the Castello Sforzesco), more as a pleasure than as a profession. Almost nothing is known of the period of his life before he knew Leonardo, in whose studio he appears in 1491. Thereafter he was one of the master's most devoted pupils and followers. In his earliest surviving work, in the

Castello Sforzesco, the influence of Leonardo, though slight, is already apparent. With the passage of time his work became increasingly Leonardesque. However, though in form and effect he was faithful to Leonardo, his own talent saved him from becoming a mere slavish imitator, even when his style most closely approached Leonardo's, as in the soft modeling and gently smiling mouths of his *Madonnas.* The *Madonna and Child* in the Poldi Pezzoli Museum, Milan, is a lovely example (but Leonardo would never have so definitely outlined the slits of the eyes showing under lowered lids). Another example, more softly modeled, is the *Virgin and Child* in the National Gallery, London. His masterpiece is the *Casio Madonna* (1500), in the Louvre, Paris, painted at Bologna, whither he had gone when the fall of Ludovico Sforza caused Leonardo to leave Milan. Of about the same period is his *Two Worshippers* (Brera, Milan). Of 1508 is a great altarpiece, now at Budapest but originally intended for Lodi. In 1514 or 1515, having followed Leonardo to Rome, he painted a fresco of the Madonna in the cloister of S. Onofrio. The fresco was formerly attributed to Leonardo himself but is now generally considered to have been entirely by Boltraffio. Other works include the subtle *Narcissus at the Fountain* (Uffizi, Florence); *Madonna and Child* and *Christ Blessing* (Carrara Academy, Bergamo); a number at Milan where, in the Ambrosiana, there is a collection of his drawings; and paintings at Cambridge, Massachusetts; Cleveland; El Paso, Texas; New York; Raleigh, North Carolina; Worcester, Massachusetts; and elsewhere. He painted a number of portraits of high quality, as that of the poet Giacomo Casio (Brera, Milan), and those at Detroit, in the Johnson Collection, Philadelphia, and in the National Gallery, Washington.

Bombelli (bôm-bel′lē), **Raffaele.** Bolognese mathematician; d. after 1572. He studied mathematics and hydraulic engineering at Bologna, and afterward was employed to drain marshes in Tuscany. When this employment was interrupted, he devoted himself to mathematics. In 1572 an enlarged edition of his work, *L'Algebra . . . divisa in tre libri* (*Algebra, Divided into Three Books;* the whole title goes on to state that with the aid of these books anybody may achieve a perfect knowledge of the theory of arithmetic), was published at Bologna. This work is a summation and completion of the work published on arithmetic and algebra up to this time. (Algebra was considered a more advanced form of arithmetic.) Among its many contributions is a simplified way of writing equations and a thorough discussion of cubic and quadratic equations. A fifth book, in the enlarged edition, includes problems of geometry. Bombelli recognized that algebra and geometry are separate branches of mathematics.

Bonaccorsi (bō-nä-kôr′sē), **Niccolò.** See **Niccolò di Buonaccorso.**

Bonaccursius Pisanus (bō-na-kėr′ṣi-us pī-sā′-nus). [Original name, **Buono Accorso.**] Classical scholar and rhetorician; b. at Pisa, c1450. He wrote commentaries on Caesar and other Latin authors.

Bonacolsi (bō-nä-kōl′sē), **Iacopo Ilario.** See **Antico, L'.**

Bonaggiunta Orbicciani (bō-nä-jön′tä ōr-bēt-chä′nē). See **Orbicciani, Bonaggiunta.**

Bonaiuto (bō-nä-yö′tō), **Andrea di.** See **Andrea di Bonaiuto.**

Bonamico (bō-nä-mē′kō), **Lazzaro.** Humanist and teacher; b. at Bassano, 1479; d. at Padua, February 11, 1552. He studied Latin and Greek at Padua under Giovanni Calfurnio and Marcus Musurus, and studied philosophy there under Pomponazzi. He was renowned for his learning and sought out by many, but except for short stays at Bologna and Rome, he taught Latin and Greek all his life at the university (studio) at Padua. In the discussions of his day over the relative merits of Latin and the vernacular as a literary language, he favored Latin. Noted above all as a teacher, he left some Latin verses, orations, letters, and a treatise on Latin.

Bondi (bōn′dē), **Giovanni.** [**Ioannes de Aquilegia.**] Teacher and writer; b. at Venzone in Friuli, toward the end of the 14th century. He was a teacher of the *ars dictaminis,* the art of writing Latin letters and official papers with ease and speed. He taught at Ascoli and there wrote on the art of writing, dedicating his work to his friends: the notaries, jurists, and scholars of the city. His works on the art of writing letters include one listing the proper titles by which persons of various rank and condition should be addressed, *Practica sive usus dictaminis,* and one on the various rules for letter-writing, *Practica sive ars dictandi in radice.* For his specialty he enjoyed a great reputation in his day, and his works were frequently copied for use in schools, by teachers, and by others who had a use for them.

Boner (bō′nėr), **Ulrich.** Swiss Dominican friar who collected 100 fables which he retold in popular language; fl. first half of the 14th century. The collection, *Der Edelstein*, appears to have been the first German collection of fables, and was possibly the first German book ever printed. It was issued in 1461.

Bonfadio (bōn-fä′dyō), **Iacopo.** Humanist and historian; b. at Gazzane, near Salò, 1509; beheaded at Genoa, July 19, 1550. He studied at Verona and Padua and served (1532–1538) as secretary to two cardinals in succession before embarking on travels and sojourns in Venice, Rome, and Naples. At Naples he was on friendly terms with Pietro Campecchi and Juan de Valdés, supporters of Protestant reform. On his return to Padua he became tutor to Pietro Bembo's son. In 1544 he went to Genoa to teach philosophy and was shortly invited to continue Uberto Foglietta's history of Genoa. The five books he wrote of the *Annalium Genuensium* cover the years 1528 to 1550. These books are noted, in addition to accuracy, for Bonfadio's lucid and succinct Latin style, a style reminiscent of that of Caesar in his *Commentaries*. Bonfadio also left verses in Latin and in the vernacular, and colorful letters that present an animated review of his own day. He was accused of sodomy and beheaded at Genoa.

Bonfigli (bōn-fē′lyē), **Benedetto.** Painter; b. at Perugia; d. there, 1496. Recorded for the first time in 1445, he matriculated in the Painters' Guild at Perugia about that time and was in Rome (1450) painting in the rooms in the Vatican that were later redecorated by Raphael. He was back at Perugia in 1453, and from that time until his death there are a number of documents that record his activity in his native city. His earliest surviving work is an *Adoration of the Magi* (c1453), National Gallery of Umbria, Perugia, of somewhat archaic composition and lively colors, and showing the influence of the Sienese painter Domenico di Bartolo. The influence of his teacher, Benozzo Gozzoli, who brought Florentine developments to Umbria, is apparent in Bonfigli's *Annunciation*, in the same gallery. In 1454 he was commissioned to decorate part of the new Chapel of the Priors at Perugia with scenes from the life of St. Louis of Toulouse. The tempera murals (now in the National Gallery of Umbria, Perugia) indicate his acquaintance with the work of Fra Angelico and Piero della Francesca; the animated scenes have a charming naïveté, and are historically important for the faithful representation of the monuments of Perugia and its general aspect in the middle of the 15th century. The series was completed in 1461. In the same year he received the commission to complete the decoration of the chapel with scenes from the life of St. Ercolano. The latter series was not quite complete at the time of his death. He also painted a group of gonfalons that are important iconographically. That of S. Bernardino (1465, National Gallery of Umbria, Perugia) represents a lively and picturesque scene in bright colors, with the crowns of roses on the heads of the ladies that were a characteristic decoration of Bonfigli's angels. A number of other works by this imaginative and persuasive local painter are in the same gallery. Predella panels at Bayonne and Chantilly are from a polyptych, two panels of which are at Munich; a panel at El Paso, Texas, is from a triptych.

Bonfini (bōn-fē′nē), **Antonio.** Historian; b. at Patrignone, c1427; d. at Buda, between 1502 and 1505. He taught at Ascoli and Recanati until 1486. At that time he went to the court of Matthias Corvinus, king of Hungary, at Buda, and at the request of the king began his history of Hungary, *Rerum Hungaricarum decades*. The work was completed after the death of the king on order of his successor, Ladislaus II. Bonfini was rewarded for it by being granted a patent in the Magyar nobility. He also wrote other, lesser historical works, orations, letters, and translations from the Greek into Latin. His history of Hungary had great influence on subsequent Hungarian writing.

Boniface VIII (bon′i-fās). [Original name, **Benedetto Caetani.**] Pope (1294–1303); b. at Anagni, c1228; d. at Rome, October 11, 1303. A headstrong and energetic man, who had studied canon and civil law, like many of his predecessors he attempted to enhance the temporal power of the papacy and engaged in struggles with, among others, the French and the Florentines during his pontificate. He issued (February 25, 1296) the bull *Clericis laicos*, which was directed against Philip IV of France (Philip the Fair), who had imposed taxes on the French clergy, and which forbade the clergy of any country to pay tribute to the secular government without the papal permission; but was forced by an enactment of Philip, which stopped the exportation of money from France, to concede that the French clergy might render voluntary contributions. He opened at Rome on October 30, 1302 (as the result of a quarrel with Philip over the imprisonment of an insolent papal legate, the bishop of Pamiers), a synod, in which he promulgated (November 18, 1302) the bull *Unam sanctam,* asserting the temporal as well as spiritual supremacy of the papacy. In 1300 he proclaimed a Holy Year of Jubilee during which thousands of pilgrims, including Dante, flocked to Rome. In 1301 he attempted to mediate between warring Bianchi (White Guelphs) and Neri (Black Guelphs) factions in Florence and encouraged Charles of Valois to enter the city, ostensibly as a peacemaker, but actually also as an instrument to exert papal influence. To Dante, Boniface was the archenemy, for his political meddling, his avarice, and his nepotism. Although Boniface was alive at the supposed date (1300) of the vision of the *Commedia* (begun possibly in 1307), Dante indicates that Boniface will occupy one of the lower reaches of Hell (*Inferno,* xix). As Boniface was about to excommunicate Philip of France for his defiance he was made prisoner at Anagni, September 7, 1303, by Nogaret, vice-chancellor to Philip, and Sciarra Colonna. Among Philip's charges was that Boniface was not the true pope because of the unusual circumstance that his predecessor, Celestine V, had abdicated with his assistance. Colonna took part in the seizure because of resentment of Boniface VIII's aggrandizement of the Caetani family. Boniface was released after three days by the populace, and died at Rome of a fever. His death was a profound psychological shock even to those who feared and distrusted him. There is a statue of Boniface at the Cathedral of Anagni, and the 13th century papal palace where Nogaret seized him still stands in that town. He was succeeded by Benedict XI.

Boniface IX. [Original name, **Pietro Tomacelli.**] Pope (1389–1404); b. at Naples; d. at Rome, October 1, 1404. He was elected by the Roman cardinals, during the Great Schism, to succeed Urban VI. He quelled rising republican sentiment in Rome, fortified the city, sought to organize the States of the Church, and declared in favor of Ladislaus, king of Naples, in his struggle with Louis II of Anjou over control of the kingdom of Naples. His efforts to restore the States of the Church and Rome kept him ever in need of money. He made perpetual the annates, by which the pope received the first fruits (a year's revenue or a specified part thereof) from the bishop, abbott, or other ecclesiastic, on his appointment to a new see or benefice, and began the practice of selling offices and indulgences. He was pope in the time of the antipopes Clement VII and Benedict XIII at Avignon, and attempted, vainly, to secure their submission to Rome. He was succeeded by Innocent VII.

Bonifazio Veronese (bō-nē-fä′zhō vā-rō-nā′zā). [Also, **Bonifazio de' Pitati** and **Bonifazio Veneziano.**] Painter; b. at Verona, c1487; d. at Venice, October 19, 1553. His father left Verona about 1505 and Bonifazio's style was formed at Venice, especially under the influence of Palma Vecchio, with whom he worked as a collaborator. He finished the *Holy Conversation,* now in the Querini Stampalia Collection at Venice, that Palma had begun, and painted a number of others on the same subject and in the same style, as those in the Pitti Palace, Florence, Ambrosiana, Milan, and at Vienna. One of his most celebrated works, *The Rich Man's Feast,* Accademia, Venice, is typical of his predilection for painting nobles and their ladies at hunting parties, picnics, and in other activities in elaborate and contrived pastoral settings. These subjects and his paintings were very popular at Venice, where he had a large workshop and many pupils (including Tintoretto) and assistants. Because his pupils and assistants executed many works to his designs, paintings executed by him alone are rare. Among the works attributed to him are a number in the Accademia, churches, and other buildings at Venice; two panels of Virtues (1532), Modena; *The Finding of Moses,* another of his best works, Brera, Milan; and a number of small decorative panels in the museums of Italy and at Lille and Berlin. Among his paintings in museums in the United States are *Joseph Lowered into the Well by His Brothers* (Cannon Collection, Princeton); *The Cumaean Sibyl* and *Virgin*

Bonifazio Veronese
Supper at Emmaus
Courtesy of The Art Institute of Chicago

and Child with Saints (Museum of Fine Arts, Boston); *Holy Conversation* (Isabella Stewart Gardner Museum, Boston); *A Miracle of St. Ambrose* (the Metropolitan Museum, New York); and paintings at Greenville, South Carolina; Los Angeles; New Haven; Sacramento; San Francisco; Santa Monica, California; Sarasota, Florida; and Washington.

Bonincontri (bō-nēn-kōn′trē), **Lorenzo.** Humanist, astrologer, and historian; b. at S. Miniato in Tuscany, February 23, 1410; d. 1491. He was a mercenary with Francesco Sforza; was a friend of Panormita and Pontano; lectured on astrology at the university (studio) at Florence and at Rome; and was astrologer at the Sforza court at Pesaro. Of an erudite and lively intellect, he spent most of his life at three leading humanistic centers: Naples, Florence, and Rome. He left a poem in Latin hexameters, dedicated to Lorenzo de' Medici, on theological and philosophical subjects, *Rerum naturalium libri ad Laurentium Medicem*, and another, also in Latin hexameters and dedicated to Ferrante of Naples, on astrology, *De rebus coelestibus ad Ferdinandum Aragonium*. A collection of lyrics of religious inspiration is noteworthy for its poetic artistry and for the inclusion of astrological references. His other extant works include writings and manuals on astrology, commentaries and studies on Ptolemy, ten books of a history, *Chronicon sive annales ab a. 903 ad a. 1458*, a history of the kingdoms of Naples and Sicily (written during the reign of King Ferrante), and a life of Muzio Attendolo Sforza. An early collection of love lyrics has been lost.

Boninis (bō-nē'nēs), **Bonino de.** See **De Boninis, Bonino.**

Bonner (bon'ėr), **Edmund.** [Also, **Boner.**] English prelate; b. at Hanley, Worcestershire, England, c1495; d. at London, September 5, 1569. He was noted for his persecution of Protestants in the reign of Mary of England. He refused to take the oath of supremacy, on the accession of Elizabeth, and was committed to prison, where he died.

Bonnivard or **Bonivard** (bo-nē-vȧr), **François de.** Swiss prelate and politician; b. at Seyssel, Switzerland, c1493; d. at Geneva, 1570. He was the hero of Byron's poem *The Prisoner of Chillon* and was the author of *Les Chroniques de Genève*.

Bono da Ferrara (bō'nō dä fer-rä'rä). Painter; active in the middle of the 15th century. He was at first a pupil of Pisanello, under whose influence he painted his signed *St. Jerome in a Landscape*, National Gallery, London. In 1450 and 1452 he was working for the Estensi at Ferrara, painting frescoes (now lost) in their palaces and pleasure villas. From Ferrara he went to Padua to paint scenes from the life of St. Christopher in the Chapel of the Ovetari in the Church of the Eremitani. This was the chapel largely decorated by Mantegna; the paintings that were not destroyed entirely were badly damaged in World War II. Other activity attributed to Bono was the painting of frescoes in the cathedral at Siena (1442 and 1461).

Bonomo (bō-nō'mō), **Jacobello.** Venetian painter; active in the second half of the 14th century. He was strongly influenced by the Gothic elements in Lorenzo Veneziano, of whom he was a not very original or talented follower. A polyptych, *Virgin and Child*, signed and dated 1385, is in the Town Hall of S. Arcangelo di Romagna. Other works attributed to him are at Fermo and Pesaro.

Bonomo, Pietro. Humanist and poet; b. 1458; d. 1546. Of an ancient family of Trieste, he was bishop of Trieste, and served the emperors Frederick III and Maximilian I and Ferdinand of Austria in various high official positions.

Bonsi (bōn'sē), **Giovanni.** Florentine painter, of whom there are notices from 1366 to 1371. In the latter year he painted his only signed and dated work, a polyptych, *Madonna and Child with Saints Onofrius, Nicholas of Bari, Bartholomew and John the Evangelist*, now in theVatican.

Bonsignori (bōn-sē-nyō'rē), **Francesco.** Painter; b. at Verona, c1455; d. at Caldiero (Verona), 1519. According to Vasari, his father was an amateur painter and his three brothers were painters. He was influential in rescuing Veronese painting from the doldrums in which it had floundered since the time of Francesco Benaglio (c1432–before 1492). His lively color, which later took on a metallic sheen and became a characteristic of Veronese painting until the end of the 15th century, was already apparent in his early *Madonna Enthroned*, in the Church of S. Paolo di Campo Marzio, Verona. Contacts with Alvise Vivarini and the Bellini led to new vigor of composition and clearer forms, but after 1488 Mantegna was the chief influence on his work. His masterpiece is his *Portrait of an Elderly Man* (1487), National Gallery, London, a work of stunning realism and noble individuality. In 1487, according to Vasari, he went to Mantua, to the court of Francesco II Gonzaga. There he painted *Christ Carrying the Cross* and *Beata Osanna degli Andreana*, in the Ducal Palace at Mantua. The last includes a figure supposed to represent Isabella d'Este kneeling before her great friend Beata Osanna. Both paintings are of vigorous draftsmanship and a certain nobility of expression, but are somewhat monotonous in color and show a marked dependence on Mantegna. His last work, an altarpiece (commissioned 1514) for the Compagnia di S. Nazaro e Celso at Verona, delivered in 1519, is notably different. Its slender, elegant figures, luminous color, and softened tones became characteristics of Veronese painting at the beginning of the 16th century. In addition to the works at Verona and Mantua, there are others in the Poldi Pezzoli Museum at Milan, the Carrara Academy at Bergamo, the National Gallery, London, the Johnson Collection, Philadelphia, and elsewhere.

Bonsignori, Fra **Gerolamo.** Painter; b. at Verona, c1440; d. at Mantua, c1519. He was the brother of Francesco Bonsignori (c1455–1519), and was a follower of Mantegna. He frescoed a *Madonna* in the Church of S. Barnaba at Mantua, and also made a large copy of Leonardo's *Last Supper*.

Bontemps (bôn-tän), **Roger.** [Pseudonym of **Roger de Collerye.**] French poet; b. at Paris, c1470; d. c1540. Of a lively, carefree temperament, his name is proverbially given to any jovial fellow.

Bonvesin de la Riva (bōn-vā-zēn′ dā lä rē′vä). Religious poet and grammarian; b. at Milan, c1240; d. 1315. He was a member of the order of the Umiliati. A highly productive writer, he wrote verse in Latin and the speech of Lombardy. His aim in writing was to do good, but he was neither a moralist nor a pedant. His *De magnalibus urbis mediolani* (1288) is a civil and religious record of his beloved city. It is based on documents, his own observation, and his educated guesses, and is valuable for its description of 13th century Milan. His other poetic works include his characteristic verses of contrasts, in one of which the Madonna and Satan are contrasted, and Satan is permitted to make a passionate defense of himself. Bonvesin could be satiric, persuasive, didactic, or frightening in his descriptions of the terrors of the next world. Although he always wrote for a purpose, occasionally the joy of simply telling a story, perhaps to illustrate a point, is evident in his work. His poetry in the language of Lombardy is marked by a simplicity and beauty that make him preeminent among Lombard poets of the 13th century.

Bonvicino (bōn-vē-chē′nō), **Alessandro.** See **Moretto da Brescia.**

Book of the Duchess, The. Poem by Geoffrey Chaucer, known also as *The Death of Blanche the Duchess*. The earliest of Chaucer's original poems of any length, it was probably written near the end of 1369, as Blanche, the wife of the duke of Lancaster, died on September 12, 1369. The poem represents the inconsolable grief of the duke, and embodies the story of Ceyx and Alcyone. The duke, John of Gaunt, married again, however, in 1372. The broader outlines of the plot come from Guillaume de Machaut's tales, *Dit du Lion* and *Dit de la Fontaine Amoureuse*.

Book of Margery Kempe (kemp), **The.** Autobiography by Margery Kempe of Lynn (d. c1438). As a human document and for its many glimpses of medieval life, it has great interest for students of English literature and history.

Book of Martyrs, The. History of the persecution of various Protestant reformers in England, by John Foxe. Written in Latin it was finished in 1559 and published in 1563. Its full title is *Actes and Monuments*. Foxe translated it into English.

Book of St. Albans (sânt ôl′bạnz). Rhymed treatise on hawking, hunting, and similar sports, printed in English in 1486. The second edition contains the popular *Treatyse on Fysshynge with an Angle*.

Bora (bō′rä), **Katharina von.** Wife of Martin Luther; b. at Löben, near Merseburg, Germany, January 29, 1499; d. at Torgau, Germany, December 20, 1552. She had been a Cistercian nun (1515–1523) at Nimptschen. She married Luther on June 13, 1525, and brought him the warm family life that was so important to the reformer in his later years.

Bordone (bôr-dō′nā), **Paris.** Painter; b. at Treviso, in July, 1500; d. at Venice, January 19, 1571. Orphaned at the age of 7, he was sent as a youth to the workshop of Titian at Venice. He did not remain there long as Titian, according to Vasari, was a reluctant teacher. Moreover, when Bordone was 18 his master deprived him of a commission he had received for a painting in the Church of S. Niccolò at Treviso. Soon after he was called to Vicenza to paint a fresco on the story of *Noah and His Children* in the Loggia of that city and came off with honor, as his work compared favorably with that Titian painted in the same place on *The Judgment of Solomon*. Both frescoes were destroyed in 1539. After his work at Vicenza he had a good reputation and received commissions from many places in the Veneto. His work appeared in the churches of Venice, Treviso,

Paris Bordone
The Cello Player
Courtesy of The Pierpont Morgan Library, New York

Belluno, and Agordino, among others, as well as at Milan and Crema. His masterpiece, *The Fisherman Presenting St. Mark's Ring to the Doge* (1535), Accademia, Venice, was of great importance to him, as it brought him fame and important commissions. He was invited to the court of France, probably in 1538, but left few authenticated works there. About 1540 he was invited to Augsburg in Bavaria to decorate the palace of the famous Fugger banking family and remained there some time. On his return to Venice his clients included Sigismund I, king of Poland, and Cardinal Granvelle, the chancellor of Charles V. In addition to his paintings on religious and mythological themes he painted a number of fairly penetrating portraits. In his later career he adopted some of the elements of mannerism; his color became warmer and his style more monumental. Known for the splendor of his color and the beauty of his female figures, his work is often vitiated by weakness of draftsmanship and uncertainty of composition. Perhaps because he was so prolific, his paintings seem trite, superficial, and sentimental. Of the many he produced, a great number have been lost, but a great number remain. Much of his work is to be found at Venice and in its environs. There are also examples from his brush at Bari, Bergamo, Florence, Genoa, Lovere, Milan, Rome, Siena, and elsewhere in Italy, as well as at Cologne, Frankfurt, London, and Paris. Documented works in the United States include those in the Isabella Stewart Gardner Museum (Boston), the Fogg Museum (Cambridge), the Johnson Collection (Philadelphia), and the Los Angeles County Museum; many others are assigned to him on solid grounds.

Borghese (bôr-gā′zā). Name of a family famous at Rome during the period of the Renaissance. Of Sienese origin, they first appear in the records in 1238. Marcantonio Borghese, a jurisconsult who became attached to the papal court early in the 16th century, established the family at Rome, where one of his sons, Camillo, became pope under the name of Paul V (1605–1621), and another, Francesco, was commander of the papal troops. The pope secured important titles of nobility for his nephew Marcantonio, and by his influence another nephew, Scipione, became a cardinal. Cardinal Scipione erected the Villa Borghese at Rome. The building, in what is now the most beautiful public park in Rome, houses what has been called "the queen of private collections." On the ground floor is the museum, with a rich collection of marbles and sculptures, many of which have been in the building since it was adopted as the seat of the collection by Marcantonio Borghese near the end of the 18th century. The art gallery, on the floor above, has been in the building since it was acquired and moved from the Borghese Palace by the Italian government in 1902. Many additions have been made to both collections over the years. Many of the treasures sold to Napoleon I by Camillo Borghese, who married a sister of Napoleon's, have been returned. Among the paintings of the art gallery are examples of the principal Italian schools of the Renaissance.

Borghini (bōr-gē′nē), **Vincenzo.** Philologist and historian; b. at Florence, October 29, 1515; d. there, August 18, 1580. He entered the Benedictine order (1531), became a teacher of grammar and eventual prior of his monastery at Florence. A learned man, he was a member of the commission that edited (bowdlerized) Boccaccio's *Decameron* (1573). In connection with this he wrote *Annotazioni e discorsi sopra alcuni luoghi del Decameron,* a learned commentary (Florence, 1574). He was an ardent admirer of Dante, and defended him against Girolamo Ruscelli; he was a lover of art and architecture who made suggestions to Vasari, and a representative of Grand Duke Cosimo I in the academy of arts. His *Discorsi* is the result of his researches into the early history of Florence, and is notable for his wise and critical use of ancient sources.

Borgia (bôr′jä), **Alfonso.** Italianized name of Alonso de Borja, who became Pope Calixtus III.

Borgia, Cesare. Duke of Valentinois; b. probably in the summer of 1475; killed before the castle of Viana, in Spain, March 12, 1507. He was the natural son of Rodrigo Borgia (Pope Alexander VI) and Vannozza Cattanei. Destined for an ecclesiastical career, he was made apostolic protonotary at the age of seven, bishop of Pamplona, and archbishop of Valencia at the first consistory his father held after becoming pope (August 31, 1492). In 1493 (September 20), he was raised to the cardinalate. Without the slightest inclination or desire for a career in the Church, he led a dissolute and disorderly life at Rome. Furthermore, his role as a prelate was far less brilliant and more circumscribed as to its future than that of his brother Giovanni (Juan), duke of Gandia and the pope's favorite. Giovanni was loaded with every temporal honor and office in the gift of the pope. On the night of June 14, 1497, Giovanni disappeared. His fully clothed body, pierced by nine dagger wounds, was hauled from the Tiber a few days later. The pope was utterly grief-stricken. A frantic investigation was begun, and then abruptly halted. The murder was attributed to Cesare, who in this manner may have opened for himself the possibility of winning Giovanni's offices and power, and who possibly frightened his father into calling off the investigation of the murder. The next year (August, 1498), Cesare requested to be relieved of his dignity as cardinal on the grounds, as he blandly put it, that he was illegitimate. Shortly thereafter he was named count (later duke) of Valentinois (hence his Italian title of Valentino) by Louis XII of France. Cesare wished to marry a daughter of the royal house of Naples, to establish his role as prince and as a first step in gaining his own state. However, King Federico of Naples and Carlotta, the daughter in question, refused to consider the idea. Louis XII, who planned to divorce his wife Jeanne in order to marry Anne of Brittany, widow of Charles VIII, was anxious to please the pope, from whom he must receive a dispensation for his divorce and remarriage. (It was for this reason that he had created Cesare Borgia duke of Valentinois.) He sought a bride for Cesare and found one in Charlotte d'Albret, sister of the king of Navarre. Cesare went to France, bearing the coveted dispensation for Louis. He rode into Chinon, where the court was sitting, with a suite of the most ostentatious, almost ludicrous splendor, in order to impress the French with the high degree of his opulence if not of his birth. Louis welcomed him warmly (October, 1498), and the following spring Cesare married Charlotte at Blois (May 12, 1499). After a brief honeymoon Cesare, with promises of support from Louis for his great plans, set out for Rome. He never saw his young bride again, or the daughter she subsequently bore him. Returned to Italy as the king's representative, with troops furnished by the king and paid for by the pope, he set out to carve out a principality in the Romagna and the Marches. The justification for this was that the vassals of the Church had not fulfilled their feudal obligations. His first target was a woman, Caterina Sforza of Forlì. Her city of Imola fell to him in November, 1499. Forlì fell the next month. Caterina retired to the fortress of Ravaldino and personally commanded its defense. The fortress fell (January 12, 1500) under the pounding of Cesare's artillery.

Caterina was taken prisoner and, according to some accounts, was violated by Cesare, but according to others was treated with courtesy. Alexander named Cesare vicar of the two cities. Louis XII, fearing too much success for Cesare, ordered the French troops withdrawn. Cesare returned to Rome (February, 1500) where he was welcomed as a hero. The pope invested him as vicar, gave him the Golden Rose (a gold rose blessed by the pope and given in recognition of special service to the Holy See), and named him gonfaloniere of the Church. Cesare sent the Spaniard Ramiro de L'Orqua to administer his vicariates, and promised that they would be governed with justice and mercy. He remained in Rome, amused himself in carnival, took part in the religious ceremonies and splendid processions that marked the Jubilee year, and even displayed his agility and prowess in bullfights (for which the Romans had little taste). (In the four years that Cesare dominated Italian history he curiously alternated periods of the most intense activity with others of almost passive indolence. The latter periods were, however, often occasioned by variations of the French king's policies or of Alexander's access to money.) On July 15, 1500, the young and handsome Alfonso, duke of Bisceglie, natural son of Alfonso II of Naples, was attacked as he was leaving the Vatican and seriously wounded. He was the beloved husband of Cesare's sister Lucrezia. She took care of him with the utmost tenderness and he appeared to be recovering. Cesare is said to have remarked that what was not accomplished at breakfast might be fulfilled at dinner. On August 18, bravos invaded the young duke's room in the Vatican and strangled him in his bed. For this murder, too, public opinion held Cesare responsible, though the motive for it was not clear. His contemporaries said he acted from excessive love for his sister; some alleged that he had incestuous relations with her, though there is no evidence to support this charge, and what is known of her character is not consonant with this allegation. (In February, 1497, Pedro Calderon, a young papal chamberlain, was slain, and the report was that Cesare had murdered him "because of something offending the honor of Madonna Lucrezia.") With his brutal rationalness, a more likely motive is that he killed the son of the late king of Naples to forestall the possibility that the pope and the Aragonese of Naples might enter an agreement that would interfere with the plans of the French king to seize Naples, and thus with Cesare's own ambitions. In the fall of 1500 he resumed his operations for the conquest of the Romagna. Money was supplied by the pope; Venetian neutrality was secured by promises of help against the Turks; Louis XII again agreed to supply troops. When Cesare's army left Rome in September there were many Roman nobles among its officers. They joined perhaps out of fear of the consequences if they didn't, but more probably out of enthusiasm for a commander who seemed to know exactly what he was doing, who acted with decision, and who won. Also in his train were jewelers, goldsmiths, and armorers, ever busy creating ornaments and armor, either for him or as gifts for those whose friendship he sought. Poets and scholars made part of his vast retinue, to sing the praises of the Borgia. Cesena and Bertinoro had already acknowledged him as lord. Giovanni Sforza, lord of Pesaro and Lucrezia's first husband, was unable to secure support to defend his state and fled to Venice. Pesaro was occupied; Rimini was ceded. Cesare called on Faenza to yield. There, however, the devotion of the people to their 17-year-old lord, Astorre III Manfredi, caused a delay. The people of Faenza defended themselves with a gallantry that was the admiration of all Italy. Cesare, impatient of wasting time as winter approached, left troops to besiege Faenza and went on. The citizens of Faenza, inspired by their love for their lord and their independence, miraculously resisted, supported to some extent by Giovanni Bentivoglio of Bologna and the Florentines. Faenza could not fight starvation. The city surrendered (April 25, 1501) after a siege of five months. Young Astorre Manfredi, in complete and cynical disregard for the terms under which he had surrendered, was sent as a prisoner to Rome. In June of the following year his dagger-pierced body was hauled from the Tiber. Cesare took no chances that a surviving popular leader might return and cause revolt in the states he conquered. Giovanni Bentivoglio of Bologna came to terms with Cesare. With his troops practically at the gates of Florence, the Florentines offered him tribute in the shape of a command. In May, 1501, Alexander named him duke of Romagna. In the middle of June he was back at Rome. By this time Alexander had found it expedient to agree, secretly, to the partition of Naples between the French and the Spanish. As evidence of his good faith to the French, he sent Cesare to accompany the French army from Rome to Naples. On the way the French entered Capua, which had capitulated after a pounding, and massacred 4,000 of the inhabitants, helpless before the brutal troops that composed the French army. Cesare was held responsible for the butchery, although in fact he was a subordinate of the French commander. He entered Naples with the French (August 1, 1501), is said to have amused himself in his dissolute way there, and was back at Rome in September. He passed the winter organizing the government of his conquered states and raising and training his own army so that he would be less dependent on troops provided by the French king. In June, 1502, he left Rome. He seemed to be headed for Camerino, but made a sudden detour and invaded the duchy of Urbino instead. Duke Guidobaldo, one of the most loyal adherents of the papacy and an ally of France, was completely taken by surprise with this betrayal and fled (June 20, 1502). Cesare added the title duke of Urbino to his other titles, and carried off many valuable works of art, including the famous tapestries of the *Siege of Troy* which he gave to the cardinal of Rouen, and books from the famous library founded by Federico da Montefeltro. The next month he took Camerino from the Varani, who were imprisoned and either died or were killed in prison. His troops were under the command of some of the most noted captains of Italy. His captains and his supposed allies included Pandolfo Petrucci of Siena, Ermes Bentivoglio of Bologna, two members of the Baglioni family of Perugia, Vitelozzo Vitelli, Oliverotto of Fermo, the duke of Gravina, and Paolo Orsini. They had helped Cesare overrun the Romagna. They had observed his decisiveness, his ruthlessness, and his success. In some cases they had seen his Spaniards devastate their territories while he looked on with indifference. The Bentivoglio thought he would turn next against Bologna. Others feared for their lives and their states. In October, 1502, the captains met at the castle of La Magione, near Perugia, and planned revolt before they "should be devoured, one by one, by the dragon." Cesare's dominion seemed about to collapse. Urbino and Camerino rebelled; Fano was threatened. Cesare, aware of what was happening, kept his nerves under complete control and coolly planned his revenge. He replaced the Spaniard Ramiro de L'Orqua, "a cruel and energetic man" who was accused of harshness and conspiracy, with Antonio del Monte, a man known for his learning, moderation, and goodness. A short time later De L'Orqua's body was found in the public square at Cesena, in two pieces. Machiavelli, the Florentine envoy to Cesare's headquarters, wrote to his masters, "The reason for his death is not properly known, beyond the fact that such was the wish of the prince who has shown that he can do or undo men according to his talents and their merits." Thus did Cesare dissociate himself from the hatred roused by his lieutenant and warn disloyal servants. "This ferocious spectacle," wrote Machiavelli, "left the people at once content and horrified." Urbino and Camerino were reconquered and subdued. He now moved swiftly against the conspirators of Magione, some of whom were already wavering and all of whom distrusted each other. They patched up their differences with Cesare, and to show their good faith seized Senigallia for him. In spite of their thorough knowledge of his methods, "in their simplicity they all were induced to come to Senigallia and fell into his hands." Having left their troops outside the city, the captains were helpless. Cesare took them prisoner (December 31, 1502). Oliverotto da Fermo and Vitelozzo Vitelli were strangled by his executioner, Don Michelotto, the same night, the duke of Gravina (an Orsini) and Paolo Orsini sometime later. Machiavelli, with the duke to try to find out his plans vis-à-vis Florence, wrote of the success of Cesare's deception with unclouded admiration; Louis XII called it "a deed worthy of the great days of Rome." At Rome the pope arrested other members of the Orsini family. Cardinal Battista Orsini died (February 22, 1503), presumably of poison. Orsini lands were seized. In Umbria the petty tyrants fled; Perugia and Città di Castello were won by Cesare, and his army was permitted to ravage the lands surrounding them. But he did not permit sacking and devastation of the states that were to be part of his duchy. On the contrary, he reorganized the administration, lowered taxes

Leonardo da Vinci
Studies of the head of Cesare Borgia
Biblioteca Reale, Turin

(he could do this since Rome supplied his money), reformed the judicial system, established a court of appeal, and insisted on impartial justice. He placed his own governor in each state and filled other offices with local men. He promoted industry, protected agriculture, and fostered printing; he erected buildings, as the palace of the court of appeals at Cesena, and had his architect and engineer, Leonardo da Vinci, plan a new quarter for Cesena (never carried out). In fact, he restored law and order in an area that had been ravaged by war, brigandage, and injustice, and protected its people from the extortions and inequities that had ever been their lot. And they were grateful, and acclaimed him as their new lord. On June 24, 1503, the first session of the court of appeals opened at Cesena, to the accompaniment of magnificent festivities, floats, and a triumphal car representing the triumph of Julius Caesar: one of Cesare Borgia's mottoes was *Aut Caesar aut nihil* (Either Caesar or nothing). Cesare, back at Rome, considered the French defeat in Naples (the French and Spanish, having decided to partition Naples, quarreled over the division, and the French were defeated in the ensuing battle, in April, 1503), and decided to approach the Spanish victors, as the French could be of no more use to him. There seemed to be nothing to stop him from winning the crown to which it was thought he aspired. All Italy, while congratulating him on his success, trembled at his name. The gathering of a new French army at Parma delayed an attack that may have been planned against Siena, Pisa, and Florence. The pope's death (August 18, 1503) and his own illness at the same time marked the end of his success. Machiavelli reports that he told him he had thought of everything that might occur when his father died, and that he had provided for every eventuality, but he never dreamed that he would be sick almost unto death himself at the same time. He was so weak he could do nothing. However, Machiavelli's observation that had not his sickness and his father's death coincided he would have established a permanent kingdom is open to question; it is doubtful that his aspirations went so far. At the beginning of September, after long negotiations with the cardinals, he put himself under the protection of the king of France and left Rome. The lords whose lands he had conquered returned and drove out his governors in many of the states. The Romagna, which had known the blessings of peace under his rule, remained loyal. Pius III, who succeeded Alexander, was not unfriendly but within a month he was dead. Cesare made a bargain with Giuliano della Rovere, the leading contender to succeed Pius. He promised him the votes of the Spanish cardinals in return for the office of gonfaloniere of the Church and vicar of the lands he had won. Once elected, Giuliano, now Julius II, ignored the bargain. In the meantime, Venice seemed about to swallow up the Romagna. Cesare was compelled to hand over most of his lands to the pope. He escaped to Naples, where the Spaniard Gonzalo de Córdoba at first treated him with honor then, at the order of Ferdinand the Catholic, arrested him as a disturber of the peace of Italy (May 27, 1504). He was compelled to yield the fortress of Forlì, the last of his conquests, and was sent a prisoner to Spain. In October, 1506, he escaped and fled to his brother-in-law, the king of Navarre. The king welcomed him as a captain of known talent and put him to work at once. Cesare was killed in the siege of the castle of Viana, March 12, 1507.

Blond, handsome (before pustules, perhaps from syphilis, disfigured his face), robust in physique, so strong he could bend a horseshoe with his bare hands, an eloquent speaker, he was also a patron of the arts who employed Pinturicchio and for whom Leonardo da Vinci served for two years as architect and engineer. Bold, firm, decisive, utterly unscrupulous, he was an able planner and organizer, but for the wherewithal to execute his vast plans he was completely dependent on the pope, as he was dependent on him also for his freedom of action and the limitations on the actions of his enemies. He blazed across the Romagna and in four years seemed to have conquered and organized it, but it all collapsed on the death of the pope. For his dissolute life, his violence, cruelty, arrogance, secretiveness, mastery of dissimulation, and the mysterious crimes that littered his path, he is the archtype of the popular national Renaissance prince. The qualities—firmness, gift for command, decisiveness and speed in action, coolness, "savage courage," ruthlessness, capacity for perfidy and murder—that enabled Cesare to overrun the Romagna, the Marches, and Umbria, convinced Machiavelli that only a prince possessed of such qualities could unite turbulent Italy in the face of her enemies. Machiavelli, in *Il principe*, was greatly influenced by the successes of Cesare, writing, "I could not suggest better precepts to a new prince than the examples of Cesare's actions." He was also aware of the Borgia's ultimate failure and the role of chance in his undoing.

Borgia, Francesco. Cardinal; b. c1441; d. November 4, 1511. He was a cousin of Alexander VI and, as did other Borgia kinsmen, profited by the relationship. He became papal treasurer (1493), bishop of Teano (1495) and of Cosenza (1499), and was made cardinal (1500). Julius II excommunicated him as a rebel and a promoter of a church council, in October, 1511.

Borgia, Saint **Francesco.** General of the Society of Jesus (1565–1572); b. at Gandia, October 28, 1510; d. at Rome, September 30, 1572. He was the son of Don Giovanni, third duke of Gandia, and Joanna of Aragon, and was the great-grandson of Pope Alexander VI. At 20 he married Eleonora de Castro, of a Portuguese house, and by her had eight children. On the death of his father (1543), he succeeded as fourth duke of Gandia, and had as well many titles and honors from the emperor Charles V. He corresponded with Ignatius Loyola and became interested in the Jesuit order that Loyola had founded. After his wife died (March 27, 1546), he settled his domestic affairs, gave up his duchy and his secular titles to his son, Don Carlos, and, having studied theology and made a pilgrimage to Rome in the Jubilee Year (1550), entered the order and was ordained. After service at Guipúzcoa, Lisbon, and Valencia, he was named commissary in Spain and the Indies. Accused by the Inquisition of heresy, he was brought before Philip II of Spain in disgrace. Pius IV called him to Rome (1560), cleared him of the charges, and he became vicar of the Society (January, 1565), and then its general (July, 1565). He was offered the cardinal's hat several times and declined each time. He was canonized by Clement X in 1671.

Borgia, Giovanni. [Called **the Elder.**] Cardinal; b. c1446; d. 1503. A cousin and intimate of Rodrigo Borgia, he was archbishop of Monreale (1483) and was raised to the cardinalate in the first consistory his cousin held (August 31, 1492) after becoming Pope Alexander VI. A member of the pope's household, he carried out such important missions for him as the negotiations with Charles VIII.

Borgia, Giovanni (Juan). Second duke of Gandia; b. 1474 or 1476; murdered at Rome, June 14/15, 1497. He was the illegitimate son of Rodrigo Borgia (Alexander VI) and Vannozza Cattanei, and inherited the title, duke of Gandia, on the death of his elder half-brother Pedro Luis (1488). He married Maria Enriquez, his brother's widow, in 1493. Giovanni was his father's favorite, and was loaded with offices, honors, and wealth by the doting pope. In 1496 he was made captain general of the Church; but neither a valiant nor a capable commander, he was defeated at Soriano (January 25, 1497) when he attempted, on behalf of the pope, to crush the Orsini. The same year he was made duke of Benevento and lord of Terracina, and seemed destined for a great future, thanks to the indulgence of his father. On the night of June 14, 1497, he left his mother's house with his brother Cesare and was never seen alive again. His dagger-pierced body was hauled from the Tiber a few days later. On investigation, it was learned that a boatman guarding his wood on a boat in the Tiber had seen several men on horseback ride to the riverbank. They left briefly; another rider, masked, rode up with a body on the crupper of his horse. With the help of two others he threw the body into the river. Why had this man not reported what was an obvious crime? He had been there many nights, he answered, and had seen scores of bodies hurled into the river at that place. Cesare, accused of the murder and of so frightening the pope that he abruptly halted the investigation he had begun, inherited his brother's honors, but the title duke of Gandia was passed on to Giovanni's son Juan II (Giovanni) (1494–1543).

Borgia, Giovanni. [Called **the Younger.**] Cardinal; b. c1474; d. at Urbino, January 16/17, 1500. A great-nephew of Alexander VI, his career in the Church was greatly advanced by the latter. He became bishop of Melfi (1494), cardinal (1496), legate of Perugia and Spoleto (1497) and of Bologna and Romagna (1498). Noted for his intelligence and his discretion, he was an intimate and confidant of Cesare Borgia.

Borgia, Giovanni. Duke of Camerino; b. 1498; d. 1527. His parentage is uncertain. He was called, and written of, as the *Infante Romano*. Some said he was the son of Alexander VI and Giulia Farnese. Others said he was Cesare's child. Hints were dropped that Lucrezia was his mother. Opinion now seems to be that, whoever his mother, Alexander was his father. Alexander named him duke of Camerino (1502) but he lost his duchy after the death of the pope and never recovered it. He was brought up for a time with his kinsman and contemporary, Rodrigo, duke of Bisceglie, by Isabella of Aragon at Bari. He appeared at the court of Lucrezia in Ferrara in 1517, and she gave him assistance and helped him to go to France, where he hoped to make his fortune, a hope that was disappointed. He returned to Rome, sought again to regain Camerino, and died at Genoa.

Borgia, Girolamo. Neapolitan humanist and ecclesiastic; b. 1475; d. 1550. He was a follower of Pontano, was an intimate of Alexander VI, served the condottiere Bartolomeo d'Alviano, and later enjoyed the patronage of Paul III. Most of his Latin verses celebrated the virtues of his patrons in extravagant terms. His *Historiae de bellis Italicis* is the history of the Italian wars from 1494 and was dedicated to Pope Paul III. Some of his Latin poems appeared in the collection *Carmina lyrica et heroica* (Venice, 1666); others exist in manuscript in various libraries. He was named bishop in 1544.

Borgia, Goffredo (Jofré). Prince of Squillace; b. 1482. He was the youngest of the natural children of Rodrigo Borgia (Alexander VI) and Vannozza Cattanei. When Alexander had resolved his quarrel with King Ferrante of Naples, through the mediation of Spain, he confirmed his new ties to Naples by marrying Goffredo, then scarcely 13 years of age, to Sancia, a natural daughter of Alfonso, duke of Calabria. The marriage took place by proxy at Rome (August 16, 1493), and was celebrated at Naples the following year (May 7, 1494). Goffredo remained at Naples and was made prince of Squillace when his father-in-law ascended the throne as Alfonso II. On the death of Sancia, who had no children, Goffredo married again and had several heirs. The date of his death is unknown.

Borgia, Lucrezia. Duchess of Ferrara; b. at Rome, April 18, 1480; d. at Ferrara, June 24, 1519. She was the natural daughter of Rodrigo Borgia (Alexander VI) and Vannozza Cattanei. From a tender age her father used her in furtherance of his and his son Cesare's political aims. Having become pope thanks partly to Cardinal Ascanio Sforza, Alexander wished to strengthen his ties with the Sforza family. He therefore annulled an existing marriage contract (executed in 1491) between Lucrezia and a Spanish nobleman of Naples and gave Lucrezia to Giovanni Sforza, lord of Pesaro and a kinsman of Ascanio and Ludovico Sforza of Milan. Lucrezia's marriage to Giovanni was celebrated with "the greatest pomp and extravagance" in the Vatican, on June 12, 1493. The bride was 13 and her husband was 27, which was not an unusual difference in age at this time. Several cardinals and Giulia Farnese, Alexander's mistress, attended the dinner given by the pope for the bride and groom following the ceremony. After the French invasion of Italy (1494–1495) and the reestablishment of the Aragonese kingdom of Naples, Alexander was moved to strengthen his ties with Naples. Giovanni, wise in the ways of the pope, saved his life by fleeing from Rome (March, 1497). Alexander had his marriage to Lucrezia annulled (December 20, 1497), on the ground that it had never been consummated and that Lucrezia was still a virgin. Unbelief and derision greeted this pronouncement. The scandal of the divorce, and Giovanni's protests and accusations, gave rise to the most sinister reports concerning Lucrezia's private life. She was next betrothed to Alfonso of Aragon, duke of Bisceglie, the natural son of Alfonso II of Aragon, the late king of Naples. The marriage took place on July 21, 1498. According to all evidence, Lucrezia loved her handsome 17-year-old husband. Papal policy changed again. Alexander and Cesare, for their own reasons, turned to France. Since the French claimed Naples, the alliance with Naples through Lucrezia's marriage was a hindrance. The young duke fled Rome in fear of his life. Lucrezia, awaiting a child, was frantic at parting from him. To console her the pope, who doted on her but who apparently neither wished nor dared to oppose Cesare, made her governor of Spoleto (August, 1499), and she went there to take possession of it. Shortly afterward, her husband joined her at Nepi, with which Alexander invested her, and both returned to Rome. There her son Rodrigo was born on November 1, 1499. Alexander seized the estates of the Gaetani, declared rebels by him, and gave his daughter Sermoneta, of which the little Rodrigo became duke. In the next year Lucrezia's husband was set upon before the gate of St. Peter at Rome by a gang of bravos (July 15, 1500). Seriously wounded, he managed to return to the Vatican, where he was tenderly cared for by Lucrezia. So well aware was she of the conditions that prevailed in Vatican circles that she prepared his food herself, lest it be poisoned. The young man seemed to be recovering when a new set of ruffians invaded his room in the Vatican. Lucrezia ran for help, but before she could return the handsome boy had been strangled in his bed (August 18, 1500). Public opinion held Cesare responsible for his death: it was alleged he had remarked that what was not accomplished at breakfast would be fulfilled at dinner. Lucrezia was heartbroken. She retired to her castle at Nepi to mourn. Her grief was soon assuaged to the degree that she returned to Rome and took part in the revels held in the Vatican. When Alexander left Rome (July, 1501) to join the army at Sermoneta, he left Lucrezia in charge of the Holy See. In the same year, he planned her third marriage. Cesare had begun his conquest of the Romagna and wanted to be sure of the good will of Ferrara. Alexander proposed to bind Ferrara by marrying Lucrezia to the widower Alfonso, eldest son of Ercole d'Este, duke of Ferrara. Ercole, and even more so Alfonso, was shaken. Aside from the fact that the Estensi were the oldest ruling family in Italy and the Borgias were upstarts, Alfonso was understandably reluctant to marry a woman whose first husband had suffered humiliation and ridicule and whose second husband had been murdered. He balked, and Ercole resisted as tactfully as he could. The French king advised him to consent; the Emperor Maximilian expressed strong displeasure and tried to prevent the marriage but he had no troops and little influence; the principal powers of Italy were also opposed on the theory that it would make the papacy of Alexander too strong. Alexander did not understate the advantages that would accrue to Ferrara as a result of the alliance, nor did he veil his threats as to the consequences of a refusal of consent by Ercole. In yielding, Ercole drew a hard bargain. Lucrezia was enthusiastic, and wrote many letters to her future father-in-law on the subject of his demands, but none to her future husband. Alexander, cajoled by Lucrezia, and determined on the alliance, was constrained to yield to Ercole's demands on the size of Lucrezia's dowry, the remission of the tribute Ferrara annually paid to the Church, the cession of certain cities to Ferrara, and the gift of benefices to the Estensi. She was married by proxy in the Vatican (December 30, 1501). Early in January she left Rome for Ferrara. Every city through which she passed entertained her and her large retinue. She stopped at Urbino, from where the Duchess Elizabetta accompanied her to Ferrara. Ercole's couriers with the retinue reported to their master that it was impossible to say exactly when they would arrive at Ferrara, as Madonna Lucrezia insisted on frequent stopovers to wash her golden hair; otherwise, she complained, she was afflicted with headaches. As the travelers neared Ferrara, Alfonso rode out in disguise to have a private glimpse of his bride. He passed two hours in her company, was instantly charmed, and galloped back to Ferrara for the official meeting. Her entry into the city (February 2, 1502) was a ceremonial procession of regal proportions and gorgeous color. In the cavalcade were members of the courts of Mantua and Urbino, ambassadors, and ecclesiastical dignitaries. Mounted archers in the red and white livery of the house of Este rode ahead; Alfonso, in red velvet, sat a horse caparisoned in crimson and gold; Lucrezia wore black velvet with a cape of gold brocade trimmed with ermine, a net shimmering with gold and diamonds on her golden hair, and about her neck a necklace of rubies and pearls. Once at her new home, Lucrezia won the hearts of all. She was praised for her beauty, but more than that, for her graciousness and her joyous spirit, for her taste and her learning. Judging from the medals that show her profile, she was not a beautiful woman, but was always spoken of as if she were. In *The Dispute of St. Catherine*, painted by Pinturicchio in the Borgia apartments in the Vatican, the saint is presumed to represent a portrait of Lucrezia, and is the face of a winsome, almost wistful, pretty blonde girl. It is not a striking, strong, nor beautiful face, but appealing. Many of her admirers wrote of an inner grace of personality by which she won admiration. The old duke was captivated, Alfonso was delighted. She harmonized beautifully with the Estense court and its tradition of culture, was tactful and gracious to courtiers, poets, artists, and citizens. All the members of the Estense family were united in their affection for her. Francesco Gonzaga, husband of Isabella d'Este was a great admirer. Isabella herself, at first outraged at the thought of her brother's marriage to Lucrezia, came to have sincere regard for her. Many of Lucrezia's letters to her sister-in-law survive in the archives at Modena. Either through wisdom or indifference she refrained from interference in political matters. Around her were gathered some of the most prominent intellects of the day. Pietro Bembo, who was said to have been in love with her, dedicated to her his *Gli asolani*, the dialogues on Platonic love. She gave him a lock of her yellow hair (now in the Ambrosiana, Milan), and wrote him a number of letters. The tone of the letters is ardent, but in the spirit of gallantry of the day. Aldus Manutius was an admirer, as were the Strozzi, father and son, who wrote extravagant poems to her in the manner of court poets. Trissino, Caviceo, and Mario Equicola were her friends. The court at Ferrara was perhaps the most brilliant in Italy, and for a time she was its center. She had an instinct for sympathetic understanding and an intuitive knowledge of how to deal with courtiers and artists. Reasonably intelligent and capable, after Alfonso became duke she served as regent of Ferrara in his frequent absences and was a credit to him. From 1512 she began to lead a retired life. She became very pious and gave herself to good works and to visiting churches and monasteries. At one time she entered a convent (she had done so on other occasions of grief or sorrow) and from there wrote to Francesco Gonzaga, advising him to give himself to God, as she had done, to obtain pardon for the sins "of our age." She bore five living children to Alfonso, including Ercole (d. 1559) who succeeded him as Ercole II, Ippolito (d. 1572) who became a cardinal, and Eleanora (d. 1575) who became a nun in the Convent of Corpus Domini (where, in the choir, Lucrezia and Alfonso were buried). At thirty-nine she already seemed old. On June 14, 1519, she bore a stillborn child. On June 22 she wrote to Pope Leo X saying she realized she would "be compelled to pay my debt to nature," and that she approached the end of her life with pleasure. As a Christian, "although a sinner," she asked the pope's blessing and commended her husband and her children to him. She died on June 24 at Belriguardo, the pleasure palace where she had been so joyously welcomed as a bride seventeen years earlier.

Some of her contemporaries, notably Sannazzaro and Pontano (Neapolitans), Matarazzo (Perugian), and Machiavelli (Florentine), accused Lucrezia of the most depraved crimes. They were quite possibly motivated

thin; ᴛʜ, then; y, you; (variable) d̦ as d or j, ș as s or sh, ț as t or ch, z̦ as z or zh; o, F. cloche; ü, F. menu; ċh, Sc. loch; ṅ, F. bonbon; ʙ, Sp. Córdoba (sounded almost like v).

by the hatred they felt for her father and her brother. On the other hand, equally reputable contemporaries who knew her well as duchess of Ferrara over a period of nearly 20 years, had nothing but praise for her goodness, her graciousness, her joyous spirit, and her irreproachable life. The latter group included Manutius, Bembo, Ariosto, Mario Equicola (chronicler of Ferrara), and Tebaldeo, among others. She was a focus of attention in her own day because of her eminent connections, and undoubtedly shared in the dissolute court life of her time. Docile to the point of stupor, she was a submissive pawn in the schemes of her father and her brother, and the evil that surrounds her name is to some extent, certainly, a reflection of their criminality and corruption.

Borgia, Pedro Luis. Prefect of Rome; b. c1432; d. at Civitavecchia, September 26, 1458. He was the nephew of Pope Calixtus III and the brother of Rodrigo Borgia (Alexander VI). Pedro Luis was loaded with princely honors and offices by Calixtus: governor of Castel Sant' Angelo, captain general of the papal militia (1456), governor of many cities of Umbria and the Papal States, prefect of Rome (1457), and vicar of Benevento and Terracina. He had such power he was called a new Caesar. Handsome, dissolute, arrogant, he was detested by the Romans. On the death of Calixtus (August 6, 1458), Pedro Luis and the other Spaniards on whom Calixtus had showered offices, wealth, and power were compelled to flee the city before the anger of the Romans.

Borgia, Pedro Luis. First duke of Gandia; b. c1458; d. 1488. He was the son of Rodrigo Borgia (Alexander VI) by an unknown mistress. For his part in the wars against the Moors in Spain, he was made duke of Gandia by Ferdinand II of Aragon (Ferdinand the Catholic), and was given a cousin of the king in marriage. On the death of Pedro Luis, his title and his wife passed to his brother Giovanni.

Borgia, Pedro Luis. Cardinal; b. c1480; d. October 4 or 5, 1511. He was a great-nephew of Alexander VI and was the brother of Cardinal Giovanni Borgia the Younger. He inherited his brother's offices and benefices on the latter's death and was made cardinal by Alexander on September 28, 1500.

Borgia, Rodrigo. Duke of Bisceglie; b. November 1, 1499; d. at Bari, 1512. He was the son of Lucrezia Borgia and Alfonso, duke of Bisceglie. When his mother was married to Alfonso d'Este (December, 1501) the child was left under the guardianship of Cardinal Francesco Borgia, since Lucrezia was not allowed to take him with her to Ferrara. On the death of Alexander VI, the boy was spirited out of Rome, and was later brought up by his aunt, Isabella of Aragon. She was the unhappy widow of Gian Galeazzo Sforza of Milan, whose death was thought to have been caused by poison. The king of Spain recognized young Rodrigo as his father's heir to the title duke of Bisceglie.

Borgia, Rodrigo. Posthumous son of Alexander VI and, possibly, Giulia Farnese; b. 1503; d. 1527. He became a monk.

Borgia, Rodrigo Lanzol y. Original name of Pope **Alexander VI.**

Borgognone (bôr-gō-nyō′nā), **Ambrogio.** See **Bergognone, Ambrogio.**

Borja (bôr′ha), **Alonso de.** Original name of Pope **Calixtus III.**

Borromeo (bōr-rō-mā′ō), Saint **Carlo.** Archbishop of Milan, reformer, and philanthropist; b. at Rocca di Arona, on Lake Maggiore, October 2, 1538; d. at Milan, November 3, 1584. Of a distinguished noble family of Milan, he received a religious education at Milan, took the clerical habit at the age of 12, and at 16 was at Pavia studying theology and law. He took his doctorate in civil and canon law in December, 1559. A few weeks later, his uncle became Pope Pius IV, called his nephew to Rome, and entrusted to him the highest and most important Church offices. The following year he was made a cardinal and named archbishop of Milan. Among his many posts of responsibility at Rome, he was his uncle's valuable assistant in the Secretariate of State, and was especially influential in reopening the Council of Trent (1562–1563). In November, 1562, his brother Federico died. This loss wrought a great change in his life. He had always been deeply religious; he now became ascetic as well, and used almost none of a great private fortune for his own needs. He was ordained (1563) and was anxious to go to Milan and take up his duties there, but was constrained by his uncle and the business of the Curia to remain in Rome. When his uncle Pope Pius IV died (December, 1565), St. Carlo was able to remove to Milan, and remained there the rest of his life. He immediately began to institute a series of reforms that were to have a profound effect on his diocese and the Church. These included administrative reforms, the calling of councils and synods, and above all regular visits to all parts of his diocese, so that the shepherd would know the condition and needs of his flock. As a result of his intimate knowledge of his diocese, he made social reforms, founded shelters for the poor and abandoned, orphanages, hospitals, schools and academies (he was especially interested in education and aware of its importance), often using his own wealth to do so. He was untiring in his ministration to his flock, and was noted for his heroic activities in the plague of 1576. And at all times his own life was severely ascetic. He was a strict disciplinarian and his reforms aroused opposition in some quarters, especially as he staunchly asserted the prerogatives of his office, and as he unsparingly disciplined orders as he felt they needed it. Twice his life was threatened by dissidents; on one occasion a hired assassin fired at him point-blank as he knelt in prayer, but the resulting wound was slight. In addition to his tireless labor in his own diocese, he made journeys to others, as to Cremona, Bergamo, and Brescia, and made journeys to the valleys of the Alps to combat superstition and Protestantism, as well as to Switzerland, Germany, and many places in Italy. He died of a fever and his body is entombed in the cathedral at Milan. His cult spread rapidly after his death, and he was canonized by Pope Paul V on November 1, 1610.

Borsa (bôr′sä). A bag or purse into which the names of those eligible to hold office at Florence were put. In theory, since the names were pulled blindly from the *borsa*, this was a completely impartial and democratic means of choosing the officials. In fact, control of the names that were put into the *borse* could give control of the government to a political elite. The rules governing admission to the list of eligibles changed from time to time; nobles were permanently excluded from the highest offices, but they were allowed to occupy some leading public posts. Many nobles in Florence accepted commoner status in order to be eligible for high political office.

Bos (bôs), **Jerom.** See **Bosch, Hieronymus.**

Boscán Almogaver (bōs-kän′ äl-mō-gä-ʙer′), **Juan.** Spanish poet; b. at Barcelona, c1493; d. near Perpignan, France, 1542. He was a courtier at the court of Charles V and served the emperor in several military campaigns. He was one of the earliest to write Spanish poems in Italian meters, thereby revolutionizing Spanish poetry. He translated Castiglione's *Il Cortegiano* into Spanish, *Los cuatro libros del Cortesano*, and wrote sonnets, odes, and blank verse. His friend Garcilaso de la Vega, who wrote a preface to his translation of Castiglione's work, also wrote in the Italian meters, and encouraged Boscán Almogaver to continue his efforts. Their works were published together by Boscán Almogaver's widow in 1543.

Bosch (bôs), **Hieronymus.** [Also, **Jerom Bos;** family surname, **van Aeken.**] Dutch painter; b. at 's Hertogenbosch, Netherlands, c1450; d. there, 1516. Popularly known for the fantastic figures in many of his works, he was also a painter of satirical genre pictures. He excelled in large representations of religious subjects, and in such works as *The Temptation of Saint Anthony* and *The Last Judgment*, surrounded his central characters with nightmarish creatures representing evil and torture. Many of his paintings are in Spanish collections. Bosch achieved in his compositions a unity between background and figures new at that time in Dutch art.

Boscoli (bôs′kō-lē), **Andrea.** Painter; b. at Florence, 1550; d. 1606. He was a pupil of Santi di Tito, and was influenced, in his studies in lighting, by the Venetians and the Flemings. To these influences he added a personal, animated touch of his own in his well-drawn figures. At Florence there is a *Visitation*, in S. Ambrogio, a *Self-Portrait* and a *St. Sebastian*, in the Uffizi. He also worked at Pisa, Rimini, Macerata, and Sanginesio.

Boselli (bō-sel′lē), **Antonio.** Painter; b. at Bergamo, c1480; d. c1536. A provincial painter, his *St. Lawrence between St. John the Baptist and St. Barnaba* is in the Carrara Academy, Bergamo.

Bosone da Gubbio (bō-zō′nā dä göb′byō). Ghibelline party leader and writer; d. after 1349. In 1300 he and his party were driven from their native Gubbio by the Guelphs, and fled to Arezzo. After a return to Gubbio, he was again exiled (1315). In the following years he served as podesta in various Ghibelline cities, as Arezzo, Viterbo, Lucca and Todi. He was imperial vicar of Pisa (1328) under Ludwig the Bavarian, and was taken prisoner by his enemies. He left some verses of little merit, a *capitolo* on the *Divina Commedia,* and a sonnet, addressed to the Hebrew poet Immanuel ben Solomon, on the death of Dante.

Bosso (bôs′sō), **Matteo.** Humanist and ecclesiastic; b. 1427; d. at Padua, 1502. Of a noble family of Verona, he studied at Milan, and then (c1450) entered the Congregation of the Canons Regular. A distinguished humanist, he enjoyed the favor of popes and cardinals, and especially of the Medici at Florence, but declined all offices, honors, and ecclesiastical positions. His writings became famous; among them are *De veris ac salutiferis animi gaudiis,* dedicated to Poliziano and Lorenzo de' Medici; a collection of Latin letters, *Recuperationes Fesulanae; De instituendo sapientiae animo;* and two other collections of letters.

Botero (bō-tā′rō), **Giovanni.** Political writer; b. at Bene Vagienna, in the Piedmont, 1544; d. at Turin, June 27, 1617. He began his studies in a Jesuit college in 1559, studied a year at Rome, and then became a teacher of philosophy and rhetoric in Jesuit schools in Italy and France. He was also active as a preacher. He appears to have been a nonconformist in some respects and was not permitted to take his final vows. On the contrary, in 1579 he was dismissed because of a sermon he preached at Milan, in which he registered his opposition to the pope's temporal power. The archbishop of Milan, St. Carlo Borromeo, a man of noble piety, extraordinary zeal, and tireless reforming ardor, heard the sermon, realized that it was not an attack on the Church, and found a position for Botero. Later (1582) the archbishop took him as his secretary and was undoubtedly influential in giving a religious cast to Botero's political thinking. On the death of the archbishop, Botero became counselor to his nephew, Federico Borromeo (the saintly cardinal in Manzoni's Italian classic, *I promessi sposi*), and went with him to Rome. In 1598 he left the service of Cardinal Borromeo and became tutor to the sons of Charles Emmanuel, duke of Savoy. In the course of his years as tutor he went to Spain (1603) with his pupils and remained there three years. He left the service of the duke in 1614. Botero left a large body of writing that was highly respected in his own time. He was a man of lively curiosity in many areas, particularly in geography, economics, and politics. It was said that he stood at the gates of Milan and questioned the customs men about the kinds of goods that were brought into the city, the variations in prices, and the duties that were paid, among other things. He attempted to draw conclusions and rules from what he learned and to draw up statistical lists, and he enjoyed discussing these matters with people of all classes. One result of this interest was his *De regia sapientia* (1583), in which he set forth his findings and conclusions. Among his other works are *Cause della grandezza e magnificenza delle città* (*The Greatness of Cities,* Rome, 1588), in which he describes the geography, choice of site, population, and many other relevant matters. His *Relazioni universali* (Rome, 1591) is a description and history of many parts of Europe where he had worked and traveled, and of other parts of the world as well. His most important political work is his *Ragion de Stato* (*Reason of State,* Rome, 1589). In the dedication he asserts that his reason for writing it is to register opposition to Machiavelli's views on how the needs of the state and the ruler must be met, views that he claimed were abhorrent. However, although never so bluntly put, and always on a more elevated plane, he often finds himself adapting Machiavelli's thought that the end justifies the means when it is for a "reason of state." Justice and ethics, he finds, should prevail in governing for good practical reasons—not for their inherent virtues. He champions morality in government because, he argues, it works. He favors uniformity of religion, again for its practical advantages. He thinks prelates should be consulted on governmental matters, but not taxed, and fears the Turks more than heretics. His book is compartmentalized into brief discussions on a wide variety of topics, as those pertaining to peace and war, economics, religion, the public good. "The public good," he wrote, "has two aspects, the spiritual and the temporal. The temporal consists of civil and political peace, the spiritual of religion and the unity of the Church of God." His book takes up all the matters that he thinks will secure and defend the public good. As did Machiavelli, on whom he modeled his book, he quotes widely from the classic Roman writers: Livy and Tacitus are his favorites. Machiavelli, who was a much better writer, discusses government and rulers from a purely political point of view. Botero, in the atmosphere of the Counter-Reformation, attempted to combine religious and political reform.

Botticelli (bôt-tē-chel′lē), **Sandro.** [Original name, **Alessandro di Mariano di Filipepi.**] Florentine painter; b. at Florence, 1445; d. there, May 17, 1510. He was the son of Mariano di Vanni di Filipepi, a tanner, and was one of the youngest of a large family. Of his older brothers, Giovanni (1421–1493) was called Botticello, "little barrel," and it is perhaps from him that Sandro (a common nickname for Alessandro) came to be called Botticelli. Another brother, Simone (b. 1443), became an ardent *piagnone* ("weeper," as the followers of Savonarola were called), and wrote a chronicle of the rise and death of Savonarola. Sandro lived with his brothers after their father died (1482) and with Simone especially from about 1493. It is perhaps from this circumstance that a tradition, of which Vasari was the source, developed that Botticelli himself was a follower of Savonarola. Although his last works were devoted to religious themes, were increasingly austere in presentation, and indicate a mind absorbed in a spiritual search, no documents exist to confirm the tradition. Vasari writes that though quick enough at his studies he was discontented at school. His father apprenticed him to a goldsmith and then put him under the painter Fra Filippo Lippi. He worked with great enthusiasm under Fra Filippo, and his early works are very close to his master's, as *Madonna and Child with an Angel* (Ospedale degli Innocenti, Florence), formerly attributed to Lippi, *Madonna and Child with Two Angels* (Galleria Nazionale di Capodimonte, Naples), *Madonna and Child with Cherubim,* and *Madonna and Child against a Rose Hedge* (Uffizi). In all these the types of the *Madonna* closely resemble the sweet girlishness of Lippi's *Madonnas;* the two last-mentioned, thought to have been painted about 1470, show Botticelli's developing individuality in their interest in line and linear design. In 1470 Botticelli had his own workshop at Florence (one of his pupils was Filippino Lippi, son of his former master). The earliest dated painting is his *Fortitude* (1470), now in the Uffizi but painted for the Hall of the Merchants. It is one of seven *Virtues* painted for the Merchants (all now in the Uffizi). The others were done by Piero del Pollaiuolo, and the influence of Pollaiuolo, who was a weak follower of his brother Antonio, is evident in Botticelli's painting from this time. In his development Botticelli passed from the tenderness and color of Lippi to a deeper concern, inspired by Antonio Pollaiuolo, with the contour and defined rendering of the human figure. Lippi and Pollaiuolo were, if not at opposite ends of the spectrum, representatives of different approaches to art—Lippi limiting himself to portraying and rendering gentle emotions with glowing color and expressiveness, and Pollaiuolo absorbed with new techniques that involved perspective and the possibilities of the human figure. Botticelli had undoubtedly studied Masaccio's frescoes in the Brancacci Chapel, but his artistic vision did not encompass Masaccio's monumentality, exaltation of the dignity of man, or his preoccupation with perspective and light. In his intellectual approach to his art his interest was less in presenting a three-dimensional natural world than in presenting an intellectualized, poetic design, in which his sinuous, nervous, living line is all-important.

For much of his painting life Florence was governed by Lorenzo de' Medici; the era was called a Golden Age for artists, who received many commissions under the patronage of the Medici family. In 1475 he designed a standard for the *giostra* (tournament) that Giuliano de' Medici gave in honor of Simonetta Vespucci, and in 1478 painted, in fresco, the Pazzi conspirators and their accomplices hanging by their necks (except for Bernardo Bandini, who was hanged by a foot as a sign of special contempt) from the Palazzo Vecchio. Of the early period is the *Adoration of the Magi* (National Gallery, London). Another on the same theme (Uffizi), ordered in 1475 and intended for S. Maria Novella, has portraits of Cosimo the Elder and his two sons, Piero and Giovanni, as the three kings, and of Cosimo's grandsons, Lorenzo and Giuliano, as well as what is traditionally held to be a self-portrait of the artist. The *Adoration* in the National Gallery, Washington, is of a slightly later date (1481–1482). In all three, the figures and composition are dominant; there is scarcely any purely decorative detail and a complete absence of the genre elements so dear to the hearts of some other painters of this subject. In 1472 he had been admitted to the Artists' Guild, and in 1481 he was called to Rome by Sixtus IV to paint frescoes on stories from the Old Testament in the Sistine Chapel. Cosimo Rosselli, Domenico Ghirlandaio, Perugino, and Signorelli were working in the chapel at the same time. Vasari writes that Cosimo Rosselli, the least gifted of the artists painting in the chapel, succeeded best in winning the pope's admiration. Botticelli, and presumably the others also, who had scorned Cosimo for his liberal use of ultramarine and gold to disguise the inadequacies of his technique, was chagrined, and thenceforth painted for more sophisticated patrons who understood his ideals. And his ideals and paintings were highly popular at Florence. There and in the neighborhood, except for the brief visit to Rome, he spent his working life. By the fall of 1482 he was back at Florence and working again for the Medici family. With Ghirlandaio, Perugino, and Filippino Lippi he painted in their villa at Spedaletto. In 1486 he painted in the Tornabuoni villa at Chiasso Macerelli, and thereafter worked for Lorenzo di Pierfrancesco de' Medici, Lorenzo the Magnificent's cousin, in the villas at Trebbio and Castello. For the same patron he made exquisite drawings in silver point and pen to illustrate the *Divine Comedy*, many of which are at Berlin and in the Vatican. The majority of Botticelli's paintings are on religious and Biblical themes. The religious paintings and the great series of *tondi* (circular paintings) of the Virgin that culminated in *The Coronation of the Virgin* and *The Madonna and Six Saints* (called *The Madonna of S. Barnaba*), Uffizi, are of the period 1484–1490. At the same time, as a child of his age and intellectually stimulated by the preoccupations of the poets and humanists with the classical world, he expressed their ideas in his paintings. His two widest known of this type are probably *La Primavera* (*Spring*), originally called *The Kingdom of Venus*, painted for Lorenzo di Pierfrancesco's villa at Castello, and *The Birth of Venus*, probably painted for the same patron. The former is thought to be Botticelli's presentation of the kingdom of Venus as described in Poliziano's *Stanze per la giostra*, written for Giuliano de' Medici. Botticelli translated the poet's imagery into the poetry of line and color. *The Birth of Venus* may derive from a combination of the Homeric *Hymn to Venus*, Ovid, and Poliziano's verses. Other paintings on mythological or classical themes, with complicated allegorical implications, include *Pallas and the Centaur* (Uffizi). Of all the interpretations to which it has been subject, the common thread is that it represents the triumph of wisdom and man's intellectual and better nature over barbarism and the animal side of his nature. Pallas, as wisdom, may represent Lorenzo de' Medici, the good government of Florence under the Medici, or Florentine superiority in general. Another in a similar vein is *Mars and Venus* (National Gallery, London). His *Calumny* (Uffizi) is a work of the late period (c1494–1495), and is his version of the celebrated painting of the Calumny of Apelles described by Lucian and introduced into Alberti's treatise on painting. Of his frescoes, those in the Louvre originally formed part of the decoration of a villa. They are notable for the delicacy of the clear color and the splendor of the draftsmanship. The fresco of *St. Augustine* at the Church of the Ognissanti, Florence, is a strong work that in the powerful expressivity of the saint's head may indicate some influence of Andrea Castagno. Botticelli also painted a number of sharply defined and illuminating portraits. There are four similar ones of Giuliano de' Medici: in the Carrara Academy at Bergamo, in the Crespi Collection at Milan, at Berlin, and in the National Gallery, Washington. Other portraits are in the National Gallery, London, the Johnson Collection, Philadelphia, the Uffizi, Florence, and elsewhere.

Botticelli had a busy workshop at Florence, and all the commissions he could fulfill. A prominent and popular painter, in 1491 he was one of a panel to consider a design for the façade of S. Maria del Fiore. In 1503 he was a member of the committee to select a site for Michelangelo's *David*. Toward the end of his life his popularity lessened. This may have had something to do with the fact that the Medici, with whom he had been linked for so long, were discredited and driven out of Florence. It was probably also because he did not embrace and express new developments in an evolving art, such as those of Leonardo da Vinci, but maintained his personal, intellectualized, and poetic individuality. Isabella d'Este, looking for a painter to decorate her *studiolo* at Mantua, learned from her agent in Florence that Botticelli was available, but he never worked for her. His last known painting, and the only one he signed, is the *Mystic Nativity*, National Gallery, London, painted at the end of 1500 or the beginning of 1501. The work is roughly in three tiers, with a group of singing angels above the shelter with the Holy Family, and groups of men being embraced by angels in the lowest register; very small devils leap in the lower corners. (One cannot really speak of a foreground in connection with Botticelli's paintings, as he was uninterested in projecting depth. It may be noted that in general he was not interested in landscape as such. When he did paint a landscape in the background it appears in miniature rather than in perspective.) An inscription on the painting, in Greek and now partly effaced, reveals Botticelli's preoccupation with the events of his time and his sincere spiritual interests. It reads, "I Sandro painted this picture at the end of the year 1500 [perhaps the beginning of 1501 according to the new calendar] in the troubles of Italy in the midtime after the time according to the 11th chapter of St. John in the second woe of the Apocalypse in the loosing of the devil for three and a half years then he will be chained in the 12th chapter and we shall see clearly . . . as in this picture." The effacement of the inscription prevents us from knowing what shall be seen clearly. Various interpretations of the painting have been offered: that it refers to the political troubles of Florence and Italy; that it refers to the martyrdom of Savonarola; that it is an expression of Botticelli's own religious devotion.

Botticelli was an enormously productive painter, but according to Vasari his activity lessened at the end of his life, and though he had earned a great deal of money he was a bad manager, and "having become old, unfit for work, and helpless, he was obliged to go on crutches, being unable to stand upright, and so died, after long illness and decrepitude . . ." It is written that he had a horror of women and marriage and that he was most drawn to those "whom he knew to be zealous students in art." From the tender expressivity and glowing color of Fra Filippo, Botticelli was attracted by the strength, movement, and definition that delighted Pollaiuolo, and developed an individual style based on clear, often cool color, masterly draftsmanship, and an energetic line. The sharply outlined, heart-shaped faces of the Madonnas and angels of his mature period are distinctively Botticellian. His approach to his art was intellectual rather than representational. He apparently welcomed and investigated new ideas and techniques and chose among them as suited him technically and metaphysically, content to be alone in his vision. Perhaps for this reason he had little impact or influence on younger painters. The Uffizi, Florence, with its large number of paintings beginning with the early *Fortitude* and ranging at least as late as the *Calumny*, has the greatest single collection of his paintings. Other works are in the Accademia, Pitti Palace, and churches of Florence; in the Louvre, Paris; the National Gallery, London; the Ambrosiana and Poldi Pezzoli Museum, Milan; the Carrara Academy, Bergamo; and elsewhere in Europe. In the United States there are works in the Metropolitan Museum, New York; the Hyde Collection, Glens Falls, New York; the Johnson Collection, Philadelphia; the Isabella Stewart Gardner Museum, Boston; the Art Institute of Chicago; the National Gallery, Washington; the Fogg Museum, Cambridge, Massachusetts; the Detroit Institute of Art; the Museum of Art, El Paso, Texas; the Portland, Oregon, Art Museum; Raleigh, North Carolina; and the Columbia, South Carolina, Museum of Art.

Botticini (bôt-tē-chē′nē), **Francesco.** Painter; b. at Florence, 1446; d. there, 1497. At first a pupil of Neri di Bicci, from whom he is supposed to have fled, he was an eclectic who adopted, in succession, the styles of Verrocchio, Andrea del Castagno, Cosimo Rosselli, Domenico Ghirlandaio, and, most especially, Botticelli. Because he imitated the others so closely his work, in the absence of documentation, is difficult to identify. His only documented work consists of parts of the predella of the Tabernacle of the Sacrament at Empoli, commissioned in 1484 and practically completed in 1491. He has variously been called a "mediocre" painter and a "fresh and pleasing minor master." Paintings attributed to him on stylistic grounds include what were perhaps his two best works, *The Three Archangels with the Little Tobias*, Uffizi, Florence, painted when he was following Verrocchio, and *Madonna and Child with the Little St. John*, Isabella

Stewart Gardner Museum, Boston. Other paintings attributed to him are in the Pitti Palace, the Accademia, and S. Spirito, Florence; at Empoli; in the Louvre, Paris; National Gallery, London; at Amsterdam, Bergamo, Modena, Prato, Turin, Venice (Ca' d'Oro); and the Metropolitan Museum, New York, Baltimore (Museum), Chicago, Cincinnati, Cleveland, and elsewhere.

Bourbon (bör-bôṅ), **Charles,** Duc **de.** [Called **Connétable de Bourbon,** meaning literally "Constable of Bourbon," but usually taken to convey the sense that he was the "Bourbon Constable," as opposed to other constables of France.] French general; b. February 17, 1490; d. at Rome, May 6, 1527. He was descended from a younger branch of the house of Bourbon (being a son of a count of Montpensier), and married Suzanne, an heiress of Bourbon, through whom he obtained the title of duke. In 1515 he was created constable of France. In 1522 (on the death of Suzanne) he went over to the enemies of France and concluded a private alliance with the emperor Charles V and Henry VIII of England. In return, he was promised, by the emperor, that he would receive the emperor's sister Eleonora in marriage, with Portugal as a jointure, and an independent kingdom which was to include Provence, Dauphiné, Bourbonnais, and Auvergne. He fled from France in 1523, aided in expelling the French from Italy in 1524, and contributed to the victory over Francis I at Pavia in 1525, in spite of which his interests were neglected in the treaty of peace between Spain and France in 1526. He was one of the commanders of the army of Spanish and German mercenaries that fell on Rome on May 6, 1527. Benvenuto Cellini, standing on the ramparts with some companions, watched the enemy close in on the walls and decided to take a few shots at the enemy before he fled to safety. Cellini and his friends fired their arquebuses. In his *Autobiography*, Cellini suggests that it was a round from his own arquebus that killed the constable. Whether or not it was his lucky aim that did it, the constable fell in the assault on the walls, and at the place that Cellini describes.

Bourbon, Charles, Cardinal **de.** French nobleman and ecclesiastic; b. c1520; d. May 9, 1590. He was one of the leaders of the Catholic League, and opposed Henry of Navarre, who had not at that time renounced Protestantism.

Bourchier (bou'chėr), **John.** [Title, 2nd Baron **Berners.**] English statesman and author; b. 1467; d. at Calais, France, March 16, 1533. He was chancellor of the exchequer in 1516. He translated Froissart's *Chronicle* (1523–1525), *Arthur of Lytell Brytayne, Huon of Burdeux, The Castell of Love,* and others.

Bourchier, Thomas. English ecclesiastic; b. c1404; d. at Knowle, near Sevenoaks, England, 1486. Originally a Lancastrian, as archbishop of Canterbury (1454–1486) he crowned Edward IV (1461) and Richard III (1483), and officiated (1486) at the marriage of Henry VII to Elizabeth of York. He drew up the terms of agreement (1458) between the Lancastrians and Yorkists.

Bouts (bouts), **Dierick** or **Dierik** or **Dirk** or **Thierry.** Dutch painter; b. c1410; d. at Louvain, Belgium, May 6, 1475. His work shows the influence of Roger van der Weyden, and of the Van Eycks. One of his masterpieces is an altarpiece in the Church of St. Peter at Louvain; his *Moses and the Burning Bush* is in the Johnson Collection at Philadelphia; and one of his portraits is in The Metropolitan Museum of Art in New York.

Bower (bou'ėr), or **Bowmaker** (bō'mā-kėr), **Walter.** Scottish cleric and writer; b. at Haddington, Scotland, c1385; d. 1449. He is believed to have been one of the authors of *Scotichronicon*, a primary source for early Scottish history.

Bowge of Court (böj), **The.** Poem (c1499) by John Skelton. It is a dream allegory in rime royal, and pictures the hazards of one who lives at court.

Bowmaker (bō'mā-kėr), **Walter.** See **Bower** or **Bowmaker, Walter.**

Braccesi (brät-chā'zē) or **Bracci** (brät'chē), **Alessandro.** Poet; b. at Florence, 1445; d. at Rome, 1503. He held office at Florence and served the republic as ambassador to Rome. Learned in Latin and Greek, he wrote Latin poetry in the manner of his friend Poliziano, translated from the Latin (among his translations is Pope Pius II's youthful tale of two lovers), and wrote a great deal of Italian poetry in the burlesque manner of Burchiello.

Bracciano (brät-chä'nō), Duchess of. See **Accoramboni, Vittoria.**

Bracciano, Duke of. Title of various members of the Orsini family, derived from their castello and the area around it on the Lake of Bracciano, about 20 miles northwest of Rome.

Braccio da Montone (brät′chō dä mōn-tō′nā), **Andrea.** Celebrated condottiere and lord of Perugia; b. probably in the castle of Montone, July 1, 1368; d. at Aquila, June 5, 1424. As a child he saw his father, a noble of Perugia, deprived of his lands and driven into exile. His aim was to recover his inheritance and add whatever he could to it. He joined John XXIII in his war against Ladislaus of Naples, defeated the latter at Roccasecca, and won back most of his patrimony. When John XXIII made peace (1412) with Ladislaus, however, he ceded Perugia to him for ten years. Braccio now fought Ladislaus and Carlo Malatesta, defended Umbria, and returned in triumph at the head of a large army to Perugia. His victories and his army, which included many exiles, made him feared throughout Italy. He suppressed his enemies at home by treachery or force, and greatly extended the area of his state to include all of Umbria, most of the Marches, and part of Capua, governing it all with an iron hand, although retaining the old communal institutions as a formality. In 1417 he took advantage of a conspiracy to occupy Rome and held the city for seventy days, at length falling back before the advance of Muzio Attendolo Sforza. Martin V sought to recover former Church lands and engaged in a duel with Braccio, in which Florence, which took Braccio's side against the pope, attempted to mediate, but each time the negotiations came to nothing. In an invasion of the Abruzzi, Braccio attacked Aquila (1424). One of the bloodiest battles of the century ensued. Braccio was wounded and died a few days later. On his death, the state he had built up by force of arms fell apart. Perugia, Assisi, Jesi, and Todi submitted to the pope.

Braccio was celebrated as a warrior, and around his name grew up a school of warfare. He built the Loggia di Braccio (1423) at Perugia, and other buildings to beautify the city. The Loggia is the earliest Renaissance work there. He was also noted for tunneling through a mountain to drain Lake Trasimeno, a remarkable engineering accomplishment. Pius II, in his *Commentaries,* wrote of him that he "was a fine figure, though his left side was paralyzed. He was pleasant and charming in address but so cruel that he laughed when he ordered men to be tortured and racked with the most excruciating punishments. . . . He did not believe in heaven or hell. He was a foe of the Church and of religion and thoroughly undeserving of the Church's burial rites." The last was added because when Braccio died he was buried in unhallowed ground, among beasts. It was only in the time of Eugenius IV that permission was granted his kinsmen to remove the body to his native Perugia.

Bracelli (brä-chel′lē), **Giacomo.** Humanist, historian, and public official; b. probably at Sarzana, toward the end of the 14th century; d. at Genoa, c1466. He studied the classics at Pavia and Milan, and became (1411) chancellor of the Republic of Genoa. Although Pope Nicholas V invited him to Rome as a secretary, he preferred to remain at Genoa and served the republic as chancellor with dignity and integrity until July 14, 1466. To the post he brought the learning and accomplishments of humanism and is an important figure in the history of humanism in the Ligurian area that embraced Genoa. He was official historian of Genoa, and wrote much about the republic, its citizens, and the area. His *De bello hispano libri V* relates, in measured Latin prose, the history of the wars of Alfonso I of Naples against Genoa. Other works are *De claris Genuensibus,* on illustrious citizens, and *Liguriae descriptio*, a work on the region.

Bradamante (brä-dä-män′tā). [Also, **Brandiamante.**] In Matteo Maria Boiardo's *Orlando Innamorato*, the sister of Rinaldo, a very Amazon of valor, and a lady of surpassing beauty. In her guise as a warrior, and armed with her enchanted spear, she fights with the Moor Ruggiero. When her beauty and her sex are revealed he falls in love with her and she with him. In Lodovico Ariosto's *Orlando Furioso*, a continuation of Boiardo's epic, Bradamante marries Ruggiero, after he has been baptized, and they become the founders of the Este house of Ferrara. Their story, with prophecies and noble deeds, is a eulogy of the Estensi, Ariosto's employers.

Bradshaw (brad′shô), **Henry.** English Benedictine monk and poet; b. at Chester, England, c1450; d. 1513. He wrote *De Antiqui-*

tate et Magnificentia Urbis Cestriae and a life of Saint Werburgh, in English verse.

Bradwardine (brad′wạr-dēn), **Thomas.** [Surnamed **Doctor Profundus.**] English prelate, theologian and mathematician; b. at Hartfield, Sussex, England, c1290; d. at Lambeth, August 26, 1349. His works include *De causa Dei, De quadratura circuli, Geometria speculativa,* and *Ars memorativa.*

Bragadin (brä-gä-dēn′), **Donato Bernardo di Giovanni.** Venetian painter; active by 1438; d. 1473. A triptych, *Madonna and Child; St. Philip; St. Agnes,* signed by him is in the Metropolitan Museum, New York.

Brahe (brä′ẹ), **Tycho.** Danish astronomer; b. at Knudstrup, in Skåne, Denmark (now in Sweden), December 14, 1546; d. at Prague, October 24, 1601. Under the patronage of Frederick II of Denmark, he built an observatory, the Uranienborg (completed 1580), on the island of Hven, off the southwest coast of Sweden. Working with improved instruments, he was able to fix more precisely the positions of the planets and the stars. He discovered (1572) a new star in the constellation Cassiopeia, discovered the variation of the moon and the fourth inequality of the motion of the moon. His discoveries and measurements paved the way for later astronomers. In 1596 he lost the patronage of the Danish king, and the following year he left Hven and went to Prague, where he entered the service of the emperor Rudolf II and settled (1599). He left works describing his astronomical observations, his instruments, and an autobiography. He is said never to have been surpassed as a practical astronomer, although he rejected the Copernican system: in his system, the earth was fixed with the sun revolving around it.

Bramante (brä-män′tā), **Donato d'Agnolo.** Architect, one of the greatest of the Italian Renaissance; b. at Asdrualdo (now Fermignano), in the duchy of Urbino, 1444; d. at Rome, April 14, 1514. Few facts are known of his early life: he was the son of poor parents; is thought to have been trained as a painter; probably went to Urbino at an early age; and may have been in contact there with Piero della Francesca, from whom, according to Vasari, he learned aerial perspective, with Laurana, Melozzo da Forlì, and Boccati. Certainly he would have seen the beautiful palace Luciano di Laurana was raising for Federico da Montefeltro, duke of Urbino, and this made a lasting impression on him. Refinement and elegance of ornamentation, a developed sense of proportion, and harmony of the elements were characteristics of all his later work. No work in Umbria, the Marches, or the Romagna, save possibly the Church of S. Bernardino, just outside Urbino, can be ascribed to him. The earliest known date concerning him is 1477, in which year he was working at Bergamo, painting frescoes in the Palace of the Podesta. About 1480 he went to Milan to seek his fortune, on the way visiting Mantua and Florence, where he saw the works of Brunelleschi and Alberti. Probably of his first years at Milan are some monumental figures of men of arms, in fresco, now in the Brera, a *Christ Bound* (Chiaravalle Abbey, near Milan), and a few minor works. The precision of line and grandness of scale in his painting were carried over to his architectural works. The earliest of these at Milan that is known for certain is his reconstruction of the small 9th century Church of S. Maria presso S. Satiro. A feature of his work here is that, lacking space, he built the choir in a perspective of planes that give the appearance of depth and unity; the space that seems to be occupied by a deeply recessed choir is an optical illusion. In this, his first known work, are first apparent the painterly means (perspective) of conveying a visual effect that are features of his later work. The second feature of S. Satiro, and one that foretold many of Bramante's conceptions, is the organization of space about a center. For the baptistery, which he reconstructed as an independent unit from a small chapel on the north transept of the church, his basic plan was a Greek cross (a square) within a circle. This was an arrangement of space that appeared in many surviving early Christian buildings. The first mention of Bramante at S. Satiro was in 1486, but he had probably been working there since the late 1470's. From 1488 he worked with Amadeo on the cathedral at Pavia, but because of the number of architects engaged there and the changes that were made as different architects were in charge, Bramante's work, except for some details of the crypt and the apses, cannot be identified. Also in the late 1480's he began work on the tribune for the east end of the Church of S. Maria delle Grazie. In effect the tribune is an independent, centrally planned unit. It is a square surmounted by a drum and lantern, with apses on three sides of the square and the long nave, already in existence, extending from the fourth side. From about 1492 Bramante began to be regularly employed in the service of Ludovico il Moro's court. He carried out a number of works for him, as in the Castello, in his favorite city of Vigevano, and, of course, in the invention of mechanical devices and contraptions for the sumptuous and elaborate festivals with which the members of the court were frequently regaled. In 1492 he began the Cloisters of S. Ambrogio for Cardinal Ascanio Sforza, Ludovico's brother, which is one of the finest of his late works at Milan. The principal elements of the cloister were the portico with columns and a great arch in the middle, somewhat in the manner of the Pazzi Chapel at Florence and Alberti's Church of Sant' Andrea at Mantua. In 1499, just before the fall of Ludovico, Bramante went to Rome. A "son of poverty," he was frugal and had saved money. He used it to give him the time to study and measure the remains of Imperial Roman buildings, for it was the great scale, severe and stark beauty of form (the marble facings had been almost entirely removed from the ruins) that appealed to Bramante's spirit. Yet one of his most perfect, and perfectly preserved, works of the early years at Rome is the small, circular Tempietto di S. Pietro in Montorio. It was a memorial, rather than a church, built for Ferdinand and Isabella of Spain on the spot where, according to tradition, St. Peter was martyred. In continuation, rather than in imitation, of the classical Roman style of the Pantheon and the Temple of Vesta at Tivoli, Bramante designed the Tempietto as a cylinder rising within a proportionately wider ring of columns, surmounted by a hemispherical dome. In a mathematical application of proportion, the height of the complete structure is twice the diameter of the largest circle of the base. The exquisite rotunda, one of the few designs that was carried out largely as Bramante planned it, is a milestone in Renaissance architecture. (But Bramante's intention of creating a circular courtyard around it to reflect its form in ever-widening circles was never fulfilled.) Another early work at Rome was the rebuilding of the Cloister of S. Maria della Pace, which he carried out for Cardinal Carafa. For the problem of reconstructing an existing cloister of two stories, Bramante adopted solutions derived from Roman amphitheaters. Through Cardinal Carafa he met the members of the papal court and was thereafter much in demand.

In 1503 Julius II was elected pope. Bramante now found a patron who was as enthusiastic, energetic, daring, and grandiose in his plans as was Bramante himself. The two aging men had undiminished appetites for glory; Julius sought the greater glory of the Church; Bramante aspired to raise structures of the splendor and beauty of ancient Rome. From the time of his accession, Julius kept Bramante (and Michelangelo and Raphael) constantly occupied with his numerous projects. For Julius he built fortresses, laid out the Via Giulia, reclaimed land, designed fountains. For others he designed or redesigned palaces, including a palace, perhaps intended for himself, that came to be known as Raphael's House (destroyed in the 17th century) from the fact that Raphael lived in it. The strongly accented horizontals and verticals that give solidity, harmony, and grace to the symmetrical façades, with their evenly spaced windows flanked by elegant columns, became the pattern for palaces and public buildings for the next two centuries. In the great plans for papal building, the idea evolved of reconstructing the buildings of the Vatican area into a harmonious and grandiose whole. In the execution of the idea Bramante built the main courtyard of the Vatican Palace, that of S. Damaso. With the example of the Colosseum before his eyes he constructed it as a series of arcades. (Raphael completed the loggias begun by Bramante, and designed the frescoes that decorate them. To protect the frescoes the arcades have been closed in so that the effect of light and shade —always important to Bramante—is lost.) A second great undertaking in the reconstruction of the Vatican area was the building of a courtyard to unite the Vatican Palace and the Belvedere, a villa about 300 yards away. This Bramante accomplished (although his work has been much obscured in later times) by building two long wings that diminished from a height of three stories to one as the ground rose up the hill to the Belvedere. A series of ramps and monumental staircases provided for the ascent from the palace to the Belvedere. Interest and variety were provided in the great expanse of the walls by varying the texture of the masonry and by placing pilasters of different form in the different registers. Niches in the walls were intended for the antique statues the pope was collecting. But his greatest undertaking for Julius was the plan to build a new Church of St. Peter's. The ancient church was falling into ruin. Julius at first thought only of restoring and rebuilding but quickly decided to tear down the ancient and hallowed church and build a new one. Bramante's enthusiasm matched the pope's. His design was accepted and work was begun in April, 1506. The demolition of part of the old church, the reliquary of so many precious Christian relics, proceeded at a feverish pace and the Romans gave Bramante the name "the Destroyer." His design for St. Peter's (the present church bears almost no resemblance to his original plan) is known from a drawing by Antonio da Sangallo (now in the Uffizi), and from a medal cast by Caradosso that has a representation of the church Bramante planned on the reverse. On a ground plan of a Greek cross a great cupola was to be raised. Four towers were to be erected at the corners of the square formed by the Greek cross. It was Bramante's classic plan for the organization of space about a center —austere, monumental, overwhelmingly impressive—and was a plan derived from the great vaulted, Imperial baths. (Bramante had known Leonardo da Vinci at Milan. The latter occupied himself for some time with plans for centrally organized buildings, and had prepared drawings of plans and elevations of such buildings. Both geniuses had given a great deal of thought to, and had probably discussed, the effective use of space as it had been employed by the ancients, and its advantages for buildings in their own age.) By the time of the pope's death (1513) little more than the foundations of the great piers to support the cupola had been raised. Bramante himself died the following year. Work was carried on (but interrupted for a period after the sack of Rome in 1527) by a series of architects, including Giuliano da Sangallo, Raphael, Antonio da Sangallo, and Peruzzi, among others. Each of them altered the basic plan. In 1546 Michelangelo was put in charge and, though he was no great friend of Bramante, asserted that wherever Bramante's successors departed from his plan they erred. The church, in its final form a Latin cross (so that the extended nave makes it impossible to see the great dome except from a distance), was consecrated on November 18, 1626. About all that was left of the ideas of Julius and Bramante was their inspiration. Bramante's Milanese works, in which he was developing his ideas for the composition and flow of space, were embellished with graceful decorative elements in modification of the exuberant Lombard style of ornamentation. His Roman works, on a grander scale under the influence of the Imperial buildings, are marked by grandeur, sobriety, and a purity of symmetry and proportion that is entirely satisfying in its outer visual effect, as well as providing light and shade, a sense of flowing space, and harmony within. Vasari writes admiringly of his profound theoretical and practical knowledge and contends that the structural faults that appeared in some of his buildings were owing to the speed that the impetuous Julius forced on him.

Bramantino (brä-män-tē′nō). [Original name, **Bartolomeo Suardi.**] Milanese painter and architect; b. c1465; d. 1530. Bramante, who left Milan in 1499, was his first teacher in the arts of painting and architecture, whence his name Bramantino, "little Bramante." Yet the earliest painting known to be by Bramantino, *The Nativity* (Ambrosiana, Milan), shows more the influence of Mantegna and the Ferrara school than that of Bramante. In it line is the symbol for form. Even his *Christ* (Lugano), which is close to the *Christ Bound* of Bramante at Chiaravalle, shows that Bramantino's orientation was different from Bramante's, and that even when he was closest to his master he maintained a certain originality and individuality. The earliest date known concerning his activity is 1503, when he executed some works in the cathedral at Milan. In 1508 he was at Rome, perhaps at the invitation of Bramante, but little is known of the work he did for Julius II there. His *Philemon and Baucis* (Cologne) may be of this period; it reveals the great impression the sight of the ruins of Rome made on him. The brief visit, which at most lasted a year and a half, put him in contact with such other artists as Pinturicchio, Perugino, and the Sansovini. The Roman sojourn led to a marked change in his development. His art became monumental, his forms broader and rounder, his flesh tones warmer, and the figures less sharply outlined. His *Adoration of the Kings* (National Gallery, London) is thought to be a work of the pre-Roman period. The later style is represented by *The Holy Family* and *Crucifixion* (Brera) and the *St. John* in the Borromeo Collection, Isola Bella. Less influenced by Leonardo than many Milanese painters, he was fundamentally a Lombard painter and had his own place between Butinone and Bergognone, representatives of the traditional manner, and the followers and imitators of Leonardo. Frescoes executed (1511) in the Carafa Chapel in S. Domenico Maggiore, Naples, are attributed to him. In 1513 he was back at Milan, working in the abbey at Chiaravalle. In 1519 he was the architect of the Trivulzio Chapel in S. Nazaro at Milan. It is notable for the simplicity and purity of its lines, for its classical conception, and for the austere elegance of its ornamentation. Though this is his only known architectural work, his interest in architecture is abundantly apparent in the complex, often classical, architecture of the backgrounds of his paintings. In many of his paintings the interest is about equally divided between the figures and the architecture that enfolds them. In 1525 he was named court painter and architect to Francesco II Sforza. Though the political upheavals of Milan—the overthrow of Ludovico Sforza, French rule, restoration of the Sforza, French rule again, and a second restoration of the Sforza—deeply affected his private and political life, he remained at Milan and continued his productivity, now for one ruler, as Trivulzio, and now for another. Besides the works mentioned, he left frescoes in S. Maria delle Grazie (some of which were destroyed in 1943) that are greatly admired and in the Castello Sforzesco at Milan. Other works in that city include a book of sketches of ancient monuments (Ambrosiana) and a series of tapestries of the twelve months made to his designs. Paintings by Bramantino are at Florence, Bergamo, Venice, Vienna, Paris, and elsewhere in Europe. His *Madonna and Child* is in the Metropolitan Museum, New York; *Lucretia*, Johnson Collection, Philadelphia; *Virgin and Child*, Museum of Fine Arts, Boston; and *Christ and the Apostles*, National Gallery, Washington. At a time when Leonardo, Raphael, and Michelangelo were putting their mark on shoals of followers and imitators, Bramantino maintained his individuality as a Lombard painter and in his turn exerted strong influence on such painters as Luini, Gaudenzio Ferrari, and Boccacino.

Brancacci (brän-kät′chē) **Chapel.** A chapel in the Church of the Carmine at Florence. It is famous for the remarkable frescoes painted there by Masaccio. The frescoes, the subject of which was to be episodes from the life of St. Peter, were commissioned by Felice Brancacci. The decoration in the chapel of the Gothic church was begun by Masolino. Having completed the decoration of the vault and upper walls, he left Florence, about 1425, and went to Hungary. When he returned in the late summer of 1427 he resumed work on the chapel and called on Masaccio to help him. In May of the following year Masolino went to Rome, and Masaccio worked alone until the fall, when he too left for Rome, leaving the work still unfinished. Masaccio died in Rome, just before his twenty-seventh birthday. The chapel remained unfinished for fifty years. Then Filippino Lippi took up the work and completed the decoration. The scenes done by Masaccio are *The Tribute Money*, *Resurrection of the Son of the King of Antioch* (completed by Filippino Lippi), and *St. Peter Enthroned*, *St. Peter Healing the Sick with His Shadow* (which contains a portrait of Masolino), *Baptism of the Neophytes*, *St. Peter Distributing Alms and the Death of Ananias*, and *The Expulsion of Adam and Eve*. Masolino, with some assistance from Masaccio, painted *St. Peter Healing the Cripple* and *Resurrection of Tabitha*, *St. Peter Preaching to the Crowd*, and *Temptation of Adam and Eve* (on the pilaster opposite Masaccio's *Expulsion*). Filippino Lippi executed *St. Peter before the Proconsul*, in which he included a self-portrait in one of the onlookers, *St. Paul Visiting St. Peter in Prison*, and *The Angel Freeing St. Peter from Prison*.

In 1690 destruction threatened the frescoes when a plan for the reconstruction of the chapel was proposed by the Marquess Francesco Ferroni. Members of the Academy of Fine Arts, with many others, appealed to Vittoria della Rovere, mother of Grand Duke Cosimo III, for help. Thanks to her vigorous action the proposed reconstruction of the chapel was abandoned and the frescoes were saved. They were again threatened when a disastrous fire swept the church on the night of January 29, 1771, and destroyed much of the old Gothic building. Again they were saved, in no small part owing to the heroic efforts of the firemen to save the paintings. A new church, in a different style, replaced the old Gothic building, but the Brancacci Chapel, which had undergone some changes in the middle of the 18th century, remained substantially unchanged.

Brancaleone (bräng-kä-lā-ō′nā), **Dandolo.** Statesman of Bolognese origin; d. at Rome, 1258. He was elected by the people podesta (captain) of Rome in 1253, with the power of enforcing justice and the command of the military forces. He repressed the nobles and forced Pope Innocent IV to recognize the power of the people, but he exercised his power with such severity that he was driven from the city. Two years later, however, he was recalled.

Brandimarte (brän-dē-mär′tā). In Matteo Maria Boiardo's metrical romance, *Orlando Innamorato*, and Lodovico Ariosto's *Orlando Furioso*, Orlando's loyal friend. He saves Orlando from a magic lake, and takes Orlando's place so that his friend can escape. He is the husband of Fiordiligi. Mortally wounded by Gradasso, he dies uttering his wife's name.

Brandon (bran′dọn), **Charles.** [Title, 1st Duke of **Suffolk.**] English nobleman; d. at Guildford, England, August 24, 1545. He was a favorite of Henry VIII, and served him on various diplomatic missions. He secretly married Henry's sister, widow of Louis XII of France.

Brant (bränt), **Sebastian.** German satiric poet; b. at Strasbourg, 1457; d. there, May 10, 1521. He studied law at Basel, and was city scribe (from 1503) at Strasbourg. He made a European reputation with his *Das Narrenschiff* (*Ship of Fools*), a long poem in rhymed couplets telling of 100 fools in a ship bound for Narragonia. By means of the fools he comments on human weaknesses and contemporary manners. The poem was first published in 1494, and subsequently appeared in many editions. Alexander Barclay (British poet, c1475–1552) based *The Shyp of Folys* on Brant's work. Brant, a pious Catholic humanist, also wrote Latin as well as German poems.

Brantôme (bräṅ-tōm), **Pierre de Bourdeilles,** Seigneur **de.** French chronicler; b. in Périgord, France, c1535; d. July 15, 1614. His *Mémoires* (1665–1666) are valued for their lively description of the chief historical persons and events of his time.

Bray (brā), Sir **Reginald.** English architect and politician; b. in the parish of St. John Bedwardine, near Worcester, England; d. 1503. He supervised the construction of, and probably designed, the Chapel of Henry VII at Westminster. He also founded Saint George's Chapel at Windsor.

Bregno (brā′nyō), **Andrea.** Sculptor and architect; b. at Osteno, on Lake Lugano, 1418; d. at Rome, 1503. Little is known of his youth or training, but the ornate and exuberant Lombard style was replaced by one that approached the classical after he arrived at Rome. There most of his work consisted of funeral monuments in which, typically, the effigy rests on a classical sarcophagus with statues of saints in niches at the sides and angels on the base. Among the monuments he designed and executed at Rome are those for a number of cardinals in various churches, as in S. Maria in Aracoeli, S. Pietro in Vincoli, S. Maria sopra Minerva, S. Maria del Popolo, where there is, in addition to monuments for two cardinals, a signed and dated (1473) altar made for Rodrigo Borgia, SS. Apostoli, where there is one of the finest examples of his style in the monument to Cardinal Pietro Riario (d. 1474) and another to Raffaello della Rovere. He also made (1481–1485) and signed the Piccolomini altars in the cathedral at Siena; a tabernacle (1490) near Viterbo; and worked with Mino da Fiesole and Giovanni Dalmata on other monuments. His compact and well-designed monuments, with their carefully carved figures and precise ornamentation, made him the most favored sculptor at Rome in the time of Pope Sixtus IV.

Bregno, Antonio. [Called **Antonio da Como.**] Lombard sculptor; native of Righeggia (Como); active from 1425; d. after 1457. He worked with his brother Paolo, an architect, in the Ca' d'Oro at Venice (1425–1426), then became associated with the Buon workshop at Venice and perhaps assisted in the execution of the *Porta della Carta* of the Ducal Palace, for which he is thought to have carved some figures of *Virtues*. Little is surely known of him and he is sometimes confused with Antonio Rizzo. The only certain work from his hand is the tomb of Doge Francesco Foscari (d. 1457) in the

Church of the Frari. Because of similarity between the figures of the tomb and those on the Foscari Arch in the Ducal Palace, work on the Foscari Arch is also attributed to him. The combination of Renaissance elements with those predominantly Gothic on the Foscari tomb show him to have been a sculptor of the transition in Venetian sculpture between Bartolomeo Buon (d. 1464) and Antonio Rizzo (d. 1499/1500).

Bregno, Lorenzo and **Giovanni Battista.** Lombard architects and sculptors who came from Osteno or Righeggia (Como) and worked in the Veneto in the early years of the 16th century. Lorenzo died in December, 1523; Giovanni Battista predeceased him. They executed a number of works together and, without fresh inspiration or warmth, followed the classicized examples of Tullio Lombardo. Their works at Venice include the monument to Benedetto Pesaro, in the Frari Church; statues of *St. Catherine* and *St. Mary Magdalen,* in the Church of SS. Giovanni e Paolo; and sculptures in other churches. They also left work, as the relief *The Meeting of the Virgin and St. Elizabeth,* in the cathedral at Treviso.

Brera (brā′rä). Art gallery, Pinacoteca di Brera, located in a monumental palace begun in 1591 on a site formerly occupied by a monastery. The gallery was founded at the end of the 18th century for the instruction of students of the Academy of Fine Arts. It has been continually enriched with works of art from churches, abbeys and suppressed religious institutions, by gifts and acquisitions. The collections comprise paintings of all Italian schools, but the gallery is particularly rich in 15th and 16th century frescoes and representatives of the Lombard and Emilian schools of the Renaissance period. In the same building is the National Braidense Library, founded in 1763. The Empress Maria Teresa declared the collection open to the public and added to it (1773) the library of the Jesuit College that had occupied the palace. Many additions have been made in succeeding years, and the library now contains more than 627,000 volumes.

Brescianino (brā-shä-nē′nō), **Andrea del.** [Original name, **Piccinelli.**] Sienese painter; documented from 1507 to 1525. He was influenced by various painters of his time, including Andrea del Sarto, Fra Bartolommeo, Albertinelli, Sodoma, Beccafumi, and especially Raphael. Although he was gifted with a delicate pictorial sense and achieved a number of works of grace with his refined draftsmanship and soft color, his own artistic personality was overshadowed by the masters he followed so faithfully. His *Madonnas* are obviously derived from Raphael; among these the outstanding ones are in the Uffizi, Florence, the Pinacoteca, Siena, and S. Lorenzo at Bibbiano (Siena). Also at Siena, in the Opera del Duomo, is a *Baptism of Christ.* A portrait in the manner of Raphael at Montpellier is attributed to him on stylistic grounds. Other works include a *Coronation of the Virgin,* Church of S. Paolo, Siena, and *Virgin and Child with SS. Catherine of Siena, Sebastian and the Infant Baptist* and *Portrait of a Young Man,* Johnson Collection, Philadelphia, and paintings at Cambridge, Massachusetts, Cleveland, Glasgow, London, Munich, Palermo, Rome (National and Borghese galleries), Turin (Sabauda Gallery), and elsewhere.

Breughel (brė′gẹl). See **Brueghel, Pieter.**

Brie (brē), **Simon de.** Original name of Pope **Martin IV.**

Brie, Théodore de. See **Bry** or **Brie, Théodore de.**

Briosco (brē-ōs′kō), **Andrea.** [Called **il Riccio,** meaning "the Curly-Headed."] Sculptor and architect, best known for his work in bronze; b. at Padua, c1471; d. 1532. He was the son of a Milanese goldsmith, and was a pupil and follower of Bartolomeo Bellano. After Bellano's death, he completed the Roccabonella monument that Bellano had begun in the Church of S. Francesco at Padua. In 1500 he designed the chapel of St. Anthony's tomb in the Basilica at Padua. Another architectural achievement was his plan for the Church of S. Giustina at Padua (1516). One of his most famous works, and one of the most richly ornamented creations of its kind, is the candlestick (the design for which was approved in 1507) for the Pascal candle, in the Basilica of St. Anthony. The monumental candlestick is magnificently decorated with ornamentation and figures representing allegorical, Christian, and mythological motifs. Other works include the monument of Abbot Antonio Trombetta (1521–1524) in the Basilica and the Della Torre monument (1516–1521) in S. Fermo Maggiore at Verona. The latter had eight bronze reliefs (in the Louvre since they were carried off by the French in

1796). In the Ca' d'Oro at Venice are four reliefs on the *Finding and Miracles of the True Cross* (1509–1511) and a tablet with *St. Martin Dividing His Raiment,* in high relief, which is attributed to Briosco on stylistic grounds. Because of his great reputation for casting his own works, and his predilection for small sculptures in the Hellenistic manner, a large number of statuettes—of creatures of mythology as well as of the natural world—are attributed to him. Examples of these smaller works are to be found in museums at Vienna, Paris, London, Florence, Padua, and elsewhere, as well as in private collections. One of the more curious of these is the *Mountain of Hell,* at Vienna. A large number of plaques and medals, with pagan or Christian motifs, are also attributed to him. Padua in Briosco's time was the center of a vibrant humanistic culture; artists, writers, and intellectual leaders were absorbed in the restoration and exaltation of the classical spirit. Briosco's art reflected the atmosphere. But in his aspiration toward the classical the naturalistic, narrative style and spirit that characterized his early work were never completely submerged. In his efforts to follow classical models he often achieved the outward form rather than the spirit of the antique.

Briosco, Benedetto. Lombard sculptor whose activities at the end of the 15th and the beginning of the 16th century were largely confined to his own region—Milan, Pavia, Cremona. In 1483 he carved a statue of S. Apollonia (now either unidentifiable or lost) in the cathedral at Milan, and in 1491 executed his statue of *St. Agnes* for the same church. Also in this year he went to work on the Certosa di Pavia, where he executed and signed a statue of the Virgin on the mausoleum of Gian Galeazzo Visconti, did part of the decoration of the tomb, and worked on the statue of the duke for one of the niches. From 1497 his collaboration on the façade of the Certosa was active. In 1501 he began to decorate the great doors that had been left unfinished by Amadeo. He designed a simple entrance with a pair of classical columns and worked on reliefs beside the entrance. In his facile, narrative style he executed a series of scenes from the history of the order of Carthusians, from the laying of the first stone of the Certosa through to the translation of Gian Galeazzo's soul to heaven. In the panels the reliefs are carefully designed, fairly intricate, and precisely modeled. In 1506 he received the commission to decorate tombs at Cremona, but did not finish the work.

Brocard (bro-kår). [Also, **Brochard, Burcardus.**] French Dominican friar; fl. at Avignon, c1332. To him is ascribed *Directorium ad passagium faciendum ad Terram Sanctam,* dedicated to Philip IV of France, which deals with reasons and plans for a crusade against the Saracens and describes routes, peoples, and conditions that would be met with. The work is important for the information it provides about the commercial and economic life of the region around Constantinople and the Greek peninsula, where he had traveled in 1307. He was in Persia after 1312, visited an island at the entrance to the Gulf of Aden, and went so far south of the equator that he considered the belief in the Antipodes to be neither false nor frivolous. (His reasons for believing he had gone south of the equator are of particular interest: he observed that the length of the days and nights at the equator are equal at all times of the year, that the stars were in different positions south of the line, and that the North Star was no longer visible.) He also concluded that the size of the inhabited part of the earth was larger than had been indicated in earlier works on geography.

Brocardo (brō-kär′dō), **Antonio.** Venetian humanist and man of letters; d. at an early age, 1531. While he was studying at Padua he hurled a few literary shafts at the almost sacrosanct Pietro Bembo. This effrontery began a war of words between the worshippers of Bembo and the supporters of Brocardo. The vituperative sonnets Aretino shot off against Brocardo so grieved him that he died soon after, thought to be a victim of a literary war. He left sonnets somewhat influenced by Petrarch, madrigals, ballate, a *capitolo,* and a canzone.

Brochard (bro-shår). See **Brocard.**

Brogni (bro-nyē), **Jean Allarmet de.** French cardinal; b. at Brogni, in Savoy, 1342; d. at Rome, February 16, 1426. He tried to heal the papal schism between Rome and Avignon (the Great Schism). He was president of the Council of Constance (1415–1417), and as such pronounced the sentence of the Council upon John Hus.

Broke or **Brooke** (brůk), **Arthur.** English translator; d. 1563. He wrote *The Tragicall*

Historye of Romeus and Iulieit (1562), one of the first English versions of the famous tragedy, and probably the version used by Shakespeare as the source for the plot of *Romeo and Juliet*.

Bronzino (brôn-dzē′nō), **Agnolo.** [Original name, **Agnolo** (or **Angiolo**) **di Cosimo Allori.**] Florentine painter; b. November 17, 1503; d. November 23, 1572. His father put him under some anonymous painters to study, but neither these nor Raffaellino del Garbo, in whose workshop he was for a time engaged, can be considered as his masters. More than a master, his spiritual father and guide was Jacopo Carucci, called Pontormo, from whom Bronzino learned the technique that formed his style without adopting the warmth and feeling that appears in Pontormo's best works. His style was also influenced by Michelangelo's mannerism. He was an extremely productive painter and executed many frescoes in the churches of Florence, in several Medici villas about Florence, in the Palazzo Vecchio for Cosimo I, at Pesaro for Guidobaldo II, at Pisa, and elsewhere. The exaggerations of elongation, agitation, and contrapposto, as well as the often esoteric symbolism of the mannerists, mark, and mar, his mythological and religious paintings. Examples of these, to name only a few, are his allegorical *Venus, Cupid, Folly and Time* (c1546), National Gallery, London; *Christ in Limbo* (1552), formerly in the museum of S. Croce, Florence, damaged in the flood of 1966; and his frescoes on *Stories of Moses,* painted between 1545 and 1564 in the Chapel of Eleonora of Toledo (wife of Cosimo I) in the Palazzo Vecchio at Florence. In 1530 he went to Pesaro at the invitation of Guidobaldo II, duke of Urbino. He painted some frescoes there which have now almost disappeared. More important, he painted Guidobaldo's portrait, now in the Pitti Palace, Florence, and revealed his great talent for portraiture. In 1539 he painted two scenes in the courtyard of the Medici palace at Florence on the occasion of the marriage of Cosimo I to Eleonora of Toledo, and the following year entered Cosimo's service as court painter. From this time dates the remarkable series of portraits of the Medici family, including the series of small portraits of illustrious Medici men, some of which are now in the Uffizi. Most admired now as a portrait painter, his portraits have a sculptural, marblelike coldness, and exhibit a loving rendering of the colors and patterns of fabrics. Of the Medici portraits, many are almost abstractions of hauteur and pride; few present the sitter in as winning a manner as that of the little *Maria de' Medici* (Uffizi). There are several other paintings by Bronzino in the Uffizi, as well as portraits in the Louvre, at Chicago; Cincinnati; Detroit; Kansas City, Missouri; Portland, Oregon; San Francisco; Toledo; Worcester, Massachusetts; the Metropolitan Museum, New York; the Cannon Collection, Princeton; the National Gallery, Washington; the Museum of Fine Arts and Isabella Stewart Gardner Museum,

Agnolo Bronzino
Copy after Bandinelli's Cleopatra
Fogg Art Museum, Harvard University
Bequest of Charles A. Loeser

Boston; and elsewhere. Bronzino was also a lover of letters and a poet who wrote lively, polished, not very original verse. A child of his age and influenced by the intellectual currents of his time, the sonnets he wrote for the beautiful Laura Battiferri, Bartolomeo Ammannati's cultivated wife, expressed the Platonism and Petrarchism that were fashionable in Florence in his day. In another key were his humorous and bawdy *capitoli*. He was a member of the Accademia della Crusca and as such defended, but without pedantry, the purity of the Italian language.

Brooke (brůk), **Arthur.** See **Broke** or **Brooke, Arthur.**

Bruce (brös), **Robert the.** See **Robert I** (*of Scotland*).

Brucioli (brö′chō-lē), **Antonio.** Florentine humanist and man of letters; d. 1556. Accused of complicity in a conspiracy (1522) against Cardinal Giulio de' Medici (later Pope Clement VII), he fled to France, but returned to Florence when the Medici were driven out (1527). A new accusation of Lutheranism was brought against him; he was tried and banished. He went to Venice, where his brothers were printers and booksellers, and where he was a friend of Gabriele Giolito, a noted publisher. A man of wide learning and intense activity, Brucioli wrote *Dialoghi della morale filosofia* (Venice, 1526–1538) and *Dialoghi faceti* (Venice, 1535), in which he popularized in the vernacular the works of Aristotle, Cicero, Pliny, and others. He also edited editions of Petrarch and Boccaccio. His greatest achievements were translations of the New Testament (Venice, 1530) and of the Bible (Venice, 1532). To his translations he later added commentaries (they amounted to seven volumes in the final edition, 1542–1546). The Protestant doctrines he expounded in his dedications to the king of France and to Renée, duchess of Ferrara, as well as those he expressed in his commentaries, caused his books to be placed on the Index.

Brueghel (brė′gėl), **Pieter.** [Also, **Bruegel, Breughel**; called **Boeren Brueghel**, meaning "Peasant Brueghel"; surnamed **the Droll** and **the Elder.**] Flemish painter; b. at Brueghel (now usually spelled Breughel), near Breda, Netherlands, c1525; d. at Brussels, 1569. He was instructed by Pieter Couke, but was more influenced by the paintings of Hieronymus Bosch. Received into the Antwerp Guild of Painters as a master painter in 1551, after a tour of France and Italy, he settled in Antwerp, and later in Brussels, where he spent the rest of his life, painting the Flemish landscape and the Flemish people and their manners and customs. Considered one of the world's great painters, his works are treasured by many of the world's great museums; his *Harvesters* is in The Metropolitan Museum of Art, New York.

Brunelleschi (brö-nel-les′kē), **Filippo.** Florentine architect and sculptor; b. at Florence, 1377; d. there, April 16, 1446. His father, a member of an old Florentine family, was a notary who often performed diplomatic missions outside Florence for the republic. He hoped his son would follow in his footsteps, but when he saw the young Filippo's ardent interest in the arts of design he apprenticed him to a goldsmith friend of his, and in 1404 Brunelleschi matriculated as a master in the guild that included the goldsmiths. In this art he became expert in design, relief, the cutting of gems, and in niello work. At the same time he continued his studies, in which he showed obvious intelligence, and his study of mathematics and geometry led him, according to tradition, to the discovery of one-point perspective. He made two paintings, now lost, to demonstrate it. To insure that the perspective was evident he made a hole in the panel at the vanishing point and asked the viewer to hold the back of the painting to his eye and look through the hole into a mirror that reflected it. In this manner the depth added by perspective was obvious. He also applied himself so industriously to the art of sculpture that when (1401) a contest was announced for the north door of the Baptistery, to balance Andrea Pisano's bronze door on the south, Brunelleschi entered it. Among the other contestants were Lorenzo Ghiberti and Jacopo della Quercia. Each entrant was given material and required to execute, within one year and within a prescribed shape and size, a relief on the subject of *The Sacrifice of Isaac*. The relief prepared by Brunelleschi was bursting with dramatic energy, in contrast to the decorative grace and refined composition of his chief rival's, Lorenzo Ghiberti's. Vasari has it that Brunelleschi recognized the superiority of Ghiberti's panel over his own, and gracefully withdrew in his favor. Others, however, recount that the judges, unable to decide between them, wished to give the commission for the door to the two jointly. This the independent and imperious Brunelleschi would not tolerate—either the commission was his alone or he would withdraw. In any case, he withdrew and gave his panel to his friend Cosimo de' Medici. It is now, along with Ghiberti's prize panel, in the Bargello at Florence. That prepared by Jacopo della Quercia has been lost. The only other surviving sculptures by Brunelleschi are two busts of prophets on the silver altar of Sant' Iacopo in the cathedral at Pistoia, and the huge wooden crucifix in S. Maria Novella at Florence. Vasari has a story on this work. Brunelleschi's good friend Donatello had made a Crucifix in wood and showed it to Brunelleschi for his opinion. Brunelleschi commented that Donatello had placed a peasant on the cross. Donatello, incensed, advised Brunelleschi to go and make a Crucifix himself. He secretly did so, and when it was finished invited Donatello to his house for dinner. On the way they stopped to shop for the meal. Brunelleschi gave Donatello the wine, cheese, eggs, and so on to carry in his sculptor's apron, and told him to go on ahead, that he would soon join him. When Donatello entered the house the first thing he saw was the Crucifix, which Brunelleschi had so placed to catch the most effective light. In amazement, Donatello flung out his arms and the provisions in his apron rolled onto the floor. Brunelleschi entered at that point, and laughingly told his friend that now their dinner was all spilt. Donatello replied that the sight of the Crucifix was food enough for him, that Brunelleschi had "represented the Christ. Mine is a common man."

After the commission for the Baptistery doors was awarded to Ghiberti, Brunelleschi and Donatello went off to Rome to study the remains of Roman sculpture. But once there, wandering among the ruins of the Imperial buildings, Brunelleschi decided to give up the art of sculpture and, as he had already worked on some buildings at Florence, to devote himself to architecture. He drew plans of the ancient buildings, measured the thickness of walls, proportions of columns and arches, the size and shapes of bricks, studied the methods of dovetailing blocks of marble, made drawings of Doric, Ionic, and Corinthian capitals, hired laborers and dug himself to excavate the bases of columns or structures that were buried in the ground so that he could examine them. While he concentrated on proportions and structural methods, Donatello was busy copying friezes and inscriptions. The two supported themselves by working in goldsmith shops. Brunelleschi particularly studied the dome of the Pantheon, for he seems to have been already thinking of the great cupola that was to be raised over the crossing of the nave and transepts of the Cathedral of S. Maria del Fiore, the church begun to designs by Arnolfo di Cambio which was approaching the stage in its construction when the cupola would be raised. Along with his own inventiveness and ingenuity, Brunelleschi's intense and intelligent study of the Roman buildings, made in the course of several visits to Rome, gave him the technical knowledge that ultimately enabled him to raise the dome. As early as 1404 the overseers of the building consulted with him and other architects on certain criticisms that were being leveled against Giovanni d'Ambrogio, the superintendent of construction. By 1418 the building had reached the stage when it was necessary to tackle the cupola. Giovanni d'Ambrogio had remained in charge, but was dismissed at this time, as his advanced age made it unlikely that he would live to complete the work. Brunelleschi had been following the construction closely, and probably had already considered and solved the problem of the dome. The method of constructing a dome, which is essentially an arch rotated on its axis, was to lay a long shaft across the opening, from the ends of which the arch springs, and build up the arch on scaffolding until the peak was reached, the keystone inserted, and the centering could be removed. In the case of the cathedral, the crossing was over 138 feet long and was at a height of 180 feet. No tree could be found to provide a shaft of such length; besides it seemed obvious that the beams of the centering would collapse of their own weight before any stone could be raised. The overseers of the cathedral and the Woolworkers Guild (the woolworkers were patrons of the cathedral) met and discussed, and asked advice, and sought architects to solve the problem of the cupola. Brunelleschi was among those consulted, but refused to tell his solution. He was determined to have the honor of raising the cupola himself, and feared, on just grounds, that if he revealed his plans someone else might have the opportunity of carrying them into execution. Again a contest was proclaimed (August 19, 1418) for a model of the cupola, with a prize of 200 florins and compensation for all who took part. Architects were called from all over Italy and outside it as well. Many suggestions were made. Brunelleschi, who had never denied that the construction of the cupola was almost impossible, and had pointed out every difficulty, also pointed out the weaknesses of the plans submitted. When he submitted his own, in which he proposed to build the cupola without centering and without scaffolding, he was hooted out of the meeting. Subsequently he built a dome for a chapel without centering or scaffolding, proving he could do it, but this dome was so much smaller than that required for the cathedral that it was hardly a fair test. Soon, as a result of private conversations with some of the overseers and others, he was invited, with Ghiberti, to submit his plan in writing and, again with Ghiberti, was given a partial contract: to raise the cupola to a height of 23 feet. He was much incensed that he must share the honors with Ghiberti, and was insulted at the doubt implied by giving him a limited commission. Vasari writes that he would have given up the whole idea of building the cupola and would have gone off to Rome but for the pleas of his friends. The first thing he had decided was that the octagonal drum from which the cupola was to rise should be raised, for reasons of proportion and so that the cupola could be seen. His plan was to build a pointed dome, instead of the purely classical hemispherical dome that he would have preferred, as a tapering dome would exert less side thrust. The design included an inner, thick shell, built on eight huge ribs rising from the eight angles of the octagonal drum, with a pair of lesser ribs between each of the eight principal ones for additional support, and an outer, thinner shell, to distribute the weight of the dome. When he had first submitted the plan he was met by extreme doubt. The committee did not see how it could be done. The story is that (like Columbus later) Brunelleschi asked the competing architects to stand an egg on end. They couldn't. He slightly dented the egg on one end and stood it up. All exclaimed they could have done that. Yes, indeed, after he had showed them how, and it was for this very reason that he refused to divulge his methods in advance. Work on the cupola began on August 7, 1420. It was completed as far as the lantern that would top it between 1434 and 1436. The "eye" opening at the top of the dome was to be closed by a lantern modeled on that of the Baptistery. In 1436 another competition was held for the design of the lantern. Brunelleschi won, but work was not begun until a few months before Brunelleschi's death (1446). His pupil and close follower, Michelozzo, carried on the construction which, in the main, was faithful to Brunelleschi's design. In the sixteen years during which work on the cupola was in progress, Brunelleschi invented a variety of methods to facilitate the work. He made devices to raise the heavy stones. He rigged a scaffolding as the dome rose to dizzying height, and provided wine and food shops atop it so that the workmen would not lose time descending to their meals. When the masons were in doubt as to the shape of a stone for a particular purpose, he cut the required model in a turnip with his pocket knife. He settled a strike by the laborers, who had demanded higher wages because of the perilous nature of the work—and he managed to nullify Ghiberti's part in the work. From the beginning, Brunelleschi and Ghiberti had been named and paid as equals. But Brunelleschi, who knew well that Ghiberti lacked the technical knowledge for the endeavor and who besides wanted the fame which his own skill deserved, resolved to get rid of him. At one point he feigned illness. When the masons came to his house to ask for instruction, he referred them to Ghiberti. Ghiberti refused to act without him, and at length was compelled to say that he could not get along without Brunelleschi. Brunelleschi's significant reply was that he could do very well without Ghiberti. Henceforth the latter's role, which he never completely lost, was lessened. (In the same year, 1425, Ghiberti had the commission for the bronze doors of the Baptistery that were later called "The Gates of Paradise.") On August 31, 1436, when the dome was closed, all Florence gathered to watch as the bishop of Fiesole climbed up to bless the great structure. The bells of the city rang out in exultation. Brunelleschi's dome, as it was henceforth called, is one of the landmarks of

Florence and one of the marvels of the age. It has been said that no other 15th century architect could have done it, and some of his methods are still unknown. No documentation exists to describe the technical problems and their day-to-day solutions.

The dome of S. Maria del Fiore is Brunelleschi's most famed monument. However, it is still closer to Gothic than to Renaissance in style. Other examples of his knowledge of Roman architecture and construction, and his adaptations of these to the needs of his age, illustrate the symmetry, proportion, and simplicity that were his great contributions in the development of Renaissance architecture. Of these, the Ospedale degli Innocenti (Foundling Hospital) is the first truly Renaissance work. He directed the work between 1421 and 1424. Noted for its simplicity and regularity, the simple, airy loggia, with its pure arches (of which the spandrels are filled with the Della Robbia *Bambini*) and broad steps, is a landmark in Renaissance architecture. (The Ospedale was completed by a collaborator, since Brunelleschi was fully occupied with his dome. The collaborator made a change of which Brunelleschi disapproved, and justified himself on the ground that he had copied it from the Baptistery. "Yes," said Brunelleschi, "there is only one fault to be found in that building and you have imitated it.") Other works in his early manner included the Old Sacristy of S. Lorenzo and the Basilica of S. Lorenzo, both built under Medici patronage. The first was carried out between 1421 and 1428; the second was completed (the façade was never completed) after Brunelleschi's death. In each he developed, on a mathematical basis, his theories of the composition of space and proportion. The church, on the ground plan of a Latin cross, has a square central crossing, a square choir, and square chapels. The Old Sacristy is a cube, horizontally divided in thirds, with round arches and square pilasters with Corinthian capitals. (His friend Cosimo de' Medici regretfully declined to build the palace Brunelleschi designed for him, on the ground that it was too magnificent and "Envy is a plant that should not be watered." In a rage of frustration Brunelleschi smashed to bits the model he had made. But his palace design, somewhat modified, was probably similar to the palace design of his follower Michelozzo, who built the Medici palace.) The Pazzi Chapel, one of Brunelleschi's masterpieces, was begun in 1430, but was not finished at the time of his death. In its elegant simplicity and severity, with its pure round arches, slender columns, and dome, it is one of the jewels of Renaissance architecture. Luca della Robbia and Desiderio da Settignano vied with each other in decorating the chapel when it was completed under the supervision of Michelozzo. The incomplete Church of S. Maria degli Angioli was perhaps the most beautiful work Brunelleschi designed, with its octagonal internal space surrounded by rectangular chapels, each with two small apses. The intention was to cover it with a circular cupola by which the light entered. The church was never completed for lack of funds. Plans for the great Church of S. Spirito were ready in 1436, but the building itself proceeded slowly, for lack of money. The walls of the façade were put up only in 1482. Again on the ground plan of a Latin cross, the church is a masterpiece in its simple elements, noble proportions, and harmonious composition of space. The three aisles are divided by Corinthian columns; the interior is surrounded by forty small chapels with circular bases. Last, in the order of time, was his design for the Pitti Palace. The original design, not carried out, called for a smaller palace, more compact and harmonious in its proportions and less fortresslike than the present palace, which was enlarged in succeeding centuries. As may be noted, most of Brunelleschi's designs were not carried to completion under his supervision or during his lifetime; changes, either more or less important, were made in his plans, so that almost no building survives that is just as Brunelleschi planned it. His great contributions lay in his understanding, gained by his own intense study, of the structural methods of the Romans. In his building he created a style in which he freely adapted and translated elements of Roman and Gothic architecture with new and lively inspiration. He adapted the use of columns and capitals (his favorite was a version of the Corinthian), pilasters, and arches, and some decorative motifs. What he created was not a mere imitation of classical architecture—the needs of his age (mainly church architecture) were not met by the solutions to the problems of space that the Romans had found—but a style in which ancient solutions were adapted to modern needs and embellished by classical elements.

Vasari speaks in his biography of Brunelleschi of the architect's unprepossessing appearance: he was slight and homely. He tells of his greatness of soul and warns that nature does not always endow those who exhibit the most distinguished talent with the grace and beauty that might be expected; that under "the clods of earth the veins of gold lie hidden." The earliest biographer of Brunelleschi was his contemporary, Antonio Manetti. Both biographers speak of his manifest intelligence, his imperious will, his tenacity, and his elevated spirit. He was a friend of the leading artists of the day. Masaccio, Donatello, Brunelleschi—the three representatives of the most advanced painting, sculpture, and architecture of the time—were friends who each contributed to the others' development. Vasari and Manetti mention a number of anecdotes to illustrate Brunelleschi's lively sense of humor and preference for the practical joke, and both speak with respect of his learning. When the architect who raised the cupola of S. Maria del Fiore died, his body was laid in state in the cathedral. The Florentines, who honored their artists and took great pride in the work they did that brought such fame to the city, passed reverently by his bier to honor him. A portrait of him, with those of Giotto, Donatello, and Antonio Manetti, in the Louvre, is attributed to Paolo Uccello by some, to his good friend Masaccio, by others. The bust in relief in the cathedral at Florence is by his pupil and adopted son, Andrea di Lazzaro Cavalcanti, called il Buggiano.

Brunello (brö-nel′lō). In Matteo Maria Boiardo's *Orlando Innamorato* and Lodovico Ariosto's *Orlando Furioso*, an ugly, exceedingly clever and successful thief. He steals Angelica's magic ring, Marfisa's sword, and Orlando's horn. Sacripante, seated on his horse, is lost in meditation. Brunello steals the horse by slipping a tree trunk under the saddle as he removes the horse. He is made king of Tingitana by Agramante for his services. After a life spent in theft and subtle knavery, he is hanged.

Bruni (brö′nē), **Leonardo.** [Called **Leonardo Aretino,** from his birthplace.] Humanist and statesman; b. at Arezzo, 1370; d. at Florence, March 9, 1444. Son of a family with no pretensions as to birth or wealth, Bruni left Arezzo and went to Florence to study. There he perfected his Latin under Coluccio Salutati and his Greek under Manuel Chrysoloras and became a teacher. Since he was a poor man, he decided to go to Rome to improve his circumstances. According to Vespasiano, he won (1405) a post as apostolic secretary to Innocent VII as the result of a letter-writing contest. He held official positions at the papal court for the next ten years, except for an interlude as chancellor of Florence, and then (1415) returned to Florence. John XXIII, lingering at Florence and undecided about whether to attend a council, finally decided to go to the Council of Constance and took Bruni with him in an official capacity. When the Council turned against John and threatened to imprison him, Bruni fled with him. In his role as statesman, Bruni went on an embassy for Martin V (1426), held many public offices (as that of a member of the Council of Ten under whose tenure Niccolò Piccinino was defeated at Anghiari in 1440), and was chancellor of Florence from 1427 until his death. Because of his wisdom, his tact and eloquence in persuasion, and his loyalty to the interests of Florence, he was highly respected and seldom challenged in public affairs.

Bruni was one of the most outstanding humanists of his age. Learned in Greek and Latin, he sought ancient manuscripts in the two languages, studied and corrected them and translated many, especially from the Greek into Latin. He also promoted the use and study of Italian. His writings embraced many areas; he wrote on education, translated Aristotle's *Ethics*, *Politics* and *Economics*, as well as several of the *Dialogues* of Plato and of the *Lives* of Plutarch. In his own *Isagogicon Moralis Disciplinae* he presented one of the earliest introductions to ethics since ancient times. He also wrote orations, dialogues, lives of Dante and Petrarch (in Italian), and histories. Of the latter, several were in the Latin manner, but his *Historiae Florentini populi*, from the origins of Florence to 1404, has been called the first history of Florence worthy of the name history, as he eliminated mythology, legend, and traditional tales in favor of a search for facts. The work was translated into Italian by Donato Acciaiuoli and was widely read in the Renaissance. Vespasiano gives an appealing picture of Bruni. He was of small stature, generally grave but with a quick temper which he held under firm control, and was gentle and pleasant in his manner. He wore, says Vespasiano, a long red cloak, with lined sleeves turned back, and over this a red mantle that reached to the ground; a red hood sheltered his head. He was so venerated in his own time that men came from afar just to look at him. When he died the Florentines revived the custom of awarding the laurel crown for him. Gianozzo Manetti stood at the head of the bier on which Bruni's silk-clad corpse was laid and pronounced the funeral oration. He was buried in the Church of Santa Croce in Florence. Bernardo Rossellino designed his mausoleum.

Bruno (brö'nō), **Giordano.** [Baptismal name, **Filippo.**] Philosopher; b. at Nola, 1548; d. at Rome, February 17, 1600. In 1562 he went to Naples to study letters and philosophy. His father was not wealthy, and it was perhaps for this reason that he entered (1565) the Dominican order—to feed his hunger for knowledge. It was at this time that he took the name Giordano. He was interested in all branches of learning, worked hard at his studies, and read the poets as well as the philosophers, the pagans along with the Christians. (His favorite work was Lucretius, a copy of which he always carried with him.) As a result of his studies he acquired an extraordinary breadth of knowledge, was ordained in 1572, and gained a doctor of theology in 1575. His studies had stirred his doubts about such articles of faith as the Trinity and the Immaculate Conception. Of an incautious temperament, he expressed and argued about his doubts and theories and was summoned before the Inquisition at Rome (1576). (As a youth he had been disciplined by his order for giving away all the sacred images except the Crucifix.) Rather than face the charges he put off the habit of his order and fled, at first to Rome itself, where he took refuge in a convent. From this time date his wanderings about Europe. He went to Liguria, Piedmont, Venice, and Lombardy, taught at Noli, and published a book, now lost, at Venice. In 1579 he went to Chambéry and then to Geneva, where he earned his living as a proofreader. He left Geneva because he found the bigotry of the Calvinists as intolerable as that of his own faith. This was to be the pattern of his wanderings. He was an eloquent man, of agreeable manners and attractive by the force of his personality. These features won him welcome when he first arrived in a new place, but the vehemence, not to say arrogance, with which he expressed his scorn for the traditional approach to learning and the establishment usually made his departure quite as welcome to his easily found patrons as his arrival had been. From Geneva he went to Toulouse, where he held the chair of philosophy (1579–1581), and then to Paris. His fame had preceded him, and at Paris he attracted the attention of Henry III. The king was interested in his theories on the art of memory and believed them to suggest memory could be acquired by magic. Bruno assured him it was done by science and not by magic. His own memory was prodigious, and he worked to develop mnemonic systems. (Ultimately, it was his theories on the art of memory and invention that led to his undoing, for all the wrong reasons.) At Paris, Bruno lectured and moved in the best circles. In 1583 he left France and went to England. There he was under the protection of the French ambassador, Count de Chastelnau, and spent a happy period. He lectured at Oxford on the immortality of the soul and on the sphere (astronomy), but found the professors at Oxford to be limited pedants, got into a dispute with them, and returned to London to the house of the count. Through his host and his own reputation he was welcomed in the most cultivated and intellectual circles and, except for the pedantry he scorned at Oxford, was very favorably impressed with the freedom of opinion he found in England. In 1585 he returned to Paris, where he again lectured. Political unrest caused him to leave that country (1586) for wanderings in Germany—to Marburg, Mainz, and Wittenberg, where he taught, to Prague (1588), Helmstadt, and Frankfurt. Usually he taught for a time, but as he found the same limited approach to knowledge and truth wherever he went, he moved on. During all these years he had been writing continually, setting forth his theories on the art of memory and his ideas of the universe and of the infinite in Italian dialogues and Latin hexameters, and expressing his utter participation in life in poetry. Some of his work, published abroad, found its way to Italy. A Venetian noble, Giovanni Mocenigo, saw one of his books in a Venetian bookseller's and became intrigued by what he considered to be hints of the occult, especially in the attainment of knowledge, in Bruno's work. He wrote Bruno a letter and invited him to Venice as his guest. One of his objects was to learn from Bruno the magic by which he had perfected his memory and the secrets of invention. The charges against Bruno before the Inquisition were still outstanding; he had been excommunicated while at Helmstadt, and he might be arrested and taken to Rome if he entered Italy. Nevertheless, he decided to go to Venice (1591), sanctuary of rebels as long as they did not interfere in Venetian political affairs. Mocenigo entertained him but was disappointed in his hope that Bruno could teach him occult science, and was utterly uninterested in Bruno's theories of the universe. In May, 1592, he had Bruno seized and denounced him to the Inquisition. Among the beliefs Bruno had expressed in his writings was his conception of the infinity of the universe, a conception, derived from Copernicus but greatly extended, that this world is not the center of the universe but is only one of many solar systems that exist to infinity and that are united in the infinite God. These statements contradicted the Aristotelian and Ptolemaic dicta that the earth is the center and that the universe is finite. Their views had become part of Church doctrine. The acceptance of Bruno's views of the infinite would destroy the basis for literal belief in some doctrines. Bruno further believed in the unity and imperishability of matter, exalted nature, saw no limit to knowledge, considered the attainment of absolute truth an impossibility (since our view of the world is governed by our position in space and time, and different positions lead to different views), believed in the transmigration of souls, doubted the dogma of the Trinity and the Immaculate Conception, and postulated pantheism. In his defense before the Inquisitors he distinguished between what he thought as a philosopher and what he professed as a Christian. His Inquisitors found themselves unable to make this distinction. He was imprisoned at Venice while the process was pending. It was not until February 9, 1600, after seven years of imprisonment, that the sentence against him was pronounced at Rome: that he was "to be punished without effusion of blood." In plain words, he was sentenced to be burned alive. He had made no extraordinary effort to defend himself; he retracted only to the extent of distinguishing between his belief as a Christian and his reason as a philosopher; he could point to written chapter and verse in which he had expressed his scorn for heretics; he did not consider himself a heretic, and had as little use for the pedantry and bigotry of reformers as for the pedants and bigots of his own faith. At the moment of hearing his sentence he did not look back. His response to the Inquisitors was, "You, perhaps, fear more to pronounce the sentence than I do to receive it." A lifelong opponent of dogmatism and pedantry, a lifelong advocate of freedom of thought and investigation, he refused to turn his back on his beliefs or to deny them. He was burned at the stake as a heretic in the Campo dei Fiori at Rome, February 17, 1600.

Wherever Bruno went he wrote and published. His poetry is instinct with a vivid sense of life as he had known it at Naples. A comedy, *Il Candelaio* (*The Light-bearer*) (1582), is a satiric attack on scholasticism by way of a timid lover, a miser, and a pedant. His philosophical writings set forth his views, separate philosophy from theology, and, in his conception of the universe, link him to modern science. The Latin work *De umbris idearum* (*On the Shadows of Ideas*) (Paris, 1582) contains an exposition of his art of memory and his theory of the unity of origin of all matter, which thereafter exists in infinite variety. Most of his future speculation is adumbrated in this work. While in England he wrote six sets of Italian dialogues: *Cena de le ceneri* (*The Ash-Wednesday Supper*), *Cabala del cavallo pegaseo* (*The Cabala of the Pegasean Steed*), *Gli eroici furori* (*The Heroic Enthusiasts*), *De la causa, principio e uno* (*On the Cause, Principle and One*), *Spaccio de la bestia trionfante* (*The Expulsion of the Triumphant Beast*), and *De l'infinito universo et mondi* (*On the Infinite Universe and Worlds*). (These were all published at London, although they were imprinted as having issued from Paris and Venice, as the English at that time were more impressed by books printed abroad. . . .) In the dialogues he attacks Aristotelian cosmology, restates his theory of the universe, develops his ideas of the functions of opposites in creating unity and harmony, stresses the importance of the observation of nature and the discovery of her laws, and scorns the sacrosanct traditions that obstruct the path to truth. Other works include *De monade*, in Latin hexameters, on the monad as the irreducible element from which the infinite varieties of matter proceed; and several works on the art of memory. Throughout his work he sees himself as a fighter in the struggle for freedom of thought, an unvanquished follower of truth, for whom death itself has no terrors.

Brusasorci (brö-sä-sôr′chē), **Domenico.** [Original name, **Domenico Riccio.**] Painter; b. at Verona, c1516; d. there, 1567. First trained by Francesco Caroto (1480–1555), in his maturity he adopted the full-blown style of Paolo Veronese. His chief works are at Verona, including altarpieces and frescoes in the churches of S. Eufemia, S. Lorenzo, S. Pietro Martire, and other churches, a *Crucifixion* in S. Fermo; frescoes in S. Maria in Organo; and the decorations of the Bishop's Palace. There is a series of frescoes in the Villa del Bene, Volargne, and another in the Villa di Caldogno, near Vicenza. Other works include *Bathsheba at the Bath*, Uffizi, Florence, in which to his traditionalism are added some Venetian influences; *Bust of a Youth*, Carrara Academy, Bergamo; and *The Last Supper*, Cannon Collection, Princeton, as well as works at Mantua, Milan (Brera and Castello Sforzesco), Trent, Venice, Paris, Baltimore (Walters Art Gallery), Providence, and elsewhere.

Brusasorci, Felice. Veronese painter; b. c1539; d. 1605. He was the son of Domenico Brusasorci, and carried on his father's work. A facile but mediocre painter, he made a long sojourn in Florence, where he was exposed to Tuscan mannerism. A fresco, *Musicians*, is in the Isabella Stewart Gardner Museum, Boston.

Bruyn (broin), **Barthel** (or **Bartholomäus**). German painter of the Cologne School; b. at Cologne, Germany, c1493; d. 1555. His early works have characteristics of the Flemish school, but his later paintings show strong Italian influence. Perhaps his greatest achievement is a series of pictures decorating a shrine in the church at Xanten.

Bry or **Brie** (brē), **Théodore de.** Flemish goldsmith, engraver, and painter; b. at Liege, Belgium, 1528; d. at Frankfort on the Main, Germany, 1598. About 1570 he established a printing and engraving house at Frankfort, his two sons assisting him. They illustrated many books, but are best known for their collection of works of travel. The first was entitled *Collectiones peregrinationum in Indiam orientalem et occidentalem* (1590), illustrated with many plates by De Bry.

Bucentaur (bū-sen′tôr). The state ship of the Venetian Republic, used in the annual ceremony of wedding the Adriatic, which was enjoined upon the Venetians by Pope Alexander III to commemorate the victory of the Venetians under Doge Sebastiano Ziani over the fleet of Frederick Barbarossa, in the 12th century. On Ascension Day of each year a ring was dropped from the *Bucentaur* into the Adriatic, with the words "We espouse thee, Sea, in token of true and lasting dominion." The ceremony was attended by the entire diplomatic corps. The ship perhaps took her name from the figure of a bucentaur (head of a man and body of a bull) in her bows. Three of the name were built. The last was destroyed by the French in 1798.

Bucer (bū′sėr), **Martin.** [Also, **Butzer**; original surname, **Kuhhorn.**] German theologian; b. at Schlettstadt (Sélestat), in Alsace, 1491; d. at Cambridge, England, February 28, 1551. He was a coadjutor of Martin Luther. Refusing (1548) to sign the Augsburg Interim (a provisional settlement of the differences between the Catholics and Protestants), he accepted, at the invitation of Thomas Cranmer, a professorate of theology at Cambridge in 1549. He is chiefly noted for his efforts to unite the different Protestant bodies, especially the Lutherans and Zwinglians, in which he was only partially successful.

Buchanan (bū̦-kan′a̤n), **George.** Scottish historian and scholar; b. at Killearn, Stirlingshire, Scotland, February, 1596; d. at Edinburgh, September 29, 1582. He was a tutor of James VI of Scotland. He published (1571) *Detectio Mariae Reginae*, a violent attack on Mary, Queen of Scots, whom he held responsible for the murder of Darnley. Among his other works are *De jure regni apud Scotos* (1579) and *Rerum Scoticarum historia* (1582).

Budé (bü-dā), **Guillaume.** [Latinized, **Budaeus.**] French humanist scholar; b. at Paris, 1467; d. there, 1540. He studied Greek under Lascaris and became one of the foremost Greek scholars of the century. He was a friend of Erasmus and a trusted official of the king. He held many important positions, including that of ambassador to Pope Leo X, and was secretary to Francis I. He persuaded the king to found the Collège de France, and his own private library became the nucleus of the Bibliothèque Nationale. He was a student of Roman law and, in his *Annotations sur les Pandectes* (1508), applied textual criticism to the study of Roman law. He was also a student of Roman coins, and was as well one of the scholars responsible for the revival of Greek learning in Europe. His many works included commentaries on the Greek language and numerous letters that are of great interest for their accounts and record of the literary life of the time. Budé was aware of, and emphasized, the need for religious reform, but did not accept the Protestant Reformation as a proper accomplishment of this end.

Buffalmacco (bö-fäl-mäk′kō), **Bonamico.** Florentine painter of the 14th century. Praised from Boccaccio to Vasari as Giotto's greatest contemporary, no authentic work of his survives. Even in Vasari's time, the frescoes attributed to him were in a very poor state of preservation.

Buggiano (bö-jä′nō), **Il.** See **Cavalcanti, Andrea di Lazzaro.**

Bugiardini (bö-jär-dē′nē), **Giuliano di Piero di Simone.** Painter; b. at Florence, 1475; d. there, 1554. He studied in the Medicean Garden under Bertoldo, and then with Mariotto Albertinelli. Affected, as were most artists, by the giants of his age—Leonardo, Michelangelo, Raphael—he yet managed to develop a style of his own, one somewhat marred by hardness of drawing and crude, metallic color. In 1508 Michelangelo called him to Rome to assist him in the painting of the Sistine ceiling, but soon sent him away, along with others he had invited to assist him. Nevertheless, Bugiardini remained a friend of the master and took great pleasure from his contacts with him. Between 1527 and 1530 he went to Bologna, perhaps to escape the dangers that then beset the last Republic of Florence. At Bologna he painted his best work, *Madonna between St. Anthony and St. Catherine*, now in the Pinacoteca, Bologna. On his return to Florence he finished *The Martyrdom of St. Catherine*, in S. Maria Novella. Despite the help of sketches from Michelangelo and models by Tribolo, it had taken him twelve years to finish the work. He painted a number of pictures of the *Holy Family*, now in various collections. Other works include *St. John*, in S. Maria delle Grazie, Milan; *Madonna and Child Enthroned with St. Mary Magdalen and St. John the Baptist*, the Metropolitan Museum, New York. Among the many portraits he left are those of Francesco Guicciardini, the historian, at New Haven; one of Michelangelo, in the Casa Buonarotti, Florence; and a portrait in the National Gallery, Washington. In addition, there are paintings at Modena, Rome (Colonna Gallery and Palazzo Venezia), Turin, Venice (Ca' d'Oro), Volterra, Copenhagen, Leningrad, Vienna, Allentown (Pennsylvania), New Orleans, Portland (Oregon), and elsewhere.

Bulgarini (böl-gä-rē′nē), **Bartolomeo.** [The so-called **Ugolino Lorenzetti.**] Sienese painter; active in the middle of the 14th century. Among his surviving works are *Assumption of the Virgin*, Pinacoteca, Siena; *Madonna of Humility*, National Gallery, Washington; *Nativity*, Fogg Museum, Cambridge; and two wings of a triptych, framed together, bearing eight small panels with single standing figures, in the Johnson Collection, Philadelphia.

Bullinger (bůl′ing-ėr), **Heinrich.** Swiss reformer and historian; b. at Bremgarten, Aargau, Switzerland, July 18, 1504; d. at Zurich, September 17, 1575. He succeeded Zwingli at Zurich and was a leader in the drawing up (1536) of the First Helvetic Confession. With John Calvin he drew up (1549) Consensus Tigurinus on the Lord's Supper, which led to the separation of Zwinglian and Calvinist theory. He also prepared (1566) the Confession of Basel or Second Helvetic Confession.

Buon (bö-ôn′), **Bartolomeo.** Venetian sculptor and architect; d. at Venice, 1464. He was the son, pupil, and collaborator of Giovanni Buon (d. 1442) and accepted the Tuscan forms that were brought into Venice by Niccolò and Pietro Lamberti to a greater extent than did his father. He worked with his father on many commissions, and finished the *Porta della Carta* of the Ducal Palace, their masterpiece, after his father's death. He directed the rebuilding of the façade and from 1441 to 1445 carved the tympanum of the great door of the School of the Misericordia at Venice. His work appeared in many other churches of Venice, and with Pantaléon he worked on the Foscari Arch in the Ducal Palace, but before it was completed the two artists were dismissed (September, 1463). In the last years of his life he worked on the Ca' del Duca, so called because Duke Francesco Sforza had gotten it from Marco Cornaro in 1461. Linked as he was to the Gothic tradition, he adopted Tuscan forms and grafted them on the older style, and developed a sculptural style that made him one of the principal Venetian sculptors of his time.

Buon, Giovanni. Venetian architect and sculptor; active from 1382; d. 1442. He probably assisted in the restoration of the Church of S. Maria dell' Orto at Venice, but his work is not identifiable. In 1422 with his son Bartolomeo and others he worked on the Ca' d'Oro, and when the project of rebuilding the Ducal Palace was undertaken he and his son were called upon to assist. Their masterpiece is the *Porta della Carta* of the Ducal Palace. The contract, of November, 1438, called for completion of the work in eighteen months, but it was unfinished on Giovanni's death in 1442, and Bartolomeo was given an additional year to complete it. Giovanni's work was decorative rather than architectural, and in its use of Gothic elements, with additions from 14th century Pisan art and a few of the new forms that had come into Venice from Tuscany, his work is close to that of the Dalle Masegne masters. The *Porta della Carta* clearly shows his decorative and sculptural interests. With its ornate pinnacles, pointed arch above the great door, and profusion of ornamentation, it is still very much in the Gothic tradition.

Buonaccorsi (bwô-näk-kôr'sē), **Filippo.** [Latin name, **Callimachus.**] Humanist, statesman, and historian; b. at San Gimignano, 1437; d. at Cracow, Poland, November 1, 1496. He was a pupil of Julius Pomponius Laetus at Rome, and with him founded the Roman Academy. In his association with Julius Pomponius, whose principal aim was to restore ancient Roman ways, he took the Roman name Callimachus. In 1468, along with other members of the academy, he was accused of immorality, impiety, and a plot against the life of Pope Paul II. Buonaccorsi fled, first to the East and then (c1470) to Poland. In Poland he was under the protection of an archbishop, and became teacher to the children of Casimir IV. He was very active on behalf of his adopted country and was entrusted with important and delicate missions, including a peace treaty with the Turks (1487). At the Congress of Rome (1490) he supported a league between the pope and Poland; but with due care for the interests of Poland, he also tried to keep the friendship of the sultan. His influence and power were great in the affairs of state in Poland, as well as in diffusing humanistic culture in that country. His many works included a history of Attila the Hun, orations, letters, and verses.

Buonaccorsi, Pietro. See **Pierin del Vaga.**

Buonaccorso (bwô-näk-kôr'sō), **Niccolò di.** See **Niccolò di Buonaccorso.**

Buonaccorso de Montemagno (dā mōn-tā-mä'nyō). [Called **the Younger,** to distinguish him from his grandfather (d. c1390), with whose works some of his are sometimes confused.] Poet, humanist, and statesman; b. at Pistoia, between 1391 and 1393; d. at Florence, December 16, 1429. He held high office at Florence, and served as ambassador to Lucca, Milan, and elsewhere. He wrote an influential *Dialogue on True Nobility,* and several of his orations are extant, but he is known primarily for his love lyrics. These, on the Petrarchan model, are informed with his own grace and originality, and are among the best of the early poems in the manner of Petrarch.

Buonarroti (bwô-när-rôt'tē), **Michelangelo.** See **Michelangelo.**

Buonconsiglio (bwôn-kōn-sē'lyō), **Giovanni.** [Called **il Marescalco,** from his father, who was a farrier.] Painter; b. at Vicenza, active from 1495; d. at Venice, between 1535 and 1537. The influence of Montagna, the most important painter at Vicenza in his time, and of Antonello da Messina, is clear especially in his masterpiece, *Pietà,* signed, and painted before 1497, now in the Municipal Museum, Vicenza. It is a work of elemental strength and great dramatic power, expressive of deep, almost wild, sorrow, and marked by his harsh, incisive style. Most of his life after 1495 was spent at Venice, but he continued his contacts with Vicenza and the towns in its vicinity, and often executed altarpieces, easel paintings, and frescoes for churches and patrons in the area. His earliest dated work (1497) is a fragment with the heads of saints, painted for the Church of SS. Cosma e Damiano at Venice and now in the Accademia in that city. Other works are in the parish church at Cornedo, in the cathedral, churches, and museum at Montagnana, in the churches and museum at Vicenza, the Accademia, Venice, National Gallery, London, and elsewhere. Traces of Bellini influence appear in the powerful, early *Pietà*. Later he seems to have tried to soften his strongly marked forms with the softer modeling of Bellini. In imitating Giorgione and Titian in his last years, the monumentality, plasticity, and personal style of his early *Pietà*, which he never equaled in later work, disappeared, and with them his individuality as a painter.

Buondelmonti (bwôn-del-môn′tē), **Cristoforo.** Ecclesiastic and humanist; active in the first half of the 15th century. A member of an ancient, noble, and powerful Florentine family, he was a priest and was interested in antiquity and archaeology. He was an ardent collector of Greek manuscripts, traveled widely in the Aegean Islands, and wrote, in Latin, a book on his travels there, *Liber insularum archipelagi* (1422).

Buoninsegna (bwô-nēn-sän′yä), **Duccio di.** See **Duccio di Buoninsegna.**

Buoninsegni (bwô-nēn-sā′nyē), **Domenico.** Florentine official and humanist; b. 1385; d. 1467. Of an ancient and wealthy family, Domenico himself was a wealthy silk merchant, a conscientious and much sought-after public official (he held the highest offices, many of them three and four times). He studied under the noted humanist Roberto de' Rossi, probably heard the lectures of Guarino da Verona when the latter was at Florence, and corresponded with him after Guarino left the city. He wrote *Storia della città di Firenze, 1410–1460*, a chronicle in the vernacular that was very well received.

Burcardus (bėr-kär′dus). See **Brocard.**

Burchard (bůr′kärt), **Johann.** Diarist; b. at Haslach, near Strasburg, Germany; d. at Rome, May, 1506. Educated in Germany, he entered upon an ecclesiastical career and went to Rome (1481). Two years later he became master of ceremonies at the papal court, and held this position until his death. The years of his service thus covered the last years of the reign of Sixtus IV, all those of Innocent VIII and Alexander VI, and the beginning of the reign of Julius II. In his position, he had intimate knowledge of what actually took place at the papal court, and recorded day-to-day events in a secret *Diary* that covers the years of his service. At the outset, he states in the *Diary* that he means to record events as a means of establishing for his own use the precedents to be followed in the bewildering number of ceremonials that took place at the papal court. Much of the *Diary* to 1494 is a collection of notes on his official duties and the manner in which he fulfilled them; even these contain a great deal of information on who came and went at the papal court, and sometimes why. After 1494 the *Diary* begins to include reports on matters outside Rome. Burchard reported facts and details of official ceremonies and ignored many other matters, but what he did report is without comment, and seemingly without any personal reaction, except when the pope offended him by ignoring protocol. His *Diary* is one of the most reliable sources for the history of the reign of Pope Alexander VI, in spite of the limited scope of its material, because in a day when rumors flew as to the crimes and general immorality of the Borgias, Burchard (whose knowledge was limited, to be sure) soberly reported only what he understood to have happened. Thus, it was generally thought that Pope Alexander VI died of poison, but Burchard, who prepared his body for burial, gives no hint of poison, and historians generally agree that Alexander died of malaria and apoplexy. As to the many murders and poisonings attributed to members of the Borgia family, especially Cesare, Burchard sometimes hints at them, sometimes repeats what is said, and at other times confirms the rumors by saying it is better not to talk about certain mysterious deaths.

Burchiello (bör-kyel′lō). [Original name, **Domenico di Giovanni.**] Florentine poet and barber; b. 1404; d. at Rome, 1449. Of a very humble family, he supported the Albizzi against the Medici and was forced to leave Florence (1434). After joining other Florentine exiles in Siena, where he was imprisoned for debt, he went to Rome (1445). He knew many of the leading literary men of his day and was the foremost exponent, if not the inventor, of a kind of nonsense verse. In his sonnets he dealt with his own unfortunate life, often in a light and even crude manner, or satirized famous or obscure men. Since they were full of topical allusions, his poems are difficult for modern readers to understand, but they were clear enough to readers of his own day. His use of bizarre language and seemingly senseless phrases started a vogue, and rhyming in this way came to be called "alla burchia." Of the several hundred sonnets attributed to him, many were undoubtedly written by others who copied his style.

Burgkmair (bůrk′mīr), **Hans.** German painter and engraver, probably a pupil of Albrecht Dürer; b. at Augsburg, Germany, 1473; d. 1531. Among his most noted works is a series of wood engravings portraying a triumphal procession of Maximilian I. He was instrumental in introducing the Italian Renaissance style into Germany.

Burlamacchi (bör-lä-mäk′kē), **Francesco.** Lucchese patriot or conspirator; b. September 14, 1498; executed September 14, 1548. Of an ancient and wealthy Lucchese family, he had been brought up to serve his state. His studies had shown him the greatness and freedom of the ancient republics of Tuscany, and he resolved to free his state and all Tuscany from the tyranny of Cosimo I de' Medici, restore Lucca to its ancient liberty, unite Italy in freedom, and renew the purity of the Christian faith in the peninsula. With others, he decided to attack Cosimo, the symbol and fountainhead, as he thought, of the enslavement of Tuscany. The carefully worked out and timed plan was delayed in execution. The delay was fatal. The plot was discovered, and Burlamacchi was arrested and imprisoned by the Signory of Lucca. Cosimo's request for the right to try him was denied; Charles V of Spain intervened; but nothing could save Burlamacchi, and he was executed. Whether he was a madman, as some thought, or a true patriot has been argued at length. He has been called a fanatic, the first martyr in the cause of Italian unification, and a harbinger of the Counter-Reformation. Fundamentally, he was a sensitive man who loved liberty and his state as the men of the Middle Ages had done. His attempt to secure liberty through the unity of all Italy against tyrants was viewed by later patriots as the forerunner of the modern movement toward unification.

Burley (bėr′li), **Walter.** [Surnamed the **Plain Doctor.**] English scholastic philosopher; b. c1274; d. c1345. He became tutor to Edward, the Black Prince. He wrote numerous philosophical treatises and commentaries, most of which are still in manuscript. His printed works include *De vita et moribus philosophorum* (probably published at Cologne, 1467) and *Tractatus de meteria et forma* (Oxford, 1500).

Busati (bö-zä′tē), **Andrea.** Venetian painter; active from 1503; d. 1528/1529? Of Slavic origin, his father was a painter from Scutari, and his two brothers were painters. Among his extant works, in which the influence of Cima da Conegliano is prominent, are *St. Mark Enthroned with SS. Andrew and Francis,* signed, Accademia, Venice; the signed *St. Anthony of Padua,* Vicenza; and the signed *The Entombment,* National Gallery, London.

Bussi (bös′sē), **Giovan Andrea.** Humanist; b. at Vigevano, 1417; d. at Rome, 1475. He studied at Paris, and at Mantua at the school of Vittorino da Feltre; taught at Genoa; and went to Rome, where he was in the service of Cardinal Nicholas of Cusa, Pius II, and Paul II. Paul II made him bishop of Aleria, in Corsica, but he never visited his see. He accompanied Cardinal Carvajal to Venice (1466 and 1467), became librarian of the Vatican Library and apostolic secretary (1472). Bussi was a fine classical scholar. He was tireless in collecting and correcting codices of ancient writers. His great contributions lay in the first editions of the ancients that he prepared for the press for the German printers Sweynheym and Pannartz, precursors of Aldus Manutius. The ancient authors so prepared and printed included Cicero, Vergil, Caesar, Ovid, Pliny, Suetonius, and Apuleius.

Bussone (bös-sō′nā), **Francesco.** See **Carmagnola, Francesco Bussone da.**

Busti (bös′tē), **Agostino.** See **Bambaja.**

Butinone (bö-tē-nō′nā), **Bernardino.** Painter; b. at Treviglio; active 1484–1507. The first and strongest influence on his development was Andrea Mantegna; Foppa and others were subsequent influences. Of his two most important works, the first is a polyptych for the Cathedral of S. Martino at Treviglio, commissioned in 1485, which he painted in collaboration with Bernardino Zenale. The record of a payment made in 1507 for the polyptych is the last notice that exists of Butinone. The grandiose character of the Treviglio altarpiece probably derives from Butinone's collaborator, who was influenced by Bramante. Berenson says of it, "It is, in the main, an offspring of Foppa's art, but less serious, more pleasing, and, above all, more gorgeous." His other important work is the fresco decoration, also carried out with Zenale, in the Church of S. Pietro in Gessate, Milan, in which scenes from the life of St. Ambrose are portrayed. The first datable work is a triptych (1484), now in the Brera, which shows the influence of Foppa. Close to it is a tondo of *St. Jerome Reading,* in the National Gallery at Parma, a small *Madonna* (Brera), and a group of Dominican saints frescoed in S. Maria delle Grazie, Milan, after 1482. A number of panels from a series on the *Life of Christ* are also attributed to him, including those in the Borromeo and Crespi Collections at Milan, in the Carrara Academy at Bergamo, at Pavia, Edinburgh, Vaduz, the National Gallery (London), and the Art Institute of Chicago. In these and in other works like them, Butinone interprets, in somewhat crude and wooden style but without losing his individuality and with great narrative integrity, the manner of Mantegna as it penetrated into Lombardy.

Butts (buts), Sir **William.** English physician; b. in Norfolk, England; d. November 22, 1545. He became physician in ordinary to Henry VIII, and appears as one of the characters in Shakespeare's *Henry VIII.*

Byrd or **Byrde** or **Bird** (bėrd), **William.** English composer and organist; b. c1538; d. July 4, 1623. He was a pupil and associate of Thomas Tallis and with him was granted a monopoly for publishing printed music in England (1575). The first composer of English madrigals, he also wrote masses and other sacred works. Among his works are *Psalmes, Sonets, and Songs* (1588), *Songs of Sundrie Natures* (1589), and *Gradualia* (1607).

C

Cabot (kab′ọ̤t), **John.** [Italian, **Giovanni Caboto;** Spanish, **Gaboto.**] Italian navigator in the English service; b. probably at Genoa, 1450; d. 1498. On his discoveries were based English claims in North America. He was the father of Sebastian Cabot (c1476–1557). He was probably a native of Genoa or its neighborhood, and in 1476 became a citizen of Venice after a residence there of fifteen years. He subsequently removed (c1484) to Bristol, England. Believing that a northwest passage would shorten the route to India, he determined to undertake an expedition in search of such a passage, and in 1496 obtained from Henry VII of England a patent for the discovery, at his own expense, of unknown lands in the eastern, western, or northern seas. He set sail from Bristol in May, 1497, in company with his sons, and returned in the same year. The expedition resulted in the discovery of what is probably Cape Breton Island and Nova Scotia. In the spring of 1498 he made a second voyage, reaching Greenland and Baffin Island, and exploring the coast as far south as the 38th parallel.

Cabot, Sebastian. Explorer; b. at Venice, c1476; d. 1557. He was the son of John Cabot (1450–1498), whom he accompanied on the voyage of 1497, when the shore of North America was discovered (his name appears with his father's in the petition to Henry VII), and it is probable that he was with him also on the voyage of 1498. In the period 1508–1509, it is said, he went in search of a northwest passage, touching the coast of Labrador and possibly entering Hudson Bay. Invited by Charles V to Spain, he was made (1519) grand pilot of Castile but gave up the post to take command of four ships which left San Lucar on April 3, 1526, to sail to the Moluccas by the Strait of Magellan. Lacking provisions, he landed on the coast of Brazil, where he had some encounters with the Portuguese; thence he sailed southward, discovered the river Uruguay, and erected a fort there. He discovered the lower Paraguay to the present site of Asunción. Convinced of the importance of this region, and joined by Diego Garcia, he relinquished the voyage to the Moluccas and dispatched a ship for reinforcements; meanwhile he established himself at the fort of Espírito Santo on the Paraná. Not receiving aid, he returned in 1530, leaving a garrison at Espírito Santo.

Cabot was subsequently in the service of Spain until c1547, when he returned to England. He was interested (1553–1556) in explorations in the Baltic, as a founder and (after 1555) life governor of the Merchant Adventurers, a company whose search for a northeast passage to the Orient opened the routes for trade with Russia. A map of the world published in 1544 is ascribed to him.

Cabral (ka̧-bräl′), **Pedro Alvares.** [Prenames sometimes abbreviated to **Pedralvarez** or **Pedralvez.**] Portuguese navigator; b. c1460; d. c1526. He was put in command of a fleet to follow up the discoveries of Vasco da Gama. According to instructions he kept far out into the Atlantic, and discovered (April 22, 1500) the coast of Brazil, which he took possession of in the name of Portugal. He continued his voyage and arrived at Calicut. He made an alliance with the ruler of Cochin, loaded his vessel with spices, and returned to Lisbon, arriving on July 23, 1501.

Caccia di Diana (kät′chä dē dē-än′ä). Poem in terza rima by Giovanni Boccaccio, composed 1336–1338. In this poem Boccaccio, who is the first to do so, adopts the rhyme scheme invented by Dante for the *Divina Commedia.* The poem tells of sixty Neapolitan ladies who go hunting under the leadership of Diana.

Caccialupi (kät-chä-lö′pē), **Giovanni Battista.** Jurisconsult; b. at San Severino in the Marches; d. at Rome, July 23, 1496. He studied at Perugia, then was professor of civil law at Siena and of canon law at Rome, where he became a consistorial advocate. He left many treatises on various facets of the law.

Cada Mosto or **Ca Da Mosto** (kä-dä mōs′tō), **Alvise** (or **Luigi**) **da.** Italian navigator; b. at Venice, c1432; d. there, c1480. In the service of Prince Henry the Navigator he explored the coast of Africa as far as Gambia, and discovered the Cape Verde Islands (1456). He was the author of *El Libro de la prima navigazione per oceano alle terre de' Nigri de la Bassa Etiopia* (1507).

Cademosto (kä-dā-mōs′tō), **Marco.** Poet and writer of the 16th century; b. at Lodi. He spent most of his life at Rome, where his genial personality won him the friendship of Pope Leo X. He wrote sonnets and other poems in the manner of Petrarch. His novelle are better than his poems. Six of these, saved during the sack of Rome (1527), remain. They are notable for his use of the popular speech.

Caesalpinus (ses-al-pī′nus), **Andreas.** [Latinized name of **Andrea Cesalpino.**] Physician, physiologist, and botanist; b. at Arezzo, June 6, 1519; d. February 23, 1603. He studied anatomy and medicine at Pisa, where he took his doctorate (1551), and later (1555) taught there and was in charge of the Botanical Garden. In 1592 he was named physician to Pope Clement VIII and went to Rome, where he was also a professor at the *Sapienza* (University). His interests embraced philosophy, in which he was a forerunner of Spinoza, mineralogy, biology, physiology, and his passion, botany. As a physiologist he was in some respects in advance of his time. He gave a theoretical description of the circulation of the blood, in which he contested Galen's theory of the function of the liver in the circulatory system, and which prepared the way for Harvey. However, his most notable achievement was contained in his work *De plantis* (Florence, 1583). In this he outlined the first truly systematic scheme of botanical classification—a classification of plants according to their fruits. Linnaeus later praised his system and made use of it.

Caetani (kä-ā-tä′nē), **Benedetto.** Original name of Pope **Boniface VIII.**

Caetano (kä-ā-tä′nō), **Cardinal.** See **De Vio, Tommaso.**

Caimi (kī′mē), **Bartolomeo.** Jurisconsult; d. 1496. Learned in canon law, he belonged to the Friars Minor and lived at Milan. His main work, printed in many editions, was a treatise in four books on the sacrament of penitence, *Interrogatorium scilicet confessionale* (Venice, 1473).

Cajetan (kaj′ȩ-tan), **Cardinal.** See **De Vio, Tommaso.**

Calandria (kä-län′drē-ä). Comedy by Bernardo Dovizi; it is an adaptation of the *Menaechmi* of Plautus, and was first presented at Urbino in 1513.

Calcagnini (käl-kä-nyē′nē), **Celio:** Humanist and writer; b. at Ferrara, September 17, 1479; d. there, April 17, 1541. He served for a time in the armies of the Emperor Maximilian and of Pope Julius II, and also served on missions and embassies for them. After a visit to Hungary, he returned to Ferrara and took the chair of belles lettres at the university, a post he held until his death. He was a friend of Ariosto and Erasmus of Rotterdam, and collected a fine library that he left to the Dominicans. Calcagnini wrote learned treatises on various subjects. One treatise (1520), *Quod coelum stet, terra autem moveatur,* on the rotation of the earth, anticipated Copernicus by more than ten years.

Calcar or **Kalkar** (käl′kär) or **Kalcker** (käl′kėr), **Jan Stephen von.** [Also, **John de Calcar** (or **Kalcker**), **Jan Stevenszoon van Calcar** (or **Kalkar** or **Kalcker**), **Jan Stephanus van Calcker.**] Dutch painter, illustrator, and designer; b. at Calcar, in the duchy of Cleve, Rhenish Prussia, c1499; d. at Naples, c1546. He is noted for his imitations of Titian and Raphael, which are almost indistinguishable from their authentic works. He illustrated the *De humanis corporis fabrica* of Andreas Vesalius.

Calco (käl′kō), **Bartolomeo.** Humanist and statesman; b. at Milan, 1434; d. there, June 18, 1508. He had a sound education and was learned in many fields. Under the Sforza he held various posts and won many honors, and with the rise to power of Ludovico il Moro (September, 1479) his influence at court greatly increased. He was secretary and councillor to Ludovico and, devoted to his lord and to his city, performed valuable services for both. In the name of Ludovico he was the patron and protector of artists and men of letters. Leonardo da Vinci, Demetrius Chalcondylas, and others were attracted to the court in his time, and he was in close contact with Poliziano and other men of letters, and is mentioned in many letters and verses of the time. A great deal of his official correspondence is in the archives at Milan.

Calco, Tristano. Milanese historian; d. c1515. He was in the service of the Sforza, and by 1478 was librarian of the Visconti-Sforza library at Pavia. In 1496 he became director of the ducal library at Milan and provost of the secret archives of the Sforza. He wrote a history of Milan, which he left unfinished in Book XXII. The first twenty books covered the history of Milan from its founding to 1313. The work is notable for its honesty and for the care with which, through thorough research and comparison of documents, he sought accuracy of fact.

Calderini (käl-dā-rē′nē), **Domizio.** Humanist; b. at Torri (Verona), c1444; d. at Rome, 1478. At 24 his reputation for learning was so great that Pope Paul II invited him to Rome as a teacher. He remained there under Sixtus IV, and became an apostolic secretary. Calderini wrote commentaries on many of the Latin writers—Vergil, Propertius, Juvenal, Martial, and others—and translated the first two books of Pausanias from Greek to Latin. He studied law, philosophy, and mathematics, and wrote Latin verses in addition to his many other writings. He died of the plague at Rome.

Calderini, Giovanni. [Latinized, **Johannes Calderinus.**] Bolognese specialist in canon law; d. 1365. He was the pupil and adopted son of Giovanni d'Andrea, took his doctorate in canon law (1326), and taught it at Bologna until 1359. He was famous at Bologna as a teacher and a writer. He left many treatises on legal matters that were widely disseminated after the invention of printing.

Calepino (kä-lā-pē′nō), **Ambrogio.** Humanist and lexicographer; b. at Calepio, near Bergamo, June 6, 1435; d. there, November 30, 1511. He followed humanistic studies, but owes his fame to the Latin-Italian dictionary, originally entitled *Cornucopiae,* that he compiled and first published at Reggio Emilia (1502) and later revised and expanded. The work passed through many editions, and became, after successive enlargements, in 1590 a polyglot of eleven languages. Despite some errors and omissions, the original work served as a model for later dictionaries, and gave the word *calepino,* meaning dictionary, to the Italian language.

Caliari (kä-lyä′rē), **Paolo.** See **Paolo Veronese.**

Calixtines (kạ-liks′tinz). [Also, **Utraquists.**] A sect of Hussites in Bohemia whose center was the University of Prague. They separated (c1420) from the more radical Taborites, a sect led by Jan Žižka, and published (1421) their confession, called the *Articles of Prague,* the leading article of which was a demand to partake of the cup (*calix*) as well as of the bread in the Lord's Supper. The articles were accepted in the main by the Roman Catholic Church at the Council of Basel (1433), and priests were permitted to administer the Eucharist in both kinds, i.e., with both bread and wine, in Bohemia and Moravia. As the Protestant Reformation gained strength in central Europe, the Calixtine sect itself split, some of its members being absorbed by Catholicism and some by Protestantism.

Calixtus III (kạ-liks′tus). [Original name, **Alonso de Borja**, Italianized to **Alfonso Borgia.**] Pope (1455–1458); b. at Xativa, Valencia, Spain, December 31, 1378; d. at Rome, August 6, 1458. He came of an old and gifted family, noted for its tenacity, strength, arrogance, and good looks. He had studied law at the University of Lerida and served Alfonso of Naples as private secretary, counselor, and confidant. He was made bishop of Valencia (1429) and cardinal (1444) for his good offices in securing an agreement between Alfonso and Eugenius IV. On the death of Nicholas V, factions in the conclave to choose a new pope were so evenly divided that none could win a majority. Alfonso Borgia, then nearing 80, was chosen as a compromise on April 8, 1455. He had long expected to be pope, as St. Vincent Ferrer had prophesied that he would be. He firmly believed in the prophesy, repeated it often, and one of his early acts as pope was the canonization of St. Vincent Ferrer, his saintly countryman. Those who believed Calixtus III would be a caretaker pope were immediately made aware of their error. He was an able administrator and firmly took the reins into his own hands. He refused to allow Alfonso of Naples to trade on their former friendship, which Alfonso had confidently expected to do. When Alfonso died, Calixtus declared that the kingdom of Naples revert to the Church, as he did not recognize Alfonso's illegitimate son Ferrante as the heir. Humanists and artists were dismissed from the court of Calixtus. Building was stopped in Rome. He devoted all his energy, his acknowledged talents, and the wealth of the Church to the promotion of a crusade against the Turks. He built a fleet, supported Hunyadi of Hungary and Scanderbeg of Albania (appointed captain-general, 1457), lived to see a victory at Belgrade (1456), but failed in his efforts to organize the crusade. A man of blameless life himself, he was blind to the sins of his nephews, on whom he lavished honors, benefits, and high positions in the Church. Neapolitans and Spaniards were so favored that the name "Catalan," by which they were commonly called, became a term of opprobrium. Rodrigo Borgia, who became Alexander VI, and Luis Juan Mila, nephews of Calixtus, were named cardinals in 1456. Don Pedro, the infamous brother of Rodrigo, was loaded with benefits. Fortresses in Rome were turned over to the Catalans. Their power became so unendurable that, on the death of Calixtus, Catalans fled for their lives before the unleashed anger of the Romans. Calixtus was succeeded by Pius II.

Callistus (kạ-lis′tus). A variant name (considered by some to be the preferable name) for the popes often listed under **Calixtus.**

Callistus Andronicus (an-drọ̄-nī′kus). Greek scholar; b. at Constantinople; d. after 1476. He fled to Italy, where he was befriended by his countryman Cardinal Bessarion. He taught Greek at Bologna (1458–1465) and Rome, and lectured on Greek language and literature at Florence. Although he was a successful teacher and numbered men who later became eminent among his pupils, his private circumstances were poor, and he became one of the earliest of the Greek scholars to go to France to improve his fortunes. There he taught at the University of Paris. He later went to England, where he died after 1476. Among his writings is a lament on the fall of Constantinople.

Calmo (käl′mō), **Andrea.** Actor and playwright; b. at Venice, 1510; d. there, 1571. Of his comedies, some are based on classical models, as his *Rodiana*, presented at Venice in 1540, and *Travaglia*, presented in 1546; others are weak imitations of Machiavelli and Ruzzante; and others, in simplicity of theme and rapidity and realism of action, are distinctly his own, as his *Spagnola* and *Saltuzza*. Calmo used an elegant, literary speech in some of his works, but in others employed the speech of the common people, with bits of dialect from the northern areas of Italy, as Venice, Bergamo, Padua, and so on, as the play required. In his use, in some of his comedies, of standard figures who improvise as they play, Calmo was the forerunner of the realistic, improvisatory commedia dell'arte. He also made a collection, in the form of rhymed letters, of a large variety of subjects and in different meters. The collection includes all sorts of bizarre and recondite information and went through twenty editions between 1547 and 1610. The letters of the first books are supposed to have been written by a member of a family of poor fishermen over the course of many years. Descriptions and recitals, in an almost archaic dialect, of poems, songs, festivals, stories, provide not only an artistic literary work but also a valuable historical record.

LUCA CAMBIASO
Holy Family with the Young St. John
Gabinetto Disegni e Stampe degli Uffizi Foto Soprintendenza

LUCA CAMBIASO
Epiphany
Gabinetto Disegni e Stampe degli Uffizi Foto Soprintendenza

LUCA CAMBIASO
The Capture of Christ
Gabinetto Disegni e Stampe degli Uffizi Foto Soprintendenza

CALVIN (kal′vin), **JOHN.** [Original name, **JEAN CHAUVIN** or **CAUVIN** or **CAULVIN.**] Protestant reformer and theologian; b. at Noyon, in Picardy, France, July 10, 1509; d. at Geneva, Switzerland, May 27, 1564. He studied at Paris, Orléans, and Bourges. Having embraced the Reformation (c1528), he was driven (1533) from Paris, published *Institutes of the Christian Religion* (Basel, 1536), in which he systematized his basic Protestant theology, and went to Geneva in 1536. The extreme nature of the reforms which Calvin, with Guillaume Farel, attempted to carry out there caused their banishment from Geneva (1538). On his return to Geneva (1541), he was welcomed and had the opportunity to put his reforms, political and economic as well as religious, into effect. Since to him the Bible was the source of God's law and thus of all law, its teachings were extended into all phases of life at Geneva. The moral principles of the Bible—thrift, honesty, industry—were applied to the commercial and industrial life. He expounded his theological system and doctrines in powerful prose, and engaged in violent controversies to defend his views and oppose contrary ones. He disagreed with Luther and caused a division in the Protestant movement. His controversy with Servetus (1553) led to the burning at the stake of Servetus. Calvin's influence and his movement spread throughout western Europe and ultimately into the New World.

CALYGORANTE (kä-lē-gō-rän′tā). In Lodovico Ariosto's *Orlando Furioso*, a giant who snares passersby in a net of unbreakable mesh. Astolfo frightens him with his magic horn and captures him in his own net.

CAMBIASO (käm-byä′zō), **GIOVANNI.** [Also, **CAMBIASI.**] Painter; b. near Genoa, 1495; d. at an advanced age, year unknown. He was a pupil of Semino and an imitator of Pordenone and Perin del Vaga, and worked especially in fresco. Of the many works he is said to have painted, some with his son Luca (1527–1585), the only surely known one is the signed painting in the church at Breccanecca (Chiavari).

CAMBIASO, LUCA. [Also, **CAMBIASI, CANGIAGIO;**

LUCA CAMBIASO
Study of Volumes
Gabinetto Disegni e Stampe degli Uffizi   Foto Soprintendenza

called **Luchetto.**] Draftsman, painter, and sculptor; b. at Moneglia, near Genoa, 1527; d. in the Escorial, near Madrid, 1585. He began his art study with his father, Giovanni Cambiaso (b. 1495), who, to make sure that the boy kept at his drawing, hid his clothes and his shoes. Probably it was native talent rather than these Spartan measures that made of Cambiaso one of the most superb draftsmen of his time. At 15, with his father, he painted scenes from the *Metamorphoses* of Ovid on the façade of a house at Genoa, went on to the *Labors of Hercules* in the Palazzo Antonio Doria, and afterward painted commissions of his own. He soon surpassed his father in accomplishment and fame, and created a style of Genoese mural decoration that dominated Genoese style in his century and laid the foundations for the style of the 17th century. Visiting Rome and Florence (1575), he fed his native inclination toward large and majestic composition by intensive study of the works of Raphael, Michelangelo, and other great painters and sculptors. His own early works tended to be in the monumental, perhaps too grandiose manner, in the style of Michelangelo and with the movement of Beccafumi. But later, on the advice of a friend, he abandoned the grandeur and monumentality of Michelangelo and in his work then approached the elegance and softer tonality of Correggio and Parmigianino. The paintings of his best period are marked by grace of design and superior loveliness of color. He often painted, with complete assurance, with a brush in each hand. In 1583, at the invitation of Philip II of Spain, he undertook the completion of certain frescoes in the Escorial, and his *Assemblage of the Blessed*, on the ceiling of the choir in the Church of St. Lawrence there, was once considered one of his most remarkable works (later criticism finds a failure of his powers in his last works). For this he received 7,000 ducats, the greatest sum paid up to that time for a single work. He died while working in the Escorial. For all the large frescoes and paintings he executed in the palaces and churches of Genoa and vicinity, or the few pieces of sculpture he left, Cambiaso's true genius and spirit are revealed in his drawings. Hundreds of these are extant, and there is scarcely a museum or school collection of note without one. Hundreds more perished. It is said his wife sometimes used them to light the fire; many were saved from the flames by his favorite and best pupil, Lazzaro Tavarone. The drawings, mostly in pen and brown ink, and sometimes with a wash, are decisive, monumental in the early years when he made many on classical and mythological subjects, vigorously plastic, and rapidly executed in pursuit of his swift flow of ideas. They are piercingly expressive and beautiful. The eye absorbs at once the well-disciplined composition. The wide variety of subjects commands respect and even awe. He often made a number of drawings on the same subject, as *The Holy Family*, *Conversion of St. Paul*, *Rest on the Flight into Egypt*, *Deposition*, and others, and each is a unique expression of his idea. Many of the drawings were studies, as his *Enthroned St. Benedict with Saints John and Luke*, a study for one of his finest paintings, now in the Baptistery of the cathedral at Genoa (drawings on the subject are in the Accademia, Venice; Louvre, Paris; Prado, Madrid; Manning Collection, New York; and elsewhere), and the *Sacrifice of Abraham*, study for a fresco formerly (destroyed by a bomb, 1944) in the Archbishop's Palace at Genoa. Others can be related to finished paintings or frescoes; many more were executed out of pure love of drawing. He is sometimes thought of as a forerunner of modern art for his manner of presenting volumes in three-dimensional geometric figures. But this technique was employed by him in his preparatory studies to arrange the space that would be occupied by volumes; he was not a "cubist" in the modern sense, despite the cubes and other solids that sometimes composed the figures of his drawings. An immediate impression of his drawings is that the idea was conceived complete and executed with incredible swiftness in unerring, flowing, living line. The Uffizi, Florence, has a rich collection of them; other great collections are those at Darmstadt and the Manning Collection, New York, but as noted earlier, Cambiaso drawings are to be found in many museums, as well as in a number of private collections. His best paintings are at Genoa.

Cambio (käm′byō), **Arnolfo di.** See **Arnolfo di Cambio.**

Cambrai (kam-brā′; French, käṅ-brā), **League of.** Alliance among Louis XII of France, the Holy Roman Emperor Maximilian I, Ferdinand "the Catholic" of Spain, Pope Julius

II, and others, formed at Cambrai on December 10, 1508. The aim of the league was to curb the power of Venice, with the plan of seizing and partitioning her territories. The league had great initial success; Maximilian I entered Venetia, and Venice had to make concessions to the pope and to Ferdinand. But Maximilian was halted before Padua and withdrew; Julius II made peace with Venice (1510) and the league disbanded. Venice had been greatly weakened but by no means crushed, and the following year was allied to her former enemies, Julius II and Ferdinand, in an attempt to drive the French from Italy.

Cambrai. Peace of. [Called the **Ladies' Peace.**] Peace negotiated at Cambrai, August 5, 1529, between Francis I of France and Charles V of the Holy Roman Empire. France abandoned Italy to the emperor, and relinquished her claim to suzerainty over Flanders and Artois; her title to the duchy of Burgundy was recognized. It was called the "Ladies' Peace" (*La Paix des dames*) because the preliminaries were conducted by Louise, mother of Francis I, and Margaret, aunt of Charles V.

Camerarius (kam-ėr-ār′i-us; German, kä-mā-rä′rē-u̇s), **Joachim.** [Original surname, **Liebhard.**] German scholar; b. at Bamberg, Germany, April 12, 1500; d. at Leipzig, Germany, April 17, 1574. He was the author of a life of Melanchthon (1556) and editor of his letters (1569).

Cammelli (käm-mel′lē), **Antonio.** [Called **il Pistoia.**] Poet; b. at Pistoia, 1436; d. at Ferrara, April 29, 1502. He held a minor post at the court of Ercole I at Ferrara, for a time, and then (1487) was made captain of the Porta S. Croce at Reggio. Either because he was a poor administrator, or because his biting satire against prominent persons failed to endear him to them, he lost the post (1497) and was compelled to seek employment from various potential patrons, as from Isabella d'Este and the marquess of Mantua. Seemingly gay and reckless, his literary work inclines to the satiric and burlesque. A tragedy in terza rima, *Filostrato e Panfilo,* was drawn from an episode in the *Decameron,* and though of slight literary merit was performed and printed several times. Over 550 of his *Sonetti faceti* are to be found in a codex in the Ambrosian Library at Milan. Among these are many that reveal the misery of his life, an indication that his gaiety and wit concealed a fundamental melancholy. One group of the sonnets concerns the devastating events that were taking place in Italy between 1492 and 1502, and show him to have been a free spirit and a patriot.

Camões (ka̤-moiṅsh′), **Luiz (Vaz) de.** Portuguese poet, the most celebrated in that language; b. in Portugal, c1524; d. at Lisbon, June 10, 1580. His epic poem *Os Lusíadas* (*The Portuguese,* 1572; commonly called *The Lusiads*), on the discovery of the sea route to India by the Portuguese navigator Vasco da Gama, is one of the masterpieces of Renaissance literature. Camões came of a family of the minor nobility and was educated at Coimbra, which he is believed to have left for Lisbon in the early 1540's. For about two years he lived in Ceuta, Africa, where he served in the army and lost the sight of his right eye, probably in a battle. At Lisbon, he was imprisoned (1552) for having wounded one of the king's equerries in a street fracas. He was pardoned (1553) on the condition of his immediate embarkation for India. He arrived in Goa in September of the same year, and went to Macao a few years later. There, according to tradition, he was responsible for the property of those Portuguese who had died or were absent from Macao. About 1560 he was back in Goa. He embarked there for Portugal in 1567, but was left in Mozambique having, again according to tradition, been shipwrecked off the coast of Cambodia on the way. At last he landed at Lisbon at the end of 1569 or the beginning of 1570, after about seventeen years of an exile that was marked by misfortunes. These perhaps account for the note of pessimism that pervades the substantial body of his poems that have been preserved. His lyric production is of extreme literary value, his sonnets being thought by many to have been unsurpassed. The sonnets, and some of the longer poems, combine an emotional intensity with perfection of style; their subjects are frequently his loves or his misfortunes. Other poems are marked by the pessimism noted above. The most reliable edition of his lyrics is considered to be *Lírica de Camões,* a scholarly work published at Coimbra in 1932 by José Maria Rodrigues and Afonso Lopes Vieira, which contains all the lyric poems actually written by Camões, omitting those that for centuries had been

DOMENICO CAMPAGNOLA
Buildings in a Rocky Landscape
Courtesy of The Pierpont Morgan Library, New York

unduly attributed to him. Of his three comedies in verse, *El-Rei Seleuco* is based on Plutarch and *Anfitriões* on the *Amphitruo* of Plautus; the third is *Filodemo.*

CAMPAGNOLA (käm-pä-nyō'lä), **DOMENICO.** Venetian painter and engraver; b. at Padua, probably c1500; d. after 1562. It is thought that he was adopted and brought up by Giulio Campagnola, from whom he took his name and of whom he was a pupil. His engravings, which show a dependence on Giulio Campagnola, Titian, and Pordenone, date from 1517, and are the earliest works of any kind from his hand. He executed many of them, as well as woodcuts and exquisite pen and ink drawings that are finished works of art; there are collections of these in the Uffizi at Florence and in the British Museum. As a painter he was a pupil and follower of Titian, whom he assisted in the decoration of the Scuola del Santo at Padua, and was also influenced by Giorgione. He worked mostly at Venice and Padua; the greatest number of his works are in the latter city. At Padua he painted some of the scenes from the lives of Christ and the Virgin in the Carmelite School, and the *Holy Conversation, Saints Francis and Anthony,* and the detached fresco *Beheading of John the Baptist* in the Museo Civico. Other works are a *Male Portrait* in the Uffizi at Florence, attributed to him, and a *Virgin and Child with SS. Catherine of Alexandria and George* in the Johnson Collection at Philadelphia.

CAMPAGNOLA, GIULIO. Painter, miniaturist, and engraver; b. at Padua, 1482; d. after 1514. His father, Gerolamo, was also an artist. Giulio was noted in his youth for his learning—he knew Latin, Greek, and Hebrew, and was a musician—as well as for his artistic gifts. He was at the court at Ferrara in 1498, was at Venice in 1507, and was mentioned by Aldus Manutius in his will (1514) as a type cutter. In painting he was a link between Mantegna and Giorgione in the development of Paduan art, and spread the elegance and refinement of Giorgione by means of his engravings. In his prints, he was influenced to some extent by Mantegna and, as were most contemporary engravers, by Dürer, but his main inspiration in his best creations was Giorgione.

Campanile (käm-pä-nē′lā). A bell tower. In Italy, the campanile is often a detached building, next to a church, erected for the purpose of containing bells. Many of the campanili of Italy are lofty and magnificent structures; that in Cremona, erected at the end of the 13th century and 387 feet high, is the highest in Italy. The campanile at Florence, next to the Duomo (Santa Maria del Fiore), designed, begun and partly decorated by Giotto in the 14th century, is world-famous.

Campano (käm-pä′nō), **Giovanni Antonio.** Humanist, poet, and ecclesiastic; b. at Cavelli (Capua), 1429; d. at Siena, July 15, 1477. At the age of 15 he attended the humanistic lectures of Lorenzo Valla at Naples. He fled from Naples when it fell to the Aragonese and went to Perugia. There he continued his studies and produced most of his literary work. In 1459 he met Pope Pius II at the Congress of Mantua, and won the pope's favor by his cultivated mind and genial temperament. Pius took him back to Rome as one of his secretaries and invested him with the bishoprics of Cotrone (1460) and Teramo (1463). It was to Campano that Pius entrusted his *Commentaries* for correction and editing. Campano fortunately thought they needed very little of either, merely suppressing such parts as he considered too frankly expressed. Thus it was that the *Commentaries* were given to a copyist almost unaltered. He went on several diplomatic missions for the popes but fell out of favor with Sixtus IV and retired to Siena. He died and was buried in the cathedral there. Campano wrote on philosophy and politics, in Latin, more than 400 letters, and lives of Braccio da Montone and Pius II.

Campeggi (käm-ped′jē), **Lorenzo.** Cardinal, reformer, and diplomat; b. at Bologna, between 1472 and 1474; d. at Rome, July 25, 1539. He studied law at Padua, married, and had five children. On the death of his wife (1509) he entered the Church. He was bishop of Feltre (1512) and held other high offices in the Church, and was given the red hat in 1517. He is known above all for the number of religious and political missions he undertook at a troubled time in Church history. His missions took him to Germany to enlist the aid of Maximilian I and the German states in a crusade against the Turks, and to England to win the aid of Henry VIII for the same purpose. In neither case was he wholly successful, but in both he won the respect of the sovereigns to whom he applied. Henry named him (1524) bishop of Salisbury, and he held the see in absentia for ten years. (In 1534 Henry's break with the Church was complete.) On his return to Rome, and on the elevation of Pope Adrian VI, he proposed specific reforms to the pope that were accepted for implementation. Campeggi ardently desired reform of the Church, in its administrative as well as its spiritual life. His reforms implied political as well as ecclesiastical change, and some of them were adopted by succeeding popes. On a second mission to Germany (1524) he attempted to unite the Catholic prelates and princes and to conciliate the Protestants. In 1528 he was associated with Thomas Wolsey in hearing the divorce suit of Henry VIII against Catherine of Aragon. He adjourned the hearing. In his missions his first policy was one of conciliation. He was one of the principal proponents of a Church council that eventually met in Trent.

Campeggi, Tommaso. Ecclesiastic; b. at Pavia, 1481; d. at Rome, January 21, 1564. He took his doctorate in philosophy at Bologna (1506) and in canon and civil law in 1512, taught canon law (1512–1514), and was archdeacon of Bologna. Pope Adrian VI sent him as nuncio to Venice, and under Pope Clement VII he took orders and was in the service of the papal court at Rome. Pope Paul III sent him (1540) to Worms to seek an agreement with the Protestants, but in this he was unsuccessful. He was at Trent for the opening of the Council and read the papal bull calling the sessions. In 1546 he gave up his bishopric of Feltre to his nephew and returned to Rome. He left many treatises on religious matters, as on the celibacy of the clergy, the authority of the pope vis-à-vis a council, and many letters in connection with the Council of Trent.

Campi (käm′pē), **Antonio.** Cremonese painter, architect, sculptor, and historian of Cremona; b. at Cremona, c1530; d. there, 1591. He was the son of Galeazzo Campi (1477–1536), with whom he studied, and worked at Milan, Piacenza, Brescia, Mantua, and Rome. At Cremona he constructed the Bedoni and Pallavicino palaces. His paintings, chiefly of religious subjects, show the influence of Giulio Romano, Pordenone, and Parmigianino, and are well esteemed both for color and for design. A man of many parts, he was known also as an architect and a sculptor, and he wrote and illustrated with original engravings a chronicle of the city of Cremona. Among his works are a *Pietà*, in the Duomo at Cremona; a *Madonna Consolatrice* and a *Madonna with Saints*, in the Church of San Pietro at Cremona. His best works are found in the Church of San Sigismondo at Cremona. Others are a *Madonna with Saints*, in the Brera at Milan, and the *Adoration of the Magi*, *Story of St. Paul*, *Birth of Christ*, and *Martyrdom of St. Lawrence*, at Milan.

Campi, Bernardino. Cremonese painter; b. at Cremona, 1522; d. there, between 1590 and 1595. Bernardino was a pupil at Cremona of Giulio Campi and thus may have been a younger brother like Antonio and Vincenzo Campi, who were also students of Giulio. There is some evidence, however, that he was the son of one Pietro Campi, also a painter and a cousin, rather than a brother, of Giulio. After his study at Cremona he went to Mantua, where he was subject to many influences, those of Giulio Romano, Correggio, and Parmigianino being especially pronounced. He was also an enthuiastic follower of Titian, and so devotedly studied the Venetian master's work that he was able to add a figure to Titian's series of Caesars which could not be distinguished as to authorship from the others. He developed a mastery of his own, however, and was, in his own right, influential on Italian painting. His skillful treatment of figures, as to both composition and perspective, is a feature of the frescoes in the cupola of the Church of San Sigismondo at Cremona, considered his masterpiece. In addition to Cremona, he worked at Piacenza, Alba, Milan, and Mantua, executing religious paintings and portraits. His *Descent from the Cross* in the Brera, at Milan, and a *Mater Dolorosa* in the Louvre, at Paris, are well known. He was the author of a treatise on painting, *Parere sopra la pittura*.

Campi, Galeazzo. Cremonese painter; b. at Cremona, 1477; d. there, 1536. He was the father of Giulio Campi (c1502–1572), Antonio Campi (c1530–1591), and Vincenzo Campi (1536–1591). He painted chiefly religious pictures, some of them in imitation of Boccaccino, whose pupil he was in his youth, and others reminiscent of Perugino. His works are to be found at Cremona, in various churches, and in the Museo Civico, at Bergamo, Brooklyn, and Vienna. His *Madonna with S. Anthony and S. Biagio*, is in the Brera, at Milan.

Campi, Giulio. Cremonese painter; b. at Cremona, c1502; d. there, 1572. He was the son and pupil of Galeazzo Campi (1477–1536), and founded a school of painting at Cremona where his brothers Antonio Campi (c1530–1591), Vincenzo Campi (1536–1591), and Bernardino Campi (1522–1590/1595), who was thought by some to be his cousin, were pupils. Giulio's earlier works enjoy a richness of Venetian coloring, the influence of Titian, that is missing in later works. The strongest influences in his art are those of Pordenone and Dosso Dossi. His best works are at Mantua and at Cremona, especially the frescoes in S. Margherita in the latter city, and his *Virgin and Child with Saints Celsus and Nazarus*, which he painted at the age of 27 for Sant' Abbondio at Cremona. Among his works are a portrait of his father and the gently melancholy *The Guitar Player*, Uffizi; a *Madonna with Saints*, Brera, Milan; *Allegory*, Poldi Pezzoli Museum, Milan; and *St. Peter*, Johnson Collection, Philadelphia. Besides the many frescoes and paintings in the churches at Cremona there is a series of frescoes in S. Maria delle Grazie, Soncino, and paintings at Turin, Budapest, London, Paris, Stuttgart, Cleveland, Pittsburgh, Worcester, Massachusetts, and elsewhere.

Campi, Vincenzo. Cremonese painter; b. at Cremona, 1536; d. 1591. He was the son of Galeazzo Campi (1477–1536), and became noted for his portraits and still lifes. His instruction in painting was chiefly at the hands of his brother Giulio, and he also worked with his brother Antonio, accompanying the latter to Spain where both were employed by Philip II in the decoration of the Escorial Palace. He varied the family tradition of painting mostly religious pictures, however, and became best known for his portraits, still lifes, and genre compositions. His color has been more admired than his design. Examples of his work survive chiefly in his native Lombardy, at Cremona, and in the Brera at Milan.

Campione (käm-pyō′nā), **Giacomo** or **Iacopo da.** Lombard architect and builder; d. 1398. He was a member of a family of architects and builders who worked in Lombardy, and worked on the construction of the cathedral at Milan as well as that of the Certosa di Pavia.

Campolongo (käm-pō-lōng′gō), **Bartolomeo.** Venetian painter; active at the beginning of the 16th century. His *Madonna Adoring the Sleeping Child* is in the Carrara Academy, Bergamo.

Canace (kä-nät′chā). Tragedy by Sperone Speroni; an undramatic horror story based on the myth of the incestuous love of the children of the wind god Aeolus.

Canale (kä-nä′lā), **Cristoforo da.** Venetian captain of the 16th century who distinguished himself (1562) for bravery in one of the many encounters with the Corsair pirates in the Adriatic. Wounded in an engagement, he had himself lashed to the deck of his vessel and directed the attack from there. The Venetians won, but Canale died the next day. He wrote a manual on naval tactics, *Della milizia marittima,* which is one of the best of the age.

Candrino (kän-drē′nō), **Lola** and **Paolo.** Workers in stucco; active in the 16th century. They came from Bologna, and executed some precious stucco decorations (*Liberation of Andromeda, Metamorphosis of Daphne, of Callistus, of Actaeon,* and others) in the transformation of the Villa d'Este at Tivoli for Cardinal Ippolito d'Este.

Cane (kä′nā), **Facino.** See **Facino Cane.**

Can Grande della Scala I (kän grän′dā del′lä skä′lä). See **Scala, Can Grande della.**

Canigiani (kä-nē-jä′nē), **Barduccio di Pietro.** Follower and secretary of St. Catherine of Siena; d. at Siena, December 8, 1382. He was a Florentine who met St. Catherine when she went to Florence to make peace between the Florentines and the pope (1377). He became one of her constant companions and was one of the secretaries who took down the *Dialogo della Divina Provvidenza,* which she dictated while in ecstasy. He became a priest after her death.

Canigiani, Ristoro. Florentine statesman and poet; d. 1380. Little is known of his life. Among the offices he held at Florence was that of ambassador to Naples (1376). He was also head of the Guelph party. In 1363 he fled to Bologna to escape the plague, and there wrote his *Ristorato,* a poem in terza rima, in forty-four cantos, which has reflections of Dante. Boccaccio speaks highly of Canigiani.

Canisio (kä-nē′syō), **Egidio.** See **Egidio da Viterbo.**

Cano (kä′nō), **Juan Sebastián del.** Spanish navigator; b. at Guetaria, Guipúzcoa, Spain, c1460; d. at sea, August 4, 1526. He was captain of the *Concepción,* one of the ships in Magellan's fleet. After the death of Magellan he assumed command. He reached the Moluccas, loaded his two remaining ships with spices, and in one of them, the *Victoria,* he reached Spain (September 6, 1522) by way of the Cape of Good Hope, thus becoming the actual commander of the first vessel to circumnavigate the earth. He died at sea on a subsequent voyage.

Cano or **Canus** (kā′nus), **Melchior.** Spanish Dominican theologian; b. at Tarrançon, Spain, January 1, 1509; d. at Toledo, Spain, September 30, 1560. He was a bitter antagonist of the Jesuits, and an influential counselor of Philip II.

Canon's Yeoman's Tale, The. One of Chaucer's *Canterbury Tales.* The canon of the tale is a ragged alchemist who has no gold but what he gets by trickery, and he and his hungry yeoman join the Canterbury pilgrims to practice their thieving arts upon them. It exposes the tricks of the alchemists.

Canossa (kä-nôs′sä), **Ludovico.** Bishop of Tricarico; b. 1476; d. 1532. He was a friend of Castiglione and lived at the court of the Montefeltri at Urbino as early as 1496. He served Pope Leo X as nuncio to England and France, and thereafter long resided at the French court, where he was among those favored by Francis I.

Cantalicio (kän-tä-lē′chō), **Giovanni Battista.** Poet, man of letters, and teacher; b. at Cantalice (Rieti), c1450; d. at Rome, 1515. As a youth he went to Rome and studied under Gasparo Veronese. In 1471 he left Rome and embarked on what turned out to be a checkered teaching career. He taught at San Gimignano, Siena, Florence, Foligno, Rieti, Perugia, and Viterbo, before he went to the courts of Guidobaldo at Urbino and the Borgia at Rome, where fortune smiled on him. Alexander VI sent him to Naples with Cardinal Giovanni Borgia at the time of the French invasion of that city (1495). There he met the Aragonese captain Gonsalo de Córdoba, who later made him tutor of his son. Julius II created him bishop of Atre and Penne in 1503. Among his writings, Cantalicio published a Latin grammar, a treatise on metrics, and commentaries on several Latin authors. He also wrote verse—eclogues and epigrams. Many of his poems are in praise (and flattery) of contemporary figures. Of all his work, only his epigrams show originality and sincerity, recorded briskly and with gusto.

Canterbury Tales, The. Work by Geoffrey Chaucer, probably begun about 1387 and presenting, through the various tales and the wide variety of tellers, a magnificent and animated picture of 14th century English life and mores. Using a typically Boccaccesque framework, at the Tabard Inn, Southwark, Chaucer joins some twenty-nine pilgrims bound for the shrine of Saint Thomas à Becket at Canterbury. The Prologue describes the vividly individualized pilgrims, ranging from an eminent jurist and a worthy knight to a plowman and a dishonest miller. The Host of the Tabard, Harry Bailey, suggests that on the journey each pilgrim tell four stories, the best to be rewarded by a supper on their return. Chaucer did not live to complete the projected series of 120 tales (outdoing the *Decameron* by a score); most of the 22 tales are in heroic couplets, a few in stanzas, and two in prose. First the Knight recounts a romance of fighting, love, and pageantry, condensed from Boccaccio's *Il Teseida*. The Host next calls upon the Monk, but Robin the Miller, already drunk, insists on his turn. With brilliant characterization he vitalizes a clever fabliau plot of an old uxorious carpenter deceived by an Oxford undergraduate who in turn is tricked by a parish clerk. Osewold, the "sclendre colerik" Reeve, formerly a carpenter, takes personal offense and retaliates with a fabliau of a thieving miller deceived by two Cambridge students. Then Roger of Ware, the uncleanly London Cook, starts a story of low London life (unfinished). The Man of Law retells the tale of the long-suffering Constance from the Anglo-Norman *Chronicle* of Nicholas Trivet. After the Shipman's fabliau comes the Prioress' miracle of a boy's devotion to the Virgin Mary; then Chaucer attempts the doggerel rime of Sir Thopas, a romance so "drasty" that the Host makes him stop. Chaucer tries again with the long prose allegory of Melibeus and his wife Prudence, a humanitarian document against the evils of war and the perversion of justice, originally by Albertano of Brescia. The Monk is not allowed to finish his "tragedies" of the falls of the great; the Nun's Priest satirically retells the barnyard beast-epic of Chauntecleer and Pertelote. Alice of Bath, looking for a sixth husband, defends her marriages, tells how she has handled her husbands, and recounts the folk tale of an old hag who becomes a beautiful maiden when her husband promises obedience. After Friar Huberd and the Summoner have chastised each other with fabliaux, the Clerk of Oxenford retells Petrarch's story of patient Griselda, who submits to her husband's every whim. The disillusioned Merchant, two months wed, bitterly tells of old January deceived by his young wife May; then the gay Squire starts an Eastern romance (unfinished). The country gentleman, the Franklin, tells of a perfect marriage based on truth and generosity. The Physician retells the old Roman "geste" of Appius and Virginia. The Pardoner shows how he wins money by preaching on "the root of all evil" and by telling his impressive exemplum of how avarice brought death to three revellers. After the second Nun's legend of the martyred Saint Cecilia, the Canon's Yeoman exposes his master's alchemical deceptions; the Manciple retells Ovid's story of Phoebus and the Crow; and as the company nears Canterbury, the Parson gives his prose sermon on Penance and the Seven Deadly Sins. In addition to the interest of the tales themselves and the vivacity with which they are presented, Chaucer's great work resulted in the establishment of English as a literary language.

Canus (kā′nus), **Melchior.** See **Cano, Melchior.**

Canzone (kän-tsō′nā). In Italian poetry, an ancient verse form, possibly influenced and modified by the Provençal *chanso*, but of older lineage, perhaps an offshoot or modification of the ballata. Dante systematized its construction and proclaimed it the most appropriate verse vehicle for the themes of love, of arms, and of moral ideas. The canzone was originally intended to be accompanied by music.

Capece (kä-pā′chā), **Scipione.** Humanist and jurisconsult; b. at Naples; d. there, December 18, 1551. He taught civil law at Naples, and was head of the Accademia Pontaniana there which, following the death of Sannazzaro (1530), met in his house. Capece was banished from Naples (1543) for his adherence to the religious ideas of Juan de Valdés and Bernardino Ochino. He went to Salerno, where he remained until 1550. Capece left many juridical works, and poetry, and is best known for two poems: *De divo Iohanne Baptista vate maximo libri tres* (Naples, 1533) and, even more famous, *De principiis rerum libri duo* (Venice, 1546). The latter was modeled on the *De rerum natura* of Lucretius, and was hailed by Pietro Bembo and Paolo Manutius as being superior to the model.

Capello (kä-pel′lō), **Bianca.** Mistress of Francesco de' Medici; b. 1548; d. at Poggio, 1587. Of a noble Venetian family, niece of Cardinal Grimani, accomplished and beautiful, she left her father's palazzo at the age of 15 to follow her Florentine lover, Pietro Buonaventuri. The affair was a matter of concern at the highest level of government; Venice tried to suppress news of the scandal and, equally uselessly, asked Florence to return the fugitive. She married Buonaventuri, and later became the mistress of Francesco de' Medici, heir to the duchy of Tuscany. When her husband was murdered, the lovers made no secret of their alliance, to the chagrin of Francesco's wife, Joanna of Austria. When Joanna died, Bianca officially replaced her (1579). Francesco had become grand duke of Tuscany following the death of his father (1574), and because of his position and Bianca's influence over him and her role in public life, the past seemed to have been forgotten. But there was great hostility, and at a great celebration at Poggio (1587) Francesco died very suddenly; it was said he had been poisoned. Bianca died a few hours later. Her story has provided material for many writers of romance and historical fiction.

Capgrave (kap′grāv), **John.** English historian; b. at Lynn, Norfolk, England, April 21, 1393; d. there, August 12, 1464. He wrote *Chronicle of England*, *Liber de Illustribus Henricis*, *A Guide to the Antiquities of Rome*, and is best known for *Nova Legenda Angliae*, the first English hagiology.

Capilupi (kä-pē-lö′pē), **Camillo.** Poet and man of letters; b. 1504; d. at Mantua, 1548. He was the brother of Lelio (1497–1563) and Ippolito Capilupi (1511–1579), and was in the service of the Gonzaga at Mantua from 1544 to 1548. His poems were printed with those of his brothers. Important documents and official correspondence written by him during his service to the Gonzaga are preserved in the archives at Mantua.

Capilupi, Ippolito. Poet, philologist, and grammarian; b. at Mantua, July 8, 1511; d. at Rome, 1579. His father Benedetto, who was secretary to Isabella d'Este, died while he was young, and he was educated by his brother Lelio (1497–1563) at Rome. An accomplished poet in Latin and the vernacular, he was also learned in the classics and translated from Latin and Greek. He served Ferrante Gonzaga at Rome, became bishop of Fano (1560), and was in the suite of Cardinal Ercole Gonzaga at some of the sessions of the Council of Trent. He gave up his bishopric to serve the king of Sweden at Rome and Naples. His translations and letters, in manuscript, are at Mantua. His poems were published, in several editions, with those of his brothers.

Capilupi, Lelio. Poet; b. 1497; d. 1563. He was the brother of Camillo (1504–1548) and Ippolito Capilupi (1511–1579), and like his brothers wrote poems in Latin and in the vernacular. His poems, some in the macaronic style, were published with those of his brothers.

Capistrano (kä-pēs-trä′nō), San **Giovanni da.** [**John of Capistrano.**] Theologian, preacher, and diplomat; b. at Capistrano in the Abruzzi, June 24, 1386; d. at Ilok, Yugoslavia, October 23, 1456. He was the son of a noble family that had come into Italy (1382) in the army of Louis I of Anjou. In 1401 he went to Perugia, where he studied civil and canon law and where he held official positions. He favored the people in their struggle against Braccio da Montone, lord of Perugia, and was imprisoned by Braccio after the battle of San Egidio. This experience changed his life, and although already married, in October, 1415, he entered the Friars Minor at Perugia. He studied theology and was ordained about three years later. As a public official he had treated the Fraticelli (a group that had broken away from the Franciscans and was considered heretical) with severity. He became a celebrated preacher, and preached against them. He was at Siena in 1423, worked with St. Bernardino of Siena in 1425, and successfully defended him before Pope Martin V when Bernardino was charged with heresy for his devotion to the Holy Name. The Observants, to which he belonged, were a group of Franciscans who wished to restore the simplicity and poverty of the rule of St. Francis. S. Giovanni Capistrano was among those who sought, vainly, to unite the groups of the order. (The Observants ultimately were recognized as a separate order.) He performed many missions for the pope, visited the Holy Land (1439), made reforms, preached and wrote, and traveled in France and Burgundy. In 1451 he was sent to Austria, at the request of Frederick III, to preach against the Hussites. His preaching aroused great enthusiasm. Pope Pius II, describing him in his *Commentaries*, says he was about 65 when he went, that he was "small of stature, thin, withered and worn, mere skin and bone, but always cheerful, powerful in intellect, unwearied in work, very learned and eloquent." He tells that the people "flocked down from the mountains as if St. Peter or St. Paul, or some other of the Apostles were passing by," and marvels that his audiences, of from twenty to thirty thousand people, listened to him with rapt attention although they didn't understand a word of his Latin sermons, and then listened to the interpretations. The sermons themselves lasted for two or three hours, and the interpretations an equal length of time. In Vienna, Pius wrote, he was "greeted as a messenger from heaven." He later went to Styria, Hungary, and Bohemia, and in 1454 he was sent to Hungary to preach and recruit for a crusade against the Turks. He led the crusading army to Belgrade, under siege by Mohammed II, in July, 1456. His own fervor and courage inspired the defenders of Belgrade to gain the victory of July 21, 1456. A few months later he died of plague at Ilok, on his way back from Belgrade. Among his writings is the *Speculum conscientiae*. Pope Pius II wrote of him that he led "on earth what may be called a heavenly life, spotless, blameless, and sinless." The process for his canonization was begun in the year of his death but was not completed until the time of Pope Alexander VIII, who canonized him on October 16, 1690.

Capitolo (kä-pē-tō′-lō). In Italian poetry, a verse form derived, either in imitation or in parody, from Dante's terza rima. Its name comes from the *capitoli* of Petrarch's *Trionfi*, in which works it was employed for the expression of didactic and moralistic poetry. Francesco Berni (1497/1498–1535) perfected the capitolo as the traditional verse form for satirical and burlesque poetry. As employed by Berni and his many followers, the capitolo might sing the praises of a trivial subject in an exaggerated and serious manner, and in elegantly polished language; subjects of the capitoli included an eel, a sausage, thistles, the urinal, peaches, the plague, and debt. The elegant and mocking seriousness with which the homeliest and most trivial subject was celebrated heightened for the authors and listeners (Berni wished his capitoli to be recited) the glee with which they were received. Other capitoli were satirical or sarcastic rhymed letters. Berni's on Pope Adrian VI finds every weak and ridiculous chink in that worthy man's character—that is, he was weak and ridiculous to the members of the society Berni frequented. Many of the capitoli were undisguisedly and enthusiastically filthy. It was practically a rule that the meaning and purpose or effect of the most ordinary topic be reversed by the exalted treatment rendered it by the poet.

Capivaccio (kä-pē-vät′chō), **Gerolamo.** Physician; b. at Padua at the beginning of the 16th century. He was professor of medicine at Padua from 1552, and went (1576) to Venice to study an outbreak of the plague. His medical works were published for the first time at Frankfurt (1603), then in several editions at Venice.

Caporali (kä-pō-rä′lē), **Bartolomeo.** Umbrian painter; b. at Perugia, c1420; d. after 1503. Called by some the greatest painter of Perugia before Pinturicchio and Perugino, he was early influenced by Benozzo Gozzoli, then by his fellow Umbrian Giovanni Boccati, Piero della Francesca, Bonfigli, and Fiorenzo di Lorenzo. Most of his works are in the National Gallery of Umbria at Perugia and in the neighborhood of that city. A *Madonna and Child with Angels* is in the Uffizi, and *Death of the Virgin* is in the Isabella Stewart Gardner Museum, Boston. Other paintings are at Naples, Padua, Udine, Berlin, Leningrad, London, and Zagreb. Caporali was also a miniaturist; examples of his illuminations are in the sacristy of S. Pietro at Perugia.

Caporali, Giovanni Battista. Perugian painter; b. c1476; d. c1560. He was the son and pupil of Bartolomeo Caporali (c1420–1503). He worked with Giannicola di Paolo at Perugia, and as a pupil and assistant of Pinturicchio painted part of the *Coronation of Mary, Apostles and Saints* in the Vatican, which is ascribed to Pinturicchio.

Cappello (käp-pel′lō), **Bernardo.** Poet; b. at Venice, 1498; d. at Rome, March 8, 1565. At Padua he became a friend and admirer of Pietro Bembo, and the collection of lyrics he left is conspicuously imitative of Bembo yet bears his own personal stamp. In 1540 he had been exiled to an island off the Dalmatian coast by the Council of Ten of Venice. He spent two years on the island, then fled to the States of the Church, became governor of Orvieto and of Tivoli, spent some time at the court at Urbino, and then (1565) returned to Rome, where he died.

Capponi (käp-pō′nē). Large and distinguished Florentine family, whose history is closely linked to that of Florence. The earliest documented member is Compagno di Uguccione, who was enrolled in the wool guild (1244) and fell in the battle of Montaperti (1260). From the beginning of a government by priorate (1282) the Capponi contributed fifty-seven priors and ten gonfalonieri to Florence. The first prior was Bonamico, son of Compagno di Uguccione. He was also the founder of the family's wealth. Bonamico's son Recco, prior many times and ambassador to Pope Boniface VIII, had five sons, each of whom became the founder of a flourishing branch of the family. The Capponi acquired wealth in the silk and wool trades, and kept and increased it in their family banking business. In 1299 their branch in Milan received the Iron Crown of Italy from Matteo Visconti, in pledge for a loan. Nearly a hundred years later (1391), when Florence was in a deadly struggle with Gian Galeazzo Visconti, the Capponi made a large, interest-free loan to Florence. A Capponi was papal treasurer in the Romagna at the end of the 15th century, and another, Neri di Gino (1452–1519), was Charles VIII's banker in Italy and was accused of betraying his country. The Capponi, of popular origin, took an active part in the political events of their day. Among the outstanding members of the family was Gino dei Neri di Recco (c1350–1421), a partisan of the Albizzi and sponsor of an expansionist policy for Florence. His son Neri di Gino (1388–1457), was a supporter of Niccolò da Uzzano, whose daughter married a Capponi (see below). Piero (1446–1496), Neri di Gino's grandson, forced Charles VIII, who had entered Florence as a conqueror (1494), to respect Florentine dignity (see below). Following the expulsion of the Medici (1494) and the establishment of the Soderini government (1502), the Capponi played an inconspicuous role in Florentine affairs, and were spared the reprisals that were meted out on the return of the Medici. Agostino di Bernardo, however, was an unyielding opponent of the Medici, took part in a conspiracy, was discovered, and was beheaded (1513). Another Medicean opponent was Niccolò di Piero (1437–1529). He was elected gonfaloniere in 1527, when the Medici were again expelled and a republic again established, but his conciliatory policy pleased no one. He was replaced by a more ardent republican, Francesco Carducci. Niccolò went to Charles V as ambassador in a fruitless effort to win the emperor's favor for the republic. He was on his way back to Florence when he became ill. He learned from Michelangelo of the preparations that were being made to defend Florence from the imperial troops, allied with Pope Clement VII to win back control of Florence for the Medici, and disapproved of them. Niccolò died, in the arms of the poet Lodovico Ariosto, at Castelnuovo di Garfagnana, a bandit-infested region of which Ariosto had been governor. In the siege of Florence (1530) by the imperial troops, some members of the family urged resistance, others advised capitulation to the overwhelming force brought against the city. When it was all over, and Florence fell again to the Medici, Capponi influence in the affairs of the city was slight.

Capponi, Gino. Florentine statesman; b. at Florence, 1350?; d. there, May 19, 1421. When the oligarchs were restored at Florence after the fall of the last democratic government (1382), Capponi, always a faithful supporter of the Albizzi party, held many public offices. He was instrumental in procuring a treaty with the Visconti by which Pisa was ceded to them, was an official in charge of the ruthless war that Florence waged against the Pisans, and an influence in securing moderate treatment of the city when it fell (1406); Pisa was spared a sack at that time. In 1409 he helped defend Arezzo against Ladislaus, king of Naples, and in 1411 he accompanied Pope John XXIII to Siena, when the latter was on his way to Rome. He also served on an embassy to Venice to make peace with the emperor Sigismund. In the last years of his life he wrote, in Italian, a chronicle of Florence that is especially valuable for its bitter account of the period of the Ciompi rebellion (1378), and a panegyric in praise of the conquest of Pisa by Florence in 1406, *Commentari dell' acquisto di Pisa.*

Capponi, Luigi. Sculptor; active at the end of the 15th century and the beginning of the 16th. A native of Milan, he worked mostly at Rome. Only two documented works of his are extant: the monument of Bishop Giovanni Brusati in the Church of S. Clemente at Rome (1484) and an altar, with a *Crucifixion* in half-relief, in the Church of the Consolation at Rome (1496). Other works in the churches of Rome seem readily attributable to him, including the monument to the Bonsi brothers in S. Gregorio al Celio and an altar frontal in the same church with legends of St. Gregory sculptured in low relief; the tomb of Luca Piccolomini (d. 1479), in the cloister of the convent of S. Agostino; and the tomb of Antonio and Piero Pollaiuolo in S. Pietro in Vincoli. Capponi, an artist in the Lombard style, may have been the first to include portrait busts of the deceased in circular niches in their funeral monuments.

Capponi, Neri di Gino. Florentine diplomat, soldier, and man of humanist letters; b. 1388; d. 1457. He was the son of the official and chronicler Gino Capponi (c1350–1421), of an ancient and eminent Florentine family. In politics he was a follower of the moderate Niccolò da Uzzano, and was one of those responsible for the recall from exile of Cosimo de' Medici (1434). As a diplomat he took part in the negotiations with the Visconti that finally led to a peace (1441). As a soldier he was credited with the victory over Piccinino at Anghiari (June 29, 1440). As a historian he worked on his father's notes and memoirs to produce his own commentaries on the affairs of Italy between 1419 and 1456, *Commentari delle cose seguite in Italia tra il 1419 e il 1456*, and wrote on the acquisition by Florence of the estates of the counts of Poppi, *La cacciata del conte di Poppi ed acquisto di quello stato per il popolo fiorentino.*

Capponi, Nicola. See **Montani, Cola de'.**

Capponi, Piero. Florentine statesman and soldier; b. 1446; d. September 25, 1496. For years he served Lorenzo de' Medici in diplomatic affairs, but after Lorenzo's death in 1492 he opposed the policies of Lorenzo's son Piero which led to French intervention in Italian affairs and, with Piero de' Medici's fall from power, became the head of the Florentine republic. Charles VIII of France rode into Florence in November, 1494, with his lance at rest, in sign that he had conquered the city. His secretary read his ultimatum to Piero Capponi. Piero snatched the document from his hands and tore it to shreds, vowing that Florence would never accept its humiliating terms. Charles threatened, "We shall sound our trumpets." "And we shall ring our bells," was Piero's defiant answer. Charles did not want to fight in the narrow streets of Florence. He agreed to ameliorate the harsh conditions of the peace. Two years later Capponi was mortally wounded in an attack on the castle of Soiana while leading the Florentine armed forces in a war with Pisa.

Capponi, Serafino. Theologian; b. at Porretta, 1536; d. at Bologna, January 2, 1616. He entered the Dominican order at Bologna (1552), and taught for the rest of his life. He was a learned commentator on St. Thomas Aquinas.

Capranica (kä-prä′nē-kä), **Domenico.** Cardinal, statesman, and humanist; b. at Capranica, May 31, 1400; d. at Rome, Aug. 14, 1458. At the age of 15 he began the study of civil and canon law at the University of Padua, where he was a pupil of Giuliano Cesarini and a fellow student of Nicholas of Cusa. He pursued his studies at the University of Bologna and became a doctor of law. Martin V, a connection of his, appointed him clerk of the Apostolic Chamber at an early age, and in 1423 named him a cardinal, but because of his youth the elevation was not published. He was papal legate to Perugia, 1430, and governed that unruly city successfully. While at Perugia his appointment to the Sacred College of Cardinals was published (November, 1430). However, since he was at Perugia he did not receive the red hat and ring. Martin died before he could present them. His successor, Eugenius IV, influenced by the Orsini, who were rivals of the Colonna family of Martin V, not only refused to acknowledge Capranica's earlier appointment as cardinal but deprived him of his benefices. His palace and valuable library, at Rome, were plundered. The Council of Basel was in session and Capranica resolved to go there and present his case. With him, he took Enea Silvio Piccolomini as his secretary. They had a perilous journey. Devious routes had to be chosen by sea because land routes were blocked. The ship was blown by a storm to the shores of Africa, blown back to Italy, and then the battered travelers crossed the Alps. At the Council he impressed all with his piety, his learning, his lack of bitterness, and his reverence for the pope. The Council named him a cardinal and bestowed on him the red hat. Subsequently he was reconciled with and acknowledged by Eugenius IV, and joined him at Florence (1434). From the time of the reconciliation he enjoyed the confidence of Eugenius, as he did of his successors Nicholas V and Calixtus III, although he courageously protested against the naming, by Eugenius, of the notorious Vitelleschi as a cardinal and Calixtus III's flagrant nepotism.

As a statesman of the Church he had negotiated a settlement with the rebelling Bolognese, governed Perugia, taken part in arranging the convention of union between the Greek and Latin churches, negotiated with the Milanese and with Alfonso of Naples. He was the friend of humanists and churchmen, had collected a valuable library of more than 2,000 volumes, and founded Capranica College in Rome, the first of the ecclesiastical colleges there. He was noted for his asceticism, his love of justice, and his great learning. Statesmen trusted and admired him. On the death of Nicholas V, many expected him to become pope, but the conclave was so evenly divided a compromise candidate was chosen in Calixtus III. When Calixtus died, three years later, Capranica seemed the certain choice, but he himself died just before the conclave opened and was deeply mourned. Francesco Sforza's ambassador in Rome, writing an hour after Capranica's death, told how the cardinal had taken his hand and expressed his grief that he must leave without having been able to show his appreciation for the friendship of Sforza and his ambassador. The moved ambassador was unable to speak. "Thus, my illustrious lord, passed from this life the wisest, most perfect, learned, and saintliest prince and prelate of the Church in our day. . . . One whose life was an exaltation of the Holy See, a pillar of peace of Italy and a mirror of religion and every sanctity, just when we were all confidently expecting to honor him as pope."

Caracciolo (kä-rät′chō-lō). One of the oldest, perhaps the oldest, of the noble families of Naples, whose history dates from the 8th or 9th century. Of the numerous branches of the family that of the Caracciolo of Avellino was one of the most important, and beginning with Domizio, at the end of the 15th century, members of that branch became the possessors of numerous titles and lordships in southern Italy. The family was noted for its loyalty to the rulers of Naples and to the Church. Notable members included Sergianni, or Giovanni (d. 1431; see below); Giovanni (b. 1487; see below), who served Florence as a general in 1529 and later served Francis I and Henry II of France; and Galeazzo (1517–1586). Of the Caracciolo cardinals, Marino (d. 1538) represented Pope Leo X at Augsburg (1518) and at Worms (1521) and opposed Pope Clement VII by favoring a Spanish policy as against the pope's vacillating French policy.

Caracciolo, Giovanni. Prince of Melfi, duke of Ascoli, marquess of Atella, and count of Forenza; b. 1487; d. at Susa, August 7, 1550. Besieged at Melfi by the French (1528), Caracciolo, who was a supporter of the empire, was wounded and taken prisoner, with his wife and children. The captain of the imperial army refused to pay his ransom, and thereafter Caracciolo went over to the French, for whom he fought in Italy and occupied Bari, Molfetta, and Barletta. After the fall of the republic of Florence, which he had served in 1529, he went to France, and served that nation until his death.

Caracciolo, Giovanni. [Known as **Sergianni.**] Grand seneschal of Naples; d. August 19, 1431. He served Ladislaus, king of Naples, and then, as the ablest of her favorites, won complete domination over Queen Joanna II, who succeeded her brother Ladislaus in 1414. Besotted with his handsome face and ingratiating manner, she practically turned over the rule of the kingdom to him, and made him grand seneschal of Naples. His influence over the queen was the scandal of the day. It caused strife with her captain, Muzio Attendolo Sforza, who was grand constable of Naples. Joanna was compelled, by her outraged subjects, to send Sergianni into exile (1418). He went to Florence, beguiled Pope Martin V with large promises, and won the pope's agreement to the coronation of Joanna. From Florence he went to Gaeta, and was able to persuade Joanna to send Sforza away. Once his hated rival was removed, he returned to Naples and was joyously welcomed by the queen. When she had been crowned his power over her was greater than ever. He suggested that she adopt Alfonso of Aragon as her heir, in the belief that he could dominate Alfonso. Alfonso soon disabused him of this notion; war broke out, Sergianni was captured (1423), and Naples was sacked and put to the torch by Alfonso's Catalan supporters. Joanna ransomed her lover, and Louis of Anjou was substituted for Alfonso as her adopted son. Sergianni now kept the queen a virtual prisoner in the castle at Aversa and assumed the reins of government. His rule was harsh, his greed was great, and his position was constantly threatened. On suspicion that Martin V planned to depose Joanna and give her kingdom to his kinsman Antonio Colonna, he hurriedly assured the pope of his loyalty (1427). The blandishments with which he had won the queen's love were now replaced by threats and even violence. For his harshness as a ruler, and for his crimes, his enemies multiplied, and he was finally stabbed by conspirators, possibly with the queen's knowledge.

Caracciolo, Fra **Roberto.** [Called Fra **Roberto da Lecce.**] Franciscan preacher; b. at Lecce, 1425; d. there, May 6, 1495. Member of a noble family, he entered the Franciscan order at an early age, and became, for nearly fifty years, one of the most celebrated preachers of Italy. He was frequently sent by his superiors to preach a series of sermons in cities that were torn by factional strife, and was sometimes accused of interfering in political matters. Presenting his message of penitence and reconciliation with God and man in the manner of S. Bernardino of Siena, he had a profound effect on his large congregations, who listened to him as to an apostle and acclaimed him as a second St. Paul. His sermons were printed in a number of editions. He was made bishop of Aquila (1475), was transferred to the see of Aquino (1477), and after 1485 acted as bishop of Lecce.

Caracciolo, Tristano. Neapolitan man of letters; b. 1437; d. 1528. He was intimately connected with the intellectual and humanistic developments of his day in Naples. In the course of his long life he saw Naples won by Alfonso of Aragon (1442) and its ultimate fall under Spanish dominion (1504). He was a friend and intimate of Pontano, and was in contact with the men of his day who played leading roles in the history and intellectual life of Naples. A youth when Alfonso won Naples, he grew up in the expansive, cultivated atmosphere of that monarch's court, and deplored the moral tone he observed there. He was a moralist, and his own writing often had a didactic purpose. He wrote lives of Sergianni Caracciolo, Pontano, Joanna I, and Ferrante, from a moralistic rather than a strictly biographical point of view. In his lives, however, he gives vivid pictures of the individuals, their temperaments and their characters, presenting figures in which "guilt and destiny are wondrously mingled" (Burckhardt). He also wrote treatises or dialogues, as *De concordia et de ineundo coniugio*, on marriage, and *De varietate fortunae*. His autobiography, *Vitae auctoris actae notitia* (1518), is more an examination of his soul than a recital of events, and reveals the development of an intellectual and moral individual. All his works, in Latin, circulated in manuscript during his lifetime, and were greatly praised by his contemporaries and friends, who had some of them printed after his death.

Caradosso (kä-rä-dôs′sō). [Original name thought to have been **Cristoforo** or **Lorenzo Foppa.**] Goldsmith, jeweler, and medalist; b. at Mondonico (near Como), c1452; d. 1527. Nothing certain is known of him before

1480, but it is thought that he was in Rome in 1477 and that he then completed for Sixtus IV and Giuliano della Rovere (later Julius II) the bronze doors for the reliquary of the chains of St. Peter, in S. Pietro in Vincoli, and bronze doors in St. John Lateran. At Rome, he was inspired by the works that survived there from imperial times, such as the Triumphal Arch of Marcus Aurelius with its elaborate reliefs. Other bronzes in the museums of Rome are attributed to him. In the service of the duke of Milan (from 1480) his duty was to acquire antique works and carved gems. In 1490 he called Francesco di Giorgio Martini of Siena to Milan, perhaps for consultation on the work of the cathedral, and in the same year he and others conveyed a *Bacchus* and other gifts to Matthias Corvinus of Hungary at the request of Ludovico il Moro. He visited Ferrara (1493), Florence, Parma, Viterbo, and Rome (1495), Piacenza (1496), and Venice (1497). One of the leading practitioners of his art, in 1503 he was at Milan again, and giving his often-sought advice on a variety of artistic matters. In 1504 and 1505 he was in contact with Isabella d'Este on the matter of selling her a vase made of forty-nine pieces of crystal bound together with silver gilt, enameled, and carved with scenes from mythology (some copies of the reliefs remain), and a silver inkstand that was considered a gem of his art. As a medalist he was greatly admired for his sense of composition and for the energy and modeling of his forms. In 1505 he was at Rome, making dies for coins and medals, as the commemorative medal of Pope Julius II with a relief of the new St. Peter's designed by Bramante on the reverse, and other medals for subsequent popes. Among his many friends were Gian Cristoforo Romano and Sabbà da Castiglione. The latter wrote that he was without a peer in his art. Baldassare Castiglione, a man of excellent taste, and Benvenuto Cellini, who bowed to no one in matters of his craft, accorded him great praise. His mark, registered with the goldsmiths' guild at Milan, was a gypsy with a dancing boy in front.

Carafa (kä-rä′fä), **Diomede.** Neapolitan statesman; b. at Naples, c1406; d. there, March 17, 1487. He was devoted to the interests of Alfonso of Aragon, and was with him at the siege by which Alfonso won the kingdom of Naples from the Angevins. Possessing great influence under Alfonso, he became even more powerful under his son Ferrante, held many positions of importance and power, was given vast estates and fiefs (as the countship of Maddaloni), and was entrusted with the education of Ferrante's son Alfonso, the duke of Calabria, and of the royal princesses. He built (1466) a magnificent and sumptuous palace at Naples, one of the finest Renaissance buildings in the city, and filled it with works of art. Many of the latter are now in the National Museum at Naples, including a huge bronze horse's head of the Roman era, gift to Carafa from Lorenzo de' Medici. He was buried in a magnificent mausoleum that he had caused to be constructed (1470) in the Church of S. Domenico Maggiore. He left some tracts on political and moral topics.

Cardano (kär-dä′nō), **Girolamo** or **Geronimo.** [Known in English as **Jerome Cardan.**] Physician, mathematician, and philosopher; b. at Pavia, September 24, 1501; d. at Rome, September 20, 1576. He was the illegitimate son of a learned lawyer. In his childhood he was battered by bouts of illness and the stigma of illegitimacy. He studied at Pavia, Milan, and Padua, and earned his medical degree in 1526, but was denied admission to the Milan College of Physicians because of his illegitimacy. He passed six years (1526–1532) at the village of Sacco, near Padua. In later life he looked back on these years, during which he married, as the happiest of his life. In that time he was not poor, he said, because he had absolutely nothing, but he gambled and practiced as a country doctor, and enjoyed life. In 1532 he returned to Milan and lived in great poverty until he began to lecture in mathematics. An attack (1536) on the evil practices of the doctors of his time, *De malo recentiorum medicorum medendi usu libellus,* did not help him in his attempt to gain admission to the College of Physicians. But through the influence of a powerful patron he was at last (1539) admitted, and almost immediately gained fame as a doctor. He became the most sought after physician in his region, and felt free to decline the patronage of Pope Paul III, as well as the post of physician to the court of Denmark (one of the reasons he gave for declining the latter post was the fear that he might have to change his religion). In 1552 he answered a call to Scotland to attend an official of high rank there. He stayed some time and left his patient improved. His return journey through Europe was a triumphal march. In the meantime, he had pursued his mathematical studies and had published (1545) his *Ars magna*, a treatise on algebra that was a milestone in the history of mathematics. In this work he published the solution of cubic equations that had been worked out by Niccolò Tartaglia. The latter had confided his solution to Cardano under a pledge of secrecy. Although Cardano gave credit to Tartaglia, and presented solutions to additional forms of the cubic equation, Tartaglia felt he had been betrayed, and a long and bitter controversy ensued. Cardano was defended by his collaborator, pupil, and former servant, Lodovico Ferrari. Ferrari had developed a solution for biquadratic equations, which Cardano also included in his *Ars magna*. His interest in science and the observation and unlocking of the secrets of nature led him to perform experiments in physics. Among other things, he demonstrated the impossibility of perpetual motion. By 1560 he was noted throughout Europe as a physician, mathematician, and physicist. He was also known as an astrologer and magician. The last years of his life were saddened by the execution of his adored son Giambattista (also a doctor), for poisoning his wife (1560), and by the roguery of his second son. The scandal caused him to leave Milan. He went to Bologna as professor of medicine, and remained there eight years. In 1570 he was accused of heresy and imprisoned for a short time. After his release he went to Rome where, despite the earlier charge of heresy, Pope Gregory XIII became his patron and gave him a pension. He was admitted to the College of Physicians at Rome.

At the age of 74 Cardano began to write his autobiography, *De vita propria liber*. In this work he produced one of the earliest psychological self-studies of a man—himself. He states at once that his autobiography is "without artifice . . . being merely a story, [it] recounts my life, not tumultuous events." He examines himself minutely, describes his physical appearance (even to counting his fifteen teeth, one of which is wobbly), states and examines his feelings, presents his habits of diet and sleep and any physical imperfections. He cast his own horoscope and discovered that he missed being a monster by a hair. He thought he was gifted with second sight and tells of many instances when, for no reason, he changed his path as he walked in the streets or alleys and in so doing escaped destruction from falling masonry, overturning drays, wild dogs, and similar accidents. A chapter is devoted to some marvelous cures he made; another to his writings. According to his own account, he left 138 books (mostly in Latin) and 111 more in manuscript. These were what he had left after burning all those of his writings that displeased him. He wrote on mathematics, astronomy, physics, medicine, and music; on methods of divination and dreams; short works on marvelous cures, gems and colors, medicinal potions, the art of healing, games of chance; he wrote theological works. He lists all the books of others in which his name is favorably mentioned. He states that early in life he resolved to make a name for himself, and also that from an early age he had conceived it to be his duty "to care for human life." He further states, "I know that the souls of men are immortal; the manner I know not." He was the first to give a clinical description of typhus, and prescribed a treatment for syphilis. "Prone to every vice except ambition," he says, "wrath is a great evil, but it passes; the misfortunes of high rank are never ending."

In addition to his great *Ars magna* (Nuremberg, 1545), his other works include a book on arithmetic, *Practica arithmetica* . . . (Milan, 1539); the treatises *De subtilitate rerum* (Nuremberg, 1550) on scientific questions, experiments, inventions—an encyclopedic review of science—with hints of magic and the first suggestions on means of instructing deaf mutes and the blind; and *De rerum varietate* (Basel, 1557), along similar lines. He was an inveterate and professional gambler. His work *Liber de ludo aleae* is a guide for gamblers, and includes computations of probabilities. He also wrote philosophical treatises on the uses of adversity and on consolation. By the variety of his interests and achievements he was admired in all quarters. He was also the target of many enemies, for his successes as well as for his dabbling in magic. His legacy to future ages is in his mathematical works. His philosophy of medicine is perhaps best expressed in his own conclusion that "a man is nothing but his mind." If anything is wrong with that, everything is wrong. If that is healthy, all the rest will be. He wrote a commentary on Ptolemy, and in philosophy falls between Bernardino Telesio, who constantly exhorted to observation and experiment, and Giordano Bruno, who soared to an infinite universe.

Cárdenas (kär′ᴛʜā-näs), **García López de.** Spanish nobleman. fl. 1540. One of Coronado's captains on the expedition of 1540 to New Mexico and beyond. With his party he was the first to see and describe the Grand Canyon of the Colorado, which he beheld about September, 1540.

Cariani (kä-ryä′nē), **Giovanni.** [Original name, **Giovanni Busi.**] Venetian painter of a Bergamasque family; b. at Fuipiano del Brembo, c1480; d. at Bergamo, after 1547. Lombard in his presentation of some elements of landscape and in his somewhat metallic color, he was later influenced by Giorgione, Lotto, and Palma Vecchio. The first work known is his *Christ with the Cross,* Carrara Academy, Bergamo, and shows the influence of the Venetians. The greatest single collection of his portraits and paintings on religious subjects, including *Madonna and Child with a Donor,* is in the Carrara Academy. Other portraits and paintings are at Brescia, Milan (Ambrosiana, Brera, Castello Sforzesco, Poldi Pezzoli Museum), Rome (Borghese and National galleries, and Palazzo Venezia), Turin (Sabauda Gallery), Venice, Vicenza, Basel, Hampton Court, Leningrad, London, Munich, Oslo, Ottawa, Paris, Strasbourg, Vienna; and there are portraits at Boston, New York, Philadelphia (Johnson Collection), San Diego, Santa Monica, California; Tucson, Arizona; Tulsa, Oklahoma; and Washington. Typical of his paintings are the brilliant, iridescent, but rather empty *Holy Conversation,* at Venice, and another at Bergamo; *Madonna and Child with Saints,* Brera; and such secular paintings as his *Lady in a Landscape,* Berlin.

Cariteo (kä-rē-tā′ō), **Il.** Name by which the poet Benedicto Gareth is known in Italian literature.

Carli (kär′lē), **Raffaellino de'.** See **Raffaellino del Garbo.**

Carlos (kär′lo̧s, -lōs), Don. Spanish prince; b. at Valladolid, Spain, July 8, 1545; d. at Madrid, July 24, 1568. He was the eldest son of Philip II of Spain and Maria of Portugal.

Carmagnola (kär-mä-nyō′lä), **Francesco Bussone da.** [Original name, **Francesco Bussone;** Count of Carmagnola.] Condottiere; b. at Carmagnola, 1380; d. at Venice, May 5, 1432. Filippo Maria Visconti noticed the courage of Carmagnola at the battle of Monza (1412) and gave him a command in his employ. Between 1412 and 1422 Carmagnola defeated the forces of Genoa, Parma, Piacenza, and other cities, and won back for Filippo Maria the territories that had broken away from the duchy of Milan on the death of Gian Galeazzo, Filippo Maria's father. In the course of his many victories for the Visconti, Carmagnola had acquired great glory and wide influence over the soldiers. Filippo Maria, ever suspicious, and especially of his most successful generals, instead of rewarding him disgraced him and deprived him of his command. Carmagnola went over to the service of the Venetians, who declared war on Milan in 1426. He was as successful against Milan as he had been against its enemies. The Venetians, however, never trusted the captains in their pay. When (1431) Carmagnola was surprised by Francesco Sforza and lost a number of his cavalry, and remained inactive thereafter for various reasons, the Venetians suspected him of having come to some sort of agreement with his former master. They summoned him to Venice and welcomed him with every mark of confidence. He was taken to the palace of the doge, delivered a speech to the Senate that was highly applauded, then, as the day drew to a close, he was surrounded, loaded down with chains, and carried off to the dungeons of the palace. He was put to the torture, and some days later, gagged so that he could not protest his innocence, was beheaded in St. Mark's Square.

Carmeliano (kär-me-lyä′nō), **Pietro.** [Also, **Peter Carmelianus.**] Humanist; b. at Brescia; d. 1527. He went to England sometime after 1470 and before 1480 and was Latin secretary and chaplain to Henry VII, and lute player to Henry VIII, who gave him forty pounds a year. He was prebendary of Saint Paul's (1517–1526), of Saint Stephen's (1524), and of York from 1498 until his death. He wrote poems on the life of Saint Mary of Egypt, on the death of the king of Scots (James IV) at the battle of Flodden, on the engagement of Prince Charles of Castile to Mary, daughter of Henry VII, and on Richard III, praising him while he lived as a perfect king, and attacking him after his death as a tyrant and a murderer. Some of his poetry was translated into English by Alexander Barclay, under the title *The Mirrour of Good Maners*, and included (1570) in Barclay's *The Ship of Fools*.

Carmina Burana (kär′mi-nạ bū-ran′ạ). Manuscript of some 300 medieval songs from the 12th and 13th centuries, composed by goliards, i.e., wandering students. Most of the songs are in Latin, some in German, and some in a mixture of the two. They are satirical, roisterous, amorous, seldom serious. The name *Burana* derives from the Abbey of Benediktbeuren where the manuscript was found.

Carnesecchi (kär-nā-sek′kē), **Pietro.** Reformer; b. 1508; beheaded, October 1, 1567. His father, a wealthy Florentine merchant, directed his son toward a career in the Church, in order to take advantage of his close friendship with the Medici. Pietro went to Rome and made rapid progress at the papal court. He became acquainted with the reforming ideas of Juan de Valdés, ideas that were quite freely discussed for a time. He at length came to subscribe to the Lutheran doctrine of justification by faith and fled (1552) to Venice. He was summoned before the Inquisition, recanted, and for a time was left in peace, but under Pope Pius V the charges against him were revived (1565). He was in Venice at the time and perhaps would have survived if he had remained in that republic of refuge, but he went to Florence to seek the aid of the Medici, on whose friendship he counted. However, Cosimo I wanted the pope's support for his own affairs. He had Carnesecchi arrested. After a year in prison he was tried, convicted, and beheaded as a heretic.

Caro (kä′rō), **Annibale.** Renaissance writer; b. at Civitanuova, Ancona, June 19, 1507; d. at Rome, November 21, 1566. He studied at Florence, where he became a friend of Benedetto Varchi, and then went to Rome as secretary to Monsignor Giovanni Gaddi. The latter gave him lucrative employment at Rome. In that city Caro became acquainted with the leading poets and writers of the city, and became part of the gay band that met in the quarter of the Bianchi, as well as a member of a more serious group dedicated to literature. His joyous spirit was freely expressed in his two chatty works, *Santa Nafissa* and *Nasea*, the latter being a discourse on noses. In 1538 he went to Naples with his patron and met other literary lights—Tansillo, Rota, Bernardo Tasso, Telesio, and Costanzo. He later served Pier Luigi Farnese, son of Pope Paul III, and went on many missions with or for him. When Pier Luigi was murdered, Caro divided his allegiance between Pier's quarreling brothers. He engaged in a famous quarrel himself, with Lodovico Castelvetro, over a canzone he had written, at the request of Cardinal Alessandro Farnese, his patron, in praise of France. Castelvetro criticized the poem as lifeless, plebeian, and ill-formed, and the battle was on. The war of polemic was waged with fury—each accused the other of attempted assassination, among other things, and it is said that Caro denounced Castelvetro to the Inquisition. Caro is best known as a letter writer and for his translation in Italian blank verse of Vergil's *Aeneid*. He began the latter at Frascati, whither he had withdrawn in weariness in February, 1563, and transformed the Latin epic into an Italian one of exquisite language, that yet preserved Vergil's spirit. His familiar letters, to the number of about a thousand, are among the best of the 16th century. They treat a wide variety of topics with ease and grace—are now brief notes, now rounded discourses, are witty and light or serious, are never dull or pedantic and always graceful, elegant, and imaginative. His prose comedy, *Gli straccioni* (*The Ragged Ones*) is about two actual and inseparable Roman brothers who dressed in rags and spent most of their lives in litigation. In the end they win their case.

Caroto (kä-rō′tō), **Gian** (or **Giovanni**) **Francesco.** Veronese painter; b. at Verona, c1480; d. there, c1555. He was Liberale da Verona's best pupil, and was distinguished among his contemporaries for his fluid line, soft color, luminous sweetness, and his landscape. A later influence on him was Andrea Mantegna, whom, in his youth, he often imitated, according to Vasari. His later work also showed his acquaintance with the work of Leonardo and Raphael. His adoption of some of their ideas was saved from mere imitation by his own sound color sense and technique. After having painted at Mantua for Isabella d'Este in 1514 and at Milan, he became court painter to the marquess of Monferrato. The masterpiece of his youth is a series of frescoes on the legend of St. Raphael in S. Eufemia, Verona. After his return to Verona from Monferrato he painted (1528) the magnificent altarpiece in S. Fermo, Verona. A number of his paintings and frescoes survive in the churches of Verona. His *The Archangels and Little Tobias* is in the museum there; other works are at Trent, in the Uffizi, the Carrara Academy (Bergamo), the Accademia (Venice), at Mantua, Modena, Turin, Volargne (frescoes, Villa del Bene), Dresden, Augusta (Georgia), Baltimore (Walters Art Gallery), Portland (Oregon), Princeton, Philadelphia (Johnson Collection), and elsewhere.

Caroto, Giovanni. Veronese painter; b. at Verona, 1488; d. 1566. He was the brother of Gian Francesco Caroto (c1480–c1555). He was more influenced by Francesco Morone than by his brother, and became known as a portrait painter. Vasari, who knew him personally, owned one of his portraits. Most of his surviving paintings are to be found in the museum and churches of Verona; others are at Pavia, Budapest, and Princeton. He had a great interest in archaeology, and ultimately devoted himself to studying it. He made drawings of all the antiquities of Verona for a book written by Torello Saraina and printed in 1540. He is also known for having been one of the first teachers of Paolo Veronese.

Carpaccio (kär-pät′chō), **Vittore.** Venetian painter; b. at Venice, probably between 1460 and 1465; d. there, before June 26, 1526. He was a descendant of an old family of sailors and fishermen who lived on the small island of Mazzorbo near Venice from the 13th century, but his immediate ancestors had moved to Venice in the 14th century. There his father, Piero, who was a furrier, had his shop. Little is known of Carpaccio's life. He had two painter sons, Pietro and Benedetto. No paintings can be certainly attributed to Pietro. Benedetto is thought to have assisted his father and to have used his drawings and designs as models for altarpieces he executed in provincial churches. In view of the number of paintings he left, Carpaccio must have had a flourishing workshop; many of his paintings show the hand of assistants. His earliest signed and dated work is one of the series of paintings he executed on the life of St. Ursula for the Scuola di Sant' Orsola at Venice. It is *The Arrival of St. Ursula at Cologne During the Siege by the Huns* (1490), and probably the first of the great pageant paintings he painted for various organizations at Venice. To have received the commission he must have been already an acknowledged and respected painter. Among the works that may have gained him such a reputation by 1490 is his *Salvator Mundi*, Conte Contini-Bonacossi Collection, Florence. Another work of his early maturity, one that shows strong Bellini influence in the modeling, the treatment of the landscape, and the presence of symbolic plants and animals, is the intensely religious *Meditation on the Passion*, the Metropolitan Museum, New York. (The later, c1505, *Burial of Christ*, Berlin, of broader modeling and more luminous color, has the same deeply religious feeling. The religious paintings of his last years are less intense.) Throughout his painting life Carpaccio's style evolved but little; it followed a continuous development that was not broken by changes of direction or technique. Bellini continued to be the chief influence, and as Bellini's forms became softer and more broadly modeled, Carpaccio's did also. The earliest documentation of his work concerned payments made (1501, 1502) for a painting that was intended for the Doge's Palace; it was destroyed by fire in 1577. He is also recorded (1507) as an assistant of Giovanni Bellini in painting the historical scenes in the Hall of the Great Council in the Doge's Palace, a work also destroyed in 1577.

Carpaccio is perhaps best known for the great cycles he painted for various schools at Venice. (The schools, as they were called, were organizations formed by various communities or groups for charitable or devotional purposes; each had its own building for meetings and worship and its own patron saint, or saints, for which the school was named, as the Scuola di Sant' Orsola, Scuola di San Marco, Scuola di San Giovanni Evangelista, etc.) The first cycle of such paintings, executed between 1490 and perhaps 1498, was for the Scuola di Sant' Orsola. The cycle included eight separate paintings depicting nine scenes from the legend of the saint. Among them is the *Dream of St. Ursula*, celebrated for the early morning light that suffuses the saint's bedroom as well as for the affectionate realism of the interior. It is a lovely example of Carpaccio's use of light, his realism in the treatment of detail, and the quality of stillness and calm that

VITTORE CARPACCIO
Adoration of the Magi
Uffizi, Florence   Alinari-Art Reference Bureau

pervades much of his painting. Other paintings in the cycle portray what might be called crowd scenes with beautiful Venetian backgrounds. In these, too, quietness is a characteristic—drama and movement are crystallized in silence. The school was suppressed by Napoleon in 1810, and the paintings are now in the Accademia, Venice. The painting *St. Ursula Taking Leave of Her Father* (National Gallery, London) is not considered to be one of the original cycle, and perhaps has nothing to do with St. Ursula at all. The second cycle is that for the Scuola di San Giorgio degli Schiavoni, an organization formed by Dalmatians living at Venice, hence its name (St. George of the Slavs). Carpaccio began work there in 1502, and painted scenes from the legends of St. Jerome, St. George (including *St. George and the Dragon*, in which an expressionless St. George on horseback charges the dragon across a field littered with gruesomely mutilated bodies and limbs), and St. Tryphon, in addition to an *Agony in the Garden* and the *Calling of Matthew*. Napoleon's decree ordering the suppression of the school (1806) was revoked, and Carpaccio's paintings can still be seen in the surroundings for which they were originally painted, in the little building that still exists much as it did when he worked there. In 1504 he began six scenes from the life of the Virgin for the Scuola degli Albanesi. These were scattered after the suppression of the community and are now in the Brera (Milan), the Carrara Academy (Bergamo), the Correr Museum and the Ca' d'Oro (Venice). His last great cycle, painted between 1511 and 1520, consisted of five scenes on the life of St. Stephen, painted for the Scuola di Santo Stefano. One of them, *The Trial of the Saint*, has been lost. The others, after the suppression (1806) of the school, were scattered

VITTORE CARPACCIO
Studies of Oriental warriors
Louvre, Paris   Alinari-Art Reference Bureau

and are now at Berlin, Paris, Milan, and Stuttgart.

The paintings of the St. Ursula cycle reveal Carpaccio at his lyrical best. His great narrative gift, richness of invention, and lovingly realistic portrayal of costume and the Venetian scene are exercised to the full. Painted over a period of years they are a record of his growing command of space, color masses, and light. In all the cycles he paid particular attention to architectural details, included many Oriental motifs (some think this is proof that he accompanied Gentile Bellini, possibly his early teacher, to Constantinople, but there is no evidence that he did so; Venice was a highly cosmopolitan city in which the presence of men in Oriental costume was a commonplace), and made of the scenes a documentary of Venice and Venetian life. They are moments exquisitely suspended in light, stillness, and glowing color. In the later cycles he increasingly repeated groupings, figures, and motifs. He left many drawings of studies and designs and some of them were used over and over again. The figure of *The Virgin Reading* (National Gallery, Washington), for example, appears without change in *The Birth of the Virgin*, now in the Carrara Academy, Bergamo. (Other paintings at Washington are *Flight into Egypt* and *Virgin and Child*.) There is also evidence of greater participation by his pupils and members of his workshop. Besides the cycles, Carpaccio left a number of single paintings in addition to those already mentioned above. *The Healing of the Obsessed* (Accademia, Venice) is one of four historical paintings on *The Miracles of the True Cross;* Gentile Bellini, by whose manner of painting historical scenes Carpaccio was influenced, painted the other three, including his *Procession in the Piazza S. Marco* (1496). In general, his subjects were on religious or historico-religious themes, or portraits. Among the exceptions is the *Story of Alcyone* (Johnson Collection, Philadelphia). In the last years of his life, Venetian painting took a new direction under the impetus of Titian, a development in which Carpaccio did not participate. He can best be studied and admired at Venice (S. Giorgio Maggiore, S. Giorgio degli Schiavoni, S. Vitale, Doge's Palace, Accademia, Ca' d'Oro, Correr Museum). Other works are at Ferrara, Florence, Rome, Paris, Lisbon, Karlsruhe, Zagreb, Zara, Atlanta (Georgia), Kansas City (Missouri), New Orleans, Tucson (Arizona), Tulsa (Oklahoma), and elsewhere. Many museums have collections or examples of the drawings he made as studies and designs for paintings, drawings that in their freedom of line, draftsmanship, delicate shading for form and volume, and degree of finish are works of art in themselves.

Carranza de Miranda (kär-rän′thä dā mē-rän′dä), **Bartolomé de.** [Original name, **Bartolomé de Carranza;** surnamed **de Miranda** from his birthplace.] Spanish churchman; b. at Miranda de Arga, in Navarre, 1503; d. at Rome, May 2, 1576. At one time a censor of the Inquisition he was imprisoned by the Inquisition on charges of heresy after the publication of his *Commentario sobre el catequismo cristiano*. He was acquitted.

Carrara (kär-rä′rä), **da.** Ancient noble and ruling family of Padua, whose name comes from the castle they possessed outside the city. From the 11th century they exercised dominion over their lands outside Padua. As the city grew, its demands conflicted with those in the country around it. Sharp struggles took place between the city and the country, between the commune and the empire; the castle of the Carrara fell to the city, and with it many of their long-held rights. The family moved into the city and took advantage of the internal struggles that were constant in Italian communes of the period. Giacomo Carrara became captain of the people (1318), and then imperial vicar. The ambitions of the powerful Scaliger family of Verona curbed the growing power of the Carrarese for a time, but they resumed their control in 1339. After a brief period of consolidation, the Carrarese adopted the policy of expansion that was common to so many of the communes of the time, and that led to the endless wars that rocked Italy. Under Francesco the Elder (ruled 1355–1388) and his heir Francesco the Younger (1391–1404), Padua had a brilliant court, where artists and men of letters were welcomed. The court was also the center for intrigue, as the Carrarese dreamed of making Padua a great territorial state. Padua's neighbors awakened the Carrarese from this dream with a shock. Carrarese ambitions came into collision with those of Venice. The Venetians took Francesco the Younger prisoner in a war and strangled him in prison (1406). The Carrarese dynasty in Padua ended with his death.

Carretto (kär-rāt′tō), **Galeotto del.** Courtier and poet; b. 1455; d. 1530. He lived at the courts of Monferrato, Milan, and Mantua, and at the last-named was on cordial terms with Isabella d'Este. He wrote sonnets, *capitoli*, and other verse for Isabella, sent her his rendering, in octaves, of Lucian's dialogue on *Timon of Athens*, which he called *Comedia de Timon greco* (1497), and dedicated his verse tragedy, *Sophonisba* (1502), to her. His other works include *Nozze di Psiche e Cupidine*, a mediocre rendering of the story by Apuleius; *Tempio d'Amore*, an allegorical drama; a rhymed chronicle of Monferrato to 1493, and a prose chronicle to 1530. In his verse, Carretto catered to the taste of the court, composing his sonnets and eclogues with facile grace.

Cartier (kȧr-tyer), **Jacques.** French navigator; b. at St.-Malo, France, 1491; d. there, September 1, 1557. He made three voyages to Canada. In the first (1534) he explored the Gulf of St. Lawrence; in the second (1535) he sailed up the St. Lawrence to Montreal; and in the third (1541–1542) he made an unsuccessful attempt at colonization in Canada.

Cartoon. In art, a design of the same size as an intended decoration or pattern to be executed in fresco, mosaic, or tapestry, and transferred from the paper on which it is drawn either by cutting out the figure and outlining it on the surface to be decorated with a sharp point or, in the case of a composition, by pricking holes in the paper and pouncing with a bag of muslin filled with charcoal dust. Cartoons were often so carefully finished that they are in themselves works of art, as are those of Leonardo da Vinci and Raphael.

Cartouche (kär-tösh′). In architecture, an irregularly shaped ornament on which may be inscribed coats-of-arms, emblems, or inscriptions. They may be decorated with garlands, flowers or foliage, and are oval, rectangular, or in the form of ribbons with the ends rolled up. The Renaissance produced many finely designed and beautiful cartouches. The cartouche may also be used to decorate the title page of a book.

Carucci (kä-röt′chē), **Jacopo.** See **Pontormo, Jacopo.**

Carvajal (kär-bä-häl′), **Juan.** Spanish cardinal and diplomat; b. at Trujillo, Estremadura, Spain, c1400; d. at Rome, December 6, 1469. Called by Pius II "a man of principle who neither sought favors nor shrank from difficult assignments," he served twenty times as papal envoy to various places in Italy and Europe. He was a steadfast supporter of the pope in his struggle with the Council of Basel and went on a mission to the Germans (1440) in an effort to keep them neutral in the struggle. Eugenius made him a cardinal in 1446. He helped negotiate the Concordat of Vienna (1448) with Frederick III, which resulted in the dissolution of the Council. Later (1455) he went to Hungary with St. John Capistrano to support that nation in its struggle against the Turks, and in 1466 he went to Venice in an attempt to get help from the republic for the same cause. From the beginning of 1469 until his death at the end of the year he was chamberlain of the Sacred College of Cardinals. He was of the highest type of ecclesiastical statesman—incorruptible, tireless, unassuming, "an ornament to the Sacred College, to the Church, and to humanity itself." (Pastor, *History of the Popes.*)

Casa (kä′zä), **Giovanni della.** See **Della Casa, Giovanni.**

Caselli (kä-sel′lē), **Cristoforo.** [Called **Cristoforo de' Temperelli.**] Painter; b. at Parma, 1461; d. there, 1521. He went to Venice before 1488 and was a pupil in the workshop of Giovanni Bellini. From his stay at Venice and his association with Bellini and Alvise Vivarini there are derived the sparkling Venetian color and the motifs of angel musicians that adorn one of his best works, *Madonna and Child Enthroned with Saints and Angels*, signed and dated (1499), and now in the National Gallery at Parma. After painting in the Church of the Carmine and in the Hall of the Great Council (1489) with Alvise Vivarini, he painted at Murano and then (1496) returned to Parma. In 1507 he frescoed the Montini Chapel in the cathedral at Parma, decorating it with arabesques and figures of the *Eternal Father* and a *Pietà*. The influence of his Venetian sojourn is evident in his work, and he was among those who introduced Venetian forms and color to the painters of Parma. Several of his paintings are in the National Gallery at Parma and in the Carrara Academy at

Bergamo. Others are at Baltimore (Walters Art Gallery), Detroit, and elsewhere.

Casentino (kä-zen-tē′nō), **Jacopo del.** See **Iacopo del Casentino.**

Casimir (kas′i-mir, kaz′-), Saint. Polish prince and patron saint of Poland; b. at Cracow, October 5, 1458; d. at Grodno. March 4, 1484. He was the son of Casimir IV, king of Poland, and Elizabeth of Austria. From early youth he cared little for honors and worldly pleasures but gave himself up to meditation and prayer. In 1471 the Hungarians, dissatisfied with their king, Matthias Corvinus, offered the crown to Prince Casimir, but rather than go to war with Matthias Corvinus he retired. When his father was occupied in Lithuania (1481–1483), which he ruled with Poland, Casimir governed Poland. He had taken a vow of chastity and refused to marry the daughter of the Emperor Frederick III. He died at the age of 26, and was canonized in 1521.

Casimir IV (of *Poland*). [Polish, **Kasimierz;** German, **Kasimir.**] King of Poland (1447–1492); b. November 29, 1427; d. at Grodno, Poland, June 7, 1492. He carried on a war of fourteen years against the Teutonic Knights, which was terminated (1466) by the peace of Toruń (Thorn), and which gave Poland possession of West Prussia, with suzerainty over East Prussia. He ruled both Poland and Lithuania, and was so impartial that he satisfied neither. Casimir was a patron of the arts and letters, a mild and tolerant ruler. In his reign many presses were established and published without restriction. Scholars who found themselves limited in other countries took refuge in Poland. Copernicus went to Cracow in 1492.

Cassaria (käs-sä′ryä). Comedy in five acts by Ariosto; it was produced at Ferrara in 1508.

Cassone (käs-sō′nā). An Italian word meaning a chest or coffer ordinarily used to store bridal linens. Cassoni of the 14th to the 16th century were often richly carved and decorated with paintings; scenes from mythology were frequently painted on the long sides and ends, and sometimes the interiors were also decorated.

Castagno (käs-tä′nyō), **Andrea del.** Florentine painter; b. at Castagno, 1421; d. at Florence, July 19, 1457. His father died while he was young, and Andrea became a shepherd. Tradition has it that, like Giotto, he drew on rocks, so great was his interest. When the owner of the lands where he lived saw the youth drawing men and animals, he took him to Florence and placed him in a workshop (perhaps that of Paolo Uccello) to learn painting. Influenced at first by Masaccio, the young painter soon asserted his own artistic personality, and turned away from the color and light of Masaccio to emphasize exactness of line, energy of design and expression, vigorous chiaroscuro, and an interest in perspective. In his sense of the dramatic and his tendency toward realism, as opposed to Masaccio's monumentality and dignity, he was rather a follower of Donatello. After Cosimo de' Medici was restored to power in Florence (1434), Andrea was commissioned (c1440) to paint on the walls of the Palace of the Podesta the likenesses of the rebels earlier hanged in effigy as traitors to their country. For this reason he came to be known as *Andreino degl' Impiccati.* Of his early work there remains only a *Crucifixion* in the Cloister of S. Maria degli Angeli. While still young, he went to Venice, where he worked with Francesco da Faenza painting the dome of the apse of the Chapel of S. Tarasio, in S. Zaccaria, depicting there *God the Father, Six Saints,* and a number of half figures and putti. The work was signed by both artists. Dated 1442, it is his earliest known work. Some cartoons for mosaics are also thought to have been prepared by him at Venice. In 1444 he returned to Florence (where he spent most of his life) and drew a cartoon for a *Deposition* for one of the stained glass windows in the cupola of the cathedral. The next year he was enrolled in the Guild of Physicians and Apothecaries. In 1449 he painted a *Madonna in Glory Between S. Miniato and S. Giuliano;* it was the only one of his altarpieces that had been preserved until it was destroyed at Berlin in 1945. Few of his panel paintings and frescoes have survived. Frescoes that he executed between 1450 and 1452 in S. Egidio, including scenes from the life of the Madonna and many portraits, were destroyed when the church was rebuilt. Some of the frescoes he executed in the Church of SS. Annunziata have also perished. In the Refectory of S. Apollonia at Florence is a *Last Supper,* as well as a *Crucifixion, Entombment,* and *Resurrection,* painted just before 1450. These are characteristic in their strong modeling and use of light and shade, superb draftsmanship, drama of composition, perspective, rather harsh color, and violent energy. Some influence of Piero della Francesca, with whom he had perhaps worked in S. Egidio, appears in the damaged upper part. The frescoes above the *Last Supper* have been detached to prevent further damage from dampness. The *sinopie* that were found underneath them, especially under *The Resurrection*, include carefully detailed drawings as well as a simple blocking in of the figures that were to appear in the finished fresco. Also in S. Apollonia, moved from another location in the convent, is a large *Pietà;* and in the Castagno Museum (Cenacolo di S. Apollonia) are nine frescoes of famous men and women, from the Villa Carducci Pandolfini at Legnaia. The figures represent Pippo Spano, a swashbuckling Florentine soldier of fortune who served in Hungary; Farinata degli Uberti, who reportedly saved Florence from destruction after the defeat at Monteperti (1260); Niccolò Acciauoli; the Cumaean Sibyl; Queen Esther; Tomyris, Queen of the Massagetae; and Dante, Petrarch, and Boccaccio. Other frescoes in the series, of Adam and Eve and of the Virgin, remain in the villa. In the Church of SS. Annunziata is a *Trinity and St. Jerome*. The fresco was badly damaged in the flood of November, 1966, and has been detached. The *sinopia* underneath shows that before he began to execute the fresco itself, Castagno had changed his mind, not only about the composition but about the mood and emotion he wished to express. Dissatisfied with the foreshortening he had attempted in the fresco he painted over it, *a secco*. The latter painting, since it is not true fresco and is thus on top of the plaster instead of combined with it, has since begun to flake off, revealing what Andrea regarded as a mistake in the original fresco. Also in the Annunziata is his fresco *St. Julian with Christ*. One of his last works (1456) is the equestrian figure of Niccolò da Tolentino, frescoed in the left aisle of the cathedral at Florence. Other surviving paintings are a *St. Sebastian* (the Metropolitan Museum, New York) and *Portrait of a Man* and *The Youthful David* (National Gallery, Washington). The latter is painted on a leather processional shield and is a fine example of the virile, animated, and slightly supernatural cast of his work. Vasari has given Andrea del Castagno an undeservedly bad name. He accused him of a violent temper and of killing his colleague, Domenico Veneziano, either out of jealousy or to prevent him from passing on the secret of painting in oils, which Andrea had learned from him, so Vasari said. However, documents prove that Domenico died four years after Andrea, although, again according to Vasari, Andrea was supposed to have confessed to the murder on his deathbed. Among Andrea's many pupils was Piero Pollaiuolo, but his influence extended far beyond his workshop, and the main elements of his style dominated Florentine painting for a number of years. Alessio Baldovinetti, Antonio Pollaiuolo, Botticelli, and Ghirlandaio all felt his influence. They were superb draftsmen, as was Andrea, and like him they used color as an ornament rather than as a basic element of the composition.

Castaldi (käs-täl′dē), **Cornelio.** Poet, humanist, and jurisconsult; b. at Feltre, 1463; d. 1537. He practiced his profession as a jurisconsult at Venice and Padua, and wrote poetry. In his poems, in Latin and Italian, he was at first a follower of Petrarch, but later became an anti-Petrarchist, in favor of less classicism and more sentiment. He was a friend of Augurello, Flaminio, Fracastoro, Navagero, and other leading men of letters of his day.

Castaldi, Panfilo. Physician and typographer; b. at Feltre, September 22, 1398; d. after August 21, 1479. He practiced medicine at Capodistria, then went to Venice (1469), and later (1472) to Milan as a typographer with the license to print in the duchy. Castaldi is credited by some with the invention of movable type in anticipation of Gutenberg, but the evidence is inconclusive.

Castanheda (käsh-tą-nyā′dą), **Fernão Lopes de.** Portuguese historian; b. at Santarém, Portugal, c1500; d. at Coimbra, Portugal, March 23, 1559. He was the author of *Historia do descobrimento e conquista da Índia pelos Portugueses*.

Castellani (käs-tel-lä′nē), **Castellano de'.** Poet, priest, and writer of sacred plays; b. perhaps at Prato, 1461; d. 1519. He was a priest, vicar of Fiesole, and an admirer of Savonarola. He was made count palatine, and was a friend of the Medici at Florence. He lectured on canon law at Pisa until 1519. His verses, *Opera spirituale*, were published at Venice (1521), and others appeared in various collections. He is best known for his sacred plays, usually representations of the life of a saint.

Castellesi (käs-tel-lā′sē), **Adriano.** See **Adriano di Corneto.**

Castello (käs-tel′lō), **Giambattista.** [Called **il Bergamasco.**] Architect and painter; b. at Gandino in Val Seriana, c1509; d. at Madrid, 1569. He went to Genoa as a youth to study. There he became a close friend of Luca Cambiaso and adopted his style. He became a respectable painter but is best known as an architect. At Genoa he was the architect of a number of palaces and was also noted for the stucco decorations he created in various palaces and other buildings. He rebuilt the Gothic Church of S. Matteo (completed 1554) and executed paintings and stucco decorations for the Church of the SS. Annunziata (1563–1564) and the cathedral (1564). He was fundamentally an architect in the manner of the early 16th century, whose characteristics were grace and a certain restraint, even coldness, as compared to the Baroque style that was developing in his day. In 1567 he went to Spain and entered the service of Philip II. The only work surely known to be his in Spain is a staircase between the church and the palace of the Escorial.

Castel Sant' Angelo (käs-tel′ sän-tän′jā-lō). [Also, **Hadrian's Tomb** or **Hadrian's Mole.**] A landmark of Rome, located on the right bank of the Tiber at the Ponte Sant' Angelo. It was probably conceived by Hadrian to serve as a tomb for himself and his successors. It was begun in 135 and completed in 139, but has undergone numerous additions and changes. It consists, fundamentally, of a huge cylinder on a square base, within which is the original winding Roman ramp with traces still of the original mosaics. Nicholas V and Alexander VI added the towers at the four corners of the base. Theodoric converted the structure, in which were deposited the funeral urns of the emperors from Hadrian to Septimius Severus, into a prison, and it became a fortress as well, connected by a secret passage to the Vatican. Cola di Rienzi fled to it for refuge in 1347. Cardinal Vitelleschi, general of Pope Eugenius IV and a governor of the Papal States, died a prisoner there in 1440. The humanists Platina and Pomponius Laetus, accused of a conspiracy against the pope, were imprisoned there (1465 and 1468); and in 1527 Clement VII escaped to it at the last moment as the invading hordes of the Constable of Bourbon surged to the Vatican. Benvenuto Cellini, who was one of those in the beleaguered fortress, describes the siege that went on for months in his *Autobiography*. It knew other prisoners, famous or infamous for their deeds, until it ceased to serve as a prison at the end of the 19th century. In the Renaissance, Papal apartments were built on the summit of the huge cylinder. Alexander VI, Julius II, and Leo X left their mark in the form of a loggia that looks out over the Tiber, the Apartments of Julius, designed by Bramante, a chapel added by Leo, and other works, and had their constructions decorated by various Renaissance painters. A bronze angel surmounts the entire edifice. This commemorates a vision (590) of Gregory the Great, who saw in the sky above the tomb the archangel Michael sheathing his sword to signal the end of a terrible plague that was wracking Rome. It is for this reason that the structure is called Castel Sant' Angelo. (The bronze angel was substituted, in 1753, for an earlier statue by Guglielmo della Porta; the earlier statue is now inside the fortress.) Today the structure houses a Military and Artistic Museum.

Castelvetro (käs-tel-vā′trō), **Lodovico.** Critic, writer, and playwright; b. at Modena, 1505?; d. at Chiavenna, February 21, 1571. He studied law at Bologna, Ferrara, Padua, and Siena, and in the last city also studied literature and produced his comedy *Gli ingannati* (1531). After a sojourn in Rome, he returned to Modena and remained there a long time, except for brief visits to Venice, Padua, Florence, Ferrara, and other cities. He was a keen critic, but tactless and arrogant. In 1553 he began a famous quarrel with Annibale Caro by criticizing the latter's canzone in praise of France, *Venite all' ombra de' gran gigli d'oro*. Castelvetro, in what he thought was a private letter, called it lifeless, plebeian (the worst criticism that could be made in that day and age), and ill-formed. The letter, or its contents, came to Caro's attention. In replying to the criticism, Caro called him an enemy of God and of man. Castelvetro had, indeed, publicly disagreed with opinions of the Church. In 1557 Castelvetro, perhaps denounced to the Inquisition by Caro, was accused of heresy, fled, and was excommunicated. He made a visit to Rome in hopes of having the ban lifted, but on learning that it would not be he fled again. When all hope of becoming reconciled with the Church had vanished, he began his wanderings—to Geneva, Lyons, Vienna, then back to Chiavenna. Among the writings of this learned and cantankerous man are commentaries on the *Rime* of Petrarch, Latin poetry, and Italian poetry. His most important work is his commentary on the *Poetics* of Aristotle, which is keen and penetrating in its analysis of Aristotle. He presents in the commentary his own theories and deductions; among them, he asserts that poetry and rhetoric are two separate arts. Frequently they had been considered as one and the same. He also asserted that poetry's main and single purpose is to give pleasure, that it has nothing to do with education or presenting moral theses. If it happens to be educative and moralistic, that may be good, but it is not the primary purpose of poetry. In a work on the grammar of Pietro Bembo, Castelvetro explored the derivation of Italian from Latin. Most of a grammar he was himself preparing was lost at Lyons in 1567.

Castiglionchio (käs-tē-lyōn′kyō), **Lapo da.** See **Lapo da Castiglionchio.**

Castiglione (käs-tē-lyō′nā), **Baldassare,** Conte. Courtier, diplomat, and man of letters; b. at Casatico, near Mantua, December 6, 1478; d. at Toledo, Spain, February 2, 1529. His father was the count of Castiglione and his mother was a Gonzaga. He received a sound education at Mantua along the lines laid down by the noted educators Vittorino da Feltre and Guarino da Verona—that is, an education that embraced the humanistic studies, Latin and Greek, athletics, and religious training. He continued his studies at Milan, where one of his masters was the noted Greek scholar Demetrius Chalcondylas, and where he was a member of the court of Ludovico il Moro and his wife Beatrice d'Este. From his education and his interests he had access to the great writers of the past, a knowledge of painting and music, athletic and military skill. He entered the service of Federico Gonzaga at Mantua, and with his lord fought the losing battle against the Spaniards in Naples (1503). Visits to Rome and Urbino delighted him with the very different charms of these two cities, and in 1504 he left Mantua to enter the service of Duke Guidobaldo at Urbino. There he was captain of fifty men of arms and active as a diplomat. The years he spent at the highly cultivated, relatively peaceful, and well-administered court of Urbino shaped his career and satisfied his chivalrous and studious temperament. He was the devoted admirer of the Duchess Elizabetta, Guidobaldo's intelligent and attractive wife. In 1506 he went on a mission to England to receive the Order of the Garter from Henry VII on Guidobaldo's behalf, and the next year went on a mission to Louis XII of France. Guidobaldo died in 1508 and was succeeded by his nephew Francesco della Rovere, whom Castiglione also served. From 1513 to 1515 he was the envoy from Urbino to Rome. On the accession of the Medici pope, Leo X, Francesco della Rovere was replaced (1516) as duke of Urbino by Leo's nephew Lorenzo de' Medici. This was in line with the custom of ruling houses of aggrandizing members of the family. Castiglione left Urbino and went back to Mantua. Two years later he was again at Rome. There he was on friendly terms with the leading men of letters and artists of the time and a member of the so-called Roman Academy, a group of kindred literary and artistic spirits. Among his close friends was Raphael. The artist's portrait of him, now in the Louvre, shows a gentle, thoughtful man, about whom there is an air of faintly questioning melancholy. Castiglione married (1516) Ipollita Torelli, of a noble family of Modena, but she died within a short time. In 1523, he fought against the French at the side of Federigo II of Mantua, and in 1524 Pope Clement VII sent him to Spain as his nuncio. (This was at the beginning of Clement's disastrous dependence on Francis I of France. The following year Francis was captured by Charles V of Spain at the battle of Pavia.) Castiglione was unable to reconcile the conflicts between Clement and Charles, conflicts aggravated by Clement's notorious vacillations and ambiguities, and was in Spain when the troops of Charles sacked Rome (1527). A suspicion that he betrayed Clement was unfounded. He never lost Clement's confidence nor the emperor's respect. Charles showed him marked favor.

In his own life Castiglione approached the ideal of the perfect courtier described in his *Il libro del cortegiano* (*The Book of the Courtier*). This work is an expression of his ideals as to what a courtier should be, the attributes he should possess, and the role he should play. In presenting the background against which the courtier plays his part, he paints for all time the manners and society of the most refined and cultivated court in Italy—a court society in which the word "prince" implied all the civilized and humane qualities, and in which each member knew his role and was delighted to play it. The society so painted was, of course, a select one. The lines between the classes were clear-cut, but the communications across them were easy. Castiglione also wrote distinguished Latin and Italian poetry, and left a number of shrewd and graceful letters. His masterpiece, and a masterpiece of European literature, is his *Il cortegiano*, a mirror that reflects through a film of idealism the nobility and knightly class that thronged the courts and served the royal and ducal sovereigns of that time. See **CorteGiano, Il.**

Castiglione, Branda da. Cardinal; b. at Castiglione d'Olona, near Milan, 1350; d. there, February 3, 1443. He studied canon law at Pavia, and then continued his studies at Rome. He held many ecclesiastical offices and was made cardinal (1411) by Pope Alexander V. He served on many diplomatic missions for the Church, as to Lombardy, Germany, Bohemia, Poland, and at the Councils of Constance, Basel, and Florence. A pious, learned, and industrious man, he worked for peace among all Christians and for the unity of the Latin and Greek churches. In 1426 he founded, at Pavia, a college for twenty-four poor students. Castiglione was noted as a patron of art and for the works of art he caused to be executed at his native city. He founded (1421) a church there and commissioned Masolino da Panicale to decorate it. The adjoining baptistery contains Masolino's masterpiece. In 1428 Castiglione called Masaccio to Rome to decorate his chapel in the Church of San Clemente, but the young artist died suddenly, before he could begin the work.

Castiglione, Branda da. Jurisconsult and orator; b. at Milan, c1415; d. at Rome, July 16, 1487. He was the grandnephew of Branda da Castiglione (1350–1443). In 1466 he became bishop of Como. He was one of Galeazzo Maria Sforza's councillors, and was at his side when the latter was murdered (1476) in church. He continued in the service of the Sforzas, served on the council, went on a mission to France, and was legate of the papal fleet against Venice (1483). He caused the College of Pavia to be decorated with splendid frescoes by masters of the Paduan school.

Castiglione, Cristoforo da. Jurisconsult; b. at Milan, 1345; d. at Pavia, May 16, 1425. He taught law at Parma, Pavia, and Siena, and was a counselor to the duke of Milan. He left a number of Latin works on the law.

Castiglione, Guarnerio da. Jurisconsult and statesman; d. May, 1460. He lectured on civil law at Pavia from 1418 to 1427, and thereafter held many positions in the service of various princes. Duke Filippo Maria Visconti charged him with settling the quarrel between Amadeus VIII of Savoy and the lord of Monferrato (1434) and also with establishing the conditions for the release of Alfonso of Naples, captured by the Genoese under Filippo Maria (1435). On the death of the duke, Castiglione had an important role in the short-lived Ambrosian republic, then linked his fortunes to those of Francesco Sforza, used his influence to have Sforza named duke of Milan, became one of his counselors, and served as his emissary to Venice to implement the Peace of Lodi (1454). He left many works on legal subjects, orations (he had served as orator for Sigismondo Malatesta, among others), and letters.

Castiglione, Sabbà da. Knight Templar and scholar; b. at Milan, 1484. He was a kinsman of Baldassare Castiglione and was a friend of Cristoforo Romano, Andrea Mantegna, and Isabella d'Este. While at Rhodes (1505–1508), which his order was defending against the Turks, he collected antique statues and fragments and sent them to Isabella for her collections. He returned to Rome (1508) and remained there until 1516. At that time he became prior of a house near Faenza and remained there until he was an old man. He left a memoir, *Ricordi*.

Castillejo (käs-tē-lye′hō), **Cristóbal de.** Spanish poet; b. at Ciudad Rodrigo, Spain, c1490; d. at Vienna, c1550.

Castillo (käs-tē′lyō), **Diego Enríquez de.** Spanish chronicler; b. at Segovia, Spain; fl. c1475. He was the author of *Annals of the Reign of Henry IV, 1454–1474*.

Castracani (käs-trä-kä′nē), **Castruccio.** Nobleman and condottiere; b. 1281; d. 1328. He was of the noble family of Antelminelli of Lucca which, having espoused the Ghibelline cause, was banished during Guelph ascendancy when Castruccio was still a youth. To retrieve his fortunes, Castruccio, an able, intelligent, and ambitious man, turned to the profession of arms and was singularly successful. He spent some time in the Ghibelline city of Pisa, swore allegiance to Henry VII when that monarch descended into Italy and cleared the way for many Ghibelline exiles to return to their homes; and when Uguccione della Faggiuola, lord of Pisa, conquered and sacked Lucca (1314) Castruccio returned with him to his native city as one of Uguccione's ablest lieutenants. A rebellion in Pisa (1316) enabled Castruccio to oust Uguccione, whom he had long planned to overthrow. The people of Lucca, delighted to be rid of the Pisan tyrant, made Castruccio lord of Lucca for life. He then became the dominant figure in Tuscany, and aspired to control of the whole region. A war over Genoa (1320) embroiled him with Florence. He seized the city of Pistoia (1325) and later in the same year won a great victory over the Florentines at Altopascio, a victory which he celebrated with a triumph of Roman proportions. The emperor Louis IV (Ludwig the Bavarian) had confirmed his position as imperial vicar of Lucca and surrounding territory in 1324. Louis wished to be crowned emperor in Rome, but the pope, John XXII, a Frenchman residing in Avignon, refused to permit the ceremony. Louis came into Italy and received the Iron Crown of Lombardy in Milan. Welcomed by the Ghibellines, as Henry VII had been, Louis proceeded south into Tuscany. There, because of the small force he had brought with him, he was under the protection of Castruccio. Louis made him (1327) duke of Lucca, with the right of succession for his sons. Castruccio went with Louis for the coronation. This took place in January, 1328, and was performed first by the Roman senate and then by two bishops. While he was in Rome, Florence took the opportunity to recapture the city of Pistoia. Castruccio sped north and won back the city after a siege, in August, 1328, but did not long enjoy his victory. He died of a fever shortly thereafter. While in Rome he had been impressed by the ancient ruins and Christian monuments, and had wished, if he died outside Lucca, to be buried in St. Peter's. As it was, he died at Lucca and was buried, in the habit of a Franciscan monk, in the Church of San Francesco there, although he had twice (1324, 1328) been excommunicated by the pope because of his support of Louis and for other offenses. With his skill at arms, his intelligence, his ruthlessness in pursuit of his own interests and the aggrandizement of his state, Castruccio Castracani was the hero of a fictional life written by Machiavelli two hundred years later. All that he had accomplished, which was domination of Tuscany, was undone after his death; the power he had acquired by skill and arms disappeared with his person.

Castro (käs′trō), **Alfonso y.** Franciscan theologian and preacher; b. at Zamora, Spain, 1495; d. at Brussels, February 11, 1558. He accompanied Philip II to England in 1554, and opposed the extreme measures of the English Catholics, strenuously condemning the burning of heretics. His most noted work is *Adversus omnes haereses.*

Castro (käs′trō; Portuguese, käsh′trö), **Inés de.** Spanish noblewoman; killed at Coimbra, Portugal, 1355. She was the favorite of Pedro, son of Alfonso IV of Portugal, who claimed to have married her after the death of his wife. She was murdered by order of Alfonso, to prevent the consequences of an unequal union. Her tragic story has been celebrated by novelists and poets, all of whom have idealized her character.

Castro (käsh′trö), **João de.** Portuguese naval commander; governor in India; b. at Lisbon, February 7, 1500; d. at Ormuz, Persia, June 6, 1548.

Castro (käs′trō), **Paolo de.** Specialist in canon and civil law; d. at Padua, c1441. He was professor of canon and civil law successively at Florence, Bologna, Ferrara, and Padua.

Cateau-Cambrésis (kȧ-tō-kän-brā-zē), **Treaty of.** Treaty among France, England, and Spain, concluded April 2–3, 1559. By it England formally acknowledged the right of France to retain Calais; but the most important sections of the treaty were those involving points of dispute between France and Spain, and in these Spain gained Savoy and territory on the French boundary with the Netherlands. The French also accepted Spanish dominance in Italy. With this treaty, the conflict that had existed between France and

Spain (with occasional anti-French intervention by England) for more than fifty years was settled.

Catena (kä-tā′nä), **Vincenzo di Biagio.** Venetian painter; b. at Venice, c1480; d. there, 1531. He was a man of wealth who evidently enjoyed planning for its disposition after his death, for he made five wills. He left several specific bequests and the residue of his property to the Scuola dei Pittori at Venice, a sum that enabled the school to buy land and erect a building on it. His wealth gave him the leisure to perfect himself in his art at his own pace and pleasure. His style developed slowly. He began in the somewhat archaicized manner and spirit of the 15th century, and was affected by the developments introduced by Antonello da Messina and transmitted to Venetian painting by Cima de Conegliano and Alvise Vivarini. His linearism was then softened by the influence of Giovanni Bellini, and ultimately, with some hesitation, he approached the softness, coloring, and grace of Giorgione (long after Giorgione's death), Titian, and Jacopo Palma the Elder. His early works, with clear outlines and strong contrasts of light and shade, reflect the Antonello influence, as in his *Holy Conversation* and *Virgin and Child with the Baptist and St. Jerome* (c1505), Accademia, and *Virgin Adored by Doge Leonardo Loredan* (c1510), Correr Museum, Venice. The latter is a vigorous work in the 15th century manner. The luminous color and soft modeling of Bellini appear in other *Holy Conversations,* as at Budapest, Glasgow, and Berlin. His masterpiece is *Christ Appearing to St. Christina in a Landscape* (c1521), Church of S. Maria Materdomini, Venice, notable for the clearly cut forms and serene landscape. Catena often derived or borrowed figures and designs from Bellini, and made such changes as suited his own style. *The Circumcision* (the Metropolitan Museum, New York) is after a Bellini painting. He also frequently made more than one version, so close as to appear to be a copy, of the same painting, as the *Supper at Emmaus,* of which there is one in the Carrara Academy, Bergamo, and another in the Contini-Bonacossi Collection at Florence; and *Christ Delivering the Keys to St. Peter,* of which one, beautifully painted and showing the influence of Palma Vecchio and Sebastiano del Piombo in its graceful feminine figures, is in the Prado, Madrid, and another in the Isabella Stewart Gardner Museum, Boston. There are similar duplications of other paintings. His *Holy Family with a Warrior Adoring the Infant Christ* (National Gallery, London) is eloquent in its grace, sensitivity, and soft landscape in the manner of Giorgione. Catena's technical proficiency and visual realism made him a fine portraitist; among the portraits is that of *Doge Andrea Gritti* (the Metropolitan Museum, New York) and *Portrait of Giangiorgio Trissino* (Louvre, Paris); a *Portrait of Count Raimund Fugger,* formerly at Berlin, was destroyed in 1945. In his own day, Catena was ranked with Giorgione and Titian. Later criticism has been less generous, while allowing that he was a sincere and gifted artist, many of whose works are suffused with a singular loveliness. In addition to those already mentioned, paintings by Catena are in the Correr Museum and Querini Stampalia Gallery, Venice; the Brera, Milan; at Dresden, Frankfurt, Edinburgh, Prague; The National Gallery, Washington; and elsewhere.

Caterina de' Medici (kä-tā-rē′nä dā mā′dē-chē). See **Catherine de Médicis.**

Caterino (kä-tā-rē′nō). Venetian painter; active in the second half of the 14th century. Caterino's works mark a departure from the Byzantine influence and a direction to an Italian style in simplicity of arrangement, drapery, and color. A triptych, *Coronation of the Virgin,* is in the Accademia, Venice. A polyptych, *Virgin and Child* (Walters Art Gallery, Baltimore) shows, in its Gothic elements, the influence of Lorenzo Veneziano. With a Venetian colleague, Caterino painted a *Coronation of the Virgin* (1372) (Querini Stampalia Collection, Venice) that owes its skill in rendering and richness of color to his colleague, Donato, who seems to have been the guiding spirit in the work. A signed *Madonna of Humility* is at Worcester, Massachusetts.

Catherine de Médicis (kath′e̤-rin de̤ mā′dē-sēs). [Italian, **Caterina de' Medici.**] Last survivor of the older branch of the Medici family of Florence founded by Cosimo the Elder (1389–1464); b. at Florence, 1519; d. at Blois, France, January 5, 1589. She was the daughter of Lorenzo de' Medici, duke of Urbino, and was the great-granddaughter of

Lorenzo the Magnificent. In 1533 she was married, through the agency of her kinsman Pope Clement VII, to the duke of Orléans, who became Henry II of France in 1547. Her first child was not born until ten years after her marriage; she ultimately had nine children, including the three kings Francis II (reigned 1559–1560), Charles IX (reigned 1560–1574) for whom she was regent from 1560 to 1563, and Henry III (reigned 1574–1589). Her daughter Marguerite of Valois married Henry of Navarre, who became king of France in 1589. In her husband's lifetime Catherine had little influence, since he was dominated by his mistress Diane de Poitiers, but afterward she had, until her death, an important though sometimes concealed share in the intrigues and party contests that distracted France, and she was held responsible for the massacre of the Huguenots on Saint Bartholomew's Day (August 24, 1572).

Catherine of Aragon. Queen of England; b. at Alcalá de Henares, Spain, in December, 1485; d. at Kimbolton, Huntingdonshire, England, January 7, 1536. She was the daughter of Ferdinand and Isabella of Spain, and was married to Arthur, prince of Wales, in November, 1501. He died on April 2 of the following year, and the next year she was betrothed to his younger brother Henry. For the next seven years Catherine was a pawn in the struggle of Henry VIII of England to win concessions from Ferdinand. She was at last married to Henry in June, 1509. In the next nine years she gave birth to six children, two sons and four daughters, the only one of whom lived was Mary, born in 1516. About 1526 Henry, who was by that time in love with Anne Boleyn and eager to have a male heir, began to take measures toward a divorce, primarily on the grounds that his union with Catherine was invalid, the relationship between them, through her earlier marriage with his brother, being considered incestuous by the Church. (Many were saying that it was because of this relationship that her children were either stillborn or died in infancy—a punishment of Heaven.) The fact was that through several circumstances papal approval of the marriage had never been actually expressed; but the divorce proceedings instituted by Henry through Wolsey were not given sanction at Rome. The pope was dependent on Charles V, Catherine's nephew, and did not wish to offend him. Hoping that Henry would tire of Anne Boleyn, the pope resorted to his usual tactics of delay. In 1534 he finally pronounced in favor of Catherine, bidding Henry to consider her his queen; by that time, however, it was too late. In 1533 the marriage had been declared void by Cranmer, archbishop of Canterbury, and Catherine had been forced into retirement, all earlier attempts at persuading her to relinquish her position voluntarily having been in vain. Henry's inability to receive the pope's sanction to his divorce and remarriage occasioned him to pronounce the Act of Supremacy (1534), declaring himself sole head of religious rules and ceremonies in his land; thus England joined the general movement of the Reformation, and established the independent Church of England. Catherine, a pious and cultivated lady, very popular with her subjects, bore her sufferings and humiliations with dignity, and died a virtual prisoner.

Catherine of Bologna, Saint. Abbess of the Poor Clares at Bologna; b. at Bologna, September 8, 1413; d. there, March 9, 1463. She was said to have the gift of prophecy and to have enjoyed visions, and left a treatise on spiritual weapons, *Le sette arme necessarie alla battaglia spirituale*, which went through many editions and translations, and collections of her revelations, as well as minor works in prose and verse.

Catherine of Genoa. [Original name, **Caterina Fieschi.**] Saint; b. at Genoa, 1447; d. there, probably September 15, 1510. She was the daughter of Giacomo Fieschi, of the powerful Genoese family. From an early age she was drawn to the religious life, and at 13 wished to commit herself formally to it, but was prevented from doing so. At 16, for political reasons, she was married to Giuliano Adorno, member of a rival Genoese family. Her profligate husband neglected her and wasted his patrimony. In 1473 she had a vision of grace and entered upon a new life of the spirit. Her husband, having been influenced by her, became a Franciscan tertiary. For a time they lived in a small house near a hospital and devoted themselves to the care of the sick and the poor in the neighborhood. From 1479 they lived in the hospital itself, serving the sick without pay. In 1490 Catherine became chief administrator of the hospital, performed heroically in two epidemics of plague, and continued her hospital work after the death of her husband (January 10, 1497). After her death, miraculous cures were said to have taken place at her tomb, and she was soon venerated as a saint. No work from her own hand is known, but her sayings and ideas were written down by her confessor, Cattaneo Marabotto, and her spiritual son, Ettore Vernazza, a Genoese lawyer, in a *Vita e Dottrina*, published at Genoa in 1551. From this work were drawn a treatise on purgatory and a collection of spiritual dialogues that supposedly represent her ideas and views. She was canonized in 1737.

Catherine of Ricci (rēt′chē). Saint; b. at Florence, April 23, 1522; d. at Prato, February 2, 1590. She took the veil among the Dominican nuns at Prato, in Tuscany, in 1535, and was subprioress or prioress from the age of 25 until her death. In 1542 her visions and ecstasies began; from Thursday noon to Friday at 4:00 P.M. of Holy Week she relived Christ's Passion. A wise, energetic, and able administrator, she was adviser to bishops, cardinals, generals of orders, and three who became popes. She was canonized 1746.

Catherine of Siena, Saint. Mystic; b. at Siena, March 25 (according to tradition), 1347; d. at Rome, April 29, 1380. She was the twenty-third child, a twin, of Iacopo Benincasa, a dyer, and his wife Lapa, and was born in a house that still stands on a steep, narrow street near the Fontebranda in Siena. On a nearby hill looms the great Church of S. Domenico that played such a role in her life. A mystic and ascetic, intelligent, ardent, fearless, and of great vitality, of extraordinary piety and untiring energy in good works, she was deeply religious from childhood, and ultimately surrendered herself completely to the will of God. Love of God and an overflowing love for all the creatures He created was the point of departure for all her activities in service to her fellowmen and to her Church. When she was seven years old she had her first vision. In the air above S. Domenico she seemed to see Christ enthroned, as in a bridal chamber. From this time her thoughts and her life were devoted to contemplation and to communion with Christ. In the same year she vowed to remain a virgin, and began to scourge herself and to spend hours in meditation and prayer. The charm and appeal of her personality were already manifest, and her young companions, drawn by her fervor, imitated her religious activities. As she neared the age of 12 her parents, especially her mother, began to think of her marriage. Catherine was urged to consider her appearance, to make herself as pretty as possible for a future husband. She resisted all efforts to interest her in her looks, and when her mother persisted, she cut off her hair. She told her parents she had made a vow of virginity and meant to dedicate her life to carrying out the will of Christ. Her father, a religious and loving man, supported her, and gave her a small room in the house for her own, a private place for her private meditations. She scourged herself with an iron chain and wore a chain about her waist. She began to eat less and less. (As she grew older eating became an agony for her.) Her mother opposed her activities but was powerless in the face of her daughter's gentle, humble manner and undeviating will. After some attempts to change her by giving her every menial task in the household, Iacopo, who intuitively understood his daughter's vocation, ordered the members of his family to respect it. She became an ardent admirer of the Dominicans, one of whom, Fra Tommaso della Fonte, was her spiritual adviser, and conceived the desire to become a member of the lay order called the Sisters of Penance of St. Dominic. A dream in which St. Dominic appeared to her and presented her with the habit of the order supported her belief that it was the will of God for her to become a member. She badgered her mother to ask the sisters, called *Mantellate*, to admit her. The women in the order were widows, and they at first refused to take a young unmarried girl, on the ground that it was unsuitable for such a one to belong to an open order whose members went out into the world on missions of charity. Catherine persisted, and during a serious illness induced her mother to go again to the sisters. In the face of such determination and devotion, they yielded and accepted her (1363). Several years of seclusion in her room in her father's house followed, during which she fasted, prayed, and communed with Christ. Of an ardent but practical spirit, she conversed with Christ in forthright fashion, according to confessions that were later incorporated into her biography by Raymond of Capua. She was unable to read and prayed, "Lord, if you want me to learn to read so that I can say the Psalms and sing your praises in the Canonical Hours, deign to teach me what I am not clever enough to learn by myself." She did learn to read. She sometimes pleaded with Christ to save a soul about to leave the world. One such had been a great sinner and was condemned. She did not want him to die unredeemed and urged Christ to help her bring him to grace and salvation before his death. Christ answered her, she said, that it was only justice that such a sinner should be punished. "Have I come to you to discuss justice or to ask for mercy?" she demanded, and persuaded Christ to allow her to save the man, who died shortly thereafter in a state of grace.

After several years, she had the vision in which occurred her mystical marriage to Christ (1368). (St. Catherine's Mystical Marriage became a favorite subject in painting in the early Renaissance and later.) Thereafter she began to go into the world, to perform acts of charity, to care for the sick, and to save souls. No disease was too loathsome for her tenderness; no effort was too great in the service of those in need. Around her gathered a group of men and women from all walks of life who became her ardent followers. Three young men, two of whom were Sienese nobles, became her devoted secretaries, and to them she dictated the letters that she now began to write and to send to people of all ranks. Her followers were members of her "famiglia," and all, though many of them were senior to her, became her spiritual pupils and children. Her goodness was a radiance in which people were comforted. She was greatly loved and so revered that people knelt before her. (For allowing this she was much criticized, but her response was that she did not notice what people were doing physically; she was aware only of their needs.) Her fame spread beyond the bounds of Siena into Tuscany and farther. Miraculous cures were ascribed to her. Souls were saved from eternal damnation by her prayers. A famous case, described in one of the most poignant of her letters, concerns a young Perugian who, on a visit to Siena, was arrested for political reasons and immediately condemned to death. He raged at man and God. Catherine went to him, prayed with him, and reconciled him to God. He asked only that she be with him in the hour of his death. She promised, and was at his side when he laid his head on the block. Before the executioner's axe fell, he smiled and murmured, "Gesù, e, Catarina."

She attempted to compose the violent quarrels that divided families, then strove to reconcile the factions in Siena. Her fame grew, and men from all over came to visit her, and her followers in spirit were drawn from many parts of Italy. She became aware of the travails that afflicted Italy and longed to ease them, and to bring back the pope from Avignon to Rome, where he belonged. The arrival of Pope Urban V (1367) was an occasion of great joy for her, but it was short-lived, as he returned to Avignon after a brief stay (1370). On the eve of his departure she had a vision that indicated to her that she was to be a messenger of peace. Unhesitatingly she took up the charge; and a program, indicated in her letters, began to evolve. There were three objectives: to pacify Italy, to call a crusade against the Turks that would unite Italy in a common cause, and to reform the Church. Her travels, her letters, and her public activity were most extraordinary for a single young woman in that age. Many grumbled and criticized the enthusiasm that was generated by the dyer's daughter. She bore criticism and persecution with the utmost serenity; called before the general chapter of the order at Florence (1374) to defend her activities, she acquitted herself completely and won official Dominican protection. She was invited to Pisa, and went there with a group of followers (1375). In that year she received the stigmata (visible to her alone, as she had asked in order to avoid a public clamor). Raymond of Capua, who became her spiritual director in that year, accompanied her. She went next to Lucca, as the pope's agent to dissuade the Lucchese from joining an antipapal league. In the same year (1376) she was asked by the Florentines to go as their envoy to seek peace between them and the pope (they were under a papal interdict for having warred against the papal legates; the interdict was bad for business). Raymond accompanied her, with others, and acted as her interpreter, as the pope did not speak Italian and she did not speak Latin. She failed at this time to secure the desired peace, and was deeply grieved by the luxury and corruption she found at the papal court. However, she made a great impression on Pope Gregory XI and was extremely influential in his subsequent decision to return the papal court to Rome. He entered the Eternal City to wild acclaim on January 17, 1377. Catherine wrote letters of encouragement to Gregory, seeking to instill in him some of her own unflinching spirit in the face of difficulties, and exhorting him to purge himself of what she called self-love. She took his measure at Avignon and realized that by himself he would not stand firm. She tactfully but frankly and definitely told him what he should do. She wrote, "I beg you to be not a fearful child but a man; open your mouth and swallow the little drop of bitter medicine." This was in reference to the opposition and intrigues of the French cardinals. At the pope's request she visited Florence and finally (July, 1378) secured peace between the commune and the pope. It was a perilous time to be in Florence, for the Ciompi revolt broke out, and at least once her very life was in danger. Gregory had died (March 26, 1378) before the peace was secured. The cardinals, a majority of whom were French, elected an Italian prelate to succeed him, Urban VI. The French cardinals quickly regretted their choice, as Urban energetically set out to make reforms. Joined by some of the Italian cardinals, they elected a new pope (September, 1378), Clement VII. They claimed that the earlier election was illegal because they had been compelled, by fear of the Romans, to elect an Italian. This was a heartbreaking development to Catherine. She had hoped for a reformer to replace the weak Gregory, but quickly realized that the violence of Urban's unfortunate personality alienated more than it reconciled. However, convinced of the canonicity of Urban's election, she supported him to the end. She sent him letters of encouragement, advice, and support. She dictated letters to the princes and rulers of Europe urging them to support the canonically elected pope. Nor did she spare the Italian cardinals who had aided the election of the antipope, sending them a letter in which she named them the "incarnate demons who chose the demon." Urban sent for her, and in November, 1378, she went to Rome. She was by this time a famous holy woman, having won fame and influence by her manifest love of humanity, the miraculous cures ascribed to her (some of which took place during her heroic service in the plagues of 1363 and 1374), her common sense, and her flaming devotion to the will of God. Urban wanted her support but was temperamentally unable to take her advice. Her devoted disciples gathered about her in Rome. By this time her body was worn out, she suffered grievously, suffering that she bore with unflagging cheerfulness. She fasted and prayed, wished that her life might be taken as a general penance. She dictated letters and comforted her followers, who could see that her death was near. On April 29, 1380, surrounded by her sorrowing followers, she murmured, "Sangue, sangue, sangue," and restored her soul to God. Mourners surged to the church where her body rested; many cures were believed to have taken place. One of the most appealing figures of her century, she was canonized by Pope Pius II, who wrote the bull himself, in 1461. Pope Pius XII named her a patron saint of Italy in 1939.

Nearly four hundred of St. Catherine's letters exist. Most of these are copies of a copy, now lost, made by her disciple Stefano Maconi, who was one of the secretaries to whom she dictated them. His copy of her letters was at one time in the Certosa di Pavia, of which he was prior. Her letters have been called "the most dynamic prose of the 14th century" (Wilkins). They are addressed to all sorts and conditions of men and women. At first their aim was to give spiritual instruction and encouragement; but as her activities widened, the subject matter of the letters changed. The tone of the letters is frank and authoritative. Completely selfless, she had no hesitation in instructing her correspondents in accordance with the dictates given to her by Christ. The style is crisp and lucid, and the language a pure Tuscan. She wrote Joanna of Naples, who had openly espoused the cause of Clement VII, urging her to support Urban VI. She wrote the English condottiere John Hawkwood, whose company of adventurers had ravaged Italy, inviting him to change his way of life and take up "the pay and the cross of Christ." The letters to members of her "famiglia" are full of tender concern and encouragement. In addition to her letters she dictated the *Dialogo della Divina Provvidenza* (*Book of the Dialogue with Divine Providence*), which was intended as her spiritual testament. In the course of the years she had from time to time, and increasingly as her life went on, gone into a state of ecstasy, in which she would become rigid and unaware of what was going on around her. It was during such trances that she dictated her book. Her secretaries took turns in taking it down. Her letters and her book are classics of Italian literature. The Church of S. Domenico at Siena is closely associated with the saint's life. The only authentic portrait of her, a fresco by her follower Andrea Vanni, is at the back of the nave. It has been much repainted. The saint's head (the body is at Rome) is also in S. Domenico. Her chapel in the church is decorated with frescoes (many of which are by Sodoma) of incidents of her life.

Catherine of Valois (val′wä, vȧ-lwȧ). Queen of England; b. at Paris, October 27, 1401; d. at Bermondsey (now part of London), January 23, 1437. She was the daughter of King Charles VI of France. She married Henry V of England at Troyes (June 2, 1420) and was crowned at Westminster Abbey (February 23, 1421). She bore Henry a son who became Henry VI. After Henry V's early death in France (1422), she returned to England and married (c1425) Owen Tudor, a Welsh squire. By him she was the mother of Edmund, earl of Richmond, who was the father of the first Tudor king, Henry VII. She is the heroine in one of the most beguiling of love scenes in all of Shakespeare: his *Henry V*.

Catholic Majesty. A title of the kings of Spain, assumed at times after the Council of Toledo, and permanently after the time of Ferdinand the Catholic (1474–1516).

Catholicon Anglicum (kạ-thol′i-kon ang′gli-kum). English-Latin dictionary, compiled c1483.

Cattanei (kät-tä-nā′ē), **Vannozza.** Mistress of Alexander VI; b. 1442; d. at Rome, November 26, 1518. Little is known of this Roman woman who, about 1466, attracted the attention of Cardinal Rodrigo Borgia (Alexander VI) and subsequently bore him four children: Cesare, Giovanni (Juan), Goffredo (Jofré), and Lucrezia. This is the order in which their names appeared in an inscription placed over her grave by the executor of her will. The inscription also noted that she was "conspicuous for her uprightness, her piety, her discretion, and her intelligence." Whatever her qualities, she held the respect, if not the love, of Alexander as long as he lived. He provided two of her three husbands and endowed her with property and money to the extent that in her last years she was able to contribute heavily to religious foundations for the salvation of her soul. She provided in her will for what was almost a state funeral, and it was attended by many of the notables of Rome, including the pope's chamberlain. A contemporary wrote, "She was buried yesterday in S. Maria del Popolo, with the greatest honors—almost like a cardinal. . . . She left all her property—which was not inconsiderable—to S. Giovanni in Laterano." The remains of the tombstone, once lost, are now in the Palazzo Venezia, Rome.

Cattaneo (kät-tä′nā-ō), **Danese.** Sculptor, architect, and poet; b. at Massa, 1509; d. at Padua, in January, 1573. He was a pupil in the school of Jacopo Sansovino at Rome, from which he fled at the time of the sack (1527) to Florence. He rejoined his master at Venice about 1530 and spent the rest of his life there. With other followers, he assisted Sansovino in the work of that master's buildings. As a sculptor, he carved (c1530) a strongly modeled *St. Jerome* for the base of the organ in S. Salvatore, of which Sansovino was the architect. His sculptural works followed the elegant, mannered 16th century Tuscan style; and in his portraits, which are among the better examples of his work as a sculptor, his tendency was to present an idealized portrait, as in the bust of Pietro Bembo (1547) in the basilica of St. Anthony at Padua. His two greatest works were of his last years: the commemorative altar in the Church of Sant' Anastasia at Verona, and the allegorical statues and marble reliefs on the funeral monument of Leonardo Loredano in the Church of SS. Giovanni and Paolo at Venice, which he completed with an assistant in 1572. Cattaneo was a friend of Vasari, to whom he seems to have supplied information on the Venetian painters for Vasari's *Vite*. He was also a poet much admired by such contemporaries as Aretino and Bernardo and Torquato Tasso. The manuscript of his epic poem, *Amor di Marfisa*, the first thirteen cantos of which were published in 1562, and two volumes of his literary works are in the Chigi Collection at Rome.

Cattani (kät-tä′nē), **Francesco.** See **Diacceto, Francesco di Zanobi Cattani da.**

Cauliac (kō-lyȧk), **Guy de.** See **Chauliac, Guy de.**

Cavalcanti (kä-väl-kän′tē), **Aldobrandino.** Florentine Dominican; b. c1217; d. at Florence, August 30, 1279. He entered the Dominican order in 1231, and served several times as prior. Named bishop of Orvieto (1272), he later gave up his see, returned to Florence, and there was instrumental in founding the great Dominican Church of Santa Maria Novella (1279). His tomb is in the right transept of the church.

Cavalcanti, Andrea di Lazzaro. [Called **Il Buggiano,** from his birthplace.] Sculptor; b. at Borgo a Buggiano, in Valdinievole, 1412; d. at Florence, 1462. He studied with Brunelleschi from his youth, and was adopted and made the heir of his master. He worked with Brunelleschi on the Sacristy of San Lorenzo, and either worked with him or finished works begun by him in the Duomo at Florence, where there is a bust by him of his master. Among his most important works is the pulpit of Santa Maria Novella, on which he carved the reliefs in the period 1443–1448. Buggiano imitated, but with imperfect understanding and artistry, Donatello's departure from the Gothic; his principal orientation was toward the Gothic style.

Cavalcanti, Bartolomeo. Humanist and diplomat; b. at Florence, January 14, 1503; d. at Padua, December 5, 1562. Exiled from Florence, he went to Ferrara and entered the service of the d'Este family. For them, as for the French at a later date, he ably carried out diplomatic missions. He wrote orations, a treatise on government, and a *Retorica*, one of the earliest in Italian on that subject.

Cavalcanti, Giovanni. Florentine historian, of whose life little is known. Imprisoned for not paying an enforced loan to the Commune of Florence, he occupied himself with writing a history, *Storia fiorentina*. The work begun in prison starts with the war against the Visconti (1423) and goes to 1440. After his release he continued his history. He was among the earlier historians who concerned themselves with internal developments as a cause of external policy, a method of presenting history adopted with brilliant success by Machiavelli. Cavalcanti was a partisan of the Medici and a member of the so-called Platonic Academy.

Cavalcanti, Guido. Florentine poet and philosopher; b. at Florence, c1259; d. there, August, 1300. He was a member of a prominent Guelph family of Florence, took an active part in civic affairs, and was the bitter enemy of the arrogant Corso Donati, leader of the Neri (Black Guelphs). A learned man, a poet with a deep philosophical bent to his art, he was outstanding in the circle of poets at Florence in his day and second only to Dante among 13th century Italian poets. In 1292 he went on a pilgrimage to St. James of Campostella, but for some reason halted at Toulouse and returned to Florence without continuing the pilgrimage. In 1300 he was one of those banished from his city in an effort to restore calm in the agitation between the Bianchi and the Neri. Dante, his close friend and admirer, was a member of the priorate by which he was exiled. In the same year his exile was revoked. He returned to Florence and died shortly after of a fever. Cavalcanti left about fifty poems: sonnets, ballate, and two canzoni. A few of his lyrics are marked by a simple joyousness, but he was not a simple man. He was concerned with the philosophical aspects of love, a love that for him meant a marriage of the ideal and the actual images, and many of his poems on the subject are complicated and analytical. Without the union of the ideal and the real images, love, as he saw it, dies. Many of his lyrics are addressed to his lady Giovanna, to whom he gave the name Primavera, "Spring." Others are addressed to his heart, whose secrets and sufferings he exposed, to his mind, and to personifications of spirits and images. His last poem, a ballata written while he was still in exile and when he felt death approaching, is addressed to the poem itself, charging it to carry his final message. His theme of love and the philosophy of love is explored with true feeling and thought, as opposed to the earlier poetry of conventional or courtly love. His sufferings and uncertainties give an air of melancholy to much of his work.

Cavalli (kä-väl′lē), **Gian Marco.** Goldsmith, sculptor, and medalist; b. near Mantua, before 1454; d. after 1506. He worked at first for Federigo I Gonzaga at Mantua, making pots, jars, and flasks modeled after the antique or to designs by Andrea Mantegna. He also made dies for the Mantuan mint. He is known to have made silver plates for Isabella d'Este, wife of Francesco II Gonzaga, and for Bishop Ludovico Gonzaga. Extant are two handsome medals surely from his hand: one of the Emperor Maximilian I, and the other of Bianca Maria. A bust of Mantegna on his tomb at Mantua and a bronze bust of the poet Spagnoli (now at Berlin) are attributed to him on stylistic grounds; but by some critics they are attributed to Melioli, among others. Most of Cavalli's life was passed in the service of the Gonzaga family, but occasionally he was too expensive even for them.

Cavalieri (kä-vä-lye′rē), **Emilio de'.** [Also, **del Cavaliere.**] Italian composer; b. at Rome c1550; d. there, March 11, 1602. He was a member of the group of Florentine musicians and poets who launched the new form of dramatic music at the end of the 16th century. His most important work was *La Rappresentazione di anima e di corpo*, the first oratorio. He was one of the first to use solo voices with instrumental accompaniment and the mode of notation called figured bass.

Cavallini (kä-väl-lē′nē), **Pietro.** Painter, mosaicist, and sculptor; b. 1250; d. at Rome, 1330. Little is known concerning this artist who flourished in the very dawn of the Renaissance. The mosaics in the apse of Santa Maria in Trastevere, Rome, executed in 1291, are credited to him, and it is known that he worked for Charles II at Naples in 1308. A number of frescoes in S. Maria di Donna Regina, at Naples, are attributed to him and his assistants. Ghiberti, who saw many of his works in Rome, noted that he united classical influences to his Byzantine tradition. He was the founder of a Roman school of painting and had many followers. There is a celebrated fresco by him, *The Last Judgment*, in the Church of Santa Cecilia in Trastevere, Rome. Cavallini is important in the history of Renaissance art for the influence he is thought to have had on Cimabue and Giotto, especially in the extent to which he departed from the Byzantine tradition and in his color.

Cavazzola (kä-vät-tsō′lä), **Paolo.** [Called **il Morando.**] Painter; b. at Verona, 1486; d. there, 1522. He was a pupil of Francesco Bonsignori and of Domenico Morone. The influence of his masters is apparent in the plasticity of his figures, his chiaroscuro, treatment of drapery, and rich metallic color. He came to surpass all his Veronese contemporaries in nobility of expression, freedom and animation of gesture, and harmonious fusing and balancing of tones. His earliest dated work, the *Cagnola Madonna* (1508), Gazzada, shows the influence of Bonsignori; and one thought to be earlier (c1506), in the museum at Verona, is reminiscent of Morone, whom he came to surpass. One of the most important works of the Veronese school is the polyptych he painted for the Church of S. Bernardino (1517) with its *Flagellation*, *Agony in the Garden*, *Way to Calvary*, and *Deposition*, now in the museum at Verona. His last dated work, *Madonna and Child in Glory* (1522), with figures of the cardinal and theological virtues and of saints, is also in the museum at Verona, and has, in the figures of the saints and virtues, a Raphaelesque grace which may have been passed to Cavazzola by Caroto, who also had some influence on him. Of his frescoes, an *Annunciation* (1510) is preserved in SS. Nazaro e Celso; and two archangels, *Michael* and *Raphael*, of his mature period, are in S. Maria in Organo, Verona. The fresco *Augustus and the Sibyl*, at 29 Via del Paradiso, Verona, is gradually disappearing. Cavazzola also left a few beautiful portraits, including *Portrait of a Gentleman* (Dresden), *Portrait of a Lady* (Cararra Academy, Bergamo), *Portrait of Giulia Trivulzio* (Milan), and *Gattamelata and His Page* or *Youthful Warrior and His Page* (Uffizi, Florence). Besides those mentioned, a number of paintings by Cavazzola are in the churches and museum at Verona and in surrounding towns. Other examples of his work are the signed and dated (1518) *Madonna and Child* (Poldi Pezzoli Museum, Milan), *S. Roch*, signed and dated (1518) and *Virgin and Child* (National Gallery, London), and *Virgin and Child in a Landscape* (Johnson Collection, Philadelphia). Other paintings are at Dresden, Frankfurt, Paris, Prague, Vienna, Chicago, and Bob Jones University (Greenville, South Carolina).

Cavendish (kav′ẹn-dish), **George.** English biographer and constant attendant of Cardinal Wolsey; b. 1500; d. c1561. He wrote *Life of Cardinal Wolsey*.

Caviceo (kä-vē′chā-ō), **Jacopo.** Priest, author, and adventurer; b. at Parma, May 1, 1443; d. at Montecchio, June 3, 1511. He was imprisoned for scandals connected to his name, escaped, and fled to Constantinople; but tiring of wandering, he returned to Parma. Next he put himself at the head of the malcontents in the clergy and was again forced to flee. He went to Rome, and there saved himself from the dagger of a would-be assassin by killing the ruffian. For his native city he went on a mission to Venice, and he held high Church posts at Rimini, Ferrara, Florence, and Siena. His best known work is a romance, in the style of Boccaccio's *Filocolo*, entitled *Il Peregrino*. It was written at Ferrara and dedicated to Lucrezia Borgia. The tale is concerned with the love of Peregrino for the beautiful Ginevra, and through a multitude of episodes recounts perilous adventures, clever tricks for escaping difficult situations, and sentimental encounters. It makes many references to living people and includes great dollops of flattery of some of them. Underneath the veil of allegory in its licentious episodes, it is supposed to contain a moral. The romance was enormously popular, went through twenty Italian editions, and was translated into French and Spanish. Because of the generally immoral tone and its wide acceptance, it was criticized by the Church in France and denounced from the pulpit.

Caxton (kaks'tọn), **William.** The first English printer; b. in Kent, c1422; d. at Westminster, London, 1491. He was first apprenticed to a London mercer, Robert Large (lord mayor of London in 1439–1440), and after his master's death (1441) went to Bruges, where he served out the remainder of his apprenticeship (1446), and then established himself as a mercer, becoming (c1465) governor of the English Association of Merchant Adventurers in that city. In 1469 he began a translation from French which he called *The Recuyell of the Historyes of Troye* (completed in 1471 at Cologne) and, to supply the great demand for copies of the book, set himself to learning the art of printing. *The Recuyell*, the first printed English book, appeared in 1475, having been printed probably at the press of Colard Mansion at Bruges. In 1475 he completed and had printed (perhaps by Mansion) a translation of a French version of the *Ludus scacchorum* of J. de Cessolis, under the title *The Game and Playe of the Chesse*. This was the second printed English book. He left Bruges in 1476 and set up his press at Westminster (the exact site is uncertain), from that time until his death being constantly engaged in translating and printing with several assistants, among whom was Wynkyn de Worde, his successor.

Cecchi (chāk'kē), **Giovanni Maria.** Playwright; b. at Florence, March 15, 1518; d. at Gangalandi, October 28, 1587. He was a man of good will, who took life as he found it. In his youth he had witnessed the siege of his beloved city (1530) in which his father was killed, the fall of the republic, and the return of Cosimo I de' Medici as grand duke and master of Florence. These events appear fleetingly in his comedies. He was a notary by profession, and several times held high office in his state. Cecchi's literary output included a collection of Florentine mottoes, proverbs, adages, and expressions, compiled in 1557; a descriptive book on Flanders, Spain, and Naples; and collections of poetry. He is remembered primarily as the earliest thoroughly Italian playwright. Of his more than fifty comedies, dramas, farces, and scenic interludes, many of the comedies follow Latin models. Others are in his own manner, as his *Assiuolo*, which was derived from neither Plautus nor Terence but from an incident, as he says, that took place at Pisa. This is his masterpiece and, though it has echoes of Boccaccio and even of Machiavelli, is marked by his own style. Even the comedies modeled after Plautus and Terence are salted with Cecchi's observations on the life of his day, and thus provide an important source for the manners and mores of his time. In his spiritual dramas, to which he turned toward the latter part of his life, he succeeded in fusing the sacred and profane with true originality, and achieved the mystery of the earlier *sacre rappresentazioni* by an ingenious blending of the miraculous with a keen observation of natural phenomena.

Cecchino da Verona (chek-kē'no dä vā-rō'nä). Painter; active 1447–1480. He was one of the last of the painters of the Veronese school who shows a marked influence of Stefano da Verona. A *Virgin Between Saints* is at Trent.

Cecco d'Ascoli (chāk'kō däs'kō-lē). [Nickname of **Francesco degli Stabili.**] Astrologer, mathematician, and poet; b. at Ascoli, c1257; burned at the stake, 1327. While teaching astrology and mathematics at the University of Bologna and elsewhere, he also wrote poetry, and his chief achievement in this art proved his undoing. In the ambitiously comprehensive poetic allegory entitled *L'Acerba*, the severity of his criticism of Dante's *Divina Commedia* led to charges of heresy. He was convicted and burned at the stake.

Cecco di Pietro (dē pye'trō). Pisan painter; d. before 1402. Among his works in the

Museo Nazionale at Pisa are a *Crucifixion*, 1386, and a *Madonna Enthroned with Child*. Other paintings are at Copenhagen, Portland, Oregon, and elsewhere.

Cecil (ses′il, sis′il), **William.** [Title, 1st Baron **Burghley** (or **Burleigh**).] English statesman; b. at Bourn, Lincolnshire, England, September 13, 1520; d. at London, August 4, 1598. He occupied a position of great power in the government of Elizabeth of England.

Cei (chā), **Francesco.** Poet; b. at Florence, 1471; d. 1505. He was known in his own day for his facile improvisations. His sonnets, canzoni, and *strambotti* celebrate his love for a Florentine lady, in some instances, and concern politics in others; in three of his sonnets he attacks Savonarola. Generally speaking, his lyrics are of slight poetic merit.

Celestine V (sel′ẹs-tīn, sẹ-les′tin, -tīn), Saint. [Also, **Coelestine;** original name **Pietro di Murrhone.**] Pope (July–December, 1294); b. at Isernia, c1215; d. at the castle Fumone, in the Campagna, May 19, 1296. A Benedictine who lived an ascetic life, he gathered about him a group of like-minded monks who afterward (c1254) became the order of Celestines. He was living as a hermit in the mountains when, after the papacy had been vacant for two years because of the struggle between the Orsini and Colonna, at the age of about 80 he was elected to succeed Nicholas IV. He was completely unfit for the burdens of the papacy by reason of his ascetic and visionary attitudes and life, to say nothing of his age. He had probably been chosen because of his age and the certainty that the opportunity to agree on and elect a new pope would soon arise. Charles II of Naples won complete influence over him and, for a time, directed the Church government. Bewildered by the intricacies of his office and, perhaps, persuaded by Boniface VIII who became his successor, Celestine abdicated. Dante, without compassion, refers to him in the *Divina Commedia* as he "who cravenly the great refusal made" (*Inferno*, iii). Celestine was kept in custody at Fumone by Boniface VIII. The latter feared that, because of his great popularity among the masses, if Celestine were left at liberty he might become the occasion of schism. Celestine was canonized in 1313 by Pope Clement V.

Celle (chel′lā), **Giovanni dalle.** See **Giovanni dalle Celle.**

Cellini (chel-lē′nē), **Benvenuto.** Sculptor, goldsmith, and silversmith; b. at Florence, November 1, 1500; d. there, February 14, 1571. When he was 58 years old he decided to dictate his autobiography, on the ground that "all men who have done anything of excellence, . . . ought, if they are men of truth and honesty, to describe their life with their own hand; . . ." There was no question in his mind that he had done things of excellence. The autobiography he began by dictating and finished in his own hand is vibrant and compelling, the swift record of a bold, gifted, and energetic man. Untroubled by self-doubt, Cellini paints a frank and sincere, if often boastful, self-portrait. He also gives a living picture of the turbulent life of the 16th century. His autobiography portrays, as perhaps no other, the utter dependence of the artist on the whims and taste of a patron, and the vicious rivalry between artists for the patron's favor. It is Cellini's autobiography, even more than his work as sculptor and goldsmith, that stands today as his monument. It is also a monument to his age. Much of the information in it is corroborated by contemporary accounts. Michelangelo, Raphael, Giulio Romano, Popes Leo X, Clement VII, and Paul III, Francis I and Cosimo I de' Medici, Pietro Bembo, Annibale Caro, Luigi Alamanni and other writers, the physician Guido Guidi, and many others whose names have come down to us, pass through his pages.

Benvenuto's father, a musician, wanted his son to be a musician. The youth dutifully took lessons and practiced the cornetto. (His musical skill later won him a place as one of Pope Clement VII's musicians.) But his heart was not in it. He was fascinated by the arts of design. He studied with Michelangelo Bandinelli, father of the sculptor Bandinelli (a rival of whom he had the lowest opinion), and with the goldsmith Marcone. At the age of 16 he left home in a fit of pique at his father and went to Pisa. He quickly found work there (he never had any trouble finding work) and remained a year. In 1517 he returned to Florence. He met the sculptor Torrigiani and was invited to go to England with him, to work on the tomb of Henry VII for Henry VIII. Cellini, always attracted by the thought of seeing new places, was on the point of accepting when Torrigiani mentioned Michelangelo, and the fact that in an argument he had broken Michelangelo's nose. Michelangelo was Cellini's hero. On hearing of this incident he gnashed his teeth and declined Torrigiani's invitation. In 1519 he left Florence because of a brawl in which he was involved and went to Rome, but returned to Florence in 1521. In 1523 he was again at Rome. There, occupied with his work as a goldsmith, he was under the patronage of Pope Clement VII and later of Pope Paul III, as well as a number of cardinals. At Rome he became a member of "a club of painters, sculptors, and goldsmiths, the best that were in Rome." His accounts of the merry supper parties and other festivities of the club give a vivid picture of the Bohemian life of the time. He also tells of studying Roman antiquities, of buying antique gems and vessels that were found by peasants, and of raising spirits in the Colosseum at night with a necromancer.

In May, 1527, occurred the siege and sack of Rome by the German troops of the renegade Frenchman, the Constable de Bourbon. Cellini writes that he and three companions went out to reconnoiter as the troops were attempting to scale the walls of the city. They stood on the ramparts and watched the enemy through the fog, knowing that it was only a matter of hours until the foreign troops would enter the city. Before they withdrew, Cellini says he decided he "must perform some worthy action." They saw a group of soldiers, took aim with their arquebuses, and fired two rounds each. Cellini aimed at one he saw who was higher than the rest, perhaps because he was on horseback, but Cellini could not be sure because of the fog. When they had fired they cautiously peered over the wall and saw a scene of indescribable confusion. They learned afterward that they had killed the Constable de Bourbon himself. (Historians agree that the constable was killed at the walls of Rome near the place that Cellini describes. Whether, as he claims, it was Cellini's own shot that killed him is impossible to say.) On leaving the ramparts and reentering the city, Cellini was claimed as a member of the pope's household and pressed into service in the defense of Castel Sant' Angelo, whither the pope and his retinue had taken refuge. He served as a bombardier and thoroughly enjoyed it; according to his own account, if it hadn't been for him the fortress would have been taken in the first hours because of the confusion, uncertainty, fear, and inefficiency of the defenders. The pope was under siege for a month. In that time Cellini asserts that he wounded the prince of Orange and almost, by accident, killed Cardinal Farnese (later Pope Paul III), who was inside the fortress. He wished he had. In October, 1538, at the instigation of Pier Luigi Farnese, illegitimate son of Pope Paul III, he was imprisoned in Castel Sant' Angelo. The charge was that during the siege of May, 1527, he had, at the pope's request, dismounted the jewels of Clement's tiara and other jewels of the papal collection, sewed them into the pope's robes, and melted down the gold. He was accused of withholding some of the jewels for himself. It was a false charge, as he was able to prove by the papal records, but he was kept in prison. The account of the madness of his jailer, who thought he was a bat and could fly, and of his escape, after many months, from Castel Sant' Angelo forms one of the most sensational sections in his sensational autobiography. In the course of his escape he broke his leg, was seized in the house to which he had crawled for asylum, and was again imprisoned at the pope's order, but this time in the Torre di Nona, one of the most notorious criminal prisons in Rome. He was finally released (after a plot to kill him had failed) through the agency of the king of France, who wanted Cellini to come to France and work for him. From then (1540) until 1545 he lived in France at the court of Francis I. He had his atelier in the Petit Nesle. In France, as in Italy, he was beset by jealous rivals, enmity, and attempts on his life. It was in France that he first turned to sculpture, and with immediate success. He writes admiringly of Francis I as a patron and man of taste, and of "the great things I wrought for him." Francis gave him a specific commission of twelve figures, as tall as the king himself, but in general Cellini executed his own ideas and then won the king's interest in them. This caused some conflict, as Francis was not accustomed to having his wishes and orders disregarded. However, Cellini was a man after the king's own heart, in daring, inventiveness, and taste. All would have been well if Cellini could have won the favor of the king's mistress, Mme. d'Estampes. But, for one reason and another, she was his enemy and he came to hate her. The records of the conversations with the king show on what easy terms he was with his patron, indicate his own independence, the value he set on himself as an artist, and the complete absence of any awe in the face of royalty—but there was not much that overawed Cellini.

In 1545 he left France for a journey into Italy, planning to return. He never did return and often bitterly regretted it. After his arrival in Florence he served Cosimo I and the Medici family until his death. The relationship was not an easy one, but none of Cellini's was, partly because of the dependence of the artist upon the generosity of his patron and partly because of the independence of the artist: he could not bring himself to truckle, refused to suffer in silence, and yielded to none when it came to matters of his art. It was for Cosimo that he made his famous bronze of *Perseus with the Head of Medusa,* now in the Loggia dei Lanzi and a sight well known to every tourist to Florence. The record in the autobiography of the modeling, and especially of the casting, of the statue is a cliffhanger in the best Cellini manner. He says that when it was shown to the public (April 27, 1554), "a shout of boundless enthusiasm went up in commendation of my work," and tells that dozens of sonnets in praise of it were nailed up. Cosimo was pleased to see his judgment vindicated by the alert and knowledgable Florentine public, but paying for it was another matter.

Cellini's autobiography, on which he was still at work in 1566, covers the period to 1562, when it abruptly stops. He continued to work for the Medici, but much time in his last years was occupied by quarrels and litigation. He was a man of boldness, violence, enormous vitality, and great gifts. In the course of his life he suffered severe illness, from disease, privation in prison, and wounds, but his robust constitution pulled him through. He describes himself as "being by nature somewhat choleric." The autobiography cites a number of instances when he killed someone who had offended his sensitive pride and had to hide or flee or was banished as a result. And as a man who "did not know the color of fear," he never refused a challenge. He married late in life and, after having fathered six illegitimate children, became the father of two legitimate ones. As a goldsmith and silversmith he made medals, vases, dies for the mint, candlesticks, ornaments of all kinds, and set jewels. He describes them, most of which have been lost, in his autobiography. His work is characterized by intricacy of ornamentation, bizarre imaginativeness, movement, and great skill. The outstanding extant example of his work in this art is the saltcellar he made for Francis I, now in the Kunsthistorisches Museum at Vienna. It is oval-shaped, over ten inches high, has a reclining nude male figure at one end and a reclining nude female figure at the other. These represent land and sea. They seem to be reclining more or less at the edge of the sea. A boat is intended to hold the salt, a small temple the pepper. The sea is filled with monsters of Cellini's imagination. The ornamental base is filled with intricately composed figures and animals. Extant works in sculpture, in addition to the *Perseus* cited above, are a bust of *Cosimo I de' Medici,* an antique *Ganymede* that he restored, *Narcissus,* and *Apollo and Hyacinth,* all in the Bargello (Museo Nazionale) at Florence; *The Nymph of Fontainebleau,* in the Louvre at Paris (one of the works Francis I did not commission but by which he was enchanted when it was completed); a white marble Christ on a black crucifix, in the Escorial at Madrid; and a bust of *Bindo Altoviti,* in the Isabella Stewart Gardner Museum at Boston. The conception and execution of most of these are described in the autobiography. This autobiography, one of the most famous of Italian classics, circulated in manuscript until it was printed in 1730. It was translated into German by Goethe. The standard English translation is by John Addington Symonds, from whose translation the above quotations have been taken.

Celtes (tsel′tẹs), **Conrad.** [Original name, **Konrad Pickel.**] German poet and scholar; b. at Wipfeld, Germany, February 1, 1459; d. at Vienna, February 4, 1508. He was an outstanding humanist and was diligent in spreading the new knowledge in his time. After the manner of wandering scholars he studied at many universities and taught at Erfurt, Rostock, Leipzig, and Vienna. Wherever he went he waged everlasting battle for humanism. He founded learned societies (*Sodalitates*) to this end, and was himself made head of the *Collegium poetarum* at Vienna by the emperor Maximilian I (1502). He wrote a poetic treatise on the art of versifying, *Ars versificandi et carminum* (1486);

and his own poems (like all of his writings, in Latin) were considered the best of the time. He was crowned poet laureate by Frederick III, the first German ever to be thus honored. He gained lasting fame by discovering and publishing (1501) the writings of Hroswitha of Gandersheim (German Benedictine nun and poet, c935–c1000).

Cene (chā′nā), **Le.** A collection of twenty-two tales by Anton Francesco Grazzini.

Cennini (chen-nē′nē), **Bernardo.** Florentine goldsmith and typographer; b. January 2, 1415; d. c1498. He first won renown as a goldsmith, and worked (1448 and 1451) with Ghiberti on the Doors of Paradise for the Baptistery at Florence. (His specific part in the creation of the doors cannot be identified.) A panel from a reredos, originally in the baptistery, of the *Annunciation of the Angel to Zachariah* and the *Visitation*, is in the Museo dell' Opera del Duomo, Florence. Cennini's great contribution, however, was in the new field of printing. He had the first printing press at Florence, and printed the commentary of Servius on Vergil's *Bucolics*, 1471, and he was the first Italian to cast his own type.

Cennini, Cennino. [Full name, **Cennino di Drea Cennini.**] Painter and writer on art; b. at Colle Val d'Elsa, c1365; d. c1440. Little is known of his painting, which has been lost or is now unidentifiable. According to his own statement, for twelve years, which was the normal period of apprenticeship, he was a pupil of Agnolo Gaddi, whose father, Taddeo Gaddi, had been the godson and pupil of Giotto. Thus Cennini considered himself a disciple of Giotto. In 1398 he is known to have been a painter for the Carrara family at Padua. He is notable for his valuable book, *Libro dell' Arte*, a comprehensive manual on the techniques of painting, the first such manual by an Italian and in Italian. It was written, perhaps at Padua, early in the 15th century. In his book Cennini describes in detail the methods of painting in fresco, tempera, size, and gum. He tells how to paint in miniature and how to apply gold to all the different kinds of painting. In his discussion of pigments he gives explicit directions for grinding them, advises the artist which ones to make himself and which ones to buy at the apothecary's, which ones to use for fresco and which to use for tempera, tells the artist how to make paper and charcoal crayons, and also lectures him lightly on his work habits and his approach to his work. The book is rich in the art terminology and methods of the 14th century, uses a charming system of measurements—"the size of a lentil," "a third the size of a bean," "as much as can be held on the point of a penknife"—and gives some notion of Cennini himself. In preparing to acquaint the reader with the proportions of a man, he says, "I omit those of a woman, because there is not one of them perfectly proportioned."

Cent Nouvelles Nouvelles (sän nö-vel nö-vel), **Les.** [English translation, "*One Hundred New Tales.*"] Collection of medieval French tales, first printed in folio, without date, from a manuscript of the year 1456. Authorship is attributed to Antoine de la Salle. The *Cent Nouvelles Nouvelles*, although in prose, bear much resemblance to the metrical, comic, or satiric medieval writings called fabliaux. Many of them are taken from the work of the Italian writers, but all of them are reworked in an original manner.

Cento novelle antiche (chen′tō nō-vel′lā än-tē′kā). [English translation, "*One Hundred Old Tales.*"] Collection of tales and anecdotes from ancient and medieval history, from Oriental and Greek mythology and legend, from the Bible, and from the popular tales of Italy, Provence, and Brittany, compiled in Italy about the end of the 13th century.

Cepeda (thā-pā′ᴛʜä), **Diego.** Spanish judge; b. at Tordesillas, Spain, c1495; d. at Valladolid, Spain, c1549. He accompanied the viceroy Blasco Nuñez Vela to Peru, and there led the judges opposing him. He joined Gonzalo Pizzaro in the battle in which the viceroy was killed (January 18, 1546) but later deserted him on the battlefield of Sacsahuaman (1548). He was sent to be tried in Spain, and, it is said, poisoned himself in prison.

Cerniti (cher-nē′tē), **Pietro dei.** See **Pietro dei Cerniti.**

Cervantes Saavedra (sėr-van′tēz; Spanish, ther-ʙän′tās sä-ä-ʙä′ᴛʜrä), **Miguel de.** Spanish novelist, poet, and dramatist; b. at Alcalá de Henares, Spain, possibly on October 9, 1547; d. at Madrid, April 23, 1616. He was of a good but impoverished family. Except that for a time he went to school at Madrid, where he published some verses (1568), nothing is known of his youth or education.

He went to Rome (1569) as chamberlain of Cardinal Acquaviva, then enlisted as a common soldier and for the next five years served in the Spanish army, based in Italy. In the naval battle of Lepanto (1571) he received the "beautiful" wounds that left his left arm and hand crippled and useless. En route home in 1575 he was captured by pirates and held at Algiers for five years, where his tireless bravery, his attempts to escape, and his help in assisting others to escape are well documented. He was released at last on payment of a ransom by his family. After a brief turn with the army in Portugal he settled down to writing; but a number of plays brought neither fame nor wealth, nor did the pastoral *La Galatea* (1585). In 1584 he married a farmer's daughter. They had no children, but his household for long included two sisters, an illegitimate daughter, and a niece. A position as a government collector, first of grain and then of taxes, took him to Seville in 1587. His work yielded valuable knowledge of Andalusians, respectable and criminal, but his bad bookkeeping put him in jail at least twice. For a while he sojourned at Valladolid, then ended his days at Madrid (1608–1616), "old, a soldier and gentleman, but poor." He had a considerable acquaintance among the writers of his day but no great reputation. The popular success of the first part of *Don Quixote* (Madrid, 1605) was a great surprise to his publisher, and probably to Cervantes. However, he dallied over the second part, first publishing the *Novelas Exemplares* (*Twelve Instructive or Moral Tales*, 1613) and the long poem *Viaje del Parnaso* (*Journey to Parnassus*, 1614). Aroused by the appearance of the spurious sequel to *Don Quixote* in 1614, he hurried his own second part to completion in 1615. In the same year he brought out his *Ocho Comedias* (*Eight Comedies*). He died of dropsy on April 23, 1616, and was buried, no one knows where, by the Franciscans, of whose Tertiary Order he was a member. *Persiles y Sigismunda*, a long prose romance, appeared posthumously in 1617. Though the beautiful dedication to this work was written only four days before his death, the book may well be largely early work. To the end of his life he was full of plans for other writings. Considering his age, illness, and financial worries, the productivity of his declining years is phenomenal.

Cesalpino (chā-zäl-pē′nō), **Andrea.** See **Caesalpinus, Andreas.**

Cesare da Sesto (chā′sä-rā dä ses′tō). Lombard painter; b. at Sesto Calende, 1477; d. at Milan, July 27, 1523. Little is known of his life. He worked some time at Rome, probably after 1510, at Naples and Messina, but most of his career was passed at Milan. He was an eclectic who achieved his style by borrowings from Leonardo da Vinci and Flemish painting and, in his later years, by adaptations from Raphael and Michelangelo. Among his works are *Adoration of the Magi*, painted at Messina and now at Naples, *St. Jerome* (Brera), and *Madonna and Child* (Poldi Pezzoli Museum, Milan). He left a number of drawings on the basis of which other paintings are attributed to him.

Cesarini (chā-zä-rē′nē), **Giuliano.** Cardinal, diplomat, and humanist; b. at Rome, 1398; d. at Varna, Bulgaria, November, 1444. Of a poor family, when he was a student at Perugia he collected candle ends to provide light for his nighttime studying. He became a professor of canon law at the University of Padua, where he numbered Domenico Capranica and Nicholas of Cusa among his pupils. Martin V elevated him to the cardinalate in 1430, and named him president of the Council called to meet at Basel in 1431. Martin died before the Council opened and Eugenius IV, his successor, sent Cardinal Cesarini to the Council. Eugenius dissolved the Council, distrusting its motives and scornful of the attendance it had drawn; but Cesarini, believing this put Eugenius in an unfavorable position, persuaded him to retract the bull of dissolution and reconcile himself with the Council. However, when the Council later openly attacked Eugenius and he withdrew to Ferrara and then to Florence, Cesarini left the Council and supported the pope. He went to Hungary (1443) as papal envoy, and took part in the battle of Varna (November 10, 1444), where a crusading army met with disaster at the hands of the Turks. The cardinal was killed as he fled after the battle. In addition to being an outstanding ecclesiastic, diplomat and man of action, Cardinal Cesarini was among those who gave enthusiastic support to humanistic studies.

Céspedes (thās′pā-ᴛʜās), **Pablo de.** Spanish painter; b. at Córdoba, Spain, 1538; d. there July 26, 1608. He was also a poet, sculptor, and architect. He was author of *Arte de la* *pintura*, a poem. His painting *Last Supper* is in the Córdoba Cathedral.

Chalcondylas (kal-kon′di-lạs), **Demetrius.** Greek grammarian and teacher; b. at Athens, 1424; d. at Milan, 1511. He left Greece in 1447 and went to Rome. From there he went to Perugia, where he taught Greek from 1450 until 1463. He also taught at Padua, went to Florence (1472) at the invitation of Lorenzo de' Medici, and then to Milan (1492), where he remained until his death. He became famous as a teacher and numbered among his pupils Poliziano, the German scholar Reuchlin, William Grocyn who became the first teacher of Greek at Oxford, and Thomas Linacre, a pioneer of humanistic studies in England. He wrote a Greek grammar, *Erotemata* (c1493), and edited the works of Homer (1488), Euripides (1493), Isocrates (1493), and Suidas (1499).

Chalcondylas, Laonicus (or **Nicolas**). Byzantine historian; b. at Athens; d. c1464. He was ambassador of John VIII Palaeologus to the sultan Murad II of Turkey during the siege of Constantinople in 1446. He wrote a history of the Byzantine Empire from c1297 to c1462.

Chaloner (chal′ọ-nėr), Sir **Thomas.** English statesman and writer; b. at London, 1521; d. there, October 14, 1565. He translated into English the homilies of Saint John Chrysostom (1544), Erasmus' *Praise of Folie* (1549), and others.

Chanca (chäng′kä), **Diego Álvarez.** Spanish physician; fl. in the late 15th century. A native of Seville, he accompanied Columbus on his second voyage (1493), and wrote an account of what he saw. His account is one of the main historical authorities for the voyage.

Chancellor (chân′sẹ-lọr), **Richard.** English navigator; d. November 10, 1556. A narrative of his first visit to Moscow, written by Clement Adams and published in Hakluyt's *Navigations*, is the first considerable account of the Russian people in the English language.

Chandos (chan′dos, shan′-), Sir **John.** English soldier; d. at Mortemer, France, January 1, 1370. He served in the siege of Cambrai and in the battles of Crécy, Poitiers, and others.

Charles (of *Anjou*). See **Charles I** and **Charles II** (of *Naples*) and **Charles II** (of *Durazzo*).

Charles (of *Burgundy*). [Called **le Téméraire; the Bold.**] Duke of Burgundy (1467–1477); b. at Dijon, November 10, 1433; killed at Nancy, Lorraine, January 5, 1477. He was the son of Philip the Good, who turned over the government of the duchy to him in 1465. He married Margaret, sister of Edward IV of England. An opponent of Louis XI of France, he joined in defeating him. He conquered Lorraine in 1475, but was defeated by the Swiss at Grandson (March, 1476), at Morat (June, 1476), and finally at Nancy (January, 1477). Two years after his death Burgundy was incorporated in France.

Charles II (of *Durazzo*). King of Naples (as Charles III), king of Hungary (as Charles II), and count of Anjou; b. 1345; d. at Buda, Hungary, 1386. Instigated by Pope Urban VI, he attacked Joanna I, queen of Naples, whom he put to death at Aversa, and whose throne he usurped and ascended in 1382. He had been adopted by her much earlier, but she later repudiated him for Louis I of Anjou. Charles defended his throne against attacks (1382–1384) from Louis. He was chosen (1385) king of Hungary, but was killed at Buda in the following year. His son Ladislaus succeeded him on the throne of Naples.

Charles IV (of *France*). [Called **Charles le Bel; Charles the Fair.**] King of France (1322–1328); b. 1294; d. at Vincennes, near Paris, 1328. He was the youngest son of Philip IV, brother of Louis X and Philip V (whom he succeeded), and (as Charles I of Navarre) the last of the Capetian line. His sister Isabella was married to Edward II of England, with whom Charles was at war over the duchy of Guienne. Isabella having been sent to France to negotiate the question, he aided her in planning the dethronement of Edward. Charles increased the power of the king and, by a policy of taxation, duties, and debasing the coinage, enriched the royal treasury. He left only a daughter. The Salic law (barring women from the succession) was invoked, and Charles was succeeded by his cousin Philip VI.

Charles V (of *France*). [Called **Charles le Sage; Charles the Wise.**] King of France (1364–1380); b. at Vincennes, near Paris, January 21, 1337; d. there, September 16, 1380. He was the son and successor of John II. He was lieutenant general or regent of France (1356–1360) during the captivity of his father in England. In this time he faced the revolt (1358) of the Jacquerie, a French peasant group who were unsuccessful in their uprising. During his reign Charles, aided by Bertrand du Guesclin, made war against the free companies (bands of armed adventurers), which he managed to suppress, and against the English. In his wars against England, France recovered all the territory that had been won by Edward III of England except Calais and Bordeaux. He was a patron of learning, and founded the Royal Library, built the Bastille, and added to the ornamentation of the Louvre, the royal palace. He was succeeded by his son Charles VI.

Charles VI (of *France*). [Called **Charles le Bien-Aimé; Charles the Well-Beloved.**] King of France (1380–1422); b. at Paris, December 3, 1368; d. there, October 21, 1422. He was the son of Charles V. Being a minor at his accession, he was placed under a regency conducted by his uncles, the dukes of Anjou, Burgundy, and Berry. He defeated the Flemings under Philip van Artevelde at Rosebecque, on November 27, 1382. In 1388 he assumed the government, but becoming subject to fits of insanity in 1392, he retired from active government. A struggle for power arose between the duke of Burgundy and the duke of Orléans, the king's brother, whom Charles had chosen to advise him. The duke of Burgundy gained the ascendancy, but died in 1404. His son Jean procured the murder of the duke of Orléans (1407), which provoked civil war, the so-called war of the Burgundians and Armagnacs. Henry V of England invaded the country and, on October 25, 1415, defeated the French at Agincourt. Supported by Queen Isabella, Charles' wife, the Burgundians concluded at Troyes a treaty (May 21, 1420) with Henry V, according to which he was to be king of France on the death of Charles. Henry V died within a few months of Charles, and his heir, Henry VI, was unable to make good the claim. Charles VI was succeeded by his son Charles VII.

Charles VII (of *France*). [Called **Charles the Victorious.**] King of France (1422–1461); b. at Paris, February 22, 1403; d. at Mehun-sur-Yèvre, near Bourges, France, July 22, 1461. The son of Charles VI of France, at his accession he found a rival in Henry VI of England, who claimed the French throne by virtue of the Treaty of Troyes (1420), which had promised Henry V of England the French throne on the death of Charles VI of France. Charles' actual power at the time he ascended the throne was limited by the fact that the English were masters of the country north of the Loire River, including the capital, and in 1429 besieged Orléans. Of an indecisive character, Charles was strongly propelled in the direction of winning his kingdom by purposeful advisers, but it was not until 1429, with the help of Joan of Arc who liberated Orléans, that Charles began to win France back from the English. He was crowned at Reims in 1429, and entered Paris in 1437. He effected a reconciliation between the Armagnac and Burgundian factions, and regained all of France except Calais from the English. Thereafter he ruled a relatively peaceful and prosperous country, influenced in many of his decisions by his mistress, Agnès Sorel. In 1438, with the Pragmatic Sanction of Bourges, he took the dramatic step of recognizing the rights of the Gallican Church and severely limited papal power in France. Pius II, who regarded him as an enemy for his support of the Angevins in Naples and for the Pragmatic Sanction, wrote that at the end of his life Charles was in mortal fear of being poisoned, and would eat hardly anything.

Charles VIII (of *France*). King of France (1483–1498); b. at Amboise, France, June 30, 1470; d. there, April 7, 1498. He was the unattractive son of Louis XI of France, and reigned, from 1483 to 1491, under his sister Anne of Beaujeu's regency. In 1491 he married Anne of Britanny. Urged on by his advisers, who thought to advance their own cause, and, as Sismondi wrote (*A History of the Italian Republics*), "Eager for glory, in proportion as his weak frame, and still weaker intellect, incapacitated him for acquiring it," he decided to invade Italy, intending from there to go on and conquer the Turks. His justification was that the rights of the Angevins to the kingdom of Naples had been acquired by his father, Louis XI. His intention to claim his so-called inheritance was furthered by Ludovico il Moro, regent of Milan. Ludovico feared demands by the kingdom of Naples that he give up his regency and permit the accession of the lawful duke, his nephew Gian Galeazzo, whose wife was the daughter of the heir to the throne of Naples. As Charles, with a highly trained and skilled army, moved into Italy, Ludovico and rulers of other north Italian states opened their gates to him. Piero de' Medici, at that time virtual ruler of Florence, betrayed his city and his trust, and freely gave up fortified places to the French. On Piero's return to Florence after this submission to Charles, he was compelled to flee by his angry compatriots. Charles entered Florence as if he were a conqueror. Piero Capponi, to whom Charles' secretary read the French sovereign's ultimatum to the Florentines, snatched the paper from the secretary's hands and tore it to shreds. Charles threatened, "We shall sound our trumpets." "And we shall ring our bells," retorted Capponi. Charles hesitated at the prospect of fighting in the narrow streets of Florence. He accepted a subsidy and went on his way, proceeding without hindrance to Rome, which, as the pope shut himself up in Castel Sant' Angelo, he entered at the end of November, 1494. On the frontiers of the kingdom of Naples he took two towns and massacred the inhabitants. Alfonso II, king of Naples, was terrified by this kind of warfare. He abdicated in favor of his son Ferdinand II. The latter was forced to flee in February, 1495, and Charles entered Naples. The ease of his march through Italy and his conquest of Naples at last aroused fear in the other states of Italy, and they formed a league against him. He left the duke of Montpensier with a strong force at Naples and returned to France with the remainder of his army, defeating on the way the numerically superior allies at Fornovo di Taro, on July 6, 1495. Guicciardini, in his *History of Italy*, describes Charles as physically weak and unhealthy from boyhood, small in stature, and ugly except for his bright glance, with such badly proportioned limbs that he appeared more a monster than a man. He writes that Charles not only knew nothing of the arts but barely knew how to read and write. He wanted power but was always influenced and swayed by his base favorites, was lazy, imprudent, and impulsive. Anything about him that appeared praiseworthy turned out to be, on closer inspection, less of a virtue than a weaker vice. Other contemporary descriptions of his character, intellect, and capacity are similar to Guicciardini's portrait. Yet Charles swept through Italy like a tornado, provoking a revolution in the policy of Italy and leaving it a helpless and tormented prey to the ambitions of the French and the Spanish crowns. The struggles between these two nations for domination in Italy ended at last in the victory of the Spanish. The success of Charles, however, had been less a demonstration of the admitted power and skill of his armies than of the condition of a peninsula divided and weakened by continual internal strife. The opportunistic politics of the Italian heads of state and their dynastic ambitions made the requisite unity as remote as the stars.

Charles IV (of the *Holy Roman Empire*). [Called **Charles of Luxembourg.**] King of Bohemia, Holy Roman emperor (1374–1378); b. at Prague, May 14, 1316; d. there, November 29, 1378. He was the son of John, count of Luxembourg, was educated at the court of Charles IV of France, returned to Bohemia and, at the age of 15, went to Italy as his father's deputy. From that time, he was embroiled in dynastic affairs; he governed Bohemia jointly with his father until a disagreement broke out between them, intervened in the Tyrol, was reconciled with his father and named his heir (1340), and fought with the French against the English at Crécy. In that battle (1346) he was wounded and his father was killed. Charles ascended the Bohemian throne and was crowned king of the Germans at Bonn (1346). He received the Bohemian crown at Prague (1347). After the elimination of various rivals, he was crowned emperor (1349). He had been several times in Italy and had considered an attempt to reestablish imperial power there. Petrarch wrote him (1351) urging him to come to Italy and restore order. Cola di Rienzi, briefly tribune of Rome, also invoked his aid. In 1354 he crossed the Alps with a small suite and went to Milan. Petrarch met him there and was disillusioned with Charles as a representative of imperial dignity. He later wrote an invective against him, but also served on missions to him at Basel and Prague, without much result. Charles found that Italy was by no means welcoming. He received the Iron Crown of Lombardy at Milan in January, 1355, and went to Rome to receive the imperial crown in April, 1355. Having received it, he immediately left the city, as he had promised the pope he would do. On his way north again he found increasing hostility, and in less than a month he hurriedly recrossed the Alps. In 1356 he published the Golden Bull, an electoral code for the empire with which he hoped to eliminate such complications as had been attendant on his own election. Charles married Blanche of Valois and sought by this and his other two marriages, by purchase, and by his adroitness at taking advantage of the quarrels among his rivals to enhance the power of Bohemia. He twice went to France: once (1365) to Avignon to discuss the return of the popes to Rome, and the second time (1369) to Paris to argue against it. While in France he took the opportunity to have himself declared king of Burgundy (1365). In 1368 he made another trip to Italy which proved inconclusive. (His entries into Italy served to disenchant poets, chroniclers, and the literati with the figure of the Holy Roman emperor, and Petrarch's reaction became generalized.) He spent the last years of his life ensuring the succession for his son Wenceslaus. Charles was the founder of the University of Prague (1348), and did much to promote the welfare of Bohemia. Under him the kingdom enjoyed great prosperity, and he has been called the father of Bohemia. He was succeeded as king of Bohemia by his son Wenceslaus IV.

Charles V (of the *Holy Roman Empire*). Emperor of the Holy Roman Empire and king (as Charles I) of Spain; b. at Ghent, Flanders, February 24, 1500; d. at Yuste, near Placiencia, Estremadura, Spain, September 21, 1558. He was the son of Philip, duke of Burgundy (later Philip I of Spain) and Joanna or Juana (Joanna the Mad), daughter of Ferdinand and Isabella of Spain, and the grandson of the emperor Maximilian I and Mary of Burgundy. Charles was under the early and emphatic influence of his aunt Margaret of Austria, who acted as regent for him in the Low Countries when he was a boy. Before he ascended the throne he appeared to be completely docile and will-less under her beneficent sway. This impression was thoroughly reversed on his accession. Another strong influence on his youth and subsequent life was that of Adrian Dedel, vice-chancellor of the University of Louvain, who was chosen as his tutor by Maximilian, and who instilled into his pupil a deep devotion to the Roman Catholic Church. (Through Charles' influence, Adrian Dedel became Pope Adrian VI, the last non-Italian pope.) Charles became king of Spain on the death (1516) of his grandfather Ferdinand V, ruling Castile as regent for his insane mother, and as heir in his own right to Aragon, Navarre, Granada, the Spanish dominions in America, Naples, Sardinia, and Sicily. When Maximilian died (1519), Francis I of France became a powerful rival of Charles to succeed him as emperor. Charles, heir to Maximilian's Hapsburg lands—in addition to all the others he had inherited—with the aid of bribery won the contest and was elected emperor of the Holy Roman Empire in the same year. He was crowned at Aachen (Aix-la-Chapelle) in 1520.

Charles immediately became embroiled in the religious struggle going on in Germany, presiding at a diet held at Worms in 1521, from which resulted the Edict of Worms, in which Charles declared his unswerving determination to stamp out the "heresy" of Luther's doctrines. Charles' seeming preoccupation with Germany, his Flemish birth and education, his ties to the German financiers resulting from his bribery of the seven electors to the imperial crown, and the high-handed methods he used in establishing his own followers in Spanish office combined to arouse feeling against him in Spain. The resentment culminated in revolts in Castile (1520–1521), which were suppressed. War broke out (1521) in Italy over the rival claims of Charles and Francis I of France to Milan, Burgundy, Navarre, and Naples. In 1525 Francis was defeated and captured at Pavia and forced to sign (January, 1526) at Madrid a treaty giving Charles great concessions. This he repudiated immediately upon his release and, joining with Milan, Venice, Florence, and Pope Clement VII, reopened hostilities. The imperial troops that Charles sent to Italy, mostly Germans, were only fitfully paid. They were expected to live off the land and the booty they could seize. They marched down the peninsula to Rome, which they stormed and entered in May, 1527, and subjected to a barbaric sack. For weeks the undisciplined barbarians ravaged the city, destroying works of art, desecrating churches, plundering palaces, seizing valuables and jewels, holding individuals for ransom or slaying them, and assaulting women. Rome had not endured such a sack since the time of the Goths. Pope Clement, with some members of his court, fled to Castel Sant' Angelo for refuge, and remained there, a prisoner, until December, when he was released and fled again, this time to Orvieto. Although Charles did not order the sack, and perhaps was not even sure of the exact whereabouts of the imperial army, it was his policy toward his troops that made it possible. The wars, carried on in Italy against the French, ended in the Peace of Cambrai, the "Ladies' Peace" (1529). By the treaty, Charles became undisputed master of Italy. He was crowned (1530) by the pope at Bologna, and was the last Holy Roman emperor to have a papal coronation. Thenceforth he wielded enormous influence in Italian affairs, ecclesiastical as well as political. He was responsible, among other matters, for the restoration of the Medici at Florence. From the time of the coronation of Charles at Bologna a heavy hand was laid on Renaissance Italy. The Spaniards suppressed what they could neither understand nor appreciate.

Charles was now forced to attend to the inroads being made on Europe by the Turks under Suleiman I (Suleiman the Magnificent). In 1535 Charles took the Ottoman city of Tunis in Africa (leading his army in person), and sacked it. For the third time, a war against Francis I broke out (1536) over Francis' claims to Milan. Charles marched into Provence, and Francis entered Savoy and Piedmont, but the struggle came to an inconclusive halt by truce in 1539. Intermittently from that time Charles fought against Suleiman and Francis, who had allied himself with the Turkish ruler. In 1538, a league formed by Charles, Venice, and the pope was defeated. In 1541, Charles sent an expedition against Algiers, in Africa, which failed. Again in 1542 war began over claims to Milan by Charles and Francis. This ended in 1544 with the peace of Crépy (Crespy), in which Francis agreed not to press claims to Milan and Naples, and Charles gave up his claims to Burgundy.

In 1530 a diet was held at Augsburg under the emperor, who reiterated that he wanted the Protestant innovations ended. It was at this diet that Philipp Melanchthon's Confession of Augsburg was first read. Later that year there was arranged, and in 1531 formally organized, the Schmalkaldic League (named for Schmalkalden, the city in Prussia where it was formed) of many of the Protestant rulers (rulers who "protested" against the emperor's edict at Augsburg) of the German states and a number of cities of the empire. But Charles was occupied with matters elsewhere and could not at the moment attempt to crush this expression of independence. By 1546 he was able to turn his attention to the German situation and, at the battle of Mühlberg (April 24, 1547), defeated and captured the elector of Saxony, John Frederick I, one of the leaders of the League. Charles in turn was attacked (1551) and forced to retreat by Maurice of Saxony, formerly one of his allies in Germany; and by the convention of Passau (1552), he recognized the Confession of Augsburg. On this basis the Peace of Augsburg was concluded (September 25, 1555), under which the states and cities acknowledging the Confession were to have the freedom of adopting the reformed religion. Devoted to Roman Catholicism himself, Charles' aim and ideal were to unite his empire in the faith. In pursuit of this ideal (which he did not realize) he did not, except in few instances, resort to persecution.

At war again, beginning in 1551, with France, now under Henry II, Charles in 1555 decided to give up his several kingships. On October 25, 1555, he took the unusual step of resigning the throne of the Netherlands, being succeeded by his son Philip II. On January 15, 1556, the crown of Spain too went to Philip, and the Hapsburg holdings in Germany and the imperial crown were resigned in favor of his brother Ferdinand I, to whom since the beginning of Charles' reign he had relinquished the sole sovereignty over these lands and who had inaugurated the Hapsburg rule in Bohemia and Hungary. Charles retired to a monastery at Yuste, Spain, where he lived until his death, without, however, abandoning all interest and influence in affairs of his former empire. Charles had sought throughout his reign to strengthen his empire and to promote peace in it by matrimonial alliances. He married Isabella of Portugal, to whom he was deeply attached, and married his sisters and his nieces to members of various European royal houses. The Medici of Florence, the Gonzaga of Mantua, the Doria of Genoa, the Piccolomini of Siena, and the Farnese, as well as the ruling houses of Portugal, France, Denmark, and Germany, were all connected to him by marriage. His natural daughter, Margaret of Parma (born before his marriage to Isabella), married first (1533) Alessandro de' Medici, duke of Florence, and second (1542)

Ottavio Farnese, duke of Parma. His natural son, Don John of Austria (born after his wife's death) was the hero of the battle of Lepanto (1571) in which the Turks were defeated. His son Philip, who succeeded him, married first Mary of Portugal and second Queen Mary I of England (he married twice more after his father's death). The rule of Charles had extended over nearly forty years, in which time he ruled over an area reaching from the Americas to eastern Europe. The Spanish conquests in Mexico and Peru by Cortés and Pizzaro brought tremendous wealth to the Spanish treasury. He and his contemporaries (Henry VIII of England, Francis I of France, Suleiman I of Turkey) form a constellation of kings that makes the first half of the 16th century outstanding in political history. Portraits of Charles by Titian, showing his long, narrow, homely face, with its adenoidal expression, are in the Prado at Madrid. An equestrian portrait of him by this master is an outstanding example of the art of portraiture.

Charles I (of *Naples*). King of Naples and Sicily (1266–1285) and count of Anjou; b. 1226; d. at Foggia, January 7, 1285. He was the son of Louis VIII of France and Blanche of Castile, and the brother of Louis IX of France. In 1248 he took part in a crusade, and was returning from it when (1253) Pope Innocent IV offered him the crown of Sicily. The kingdom of Sicily, which comprised the island of Sicily and Naples, was a feudatory of the papacy over which the papacy had lost control to the heirs of the Hohenstaufen emperor Frederick II. The pope surrounded his offer to Charles with so many conditions and restrictions that Charles declined it. Ten years later Pope Urban IV, in fear of Manfred, the illegitimate son of Frederick II, renewed the offer to Charles, and with more favorable conditions. Charles accepted the offer from Pope Clement IV, Urban having died before the terms were satisfactorily completed. The popes concerned, at this time, feared the French less than the German Hohenstaufens. The French kings, beginning with Louis IX, now came to regard Sicily as an appendage of the French throne. This was the origin of the claim of the counts of Anjou to Sicily and Naples. Charles was crowned at Rome in 1266. In February of the same year he marched against Manfred and defeated and killed him at the battle of Benevento, February 26, 1266. Thereafter he fought up and down Italy with such success that none dared oppose him. Conradin, last of the Hohenstaufens, came into Italy to win back his lands of Sicily from the usurping Charles. Charles met him at Tagliacozzo, August 23, 1268, defeated and captured him, and had him beheaded at Naples. Charles was now without a rival to the throne of Sicily. He was vicar of Tuscany. His power in Italy seemed unlimited as one state after another fell into the Guelph column of pope and Charles. This had not been accomplished without great cost in money and men. He continued his conquests, capturing Durazzo and having himself made king of Albania. This was the beginning of his ambitious plan to capture the Byzantine Empire. In 1270 he joined his brother Louis IX in a crusade against Tunis, and took the opportunity to add to his conquests. In his government of Sicily he replaced the local officials, from top to bottom, with Frenchmen, and to support his wars he levied crushing taxes. The resentment and rage that this combination roused in his subjects led to an uprising at Palermo, in March, 1282, known as the Sicilian Vespers. The revolt spread rapidly throughout Sicily. Thousands of Charles' French officials were slain. The hatred of the French led to a wish for a return of the Hohenstaufens. The Sicilians invited Pedro III, husband of Manfred's daughter Constance, and son of James I of Aragon, to drive the French out and take the throne himself. With the island in an uproar, Charles fell back on Naples. Pedro's forces controlled Sicily. Charles set out for France to raise an army and money, but died on the way, at Foggia. It was, thus, from this period that the counts of Anjou dated their claim to Naples and Sicily—a claim that had been established with papal consent—and also that the Aragonese dated their claim—a claim established on the invitation of the inhabitants. The rival claims kept Naples and Sicily in a state of warfare and turmoil for over two hundred years. It is also from this period that the kingdom of Sicily was divided into a kingdom of Sicily and one of Naples, not to be reunited until 1816. Charles was an extremely able commander and a capable statesman. For a time he was almost unopposed in Italy, but his very success aroused fear in the hearts of those who had called on him for aid. He was succeeded on the throne of Naples by his son, Charles II.

Charles II (of *Naples*). King of Naples (1285–1309); b. c1250; d. 1309. He was the son of Charles I of Naples, count of Anjou and Provence. Following the uprising known as the Sicilian Vespers (1282), he was captured (1284) by the forces of Pedro III of Aragon during a naval battle. Pedro had been invited by the Sicilians to become their king in place of Charles I, whose harsh rule had caused the Sicilian Vespers. In 1285 Charles I died. Three years later Charles II was released by his captors, on condition that he give up his claim to Sicily and content himself with the throne of Naples. On being released, however, he disregarded his promises, and the early part of his reign was occupied in trying to win back Sicily from the Aragonese. The war ended in the Peace of Caltabellotta (1302), by the terms of which Charles abandoned his claim to Sicily. He also consented to the marriage of his daughter to Frederick of Aragon, son of Pedro III and successor of Pedro's brother James as king of Sicily. Charles was succeeded on the throne of Naples by his third son, Robert.

Charles II (of *Navarre*). [Called **Charles the Bad.**] King of Navarre in the period 1349–1387 and count of Évreux; b. 1332; d. 1387. His reign was marked by intrigues and territorial disputes, notably with John II of France, his father-in-law, who took Charles prisoner in 1356. Released (1357), Charles was active (1358) in suppressing the peasant revolt of the Jacquerie.

Charles (of *Valois*). Count of Valois, of Maine, and of Anjou; b. March 12, 1270; d. at Perray, France, December 16, 1325. He was the third son of Philip III, king of France. He was unsuccessful in an attempt to claim the throne of Aragon, but fought successfully against England and Flanders. In 1301 he crossed the Alps and went into Florence, at the request of Pope Boniface VIII, to subdue the Bianchi (White Guelphs). The Bianchi put up no resistance, having convinced themselves, in the face of all the evidence, that Charles was coming to help them. With the aid of Charles the Neri (Black Guelphs) returned to Florence, destroyed or confiscated Bianchi property, and drove many of the Bianchi, including Dante, into exile. Dante mentions Charles, as the destroyer of Florentine liberty, in the *Divina Commedia* (*Purgatorio*, xx). In 1309 he sought to become Holy Roman emperor to succeed Albert I, but was rejected by the electors in favor of Henry VII.

Charles (of *Viana*). [Also, **Charles IV** (of *Navarre*).] Spanish prince; b. 1421; d. 1461. From his mother and from his maternal grandmother, he inherited Navarre, but upon his mother's death, his father seized power there. Charles submitted, but when his father's second wife interfered in Navarrese affairs, civil war ensued, in the course of which Charles was imprisoned by his father. Released upon his promise not to claim his crown until his father's death, Charles nevertheless resorted to arms, was defeated, and took refuge with Alfonso V, king of Aragon, Naples, and Sicily. Following Alfonso's death in 1458, Charles of Viana's father became John II of Aragon, and offered his son the crown of Naples and Sicily, which the latter refused. Reconciled with his father in 1459, Charles returned to Navarre, but upon his proposing to marry a princess of Castile, he was again imprisoned by John. This led to a popular insurrection, and Charles was released, but died soon afterward. Charles of Viana was a poet and a scholar, who translated Aristotle's *Ethics* into Spanish and wrote a chronicle of the kings of Navarre.

Chartier (shär′tyā), **Alain.** French poet and man of letters; b. at Bayeux, France, c1385; d. c1430 or 1433. He wrote *Le Quadrilogue invectif*, *L'Espérance*, *La Belle Dame sans mercy*, and numerous other works. His poetry consists mainly of allegorical love poems and moral verse.

Chastelard (shä-te̤-lär), **Pierre de Boscosel de.** French poet; b. in Dauphine, France, c1540; executed at the Tolbooth, Edinburgh, 1563. Violently in love with Mary, Queen of Scots, he followed her to Scotland. He was executed after being twice found in the queen's bedchamber.

Chastellain or **Chastelain** (shä-te̤-laṅ), **Georges.** Flemish chronicler and poet; b. near Aalst, Flanders c1405; d. 1475. He was the author of *Chronique des ducs de Burgogne*, among other works.

Châteaubriant (shä-tō-brē-äṅ), Comtesse **de.** [Title of **Françoise de Foix.**] Mistress of Francis I, king of France; b. c1490; d. at Châteaubriant, France, October 16, 1537.

Chaucer (chô′sėr), **Geoffrey.** English poet; b. c1344; d. 1400. He was the son of the wealthy vintner John Chaucer, whose family had long been wholesale importers and merchants of wine and collectors of the king's customs. Chaucer was early in a courtly environment, probably as a page. Our first certain record, dated London, May, 1357, reveals him in the service of Elizabeth, countess of Ulster and wife of Prince Lionel, son of King Edward III. It was probably in the household of John of Gaunt, Lionel's younger brother, that Chaucer met his wife Philippa (d. 1387). In the winter of 1359–1360 he was with the English army invading France, was taken prisoner near Reims, and was then ransomed. Perhaps during the period 1361–1366 he obtained legal training at the Inns of Court. There is a convincing tradition that he studied at the Inner Temple, which offered an education sufficiently broad to prepare Chaucer for his later career at court and in business. In 1367 he was a yeoman in the King's Household (dilectus vallectus noster) with a pension of twenty marks for life, and the following year was listed as "esquire." In 1369 he was with an English army raiding in France, probably under John of Gaunt, by that time duke of Lancaster. Later that year John's wife, the Duchess Blanche, died of the pestilence, and Chaucer wrote his first long poem, *The Book of the Duchess,* an elegy in the form of a conventional French love-vision, praising Blanche and consoling the bereaved duke. From 1368 on, Chaucer undertook seven or more diplomatic missions to the Continent, to arrange for commercial treaties, for a marriage for Prince Richard, for help in the French war, and on secret business. He was envoy in 1373 to Genoa and Florence and in 1378 to Milan. In the latter place he visited the court of Bernabò Visconti and must have noted with some admiration the flourishing city and the paved streets, at a time when the streets of London were mires of mud. He probably met neither Petrarch nor Boccaccio on his Italian journeys, but he came to know their writings, as well as those of Dante, and Italian influences appear in his next poems, such as *The House of Fame* and *The Parliament of Fowls.* From 1374 to 1384 he was active in business affairs and held official positions. In 1385 he became justice of the peace for Kent, and in the following year a member of Parliament for Kent, the customs position he had held since 1374 being terminated. He moved from London to the countryside (probably Greenwich), and his new activities apparently afforded him leisure to bring to completion two long narratives based on poems by Boccaccio, *Troilus and Criseyde* and the story of Palamon and Arcite (later *The Knight's Tale*). Soon he started *The Legend of Good Women* and also *The Canterbury Tales.* From 1389 to 1391 he was clerk of the king's works, in charge of building and repairs for the Tower of London, Westminster Palace, and eight other royal residences scattered from Surrey to Worcester. From 1391 until 1398 he was deputy forester of North Petherton Forest, Somersetshire, and probably lived chiefly in the Park House, where he may have composed most of *The Canterbury Tales.* In 1391 he composed *The Treatise on the Astrolabe* for his "little son Lewis." (Another son, Thomas, became prominent in the next century.) In 1395–1396 at London, Chaucer seems to have been briefly in attendance upon Henry of Derby, son of John of Gaunt, who was later crowned Henry IV. As king, in 1399, Henry renewed the annuity to Chaucer and added another of forty marks, and the poet leased a house in the garden of St. Mary's Chapel, Westminster Abbey. The traditional date of his death is October 25, 1400, and he was buried in that part of the Abbey which has become the Poets' Corner. *The Book of the Duchess* (c1369) shows Chaucer's familiarity with Roman poetry (especially Ovid) and his intense preoccupation with courtly writings: the *Roman de la Rose* (of which he translated at least part), and poems by Deschamps, Froissart, and Machaut (poets whose lyrics and complaints he imitated). After 1373 came *The House of Fame, Anelida and Arcite,* and *The Parliament of Fowls,* with continued admiration of Roman poetry and courtly conventions, but with a new handling of detail and sensuous imagery learned from Dante and Boccaccio, and with a transition from French octosyllabics to the rime royal, which he invented. He translated the *De Consolatione Philosophiae* of Boethius, whose ideas are reflected in *Troilus and Criseyde* (c1385) and the story of Palamon and Arcite (later *The Knight's Tale*), poems retelling long romances by Boccaccio. The *Troilus* excels in characterization; *The Knight's Tale* and *The Legend of Good Women* show growth of narrative power and mastery of the decasyllabic or heroic couplet, which he was the first to use in English. *The Canterbury Tales* (c1387–1400) reveal wider reading, freedom from earlier conventionalism, and greater control over materials. In his fullest maturity Chaucer exercised an unsurpassed combination of narrative skill, powerful characterization, mastery of cadence, vivid realism, poetic intensity, and rich humor.

Chaucer, Thomas. English statesman; b. c1367; d. March 14, 1434. He is thought to be the son of Geoffrey Chaucer. He was present at the battle of Agincourt (1415).

Chaucer's Dream. Name at one time given by some to *The Book of the Duchess*, in which the poet relates his dream.

Chaucer's Dream. Title given to an independent poem, first printed by Thomas Speght in the 1597 edition of the works of Geoffrey Chaucer. This poem is not now assigned to Chaucer.

Chauliac (shō-lyȧk), **Guy de.** [Also, **Cauliac, Chaulieu**; in Italy, **Guido de Cauliaco.**] French surgeon; b. c1300; d. c1370. He wrote a noted treatise on surgery, *Chirurgia magna* (1363). He left a description of the great plague of 1348.

Cheke (chēk), Sir **John.** English scholar of Greek; b. at Cambridge, England, June 16, 1514; d. at London, September 13, 1557. A zealous Protestant, on Mary Tudor's accession he was accused of treason but was pardoned. He was again thrown in the Tower and was induced to renounce his Protestant beliefs. He wrote numerous works in Latin and English.

Chepman (chep′mạn), **Walter.** Scottish printer and merchant of Edinburgh; b. c1473; d. c1538. He established the earliest Scottish press.

Chiaroscuro (kyä-rō-skö′rō). The general distribution of light and shade in a picture, whether painted, drawn, or engraved. The word comes from two Italian words meaning, respectively, light and dark. The contrast of light and shade may be used as an element of composition, to produce depth and modeling, to throw certain parts of the picture into relief, or to create a focal point. By means of chiaroscuro, among other things, two-dimensional surfaces attain a three-dimensional effect.

Chierico (kyā′rē-kō), **Francesco d'Antonio del.** See **Del Chierico, Francesco d'Antonio.**

Chierigati (kye-rē-gä′tē), **Francesco.** Bishop of Teramo; b. at Vicenza, 1479; d. at Bologna, December 6, 1539. He was named bishop of Teramo by Pope Leo X. In 1522 he went to Nuremberg to seek aid for a war against the Turks and also to seek implementation of the Edict of Worms (1521) by which Luther was placed under the imperial ban. Chierigati was noted for his speeches urging reform of the abuses in the Church.

Chigi (kē′jē), **Agostino.** [Called **Il Magnifico.**] Roman banker; b. c1465; d. at Rome, 1520. Of an ancient and noble Sienese family, he held the contracts for the salt mines and the alum mines at Tolfa, sources of great wealth for the Church; and through his house he had dealings throughout Europe. With his vast wealth he aided Cesare Borgia in his wars to carve out a kingdom and endowed the prodigal Leo X. He was a friend of Bembo, of Aretino, who was in his service, and of Giovio, among many others; opened a press from which issued (1515) an edition of Pindar that was the first Greek book printed at Rome; and was the patron of Raphael and Sodoma. He commissioned the artists to decorate the palace he had outside the gates of Rome (now known as the Farnesina, from the Farnese who acquired it in 1579), as well as his chapel in Santa Maria del Popolo, where he is buried. He was the archetype of the wealthy, cultivated Maecenases of the Renaissance.

Chioggia (kyôd′jä), **War of.** Climax of the struggle between Venice and Genoa for trade supremacy in the eastern Mediterranean. The War of Chioggia (1378–1380) found Venice attacked in her mainland possessions by the lord of Carrara and by the Hungarians, and attacked from the sea by the Genoese. While the Venetian fleets were attacking the Genoese in the Mediterranean, the Genoese decided to attack Venice at home. They took Chioggia, a city on an island about fifteen miles from Venice (August, 1379), and threatened Venice itself. The Venetians recalled their fleets and blocked the channels of the lagoons. The heavy Genoese vessels, commanded by men who were unfamiliar with the tricky channels of the lagoons, could not maneuver and could not escape, as Venetian vessels were standing off the one open channel. There was great suffering in Venice, as supplies by sea were cut off. With the return of the Venetian fleets of Vettore Pisani and Carlo Zeno, the Genoese found themselves blockaded in Chioggia and under siege. They were forced to surrender (June, 1380), and the Venetian victory decided the ascendancy of Venice over Genoa thenceforth in the trade with the Levant, although Genoa continued to be a leading maritime center.

Christian II (of *Denmark* and *Norway*). [Called **Christian the Cruel.**] King of Denmark and Norway in the period 1513–1523; b. at Nyborg, Denmark, July 2, 1481; d. at Kallundborg, Denmark, January 25, 1559. In 1515 he married Isabella, sister of the emperor Charles V. He was called "the Cruel" for his massacre of the Swedish nobility at Stockholm (1520) when he conquered Sweden. Gustavus Vasa liberated Sweden, and Christian was deposed (1523) and then driven out of Denmark. He went to Norway (1531), was captured (1532), and remained a prisoner until his death.

Christian III (of *Denmark* and *Norway*). King of Denmark and Norway in the period 1534–1559; b. 1503; d. at Kolding, Denmark, January 1, 1559. He introduced the Reformation into Denmark and Norway, destroyed the influence of the Hansa towns in his dominions, and reduced Norway to a province.

Christine de Pisan (krēs-tēn dẹ pē-zäṅ). [Real name, **Christine de Pizan,** from Pizzano, near Bologna, from her father, Thomas de Pizan, who was a councillor of the Venetian republic and also noted as an astrologer. French students mispronounced and misspelled Pizan.] French writer, of Italian parentage; b. at Venice, c1364; d. c1431. Her father moved to the French court (c1368) as astrologer and physician to King Charles V, taking his family with him. Christine was brought up in an Italian house surrounded by French influences. She married a royal secretary at the age of 15. He died (1389), leaving her a poor widow with three children. Her father also having died, she wrote, "Alone I am, and alone I will be," and began a literary career by which she managed to support herself and her family. She is thus of interest to modern historians of literature from the fact that she was one of the first European writers to secure a living from her writing (from the Roman era through to the Renaissance, writing was usually an avocation rather than a vocation, and was practiced by people whose actual support came usually from the Church or royal patronage). In her poetry are echoes of Dante and Boccaccio, as well as of Petrarch and Cecco d'Ascoli. She laments the unhappy state of the kingdom of France, and defends and exalts feminine virtue, especially in *Cité des Dames* and *Livre des Trois Vertus.*

Christus (kris'tus), **Petrus.** [Also, **Pieter Christophsen Cristus.**] Flemish painter; b. at Baerle, a village in Brabant, c1400; d. at Bruges, in Flanders, 1473. He is thought to have studied with the Van Eycks, and it was from them that his style was derived. Little is known of his career until in 1444 he purchased citizenship at Bruges, and became a member of the Guild of St. Luke. Among the few works attributed to him with certainty are portraits (*Marco Barberigo,* National Gallery, London), a *Pietà* (Brussels), *Nativity* (National Gallery, Washington), and a *Deposition from the Cross* (the Metropolitan Museum, New York).

Chrysoloras (kris-ọ̄-lō'rạs), **Manuel.** Greek scholar and teacher; b. probably at Constantinople, c1355; d. at Konstanz (Constance), Germany, April 15, 1415. He was sent to Italy by the Byzantine emperor to seek the help of the Christian world against the Turks. His political mission was fruitless, but he was visited by some eminent Florentines while he was in Venice, and later journeyed to Florence at their request. In Florence he met Coluccio Salutati, who was instrumental in having him named (1397) professor of Greek at the University of Florence, a post he held until 1400. In this position, Chrysoloras was largely responsible for introducing, and thus preserving and encouraging, the Greek studies in Italy. He was the first true teacher of Greek in Italy. He numbered among his pupils Poggio Bracciolini, Leonardo Bruni, Francesco Barbaro, Gianozzo Manetti, Carlo Marsuppini, and Ambrogio Traversari. He later lectured at Rome, Padua, Milan, and Venice, thus broadening the area where an interest in Greek studies was aroused. Among his works are a Greek grammar and a Latin translation of Plato's *Republic.* He went to the Council of Constance in an official capacity, but died soon after his arrival there.

Churchyard (chėrch'yärd), **Thomas.** English poet, page to Henry Howard, earl of Surrey, vagrant, hanger-on at court, and soldier; b. at Shrewsbury, England, c1520; d. at London, April 4, 1604. Between 1560 and 1603 he wrote a considerable amount of prose and poetry, much of it of autobiographical interest and referring to current happenings. Some of his works are *The Worthines of Wales* (1587), a long historical poem; *Shore's Wife*, a tragedy; the story of Cardinal Wolsey; and a volume of prose and poetry, *Churchyard's Challenge* (1593). As a soldier he saw service in Scotland, France, Ireland, and the Low Countries, and he drew on his own military experience in *Wofull Warres in Flanders* (1578) and *General Rehearsal* (1579). Specimens of his verse are to be found in volumes with such curious titles as *Churchyard's Chips, Churchyard's Chance, Churchyard's Charge*, and *Churchyard's Good Will*, and he is represented in a number of Elizabethan anthologies. He wrote to the very end of his long life.

Ciborium (si-bō′ri-um). **1.** In Church architecture, a permanent canopy, together with its supports, over a high altar. Ciboria came to be treated as architectural features in church interiors. They were often of marble and richly ornamented. That by Arnolfo di Cambio above the high altar of St. Paul Outside the Walls, Rome, is a splendid example of 13th century Tuscan art.

2. An ecclesiastical vessel designed to contain the sacred wafers or consecrated bread for the eucharist. The vessel, often shaped like a chalice with a dome-shaped cover, is frequently of precious metal and richly ornamented.

Cicognara (chē-kō-nyä′rä), **Antonio.** Painter; b. at Cremona; active in the second half of the 15th century. He was an assistant of Cosmè Tura in painting the Hall of the Months in the Estense Palace of Schifanoia at Ferrara, and was for a time deeply influenced by Tura. His best works are those in which he most closely imitated his Ferrarese master. After 1484, when Tura's popularity waned at the Estense court, Cicognara drew closer to Lorenzo Costa, as in the *St. Catherine and a Worshiper* (Carrara Academy, Bergamo), *Prayer Before a Tomb* (Isabella Stewart Gardner Museum, Boston), and others.

Cid (thēᴛʜ), **Crónica del.** [English translation, *Chronicle of the Cid*.] Name of one of the Spanish accounts of the Cid (date of writing unknown, but printed in 1512). It is the same in substance as the history of the Cid in the *Crónica general ó estovia de España* composed and compiled (c1260) by King Alfonso X of Spain.

Cieco (che′kō), **Francesco.** [Called **Il Cieco di Ferrara,** because he was blind.] Poet; d. 1505. Little is known of this poet of the second half of the 15th century. By some he has been identified as Francesco Bello. Others identify him as Francesco Orbo da Fiorenza, the author of *Laude di Venezia* and *Torneamento di Giovanni Bentivoglio*. He was in the service of the Bentivoglio at Cento, then was at Ferrara (1471–1479) and next at the court of the Gonzaga at Mantua. He wrote a romantic epic, *Il Mambriano*, on the pattern of Boiardo's *Orlando Innamorato*. As did Boiardo, he drew on the Carolingian and Arthurian cycles, as well as on classical antiquity, but was not as successful as Boiardo in fusing them into a harmonious whole. Rinaldo and Astolfo, as they do in the Orlando romances of Boiardo and Ariosto, play important roles. The Mambriano of the title is a king of Bithynia.

Cieza de León (thyā′thä dā lā-ōn′), **Pedro de.** Spanish soldier; b. at Llerena, Spain, c1518; d. at Seville, Spain, 1560. He was the author of *Crónica del Perú* and of *Historia de la Nueva España*, among other works.

Cima da Conegliano (chē′mä dä kō-nā-lyä′nō), **Giovanni Battista.** Painter; b. at Conegliano in the Veneto, c1459; d. there, c1517. Little is known of his early life and training. Some scholars believe he had his early training at his native place, possibly with the painter Girolamo da Treviso il Vecchio (Girolamo Pennacchi). His earliest dated (1489) work is the altarpiece *Madonna with SS. James the Apostle and Jerome*, painted for the Church of S. Bartolomeo at Vicenza and now in the Municipal Museum at that city. However, this highly finished and accomplished work must have been preceded by others, whose chronology is not documented. Among the presumed earlier works are a number of *Madonnas*, as those at Bologna, Bergamo, and in the Johnson Collection at Philadelphia. These are very much in the manner of Giovanni Bellini, if somewhat more austere, and presuppose contact with Bellini, perhaps in visits to Venice. The first two of the *Madonnas* mentioned are painted from the same cartoon, and vary only as to size and the amount of landscape background. In them Cima presents the Christ Child in what appears to be a new pose: the Holy Infant stands almost sternly erect, with His arms folded across His chest. Throughout

CIMA DA CONEGLIANO
St. Jerome
Gabinetto Disegni e Stampe degli Uffizi
Foto Soprintendenza

his painting life Cima frequently used the same cartoon more than once, sometimes painting four or five from the same one, or handing it over to his assistants. The Bellini influence shows clearly in these and other early *Madonnas*, as well as in the polyptych at Olera, near Bergamo, which some think may be his earliest work; the *Madonna and Child*, at Detroit; and that at Berlin with its lovely landscape. His *Madonna and Saints* (Brera, Milan) is thought to have been painted soon after the Vicenza altarpiece of 1489. Cima is recorded at Venice in 1492, and was probably there well before that date. He may have assisted in the workshop of Alvise Vivarini, where he was introduced to the compositional methods of Antonello da Messina as transmitted by Vivarini, for the influence of Antonello is also clear in his work. The influence of his contemporary, Bartolommeo Montagna, the most important painter of Vicenza in his day, is also apparent in some of Cima's work, and he may have come in contact with him at Venice, where Montagna was painting frescoes in the Scuola Grande di S. Marco, or at Vicenza. Echoes, either isolated or recurrent, of Carpaccio and Giorgione, as well as of the painters previously mentioned, also appear. Whatever elements he chose from other painters were reshaped into his own individual pictorial language. His style evolved little; it has been said that one of the difficulties in fixing the chronology of his work is that the differences between the first dated painting (1489) and the last (1516) are so slight. Characteristic of his paintings are the affectionately limned landscapes reflecting his love for the soft countryside and low hills of his native Conegliano. (In the cathedral at Conegliano is his *Madonna and Child with SS. John the Baptist, Nicholas, Catherine, Apollonia, Francis, and Peter,* 1493, with its two angel musicians at the foot of the Madonna's throne in the manner of Bellini.) In clear, transparent color he expresses his joy in nature and creates a lovingly idealized world. In the golden light of his paintings he communicates a serene and optimistic sense of life. In the works on mythological themes, as *Endymion Sleeping* and *The Contest of Apollo and Marsyas* (National Gallery, Parma), his joy in nature is exquisitely portrayed in the landscape. His *Madonnas, Saints,* and other paintings on religious themes are instinct with reverence and contrition; he was completely at ease in expressing an innate spirituality in the context of his age. Cima's paintings are in the churches of S. Maria dell' Orto, S. Giovanni in Bragora (*Baptism*), and S. Maria del Carmine, at Venice, as well as in the Accademia (*Pietà, Archangel Raphael, Madonna Enthroned and Saints* with its charming landscape, among others). His paintings are also to be found in the Ambrosiana, Brera, and Poldi Pezzoli Museum, Milan; Uffizi, Florence; at Bergamo, Pavia, Modena, and Treviso; the National Gallery, London; Louvre, Paris; in museums at Berlin, Frankfurt, Dresden, Moscow, and Leningrad; at Detroit, Baltimore, Cleveland; the Metropolitan Museum, New York; the Johnson Collection, Philadelphia; the National Gallery, Washington; and elsewhere.

Cimabue (chē-mä-bö'ā), **Giovanni.** [Original name, **Cenni di Pepo.**] Florentine painter, active in the second half of the 13th century and the early years of the 14th century. Little is known of his life. According to some, he is "The Father of Modern Painting." Increasingly, however, it is maintained that he is the last great painter in the Byzantine tradition. The reasons for the two views probably lie in the fact that he worked in the Byzantine style but modified and softened it, without, however, breaking away from conventionalized Byzantine composition. His modifications were in a more fluid outline, in his attempts at relief, and in his use of softer color. Giotto, his great pupil, is more generally considered to have made the break from the Byzantine tradition. Cimabue went to Rome (1272) and saw the work of the Roman school, with its classical elements. He was a mosaicist as well as a painter, and evidence of mosaic technique is strong in his painting. At Pisa he worked on the mosaic of St. John in the apse of the cathedral (1301 and 1302), and in Florence may have executed mosaics in the Baptistery. Most of his extant painting is in the Upper Church of the Basilica of San Francesco at Assisi. There, in the apse, transept, and vault are some frescoes, now dim and partially destroyed, by him and his assistants, painted probably between 1277 and 1281. In the Lower Church of the same basilica is a fresco of *Madonna with St. Francis and Angels,* which is also attributed to him. Other work credited to him includes a *Virgin,* in the Church of Santa Maria dei Servi at Bologna; a *Madonna Enthroned,* Uffizi, Florence; a *Crucifix,* Arezzo; paintings at New York (Frick Collection), Paris, Turin, and Washington; and a *Crucifix* in S. Croce, Florence. A large part of the S. Croce *Crucifix* was ruined by oil and mud in the disastrous floods of November, 1966.

Cino da Pistoia (chē'nō dä pēs-tō'yä). [Original name, **Guittoncino de' Sinibaldi.**] Jurist and poet; b. at Pistoia, c1270; d. there, c1336. He studied law at Bologna, and afterward traveled and studied in France. He became an admirer but not an imitator of the French system. He taught law at Bologna, Siena, and Perugia, and was the master of, among others, the famed Bartolus. Among his many legal works the greatest is his commentary on the Justinian Code, *Lectura in codicem.* His philosophy of law was to adapt it to the needs of the time and to favor the rights of the state and civil law over canon law. In this he marked a turning away from an ancient and medieval to a modern view of law and its function. He was the greatest jurist of his time. Cino was also a poet. About 200 of his verses survive. He was acquainted with Dante and Petrarch and acknowledged by them as a poet. He followed the school adapted from the Provençal troubadours, the *dolce stil nuovo,* in the songs he sang of his hopeless love for various ladies, who may have been real but may equally well have been imaginary symbols for his outpourings. His gift for painting the melancholy moods of love is expressed with tenderness, musicality, and a wealth of imagery. At one time he was allied with the fortunes of the emperor Henry VII, and two of his songs mourn the death of that monarch, another that of Dante, with whom he had corresponded. Most of his verses sing the pangs of love, but a few are on contemporary matters.

Ciompi (chôm'pē). Popular name given to the woolworkers of Florence. In 1378, encouraged by divisions among the greater guildsmen, they revolted in an attempt to win the right to organize into guilds. Their object was to obtain a measure of participation in the government. As a result of their revolt, the Ciompi organized two guilds, but the degree of their influence on the government and against the power of the greater guilds was slight. The work of their revolution was undone by September of 1378. The regime that followed them until January of

1382 did rule as the most sustained democratic experiment in Florentine history. While the workers did not have representation in this government, the lesser guildsmen did have a substantial share of the offices.

Cione (chō′nā). See **Orcagna, Andrea; Jacopo di Cione; Matteo di Cione; Nardo di Cione.**

Cipolla (chē-pôl′lä), **Bartolomeo.** Jurisconsult; b. at Verona; d. after 1467. He studied at Bologna, took his doctorate at Padua (1446), and taught at Padua from 1458. From his lectures at Padua he compiled his *Tractatus de servitutibus praediorum* (*urbanorum et rusticorum*) on urban and agricultural labor, a noted work that was translated into Italian. Another noted work was his *Tractatus cautelarum*. A letter, dated Padua, 1467, is in the library at Trent.

Ciriaco d'Ancona (chē-rē′ä-kō dän-kō′nä). [Original name, **Ciriaco di Filippo Pizzicolli.**] Humanist and collector; b. at Ancona, 1391; d. at Cremona, 1452. From the age of nine he traveled with merchants; later he began his own career as a merchant and continued his travels. His journeys took him to Egypt, the islands of the Aegean, Sicily, Dalmatia, Greece, and many of the cities of Italy. An enthusiast for classical studies, he taught himself Latin and Greek and gave himself up to his compulsion for collecting inscriptions, gems, coins, fragments of statuary, and manuscripts wherever he went. His ardor for collecting was uncritical and his knowledge uneven; some of the finds he treasured were spurious, as his detractors were quick to point out. His passion for collecting seemed excessive, but when asked why he hunted and traveled so feverishly he replied, "I go to awake the dead." In 1433 he joined the suite of the Emperor Sigismund at Siena and traveled with him to Rome, where he expounded on the ruins for the edification of the emperor. His large and valuable collection of epigraphs perished in a fire in the Sforza library at Pesaro. He is an outstanding example of the ardent, and often uncritical, early humanist collector, but his pioneering work in many fields has been of great importance to the work of later scholars. His drawings of the ruins in Greece have assisted archaeologists, and his collections of epigraphs laid the basis for modern epigraphy. His early work was of great importance in helping to make possible the serious studies and preservation of the works of antiquity.

Ciuffagni (chö-fä′nyē), **Bernardo.** Sculptor; b. at Florence, 1381; d. there, 1457. In 1407 he was working as an assistant to Lorenzo Ghiberti. Two years later he received a commission to execute two sculptures in marble for the façade of the cathedral at Florence and worked on them a number of years. From 1410 to 1415 he carved his *St. Matthew* for the cathedral. The other Evangelists were carved by Donatello (*St. John*), Nanni di Banco (*St. Luke*), and Niccolò di Pietro Lamberti (*St. Mark*). Other works included a statue of *Joshua* for the campanile (completed by Nanni di Bartolo) and a *St. Peter* for the Butchers' Guild at Orsanmichele. A *David*, also for the façade of the cathedral, completed in 1433, shows the effect that Donatello's realism had on the sculptors working at that time, but is pedestrian in the formality of pose and lack of expressiveness. Little is known of Ciuffagni's work after this time.

Civerchio (chē-ver′kyō), **Vincenzo.** Brescian painter; b. c1470; d. c1544. He worked at Brescia in 1493, executing frescoes (since destroyed) in the cathedral. In the same city he painted (1495) a triptych, now in the Pinacoteca, and a *Deposition* (1504). In 1519 he was at Crema and in 1525 painted a polyptych for the parish church of Palazzolo sull'Oglio. Many other works are ascribed to him, among them: *St. Francis* and an altarpiece with the Madonna, Carrara Academy, Bergamo; a *Pietà* (1539) in S. Giovanni sopra Lecco, Lecco; a *Baptism* (1539) in the Tadini Gallery, Lovere; *Madonna Adoring the Child*, Brera, Milan; *Circumcision*, Johnson Collection, Philadelphia; other works at Milan, and elsewhere. An uneven painter, his early works are obviously derived from Vincenzo Foppa but with a more agitated line and a certain dryness of tone that recalls Butinone. For a time he was influenced, as were most of the Lombard painters, by Leonardo, as indicated by his *St. Sebastian* (Brescia). As he grew older, provincial and archaicized elements became more apparent in his work; he slipped back, so to speak, and repeated outmoded forms; his color and modeling were less assured and firm. From a highly promising beginning his work deteriorated noticeably to repetitions of earlier designs and motifs.

Civitali (chē-vē-tä′lē), **Masseo.** Sculptor and worker in intaglio; nephew of Matteo Civitali (1436–1501). Much of his work has been lost, but some examples remain at Lucca, as the doors of the cathedral, on which he worked as an assistant, an *Assumption* in the Church of S. Frediano, and a *Redeemer* in the museum. A terra-cotta figure of the *Virgin Annunciate* is at Amsterdam; the *Angel of the Annunciation* from the same group is in the Metropolitan Museum, New York.

Civitali, Matteo di Giovanni. Sculptor and architect; b. at Lucca, June 5, 1436; d. there, October 12, 1501. He was an associate of Antonio Rossellino, and may have been trained in his workshop. In his approach to his art he was similar to the followers of Donatello, as typified by Rossellino; he achieved an exquisite technique of carving delicate forms and imbued his work with an almost hieratic, spiritual expressivity. Much of his work was executed for the churches of Lucca, but he also had commissions at Pisa and Genoa. In the latter city he carved six vigorous and original statues of prophets and six low reliefs for the cathedral. His first great tomb in the cathedral at Lucca was that of the humanist Piero da Noceto (d. 1467) and was completed in 1472. Piero's son, who commissioned the tomb, wanted to honor his father with a monument similar to those of the humanists Bruni and Marsuppini at Florence. Civitali's construction emphasized architectural features and was ornamented with a *Madonna* in a tondo in the lunette, some busts and putti, as well as a fairly elaborate frieze on the base of the monument. Civitali's great patron at Lucca was Domenico Bertini. For him he carved the Altar of the Sacrament, in the cathedral, begun in 1473, completed after 1476. The angels from the altar are still in the cathedral; the signed tabernacle is in the Victoria and Albert Museum, London. For Bertini also he designed and executed the *Tempietto* and *St. Sebastian* of the *Santo Volto*, an exquisitely carved, small, free-standing chapel to house a wooden crucifix much venerated by the Lucchese. (The legend is that the statue was carved by St. Nicodemus and an angel, that it was brought from Palestine to Luni in a crewless boat, and that it was then transported to Lucca in a chariot drawn by wild bulls.) The monument of Bertini, with its beautifully modeled bust, is also in the cathedral. Other works by Civitali in the cathedral are the Altar of S. Regolo (1484–1485), which he designed and carved, and a pulpit (1495–1498). Many of his works have been broken up and scattered or lost. With his exquisite taste and high degree of technical proficiency, Civitali was the leading marble sculptor outside Florence in the 15th century.

Civitali, Nicolao di Matteo. Sculptor; b. at Lucca, 1482; d. there, 1560. He was the son of Matteo Civitali (1436–1501). He worked at Pietrasanta, Pontremoli, Garfagnana, and at Lucca. In the Church of the Servi at Lucca is an altar of his design.

Civitali, Vincenzo. Architect and sculptor; b. at Lucca, 1523; d. 1597. He was the son of Nicolao di Matteo Civitali (1482–1560), and served Lucca as a military architect. He also was the architect of buildings for the commune, most important of which was his enlargement of the Palazzo Pretorio. He worked at Rome, where he executed statues and ornamental decorations.

Claudio da Correggio (klou′dyō dä kôr-red′jō). See **Merulo, Claudio.**

Clavius (klä′vẹ-ůs), **Christopher.** German mathematician and astronomer; b. at Bamberg (Bavaria), 1537; d. at Rome, 1612. He became a Jesuit in 1555, studied at Coimbra in Portugal, and taught mathematics in the Jesuit college at Rome. He corresponded with Tycho Brahe and was a friend of Galileo at Rome. Among his many writings, one of the most important was his Latin edition of the *Elements* of Euclid, with the original notes. He also collaborated in the reform of the Gregorian calendar (1582). His works were printed in many editions.

Clement IV (klem′ẹnt). [Original name, **Guy Foulques.**] Pope (1265–1268); b. at St.-Gilles, Gard, France; d. at Viterbo, November 29, 1268. He held a high position at the court of Louis IX of France, but renounced the world on the death of his wife and entered the Church. He became bishop of Puy in 1256, archbishop of Narbonne in 1259, cardinal in 1261, and was on a journey to England as papal legate when he was unanimously elected pope by the College of Cardinals, to succeed Urban IV. Clement was an able statesman who sought to strengthen the papacy and to weaken the power of the Hohenstaufens in Italy and to break up the

Ghibelline party. He confirmed an agreement, initiated by his predecessor, Urban IV, with Charles of Anjou, brother of Louis IX, by which Charles was given the throne of the kingdom of Sicily as Charles I. He crowned Charles at Rome, 1266, and gave him financial aid for the conquest of Sicily. When Conradin, the last of the Hohenstaufens, marched into Italy to win back Sicily (1268), Clement retired to the fortified city of Viterbo. Watching the young monarch as he marched past to Rome, Clement remarked that he would vanish as the golden dust raised by his army. Conradin was defeated and executed by Charles. Clement died a few months later and was succeeded by Gregory X.

Clement V. [Original name, **Bertrand d'Agoust** or **Bertrand de Got.**] Pope (1305–1314); b. at Villandraut, in Gascony, France, 1264; d. at Roquemaure, in Languedoc, April 20, 1314. He was elected (1305) to succeed Benedict XI, who had died July 7, 1304. The election was delayed because the French and Italian cardinals were about evenly matched in the conclave. Through the influence of Philip IV (known as Philip the Fair), the French cardinals prevailed. Clement was crowned at Lyons and never left France. To please Philip he removed the papal residence to Avignon in 1309. For the same reason, he dissolved the order of Templars in 1312. In the hope that the restoration of imperial power in Italy would regain for him the papal lands there, Clement encouraged Henry VII in his descent into Italy in 1310. But the French court was opposed to any increase in Henry's power, and Clement failed him. He did not act when troops of Robert of Naples invaded Rome. With the withdrawal of papal support, many towns that had welcomed Henry rose against him. Clement was succeeded by John XXII.

Clement VI. [Original name, **Pierre Roger.**] Pope (1342–1352); b. at Maumont, France, 1291; d. at Avignon, December 6, 1352. He established the jubilee for every fifty years, and purchased Avignon in 1348 from Joanna I, queen of Naples. During his pontificate Cola di Rienzi attempted to reestablish the republic at Rome, and initially Clement recognized him, but later, fearing Rienzi's call for a universal empire under the leadership of Rome, supported the barons against him, and charged him with heresy. Clement VI was succeeded by Innocent VI.

Clement VII. [Original name, Count **Robert of Geneva.**] Antipope (1378–1394); b. c1342; d. at Avignon, France, September 16, 1394. He was elected, September 20, 1378, at Anagni, Italy, by a group of dissident cardinals who opposed Urban VI; and he established his court at Avignon. With his election began the Great Schism that divided the Roman Catholic Church into two principal parties, each of which supported a different pope. He was succeeded by Benedict XIII.

Clement VII. [Original name, **Giulio de' Medici.**] Pope (1523–1534); b. at Florence, May 26, 1478; d. at Rome, September 25, 1534. He was the illegitimate son of Giuliano de' Medici, born a month after his father was slain in the Pazzi Conspiracy. Before he was a year old he was taken into the household of his uncle, Lorenzo the Magnificent, brought up with Lorenzo's children, and shared in the broad and humanistic education that was provided for his cousins. Destined for the Church, the bar of his illegitimacy was removed by various decrees and dispensations. He was given many honors and benefices, and his cousin Giovanni de' Medici, having become Pope Leo X, named him archbishop of Florence in May, 1513, gave him the red hat in September of the same year, and named him vice-chancellor of the Church in 1517. Under Leo he had great influence; the pope gladly handed over to him much of the shaping and implementation of papal policy. On the death of Lorenzo II de' Medici, who had been Leo's representative as effective head of the Florentine government, Cardinal Giulio was sent to Florence in his place and governed judiciously and successfully. From the long conclave following the death of Pope Adrian VI, Leo's successor, Cardinal Giulio emerged as pope and took the name Clement VII. Many hoped that the merry days of Leo would now return to Rome. Clement was faced with the gravest problems at once. Foremost among these was the Protestant Revolt. He needed the support of Emperor Charles V in curbing it, and had supported the Edict of Worms (1521) by which Luther was proscribed; but Clement could never agree with the emperor as to the best means of halting the revolt, and refused to the end to call a council, as

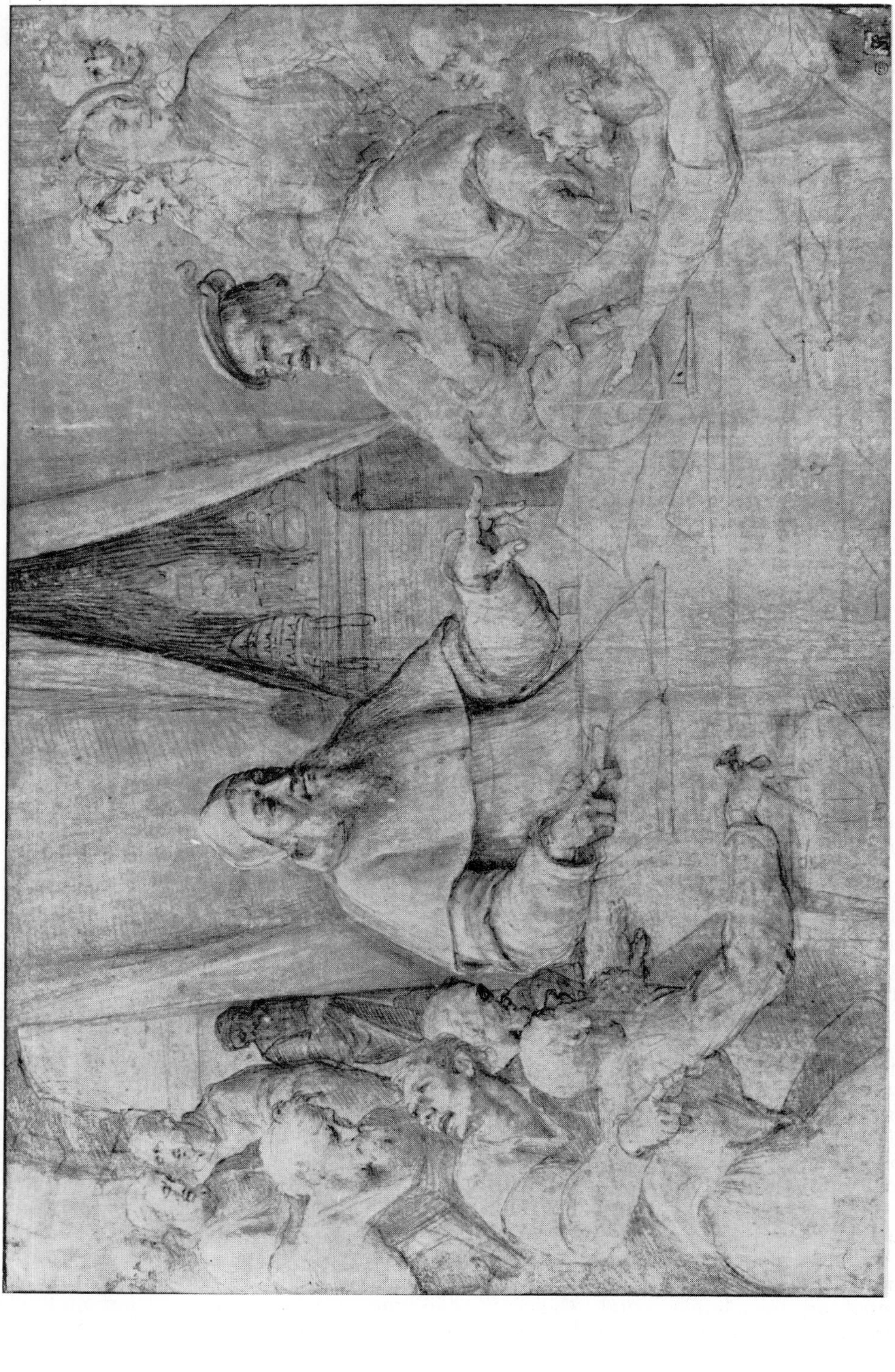

Sebastiano del Piombo
Pope Clement VII and Emperor Charles V
The British Museum, London

thin; ŦH, then; y, you; (variable) d̮ as d or j, s̮ as s or sh, t̮ as t or ch, z̮ as z or zh; o, F. cloche; ü, F. menu; ċh, Sc. loch; ṅ, F. bonbon; ʙ, Sp. Córdoba (sounded almost like v).

the emperor and many others wished to do. Furthermore, his dealings with Charles were complicated by his political aims. Charles had supported his election as pope, expecting that he could count on him in his war with Francis I. Clement was his ally in the war that ended with the disastrous defeat of the French and the capture of Francis at Pavia (1525). Immediately, fearing that a complete collapse of France would add to the power of the already dangerously powerful emperor, Clement secretly negotiated with Francis. (Francis had been released by his captors on signing the Treaty of Madrid, 1526, by which he agreed to abandon all his claims in Italy. As soon as he was freed he repudiated the treaty, on the ground that he had signed it under duress.) Clement joined Francis, the Sforza of Milan, Florence, and Venice in the League of Cognac (May 22, 1526). In September, Cardinal Pompeo Colonna, a vassal and ally of Charles V, entered Rome, raised the cry of "Colonna and Liberty," and plundered the Vatican. Clement saved himself in Castel Sant' Angelo. Charles repudiated this act of his vassal, and Clement was persuaded to withdraw from the alliance with France and Venice. Shortly thereafter a band of thousands of German adventurers entered Lombardy under the command of the German captain George de Frundsberg. They were without provisions, were not paid, and lived off the tormented land. Frundsberg died and the undisciplined troops insisted on marching on Rome for the rich plunder it offered. The Constable of Bourbon, a renegade French noble who had a command under Charles, took command of the Germans and they set out for Rome. The duke of Urbino, in command of Venetian and papal forces, followed the "barbarians" as they marched toward the Eternal City, but never engaged them. Clement, who considered himself safe and had dismissed troops guarding the city, was totally unprepared for the arrival of the horde from the north. The imperial troops approached the walls of Rome and, on May 6, 1527, entered the city. Clement just had time to fly to the Castel Sant' Angelo with some of his suite. The Germans put Rome to the most terrible sack it had endured since the declining days of the Empire. As Lutherans, their worst fury was vented on the churches and religious establishments: vestments, ornaments, vessels, and other priceless treasures were destroyed. Prelates were seized, tortured, and held to ransom. Women, including nuns, were violated, houses and palaces plundered and burned. Benvenuto Cellini, who was in Castel Sant' Angelo with Clement, describes in his *Autobiography* what those inside the refuge could see of the burning and pillaged city. Clement was a virtual prisoner until December, when he fled, first to Orvieto, then to Viterbo. He reentered Rome on October 6, 1528. In the meantime, the leaderless Germans had despoiled the city. Plague struck. Between the sack and the plague the population of the city was nearly halved. Perforce, Clement was reconciled with Charles, who disclaimed responsibility for the sack of Rome which had horrified all Europe. But Charles was the one to profit from it. Clement entered into negotiations with him and arrived at the terms of an agreement signed at Barcelona (June 29, 1529). By its terms Charles acknowledged the Sforza at Milan (but the duke was his puppet), restored the Papal States to the pope (he had contemplated assuming the temporal power himself), promised to restore the Medici (who had been expelled from Florence while Clement was shut up in Castel Sant' Angelo), by force of arms if necessary, and, to cement the alliance, gave his illegitimate daughter Margaret to Alessandro de' Medici, the illegitimate son of Lorenzo II and one of the last available males of the older branch of the house of Medici. In fulfillment of his agreement, Charles sent an imperial army against Florence in the autumn of 1529. The Florentines resisted. Since the city could not be taken by storm it was put under siege by the prince of Orange, commander of the imperial forces. Totally friendless, all the Italian states having come to terms with the emperor, the Florentines with unparalleled unanimity and heroism prepared to withstand. Their own commander, Francesco Ferrucci, undertook to keep the supply routes to the city open; for months, by his courage and skill, he was able to do so. Greatly outnumbered by the imperial troops, Ferrucci was wounded, captured, and murdered at Gavinana on August 3, 1530. The starving city could do no other than surrender (August 12), but to the emperor, not to the pope who had turned the army that had humiliated him at Rome against his own city. This flash of defiance against Clement did no good. He had crowned Charles at Bologna earlier in the year. He thus advertised his surrender to the emperor, but Charles kept his part of the bargain, and Florence was effectively given to Clement. In 1532, Alessandro de' Medici was named hereditary duke of Florence. Yet Clement could even now not abandon his idea of balancing Charles and Francis against each other. In a gesture to France he went to Marseilles (1533) to officiate at the marriage of his very young kinswoman, Catherine de' Medici, to Henry, the son and heir of Francis I.

The struggle between France and the emperor Charles V for control in Italy and the Protestant Revolt were not the only problems Clement had to face. In 1527 Henry VIII of England requested that his marriage of eighteen years with Catherine of Aragon be annulled. Catherine was the aunt of Charles V, and Clement was in no position to offend him. He took refuge in his most disastrous method of dealing with crises—delay. He instructed his legate, Cardinal Lorenzo Campeggio, to put off reaching a decision on the matter in the hope that Henry would lose interest in Anne Boleyn. Campeggio delayed, but Henry would not wait. He married Anne Boleyn (1533), and set in train a series of acts of Parliament that brought the Protestant Reformation to England.

Clement's pontificate was an almost unrelieved disaster. His policy of playing off Francis I against Charles V may have been sound, but his hesitations, indecision, and changes of mind, which were the despair of his advisers, made the implementation of any policy impossible. His reaction to the most urgent call for action was inaction. He tried to deal with the Protestant Revolt as a political problem, and seemed far too little concerned with its great spiritual significance. The measures he took to contain it were ineffective. He realized the need for Church reform but took few steps in that direction. His devotion to the interests of his family caused him to subject his city of Florence to a cruel siege and to back a restoration of the Medici that destroyed the last vestiges of republican government. He was an able and intelligent man who, as deputy for Leo, had successfully fulfilled important missions. Under the burden of final responsibility as pope, he fell a prey to conflicting opinions and consequent indecision. The threads of his diplomacy became hopelessly tangled, and his ablest advisers could not force him to adopt a single direction. A cultivated man, moderate in his personal life, he encouraged the arts and letters but was not an extravagant and indiscriminate Maecenas. He was the patron of Raphael and of Sebastiano del Piombo, whose portrait of him is in the Galerie Nazionale di Capodimonte at Naples. He commissioned Michelangelo to make the glorious Medici tombs in the New Sacristy of S. Lorenzo at Florence and also commissioned the Laurentian Library. He was succeeded by Paul III.

Clement (klā-mäṅ), **Jacques.** [Also, **Jacob Clemens;** called **Clemens non Papa,** meaning "Clement not Pope," to distinguish him from Pope Clement VII.] Flemish composer, principally of sacred music; d. before 1558. He was chief chapel master to Emperor Charles V. He is noted for his use of counterpoint and for his setting of certain psalms to popular tunes.

Clerk's Tale, The. Tale told by the Oxford student in Chaucer's *The Canterbury Tales.* It is founded upon Boccaccio's story of the patient Griselda, which the clerk states he read in Petrarch's version, to which several harrowing incidents from folk tale are added.

Clesius (klē'sẹ-u̇s), **Bernardinus.** [Name given to him by the humanists; real name, **Bernardo Cles.**] Cardinal and statesman; b. in the castle of Cles, in the Trentino, March 11, 1485; d. at Bressanone, July 28, 1539. After he had taken his doctorate at Bologna, he was named (1514) bishop of Trent. The emperor Conrad had made the bishopric of Trent into a principality (1027) and its rulers were prince-bishops. Clesius's elevation, celebrated by magnificent ceremonies, marked the beginning of a line of native Tridentine bishops after a long series of Germans, and he became one of the most distinguished bishops of Trent. In 1530 he was at Bologna for the coronation of Charles V, and was given the red hat at that time by Pope Clement VII. In 1539 he became administrator of the see of Bressanone, hitherto also held by Germans. As an administrator and prince he won back control of Riva, enlarged the bishop's jurisdiction, reorganized the episcopal archives, arranged for the compilation of the Codex Clesiano, published the statutes of Trent, reopened the mint, and coined money stamped with his own likeness. He strongly opposed religious and political reform and was a devoted partisan of the emperors. He spent part of his life in Germany, where he acted as astute chancellor and intimate adviser of Ferdinand, king of the Romans (brother of Charles V). He was a generous patron of Italian humanism and art, diffused Italian culture in the Trentino, and encouraged it with his support in his diocese. He was in touch with Erasmus and German humanists as well as with such Italians as Bembo, Aretino, Vergerio, and others. His own love of splendor had a profound effect on the artistic development of the region, and his encouragement of building changed Trent from a medieval city to one with the aspects of the Italian Renaissance. Castles, churches, and palaces rose in Trent. The palace he caused to be constructed for himself was a magnificent edifice, worthy of his imperial guests, and filled with art treasures and decorated by outstanding painters of the time. He had planned also to restore and reconstruct the bishop's palace at Bressanone but died before he could carry out his plan. Many of his letters are preserved in the state archives at Trent.

Clizia (klē'tsyä). Comedy by Niccolò Machiavelli, written after 1512 during his enforced retirement from political life. Nicomaco, a sober, industrious, and dignified old man, has fallen in love with Clizia, a beautiful young girl. Clizia (who never appears on stage) was left as a child with Nicomaco and his wife Sofronia and, since her father never returned to fetch her, has been carefully brought up by them. His love for Clizia transforms Nicomaco into a besotted old fool, a transformation that has not escaped his wife's notice. Their son Cleandro is also in love with Clizia. Nicomaco, scheming to enjoy the delights of the young girl, plans to marry her to his servant Pirro, who has agreed that Nicomaco can take his place on the wedding night. Sofronia, aware of his plans, wishes to marry her ward to a less cooperative husband, and has chosen Eustachio, bailiff of their farm, as her husband. Cleandro knows that his mother will not consent to his own marriage to a girl of unknown heritage, and seeks to prevent Clizia from marrying either. In a drawing of lots to see whose candidate wins, Pirro is chosen and Nicomaco is ecstatic over his prospects. But he has reckoned without his wife. She substitutes a strapping young man dressed in Clizia's clothes at the wedding. The hilarious, and painful, results when Nicomaco attempts to carry out his plans in the darkened bridal chamber can be imagined. Sofronia has made Nicomaco ridiculous by her cleverness, and henceforth he is willing to do whatever she says, if only he can be spared public disgrace. To make all tidy, Clizia's father, who turns out to be a wealthy Neapolitan gentleman, appears. He acknowledges his daughter and graciously gives her to Cleandro in marriage. Machiavelli drew the model for his comedy from Plautus, but he has rendered it immutably Florentine by his setting, his crisp and biting dialogue, and his Florentine realism.

Clopinel (klo-pē-nel), **Jean.** See **Jean de Meung** (or **Meun**).

Cloridano (klō-rē-dä'nō). Friend of Medoro in Ariosto's *Orlando Furioso.* The two venture into the field of battle to find among the heaps of slain the body of their lord.

Clorinda (klō-rēn'dä). In Torquato Tasso's *Gerusalemme liberata,* an Amazon who comes to aid the pagans besieged in Jerusalem by the Crusaders. Tancred sees her at a fountain and falls in love with her. She meets him and prepares to fight him in single combat but he refuses her challenge. "Thy conquest lies in those fair eyes," he tells her, bares his breast to her lance, but is swept away by his fellow knights as the battle surges around them. In the battle before the walls of Jerusalem, Clorinda is limited to shooting arrows from the ramparts, and chafes at her inactive role. She proposes a night sortie to the crusading camp. The eunuch who has attended her since childhood pleads with her not to go, and tells her the story of her life. Fair and white as she is, she is the daughter of a black Ethiopian king and his wife. Her mother, a Christian, fearing her jealous husband's suspicion of the white child, had given Clorinda to the eunuch to care for, and had begged him to have her baptized. Under his care, she had had many miraculous escapes, had been nursed by a tiger, but he had never carried out his promise to have her baptized; now he is troubled by strange dreams. Clorinda too has been troubled by dreams, but resolves to carry out her plan to invade the

Christian camp and set fire to their siege tower. Under darkness and in disguise, she enters the camp and sets fire to the tower. In the chase that follows she remains outside the walls to allow her companions to escape. Tancred pursues her and in a furious struggle mortally wounds her. He lifts her helmet and discovers his beloved Clorinda. Before she dies he accedes to her request for baptism.

Clouet (klö-e), **François.** [Called **Janet** or **Jehannet.**] French painter; b. at Tours, France, c1516; d. c1572. He was the son and pupil of Jean Clouet (c1485–c1541), whom he succeeded as painter to the king in the reign of Francis I (a position he also held under Henry II and Charles IX).

Clouet, Jean. [Called **Jehan, Jehannot, Jehannet.**] Portrait painter at the French court; b. c1458; d. c1541. He was the father of François Clouet.

Clovio (klō′vyō), **Giorgio Giulio.** [Original name, **Clovich;** called **Macedo** or **il Macedone,** because it was thought that he came from Macedonia.] Miniaturist, illuminator, and painter; b. in Croatia, 1498; d. at Rome, 1578. He came to Venice in 1516, went to the court of Louis II of Hungary for a time, and then to Rome, where he was taken prisoner in the sack of 1527. He succeeded in escaping and went to Mantua, where he entered the Convent of S. Rufina. He entered the priesthood and was called to the papal court at Rome by Paul III and had many highly placed patrons for his art, which he is thought to have studied with Giulio Romano at Rome and Girolamo dai Libri at Verona. Among his patrons were the cardinal of Trent, Grand Duke Cosimo I de' Medici, and Pope Julius III. Many illuminated codices are attributed to him, among them two missals in the Vatican; an illuminated life of Federico, duke of Urbino; and a book of hours with twenty-six illuminations and twelve miniatures commemorating victories of Charles V (British Museum). He was highly admired as the "prince of illuminators" by his contemporaries. Later criticism has held that he did not understand that the limits of illumination cannot be exceeded without changing its character, and that he was to a great degree responsible for the decline of illumination in the middle of the 16th century.

Cobham (kob′ạm), **Eleanor.** Second wife of Humphrey, duke of Gloucester; d. c1443. She had dealings with Roger Bolingbroke, who professed the black art, and was tried for a conspiracy to kill the king by magic, that her husband might have the crown.

Cocchi (kōk′kē), **Pompeo di Piergentile.** Perugian painter; active from 1509; d. 1552. He was a follower of Domenico Alfani, and later fell under the influence of Raphael. A *Crucifix*, dated 1522, and another with a *Pietà* (intended to be shown for consolation to those condemned to death) are in the National Gallery of Umbria at Perugia.

Coccio (kō′chō), **Marcantonio.** See **Sabellico, Marcantonio.**

Cochlaeus (kok-lē′us), **Johannes.** [Original name, **Johann Dobenek** or **Dobneck.**] German Roman Catholic humanist, theologian, and controversialist; b. at Wendelstein, near Nuremberg, Germany, 1479; d. at Breslau, January 11, 1552. He became secretary to the duke of Saxony in 1528, and canon at Breslau in 1539. He was a participant at the Diet of Augsburg (1530), shared in composing the Refutation of the Augsburg Confession, and came to be regarded as a leading opponent of the Reformation.

Cock (kôk), **Hieronymus.** [Also, **Kock.**] Flemish painter, engraver, and publisher of prints; b. at Antwerp, Belgium, 1510; d. there, 1570. He studied at Rome and is believed to have assisted Vasari in writing the lives of Dutch artists. He was the first in his country to go into the business of engraving and selling prints in a large way.

Cocxie (kok′si), **Michiel.** See **Coxcie** or **Cocxie** or **Coxie, Michiel.**

Codronchi (kō-drông′kē), **Giovanni Battista.** Physician; b. at Imola, 1547; d. there, 1628. He was one of the earliest to treat forensic medicine as a separate discipline. His famous *Methodus testificandi* was appended to one of the earliest works that dealt with lesions of the vocal apparatus, *De vitiis vocis libri duo.*

Codrus Urceus (kō′drus ör′sẹ-ůs), **Antonius.** [Real name, **Antonio Urceo.**] Humanist; b. at Rubiera, August 14, 1446; d. February 11, 1500. He learned Greek at Ferrara and was noted as a Hellenist. From 1470 he was tutor, for ten years, to the son of Pino Ordelaffi of Forlì, and then went to Bologna as a professor. In some of his writings he abused the Church and the clergy in outrageous terms;

he was superstitious and frightened by omens; he told his pupils that no one knew what happened after death; but in his will he commended his soul to God. He left prose works, learned letters, and poetry in several forms.

Coelho (kwā′lyö), **Gonçalo.** Portuguese navigator, fl. 1488–1506. He explored the coast of Brazil as far as Rio de Janeiro.

Coelho Pereira (pẹ-rā′rạ), **Duarte.** Portuguese soldier; b. c1485; d. at Olinda, Pernambuco, Brazil, August 7, 1554. He is said to have been the first to reach Cochin China. In 1530 he destroyed a French settlement on the coast of Brazil. He was granted the captaincy of Pernambuco and made it the most flourishing colony in Brazil.

Coello (kō-ā′lyō), **Alonzo Sánchez.** Spanish painter; b. at Benifayro, near Valencia, Spain, c1531; d. at Madrid, c1588. He was especially noted for his portraits. He worked at the court of Philip II of Spain, succeeding his teacher, Antonio Moro (Sir Anthony More).

Coeur (kėr), **Jacques.** French merchant and financier; b. at Bourges, France, c1395; d. on the island of Chios, November 25, 1456. He had charge (c1436 *et seq.*) of the coinage and financial affairs of the state and effected important reforms. His own money and agents were often used to support French interests, and one of the results of his policies was the eviction of the English from Normandy. He was imprisoned (c1451–c1455) on the false charge of having poisoned Agnès Sorel, the king's mistress, and his fortune was seized by the king. He escaped, entered the service of Pope Calixtus III, and was in charge of a fleet in the papal campaign against the Turks when he died.

Coffer. In architecture, an ornamental sunken panel or compartment in a ceiling or soffit. The coffers are usually enriched with moldings, which may be plain, painted or gilded, and have a rosette, pomegranate, star or other ornament in the center. Many Renaissance buildings have handsome coffered ceilings, as some of the salons in the ducal palace at Mantua.

Cognac (ko-nyȧk), **Holy League of.** League concluded on May 22, 1526, among Pope Clement VII, Francis I of France, and the cities of Milan and Venice, against the emperor Charles V. Henry VIII of England was in sympathy with the league, but contributed nothing to its effectiveness. In the following year the forces of Charles overran Italy and sacked Rome.

Cola dell' Amatrice (kō′lä del ä-mä-trē′chā). [Original name, **Nicola Filotesio.**] Painter and architect; b. at Amatrice, 1489; d. after 1547. He was a native of Amatrice, in the Abruzzi, and was active in the first half of the 16th century. Most of his life and work was carried out at Ascoli Piceno, where he was a citizen and (1521) public architect. His activity is recorded there up to 1547. As a painter he began by following in the footsteps of Carlo Crivelli, as in his *St. James of the Marches* (National Gallery of the Marches, Urbino), *Four Saints* (Church of S. Angelo Magno, Ascoli Piceno), and others. Later he was influenced by the Umbrians and by Lo Spagna. Many of his works are in the art gallery at Ascoli Piceno, including his *Mater Dolorosa* and *St. John the Evangelist*, both of which are so sharply defined in form and the lines of the drapery as to seem carved. A *Madonna and Four Saints* (1514), at Ascoli, and an *Assumption*, signed and dated (1515), in the Vatican, reflect various influences resulting from a visit to Rome. Other works at Ascoli Piceno include a statue of Pope Paul III (Palazzo del Popolo) and paintings in the churches of S. Francesco and S. Agostino. As an architect, Cola designed (1527) the façade of the Church of S. Bernardino at Aquila and several works at Ascoli Piceno.

Cola da Camerino (dä kä-mā-rē′nō). See **Arcangelo di Cola da Camerino.**

Colantonio (kō-län-tō′nyō). Neapolitan painter; active from c1440 to 1470. He is thought to have been the teacher of Antonello da Messina at Naples. A panel, *St. Jerome in His Study*, now in the museum at Naples, comes from the Neapolitan Church of S. Lorenzo Maggiore, and is part of a large Franciscan retable. Pilasters at the sides of the central panel, *The Delivery of the Rule of the Order*, carry figures of Beati of the Franciscan order.

Coleberti (kō-lā-ber′tē), **Pietro.** Painter of Piperno; active in the first half of the 15th century. An unpolished painter in the international Gothic style; of more industry than inspiration, his work yet has a certain archaic charm. A series of frescoes on the life of St. Catherine of Alexandria, signed and dated (1430), is at Roccantica, near Rome.

Colet (kol′ẹt), **John.** English theologian and

humanist; b. at London, c1467; d. there, September 16, 1519. He studied in Italy and France, and was the intimate friend of Erasmus, whom he accompanied on a pilgrimage to Canterbury (1514). Other humanists in the group of which he was a member were Sir Thomas More, Grocyn, and Linacre. Colet was one of the chief promoters of the "new learning" of the Renaissance and indirectly of the Reformation.

Colette (ko-let), Saint. Flemish religious; b. at Corbie, France, January 13, 1381; d. at Ghent, March 16, 1447. Permitted by Pope Benedict XIII to enter the Poor Clares, and authorized by him to found new convents and promote reform of the order, she founded seventeen convents during her lifetime, the nucleus of the Colettine Poor Clares. She was canonized in 1807.

Coligny or **Coligni** (ko-lē-nyē), **Gaspard de.** French general and Huguenot leader; b. at Châtillon-sur-Loing, France, February 16, 1519; killed in the Saint Bartholomew's Day massacre, at Paris, August 24, 1572. He openly embraced Calvinism, and did not hesitate to use his official position as admiral of France where this could be of help to the Huguenots. Detested by Catherine de Médicis, he was murdered in his chamber, falling as the first victim of the Saint Bartholomew's Day massacre.

Colines (ko-lēn), **Simon de.** French printer; d. 1546. His work was carried on at Paris, where he was the collaborator and successor of Henri Estienne, the Elder. It is thought that he was a type designer.

Colines (ko-lēn), **Simon de.** French printer;

Colle, Raffaello.

Collenuccio (kōl-lā-nöt′chō), **Pandolfo.** Historian, poet, scientist, and statesman; b. at Pesaro, January 7, 1444; executed there, July 11, 1504. He studied law at Padua, and then entered the service of the Sforza at Pesaro. For his patrons he performed many diplomatic missions and carried out numerous charges, until he was expelled from Pesaro by his lord, Giovanni Sforza. His great reputation as a lawyer, man of letters, and skillful diplomat opened the doors of the most brilliant courts of Italy to him. Among others who availed themselves of his talents were Lorenzo the Magnificent at Florence, Ercole I d'Este at Ferrara, the emperor Maximilian, and Pope Alexander VI. He successfully concluded many delicate negotiations for his patrons. When Cesare Borgia made himself master of Pesaro and forced Giovanni Sforza into exile, Collenuccio was able to persuade him to restore Giovanni's goods. Otherwise, as he was in the service of another, he supported the cause of Cesare Borgia in the Romagna. On the fall of Cesare, the Sforza returned to Pesaro, and when Collenuccio returned to Pesaro, Giovanni Sforza had him imprisoned and then executed. Collenuccio wrote a history of Naples, Latin and Italian poems, and made the translation *Anfitrione*, of the comedy of Plautus. In his many-sided interests and activities Collenuccio was a typical man of the Renaissance.

Colleoni (kôl-lā-ô′nē), **Bartolomeo.** Captain; b. at Solza, near Bergamo, 1400; d. November 4, 1475. He was of an ancient and noble family which exercised a minor sovereignty over the province of Bergamo. Considered the foremost tactician and disciplinarian of the 15th century, he was often in the pay of Venice, but changed sides, as did all the captains, as it suited his interest. In his youth he served Filippo Arcelli of Piacenza as a page. He then entered the armies of Braccio da Montone, who was at the time (1419) in the pay of Alfonso of Aragon. Colleoni was the last of the great captains trained by Braccio, who trained so many of the warriors of the 15th century. In 1424 Colleoni switched to the armies of Braccio's rival and former comrade in arms, Muzio Attendolo Sforza, and in the same year took part in Braccio's defeat at the battle of Aquila (Braccio himself meanwhile having changed sides). Colleoni won great fame in that battle; and as Muzio Attendolo had been drowned, Colleoni emerged as a leader. He next entered the pay of Venice in the wars against the Visconti, in which he won more laurels. He fought at the side of Gattamelata in southern and central Italy, and again for Venice; and he fought with Francesco Sforza in the wars concluded by the Peace of Cremona (1441). Thereafter he was among the leading captains of the age and played a part in the major engagements from Verona to Brescia. Venice rewarded him well for a time, to keep him in its pay, but when the republic became niggardly in its recognition Colleoni entered the pay of the Visconti (1442). The Visconti began to suspect him and cast him into prison, but he escaped. (His employers often suspected him of being about to go over to the other side. The Venetian Council of Ten at one time conspired to have him assassinated.) He returned to the service of Venice (1448) and for the next six years had a brilliant career. In 1454 he was finally given top command of the Venetian land forces and retained the post until his death. He was installed in a castle of almost regal splendor, and remained faithful to Venice despite the requests of Pope Pius II for his services. Venice, always distrustful of her captains, kept a close watch on him, and he died in an atmosphere of intrigue and espionage. He was a patron of the arts. The most notable works that celebrate his greatness are the statue by Verrocchio and Leopardi at Venice, considered among the best equestrian statues in existence; the castle at Malpaga, near Bergamo, with its frescoes; and the Colleoni Chapel in the Alta Città at Bergamo, with the tombs of Bartolomeo and his daughter Medea. Colleoni had amassed great wealth, and left most of it to Venice on condition that a monument to him be erected on the Piazza San Marco. The equestrian statue, designed and begun by Verrocchio and finished by Leopardi, was not, however, placed in the piazza; it stands in the Campo dei SS. Giovanni e Paolo. The Venetians had a rule against cluttering the piazza with monuments, and easily convinced themselves that Colleoni's condition would be fulfilled if the statue was placed in a nearby square. The statue was cast in 1496, and is the second equestrian statue of the Italian Renaissance, Donatello's *Gattamelata* at Padua being the first. It characterizes with striking naturalism the haughty and formidable mercenary soldier. The rich marble pedestal has Corinthian columns and entablature. The Colleoni Chapel in the old city at Bergamo was built between 1470 and 1476 by Amadeo, the architect of the Certosa di Pavia. It was frescoed in the 18th century by Tiepolo.

Colleoni, Girolamo. Painter of Bergamo, active in the second quarter of the 16th century. His *Madonna and Child* is in the Carrara Academy, Bergamo.

Collerye (kol-rē), **Roger de.** See **Bontemps, Roger.**

Colloquies. Prose work (1516; later editions 1519, 1522, 1536) in Latin by Erasmus, in which he bitterly and satirically attacks evil practices in the Catholic Church and improper conduct on the part of priests. In a single year, 24,000 copies were sold. In this work, according to the monks, "Erasmus laid the egg that Luther hatched."

Colombini (kô-lôm-bē′nē), **Giovanni.** Sienese religious; d. July 31, 1367. He was a wealthy Sienese merchant who became oppressed by his sins and decided to give his possessions to the poor. In 1355 he gave away his money, to the dismay of his wife. When he reminded her that she had often charged him to be more charitable, she replied that when she prayed for rain she did not want a flood. To chastise himself, Colombini did manual labor in the Palazzo Pubblico at Siena, rode about the city on an ass, and asked his companions to shout accusations against him in the Campo. He opposed books and learning, preached the abolition of the privileges of wealth, and advocated democracy. By his example and his preaching he won many followers, among them three members of the prominent Piccolomini family; but the government of Siena exiled him as a disturber of civic peace. He went to Arezzo, with some of his followers, and thence to other cities of Tuscany, preaching and singing songs of praise composed by his companions. When plague broke out in Siena, 1363, it was thought to be a judgment against the city, and he was recalled. In 1367 his activities were finally approved by Urban V, who recognized him as the founder of a fraternity for laymen called the Gesuati (Order of *pauperes Christi*). His letters are witnesses to his religious fervor. He was beatified by Gregory XIII.

Colonna (kō-lôn′nä). Ancient, noble Roman family whose origins are obscured by the mists of time but who, by the 11th century, were already powerful at Rome, with vast possessions outside of Rome and strongholds within it. They were often driven from Rome and lost their lands, their fortresses, and palaces, but they always returned, rebuilt, and regained power. From the Middle Ages, the history of the family is intimately linked to the history of Rome. From early times they were rivals of the equally powerful Orsini family. Their wealth and influence were increased by their connections with the Church and their offices in the city; they contributed many cardinals to the former and officials and captains to the latter. An early cardinal was Giovanni (d. 1216), raised to the Sacred

College in 1193, noted for his piety and as a protector of St. Francis of Assisi and his order. A second Giovanni (d. 1244) became cardinal in 1212. He was papal legate on the fifth crusade, and brought back to Rome the highly venerated Column of the Redeemer (the column to which it is thought Christ was bound for scourging, now in the Church of S. Prassede). After fighting against Ezzelino da Romano in the March of Ancona, he suddenly switched over to the emperor's Ghibelline party, and the Colonnesi were thereafter almost always supporters of that party. Pope Gregory IX threatened to depose him, but Giovanni died before he could do so. For a time the family fortunes were in eclipse for having thus opposed the pope. Nicholas III (an Orsini) restored their fortunes in order to curb the power of his enemies. He named Giacomo Colonna a cardinal (1278), and made his brother Giovanni senator of Rome. In 1289 Giovanni's son Pietro became a cardinal. The two cardinals quarreled with Boniface VIII. They asserted that his pontificate was illegal, as the abdication of his predecessor, Celestine V, was illegal. They also supported Philip the Fair of France, the pope's arch foe. On May 3, 1297, Stefano Colonna, brother of Cardinal Pietro, leaped from an ambush with his followers and seized the papal treasure, which was being transferred from Anagni to Rome. Boniface called the Colonna cardinals into his presence, demanded that Stefano be given up as a prisoner, and that, along with restoring the treasure, the Colonnesi hand over their strongholds of Palestrina, Zagarolo, and Colonna. The treasure was returned, but the Colonnesi wrote out a proclamation that they daringly deposited on the altar of St. Peter's itself. They asserted that Boniface was not the true pope and called for a council. Boniface promptly declared the Colonna cardinals deposed from their offices. He condemned them, as well as members of the family and their descendants. He waged war on them, drove them from their strongholds, seized their most important fortress, Palestrina, and razed it. Their goods were confiscated, and they were banned from office and from the lands of the Church. Their power was at a low ebb. But Boniface was seized by Sciarra Colonna at Anagni on September 7, 1303, and though liberated by the people a few days later, he died of rage the next month. In exchange for their support at the long conclave at Perugia, from which the Frenchman Clement V emerged as pope (June 5, 1305), Clement fully restored the two cardinals, enriched them with ecclesiastical benefices, and rewarded them in other ways. Giacomo died at Avignon (whither Clement had moved the papal seat at the French king's request), on August 14, 1318. He was buried in S. Maria Maggiore at Rome, where there is a portrait of him in mosaic, executed in 1295. Pietro also died at Avignon (1326) and was buried in S. Maria Maggiore. Stefano was the most distinguished lay member of the family at the end of the 13th and well into the 14th century. After the death of Boniface he restored the family fortunes, forced the Caetani (Boniface's family) to indemnify the Colonnesi, and made it possible for the family once more to assume a leading role at Rome. He was named imperial vicar and was knighted by the Roman people (1326). He and his brother Sciarra went separate ways when the emperor Louis IV came to Rome. Stefano abandoned his Ghibelline loyalties; Sciarra, faithful to the traditions of his house, remained a Ghibelline and was at the emperor's side when Louis was crowned (1328). After Louis had declared Pope John XXII deposed (for opposing him), Giacomo, Stefano's son, daringly entered a Rome that was occupied by German troops and read Pope John's condemnation of the emperor. When Louis left Rome, Sciarra was banished. He died in exile, grieving in his last illness, that he was tamely dying in bed (1329). The fighting between the Colonnesi and the Orsini, in which all the nobles took part on one side or the other, brought Rome to a state of anarchy. As the only hope of restoring order, the Roman people made Stefano virtual ruler (1339). A noble Roman, he was the friend of Petrarch and died at an advanced age between 1348 and 1350. A second Stefano, grandson of Sciarra, and his brother Agapito were elevated to the Sacred College by Urban VI (1378). With the election of Oddone Colonna as Pope Martin V (1417) the family prospered mightily. Queen Joanna II of Naples was persuaded to name the pope's brother Giordano duke of Amalfi and prince of Salerno; his brother Lorenzo became count of Amalfi. These were but small additions to the vast possessions about Rome and in southern Italy that the Colonnesi, in the various branches of the family, now held. Of Lorenzo's three sons, Antonio became prince of Salerno and count of Alba; Odoardo count of Celano; and Prospero became a cardinal (1430). Prospero (d. 1463) was a friend of humanists (Poggio Bracciolini dedicated his treatise on avarice to him) and ardently interested in humanism himself; he founded a valuable library. (His vote in the conclave of 1458 was the last needed to elect Enea Silvio Piccolomini as Pius II. Pius admired him as a patron of learning but thought he was too much under the influence of his mother and the Ghibellines.) Eugenius IV, Martin's successor, ordered the Colonnesi to return the papal treasure, and hand over certain lands. They rebelled, drove the pope from Rome, were excommunicated, and their fortress at Palestrina was again destroyed (1437) by Orsini partisans of the pope. Members of the family supported Alfonso of Aragon in his struggle with René of Anjou for control of the kingdom of Naples. Pius II made Girolamo Colonna prefect of Rome with a hereditary right to the office. (Girolamo, fighting the Orsini, was killed at Rome in April, 1482.) Antonio, Martin's nephew, died in 1471. Of Antonio's many children, Prospero (b. 1452) took an active part in events of his age. Under Sixtus IV the old rivalry between the Colonnesi and Orsini erupted again. The pope and the Orsini supported Girolamo Riario, the pope's nephew. The Colonnesi opposed his activities in the Romagna. With the pope's encouragement, the Orsini plundered the Colonna palace in Rome and devastated other palaces of the family. Lorenzo Oddone Colonna was put to the torture and beheaded in Castel Sant' Angelo. War followed, in which the Colonnesi party was led by Prospero and his cousin Fabrizio. After the death of Sixtus, the Romans rose up and recalled the Colonnesi. (They were generally regarded as the popular party.) When the French descended into Italy (1494), Fabrizio facilitated their advance into Naples. Afterward, with his cousin Prospero, he went over to the side of the Spanish. For their services, Prospero and Fabrizio were invested with lands in the kingdom of Naples. Fabrizio's son Ascanio took part in the siege and sack of Rome (1527), as the family allied itself to the cause of Spain. Cardinal Pompeo Colonna, a soldier at heart, was the enemy of popes Julius II and Leo X, and of the Medici. For most of the 16th century the family were partisans of the emperor. Marcantonio II, the son of Ascanio, was excommunicated by Paul IV and deprived of his lands. They were restored by Pius IV, and Marcantonio led the papal forces at the battle of Lepanto (1571). The holdings of the Colonnesi in 1252 had included the mausoleum of Augustus, transformed into a fortress, and Monte Citorio, at Rome. Outside Rome they held Palestrina, formidable fortress and principal seat of the family, Zagarolo, La Colonna, Capranica, Pietra Porzia, Gallicano, San Giovanni, and San Cesareo. In the course of the years their holdings were frequently lost and regained, and to them were added donations by sovereigns and popes. As the centuries passed, they sold some of their lands to other prominent families, but it is thought that the Colonnesi family has occupied the same quarter of Rome for seven centuries. During those centuries members of the family were prominent in affairs of the Church, of the state, and in arms, and have remained so down to the 20th century.

Colonna, Fabrizio. Soldier; d. 1520. Of the main branch of the famous Roman Colonna family, he was destined for the Church but preferred the arts of war. He took part in the battle by which Otranto was won back from the Turks (1481), fought, with other members of his family, against the Orsini, and was an ally of Pope Innocent VIII in the wars (1485–1486) against King Ferrante of Naples. He at first helped Charles VIII of France to take Naples, then switched his allegiance to Ferdinand II, king of Naples, and helped chase the French out (1495). He was rewarded by the investiture of Tagliacozzo, numerous other fiefs, and a substantial annual pension. In 1501 he was taken prisoner when the French returned, was released, and thereafter entered the service of Spain, along with his cousin Prospero. The Spanish rewarded him for his military feats in their behalf with fiefs in the Abruzzi. In the battle of Ravenna (1511), as a commander of Spanish forces, he was wounded and taken prisoner by Alfonso I d'Este. Alfonso treated him well and released him without ransom. From this cause, Fabrizio sought to bring about a reconciliation between Julius II and the Estensi. When the Estensi, at Rome under a safe conduct, were about to be treacherously imprisoned, Fabrizio braved the wrath of the warlike pope to help his former captor escape. In 1515 Ferdinand the Catholic made him grand constable of Naples, a position that was passed on in the family of the Colonna of Paliano (to which branch Fabrizio belonged) for generations. Machiavelli so admired his skill in arms that he made him one of the speakers in his dialogue on the art of war. By his wife, Agnesina da Montefeltro, Fabrizio had Federico, who predeceased him; Ascanio, who succeeded him; and Vittoria, the poet and friend of Michelangelo, who became the marchioness of Pescara.

Colonna, Francesco. Dominican friar; b. at Venice, c1432; d. there, c1527. He wrote *Hypnerotomachia Poliphili*, on the dream and struggle of Poliphil. The work, written at Treviso (1467), in a peculiar mixture of archaized Italian and Italianized Latin, is interesting as an allegory in which humanistic ideas—as of free will, the supremacy of the intellect, and the sensuous enjoyment of beauty (all fully developed in the Renaissance)—struggle with the principles of piety of the Middle Ages. The allegory is expressed in a search by Poliphil for a nun who is the object of his love. The search is successfully conducted in a dream, from which Poliphil wakens to find himself alone. The dream is a salmagundi of classical and theological allusions, a storehouse of exotic facts, descriptions of 15th century architecture, painting, and sculpture, details of gardens and the celebrations of festival days, and a loving survey of jewelry, banquets, the virtues of athletics, and the joys of beautiful women. The work, dedicated to Duke Guidobaldo of Urbino, was beautifully produced by Aldus Manutius, and was illustrated with rare woodcuts by unknown artists.

Colonna, Giacomo. Bishop of Lombez; d. 1341. He was the son of Stefano Colonna (d. between 1348 and 1350) and the brother of Cardinal Giovanni (d. 1348). John XXII named him bishop of Lombez in 1328. He was the patron and friend of Petrarch for many years.

Colonna, Giovanni. Cardinal; d. 1348. He was the son of Stefano Colonna (d. between 1348 and 1350) and the brother of Giacomo, bishop of Lombez (d. 1341). He was named cardinal by John XXII before he was 30. As were other members of his family, he was the friend and patron of Petrarch for many years. A metrical letter addressed to him by Petrarch (1347) concerns a dog that the cardinal had given him and describes his pleasure and satisfaction with the gift.

Colonna (or **delle Colonne**), **Iacopo.** Sculptor; b. 1504; d. at Bologna, before 1540. He worked at Venice, Forlì, Bologna, and Padua. The few of his works that remain, as at Venice and Padua, show him to have been a conventional follower of Sansovino.

Colonna, Marcantonio II. Soldier; b. at Civita Lavinia, 1535; d. at Medinaceli, Spain, August 1, 1584. A member of the prominent Roman family, he fought with Spanish troops at Siena (1553–1554), took advantage of a quarrel between his father, Ascanio, and Pope Julius III to seize his father's lands, quarreled with and was excommunicated by Pope Paul IV because in the struggle between the pope and Spain he took the Spanish side. On good terms with Pius IV, he was named captain-general of the pontifical fleet by Pius V in 1570. In 1571 he was lieutenant under Don John of Austria, commander of the Italian and Spanish fleets, and at the battle of Lepanto (October 7, 1571), as commander of the Papal forces, Marcantonio withstood the main thrust of the Turkish fleet. For the victory, Colonna was welcomed at Rome with a triumph that recalled those of ancient Rome. His desire to pursue the war against the Turks was not fulfilled, and peace was made in 1573. Philip II, the emperor, appointed him imperial vicar of Sicily, where Colonna proved an able administrator. He died on a mission to Spain. His letters concerning the preparations for an allied fleet to oppose the Turks survive.

Colonna, Oddone. Original name of Pope **Martin V.**

Colonna, Pompeo. Cardinal; b. at Rome, 1479; d. at Naples, 1532. The son of Prince Girolamo Colonna, of the noble Roman family, at a very early age he took part in the skirmishes with the Orsini at Rome and in other struggles. His uncle, Cardinal Giovanni Colonna, wished him to follow an ecclesiastical career. Through him Pompeo received offices and benefices. He passed his life as a prelate but he was a soldier at heart. In August, 1511, in response to rumors that Pope Julius II was dying, Pompeo, perhaps disappointed in his hope of being made a cardinal, went to the Campidoglio at Rome and roused the people to throw off the yoke of the priests and regain their liberty. Julius recovered and Pompeo was accused of disloyalty, deprived of his offices, and forced to retire from Rome. When Julius died (1513), Pompeo returned to the city and was acclaimed by the people. Deeply interested in the intellectual movements of his age, his happiest years were in the time of Pope Leo X, who shared his interest in letters, was his friend, and gave him the red hat (1517). He had a splendid palace at Rome and lovely villas outside the city, where he gave sumptuous banquets, arranged almost royal hunts, and where cardinals and nobles were accustomed to meet with men of letters. (His own writing included an *Apologia mulierum*, dedicated to his cousin Vittoria.) He traveled in Spain and France, and was sent by the emperor Maximilian to Flanders to woo his grandson, the future Charles V, away from an alliance with the French. Although a friend of Leo, Cardinal Colonna was opposed to Giulio de' Medici, but supported him in the conclave of 1523 either out of fear that an Orsini might be elected or because of simony. Giulio, as Clement VII, made him vice-chancellor, gave him the magnificent Riario Palace, and many benefices which the cardinal gave up to his relatives and friends. But the cardinal remained an enemy of the pope, and was one of the principal intriguers with the Spanish. In September, 1526, he entered Rome with a band he had collected, and to the cry of "Empire, Colonna, and Liberty!" plundered the Vatican and the basilica of St. Peter's itself. His attempt to raise rebellion failed because the imperial envoy concluded a pact with the pope. Under the pact Colonna was promised amnesty; however, the pope refused to honor the amnesty, deprived him of every ecclesiastical dignity, and, in his turn, saw Colonna's houses plundered and burned. In the following year Colonna was openly on the side of the Spanish in the war against the pope, but he was horrified at the sack of Rome (May, 1527), and did what he could to alleviate the suffering caused by it. He answered Clement's call from Castel Sant' Angelo, where the pope had taken refuge, and worked efficiently for his liberation. The pope forgave him his earlier disloyalty and restored him to his honors. In 1530 he replaced the prince of Orange as vicar of Naples. At Naples he vigorously set about his administration, and soon became hated for his harshness and repressive fiscal policies. His death there was said to have been the result of poison.

Colonna, Prospero. Cardinal and humanist; d. March 24, 1463. A member of the wealthy and powerful Roman family, he was the brother of Antonio, prince of Salerno and count of Alba, and of Odoardo, count of Celano. He was given the red hat in 1430. He was an outstanding humanist, had a valuable library, and was a friend of the leading humanists of his day.

Colonna, Prospero. Distinguished soldier; b. 1452; d. at Milan, December, 1523. He was the son of Antonio, prince of Salerno, of the famous Roman family. He fought vigorously in the wars against the Orsini and Pope Sixtus IV, was declared a rebel, and was banished from Rome by the pope (1482). In the war of Sixtus and Venice against Ferrara (1482–1484) he was in the army of Alfonso of Aragon against the pope, and defended the Colonna territory of Paliano against the Orsini and Girolamo Riario in 1484. The next year he joined the pope against Ferrante of Naples. When Charles VIII of France marched through Italy (1494), Prospero and his cousin Fabrizio assisted his conquest of Naples, but the following year they both went over to Ferdinando II, king of Naples, and helped him chase the French from the kingdom. Later, with the knowledge and consent of Ferdinando, then in exile, the cousins went over to the Spanish, and thereafter remained loyal to the empire in the long struggle between the French and Spanish for domination of Italy. While in the service of Massimiliano Sforza, attempting to prevent the French from invading Milan, he was taken prisoner at Villefranche (1515). On his release he resumed service for the empire and was named imperial commander in Italy by Charles V. In 1521 he forced the French to retire from Milan; the following year he defeated them at Bicocca, and drove them out of Genoa. His last battle (1523) was another attempt to prevent a French invasion of Milan.

Colonna, Stefano. Roman senator, count of Romagna; d. between 1348 and 1350. He was one of the outstanding figures of this leading Roman family. He was senator in 1292, became an implacable enemy of Boniface VIII, who excommunicated the Colonnesi, seized their lands and razed their stronghold, Palestrina, and later won from the Roman Senate a decree by which the Caetani (family of Boniface) made restitution. The rivalry between the Colonnesi and Orsini involved all the Roman nobility and kept Rome in a continual state of warfare. Stefano invoked the aid of Henry VII, and accompanied him when he entered Rome. In the contest between the Orsini and the Ghibellines of the emperor's party (1310), Stefano was seriously wounded. In 1316 he was vicar of Rome, and in 1339 he was given dictatorial power by the people as the only man who might be able to restore order. The Colonnesi sought to overthrow Cola di Rienzi, who had seized power in Rome. In a battle with Rienzi's men at the gate of San Lorenzo on November 20, 1347, the Colonnesi were routed. Two of Stefano's sons were killed. He is said to have received the news of their deaths without tears and with the resigned remark that it was better to die than to bend to the yoke of a tyrant. Petrarch, of whom various members of the Colonna family had been patrons, met Stefano when he visited Rome in 1336. The two took walks together to view the ancient ruins and discussed history and the glory of ancient Rome. Of Stefano, Petrarch said that "he never grows old, while Rome ages continually."

Colonna, Vittoria. Poet; b. at Marino, near Rome, 1490; d. at Rome, February 25, 1547. She was the daughter of Fabrizio, grand constable of Naples, by his marriage with Agnesina di Montefeltro, daughter of Federico, duke of Urbino. As a daughter of one of the oldest, wealthiest, and most powerful houses of Italy, she was betrothed, for reasons of state, when four years old to a boy of the same age, Fernando Francesco d'Avalos, the only son of the marquess of Pescara, an Aragonese house. She received a good education and was well grounded in Latin literature. The beautiful, intelligent, and cultivated young woman was married at Ischia to the young marquess of Pescara at the age of 19, and for her it was a love match. Her husband had political and military ambitions, and in 1511 was wounded and taken prisoner by the French at the battle of Ravenna. Released soon afterward, he returned to his wife, but left her again in 1515 for military duty in Lombardy. She never saw him again. Weakened by wounds and illness, he died in 1525.

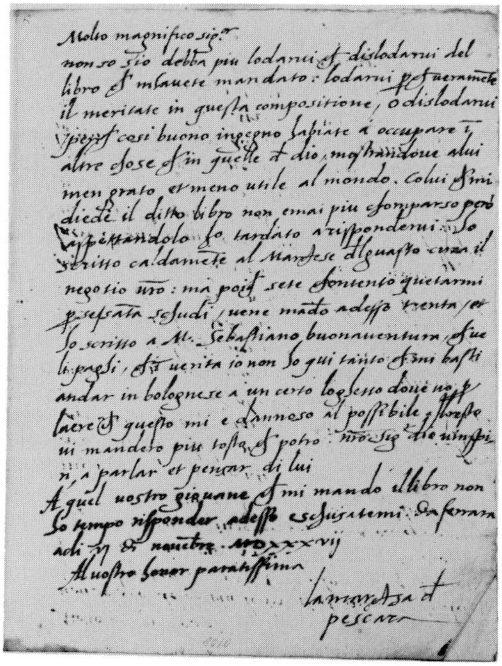

Letter (1537) from Vittoria Colonna
to Pietro Aretino
Courtesy of the Isabella Stewart Gardner Museum,
Boston

Vittoria heard the news at Viterbo and was prostrated with grief. She abandoned the interest in political affairs that had been nourished by her husband's ambitions, began an ascetic life devoted to good works, and gave more attention to the poetry that had been of interest to her since her youth. (One of her earliest and best poems had been written to her husband when he was a prisoner in 1511.) She wandered about Italy, often staying in convents, as at Viterbo and Orvieto, and finally in semimonastic seclusion at Rome. The blatant corruption of the Church troubled her sorely. She was in contact with such advocates of reform as the Englishman Cardinal Pole, Cardinal Contarini, Jacopo Sadoleto, and others, but remained a faithful daughter of the Church. Her intellectual activities are those by which she is best known. She was the friend and confidante of Michelangelo especially, with whom she shared deep concern for the state of the Church and with whom she enjoyed a profound and pure friendship. She was, as well, the center of a group of leading men of letters that included Bembo, Sannazzaro, Bernardo Tasso, Castiglione, Guidiccioni, and was a correspondent of the infamous Aretino, among many others. Many letters, diaries, and documents of the time speak with admiration of this gifted, beautiful, and spiritual woman. Her friendships and her influence alone ensure her place in the history of Italian literature. Her poetry falls into two groups, of which one is devoted to sonnets in memory of her husband, whom she came to idealize as a saint (she was perhaps unaware of his treachery to the Italians, whom he openly despised as a Spaniard), and with whom she longed to be reunited in a better world. The second and larger group of her poems are on sacred and moral themes. In style she was a disciple of the purist Bembo. In her treatment of her moral themes she reveals herself as one striving and longing for spiritual release. A later age has found her personality, her friendships, and her influence more remarkable than her poetry.

Coltellini (kôl-tel-lē′nē), **Michele di Luca dei.** Ferrarese painter; b. at Ferrara, c1480; d. c1542. He was a minor painter whose first known work, the signed and dated (1502) *Death of the Virgin* (Pinacoteca, Bologna), shows the influence of Ercole Roberti of Ferrara in its types and dated 15th century forms and motifs. Later influences were those of Lorenzo Costa, Francia, and Perugino; that of Costa became so apparent after 1503 that it seems likely that Coltellini followed him to Bologna. A *Presentation in the Temple* by Coltellini is in the Carrara Academy at Bergamo.

Colucci (kō-löt′chē), **Angelo.** Humanist and poet; b. at Jesi, 1474; d. 1549. He was secretary to popes Leo X and Clement VII, and became bishop of Nocera in 1537. He became the leading light of Roman humanism. A noted Greek and Latin scholar, he wrote Latin verse of classical excellence and was among the first to study the origins of Italian and Provençal poetry, as well as among the very first to study ancient Portuguese poetry. He had a magnificent collection of manuscripts (badly damaged in the sack of Rome, 1527), many of which are now in the Vatican Library.

Columbus (kǫ-lum′bus), **Bartholomew.** [Spanish, **Bartolomeo Colón.**] Brother of Christopher Columbus; b. probably at Genoa, c1445; d. at Santo Domingo, on the island of Hispaniola, May, 1515. He was with Bartolomeu Dias on the West African coast (1486–1487), and went to England in 1488 in a vain attempt to interest Henry VII in his brother's project. He returned to Spain in 1493, after Christopher Columbus had sailed on his second voyage, but followed him, in command of a supply fleet, to the settlement of Isabella. Columbus made him *adelantado* (governor), and from 1496 to 1498 he governed the island during his brother's absence, founding the city of Santo Domingo in 1496. He subdued an Indian revolt, marched to Xaraguá in 1497, and in 1498 had the first trouble with the rebel Francisco Roldán. In 1500 Francisco de Bobadilla, the royal commissioner sent to restore order, deported him as a prisoner to Spain, where he was released with the admiral. He was with his brother on the fourth voyage (1502–1504) and was the leader where active work was required. In the struggle to subdue a new rebellion at Jamaica, he was wounded. After the admiral's death he seems to have been at Rome, and in 1509 he accompanied his brother and nephew, both named Diego Columbus, to Hispaniola, where he held important and lucrative offices.

Columbus, Christopher. [Italian, **Cristoforo Colombo;** Spanish, **Cristóbal Colón;** Latin, **Christophorus Columbus.**] The most famous discoverer of America; b. probably at or near Genoa, c1446; d. at Valladolid, Spain, May 20 or 21, 1506. There has been much dispute concerning the place of his nativity and even his nationality, but it is generally accepted that he was the son of Genoese wool combers. He received a fairly good education, and certainly, like a true Genoese, took to the sea at an early age. In 1473 or thereabouts he was in Portugal, where he married and had a son, Diego; he also lived for a time on the island of Porto Santo, near Madeira. It is probable that he sailed with some of the Portuguese expeditions to the African coast; he is known to have visited Ireland, and there is some doubtful testimony that he voyaged as far as Iceland. Being among those who understood that the earth is round, he had already formed the conviction that Asia might be reached by sailing westward, and he tried to get the backing of the king of Portugal for an expedition in that direction. Failing in this, he went to Spain (c1484) and offered the enterprise to its monarchs, Ferdinand and Isabella, but the advisers whom they deputed to examine the project reported adversely. Columbus sent his brother Bartholomew to England in 1488 in a vain effort to interest Henry VII. Oppressed by poverty, Christopher was about to go to France when he obtained a personal interview with the Spanish royal couple at Granada, but the rewards he demanded in case of success of the projected voyage were so excessive that they declined to aid. Columbus was about to leave Granada when some of his friends induced the queen to reconsider; and on April 17, 1492, Ferdinand and Isabella agreed over their signatures that Columbus should be admiral in all regions that he might discover, and viceroy in all countries that he might acquire for Spain, with full powers and a generous share of the revenues, and that these honors and powers should pass to his heirs. Partly with royal aid, partly with the help of the Pinzóns, merchants of Palos, three small ships were fitted out: the *Santa Maria*, the *Niña*, and the *Pinta*, with the first named as flagship. With crews totaling either 90 or 120 men (accounts differ), the little vessels left Palos on August 3. After touching at the Canaries they continued westward into the unknown, and on October 12, 1492, came to a small island called by its natives "Guanahani," but christened by Columbus "San Salvador"; it was one of the islands now called the Bahamas, but exactly which one is not known with certainty (some believe it to have been Watling Island). After landing and claiming the island for Spain, he sailed on, discovering and claiming other islands, obtaining small quantities of gold and other products. He coasted the northern side of Cuba and of Hispaniola, and at a point on the shore of the latter island, which he called Española, the *Santa María* was wrecked. Here he built a fort that he called La Navidad; and leaving 40 men there, he returned to Spain in the *Niña*. After pausing to visit the king of Portugal he reached Palos on March 15, 1493, and was summoned to the Spanish court, where he was received with great honor, confirmed in his privileges, and given ample means for a new expedition. On September 25, 1493, he sailed from Palos again with 17 vessels and 1,500 men. On November 3 he discovered the island of Dominica, and thereafter touched at several of the Caribbees before making his way to La Navidad, where he found that his colony had been wiped out by the Indians. On a new site he founded Isabella, the first European town in the New World, and continued his explorations. Ill conduct by the Spaniards turned the original friendliness of the Indians into hostility; there were many bloody clashes, and Columbus proposed to enslave all hostile natives. The Spanish colonists also were restive under Columbus' rule, and conveyed their complaints to Spain, from which a commission was sent to investigate the state of affairs in Española. Columbus sailed to Spain, leaving his brothers in charge, and was well received by the king and queen, who dismissed the charges against him. He sailed westward again in 1498, and for the first time came to the mainland of South America, making a landfall near the mouth of the Orinoco. When he came to Española he found that a new town, Santo Domingo, had been founded by Bartholomew in his absence and was in the hands of rebels with whom he had to make humiliating terms. When word of these troubles reached Spain, Francisco de Bobadilla was sent to Española as royal commissioner, and presently the great admiral and his brothers were sent to Spain in chains. Arriving there in October, 1500, they were promptly released, but Columbus could not obtain a reinstatement of his dignities. He did obtain four caravels in which he sailed westward again, intent on circumnavigating the globe. In 1502 he sailed down the coast of Central America from Honduras to Panama, vainly seeking a westward passage. Defeated, he turned eastward, and at Jamaica his ships, worm-eaten, became unnavigable. By means of a canoe his plight was after a while made known in Española, but not until June, 1504, were he and his men rescued. Once more the weary admiral returned to Spain (November 7, 1504), but before the year was out Isabella died, and his petitions for reinstatement were ineffective. He passed his remaining days in poverty and neglect. Columbus was, of course, acquainted with the legends of Saint Brendan's Isle and of Hy-Brasil and with other Irish accounts of a land beyond the western ocean; similar legends were probably current in other countries, though there was by no means so extensive a knowledge of pre-Columbian transatlantic voyages then as modern scholarship has developed. His great merit was that, having a scientific mind at the moment of history when the scientific approach became both possible and imperative, and having indomitable courage as well, he established once and for all the existence of lands westward across the Atlantic from Europe. But the Admiral of the Ocean Sea died believing that he had reached India, quite unaware that he had opened a New World to the peoples of Europe.

Columbus, Diego. [Italian, **Giacomo Colombo**; by Latin writers called **Jacobus.**] Brother of Christopher Columbus; b. probably at Genoa, c1450; date and place of death unknown. He accompanied Christopher Columbus on the second voyage (1493) and was at times left in command at the settlement of Isabella or at Santo Domingo, on the island of Hispaniola. He was sent to Spain in chains with his brothers in 1500, and about that time became a priest. In 1509 he accompanied his nephew Diego Columbus to Santo Domingo, and probably died soon after.

Columbus, Diego. [Spanish, **Diego Colón.**] Son of Christopher Columbus; b. probably at Lisbon, Portugal, c1476; d. at Montalvan, near Toledo, Spain, February 23, 1526. In 1492 Queen Isabella made him a page at the Spanish court, where he remained until after his father's death. He was confirmed in 1509 as admiral of the Indies and governor of Hispaniola, but without the title of viceroy. He arrived at Santo Domingo on July 10, 1509, but the conflicting claims of jurisdiction and dissatisfaction with his rule soon made the position an uneasy one. Diego Velásquez, whom he sent to conquer Cuba in 1511, virtually threw off his authority. The establishment of a royal audience at Santo Domingo restricted his power, and though in a visit to Spain he obtained new favors (1520), he was finally called back by the Council of the Indies in 1523 to answer charges against him. His wife was left in charge of the government, but Diego followed the court, vainly seeking redress, until his death.

Columbus, Ferdinand. [Spanish, **Ferdinando Colón.**] Illegitimate son of Christopher Columbus; b. at Córdoba, Spain, August 15, 1488; d. at Seville, July 12, 1539. His mother was Doña Beatrix Henríquez, a lady of Córdoba. The child was made a page to Queen Isabella in 1498, was with his father on the fourth voyage (1502–1504), and by the admiral's will received an ample income, afterward increased by royal grants. He amassed a library of over 20,000 volumes, which passed by will to the cathedral chapter of Seville, where it was known as the "Columbina"; only about 4,000 volumes remain. A history of the Indies by him is lost, as is the Spanish original of his biography of his father.

Columbus, Luis. [Spanish, **Colón**; titles, Duke of **Veragua.** Marquess of **Jamaica.**] Son of Diego Columbus and grandson of Christopher Columbus. In 1536 he gave up all claims to the title of viceroy of Hispaniola (inherited by the grant to his grandfather by Ferdinand and Isabella), receiving in return the island of Jamaica in fief, a large pension, lands in Veragua (in what is now Panama), and the titles of duke of Veragua and marquess of Jamaica. He was captain-general of Hispaniola from 1540 to 1541. In 1559 he was imprisoned for having three wives, and in 1565 banished to Oran. His descendants were the dukes of Veragua.

Colyn Clout (kol′in klout; kō′lin). Poem (c1520) by John Skelton, a satire against the clergy of his time.

Comines or **Commines** or **Commynes** or **Comynes** (ko-mēn), **Philippe de.** [Title, Sieur **d'Argenton.**] French chronicler and statesman; b. in Flanders, c1447; d. at Argenton, Deux-Sèvres, France, October 18, 1511. He entered the service of Charles the Bold of Burgundy, and then (1472) went over to Louis XI of France, in whose household he rose to the dignity of confidant and counselor. He served Louis well in the intrigues against the duke of Burgundy, in dealings with England and the Italian states, and was well rewarded by his sovereign. His fortunes fell after the death of Louis. He entered into court intrigues, took part in a plot, and was arrested (1486) and imprisoned for over two years. After Charles VIII released him he never again had as much influence as he had enjoyed under Louis XI. Forced to give up his political life, he began his *Mémoires*, which were written between 1489 and 1498. These give a vivid, but balanced account of the reigns of Louis XI and Charles VIII, and are marked by his awareness of the significant event. Charles VIII had no use for Comines' advice concerning his expedition into Italy, a country that Comines knew well. Comines describes Charles as "weak, willful, and surrounded by foolish counselors," and says of him in regard to the Italian expedition that Charles was a fledgling, "provided with neither money nor good sense." Nevertheless, the expedition succeeded, as Comines thought, by the grace of God. His *Mémoires* are invaluable as an eyewitness account of events of his day.

Commandino (kôm-män-dē′nō), **Federico.** Mathematician; b. at Urbino, 1509; d. 1575. After the death (1534) of Pope Clement VII, in whose service he had been, he went to Padua to study Greek and medicine. He practiced medicine for a time at Ferrara then, under the patronage of Guidobaldo, duke of Urbino, gave himself up entirely to the study of mathematics, and translated the principal scientific works from Greek to Latin. His great contribution lay in thus making available the works of Archimedes, Aristarchos of Samos, Ptolemy, and the *Collection* of the 14th century Alexandrian geometer Pappus. He also translated Euclid's *Elements.* His original scientific works were *Horologiorum descriptio* (Rome, 1562) and *Liber de centro gravitatis solidorum* (Bologna, 1562).

Commendone (kôm-men-dō′nā), **Francesco Giovanni.** Cardinal and diplomat; b. at Venice, March 7, 1523; d. at Padua, December 26, 1584. He finished his law studies at Padua, and from 1550 was almost continuously in the service of the Holy See, beginning as one of the secretaries of Pope Julius III. He traveled all over Europe on business for the Church, as to Brussels, to England to win acknowledgment from Queen Mary of the English throne's dependence on Rome (a mission in which he succeeded partly because his fluent command of English made him accessible to the queen), to the Low Countries, and to the courts of Urbino, Ferrara, and Parma, as well as to Venice. In 1560 he went to Germany to seek agreement to the reopening of the Council of Trent, and invited the Protestants to attend; they refused. In 1564 he went to Poland and won the king's recognition of the Decretals of Trent, and permission for the Jesuits to enter the kingdom. Many of the dispatches from his missions have been published.

Commentaries of Pius II. A record of the memorable events of the reign of Pope Pius II (*Pio II Comentarii rerum memorabilium quae temporibus suis contigerunt*), written, in Latin, during his pontificate, and comprising thirteen books. Modeled on Caesar's *Commentaries,* Pius wrote parts of the work in his own hand and dictated the rest to secretaries. He turned the material over to his secretary, Antonio Campano, for correction and editing for, as he said, "we set down the important and the unimportant alike, we are without eloquence, and have woven together a rude and unorganized narrative." Campano made a few changes, suppressed such parts as he thought too frankly expressed, and in this form gave it to Johannes Gobellinus, a German cleric and copyist. Gobellinus copied the manuscript he received and signed his name to it, as was the custom of the time. Since the memoir is written in the third person (Pius always speaks of himself as "Aeneas," "the Pope," "Pius"), and since it was signed by Gobellinus, it was long thought that Gobellinus was the author. The original manuscript was found, soon after 1883, by the Catholic scholar Ludwig Pastor, in the Vatican Archives. Comparing this with the authorized version, published 1584, it was found that the original had been cut, perhaps at the instigation of Francesco Bandini de' Piccolomini, archbishop of Siena, who, in the more restrained atmosphere of the Counter-Reformation, feared lest this frank record might damage the reputation of his great humanist kinsman.

The *Commentaries* do not reveal Pius as a modest man. Nowhere do we find an admission of an error of judgment or policy. "Pius," "Aeneas," "the Pope," always appears as brave, wise, good, and greatly beloved, as well as a man who could move audiences to tears by his eloquence. Nevertheless, his description of his work as being "without eloquence" and "rude and unorganized" is modest. The *Commentaries* supply a vivid record of the principal events and figures of mid-15th-century Europe. They abound in brisk portraits of his contemporaries. Cosimo de'

Medici, who was over 70 when Pius saw him in Florence in 1459, "was of fine physique and more than average height; . . . Nothing went on in Italy that he did not know." Federico da Montefeltro "was an able and eloquent man, but blind in one eye, which he had lost in a tournament." Francesco Sforza "sat his horse (at 58) like a young man; . . . He had great physical and intellectual gifts." Alfonso I (Alfonso V of Aragon), "a great king . . . who had subdued many provinces of Italy and defeated the most powerful generals, was finally conquered by love and like any captive of war was a slave to a weak woman." Of an obstinate cardinal, "When the pope could make no impression on him by arguments (he is so dull as to be incapable of reasoning) he disregarded him as being weak-minded." He gave such a devil as he considered Sigismondo Malatesta his due, "vigorous in body and mind, eloquent, and gifted with great military ability. . . . whatever he attempted he seemed born for, . . ." yet, he was a "prince of all wickedness," "outdid all barbarians in cruelty, . . . hated priests and despised religion . . ."

He had traveled in Switzerland, Germany, Austria, France, England, and Scotland, to say nothing of crisscrossing Italy, and was a tireless sightseer. Everything interested him. Was there a shrine, an abandoned castle or monastery, an ancient fortress, or archaeological site anywhere near the path of one of his journeys, he went to see and investigate. He writes of the village of Strood, in Kent, England, where men were said to be born with tails to punish them for having cut off the tail of Thomas à Becket's horse. He is skeptical about the genesis of the herb carolina, said to have been miraculously provided to cure Charlemagne's army of a pestilence, calling it "a mere tale invented by Charlemagne's admirers." Often, as background for some event of his own time, he gives the history of families or kingdoms, or relates recent occurrences, as the battle of Agincourt and events of the life of Joan of Arc, all of which took place in his own lifetime. The pages bristle with accounts of the raids, sieges, and campaigns going on in Italy, the condottieri and captains who led them, the plunder that was taken, and the lives that were lost.

He delighted in nature. "Masses of flowering broom gave much of the country a golden hue. . . . The world was green in that month of May and not only the meadows but the woods were smiling and birds were singing sweetly." "Nearby (Abbadia, near Siena), an abundant spring gushes from the rock, and after he had lunched beside it, Pius heard embassies and petitions there." "Sometimes too Pius held a consistory with the cardinals under the chestnuts and heard embassies in the meadow." He also took delight in the pageantry of processions and describes with relish the ingenious and elaborate decorations of the palaces along the routes. The ceremonies attendant on his own coronation, with banners and flags painted by Benozzo Gozzoli, win a colorful and enthusiastic description, as do those that took place when St. Andrew's Head was brought to Rome (1462).

The *Commentaries* reflect the age in which they were written, an age that was more worldly than spiritual. Pius tells, in minute detail, of an argument he heard on a theological question, and comments, "It was a noble and delightful experience to hear brilliant and profoundly learned men arguing together." At the same time they reveal a warmly human personality and a highly articulate and intelligent man, who wrote of his world as he saw it. It was a world bursting with vitality and boiling with the intellectual and political struggle to take Europe out of the limitations of the Middle Ages.

Commines or **Commynes** (ko-mēn), **Philippe de.** See **Comines** or **Commines** or **Commynes** or **Comynes, Philippe de.**

Compagni (kōm-pä′nyē), **Dino.** Florentine chronicler, merchant, and public official; b. at Florence, 1260; d. there, February 26, 1324. He was a contemporary of Dante but not as ardent a member of the Bianchi (White Guelphs), and was not expelled from Florence when (1301) the Neri (Black Guelphs) returned to power. Fundamentally, he was a merchant and public official (he served as prior and gonfalonier of justice). He is noted for his *Cronica delle cose occorrenti ne' tempi suoi* (c1310), a record of his own times. It is concerned with the struggles between the Bianchi and Neri, especially about the year 1300; it shows him to have been a patriot and justifies his role in the struggles. The *Cronica* was not published for about 400 years after Compagni's death. In its immediacy, detail, and religious conviction, the *Cronica* is an indispensable source for the history of the period.

Compère (kôṅ-per), **Loyset.** French composer noted for his contrapuntal music; d. at St.-Quentin, France, August 16, 1518. He was chorister and chancellor of the cathedral at St.-Quentin.

Complaint of Mars. Poem by Geoffrey Chaucer, written probably c1379. It is full of astronomical allusions, and contains the story of "the broche" that Vulcan wrought at Thebes. It is supposed to be sung on Saint Valentine's Day by a bird. A *Complaint of Venus* is sometimes appended to it, but is of a later period, is of a totally different character, and is a translation from the French.

Complaint of Venus, The. Poem by Geoffrey Chaucer, translated by him late in life from the French. It is made up of three independent ballades. The title was given by the copyists as a counterpart to the *Complaint of Mars,* to which it is sometimes appended.

Complaint to His Empty Purse. Poem by Geoffrey Chaucer, sometimes attributed to Thomas Hoccleve. It is believed that it was written sometime before 1399, but that in that year Chaucer appended a dedicatory postscript and sent the poem to Henry IV, on that monarch's accession to the English throne. Chaucer is known to have received an annuity from the king within a very short time after his taking the throne.

Complaint Unto Pity. Poem by Geoffrey Chaucer, printed before 1532 and perhaps written c1367.

Comynes (ko-mēn), **Philippe de.** See **Comines** or **Commines** or **Commynes** or **Comynes, Philippe de.**

Concordat of Francis I. Convention concluded in 1516 between Francis I of France and Pope Leo X. It replaced the Pragmatic Sanction of Bourges, a modification of the reformatory decrees of the Council of Basel, which had been adopted at the Assembly of Bourges in 1438, but which had never been recognized by the pope. It reestablished the annates (a fee on a bishopric payable to the pope), referred the *causae majores* to Rome, and gave to the king the right of nominating bishops, subject to papal confirmation. The movement toward making agreements with the French crown from the Pragmatic Sanction of Bourges to this Concordat was in part a consequence of pressures on the papacy, first by Church councils and then by Spain, inducing the Church to sacrifice time-honored prerogatives in order to win the support of the French king.

Condolmieri (kōn-dōl-mye'rē), **Gabriele.** Original name of Pope **Eugenius IV.**

Conecte or **Connecte** (ko-nekt), **Thomas.** French Carmelite monk; b. at Rennes, France, in the latter part of the 14th century; burned at Rome 1433. He was famous as a preacher of moral reforms among the clergy and laity. He was put to death on a charge of heresy.

Conegliano (kō-nā-lyä'nō), **Cima da.** See **Cima da Conegliano, Giovanni Battista.**

Conrad (kon'rad), Saint. Franciscan tertiary; b. at Piacenza; d. 1351. He was of a noble family of Piacenza, was married to a lady of equally good family, and seemed destined for a happy life. On a hunting expedition he ordered his servants to set fire to a thicket in which he thought his quarry had taken refuge. The wind fanned the flames and set fire to and destroyed the harvest in nearby fields. A woodsman was charged with the destruction and was sentenced to death. Conrad, who had escaped the flames, confessed that he was responsible for the fire. To pay for the damage, he sold his property and goods and was reduced to poverty. Reflecting on the evanescence of worldly happiness, he and his wife began to think of the salvation of their souls. She joined the Poor Clares and he became a Franciscan tertiary. He won such a reputation for saintliness that people began to seek him out. To avoid this he went to Sicily, where he alternated between caring for the sick in hospitals and meditation in a hermitage. When he felt himself tempted by the desires of the flesh, he did as St. Francis had done: rolled in thorn bushes.

Conrad IV. King of the Germans; b. at Andria, April 25 or 27, 1228; d. at Lavello, May 21, 1254. He was the second son of Frederick II, whom he succeeded in 1250. The imperial crown was contested by William, Count of Holland, who maintained himself by the aid of the Guelphs. In 1251 Conrad undertook an expedition into Italy to enforce his rights of succession to the crown of Sicily. He is said to have died of poison, leaving his infant son Conradin as the last heir of the line. The throne was occupied as regent by Conrad's illegitimate brother Manfred. The imperial throne was vacant, the Great Interregnum, until the election of Rudolph of Hapsburg, 1273.

Conradin (kon′ra̤-dēn; German, kon′rä-dēn). [Also, **Conrad V**; called **Conrad the Younger.**] Duke of Swabia; b. near Landshut, Germany, March 25, 1252; beheaded at Naples, October 29, 1268. He was the son of Conrad IV of Germany, and the tragic last survivor of the house of Hohenstaufen. In 1268 he marched into Italy to win back his kingdom of Sicily from the usurping Charles of Anjou. Conradin was received with rapture by the Ghibellines of Lombardy and Tuscany and marched south to Rome. His principal adviser was a young man only three years older than he. His army met Charles at Tagliacozzo on August 23, 1268, and, although superior in numbers, was defeated. Conradin escaped but was betrayed, captured, and beheaded at Naples.

Consensus Genevensis (ko̤n-sen′sus jen-ḛ-ven′-sis). Confession of faith drawn up by Calvin which was dedicated (January 1, 1552) by the pastors of Geneva to the syndics and council of the city. It was occasioned by Calvin's dispute with Bolsec, who denied the doctrine of reprobation, and was designed to unite the Swiss churches on the subject of predestination, but failed to acquire symbolic authority outside Geneva.

Consensus Tigurinus (tig-ṳ-rī′nus). Confession of faith drawn up in 1549 at Zurich (Latin, Tigurium) by Calvin, in concert with Bullinger and the pastors of Zurich, for the purpose of uniting the Swiss churches on the doctrine of the Lord's Supper. It was published in 1551 and was adopted by all the Reformed cantons of Switzerland except Berne.

Console. In architecture, a bracket, usually in the form of a reversed S-curve, used to support a cornice, shelf, dais, statue, urn, or the like.

Constance, Council of. Ecclesiastical council called, with great reluctance, by the antipope John XXIII. It met in Konstanz (Constance), Germany, in 1414 to: try to end the Great Schism, in which there were at that time three who claimed to be pope (Gregory XII, Benedict XIII, and John XXIII); provide for reform of the Church; and suppress the Hussite heresy in Bohemia. John fled the hostile Council in March, 1415. Benedict XIII, the Avignon antipope, also fled, but he never relinquished his claim to the papal chair. He and John were tried by the Council and deposed. Gregory sent legates acceptable to the Council and formally abdicated to it (July, 1415). The Council governed until 1417. At that time it elected Martin V, and the Great Schism ended. This Council, as opposed to the Council of Pisa (1409), was considered canonical from the time that the legates sent by Gregory XII convened it (1415). Before being dissolved (1418), the Council condemned John Hus (1415) and Jerome of Prague (1416) to death. Not surprisingly, these executions had a disturbing effect upon clerics and literary men at the Council.

Constantine XI Palaeologus (of the *Byzantine Empire*) (kon′sta̤n-tēn, pā-lḛ-ol′o̤-gus). Last Byzantine emperor (1448–1453); b. 1394; d. May 29, 1453. He was the son of Manuel II and the brother of John VIII, whom he succeeded. During his reign the Turks under Mohammed II besieged Constantinople. The defenders, led by Constantine, put up a heroic resistance for two months, though outnumbered twenty to one, but the city fell on May 29, 1453. Constantine was killed with the last of his men in the desperate final struggle.

Contarini (kôn-tä-rē′nē). Ancient noble family of Venice, documented from the 11th century. They were noble merchants who expanded Venetian commercial interests in the East. One branch of the family had such possessions in Syria that it came to be known as the Contarini dal Zaffo from the city of Jaffa. Branches of the family at Venice held vast possessions and estates gained in the 14th and 15th centuries. Luca Contarini, who lived at the end of the 14th and the beginning of the 15th centuries, was an eminent jurisconsult, statesman, philosopher, and lecturer at the University of Padua. Iacopo was doge (1275–1280), as was Andrea (d. 1382). During the latter's dogeship Venice fought Trieste, the Carrarese of Padua, and the war with Genoa that ended with victory at Chioggia. Other members of the family were eminent statesmen, diplomats, and men of letters.

Contarini, Ambrogio. Traveler; d. at Venice 1499. Of an ancient noble Venetian family, in 1474 he was sent on an embassy to the sovereign of Persia, in connection with the war against the Turks. In February of that year he set out. He crossed the Alps by the Brenner Pass, traveled across Austria, Poland, the Ukraine, and into the Crimea. Crossing the Black Sea, he next went into Caucasia and arrived at Tabriz in Persia in August of 1475. The Persian ruler was at Isfahan, where Contarini joined him. At first welcomed, he was abruptly asked to leave in June, 1476, and set out for home, passing through southern Russia on his way and arriving in Venice in April, 1477. He left an account of his travels. Though not an in-depth analysis, it is generally accurate. It was printed in 1486 and later included in the second volume of Ramusio's great collection of travel writings, *Delle Navigationi et Viaggi*.

Contarini, Andrea. Doge of Venice (1368–1382); b. c1300; d. 1382. During his reign the Venetians waged war against Trieste (1366), against the Carrarese family of Padua (1372–1374), and against Genoa in the War of Chioggia (1377–1381), so called because of the Genoese seizure of the Venetian city that precipitated the war. The latter struggle, marked by deeds of military and civic heroism, was brought to an end under the walls of Chioggia with a Venetian victory. Contarini himself set the example of patriotism by melting down his gold and silver plate and pledging his estate to raise funds for the prosecution of the war.

Contarini, Gaspare. Cardinal and reformer; b. at Venice, October 16, 1483; d. at Bologna, August 24, 1542. Of a distinguished Venetian family that had contributed magistrates, ecclesiastics, and six doges to the republic, he served Venice at home, and abroad as ambassador to Charles V (1521–1528) and to the papal court of Clement VII. In both cases he suffered a degree of personal humiliation and attack, since he was defending Venetian opposition to Charles and Clement. Pope Paul III raised him, although a layman, to the cardinalate, and he soon made his influence felt in the Curia. He was greatly troubled, as were his friends Vittoria Colonna and Michelangelo, by the corruption in the Church; he vigorously set about correcting it, and became a leading figure within the Church to plan and promote reform. He sought, unavailingly, reconciliation with the Protestants. In 1536 he headed a commission to prepare for a council that would take up internal reform. In the recommendations he drew up, *Consilium de emendanda Ecclesia*, he courageously pointed out abuses, made specific suggestions by which they could be purged, and urged the calling of a council. Reforms he considered urgent were moral regeneration of the clergy, regulation of the distribution and transfer of benefices, reform of the monastic orders, and inspection and regulation of schools and books. He also supported papal recognition of the Jesuits as a reforming order. His recommendations were well received at the Consistory of March, 1537, but implementation was slow. However, as bishop of Cividale di Belluno, he put his recommendations into effect in his own diocese. An earlier work, *De officio episcopi*, describes the abuses of the clergy as he saw them, and outlines the ideal behavior and motivation of a bishop. He played a prominent part at the Diet of Ratisbon (Regensburg, 1541), but his influence declined somewhat as his doctrine appeared to be too sympathetic to the Protestants. His defense of a double view of justification did not win the Lutherans and pleased neither the Italian nor German Catholics. It was most unsatisfactory to the emperor. But he kept the confidence of the pope and was acting as his legate at Bologna when he died. His *De potestate pontificis* and *Confutatio articulorum seu quaestionum Lutheranarum* are defenses of papal power against attacks by Venice and the Protestants.

Conte (kôn′tā), **Jacopino del.** See **Iacopino del Conte.**

Conti (kôn′tē), **Bernardino de'.** Lombard painter; b. at Pavia, 1450; d. 1525 or 1528. At first a follower of Vincenzo Foppa and Civerchio, he later tried to achieve the manner of Leonardo da Vinci; but with his often hard and mannered style and his turbid color, he was one of the less gifted of that master's Lombard followers. Signed and dated paintings by Bernardino de' Conti exist from 1496 to 1523, the earliest signed work being an effigy of Francesco Sforza, now in the Vatican. A capable portraitist, he left a number of portraits of historical and iconographic interest, among them one of the historian Corio (now in the Musée Jacquemart-André, Paris), *Male Portrait* (Uffizi, Florence), and *Portrait of a Young Man* (Johnson Collection, Philadelphia). Other portraits are at Berlin; Bologna; Brooklyn; Detroit; Cedar Rapids, Iowa (Coe College); Seattle; and San Marino, California. He also painted a number of *Madonnas*, all inspired by Leonardo; examples of these are to be found in the Carrara Academy, Bergamo (1501), and the Ambrosiana, Poldi Pezzoli Museum, and the Brera, Milan; and at Karlsruhe, Munich, and Worcester, Massachusetts.

Conti, Giusto de'. Poet; b. 1379; d. at Rimini, November 19, 1449. Little is known of his life. He probably studied law at Bologna, where he fell in love with the lady who became the inspiration for his poems. Nicholas V sent him as ambassador to Rimini, where he died. He was an imitator of Petrarch before the form of the Petrarchan sonnet and canzone had become so rigidly fixed as to have the force of law. Thus his imitation was not so slavish. His *La bella mano*, a collection of lyrics, is marked by delicacy, sensitivity, and sincerity.

Conti, Natale. Humanist; b. at Milan, 1520; d. 1582. He was learned in Greek and Latin, and presented the harvest of his learning in his *Mythologiae sive explicationes fabularum*, an influential compilation on mythology and its meanings. He also wrote poems on love and other subjects, and a history of his own times that has no great merit. His *De venatione*, in four books of hexameters, was dedicated to Giuliano della Rovere (Pope Julius II).

Conti, Niccolò dei. Venetian nobleman and traveler; b. c1395; d. 1469. He began to travel on business as a young man. About 1414 he set out on a journey that was to take him to regions few, if any, Europeans had seen up to that time. He visited Damascus, where he learned Arabic, then joined a caravan that took him to Baghdad, adjacent regions of Arabia, and Persia, and went on by sea to India, and even reached Sumatra and Java, before returning by way of Indo-China, Burma, the Red Sea, Mecca, and Egypt to his native city. He was gone on his travels for twenty-five years. On his return to Venice he continued his mercantile enterprises, greatly aided by the knowledge he had gained of markets and products on his travels, began to amass wealth and then to enjoy it. At the same time, he undertook many duties for the Republic of Venice. It had been necessary for him in the course of his journeying through infidel regions to renounce Christianity, and as penance for this sin it is said that Pope Eugenius IV required him to tell the story of his wanderings and explorations to Poggio Bracciolini, the pontiff's secretary, who wrote them down. Belatedly they were published (1723) as part of a late edition of Poggio's *Historiae de varietate fortunae*, and were enormously popular.

Conti, Sigismondo de'. Poet and humanist; b. at Foligno, 1432; d. there, February 13, 1512. He studied Greek and Latin at Rome under the outstanding teachers of his day, served his own city in public office many times, and then was called to Rome to serve Pope Paul II. He remained in Rome most of his life, in the service of Popes Paul II, Sixtus IV, Innocent VIII, Alexander VI, and Julius II. His duties under the popes sometimes took him outside Rome and even outside Italy. Conti knew the leading literary men of his day; Bembo admired his Latin letters. He left many lyrics and learned writings, but his best work is the history of his own times, *Historiarum sui temporis*, in seventeen books.

Contile (kôn-tē'lā), **Luca.** Writer and courtier; b. at Celona, in Val di Chiana, 1505; d. at Pavia, October 28, 1574. He completed his studies at Siena, and then entered the service of various princes—service that took him to many parts of Italy and Europe, that made him thoroughly familiar with court life as he served at one court after another, and that gave him an acquaintance with the main literary circles of the time. It is for the manners and attitudes of these circles in his age as he describes them that his work is of interest. He wrote *Dialoghi spirituali* (1543), reflecting the atmosphere of reform at this time, comedies, allegorical eclogues, lyrics in the Petrarchan manner that are typical of court poetry, and a collection, *Le sei sorelle di Marte* (1566), in which he proposed a confederation of Venice and Philip II for the triumph of the Catholic Church. He also left letters that add to the picture of his age. Some of these are in the library at Siena.

Contrapposto (kōn-trä-pôs'tō). An Italian word meaning "opposed," "placed opposite." It was applied to a manner, popular in the 16th century, of depicting different sections of the body in opposite directions, as the shoulders turned sharply in one direction and the hips and legs in the opposite direction. Such twisting gave great opportunity to show the painter's knowledge of anatomy. Michelangelo, whose interest in portraying the nude was a fundamental of his art, was a leader in the use of *contrapposto*, and it was taken up, imitated, and exaggerated to the point of distortion by the mannerists.

Convivio (kôn-vē′vyō), **Il.** [*The Banquet*.] Unfinished prose work of Dante that has been called "the first great work written in Italian prose." Begun perhaps c1304, the banquet of which Dante writes is a feast of knowledge, for, as he quotes Aristotle, "it is the nature of man to desire to know." In the years following the death of Beatrice he had studied philosophy, particularly Boethius' *On the Consolation of Philosophy*, a medieval work, and Cicero's *De amicitia*; he had engaged in Florentine political life and suffered exile. As a development of his youthful work *Vita Nuova*, *Il Convivio* is the work of his manhood; and the new love, in addition to but not replacing the old, is philosophy. His original intention was to choose fourteen of his canzoni (songs), written at various times, and explain and interpret them in prose, bringing to the task his wide store of learning and employing it in an encyclopedic manner. He completed four of the contemplated books and then, for reasons unknown, about 1307 he left the work unfinished. The first book, prefatory to an examination of his fourteen canzoni, includes a justification of his use of Italian and parallels his *De vulgari eloquentia*, a treatise of Italian as a literary language. Book two begins with the first canzone he chose to discuss and has for its general topic philosophy, as do the canzone and interpretive material of the third book. The fourth book is on nobility. As in all his works, Dante gives immediacy with his many references to men and events of his day, and remains unfailingly perceptive as to his own state and experience. No matter how exalted or erudite the theme, one is always aware of the man and the spirit that created the work.

Conyers (kon′yėrz), Sir **William.** See under **Robin of Redesdale.**

Conyngton (kon′ing-to̩n), **Richard.** English schoolman; d. 1330. A graduate of Oxford, he was chosen, in 1310, provincial of the Franciscan order in England. His best-known work is a commentary on the *Sentences* of Peter the Lombard.

Cook's Tale, The. One of Chaucer's *Canterbury Tales*. It is unfinished and perhaps would have been suppressed if Chaucer had revised his manuscript. A spurious ending was added to it in the folio of 1687.

Coornhert (kōrn′hert), **Dirck Volckertszoon.** Dutch author and poet; b. at Amsterdam, Netherlands, 1522; d. at Gouda, Netherlands, 1590. After 1540 he lived at Haarlem as an engraver and etcher, and became there notary (1561) and secretary to the city (1562). He wrote a vast number of tracts and pamphlets against religious freedom, the great question of the day.

Copernicus (kō̩-pėr′ni-kus), **Nicolaus.** Founder of modern astronomy; b. at Thorn, on the Vistula, February 19, 1473; d. at Frauenburg, May 24, 1543. (The territory of his birth was in dispute between Poland and Germany; Copernicus is usually thought of as a Pole.) His father died when he was a child, and he was protected and encouraged by his uncle, a bishop who had been educated in Italy. From 1491 to 1494 Copernicus studied astronomy at the University of Cracow. From 1496 to 1500 he studied law at Bologna. In 1497, through the influence of his uncle, he had been appointed canon of the chapter of Frauenburg. In 1500 he lectured on astronomy and mathematics at Rome and, after a short visit to his uncle, returned to Italy and studied medicine at Padua and law at Ferrara, where he became (1503) doctor of canon law. In 1506 he returned to his uncle's bishopric and, from 1512 to 1543, remained at Frauenburg, where he performed his duties as canon and practiced medicine. Learned in Latin and a profound student, he had studied all the available material on astronomy and had found it unsatisfactory. He sought to find better answers on a theoretical basis. His own theories evolved from his mathematical studies. His first, unpublished, expression of his theories attracted the attention of Pope Clement VII, not adverse attention; others encouraged him to go on with his work. A young German mathematician, Georg Joachim Rhaeticus, came to Frauenburg to talk with Copernicus and remained to work with him for two years. It was Rhaeticus who published, in the name of Copernicus, the *Narratio primo* (Danzig, 1540; Nuremberg, 1541), a foretaste of Copernicus' conclusions. The favorable reaction to this effort encouraged Copernicus to finish his great work, *De orbium coelestium revolutionibus* (1543).

This work, in presenting a solar system now called Copernican for its author, revolutionized astronomy. It argues that the sun is the center of the universe, that the earth is a planet that moves about it as do the other planets, and that the earth rotates on its axis daily. He dedicated it to Pope Paul III. A devout Catholic, Copernicus had no wish to challenge Church doctrine. A gentle man, he was also a fearless seeker of the truth. And at first, indeed, it was not the Catholic Church but the Protestants, including Luther, who condemned him. But he did not live to know this. Rhaeticus had been unable to see the work through the press and it was delayed. It was not until a few hours before his death that an advance copy of the great work was put into its author's hands.

Copland (kōp′lạnd), **Robert.** English printer, publisher, poet, and translator; fl. 1508–1547. He may have worked for Caxton, and he undoubtedly was employed by Wynkyn de Worde. The first book carrying his name is *The Boke of Justices of Peas* (1515). The best known of his own works are two poems, *The Hye Way to the Spyttel Hous* (c1536) and *Jyl of Breyntford's Testament.*

Coppeta (kōp-pä′tä), **il.** See **Beccuti, Francesco.**

Coquillart (ko-kē-yȧr), **Guillaume.** French poet; b. in Champagne, France; d. c1490. He was the author of *Les Droits Nouveaux,* in octosyllabic verse, and other poems.

Corbel (kôr′bel). In architecture, a piece of stone, wood, or metal projecting from the vertical face of a wall and serving as a bracket to support a structural member or ornamental element. Corbels were much used in medieval architecture, of various shapes and wide variety of ornamentation.

Corbinelli (kôr-bē-nel′lē), **Angelo.** Florentine humanist; b. c1373; d. 1419. He was a close friend and protégé of Coluccio Salutati, who encouraged him to pursue his humanistic studies. He attended (1410–1414) the lectures of Guarino da Verona at the University of Florence, and became one of his many correspondents when Guarino left the city. Angelo held various offices in the service of the republic.

Corbinelli, Antonio. Florentine humanist; b. c1377; d. at Rome, 1425. Member of a wealthy and powerful Florentine family, among his several brothers was Angelo Corbinelli (c1373–1419). He had studied under Giovanni Malpaghini, Chrysoloras, and Guarino da Verona. He knew Latin and Greek, was on close terms with Guarino, whom he had helped to obtain a professorship at Florence, and with such prominent humanists as Ambrogio Traversari, Niccolò Niccoli, Giovanni Aurispa, Francesco Barbaro, and others. His splendid collection of classical manuscripts was one of the best in Europe at the time. It included such Greek writers as Homer and Pindar, Aeschylus, Euripides, Sophocles and Aristophanes, Herodotus and Thucydides, along with others. He left his rich collection to the Florentine Badìa. Antonio held many official posts for the Florentine Republic, as did his brothers.

Corbinelli, Jacopo. Humanist; b. at Florence, 1535; d. near the end of the 16th century. Exiled on political grounds from his native city, he went to Paris and was given asylum by Catherine de' Medici and King Henry III. A learned and intelligent man, he began a translation of the chronicles of Villehardouin into Italian. He is best known for his scholarly editing and annotating of ancient texts. He published, at Paris, Boccaccio's *Corbaccio* and Giusto de' Conti's *Bella mano* and, most important of all, an edition in its original form of Dante's *De vulgari eloquentia* (Paris, 1577). The authenticity of this work, the manuscript of which was discovered by Trissino, had been questioned by some.

Corbizzi (kōr′bēt-tsē), **Jacopo.** Florentine humanist and official. Of an ancient Florentine family, he was a close friend of Antonio Corbinelli (c1377–1425), perhaps had studied Greek under Chrysoloras, and did study (1410–1414) rhetoric and Greek under Guarino da Verona at the University of Florence. He held a number of lesser offices under the republic.

Córdoba or **Córdova** (kôr′ᴛʜō-bä), **Francisco Hernández** (or **Fernández**) **de.** Spanish soldier and explorer; d. at Santo Espíritu, Cuba, in May or June, 1517. He went to Cuba with Velásquez in 1511, acquired wealth there, and commanded an expedition as a private speculation. He discovered Yucatán, followed the coast beyond Campeche, and noticed signs of a higher civilization than had before been found in America.

Córdoba or **Córdova, Francisco Hernández** (or **Fernández**) **de.** Spanish soldier and explorer; b. c1475; d. at León, Nicaragua, in

March, 1526. In 1514 he went to the Isthmus of Panama with Pedrarias (Pedro Arias de Ávila). Sent to take possession of Nicaragua in defiance of the rights of the discoverer Gil Gonzalez Dávila, he founded several towns, explored Lake Nicaragua and found its outlet.

Córdoba, Hernández Gonzalo de. See **Gonzalo de Córdoba, Hernández.**

Corinto (kō-rēn′tō). A pastoral idyll by Lorenzo de' Medici, in which the passionate shepherd Corinto sends a message on the wind to the nymph Galatea, the object of his love. With pride he describes his own young strength, his wealth in cattle and flocks, and asks her not to scorn them. In his garden are roses, some in bud, others just coming into lovely bloom, and yet others whose petals are already dropping. Like the budded rose, youth is soon gone; therefore, "*Cogli la rosa, o ninfa, or che è il bel tempo*" (Pluck the rose, o nymph, while it is loveliest).

Corio (kō′ryō), **Bernardino.** Historian; b. at Milan, March 8, 1459; d. c1514. His patron, Ludovico il Moro, commissioned him to write a history of Milan, *Patria historia;* gave him a pension and other benefits; and opened the archives of the city to him. The eclipse of Ludovico and the entrance of the French into the city deprived Corio of these advantages, and he withdrew to his villa outside the city. His *Patria historia,* written in an unpolished Italian studded with Latinisms, is the story of Milan from its beginnings to 1499. The earlier sections are based on legends and fables, but in the later sections it is full, detailed, careful, and based on archival material. It presents with lively immediacy the events of the city (Corio was an eyewitness to the murder of Galeazzo Maria Sforza, for example), the manners and customs, and luxury of Milan (three pages are devoted to the description and menu of a marriage feast—roasted boars and peacocks, sugared and gilded peeled oranges, silver utensils), and includes vivid word-portraits of Milan's eminent men. It is perhaps partial to the Visconti and Sforza but is of inestimable value for its use of sources and inclusion of documents, many of which were later scattered and lost.

Cornaro (kôr-nä′rō), **Caterina.** Queen of Cyprus; b. at Venice, 1454; d. there, July 5, 1510. She married, in 1472, James of Lusignan, king of Cyprus, on whose death in 1473 she succeeded to the throne. In 1489, some years after the death of the last of the Lusignan line, she ceded Cyprus to her native Venice.

Cornaro, Luigi or **Lodovico.** Venetian nobleman, b. c1467; d. 1566. He suffered ill health as a young man, because of intemperance, and lost all faith in the physicians and the medicines of his time. He resolved to change his habits and did so. The result was a vast improvement in both his health and his spirits, and he decided to record the regimen, of his own devising, by which this had been accomplished for the benefit of others. He wrote the first of his four essays on a healthful life, *Discorsi della vita sobria,* when he was 81 years old. Two others followed, at age 86 and age 91, and the last was written when he was 95. The *Discorsi* describe in detail the rules he evolved, for diet and exercise, to improve his health and lengthen his life. He asserts, in his works, that there are many who can attest to the fact that he can mount his horse unaided, can climb stairs or hills with vigor, is cheerful, of sound memory and untroubled mind—all owing to his careful habits. Also, and most importantly, for himself he found life endlessly interesting and enjoyable. He says he never knew how beautiful the world is until he grew old. In addition to his good health, or because of it, he was able to improve the fields around his house by proper drainage, and thus contributed to the glory of God and the welfare of mankind; enjoyed the company of learned friends and a wide correspondence; and was grateful for the immortality granted him by the existence of his eleven grandchildren, all apparently gifted and healthy. His *Discorsi* were immensely popular, were widely translated, and went through many English editions.

Cornaro, Marco. Venetian merchant and public official; b. at Venice, 1412. At the age of 18 he was admitted to the Grand Council, and from that time took an active part in Venetian affairs. He held many official posts, including (1457) one in charge of the waterways. In this connection he made a landmark study of the rivers, lagoons, and canals, examining the problems inherent in them from all angles. He was also a pioneer in arousing interest in and exploitation of the minerals to be found in the mountains of mainland Venice.

Cornazzano (kôr-nät-tsä′nō), **Antonio.** Poet and writer; b. at Piacenza, 1429; d. at Ferrara, 1484. One of the most productive versifiers of his time, he wrote sonnets, canzoni, *capitoli*, and other lyrics, and was noted as an extemporaneous versifier. A courtier, he spent his life among princes and rulers, as at the court of Francesco Sforza, for whom he wrote the *Sforzeide*. In Italian, it is in twelve books and is modeled on Vergil's *Aeneid*. He was also at the courts of Bartolomeo Colleoni, the famous condottiere, and of Ercole I d'Este at Ferrara. He wrote a life of the Virgin, *Vita di Nostra Donna*, in terza rima, novelle, a treatise on the art of war (in Latin), and a collection of tales called *I Proverbi*. These are sixteen droll and licentious stories, each of which is supposed to relate the origin of some proverb.

Corneo (kôr′nā-ō) or **Della Corgna** (del′lä kôr′nyä), **Pier Filippo.** Jurisconsult; b. at Perugia; d. 1462. He took his doctorate in law at Perugia, and then taught there, at Ferrara and at Pisa, and again at Perugia. He was famous as a teacher and was celebrated for his opinions, four books of which were published. His lectures on the *Digestum vetus* and the *Codex* were also published.

Corneto (kôr-nā′tō), **Adriano di.** See **Adriano di Corneto.**

Cornice. In architecture, a molded ornamental projection that crowns or finishes the walls of a building. In some Renaissance palaces the cornice was proportioned to shade the face of the building during the heat of the day.

Cornwall (kôrn′wôl, -wa̤l), 1st Duke of. Title of **Edward**, the Black Prince (1330–1376).

Coronado (kor-ǫ-nä′dō; Spanish, kō-rō-nä′-ᴛʜō), **Francisco Vásquez de.** Spanish explorer of the American Southwest; b. at Salamanca, Spain, 1510; d. at Mexico City, 1554. He led an expedition to search for the Seven Cities of Cibola and their wealth, which took him as far as eastern Kansas.

Coronado, Juan Vásquez de. Spanish administrator; b. at Salamanca, Spain, c1525; drowned at sea, October, 1565. In 1562 he was appointed alcalde (mayor) in Costa Rica; he explored the whole country and founded Cartago. In recognition of his work he was named hereditary captain-general of Costa Rica.

Correggio (kôr-red′jō). [Original name, **Antonio Allegri**, called **il Correggio** from his birthplace.] Emilian painter; b. at Correggio, 1494; d. there, March 5, 1534. Little is known of his early life and training. His uncle, Lorenzo, was a painter and probably taught him the rudiments of his art. The little city of Correggio is about halfway between Parma and Modena, and not far from Mantua and Ferrara; its princes or members of its ruling family had contact with the Gonzaga and Estensi in the latter cities. (Niccolò da Correggio, 1450–1508, for example, was one of Isabella d'Este's favorite courtiers at Mantua.) Through them painters came to Correggio, and the influence of the Ferrarese school was especially strong. The young painter was in the workshop of Francesco Bianchi Ferrari at Modena from 1503 to 1505. There he acquired clarity of contour and smooth, gemlike color. At Modena also he came in contact with the works of Francesco Francia (1450–1517) and Lorenzo Costa (1460–1535), and responded to their strong feeling for color. Between 1506 and about 1510 he worked at Mantua, where he was at first influenced by the classicism, linearity, and sculptural qualities of Mantegna. The Mantegna influence is evident in the *Madonna with St. Elizabeth* (c1512), Johnson Collection, Philadelphia, especially in the carved, anxious face of the aged St. Elizabeth. An early documented painting is the *Madonna of S. Francesco*, an altarpiece commissioned (August, 1514) for the Church of S. Francesco at Correggio and now at Dresden. In it the influences under which Correggio painted are lessened as he began the establishment of his own style and painting technique. Of about the same period is the panel of *Four Saints: Peter, Martha, Mary Magdalen, and Leonard*, the Metropolitan Museum, New York. Other early works under the Mantegna spell, but softened as to line and warmed with Correggio's color include *The Marriage of St. Catherine* (c1510–1512), Kress Collection, New York. A slightly later painting (c1513–1514) on the same subject, at Detroit, indicates that Correggio had by this time seen the paintings of Leonardo da Vinci. Leonardo's softening of forms by light and shadow and a misty overlay on color and line matched Correggio's temperament. Henceforth his painting technique continued to develop along this line. His forms became softer, marvelous color glowed, an enchant-

CORREGGIO
Study for the Virgin in *The Coronation of the Virgin,* Parma
Cabinet des Dessins Musée du Louvre   Cliché Musées Nationaux

ment with the movement and play of light seemed to possess him. In the Detroit painting the faunlike smile, arched body, and pointing hand of John the Baptist seem clearly derived from Leonardo; the landscape background and pyramidal composition of his *Madonna and Child with the Infant St. John* (c1515–1516), Prado, Madrid, seem to have been suggested by Leonardo's *Virgin of the Rocks.* Other paintings of *The Marriage of St. Catherine* are in the National Museum, Naples, and the Louvre, Paris. Of the last, Vasari wrote that the heads were so beautiful they seemed to have been made in Paradise. Another favorite subject was the *Holy Family*, of which one example is presently in the Los Angeles County Museum, and another, and perhaps the best on the theme, is at Hampton Court.

Of the many individual qualities that distinguish Correggio's painting his sinuous line, preoccupation with light, affinity for feminine charm, marvelous color, and often agitated movement are outstanding. A *Madonna and Child*, called also *La Zingarella* and *Madonna with the Rabbit*, National Museum, Naples, with the sweeping arc of the Madonna's head and her arm as it envelops the Child, and the serpentine curves of her skirt, is an obvious example of his love of the movement and grace of line. The *Madonna Adoring the Child* (c1522), Uffizi, is one of the earliest marked expressions of his absorption with light. The light from the Divine Child reflects from His kneeling mother's tender profile and her beautiful hands outstretched in wonder and surrender. The painting is a forerunner of *The Adoration of the Shepherds* (c1530), Dresden, originally painted for the Church of S. Prospero at Reggio, and removed, to the great grief of the people, by Francesco I of Modena in 1640. Again the radiance of the Holy Infant illuminates and gives form to the worshippers in the human and touching scene. The painting is sometimes known as *Night*, and is one of the finest nocturnes of 16th century painting. In another painting, *Madonna with St. Jerome* (c1527–1528), also called *Day*, National Gallery, Parma, magnificent color gleams in the full sunshine of high noon. It was painted for the Church of Sant' Antonio, Parma, and is among Correggio's most popular paintings. The Madonna with her lowered lids and soft, half smile is typical; Vasari wrote that the joyous smile of the attendant angel is so contagious that whoever looks at him must smile back. The painting is a lovely example of the happy, life-embracing spirit that pervades Correggio's work. In paintings on mythological themes Correggio yields to his sensuous delight in representing the texture of tingling, blushing human flesh. His *Danaë* (c1531–1532), Borghese Gallery, Rome, was one of a series on the *Loves of Jove* commissioned by Duke Federigo II Gonzaga and intended as a gift for the Emperor Charles V. Others in the series are *Io* and *Ganymede* (Vienna) and *Leda* (Berlin). The *Allegory of Virtue* and *Allegory of Vice*, now in the Louvre, came from the *studiolo* of Federigo's mother, Isabella d'Este.

Correggio painted three great frescoes at Parma, in which his restless movement and love of depicting curly-haired children in the form of cherubs and angels and painting rosy clouds of color are given free rein. The first of these, painted 1518, was the decoration of the cupola of the Camera di S. Paolo for the abbess of the convent. The cupola gives the illusion of a screen with oval windows, through which may be seen pairs of cherubs with trophies of the chase, or swinging garlands, or tumbling in what appears to be sheer excess of spirits. The abbess, Donna Giovanna Piacenza, who commissioned the work, was restive under the cultural restraints imposed by the Church and did not insist on devotional paintings. Some interpret Correggio's cupola as an allegory of the abbess' coat of arms. This carried three crescent moons, and since Diana, the moon, is also the goddess of the hunt, the pairs of cherubs with their trophies bear out the theme. Between 1520 and 1525 he painted the frescoes in the cupola of the Church of S. Giovanni Evangelista. The Redeemer is in the center; around the rim tumbling, flying cherubs support the Apostles on puffs of cloud. The fresco was severely damaged after the French removed the copper sheathing of the dome in the 18th century. The last fresco (1526–1530), in the cupola of the cathedral, presents angels swirling in all positions about the Virgin in *The Assumption of the Virgin* at the center. The waves of figures in vigorous motion proceed in ever-widening circles to a ring of Apostles and athletic youths on the rim. Individual figures, which can hardly be isolated from the confusion and movement presented to the spectator below, are beautifully painted and are marvels of foreshortening when seen in detail in reproduction.

Vasari lamented that Correggio had never been to Rome to see the marvels of antiquity and the great works of such "modern" masters as Michelangelo and Raphael. He thought Correggio might have been their equal if he had had the advantages of a visit to Rome. As far as is known he did not go to Rome; it is assumed that he did, although no documents exist to support the assumption. He passed his life in and about Correg-

CORREGGIO
Virgin Ascending
Study for the Virgin of *The Assumption* in the cupola of Parma Cathedral
The British Museum, London

gio and Parma, married (1519) a beautiful girl who, according to tradition, was the model for *La Zingarella*, had one son, Pomponio Allegri, who became an indifferent painter, and two daughters. In his short and highly productive career he was never led into paths alien to his temperament by Michelangelo's monumentality or Raphael's smooth (perhaps even bland) harmonies. He obviously knew the work of Leonardo and Raphael, as appears in his exquisitely toned and atmospheric use of Leonardo's sfumato and the broader forms of Raphael in his work after 1516 (when he may have seen Raphael's *St. Cecilia* at Bologna), but his painting was a free expression of his own spirit; he was never an imitator of nor dominated by another master. The elements of other painters that appealed to his temperament were metamorphosed and fused in what remained a unique artistic vision. Masterly in draftsmanship, color, and representation of light, there are movement and exuberance in much of his painting that are missing from the works of more disciplined artists, and that add to the charm of Correggio's.

The frescoes at Parma, with their restless, impulsive movement and myriads of tumbling figures, are perhaps the most spectacular of Correggio's works. The National Gallery there has a number of examples of his panel paintings. Other paintings by Correggio are in the Castello Sforzesco and the Brera (Milan), the Uffizi (Florence), National Museum (Naples), Estense Gallery (Modena), Prado (Madrid), National Gallery and Victoria and Albert Museum (London), Louvre (Paris), and elsewhere.

Correggio, Niccolò da. See **Niccolò da Correggio.**

Correr (kôr′rer), **Angelo.** Original name of Pope **Gregory XII.**

Correr, Gregorio. Venetian humanist; b. at Venice, 1411; d. at Verona, November 19, 1464. Of a prominent Venetian family, he was educated by Vittorino da Feltre at Mantua, and then went to Rome with his uncle, Cardinal Antonio Correr. His uncle influenced him to enter upon an ecclesiastical career. Named an apostolic protonotary by Pope Eugenius IV, he went to the Council of Basel (1433) where, drawing on Salviano's *De gubernatione Dei,* he pronounced against some of the papal claims. He returned to Italy after the Council, spent some time at Florence where the Curia was sitting, and then (after 1443) went to Venice, where he was attacked by his ecclesiastical enemies and rivals. Venice supported him and chose him patriarch, but he was able to claim his office only after long negotiations with Pope Paul II, and died before he could take possession of it. He left many works on educational matters and teaching, as a poem in hexameters, *Quomodo educari debeant pueri,* and *Idea dell' ottimo precettore nella vita di Vittorino da Feltre.* He also made a Latin version of *Aesop's Fables,* and wrote *Soliloquium,* an autobiography that is interesting for its psychological insight. A tragedy in Latin verse, *Progne,* was written when he was 18, and is a dramatization of the story of Tereus and Procne.

Corsignano (kôr-sē-nyä′nō). Village near Siena; its name was changed to Pienza in 1462, in honor of Pope Pius II, whose birthplace it was. See **Pienza.**

Corsini (kôr-sē′nē), **Amerigo.** Florentine humanist; b. 1452; d. 1501. He was a member of a wealthy Florentine family that had been prominent in trade, the Church, and the republic since the middle of the 13th century. He was a pupil and friend of Marsilio Ficino. Learned in the law, he left *Constitutiones synodales Ecclesiae Florentinae.*

Corsini, Filippo. Florentine humanist and statesman; b. 1334; d. 1421. Having completed his studies in civil law, he served Florence many times as ambassador and was gonfaloniere five times. He was active in promoting an Italian league to protect the cities against the ravages of the free companies (mercenary bands), was active in attempts to heal the schism in the Church, and was a principal agent in the restoration of the Florentine university (studio).

Corsini, Matteo. Florentine diarist and friend of Petrarch; b. 1322; d. 1402. He left familiar memoirs and a *Rosaio della vita.*

Corso (kôr′sō), **Rinaldo.** Humanist and ecclesiastic; b. at Verona, 1525; d. 1580. He was for a long time in the service of the court at Correggio; later he entered upon an ecclesiastical career, and became bishop of Policastro. He was a student of letters and of law, wrote love poetry, a tragedy, *Panthia,* and published, among other things, a kind of Italian grammar, *Fondamenti del parlar toscano* (Venice, 1559), that set the pattern for such works.

Cort (kôrt), **Cornelis.** Dutch engraver; b. at Hoorn, Netherlands, after 1530; d. at Rome, 1578. He worked (c1565) at Venice for Titian, doing copperplates, went to Bologna, and then to Rome, where he established a school whose exponent was Agostino Carracci. His works include engravings after Titian, Raphael and other masters.

Cortegiana (kôr-tā-jä′nä), **La.** Comedy by Aretino. More original and animated than most comedies then being written, it describes in brutal detail the scandalous life of the Roman court. Francis I sent him a chain of gold in thanks for his copy of the play.

Cortegiano (kôr-tā-jä′nō), **Il.** [Full Italian title, **Il libro del cortegiano; The Book of the Courtier.**] A treatise in four books on what constitutes the perfect courtier, by Baldassare Castiglione. It purports to be a report of conversations that took place on four successive evenings in the Duchess Elizabetta's drawing room in the Ducal Palace at Urbino. It was the custom for the members of the court and visitors to gather in the duchess' magnificent room each evening for recreation, dancing, music, games, or conversation. In his introduction to the work Castiglione says that the question of the perfect courtier arose, and it was resolved to make that the subject for discussion on the evening when his book opens. The participants in the discussion, nineteen men and four ladies, are all historical personages, of varying degrees of importance. All were friends of Castiglione. The stylist Pietro Bembo, Giuliano de' Medici, and L'Unico Aretino are among them. Castiglione does not include himself, although he had been present on many such occasions. The rules for the discussion were that one person should be chosen by the duchess' friend and companion Emilia Pia to present his ideas, with the others free to interrupt: to protest, comment, or disagree as the spirit moved. By the comment, questions, additions, and dissents that are offered, the work has the air, on the whole, of an urbane and intelligent conversation.

On the first evening (Book I) the attributes of the perfect courtier are presented. First of all, he must be of noble birth. This point is immediately protested, for a noble spirit, it is pointed out, can arise from humble birth. The protest is at length overruled, on the ground that the tradition of his birth spurs the courtier to live up to, and strive to excel, the noble actions of his ancestors. The courtier must be well-built and shapely, completely loyal, and brave. He must excel in arms and be a good horseman; must be possessed of sound learning and broad culture; be skilled in swimming and athletic games and exercises; must be qualified in drawing, painting, and music; and must know how to make himself agreeable in social intercourse, especially to ladies. Above all, the courtier must avoid affectation in any of its aspects. Throughout the conversations on this and the following evenings, it is remarked over and over again that the acts of the perfect courtier, his attitudes, and enjoyments must be accommodated to the time, place, and circumstances; and in all he does he must display grace and such ease in his particular accomplishments that he appears to toss them off without being aware of the skill that they require and represent. Frequent references to the classical writers, drawn in naturally, are made to illustrate various points made about the attributes of the courtier.

The second book, comprising the conversation on the following evening, takes up a variety of topics, such as the games, music, and conversation suitable to the courtier. Again there is the emphasis on the proper time and place. The courtier, military man though he must be, should not carry his campaign manners into the drawing room. Many other examples of time and place are given. In the matter of games, music, and dancing, the courtier is given the practical advice not to engage in any activity in which he cannot show off to advantage. The latter part of Book II treats of jokes and jests. All are in favor of humor, and all agree that humor may bite but should not wound. Humor is divided into several categories, each of which is copiously illustrated. Some of the jokes don't sound very funny to a modern reader; some of them are fairly broad. Others depend on witty turns of phrase, and might be difficult to teach to the courtier if he did not happen to be endowed with a lively wit. The type of humor to be engaged in depends on the circumstances. Practical jokes are, in general, frowned upon.

The third book is concerned with the qualities and attributes of the perfect court lady. There is a strong tendency on the part of some of the speakers to regard a woman as so inferior to a man that it almost doesn't matter about her attributes as long as she is chaste, or has the reputation for being so. Others, notably the principal speaker, champion the ladies in most chivalrous fashion. An interesting and rather stultifying view is that woman is an imperfect rendering by nature of man; that nature seeks perfection in all her creatures, and would, if she could, produce nothing but men. The weaknesses of this theory are quickly made clear. The discussion is of additional interest for the frankness between the sexes with which it is carried on, for the arguments in favor of a double standard of morality, and for the rather unrealistic views of the champions of the ladies. Again, there are many examples—from legend, ancient, and contemporary times—to illustrate the manner, especially, in which ladies have protected their virtue. These are necessary to combat one misogynist's view that women are naturally weak, venal, deceitful, and a prey to their senses.

The last book treats the purpose and aim of the courtier and is a discussion of the manner in which he should guide and influence his prince for good ends. The points that are made add up to making the courtier in most ways superior, as a human being, to his prince. Thus it develops that the courtier, if he is to exert so much influence, must be an older, experienced man. This being so, he should eschew love, according to some of the speakers, as for an older man to be in love makes him ridiculous. Here Pietro Bembo rises to the defense of love. He makes an eloquent oration on Platonic love which, for the purposes of discussion, he defines and describes in ideal fashion. In this speech are repeated some of the ideas expressed in Bembo's dialogues, *Gli Asolani*. (The question of love as a concept of beauty greatly occupied the minds of these cultivated circles, but those who so ardently upheld the beauties of Platonic love did not for an instant consider that the principles should be applied in their own lives. Bembo himself was the father of several illegitimate children.) With this exalted hymn to Platonic love *The Book of the Courtier* ends.

The work, begun in 1509, finished about 1518, and published at Venice in 1528, had an immediate success. It was translated and read all over Europe, had deep influence on the society of other courts, and literary influence as well. The style is natural and unaffected. In an introduction to Book I, and in the discussions of that book, Castiglione presents his view of the Italian language. His sensible attitude is that language should communicate. There is, therefore, no value in using words found in Boccaccio and Petrarch whose meanings are no longer generally understood. To insist on words from these great poets and artists is pedantic, awkward, and confusing. He knows that every noble city of Italy has its own characteristic speech. He would choose the most vivid, exact, and generally used words, whether they are close to Latin or have departed from it, as his Italian language. He would not limit himself to Tuscan, and deprive himself of the richness available in other dialects, nor did he. The question of what should constitute the Italian language was one that exercised many of the literary men of his time, when the vernacular was asserting itself as a literary language at least as available as Latin. Throughout the four books there are leavening touches of humor, interruptions and remarks that give the speakers individuality, asides and protests that characterize them psychologically. Throughout also there is an overtone of sadness, although the conversations are lively. Castiglione made it a premise of his work that the courtier and court lady being described were ideal, not actual. The sadness comes from his knowledge that courts such as he had known at Urbino, where so many gallant and cultivated spirits flourished, were disappearing. By the time he had finished his work several of those who had participated in his supposed conversations had died. The world he had known and loved was threatened on every side, and was visibly disappearing.

Cortés or **Cortez** (kôr-tez), **Hernando** or **Fernando.** [Title, Marquess of the **Valley of Oaxaca** (Marqués **del Valle**).] Spanish soldier, conqueror of Mexico; b. at Medellín, Estramadura, Spain, 1485; d. at Castillejo de la Cuesta, an estate near Seville, Spain, December 2, 1547. In 1518 Velásquez placed him in command of an expedition to follow up Juan de Grijalva's discoveries in Mexico. In August, 1519, he began his march to Tenochtitlán, or Mexico City. On November 8, he marched over the causeway to Tenochtitlán, Montezuma coming out to greet him, though he had earlier protested the invasion. At rumors of an uprising, Montezuma was taken hostage, and was later killed during the course of uprisings against the Spaniards. Cortés and his men escaped secretly from the city, but returned to besiege it. After the fall of the city in 1521 Cortés was empowered by the emperor to conquer all of Mexico.

Cortés, Martín. [Title by inheritance, Marqués **del Valle.**] Son of Hernando Cortés; b. in Mexico, 1532; d. in Spain, August 14, 1589. He served with distinction in the army of Philip II in Flanders and England.

Cortese (kôr-tā'zā), **Gregorio.** Humanist and Benedictine theologian; b. at Modena, 1489; d. at Rome, September 29, 1548. He took his doctorate in law at Padua (1500), then entered the service of Cardinal Giovanni de' Medici (later Pope Leo X), but in 1506 he entered a monastery near Mantua and applied himself zealously to the work of the order of the Benedictines in Italy and in France. He also taught and encouraged the study of Latin, Greek, and Italian. In 1542, his friends Cardinals Contarini and Sadoleto having smoothed the way, he was made a cardinal, and was an ornament to the office until the end of his life. Some of the many writings he left have been edited and published; others are in Vatican City.

Cortese, Paolo. Poet and man of letters; b. at Rome, 1465; d. 1510. He was the brother of Alessandro Cortese, also a poet, who died young, and succeeded Platina as an apostolic secretary (1481). He corresponded with Poliziano on the best language and style for literary work. Cortese favored the Ciceronian manner. His chief writings had to do with questions of Latin style and the use of Latin as the best vehicle for literary composition. He was also the author of an influential biographical collection on the writers of his time, *De hominibus doctis*.

Corvinus (kôr-vī′nus), **Matthias.** See **Matthias Corvinus.**

Coryate or **Coryat** (kôr′yạt, -i-ạt), **Thomas.** English traveler; b. at Odcombe, Somersetshire, England, c1577; d. at Surat, India, in December, 1617. After a period at court as a jester, he made a journey through France, Savoy, Italy, Switzerland, and other countries of the Continent in 1608, an account of which was published in 1611 under the title *Coryat's Crudities, hastily gobled up in Five Months Travells in France, Savoy, Italy, Rhetia, Helvetia, High Germania and the Netherlands.* In Italy he visited the cities of Lombardy and Venetia–Turin, Milan, Cremona, Parma, Padua, and Venice, among others–told the time of arrival and departure from each, the places passed through on the way, and the means of travel. His book is as interesting as a revelation of his own curious character as it is for the bizarre incidents that befell him and the information it presents. It is, in a manner of speaking, the first English guidebook to Italy. He surveyed and reported on monuments and antiquities, religiously copied Latin inscriptions that appeared thereon, and relates items of historical interest; "did eat fried Frogges" in Cremona that "did exceedingly delight my palat," "observed that many of their women goe onely in their smocks and shirts in divers places of the countrey without any other apparrell at all by reason of the extreme heat of the climate; and many of their children which doe weare breeches, have them so made, that all the hinder parts of their bodies are naked, for the more coolnesse of the arye." He regretted the Italian custom of putting cheese on meat dishes, and the fact that he was compelled to forgo so much "good fare" because of it. He describes in detail the manner in which the Italians used a fork to anchor meat while they cut it from the common dish so as not to touch it with their fingers, and is credited with introducing to England the use of forks, which he had seen only in Italy. Venice was his favorite city, and he describes its beauty, luxury, and wantonness with undisguised wonder and relish. In 1612 he started on a tour of the East, and visited Palestine, Persia, and India, in which last-named country he fell a victim to disease.

Cosa (kō′sä), **Juan de la.** Spanish navigator; b. c1460; d. near Cartagena, in what is now Colombia, 1510. One of the most skillful navigators of his time, he was with Columbus as master or pilot of the *Santa María* and during the exploration of Cuba (1498). He made at least five voyages to the northern coast of South America. His map of the New World, made in 1500, is the oldest known. Two or three of his charts are also in existence.

Cosimo (kō′zē-mō), **Piero di.** See **Piero di Cosimo.**

Cosmati (kôz-mä′tē). Name applied to a group of craftsmen in Rome who specialized in a particular kind of geometric mosaic work used in architectural decoration. The work, called Cosmati work or Cosmatesque, consisted of geometric patterns in marble mosaic and was used especially in ecclesiastical edifices to adorn doorways, arches, backgrounds, architraves, twisted columns, and pavements, among other elements, and to decorate ecclesiastical furnishings, as thrones, tables, and so on. Stars, checks, diamonds and circles, in different-colored marbles, were some of the figures employed. The craftsmen, to whom the name Cosmati was applied, flourished from the beginning of the 12th century and enjoyed their most popular and productive period from then until the beginning of the

14th century. The outstanding members of the group were Lorenzo (fl. 12th century), Jacopo (fl. 1205–1210), Cosimo (fl. 1210–1235), Luca (fl. 1231–1235), Jacopo (fl. 1231–1293), Adeodato (fl. 1294), and Giovanni (fl. 1296–1303). Examples of their work are the Cloister of St. John Lateran, the bishop's seat in the Basilica of St. Lawrence-Without-the-Walls, the Cloister of St. Paul-Without-the-Walls, all at Rome, and the pavement of the cathedral at Anagni (1277). The *Three Princesses*, a sculpture in high relief by Tino di Camaino (Yale University Art Gallery) has a brilliant Cosmatesque background.

Cossa (kôs'sä), **Baldassare.** Original name of the antipope **John XXIII.**

Cossa, Francesco del. Painter; b. at Ferrara, 1436; d. at Bologna, 1478. His artistic development was influenced by the Paduan school of Squarcione, and especially by the linear relief and classicism of Squarcione's greatest pupil, Andrea Mantegna. The amplitude and dignity of some of his figures may derive in part from the work of Piero della Francesca, which he must have seen at Ferrara. The first documented work by Cossa was a *Deposition* (1456), now lost, for the high altar of the cathedral at Ferrara. In 1467 he made the cartoons for a *Madonna Enthroned with Four Angels,* painted on glass, for the Church of S. Giovanni in Monte, Bologna. (He made other designs for paintings on glass for the same church.) In 1469 and 1470 he was working in the Schifanoia Palace at Ferrara for Duke Borso d'Este. An additional story containing many rooms and great salons had been built on the late 14th century palace by Borso. Cossa, with other artists, was engaged at ten *bolognini* per square foot to paint a series of panels on the months in the great hall that came to be known as the *Salone dei Mesi.* The underlying theme that united the twelve scenes is astronomical and astrological; the unstated purpose of the decoration is the exaltation of the just and liberal duke who commissioned the work. The paintings were lost to view under coats of whitewash until early in the 19th century. Those on the west and south walls have practically disappeared; those on the north wall, painted in part, it is thought, by Ercole de' Roberti, are in the best condition. Cossa painted those on the east wall. Extensive restoration was completed in 1954. Each wall was divided into fields, separated by pilasters; the fields were in turn divided into three horizontal bands. In the lowest, and deepest, band was a scene or scenes devoted to the activities typical of the month. In these Borso had a prominent place. In the narrow middle band appeared a sign of the zodiac flanked by one or two figures whose significance is often obscure; and in the topmost band was the scene of a *Triumph* of the god or goddess presumed to prevail over the month. Cossa painted *March, April,* and most of *May* on the east wall. The first panel represents Duke Borso, mounted and surrounded by his courtiers, in the center of a hunting party. A vignette to one side shows him listening to a suppliant. In the background are peasants pruning the vines, on one side, and great classical arches on the other. In the middle band is the sign of Aries, and above it the *Triumph of Minerva,* with learned humanists and jurists on one side of the car on which the goddess is seated, and industrious women—weavers and seamstresses—on the other. In *April,* Duke Borso rewards his buffoon, Scocola, with a gift of money. The Ferrarese celebrated the day of their patron saint, St. George, with a race—of horses, donkeys, men, and women. Cossa painted the strain and movement of the race, eagerly watched by courtiers and their ladies from their balconies, in the background. Taurus is the zodiacal sign above, and the *Triumph of Venus* appears in the topmost band. Venus, seated on her car, which is drawn by a pair of swans, shackles a cavalier. The Three Graces dance in the background, loving couples surround the car, and rabbits (symbol of fertility) nibble everywhere. The lower band of *May* is severely damaged (a door was cut through it, for one thing). Gemini is the zodiacal sign, and the *Triumph of Apollo* is represented at the top. The frescoes, possibly influenced by those of Piero della Francesca at Ferrara (now lost), present in clear, light color a lively description of mid-15th-century court and country life at Ferrara. Here are their costumes, their hounds, falconers, horses with elaborate trappings, country and court activities; and here is a composite portrait of Borso, the genial and just ruler. On March 25, 1470, Cossa wrote a letter to Duke Borso, explaining that he had used only the best paints and much gold, which he had paid for himself, and that furthermore he had painted almost entirely in fresco (which is probably why his paintings have survived), and that he would like to be paid. He would also like his pay to reflect his superiority as a painter and wrote that it wounded him grievously to be treated on a par with "the worst dauber in Ferrara." Borso denied his request and Cossa, who by this time had made a name for himself, left Ferrara for Bologna. Henceforth, though he kept his Ferrarese citizenship and maintained a house at Ferrara, he worked at Bologna.

The chronology of his paintings is uncertain. From before 1472 are his altarpiece for the Church of the Osservanza, Bologna; an *Annunciation*, now at Dresden, which, with its almost photographic representation of architectural details and of the decoration on the great arches that form the background, and the linear relief of the forms, is reminiscent of Mantegna; and a *Nativity*, also at Dresden. Of 1472 is the first notice of him at Bologna. In that year he was occupied with the restoration of, and some additions to, the highly venerated *Madonna del Barracano* at Bologna (now greatly damaged). Of about the same period was the finest religious painting by Cossa that has survived, the Griffoni polyptych of *St. Vincent Ferrer*, painted for a chapel in the Basilica of S. Petronio at Bologna and later broken up and scattered. The central panel, *St. Vincent Ferrer*, is in the National Gallery, London; a *Crucifixion*, with the harsh, intense strength of an Andrea del Castagno, is in the Lehman Collection, New York; panels of saints, in an energetic and monumental style, are in the Brera, Milan, and the National Gallery, Washington; and the predella of three panels with the *Miracles of St. Vincent Ferrer* is in the Vatican. Other works executed at Bologna include a *Portrait of a Man*, Haarlem; cartoons for *St. Petronius* and *St. Ambrose* that were executed in intarsia; a signed and dated (1474) *Madonna Enthroned with SS. Petronius and John the Evangelist*, Pinacoteca, Bologna; and (c1477) fresco decorations, of figures of Evangelists, Prophets, Doctors of the Church, and an *Annunciation*, in the vault of the Garganelli Chapel in S. Pietro, Bologna, now lost. At the height of his powers Cossa was struck down by the plague. His work is full of energy, passion, and movement in the panel paintings, and shows a marked narrative gift, broad planes, clear color, and a taste for landscape in the frescoes at Schifanoia. With Cosmè Tura, to whose work his own was often compared —for its barren landscapes, ruined buildings, strongly defined forms, and glowing color— and Ercole de' Roberti, his younger contemporary, he formed the great triad of Ferrarese painting at its height. The characteristics of the school are energy, intensity, sharply defined contours, swiftness of movement, a bent for classicism and intellectual symbolism, and strong color, along with great originality. Cossa is also considered to be one of the founders of the Bolognese school of painting.

Costa (kō'stä), **Lorenzo.** Painter; b. at Ferrara, 1460; d. at Mantua, 1535. He was trained in the Ferrarese school, and was especially influenced by Cosmè Tura, Ercole de' Roberti, Francesco del Cossa, and later by Francesco Francia at Bologna. A man of broad interests and intellectual activity, much of his painting life was affected by his attempts, not always successful, to assimilate elements of these painters as well as of others. His *St. Sebastian*, Dresden, stylistically recalls the work of Tura. With its harsh, quivering outlines and the irregular, anguished features of the saint, the painting shows marked influence of Tura but lacks that painter's robust vigor. (Some critics doubt that this is a painting of Costa's, and attribute it to a lesser follower of Tura. Because of his similarities to the painters he followed, the attribution to Costa of a number of paintings is disputed.) By 1483 Costa was at Bologna, decorating rooms in the Bentivoglio Palace and working for Giovanni II Bentivoglio, lord of Bologna. The amplitude and dignity of a youthful *St. John the Evangelist*, painted at Bologna between 1483 and 1485, and now in the Carrara Academy, Bergamo, are reminiscent of Piero della Francesca, whose work Costa must have seen at Ferrara. In 1488 he painted the sons and daughters of Giovanni II gathered about the throne of the Virgin, in the Bentivoglio Chapel in S. Giacomo Maggiore at Bologna. In the same chapel are two paintings on themes from Petrarch, *The Triumph of Fame* and *The Triumph of Death;* in the latter Death seems even bonier than most skeletons as he rides in his cart. His portrait of Giovanni II (c1490), now in the Uffizi,

LORENZO COSTA
A Group of Four Women
The British Museum, London

is a beautiful work, secure in form and plasticity, and of considerable insight. In the years between about 1490 and 1500 he produced some of his most successful paintings; his forms became broader, more sculptural and plastic, and his color attained the warmth and richness of his Venetian models. All the elements of his best painting appear in his masterpiece, the altarpiece in the Baciocchi Chapel in the Basilica of S. Petronio at Bologna, *Virgin and Child with Saints* (1492) (Costa executed many paintings, of varying degrees of interest, on this theme). In 1499 he completed *The Adoration of the Magi* (Brera, Milan). The signed and dated panel was the predella of a *Nativity* painted by

Francia. When Giovanni II was forced to flee Bologna before the arrival of the papal armies under Julius II (1506), he took the altarpiece with him. (In 1503 Costa had been a member of a Bolognese embassy to Rome on the election of Julius.) The central portion was restored to Bologna, and is now in the Pinacoteca. Costa's predella, in which the harshness of the Ferrarese school is softened under the dominating influence of Francia, went to Milan, where it has remained. Of 1502 is his signed and dated *St. Petronius Enthroned* (Pinacoteca, Bologna), in which he returned to the models of Ercole de' Roberti. In 1504 his reputation was such that Isabella d'Este, a noted connoisseur and collector, asked for a painting. Of the same year is the *Pietà* now at Berlin, and of the following year are the polyptych in the National Gallery, London, and *The Marriage of the Virgin* in the Pinacoteca, Bologna. In 1506 he was invited to replace Mantegna (d. 1506) as court painter to Francesco Gonzaga at Mantua. For Francesco's wife, Isabella d'Este, he painted the *Story of Comus*, originated by Mantegna, and *The Kingdom of the Muses* (also called *Isabella Crowned by Love*), both now in the Louvre. The latter has one of the loveliest of Costa's airy, feathery landscape backgrounds. He worked on the decoration of the Gonzaga Palace of San Sebastiano near Mantua, painted a *Holy Family* that was sent to the French court in 1510 (now in the Barberini Gallery, Rome), and eight panels on stories from the Old Testament, now scattered in collections at Rome, Bergamo, and the National Gallery, London. Francesco Gonzaga was devoted to him, and when he was taken prisoner by the Venetians (1509), entrusted his wife, horses, and "dear painter" to the care of a friend. In the next years Costa, worn out and ill, worked little, and was soon overshadowed by the arrival at the court of Mantua of a flashy and energetic rival, Giulio Romano. Nevertheless, he continued to paint for the Gonzaga family. Of 1518 was his *Venus* (Scarselli Collection, Bologna), intended for Francis I of France; of 1520 a portrait of the Mantuan humanist and chronicler Mario Equicola; of 1522 a great altarpiece glorifying Federigo Gonzaga, who had just been named general of the pontifical armies (Prague); and of 1525 the altarpiece for the Church of S. Silvestro at Mantua, where the painter was buried in 1535. It may perhaps be said of Costa that what natural gifts he had were vitiated by his restless search for new elements in the development of an individual style, elements that he seldom assimilated. Often his figures are stiff and awkward and not well articulated. His preference was for symmetric compositions, with simple architectural backgrounds; his color was at times clear and light and at others rather acid. In his best works his very awkwardness is a strength, and he is interesting for the different experiences he reflects. Many of his paintings are to be found in the churches and galleries of Bologna; others are at Mantua, Ferrara, Berlin (*The Virgin and Child with Saints* was destroyed in a fire in the last days of the war, 1945; the predella from this work, *Miracle of the Catafalque*, is in the National Gallery, Washington), Baltimore (*SS. Naborre and Felicia Enthroned*, part of a predella), Johnson Collection (Philadelphia), Metropolitan Museum (New York), and elsewhere.

Costanzo (kō-stän′tsō), **Angelo di.** See **Di Costanzo, Angelo.**

Coster or **Koster** (kos′tėr), **Laurens Janszoon.** [Original name, **Laurens Janszoon;** surnamed **Coster** or **Koster**, meaning "the Sexton."] Citizen of Haarlem, Netherlands, who, according to Hadrianus Junius in his *Batavia* (1588), invented the art of printing with movable types (c1440). The claims of Coster (whose identity is uncertain) to the discovery have been maintained with great confidence by the Dutch and in other quarters, but may be invalid.

Cota de Maguaque (kō′tä dā mä-gwä′kā), **Rodrigo.** Spanish poet; b. at Toledo, Spain; fl. in the 15th century. He was the reputed author of the first act of the celebrated drama *Celestina* (1480), of the satire *Coplas de Mingo Revulgo*, and of *Diálogo entre el Amor y un Caballero viejo*.

Cotta (kôt′tä), **Giovanni.** Humanist and poet; b. at Vangadizza, Legnago, 1480; d. at Viterbo, 1510. Of a modest family, he went to Lodi for a time, and then to Naples, where he was a friend of Pontano and a member of the circle of poets and literary men known as the Accademia Pontaniana. In 1507 he became secretary to a Venetian general, in whose service he remained until the general was taken prisoner by the French (1509). Cotta tried to secure his release, but was unsuccessful, and died of the plague at Viterbo (1510). He was noted for his humanistic culture, but his name is best known for his ardent, graceful Latin lyrics in the manner of Catullus.

Council of Salamanca (sal-ạ-mang′kạ). [Also, **Junta of Salamanca.**] Meeting held at Salamanca, Spain, apparently in the winter of 1486–1487, to consider the projects of Columbus.

Council of Seville (sẹ-vil′). [Spanish, **Consejo de Sevilla;** also, **Casa de Contratación de las Indias.**] Office established at Seville, Spain, in 1503 for the regulation of commerce with the Indies.

Council of Ten. In the republic of Venice, a secret tribunal instituted in 1310 that developed its powers gradually and continued until the overthrow of the republic in 1797. It was composed at first of ten and later of seventeen members, and exercised unlimited power in the supervision of internal and external affairs, often with great rigor and oppressiveness. It had its own secret police and inquisitors; its sessions were secret and its judgments final.

Courtenay (kôrt′ni, kōrt′ni), **Edward.** [Title, Earl of **Devonshire.**] English nobleman; b. c1526; d. at Padua, September, 1556. He aspired to the hands of both Mary and Elizabeth of England. He was suspected of complicity in Thomas Wyatt's rebellion and sent to the Tower, but was paroled and exiled.

Courtenay, Henry. [Titles, Marquess of **Exeter,** Earl of **Devonshire.**] English nobleman; b. c1496; beheaded on Tower Hill, London, December 9, 1538. He was arrested on a charge of treason in November, 1538, tried, condemned, and executed.

Courtenay, William. English prelate, archbishop of Canterbury (1381–1396); b. at Exeter, England, c1342; d. at Maidstone, Kent, England, July 31, 1396. He was an opponent of Lollardism and the prosecutor of Wycliffe.

Cousin (kö-zaṅ), **Jean.** French painter, engraver, and sculptor; b. at Soucy, near Sens, France, c1500; d. at Sens, France, c1590. He was noted especially for his paintings on glass and his miniatures.

Cousin, Jean. [Called **Jean the Younger.**] French painter and writer on art; b. at Sens, France, c1522; d. 1594. Although he was a noted portraitist, his most important achievements were, like those of his father, Jean Cousin (c1500–c1590), in the art of stained glass, and the work of the two men is often confused. It is known that he was the artist of the windows of the castle of Fleurigny at Sens. He was also author of *Livre de Perspective* and of *Livre de Pourtraicture.*

Coverdale (kuv′ėr-dāl), **Miles.** First translator of the whole Bible into English; b. in the North Riding of Yorkshire, England, 1488; d. in February, 1568. He was ordained a priest in 1514. In 1535 his translation of the Bible from Dutch and Latin into English appeared at Zurich with a dedication to Henry VIII. In 1538 he was sent to Paris to superintend a new English edition; this was known as the "Great Bible," and in 1540 he edited another Great Bible, known as "Cranmer's Bible." He became identified with the Reformers when he repudiated celibacy to marry.

Covilhão (kö-vē-lyouṅ′), **Pedro de.** [Also, **Covilham** or **Covilhã.**] Portuguese navigator; b. at Covilhã, Portugal, c1450; d. in Ethiopia, c1540. He was sent by John II of Portugal to Asia to search for the legendary Prester John. He visited the principal towns of Ethiopia and Malabar, and sent home a report of his journey. He was forced by the prince of Ethiopia to remain in the country. His report is said to have been of use to Vasco da Gama.

Coxcie or **Cocxie** or **Coxie** (kok′sē), **Michiel.** Flemish painter; b. at Mechlin in the Low Countries, 1499; d. there, March 5, 1592. His best-known work is a copy of the *Adoration of the Lamb* by the brothers Van Eyck.

Cozzarelli (kôt-tsä-rel′lē), **Giacomo.** Sienese sculptor; b. at Siena, 1453; d. 1515. He worked in bronze, wood, and terra-cotta. He was a pupil of Francesco di Giorgio, whom he assisted in the Church of the Osservanza. He left no signed or documented works. His contemporary and friend, Sigismondo Tizio, is the authority for assigning to Cozzarelli a *Pietà*, a group in polychrome terra-cotta, originally in the Osservanza and now in the cathedral museum. To this group must belong his touching and delicate *St. John the Evangelist,* also in the cathedral museum. The *Pietà* was commissioned by Pandolfo Petrucci, lord of Siena, for his own tomb; and for delicacy, dignity, and serenity it is among the loveliest of its kind in a time that erred on the side of violent emotions and contorted gestures. Cozzarelli also made the bronze bells for Petrucci's palace. Other works, in wood and terra-cotta, in and about Siena are attributed to him, including a terra-cotta *St. Sigismund* in the Church of the Carmine and a bust of St. Catherine over the door of her Oratory, at Siena, and a *Christ*, in wood, in the Louvre.

Cozzarelli, Guidoccio. Sienese painter and miniaturist; known from 1450 to 1495, which is the date on his *St. Sebastian,* in the Pinacoteca, Siena. He is known to have worked in the cathedral at Siena: on a tabernacle in 1450; on frescoes, with other painters, in the cupola in 1481; and on the pavement in 1483, for which he completed the design of the Libyan Sibyl. In 1480–1481 he illuminated antiphonaries now in the library of the cathedral. A number of his paintings and illuminations are to be found in the churches in and about Siena. In his art he appears to have been a follower of Matteo di Giovanni, and in his best works so achieved the sensitive drawing and subtle color variations of his master that their works are sometimes confused. His *Virgin and Child with SS. James and Bernardino* and a cassone panel, *Camilla Engaged in Battle,* are in the Johnson Collection, Philadelphia; *Virgin and Child with Angels* and *Virgin and Child with Saints* are in the Museum of Fine Arts, Boston. Many other examples of his painting are in museums in Europe and in the United States at Amherst, Massachusetts; Atlanta, Georgia; Baltimore (Walters Art Gallery); Brooklyn; Columbia, South Carolina; Coral Gables, Florida; Madison, Wisconsin; New York; Princeton; Tucson, Arizona; and Williamstown, Massachusetts.

Crabeth (krä′bet), **Dirk.** Dutch painter on glass; b. at Gouda, Netherlands; d. c1601. He was the brother of Wouter Crabeth.

Crabeth, Wouter. Dutch painter on glass; b. at Gouda, Netherlands; d. c1581.

Craig (krāg), **Sir Thomas.** Scottish jurist and Latin poet; b. 1538; d. at Edinburgh, February 26, 1608. He was the author of a treatise on feudal law, *Jus feudale* (1603), still a standard authority in Scotland.

Cranach (krä′näċh), **Lucas.** [Also, **Kranach, Kronach.**] German painter and engraver; b. at Kronach, near Bamberg, Germany, 1472; d. at Weimar, Germany, October 16, 1553. His best-known works are altarpieces in Weimar, Wittenberg, and elsewhere.

Cranach, Lucas. [Called **Lucas Cranach the Younger.**] German painter; b. at Wittenberg, Germany, October 4, 1515; d. at Weimar, Germany, January 25, 1586. He was the son of Lucas Cranach (1472–1553).

Cranmer (kran′mėr), **Thomas.** English ecclesiastic and reformer, one of the most notable of the archbishops of Canterbury; b. at Aslacton, Nottinghamshire, July 2, 1489; burned at the stake, March 21, 1556. He is remembered as one of the engineers of Henry VIII's divorce from Catherine of Aragon, as a leading figure in the movement for moderation within the then newly founded Anglican Church, and as a staunch advocate of royal supremacy in ecclesiastical affairs. Upon the death of Henry (1547) Cranmer receded into the background of politics. During the reign of Edward VI (1547–1553), he supported many of the measures in reforming the Church and doctrine. As the young sovereign was about to die, he was persuaded to approve of the royal will that sought to modify the royal succession. After the collapse of the movement to enthrone Lady Jane Grey and the accession of Mary, Cranmer was one of the first to be investigated for his past actions. Charged with treason because of his aid to Lady Jane Grey, Cranmer pleaded guilty and was sentenced to death but pardoned. In the next year (1554) he was examined for heresy. Although his defense of himself won the admiration of his examiners, his case was transferred to a papal court. Maintaining his belief in judicial independence from papal authority, Cranmer refused to plead and was therefore condemned for heresy. He was degraded in 1556. Then followed a series of seven recantations by which he repudiated one after another of his past works as archbishop. In one of these he even acknowledged his submission to the pope (using, not without a degree of casuistry, the justification that, both king and queen now being Roman Catholic, his belief in royal supremacy in ecclesiastical matters left him no choice but to accept their position, which obviously entailed a reversal of his actual former position). Two days before his execution it was arranged that he should make a final recantation in which he would declare his belief in every article of the Catholic faith and confess by repudiating his writings, particularly those against the sacrament of the altar. On the day of execution, Cranmer made use of his final opportunity to confess his sin in having signed the previous recantations, and offered to have that hand of his that made the signature to be first burned. Cranmer was married twice, before clerical marriage was allowed. It is said that during that time he used to carry his second wife about in a chest, perforated with air holes to let her breathe; and on one occasion, she and the chest were removed by an unknowing porter and deposited wrong side up, and thereupon she was compelled to disclose her situation by a scream. Of Cranmer's writings, the principal ones include *A Book on Henry VIII's Divorce, against marriage with a Brother's Widow; Preface to the Bible* (1540); *A Short Instruction into Christian Religion* (commonly called his *Catechism*); *Answer to the Devonshire Rebels; A Defense of the True and Catholic Doctrine of the Sacrament* (1550); *A Confutation of Unwritten Verities.*

Credi (krā′dē), **Lorenzo di.** See **Lorenzo di Credi.**

Crescenzi (krā-shen′tsē), **Pietro.** Jurist and writer on agriculture; b. at Bologna, 1230; d. there, c1307. He followed his profession as a jurist from 1269 until 1299, then returned to Bologna and began his famous work, *Liber ruralium commodorum*, a treatise on agriculture. It is based on ancient sources, with the addition of much material gathered from his own experience. The work became well known outside of Italy and was translated into French, German, and English. An Italian translation of it, by an unknown Tuscan, is valuable as a source of Tuscan agricultural terms. The work was printed in 1471, one of the earliest books to be printed.

Crétin (krā-tan̂), **Guillaume.** French poet; fl. late 15th and early 16th centuries. The extreme reverence in which he was held by his contemporaries caused Rabelais to ridicule him.

Cristiani (krēs-tyä′nē), **Giovanni di Bartolommeo.** See **Giovanni di Bartolommeo Cristiani.**

Cristoforo da Bologna (krēs-tō′fō-rō dä bō-lō′nyä). Bolognese painter; active in the last quarter of the 14th century and the beginning of the 15th. A painter of merit, his work is characterized by his sense of drama and a somewhat crude realism. A panel, horizontally divided, has a *Crucifixion* in its upper register and *Mourning over the Body of Christ* below. It is at Ferrara.

Cristus (kris′tus), **Petrus.** See **Christus, Petrus.**

Crivelli (krē-vel′lē), **Carlo.** Painter; b. at Venice, probably between 1430 and 1435; d. perhaps at Ascoli, before August 7, 1500. The first recorded notice of him is of March 7, 1457, at which time he was already known as a painter. On this date he was charged with abducting the wife of a sailor and of holding her for several months. He was sentenced to serve six months in prison and was fined 200 lire. The escapade, thought to have occurred while he was still a fairly young man, may have had far-reaching results on his development as a painter, for he left Venice at some time after his release from prison and was not exposed to the developments that revolutionized Venetian painting in the second half of the 15th century. Elements in his early paintings indicate that he had had some contact with developments of the Paduan school as they were evolved by Squarcione and his celebrated pupil, Andrea Mantegna, and that either at Venice or at Padua he knew another of Squarcione's pupils, Giorgio Schiavone. When, at an unknown date, he left Venice, Crivelli went to Zara, and he may have gone there with Schiavone, who was in the city as early as 1461. In September, 1465, Crivelli became a citizen of Zara, which would imply that he had been a resident for some years. Whatever work he may have done at Zara has been lost. By 1468, and probably somewhat earlier, he was in the Marches, and remained in the region for the rest of his life. In 1478 he had a house at Ascoli, but he moved from city to city in the Marches as his commissions required, painting at Massa Fermana, Porto S. Giorgio, Ascoli Piceno, Fermo, Camerino, Matelica, Fabriano, and Pergola. In 1490 he was made a knight by Prince Ferdinand of Capua (later, King Ferdinando II of Naples). The tradition that he died at Fermo in 1495, and was buried in the Church of S. Francesco there, is unsupported by documentation. Some think he died at Ascoli; in any event, his wife was a widow by August 7, 1500.

A signed *Madonna and Child* (Castelvecchio Museum, Verona) is thought to have been painted before 1468. It has motifs derived from Mantegna and the Paduan school, such as the putti with symbols of the Passion, musician angels, a glimpse of a meticulously painted Mantegnesque landscape, and the decorative garland of fruit sometimes shown in the works of Mantegna and Squarcione and which became a distinguishing mark of Crivelli's. His earliest extant signed and dated work is a polyptych, *Madonna and Child with Saints* (1468) in the Church of S. Silvestro, Massa Fermana. A masterpiece, it contains the elements that were continuous, and continuously developed, in Crivelli's highly individualistic style. His spirit was essentially Gothic. Features of his style are calligraphic curves of drapery, a predilection for richly patterned fabrics—gold brocade, cut velvet, damask, gold backgrounds with intricate designs—jewels in collars, aureoles, and crowns, and garlands of fruit (sometimes with the quirky addition of a single cucumber) for purely decorative purposes. His paintings are distinctive in their "lininess." His vibrant, subtle line is an abstraction for its own beauty rather than for form. Often the Madonna is set against a tapestry, drapery, or panel, with bits of landscape showing at either side, and above her head the garland of fruit. The heads of his Madonnas are almost stylized—long ovals, with high foreheads over nearly closed eyes that are strongly outlined, thin noses, and small mouths. The heads are painted with little relief, and are sensitive and human in their pure spirituality and timidity. These features are all present in another of his masterpieces: the signed *Madonna and Child* (c1480), Municipal Gallery, Ancona. Other paintings of the *Madonna and Child* include those in the Carrara Academy, Bergamo (1475–1480), with jewel-like precision of detail, the signed and dated one in the Vatican, and the *Madonna della Candeletta* (c1490), part of a polyptych, in the Brera, Milan. An unpredictable fantasy is often apparent. In the beautifully preserved *Madonna and Child* at the Metropolitan Museum, New York, the Child is looking at a large fly on the ballustrade before Him; in the Washington *Madonna,* the arms of Her throne are sinuous dolphins; a fantastic helmet lies at the base of the sarcophagus from which Christ rises in the *Resurrection,* at Zurich; a peacock perches on the cornice of the Virgin's house in the *Annunciation* in the National Gallery, London. The last painting is a splendid example of Crivelli's love for intricate patterns, painted with exquisite verisimilitude, and for ornamentation, as in the decorated ceiling and ornate frieze of the Virgin's room, and the details of the street outside in which the Angel stands. Signed and dated (1486) the picture includes St. Emidius, the patron saint of Ascoli Piceno, standing beside the Angel of the Annunciation and holding a city in his hands. It was painted to celebrate the granting by Pope Sixtus IV of some rights of self-government to the people of Ascoli Piceno; news of the concession reached the city on Annunciation Day. Another marked feature of Crivelli's style is the sharp definition of details, as the grain of the wood, the shapes of bricks in a wall and of various vessels on a shelf in the *Adoration of the Shepherds* (Strasbourg), a work of his late maturity. He painted a number of polyptychs. That of Porto San Giorgio (near Fermo) signed and dated (1470), has been dismembered. Its parts are scattered; the central panel, *Madonna and Child,* is in the National Gallery, Washington; the dynamic *St. George,* with its fantasy and aggressive vitality, is in the Isabella Stewart Gardner Museum, Boston. Panels of saints from the polyptych are in the National Gallery, London, at Tulsa and at Cracow; and a *Deposition* that formed the apex is at Detroit. Another signed and dated polyptych (1473) is in the cathedral at Ascoli Piceno. The Madonna of the central panel is stylized and fragile against a richly ornamented background; Crivelli's tormented line depicts the saints in some of the numerous side panels, but is carefully disciplined in the rendering of hands and feet; the mourners in the *Lament over the Dead Christ* that appears over the central panel grieve with wild realism. Crivelli was fully capable of achieving naturalism by relief when it suited him. Parts of another dismembered polyptych, painted for the Church of S. Lucia, Montefiore dell' Aso, include a *Madonna Enthroned with Angels* and a *St. Francis* (Brussels), *Dead Christ Supported by Angels* (National Gallery, London), and panels of *St. John the Evangelist* and *St. Peter* (Detroit). The signed and dated (1476) Demidoff Altarpiece, with its twelve panels of saints in three tiers surrounding the *Virgin and Child,* is in the National Gallery, London. Parts of another polyptych, the other panels of which are not identifiable, are in the Castello Sforzesco, Milan; the Yale University Art Gallery, New Haven; at El Paso, Texas; and at Amsterdam. His last dated work is *The Coronation of the Virgin* (1493), in the Brera, Milan. All of Crivelli's paintings are on religious subjects, and all are executed in brilliant tempera in color that glows and sparkles for the sake of its beauty rather than as a means to naturalism. A large number of his paintings are extant. Besides those mentioned, there are paintings in the Accademia, Venice; the Brera and Poldi Pezzoli museums, Milan; Castel Sant' Angelo, Rome; at Florence, Urbino, Verona, Berlin, Budapest, Frankfurt, Paris, Tokyo, and elsewhere. Many museums in the United States possess one or more Crivellis, some of which are panels from polyptychs, including museums at Baltimore, Brooklyn, Boston, Cambridge, Chicago, Cleveland, Denver, New York, Philadelphia, Portland (Oregon), San Diego, Washington, D.C., Williamstown, and Worcester.

Crivelli, Vittore. Venetian painter; b. at Venice, c1440; d. c1502. He was the brother of Carlo Crivelli, whom he followed to Zara in Dalmatia. He was at Zara at least until 1476, when he acquired a house in the city, but by 1481 was in the Marches, where his brother had been for some time. All of Vittore's work, in many polyptychs and altarpieces he painted for churches in the Marches, was dependent on his gifted brother's style, and was successful to the degree that he closely imitated Carlo. In Vittore's hand, Carlo's energetic line is often harsh, and Carlo's brilliant color becomes unpleasantly strident. Some of his best work consists of the little scenes he painted for predella panels, some of which were brisk and clear, as those he painted for a polyptych for the Church of S. Elpidio, signed and dated 1496. He left a number of religious paintings in the churches of the Marches. Among his works is a polyptych, signed 1489, in the Museum of Art, Philadelphia, and a *Madonna and Child Enthroned with Angels and a Donor,* the Metropolitan Museum, New York.

Croke (krůk) or **Crocus** (krō′kus), **Richard.** English scholar and diplomat; b. at London, probably in 1489; d. there, August, 1558. His most notable publications are an edition of Ausonius (1515) and a translation of the fourth book of Theodore Gaza's Greek grammar (1516).

Cromwell (krom′wel), **Thomas.** [Title, Earl of **Essex.**] English statesman; b. probably c1485; d. at London, July 28, 1540. The son of a blacksmith, he served in his youth in the French army in Italy, and after his return to England became a lawyer. He was appointed collector of the revenues of the see of York by Wolsey in 1514, became a member of Parliament in 1523, was appointed privy councillor by Henry VIII in 1531, and was made chancellor of the exchequer in 1533. In 1535 he was appointed vicar-general of the king to carry into effect the Act of Supremacy, in which capacity he began in 1536 the suppression of the monasteries and the confiscation of their property. He became lord privy seal in 1536 and lord high chamberlain of England in 1539, and was created earl of Essex in 1540. In 1539 he negotiated the marriage of Henry VIII to Anne of Cleves, which took place in January, 1540. Having fallen under the king's displeasure, partly on account of his advocacy of this marriage, he was attainted by Parliament and beheaded on the charge of treason.

Cronaca (krō′nä-kä), **Il.** [Real name, **Simone Pollaiuolo.**] Architect and sculptor; b. at Florence, 1457; d. there, 1508. He was a nephew of Antonio and Piero Pollaiuolo. His sobriquet "Il Cronaca" (meaning "the Chronicler") stemmed from his habit of storytelling. On account of some misdemeanor (the details of which are now lost) he was obliged to flee from Florence to Rome, where he busied himself with study of the ancient monuments. On his return to Florence he was named (1491) overseer in charge of completing the Strozzi Palace, began by Benedetto da Maiano. For it he designed a spacious courtyard and a cornice celebrated for its classic simplicity and vigor. In 1495 he was named overseer of the works of the cathedral and of the Palazzo Vecchio. For the latter he designed the great Hall of the Five Hundred, later completely redesigned by Vasari. A few years before his death he built his masterpiece, the Church of S. Salvatore al Monte, also known as S. Francesco al Monte. With its single nave lined by chapels, its simplicity of line and geometric composition of space, Cronaca recalled the influence of Brunelleschi on his early training.

Crotus Rubianus (krō′tus rö-bi-ā′nus). [Original name, **Johann Jäger.**] German humanist and sometime friend of Luther; b. near Arnstadt, Germany, c1480; d. after

1539. He taught school at Fulda (1510–1515), visited Italy (1517–1520), and espoused the Reformation, but then deserted it to become a canon at Halle in 1531. He is chiefly remembered for having written most of the letters in the famous satire *Epistolae obscurorum virorum* (1515). This (*Letters of Obscure Men*) is a collection of forty-one anonymous letters satirizing the ignorance, hypocrisy, and licentiousness of the Roman Catholic monastics at the time of the Reformation. The letters were addressed to Johann von Reuchlin, the German humanist. They were occasioned by the controversy between Reuchlin and Johannes Pfefferkorn, a converted Jew, who advocated the destruction, as heretical, of the whole Jewish literature, except the Bible, and who was supported by the Dominicans of Cologne.

Crowley (krō′li), **Robert.** [Also, **Crole, Croleus.**] English author, printer, and divine; b. in Gloucestershire, England, c1518; d. at London, June 18, 1588. He set up (c1549) a printing press at Ely Rents, in Holborn, which he operated for three years. His typographical fame rests chiefly on three impressions he made in 1550 of the *Vision of Piers Plowman.* Among his notable works are *An Informacion and Peticion agaynst the Oppressours of the Pore Commons of this Realme* and *Pleasure and Payne, Heaven and Hell: Remember these Foure, and all shall be Well.*

Cruciger (krö′si-jėr; German, krö′tsē-gėr), **Kaspar.** [Also, **Creutziger, Creutzinger.**] German Protestant theologian; b. at Leipzig, Germany, January 1, 1504; d. at Wittenberg, Germany, November 16, 1548. He was a coworker with Luther in the translation of the Bible.

Cujacius (kū̦-jā′shus). [Original name, **Jacques Cujas.**] French jurist; b. at Toulouse, France, 1522; d. at Bourges, France, October 4, 1590. He wrote commentaries on the Institutes of Justinian, the Pandects and Decretals, including emendations of the text of legal and other manuscripts, under the title of *Observationes et emendationes.*

Cunha (kö′nya̤), **Tristão da.** Portuguese navigator and diplomat; b. c1460; d. c1540. He led expeditions to Africa and to India. Among his discoveries was a group of three islands in the South Atlantic Ocean, one of which is known by his name.

Cunningham (kun′ing-a̤m, -ham), **Alexander.** [Title, 5th Earl of **Glencairn.**] Scottish leader in the Reformation; d. November 23, 1574. He was a signer of a letter (1557) inviting John Knox to return from Geneva, and was active in the rebellion against Mary, Queen of Scots.

Cusanus (kū-zā′nus), **Nicolaus.** See **Nicholas of Cusa.**

D

Daddi (däd′dē), **Bernardo.** Florentine painter; d. 1348. Little is known of his life. He joined the Guild of Physicians and Apothecaries when Giotto did (1327) and later aided in founding the Company of St. Luke, an artists' guild. A younger contemporary and possible pupil of Giotto, he was not directly influenced by that master but followed the Sienese school, especially in the brilliance of his color, strong decorative effect, and the quality almost of miniature painting that marked his work. He produced many small panel paintings, in which his delicate charm shows to best advantage, altarpieces, and narrative predella panels. A general impression of Daddi is of rather archaic figures against gold backgrounds (common to many 14th century paintings), and resplendent color. Among his works are a *Virgin Between Two Saints,* signed and dated (1328), and *Madonna and Child with Saints* and other panels from the dismembered Pancrazio polyptych of which it was a part, Uffizi, Florence; frescoes of the Martyrdoms of St. Lawrence and St. Stephen (1330), S. Croce, Florence; and a large and often restored *Madonna* (1347) in Andrea Orcagna's tabernacle in Orsanmichele, Florence. His *St. Paul and Wor-*

shippers, National Gallery, Washington, is typical of 14th century painting in the presentation of the divine figure on an awesomely larger scale than that in which the human figures are delineated. A number of works by Daddi are at Florence, in the Accademia, Bigallo, cathedral, churches, and other collections, and in the neighborhood. Other paintings (often panels from dismembered polyptychs) of this ardent and delightful master are at Fiesole, Milan (Poldi Pezzoli Museum), Naples, Parma, Pisa, Pistoia, Prato, Rome (Vatican), Siena, Turin; in a number of European museums outside Italy, as at Berlin, Hampton Court, Munich, Paris, Vienna, and Zurich; and at Baltimore (Walters Art Gallery), Boston (Museum of Fine Arts and Isabella Stewart Gardner Museum), Cambridge (Massachusetts), Chicago, Columbia (South Carolina), Kansas City (Missouri), Minneapolis, New Haven, New Orleans, New York (the Metropolitan Museum and the New York Historical Society), Philadelphia (Johnson Collection), and San Francisco.

Dafne (däf′nā). In Torquato Tasso's pastoral play *Aminta*, a shepherdess who encourages Aminta in his love for Silvia, and warns the latter of the empty old age that faces one who denies love.

Dafydd ap Gwilym (dä′viᴛʜ äp gwi′lim). See **David.**

D'Alcamo (däl-kä′mō), **Cielo.** Poet of the so-called Sicilian school; active in the first half of the 13th century. His *contrasto* beginning "*Rosa fresca aulentissima*," is a poetic dialogue or dispute (hence, *contrasto*) between a lover and his lady, and is one of the earliest documents of Italian literature. Its thirty-two stanzas are written in the vulgar tongue of the Italian troubadours, a combination of an Italian dialect, French, and Provençal.

Dalla Spado (däl′lä spä′dō). See **Marescalco, Pietro.**

Dalle Masegne (däl′lā mä-zā′nye), **Iacobello** and **Pier Paolo.** Venetian sculptors and architects; active between 1383 and 1409. They worked at Mantua, where the notices of them date from 1383; built and decorated the tomb of Giovanni da Legnano at Bologna, soon after 1383, and the marble altarpiece in the choir of the Church of S. Francesco in the same city (1388). For the basilica of St. Mark's at Venice they carved the iconostasis surmounted by fourteen figures: the Virgin and St. John and the Twelve Apostles (1394). Commissions took them back to Mantua (1394–1397), to Milan, Pavia, and back to Venice.

Dalmasio (däl-mä′zyō), **Lippo.** See **Scannabecchi, Dalmasio.**

Dalmata (däl′mä-tä), **Giovanni.** See **Giovanni Dalmata.**

D'Ambra (däm′brä), **Francesco.** Playwright; b. at Florence, July 29, 1499; d. at Rome, 1558. He wrote Italian comedies, based on Latin models, but distinguished by his own freshness of language, facility, rapidity of action, and a number of newly invented (and often preposterous but carefully controlled) episodes. His *Il Furto* was given a lavish presentation at Florence, 1544, and his *Bernardi* was presented for Duke Cosimo I de' Medici, 1547.

Dandolo (dän′dō-lō), **Andrea.** Doge of Venice (1343–1354); b. 1310; d. Oct. 7, 1354. He joined (1343) the Crusade proclaimed by Clement VI against the Turks, which ended in a peace advantageous to Venice in 1346. He waged almost continuous war with Genoa (1348–1354), rival of Venice for supremacy on the sea. A professor at Padua before he became doge, he wrote a *Chronicon Venetum*, a Latin chronicle of Venice, which terminates with the year 1339. A friend of Petrarch, he presented him with a palace in 1347 in the name of the Republic of Venice.

Daniele da Volterra (dä-nyel′lā dä vôl-ter′rä). [Original name, **Daniele Ricciarelli.**] Painter and sculptor; b. at Volterra, c1509; d. at Rome, 1566. He was at first a pupil of Sodoma and then of Baldassare Peruzzi. He went to Rome while still fairly young and there was an assistant to Pierino del Vaga. His earliest work, *Justice*, in the museum at Volterra, is closest to Sodoma. At Rome he finished the work begun by Pierino del Vaga in the Chapel of the Crucifix in the Church of S. Marcello; and painted a beautiful frieze with stories from the life of Fabius Maximus in the Massimo palace, and friezes in the Farnese palace. His *Deposition*, now badly damaged, in the Orsini Chapel in the Church of the Trinità dei Monti, is considered one of his finest works. It is notable for its harmonious composition and for the nobility and flow of gesture and intensity of expression. For the Della Rovere chapel in the same church he made an *Assumption*, also badly damaged, which is the equal of the *Deposition*. At the request of Pope Paul IV he painted draperies on the nude figures of Michelangelo's *Last Judgment* in the Sistine Chapel and because of this was given the nickname "Braghettone," meaning that he provided pants for the naked. After the death of Pierino del Vaga (1547), he carried out the decorations in the Sala Regia in the Vatican. Also at Rome is his *Baptism of Christ* in a chapel of the Church of S. Pietro in Montorio. As a painter deeply influenced by Michelangelo, his work was marked by admirable balance and harmony of composition, fine knowledge of anatomy and, like Michelangelo, pleasure in portraying it, a smooth painting technique and a tendency toward monumentality. Of his sculptural works, few were carried to completion. Among those remaining is a splendid portrait bust of Michelangelo.

Dante (dän'tā). [Full name, **Dante Alighieri.**] Most celebrated of Italian poets and the one who gave the Italian language its definitive form; b. at Florence, May, 1265; d. at Ravenna, September 14, 1321. In his Latin letters he gives his name variously as Dantes Alagherius and Dantes Alagherii. His family can be traced back to Adamo of Florence, the father of Cacciaguida who is mentioned in the *Divina Commedia* (*Paradiso*, xv, 139–144), as having been killed during the Second Crusade in 1147. The family was of the lesser nobility, not wealthy but comfortable, and, like them, Dante lived on the income from a small property. Dante's first meeting with Beatrice Portinari, who was to become the object of his "courtly," artistic, ideal, moral, spiritual, and symbolic love and the source of his poetic inspiration, can be dated as May 1, 1274. (His first extant sonnet in honor of Beatrice was written in 1283, and published in his first work, the *Vita Nuova* (c1292), a work, in Italian, of verse and prose celebrating his love for a real or an idealized Beatrice. Shortly after the death of Beatrice in 1290, Dante married Gemma Donati, to whom he had been betrothed as a boy in 1277. Gemma was the mother of Dante's four children, Piero, Jacopo, Giovanni, and Antonia, the first two of whom wrote commentaries on the *Divina Commedia;* the last became a nun in Ravenna with the name Sister Beatrice. Dante does not mention his wife's name in any of his works, and she did not accompany him into exile.)

Dante's elementary education was entrusted to a professional teacher named Romano; but he attributes his higher intellectual inspiration to Brunetto Latini, though it is not certain that Latini was actually his teacher. Latini (1230–1294) was one of the earlier intellectuals who was not a member of the clergy. He was the first chancellor of Florence, and he compiled *Il Tesoro* (*The Treasure*, originally written in French because he was in exile in France at the time), an encyclopedia of what was then known in various fields of knowledge. It had wide circulation in Europe. In the *Divina Commedia,* Dante meets him and is asked by Latini to remember *Il Tesoro,* that Latini's name may live on through his work (*Inferno*, xv). In his *Il Convivio* (*The Banquet*), a prose work in Italian that he never completed, Dante relates that he spent three years in the "Schools of the friars (*religiosi*) and the disputations of the philosophers." It was, however, to his lifelong habit of insatiable reading in such of the ancient classics as were available in his time, the patristic writings, contemporary poets and chroniclers, and scholastic philosophers and theologians that he owed the extraordinarily wide knowledge that is revealed in his works. He was one of the earliest of those not connected with the clergy to command such learning. A great poet, celebrated for his vision and one who is generally considered to be the supreme example of integral Christian humanism, Dante yet eschewed the role of the contemplative spectator who viewed life from the seclusion of his study. He was an active participant in the politics and problems that agitated his world. The circumstances of his life, his political and spiritual attitudes and convictions, the problems and politics of his time are inseparably loomed in the fabric of his work, and especially in his masterpiece of world literature, the *Divina Commedia.*

As a young man Dante was trained as a soldier, and took part in the battle of Campaldino (1289), in which the Guelphs of Florence defeated the Ghibellines of Arezzo. In 1295 he began to play an active role in Florentine political life. The documents show that he took a firm stand against any outside,

First page of a 14th century *Commentary* on Dante's *Divine Comedy*, with miniature portrait of Dante in an illuminated initial
Courtesy of the Isabella Stewart Gardner Museum, Boston

including papal, interference in the city government. His family had usually been aligned with the Guelphs but had not played a prominent role in Florentine affairs. Membership in one of the greater guilds was a requirement for the exercise of political rights in Florence. Dante joined the guild of Physicians and Apothecaries (the guild included many besides those of its name; Dante registered as a poet). Florence was, as usual, wracked by factions. Dante took the part of the Bianchi (the Whites, the Guelph faction of the newly rich banking and commercial bourgeoisie) as against the Neri (the Blacks, the Guelph faction of the ancient nobility). The policy of the Bianchi purported to be maintenance of the independence and liberties of Florence against encroachments by the pope and the tyranny of the Neri. In 1300 he was elected by the Bianchi as one of the priors, the group that governed Florence, and served the regular two-month term. It was in this office, as prior, that he was called upon to banish one of his dearest friends, Guido Cavalcanti, in an effort to curb the factious political rivalry of the Neri and Bianchi. Shortly after his tenure of office he went to Rome to make the pilgrimage of the Holy Year of Jubilee proclaimed by Pope Boniface VIII. It seems to have been this experience of visiting the center of Christendom and the "capital of the world" that filled Dante with the vision of humanity in history and in eternal life which is the subject matter of the *Divina Commedia.* (Dante called it simply *Commedia, The Comedy;* it was a later age that gave it its adjective.) During Dante's absence from Florence on an embassy to Pope Boniface VIII in 1301, the party of the Neri, supported by Charles of Valois and then by Boniface, regained control of Florence, drove the Bianchi from office, confiscated or destroyed their property, and condemned hundreds to exile or death. Dante, whose house was among those destroyed, was called to trial in January, 1302. The trials were a travesty, since they had only one purpose, to get rid of the Bianchi. Rather than undergo the expected condemnation Dante, like many others, left the city. As he did not appear for his trial the Neri condemned him (March, 1302) to death by fire. The Bianchi exiles fled to Ghibelline communes and were welcomed as opponents of the Guelph commune of Florence. Dante went to Arezzo, where many militant Bianchi had gathered under the protection of their former Ghibelline enemies. They dreamed of revenge and plotted to return. Dante, at first a passionate supporter of the cause, tired of their intrigues, their incompetence, and their internal quarrels and withdrew from their deliberations, determined, as he says in the *Divina Commedia* (*Paradiso,* xvii, 69), to become a party all by himself. His resentment at his betrayal by his beloved but stony-hearted city is reflected in the passionate mood of the *Pietra* (*Stone*) sonnets. But Florence was his home; he longed to return to it, ever remained a Florentine, and considered himself a stranger and a beggar as he wandered from court to court in Italy. (In May, 1315, an amnesty was offered to the exiles. In the same month Dante wrote a letter to a Florentine friend who had advised him of the amnesty and gave his reaction to it. He scorned to return under the conditions of the amnesty: the payment of a fine and submission to the oblation. The last was a ritual by which a criminal or prisoner was publicly shriven of his guilt. If, as he says, he were willing to fulfill the conditions it would be an admission of guilt that he did not own. He could gaze upon the sun and stars anywhere, could contemplate truth under any sky, could earn his bread, and would return to Florence on honorable terms or not at all. He never went back.) His travels throughout Italy, where he found no less than fourteen dialects, suggested to him a work, in Latin, on "courtly" vernacular diction, *De vulgari eloquentia.* In it he distinguished the noble words of Italian and sought to establish Italian as a national and literary language. His philosophical reading and reflection prompted him to write *Il Convivio,* a collection of ethical essays in which he hoped to discuss in detail fourteen moral questions. In 1307 he left both works unfinished, and appears to have gone for a period of study in the University of Paris. When Henry VII succeeded as king of Germany (1308), and then as emperor (1309, crowned, 1312), he planned, having secured his power in Germany, to descend into Italy and reestablish imperial power there. This renewed in Dante the hope of seeing realized a world society under the triple universal authority of law, truth, and grace, organized by the efforts of the emperor (*imperium*), the university (*studium*) and the Pope (*sacerdotium*), and renewing the highest traditions of Rome, Athens, and Jerusalem in the spheres of civilization, culture, and religion. He hastily returned to Italy and sent a letter (1310) to the princes and people of the tormented peninsula proclaiming in ecstatic accents his welcome to Henry as a savior and restorer of peace and order. In his enthusiasm he declared that a new day was dawning, that

Henry came as a bridegroom to restore justice and deliver the oppressed from the yoke. He urged his readers to welcome Henry as the King appointed by God, for that the Roman Prince (the emperor) is lord of all the earth is recognized by Holy Church itself, he wrote. A later letter (March 31, 1311) denounces the Florentines, "blinded by greed," for resisting Henry. Again Dante states his belief that the emperor is the elect of God, and predicts doom to the iniquitous Florentines for defying him. A third letter (April 17, 1311), is addressed to Henry, and chides him for the delay in his entrance into Tuscany, for, as he writes, Henry is wasting time subduing Milan and Cremona when the root of the evil is Florence. In this letter, too, Dante expresses his conviction that the empire is sanctioned by God, is universal and not bounded by the limits of Italy or even by the coastline of "three-cornered Europe." About this same time he wrote *De monarchia*, a political treatise in Latin in which he expanded the ideas of the letters concerning the divine origin of Church and Empire and set forth his theory of the proper Church-State relationships. Earlier, in the *Divina Commedia* (*Purgatorio*, vi, 76), he had addressed an appeal to Henry's predecessor, Albert (c1250–1308), to assert the imperial power. He described the strife between Guelphs and Ghibellines that was ravaging the communes of the peninsula, mentioned the Montagues and Capulets of Verona, among other rival families, and called upon Albert to stanch the wounds of bleeding Italy. Albert was too occupied asserting his power in Germany to heed the poet's call. Henry died of a fever in Italy before he could know that the time of a universal empire beside a universal Church had passed and could not return. Unlike their eminent exile, the Florentines were the last who wished for a revival of imperial power in Italy. Another issue, of grave and lasting consequence, was the removal (1305) of the papal court to Avignon. Dante, who considered Rome the capital of Italy and of Christendom, was one of the earliest to protest and condemn the move. He wrote (May or June, 1314) the Italian cardinals urging a return to Rome and condemning them for depriving that city of its light (the pope). The years after 1314 were filled with the completion of the *Divina Commedia* (begun, perhaps, in 1307). He interrupted the work in 1319 to compose two Latin eclogues which are as classical in form as they are poetical in inspiration. On January 20, 1320, in the presence of the lord of Verona, Can Francesco della Scala (the Can Grande who patronized the arts and was, especially, Dante's protector), and of high ecclesiastical authorities, in the Chapel of Saint Helen, he formally defended, in Scholastic Latin, a *Quaestio de aqua et terra* in order to establish his position as an authorized teacher. An embassy to Venice undermined his health. He died at Ravenna, where he had spent the last three years of his life, and his bones were placed in a sarcophagus there.

Dante was recognized and became part of the Italian ambience in his own lifetime. Peasants, blacksmiths and donkey drivers chanted his verses at their work. Giovanni Villani, a chronicler of Florence and Dante's contemporary (d. 1348), described him in his chronicle as a great scholar, a great poet and philosopher, a noble orator and "supreme in rhyme, with the most polished and beautiful style which has ever been used in our language." Villani speaks of the *Commedia* in terms of the highest praise, reflecting its reception in its own time, and adds that though Dante was somewhat haughty, owing, no doubt, to his great knowledge, his name deserves to be recorded in the chronicle, "although indeed his noble works left to us in writing are the true testimony of him." Pius II, writing a hundred years later, put Dante at the peak of the trinity of Dante, Petrarch, and Boccaccio, saying of him that his "great poem with its noble description of Heaven, Hell, and Purgatory breathes a wisdom almost divine, though, being mortal, he sometimes erred." Some have termed the *Divina Commedia* the swan song of the Middle Ages. To others, Dante and his works herald a new day. By tradition, training, predisposition, and temperament, Dante was a man of the Middle Ages in his spiritual outlook. His intellectual approach and outlook, his interest in human nature and his profound understanding of it, his delight in the natural world, and his revelation of the inner man with all his passions and yearning, presaged a new era—if not a Renaissance, an avenue to it.

The people of Florence long wished to regain the bones of their most celebrated citizen, but to no avail. In 1519 a mission from Florence under the sponsorship of Leo X (a Medici pope) arrived at Ravenna to recover Dante's remains. When the sarcophagus was opened it was empty. Some years earlier the family of the lord of Ravenna, who had been Dante's patron and benefactor, was driven out. A cardinal threatened to burn Dante's bones and the monks, to forestall him, hid them. They were so well hidden that they were not found again until 1865, when workmen turned up a box with an inscription saying that the contents were the bones of Dante. Scientists examined them and agreed that this was indeed the case. They lay in state for three days and thousands of people filed by to honor the poet. The Florentines annually send Tuscan oil for the votive lamp at Dante's tomb and have an empty sepulchre waiting in the Church of Santa Croce. Among the representations of Dante the most authentic painting of him is that by his friend Giotto, still to be seen on the wall of the Bargello (Museo Nazionale) at Florence. The so-called death-masks have no authentic value. The bibliography on Dante's period, life, and works is immense. See **Divina Commedia, Vita Nuova, Il Convivio.**

Dante da Maiano (dä mä-yä'nō). Tuscan poet; active in the second half of the 13th century. His name comes from the village of Maiano, near Florence, where he was born. He left several sonnets in the Provençal tradition.

Danti (dän'tē), **Egnazio**, Fra. Mathematician, cosmographer, and architect; b. at Perugia, in April, 1536; d. at Alatri, October 19, 1586. He was the son of Giulio Danti (1500–1575) and the brother of Vincenzo Danti (1530–1576). Originally named Pellegrino, he took the name Egnazio when he entered the Dominican order (1555) at Perugia. In 1562 he went to Florence and spent the next twelve years in the service of Grand Duke Cosimo I, among other things, in painting a celebrated series of maps for the *Guardaroba* (in this case, a place where precious objects were kept) in the Palazzo Vecchio. He taught mathematics to the sons of Cosimo and to those of other eminent Florentines, and (1571) became public lecturer in mathematics at the studio (university). In the meantime, he published a number of treatises, as on the use and manufacture of the astrolabe, the sphere and its use, and he translated the *Sphere* of Proclus (5th century Greek Neoplatonic philosopher), and some of Euclid. After the death (1574) of Cosimo, Danti was forced by criticism and persecution to leave Florence. In 1576 he was given the chair of mathematics at Bologna, and during his stay at Bologna published his *Scienze matematiche ridotte in tavole* (1577), *Anemographia* (1578), and other writings. Also at Bologna he built the chapel for the relics in S. Domenico. In 1577 he made a relief map of the contado of Perugia, which was printed at Rome. Thereafter, for the pope, he made maps of Bologna, the Romagna, Umbria, and other papal dominions. He was named pontifical cosmographer (1580) by Pope Gregory XIII, and was invited to take part in the reform of the calendar. In 1583 he was made bishop of Alatri. He assisted as architect and engineer in restoring the port at Fiumicino, and was called to Rome to help in the engineering feat of raising the obelisk in Piazza S. Pietro. In addition to his many works and treatises, he was a skilled maker of instruments; some of those made by him are in the Museum of Ancient Instruments at Florence.

Danti (dän'tē) or **Dante** (dän'tā), **Giovanni Battista.** Mathematician and inventor; b. at Perugia, 1478; d. at Venice, 1517. He taught mathematics at Venice, and was a military engineer. He thought out and built a flying machine, consisting of two large wings mounted on a special apparatus. It was recorded that he made many attempts at flight on Lake Trasimeno, launching himself from nearby buildings. His first public experiment took place at Perugia, in 1503, and won him great fame. He was acquainted with Leonardo da Vinci, who was also intrigued by the possibility of flight.

Danti, Giulio. Architect, goldsmith, and founder; b. at Perugia, 1500; d. there, 1575. As an architect he assisted in the raising of the Rocca Paolina (1547) at Perugia, and other works. With his son Vincenzo he executed (1553–1556) the bronze statue of Pope Julius III outside the cathedral at Perugia. A number of his works as a goldsmith are extant, including several crosses, as those at Visso (Macerata) and Todi. He also made, on a design by Galeazzo Alessi, the bronze tabernacle for the host in the lower church of the Basilica of S. Francesco at Assisi. Of his three sons, Egnazio (1536–1586) was a mathematician, cosmographer, and architect; Girolamo (1547–1580) was an indifferent painter; and Vincenzo (1530–1576) was a sculptor, goldsmith, and military architect.

Danti, Pier Vincenzo. Perugian mathematician and goldsmith; d. at Perugia, 1512. He entered the Goldsmiths' Guild at Perugia, in December, 1488. He was the founder of a family of mathematicians and artists, including his son Giulio (1500–1575), and his grandsons Egnazio (1536–1586) and Vincenzo (1530–1576).

Danti, Vincenzo. Perugian sculptor and goldsmith; b. at Perugia, 1530; d. there, May 26, 1576. He was the son of Giulio Danti (1500–1575), was trained as a goldsmith at Perugia and Rome, and was enrolled in the Goldsmiths' Guild at Perugia in January, 1548. He and his father had the joint commission for the forceful bronze statue of Pope Julius III, finished, and signed (1566) by Vincenzo alone, and placed outside the cathedral at Perugia. In 1557 he went to the court of Cosimo I at Florence, and thereafter worked mainly at Florence, with intermittent periods at Perugia, as architect, engineer, and sculptor. In 1564 he helped prepare the decorations for the splendid funeral that the Florentines gave Michelangelo, and the following year worked on the decorations for the marriage of Francesco, Cosimo's son, to Joanna of Austria. In his stay at Florence, as well as from casts of Michelangelo's work that he had studied at Perugia, he was deeply influenced by the great master. His work in marble reflects that influence. The first of these at Florence was his *Honor Conquering Falsehood* (c1561), now in the Bargello. Of about the same time are three figures over the entrance to the Uffizi. He then returned to working in bronze and made two bas-reliefs, *Moses and the Brazen Serpent* and a relief for the safe door of the Guardaroba, both now in the Bargello. His masterpiece is the bronze group of three figures, *The Beheading of John the Baptist* (1571), Baptistery, Florence. In this elegantly executed and well-proportioned work, as in all his marble sculpture, a certain rigidity of contour interferes with and adds stiffness to the fluidity of movement expressed by Michelangelo that Danti tried in vain to achieve. Michelangelo was his hero and model, and he expressed his admiration in the opening statement of his treatise, *Trattato delle perfette proporzioni* (1567), to the effect that Michelangelo, as sculptor, painter, and architect, surpassed all modern artists, and possibly all ancient ones as well. Works in the National Gallery of Umbria at Perugia include a gesso relief, possibly the model for a bronze relief never executed, of *The Expulsion of the Traders from the Temple*, an *Allegorical Figure*, and *Saturn devouring his Children*. A late work, a bronze statuette of *Venus Anadyomene* is in the Palazzo Vecchio, Florence, a marble *Venus*, in the Pitti Palace, *Leda and the Swan*, in marble, is in the Victoria and Albert Museum, London, and a relief, *Descent from the Cross*, is in the National Gallery, Washington.

Da Ponte (dä pôn′tā), **Jacopo.** See **Bassano, Jacopo.**

Dati (dä′tē), **Giuliano.** Ecclesiastic and poet; b. 1445?; d. December 29, 1524. He was deacon of St. John Lateran at Rome, and was later named a bishop. He wrote an Italian poem, *Lettera delle isole nuovamente ritrovate*, taken from the letter of Columbus announcing the discovery of the New World. His other works are on the saints and figures of legend.

Dati, Gregorio. Merchant, public official, historian, and writer; b. at Florence, April 15, 1362; d. there, September 12, 1435. In his business as a merchant he traveled widely in Italy and spent some time in Spain. He was also active in public affairs at Florence and served several times as a public official. His two principal works are *Istoria di Firenze*, which is a history, in nine books, that covers the period 1348 to 1406, and his *Libro segreto*, a kind of personal memoir or collection of personal and business notes. Together they give a living picture of the Florence of his day, and reveal an acute observer who recorded events without prejudice and with keen relish and understanding of human nature.

Dati, Leonardo. Florentine poet and humanist writer; b. 1418; d. at Rome, 1472. He was in the service of Cardinals Orsini and Condulmieri, and then of four popes—Calixtus III, Pius II, Paul II, and Sixtus IV, and was made bishop of Massa in 1467. He wrote poetry and epistles in Latin, eclogues, a tragedy, *Hiempsal*, in the manner of Seneca, and *Trophaeum anglarium*, a description of the Battle of Anghiari in an elegant Vergilian style.

Datini (dä-tē′nē), **Francesco. [Francesco di Marco da Prato.]** Florentine merchant; b. at Prato, c1335; d. there, 1410. Orphaned by the Black Death in 1348, he went to Florence and worked as an apprentice in a number of shops. In 1350, at the age of 15, he went to Avignon to seek his fortune. There he applied the knowledge of business he had gained in the shops of Florence, added new systems to it, and by 1370 had established a thriving retail and wholesale trade, supplying the wants of the luxurious papal court at Avignon and the surrounding area. At the same time, he expanded his business into the manufacture and sale of arms, and into money and banking. In 1383 he returned to Prato, leaving a partner in charge at Avignon, and soon thereafter moved his headquarters to Florence, continuing to maintain warehouses at Prato. Engaged now in transactions of every kind, he had partnerships, branches, or contacts in France, England, Spain, Germany, Italy, and throughout the Mediterranean area. He wrote copious letters of instruction to his partners, agents, and correspondents, kept copies of them, and preserved letters received, bills of exchange, account books, bank drafts, checks, and other commercial records. From Florence he also wrote numerous letters to his wife (whom he had married at Avignon in 1376), full of instruction and information on business matters, and with many illuminating items of social and domestic life. The records, over 200,000 items including about 150,000 letters, are preserved in the Datini Palace at Prato and form one of the most precious sources for the economic, commercial, and industrial life of the time. Under his will Datini, who had no children, left his wife an income. All the rest of his fortune was left to found the Ceppo dei poveri di Francesco di Marco, a charitable institution at Prato still in existence.

Davanzati (dä-vän-zä′tē), **Bernardo.** Florentine humanist and writer; b. at Florence, August 31, 1529; d. there, March 29, 1606. His attempts at a mercantile career in Lyons having met with little success, he returned to Florence and gave himself up to study and writing. To prove that Italian was a suitable language for conveying Latin thought, he translated the *Annals* of Tacitus into Italian, and used fewer words than had Tacitus. In fact, his desire for brevity sometimes made him so concise as to be obscure. He also wrote treatises on economics and agriculture, orations, and other works, including a summary of the work by Nicholas Sanders on the schism in England, all notable for his succinct and sober style.

Davanzati, Chiaro. Florentine poet; b. between 1230 and 1240; d. c1280. To his lyrics, modeled after the Provençal poets and Guittone d'Arezzo, he added his own imprint by means of simple and graceful images, new themes, sincere sentiments drawn from real experiences, and his ardent patriotism. In these respects his sonnets and canzoni are in the *dolce stil nuovo* hailed by Dante, as distinct from the conventional treatment of such themes by the Provençal poets.

Davanzati, Giuliano. Florentine humanist and lawyer; b. 1390; d. 1446. He took his doctorate in civil law at Bologna, and taught there (1415–1417). On his return to Florence he entered public life and thereafter served the Republic in many capacities. He was one of the leading lawyers of his time, as well as an ardent student of the classics.

David. [Welsh, **Dafydd ap Gwilym** or **Gwillum.**] Welsh 14th century poet and anticlerical songwriter, contemporary with Edward III; b. probably at Bro Gynin, in Llanbadarn Vawr parish, Cardiganshire, Wales, c1340; d. c1400. His dates and the places of his birth and death are uncertain. He knew Latin and Italian and is believed to have lived and studied in Italy. He wrote some 147 poems to Morvid (also variously Morvydd or Morfudd or Morfid) of Anglesey, who loved him and with whom he eloped after she had, against her will, married another. Her husband, a wealthy old man, is satirized in David's poetry as "Little Hunchback." Fined and imprisoned for his romantic adventure, David was saved by the men of Glamorgan who paid the fine for him, a favor he returned by celebrating the county in his verse. His collected work consists of 262 poems. Much of his poetry, in manuscript form, is in the British Museum.

Davies (dā′vēs, -vis), **Richard.** Welsh clergyman; b. at Plas y Person, Wales, c1505; d. in Wales, November 7, 1581. With William

Salisbury he translated the New Testament into Welsh (1567); he was responsible for Deuteronomy and 2 Samuel in the revision of the "Great Bible," known as the "Bishops' Bible" (1568).

Dávila (dä′bē-lä), **Pedrarias.** See **Pedrarias.**

Da Vinci (dä vēn′chē), **Leonardo.** See **Leonardo da Vinci.**

Dazzi (dät′tsē), **Andrea.** Humanist and poet; b. at Florence, 1473; d. there, 1548. He taught Greek at the University (studio) at Florence until a disease of the eyes compelled him to give up his post. His poetic works were collected and published by his son (Florence, 1549). The collection included Latin epigrams, elegies (in which he celebrated his love for Fulvia), and eight *Selve* on myths, praise of his patrons, and the sad state of his own age. The final work of the collection is *Aeluromiomachia,* in three books of hexameters, on the battle of the cats and mice—a derivation from Homer's *Batrachomyomachia.*

De Alenis (dā ä-lā′nēs), **Tommaso.** See **Aleni, Tommaso.**

De' Barbari (dā bär′bä-rē), **Iacopo.** [Known in Germany, where he spent much of his working life, as **Jacob Walch.**] Venetian painter and engraver; b. about the middle of the 15th century; d. probably at Brussels, before 1516. He worked at Augsburg, where he was portrait and miniature painter for the emperor (1500), at Wittenberg in Saxony in the employ of Frederick the Wise (1503–1505), at Nuremberg, Frankfurt, and in the Netherlands, where he was in the service of the Archduchess Margaret, regent of the Netherlands and aunt of the future emperor Charles V. As a painter he was influenced by Alvise Vivarini and the tradition of Antonello da Messina, and also by Dürer. The influence of the latter is apparent in a painting of *Christ,* at Weimar, and in his *Galatea* at Dresden. A *Still Life,* now at Munich, is signed and dated (1504); *Old Man Embracing a Young Girl* (1503) is in the Johnson Collection, Philadelphia. Other paintings are at Berlin, London, Paris, Vienna, and elsewhere. As an engraver he achieved a remarkable technique, and worked as an original artist rather than solely as a copier. Among his engravings is a series of thirty, and two woodcuts, almost all dating from 1504. Among these, his *Apollo Drawing the Bow* is a masterpiece of the engraving art of the time. Other notable prints in the series are a *St. Sebastian, Madonna of the Fountain,* and *Victory and Glory.* De' Barbari's individualized signature included a caduceus.

De Bardi (dā bär′dē), **Giovanni di Antonio Minelli.** Paduan sculptor and architect; b. about the middle of the 15th century; d. 1527. From 1472 he is known to have been working in the Basilica of St. Anthony of Padua at Padua. Between 1487 and 1490 he made the terra-cotta statues of Christ and of three Apostles that are now in the Museo Civico at Padua. In 1500 he was carrying out the plans of Riccio for the chapel of St. Anthony in the Basilica, and several of the sculptural decorations in it were executed by him, perhaps with the aid of his son Antonio. He worked in the Basilica until 1519, and thereafter in the convent. Among his works are a *Deposition of Christ* (1483–1487), formerly in the Church of S. Agostino and now at Boston; a polychrome stucco relief of *The Baptism of Christ;* and a polychrome terra-cotta *Pietà* at Vicenza. His work is delicate and decorative and characterized by a mannered exaggeration of line and drapery.

De Boninis (dā bō-nē′nēs), **Bonino.** Typographer and publisher; b. at Curzola in Dalmatia, 1454; d. 1528. Because of his Dalmatian origin he signed himself "de Ragusia." He was an ecclesiastic, and was dean of the cathedral at Treviso. His first known work is the edition (Venice, 1478) of *De divinis institutionibus* of the 4th century Christian apologist Lactantius Firmianus. At Verona he printed a *Grammatica* and, among other books, a Latin and an Italian edition of *De re militari* by Valturio (1483). He also worked at Brescia (1483–1491), where he was the first to print Greek characters, and where he printed an edition of the *Divina Commedia* (1487) illustrated with wood-engravings. He went later to Lyons, where he devoted himself to publishing works of a religious nature and to the book business he carried on with Giorgio Serre, a bookseller of Avignon. Wherever he went he served the Council of Ten of Venice as an informer on foreign matters, whether they concerned events in Italy or outside the peninsula.

Decameron (dẹ-kam′ẹ-rọn). [Italian, **Il Decamerone; Principe Galeotto.**] Collection of one hundred tales, by Giovanni Boccaccio, written probably between 1348 and 1353.

Woodcut (*Inferno*, xvii) from the 1487 edition of Landino's *Commentary* on Dante's *Divine Comedy*
Courtesy of the Isabella Stewart Gardner Museum, Boston

thin; ᴛʜ, then; y, you; (variable) ḏ as d or j, ș as s or sh, ț as t or ch, ẓ as z or zh; *o*, F. cloche; ü, F. menu; ċh, Sc. loch; ṅ, F. bonbon; ʙ, Sp. Córdoba (sounded almost like v).

The tales are enclosed in a framework device giving a fictional account of how they came to be told: in the year 1348, when Florence was devastated by the Black Death (of which Boccaccio gives a vivid description), a gay company of seven young ladies and three young gentlemen retire to villas and pleasant gardens above the city, near Fiesole, where through the hot afternoon hours of ten summer days they pass the time by telling stories, one each on each day, under some general heading or subject matter proclaimed by the one who is elected king or queen for the day. The *Decameron* is a masterpiece of prose style and narrative art. It became a model for Italian prose for centuries after, and enjoyed great popularity throughout Europe. Not even the major part of the stories contained in it were invented by Boccaccio, but all are cast in a manner quite his own. Included are the tales of the day from the French *fabliaux*, from incidents of actual life, or from whatever source was open to the author. The collection has had, through the years, the reputation of being overly licentious, but the tales reflect the mid-14th century in its moral as well as its immoral aspects. They present a kind of "human comedy," rich in the variety of characters that people it, a "natural" world quite untouched by any sense of otherworldliness as might be expected in a work written in the years immediately following the disaster of the Black Death and less than half a century after Dante's *Divina Commedia*. The characters of the tales are drawn from all classes and conditions of men, no area of activity is considered sacrosanct; they may be scoundrels or near-saints; they may be ingeniously nimble in escaping the predicaments in which circumstances have placed them; some are fools, others are of great wisdom; all are portrayed with a deep understanding of human psychology and with an encompassing tolerance. The tales are not told for the purpose of teaching a lesson or pointing a moral. Both the proem of the work with its dedication to the "idle ladies" (as its ideal public), and the framework where the author speaks out in his own person in defense of a serene and objective art free from allegory, moralism, and didacticism, give ample evidence that Boccaccio was aware that this "new" art might well be attacked by those who demand that literature should do more than entertain, a fear which history has shown to be not without some ground. The collection of tales is also entitled *Principe Galeotto*, an appellation which the deputies appointed for correction of the *Decameron* considered as derived from the fifth canto of Dante's *Inferno*, Galeotto being the name of the book which was read by Paolo and Francesca. Few works have had an equal influence on literature. From it Chaucer adopted the idea of the framework of his tales, and the general manner of his stories, while in some instances, he merely versified the novels of the Italian. In 1566, William Paynter printed many of Boccaccio's stories in English, in his work called *The Palace of Pleasure*. This first translation, containing sixty tales, was soon followed by another volume, comprising thirty-four additional tales. Shakespeare made considerable use of the tales as he found them in Paynter.

Decembrio (dā-chem′bryō), **Angelo.** Humanist; b. c1415; d. after 1466. He was the son of Uberto Decembrio (c1350–1427) and the brother of Pier Candido (1392–1477). He studied at Milan under Gasparino Barzizza and at Ferrara under Guarino da Verona. For a time he had a school at Milan, then was attached to the courts of the Estensi at Ferrara and of Alfonso I at Naples. On the death of the latter he went to Spain and became one of the first humanists to make a systematic search of the libraries there for manuscripts. The most impostant of his writings is *Politia literaria*, a full description of the circle about Guarino da Verona at Ferrara.

Decembrio, Pier Candido. Humanist; b. at Pavia, October 24, 1392; d. at Milan, November 12, 1477. He was the son of Uberto Decembrio (c1350–1427) and the brother of Angelo (c1415–1466). In 1410 he was imprisoned with his father, but was released the following year and went to Genoa. In 1419 he became secretary to Filippo Maria Visconti, and remained in Milan until 1450. In that year he was invited to Rome by Nicholas V, and remained there under Calixtus III. Following that period of service to the popes he went to the court of Alfonso I of Naples and on that monarch's death, remained for a time at the court of his son Ferrante. His last post was at the court of the Estensi at Ferrara. In all his posts he performed literary and diplomatic services. Among his writings are translations from the Greek to Latin, including Plato's *Republic*, and, for his Visconti patrons, translations of Caesar's *Gallic Wars* and Polybius' *Punic Wars* into Italian. He wrote biographies of Francesco Sforza and Filippo Maria Visconti. The latter, on the model of Suetonius, is a vivid picture of "the habits and vices of a tyrant." His letters provide a valuable source for the political and literary history of his times.

Decembrio, Uberto. Lombard humanist; b. at Vigevano, c1350; d. at Treviglio, April 7, 1427. He served as secretary to Petros Philargos (the future pope Alexander V) and accompanied him to Prague (1393–1395) on an embassy. He was later in the service of the Visconti at Milan. A follower of Salutati, he was one of the earliest humanists in Lombardy. Among his works are some Latin moral treatises and a few letters that are interesting for the picture they give of humanistic studies in his era. He was the father of Angelo Decembrio (c1415–1466) and of Pier Candido (1392–1477).

Deciani (dā-chä′nē), **Tiberio.** Criminologist; b. at Udine, August 3, 1509. In 1549 he was named to the chair of criminal law at the University of Padua, where his lectures attracted large audiences. In 1552 he held the chair of Roman law, and in 1570 that of canon law. He won great fame in resolving many important legal questions. His most important work, *Tractatus criminalis utriusque censurae* (Venice, 1590), is a treatise in nine books in which he discusses crime in general and in particular, its sources, and procedures for dealing with it according to law.

Decio (dā′chō), **Filippo.** [Latinized, **Philippus Decius.**] Jurisconsult and orator; b. at Milan, 1454; d. perhaps at Siena, October 12 or 13, 1535. He studied at Pavia and took his doctorate at Pisa, where he then taught civil law. He lectured at Siena, Pisa, Padua, and Pavia. A skillful speaker and keen polemicist, he won renown, and the dislike of his contemporaries, for his part in many disputations. In 1512 he was excommunicated and fled to France, where he taught at Valence. The ban was lifted in 1515 and he returned to Pavia and then went to Pisa. He left commentaries on many Roman legal works, many opinions, and other legal works as *De actionibus* (Pavia, 1483), *De iure emphiteutico* (Pavia, 1476, 1489), and *Apophthegmata singularia iuris* (Pavia, 1489).

Decretals of the Pseudo-Isidore (sū′dọ̄-iz′-i-dôr). See **False Decretals.**

Dedekind (dā′dẹ-kint), **Friedrich.** German poet and pastor; b. at Neustadt an der Leine, Germany, c1525; d. 1598. He is remembered for his satirical Latin poem *Grobianus* (1549), directed at gluttony and drunkenness. The idea was derived from the chapter on "Grobe Narren" in Sebastian Brant's *Narrenschiff* (*Ship of Fools*, 1494). Dedekind's mock epic was translated in 1551, with emendations, into German. An English translation appeared in 1605.

Dee (dē), **John.** English mathematician and astrologer; b. at London, July 13, 1527; d. at Mortlake-Surrey, England, in December, 1608. He was astrologer to Mary Tudor, and gave exhibitions of magic at the courts of various princes. His most notable work is *Monas Hieroglyphica*. His reputation is primarily that of a magician, but he was also a sober mathematician who advocated the adoption of the Gregorian calendar, and who did geographical descriptions of the new lands in America.

Defendente Ferrari (dā-fen-den′tā fer-rä′rē). See **Ferrari, Defendente.**

De Ferrariis (dā fer-rä′rē-ēs), **Antonio.** [Called **Il Galateo.**] Physician and humanist; b. at Galatona, 1444; d. at Gallipoli, November 12, 1517. He was well-grounded in Latin and Greek and knew Spanish. At Naples he was a member of the Accademia Pontaniana, boon companion of Ermolao Barbaro, physician and secretary of Alfonso, Duke of Calabria, whom he accompanied on his military campaigns, and a loyal supporter of the Neapolitan Aragonese dynasty. The moral and social ideas expressed in his more than seventy literary works were influential in the Renaissance. Of his many works, most circulated widely in manuscript; some have been published in other collections as representative of the writers of the region of Otranto; and others are still unpublished.

De Fonduti (fôn′dö-tē) or **Fondulo** (fôn′-dö-lō), **Agostino.** Sculptor and architect of Crema; active at the end of the 15th and the beginning of the 16th century. In 1483 he undertook to finish the group, *Pietà*, in the

Church of S. Maria di S. Satiro at Milan, and to decorate the new sacristy of the church (which Bramante had begun remodeling in the 70's), with a frieze of heads and putti, and thirty-six figures in terra-cotta. The work was completed in 1488 (the frieze remains; the thirty-six figures were removed from the cornice of the cupola in 1764). In 1484 he worked, with Giovanni Battaglio of Lodi, on the building and decoration of a palace at Piacenza, and in 1502 he was commissioned to make statues of the Apostles for the Church of S. Celso at Milan. In 1513 and 1517 he worked at Castelleone. Among the works attributed to him are the decorations on the outside of the apse of S. Maria delle Grazie at Milan. His masterpiece is the lovely frieze of S. Satiro.

Dei (dā′ē), **Andrea.** Sienese chronicler, of the 14th century. He wrote a chronicle of Siena from 1186 to 1348, which was later continued to 1384 by another writer. Some of the chronicle seems to have been drawn from earlier works, but much of it is a brief and factual record of offices and public events. It has been a valuable source for later historians of Siena.

Dei, Benedetto. Historian; b. at Florence, March 4, 1418; d. there, August 2, 1492. In early life he was a public official at Florence, but after taking part in an abortive conspiracy against Luca Pitti he was forced to flee the city, and began on his travels. These took him to Africa and Asia, and finally to Constantinople, where he remained some years and where he was on very friendly terms with the Sultan. He returned to Florence, 1486, and entered the service of the Medici, later moving on to other courts in Italy. His travels furnish material for a chronicle he wrote and for his *Le memorie storiche*. These make up a collection of interesting and varied items of information on geography, finance, art, politics, and so on, and are particularly valuable for material on the Ottoman Empire. He also wrote poems, in one of which he makes an ardent defense of the faith, in reply to a sonnet by Luigi Pulci.

Dei, Pier or **Pietro d'Antonio.** See **Della Gatta, Bartolomeo.**

Delattre (dẹ-lätr), **Roland.** Original name of **Orlandus Lassus.**

Del Balzo (del bäl′tsō), **Iacopo.** Neapolitan nobleman; d. September 21, 1384. He was the nephew of Luigi (Louis) of Taranto, the second husband of Joanna I of the Kingdom of Naples, and was known as "the first lord of the Kingdom." From his grandfather and his uncles he inherited the titles: Prince of Achaia, Despot of Romania, Lord of Albania, and Emperor of Constantinople. In 1373 he waged war on Joanna but made peace with her murderer and successor, Charles III, who gave him his cousin Agnese of Durazzo, widow of Can Grande della Scala, in marriage and restored Taranto and the island of Corfu to him. Iacopo named his cousin, Louis of Anjou, who had been adopted by Joanna and was at war with Charles in an attempt to gain the throne, as his heir.

Del Barbiere (del bär-bye′rā), **Domenico.** [Called **Domenico Fiorentino.**] Painter, sculptor, and engraver; b. at Florence, c1506; d. after 1565. He worked with Rosso Fiorentino and Primaticcio at Fontainebleau for Francis I between 1533 and 1550. His contributions were stucco decorations and statues for the garden. He continued to work in France at least until 1565, when the last notices of him are known, and left examples of his work at Troyes, Bar-sur-Aube, and in the Louvre, among others.

Del Bene (bā′nā), **Bartolomeo.** Poet; b. at Florence, 1514; d. in France, after 1587. He passed most of his life at the courts of the French kings and princes, where he often wrote lyrics for festivals and entertainments, and was a protégé of Catherine de Médicis and of Henry III. His poems, in the meters of Horace and in his own metrical variations, are flattering, didactic, jerky, and often original.

Del Bene, Sennuccio. Florentine poet of the first half of the 14th century; d. 1349. He was a partisan of the Bianchi (White Guelphs), and was exiled in 1311, but was restored to his city in 1326. Del Bene's poetry, little of which remains, is in the *dolce stil nuovo* of Dante, and includes a canzone on the death of the emperor Henry VII that appears under Dante's name in many manuscripts. He was a friend of Petrarch, who lamented his death and mentioned his name in one of his *Trionfi*.

Del Carretto (kär-rāt′tō), **Galeotto.** See **Carretto, Galeotto del.**

Del Chierico (kyā′rē-kō), **Francesco d'Antonio.** Miniaturist; active at Florence in the second half of the 15th century. In his work as an illuminator he departed from the practice of earlier times of decoration of capitals and borders. He came closer to the painters by utilizing entire, or nearly entire, sheets of the parchment for depicting scenes or illustrations. In his delicacy and clarity of color he was a follower of Fra Angelico. His tendency to make his illuminations illustrations is especially marked in the great liturgical books he illuminated for S. Maria del Fiore (the cathedral) at Florence between 1463 and 1471. In other books he often continued the decorative manner of earlier illuminators, painting decorations of exquisite delicacy and refinement. Among his patrons were the Aragonese of Naples, the dukes of Urbino, King Matthias Corvinus of Hungary, and, above all, Piero de' Medici. His only signed work is a *Plutarch* he illuminated for Piero de' Medici. The *Plutarch,* some liturgical books, and a *Libro d'oro* he illuminated for Lorenzo the Magnificent are in the Laurentian Library at Florence.

Del Colle (kōl'lā), **Raffaello.** [Called **Raffaelino.**] Painter; b. at Sansepolcro towards the end of the 15th century; d. there, 1566. According to Vasari, he was a pupil of Giulio Romano, with whom he worked on the decoration of the *Sala di Costantino* in the Vatican between 1523 and 1525. His work there cannot be distinguished from that of other assistants of Giulio Romano. For Francesco Maria I, duke of Urbino, he worked at Pesaro then, after 1530, lived for a long time at Sansepolcro and completed a number of paintings, now in the gallery at Città di Castello. Except for these paintings, most of Del Colle's work was as a collaborator with some more noted painter. Among others, he assisted Vasari, and helped Bronzino with the designs of the story of Joseph for the tapestries for the Palazzo della Signoria at Florence. His dependence on Raphael shows him to have been lacking in originality, but his imitations of the great Umbrian helped to spread the school of Raphael in Tuscany.

Del Conte (kôn'tā), **Jacopino.** See **Iacopino del Conte.**

Del Cossa (kôs'sä), **Francesco.** See **Cossa, Francesco del.**

Del Fora (fō'rä), **Gherardo.** See **Gherardo di Giovanni del Fora.**

Del Garbo (gär'bō), **Dino.** Physician; d. at Florence, in September, 1327. His father was a professor of medicine at Bologna, and he studied there under his uncle, also a physician. After teaching at Siena he practiced at Florence and became a physician of great renown. He took part in a bitter dispute with Cecco d'Ascoli concerning Guido Cavalcanti, and was blamed by some for having brought on a charge of heresy against Cecco through his accusations. His most important work was *Dilucidarium Avicennae* (Ferrara, 1492). His son, Tommaso (d. c1370), was a friend of Petrarch, Franco Sacchetti, and Giovanni Villani. He was also a noted physician. He wrote a highly respected work on disease, *Consiglio contro la pestilenza,* and a *Summa medicinalis* (Venice, 1506).

Delitio (dā-lē'tyō), **Andrea.** [Also, **De Litio, De Lisio, Delisio, Delisiis.**] Painter of Guardiagrele in the Abruzzi; active in the second half of the 15th century. A fresco, *S. Cristoforo,* in the cathedral of Guardiagrele is dated 1473. Frescoes in the cathedral and other churches at Atri and at Isola del Gran Sasso are attributed to him, as well as a painting of *S. Silvestro* at Mutignano, detached frescoes in the museum at Aquila, a triptych, *Madonna and Child Enthroned,* Walters Art Gallery, Baltimore, and a predella panel, Rhode Island School of Design, Providence. The flat tones and solid forms of his work are similar to those of Piero della Francesca and Benozzo Gozzoli.

Dell' Abate (del-lä-bä'tā), **Niccolò.** Painter of the Emilian school; b. at Modena, 1509; d. in France, 1571. He worked in Modena until 1548, and in Bologna until 1552. In the latter year, on the advice of Primaticcio, he was invited by Henry II to come to Fontainebleau. The frescoes he executed there, to designs by Primaticcio, have almost all perished. He painted in the castle of Beauregard, near Blois, and, among others at Paris, in the royal palace. His earlier work in Modena and Bologna was first derived from Dosso Dossi and Correggio. Later he was influenced by the elegant mannerism of Parmigianino, and finally, in France, by his close association with Primaticcio. In France, where he remained to the end of his life, he was an outstanding representative of Italian mannerism, and a founder of the so-called school of Fontainebleau. Early works at Modena included a frieze in the ducal palace (1546), frescoes in the fortress of Scandiano that have been detached and are now in the Estense Gallery at Modena, and a *Martyrdom of Saints Peter and Paul,* now at Dresden. At Bologna he painted a frieze for a hall in the university library that is especially interesting for its faithful representation of courtly life in the 16th century. A *Portrait of a Young Man with a Cap,* in the Uffizi, is attributed to him. His son Giulio Camillo worked with him at Fontainebleau, and his work is sometimes confused with that of his father.

Della Casa (del′lä kä′zä), **Giovanni.** Poet and ecclesiastic; b. in the Mugello, near Florence, June 28, 1503; d. at Montepulciano, November 14, 1556. Of a noble Florentine family, he was educated at Bologna and Florence and subsequently, more for material reasons than because of any spiritual vocation, he entered the Church. He went to Rome (1529) and quickly won the position of apostolic secretary. During this time at Rome he wrote *capitoli* in the manner of Berni (*Del forno, the Oven,* was notorious). These reveal his attitude toward life. In 1541 he was at Florence, and in 1544 he returned to Rome and was made Archbishop of Benevento, but he never visited his diocese. His work for the church was varied and important, as he served as papal nuncio at Venice, attended the Council of Trent, and made an eloquent oration in which he tried to arouse interest in the league, proposed by Paul III, of the Italian powers and France against Spain. In the midst of his heavy and varied ecclesiastical duties he continued to write. He left a number of Latin and Italian poems. Those of his later years are somber and melancholy, and often express regret for his wastrel youth. Some of his grave and dignified sonnets proceed rather from his brain than from his heart. His most famous work, written between 1551 and 1555, is his *Galateo,* a treatise on the subject of good manners, set forth with good sense, humor, and in a graceful style. The point of departure is that good manners are important as an aid to advancement and ease in society. His recommendations of what to avoid are specific, as not to gobble at table or talk with one's mouth full. His strictures apply as well to topics of conversation, methods of telling a story, avoidance of affected foreign ways, comments on personal habits and mannerisms, and proper dress. The treatise is of interest for its relation of customs that later fell into disuse, as well as for the specific and encompassing advice that Della Casa gives to who would be a gentleman. The work was immensely popular and was widely translated.

Della Corgna (kôr′nyä), **Pier Filippo.** See **Corneo, Pier Filippo.**

Della Fonte (fôn′tā), **Bartolomeo.** [Full name, **Bartolomeo di Giampetrino della Fonte**; Latin name, **Fontius.**] Florentine humanist; b. at Florence, 1445; d. there, in October, 1513. He studied under Cristoforo Landino and Argyropolos at the *Studio* (University) and had private lessons with Bernardo Nuzzi. Between 1468 and 1472 he was at the court of Duke Borso d'Este at Ferrara, then returned to Florence. He taught at Florence and at Rome, went to Hungary in 1489 to rearrange the library of King Matthias Corvinus, returned to Florence after several months, and remained there the rest of his life. He wrote commentaries on various Latin authors, prepared the first edition (1478) of the work of the 1st century encyclopedist, Aulus Cornelius Celsus, translated Apollonius Rhodius and other Greek writers, and edited the text of books xxi–xxvi of Livy. His most rewarding work for later readers is the collection of his letters, with their many affectionate and revealing glimpses of the humanists of Florence and other places whom he knew and with whom he corresponded.

Della Gatta (gät′tä), **Bartolomeo.** [Real name, **Pier** or **Pietro d'Antonio Dei.**] Camaldolese monk, painter, miniaturist, and architect; b. at Florence, 1448; d. at Arezzo, 1502 or 1503. He entered the Camaldolese monastery at Florence as a youth and there worked as an illuminator. When he was about 20 he transferred to a monastery at Arezzo, and after that began his career as a painter. He went to Rome to help Signorelli with the frescoes, *The Promulgation of the Laws* and the *Death of Moses,* and perhaps assisted Perugino on *Christ Giving the Keys to St. Peter,* all in the Sistine Chapel. He returned to Arezzo, where he was made abbot of the convents of S. Clemente and S. Maria in Gradi, and where he executed a number of paintings. Besides being a miniaturist and a painter, he was a musician, a builder of organs, and a gifted architect; the Church of the Annunziata at Arezzo was built to his designs at the end of the 15th century. In his painting, Bartolomeo della Gatta combined elements of Florentine art with the solid dignity of Piero della Francesca and the drama of Luca Signorelli to achieve his own style, one marked by delicacy and precision. His followers constituted a small local school that flourished at the beginning of the 16th century. Among his Aretine followers were: Matteo Lappoli, Domenico Pecori, and Angelo di Lorentino. Many of his paintings are in and around Arezzo, where he spent so much of his life. They include: *St. Roch,* in the Pinacoteca, and *St. Jerome,* in the cathedral. Other works are *St. Michael the Archangel, St. Francis Receiving the Stigmata,* and a *Madonna and Saints,* Pinacoteca, Castiglione Fiorentino, and an *Assumption,* S. Domenico, Cortona.

Della Paglia (päl′yä), **Antonio.** See **Paleario, Aonio.**

Della Porta (pōr′tä), **Antonio.** [Called **il Tamagnino.**] Sculptor; active at the end of the 15th century and the beginning of the 16th. In 1491, with other sculptors and their many assistants, he began work on the façade of the Certosa di Pavia, and worked there until 1498. In those years he completed eight statues of saints and busts of four prophets. In 1499 and the following year he was in Brescia, where he executed six imperial busts on the west side of the Loggia (or Palazzo del Comune, built between 1492 and 1574), and did some low reliefs for the Renaissance church of S. Maria dei Miracoli. By 1501 he had a workshop at Genoa, where in succeeding years he carved the decoration for a chapel in S. Teodoro, and made the elaborately carved doorways for several palaces with his associate Pace Gaggini. The two worked together in the Certosa di Pavia and also in France. Della Porta is especially known for the variety and richness of his ornamentation. He was one of the most virile sculptors of the early 16th century in northern Italy. Other works include statues of Luciano Grimaldi (d. 1479) and Antonio Doria, both in the Palazzo S. Giorgio at Genoa, and his masterpiece, the bust of Accelino Salvago (1500), now at Berlin.

Della Porta, Giambattista. See **Porta, Giambattista della.**

Della Porta, Giovanni Giacomo. Sculptor and architect; b. at Porlezza, near Como, c1485; d. at Genoa, 1555. After working at Genoa between 1513 and 1516, he went into Lombardy, and was a pupil of Cristoforo Solario at Milan. For him he designed the tomb of Beatrice d'Este and Ludovico il Moro for the Church of S. Maria delle Grazie (the tomb was removed to the Certosa di Pavia), and he worked with him on the cathedral. He also worked on the Certosa di Pavia and on the tomb of Gian Galeazzo Sforza. In 1531 he went to Genoa and worked on the chapel of St. John the Baptist in the cathedral, for which, with his nephew Guglielmo and Niccolò da Corte, he constructed the altar and ciborium. With a number of assistants from his workshop he constructed the great Altar of the Apostles in the Cibo chapel in the same church, and carved the statue of Luke the Evangelist and perhaps also that of St. Mark, for the presbytery. With other Lombard associates he carried out important commissions for clients in Milan and even in Spain. At Genoa he made the portal of the Palazzo Salvago (1532) and carved the statues for the Palazzo S. Giorgio.

Della Porta, Guglielmo. Sculptor; b. at Porlezza, near Como, 1500?; d. 1577. He was the nephew of Giovanni Giacomo Della Porta, and went to Genoa with him. As an assistant of Perin del Vaga he worked on the stucco decorations in the halls and salons of the Doria palace at Genoa. He assisted his uncle in carving the sixteen statues of prophets for the plinth of the ciborium in the chapel of St. John the Baptist in the cathedral at Genoa. Works distinctively by him, in his collaboration with his uncle and Niccolò da Corte, are a statue of *Abraham* in the Cibo chapel in the cathedral, and a statue of Ansaldo Grimaldi in the Palazzo S. Giorgio. His most noted work is a *St. Catherine* now in the Academy of Fine Arts at Genoa. After 1537 he went to Rome, where he was a protégé of Michelangelo, who secured for him (1549) the commission to execute the tomb of Pope Paul III for the basilica of St. Peter. Of the two allegorical statues on the tomb the originally nude figure of *Justice* (it was clothed in bronze in 1593 by Guglielmo's son Teodoro) is said to be a portrait of Giulia Farnese, Paul III's sister. Guglielmo's art reached its greatest development after he went to Rome, and is best shown in the monument of Paul III, but he continued to use his creative imagination and his sculptor's skill to design decorations for the floats for festivals and for masquerades.

Della Quercia (kwer′chä), **Jacopo.** Sienese sculptor; b. c1374; d. 1438. He was the son of a goldsmith and woodcarver, from whom he probably received his early training. By 1401 he considered himself well-enough established as a sculptor to enter the contest for the second bronze doors of the Florentine Baptistery. Lorenzo Ghiberti and Filippo Brunelleschi were his principal rivals among the contestants. Ghiberti won and Della Quercia's entry, on the prescribed subject *The Sacrifice of Isaac,* has been lost, and with it an early work of one of the three most influential sculptors of his day. Earlier works that would have qualified him to enter the contest must have existed, but none are now known with certainty. His earliest known work (c1406) is the marble tomb of Ilaria del Carretto (d. 1405) in the cathedral at Lucca. She was the wife of Paolo Guinigi, lord of Lucca. When the rebellious Lucchese drove him out of the city (1429) they vented their hatred of him and his family by removing the tomb from its place, and would have broken it up, but were so moved by the beauty of the figure of Ilaria and the ornamentation of the tomb that they did not destroy the whole, and not long afterward the tomb was set up again in the cathedral. The serene effigy of the youthful Ilaria, her hands crossed and her feet resting on a dog (to symbolize her fidelity to her husband), is one of Della Quercia's most celebrated works. The effigy rests on a sarcophagus which, with its carved putti holding garlands, is derived from classical models. Other works by Della Quercia include *Virgin and Child,* cathedral, Ferrara, completed in June, 1409; the tomb slabs for the Trenta family at Lucca, and the Trenta altar with the Virgin and Child surrounded by four saints in the Church of S. Frediano, Lucca. In 1409 he was commissioned by the Council of Siena to carve marble plaques representing the cardinal and theological virtues and scenes from the Old Testament in low relief for the fountain in the Campo at Siena, known as the Fonte Gaia. He worked on the fountain, with interruptions, from 1414 to 1419. It is a great rectangular basin jutting out from a wall; the principal reliefs adorned the wall. According to Vasari, the Sienese were so pleased with the life and beauty with which he endowed the marble forms that ever afterward he was known as Jacopo della Fonte (Of the Fountain). The surviving original sections, much worn and weathered, were removed to the Palazzo Pubblico at Siena in the 19th century. The marbles now in the fountain are reproductions. Between 1417 and 1431 he was one of the sculptors working on the bronze reliefs for the Baptismal font at Siena. He had been commissioned (1417) to make two of the reliefs for the font but when (1423) his first relief, *Zacharias in the Temple,* was still unfinished, the commission for his second relief was transferred to Donatello. It was Della Quercia's custom to be working on several commissions, and often in different cities, at the same time. This would account for the length of time it took him to finish any given commission. From 1425 until his death he was decorating the doorway of the Basilica of S. Petronio at Bologna with five narrative reliefs on each of two pilasters, five reliefs on the architrave, and on the tympanum a group of three life-size, free-standing figures: the Virgin and Child between St. Petronius and St. Ambrose (the latter executed by another sculptor in 1510). At the same time, or in the same period, he carried out some of the decoration of the Casini Chapel in the cathedral at Siena and worked on the Bentivoglio monument in the Church of S. Giacomo Maggiore, Bologna. A group of the Angel of the Annunciation and the Virgin Annunciate, in wood, is in the cathedral at S. Gimignano. Della Quercia's style was influenced somewhat in his later years by the realism of Donatello, but in general his vigorous and passionate forms are closer to those of northern Europe, and project the drama and movement of the late Gothic. Although he was influenced to some degree by the fragments of classical sculpture that were coming to light and were available, his approach to his art was energetic, and even agitated, in a manner that gave a foretaste of Michelangelo. The flexibility and animation of his sculpture, his massive forms and dramatic movement, had a deep impact on the development of Renaissance sculpture.

Della Robbia (rôb′byä), **Andrea.** Florentine sculptor and ceramist; b. October 20, 1435; d. August 4, 1525. He was the nephew and most gifted pupil of Luca della Robbia

(1399 or 1400–1482), and in his uncle's old age gradually took over control of his workshop. He carried Luca's innovations in the art of modelling in terra-cotta further by creating retables, fountains, and friezes in enamelled terra-cotta. The white and blue medallions with the figures of infants in swaddling clothes (*bambini*) that decorate the loggia of the Ospedale degli Innocenti (Foundling Hospital) at Florence, are among the best known of the Della Robbia terra-cottas, but as art are nowhere equal to Luca's dancing children of his *Cantoria*, in the Cathedral Museum, Florence. Nor was Andrea's color sense as refined as that of his uncle. The effects he achieved in his multicolored decorative borders of flowers and fruits are sometimes rich and sometimes rather garish. He executed the decorations of the Loggia di S. Paolo at Florence and a long series of bas-reliefs for the churches of Arezzo, Prato, Pistoia, Siena, and other cities. He very rarely worked in marble; a marble *Pietà* is in the Church of S. Maria delle Grazie, near Arezzo. Andrea's chief contribution was to adapt the processes Luca had extended to sculpture in enamelled terra-cotta to more uses. In the process he created a ceramic industry that endured for nearly a hundred years, and debased the quality that Luca had achieved for sculpture in this medium.

Della Robbia, Giovanni. Florentine sculptor and ceramist; b. 1469; d. c1529. He was the son of Andrea della Robbia (1435–1525) and the great-nephew of Luca della Robbia (1399 or 1400–1482), and practiced chiefly the art of terra-cotta sculpture. He executed medallions, retables, friezes, and lavabos, and his work adorned, among other sites, the churches of S. Croce and of S. Maria Novella at Florence, the Church of S. Girolamo at Volterra, and the Ceppo Hospital at Pistoia.

Della Robbia, Girolamo. Florentine architect, sculptor, ceramist, and painter; d. c1566. He was the son of Andrea della Robbia (1435–1525), and greatly extended the use of enamelled terra-cotta to architectural use. About 1520 he was taken to France by some Florentine merchants and there found employment during the remainder of his life under four kings of the house of Valois. On his arrival he was employed by Francis I to build the Château de Madrid in the Bois de Boulogne, which he decorated throughout with glazed terra-cotta (this palace was leveled in the French Revolution, and its beautiful terra-cottas were used to mend roads).

Della Robbia, Luca. Florentine sculptor; b. at Florence, 1399 or 1400; d. there, February 20, 1482. Little is surely known of his early life and training. Some art historians recognize elements of the style of Nanni di Banco (d. 1421) in his work, as well as those of Ghiberti (d. 1455), with the latter of whom he may have worked. He was a member of the Guild of Stonemasons and Woodcarvers, held offices in his guild, and on several occasions carried out official missions for it. He and his brother Marco owned a house at Florence, and Luca, who never married, lived in it with his brother and his nephews and nieces. Of a deeply religious nature, he devoted much time to charitable work. His spirit—serene and restrained—is reflected in his work. By 1431 he was already a marble sculptor of reputation. Of that year is his first documented commission. It was for the *Cantoria (Singing Gallery)*, finished in 1438. It was moved from its place over the door of the north sacristy in the cathedral at Florence in the 17th century, and was taken apart. What remained has been reassembled and is now in the Cathedral Museum. The *Cantoria* comprised ten panels of reliefs: four, separated by pilasters, on the front of the gallery proper superposed on four between supporting consoles, and one on each of the short ends of the gallery. The reliefs, of groups of singing, instrument-playing, and dancing children, illustrate in their separate panels Psalm 150, with its exhortation to praise the Lord with the sound of the trumpet, with the psaltery and harp, with the timbrel and dance, with stringed instruments and organs, and with the loud cymbal. The words of the Psalm, in Latin, appear across the cornice and base of the gallery proper and on the base of the consoles supporting it. Vasari wrote of the *Cantoria* that it represents the "agreeable actions that constitute the charm of music," and charming is an appropriate word for the grace, simplicity, and highly finished forms of the musical children. Each of the reliefs constitutes a separate scene; they are not united as a composition but as an expression of the various phrases of the Psalm. The architectural design in which they were set may have been the work of Luca's friend Brunelleschi, and the flow and movement of the dancing children in those that are thought to have been the last to be carved reflect the influence of Donatello's *Cantoria* in the cathedral and the dancing children, of much more abandoned movement, of his pulpit at Prato, both of which were executed after Luca had begun his first reliefs. Between 1437 and 1439 he was at work on five reliefs for the campanile. The five—*Grammar, Logic, Music, Arithmetic, Harmony*—were to complete the set of reliefs on the Arts and Sciences begun by Giotto and Andrea Pisano. In 1439 he was commissioned to carve marble altars for two chapels in the cathedral. Only two unfinished reliefs, *St. Peter Delivered from Prison* and *The Martyrdom of St. Peter,* now in the Bargello, resulted from this commission.

The Della Robbia name is inevitably associated with enamelled terra-cotta. Luca della Robbia did not invent the process of glazing terra-cotta; it had long existed in majolica ware, but he was the first to adapt the process to monumental sculpture. Terra-cotta, so much lighter than marble, was more practical for some uses; and it had the advantage that it could be colored with enamels, with the same effect as was achieved by painting marble statues, as was not infrequently done. Of the many terra-cotta reliefs Luca ultimately modeled, most had very little color. The Madonnas are milky white, a little color was used for the eyes, gilding was applied to haloes, and a clear blue, characteristic of Luca, was used for the backgrounds. His color sense was impeccable. The wreaths of flowers or fruits with which he often framed his plaques, lunettes, and coats-of-arms, shine with clear, delicate harmonious color. His successors, his nephew Andrea (1435–1525), who was his pupil and assistant, and who assumed control of Luca's studio when the latter was growing old, and his great-nephew Giovanni (1469–c1529), lacked Luca's taste and refinement. Under them the art of sculpture in enamelled terra-cotta was transformed to a decorative ceramics industry. It was an industry associated with the Della Robbia name for nearly a century, after which it died out. A marble tabernacle, executed between January, 1441, and 1443, and now at Peretola, has an enamelled terra-cotta background, and is the first documented use by Luca of glazed terra-cotta as a sculptural medium. The enamelled terra-cotta roundels, in the Pazzi chapel, of the twelve Apostles and the larger one of St. Andrew, of which the dates are not known, may have been begun before the Peretola tabernacle. At the instance of Brunelleschi, the architect of the Pazzi Chapel and of the dome of the cathedral at Florence, Luca was commissioned (1442) to mold the terra-cotta *Resurrection* (completed 1445) for the lunette over the doorway to the north sacristy in the cathedral. The relief, still in place, is notable for the nobility of the strongly modeled Christ and for the grandeur and power of the composition. A few years later he made the *Ascension* (1446–1451) over the door to the south sacristy. In this, with its many figures, Luca added more color in the green trees and brown earth against his typical blue background. Other major works in terra-cotta included the *Visitation* (1445), S. Giovanni Fuorcivitas, Pistoia; the decoration of the Chapel of the Crucifix in S. Miniato (1445–1448); two freestanding angels holding candelabra, now in the sacristy of the cathedral at Florence (1448–1451); a lunette for the Church of S. Domenico at Urbino (1450); altars in the Church of S. Maria at Impruneta; the ceiling with the allegorical figures of the four cardinal virtues—Prudence, Justice, Fortitude, and Temperance—surrounding the Holy Ghost, in the Chapel of the Cardinal of Portugal in S. Miniato; and his last major work, the altarpiece of Pescia, completed after 1472. He had completed his last documented marble work in 1456 or 1457; it was the monument of Benozzo Federighi, Bishop of Fiesole, now in S. Trinità, Florence. The monument, with its exquisitely carved effigy of the bishop and a relief with a *Pietà,* has an enamelled terra-cotta surround. Luca also worked in bronze. Two bronze angels, originally made for the *Cantoria,* are in the Musée Jacquemart-André at Paris. The bronze door to the north sacristy in the cathedral, with its heads of Apostles and ten reliefs, was originally a commission to three sculptors, but was carried to completion by Luca over a period of 30 years (completed c1469). In the meantime, Luca and his studio completed a great number of smaller works in terra-cotta, including a series of serene, gentle, youthful Madonnas, several of which are in the Bargello at Florence; others are at Berlin, the Metropolitan Museum, New York, and elsewhere. He molded coats-of-arms framed with wreaths of flowers for several guilds and for leading Florentine families. Of these, the coat-of-arms for the Physicians' and Apothecaries' Guild (1455–1465), now in Orsanmichele, is among the most richly colored of his terra-cottas. The large medallion with the arms of René of Anjou surrounded by a wreath of fruit and flowers, now in the Victoria and Albert Museum, London, is another example of his more richly colored creations. His chief patrons were the Overseers of the cathedral, the churches, hospitals, guilds, and leading families of Florence, and the finest examples of his work are to be found in that city. His innovation was in the adaptation of glazed terra-cotta to the uses of sculpture and architectural decoration (as in the Pazzi Chapel). His spirit looked back to the serene and simple forms of the school of Andrea Pisano. He indicates no interest in the problems of perspective and anatomy that so occupied his great contemporaries—Masaccio, Brunelleschi, Donatello. His approach to composition depended on symmetry and balance. The backgrounds of his reliefs, whether in bronze, marble or terra-cotta, are more often than not unadorned flat planes, lacking in the architectural details in perspective that give such depth and so intensify the foreground drama of Donatello's reliefs. In comparison to Donatello's drama and ultimate realism, are Luca's gentle Madonnas, joyous children, and noble Apostles. His artistic vision is ennobled by his spirit of reverence.

Della Rovere (rō′vā-rā). Family that originated in Savona, in Liguria, whose fortunes rose rapidly when Francesco (b. 1414) became Pope Sixtus IV (1471). Among the benefits he conferred on members of his family were ecclesiastical benefices, temporal offices, the investiture of fiefs of the Church, and advantageous marriages. The sons of his brother Raffaele were: Leonardo, who married a natural daughter of King Ferrante of Naples and was made duke of Sora; Giuliano, who was made a cardinal and became Pope Julius II; Bartolomeo, who became bishop of Ferrara; and Giovanni, who became lord of Senigallia and vicar of Mondavio, and married Giovanna, daughter of Federico da Montefeltro, duke of Urbino. Giovanni was prefect of Rome and a captain general of the Church. He was a good prince (he succeeded his brother as Duke of Sora), and won the affection of his subjects. It was through him that the Della Rovere became dukes of Urbino, for his son Francesco Maria (1490–1538), was the heir of his uncle, Guidobaldo I of Montefeltro, and succeeded him as duke of Urbino in 1508. Francesco Maria made highly advantageous marriages for his daughters; his son Giulio (1533–1578) was a cardinal and archbishop of Ravenna; his son Guidobaldo II (1514–1574) succeeded him as duke of Urbino. Guidobaldo II held a sumptuous court at Pesaro, to pay for which he levied heavy taxes. His subjects rebelled and sought agreements guaranteeing their rights. Guidobaldo imprisoned the ambassadors his subjects sent to him, confiscated their goods, and hanged them. He was succeeded by Francesco Maria III (1548–1631), who was a student of humanism and philosophy, and a fellow pupil of Tasso. Francesco Maria III was a brave fighter at the battle of Lepanto (1571), and when he became ruler (1574), set out to reform the administration of his duchy. He abolished some taxes and dismissed corrupt ministers. By his second wife, Livia della Rovere (1585–1641), he had a son, Federico Ubaldo (1605–1623), whose dissolute life caused his early death. Francesco Maria III, the last of his line, yielded to the urging of Pope Urban VIII and turned over his duchy to a representative of the Church.

Della Rovere, Francesco. Original name of Pope **Sixtus IV**.

Della Rovere, Giuliano. Original name of Pope **Julius II**.

Della Scala (skä′lä). See **Scala, della.**

Della Valle (väl′lā). Ancient Roman family that was prominent especially in the 15th and 16th centuries. Members of the family were among the most loyal supporters of the Colonnesi, largely because their own enemies were supporters of the Orsini. For centuries they lived in the quarter of Rome where their name is preserved in the Church of S. Andrea della Valle. Among the outstanding members of the family was Paolo (d. 1440), a physician consulted by popes Alexander V and Martin V. Niccolò was a consistorial advocate and a humanist of note, especially in the pontificate of Pius II. He was learned in Greek, translated *Hesiod*, and had begun the translation of the *Iliad* at the time of his early death (1473). Andrea (d. 1534) was the most noted of the family. He was bishop of Crotone and of Miletus, and was made a cardinal by Leo X. Leo and Clement VII entrusted important missions to him and gave him rich benefices. He acted as intermediary for Clement in his negotiations with the Colonnesi, and played an important part in the struggle between Clement and Charles V. Although he was on the emperor's side, in the sack of Rome he was seized in his palace and compelled to pay a heavy ransom.

Della Viola (vyō′lä), **Alfonso.** Musician; b. at Ferrara, c1508; d. there (?), c1570. He was an accomplished composer of motets and madrigals, but his greatest work was the music he wrote to accompany the tragedies and pastorals that were produced at the court of the Estensi at Ferrara or in the palaces of the Ferrarese nobles. In the work of this Ferrarese master is to be found the beginning of an operatic form, a combination in which the music supports the drama and is integral to it. The first instance in which the combination was presented was in the music he wrote for Giambattista Cinzio Giraldi's tragedy *Orbecche*, presented in Giraldi's house in 1541. Soon afterwards Della Viola began to write music for pastorals, the first being for Agostino Beccari's *Sacrificio*, presented for the Estensi in the spring of 1554. In it occurs an early example of a single voice part to carry the melody. Some of Della Viola's music from the *Sacrificio* is extant, as well as two books of madrigals and some madrigals that appear in other collections.

Delle Greche (del′lā gre′kā), **Domenico.** See **Campagnola, Domenico.**

Delle Massegne (mäs-zā′nye). See **Dalle Masegne.**

Delli (del′lē), **Dello.** Florentine painter; b. c1404; d. at Valencia, Spain, 1471. After working at Venice (1427) and Florence, where he was enrolled as a painter in 1433, he went to Spain in the latter year. The only work that can be attributed to him with any certainty is in Spain. In the cathedral at Salamanca there is a *Last Judgment*, heavily repainted, and an altarpiece with fifty-three scenes on incidents from the Gospels. These show him to have been a painter in the manner of Bicci di Lorenzo, with some touches of the international Gothic. Vasari admired his skill at portraying human anatomy.

Dell' Indaco (del-lēn′dä-kō). See **Indaco.**

Deloney or **Delone** (dẹ-lō′ni), **Thomas.** English weaver, balladist, pamphleteer, and realistic prose fictionist; b. probably at London, c1543; d. c1607. Author of more than fifty ballads, and of three popular narratives, *Thomas of Reading*, or *The Six Worthy Yeomen of the West*, *Jack of Newbury*, and *The Gentle Craft*. The last served as the basis of Thomas Dekker's *The Shoemaker's Holiday*.

Del Pacchia (päk′kyä), **Girolamo.** Sienese painter; b. at Siena, 1477; d. in France, c1535. A youthful sojourn in Florence left lasting influences on his style. He was at Rome, from 1500, returned to Siena, and then (c1530) fled to France, where he remained until his death. His painting shows the influence of various Florentines—Fra Bartolommeo, Andrea del Sarto, and, especially, Piero di Cosimo. At Siena he had been influenced by Pacchiarotto, with whom he was for a time confused, and later by Raphael. A number of his works are to be found at Siena, in the Accademia, and frescoes in the churches of S. Caterina and S. Bernardino. Other paintings of this eclectic who also drew on the Umbrians and on his fellow-townsman Sodoma, indicate his ability to produce solid forms and his predilection for clear color. Examples of his work are to be found in the Uffizi, in the Vatican, Naples, the Museum of Fine Arts, Boston, New Haven, and elsewhere.

Del Pecora (pe′kō-rä), **Iacopo.** [Also called **Iacopo da Montepulciano.**] Tuscan poet; active at the end of the 14th and the beginning of the 15th century. A native of Montepulciano, where his family held the lordship, he took part in the factional disputes that wracked so many Italian towns. In 1390 he supported Siena against Florence and was condemned and imprisoned by the Florentines. He remained in prison until 1407. He wrote love poetry and *laudi* (songs on spiritual themes). Among his best works is *Fimerodia*, an allegorical and moral poem in thirty-eight cantos in terza rima, modeled on the *Divina Commedia* of Dante, with elements of Petrarch's *Trionfi* and echoes of the lesser works of Boccaccio.

Del Rosso (rôs′sō), Fra **Paolo.** Florentine Knight of St. John and soldier; active in the first half of the 16th century; d. 1569. He was an exile from the Medici regime, was accused of treason against Grand Duke Cosimo I, and was imprisoned at Florence for a time. He was freed in 1566 and died a few years later. His literary works included a translation of Suetonius; a treatise on the correct way of writing the Tuscan language, *Regole, osservanze e avvertimenti sopra lo scrivere correttamente la lingua toscana*, published at Naples in 1545; a commentary on a work of Guido Cavalcanti; lyrics that are scattered in various collections; and a rather unsuccessful didactic poem *Fìsica*.

Del Sarto (sär′tō), **Andrea.** See **Andrea del Sarto.**

Del Tasso (täs′sō). Family of woodcarvers, sculptors, and architects that originated in San Gervasio, near Florence, and that by the end of the 15th century had settled in Florence in the quarter of Sant' Ambrogio. Chimenti, or Clemente, "the Elder" (1430–1516), carved various works for the Church of Sant' Ambrogio in 1483 and 1484, and in 1488 carved the walnut choir for a chapel in S. Pancrazio at Florence. When Benedetto da Maiano died (1497), Chimenti and his son Leonardo took over his workshop in the Via dei Servi and ran it for several years. Leonardo carved the wooden statue of St. Sebastian in the Church of Sant' Ambrogio (1500). Of Chimenti's two brothers, Cervagio worked in the Palazzo Vecchio and Domenico the Elder (1440–1508) worked at Perugia, where (1490) he carved the choir, begun by Giuliano da Maiano and left incomplete at his death (1490), in the cathedral. By about 1493 Domenico completed the carving of the benches for the Audience Hall of the Exchange at Perugia. Domenico's three sons were also stone- and woodcarvers, and his grandson Giovan Battista (1500–1555) became the most noted of all the members of the family; one of his works is a woodcarving to designs by Michelangelo in the Laurentian Library at Florence. About 1548 Giovan Battista worked as an architect on the enlargement and embellishment of the Palazzo Vecchio and carried out all the woodcarving for the new hall. He also built the loggia of the Mercato Nuova. He had three sons, carvers like himself, who worked with him. Of the many carvers in the family, Domenico the Elder and Giovan Batista (called Maestro Tasso) contributed original ideas to the art of woodcarving, broadening the treatment and adding new motives to the traditional repertoire. Their enrichment of the art influenced woodcarving in Tuscany and Umbria for the next fifty years. Cellini praised Giovan Battista for his bold attempts to create new forms and for his skill in overcoming technical difficulties, for his imaginative approach to a traditional art, and for the delicacy with which he embellished it.

Del Virgilio (del vēr-jē′lyō), **Giovanni.** Grammarian and poet; b. at Bologna in the last quarter of the 13th century; d. after 1327. In 1319 he taught Latin poetry at Bologna, after 1323 he taught grammar at Cesena, and by 1326 was back at Bologna. After 1327, when he sent an eclogue to Albertino Mussato, no further dates are known concerning him. His *Diaffonus* is a collection of five poetic letters addressed to Nuzio da Tolentino, a judge at Bologna in 1314. The collection is of great interest and importance for the picture the letters give of Bolognese intellectual and social life at the beginning of the 14th century. He also wrote a commentary on Ovid's *Metamorphoses* and translated parts of it into the Venetian dialect. A great deal of Del Virgilio's interest derives from his correspondence with Dante. He invited the poet to write on contemporary subjects, as the deeds of Henry VII, Can Grande della Scala, or Robert of Anjou, when Dante was in his last refuge at Ravenna, and invited the poet to take the chair of Latin poetry at Bologna. Dante wrote two Latin eclogues in reply, but by the time his last response to Del Virgilio had been received, the great poet was already dead. Del Virgilio wrote a poetic epitaph.

Del Viva (vē′vä), **Guittone.** See **Guittone d'Arezzo.**

De Marchi (dā mär′kē), **Francesco.** Military engineer and architect; b. at Bologna, 1504; d. at Aquila, 1576. As a youth he served in the army of Prospero Colonna, and then successively under other noted commanders. His varied service as an artilleryman gave him a good opportunity to study the effectiveness of various kinds of fortifications. He served Alessandro de' Medici at Florence, Pope Paul III at Rome, accompanied Ottavio Farnese in the Abruzzi, and then at Rome (1542) prepared an atlas that ultimately had 161 illustrations of his designs for fortifications. He worked on the walls at Rome, helped Sangallo in the execution of architectural works, fought at the side of the Farnese, rebuilt the walls of Parma, and then went to Flanders, where Philip II loaded him with honors. He entered the service of Margaret of Parma, regent of the Netherlands for Philip II, and worked on the fortifications of Valenciennes and Malines. His treatise, *Della architectura militare*, was a great step forward in the art of military fortification. His book was admired and widely plagiarized, and became almost better known under the names of those who plagiarized it. He wrote a great deal on the subject of the efficiency of fortifications; many of his letters are in the archives at Parma.

De monarchia (dā mō-när′ki-ạ). Political treatise in Latin by Dante, in which he set forth his ideas concerning a universal empire and a universal Church. He believed both to be of divine origin and the only cures for the ills of Italy and the world.

De partu Virginis (pär′tö vėr-jin′is). Christian epic, in Latin, on the birth of Christ, by Jacopo Sannazzaro. In this work, with overtones of Vergil, Ovid, and Theocritus, the poet employs classical allusion and mythology in what is, essentially, a religious work.

De' Pasti (päs′tē), **Matteo.** Medalist, architect, and sculptor; b. at Verona; d. at Rimini, 1468. Little is known of him before 1441. In 1446 he was at Rimini with Leon Battista Alberti, and was the architect who carried out Alberti's plans for enlarging and rebuilding the Church of S. Francesco (Tempio Malatestiano), commissioned by Sigismondo Malatesta. He collaborated with Alberti until the latter left (1450), after which De' Pasti carried on the work alone. He is responsible for some of the decoration of the interior of the church, and perhaps also for the tomb of Isotta (Isotta degli Atti), Sigismondo's third wife. The tomb rests on elephants, symbol of strength, and is decorated with roses, symbol of art and love, the symbols of the Malatesta. The intertwined initials $ are carved on numerous surfaces throughout the church. Some critics, notably Pope-Hennessey, believe that the finest reliefs in the Tempio, those in the chapel of Isotta, the chapel of the Planets, and the reliefs of the Liberal Arts, are by De' Pasti. They are ascribed to him on the ground of their superiority over those known to have been executed by Agostino di Duccio, but no documentary evidence for crediting them to Matteo exists. De' Pasti was a contemporary of Pisanello, a great medalist, and himself created medals that are among the most beautiful examples of the medalists' art of the 15th century. Among those surviving are medals of Sigismondo and Isotta, of Guarino da Verona, Leon Battista Alberti, Timoteo Maffei, and of his brother Benedetto De' Pasti.

De Predis (pre′dēs), **Ambrogio.** See **Predis, Giovanni Ambrogio de'.**

De' Ricci (rēt′chē), Saint **Catherine.** See **Catherine of Ricci,** Saint.

De Rosa (rō′zä), **Loise.** Master of the Household of kings and queens of Naples from Ladislaus (1377–1414) to Ferrante I (c1431–1494); b. c1385; d. c1475. Between 1467 (when he was 82 years old) and 1475 he produced in his own hand three pieces of writing now preserved at Paris. They were a kind of autobiography, a piece in praise of Naples, and a chronicle of that city. Written without any pretensions as to syntax or literary style, they are of interest for preserving the middle-class Neapolitan speech of the 15th century.

De Rossi (rôs′sē), **Vincenzo.** Sculptor; b. at Fiesole, 1525; d. 1587. He was a pupil of Baccio Bandinelli and spent the major part of his working life at Florence. There he carved statues for the Palazzo Vecchio, for which he made the cycle, *The Labors of Hercules,* in the Hall of the Five Hundred and a statue for Francesco I's study, and made statues and reliefs for the cathedral. His *Dying Adonis,* in the Bargello, attributed by some to Vincenzo Danti and formerly attributed to Michelangelo, is his best work. Among the other works of this mannerist sculptor is the group *Paris and Helen* in the Boboli Gardens, and some sculptures in the Church of S. Maria della Pace at Rome.

De Russi (rös′sē), **Franco di Giovanni.** Miniaturist; active at Ferrara about the middle of the 15th century. He was one of the illuminators of the celebrated two-volume *Bibbia di Borso,* the Bible of Duke Borso of Ferrara.

De Saliba (sä-lē′bä), **Antonellio.** See **Saliba, Antonello da.**

Deschamps (dā-shäṅ), **Eustache.** [Called **Morel Deschamps.**] French poet; b. at Vertus, in Champagne, France, in the first part of the 14th century; d. early in the 15th century. He was the author of ballades, rondeaux, virelais, a long poem, the *Miroir de mariage,* and *L'Art de dictier et de fere chancons, balades, virelais et rondeaulx* (a treatise on French rhetoric and prosody).

Desiderio da Settignano (dā-sē-dā′ryō dä set-tē-nyä′nō). Florentine sculptor; b. at Settignano, near Florence, 1428 or 1431; d. at Florence, in January, 1464. His father was a stonecutter, as were his older brothers. He matriculated in the Guild of Stonemasons and Woodcarvers in 1453, and by that date had already gained a reputation as a sculptor, for in that year he was one of the assessors named to judge the reliefs carved by Buggiano, Brunelleschi's pupil, for a pulpit in the Church of S. Maria Novella. Aside from his father and his brothers, it is not known what master gave him his early training. He was undoubtedly influenced by the work of his older contemporary Donatello, but if he had any direct contact with him it must have been brief and when Desiderio was very young, as Donatello left Florence for Padua in 1443. The influence of Donatello, however, is particularly apparent in Desiderio's use and refinement of *rilievo schiacciato* (flattened relief), a manner that Donatello had begun to develop with his *St. George* (1416). Desiderio's refined and subtle handling of this type of very low relief is characteristic of many of his works, as the marble *Madonna and Child* (1450), Pinacoteca, Turin, the marble tondo with the heads of Christ and St. John as children, Louvre, Paris, thought to be an early work (perhaps 1450–1453), the *Panciatichi Madonna* (c1453), Bargello, Florence, and especially the sweetly joyous *Foulc Madonna* (c1461), Museum of Art, Philadelphia, and the *St. Jerome* (c1461–1464), National Gallery, Washington, with its rocky landscape background clearly projected in relief that seems almost reduced to line. In his busts and reliefs of women and children Desiderio was a master at capturing a fleeting expression; the delicacy and sensitivity of his finely bred young women and smiling children is unsurpassed. Examples of these include the bust of a girl in the National Gallery, Washington, another in the Morgan Library, New York, one of *Marietta Strozzi*, Berlin, one in the Bargello, and others. The chronology of his works is uncertain, but it is thought that the frieze of cherubs in relief in the Pazzi Chapel is among the earliest of them. Among his celebrated free-standing statues is the marble *S. Giovannino,* Bargello, called the Martelli St. John. The young saint of this work is realistically portrayed as slender to the point of emaciation; his expression, unlike those of Desiderio's tender and innocent young women and children, is one of profound melancholy. This work is sometimes attributed to Donatello. Another work of Desiderio's that derives from Donatello is the polychrome wood statue of *St. Mary Magdalen* (c1455), in the Church of S. Trinità, Florence. In general, Desiderio's vision was one of tenderness and joy, as opposed to the tragic realism of Donatello. Desiderio's two major works are at Florence: the *Marsuppini Monument* (c1453–1455), erected in S. Croce to honor the humanist Carlo Marsuppini (d. 1453), and the *Altar of the Sacrament* (completed 1461) in S. Lorenzo. In both of these two masterpieces, comprising reliefs and free-

Desiderio da Settignano
Design for an Altar
Uffizi, Florence Alinari-Art Reference Bureau

standing statutes, the sculptural decoration is conceived as part of the architectural design. At the apex of the tabernacle in the *Altar of the Sacrament* is a statue of the *Child Christ Blessing* which is probably one of the most winning and spiritual statues of the Infant Christ in Florentine sculpture. In the same *Altar* the tabernacle is flanked by angels bearing candelabra. The heads of the lightly smiling angels are as delicate as porcelain. Each of the figures of the monument is an exquisite work in itself; together they form a beautiful and harmonious ensemble. Desiderio married and had children; he and his brothers had a workshop near the S. Trinità bridge. In his short life he achieved such mastery of his art that he is considered among the great sculptors of the Renaissance. His work is marked by elegance, refinement, and subtlety; his vision of life as expressed in his art is one of joy and tenderness. Several of his works are in the Bargello, Florence; others attributed to him are in the Louvre and Musée Jacquemart-André, Paris, at Vienna (a delightful *Laughing Putto*), and the National Gallery, Washington.

Despenser (dẹs-pen′sėr), **Edward le.** British knight; d. 1375. He fought at Poitiers and under Pope Urban V. He was a Knight of the Garter, and a patron of Froissart, the chronicler.

Despenser, Henry le. [Also, **Spencer.**] British bishop and soldier; b. c1341; d. August 23, 1406. He defeated the peasants at North Walsham during the Peasants' Revolt. He was denounced by Wycliffe for being a soldier and a bishop at the same time. He suppressed the Lollards.

Desportes (dā-pôrt), **Philippe.** French poet, clergyman, and diplomat; b. at Chartres, France, 1546; d. October 5, 1606. A disciple of Ronsard, he was called by his contemporaries "the French Tibullus."

Devereux (dev′ėr-ö, -öks), **Walter.** [Titles, 1st Viscount of **Hereford,** 3rd Baron **Ferrers.**] English soldier and courtier; b. before 1490; d. September 27, 1558. He was the grandfather of Walter Devereux (c1541–1576).

Devereux, Walter. [Titles, 1st Earl of **Essex,** 2nd Viscount of **Hereford.**] English nobleman; b. in Carmarthenshire, Wales, probably in 1541; d. at Dublin, September 22, 1576. He raised troops to assist in suppressing the rebellion under the earls of Northumbria and Westmorland, for which he was created Earl of Essex.

De Vio (dā vyō), **Tommaso.** [Known as **Cardinal Caetano,** from his see at Gaeta.] Dominican cardinal and scholar; b. at Gaeta, February 20, 1468; d. at Rome, October 10, 1533. He entered the Dominican order at the age of 16; studied at Naples, Bologna, and Padua; taught at Padua, Milan, and Rome; was named general of the Order in 1508; and named cardinal by Leo X in 1517. A learned and energetic man, he advised Pope Julius II to make reforms in the Church; took an active interest in the scientific developments of the day; wrote a great deal; and served on many missions for the Church, as legate in Germany (1518). He went to Germany to organize a crusade. Instead he had to deal with two grave problems: Martin Luther and the succession of the Holy Roman Empire. Luther was called before his tribunal and Cardinal Caetano dealt kindly with him, but it was too late to win him back to Catholicism. The cardinal was instrumental, in the solution of his second problem, in securing the election of Charles V as Holy Roman emperor. He returned to Rome, and was saddened by the worldly atmosphere of the Curia. He would have withdrawn to his see at Gaeta, but the Lutheran question demanded his attention at Rome. Pope Adrian VI, Leo's successor, sent him on missions to Hungary, Poland, and Germany. On the election of Clement VII (1523), Cardinal Caetano withdrew from Rome and devoted himself to study, writing, and good works. His writings fall into three periods and classes: philosophical, written during his years as a teacher; theological, written as general of the Dominican Order; and exegetic, from the last years of his life. Among his theological writings is his commentary on the *Summa Theologica* of Thomas Aquinas. It reveals his inclination to return to the old, literal doctrine, with such adaptation as might be necessitated by the modern age.

De vita propria (vē′tạ prō′pri-ạ). Autobiography of Girolamo Cardano (1501–1576), significant as an early instance of a biography with psychological overtones.

De vulgari eloquentia (vul-gä′rē el-ō-kwen′-ti-ạ). Incomplete Latin work by Dante in which he advocates Italian as a literary language.

Diacceto (dyä-chā′tō), **Francesco di Zanobi**

Cattani da. Florentine humanist; b. at Florence, 1466. He was a favorite pupil and friend of the philosopher Marsilio Ficino, the latter's spiritual heir and successor as head of the so-called Platonic Academy. A group of followers and pupils gathered about him after the death of Ficino, but the spark provided by Ficino was absent, and the Platonic Academy lost its élan. Diacceto wrote *De Amore* and *Panegyricus in Amorem,* and also translated them into Italian.

Diamante (dyä-män′tā), Fra. Painter; b. at Terranuova, Val d'Arno, c1430; d. after 1498. He became a Carmelite monk and was trained under Fra Filippo Lippi, with whom he often collaborated. He is first recorded (1452) to have assisted Fra Filippo in decorating the choir in the cathedral at Prato, and often worked with him thereafter. He assisted him in painting the frescoes at Spoleto and completed them after the death of his master (1469). A triptych, *Coronation of the Virgin,* now in the Vatican, by Fra Filippo, was also a work in which Fra Diamante collaborated. In 1472 he was enrolled in the Company of St. Luke (the artists' guild) at Florence, and in 1481 he was one of a number of artists decorating the Sistine Chapel at Rome. Of the work he did with Fra Filippo, to the latter's cartoons, and in the Sistine Chapel, it is difficult to isolate that of Fra Diamante, identification occasionally being made possible by his awkward and sharply outlined figures. In his own right he was an indifferent painter.

Fra Diamante
Visitation
Gabinetto Disegni e Stampe degli Uffizi
Foto Soprintendenza

Diana (dyä′nä), **Benedetto.** [Original name, **Benedetto Rusconi.**] Painter; b. at Venice, c1460; d. there, 1525. He was trained in the tradition of Carpaccio and, especially, Giovanni Bellini, who had the strongest influence on him. A minor Venetian painter, his work has rather a hard outline but is enlivened by his Venetian sense of color. Among his several works in the Accademia, Venice, is *Virgin and Child Enthroned with Four Saints.* Other works at Venice are in the Ca' d'Oro, S. Francesco della Vigna, S. Zaccaria, and at Murano. *Salvator Mundi* is in the National Gallery, London, *God the Father,* in the Cannon Collection, Princeton, and there are examples of his work at Cremona, Pavia, Turin, Verona, Amsterdam, and elsewhere.

Diana Enamorada (dyä′nä e-nä-mō-rä′ᴛʜä). [English translation, "*Diana Enamored.*"] Chief work of Jorge de Montemayor. An important pastoral romance, it was the most popular one published in Spain after *Amadis of Gaul.* First printed at Valencia in 1542, it had been left unfinished but was continued by others. It was modeled to some degree on Jacopo Sannazzaro's *Arcadia.*

Diane de France (dyån dẹ fräṅs). [Title, Duchesse **de Montmorency et d'Angoulême.**] Illegitimate daughter of Henry II of France; b. in Piedmont, Italy, 1538; d. January 3, 1619. She played an influential part in French politics during the reigns of Henry III and Henry IV.

Diane de Poitiers (dẹ pwå-tyā). [Titles, Comtesse **de Brézé,** Duchesse **de Valentinois.**] Mistress of Henry II of France; b. September 3, 1499; d. at Anet, in Orléanais, France, April 22, 1566. She was noted for her influence at the French court.

Dias (dē′ạsh), **Bartolomeu.** [Also, **Díaz.**] Portuguese navigator; b. c1450; d. in May,

BENEDETTO DIANA
Youthful Apostle Standing Blessing
Gabinetto Disegni e Stampe degli Uffizi
Foto Soprintendenza

1500. He was a gentleman of the royal household, and in 1487 was made commander of one of two small vessels (João Iffante commanding the other) meant to explore further the coast of Africa. They passed the farthest point attained by Diogo Cão on the west coast of Africa (1482–1484), followed the coast to the present-day Diaz Point, and thence sailed south in the open sea for thirteen days in wind and storm, suffering greatly from cold. They turned eastward in search of land, and, not finding it, bore to the north, striking the coast at Mossel Bay, east of the Cape of Good Hope, and following the coast to a point beyond Algoa Bay. The sailors refused to go farther; and, after taking possession of the land for Portugal, they returned (1488) around the cape, named by him or by King John II of Portugal Cabo da Boa Esperanza (Cape of Good Hope), and reached home in safety. Some accounts say that Dias was driven beyond the cape by a storm without observing it; in any case, he and his companions were the first to double the south end of Africa. In 1497 Dias sailed with the expedition of Vasco da Gama, but remained trading on the West African coast. In 1500 he commanded a ship in the fleet commanded by Pedro Álvares Cabral that discovered Brazil; Dias was lost in a storm after leaving the Brazilian coast, probably off the Cape of Good Hope.

Díaz del Castillo (dē´äth del käs-tē´lyō), **Bernal.** Spanish soldier and author; b. at Medina del Campo, Spain, c1492; d. in Guatemala, c1581. He went to Darien with Pedrarias (1514), was with Francisco Fernández de Córdoba in the discovery of Yucatán (1517), and with Juan de Grijalva in Mexico. He joined Cortés and served through the conquest of Mexico (1519–1521). He settled in Guatemala, where he began writing *Historia verdadera de la conquista de Nueva España,* which includes his firsthand report of the conquest of Mexico, and contradicts in many ways that of Francisco López de Gómara.

Di Costanzo (dē kō-stän´tsō), **Angelo.** Historian and poet; b. at Naples, c1507; d. 1591. He was a member of a noble family of Naples. Encouraged by Sannazzaro, he began to collect material for a history of the kingdom of Naples, with the intention of correcting the errors in the work of Pandolfo Collenuccio. The work he wrote, *Istoria del Regno di Napoli,* in twenty books, is based on his own researches. Lucid and well-written as to style, it covers the history of Naples from 1250 to 1486. The entire work was published at Aquila in 1581 (the first eight books had appeared at Naples, 1572). Di Costanzo also left Latin verses. In his sonnets his agile intellect and interest in epigrammatic style frequently overwhelmed his content, and the poems are sometimes more mannered than felt, but in other verse, as on the death of a son, he expressed true sentiment.

Dicts and Sayings of the Philosophers, The. Prose work (1477) translated from the French of Guillaume de Tignonville by Anthony Wydeville. Printed in November 1477, on Caxton's famous Westminster press, it is historically important as the first book printed on English soil, and the first book printed in England with a date. The French title of the work is *Les Ditz moraulx des philosophes.*

Digby (dig´bi) **Plays.** Collection of four

late 15th-century religious plays which exist in manuscript form in the Oxford Bodleian Library. They are: *The Massacre of the Innocents and the Flight into Egypt* (also known as *The Killing of the Children*); *Conversion of Saul; Mary Magdalene;* and *Mind, Will, and Understanding.*

Digges (digz), **Leonard.** English mathematician; d. c1571. He inherited a comfortable fortune which enabled him to devote himself to scientific pursuits. His chief work is *A Booke named Tectonicon, briefly showing the exact measuring and speedie reckoning all manner of land, squares, timber, stone . . .* (1556).

Digges, Thomas. English mathematician; d. August 24, 1595. He was the son of Leonard Digges (d. c1571). His works include *A Geometrical Practice, named Pantometria* (1571), *A Prognostication . . . contayning . . . Rules to judge the Weather by the Sunne, Moone, Stars . . .* (1578), and *An Arithmeticall Militare Treatise, named Stratioticos* (1579).

Dipsodes (dip′sōdz). People in François Rabelais' *History of Gargantua and Pantagruel.* They are ruled by King Anarche, and many of them are giants. Pantagruel subdues them.

Diptych (dip′tik). A pair of pictures or carvings on two panels hinged together.

Di Tarsia (dē tär′syä), **Galeazzo.** See **Tarsia, Galeazzo di.**

Dittamondo (dēt-tä-mōn′dō). Allegorical work by Fazio degli Uberti. It was written between 1350 and 1360, and is modeled on the *Divina Commedia.* The work tells of imaginary travels, under the guidance of an ancient geographer. At Rome, a tattered and battered lady, symbolizing Rome itself, points out to the travelers the ruins of the ancient city, describes the old triumphs, and tells how Rome used to look, so that the travelers may realize "how beautiful it was."

Divina Commedia (dē-vē′nä kôm-mā′dyä). **[The Divine Comedy.]** Celebrated epic poem by Dante. The original title, *Comedia* (Italian, *Commedia*), comes from Dante's Latin inscription, "Here begins the Comedy of Dante Alighieri, a Florentine by birth but not by conduct." *Divina* was added to the title page in 1555 by an admiring editor and has remained part of it ever since. To Dante the word *commedia* meant simply, perhaps, a people's song, and because he wanted to make it accessible to as wide an audience as possible he wrote it in Italian. He was also putting into practice his own theory, expressed in *De vulgari eloquentia* and elsewhere, that Italian could be a literary language. The poem can be interpreted as a struggle toward salvation through the exercise of free will. Only those whom Dante saw in Limbo had no choice. The *Divina Commedia* "is the work of a scholar, poet, political commentator, literary critic and prophet, with perhaps something of the gossip columnist as well. The *Comedy* may be—and has been—called a picture of the late Middle Ages, a spiritual autobiography, a popularization of Thomistic theology, and an ethical guide." (Introduction, *The Divine Comedy*, Crofts Classics edition, edited and translated by Thomas G. Bergin.) Above all, it is a masterpiece of art inspired with poetic passion. Dante's theology, politics, artistic creed, and profound understanding of human nature form the solid structure of the poem. His wide knowledge, artistic imagination, and descriptive powers ornament it. Scholars, poets, and historians have studied it for centuries, have identified many of the figures referred to in it, have explained the symbolism and the theology, and have interpreted it line by line. No scholar, critic, historian, or other has found the key to the sublimity of the poetry. No translator has been able to render it into poetry of equally transcendent beauty and music in another language.

The poem is in three parts: *Inferno* (Hell), *Purgatorio* (Purgatory), and *Paradiso* (Paradise). It seems probable that the *Inferno* was begun some time after Dante's return from a pilgrimage to Rome in the jubilee year 1300, that the *Purgatorio* was finished about 1314, and that the composition of the *Paradiso* occupied the next five or six years of his life. The poem consists of 14,233 eleven syllable lines arranged in tercets with the rhyming scheme, invented by Dante for this work, known as terza rima, a b a, b c b, c d c, and so forth. After an introductory canto, the remaining ninety-nine cantos are equally divided among the three parts. Read simply as a myth for the imagination, the poem describes a journey, supposed to have taken place in the year 1300, to the abodes of the dead. Thus, in the *Inferno,* Beatrice, the love of Dante's youth and the inspiration of his life, sends Vergil to guide him through the many circles of Hell, each lower and more fearsome than the last, and each presided over by some horrendous monster. He visits the spirits of the heroes, heroines, and philosophers of antiquity who are enjoying a high but purely human happiness in the Noble Castle of Limbo. Since they antedated the birth of Christ and were ignorant of the true religion, they are consigned to Limbo, being innocent. The souls of the unbaptized are with them. From Limbo he enters the circles of Hell, Vergil guiding, informing, and protecting him. It is peopled by figures from mythology, from ancient, recent, and contemporary history. By his inclusions Dante passes graced, committed suicide. He assures Dante he was never disloyal to Frederick and begs him to clear his name (*Inferno*, xiii). There is Celestine V "who cravenly the great refusal made" (abdicated 1294, *Inferno*, iii), and Rinaldo degli Scrovegni of Padua. The latter appears in one of the lowest depths of Hell, the circle reserved for usurers (*Inferno*, xvii). He was notorious for that crime and his son Enrico, to atone for his father's guilt, built the Scrovegni Chapel at Padua and commissioned Giotto to paint it. Dante also places his archenemy Pope Boniface VIII in one of the lower reaches of Hell (*Inferno*, xix). Historical and political events are men-

The Judgment Seat of Minos: the Punishment of Lust
Engraving by Baccio Baldini, to a design by Botticelli, for Landino's *Commentary* on Dante's *Divine Comedy*, 1481
Courtesy of the Isabella Stewart Gardner Museum, Boston

judgment on people and events of his own and recent times. Not all of the shades in the *Inferno* are entirely evil, some were highly regarded while they lived. Such a one is the noble Farinata degli Uberti (d. 1264), a Florentine, and Ghibelline, statesman and soldier who, after a Ghibelline victory over the Guelphs, alone, as he proudly tells Dante, prevented the vengeful Ghibellines from razing Florence to the ground (*Inferno*, x). He is being punished to eternity for affirming that the soul dies with the body. Dante sees Piero della Vigna, who had been in the service of Frederick II and, finding himself dis- tioned, as the siege of Caprona, 1289 (*Inferno*, xxi), and the battle of Campaldino, 1289 (*Inferno*, xxii, *Purgatorio*, v), in both of which Dante fought, and the expulsion of the Neri from Pistoia by the Bianchi followed shortly by the triumphant return to power of the Neri in Florence (*Inferno*, xxiv). There are bitter references to Florence, the beloved city from which Dante had been banished: "Can any of its townsmen be called just?" (*Inferno*, vi); Florentines, a "race of ingrates envious," "jealous, niggardly and blind." (*Inferno*, xv); "Rejoice, my Florence, . . . in darkest Hell your name is known." (Inferno, xxvi); Florence "is stripped the more of good and seems disposed to suffer sorry ruin." (*Purgatorio,* xxiv); even in Paradise Dante cannot forget his city, "Your city . . . whose spite has occasioned so much woe . . ." (*Paradiso,* ix). Italy, too, is apostrophized, "Servile Italy, woe's hostelry, / Ship without steersman in a mighty storm . . ." (*Purgatorio,* vi), in a reference to the lack of an emperor who could restore peace to the peninsula. Following a carefully worked out system of sins based on Aristotelian and Ciceronian ethics, with subdivisions borrowed from patristic and scholastic ideas and with elements taken from the Roman law and the "code of chivalry," the pilgrim (Dante) sees the torments of every type of sinner in the *Inferno.* At the center of the earth, in the mouths of the three heads of Satan, he finds Judas, the traitor to the Founder of a universal faith, and Brutus and Cassius who betrayed Caesar's efforts to establish a rule of universal law, as well as Bocca degli Abati who betrayed his fellow Florentines at Montaperti, and other traitors. What, however, gives passion to the poetic vision is the meaning which is addressed to the reader's mind. The great inverted cone of Dante's Hell is, allegorically, the human heart, and the poet's pilgrimage is a vision of human nature in the utmost depths of its possible degradations.

In the same way, the seven-story mountain of Dante's *Purgatorio* is a vision of the human will struggling upwards in humanity's historical efforts to reach, by culture and civilization, the highest happiness and peace that men can hope for in a reign of light and law. A new theme in the *Purgatorio* is the efficacy of the prayers of the living to help those in Purgatory ascend the seven-story mountain, which is composed of the seven terraces of Pride, Envy, Anger, Sloth, Avarice, Gluttony, and Lust. Manfred (d. 1266) asks Dante to find his daughter and implore her to continue her prayers for him, that he may reach Paradise (*Purgatorio,* iii); Dante's friend Forese Donati has ascended part way up the seven-story mountain thanks to the prayers of his wife (*Purgatorio,* xxiii). The political comments and talks with figures long or recently dead continue; "The empty-headed folk" (*Purgatorio,* xiii) are the Sienese; Provenzano Salvani, captain of Sienese forces in the defeat of the Florentines at Montaperti (1260), whose sin is pride, is spared Hell because he publicly begged in Siena to get money to ransom a friend (*Purgatorio,* xii). He, too, is grateful for the prayers of the living. Charles of Valois (still living when Dante wrote) comes with the lance of Judas because he betrayed Florence to the Neri (1301, this led to Dante's exile) (*Purgatorio,* xx). Pope Martin IV (d. 1285) is in the sixth terrace to purge himself of gluttony (*Purgatorio,* xxiv). As they near the top of the seven-story mountain Vergil tells Dante that his will "is free and upright, full of health: / It would be wrong to act not as it bids; / Mitre and crown I give you o'er yourself." (*Purgatorio,* xxvii). Vergil cannot enter Paradise, he leaves Dante when Beatrice comes to guide him (*Purgatorio,* xxx). Paradise, like the other divisions of the world of the dead, has its gradations. Dante accounts for gradations in blessedness on the grounds that all have not equal capacity to receive it. Thus, though all in Paradise are blessed, they occupy different ranks of its nine divisions according to their capacity. Thus, too, in Paradise, there are some unexpected spirits, as Rahab (*Paradiso, ix*), a harlot, but blessed because she helped Joshua take Jericho. In this canticle Dante, in richly varied symbols and in the figures he chooses, develops to the full the medieval system of theology, stills his doubts, and finds all his questions answered. This canticle, too, can be enjoyed as a myth, in which Dante meets the lovely Piccarda (*Paradiso,* iii), the emperor Justinian (vi), Saint Thomas Aquinas (x), and many others, but what accounts for the passionate poetry and inimitable music in this part is the poet's all-but-mystical vision of the efficacy of supernatural religion in elevating humanity to consummation in the perfect peace and possession of ultimate goodness, truth, and beauty. Thus the poem is about redemption in the widest sense. The six guides who lead Dante (that is, "fallen" humanity) from the "dark wood" of sin, through the "divine forest" of innocence and upwards to "the light which in itself is true" and "the love which binds in a single volume the scattered leaves of all the universe," are Vergil, Cato, Statius, Matilda, Beatrice, and Bernard. Vergil is a symbol of reason in the form of Hellenic philosophy and Roman law (*ordinatio rationis*); Cato (a combination of Cato the Censor and Cato the Stoic, who preferred liberty with death to tyranny) is a symbol of reason in the form of conscience (*dictamen rationis*). Beatrice represents the role of grace, that is, of divine revelation and redemption and, hence, the ministry of the Church (*Sacerdotium*) as Vergil represents the authority of the State (*Imperium*). Bernard stands to Beatrice somewhat as Cato stands to Vergil. He is a symbol of mystical intuition or the religious light and force of holiness that come from direct communion with God. Statius (a combination of the historical figures of the pagan poet, author of the *Thebaid* and *Achilleid*, and of Statius, the converted rhetorician and teacher of Toulouse) stands for the Christian school (*Studium*) as the *bella donna* Matilda stands for the Christian home, for the role of love in the "age of innocence," for parental guidance in the period of childhood. The root idea of the whole poem is, as Dante tells us in a Latin letter to Can Grande (a protector and patron to whom Dante dedicated the *Paradiso*), that of human responsibility in the face of divine justice. The individual is responsible for his personality, for his inner freedom from the tyranny of ignorance and passion; the parent is responsible for the ministry of love, the teacher for the ministry of truth, the ruler for the ministry of justice, the priest for the ministry of grace, the saint for that holiness which is the nearest image we can know in history of the very life of God. Dante's sinners and saints suffer or rejoice because of the failure or fulfilment of their commission to reach and reveal some image of the divine, whether this be freedom, truth, goodness, beauty, justice, love, or holiness. It is this profound sense of the meaning of man and of history set to incomparable music and illumined and lifted up by spiritually interpretive intimations of the mystery of man's immortal destiny that has put the *Commedia* in the very forefront of the world's supreme works of art. The poem has been translated into all the great languages of the world, including Japanese and Arabic. Of the many translations, not one conveys the subtle and varied music of the original. The Carlyle-Wicksteed prose version, with its excellent introductions and notes to each canto may, however, serve as a good introduction to the poem.

Does (dös), **Jan Van der.** See **Dousa, Janus.**

Dolce (dôl′chā), **Lodovico.** Miscellaneous writer and poet; b. at Venice, c1508; d. there, c1568. Of a noble family that had fallen on evil days, he studied at Padua and then, as it was a case of necessity, went into the service of the Venetian printer Gabriele Giolito as a proofreader. In addition to his work as proofreader, he translated, patched up, plagiarized, and edited for Giolito's press. He wrote adaptations of classical tragedies, as his *Giocasta,* in which he unsuccessfully attempted to remodel the originals. He also wrote many treatises, *capitoli,* and occasional poems that appear in many collections. His most successful works are his five comedies. These are often licentious but not, as he said, as licentious as the age in which he lived. Also in the rank of his best work is his poem in twenty-three cantos that he drew from *Reali di Francia.* Dolce was, in general, a hack writer, one of the satellites in the orbit of Aretino at Venice. He died in great poverty.

Dolce stil nuovo (dôl′chā stēl nwō′vō). The "sweet new style" of poetry first mentioned by Dante (*Purgatorio,* xxiv) and afterwards always so characterized. It was a departure from the conventional and "courtly" style of the Provençal poets, hitherto much imitated by the Italians, in its spontaneity and in that, according to Dante, real as opposed to conventional love is its true inspiration.

Dolet (do-le), **Étienne.** French scholar and printer; b. at Orléans, France, 1509; hanged and burned at Paris, August 3, 1546. He obtained the right from Francis I to publish certain works, but, because he entered into religious controversy, was accused of publishing atheistic material. He was imprisoned twice but released; a third time he was found guilty and executed.

Domenichi (dō-mā′nē-kē), **Lodovico.** Writer; b. at Piacenza, 1515; d. at Pisa, 1564. He was an early example of a versatile and facile but not highly gifted writer who earned his living by his pen. In the course of so doing he suffered many hardships, and was even accused of heresy. He was a proofreader (1543–1546) for the publisher Giolito at Venice, then went to Florence, where he worked for the publisher Torrentino and translated Giovio's histories for Cosimo I. He produced a vast quantity of writing, much of it mediocre and often not even original, as he published under his own name a collection of jests, witty sayings, etc., that had been put together by Poliziano. He also rewrote the

Woodcut (*Paradiso*, i) from the 1487 edition of Landino's *Commentary* on Dante's *Divine Comedy*
Courtesy of the Isabella Stewart Gardner Museum, Boston

thin; ᴛʜ, then; y, you; (variable) ḏ as d or j, ș as s or sh, ț as t or ch, ẓ as z or zh; o, F. cloche; ü, F. menu; ċh, Sc. loch; ṅ, F. bonbon; ʙ, Sp. Córdoba (sounded almost like v).

works of others, including a revision, with the intention of polishing the language, of Boiardo's *Orlando Innamorato*. Included in his voluminous production is a book of manners for women, a dialogue on the nobility of women, sonnets, *capitoli*, dialogues, comedies, and translations.

Domenico di Bartolo (dō-mā′nē-kō dē bär′tō-lo). Sienese painter; b. at Asciano, c1400; d. before February, 1447. He may have studied under Taddeo di Bartolo, but works thought to be early, as the *Madonna*, Church of S. Raimondo, and *Madonna and Angels*, Pinacoteca, Siena, seem to point to Sassetta as his first teacher. He was enrolled in the Painters' Guild at Siena in 1428. A painter of the transition from the Gothic style to that of the Renaissance, his first dated work, *Madonna* (1433), Pinacoteca, Siena, is less pronouncedly caligraphic than Gothic painting, and has elements of the Renaissance in the vigor and plasticity of its forms. A drawing of the Emperor Sigismund with members of his court, executed (1434) as a design for the pavement of the cathedral at Siena, is also Renaissance in spirit and form. Many of the frescoes and panels known to have been painted by Domenico have been lost. Among the surviving examples are a signed and dated (1437) *Virgin and Child*, Johnson Collection, Philadelphia, and a polyptych, *Madonna and Child with Saints*, signed and dated (1438), in the National Gallery of Umbria at Perugia. The latter painting, with its five predella panels with scenes from the life of John the Baptist, is carefully executed technically and pleasingly decorative. His major surviving work is the series of frescoes he painted in the Ospedale della Scala at Siena (1440–1443). In these he was among the earliest to unite his figures in a grandiose, detailed, and carefully executed architectural background shown in perspective. The scenes represent the works of mercy carried out in the hospital, including *Care of Orphan Children, Marriage of Orphan Girls, Distribution of Alms, Reception and Care of the Sick*, and others. In painting the episodes, crowded with figures, many of which are portraits, Domenico presented a picture of contemporary costume, customs, furniture, and decoration with imagination and narrative skill. In this series Domenico united his typically Sienese sense of decoration with the plasticity and relief, obtained by light and shade, of the Florentine style. Other paintings are at Bridgeport (Connecticut), Princeton, and Washington.

Domenico di Giovanni (jō-vän′nē). See **Burchiello.**

Domenico di Michelino (mē-kā-lē′nō). [Original name, **Domenico di Francesco.**] Florentine painter; b. 1417; d. April 18, 1491. Vasari wrote that he was a pupil of Fra Angelico, and he was probably under Zanobi Strozzi before that. An authenticated work by Domenico is a panel in the cathedral at Florence that shows Dante, holding an open book, standing before a representation of the mountain of Paradise. Works attributed to him include *St. Bernardino of Siena* and *Tobias and the Three Archangels*, Accademia, Florence; *St. Vincent Ferrer*, National Gallery, Parma; and an *Annunciation*, Johnson Collection, Philadelphia, and paintings at Prato, Rome (Vatican), Chambéry, Dublin, London, Strasbourg, New Haven, Providence, Tucson (Arizona), Williamstown (Massachusetts), Worcester (Massachusetts), and elsewhere.

Domenico di Paris. [Called **Domenico del Cavallo, "Domenico of the Horse."**] Paduan sculptor; active in the second half of the 15th century. The dates of his birth and death are not known. Evident in his work is the influence of Donatello, who was at Padua in the period 1443–1453. He worked at Ferrara as an assistant of Niccolò Baroncelli, and when the latter died (1453), Domenico and others completed (1454) the work he had begun on the horse of the equestrian statue of Borso d'Este. In 1464 he executed two bronze statues for the cathedral at Ferrara: a *St. George*, with armor reminiscent of that of Donatello's *Gattamelata*, and a *St. Maurelius*. In the d'Este palace of Schifanoia he molded the stucco frieze of putti, coats of arms, and allegorical figures in the great antechamber.

Domenico da Prato (dä prä′tō). Latin scholar and writer; b. at Prato, c1370; d. c1433. He went to Florence as a youth and became a notary and a Latin scholar. He wrote (c1420) an invective against the humanists. In it he defended the use of the vernacular language, citing Dante's vernacular as more genuine than the Latin and Greek of such humanists as Niccolò Niccoli. He also wrote a patriotic poem about the Florentine resistance to Filippo Maria Vis-

Domenico di Michelino
Magus on a Horse and Heads of Young Monks
Study for an *Adoration of the Magi,* Strasbourg
The British Museum, London

conti of Milan, and love sonnets in the Petrarchan manner.

Domenico da Tolmezzo (tōl-med′dzō). Painter and sculptor in wood; b. at Tolmezzo (Friuli), c1448; d. 1507. He and his brother were known as sculptors of large wooden polyptychs, a number of which survive, as at Forni di Sopra, Illeggio, Invillino, Terzo, and Zuglio Carnico, all in the province of Udine. A painted polyptych is in the Museo Civico at Udine, and there are frescoes in the Church of S. Toscana, Verona.

Domenico Maria da Novara (mä-rē′ä dä nō-vä′rä). Italian astronomer; b. 1454; d. 1504. He was one of Nicholas Copernicus' teachers at the university of Cracow.

Domenico Veneziano (ve-nā-tsyä′nō). Florentine painter; active from 1438; d. at Florence, 1461. He was of Venetian origin but is classed as a Florentine from the many Florentine elements in his work. In 1438 he wrote a letter from Perugia to Piero de' Medici, asking to be allowed to paint an altarpiece for him, and was at Florence in the same year. In the following year he was working with the young Piero della Francesca in the Church of S. Egidio, where Domenico continued to work until 1445. The frescoes the artists painted there have been lost. Though he probably received his early training in northern Italy, his few surviving works are dominated by Florentine influences, as in his use of perspective and treatment of landscape, and in the sculptural qualities of his figures. His distinguishing features are his special sense of light, which was not a Florentine preoccupation in his time, and the luminosity of his color. His principal surviving work is a signed altarpiece in the Uffizi, *Madonna Enthroned*, called the St. Lucy Altarpiece because it was originally intended for the Church of S. Lucia de' Magnoli at Florence. A splendid example of Domenico's mature style, it reveals all the features of his individuality—his manipulation of light to suffuse and penetrate his figures with luminous color, his diversity of expression and strongly modeled figures, and his elegance of line. A predella panel from the altarpiece, *St. John in the Desert*, National Gallery, Washington, has the single figure of the nude young saint against a stark and desolate background, all bathed in an almost white light. Other predella panels from the altarpiece are at Berlin and at Cambridge, England. His only other signed work was a fresco formerly in a tabernacle in the Via de' Cerretani at Florence. Three fragments of the fresco, including a signed *Madonna*, are in the National Gallery, London. The fresco *St. John the Baptist and St. Francis*, S. Croce, Florence, is notable for its vigorous design and for such violent energy that Vasari assigned it to Andrea del Castagno; others have attributed it to Antonio Pollaiuolo. Domenico was among the first to practice glazing tempera paintings with oil. According to Vasari, Andrea del Castagno murdered him so that he could not reveal the secret of painting in oil. Domenico's death four years after that of Andrea's casts some doubt on the validity of Vasari's tale. Domenico's innovation of painting in oil, although he was not the first to do so, came to have important consequences in the effects of tones and harmonies that could be achieved by the more fluid and slower drying medium. He was a painstaking painter and produced few works. Among those attributed to him are several in the National Gallery, Washington, including a profile portrait in flat planes, and a profile *Portrait of a Girl*, the Metropolitan Museum, New York. Perhaps his most beautiful painting, and one of the loveliest *Madonnas* of the period, is his *Madonna and Child*, in the Berenson Collection, near Florence. In developing his highly individualistic style, characterized especially by his use of light and by the variety of tones and values that he multiplied for contrast and harmony, Domenico learned something from Masaccio and Fra Angelico, but his work does not resemble theirs. In his turn he influenced Baldovinetti and the Pollaiuoli brothers; his greatest influence, however, was on Piero della Francesca, through whom his treatment of light and use of clear, illuminated color was passed to other painters.

Dominici (dō-mē′nē-chē), Fra **Bartolommeo.** Dominican; b. at Siena, 1343; d. at Rimini, July 3, 1415. A learned and pious man, he was chosen confessor and spiritual director by St. Catherine of Siena. He accompanied her on many of her journeys, including that to Avignon, and was with her when she died at Rome. He was a master of Sacred Theology and won many honors in the Dominican Order.

Dominici, Domenico. Theologian and reformer; b. at Venice, 1416; d. at Brescia,

1478. He took his degree at Padua, is thought to have taught theology at Bologna and Rome, and in Rome won the respect of Popes Eugenius IV and Nicholas V. He was made bishop of Torcello in 1448. As official speaker at the conclave of 1458 (from which Pius II emerged as Pope), Dominici proposed reforms of the Church, and later incorporated his proposals in *Tractatus de reformatione Romanae Curiae.* His proposals were not adopted by either Pius II nor his successor Paul II. Dominici's public battle for reform perhaps cost him the red hat of a cardinal.

Dominici, Giovanni. Dominican preacher, cardinal, and writer; b. at Florence, 1357; d. at Buda, 1419. He was a learned and pious man, and an enemy of humanism for its harmful effects on the Christian life. A vigorous preacher, many of his sermons dealt with the evils of classical studies. He entered the Dominican Order at the age of 17 and determined to be a preacher and to work for reform in the Church. In 1391 he was named general of his order. In 1399 he was expelled from Venice, where he had been teaching theology, for supporting the activities of the fanatic, mystic, and short-lived Bianchi in defiance of the Venetian Signory. The Florentines invited him to the university (1403), and later (1406) sent him to Rome. Gregory XII named him archbishop of Ragusa, 1407, and cardinal the following year. Under Martin V he went to Bohemia and sought, vainly, to stamp out the Hussite heresy. Cardinal Dominici left many Latin and Italian writings. His collections of Latin sermons show his learning and his robust individuality. His *Lucula Noctis,* a Latin treatise on pagan authors, directed against the humanist chancellor of Florence, Coluccio Salutati, takes as its point of departure the thesis that a Christian cannot rightly pursue classical studies. His writings in the vernacular include *Governo di cura familiare, Libro d'amore di carita,* and many letters, and are more immediate in their impact. He also left a number of hymns.

Donatello (dō-nä-tel′lō). [Full original name, **Donato di Niccolò di Betto Bardi.**] Florentine sculptor, one of the greatest artists of the Renaissance; b. at Florence, 1386; d. there, December 13, 1466. He trained as a marble sculptor in the workshop of the Cathedral, and worked under Ghiberti on the bronze doors for the Baptistery between 1404 and 1407. His life divides into three periods: the first, at Florence, where he was highly successful, continually busy, and where he worked until 1443; the second from 1443, when he moved his workshop to Padua, where he remained until 1453; and the third, after 1453, when he was back at Florence, moved on restlessly to Siena for a time, and then returned to Florence where he remained until his death. In the first and longest period he mastered the technical problems of his art and continued to refine his technical mastery as long as he lived, progressed from Gothic to a thorough understanding of classical Roman sculpture, and went on from this to the realistic expression of form and emotion on which he increasingly insisted. In this same period he developed a new manner of carving in relief and made the earliest of the Renaissance statues that were intended to be viewed in the round. The second period centers around his great bronze *Gattamelata* monument at Padua which was the first equestrian statue to be cast since Roman times, and the bronzes he executed for the high altar of the Basilica of St. Anthony of Padua. In the third period Donatello's passionate humanity and turbulent emotions are expressed in a shattering realism, as in the wooden *St. Mary Magdalen,* in the Baptistery at Florence, that has all the anguish of tragedy.

By 1408 Donatello was already well enough established to receive a commission for a statue of *St. John the Evangelist* to be placed in one of the niches beside the central door of the Cathedral. At this same time, Nanni di Banco was commissioned to do the *St. Luke,* Niccolò di Pietro Lamberti the *St. Mark,* and, at a later date, Bernardo Ciuffagni the *St. Matthew.* This marble *St. John* (now in the Museo dell' Opera del Duomo) and a marble *David with the Head of Goliath* (also commissioned in 1408, and now in the Bargello) are the earliest documented works from his hand. Both are the works of one who is already a master of his art, and both bespeak his interest in and preoccupation with realism, an innovation in the art of sculpture of his day and a hallmark of his work. *David* has all the unconscious arrogance of youth; *St. John* wears his intensity with the wearier wisdom of maturity. The *David* was commissioned for the Cathedral but was bought (1416) by the Signory and exhibited in the Palazzo Vecchio as an allegory of the triumph of justice over force—this may have been in reference to the purely fortuitous death of Ladislaus of Naples, whose operations north of Rome posed a serious threat to Florence. Vasari says that Donatello and his good and dear friend Brunelleschi went off to Rome together (c1403), and that there Donatello studied the ancient statues and fragments of Roman work while Brunelleschi measured the remains of Roman buildings. By 1411 Donatello thoroughly understood the Roman sculpture, as appears in his work. In that year he was commissioned to execute a *St. Mark* by the Linen Drapers' Guild for their tabernacle in the Oratory of Orsanmichele. His *St. George,* commissioned (1416) by the Armorers for their tabernacle in Orsanmichele (now in the Bargello), is in the classical spirit, Donatello having by this time shed the last traces of Gothicism. In the years from about 1415 on he made marble statues of four Prophets for the Campanile. These included his favorite work: the statue of the Prophet Habakkuk, portrayed as a worn, somewhat battered, and baldheaded old man, popularly called *Zuccone* (*Pumpkin-head*). Vasari records that from time to time he cried out to the statue, "Speak! Why wilt thou not speak?" The four Prophets are individualized to the point of portraiture, and according to an ancient tradition, again recorded by Vasari, the heads of Donatello's Prophets are portraits. The statues are now in the Museo dell' Opera del Duomo. Other works executed in this period are the *Marzocco* (Lion of Florence) (1418–1420), a sandstone figure made for the papal apartments in S. Maria Novella and finished in time for the visit of Pope Martin V and now in the Bargello; a gilt bronze statue of *St. Louis of Toulouse* (1423), his first bronze statue, cast for Orsanmichele; and the bronze *David* (c1430–1432), naked except for a flowered hat, whose smooth flesh once gleamed in the courtyard of the Medici Palace and now graces the Bargello. In this same period he executed a number of reliefs, in marble and in bronze, and invented his own method of carving or modeling them. Rather than carving what were almost detached statuettes set in deeply recessed frames, Donatello achieved the effect of spatial depth through the use of linear perspective and shallow surface modeling. His marble relief of *St. George and the Dragon,* on the base of the tabernacle of his Orsanmichele *St. George,* is the first example of *rilievo schiacciato* (flattened relief) in Italian sculpture. Other examples of this type of flattened relief are the marble *Ascension and Delivery of the Keys to St. Peter* (1428–1430), in the Victoria and Albert Museum, London, and the marble *Feast of Herod* (c1433–1435) at Lille. The bronze reliefs on scenes from the legend of St. Anthony that were executed later for the high altar of the basilica at Padua are striking examples of the use of linear perspective, almost as in painting, to give the illusion of depth. In his last bronze reliefs, those with scenes of the Passion executed on the pulpits in the Church of S. Lorenzo, Donatello achieves the effect of the third dimension less with linear perspective than by an indistinct line for the figures in the background. Features and outlines of figures behind the picture plane are indicated, not incised; modeling on the figures in the background is slight. This manner is particularly evident in the *Lamentation.* The limestone relief of the *Annunciation* (c1428–1433) in the Cavalcanti Chapel in the Church of S. Croce at Florence, is more deeply cut, returning to the manner of semidetached figures. In this the touchingly girlish Virgin appears about to step out of the scene but, arrested by the voice of the Angel of the Annunciation, half turns to face him. The motion is fluid in the stone. Other deeply cut reliefs are the riotously ebullient dancing children of the *Cantoria* (*Singing Gallery*) (1433–1439), originally intended for the cathedral and now in the Museo dell' Opera del Duomo, and the equally boisterous dancing cupids on the outdoor pulpit of the cathedral at Prato (1433–1438). Both these last are modeled after Roman sarcophagi reliefs but the energy displayed by the agitated, swinging movements of Donatello's dancers is totally unrelated to classical serenity and detachment.

In 1443 Donatello moved his workshop to Padua, perhaps because of the opportunity there of creating a major work in bronze. This was the monument of the Venetian captain Gattamelata. The equestrian monument he created, based on an antique statue of Marcus Aurelius that was still standing in Rome, was the first bronze equestrian statue cast since Roman times. The statue is remarkable for any time for the spirited war charger, the portrait Donatello presents of Gattamelata as the epitome of a coldly determined warrior, and for the infinitely detailed decoration of the accoutrements of horse and rider. Donatello also worked on a number of commissions for the basilica of St. Anthony at Padua, including a high altar. The various parts of the altar were not assembled in his lifetime, and its original design is unknown, though a handful of scholars have arranged the seven bronze statues, the four reliefs with miracles from the saint's life, and the Crucifix that were parts of the original design, in various positions that seem likely to them. The Paduans unreservedly admired Donatello's work. In 1453 he left their city. It was necessary for the perfection of his art, he asserted, to subject it to the knowledgeable faultfinding of his traditionally critical fellow-Florentines. In the next years he produced his dramatic *Judith and Holophernes* (c1460), now in front of the Palazzo Vecchio, stunning in its emotional impact, and remarkable for its success as a complete work of art whether viewed from the front or the back or from either side. Shortly after his return to Florence he carved his wooden *St. Mary Magdalen* (1455) in the Baptistery, a figure of unrelieved tragedy. For a period in the last ten years of his life he went to Siena (1457–1461), where he undertook some commissions, as for the doors of the Baptistery, which he did not carry out, and a bronze St. John the Baptist for the cathedral (1457). Cosimo de' Medici was his loyal and appreciative patron, and in his last years Donatello was almost exclusively in his service; for him he worked on the pulpits in S. Lorenzo, as he had also worked for him in the Old Sacristy of the church. Vasari writes that Donatello cared little for money, that he had a basket suspended from the ceiling of his house and that whoever needed money could let down the basket and help himself. Cosimo de' Medici charged his son Piero with the responsibility of caring for his old friend, and in his will left Donatello a farm in the belief that the revenues from it would provide for the aged sculptor. In a few months Donatello appeared to Piero and begged to be relieved of the property: the tenants were continually running to him with complaints and demands. Piero laughed, agreed to take back the farm, and instead gave him a pension. Within a short time Donatello followed Cosimo to the grave. The funeral the Florentines gave him was of a magnificence not equaled again in honor of an artist until the death of Michelangelo. And, as Cosimo had requested that his friend he buried near him, the sculptor's grave is in the Martelli Chapel of the Church of S. Lorenzo, the favorite church of the Medici family.

Acknowledged as the greatest sculptor of the 15th century, Donatello broke the grip of the static art of the early Middle Ages. Progressing from an early Gothicism through classicism, he added the qualities of realism and unadorned naturalism to his art. No technical problem dismayed him. By his own intellect and invention he solved the difficulties of the art and augmented the skill of his chisel with his own turbulent emotions and passionate humanity. In releasing the figure from the living stone or wood he made his material a partner rather than an inanimate substance on which he imposed his will. A master with the chisel, Donatello turned from carving stone to modeling bronze, possibly because chasing the modeled figure gave the opportunity for achieving a variety of textures. As Vasari said in connection with another sculptor, "the chisel cannot easily reproduce hair and feathers," but the texture of hair and feathers, as well as others, could be chased or cut in bronze. Ultimately, to free himself from the technical demands of casting in bronze he turned to carving in wood. He left a large body of work and had an enormous influence on succeeding sculptors and painters, as on his pupil Verrocchio, and on Antonio Pollaiuolo, Desiderio da Settignano, and the painters Masaccio and Andrea del Castagno. Donatello, Brunelleschi, and their much younger contemporary Masaccio were friends, and each in his field, sculpture, architecture, and painting, marked a watershed in the history of his art. Other great works of Donatello are the tomb (with Michelozzo) and the bronze effigy of John XXIII in the Baptistery at Florence (1425–1427); the *Assumption of the Virgin*, a marble relief from the tomb of Cardinal Brancacci in the Church of S. Angelo a Nilo at Naples (1427–1428); a *Tabernacle of the Sacrament* in St. Peter's at Rome; painted stucco decorations and bronze doors for the Old Sacristy of S. Lorenzo at Florence; a bronze statue, *Atys-Amorino* (c1440) in the Bargello; and the marble relief known as the *Pazzi Madonna* (c1422) at Berlin, of which various copies exist, some attributed to Donatello himself. There is an early (c1412) wooden *Crucifix* in the Church of S. Croce at Florence, and a later (1444–1447) bronze one in the Basilica of St. Anthony at Padua. In 1434 Donatello and Ghiberti submitted designs on the subject *The Coronation of the Virgin* for a stained glass window for the drum of the dome of the cathedral. Donatello's design was accepted (April, 1434), and having been executed by the glaziers Domenico di Piero of Pisa and Angelo Lippi, was installed four years later. It was removed for safety during World War II, cleaned, and scholars had the best opportunity in more than 500 years to study its bold and assured design. Even in this medium that was alien to him Donatello's work was not a matter of just decoration. In the area in which he devoted his life, each of his efforts, whether in stone, bronze, or wood, is an event.

Donati (dō-nä′tē), **Alessio di Guido.** Florentine poet of the 14th century. His few remaining ballate and madrigals exquisitely express his sincere love of nature and his appreciation for the songs of the people. His lyrics are notable for their realism and passion.

Donati, Corso. Florentine politician; d. October 6, 1308. Of an ancient and powerful feudal family, arrogant, reckless, and courageous, he was one of the conspicuous figures in the Florentine factions of the time of Dante. Dino Compagni, who described this period in which he lived with great vividness, says that the people called Corso "the Baron," and when, clad in full armor he rode through the streets on his charger, they greeted him with shouts of "Viva il Barone!" But their feelings toward Corso varied: when he was quarreling with his own class, the magnates, he had the sympathy of the people; when, on the other hand, he played the role of lord of Florence with too much verve, the people turned against him. Exiled in 1299 for his lordly disregard of justice, he broke his banishment (1301), became a rebel thereby, and with a band of supporters forced his way into the city. This was easy for him to do as Charles of Valois, in the name of Pope Boniface VIII, was at that time in control of the city, and supported the Neri, of which party Corso was a leader. Once in the city, Corso sacked the houses of his enemies, opened the prisons, overturned the government of the Bianchi and set up his own. He terrorized the city for five days. The new government was composed of members of the Neri. Corso was too rash and quick-tempered even for members of his own party. They controlled Florence, exiled the Bianchi, including Dante, and put their own men in public office. Corso found that he no longer had great influence with his own party and began plotting against it. In 1308, rather than submit to a trial because of irregularities that had turned up concerning his finances, he tried to raise rebellion in Florence. His attempt to rally the people behind him in this purely personal cause failed. He fled the city but was overtaken. He refused to submit and was stabbed.

Donato (dō-nä′tō). Venetian painter; active in the second half of the 14th century. With his colleague Caterino, he painted a *Coronation of the Virgin* (1372), now in the Querini-Stampalia Palace at Venice. The skill in rendering and luminous color are due to Donato. Also owing to him is the Byzantine richness of the gold-threaded fabrics and general Byzantine splendor. He was more influenced by the Byzantine manner than Caterino. A *Crucifixion* by Donato is in the Accademia at Venice.

Dondi (dôn′dē), **Giovanni.** Humanist, physician, alchemist, astrologer, and poet; b. at Chioggia, 1318; d. at Genoa, 1389. He was the son of Iacopo Dondi (1293–1359). He was professor of astronomy at Padua (c1350), lectured on medicine at Florence (1367–1370), served as Paduan ambassador to Venice (1371), and spent much time at Pavia between 1379 and 1388. From 1348 to 1364 he worked on the construction of an astronomical clock, more complicated than his father's, which was put in the castle at Pavia by Gian Galeazzo Visconti. His *Planetarium* tells how to construct such a clock. As did his father, Giovanni wrote on the extraction of salt from the hot springs of Padua. Having completed his acute scientific observations with regard to the springs, he expressed the belief that such things were controlled by the stars. He was a poet and a friend of Petrarch's. The latter left him fifty ducats with which to buy a gold ring in his memory.

Dondi, Iacopo. [Called **Dondi dall' Orologio.**] Physician, alchemist, and astrologer; b. at Padua, before 1293; d. 1359. He practiced medicine at Chioggia, where he was municipal physician (1313), then went to Padua where he set himself up as an alchemist and astrologer. He wrote theoretical treatises on these subjects, and one on how to extract salt from the hot springs of Padua. He constructed an elaborate astronomical clock (whence his sobriquet), one of the first to be made with weights, which was set up in a tower at Padua in 1344. This clock was lost, but a copy of it was set up in the Piazza dei Signori in 1434.

Doni (dô′nē), **Antonfrancesco.** Writer; b. at Florence, 1513; d. at Monselice, in September, 1574. At an early age he entered a monastic order at Florence, not, apparently, from any deep religious conviction, for he was compelled to leave (1540) the order in disgrace. Since he could not deny his earlier vows he continued to be a lay priest, a fact that chafed him continually but had no effect on his disorderly life. For a time he studied law at Piacenza, where he met and became friendly with Lodovico Domenichi. The friends were the moving spirits of a disorderly literary society, the Accademia Ortolana, whose wild activities shortly caused the suppression of the group. The law did not appeal to Doni's restless and bizarre temperament, however, and he left Piacenza to wander about in search of a patron. Failing in this, he went to Florence. Here he set up a printing press and printed the work of other writers as well as his own. For some reason he quarreled with Domenichi—a quarrel that he kept alive and hot by a series of scandalous invectives leveled at his old friend throughout his life. His Florentine stay was of short duration. He traveled about again and finally settled at Venice (1547). At Venice he wrote steadily, on any and all subjects, and in every form, not for his great love of literature but to earn money. His early years at Venice were difficult, and he produced steadily, and with great facility, to support his Bohemian and scandalous life. The pieces he turned out were seldom revised but were sent off to the printer at once. No evidence of research or learning informed them. Even so, they were acceptable, the novelle especially, to a wide public for the picturesque style, rapidity of action, and curious twists he brought to them. He published letters, poems, novelle, proverbs, comedies, dialogues, and treatises on the art of design and on music, among others. He carried on a violent quarrel with Aretino, once his friend, wrote a pamphlet against him in which he called himself the earthquake that would destroy the Antichrist of the age, and also an invective, *La vita dell' infame Aretino*. At Venice he was a member of the society known as the Pellegrini, which included and was supported by some eminent and respectable men, and which carried on many good works as well as indulging in wildly festive occasions. Evidently Doni at length earned enough money to live in comparative luxury. He took up residence in an abandoned castle keep near Venice, from which, almost naked, he issued at night and prowled or raged about the countryside, singing his own and other poets' songs. His most important works are *I marmi* and *I mondi*. The first is a collection of conversations he pretends to have overheard as he hovered over the marble steps of the cathedral at Florence. For he informs the reader in an introduction that at night he could take wing and fly over the cities of Italy, and that roofs were swept from the houses so that he could look in and see what all kinds and classes of men were doing. By this device were revealed to him the great contrasts that exist in the world and the many vagaries of human nature. The conversations he overheard at Florence covered topics of all kinds and were carried on by men from all walks of life. They were often amusing, sometimes took up scientific topics (as, in one, it was decided that the earth revolved), sometimes were on literary matters and present Doni's own rather acute literary criticism, concerned the arts, told stories, recited poems, and were threaded throughout with Doni's ironic view of human nature and his realistic and disillusioned appraisal of it. *I mondi* is an imaginary description of seven worlds and seven infernos. The sixth world is reminiscent of Thomas More's *Utopia*, which he had printed in a translation. Doni is, in respect to his interest in and writing upon all topics of his day, and in his ability and facility in writing in all styles and on all subjects, a forerunner of the journalist of a later day. He is an early example of one who earned his living solely by his pen and without the continuous benefit of a patron, although he never gave up looking for one.

Doni, Dono. Painter; b. at Assisi, near the beginning of the 16th century; d. 1575. The chief influences on his work were Giulio Romano and Michelangelo. A good draftsman, he was weak in coloring and composition, having a tendency to overcrowd his scene. The frescoes he painted with Raffaellino del Garbo (1545) at Perugia have been destroyed. Extant works are a *Calvary* (1561) in the refectory of the Convent of S. Maria degli Angeli, Assisi, an altarpiece for the cathedral at Assisi, and a *Pietà* in the cathedral at Gubbio.

Don John of Austria. See **John of Austria.**

Dono (dô′nō), **Paolo di.** Original name of **Paolo Uccello.**

Don Quixote (don kę̄-hō′tē, kwik′sǫt; Spanish, dōn kē-hō′tā). [Full Spanish title, **Don Quixote de la Mancha.**] Spanish satirical romance by Cervantes, printed at Madrid in two parts, 1605 and 1615. The book is named after its hero, a Spanish country gentleman, who is so imbued with tales of chivalry that he saddles up his nag, Rosinante, and sets forth with his squire Sancho Panza in search of knightly adventure to honor his lady Dulcinea del Toboso, really an ordinary country girl. At the beginning of the work Cervantes announces it to be his sole purpose to break down the vogue and authority of books of chivalry, and at the end he declares anew that he had "had no other desire than to render abhorred of men the false and absurd stories contained in books of chivalry," exulting in his success as an achievement of no small moment. The work was considered at first to be no more than hilarious satire (the Spanish themselves were notoriously slow to value the book properly), but in time perceptive readers of all countries saw beyond the surface laughter to the thoughtful and skillfully handled treatment of the idealist in a materialistic world, so that its comedy becomes the comedy of irony, not too far removed from something akin to tragedy. Translations of *Don Quixote* have appeared in every European language.

Doolin de Mayence (do-o-laṅ dẹ mȧ-yäṅs). [Also, **Doon de Mayence.**] French *chanson de geste* of the 14th century, adapted as a prose romance in the 15th century. Doolin, or Doon, was the son of Guy of Mayence, and the ancestor of Ogier the Dane. His name is attached to a whole cycle of the Charlemagne *chansons de geste,* those dealing with the false knights, the family of Ganelon; included here are such chansons as *The Four Sons of Aymon.*

Doon de Mayence (do-ôṅ dẹ mȧ-yäṅs). See **Doolin de Mayence.**

Doralice (dō-rä-lē′chā). In Lodovico Ariosto's *Orlando Furioso,* the daughter of the king of Granada. She becomes the wife of Mandricardo, but is also loved by Rodomonte, to whom she had been betrothed. After the death of Mandricardo she is willing to give herself to his conqueror, Ruggiero.

Doria (dō′ryä). Ancient noble family of Genoa; to the middle of the 14th century, when the institution of the dogate was established (1339), they were among the most powerful feudal nobles of the region. Ghibellines, they played an energetic part in the struggles with the Guelphs, and from early in the 12th century, when the first of the name appears in documents, were conspicuous in the naval and military affairs of Genoa. Members of the large family had vast possessions and great wealth; they served as admirals against the Moors in Spain, at the siege of Acre as allies of Philip Augustus of France and Richard the Lion-Hearted, and in the crusades of Louis IX (1248, 1270); for Genoa, they acted as ambassadors and captains of the people. At the end of the 13th century (1299), war broke out between the Ghibelline Doria family and the Guelph Spinola family. Genoa's streets ran with blood. When at last peace was restored (1335), a popular revolt broke out against the oligarchic families that had caused such strife. The result led to the establishment of a dogate (1339), in which Simone Boccanegra was the first doge. From that time until 1528, the members of the Doria family were excluded from political activity at Genoa. Many times they sought to regain power but were unsuccessful. In the meantime, they continued to contribute eminent naval men to the Genoese navy. With Andrea Doria (1466–1560), who was given the title *Liberator and Father of his Country* for expelling

LEONE LEONI
Profile studies of the head of Andrea Doria
Courtesy of The Pierpont Morgan Library, New York

the French and setting up the Genoese republic (1528), the family once again became prominent in public affairs.

DORIA, ANDREA. Genoese admiral and statesman; b. at Oneglia, November 30, 1466; d. at Genoa, November 25, 1560. At the age of 19 he went to Rome, where his kinsman Domenico Doria was captain of Pope Innocent VIII's guard, and began his military career. From this time to the first decade of the 16th century he was a soldier in the pay of various princes, except for a pilgrimage he made to the Holy Land. After the battle of Ravenna (1512) he helped drive the French out of Genoa, and when they returned drove them out again. With the victory at Marignano, Francis I regained control of Lombardy and once again sought to win Genoa, but settled for an agreement by which the doge of Genoa acted as his vicar. Doria now served the French. When Francis was defeated and taken prisoner following the battle of Pavia (1525), and efforts to free him proved fruitless, Doria went into the service of Clement VII. In 1528, weary of French intrigues, the hostility of the French court, and the difficulty of collecting his pay, but more than any of these things resentful because the French refused to hand over Savona to Genoa, as they had promised, he switched to the support of Charles V. The emperor, who had been endeavoring to lure him from the French, guaranteed the liberty of Genoa (although as a dependency of the empire) and its right to control of Savona. With these terms, Doria triumphantly entered the city, September 9, 1528, and was acclaimed as *Liberator and Father of his Country*. Although he refused the office of doge and kept republican forms of government, he was, in fact, the first citizen and unofficial lord of Genoa. Having repulsed a final attempt (1529) of the French to regain Genoa, he thereafter served Charles V, by whom he was invested with the principate of Melfi (1532). For Charles, he led an expedition against the Turks, fought the Barbary pirates, and took an active part in the wars that continued between Charles and France. He was the most famous naval commander of his age. In 1547 a conspiracy of the Genoese Fieschi family against Doria failed, but not before it had taken the life of Gianettino Doria, a son of Andrea's cousin, and Andrea's designated heir. Another conspiracy in the following year failed also. Andrea's wrath towards members of the Fieschi and the Cybo families responsible for the conspiracies, was implacable, but his responsibility for the death of Pier Luigi Farnese, suspected accomplice of Giulio Cybo, was not proved. Ambitious and unscrupulous, he loved his city and governed it well. Though as greedy for power as any condottiere, he realized that an official prince would only arouse factional passions and cause more bloodshed. He therefore contented himself with the power and eschewed the title, and managed to preserve Genoa as a republic in the face of the expanding empire of Charles V by making himself indispensable to the emperor and by linking Genoese interests to those of Spain. Lacking an heir, Andrea concentrated his hopes on Gian Andrea, the son of Gianettino, and transferred many of his honors and some of his power to him. The young man was unworthy, or perhaps unprepared, for either the power or the position, and made a poor showing at the battle of Lepanto. Andrea himself continued in active service to the republic to the end of his life. One of his last accomplishments was the restoration of the island of Corsica to Genoa (1559).

Doria, Percivalle. Genoese troubadour of the 13th century. He was a Ghibelline and supported Frederick II. Manfred, Frederick's son, named him imperial vicar in the March of Ancona and the duchy of Spoleto. Two Italian love lyrics and a poem in praise of Manfred, in Provençal, survive.

Doria Pamphili (päm-fē′lē) **Gallery.** Art gallery in the Palazzo Doria at Rome. The building was erected for Cardinal Doria in the 15th century and was largely reconstructed in the 18th century. The façade of the palace is on the Via del Corso; the entrance to the gallery is from the Piazza del Collegio Romano at the back. The palace passed ultimately to the Pamphili family. The gallery is especially rich in 16th and 17th-century paintings, with important examples of the works of such painters as Correggio, Parmigianino, Dosso Dossi, Beccafumi, Veronese, Tintoretto, Titian, and others.

Dosio (dō′syō), **Giovanni Antonio.** Architect and sculptor; b. at Florence or San Gimignano, 1535; d. at Rome or Naples, 1609. He was for a time at Rome, working with the sculptor Raffaello da Montelupo. Between 1566 and 1575 he carried out the sculptural decoration, in general cold and reserved, on several funeral monuments at Rome. In 1569 he published his *Urbis Romae* . . . , which is celebrated for its clear illustrations of the ancient ruins. (The original drawings are at Florence and Berlin.) In 1574 he assisted Ammannati in the completion of a Medici villa, and from 1576 to 1590, except for a brief trip to Rome, was at Florence. There he was occupied as an architect. In his church architecture his style follows the Roman manner, as in the Gaddi Chapel in S. Maria Novella (1576–1579), with its overtones of the influence of Michelangelo. In his civic architecture he returned to the Golden Age of the Florentine palace style, as in the Palazzetto Larderel (1580), in the Via Tornabuoni. In 1591 he was at Naples as architect for the Carthusian church of S. Martino, and was again at Naples in 1609. More celebrated as an architect than as a sculptor, Dosio was an eclectic who at times contrived to blend separate elements into a harmonious whole, as in the Palazzetto Larderel and the Church of the Carthusian monastery of S. Martino at Naples.

Dossi (dôs′sē), **Battista.** [Original name, **Battista Luteri.**] Ferrarese painter; mentioned 1517–1553. He was the brother of Dosso Dossi, with whom he lived and worked at Ferrara. He assisted his brother in some of his paintings but spent his time principally in carrying out minor commissions for the insatiable Estense court: painting standards, coats of arms, molding stucco decorations, making wax models for goldsmiths and for artillery makers. Among his known paintings are a *Holy Family with the Young St. John,*

Carrara Academy, Bergamo, and a *Nativity*, Borghese Gallery, Rome.

Dossi, Dosso. [Original name, **Giovanni Luteri.**] Painter; b. c1479; d. probably 1542. He may have begun his training under Lorenzo Costa, but was later more influenced by the Venetians Giorgione and Titian. He appears as a painter for the first time at Mantua (1512). From there he went (1516) to Ferrara, where, except for brief intervals, he passed the rest of his life and was the last outstanding representative of the Ferrarese school. At Ferrara he soon became official court painter, and for the Estense dukes painted portraits (the splendid one of Ercole I d'Este in the Estense Gallery at Modena is thought by some to be a copy of a Dossi original), panels to decorate the rooms of palaces, scenery for the comedies the Estensi delighted in, cartoons for tapestries, designs for majolica, and altarpieces for the churches of Ferrara and the duchy. His brother Battista worked with him, and in 1531 the two were called to Trent by the bishop to work in the Castello del Buon Consiglio. They worked there until early in 1532. In the following year they painted altarpieces for the cathedrals of Modena and Reggio, commissioned to do so by Alfonso I d'Este to celebrate the recovery of those two cities from the pope. The influence of Giorgione is strong in Dossi's *Circe*, Borghese Gallery, Rome, in which the enchantress, clad in damask and gold, is shown against a typically Giorgionesque landscape background. Also in the manner of Giorgione is his *Nymph Pursued by a Satyr*, Pitti Palace, Florence. He became fascinated by the play of light from jewels and gilding and approached the richness in color of Titian without achieving Titian's dramatic contrasts, movement, and composition. In his own imaginative and glittering compositions, Dossi limited himself to portraying figures in the round, and to adorning his paintings with gleaming jewels, gorgeous materials, and tapestries. His love of color was pronounced and occasionally, with the luminosity of his precious stones, richly costumed figures, gilded borders and luxuriant embroideries, the total effect is majestic. With the passage of time Dossi's forms, never expertly modeled, became more monumental and increasingly he became preoccupied with the decorative effects of jewels, ornate costumes, splendid color, and magic landscapes. His *St. Sebastian*, Brera, Milan, shows the saint partially draped with a green mantle that hangs from a fruit-bearing lemon tree; in the background, framed, is an autumnal landscape. Other paintings incorporate the motif of brightly colored fruit-bearing trees. His fantasy served him well in designing illustrations for the epic, *Orlando Furioso*, in which his friend Ariosto mentions him as one of the painters of Ferrara. Dossi left a number of works, some of those from the last period of his life being finished by assistants. Many of his paintings are in the Estense Gallery at Modena; others are in the Borghese, Capitoline, Doria Pamphili, and Colonna galleries and in the National Gallery of Ancient Art at Rome; in the Uffizi, Florence; and at Parma, Bergamo, Allentown (Pennsylvania), Amherst (Massachusetts), Cambridge (Massachusetts), Cleveland, Coral Gables (Florida), Detroit, Hartford, Milwaukee, New York, Philadelphia (Johnson Collection), Providence, Washington, Worcester, and elsewhere.

Douglas (dug'ḷạs), **Gawin** (or **Gavin**). [Also, **Gawain Douglas.**] Scottish poet and bishop; b. c1474; d. at London, in September, 1522. He prepared a translation of the *Aeneid* into Scottish verse and wrote *The Palice of Honour*, *King Hart*, and *Conscience*.

Dousa (dö'sạ), **Janus.** [Latinized name of **Jan van der Does.**] Dutch scholar, poet, historian and patriot; b. at Noordwijk, near Leiden, Netherlands, December 6, 1545; d. there, in October, 1604. He published *Annals of Holland* (1599), and others.

Dovizi (dō-vēt'tsē), **Bernardo.** [Called **Il Bibbiena.**] Cardinal and playwright; b. at Bibbiena, August 4, 1470; d. at Rome, November 9, 1520. He spent his youth in the service of the Medici, and was the special friend of Cardinal Giovanni, with whom he traveled in Europe, spent some time at Urbino, and returned to Rome. When Giovanni was elevated to the papacy Bibbiena's fortunes reached a peak. Such was his influence on the pope that he was called "the other pope." In a war of the papacy against Urbino, Bibbiena was legate to the pontifical army and carried out his office with vigor. On his return from a mission to France (1519), he unexpectedly died at Rome (1520). Poison was suspected but never proved. Bibbiena was a man of learning, lively spirit, and interest in the artistic and literary developments of his day. Raphael, whose patron he was, has left a penetrating portrait of him, now in the Pitti Palace at Florence. Castiglione, in his *Il Cortegiano*, portrays him as the witty and discreet man he was reputed to be. Il Bibbiena's famous comedy, *Calandria*, is based on the *Menaechmi* of Plautus, but instead of twin boys, the twins are a boy and a girl who exchange clothes. This gives rise to all kinds of complications and amusing incidents. The plot is swiftly and surely developed; the characters breathe. The play, with an introduction by Baldassare Castiglione, was first presented (1513) at the court of Urbino. It was an enormous success, and was later presented at Rome for the Pope and Isabella d'Este (1518). Despite its obvious derivation, the play is thoroughly original in its development and style, and enough of a break with the classical model to have formed the basis of a true Italian comedy. The message of the comedy, presented by way of all sorts of immoral episodes, is that "man never makes a plan but that fortune makes a different one."

Drake (drāk), Sir **Francis.** English naval hero; b. probably at Tavistock, Devonshire, England, c1540; d. off Portobelo, Panama, January 28, 1596. In 1567–1568 he commanded a small vessel, the *Judith*, one of two which escaped from the destruction of Sir John Hawkins' fleet by the Spanish in the Gulf of Mexico. Under Elizabeth's commission as a privateer, he visited the West Indies and the Spanish Main in 1570 and 1571, and became convinced that the towns there would fall an easy prey to a small armed force. Accordingly, in 1572, he fitted out what was properly a freebooting expedition, England being then at peace with Spain. With only three vessels and 100 men he took the town of Nombre de Dios on the Isthmus of Panama and an immense treasure; but he was badly wounded in the attack, and his men abandoned both the town and treasure. Soon after, he burned a Spanish vessel at Cartagena, in what is now Colombia, captured many ships, and intercepted a train loaded with silver on the isthmus. He also crossed to Panama, and was the first English commander to see the Pacific. From his return, in August, 1573, to September, 1576, Drake served under Walter Devereux, 1st Earl of Essex, in Ireland. In December, 1577, with the express purpose of penetrating to the Pacific through the Straits of Magellan, he started on another freebooting expedition with five ships and 166 men. Two ships were abandoned on the west coast of South America, and after the passage of the Straits of Magellan, which took sixteen days, his ship became separated from the other two, which returned to England. Drake continued in the *Golden Hind*, obtained an immense booty on the Pacific coast of Spanish America, crossed the Pacific, and returned to England by way of the Cape of Good Hope, arriving in September, 1580, with a vast treasure. This was the first English circumnavigation of the globe. Queen Elizabeth knighted Drake on his own ship, and ordered that the *Golden Hind* be preserved as a monument. (It rotted and was broken up some hundred years later.) Drake was mayor (1581) of Plymouth. In 1584–1585 he was a member of Parliament. From 1585 to 1586 he commanded a powerful expedition to the West Indies and the Spanish Main, in which he took and ransomed Santo Domingo and Cartagena, ravaged the coasts of Florida, and on his way back brought off the remnant of the English Virginia colony founded by Sir Walter Raleigh in 1585. In 1587 he made a descent on the coast of Spain, and in the Bay of Cádiz destroyed numerous unfinished vessels intended for the Spanish Armada, besides capturing a rich Portuguese East Indiaman. In July, 1588, as a vice-admiral, he commanded under Lord Charles Howard in the combat with the Spanish Armada, capturing a large Spanish galleon; and the next year he was one of the commanders in a descent on the Spanish and Portuguese coasts, which proved unsuccessful. For several years thereafter he was engaged in peaceful pursuits, and in 1593 he was again elected to Parliament. In 1595 he commanded another West Indies expedition, which met with little success, and in which both he and Sir John Hawkins died.

Dream, Chaucer's. Poem, probably spurious, added by Speght in 1598 to his edition of Chaucer. The proper title is *The Isle of Ladies*. (It is not the same as *The Dream of Chaucer*, which is genuine.)

du Bellay (dü be-lā). See **Bellay.**

Ducas (dū′kạs), **Michael.** Byzantine historian; active in the second half of the 15th century. He wrote a history of the Byzantine Empire for the period between 1341 and 1462.

Duccio di Buoninsegna (döt′chō dē bwô-nēn-sā′nyä). Sienese painter, founder of the Sienese school of painting; b. c1260 at Siena; d. 1319. Judging from the number of fines he is recorded to have paid, he led a somewhat irregular life. This did not, however, interfere with his reputation as a painter in his own day. Duccio transmuted the Byzantine style and founded the Sienese school with a flowing line and slender, elongated figures that are characteristic of him and his many followers. His colors glow. His lovely slant-eyed Madonnas have an air of mystery and languor, quite distinct from the remote and majestic Madonnas of the Byzantine tradition. All elements are softened. Decorative and narrative qualities are enhanced. His masterwork, commissioned in 1308 and completed in 1311, is a *Maestà*. This great work was destined for the cathedral at Siena, and because it was to be visible from both sides of the high altar on which it was to be placed, it was painted on both sides. On the back were a number of panels. Many devout and fascinated Sienese followed the progress of the work, which was all to be carried out by Duccio himself. When it was completed the painting, including the predella, was carried from Duccio's house to the cathedral in a procession in which the most prominent men of Siena marched. Bells pealed, silver trumpets were sounded, and drums rolled, as the procession wound its way to the cathedral. In after years the work was taken apart and its many panels scattered. The main panel, with the *Madonna*, is in the Opera del Duomo at Siena, with a number of the panels on which are painted scenes from the life of Christ. Other panels are at Berlin, London, New York (Frick Collection), and Washington. To achieve the reputation that won him the contract, as Siena's greatest painter, for the *Maestà*, Duccio (who at some time worked as a mosaicist), had earlier painted cassoni panels and covers for the account books of the city, and had painted, for S. Maria Novella at Florence, an elaborate *Madonna* (1285), now in the Uffizi. This last is probably the *Rucellai Madonna*, which for centuries was attributed to Cimabue. Duccio's earliest surviving work is probably the now damaged *Virgin Enthroned and Three Franciscan Monks* (c1278), Pinacoteca, Siena. Other works are a triptych, *Madonna with St. Dominic and St. Agnes*, National Gallery, London, a repainted and restored *Madonna* at Perugia; and paintings at Massa Maritima (cathedral), Berne, Hampton Court, Boston (Museum), and South Hadley (Massachusetts).

Dudley (dud′li), **Edmund.** English politician; b. c1462; executed at London, August 18, 1510. He was employed as a fiscal agent by Henry VII, and incurred popular odium by the rigor with which he enforced the extortionate claims of the crown. After the death of Henry VII he was beheaded on a charge of treason.

Dudley, Lord **Guildford.** English nobleman; executed at London, February 12, 1554. He married Lady Jane Grey, and was implicated in his father's attempt to place her on the throne on the death of Edward VI (July 6, 1553), and was executed on the charge of treason.

Dudley, John. [Titles, Duke of **Northumberland**, Earl of **Warwick**, Viscount **Lisle.**] English politician and soldier; b. c1502; beheaded August 22, 1553. With the object of transferring the crown from the Tudors to his own family he persuaded Edward VI, one of whose regents he had been, to grant letters patent excluding Mary and Elizabeth Tudor from the succession, and appointing Lady Jane Grey, Edward's cousin, heir presumptive. He then married Lady Jane to his son, Guildford Dudley. Upon the accession of Mary he was executed for treason.

Dudley, Robert. [Title, Earl of **Leicester.**] English courtier, politician, and general; b. June 24, 1532; d. at Cornbury, Oxfordshire, England, September 4, 1588. He was a favorite of Queen Elizabeth, and tried to gain the consent of the great nobles to a marriage. Failing this he hoped to marry Mary, Queen of Scots. Because of his intrigues, he was often out of favor with the queen, and as often restored to grace. He was a patron of the arts, especially of the drama. The Earl of Leicester's company of players was licensed by the queen to play at London in 1574. This was the company that later included the Burbages and Shakespeare, and for which the first London theater, the Theatre, was built (1576).

Dudone (dö-dô′nā). In Lodovico Ariosto's *Orlando Furioso*, a Danish knight who defeats Agramante's fleet.

Dufay (dü-fā), **Guillaume.** Flemish composer and contrapuntalist; b. at Hainault, Belgium, c1400; d. at Cambrai, France, November 27, 1474. He originated improvements in musical notation, such as the use of white notes.

Du Guesclin or **Duguesclin** (dü-ge-klaṅ), **Bertrand.** French military commander, constable of France, distinguished in the campaigns against the English and Pedro el Cruel (Peter the Cruel of Castile and Leon); b. near Rennes, in Brittany, c1320; d. at Château-neuf-de-Randon, in Languedoc, July 13, 1380. After having made a soldier's reputation for himself in tournaments and in fighting for Charles de Blois, he helped in the defense of Rennes, besieged (1356–1357) by Henry of Lancaster. He was captured at Melun in 1359 by Sir Robert Knollys, but covered himself with glory. At Cocherel in 1364 he beat the forces of Navarre and captured Jean de Grailly, the Captal de Buch, Navarre's most famous soldier. At Auray the same year, Charles de Blois was killed and Du Guesclin was captured by Sir John Chandos. He was ransomed for 100,000 crowns, since his aid, as France's leading soldier, was necessary to preserve internal order. The Treaty of Brétigny (1360) had brought a temporary pause in the Hundred Years' War and bands of discharged soldiers, the so-called free companies, were pillaging the country. Du Guesclin organized them into an army and took them into Spain to fight for Henry of Trastamara (later Henry II of Castile) against Pedro el Cruel, but after success in 1366, he was defeated by Edward, the Black Prince of England, Pedro's ally, at Navarrete. He was again ransomed and in the battle of Montiel (1369) defeated Pedro and put Henry on the throne. Under Charles V of France he fought (1370–1379) in the campaigns to clean the English out of southern and western France, winning for the French throne Poitou, Guienne, Auvergne, and Brittany. He died in a campaign to suppress disorders in Languedoc.

Duke of Exeter's Daughter (ek′sẹ-tėrz). Name given to the rack which the Duke of Exeter introduced as an engine of torture in the Tower of London in 1447.

Dulcinea del Toboso (dul-sin′ẹ̄-ạ del tō-bō′zō; Spanish, döl-thē-nā′ä del tō-bō′sō). Lady beloved by Don Quixote in Cervantes' romance. Her real name was Aldonza Lorenzo, but Don Quixote was of the opinion that Dulcinea was more uncommon and romantic (from the Spanish *dulce,* meaning "sweet"); and, as she was born at Toboso, he made her a great lady on the spot with the *del.*

Dumoulin (dü-mö-laṅ), **Charles.** [Latinized surname, **Molinaeus.**] French jurist; b. at Paris, 1500; d. 1566. He became a Calvinist, was involved in many controversies, denounced feudal privileges, and exalted the monarch as the sole source of legal authority. He wrote *Sommaire du livre analytique des contrats, usures, rentes constituées intérêts et monnoyes,* and *Extricatio labyrinthi dividue et individui.*

Dunbar (dun-bär′), **William.** Scottish poet; b. probably in East Lothian, Scotland, c1460; d. c1525. He is one of the Scottish Chaucerian school. His works include *The Thissil and the Rois* (1503), a prothalamium in honor of James IV and Margaret Tudor; *The Golden Targe,* a dream allegory on beauty and love; *Dance of the Seven Deadly Sins, Merle and Nightingale, The Two Mariit Wemen and the Wedo,* a lusty discourse that outdoes Chaucer's wife of Bath; and *Lament for the Makaris,* an elegy on the poets (makers) who preceded him.

Dunois (dü-nwȧ), **Jean.** [Title, Comte **de Dunois;** called the **Bastard of Orléans.**] He was the natural son of Louis, Duke of Orléans (1372–1407) and Mariette d'Enghien; b. at Paris, November 23, 1402; d. at St.-Germain-en-Laye, near Paris, November 24, 1468. He was celebrated for his gallantries and for his military prowess. He campaigned against the English, holding out at Orléans (1429) until Joan of Arc arrived and drove them off. He carried on the fight after she was killed and by 1436 had retaken Paris. In 1440 he was for a time in league with the nobles against his uncle Charles VII, but after the truce of 1444 was broken campaigned vigorously against the English, taking many cities (1449–1451), and driving the English out of northern France altogether. Charles made him a prince of the royal blood, but Louis XI, when he came to the throne in 1461, stripped him of his honors. Dunois joined the League of the Public Good, a group of nobles in revolt against Louis' attempt to consolidate an absolute monarchy.

Duns Scotus (dunz skō′tus), **John.** [Called **Doctor Subtilis.**] Scholastic theologian, one of the most influential in the history of medieval Europe; b. at Duns, Scotland, c1265; d. at Cologne, Germany, November 8, 1308. He was the founder of the scholastic system called Scotism, which long contended for supremacy among the schoolmen with the system called Thomism, founded by Thomas Aquinas. Nothing is known with certainty concerning his personal history. According to the commonly accepted tradition, he was born c1265 at Duns (or Dunse), Berwickshire, Scotland (hence his surname Scotus, or Scot), was a fellow of Merton College, Oxford, became a Franciscan friar, was chosen professor of theology at Oxford in 1301, removed in 1304 to Paris, where, in a disputation on the Immaculate Conception of Jesus Christ by the Virgin Mary he displayed so much ingenuity and resource as to win the title of Doctor Subtilis, and where he rose to the position of regent of the university. His name, Duns, Dunse, or Dunce, came to be used as a common appellative, meaning "a very learned man," and, being applied satirically to ignorant and stupid persons as being as sensible as the extreme scholastics, gave rise to "dunce" in its present sense. Scotism, the movement he founded, was an extreme form of realism and anti-intellectualism. Instead of the middle of the road between faith and reason sought by Saint Thomas Aquinas, Duns Scotus restricted the sphere of rational thought, thus eventually driving the wedge between philosophy and religion that emancipated the philosophers from strict adherence to religious subjects, an effect opposite to the one Scotus sought. The argument concerning the Immaculate Conception found the Thomists on one side and the Scotist Dominicans on the other; the latter were joined by the Franciscans, the Jesuits, and the Sorbonne theologians; the feud was not dissolved until 1854. Scotus held that true knowledge could be reached only through revelation from God. As a corollary to this, he held that the existence of God was essentially unprovable (it must be presupposed) and that God's nature was incomprehensible to man.

Duplessis-Mornay (dü-ple-sē-môr-nā). See **Mornay, Philippe de.**

Duprat (dü-prȧ), **Antoine.** French cardinal and politician; b. at Issoire, Puy-de-Dôme, France, January 17, 1463; d. at Rambouillet, France, July 9, 1535. He became chancellor and prime minister in 1515.

Durand (dü-räṅ), **Nicolas.** See **Villegaignon,** Chevalier **de.**

Durandarte (dö-rän-där′tā). Legendary Spanish hero whose exploits are related in old Spanish ballads and in *Don Quixote*. He was the cousin of Montesinos, and was killed at the battle of Roncesvalles. One of the ballads, a fragment, can be traced to the *Cancionero* of 1511, and one, *Durandarte, Durandarte,* to the old *Cancioneros Generales.*

Dürer (dü′rėr), **Albrecht.** German painter, draftsman, and engraver; b. at Nuremberg, Germany, May 21, 1471; d. there, April 6, 1528. The son of an able goldsmith, he learned that craft from his father before entering the studio of the painter Michel Wohlgemut in 1486. In 1490 he traveled to Colmar (to study under Martin Schongauer), to Basel, and to Strasbourg. In the spring of 1494 he was back at Nuremberg, where he married. He went to Venice in the fall of the same year, drawn there, perhaps, by the presence of his friend, the humanist Wilibald Pirckheimer, who was studying at Padua. At Venice he studied the works of Mantegna and Bellini, and was deeply interested by the classical aspects of Mantegna's work and by its linearity, an interest that was later reflected in some of his own work. He returned to Nuremberg in the spring of 1495, and set up his own studio there in 1497. He made another visit to Venice in 1505. This time he remained two years and in the course of his stay met Giovanni Bellini. He was a warm admirer of that painter and wrote of him that Bellini was still the best in the art of painting. His *Madonna of the Rose Garlands,* painted for the German merchants at Venice, and *Christ Among the Doctors,* were among the works painted at this time. Through his visits to Venice, his study and observation of the work that was being done there, Dürer became the vessel through which the developments that had taken place in Italian Renaissance painting were channeled to northern Europe. By this means the Gothic tradition that was then followed, especially in Germany, was gradually replaced. In its turn, his work, especially the animated line of his incisive engravings, influenced the Italians. Back at Nuremberg, his period (1505–1520) of greatest activity ensued, during which especially he brought to superbly powerful perfection his drawings, copper engravings, and woodcuts. Nuremberg at that time was a center of intellectual activity; Humanism and Protestantism were in the air. Dürer was profoundly interested by the work of the scholars and engaged in intellectual activity himself. He studied mathematics, geometry, and Latin and humanist literature. These studies undoubtedly influenced the great intellectual content of his work, for in addition to the immediate visual impact of his works, more especially the graphic ones, is the deep meaning they are intended to convey. Humanism stimulated him intellectually. Protestantism disturbed him spiritually. He was court painter to the Emperor Maximilian I, and later to Charles V, and painted their portraits. He was also a friend of their religious opponents, Luther and Melancthon. Affected as he was by the unrest of the Reformation, it is believed that he remained a Catholic. The Christian tradition certainly gave him by far the greater number of his subjects, as shown by his numerous paintings, engravings, and woodcuts deriving from the stories of the Fall, the Nativity, the Flight into Egypt, the Passion, and the lives of the early Christian saints and martyrs. It was said by some Italian painters that if he had been an Italian, Dürer would have been the greatest of Italian artists. Although his work in all media is often Gothic in derivation, markedly different from the pictures of the Italian High Renaissance, to the Gothic elements in his painting were also added those derived from Mantegna, Bellini, and other Italian masters. His portraits of this period are solid, shrewd, uncompromisingly realistic; his copperplates and woodcuts are full of energy, crowded with invention, sometimes revealing his interest in the antique, sometimes grim, or even grotesque. Contrasting with all this vehemence and exuberance are many painted landscapes and drawings of small animals or patches of grass and flowers, of a calm and touching beauty. In 1520 he went to the Netherlands to secure from the new emperor, Charles V, the continuation of his post and pension as court painter. He visited many cities of the Netherlands and Germany on the way. Everywhere he was received with enthusiasm and respect, and he improved the opportunity of his stay in the Netherlands to learn from the works of the Van Eycks, whose spiritual influence is evident in some of the work of his own last years, especially in the *Four Evangelists*, Munich, which some consider his masterpiece. Others give that title to his *Adoration of the Magi* (1504) in the Uffizi. This work, commissioned by the Elector of Saxony, Frederick the Wise, and intended for the church of Wittenberg, is probably the central panel of an altarpiece, other parts of which are at Frankfurt, Cologne, and Munich. Painted between his Italian journeys, though intensely original it has echoes in the architecture and background of the work of Mantegna. But it is perhaps a futile critical exercise to try to name as a masterpiece any particular creation of one whose work was all masterly. Dürer was not, certainly, one of the great colorists, but as a draftsman, as a portraitist, and as a designer, he is among the very greatest in the history of art. That his accomplishments were the reflection of a keen intelligence is shown by his writings: on measurement (1525), fortifications (1527), proportion and artistic theory (1528), and accounts of his journeys to Venice and the Low Countries. The most notable Dürer paintings known today are *Virgin and Child with Saints Anthony and Sebastian* and a *Crucifixion*, at Dresden; *Martyrdom of the Ten Thousand* and a *Madonna*, at Venice; *Virgin Crowned by Two Angels* and a portrait of Hieronymus Holzschuber, at Berlin; the *Adoration of the Magi*, Uffizi; *A Young Man*, and portraits of Oswald Krell and Michel Wohlgemut, at Munich; and self-portraits at Leipzig, Madrid, and Munich. In the graphic arts Dürer attained the pinnacle of mastery. His greatest influence was exercised through his woodcuts and copper engravings. These works, as opposed to the great altarpieces and easel paintings, were easily carried from place to place. In this manner his line, designs, imaginative themes, and his technique circulated all over Europe. Even the Italians were influenced by them (and sometimes pirated them). He made several series of woodcuts, as the *Apocalypse* (1498), of which he was also the printer and publisher, the *Great Passion* (1498–1510), the *Little Passion* (1509–1511), and the *Life of the Virgin* (1501–1511). On his many engravings, among the best known are *Sea Monster* and *Prodigal Son* (1497), *Knight, Death and the Devil* (1513), *St. Jerome* and *Melancholia* (1514). Precious collections of his drawings and engravings are in the Albertina, Vienna, and the British Museum, as well as at Berlin, Florence, Milan, and Paris.

Durindana (dö-rēn-dä′nä). In the Italian versions of the Carolingian cycle, the sword of Orlando (Roland). It possessed magic qualities, was made by the supernatural smiths, and was once owned by Hector. In Matteo Maria Boiardo's *Orlando Innamorato* and Lodovico Ariosto's *Orlando Furioso,* it is one of the treasures that the Saracen Gradasso seeks in his invasion of France. In Luigi Pulci's epic, *Morgante maggiore,* the sword is returned to Charlemagne after the death of Orlando at the Pass of Roncesvalles.

Dymoke (dim′ọk), Sir **Thomas.** English soldier; b. c1428; beheaded at London, 1471. He was attached to the Lancastrian faction in the Wars of the Roses. Captured by Edward IV at Edgecote, he was taken to London and beheaded.

E

Éboli (ā′ʙō-lē) Princesa **de.** [Title of **Ana de Mendoza.**] Daughter of Don Diego Hurtado de Mendoza, viceroy of Peru; b. 1540; d. at Pastrana, Spain, February 2, 1592. According to some authorities she was the mistress of Philip II of Spain.

Ecatommiti (ā-kä-tôm′mē-tē), **Gli.** A collection of 110 tales by Giambattista Cinzio Giraldi, written in the vernacular, and around a Boccaccesque framework of a group of people traveling from Rome to Marseilles to escape the plague after the sack of Rome in 1527. The stories are on a wide variety of themes, some are adapted from popular stories, many depict tragic and horrible events, some of which were drawn from life. Though they sometimes deal with lust and immorality, they are not licentious for the sake of licentiousness, but to point a moral. Some of these stories were adapted and appeared in Painter's *Palace of Pleasure,* from which Shakespeare in his turn drew for his *Othello* and *Measure for Measure.*

Eck (ek), **Johann.** [Original surname, **Mayr** (or **Maier**), and hence sometimes written, in full, **Johann Maier von Eck.**] German Roman Catholic theologian; b. at Eck (now Egg), in Swabia, November 15, 1486; d. at Ingolstadt, in Bavaria, February 10, 1543. He was a notable opponent of Luther and the Reformation.

Écorcheurs (ā-kôr-shėr), **Les.** Bands of armed adventurers who ravaged France and Belgium in the 15th century, beginning c1435. They were called Écorcheurs, or flayers, probably because they "not only waylaid and plundered their victims, but stripped them of every vestige of clothing, leaving them nothing but their shirts."

Eden (ē′dẹn), **Richard.** English translator; b. c1521; d. 1576. His name as a translator is appended to many books on geography, travels, navigation, and the like. Among these are *A Treatyse of the Newe India,* which is the first intelligible description in English of America, and *Decades of the Newe World* (1555, mainly a translation of Peter Martyr's work).

Edward. [Titles, 1st Duke of **Cornwall** and Prince of **Wales,** Prince of **Aquitaine and Gascony;** called the **Black Prince;** occasionally known as **Edward IV** and **Edward of Woodstock.**] Eldest son of Edward III and Philippa of Hainaut; b. at Woodstock, England, July 15, 1330; d. at Westminster, June 8, 1376. He was the first man in England to hold a dukedom; a notable soldier, he fought at Crécy, at the siege of Calais, and for the victory at Poitiers. He was the father of Richard II of England.

Edward IV (of *England*). King of England (1461–1470 and 1471–1483); b. at Rouen, France, probably April 28, 1442; d. April 9, 1483. He was the son of Richard Plantagenet, 3rd Duke of York, and Cecily Neville, daughter of the earl of Westmorland. He was known as the Earl of March before his accession. In the Wars of the Roses, he defeated the forces of Henry VI at Mortimer's Cross (1461) and had himself proclaimed king March 4, 1461. In the struggles that followed he was deposed in 1470, and Henry was briefly restored, but was again defeated, imprisoned in the Tower where he subsequently died, probably murdered at Edward's order, and Edward became king again. Except for the quarrels with his cousin, the earl of Warwick, and his brother, the duke of Clarence, his domestic position was secure. In 1475 he received a subsidy from Louis XI for withdrawing from a French war. The subsidy enabled him to bypass Parliament when he needed money, and his rule assumed the tone of a Renaissance despotism. He was a patron of the New Learning and a friend of Caxton. By his wife Elizabeth Woodville he had two sons, Edward V and Richard of York, the Tower princes, and five daughters. In his later years he was profligate and self-indulgent. Of his many mistresses Jane Shore was the most notorious.

Edward V (of *England*). King of England from April to June, 1483; b. in Westminster Abbey, London, November 2 or 3, 1470; murdered in the Tower of London, 1483. He was the son of Edward IV by Elizabeth Woodville. He succeeded to the throne under the regency of his uncle Richard, duke of Gloucester who, it was later alleged, secretly put him and his brother to death and usurped the government as Richard III. The mystery surrounding the deaths of Edward and his younger brother Richard, duke of York, has never successfully been solved. It has been asserted since the time of Henry VII, who had most to gain by the assertion, that Richard III procured their deaths through Sir James Tyrell after the Tower's constable, Sir Robert Brackenbury, refused to kill them.

Edward VI (of *England*). King of England (1547–1553); b. at Hampton Court, England, October 12, 1537; d. at Greenwich, near London, July 6, 1553. He was the son of Henry VIII and Jane Seymour. During his reign the forty-two articles of religion, and the Book of Common Prayer, compiled by Thomas Cranmer, were published.

Edward of Woodstock (wu̇d′stok). See **Edward** (1330–1376).

Edwards (ed′wạrdz), **Richard.** English dramatist; b. in Somersetshire, England; c1523; d. October 31, 1566. He wrote a drama *Damon and Pythias*, and a number of poems, some of which appeared in *The Paradyse of Daynty Devises*.

Egidio da Viterbo (ā-jē′dyō dä vē-ter′bō). [Also, **Egidio Canisio**; known in English as **Giles of Viterbo.**] Theologian and philosopher; b. at Viterbo, c1465; d. November, 1532. A famous preacher and theologian, he was noted for his learning, his Latin orations, and for his knowledge of languages. As to the latter, he is said to have known Latin, Greek, Hebrew, Chaldee, Turkish, Persian, and Arabic. In 1488 he entered the Augustinian Order, of which he was made general in 1507. In the address he made at the opening of the Fifth Lateran Council (1512), he courageously detailed the evils and corruption existing in the Church, and suggested methods to eradicate them. A follower of Marsilio Ficino, he attempted to reform Catholic theology on the basis of Plato, at the Lateran Council. Leo X elevated him to the College of Cardinals (1517) and he went as papal legate to the court of Charles V to win that monarch's help for a crusade against the Turks, a mission that was fruitless. A great and serious student, author of a commentary on the Book of the Sentences from a Platonic view, his writings also include many on miscellaneous topics, some lyrics, as well as many on theology.

Elisabeth von Lothringen (ā-lē′zä-bet fon lōt′ring-ẹn). [Also, **Elisabeth von Nassau.**] German princess and author; b. in Lorraine before 1400; d. at Saarbrücken, Germany, January 17, 1456. She undertook to adapt into German prose four French *chansons de geste*. These are notable as marking the transition from medieval epics to the prose novel of modern times.

Elizabeth I (of *England*) (ẹ-liz′ạbẹth). See **Elizabeth** (of *England*) (1533–1603).

Elizabeth (of *England*). [Also, **Elizabeth I, Elizabeth Tudor**; sometimes called **the Virgin Queen.**] Queen of England (1558–1603); b. at Greenwich Palace, London, September 7, 1533; d. at Richmond, Surrey, March 24, 1603. The daughter of Henry VIII and Anne Boleyn, to marry whom Henry divorced Catherine of Aragon, Elizabeth was regarded as illegitimate by Catherine's adherents and by Pope Clement VII. Thus her right to the throne was in question throughout the reign, and many plots against her were based on this question of usurpation, although her succession was set by act of parliament and Henry's will, which established that Henry should be followed by Edward VI, then Mary Tudor, and then Elizabeth, and she supported Mary's claim to the throne on the death of Edward VI. Elizabeth was educated by teachers who followed the new Humanism; she was expert in languages, modern as well as Greek and Latin, and was known as an eloquent speaker. Raised a Protestant, she followed a policy of tolerance after her accession. Her foreign policy was marked by an avoidance of open war, but she pursued a policy of aggressive resistance to the spread of the power of Spain. Unofficial war was waged constantly by privateers, bringing great fortunes to the royal treasury. During nearly thirty years of her reign England was at peace, until Philip II of Spain resolved to put a stop to English privateer raids on his shipping and to English support of the Dutch rebels, and dispatched the Invincible Armada; but the fleet of the Armada was caught off Calais and destroyed (1588). When Mary, Queen of Scots, fleeing the wrath of the Scots after becoming embroiled with John Knox, sought refuge in England, Elizabeth kept her in custody for nearly twenty years, and then reluctantly approved her execution because of the many plots to rescue Mary and to revive her claims to the thrones of both England and Scotland. Under Elizabeth English coinage was standardized on a silver basis; a Statute of Artificers, a labor code, was enacted; and the Poor Laws of 1597 made parishes responsible for their own poor, and set heavy penalties for vagabondage. The acts of uniformity and of supremacy establishing the Church of England were passed by parliament; the Archbishop of Canterbury drew up the Thirty Nine articles of convocation, and edited a new edition of the Bible known as the "Bishop's Bible." Elizabeth's spinsterhood, and the question of the succession, were recurring and continuing problems. Several diplomatic marriages were suggested but she would not risk her hold on the throne by making a foreign marriage, nor could she risk the scandal of a marriage to Robert Dudley, who was perhaps her one real love. Her affair with Robert Devereux, earl of Essex, towards the end of her life, ended unhappily with his rebellion and execution (1601). Elizabeth died, in 1603, the only English ruler of adult years since the Norman Conquest in 1066 who had not married. She recognized clearly the problem that would face the kingdom at her death and part of her reluctance to order the execution of Mary, Queen of Scots, is traceable to the fact that Mary's son, James VI of Scotland, was the logical successor to the English throne. On Elizabeth's death, he became James I of England.

The four and one half decades of Elizabeth's reign mark probably the most brilliant period in English history. The long period of official peace with other nations built up about Elizabeth a colorful court whose energies were turned to other matters than war, although freebooting and soldiering expeditions by her military captains gave glamour to their names. Literature reached a golden age in this time, a period marked with Elizabeth's name, although much of the so-called Elizabethan literature (for example much of the body of dramatic literature) dates from the period of the first Stuart kings (1603–1642). Such poets as Spenser, Drayton, and Gascoigne, playwrights like Marlowe, Greene, Lyly, and Shakespeare, essayists, romancers, and critics of the stamp of Raleigh, Bacon, and Sidney make the period incomparable in its brilliance. Elizabeth's captains and advisers, the Cecils, Dudley, the Walsinghams, Raleigh, Hawkins, Drake, the Bacons, while not uniformly successful, were nevertheless instrumental in carrying out her policies. England became in Elizabeth's time a world power, not yet as strong as Spain but soon to surpass her; the English navy grew to be second to none; commerce expanded and colonies were established where such explorers as Frobisher and Drake had gone.

Elizabeth of Valois (vȧ-lwȧ′, val′wä). [Also, **Isabella of Valois**; French, **Élisabeth de France**; Spanish, **Isabel.**] Queen of Spain; b. at Fontainebleau, France, April 13, 1545; d. at Madrid, October 3, 1568. She was the daughter of Henry II of France and Catherine de Médicis. She was betrothed to Don Carlos, son of Philip II of Spain, but after the death of Mary Tudor, Philip's second wife, she married the father in preference to the son.

Elizabeth Woodville (wu̇d′vil). Queen of Edward IV of England; b. probably in 1437; d. at Bermondsay, June 8, 1492. After the death of her first husband, she married in 1464, Edward IV by whom she became the mother of Edward V and Richard, Duke of York, both murdered in the Tower, and Elizabeth, queen of Henry VII.

Elphinstone (el′fin-stōn, -stọn), **William.** Scottish prelate and statesman; b. at Glasgow, 1431; d. at Edinburgh, October 25, 1514. He graduated with the degree of M.A. at the University of Glasgow in 1452, and subsequently studied law at the University of Paris, where he lectured for a time on this subject. He returned to Glasgow in 1474, was appointed bishop of Aberdeen in 1483, became lord privy seal in 1492, and in 1494 obtained a papal bull for the founding of King's College at Aberdeen, which was completed in 1506.

Elsevier (el'zẹ-vēr). See **Elzevir.**

Elyot (el'i-ọt, el'yọt), Sir **Thomas.** English scholar and diplomat; b. probably in Wiltshire, England, before 1490; d. at Carlton, Cambridgeshire, March 20, 1546. He was educated at home and thereafter held several public offices. In 1531 he published *The Boke named the Governour,* which related to the education of statesmen and was dedicated to Henry VIII. This secured royal patronage, and he was appointed ambassador to the emperor Charles V. In 1535 he was again sent to the emperor, following him to Naples. He was member of Parliament for Cambridge in 1542. He also wrote *Of the Knowledge which maketh a Wise Man* (1533), *Pasquil the Playne* (1533), *The Castel of Helth* (a lay medical guide, 1534), *Bibliotheca* (a Latin and English dictionary, 1538), *The Defence of Good Women* (1545), and others.

Elzevir or **Elsevier** or **Elzevier** (el'zẹ-vēr). Family of Dutch printers, celebrated especially for their editions of classical authors, and of French authors on historical and political subjects. Louis, the founder of the family was born (c1540) at Louvain, near Brussels, and died at Leiden, February 4, 1617. He had seven sons, five of whom followed his profession.

Emanuel I (of *Portugal*) (ẹ-man'ū-ẹl). [Also, **Emmanuel, Manuel;** Portuguese, **Manoel;** called **the Great** and **the Happy.**] King of Portugal; b. May 31, 1469; d. at Lisbon, December 13, 1521. He was a cousin of John II, whom he succeeded in 1495. He promoted the expeditions of Vasco da Gama, Cabral, Corte-Real, and Albuquerque.

Emilio (ā-mē'lyō), **Paolo.** [Latinized, **Paulus Aemilius.**] Historian; b. at Verona; d. at Paris, May 5, 1529. He was summoned to France in the reign of Charles VIII to write a history of French royalty, *De rebus gestis Francorum.*

Encina or **Enzina** (en-thē'nä), **Juan de la** (or **del**). Spanish poet; b. at or near Salamanca, Spain, c1469; d. at Salamanca, 1534. Often considered the founder of the modern Spanish drama, he published a collection of his dramatic and lyric poems *Cancionero.* His dramatic pieces are transitional between the church dramas and the secular theater.

Enciso (en-thē'sō), **Martín Fernández de.** Spanish lawyer; b. at Seville, Spain, c1470; d. after 1528. He went to America with Bastidas in 1500, and in the next fourteen years took part in colonizing expeditions. He returned to Spain and published *Suma de geografia* (1519) which gives the first account in Spanish of the New World.

Enzina (en-thē'nä), **Juan de la** (or **del**). See **Encina** or **Enzina, Juan de la** (or **del**).

Enzo (en'tsō). Warrior and poet; b. between 1220 and 1225; d. at Bologna, 1272. He was an illegitimate son of the emperor Frederick II (1194–1250), married a Sardinian princess, and was made king (1239) of Sardinia by his father. He was a gallant fighter in the wars his father waged with the popes, was defeated and taken prisoner (1249) in a war against the Bolognese, and was imprisoned at Bologna until his death. His confinement was not strict and he was able to cultivate his literary interests. In a poem attributed to him he salutes Tuscany and dreams of his homeland in Apulia, where his heart dwells night and day, as his spirit dwelt in the great days of chivalry.

Epistolae Obscurorum Virorum (e-pis'tọ-lē ob-skū-rō'rum vi-rō'rum). [English translation, *Letters of Obscure Men.*] Collection of forty-one anonymous letters, first published in 1515, satirizing the ignorance, hypocrisy, and licentiousness of the Roman Catholic monastics at the time of the Reformation, and addressed to Johann Reuchlin, the German humanist. It was occasioned by the controversy between Reuchlin and Johannes Pfefferkorn, a converted Jew, who advocated the destruction, as heretical, of the whole Jewish literature, except the Bible, and who was supported by the Dominicans of Cologne. The letters, written in bombastic dog-Latin that sharpened the sting of the satire, were in reply to a collection published by Reuchlin in 1514, *Epistolae Clarorum Virorum* (*Letters of Illustrious Men*). Pretending to support the Dominicans, they in fact attacked them and supported Reuchlin. The authorship of the letters is attributed by some to Ulrich von Hutten and Crotus Rubianus.

Equicola (ā-kwē'kō-lä), **Mario.** Humanist

and courtier; b. at Alvito, near Caserta, c1470; d. 1525. He studied at Naples and then with Ficino at Florence. Later he served many times as ambassador for Cardinal Ippolito d'Este and Duke Alfonso I of Ferrara. From Ferrara he went to Mantua, and was one of Isabella d'Este's courtiers. He, like Castiglione, idealized the role of a courtier and attempted to act the role as he envisioned it. He wrote a work embodying his ideas of the courtier and the ideal man, *De natura de amore*, begun in 1495 and finished thirty years later (Venice, 1525). He began the work in Latin but changed to the vernacular as a more suitable means of expressing his age and addressing his public. He also wrote a chronicle of Mantua, and a work on how to write verse in the vernacular.

Erasmus (ẹ-raz'mus), **Desiderius.** [Original name, **Gerhard Gerhards.**] Dutch classical and theological scholar and satirist; b. at Rotterdam, Netherlands, probably October 28, 1465; d. at Basel, Switzerland, July 12, 1536. He was the illegitimate son of Gerhard de Praet, a priest, was left an orphan at the age of 13, and was defrauded of his inheritance by his guardians, who compelled him to enter the monastery of Stein. He was ordained a priest in 1492. Under the patronage of the bishop of Cambrai, whose service he entered in 1494, he was enabled to study at the University of Paris. He subsequently visited the chief European countries, including England (1498–1499, 1505–1506, 1510–1514), where he met John Colet, who stirred his interest in the Church fathers, Thomas More, who became his lifelong friend, and other English humanists. While in England he wrote his famous *Moriae encomium* (*Praise of Folly*), a satirical work that, among other things, exposed the corruption and sloth of the clergy and later led to an acceleration of reform of the clergy. Its delightful satire does not spare human weakness outside the clergy. In Italy he worked at Venice with Aldus Manutius in the preparation of some of his own texts. His travels and writing brought him into contact with most of the scholars of Europe. In 1521 he settled at Basel, whence he removed to Freiburg in 1529. At Basel he was editor of the press of Johann Froben, which under Erasmus' lead became the first press of the Continent. Froben died in 1527 and Erasmus moved on. In this period were published a number of his series on the Church Fathers. Refusing all offers of ecclesiastical preferment, he devoted himself wholly to study and literary composition. He aimed to reform without dismembering the Roman Catholic Church, and at first favored, but subsequently opposed, the Reformation, and engaged in a controversy with Luther. A well-known saying is that Erasmus laid the egg that Luther hatched, but where Luther's reform spread to a fanatical evangelism, Erasmus desired reform from within. He wished to apply high intellectualism to wipe out the superstition he found fostered by the clerics, and to limit their power. His method, however, appealed only to his own level of humanistic learning; his satirical and humorous pen never reached the lower clergy with its message, and his friendship with the pope or Henry VIII of England was of no avail in such a struggle. His chief performance was an edition of the New Testament in Greek with a Latin translation, published in 1516. Besides this edition of the New Testament his most notable publications are the abovecited *Moriae encomium*, *Colloquies*, the *Adagia*, and the *Institutio principis christiani*.

Ercilla y Zúñiga (er-thē'lyä ē thö'nyē-gä), **Alonso de.** Spanish soldier and poet; b. at Madrid, August 7, 1533; d. there, November 29, 1594. He went to Chile with Jeronymo de Alderete, and lived an adventurous life there until 1562 when he returned to Spain. He published *La Araucana*, one of the finest epic poems in the Spanish language.

Ercole da Ferrara (er'kō-lā dä fer-rä'rä). See **Roberti, Ercole de'.**

Eric XIV (er'ik) (of *Sweden*). King of Sweden (1560–1568); b. December 13, 1533; d. February 26, 1577. He was the son of Gustavus Vasa, whom he succeeded in 1560. He elevated his mistress, Katrina Månsdotter, to the throne, after having made unsuccessful overtures of marriage to Queen Elizabeth of England and Mary, Queen of Scots. His violence and misgovernment caused his deposition (1568) by a conspiracy of the nobles headed by his brothers John and Charles. He was, according to the traditional story, put to death in prison by poison.

Erizzo (e'rēt-tsō), **Sebastiano.** Man of letters and scholar; b. at Venice, June 19, 1525; d. May 5, 1585. Of a patrician family, he was a senator and a member of the Council of Ten at Venice. His literary work included the translation of some of Plato's *Dialogues*, and commentaries on three canzoni of Petrarch, among others. He is best known, however, for his collection of novelle, *Sei giornate*, a youthful work completed soon after 1554 and published in 1567. It reveals, through the long, didactic, moralizing speeches put into the mouths of six youths who, in six days, relate the thirty-six stories in the collection, an early evidence of Catholic reaction to the corruption in the Church.

Erminia (er-mē′nyä). In Torquato Tasso's *Gerusalemme Liberata* (*Jerusalem Delivered*), the daughter of the king of Antioch. When the Crusaders under Godfrey of Bouillon captured the city she was taken prisoner and fell in love with her captor, Tancred. The Crusaders released her to the pagan king of Jerusalem and when, some time later, they arrived before the walls of the city, she stood on the walls with the pagan king and identified various knights for the king. She saw Tancred and pretended to hate him so that they "thought she wished to kill, who longed to kiss." Seeing the Amazon Clorinda fighting with Tancred, she is relieved when he is swept away by his fellow knights. After failing in an attempt to reach his tent and tend his wounds, she flees to the forest and becomes a shepherdess, and carves Tancred's name on many a tree. In the end, returning to the fallen city, she finds Tancred in a deep swoon from a wound and sets to work to cure him by her magic arts.

Erskine (ėr′skin), **John.** [Called **Erskine of Dun.**] Scottish religious reformer, and one of the leaders of the Reformation in Scotland; b. at Dun, near Montrose, Scotland, 1509; d. March 12, or June 17, 1591. He was the first to encourage Greek learning and a knowledge of the Greek language in Scotland. He invited John Knox to return to Scotland to promote the cause of the Protestant Reformation. He helped to compile the *Second Book of Discipline*.

Escalera (es-kä-lā′rä), **Antonio de.** Spanish priest; b. at Toledo, Spain, 1506; d. at Ciudad Real de Guayra, September 6, 1575. He went to Paraguay with Cabeza de Vaca in 1540, and was active as a leader of explorations and conquests. He wrote several memoirs relating to the Spanish conquest.

Espinosa (es-pē-nō′sä), **Gaspar de.** Spanish lawyer and soldier; b. at Medina del Campo, Spain, c1475; d. at Cusco, Peru, in August or September, 1537. He went to Darien with Pedrarias's expedition. Balboa was tried before him. Espinosa led many expeditions against the Indians, and founded Panama (1518).

Este (es′tā). One of the oldest and most celebrated of the princely houses of Italy, famous for the patronage of art and letters that made the court of Ferrara one of the most brilliant in Italy for 200 years; noted for generations for the number of bastards it produced, many of whom succeeded as rulers of Ferrara, and for the lurid crimes that stained its history. The family traces its origin to Oberto I Obertenghi, who was granted a patent by Berengarius II (king of Italy, 950–961) in 951. Oberto (died before October 15, 975) left several sons. His grandsons were carried off as prisoners to Germany, but one of them, Alberto Azzo I, was released and reinstated by the emperor Henry II in 1018, and from that time the family began to achieve prominence. Alberto's grandson, Alberto Azzo II (c996–1097), was invested by the emperor Henry III with Este and other Italian fiefs as marquess of Italy (Margrave of the Empire), was created duke of Milan, and adopted the name of Este from his castle near Padua. His first wife was Cunegund, sister of Guelf (Welf) III, duke of Carinthia and marquess of Verona. Their son Guelf (Welf) IV was adopted by Guelf III as his heir, and became duke of Bavaria under emperor Henry IV. The German branch of the family, represented by the houses of Brunswick and Hanover (which became the royal house of Great Britain), is descended from Guelf IV. By his second wife, Alberto Azzo II had several sons, and it was one of these, Folco I (d. c1136) who was the founder of the Italian branch. This branch continued with Obizzo I (d. 1193), son of Folco I, who fought against Frederick Barbarossa, was the first marquess of Este, and became powerful in Italian politics. His successor and grandson, Azzo VI (1170–1212) became overlord of Ferrara (1208) and head of the Guelph party there. His son Aldobrandino (d. 1215), lost his castle at Este to Padua, and a second son, Azzo VII Novello (d. 1264), submitted to the rival Ferrarese family, the Torelli, broke with the emperor Frederick II, whose loyal ally his father had been, fought against Ezzelino da Romano, Frederick's general, and defeated him, and at length with the help of Pope Gregory IX, he and the Guelphs regained control of the city. Obizzo II (1247–1293), a natural son of Rinaldo and the grandson of Azzo Novello, was named as Azzo's heir, and was one of the earliest of the many bastards who became lords of Ferrara. He became hereditary lord of Ferrara, and lord of Modena (1288) and of Reggio (1289). Obizzo was a tyrant, and after his death his sons and grandsons fought for control of Ferrara. Under his son Azzo VIII (d. 1308), Modena and Reggio rebelled. Azzo VIII had named his grandson Folco, legitimate son of his own natural son Fresco, his heir. Fresco, as regent, became involved in a struggle with his uncle Francesco and his cousins for Ferrara. Venice supported Fresco, Pope Clement V supported Francesco; and Fresco, outnumbered by the army of the papal legate gave up his and his son's claims to Ferrara to the Venetians. However, the papal army entered Ferrara and the city was won by the pope, who handed over its government to the Angevin, King Robert of Naples. Francesco was murdered by the king's men (1312), the Angevins were driven out by the Ferrarese (1317), the Estensi were recalled and were reconciled (1332) with the pope. He made three Estense brothers his vicars in the dominions of Ferrara (which the pope claimed as part of the Papal States): Rinaldo (d. 1335), Obizzo III (1294–1352), and Niccolò I (d. 1344). In the second half of the 14th century Petrarch was welcomed to Ferrara (1370) by Niccolò II (1338–1388), older brother of Petrarch's friend Ugo d'Este (1344–1370). At the end of the century members of the Strozzi family of Florence emigrated to Ferrara, where their branch produced the poets Tito Vespasiano Strozzi and Ercole Strozzi. Other families that flourished in the ambience of the Ferrarese court were the Boiardo and Ariosto. Obizzo III had a number of children (later legitimized) by a beautiful Bolognese lady whom he married on her deathbed (she was then buried with every honor). Of these, Alberto V was the father of a natural son, Niccolò III (1383–1441) who became lord of Ferrara and followed a policy of playing off his powerful neighbors against each other; a policy made necessary by the size and vulnerable location of Ferrara. Niccolò III acknowledged between twenty and thirty illegitimate children. He was succeeded, first, by his natural son Leonello (1407–1450), a cultivated prince justly noted for his patronage of arts and letters; second, by his natural son Borso (1413–1471), also a great patron, who became duke of Modena and Reggio in 1452, and just before his death fulfilled a lifelong ambition to be invested as duke of Ferrara; and third, by Ercole I (1431–1505), Niccolò's son by his third wife. Ercole continued the patronage of letters begun under his older half brothers, Boiardo being a close friend and one of his ministers and Ariosto receiving his aid. Ercole's daughter, Beatrice (1475–1497), was a noted noblewoman who has been credited with great diplomatic talents that she employed in the service of her husband, Ludovico il Moro, duke of Milan. Her sister Isabella (1474–1539), was the wife of Francesco Gonzaga, marquess of Mantua, and was one of the great Renaissance diplomats and patrons of art; Raphael and Andrea Mantegna were among those residing at her court and Baldassare Castiglione was one of her advisers. The heir of Ercole I was his son Alfonso I (1476–1534), whose second wife was Lucrezia Borgia. He was a famous commander of artillery. He at first sided with the pope against the Venetians, but after the treaty between Venice and the pope found himself fighting against the papal forces. He lost and regained Modena and Reggio and received the aid of the emperor Charles V in retaining them against papal wishes. His brother Ippolito I (1479–1520), Cardinal d'Este, was Ariosto's patron. Ercole II (1508–1559), succeeded Alfonso I to the dukedom. His wife was Renée, daughter of Louis XII of France, and was a source of great embarrassment to him because of her Protestant leanings and apparent conversion to Calvinism. His brother, Ippolito II (1509–1572), Cardinal d'Este, was archbishop of Milan and built the Tivoli palace near Rome known as the Villa d'Este. Alfonso II (1533–1597), patron of Tasso, attempted reforms in the Ferrarese army and in agriculture. He had no sons, and when he named as his successor his cousin Cesare (1533–1628), Clement VIII effectively achieved the elimination of the house of Este as an Italian power. He refused to recognize Cesare's rights, on the dubious ground of illegitimacy, and obtained cession of the Este possession of Ferrara to the papal dominions through treaty with Alfonso's sister Lucrezia. The family continued as dukes of the imperial fiefs of Modena and Reggio through the line founded by Cesare and recognized by the emperor Rudolf II. They moved their possessions, including their famous library (now the Biblioteca Estense) to Modena. Mary Beatrice, wife of James II of England, was a member of the family, her father being Alfonso IV (1534–1662), but the family was in eclipse and the male line died out with Ercole III Rinaldo (1727–1803). Monuments to Estense taste in architecture are the Castello Estense (or the Castello Vecchio), begun in 1385 for Niccolò II, and once the palace of the dukes; the campanile of the cathedral; the Palazzo del Paradiso of the University (founded 1391); the Church of S. Francesco; the Palazzo Schifanoia, built at the end of the 14th century and decorated by Cosimo Tura and Francesco Cossa; and the Palazzo dei Diamanti (so-called from the diamond-shaped bossages that adorn it), begun in 1492 for Sigismondo d'Este (now museums and an art gallery). Of the beautiful villas of Belfiore and Belriguardo, pleasure palaces enjoyed by the cultivated and often carefree courtiers of the Ferrarese court from the time of Leonello and especially in that of the Duchess Lucrezia, no trace remains.

Este, Alfonso I d'. Duke of Ferrara, Modena, and Reggio; b. at Ferrara, July 21, 1476; d. there, October 31, 1534. He was the son of Ercole I, duke of Ferrara, and Leonora of Aragon, and was the brother of Isabella and Beatrice d'Este. Before he was a year old he was betrothed to Anna Sforza, daughter of Galeazzo Maria Sforza, duke of Milan. He was married to her in 1491; the gentle, well-loved girl died childless on November 30, 1497. At the end of the year 1500 Pope Alexander VI proposed to Ercole I that Alfonso marry his daughter Lucrezia Borgia. This alliance was inspired by the pope's wish to keep Ferrara friendly while his son Cesare Borgia subjugated, in the name of the Church, lands in the Romagna. Ercole and all the members of his family were appalled at the prospect of allying their ancient house to the upstart Borgias. Ercole resisted the match as long as he dared. But the activities of the pope's son presented a threat to Ferrara, and rather than risk the pope's enmity Ercole felt himself compelled to accept the marriage. He drove a hard bargain in giving his consent, and the pope at length grudgingly agreed to his demands. Alfonso, however, balked at marrying the notorious Lucrezia. His hesitation was understandable: both her previous marriages had been terminated to suit changes in papal policy; her first husband had been publicly humiliated and her second husband had been murdered. It was only when his father threatened to marry her himself if Alfonso persisted in his refusal, that Alfonso gave way. The marriage took place at Rome at the end of December, 1501, with Alfonso's brother Ferrante standing in as his proxy. Lucrezia set out for Ferrara with her retinue in January. Alfonso rode out from Ferrara in disguise to intercept his bride on her way and find out what she was like before her ceremonial entry into Ferrara. He spent two hours in her company and was completely charmed by her. She ultimately bore him five children, and when she died (June 24, 1519) he grieved deeply over the loss of his dear friend and companion. Some time after Lucrezia's death he took Laura Dianti as his mistress. She bore him a son, Alfonso, marquess of Montecchio, who founded the line of the Estense family at Modena.

On the death of Ercole I (1505), Alfonso succeeded as duke. Much of his long reign was occupied by war. The chief threats to his state were Venice, the ancient enemy, and the popes. Julius II, Leo X, and Clement VII each tried to win Ferrara. Alfonso defended it with valor and skill. He had helped Julius II defeat the Venetians in 1509, but when the pope subsequently allied himself with Venice to drive out the French he declared Alfonso, an ally of France, a rebel who had forfeited his duchy, excommunicated him, and laid Ferrara under an interdict (1510). Alfonso fought back. He helped the Bolognese to drive out Julius (1511). They pulled down from its place above the door of S. Petronio the great bronze statue of Julius that Michelangelo had made and gave it to Alfonso. He preserved the head, which he kept in his own collection, but broke up and melted down the rest of the statue, and from it cast a cannon that he named the *Giulia*. Alfonso aided Gaston de Foix to defeat the papal forces at the battle of Ravenna (April, 1512), but the French drew little profit from the victory, and were soon forced to retreat from Italy. Alfonso went to Rome to make his peace with Julius. The pope absolved him, but took away Reggio. No agreement could be reached and Alfonso feared for his safety. At the battle of Ravenna he had captured Fabrizio Colonna and had treated his prisoner with great consideration. Now, in his hour of need, Fabrizio defied the pope and helped Alfonso to escape from the city in disguise. He conducted him to Marino and entertained him there until he could withdraw into Lombardy and thence back to Ferrara to prepare its defenses. Julius died before he could take any steps concerning Ferrara. Leo X, who succeeded him, made many fair promises to Alfonso, among them that he would restore Modena and Reggio to him, but Leo did not keep his promises. On the contrary, he became as dangerous an enemy as Julius had been. The emperor Charles V promised Ferrara to the pope, and Leo excommunicated Alfonso. Again, Alfonso was saved by the pope's death. He was so grateful that he had a coin struck with his own head on one side, and on the reverse a representation of a shepherd rescuing a lamb from the mouth of a lion, and the inscription, *De manu leonis.* Adrian VI absolved him and promised to restore his lands, but died before he could accomplish it. The new pope, another Medici, Clement VII, had designs on Ferrara. Alfonso, seeking to steer a safe course through the tortuous seas of French and Spanish ambitions in Italy, aided the imperial forces to pass the Po, and when they sacked Rome (May, 1527) took the opportunity to take back Modena and Reggio. Shortly afterward, in an approach to France, he betrothed his heir Ercole to Renée, daughter of the late king, Louis XII. When Clement and Charles V made peace, Alfonso was able to get his envoys to the emperor first, and forestalled Clement in his demands for Ferrara. The emperor confirmed Alfonso's title to Ferrara, Modena, and Reggio, and the pope was forced to accept his decision.

Alfonso was an able administrator, firm, economical, and calm. He was noted for his interest in artillery, and the fine examples of it produced under him were famous throughout Europe. He made Ferrara one of the best fortified cities of Italy and skillfully defended it on many occasions. In general, he was noted for his impartial administration of justice, but showed himself unrelenting and vindictive in the punishment he meted out to his brothers Ferrante and Giulio (see **Este, Giulio d'**) and singularly unconcerned in bringing to justice the murderer of Ercole Strozzi (see **Strozzi, Ercole**). He cared little for extravagant display and spectacular ceremonies, but loved the performances of plays for which Ferrara was noted, and gave enthusiastic encouragement to drama. In his time Ferrara was a center of the arts and letters under his wife Lucrezia; many of the most gifted men in Italy were drawn to Ferrara, rather through its tradition than through Alfonso's own achievements. But he understood and appreciated the arts, was an accomplished violinist, and was a generous and sympathetic patron of Ariosto. He was also a patron of the painter Dosso Dossi, and commissioned Titian to make several paintings on mythological subjects for him, Alfonso himself choosing the subjects and telling the painter exactly what he wanted. He encouraged the manufacture of majolica, threw pots himself, and pursued his interest in the mechanical arts. Under Alfonso, Ferrara continued to be one of the most brilliant courts in Italy, and as he was not extravagant, it was also a prosperous duchy.

Este, Alfonso II d'. Duke of Ferrara, Modena, and Reggio; b. at Ferrara, November 28, 1533; d. there, October 27, 1597. He was the son of Ercole II, duke of Ferrara, and Renée of France. He received an excellent literary and courtly education in the manner of the time, knew Latin and French, and was a devotee of the hunt, of tourneys, plays, and festivals. Perhaps due to his mother's influence he was always warmly attached to France. In defiance of his father's orders, he went there when he was 18 and distinguished himself in the wars of his cousin, Henry II. Alfonso's father made peace (May, 1558) with the emperor through the good offices of Cosimo I, duke of Tuscany. To strengthen relations with Cosimo (who guaranteed the peace) Alfonso was married to Cosimo's daughter Lucrezia, but three days later returned to France, continued fighting in Henry's wars and was at the French king's side when he received the injury in a tourney from which he died a few days later (July 10, 1559). He was in Lorraine when his father died (October, 1559) and returned immediately to Ferrara to assume the government of the duchy. One of his first acts was to release his great-uncle

Giulio from the prison in the castle where he had been entombed for fifty-three years, a victim of Alfonso's grandfather Alfonso's wrath. Alfonso came to power in Ferrara in the same year in which the Treaty of Cateau-Cambrésis brought peace and Spanish domination to Italy. The long, peaceful reign of this brave and generally intelligent prince was embittered by a sterile rivalry with Florence for prestige and precedence in affairs of the peninsula. His wife Lucrezia having died (April, 1561), Alfonso married (1565) Barbara of Austria, daughter of the emperor Ferdinand I. The result of tying his fortunes to those of the emperor in order to establish his precedence over Cosimo was that he annoyed the pope, who was already displeased with him for his toleration of the Jews and the Moors, and for his failure to press the Inquisition at Ferrara. In 1567 Pope Pius V issued a bull that prohibited the investiture of illegitimate heirs with church lands. This was aimed directly at Alfonso and Ferrara. He had no children, legitimate or illegitimate, but he had a cousin Cesare, a grandson of Alfonso's grandfather Alfonso I and his mistress Laura Dianti. In succeeding years and under successive popes Alfonso tried to reach an agreement by which Cesare could be his heir to Ferrara. His efforts were fruitless. (His wife Barbara died in 1572. He married Margherita Gonzaga in 1579 but she too remained childless, and it was thought Alfonso's inability to father children resulted from an accident in his youth.) He won a promise from the emperor Rudolf II to invest Cesare with the imperial fiefs of Modena and Reggio, but his last years were saddened by the uncertainty of the succession of Ferrara. The popes, knowing there was no legitimate heir, refused to accept anything less. With the death of Alfonso the male line of the house of Este at Ferrara was extinct. The duchy devolved to the Church and ceased henceforth to play a significant role in Italy. Modena and Reggio passed to Cesare, who founded the branch of the family in those cities. Alfonso had presided over a brilliant court; he was a patron of art and letters. Tasso was a member and an idol of that court. The poet read his newly completed *Gerusalemme Liberata* to the duke and his sister Lucrezia in the summer of 1575, and Alfonso was as patient as possible with Tasso to prevent him from going to Florence and dedicating his great poem to the Medici. The rumor that Tasso's romantic interest in Alfonso's sister Leonora won the duke's displeasure was not true. Tasso was finally confined in the hospital of S. Anna because his mental condition was such that it was dangerous for him and for others as long as he remained at liberty. To maintain his splendid court Alfonso had recourse to heavy taxes and fines, and the chasm between the luxurious life of the court and the overburdened poor widened ominously. With the death of Alfonso the court that had been one of the most brilliant in Europe for 200 years went into eclipse.

Este, Baldassare d'. [Also called **Baldassare da Reggio.**] Ferrarese painter; d. c1504. He was one of the illegitimate sons of Niccolò III d'Este, and thus was the half brother of Leonello, Borso, and Duke Ercole. Highly esteemed at Ferrara as a painter in his own day, possibly because of his court connections, he won fame at Milan as a portrait painter. There he painted portraits of Duke Galeazzo Maria Sforza and of his duchess Bona of Savoy. He returned to Ferrara in 1469 and was warmly welcomed by brother Borso, of whom he became the chief portrait painter. Borso commissioned him to repaint the heads of a number of the portraits that appeared in the panels in the Hall of the Months in the Schifanoia palace. In carrying out the commission, Baldassare is said to have repainted thirty-six heads of Borso alone. On the death of Borso (1471) and the accession of Ercole, who was legitimate, the climate of Ferrara changed for Baldassare. He no longer had a salary, and received fewer commissions. Before 1489 he was given an official position at Reggio under the poet Boiardo. Having left Reggio because of a criminal attack on his daughter, after 1497 he was captain of a fortress outside the walls of Ferrara. Of the portraits and altarpieces he is known to have painted, there remains a *Profile Portrait of Borso d'Este*, Milan (Castello Sforzesco) and a *Portrait of Francesco Gonzaga as a Boy*, National Gallery, Washington.

Este, Beatrice d'. Duchess of Bari and of Milan; b. at Ferrara, June 29, 1475; d. at Milan, January 3, 1497. She was the daughter of Ercole I, duke of Ferrara, and Leonora of Aragon, and was the sister of Isabella d'Este and Alfonso I of Ferrara. As a child she was taken to Naples by her mother and remained eight years at the court of her grandfather, King Ferrante. At Naples and at Ferrara she was carefully educated; she learned Latin, Greek, and Roman history, was taught dancing at an early age, and had lessons on the lute and the viol. At Ferrara she was surrounded by some of the most learned men and gifted poets of the day. Ludovico il Moro, wishing to ally himself with Ferrara, asked for the hand of her sister Isabella, but she had already been betrothed to Francesco Gonzaga of Mantua. Ercole proposed that Ludovico marry Beatrice instead. The marriage was twice postponed, as Ludovico was deeply in love with his cultivated mistress, Cecilia Gallerani. At the end of December, 1490, in the midst of a terribly severe winter, Beatrice and her mother set out for Milan for the wedding. The marriage of the 15-year-old Beatrice to the 38-year-old Ludovico took place at Pavia on January 17, 1491 (the date was chosen by Ludovico's astrologer), and was followed by a splendid ceremony at Milan. The lawful duke of Milan was Ludovico's nephew Gian Galeazzo Sforza. His wife was Isabella of Aragon, granddaughter of King Ferrante, who had been Beatrice's playmate at Naples. However, Ludovico was effective ruler of Milan, and he and Beatrice were the center of a brilliant court. (Isabella was aware of the secondary place that she and her husband occupied, and in time complained bitterly to her father. This led to a rupture of the friendly relations between Milan and Naples, and was one of the causes why Ludovico encouraged Charles VIII of France to invade Italy.) Beatrice, with her high spirits and enthusiasm for every pleasure became the soul of the court, and Ludovico found himself entranced by her accomplishments, her liveliness, and her energy. He made provision for his mistress (married her to a count and gave her a splendid house), and devoted himself to his young wife. Their brilliant and extravagant court was the gayest in Italy. Ludovico and Beatrice were both music lovers; she had her own singers who accompanied her when she journeyed outside Milan. Poets, men of letters, the finest artists and architects came to Milan. Beatrice reveled in the hunting parties (where she showed reckless courage), the ceremonies and festivals for which Leonardo da Vinci supplied the decorations, the plays and other entertainments, and the card games, in which she was a consistent winner. Her wardrobe and jewels were magnificent. In May, 1493, when she was not yet 18, she served as her husband's envoy on a delicate mission to Venice (and was pleased to write him that as she walked in the square at Venice, the bystanders pointed to her jewels and her clothes and said that "was the wife of Signor Ludovico"). Later she was with him when he made arrangements for peace after the withdrawal of Charles VIII from Italy (1495) and was reputed to have shown much skill and courage in the negotiations. She bore two sons: Ercole (Massimiliano) and Francesco. The last year of her life was saddened when Ludovico took a new mistress, Lucrezia Crivelli. Yet when Beatrice so unexpectedly died in childbirth he was heartbroken; and no one questioned the sincerity of his grief. The funeral monument he had prepared for her and for himself, was placed in his favorite Church of S. Maria delle Grazie. It was later broken up, and her effigy is in the Certosa di Pavia. The representation of her that Leonardo da Vinci added to an existing fresco in the refectory of S. Maria delle Grazie has almost entirely disappeared. It is the only portrait Leonardo is known to have painted of his patron's wife.

Este, Borso d'. First duke of Modena and Reggio, and of Ferrara; b. 1413; d. in the Castello Vecchio at Ferrara, August 19, 1471. He was the third son of Niccolò III d'Este and his Sienese mistress Stella dell' Assassino. His own brothers were Ugo, beheaded for adultery with his father's wife, and Leonello. As a youth he fought in the service of Venice and of Milan. When Leonello succeeded Niccolò III as lord of Ferrara (1441), Borso, a loyal and affectionate brother, returned to Ferrara and became his trusted adviser. On the death of Leonello (1450), he succeeded as 14th marquess of Ferrara, although Leonello had left a legitimate son, Niccolò, for whom his partisans unsuccessfully sought to gain the succession. In 1452 the emperor Frederick III passed through Ferrara on his way to his coronation at Rome. Borso entertained him lavishly. On the way back from Rome Frederick stopped again at Ferrara and rewarded him; he invested Borso as duke of the imperial fiefs of Modena and Reggio (Frederick sold titles wholesale on his Italian journey). The investiture took place on Ascension day, before the cathedral at Ferrara, and was a magnificent display of the sumptuous costumes and splendid ceremony that Borso loved. Enea Silvio Piccolomini (later Pius II) gave an address, in Italian as Borso was not learned in Latin. Borso followed the policy of his predecessor brother and of his father: the keynote of his reign was peace. Under him Ferrara was free from war and became a meeting ground for those who would mediate the quarrels of the other Italian states. In 1459 Pius II visited Ferrara on his way to the Congress of Mantua which had been called to promote a crusade against the Turks. Borso rode out to meet him (accompanied by seven Estense bastards, none of whom was his), and did homage to the pope. His welcome was not disinterested: his dearest wish was to be invested by the pope as duke of Ferrara. Borso promised great things for the pope's crusade, in the hopes of attaining his wish (but did not deliver when the time came). The earlier warm relations he enjoyed with the pope cooled. Pius suspected him of secretly favoring the enemies of King Ferrante of Naples, whom Pius had recognized as the legitimate king. He was also offended by Borso's demands for the remission of the tribute annually paid by Ferrara to the Church. Pius clearly understood the reasons for Borso's lavish welcome, and commented that Borso would have attained some of his desires if he had known how to ask for them. In 1466 Borso aided the Florentine exiles who were attempting to overthrow Piero de' Medici. The attempt was unsuccessful and relations with the Medici became somewhat strained. Two years later a plot against Borso's life was exposed to him by his brother Ercole, whose aid the conspirators had sought to enlist. Whether there was a serious plot was doubtful, but those accused lost their lands and their heads. In 1471 Borso's dearest wish was realized. Pope Paul II invited him to Rome for his investiture as duke of Ferrara. Borso set out for Rome in March with a large and sumptuously clad suite—hounds, horses in gorgeous trappings, pages in livery, archers, trumpeters and musicians, courtiers and prelates, doctors of the university and ambassadors robed in sable and crimson velvet, gold brocade mantles trimmed with ermine, scarlet silk, and wearing magnificent jeweled collars about their necks, accompanied him. The journey from Ferrara to Rome took twenty days, as Borso was honored and entertained in cities on the way. Borso, "all joyous and jocund and lordly, . . . adorned with gold and gems," rode "on that great charger that flashed back the light gleaming in those wondrously worked and precious trappings." The investiture, in the presence of cardinals and prelates, foreign ambassadors, noble men and ladies of many courts, took place on Easter Sunday (April 14, 1471), in St. Peter's Basilica. "Both the chief actors (Borso and Pope Paul)—old men, broken down in health and walking already in the shadow of the grave—entered into the spirit of the pageantry with a kind of mystical enthusiasm" (Gardner, *Dukes & Poets in Ferrara*). Borso spent many festive, ceremony-filled days at Rome. On his return to Ferrara he was seriously ill. His nephew Niccolò (Leonello's son) swept into the city in an attempt to win control but was repulsed by the energy of Ercole, who as the presumed successor of Borso had the most to lose. Borso recovered enough to order both Niccolò and Ercole to retire from the city. Niccolò went to Mantua; Ercole, who left briefly, soon returned to Ferrara to make his preparations, as Borso was obviously dying. On the 19th of August Borso died. Ferrara was bowed in mourning. "It seemed," wrote the chronicler, "that our Saviour God had died a second time." He was buried in the Carthusian monastery of S. Cristoforo that he had founded.

The genial Borso was an experienced soldier and an able administrator. He preserved peace, maintained order within his state and friendly relations with his neighbors. Ferrara flourished. He upheld the laws and was praised for his justice, although he was not always aware of the injustices perpetrated by his favorites and officials. His liberality was proverbial, "Whoso would find Heaven open, let him experience the liberality of Duke Borso." When punishment was in order he was rigid, yet he could forgive a true penitent and be forbearing to an enemy. He increased the revenues of his state without raising taxes. He did so by relentless collection of taxes ("Suck all the juice you can") and by the imposition of a number of fines, such as that for blasphemy, which were rigorously collected. (The system of farming out the collection of taxes and fines, as well as some other fiscal duties, to favorites, friends, or the highest bidder, transferred the onus of a harsh system from Borso to his officials, who were often desperately and dangerously hated, while Borso was hailed for his generosity.) He was truly religious; his personal life was blameless; he raised the moral tone of the court. He never married, and it was said he begot no children so that no son of his could interfere with the succession of his beloved younger brother Ercole. Not a scholar himself (his passions were the hunt, field sports, the pleasures of country living, and elaborate and spectacular ceremonies and processions), he was a generous patron of art and letters. Since he did not know Latin, works were translated into Italian for him. In place of the Latin and Greek epics so loved by the humanists, Borso and his carefree courtiers enjoyed the tales of Lancelot and Guinevere, of Tristan and Isolde. Their preference for the romances of the Knights of the Round Table prepared the ground for the later great works of Boiardo and Ariosto. Among those who enjoyed his patronage were Battista Guarino (son of Guarino da Verona), Lascaris and other Greek exiles, Tito Vespasiano Strozzi, who wrote elegant Latin verse, translated some of Petrarch's *De vita solitaria* for Borso, and served as one of his Twelve Councillors (in which position he was thoroughly detested by the people). Boiardo wrote his first works—a book of Latin eclogues and one of Italian lyrics—in Borso's time. A school of Ferrarese painting, influenced by Jacopo Bellini, Andrea Mantegna, and the Flemish painter Roger Van der Weyden, came to be identifiable from the time of Borso. He invited Piero della Francesca to Ferrara, "where he painted many apartments in the palace," but, adds Vasari, "not one of his pictures is still to be seen." He added to Schifanoia, originally built as a hunting lodge in 1391, and lived there in the summer. Between 1467 and 1470 Cosimo Tura and Francesco Cossa, definitively Ferrarese painters, frescoed the walls of the great hall in Schifanoia. The decorations, which are in three courses, included panels on the twelve months of the year, the signs of the zodiac, allegorical figures, scenes of country and city life, of the court and of the camp, and scenes from the life of Borso, the jovial, presiding genius of it all. The decorations present a pageant of Ferrarese life of the time. Frescoes, somewhat damaged, remain on only two of the four walls originally painted. Borso also encouraged the minor arts. His Bible, the *Bibbia di Borso*, is one of the marvels of the art of the miniaturist. Begun in 1455, illuminators worked seven years to decorate its more than 600 parchment pages. (It is now in the Biblioteca Estense at Modena.) Pius II, as Enea Silvio Piccolomini, wrote of Borso as he knew him in 1445, "The Ferrarese worship him almost as God. He is more handsome than words can tell, genial and modest, distinguished for his liberality, robust in his body and without any blemish." As shown in the frescoes at Schifanoia, his good looks passed; he became heavy and coarsened as he grew older, but he kept to the end his geniality, his liberality, his love of pomp and display. He spent lavishly on the finest horses, falcons, and hunting dogs in Italy. He loved and bought gorgeous raiment and dazzling jewels; huge hunts and long delightful stays in the country gave him the greatest pleasure; and he enjoyed all these without weakening his treasury. Ferrara was never again to know the serene and happy days of Leonello and Duke Borso. "No sovereigns of the 15th century shed so little blood as did these two."

Este, Ercole I d'. Second duke of Ferrara, Modena, and Reggio; b. at Ferrara, October 26, 1431; d. there, January 25, 1505. He was the son of Niccolò III d'Este and his third wife Ricciarda di Saluzzo, and was Niccolò's first legitimate son. He was sent to Naples (1445), a few years after his older half brother Leonello succeeded (1441) Niccolò as marquess of Ferrara, to remove him as a possible rival. (His younger brother Sigismondo was politely banished from Ferrara for the same reason.) Ercole remained at the court of Naples, where he had a great reputation for gallantry and courtesy, until 1463. In that year he was recalled to Ferrara by his half brother Borso, who had succeeded Leonello in 1450, and was made governor of the duchy of Modena. He took part in the war that the Florentine exiles waged, ineffectively, against Piero de' Medici in 1467, and received a wound at the battle of Molinella that caused him to walk with a limp the rest of his life. As his brother Borso was dying, an attempt was made by Niccolò, legitimate son of Leonello, to get into a position to seize power. Borso recovered enough to order him, as well as Ercole, out of the city. Ercole soon returned, and by the time Borso actually died

(August 19, 1471), had made his preparations. In the company of 600 soldiers, he gathered the nobles and courtiers of Ferrara about him and, robed in the ducal regalia, went with them to the cathedral, where he announced Borso's death and proclaimed himself as his successor. Niccolò, who had lived a rather dissolute life and was not nearly so clever as Ercole, later (1476), entered the city with 700 soldiers when Ercole was absent and tried to raise rebellion against him. His attempt was a complete failure; the Ferrarese were loyal to Ercole. Ercole's brother Sigismondo and his half brother Rinaldo crushed the rebels in a brief and bloody struggle. Niccolò escaped, but was captured and beheaded (September 3, 1476). Ercole had learned of the attempted revolt but the number of soldiers who had come into the city with Niccolò being exaggerated, he hesitated and did not return at once. It was thanks to the energy and courage of his wife and his brothers that the rebellion was so quickly put down. In succeeding days, after he had returned, prisoners were killed, mutilated, or given up to ransom for their part in the uprising. It was thought that Venice was back of Niccolò's attempt, as the Serene Republic, hoping to win Ferrara for itself, welcomed disorders within the city that would give Venice an excuse for interfering.

In 1473 Ercole had married Leonora of Aragon, daughter of King Ferrante of Naples. Matteo Maria Boiardo, Ercole's friend and minister, was one of those who went to Naples to fetch Leonora to Ferrara. She was entertained nobly in many cities on her journey to Ferrara, the festivities and banquet provided by Cardinal Pietro Riario at Rome being notable for their extravagant luxury. Corio describes the changes of costume during the course of the meal, the livery of the pages, the silver gilt oranges and castles of sugar, the game and fruit that loaded the tables. Leonora was a highly cultivated lady, of great piety, courage, and force of character, who brought charm to Ercole's court and elevated its moral tone. She had the complete confidence of her husband, governed his duchy wisely in his absence, and won the devotion of his subjects by her own piety, gentleness, and generosity. Extant letters from Ercole testify to his profound attachment and admiration for his wife, his trust in her judgment, and his belief that theirs was an affectionate and equal partnership. She bore him Isabella (1474–1539), Beatrice (1475–1497), Alfonso (1476–1534), Ferrante (1477–1540), Ippolito (1479–1520), and Sigismondo (1480–1524). Except for one lapse, when Leonora stayed too long visiting her father in Naples, Ercole was faithful. Leonora died in October, 1493, and was deeply mourned by the Ferrarese. Ercole was not at her side. He had wanted to start back from Milan when he heard of the seriousness of her illness, but was detained by Ludovico il Moro, who urged him to wait for a more favorable position of the stars.

Because of its location and size, Ferrara was vulnerable to the ambitions of its neighbors. As had his father and his older brothers, Ercole sought to remain on friendly terms with the other states, especially Naples and Milan. He betrothed (1477) his infant son Alfonso to Anna Sforza, daughter of Galeazzo Maria Sforza, duke of Milan, promised his daughter Isabella to Francesco, son of the marquess of Mantua, and his daughter Beatrice to Ludovico il Moro of Milan. But he was not successful in keeping Ferrara at peace. Following the Pazzi Conspiracy (1478) at Florence, he aided the Florentines in the war Sixtus IV and Naples waged against them, and thus won the enmity of the pope. In 1482 Sixtus and Venice waged war on him. The war went badly for Ferrara; her enemies were at the walls. When the pope was forced to withdraw some of his troops to protect Rome, Ercole hoped to recover some of the lands he had lost to Venice. Suddenly Ludovico il Moro, one of Ercole's allies, entered into secret negotiations with the Venetians and made a peace with them by which it was agreed that Venice would keep the lands she had won from Ferrara. Ercole could do nothing but accept the peace, made at Bagnolo (August 7, 1484). This was the last war of Ercole's reign. By skill, or as some said, by double dealing, he managed to keep Ferrara out of the wars that despoiled Italy. In 1493 he joined the League of Rome, Venice, and Milan, but when Charles VIII invaded Italy (1494), he remained neutral, furnishing provisions to both sides alike. He refused to join the league of 1495 against France, and advised that Charles VIII be allowed free passage to leave Italy. His second son, Ferrante, was in the service of Charles. His eldest son, Alfonso, was sent with 150 men to aid the Milanese; he had sons in both camps at the battle of Fornovo (July 6, 1495). Nevertheless, he kept the friendship of Charles VIII, accompanied him back to Lyons, and was one of the mediators for the restoration of peace. When Louis XII marched into Milan in 1499 he saw to it that Ferrara did not suffer any evil consequences; Louis was his ally. Shortly thereafter, he was threatened by the activities of Cesare Borgia in the Romagna. Before the end of 1500 Alexander VI proposed that his daughter Lucrezia Borgia become the wife of Ercole's son and heir Alfonso. Ercole and the members of his family were appalled. The Estensi were among the oldest princely families of Italy. The Borgias were Johnny-come-latelies. Lucrezia had already had two husbands, the first of whom was publicly humiliated and the second murdered. The scandals connected with her name rang up and down Italy. Ercole resisted the marriage with all his might. He appealed to his ally, Louis XII, for support. Louis, however, was at the moment in need of a dispensation from the pope that would allow him to divorce his wife and marry his predecessor's widow (for her lands). His best advice to Ercole was to drive a hard bargain. Ercole proceeded to do so. He made such terms as he thought the pope could not possibly accept, yet he did not dare to refuse the pope and make Ferrara a prey to the pope's powerful son Cesare. He asked for the remission of the tribute Ferrara annually paid the Church, for 200,000 ducats as Lucrezia's dowry, for the cession of Cento and La Pieve to Ferrara, for the right to name the bishop of Ferrara, and for benefices for members of the Estense family. He and the pope haggled over the arrangements, but with Lucrezia enthusiastically seconding Ercole's demands, the pope gradually conceded all of them and Ercole was forced to accept the marriage. The other principal in the affair, Alfonso, resisted. Nothing, he said, would induce him to marry Lucrezia. In fear for his state, Ercole threatened that if Alfonso refused to marry Lucrezia, he would marry her himself. Alfonso yielded. The marriage by proxy at Rome was followed by one at Ferrara on February 2, 1502. Ercole came to be truly fond of his daughter-in-law, as did all the Estensi, but the political benefits of the alliance came to nothing, for Pope Alexander VI died the following year. Julius II invited Ercole to enter a league with the papacy and France against Venice, but before anything much could be done about it Ercole died.

Ercole was an able administrator and a lover of peace, but was less fortunate in keeping it at Ferrara than his brothers. He was also more cruel and unscrupulous than they, and less generous. He raised taxes and relentlessly collected them, even in times of famine or plague. Not a scholar himself, he was a generous patron of letters and the arts. He added to the Estense library and supported the university. Battista Guarino was a professor of letters; Aldus Manutius and Giovanni Pico della Mirandola were students. Printing was introduced at Ferrara during his reign. He was an enthusiast for vernacular poetry; Boiardo was his friend and favorite poet; the poet Antonio Tebaldeo was his secretary. A translation of the *Menaechmi* of Plautus was produced at Ferrara in 1486, and led to a revival of the drama. Thereafter no festivity at Ferrara was complete without a performance of one of the plays of Plautus or Terence; Ercole had a passion for the plays. Between the acts, *moreschi* (*ballets*) with elaborate costumes, plots, and casts were given that sometimes seemed more interesting and important than the comedies themselves. While Ercole and his court enjoyed the plays and the sumptuous ceremonies that they loved, the life of his people was hard. His officials were sometimes cruel and unjust, and the system of collecting taxes by farming them out led to great and uncontrolled abuses. Ercole himself became more benign as he aged, and much more pious, as his fellow townsman Savonarola admitted. He was exceedingly superstitious. In the Church of Sant' Antonio was the tomb of the Blessed Beatrice d'Este, and he professed to have heard groans from her tomb on several occasions when Ferrara, or a member of the Estense family, was threatened with disaster. Ercole had a passion for building, and planned to add a whole new section, the *Addizione Erculea*, with wide straight streets and noble palaces, in the heart of Ferrara. By 1490 he had begun extending the walls for this section, which was never completed. Two years later, many Jews, expelled from Spain, found refuge at Ferrara, where they were protected.

Este, Ercole II d'. Duke of Ferrara, Modena, and Reggio; b. at Ferrara, April 4,

1508; d. there, October 5, 1559. He was the son of Alfonso I, duke of Ferrara, and Lucrezia Borgia, and succeeded to his father's dignities in October, 1534. As with his father, one of Ercole's most pressing problems concerned his relations with the pope. These were improved by a series of agreements and payments. Ercole was confirmed in his dominions and Paul III underscored the reconciliation by visiting Modena, Reggio and Ferrara (1543). However, Ferrara was traditionally linked to France, and in January, 1528, Ercole had married Renée, daughter of Louis XII. This marriage to the brilliant but physically deformed Renée brought new complications for Ercole vis-à-vis the pope. She was openly and increasingly attracted to Calvinism (Calvin visited Ferrara), and made Ferrara a center of Protestant propaganda. Vittoria Colonna, who wished for reform of the Church but never abandoned her Catholicism, was her friend, and Bernardino Ochino, celebrated preacher, reformer, and ultimately a convert to Calvinism, preached at Ferrara at her invitation. The pope could not regard these developments with equanimity, and in 1554 at his request, Ercole was compelled to confine his wife to her quarters in the palace. In the meantime, Ercole had continued his policy of keeping friendly relations with the emperor and the French. He sent troops to aid Charles V in the war of the Schmalkaldic League, and in 1548 did homage to the new king of France, Henry II. But his neutrality was compromised when Henry took up arms against the emperor (1551) and Ercole's son Alfonso defied his father and hurried off to France to fight at the side of his cousin Henry. In the wars that followed, Ercole and the pope made an alliance with France, but this was ineffective, and left Ferrara exposed to the imperial army. The pope, abandoned by the French, made peace and Ercole was compelled to do the same. With the good offices of Cosimo I de' Medici, duke of Tuscany, he made a piece (May 18, 1558) by which his lands were restored and the peace was guaranteed by Cosimo. To cement the relationship with the Medici, Ercole's son Alfonso was married to Cosimo's daughter Lucrezia. Ercole was a patron of art and literature, and under him the court of Ferrara continued to be a center of learning, but its splendor was somewhat dimmed because of the religious interests of his wife. She bore him: Alfonso II, his successor; Luigi (1538–1586) who became archbishop of Ferrara and a cardinal, and who was Tasso's early patron; Anna (b. 1531) who married the Duc de Guise; Lucrezia (1535–1598), who married the duke of Urbino; and Leonora (1537–1581), who was supposed to have won the love of Tasso.

Este, Giulio d'. Member of the Estense family; b. at Ferrara, 1478; d. there, 1561. He was the natural son of Ercole I, duke of Ferrara, and was brought up in his household with Ercole's legitimate children (Isabella, Beatrice, Alfonso, Ferrante, Ippolito, and Sigismondo). When he was a young man his brother Alfonso married Lucrezia Borgia, who brought with her to Ferrara a young and beautiful lady, Angela Borgia. She captured many hearts at Ferrara, including that of Cardinal Ippolito d'Este, Giulio's brother. When the cardinal was wooing her with ardor she told him that his entire person was not the equal of Giulio's beautiful eyes. Ippolito was furiously jealous. He laid an ambush for Giulio. As Giulio was returning from the hunt, Ippolito had him seized and flung to the ground, and he himself watched as his servants drove sharp stakes into Giulio's eyes. Giulio managed to return to Ferrara and went before Duke Alfonso to demand justice. The sight of one of his eyes was saved; Ippolito was banished, but soon returned and regained his great influence over his brother. Giulio vowed revenge. Another brother, Ferrante, was jealous of Alfonso and wished to usurp his place. Giulio and Ferrante plotted to kill both Ippolito and Alfonso. Ippolito became suspicious. He seized two men who turned out to be confederates of Giulio and Ferrante. They revealed the whole conspiracy. They and others who were involved were beheaded. Ferrante went to Alfonso, threw himself on his knees before his brother and begged his forgiveness. Alfonso was so enraged he struck him in the face with his stick and blinded him in one eye. Giulio fled to his sister Isabella at Mantua. Alfonso demanded that she give him up. She was most reluctant, as she had a deep affection for all the members of her family, but was compelled at last to surrender him. Alfonso had his brothers tried and they were condemned to death (1506). A scaffold was erected in the square, members of the court, ambassadors, professors, and many others assembled to watch the execution. At the last minute Alfonso commuted their sentences to life imprisonment, and his brothers were led away to the dungeons beneath the castle. There they languished, while their brother and his court carried on the festivities for which Ferrara was noted above them. Alfonso died in 1534 and was succeeded by his son Ercole II, who refused to pardon his uncles. Ferrante died in prison in 1540. Ercole II died in 1559 and was succeeded by Alfonso II. One of the new duke's first thoughts was of his great-uncle in the dungeon. He released him. Giulio, then a man of 81, had spent fifty-three years in prison. (It does not seem possible that he could have lived that many years in the prison dungeons that are shown at Ferrara; perhaps he had somewhat more comfortable quarters.) Even at that age a man of fine physique, he went about Ferrara on a high-spirited horse, eagerly visited the haunts of his youth, and the convents, where the nuns kissed the old man to his joy, and inquired everywhere for his friends, who had been dead for fifty years. The sight of the ardent old man in his old-fashioned clothes moved those who saw him. He enjoyed his freedom somewhat more than a year before death carried him off.

Este, Ippolito I d'. Cardinal; b. at Ferrara, November 20, 1479; d. there, September, 1520. He was the third son of Ercole I, duke of Ferrara, and Leonora of Aragon, and was the brother of Isabella and Beatrice d'Este. His father decided on a career in the Church for him. At five he was an abbot; at seven, through the influence of his aunt, Beatrice of Aragon, who was the wife of Matthias Corvinus, King of Hungary, and over the protest of Pope Innocent VIII, he was named archbishop of Estergom in Hungary; in 1493 he was given the red hat by Alexander VI; and at 17 he was archbishop of Milan. He also held a number of bishoprics, abbacies, and other benefices. But he was a churchman by his father's choice, not by his own. His interests led him to soldiery and warfare, to purely secular and often corrupt pleasures. In 1509 he took an active part in the war of the pope against Venice, traditional enemy of Ferrara. Later, when the pope turned against Ferrara, Ippolito, in the absence of his brother Duke Alfonso, armed Ferrara and defended it. He was a brilliant, cultivated, and corrupt prince of the Church. He was genuinely interested in mathematics and astronomy, and surrounded himself with men of letters and science. Unfortunately for Ariosto, who was in his service, he did not share his father's and his brother's sincere love and appreciation of poetry. Ariosto dedicated, in the most fulsome manner, his *Orlando Furioso* to Ippolito, but complained in his *Satires* that his prince did not appreciate his poetry. When (1517) Ippolito went again to Hungary, Ariosto left his service rather than accompany him to what he considered a barbaric country. Ippolito did not care much for it himself. Like other members of his family, he had a passion for festivals and performances, and loved magnificence and display. His position as a prelate did not prevent him from paying court to Angela Borgia, a young lady who came to Ferrara with Lucrezia Borgia, and who captivated Ippolito. She mocked him by saying that his brother Giulio's beautiful eyes were worth more than Ippolito's entire person. In his jealousy he took a terrible revenge (see **Este, Giulio d'**) that led to the life imprisonment of two of his brothers. A penetrating portrait of him by Titian is in the Pitti Palace at Florence.

Este, Ippolito II d'. Cardinal; b. at Ferrara, August 25, 1509; d. at Tivoli, December 2, 1572. He was the son of Duke Alfonso I of Ferrara and Lucrezia Borgia. Destined for the Church, at 10 he became archbishop of Milan when his uncle Ippolito I resigned in his favor. Later he became archbishop of various French archdioceses, and was the leader of the French party in the Sacred College, having been given the red hat in 1538 largely through the influence of Francis I. In 1560 and 1561 he was Pius IV's legate to Catherine de Médicis at France to try to calm the religious disorders in that country and to prepare for the reopening of the Council of Trent. He was a skillful diplomat, and was several times the French candidate for the papal throne, but at a time when the Church was struggling to reform itself his worldliness made him unsuitable. He was an enthusiastic patron of the arts and of science, an ardent collector of works of art and had assembled a peerless collection in his palace at Rome. For him, Pirro Ligorio built (1550) the Villa d'Este at Tivoli, outside Rome, a Renaissance masterpiece noted for its magnificent park with its beautiful and ingenious fountains.

Este, Isabella d'. Marchioness of Mantua; b. at Ferrara, May 18, 1474; d. at Mantua, February 13, 1539. Known throughout Europe in her own day for her learning, taste, and diplomatic skill, she was called "the first lady of the world" by her admiring contemporaries, and is one of the great personalities of the Renaissance. She was the daughter of Ercole I, duke of Ferrara, and Leonora of Aragon, whose court at Ferrara was a center of art and culture. From childhood she met the foremost scholars, poets, men of letters, and artists of the day in her father's house. She had an excellent classical education that began with her first teacher, Battista Guarino, who taught her Latin. She learned to dance and to play various instruments, and delighted her family and friends when she sang and accompanied herself on the lute. At the age of six she was betrothed to Francesco Gonzaga of Mantua. She was married to him in a magnificent ceremony at Ferrara on February 11, 1490, and the next day sailed up the Po in a richly carved and gilded bucentaur (a state river barge) accompanied by a flotilla of gaily decorated boats, and entered Mantua in triumph on February 15, 1490. She was not yet 16. The first years of her marriage were happy. At a later date she wrote her husband that she had been married so young that she could not remember when she did not love him. He indulged her in her passion for collecting, deferred to her superior taste, discrimination, and intelligence, and valued her advice in matters of state. In the course of time she bore him six children, and was very disappointed when the first two were girls. Girls being considered unworthy of it, the cradle she had prepared for the heir of Mantua was not used until 1500 when her adored Federigo was born. But by 1495 Francesco had taken a mistress, the first of many, who subsequently bore him two daughters. Isabella pretended to be unaware of his infidelities. Florio Dolfo, a Bolognese humanist whose friendship with Francesco entitled him to some plain speaking, wrote to him, "she prudently feigns neither to see nor hear those actions of yours which must be hateful and injurious to her." Wounding to her pride and to her affections as his infidelities were to his young wife, Isabella was unwavering in her loyalty and in her efforts to help him and to defend his state. In his frequent absences she governed it with wisdom and justice. To affairs of state and diplomacy she brought tact, discretion, charm, and persistence. Her purpose was simple and straightforward: to defend and protect Mantua and the interests of her family there, at Ferrara, and at Milan and Urbino, but the means of accomplishing it were devious and complicated. Then, as now, idealism and morality were not allowed to interfere with political necessity. She tried to help Ludovico il Moro, duke of Milan and husband of her sister Beatrice, but when she saw his cause was hopeless (1500) she turned to wooing the friendship of the French king who had conquered him, while at the same time she gave asylum at Mantua to the exiles from Milan (including two of Ludovico's mistresses). Louis XII knew her by reputation and was anxious to meet her. In 1507 she visited Milan at his invitation and laughed and danced in the *castello* at Milan where, just over ten years earlier, she had enjoyed the festivities provided by her sister, now dead, and her brother-in-law Ludovico, now a captive of her host. Early in 1502 she went to Ferrara to do the honors for her brother Alfonso's bride, Lucrezia Borgia, although she had been as opposed as other members of her family to the marriage. As she wrote to Francesco, the sight of her dead mother's ruby necklace (Ercole's gift to his new daughter-in-law) encircling Lucrezia's neck brought tears to her eyes. Relations with Lucrezia were never close. The latter, though not nearly so learned and far less radiant as to personality, was so amiable and gracious that she won the devotion of some of Isabella's own courtiers, and some said that Francesco's interest in Lucrezia came to pass the bounds of mere friendship. Isabella distrusted Lucrezia's wily brother, Cesare Borgia, but for reasons of policy agreed to the betrothal of her infant son Federigo to Cesare's daughter, and congratulated him on his successes in the Romagna. But she wrote that the people of Faenza had "redeemed the honor of Italy" by resisting him, and gave asylum to Duke Guidobaldo of Urbino when Cesare treacherously seized his duchy. Guidobaldo's wife Elizabetta Gonzaga was Isabella's dearest friend, beloved companion, and recipient of many of Isabella's warm letters; she was visiting in Mantua at the time of Cesare's attack on Urbino. Isabella hospitably welcomed both and kept them as long as she could without arousing the pope's wrath. With the death

LEONARDO DA VINCI
Isabella d'Este
Cabinet des Dessins Musée du Louvre Cliché Musées Nationaux

of Alexander VI and the arrest of Cesare by the Spanish, the plans for the marriage of Isabella's son and Cesare's daughter were thankfully cancelled. Her husband, who fought as one of the generals of Julius II, was surprised and captured by the Venetians in the summer of 1509. During the period of his captivity at Venice (August, 1509–July, 1510), Isabella governed Mantua. She sent envoys everywhere, including to the sultan of Turkey, in an effort to secure Francesco's release. To win the help of Julius, she betrothed her daughter Leonora, noted for her beauty, to Francesco Maria della Rovere, the young new duke of Urbino, who was the pope's nephew, and was even prevailed upon to send her beloved Federigo to Rome as a hostage for Francesco. When her husband at length returned from Venice he lived in semi-retirement. His health was ruined by syphilis. He was timid, irresolute, and morose. He depended on Isabella but was no help in running the state, for while she pursued her policies with the utmost tact, discretion, and skill, he was promising support and devotion on all sides in a desperate attempt to avoid being on the wrong side. Isabella was the effective ruler of the state. "Here," wrote Mario Equicola to her brother Alfonso, "you may rest assured that everything is referred to Madama, and not a leaf is allowed to stir without her knowledge and consent." Following the death of Francesco (1519) her great ambition was to have Federigo appointed captain general of the Church. Baldassare Castiglione, who often acted as her ambassador, made many representations to Pope Leo X in Federigo's behalf. He told Leo, who asked who would govern Mantua if Federigo was off fighting for the Church, that Madama had already shown herself perfectly capable of governing the state. When (1521) the news was announced that Federigo had been named captain general, Mantua was delirious with joy. But Isabella, who had been the leading statesman of Mantua for years, as well as the leader in the arts and learning, was humiliated in her own family. Federigo, who had listened so willingly to her advice, fell passionately in love with a young married lady of Mantua, Isabella Boschetti, and openly took her as his mistress. The ill-bred and arrogant young woman pointedly exhibited her influence over Federigo at the expense of his mother. Isabella turned more and more to her second son, Ercole, who shared her learned interests to the full. She decided to go to Rome to escape the humiliations inflicted by Federigo's mistress and to procure the red hat of a cardinal for Ercole. She set out for Rome in January, 1525. Her house there soon became a meeting place for men of letters; wherever Isabella was soon became a center of culture. Whenever the opportunity arose, she reminded Pope Clement VII that she wanted a red hat for Ercole. In the spring of 1527 northern Italy was in turmoil. German and Swiss pikemen under the command of Charles V's generals were ravaging Lombardy and were headed for Rome. Isabella received urgent messages from Mantua begging her to return, but she had not yet received Ercole's red hat. Her third son, Ferrante, was with the imperial army, and the Constable de Bourbon, commanding it, was the son of a Gonzaga kinsman. As the imperials approached Rome she had her palace fortified and laid in provisions. She got word to Ferrante and the Constable de Bourbon to protect her palace in the event that Rome was overrun. Just before the pikemen arrived at the gates of Rome Clement tried to raise troops to protect the city. To get the money to pay them he created five new cardinals, each of whom paid 40,000 ducats. One of the new cardinals was to be Ercole, and Clement gave Isabella his red hat. But it was too late to protect Rome. The imperials breached the walls and stormed into the city. Never was such destruction caused by so-called civilized men as that which the German and Swiss troops wreaked on defenseless Rome. Isabella's was one of two palaces that were not plundered and burned (the other was the *Cancelleria*). The garrison she had had the good sense to order into it defended it, and as soon as he arrived her son Ferrante protected it. Always generous to refugees, Isabella is said to have sheltered 3,000 of them—ambassadors, prelates, noble men and women—in her palace during the sack of Rome. At the end of a week (May 13), in great peril although she was escorted by Ferrante and Spanish and Italian guards, she left the city. She reached Ferrara on June 9, and Mantua, where she was welcomed with tears and wild acclamation, on June 14. At Mantua, she gave the red hat of a cardinal to Ercole with her own hands. To the end of her life she followed political events with the greatest interest. At the end of 1529 she went to Bologna for the festivities in connection with the coronation of Charles V by Clement VII. The emperor was particularly courteous in his attentions to her, and many felt that of the important people at Bologna for the coronation, Isabella was outranked only by the emperor and the pope. It was thanks to her advice that Federigo had been on the winning side in the struggle between France and Spain for domination in Italy, and it was at Bologna that Charles told her of his intention of raising Federigo's marquisate to a duchy. And so it was that on April 8, 1530, during a visit of Charles V to Mantua, in a ceremony on the steps of the cathedral Federigo was invested by the emperor as duke of Mantua.

Affairs of state by no means exhausted Isabella's great energy or her wide-ranging intellect. She never permitted her marriage or the rearing of children to interfere with her education. For most of her life she continued to study Latin, in which she became highly proficient. At Mantua, where art and learning already flourished, she gathered about her a group of distinguished men of letters that Paolo Giovio called the "Accademia de Santo Pietro." Included in this group were Mario Equicola, chronicler of Mantua; Battista Spagnoli, the Carmelite poet; Matteo Bandello, an ecclesiastic who wrote very worldly stories; and Baldassare Castiglione, Isabella's friend, courtier, ambassador, and agent. Her witty and lively friends Francesco Berni and Bernardo Dovizi (Cardinal Bibbiena) delighted to visit her, and kept her informed of what was going on in the world when they were away from Mantua. She had read some of Boiardo's *Orlando* at an early date, and in 1491 begged him to send her the latest verses in manuscript. Ariosto read parts of *his Orlando* to her to amuse her when she was ill, and later gave her copies of the first (1516) and the last (1532) editions of his great poem. Pietro Bembo sent her his poems, Trissino sang her praises in his *Ritratti*, and Girolamo Vida dedicated his *Bombyx* to her. Poetry was her great love and the poets Antonio Tebaldeo and her kinsman, the perfect courtier Niccolò da Correggio, were among her favorites. The shelves and cabinets of her *studiolo*, and later of her rooms known as the *Paradiso*, were filled with examples of the works of her friends that they had dedicated and presented to her. Aldus Manutius sent the first copy of Petrarch from his press to her (for good luck), its parchment pages personally chosen, one by one so that each would be the best, and she had a complete collection of the Aldine classics. Her library also included many fine Greek and Latin codices, as well as richly illuminated and bound French and Spanish romances. She carried on an enormous correspondence (over 2,000 of her letters are extant), with members of her family, friends, princes, prelates, ambassadors, agents, painters, jewelers, and any number of the artists and artisans who served her. Her personal letters are lively and frank, warm and affectionate, and often sparkle with her slightly ironic humor. (In the summer of 1492 she was invited to visit Milan but felt she did not have clothes of sufficient splendor to make an impression worthy of the marquess of Mantua, but wrote to him, "Of course, if you wish it, I will set off alone, in my chemise, but this I think you will hardly desire." As it turned out, by the middle of August she was able to put together an ensemble glorious enough to do him honor and set out for Milan.) Her business letters are crisp and imperious, and the diplomatic ones show that no flattery was too fulsome if it would gain her end. *In toto*, the letters present a vivid picture of the political, artistic, and literary life of an age, and equally important, they paint a portrait of a fascinating personality. Throughout her life she had a passion for beauty, and devoted herself to collecting it for her own pleasure. Lorenzo da Pavia, maker of fine musical instruments, and friend of poets, humanists, and painters, was her friend and correspondent for over twenty years. He made a lute and a clavichord for her, and often served as her agent in adding to her collections of pictures, antiques, amber rosaries, ivory crucifixes, enamels, cameos, Murano glass, crystal, oriental fabrics, inlaid cabinets, etc. Cristoforo Romano, the sculptor, was another who found beautiful objects for her. He made a famous medal of her that she added to her large collection of medals. Niccolò Pellipario of Casteldurante, who lived at Urbino between 1520 and 1530, made her fine majolica dinner services. Goldsmiths and silversmiths, jewelers and potters, architects, antiquarians, diplomats, priests, and soldiers were delighted to serve her. At an early age she was a conoisseur of painting and began her collections. Leonardo da Vinci visited Mantua in 1499 and drew a red chalk profile sketch (now in the Louvre) preparatory to painting a portrait, which he never did; nor did he ever fill her request to paint even a little picture for her. Perugino was dilatory, as were Titian and Bellini. She was not a patient woman but nothing could hurry the artists; her letters to them express her eagerness to have the pictures they are working on for her. Mantegna, Bonsignori, Francia, Dossi,

Costa, in addition to those already mentioned, were among the painters who carried out commissions for her. She was among the first to recognize the excellence of some of the greatest artists of her day, but she was not always able to secure pictures from them. Raphael did a portrait of her son Federigo (largely through the influence of Pope Julius II), but was unable to fill any other commissions for her. Francia painted a portrait of her as a young woman which Titian later copied. The latter's copy is at Vienna. The Francia original is lost, as are the many other portraits, including one by Mantegna, that were painted of her until, as she wrote, Italy must be weary of looking at her face. Her collection of paintings, small but choice, was sold early in the 17th century. The catalog lists many that have since been lost. She was an eager collector of antique sculpture. Her friends, who traveled widely, were always on the lookout for examples for her, but the rage for collecting antiques was such that they were few and expensive. Sabbà da Castiglione, a Knight Templar, was on the island of Rhodes from 1505 to 1508, defending it against the Turks. He collected antique statues and fragments on the islands and sent them to Isabella at Mantua. When Urbino was seized by Cesare Borgia she remembered that he had once given Guidobaldo two pieces of sculpture: an antique torso and a cupid carved by Michelangelo. Sure that Cesare would have carried them off when he stripped the palace at Urbino, she wrote to her brother, Cardinal Ippolito, at Rome. Without any beating about the bush she described the statutes, said she rather thought Cesare did not really appreciate the antique, and asked Ippolito to use his good offices to secure the statues for her. Cesare, who had indeed stolen them from Urbino, graciously gave them to her. Later, when Guidobaldo was restored, he asked twice for the return of these treasures, then politely put himself at Isabella's service. She never returned them. In 1506 Mantegna, who had been court painter at Mantua for forty years, was old, ill, and in debt. He applied to Isabella, for whom he had fulfilled several commissions, for help. She offered to buy his treasured antique bust of the *Empress Faustina*, which he had on many occasions refused to sell. It was not often necessary for her to stoop so low to acquire a desired object, but when it was she did not hesitate. She herself felt that she was continually hampered in adding to her treasures by lack of money. She had a magnificent collection of jewels that often served in lieu of cash, for when funds were low, or when Francesco needed money, the jewels were pledged in return for loans from Venetian bankers. Even her gowns of rich fabric had sometimes to be pawned, but this was all in the manner of the time—sometimes the papal tiara was pawned. On a visit to Milan when her brother-in-law Ludovico still enjoyed a full treasury, he showed her the wealth his vaults contained. She could not repress a sigh of envy when writing to her husband, "Would to God that we, who are so fond of spending money, possessed as much!" Fortunately, there were also times when money was plentiful, and then the orders for jewels, fabrics, furs, paintings, ornaments, hangings, and every other object for the elegant enjoyment of life flew about Italy.

From the time of her arrival at Mantua Isabella made a nest for herself and her treasures. At the age of 17 she wrote to Luca Liombeni, a Mantuan painter who was decorating her *studiolo* in the palace, that she knew he was slow at his work, but if her *studiolo* was not ready by the time she returned to Mantua she would shut him up in the dungeons "and this is no jest." Variations on the phrase, "For God's sake, be diligent," appear frequently in her letters. As her collections grew she moved into larger quarters and finally, into three rooms finished especially for her use and refuge. These rooms, the *Apartamento del Paradiso*, were decorated by the finest artists. Scattered over the walls and exquisite ceilings are the various devices that Isabella enjoyed inventing. These included her famous motto: *Nec spec nec metu* (*With neither hope nor fear*); the magical numbers XXVII, which some thought meant that she had conquered all (*vinte; sette*); and the musical notes and rests she loved to use as decorative motifs in her hangings and dress stuffs. The lovely rooms, with their precious collections, were pillaged and ruined in the sack of Mantua (1630), but the beautiful ceilings and lovely marble doorway of Cristoforo Romano remain. Another reminder of Isabella in the ducal palace is the set of apartments, built to a miniature scale, begun in her time as living quarters for the dwarfs that so charmed the Estensi and the

Gonzaga. Visitors to the palace nowadays are shown the spot that served as a cemetery for beloved dogs and other small animals that were buried with due ceremony. It was said of Isabella that her presence or approach was always announced by the barking of her little dogs. As long as she lived Isabella maintained her lively interest in the world, and being blessed with wonderful vitality continually sought to satisfy her curiosity about what went on in it. She traveled as much as she could, to Venice, Milan, and Florence, to Rome, where on her first visit (1514) Bibbiena's *Calandria* was performed in the Vatican for her entertainment, to Naples, and on pilgrimage to France. Wherever she went she was treated like visiting royalty. (To avoid the festivities put on in her honor, she sometimes traveled incognito and indulged her passion for seeing the sights.) Everybody in her own day admired Isabella's learning. Many considered her beautiful. Her taste in dress, hats, perfumes, and ornaments set the fashion. Artists in all media, men of letters, and skilled craftsmen served her willingly, although Mantua was not a wealthy court. Her seal of approval was worth more than money. She won and kept friends in all walks of life, and ever showed herself loyal and affectionate to the members of her family. Along with her enjoyment of the refinements of the mind and the elegancies of life, she could enjoy the broadest buffoonery, the most boisterous frivolity. Her personal life was above reproach, but she was sometimes reproached for the scandalous behavior that she permitted the pretty ladies of her household. Formidably intelligent as she was, advanced enough to admire the philosopher Pietro Pomponazzi, to whom she entrusted her son Ercole, she could also entertain a dependence on astrology, as did most of her highborn contemporaries. Not notably spiritual, she followed the religious practices of her day as a matter of course, was the intimate of a holy woman of Mantua, Suor Osanna Andreasi, who died in her arms (June, 1505), and persuaded Leo X to beatify her in 1515. In her intelligence and learning, her curiosity and enthusiasm, her notable taste and ebullient personality, she embodied the qualities and contradictions of the Renaissance at its peak.

Este, Leonello d'. Thirteenth marquess of Ferrara; b. 1407; d. at his villa of Belriguardo (near Ferrara), October 1, 1450. He was the natural son of Niccolò III d'Este by his mistress Stella dell' Assassino, and was the brother of Ugo and Borso. As a youth he was sent to learn the military arts from the noted condottiere Braccio da Montone. By nature a scholar and a poet, when he returned to Ferrara he resumed his intellectual interests. At Leonello's suggestion, Niccolò invited the scholar and teacher Guarino da Verona to Ferrara to be his tutor (1429). The celebrated humanist was his companion and teacher for seven years, and deeply influenced Leonello as a scholar and a prince. Niccolò stipulated before he married his third wife (1431) that even if she should bear him a son, Leonello was to succeed him. On the death of Niccolò (1441), Leonello became lord of Ferrara, and under him Ferrara entered upon a golden age. He followed his father's policy of keeping apart from the quarrels of the Italian states. Ferrara prospered in the years of his peaceful reign and became a center of literature and poetry, a position it held for generations. Leonello's contribution to its cultural life was his enthusiastic encouragement and his participation as a collector, humanist, and poet. He knew Greek, wrote good Latin prose and verse, and was the inspiration of discussions on classical and philosophical subjects. Angelo Camillo Decembrio describes the cultivated and easy intercourse of Leonello and his scholarly friends and their discussions in his *De politia literaria*. He reformed and reorganized the university and engaged distinguished professors for it, including Theodore Gaza who taught Greek. Leon Battista Alberti was one of his friends. Leonello encouraged him rather in his writing than in his architectural talents, even complimenting Alberti on his Italian works, for Leonello's objection to vernacular writing vanished when the vernacular was good Italian. His older half brother Meliaduse (1406–1452) shared his scholarly interests and was his affectionate companion; his brother Borso was not a scholar but was a trusted adviser on other matters (all the children of Niccolò, no matter who their mothers were, appear to have shared an affectionate and loyal family feeling). A lover of music, Leonello secured a choir from France for the chapel in his palace. Pisanello, who was his favorite painter, has left two portraits of him and several medals with profile portraits. A portrait by

Giovanni da Oriolo (the only certainly identified work by this Faentine painter) is in the National Gallery at London. Leonello's first wife was Margherita Gonzaga (d. 1439) who, having been educated at Mantua, by Vittorino da Feltre, could meet her husband on equal intellectual terms. Their son was Niccolò. In 1444 he married Maria of Aragon, a natural daughter of King Alfonso of Naples, who died childless in 1449. In the time of Leonello Ferrara was an island of peace and prosperity. The annals of its court are an idyll of learned and philosophical discussions at the court and manly pleasures in its pastoral environs. The Ferrarese chronicler wrote of Leonello that he was pious, loved justice, and was liberal to the needy; ". . . patient in adversity, moderate in prosperity. He ruled his peoples in peace with great wisdom."

Este, Niccolò III d'. Twelfth marquess of Ferrara; b. 1383; d. at Milan, December 26, 1441. He was the natural son of Alberto V d'Este, whom he succeeded (1393) under the protection of Venice, as he was only nine years old. On the death of Gian Galeazzo Visconti (1402), he took advantage of the collapse of Visconti power in the Milanese dominions to establish his own rule at Ferrara, which he held from the pope, and of Modena and Rovigo, as well as of a number of smaller cities. In 1409 he caused the tyrant of Parma and Reggio to be slain in an ambush and added those two cities to his domain, but ceded Parma to Milan in 1420. His policy in succeeding years was to consolidate his state and to maintain a balance between his powerful neighbors: Venice always cast covetous eyes on Ferrara, and the popes never relinquished their claim to it. Under Niccolò, Ferrara was at peace and the encouragement of art and letters that made it one of the most brilliant courts in Italy began. Niccolò had such renown as a peace-loving ruler that he was called on at various times to mediate between the quarreling states in Italy. Relations with Milan were close, and he was invited there to mediate a quarrel with Venice. While there to do so, he died; poison was suspected.

Niccolò was an able administrator who reorganized, enlarged, and consolidated his state. His character was a mixture of qualities which to moderns seem immiscible: he was sincerely religious, cruel, sensual, prudent, superstitious, and open to the intellectual developments of his day. In 1413 he went on a pilgrimage to Jerusalem, a journey that lasted three months and included numerous stopovers to see the sights. While in Jerusalem (May 15–19), he dubbed several members of his retinue knights at Mass at the Holy Sepulchre, girding on their swords himself; on Mount Cavalry he fastened on their golden spurs. Although a knight, he had never had the golden spurs. While on Mount Cavalry he had one golden spur fastened on his left foot (as being the more important), and said he would wait until he came to S. Jacopo of Galicia to have the second spur fastened on his right foot. Later, he made pilgrimages to Vienne in France, to the Santa Casa at Loreto and to the Annunziata at Florence. There was no question of the spiritual satisfaction he derived from his journeys to the Holy places. He was married three times. His first wife bore him no children. His second wife was the much younger Parasina Malatesta, who bore him two daughters. His firstborn son Ugo (1405–1425), child of his Sienese mistress Stella dell' Assassino (who was also the mother of his sons Leonello and Borso), fell in love with her and became her lover. The lovers were betrayed. Niccolò was taken to a mirror that reflected the scene across the court; in it he saw his son embracing his wife. He had them arrested (on the night of May 20/21, 1425) and placed in the dungeons of the castle (or as some say, in the clock tower of the castle). They were both beheaded on the night of May 21st. Niccolò was said to have raved through the castle all night, gnawing at a stick in a frenzy of grief over the loss of his favorite son. His third wife, whom he married in 1431, bore him his only legitimate sons, Ercole and Sigismondo, but he had stipulated before he married her that even in the event she bore him a son, Leonello, who had been legitimized in 1429 by Pope Martin V, would be his heir. Niccolò's wives were the least of his concerns. The Ferrarese chronicler relates, with a note of pride, that he had 800 mistresses, and that he would have reached a thousand if he had lived long enough. The mothers of his children ranged from noble ladies of his court to peasant girls. His illegitimate children (he acknowledged between twenty and thirty of them) were brought up with his legitimate children in his palaces, and married into the princely houses of Italy on a par with his legitimate children. His legitimate daughters Ginevra (1419–1440) and Lucia (1419–1437) married Sigismondo Malatesta (who was said to have killed her) and the condottiere Carlo Gonzaga. Of his natural daughters, Isotta (1425–1456) had Oddantonio da Montefeltro as her first husband, and after he was murdered (1444), married Stefano Frangipani; Beatrice (1427–1497) married, first, Niccolò da Correggio, and second, Tristano Sforza, son of Francesco Sforza, Duke of Milan; Margharita (d. 1452) married Galasso Pio of Carpi; and Bianca Maria (1440–1506) married Galeotto Pico della Mirandola. An able and enlightened prince, he chose men of learning to serve him, reorganized and reopened the university, brought Guarino da Verona to Ferrara to serve as tutor to his son Leonello, and himself collected a valuable manuscript library. Many scholars and artists were drawn to the city by its cultivated atmosphere. Pisanello painted portraits of his children. Michele Savonarola came from Padua to be his physician. Giovanni Aurispa, great collector of codices, was tutor to his son Meliaduse. For the Council of Ferrara (1438), at which it was hoped to unite the Greek and Latin churches, humanists, prelates and learned men swarmed into Ferrara. Enea Silvio Piccolomini (later Pope Pius II) was one of those present. He remarked upon the brilliance of the court, the intelligence of the children, and the number of them that were bastards. As he had stipulated, Niccolò was succeeded by his son Leonello (1441) rather than by his much younger legitimate son Ercole.

Este, Niccolò di Leonello d'. Prince of the Estense family; b. 1438; d. at Ferrara, September 3, 1476. He was the son of Leonello d'Este, marquess of Ferrara, and his wife Margherita Gonzaga of Mantua. A child when his father died (1450), he was on warmly affectionate terms with Borso, his uncle and the successor of his father. Niccolò was fond of hunting and given to pleasure, and was away from Ferrara a great deal. As he grew older a party grew up that tried to win control of Ferrara, Modena, and Reggio for him as Leonello's legitimate son. But Borso was immensely popular at Ferrara, and though Niccolò pleaded with the sovereigns of various states for aid in gaining his rightful place as lord of Ferrara, he won little more than sympathy, and not a great deal of that. In 1471 he had made an attempt to take over Ferrara but obeyed when his uncle Borso ordered him from the city. Another uncle, Ercole, succeeded Borso, and sent Niccolò Ariosto, father of the poet, to Mantua to make an end of Niccolò once and for all. His plot was exposed when the servant charged with administering poison to Niccolò fell ill and thought that by mistake he had poisoned himself. In his panic he confessed all. Niccolò sought vengeance in vain. Ercole rewarded Niccolò Ariosto even though he had failed in his mission. At length, Niccolò resolved on a daring coup. In 1476 he sailed a small fleet of boats up the Po to Ferrara. The boats were apparently loaded with hay, but hidden under the hay were 700 soldiers. These entered Ferrara through a weakened place in the walls and surged into the main square led by Niccolò. Ercole heard of their invasion when he was outside the city, and thinking that there were many more men involved, hesitated to return. But his brothers Sigismondo and Rinaldo went into action at once. The Ferrarese ignored Niccolò's call to throw off the yoke of Ercole. After a brief and bloody struggle the invaders were overcome. Many captives were taken. They were hanged from the balcony and windows of the Palazzo della Ragione. Niccolò escaped, but was captured and privately beheaded (September 3, 1476). His head was sewn back on his body, which was then dressed in regal robes, and he was given a state funeral in the cathedral in the presence of the courtiers, doctors of the university, prelates, and foreign ambassadors. He was buried in the family tomb in the Church of S. Francesco.

Estienne (es-tyen) or **Étienne** (ā-tyen), **Charles.** [Latinized, **Stephanus.**] French printer, bookseller, physician, and scholar; b. at Paris, c1504; d. 1564. He was the third son of Henri Estienne (c1460–1520), and the brother of François and Robert. He studied medicine at Paris, where he took his degree, and he taught Jean Antoine de Baïf, who later became a distinguished poet and a member of the Pléiade. In 1551, Robert having left Paris for Geneva, he took full charge of the printing business, and was made king's printer. Ten years later he was bankrupt, and it is believed that he died in a debtor's prison. His works have been praised as models of typography and correctness. He published *De* *dissectione partium corporis humani libri tres* (1548), an important work on anatomy with valuable woodcuts; *Dictionarium historicum ac poëticum* (1553), the first French encyclopedia; *Praedium rusticum* (1554), a volume of pamphlets on agriculture by ancient authors; and an edition of Cicero (1557). In 1543 he translated an Italian comedy, *Gli ingannati* (under the title *Le Sacrifice*), important for its influence on French comedy, and ten years later he brought out *Paradoxes*, an imitation of the "scandalous" *Paradossi*, by the Italian wit Ortensio Landi.

Estienne or **Étienne, François.** [Latinized, **Stephanus.**] French printer and bookseller; b. 1502; d. 1550 or 1553. He was the first son of Henri Estienne (c1460–1520), founder of the family and the firm. After his father's death in 1520, he continued the business in partnership with his stepfather, Simon de Collines.

Estienne or **Étienne, Henri.** [Latinized, **Stephanus.**] French printer, bookseller, and founder of a family of scholars and printers; b. at Paris, c1460 or 1470; d. there, 1520. Between 1501 and 1503 he opened a printing establishment near the University of Paris. He did much to promote learning by bringing out at least 120 works in the fields of science, theology, and the classics, his first publication being an edition of the *Ethics* of Aristotle. His device, on his title pages, was *Plus olei quam vini* (*more oil than wine*). He had three sons, François, Robert, and Charles, and his second son, Robert, also had three sons, all printers. After his death, his business was continued by his foreman, Simon de Collines, who married his widow a year later. His name frequently appears in its English form, Stephens, and he is so listed in some works of reference.

Estienne or **Étienne, Henri.** [Latinized, **Stephanus.**] French printer and scholar; b. at Paris, 1529; d. at Lyons, France, in March, 1598. He was the son of Robert Estienne (1503–1559) and the grandson of Henri Estienne (c1460–1520). He established (c1556) a press at Paris and on his father's death in 1559 appears to have moved to Geneva and taken charge of his father's establishment. He edited and printed numerous editions of the Greek and Latin classics, compiled the *Thesaurus linguae Graecae* (1572), and wrote *Apologie pour Hérodote* (1566), *Traité de la conformité du Français avec le Grec*, *Précellence de la langue française*, and *Nouveaux dialogues de langue française italianisé*.

Estienne or **Étienne, Robert.** [Latinized, **Stephanus.**] French printer and scholar; b. at Paris, 1503; d. at Geneva, Switzerland, September 7, 1559. He was the son of Henri Estienne (c1460–1520). He became head (c1526) of a printing establishment at Paris, was appointed (1530) royal printer to Francis I, and settled (c1552) at Geneva. He published numerous editions of the Greek and Latin classics, many of which were enriched with notes by himself, various editions of the Bible (especially of the New Testament, 1550), and a Latin-French dictionary (the first of the kind) compiled by himself, entitled *Thesaurus linguae Latinae* (1532).

Eugenius IV (ū-jē′ni-us). [Original name, **Gabriele Condolmieri.**] Pope (1431–1447), b. at Venice, 1383; d. at Rome, February 23, 1447. Of a noble Venetian family, he renounced the world as a young man and entered the Augustinian monastery of San Giorgio in Alga, near Venice. Gregory XII, his maternal uncle, fostered his career in the Church, named him bishop of Siena and (1408) cardinal. His pontificate began inauspiciously. The cardinals, who had become powerful during the Great Schism, compelled him to sign certain capitulations intended to increase their power at the expense of the pope, on his election in January, 1431. He offended the powerful Colonna family of Rome, whose kinsman, Martin V, predecessor of Eugenius, had done much to aggrandize his family. Most serious of all, he became embroiled in a struggle with the conciliar movement which, during the Great Schism, had developed the theory that the popes should be subject to councils. Against his will he called a council which opened in Basel in July, 1431. Attendance was sparse and Eugenius dissolved it and transferred it to Bologna. The members, however, evaded hearing the bull of dissolution, defied the pope, and continued to meet. Forced to flee from Rome when the States of the Church were invaded by Francesco Sforza, Eugenius, through the influence of Sigismund of Germany, became reconciled with the council and rescinded the bull of dissolution. He later made a treaty with Sforza by which the latter became an ally of the papacy. Eugenius was again compelled to flee Rome (1434) when revolution broke out there. He escaped in disguise and went to Florence, where he came in close contact with the artistic and intellectual developments taking place there. He established his court at Florence and energetically set about reform of the monastic orders, a matter close to his heart. In 1437 he again ordered the Council of Basel dissolved. The following year he convened his own council at Ferrara. Many members from Basel joined him there. A few remained in Basel and continued to meet. Eugenius excommunicated them. They deposed Eugenius and elected Amadeus VIII of Savoy as pope, under the name Felix V. Felix won little support but the council continued to be a source of difficulty. Eugenius met (1439) with John VIII Palaeologus of the Byzantine Empire in Florence, whither his council had transferred from Ferrara, and a convention of union between the Greek and Latin Churches was signed. The meeting was celebrated with splendid ceremonials and processions; the Florentines were fascinated by the exotic costumes of the eastern representatives; echoes of the Council of Florence and the interest it aroused appear in the works of Piero della Francesca and Benozzo Gozzoli, to name but two. The convention of union, although soon abrogated, enhanced the power of the pope. Contact with the Greeks stimulated interest in and study of the Greek language and Greek philosophy, and increased intellectual commerce between East and West.

In 1443 Eugenius called for a crusade against the Turks. It was a disaster. The same year he made peace with Alfonso, King of Naples, and recognized the right to the succession of Alfonso's illegitimate son Ferrante. By so doing, Eugenius won the obedience of Alfonso, strengthened the papacy, and greatly weakened the already crumbling Council of Basel. In effect, he emerged from his long struggle with the council as a victor. The conciliar movement was discredited and some semblance of unity was restored to the Church, although the antipope Felix V continued to claim papal authority until 1449. In September, 1443, Eugenius returned to Rome after an exile of nearly ten years. He found it devastated from civil war and invasion, and began the work of restoration.

Eugenius has been described as a man of saintly life, dignified, austere, somewhat aloof; thin, tall, and handsome. His asceticism was never called into question. Unlike his predecessor, and many who came after him, he was not accused of nepotism. He was successful in the main struggle of his pontificate—that with the Council of Basel. Eugenius was among the earliest of a line of popes who embraced and encouraged the intellectual and artistic activities of 15th-century Italy, in his support of art and artists and the encouragement of humanists at his court, and was himself the possessor of a substantial library of 340 volumes. He was succeeded by Nicholas V.

Euse (dėz), **Jacques d'.** Original name of Pope **John XXII.**

Eusebio da S. Giorgio (ā-ö-sā′byō dä sän jôr′jō). Painter; b. at Perugia, c1465; d. after 1540. He was a pupil of Perugino, whom he assisted in painting the altarpieces of S. Pietro (1495) and S. Agostino (1520) at Perugia, and a follower and collaborator of Pinturicchio. On the arrival of Raphael at Perugia (c1500) he became one of Raphael's earliest and most ardent followers. His best work, *Adoration of the Magi* (1505), National Gallery of Umbria, Perugia, is obviously derived from Pinturicchio in its figures and groupings. A *Madonna and Child* (c1508), in the same gallery, reflects his admiration for Raphael. Other works include signed frescoes (1507) in S. Damiano, near Assissi, a signed and dated (1512) *Madonna and Child*, S. Francesco, Matelica, and paintings at Boston, Detroit, Minneapolis, Philadelphia (Johnson Collection), and elsewhere. He also carved a number of statues in wood.

Eustachi (ā-ö-stä′kē), **Bartolomeo.** Anatomist, one of the founders of modern anatomy; b. at San Severino, in the Marches, between 1500 and 1510; d. on the way from Rome to Fossombrone, August, 1574. He was a student of the humanities, knew Greek, Arabic, and Hebrew, and is thought to have studied medicine at Rome. In 1539, after practicing medicine at his birthplace for a short time, he went to the court of Duke Guidobaldo della Rovere at Urbino, where he took up the study of mathematics. In 1549 he accompanied Cardinal Giulio della Rovere, the duke's brother, to Rome. He became a member of the medical college there, papal physician, and professor of anatomy at the newly reorganized university (Sapienza). He held these posts until his death. His fame now rests on his work in anatomy. In a series of treatises, *Opuscula anatomica,* he described the eustachian tube and valve, the suprarenal gland, thoracic duct, uterus, and the kidneys, and discussed the cardiovascular system. His treatise on the teeth is a pioneer work on their anatomy. Famous is the set of fifty-four anatomical drawings he made with an assistant, beginning in 1552, *Tabulae anatomicae Bartholomei Eustachii.* The drawings were engraved on copper, but were not discovered and published until a century and a half later. Together with his *Opuscula anatomica,* they were published at Rome, 1714.

Everaerts (ā′vėr-ärts), **Jan Nicolai.** Original name of **Johannes Secundus.**

Extrados (eks-trā′dos). In architecture, the outer curve or curved surface of an arch or vault.

Eyb (īp) or **Eybe** (ī′bẹ), **Albrecht von.** See **Albrecht von Eyb** (or **Eybe**).

Eyck (īk), **Jan van.** Flemish painter; b. at Maeseyck, near Maastricht, Flanders, c1390; d. at Bruges, before July 9, 1441. He and his older brother, Hubert, perfected an oil and varnish technique that preserves the brilliant color of the original paint and permits, because of the fluidity of the medium, the execution of the most minute details. The names of the brothers are linked in the altarpiece in S. Bavon, Ghent, the world-famous *Adoration of the Lamb,* which, according to an inscription, was begun by Hubert and finished by Jan. Most critics believe that Jan executed the major portion of the work. From the time of its completion in 1432, six years after the death of Hubert, the painting has been acclaimed. The large and complex altarpiece, painted on both sides, including the wings, contains 20 minutely detailed paintings. The *Adoration of the Lamb* forms the central panel of the lower register of the inside of the painting, the side exposed when the wings are open. Painted with unblinking realism are dozens of figures, richly textured fabrics, jewels, flowers, musical instruments and angel musicians, a cavalcade of mounted worshippers, meticulously detailed background buildings and landscapes. The painting has suffered numerous vicissitudes; one panel, *The Judges of the Just,* was stolen in 1934 and has never been recovered; the panel now in its place is a copy. The work suffered some damage in the course of the centuries; especially dangerous were the Iconoclasts of Protestantism, when the painting had to be hidden. It has endured numerous restorations. Before he completed the Ghent altarpiece Jan was already a noted artist. He worked for Count John of Holland at the Hague, and in 1425 became court painter to Philip the Good, duke of Burgundy. Besides painting for Philip, he served as the duke's agent—in Spain (1427) and Portugal (1428) in connection with marriage negotiations, as well as on other occasions. In 1430 he moved to Bruges, from Lille where he had lived from 1425, and spent the rest of his life at Bruges. A number of works have been attributed to Jan van Eyck. Among his signed and dated paintings is the *Marriage of Giovanni Arnolfini and Giovanna Cenani* (1434), National Gallery, London, with the meticulously detailed and realistic interior (studded with objects of symbolic import) that became a feature of Flemish painting. Other signed and dated works are *Portrait of a Man* (1432), and *Man in a Red Turban* (1433), also in the National Gallery, London; *Madonna with Canon Van der Paele* (1434) and *Portrait of his Wife* (1439), Bruges; and *St. Barbara* (1437), a drawing, and *Madonna of the Fountain* (1439), Antwerp; and paintings at Melbourne and Dresden. Works attributed to him are at Berlin, Paris, Vienna, New York, Philadelphia (Johnson Collection), and Washington. Among Jan's great achievements were his extension of space through atmospheric perspective, the multiplication of images, and wealth of finely rendered detail. His work was greatly admired in Italy (Ciriaco d'Ancona, Bartolommeo Facio, and others record his fame in their writings) and appeared in Italian collections. Antonello da Messina is thought to have seen it at Naples and to have been greatly influenced, as were other Italian painters, by his technique and his style.

Ezzelino da Romano (āt-tsä-lē′nō dä rō-mä′nō). Ghibelline captain; b. at Onaro, near Treviso, April 26, 1194; d. September, 1259. As a loyal supporter of Emperor Frederick II, whose illegitimate daughter he married, he was an enemy of the papacy and the Guelphs, and was excommunicated by Pope Innocent IV in 1254. He conquered Verona, Vicenza, Padua, and other cities in the north of Italy, where for a time he was unopposed as the dominant figure of the area. This situation was temporary, however; he lost Padua and was defeated in an attempt to take Milan. He was notorious for his cruelty, exerting both fear and fascination upon his contemporaries. He was the central figure of the first political tragedy composed since antiquity, Mussato's *Ecerinide*.

F

Faber (fä'bėr), **Johann.** [Called **Malleus Haereticorum,** meaning "Hammer of Heretics"; original surname, **Heigerlin.**] German controversialist and opponent of the Reformation; b. at Leutkirch, Württemberg, Germany, 1478; d. at Vienna, 1541. He was appointed canon of Basel and, in 1518, papal protonotary. He did not oppose reform and sided with Erasmus and corresponded with Zwingli, but he refused to go as far as Luther's reforms went. In 1524 he published an attack on Luther, *Malleus in haeresin Lutheranam*. He became (1526) court preacher to Ferdinand I and was the emperor's envoy to Spain and England in the following years. In 1531 he became bishop of Vienna.

Fabriano (fä-brē-ä'nō), **Gentile da.** See **Gentile da Fabriano.**

Fabricius (fä-brē'tsē-ůs) **Georg.** [Original surname, **Goldschmid.**] German scholar, poet, and archaeologist; b. at Chemnitz, Saxony, April, 1516; d. at Meissen, Saxony, 1571.

Fabrizi (fä-brēt'tsē), **Aloise Cinzio delli.** Physician and poet; b. at Venice in the beginning of the 16th century. His *Libro della origine delli volgari proverbi* (1526), dedicated to Pope Clement VII, is a direct descendant of Antonio Cornazzano's *I Proverbi*. Some of the material is drawn from such authors as Boccaccio and Poggio, some from popular tales and legends. The terza rima in which it is written is difficult and tedious; the language has elements of dialect and crude Latinisms. The subject matter is undisguised obscenity, is crammed with obscene episodes and salted with crude satires, especially on the clergy and on women. It was enormously popular but called forth such opposition from the clergy that Venice suppressed it. It is a clue to the age that such a work could have been dedicated to a pope.

Fabyan (fā'bi-ạn), **Robert.** English chronicler; d. probably February 28, 1513. He wrote a chronicle of England from the arrival of Brutus to his own day, entitled *The Concordance of Histories*.

Façade (fạ-säd'). In architecture, the chief exterior face of a building, usually containing the main entrance to the building, or any one of its principal faces if it has more than one. The façade of the Church of S. Maria Novella at Florence was designed by Leon Battista Alberti for the building already in existence. The façade was often the last architectural feature to be completed and was sometimes not added for many years, or was changed. The present façade of Santa Maria del Fiore (the Duomo) at Florence was completed in 1887 and replaces one that had been demolished in 1587. The building itself was erected roughly between 1296 and 1434. The façade of S. Lorenzo at Florence, designed by Michelangelo at the request of Pope Leo X, was never constructed; the church remains with an unfinished masonry wall.

Facino Cane (fä-chē'nō kä'nā). Condottiere; b. at Casale Monferrato, between 1350 and 1360; d. at Pavia, May 16, 1412. Of a noble family, he learned the art of war fighting for Joanna I of Naples against Charles of Durazzo. He served as a mercenary captain for the Carrara family at Padua, the Visconti of Milan, and the marquess of Monferrato against the Greeks. He was Gian Galeazzo Visconti's most able general, and was in his service when the latter died. Facino took immediate advantage of this circumstance to secure what areas he could. By 1409, after various reverses, he had made himself effective ruler of Milan, and in 1410 took Pavia, although he permitted Filippo Maria Visconti to remain as titular count. As Facino was dying he advised his wife Beatrice di Tenda to marry Filippo Maria, in order to protect the great inheritance of treasure, cities, and troops he would leave in her hands.

Facio (fä′chō), **Bartolommeo.** [Also, **Fazio.**] Humanist and historian; b. at Spezia, c1400; d. at Naples, November, 1457. Following a period (1420–1426) of study under Guarino da Verona, he became the private teacher of the sons of the Doge Francesco Foscari at Venice. He later taught and studied at Florence, Genoa, and Lucca. Having returned to Genoa, he was sent by that republic as ambassador to the court of Alfonso I of Naples, and decided to remain in Naples. There he was tutor to Alfonso's son Ferrante and secretary and historian for Alfonso. His major work is the history of Alfonso, in ten books. Another work is *De viris illustribus;* included among the notable men in this work are contemporary poets, painters, sculptors, captains, princes, and so on. This work, not written to flatter a patron, presents a balanced assessment of the men whose lives he described. Facio ventured to criticize Lorenzo Valla's history of Ferdinand of Aragon on philological grounds. He said he found hundreds of errors in Valla's work. Pure Latin was Valla's special preserve. In response to Facio's criticism he shot off a series of invectives, not in defense but in attack. Facio replied in kind and the verbal duel raged for some time. Facio also wrote some important moral dialogues.

Faerno (fä-er′nō), **Gabriele.** Cremonese humanist; d. at Rome, November 17, 1561. From 1549 he had a post at the Vatican Library and devoted himself to the study of Latin literature. After his death Pope Pius IV, his patron, caused some of his works to be published. These included one hundred short compositions in different meters, *Fabulae centum* (Rome, 1564), and emended texts of the *Philippics* of Cicero (Rome, 1563) and the *Comedies of Terence* (Florence, 1565), among others.

Fair Maid of Kent. Epithet of **Joan**, wife of Edward, the Black Prince.

Faitinelli (fī-tē-nel′lē), **Pietro de'.** Notary and poet; b. at Lucca, 1290?; d. c1349. He was a notary of Lucca and a Black Guelph. As such, he was exiled (1314) to Venice when the Ghibellines gained power in Lucca. He was recalled to Lucca in 1331. His verses are on political themes or are of a didactic and moralizing character. Some of his political verses are in praise of his fellow countryman, Castruccio Castracani; others lament his exile and the passing of the old order. One canzone and seventeen sonnets are extant.

Falieri (fä-lye′rē), **Marino.** [Also, **Faliero, Falier.**] Doge of Venice; b. at Venice, 1278 (or 1274); executed there, April 17, 1355. A member of one of the oldest and noblest families of Venice, he had performed many services for the Republic. In 1346 he commanded the victorious Venetian troops at the siege of Zara in Dalmatia, and in 1354 he was elected doge. Soon after, Venice was disastrously defeated by the Genoese. The patricians turned against him and his family, and he conspired with the plebeians against the patricians, with a view to usurping the supreme power in the state. The conspiracy was discovered. He was captured, with other participants in the conspiracy. At his trial he confessed all and was convicted of treason and executed by the Council of Ten. In the Hall of the Grand Council in the Palace of the Doges at Venice, where the portraits of the doges are displayed, the place of his portrait is occupied by a tablet.

Falletti (fäl-lāt′tē), **Girolamo.** Humanist and diplomat; b. at Trino, c1518; d. at Padua, October 3, 1564. He studied at the University of Louvain, and then at Ferrara, where he took his doctorate in law. He entered the service of Ercole II, duke of Ferrara, and carried out many missions and embassies for him, as ambassador to Charles V, to Sigismund, king of Poland, to Rome for the election of Pope Julius III, and to the Republic of Venice. He left historical works, as his *Guerra di Germania al tempo di Carlo V* (Venice, 1552), and the manuscript of his history of the Estensi, *Storia dei principi d'Este*, as well as translations from the Greek.

Falloppio (fäl-lōp′pyō) or **Falloppia** (-pyä), **Gabriele.** [Latinized, **Gabriel Fallopius.**] Anatomist; b. at Modena, 1523; d. at Padua, October 9, 1562. He studied the humanities under Castelvetro and Francesco Porto, and began his studies in medicine and anatomy by himself. He was so successful that he was asked to give a public demonstration at the age of 21. In the meantime, he had become a canon of the cathedral at Modena. He went to Ferrara to complete his medical studies and took his doctorate in 1547. Thereafter he taught anatomy at Ferrara, was professor of anatomy at Pisa (1548–1551), and then, until his death, was professor of anatomy, surgery, and "simples" (medicinal herbs and plants) at Padua. He had many famous patients, including Eleonora d'Este, and made many journeys, such as to the court of Julius III at Rome, to the court of Francis II in France, and to Greece. In his own time he was noted not only as a physician, but as a surgeon, pharmacologist, chemist, and naturalist as well. He is known today as an anatomist. His *Observationes anatomicae* was written in 1556 and 1557 and was published at Venice in 1561. It is distinguished for the keenness of his observation and for the descriptions of organs hitherto unknown, or little known and understood. Among the organs described are the fallopian tubes, which he described as resembling small trumpets (his word *tuba*, "trumpet," was converted into *tubo*, "tube"), the sphenoid sinus and several nerve systems. He detailed the anatomy of the middle and inner ear, and gave names to parts of the body described by him, as the vagina, placenta, and various muscles. Other works left by Falloppio on specific anatomical or medical subjects, as his *De morbo gallico*, on syphilis (Padua, 1563), derive from the lecture notes taken by his students. Falloppio ranks with Vesalius and Eustachi as one of the great anatomists of the age.

False Decretals. [Also, **Decretals of the Pseudo-Isidore**, and **Pseudo-Isidorian Decretals.**] Certain spurious papal letters, published in France between 847 and 852, included in a compilation of canon laws by an ecclesiastic whose identity remains unknown, but who used the name Isidore Mercator. The term is sometimes applied to the whole compilation, but this in fact contains much authentic material, including a dissertation by the Pseudo-Isidore on early Church history and the Council of Nicaea, the canons of fifty-four Church councils, and a number of verified letters of popes from the 1st to the 8th centuries. The false material consists of fifty-eight letters or decrees supposedly written by popes from Clement I (88–97 A.D.) to Melchiades (311–314), one purported canon of an early council, and a number of forged letters attributed to various popes between the reigns of Silvester (314–335) and Gregory II (715–731). The apocryphal character of these documents is now universally acknowledged. The Pseudo-Isidore's method was simple: in old records he found references to papal letters and decrees, the texts of which had disappeared, and he proceeded to write his own versions of these lost documents. In the material that he invented he sprinkled phrases and sentences from authentic documents. The compilation as a whole had great authority in the Middle Ages, being much quoted in textbooks and much cited by teachers of canon law. However, with the development of philology as a scientific method, the result of the enormous interest in the Renaissance in the study of the classical languages and literature, anachronisms began to be noted in the Pseudo-Isidorian text. Nicholas of Cusa (1401–1464), cardinal, distinguished theologian, and enthusiastic scholar, and his colleague, the equally distinguished Cardinal Juan de Torquemada (1388–1468) were among the first to expose the Pseudo-Isidorian Decretals as false in many respects. Time and again the forged letters quote from or cite documents which were not written until long after the dates assigned to these letters. Cunning as was the scholarship that went to the making of this great forgery, it gradually fell apart under the examination of later scholars, Catholic and Protestant, beginning in the middle of the 15th century. By the early 19th century the False Decretals had been definitely distinguished from the genuine components of the compilation, and the approximate date of their publication had been established, together with the strong probability that they were written in northern France. The purpose behind the work, moreover, became clear. In the early centuries the Church in Western Europe, and nowhere more than in France, was constantly harassed by the secular power, which intervened in ecclesiastical appointments, convened and dominated councils, subjected churchmen to the secular courts, and occasionally seized coveted Church property. The Pseudo-Isidore wrote at a time when the empire of Charlemagne was falling apart, and resistance which would have been futile while he lived could now be attempted against the lesser kings and dukes who followed him. The true purpose of the compilation of which the False Decretals were a part was thus simply to support, by the authority of ancient papal writings, the bishops in their struggle against secular interference. Since the papal writings did not exist, the Pseudo-Isidore made them up, and centuries later his invention was exposed by distinguished members of the Church and scholars.

Fanini (fä-nē'nē) *or* **Fannio** (fän'nyō), **Fanino.** Reformer; b. at Faenza, c1520; d. at Ferrara, August 20, 1550. He was a baker by trade, and had a great desire for learning. Of a lively and curious temperament, he became deeply interested in the religious questions that agitated his age. He read the books on these matters that circulated freely in Italy between 1534 and 1549, and may have been in touch with the reformer Bernardino Ochino. It was not long before he wholeheartedly took up the cause of the Reformation. His propagandizing in Faenza was at first of such effect that Ignatius Loyola sent in one of his companions to counteract it. Accused of heresy (1547), Fanini was convicted and imprisoned, but he soon renounced his heretical views and was restored to liberty. However, in 1549 he was again charged, imprisoned, and sentenced to death by the Inquisition. Renée of France (duchess of Ferrara) interceded in an attempt to save him, to no avail. He was hanged at Ferrara on August 20, 1550, and came to be considered a martyr of the Reformation.

Farinata degli Uberti (fä-rē-nä'tä dā-lyē ö-ber'tē). Member of a prominent Ghibelline family at Florence in the 13th century. In 1258 the victorious Guelphs destroyed the houses and towers of his family in the city and left the ruins as a reminder that they had overcome the Ghibellines. (The ruins were cleared some time later and became the site of the present Piazza della Signoria.) Leading Ghibellines went into exile. Farinata, with others, went to Siena, a Ghibelline city, and later took part in the Battle of Montaperti (1260), in which the Sienese inflicted a disastrous defeat on the Florentines. The Ghibelline exiles returned to Florence and took over the government. Manfred, whose German horsemen had been decisive in the Sienese victory, and other Ghibellines wanted to destroy Florence, that she might never again threaten the Ghibelline cities. Chroniclers relate that Farinata alone defended his city and prevented its destruction. For this act Dante immortalized him in the *Divina Commedia.* In that work, Dante finds him in one of the lower reaches of Hell, and tells him the Florentines hate his family for the blood they have caused to be shed. Farinata proudly replies: "I alone stood forth defending Florence when the cry went out to raze her walls and blot her from the earth." (*Inferno,* x)

Farinato (fä-rē-nä'tō) or **Farinati** (-tē), **Paolo.** Painter; b. at Verona, 1524; d. 1606. He was a pupil of his father and then of Niccolò Giolfino, and in the development of his mannerism was particularly influenced by Giulio Romano. To about 1570 he employed the mannerist elements of *contrapposto,* exaggerated chiaroscuro, and motifs and composition as treated by the central Italian schools, to produce tight and agitated works. After 1570 his compositions became broader, his forms ampler, and his color more lively. In this change he was influenced by Paolo Veronese, who had been his friend since 1552 when, with others, they had undertaken to paint for the cathedral at Mantua under the patronage of an Estense cardinal. After 1590 Farinato's artistic powers, but not his productivity, declined. A number of the many altarpieces, panels, and frescoes he produced in a long career are to be found in the museum at Verona and in churches in the city and its neighborhood. Other surviving works include a *St. Martin* (1552), cathedral, Mantua, *Deposition,* Pinacoteca, Bologna, *Madonna and Child,* Poldi Pezzoli Museum, Milan, and a *Coronation of the Virgin* distinguished for its good state of preservation and marked by mannerist elongation, in the Cannon Collection, Princeton. Other examples of his painting are at Arona (SS. Gratiniano e Felino), Florence, Frassino, Garda, Lovere, Milan (Brera), Piacenza (S. Sisto), Siena, Venice (Ca' d'Oro, S. Zaccaria), and in a number of churches in towns in Italy, as well as at Bonn, Paris, Prague, Vienna, New Haven, New York (Historical Society), Worcester (Massachusetts), and elsewhere. His many drawings are scattered in several great European collections.

Farnese (fär-nā'zā). Celebrated family whose origins are obscure, but were probably modest. The area of their activities and possessions was north of Rome, between Lake Bolsena and the Tyrrhenian Sea. They took part in the struggles between Viterbo and Orvieto, were noted for generations for their loyalty to the popes, as well as for their instinct for participating only in those struggles that would bring most profit to them. From the Middle Ages they increasingly acquired honors, wealth, and power, and produced a line

PAOLO FARINATO
Saints Adoring the Virgin and Child
Courtesy of The Pierpont Morgan Library, New York

thin; ᴛʜ, then; y, you; (variable) ḏ as d or j, ș as s or sh, ţ as t or ch, ẓ as z or zh; o, F. cloche; ü, F. menu; ċh, Sc. loch; ṅ, F. bonbon; ʙ, Sp. Córdoba (sounded almost like v).

of daring and acute warriors. The names Pietro and Ranuccio recur in the family for four centuries. Pietro III aided Florence against Henry VII (1311); Pietro IV freed Bologna (1354); Pietro V was the Florentine general in the victorious war against Pisa (1363). Pope Eugenius IV furthered the fortunes of the Farnese, made possible their acceptance as one of the great families of Rome, enriched them with lands, and delegated authority to Ranuccio the Elder (senator, 1417). Pier Luigi I married the cultivated Giovannella Caetani, sister of the duke of Sermoneta, and thereby entered the Roman nobility. In the next years the Farnese, while clinging to their traditional lands about Lake Bolsena (in which, on the island of Bisentina, they had the family tomb), and continuing as men of arms, adopted and furthered the new humanistic culture and became patrons of the arts and learning. Alessandro Farnese, son of Pier Luigi and Giovannella Caetani, became the first Farnese pope, as Paul III. His sister Giulia was the famous "La Bella," notorious in worldly Rome for her liaison with Pope Alexander VI. She had married Orsino Orsini (1489) and was the mother of a daughter, Laura, who married a nephew of Julius II. In a short time the Farnese were connected to many of the leading houses of Rome. Alessandro's sons Paolo and Ranuccio died young, but his other two children Pier Luigi II and Costanza played a conspicuous part in the life of the city, especially after Alessandro became pope. His reign of fifteen years gave him ample time to build up his family, his branch of which had been threatened with extinction until he had his children legitimized. In 1545 he invested his son Pier Luigi with the duchy of Parma and Piacenza. This was in addition to lands already given to increase the family holdings around Lake Bolsena. The duchy remained a fief of the Church, in theory, but was made hereditary. Pier Luigi was assassinated (1547) by the nobles in his realm that he tried to dominate. His son Ottavio (1520–1586) succeeded him. Ottavio married Margaret of Parma, natural daughter of Charles V. He was compelled to struggle with the pope and with his father-in-law to take possession of his duchy. Thereafter he was a mild and wise ruler who was beloved by his subjects. He was succeeded (1586) by his son Alessandro (see below). Pier Luigi's son Alessandro (1520–1589) became a cardinal at the age of 14. A highly cultivated man, friend of poets, humanists, and artists, he completed the magnificent Farnese palace in Rome that had been founded early in the reign of Pope Leo X. Sangallo the Younger began it, Michelangelo continued it, and Giacomo della Porta completed it. A third son, Orazio, married Diane de France, natural daughter of Henry II of France. With Pier Luigi the Roman phase of the Farnese family came to an end. Its members became more concerned with their ducal possessions than with the papacy, and as Spanish domination of Italy waxed their influence waned. Members of the family continued to govern the duchy until 1731, when the male line came to an end.

Farnese, Alessandro. Original name of Pope **Paul III.**

Farnese, Alessandro. General and statesman, governor-general of the Netherlands under Philip II of Spain, and duke of Parma and Piacenza; b. at Rome, August 27, 1545; d. at St. Waast, near Arras, December 3, 1592. He was the son of Ottavio Farnese and Margaret of Parma, natural daughter of Charles V. His father struggled for years to win control of his duchy of Parma, Piacenza, and Guastalla. Alessandro was brought up by his mother in Spain, and went with her to the court at Brussels when she became governor of the Netherlands. In 1565 he married the princess Maria of Portugal at Brussels, but thereafter established his home at Madrid. Thus his orientation from his early years was Spanish rather than Italian, and he passed his life in service to Spain. He was a nephew of the Spanish king and of Don John of Austria, and served with distinction under the latter at the battle of Lepanto (1571). In 1577 he led an army to the aid of Don John, at that time governor of the Netherlands, and gave brilliant evidence of his energy, decisiveness, and military skill. It was largely thanks to him that an unfavorable position for Spain in the Netherlands was reversed by the Spanish victory at Gembloux (1578) over the Flemings and the duke of Orange. A few months later, when Don John died, Farnese succeeded him as governor-general. His career thereafter was a successful mixture of political sagacity and military skill. He was among the ablest generals of his time, and in political matters was decisive, keen, and possessed to a high degree the family characteristic of being a good fisherman in troubled waters. For him, the strife between the Catholics and Protestants, the Flemings and the Walloons, presented an opportunity. He subdued and won back to Spanish domination Brabant and Flanders, captured Antwerp after a siege, and other cities, and thus consolidated the Spanish hold on the southern provinces. He was prepared to go ahead and win back Holland and Zeeland, but Philip II was obsessed with the idea of an attack on England and threw all his resources into preparing the Armada for it. The moment for the reconquest of the Netherlands was lost, and from this time, though there were still brilliant successes, Farnese suffered from lack of support and money. He was ordered on specific missions, fulfilled them successfully, but could not take advantage of the success for lack of money, and several times was forced to withdraw after a victory. In 1590, at the head of a Spanish army sent to support the Catholic League in France, he forced Henry of Navarre to raise the siege of Paris, but then he himself was forced to withdraw. Two years later he relieved besieged Rouen, but in doing so received the wound that brought his death in an abbey at St. Waast. In 1586 he had succeeded his father as duke of Parma and Piacenza, and requested permission to go to Italy and govern his duchy, but Philip II could not spare his ablest general and refused his request. Some of the correspondence between Farnese and Philip II has been published. A great deal more remains in the state archives at Parma. (The Farnese family originated near Viterbo and, through papal alliances, had won lands around Parma. The family tomb, which contains Alessandro's ashes, is in that city.) Other important Farnese documents are at Naples.

Farnese, Giulia. Mistress of Alexander VI; b. c1475; d. at Rome, March, 1524. In May, 1489, Cardinal Rodrigo Borgia was a witness to her marriage contract with Orsino Orsini, signed in the Borgia palace at Rome. Shortly after the cardinal became pope (August, 1492), Giulia was delivered of a girl, Laura, the new pope's daughter. One of the most beautiful young women of Rome (she was called "La Bella"), through Giulia's influence her brother Alessandro (later Paul III) was raised to the cardinalate. Some say she was the mother of the pope's last two children: Giovanni, called the "Infante romano" (1498–1547), and Rodrigo, born shortly after the pope's death. No authentic portrait of her exists, but a picture of the Virgin in the Borgia apartments, painted by Pinturicchio, is presumed by some to be a portrait of her.

Fastolf (fas′tolf), Sir **John.** English soldier and benefactor of Magdalen College, Oxford; b. c1378; d. at Caister, England, November 5, 1459. He is supposed by some to be the original of Shakespeare's Sir John Falstaff, the evidence being slight but definite. He was connected with Lollardry.

Fauchet (fō-she), **Claude.** French antiquary and historian; b. at Paris, July 3, 1530; d. there, 1601. He wrote *Les Antiquitez gauloises et françoises* (1579), and *Recueil de l'origine de la langue et poésie françoise* (1581).

Faust (foust), Doctor **Johann.** [Latinized, **Faustus.**] Person born at Kundling (Knittlingen), Württemberg, or at Roda, near Weimar, Germany, and said to have lived c1480–c1538. He was known as an elderly scholar, a magician, astrologer, and soothsayer, who boasted of performing wonders. His legend is that he made a pact with the Devil. In return for twenty-four years of youth, love, pleasure, and magic power he sold his soul to the Devil, and was carried off to Hell when the time was up. Any number of plays, epic poems, and operas have been based on the Faust legends, which were gathered together and published in a book that appeared at the Book Fair at Frankfurt on the Main in 1587.

Fazio (fä′tsvō), **Bartolommeo.** See **Facio, Bartolommeo.**

Fazio degli Uberti (dā′lyē ö-ber′tē). Florentine lyric poet; b. probably at Pisa, c1307; d. at Verona, c1368. He was a Ghibelline, a descendant of that Farinata degli Uberti who had single-handedly saved Florence when his Ghibelline allies wanted to destroy it. Fazio degli Uberto spent most of his life in exile, as the Guelphs gained the ascendancy in Florence. He was in the service of the Visconti at Milan, the Scaligeri at Verona, and the Carrarese at Padua. His best works are political poems inspired by his Ghibellinism. He also wrote imaginative and personal love lyrics and an allegorical work, *Dittamondo* (1350–1360), in terza rima. This Dantesque (it was inspired by the *Divina Commedia* and written in Dante's rhyme) and encyclopedic work is less successful as poetry than his lyrics, but is a source for many legendary tales. Some say Fazio, sobered by the Black Death of 1348, began to lead a more regular life and describes his conversion in the *Dittamondo.*

Fedele (fā-dā′lā), **Cassandra.** Poet and humanist; b. at Venice, c1465; d. there, March 24, 1558. She received a humanist education and was so well versed in Latin and Greek that she was regarded as a prodigy. She wrote elegant Latin verse, composed orations, and was learned in theology and philosophy. Her accomplishments won her the esteem of the most learned men and of such princes as Louis XII, Ferdinand the Catholic, and Ludovico il Moro. Venice so prized her as an ornament of its intellectual scene that when Queen Isabella of Aragon invited her to her court (1488) the Venetian senate refused to let her go to Spain, on the grounds that Venice could not spare such a learned woman. She married Giammaria Mappelli, a physician of Vicenza, and went with him to Crete. She returned to Venice where, after the death of her husband (1521), she was in reduced straits. Paul III named her superior of the Ospitale di S. Domenico at Venice, and she remained there until her death. Her letters and orations were published at Padua in 1636.

Federico I (fā-dā-rē′kō) of Aragon. King of Naples (1496–1501); b. c1451; d. at Tours, France, November 9, 1504. He was the second son of Ferrante of Aragon, king of Naples, and Isabella di Chiaramonte. As a young man he spent a number of years at the court of Charles the Bold of Burgundy and then at the court of Louis XI of France. His wife was Anne of Savoy, granddaughter of Louis. Because of his supposed sympathy for France, the Neapolitan barons expected him to support them when they revolted (1485) against his father and sought to place a French king on the throne of Naples. Federico, however, was loyal to his father, and later to his brother Alfonso II, and to his nephew Ferdinando I, in their struggles against the barons. He succeeded Ferdinando as king (October 7, 1496), and found his kingdom, threatened by France and Spain, in a most precarious position. The Italian states, always absorbed by their own interests, and the emperor Maximilian (too poor to do anything useful) denied him their support. Ferdinand the Catholic and Louis XII by the secret treaty of Granada had agreed to divide the kingdom of Naples between them, Ferdinand the Catholic having perfidiously assured Federico that the army he was sending to Naples was to defend Federico's interests. In June, 1501, the French were at Rome and the Spanish had landed in Calabria. Capua capitulated, and the French massacred the inhabitants. Federico, more embittered by the betrayal of his Spanish relatives than by the savagery of the French, signed a treaty with the latter (July 25, 1501) renouncing his rights to the kingdom of Naples in favor of Louis XII and withdrew to France. There Louis invested him with the countship of Maine, and there he died a few years later. With Federico, through no fault of his own, the stormy history of the dynasty of Aragon as rulers of an independent kingdom of Naples came to a close.

Federico da Montefeltro (dä mōn-tā-fel′-trō). Duke of Urbino, soldier, statesman, scholar, distinguished patron of arts and letters; b. at Gubbio, June 7, 1422; d. at Ferrara, September 10, 1482. The question of his parentage has been disputed. Pius II, writing of him in his *Commentaries*, said that he was the legitimate son of Bernardo della Carda, but that it suited his aims to call himself the illegitimate son of Guidantonio, count of Montefeltro and Urbino (d. 1442). He is generally accounted to have been Guidantonio's natural son. As a youth he was sent as a hostage to Venice while negotiations between Venice and Pope Eugenius IV were going on concerning the Colonna family, of whom the count of Montefeltro had been an adherent and whom the pope sought to bring to heel. After more than a year at Venice, where the doge, Francesco Foscari, foretold his future greatness, plague broke out and Federico received permission to withdraw to Mantua. There, along with the noble sons of the house of Gonzaga and the sons and daughters of other princely houses, he was a pupil of the celebrated teacher Vittorino da Feltre. The influence of the great teacher, both on his love for scholarship and on his humane temperament, was incalculable. At the age of 15 he was married to Gentile Brancaleone (to whom he had been betrothed at the age of eight), heiress of the lands of Mercatello and S. Angelo in Vado. Following his marriage (December 2, 1437) he became administrator of his wife's estates. The following June (1438), having inherited 400 men at arms from his uncle, he set off to join the condottiere Niccolò Piccinino as a soldier. In 1439 his war with Sigismondo Malatesta began. The causes for it lay in Sigismondo's attempts to win for himself lands that belonged to the counts of Montefeltro. Federico became the implacable enemy of Sigismondo; their strife lasted, with interruptions, for twenty-four years, and ended with Federico triumphant. He immediately recaptured S. Leo, the crenellated aerie that was the ancient capital of Montefeltro, and was besieging Pesaro when he learned of the murder of Oddantonio da Montefeltro, his half brother and the reigning count of Montefeltro and Urbino (July, 1444). He returned to the city and was chosen lord by the people in exchange for certain guarantees of the peoples' privileges which, judging by his long reign, uninterrupted by civil strife, he scrupulously observed. His state included Urbino, Montefeltro, Gubbio, Cagli, the fiefs inherited by his wife, and a number of fortified villages. Fighting in the service of the princes of Italy and on his own behalf against Sigismondo Malatesta, he was often away from home. He entered the service of Francesco Sforza, persuaded Galeazzo Malatesta to cede Pesaro to Francesco's brother Alessandro (1445), bought Fossombrone, and was excommunicated by Eugenius IV for having supported Francesco Sforza in his campaign to win the Marches. Pope Nicholas V absolved him in 1450. In the same year Federico gave a tournament to celebrate the elevation of Francesco Sforza as duke of Milan. It was in this tournament (having been warned by many portents not to take part) that Federico lost his right eye and had his nose broken. Captain for the Florentines (1451), he then passed to the service of Alfonso I of Naples, and next supported Pius II and Alfonso's heir Ferrante in the war against the Angevin claimants to the throne of Naples. He became celebrated as a captain, as much for his loyalty to those he served as for his vigor and success in battle. He was the pope's captain in the pope's, and his own, war on Sigismondo Malatesta. The pope wrote him, "Proceed then, conquer, destroy, and consume this accursed Sigismondo, and in him neutralize the poison of Italy." Energetically executing Pius II's command, he took Senigallia from Sigismondo (August, 1462), and the following year took Fano after a siege of four months (September, 1463). Sigismondo tried by all means to woo him from the pope's side, but Federico, with every reason to distrust Sigismondo, passed on his communications to the pope and remained firm. In the winter of 1462–1463 he blockaded Rimini. Many of Sigismondo's cities had already surrendered. The detested Malatesta, beaten on every front, was forced to yield. A few years of peace followed.

When his wife Gentile died (c1457), Federico became betrothed to Alessandro Sforza's daughter Battista, whom he married at Urbino on February 10, 1460. The cultivated, highly intelligent, and gentle daughter of Alessandro and the poetess Costanza da Varano, Federico called her "the delight alike of my public and my private hours." She was left in charge of his state in his frequent absences, and governed it with firmness and good sense. In 1466 he was commander of the Italian League against Venice and defeated Colleoni at the battle of La Molinella, in which field artillery was used for the first time (1467). On the death of Sigismondo Malatesta (1468), Pope Paul II sought to make good the Church's claim to Rimini. Federico, fearing the growth of papal power on his borders, supported Sigismondo's son Roberto and defeated the pope's army (August, 1469). In the service of Florence, Federico overran rebellious Volterra (1472), thought to be an impregnable fortress; contrary to his orders and his policy, the hapless city was sacked by his victorious troops. Pope Sixtus IV, in need of his services for his ambitions in the Romagna, created Federico duke of Urbino (1474), and arranged the marriage of his nephew Giovanni della Rovere with Federico's daughter Giovanna. In the same year Federico received the Order of the Garter from Henry VII of England and the Order of the Ermine from Ferrante of Naples. As commander of the papal forces, he fought against Florence (1479), but in the war for Ferrara (1482), he was captain of the league which included Florence, against Venice and the pope. In this war, according to Vespasiano, the Venetians offered him 80,000 ducats a year to stay at home. One of Federico's officers remarked, "Eighty thousand ducats is a good price simply for staying at home." "To keep faith is still better, and is worth more than all the gold in the world," was Federico's unhesitating reply. A great procession, composed of his sorrowing subjects, accompanied him when he left Urbino for the war in behalf of Ferrara. He never returned. He left his state three times as large as it had been when he succeeded to it. One of the most celebrated captains of his day, Federico sold his services to now one side, now another. He fulfilled each of his contracts with a loyalty that was almost unheard of, and used the money that he earned to promote the arts of peace in his own state.

For it is as a wise and merciful ruler, a man of letters, and a patron of the arts that Federico is distinguished in the history and development of the Renaissance. By just laws, scrupulously administered, he kept order in his duchy. He is said to have mingled freely with his citizens, stopping to talk with them on his daily rides and walks in his domain, learning their needs and their grievances, which he at once filled or set right. The cast of his mind was truly scholarly. He was learned in Latin and in sacred and secular letters. He studied logic, philosophy, and theology, and could converse and argue on these subjects with the most learned men. Around him and his dearly loved Battista was gathered a court devoted to learning and the arts, a court in which discipline, and physical and military exercises had their part. Humanists and poets were welcomed there. He founded the richest library of the west at Urbino, and in the course of fourteen years kept thirty to forty copyists employed to transcribe manuscripts for it. (Except for the volumes that were lost or destroyed in the disturbances of 1502 and 1517, the library is now in the Vatican.) His taste was wide-ranging. Works in his library included the Latin poets, orators, grammarians, and historians; the Greek writers in Latin translation; the works of the doctors and fathers of the Church, Greek as well as Latin, ancient and medieval; works on canon law; a sumptuous two-volume Bible, bound in gold brocade with silver fittings; works on astrology, geometry, arithmetic, natural philosophy, architecture, painting, music, sculpture, medicine; all the works of Dante and Petrarch in Latin and in the vernacular, and the works of Boccaccio in Latin; the writings of Pope Pius II and of all the writers and humanists and poets of his age, including Coluccio Salutati, Leonardo Bruni, Fra Ambrogio Traversari, Gianozzo Manetti, Panormita, Filelfo, Pontano, Vergerio, and a dozen others; books in Greek including the writings of Homer, Aristotle, Plato, and the poets, Herodotus, Thucydides, and Pausanias. In sum, the best that was available of Greek or Latin writers, and commentaries thereon, was to be found in the library at Urbino, along with medieval and contemporary writers, and books in Hebrew. Each of the books in his library was itself a work of art, bound in crimson, with fittings and clasps of silver, "beautifully illuminated and written on parchment." Vespasiano, who helped the duke create his library and served as his librarian, listed the books in it; he found on comparing it with the catalogues of the libraries of the Vatican, San Marco at Florence, Pavia, and the University of Oxford, that of them all, Federico's was the only one that was complete. That he liked to be represented as a man of learning is evident from some of his portraits, in one of which he had himself portrayed by Justus of Ghent, the Flemish painter, in full armor, seated before a lectern, his little son Guidobaldo at his side, reading. In another he is shown, again with Guidobaldo, listening to a humanist lecture. His state was happy and prosperous. He continued the construction of the cathedral (begun by Guidantonio in 1439) and caused many other buildings to be constructed, including palaces at Fossombrone, Cagli, and Gubbio. Foremost among the palaces was the ducal palace, the *Corte*, at Urbino, begun in 1454. For this he employed the Dalmatian architect Luciano Laurana who designed a palace that is a monument to the taste of the duke and the skill of the architect. Incorporating what remained of older structures, it is a collection of spacious rooms and halls exquisitely decorated with stuccoes and frescoes, around a gracious courtyard on the piazza, and with a façade of noble turreted towers and loggias facing the approaches to Urbino. The architects, for Laurana was neither the first nor the last but had, perhaps, the distinguishing influence, mastered the difficulty of building a palace on the face of what is almost a sheer rock cliff. Melozzo da Forlì was among those who painted its frescoes; Ambrogio da Milano, Baccio Pontelli (who succeeded Laurana), and Domenico Rosselli made sculptures for it; Francesco di Simone Ferrucci executed friezes and stuccoes. Flemish masters designed the magnificent tapestries showing the siege of Troy that were among the glories of the palace. Justus of Ghent came from Flanders to paint portraits of Federico and other members of his court. Piero della Francesca, of whom Federico was an admiring patron, painted, according to Vasari, "Many beautiful pictures of small figures, most of which have been ruined or lost because of wars that have ravaged that State." Of the works painted by Piero for Federico, *The Flagellation*, now in the Ducal palace (which is a museum), was painted for the old sacristy of the cathedral; *The Montefeltro Altarpiece*, also called *the Brera Altarpiece* (painted about 1475 and so-called because it is now in the Pinacoteca di Brera at Milan), has a characteristic left profile portrait of Federico. The altarpiece may have been painted to commemorate the birth of Federico's son Guidobaldo or, as some think, in memory of Battista, who died in 1472. The finest workers in *intarsia* paneled his *studiolo* in the palace, working to designs by Botticelli. The brilliant court that assembled within the splendid structure was free of dissipation and vice. Federico was a disciplined and pious man; he demanded high standards from those surrounding him. There was no court in Italy the equal of his. Castiglione, who served it, called it "the light of Italy." The sons of leading families were sent to Urbino to be reared; among these were Giovanni della Rovere, Francesco Orsini, Girolamo and Pierantonio Colonna, Andrea Doria, and Gian Giacomo Trivulzio. By his wife Battista, whom he called "the ornament of my house and the devoted sharer of my fortunes," Federigo had nine children. (His first wife produced no children.) The first of these children, a daughter, was born when her mother was 14 years old. Seven more daughters followed her. Their longed-for son was born in January, 1472. Battista, who had vowed her life in return for a son, died on July 6 of the same year, mourned alike by her husband and his subjects. Of his children, Guidobaldo married Elizabetta Gonzaga of Mantua; Elizabetta (born 1461 or 1462) married (1475) Roberto Malatesta, for whom, despite wars against him, Federico came to have great respect and to whose care he commended his duchy in his will (Roberto, who died within a few days of Federico, was found to have returned the compliment in his will); Giovanna married (1474) Giovanni della Rovere, through whom the della Rovere dynasty was founded at Urbino in her son Francesco Maria della Rovere; Agnesina married (1474) Fabrizio Colonna and was the mother of Vittoria; Violante married Galeotto Malatesta; Costanza married Antonello Sanseverino, prince of Salerno. A natural son, Bonconte, died at Naples of the plague at the age of 14; a second natural son, Antonio, accompanied his father on his campaigns. He married Emilia Pia, who was the devoted companion of Duchess Elizabetta, wife of Guidobaldo. A natural daughter, Gentile, married Agostino Fregoso of Genoa; her sons, Federigo and Ottaviano, were often at the court at Urbino. Existing portraits of Federico, in addition to those mentioned above, include the famous diptych by Piero della Francesca in the Uffizi, showing Federico with his allegorical Triumph on the reverse, in one half of the diptych, and Battista with her allegorical Triumph on the reverse, in the other half. Because of the loss of his right eye, Federico is always shown in left profile, thus concealing the loss, but emphasizing his broken nose. Men of his own time recognized the constellation of noble qualities that illuminated and animated Federico; he was mild, just, pious, and wise, "courteous, eloquent, and true." Poggio wrote that he was "considerate of his soldiery, compassionate to the enemy"; "A Mars in the field, a Minerva in his administration," "the model of our age." Vespasiano called his court "a refuge for all men of worth"; and another contemporary called him "equally learned in every branch of study, patient under reverses, most moderate in prosperity, the bravest of generals." Amid the accounts of intrigue, murder, poisonings, terrible vengeances, wholesale massacre, perfidy, and treason that blackened the annals of many courts of his time, the record of the court of Urbino reflects a vision of grace—serene, industrious, just, and cultivated, with a ruler in Federico who epitomized for his contemporaries the ideal of the Renaissance prince.

Federighi (fā-dā-rē′gē), **Antonio.** Sienese sculptor and architect; d. 1490. He was an assistant to Jacopo della Quercia in various works for the cathedral at Siena, and for a long time retained the marks of his master's style. Among his works for the cathedral is his *Sibilla Eritrea*, one of the many designs carved for the marvelous marble pavement.

In 1451 he went to Orvieto as chief of the works of the cathedral. He remained there until 1456, when he returned to Siena and worked on figures of saints for the Loggia di Mercanzia. He also carried out architectural projects in this period, as the Loggia of Pius II and the richly decorated Palazzo delle Papesse (a palace built for a sister of Pius II who was thought to have such influence on him that she was called "Popess"). Other works include a Moses and two putti in the Museo dell' opera dell' Duomo at Siena, and a stoup at Orvieto. In his later period he attempted to adapt classical models in his sculpture without spectacular success.

Federmann (fā′dėr-män), **Nicholas.** [Old spellings, **Fredeman, Frideman.**] German traveler in South America; b. at Ulm, in Swabia, Germany, 1501; d. either in a shipwreck or at Madrid, Spain, c1543. He made extensive explorations of the interior of Venezuela, of which he wrote an account. He also made independent explorations north of the Orinoco River.

Fedra (fed′rä). See **Inghirami, Tommaso.**

Fei (fā′ē), **Paolo di Giovanni.** Sienese painter; active between 1372 and 1410. He was influenced by Simone Martini, the Lorenzetti and, in the latter part of his career, by Bartolo di Fredi. His *Nativity of the Virgin* is one of a number of works in the Pinacoteca, Siena. Other works in that city include a *Virgin with Child,* cathedral, and paintings in S. Maria della Scala and S. Bernardino. A *Madonna and Child* with characteristic gold background is in the Metropolitan Museum, New York, and *Assumption of the Virgin* is in the National Gallery, Washington. Other paintings by this typically Sienese painter are at Asciano, Modena, Naples, Poggibonsi (S. Lucchese), Rome (Vatican), Altenburg, Amsterdam, Brussels, Cologne, Rotterdam, Atlanta (Georgia), Memphis (Tennessee), and San Diego (California).

Felice da Cantalice (fā-lē′chā dä kän-tä-lē′chā), Saint. Ecclesiastic; b. at Cantalice (Rieti), 1513; d. at Rome, May 18, 1587. Of humble origin, he entered the Order of the Capuchins at the age of 30 as a lay brother, at Fiuggi, then went to Rome as a postulant. He discharged his religious duties faithfully and came to be greatly beloved by the Romans of his time for his modesty, goodness, and genial temperament. He was canonized by Clement XI in 1712.

Felix (fē′liks). Name taken by Amadeus VIII when he was elected (1439) pope by the Council of Basel. See **Amadeus VIII.**

Feltre (fel′trā), **Vittorino da.** See **Vittorino da Feltre.**

Ferdinand I (fėr′di-nand) (of *Aragon*). [Called **Ferdinand the Just.**] King of Aragon (1412–1416); b. c1379; d. 1416. He served as co-regent with his sister-in-law, Catherine, widow of Henry III of Castile, daughter of John of Gaunt, and mother of John II, the infant king of Castile, Ferdinand having refused the throne on the invitation of the Cortes. He was a prominent supporter of the antipope Benedict XIII at the beginning of the Council of Constance (1414–1418), but after the abdication of Gregory XII and the deposition of John XXIII, he was induced by the emperor Sigismund to withdraw his support in the interest of the unity of the Church.

Ferdinand V (of *Castile*). [Called **Ferdinand the Catholic**; additional titles, **Ferdinand II** (of *Aragon and Sicily*), **Ferdinand III** (of *Naples*).] King of Castile; b. at Sos, in Aragon, Spain, March 10, 1452; d. at Madrigalejo, in Estremadura, Spain, January 23 (or, according to some authorities, February 23), 1516. He was the son of John II of Navarre and Aragon, who associated him with himself in the government of Aragon in 1466, and in 1468 declared him king of Sicily. In October, 1469, he married Isabella, sister of Henry IV of Castile and heiress of that throne. Ferdinand and Isabella were, on the death of Henry in 1474, recognized as joint sovereigns of Castile by the nobles and the junta of Segovia; but a strong party, including the marquis of Villena, the Grand master of Calatrava, and the archbishop of Toledo, supported by Alfonso V of Portugal and Louis XI of France, declared in favor of Juana "la Beltraneja" (i.e., daughter of Beltran), whom Henry had in his will acknowledged as his legitimate child and designated as his successor. Ferdinand defeated Alfonso at Toro, with the result that the whole of Castile submitted to Isabella and her consort in 1479. He succeeded his father in Aragon in the same year (Navarre going to his sister Leonora de Foix). In 1482 he resumed the war against the Moors, which resulted in the conquest of Granada in 1492. For his expulsion of the Moors from Granada, he was given the title "the Catholic" by the pope. Machiavelli, in *The Prince*, writes of Ferdinand as a splendid example of the qualities he himself urged, sometimes ironically, in a prince. As to the wars against the Moors, "always making use of the pretext of religion, he adopted the piously cruel policy of driving the Moors from his kingdom and despoiling them." In this way, wrote Machiavelli cynically, Ferdinand built up a fine personal army for a pious purpose, occupied the minds of the nobles with patriotism and piety so that without their realizing it he had brought them under his control, and thus consolidated his own power in what was accepted as a very worthy cause. By the treaty of Barcelona of January 19, 1493, Ferdinand promised Charles VIII of France (in return for great territorial concessions) that he would not go to the aid of the Aragonese of Naples nor oppose Charles in any way in his invasion of Italy to claim Naples. Yet in 1495 he joined the emperor, the pope, and the states of Milan and Venice against Charles. By a treaty with Louis XII, successor of Charles, Ferdinand agreed to divide the kingdom of Naples with the French king. However, when the time to implement the treaty came, the Spanish contested the line of division and wound up by defeating the French and driving them out of Naples (1503). Ferdinand himself ascended the throne of Naples (1504). After the death of of Isabella (November 26, 1504), and the death of Philip I, husband of their daughter Juana, he was proclaimed regent of Castile, since Juana had gone mad when her husband died in 1506. In an attempt to circumvent the claims of Philip's line (the Hapsburgs), he married (1505) Germaine de Foix, but their only son died in infancy, and Philip's son inherited as Charles I (Charles V of the Holy Roman Empire). In 1511 he formed an alliance with Venice and Pope Julius II (the Holy League) for the expulsion of the French from Italy. Navarre, on the other hand, entered into an alliance with France. This gave him a pretext for invading Navarre, which was conquered in 1512, and incorporated with Castile in 1515. He thus united under his sway the four kingdoms into which Spain was at this time divided (Aragon, Castile, Granada, and Navarre), besides Sicily and Naples. The chief events of his reign, besides those already mentioned, were the establishment of the Inquisition at Seville (1480); the annexation to the crown of the grand-mastership of the military orders of Calatrava (1487), Alcantara (1494), and San Jago (1499); the expulsion of the Jews (1492) which brought commercial life in Spain to a standstill; the expulsion of the Moors (1502) who had brought to Spain their advances in science and agriculture and had fostered them in Granada for 800 years; and the discovery of America by Columbus (1492). The end and aim of Ferdinand was power and the consolidation of it in a nation of Spain. He was not sensitive to the means he used, and was unscrupulous, cruel, wily, and faithless, all in the name of a religion and piety which he avidly embraced. "A certain prince . . . preaches nothing but peace and faith and yet is the enemy of both, and if he had observed either he would already on numerous occasions have lost both his state and his renown." Thus Machiavelli cites Ferdinand as a great example of what a prince must be, as opposed to what he must seem to be, and of the qualities, regrettably wicked, that a successful prince must possess.

Ferdinand I (of the *Holy Roman Empire*). Emperor of the Holy Roman Empire (1558–1564); b. at Alcalá de Henares, Spain, March 10, 1503; d. at Vienna, July 25, 1564. He was the younger brother of the emperor Charles V. In 1521 he married the princess Anna of Hungary, and on the death (1526) of her brother, Louis II, he was elected king of Bohemia and Hungary. His title to the throne of Hungary was disputed by John I (John Zápolya), who, supported by the Turks, obtained possession of a part of the country. The struggle continued under Zápolya's successor John II (John Sigismund), truce following uneasy truce. Ferdinand retained only a small part of Hungary and paid tribute to the Turks for that. He became in 1521 president of the council of regency appointed to govern Germany during the emperor's absence in Spain, was elected king of the Romans in 1531, and became emperor on the abdication of Charles V in 1558. He exerted himself, but with little success, to settle the religious disputes between the Protestants and the Roman Catholics in Germany. He fought in the war of the Schmalkaldic League (1546–

1547) but after that maintained a more neutral position. He negotiated the treaty between the emperor and the elector Maurice of Saxony in 1552, and was responsible for the peace of Augsburg (1555). In 1519 Charles and Ferdinand succeeded Maximilian I in the Austrian dominions, and in 1521–1522 Charles relinquished his share in this sovereignty to his brother.

Ferdinand III (of *Naples*). See **Ferdinand V** (of *Castile*).

Ferdinand I (of *Portugal*). King of Portugal (1367–1383); b. c1345; d. 1383. He was the son and successor of Pedro I of Portugal. On the death (1369) of Pedro el Cruel, king of Castile and Leon, he claimed the throne of Castile, which was seized by Henry II (Henry of Trastamara), illegitimate brother of Pedro. He renounced his claim in 1371, after some indecisive fighting, agreeing to marry Henry's sister (having earlier agreed to marry the daughter of his ally, the king of Aragon). But he fell in love with the wife of one of his courtiers, dissolved her marriage, and made her his queen. He then allied himself with John of Gaunt to unseat Henry, but their campaign failed. He backed the Englishman again after Henry's death in 1379, then made a separate peace, the heir to the Portuguese throne marrying John I of Castile. But the Portuguese had had enough of his intrigues and on his death a revolution placed on the throne his natural brother, John, grand master of the order of Aviz. Ferdinand was the last of the direct Burgundian line, which had reigned in Portugal from c1112.

Ferdinand I (of *Tuscany*). See **Medici, Ferdinando I de'.**

Ferdinand the Catholic. See **Ferdinand V** (of *Castile*).

Ferdinand the Just. See **Ferdinand I** (of *Aragon*).

Ferdinando (fer-dē-nän′dō) **I** (of *Naples*). See **Ferrante,** King of Naples (1458–1494).

Ferdinando II (of *Aragon*). [Called **Ferrandino** or **Ferrantino;** his grandfather, Ferrante, was Ferdinando I.] King of Naples (1495–1496); b. at Naples, June 26, 1467; d. there, October 5, 1496. Well educated by outstanding humanist teachers, his friend and counselor, constant in adversity as well as in prosperity, was the poet il Cariteo. His first military and political experience came when he helped his grandfather Ferrante, whom he dearly loved, and his father crush the conspiracy of the barons (1485). On the invasion of Italy by Charles VIII, Ferrandino was sent with an army against him but, lacking sufficient troops and deserted by such possible allies as the Orsini, Florentines and the pope, he was forced to fall back on Naples. His father, Alfonso II, knowing himself hated by his subjects, abdicated (January 23, 1495) in the hope that they would support Ferrandino against the French. Ferrandino fought with reckless heroism against the French, but his troops melted away, Capua and Gaeta fell, Naples rebelled. Ferrandino fled to Ischia and then to Messina, gathered a new army which he led into Calabria, and began the struggle to win back his kingdom. The Neapolitans, who had at first welcomed the French, soon lost their enthusiasm for their new rulers. Charles, in the face of a league being formed against him by the Italian states, was persuaded to leave Naples but left a garrison of French troops there on his departure. The Neapolitans rebelled. Ferrandino, aided by Venice, at the usual extortionate price, and by the king of Aragon, whose granddaughter Isabella he married (she was his own aunt and he loved her with a passion), continued his fight against the remaining French troops and the barons, and won his victory (July 20, 1496). Worn out by three years of grinding warfare, he did not live to enjoy it. A soldier of indomitable courage, he was at the same time a lover of letters and of music, and was the first of the house of Aragon in Naples to win the hearts of his people. He was succeeded by his uncle, Federico.

Fernández de Enciso (fer-nän′deth dā en-thē′sō), **Martín.** See **Enciso, Martín Fernández de.**

Ferrabosco (fer-rä-bōs′kō), **Alfonso.** Musician; b. at Bologna, 1543; d. there, August 12, 1588. He went to England about 1560, and served (1562–1578) as a musician at the court of Queen Elizabeth. Many of the madrigals he composed in this period are to be found in English collections. He left the court of Elizabeth for that of the duke of Savoy, and continued to compose madrigals, two books of which were published by him in 1587.

Ferramola (fer-rä-mō′lä), **Floriano.** Brescian painter; active at the end of the 15th century. Part of a fresco transferred to canvas, of the Piazza Maggiore at Brescia, is in the Victoria and Albert Museum, London; other signed and dated paintings are at Lovere and a lunette in the Church of the Carmine at Brescia. An undistinguished painter, he was at his best when he was most successful in imitating Vincenzo Foppa, of whom he was a follower.

Ferrante (fer-rän′tā) (of *Naples*). [Also, **Ferdinando I.**] King of Naples (1458–1494); b. in Catalonia, Spain, c1431; d. at Naples, January 25, 1494. He was the natural son of Alfonso V of Aragon (Alfonso I of Naples) and a woman of Barcelona. (But some said he was not Alfonso's son at all, but the son of a Moor. Others said Alfonso's wife had the mother of Ferrante smothered; that Alfonso sent his wife back to Spain and never saw her again.) Alfonso, having won the kingdom of Naples (February, 1443), declared his son Ferrante duke of Calabria and his heir and successor to the throne (March 3, 1443). To win support from the powerful nobles for Ferrante, Alfonso gave Isabella di Chiaramonte, granddaughter of the Prince of Taranto, to his son in marriage (1446). But Alfonso could not smooth his son's path to the throne. In an Italy where practically every second prince was illegitimate, and nobody thought a thing about it, Ferrante alone was always known as "the Bastard." Whether it was bitterness at the slurs continually cast on his birth or from some other cause Ferrante, although a sound administrator and a sagacious observer of the Italian political scene, was suspicious, revengeful, perfidious, and cruel to the point of ferocity. His long reign began (1458) with a war to secure his throne. Aided by Pope Pius II, who recognized the legitimacy of his claim (Pope Calixtus III had not, and had asserted that Naples reverted to the Church on the death of Alfonso), and by the pope's generals, Federico da Montefeltro and Alessandro Sforza, he repulsed the Angevin claimant, Jean of Anjou, and crushed his own nobles who, led by the princes of Rossano and Taranto, had called in the French against him. He killed Jacopo Piccinino, the former general of his enemies, following a banquet given at Naples in Jacopo's honor; arrested and imprisoned the prince of Rossano (who died a violent death in prison); and the Prince of Taranto died. By 1464 his throne was secured. The people of Naples were in ferment because of the repressive taxes levied to support his father's extravagance and because of their hatred of the haughty Spaniards brought in by Alfonso to fill all the important posts. Ferrante reorganized the fiscal policy of his kingdom, encouraged the Spaniards to leave, corrected some feudal abuses, promoted commerce and agriculture, attempted to protect the rights of his people, and unceasingly sought to strengthen his kingdom within and to protect it from without. In 1465 he reopened the university and saw that it was staffed with professors of high standing. He continued work on the Arch of Triumph (celebrating Alfonso's victory) of the Castel Nuovo, the finest Renaissance monument at Naples. During part of his reign the arts of peace were fostered. A true southern Italian and Latin culture developed, outstanding representatives of which were Panormita (1394–1471), Sannazzaro (1456–1530), and Pontano (1426–1503, one of the few who won and kept Ferrante's trust). The literature of the period reflected the life, needs, habits, and characteristics of the area.

In external affairs, Ferrante avoided his father's mistake of trying to dominate Italy. He tried instead to strengthen his realm by allying his house, through his numerous legitimate and illegitimate children, with the leading houses of Italy and elsewhere. Already good relations with Milan were further strengthened by the marriage of his son Alfonso, duke of Calabria, with Ippolita, daughter of Francesco Sforza. He himself married (1477, his first wife having died in 1465) Giovanna, sister of Ferdinand the Catholic. He was sometimes at odds with the popes, twice sent his armies to the very gates of Rome, but supported Sixtus IV in his war against Florence following the Pazzi Conspiracy. However, when Lorenzo the Magnificent risked his life to come to Naples, Ferrante, after some bargaining, made peace with Florence without reference to the pope (1480). This was probably the high point of Ferrante's reign. Peace at home, prosperity, a brilliant court in magnificent surroundings, and the peace with Lorenzo won for him the epithet "Judge of Italy." To this epithet was added that of "Savior of Italy and of Europe" when his son, the duke of Calabria, won back Otranto from the Turks (September, 1481, although in fact it was the death of the Sultan, Mohammed II, that caused the Turks to retire). Venice was his archenemy, because the Serene Republic prevented the expansion of Naples in the only direction open to it—the East; because Venice continually wavered on the edge of support for the Angevin claims to the throne of Naples; and because of Venetian threats to let loose the Turks on southern Italy. His war to support Ferrara against Venice and the pope (1482) was an enormous drain on the economy of his kingdom. He was forced to borrow huge sums from Florentine bankers, even to pawn the jewels of the crown and books of the royal library. The heavy taxes he now levied erased his earlier fiscal reforms. Finally, his barons conspired against him, revolted, and were savagely crushed (1485). In August, 1489, Pope Innocent VIII asserted that he had not observed the terms of a treaty of 1486, declared him deposed, and opened negotiations with Charles VIII of France. His relations with Milan became tense because Ludovico il Moro had usurped the place of Gian Galeazzo Sforza, husband of Isabella, Ferrante's granddaughter. In fear of being without allies in Italy, Ludovico turned to Charles VIII (and ultimately opened the gates of Italy to the French). The Neapolitan barons, scattered through the courts of Italy and Europe, spent their time persuading the enemies of Naples that the kingdom would be easy to conquer. With the death (1492) of Lorenzo de' Medici, the "balance of Italy," the one force that had held in check the conflicting ambitions of Naples and Milan, states of almost equal power, was removed. Innocent VIII died the same year and "though," as Guicciardini wrote, "otherwise of no value to the commonweal," he at least no longer interfered in the affairs of Italy to upset the peace. When his successor, Alexander VI, was elected, Ferrante "told his wife with tears—which he was unaccustomed to shed even at the death of his children—that a pope had been elected who would be fatal to Italy and the whole Christian world." The days ahead were ominous. Ferrante, who had been a strong ruler and a good administrator, almost alone of the more powerful princes, realized what it would mean to all of Italy to invite the French, as Ludovico was about to do, into Italy to attack the kingdom of Naples. He warned Ludovico to consider well how many times foreign powers had been called into Italy because of internal strife, and to remember that the effects of their oppressive and tyrannical acts had never been effectively obliterated. Ferrante was preparing to head off the invasion of the French by negotiation with Milan when he suddenly died. He was succeeded by his son Alfonso II. In addition to the epithets applied to Ferrante, as noted above, he was known by his contemporaries as "faithless." Guicciardini speaks of his "unbelievable guile and dissimulation." His reputation for treachery and cruelty was almost unparalleled in the bloodstained pages of the history of the Italian states and princes. Free from personal profligacy, he concentrated all his energies on destroying his enemies, of which he had many. He captured them by treachery, kept some in cages, and killed others, whom he then caused to be mummified, dressed in costume, and placed on exhibition in a kind of museum. Those who served him most faithfully were the leading victims of his suspicion and found, after a lifetime of service, their estates confiscated and their lives forfeited.

Ferrara (fer-rä′rä), **Antonio da.** See **Antonio da Ferrara.**

Ferrara-Florence, Council of. Church council which, opening at Ferrara in 1438, was transferred to Florence in 1439 on account of a plague at Ferrara. It proclaimed (1439), under Pope Eugenius IV, the union of the Greek and Roman churches. The last sitting was at Rome in 1445. Many distinguished Greeks attended the council, including John VIII Palaeologus, whose principal interest was to win support from the west in his struggles against the Turks. In his train were some of the most eminent Greek scholars (Georgius Gemistus Plethon) and churchmen (Bessarion, later cardinal) of the time. The accord reached by the council was short-lived.

Ferrari (fer-rä′rē), **Bartolomeo.** Ecclesiastic; b. at Milan, 1499; d. there, November 24, 1544. Of a distinguished Milanese family, he studied law at Pavia and then became a priest and devoted himself to works of piety. In 1530, with others, he founded the order of the Barnabites (Regular Clerks of St. Paul, called Barnabites from the monastery of St. Barnabas at Milan where the order was founded).

Ferrari, Defendente. Piedmontese painter; b. at Chivasso (Piedmont); active between 1511 and 1535. Little is known of his life and training. His career was passed mainly in the western Piedmont, where many of his works are still located. A contract for a polyptych, dated 1530, is the only known documentation of his work as an artist. To the Lombard elements of the school of Vincenzo Foppa that were passed on to him by his local master were added Flemish elements. These had crossed the Alps into the Piedmont and their Gothicized manner was maintained in that area despite the artistic developments that had taken place in other parts of Italy in the Renaissance. Defendente was a leading representative of this fusion of northern Gothic and new Renaissance influences. The types of the Madonnas and saints that appear in his large polyptychs (that were often enclosed in ornate frames made in his own workshop), are close to those of northern art, while Renaissance architectural motifs constitute the backgrounds. His narrative gift is evident in predella panels, in which his choice of detail and treatment of light and color are more northern than Italian. He left a number of altarpieces in the churches of the Piedmont. At Turin there is a polyptych in the cathedral and an important collection of panel paintings and predella panels in the Sabauda Gallery, the Albertina, and the Municipal Museum. Other works are at Vercelli, in the Carrara Academy, Bergamo, Brera, Milan, Pavia, Rome (Vatican), Philadelphia (Johnson Collection), New York, Baltimore (Walters Art Gallery), Cambridge, Denver, Madison (Wisconsin), Worcester (Massachusetts), at London, Paris, and elsewhere.

Ferrari, Gaudenzio. Painter; b. at Valduggia (Piedmont), 1471; d. at Milan, January 31, 1546. Most of his life was passed in his native region. After spending part of his childhood at Varallo, he went to Milan, where he worked under a painter whose activity is unknown. More than by his teacher, he was probably influenced to some extent, as were so many, by Leonardo da Vinci and his pupils, especially by Bramantino. His early works, *Eternal Father* and scenes from the lives of St. Anne and St. Joachim, Turin, as well as the frescoes (1507, 1513) in the Church of the Madonna delle Grazie at Varallo, are especially reminiscent of Bramantino. He was subject also to Flemish and northern influence as it existed in the Piedmont. Out of many elements he forged his own style, one characterized by exuberant and realistic decoration, a sense of movement, and by the spontaneity of his imagination. The *Crucifixion*, Church of the Madonna delle Grazie, Varallo, is an outstanding example of this style. Many more frescoes by Gaudenzio and his school are in the numerous chapels of the Sacro Monte, near Varallo. He worked at Arona (S. Maria), Vercelli (S. Andrea, S. Cristoforo), Como (cathedral), and Novara, painting frescoes and altarpieces. His frescoes on the life of the Virgin in the Church of the Madonna dei Miracoli at Saronno, begun in 1534, constitute one of his most important undertakings. The *Assumption* in the dome of the church, where the Virgin is surrounded by a whirling wheel of angels, is close to Correggio's *Assumption* in the cathedral at Parma. After 1539 Gaudenzio settled at Milan. The painting of this period, as in S. Maria delle Grazie, is somewhat heavier and coarser than in his earlier works, and lacks their vigor and exhilaration. A series of frescoes on the childhood of the Virgin, begun in 1545 in S. Maria della Pace, in which he seemed to recapture his robust earlier style, was incomplete at the time of his death. Other examples of his painting are in the Poldi Pezzoli Museum and the Brera, Milan, the Carrara Academy, Bergamo, at Berlin, London, Paris, Boston, Detroit, Notre Dame (Indiana), and Sarasota (Florida).

Ferrari, Giovanni Matteo. [Also, **Giovanni Ferrario** or **De Gradibus.**] Physician; b. at Grado, at the end of the 14th century; d. at Milan, c1472. He was a physician at Milan, professor at Pavia, and court physician to Francesco Sforza. Noted as a diagnostician, he was among the first to emphasize the importance of anatomical studies and made, as a result of careful clinical observation, valuable contributions to them. His most important work, *Practica vel commentarius in IX Rhazis ad Almansorem*, contains a commentary on the Persian physician Rhazes (c850–c925), and has many of his own observations. The work went through many editions and was widely translated.

Ferrari, Lodovico. Mathematician; b. at Bologna, February 2, 1522; d. there, October, 1565. At the age of 15 he entered the household of Girolamo Cardano, the celebrated mathematician and physician, as an amanuensis. Cardano taught him Latin, Greek, and mathematics, and he became a collaborator in his master's work. In 1540 he succeeded Cardano as public lecturer on mathematics at Milan. It was the custom of the time for professors to challenge each other, or to engage in disputation on scholarly subjects. In response to one such public challenge, Ferrari presented a formula for the solution of biquadratic equations, the solution of which had hitherto resisted discovery. Cardano published his solution in his great work on algebra, *Ars magna* (1545). In the same work, Cardano published a formula for the solution of the cubic equation that had been worked out by Niccolò Tartaglia. This brought on a quarrel with Tartaglia, who had confided his formula to Cardano on a pledge of secrecy. In the quarrel that ensued, Ferrari defended Cardano. His published writings on this issue made him famous, and he received many offers. He accepted a post at Mantua that made him a wealthy man, but left Mantua after a time, and went as professor of mathematics to Bologna, where he died. Cardano believed that he was poisoned by his sister, who was greedy for his money. Among Ferrari's inventions was a device by which circular motion can be converted to rectilinear motion.

Ferraris (fer-rä′rēs), **Antonio de.** See **Antonio de Ferraris.**

Ferraù (fer-rä-ö′). In Matteo Maria Boiardo's *Orlando Innamorato*, a fiery, hot-tempered, brave Saracen, who falls in love with Angelica, a princess of Cathay, and slays her brother Argalia. He is dark and rough. Angelica prefers blonds.

Ferreira (fẹr-rā′rạ), **António.** Portuguese poet; b. at Lisbon, Portugal, 1528; d. there, in November, 1569. He wrote the first original and complete tragedy in Portuguese, *Inês de Castro* (1587), the best work of its kind in the 16th century. He also wrote two comedies, *Bristo* and *O Cioso*. All his works were printed posthumously. His poems were published by his son in 1598 under the title *Poemas lusitanos*.

Ferrer (fer-rer′), Saint **Vincent.** See **Vincent Ferrer,** Saint.

Ferretti (fer-rāt′tē), **Domenico.** Jurist and diplomat; b. at Castelfranco, November 14, 1489; d. at Avignon, 1552. He studied canon and civil law at Pisa and Siena; then went to Rome, where he was secretary first of Cardinal Salviati and next of Pope Leo X. After some time he went to Monferrat and then to France. He taught law at Valence and served Francis I, for whom he carried out diplomatic missions to Venice and Florence. Among other things, he accompanied Charles V on an expedition to Africa, was later at Lyons, then Florence, and ended his life at Avignon as a professor of law and a councillor. He left many treatises on legal subjects and a commentary on Cicero.

Ferretti, Giulio. Statesman and jurisconsult; b. at Ravenna; d. at S. Severo in Apulia, 1547. He held many important official positions, including the administration of justice in southern Italy under Charles V's vicar there. Maritime and international law were among his legal preoccupations, and in his *De gabellis et publicanis* . . . (1547), which is a treasury of the ideas on public finance of his time, he discusses problems of economics and finance.

Ferrucci (fer-röt′chē), **Francesco.** Hero of the siege of Florence, 1530; b. at Florence, August 14, 1489; d. at Gavinana, August 3, 1530. He grew up in the Florence of Savonarola and the republic, and was influenced by these factors all his life. At first engaged in a bank, this work did not appeal to his adventurous spirit and he withdrew. He served as podesta of several cities, and then became a member of the Bande Nere, where he learned the art of war. In 1528 he was taken prisoner while fighting with the French against the Spanish at Naples. Freed, he defended Prato against the combined forces of the pope and the emperor Charles V. To the efforts of Pope Clement VII and Charles V to subdue and capture Florence (1530) he was a fierce and dangerous obstacle. A proud man, jealous of his honor, and of the highest patriotism, he rallied the untrained militia of Florence and inspired it with his words and actions. He became the hope, the only hope, of beleaguered Florence. Since the forces of the Prince of Orange were camped about the city, it was of the utmost importance to Florence to keep the supply routes open. Ferrucci was put in command of Empoli to keep the line to Pisa open. He successfully defended it and made numerous sorties against the enemy, and kept supplies flowing into the besieged city. But the forces of the Prince of Orange were being augmented continually. More troops began to come from the direction of Siena. Ferrucci daringly took this time to recapture Volterra (April, 1530), and held this nearly impregnable town. While he was doing so, the Imperialists took Empoli (June, 1530) and cut the supply line. Florence was starving. Ferruci, who had defended the countryside to keep the lines open, was called on to relieve the starving city. He advanced circuitously, by way of Pisa, with 3,000 infantry and 300 horse. Inside the city, the hired captain Malatesta Baglioni refused to move out to his aid, and had already begun secretly treating with the enemy. The Prince of Orange learned of Ferrucci's plans through intercepted letters and moved against him. He cut him off at Gavinana, a mountain town near Pistoia. In the fierce battle the Prince of Orange was killed. Gavinana was won and lost several times by the forces of Ferrucci. In the end, the great superiority of the enemy troops decided the day. Ferrucci was wounded and captured with the survivors of his force. He was taken before Maramaldo, a Neapolitan captain of the Imperial troops, and was brutally murdered. He was the greatest military leader Florence ever produced. With him fell the liberty of Florence and the freedom of Italy.

Ferrucci, Francesco di Simone. Sculptor; b. at Fiesole, 1437; d. after 1492. He may have been a pupil of his father Simone di Nanni (1402–1465), who was a follower of Ghiberti. He became a follower of Desiderio da Settignano, as appears in the friezes carved in the Badia at Fiesole (1460–1466), and in the monument of Barbara Manfredi in S. Biagio at Forlì (1467–1480). In the latter there is a suggestion of the influence of Verrocchio in an increase of curving movement. Other works include the delicate stucco ornamentation in the ducal palace at Urbino (1470–1480); a tondo with a portrait of Lemmo Balducci (1472); monument of the Tartagni family in S. Domenico at Bologna (after 1477); the tombs of the Oliva at Montefiorentino (1485–1488); and works at Perugia, Norcia, Prato, Venice, and elsewhere.

Festa (fe′stä), **Costanzo.** Italian composer of the Roman school; b. c1500; d. April 10, 1545. His works, consisting of various forms of liturgical music, include a number of madrigals.

Fiammetta (fyäm-māt′tä). **1.** Fictitious name given by Giovanni Boccaccio in some of his works (*Elegy of Madonna Fiammetta*, and others) to Maria d'Aquino, natural daughter of King Robert of Naples, a lady courted by the Italian novelist in early years (c1335–1340) spent in that city. **2.** Italian romance (*Elegy of Madonna Fiammetta*) by Boccaccio in which Fiammetta tells the story of her desertion by her lover Panfilo. With psychological insight Fiammetta describes the various states of her mind and her emotions as she descends from the hope of Panfilo's return to the despair in which she realizes it will never come about.

Fibonacci (fē-bō-nät′chē), **Leonardo.** See **Leonardo da Pisa.**

Ficino (fē-chē′nō), **Marsilio.** Platonic philosopher; b. at Figline in Valdarno, October 19, 1433; d. at his villa at Careggi, near Florence, October 1, 1499. He was the eldest son of Cosimo de' Medici's physician. His early education included study of Latin grammar and rhetoric, and he was familiar with such Latin authors as Vergil and Cicero. He became interested in philosophic studies in his youth, studied at Florence and at Pisa (1449–1451), and spent about a year at Bologna, where he studied medicine. He practiced medicine for a time, and wrote treatises on it, and then abandoned it in favor of his Platonic studies. A deeply religious man (he took orders in 1473), he was perhaps drawn to Plato because that philosopher put such emphasis on the spirit, making a clean separation between soul and body, spirit and matter. Cosimo de' Medici, who had been deeply impressed by discussions with Georgius Gemistus Plethon at the sessions of the Council of Ferrara-Florence, which had adjourned to Florence in 1439, and had at that time envisioned an Academy similar to Plato's, became interested in the young scholar and encouraged him by giving him (1462) a large collection of Greek Platonic and Neoplatonic manuscripts. Ficino had begun his study of Greek in 1456, and in a short time made such progress that he was translating the Orphic and Homeric Hymns, Proclus (Greek Neoplatonic philosopher, c410–485), and others. Cosimo also provided him with a villa at Careggi, outside Florence, and he began his translation of the *Dialogues* of Plato. (His Italian translation of the *Dialogues* ranks among the best.) On the death of Cosimo (1464), his son Piero, and after him his grandson Lorenzo the Magnificent, continued to aid and befriend Ficino. The villa at Careggi became a meeting place for those interested in Platonic studies, meetings which were the forerunner of the so-called Platonic Academy. The latter was never an organized institution; rather, it consisted of a group who shared a common interest and participated in discussions of that interest under the guidance of Ficino. Their talks took place as the spirit moved. They listened to speeches, attended public lectures given by Ficino, and celebrated Plato's birthday. Many influences were brought to bear on the discussions and speeches, and on the Platonism that evolved from them. These influences included the Neoplatonists (who contributed most to what the members of the Academy thought was their Platonism), Aristotle and the Arabic commentators, the Church Fathers, and the Scholastics. Among the many scholars and literary men who took part in the Platonic Academy were Lorenzo de' Medici, the poet Poliziano, the philosopher Pico della Mirandola, and Cristoforo Landino. It was thus a group of those with a lively interest in Platonism, but whose members were not at all necessarily philosophers, and it was held together for over thirty years by the personality and inspiration of Ficino. He made Latin translations of many Platonic and Neoplatonic manuscripts and wrote commentaries on them. In 1469 he wrote his commentary on Plato's *Symposium*, which he called *Libro dello amore*. It is in the same form as the original dialogue but expresses Ficino's ideas on love, the subject of the *Symposium*. In Ficino's conception, love is the desire for beauty, ultimately, the beauty of God. In his cosmology Ficino postulated a universe of ascending order, from the beasts to God in five gradations, with man in the middle. The unifying principle of the five gradations was love, which has the power to change and ennoble whatever it embraces. Always working to reconcile Platonism and Neoplatonism with Christianity, he contended that if it were not for religion, which he believed was natural to man, men would be little different from beasts.

His major work was the *Theologia Platonica*, with the subtitle *On the Immortality of the Souls*, written some time after 1469 and revised later. In it Ficino sought to prove the immortality of the soul by reason. The question of immortality was much debated and considered in an age when man with his infinite possibilities had come to be regarded as the center of the universe. Basic to Ficino's ideas on immortality was his concept of contemplation. For him, contemplation was a spiritual experience, in which the soul withdraws from the body, and is thus freed from the pressures and temptations to which the physical man is subject. Having withdrawn, the soul is free to contemplate in a pure state the divinity in itself and the Divine Being from which its own divinity arises. In the contemplation of divinity the soul achieves true knowledge. According to Ficino, knowledge and enjoyment of God is the ultimate end of human existence. Since only a few men could, through contemplation, achieve this knowledge and enjoyment, and then only for brief periods in this life, it follows that it must be attained by many and in a permanent manner in an afterlife, hence the immortality of the soul. Otherwise the point of human existence is lost. Another fundamental strand of Ficino's thinking was his conception of "Platonic," or "Socratic," love. By the term Ficino defined the bond that arises from shared participation in the contemplative life, souls joined by their love and contemplation of God. This concept had immense intellectual and philosophical appeal in his own and the age immediately following it. Bembo gives his view of Platonic love in *Gli Asolani;* Castiglione ends his *Cortegiano* with an impassioned description of it as perfect love.

Ficino's *De vita libri tres* (1489) is a treatise on medicine and theology. He also wrote on astrology (which he defended), wrote commentaries on Plato (1496), translated Iamblichus (Syrian Neoplatonic philosopher, d. c330) and other Neoplatonists (1497), and Dionysius the Areopagite (Athenian Christian convert of the 1st century). He was a musician and music theorist. He had a wide correspondence with men in the main centers in Italy, and in France, Germany, Poland, and Hungary. Through his letters and his writings his ideas filtered to most of Europe. The Medici were his patrons, members of the Medici circle were his friends and followers, but he did not concern himself with politics and had friendly contacts in the opposing camp and was not harried when the Medici were overthrown. He was at first much impressed by Savonarola but turned against him for his authoritarianism and fanaticism. Ficino felt his ideas deeply—they defined the manner and goal of his life—and expressed them clearly. For his revival of Platonism, rather than for the originality of his ideas, he was a major figure in the history of philosophy. Renowned and admired in his own time, he remained an important influence in the field of philosophy for nearly two hundred years. A portrait bust of him by Andrea di Piero Ferrucci (1465–1526) is in the Duomo at Florence.

Fiennes (fi-enz′, fīnz), **James.** [Title, Baron **Saye and Sele.**] English nobleman; d. July 4, 1450.

Fiennes, Thomas. [Title, 9th Baron **Dacre.**] English nobleman; b. 1517; executed at Tyburn, London, June 29, 1541. He was one of a party of youths who engaged in a poaching frolic in the park of Mr. Nicholas Pelham at Laughton on April 30, 1541, and one of the park keepers was mortally wounded in the scuffle. The whole poaching party was, apparently under pressure from the king, prosecuted for murder, and Lord Dacre and three of his companions were condemned to death.

Fieravanti (fye-rä-vän′tē), **Aristotele.** Architect; b. at Bologna between 1415 and 1420; d. at Moscow, c1486. He was the nephew of Fierarvante Fieravanti (c1390–c1430). He was named engineer of the commune of Bologna and carried out many projects there, such as moving the Torre della Magione and straightening several campanili. He worked at Milan, Parma, Mantua, and again at Bologna, where he again became (1464) engineer of the commune, and was recognized as an outstanding architect. In 1467 he spent six months in Hungary at the king's request. From there he went to Rome, Naples, Milan, and then, at the invitation of Tzar Ivan III, to Moscow. He remained in that city until his death. His feats of engineering and his architectural works are mentioned in many documents of the time, but no work that can be definitely ascribed to him now exists in Italy. In the Church of the Assumption at Moscow he combined the simplicity and some of the motifs of Renaissance architecture with the Russian Byzantine style.

Fieravanti, Fieravante. Architect and engineer; b. at Bologna, c1390; d. c1430. He constructed fortifications at Perugia and Bologna, and carried out hydraulic works at Lake Trasimeno. Between 1425 and 1430 he worked at Bologna on the reconstruction of the Anziani palace.

Fieschi (fyās′kē), **Sinibaldo de'.** Original name of Pope **Innocent IV.**

Fiesco (fyās′kō), **Ottoboni.** Original name of Pope **Adrian V.**

Fiesole (fye′zō-lā), Fra **Giovanni da.** See **Angelico,** Fra.

Filarete (fē-lä-re′tā). [Original name, **Antonio di Pietro Averlino** or **Averulino;** his humanist nickname, **Filarete,** is an approximation from the Greek, meaning "Lover of Virtue."] Sculptor and architect; b. at Florence, c1400; d. at Rome, c1470. He may have been an assistant of Lorenzo Ghiberti in the execution of the bronze doors of the Baptistery at Florence. In 1433 he was at Rome, commissioned by Pope Eugenius IV to make the great bronze door for the Basilica of St. Peter's. Filarete worked on the door for twelve years, adding events as they occurred and refining his style under the influence of the Roman monuments. The bronze door is his principal work as a sculptor. Work he is thought to have been carrying out on the tomb of Cardinal Antonio Chiaves (d. 1447) was left incomplete when he was forced to leave Rome on the accusation that he was planning to steal a relic. He went to Florence (1448), and then to Lodi, Rimini, Padua, Piacenza, and Mantua, and settled for a time at Venice (1449). From this period is the beautiful processional cross of Bassano. His reputation as an architect dates from about this time. Piero de' Medici recommended him to Francesco Sforza for work on the *castello* at Milan (1451). His effort to make changes in the building was resisted by local engineers and artisans and he left the work after a few months. In 1456 Francesco Sforza asked him to design a hospital at Milan, and this Ospedale (now the university) is the main witness to Filarete's gifts as an architect. In his plan he sought to reproduce classical forms as opposed to the Gothic forms, which he considered "barbarous," of the Lombard craftsmen. The work was almost entirely carried out under his supervision and in the main followed his plan (later largely altered and rebuilt). In 1465, before it was complete, he abandoned the work and no further certain notice of him is known. Some think he may have given up on the hospital because of the notorious jealousy of the Lombard artisans and the conflicts that arose with them. They were devoted adherents of the Lombard style and could resist, in a number of ways, the more austere Florentine and classical effects Filarete sought. Throughout his Milanese period Filarete enjoyed the confidence of the duke who, when objections from the Lombards became too strenuous, sent his architect to work in other parts of his dominions. Filarete showed his appreciation by dedicating a copy of his *Trattato d'architettura*, written between 1460 and 1464, to the duke. In its second section, the treatise describes an imaginary star-shaped city, named *Sforzinda* in honor of his patron. In writing about it Filarete had the opportunity to express his ideas, sometimes highly original, and often confused, on art and architecture. In the course of his life Filarete had fulfilled commissions that required great skill, technical knowledge and artistry, as the bronze door of St. Peter's and the Ospedale at Milan; what he lacked in natural endowment he made up in intuition and practical experience.

Filelfo (fē-lel′fō), **Francesco.** Humanist; b. at Tolentino, near Ancona, July 25, 1398; d. at Florence, July 31, 1481. He studied at Padua (where, at the age of 18, he was appointed professor of eloquence), Venice and Vicenza, and in 1420 went to Constantinople with a diplomatic mission from the Venetians. There, where he remained seven years, he learned Greek under John Chrysoloras, whose daughter Theodora he married, and enthusiastically collected Greek manuscripts. In 1429 he was back at Florence and lecturing in the university there. He won great renown at Florence for his learning, and his lectures were attended by large audiences. He also made translations from the Greek and gave lectures on Dante. Pius II, writing of him at a later date, called him "a distinguished author of satires and a poet learned in Latin and Greek." However, with his satires and his power of invective he also made many enemies for, as Vespasiano noted, he did not always keep his pretty wit in order. He engaged in a feud with Carlo Marsuppini at the university and lost some of his own popularity in abusing one whom he considered a rival. More serious was the enmity he incurred from Cosimo de' Medici. When the latter's power was threatened (1433), Filelfo advocated his death rather than exile. Cosimo was exiled, but on his triumphant return (1434) Filelfo was banished. After a brief stay at Siena, where he taught, he went to Milan to the court of Filippo Maria Visconti, and was highly honored there. Francesco Sforza, who succeeded (1450) as duke of Milan, continued the patronage he had enjoyed under the Visconti. Among his duties for the lords of Milan was the making of speeches on special occasions, as at betrothals, in honor of famous men, or against state or princely enemies. These speeches were studded with quotations from classical literature, as the presence of such quotations was considered a mark of learning. In other respects, they were so larded with praise of the man in whose honor they were given, or so bitter in abuse of an enemy, and so long as to seem unendurable to a modern audience. But they were well attuned to the practice of the times. He also taught at the university, wrote on political events, and continued his translations from the Greek. In 1474 he went to Rome at the invitation of Sixtus IV but his restless spirit soon grew discontented there. Though he had continued his enmity of the Medici in his writings for many years, the old controversy finally waned and disappeared, and he longed to return to Florence. Describing himself as a harmless old man of more than 80 years, he asked leave to return. Lorenzo de' Medici revoked his banishment and invited him to return to the university to teach Greek. He died a few weeks after his arrival in Florence. Filelfo was noted for his learning, for his daring moral ideas, for his enthusiasm in teaching and promoting classical studies, and for his work in collecting, preserving and classifying examples of ancient literature. He was nearly equally noted for his biting satire and virulent invective. He wrote letters, many of which were polemics against his or his patrons' enemies or were demands for money, dialogues, poems in the vernacular, a summary of ethics based on Aristotle, a collection of epigrams gathered over many years and an incomplete epic poem, *Sphortiad*, on the deeds of Francesco Sforza.

Filelfo, Giammaria. Humanist and writer; b. 1426; d. 1480. He was the son of Francesco Filelfo (1398–1481) and spent his life wandering about central and southern Italy writing Latin verses in praise of various princes. He visited the court of King René in Provence and was given the laurel crown by that otherwise discriminating monarch. When necessary or profitable, he improvised in Latin and Italian. In a work in praise of Federico da Montefeltro, a mixture of mythology, allegory, history, and geography, he compares the noble duke to Mars. He left a collection of verses, on various subjects and in praise of various people, including, besides Federico, Gentile Bellini, and many others.

Filippino (fē-lē-pē′nō). See **Lippi, Filippino.**

Filippo (fē-lēp′pō), Fra. See **Lippi,** Fra **Filippo.**

Filocolo (fē-lō′kō-lō). Prose romance in Italian by Giovanni Boccaccio (1337–1339). Based on a story of French origin, it narrates Florio's search for Biancofiore. To the original tale Boccaccio added many incidents of his own invention. In describing the travels undertaken by Florio, and his adventures during the course of them, Boccaccio includes items and information on a wide variety of subjects—geography, battles, astronomy, metamorphoses, and complete stories that evolve from some of the episodes. One of these episodes occurs when Florio and his companions are shipwrecked at Naples. To pass the time, Florio and his companions each tell a story involving a problem of love. Fiammetta renders the decision solving each problem. The framework and some of the stories themselves foretell the Decameron. Boccaccio created the name *Filocolo* from two Greek words meaning "love" and "labor" since Florio's search is a labor of love. The form of the romance, the episodes and stories in it, had great influence on the development of the novel. Chaucer made free use of it.

Filosseno (fē-lōs-sā′nō), **Marcello.** [Latin name, **Marcellus Philoxenus.**] Poet; b. probably c1450; d. at Treviso, c1520. He was a Servite brother, visited many of the courts of Italy, and was for a long time at Rome during the pontificate of Alexander VI. His mannered *strambotti* and sonnets were collected under the title *Silve.* He also left verses in Italian, *Carmina, Hymni,* and some orations, *De laudibus Bononiensium,* that were declaimed (1488) to a general convocation of the Servite order, and that were printed in Latin and Greek. He is said to have been crowned poet on the Campidoglio at Rome.

Filostrato (fē-lōs′trä-tō). Romance in Italian verse by Giovanni Boccaccio (1339–1340). It is Boccaccio's version of the Troilus and Cressida story. In it he develops the characters of the two lovers and the friend of the hero. Chaucer borrowed freely from this work for his *Troilus and Cressida.*

Finck (fingk), **Heinrich.** German composer of motets and songs; b. 1445; d. at Vienna, June 9, 1527. He was a member of the Warsaw court chapel and subsequently (c1507 *et seq.*) *Kapellmeister* (choir leader) at Stuttgart.

Finck, Hermann. German organist and composer; b. at Pirna, Saxony, Germany, March 21, 1527; d. December 28, 1558. He was noted for the treatise *Practica Musica* (1556). He was organist (1557 *et seq.*) at Wittenberg, and composed part-songs and motets.

Finiguerra (fē-nē-gwer′rä), **Maso.** Goldsmith, niellist, and engraver; b. at Florence, 1426; d. 1464. The son of a goldsmith, he learned his father's craft, and later was working in niello (1449). He made designs for intarsia panels for the sacristy in the cathedral at Florence, and towards the end of his life, perhaps about 1460, turned to engraving, and was among the earliest of the Italians to practice this art. He was associated with Antonio Pollaiuolo. Among his prints is a series on the planets that includes much astrological lore. Drawings by him are in the Uffizi at Florence and in the British Museum.

Fioravanti (fyō-rä-vän′tē), **Leonardo.** Physician; b. at Bologna, 1518; d. there, September 4, 1586. He traveled in Spain and took ship to Africa, then returned to Italy and practiced his profession at Palermo, Naples, Rome, Venice, and Bologna. He was opposed to bloodletting, performed the first splenectomy, and concocted a protection against arsenic poisoning. One of his many works concerned control of the plague, *Del reggimento della peste* (Venice, 1565), another was on science in general, *Lo specchio di scienza universale* (Venice, 1564); others dealt with medicine, surgery, physics, and alchemy.

Fiordiligi (fyōr-dē-lē′jē). In Matteo Maria Boiardo's *Orlando Innamorato* and Lodovico Ariosto's *Orlando Furioso,* beloved by Brandimarte, Orlando's loyal friend. She and Rinaldo, journeying together, are overtaken by darkness. They lie down in the woods to sleep. Rinaldo, having drunk of Merlin's Well, is impervious to women. Fiordiligi, as dawn breaks and lightens Rinaldo's lithe form and handsome face, is shaken with a momentary disloyalty to Brandimarte. Separated from Brandimarte, she searches long for him, and after his death takes up her abode in his tomb. She lives there until her death, which occurs shortly thereafter.

Fiordispina (fyōr-dē-spē′nä). In Matteo Maria Boiardo's *Orlando Innamorato* and Lodovico Ariosto's *Orlando Furioso*, a princess. She falls in love with Bradamante, being deceived by Bradamante's armor and taking her for a knight.

Fiorentino (fyō-ren-tē′nō), **il.** See **Niccolò di Forzore Spinelli.**

Fiorentino, Vespasiano. See **Vespasiano da Bisticci.**

Fiorenzo di Lorenzo (fyō-ren′tsō dē lō-ren′tsō). Perugian painter; b. at Perugia, c1440; d. there, between 1522 and 1525. His early painting is in the manner of Benozzo Gozzoli and Alunno; he next adopted the more animated and energetic style of Pollaiuolo and Verrocchio; and was ultimately influenced by his great fellow-townsmen, Perugino and Pinturicchio. Only two signed works are known. The *Madonna of Mercy* (1476) is a detached fresco, originally in the Hostel of S. Egidio and now in the National Gallery of Umbria at Perugia. In the same gallery is his signed and dated (1487) altarpiece, *Virgin and Child with SS. Peter and Paul and Cherubim.* Paintings in the gallery at Perugia record the succession of influences to which he was subject as he followed now one and now another of the painters of his day. His earliest painting is thought to be a *Madonna and Child* of the period 1460–1470; generally provincial, it also shows the influence of Alunno and Caporali, who in their turn had been influenced by Benozzo Gozzoli. The influence of Perugino first appears in his frescoes on *St. Romano and St. Roch* (1478), Church of S. Francesco, Deruta (near Perugia), and continues strong in the polyptych, *Madonna and Child with Saints* (1487–1493), in the gallery at Perugia. A *Virgin and Child with Angels,* National Gallery, London, is of about the same period as the Deruta frescoes. Other paintings by this pleasant painter whose work reflects so many influences, are *Saint Jerome Doing Penance,* Yale University Art Gallery, New Haven, and *Virgin and Child with St. Jerome* and *St. Sebastian,* Museum of Fine Arts, Boston. St. Sebastian was a favorite subject with Fiorenzo; the saint appears in several of his altarpieces and in panels in the Palazzo Venezia, the Spada Gallery, and Castel Sant' Angelo at Rome, among others.

Fiori (fyô′rē), **Federico.** See **Barocci, Federico.**

Firenzuola (fē-ren-tswō′lä), **Agnolo.** Tuscan writer; b. at Florence, 1493; d. at Prato, June 27, 1543. He spent his youth at Siena and Perugia, where he studied law and entered wholeheartedly into the gay student life. After taking monastic orders he went to Rome. There he was given ecclesiastical benefits by Leo X and Clement VII that enabled him to lead the worldly life he preferred. He was on friendly terms with the leading poets and wits of his day, as Berni and Molza. His life at Rome was interrupted by an illness and he withdrew to Prato. There, as abbot of the Abbey of San Salvatore, he spent many pleasant and tranquil years, and gathered literary men about him in an Accademia. Towards the end of his life he lost the prebendary, and died at last poor and forgotten. In the meantime he had enjoyed himself and his writing. His novelle are on much the same subjects as those of his contemporaries, and are often not much more than humorous anecdotes on the foibles and vices of the clergy. This was one of the most popular themes of the day, and often used by literary clergymen. His *Sopra le belezze delle donne* discourses on the qualities that make for beauty in women, not character qualities only but physical attributes as well. The scene of the discourse is Prato, and many actual ladies are mentioned in the selection of each physical feature and the definition of its beauty, in giving examples of social graces, matters of dress and ornamentation, etc. He also wrote love poetry in the manner of Petrarch, comedies, and *Discorsi degli animali,* fables. His writing is gay, expressive of his awareness of the beauty of the world and of his intention to enjoy it.

Fisher (fish′ėr), Saint **John.** English prelate and scholar, bishop of Rochester, and a leader of the papal party; b. at Beverley, Yorkshire, England c1459; beheaded on Tower Hill, London, June 22, 1535. He graduated at Cambridge (B.A., 1487), and became vice-chancellor of the university in 1501, and professor of divinity in 1503. He was elected chancellor of the university in 1504 (and repeatedly reelected), and became bishop of Rochester in October of the same year. From

1505 to 1508 he was president of Queen's College. He was one of the most prominent supporters of the new learning, and a friend of Erasmus (who visited Cambridge at his invitation), but was hostile to the Reformation. He opposed the doctrine of royal supremacy and the divorce of Henry VIII, and was the confessor and chief advisor of Queen Catherine of Aragon. He was duped by the Nun of Kent, Elizabeth Barton, and was condemned to imprisonment and forfeiture of goods, but escaped with a fine of 300 pounds. During his imprisonment Pope Paul III made him a cardinal. His refusal to comply with the Act of Succession and the Act of Supremacy, by which Henry VIII became head of the church in England and by which Catherine's offspring were declared illegitimate, led to his conviction of treason and his execution. He was beatified in 1886 and canonized in 1935.

Flacius Illyricus (flā′shi-us i-lir′i-kus), **Matthias.** [Original name, **Matthias Vlacich.**] German Protestant scholar and controversialist; b. at Albona (now Labin), in Istria, March 3, 1520; d. at Frankfort on the Main, Germany, March 11, 1575. He was a pupil of Luther at Wittenberg, and was professor of Hebrew there from 1544 to 1549, when he withdrew on account of his opposition to the Augsburg and Leipzig interims. In 1557 he was appointed to a professorship at Jena, but was deprived (1561) of his office on a charge of Manicheism. He was the principal collaborator on the *Centuriae Magdeburgenses* (Basel 1559–1574), the first history of the church written from the Protestant point of view. Its plan was conceived by him. He also wrote the *Clavis scripturae sacrae* (1567), which forms the basis of Biblical hermeneutics.

Flaminio (flä-mē′nyō), **Marcantonio.** Poet and humanist; b. at Seravalle, 1498; d. at Rome, February 17, 1550. A highly gifted youth, he published his first volume of Latin poems in 1515. Armed with them he went to Rome and was welcomed at the court of Leo X. He was soon on warm terms with all the wits and scholars of his time, and came to share the interest of various individuals, inside and outside the Church, in bringing about Church reform. Among these were the Cardinals Pole and Contarini, Juan de Valdés, and Vittoria Colonna. He joined two religious societies, that of the Oratory of the Divine Love, founded by Cardinal Contarini, at Rome, and another at Venice. He was in the service of Alexander Farnese, whom he honored in his poetry, secretary to the bishop of Verona for a number of years, and for a short time secretary to Cardinal Pole. The latter took him to the Council of Trent, where he was offered the secretaryship of the Council, a post he declined. He later declined to accept a bishopric. Concerned about the corruption in the Church, he remained firm in the faith. The last poems of his life are mainly on spiritual themes, sincerely Christian in their sentiments. His *De rebus divinis carmina* is a collection of these. He had earlier paraphrased about thirty Psalms in Latin verse. *Lusus Pastorales*, from the first and longest period of his life as a poet, is a collection of glowing, elegant, lyrical love poems in the manner of Horace and Catullus, marked by Flaminio's style, simplicity, and purity. Flaminio is one of the more endearing, least cynical, poets of his age. He did not seek to advance himself by flattery of patrons, he remained singularly unambitious. He loved the peace and quiet of the country and the activities and sports of country life, often expressed envy, when in Rome, of his friends who could be elsewhere, and withdrew from the city as often as possible. He was one of the most prolific and one of the most winning of the Latin poets of his time. He wrote a number of hymns, and left a valuable collection of Italian letters in which are recorded his attitudes toward the Church, and sentiments expressive of Reformation ideals. These caused him to be suspected of heresy, and his poems were placed on the Index in 1599.

Flete or **Fleet** (flēt), **William.** Hermit and mystic; b. probably near Fleet, in Lincolnshire, England, c1310; d. probably at Lecceto, 1382. He entered the Augustinian Order (c1323), had a degree from Cambridge, and left England (1359) to enter the Augustinian monastery at Lecceto, not far from Siena. He was a noted ascetic, spent most of his time in the woods, fasted, drank no wine, and was revered by the people for his penances. He became the devoted friend and confidant of St. Catherine of Siena. She tried to persuade him to give up his life as a hermit and to enter the world to serve God's creatures. She wrote him that it was not so necessary to mortify the flesh as to slay the will. But he would not give up the life of a hermit that he had chosen, and they remained good friends. Six of her letters to him are extant. He left a spiritual treatise, *De remediis contra temptaciones*, and towards the end of his life sent three letters to England urging reform and a return to the early Christian purity in religion.

Florensz (flôr′ents), **Adrian.** Original name of Pope **Adrian VI.**

Florigerio (flō-rē-je′ryō), **Sebastiano.** Painter; b. at Conegliano, c1500; d. after 1543. In 1525 he went to Udine and entered the workshop of Pellegrino di S. Daniele. He worked for this master a number of years, often without pay, in return for the promise that he would receive the hand of Pellegrino's daughter in marriage. In 1529 he went to Padua, then to Cividale, and returned at length (1543) to Conegliano. In the agitated movement and inflated forms of his paintings Florigerio seems to reflect the influence of Pordenone. Among the surviving works of this modest painter are the altarpiece of *St. George*, Church of S. Giorgio, Udine, a *Portrait of Raffaele Grassi*, Uffizi, and paintings at Padua, Venice (Accademia), Berlin, Munich, New Haven, and Tucson (Arizona).

Foglietta (fō-lyāt′tä), **Uberto.** Historian; b. at Genoa, c1518; d. at Rome, September 5, 1581. Of a distinguished family, he was compelled for financial reasons to interrupt his legal studies and went to Rome (c1538). He was well received at the papal court and became an abbreviator and apostolic protonotary. After publishing a short work on philosophy, he wrote *Delle cose della repubblica di Genova*, in two books, in which he denounced the old nobility for its activities against the new nobility. The work was acclaimed, but as the old nobility was in power, a charge was brought against him and he was exiled from Genoa. He stayed at Rome and began writing a history of his own times, fragments of which, including the narrative of the Fieschi conspiracy, remain. From 1564 to 1576 he was in the service of various princes and wrote histories for them. His *Tyburtium* describes the beauties of Cardinal Ippolito d'Este's villa at Tivoli. His *Clarorum Ligurum elogia* (Rome, 1573), on the lives of distinguished Genoese, was written to show his undying patriotism. In 1576, the struggle between the old and new nobility having come to an end, he returned to Genoa and was chosen official historian. He wrote a history of Genoa from its origins to 1527, *Historiae Genuensis Libri XII*; it was published (1585) by his brother Paolo, who brought the history down to 1575.

Fogolino (fō-gō-lē′nō), **Marcello.** Painter; b. at Vicenza, c1480; d. after 1548. His father Francesco was a follower of Montagna at Vicenza, and a brother Matteo is known from documents to have been a painter also. Marcello worked at Vicenza where (1519) he painted an *Adoration of the Magi*, now in the Museo Civico at Vicenza, and worked at Pordenone and at Trent, where among his other surviving works are the frescoes in the Castello del Buonconsiglio. The chief influences on his work are those of Montagna and Romanino.

Foix (fwȧ), **Françoise de.** See **Chateaubriant,** Comtesse de.

Foix, Gaston, Comte **de.** [Surnamed **Phoebus.**] Count of Foix (1343–1391); b. 1331; d. 1391. He derived his surname either from the beauty of his person or from a golden sun which he bore in his escutcheon. He fought against the English in 1345, and assisted in the rescue of the royal princesses from the Jacquerie at Maux in 1358. He maintained a splendid court, which has been described by Froissart, and was passionately fond of the chase, on the subject of which he wrote a treatise known as *Miroir de Phébus des déduicts de la chasse*.

Foix, Gaston de. [Title, Duc **de Nemours.**] French general; b. 1489; d. at Ravenna, April 11, 1512. He was a nephew of Louis XII, and was created Duc de Nemours in 1505. At the age of 22 he was placed at the head of the French army in Italy that was opposing the pope, the Venetians, and the Spanish. The Spaniards under Raymond de Cardona were besieging Bologna. He drove them out (February 5, 1512). Brescia had rebelled against the French. He turned against the Venetians and retook Brescia (February 19, 1512), and put it to the sack. The armies of Spain and of the pope again advanced into the Romagna. On Easter Sunday, April 11, 1512, he forced them to give battle, and in one of the most murderous battles the Italians had ever known he defeated them. The Italians were accustomed to the bloodless skirmishes of their mercenary captains, and were appalled at the slaughter in the battle of Ravenna—20,000, it was reported, were left dead on the field. However, the Spanish retreated in good order, and in pursuing them Gaston was killed. The great French victory turned into a disaster soon after the loss of the brilliant captain.

Foix, Germaine de. Queen of Aragon and Naples; b. 1488; d. 1538. She was the niece of Louis XII of France, and after the death of Isabella the Catholic, a marriage was arranged with Isabella's widower, Ferdinand the Catholic. Louis ceded to her all his claims to the kingdom of Naples as a wedding gift and as her dowry. The marriage (1505) was intended to produce an heir to the throne of Castile, but the only child, Juan, died in infancy, leaving as heir the son of Juana and Philip I, who later reigned as Charles I of Spain (the emperor Charles V).

Folchetti (fôl-kāt′tē), **Stefano.** [Called **Stefano da San Genesio.**] Painter of the Marches; active between 1492 and 1513. A modest provincial painter who worked mostly in and about his native town of San Genesio, the chief influence in his early painting was Crivelli. In later works the linearity and definition of Crivelli were softened by the influence of Umbrian painting. His earliest known work was a signed and dated (1494) *Madonna and Saints,* at San Genesio. Several frescoes and paintings are in churches in and near San Genesio, and an *Adoration of the Shepherds* is in the Johnson Collection, Philadelphia.

Folengo (fō-leng′gō), **Teofilo.** [Pseudonyms, **Merlino Cocai, Limerno Pitoco.**] Poet; b. at Cipada, near Mantua, November 8, 1496; d. at Campese di Bassano, December 9, 1544. Of a good family, he was educated at home and then went to Bologna, where he heard the lectures of Pomponazzi. His student life was wild, profligate, and dangerous, and ended in his expulsion from the university. Some time after 1513 he entered the Benedictine order, but fled the convent he had entered at Brescia, in 1524. Ever after his most cutting sarcasm was leveled at the abuses and hypocrisy of the monastic orders and the clergy. However, clearly as he saw and despised the corruption of the clergy, he was a religious man, and sought to return to the order. He and his brother were required to enter upon a solitary hermit's life, which they did in 1530, at Capo di Minerva near Sorrento. In 1534 they were readmitted to the order. Folengo had begun composing macaronic verse in his student days at Bologna. He developed this imitation language that parodied Latin into an artistic medium of expression. His masterpiece in the macaronic verse is his *Baldus,* also known as *La macaronea.* The first edition of the work, published, 1515, under the name Merlino Cocai, was in seventeen cantos. A second and better edition contained twenty-five cantos. There were two later, slightly different editions. The work, a kind of burlesque continuation of the Carolingian legends, is highly comic, often shrewd, generally satirical and ribald. It tells of Baldus, the grandson of a king of France. Motherless, and abandoned by his father to the care of the peasant Berto, Baldus of the noble lineage is reared in a crude peasant atmosphere. His knightly instincts of chivalry and arms are perverted to brawls and raffish adventures. Fearlessness and valor are expended on tricks. Baldus gathers about him a band of comrades, literary descendants of Pulci's Morgante and Margutte, and also one Falchetto, who is half man and half dog. They share a great many adventures. Baldus is imprisoned, and for a time his companion Cingar takes the leading role. The comrades free Baldus and together go on a preposterous journey, winding up in the Inferno. Finally they are all gathered in an enormous pumpkin, in which are confined all those who waste their time in foolish pursuits, notably, philosophers and poets. Thus Folengo caricatures the courtly world and its cultural preoccupations and presents in sharp contrast the realism of life as he sees it, with all its venality and grossness. Folengo's false language is a fitting vehicle for expressing the falseness he observes in the world.

Other works by Folengo are *La moschaea,* on the battle of the ants and the flies, and patterned on Homer's *Batracomyomachia. Orlandino* is a burlesque epic of Orlando's youth, published under the pseudonym Limerno Pitoco. *Caos del Triperuno* is an allegorical autobiography, of the chaos created in the three-in-one man; and *Umanità del Figliuol di Dio,* which was written to atone for his early *Baldus,* is a religious work. But *Baldus* is his masterpiece, and most scarifyingly and comically expresses his contempt for the affectation and hypocrisy he saw in the Renaissance, and his leanings toward the tendencies of the Counter-Reformation. In his burlesque and ribald satire, Folengo is a forerunner of Rabelais, who knew his work well.

Folgore da San Gimignano (fōl-gô′rā dä sän jē-mē-nyä′nō). Minstrel; active 1305–1316. Little is known of his life. He sang songs, some of which he composed himself, in courts and halls to entertain and amuse. Two extant works of his composition are: a series of sonnets on the months of the year and the pleasures to be enjoyed in each month; and a similar series on the days of the week, in which he describes the chase, various games, and so on. He also sang of great deeds in the days of chivalry, and occasionally lamented the passing of chivalry.

Folz (folts), **Hans.** German Meistersinger; born at Worms, Germany, c1450; d. at Nuremberg, Germany, c1515. He was a forerunner of Hans Sachs. He is known for his Shrovetide plays, his *Schwänke* and *Spruchdichtung*. He was a barber and surgeon at Nuremberg.

Fonduti (fôn′dö-tē) or **Fondulo** (fôn′dö-lō), **Agostino de.** See **De Fonduti, Agostino.**

Fonseca (fōn-sā′ka), **Juan Rodríguez de.** Spanish ecclesiastic and administrator; b. at Toro, near Seville, Spain, 1441; d. at Burgos, Spain, November 4, 1524. He was successively archdeacon of Seville, bishop of Badajoz, Palencia, and Conde, archbishop of Rosario in Italy, and bishop of Burgos, besides being head chaplain to Queen Isabella and afterward to Ferdinand. He is known principally for the control he exercised over all business relating to the New World. This began with the preparations for the second voyage of Columbus in 1493 and, except during the regency of Ximenes, was continued until his death. The Council of the Indies was organized by him in 1511, and he was its first chief. Bishop Fonseca opposed Columbus (whose administration he ordered Bobadilla to investigate), Cortés, and Las Casas in many matters, and he used his position unscrupulously for the benefit of himself and his friends.

Fontana (fōn-tä′nä), **Prospero.** Painter; b. at Bologna, 1512; d. there, 1597. He worked at Genoa, Rome, where he painted (1552) a portrait of Julius III and decorated (1553) a villa on the Via Flaminia, France, where he worked at Fontainebleau for a short time, and Bologna. His early taste for the harmony and balance of Raphael was overcome, in his later career, by enthusiasm for the motion and violence of Michelangelo, of whom he became a mannerist imitator. One of his better works is a *Deposition*, Pinacoteca, Bologna; other examples of his work are to be found in the churches of his native city.

Fonte (fôn′tā), **Bartolomeo della.** See **Della Fonte, Bartolomeo.**

Fonte, Fra **Tommaso della.** See **Tommaso della Fonte.**

Foppa (fôp′pä), **Vincenzo.** Lombard painter; b. at Brescia, between 1427 and 1430; d. there, 1515 or 1516. Little is known of his training. His earliest known work, a signed and dated *Crucifixion* (1456), Carrara Academy, Bergamo, and a *St. Jerome*, also among his early works, in the same gallery, indicate that the first influences were of the local Brescian school that derived from Jacopo Bellini and Pisanello. Frescoes he is known to have executed at Genoa (1461, 1478) and at Pavia (1462), as well as a number of altarpieces he painted at Pavia, have been lost. One set of frescoes, however, has survived. This is a series on legends from the life of St. Peter Martyr, painted in the Portinari Chapel in the Church of S. Eustorgio, Milan. They constitute a masterpiece of 15th-century Lombard painting, and form a precious ornament for a chapel (built 1462–1468) that is a jewel of Renaissance architecture. In them Foppa fused the defined forms and perspectives of Tuscan painting with the naturalistic Lombard style. His robust, vigorous types and the simple grandeur of the frescoes indicate that he was acquainted with the forms of Giovanni Bellini and Mantegna. As compared to his earlier surviving work, the frescoes signalize a new departure in hitherto rather provincial Lombard painting. They illustrate his virile, monumental, individual style in its fully developed state. It is a style marked by precise draftsmanship, a developed plastic sense, and ease with perspective and foreshortening. The northern Gothic elements that had persisted in Lombard painting have disappeared. Characteristically, his color is muted, with silvery grays and cool greens predominating, without diluting the general impression of strength. A master of his purpose and means in pictorial expression, Foppa's art came to dominate Lombard painting until the impact of Leonardo da Vinci's style made itself felt at Milan towards the end of the 15th century.

Foppa had many pupils, including Ambrogio Bergognone and Vincenzo Civerchio, and influenced a number of minor painters. Between 1462 and 1463 he was at Milan on the invitation of Francesco Sforza, who was often his patron, and it was perhaps in this period that he painted frescoes in the Medici bank at Milan; *Boy Reading*, London, and *The Judgment of Trajan*, Berlin, are all that remain from this series. He was often occupied at Pavia between 1456 and 1490, but left it at intervals to work at Milan, Bergamo, Brescia, and Genoa. In the summer of 1490 he moved to Brescia and painted in the Church of S. Maria del Carmine, where his *Evangelists*, in the grand manner of the Portinari frescoes, survives. Among the works he executed at Milan is a series of windows, with stories from the New Testament, in the cathedral. Other paintings are in the Brera (a *St. Sebastian* notable for its sense of action), Castello Sforzesco, and the Poldi Pezzoli Museum (*Holy Family* and *Portrait of Francesco Brivio*), Milan, at Pavia, Brescia, Monza (cathedral), Savona, Berlin, Budapest, London, Cambridge (Massachusetts), Denver, Detroit, Louisville (Kentucky), Minneapolis, New Orleans, New York, Philadelphia (Johnson Collection), Princeton, Raleigh (North Carolina), Washington, and Worcester (Massachusetts).

Fordun (fôr-dun′), **John of.** Scottish chronicler; d. after 1384. He wrote a history of Scotland down to his own times, entitled *Chronica gentis Scotorum*, which was continued by Walter Bower under the title of *Scotichronicon*.

Forlì (fôr-lē′), **Melozzo da.** See **Melozzo da Forlì.**

Fortebraccio (fôr-tā-brät′chō), **Braccio.** See **Braccio da Montone.**

Forteguerri (fôr-tā-gwer′rē), **Antonio.** Man of letters; b. at Pistoia, 1463. Of a noble family of Pistoia, he left a collection of sonnets, canzoni, and sestinas, *Amatorius liber*, supposedly inspired by his love for an unnamed lady and modeled on Petrarch. His lyrics are more noted for their aristocratic refinement than for depth of feeling.

Forteguerri, Giovanni. Man of letters and statesman; b. at Pistoia, 1508; d. there 1582. He was of the noble Forteguerri family of Pistoia that produced a number of men of letters. He served Cosimo I de' Medici as chancellor of Pistoia for a number of years. Between 1556 and 1562 he wrote a collection of tales, *Novelle*, to amuse himself. These follow the well-known Boccaccesque formula of a number of young men and women together who entertain themselves by telling stories. The eleven tales of the collection are often obscene, despite the dutiful pointings of morals and pious injunctions with which they are sprinkled. The most successful are the ones in which the author devotes his attention and meager talent to the earthy gaiety and common sense of the peasant.

Forteguerri, Niccolò. Cardinal, diplomat, and philanthropist; b. at Pistoia, October 7, 1419; d. at Viterbo, December 21, 1473. He studied canon law at Siena and Bologna and took his doctorate at the latter university. His ecclesiastical career was greatly forwarded by Enea Silvio Piccolomini who, when he became Pope Pius II, named him bishop of Teano, then apostolic treasurer, and (1460) gave him the red hat. A loyal supporter of Pius, and an able diplomat, he served the Church well in the struggles between the pope and such princes of Italy as Sigismondo Malatesta (1460–1463), and was present at the taking of Fano from the latter in September, 1463. Later, under Paul II, he gave energetic assistance in the pacification of the states of the Church. In 1473 he founded a school at Pistoia for the education of the young, and beside it founded a library that was richly stocked, the *Biblioteca Forteguerriana.* His monument, by Mino da Fiesole, is in the Church of S. Cecilia at Rome.

Forteguerri, Scipione. Humanist; b. at Pistoia, 1466; d. 1515. He was among the first to praise the Greek language and literature, in which he was learned, above Latin, as he did, especially in his oration, *De laudibus litterarum graecarum* (Venice, 1504). He was a friend of Erasmus of Rotterdam, whom he met at Venice, and was one of the most industrious assistants of Aldus Manutius at Venice in the preparation of Greek texts. In his enthusiasm for things Greek, he gave himself a Greek name, Carteromaco.

Fortescue (fôr′tẹs-kū), Sir **John.** English jurist; b. c1394; d. c1476. He was made chief justice of the King's Bench in 1442. As a Lancastrian he followed Queen Margaret to Flanders in 1463, returned to England in 1471, was captured at the battle of Tewksbury, and accepted a pardon from Edward

IV. His most notable works are *De laudibus legum Angliae*, first printed in 1537, and *On the Governance of the Kingdom of England* (also entitled *The Difference between an Absolute and Limited Monarchy* and *De Dominio regali et politico*) first printed in 1714.

Fortini (fôr-tē′nē), **Pietro.** Sienese writer of novelle; b. c1500; d. c1562. His work consists of eighty-one tales, in two collections: *Le giornate delle novelle dei novizî*, a group of forty-nine stories, in Boccaccesque framework, describing the daily lives of five young women and two young men in the course of a week; and *Le piacevole ed amorose notti dei novizî*, a collection of thirty-two tales. The works were written toward the end of Fortini's life, after the siege (1555) of Siena. They present a portrait of the manners and customs of gay and carefree Siena, contain some bright satire, portray some delightful comic characters and preserve the speech spoken at Siena.

Fortunio (fôr-tö′nyō), **Gianfrancesco.** Sixteenth century humanist and grammarian; died early in the century. He was a Dalmatian by birth, who had been brought to Italy, and was a pupil of Marcantonio Sabellico (1436?–1506). He is known above all for his interest in the study of Italian grammar, and for his work on it, *Regole grammaticali della volgar lingua* (Ancona, 1516). The principles adopted by Fortunio were followed by many later grammarians.

Foscari (fôs′kä-rē). One of the most ancient of the noble Venetian families, noted for its promotion of Venetian commercial interests in the eastern Mediterranean. From 1207 to 1276 members of the Foscari family shared the overlordship of the island of Lemnos. In the 14th century Niccolò Foscari was made a knight by Can Grande della Scala (1328), and was invested with the title of count and with fiefs by King John of Bohemia. At the same time, family possessions in Greece were increased and were held until the 17th century. Thus the Foscari had rich and large holdings in and about Venice. Members of the family contributed many able men to public office. The family name is best known from the tragic history of the doge Francesco Foscari (see below).

Foscari, Francesco. Doge of Venice (1423–1457); b. 1373; d. October 31, 1457. From 1401 to his death he held the highest offices in the gift of the Republic of Venice. He was an enthusiastic proponent of a policy of Venetian expansion on the mainland, and favored the war against Francesco da Carrara at the beginning of the 15th century that resulted in Venetian victory and control over Padua. In the course of the next twenty years Venice made great acquisitions on the mainland, acquisitions in which Foscari had a prominent part. When the doge, Tommaso Mocenigo, was dying (1423), he reviewed the condition and wealth of Venice, and strongly advised the Venetians to consolidate the gains they had already made rather than to engage in further wars of conquest. Venetian prosperity, he reminded his hearers, was based on peaceful commerce. He warned the Venetians against electing the warlike Foscari as his successor. Nevertheless, Foscari was elected, after a sharp contest for the position with Piero Loredan, who was inclined to follow Mocenigo's advice. Foscari was not so inclined. For the next thirty years the Republic of Venice was more or less continually at war. To the degree that territory was added to Venetian control the wars were successful. They were also costly and exhausting, and led to the formation of a league against Venice by the other Italian powers, jealous and fearful of Venetian domination over north Italy. Francesco Foscari's personal tragedy began in 1445 when his only surviving son, Jacopo, was denounced to the Council of Ten for having accepted bribes. He escaped before he could be arrested, but was tried in absentia and sentenced to be banished for life. He refused to embark for Nauplia, the place of his exile; his property was confiscated, and a sentence of death between the two columns on the piazzetta was passed. Further crimes were charged to Jacopo (whose sentence had been lightened to confinement at Treviso), including the stabbing (January, 1451) of one of the senators who had tried him originally. He was arrested, put to the torture, found guilty on no good evidence, and banished to Canea in Crete. In 1456 he was brought back from Canea to answer to the Senate on charges of having appealed to the duke of Milan to intercede on his behalf, so that he could return to his longed-for home. He was again banished, but before he left was allowed to see his heartbroken father, his mother, wife, and children. He begged his father to secure permission for his return to his beloved Venice. Francesco could reply only that he must obey the law. Six months later Jacopo died in Canea. From that time the doge retired from public life and public duties, sunk in grief. The government was paralyzed, and at length the Ten asked him to retire, offering him a pension. He refused. On a second appeal being made he again refused. The Senate found itself compelled to threaten: he must resign and leave the palace within a week or his property would be confiscated. Late in October, 1457, he yielded. He pulled the ducal ring from his finger and silently handed it to the representative of the Ten. The ring was smashed to pieces; the ducal cap was removed from his head. As the old hero (he was then 84) of the republic started to leave one of his sorrowing retinue suggested that he depart from the ducal palace by an inconspicuous stairway. "I will go down by the same steps I came up as doge," he replied. A few days later he was dead. Over the protests of his wife, who decried the hypocrisy, the Senate gave him a magnificent state funeral. Clothed in his ducal robes, with the ducal cap again on his head, he lay in state as the great of the city attended. Except that he was reckless, careless, fond of good living, and passionately attached to Venice, no crime was ever satisfactorily proved against Jacopo. The suspicion has persisted that the original accusation, made by a Florentine, was part of a plot by members of the Venetian aristocracy, especially the Loredan family, to humble Francesco, who had assumed so great a role in the affairs of Venice and in the affections of the people, and who lived in royal splendor in his palace on the Grand Canal. (Now the Institute of Commerce, the palace was purchased from the Giustiniani family by Francesco in 1437.)

Foscarini (fôs-kä-rē′nē), **Ludovico.** Statesman and humanist; active in the 15th century. He held many administrative positions for Venice between 1439 and 1488, beginning with that of podesta of Feltre (1439) and ending as procurator of Venice (1488), with others in between. He also played a role on the international scene, and defended the honor and interests of Venice at the papal court of Paul II (1464). With all his official duties, he maintained his deep interest in literary studies, and had a wide correspondence, most of which is unpublished, with the leading men of letters of his time.

Fouquet (fö-ke) or **Foucquet, Jean** (or **Jehan**). One of the earliest painters of the French school, court painter to Louis XI; b. at Tours, France c1415 or 1420; d. c1480. In 1461 he painted the portrait of Charles VII. He made a new departure toward naturalism from the Gothic tradition, and was acclaimed for his rendering of the peculiar light effects of the region around Paris. His work shows signs also of the influence of a trip (c1445) to Italy, particularly in the decorative use of perspective and architectural details. Fouquet had been all but forgotten until some of his paintings were exhibited early in the 20th century.

Fournier (för-nyā), **Jacques.** Original name of Pope **Benedict XII.**

Foxe (foks), **John.** English martyrologist; b. at Boston, Lincolnshire, England, 1516; d. at London, April 18, 1587. He studied at Magdalen College, Oxford, where he took a B.A. in 1537, became a full fellow in 1539, and obtained an M.A. in 1543. He resigned his fellowship in 1545, became in 1548 tutor to the orphan children of Henry Howard, Earl of Surrey (a post which he retained five years), and in 1550 was ordained a deacon. At the accession of Queen Mary he fled to the Continent to avoid persecution as a Protestant, and lived during her reign chiefly at Frankfort on the Main and at Basel, where he was employed as a reader of the press (proofreader) in the printing office of Johann Herbst (Oporinus). He returned to England in 1559, was ordained a priest in 1560, and in 1563 was made a prebendary in Salisbury Cathedral and given the lease of the vicarage of Shipton. His chief work is *Actes and Monuments*, of which four editions appeared during his lifetime (1563, 1570, 1576, and 1583), and which is popularly known as Foxe's *Book of Martyrs*; a Latin version preceded (1559) the English edition. The book was attacked by the Roman Catholics almost immediately, among them Robert Parsons, but despite its many inaccuracies remains a monument to Foxe's energy.

Foxe or **Fox, Richard.** English prelate; b. at Ropesley, near Grantham, Lincolnshire, England, 1447 or 1448; d. probably at Winchester, England, October 5, 1528. He studied at Oxford, Cambridge, and Paris. While at Paris he entered the service of Henry, Earl of Richmond, soon after whose accession in 1485 as Henry VII he was appointed lord privy seal. He became suffragan bishop of Exeter in 1487, being transferred to the see of Bath and Wells in 1492, to that of Durham in 1494, and to that of Winchester in 1501. He founded Corpus Christi College, Oxford.

Fracastoro (frä-kä-stō′rō), **Girolamo.** Physician and poet; b. at Verona, 1478; d. at his villa near Verona, August 8, 1553. He studied medicine at Padua, where he was a fellow-student of Nicolaus Copernicus, and later was on terms of warm friendship with some of the outstanding scientific spirits of his day. In 1510 he retired to his villa outside Verona and gave himself up to the study of philosophy, medicine, and astronomy. A well-known physician, he received distinguished patients from Italy and elsewhere, including Pope Paul III and Marguerite of Navarre, and his villa was a meeting place for scientists and men of letters, for Fracastoro did not limit himself to scientific interests. His many-sided mind embraced poetry and music as well. His most celebrated work is the poem *Syphilis sive de morbo gallico* (published at Verona, 1530). Its fame rests rather on its contribution to the history of medicine than on its Vergilian verse. From this work, dedicated to Pietro Bembo, the disease received the name by which it has been known ever since. It had become virulent in the beginning of the 16th century following the arrival in Italy of French armies, and was called by the Italians the French sickness. Fracastoro sought causes of the disease. After proposing and abandoning various hypotheses, including one that it had come from the New World, the poem relates the story of the shepherd Sifilo. He, having been unfaithful to Apollo, was punished by having his body break out in sores. Through the medium of describing the course and cure of the mythical shepherd's disease, as well as others, Fracastoro gives a clinical description of the affliction and suggested cures. Among the latter, in addition to dietary and exercise regimes, are guaiacum, a resin from the New World, and the age-old panacea mercury. Fracastoro the poet writes with the keen observation of a scientist. He also wrote distinguished works on mathematics, astronomy, cosmography, physics, botany, and geography. Other works include *De contagione et contagiosis*, in which he describes contagious diseases, the means by which they are spread, the organs they attack, and in which he implicitly recognizes the spread of disease by germs in the atmosphere. His many Italian letters on scientific topics provide an invaluable picture of the state of science in his day.

Frances of Rome (fran′sẹs), Saint. [Original name, **Francesca Bussa di Leoni.**] Roman noblewoman; b. 1384; d. March 9, 1440. She married at the age of 12, and became known for her charity and piety. In 1425 she founded a congregation of women for promoting charitable works. This was affiliated with the monastery of Santa Maria Nuova, and later became the Benedictine Oblate Congregation of Tor di Specchi (1433). Its members led religious lives outside the cloister. On the death (1436) of her husband she became superior of the congregation. She was canonized by Pope Paul V in 1608.

Francesca (frän-chā′skä), **Piero della.** See **Piero della Francesca.**

Francesco d'Antonio di Bartolommeo (frän-chās′kō dän-tō′nyō dē bär-tō-lôm-mā′ō). Florentine painter; b. 1394; d. after 1433. He joined the Physicians' and Apothecaries' Guild (which included artists) in 1429. In the early part of his career he was most influenced by Lorenzo Monaco but later changed from Lorenzo's austerity to the more decorative manner of Gentile da Fabriano, and ultimately was influenced by the developments in Florentine painting that were introduced by Masaccio and Domenico Veneziano. His lyrical decorative quality has affinity with the Sienese painters of his time. He painted frescoes and panels. A figure in fresco of *St. Ansanus*, Church of S. Niccolò, Florence, reflecting the influence of Gentile da Fabriano, is attributed to him, as is a *Coronation* in the Church of S. Francesco, Figline. Two panels, originally painted (1429) as organ shutters for Orsanmichele, are in the Accademia, Florence, and a panel, *The Virgin and Child with Six Angels and Two Cherubim*, is in the National Gallery, London. Other paintings are at Arezzo, Pisa, Barcelona, Budapest, Cambridge (England), Cologne, Copenhagen, Paris (Bibliothèque nationale), Baltimore (Walters Art Gallery), Birmingham (Alabama), Denver, Kansas City (Missouri), Los Angeles, Montgomery (Alabama), New York (Historical Society), Seattle, and Tucson (Arizona).

Francesco da Barberino (dä bär-bā-rē′nō). See **Barberino, Francesco da.**

Francesco di Bartolo da Buti (dē bär′tō-lō

dä bö′tē). Grammarian; b. at Buti (Pisa), c1324; d. at Pisa, July 25, 1406. He held a number of public offices at Pisa, taught grammar and rhetoric at the studio (university), lectured on the *Divina Commedia,* and wrote a commentary on it that was the first entirely in Italian. He was famed in his time at Pisa and beyond as a teacher. A number of manuscript copies of his writings are preserved.

Francesco de' Franceschi (dā frän-chās′kē). Venetian painter; active 1443–1468. He was a contemporary of Giambono, and like his fellow-Venetian was influenced by the international Gothic style, to which he added the rich decorative details of fabrics so loved by the Venetians. A polyptych in the Museo Civico at Padua has a figure of St. Peter in the central panel, with a *Crucifixion* above, and dates from 1447. A panel of a *Holy Doctor* is in the Palazzo Venezia at Rome; two panels on the legend of St. Mammas are in the Yale University Art Gallery, New Haven. Other paintings are at Città di Castello, Venice (Accademia, Correr Museum, and Ca' d'Oro), Verona, Budapest, Detroit, and St. Louis (Missouri).

Francesco di Gentile da Fabriano (dē jen-tē′lā dä fä-brē-ä′nō). Umbrian painter; active between c1460 and c1480. An eclectic painter, he first painted somewhat in the late Gothic manner of Gentile da Fabriano. These elements were later modified by the influence of Carlo Crivelli and Melozzo da Forlì. Because of his eclecticism attribution to him of paintings is difficult, but there is a signed *Madonna* in the Vatican that dimly reflects Crivelli. Other works attributed to him are at Matelica, Perugia, Rome (Palazzo Venezia), and a *Virgin and Child* in the Johnson Collection, Philadelphia.

Francesco di Giorgio Martini (dē jôr′jō mär-tē′nē). Sienese painter, sculptor, illuminator, architect, and engineer; b. at Siena, 1439; d. there, before February 9, 1502. As a painter he was trained by his fellow-townsman Vecchietta, whose delicate lyricism is somewhat modified in Francesco's Madonnas and other paintings by Florentine influences. An additional influence on his painting was that of Neroccio di Landi, with whom he shared a studio until 1475. His earliest known work (1464) is a wooden statue of *St. John the Baptist,* now in the Pinacoteca, Siena, a virile, realistic, heavy figure that shows the influence of Donatello. He was a prodigious and productive worker, and his achievements in the several fields in which he was active overlapped. In his first period at Siena (before 1475) he served as engineer on the fountains and aqueducts of the city, and continued active on the public works of Siena throughout his life. Of this period are a *Coronation of the Virgin,* now lost, painted for the Ospedale della Scala where, as architect, he was in charge of the construction of a new choir and ceiling in the church. A second painting on the same subject and of the same year (c1475) is in the Pinacoteca. His only signed and dated (1475) painting, a *Nativity,* is in the same gallery, and is reminiscent of Vecchietta in its elongated figures and delicate heads. Perhaps in 1475, when he broke off his association with Neroccio, he went to Urbino to enter the employ of Federico da Montefeltro; in any case, he was there by November, 1477, and prior to this had executed a bronze relief, *Deposition,* now in the Church of the Carmine, Venice, in which Federico appears as one of the donors. Other reliefs associated with this one are a dramatic and iconographically unusual *Flagellation,* National Gallery of Umbria, Perugia, and a *Lycurgus and the Maenads,* or, as it is also known, *Allegory of Discord,* stucco casts of which are in the Victoria and Albert Museum, London, and at Siena, the original being lost. The principal capacity in which he served Federico was as military architect and engineer, constructing fortifications about the small cities of the duchy of Urbino. Work he did in the palace itself, as sculptor or decorator, is not certainly identifiable, but a series of bas-reliefs of military machines, arms, and trophies on the façade of the palace is attributed to him. While in the employ of Federico he undertook (1484–1485) the design of his most successful and important building, the Church of S. Maria del Calcinaio at Cortona. The church, unfinished until long after his death, was built largely according to his plans and is a notable example of 15th century Sienese architecture. In his years at Urbino he had made frequent trips to other places to give advice on fortifications, back to Siena to execute public works, and back to Urbino. Federico, who called him "my most delightful architect," also occasionally employed him on missions of state. He remained at Urbino following the death

FRANCESCO DI GIORGIO MARTINI
Bridge of inflated skins; a folding bridge; two men with water wings and paddles
The British Museum, London

of Federico (1482) until 1485, when he was recalled to Siena and became official engineer of the city. In 1489 he began work on two bronze candelabra-bearing cherubs for the high altar of the cathedral at Siena. Two tall, slender, sweeping bronze angels for the high altar were begun in 1495 and completed in 1497, and in 1499 he was named chief of the works of the cathedral. In the meantime, his fame as a military engineer had spread. The signory of Siena received numerous requests for his advice and presence. He was called to Naples by Alfonso, duke of Calabria, in 1491, 1492, and 1495, and was urgently requested to go there at other times. In 1495, after Alfonso, who had become king of Naples, abdicated in the face of the French invasion under Charles VII, Francesco served his successor Ferrantino. He devised a system of tunneling and mine-laying to recover Castelnuovo from the French. His advice on fortifications was sought by communes up and down Italy, and at the end of the century he returned to Urbino to advise on the defense against Cesare Borgia. In 1490 he was invited by Gian Galeazzo Sforza to make a design and model for the dome of the cathedral and went to Milan. There he came in contact with Leonardo da Vinci, with whom he went to Pavia to inspect the cathedral then in course of construction there. And he was the only non-Florentine invited to submit a design for the façade of the cathedral of that city (no design was adopted at the time). In the course of one, or perhaps of several, of his journeys to Naples he made drawings of buildings he saw in cities he passed through. Twenty sheets of the drawings, *Taccuino del Viaggio*, with architectural details, plans of buildings, and an occasional swiftly drawn figure, are in the Uffizi, Florence. His *Trattato di architettura* is one of the most important architectural discussions of the 15th century. The treatise, begun perhaps at Urbino (c1482), and added to later, treats general architectural principles, discusses and describes palaces, cities, religious architecture, fortifications, harbors, and machinery. An interesting plan in it is for a stable to house 300 of Federico da Montefeltro's horses. Nothing more is known of this huge stable.

Francesco left a number of paintings that, despite some Florentine influences, are typically Sienese in their lyricism, rhythm, types, and light. A number of examples are at Siena, in the Pinacoteca and churches. Others are at Florence, Perugia, London, Paris, Atlanta (Georgia), Baltimore (Walters Art Gallery), Boston, Cambridge, Coral Gables (Florida), Kansas City (Missouri), Los Angeles, New Haven, New York, Portland (Oregon), and Washington. Pages illuminated by him are in the Basilica of the Osservanza and the Pinacoteca, Siena. Several bronze reliefs, including the *Judgment of Paris* and *St. Jerome in the Wilderness*, are in the National Gallery, Washington. Besides the Church at Cortona, other important architectural works included the remodeling of the Palazzo degli Anziani (Palazzo del Comune) at Ancona and plans for the Palazzo della Signoria at Iesi. The Church of S. Bernardino dei Zoccolanti, just outside Urbino, which holds the tombs of Federico and Guidobaldo da Montefeltro, is also attributed to him. His last architectural undertaking (1500) involved repairing the cracking dome of the Church at Loreto.

Francesco da Rimini (dä rē′mē-nē). Umbrian painter; active between 1330 and 1348. Many of the frescoes he painted in the Convent of S. Francesco at Bologna are still in position, in fragmentary condition. A detached fresco mounted on canvas of *St. Francis* is in the Pinacoteca, Bologna, and his *The Magdalen and Other Saints* is in the National Gallery of Umbria at Perugia.

Francesco di Stefano (dē stā′fä-nō). See **Pesellino.**

Francesco di Vannuccio (dē vän-nöt′chō). Sienese painter; active between 1361 and 1388. The earliest reference to him is of 1361, when he was paid for work painted at Montalcino. He is known to have worked in the cathedral at Siena also. His only signed work (1370) is an animated and expressive *Crucifixion*, Berlin; one similar to it is in the Johnson Collection, Philadelphia. Other paintings are at Siena, Montepulciano, Greenville (South Carolina), and elsewhere.

Francesco Maria della Rovere (mä-rē′ä del′lä rō′vā-rā). Duke of Urbino; b. 1490; d. at Pesaro, October 20, 1538. He was the son of Giovanni della Rovere, prefect of Rome, and of Giovanna, daughter of Duke Federico da Montefeltro. On the death of his father (1501), he went from Senigallia to the brilliant court of his uncle, Duke Guidobaldo of Urbino. On the suggestion of Julius II, who was also Francesco Maria's uncle, Guidobaldo adopted him as his heir and was succeeded by him in 1508. Francesco Maria was devoted to the military arts from childhood. Julius named him captain general in the papal army in the war against Venice (1509) and again against Ferrara (1511). He was at Bologna when the Bolognese rebelled against Julius (1511), and withdrew in such haste that he abandoned his artillery and baggage. He blamed the disaster on the treachery of Cardinal Alidosi, legate and confidant of Julius, and the next day slew the legate with his own hand at Ravenna (May 22, 1511). (Francesco Maria's apologists regretfully acknowledge his quick temper.) He was brought to justice but was absolved through the intervention of the pope, and was awarded Pesaro, Sforza heirs having failed, which he made his seat. Leo X confirmed his as captain general but then replaced him, first with Giuliano then with Lorenzo de' Medici. When Francesco Maria balked at fighting the French in Lombardy under Lorenzo, Leo declared him a rebel, deposed him and sent an army to seize the duchy of Urbino for Lorenzo de' Medici. The duchy was quickly taken (1516), but Francesco Maria reconquered it the following year and held out eight months in the face of the papal army besieging him. The struggle ended in an agreement, under which Francesco Maria withdrew to Mantua. Following the death of Leo, he regained his duchy (1521), with which he was formally invested (1523) by Adrian VI. Francesco Maria was noted in his own day as a captain. He served the Venetians against the French in Lombardy, but had no part in the defeat of Francis I at Pavia (1525), and was routed in an assault on Milan (1526). When the Constable of Bourbon, at the head of a pillaging army of German and Swiss troops, began his descent from Milan to Rome, Francesco Maria followed with his army, but always prudently in the rear and never gave battle. On him had been pinned the hopes of defending Rome. In the face of his strategy of delay, the imperial troops entered Rome (May, 1527) and subjected it to the most horrible sack it had endured since the days of the barbarians. Guicciardini could not be scornful enough of Francesco Maria. "His only tactics consisted in the selection and occupation of impregnable positions; whatever his numerical superiority, he evaded fighting; . . . and by his obstinacy in refusing to risk anything, he made certain of losing all." As the duke of Urbino, Francesco Maria was a good and just administrator. He was honest and pious, but the elegance and high level of culture that had prevailed at Urbino in the lifetimes of Federico and Guidobaldo da Montefeltro was absent in the period of Francesco Maria's rule. As his military skill could not be compared to that of his grandfather, Federico da Montefeltro, the range of his intellectual and artistic interests nowhere equaled that of Federico and Guidobaldo. He was succeeded by his son Guidobaldo II (1514–1574).

Francesco Neri da Volterra (nā′rē dä vôl-ter′rä). Pisan painter of the mid-14th century. He was influenced by the Florentine school of Giotto and Orcagna. In 1346 he was at Pisa where he is supposed to have repainted some of the frescoes in the Camposanto.

Francheschi (fräng-kās′kē), **Piero dei.** See **Piero della Francesca.**

Francia (frän′chä), **Francesco.** [Original name, **Francesco Raibolini.**] Bolognese painter and goldsmith; b. at Bologna, c1450; d. there, 1517. He trained first as a goldsmith, and was enrolled in the Goldsmiths' Guild in 1482. Painting was a second career that came to supersede the work as a goldsmith, but the earlier training is apparent in the delicacy and precision of his work as a painter. By 1490 he had a workshop and many assistants and pupils. Of the early period are two small altarpieces, such as formed part of the household equipment of newlyweds, now in the Pinacoteca, Bologna. Giovanni II Bentivoglio, lord of Bologna, invited him and the Ferrarese painter Lorenzo Costa to decorate his palace and the chapels he founded in a number of Bolognese churches. In addition to painting, Francia was named Master of the Mint by Giovanni II (a position which, by the grace of his own personality, he held as long as he lived despite the overthrow of his Bentivoglio patron), and designed and cast medals. A tireless worker, as official artist he made jeweled cups, silver and gold plate, ornamented silver lamps, jeweled collars, and decorated horse armor (celebrated was a flaming forest from which animals of every kind were fleeing, that he painted on horse armor for the lord of Urbino). He was esteemed as a portrait painter, and included portraits in many of his religious paintings. In the religious paintings he expressed his own simple and sincere piety in sweetly submissive worshipers, pure virgins, and earnest saints. He was influenced in his art by the Ferrarese school, and especially by Lorenzo Costa, with whom he enjoyed a long and friendly association. Among the earliest signed works is the *Felicini Altarpiece*, Pinacoteca, Bologna, dated 1494 by some, 1490 by others. A separate panel, *Dead Christ Supported by Two Angels*, in the same gallery, has been recently restored and is identified as the finial of the altarpiece. In general, his figures are carefully outlined; his color is clear and of enamel-like brilliance,

FRANCESCO FRANCIA
Judith and Holofernes
Courtesy of The Pierpont Morgan Library, New York

especially in such early works as a *Crucifixion*, Pinacoteca, Bologna, *Nativity*, Liverpool, and *St. Stephen*, Borghese Gallery, Rome. His style was modified somewhat by the broader forms of Ercole de' Roberti, the compositional treatment of Antonello da Messina, and the soft Umbrian style of Perugino and then of Raphael, but on the whole his style evolved but little; he remained a 15th-century painter and continued to express his own unquestioning faith in grave, devout, innocent saints and Madonnas. Toward the end of his career his style deteriorated somewhat, and after 1516, when Raphael's *St. Cecilia* was placed in the Church of S. Giovanni in Monte at Bologna, Francia's followers deserted him to adopt the broad forms and harmonies of 16th-century painting as it appeared in Raphael's art. Francia lived at a time of great upheaval in Bologna. Pope Julius II marched in at the head of an army and drove out Giovanni II (1506) and the Bolognese, by way of rejoicing, sacked the splendid Bentivoglio palace and destroyed many of the works of Francia that were in it. A number of his works are to be found in the churches of Bologna, including a series of frescoes on the life of St. Cecilia in the Oratory of S. Cecilia; Francia's son Giacomo assisted him in the execution of this series. Among the many paintings by him now in the Pinacoteca, Bologna, is an *Adoration* painted for the Bentivoglio Chapel in the Church of the Misericordia (which was the site of several of his works). Giovanni II took the painting with him when he was forced to flee from Bologna. This central panel, by Francia, was restored to Bologna, but the predella, painted by Lorenzo Costa, remained at Milan and is now in the Brera. Other works are in the Church of S. Frediano, Lucca, the cathedral, Ferrara, the Carrara Academy, Bergamo, the National Gallery, Parma, the Poldi Pezzoli Museum, Milan, the Uffizi, Florence, and at Rome, London, Paris, Berlin, the Metropolitan Museum, New York, Isabella Stewart Gardner Museum, Boston, Johnson Collection, Philadelphia, National Gallery, Washington, Yale University Art Gallery, New Haven, and elsewhere.

Francia, Giacomo. Bolognese painter; b. before 1486; d. 1557. He was the son of Francesco Francia (c1450–1517), and assisted his father in painting the frescoes on the life of St. Cecilia in the Oratory at Bologna. He won a reputation as an engraver in his own day, but his painting was in general a weak and conventional imitation of his father's. Several works by him are in the Pinacoteca at Bologna and a *Virgin and Child with SS. Gregory and Lawrence* is in the Johnson Collection, Philadelphia.

Franciabigio (frän-chä-bē′jō). [Original name, **Francesco di Cristofano Bigi.**] Painter; b. at Florence, c1482; d. there, 1525. As pupil or assistant he worked with Mariotto Albertinelli and Piero di Cosimo, and then set up a workshop with his young fellow-artist Andrea del Sarto. For about two years (1508–1511?) the two worked together, but no works in which they collaborated survive. The work of Franciabigio, the less gifted of the two, reflects the influence of several of his contemporaries. The classicism of Raphael, with its harmony and balance, in Franciabigio is modified by his energy and force while retaining, especially in a number of Madonnas, the types of Raphael. His painting was also influenced by the softer modeling of Leonardo, and ultimately he essayed the monumentality of Michelangelo, but without indulging in exaggerations that were alien to his balanced temperament. In his best works the elements he derived from these and such other artists as Piero di Cosimo and Ghirlandaio are fused into a graceful style that leans more toward 15th-century painting than that of the 16th century. In other works his manner is so derivative that attribution to him is disputed. His earliest surviving work is a tondo, *The Madonna and Child with St. John* (c1503), Uffizi, Florence. Other early works are the *Temple of Hercules* (c1505), Palazzo Davanzati, Florence, and a *Holy Family* (c1507), Accademia, Florence. Among the frescoes he painted in the churches of Florence is a *Last Supper* (c1511), Convent of S. Maria de' Candeli, a gentle and poetic work. The fresco was severely damaged by the flood of November, 1966, and has been detached, remounted, and cleaned. Another *Last Supper*, in the monastery of the Calza, dates from 1514. Other surviving frescoes include two scenes of the life of John the Baptist in the Cloister of the Confraternity of the Scalzo at Florence. Andrea del Sarto had the original commission to paint the monochrome series in the cloister. When he left for France (1518) all the panels were complete except two; Franciabigio, as the second most famous painter in Florence at the time, was given the commission to paint the last two panels. In them his manner is close enough to the artistry of his erstwhile friend and later rival to withstand comparison. In an earlier fresco, *Marriage of the Virgin*, SS. Annunziata, Florence, the results were less fortunate. In that case Franciabigio's fresco was on the wall opposite Andrea del Sarto's *Birth of the Virgin*, and the difference in their gifts and style at that time is marked. Enraged that the scaffolding had been removed from his fresco before he was ready, Franciabigio damaged his work. In his day he was much esteemed as a portrait painter. A number of portraits, in the manner of Raphael, survive. Examples of his work are in the Sabauda Gallery, Turin, Borghese and National galleries, Rome, the Medici villa at Poggio a Caiano (*The Triumph of Caesar*), Brussels, London, Hunter College, New York, Pittsburgh, and elsewhere.

Francis I (of *France*). King of France (1515–1547); b. at Cognac, France, September 12, 1494; d. at Rambouillet, France, March 31, 1547. He was the son of Charles, count of Angoulême, and cousin-german of Louis XII. His mother was Louise of Savoy, an extremely able diplomat, who was widowed two years after Francis was born. When Louis XII became king in 1498, Francis became heir presumptive, and his education and that of his sister, Marguerite d'Angoulême (who reigned as Marguerite de Navarre and who is credited with writing the collection known as the Heptameron), were well looked after by both mother and cousin. In 1514 Francis married Claude de France, the daughter of Louis XII. Within the year he himself was king. In the same year (1515) he conquered Milan by the victory of Marignano (September 13–14), and claimed its sovereignty by inheritance through his great-grandmother Valentina Visconti. In 1516 he concluded a concordat with Pope Leo X which rescinded the pragmatic sanction of 1438, and vested in the crown the right of nomination to fill vacant benefices. He was an unsuccessful candidate for the imperial dignity in 1519, attempted (1520) at the Field of the Cloth of Gold to make an alliance with Henry VIII of England against Charles V, the successful candidate, but failed to get a definite commitment from England. The remainder of his reign was chiefly occupied by four wars against the emperor Charles V, who advanced claims to Milan and the duchy of Burgundy. During the first war, which broke out in 1521, Francis was taken captive at Pavia (1525), when in the face of all advice he insisted on carrying on the siege and on remaining with his army. He was taken prisoner by the imperial troops and was kept in captivity until he was prevailed upon to sign the peace of Madrid (1526) by which he ceded Burgundy and renounced his claims to Milan, Genoa, and Naples. It was during his captivity that he wrote to his mother, "nothing remains to me but honor and life." Having been liberated following the signing of the peace, Francis proceeded to ignore its terms, and was determined to defeat the Spanish. During the second war, which broke out in 1527, he was supported by Pope Clement VII, Venice, and Francesco Maria Sforza, duke of Milan. It was concluded by the peace of Cambrai in 1529, the so-called Paix de Dames, or "Ladies' Peace," signed for Francis by his mother, Louise of Savoy, and for Charles by his aunt, Margaret of Austria. The third war broke out in 1536, and was ended by the truce of Nice in 1538. The fourth war, which broke out in 1542, was terminated with the peace of Crépy in 1544, which left him in possession of Burgundy while the emperor retained Milan. During the last two wars his principal ally was Suleiman the Magnificent, sultan of Turkey. Francis has been called the typical Renaissance ruler. He built up about him a brilliant court and thus brought the nobility within the circle of the crown, where he could control them. He made the clergy subservient to his wishes by his power of appointment, granted by the Concordat of 1516. He ruled by a council of favorites, and not once during his reign were the estates called into session. Women played an important part in his reign. Besides his sister Marguerite and his mother, Francis was influenced by several mistresses. The last of these, whom he created duchesse d'Etampes, completely dominated him. Among the luminaries in the arts attracted to him were the poet Clément Marot, the Italian artist Benvenuto Cellini, who was at swords' points with la duchesse and blamed any misunderstandings he might have with Francis on her, and the satirist François Rabelais. Andrea del Sarto and Leonardo da Vinci also were present at Francis' court. Francis instituted the royal readers in the classics, mathematics, and the like who formed the nucleus from which the Collège de France was founded. The palace at Fontainebleau and the buildings at St.-Germain, Chambord, and Villers-Cotterets were products of his era. Among the statesmen who handled affairs for Francis were Anne de Montmorency and Philippe de Chabot. During his reign the exploration of Canada was begun by Jacques Cartier; French orientation towards Canada was thus established. Francis married twice: his first wife, Claude de France, was the mother of Francis' successor, Henry II, of Madeleine, first wife of James V of Scotland, and of Margaret, wife of Emmanuel Philibert, duke of Savoy. In 1530, during the period of peace (1529–1536) that followed the treaty of Cambrai, Francis married Eleanor, sister of the Emperor Charles V.

Franciscus Vieta (fran-sis′kus vī-ē′tạ). Latinized name of **Viète, François.**

Franck (frängk), **Sebastian.** [Also: **Frank;** called **Sebastian Franck of Wörd.**] German popular writer and mystical theologian, an adherent of the Reformation; b. at Donauwörth, Bavaria, Germany, c1499; d. probably at Basel, Switzerland, c1542. He wrote *Chronika* (1531), *Weltbuch* (1534; a cosmography), *Sprichwörtersammlung* (1541), and others.

Franco (fräng′kō), **Battista.** [Called **Semolei.**] Painter and engraver; b. at Venice, c1498; d. there, 1561. At 20 he went to Rome to study the works of Michelangelo, and there made engravings of the works of Raphael, Giulio Romano, and others. He became an excellent draftsman and engraver, but was a weak colorist. At Rome he helped prepare the decorations for the triumphal entry of Charles V (1536), and at Florence worked on the elaborate decorations contrived for the marriage to Cosimo I to Eleonora of Toledo. Returned to Rome, he executed some frescoes and then went to Urbino, where he painted a copy of Michelangelo's *Last Judgment* in the dome of the old cathedral (later destroyed), and made de-

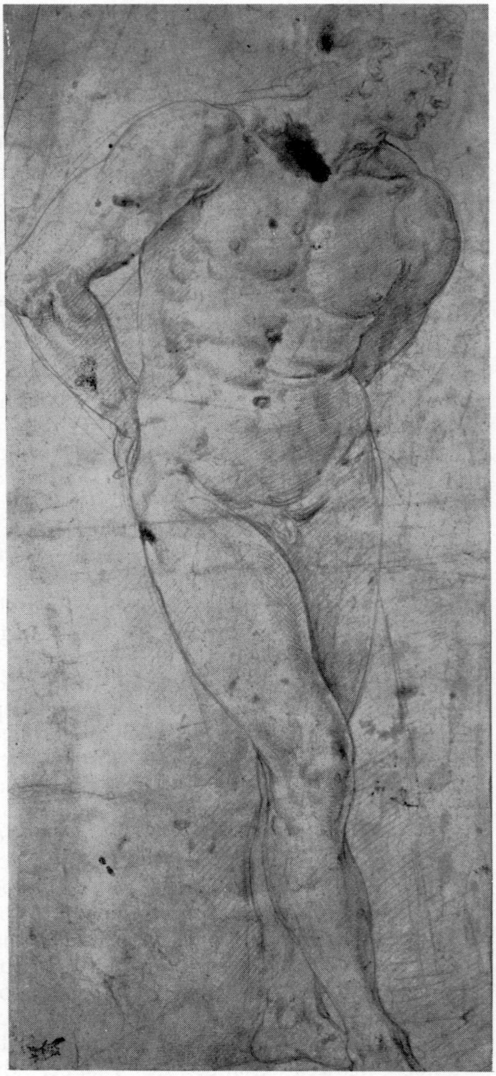

Battista Franco
Standing Male Nude
Courtesy of The Metropolitan Museum of Art, New York, Rogers Fund, 1962

signs for majolica ware. A successful engraver and designer, he was an indifferent painter.

Franco, Matteo. Florentine priest and poet; b. at Florence, 1447; d. at Pisa, 1494. A genial parish priest of humble origin, he won the hearts of the Medici, especially of Lorenzo, and received many benefits from them, often as a result of impudent poetic requests. He wrote humorous verse on the everyday events of his parish and engaged in a literary duel, begun at least, in jest, with Luigi Pulci. His loyalty to the Medici, especially to Lorenzo's wife Clarice and her children, was unwavering.

Franco, Niccolò. Minor poet; b. at Benevento, September 13, 1515; hanged at Rome, March 10, 1570. Of a humble family, he vainly sought a patron in Isabella of Capua, at Naples. Going on to Venice, he wrote *Tempio d'Amore*, in praise of the Venetian ladies, a work that was largely pilfered. Aretino befriended him and then, as so often happened, turned on him. Franco tried for vengeance in his *Pistole vulgari*, weak imitations of Aretino's *Lettere*. After a brawl with a friend of Aretino's, in which Franco was wounded, he left Venice (1540), and thereafter issued a series of venomous sonnets against Aretino, and followed these with his *Priapea*. In this he made the mistake of reviling Paul III. None of these efforts improved his fortunes. He attached himself to the count of Popoli as secretary, and when a relative of the count was elected as Pope Paul IV, Franco attempted, in vain, to have the ban of excommunication under which he had been put for his *Priapea* lifted. He went to Rome (1558) and was immediately arrested, but was freed after about two years. He then launched a diatribe against Paul IV, and was, under Pius V, handed over to the Inquisition, tried, convicted, and hanged. He wrote a great deal, but not very well. He affected to scorn Petrarch, in his *Dialoghi piacevoli* and *Petrarchista*, but his own lyrics clearly show that Petrarch was his model.

Franco, Veronica. Venetian courtesan and poetess; b. 1546; d. 1590. One of the most famous of 16th-century Venetian courtesans, she was renowned not only for her beauty but for her intellectual gifts, which made her a stimulating companion to the men of letters and artists of her day. Her friends, lovers, and admirers were drawn from the great and near-great. Among them was Tintoretto, who painted her portrait. Henry III, the young king of France, visited her in 1574. In 1580, perhaps because of a serious charge brought against her by the Church, which was later resolved in her favor, she gave up her life as a courtesan and devoted herself to good works, even going so far as to establish a society for the rehabilitation of fallen women. Her *Terze Rime*, published at Venice, 1575, is a collection of love lyrics, some of which are lyrical expressions of sincere sentiments, and others which are tinged with a crude but realistic sensuality that proclaims her independence of the Petrarchan tradition. Others of her poems, mostly sonnets, appear in collections of the time.

Franco Bolognese (bō-lō-nyā'zā). Miniaturist of Bologna; active in the 13th century. Dante mentions him in the *Divina Commedia* (*Purgatorio*, xi) as having surpassed his teacher, Oderisi da Gubbio, but none of his work is now surely known. He is thought to have worked at Bologna and, like his master, to have abandoned the Byzantine style.

Francucci (fräng-köt'chē), **Innocenzo.** See **Innocenzo Francucci da Imola.**

Franklin's Tale, The. One of Chaucer's *Canterbury Tales*. It is said in the prologue to be from a Breton lay. The story tells of the conditions which Aurelius must fulfill to win the embraces of Dorigen, wife of Arverigus. The conditions are fulfilled by magic, but Aurelius releases Dorigen from her promise. The story appears in the fifth novel of the tenth day in Boccaccio's *Decameron*, and is introduced also in his *Filocolo*.

Fray Marcos (frī mär'kōs). See **Niza, Marcos de.**

Frederick I (of *Brandenburg*). [Family name, **Hohenzollern.**] Margrave of Brandenburg; b. at Nuremberg, Germany, c1372; d. September 21, 1440. He first appears in history in 1396, when he saved the life of King Sigismund of Hungary, at the battle of Nicopolis. In 1397 he became burgrave of Nuremberg, a position formerly held by his father. By his father's death he came into possession of Ansbach, Bayreuth, and other territories, which he shared with his brother, John, whose death in 1420 made him the sole ruler. In 1409, again serving under Sigismund, he supported his candidacy for the German crown and helped him against the Hungarian rebels. In 1417, on April 18, Sigismund made him both elector and margrave of Brandenburg at the Council of Constance. These positions made the Hohenzollerns the ruling family in Prussia and made

Frederick the founder of the Prussian line.

Frederick I (of *Denmark and Norway*). King of Denmark and Norway (1523–1533); b. c1471; d. 1533. The son of Christian I and uncle of Christian II, he was chosen by the nobility to succeed the latter, who had been driven out because of his cruelty. During his reign Lutheranism was declared (1527) the state religion. He captured (1532) Christian II, who attempted to regain the Danish throne.

Frederick II (of *Denmark and Norway*). King of Denmark and Norway (1559–1588); b. at Haderslev, Denmark, July 1, 1534; d. at Antvorskov, April 4, 1588. He was the son of Christian III, and one of Denmark's most popular kings. After fighting against Sweden in the bitter Scandinavian Seven Years' War (1563–1570), which ended in the peace of Stettin and Frederick's victory, he reigned in peace. He built up the Danish navy, wiped out the pirates along the Danish coast, restored the financial stability of the kingdom, and encouraged industry and science. He was the patron of the astronomer Tycho Brahe, giving him an allowance and deeding an island off the coast to him.

Frederick III (of *Germany*). [Called **Frederick the Handsome.**] King of Germany as a rival to Louis IV (1314–1326); b. 1286; d. at Gutenstein, Germany, January 13, 1330. He was the son of Albert I, whom he succeeded as duke of Austria in 1308. He was chosen king of Germany in opposition to Louis IV (later Holy Roman emperor). Louis contested his election, fought against him and defeated him at Mühldorf in 1322. Frederick was captured, but was released in 1325. He renounced the kingship and promised either to obtain the consent of his brother Leopold to Louis' kingship or to return to his captivity. Leopold refused and Frederick returned voluntarily to his captor in Bavaria.

Frederick IV (of *Germany*). See **Frederick III** (of the *Holy Roman Empire*).

Frederick II (of the *Holy Roman Empire*). [Also, **Frederick II** (of *Germany*).] Emperor of the Holy Roman Empire (1220–1250); b. at Jesi, near Ancona, December 26, 1194; d. at Fiorentino (Firenzuola), December 13, 1250. He was the son of Henry VI and Constance, heiress of the Two Sicilies. Left an orphan in 1198, he was brought up under the wardship of the pope as feudal superior of the Two Sicilies. He assumed the government of the Two Sicilies in 1208. In 1212 he was brought forward by the pope as an aspirant to the crown of Germany in opposition to King Otto IV, with whom the pope had quarreled. Frederick was elected by the Ghibelline party, the traditional supporters of the house of Hohenstaufen, which he represented. He was crowned at Aachen in 1215, Otto having been totally defeated at Bouvines in the previous year. He was crowned emperor at Rome by Pope Honorius III in 1220. He continued the policy of his house of attempting to perfect the union of Italy, "the garden of the Empire," and Germany into one empire. In this he was opposed by the pope and the Lombard League. He conducted (1228–1229) a crusade to the Holy Land in tardy fulfillment of a pledge to the pope, and procured the cession of Jerusalem, Bethlehem, and Nazareth from the Saracens. Frederick maintained a court of oriental splendor at Naples. He surrounded himself with poets, artists, and men of letters. One of his chief ministers, Pier della Vigna, was himself a poet. A cultivated man, he gathered cultivated men about him, fostered the arts, founded the University of Naples (1224), and was the patron of science and philosophy. He is said to have spoken Latin, Italian, German, French, Greek, and Arabic. He loved letters, was a poet himself, and wrote *De arte venandi cum avibus*, a treatise on hawking that also describes the anatomy and habits of birds. He ruled his Sicilian domain (he passed most of his life in Italy, where he seemed more comfortable) with an iron hand, through constant wars with the Lombard League and the popes. He crushed the barons, subdued the Saracens, recovered his lands, began a series of needed legislative reforms, reorganized the finances, made the traffic in oil, wine, and salt an imperial monopoly, imposed excise taxes, attempted the destruction of the feudal system, and centralized authority in the person of the monarch. He seemed, in many respects, the forerunner of the cultivated, enlightened, and thoroughly autocratic Renaissance princes. He was cruel in pursuing his objectives and wise and enlightened in some of his political, juridical, and economic administrative reforms. Salimbene of Parma, a contemporary chronicler, wrote of him that he was absolutely without faith in God, was covetous, sensual, prodigal, crafty, and hot-tempered, and at the same time, powerful, merry, energetic, agreeable, handsome and well-formed. "I have seen him," writes Salimbene, "and sometimes I loved him." Like other Hohenstaufens, he exercised a fatal fascination over enemy and friend. Burckhardt, foremost historian of the Renaissance, began his study with the reign of this charismatic personality. After Frederick's death in 1250 an unparalleled opportunity was given to the North Italian city-states to develop in relative autonomy.

Frederick III (of the *Holy Roman Empire*). [Also, **Frederick IV** (of *Germany*).] Emperor of the Holy Roman Empire (1440–1493); b. at Innsbruck, Austria, September 21, 1415; d. at Linz, Austria, August 19, 1493. He was the son of Ernest of Hapsburg, duke of Styria and Carinthia, and after his father's death quarreled with his brother Albert over the government of Styria and Carinthia until Albert's death (1463). As head of the Hapsburg house, he was chosen king of the Germans in 1440. Under the influence of his secretary, Enea Silvio Piccolomini (later Pius II), he made a secret agreement with Pope Eugenius IV (1445) that bound the Germans to the Church. In return Frederick was to receive a money payment and the imperial crown. Without consulting the German Diet, he signed the Concordat of Vienna (1448) with Pope Nicholas V that confirmed the earlier agreement and restored revenues and privileges to the pope of which he had been deprived by the Council of Basel. In January, 1452, Frederick crossed into Italy to be crowned by the pope. He was royally entertained in the cities he passed through on his way to Rome. At Ferrara, the marquess Borso d'Este "sent 16 different kinds of wine, as much bread as two men could carry, ten chests of confectionary, three of wax lights, thirty capons, two live calves, and provender enough to load ten men." (Borso's gifts of provisions and the entertainment he offered Frederick did not arise from pure and disinterested hospitality; he hoped that Frederick would invest him as duke of Ferrara. For a suitable payment and other considerations, Frederick did so invest him on his way back from Rome.) Other cities honored him with generous attentions. Arrived at Rome, Frederick met his bride, Leonora of Portugal. His marriage had been arranged by Enea Silvio to take place at the same time as his coronation. One of Pinturicchio's delightful panels in the Piccolomini Library in the cathedral at Siena is a representation of Enea Silvio presenting Frederick to his bride a few days before the wedding. The wedding took place on March 16, 1452, and the coronation three days later. Frederick was the last Holy Roman Emperor to be crowned by the pope at Rome. The splendid festivals and ceremonies that were held in the days preceding the wedding and coronation are described in detail in the *Commentaries* of Pius II. Frederick left Rome for Naples, but was compelled to hurry back on news that his ward Ladislaus (heir to Bohemia, Hungary, and Austria) had tried to escape from Rome, whither he had perforce accompanied Frederick. On his way back to Germany Frederick distributed titles and fiefs on every hand. His rapacity in selling the titles aroused the contempt of the Italian princes who sought them. Frederick further eroded his reputation as a monarch by going into the shops at Venice in disguise in order to avoid paying imperial prices. Avaricious and incompetent, he had left Germany in disorder and returned to find it in turmoil. The Germans resented his agreement with the pope and his indifference to the dangers threatening from the Turks. After the death of his brother Albert (1463) he united upper and lower Austria under his rule, but could not protect them from attacks by George of Podiebrad and Matthias Corvinus, who had seized Bohemia and Hungary on the death of Ladislaus. In furtherance of his ambitions for the Hapsburgs, he married his son Maximilian to Mary, daughter of Charles the Bold, duke of Burgundy, and added this rich territory to Hapsburg dominions. In 1486 Maximilian was elected king of the Romans, and in 1490 Frederick turned over the responsibilities of the government of the Empire to him. He then retired to Linz and gave himself up to his study of the natural sciences and alchemy. He was sincerely interested in learning, and for all his rapacity and weakness, was mild and just, and unquestionably strengthened the Hapsburgs. He attached the initials AEIOU to documents and ornaments. They stood for: *Austriae est imperare orbi universo,* by which he expressed his conviction that Austria would rule the world.

Frederick I (of the *Palatinate*). [Called **Frederick the Victorious.**] Elector palatine (1451–1476); b. August 1, 1425; d. at Heidelberg, Germany, December 12, 1476. He was regent for his nephew Philip after Louis IV's death in 1449, and in 1451 was accorded recognition as elector, with the understanding that Philip would succeed him.

Frederick II (of the *Palatinate*). [Called **Frederick the Wise.**] Elector palatine (1544–1556); b. December 9, 1482; d. February 26, 1556. He commanded the imperial army for Charles V against the Turks in 1529 and 1532. In 1545 he joined the Schmalkaldic League of Protestant supporters, but soon submitted to Charles V.

Frederick III (of the *Palatinate*). [Called **Frederick the Pious.**] Elector palatine (1559–1576); b. at Simmern, Germany, February 14, 1515; d. at Heidelberg, Germany, October 26, 1576. He was originally an adherent of the Lutheran faith, but eventually joined the Reformed (Calvinist) communion, and in 1563 published the Heidelberg Catechism throughout his dominions.

Frederick I (of *Saxony*). [Called **Frederick the Warlike.**] Elector and duke of Saxony; b. at Altenburg, Germany, March 29, 1369; d. there, January 4, 1428. He was made elector and duke of Saxony in 1423 as a reward for his services to the emperor Sigismund in the Hussite war. His army was defeated by the Hussites at Aussig in 1426. He founded the University of Leipzig in 1409.

Frederick II (of *Saxony*). [Called **Frederick the Meek.**] Elector and duke of Saxony; b. August 22, 1411; d. at Leipzig, Germany, September 7, 1464. He was the son and successor of Frederick I (1369–1428). His reign was marked by struggles with the Hussites and with neighboring rulers.

Frederick III (of *Saxony*). [Called **Frederick the Wise.**] Elector of Saxony; b. at Torgau, Prussia, January 17, 1463; d. at Annaburg, near Torgau, May 5, 1525. He succeeded to the electorate in 1486; founded (1502) the University of Wittenberg, and appointed as professors there Martin Luther and Melanchthon. Leo X hoped that the imperial crown would go to him in the election of 1519, but he declined it and advocated the election of Charles V. When Luther was proscribed, Frederick protected him by seizing him as he was returning from Worms and hiding him (1521–1522) in the castle of Wartburg.

Frederick the Handsome. See **Frederick III** (of *Germany*).

Frederick the Meek. See **Frederick II** (of *Saxony*).

Frederick the Pious. See **Frederick III** (of the *Palatinate*).

Frederick the Victorious. See **Frederick I** (of the *Palatinate*).

Frederick the Warlike. See **Frederick I** (of *Saxony*).

Frederick the Wise. See **Frederick II** (of the *Palatinate*), and **Frederick III** (of *Saxony*).

Fredi (frā′dē), **Bartolo di.** See **Bartolo di Fredi.**

Fregoso (frā-gô′sō). [Also, **Campofregoso.**] Rich and powerful merchant family of Genoa that began to assume a prominent place in Genoese affairs in the 13th century with Rolando, a governor of several small states. With his son Domenico (1325?–1390?) the family rapidly came to the forefront. In August, 1370, he deposed Gabriele Adorno, the vicar, and had himself declared doge. Henceforth the rivalry between the Adorno and the Fregoso families was bitter and bloody, and kept Genoa in turmoil for nearly two centuries. Members of the two families, both of which had sprung from the people and gained power through wealth, contested each other with every violent means available and often sought the help of foreigners in their struggles. Ambitious and partisan, unrelenting in their factious strife, the Fregosi were at the same time patrons of letters and devotees of the new studies of humanism. Thirteen members of the family served, for longer or shorter times, as doges of Genoa. The rule of Domenico (he was deposed in 1378) was notable for the war his brother Pietro carried on against Cyprus, for the suppression of the pirates, and for the beginning of the war of Chioggia with Venice. His son Giacomo, who served briefly as doge (August, 1390–April, 1391), was primarily a scholar. Domenico's brother Pietro (1329–1404), having distinguished himself in the war of Cyprus (1373), seized the ducal palace (June, 1393) but was expelled. He had many warlike sons. Of these, Battista, governor of Corsica, forced Alfonso of Aragon (future Alfonso I of Naples) out of the island (1421), seized Alfonso's ally, and sent him to Genoa where he was beheaded. Giovanni, Bartolomeo, and Spinetta were admirals, captains, and governors whose activities ranged over a wide area; Tommaso (1402–1485) was doge three times between 1414 and 1442. He lived in magnificent splendor, ruled harshly, and was unpopular at home and threatened from abroad. All the members of the family who became prominent in the future were descended from these sons of Pietro I. Battista was the father of a second Tommaso, governor of Savona, who was beheaded (1459) for having tried to turn over Genoa to the French; Pietro II (1412–1459), doge (1450–1458), who was killed in a popular uprising; and Paolo (1430–1498), archbishop of Genoa, warrior, and statesman (see below). Other conspicuous members of the violent family were Battista II (1453–1504), doge from 1478 to 1483, when he was deposed by his uncle Paolo; Spinetta II, doge for 14 days in July, 1461; Antoniotto, poet, supporter of the Sforza family, and founder of the Milanese branch of the family (see below); Giano I (1405–1447), doge, and distinguished in his family for dying in office; and a third Tommaso, a restless warrior who fought the Sforza in Corsica. Cesare, the protector of the writer Bandello and himself the author of a poem in praise of Marguerite of Navarre, was a valiant captain who, being exiled after 1528, went into the service of Venice and Piedmont and was killed in 1541. Ludovico succeeded his brother Giano I as doge (1447) but was deposed (1450) by his cousin Pietro, and then served in the office twice more, alternating with his cousins Paolo and Spinetta up to 1463. Ludovico's son was Agostino (d. 1487), who married Gentile, the natural daughter of Federico, duke of Montefeltro. Agostino was a soldier in the service of the Church. He lost (1487) Sarzana to the Florentines, a city his ancestors had sold to Piero de' Medici and then treacherously taken back. Among Agostino's many sons were Ottaviano and Federico (see below). After 1528, when Genoa had become allied to the emperor Charles V, a new constitution was adopted. One of its provisions was that members of the Adorno and Fregoso families should be forever prohibited from holding public office. Henceforth the Fregoso family played a minor role in Genoese affairs.

Fregoso, Antoniotto. Genoese courtier and poet; d. after 1532. He was the natural son of Spinetta II of the turbulent Fregoso family of Genoa. In the service of the Sforza at Milan from 1464, he became a knight (1478) and a courtier of Ludovico il Moro. When the latter was taken prisoner by the French (April, 1500), Antoniotto retired to a villa at Colturano and gave himself up to a life of solitude (which won him the nickname, *Il Fileremo*). He left a number of sonnets and allegorical poems. Of the latter, his *Doi filosofi* (Milan, 1506) describes a fantastic journey made to listen to the laughter of Democritus ("the Laughing Philosopher") and the weeping of Heraclitus ("the Weeping Philosopher"). It was highly regarded in its day and was translated into French and Spanish. A second allegorical poem was *La cerva bianca* (Milan, 1510), another fantasy, of a hunt in which a nymph, changed into a white deer by Diana, is pursued and is at last restored to her true form.

Fregoso, Federico. Genoese cardinal; b. 1480; d. at Gubbio, July 29, 1541. He was the son of Agostino Fregoso and Gentile, natural daughter of Federico da Montefeltro. Named archbishop of Salerno in 1507 (and later forced by the Spanish to renounce it), in 1508 he became administrator of Gubbio, and was often at the cultivated court of his uncle, Duke Guidobaldo, at Urbino. Proficient in eastern languages, a student of philology, he studied the sacred texts and was an early and discriminating collector of Provençal poetry. He contributed his diplomatic gifts to aid his brother Ottaviano in the government of Genoa, and his military talent to driving the corsairs back to Bizerte (a feat memorialized by Ariosto). Pope Leo X did not look with favor on him, but Paul III recognized his qualities and gave him the red hat (1539). A cultivated man and a scholar, Federico was a friend of the outstanding men of letters of his day: Pietro Bembo and Jacopo Sadoleto were particular friends. At Urbino he often took part in the entertainments and discussions that were held in the evening room of the ducal palace, and that were presided over by the Duchess Elizabetta. Castiglione names him in this connection in his *Il Cortegiano*.

Fregoso, Ottaviano. Genoese courtier, soldier, and statesman; b. 1470; d. at Ischia, 1524. He was the son of Agostino Fregoso and Gentile, natural daughter of Federico da Montefeltro. Educated at the cultivated court of his uncle, Duke Guidobaldo, at Urbino, the elegant and refined atmosphere of that court, free from ostentatious luxury and dissipation, made a lasting impression on him.

He and his brother Federico are named by Castiglione as being among the noble courtiers who took part in the discussions that are so vividly described in his *Il Cortegiano*. Ottaviano had hoped, through Charles VIII of France, to free Genoa from the domination of the Sforza ruler but saw the lordship of Ludovico il Moro succeeded by that of Louis XII in 1499. He returned to Urbino, and when the duchy was attacked and fell to Cesare Borgia (1502), he displayed conspicuous valor in defending S. Leo, the old capital of the county of Montefeltro. For Francesco Maria della Rovere, who followed Guidobaldo (d. 1508) as duke of Urbino, he was ambassador to France. He served Julius II, who named him a general of the Church, in the wars of the League of Cambrai and the Holy League. He twice (1507 and 1510) tried to gain possession of his native Genoa and failed each time. In 1513 when the French fled Genoa he was named doge, and occupied his brief tenure by destroying the fortress Louis XII had caused to be built. Continual conspiracies by the recalcitrant Genoese harried his brief rule. With the accession of Francis I to the throne (1515), Ottaviano concluded that further resistance to the French was useless. He proposed that the title of doge be abolished, and he was retained as governor of Genoa for the French. As such he was a wise and moderate ruler. The few years of relative peace were interrupted when the French were defeated by the Spanish (1522). The marquess of Pescara overran Genoa and mercilessly sacked it. Ottaviano was taken prisoner and was sent first to the castle at Aversa, and then to Ischia. There, already ill when he was made prisoner, he died.

Fregoso, Paolo. Genoese archbishop, warrior, and statesman; b. 1430; d. at Rome, March 19, 1498. He was the son of Battista Fregoso and the grandson of Pietro I (1329–1404). An adventurous, warlike, and political prelate, restless and wildly partisan, his ambition knew no bounds and he was totally lacking in scruples. Gifted with an active and intelligent mind, he was typical of the turbulent members of his family who pursued power and culture at the same time and achieved both. Against his will, and on the insistence of his brother Pietro II (1412–1459), he became archbishop of Genoa, but when Genoa fell under French control and his brother was killed (1459) he entered upon an active political career. He cooperated briefly with Prospero Adorno, of the family that was by long tradition an enemy of his own, to drive out the French. Almost at once he quarreled with the Adorni and aided his kinsmen to lay siege to the ducal palace. For two brief periods (1462, 1464) he replaced Ludovico Fregoso as doge. Ludovico's violent and disorganized rule gave Francesco Sforza the chance he was looking for, and with the blessing of Louis XI he seized Genoa (1464). Paolo fled. For some years he was a roving soldier. He returned to Genoa when his nephew Battista II had overthrown his old rival Prospero Adorno. At Battista's suggestion, Pope Sixtus IV raised Paolo to the Sacred College (1480) and named him head of the forces to drive the Turks from Otranto. The Turks left in 1481, but rather as the result of the death of the sultan, Mohammed II, than as a result of Italian military prowess (although Alfonso, duke of Calabria, gladly took the credit for driving the Turks from Italy). Paolo would have pursued the Turks but was prevented by the pope from doing so. He left the fleet, of which he had been papal commander, at Civitavecchia and returned to Genoa. There he was warmly welcomed. At once he organized a conspiracy against his nephew, forced him aside, and had himself proclaimed doge for the third time (1483). His five-year reign is described by contemporary chroniclers as one of unparalleled violence, and weakness in the face of the unrelenting efforts of the deposed Battista II to regain power. His son Fregosino, noted for his dissolute life, shared Paolo's power and contributed greatly to his unpopularity. Unable to dispel the threats of his adversaries, late in 1487 he yielded the signory of Genoa to Ludovico il Moro, retaining his position under the title of governor. But a popular uprising of January, 1488, forced him to flee. Ludovico il Moro banished the Fregosi. Paolo, now his enemy, joined the Aragonese fleet and took part in a number of actions. At length he joined Charles VIII and departed with him for France, but later returned to Rome, where he died.

Fresco (fres′kō). A method of painting on walls that have been prepared with a coating of wet plaster. According to Cennino Cennini, who described it in his book *Libro dell' Arte*, written in the 15th century, the method was as follows. The wall to be painted was first coated with plaster. This first layer of rough plaster was called the *arriccio*. In the 14th century paper was scarce and costly. The artist sketched his design, in charcoal, directly on the rough plaster surface. He next went over it with ochre and made any changes in the composition that occurred to him; and finally drew his completed composition in *sinopia*, a red pigment, from which the drawing itself is called a *sinopia*. These *sinopie* are the only drawings that exist from the hands of the early artists. They did not expect that the drawings would ever be seen again, once the fresco was completed, and drew with great spontaneity and verve. The drawings are free from the conventions that appear in the frescoes, often exhibit much finer draftsmanship than the finished work, are sometimes quite finished, and at others just blocked in to indicate the arrangement of figures in the space to be filled. After the *sinopia* was completed to the artist's satisfaction he was ready for the next step. The first layer of plaster was well wetted and a second very thin layer, "of the consistency of ointment," was spread on. The amount of the second layer, called the *intonaco*, that was spread was limited to the amount of the surface that the painter could paint in one day, as the *intonaco* dried over night. To the wet *intonaco* the painter applied the undercoating, which Cennini describes as "a little ochre without tempera, as liquid as water," with special features as the eyes and mouth and shading for modeling having a specially prepared undercoating. Having carried out this step the artist was ready to apply his colors. In true fresco, the process here described, water soluble pigments become chemically immixed with and part of the plaster. Only earth pigments dissolved in water attain the desired chemical reaction. When the plaster dried the color was of great brilliance and durability. The artist, or craftsman, as he was considered in the 14th century and most of the 15th, carried out all the various steps himself; he mixed the plaster, usually to his own private formula, ground his pigments, drew the *sinopia*, applied the *intonaco*, and painted. As the demand for frescoes increased, some of the time-consuming work was delegated to assistants, and in many cases assistants were employed to paint the designs executed by the artist. In the 15th century paper became less costly and a somewhat quicker method of putting the composition on the wall was developed. The design intended to fill the space was drawn to exact scale on large sheets of paper. This was the cartoon. When the *arricio* was dry the artist transferred the design to the plaster by tracing from his large sheets. This was usually done by pouncing (pricking holes in the cartoon and dusting them with charcoal dust to leave a dotted outline of the composition on the plaster). The outline having been transferred to the wall, the painter proceeded as described above (first dusting off any specks of charcoal "with a brush of feathers"). A third method was to lay out the design on paper of a convenient size, divide the paper into squares, and, through a proportional enlargement of squares on the wall, transfer the composition to the surface to be painted. To paint in fresco requires speed, skill, a sure hand, and great self-confidence, as the plaster dries quickly and cannot be repainted or corrected. (Although, as Cennini says, some retouching is essential for details after the plaster is dry. Such retouching, however, is not chemically bound to the plaster and has a tendency to flake off. Painting on dry plaster is called *fresco a secco*.) The method was widely used for covering large surfaces. Great examples are the frescoes of Giotto at Padua, those of Masaccio in the Church of the Carmine at Florence, of Piero della Francesca in the Church of San Francesco at Arezzo, and of Michelangelo on the ceiling of the Sistine Chapel in the Vatican. Thousands of frescoes on a less ambitious scale covered the walls and vaults of churches and many palaces throughout Italy. Michelangelo said true fresco was the only kind of painting worthy of men. A great disadvantage of it is that the plaster has a tendency to crack, because of changes in temperature, settling of the building, bombardment, and so on, and the cracking may cause patches to fall, thus completely destroying larger or smaller areas of the fresco. Water on the surface is far less harmful than water seeping in from the back, in which case the surface flakes and crumbles. A delicate and highly skilled process has been developed for detaching frescoes that are in danger of disintegration because of dampness in the wall behind them. The process, employed since the 17th century with indifferent success, was perfected after the disastrous flood at Florence, November 4, 1966. By it, works of art that are threatened with destruction are peeled from the wall on which they are painted and attached to new surfaces that are impervious to dampness and to heat and cold. With this method marvelous 14th-century (and later) drawings in *sinopia*, hidden for four or five hundred years, have been revealed, and the frescoes themselves have been saved.

Frescobaldi (frās-kō-bäl′dē), **Dino.** Poet; b. at Florence, c1270; d. c1316. He composed love lyrics in the *dolce stil nuovo* that are among the best in that tradition. His lyrics are influenced by Guido Cavalcanti in their melancholy strain.

Frescobaldi, Leonardo. Writer; b. at Florence, 14th century; d. after 1405. With several of his fellow-townsmen he made a journey to Egypt and the Holy Land, about 1384. On his return to Florence he held several public offices, including that of ambassador to the pope (1396). The last that is known of him is that he took part in the siege of Pisa (1405). His account of his journey to the Holy Land, *Viaggi in Terra Santa*, presents detailed descriptions of the social and economic life of the lands he visited, and is the most valuable of its age in geographical information.

Frescobaldi, Matteo. Florentine poet; b. at Florence, 1297?; d. there, 1348. He was the son of Dino Frescobaldi (c1270–c1316), and composed love lyrics, and canzoni on moral and political themes.

Frezzi (frāt′tsē), **Federico.** Dominican theologian and poet; b. at Foligno, 1346?; d. at Constance, May, 1416. Of humble parentage, after a rather dissolute youth he entered the service of Ugolino III Trinci, at Foligno, began his studies, and took the habit of the Dominicans. He rose in the ranks of the order and became one of the leading theologians of his time. In 1404 he became bishop of Foligno, and in 1416 he went to the Council of Constance, from which he never returned. His one remaining literary work is his *Quadriregio*, a poem in terza rima, in seventy-four cantos. The four regions of the title are the realms of Love, Satan, Vice, and Virtue. The purpose of the poem is to show that man is too susceptible to earthly love, which really causes nothing but grief and pain, and that he would do better to elevate his spirit by a search for the Divine Truth, which, after much struggle, he might attain. Cupid and Minerva are the guides of the poet through the four realms. Obviously, it is derived from Dante, Petrarch, and other early poets, but has its own attributes in its easy and harmonious style, and its individuality in the sincerity of its ideas. It is one of many examples, from the early days of humanism, of the use of pagan symbols to express Christian ideas.

Friar's Tale, The. One of Chaucer's *Canterbury Tales*. It is the story of a summoner who, when he was riding to oppress a poor widow, met a foul fiend and entered into a compact with him. The fiend finally carried him off. Hubert, the friar who tells the tale, is a "limitour," that is, one licensed to hear confessions and perform offices of the church within a certain district. He is "wanton and merry, a full festive man."

Frith (frith), **John.** English Reformer and martyr; b. at Westerham, Kent, England, 1503; executed at London, July 4, 1533. He went abroad in 1528 to avoid religious persecution, resided for a time at the University of Marburg, and was associated with Tyndale in his literary work. He returned to England in 1532, was arrested for heresy by order of Sir Thomas More, and was burned at the stake in Smithfield, London. During his imprisonment he wrote *A Boke made by John Fryth, prysoner in the Tower of London, answerynge to M. More's Letter* . . . (1533).

Frobisher (frō′bi-shėr), Sir **Martin.** English navigator; b. c1535; d. at Plymouth, England, November 22, 1594. He was of a family of Welsh origin settled at Altofts in the West Riding of Yorkshire. He commanded an expedition, consisting of two ships of less than twenty-five tons each, a pinnace of ten tons, and a total crew of thirty-five, in search of the Northwest Passage in 1576, on which he discovered, in the *Gabriel*, the only ship remaining, the bay since known as Frobisher Bay. One of his sailors having brought home a piece of ore supposed to contain gold, he was sent out again in command of two expeditions in search of gold, in 1577 and 1578. These were larger and better equipped expeditions, the queen herself taking an interest and lending a ship of the royal navy. On both occasions, however, the ore which he brought home proved to be worthless. He fought with distinction with Drake in the West Indies in 1585 and against the Spanish

Armada in 1588. He was in Raleigh's expedition to raid Spain in 1592 and received a mortal wound at the relief of Brest in 1594.

Froissart (frwȧ-sȧr), **Jean.** French chronicler; b. at Valenciennes, France, 1338; d. at Chimay, Belgium, c1410. Nothing is known of his family or early life beyond the few facts to be gleaned from his own writings. In 1360 he was welcomed to England by his countrywoman Queen Philippa of Hainaut, wife of Edward III. In 1365 he visited Scotland, and in May, 1368, he was at Milan in the company of Petrarch and Chaucer. After several years spent in travel, Froissart decided to enter the church (c1372). The period of his activity as a chronicler extends from 1367 to 1400. His great work is the *Chronique de France, d'Angleterre, d'Écosse et d'Espagne,* relating the events of history from 1325 till 1400. It was published before the close of the 15th century, and was thus among the first books to be printed.

Fuenleal (fwen-lā-äl′), **Sebastián Ramírez de.** Spanish ecclesiastic and administrator; b. in the province of Cuenca, Spain, c1480; d. at Valladolid, Spain, January 22, 1547. He was successively inquisitor of Seville, member of the audience of Granada, bishop of Santo Domingo (now Hispaniola) in the West Indies (1524), and president of the audience of that island (1527). From 1531 to 1536 he ruled Mexico as president of the audience of New Spain. He was friendly to Cortés. Returning to Spain, he was successively bishop of Túy and León, and in 1542 was made bishop of Cuenca and president of the audience of Valladolid.

Fugger (fůg′ėr). Swabian family of ennobled merchants, famous in the 16th century. It traces its descent from Johann Fugger, a weaver who lived at Graben, near Augsburg, in the first half of the 14th century. His son Johann became a citizen of Augsburg. After his death in 1408, his sons Andreas (d. 1457) and Jakob (d. 1469) carried on the family business. Lukas, Andreas' son, was a well-known Augsburg politician and moneylender, rich enough to be ruined by the default of Louvain on a note held by him. His brother Jakob obtained the right to display family arms. Ulrich (1441–1510), Georg (1453–1506), and Jakob (1459–1525), sons of Jakob (d. 1469), widened the scope of the family's business. Ulrich became banker to the Hapsburgs and obtained control of several lands in Germany through his mortgage holdings; Jakob obtained mines in the Tirol and in Hungary and traded in spices and textiles with India and Europe. The Fuggers reached their greatest influence and wealth under Raymund (1489–1535) and Anton (1493–1560), sons of Georg. Before his death Jakob had backed with his great wealth the successful candidacy (1519) of Charles V as Holy Roman emperor. To Jakob's heirs and nephews, Charles granted many concessions in mining and in rents; he raised them to the nobility in 1530 and in 1534 they obtained the right to coin money. They further expanded the family's business horizon to the New World and extended the family's land holdings. Both brothers were patrons of the arts and supporters of the charities and other works of the Roman Catholic Church. Among later descendants of the Fuggers were several scholars and writers, art patrons, and soldiers.

Fulda (fůl′dä), **Adam von.** German music theorist, composer, and monk; b. c1450; date of death not known. He was the author of *Tract on Music* (1490) and a composer of motets.

Fumani (fö-mä′nē), **Adamo.** Poet; b. at Verona; d. 1587. A canon at Verona, he was a man of letters who enjoyed the friendship of such other humanists and men of letters as Fracastoro, Flaminio, and Berni. At the Council of Trent he was secretary to Cardinal Navagero. He translated the works of Basil (329–379), saint and rhetorician, from the Greek, set a treatise on logic in Latin hexameters, and left poems in Latin and in Italian. His poems appeared in anthologies of his day.

Fungai (föng-gä′ē), **Bernardino.** Sienese painter; b. at Siena, c1460; d. there, 1516. He was subject to any number of influences: Sienese, Florentine, and Umbrian, and in certain narrative scenes, such as those on cassoni panels, revealed a lively, delicate, and imaginative personality. Other works are often heavy and inflated. He was among the last representatives of the declining Sienese school, clung to rather archaic forms and made little attempt to understand and adopt the developments of other schools. Many examples of his work are to be found at Siena, as in the Pinacoteca, and in the churches—S. Domenico, S. Girolamo, the Servi, and others—and in the country about Siena. Other works are at Bergamo, Florence, Cologne, Leningrad, London, Baltimore (Walters Art Gallery), Cambridge (Fogg Museum), Columbia (Missouri), Coral Gables (Florida), Hartford, Houston, New Haven, New Orleans, New York, Richmond (Virginia), Washington, D.C. (Howard University), and elsewhere.

Fust (föst) or **Faust** (foust), **Johann.** German printer; d. probably at Paris, 1466 or 1467. He was the partner of Gutenberg from c1450 to 1455. In the latter year the partnership was dissolved, and Fust obtained possession of the printing press constructed by Gutenberg. He continued the business with his son-in-law Peter Schöffer.

G

Gabriele (gä-brē-el′ā), **Trifone.** Humanist; b. at Venice, c1470; d. 1549. His early career had been in the Church; he then served Venice in various official posts, until he gave up both these careers and devoted himself to literary studies. He was equally noted for his virtuous life and for his learning, and for the latter was called the Socrates of his age. Ariosto, Bembo, Varchi, Speroni, and Giannotti were among his admirers, and often sought his advice and praised him in their own works. His work, which circulated in manuscript, included lyrics, commentaries on the *Divina Commedia* and the *Canzoniere* of Petrarch, and an Italian grammar. The last named, *Institutione della grammatica volgare,* though not published was a source for a great deal of the work on grammar by Trifone's relative, Giacomo Gabriele.

Gabrieli (gä-brē-el′lē), **Andrea.** Italian composer, organist at St. Mark's, Venice; b. at Venice, c1510; d. there, 1586. He was noted for his mastery of counterpoint; he wrote madrigals, psalms, motets, and other works.

Gabrina (gä-brē′nä). In Lodovico Ariosto's *Orlando Furioso,* a faithless lady saved by Orlando. She returns Zerbino's kindness by accusing him of a murder. Eventually, she is hanged.

Gaddi (gäd′dē), **Agnolo.** Florentine painter; active at least from 1369; d. October 16, 1396. He was the son of Taddeo Gaddi (c1300–1366?), and received his training in his father's workshop. To the Giottesque tradition of painting, which he followed closely, he added more expressive faces and contributed his own narrative gift. He had a prosperous workshop at Florence, with many pupils and assistants. In 1369 he is known to have been working in the Vatican. Much of his work was carried out at Florence and Prato. From his hand are frescoes on the *Legend of the True Cross,* in the Church of S. Croce, and frescoes on the legends of several saints, painted after 1374, in the Castellani Chapel in the same church. In the Uffizi is a *Crucifixion,* which may have been the central panel of an altarpiece. He worked (1391–1392) with Niccolò di Pietro Gerini at Prato. His fresco cycle there in the Chapel of the Holy Girdle in the cathedral (painted c1392–1395), tells the story of the Holy Girdle. The story is that St. Thomas refused to believe in the Assumption of the Virgin and opened her tomb to investigate. He found it full of flowers, and on looking up saw the Virgin. She untied her girdle and handed it to him. There are frescoes and panels in other churches (S. Ambrogio, S. Maria Novella, S. Miniato al Monte) and collections at Florence, and at Empoli, Perugia (Museo dell' Opera del Duomo), Amsterdam, London, Munich, Paris, Vaduz, Birmingham (Alabama), New Haven, New York, Tucson (Arizona), and Washington.

Gaddi, Taddeo. Florentine painter; b. at Florence, c1300; d. 1366? He was the son of Gaddo Gaddi, a painter and mosaicist, all of whose work has been lost. The family was prominent in Florence in affairs of the state and of the church. Taddeo, who was Giotto's godson, became the master's pupil and worked with him for twenty-four years. He joined the Guild of Physicians and Apothecaries in 1327, at the time when Giotto joined it. Influenced by Giotto in his interest in the figure, he was, according to critics, less successful in his composition and in his rendering of architectural backgrounds, yet there is great charm in his fragile, airy temples. He was also less successful in focusing the drama of his subject matter. He continued and increased the interest in the world of nature that has its marked beginnings with Giotto. According to Vasari, he "continued Giotto's manner." According to Gaddi himself, after the death of Giotto, "this art (painting) has grown and continues to grow worse day by day." Gaddi's earliest surviving work is probably *Christ Among the Doctors*, part of a fresco cycle in the Church of S. Croce, Florence. In the Baroncelli Chapel of the same church is a fresco cycle on Joachim and the life of the Virgin (1332–1338), which is one of his most important works. In the Camposanto at Pisa he painted (1342) a fresco cycle on the stories of Job. The frescoes were seriously damaged in the Allied bombardment, July, 1944. Also at Pisa are remains of frescoes in the Church of S. Francesco. A *Last Supper*, painted with assistants, in the refectory of S. Croce, Florence, is an early instance of paintings on this subject, which became so popular in succeeding years. Gaddi's *Last Supper* established an arrangement of the disciples—with Judas sitting alone on one side of the table, facing the other disciples—that was followed until the time of Leonardo da Vinci. Other works include a polyptych, *Madonna and Four Saints* (1353), in the Church of S. Giovanni Fuoricivitas, Pistoia; A *Madonna* (1355), Uffizi, a number of panels in the Accademia, and in churches of Florence; triptychs at Berlin and Brooklyn; a *Madonna*, New York Historical Society; *Madonna and Child Enthroned with Saints*, The Metropolitan Museum of Art, New York; a *Pietà*, Yale University Art Gallery, New Haven, and panels at Bloomington (Indiana), Indianapolis, and Williamstown (Massachusetts). Of the numerous altarpieces he painted, many are now lost. Three of Taddeo's sons, Giovanni, Niccolò, and Agnolo, became painters in his workshop.

Gaetano (gä-ā-tä′nō), **Giovanni.** Italian navigator in the service of Spain; fl. c1542. He was sent on the expedition from Mexico to the Philippines commanded by Lopéz de Villalobos. To this expedition the discovery of the Hawaiian Islands is attributed.

Gaetano of Thiene (tye′nā), Saint. Lawyer and religious reformer; b. at Vicenza, October, 1480; d. at Naples, August 7, 1547. He studied law at Padua, and at the age of 24 became doctor of canon and civil law there. He subsequently served Pope Julius II. On the death of Julius he withdrew from the papal court and devoted himself to good works. A special interest was in hospitals for the incurable. He founded an association of pious priests known as the Oratory of Divine Love. He was himself ordained a priest in 1516, and promoted the ideas of the association at Vicenza, Verona, and Venice. In 1523 he founded a new congregation, approved by Pope Clement VII in 1524, which later became known as the Theatines from one of its members, Cardinal Pietro Caraffa, bishop of Chieti (Latin, *Theate*). Gaetano of Thiene was canonized by Clement X in 1671.

Gaffurio (gä-fö′ryō), **Franchino.** Priest and musicologist; b. at Lodi. He studied music and theology, was choirmaster at Cremona (1481), Bergamo, and then (1484) of the cathedral at Milan. Under Ludovico il Moro he occupied at Milan the first chair of music ever founded in Italy. He wrote treatises on music and several works on harmony, and composed a number of masses, hymns, and motets. His works were noted for their spontaneity and freshness. A painting attributed to Leonardo da Vinci, in the Ambrosiana, Milan, is thought to represent him.

Gaguin (gȧ-gaṅ), **Robert.** French chronicler; b. at Calonne-sur-le-Lys, France, c1425; d. near Nieppe, France, July 22, 1502. He became (1463) professor of rhetoric at the University of Paris, and was employed in diplomatic missions by Louis XI, Charles VIII, and Louis XII. He was the author of *Compendium supra Francorum Gestis, a Pharamundo usque ad annum 1491* (Paris, 1497).

Galafrone (gä-lä-frō′nā). In Matteo Maria Boiardo's *Orlando Innamorato* and Lodovico Ariosto's *Orlando Furioso*, the king of Cathay. His capital of Albracca is besieged by Agricane, a king of Tartary, who seeks thus to win Galafrone's daughter Angelica, the fairest of women.

Galateo (gä-lä-tā′ō), **Il.** See **De Ferrariis, Antonio.**

Galateo, Il. A treatise on good manners by Giovanni della Casa (1551–1554). It was instantly popular for its style, good sense, and humor, went through many editions, and was translated into English in 1576.

Galeota (gä-lā-ō′tä), **Francesco.** Neapolitan poet; d. 1497. A Neapolitan nobleman, he was a member of the so-called Neapolitan Academy, a friend and contemporary of Pontano, Sannazzaro, of Guardati especially, and of other leading literary figures at the court of Naples. An avid traveler, he went on many diplomatic missions for the court, as to France, and visits to Provence and Catalonia, as well as on adventurous journeys on his own account. Galeota wrote *strambotti* in the manner of Petrarch, and also imitated the Ovidian forms. His most successful lyrics were ballate, which are lively and of individual inspiration.

Galileo (gä-lē-lā′ō). [Full name, **Galileo Galilei.**] Physicist and astronomer; b. at Pisa, February, 1564; d. at Arcetri, near Florence, January 8, 1642. He was descended from a noble but impoverished Florentine family. After studying (1581–1586) at the University of Pisa without taking a degree, he became professor of mathematics there (1589–1591), later serving at Padua (1592–1610) and Florence. He discovered (1583), while watching a lamp swing in the cathedral at Pisa, that its oscillations could be used to time his pulse; from this he deduced the isochronic nature of the swing of the pendulum, which he later demonstrated might be used to measure time. In 1586 he invented the hydrostatic balance, an instrument for determining the specific gravities of substances by comparing their weights in and out of water. He also developed an experiment to determine the speed of light; a flash was to be timed from two points, but the timing mechanisms then in use were too inaccurate to measure the extremely small time intervals involved, and the experiment came to nothing. According to a famous story, he dropped bodies of various weights from the Leaning Tower of Pisa and thus showed that all bodies would fall with equal velocities in a vacuum. He continued his experiments with falling bodies with the use of the inclined plane, from which experiments he developed theories relative to motion that were later to be demonstrated as laws by Isaac Newton. He showed also that the parabola of a projectile's flight was made up of a horizontal and a vertical component, and that the latter was ruled by the same forces that governed falling bodies. He invented the first thermometer (1597), and the first telescope (1609). With this instrument, magnifying to about thirty diameters, Galileo discovered (1610) that Jupiter had satellites (he saw four of them), that Saturn was surrounded by rings, that the moon's surface was mountainous and not smooth, that Venus went through phases like the moon (due to its position between Earth and Sun). He noted (c1610) the existence of sunspots and developed thence the idea that the sun rotated on its axis; and he stated that given a better telescope, an observer might resolve the Milky Way into individual stars. His publication of *Letters on the Solar Spots* (1613) embodied his acceptance of the Copernican system of the universe, which made of the earth a mere planet circling about the sun instead of the fixed center of the universe (which it was according to the Ptolemaic theory). He was summoned to Rome where, in 1616, his doctrines, which he had attempted to justify by Biblical quotation, were condemned as heretical by the pope. An essay on comets, *Saggiatore*, which he published in 1623, was well received, however, despite several oblique defenses of the Copernican system. But his publication of *Dialogo dei due massimi sistemi del mondo* (*Dialogue on the two chief systems of the universe*, 1632) caused a storm. It was acclaimed all over Europe, but its advocacy of Copernicanism, despite the papal injunction of 1616, brought down the wrath of the Church on his head. The book was banned by Rome and Galileo was called (1633) before the Inquisition. There, under the threat of torture, he was forced to abjure his belief that the earth moves around the sun; the familiar legend states that as he arose after his recantation he murmured: "Eppur si muove" (Nevertheless, it moves). As a result of his quarrel with the Church, he was removed from his academic posts and retired to his home at Arcetri. There, despite almost total blindness, he discovered (1637) the moon's libration (presentation of more than half its surface to the view of observers on earth). Galileo's *Dialoghi delle nuove scienzi* (1638) summed up his experiments and theories on mechanics. Galileo established the method of modern science, a deductive-inductive method that verifies theory by practical experiment and surrenders the rationalized, universal "proofs" of scholasticism for the amassing of data, later to be systematized by theory, in limited fields.

Galizzi (gä-lēt′tsē), **Girolamo da Santacroce.** See **Santacroce, Girolamo da.**

Gambara (gäm′bä-rä), **Veronica.** Poet; b. at Pratalboino, near Brescia, June 30, 1485; d. at Correggio, June 13, 1550. Of a noble family, she was highly educated, and numbered the leading literary men of her day among her friends. In 1509 she married the lord of Correggio, and by him had two sons. Her husband died in 1518, and she was left to bring up her sons and manage her husband's small state. Her house became a salon where the outstanding men of her day gathered. Charles V twice visited her; she was on good terms with Francis I, and numbered Bembo and Vittoria Colonna among her intimates. Like the latter, she was noted for her virtuous life. Her poems, in an elegant Petrarchan manner, are mostly concerned with her affection for her husband, and lack the spark of life. They are more correct than lyrical or passionate. More sincere and moving are a few she wrote on the devastation of Italy and on her native and loved cities, Brescia and Correggio. About fifty of her poems, mostly sonnets, survive. A number of her letters, including those to the infamous Aretino, are extant. They contribute largely to the literary history of the day.

Gamboa (gäm-bō′ä), **Pedro Sarmiento de.** See **Sarmiento de Gamboa, Pedro.**

Gan (gän) or **Gano** (gä′nō). In the Italian versions of the Carolingian cycle, the traitor Ganelon. In Luigi Pulci's *Morgante maggiore* he plays his treacherous role that culminates in the ambush of Orlando in the Pass of Roncesvalles, but meets his just deserts when Charlemagne arrives and causes him to be hanged. He appears briefly in Matteo Maria Boiardo's *Orlando Innamorato*, but since this is a romantic epic of love and not of treachery, Gan plays a small part.

Gandía (gän-dē′ä), Duke of. See **Borgia, Pedro Luis; Borgia, Giovanni; Borgia,** Saint **Francesco.**

Gandini (gän-dē′nē), **Giorgio.** [Called **Gandini del Grano.**] Painter; b. at Parma, c1480; d. there, 1538. He was a pupil and follower of Correggio, and his work shows the profound influence of that master. Correggio died in 1534, and the following year Gandini was commissioned by the Overseers of the cathedral to finish the paintings Correggio had begun, but death overtook Gandini also and the work was carried on by Girolamo Bedoli Mazzola. Gandini's masterpiece is an altarpiece, *Madonna and Child, and Saints,* now in the National Gallery, Parma. His few surviving works are illustrative of his draftsmanship and sense of color, while at the same time they reveal his weakness in overcrowding his compositions. A *Madonna and Child, with St. Michael and the Devil Contesting for Souls,* in the same gallery, is notable for meticulous and delicate rendering of details, although again the composition is excessively crowded.

Garbo (gär′bō), **Dino del.** See **Del Garbo, Dino.**

Garbo, Raffaellino del. See **Raffaellino del Garbo.**

Garcilaso de la Vega (gär-sē-lä′sō dā lä bā′gä). Spanish poet; b. at Toledo, 1503; d. at Nice, 1536. He served Charles V as soldier and courtier, but fell into disfavor with the emperor and was banished. Thereafter he went to Naples for a time; then pardoned, he served Charles in the expedition to Tunis (1535). He was a friend of Boscán Almogaver, whom he encouraged to write Spanish poems in Italian meters. His own poems, some modeled after Sannazzaro, Horace, and Vergil, were more successful as poetry than those of his friend. His most enduring theme —he wrote sonnets, eclogues, odes, and elegies—is his hopeless love for a married lady, a theme which he presents with sincerity and deep feeling. With his gifted use of Italian and classical models he had profound influence on Spanish poetry. His works were published with those of his friend Boscán Almogaver in 1543 by the latter's widow.

Garcilaso de la Vega. [Called **"el Inca,"** meaning "the Inca."] Peruvian soldier, historian and translator; b. at Cusco, Peru, c1539; d. at Córdoba, Spain, c1616. He was the son of Sebastián Garcilaso de la Vega y Vargas, who served under Cortés and Pizarro, and an Inca princess (whence his epithet "el Inca"). He went (c1560) to Spain, was given a pension by Philip II, and was a captain in the Spanish army fighting the Moors. He later settled at Córdoba and devoted himself to literature. His works are *La Florida del Inca; historia del adelantado Hernando de Soto* (1605) and his history of Peru, *Commentarios reales que tratan del origen de los*

Incas (part 1, 1609; part 2, 1617, both parts being translated into English, 1688 and 1869–1871, and into French, German, and Italian). In 1590 he translated the *Dialoghi di amore* of Leon Hebro. His account of De Soto's conquest of Florida was for a long time regarded as more fiction than fact, but it was used to advantage by historians such as Robertson and Prescott, by Marmontel for his historical novel *Les Incas*, and by Sheridan for his *Pizarro*. He has been called "the first South American in Spanish Literature." His birth date is variously given as about 1530, 1536, 1539, and 1540, the same uncertainty existing about his death, which is placed as early as 1568, and as late as 1620, with 1616 being given some preference.

Garcilaso de la Vega y Vargas (ē bär′gäs), **Sebastián.** Spanish soldier; father of Garcilaso de la Vega; b. c1500; d. 1559.

Gardiner (gärd′nėr, gär′dẹn-ėr), **Stephen.** English prelate and politician; b. at Bury St. Edmunds, England, between 1483 and 1490; d. at London, November 12, 1555. He studied at Trinity Hall, Cambridge, of which society he was elected master in 1525. In 1528 he was sent by Henry VIII on a mission to the Pope in reference to the proposed divorce between the king and Catherine of Aragon. He was made Secretary of State in 1529, was appointed bishop of Winchester in 1531, and was elected chancellor of the University of Cambridge c1540. Although constantly employed on diplomatic missions to the courts of Rome, France, and the emperor, his chief service to Henry consisted in a learned defense of the Act of Supremacy, published in 1535 under the title *De vera obedientia oratio*. In the reign of Edward VI he resisted the ecclesiastical policy of Cranmer, in consequence of which he was committed to the Tower of London, and, in 1552, deprived of his bishopric. He was restored to liberty at the accession of Queen Mary, who appointed him lord high chancellor of the realm in 1553. In conjunction with Bonner he was the chief instrument in bringing about the persecution of the Protestants in the early part of Mary's reign.

Gareth (gä-ret′), **Benedicto.** [Called, **il Cariteo.**] Neapolitan poet; b. at Barcelona, c1450; d. at Naples, 1514. He went to Naples about 1467 and was soon on friendly terms with the leading literary men of the court, as Pontano and Sannazzaro. An accomplished musician and a brilliant conversationalist, he was known as the Darling of the Graces, whence his name Il Cariteo. He held various official positions at the court, including that of Secretary of State (in which office he succeeded Pontano), and fled with his king into exile on the arrival of Charles VIII of France. When Naples fell to Ferdinand the Catholic, he returned to the kingdom. Gareth is best known for his collection of lyrics, *Endymion*. These, to the number of about 200, show the influence of Petrarch as well as that of the Latin lyricists. Many of them are in honor of his poetic inspiration, to whom he gave the poetic name Luna. Written as court poetry, these lyrics, and others he wrote in terza rima, are marked by high-flown language, allusiveness, and a striving for elegance.

Gargantua (gär-gan′ṭū-ạ; French, går-gäṅ-tü-å) **and Pantagruel** (pan-tag′rö-el; French, päṅ-tå-grü-el), **The Life of.** Satirical work in prose and verse by François Rabelais. Rabelais edited and perhaps in part rewrote a prose romance, *Les Grandes et Inestimables Chronicques du Grant et Énorme Géant Gargantua*. This work, the author of which is unknown, and no earlier copies of which exist, probably gave him the idea of his own famous book. The next year (1532) followed the first installment of this, *Pantagruel Roi des Dipsodes Restitué en Son natural avec ses Faicts et Proueses Espouvantables*. Three years afterwards came *Gargantua* proper, the first book of the entire work as we now have it. Eleven years, however, passed before the work was continued, the second book of *Pantagruel* not being published until 1546, and the third six years later, in 1552, just before the author's death. The fourth or last book did not appear as a whole until 1564, although the first sixteen chapters had been given to the world two years before. This fourth book, the fifth of the entire work, from the length of time which elapsed before its publication and from certain variations which exist in the manuscript and the first printed editions, has been suspected of spuriousness. Gargantua is a giant with an enormous appetite, and his name has become proverbial for an insatiable eater. There was a chapbook, popular in England in the 16th century, giving the history of the giant Gargantua, who accidentally swallows five pilgrims, staves and all, in his salad.

Garofalo (gä-rō′fä-lō). [Original name, **Benvenuto Tisi**, called **il Garofalo** from his birthplace near Ferrara.] Painter; b. c1481; d. at Ferrara, July 6, 1559. He was one of the leading painters of the Ferrarese school, and was called "the Raphael of Ferrara." He received his early training under a local painter, Domenico Panetti, but his work shows that painters with whom he came in contact later had more influence on his development, as Boccaccio Boccaccino, who was painting in the cathedral at Ferrara in 1499 and 1500. The grace and freshness that appear in Garofalo's early works probably derive from Boccaccino's training and influence. Other influences on him were those of the Ferrarese painters, especially Lorenzo Costa. In 1506 he painted a ceiling for Lucrezia Borgia at Ferrara, and in 1507 and 1508 he is presumed to have been with Boccaccino at Cremona. In the same period he visited Venice and other cities, including Mantua, where Lorenzo Costa had recently succeeded Mantegna as court painter. It is thought that in 1515 and 1516 he was at Rome, where he was deeply impressed by the painting of Raphael, whose full-bodied figures and spacious compositions he adapted to his own style, as in the *Madonna and Saints*, Estense Gallery, Modena. His blond Madonnas have a characteristic sweet and gently pensive expression that is strongly reminiscent of Raphael. Frequently, misty, slightly fantasized landscapes form the backgrounds to his paintings, as in the mythological scene, National Gallery, London, and the typically graceful *Annunciation*, Uffizi. His paintings are also noted for their gay, harmonious color. Among the works that illuminate the classicized majesty of his artistic approach are the beautiful frescoes on the ceiling of Ludovico il Moro's palace (now the Spina Museum) at Ferrara and the frescoes on the ceiling of the Seminario. In 1537 he collaborated with Dosso Dossi and Girolamo da Carpi in the decoration of the Estense villa, Belriguardo (now lost), and some influence of Dossi appears in such of his paintings as the *St. Sebastian*, National Museum, Naples. In his career he absorbed elements from the great masters of his age, but Raphael was perhaps his chief inspiration. His ideal in painting was expressed in gentle harmonies and without passion. A number of works ascribed to him survive; examples at Ferrara are in the Church of S. Francesco, the Pinacoteca, and the cathedral, in addition to those mentioned above. Others are at Rome (Borghese, Capitoline, Doria, and National galleries, and the Vatican), in the Accademia, Venice, Carrara Academy, Bergamo, Uffizi, Florence, National Gallery, Parma, Brera, Milan, and at Bologna, Padua, Turin (Sabauda Gallery), Amsterdam, Budapest, Dresden, Leningrad, London, Munich, Paris, Vienna, Atlanta (Georgia), Baltimore (Walters Art Gallery), Birmingham (Alabama), Chicago, Columbus (Ohio), Coral Gables (Florida), Dallas, Detroit, El Paso, Los Angeles, New Orleans, New York, and elsewhere.

Gasca (gäs′kä), **Pedro de la.** Spanish lawyer; b. at Barco de Avila, in Castile, Spain, 1485; d. at Valladolid, Spain, in November, 1567. In 1546 he was sent to Peru as president of the audience, with extraordinary powers, to put down the rebellion of Gonzalo Pizarro. He managed by peaceful means to win over many of the rebels. Centeno, Valdivia and Benalcazar joined him; and Pizarro's forces finally deserted on the field of Sacsahuana, near Cusco, on April 9, 1548. Pizarro and his lieutenant, Carbajal, were captured and executed, and Gasca treated the rebels with great severity. While the country was still in a state of confusion he slipped away (January, 1550), leaving the government in the hands of the audience. On his return to Spain he was made bishop of Valencia, and in 1561 was promoted to the see of Siguenza, which he occupied until his death.

Gascoigne (gas′koin), **George.** English poet; b. probably in Bedfordshire, England, c1535; d. at Stamford, England, October 7, 1577. He was educated at Trinity College, Cambridge, studied law at Gray's Inn, and was member of Parliament (1557–1559) from Bedford. His *Posies of G. Gascoigne* (1575) included *Jocasta*, a tragedy in blank verse which is supposedly the second of its kind in English, and *Certayne Notes of Instruction concerning the making of verse or ryme in English*, held by some to be the first English critical essay. Other works by him include *The Steele Glas* (1576) and *The Droomme of Doomesday* (1576).

Gascoigne, Sir **William.** English judge; b. c1350; d. 1419. He was made chief justice of the King's Bench by Henry IV (c1400). According to a tradition, followed by Shakespeare in *Henry IV*, he committed Prince

Henry to prison when the latter struck him for venturing to punish one of the prince's riotous companions.

Gasparino da Barzizza (gäs-pä-rē′nō dä bär-tzē′tzä). See **Barzizza, Gasparino.**

Gatta (gät′tä), **Bartolomeo della.** See **Della Gatta, Bartolomeo.**

Gattamelata (gät-tä-mā-lä′tä). [Original name, **Erasmo da Narni.**] Condottiere; b. c1370; d. at Padua, January 16, 1443. He served under Braccio da Montone, and was captured in the defeat at Aquila (June 20, 1424) but escaped and went into the service of Niccolò Piccinino, who was at that time in the pay of Florence. When Piccinino went over to Milan, however, Gattamelata remained in the service of Florence. He served Pope Martin V (1427) against rebellious Bologna, and in 1434, with the consent of Eugenius IV, went into the pay of the Venetians, the pope's allies, remaining in the Romagna to face the forces of the hostile Visconti. In April, 1437, as he was moving against Milan, he was isolated and surrounded as a result of the collapse of a bridge over the Adda, but defended himself and crossed the river on horseback. In fighting against Piccinino he was outnumbered (September, 1438) and made a famous successful retreat from Bergamo, leading his forces in safety through hostile territory to Verona. Confirmed by the Venetians as their captain general, he tried to relieve Bergamo by a fleet drawn overland to Lake Garda, but the fleet was defeated and he fell back on Padua. He next joined with Francesco Sforza, general of the league against the Visconti, and defeated Piccinino (November, 1439). Piccinino, besieged in the castello of Termo, escaped and took Verona, but a few days later Gattamelata and Sforza retook it. This was the last action in which Gattamelata took part. He suffered two apoplectic strokes, and though he retained his title of captain general for another two years he did not fight again. Gattamelata was a brave and vigorous soldier and, what was rare in those days, was loyal to those who paid him. He was honest and endowed with a rough eloquence. The Venetians honored their general and gave him a state funeral. They were also thought to have some interest in the great equestrian monument executed by Donatello at Padua to commemorate his exploits. For brave and honest soldier that he was, Gattamelata's name would probably have disappeared in the mists of history except for this remarkable bronze monument, with the warrior astride his charger, that stands before the Basilica of St. Anthony at Padua.

Gatti (gät′tē), **Bernardino.** [Called **il Soiaro.**] Painter; b. probably at Pavia or Cremona, c1495; d. at Cremona, 1575. He was an eclectic who freely borrowed the elements, figures, and models of other painters, but he was especially dependent on Correggio. He had collaborated with the Campi painters of Cremona, and with Boccaccino at Cremona and Milan, and drew on them. His earliest known work, *Christ Risen* (1529), cathedral, Cremona, leans heavily on Correggio and Pordenone. All his works are derivative amalgamations of the elements and even the models of other painters with, as noted above, special dependence on Correggio. Among his surviving paintings are a *Madonna in Glory* (1530), cathedral, Pavia; a *St. George*, Church of the Madonna di Campagna, Piacenza; and an *Assumption*, cathedral, Cremona.

Gaudenzio Ferrari (gou-den′tsyō fer-rä′rē). See **Ferrari, Gaudenzio.**

Gavazzi (gä-vät′tsē), **Giovanni di Giacomo.** Painter of Bergamo; active at the beginning of the 16th century. An *Adoration of the Magi* and a number of panels of saints by this local painter are in the Carrara Academy at Bergamo.

Gaza (gä′dzä; Anglicized, gā′zạ), **Theodorus.** Byzantine humanist; b. at Salonika, in Macedonia, c1400; d. at Salerno, 1478. He left Greece (1444) after his native town had been overrun by the Turks, and went to Italy. He taught Greek at Ferrara (1447) and philosophy at Rome (1450). Pope Nicholas V, for whom he prepared many translations, was his patron. When the pope died, Theodorus went to the court of Alfonso I of Naples. His fellow countryman, Cardinal Bessarion, became his next patron, and gave him the Abbey of San Giovanni di Piro at Salerno. Theodorus was noted above all as a translator. His translations included Aristotle, Theophrastus, Dionysius of Halicarnassus, Alexander of Aphrodisias, and others. His best known work was a Greek grammar, printed by Aldus Manutius in 1495. In the controversy between the followers of Aristotle and those of Plato, he defended Aristotle.

Bernardino Gatti
St. Catherine of Alexandria Being Blessed by the Infant Christ and Crowned by the Virgin and Two Angels
The British Museum, London

Gaza was among the more important of the Greek exiles who spread Greek learning in Italy.

Geertgen van Haarlem (gärt′gẹn vän här′-lẹm). [Also, **Geertgen tot Sint Jans.**] Dutch painter; b. at Leiden, Netherlands, c1463 or 1465; d. at Haarlem, Netherlands, c1493 or 1495 (all dates are conjectures; according to different accounts he was 28, or 30, when he died). Some of his works (and some believed to be by him because of resemblance to his known paintings) are *Legend of the Bones of Saint John, the Baptist* (Vienna Gallery), *View of Haarlem Cathe-*

dral, Crucifixion, Adoration of the Magi, The Virgin's Kindred (the two latter at Amsterdam), *The Raising of Lazarus* (Louvre), *Christ in the Tomb, Nativity* (National Gallery, London), a night scene, *The Man of Sorrows* (Utrecht), *Saint John the Baptist* and *Virgin and Child* (both Berlin); the last three are doubtful. The artist is also called Geertgen tot Sint Jans because he lived with the Knights of Saint John at Haarlem, although he was not a member of their order.

Geiler von Kaiserberg (gī′lėr fon kī′zėrs-berk), **Johannes.** German preacher, famous for his sermons (1487 *et seq.*) at the cathedral of Strasbourg; b. at Schaffhausen, Switzerland, 1445; d. at Strasbourg, in Alsace, 1510. An outstanding mystic of his time, he was also a merciless satirist of ecclesiastical corruption. His name is often connected with Sebastian Brant, on whose *Narrenschiff* (1494) he delivered a series of sermons. Most of the writings attributed to him were set down by others.

Gelli (jel′lē), **Giambattista.** Florentine writer and moralist; b. at Florence, August 12, 1498; d. there, July 24, 1563. He was the son of a vintner and followed the trade of shoemaker himself. He was aware of the vast amount of knowledge that existed and distressed that it was available to so few. It became an object with him to disseminate some of the treasure to the benefit of the less educated masses. At the age of 25 he began to study Latin, and followed this with the study of philosophy and letters. His efforts met with success. He was a member of the Florentine Academy, of which he was also a founder, and official lecturer on Dante there from 1553 to 1563. He wrote two comedies, *Sporta* and *Errore*, both of which turn on a broad joke. They are presented in racy and fresh Italian, but are transparently patterned after Machiavelli's comedies. His chief works are *I capricci di Giusto bottaio* and *La Circe*. The former consists of ten essays by Giusto the Cooper, in which he expresses his views on a number of topics in vigorous and trenchant Italian. These include soliloquies on old age, death, immortality, and the contrast between the soul and the body. The second tells of eleven men who have been transformed into animals—goat, lion, snake, elephant, calf, and so on—by Circe. Ulysses persuades the enchantress to turn them into men again, but cannot persuade the animals that this would be to their advantage. Ten of them insist that they are happier as they are than they were in the miserable world of men. The eleventh, an elephant, had been a philosopher in his human state, and wishes to return to it so that he can continue his search for truth. In the course of the dialogues, in which Ulysses tries to convince the animals, Gelli draws on the classical writers and philosophy, Medieval thought, the Church Fathers, and contemporary life. He was an admirer of Savonarola, who had been burned as a heretic before Gelli was born, was suspected of heresy himself for some of the sentiments he expressed, and his *Capricci* was placed on the Index (1562). Gelli's works are spontaneous and balanced, and written in vigorous and colloquial Italian. He was one of the few in that day when Latin was so widely used, to write in the vernacular.

Gelosia (jā-lō-sē′ä). Comedy by Anton Francesco Grazzini; in a prologue to the play, Grazzini criticizes the writers of this time for clinging, in plot and manner, to the models of the classical writers. Florence, he claimed, was not Athens or Rome, and its inhabitants, as characters in plays, should not be treated or portrayed as ancient Athenians and Romans. He expressed himself as bored to death with the ancient plot of the lost heir, and declared he had had enough of mistaken identity as a subject for a play.

Gemistus Plethon (jẹ-mis′tus plē′thon), **Georgius.** Byzantine philosopher and scholar; b. at Constantinople, c1355; d. in the Peloponnesus, c1450. At an early age he went to Brusa to study philosophy, and there came in contact with the theories of Zoroastrianism. Later he went as a judge to the Morea, in the Peloponnesus. The Peloponnesus, as all of Greece, was in a state of chaos. Gemistus Plethon concluded that the old laws and religion had failed. In his brooding over the failure he conceived the idea of creating a new order, derived from Platonism, of which he was an ardent exponent, and the beliefs of the ancients. He expressed his ideas in *Nomoi*, a description of a society and a religious system based on what he thought was Platonism (actually, it was Neoplatonism, a mystic philosophy that early Christian and medieval scholars had evolved), and a mixture of Greek mythology. Gemistus Plethon became famous as a teacher and Platonic philosopher. Among his pupils and adherents was Cardinal Bessarion. In 1438 he accompanied John VIII Palaeologus to the Council of Ferrara in an official capacity. The Council, called to reconcile differences between the Eastern and Western Churches (with the more immediate aim of securing western aid against the Turks), adjourned to Florence (1439). There Gemistus was warmly welcomed, rather as a renowned scholar than as a theologian. He met Cosimo de' Medici, among many others, and it was from this meeting that Cosimo became interested enough in Platonic studies to envision the founding of a Platonic Academy (a dream that was not fulfilled). Gemistus was enormously influential in arousing interest in Plato in the west. For this he was considered heretical, as the system of Aristotle, as it was then understood, was considered orthodox by the Church. The dispute over the various truths, from a theological as well as a philosophical standpoint, of Aristotle and Plato raged for years. However, the interest that Gemistus aroused in Plato led Florentine and other scholars to study that philosopher with a keener critical sense and, eventually, with the publication of Greek texts, to strip away the layers of mysticism with which he had been enshrouded. By 1441 Gemistus was back at Mistra in the Peloponnesus. In his last years he was under attack by the Patriarch of Constantinople as a heretic because of his championship of Plato. The Eastern as well as the Western Church had adopted Aristotle. On his death (c1450) Gemistus was buried at Mistra, but Sigismondo Malatesta, an ardent admirer, dug up his bones and removed them to Rimini. There he placed them in one of the sarcophagi of the Tempio Malatestiano.

Genga (jeng'gä), **Girolamo.** Painter and architect; b. at Urbino, c1476; d. there, August 11, 1551. As a painter he was a pupil and imitator of Luca Signorelli, but felt the influence also of Perugino, Sodoma, Raphael, and other masters. Among his works are *The Dispute over Original Sin* (1515), Berlin; *St. Augustine Baptizing a Neophyte*, Carrara Academy, Bergamo; *The Martyrdom of St. Sebastian* (1535), Uffizi, Florence, one of his best works; *Madonna, Saints, and the Eternal Father* (1513–1518), Brera, Milan; *Madonna and Child Enthroned, with Saints*, Vatican; and a number at Siena. He was one of the painters who decorated (1530) the Imperiale, the ducal villa at Pesaro begun by the Sforza duke and then passing to the duke of Urbino. He also worked on the villa as architect for the duke of Urbino, restoring, rebuilding, and adding to it. Architecturally, his varied, lively, imposing buildings derive from classical models. A notable edifice is the Church of S. Giovanni Battista at Pesaro, begun 1543, impressive for its noble façade and for the grandeur and solemnity of the interior.

Gengenbach (geng'ẹn-bäċh), **Pamphilus.** Swiss printer and author; b. at Basel, Switzerland, c1480; d. there, 1525. A colorful figure of the Renaissance, he joined the Reformation and wrote, in German, didactic and satirical poems and a number of moralizing plays that were very popular in their day.

Gennadius (jẹ-nā'di-us). [Original name, **Georgios Scholarios.**] Greek scholar and prelate; b. c1400; d. c1468. After the Council of Ferrara-Florence (1438–1439) in which an accord was reached on union between the Greek and Roman churches, he was one of the chief opponents of the union, although he had earlier supported it. He became patriarch of Constantinople in 1454, the first after the conquest of the city by the Turks, but resigned (in 1456 or 1459), and spent the rest of his days as a monk, studying and writing in defense of the Greek church.

Gentile da Fabriano (jen-tē'lā dä fä-brē-ä'nō). Painter, first great master of the Umbrian school; b. at Fabriano, between 1360 and 1370; d. at Rome, before October 14, 1427. He was the son of a comfortable family that had been established at Fabriano for several generations. His father, who became a monk in 1397, was reputed to have been a scholar and an astrologer. Little is known of the son's early training. He was undoubtedly familiar with the work of his fellow-townsman Allegretto Nuzi, and by 1408 had himself acquired an acknowledged reputation, for in that year he was at Venice executing a commission for an altarpiece (now lost). He remained at Venice a number of years, painting in the Hall of the Great Council there, went to Brescia to decorate a chapel for Pandolfo Malatesta (1416–1419), and then to Rome (1419) at the invitation of Pope Martin V. Martin V was the pope whose election ended the Great Schism; he returned to a Rome that was almost a ruin, and at once began to rebuild and ornament the city. The paintings Gentile wrought in St. John Lateran perished, as did those in the other places mentioned above. He was at Florence (1421) where he was enrolled (1422) in the Physicians and Apothecaries' Guild, which included painters (because the apothecaries supplied their colors). He also worked at Siena and Orvieto; again at Fabriano, Florence, and Rome. He was the foremost painter in the international Gothic style in his time and, according to some critics, Italianized it. The calligraphic curves of drapery, jewel-like colors, intense interest in the details of the world of nature, crowded compositions, and imperviousness to the demands of space that characterize the style reach a height in Gentile's charming renderings of an Italian fairyland. Generations later, Michelangelo, according to Vasari, said of one of Gentile's paintings that it was like the painter's name, "*gentile*." One of the loveliest examples of his special characteristics is his *Adoration of the Magi*, ordered by Palla degli Strozzi for S. Trinità at Florence, signed and dated 1423, and now in the Uffizi. The panel is crowded with richly dressed adorers and their suites. Every inch of space is filled; walled towns in miniature crown the hills that reach up into the three lunettes that form the top of the panel; beyond one of them there is even a stretch of sea and a small boat. Birds, dogs, a camel, monkeys, and a leopard, as well as numerous horses and mounted processions, attend the throng that approaches the Holy Child. Those worshiping, their richly patterned garments glowing with color and liberally sprinkled with gold, seem to have stepped from an exquisite

Gentile da Fabriano
Two Studies of a Madonna and Child
Biblioteca Ambrosiana, Milan

and brilliant miniature. Natural attitudes, as the servant kneeling to remove a king's spurs, a second king about to doff his crown, the ladies gossiping behind the Madonna, make of this work a charming illustration of a domestic scene. The whole is enclosed in an elaborate Gothic frame, the pilasters of which are painted with flowers—anemones, roses, and violets. A second dated work is a fresco of the *Madonna* in the cathedral at Orvieto (1425); and a third is a polyptych, the Quaratesi altarpiece, originally for the Church of S. Niccolò at Florence, signed and dated 1425, and now broken up and scattered: the central panel, *Madonna and Child with Angels*, is at Hampton Court, London; four scenes from the predella on the life of St. Nicholas of Bari are in the Vatican, and other panels from the altarpiece are in the Uffizi and the National Gallery, Washington.

Gentile's paintings, charming and of infinite appeal, are essentially narrative and decorative. The subjects are religious but the execution evokes a delight in his enchanted world rather than a spiritual response. The sinuous Arabic lettering that adorns the haloes of his holy figures in some cases cannot be accounted for on strict theological grounds; as decoration it is highly effective. His influence was enormous in the Marches and Umbria, and even on the Venetian school through his pupil Jacopo Bellini. Giovanni di Paolo, a prolific painter, was the Sienese most influenced by him, and there were many, often delightful, provincial painters who were followers of his school. Other works by Gentile da Fabriano are: *Coronation of the Virgin*, Brera, Milan; *Madonna and Child with Angelic Musicians*, National Gallery of Umbria, Perugia; *Madonna Adoring the Child*, Museo Civico, Pisa; *Madonna and Child with Two Angels*, Capitolo del Duomo, Velletri; *Madonna and Child*, Jarves Collection, Yale University; *Madonna and Child with Angelic Musicians*, The Metropolitan Museum of Art, New York; *Madonna and Child with Two Angels*, National Gallery, Washington; a brilliant, fairly late work, *Madonna and Child with Saint Lawrence and Saint Julian*, Frick Collection, New York; a signed early *Madonna and Child* is at Berlin, and a panel from the predella of the Uffizi *Adoration* is at Paris.

Gentili (jen-tē′lē) or **Gentile** (jen-tē′lā), **Antonio.** [Called also, **Antonio da Faenza.**] Goldsmith, sculptor, and engraver; b. at Faenza, 1519; d. at Rome, October 29, 1609. For Cardinal Alessandro Farnese he made a cross and two candlesticks, intended for the high altar of St. Peter's and now in the Treasury, and a design for a fountain at Ronciglione (near Viterbo), often attributed to Vignola. No other works by him are known with certainty. The figures on the pieces made for the Farnese cardinal reveal his virtuosity as an original sculptor.

George (of *Saxony*). [Called **George the Bearded.**] Duke of Saxony, son of Albert the Brave, whom he succeeded in 1500; b. August 27, 1471; d. April 17, 1539. He was educated for the priesthood, and is chiefly noted for his opposition to the Reformation, which was favored by his uncle, the elector of Saxony. He attended the disputation between Eck and Luther at Leipzig (July 4–14, 1519) and subsequently himself engaged in debate with Luther. He sought in vain to prevent, by imprisonment and execution, the spread in his dominions of the principles of the Reformation which were adopted by his brother Henry, who succeeded him in the duchy.

George of Podiebrad (pô′dye-brät). King of Bohemia (1458–1471); b. in the 12th-century castle at Podiebrad, on the Elbe River in Bohemia, April 6, 1420; d. March 22, 1471. A Bohemian nobleman, he was a soldier and a leader of the conservative or moderate Hussites, known as the Utraquists, as opposed to the radical wing, known as the Taborites. During the Interregnum (1440–1453), Bohemia was wracked by religious strife and civil war. George made himself master of Bohemia, won control of Prague (1448), and by 1452 forced his enemies to acknowledge him as administrator of Bohemia. He continued as the effective ruler after the accession of Ladislaus Posthumus (Ladislaus V, duke of Austria and king of Hungary) as Ladislaus I of Bohemia (1453). George had been largely responsible for his election and the end of the Interregnum. When Ladislaus died of the plague (1457) George was elected king (March 2, 1458). He was acknowledged as such by both the pope and the emperor, and the Bohemian dependencies of Moravia, Silesia, and Lusatia recognized the central authority at Prague. Pope Pius II, impatient with the Hussite heresy, asked him to renounce the Compactata. These were a series of agreements drawn up at the Council of Basel and accepted in 1436 by which the Utraquists were recognized as Catholics with the right to their own forms of communion. George, who had come to power as leader of the Utraquists, refused to renounce the Compactata, and hoped to avoid an open breach with the papacy. He had restored peace and order in Bohemia, had created a nation recognized throughout Europe, and had tried to damp down religious strife by conciliation while remaining loyal to the Utraquists. Pius II abolished the Compactata (1462), and Pope Paul II, his successor, deposed George and excommunicated him (1466). A year later George was in conflict with the emperor, Frederick III, and with Matthias Corvinus, king of Hungary, both his former allies. Matthias had some success against him and was elected king of Bohemia and margrave of Moravia (1469), but George finally expelled him and compelled him to sue for peace. In this contest George received Polish aid in return for his promise to name Ladislaus, son of Casimir IV, king of Poland, as his successor to the Bohemian throne, thus passing over his own sons. George was the only native Bohemian ever to become king of his country, and the only non-Roman Catholic.

George of Trebizond (treb′i-zond). Byzantine scholar and humanist; b. in Crete, 1396; d. at Rome, 1484. He learned Latin at Venice under Vittorino da Feltre and Guarino da Verona, and began to copy Greek codices there for distinguished patrons. He taught Greek at Mantua and at Venice, and served as interpreter at the Council of Florence (1438–1439) when John VIII Paleologus met with Eugenius IV for the purpose of effecting a union between the Eastern and Western Churches. When Eugenius returned to Rome, George of Trebizond went with him and became (1444) an apostolic secretary. Nicholas V, in his uncritical enthusiasm for ancient literature, kept him busy making translations from the Greek into Latin. He translated Aristotle, Plato, Ptolemy, Eusebius, John Chrysostom, and others into Latin. At a time when there were very few with his knowledge of Greek language and literature he enjoyed great fame and prestige as a scholar, translator, and lecturer. However, he was so greedy for the fees he earned by his translations that he worked very fast and made many errors. Poggio and Aurispa attacked him violently on this account. He lost the patronage of Nicholas and went to Naples. Under Calixtus III and Pius II he again served as secretary and was again forced to leave Rome (1459) owing to various unpleasantnesses. He wrote a comparison of Aristotle and Plato in which he advocated the Aristotelian system of philosophy. This was in opposition to his contemporary Georgius Gemistus Plethon, and was cogently attacked by Cardinal Bessarion, a far better Greek scholar than he was. In 1466 he returned to Rome and remained there in obscurity to the end of his life. He was a pioneer in bringing a knowledge of the Greek language to Italy and in reviving and stimulating an interest in ancient Greek literature and philosophy.

Georges d'Amboise (zhôrzh däṅ-bwȧz). See **Amboise, Georges d'**.

Geraldini (je-räl-dē′nē), **Alessandro.** Prelate, scholar, and diplomat; b. in Umbria, 1455; d. in Santo Domingo, 1525. He served as a soldier, subsequently took orders, and was made (c1485) religious tutor to various younger members of the Spanish royal family, including the daughters of Queen Isabella. He met Columbus at court, and favored his projects. In 1520 he was appointed bishop of Santo Domingo. His *Itinerarium ad regiones sub aequinoctiali plaga constitutas* (published at Rome, 1631), describes his journey to Santo Domingo and the island itself, and records his experiences as an explorer in the New World, as a diplomat, and his interests as a humanist.

Gerardo di Bologna (jā-rär′dō dē bō-lō′nyä). Carmelite friar; b. c1250; d. at Avignon, April 17, 1317. From 1297 until his death he was general of the order. He is one of the Carmelites noted for his adoption of the Aristotelian-Thomistic theology. His own work, *Summa Theologiae*, based to a degree on Thomas Aquinas, presents his lively disagreement on some points.

Gerini (jā-rē′nē), **Lorenzo di Niccolò.** Florentine painter; active between 1392 and 1411. He was the son of Niccolò di Pietro Gerini and assisted him at Prato (1392) and on the altarpiece, *Coronation of the Virgin and Saints,* painted for the Church of S. Felicita and now in the Accademia, Florence. Spinello Aretino, with whom he sometimes collaborated, contributed the design for the triptych. His first independent work is a triptych of *St. Bartholomew*, signed and dated (1401) and painted for the Palazzo Communale, S. Gimignano. Other works now in the museum at S. Gimignano include a polyptych of St. Gregory and St. Fina, with scenes from the life of St. Fina on the side panels and on the back. Lorenzo di Niccolò was more influenced by Agnolo Gaddi than by his father, was less productive than his father, and was a better draftsman. A number of works attributed to him are to be found at Florence (Accademia, Bargello, S. Croce, S. Felicita) and in the neighborhood (Settignano, Arcetri). An elaborate triptych with the *Coronation of the Virgin* in the central panel, five saints in each of the side panels, a five-part predella, and pinnacles over each of the three main panels, is over the high altar of S. Domenico, Cortona. The Gothic atmosphere is enhanced by the sharply pointed pinnacles of the frame. The types and forms of the figures reflect the Gaddi influence. Other works are at Parma, Pisa, Rome (Vatican), Altenburg, Zurich, Boston, Brooklyn, Denver, New Haven, New York, Raleigh (North Carolina), St. Louis (Missouri), and elsewhere.

Gerini, Niccolò di Pietro. Florentine painter; documented from 1368; d. at Florence, 1415. He perhaps received his first training under Taddeo Gaddi, Giotto's pupil, and then was influenced by Jacopo di Cione, Andrea Orcagna's brother, from whom are derived the Orcagnesque characteristics in his work. He was an independent master by 1368, in which year his name was on the rolls of the Physicians' and Apothecaries' Guild. An industrious rather than a gifted painter, he had a large and active workshop, in which he trained a number of assistants in the tradition of Giotto, with the result that the tradition was maintained by many painters in spite of the Renaissance developments that were being introduced into Florentine painting by such an artist as Masaccio. Many works are attributed to Niccolò. The decoration of the sacristy in S. Croce is believed to be his earliest work. A *Madonna* (1372) in the same church shows a plasticity derived from Giotto through Taddeo Gaddi. In 1386 he began frescoes in the Oratory of the Bigallo at Florence with Ambrogio di Baldese; a triptych, *The Baptism,* National Gallery, London, is of the following year. He worked with Agnolo Gaddi at Prato (1391–1392); frescoed the chapter room of S. Francesco at Pisa (1392); then worked alternately at Prato and Florence. The triptych, *Coronation of the Virgin and Saints,* Accademia, Florence, was painted in 1401 with his son Lorenzo to Spinello Aretino's design. In 1408 and 1409 he frescoed the pilasters in Orsanmichele. In the meantime, he and his workshop were producing a great number of altarpieces and other paintings. In addition to works in the Accademia and several churches at Florence and in the neighborhood, there are examples of his painting at Empoli, Fiesole, Parma, Pisa (frescoes in S. Francesco), Pistoia, Prato (frescoes in S. Francesco), Rome (Vatican and Capitoline), Verona, Baltimore, Birmingham (Alabama), Boston (Isabella Stewart Gardner Museum and Museum of Fine Arts, where there is a *Virgin and Child* that is one of his best works), Chicago, Colorado Springs, Denver (*Four Crowned Saints,* companion to the *Scourging of the Four Crowned Martyrs,* Johnson Collection Philadelphia), Greenville (South Carolina), New Haven, and elsewhere.

Gerusalemme liberata (je-rö-sä-lem′mā lē-bā-rä′tä). [English, "Jerusalem Delivered."] Heroic epic in twenty cantos by Torquato Tasso. He conceived the idea of such an epic, on a Christian and historical theme, in his youth. The theme is the reconquest of Jerusalem from the Saracens by Godfrey of Bouillon, whence the name that Tasso originally gave it, *Il Goffredo.* The title *Gerusalemme liberata,* by which it is known, was given to it by friends who published an unauthorized edition in 1581. The work is modeled on Homer and Vergil, as in the catalogue of crusading knights in Canto II; Erminia identifying the crusaders from the walls of Jerusalem for the benefit of the pagan king; the violation of a truce; and the use and kinds of metaphor, to mention a few obvious comparisons. However, Tasso's poem is informed by his own spirit and imagination, is fanciful in its episodes, theaded with the mystery and wonder of magic. Its fundamentally religious and human theme is in contrast to the pure joy in arms and the superhuman quality of Homer's epic. Tasso adapted historical characters and events and added imaginary ones as his muse dictated. He creates all his characters, in the sense that they are moved by inescapably human and conflicting emotions. The epic, covering a period of forty days, proceeds from the arrival of the crusading forces before Jerusalem through a series of heroic attacks, pitched battles, and single combats. An infernal council presided over by Pluto looses demons to cause dissension in the crusaders' camp. A terrorizing enchanted forest delays them. The wondrous magic of Armida's bower enchains Rinaldo. Tancred is unmanned by his love for the pagan princess Clorinda. The Christian spirit overcomes pagan armies and sorcery and Jerusalem is reconquered and liberated. Tasso, like Boiardo and Ariosto before him, made his poem a vehicle for praise of the House of Este, of whom his Rinaldo is supposed to be an ancestor. Unlike them, he had no temperament for playful fancies, brilliantly witty invention, or satire. His cast of mind turned him to an expression, in elegiac, lyrical, and melodic accents, of accounts of men at arms moved by a deeply religious impulse to overcome the powers of darkness, whether they appeared in an infernal council, an enchanted forest, a magical garden, or the bravery of men doomed by their unbelief. His luminous and melodic verses became enormously popular with his countrymen from all walks of life. For years gondoliers on the canals of Venice sang his verses to each other. Immediately successful and soon translated, *Gerusalemme liberata* brings to full circle the masterpieces of Italian Renaissance literature.

Gesner (ges′nėr), **Konrad von.** [Also, incorrectly, **Gessner.**] Swiss naturalist and scholar; b. at Zurich, Switzerland, March 26, 1516; d. there, December 13, 1565. He became (1537) professor of Greek at Lausanne, and was afterward professor of physics at Zurich. Among his works are *Bibliotheca universalis* (1545–1555), *Historia animalium* (1550–1587), and *Opera botanica* (published by Schmiedel 1753–1759).

Gessart (ges′ärt), **Jan.** See **Mabuse.**

Gesso (jes′ō). A coating applied to wood or canvas to serve as a ground for painting or gilding. It consists of a preparation of chalk or plaster of Paris and glue. Such an undercoating enhances the brilliance of the pigments. Gesso is also used as a material for sculpture.

Getto di Jacopo (jet′tō dē jä′kô-pō). Pisan painter; active at the end of the 14th and the beginning of the 15th centuries. A panel of six saints, over which there is an *Annunciation*, reflects Florentine influence. It is signed and dated 1391, and is in the Museo Nazionale, Pisa.

Gherardesca (gā-rär-dās′kä), **Ugolino della.** See **Ugolino della Gherardesca.**

Gherardi (gā-rär′dē), **Giacomo.** Statesman and man of letters; b. at Volterra, July 25, 1434; d. September, 1516. A learned and discreet man, he had completed his studies at Florence, been secretary to a cardinal (until 1479), and then apostolic secretary. In his positions he successfully carried out important and delicate diplomatic missions. Lorenzo the Magnificent, whose policy was to keep peace in Italy as a protection from the interference of foreigners, briefed him before he went to Ludovico Il Moro at Milan on the matter of the kingdom of Naples, and later put him in charge of his son Giovanni's education. (Giovanni was the future Pope Leo X.) Gherardi had an intimate knowledge of political and literary affairs of his day. His *Diarium Romanum* is a valuable source on life at Rome in the years 1479 to 1484. Also notable are his diplomatic despatches and his many letters.

Gherardi, Giovanni. [Called **Giovanni da Prato.**] Poet; b. at Prato, c1367; d. at Florence, between 1443 and 1446. A disciple of Dante, Petrarch, and Boccaccio, he gave readings of their works in the cathedral at Florence from 1417 to 1425. His own works, full of echoes of the three masters, include *Il Paradiso degli Alberti*, the tale of an imaginary voyage to Crete and Cyprus. The traveler returns to Tuscany and, in the villa of the Alberti and the nearby castle of the Poppi, discusses with Luigi Marsigli, Coluccio Salutati, and others, the glorious culture of the past and its rediscovery in their own age. The conversations recorded in this work are thought by some historians to reflect the authentic origins of humanism. His *Philomena*, in terza rima, is an allegory of the poet's progress from the wood of ignorance to the mount of knowledge under the guidance of the seven virtues.

Gherardo di Giovanni del Fora (gā-rär′dō dē jō-vän′nē del fō′rä). Florentine painter, mosaicist, engraver, and illuminator; d. 1497. Of his painting, a fresco, *Virgin and Child with Saints*, is at Florence. He and his brother Monte (d. 1529) both worked as mosaicists in the cathedral at Florence. Both worked as miniaturists, and it is in this area that their work is best known. Because they

COLOR PLATES

The color plates on the following pages reproduce paintings that were executed over a span of about 250 years. The subject of the first seven plates is the same, with the dual purpose of illustrating the developments that took place in the art and techniques of painting and of illustrating the changes that took place in the painters' approach to the subject. Placed as they are in chronological sequence, the developments in technique in these seven paintings are obvious. The changes in approach range from serene religiosity (Giotto) and mystic austerity (Lorenzo Monaco), through secular splendor (Gentile da Fabriano), the introduction of portraits to honor prominent men (Botticelli's portraits of the Medici), and the solution of painterly problems (Leonardo da Vinci), to a deep feeling for pastoral landscape (Giorgione) and an intense preoccupation with light and movement (Tintoretto). Together, the ten plates represent a wide range of technique, style, painting personality, and artistic achievement.

1. GIOTTO. *Adoration of the Magi*. Scrovegni Chapel, Padua. Alinari-Scala

2. LORENZO MONACO. *Adoration of the Magi*. Uffizi, Florence. Alinari-Scala

3. GENTILE DA FABRIANO. *Adoration of the Magi*. Uffizi, Florence. Alinari-Scala

4. SANDRO BOTTICELLI. *Adoration of the Magi*. Uffizi, Florence. Alinari-Scala

5. LEONARDO DA VINCI. *Adoration of the Magi*. Uffizi, Florence. Alinari-Scala

6. GIORGIONE. *The Adoration of the Shepherds*. National Gallery of Art, Washington, D.C. (Kress Collection)

7. TINTORETTO. *Adoration*. Scuola di San Rocco, Venice. Alinari-Scala

8. MICHELANGELO. *Creation of Adam*. Sistine Chapel, Vatican. Alinari-Scala

9. RAPHAEL. *The Mass of Bolsena*. Stanza di Eliodoro, Vatican. Alinari-Scala

10. TITIAN. *Sacred and Profane Love*. Borghese Gallery, Rome. Alinari-Scala

1. GIOTTO. *Adoration of the Magi*. Scrovegni Chapel, Padua.

2. LORENZO MONACO. *Adoration of the Magi*. Uffizi, Florence.

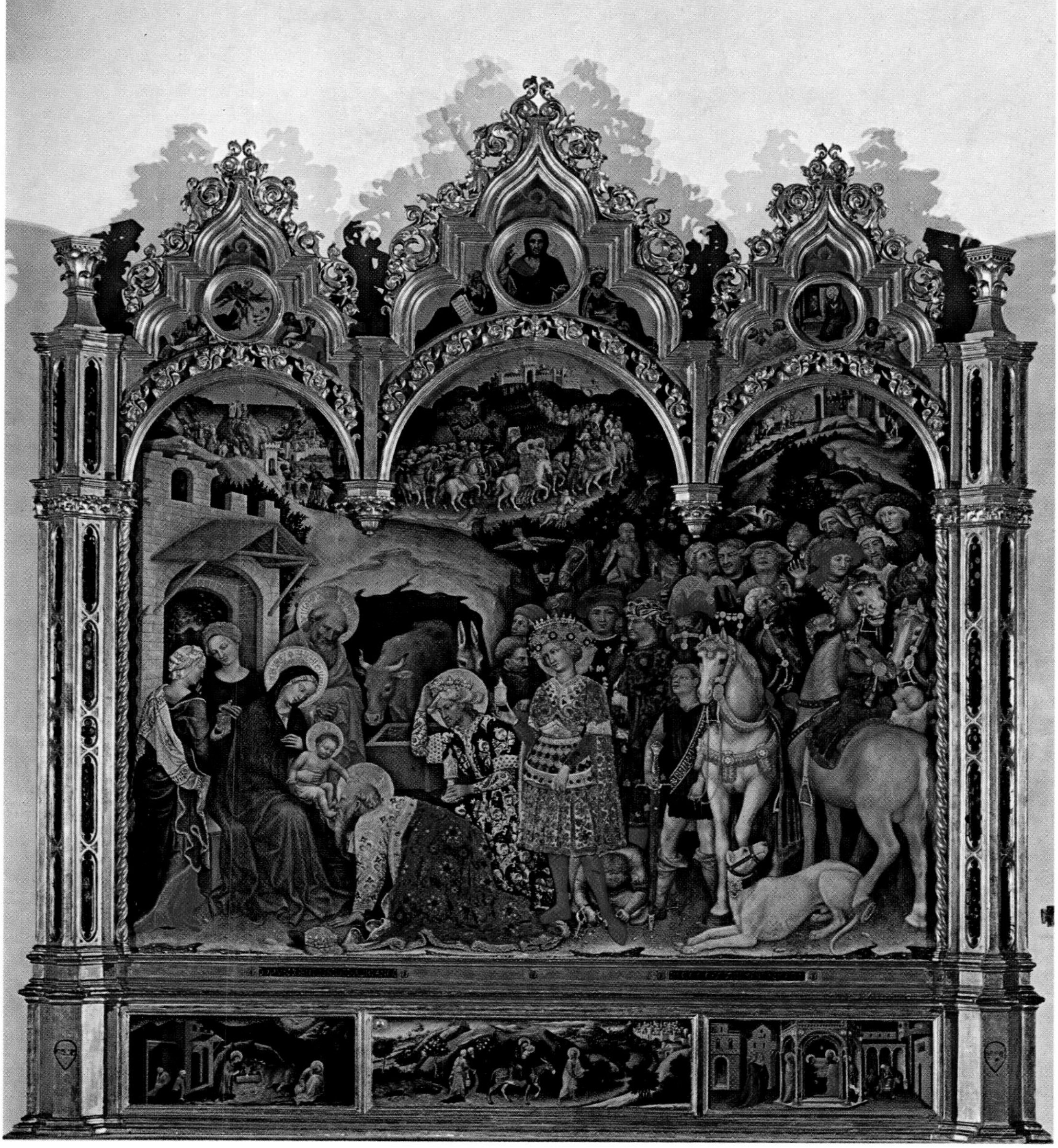

3. GENTILE DA FABRIANO. *Adoration of the Magi*. Uffizi, Florence.

4. SANDRO BOTTICELLI. *Adoration of the Magi*. Uffizi, Florence.

5. LEONARDO DA VINCI. *Adoration of the Magi*. Uffizi, Florence.

6. GIORGIONE. *The Adoration of the Shepherds*. National Gallery of Art, Washington, D.C. (Kress Collection)

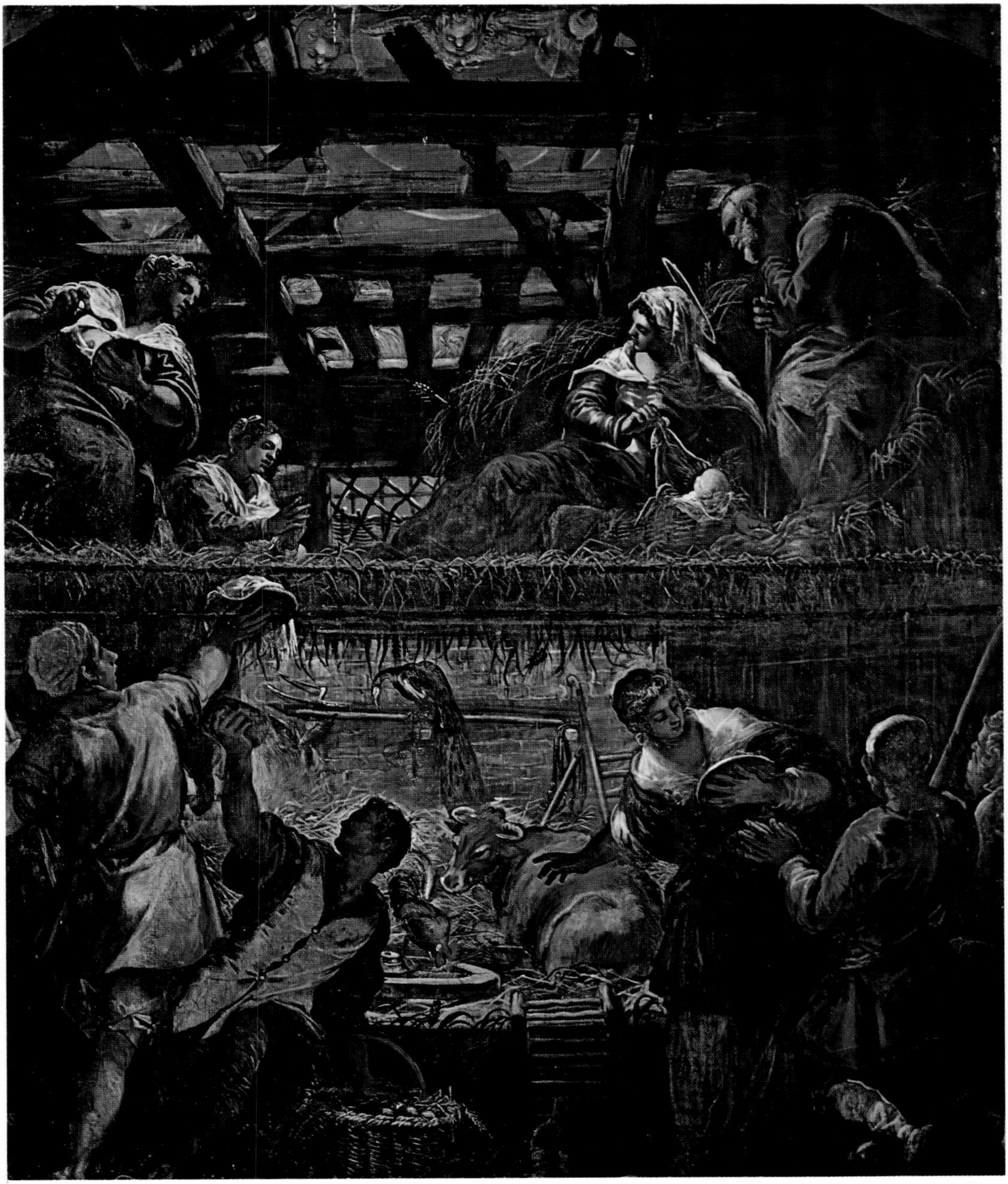

7. TINTORETTO. *Adoration*. Scuola di San Rocco, Venice.

8. MICHELANGELO. *Creation of Adam*. Sistine Chapel, Vatican.

9. RAPHAEL. *The Mass of Bolsena*. Stanza di Eliodoro, Vatican.

10. TITIAN. *Sacred and Profane Love*. Borghese Gallery, Rome.

worked together, it is difficult to separate their work, which shows the influence of Flemish illuminators. Examples of their work are a Missal in the Museo Nazionale, a Psalter in the Laurentian Library, and an Antiphonary in the cathedral, all at Florence, as well as examples at Lisbon, Aosta, and elsewhere. Gherardo was known as an engraver, but none of his prints is certainly identifiable. Monte was also a painter; an *Annunciation* by him is in the Galleria Estense at Modena.

Ghibellines (gib′e̤-linz, -lēnz, -līnz). Imperial party of Italy, opposed to the Guelphs, the papal party. See **Guelphs.**

Ghiberti (gē-ber′tē), **Lorenzo.** Florentine sculptor; b. at Florence, c1378; d. there, December 1, 1455. He was brought up by, and trained in the workshop of, the goldsmith Bartolo di Michele, called Bartoluccio, and may have been his son, for in a number of documents he signed himself Lorenzo with the addition of variations of Bartolo's name. He received a good education and knew Latin. In 1400, because of the unstable political situation at Florence and an outbreak of the plague, he went to Pesaro with a fellow artist and worked as a painter for the Malatesta. On learning of the competition that was to take place for the second set of bronze doors for the Baptistery (the first set had been executed by Andrea Pisano and set in place in 1336), he returned to Florence to enter the competition (1401). Filippo Brunelleschi and Jacopo della Quercia were his principal rivals among the contestants. According to Brunelleschi's biographer the committee appointed by the Calimala (the Merchants' Guild, which had charge of the Baptistery and had organized the contest) could not decide between the entries submitted by Brunelleschi and Ghiberti, and proposed to give the commission to the two jointly. Brunelleschi, however, wanted the commission for himself or not at all, and it was awarded to Ghiberti. In the autobiographical section of his *Commentarii*, Ghiberti makes no mention of any such doubts on the part of the committee. He wrote, "To me was conceded the palm of the victory by all the experts and by all those who had competed with me." All the contestants were required to execute a relief on *The Sacrifice of Isaac*, and were given one year in which to do it. Ghiberti's graceful, rhythmical panel, with figures derived from ancient reliefs or models, is now in the Bargello, as is Brunelleschi's; Della Quercia's has disappeared. Ghiberti was awarded the contract (1403) for what is now the North Door, and Bartolo's workshop, where it was to be cast, became a leading bronze foundry at Florence. The two wings of the door included twenty-eight quatrefoil panels, of which twenty were narrative reliefs on stories from the New Testament and eight were reliefs of single figures of the four Evangelists and the four Doctors of the Church. Ghiberti worked on the door until 1424, when it was set in place in the entrance opposite the cathedral, where the Gate of Paradise is now. In the course of those years definite changes took place in his style. The earliest reliefs, beginning with the *Annunciation*, which is thought to be the first, are still strongly Gothic, close to the trial panel in spirit and linked to the painting of Lorenzo Monaco. The last reliefs, such as *Christ Carrying the Cross*, are broader in approach, more realistic, more harmonious and balanced in composition, and in their more classical feeling reflect the influence of a visit he had made to Rome and the observations he had there made of imperial reliefs on arches and buildings. In some of the panels Ghiberti united his scene with an architectural background. At the corner of each panel was a tondo with a small sculptured head; between the heads the panels were framed with ivy leaves. The door jambs were decorated with a frame of many kinds of leaves. In the years from 1403, when he was awarded the contract, to April, 1424, when the door was set in place, Ghiberti was engaged on many other projects. In 1404 he designed cartoons for stained glass windows for the cathedral (between 1434 and 1443 he made most of the designs for the stained glass windows that were ordered for the cathedral; among these were the *Assumption* in the façade, and three in the choir). In 1409 he matriculated in the Goldsmiths' Guild. In 1414 he completed the monumental bronze statue of *St. John the Baptist* for the tabernacle of the Merchants' Guild in Orsanmichele. (According to the contract, the statue was to be cast at his own risk; the great statue, one and a half times lifesize, was cast in a single piece.) In 1419 the Cambio (Bankers' Guild) commissioned a bronze statue of *St. Matthew* for Orsanmichele. It was completed in 1422, and a few years later (1427–1428) he completed a bronze *St. Stephen* for the Lana (Wool Guild). The three statues, powerful and refined, show what Ghiberti could do in creating monumental sculpture; they are the only examples of his work on this scale; his preference was for the finer sculpture of reliefs that approached goldsmith's work in detail and finish. In 1417 he accepted a commission to do two bronze reliefs, *Baptism of Christ* and *St. John the Baptist before Herod,* for the Baptismal font at Siena. (Donatello and Jacopo della Quercia also furnished panels for the font; hence the three leading sculptors of the time are represented.) This was the only time he executed an important work for a client outside Florence, for although he traveled to Rome (once before 1416 and once between 1425 and 1430), and visited Venice (1424–1425; 1430) and other places, he was a Florentine to the bone and lived and worked in his native city. Also in this period (1403–1424) he married, and had two sons: Tommaso (b. 1417) and Vittorio (b. 1418) who worked with him and carried on the workshop after Lorenzo's death.

In January, 1425, he received the commission to make the East Door of the Baptistery. As finally carried out, the two wings of the door, which came to be known as the "Gate of Paradise," included ten large square reliefs with scenes from the Old Testament. In some of the panels as many as four scenes are represented, the scenes being differentiated by placing them on different planes. Gilding on the entire panel heightens the capacity to reflect light and enhances the relief. At the corners of each panel he placed a tondo with a sculptured head, as he had done with the North Door. In both doors he included a sculptured portrait of his own head, and the difference in these, done about thirty years apart, shows the extent to which his skill at modeling and his sense of realism in portrayal had developed. The heads are separated by statuettes in niches on the upright sides and reclining figures at the top and bottom, to form a frame for the panels. In this work, which was the crowning achievement of Ghiberti's work and life, he showed himself a master of the pictorial relief. With melodious understatement he presents the sweep and flow of draperies, the rhythm and sway of figures. His scenes, frequently presented against elaborate architectural backgrounds depicted in linear perspective, as in the *Solomon* panel, bespeak refinement, elegance, and harmony, rather than drama. In his *Commentarii* he wrote that in the execution of the panels he "strove to imitate nature as closely as I could, and with all the perspective I could produce. . . . The scenes are in the lowest relief and the figures are seen in the planes; those that are near appear large, those in the distance small, as they do in reality." The reliefs were completed in 1447; the door, with the frames of heads and statuettes, was set in place in 1452. (The ornamental frieze for the jambs was completed by his son Vittorio.) Ghiberti had succeeded Bartolo as head of the workshop and carried out a number of other projects while he was working on the East Door. Among these was a reliquary of the three Martyrs, SS. Protus, Hyacinth, and Nemesius (1428), now in the Bargello; a tabernacle for Fra Angelico's Linaiuoli triptych (1432); and a reliquary of St. Zenobius (1442), now in the cathedral. (Lost works of the period when he was working on the doors include a morse and a mitre in gold for Pope Martin V [1419], a gold and jeweled mitre for Pope Eugenius IV, and the mounting of an antique carved cornelian for a member of the Medici family. On the whole he did not work often for the Medici or other great families of Florence.) Before he began the Gate of Paradise he had been charged, along with Brunelleschi, with designing and executing a plan for the erection of the great dome of the cathedral. Ghiberti had no visible qualifications as an architect; his association with Brunelleschi was productive of nothing but friction; in 1425 he was relieved of his commission, but without in any way impairing the great reputation he enjoyed as one of the leaders in Florentine art.

Toward the end of his life Ghiberti wrote his *Commentarii,* in three sections. In the first he tells about ancient art, drawing on Vitruvius and Pliny for much of his material. The second section deals with the lives of artists of the 14th century. In it Ghiberti describes works of art he himself had seen. This section also contains his autobiography and a listing of his own work, with emphasis on his works as a goldsmith and his reliefs for the Gate of Paradise, which he realized was his most important work. The third section, again drawing on the ancient Roman writers, and on Arabian scholars as well, is on the theory of art. The *Commentarii* constitute the earliest attempt at describing the lives of the artists, and an early and important description of antiquities and discussion of the theory of art. In his career Ghiberti had been eminently successful, as artist and businessman. He was a man of considerable means. His shop was a leading bronze foundry and employed and trained many artists. Among these were Donatello, Michelozzo, Benozzo Gozzoli, Paolo Uccello, and a number of others. He was always busy, usually fell behind his deadlines, but managed to keep the respect and commissions of the great guilds who were his chief patrons. A true artist, he was also a true Florentine, witty, shrewd, supple, and well aware of his worth; in concluding his autobiography in the *Commentarii* he writes, "Few things of importance were made in our country that were not designed and planned by me."

Ghiberti, Vittorio. Florentine sculptor; b. at Florence, 1418; d. there, November 18, 1496. He was the son of Lorenzo Ghiberti (c1378–1455) and worked with him from an early age, succeeding as head of the workshop when Lorenzo died. He worked with his father on the Gate of Paradise, the third bronze door of the Baptistery, and completed the ornamental friezes of the door jambs.

Ghini (gē′nē), **Luca.** Botanist and physician; b. at Croara d'Imola, c1490; d. at Bologna, May 4, 1556. He was a doctor of medicine and a professor at the university at Bologna. A man of broad learning, he became better known as a botanist than as a physician. In 1544 he went to Pisa at the invitation of Cosimo I de' Medici, and founded the botanical gardens of Pisa and Florence. Rather than study and comment on the ancient writers, he observed plants in their natural surroundings. He was the first to preserve plants by pressing them between sheets of paper. He prepared herbals of particular areas, as the island of Elba and the Tuscan Apennines. His disciples included Ulisse Aldrovandi and Pierandrea Mattioli.

Ghirlandaio (gēr-län-dä′yō), **Benedetto.** Florentine painter; b. 1458; d. July 17, 1497. He was the brother of Domenico (1449–1494) and David Ghirlandaio (1452–1525) and sometimes assisted Domenico in his painting. At first a miniaturist (a *Vision of Jeremiah*, from the Urbino Bible, now in the Vatican, is attributed to him), after 1480 he turned to painting because of weakness of his eyesight. After the death of Domenico he wandered about Europe and then lived for a time in France, from which he returned loaded with honors and gifts. His only signed work, *Nativity*, is a product of his French sojourn and was probably painted about 1494. It is at Aigueperse. Other works attributed to him are *Way to Calvary*, Louvre, Paris, and part of the *Crossing of the Red Sea*, Sistine Chapel, Rome.

Ghirlandaio, David. Florentine painter; b. 1452; d. 1525. He was the brother and principal collaborator of Domenico Ghirlandaio (1449–1494). In his early works, such as the *Deposition*, Ognissanti, Florence, and *SS. Sebastian and Roch*, Municipal Museum, Pisa, his style is somewhat crude and heavy, with elements of Castagno and Verrocchio. But the over-riding influence in his work is that of his brother Domenico. After the latter's death he devoted himself to work in mosaic; examples in this medium are *Virgin Seated Flanked by Two Angels* (1496), Cluny Museum, Paris, and *Annunciation* (1510) over the central doorway of SS. Annunziata, Florence. Among his known works is the fresco *Crucifixion*, now in S. Apollonia, Florence. The greater part of the frescoes in S. Martino dei Buonomini, Florence, is attributed to him, as are frescoes in the Palazzo Vecchio, S. Croce, S. Lorenzo, S. Maria Novella, and other churches in and about Florence. Other paintings attributed to him are at Rome (Vatican), Venice (Ca' d'Oro), Altenburg, Berlin, Philadelphia (Johnson Collection), and elsewhere.

Ghirlandaio, Domenico. [Original name, **Domenico di Tommaso di Corrado di Doffo Bigordi.**] Florentine painter; b. at Florence, 1449; d. there, of the plague, January 11, 1494. He was the foremost member of a family of Florentine artists. His father, Tommaso, was a goldsmith, noted for making ornamental garlands for the heads of Florentine ladies, for which reason he was called il Ghirlandaio, a name adopted by his sons. He apprenticed Domenico to a goldsmith, but as the youth was patently more interested in drawing and the pictorial arts, he soon devoted himself to them. In his youthful works he was a follower of Baldovinetti, whose pupil he probably was, and of Verrocchio,

DOMENICO GHIRLANDAIO
Pope Honorius III Approving the Rule of St. Francis
Study for the fresco in the Sassetti Chapel, S. Trinità, Florence
Kupferstichkabinett, Berlin

with some indication of the influence of Andrea del Castagno, as in the *Last Supper* (1480) in the Ognissanti at Florence, which is derived from Castagno's painting on the same subject in the Church of S. Apollonia. After 1481 he was less dependent on earlier influences. Brilliant, luminous color, a crisp freshness of features and gestures, and remarkably acute portraiture are characteristics of his work. He became the most popular painter in Florence in his day, had a large and busy workshop, and, since he had more commissions than he could fulfill, turned over a great deal of work to his assistants and pupils. In the course of filling the many orders he received his compositions at times became formalized and sterotyped, and somewhat empty of feeling. He painted at S. Gimignano (1475), at Rome (1475; 1481–1482), at Pisa, and for churches and abbeys in the neighborhood of Florence as well as for many churches in the city itself. His earliest known work (c1473) is a fresco of *The Madonna of Mercy*, in the Vespucci Chapel in the Church of Ognissanti. In this work he established the precedent later followed in his frescoes of painting portraits of eminent living Florentines as spectators or participants in religious events; a practice that contributed more to historical than to artistic interest. *The Madonna of Mercy* has portraits of old Amerigo Vespucci, who founded the chapel, and members of his family, including the grandson Amerigo who gave his name to a continent. Also included are other prominent Florentines or members of their families, as Antonio, Archbishop of Florence, and Simonetta Vespucci. (The latter had married into the Vespucci family in 1468. She was beloved by Giuliano de' Medici and honored by him with a famous tournament in 1475. Poliziano wrote his *Stanze per la giostra* on the occasion of the tournament, and Botticelli later drew inspiration for his *Primavera* from them.

She died in 1476.) In 1475 he frescoed the chapel of S. Fina in the cathedral at S. Gimignano, and in the same year, with his brother David, was painting in the library of Sixtus IV at Rome. In 1481, perhaps with his brother Benedetto, he began frescoing the walls of the Sistine Chapel in the Vatican with Botticelli, Cosimo Rosselli, and Perugino. Domenico's fresco, *The Calling of the Apostles Peter and Andrew*, abounding in portraits of Florentines at that time in Rome, is reminiscent of Masaccio in its monumentality. He also painted a *Resurrection*, later repainted, and supplied the cartoon for *The Crossing of the Red Sea;* the fresco is variously attributed to Cosimo Rosselli or to Domenico and Benedetto. Among the finest examples of his fresco painting is the cycle on the life of St. Francis in the Sassetti Chapel in the Church of S. Trinità, Florence, executed (1485) with his brother David and assistants. In brilliant color, against a background of the area around S. Trinità, he painted portraits of members of the Sassetti family, of Lorenzo de' Medici and members of his family and his circle, including the poets Poliziano and Matteo Franco, as spectators to the various scenes on the life of the saint. Flanking the altarpiece, *The Adoration of the Magi,* are portraits of the kneeling donor, Francesco Sassetti, and his wife. Another great fresco cycle is that on the lives of the Virgin and St. John the Baptist in the choir of S. Maria Novella (1486–1490), again rich in portraits, including those of the philosopher Marsilio Ficino, the humanist Cristoforo Landino, and a self-portrait. In the broad and spacious compositions of the frescoes, painted in glowing color, the world of the rich, proud, and self-satisfied Florentine burghers is magnificently and convincingly presented; this was a world Domenico knew well and passed a good deal of his career in preserving. His art in religious scenes is restrained; it comes alive in his well-drawn, acute portraits. He was happiest in the broad reaches of fresco; Vasari writes that he expressed a wish to have the whole circuit of the walls of Florence to paint his stories on. In his vast compositions he looked back to the monumentality of Masaccio; in his fidelity to detail, as the *St. Jerome*, Ognissanti, there is an element of Flemish painting. In contrast to the scope, complexity, and animation of the frescoes, his panels in tempera (he never painted in oil) are brilliant in color but flat and conventional, seemingly often painted according to formula. Ghirlandaio trained many painters in his workshop who continued to paint in his manner, but they were not the painters who brought Florentine painting into its new phase. His most famous pupil, or apprentice, was Michelangelo, who drew little from his master. Ghirlandaio is also known to have been a mosaicist, working (1490) with his brother David on a mosaic, *The Annunciation*, for the cathedral, and later on mosaics at Pistoia. A miniature, *The Testing of the True Cross*, signed by him, is in

DOMENICO GHIRLANDAIO
Girl Pouring Water
Study for the fresco of *The Birth of the Virgin*,
S. Maria Novella, Florence
Gabinetto Disegni e Stampe degli Uffizi
Foto Soprintendenza

the Vatican Library. Many works Ghirlandaio is known to have executed have perished. Among the remaining examples are a beautifully preserved *Adoration of the Magi* (1488), Ospedale degli Innocenti, Florence; *Visita-*

tion (1491) and a touching *Portrait of an Old Man with his Grandson,* Louvre, Paris; and paintings in the cathedral at Lucca, in the Uffizi, Florence, the National Gallery, London, the Metropolitan Museum, New York, the National Gallery, Washington, Detroit, and elsewhere.

Ghirlandaio, Michele di Ridolfo. [Original name, **Michele Tosini.**] Painter; b. 1503; d. 1577. A pupil of Lorenzo di Credi, he became an assistant of Ridolfo Ghirlandaio, whose name he took. He collaborated with Vasari in the decoration of the Palazzo Vecchio, and imitated the exaggerations of Michelangelo in allegorical figures in the Borghese and Colonna galleries, Rome. Of 1570 are the frescoes of the Church of the Madonna della Quercia, Viterbo. His best works are the broad and solidly constructed *Nativity* and the *Archangels,* Abbey of Passignano, near Florence, and some portraits close to the work of Parmigianino in the Pitti Palace and Accademia. There are altarpieces in several churches in and about Florence, and other paintings at Fiesole, Fucecchio (S. Giovanni Battista), S. Gimignano, Berlin, Greenville (South Carolina), San Marino (California), and elsewhere.

Ghirlandaio, Ridolfo. Florentine painter; b. 1483; d. 1561. He was the son of Domenico Ghirlandaio (1449–1494), and was trained in his father's workshop. His father's was the earliest influence on his painting, but he was an eclectic, and borrowed from Lorenzo di Credi, Piero di Cosimo, Perugino, Leonardo da Vinci, Raphael, Fra Bartolomeo, Andrea del Sarto and Pontormo, and finally, Michelangelo and Bronzino. He left a number of paintings, but is best known for his portraits. Examples of his work are in the Uffizi, Accademia, Pitti Palace, and in a number of churches at Florence, at Pistoia, Prato, Budapest, Leningrad; in the Louvre, Paris, National Gallery, London, the Metropolitan Museum, New York, at New Haven, and elsewhere. A splendid *Portrait of a Gentleman of Florence* that reflects the influence of Piero di Cosimo is in the Art Institute of Chicago. Other portraits are at London, in the Johnson Collection, Philadelphia, the National Gallery, Washington, at Minneapolis, Stockton (California), Williamstown and Worcester (Massachusetts).

Ghisi (gē′sē), **Giorgio.** Engraver; b. at Mantua, 1520; d. there, December 15, 1582. Esthetically and technically, he was a follower of Marcantonio Raimondi. In 1540 he went to Rome, where he fell under the influence of Michelangelo, and engraved the artist's Sistine Ceiling and *Last Judgment* in a series of ten plates, but he was not equal to the task of interpreting Michelangelo. He also reproduced some of the works of Raphael, but was more comfortable in copying lesser painters, as Giulio Romano. He returned to Mantua in 1576, and died there.

Ghissi (gēs′sē), **Francescuccio di Cecco.** Marchigian painter; active in the second half of the 14th century. He was a follower of Allegretto Nuzi, and the most important painter of the school after Nuzi. His work is characterized by a certain air of mysticism, by the importance he gives to decorative detail, and the meticulous care with which he renders fabrics (without, however, any plastic folds). Through him many painters of the Marches were influenced to the international Gothic style. The *Madonna of Humility* was his favorite subject. One, signed and dated (1359), is in the Church of S. Domenico, Fabriano; another signed and dated example (1374) is at Montegiorgio, and other examples are at Fermo, Ascoli Piceno, and in the Vatican.

Giacomino Pugliese (jä-kō-mē′nō pö-lyā′zā). Poet. Little is known of the life of this poet of the so-called Sicilian school, who lived c1200–1250. Eight of his love lyrics survive, and are notable in the period for an unusual realism, and for freshness of language and ease of rhythm. Among them is a passionate lament on the death of his lady.

Giacomino da Verona (dä vā-rō′nä). Franciscan friar and poet, of the second half of the 13th century. He wrote poems in crude but vigorous language on religious subjects. His *De Ierusalem celesti* and *De Babilonia civitate infernali* contain strange and wonderful descriptions of Paradise and of the Inferno.

Giacomo da Lentino (jä′kō-mō dä len-tē′nō). Poet of the so-called Sicilian school; b. at Lentini, Sicily (but some say he was of Tuscan origin), c1180/1190; d. c1240. He studied at Bologna and then became attached to the court of Frederick II at Palermo, where he was one of the emperor's notaries. Among his forty extant love lyrics are some of the earliest (perhaps the earliest) examples of the sonnet. Dante speaks of him as "the Notary"

(*Purgatorio*, xxiv) held fast in the traditional style, which was being supplanted by his own *dolce stil nuovo* ("sweet new style").

Giacomo da Recanati (dä rā-kä-nä'tē). Marchigian painter; d. after 1466. He was a follower of Pietro da Montepulciano, and through him was influenced by Gentile da Fabriano. A *Madonna and Angels*, perhaps the central panel of a polyptych, signed and dated (1443), is in the cathedral at Recanati.

Giacomo da Riva (dä rē'vä). Veronese craftsman-painter; active between 1374 and 1418. He worked in the churches of Verona, where he left a signed and dated fresco (1388) of the *Madonna*.

Giambellino (jäm-bel-lē'nō). Name by which Giovanni Bellini is sometimes known; see **Bellini, Giovanni.**

Giambologna (jäm-bō-lō'nyä). [Also, **Giovanni da Bologna, John of Boulogne.**] Sculptor; b. at Douai, 1529; d. at Florence, 1608. He was trained in Flanders in the studio of Jacques Dubroeucq, who had spent some time in Rome, and while still quite young went himself to Rome to study. There he made clay and wax models of all the most famous statues, and came into contact with Michelangelo, who encouraged him in this method of study and preparation. About 1557 he left Rome to return to Flanders (he was sometimes called "il Fiammingo," because of his origin), but stopped at Florence to study the work of Michelangelo and other Renaissance sculptors there. At Florence he met a noted collector and patron, Bernardo Vecchietti, who was impressed with his work and offered to subsidize his studies. The patronage of Vecchietti, through whom he was introduced to Francesco de' Medici, changed his plans. He remained in Italy the rest of his life, became the greatest sculptor of his age, and had a deep influence on subsequent sculpture in Italy and abroad. In 1560 he was one of the contestants for the *Neptune Fountain* at Florence; others were Bandinelli, Cellini, and Ammannati. Bandinelli was eliminated by death and Ammannati was awarded the commission. However, Giambologna's model won him (1563) the commission to execute the bronze *Neptune Fountain* at Bologna. In the massive figure of a heroic Neptune, Giambologna developed the twisting pose, the forceful energy and electrifying animation of his elegant mannerist sculpture that marked his subsequent works. The vitality of the principal figure is also apparent in the figures of putti and sea goddesses that adorn successive descending levels of the pyramidal fountain. His best known work is his bronze *Mercury*, with the soaring god balanced on one winged foot in an extravagant display of Giambologna's virtuosity. His first version of the *Mercury* has been lost; the celebrated surviving version is in the Bargello, Florence. In 1565 he returned to Florence to assist in the execution of the elaborate decorations for the marriage of Francesco de' Medici to Joanna of Austria. For this occasion he made a plaster model (exhibited during the festivities and carved in marble at a later date) of *Florence Triumphant over Pisa*, Bargello, in which, with daring assurance, he left openings in the block for the play of light and shadow about the limbs of the figures. Such openings, which required the most delicate balancing of forces within the block to prevent collapse, had not been seen since Hellenistic times. Another work embodying the same idea of open spaces in the block is his marble *Samson and a Philistine*, Victoria and Albert Museum, London, also commissioned by Francesco de' Medici (who was not much of a ruler, when his time came, but was a good patron). Among his other works are a *Fountain of Oceanus*, with three river gods, Boboli Gardens, Florence (the figure of *Oceanus* is in the Bargello; that presently on the fountain is a copy). His marble *Rape of the Sabines*, Loggia dei Lenzi, Florence, is a masterpiece of design for a composition that was equally effective from any view, of superb technique, and of masterly control of space and spaces. In the execution of the work Giambologna was interested in solving the problem of presenting three figures in action, and, as he said, in broadening the knowledge and study of art. He proposed several names for the group, as it was the working out of the problem, not its subject matter, that had concerned him. A wonderfully expressive bronze relief in the base fixed the ultimate title as *The Rape of the Sabines*. Among his other reliefs are those with religious themes: on the Altar of Liberty at Lucca, for the Grimaldi Chapel at Genoa, and in the Chapel of S. Antonino, S. Marco, Florence. Other works include the colossal allegorical figure of the *Appenines*, carved from the living rock at Pratolino, and the equestrian statues of

Cosimo I (1594), Piazza della Signoria, and of Ferdinando I, Piazza della Annunziata, Florence. He was noted also for his carvings and bronzes of animals and birds, sometimes used as decorative elements on his fountains, and for bronze statuettes, produced by himself and in great numbers in his workshop. The statuettes, such as those of *Apollo*, Palazzo Vecchio, and *Astronomy*, Vienna, because of the ease with which they could be handled and shipped around, spread his style throughout Europe, and the form was imitated for a number of years following his death. The acknowledged successor of Michelangelo, Giambologna was in love with his art—its problems, their solutions, and the possibility of stretching its range. He was the last great representative of Florentine Renaissance sculpture or, as it might be put, the herald of the Baroque.

Giamboni (jäm-bō′nē), **Bono.** Translator from Latin and French; b. at Florence, c1230; d. c1300. He translated Brunetto Latini's *Le Trésor* into Italian, Vegetius' *Art of War*, and some medieval works. His own, *Introduzione alle virtu*, is an allegory in which the author is led by Philosophy to Faith. It draws material from many sources. His chief importance lies in his contribution as a prose translator.

Giambono (jäm-bō′nō), **Michele.** [**Michele (di Taddeo) Bono**; called **Giambono.**] Venetian painter; active between 1420 and 1462. A painter in the international Gothic style, he was influenced by Jacobello del Fiore and by Gentile da Fabriano, and was typically Venetian in his love of rich fabrics and glowing backgrounds. His polyptych, *St. James the Greater*, is in the Accademia, Venice; *Madonnas* from his hand are at Bassano, Venice (Ca' d'Oro and Correr Museum), Rome (National Gallery), and Verona. Other examples of his work are *A Saint with a Book*, a panel from an altarpiece, National Gallery, London; *An Episcopal Saint*, Isabella Stewart Gardner Museum, Boston; *The Man of Sorrows*, the Metropolitan Museum, New York: and paintings at Fano, Padua, Pavia, S. Daniele del Friuli (S. Antonio), Zara (S. Francesco), Baltimore (Walters Art Gallery), Detroit, Washington, and elsewhere.

Giambullari (jäm-böl-lä′rē), **Bernardo.** Florentine poet; b. 1450; d. c1525. He was the father of Pier Francesco Giambullari (1495–1555). With equal facility, he wrote spiritual hymns and carnival songs, religious poems, and novelle with rustic settings.

Giambullari, Pier Francesco. Historian and man of letters; b. at Florence, 1495; d. there, August 24, 1555. He was the son of Bernardo Giambullari (1450–c1525). He knew Hebrew and Chaldee (Aramaic) as well as Latin and Greek, and became a protégé of Pope Leo X. The pope gave him ecclesiastical benefices and named him librarian of the Laurentian Library at Florence. At Florence he was an active member of the Florentine Academy. From young manhood he wrote love lyrics, carnival songs, and later, commentaries on Dante. He was deeply interested in language, and took part in the controversy of his day over the relative merits of Tuscan and Latin. But as regarded both Italian and Latin he deplored the corruption of the former and the barbarization of the latter. His chief works are *Della lingua che si parla e scrive in Firenze*, an early Tuscan grammar, and *Historia dell' Europa*. Although he completed only the section of his history dealing with Carolingian Italy, in its conception, this work is an early general history in Italian, and is notable as an attempt to deal with the Middle Ages. In its own day it was noted for the elegance and purity of the language in which it was written. Although he drew on earlier sources, he made an effort to compare and examine them for accuracy. Nevertheless, the work is more important for its language than for its historical accuracy.

Giampetrino (jäm-pā-trē′nō). [Original name, **Gian Pietro Rizzi.**] Milanese painter; active in the first half of the 16th century. Nothing is known of his life, including the date of his birth or the date of his death, and he left no signed works. His character as a painter must be deduced on stylistic grounds, and a number of paintings are attributed to him on these grounds. One of the best representatives of the Lombard school, it is thought that he may have been a pupil of Leonardo da Vinci. In any case, he was profoundly influenced by the master in his grace and sweetness. Works attributed to him are to be found at Milan, where there is an unfinished half figure of *The Magdalen* (apparently his favorite subject) and another of the *Madonna*, in the Brera. Other works are in the Ambrosiana, the Poldi Pezzoli Museum and churches of Milan. Paintings attributed to him are in collections at Bergamo, Florence,

Turin, London, Amsterdam, and Vienna, and include a *Virgin and Child with the Infant Baptist* in the Johnson Collection, Philadelphia, and paintings at Cambridge (Massachusetts), Lewisburg (Pennsylvania), Madison (Wisconsin), Minneapolis, Oberlin (Ohio), Portland (Oregon), Seattle, Waco (Texas), Washington, and elsewhere.

Gianfrancesco da Tolmezzo (jän-frän-chäs′kō dä tōl-med′dzō). Painter; native of the Friuli; b. c1450; d. after 1510. He was a follower of the Vivarini and was influenced by the Veronese painters. Most of the works of this provincial painter are in and about Udine. A signed *Madonna and Child* is in the Accademia, Venice.

Gianni (jän′nē), **Lapo.** Florentine lyric poet; b. at Florence, 1270; d. c1330. He was a friend of Dante and Guido Cavalcanti. Dante mentions him in his *De vulgari eloquentia.* Gianni wrote in the style Dante called *il dolce stil nuovo*, but his lyrics are less conventional and "courtly" and more lighthearted than those of the somewhat melancholy Cavalcanti.

Giannicola di Paolo (jän-nē-kō′lä dē pä-ō′lō). Perugian painter; b. c1460; d. 1544. He was a pupil and follower of Perugino, whom he assisted in painting frescoes in the Cambio at Perugia (from 1513). He worked almost exclusively at Perugia; among his patrons was Gian Paolo Baglioni, one of the Baglioni tyrants of Perugia, for whom he painted effigies of the traitors in the uprising of 1500. An *Annunciation* attributed to him, National Gallery, London, shows the influence of Perugino. Later he became a follower of Raphael and then of Andrea del Sarto and Sodoma. His best work, the *All-Saints Altarpiece* (1506–1507), painted for the Baglioni Chapel in the Church of S. Domenico and now in the National Gallery of Umbria at Perugia, shows the influence of Raphael and Pinturicchio. By 1528 he had painted stories of the life of St. John the Baptist in the Cambio and these works, among his best, have elements of Florentine painting in the manner of Andrea del Sarto. The *Madonna and Child,* Louvre, is the central panel of an altarpiece, the predella panels of which are in the National Gallery, Perugia, where there are other examples of his work.

Giannotti (jän-nōt′tē), **Donato.** Political writer and historian; b. at Florence, November 27, 1492; d. at Rome, December 27, 1573. He earned his doctorate in law and, after teaching at Pisa, was called to serve the Chancellery at Florence (1527) when the Medici had been driven out and the Republic briefly restored. An ardent republican, he fulfilled his office with zeal, with the result that when the Medici returned to power (1531) he was banished. Aside from some youthful Latin and Italian verse, and two comedies, his writings were concerned with political matters. His *Trattato della Repubblica fiorentina,* written in exile, shows his republican convictions. Another work, *Dialogo della Repubblica dei Veneziani,* is an analysis of the Venetian government. Giannotti advocated for Florence a government on the Venetian plan, the *governo misto* of an oligarchic council representing the limited number of citizens. The difficulty was that the Venetian system had been slowly developing for centuries. It could not be introduced to the citizens of Florence at a moment's notice. Giannotti at length entered the service of Pius V. His *Discorso delle cose d'Italia* advises the Pope, to whom it was addressed, to form an alliance with the French, as a bulwark against Charles V. As a statesman, he did not envision a united Italy free of foreign influence. Rather, he sought the influence of one foreigner to counteract that of another. From time immemorial, such policies had led to invasions of Italy. His works on politics, cited above, are of value for the exact and detailed descriptions of the Florentine and Venetian systems of government, and for the histories of these systems.

Giasone del Maino (jä-sô′nā del mī′nō). Jurist and teacher; b. at Pesaro, 1435; d. at Pavia, 1519. He studied law at Pavia, served as professor of law there (1467–1485), and also at Padua. His fame as a jurist and teacher was great (the king of France and his entire suite attended one of his lectures at Pavia), and he numbered among his students several who became eminent in the law.

Giberti (jē-ber′tē), **Gian Matteo.** Ecclesiastic and diplomat; b. at Palermo, September 20, 1495; d. at Verona, December 30, 1543. About 1513 he went to Rome with his father, a Genoese, where he became friendly with Giulio de' Medici, the future Pope Clement VII. He won Clement's confidence and became one of his most trusted and influential advisers. Giberti, a power in the Curia, oriented papal policy toward France and against the empire of Charles V. His policy was disastrous. The French were defeated at Pavia (1525). Rome was sacked (1527). Giberti himself took refuge in Castel Sant' Angelo with Clement and watched the pillaging of Rome. He was later given as a hostage to the Spanish by Clement. His anti-imperial policy having failed, Giberti retired to Verona (1528), of which Clement had named him bishop, and became active in attempted reform of the clergy and populace there. Paul III, who valued his ability, was prevented from giving him the red hat through the opposition of Charles V, who clearly remembered Giberti's anti-imperial policy.

Gilbert (gil′bėrt), Sir **Humphrey.** English soldier and navigator; half brother of Sir Walter Raleigh; b. at Compton, near Dartmouth, England, c1539; drowned off the Azores, September 9, 1583. He served in Ireland where he defeated McCarthy More in 1569, and was made governor of the province of Munster, and in the Netherlands in 1572, where he unsuccessfully besieged Goes. In 1578 his expedition seeking to discover the Northwest Passage to the Far East was a failure. In 1583 he set out again with five ships; he sighted the northern shore of Newfoundland, and on August 5 landed at the site of the present city of St. John's, where he established the first English colony in North America. On the return voyage the ship in which he sailed foundered in a storm, and he was drowned. He wrote a *Discourse of a Discovery for a New Passage to Cataia,* and sponsored a scheme for the founding of an academy and library at London (published by Furnivall, 1869, as *Queen Elizabethes Achademy*).

Gilles de Laval (zhēl dẹ lȧ-vȧl). See **Retz,** Baron **de.**

Gilpin (gil′pin), **Bernard.** English clergyman; b. at Kentmere, Westmorland, England, 1517; d. at Houghton-le-Spring, Durham, England, March 4, 1583. He became archdeacon of Durham in 1556, and was afterward appointed rector of Houghton-le-Spring; both of these positions he held until his death. He gained great popularity by his charities and gratuitous ministrations among the poor (whence he is sometimes called "the Apostle of the North").

Ginevra (jē-ne′vrä). In Lodovico Ariosto's *Orlando Furioso,* a Scottish princess beloved by Ariodante. She is falsely accused of unchastity and condemned. Rinaldo saves her, reveals the falseness of her condemnation, and she marries Ariodante.

Giocondo (jō-kōn′dō), Fra **Giovanni.** Architect, engineer, and humanist; b. at Verona, c1433; d. at Rome, July 1, 1515. Member of a religious order, he was a man of many accomplishments and interests, as in the fields of philosophy, classical literature, and archaeology, and is one of the most interesting figures of northern Italy of his time. He published editions of the letters of Pliny, Caesar's *Commentaries,* and Vitruvius, and collected about 2,000 Latin inscriptions in a work that he dedicated to Lorenzo the Magnificent. Like Leon Battista Alberti, he became noted as an architect, and like his predecessor, he was a theorist who left it to others to carry out his designs. It is on this account that it is difficult to pinpoint his architectural achievements. From 1489 to 1495 he was in the employ of King Alfonso II of Naples and the duke of Calabria. He accompanied Charles VIII back to France when that monarch withdrew after his successful invasion of Italy, and served as architect to the king. The Pont Notre-Dame, over the Seine at Paris, is a legacy of this employment. The elegant Loggia del Consiglio at Verona was designed by him, and he drew the plans for the fortification of Treviso and Padua when the emperor Maximilian waged unsuccessful war against Milan and Venice. To him is assigned the design for the quarter and the bridge of the Rialto at Venice. In 1514 he was called to Rome to help Raphael in carrying on the construction of St. Peter's. He died the following year.

Giolfino (jôl-fē′nō), **Bartolomeo.** Veronese sculptor; b. c1410; d. c1496. His youthful works were in the Venetian Gothic tradition. An altarpiece (1470), carved in wood, now in the Accademia, Venice, shows the influence of Florentine sculptors who worked at Verona at the beginning of the 15th century.

Giolfino, Niccolò. Veronese painter; b. 1476; d. 1555. He was the outstanding member of a family of Veronese painters and sculptors. A pupil of Liberale da Verona, he combined the Gothic tendencies of his master with the intensity of Mantegna and the Ferrarese school and ultimately adopted some of the exaggeration and over-ornamentation of the baroque. Most of his surviving paintings and

Niccolò Giolfino
Betrayal of Christ
Courtesy of The Metropolitan Museum of Art, New York, Hewitt Fund, 1917

frescoes are in the museum and churches (S. Anastasia, S. Bernardino, S. Maria in Organo, S. Maria della Scala, and the cathedral) at Verona. There is a *Madonna and Child*, Carrara Academy, Bergamo, and paintings at Rome (National Gallery and Palazzo Venezia), Vicenza, Princeton, and elsewhere. He was active as a painter of cassoni and furniture panels; among the number of these extant are *Triumph of Silenus* and *Silenus Asleep*, Johnson Collection, Philadelphia, and others on mythological or historical subjects at Bloomington (Indiana), Oberlin (Ohio), and elsewhere.

Giolito (jō-lē′tō), **Gabriele.** Venetian printer and bookseller; b. at Venice, between 1500 and 1510; d. 1578. He was the son of Giovanni, called Il Vecchio, who was also a printer, and the grandson of Bernardino, who founded the family business at Venice in 1483. Gabriele joined his father in the business in 1536, and from then until his death dominated the printing field. His shop was at Venice, with branches at Naples, Bologna, Ferrara, and other cities. His press, La Fenice, so-called from its phoenix colophon, published the outstanding writers of the age: Aretino, Bembo, Bernardo Tasso, Lollio, Antonfrancesco Doni, and many others. He published twenty-two editions of Petrarch between 1542 and 1560, nine of the *Decameron*, and twenty-eight of Ariosto's *Orlando Furioso*, to say nothing of editions of other works by the same writers. The backbone of his business was books in Italian. Giolito did not hold with the dictum among the purists of his time that only Latin and Greek could properly express serious literature. The onset of the Counter-Reformation caused a change in his list. From the licentious novelle and verses of the first half of the 16th century he switched to translations from the Latin and Greek Church Fathers and, more particularly, to books of instruction and practical religion. In adapting himself to the times he assured the continued success of his business. In 1545 he published the first of several anthologies of such contemporary poets as Bembo, Ariosto, Veronica Gambara, Vittoria Colonna, and many others. These little anthologies were highly popular, were transported across the Alps, and introduced the Italian poets to other areas of Europe and to England. Giolito's press was carried on by his two sons, but they had not their father's gift. The last edition from the Fenice Press was in 1606.

Giordano da Pisa (jôr-dä′nō dä pē′sä) or **da Rivalto** (rē-väl′tō). Dominican friar and preacher; b. at Pisa, c1260; d. at Piacenza, August 19, 1311. He entered the Dominican order about 1280, studied at Pisa, Bologna, and Paris, and then traveled about Europe, preaching and studying. He carried out many missions for his order, and was on his way to teach at Paris when he fell ill and died. He was noted throughout for his eloquence. His sermons are preserved from the notations of listeners, sometimes quite fully and at other times only in the main points. Several manuscripts are extant, and some collections of his sermons were printed. The examples that survive are among the most notable in the Italian prose of the 13th century. They are vigorously expressed, and of glowing simplicity, and are valuable for the information in them on the life and state of culture of the time. Giordano was beatified in 1833.

Giorgio (jôr′jō), **Francesco di.** See **Francesco di Giorgio Martini.**

Giorgione (jôr-jō′nā). Venetian painter; b. at Castelfranco, c1477; d. of the plague, at Venice, 1511. Almost nothing is certainly known of his life. By the time of his early death he had already become famous, and that in an age rich in Venetian painters. The numerous legends about his life that sprang up and multiplied immediately following his death obscured his true artistic personality and achievements. He was known to have been an attractive, sociable man with a zest for life; one who loved music and played the lute so well he was in demand as a musician. Of his artistic formation little is known. Giovanni Bellini, the dean of Venetian painters, was certainly an influence on his development. The classicism of such central Italian painters as Francia and Lorenzo Costa is reflected in his work, as are the intellectual preoccupations of the Paduan humanists. The fusion of tones in his misty landscapes and firmly modeled figures is perhaps a legacy from Leonardo da Vinci, who was at Venice in 1500; individual color is overlaid by a pervading tone without losing its warmth and luminosity. He painted on religious themes, endowing his divine figures with a universal humanity, and introduced subjects from mythology and fantasy to traditional Venetian painting, hitherto, except for portraits, limited to religious subjects. He left no signed works. The number attributed to him varies from a scant half dozen to over forty. Art historians generally agree that the altarpiece in the Church of S. Liberale at Castelfranco is a work of his hand. This *Madonna and Child Enthroned with Saints Liberale and Francis*, in the manner of Giovanni Bellini, is thought to be an early work, perhaps prior to the first date known concerning his career. That date (1507) concerns payment ordered by the Council of Ten for painting, now lost, executed in the Ducal Palace at Venice. By inference, he must have been an established painter to have won such an important commission. In the following year he was commissioned to fresco the newly rebuilt Hall of the German Merchants (Fondaco dei Tedeschi) at Venice, work that has disappeared. Paintings thought to be early are two panels in the Uffizi, Florence: *The Testing of Moses by Fire and Gold* and the *Judgment of Solomon*. The classical restraint of the figures in the first was abandoned in his later style, but in the landscape (thought to have been painted by Giorgione himself while much of the rest of both paintings was done by a collaborator), Giorgione establishes his lyrical mastery of landscape painting; the frond-

GIORGIONE
Landscape
Louvre, Paris Alinari-Art Reference Bureau

like trees and palpable atmosphere of the out-of-doors are constants of his renderings of nature. Other works the critics agree on, generally speaking, are *Adoration*, the National Gallery, Washington, *Judith*, Leningrad, *The Three Philosophers*, Vienna, and *The Tempest*, Accademia, Venice. The difference between the Castelfranco altarpiece and *The Tempest* signals the revolution Giorgione was to bring about in Venetian painting. The time that had elapsed between the execution of the two works was necessarily short. In that time Giorgione's artistic vision was transformed. The Castelfranco altarpiece, exquisitely painted and with Giorgione's own ambience, is nevertheless a conventional composition in the Bellini manner, with glimpses of an idyllic landscape forming a background to the upper part of the Madonna's throne; the meaning and the spirit are clear. In *The Tempest* a nude woman is seated on the ground under trees and is nursing an infant. Nearby a young man—a soldier?—watches her. In the background are a bridge over a stream, the towers and walls of a city (perhaps his native Castelfranco), and over all hang dark clouds just now rent by a streak of lightning. Various meanings have been ascribed to the painting. It is an exquisite landscape with figures, aromatic with Giorgione's sensitivity and lyrical feeling for atmosphere, vibrant with life and luminous color, tranquil in its action, dramatic in the darkening tones that foretell the storm. The painting, perhaps among his early works, marks a turning point in Venetian pictorial taste, as well as a milestone in artistic self-expression. The meaning of *The Three Philosophers* has also proved elusive; again it is a group of figures in a landscape: two men stand under a tree talking, while a third, seated under the tree, seems to be looking at something in the distance, all against the subdued radiance of an ideal landscape.

Giorgione's influence on his fellow Venetians was immense. Titian, his contemporary, was especially influenced by him in his earlier years, and some works are variously attributed to Giorgione or to Titian or to a collaboration of the two; Giorgione's *Venus*, Dresden, was largely finished by Titian. In Titian the tranquil, idyllic, and often somewhat melancholy vision of Giorgione is infused with drama and rich color. Tintoretto was also deeply influenced by Giorgione. Besides those mentioned, paintings attributed to Giorgione are *Holy Conversation*, *Old Woman*, and *Feminine Nude*, Accademia, Venice; *Leda and the Swan* and *Idyll*, Municipal Museum, Padua; *Double Portrait*, Palazzo Venezia, Rome; and paintings at Vienna, Berlin, Dresden, Madrid, the National Gallery and Hampton Court, London, and elsewhere. Frescoes in a poor state of preservation in a house at Castelfranco are attributed to him on solid grounds. Many painters felt themselves liberated by the example of Giorgione. His technique, his identification with nature, and his capacity to express a personal vision enlarged and transformed Venetian painting. He was so closely imitated that in a number of cases it is impossible to distinguish the works of the Giorgionesque school from those of the master himself.

Giottino (jôt-tē′nō). A nickname meaning "little Giotto." Some consider that the name applies to Maso di Banco, a pupil and close follower of Giotto.

Giotto (jōt′tō). [**Giotto di Bondone** (dē bōn-dō′nā).] Florentine painter, sculptor, and architect; b. at Colle di Vespignano, in the Mugello, a few miles north of Florence, c1267; d. at Florence, January 8, 1337. Giotto was the son of Bondone, a peasant and small landholder. According to a pretty tale of Vasari, Cimabue came upon him when he was a lad tending his father's sheep and observed that he was drawing a sheep with a sharp rock on a flat stone. Cimabue was so struck, according to the story, by the child's talent that he took the boy into his own workshop at Florence as an apprentice. Whether or not it was under these circumstances that Giotto became the pupil of Cimabue, it is generally accepted that he was a pupil of that master, was influenced by him, and came to outstrip him to such an extent that Giotto represents the break between Byzantine and Italian Renaissance painting. With Giotto painting speaks a new language, one derived, to be sure, from its Byzantine parent. Byzantine painting and mosaic had become rigidly stylized in the course of the centuries that it dominated. Figures, brilliant especially in the mosaic, were hieratic and two-dimensional. Symbols, attributes, and methods were traditional. In his work Giotto humanized the figures, gave them density and mass. Influenced perhaps by the Pisan school of sculpture, Giotto's figures have modeling, dimension, and movement. These effects are achieved by variations in color as well as by line. Because of his emphasis on the figure, some have attributed to him the development in Florence of the foremost school of figure-painting. Giotto also brought drama to his painting by his use of space as an element of composition and by his attempts at perspective to produce an illusion of space. The figures, fluid, lifelike, dignified, and human, and the tensions created by their place in the composition are dominant in Giotto's work. His symbols or elements are often from everyday life. Closely observed details of the realm of nature have their role. Man is portrayed in an eloquent and devotional manner but is man, not a divine symbol. This holds true even in paintings on the most revered of religious subjects. (Only the paintings he did on religious themes survive; all others, such as a cycle he did at Padua on astrological themes, have been lost.) The principal evidence of the Byzantine tradition from which his work emerged lies in his characteristic use of line and outline. He was regarded as a leading painter in his own lifetime. Dante acknowledges his fame in the *Divina Commedia*. Petrarch called him "the first painter of our age." Cennino Cennini said of him that he "translated the art of painting from Greek (here meaning Byzantine) into Latin." And Ghiberti said he made art "natural." Later generations have agreed that Giotto was the founder of a national Italian school of painting. A school grew up about him and his workshop. Among his disciples were Stefano, Taddeo Gaddi and Maso di Banco. His pupils and those who followed in succeeding generations imitated their master so closely that for centuries scores of paintings were attributed to Giotto. Art historians and scholars have been working over the list of attributions for years, and have now assigned many of those formerly credited to Giotto to the Giotteschi—painters in the manner of Giotto.

It is thought that Giotto first went to Rome some time before 1290, that there he saw the works of the Roman school, which exhibited some classical elements, and was influenced by them. He worked in Florence (where he married, had a family, owned property, had his workshop, and to which he always returned), in Assisi, Rimini, Padua, Naples, and Milan. The pope at Avignon was on the point of inviting him to that city when the painter died. The work he did at Rimini (c1303) has perished. For King Robert of Naples, with whom he was on familiar terms (and it must be remembered that at this period painting was a craft, not an art, in the general view, and that painters did not usually mix with princes on anything like equal terms), he painted the Royal Chapel and in the Castelnuovo (1329–1333). Petrarch saw the Neapolitan work soon after it was completed and advised all who visited Naples to see it. This work too has been lost, at the hands of man, nature, and time, as has the work he did in his last years (1335–1336) at Milan.

Of the works definitely assigned to the master, the best preserved, the least restored and the best lighted is the great series of frescoes he did, with the help of assistants, in the Scrovegni Chapel at Padua (1304–1306), dedicated to the Virgin. The chapel (also called the Arena Chapel because it is built on the site of a Roman arena), was erected by Enrico Scrovegni to atone for his father's sin of usury (mentioned in the *Divina Commedia*), as well as to preserve his inheritance. (According to canon law, the estate of a usurer should have been forfeited to the Church. Enrico was able to keep most of his inheritance in return for his promise to erect the chapel.) Almost the entire interior of the barrel-vaulted chapel is frescoed. The walls on both sides of the nave and on both sides before the apse are divided into four tiers. On the lowest tier, on the walls of the nave, are depicted the seven virtues with, opposite them, the seven vices. The second and third tiers contain twenty-six scenes from the life of Christ. The fourth tier has fourteen scenes of the life of the Virgin. The entire entrance wall is covered with *The Last Judgment*. The chapel glows with the clear, soft pinks, blues, and greens of the frescoes. The episodes are tense with drama or winning in gentle, grave appeal.

Another famous series of frescoes is in the Upper Church of the Basilica of San Francesco at Assisi, painted probably between 1291 and 1297. These include twenty-eight episodes from the life of St. Francis. They have traditionally been attributed to Giotto. Art historians have been whittling away at the attribution for generations. Almost no one now believes that the entire cycle was painted by Giotto, even with assistants. Some think he did not actually paint any of the episodes of the series. Many believe that some of the episodes are by Giotto's hand, others by Giotto and assistants, and some by assistants only. Of the badly mutilated frescoes in the same Upper Church (the basilica is constituted of two churches, one above the other), on Old and New Testament themes, those depicting the stories of Isaac are believed by many art historians to be by Giotto. The fact that, on stylistic grounds, the argument still rages as to how much, if any, of the work of the St. Francis cycle was done by Giotto is evidence that the cycle is, at the very least, very close to the master's work. Tourists who visit the basilica will be told, and will unquestioningly believe, that the frescoes are by Giotto and his assistants.

Other works attributed to Giotto and accepted generally as from his hand, are a crucifix, painted on wood (c1290) for the Church of S. Maria Novella at Florence, and now in the sacristy of that church; *Madonna Enthroned*, painted (c1310) for the Ognissanti and now in the Uffizi; episodes from the life of St. Francis in the Bardi Chapel and episodes from the lives of St. John the Baptist and St. John the Evangelist in the Peruzzi Chapel, both in the Church of S. Croce at Florence. These frescoes are thought to have been painted some time after 1317. They have suffered great mutilation, from being whitewashed, from clumsy cleaning and ill-advised restoration in the past. Recent cleaning and restoration show them to be among Giotto's most mature works. (Works by Giotto in two other chapels in this church have been lost.) A work that was famous in its own time was the *Navicella*, a mosaic executed in Rome. It represented a ship (the Church) on a stormy sea, and was commissioned (c1298) by a friend of Pope Boniface VIII, whose pontificate was tempestuous. It has been so often restored that the hand of the master is no longer visible in it. A *Madonna and Child* is in the National Gallery, Washington.

Giotto was a prominent and popular figure in Florence. He was short and remarkably homely, a fact that endeared him to the Florentines rather than otherwise. His fellow townsmen delighted in his quick, often earthy, wit and admired his shrewdness in business affairs. He had no love for poverty and is the reputed author of a canzone on that subject in which he lists all its disadvantages. In 1327 the Guild of Physicians and Apothecaries opened its rolls to artists and Giotto joined it. In 1334 he succeeded Arnolfo di Cambio as master of the works of Santa Reparata (the Duomo, known since the 15th century as Santa Maria del Fiore). At the same time he was named architect in charge of the walls and fortifications of the city. He designed the campanile, known forever after as Giotto's Campanile (with Brunelleschi's dome, one of the landmarks of Florence), the foundation of which was laid on July 19, 1334 (completed 1359), and executed some of the sculptures on the origin of the arts that adorn its lowest courses. The famous portrait of Dante, with whom Giotto was acquainted and possibly on terms of friendship, in the Bargello (Museo Nazionale) is considered to be the only authentic portrait of the poet. It has long been attributed to Giotto, but some now contend it is a work of his pupils. Giotto was buried in the Church of S. Croce at Florence. More than a century after his death, Lorenzo the Magnificent commissioned Benedetto da Maiano to execute a medallion with a representation of him. It is inside the Duomo at Florence and bears a Latin inscription by the poet Angelo Poliziano that begins, "I am he by whom the extinct art of painting was revived."

Giovanna I (jō-vän′nä) and **Giovanna II**, queens of Naples. See **Joanna I** and **Joanna II**.

Giovanni d'Alemagna (jō-vän′nē dä-lā-mä′-nyä). Painter of German origin, whence his name; known from 1441; d. at Padua, 1450. He was a collaborator of Antonio Vivarini, whose sister he married, at Padua and Venice. No works by Giovanni alone are known. His works with Antonio include a polyptych with *St. Jerome* (1441), now at Vienna, altarpieces (1443–1444) in S. Zaccaria, Venice, a *Madonna Enthroned* (1446), Accademia, Venice, and another in the Poldi Pezzoli Museum, Milan. He was commissioned (1448) to work in the Ovetari Chapel in the Church of the Eremitani at Padua, and was working there at the same time as Andrea Mantegna. The only work there identified as his includes some ornamental bands and putti; in this work, too, he was Vivarini's collaborator.

Giovanni da Anagni (dä ä-nä′nyē). Specialist in canon law; d. probably January 17, 1457. He taught for many years at Bologna, and also performed various missions for the Bolognese senate. On the death of his wife he entered upon an ecclesiastical career, and was made canon and subsequently archdeacon of the cathedral of Bologna.

Giovanni di Bartolommeo Cristiani (dē bär-tō-lôm-mā′ō krēs-tyä′nē). Painter of Pistoia; active between 1367 and 1396. He was a close follower of the Florentine school, and shows especially the influence of Orcagna. An altarpiece, *St. John the Evangelist*, is in S. Giovanni Fuoricivitas, at Pistoia, and several panels on the legend of St. Lucy are in the Metropolitan Museum, New York.

Giovanni delle Bande Nere (del′le bän′dā nā′rā). See **Medici, Giovanni de'.**

Giovanni del Biondo (del byôn′dō). Florentine painter; active in the second half of the 14th century. Not from Florence originally, he came perhaps from the Casentino, and became a citizen of Florence in 1356. A productive craftsman and minor artist, he was influenced by Andrea Orcagna and Giovanni da Milano, and painted a number of works marked by an individual toughness and sincerity. Among them are a number at Florence, as the rigid, yet individualized, *Saints* of a polyptych (1363) in S. Croce, and the Tuscan *Presentation in the Temple* (1364), Accademia, as well as other paintings in S. Croce, S. Felicita, S. Maria Novella, the cathedral, an *Annunciation* (1385), Ospedale degli Innocenti, and others. In addition, there are paintings at Fiesole (cathedral), Figline (S. Francesco), Rome (Vatican), San Giovanni Valdarno, San Miniato al Tedesco (S. Domenico), Siena, and at Allentown (Pennsylvania), Baltimore (Walters Art Gallery), Buffalo, Cambridge, Charlotte (North Carolina), Detroit, Los Angeles, Memphis, Muncie (Indiana) (Ball State Teachers College), New Haven, New Orleans, Philadelphia (Johnson Collection), Sarasota (Florida), and elsewhere.

Giovanni da Bologna (dä bō-lō′nyä). Bolognese painter; active in the second half of the 14th century. No evidence of Byzantine influence occurs in his work; rather, he was influenced by the Gothic elements of Lorenzo Veneziano. A panel of *St. Christopher* (1377), originally painted for the Collegio dei Mercanti at Venice, is now in the Museo Civico at Padua. There is a signed *Madonna of Humility* in the Accademia at Venice, and another in the Brera at Milan. Other paintings are at Bologna, the Correr Museum, Venice, and at Denver.

Giovanni dalle Celle (dä′lā chel′lā). Tuscan religious; b. near Volterra, c1310; d. c1396. Of a noble Tuscan family, some time before 1347 he entered the monastery at Vallombrosa, near Florence. He became abbot of S. Trinità, in Florence, after 1351, and shortly thereafter retired to the cells above the monastery at Vallombrosa, whence his name. A cultivated man who is said to have translated Cicero and Seneca, he won many followers through his tolerance, wisdom, and discretion, at the same time being unsparing of himself. In his wide correspondence with other religious leaders he showed himself to be rather suspicious of visions and disapproving of extremists. He wrote on the problem of the Fraticelli, a dissident group of Franciscans recently condemned as heretics. He became an adherent of St. Catherine of Siena, without, however, abandoning his right to disagree with her, as he disagreed with others when that seemed the proper course. At the time, her activities had not been approved by the Church and he wrote, "It will be glorious for me to be called a heretic with her." Much of his correspondence has been preserved and provides a vivid picture of conditions of the Church and of Florence in his time; his letters reveal an intense appreciation of the demands of public life upon a Christianized laity. He was later beatified.

Giovanni di Francesco (dē frän-chās′kō). Painter; active at Florence in the second half of the 15th century. In 1458–1459 he frescoed a lunette in the Church of the Innocenti at Florence. With this as a criterion other works have been ascribed to him, including the Carrand triptych, Bargello, a predella with stories of St. Nicholas, Casa Buonarroti, possibly from the triptych, a cross painted for S. Andrea a Brozzi, frescoes in S. Maria Maggiore and S. Trinità, Florence, and an *Adoration of the Magi*, Montpellier. These paintings reveal him as a pleasing minor master who was influenced in his artistic development by Domenico Veneziano and, especially, by Andrea del Castagno. Other paintings are at Prato (cathedral), Edinburgh, Karlsruhe, London, Detroit, Philadelphia (Johnson Collection), and elsewhere.

Giovanni da Milano (dä mē-lä′nō). Florentine painter who came originally from Como, in Lombardy. He is known to have worked as an apprentice in Florence in 1350, to have joined the Physicians' and Apothecaries' Guild in 1363, and to have become a citizen in 1366. He was familiar with the school of Giotto but, though less lyrical and mystical, equally influenced by the Sienese school, especially in his brilliant color. His attention to homely detail and a slight elongation of figures are characteristic of the northern painters. The humanity of his realism in costumes and features is rendered with a spiritualizing seriousness. His most important surviving work is a series of frescoes on the lives of St. Mary Magdalene and the Virgin, in the Rinuccini Chapel, S. Croce, Florence. Like Giotto, Giovanni aimed at the dramatic moment. The grandeur and rhythm of his composition are his own. Also from his hand are a *Pietà*, Accademia, Florence, and some panels from a polyptych, *Saints, Martyrs and Virgins*, Uffizi, Florence. His polyptych at Prato of the *Virgin Enthroned* is notable for the brilliance of its color and its loving detail. Other works are at Amsterdam, London, New York, Rome (Vatican and National Gallery), Turin, and Williamstown (Massachusetts).

Giovanni da Modena (dä mō′de-nä). [Real name, **Giovanni di Pietro Faloppi.**] Painter; active in the first half of the 15th century. An often repainted fresco of the *Last Judgment* (1420) from his hand is in the Basilica of S. Petronio at Bologna; a *Crucifixion* is in the Palazzo Venezia at Rome.

Giovanni di Niccolò (dē nēk-kō-lô′). Pisan painter; active in the middle of the 14th century. In 1358 he held public office at Pisa. In his taste for rich decoration and in his refinement of execution, he shows the strong influence of Simone Martini. A signed polyptych, *Madonna and Child*, is in the Museo Nazionale at Pisa, as are other *Madonnas* from his hand.

Giovanni da Oriolo (dä ō-ryō′lō). [Also, **Giovanni di Giuliano.**] Painter; b. at Oriolo, near Faenza; active from 1439; d. between 1480 and 1488. An imitator of Pisanello and an early representative of the Ferrarese school, he was employed at Ferrara by Leonello d'Este, c1447. His signed *Portrait of Leonello d'Este*, National Gallery, London, is his only identified painting.

Giovanni di Paolo (dē pä-ō′lō). [Also known as **Giovanni dal Poggio.**] Sienese painter; b. at Siena, c1403; d. 1482. He may have been a pupil of Paolo di Giovanni Fei. In his ornamentation and genre detail he felt the influence of Gentile da Fabriano, who was at Siena between 1424 and 1426, as appears in an *Adoration of the Magi*, Cleveland, companion panels of which are at Berlin, the Vatican, the National Gallery, Washington (*Annunciation*), and the Metropolitan Museum, New York (*Presentation in the Temple*). He was active at Siena from 1420, by 1423 was a well-known painter there, painted his earliest surviving signed and dated (1426) work, and in 1428 was enrolled in the Painters' Guild at Siena. The predominant influence on him came to be that of his slightly older fellow-townsman, Sassetta. His life span covered a period when great changes were taking place in the art of painting, as the use of modeling and light to produce form, and the rediscovery of the principles of perspective. Some elements of his later work indicate a visit to Florence, but on the whole he looked back to 14th-century painting, and was little influenced by the new developments. A naïve and delicious master, he painted traditional themes with sincere religious fervor. In his predella panels his gift for exuberant narrative is apparent. Typical of his style is a group of six scenes from an altarpiece on the life of St. John the Baptist in the Art Institute of Chicago. Of these, *St. John Going into the Desert* presents a charming example of his taste for landscape—steep paths rapidly ascending beetling mountains that tower over a plain laid out in a checkerboard of fields; his tufted trees resemble those of Sassetta. Of his Madonnas and saints, the types have round faces, long sharp noses, tiny mouths, thin spread-out hands, and elongated figures. In a number of paintings he shows a lively interest in genre detail. His art is imbued with a poetic spirituality and mystical intensity. His work was uneven, especially in his later years, but carefully painted and animated. A prolific painter, many of his paintings are at Siena: in the Pinacoteca, churches, cathedral, and the archives.

Others are scattered in museums and collections, as at Florence, Modena, Palermo, Parma, Pienza, Berlin, Budapest, Cologne, Frankfurt, London, Paris, and elsewhere in Europe. There are examples of his work also in a number of museums in the United States, as the Walters Gallery, Baltimore, Museum of Fine Arts and Isabella Stewart Gardner Museum, Boston, Fogg Museum, Cambridge, Art Institute of Chicago, Cleveland, Detroit, El Paso, Houston, Kansas City, Missouri, Minneapolis, New Haven, the Metropolitan Museum and the Frick Collection, New York, Johnson Collection, Philadelphia, St. Louis, and the National Gallery, Washington.

Giovanni da Pesaro (dä pā-zä′rō). Marchigian painter; active in the second half of the 15th century. A *Madonna of Mercy*, signed and dated (1462) is at Candelare, near Pesaro, and a *Martydom of St. Biagio* is in the Palazzo Venezia, Rome.

Giovanni di Piermatteo (dē pyer-mät-tā′ō). See **Boccati, Giovanni.**

Giovanni dal Ponte (däl pōn′tā). [Real name, **Giovanni di Marco.**] Florentine painter; b. 1385; d. 1437. A traditional painter who could not help but be somewhat influenced by the developments taking place in Florentine painting, he yet continued to paint in the manner of such older painters as Spinello Aretino and Bicci di Lorenzo. He was enrolled in the Company of St. Luke (the Painters' Guild) in 1408, and counted such prominent families as the Strozzi, the Tornabuoni, and the Rucellai among his patrons. For a time he worked at Arezzo where he became familiar with the work of Spinello Aretino. Traces of the international Gothic style in his work remain in a slight elongation of the figures. In the handling of drapery and folds he followed the earlier Tuscan manner and eschewed the graceful arabesques of the international Gothic. Among the many works from his hand are a number of cassoni panels, as at Madrid, New Haven, and Paris (Musée Jacquemart-André), *Madonna and Child*, Pisa, a triptych, *Annunciation* (1435), Vatican, panels at Fiesole, predella panels in the Uffizi, a triptych, *Coronation of the Virgin*, Accademia, and frescoes in several churches at Florence, and paintings at Brussels, Budapest, Cambridge (England), Chantilly, London, Cambridge (Massachusetts), Columbia (South Carolina), Philadelphia (Johnson Collection), San Francisco, and elsewhere.

Giovanni da Prato (dä prä′tō). See **Gherardi, Giovanni.**

Giovanni da Ravenna (dä rä-ven′nä). See **Malpaghini, Giovanni di Iacopo.**

Giovanni di Riolo (dē ryō′lō). Emilian painter; active in the first half of the 15th century. A conservative painter in the Gothic manner, he left a signed and dated (1433) polyptych, *Madonna*, at Imola.

Giovanni da Udine (dä ö′dē-nā). Painter, architect, and designer of ornamental stuccos; b. at Udine, October 15, 1487; d. at Rome, 1564. His master from 1502 was Giovanni Martini da Udine. Later, at Rome, he worked with Raphael, assisting him in the painting of *St. Cecilia* (1516) and in painting the scenes of the *Fable of Psyche* (1517) in the Chigi villa (now the Farnesina). He became fascinated by the grotesques on the Imperial ruins of Rome and made up his mind to imitate them. As a result of numerous experiments he discovered the secret of white Roman stucco: marble powder and travertine lime. Raphael entrusted to him the task of decorating with stuccos the areas surrounding the paintings in his new Loggia in the Vatican. With endless invention and grace Giovanni created an exquisite decoration in which he united totally disparate elements in a harmonious whole, drawing inspiration for his motifs from Roman decoration and from the miniaturists' repertoire and imposing on them his own style. He created what was essentially a new kind of decoration—of stucco vignettes and ornamentation—that became enormously popular. Other examples of his work in this medium are in Castel Sant' Angelo, the Villa Madama, and the Borgia Apartments in the Vatican. Cardinal Giulio de' Medici (later Clement VII) employed him to work on the Villa Madama (1520), recalled him to Rome, from which Giovanni had departed for Udine after the death of Leo X, in 1523 when he became pope, and later (1532) sent him to Florence to make stucco decorations in the new Sacristy of S. Lorenzo. He later returned to Udine, where, after 1539, he was active as an architect, building clock towers, fountains, staircases, windows, and doors for public buildings in his native town. From 1550 he was general architect of all public works at Udine.

Giovanni Acuto (ä-kö′tō). Italian name for Sir John Hawkwood, the Englishman who formed The White Company and went into Italy as a leader of mercenaries. See **Hawkwood, Sir John.**

Giovanni Agostino da Lodi (ä-gôs-tē′nō dä lō′dē). [Also known as **Pseudo-Boccaccino.**] Painter. Nothing is certainly known of his life or training. His artistic personality has been deduced by grouping together a number of paintings that seem to have been executed by the same hand and that were once attributed to Boccaccino. A panel in the Brera signed with the name of Giovanni Agostino da Lodi has marked affinities with these, and has led to the conclusion, not universally accepted, that Giovanni Agostino da Lodi and the Pseudo-Boccaccino are the same painter. An eclectic, the strongest influence in his work is that of Boccaccino. Traces of Bramantino, Leonardo (as in *The Washing of the Feet*, dated 1500, Accademia, Venice), and Solario indicate that some of his artistic activity took place in Lombardy. The influences of the Venetians—Vivarini, Cima da Conegliano, and even Giorgione—indicate a move to the Veneto, where works attributed to him are to be found. Examples of his work are at Brescia and Cremona (two versions of a bust of *St. Jerome*), at Milan (Ambrosiana, Brera, Castello Sforzesco), Modena, Naples, Pavia (cathedral), Turin, Venice, Verona, Altenburg, Berlin, Vienna, Allentown (Pennsylvania), Baltimore (Walters Art Gallery), Cleveland, El Paso, New York, and elsewhere.

Giovanni Antonio da Brescia (än-tō′nyō dä brā′shä). Engraver, active in the first quarter of the 16th century. He made prints after designs by Mantegna, whose authorship he acknowledged, and did them perhaps with the permission of Mantegna. The artist may have wished to extend knowledge and appreciation of his work through engravings. Giovanni Antonio copied, as did many of his contemporaries, the works of Dürer. Three (1505, 1507, 1509) are extant. In 1509 or 1510 he went to Rome. There he was influenced by the work of Marcantonio Raimondi, and copied many of his prints.

Giovanni Battista da Faenza (bät-tēs′tä dä fä-en′dzä). See **Bertucci, Giovanni Battista.**

Giovanni Dalmata (däl-mä′tä). [Original name, **Ivan Duknovic.**] Sculptor and architect; b. at Trau, Dalmatia, whence his name, c1440; d. after 1509. He was trained in the workshop of Giorgio da Sebenico, and worked at Rome, Hungary, Venice, and Ancona. At Rome he collaborated with Andrea Bregno on the Tebaldi (d. 1466) and Ferrici (d. 1478) tombs in S. Maria sopra Minerva, and on the tomb of Cardinal Pietro Riario (d. 1474) in SS. Apostoli. He worked with Mino da Fiesole in the execution of an altar in S. Marco (1474) and the monument of Pope Paul II (d. 1471). Giovanni, who perhaps designed the monument, Mino da Fiesole, and many assistants worked on the many figure sculptures of the elaborate tomb, the sarcophagus, effigy, and other parts being by Giovanni's own hand, easily distinguishable for his individuality and virility. The tomb was broken up, the base is now in the Louvre, other parts of it are in the Vatican. The tomb of Cardinal Roverella, executed 1476–1477, Church of S. Clemente, Rome, is by Giovanni alone. Under Pope Paul II he was official sculptor of the pope, and for him designed many medals and carried out architectural works, as in the Palazzo Venezia, for which he built the Loggia and the doors. In 1481 he went to the court of King Matthias Corvinus of Hungary, and remained there until shortly after the king's death (1490). In 1498 he was at Venice, and in 1509 he was at Ancona, where he made the tomb of Blessed Girolamo Giannelli.

Giovanni Fiorentino (fyō-ren-tē′nō), **Ser.** Florentine prose writer of the second half of the 14th century. He was a notary who withdrew to the country, for reasons now unknown, and wrote (1378) *Il Pecorone* (*The Numbskull*). It is a collection of fifty stories related, in twenty-five days, by a monk and a nun—a device copied from the *Decameron.* A ballata, of some poetic freshness, follows each two stories. The tales themselves are, in general, retelling of familiar material. That of Gianetto, or the pound of flesh, reappears in Shakespeare's *Merchant of Venice.* The title, *Il Pecorone*, comes from a burlesque sonnet at the end of the collection.

Giovanni Francesco da Rimini (frän-chās′kō dä rē′mē-nē). Painter; b. at Rimini, c1425; d. at Bologna, before 1470. He was influenced by Benozzo Gozzoli and Benedetto Bonfigli, and was active at Bologna, where there is a signed and dated (1459) *Madonna and Child* in the Church of S. Domenico. Other works include *The Virgin and Child with Two An-*

gels, signed and dated (1461), National Gallery, London, a *Madonna and Child Enthroned*, National Gallery of Umbria, Perugia, and paintings at Pesaro, Rome (Vatican), Spoleto, Urbino, Liverpool, Paris, Atlanta (Georgia), Baltimore (Walters Art Gallery), Brooklyn, and elsewhere.

Giovanni Maria da Brescia (mä-rē′ä dä brā′-shä). Engraver; active in the first quarter of the 16th century. He was a Carmelite; was a mediocre draftsman, but preserved in his *Triumph of Trajan* a lost work of Foppa.

Giovanni Martini da Udine (mär-tē′nē dä ö′dē-nā). [Original name, **Giovanni Mioni.**] Venetian painter; b. c1453; d. September 30, 1535. He was the son of Martino da Tolmezzo and the nephew of Domenico da Tolmezzo, and was influenced by Alvise Vivarini and other Venetians. Several of his paintings are at Udine, in the museum, cathedral, and S. Pietro Martire, and in churches in neighboring towns. Others are at Bassano del Grappa, Milan (Brera), Venice (Correr Museum), Verona, National Gallery, London, Walters Art Gallery, Baltimore, and elsewhere. He was also noted as a carver of wooden ecclesiastical furnishings.

Giovannino de' Grassi (jō-vän-nē′nō dā gräs′sē). Lombard architect, sculptor, miniaturist, and draftsman; d. 1398. He carved reliefs, designed stained glass windows, and acted as engineer for the cathedral being built at Milan. His son Salomone, also an artist, was charged with preserving his many drawings and the wooden model of the cathedral he made. No paintings from his hand are extant. As a miniaturist, he, with his son, illuminated a prayer book for Gian Galeazzo Visconti, and he illustrated an encyclopedia of natural history that is now in the Casanatense Library at Rome. Pages from his sketchbook bearing delightful drawings of animals are preserved in the town library at Bergamo. Giovannino de' Grassi worked in the international Gothic style but with fewer Gothic elements and a greater tendency toward naturalism.

Giovannino de' Grassi
Three Tigers
Biblioteca Civica, Bergamo

Giovannino di Pietro (dē pye′trō). See **Zanino.**

Giovenone (jō-vā-nô′nā), **Girolamo.** Painter; b. at Vercelli, c1490; d. 1555. He was active at Vercelli, where his earliest signed and dated (1513) work is in the museum. The influence of Defendente Ferrari, whose pupil he may have been, appears in his early work; that of Gaudenzio Ferrari in his later work. A number of his paintings are in the museum and churches (S. Cristoforo, S. Francesco, S.

Giuliano) at Vercelli, and in churches in the neighborhood. Other examples of his work include a signed and dated (1527) *Madonna and Child*, Carrara Academy, Bergamo, and paintings at Milan (Castello Sforzesco), Pavia, Turin (Sabauda Gallery and Municipal Museum), London, Baltimore (Walters Art Gallery), Boston, Madison (Wisconsin), and elsewhere.

Giovio (jō′vyō), **Paolo.** [Latinized, **Paulus Jovius.**] Historian; b. at Como, April 19, 1483; d. at Florence, December 10, 1552. He studied at Pavia, and under Pomponazzi at Padua, practiced medicine for a time and, above all, traveled. In the course of his restless life he visited many of the cities of Italy, witnessed the sack of Rome (1527) from the Castel Sant' Angelo, where he was shut up with Pope Clement VII, saw the coronation of Charles V at Bologna (1530), visited Germany, and journeyed to France (1533) for the marriage of Catherine de' Medici to the future Henri II of France. He was also an eyewitness to some of the land and naval battles described in his *Historiarum sui temporis*. He had already begun this history of his times when he went to Rome in 1513. Leo X was delighted with it and gave him a warm welcome. The history begins with the year 1494 and is carried to 1547. The early chapters perished in the sack of Rome. Giovio became friendly with Giulio de' Medici who, when he was elevated to the papacy as Pope Clement VII, named Giovio bishop of Nocera (1528). Giovio had also served Adrian VI, whom he later satirized unmercifully. He is said to have retired to Como in disgust when he was not made a cardinal. In Como he built a palace and garden, and began his museum. The palace was decorated with frescoes, many of them executed by his friend Giorgio Vasari, whom he encouraged to write the celebrated and invaluable *Vite de' più eccelenti architetti, pittori e scultori italiani*. Princes and prelates from all of Italy and Europe made gifts to his museum. Giovio's *Elogia*, a series of biographies of eminent Italians, Greeks, Germans, French, and English, living and dead, was supposedly a collection made to explain the portraits in his museum. Giovio was a witness to many of the events he described in his history, and was acquainted with many of the figures whose biographies he wrote. He was an acute observer, a fluent and witty writer, unscrupulous in his application of ridicule when he wished. His histories and biographies were not, as earlier ones had been, mere recitals of events. He fleshed out his work with analyses and study of causes and character. He said he could write with a golden or a silver pen. The gold was used for those he admired or wished to please; the silver was used for malice or vengeance—ridicule, scorn, or satire.

Giraldi (jē-räl′dē), **Giambattista Cinzio.** Man of letters; b. at Ferrara, November, 1504; d. there, December 30, 1573. He taught medicine and philosophy at the University of Ferrara and humane letters at Turin and Pavia and, after 1560, at Mondovì. His *Gli ecatommiti* is a collection of 110 tales, in a Boccaccesque framework. The tellers of the stories are the members of a group traveling from Rome to Marseilles to escape the plague that ravaged Rome after its sack in 1527. The introduction to the stories describes, in vivid and horrifying detail, the sack of the city. The stories, on various themes and revelatory of his understanding of human nature, differ in tone from the majority of the licentious novelle of his time. His treatment of tragic and horrible events, some of which were drawn from life, of lust and crime, show that he knew the difference between good and evil. They deal in detail with the manners and customs and misdeeds of a class that fascinated those who did not belong to it, and thus, though awkwardly constructed and written, were enormously popular and widely translated. Shakespeare drew on his plots for *Othello* and *Measure for Measure*. Giraldi was also a tragic poet. His model for his many tragedies was Seneca. He chose horrifying subjects for his plots, drew some of them from his own novelle, and some from the classical writers. He interrupted the action with long static speeches in the Senecan style, so that despite the horror of the plots the plays are not dramatic. He professed to follow the dramatic rules laid down by Aristotle in the *Poetics*, but thought that Seneca had improved on the Greeks. Passion, crime, and bloodshed, in that order, are the ingredients of his *Orbecche*, written and produced at Ferrara in 1541. It is one of the first modern tragedies on the classical model. (Earlier ones had been adaptations and translations of the classical tragedies.) In the tragedy, Orbecche innocently informs her father Sulmone of his wife's adultery. Sulmone kills his wife Selina. Selina's ghost bedevils Orbecche, who, secretly marries Oronte. Sulmone learns of it through the agency of Selina's ghost, slays Oronte because of his humble birth, as well as Orbecche's children by him, and presents the head and hands of Oronte to Orbecche. Orbecche kills her father and then herself. Giraldi wrote a number of other tragedies. He also wrote two works in which he expressed his views on tragedy, comedy, and the epic, *Intorno al comporre delle comedie e delle tragedie*, and *Intorno al comporre dei romanzi*. In these works he supports the use of the vernacular as a fitting language for the drama. His *Egle* is a pastoral drama of classical derivation.

Giraldi, Giglio Gregorio. [Latinized, **Lilius Gregorius Gyraldus.**] Poet and humanist; b. at Ferrara, June 14, 1479; d. at Rome, February, 1552. In 1514 he went to Rome and entered the service of Pope Leo X as an apostolic protonotary. He remained in this post under Clement VII, and in this time wrote on various learned subjects. After the sack of Rome (1527) he withdrew to Florence and his last years were spent in poverty. Among his writings, the dialogue *De poetis nostrorum temporum* is valuable for its notices of 16th-century Latin poets. His *De deis gentium* was an influential work on mythology in which he set forth the classical myths and gave interpretations. He also left Latin poems and scholarly works.

Girolamo di Benvenuto (jē-rō′lä-mō dē ben-vā-nö′tō). [Also called **Gerolamo del Guasta.**] Painter; b. at Siena, September 23, 1470; d. there, 1524. He was the son and pupil of Benvenuto di Giovanni, with whom he collaborated in Benvenuto's last works. The strongest influence on his work was his father's but in Girolamo, Benvenuto's qualities appear coarsened. An early work, *Assumption* (1498), Diocesan Museum, Montalcino, has elements of the Umbrian school, as well as being very similar to one painted by his father (the Metropolitan Museum, New York), with the exception that Benvenuto's types are more delicate, refined, and elegant than Girolamo's. A later work, a fresco of *The Last Judgment* (1510) for the Basilica of the Osservanza at Siena, has echoes of Signorelli. A number of his works are to be found at Siena, including a *Deposition* and other panels in the Pinacoteca,

Girolamo di Benvenuto
Libyan Sibyl
The British Museum, London

Stigmatization of St. Catherine, in the Oratory, and paintings in other churches. Other works are in churches in the neighborhood, at Montalcino, Montepulciano, Rome (National Gallery and Castel Sant' Angelo), Venice (Ca' d'Oro), Berlin, Dresden, Dublin, Paris, Baltimore (Walters Art Gallery), Cambridge, Denver, Detroit, Hartford, Lewisburg (Pennsylvania), New Haven, New Orleans, Tulsa, Washington, and elsewhere.

thin; ŦH, then; y, you; (variable) d̦ as d or j, s̜ as s or sh, t̜ as t or ch, z̜ as z or zh; ȯ, F. cloche; ü, F. menu; ċh, Sc. loch; ṅ, F. bonbon; ʙ, Sp. Córdoba (sounded almost like v).

Girolamo da Carpi (dä kär′pē). [Also called **Girolamo dei Sellari.**] Painter and architect; b. at Ferrara, 1501; d. there, 1556. His father, Tommaso, was a painter who came from Carpi. Girolamo, an elegant, eclectic mannerist, had at first studied the works of Correggio at Modena and Parma, then fell under the influence of Parmigianino. When he returned to Ferrara he was subjected to the influence of the Ferrarese school, as Dosso Dossi and Garofalo, with the latter of whom he sometimes collaborated. He was much employed by the Estense court in the decoration of their palaces and villas, but the work he did in them has perished except for mural decorations in the Castello at Ferrara. Some of his finest paintings, originally at Ferrara, are at Dresden. Between 1549 and 1554 he was painting at Rome, and the *Adoration of the Child,* now in the Uffizi, Florence, with its background of Roman buildings, was probably painted in this period. Examples of his work now at Rome are in the Capitoline Museum, Doria Pamphili Gallery, and Palazzo Spada. He was noted as a portraitist; a number of his portraits are at Modena, Ferrara, and elsewhere. As an architect, in the style of Bramante and Peruzzi, he was employed by Cardinal Ippolito d'Este, designed a number of palaces at Ferrara, the towers and loggia of the Castello, and the Church of S. Francesco. Under Julius III he continued construction of the Belvedere (begun by Bramante) in the Vatican.

Girolamo da Cremona (dä krā-mō′nä). Miniaturist and painter, of Cremona; active between 1467 and 1483. While still very young he began as a miniaturist, working on the precious Missal of Barbara of Brandenburg (wife of Ludovico III Gonzaga), now in the museum at Mantua. In his solidly constructed figures, vigorously modeled heads, and clear, intense color he reveals himself as a follower of Mantegna. From 1467 to 1473 he worked with Liberale da Verona in the cathedral library at Siena, where he executed a great many miniatures for a number of antiphonaries. Other miniatures are at Chiusi, the Bargello and the National Library, Florence. He is best known for his miniatures, and was called by Bernard Berenson "the most intellectual, imaginative, and accomplished of Italian miniaturists." In his painting, where the influence of Liberale appears as well as that of Mantegna, he loses some of the grace and delicacy of the miniatures. Examples of his painting are in the National Gallery of Umbria at Perugia, the cathedral, Viterbo, and in the Palazzo Venezia and the Church of S. Francesca Romana, Rome.

Girolamo dai Libri (dī lē′brē). Veronese painter and miniaturist; b. at Verona, 1474; d. there, July 2, 1555. His father, Francesco (1451– after 1502), was a gifted miniaturist in the local Gothic tradition. Girolamo was at first strongly influenced in his painting by the techniques of miniature painting he had learned from him. Later the chief influence on this tender and witty painter was that of Mantegna, and to a lesser extent, those of Francesco Morone and other Veronese painters. His Centrego altarpiece (1502), in the Church of S. Anastasia, Verona, in its ample scale and composition shows that he had freed himself from the limitations of miniature painting, as does a *Deposition* at Malcesine. He painted a number of altarpieces. The central panel of a triptych, *The Virgin and Child with St. Anne,* is in the National Gallery, London. Notable in the paintings of Girolamo are his poetic, imaginative, and spacious landscapes, and his warm color. A number of his paintings and miniatures are in the museum at Verona. Other paintings are in several churches in the city and in the neighborhood, and at Bergamo, Venice (Accademia), London, Cleveland (miniature), New York, and elsewhere.

Girolamo del Pacchia (del päk′kyä). See **Del Pacchia, Girolamo.**

Girolamo del Santo (del sän′tō). Painter; b. at Brescia, c1498; d. c1563. His *Madonna Enthroned with Child* is in the Poldi Pezzoli Museum, Milan.

Girolamo da Treviso il Vecchio (dä trā-vē′zō il vek′kyō). See **Pennacchi, Girolamo.**

Girolamo da Udine (dä ö′dē-nā). Painter; documented from 1506; d. 1512. In 1511 he was commissioned to paint a chapel at Udine; work there was completely repainted. The only certain work known to be from his hand is a signed *Coronation of the Virgin,* in the museum at Udine. In this his imitation of the types of Cima da Conegliano is modified by his sense of composition. Other works attributed to him on stylistic grounds are at Padua and Worcester (Massachusetts).

Girolamo da Vicenza (vē-chen′tsä). Painter of Vicenza; active between 1480 and 1510. He was active at Vicenza, where he seems to have been associated with Bartolomeo Montagna, and at Venice. His *Christ Carrying the Cross* is in the Carrara Academy, Bergamo, *Martyrdom of St. Sebastian,* in the Musée Jacquemart-André, Paris, and *The Death and Assumption of the Virgin,* his only signed and dated (1488) work, in the National Gallery, London.

Girolamo Marchesi da Cotignola (mär-kā'zē dä kō-tē-nyō'lä). See **Marchesi, Girolamo.**

Giuliano (jö-lyä'nō), **Pedro.** Original name of Pope **John XXI.**

Giuliano da Maiano (dä mī-ä'nō). [Original name, **Giuliano di Leonardo d'Antonio.**] Architect, sculptor, and worker in intarsia; b. at Maiano (Fiesole), c1431; d. at Naples, 1490. He was the brother of the sculptor Benedetto da Maiano (1442–1497), with whose career his own was closely connected. Giuliano frequently served as the architect for tabernacles, shrines, chapels, and other structures, while Benedetto carried out the sculptural works contained in them. Giuliano altered and restored the cathedral at S. Gimignano (1466), and two years later designed the Chapel of S. Fina in the cathedral; Benedetto later made the altar for the chapel. The cathedral at Faenza was begun (1474) according to Giuliano's design, one inspired by Brunelleschi's Church of S. Lorenzo at Florence. Giuliano designed the tabernacle for *The Madonna of the Olive* (1480), now in Prato; Benedetto executed the terracotta Madonna for it. As an architect, Giuliano followed the style of Brunelleschi, with its refined and elegant architectural elements. His finest work as an architect is perhaps the Spannochi Palace at Siena. For King Ferrante of Naples, he served as architect for, among other things, the Porta Capuana (Capuan Gate) at Naples.

Giuliano da Rimini (dä rē'mē-nē). Riminese painter; d. before 1346. In his work the influence of the earlier Roman school of Pietro Cavallini is subordinate to that of Giotto. His only extant signed work dates from 1307, and is now in the Isabella Stewart Gardner Museum, at Boston. It is a panel of the *Virgin Enthroned, with Saints.* A series of frescoes in the refectory of the abbey at Pomposa (near Ferrara) is attributed to him. They include a *Last Supper,* in which the Apostles are seated at a round table.

Giuliano di Simone da Lucca (dē sē-mō'nā dä lök'kä). Tuscan painter, documented from 1389. At the foot of the Madonna's throne in his *Madonna and Child Enthroned with Saints,* National Gallery, Parma, is a prone figure of Eve; nearby is an undulating serpent with a woman's head. Similar paintings of the Madonna with Eve and a serpent at her feet are at Leghorn and Paris. The only other work known by him is a signed and dated (1389) polyptych in S. Michele, Castiglione Garfagnana.

Giuliano Fiorentino (fyō-ren-tē'nō). Tuscan sculptor; active in the first quarter of the 15th century. He was a sculptor of the transition from Gothic to Renaissance sculpture. He is identified with the sculptor called il Facchino who worked (1407) under Ghiberti on the bronze doors for the Baptistery. Other works included a statue (1410–1422) for the façade of the cathedral of Florence, and twelve bas-reliefs (1418–1424) in alabaster with stories from the Old and New Testaments, carved in Valencia, Spain, for the façade of the cathedral.

Giulio Romano (jö'lyō rō-mä'nō). [Original name, **Giulio Pippi.**] Painter and architect; b. at Rome, in 1492 according to Vasari, but in 1499 according to others; d. at Mantua, November 1, 1546. The only important artist of the Renaissance to be born at Rome, he grew up in the shadow of Imperial ruins, a fact that profoundly influenced his work. The impression made on him by the reliefs of the Column of Trajan and the ruined shells of ancient buildings appears in much of his work. While still a youth he worked in the studio of Raphael, whose most faithful pupil and assistant he became, painting from his cartoons and drawings. He may have made drawings for *The Fire in the Borgo* in the *Stanza dell' Incendio* in the Vatican, in the execution of which he assisted Raphael. In 1517 he finished the monochrome figures (later repainted) on the dado in the same room. Between 1516 and 1518 under Raphael's direction he supervised the decoration of Raphael's new *loggie* in the Vatican and painted several of the frescoes himself, including the grandiose and catastrophic *Jacob's Dream* and *The Deluge.* In 1518 he finished a large part of the paintings intended for Francis I as well as the scenes of *The Fable of Psyche* in the Chigi Villa (now the Farnesina). His hand is obvious in almost all of the paintings of Raphael's last years, including such works as *The Transfiguration*, Vatican, to which, according to Vasari, Raphael put the finishing touches with his dying breath—a legend. Other works of Raphael in which he assisted are *St. Michael* and *Holy Family*, Louvre, Paris, painted for Francis I. Several hundred of his splendid drawings survive. Those executed while he was still under the aegis of Raphael are meticulous, disciplined figures. Those executed later are notable for their animation, fantasy, and spontaneity—qualities that were frequently lost when the matter of the drawings was committed to paint. By talent and temperament he tended toward mannerism, with a hard touch and a reddish color, and a strong chiaroscuro relief obtained with dark shadows and metallic highlights. His spirit and ideas were far from the serenity and balance of Raphael. His early and continued training in Raphael's studio was of profound importance for his technique but had little effect on his essentially violent temperament, nor had he much contact with other painters who influenced him. After the death of Raphael (1520) he inherited Raphael's studio and the commissions then in process of execution in it. Clement VII called on him to finish the decorations of the *Stanze*. Following the general scheme of Raphael he executed the stories of Constantine in the *Sala di Costantino* with the assistance of Francesco Penni and Raffaellino del Colle, who often worked with him. Perhaps the earliest of his works is the *Madonna and Child with the Infant St. John*, Louvre. Other works of his Roman period include a *Holy Family*, called *La Perla*, Prado, Madrid, one of his best easel paintings (when the painting came into the possession of Philip IV of Spain he called it "a pearl among pictures"); *The Martyrdom of St. Stephen*, Church of S. Stefano, Genoa, with its atmosphere of terror and background of identifiable Roman ruins; and works at Naples, the Barberini Palace and Church of S. Maria dell' Anima, Rome, and Moscow. A *Portrait of Bindo Altoviti*, National Gallery, Washington, is attributed to him; the soft, rather effeminate youth of the portrait is in sharp

GIULIO ROMANO
River-God Holding a Cornucopia
The British Museum, London

fat, fāte, fär, fâll, ȧsk, fãre; net, mē, hėr; pin, pīne; not, nōte, möve, nôr; up, lūte, pu̇ll; oi, oil; ou, out; (lightened) ẹlect, agọny, ụnite; (obscured) errạnt, ardẹnt, actọr; ch, chip; g, go; th, contrast to the bust of Bindo Altoviti, the man, by Cellini, in the Isabella Stewart Gardner Museum, Boston.

He also served Raphael in the capacity of architect, carrying out the latter's plans for the villa, now known as the Villa Madama, for Cardinal Giulio de' Medici (later Clement VII), where he did much of the painting and decorating as well. Other buildings he worked on at Rome included the Villa Lante, with its classically simple, elegant and charming façade, and the Palazzo Maccarani (now Di Brazzà), still in the Bramante tradition of elegant austerity and the separation of architectural elements. In 1524 he went to Mantua, where he was presented to Federigo Gonzaga (Isabella d'Este's son) by Baldassare Castiglione. At Mantua he soon established himself as court architect, was awarded many honors by Federigo, and was made a citizen of Mantua. He held a number of city offices and perquisites from which he received revenues. Under Federigo and his successor, Cardinal Ercole Gonzaga, Giulio practically rebuilt Mantua and protected it from the periodic flooding of the Mincio. His greatest achievement was the Palazzo del Tè (1526–1535), a pleasure villa for Federigo on the outskirts of Mantua. In this, his architectural masterpiece, he had the opportunity to plan the entire building and design the interior decoration as a unit. The square building built around a courtyard, seemingly in the style of a classical Roman villa, incorporates Giulio's sophisticated fancies in its asymmetries. Every inch of the interior carries decoration designed by Giulio and executed with assistants. Mythological and other stories are frescoed on the walls, vaults, lunettes and ceilings. Friezes and medallions form additional decoration. Lifesize pictures of Federigo's favorite stallions are frescoed on the walls of the largest salon (there are no bedrooms as the villa was intended for day excursions). Among the mythological scenes is a terrifying rendering of the defeat of the Giants who had besieged Olympus. Over the chimneypiece Giulio painted the Giants hurtling downward so that when the fire was lighted they seemed to be falling into it. The whole somewhat disturbing and entirely fascinating building is a superb example of mannerist architectural style. When Charles V was to visit Mantua, Giulio was charged with connecting the ducal palace to the *Castello*. He did it by a series of rooms, loggias, courtyards, galleries, and monumental staircases to make of the palace, with its more than 500 rooms, a luxurious court residence exceeded in size only by the Vatican among Italian palaces. He built other buildings in the countryside but little remains of them with the exception of the reconstruction of the Basilica of S. Benedetto in Polirone. He carried out a similar reconstruction of the cathedral at Mantua for Cardinal Ercole. Paintings of his Mantua years include a *Nativity*, Louvre; *Madonna of the Basin*, Dresden; mythological works, London, and others; a portrait presumed to be of Isabella

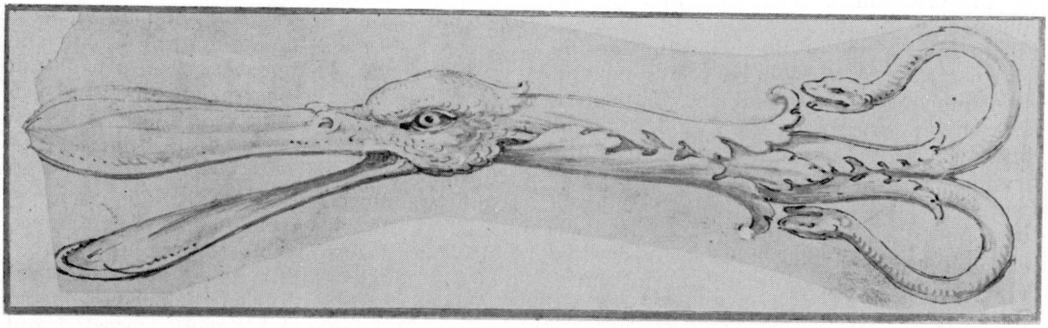

GIULIO ROMANO
Design for a pair of tongs
The British Museum, London

d'Este, Hampton Court, is attributed to him. He made cartoons for tapestries, designs for cups, bowls, platters, other vessels, belts, and ornaments. His own house still stands at Mantua. In designing it he combined architectural elements, such as pediments over windows within arches, in a manner far from the separation of elements that imparted such elegance to the style of Bramante. His combination of textures gives the façade a somewhat busy air. A vigorous, ingenious, endlessly inventive artist, he overflowed with ideas, which he sometimes expressed with elegance, sometimes with vulgarity, but usually with exuberance, whether in painting or in architecture.

Giunta Pisano (jön′tä pē-sä′nō). Painter, active in the first half of the 13th century. Frescoes, now much mutilated, in the nave of the Lower Church of the Basilica of San Francesco at Assisi are attributed to him. A *Cross* (1236), said to have been painted for Fra Elia, is now lost. Other crosses signed by him are at Assisi (S. Maria degli Angeli), Bologna (S. Domenico), and Pisa (Museo Nazionale di S. Matteo).

Giustiniani (jös-tē-nyä′nē), **Agostino Pantaleone.** Ecclesiastic and philologist; b. at Genoa, 1479; lost at sea, 1536. He published a polyglot edition of the Psalter in 1516.

Giustiniani, Bernardo. Statesman, humanist, and historian; b. 1408; d. 1489. He was educated at Venice by Guarino da Verona, Filelfo and George of Trebizond. Learned in law, poetry, and history, he was a man of wide humanist culture, and one who served his state well. Among his various public duties, he served as captain of Padua, ambassador to Louis XI of France, and to popes Paul II and Sixtus IV, and as a member of the Council of Ten. His great interest was in history, and to that interest he devoted his leisure time. He wrote a life of his uncle, San Lorenzo, and a long and celebrated history of Venice, *De origine Urbis Venetiarum* . . . , which, for his willingness to discard popular tradition in favor of documents, earned him the title "Father of Venetian history."

Giustiniani, Leonardo. Statesman, humanist, and poet; b. at Venice, 1388; d. there, in November, 1446. He was a member of a noble Venetian family, and studied under Guarino da Verona. A man of excellent taste, gifted with eloquence and endowed with a broad culture, he enjoyed a wide acquaintance among the humanists of his time. He collected a rich library of Greek and Latin manuscripts, as well as manuscripts in Italian. His career was in the service of the Republic; he played an important part in the war between Venice and the Visconti of Milan; and was chosen (1428) a member of the Council of Ten. Humanism was an avocation with him. He was learned in Latin and Greek, translated some of Plutarch, wrote gay lyrics, many *laude* (songs of praise, commendation, etc.), and wrote Latin letters that are among the most sincere and spontaneous of the day. His fame, however, rests on his popular songs in the Venetian dialect, set to music of his own composing, that completely capture the folk spirit and became enormously popular.

Giustiniani, Paolo. Dominican; b. at Genoa, 1444; d. at Buda, 1502. Member of an illustrious Genoese family, he was active at Rome in the Curia, and was the pope's legate to Hungary.

Giusto (jös′tō), **Andrea di.** See **Andrea di Giusto.**

Giusto d'Andrea (dän-drā′ä). Painter; b. at Florence, 1440; d. there, 1496. He was the son of Andrea di Giusto and, like his father, was not of the first rank. He was a pupil of Neri di Bicci from 1458 to 1460, then worked with Filippo Lippi; and about 1465 assisted Benozzo Gozzoli at S. Gimignano and Certaldo. The great number of paintings he churned out appear in churches and galleries in Tuscany and beyond its confines. They show him to have been a diligent but mediocre painter, who repeated, without understanding, the forms of contemporary masters. An *Annunciation*, at Yale University, New Haven, is the standard arrangement of this subject, with receding arches that are somewhat successful in achieving spatial values. It is one of his more animated and less labored works. Painted by him to designs by Benozzo are some figures of saints and some architectural painting in the chapel of S. Agostino at S. Gimignano. Also at S. Gimignano are parts of a fresco on *The Martyrdom of St. Sebastian*, in the cathedral. The design for the fresco was by Benozzo. Other examples of his work are several panels attributed to him in the Accademia, Florence, some works at Fiesole, Parma, Pisa, and at San Miniato al Tedesco.

Giusto Menabuoi da Padova (mā-nä-bö-ō′ē dä pä′dō-vä). Paduan painter; d. before April 30, 1393. He was originally from Florence, where his name was on the roster of painters, but passed most of his life at Padua. An undistinguished provincial painter, his work is appealing for its decorative qualities and for its warm, bright colors. Influences of Giovanni da Milano, the Sienese, and the Paduan painters appear in his work. His most important undertaking is a series of naïvely inventive frescoes, of nearly 100 scenes, in the Baptistery at Padua, executed 1376–1378. They represent scenes from the Old and the New Testaments. Frescoes he painted in the Chapel of Beato Luca Belludi, in the Basilica of St. Anthony at Padua, have been so much repainted as to almost destroy his work. Other works are two figures of *Madonna Nursing the Holy Child*, Scrovegni Chapel, and an elaborate polyptych, *Madonna and Child Enthroned*, with two tiers of saints in side panels, on the altar of the Baptistery, Padua. A signed and dated (1367) triptych, *Coronation of the Virgin* is at London, and panels from a polyptych are at Athens, Georgia.

Glareanus (glä-rā-ä′nůs). [Original name, **Heinrich Loriti.**] Swiss humanist; b. at Mollis, Switzerland, 1488; d. at Freiburg im Breisgau, Germany, 1563. He was crowned (1512) poet laureate by the emperor Maximilian I, became (1521) professor of belles lettres at the Collège de France, and subsequently founded a school for belles lettres at Freiburg im Breisgau. He favored the Reformation for a time, but was induced by the disturbances at Basel in 1529 to withdraw his support. He published *De geographia liber* (1527), *Helvetiae descriptio* (in verse), numerous studies on Latin authors, and other works.

Gobellinus (gō-bel-lī′nus), **Johann.** German cleric and scribe who was commissioned to make a copy of the *Commentaries* (*Pio II Comentarii rerum memorabilium quae temporibus suis contigerunt*) of Pope Pius II. He made a faithful copy and signed his name to it, as was the custom of copyists at the time. Because his name was signed to the *Commentaries,* it was for long thought that he had written them. It was not until 1883 that a codex was discovered in the Vatican that was partly written in Pius II's own hand and partly in that of his secretary, Giovanni Antonio Campano, and proved that Pius had written or dictated the *Commentaries* himself.

Golden Bull. Bull published at the Diet of Nuremberg by the emperor Charles IV in 1356. It was so named from its golden seal. It fixed the seven princes who had the right to elect the German kings, the so-called kings of the Romans. The seven princes were: the archbishops of Mainz, Trier, and Cologne, the king of Bohemia, the count palatine of the Rhine, the duke of Saxony, and the margrave of Brandenburg. Until the time of Maximilian I (1493–1519), the kings of the Romans were not called Holy Roman Emperors until after coronation by the pope. The Golden Bull also regulated the procedures and ceremonies connected with the election, and established the rule of primogeniture for the electors.

Golden Legend. Collection of biographies of saints, compiled by Jacobus of Voragine (or Varagine) in the 13th century. The book, arranged as a calendar of the Christian year, was one of the most popular works of the Middle Ages and held its audience until the critical eye of the Renaissance examined its improbabilities and pedestrian style and brought it into disrepute as real biographical history. Renaissance painters, however, continued, as earlier painters had done, to draw the subject matter of many paintings from the Golden Legend. (Its original name, *Legenda sanctorum,* was soon changed, and the work came to be called *Legenda aurea.*) Though its reputation as a devotional inspiration is somewhat impaired, the work remains a storehouse of medieval folklore. It was translated from the original Latin into the several vernacular tongues of Europe before the 16th century. An English translation was printed (1483) by Caxton.

Golden Rose. Jewel consisting of roses and buds on one stem, all of gold, and set with sapphires or other gems, given by the pope to a church or sovereign, general, or other distinguished person, as a mark of esteem, for loyalty to the Holy See.

Goldschmid (golt′shmēd), **George.** Original name of **Fabricius, Georg.**

Gómara (gō′mä-rä) or **Gómora** (gō′mō-rä), **Francisco López de.** Spanish historian; b. at Seville, Spain, 1510; d. after 1559. He was a priest, and in 1540 became secretary and chaplain to Hernando Cortés, but it does not appear that he was ever in America. His *Historia general de las Indias* was first published at Saragossa (1552–1553) in two folio parts; the second part, which relates to Mexico, appeared in later editions with the separate title *Crónica de la Nueva España con la Conquista de Mexico*. Gómara's work was very popular, and there are many editions in Spanish, French, Italian, and English.

Gonfaloniere (gōn-fä-lō-nye′rā). A chief magistrate in several Italian states; at Florence, the first among the priors that formed the governing body. The eight priors and the gonfaloniere served for a term of two months. The name gonfaloniere is also applied to an official appointed by the pope, who bore the standard of the Church. The term, in all its senses, is an extension of the word *gonfalone*, a standard or banner.

Góngora Marmolejo (gông′gō-rä mär-mō-le′hō), **Alonso de.** Spanish soldier and historian; b. at Carmona, Seville, Spain, c1510; d. in Chile, in January, 1576. He served in Peru, went to Chile in 1549 and took an active part in the Araucanian wars, was a captain, but never had any important commissions. In his latter years he lived at Santiago. His *Historia de Chile*, written between 1572 and 1575, is preserved in the original manuscript at Madrid. It was first published in 1850, in the *Memorial historico Español*, and republished in the *Colección de historiadores de Chile*, 1862. It gives the history of Chile down to 1575, and is the best of the early works on that subject.

Gonzaga (gōn-tsä′gä). An illustrious family of Mantua, members of which, as captains general, marquesses, and dukes, ruled Mantua from 1328 to 1707. Luigi Gonzaga (1267–1360), member of an old Mantuan family, established the family power in 1328 when he overcame the captain general Passarino Bonacolsi. Luigi was elected captain general in his place. He was succeeded by his son Guido, captain general from 1360 to 1369. Jealousy among Guido's three sons led to the murder of his heir, Ugolino (1362), and the Mantuans elected a second son, Ludovico (called Ludovico II) to succeed Guido. By the time Ludovico II assumed power Mantua was rich and prosperous and the Gonzaga family had acquired great wealth. Ludovico (captain general, 1369–1382) was followed by his son Francesco I (captain general, 1382–1407), who defeated the forces of Gian Galeazzo Visconti (1397), and served as a captain in the pay of Venice. Gianfrancesco (1395–1444), a child when his father Francesco died and left him a ward of Venice, was nevertheless made captain general and Mantua was governed during his minority by regents. He became the first marquess of Mantua under a patent granted by the Emperor Sigismund (1433). Two of his four sons died at early ages. Ludovico, his heir, jealous of his father's preference for his brother, Carlo, flung himself out of Mantua and entered the service of Milan. Since his father was in the pay of the Venetians, historic rivals of Milan, this was a political embarrassment. In due course, Gianfrancesco was reconciled with Ludovico, who succeeded him as Ludovico III, second marquess of Mantua (1444–1478). Because of the history of rivalry for the succession between sons of the family, it became a tradition for the eldest son to become a man of arms and the heir, and for second sons to enter the Church. Ludovico III's second son, Francesco, became the first Gonzaga cardinal (1461). (The family, consisting of many branches holding various areas as lands were divided among the sons by will, contributed ten cardinals to the Church, in addition to many other prelates.) Under Ludovico III the court of Mantua was one of the most brilliant of Italy. His realm was prosperous through its cloth trade, the laws were administered equitably, and a great building program was begun. Educated by the famous teacher Vittorino da Feltre, Ludovico was, in addition to being an able general, a highly cultivated man. He was the patron of artists, as Mantegna, men of letters, architects, and poets. He married the German princess Barbara of Brandenburg, thus allying his house with the emperor. Their eldest son was Federigo I (b. 1442), who succeeded as third marquess of Mantua (1478). He also was a soldier and a builder, and married a German princess, Margaret of Bavaria. Their eldest son was Francesco II (b. 1466), the fourth marquess of Mantua. He married Isabella d'Este and succeeded to the marquisate in 1484. He was often at war, as a captain in the service of one prince or republic or another, and is remembered as the victor, as he was considered in Italy at that time, over Charles VIII at Fornovo (1495), and for his famous stable. His wife Isabella, a great patron of the arts and a notable and avid collector, overshadowed him in cultivation, intelligence, and statecraft, and was frequently left in charge of the government. Federigo II became the fifth marquess of Mantua on the death of his father (1519). His younger brother Ercole became the second Gonzaga cardinal, thanks largely to Isabella's efforts in behalf of her son, and was an illustrious prince of the Church. Federigo II supported the imperial party as against the French in the wars between the Emperor Charles V and France (this was his mother's policy), and in consequence Mantua emerged from the struggles between Spain and France that left much of Italy in ruins and completely disorganized, stronger than ever for having supported the winning side. As a reward for his support, Charles V made Mantua a duchy and created Federigo II the first duke (1530). His son Francesco (d. 1550) became the second duke (1540) but died at the age of 17, and was succeeded by his brother Guglielmo I (d. 1586), under whom Mantua achieved new heights of splendor and prosperity. The last duke in the male line of the Gonzaga died in 1627. After a bloody struggle, in which Mantua was sacked and many of its treasures destroyed or carried off, a French branch of the family gained control. The last duke of this branch went into exile (1707) and Mantua was annexed to Austria (1708).

Because of the location of Mantua, it was vulnerable to the ambitions of Venice and the Visconti and Milan. In general, the Gonzaga maintained the independence of their territory by judicious shifting of alliances and the maintenance of a balance between its two powerful neighbors. Thanks to this policy, and perhaps also to the continuity of the succession in a family that produced capable and, on the whole, judicious rulers, Mantua was one of the most stable and prosperous princedoms of the peninsula. The Gonzaga presided over a highly cultivated and splendid court. They were patrons of art and literature, and great builders who transformed Mantua. They gave to it such outstanding examples of Renaissance architecture as the Church of S. Sebastian, the basilica of S. Andrea, and the Palazzo del Tè. Andrea Mantegna, Leon Battista Alberti, and Giulio Romano were outstanding contributors to the magnificence of the city. Poliziano visited there, as well as Petrarch. Baldassare Castiglione was an adviser. Titian, Tintoretto, and Correggio were represented in the great art collections. Under the Gonzaga the economy flourished and the laws were administered with a justice that was rare. The ducal palace was renovated and added to, to make of it a bewildering complex of more than 500 rooms and fifteen courtyards. Among the many rooms is a set of apartments, including the staircases and chapel, all built to a miniature scale, for the comfort of the dwarfs that the Gonzaga kept for their entertainment and whom they tended and regarded with great affection. Also in the palace, in addition to splendid halls with magnificent ceilings, is the *Sala degli Sposi*, decorated by Mantegna, and including in its scenes portraits of members of the family of Ludovico III. The *Paradiso* is a set of exquisite rooms in the palace in which Isabella d'Este housed her priceless collections, and to which she withdrew for reflection, the writing of the thousands of letters (many of which are extant) on all sorts of subjects, and solace for her spirit. The rooms, which were ruined in the sack of 1630 and again despoiled by the French (1797), have been restored, but the precious collections were sold and scattered in the 17th century. See separate entries below.

Gonzaga, Cecilia. Daughter of Gianfrancesco Gonzaga (1395–1444) and Paola Malatesta da Rimini. Her father desired to marry her to Oddantonio da Montefeltro of Urbino. The marriage was distasteful to her and she refused. Supported by the famous teacher Vittorino da Feltre in her refusal, she was finally allowed to enter a convent, where she took the name Suor Chiara, and where she remained thirty years.

Gonzaga, Cesare. Knight of St. John of Jerusalem; b. 1475; d. 1512. He was a member of a younger branch of the Mantuan house of Gonzaga, and was a cousin and close friend of Castiglione, with whom he was at the court of Guidobaldo da Montefeltro at Urbino in 1504. After the death of Guidobaldo (1508), he remained for some time in the service of Francesco Maria della Rovere, Guidobaldo's successor. He also served as Pope Leo X's ambassador to Charles V.

Gonzaga, Curzio. Poet and humanist; b. at Mantua, c1536; d. April 5, 1599. Though destined for the Church, he devoted himself instead to arms and the study of poetry. His kinsman, Cardinal Ercole Gonzaga, sent him

(1559) as a delegate for the peace of Cateau-Cambrésis (by which, among other things, the French accepted Spanish dominance in Italy), and later took him to Rome. Curzio made a long stay there and took an active part in the city's literary life. He was a member of the academy founded at Rome by Cardinal Borromeo, and was a friend of Tasso. His chief work is the poem of chivalry *Il Fidamante* (Mantua, 1583), a poetic account of the great deeds performed by the lover of a beautiful but cold-hearted lady. He also wrote a comedy, *Gli inganni* (Venice, 1592), and published his lyrics.

Gonzaga, Elizabetta. Duchess of Urbino; b. 1471; d. January 28, 1526. She was the daughter of the Marquess Federigo Gonzaga of Mantua, and the youngest sister of his successor, the Marquess Francesco Gonzaga. In October, 1489, she married Guidobaldo, duke of Urbino. In January, 1502, Lucrezia Borgia passed through Urbino on her way to be married to her third husband, Alfonso d'Este, at Ferrara. Pope Alexander VI required the duchess to accompany his daughter Lucrezia to Ferrara. Following that arduous journey in the middle of winter, Elizabetta went to Venice with Isabella d'Este, and then returned with her to Mantua. Thus she was away from Urbino when her husband's state was treacherously attacked and taken by Lucrezia's brother, Cesare Borgia. On the fall of Cesare (August, 1503), she and Guidobaldo returned to Urbino. Because of his health and the semi-retired life he led, she was the presiding genius of the urbane and elegant court that was maintained at Urbino. Castiglione has immortalized the atmosphere of the court, his adored duchess, and the evenings passed in her salon in the ducal palace in his *Il Cortegiano*. The sparkling Emilia Pia, widow of Guidobaldo's half brother Antonio, was Elizabetta's constant companion. In addition, she enjoyed the ardent and unswerving affection of her sister-in-law, Isabella d'Este. Of indifferent health herself, she was devoted to her ailing husband and cared for him in his many illnesses with unfailing tenderness. Highly cultivated, grave, and gracious, she won the devotion of those around her, was on good terms with her husband's adopted successor, Francesco della Rovere, and maintained affectionate relations with him following her husband's death (1508) until her own. A portrait of her by Raphael is in the Uffizi at Florence.

Gonzaga, Ercole. Cardinal; b. 1505; d. at Trent, March 8, 1563. He was the second son of Francesco II Gonzaga and Isabella d'Este. In the Gonzaga tradition of second sons, he was destined for a career in the Church. In 1521 he was made a bishop, and then went to Bologna to complete his studies under Lazzaro Buonamici, one of the foremost teachers of the day. He was an industrious and able student, and completed his studies in 1525. The following year he was at Rome, and through the tireless efforts of his mother received the red hat of a cardinal (1527). A highly cultivated man, he was also extremely able and was noted for his integrity, and wielded great influence at the papal court. In 1540 his brother Federigo died, and he assumed the regency with Margherita of Monferrato, Federigo's wife, during the minority of his seven-year-old nephew Francesco. He was a just and able administrator; chose capable men for high posts, put the financial affairs of Mantua in order, promoted industry, and attempted to curb the luxury that was enveloping the court. He encouraged art and letters, was a friend of Bembo, Sadoleto, and other leading humanists; he concerned himself with the education of the young members of the family, gave them the best teachers, and instilled in them a love of learning. His constant care was for the well-being of Mantua. In 1550 the young duke died and Cardinal Ercole took up again his beneficent, enlightened, and effective administration of Mantua. In this period he established standards for weights and measures and saw that they were observed. Known for his integrity, ability, and purity of life, he was favored by many in the conclave following the death of Pope Paul IV (1559), but the Farnese opposed him and Pius IV was elected. When the Council of Trent reconvened (1561) he was one of the pope's five representatives. As president of it, his aim was moderation and conciliation. Among his writings on ecclesiastical subjects are his *Responsio ad cardin. a Lotheringia nomine synodi Tridentinae* (Pavia, 1563), and *Le costituzioni per il clero* (Mantua, 1564). Intelligent, of unquestioned integrity and purity, firm, and just, Cardinal Ercole was an outstanding prince of the Church as well as a statesman of the first rank. His life and deeds formed a link between the brilliant Renaissance court of his mother Isabella d'Este and the austere beginnings of the Counter-Reformation.

Gonzaga, Federigo I. Third marquess of Mantua; b. 1442; d. at Mantua, 1484. He was the son of Ludovico III and Barbara of Brandenburg. According to contemporary accounts, he was loth to marry the German princess, Margaret of Bavaria, his father had chosen for him and fled Mantua with six servants. He set out for Naples, was robbed on the way, and fell ill when he arrived at Naples. His servants kept his identity a secret and loyally ministered to him and sustained him by engaging in all sorts of menial work. His distracted mother sent couriers throughout Italy in an attempt to learn what had become of him, while his father refused to have his name mentioned. The couriers arrived at last at Naples, and through the cooperation of the king the "seven men of Lombardy" were brought before the couriers, lacking Federigo who was ill. They gave false names but were recognized by the messengers of the Marchioness Barbara. Federigo returned to Mantua and by the pleas of his mother was forgiven by Ludovico and married (1463) Margaret of Bavaria. It was for this couple that Andrea Mantegna painted the *Sala degli Sposi* in the ducal palace, a glory of Mantua and one of the greatest of Renaissance treasures. Federigo, a soldier and a builder, fought in behalf of Milan (1478). Before he died he contracted for his son Francesco a marriage with Isabella d'Este, who became one of the most famous women of her day. Federigo was succeeded by Francesco as marquess of Mantua.

Gonzaga, Federigo II. First Duke of Mantua; b. May 17, 1500; d. at Marmirola, June 28, 1540. He was the son of Francesco Gonzaga and Isabella d'Este of Ferrara. As a child he was sent to Rome as a hostage of Pope Julius II in return for the pope's good offices in securing the release of his father (1510) from the Venetians. The pope became devoted to his winning hostage. After several years he was restored to his family. He succeeded his father as marquess of Mantua on April 3, 1519. After fighting against the French at Pavia (1522) and serving as captain of the papal armies, he adopted a policy of support of Charles V, the emperor, largely on the advice of his mother. Because of this support of the imperial cause, Mantua emerged from the wars between the French and the empire, fought on Italian soil, stronger than ever. To reward him, Charles raised Mantua from a marquisate to a duchy, and in a magnificent ceremony before the doors of the cathedral at Mantua proclaimed him duke on April 8, 1530. Federigo had married (October, 1531) Margherita, daughter and heiress of the marquess of Monferrato, and thus united that marquisate to his own. It became a duchy in 1536, but as Savoy continued to claim it this apparent addition to the power of the Gonzaga became a source of strife in the future. Federigo, in the tradition of his family, was a builder and patron of the arts. Giulio Romano, who worked long and effectively at Mantua, decorated halls in the ducal palace. Federigo had the Palazzo del Tè built on designs by Giulio Romano. It was to serve as a summer palace. Among the many splendidly decorated rooms is one that has six pictures, lifesize, of Federigo's favorite horses. Another room shows the giants attacking Olympus, the scenes painted by Giulio Romano. Federigo's children were: Francesco, the heir, Guglielmo, Ludovico, and Isabella.

Gonzaga, Feltrino. Mantuan soldier; d. at Padua, 1374. He was the son of Luigi Gonzaga, and the brother of Guido and Filippino Gonzaga. With his brother Filippino, he was named imperial vicar of Reggio (1349). After the death of Filippino he seized Reggio for himself and fortified it, and refused to give it up. His nephew Ugolino tried unsuccessfully to dislodge him (1359). Feltrino's rule was harsh. The Reggians rose up against him during the wars with the Visconti of Milan and Feltrino was forced to flee to Padua (1371). His son Guido sold Reggio to the Milanese for 50,000 gold florins. From the castles and their surrounding territory that Guido kept for himself arose a new branch of the family.

Gonzaga, Ferrante. Mantuan soldier and count of Guastalla; b. 1507; d. November 15, 1557. He was the third son of the marquess Francesco II Gonzaga and Isabella d'Este, and was early directed toward a military career, a career which, on the advice and policy of his mother, he made in the service of the emperor. He took part in the imperial expedition against Rome and was able to save his mother, who was visiting there and was in danger during the sack (1527). In 1530 he succeeded the Prince of Orange as commander of the imperial troops and reduced Florence. He fought in the Romagna, in Lombardy, accompanied Charles V when he visited Mantua for the second time (1532), and was in the imperial expedition against Tunis. Charles made him vicar of Sicily and later, for his brilliant action in an invasion of Provence (1536) made him count of Guastalla (October 3, 1539). In 1540, with his brother, Cardinal Ercole, and his sister-in-law, Margherita, he was a member of the regency that governed Mantua in the minority of his nephew, Francesco III. His career was one of unchecked success until Charles V named him governor of the Duchy of Milan. Then fortune went against him. He had financial difficulties, and he gave Charles poor advice, and was unsuccessful in a war he had undertaken against the French at Parma. Charles dismissed him and he went to Guastalla, removed agents there who had been faithless, and set about reorganizing his state. In 1557, Philip II, son and successor of Charles V, sent him to Flanders. There he took part in the campaign and victory over the French at St. Quentin (1557). Worn out by the hard campaigns of his life, he fell sick and died. He left the countship of Guastalla to his eldest son Cesare.

Gonzaga, Filippino. Mantuan soldier; d. 1356. He was the son of Luigi Gonzaga, and the brother of Guido and Feltrino Gonzaga. An expert in the art of war, he defeated the forces of the Visconti (September, 1348), sent against Mantua, and, with his brother Feltrino, was named imperial vicar of Reggio (1349).

Gonzaga, Francesco. Cardinal; b. at Mantua, 1444; d. at Bologna, October 22, 1483. He was the son of Ludovico III Gonzaga and Barbara of Brandenburg. Pope Pius II, in Mantua (1459) for the Congress held there to raise a crusade against the Turks, was charmed by the cultivated Gonzaga family. In 1461 he made Francesco a cardinal. (The return of Francesco from Rome, with the red hat, is shown in a Mantegna painting in the *Sala degli Sposi* in the ducal palace at Mantua.) In 1466 he became bishop of Mantua, and in 1471 was named papal legate of Bologna. As cardinal legate he returned to Mantua (1472), bringing Leon Battista Alberti and the poet Poliziano with him, and during Poliziano's stay at Mantua the poet's *Orfeo* was performed. Francesco shared his father's love of art and letters; on his way to Mantua in 1472 he had requested that Mantegna be sent to meet him so that he could show him his collection of antiques. An intelligent, urbane, and charming man, he was known for his kindness, his generosity, and his good character, and was very influential at Rome; he was also sometimes criticized for his worldliness.

Gonzaga, Francesco I. Captain general and lord of Mantua; b. c1366; d. March 17, 1407. He was the son of Ludovico Gonzaga (d. 1382). In fulfillment of the terms of a peace between the Milanese and the Mantuans, made by the Emperor Charles IV in 1368, Francesco married Agnese, daughter of Bernabò Visconti, at Milan in 1380. She brought him a dowry of 50,000 florins. Francesco was his father's heir but did not succeed immediately on his father's death, as he was too young. He assumed the rule of Mantua in 1388. He was loyal to the treaty with Milan and seemed to be on good terms with Gian Galeazzo Visconti even after the latter had seized and put to death Bernabò, the father of his wife. But Gian Galeazzo had ambitions for winning control of all Italy, either by arms or by intrigue. Allegedly by an infamous plot, involving forged letters, he made Francesco believe that his wife was unfaithful and was planning his murder. Francesco believed the reports, had Agnese tried, condemned, and secretly beheaded in the palace (February 7, 1391). A secretary was strangled in prison for his alleged part in her infidelities. It was only later that Francesco discovered that he had been duped. Thereafter, he entered a league against the Visconti. In April, 1397, Gian Galeazzo sent his armies against Mantua, claiming vengeance for the death of Agnese. Francesco and his allies held off the Milanese, destroyed Gian Galeazzo's flotilla on the Po (August, 1397), pursued his generals, and took 8,000 prisoners. In May, 1398, a truce of ten years was proclaimed. In 1405 Venice offered Francesco the position of captain general, and for his employers he won Verona and Padua. In addition to being a great captain in the tradition of the Gonzaga, Francesco was a patron of the arts and a builder. He added to the *Castello* (the ducal palace) begun by the Bonacolsi family in the

13th century. He was a good ruler who reformed the statutes of the city and saw to it that they were administered evenly. In 1403 the Emperor Wenceslas III gave him a patent as marquess of Mantua, but as Francesco did not care to pay the sum demanded by the greedy and needy Wenceslas in return, he did not take up the patent. Francesco was succeeded by his son Gianfrancesco, whom he left as a ward of Venice.

Gonzaga, Francesco II. Fourth marquess of Mantua; b. 1466; d. March 29, 1519. He was the son of Federigo Gonzaga and Margaret of Bavaria, and succeeded his father (July 24, 1484) at the age of 18. He was brought up in a court that was a center of culture, and was himself a cultivated man. In the tradition of the marquesses of Mantua he became a soldier and fought for others. He was unquestionably brave, but won an undeserved reputation as a general. His great interest was in the breeding and training of horses, and those from his stables were famous throughout Europe. In the horse races that were such a feature of the many festive occasions in Italy, the horse from Mantua usually won the prize. With his flat face, protruding eyes, and thick lips, Francesco was an exceedingly homely man, but his looks were redeemed, at least in his young manhood, by his amiable and affectionate disposition. In February, 1490, he married Isabella d'Este, to whom he had been betrothed when he was 15 and she was six. Soon he was completely overshadowed by his brilliant wife (not yet 16 when he married her) in intelligence, statecraft, and as a patron. He did not seem to resent it and gave her a free rein in pursuit of her often costly interests. The first years of the marriage were happy, but after 1495 he quite openly took a mistress, the first of many. Because of its location, Mantua was constantly compelled to preserve its position in the face of the ambitions of its two powerful neighbors: Venice and Milan. Francesco, with the help of his wife, managed to maintain some sort of balance between them. Charles VIII of France, descending into Italy at the head of a highly trained army, offered him a command but he declined it. Instead he became general of a league of the emperor Maximilian, Ferdinand of Spain, the pope, the Venetians (in whose pay he was at the time), and Ludovico il Moro, duke of Milan, against Charles. The French king, who had marched unopposed to Naples, found himself threatened by the league and determined to quit Italy. The aim of the league was to prevent him from escaping. At the battle of Fornovo (July 6, 1495) Francesco fought like a lion; three horses were killed under him. His forces greatly outnumbered the French and were at first successful. The French abandoned their camp and Francesco's troops, especially the stradiots (Dalmatian mercenaries), instead of pursuing the French across the swollen Taro River, gave themselves up to plundering the French camp. The booty taken included a thorn from the Crown of Thorns, the shattered sword of the French king, and a book filled with portraits of beautiful Italian ladies who had taken the fancy of Charles. In the meantime, the French army escaped almost intact. In a letter to his wife immediately following the battle Francesco showed, by his bitterness concerning the stradiots, that he realized the league had missed a great opportunity. Quite soon, however, he and the Italians convinced themselves that they had won a great victory. Francesco had a chapel of victory erected at Mantua. Mantegna painted a picture—*The Madonna of Victory*—to celebrate it. Francesco's portrait appears in the painting, which was originally in the Church of S. Andrea at Mantua but is now in the Louvre. And Sperandio made two medals on which Francesco was inscribed as the liberator of Italy. Guicciardini, however, with his usual wry realism, wrote that since the object of the league was to destroy the French army, and since in fact it successfully escaped, the claim of victory was at best a dubious one. At this time, Francesco's reputation was great. He became captain general of the Venetian armies, but fell from favor when he aided the king of Naples, and was dismissed. Thereafter he served Louis XII of France and the pope, and was a general in the army that defeated the Venetians at Agnadello (1509). In the same year he was surprised by the Venetians and carried off a prisoner to Venice. He remained there (August, 1509–July, 1510) while his wife governed his state and made tireless attempts to secure his release. This was at last accomplished through the influence of Pope Julius II, who in return received Francesco's son Federigo as a hostage. On his return to Mantua he lived in semi-retirement. His health was ruined by syphilis. He was morose and difficult. His fear of a war in which he would be on the wrong side kept him in continual agitation. Isabella was effective ruler of his state, and when he was dying he acknowledged his debt to her and advised his sons to trust to her. She had often ruled his state, with wisdom and justice. Once, while a prisoner of Venice, a reference to him as marquess of Mantua was made. It was said he corrected the speaker, assuring him that the marquess was governing at Mantua—to such an extent did he identify Isabella with the welfare of his state. His sons were Federigo, who succeeded him, Ercole, who became a cardinal, and Ferrante, a soldier who fought for Charles V. Under Francesco and Isabella the court at Mantua, always highly civilized, was particularly brilliant, intellectually and artistically.

Gonzaga, Francesco III. Second duke of Mantua; b. March, 1533; d. at Mantua, February 21, 1550. He was the son of Federigo II and Margherita of Monferrato. He was only seven when his father died, and Mantua was governed under the regency of his mother, his uncle, Cardinal Ercole Gonzaga, and his warrior uncle, Ferrante Gonzaga. On his early death he was succeeded by his brother Guglielmo.

Gonzaga, Gianfrancesco. First marquess of Mantua; b. 1395; d. at Mantua, November, 1444. He was the son of Francesco Gonzaga and his second wife, Margherita Malatesta da Rimini. On the death of Francesco the Mantuans decided on a government by succession and Gianfrancesco, left as a ward of Venice by his father, was assured of inheriting it. He succeeded his father on March 20, 1407, but because of his youth his uncle Carlo Malatesta and Bartolommeo of Perugia, the *podestà*, ruled for a time. As he grew older he took over the reins of government. He married Paola Malatesta, the daughter of his uncle Carlo, in festivities that included jousting and splendid feasts. (It was perhaps from Paola that the hereditary defective spine that plagued later members of the family sprang.) In 1411 he entered the service of Venice against the emperor Sigismund. As a soldier in the tradition of the Gonzaga, he fought against Braccio da Montone (1418) and against Filippo Maria Visconti (1426). In the same year (1426) he fought against his uncle Carlo at Cremona and took him prisoner. Reconciled with Sigismund, the emperor visited Mantua and confirmed the title of Marquess of Mantua (previously offered to his father by Wenceslas III in 1403). In a magnificent ceremony on the cathedral steps at Mantua, Gianfrancesco received the mantle and ring of his marquisate from Sigismund (September 22, 1433). Gianfrancesco was a liberal spender, a cultivated man who wished to secure the best education for his children. In pursuance of that aim he brought the noted teacher, Vittorino da Feltre, to Mantua (1423). He paid him a salary of 240 gold florins a year and built him a house, *La Giocosa*, where the master lived with his pupils, including those poor youths of good intelligence that he taught for the pure love of learning. When, as often happened, Vittorino found himself in need of funds, he did not hesitate to approach his patron, who was proud to know that scholars from all over Europe attended Vittorino's school at Mantua. Gianfrancesco was a patron of the humanists and founded the *Studio pubblico* (university) at Mantua. Reconciled with his eldest son, Ludovico, with whom he had earlier quarreled, he left Ludovico the marquisate and divided the rest of his lands among his other sons. Each of the Gonzaga lords of Mantua increased his territory and then fragmented it in his will.

Gonzaga, Giulia. Countess of Fondi; b. probably at Gazzuolo, 1513; d. at Naples, April 19, 1566. She was the daughter of Ludovico di Sabbioneta, member of a branch of the Gonzaga family of Mantua. Noted for her intelligence and her extraordinary beauty, she was married at 14 to a 40-year-old widower, Vespasiano Colonna, count of Fondi. He died (1528) and she governed his state. Her youth, her beauty, and her famed chastity gave rise to many legends concerning her. She had many suitors but disdained them all. The leading men of letters of her day were drawn to her court by her cultivated mind and her charm of manner. These included Molza, Flaminio, Berni, and Vergerio. Ariosto and Bernardo Tasso sang her praises. In July, 1534, Khair-ed-dīn Barbarossa (Barbarossa II) attacked Fondi at night, with the intention of seizing Giulia and sending her as a gift to the sultan, Suleiman I the Magnificent. She shut herself up in the castle. Cardinal Ippolito de' Medici galloped up to her rescue, and the Turks withdrew. Of great piety, she was deeply concerned over the laxness and corruption of the Church, and shared this concern with Vittoria Colonna and others who worked for reform but did not break away from the Church. In December, 1535, she entered the convent attached to the Church of S. Francesco at Naples. Her activities in behalf of reform caused her to be suspected of heresy, and she fell under the scrutiny of the Inquisition. She was advised to flee, but refused, and ultimately died at the convent.

Gonzaga, Guglielmo. Third duke of Mantua and Monferrato; b. c1537; d. at Goito, August 14, 1586. He was the second son of Federigo Gonzaga and Margherita of Monferrato and was destined for an ecclesiastical career, in the tradition by which second sons entered the Church. On the death of his brother Francesco, however, he succeeded as duke, under the regency of his mother and his uncle, Cardinal Ercole Gonzaga. He married the Archduchess Eleonora of Austria, daughter of the emperor Ferdinand (April, 1561). Guglielmo, who inherited the family spinal defect, was a firm and capable ruler, pious, prudent, loyal, and just, and a lover of music and architecture. Under him Mantua reached ever new heights economically and politically. He was also a brave man who stayed in his city during the plague of 1567 and converted convents and churches into hospitals to care for his stricken people. He shrewdly fended off foreign attempts against his state, consolidated his realm, and allied his house by marriage to the principal dynasties of Europe. Under his son and successor, Vincenzo I (ruled 1587–1612), all forms of art flourished at Mantua; the court was one of splendor and prodigality; soon, however, Mantua entered upon a period of political and economic decline.

Gonzaga, Guido. Mantuan captain general; d. 1369. He was the son of Luigi Gonzaga, whom he assisted to become lord of Mantua (1328) and whom he succeeded (1360). He entertained Petrarch, who was visiting Vergil's city in 1349, and won the friendship of the poet. Of Guido's three sons, Francesco and Ludovico were jealous of their father's preference for Ugolino and assassinated him as he was at supper. Guido, to avoid an open break and a disturbance, had Ugolino secretly buried and forgave his sons. Equicola, a chronicler of Mantua, said of Guido that he was "a peaceful, quiet, modest and religious man, and above all faithful to his word."

Gonzaga, Isabella. See **Este, Isabella d'.**

Gonzaga, Ludovico. The third son of Federigo II Gonzaga (1500–1540) and Margherita of Monferrato. He went to France and became the founder of the French branch, the Nevers-Gonzaga, descendants of which won power in Mantua in 1630 and ruled until 1707.

Gonzaga, Ludovico II. Captain general and lord of Mantua; d. at Mantua, 1382. He was the son of Guido Gonzaga, and the brother of Ugolino and Francesco Gonzaga. He and his brother Francesco were jealous of Ugolino. At a supper in his own castle, to which Ugolino had invited them, they killed him (1362). Guido, though heartbroken over the loss of his favorite son, forgave them, and the Church also pardoned them as they claimed they had killed their brother in the course of a passionate quarrel. Bernabò Visconti made war on Ludovico and the Gonzaga (1368), to avenge, as he claimed, the death of his daughter's husband Ugolino. Under the auspices of the emperor Charles IV, a peace concluded the war for a time. By the terms of the peace, Ludovico's son Francesco was to marry Agnese Visconti, another of Bernabò's many daughters. On the death of his father Guido and his brother Francesco (1369), Ludovico was elected captain general of Mantua as Ludovico II (Luigi being the first). His first acts were to secure the city by reconstructing and repairing its fortifications. He freed Mantua from debt, promoted its prosperity, and showed himself to be liberal and upright in conduct while in power. He was succeeded by his son Francesco.

Gonzaga, Ludovico III. Second marquess of Mantua; b. 1414; d. at Goito, June 11, 1478. He was the son of Gianfrancesco Gonzaga and Paola Malatesta da Rimini, and was one of the foremost patrons of art and letters of his age. At the age of 19 he married Barbara of Brandenburg, the niece of the emperor Sigismund. Ludovico quarreled with his father because of the latter's obvious preference for his brother Carlo. He left his wife Barbara at Mantua where, at that point childless, she suffered humiliation at the hands of the favored Carlo's wife, and entered the service of Milan. This embarrassed his father in his relations with Venice. Ludovico was disinherited and Carlo was named heir to the marquisate (1436). Ludovico had been educated by Vittorino da Feltre, and through the good offices of his beloved master, his quarrel with his father was resolved. He returned to Mantua, Barbara gave him a son, and on the death of his father (1444) he succeeded as marquess. In the consolidation of his state Ludovico inherited the lands of his highly gifted brother Gianlucido, who died young (1446), and later the estates of his brother Alessandro (d. 1466). In the struggle between Milan and Venice following the death of Filippo Maria Visconti (1447), Ludovico had at length become allied to the new duke of Milan, Francesco Sforza, and a marriage between the Milanese duke's son Galeazzo Maria Sforza and Ludovico's daughter Dorotea was arranged. Earlier, Ludovico's daughter Susanna had been the candidate, but as she grew up a defect of the spine became apparent and her engagement to Galeazzo Maria was cancelled. The marriage with Dorotea never took place either, as the Sforza found what they considered a more advantageous match in Bona of Savoy. Ludovico's brother Carlo, now jealous in his turn of Ludovico, had at first helped Francesco Sforza to become lord of Milan and then turned against Sforza and encouraged the Venetians to fight him. In a great battle in which Carlo led the Venetians, Ludovico defeated him (1453). Carlo fled to Ferrara, where he died on December 21, 1456. In 1459 Ludovico welcomed Pope Pius II to Mantua when the Congress to raise a crusade against the Turks met there. Pius II, an outstanding humanist and man of letters, was charmed by the cultivated Ludovico, and invited him to enter the service of the papacy. Ludovico, fearing to incur the wrath of Venice, declined the offer. Later, rebuffed by Venice, he entered a league with the kingdom of Naples and the duchy of Milan, and when Galeazzo Maria Sforza was murdered (1476) Ludovico went to Milan at the request of the Duchess Bona and reestablished order. He was a great patron of the arts, a builder, and a man of letters. Under him the court of Mantua was one of the most brilliant of Italy. He was the patron of his master Vittorino da Feltre and often aided him. He added to the palace and engaged the best of the artists of the day to decorate the new apartments that were made in it. These included Andrea Mantegna, who painted the famous *Sala degli Sposi* for Ludovico's son Federigo and his bride. Ludovico built roads, aqueducts, and canals, drained marshes, and constructed the great hospital of S. Leonardo. Under him the cloth industry prospered and printing was introduced at Mantua. The marquisate was prosperous and relatively peaceful. He engaged in great building projects and caused the Church of S. Sebastian and the Basilica of S. Andrea (1472) to be built by Luca Fancelli on designs by Leon Battista Alberti. Guarino da Verona, Francesco Filelfo, Platina, and scores of grammarians, painters, men of letters, and miniaturists enjoyed his patronage. He was amiable and kind as to character, devoted to his marquisate and its welfare—an outstanding example of a Renaissance prince. Giovan Pietro Arrivabene sang the praises of his patron in the elegant Latin poem *Gonzagidos*. Ludovico's sons were: Federigo, his heir; Francesco, who became a cardinal at the age of 17; and Gianfrancesco. One of the scenes in the *Sala degli Sposi* painted by Mantegna, shows Ludovico and members of his family; another shows Ludovico welcoming his son Francesco on his return from Rome with the cardinal's hat.

Gonzaga, Luigi. Mantuan captain general; b. 1267; d. 1360. A member of an ancient family, he was the founder of that family's power at Mantua. In July, 1328, he sent his son Guido to Can Grande della Scala of Verona for aid against Passarino Bonacolsi, captain general of Mantua. A plot was hatched, and on August 16, 1328, the Gonzaga, with their allies, rose up in Mantua. Passarino, thinking to quell the disturbance by his presence, rode into the piazza. He, his sons, and other kinsmen and partisans were taken prisoner, and the whole race of the Bonacolsi was wiped out. The people of Mantua gave the government into the hands of Luigi by election (1329), making him captain general and lord of Mantua, and giving him the right to name his successor. Ludwig the Bavarian (Emperor Louis IV) named him imperial vicar (1329), Charles IV, Ludwig's successor, gave him the estates of the Bonacolsi and made him vicar of Cremona, Reggio, and Asola (1331), and he further extended his realm to the banks of Lake Garda. Active participation in the wars of Italy and advantageous marriages, as with the d'Este of Ferrara, the Beccaria of Pavia, and the della Scala of Verona, consolidated his power. His three sons were Guido, who succeeded him, Filippino, and Feltrino.

Gonzaga, Ugolino. Mantuan soldier; d. 1362. He was the son of Guido, and the grandson of Luigi Gonzaga who had founded the family power. He was said to have been the lover of the wife of Luchino Visconti of Milan, and when this became known the Visconti used it as a pretext for war against Mantua, although their real aim was to win back parts of Brescia and Verona that the Gonzaga had seized. The war broke out in 1348 (it lasted, with intervals, until 1403). Ugolino defeated the Milanese at Montechiaro and captured Bernabò Visconti's castle (1357). An interruption in the fighting occurred and he went to Milan to arrange a peace. One provision of the peace was that Ugolino should marry Caterina, Bernabò Visconti's daughter. Returned to Mantua, he shared in the government with his father. His brothers, Ludovico and Francesco, were jealous of their father's preference for Ugolino. At a supper to which he invited them at his castle they murdered him. Their father was deeply grieved, but rather than come to an open break with his sons he forgave them, had Ugolino secretly buried, and sent Caterina back to Milan. From this time, Francesco (d.1369) and Ludovico were virtual rulers of Mantua.

González Dávila (gōn-thä′leth dä′bē-lä), **Gil.** Spanish conquistador; b. at Ávila, Spain, c1470; d. there, c1528.

Gonzalo de Córdoba (gōn-thä′lō dā kôr′-ᵺō-bä), **Hernandez.** [Called **the Great Captain.**] Spanish general; b. at Montilla, near Córdoba, Spain, March 16, 1453; d. at Granada, Spain, December 2, 1515. He served with distinction in the wars against Portugal and the Moors, and conducted the negotiations that finally resulted in the union of Granada with Castile. According to Guicciardini, when he came into Italy it was thought that his nickname "Great Captain" was just Spanish boastfulness, but he soon proved his right to it by his brilliant victories. In 1495 he expelled the French from Naples, for which service he was created duke of Sant' Angelo by Ferdinando II. He helped the pope defeat the Orsini and in 1497 conquered Ostia, taking it from Pope Alexander's enemy, the cardinal of San Pietro in Vincoli (Giuliano della Rovere, later Julius II). For this Alexander gave him the Golden Rose. When later the French and Spanish quarreled over the division of the kingdom of Naples, he defended Barletta against the French, and defeated them at Cerignola and on the Garigliano in 1503. On the death of Alexander VI, his son Cesare Borgia fled to Naples, where he was at first courteously treated by Gonzalo de Córdoba, who later, on orders from Ferdinand the Catholic, arrested him and sent him as a prisoner to Spain. Gonzalo de Córdoba was named governor of Naples by Ferdinand but fell from the king's favor (1507) when Ferdinand became suspicious of the power he seemed to be acquiring in Naples.

Gordon (gôr′dọn), **Adam.** English outlaw; d. 1305. He established himself near the village of Wilton in 1267, and attacked those especially who were of the king's party. He engaged with Prince Edward (afterward King Edward I) in single combat, and the latter so admired his courage and spirit that he promised him his life and fortune if he would surrender. Gordon consented, and was ever after an attached and faithful servant to Edward.

Gordon, Sir **Adam de.** Scottish statesman and soldier; d. 1333. He was at first a partisan of Edward II, but after the battle of Bannockburn adhered to Bruce.

Gossaert (gos′ärt), **Jan.** See **Mabuse.**

Got (gō), **Bertrand de.** Original name of Pope **Clement V.**

Goudimel (gö-dē-mel), **Claude.** French composer and teacher of music; b. at Besançon, France, 1510; killed at Lyons in the massacre of the Huguenots, August 27, 1572. He set to music some of the Psalms in their French version by Marot and Beza (1565).

Goujon (gö-zhôṅ), **Jean.** French sculptor of the Renaissance period; b. c1515; d. probably between 1564–1568. He worked with Pierre Lescot on the decoration of Saint-Germain l'Auxerrois, and with the architect Bullant at Rouen. The *Victory* of Écouen is well known. From 1547 to 1550 he worked with Pierre Lescot on the reconstruction of the Louvre. To this period belong the *escalier* (staircase) of Henry II, the figures of the oeils-de-boeuf, the *Caryatides du Louvre*, and the figures of the *Fontaine des Innocents*. In 1550 he worked on the chateau of Diane de Poitiers. The *Diane Chasseresse* which stood in the courtyard is now in the Louvre.

Gourgues (görg), **Dominique de.** French

adventurer; b. at Mont-de-Marsan, Landes, France, c1530; d. at Tours, France, 1593. He commanded a successful expedition (1567) against the Spaniards in Florida.

Gower (gou′ėr, gōr, gôr), **John.** English poet; b. c1325; d. in the priory of Saint Mary Overies, Southwark (now in London), 1408. His principal work, the *Confessio amantis* (written in English, probably in 1386), was originally dedicated to Richard II, but in 1394 he changed the dedication to Henry of Lancaster (afterward Henry IV). Caxton printed it in 1483. Among his other works are *Speculum meditantis* (found 1895, under the title *Mirour de l'omme*), and *Vox clamantis* (written in Latin, begun in 1381). After the accession of Henry IV, Gower wrote *Cronica tripartita.* It treats of occurrences of the time, and the strength of its aspirations and teaching caused Chaucer to call him "the moral Gower."

Gozzoli (gōt′tsō-lē), **Benozzo.** See **Benozzo Gozzoli.**

Gradasso (grä-däs′sō). In Matteo Maria Boiardo's *Orlando Innamorato* and Lodovico Ariosto's *Orlando Furioso,* a king who invades France to secure Orlando's magic sword Durindana and Rinaldo's horse Baiardo. He agrees to fight Rinaldo in single combat for the sword and horse. If he loses he is to release his prisoners and return to Africa. Rinaldo is spirited away by the magic of Angelica and prevented from meeting Gradasso. The latter attacks Paris, seizes many of the peers, and claims his prize. Astolfo, receiving a message to deliver the horse in accordance with the terms, indignantly refuses. He engages Gradasso in single combat and is victorious. Gradasso abides by the conditions he had laid down with Rinaldo, releases his prisoners, and returns to his kingdom of Sericania. In a later combat he is slain by Orlando.

Grafton (gråf′tọn), **Richard.** English chronicler, printer to Edward VI both before and after his accession to the throne; d. c1572. He instigated, together with Edward Whitchurch, the printing at Antwerp of Thomas Matthew's Bible, had printed (1538) the Coverdale New Testament translation, printed and published (1539) at London, the folio Bible called "the Great Bible," issued (1549), the first Book of Common Prayer, and printed *Actes of Parliament* (1552, 1553).

Granacci (grä-nät′chē), **Francesco.** Florentine painter; b. perhaps at Villamagna (Florence), 1469; d. 1543. He was a fellow-pupil of Michelangelo in the studio of Domenico Ghirlandaio. At the end of the century he felt the influence of Leonardo and Perugino. Although there are traces of Raphael and Michelangelo in his work he remained an archaizing painter, pleasing in his types and the ivory cast of his color, but definitely a painter in an earlier tradition. Well provided for in his later years, he was not compelled to earn his living by his brush and painted as he chose. Several examples of his work are in the Accademia, Florence. A panel in the Uffizi, *Joseph Presents his Father and Brother to Pharaoh,* is one of a series painted for the nuptial chamber of Pierfrancesco Borgherini; others in the series were painted by Andrea del Sarto, Pontormo, and Bacchiacca. Other works are at Montemurlo, Villamagna, Castelfiorentino, Dublin, Berlin, the Johnson Collection, Philadelphia (*St. Julian Meeting his Wife, after Killing his Parents*), Baltimore (Walters Art Gallery), Charlotte (North Carolina), Portland (Oregon), Sarasota (Florida), and elsewhere.

Granada (grä-nä′ᴛʜä), **Luis de.** Spanish preacher and religious writer; b. at Granada, Spain, 1504; d. at Lisbon, Portugal, 1588. He was head of the Dominicans.

Granvella (gräm-bā′lyä), Cardinal **de.** [Title of **Antoine Perrenot;** French, Cardinal **de Granvelle.**] Spanish ecclesiastic and statesman; b. at Besançon, France, August 20, 1517; d. at Madrid, September 21, 1586. He was made chancellor of the empire by Charles V in 1550, and negotiated the marriage of Philip, Charles' son, and Mary I of England (1554). He was the chief councilor to Margaret of Parma in the Netherlands (1559–1564) and by his introduction of Spanish troops and the Inquisition into the Netherlands made the Spanish highly unpopular. He was made viceroy of Naples in 1570 and president of the council of Italy and Castile in 1575.

Grassi (gräs′sē), **Giovannino de'.** See **Giovannino de' Grassi.**

Gravina (grä-vē′nä), **Pietro.** Humanist and poet; b. at Palermo, 1452; d. 1526. A Latin poet at Naples, he was a friend of Pontano, Sannazzaro, Il Cariteo, and other leading humanists. He wrote epigrams, elegies, and other verse.

Gravina, Duke of. Title of various members

of the Orsini family. The first to be named duke of Gravina was Francesco Orsini, elevated in 1435 by Pope Eugenius IV. A later duke, Paolo Orsini, was strangled (1503) at the order of Cesare Borgia.

Gray (grā), Sir **Thomas.** English writer (in Latin); d. c1369. He was the author of *Scalachronica,* a historical work in five parts, covering English history to c1362; it is valuable as a source for the reigns of Edward I, Edward II, and the early part of the reign of Edward III.

Grazzini (grät-tsē′nē), **Anton Francesco.** [Called **il Lasca.**] Poet and dramatist; b. at Florence, March 22, 1503; d. there, February 18, 1584. He was the son of an ancient and honorable family, and entered the Guild of Physicians and Apothecaries at Florence as an apothecary, a profession that he followed all his life. As far as is known, he spent his entire life at Florence. In the Accademia degli umidi, of which he was a founder, all the members took the name of a fish. He was known as Il Lasca, "the roach." He was also a founder of the Accademia della crusca, but withdrew from both later as the results of quarrels. Among his writings are somewhat insipid Petrarchan lyrics, and lively, good-humored, sometimes pointed, sonnets, canzoni, carnival songs, ballate, capitoli, etc. He was not averse to taking sharp aim at such of his literary adversaries as Gelli and Giambullari. His most important works are *Le Cene* and his comedies. His *Cene* is a collection of twenty-two tales, told by five youths and five maidens during three days of carnival. A snowfall at Florence leads to a gay snowball fight carried on by the young men in the square, as the maidens watch. Afterwards, before a roaring fire, they tell their stories. The tales are largely concerned with the trickery and practical joking, often brutal and vicious, of three main characters. Some of the stories are horrible tales of lust and crime. They are in the racy Tuscan idiom and crackle with the rather sardonic Florentine brand of humor. In his approach to comedy, Grazzini departed from the classical models, on the ground that the Florentines did not live and move in the atmosphere of ancient Rome and Athens. Therefore, he concluded, it was ridiculous to imitate the ancients. His comedies, of which there were many, all written before 1560, are set in the modern age. His contention was that comedy should be "the mirror of life." The theme of mistaken identity (lost heirs, slaves who turn out to be princes, and so on) earned his particular scorn. He wrote that when a play opened with a city under siege, with the loss or theft of children, everybody knew what was going to happen. In his own comedies the plot is all-important; characterization is sketchy. As a rule, the plot hinges on a clever, startling, or amusing trick—as one by which a wife gets revenge for her husband's infidelity, or an elderly man seeking a young wife is duped and made ridiculous. The comedies, including *Gelosia, Spiritata, Strega,* and so on, are witty, natural, and fast-moving, and support Grazzini's contention that it was past time to abandon classical themes and situations. Grazzini edited and published Francesco Berni's *Capitoli,* 1548, many of which the author himself had never written down. He also made a famous collection of *Canti carnascialeschi.*

Great Interregnum (in-tėr-reg′num). Period from 1254 to 1273 in which there was no Holy Roman Emperor because of an unsuccessful attempt to unite the Germans under one king. It ended with the election of the first of the house of Hapsburg, Rudolf I, after which the attempt to unify Germany under one crown remained in abeyance.

Great Schism. Period (1378–1417) in Roman Catholic history during which different parties in the Church adhered to different popes. The end of the so-called Babylonian Captivity at Avignon came in 1376 when Gregory XI left France to return to Rome. He died (1378) and the Roman populace, fearful that the papacy would again leave Rome, demanded the election of an Italian as pope. The Conclave elected Urban VI (April, 1378), but the cardinals, most of whom were French, greatly resented his efforts to curb their power and claimed they had been compelled by force to elect him. They revolted against him, and a number of them met (August, 1378) at Anagni, declared his election illegal, and chose in his place Clement VII, who in 1379 established his court at Avignon. The Avignon papacy was supported, primarily for political reasons, by France, Castile, Aragon, Naples, and Scotland. Clement was succeeded by Benedict XIII; Urban by Boniface IX, Innocent VII, and Gregory XII. Within the Church a conciliar movement was developing, which called for reform and maintained that the pope was subject to the decisions of a general council. The movement gained strength as the schism continued. In 1409 a Council was called at Pisa, whose members deposed both Gregory and Benedict and elected the cardinal of Milan as Alexander V. Alexander died in 1410 and John XXIII was chosen in his place. Since neither Gregory nor Benedict recognized the authority of the Council, there were now three claimants for the tiara. John XXIII, as the choice of the Council, won wide adherence but was unable to restore peace to the Church or to Italy. Ladislaus, king of Naples, captured Rome (1413), and John fled to Florence. In 1414, under the influence of Sigismund, uncrowned Holy Roman Emperor, John reluctantly called the Council of Constance. Arrived at Constance, he soon realized that all parties were against him, fled, and was deposed by the Council. Gregory XII formally abdicated, July, 1415. Benedict fled, without, however, recognizing the authority of the Council to depose him. The Holy See was declared vacant, and the Council ruled until 1417 when, on the election of Martin V, the Great Schism ended. It left long-lasting effects, especially on demands for Church reform, the proliferation of religious nonconformity, and on the dependence of the pope on temporal power.

Gregorio da Rimini (grā-gō′ryō dä rē′mē-nē). Augustinian; d. at Vienna, 1358. He studied at Paris, and entered the order of the Augustinian hermits after having taught at Bologna, Padua, and Perugia. In 1357 he was named general of the order. He was noted for his piety and his strict adherence to the rules of the order. His works include treatises on theology and on his order.

Gregory X (greg′ọ-ri). [Original name, **Teobaldo Visconti.**] Pope (1271–1276); b. at Piacenza, 1210; d. at Arezzo, January 10, 1276. Following the death of Clement IV (1268) the conclave for the election of a new pope was deadlocked for nearly three years. Gregory was at Acre, in Syria, at the time of his election, and was greatly saddened by the loss of many holy places, only lately won, to the infidels. On his return to Italy he sought to reconcile the Guelphs and Ghibellines to restore peace to the peninsula and to win support for a crusade. The treaty of reconciliation he effected was short-lived and he placed Florence under an interdict for its defiance. He also tried to bring peace to Germany and supported the election (1273) of Rudolf of Hapsburg as German king, and planned to have him come to Rome to receive the imperial crown. His support of Rudolf was to offset the dominance of Charles I of Naples in Italy. Gregory called the Council of Lyons (1274) to consider and prepare for a crusade and to make reforms in the Church. Some reforms were effected, including the establishment of regulations for papal elections, restrictions on the orders of Mendicant Friars, protection of the Franciscans and Dominicans, and the acceptance of the renunciation of schism by the Byzantine emperor Michael VIII Paleaologus (this was also short-lived). On his slow journey back from the Council he died at Arezzo. He was succeeded by Innocent V.

Gregory XI. [Original name, **Pierre Roger de Beaufort.**] Pope (1370–1378) who ended the so-called Babylonian Captivity at Avignon, 1376; b. near Limoges, France, 1331; d. at Rome, March 26, 1378. In 1375 the Florentines revolted against the rule of the papal legates, who they believed denied them rights to import needed grain, and warred against the pope's lieutenants. Gregory excommunicated them and sent arms against them. St. Catherine of Siena, in writing to plead for peace and to urge reform of the Church, told him he was right in trying to win back the territory that had been lost to the Church, "but you are even more bound to win back the lambs which are the Church's real treasure." She was equally outspoken in her messages to the Florentines. The latter sent her as their emissary to negotiate peace with Gregory at Avignon. In this she failed, at this time, but she made a great impression on the pope, a good but rather weak man. Her fame had preceded her. She urged the pope to restore the Curia to Rome, to free it of French influence, and to restore its independence. She sought by her not negligible means to inspire him with the courage to overcome the hostility of the French cardinals to a move to Rome. Reluctant but persuaded, Gregory left Avignon in the fall of 1376; reached Italy in December; and entered Rome on January 17, 1377. He was succeeded by Urban VI.

Gregory XII. [Original name, **Angelo Cor-**

RER.] Pope (1406–1415); b. at Venice, c1327; d. at Recanati, October 18, 1417. He was elected by the Roman cardinals, during the Great Schism, in opposition to the antipope Benedict XIII, who reigned in Avignon. Gregory promised to resign if Benedict also resigned. He also promised to create no new cardinals, but did so. Some of the older cardinals deserted him and, with the French cardinals, called for a council to end the schism. The Council met at Pisa, 1409, and deposed both Gregory and Benedict and elected Alexander V. Neither Gregory nor Benedict recognized the Council's authority, and there were thus three men who claimed to be pope. John XXIII, who had succeeded Alexander, called the Council of Constance in a further attempt to unite the Church. Gregory abdicated to the Council, in 1415. The Council ruled until 1417, when Martin V was elected and the schism was ended. Gregory was named cardinal bishop of Oporto, in Portugal. His death soon after the election of Martin was thought to be added proof that Gregory had been the true pope (as canon law had decided), as a new pope could not reign while the old one still lived. Gregory's reign was filled with confusion, a falling away of his supporters, and a growing sentiment in favor of councils to which the popes would be subject. His last words were said to be, "I have not understood the world, and the world has not understood me."

Grey (grā), **John.** [Title, 8th Baron **Ferrers of Groby.**] English soldier; b. 1432; d. at the second battle of St. Albans, February 17, 1461. He was the elder son of Edward Grey (1415–1457). He married (1450) Elizabeth Woodville (later queen of Edward IV) and died fighting for Henry VI in the second battle of St. Albans.

Grey, Reginald de. [Title, 3rd Baron **Grey de Ruthin.**] English statesman and soldier; b. c1362; d. September 30, 1440. He was close to Richard II in a military capacity and to Henry IV as a trusted adviser.

Grey, Thomas. [Title, 1st Marquis of **Dorset.**] English nobleman; b. 1451; d. September 20, 1501. He was the son of Sir John Grey, 8th Baron Ferrers of Groby, and Elizabeth Woodville. He was created Earl of Huntingdon in 1471, and Marquis of Dorset in 1475. In 1471 he took part in the murder of Prince Edward, son of Henry VI. On the accession of Richard III he fled, and joined the party of Henry of Richmond (afterward Henry VII) and remained on the continent until after the battle of Bosworth.

Grey, Thomas. [Title, 2nd. Marquis of **Dorset.**] English courtier, favorite of Henry VIII, statesman and soldier; b. June 22, 1477; d. October 10, 1530. He was the third son of Thomas Grey, 1st Marquis of Dorset (1451–1501). Although none too successful a general, he maintained his popularity at court by jousting, and became steward of many manors and abbeys, and warden of several forests.

Grey, William. Bishop of Ely; d. at Ely, August 4, 1478. He was educated at Oxford and became a doctor of divinity in that university. A member of the family of Lord Grey of Codnor, family connections secured him many benefices in England. He was a classical scholar and humanist, a man of great learning, and he spent much time abroad. Vespasiano, who knew him as a client at Florence, says he went first to Cologne, where he studied logic, philosophy, and theology, and that then, perhaps after 1442, he wished to improve his classical learning and, as he knew he could do this only in Italy, decided to leave Cologne. Vespasiano also tells how, because of his great wealth and the fear that he might be taken on the road and held for ransom, he kept his departure a secret and left for Italy in the guise of a pilgrim. He says Grey told him the story himself when he came to Florence and ordered books from Vespasiano. From Florence, Grey went to Padua, and then to Ferrara, where he profited by the teaching of Guarino da Verona who was then at the court of the Estensi. Wherever he stayed he maintained a princely establishment and a large retinue. In 1449 Henry VI named him his proctor at the Roman Curia. Grey went to Rome and made a favorable impression on the humanistic Pope Nicholas V, who named him (1454) bishop of Ely. He was installed in his cathedral a few years later. For the next twenty years he devoted himself to the duties of his diocese and to his studies. In general, he avoided political involvement in the Wars of the Roses. He assembled a rich collection of codices that he had had copied while in Italy. Many of these were exquisitely illuminated. He gave about 200 of them as the nucleus of a library to Balliol College, Oxford. Some of them were destroyed in the reign of Edward VI, and many of the miniatures were mutilated, but over 150 of his codices are still in the possession of the college.

Grien (grēn), **Hans Baldung.** See **Baldung, Hans.**

Grifone (grē-fō′nā). In the *Orlando* romances of Matteo Maria Boiardo and Lodovico Ariosto, a knight called "the White." He is the brother of Aquilante "the Black." He and his brother fight Orrilo, an invincible man whose wounds heal instantly. Grifone is the lover of the faithless Orrigille. Astolfo persuades him to go to France to defend Paris from the Infidels.

Grijalva (grē-häl′bä), **Juan de.** Spanish soldier, discoverer of Mexico; b. at Cuéllar, Spain, 1489 or 1490; d. in Nicaragua, January 21, 1527. He was a nephew of Diego Velásquez, who was with him in Hispaniola and Cuba. He was chosen to follow up Córdoba's discovery of Yucatán. In 1523 he went with Garay to the coast of Mexico, and later took service with Pedrarias (Pedro Arias de Ávila) at Panama. It was he who dubbed Mexico "New Spain."

Grimani (grē-mä′nē). Eminent Venetian family, members of which were early promoters of Venetian (and their own) commercial interests in the east and on the island of Candia (Crete). The family reached the height of its power and influence at Venice in the 15th and 16th centuries. Prominent members of the family followed the sea; others were eminent in the Church. For more than a century, the patriarchate of Aquileia descended in this family.

Grimani, Antonio. Doge of Venice; b. 1436; d. at Venice, May 7, 1523. Member of an eminent Venetian family, he at first followed the sea. As a statesman, he served on various embassies for the republic and, after having fought against Charles VIII in 1495, a few years later became an ardent supporter of the French league. After a disastrous defeat at Zonchio (1499), he was stripped of his offices, which included those of General of the Sea and Procurator of St. Mark. He went to Rome, where his son Domenico was a cardinal, and sought to rehabilitate his name and his fortunes. Returned to Venice (1509), his honors were restored. In 1521 he was elected doge but his uncertain policy, first of support for France and then of alliance with Spain, was ineffective.

Grimani, Domenico. Cardinal, diplomat, and humanist; b. at Venice, c1461; d. at Rome, August 27, 1523. He was the son of Antonio, who became doge of Venice in 1521. In 1497 he was named patriarch of Aquileia. He was a friend of Pope Julius II, was a generous patron and protector of the arts, and collected a rich library (later destroyed by fire). His name is now best known in connection with a famous breviary, the Grimani Breviary. This jewel of the art of illumination is a 14th-century, Flemish-illuminated manuscript of over 800 double-columned pages. Each of the pages is richly decorated. In addition, there are eighty-six miniatures, brilliantly executed and in fine condition, on subjects from the Old and New Testaments and the lives of the saints. Cardinal Domenico Grimani left the breviary to the republic of Venice with the proviso that his nephews, Cardinal Marino Grimani (d. 1546) and Giovanni, patriarch of Aquileia (d. 1593) should have the use of it in their lifetimes. In 1594 it was deposited in the treasury of the Basilica of St. Mark, and in 1801 was transferred to the *Biblioteca Marciana*, where it now remains.

Grimoard (grȧm-wȧr), **Guillaume de.** Original name of Pope **Urban V.**

Gringore (grañ-gôr) or **Gringoire** (grañ-gwȧr), **Pierre.** French satirist and dramatic writer; b. in Normandy, c1480; d. c1539. Among his works are *Saint Loys* (a mystery), *Les Folles Enterprises* (a series of monologues), *La Chasse du cerf des cerfs*, and *Le Coqueluche*.

Grocyn (grō′sin), **William.** English humanist; b. at Colerne, Wiltshire, England, c1446; d. at Maidstone, Kent, England, 1519. He was a friend of Linacre, More, Colet, and Erasmus, was an ardent promoter of the New Learning, though an adherent of the old religious faith, and is reputed to have been the first teacher of Greek at Oxford. With the exception of a letter to Aldus Manutius and an epigram (on a lady who threw a snowball at him), no writings of his have survived.

Grolier de Servier (gro-lyā dẹ ser-vyā), **Jean,** Vicomte **d'Aguisy.** [Also known as **Jean Grolier.**] French bibliophile; b. at Lyons, France, 1479; d. 1565. He was of a rich family, and became treasurer under Francis I. He owes his reputation to his passion for fine books (in point of subject, binding, printing, and paper). He designed many of his own ornaments and supervised the binding. The Grolier Club of New York was named for him.

Groot (grōt), **Gerhard.** [Latinized, **Gerhardus Magnus.**] Dutch reformer; b. at Deventer, Netherlands, in October, 1340; d. there August 20, 1384. He was the founder of the society of "Brethren of the Common Life."

Grossi (grō′sē), **Bartolommeo de'.** See **Bartolommeo de' Grossi.**

Groto (grō′tō) or **Grotto** (grōt′tō), **Luigi.** [Called **il Cieco d'Adria,** "Blind man of Adria."] Poet and orator; b. at Adria, September 7, 1541; d. at Venice, December 13, 1585. He lost his sight eight days after his birth, but his mother, realizing as he grew older that he was possessed of a keen intelligence, gave him every advantage in securing an education. He wrote tragedies, comedies, Latin verse, pastoral fables, and other verse, of no great poetic merit, was known in his day as an orator, and was often chosen to give the oration on important occasions.

Grün (grün), **Hans Baldung.** See **Baldung, Hans.**

Gryphius (grif′i-us; German grē′fẹ-u̇s), **Sebastian.** [Original surname, **Greyff.**] German printer; b. at Reutlingen, Germany, 1493; d. at Lyons, France, September 7, 1556. He settled at Lyons and revived the art of printing there. His Latin Bible of 1550 is an excellent example of his work.

Guardati (gwär-dä′tē), **Tommaso.** [Called **Masuccio Salernitano.**] Fifteenth-century writer; b. at Salerno; d. there. A nobleman of Salerno, he spent many years at Naples in the service of Roberto Sanseverino, and was an active and beloved member of the court circle. His *Novellino* was dedicated (1475) to Ippolita Sforza, wife of Alfonso, the future king of Naples. The *Novellino* consists of fifty stories, divided into ten books of five stories each. Though provided with a slender connecting link, in the manner of the *Decameron,* each of the stories is an independent unit. Each has its own dedication, to a prince, prelate, soldier, or member of the royal family, and each ends with an often satirically expressed moral. Some of them are coarse or licentious, again in the manner of Boccaccio, with the difference that Guardati makes clear his own disapproval and indignation at the vices of his age. He attacks the frauds, immorality, and falsity of the monastic orders unsparingly, revealing the hypocrisy prevailing in some of them with utter frankness and contempt. The duplicity of women figures in other stories, and some relate the nobility of princes, concern chivalric deeds, or detail the pathos, violence, and humor in the lives of the common people. His tale of Mariotto and Gianozza, laid in Siena, is a forerunner of *Romeo and Juliet.* The language of the *Novellino* is an Italian of the south, larded with dialect and regionalisms. As his tales deal with accepted attitudes of both the nobles and the common people, Guardati's stories are a revelation of the manners and customs of his age.

Guariento (gwä-ryen′tō). [Called **Guariero** by Vasari.] Paduan painter; d. before September, 1370. Byzantine influence has almost disappeared in his work, and there is little evidence of the influence of the Venetian school. On the contrary, he was strongly influenced by the frescoes Giotto had executed early in his century in the Scrovegni Chapel at Padua, especially in solidity of form and individuality of faces. He appears to have been the center of a school of painting at Padua, and a vessel for transmitting Giotto's Tuscan style in the region. But all painters in the area must have been deeply influenced by Giotto's frescoes. Among the known works of Guariento are panels with scenes from the Old Testament and panels with groups of militant angels, the *Celestial Militia,* in the Museo Civico at Padua. The arrangement in ranks and the richness of dress in the latter are somewhat Byzantine, but the faces are purely Italian. Works executed in the Church of the Eremitani at Padua were largely destroyed by bombs in 1944; a *Coronation of the Virgin* there has been restored. In the Museo Civico at Bassano, about twenty-five miles from Padua, are a *Crucifix,* in the manner of Giotto, signed by the artist, and a fresco of the *Virgin with Saints.* Only traces remain of his fresco *Paradise,* in the Hall of the Great Council in the Doges' Palace at Venice.

Guarini (gwä-rē′nē), **Battista.** Poet and diplomat; b. at Ferrara, December 10, 1537; d. at Venice, October 7, 1612. He was a descendant of the famous teacher, Guarino da Verona (c1374–1460), was educated at Pisa and Padua, and taught moral philosophy at the University of Ferrara. His income and estates were sufficient to allow him to live a life independent of the favor of princes, but his ambition and "honor" induced him to seek it. In 1567 he entered the service of Alfonso II, duke of Ferrara, and remained until 1583, serving, in that time, as ambassador to Venice, Rome, Turin, and Poland. His younger contemporary, Torquato Tasso, was Alfonso's court poet, and his position became a source of envy to Guarini. His resentment caused him to leave Ferrara in 1583. He retired to his villa and engaged in literary work. His retirement should have been satisfying, as he enjoyed the society of learned men from Padua and had completed his *Pastor fido*, his most important work, and his comedy *L'Idropica*, but in 1585 he returned to Ferrara as the duke's secretary. In 1588 he left again, rousing the wrath of Alfonso. A reconciliation was effected and he returned in 1595, but left, 1599, to enter the service of the grand duke of Tuscany. In comfortable circumstances, he was yet a fractious and ambitious man, and spent the last years of his life in litigation and family quarrels. His jealousy of the tragic Tasso was petty and unfounded. His works include *Rime*, in the Petrarchan manner, a treatise on political liberty and a dialogue on the duties of princely secretaries, many works left incomplete or later lost, the comedy *L'Idropica*, and his most important work, *Pastor fido*. This drama, in a pastoral setting, is one of the earliest of the Arcadian genre. It is of the love of Mirtillo and Amarilli, with two lesser love stories supporting it. The action is interrupted repeatedly by songs of love, its hopes, frustrations and the joys of its fulfillment. (It is for the presence of so many songs concerning the action that *Pastor fido* and Tasso's *Aminta* are often cited as the forerunners of opera.) The idyllic setting, far from the pressures of the world of affairs, is the background against which love disports in all its sensuous delights. The play, begun in 1580, was completed in 1583, published at Venice, 1590, and first presented at Crema in 1595. The summation in drama of the polished decadence of 16th-century Italian court life, it was the model, with Tasso's *Aminta*, for a long series of pastoral dramas.

Guarino (gwä-rē′nō), **Battista.** Humanist and educator; b. at Ferrara, 1434; d. there, July 31, 1503. He was the son and successor of Guarino da Verona (c1374–1460). In his treatise on teaching, *De ordine docendi*, he expounded on and preserved his father's methods. For Duke Ercole of Ferrara he translated some of the comedies of Plautus into Italian.

Guarino da Verona (dä vā-rō′nä). [Also, **Guarino Veronese.**] Educator and humanist; b. at Verona, c1374; d. at Ferrara, December 4, 1460. Pius II, to whom he had taught Greek, said of this celebrated educator that he "had been the teacher of almost all who have attained distinction in the humanities in our day." His fame derived from the school he established (1429) at Ferrara. The background for his educational program and his excellence as a teacher was extensive. Early in his career a notary who had studied under Giovanni Malpaghini at Padua, he then went to Venice to become a teacher. There he met the eminent Greek teacher Manuel Chrysoloras, who was at the time on a mission from Constantinople. Guarino returned to Constantinople with him to learn Greek, and stayed there five years. While there he collected many ancient manuscripts that he took back to Italy with him in 1409. He found few opportunities in his native Verona on his return and went to Bologna. There he met Leonardo Bruni. Bruni recommended him for the university at Florence and Guarino taught there for about five years. Next he went to Venice and established a school for young noblemen. Vittorino da Feltre and George of Trebizond were associated with him. He taught the former Greek and the latter Latin. In 1419 he moved his school to Verona but was forced by plague to evacuate that city. In 1429 he went to Ferrara to tutor young Leonello d'Este, along with other princely sons and daughters, as well as poor boys whom he took into his own home and supported at his own expense. From this arose his famous school. He served as interpreter for the Greeks at the Councils of Ferrara and Florence, 1438–1439, whither they had come to discuss a union with the Western Church, but most of his remaining thirty years were spent at Ferrara running his school. Guarino's principal innovations in education consisted in a change in the curriculum. For the traditional trivium and quadrivium of the Middle Ages he substituted a graduated course of studies in three parts. The elementary course covered the elements of Latin. The grammatical course took up an advanced Latin, prosody and metrics, the elements of Greek, and history and literature, all based on ancient texts. The third course, Rhetoric, was devoted to the orations of Cicero and other Latin orators and to the Greek philosophers Plato and Aristotle. By these courses Guarino provided a thorough classical, or humanistic, education. Along with the course of studies Guarino, a man of upright and pious life himself, insisted on a strict adherence to religious principles in his pupils. He developed, or caused to be developed, teaching manuals for the different courses. The manuals were models of clarity and simplicity, and were widely adopted. He wrote the first systematic treatise on Latin grammar. His school became famous throughout Europe. Pupils came from all Italy and from as far away as England, as well as France, Bohemia, Poland, Germany and Hungary. When Leonello d'Este, his pupil and patron, died (1450), his successor Borso d'Este, after a slackening of interest, continued to maintain the school. The amount of work that Guarino produced inspires awe. In addition to the teaching manuals, he wrote more than seventy orations for all kinds of occasions—betrothals, deaths, welcomes, farewells, state ceremonies, etc. The more than 900 letters he wrote in the course of fifty-five years give an intimate picture of the life of his times and the activities of the humanists. He wrote verse, translated and edited, in whole or in part, the works of Livy, Plautus, Pliny the Elder, and Catullus. He translated some of Plutarch's *Lives* from the Greek. For Pope Nicholas V he translated all of Strabo and had received 1,000 gold florins for the two sections he had completed before the pope died. He wrote commentaries on Juvenal, Martial, Persius, Aristotle, and Cicero. Vespasiano says of him that he lived for some time in "easy circumstances with his wife and children, taking no heed of aught else but letters." Pius II wrote, "No scholar of our age has left a higher reputation."

Guazzalotti (gwät-tsä-lōt′tē) or **Guacialotti** (gwä-chä-lōt′tē), **Andrea.** Medalist and smith; b. at Prato, 1435; d. November 8, 1495. He worked for Niccolò Palmieri, bishop of Orte, of whom he made several medals that he signed. Much of his work as a medalist was done at Rome. The medals made there include those of the popes Nicholas V, Calixtus III, Pius II, and Sixtus IV. The Pazzi Conspiracy of Florence (1478) is commemorated by four medals. The modeling and style of his work is vigorous and virile; the designs of the reverses show the influence of Pisanello.

Guelphs or **Guelfs** (gwelfs). The names Guelph and Ghibelline were first used in Italy in Florence (1216), in connection with an Easter murder there. From Florence the names spread throughout the peninsula. They come from the names of two 13th-century emperors. In 1212, Pope Innocent III, in a power struggle with the Holy Roman emperor, commanded the Italians to repudiate the emperor Otto and to support Frederick of Hohenstaufen (who became Frederick II). Otto was a member of the Welf or Guelph family. The Welfs (Guelphs) were a powerful family of Germany, so called from Welf I in the time of Charlemagne. His descendants, several of whom bore the same name, held great possessions in Italy. Those who defied the pope to support Otto were called Guelphs. Frederick came of a family that controlled the castle of Waiblingen, in Swabia. Waiblingen was an impossible name for Italians. They transformed it to Ghibellino. Those who supported the pope and Frederick came to be known as Ghibellines. However, when Frederick, with the pope's support and that of the Ghibellines, became emperor he quickly made it apparent that he meant to be supreme in temporal matters. Innocent, who had expected more docility, reversed himself and denounced Frederick. Otto was well out of the way by this time. The names Guelph and Ghibelline now came to signify those who supported the pope, that is the Guelphs, and those who supported the emperor whom the pope had originally asked them to support, that is the Ghibellines. The question of papal versus imperial supremacy soon ceased to be the compelling reason for the division into Guelphs and Ghibellines in the various communes of Italy. Their main interest became which authority, pope or emperor, could do them the most good. The communes were Guelph or Ghibelline according to their own interest, were not often of much help to either pope or emperor in his interest, and readily switched sides if it seemed advantageous to do so. Siena, constantly threatened by Florence, was Ghibelline. Florence, nominally a supporter of the pope as a Guelph commune, was frequently at odds with the papacy. Within the commune itself there were always parties and factions warring for control. In Florence the Ghibellines intrigued with the emperor or his agents to overthrow the ruling Guelphs time and again, with brief successes. Ultimately the Guelphs were successful and the Ghibellines practically annihilated. The Guelphs in Florence then split into the Blacks (Neri) and the Whites (Bianchi). These names came from two factions in Pistoia, a commune that had been under Florentine control. One faction of Guelphs in Florence drove out the Whites of Pistoia and established the Blacks in control there. From this, that Guelph Florentine faction came to be known as Blacks and their opponents in Florence as Whites. The Blacks and Whites of Florence represented a split in the upper classes there. Dante was a White and suffered exile (1302) when the Black Guelphs won control.

Guerino Meschino (gwā-rē′nō mās-kē′nō). Hero of a romance of the Middle Ages, of uncertain authorship and date, first printed in Italian at Padua in 1473.

Guesclin (ge-klañ), **Bertrand Du.** See **Du Guesclin** or **Duguesclin, Bertrand.**

Guevara (gā-bä′rä), **Antonio de.** Spanish historical writer; b. in the province of Vizcaya, Spain, c1490; d. 1545. He was one of the official chroniclers to Charles V. He wrote *Reloj de Principes* (*Dial for Princes,* 1529), *Decada de los Cesares* (*Lives of Ten Roman Emperors,* 1539) and *Epistolas Familiares* (1539–1545). Guevara also wrote a number of works on theology, navigation, and court life.

Guicciardini (gwēt-chär-dē′nē). An old Florentine family, originally from the Mugello, that by 1200 possessed houses in Florence. The family early became wealthy through commerce; branches of the business of the house were at Lyons, Antwerp, London, and Naples. In addition to their interest and success in commerce, the family had a tradition of public service at Florence; the names of the Guicciardini recur at frequent intervals in the annals of the city. Members of it served as prior (forty-four times), gonfaloniere (sixteen times), and on countless missions and embassies in Italy and beyond. Politics was their passion for generations. Francesco Guicciardini, the statesman and historian, was proud to be a member of this family, and never missed a chance to record, in his *Storie fiorentine* and in his *Storia d'Italia,* the name of a Guicciardini who had played a part in public affairs.

Guicciardini, Francesco. Historian and statesman; b. at Florence, March 6, 1483; d. at Santa Margherita in Montici, May 22, 1540. Guicciardini's fame rests on his histories, particularly on his *Storia d'Italia,* written for his own instruction, published long after his death, and titled by his editor. The basis for his histories, as for his other writings, was lifelong involvement in affairs of state.

Guicciardini was the third son of a father who had a large family (eleven children), a cultivated mind, and a limited property. Francesco could expect no inheritance. Motivated by an overmastering ambition, and mindful of the long and honorable part his forbears had played in Florentine history, he determined to make his own way in the world. He studied Latin, Greek, philosophy, and mathematics, and then, from 1498 to 1505, pursued his legal studies at Ferrara, Padua, and Pisa. (He had, on the advice of his father, declined an opportunity for a career in the Church. His father, whom he seems to have admired, did not want to see the Church used as a vehicle for Francesco's ambition.) In 1505 he received his doctorate in civil law at Pisa. In his years of study he devoted himself with the utmost concentration to his work; he eschewed the pleasures normally associated with youth, and later stated with satisfaction that he never wasted time. His habit of never being diverted from his main object persisted throughout his life. In 1506 he began his legal career at Florence and was immediately successful. His clients included the leading families of Florence and many civic organizations. When (1511) he was asked to serve as Florentine ambassador to the court of Ferdinand the Catholic of Spain, he considered declining the post lest such an interruption as a protracted stay in Spain interfere with his career. However, he accepted, and left Florence in January, 1512. He remained in Spain until January, 1514. The experience was an eye opener. Ferdinand was an able, decisive, and dissembling autocrat, the ruler of the most powerful nation of Europe at the time. Guicciardini observed his use of power. If, at this age, he needed any lessons on what moves men he learned them at Ferdinand's court, and he remembered them. While he was in Spain the republican government of Piero Soderini at Florence was overthrown and the Medici were restored. Guicciardini, whose wife's family, as well as his own, had been openly hostile to Soderini, was now in sympathy with the party that ruled Florence. Pope Leo X named him (1516) governor of the papal city of Modena, recently won from Ferrara, and thus he began twenty years in the service of the popes. The territory embraced by Modena had been devastated by war; all agencies of government had collapsed. Guicciardini, decisive and resolute in action, set about to restore order. It was a task exactly suited to his temperament and ability, and one in which he was supported with sufficient power. He spared neither prince nor priest in his administration of the law. What was even more unusual, he was not susceptible to bribery. To his charge of Modena, Leo X added Reggio (1516) and Parma (1521), and made Guicciardini commissioner-general of the papal armies. In all three of these areas Guicciardini's purpose was to restore order and security, and to revive the economic life of the territory. When (1521), soon after he arrived at Parma, the troops of Francis I laid siege to the city, it was thanks almost alone to his ability and the force of will by which he kept the mercenaries from deserting that the French were compelled to retire. Inevitably, the vigorous action he took aroused the enmity of those standing most in need of control, but the people came to respect him and to value his ability to keep order. In 1523 Leo X's cousin, Giulio de Medici, ascended the papal throne as Clement VII, and Guicciardini had a master who was also his friend, and of whom he was the trusted adviser. Clement named him (1524) governor of the Romagna, an area completely disorganized by wars and faction. He reorganized the judicial and fiscal departments, but before he could complete his task was called (1526) to Rome to help Clement devise a policy with regard to the foreign powers that were struggling for control of Italy. In 1525 the Pope's ally, Francis I, was defeated by the troops of the emperor Charles V at Pavia and taken prisoner. Milan was occupied. Charles had raised the imperial emblem at Naples. As between coming to terms with Charles or openly contesting him in Italy, Clement could not decide. In Guicciardini's view, it was of the utmost importance to neutralize the ominous power of Charles V. He urged Clement to form an anti-imperial league. His advice (others agreed with him) was adopted in the League of Cognac, a league of the pope, Francis I, Milan, and Venice, against Charles V. Guicciardini left Rome to join the armies, with full power to direct military operations. The plans so carefully prepared were frustrated by treachery and delay. Charles' armies marched south from Lombardy. Guicciardini was able to prevent them from sacking Florence, but in May the imperial troops under the Constable of Bourbon entered Rome and for seven days put it to the sack. Clement himself took refuge, with many others, in the Castel Sant' Angelo, and finally surrendered. Guicciardini returned to Florence. The city had expelled the Medici and was once more a republic. The Florentines accused him of having betrayed them, notwithstanding he had saved them from a sack. Early in 1530 he was threatened with arrest and, in March, 1530, was condemned. He fled the city. In August of the same year the Medici were restored, through the agency of Charles V and Pope Clement, now on the same side. The pope sent Guicciardini to Florence to help the Medici and to discipline the leaders of the revolt against their rule. His severe punishment of his fellow Florentines—torture and death—is a stain on his record; hitherto he had been stern but just; here he was revengeful. However, though he favored an aristocratic government, he was opposed to the personal tyranny that became the government of Florence under the Medici. He lost their confidence on this account, and withdrew from the city in 1537. He retired to his villa at Montici to write his *Storia d'Italia*, the product of his experience, knowledge, observation, political views, and analytical mind.

Throughout his life, Guicciardini was accustomed to reduce his thoughts and observations to writing, not with the intention of publication, but as a means of viewing events from a slight distance and of analyzing their causes. Since he did not suffer from self-delusion, his accounts and memos written to himself are dispassionate and searching. Among his many works, none published until after his death, is his *Storie fiorentine,* written in 1508 and 1509, before he had begun his political career. It covers the period from 1378 to 1509, but is rather sketchy in the early sections. From 1492 to 1509, the history of Florence is presented in great detail. It is livelier and more personal than his later works, less sure in his judgments. It was not published until 1859. His *Dialogo del reggimento di Firenze,* written probably between 1521 and 1525, is a discussion of the government he thinks most suitable to Florence. It is his political conviction that the best government for Florence is an aristocracy. The form he advocates is a variation of the Venetian system. His *Ricordi politici e civili* is a collection of aphorisms, generally on politics but also including conclusions he had come to about the nature of man. All men, he said, are moved by a desire for power, however they may drape their motives with high-sounding phrases. Problems must be approached in their modern context: "How mistaken are those that quote the Romans at every step." No one should overlook the part played by chance in human affairs: "No one who considers well can deny that in human affairs fortune has enormous influence, . . ." As most men are neither very good nor very prudent, a leader must be severe rather than kind, "and anyone who thinks otherwise is mistaken." "Small and almost imperceptible beginnings are often the occasion of great disaster or of great prosperity." In 1529 he wrote his *Considerazioni sui Discorsi del Machiavelli,* a series of commentaries on his friend's discourses on Livy. In this he points out errors he thinks Machiavelli has made in his interpretations of Roman history. Here again, as in so many instances, he expresses the view that new problems demand new solutions, and must be considered in the context of their times. Since the circumstances and conditions have changed, Roman solutions cannot be applied. Historic parallels are useful possibly as guides, but cannot be adopted in new conditions. His work on the history of Florence, published in 1945 and titled *Cose fiorentine* by its editor, was to have been a history of Florence from 1375. He left it unfinished. From 1537 to 1540 he devoted himself to his *Storia d'Italia,* his great work.

For this work Guicciardini has been called the first great modern historian. The history covers the years 1494 to 1532, years in which he played a crucial role at the center of events. The history is modern in its overall view of the relationships of various areas of Italy to each other. It weighs and considers the interaction of events as between the cities and states of Italy as well as of nations beyond the Alps. It is based on his own knowledge and experience and on documents and official correspondence. (When he returned to Florence in 1530 he removed the archives of the committee that dealt with foreign affairs to his own house.) In his work he investigates and explains causes and motives, to show how one event led to another, and often, to show how the outcome was decided almost by accident. Time and again he comments on the small details that frustrated large plans. Frequently, too, he remarks on the part that chance played in the events he describes. He has no illusion that the justice of the cause will bring success, for he has observed too often that the wicked, unjust, and cruel are as likely, if not more so, to attain success in their undertakings as the good and the just. His analyses of men are unsparing. He has seen too often the timidity, self-interest or greed that has formed decisions and policies. The history, first printed in 1561, met with instant recognition, was translated into Latin, French, German, Dutch, Spanish, and English, and had great influence in the approach and elaboration of future histories.

Guicciardini has been represented as a cold, relentlessly realistic, ambitious man, an unattractive and somewhat sinister personality. He was moved by a powerful desire for "honor," for the rewards that go with it, and for recognition that he had achieved it. He was dispassionate and coldly analytical; these are the great virtues of his *Storia d'Italia.* He married—not for love, possibly for wealth, and certainly for the power of the connection. (In his *Ricordanze,* an informal diary, he tells how his bride came to him at night, on horseback, because the match between two such families might lead to a disturbance.) On the other hand, he used his indubitable political and administrative talents with the utmost probity, and was utterly scrupulous in private as well as in public affairs. He made his fortune honestly. His support of the Medici had the advantage of furthering his career as well as of implementing his political conviction that the best government was by a prince, in conjunction with the advice and counsel of the "wise and the prudent." Of "the people," he said it is a creature that is mad, "full of a thousand errors and a thousand confusions, without taste, discrimination or stability." He was disgusted by the corruption that was manifest in the clergy, scorned the greed and loose-living of the priests, and held the Church, too weak to unite Italy but strong enough to prevent its unification, responsible for the disunity and ruin of the peninsula. Yet he admitted that his positions under the popes forced him to desire their greatness, for his own personal interest, "and if it had not been for this I should have loved Martin Luther as myself." This was not a statement of sympathy for Luther's cause. It was that he considered that Luther would "reduce this band of rogues [the corrupt clergy] to their proper state, that is, either deprived of their vices or of their power." Refreshing, especially in consideration of the turbulence and corruption of his time, is his self-knowledge. His power to observe with clear and even cynical eyes, to analyze and evaluate motives and their results, to make the connection between events, and to write it all down in a perhaps difficult but unembroidered prose, makes him the great historian he is now considered. The Italian critic Francesco de Sanctis, writing in the middle of the 19th century, reviled Guicciardini for his cynicism and his self-interest, yet called his history "from the point of view of intellectual power, the most important work to have issued from an Italian mind."

Guicciardini, Lodovico. Historian, geographer, statesman, and man of letters; b. at Florence, June, 1523; d. at Antwerp, 1589. He was the nephew of Francesco Guicciardini (1483–1540). He served Cosimo I de' Medici in several capacities, traveled widely, and finally settled at Antwerp, where he had the confidence of the duke of Alba. Through the betrayal of a friend, to whom he had confided a dangerous secret, he was imprisoned. On his release he lived retired from public affairs. His chief writings were two works on the Low Countries, published in the same year (1567) in Italian and French, and later translated into Latin. These works, informed with his keen observation, are notable for the inclusion of details of the economic life of the Low Countries. He also made a collection of witty sayings, jokes, and anecdotes, *L'hore di ricreatione*, which was reprinted many times and translated into French.

Guicciardini, Piero. Florentine statesman; b. 1370; d. 1441. A member of the old and powerful Guicciardini family, he favored the Medici party at Florence, and saw it win power in the last years of his life. He was gonfaloniere three times, served as ambassador many times, and was given the title of Count Palatine by the emperor Sigismund in 1416.

Guidi (gwē′dē), **Guido.** Physician; b. at Florence about the beginning of the 16th century; d. at Pisa, May 26, 1559. Francis I, on the advice of Luigi Alamanni, called him to Paris in 1542 and gave him a pension and a professorship at the Collège de France. (In Paris he was a friend of Benvenuto Cellini.) On the death of Francis (1547) he returned to Italy and became professor of philosophy and medicine at the University of Pisa. The Vidian artery and canal, which he described, are named for him. He also described the palatine bone and the sphenoid bone. His anatomical findings are described in *De anatomia corporis humani*, published in 1611. He commented upon the works of Hippocrates and Galen, wrote on fevers, *De febribus*, on healing, *De curatione*, and on the art of medicine, *Ars medicinalis*.

Guidiccioni (gwē-dēt-chō′nē), **Giovanni.** Ecclesiastic, poet, and diplomat; b. at Lucca, February 25, 1500; d. at Macerata, July 26, 1541. He took orders in 1518, studied at Pisa, Padua, and Bologna, and earned his doctorate in law at Ferrara (1565). His patron, Cardinal Alessandro Farnese, took him on many missions and journeys and, when he became Pope Paul III, charged Guidiccioni with important business. Among other positions, he was governor of Rome, bishop of Fossombrone, and commissioner-general of the papal armies. His *Orazione* (1533) was a defense of those who had rebelled against the greed of the nobles. In it he warned the nobility against oppression of the people. His *Lettere di negozi*, sincerely and simply expressed, are of great value as a record of the momentous events in which, by virtue of his position, he took part. He wrote Petrarchan lyrics, but as a poet is best known for the fourteen sad sonnets he composed in which he compared the pride and glory of ancient Rome with the shame of the city of his time. The sonnets eloquently proclaim the depth of his feeling.

Guido delle Colonne (gwē′dō del′le kō-lō′nā). Poet of the Sicilian school, and jurist; b. probably at Messina; d. after 1287. He was a jurist by profession. His *Historia destructionis Troiae* (1287) is a Latin prose adaptation of the *Roman de Troie* of Benoît de Sainte-Maure, a 12th-century French trouvère. The *Historia,* in an English translation, was the first book printed by Caxton and the first printed book in English. Shakespeare probably used it as a source for his *Troilus and Cressida.*

Guido da Como (dä kō′mō). Sculptor; active in the middle of the 13th century. He executed (1246) the baptismal font at Pisa, and the pulpit in the Church of S. Bartolomeo in Pantano at Pistoia. These are delightful, archaic and Gothic in feeling, and are fine examples of early Lombard sculpture. Other works attributed to him are at Lucca, Pisa, and Pistoia.

Guido da Pisa (pē′zä). Narrative writer of the first half of the 14th century. A Carmelite, he was a great admirer of Dante, and wrote a poetic epitome, in terza rima, of the *Inferno,* and a Latin commentary on it. His *Fiore d'Italia* (first printed at Bologna, 1490), is a notable compilation of stories from the Old Testament and from Greek mythology. Two sections of it have been published many times. That called *I fatti d'Enea* is still published and used in schools, for its language and for the stories in it as well.

Guido della Polenta (del′lä pō-len′tä). See **Polenta, Guido della.**

Guido da Siena (dä sye′nä). Thirteenth-century Sienese painter, one of the earliest of the Sienese school. He is one of the last representatives of the Byzantine school of painting, a tradition which in his work is modified by his interest in modeling and relief. A large painting of the Madonna, inscribed with his name and dated 1221 (although some interpret the date as 1271) is in the Palazzo Pubblico at Siena. A number of panels in the Pinacoteca are ascribed to him, as is the *Virgin of the Vow* in the cathedral. Other works are at Arezzo, Florence (Accademia), Grosseto, Cambridge (Massachusetts), New Haven, Princeton, and elsewhere.

Guidobaldo da Montefeltro (gwē-dō-bäl′dō dä mōn-tā-fel′trō). [Original name, **Guido Paolo Ubaldo da Montefeltro.**] Duke of Urbino; b. at Gubbio, January 24, 1472; d. at Fossombrone, April 11, 1508. He was the son of Federico da Montefeltro and Battista Sforza, and owed his name and his birthplace to his mother's prayers to S. Ubaldo of Gubbio for a son. From childhood he showed himself to be gentle in disposition, prudent and studious in temperament. Soundly educated by Ludovico Odasio, a distinguished scholar of Padua, he was proficient in Latin and Greek, read classical literature and the poets and, as he grew older, became increasingly attracted by the study of philosophy, ethics, and history. As a youth he was skilled in athletic and military games, but the early onset of gout put an end to these activities. Much of his life was passed in painful and incapacitating illness. His father died (September 10, 1482) when he was ten, and he was at once invested with the duchy of Urbino. His older cousin, Ottaviano Ubaldini, was his companion and councilor. By the terms of a contract Federico had with Naples, Florence, and Milan, the command they had entrusted to him for the war against Venice and the pope in defense of Ferrara was to be passed to his son if Federico should die before the contract expired. The command was in fact transferred to the ten-year-old boy, formally if not actually. But Guidobaldo, because of precarious health and bad luck, as his contemporaries agree, was not destined for the fame in arms won by his father. In a war for Alexander VI against the Orsini he was wounded and taken prisoner (January 23, 1497). The pope refused to act in his behalf and he was finally ransomed for 40,000 ducats. His part in other wars of the time was slight and ineffectual, but his valor and his military skill were never in question. His gifts were in the just administration of his duchy and in scholarly pursuits. A loyal supporter of the Church and of the pope's alliance with Louis XII of France, he hoped and expected that for these reasons his duchy would be spared the attentions of Cesare Borgia, the pope's son. As evidence of his support of Louis, and in the expectation of his protection, Guidobaldo sent men to join Louis on his expedition into Naples. At about the same time, he refused to send men to Arezzo to aid Cesare's captains, as Florence, of which Arezzo was a dependency, was also an ally of France. Cesare, streaking across the Romagna like a flaming arrow, unknown to the pope made a detour in the Romagna, entered the duchy of the unsuspecting duke, and blocked the passes into, or out of, the duchy. Guidobaldo was in the garden of a convent where he had been dining with a learned monk when he heard the news. Exclaiming that he had been betrayed (and by the son of his supposed ally), he immediately prepared for flight and escaped the same night with a few attendants (June 20, 1502). On his way to an asylum, his party was attacked and the gold he had brought with him was lost. A week later he reached Mantua and described his dramatic escape in a letter to Cardinal Giuliano della Rovere of June 28, 1502, in which he concluded, "I have saved nothing but my life, a doublet and a shirt." In October he returned briefly to Urbino, but left again in December, after accepting the agreement Cesare imposed on him by which he was allowed to keep his fortified S. Leo and three other fortresses in the duchy. Before leaving, he advised his people, who begged him to resist, not to strive against Cesare at this moment when he seemed invincible, in order to spare them the sack he knew to be inevitable if they did. He further suggested that they dismantle the fortified castles. Machiavelli cites this in *The Prince*, and says, "a prince who has more to fear from his own people than from foreigners, should build forts, and one who has more to fear from the foreigners should not build them." "The best fortress a prince can have," he continues, "is simply in not being hated by his people." Guidobaldo, secure in the love and fidelity of his people, knew that Cesare would need fortresses to govern them. He went first to S. Leo but, with Cesare's reputation for treachery and Guidobaldo's knowledge that many of those who surrendered to Cesare in good faith ended up with a bowstring around their throats, he fled from there to Mantua. Cesare entered Urbino and allowed his captain to open the palace to plunder. Earlier, in the June invasion, he had carried off to Forlì many of the valuables in the palace, including the precious library, and the tapestries of the Siege of Troy, which he gave to the cardinal of Rouen. The following summer (August,1503), Pope Alexander VI died. Cesare's principality in the Romagna collapsed. Guidobaldo returned to his duchy (August 28, 1503). "He was met," wrote Castiglione, "by swarms of children bearing olive boughs, and hailing his auspicious arrival; by aged sires tottering under their years, and weeping for joy; by men and women; by mothers with their babes; by crowds of every age and sex; nay, the very stones seemed to exult and leap." By a beautifully molded instance of irony, Julius II (the former cardinal, Giuliano della Rovere) named Guidobaldo captain general of the Church to win back the states of the Romagna that Cesare had taken when he held that position, and word went out that he who sought the ear of Julius must court the duke of Urbino. (It happened that Guidobaldo, waiting in an antechamber for an audience with the pope, was accosted by Cesare. The latter fell to his knees, begged forgiveness for his crimes, promised to return what he had stolen from Urbino, and beseeched Guidobaldo to use his good offices in his behalf with the pope.) Cesena and Forlì surrendered without a fight. Guidobaldo recovered many of the treasures of the palace. His remaining years were passed at Urbino, except for long visits to Rome, whither the pope invited him to woo him from a too strong attachment to Venice, which had received and sustained him on his two flights from Cesare. In his absences, his duchess, Elizabetta, governed his state. At home, he devoted himself to the administration of his duchy, where he was universally loved, and to his scholarly interests.

In October, 1489, Guidobaldo had married Elizabetta Gonzaga, youngest sister of the Marquess Francesco Gonzaga of Mantua. The elegant and refined court over which he and his duchess presided has been immortalized in *Il Cortegiano*, the work of their famous courtier Baldassare Castiglione. The court was as notable for its freedom from ostentatious luxury, dissipation, and vice, for its discipline, justice, and wisdom in government, as it was for its urbane and cultivated atmosphere. The leading literary and political figures of the day were delighted to be received at Urbino, and some of them stayed years there. Because of Guidobaldo's poor health and semi-retired life, his duchess, who was not of robust health herself, was the presiding genius of the cultivated circle that made the court at Urbino a model (never copied) of its day. When it had become obvious to Guidobaldo that he would not have an heir (his impotence was attributed to sorcery), he had agreed with the then Cardinal Giuliano della Rovere to adopt his and the cardinal's nephew, Francesco Maria della Rovere, as his son and heir. Early in 1508, overcome by a painful illness, Guidobaldo was carried to Fossombrone, in the hope that the air there would aid in a recovery. It was all useless. To his sorrowing attendants, including the faithful Elizabetta, he recited some verses of Vergil indicating his longing for the release of death, and died. He was succeeded by his adopted heir, who founded the della Rovere dynasty at Urbino.

Guidone Selvaggio (gwē-dô′nā sel-väj′jō). In Lodovico Ariosto's *Orlando Furioso*, the half brother of Rinaldo. Unaware of the relationship, he and Rinaldo fight, but are so evenly matched that neither gains the upper hand. Darkness interrupts their struggle, and Rinaldo offers to share his tent with Guidone. As they return to the tent, Rinaldo tells him his name and Guidone realizes that they are brothers. He makes himself known to Rinaldo and accompanies him to the attack on the Infidel camp.

Guillaume de Machault (or **Machaut**) (gē-yōm dẹ mȧ-shō). French poet and musician; b. c1284; d. after 1370. Chaucer's indebtedness to him is marked. Author of *La Prise d'Alexandre*, *Voir Dit*, and numerous ballades and long poems.

Guinizelli (gwē-nē-tzel′lē), **Guido.** Bolognese poet and jurist; b. at Bologna between 1230 and 1240; d. 1276. He practiced his profession as a jurist in Bologna until, as a Ghibelline, he was banished (1274) with other members of the party. He died in exile. As a poet he was a follower of Guittone d'Arezzo, and his early poems are closely imitative in theme and manner. His later works, including some lyrics of great beauty, show his own mastery and idealism. He was among the earliest to express the idea, developed by Dante, that nobility and love are inseparable. Dante acknowledged his influence and called him "il padre mio." About twenty canzoni and sonnets by Guinizelli are extant.

Guittone d'Arezzo (gwē-tô′nā dä-ret′zō). Tuscan lyric and didactic poet; b. at or near Arezzo, c1225; d. c1294. About 300 of the poems of this prolific Tuscan poet are extant. The love poems of his youth are conventional imitations of the Provençal poets. On the occasion of the defeat of the Florentine Guelphs at Montaperti (1260) he wrote a canzone expressing his grief, the first political poem before Dante. In later years, as a consequence of his joining (1268) the Cavalieri di Santa Maria (Knights of the Blessed Virgin Mary, also called *frati gaudenti*), the conventional theme of courtly love is replaced in his poetry by moral and religious themes which, since he felt them deeply, speak more sincerely. In addition to his poems he wrote many letters, often on the same themes as those of his poems. Saddened by the disturbed state of the world, in 1293 he gave his property to found a monastery, and died the following year.

Gusnasco (gös-näs′kō), **Lorenzo.** [Also called **Lorenzo da Pavia.**] Maker of fine musical instruments; d. 1517. He was famous throughout Italy for the beautiful instruments he made, and was a friend of Giovanni Bellini, Andrea Mantegna, Pietro Bembo, Aldus Manutius, Leonardo da Vinci, and Isabella d'Este. He made organs, viols, lutes, and clavichords, and made an organ for Matthias Corvinus, king of Hungary, and one for Leo X. For his instruments he used the finest woods and metals, and took as much pleasure in the beauty of form as in the beauty of tone. In 1494 he moved to Venice, and from there advised Isabella d'Este, whose friend and correspondent he was for twenty years, on treasures she might add to her precious collections. He made her lutes and a clavichord, and acted often as her agent for buying cameos, antiques, glass, pictures, books, tapestries, and so on for her collections.

Gustavus Vasa (gus-tā′vus, -tä′-, vä′sạ). [Also, **Gustavus Eriksson, Gustavus I.**] King of Sweden (1523–1560); b. at Lindholmen, in Uppland, Sweden, May 12, 1496; d. at Stockholm, September 29, 1560. He was the son of Erik Johansson (hence called Gustavus Eriksson) of the house of Vasa, and was descended on his mother's side from the house of Sture, two of the most influential noble families in Sweden. He received a careful education, chiefly at the court of his kinsman, the regent Sten Sture the younger, under whom he served (1518) against the Danes at the battle of Brännkyrka. In the negotiations which followed this Swedish victory, he was sent as a hostage to Christian II of Denmark, by whom he was treacherously carried off to Denmark. He escaped (1519), and on the massacre of Stockholm, in which ninety of the leading men of Sweden, including the father of Gustavus, were executed by Christian II, headed (1520) a revolt of the Dalecarlians. He captured Stockholm in 1523, the year in which a diet at Strengnäs chose him (June 6) king, and repudiated the Kalmar union with Denmark. He favored the Reformation in opposition to the Roman Catholic clergy, who had supported the Danes during the war for freedom; and at the Diet of Vesteräs, procured (1527) the passage of measures placing the lands of the bishops at his disposal, and granting the liberty of preaching the new doctrine. During the reign of Gustavus Vasa the New Testament was translated (1526) into Swedish by Olaus Petri. The power of the Hanseatic League, crippling to the new Swedish state, was broken (1537) with a victory over Lübeck. Royal power was consolidated; several revolts were suppressed, and in 1544 the line of Vasa was declared hereditary in the rule of Sweden.

Gutenberg (gö′tẹn-bėrg; German, gö′tẹn-berk), **Johannes** (or **Henne**). [Original surname, **Gensfleisch.**] German printer, usually considered to have been the inventor of printing; b. at Mainz, Germany, c1400; d. probably at Mainz, c1468. His claim to the invention of printing has been much disputed, especially by proponents of the priority of Laurens Janszoon Coster. Gutenberg was the son of Frielo Gensfleisch and Else Gutenberg (or Wyrich, Gutenberg being an adopted place name), and took his mother's name. In 1420 his father was exiled, and various legal proceedings growing out of this show that Gutenberg was at Strasbourg in 1434. The claim that he was the inventor of printing rests in large part on a legal decision handed down at Strasbourg on December 12, 1439. From this it would appear that he entered into partnership with certain persons to carry on various secret operations, one of which involved the use of a press with an attachment conjectured to have been a type mold. In 1450 he formed a partnership with Johann Fust, a moneylender, which terminated in 1455. Fust demanded payment of money loaned. In default of this, he seized all of Gutenberg's types and stock, and carried on the business himself, with Peter Schöffer (later his son-in-law) as manager. Gutenberg continued his work with inferior types. None of the work ascribed to Gutenberg bears his name and much of the ascription of books to him is conjectural. It is generally agreed that he printed the Mazarin Bible (so-called because the first copy described was in the library of Cardinal Mazarin), which is also known as the 42-Line Bible; some claim, however, that Schöffer and Fust are responsible for the book.

Guzmán (göth-män′), **Fernando** (or **Fernán**) **Pérez de.** Spanish poet and chronicler; b. 1405; d. 1470. He served for a time at the council board and in the army of John II, king of Castile, but eventually retired to private life and devoted himself to literature. His chief work is *Cronica del señor don Juan Segundo deste nombre, rey de Castilla* (1564).

Guzmán (gös-män′), **Gonzalo Nuño de.** Spanish administrator; b. at Portillo, Spain; d. at Santiago de Cuba, November 5, 1539. He was one of the conquerors of the island of Cuba, regidor of Santiago, and after the death of Velásquez became the island's second governor, on April 27, 1527.

H

Habsburg (haps′bėrg, häps′bu̇rk). See **Hapsburg.**

Haller (häl′ėr), **Berthold.** Swiss preacher; b. at Aldingen, near Rottweil, Württemberg, Germany, 1492; d. at Bern, Switzerland, February 25, 1536. He was influential in establishing the Reformation at Bern.

Hamilton (ham′il-tọn), **John.** Scottish cleric; b. c1511; executed at Stirling, Scotland, April 6, 1571. He was the illegitimate son of James Hamilton, 1st Earl of Arran (c1477–1529), and was noted for his efforts to prevent the growth of Protestantism in Scotland. He became archbishop (1546) of St. Andrews, and was president (1552) of the council that established the catechism later known as Hamilton's Catechism. To improve the standing of Catholicism, he endowed St. Mary's College, St. Andrews, but he aroused hatred by his burning of heretics and his alleged immorality. He was tried (1563) for hearing Mass, but remained a stout supporter of Mary. He granted a divorce (1567) to Bothwell and Lady Jane Gordon. Hamilton assisted the queen in her escape (1568) from Lochleven. Declared a traitor, he was accused of being accessory to the murder of Darnley and of complicity in the murder of Moray, and was hanged in his vestments at the Stirling market place.

Hamilton, Patrick. Scottish reformer; b. c1504; burned at St. Andrews, February 29, 1528. Through his mother he was a grandson of James II of Scotland. He adopted and advocated the doctrines of the Reformation, especially following a period of study at Wittenberg, where he met Luther, and at Marburg, where he knew Tyndale. He returned to Scotland, was examined by the archbishop and bishops of St. Andrews, and was put to death the day of his conviction as a heretic.

Hampton Court (hamp′tọn). English royal palace on the Thames, about twelve miles from Charing Cross, London, built by Cardinal Wolsey. Much of the battlemented, red brick, Tudor construction, surrounding three courts, still remains. The total property originally consisted of about 1,000 acres of more or less barren land belonging to the Knight Hospitallers of Saint John of Jerusalem. It was leased from the Priory of Saint John in 1515 by Thomas Wolsey, archbishop of York and primate of England, who erected the original Gothic palace. In 1526 he surrendered the estate to Henry VIII, who added the chapel and great hall in the period 1531–1535. In the reign of William III, the great façade, modern state apartments, and a gallery for the cartoons of Raphael (since moved to the Victoria and Albert Museum) were added by Sir Christopher Wren. The front on the French gardens is later, in the Renaissance style. The great hall is 106 by 40 feet and 60 feet high. The state apartments are filled with paintings. Hampton Court is most intimately associated with James I and William III, and was a place of imprisonment of Charles I.

Hapsburg (haps′bėrg; German häps′bůrk), **House of.** [Also, **Habsburg;** original name, **Habichtsburg,** meaning "Hawk's Castle."] German princely family which derived its name from the castle of Habsburg, in Switzerland, and which furnished sovereigns to the Holy Roman Empire, Austria, and Spain. The title Count of Hapsburg was assumed by Werner I, who died in 1096. Count Rudolf was elected emperor as Rudolf I in 1273 and acquired Austria, and founded the imperial line which reigned during the periods 1273–1291, 1298–1308, and 1438–1740. The title Archduke of Austria was revived in 1453. In 1477 the emperor Maximilian I acquired the domain (except the duchy) of the ducal house of Burgundy by marriage with the heiress Mary, and in 1490 had all the Hapsburg possessions united in his hands by the abdication of Count Sigismund. His son, Philip I of Spain, married Joanna (Juana) the Mad, queen of Aragon and Castile. Their eldest son became king of Spain as Charles I in 1516, and emperor as Charles V in 1519; their second son, Ferdinand I, received the Austrian crown, to which he added, by election, the kingdoms of Bohemia and Hungary. The Spanish line was continued by Charles' son Philip II, and reigned from 1516 to 1700. On the abdication (1556) of the imperial crown by Charles V, he was succeeded by his brother Ferdinand, who continued the imperial line, the last male representative of which was Charles VI. On the death of Charles VI (1740), his daughter Maria Theresa succeeded to the Austrian inheritance by virtue of the pragmatic sanction. She married Francis I, grand duke of Tuscany, of the house of Lorraine, who became emperor in 1745, and founded the Hapsburg-Lorraine line, members of which ruled as emperors of the Holy Roman Empire until its abolition in 1806, and until 1918 ruled as emperors of Austria.

Harcadelt (här′kä-delt), **Jacob.** See **Arcadelt, Jacob.**

Hardyng or **Harding** (här′ding), **John.** English chronicler; b. 1378; d. c1465. As a youth he was a member of the household of Harry Percy (Hotspur), and was present at the battle of Shrewsbury (1403). He fought also at Agincourt (1415). His chronicle is written in English verse, and comes down to about 1436. He forged certain documents for Henry V relating to the feudal relations of the Scottish and English crowns.

Hastings (hās′tingz), **George.** [Titles, 1st Earl of **Huntingdon,** 3rd Baron **Hastings of Hastings.**] English nobleman; b. c1488; d. 1545. He was a favorite of Henry VIII and as one of the leaders of the king's forces helped (1536) suppress the insurrection of the Pilgrimage of Grace.

Hastings, John. [Titles, 2nd Baron **Hastings,** Baron **Bergavenny.**] English nobleman; b. May 6, 1262; d. February 28, 1313. He was a claimant (1290) to the throne of Scotland. He married (1275) Isabella de Valence, niece of Henry III, served in Scotland (1285), Wales (1288), and Ireland (1295), and commanded the Durham troops at the siege of Carlaverock (1300). Hastings attended (1301) the Parliament at Lincoln, and signed the baronial letter denying the right of Pope Boniface VIII to judge the dispute with Scotland.

Hastings, John. [Title, 2nd Earl of **Pembroke.**] English soldier; b. 1347; d. en route between Paris and Calais, April 16, 1375. He accompanied (1369) the earl of Cambridge to France to reinforce Edward, the Black Prince, in Aquitaine, participating in the capture of Bourdeille and Limoges. As lieutenant of the king's forces in Aquitaine, he was imprisoned (June 23, 1372) while making an unsuccessful attempt to relieve the siege of La Rochelle. He married Margaret, the fourth daughter of Edward III, and in 1368 Anne, Sir Walter de Manny's daughter.

Hastings, Laurence. [Title, 1st Earl of **Pembroke.**] English soldier; b. c1318; d. August 30, 1348. He accompanied (1345) the earl of Derby to Gascony, where he was present at the siege of Bergerac and the capture of Aiguillon and La Réole. He was appointed (June, 1347) with the earl of Northampton to command the fleet at Calais, where they were victorious.

Hastings, William. [Title, Baron **Hastings.**] English Yorkist nobleman; b. c1430; executed in the Tower of London, June 14, 1483. In 1475 he was sent to France with an invading army, and a treaty of peace followed. He swore allegiance to Edward's eldest son, but was on bad terms with the queen. After the king's death, Gloucester (later Richard III), failing to win his agreement to his plans, charged him with treason at a council held in the Tower, and he was taken out and beheaded at once. Shakespeare dramatized Sir Thomas More's account of this in *Richard III*.

Hawes (hôz), **Stephen.** English poet and courtier of Henry VII; b. c1476; d. c1523. He wrote (c1506) an allegorical poem, *The Passetyme of Pleasure, or the History of Graunde Amour and la Bel Pucel, conteining the knowledge of the Seven Sciences and the Course of Man's Life in this Worlde*, printed by Wynkyn de Worde in 1509.

Hawkins or **Hawkyns** (hô′kinz), Sir **John.** English naval hero; b. at Plymouth, England, 1532; d. at sea off Puerto Rico, November 12, 1595. In 1562, 1564, and 1567 he carried cargoes of slaves from Africa to the West Indies and the Spanish Main. Several English noblemen, and, it is said, Queen Elizabeth, had a financial interest in these voyages. The trade was a violation of Spanish law, and ultimately Hawkins was attacked (September 24, 1568) by a Spanish fleet in the harbor of Veracruz, and escaped with difficulty, after losing all his ships except the *Minion* (under him) and the *Judith* (owned and commanded by his cousin Francis Drake). In apparent disgrace, Hawkins, with the connivance of Lord Burleigh (William Cecil), the secretary of state, undertook negotiations with the Spanish to enable them to invade England and overthrow Elizabeth. For these supposed services he was granted a Spanish title and a large sum of money. In 1573 he was made treasurer of the English navy, and shortly thereafter comptroller. As rear admiral he took a prominent part in the defeat of the Spanish Armada (August, 1588), and was knighted. He was with Frobisher on the Portuguese coast in 1590 in an attempt to meet the Spanish silver fleet, but the expedition failed in its purpose. He died while second in command in Drake's unsuccessful expedition to the West Indies.

Hawkwood (hôk′wu̇d), Sir **John.** [Called **Giovanni Acuto** by the Italians.] English leader of condottieri; b. at Hedingham Sibil, Hinckford, Essex, England, c1320; d. at Florence, March 16/17, 1394. He was of good family and by 1359 was in Gascony at the head of a band of freebooters who supported themselves by pillage. He and his men took Pau, and then headed toward Italy. On the way they exacted tribute from Pope Innocent VI, whose papal court was at Avignon. Hawkwood entered the pay of the Marquis of Monferrato for the war against the Visconti and, under the name of the White Company, ravaged and plundered Lombardy. After he defeated a company of Hungarians in the Visconti pay, the Visconti made peace (1363). The White Company was, in turn, in the pay of Pisa, the Visconti, Pope Gregory XI, again for the Visconti, Florence, Padua, and again and last, Florence. While in the pay of the pope he, at the order of Cardinal Robert of Geneva (later the antipope Clement VII), took Cesena (1377) and put its population to the sword. In the pay of the Visconti he married one of Bernabò Visconti's daughters. Florence paid him not to ravage its territory. When not serving for pay the White Company supported itself by pillaging and burning the countryside. He ended his days, from 1380, in the pay of Florence, died there and was given a magnificent funeral in the Duomo. While he was still living the Florentines had engaged to have a statue of him placed in the cathedral. The design had been made. After he died the Florentine government compromised by having Paolo Uccello paint a fresco showing him mounted on his horse, in such a manner that it looked like a statue. It is in the cathedral, and was quite a money saver as compared to a bronze monument. Hawkwood had finally become the permanent military adviser and captain general of Florence. He was a good organizer and on the whole faithful to his employers. Fra Filippo Agazzari called him "a very wicked English knight," and St. Catherine of Siena wrote to him, urging him to enter the pay of Christ and take up the Cross. His was among the first of the bands of adventurers who ravaged Italy as freebooters, doing more damage when they were not engaged in fighting than when they were.

Heinrich der Vogeler (hīn′rich dėr fō′gẹ-lėr). German poet; active late in the 13th century. He wrote (c1300) the epic *Dietrichs Flucht*.

Heinrich von Freiberg (fon frī′bėrk). Middle High German poet; fl. early 14th century. A native of Saxony, he was one of the last court poets. He is known chiefly for having completed Gottfried von Strassburg's *Tristan und Isolde*.

Heinrich von Meissen (fon mī′sẹn). [Called **Frauenlob**, meaning "Praise of Women."] Middle High German lyric poet; b. at Meissen, Germany, 1250; d. at Mainz, Germany, 1318. He was a wandering singer who lived in all parts of Germany. He is said to have founded at Mainz the first school of so-called Master Singers, and himself marks the transition from the Minnesingers to the later Meistersingers. It is said that the women of Mainz bore him to his grave, where, at the cathedral, his monument is still to be seen.

Heinrich von Morungen (fon mō′rùng-ẹn). German Minnesinger, a native of Thuringia; active in the 13th century. Although he was one of the poets who brought the art of the French troubadours to Germany, his work is nevertheless not entirely derived from them.

Heinrich von Mügeln (fon mü′gẹln). German author; active in the 14th century. He spent most of his life at the court of Emperor Charles IV at Prague. He was a Minnesinger and one of the earliest Meistersingers. He was also a forerunner of humanism.

Helier (hē′lyėr), **Wat** (or **Walter**). See **Tyler, Wat** (or **Walter**).

Hemling (hem′ling), **Hans.** See **Memling, Hans.**

Henry II (of *Castile*). [Additional title, Count of **Trastamara.**] King of Castile (1369–1379); b. 1333; d. in May, 1379. He was the natural son of Alfonso XI, and before his accession to the throne was known as the count of Trastamara. Charles V of France sent him an army made up of members of the free companies under the command of Bernard Du Guesclin, the celebrated captain. With this army Henry expelled his half brother Pedro the Cruel and seized the throne. The next year (1367) Pedro, aided by Edward, the Black Prince, defeated him at Nájera, but when Edward withdrew, Henry defeated and killed Pedro (1369) and kept the crown. Henry was succeeded by his son John I.

Henry III (of *Castile*). [Called **Henry the Sickly.**] King of Castile (1390–1406); b. 1379; d. 1406. He was the son of John I, and married (1388) Catherine, daughter of John of Gaunt, duke of Lancaster, and Constance, daughter of Pedro the Cruel. In 1403 he recognized Benedict XIII as pope in opposition to Boniface IX. He was succeeded by his son John II.

Henry IV (of *Castile*). [Called **Henry the Impotent.**] King of Castile (1454–1474); b. at Valladolid, Spain, January 6, 1425; d. at

Madrid, December 12, 1474. He was the son of John II. He married Juana of Portugal, the legitimacy of whose daughter, Juana (called la Beltraneja after her reputed father, the court favorite Beltrán de la Cueva), was questioned by the Cortes. Henry was deposed (1464) by a revolt, but his successor died the following year and he regained the throne. He adopted as his heiress his half sister Isabella of Castile, who married Ferdinand of Aragon in 1469, and succeeded Henry as queen of Castile.

Henry IV (of *England*). [Called **Henry of Bolingbroke, Henry of Lancaster.**] King of England (1399–1413); b. at the castle of Bolingbroke, near Spilsby, Lincolnshire, April 3, 1367; d. at Westminster, March 20, 1413. He was the son of John of Gaunt (fourth son of Edward III) and Blanche, heiress of Lancaster, and was the first king of England of the house of Lancaster. In July, 1399, while Richard II was absent in Ireland, Henry gathered to him many of the nobility, who hated Richard's usurpations, and took possession of the kingdom. Richard rushed back from Ireland, but, deserted by his forces, fled to Wales, where he was captured. On September 29, 1399, Richard resigned the throne, but Parliament gratuitously insulted him the next day by voting his abdication and proclaiming Henry king. Henry's reign was marked by a more scrupulous adherence to constitutional government and by the adoption (1401) of a special statute against the Lollards. His first wife, Mary de Bohun, bore him six children, including his successor Henry V.

Henry V (of *England*). King of England (1413–1422); b. at Monmouth, probably August 9, 1387; d. at Vincennes, France, August 31, 1422. He was the son of Mary de Bohun and Henry IV, whom he succeeded on March 20, 1413. In October 25, 1415, he defeated a vastly superior French army at Agincourt, and in 1420, by the Treaty of Troyes, achieved his principal aims in France: he was to marry Catherine of Valois, daughter of Charles VI of France; he would serve as regent for the insane king; and he was to be the king's heir, the dauphin being specifically excluded. On June 2 he married Catherine; in December he made a triumphal entry into Paris. He returned with his queen to England to have her crowned and to have the treaty ratified. Forced to return to France (1421) to put down a revolt, he weakened his health and died the following summer. Henry, like his father, observed and strengthened constitutional government: the consent of Parliament to a law was made necessary for its validity and Parliament obtained the right to draft bills without amendment; the privy council became a permanent body. Henry is often considered the ideal knightly king, and he modeled himself deliberately in the image of King Arthur and Godfrey of Bouillon. Pius II called him ". . . an illustrious man and easily foremost among the sovereigns of his time . . . ; he governed subject peoples justly; he forbade the English to have featherbeds. They say he intended, if he obtained sovereignty over all France, to abolish the use of wine and plow up all the vineyards; for he thought nothing weakened men so much as feathers and wine." Henry is said, on doubtful authority, to have been wild and dissolute in his youth, and is so represented by Shakespeare; but Shakespeare took him as the model king and as the culmination of English greatness before Elizabeth. He was succeeded by his son Henry VI. Seldom in England, he stands in the company of Richard I, also virtually never on the island, as one of the most popular of kings. Both engaged in futile and costly wars that won them monumental public acclaim.

Henry VI (of *England*). King of England (1422–1461 and 1470–1471); b. at Windsor, December 6, 1421; d. at London, May 21, 1471. He was the son of Henry and Catherine of Valois. By the Treaty of Troyes (1420), Henry V became heir to the French throne; when he and his father-in-law, Charles VI of France, died within a few months of each other, the infant Henry VI inherited both kingdoms under the treaty. He was opposed by Charles' son, the dauphin (later Charles VII), in France. In 1429 Joan of Arc came to the aid of the French king, drove the English from their positions around Orléans, and started the retreat of the English from France. Henry had been crowned at Paris in 1431 but by 1453 the English retained nothing but Calais. In that same year Richard, duke of York, Henry's cousin and nearest kinsman, became regent when Henry suffered the first of several attacks of insanity. Henry's wife Margaret contested with York for the regency and for the protection of her infant son Prince Edward. Henry recovered his sanity and dismissed York, but from this time began the bitter struggle between the Yorkists (whose badge was a white rose) and the Lancastrians (Henry's party, whose badge was a red rose) that came to be known as the Wars of the Roses. Of the battles that ensued, beginning in 1455, a decisive one was at Towton (March 29, 1461), in which the Lancastrians were routed. Henry fled but made an attempt to return; other battles followed; he was restored briefly (1470). His son Edward was killed at the battle of Tewkesbury (May 4, 1471) and Henry died soon afterward in the Tower, probably murdered. He was succeeded by Edward IV, of the house of York, who had also reigned between 1461 and 1470.

Henry VII (of *England*). [Frequently called **Henry Tudor;** before his accession known as the Earl of **Richmond.**] King of England (1485–1509); b. January 28, 1457; d. at Richmond, near London, April 21, 1509. He became head of the house of Lancaster on the death of Henry VI in the Tower of London in 1471. Because Henry VI's Yorkist successors (Edward IV and Richard III) distrusted him as a Lancastrian, he prudently spent the years 1471 to 1485 in exile. In the latter year he returned to England and was victorious at Bosworth Field (August 22, 1485) where King Richard III was killed. Henry was crowned king October 30, 1485. Henry VII traced his descent on his mother's side back to John of Gaunt, duke of Lancaster, fourth son of Edward III; his father, Edmund Tudor, earl of Richmond, was the son of Owen Tudor and Catherine of Valois, widow of Henry V of England. When Henry married (January 18, 1486) Elizabeth, eldest daughter of Edward IV, he united in his own person the titles of the houses of Lancaster and York. Edward's brothers being dead (George, duke of Clarence, murdered in 1478, and Richard III dying at Bosworth) and his sons (Edward V and Richard, duke of York) being slain in the Tower, Henry Tudor stood as undeniably having the best claim to the throne. (It is because of this circumstance, that death had so conveniently removed possible rivals, that supporters of Richard III point suspiciously toward Henry VII in the matter of the death of the Tower princes.) In succeeding years Henry overcame other claimants to the throne as well as dealing with a number of impostors and with frequent revolts. His policy was to avoid war and to build up the internal economy and the royal treasury. He withdrew from a war with France (1492) for an indemnity of 750,000 crowns. He reconciled Scotland through the marriage of his daughter Margaret to James. His eldest son, Arthur, married Catherine of Aragon on November 15, 1501. Arthur died on April 2, 1502, and Henry, wishing to preserve the Spanish connection, made several attempts to match Catherine again, including himself as a suitor after the death of Elizabeth of York in 1503; Catherine eventually married Arthur's younger brother Henry, after the latter ascended the throne as Henry VIII, the marriage being perhaps the most fateful in English history. Another of Henry's daughters, Mary, married Louis XII of France in 1514. Henry strengthened the monarchy while outwardly conforming to many of the limitations imposed on royal power over the preceding 270 years. He put his trust in able men, regardless of their status, raising them to the nobility when necessary and, by making them dependent on him, controlled them more effectively. His council, sitting in the Star Chamber, became the supreme court of the land (and a lucrative one in fees), and its powers were strengthened by statutes. Laws were passed controlling economic life; wages and prices were made subject to law. He reestablished ancient taxes and fees where he could, and saw to it that they were collected. He himself checked the accounts of the treasury (to which he diverted much of the business of the exchequer) and won the reputation of being extremely tightfisted. In his reign Ireland was made a vassal state under the English crown (1495). His enforcement of the Statute of Liveries eventually broke down the private armies of retainers maintained by the nobility. The severe fines and other punishments made the royal military force paramount in the nation and permitted economies in the military budget. Henry's reign is notable as the period when English overseas exploration began (Cabot's voyages of 1496 and later) and when the New Learning came to England (John Colet's lectures at Oxford, 1496–1504). He left his son and successor, Henry VIII, a full treasury, enabling him to cut a dashing figure on the European diplomatic scene during the early years of his reign.

Henry VIII (of *England*). King of England (1509–1547); b. at Greenwich, June 28, 1491; d. at Westminster, January 28, 1547. He was the second and only surviving son of Henry VII and Elizabeth of York. Well educated in the New Learning by such teachers as poet laureate John Skelton, he had great respect for scholarship and was himself an accomplished linguist, a poet, and a musician on the lute, organ, and harpsichord. He was also a fine horseman, swordsman, runner, and wrestler, all accomplishments that led to his early popularity. He was handsome, of powerful physique, and proud of his well-formed legs. After the death of his older brother Arthur, he became (1503) prince of Wales. He succeeded his father on April 22, 1509, and on June 3 married his betrothed, Catherine of Aragon, widow of his brother, for which marriage negotiations had been proceeding, principally concerned with her dowry, for some five years. He entered freely into European politics and sought to keep the balance of power between Francis I, who became king of France in 1515, and Charles I of Spain who, as Charles V, became Holy Roman emperor in 1519. In 1513 he had gone to France and defeated the French, with the aid of the previous emperor, Maximilian I, at Guinegate (the Battle of the Spurs), on August 16, 1513. After the election of Charles V there were many conferences, as with Charles in England in 1520, and with Francis, later in the same year, at Calais at the Field of the Cloth of Gold. His wars in France exhausted the Treasury, and in the resolution of the struggle between Francis and Charles he was unable to play a decisive role. At home he sought to bring Scotland under English domination, and defeated James VI at Solway Moss (1542) but could not bend the Scots to his will. His foreign policy, apart from its resulting in a strong English navy, was a failure. He had dissipated his father's fortune in fruitless adventures, and England, instead of becoming the power on the Continent he had wished it to be, was of little consequence in the continental struggle for power. Calais alone still remained in English hands, but so weak was England that in ten years Calais would be lost.

His combined desires for an heir (Catherine of Aragon had borne him a daughter, Mary) and for Anne Boleyn led him to seek a divorce from Catherine of Aragon, on the ground that a dispensation should never have been granted to him, as it had been, to enable him to marry his brother's widow. He was a firm adherent of the Church of Rome. His book *Assertio septem sacramentorum contra M. Lutherum* (1521), a vigorous defense of the sacraments against Luther's doctrines, had won for him the title of Defender of the Faith (Fidei Defensor) from Pope Leo X. But his position as head of the English nation was paramount in his thoughts and in 1527 he began proceedings for a divorce from the 42-year-old Catherine, alleging the invalidity of the marriage with a deceased brother's wife, despite the papal dispensation. Pope Clement VII, well aware of the immediate power of the emperor, whose cousin Mary would become illegitimate if the marriage with Catherine were annulled, and of the distance separating him from England, temporized, as was his custom. Henry gathered opinions from various English and foreign universities, and with these opinions that the dispensation had been illegal to back him, Cranmer, who had replaced the unfortunate Wolsey, held that the marriage was invalid and that the pope had been incompetent to grant a dispensation. Anne Boleyn, who had managed her part in the affair very cleverly, was carrying Henry's child, and a marriage had to be arranged quickly. Cranmer secretly performed the ceremony on January 25, 1533, and on May 23, as archbishop of Canterbury since March, declared the marriage with Catherine void and that with Anne Boleyn valid (May 28, 1533). Elizabeth, the future queen, born on September 7, 1533, was thus legitimatized. Meanwhile Henry had been carrying on a war of nerves with the pope, who was particularly unsuited to this, or any other kind, of war. He convoked Parliament in November, 1529, and with his new chancellor, Thomas More, as speaker, worked on the anticlerical feelings of the assembly. Acts limiting the power of the clergy were passed; the annates paid to Rome were reduced to five percent; he fined the convocation of the clergy at Canterbury and York for acting on papal authority without the king's consent. Clement could not sit idly by while this defiance of the Church was taking place. In September, 1533, he excommunicated Henry. Earlier in 1533 the king had caused to be passed an act (essentially a renewal of an old statute of the second half of the 14th century) whereby spiritual appeals had to be made to Canterbury or to the king. In 1534 a group of thirty-two religious bills were passed by Parliament, which among other things cut Rome off from English revenue, declared that episcopal and archiepiscopal offices were to be filled by royal nomination and election by chapters, authorized an oath to the crown before consecration, established dispensations in the hands of the archbishop of Canterbury, and gave the king control of canons. The Act of Supremacy, at the end of the same year, appointed the king (and his successors) protector and only supreme head of the church and clergy of England. In addition to the clerical acts, Parliament passed an act of succession, declaring the children of Henry's second marriage heirs to the throne and requiring an oath to uphold the succession, on pain of conviction of treason, from all subjects. Both Thomas More, the chancellor, and John Fisher, bishop of Rochester, refused to take the oath, because of a rider attached to it, and in 1535 both were beheaded. At the instance of his new adviser, Thomas Cromwell, who was made vicar general or vicegerent of the king in matters ecclesiastical in 1535, Henry first suppressed the smaller (1536) and afterward the larger (1539) monasteries, whose property was confiscated, and in the case of the buildings and libraries was in many instances destroyed. In 1536 occurred the Pilgrimage of Grace, an uprising of Roman Catholics in the north of England; their leaders were tried and executed. In 1535 Coverdale's Bible and in 1539 the Great Bible, its successor, were printed, in English. The Ten Articles of Faith, put forth in convocation in 1536, contained far too much Protestantism for Henry, and in 1539 he procured the enactment of the Statute of Six Articles, a definition of heresy that adhered closely to Roman Catholic doctrine. But this could not hold back the flood he had released, and the Reformation flowed on to its full tide under his successors.

Henry's marriage to Anne Boleyn ended on May 19, 1536, when she was executed for adultery. The next day he was married for the third time, to Jane Seymour. She gave birth to the future Edward VI and then died on October 24, 1537. Henry's fourth wife (January 6, 1540) was Anne of Cleves. Their divorce took place on June 24, 1540. On August 8, 1540, he married Catherine Howard, the day Cromwell was executed for being too zealous a Protestant. Catherine Howard was beheaded in less than two years (February 12, 1542) for adultery, apparently a more justifiable charge than the one against Anne Boleyn. Henry's sixth wife was Catherine Parr. They were married on July 12, 1543. Catherine Parr, who had survived two husbands before she was married to Henry, survived him and married again. By his six marriages, Henry had three children: Mary, daughter of Catherine of Aragon, who reigned as Mary I; Elizabeth, who was the daughter of Anne Boleyn; Edward VI, the son of Jane Seymour, who was Henry's immediate successor.

Henry's reliance on Parliament, especially during his struggle with Rome, resulted in a widening of that body's powers and of its membership to include Wales and other regions. Under Henry the power of the crown was further centralized and that of the feudal nobility was reduced in proportion. The councils of the North and of Wales, similar to the Star Chamber court (and like it established under Henry VII), became powerful weapons against feudal barons who resisted the royal authority. The great distribution of church lands led to further close adherence to the crown by recipients of the royal favor. Despite personal scandal he remained popular, having accomplished a relatively easy transition from a medieval to a state church with a minimum of violence and bloodshed. His intention throughout his reign was to strengthen his country and the position of the monarch. It was his boast that he did nothing unconstitutional, but often the constitutionality of his acts depended on laws enacted after the acts they legitimized.

Henry II (of *France*). King of France (1547–1559); b. at St.-Germain-en-Laye, March 31, 1519; d. at Paris, July 10, 1559. He was the son of Francis I, whom he succeeded, having become dauphin (1536) when his brother Francis died. In 1533 he married Catherine de Médicis, the last survivor of the elder branch of the Florentine house of Medici. His wife had not much influence during his reign as he came to be dominated by Anne de Montmorency, constable of

France, and Diane de Poitiers, his mistress. Henry conquered the bishoprics of Metz, Toul, and Verdun from Germany in 1552, and captured Calais and Guines, the last English possessions in France, in 1558. He was mortally wounded at a tournament in honor of the marriage of his daughter Elizabeth to Philip II of Spain and his sister Margaret to Emanuel Philibert of Savoy, events growing out of the treaty of Cateau-Cambrésis, by which France lost Savoy, territory bordering the Netherlands, and all claims in Italy to Spain. Three of his sons became kings of France: Francis II, Charles IX, and Henry III; a daughter married Henry of Navarre, who became Henry IV of France.

Henry VII (of the *Holy Roman Empire*). Count of Luxemburg and emperor of the Holy Roman Empire (1309–1313); b. 1269; d. at Buonconvento, near Siena, August 24, 1313. He was the son of Henry III, count of Luxemburg, succeeded Albert I as German king (1308) and was elected emperor in 1309. He granted the Swiss cantons documentary confirmation of their immediate feudal relation to the empire, and their consequent independence of Austria, in 1309. Handsome, and of a generous and romantic nature, he dreamed of restoring the age of chivalry and especially of reviving imperial power in Italy. Having secured order in Germany he descended into Italy in 1310, was welcomed by both Guelphs and Ghibellines and ecstatically so in a letter of Dante, who idealized the order of the ancient empire. In the *Divina Commedia* (*Paradiso*, xxx) Dante speaks of him as one who came to guide an Italy as yet unfit for him. Henry was crowned with the Iron Crown of Lombardy in Milan (1311), and later with the imperial crown at Rome (1312) by the cardinals, the pope being in Avignon. He was quite promptly awakened from his dream of being above partisan strife. Milan revolted against him. He subdued that city and Cremona and allied himself with the Ghibellines, but hesitated to march against Florence, where the Neri (Black Guelphs) were preparing to resist him. Dante wrote him again, chiding him on his delay, and pointing out to him that he was wasting his time on Milan and Cremona when it was Florence that was at the bottom of the resistance against him. Henry died of a fever at Buonconvento, near Siena. The dream of a universal empire that would restore universal order and would rule in harness with, but always subject to, a universal Church, died with him. A virtuous prince, he was one of the very few of his contemporaries for whom Dante reserved a place in Paradise. On his death, Louis IV of Wittelsbach and Frederick III of Germany were rivals for the imperial crown. Louis was eventually successful.

Henry I (of *Navarre*). [Called **Henry the Fat**; additional title, Count of **Champagne.**] King of Navarre (1270–1274); b. c1210; d. July, 1274. He was succeeded by his daughter Jeanne, whose marriage (1284) to Philip IV of France joined Navarre to the French crown.

Henry II (of *Navarre*). Titular king of Navarre; b. at Sanguesa, Spain, April, 1503; d. at Pau, France, May 25, 1555. He was the son of Jean d'Albret and Catherine de Foix, heiress of Navarre. His attempt to claim the throne (1521) was frustrated by the troops of the emperor Charles V. He married (1526) Marguerite de Valois, sister of Francis I of France, and was the father of Jeanne d'Albret, mother of Henry IV of France (Henry of Navarre).

Henry (of *Portugal*). [Called **Henry the Navigator.**] Portuguese prince; b. at Oporto, Portugal, March 4, 1394; d. at Sagres, Portugal, November 13, 1460. He was a younger son of John I of Portugal, distinguished for his encouragement of science and geographical discovery. The expeditions sent out by him rounded Cape Bojador in 1433, and discovered Madeira, the Azores, the Senegal, and other places. He is responsible in the main for stimulating the interest in exploration and discovery that led the Portuguese to the Indies and the New World in the years following his death. While he made no voyages himself, he was the focus of the new geographical study and his home at Sagres was a clearinghouse for information about new lands, map improvements, shipbuilding innovations, and the like.

Henry I (of *Portugal*). King of Portugal (1578–1580); b. at Lisbon, January 31, 1512; d. 1580. An ecclesiastic (appointed cardinal, 1542), he was a weak ruler and left no offspring. The dynastic quarrel that followed his death led to the absorption of Portugal by Spain under Philip II.

Henry of Marlborough (märl′bur-ǭ, -brǫ, môl′-). English chronicler; fl. c1420. His annals (in Latin) cover the history of England and Ireland for the period 1133–1421.

Henry the Fat. See **Henry I** (of *Navarre*).

Henry the Impotent. See **Henry IV** (of *Castile*).

Henry the Navigator. See **Henry** (of *Portugal*).

Henry the Sickly. See **Henry III** (of *Castile*).

Henryson (hen′ri-so̤n), **Robert.** [Also, **Henderson.**] Scottish poet; b. c1430; d. c1506. He wrote *Testament of Cresseid* (a sort of tragic sequel to Chaucer's *Troilus and Cressida*), *Robene and Makyne* (said to be the earliest English pastoral poem), *Morall Fabillis of Esope the Phrygian* (probably written between 1470 and 1480), and other works. The fables include "The Taill of the Uponlandis Mous and the Burges Mous" ("The Country Mouse and the City Mouse").

Heptameron (hep-tam′e̤-ro̤n). Collection of stories by Margaret of Angoulême, queen of Navarre (1492–1549), supposed to have been related during seven days, modeled on the *Decameron* of Boccaccio.

Herbert (hėr′bėrt), Sir **William.** [Title, 1st Earl of **Pembroke** of the first creation (1468).] English Yorkist leader; beheaded at Northampton, England, July 28, 1469. A soldier from his youth, he was knighted (1449) by Henry VI, served notably against Jasper Tudor in the Wars of the Roses, and was made privy councilor and chief justice (1461) of South Wales by Edward IV, later becoming chief justice (1467) of North Wales. Defeated and captured (1469) by rebel supporters of Henry VI, he was executed.

Herbert, William. [Titles, 2nd Earl of **Pembroke,** Earl of **Huntingdon.**] English army captain; b. March 5, 1460; d. 1491. He was the son of Sir William Herbert (d. 1469). Captain (1475) of English forces in France, he was appointed (1483) justice of South Wales. He surrendered (1479) the earldom of Pembroke to the king in exchange for the earldom of Huntingdon.

Herbert, Sir **William.** [Title, 1st Earl of **Pembroke** of the second creation (1551).] English soldier and diplomat; b. c1501; d. at Hampton Court, England, March 17, 1570. He was the son of an illegitimate son of Sir William Herbert (d. 1469). He married Anne Parr, sister of Henry VIII's sixth queen, Catherine Parr, became (1546) a gentleman of the privy chamber and later an executor of Henry VIII's will, and was a member of Edward VI's council. He acted with Northumberland in support of Lady Jane Grey, but declared (July 19, 1553) for Mary Tudor. He commanded the forces (1554) which overcame Sir Thomas Wyatt's rebellion against the queen's marriage to Philip of Spain. He supported the Protestant party under Queen Elizabeth, and was appointed (1568) lord steward under her: a very supple man.

Herlin (her′lin), **Friedrich.** [Also, **Herlen, Hörlin, Herlein.**] German religious painter; active in the latter half of the 15th century. He is known to have lived and worked in the Bavarian part of Swabia, and especially at Nördlingen after 1467, but his paintings display the influence of Roger van der Weyden and of the Van Eycks so strongly as to compel the inference that he studied in the Netherlands. Most of the surviving known works of Herlin, including a *Virgin Enthroned,* a *Magdalene,* a *Crucifixion,* and several saints, are in the Church of Saint George at Nördlingen.

Hermandad (er-män-däᴛʜ′). [Original name, **Santa Hermandad.**] In Spain, originally, a voluntary organization for the maintenance of public order. The first Hermandad was formed in Aragon in the 13th century, and another in Castile and Leon a few years later, chiefly to resist the exactions and robberies of the nobles. They soon assumed general police and judicial powers, under royal sanction; and at the end of the 15th century the organizations were united and extended over the whole kingdom. The Hermandad was soon after reorganized as a regular national police, which was superseded in later times by a civil guard on the model of the French gendarmerie.

Hernández (er-nän′deth), **Francisco.** Spanish naturalist; b. at Toledo, Spain, 1514; d. c1578. He traveled in Mexico from 1570 to 1576, and prepared sixteen fo̤lio volumes on plants, animals, and minerals; portions were published in 1648, 1651, and 1791.

Hernández Girón (hē-rōn′), **Francisco.** Spanish adventurer; b. at Cáceres, in Estremadura, Spain, c1505; executed at Lima, Peru, December 7, 1554. He went to America in 1535, took part in the conquest of New Granada, and fought on the royal side in Peru during the rebellion (1545–1548) of Gonzalo Pizarro. On November 12, 1553, he headed a revolt at Cusco; he defeated the royalists under Alonzo de Alvarado at the battle of Chuquingua (May 21, 1554), but later his forces were outnumbered. He was captured and beheaded.

Herrada (er-rä′ᴛʜä), **Juan de.** See **Rada, Juan de.**

Herrera (er-rā′rä), **Fernando de.** [Called **el Divino.**] Spanish lyric poet; b. at Seville, Spain, 1534; d. there, 1597. He was a friend of Cervantes, who wrote a sonnet in his honor. His poetical works were published by his friend the painter Francisco Pacheco, in 1582 and 1619. He also wrote *Relación de la guerra de Chipre, y suceso de la batalla naval de Lepanto* (1572), and *Vida y Muerte de Tomás Moro* (1592).

Heywood (hā′wu̇d), **John.** English epigrammatist and dramatist; b. c1497; d. at Mechelen (Malines) Belgium, c1580. He was a sort of court jester, though of good social position, and known for his powers of repartee. He was a favorite with Queen Mary but when Elizabeth ascended the throne he retired to Mechelen, where he is supposed to have died. He wrote three interludes in which for the first time characters were personal and not mere abstractions. He thus paved the way for English comedy. The best known of the interludes is *The Playe called the foure P P: a newe and a very mery interlude of a palmer, a pardoner, a potycary, a pedler,* printed between 1543 and 1547. His *Epigrams and Proverbs* (1562) show both wit and humor, and were very popular. He wrote also *The Play of Love, The Play of Wether,* and *Witty and Witless;* probably also by him are the plays *The Pardoner and the Friar* and *A mery play Betwene Johan Johan the husbande, Tyb his wife, and Syr Jhan the preest.*

Higden (hig′dẹn) or **Higdon** (-dọn), **Ranulf.** English chronicler; b. c1299; d. at Chester, England, c1363. He was the author of a general history entitled *Polychronicon.*

Hilliard (hil′yạrd), **Nicholas.** English miniature painter; b. at Exeter, England, 1537; d. at London, 1619. He was originally a goldsmith, became court painter to Queen Elizabeth, and is classed as the first English miniaturist.

Hinojosa (ē-nō-hō′sä), **Pedro de.** Spanish soldier; b. at Trujillo, Spain, c1490; murdered at Chuquisaca, Upper Peru (now Sucre, Bolivia), May 6, 1553. He was a follower of Pizarro in Peru, fought against the Almagros in 1538 and 1542, followed the rebellion of Gonzalo Pizarro in 1545, and as captain of his ships took Panama and Nombre de Diós. Gasca induced Hinojosa to desert to the royal side with his whole fleet (November 19, 1546), and this defection insured the defeat of the rebellion. Gasca gave him the command of his army, and subsequently he was made governor of Charcas (or Upper Peru, now part of Bolivia) where he received rich grants. He was murdered there by conspirators.

Hipsch Martin (hipsh mär′tēn). See **Schongauer, Martin.**

Hobertus (hō-ber′tus), **Jacob.** See **Obrecht, Jacob.**

Hobrecht (hō′breċht), **Jacob.** See **Obrecht, Jacob.**

Hoccleve (hok′lēv), **Thomas.** See **Occleve, Thomas.**

Hofhaimer (hōf′hī-mėr) or **Hoffheimer** (hof′hī-mėr), **Paul** (or **Paulus**) **von.** German organist and composer; b. at Radstadt, Germany, January 25, 1459; d. at Salzburg, Austria, 1537. His works include organ pieces, part-songs, and musical settings for thirty-five odes of Horace.

Holbein (hol′bīn), **Hans.** [Called **Holbein the Elder.**] German painter; b. at Augsburg, Bavaria, Germany, c1460; d. there, 1524. His two painter sons, Hans Holbein the Younger and Ambrosius, worked in his shop at Augsburg until he moved to another city (1514). He represented the realistic tendency of the Swabian school and was later influenced by developments of the Italian Renaissance. His *Altar of Saint Sebastian* (1516), at Munich, is sometimes called his masterpiece. A sketchbook with studies for portraits is at Berlin.

Holbein, Hans. [Called **Holbein the Younger.**] German painter, renowned for his portraits, and wood engraver; b. probably at Augsburg, Bavaria, Germany, c1497; d. of the plague at London, 1543. He was the son of Hans Holbein (c1460–1524), and worked in his father's shop until 1514. He went to Basel, Switzerland (1515), left it for a time to visit Lucerne, and may have visited Italy. In 1519 he was back at Basel, where he married, became a Swiss citizen, matriculated in the Painters' Guild, painted some portraits, and worked as an illustrator for publishers.

He began painting a series of frescoes on appropriate civic subjects in the Council Chamber of the City Hall in 1521. Owing to frequent disturbances caused by religious unrest and to his own absences, these were not completed until 1530. In 1523 he painted the first of several portraits of Erasmus, whom he probably met through the publisher Froben (Erasmus was the editor), and with these made an international reputation as a portraitist. About 1526 he visited Antwerp to see the Flemish painter Quentin Massys, and afterward went to England. Erasmus had given him an introduction to Sir Thomas More and the two became good friends. The portrait, *Sir Thomas More*, Frick Collection, New York, was painted (1527) during this visit to England. In the same collection is his *Sir Thomas Cromwell* (1533), who (1535) was one of those responsible for the death of More. In 1528 he went back to Basel, but the city was torn by the strife of the Reformation. He returned to England (1532) and remained there the rest of his life. In 1533 he painted *The Ambassadors*, National Gallery, London, and in the next several years painted a number of half-length portraits of German merchants of the Steelyard. About 1536 he became court painter to Henry VIII. The king required him to make some designs for goldsmiths and decorations of various kinds, and occasionally sent him on private missions to paint portraits of ladies he was considering honoring with his hand, as the *Duchess of Milan* (1538), National Gallery, London, and *Anne of Cleves* (1539 or 1540), Louvre, Paris, who was briefly Henry's fourth queen. A portrait of his fifth queen, *Catherine Howard*, is at Toledo, Ohio. He painted a number of portraits of Henry (one at Rome) and of various members of his court. In his later life he began painting portraits from sketches he had made earlier, and some of the portraits painted in the absence of the sitter are less compelling, without, however, a lessening of the realism and fluidity for which his portraits were noted. A series of more than eighty sketches for portraits in red chalk and India ink is in the Royal Library, Windsor, and reveal his mastery at capturing the essence of his sitter. Among his works is a series of designs for wood engraving, *The Dance of Death*, engraved by Hans Lützelburger and published in 1538 and 1547, and the title pages he designed for Coverdale's and Cranmer's Bibles. He painted decorations on a number of houses and buildings at Basel for which the sketches survive but the decorations have perished. Works he painted on religious subjects include *The Last Supper*, *The Dead Christ*, eight Passion pictures, and others (all in the museum at Basel), *The Nativity* and the *Adoration of the Magi* (at Freiberg im Breisau), *Madonna* (at Darmstadt), and *Madonna and Saints* (at Solothurn). But he is best known as a painter of realistic and perceptive portraits, and representations of his sober, concentrated sitters appear, besides those mentioned, in museums of Germany, in the Uffizi at Florence, The Hague, and in a number of museums in the United States, as the Museum of Fine Arts and the Isabella Stewart Gardner Museum, Boston; the Johnson Collection, Philadelphia; the National Gallery, Washington; the Metropolitan Museum, New York; and in museums at Los Angeles, Detroit, and St. Louis.

Holinshed (hol′inz-hed, -in-shed) or **Hollingshead** (hol′ingz-hed), **Raphael.** English chronicler; b. probably at Sutton Downes, Cheshire, England; d. c1580. He is said to have been educated at one of the universities, possibly Cambridge. His great work, *The Chronicles of England, Scotland, and Ireland*, was begun for Reginald Wolfe, a London printer, whose service he entered as translator early in the reign of Elizabeth. A second and enlarged edition, edited by John Hooker, was published after Holinshed's death (1587). The work furnished Shakespeare with plots for *King Lear*, *Macbeth*, and some of the historical plays.

Holland (hol′ạnd), **John.** [Titles, Duke of **Exeter**, Earl of **Huntingdon.**] English soldier and political leader; b. c1352; beheaded at Pleshey, England, January 16, 1400. He was a half brother to Richard II through his mother's marriage to Edward, the Black Prince. He served (1386) under John of Gaunt in Spain, and was made (1389) chamberlain of England for life. After supporting (1397) Richard II against Gloucester and Arundel, he was made duke of Exeter and given large grants of land, which he was forced to give up after the king was deposed in 1399. Defeated in a conspiracy to restore Richard II, he was captured by the countess of Hereford and beheaded.

Holland, John. [Titles, Duke of **Exeter,** Earl of **Huntingdon.**] English commander; b. March 18, 1395; d. August 5, 1447. He was the second son of John Holland (c1352–1400), duke of Exeter. He distinguished himself at Agincourt (1415), and was commander of the fleet that defeated (1417) the Genoese off Harfleur, thus making possible Henry V's second expedition to France. He engaged (1436) in the defense of Calais, and was commander of the expedition sent (March, 1438) for the relief of Guînes.

Holy League. League between Pope Julius II, Ferdinand the Catholic, and the states of Venice and Switzerland, formed in 1511 for the purpose of expelling Louis XII of France from Italy. It was subsequently joined by Henry VIII of England and by Emperor Maximilian I. It was dissolved on the death of Julius in 1513.

Holy Roman Empire. Realm ruled by various emperors who claimed to be the representatives of the ancient Roman emperors, and who asserted (in theory) authority over the states and countries of west central Europe. It was called "holy" from the theoretical interdependence of the empire and the Church (it has been a classroom witticism for generations that the Holy Roman Empire "was neither Holy, nor Roman, nor an Empire"; and, indeed, it was for most of its history more nearly a concept than a political entity). It comprised in general the German-speaking peoples in central Europe, and it had for a long time a close and uncomfortable connection with Italy. Various regions outside of Germany proper were at different times nominally under the empire. It began with Charlemagne, king of the Franks, who was crowned emperor of the West (800), and was succeeded by various Carolingian emperors. By the treaty of Verdun (843) the Carolingian dynasty continued in the east part of Charlemagne's empire (i.e., Germany). The German nation grew from the union of Thuringians, Franks, Saxons, Bavarians, Swabians, Lorrainers, and others. The Saxon line of German kings began with Henry the Fowler in 919. The lasting union of Germany with the empire began in 962, when Otto I, king of Germany, became Roman emperor. The Saxon line of emperors continued until 1024. The Franconian line (Conrad II, Henry III, Henry IV, Henry V) reigned from 1024 to 1125; the Hohenstaufen or Swabian line (Conrad III, Frederick I, Frederick II, Conrad IV) from 1138 to 1208 and from 1215 to 1254. There was an interregnum from 1254 to 1273. Emperors from the Hapsburg, Luxemburg, and other houses reigned from 1273 to 1437. The continuous line of Hapsburg emperors, who were powerful Austrian rulers, began in 1438. After Maximilian I and Charles V the empire degenerated through the 17th and 18th centuries, and Francis II (Francis I of Austria) abdicated as the last emperor in 1806. The emperors were elected. The number of electors was fixed at seven by the Golden Bull of 1356: the archbishops of Mainz, Trèves (Trier), and Cologne, the count palatine of the Rhine, the king of Bohemia, the duke of Saxony, and the margrave of Brandenburg. Bavaria and Hanover were respectively made electorates in 1623 and 1692, and in the years immediately before the fall of the empire Württemberg, Hesse-Cassel, and Salzburg. By Maximilian I the empire was divided into ten circles or districts: Burgundian, Westphalian, Lower Rhine, Upper Rhine, Lower Saxon, Upper Saxon, Franconian, Swabian, Bavarian, and Austrian.

Honorius IV (hǫ-nō′ri-us). [Original name, **Giacomo Savelli.**] Pope (1285–1287); b. at Rome, c1210; d. there, April 3, 1287. He was the grand-nephew of Pope Honorius III, and the successor of Martin IV. He was succeeded by Nicholas IV.

Hooper (hö′pėr, hu̇p′ėr), **John.** English Protestant bishop and martyr; b. in Somersetshire, England, c1495; burned at the stake at Gloucester, England, February 9, 1555. He fled from England to escape prosecution for heresy in 1539, and resided (1547–1549) at Zurich. In the latter year he returned to England, and was subsequently consecrated bishop of Gloucester (after a struggle against the wearing of vestments, yielding only when he was committed to the Fleet Prison) in 1551. In 1552 he became bishop of Worcester. On the accession of Mary he was imprisoned, accused of heresy, and, having refused to recant, executed.

Hopkins (hop′kinz), **John.** English clergyman and schoolmaster; b. probably in Gloucestershire, England, c1520; d. at Great Waldingfield, Suffolk, England, in October, 1570. With Thomas Sternhold he was the author of metrical versions of the Psalms. The 1549 edition contained 44 psalms, 7 of them by Hopkins; the first complete edition, the *Whole Booke of Psalmes* (1562), contained 150, 56 by Hopkins, 43 by Sternhold, and 51 by seven other versifiers.

Hotman (ot-män), **François.** [Latinized, **Hotmanus.**] French jurist and Huguenot leader; b. at Paris, August 23, 1524; d. at Basel, Switzerland, February 12, 1590. *Franco-Gallia* (1573), considered his greatest work, is a plea for representative government and for an elective monarchy.

Hotspur (hot′spėr). Epithet of **Percy,** Sir **Henry** (1364–1403).

House of Fame, The. Poem by Chaucer, in which the influence of Dante is marked. Its general idea is from Ovid, though the first book follows Vergil.

Howard (hou′ard), **Catherine.** Fifth queen of Henry VIII; executed February 13, 1542. She was a niece of Thomas Howard (1473–1554), 3rd duke of Norfolk, and married Henry July 28, 1540. She was convicted of adultery and condemned as a traitor.

Howard, Charles. [Titles, 2nd Baron **Howard of Effingham,** 1st Earl of **Nottingham.**] English sailor, statesman, and courtier, commander at the defeat of the Spanish Armada (1588); b. 1536; d. at Harling, England, December 13, 1624. He was a son of William Howard (c1510–1573). He was ambassador to France (1559), and lord chamberlain (1574–1585). He was a commissioner for the trial (1586) of Mary, Queen of Scots, although he was not present at the trial. As lieutenant general and commander in chief of the land and sea forces he was responsible for the Armada's defeat. He shared joint command with the earl of Essex in the Cádiz expedition (1596) in which Spanish shipping was destroyed, and served as lord lieutenant of England during the Spanish invasion alarm (1599). Among the important commissions he served on was one for Essex's trial for treason (1601), one for the union with Scotland (1604), and one for the trial of those in the Gunpowder Plot (1606).

Howard, Henry. [Title (by courtesy), Earl of **Surrey.**] English poet; b. c1517; beheaded on Tower Hill, London, January 21, 1547. He was a son of Thomas Howard (1473–1554), and was known in youth as "Henry Howard of Kenninghall," from an estate owned by his grandfather in Norfolk. He received an unusually good education, and from 1530 to 1532 lived at Windsor with the young Henry Fitzroy, duke of Richmond, the natural son of Henry VIII, accompanying the king to France in 1532. He remained at the French court for about a year, returning for the marriage of his sister Mary to Richmond. In 1541 he was installed Knight of the Garter, and in 1543 joined the English forces at Landrecies with special recommendations from Henry VIII to the emperor Charles V, and a little later was appointed cupbearer to the king. Present at the surrender of Boulogne, he became its governor in 1545, but was recalled to England the next year. Henry VIII was ill, and, when his death was near, Surrey's father, Thomas, 3rd duke of Norfolk, was suspected, as premier duke, of aiming at the throne. A month before the king's death both Norfolk and Surrey were arrested, and the former, as a peer of the realm, was tried by his peers. The latter, however, who had only a courtesy title, was tried by a jury picked for the occasion, who found that he "falsely, maliciously, and treacherously set up and bore the arms of Edward the Confessor, then used by the prince of Wales, mixed up and joined with his own proper arms." He had borne these arms without question in the presence of the king, as the Howards before him had done since their grant by Richard II. He was tried for high treason and beheaded. His poems were first printed as "Songes and Sonettes" in *Tottel's Miscellany* in 1557, with those of Sir Thomas Wyatt. He was the first English writer of blank verse (unrhymed iambic pentameter), translating the second and fourth books of the *Aeneid* into this form, and with Wyatt he introduced the sonnet into English literature.

Howard, John. [Title, 1st Duke of **Norfolk;** called **Jack of Norfolk.**] English commander; b. c1430; killed at Bosworth Field, August 22, 1485. He was the 1st duke of Norfolk of the Howard line (1483), and was the father of Thomas Howard (1443–1524). He was a trusted councilor of Edward IV, and was created earl marshal of England by Richard III. Appointed (1483) admiral of England, Ireland, and Aquitaine, he led (1485) the vanguard of archers at the battle of Bosworth Field, where he fell.

Howard, Thomas. [Titles, Earl of **Surrey,** 2nd Duke of **Norfolk.**] English soldier and politician; b. 1443; d. May 21, 1524. He defeated the Scots at Flodden Field on September 9, 1513.

Howard, Thomas. [Titles, Earl of **Surrey,** 3rd Duke of **Norfolk.**] English soldier and politician; b. 1473; d. at Kenninghall, Norfolk, England, August 25, 1554. On the marriage of his niece, Catherine Howard, to Henry VIII in 1540, he gained great influence at court. After her execution (1542) for treason he was in danger, and was ultimately condemned to death himself on a charge of treason through the influence of his rival Edward Seymour (whose sister Jane had been Henry's third queen), but was saved by the death of Henry.

Howard, Thomas. [Title, 4th Duke of **Norfolk.**] English politician; b. March 10, 1536; executed on Tower Hill, London, June 2, 1574. He was the son of Henry Howard (c1517–1547), earl of Surrey, and inherited his title from his grandfather Thomas Howard (1473–1554). He was the first subject in England under Elizabeth, inasmuch as there were no princes of the blood and he was the possessor of the highest title of nobility. He aspired to become the husband of Mary, Queen of Scots, was jailed (1569–1570) for his intrigue, but released when he promised to give up the idea. But he was implicated in the Ridolfi conspiracy for her liberation and assumption of the English crown, in consequence of which he was executed for treason.

Howard, Lord **William.** [Title, 1st Baron **Howard of Effingham.**] English soldier and politician; b. c1510; d. at Hampton Court, January 12, 1573. He was the son of Thomas Howard (1443–1524). He was recalled from an embassy in France and charged with concealment of immoral acts committed by Catherine Howard, Henry VIII's fifth queen, but was pardoned (1541). Under Mary he was created Baron Howard of Effingham for his defense (1554) of London against Sir Thomas Wyatt. Although under suspicion for friendship with Elizabeth, he was appointed lord chamberlain (1558), an appointment confirmed by Elizabeth.

Hübsch Martin (hüpsh mär′tēn). See **Schongauer, Martin.**

Humanism. A term coined by 19th-century German scholars and applied to the areas of interest and professional activities of Renaissance humanists. One large group of humanists consisted of the professional writers of official documents, attached to the Church and to the courts of princes, rulers, and states, for the official language of the Church, of courts, and of international diplomacy had continued to be Latin throughout the Middle Ages. The other principal group of humanists comprised the teachers and students of the *studia humanitatis*—the humanities. By the 15th century these, the disciplines of the humanities, were: Grammar, Rhetoric, Poetry, History, and Moral Philosophy. Enormous impetus was given to the intellectual ferment that came to be known as humanism by the so-called Revival of Learning. The sequence of events or specific incidents that led to the latter cannot be identified with exact occurrences or moments. Undoubtedly, the development of an urban society, expanding commerce, the rise of a wealthy merchant class, the increased complexity of government and business life, as well as a close identification of the Italians with their heroic Roman past and a general dissatisfaction with the clerical-dominated culture of the Middle Ages, were among the factors that caused scholars to look back and seek out the writings of the ancients as models and guides for their increasingly complex world. The conditions that made Italy ripe for humanism in the 14th century did not prevail in other parts of western Europe, for the feudal system had never taken firm root in Italy. At the beginning of the 14th century Paduan lawyers, before whom many intricate problems were coming up, began to seek manuscripts of the Roman code, to learn what the original intention of the codifiers was, rather than what interpretations medieval clerical scholars had put upon it. The use and study of Latin had never disappeared—Grammar (meaning Latin grammar) and Rhetoric were part of the medieval curriculum—and some examples of the ancient Latin authors had been continuously studied throughout the medieval period. Some of the works of Cicero and Seneca were familiar to learned men, who were mostly of the clerical ranks. Dante (1265–1321) takes Vergil as his guide in *The Divine Comedy,* in which the model for the journey through the Inferno, Purgatory, and Paradise comes from the sixth book of Vergil's *Aeneid.* Petrarch (1304–1374), an early and great humanist, was a champion of the ancient authors. He had been interested in Cicero since childhood and, when a student of law at Bologna, began collecting his own manuscript library with Vergil and Cicero's *Rhetoric*. To these he added Servius Statius and the *Odes* of Horace. On his many journeys he bought manuscripts, or copied them with his own hand. His library at the time of his death included, in addition to the above, Seneca, Livy, Sallust, Suetonius, Ovid, Juvenal, and Lucian, among others. He could but admire his copies of Plato and Homer in the original Greek, as he could not read that language. Because of the fame he enjoyed in his own time, as a writer of letters, poems, treatises and epics in elegant Latin, and his constant exhortation to read the ancient authors in their original glory, his influence on the study and acquisition of the ancient authors was enormous. A search for ancient manuscripts began in the 14th century and reached fever pitch in the 15th century. Monastic and other libraries were ransacked. Poggio (1380–1459), in an official capacity at the Council of Constance (1415), searched the libraries of South Germany and Burgundy and found forgotten works of Servius Statius, Lucretius, Quintillian and others, as well as some forgotten orations of Cicero. Pope Nicholas V (1397–1455), one of the foremost collectors of ancient manuscripts and books, required his legates to search for manuscripts in the different posts to which they were sent. In the period, almost all of the works of the ancient Latin writers that we now possess were rediscovered, copied, and diffused. When, toward the end of the 14th century, the Turks began pressing in on the Byzantine Empire, Greek scholars fled to Italy and brought with them manuscripts of the ancient Greek writers. Florence, the center from which humanism radiated, offered (1396) courses in Greek literature under the scholar Manuel Chrysoloras. Greek manuscripts were hunted as ardently as Latin, and translated into Latin, as the study and knowledge of Greek was much more limited. In this way the whole body of ancient Greek writings—literary, historical, mythological, philosophical, scientific and so on—was rediscovered, preserved, and made available on a wide scale. It is this interest in, search for, and study of the ancient writers to which the phrase Revival of Learning particularly applies. The results of it, which permeated all fields of knowledge, activity, and education, were the contributions of the humanists. As the material became available the humanists studied it for its language and style. The ancient writers became the models for excellence in writing and speaking. The humanists compared manuscripts, subjected them to textual criticism and edited them. Concentration on the manuscripts led to the study of grammar, orthography, vocabulary and rhetoric. Lorenzo Valla (1440) proved by a comparison of the vocabulary of the 4th century with the language of the *Donation of Constantine* that this document was a forgery and could not have been written before the 8th century. In order to understand the references and allusions in the ancient works, ancient history, coins, inscriptions, mythology, and archaeology developed as branches of study. Commentaries on ancient works were written to explain difficult parts or to interpret the works as a whole for a later age. Such outstanding scholars as Poggio and Manetti (1396–1459) added the study of the Hebrew language and literature to their Latin and Greek studies. Collections of Hebrew manuscripts were undertaken and formed a valuable part of such libraries as that of Federico da Montefeltro at Urbino and the Vatican Library. These studies all had as their starting point a literary interest but, as has been seen, gave rise to other studies.

The movement of humanism was parallel in its beginnings to the clerical and Church-engendered culture of the Middle Ages. The earlier humanists were medieval in their spiritual outlook and humanist in their intellectual interests, and saw and felt no conflict between them. Continued absorption by the educated in ancient writers led to a victory of the ideas of the ancients over the ecclesiastical domination of men's minds that had existed for centuries. In the works of the classical authors the humanists found a new concept of man, of his value and dignity, and of his place in the universe of here and now. This was in opposition to the medieval concept of man as unworthy, whose best hope of salvation and happiness lay in an afterlife. The emphasis of the humanists came to be on man and his possibilities in this world. Ultimately, humanism led to an examination, conscious or not, of the precepts and practices of the Church, an examination that led to criticism (since the precepts and practices were observed to be so disparate), skepticism, and eventual ridicule and reform. However, the attacks of the humanists, most of whom remained sincerely devoted to Catholicism, would have been of little effect on a strong and incorrupt Church.

As results of humanistic studies, the purity of the Latin language was restored, Latin was used by all who had any pretensions as literary men (although some writers wrote in Italian as well as Latin), Latin models and forms, in verse, prose, and oratory, epistles and epigrams, were followed as the only true manifestations of a cultivated writer. Because of this the use of the vernacular, which had reached such a height with Dante, was abandoned by any writer for the works he wished to be considered seriously. Thus the development of vernacular tongues and national styles was delayed. Another development that took place in the age of humanism was the writing, on the ancient models, of collections of lives of illustrious men and of biographies or histories of men still alive or only recently dead. Whereas *Lives* of the saints had served in the Middle Ages as examples of conduct and means of inspiration, in the humanistic era biographies of men of the world of action became extremely popular. One object of the biographies, most of which were commissioned, was to insure the subject's fame in history. For, perhaps because the medieval idea of happiness in an afterlife had become dimmer, men were obsessed with the idea of perpetuating their names and glory in history. It was also thought that the biography of a famous man, whatever the reason for his fame, whether it be learning, artistic genius, or administrative skill, could serve as instruction, could give living and understandable examples of conduct in the affairs of this world, could indicate valor, shrewdness, or skill under difficult conditions. Since most of the biographies were commissioned they can hardly be called detached and impartial in their treatment of the subject. Panormita and Facio could hardly be expected to see with clear eyes or write in unadorned words of the extravagance, for example, of Alfonso I, who was maintaining them in great honor at his court. Many of the biographies are servile in their praise. In most of them are found nuggets of factual information that might otherwise be lost, and they reveal as well a standard of conduct that was considered praiseworthy and possible at the time. For a considerable period, the ability of the poet-historian to give or withhold immortality through his work was a source of his influence, honor, and emoluments at princely courts. The discovery of the *Familiar Letters* of Cicero, among others, gave impetus to a vast amount of letter-writing. Collections of letters appeared; they were written to be read, not just by the addressee but by a wide audience, as models of the classical style, founts of classical erudition, and as means of instruction and information. Many of them are in the nature of essays, on a wide variety of topics. The biographies and letters, as well as the orations, treatises, and dialogues on a large number of subjects, poetry, official documents, eulogies and elegies, were written in Latin of classical purity and closely imitated Latin style, form, and matter. The ideal of the humanists was not slavish imitation of the ancients but to use them as models of excellence. Originality was also valued. To the extent that lesser figures fell into slavish imitation they failed to produce works of great artistic creativity. Petrarch expected his fame to rest on his Latin verse and writings in the Latin style and language, but less than a century after his death Pius II, a humanist pope of great learning, taste, and discrimination, said his "equal would be hard to find if his Latin works were comparable to those he wrote in Italian." Nonetheless, some of Petrarch's Latin writings were works of poignant insight into the moral problems of his day, and were written in a pungent style. Valla, Alberti, and Pontano were known for their ironic wit and iconoclasm. The Latin verse of Panormita, Poliziano, and Pontano revealed a resourceful new use of this ancient language. And at the same time it must be appreciated that in their many works the humanists preserved a record of the expanding range of the ideas of their own times; much historical and biographical information, and a record that covers the whole spectrum of the problems and, above all, the possibilities inherent in man are found in their works.

Whether they served as writers or teachers or both, the humanists wandered from court to court and university to university in Italy, wherever the prestige or rewards were highest. A humanist such as Gianozzo Manetti, for example, served Florence as ambassador to Naples and governor of Pescia and Pistoia, and was attached to the courts of Nicholas V at Rome and Alfonso I at Naples. Poggio was an apostolic secretary under eight popes. The humanists depended for a livelihood on the favor of patrons or the popularity they could win in a university, and so were in constant competition with each other. The manner of competing came to be, in many cases, scurrilous, often libelous, attacks on rivals, attacks which, in attempting to destroy others destroyed all. With the invention of printing knowledge of the past, hitherto almost the exclusive possession of the humanists, became much more widely available; dependence on the humanists came to an end. There was, in addition, a growing distaste for the ribaldry and indecency of some of the Latin verse produced by the humanists and for their satirical attacks on men and institutions which, in the stricter atmosphere of the Counter-Reformation, led to a strong reaction against them. The day of the humanists, so brilliant at its noon, drew to a close in the 16th century in a more subdued atmosphere. Many individuals were criticized for their excesses. Others suffered for the boldness of their speculation. Many others took note of the change in the wind, settled down, and became expert practitioners of the individual disciplines of the humanities.

As has been stated, the results of humanism were felt in all fields of activity. Men imbued with the works and ideas of ancient authors, artists, architects, statesmen, and scientists began to collect fragments of ancient statuary, coins, inscriptions, and jewelry; to measure ancient ruins; to feel new ideas germinating in them as to the role of the state and the place of nature, with the possibilities for its conquest, in the life of man. Because examples of ancient painting were almost nonexistent, painting in the great era of humanism was less affected by ancient models than was literature, although the remains of ancient sculpture that were found had an important influence on that art, and subsequently on painting. Descriptions of ancient paintings also had their effect; Botticelli followed Julian's description of a painting by the Greek Apelles in his "La Calunnia." The new concepts of man as the possible master of nature and of man with unlimited capacity for perfectibility were reflected in the works of artists beginning at least as early as Masaccio (1401–1428), who was a friend of the outstanding humanists of his day and whose works represent man in supreme dignity.

Humanism had a particular effect on education. Having found a new concept of man, the humanists set themselves the task of determining how he could best fulfill his possibilities, and what sort of education would prepare him to do so. Leon Battista Alberti (1404–1472), in the first book of his dialogue *Della Famiglia,* discusses the education of children and its purpose, which is to train their bodies as well as their minds, to develop all their inherent capacities for a happy and independent life, and to imbue them with a sense of service and responsibility in the world outside the study: the world of men and their activities. Vittorino da Feltre established (1423) a school at Mantua, at the court of the Gonzaga, in which, in addition to the humanities and sciences, physical exercises were a regular event, deportment and manners were stressed, along with religious education. Furthermore, the school was not limited to the sons and daughters of the court. Poor boys who could be expected to profit by such an education lived in his house and were taught along with the courtiers' children. Eminent families from all over Italy, and even outside Italy, sent their sons to be educated at Mantua. Six years later Guarino da Verona established a similar school at Ferrara. The spread of humanistic studies was rapid. Lawyers, physicians, bankers, merchants, clerics, and many in other ranks had had the benefit and felt the influence of a humanistic training. Students came from all over Europe to study in the Italian universities, to study the humanities as well as law and medicine. They returned to their homes and spread the new methods and concepts of scholarship. Ambassadors, agents, cultivated merchants, and teachers from Italy went to cities in Europe and took their humanistic training and practices with them. Great humanists such as Erasmus (1465–1536), Sir Thomas More (1477–1535), and Montaigne (1533–1592) appeared. National conditions and traditions produced modifications in different countries, but the origin and fundamental methods of humanistic studies came from Italy—the fount of classical learning and the teacher of Europe for 300 years.

Humphrey (hum'fri). [Titles, Duke of **Gloucester** and Earl of **Pembroke**; called "the Good Duke Humphrey."] English soldier and statesman; b. 1391; d. at Bury St. Edmunds, England, February 23, 1447. He was the youngest son of Henry IV by his first wife, Mary de Bohun. He studied at Balliol College, Oxford, and was noted as a patron of learning and a collector of books. He was the founder, by his gifts of books, of the library of that university. In 1420 he was appointed lieutenant of England, and held that office until the return of Henry V in 1421. On Henry's death Gloucester, though only deputy for his brother, the duke of Bedford, became, in effect, protector of the young King Henry VI. In 1422 he married Jacqueline, only daughter of William VI, count of Hainaut, to whose estates she had succeeded, but of which she had been deprived. In 1424 he conquered Hainaut and was proclaimed its count. In 1428 his marriage with Jacqueline was annulled, and he soon married his mistress, Eleanor Cobham. His protectorate, which was throughout unfortunate, was terminated by the coronation (November 6, 1429) of Henry VI. In 1441 he was disgraced through the dealings of his wife with the astrologer Bolingbroke. In 1447 he was arrested by order of the king, and in a few days died.

Hundred Years' War. Series of wars between England and France, c1338–1453. The English, generally victors in these wars down to c1430 (Crécy, Poitiers, Agincourt), and rulers of a great part of France, were finally expelled entirely, except from Calais, which they retained for about a century longer.

Hunyadi or **Hunyady** (hö'nyô-dē), **János.** [English, **John Hunyadi.**] Hungarian general; b. at Hunyad, in Transylvania, c1387; d. at Zemun, in what is now Yugoslavia, August 11, 1456. He was a military leader and councilor of Sigismund, attending the monarch when he successfully sought to become (1411) emperor. Albert II of Germany, Sigismund's successor, entrusted him with a frontier region, where he defended (1437–1438) the outposts of the empire against the Turks. When Albert died (1439), Hunyadi supported Ladislaus III for the Hungarian throne and in return was appointed (1442) *voivode* (governor) of Transylvania. He entered into a series of victorious campaigns against the Turks, defeating them (1441–1442) in several great battles. In 1443 he embarked on an expedition that drove the Turks from the Adriatic and in 1444 with Ladislaus began a campaign aimed at supporting Constantinople; they were defeated at Varna (November 10, 1444), Ladislaus dying in the battle. In 1446 Hunyadi was elected regent of Hungary for Ladislaus V, who was being held against his will by Frederick III of Germany. Hunyadi marched against Frederick but was forced to return to battle the Turks. At Kossovo (October, 1448) he was defeated through the machinations of men he had counted as allies. Constantinople fell to the Turks in 1453 and Hunyadi began, unsupported by his own nobles, to rally an army for the defense of Hungary. The result was his most celebrated exploit, the successful defense of Belgrade against Mohammed II in 1456. The Turks broke off the siege and retired, but Hunyadi died of plague three weeks afterward. His life, and legends accreting to it, became a national legend and Hunyadi the national hero.

Hurtado de Mendoza (ör-tä'ᴛʜō dā men-dō'-thä), **Diego.** See **Mendoza, Diego Hurtado de.**

Hus (hus; Czech, hös), **John.** [Also, **Huss,** Czech, **Jan Hus.**] Czech preacher and reformer; b. at Husinec, in Bohemia, c1369; burned at the stake at Konstanz (Constance), Germany, July 6, 1415. He preached in Czech and became (1402) preacher of the Bethlehem Chapel at Prague. This was the center of the local movement to reform the clergy and the monastic orders. He protested the burning of Wycliffe's writings and was excommunicated (1409) by the archbishop of Prague. In 1411, when Prague was placed under an interdict because of him, he left the city and went into hiding. Hus had denounced the bull of John XXIII declaring a crusade against King Ladislaus of Naples and proclaiming indulgence for all who joined it. He vehemently opposed such an abuse of indulgences. While he was in seclusion he wrote some of his most important works, particularly the tract on *Simony* and *De ecclesia.* When the Council of Constance met in 1414, Hus was offered a safe-conduct by the emperor Sigismund. Hus accepted the invitation to appear before the Council, hoping thus to be able to answer to charges of heresy. Nevertheless, he was arrested shortly after his arrival on orders of John XXIII. The charges against him were prepared by his enemies and centered on views that he had never held. The Council ordered him to recant unconditionally, which his conscience would not permit him to do, especially since he did not subscribe to the doctrines imputed to him and recantation would imply he had held those doctrines. He was, accordingly, burned at the stake as a heretic. Around his name gathered a great number of followers who, like him, at first sought to reform the Church from within and then to question Church doctrines. This group, that increased rapidly, came to be known as Hussites and constituted what was called the Bohemian Heresy. The Council of Basel (1431 *et seq.*) tried to deal with it, to little avail. Popes from Martin V on sought unsuccessfully to suppress it. Hus, in his denunciations of the abuses of indulgences, was one of the most articulate of Martin Luther's forerunners.

Hussites (hus′īts). Followers of John Hus. The Hussites organized themselves immediately after Hus's death into a politico-religious party, and waged fierce civil war in Bohemia from 1419 to 1434. A compromise was effected by negotiations (1433–1436) with the Roman Catholic council sitting at Basel. The Hussites were divided in doctrine into radical and conservative sections called Taborites and Calixtines (or Utraquists). The former (named for the city of Tabor) finally became merged with the Bohemian Brethren, and the latter (who took their name from the chalice or from their doctrine of the double communion, *sub utraque specie,* that is, the wine and the bread) partly with the Lutherans and partly with the Roman Catholics.

Hutten (hu̇t′en), **Ulrich von.** German humanist; b. at Castle Steckelberg, near Fulda, Germany, April 21, 1488; d. on the island of Ufenau, on the Lake of Zurich, Switzerland, August 23, 1523. Intended for the Church, he was placed (1498) in the monastery of Fulda, whence he fled in 1505. He subsequently studied the humanities at various German and Italian universities, including those of Frankfort on the Oder and Pavia. He served in the imperial army in 1513, was crowned poet by the emperor Maximilian I at Augsburg in 1517, entered the service of the archbishop of Mainz in 1518, joined the Swabian League against Ulrich, duke of Württemberg, in 1519, and in 1522 fought unsuccessfully in association with Franz von Sickingen at the head of the nobility of the Upper Rhine against the spiritual principalities. He was a friend and supporter of Luther, one of the authors of the *Epistolae obscurorum virorum,* and one of the principal satirical writers of his time. His Latin dialogues, modeled on Lucian, included *Phalarismus* (1516), an attack on tyrants; *Vadiscus* (1520), an attack on the papacy; and *Inspicientes* (1520), which was a paeon to the emperor and the German spirit. By writing in German, after 1520, he introduced the dialogue form into the popular German literature.

I

Iacobello del Fiore (yä-kō-bel′lō del fyō′rā). Venetian painter; d. before November 8, 1439. To the Byzantine style of Paolo Veneziano he united some elements of the international Gothic, but in his hieratic conception he remained essentially Byzantine. His *Coronation of the Virgin* and *Madonna of Mercy* are in the Accademia at Venice. Among his best works is a *Coronation of the Virgin* in the cathedral at Teramo. Other examples of his work at Venice are in the Correr Museum, Ducal Palace, and S. Alvise, S. Giovanni in Bragora, and S. Trovaso. In addition, there are paintings at Chioggia, Fermo, Pavia, Pesaro, Budapest, Stockholm, Stuttgart, Vienna, Philadelphia, Washington (Dumbarton Oaks), and elsewhere.

Iacopino del Conte (yä-kō-pē′nō del kôn′tā). Painter; b. at Florence, 1510; d. at Rome, January 9, 1598. A mannerist, he was a pupil of Andrea del Sarto, but was deeply influenced by the sculptural quality and agitated movement of Michelangelo. Other influences were those of Sebastiano del Piombo, Pontormo, and Francesco Salviati. His principal works are frescoes on scenes from the life of John the Baptist in the Oratory of S. Giovanni Decollato, Rome. (The church was in charge of the Florentine Confraternity of S. Giovanni, which was charged with giving assistance and comfort to those condemned to death, and had the privilege of freeing one of the condemned each year, the liberation being carried out in a ceremony of great solemnity. Michelangelo was a member of the Confraternity.) Of the frescoes, *The Annunciation of the Birth of the Baptist to Zaccariah* (c1535) has some indications of the pictorial freedom of Andrea del Sarto, indications that are overshadowed by the predominantly architectonic, and Michelangelesque, arrangement of the groups of figures, and by their solemn and grandiose expressions and gestures. In the *Preaching of the Baptist* (1538) and *The Baptism of Christ*, the agitated movement and sculptural quality more markedly recall Michelangelo. The frescoes are evidence that Iacopino, a strong artistic personality in his own right, carried on the Tuscan tradition so faithfully and with such individuality, as opposed to imitation, that his work, in its power, has formerly been confused with that of Michelangelo. Other works attributed to him are *Madonna and St. Elizabeth*, Contini-Bonacossi Collection, Florence, with typical mannerist characteristics; and the powerful and significant *Three Fates*, Pitti Palace, Florence. He was a vigorous and incisive portraitist, one of his earliest portraits being of Michelangelo, now at Paris. Other portraits include that of his friend Ignatius Loyola, a portrait of Paul III and a cardinal, Church of S. Francesca Romana, Rome, of S. Carlo Borromeo, Torlonia Gallery, Rome, portraits in the Metropolitan Museum, New York, and in the Johnson Collection, Philadelphia.

Iacopo del Balzo (yä′kō-pō del bäl′tsō). See **Del Balzo, Iacopo.**

Iacopo de′ Barbari (dā bär′bä-rē). See **De Barbari, Iacopo.**

Iacopo da Bologna. (dä bō-lō′nyä). See **Avanzi, Iacopo degli.**

Iacopo del Casentino (del kä-zen-tē′nō). [Original name, **Iacopo Landini.**] Painter; b. at Florence, 1297; d. at Pratovecchio, 1358 or 1368. In 1339, with Bernardo Daddi and other Florentine painters, he helped to found the Corporation of St. Luke—the painters' guild. Of the paintings by him mentioned in the ancient sources, one of the best preserved is his *Madonna of the Marketplace*, in the Hall of the Wool Guild. A fundamental work is a signed triptych in the Uffizi, Florence, of *The Virgin Enthroned; St. Francis Receiving the Stigmata;* and *The Crucifixion*. From the grandiose and monumental style of Giotto, which he followed in his earlier years, he turned to a softer and more intimate manner under the influence of Bernardo Daddi. Though essentially Florentine, his style has marked reflections of Sienese painting, especially of Duccio and his school. Critics have ascribed such a large number of works to him, using his known works as a standard, that he would appear to have been a very productive painter. Among these is a *Presentation of Christ*, National Gallery, Washington; a triptych, Arezzo; and a triptych, *Madonna Enthroned*, Milan. In addition to paintings at Florence, in other cities of Italy and Europe, there are examples of his work at Ann Arbor (Michigan), Boston, Cleveland, El Paso and Houston (Texas), Kansas City (Missouri), New Haven, New York, and Tucson (Arizona).

Iacopo della Lana (del′lä lä′nä). Commentator; b. at Bologna, c1290; d. c1365. He composed, perhaps at Venice, the first complete commentary, in Italian, on Dante's *Divina Commedia*. It was a thorough analysis and interpretation of the poet's meaning as well as an exposition of the poet's great learning. The commentary was widely read and was translated into Latin.

Iacopo da Lentino (dä len-tē′nō). See **Giacomo da Lentino.**

Iacopo da Montagnana (dä mōn-tä-nyä′nā. [Original name, **Jacopo Parisatti da Montagnana.**] Painter; b. at Montagnana (Padua), between 1440 and 1443; d. after 1499. His first teachers at Montagnana are unknown. He went early to Venice and became a workmanlike and productive follower of the school of Giovanni Bellini. By 1469 he was enrolled in the company of painters at Padua. He painted a number of altarpieces, triptychs, and other panels, including a fine diptych of the *Annunciation*, Accademia, Venice, a triptych with the *Annunciation between*

Archangels (1496), Archbishop's Palace, Padua, *Pietà*, Budapest, *and SS. Nicholas of Bari and Catherine of Alexandria*, Columbus, Ohio. He worked at Padua, where he began (1469) an altarpiece for the Basilica of St. Anthony (it was finished by Girolamo del Santo in 1518). Many of his frescoes survive, as *The Marriage of St. Catherine* (1487), executed for the Cloister of the Novitiate of the Basilica and now in the Museo Antoniano; several in the Archbishop's Palace and in the shrine of St. Anthony; and others at Monte Ortone, Belluno, and elsewhere.

Iacopo del Sellaio (del sel-lī′ō). Painter; b. at Florence, 1442; d. there, 1493. He was the son of a saddler (*sellaio*), whence his name. According to Vasari, he was a pupil of Fra Filippo Lippi. However, he was an eclectic who borrowed freely from others, and his work shows rather the influence of Botticelli, a fellow pupil under Fra Filippo, and, to a lesser degree, that of Ghirlandaio. He was listed on the rolls of the Corporation of St. Luke (the painters' guild) at least as early as 1460. He painted a number of solemn altarpieces and other works and had a tendency to make a number of versions of the same subject. Thus, there are versions of the *Madonna Adoring the Child* in the Metropolitan Museum, New York, at Baltimore, Indianapolis, New Haven, the Johnson Collection, Philadelphia, and elsewhere. He made several paintings of St. Jerome kneeling in penitence, placing the saint against a broad landscape that bristles with crags, with often a glimpse of the sea or a lake in the distance in whose waters the towers of a city are reflected. Examples of these are at Budapest, El Paso, Texas, the Horne Museum, Florence, New Haven, the Louvre, Princeton, and elsewhere. Other works include a *Crucifixion* (c1490) in the Church of S. Frediano, Florence, a signed *Annunciation* (1472), S. Giovanni Valdarno, another (c1473) in the Church of S. Lucia de' Magnoli, Florence, a *St. Sebastian* (1479), at New Haven; and works at Arezzo, Bergamo, Empoli, Florence (Uffizi, Pitti, Accademia, churches), Leningrad, London, Munich, Birmingham (Alabama), Memphis, Washington, and elsewhere. He painted a number of cassoni panels, portraying scenes from mythology, Roman history, the Bible, and allegories, with wit and charm. Among these is the series of *Triumphs*, Bandini Museum, Fiesole, and panels in the Uffizi, the Museum of Fine Arts, Boston, Brooklyn Museum, Art Institute of Chicago, Cleveland, Johnson Collection, Philadelphia, and elsewhere.

Iacopo da Valenza (dä vä-len′tsä). Painter; active at Venice from 1485 to 1509. He was a native of Friuli who became a close follower and assistant of Alvise Vivarini at Venice. Several examples of his work are at Venice—in the Correr Museum, the Accademia, and the Church of S. Maria della Salute. His *Christ Blessing* is in the Carrara Academy, Bergamo, *Madonna Adoring the Child* is at Columbus, Ohio, and there are paintings at Berlin, Bonn, Budapest, Darmstadt, New York (Kress Foundation), and elsewhere.

Ignatius of Loyola (ig-nā′shus, loi-ō′lä), Saint. [Original name, **Iñigo de Oñez y Loyola.**] Spanish Roman Catholic ecclesiastic, soldier, and mystic, founder of the Society of Jesus (Jesuit Order) and one of the leaders in the Counter-Reformation; b. at Casa Torre of Loyola, Azpeitia, Guipúzcoa, Spain, December 24, 1491; d. at Rome, July 31, 1556. After pasing his childhood at home, he became, while still a boy, a page of an official of Ferdinand the Catholic. He followed the court, eventually to Madrid, and learned the ways and customs of knighthood. When his master fell from favor he was attached to the household of the duke of Nájera and viceroy of Navarre (1516), and under him saw military service. A good soldier, he rose to the rank of captain. He was so seriously wounded (May 20, 1521) while defending the castle of Pampeluna in Navarre against the troops of Francis I that he was crippled for life. During his long recovery he read the only books that he was able to obtain, a *Life of Christ*, by Ludolphus of Saxony, and a popular devotional book, the *Flowers of the Saints*. The result was a complete change in his life, character, and outlook. He gave himself up to mysticism, renounced the material world and all its pleasures, gave up his army career, and, as soon as he was strong enough to do so, made a pilgrimage, barefoot, to the shrine of the Virgin at the Benedictine monastery of Montserrat. There, on March 21, 1522, he put away his arms, gave away his clothing and possessions, and swore himself a knight to the Virgin. From there he went to Manresa, where he practiced great austerities, and where he wrote (1522) his chief work, *Ejercicios espirituales* (printed 1548).

He went thence to the Holy Land but was prevented by the hostility of the Turks from going to Jerusalem. On his return he studied Latin, philosophy, and theology at Barcelona (1524), Alcalá (1526–1527), Salamanca (1527), and Paris (1528–1535). He was twice imprisoned on suspicion that he was a member of the *Alumbrados* (a group that claimed to receive enlightenment directly from the Holy Spirit). At Paris, in 1535, after having received his master's degree, he organized what was to become the Society (or Company) of Jesus five years later. The goal of the Society was the defense and propagation of the faith. During his stay at Paris he met six men, Pierre Lefèvre (Faber), with whom he roomed, Francis Xavier, professor of philosophy at St. Barbara, Diego Lainez, a Castilian who came to Paris after hearing about Ignatius at Alcalá, Alfonso Salmeron, from Toledo, Simon Rodriguez, a Portuguese, and Nicholas Bobadilla, who had already finished his studies. These men were to become the first fathers of the society he founded. On the day of the Feast of the Assumption (August 15) in 1534, this group of seven gathered in the chapel of the Church of Saint Mary of Montmartre, dedicated themselves to the great work of converting sinners and heathens, took vows of chastity and poverty, and solemnly agreed to go to the Holy Land as missionaries or to take care of the sick, or to go to Rome to undertake any task that might be pleasing to the pope. In 1536 they met at Venice, where Loyola had been for a year, and went on to Rome. At La Storta, just outside Rome, Loyola had a vision (November, 1537) that promised he would find favor at Rome. While waiting at Venice for his comrades to join him, Loyola had been ordained as a priest in June, 1537, but he said his first Mass on Christmas, 1538, at Rome in the Church of S. Maria Maggiore. On September 27, 1540, Pope Paul III officially recognized the Company of Jesus. Loyola was the first general, or superior, of the Order, a post to which he was unanimously elected in April, 1541, and which he held until his death, although he tried to resign in 1547 and 1550, his offer being rejected both times. He died of fever, unexpectedly, without being able to receive the last sacraments. He was beatified in 1609 by Pope Paul V, and canonized by Pope Gregory XV in 1628. He was the author of the *Constitutions of the Order*, which was issued in final form after his death, and of *The Book of the Spiritual Exercises* (mentioned above under its original title, *Ejercicios espirituales*), the title coming from a work written in 1500 by Abbot Garcias de Cisneros, which had influenced and interested him. It has been called a world-moving book, and has been translated, from its original Spanish, into Latin, English, and other languages, two Latin versions of it appearing while Loyola was alive. A great believer in unquestioning obedience, possibly as a result of his military experience, he wrote an important *Letter on Obedience* (1553) to the Portuguese Jesuits. Loyola's insight into the psychology of religious experience remained fundamental for his times and was expanded by his followers, who became the leading educational theorists of early modern Europe. Of interest is the fact that his Order educated some of the most formidable figures of the Enlightenment, and that they became its bitter critics. There are many lives of Loyola, in English, French, German, and Spanish, and there are many editions of his works. Rubens and Titian painted his portrait.

Immanuel ben Solomon (i-man′ṳ̄-e̤l ben sol′o̤-mo̤n). [Called **Manoello Giudeo.**] Hebrew poet and humorist; b. at Rome between 1268 and 1272; d. after 1328. He lived in several cities of Italy, and acted as teacher or tutor in various wealthy Hebrew families. His chief work, the *Maḥbaroth*, is a collection, in prose and verse, of twenty-eight episodes. The collection contains works of the greatest variety, love lyrics, festival songs, jokes, witty sayings, letters, riddles, elegies, and some pieces of religious import. In general, the pieces are purely for entertainment, and are presented with liveliness, keen wit, and a startling inversion, at times, of Biblical phraseology. Together, they present a lively picture of the intellectual and social life of the time. He also wrote some Italian poems. In his writings he was influenced by the writings of Spanish Hebrews, but also by the Italian poets of his time. The love lyrics are in the *dolce stil nuovo*. He may have known Dante, whom he admired and imitated, and he was certainly acquainted with Cino da Pistoia.

Imola (ē′mō-lä), **Innocenzo da.** See **Innocenzo Francucci da Imola.**

Indaco (lēn′dä-kō), **l'.** [**Iacopo di Lazzaro**

DI PIETRO TORNI, called L'INDACO.] Painter; b. at Florence, 1476; d. c1534. He was a pupil of Domenico Ghirlandaio, worked at Rome with Pinturicchio, and may have been one of Michelangelo's assistants at Rome. No surely identifiable work from his hand is extant. With his brother Francesco (b. 1492), also a painter, who worked at Arezzo, Montepulciano, and Rome, L'Indaco was in Spain (1520–1522), where works at Murcia and Granada are attributed to the brothers.

INFERNO (ēn-fer′nō). First part of Dante's *Divina Commedia.* It consists of a general introductory canto to the whole poem followed by thirty-three cantos in terza rima. Under the allegory of an imaginary journey to the center of the earth, the poet gives us a passionate vision of the wilfulness of the human heart from the less culpable sins of sensuality, through the graver irrationality of the rejection of revelation, to the injustice of deliberate violence and the malice of calculated fraud and infidelity. In certain episodes, as that of the death of Conte Ugolino and his sons (canto xxxiii), the poetry and music are directly related to the tragedy in its literal sense. For the most part, however, as in the journey of Ulysses (canto xxvi), it is the deeper meaning symbolized by the myth which is the center of the poet's vision, the source of his feeling, and the stimulus to creative fancy.

INFESSURA (ēn-fes-sö′ra), **STEFANO.** Chronicler; b. at Rome, 1436; d. in January, 1500. He studied law, taught it at the University of Rome, and held public office. He was close to those in positions of power at Rome. He is best remembered for his *Diario della città di Roma,* written in a crude Latin mixed at times with an inelegant Italian. The *Diario* covers the period from the time of Boniface VIII to 1494. The earlier parts of the work are sketchy, but from the time of Pope Martin V the *Diario* is fuller and more detailed. Infessura was an ardent supporter of the Colonna family, and as ardent a denigrator of their enemies, especially Pope Sixtus IV. These personal attitudes are reflected in his history and thus, as a source, it is often undependable. It is valuable, however, for the living picture it presents of the city of Rome.

INGEGNERI (ēn-je-nyā′rē), **MARCO** (or **MARC**) **ANTONIO.** Italian composer, teacher of Monteverdi; b. at Verona, c1545; d. at Cremona, July 1, 1592. His church music includes a group of twenty-seven responsoria for Holy Week which were long thought to be by Palestrina.

INGEGNO (ēn-jā′nyō). [Real name, **ANDREA ALOISI;** called **IL INGEGNO** and **ANDREA D'ASSISI.**] Painter; mentioned as such in documents of 1484–1490 and 1501–1516. In the latter period he filled commissions at Assisi, whence his name Andrea d'Assisi. Vasari mentions him as one of Perugino's best pupils, but no work surely from his hand survives and little is known of his life or artistic personality. A *Madonna and Child* in the Vatican is attributed to him.

INGHIRAMI (ēng-gē-rä′mē), **TOMMASO.** [Called **FEDRA.**] Poet, scholar, and orator; b. at Volterra, 1470; d. at Rome, September 6, 1516. He was secretary of the Sacred College of Cardinals and librarian of the Vatican Library. For his style and manner in his philological works, poems, and funeral orations, his contemporaries gave him the name "Cicero." For his success in enacting the role of Phaedra in Seneca's *Hippolytus* they named him "Fedra." Very similar portraits of him by Raphael, showing Inghirami in the scarlet robe and cap of his Office as secretary, are in the Pitti Palace at Florence and the Isabella Stewart Gardner Museum at Boston.

INNOCENT IV. [Original name, **SINIBALDO DE' FIESCHI.**] Pope (1243–1254); b. at Genoa; d. at Naples, December 7, 1254. He inherited from his predecessors a feud with the emperor Frederick II, who had been excommunicated by Gregory IX in 1239. After the death of Frederick in 1250, and of his son the emperor Conrad IV in 1254, the struggle was continued with Manfred, illegitimate son of Frederick, and uncle and guardian of Conrad's son, Conradin of Sicily. Manfred inflicted a decisive defeat on the papal troops five days before Innocent's death. Innocent was succeeded by Alexander IV.

INNOCENT V. [Original name, **PIETRO DI TARANTASIA.**] Pope (January 20 to June 22, 1276); b. at Tarentaise, in Savoy, 1225; d. at Rome, June 22, 1276. He was a learned Dominican and the first of his order to become pope. He succeeded Gregory X and was succeeded by Adrian V.

INNOCENT VI. [Original name, **ÉTIENNE AUBERT.**] Pope (1352–1362); b. at Mont, near Limoges, France; d. at Avignon, September

Woodcut (*Inferno,* vii) from the 1487 edition of Landino's *Commentary* on Dante's *Divine Comedy*
Courtesy of the Isabella Stewart Gardner Museum, Boston

thin; ᴛʜ, then; y, you; (variable) d̦ as d or j, ș as s or sh, ț as t or ch, z̦ as z or zh; o, F. cloche; ü, F. menu; ċh, Sc. loch; ṅ, F. bonbon; ʙ, Sp. Córdoba (sounded almost like v).

12, 1362. He had been named cardinal in 1342, and succeeded Clement VI on the papal throne (1352). He kept the papal court at Avignon. He was an upright man who tried to reform the clergy and the court. The main quarrel of his pontificate was with Charles IV, whom he had had crowned (1355) at Rome, over the Golden Bull (1356). This was a code for the election of the emperor. Innocent opposed it on the ground that it infringed papal rights. Innocent sought in vain to restore peace between Castile and Aragon, to promote a crusade, and to reunite the Church in the East and West. He absolved Cola di Rienzi of a charge of heresy (1352) and sent Cardinal Albornoz into Italy with him to attempt a recovery of papal lands and to restore order. Innocent was succeeded by Urban V.

Innocent VII. [Original name, **Cosimo dei Migliorati.**] Pope (1404–1406); b. at Sulmona, Abruzzi, 1336; d. at Rome, November 6, 1406. He was the pope elected by the Roman cardinals while the antipope Benedict XIII was at Avignon. Innocent was a lover of science and the arts, and wished to restore the University at Rome. He was succeeded by Gregory XII.

Innocent VIII. [Original name, **Giovanni Battista Cibo.**] Pope (1484–1492); b. at Genoa, 1432; d. at Rome, July 25/26, 1492. Member of an eminent Genoese family, he passed a dissolute youth at the Aragonese court at Naples. He was the father of at least two illegitimate children (whom he recognized) before he reformed his manner of life and entered the priesthood. He studied at Padua and Rome, entered the service of Cardinal Calandrini, and was made bishop of Savona (1467) and of Molfetta (1472). Cardinal Giuliano della Rovere (later Julius II), whom he greatly admired, furthered his career with the view to controlling him, and was responsible for his elevation to the cardinalate (1473). Through intrigue and bribery, Cardinal della Rovere secured his election as Innocent VIII (1484) to succeed Sixtus IV. Thereafter, Innocent, instrument of the fiery cardinal, became embroiled in his warlike projects. War with Ferrante of Naples was more or less continual; Rome itself was threatened; peace treaties were soon violated. Innocent excommunicated Ferrante, deposed him, and supported French claims to Naples. He won the support of Lorenzo de' Medici and became practically Lorenzo's client. (His son Franceschetto Cibo was married to Lorenzo's daughter Maddalena in a magnificent ceremony in the Vatican in January, 1488; the following year he raised Lorenzo's 14-year-old son Giovanni to the cardinalate.) At length, helpless before the turmoil Ferrante was creating in the Romagna, he made peace with the king, reinstated him, and to cement the peace married a niece to an illegitimate son of the duke of Calabria, Ferrante's son. Innocent was vigilant against heresy. He condemned 13 of the 900 theses proposed for debate by Pico della Mirandola, as heretical, and he authorized an inquisition against witchcraft in Germany. He worked, with conspicuous lack of result, for a crusade against the Turks. At the same time, he received an annual sum of 40,000 ducats from the sultan Bajazet II as a payment for keeping the sultan's rival brother, Djem, a prisoner. The sultan sent the pope the Sacred Lance, said to have pierced the Saviour's side, a gift that was received amid solemn ceremonies at Rome. Mild and benevolent, he was weak and vacillating, incapable of curbing the scandalous conduct of his libertine son or of members of his court. He could keep order neither in the Curia nor the city. Endless wars so exhausted the papal treasury that he was forced to pawn the papal mitre itself, and resorted to the creation of new offices and the sale of them to the highest bidder. He was interested in building, and made important restorations. He erected the Villa Magliana, and caused the Belvedere to be built near the Vatican palace. (The paintings by Pinturicchio and Mantegna with which it was decorated have been lost.) He was a patron of artists and men of letters, improved the Roman *Sapienza,* and encouraged translations. Innocent's magnificent Renaissance monument in the Basilica of St. Peter is the work of Antonio Pollaiuolo. He was succeeded by Alexander VI.

Innocenzo Francucci da Imola (ēn-nō-chen′tsō frän-köt′chē dä ē′mō-lä). Painter; b. at Imola, c1494; d. c1550. According to Vasari he was at Florence a number of years with Mariotto Albertinelli, after which he returned to Imola, where he was active. His *Annunciation,* signed and dated (1515), Church of the Servi, Imola, is reminiscent of a painting on the same subject by Albertinelli in the Uffizi. He did not limit himself to an imitation of Albertinelli, however, but was also influenced by Fra Bartolommeo and Andrea del Sarto. *Madonna and Four Saints*, formerly Crespi Collection, Milan, reveals his effort to adopt the Tuscan style. He was also influenced by Francia, with whom he had been associated at Bologna in 1508, as is shown in his *Marriage of St. Catherine*, Karlsruhe. One of his best works, *Virgin in Glory and St. Michael*, Pinacoteca, Bologna, reflects with delicacy the influence of Raphael. There are several other examples of his work at Bologna, and another *Marriage of St. Catherine* is in the Vatican.

Inquisition. Name given to a tribunal of the Roman Catholic Church established in 1229 at the Synod of Toulouse, by Pope Gregory IX. Its purpose was to discover and to punish heretics and heresy. In the 12th and 13th centuries the Inquisition was directed chiefly against the Cathari, the Waldenses, and the Albigenses; in the 14th century its activity was directed against Franciscan heretics.

Inquisition, Spanish. Tribunal established in Castile in 1478 by Ferdinand V of Castile and Isabella, with the approval of Pope Sixtus IV. It was nominally under papal control, but operated in fact as an agency of the Spanish crown. The tribunal began to function at Seville in 1481, the first inquisitor-general being Tomás de Torquemada. He was followed by Diego Deza, from 1499 to 1506, and by Francisco Jiménez de Cisneros, from 1507 to 1517. The Spanish Inquisition was directed chiefly against Jews and Moors. It was so severe that it directed its power not only against words and actions but also against the thoughts that the accused was supposed to have and against his intentions, real or imaginary. The accused was commanded to appear before the tribunal, immediate arrest following if he did not obey the order. He might be charged with blasphemy, sorcery, witchcraft, infidelity, polygamy, seduction, rape, or Judaism. He was not told who accused him, and he was not always told what was the charge against him. He was kept in prison at the pleasure of his judges, who were often in no hurry to bring him to trial, being content to keep him under restraint. He was subjected to constant cross-examination in an attempt to make him confess, and, if questioning failed, various forms of torture were sometimes employed. The sessions of the Inquisition were secret, and the sentence was proclaimed publicly at what was shown as an auto-da-fé (act-of-faith), and carried out by the secular authorities. The Spanish Inquisition was abolished in 1820, its place being taken in 1823 by an independent body known as the Tribunal of the Faith, which itself finally disappeared in 1835.

Intarsia (in-tär′syä). An Italian word, from *intarsiare*, to inlay, applied to the execution of designs in inlaid wood.

International Gothic. A late phase of the Gothic style of painting, resulting from a fusion of elements from France and Flanders with those of Germany, Bohemia, and North Italy. It originated late in the 14th century and carried over into the 15th century, and was characterized by a pronounced linearity in the rendering of drapery and figures. The marked line often seems just slightly contorted. The drawing is not as conventional as in the Gothic style but is less naturalistic than that which developed in the Renaissance. Other features of the style are a close attention to realism in detail without an overall aim at realism, great care in the rendering of individual parts and of such natural items as foliage, birds, and animals, and enamel-like coloring. The style evolved from French miniature painting and from the refined Sienese style of Simone Martini, who worked at Avignon and whose influence was widespread. It retained the refinement, elegance, precision, and fairy tale quality of the miniaturists and the Sienese, and presented an enchanted world, in which considerations of space were unimportant, in glowing color. Gentile da Fabriano and Lorenzo Monaco are outstanding examples of painters in the international Gothic style.

Intrados (in-trā′dos). In architecture, the inner curve or curved surface of an arch or vault.

Iocondo (yō-kōn′dō). In Lodovico Ariosto's *Orlando Furioso*, a man whose masculine splendor surpasses even that of Astolfo. Like Astolfo and others, he learns that his loving wife cannot resist another man when he is absent, even if the other man is ugly. The canto containing the story of Iocondo was the first one translated into English, by Sir John Harrington. It was done for the delectation of the ladies at Queen Elizabeth's court.

Irala (ē-rä′lä), **Domingo Martínez de.** Spanish soldier; b. at Vergara, Guipúzcoa, Spain, 1487; d. at Itá, near Asunción, Paraguay, 1557. In 1537 he was made governor of the Spanish colonies on the Plata and Paraguay rivers. He conducted many important expeditions, and first opened communications between Paraguay and Peru.

Isaac (ē′zäk), **Heinrich.** [Also, **Arrigo Tedesco.**] Early contrapuntal composer and organist; b. probably in Flanders, c1450; d. 1517. He spent the years 1484–1492 at Florence in the service of Lorenzo de' Medici. In that time he composed madrigals, the music for *San Giovanni e San Paolo*, a drama by Lorenzo, and the music for the elegy Poliziano wrote on the death of Lorenzo. He was active also at Rome and Innsbruck, as well as in Switzerland. His works include much church music and songs in various languages.

Isabeau of Bavaria (ē-zä-bō′). [Also, **Elizabeth, Isabella.**] French queen; b. 1370; d. in September, 1435. She was married (July 17, 1385) to Charles VI of France, being crowned with him at Paris on August 22, 1389. When Charles became insane (August, 1392) she took over the reins of government, acting as regent. At this time also she became openly the mistress of Louis, duke of Orléans. Politically she wavered between the conflicting factions of Armagnacs and Burgundians. In the Hundred Years' War, she sided generally with the enemies of France (the English and the Burgundians). She was chiefly responsible for the Treaty of Troyes (May 21, 1420), by which she surrendered France to England and disinherited her own son. Her daughter, Catherine of Valois, married Henry V of England, and another daughter, Isabella of France, became the wife of Richard II. She, her husband, and Catherine all appear as characters in Shakespeare's *Henry V*, and Isabella appears as "Queen" in *Richard II*.

Isabella I (ē-sä-bel′lä) (of *Castile*). [Called **Isabella the Catholic.**] Queen of Castile (1474–1504) and through her marriage to Ferdinand of Aragon also queen of Aragon (1479–1504); b. April 22, 1451; d. at Medina del Campo, Spain, November 24, 1504. She was the daughter of John II of Castile. When her brother Henry IV succeeded his father (1454), Isabella's mother took her to Arevals and educated her in seclusion. Her brother brought her to his court at a later time, and she was urged by his enemies to accept the crown of Castile once they had overthrown him. Isabella, by nature and education possessed of a high moral sense, rejected their proposals in a rare instance of loyalty at a time when family feuds kept so many princely houses in turmoil. Her brother, called Henry the Impotent, named her (1468) his legal heir, and on his death (1474) she succeeded him as queen of Castile and Leon. In the meantime she had had many princely suitors and had married Ferdinand of Aragon (1469). It was through the joint rule of Ferdinand and Isabella over both Aragon and Castile that Spain became a single political unit under the rule of a single royal house. Isabella imposed her standards of morality on the court, and lifted it from the debasement to which it had descended. Deeply religious, her zeal was excessive in the proscription of the Jews and the introduction of the Inquisition into Spain. She is probably best known to most American readers from the fact that she supported Christopher Columbus (even to the point of offering to pawn her jewels if the treasury could not support his needs) at a time when few others were willing to give his proposed journey of exploration a serious hearing. It was unquestionably largely through her efforts that Columbus was finally enabled to sail, and that America was discovered in 1492. Isabella was the mother of Joanna, and the grandmother of the emperor Charles V.

Isabella d'Este. See **Este, Isabella d'.**

Isabella of Aragona. Duchess of Milan and of Bari; d. at Bari, February 11, 1524. She was the daughter of Alfonso, duke of Calabria (who became King Alfonso II of Naples), and of Ippolita Sforza. A beautiful, spirited girl, she was married (1489) to Gian Galeazzo Sforza, duke of Milan. (Leonardo da Vinci planned and organized the decorations for the festivities celebrating her marriage at Milan.) Her husband's power, but not his title, was usurped by his uncle, Ludovico il Moro. Gian Galeazzo, docile, weak, and somewhat stupid, was completely dominated by his uncle. Isabella understood the situation perfectly, and deeply resented the secondary place that she and her husband were forced into at the court of Milan. Her resentment was exacerbated when Ludovico married Beatrice d'Este (1491), her childhood playmate who had lived some time at Naples, for Beatrice was by all odds the center of the brilliant court. Isabella's humiliation, of which she complained in letters to her father, was a basic reason for the enmity that now rose between Naples and Milan, former allies. Ludovico, finding himself isolated in Italy, turned to France and offered Charles VIII free passage through Italy for the conquest of Naples. As a result, Isabella witnessed the fall of the house of Aragon at Naples and of that of the Sforza at Milan. She is one of the most tragic figures of her time, who, after the death of her husband and the decline of her own family found herself friendless. She later signed her letters, "Isabella of Milan, alone in misfortune." Her son Francesco, the legitimate heir to Milan (called "il Duchetto"), was taken from her by Louis XII so that he could not become a rallying point for those favoring the return of the Sforza. He was sent to France, where he became a priest and died at an early age. Her daughter Bona married (1517) Sigismund I, king of Poland. Isabella retired to Bari, which Ludovico had given her. There, for some time, she cared for Rodrigo Borgia, son of Lucrezia Borgia and of Isabella's half brother Alfonso.

Isabella of France. Queen of Edward II of England, and daughter of Philip IV of France; b. 1292; d. at Hertford, England, August 23, 1358. She and Edward were married at Boulogne on January 25, 1308. Her first son (afterward Edward III) was born on November 13, 1312, at Windsor. Edward II, under the influence of his several favorites, treated her badly. Driven from England by the influence of the Despensers, she raised an army, and with Roger Mortimer, probably her lover, in command, landed (September 24, 1326) at Harwich, beginning the campaign which terminated with the deposition (January 7, 1327) of Edward II by the Parliament at London and the recognition of Edward III, then 14 years old. Isabella and Mortimer ruled in his name. In 1330 Edward III and Henry of Lancaster conspired against her, and she was arrested with Mortimer at Nottingham, on October 18. Mortimer was executed.

Isabella of France. Queen of England; b. at the Louvre, Paris, November 9, 1389; d. at Blois, France, September 13, 1409. She was the second daughter of Charles VI of France and Isabeau of Bavaria, and as the second wife of Richard II was queen of England. The marriage contract was signed on March 9, 1396, when she was seven years old. After Richard's death she was restored to France (July, 1401), and in June, 1404, married Charles d'Orléans, count of Angoulême.

Isabella of Portugal. Queen of Spain and Empress of the Holy Roman Empire; b. at Lisbon, 1503; d. at Toledo, 1539. She was the daughter of Manuel, king of Portugal, and Maria of Castile. In 1526 she married Charles V, Holy Roman Emperor. He was deeply attached to his beautiful wife, who bore him Philip II, his successor, and Juan, Fernando, and Maria, who in her turn became empress as the wife of Maximilian II.

Isabella of Valois. See **Elizabeth of Valois.**

Island of the Seven Cities. See **Seven Cities, Island of the.**

Ismeno (ēs-mā′nō). In Torquato Tasso's *Gerusalemme liberata*, a pagan sorcerer who advises his king to steal the image of the Virgin from the Christian temple in Jerusalem.

Issabella (ē-zä-bel′lä). In Lodovico Ariosto's *Orlando Furioso*, the daughter of a king of Galicia. She is rescued from a band of outlaws by Orlando. When Zerbino, her lover, is slain by Mandricardo, she vows to dedicate herself to religion. Rodomonte comes upon her as she is journeying with the body of Zerbino, and falls in love with her. He attempts to woo her and persuade her to break her vow of chastity. To preserve her chastity, she pretends to Rodomonte that she has prepared a magic potion that makes one's flesh impervious to the sword or lance. She anoints her own breast and neck with the potion and invites Rodomonte to strike her, to prove its efficacy. He does so, and cuts off her head. Overcome by sorrow and remorse, he builds a splendid tomb for her.

Italia liberata dai Goti (ē-tä′lyä lē-bā-rä′-tä dī gō′tē). Epic in blank verse by Giangiorgio Trissino, treating the struggle between the Goths and the Byzantine Greeks for control of Italy. He worked twenty years on what he intended to be a Homeric epic. The result was a forced literary exercise.

J

Jacobello di Antonello (yä-kō-bel′lō dē än-tō-nel′lō). [Also, **Jacobello da Messina.**] Painter; documented from 1479 to 1508. He was the son and follower of Antonello da Messina. Of his three known paintings, a signed *Madonna and Child* (1490) is in the Carrara Academy, Bergamo.

Jacobus de Voragine (ja-kō′bus dē vō-raj′i-nē). [Also, **Jacobus de Varagine; Jacopo de Voragine.**] Italian ecclesiastic; b. at Varazze, near Genoa, 1230; d. 1298. He entered the Dominican order in 1244, and became archbishop of Genoa in 1292. He was noted for his sermons and for a chronicle of Genoa to his own time, but above all for his collection of lives of the saints. This later became known as the *Legenda Aurea* (*Golden Legend*). The lives as compiled by Jacobus have almost no historical basis, but are recordings of the legends that grew up concerning the saints. His collection became the most popular of its kind in the Middle Ages. Many of the legends recounted are the subject of Renaissance paintings.

Jacometto Veneziano (yä-kō-met′tō ve-nā-tsyä′nō). Venetian painter and miniaturist; active from c1472; d. before 1498. His style was, at times, close to that of Antonello da Messina and Alvise Vivarini, and his work has sometimes been attributed to them. Two portraits in the National Gallery, London, are ascribed to him; a *Portrait of a Lady* is in the Johnson Collection, Philadelphia.

Jacopo de' Barbari (yä′kō-pō dā bär′bä-rē). See **De Barbari, Iacopo.**

Jacopo del Casentino (del kä-zen-tē′nō). See **Iacopo del Casentino.**

Jacopo di Cione (dē chō′nā). Florentine painter; d. c1398. He was the younger brother of Andrea Orcagna and Nardo di Cione, entered the guild in 1368 or 1369, and was influenced by his famous brother Andrea. He worked with Andrea on the panel *St. Matthew*, with scenes from his life, now in the Uffizi, Florence. Andrea did the central panel (1367) and Jacopo finished some of the scenes (1368); also executed with Andrea is the *Madonna and Child with Angels*, National Gallery, Washington. He also sometimes worked with or was assisted by his brother, Nardo, and Niccolò di Pietro Gerini. In the triptych, *Madonna and Child with St. Gregory and Job* (1365), S. Croce, Florence, he worked with Nardo, whom he assisted on the frescoes of St. Thomas in the vault of the Strozzi Chapel, S. Maria Novella. Niccolò di Pietro Gerini assisted him in the triptych, *Coronation of the Virgin* (1370–1371), National Gallery, London, the predella panels of which are scattered among Philadelphia (Johnson Collection), Providence (Rhode Island School of Design), Radensleben, and Rome (Vatican). Other surviving works of Jacopo include a *Madonna* (1362), Brussels, *Coronation of the Virgin*, and others, Accademia, Florence, paintings in the Uffizi, Bigallo, and frescoes in the Palazzo Vecchio and S. Trinità, Florence.

Jacopo da Lentini (dä len-tē′nē). See **Giacomo da Lentino.**

Jacopo di Michele Gera (dē mē-kā′lā jā′rä). Pisan painter; active in the second half of the 14th century. In 1389 he painted banners for the cathedral at Pisa, and in 1390 executed figures in the cupola of the cathedral. He was influenced by the Sienese, especially by the Lorenzetti, in the richness of the decorative detail in his *Mystical Marriage of St. Catherine*, in the Palazzo dei Priori at Volterra. A signed *Madonna and Saints* is in the Museo Nazionale at Pisa.

Jacopo di Paolo (dē pä-ō′lō). Bolognese painter; active from 1380 to 1426. An undistinguished painter, he followed the manner of the 13th century and was uninfluenced by developments of the 14th century. A number of panels and a detached fresco are to be found in the Pinacoteca at Bologna.

Jacopo della Quercia (del′lä kwer′chä). See **Della Quercia, Jacopo.**

Jacopo di San Secondo (dē sän sā-kôn′dō). Violinist at the court of Ludovico il Moro at Milan. After the fall of Ludovico (1500) he went to Rome, where he was a friend of Raphael and Castiglione. He is said to have been the model for the Apollo in Raphael's *Parnassus* in the *Stanza della Segnatura* in the Vatican.

Jacopo da Verona (dä vā-rō′nä). Paduan painter; b. 1355; d. after 1442. Originally from Verona, where he was working in 1404, he went to Padua and was influenced, especially in his predilection for architectural backgrounds and his preoccupation with homely detail, by Altichiero Altichieri. He painted undistinguished frescoes in the churches of Padua.

Jacopone da Todi (yä-kō-pō′nā dä tō′dē). Poet and jurist; b. at Todi, c1230; d. December 25, 1306. He studied law at Bologna but turned to religion following the death (c1268) of his wife, and joined the Franciscan order. In the order he staunchly upheld the principles of poverty laid down by St. Francis, and was a violent enemy of corruption and laxness in the clergy. He expressed his feelings in the latter regard in several poetic attacks on Pope Boniface VIII. Boniface excommunicated him in 1297, and he was imprisoned. Benedict XI pardoned and released him in 1303. Jacopone wrote many *laude* (hymns, songs of praise or exhortation) in which he reveals the emotions of his soul and his longing for God. He was a mystic, and highly gifted in the expression of his religious experience in verse.

Jacqueline of Bavaria (jak′we̤-lin, -lēn, ba̤-vãr′i-a̤). [Also, **Jacqueline of Holland**; German, **Jakobaa.**] Daughter of William VI of Holland; b. 1401; d. at Teilingen castle, on the Rhine, 1436. She succeeded her father in Holland and Hainaut in 1417.

James II (of *Aragon*). King of Aragon (1291–1327); b. c1260; d. 1327. He succeeded his brother, Alfonso III. He was king of Sicily (1285–1291) but surrendered his claim and was rewarded by the pope for so doing by being made king of Corsica and Sardinia. He founded the University of Lérida in 1300. He was succeeded by his son, Alfonso IV.

James I (of *Majorca*). [Titles, Count of **Roussillon** and **Cerdagne,** Lord of **Montpellier.**] King of Majorca (1276–1311); b. 1243; d. 1311. He was the son of James I of Aragon. In 1278 he was compelled to submit to his brother, Pedro III of Aragon, and in 1285 he was deprived of his territories by Pedro's son, Alfonso, for having aided the French against Pedro. Ten years later he was restored to his privileges by James II of Aragon.

James II (of *Majorca*). [Titles, Count of **Roussillon** and **Cerdagne,** Lord of **Montpellier.**] King of Majorca (1324–1349); b. 1315; d. 1349. He was the grandson of James I of Aragon. In 1329 he became a vassal of the Aragonese crown.

James I (of *Scotland*). King of Scotland (1406–1437); b. at Dumfermline, Scotland, 1394; d. at Perth, Scotland, February 20, 1437. He was the son of Robert III and Annabella Drummond. He was captured (c1406) by the English while on the way to France and held in captivity until 1423. He repressed the great feudal lords of Scotland, with the assistance of the clergy and the burghs, and maintained peaceful relations both with England and with France. He was murdered at Perth. He was the author of *The Kingis Quair*, an allegorical poem on his courtship while in England of his future wife, Jane Beaufort.

James II (of *Scotland*). King of Scotland (1437–1460); b. October 16, 1430; d. at Roxburgh, Scotland, August 3, 1460. He was the son of James I and Jane Beaufort, daughter of the earl of Somerset. He continued his father's policy of repressing the great feudal lords, and on February 22, 1452, stabbed with his own hand William Douglas, 8th earl of Douglas, who had entered into a treasonable alliance with the earls of Crawford and of Ross, and whom he had enticed to Stirling by a safe-conduct. He was accidentally killed by a wedge from a bombard at the siege of Roxburgh.

James III (of *Scotland*). King of Scotland (1460–1488); b. July 10, 1451; d. June 11, 1488. He was the son of James II and Mary of Guelders. He favored men of less than noble rank to the neglect of the great feudal lords, which provoked a rising of the latter under his son James. He was defeated and killed at Sauchieburn.

James IV (of *Scotland*). King of Scotland (1488–1513); b. March 17, 1473; d. September 9, 1513. He was the son of James III and Margaret of Denmark. He headed the rebellious nobles who defeated and killed his father at the battle of Sauchieburn. He married Margaret, daughter of Henry VII of England. He died at Flodden in an invasion of England during an absence of Henry VIII in France.

James V (of *Scotland*). King of Scotland (1513–1542); b. at Linlithgow, Scotland, April 10, 1512; d. at Falkland, Scotland,

December 14, 1542. He was the son of James IV and Margaret, daughter of Henry VII. He was a vigorous administrator, protected the poor against oppression by the nobles, and mingled with the commons, whence he is sometimed called "the king of the commons." He was succeeded by his week-old daughter, Mary, Queen of Scots.

Jasper of Hatfield (jas′pėr, hat′fēld). See **Tudor, Jasper.**

Jean de Meung (or **Meun**) (zhäṅ dẹ mėṅ). [Pseudonym of **Jean Clopinel.**] French poet; b. at Meun-sur-Loire, Orléanais, France, c1250; d. at Paris, c1305. He is known chiefly as having continued, after a lapse of forty years, *Le Roman de la rose*, a poem undertaken c1237 by a young poet, Guillaume de Lorris, and left incomplete at the time of his death. To the 4,000 lines of Guillaume, Jean de Meung added almost 19,000. His satirical, critical verses on clergy, nobility, and especially women and their wiles contrast with the courtly approach of the earlier part. His translations into French include the *De re militari* of Vegetius (1284), the correspondence of Héloïse and Abelard, and the *Topographia Hiberniae* of Giraldus Cambrensis (Giraldus de Barri). Between 1291 and 1296 he wrote his *Testament*, a curious piece of work replete with sarcasm and criticism, especially of the women and of the mendicant orders of his day.

Jeres (hā′rās), **Francisco de.** See **Xeres, Francisco de.**

Jerome of Prague. Bohemian religious reformer; b. at Prague, c1365; burned at Konstanz (Constance), Germany, May 30, 1416. He studied at Oxford, where he became acquainted with the doctrines of Wycliffe. After traveling and studying at Cologne, Heidelberg, and Jerusalem, he returned to Prague. There his advocacy of Wycliffe and his opposition to the archbishop of Prague, especially in the matter of the sale of indulgences for the pope's war against the king of Naples, led to his becoming known as a radical. He was an associate and follower of John Hus, whom he accompanied to the Council of Constance in 1415, but recanted after he was arrested. In 1416 he resumed his advocacy of his former doctrines before the council, was condemned for heresy, and burned immediately.

Jerusalem Delivered. See **Gerusalemme liberata.**

Jiménez de Cisneros (hē-mā′neth dā thēs-nā′-rōs), **Francisco.** [Also, **Jimenes** (or **Ximenes**) **de Cisneros.**] Spanish cardinal and statesman; b. at Torrelaguna, Spain, 1436; d. at Roa, Spain, November 8, 1517. After becoming a Franciscan monk in middle life, he obtained appointment as confessor to Queen Isabella (1492), and later as Franciscan provincial. He served in many high offices, became a cardinal (1507), and was regent of Spain (1516–1517) for Charles I (later, Emperor Charles V). He printed the Complutensian polyglot Bible and founded (1500) the University of Alcalá de Henares.

Jiménez de Quesada (dā kā-sā′ᴛʜä), **Gonzalo.** [Also, **Ximenes de Quesada.**] Spanish conqueror of Colombia; b. c1500; d. 1579. He was chief justice (1535 *et seq.*) of Santa Marta colony in New Granada (now Colombia), and founded (1538) Bogotá as a Spanish possession. Chosen (1565) *adelantado* (governor) of New Granada, he led an expedition to the Orinoco Valley in search of El Dorado.

Joan (jōn). [Called **Joan Make-peace; Joan of the Tower.**] Queen of Scotland (1329–1362); b. in the Tower of London, about July, 1321; d. August 14, 1362. She was the youngest child of Edward II of England and Isabella of France. Her marriage to David, heir to Robert Bruce, was one of the conditions of the peace of Northampton (1328). The Scots called her Joan Make-peace.

Joan. [Called the **Fair Maid of Kent.**] Wife of Edward, prince of Wales, the "Black Prince"; b. 1328; d. at Wallingford Castle, Berkshire, England, August 7, 1385. She was the daughter of Edmund of Woodstock, earl of Kent, sixth son of Edward I. Froissart called her "in her time the most beautiful of all the kingdom of England and the most loyal." By Edward, who was her second husband, she was the mother of Richard II. By her exertions in 1378 proceedings against Wyclif at Lambeth were arrested. She also exerted all her influence to heal the breach between Richard II and John of Gaunt.

Joan of Arc. [French, **Jeanne d'Arc;** called by the English the **Maid of Orléans,** by the French **La Pucelle.**] French national heroine; b. at Domremy (now Domremy-la-Pucelle), France, c1412; d. at Rouen, France, May 30, 1431. She was the fourth child of a peasant proprietor, Jacques d'Arc, who occupied a position comparable to that of mayor of a present-day French village. In her time the English and their allies, the Burgundians, were masters of the whole of France north of the Loire, and the queen mother, Isabella, supported the claim of Henry VI of England to the throne of France, in opposition to her son the dauphin of France (later Charles VII). There was a prophecy made by Marie d'Avignon to Charles VI that "France ruined by a woman would be restored by a maid from the border of Lorraine." The young girl was undoubtedly familiar with this saying. Deeply religious, from the age of 13 she believed she heard divine voices speaking to her, among them those especially of St. Catherine and St. Margaret, whose words were sometimes heralded by the voice of St. Michael. In May, 1428, the supernatural voices commanded her to go to the dauphin of France and help him to reconquer his kingdom. It was not easy to convince the agents of the validity of her mission but eventually she gained access to the court of the dauphin at Chinon in 1429. She recognized the dauphin, who had taken a place among his knights, and told him she had come at God's command to help him. The timid and irresolute dauphin was convinced. Clad in white armor, Joan rode at the head of about 4,000 troops and raised the siege of Orléans on May 8, 1429. By gaining the victory of Patay on June 18, 1429, she enabled the dauphin to enter the city of Reims in triumph. In that city, where the kings of France were crowned and consecrated with the holy oil, she stood beside the dauphin when he was crowned Charles VII of France, on July 17, 1429. On May 24, 1430, while making a sally against the Burgundians at Compiègne unassisted by Charles' armies (Charles had relapsed into his former timid indolence and was seeking to treat with the Burgundians), she was captured by one of John of Luxemburg's men. John of Luxemburg sold her to the duke of Burgundy, who turned her over to his close friend and ally, John of Lancaster, duke of Bedford, for 10,000 gold francs. At the same time, John of Luxemburg consented to let the duke of Bedford and the cardinal of Winchester have her tried under the jurisdiction of the University of Paris, which was at that time under the domination of the English. Charles made no move to assist her. The English were anxious to crush the great influence she had acquired with the French people, who already regarded her as a saint. It was to discredit her that she was tried on charges of heresy and sorcery. She was burned at the stake as a heretic on May 30, 1431. The rehabilitation trial which reversed the verdict of the earlier court was ordered by Charles VII in 1450, but owing to political and ecclesiastical intrigues the actual hearings did not take place until 1455. Hearings begun at Rome in 1869 led to her beatification (April 11, 1909) by Pope Pius X and her canonization (1920) by Pope Benedict XV. She was made patron saint of France in 1922.

Joanna I (jō-an′a). [**Giovanna.**] Queen of Naples (1343–1382); b. c1327; killed at Aversa, 1382. She was the granddaughter of Robert of Naples, whom she succeeded on the throne of Naples in 1343. She procured the murder of her first husband, Andrew, prince of Hungary, in 1345, and in 1346 married Prince Louis of Tarentum. She was expelled from her kingdom by Louis, king of Hungary, who invaded Naples to avenge the death of his brother Andrew. She went to Provence for refuge and sold (1348) her land of Avignon to Clement VI in return for a pardon. She returned to Naples and was restored to power in 1352. Prince Louis of Tarentum died in 1362 and Joanna had two husbands after him, but had no direct heirs. She named Louis I, duke of Anjou, her heir. She was captured and put to death at Aversa by the usurper Charles III, duke of Durazzo, whom she had earlier adopted and later disinherited.

Joanna II. [**Giovanna.**] Queen of Naples (1414–1435); b. 1371; d. February 11, 1435. She was the daughter of Charles III, king of Naples and Hungary, and the sister of Ladislaus, king of Naples, whom she succeeded (1414). Her life was a scandal. Naples suffered as her lovers succeeded each other and sought control of the kingdom. At the time of her accession she was under the influence of her lover Pandolfo Piscopo (called Alopo), and the constable Muzio Attendolo Sforza. James of Bourbon, whom she married in 1415, tried to seize power and killed Alopo. The barons rebelled, captured James and imprisoned him. Sforza, back in power, reestablished Neapolitan power in Rome, but while he was absent the queen's new lover, Giovanni Caracciolo, obtained influence over her. He opposed Sforza's nomination of Louis III of Anjou as heir of the childless queen, and convinced her that Alfonso V of Aragon was a better choice. The resulting war ended in Alfonso's victory and she adopted him (1420) as her heir. However, he began to assume too prominent a place in the government and Joanna was forced to turn to Sforza for help to keep him from usurping the throne. She now adopted Louis III of Anjou. He was killed fighting the prince of Taranto (1434) and she adopted his brother René. When Joanna died, Alfonso seized the kingdom from René.

Jodelle (zho-del), **Étienne.** [Title, Sieur **de Lymodin.**] French dramatic poet; b. at Paris, 1532; d. there, July, 1573. He was a member of the Pléiade, and the founder of classical French tragedy and comedy. He wrote the tragedies *Cléopâtre Captive* (1552) and *Didon se sacrifiant* (1553) and the comedy *Eugène*.

Jodocus Pratensis (jō̤-dō′kus pra̤-ten′sis). Latin name of **Josquin des Prés.**

Johannes ab Horologio (jō-han′ēz, -e̤s, äb hō-rō-lō′jō). See **Dondi, Giovanni.**

Johannes Secundus (sē̤-kun′dus). [Original name, **Jan Nicolai Everaerts.**] Dutch Poet; b. at The Hague, Netherlands, in November, 1511; d. at Utrecht, Netherlands, 1536. He was noted for his Latin lyrics, elegies, and other works. His *Basia* was published in 1539.

John XXI. [Original name, **Pedro Giuliano;** also known as **Petrus Hispanus.**] Pope (September, 1276–March, 1277); b. at Lisbon, c1215; d. at Viterbo, March 20, 1277. He succeeded Adrian V. A physician and philosopher, he favored the University of Paris and encouraged learning. He wrote several medical treatises and a textbook on logic (*Summulae logicales*). In his ecclesiastical career he had been archbishop of Braga. John XXI was killed at Viterbo when the roof of his palace there collapsed. He was succeeded by Nicholas III. Although he was, strictly speaking, John XX, this pope was crowned as John XXI and is so listed by the most authoritative papal catalogs. There is thus no Pope John XX, and the double numbering which sometimes begins with Pope John XV is ended.

John XXII. [Original name, **Jacques d'Euse.**] Pope (1316–1334); b. at Cahors, France, 1249; d. at Avignon, December 4, 1334. He succeeded Clement V, made his residence at Avignon, and was subservient to the interests of the French court. He opposed the emperor Louis IV (Louis the Bavarian), whom he excommunicated and declared forfeit of all rights to the German crown, and supported Robert of Naples. Louis installed Nicholas V as antipope at Rome in 1328, but on retiring from Italy was unable to prevent Nicholas from falling into the hands of John. He was succeeded by Benedict XII.

John XXIII. [Original name, **Baldassare Cossa.**] Antipope (1410–1415); b. at Naples, c1370; d. at Florence, December 22, 1419. He served as a corsair in his youth, and afterward studied at the university of Bologna. He was created a cardinal (1402) by Boniface IX. During the Great Schism (1378–1417) John was one of a group of Roman cardinals who broke away from Gregory XII. They were joined by the French cardinals of the antipope Benedict XIII and were instrumental in calling the Council of Pisa. The Council met in 1409, declared both Gregory and Benedict deposed and elected Alexander V, whose candidacy was promoted by John. Alexander died the following year and John succeeded him. He was supported by many princes of Italy and by France, England and parts of Germany. He established his court and energetically set about restoring order, but was compelled to flee to Florence when Ladislaus, king of Naples and his former ally, captured Rome (1413). Since neither Gregory nor Benedict recognized the authority of the Council to depose them, there were three who claimed to be pope. This increased the demand for a council to end the schism and unite the Church. Under the influence of Sigismund, whom John had helped to elect emperor, John was persuaded to call a council at Constance, in 1414. Judging the temper of the Council to be against him, he fled Constance in disguise (March, 1415), was surrendered by the prince with whom he had taken refuge, arrested, and imprisoned. He was tried and deposed in May, 1415. He made no attempt to defend himself, humbly submitted to the will of the Council, and ultimately freely renounced any claim he might have had to the papal chair. He passed the next few years under the guard of German jailers, whose language he did not know and with whom he communicated by signs, and occupied his time in writing verses on the ephemeral nature of worldly concerns. In 1418 he was ransomed for 38,000 florins and went to Florence to ask forgiveness of Martin V, the pope whose election ended the Great Schism. Martin created him cardinal bishop of Tusculum, in June, 1419, but John died soon after. Cosimo de' Medici the Elder commissioned Donatello to make a monument for John. It is in the Baptistery at Florence.

John I (of *Aragon*). [Spanish, **Juan.**] King of Aragon (1387–1395); b. December 27, 1350; d. 1395. He succeeded his father, Pedro IV, was a patron of learning, and maintained a brilliant court. He was succeeded by his brother Martin I.

John II (of *Aragon*). [Spanish, **Juan.**] King of Aragon (1458–1479) and of Navarre (1425–1479); b. June 29, 1397; d. January 20, 1479. He was the son of Ferdinand I. He married Blanche of Navarre, through whom he claimed Navarre, but his claim was contested after her death in 1441 by their son, Charles, prince of Viana. Charles died in 1461 but John was faced with continued denial of his claim. He married Juana Henríquez in 1447; their son Ferdinand married Isabella of Castile. His son Ferdinand inherited Aragon; his daughter Leonora de Foix inherited Navarre.

John (of *Bohemia*). [Called **John of Luxemburg, John the Blind.**] King of Bohemia (1310–1346); b. c1296; killed at the battle of Crécy, August 26, 1346. Of the house of Luxemburg, he became count of Luxemburg in 1309. He fought (1322) at the battle of Mühldorf for Louis IV. He fought in numerous wars and formed many alliances, eventually becoming estranged from the emperor. His alliance with King Philip VI of France called him to aid against the English and, though blind, he demanded to be led into the thick of the fighting at Crécy, where he died. His son Charles of Luxemburg became Charles IV of the Holy Roman Empire.

John (of *Burgundy*). [Called **John the Fearless.**] Duke of Burgundy (1404–1419); b. at Dijon, May 28, 1371; assassinated at Montereau, France, September 10, 1419. He was the son of Philip the Bold, whom he succeeded in 1404. He and Louis, duke of Orléans, younger brother of the insane King Charles VI of France, struggled for the regency of the kingdom. Both before and after the assassination of the duke of Orléans in 1407 (procured by John) civil war was waged between the Burgundians and the Orléanists (or Armagnacs), especially in the period 1411–1412. Compromise settlements were reached several times but not until 1418 did John take Paris. His opponent, the Dauphin Charles (later Charles VII), fled but a reconciliation was attempted and during a parley on the bridge of Montereau John was cut down and slain by the dauphin's escort. He was succeeded by his son Philip the Good.

John I (of *Castile*). King of Castile (1379–1390); b. in August, 1358; d. at Alcalá de Henares, Spain, October 9, 1390. He was the son of Henry II. On his accession he was faced by an English rival to the throne, John of Gaunt, who claimed the kingship through his wife Constance, the daughter of Peter the Cruel (the king who had been deposed and slain by Henry II's father). John of Gaunt's ally, Portugal, went to war with John I, and he attempted to resolve his difficulties by matrimonial alliances. He married (1382) a daughter of the king of Portugal, and arranged the marriage of his son to John of Gaunt's daughter. The marriages added to the tangle of conflicting claims and brought more wars, because of his wife's claim to the Portuguese throne after 1383, when her father, Ferdinand I, died. John was defeated (August 14, 1385) by John I of Portugal. He was succeeded by his son Henry III.

John II (of *Castile*). [Spanish, **Juan.**] King of Castile (1406–1454); b. March 5, 1405; d. in June, 1454. He was the son of Henry III of Castile and Catherine, daughter of John of Gaunt. His early reign was under a regency and later he was under the influence of favorites. By his second wife, Isabella of Portugal, he was the father of Isabella I, wife of Ferdinand V.

John I (of *France*). [French, **Jean**; called **John the Posthumous.**] Posthumous son of Louis X; b. November 15, 1316; d. November 22, 1316. Louis' brother Philip acted as regent in the period from the death of the king and, when the infant king was born and died within a week, himself became king as Philip V.

John II (of *France*). [French, **Jean**; called **Jean le Bon,** "John the Good."] King of France (1350–1364); b. 1319; d. at London, April 8, 1364. He was the son and successor of Philip VI. He was defeated and captured by the English under Edward the Black Prince at Poitiers in 1356, and was restored to liberty by the peace of Brétigny in 1360 on condition that he pay a ransom of 3,000,000 crowns. He left his son as hostage, instituted heavy taxes, and married his daughter to a Visconti of Milan in return for a large gift. These expedients, however, failed to raise more than a fifth of the ransom, and when his son escaped in 1363 John left France for England. He died there within a few months and was succeeded by his son Charles V.

John I (of *Portugal*). [Portuguese, **João**; called **John the Great.**] King of Portugal (1385–1433); b. at Lisbon, April 22, 1357; d. August 11, 1433. He was the illegitimate son of Pedro I. He became grand master of Aviz in 1364, and was in 1385 elected to succeed his legitimate brother Ferdinand I, to the exclusion of Ferdinand's daughter Beatrice, wife of John I of Castile. John of Castile sought to enforce his wife's claim, but suffered a decisive defeat, August 14, 1385. John the Great married Philippa, daughter of John, duke of Lancaster. Among his sons were his successor, Edward, and Prince Henry the Navigator.

John II (of *Portugal*). [Called **John the Perfect.**] King of Portugal (1481–1495); b. 1455; d. in October, 1495. He was the son of Alfonso V. During his reign Bartolomeu Dias discovered the Cape of Good Hope (1486). In 1494 John concluded with Spain the treaty of Tordesillas, establishing the limits of each country in their colonizing and modifying the papal decision of the year before. The line of demarcation was moved westward, a shift that eventually made Brazil a Portuguese colony.

John III (of *Portugal*). King of Portugal (1521–1557); b. at Lisbon, 1502; d. 1557. He was the son of Emanuel I. He introduced the Inquisition (c1526), and in general permitted clerical opinion to hold sway to the detriment of trade and prosperity. The slow degeneration of the court was not matched abroad, where Portuguese explorers pushed farther into the East Indies.

John (of *Saxony*). [Called **John the Constant.**] Elector of Saxony; b. June 30, 1468; d. August 16, 1532. He was coregent with his brother Frederick III (Frederick the Wise) until the death of the latter (May 5, 1525). He was one of the original Protestant leaders at the Diet of Speyer (1529), and was an organizer of the Schmalkaldic League (1531).

John III (of *Sweden*). King of Sweden (1568–1592); b. 1537; d. November 17, 1592. He was the second son of Gustavus Vasa. He deposed and murdered his brother Eric XIV, whom he succeeded. Originally a Protestant, he became (1578) a Roman Catholic, but failed in his efforts to make a Roman Catholic country of Sweden.

John VI Cantacuzene (kan-ta̤-kṳ̄-zēn′) (of the *Byzantine Empire*). Byzantine emperor (1347–1355) and historian; b. at Constantinople, c1292; d. in Greece, 1383. He was an adviser of Andronicus III and, when Andronicus died (1341), became acting regent for John V Palaeologus. A court intrigue forced him to flee to Thrace, where in 1341 he proclaimed himself emperor. He was victorious in the ensuing civil war and, entering Constantinople in 1347, had himself made coemperor with John V, thereby retaining the rule during John's minority. The civil war had been fought to a great degree with foreign, European mercenaries and Cantacuzene's lack of money with which to pay them resulted in their seizing much territory. In 1355 Cantacuzene, who had made disastrous bargains with the Turks and whose turbulent reign had made him unpopular, retired to a monastery. Thereafter, under the literary name of Joasaph Christodulus, he devoted himself to literature. He wrote a history, commentaries, and treatises.

John V Palaeologus (pā-lē-ol′ō-gus) (of the *Byzantine Empire*). Byzantine emperor; b. 1332; d. 1391. He became emperor in 1341 on the death of his father. His reign was wracked by internal troubles which so weakened it that John was forced to become (1381) a vassal of the Ottoman Turks. He was succeeded by his son Manuel II.

John VII Palaeologus (of the *Byzantine Empire*). Byzantine emperor (1390) and coemperor (1398–1412); b. 1360; d. 1412. He was the son of Andronicus IV. He revolted and seized Constantinople (1385) and had himself made emperor. After the accession of his uncle Manuel II, John was for a time (1398–1412) co-emperor.

John VIII Palaeologus (of the *Byzantine Empire*). Byzantine emperor (1425–1448); b. 1390; d. 1448. He was the son and successor of Manuel II. He managed to retain

Constantinople during his reign although it was completely surrounded by the Turks and underwent a siege in 1432. In an effort to find help against the Turks and to preserve the rapidly shrinking Byzantine Empire, John turned to the West. The idea, often discussed, of uniting the Latin and Greek churches was revived. John met Pope Eugenius IV at Ferrara to discuss the union. The Council adjourned to Florence and there (1439) an agreement of union was ratified. John brought with him to Italy leaders of the Greek Church and a great retinue. The splendor of their costumes appears in paintings of that age, especially in Benozzo Gozzoli's *Procession of the Magi*, in the Medici Riccardi Palace, where John is pictured as one of the three kings. The agreement signed with such ceremony at Florence was of short duration. Since it was followed by no crusade against the Turks, as the Byzantine party had expected, there was great objection to it by the Orthodox ecclesiastics in Constantinople, and it came to nothing. John was succeeded by his brother Constantine XI, the last Byzantine emperor.

John Capistran (ka̤-pis′tra̤n), Saint. See **Capistrano,** San **Giovanni da.**

John Frederick (of *Saxony*). [Called **John Frederick the Magnanimous.**] Elector of Saxony; b. at Torgau, Saxony, Germany, June 30, 1503; d. at Jena, Thuringia, Germany, March 3, 1554. He was the son of John the Constant, whom he succeeded in 1532. He was one of the leaders of the Schmalkaldic League. At Mühlberg, on April 24, 1547, he was defeated by the emperor Charles V, captured, and was forced to renounce the electorate.

John of Austria. [Generally called Don **John of Austria;** Spanish, Don **Juan de Austria.**] Spanish general; b. at Regensburg, Bavaria, Germany, February 24, 1547; d. near Namur, Belgium, October 1, 1578. He was the illegitimate son of the emperor Charles V by Barbara Blomberg. Brought up without knowledge of his parentage, he was acknowledged in Charles' will and recognized by Philip II as a prince of the royal blood. He fought against the pirates of Algeria in 1568, defeated the Moriscos in Granada (1569–1570), gained a tremendous naval victory as admiral of the combined fleets of the Holy League over the Turks at Lepanto (October 7, 1571), captured Tunis (1573), and was governor of the Netherlands from 1587 until his death. He granted the "perpetual edict" in 1577, which gave the Dutch many concessions. He soon found that the real power in the Netherlands was William of Orange (William I), and in 1578 declared war against the insurgent provinces. He, aided by Alessandro Farnese, beat the patriots severely at Gembloux (January 31, 1578), but further aid from Spain was not forthcoming and he died before he could follow up his victory.

John of Capistrano (kä-pēs-trä′nō̤), Saint. See **Capistrano,** San **Giovanni da.**

John of Gamundia (ga̤-mun′di-a̤). Astronomer and mathematician; d. 1442. He is remembered chiefly for the calendars he made.

John of Gaunt (gänt, gônt). [Title, Duke of **Lancaster.**] English statesman; b. at Ghent Belgium, March, 1340; d. at London, February 3, 1399. He was the fourth son of Edward III. His name comes from an English version of Ghent. In 1342 he was created earl of Richmond, and in 1359 married his cousin Blanche, second daughter of Henry, duke of Lancaster. On the death of Henry (May, 1361) and his eldest daughter Maud, duchess of Bavaria, he succeeded by right of his wife to the rank and possessions of the dukes of Lancaster. In 1367 he accompanied his brother, Edward, the Black Prince, on the Spanish expedition against Henry of Trastamara and in aid of Pedro the Cruel. Blanche died in 1369, and in 1371 he married Constance, Pedro's eldest daughter. Pedro was defeated and killed by his half brother, and returning to England in 1372, John of Gaunt styled himself king of Castile by right of his wife. He was constantly engaged in the stuggle with France, but although a brave knight he was never a competent general, and his repeated failures contributed much to his increasing unpopularity. The Black Prince died June 8, 1376, and the Good Parliament, which under his patronage had undertaken to reform abuses, was dissolved. On July 6, the supreme power passed into the hands of Lancaster, Edward III being more or less incompetent to rule because of his early aging. His most powerful opponent, William of Wykeham, bishop of Winchester, was disgraced. In the struggle with the clerical party Lancaster was drawn into an alliance with the Reformers, especially with Wycliffe, whom he defended before the convocation at Saint Paul's, February 19, 1377. His brutal behavior excited a riot in London; his palace, the Savoy, was attacked, and he was forced to take refuge with Prince Richard and his mother, the widow of the Black Prince, at Kennington. Edward III died June 21, 1377, and Richard II became king, and Lancaster's political power declined. He was engaged in futile expeditions to France and Scotland. While absent in the north his extreme unpopularity was shown by the destruction of his palace of the Savoy in Wat Tyler's insurrection, June 13, 1381. He made a futile attempt (1386–1389) to take the throne of Castile but his separation from English politics brought him back into Richard's favor. Richard created him duke of Aquitaine on March 2, 1390, and he assisted in negotiating the French truce on May 24, 1394. He never recovered from the shock of the exile of his son Henry (later Henry IV). From John of Gaunt and Blanche were descended Henry IV, Henry V, and Henry VI; his children by Catherine Swynford, legitimatized after their marriage in 1396, were the ancestors of Henry VII. John of Gaunt was a patron of Chaucer.

John of Lancaster (lang′kạs-ter). [Title, Duke of **Bedford.**] Regent of England and France; b. June 20, 1389; d. at Rouen, September 14, 1435. He was the third son of Henry IV of England by Mary, daughter of Humphrey Bohun, Earl of Hereford. He was knighted at his father's coronation as one of the original knights companions of the Bath, and in 1403 was made constable of England and warden of the East Marches. In May, 1414, he was created duke of Bedford and earl of Kendal and later earl of Richmond. He commanded the troops in the north until the death of Henry IV (March, 1413). On August 15, 1416, the fleet under his command won a great victory over the French in the English Channel, and succeeded in relieving the besieged town of Harfleur; and in 1417 his expedition into Scotland was successful. At the death of Henry V (August, 1422) he assumed the regency. He went to France to prosecute English claims there, leaving Humphrey, duke of Gloucester, as regent in England. To secure the alliance of Philip, duke of Burgundy, Bedford married his daughter Anne in 1423. His administration of France continued both successful and beneficial until the siege of Orléans (1428–1429), which marks the appearance of Joan of Arc and the decline of English supremacy. Charles VII was crowned king of France at Reims on July 17, 1429, and Joan of Arc unsuccessfully assaulted Paris on September 8, 1429. She was betrayed to the English, and executed on May 30, 1431. Anne, duchess of Bedford, died November 13, 1432, and Bedford sacrificed the alliance of Philip, duke of Burgundy, by marrying Jacqueline, daughter of Pierre, Count of St.-Pol, April 20, 1433. Philip entered into an alliance with the French king, thus thwarting Bedford's hopes, and terminating the French dominion of the English king.

John of Leiden (lī′dẹn). [Original name, **Jan** (or **Johann**) **Bockelson** (or **Bockold**).] Anabaptist fanatic; b. at Leiden, Netherlands, c1510; put to death at Münster, Germany, January 23, 1536. He succeeded Matthiesen as leader of the Anabaptists at Münster (1534), and overthrew the regular authorities. He was imprisoned by the bishop of Münster in 1535, and with the other leaders of the revolt was tortured and finally killed. He is the subject of Meyerbeer's opera *Le Prophète.*

John of London. [Also, **John Bever.**] English chronicler; d. 1311. He was a monk of Westminster Abbey, and was the author of *Commendatio lamentabilis in transitum Magni Regis Edwardi Quarti*. He is supposed to have been the author of *Flores Historiarum* (from 1265 to 1306).

John of Luxemburg (luks′ẹm-bėrg). See **John** (of *Bohemia*).

John of Nepomuk (ne′pô-mök), Saint. Bohemian ecclesiastic, patron saint of Bohemia; b. at Pomuk (Nepomuk), in Bohemia, c1340; drowned in the Moldau (Vltava) River in 1393 (according to legend, 1383). He opposed King Wenceslaus IV, who had him tortured and drowned. His opposition to Wenceslaus is agreed upon, but not its content. According to one story, he refused to divulge the queen's confession to the king; another says that he refused to sanction the transformation of a lesser building to a cathedral.

John of Peterborough (pē′tėr-bur-ọ̄). Alleged author of the *Chronicon Petroburgense*; fl. 1380. He was probably an imaginary person.

John of Swabia (swā′bi-ạ). [Called **Johannes the Parricide.**] German prince; b. 1290; d. 1368. He was the nephew of King Albert I of Austria, whom he murdered in Switzerland, May 1, 1308, for withholding his hereditary domains.

John of the Cross, Saint. [Spanish, San **Juan de la Cruz;** original name, **Juan de Yepis** (or **Yepes**) y **Álvarez.**] Spanish mystic; b. at Fontiveros, Avila, Spain, June 24, 1542; d. at Úbeda, in Andalusia, Spain, December 14, 1591. His chief works are *Ascent of Mount Carmel, Dark Night of the Soul, Spiritual Canticle,* and *Living Flame of Love.*

Joinville (zhwaṅ-vēl), **Jean de.** French chronicler; b. at Joinville, in Champagne, France, c1224; d. on his ancestral estates, July 16, 1317. In 1250 he drew up the articles of his *Credo.* The great work to which he has left his name is the *Histoire de Saint Louis,* a personal appreciation of Louis IX, that remains the best source on the period, its customs, its events, and its people.

Joscelyn or **Josselin** (jos′ẹ-lin), **John.** One of the earliest students of Old English; b. 1529; d. at High Roding, Essex, England, December 28, 1603. He was Latin secretary to Matthew Parker, archbishop of Canterbury, and at his suggestion made collections of Old English documents which he annotated.

Josquin des Prés (zhos-kaṅ dā prā). [Latinized, **Jodocus Pratensis, Josquinus a Prato.**] Flemish composer; b. c1445; d. at Condé, France, August 27, 1521. He was preeminent in the Netherlands school of contrapuntalists and was the author of masses, numerous motets, and others.

Josselin (jos′lin), **John.** See **Joscelyn** or **Josselin, John.**

Jovius (jō′vi-us), **Paulus.** Latinized name of **Giovio, Paolo.**

Juan de la Cruz (hwän dā lä kröth′), San. Spanish name of Saint **John of the Cross.**

Julius II (jöl′yus). [Original name, **Giuliano della Rovere.**] Pope (1503–1513); b. at Albissola, near Savona, December 5, 1443; d. at Rome, February 20/21, 1513. A greathearted and fiery spirit, he was perhaps the greatest of the papal patrons of art, letters, and architecture. He was the son of a poor family of Liguria, was educated by the Franciscans, and studied law at Perugia. His paternal uncle, Sixtus IV, made him cardinal of S. Pietro in Vincoli (December, 1471), gave him many benefices, and entrusted many important missions to him. He was legate to the Marches (1473), restored order in Umbria (1474), and was legate to Avignon and France (1476), where he won the respect and friendship of Louis XI. He was again legate to France, and to the Low Countries (1480–1482), where he vainly endeavored to restore peace. Aware that he could not be elected himself in the conclave of 1484, he supported the election of Innocent VIII, and thereafter had great influence with that weak pope. He had been unfriendly to the Aragonese of Naples, but was reconciled to them, and they supported his candidacy in the conclave of 1492, in which Alexander VI was elected. The cardinal had made no secret of his enmity to Alexander, and left Rome in fear of his life. He went to France (June, 1494) and encouraged Charles VIII to undertake the expedition into Italy that the monarch had already almost decided upon. The cardinal accompanied the king on the march and when, according to Guicciardini, the king began to hesitate in carrying out his planned undertaking, Cardinal Giuliano exhorted him to forge ahead. On the march he discussed with Charles the possibility of calling a council to depose Alexander. Later, however, he welcomed Cesare Borgia at Avignon, helped him to attain a French bride, and looked with favor on his enterprise in the Romagna. But he refused to return to Rome, as Alexander ordered him to do, as long as Alexander lived, on the ground that he could not trust his life to the word of a gang of "Catalans." Following the brief reign of Pius III (less than a month), Cardinal Giuliano, by agreement with Cesare Borgia for the votes of the Spanish cardinals, and with the aid of a little judicious simony, was unanimously elected and took the name Julius II (October 1, 1503).

Under his uncle and later pontiffs, he had become thoroughly familiar with the conditions and possibilities of papal authority. At last he could apply his great and restless energy, his administrative skill, his knowledge, and his fiery spirit to the defense and glorification of the Church. For him, the salvation of the papacy rested less in a spiritual renewal of the Church than in a reaffirmation and assertion of its political greatness and in a magnification of its external splendor. His acts as spiritual leader included the publication of a bull in 1510 (but dated January 14, 1505 and confirmed in the Lateran council, February 16, 1513) that declared void papal election as a result of simony. He anathematized any who interfered with papal authority or appealed from the pope to a council. He encouraged the religious orders and sent out missions, and sought, but without fanaticism, to repress heresy. He considered reform of the Church; founded the Capella Giulia, the school for choristers in St. Peter's; collected and spent money, had ships fitted out, and planned personally to lead a crusade against the Turks when he had restored peace in the Christian world. But his immediate concern was in the political field. He restored peace and order at Rome, which he thereafter governed with wisdom and justice. Nepotism, rampant and rotting to the fabric of the papacy under his predecessors, was not a weakness of Julius. He took appropriate sanitary measures, promoted agriculture, and reorganized the currency (the *giulio*, a coin of fixed weight and fineness, was named for him). The states of the Church were in disarray, for the principality Cesare Borgia had constructed collapsed on the death of Alexander. Italy was occupied by foreigners: the French were in Lombardy, the Spanish in Naples. The Church itself was threatened. He turned his attention to restoring the temporal authority of the pope and to making of him "the lord and master of the world." He soon got rid of Cesare Borgia, whatever his secret arrangements with him may have been before the conclave, and seized the fortresses of the Romagna that had remained loyal to him (1504). Giampaolo Baglioni of Perugia, who had broken every law of man and God, was nevertheless overawed by the majesty of the pope and submitted to him without a struggle. Machiavelli was thoroughly exasperated by this pusillanimity; he considered that Giampaolo would have won immortal glory if, when he had Julius in his power, he had taken advantage of the opportunity to rid the world of the warlike pope. Giovanni Bentivoglio, threatened with excommunication, interdict, and a French attack, fled from Bologna with his family (1506) and Julius was welcomed to the city as a liberator from tyranny. In his *Iter Julii Secundi* (*Journey of Julius II*) Adriano di Corneto describes the impressive entry of the pope into Bologna. He returned to Rome in triumph in March, 1507. The Venetians, who had seized Faenza and Rimini on the overthrow of the Borgia, defied the pope and refused to restore those cities to the Church. Julius allied himself with the emperor Maximilian and the king of France in the League of Cambrai (December, 1508) and hurled excommunication and interdict at Venice. Defeated at Agnadello by the forces of the League (May, 1509), Venice gave up the cities. Julius, now fearful of French power in Italy, and chafing under the arrogance of Louis XII who, he said, was turning the pope into his chaplain, now concluded an agreement with the Venetians and the Swiss to drive out the French. (As a result of this alliance with the Swiss, Julius established the colorful Swiss Guard.) Again he personally led an army, this time against Ferrara, an ally of France and a rebellious vassal of the Church. The army occupied Modena. At Bologna Julius fell ill and just missed being captured by the French. Nevertheless, in the dead of a severe winter, amid a hail of bullets, he remained with the army besieging Mirandola, the key to Ferrara, and himself climbed a ladder to enter the city through a breach in the walls (January 20, 1511). But Bologna was lost through the misgovernment of Alidosi, the papal legate and a man dear to the heart of Julius, and through the inactivity of the duke of Urbino (nephew of Julius) who later, in Ravenna, killed the legate almost under the pope's eyes. In the meantime, the king of France called a synod at Tours to revive the Gallican Church. This was followed, with the assistance of some rebellious cardinals, by a council called at Pisa (May 16, 1511) to consider reform of the Church in its head and its members. Julius answered by convoking the Fifth Lateran Council (July 25, 1511). In the next month Julius was felled by a severe illness, and it was rumored that he was dead. Members of the Orsini, Savelli, and Cesarini families swarmed into Rome, where Pompeo Colonna raised the cry of "Liberty." The revolt collapsed and Julius, far from dead, deprived the participants of their honors. Having turned against the French, he sought the aid of other foreigners to drive them out. He formed the Holy League with Spain and Venice (October, 1511) for this purpose. Henry VII of England joined it later, as did the emperor Maximilian (who at this time was under the delusion that he himself might become pope). The French reconquered Brescia, defeated the League in a savage battle at Ravenna (April 11, 1512), and occupied the Romagna. The schismatic council at Pisa, transferred to Milan, declared Julius deposed. His mighty spirit did not even quiver under these blows. He opened the Lateran Council (May 3, 1512) in which the unity of the Church and the supreme authority of the pope were confirmed. The French, attacked on all sides, were forced to withdraw from the Romagna, from Lombardy, and from Italy itself. The pope had such a triumph at Rome as not even Caesar had enjoyed. Members of the Holy League met at Mantua (August, 1512) to reorganize Italy. Massimiliano Sforza was restored at Milan and the Medici (thanks to Cardinal Giovanni, who had been an energetic supporter of the pope) were restored at Florence. Julius longed to punish Ferrara and wipe out French influence there, and he earnestly desired recognition by the emperor of the Lateran Council. In return for concessions at the expense of Venice, the emperor recognized the Council and gave it his obedience. The pope now began to feaı Spanish power in Italy, and was considering how he could eradicate it when death overtook him.

Most of the pontificate of Julius was occupied by war. The pope himself, in armor under his pontifical robes, preceded by the Host and numerous cardinals, led the papal armies in the field. But war and politics did not exhaust his enormous energy. For the glorification of the Church he was an enthusiastic and magnificent Maecenas. A man of great talents, wide interests, and fine taste, while still a cardinal he had collected a library, that went to the Vatican with him. He had restored his two churches, S. Pietro in Vincoli and the Basilica of the Santi Apostoli, raised a bishop's palace at Avignon, so walled his abbey at Grottoferrata that it resembled a fortress, and erected a solid and magnificent fortress at Ostia (1483) that Alexander VI in vain had sought to win from him. As pope he protected studies and the university, founded the first Arab printing press at Fano, was patron and friend of Sigismondo de' Conti, his secretary and historian, of Sadoleto, Bembo, and other celebrated men of letters. He had the gift of recognizing greatness in its early stages and harnessed it for the splendor of the Church. He commissioned Michelangelo (at that time about 30) to make a monumental tomb for him. Michelangelo designed a gigantic and powerful structure, with over forty figures. The pope, whose great spirit demanded a vast scale in all his undertakings, was delighted, and Michelangelo went off to the quarries of Carrara to select his marble (April, 1505). At first Julius visited Michelangelo often in his studio near the Vatican. Then he seemed to lose interest in the tomb. (The monument, never completed according to its planned design, with the powerful and majestic figure of *Moses* that embodies the spirit of Julius himself, is in S. Pietro in Vincoli at Rome.) He had resolved to pull down the ancient basilica over St. Peter's grave, and to raise a mighty new one in its place. (Some said he did this to build a basilica worthy of the planned tomb.) He entrusted the designing of the new basilica to Bramante, a man as old and energetic as Julius himself. Bramante was called "the Destroyer" because of his enthusiasm for pulling down buildings, and there were outcries in Rome at the thought of destroying the old church of holy memory and remains. But Julius was never one to be deterred by outcries, and he and Bramante went ahead with undiminished enthusiasm. Bramante's orders were to design a building that "in grandeur and beauty" would surpass every other. The first stone was laid on April 18, 1506, and by the time of the pope's death the pillars of the great arches that would support the dome had already been raised. (After many interruptions, changes of architect and design, the basilica was dedicated in 1626). The new structure was to be paid for by taxes, contributions, and the sale of indulgences, all of which were contributing causes of the Reformation disaffection. Having begun the basilica, Julius insisted that Michelangelo abandon the tomb for a time and paint the ceiling of the Sistine Chapel. Michelangelo protested that he was not a painter. Julius assured him he knew better what Michelangelo could do than Michelangelo did himself. Michelangelo fled to Florence (April, 1506). Yet there was an attraction between these two fierce spirits. Julius admired the difficult young sculptor and determined to bend his genius to the splendor of the Church. Michelangelo did not admit that he admired the forceful old pope but he could not resist him. He joined Julius at Bologna soon after and there made a bronze statue of the pope, three times life-size. The statue showed Julius seated, with one hand upraised. When he was asked whether Julius was in the act of blessing or cursing, Michelangelo said the hand was raised in warning to the Bolognese. As to the other hand, Julius instructed him to place a sword in it rather than a book as "I know nothing of letters." The statue was placed above the door of S. Petronio (February, 1508). (Later, December, 1511, when the Bolognese had become disenchanted with Julius, they pulled down the statue and broke it up. The fragments were sent to Alfonso d'Este of Ferrara, who cast a cannon from them, set it up before his palace, and named it the *Giulia.*) Julius at last prevailed on Michelangelo to take up the work on the Sistine ceiling (autumn, 1508). In the course of the next four years the pope and the artist had many a royal battle over the pace at which the work progressed. The pope did the artist the honor of fighting with him on equal terms. He climbed up to the narrow bridge under the ceiling where Michelangelo was lying on his back as he worked, to inspect his progress, and is said to have threatened, at least once, to throw the painter off. The goaded artist replied in equally unrestrained terms, but kept working, and in October, 1512, the glorious ceiling, one of the greatest artistic creations of all time, was finished. Julius was more than vindicated. When he moved into the Vatican palace the proud spirit of Julius was exacerbated by the paintings and portraits in the Borgia apartments. He could not bear to be surrounded by images of the detested Borgia of "wicked and cruel memory," and determined to move into other rooms. He dismissed the suggestion that the Borgia paintings by Pinturicchio could be removed, on the grounds that to do so would be improper. The new rooms (in the old palace of Nicholas III, partially rebuilt by Nicholas V) had been decorated by Piero della Francesca, Luca Signorelli, and others. Julius ordered them replaced. He employed Perugino, Sodoma, Peruzzi, Bramantino, and others, and they worked there in 1508. But when, perhaps late in 1508, the 25-year-old Raphael arrived in Rome, the delighted and impetuous Julius dismissed the other painters and entrusted the entire project to Raphael. Most of the earlier works were destroyed and Raphael set out to put in their place the combination of a classical program and a historical view that magnified the power of the papacy. The *Stanze,* as these rooms are called, are four connected chambers in a row, in the north wing of the Vatican. They are known as the *Stanza dello Incendio, Stanza della Segnatura, Stanza di Eliodoro* and *Sala di Costantino.* The *Stanza della Segnatura,* the second room but the first in which Raphael worked, was so called because the ecclesiastical tribunal of that name had held its hearings there. It was intended to be the library of Julius. The names of the other *stanze* derive from the subject of a painting in each. Julius is represented in several of the paintings that decorate them, as in *The Disputation of the Sacrament* and *Gregory IX Approving the Decretals,* in the *Stanza della Segnatura,* and *The Expulsion of Heliodorus* and *The Mass of Bolsena* in the *Stanza di Eliodoro.* In *The Mass of Bolsena* the kneeling pope's great uplifted head reveals intensity and absorption in the religious ceremony and the miracle, but no trace of unlikely humility. In all the portraits Julius appears with flowing beard, for he had vowed he would not shave again until Italy was liberated from the barbarians. The Sistine Ceiling, the Basilica of St. Peter's, and the *Stanze* of Raphael are among the greatest monuments of a great age. They are also monuments to Julius' taste, energy, grandeur of conception, and ability to make artists do their best work. They are not, however, the only contributions he made to the art and architecture of Renaissance Rome. His own palace, erected in the 15th century near his church of the Santi Apostoli, was incorporated in a 17th-century palace that now houses the Colonna Gallery. In the Vatican palace the courtyard of S. Damaso and the Belvedere were begun to designs by Bramante. Ancient statues that had been found at Rome were exhibited in the garden of the Belvedere. On January 14, 1506, workmen digging came upon some colossal figures. When he heard of it Julius sent Giuliano da Sangallo to look at them. Michelangelo was one of the party. Sangallo recognized the find as the *Laocoön* described by Pliny. Julius bought the group and put it in the Belvedere. There, with the *Apollo Belve-*

dere and others, it formed the nucleus of a great collection. Around ancient and medieval Rome a new Renaissance Rome arose, with new streets flanked by beautiful buildings. One of these, the Via Giulia, was the first straight street laid out in Rome for centuries. Bramante enlarged the choir, Pinturicchio painted frescoes, and Andrea Sansovino made the sepulchral monument to Cardinal Ascanio Sforza in the Church of S. Maria del Popolo, the favorite church of Julius, as it had been of his uncle Sixtus. (The cardinal had been a bitter enemy of Julius, or vice versa, but the pope was never one to vent personal spite. He was of that breed of strong men who joyfully test their strength in endless battle but scorn to use it for personal vengeance.) Bramante designed a fortress at Civitavecchia for Julius, the Apostolic palace at Loreto (begun 1510, never finished), and the marble façade of the Santa Casa (the House of Mary) there. Churches, palaces, and fortresses everywhere bear witness to his generosity and his unlimited interest in the glorification through worldly splendor of the Church. Impatient, impetuous, strong-willed, gifted, energetic, and majestic, Julius was one of the great personalities of the culminating Renaissance. He was a driver, and those about him, whether architects, artists, soldiers, or clerks, could never work fast enough to suit him. They called him the *Pontefice terribile;* his drive and vital energy were described, with admiration, as *terribilità*. He drove himself. His anger was never hidden, nor his goodwill concealed. All his qualities were larger than life. The Italians, exhausted by his wars and his vitality, hoped for a less strenuous successor and breathed a sigh of relief when the mild and pleasure-loving Leo X was elected. To him Julius bequeathed a papacy in which the temporal power was restored by his reconquest of the Romagna, Umbria, and the Marches, and his addition of Parma and Piacenza to the states over which the Church had control. He left Leo a full treasury, the commencement of great enterprises, and a city where order and law had been secured. He also left Leo the terrible heritage of an Italy that France and Spain had successfully invaded.

Julius Pomponius Laetus (pôm-pō′ni-us lē′-tus). See **Laetus, Julius Pomponius.**

Justus of Padua (jus′tus; paḍ′u-ạ). See **Giusto Menabuoi da Padova.**

K

Kalkar (käl′kär) or **Kalcker** (käl′kėr), **Jan Stephen von.** See **Calcar** or **Kalkar, Jan Stephen von.**

Kallistos Andronicus (kạ-lis′tos an-dron′i-kus). See **Callistus Andronicus.**

Kemp or **Kempe** (kemp), **John.** Archbishop of Canterbury (1452–1454); b. near Ashford, Kent, England, c1380; d. at Lambeth, March 22, 1454. He was a principal counselor of Henry VI and an opponent of the Yorkist faction, but never committed himself to either Lancastrians or Yorkists.

Kennedy (ken′ẹ-di), **Walter.** Scottish poet and churchman; b. at Carrick, Ayrshire, Scotland, c1460; d. c1508. He wrote *The Passion of Christ*, a long poem.

Ker (or **Kerr**) **of Ferniehirst** (kär, kār, kėr; fėr′ni-hėrst), **Andrew.** Scottish border chieftain; b. c1471; d. in Scotland, 1545.

Kerle (ker′lẹ), **Jacob van.** [Also, **Jacques de Kerle.**] Flemish composer; b. at Ypres, in Flanders, c1531; d. at Prague, January 7, 1591. Among his works are hymns, masses, and motets.

Kingmaker. Epithet of **Warwick,** Earl of.

Kirkcaldy (kėr-kôl′di, -kô′di) **of Grange,** Sir **William.** Scottish soldier and knight; b. c1520; executed August 3, 1573. During the reign of Mary, Queen of Scots, he alternately supported and opposed her, being remembered especially as an opponent of her marriage to Darnley and as one of the conspirators against Rizzio. In the end, however, as governor of Edinburgh Castle, he held the town and castle for Mary until they were taken (May 28, 1573) by Sir William Drury.

Knight's Tale, The. One of Chaucer's *Canterbury Tales*. It is Chaucer's version of Boccaccio's *Teseide,* on the rivalry between Palamon and Arcite, prisoners at Athens, for the love of Emilye, sister of the wife of Theseus. Palamon is defeated by Arcite in a combat for her hand but Arcite is killed, thrown from his horse, and Palamon wins Emilye.

Knollys (nōlz), Sir **Francis.** English statesmen; b. c1514; d. July 19, 1596. With Henry Scrope he was charged with the care of Mary, Queen of Scots, and later was one of the commissioners at her trial.

Knollys or **Knolles,** Sir **Robert.** English soldier; b. in Cheshire, England, c1317; d. at Sculthorpe, August 15, 1407. He was one of the principal leaders of the companies of free lances, and in 1358 commanded the "Great Company" in Normandy. In Wat Tyler's rebellion (June, 1381), Knollys was in command of the forces of the city of London, and rode with Richard II to the interview at Smithfield.

Knox (noks), **John.** Scottish reformer, one of the principal figures of the Reformation during the 16th century; b. at or near Haddington, East Lothian, Scotland, in 1505, 1513, or 1515; d. at Edinburgh, November 24, 1572. He became a Roman Catholic priest, and apparently studied under John Major, whose theory that government derives from the people Knox later supported against Mary, Queen of Scots. Knox became attached to Wishart and espoused Protestantism. He was chaplain to Edward VI, and had a part in the revision of the Book of Common Prayer. At the accession of Mary Tudor he fled to the Continent. At Geneva he met Calvin and other leading Protestants. The connection with Calvin remained firm and he often approached him for advice. In 1555–1556 Knox was permitted to preach in Scotland, and at this time probably made the influential ties that brought him to prominence in the Scottish Reformation. After the Treaty of Edinburgh (1560) the French troops of the absent Queen Mary left, and the Protestants remained in control of Scotland. The Scottish estates adopted the Confession of Faith written by Knox and others and anti-papal legislation followed, including the death penalty for celebrating Mass. In 1561 Mary arrived to take possession of her realm. She was a Catholic and insisted on hearing Mass. Mary's charm and diplomacy caused defections in the ranks of Knox's followers but her actions (her confidence in Rizzio, her marriage to Darnley, and his murder) gave Knox ammunition for his attacks on the modern "Jezebel." After her capture and imprisonment by insurgent nobles Knox appeared at the assembly that dethroned her and placed her son on the throne as James VI. Even the civil war failed to shake the solidly established Calvinism of the Scottish church. Knox's major written work is *The History of the Reformation of Religioun within the Realme of Scotland.* He also wrote the tract *First Blast of the Trumpet Against the Monstrous Regiment of Women* (1558), intended as an attack upon Mary Tudor, Catherine de Médicis of France, her daughter-in-law Mary, Queen of Scots, and Mary's mother Mary of Guise.

Kochanowski (kô-hä-nôf′skē), **Jan.** Polish courtier and poet; b. at Sycyna, in Sandomierz commune, Poland, 1530; d. at Czarnolas, Poland, 1584. Influenced by what Ronsard and the Pléiade had done in France with the French language, he abandoned Latin for Polish, thus establishing a precedent for the use of the vernacular as a literary instrument. He was the outstanding representative of the humanist trend in Polish Renaissance literature. His works include, besides the lyric cycle *Threnodies,* one play, *The Dismissal of the Grecian Envoys.*

Kock (kok), **Hieronymus.** See **Cock, Hieronymus.**

Kranach (krä′nȧch), **Lucas.** See **Cranach** or **Kranach** or **Kronach, Lucas.**

Kronach, Lucas. See **Cranach** or **Kranach** or **Kronach, Lucas.**

Kyle (kīl), **John Stewart,** Lord of. See **Robert III** (of *Scotland*).

L

Labazares (lä-bä-thä′räs), **Guido de.** See **Labezares, Guido de.**

Labé (là-bā), **Louise.** [Called **La Belle Cordière,** "The Beautiful Ropemaker."] French poetess; b. at Lyons, France, 1526; d. near there, in March, 1566. In her youth she was a soldier, and was sometimes called Captain Loys. The wife of Ennemond Perrin, a ropemaker, she made her home a meeting place of poets, artists, and others. Jealousy, both masculine and feminine, and the strict prudery of Calvinism caused her name to be blackened. The most important French poetess of the 16th century, she was the author of elegies, sonnets, and a prose work, *Débat de la folie et de l'amour.*

La Belle Cordière (là bel kôr-dyer). See **Labé, Louise.**

Labezares (lä-bä-thä′räs), **Guido de.** [Also, **de Labazares.**] Spanish commander in Florida and the Philippines; b. in Vizcaya, Spain, c1510; d. in the Philippine Islands, c1580.

La Boétie (là bo-ā-sē), **Étienne de.** French writer; b. at Sarlat, Dordogne, France, November 1, 1530; d. at Germignan, near Bordeaux, France, August 18, 1563. He wrote treatises on politics (he was a judge) and religion, and sonnets on the Petrarchan model. He was a friend of Montaigne.

Ladies' Peace. Another name for the Peace of Cambrai, concluded August 5, 1529, so named because the preliminaries were conducted by Louise, mother of Francis I of France, and Margaret, aunt of Charles V of the Holy Roman Empire.

Ladislaus (lad′is-lôs). King of Naples (1386–1414); b. at Naples, February 11, 1377; d. there, August 6, 1414. He was the son of Charles III, king of Naples and Hungary, and Margaret of Durazzo. When his father was assassinated at Buda (1386), he succeeded to the throne of Naples under the regency of his mother. His claim to Naples was disputed by Louis II of Anjou, who was supported by Popes Urban VI and Clement VII. Boniface IX recognized the claim of Ladislaus and crowned him at Gaeta (1390). Louis did not recognize him and occupied Naples and much surrounding territory but was driven out of Naples and of the entire kingdom by Ladislaus (1399). Ladislaus went (1403) to Zara and proclaimed himself king of Hungary but was forced to return to Naples to suppress the barons, who were revolting again as they had done at the beginning of his reign. In 1408 he occupied Rome, was driven out by the antipope John XXIII, later came to terms with John, who invested him with Church possessions, quarreled with John, again occupied Rome, and sacked and burned it. John fled to Viterbo (1413). Ladislaus wanted to unite all Italy under his sway. Florence took up arms against him and the conflict was settled by a peace treaty. Ladislaus was preparing to go into action to consolidate and extend his conquests when he was taken ill at Narni, returned to Naples, and died there. He was succeeded by his sister Joanna II.

Lady Chapel. A chapel dedicated to the Virgin Mary, generally placed behind the high altar, at the extremity of the apse or the eastern end of the church.

Laetus (lē′tus), **Julius Pomponius.** Humanist; b. in Lucania, 1428; d. at Rome, 1497. He was an illegitimate offspring of the noble Sanseverini family of Salerno. In his enthusiasm for antiquity he gave himself the Latin name by which he is known. His original name is unknown. After spending his early years in Salerno, he went to Rome (c1450) to attend the lectures of Lorenzo Valla. There he became saturated with the spirit of the ancient Romans. It is said that he was so moved by the ruins that he sometimes burst into tears at sight of them. He tilled his fields and cultivated his vineyard in the manner recommended by Cato, Varro and Columella, diverted himself with fishing and hunting birds, and lived the simple, frugal life of a Roman sage. His house on the Esquiline and his garden on the Quirinal became the centers of a group of fellow-enthusiasts who called themselves the Roman Academy. They met to promote Latin studies and the Latin way of life, annually celebrated the founding of Rome, and held banquets at which they recited Latin poems or speeches or produced Latin plays (the earliest to do so). Included in the group, of which Laetus was the revered leader, were Pontano, Sannazzaro, Platina, Sabellicus, and the future pope, Paul III. Laetus lectured at the University of Rome on the chief Latin authors, and prepared new editions of their works. For his lectures he rose before daybreak and, by the light of his lantern, went to the lecture hall. No matter how early the hour it was always full of eager listeners, some of whom, it is said, went there at midnight to be sure of a place. In 1466 Laetus left Rome, because he had not been paid, and went to Venice. In 1468 a supposed conspiracy by the humanists against Paul II was discovered in which Laetus was implicated. The Venetians returned him to Rome (March, 1468), where he was imprisoned in Castel Sant' Angelo. No evidence turned up against him, and he refused to testify against his friends. He was finally released in April, 1469. He was restored to favor under Sixtus IV, accompanied the affianced bride of Ivan III to Moscow (1472), and resumed his teaching at the University of Rome in 1473. He remained there until his death. Laetus, a man of broad tolerance, a strong sense of justice, and an unwillingness to flatter, was greatly admired in his own time for his store of ill-assorted learning and the enthusiasm for learning and Latinism that he communicated to his pupils. He left few writings but had an important influence on his followers. When he died forty bishops attended his funeral, and his corpse was crowned with the laurel.

Lafayette (là-fà-yet), **Gilbert Motier de.** French marshal; b. c1380; d. February 23, 1462. He was one of the chief counselors of Charles VII. He contributed to the victory of Joan of Arc at Orléans in 1429.

La Hire (là-ēr). [Pseudonym of **Étienne de Vignoles.**] French general; b. c1390; d. at Montauban, France, January 11, 1443. He distinguished himself in the war of Charles VII against the English, and aided Joan of Arc at the battle of Patay (1429).

Lambert (lam′bėrt), **John.** [Original name, **John Nicholson.**] English priest and Protestant martyr; burned at Smithfield, London, November 22, 1538. He was tried before Henry VIII and the peers on November 16, 1538, and condemned for denying the real presence.

Lamberti (läm-ber′tē), **Niccolò.** Florentine sculptor and architect; d. at Florence, 1451. By 1388 he was among the sculptors working for the cathedral at Florence and in 1401 he took part in the competition for the bronze doors of the Baptistery, a competition in which Ghiberti was the victor. Beginning in the last decade of the 14th century he worked with Giovanni d'Ambrogio and others on the *Door of the Mandorla* of the cathedral. He carved (1403–1406) a *St. Luke* for Orsanmichele, now in the Bargello, and a *St. Mark* (1415) for the façade of the cathedral. In comparison with Donatello and Ghiberti, Lamberti began to seem old-fashioned at Florence. The Venetians had earlier invited him to their city, and in 1416 he went there. Among his notable works at Venice was the sculptural decoration of the cusps and arches of the Basilica of S. Marco; the summit of the central cusp was crowned by a figure of St. Mark, with worshiping angels ascending the arches of the cusp on either side. Also at Venice, he supervised the restoration of S. Marco, which had been damaged in a fire in 1418, and called his son Pietro and Paolo Uccello to help him. In his position as overseer of such important works at Venice, and with the large number of Tuscan and Lombard assistants who came to help him, Lamberti came to dominate Venetian sculpture for a time, and introduced to Venice and the Venetian mainland the transitional style between Gothic and Renaissance. As an architect he was highly regarded by Brunelleschi, and worked for the cathedral at Prato, but his work as an architect is difficult to identify. From Venice he went to Bologna, where he executed the tomb of Alexander V, since disappeared, and thence to Florence, where he died.

Lamberti, Pietro. Sculptor; b. at Florence, 1393; d. at Padua, 1435. He was the son of Niccolò Lamberti (d. 1451), under whom he was trained at Florence, and with whom he collaborated (c1410), and probably carried out most of the work, on a statue of *St. James* for Orsanmichele. By 1416 he was working with his father at Venice. About 1420 he returned briefly to Florence to execute the tomb of Onofri Strozzi in S. Trinità and in 1424 he replaced his father as overseer of the new wing of the Ducal Palace at

Venice. Thereafter he passed his career at Venice and its territories on the mainland. Among his works at Venice were sculptural decorations for the façade and central cusp of the Basilica of S. Marco and the monument of Doge Tommaso Mocenigo (1423) in the Church of SS. Giovanni e Paolo. A beautiful group, *The Judgment of Solomon*, above the capital, *Justice*, on the Ducal Palace is attributed to him by some art historians (others question the attribution). He and his assistants executed much sculptural decoration for the Ducal Palace, and to him are ascribed two of the four *Virtues* of the Porta della Carta (an entrance to the palace). In the environs of Venice he executed the Fulgosio monument in the Basilica of St. Anthony at Padua and the Serego monument in the Church of S. Anastasia at Verona. As his father had introduced the transitional style to Venice and supplanted the Gothic, Pietro was responsible for bringing to Venice Renaissance sculpture as it was developing in Tuscany.

Lamberti, Simone. Modenese painter; active in the middle of the 15th century. A polyptych, *St. Peter the Martyr and Legends of his Life*, signed and dated (1450) and notable for its realism, is in the National Gallery at Parma.

Lamola (lä′mō-lä), **Giovanni.** Humanist; b. near Bologna, c1407; d. at Bologna, December, 1449. He studied under Guarino da Verona, Vittorino da Feltre, Gasparino Barzizza, and Francesco Filelfo, at Verona, Mantua, Milan, and Florence. Thereafter he lived at Bologna, where he taught. In 1427 he discovered a famous codex of Celsus (Roman encyclopedist of the first century) in the Basilica of St. Ambrose at Milan. About the same time, he made a copy of a famous codex of Cicero, which is now lost. He left essays and panegyrics on a wide variety of topics and some letters.

Lampridio (läm-prē′dyō), **Benedetto.** Humanist and teacher; b. at Cremona; d. at Mantua, 1540. He taught Greek and Latin at Rome, where he was one of many poets and humanists in the suite of Pope Leo X. In 1536 he went to Mantua, where he was the teacher of Francesco Gonzaga, the son of Duke Federigo II. His works include a number of odes in Pindaric and Horatian meters, epigrams, letters, and verses.

Lampugnani (läm-pö-nyä′nē), **Giovanni Andrea.** Conspirator who organized the plot in which Galeazzo Maria Sforza, duke of Milan, was murdered, on December 26, 1476, in the Church of S. Stefano at Milan. It is thought that he had personal reasons for the tyrannicide. He was also imbued by his humanist teacher with a fervor for the revival of the liberties of ancient republican Rome. Associated with him in the plot were Carlo Visconti and Girolamo Ogliati. Only the last seems to have been inspired by purely idealistic motives. The three were, however, examples of tyrannicides of the 15th and 16th century who longed for the return of an idealized Rome and thought to restore it by murder. Lampugnani expected that once the death of the tyrannous duke was known the people would rise up and establish a republic. Instead, he was felled by a blow from one of the duke's guards; his body was dragged through the streets of Milan; and the house of his parents was put to the sack.

Lana (lä′nä), **Iacopo della.** See **Iacopo della Lana.**

Lancaster (lang′kạs-tėr), **Edmund.** [Title, Earl of **Lancaster**; called **Crouchback.**] Second son of Henry III of England and Eleanor of Provence; b. January 16, 1245; d. at Bayonne, France, in June 1296. He took the cross in 1268 and went to Palestine in 1271. His nickname was due either to this crusade (from the cross on his back) or to personal deformity.

Landino (län-dē′nō), **Cristoforo.** Florentine humanist; b. at Florence, 1424; d. there, September 24, 1492. He was the grandnephew of the organist Francesco Landino, and was a member of the group of cultivated and talented men surrounding Lorenzo de' Medici. From 1458 until his death he held the chair of poetry and oratory at the university (*Studio*) at Florence. Among his writings is the Latin philosophic treatise *Disputationes camaldulenses* (c1475), in four books. This is supposedly a record of a discussion that took place during four days in the summer of 1468 on, among other things, the relative merits of the contemplative and the active life. Lorenzo de' Medici, Leon Battista Alberti, and Marsilio Ficino are supposedly the members who contribute to the discussion. They agree that the contemplative and active life are equally important and conclude that contemplation should precede action. In his philosophy and his literary interpretations, Landino followed the Platonic ideas of Marsilio Ficino. Landino also wrote a commentary on the *Divina Commedia*. In a preface to his commentary he provides a brilliant discussion of the origin and nature of poetry. Botticelli provided designs for the engravings placed at the head of 19 of the 100 cantos for Landino's edition. A copy of this edition (1481) is in the Isabella Stewart Gardner Museum at Boston.

Landino, Francesco. [Also, **Francesco Cieco,** "the Blind."] Florentine blind organist and composer; b. at Florence, 1325; d. there, 1397. In spite of his blindness, he was an accomplished organist from boyhood. He became organist in the Church of S. Lorenzo at Florence and composed many works. His madrigals are notable for their freshness and melodic invention. He also wrote a philosophical poem defending the theories of the English scholastic philosopher, William of Ockham.

Lando (län′dō), **Ortensio.** Humanist; b. at Milan, c1512; d. c1553. In the service of various patrons he satisfied his love of travel on missions throughout Italy and to Germany, Switzerland, and France. He was a curious and keen observer, and combined his findings with a broad, but unorganized erudition, in presenting his *Paradossi* (*Paradoxes*), and in his generally satirical works. His *Forcianae quaestiones* consists of a dialogue on local customs and one on women. *Cicero relegatus et Cicero revocatus* is a condemnation of Cicero followed by a defence. Other works, which indicate the trend of his mind, include a collection of funeral orations for animals in which various writers are parodied. A dialogue on the Scriptures was placed on the Index by the Church. In addition to his many writings in Latin and Italian, he translated Thomas More's *Utopia*.

Landucci (län-döt′chē), **Luca.** Florentine diarist, who lived between 1436 and 1516. He left a *Diario fiorentino dal 1450 al 1516* which is of great interest for details he recorded of Florentine life. He tells of festivals, describes churches and palaces, enumerates taxes, and records births and deaths at the zoo. He was a witness of the arrival of Charles VIII of France into Florence and the restoration of the Florentine republic. He was a devoted follower of Savonarola, was against the Medici rule and in favor of a republic, yet civic pride compelled him to describe with gusto and in detail, the triumphal entry into Florence of Leo X after his elevation to the papacy.

Langey (läṅ′zhā), **Guillaume du Bellay,** Seigneur **de.** French general and diplomat; b. at Château de Glatigny, France, 1491; d. near Lyons, France, 1543. He wrote a Latin allegorical poem, *Peregrinatio humana* (1509) and his memoirs, *Ogdoades*. The latter were translated into French.

Langland (lang′lạnd) or **Langley** (lang′li), **William.** English poet; b. probably in S. Shropshire, England, c1332; d. c1400. He is the supposed author of *The Vision of William concerning Piers the Plowman*, and probably of a poem entitled by Skeat *Richard the Redeless*.

Langley (lang′li), **Edmund de.** [Title, 1st Duke of **York.**] Fifth son of Edward III of England, and Philippa of Hainault; b. at King's Langley, Hertfordshire, England, June 5, 1341; d. August 1, 1402. Created 1st duke of York he became a member of the council of regency on the accession of Richard II, and was regent during the absence of the king (1394–1396). Through his second son, Richard, earl of Cambridge, he was great-grandfather of Edward IV. The Yorkists in the civil strife known as the Wars of the Roses were called after him and his descendants.

Langtoft (lang′toft), **Peter of.** English chronicler; b. probably at Langtoft, in the East Riding of Yorkshire, England; d. c1307. He was the author of a history of England to the death of Edward I, in French verse.

Languet (läṅ-ge), **Hubert.** French Huguenot, political writer and diplomat; b. at Viteaux, in Burgundy, France, 1518; d. at Antwerp, Belgium, September 30, 1581. He was the author of *Vindiciae contra tyrannos* . . . and others.

Lanino (lä-nē′nō), **Bernardino.** Painter; b. at Mortara, c1511; d. at Vercelli, 1583. After 1530 he was in the workshop of Gaudenzio Ferrari at Vercelli, and in 1540 he married the daughter of the painter Girolamo Giovenone. The influence of Gaudenzio Ferrari appears in the warm dark colors, compositional plan, and movement in one of his best works, the early fresco, *Martyrdom of St. Catherine*, Church of S. Nazaro Maggiore, Milan. In a second period of his development, from about 1546 to 1568, his palette changed quite markedly to clear, cool tones, in which a silvery gray predominated. The movements of the figures in this period are less agitated, more graceful and composed. A signed and dated (1554) *Baptism of Christ*, Brera, Milan, and a signed and dated (1558) *Deposition*, Galleria Sabauda, Turin, are typical of this period. After 1568 his artistic vision weakened and his invention faltered, his paintings became empty repetitions of earlier works and lacked their ingenuous freshness. Many of his panels and frescoes survive in the museum and churches at Vercelli and in the vicinity. Others are at Legnano (S. Magno), Milan (Brera, Poldi Pezzoli, S. Ambrogio), Novara (cathedral), Saronno (S. Maria dei Miracoli), Turin, and elsewhere. At Bloomington, Indiana, there is a *Madonna and Child*, similar to one at Naples; there is a signed and dated (1552) *Madonna and Child Enthroned* at Raleigh, North Carolina, and a *Nativity*, in the Ringling Museum, Sarasota, Florida.

Lapo (lä′pō), **Arnolfo di.** See **Arnolfo di Cambio.**

Lapo da Castiglionchio (lä′po dä käs-tē-lyōn′-kyō). [Called **the Elder.**] Humanist and ecclesiastic; d. June 27, 1381. He was a friend of Petrarch and a student of letters, but abandoned his literary interests to devote himself to the study of canon law. After obtaining a doctorate at Bologna he returned to Florence. There he served the Republic in many offices, political as well as ecclesiastic. The revolution of 1378 drove him into exile and he went to Padua to teach. In 1380 he went to Rome in the service of Charles II of Durazzo and was honored by Pope Urban VI, who named him consistorial advocate and senator. Lapo left Latin letters, orations, treatises and legal works, and a notable collection of letters in model Tuscan.

Lapo da Castiglionchio. [Called **the Younger.**] Humanist; d. 1438. He was the grandson of Lapo da Castiglionchio the Elder, a pupil of Filelfo, and enjoyed a good reputation among the humanists of his day. His translations, of many of Plutarch's *Lives*, the *Orations* of Demosthenes and Isocrates, among others he made from Greek to Latin, were notable for their fidelity to the original and for their high literary quality. His own orations and letters were much esteemed in his time.

La Salle (là sàl), **Antoine de.** [Also, **La Sale.**] French poet; b. c1388; d. c1462. Of the three works attributed to him, only the romance *Petit Jehan de Saintré* is certainly of his authorship, but he is often named as author of the satirical *Les Quinze Joyes de mariage*, and the collection known as *Cent nouvelles nouvelles*.

Lasca (läs′kä), **il.** See **Grazzini, Anton Francesco.**

Lascaris (las′ka̤-ris), **Andreas Joannes** (or **Johannes** or **Janos** or **Janus**). [Called **Rhyndacenus.**] Greek scholar; b. at Rhyndacus, in Asia Minor, 1445; d. at Rome, December 7, 1534. Possibly the younger brother of Constantine Lascaris, after the fall of Constantinople (1453), he went to the Peloponnesus and then to Venice. His fellow-countryman, Cardinal Bessarion, befriended him and sent him to the University of Padua. In Florence, where he taught Greek, Lorenzo de' Medici became his patron. For him he collected, from Italy and the Near East, many precious manuscripts for the Medicean Library. When Charles VIII of France entered Italy (1494), Lascaris joined his train, hoping to persuade him to organize a crusade against the Turks. He later went to France, taught Greek at Paris, and served (1503 and 1505) as French ambassador at Venice. Leo X invited him to Rome to teach Greek, and he spent his last years there. His most notable work is an edition of the Greek anthology (1494). He also edited the Greek scholia on the *Iliad*, and other works.

Lascaris, Constantine. Byzantine scholar and teacher; b. at Constantinople, 1434; d. at Messina, 1501. He was taken prisoner in the fall of Constantinople (1453) to the Turks, but escaped and went to Rhodes, Crete, and finally to Italy. In Italy he became a famous teacher of Greek. One of his pupils was Ippolita, the daughter of Francesco Sforza, for whom he wrote a Greek grammar. This was the first book printed in Greek characters (1476). When his pupil went to Naples to marry, Lascaris followed her, then went to Messina to teach Greek. Among the many who came to study with him was the scholar and stylist Pietro Bembo. Fearful lest the Greek heritage perish with the Byzantine empire, Lascaris was tireless, and largely successful, in his efforts to secure and preserve Greek manuscripts. A true scholar, he remained in Messina, in humble conditions, as a teacher of Greek to the monks for thirty-five years.

Las Casas (läs kä′säs), **Bartolomé de.** [Called **Apostle of the Indians.**] Spanish Dominican; b. at Seville, Spain, 1474; d. at Madrid, in July, 1566. He was celebrated as a defender of the Indians against their Spanish conquerors. He published *Breuissima relacion de la destruycion de las Indias* (*Destruction of the Indies*), *Historia de las Indias,* and others.

Lasseran-Massencome (làs-räñ-mà-säñ-kom), **Blaise de.** See **Montluc, Blaise de Lasseran-Massencome,** Seigneur **de.**

Lassus (las′us), **Orlandus.** [Also, **Orlando di Lasso, Orlande de Lassus;** original name, **Roland Delattre.**] Belgian composer; b. at Mons, in Hainault c1530; d. at Munich, June 14, 1594. As a composer he was second only to Palestrina in the 16th century. He composed the famous music for the Seven Penitential Psalms, and over 2,000 other works, chiefly sacred, including between 50 and 60 masses, and a number of madrigals, songs, and other works.

Latimer (lat′i-mėr), **Hugh.** English prelate and reformer; b. at Thurcaston, Leicestershire, England, c1485; burned at Oxford, England, October 16, 1555. He was cited to appear before the bishop of London on a charge of heresy in 1532 but recanted. On the accession of Mary Tudor he was arrested and committed to the Tower of London (1553). He was sent to Oxford with Nicholas Ridley and Thomas Cranmer to defend their doctrines regarding the Mass before the divines of Oxford and Cambridge (March, 1554). He was excommunicated, and was burned with Ridley. His words to Ridley as the torch was applied to the faggots have become famous: "Be of good comfort, Master Ridley, and play the man; we shall this day light such a candle, by God's grace, in England, as I trust shall never be put out."

Latini (lä-tē′nē), **Brunetto.** Poet, scholar, and diplomat; b. at Florence, 1230; d. there, 1294. Latini, a notary by profession and a Guelph by political conviction, played an active part in Florentine affairs. He was Florentine ambassador to the court of Alfonso X at Castile (1260). Following the defeat of the Florentines at Montaperti (1260) by the Sienese and the restoration of the Ghibellines, he went into exile in France and remained there seven years. While there he composed *Le Trésor,* a long work that constituted an encyclopedia of what passed for knowledge in his day. The work was translated into Italian and known as *Il tesoro.* He returned to Florence when the Guelphs were restored to power. Latini also had a role in the revival of interest in classical literature, translating Cicero's *De inventione* into Italian and writing a commentary on it. Dante memorialized him (*Inferno,* xv) as his kind preceptor. Latini's unfinished allegory, *Il tesoretto,* is thought to have influenced Dante.

Laudonnière (lō-do-nyer), **René Goulaine de.** French Huguenot; active in the 16th century. In 1564 he was sent to carry aid to the Huguenot colony in Florida that went out in 1562. Finding the settlement abandoned, he built (June, 1564) Fort Carolina on the St. John's River in Florida. The fort was stormed and the garrison massacred (September 21, 1565) by the Spaniards. Laudonnière escaped, with a number of others, to England, and afterward returned to France. He wrote *L'Histoire notable de la Floride, contenant les trois voyages faits en icelle par des capitaines et pilotes français* (1586).

Laurana (lou-rä′nä), **Luciano.** Dalmatian architect; b. at Zara, between 1402 and c1425; d. at Pesaro, 1479. Little is known of his artistic education or his early work. The first notices of him are of May, 1465, when he worked for a short time at Mantua, whither he had been called by Barbara of Brandenburg, wife of Ludovico III Gonzaga. He was at Pesaro briefly, and by 1467 was at Urbino, where work on the palace of Federico da Montefeltro was by then well started. He remained at Urbino until September of 1472, when he left for Naples and the service of King Ferrante. Two years later he was at Pesaro. Of the work he may have done at Mantua, Pesaro, and Naples, little is certain, having been destroyed, or changed, or unidentifiable. What surely remains from him is the magnificent ducal palace at Urbino. In the case of this building, Laurana added to an existing nucleus of two Gothic palaces, creating around them one of the most splendid of Renaissance buildings—a palace that Baldassare Castiglione, who knew it well and wrote of it in his *Il Cortegiano,* said was "not a palace, but a city in the form of a palace." The façade, presented to the approach to Urbino, is of two tall, slender towers, capped by gracefully curved and pointed turrets that frame three superposed single-arched loggias. One seems to be approaching a palace out of a fairy tale. In his style, Laurana was influenced by Leon Battista Alberti and by Brunelleschi. He was an outstanding proponent of the classical rhythm in architecture.

Laurentius Justinianus (lô-ren′shi-us jus-tin-i-ā′nus). See Saint **Lawrence Justinian.**

Laval (là-vål), **Gilles de.** See **Retz,** Baron **de.**

La Valette (là vá-let), **Jean Parisot de.** [Also, **Valette.**] Grand Master of the Knights of Malta (1557–1568); b. 1494; d. 1568. He is famous for his conduct of the successful defense of Malta against the Turks in 1565. He built Valletta, the capital city of Malta, which was named for him.

Lawrence Justinian (lô′rẹns, lor′ens jus-tin′-i-ạn), Saint. [Latin, **Laurentius Justinianus.**] Italian Augustinian canon regular; b. 1381; d. January 8, 1456. At the age of 19 he entered an Augustinian monastery near Venice. This later became a convent of secular canons living in community, of which Lawrence was chosen prior and then superior general. He was consecrated bishop of Castello (1433), and in 1451 became patriarch of Venice, on transference of the patriarchate from Grado by Pope Nicholas V. He was known for his liberality and charity toward the poor.

Learmont (lir′mont), **Thomas.** See **Thomas the Rhymer.**

Lefèvre d'Étaples (lẹ-fevr dā-tàpl), **Jacques.** [Also, **Jacobus Faber,** surnamed **Stapulensis.**] French scholar and reformer; b. at Étaples, France, c1450; d. at Nérac, Lot-et-Garonne, France, c1537. He visited Italy (1492) and came into contact with Florentine Neoplatonism. Returned to France, he was an associate of Guillaume Budé and taught Greek at Paris. He wrote commentaries on the Psalms and on the Epistles of St. Paul which, closely following the text and with a humanistic tendency, brought him into conflict with orthodox theologians. He fled when the Sorbonne declared some of his writings heretical, but under the protection of the king and Margaret of Navarre he was able to return. He wrote commentaries on the works of Aristotle, and translated the New Testament (1523) and the whole Bible (1530) into French. He was associated with others in his desire for reform of the Church and a return to the teachings of the Gospels.

Legazpe (lā-gäs′pā) or **Legaspi** (lā-gäs′pē), **Miguel López de.** See **López de Legazpe** (or **Legaspi**), **Miguel.**

Legend of Good Women, The. Unfinished poem by Geoffrey Chaucer. The Prologue, a courtly love-vision influenced by such poets as Deschamps, Machaut, and Froissart, introduces some ten "legends" of martyrs of Cupid, beginning with Cleopatra. Chaucer adapted from Ovid and from medieval redactors, especially Boccaccio, most of these stories of classical heroines who suffered or died out of devotion to their lovers. The *Legend* reveals Chaucer's growing mastery of the heroic couplet and of brief narrative.

Leland or **Leyland** (lē′lạnd), **John.** English antiquary; b. at London, September 13, c1506; d. April 18, 1552. He was appointed king's antiquary by Henry VIII in 1533, with a commission to search for English antiquities in all libraries and other places where they might be found, and for this purpose journeyed for six years (1536–1542), through England, making exhaustive researches and minutely recording his observations. He was adjudged insane in 1550. Most of his work was left in manuscript at his death. His *Itinerary* was published in 1710, and his *Collectanea* in 1715.

Lello da Velletri (lel′lō dä vel-lā′trē). Painter; b. at Velletri; active about the middle of the 15th century. He is known by one signed work, *Madonna and Child with Saints,* in the National Gallery of Umbria, at Perugia. It shows him to have been a painter in the international Gothic style and a close follower of Gentile da Fabriano's last manner.

Lemaire or **Le Maire** (lẹ mer), **Jean.** [Also, **Lemaire** (or **Le Maire**) **de Belges.**] Belgian poet and historian; b. at Belges, or Baria, in Hainaut, 1473; d. c1525. After 1504 he was secretary and librarian to Margaret of Austria, who was regent of the Netherlands after 1507. His most important work is his *Illustrations de Gaule belgique* (1812). His *Epistres de l'amand verd,* written to his patroness, were very influential in establishing verse as a French literary form.

Lena (lā′nä). Comedy by Ariosto (1530).

Leo X (lē′ō). [Original name, **Giovanni de' Medici.**] Pope (1513–1521); b. at Florence, December 11, 1475; d. at Rome, December 1, 1521. He was the second son of Lorenzo the Magnificent and Clarice Orsini, and was destined from childhood for the Church.

He received the tonsure before he was 8, held many benefices in Tuscany and France, and was given the red hat (March 9, 1489) by Innocent VIII before he was 14, with the provision that he should not assume his office for three years. His father's friend, the poet Poliziano, was his tutor for three years, after which, at his mother's request, the poet was replaced by masters of lesser renown. At his father's brilliant court he was in contact with some of the most gifted minds of the time. He continued his education at Pisa (1489–1491), where he studied theology and canon law, and where one of his fellow-students was Cesare Borgia. In 1492 he left Florence to take up his position in the College of Cardinals. He carried with him a letter from his father in which Lorenzo counseled the youth to lead a "pious, chaste and exemplary life." This, Lorenzo acknowledged, would be the more difficult "as you are now to reside in Rome, that sink of all iniquity." Since Giovanni is the youngest who has ever been raised to the rank of cardinal, "it will be more advisable for you to listen to others than to speak much yourself." He should avoid ostentation and "any imputation of hypocrisy." Furthermore, he should live within his means, eat plain food, get up early, and take sufficient exercise. Lorenzo also points out to the young cardinal that in his new position he will be able to favor his family and his city, "I doubt not but that this may be done with equal advantage to all: observing, however, that you are always to prefer the interests of the Church." Within a month Lorenzo had died, and Cardinal Giovanni returned to Florence, where he lived for a time at his brother's court. Mild, humane, and gracious, he was well aware that the Medici had gained and kept power at Florence while claiming to be nothing other than private citizens. He disapproved and was distressed by his brother Piero's arrogance and discreetly withdrew to his villas and benefices in Tuscany. His attempts to save Florence and protect the interests of his family in the face of the French invasion (1494) were in vain, and he fled Florence with his brothers (November, 1494). He went first to Urbino, then traveled in the Low Countries, Germany, and France. In 1500 he returned to Rome and devoted himself to letters and music. (He had not supported Alexander VI in the conclave of 1492, was never on friendly terms with him, and played a small part in Church affairs under him.) He opened the rich library in his palace of S. Eustachio (Palazzo Madama) to students, restored his diaconal church of S. Maria in Dominica, gave the façade to S. Cristina in Bolsena, and gathered artists, musicians, and men of letters about him. All the while, he cordially received all visitors from Florence and won them by his gracious reception. On the elevation of Cardinal Giuliano della Rovere as Julius II he took a more active part in ecclesiastical affairs. Julius named him legate of Bologna and the Romagna (1511). He was taken prisoner by the French at the battle of Ravenna (April, 1512) but escaped. In the same year, the French were driven out of Italy, and members of the Holy League met at Mantua to reorganize Italy. With the support of the pope, whose policies Cardinal Giovanni had loyally and energetically supported, the Medici were to be restored at Florence. An army was sent to overcome Florentine resistance. Prato was taken and sacked, the Soderini government of Florence yielded in panic, and, according to a popular saying, backed up by imperial troops Cardinal Giovanni entered Florence with his purple stockings stained by the red blood of Prato. As head of the family, he now became the effective ruler of Florence and sought at once to heal the political wounds by his mild and judicious course, at the same time, quietly getting rid of those who had been active in the republican government, one of whom was Machiavelli. He also revived the *parlamento* and the *balìa*, devices by which the Medici had maintained control in former years.

On February 21, 1513, the warlike Julius died. In an election that took place almost without simony, Cardinal Giovanni was elected as Pope Leo X, although he was still so young (his poor health worked in his favor). Exhausted Italy breathed a sigh of relief and hailed the elevation of the cultivated, mild, and supposedly peace-loving cardinal. Grave political and ecclesiastical questions immediately confronted him. He first dealt with family affairs. In August, 1513, he made his nephew Lorenzo his agent as head of the government at Florence, and gave him constant instructions from Rome as to his conduct of the government. To give Lorenzo his own state, he declared Francesco Maria della

Rovere, duke of Urbino, a rebel and deposed him (1516), naming Lorenzo duke in his place. Francesco Maria regained his duchy and a costly war ensued that ended equivocally (September, 1517). Lorenzo died in 1519, and the duchy was claimed for the Church. Leo sent his cousin, Giulio de' Medici (later Pope Clement VII), to govern Florence in Lorenzo's place. The war for Urbino had been a heavy drain on the papal treasury, already emptied of the wealth Julius had left by maladministration and papal extravagance. To meet the demands for money, Leo negotiated loans, increased duties, pawned treasures, sold offices, and appropriated funds intended for the building of St. Peter's. In 1517 a conspiracy of several cardinals was exposed, and the suspicion was not without foundation that the extent and seriousness of the plot, allegedly against the pope himself, was exaggerated so that Leo could demand great sums from the conspirators as amends. Cardinal Alfonso Petrucci was put to death in prison. His fellow conspirators (Cardinals Adriano Castellesi, Francesco Soderini, Raffaello Riario, and Bandinello Sauli) were compelled to pay enormous fines. At the same time, Leo named thirty-one new cardinals (July 1, 1517), some of whom were worthy of the honor but many of whom were given it for political or financial reasons. The practice of preaching indulgences did not originate with Leo. The Germans had always resisted it: they hated to see the money derived therefrom going over the Alps to Rome. By a complicated arrangement with the banking house of Jacob Fugger, Albrecht of Brandenburg, archbishop of Magdeburg, raised the money to be named archbishop of Mainz, on condition that he allow the preaching and purchase of indulgences to take place in his dioceses. (One half the proceeds was earmarked for the Fugger banking house.) Leo authorized it and in January, 1517, the Dominican friar Johann Tetzel began preaching. Resentment, long brewing over the corruption of the clergy, the financial exactions of Rome, the worldliness and immorality there, boiled over. It culminated in the ninety-five theses that Luther nailed to the church door at Wittenberg (October 31, 1517). Leo tried to silence him by indirection. This failed, and on June 15, 1520, he issued the bull, *Exsurge Domine*, condemning Luther on forty-one counts. Luther publicly burned it; he was excommunicated (January 3, 1521). Leo apparently failed to realize the gravity of the situation and the consequences that might result. The means he used to calm the storm were ill-conceived and ineffectual. The Reformation had arrived.

Political events in Italy revolved around the attempts of France and Spain to win control of the kingdom of Naples and the duchy of Milan, a state of affairs that the Italian princes blindly refused to recognize. Leo's fear was that one of them might come to control both "the head and the tail of Italy." To circumvent this, as well as to advance his family, he proposed to create a state for his brother Giuliano that would include Parma, Piacenza, Modena, and Reggio, and some said he contemplated adding Naples and Milan as well. After the victory of Francis I over the Milanese and the Swiss at Marignano (September, 1515), Leo met with the French king at Bologna, abandoned the idea of a state for Giuliano (who died the following year), promised to restore Modena and Reggio to the Estense allies of the French (a promise he did not keep), and to invest Francis with the kingdom of Naples on the death of Ferdinand the Catholic. He arranged a concordat with Francis that ended the Pragmatic Sanctions. By its terms the king could name bishops, abbots, and priors in France, with the pope retaining the right of veto and the right to name other ecclesiastics. In 1519 the emperor Maximilian I died and Francis and Charles I of Spain contested the succession. If Charles won, Spain, the Sicilies, and lands in the New World would be added to the dominions of the emperor. Leo supported Francis, hoping perhaps that when the king saw it was impossible for him to be elected he would throw his support to a third candidate. Since Leo did not support him until his election was assured, the new emperor, Charles V, owed him nothing. To strengthen papal control in Modena and Reggio Leo had named Francesco Guicciardini governor of those states and given him authority to restore order. To crush the petty tyrannies that still remained in Umbria he lured Giampaolo Baglioni of Perugia to Rome, had him put to death (1520), and claimed Perugia for the Church. Compelled by the need for the emperor's help in putting down the Lutheran revolt, he repudiated his alliance with Francis and made one with Charles V (May 8, 1521), directed against heretics, the Turks, the French, and the Venetians. By its terms, the Church was to receive Parma, Piacenza, and Ferrara, and Medicean control of Florence was guaranteed. Celebrating the imperial and papal victory over the French at Milan, Leo, whose health had never been robust, caught a chill and died a few days later.

In furtherance of his spiritual obligations, Leo approved the Oratory of Divine Love, founded by Gaetano of Thiene, supported reform of the religious orders, condemned magic and divination, and protected the Jews. He continued the work of the Fifth Lateran Council, begun by Julius (July, 1511), and concluded it on March 16, 1517. This accomplished the end of the Gallic schism and the Concordat with France, and condemned doubts on the immortality of the soul. A few faltering steps toward reform of the Church were considered, but nothing like the far-reaching reform, and implementation thereof, that was required both for the good of the Church and to arrest Lutheranism. His pontificate was occupied more with temporal than religious concerns. He lived as a secular prince. His personal life was free of the scandals that blackened the pontificates of some of his predecessors. His doctrine was never in question; his piety seemed based on temperament and upbringing rather than rooted in any profound religious feeling.

Leo had become pope through his energy and the exercise of his considerable intelligence. Having attained to the summit, his energy waned. He is said to have remarked, "Since God has given us the papacy, let us enjoy it." He was the patron of humanists, men of letters, poets, musicians, and artists. Bembo, Sadoleto, and Colucci were his secretaries; Bernardo Dovizi (Cardinal Bibbiena) was an influential and often slippery adviser; Castiglione was his friend; Molza, Benedetto Accolti, Sannazzaro, Vida, Giovio, and Trissino enjoyed his patronage, as did a host of other poets, men of letters and humanists of lesser rank, as well as improvisers, musicians, and buffoons. He was somewhat cool to Ariosto but when the poet's *Suppositi* was given an elaborate performance in the Vatican (March 6, 1519), the pope himself stood at the door to greet the spectators. He brought out Dovizi's *Calandria* (1518) and permitted a performance of Machiavelli's *Mandragola* at Rome. Under him Rome became the intellectual and artistic center of Italy, and his age is sometimes called "Leonine" after him. His reputation as a protector and promoter of learning and culture has been somewhat exaggerated. He attempted to reform the Roman Sapienza (university), founded a Greek printing press at Rome, encouraged Hebrew and Arabic studies, combed Europe for books for his own and the Vatican Library, and encouraged Raphael to prepare an archeological plan of Rome. (Raphael's portrait of him is in the Pitti Palace at Florence.) He wanted to beautify Rome and made a number of improvements, but his lack of money caused him to interrupt some of the great works begun under Julius. Raphael and his assistants continued work on the *Stanze* in the Vatican under Leo, but those they painted for him lacked the grandeur of conception of those done under Julius. He commissioned Michelangelo to design the façade (never built) and the New Sacristy of S. Lorenzo at Florence. Again, the work done by Michelangelo for Leo did not come up to the great standards of that completed (the Sistine Ceiling) or begun under Julius. In a time that called for wisdom, resolution, and expert diplomacy in political matters, and the utmost concern for the state and fate of the Church, Leo responded with subtle intrigue, caution, and irresolution, a self-indulgent surrender to the pleasure-loving side of his nature (he was inordinately fond of hunting, delighted in lavish spectacles, and spent long periods in the country enjoying life), and a determination to advance the interests of his family. Rome under Leo was gay, stimulating, and brilliant, for certain people. Such features were of little profit to the Church, which in his age was irrevocably sundered. He was succeeded by Adrian VI.

Leo Africanus (lē′ō af-ri-kā′nus). [Original name, **al-Hassan ibn-Mohammed**; name assumed on conversion to Christianity, **Johannes, Leo.**] Moorish geographer and traveler; d. after 1526. He was the author of a description of Africa (published in Italian in 1588). In the course of his travels he was captured (c1520) by pirates and sent as a slave to Rome. Here he learned Italian and Latin and was converted by Pope Leo X to Christianity.

León (lā-ōn′), **Juan Ponce de.** See **Ponce de León, Juan.**

León, Luis Ponce de. See **Ponce de León, Luis.**

Leonardi (lā-ō-när′dē), **Camillo.** Physician of Pesaro. He wrote *Speculum lapidum* (*Mirror of Stones*, or *Gems*), published at Venice in 1502. Its three parts include descriptions of nearly 300 minerals and the astrological meanings of figures engraved on gems. The purpose of the work is to describe the astrological and magical properties of gems but, as sometimes happened, an effort to master magic led to careful, even scientific observation.

Leonardi di Monte l'Abate (lā-ō-när′dē dē môn′tā lä-bä′tā), **Giangiacomo,** Count. Military engineer; b. at Pesaro, November, 1498; d. there, January 2, 1562. He studied at Bologna and took his doctorate in law at Ferrara. However, he preferred a military career and entered, in turn, the service of various captains. When Pavia was under siege by the French (1525) he fortified it. He served Francesco Maria della Rovere, and was enfeoffed by Guidobaldo della Rovere with Monte Abate (1540) and granted the title of count. He directed the construction of the walls of Senigallia, and in 1553 erected fortifications at Rome. From 1558 he divided his time among Pesaro, Urbino, and Monte Abate. He left some works on military engineering.

Leonardo da Besozzo (lā-ō-när′dō dä bā-zôt′-tzō). Fifteenth-century Lombard painter and miniaturist. He was the son and pupil of Michelino da Besozzo, and was working with his father at Milan in 1421. At that time he must have been very young, for he was reportedly still alive in 1488. Some time after 1421 he went to Naples, where he carried out his most important work: a signed (c1442) series of frescoes on the life of the Virgin in the Church of S. Giovanni a Carbonara. The frescoes show him to have been a typical Lombard painter of his time, who combined elements of the Gothic style, that is, an attention to line and detail, with Renaissance realism. In 1454 he was one of Alfonso I's official court painters. His duties included painting coats of arms of the royal house in the cathedral, and painting flags and banners to decorate the royal kitchens for a feast. As a miniaturist he illuminated a universal history with thirty-eight panels, demonstrating his pleasing and animated narrative style.

Leonardo of Chios (kī′os). Dominican; b. at Chios; d. in the second half of the 15th century. He studied at Padua and was named bishop of Mytilene, on the island of Lesbos, by Pope Eugenius IV. He sent a notable eyewitness account to Pope Nicholas V (August, 1453) of the capture of Constantinople by the Turks. Later, he described the conquest of Lesbos by the Turks in a letter to Pope Pius II.

Leonardo da Pisa (dä pē′sä). [Also, **Leonardo Pisano, Leonardo Fibonacci.**] Italian mathematician; b. at Pisa, c1170; d. after 1240. The greatest mathematician in the Christian world of the Middle Ages, he studied Greek and Arabic mathematics and wrote treatises on the application of algebra to geometry. In one of his most important books, *Liber abaci* (composed 1202), he advocated the adoption of Arabic notation. Another important work was *Practica geometrica* (written 1220). In 1225 he wrote two shorter works, *Flos* and *Liber quadratorum.*

Leonardo (Malatesta) da Pistoia (mä-lä-tes′tä dä pēs-tō′yä). Florentine painter; b. 1483; d. after 1518. He was a follower of Fra Bartolommeo and Raphael. Among his surviving works are a signed and dated (1516) *Madonna and Child and Saints,* Volterra, *Madonna and Child,* signed and dated (1516), Berlin, a *Madonna and Child,* Boston, which is a copy of a Raphael work, and paintings at New Haven and Philadelphia (Johnson Collection).

Leonardo da Vinci (dä vēn′chē). Painter, sculptor, musician, engineer, and scientist; b. at Anchiano in the community of Vinci, near Florence, April 15, 1452; d. at Cloux, near Amboise, France, May 2, 1519. He was considered by many to have been the first man of the modern age to anticipate what science and invention would achieve in man's struggle against nature. He anticipated Galileo's, Newton's, and Harvey's discoveries, and man's conquest of the air. He devoted his life to an attempt to penetrate and interpret the secrets of the universe, and at the end of it felt that he had failed, both to complete his studies and to cause men to acknowledge their validity. Most of his discoveries were ignored, forgotten, and had to be discovered all over again in following centuries. He has been called a "universal man of the Renaissance" but he was in fact a man for all ages. The red chalk self-portrait in the Royal Library at Turin is that of a man who endured the disappointments of the present and steadfastly maintained a vision of the future. He was the illegitimate son of Ser Piero da Vinci, a notary at Florence, and Caterina, a country girl of Anchiano. His father married and the child Leonardo, acknowledged as his son, spent his boyhood in his family's house. (A substantial stone house on a hilltop near Vinci is pointed out as the house.) From an early age he preferred an investigation of the marvels of nature to the study of his schoolbooks. He wandered about the hills of his native region, followed the courses of brooks and streams, explored caves (later in life he described his fear of a mysterious cavern he had explored in his youth and told how his curiosity had overcome his fear), made sketches of the natural wonders that interested him, and was irresistibly drawn to the fantastic. Vasari tells of a painting he executed on a wood panel while still a boy, at his father's request. It was a weird and fearful fire-breathing monster that he had created by combining the most startling features of bats, hedgehogs, crickets, snakes, grasshoppers, and lizards; he showed it emerging from a smoking cavern. Ser Piero moved to Florence and about 1469 Leonardo entered Andrea Verrocchio's workshop. For a time also he drew the statues that Lorenzo de' Medici had set up in the garden of San Marco as a school for Florentine artists. (At a later date Michelangelo worked there.) With Verrocchio he learned many crafts: painting, goldsmithing and casting of monuments, construction, and engineering. He also came into contact with the many distinguished men who visited the workshop and was stimulated by their discussions of the philosophical, technical, artistic, and scientific theories of the time. In 1472 he was accepted into the Painters' Guild, but he still remained Verrocchio's co-worker. The earliest known work from his hand is a drawing of a landscape, Uffizi, dated August 5, 1473. The earliest of his painting that has survived is the angel in profile of the two angels in Verrocchio's *Baptism of Christ* (c1475), Uffizi, Leonardo's angel is distinctive in the softness of the modeling, in the reach for ideal beauty, and in poetic spirituality. It is the work of one who was already highly accomplished in his art. Vasari writes that when Verrocchio saw Leonardo's angel he gave up painting forever, chagrined that he should be so far excelled by a mere youth. Leonardo may have painted some of the landscape background as well, for there is an atmosphere and originality in the forms that were not found in Verrocchio's conventional landscapes, but it is in the figures that the contrast between that done by Leonardo and those done by Verrocchio, or possibly others, is most marked. Also of the early period are two *Annunciations*, one in the Uffizi and one in the Louvre. Other early works are the portrait, *Ginevra de' Benci* (c1478), National Gallery, Washington, and the unfinished panels of *St. Jerome*, Vatican, and of the *Adoration of the Magi*, Uffizi. The last-mentioned, one of the earliest of his masterpieces, was for a complicated altarpiece commissioned by the monks of San Donato di Scopeto in 1481. It is an involved, significant, and dramatic composition. A semicircle of adoring figures encloses the triangle formed by the Holy Family and kneeling kings, causing a flow of adoration toward the Child. The intensity of the facial expressions and the thrust of the gestures of the worshipers impart tension and urgency to what had usually been treated as an idyllic scene. In the background are archeological and imaginary ruins and rearing horses from another world. Since the panel is in monochrome the sfumato, with its fugitive shadows, adds an unearthly luminosity to the effect. For reasons unknown, Leonardo never finished the painting. Perhaps also of the period when he was associated with Verrocchio are the *Benois Madonna*, Hermitage, Leningrad, with its young mother lost, and caught, in a laughing moment with her child, and the *Madonna with a Vase of Flowers*, Alte Pinacothek, Munich. The first of these may be one of the paintings of which Leonardo wrote, late in the year 1478, "I have started to paint the two Marys."

With his wide-ranging gifts and insatiable curiosity, Leonardo never confined himself to painting. He was fascinated by the forces and features of nature, by causes and structures, and was continually studying and experimenting. He became an accomplished musician and a winning improviser. For his own interest and use he made a silver lyre in the form of a horse's head and showed it to Lorenzo de' Medici. According to one story, Lorenzo, wishing to please Ludovico il Moro whom he knew to be fond of music, sent Leonardo to Milan to present the lyre to Ludovico in per-

Leonardo da Vinci
Study in perspective for *The Adoration of the Magi*, Uffizi
Uffizi, Florence   Alinari-Art Reference Bureau

thin; ᴛʜ, then; y, you; (variable) ḏ as d or j, ş as s or sh, ţ as t or ch, ẓ as z or zh; *o*, F. cloche; ü, F. menu; ċh, Sc. loch; ṅ, F. bonbon; ʙ, Sp. Córdoba (sounded almost like v).

son. (Ludovico had given Lorenzo at least moral support in his war with Naples.) Lorenzo does not seem to have recognized Leonardo's genius; he never commissioned a painting from him. Leonardo felt he was cut off from his patronage by the humanists of the Platonic Academy. He did not read the Greek and Latin philosophical treatises that absorbed their attention, but, in the manner of the Aristotelians, pursued his scientific researches, and was relatively ignored. "They go about, in fine raiment and jewels, pompous and puffed up, not from the fruits of their own labors but from those of others; my own labors they refuse to recognize." At about the same time (1481), Verrocchio left Florence, and several of Leonardo's fellow-artists—Ghirlandaio, Cosimo Rosselli, Botticelli, Perugino—were invited to Rome to paint in the Sistine Chapel. Leonardo did not find a rewarding outlet or sufficient acknowledgment of his manifold gifts in his native Florence. He went to Milan, probably about 1482, and sought to enter the service of Ludovico il Moro who was, in all but name, lord of Milan. In a memorandum to Ludovico he set forth the various ways in which he could assist him. He could make light, portable, demountable bridges, siege engines, bombards, means of storming fortifications, mines and tunnels to blow up fortresses, armored cars, mortars and catapults, and other engines of war. The emphasis on his military skill was owing to the disturbed political situation of Milan and of all Italy. For times of peace he wrote that he could give the utmost satisfaction, "well bearing comparison with anyone else, in architecture, in the designing of buildings, . . . and in the conducting of water from one place to another." (The patterns, power, and possibilities of water always deeply interested him—his notebooks have many sketches illustrating the flow of water, the courses of streams, torrential rainstorms, deluges, as well as canals and illustrations of the uses of water power.) "Item. I shall carry out sculptures, in marble, bronze, and clay, and similarly paintings of every possible kind, to stand comparison with anyone else, be he who he may." Moreover, he would undertake the execution of the bronze equestrian monument of Francesco Sforza that Ludovico had long desired. And if anyone doubted his ability to execute the works he described, "I am ready at any time to put it to the test in your park or at whatever place shall be most convenient to Your Excellency, to whom I most humbly commend myself. . . ."

The hopes of great accomplishment at Milan were not immediately fulfilled. For a time he was associated with Ambrogio de Predis, a Milanese painter who was familiar with the conditions and requirements of artists at Milan. An important painting of the Milanese period before 1493, or perhaps even of the earlier Florentine period, is *The Virgin of the Rocks*, Louvre, Paris. Another on the same subject in the National Gallery, London, is considered to be the painting executed in fulfillment of a contract with the Confraternity of the Immaculate Conception of St. Francis at Milan. The contract had been given to Leonardo and Ambrogio and

LEONARDO DA VINCI
Study for *The Virgin of the Rocks*, Louvre
Biblioteca Reale, Turin

Evangelista de Predis, and was to be completed in December, 1483. Leonardo was to paint the central panel of the altarpiece himself; Ambrogio was to paint the side panels. The execution of the painting dragged on for years. Leonardo left Milan and it was still incomplete; it was the object of litigation at least until 1508, and much of it was painted by others. The Louvre painting, executed by Leonardo himself, is earlier and may have been copied to fulfill the contract with the Confraternity. In any case, the painting of the Virgin in the shadowy grotto, with a beautiful enigmatic angel kneeling at her side, and the exquisite children, really beautiful babies, is suffused with the mystique and technical mastery that give such significance, atmosphere, and mystery to his paintings. In the seventeen years he spent at Milan, Leonardo carried out a wide variety of projects for Ludovico il Moro; painting was almost incidental. Among his many services was the preparation of decorations for great ceremonial occasions, as the festivities (1490) to celebrate the marriage of young Gian Galeazzo Sforza, the legitimate ruler of Milan, to Isabella of Aragon. On this occasion he constructed a representation of the heavens, with the seven planets, signs of the zodiac, and the stars twinkling in them; and he designed the settings and costumes for the pageant that was unfolded for his *Festa del Paradiso*. His ingenuity knew no bounds in creating decoration, diversions and "Prophecies" (in the nature of riddles) for the entertainments in which the court of Ludovico and his young wife, Beatrice d'Este, delighted. And he seems to have enjoyed using his great talents in this fashion. Through much of his stay at Milan he was occupied at intervals in the design and construction of the clay model of the enormous equestrian statue of Francesco Sforza that he had mentioned in his memorandum. Many preparatory sketches, indicating how his ideas for the monument changed, survive. The clay model was at last completed (1493) and set up in the courtyard of the *castello*. It won instant admiration and henceforth Leonardo's fame at Milan and beyond was secure. The model was praised as beyond anything that had been seen up to this time. (But the bronze intended for casting the statue was diverted to the casting of cannon; and when the French drove Ludovico out of Milan, French archers used the model as a target. Though the duke of Ferrara begged to be given the ruined model it was ultimately destroyed.) In 1495 he began *The Last Supper*, in the Refectory of the Convent of S. Maria delle Grazie at Milan. The painting is world famous as a masterpiece of pictorial invention and psychological interpretation. Leonardo worked on it for at least two years. Ludovico and the prior of the Convent were impatient with his slow progress. Matteo Bandello, a Milanese who became a bishop but who was more noted as a writer than as an ecclesiastic, was accustomed, as were many, to go to the Refectory to watch Leonardo paint. He wrote that some days Leonardo rushed in in the heat of the day, stood on the scaffold and painted furiously for hours. Other days when he was in the Refectory, he studied the painting for a long time, took up his brush, added one or two strokes, and left. And some days passed when he did not work on the painting at all. The prior complained, and Leonardo assured him and Ludovico that each day he spent many hours at work, even when he was not physically present. As always, he was solving the problems in his mind before expressing the solutions in paint. The prior was especially disturbed because he did not paint in the head of Judas. Leonardo explained that he was seeking a suitable model, but that if the prior continued his complaints he would use the prior as his model. It was well known that he often followed extraordinary looking people about the streets until he knew their features well enough to make sketches. Pages in his notebooks are devoted to such sketches, often of grotesque old men. He said he was searching in the most evil sections of the city for his Judas. It is said that failing to find a model for Christ he left that head unfinished. He was continually experimenting with new techniques and media. For *The Last Supper* he used oil tempera rather than working in fresco. After a time the painting cracked and flaked, as oil tempera did not bond to the surface, nor that to the wall. Further damage resulted through wanton insensitivity (a door was cut through the lower half of the center of the painting), warfare, faulty restoration, and repainting. In World War II the wall of the Refectory opposite the painting was badly damaged by a bomb, but *The Last Supper*, protected by sandbags—it was too fragile to move—survived, and is now under expert care to avoid further damage. The painting, which supposedly represents the moment at the Passover when Christ said, "One of you shall betray me," is designed to appear as an extension of the room where the monks of the Convent ate, with openings painted to reveal a serene landscape at the back. Thus the

LEONARDO DA VINCI
Bust of a youth, thought to be a study for the St. James in *The Last Supper*, S. Maria delle Grazie, Milan, and below, sketches for the tower angle of a castle.
Royal Library, Windsor Castle Reproduced by gracious permission of Her Majesty the Queen

monks at their tables looked at what was, in effect, a table across the end of the room, where the Apostles, arranged in groups of three on either side of Christ, express their shock, despair, or disbelief in highly individualized expressions and gestures. Thousands of words have been written on the technique, composition, psychological significance, iconography, and influence of the painting. At Milan Leonardo was also engaged in architectural and engineering tasks, both military and civil. He planned cities and fortifications; he made a number of sketches of centrally planned churches and for the dome of the cathedral, and went to Pavia with Bramante, his friend, and Francesco di Giorgio Martini to advise on the construction of the cathedral there. As far as is known, none of his important architectural designs were ever executed. He designed pageants, built the first revolving stage, and worked on projects for the diversion of rivers, developing a canal system with locks which are still in operation. (In the Museo Nazionale della Scienza e della Tecnica at Milan are models of the inventions and scientific work of Leonardo; these, most of which were never constructed in his lifetime, have been built according to the specifications in the innumerable sketches he left.) He studied mathematics with Luca Pacioli, and designed the illustrations for a book, *De Divina Proportione*, written by this famous mathematician. "There is no certainty," he said, "where you cannot apply one of the mathematical sciences." He planned and began, but never completed, treatises on painting, anatomy, flight, and other subjects. He filled his notebooks with mathematical, anatomical, botanical, and geophysical observations; with studies in optics, hydraulics, mechanics, both practical and theoretical, with precepts for painters, and with philosophical reflections. He went to the hospitals and whenever possible took possession of the newly dead, dissected them and made exact and beautiful anatomical drawings, as of the muscles, the nervous system, the heart, a fetus in the womb, and many others. He told Cardinal Louis of Aragon, who visited him in his last years at Cloux, that he had dissected the bodies of more than thirty men and women. More than 7,000 pages of his notebooks are preserved. All are written in left-handed mirror script. This storehouse of knowledge, in its original form illegible to the general reader, has been carefully studied, transcribed, and edited during the past century. (In February, 1967, announcement was made concerning 700 pages of manuscript and drawings in the National Library of Madrid that have never been transcribed and published. Among the inventions described is a device to convert rotary motion into reciprocating motion, a variety of gears and cams, link and chain drives, and many others.) The *Codice Atlantico*, Ambrosiana, Milan, is the most important collection of his notes and drawings. It is a selection cut from Leonardo's several notebooks by a Milanese sculptor who bought many of the papers of Leonardo from the heirs of Francesco Melzi, to whom Leonardo had willed them. The *Codice Atlantico* contains over 4,000 sheets, of various sizes and dates, with notes and sketches on a wide variety of subjects, and with his reflections and observations on his friends, his pupils, and his reading.

After 1497 Ludovico il Moro was almost totally absorbed in military preparations as Louis XII of France threatened to claim Milan. Leonardo was neglected and had on several occasions to remind Ludovico that he needed money. In lieu of cash, Ludovico presented him with a house and vineyard outside the walls of the city. In 1499 the armies of Louis XII marched into Milan. Ludovico fled. Leonardo went to Mantua, where he made the red chalk sketch of Isabella d'Este now in the Louvre. She tried in vain to secure a painting from him. He went on to Venice briefly, where he considered the problem of underwater destruction of enemy fleets but suppressed his findings as too dangerous, and the following year (1500) returned to Florence. In 1502 he became military engineer for Cesare Borgia, and for nearly a year traveled about the areas of Italy that the Borgia had conquered and was in process of consolidating. He drew maps of strategic zones which are the first examples of modern cartography. In the service of Cesare he met Machiavelli at Urbino and later, on his return to Florence, they became good friends. He designed such weapons as an armored tank, guided projectiles, and breechloading cannons. He studied the flight of birds and designed flying machines, conceiving the problem of flight in the modern sense of aerodynamic reciprocity. At Florence from 1500 to 1506 he painted the panel of *The*

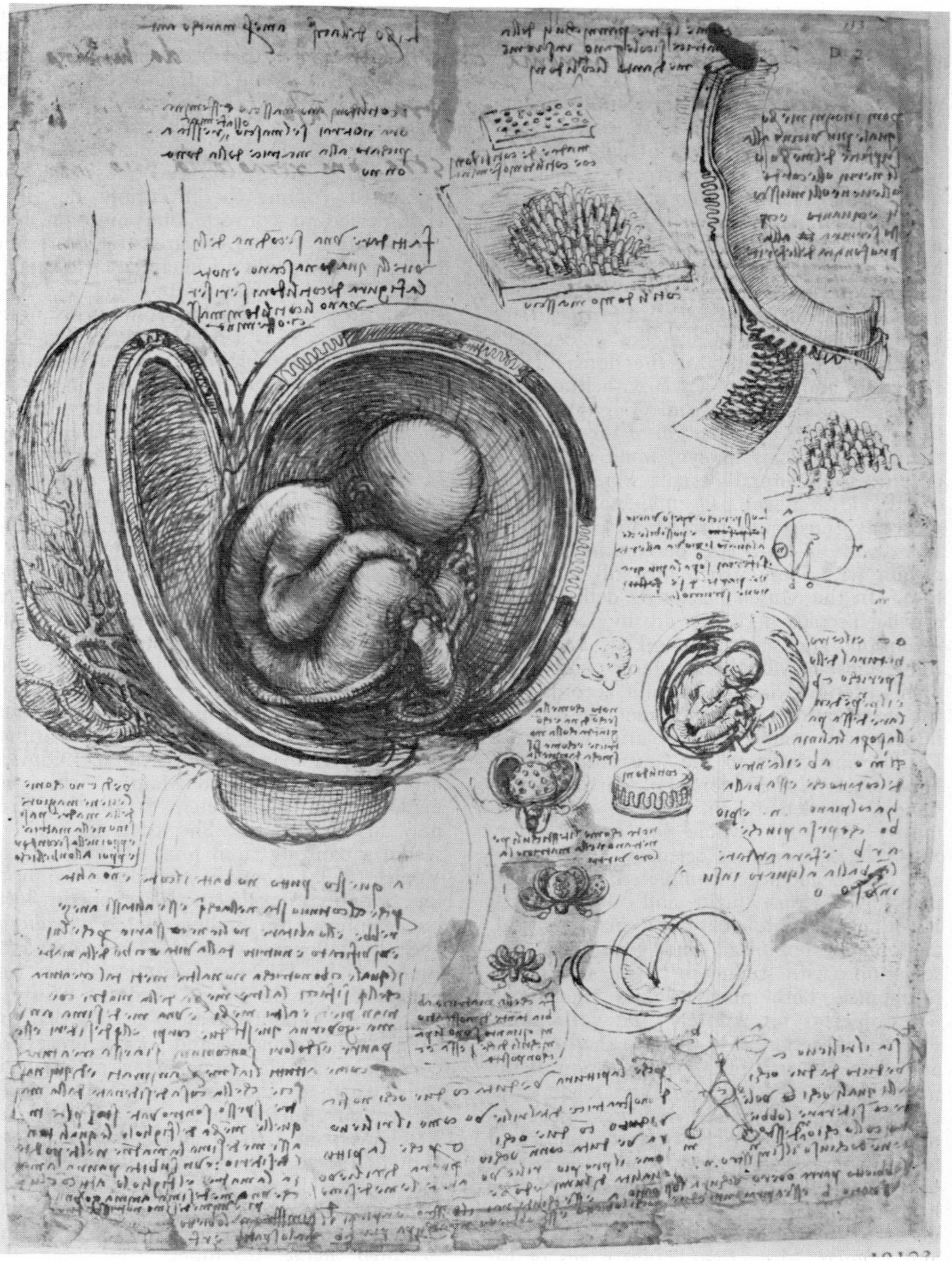

Leonardo da Vinci
Drawing of an embryo in the uterus
Royal Library, Windsor Castle   Reproduced by gracious permission of Her Majesty the Queen

LEONARDO DA VINCI
Studies of Nudes
Louvre, Paris   Alinari-Art Reference Bureau

Virgin with St. Anne, Louvre. A cartoon on the same subject, but for a different painting that was apparently never executed, is in the National Gallery, London. It may be the cartoon of which Vasari wrote that when it was finished "men and women, young and old, continued for two days to crowd into the room where it was exhibited, as if attending a solemn festival; and all were astonished at its excellence." The knowledgable Florentines were appreciative as the Milanese had never been. Of the same Florentine period is the portrait of *Mona Lisa* (or *La Gioconda*), famous and much discussed for the smile which gives it life; great for the simplicity and dignity of composition and for the mountain landscape which opens the background into infinite distances. In the same period at

Florence he was commissioned, on the recommendation of his friend Machiavelli, to paint a fresco in the Council Hall of the Palazzo Vecchio. Michelangelo was commissioned to paint a fresco on the opposite wall of the same hall. Both painters finished their cartoons, Michelangelo's on a group of Florentine soldiers surprised while bathing, and Leonardo's on *The Battle of Anghiari*—a scene of mounted men in furious combat. The cartoons were exhibited and became a school for young painters. Leonardo experimented with a method by which the color, after it was applied, was to be bonded to the wall by heat. The experiment failed and his work was ruined. (Michelangelo did not even begin to paint from his cartoon—thus the marvellous comparison that the works of these two geniuses might have provided was never brought into being.) Leonardo's cartoon was later lost. Knowledge of part of his intention survives in drawings he left and in a copy of part of the cartoon, *The Battle of the Standard,* that Peter Paul Rubens made of an earlier copy. In 1506 Leonardo returned to Milan in the service of the French king. More and more interested in scientific problems, he left his paintings to be finished by his pupils. Of his earlier days at Milan one of his most successful followers was Boltraffio. Later pupils, most of whom are obscure, imitated his work without understanding it, and produced saccharine versions of his ideal beauty. But despite imitation and vulgarization, painting was never the same after Leonardo. One of his most significant developments was in the atmosphere he produced by the use of *sfumato,* by which is meant the submerging of outlines in the atmosphere—the mass of air—that envelops all things. As the light lessens the outlines disappear, but as the light lessens there is a consequent loss of color, which accounts for the almost subterranean atmosphere of such works as *The Virgin of the Rocks.* To superb intuitive draftsmanship, he added intellectual clarity and science, a deeply personal and strongly idealized sense of beauty, and an intense effort to reveal in his painting the secrets he had forced from nature in his scientific studies. In 1513, at the age of 61, he went to Rome, but he did not get the support he expected from Giuliano de' Medici, the pope's kindly, cultivated, but weak, younger brother. The pope listened to secret and false accusations by enemies and forbade Leonardo the use of the hospital for dissections (on the ground that they defiled the temple of the soul). Leonardo passed his time creating baubles. Raphael and Michelangelo were the favored artists. In 1516 he accepted the invitation of Francis I to go to France as "first painter and engineer to the King," and left Italy forever. He painted only one more panel, *St. John,* Louvre, but was engaged in architectural and canal-engineering projects. Francis I gave him a free hand, but little of the work he planned was carried out. He again staged a great festival with a repetition of the scenery of Milan in 1490. He was honored and admired, received many distinguished guests, and was frequently visited by the enthusiastic King Francis I.

Other paintings attributed to Leonardo by tradition and by some, but not all critics, include the *Madonna Litta* or *Nursing Madonna,* Hermitage, Leningrad; *Lady with an Ermine,* Cracow, Poland, a portrait identified by some as of Cecilia Gallerani, one of Ludovico il Moro's mistresses, and by others as Beatrice d'Este, his wife; *La Belle Ferronière,* Louvre; *Portrait of a Musician,* Ambrosiana, Milan, thought to be Franchino Gaffuri; *Portrait of a Lady,* Ambrosiana, Milan, perhaps Beatrice d'Este. Some paintings he is known to have completed have been lost. And patrons who ordered work from him, in Milan as in Florence, were continually being disappointed. Perhaps, having solved the problems presented in his mind by a given painting, he lost interest and failed to complete a work nobly begun; or his experiments ended in disaster; or he became entirely absorbed in some aspect of science and never even started a commissioned work. Besides the sketches in the notebooks he left a large number of drawings, rich collections of which are at Windsor, the Louvre, and the Uffizi.

Writers have wrestled with the complex and mysterious personality of Leonardo da Vinci from the time of his death in the château of Louise of Savoy to the present. Contemporary writers were unanimous in praise of his extraordinary beauty as a youth. Vasari wrote that he was "so pleasing in conversation that he won all hearts." (Among other things, during the war between Florence and Pisa he persuaded Machiavelli, who in his turn persuaded the Florentine Signory, that it was feasible to divert the Arno River from its bed and thus leave Pisa without a passage inland.) He loved to dress in luxurious garments, but led an austere personal life, and spent much of it alone, for he said, "You own yourself when you are alone." He seems to have had no deep attachments to women, but was much attracted by handsome young men (many sketches of young men with beautiful heads of curly hair are extant), and usually had one or more living in his household, as the scoundrelly Salai, whom he mentioned in his will as a servant. In later life his devoted pupil and friend was the young Milanese, Francesco Melzi, who accompanied him to France and who inherited his drawings and papers. His love of the creatures of nature was proverbial. It was said that he bought caged birds in the market in order to set them free. The principal evidence for his interest in the human condition and affection for mankind lies in his drawings and his paintings. There are no references to deep affections in his voluminous writings. Perhaps because of his ingenuity in science he was regarded and feared by some of his contemporaries as a magician. In consideration of his pioneering experiments and accomplishments in science and his development of the art of painting to a perfection and significance that defies words, he may well have been termed a magician.

Leone (lā-ô′nā). In Lodovico Ariosto's *Orlando Furioso*, the son of the emperor Constantine. He falls in love with Bradamante, and his father arranges a match for him, but he renounces his love out of admiration for Ruggiero, who also loves Bradamante.

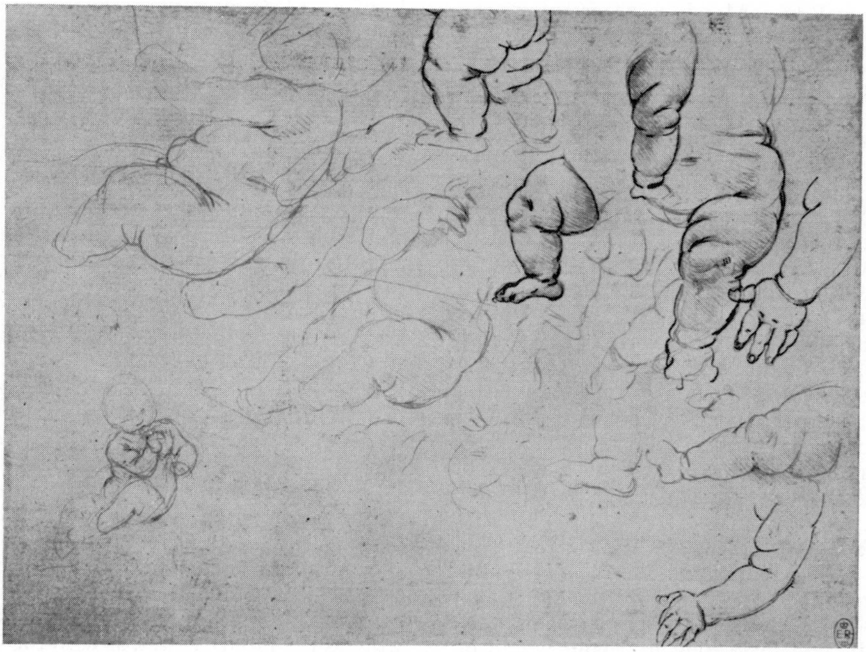

Leonardo da Vinci
Studies of a Child
Royal Library, Windsor Castle
Reproduced by gracious permission of Her Majesty the Queen

Leoni (lā-ô′nē), **Francesca Bussa di.** See Saint **Frances of Rome.**

Leoni, Leone. Medalist and sculptor; b. at Menaggio (Como), 1509; d. at Milan, July 22, 1590. From 1537 to 1540 he was employed at the papal mint. In the last year he was sent to the galleys after a fight with a fellow employee, but was later released thanks to the influence of Andrea Doria. Thereafter, except for a period in Spain, he worked for the mint at Milan. He made a number of medals of Andrea Doria, with a strongly modeled portrait of the admiral on the obverse and a self-portrait, surrounded by the chains from which Doria had freed him, on the reverse. He was one of the most distinguished medalists of his century, noted for the clarity, precision, and firmness of his line, and for his gift for portraiture. Among the medals in which these qualities are apparent (a number of them are in the British Museum), are those of Aretino, Charles V, Philip II, and Michelangelo. The last-named, finished at Rome, March, 1561, is among the best extant portraits of the master. Through the good offices of Ferrante Gonzaga, count of Guastalla, he entered the service of Charles V, became the emperor's favorite sculptor, and received many honors from him. Among his works for the emperor one of the most famous is Charles V conquering Furor, in the Prado, Madrid. The influence of Michelangelo and Sansovino is apparent in his monument to Gian Giacomo Medici in the cathedral at Milan. Other works included a monument of Ferrante Gonzaga at Guastalla, and a bronze statue of Vincenzo Gonzaga in the Church of the Incoronata at Sabbioneta. In his last years he designed a dossal for the Escorial in Spain, a work that was executed by his son Pompeo (c1533–1608), and worked on his house at Milan, which, filled with works of art and antique marbles, was a veritable museum.

Leoni, Pompeo. Sculptor and medalist; b. c1533; d. at Madrid, October 13, 1608. He was the son and pupil of Leone Leoni (1509–1590), was a sculptor favored by Philip II, and lived long in Spain, where he executed the sculptures designed by his father for the Escorial. The grandiose groups he executed for the tombs of Charles V and Philip II in the Escorial reflect the oppressive regality and sombre religious spirit of his royal patrons. Pompeo Leoni bought many of the papers of Leonardo da Vinci from the heirs of Francesco Melzi, the friend and pupil to whom Leonardo had left them. He cut selections from the drawings and notes of Leonardo's papers and arranged them together, intending them as a gift for his Spanish patrons. The gift, never delivered, forms the largest single collection from Leonardo's notebooks, the *Codice Atlantico*, and is now in the Ambrosiana, Milan.

Leonico Tomeo (lā-ō-nē′kō tō-mā′ō), **Niccolò.** Humanist; b. at Venice, 1456; d. at Padua, 1531. He studied Greek at Florence under Demetrius Chalcondylas, who had been his master at Padua. He took his doctorate (1485), and thereafter fixed his residence at Padua. There he lectured on Aristotle for ten years, after which he became a private teacher. He was versed in Greek, Latin, and Italian, and urged the study of philosophy from the Greek texts.

Leopardi (lā-ō-pär′dē), **Alessandro.** Goldsmith, bronze founder, and architect; b. at Venice, 1466 or earlier; d. there, between June, 1522, and March, 1523. Early notices speak of him as a master employed by the mint and also praise his skill as a sculptor. Banished (1487) from Venice for forgery for five years, he was recalled the following year to finish casting the bronze equestrian statue of Bartolomeo Colleoni begun by Verrocchio and left incomplete at the time of Verrocchio's death. Leopardi finished the casting and also designed the pedestal. He inscribed his name on the work and was called ever after "del Cavallo" (*Of the Horse*). In 1503 he and Antonio Lombardo were commissioned to work in the Zeno Chapel in S. Marco, but two years later he left the work because of a dispute. In 1505 he began the central bronze socket for the standards in the Piazza S. Marco, and a few years later executed two lateral ones. These three signed bronze bases, richly ornamented with magnificent friezes of gods, satyrs, sirens, tritons, and so on, are the only sculptural works that can certainly be ascribed to him, but even here, it is not certain whether his signature refers to his work as the bronze caster, as with the Colleoni statue, or whether he was the designer and executor of the reliefs as well. As an architect he made a model (1507) for the restoration of the Scuola Grande della Misericordia, inspected the fortifications of Padua and Treviso, and with three other architects was invited (1514) by the Venetian Signory to submit models for new buildings to replace those on the Rialto that were destroyed by fire in that year. In 1521 he was named overseer for the plan and construction of a new church for the Convent of S. Giustina at

Padua. The church was completed, largely following his plans, after his death, and is his only surviving architectural work.

Lescot (les-kō), **Pierre.** French architect; b. at Paris, c1510; d. September 10, 1578. About all that is known of his personal history is derived from a poem by Ronsard, and the accounts of the royal buildings. He was practically the first architect of France to employ the classical forms in a truly classical way, previous attempts being largely influenced by Gothic forms. His work is considered the best that the Renaissance produced in France. He was made architect of the Louvre August 3, 1546, and retained the office as long as he lived. That part of the Louvre which was built by Lescot consists of the western side south of the Tour d'Orloge, which stands upon the foundations of the great hall of Philippe Auguste, and, with a lower roof, remains just as Lescot left it; the Pavillon du Roi, remodeled; and the western half of the south side, also remodeled.

Leslie (les′li, lez′li), **John.** Scottish Roman Catholic prelate and historian; b. September 29, 1527; d. at Guirtenburg, near Brussels, May 30, 1596. Bishop of Ross, he was a partisan and influential adviser of Mary, Queen of Scots. He wrote a history of Scotland, partly in Latin (1578) and partly in Scots (published 1830), and various other works.

Leslie, Norman. [Title, Master of **Rothes.**] Scottish soldier; d. in France, August 29, 1554. He was a leader in the party that assassinated (1546) the Scottish prelate and statesman, Cardinal Beaton, who was a violent opponent of the Reformation. Although he had no personal part in the act of murder, Leslie was denounced as a rebel, and carried captive (1546) to France. He escaped to England, and was pensioned by Edward VI. He fled (1553) to France at the accession of Mary Tudor, and entered the service of Henry II of France. He died of wounds received in an action at Renti (near Cambrai).

Lethington (leth′ing-to̤n), Lord. See **Maitland,** Sir **Richard.**

Leto (le′tō), **Giulio Pomponio.** See **Laetus, Julius Pomponius.**

Levi ben Gershon (lē′vī ben gėr′sho̤n). [Also, **Gersonides.**] Jewish philosopher, rationalist, mathematician, astronomer, and Biblical scholar; b. at Bagnols, in Languedoc, France, 1288; d. probably at Perpignan, France, April 20, 1344. He wrote books on trigonometry and a treatise on the parallel axiom. In astronomy he invented the Jacob's staff, an instrument for measuring visual angles, and the camera obscura, with the aid of which he made several new observations. He wrote commentaries on the Bible, the Talmud, on Aristotle, and on the commentaries of Averroës on Aristotle. His chief work is *Milhamoth Adonai* (*The Wars of God*), on which he worked for twelve years (1317–1329), and in which he presents his religious philosophy. It deals with the immortality of the soul, prophecy, divine knowledge, providence, miracles, and the creation of the world. At the instigation of Pope Clement VI, a Latin translation of part of the work dealing with astronomy as it was understood by the Arabs was made during his lifetime and published in 1342. He came from a long line of pious scholars, and his Biblical commentaries gave him a certain standing in the Jewish community, but it does not appear that he ever officiated as a rabbi or was offered a rabbinical post. It may be that his reputation as a rationalist and his tendency to depart from strict orthodoxy operated against him. He spent some time at Avignon and Orange, and is generally believed to have died at Perpignan. His theories and his inventions had a great influence on modern astronomy. His great work, which is modeled after the *Moreh Nebuhim* of Maimonides, was not published until 1560.

Leyland (lē′la̤nd), **John.** See **Leland** or **Leyland, John.**

L'Hospital (lo-pē-tȧl), **Michel de.** [Also, **L'Hôpital.**] French statesman; b. at Aigueperse, in Auvergne (now Puy-de-Dôme), France, c1505; d. March 13, 1573. He was sent (1547) on a mission to the Council of Trent, which was at that time sitting at Bologna. He was made superintendent of the royal finances in 1554, and in 1560 became chancellor of France. He caused the States-General to be assembled at Orléans in 1560, and procured the passage in 1562 of the Edict of January, which granted toleration to the Huguenots. His liberal policy was, however, distasteful to the Guises, and civil war broke out in 1562 in spite of his efforts to maintain peace. He was dismissed from office in 1568.

Liberale da Verona (lē-bā-rä′lā dä vā-rō′nä). Painter and miniaturist; b. c1445; d. between

1526 and 1529. He studied under local painters and was first influenced by Jacopo Bellini, who was painting at Verona in 1463, and later by Mantegna. His early works at Verona have disappeared. Between 1467 and 1469 he was at Monteoliveto, near Siena, where he illuminated a number of liturgical works, now at Chiusi. Between 1470 and 1474 he was at Siena, illuminating codices for the Piccolomini Library in the cathedral. After this he traveled about and probably visited Florence and Venice, for his *St. Sebastian*, Brera, Milan, has elements of Florentine figure painting, and the saint is set against a background of a Venetian canal. Reacting to a number of influences, he evolved a highly personal style, in which warm color and a flexible line reveal an emotionalism that counteracted the colder classicism of Mantegna. Vasari called him "generous, fiery, and lovable." On his return to Verona he was very active and had a number of pupils and assistants, including Giolfino and Caroto and Torbido. Many of his frescoes and panels survive at Verona, as in the churches of S. Anastasia, S. Lorenzo, S. Toscana, S. Fermo, the cathedral, and in the art gallery. Versions of his *Madonna Adoring the Sleeping Child* are at Verona, Vicenza, Budapest, Leipzig, and Columbus, Ohio. Examples of his work are in the National Gallery, London, the Johnson Collection, Philadelphia, the Isabella Stewart Gardner Museum, Boston, the Cannon Collection, Princeton, and elsewhere.

Libri (lē′brē), **Bartolomeo di Francesco.** Florentine printer of the 15th century. He used a clear and graceful typeface, printed many books in the vernacular, and adorned them with woodcuts. His earliest known work was an edition of Leonardo Dati's *La Sfera*, of November, 1482; his last was a legal treatise of April, 1500. About 120 volumes are known to have issued from his press, including the first edition of Jacopo Passavanti's *Specchio di vera penitenza*, and many works of Savonarola.

Libri, Girolamo dai. See **Girolamo dai Libri.**

Licinio (lē-chē′nyō), **Bernardino.** Painter of the Venetian school; b. perhaps at Poscante, c1489; d. at Venice, 1565. An eclectic of indifferent talent, he borrowed freely from his great Venetian contemporaries—Giorgione, Palma Vecchio, Pordenone, Paolo Veronese—and was most successful at portraiture. Among his works are *The Madonna and Child with St. Francis*, Uffizi, *The Holy Family with the Infant St. John*, Museum of Fine Arts, Boston, paintings at Brescia, Lucca, Milan (Brera), Venice (Accademia, Ca' d'Oro, S. Maria dei Frari), Hampton Court, Leningrad, Madrid, Waterford, Connecticut (Mr. Nelson White), and portraits at Bergamo, Florence (Uffizi), Padua, Rome (Borghese Gallery, Palazzo Venezia), Venice (Accademia), Vicenza, Munich, Paris, Birmingham (Alabama), Philadelphia (Johnson Collection), San Diego, and elsewhere.

Lidia (lē′dyä). In Lodovico Ariosto's *Orlando Furioso*, a daughter of the king of Lydia. Astolfo finds her in the Infernal regions, and learns that she is there in punishment for her cruel treatment of her lover.

Liebhard (lēp′härt), **Joachim.** Original name of **Camerarius, Joachim.**

Ligorio (lē-gō′ryō), **Pirro.** Architect and painter; b. at Naples, c1510; d. at Ferrara, October 30, 1583. He went to Rome at an early age and devoted himself to the study of the antique, and was also engaged in the workshop of a painter. From 1549 he worked as an architect for Cardinal Ippolito d'Este on the Villa d'Este at Tivoli, and directed the excavation of Hadrian's Villa. Many buildings and constructions were undertaken by him. Among them is the Casino of Pius V (so-called because it was completed in his time) in the Vatican Gardens, and various palaces at Rome. He followed Michelangelo as chief architect of the Basilica of St. Peter's but when he wished to change Michelangelo's plans in some respects he was dismissed from his post. He took up the study of antiquity again, and in 1553 published his *Libro delle antichità di Roma*, somewhat marred by his free interpolations. In 1568 he went to Ferrara on the invitation of Alfonso II d'Este, and there became the duke's antiquarian. He remained at Ferrara until his death. Many manuscripts from his hand are extant, as at Modena, Naples, Turin, Rome, Oxford, and Paris.

Ligozzi (lē-gōt′tsē), **Jacopo.** Painter; b. at Verona, c1547; d. at Florence, March 26, 1626. He was trained by his father and perhaps also by Giovanni Antonio Badile. When he moved to Florence (1578) he fell under the influence of the followers of Michelangelo and Bronzino, and sought, sometimes successfully, to combine Venetian color and

Pirro Ligorio
The Death of Hippolytus
Courtesy of The Pierpont Morgan Library, New York

Florentine plasticity. He was noted as a miniaturist, and for the Medici and Ulisse Aldrovandi made the superbly exact illustrations for the latter's works on natural history. Under Ferdinand II de' Medici he was superintendent of the collections of the Uffizi. Many of his frescoes survive in churches at Florence, as in the Annunziata, Ognissanti, S. Maria Novella, and S. Croce. Others are at Lucca, Pescia, S. Gimignano, Pisa, and elsewhere.

Lilio (lē′lyō) or **Giglio** (jē′lyō), **Luigi.** Scientist and student who suggested reforms in the Julian calendar; b. c1510 at Cirò (Catanzaro); d. 1576. He studied medicine at Naples with his brother Antonio, and then was in the pay of Count Carafa, lord of Cirò. His *Compendium novae rationis resti-*

tuendi kalendarium, which had not been published by the time of his death, presents a plan for the reform of the calendar. It was presented to Pope Gregory XIII by his brother Antonio. After analysis and discussion by some of the most learned men of the day it was given to the most famous scientists in Europe. It was adopted 1582 and the new calendar embodying the reforms is the Gregorian calendar.

Limerno Pitoco (lē-mer′nō pē-tō′kō). Pseudonym of Teofilo Folengo, under which he published his *Orlandino*. Limerno is an anagram of the name of the magician Merlin.

Linacre (lin′ạ-kėr), **Thomas.** English physician and classical scholar; b. probably at Canterbury, 1460; d. at London, October 20, 1524. He was a pioneer in the New Learning of the Renaissance in England, the projector and one of the founders of the College of Physicians at London, and the founder of lectureships at Oxford and Cambridge. He was elected fellow of All Souls College, Oxford, in 1484, and traveled in Italy. In Florence he studied under Poliziano and the Greek Chalcondylas. At Padua he took the degree of M.D. Returned to Oxford, he taught Greek, and had among his pupils Thomas More and Erasmus. Soon after Henry VIII came to the throne, Linacre was appointed one of his physicians and thereafter lived chiefly at London. He received priest's orders in 1520. He published grammatical works and translations, especially of Galen, from Greek into Latin.

Lindsay (lin′zi), **Alexander.** [Title, 4th Earl of **Crawford;** called the **Tiger Earl** and **Earl Beardie.**] Scottish nobleman, warden of the Marches in 1451; d. 1454. He raised a force against James II of Scotland after the murder of his ally William Douglas, 8th earl of Douglas (February 21, 1452), but was defeated at Brechin on May 18, 1452.

Lindsay, David. [Titles, 5th Earl of **Crawford,** 1st Duke of **Montrose.**] Scottish nobleman and politician; b. c1440; d. cDecember 25, 1495. The son of Alexander Lindsay (d. 1454), he was appointed (1476) lord high admiral, master (1480) of the household, lord chamberlain (1483), and joint high justiciary (1488) of north Scotland. He was created (1488) duke of Montrose, the first instance in which the dignity of duke was given to a Scotsman not of royal blood.

Lindsay, Sir **David.** [Also, **Lyndsay.**] Scottish poet and diplomat; b. 1490; d. before April 18, 1555. He was appointed (c1529) Lyon king at arms. His poetry, in the Chaucerian tradition, attacked the vices of the church and is considered as one of the factors that aided the Reformation in Scotland. He was the author of *The Complaynt to the King* (1529), *Ane Satyre of the Three Estaits* (1540, a dramatic poem satirizing abuses in church and state, acted again in 1555), *The Monarchie* (1543, his last and longest poem), and *The Register of the Arms of the Scottish Nobility and Gentry* (first published in 1821).

Lindsay, Patrick. [Title, 6th Baron **Lindsay of the Byres.**] Scottish statesman; d. December 11, 1589. He is said to have been the first of the nobles to give open support to the cause of the Reformers. He played a prominent part in the affairs of Scotland during the reign of Mary, Queen of Scots, and the regencies of Murray and Morton. He supported the plot for the murder of Rizzio, and was guardian with Lord Ruthven of Queen Mary in Lochleven Castle. He was deputed to obtain her signature to the deed of abdication, and decided by his skill the result of the battle of Langside, in which her adherents were defeated.

Lindsay, Robert. Scottish writer; b. at Pitscottie, Fifeshire, Scotland, c1500; d. c1565.

Lippi (lēp′pē), **Filippino.** Painter; b. probably at Prato, 1457 or 1458; d. at Florence, April 18, 1504. He was the son of Fra Filippo Lippi and the nun Lucrezia Buti, was brought up at Prato, went to Spoleto with his father and was there when the latter died. Thereafter, at about the age of 12, he went alone to Florence and was for a time with his father's assistant Fra Diamante. By 1472 he was working under Botticelli. A group of paintings formerly assigned to an unknown painter whom Bernard Berenson named "Amico di Sandro" because of their closeness to Botticelli's work in their delicate tones and linearity, have been classified as youthful works of Filippino. Among these are *Adoration of the Kings*, National Gallery, London, and *The Adoration of the Child*, Uffizi. By 1480 he was working as an independent artist and soon after produced one of his most beautiful paintings, *Apparition of the Virgin to St. Bernard*, now in the Badia, Florence. The sensitivity with which the saint's fear

FILIPPINO LIPPI
Madonna with Dead Christ on Her Knees
Fogg Art Museum, Harvard University. Bequest of Charles A. Loeser

and wonder are rendered as he beholds the serene Virgin makes this one of Filippino's most spiritual expressions. Here his nervous line gives life and movement to the painting without dominating it, and the composition, though filled with details, remains solid in the clear, bright colors that came to be qualities of his painting. From this point Filippino had passed outside Botticelli's influence. After painting in the Palazzo Vecchio (1482) he was given the commission (1484) to complete the frescoes in the Brancacci Chapel of the Church of the Carmine that had been begun by Masolino and continued by Masaccio. He was then about 27 years old, the age of Masaccio when he worked in the Chapel. Filippino completed the figures in *The Raising of the Son of the King of Antioch* and all of the panel of *St. Peter in Prison*, on the left wall. On the right wall he frescoed *The Angel Freeing St. Peter from Prison, SS. Peter and Paul before the Proconsul*, and *Crucifixion of St. Peter*. In the work he obviously tried to continue in the manner of Masaccio. Some critics (but not all), noting his forceful, individualized figures, among which are many portraits including those of Botticelli, Antonio Pollaiuolo, and himself, consider his work in the Brancacci Chapel as his masterpiece. Later frescoes were those in the Strozzi Chapel of S. Maria Novella, with the stories of St. Philip and St. John the Evangelist. These were commissioned in 1487 but not begun for over ten years and completed only in 1502. By this time his style had undergone considerable change. In the meantime he had been at Rome (1488–1493) decorating the Caraffa Chapel in S. Maria sopra Minerva with frescoes on the Virgin and St. Thomas. At Rome he became fascinated by Roman antiquities, made many drawings, and ever after included details from the antique in his paintings, without regard to their appropriateness. Vasari writes that "he never did any work whatever without using Roman antiquities . . . helmets, banners, trophies, vases, temple ornaments, . . . the toga, swords, and scimitars." He writes as if it were a matter for congratulation; but Vasari also spoke admiringly of Filippino's penchant for dressing his figures in the antique style or bizarre costumes. Filippino was a busy and highly respected artist in his day. Vasari writes of his "fresh and animated color," still admirably preserved in many of his works, and of the abundance of his invention. Later critics have sometimes felt that his creations were better imagination than art. In his development the principal channel for his father's influence had been Botticelli. Later he was deeply affected, as were many, by the work of Leonardo da Vinci, and attempted to follow in his manner to the detriment of his native gifts. In the last fifteen years or so of his life his line became increasingly agitated, his figures were elongated and not always well drawn, and his compositions were crowded with details from the antique or from his fancies. He was in these respects a forerunner of 16th-century mannerism. Much of his work has great charm, along with a certain amount of theatricality. Among his many works is a *Madonna and Saints* (1485), Uffizi, which was originally a commission to Pollaiuolo and then to Leonardo. The latter drew the cartoon but never executed the painting. A number of works by Filippino survive, some of them signed and dated. They are in the Uffizi, Accademia, and the Annunziata, Florence (his last painting, *Deposition*, begun for the Annunziata in 1503, was finished by Perugino); in the Church of S. Domenico, Bologna (a *St. Catherine*, with attempts at the manner of Leonardo, signed and dated, 1503); at Prato, Lucca, Genoa, Naples, Copenhagen, the National Gallery, London, Berlin (several there were destroyed in 1945), and at Cambridge (Massachusetts), Cleveland, Denver, El Paso, Memphis, New Haven, the Metropolitan Museum and the New York Historical Society, New York, Raleigh (North Carolina), the National Gallery, Washington, and elsewhere.

Lippi, Fra **Filippo.** Florentine painter; b. at Florence, c1406; d. at Spoleto, October 9, 1469. As a child (Vasari says he was eight years old) he was placed in the Convent of the Carmine at Florence, although as subsequent events proved he had absolutely no vocation for the monastic life. He took his vows as a Carmelite (1421), was listed among the brothers as a painter (1430), and seems to have left the Convent (c1432), but never put off the habit or gave up his title. In his youth he saw Masolino, and after him Masaccio, painting the famous frescoes in the Brancacci Chapel of the Convent. Possibly he was Masaccio's pupil, and he was in any case greatly influenced by him in his early work, as in the remains of a fresco, *Confirmation of the Carmelite Order* (c1432), in the Cloister of the Carmine, and *Madonna of Humility and Angels*, Trivulzio Collection, Castello Sforzesco, Milan, which are attributed to him. Other early influences on his development were those of Lorenzo Monaco and Fra Angelico. The influence of the former appears in the Gothicized elements such as the fantastic rocky crags in the background of his *Madonna Adoring the Child*,

Berlin, painted for the Medici, and *Madonna Adoring the Child with St. Bernard and the Infant St. John* (c1463), commissioned by Lucrezia Tornabuoni, mother of Lorenzo the Magnificent, and now in the Uffizi. The example of Fra Angelico, whose *Adoration of the Magi*, National Gallery, Washington, he finished, introduced him to early Renaissance developments and perhaps influenced his love of color and strong outlines. He soon became the favorite painter of the Medici, who remained his protectors and benefactors throughout his life, and commissioned paintings from him for themselves and as gifts for the pope, the king of Naples, and others. Fra Filippo, a genial soul who enjoyed the pleasures of the flesh, was not especially appreciative of their kindness. They were forced to cajole, to threaten, even to pay him in advance. Even so he often failed to fulfill his obligations—at least, when he said he would. Vasari writes that he could never work when he was in love. He recounts that once Cosimo de' Medici, in order to force him to finish a painting, locked him in the room where he was working. Fra Filippo, overcome by his appetites, escaped from the upper chamber by means of knotted sheets and disappeared for days. Thereafter Cosimo, fearful that his painter might injure himself in a similar escape, concluded that artists were not beasts of burden who could be compelled and ceased to harass him. In 1434 Filippo was at Padua, where he might have followed his patron into exile, but the work he did there has perished. His first certain dated work (1437) is the *Tarquinia Madonna*, painted for Cardinal Vitelleschi, Pope Eugenius IV's general, and now in the Barberini Palace, Rome. In 1442 he was named Rector of S. Quirico at Legnaia, near Florence. Between 1441 and 1447 he painted the *Coronation of the Virgin* for the nuns of S. Ambrogio, now in the Uffizi, in which he included a portrait of himself as a kneeling monk. In 1450 he was charged with forging an assistant's signature on a receipt, confessed, and was imprisoned briefly. The following year a suit was brought against him for turning over to a pupil a painting he had contracted to do himself. In 1455 he was deprived of his ecclesiastical benefices but the following year, notwithstanding the scandal, he was named chaplain of the Convent of S. Margherita at Prato. In the meantime, he had begun (1452) painting scenes from the lives of St. John the Baptist and St. Stephen in the cathedral at Prato. The frescoes, of which the *Funeral of St. Stephen* is signed and dated (1460), were not completed until 1464, and then only as the results of threats from Carlo de' Medici, and with the generous participation of assistants. The frescoes at Prato constitute his most important monumental work. Other work at Prato includes the *Madonna del Ceppo* (1453), painted for the Ospedale del Ceppo and now in the Municipal Gallery; much of it was painted by his assistant Fra Diamante to Filippo's design. Also in the Gallery is a *Nativity*. For all his dilatoriness and irregular life, Fra Filippo was a favorite painter of the ecclesiastical authorities and was highly regarded as an artist. In 1456 the authorities of the Convent of S. Margherita allowed the nun Lucrezia Buti to serve as a model for a Madonna he was painting. He fell violently in love with her. On the Feast of the Holy Girdle he carried her away—no force seems to have been needed—to his house. She was soon joined by her sister Spinetta, also a nun; three other nuns of the Convent chose the perils of the world at the same time. In 1457 or 1458 Lucrezia's son Filippino was born. The model for the popular *Madonna and Child*, with the Child supported by two angels, Uffizi, was, according to all accounts, Lucrezia. Having been forgiven and reinstated in the Convent, she fled again to Filippo. He was ultimately freed from his vows and married her, and she bore him a daughter, Alessandra, in 1465.

Through the influence of Piero de' Medici he was commissioned (1468) to fresco the apse of the cathedral at Spoleto. He worked on it until his death, but as his health was failing much of the work was carried out by assistants, chief of whom was Fra Diamante, who finished the work after Fra Filippo's death. Only the *Coronation of the Virgin* in the vault is largely from his hand. When Lorenzo de' Medici learned of his death he asked the authorities of Spoleto to send his body to Florence for burial. They politely declined to do so, on the ground that Florence held the tombs of many famous men, whereas Spoleto had but few. Lorenzo caused a beautiful monument to be erected in the cathedral at Spoleto where, with an inscription by Poliziano, it remains to this day.

In some senses Fra Filippo bridges the transition from the international Gothic style of Lorenzo Monaco and the early Renaissance manner of Fra Angelico to fully developed 15th century Tuscan painting. His attitude toward life and the religious pictures that the times required of him was utterly at variance with theirs. The spirituality that pervades the works of the earlier masters is replaced in Fra Filippo by a naturalism that reflected the world and the people of his day (the impudent angel facing the spectator as he supports the Holy Infant in the Uffizi *Madonna and Child* could be a street Arab of Florence; his Madonnas are frequently winsome rather than spiritual). In like manner the element of fantasy in the details of Lorenzo Monaco, for example, is lacking in the genre details of Fra Filippo's realistic interiors and contemporary costumes. His use of line to create form is reflected in the subsequent work of Botticelli, whose line is artistry of the highest. Charm, grace, warm color, good draftsmanship (except for the extremities which, after his rendering of hands had been criticized, he contrived to hide under draperies), and lyricism mark much of Fra Filippo's easel painting. In his great frescoes at Prato he showed an interest in drama and movement that no longer held any signs of the dignity and nobility of Masaccio. For although Fra Filippo was a leading painter of his time and had great influence on his immediate successors with his innovative naturalism, he was not the vehicle through which the revolutionary developments of Masaccio were passed to Florentine painting. Besides those already mentioned, other works are an *Annunciation*, S. Lorenzo, Florence, in which he ignored traditional iconography by showing three angels rather than the usual one; *Madonna and Child*, with the Birth of the Virgin in the background, a tondo in the Pitti Palace; several works in the Uffizi and in the Medici-Riccardi Palace, Florence; paintings in the National Gallery, London, the Louvre, Paris, the Hermitage, Leningrad, at Berlin, Rome, Venice, and Turin, and at Baltimore, Cambridge, New Orleans, in the Metropolitan Museum and in the Frick Collection, New York, the National Gallery, Washington, and elsewhere.

Lippo di Dalmasio (lēp′pō dē däl-mä′syō). See **Scannabecchi, Dalmasio.**

Lippo Vanni (vän′nē). See **Vanni, Lippo.**

Little Masters. A name given to a group of 16th-century German artists, all of them followers of Albrecht Dürer.

Littleton (lit′l-tọn), Sir **Thomas.** English jurist; b. at Frankley, Worcestershire, England, c1407 (some authorities say 1422); d. there August 23, 1481. He was made justice of the Common Pleas, April 27, 1466, and was the author of a famous work (in the French then standard in English law) on tenures, which, with Edward Coke's commentary, was long the authority on the English law of real property.

Loaisa or **Loaysa** (lō-ī′sä), **García Jofre de.** Spanish sea captain; b. at Placencia, Cáceres, Spain, c1485; d. July 30, 1526.

Lobeira (lö-bā′rạ) or **Loveira** (lö-vā′rạ), **Vasco de.** Portuguese writer and soldier; b. at Oporto, Portugal, about the middle of the 14th century; d. at Elvas, Portugal, c1403. He was a reputed author of the famous romance *Amadis of Gaul*.

Loggia (lō′jä). In Italian architecture, a gallery or arcade in a building, properly at the height of one or more stories, running along the front or part of the front of the building, and open on at least one side to the air, on which side is a series of pillars or slender piers. Such galleries provide an airy and sheltered resting place or outlook and are very characteristic of Renaissance palaces. Among famous loggias is that at Florence, the *Loggia dei Lanzi*, and those of the Vatican decorated by Raphael and his pupils.

Logistilla (lō-jēs-tēl′lä). In Lodovico Ariosto's *Orlando Furioso*, an enchantress, who represents Reason or Virtue. She is the sister of the wicked enchantresses Alcina and Morgana, with whom she is continually at war. The lovers whom Alcina, Circe-like, has transformed into different shapes, are received by Logistilla after they have regained their natural shapes and are sent to their homes. Logistilla gives Astolfo a magic horn whose blast terrifies all who hear it.

Logroño (lō-grō′nyō), **Pedro.** Spanish priest; b. at Guadalajara, Spain; d. probably in Mexico, after 1567. His *Manual de los adultos para bautizar* (known only in a fragment) is probably the oldest existing book published in America. It was printed at Mexico City in 1540.

Lola (lō′lä), **Francesco.** Painter; active in the first quarter of the 15th century. His frescoes in S. Petronio, Bologna, executed in 1419, are in the international Gothic style.

Lollards (lol′ạrdz). English followers of John Wycliffe, adherents of a widespread movement, partly political and socialistic, and in some respects anticipating Protestantism and Puritanism, in the 14th and 15th centuries. They were also called "Bible men," from their reverence for the Bible. They differed on some points both among themselves and from Wycliffe, but in the main condemned the use of images in churches, pilgrimages to the tombs of saints, the temporal lordship of the clergy, the hierarchical organization, papal authority, religious orders, ecclesiastical decorations, the ceremony of the Mass, the doctrine of transubstantiation, waging of wars, and capital punishment. Some of them engaged in seditious proceedings, and they were severely persecuted for more than a hundred years, especially after the adoption of a special statute (*De haeretico comburendo*) against them in 1401. Under Henry IV the place of origin and intellectual center of the movement was cut off by close clerical supervision of Oxford University; after that its principal followers were found among the landed gentry and the lower classes. Persecution became more severe under Henry V and in 1414 an uprising took place under the leadership of Sir John Oldcastle, formerly one of Henry's companions. Oldcastle was eventually captured and executed (1417) according to the statute, one of the few who actually was burned. The movement continued, but gradually it lost force, although its doctrines, and its critical spirit towards Roman Catholicism, survived in the Reformation. At the peak of the movement, probably one Englishman in four was a Lollard. The name comes from a Dutch word meaning one who mumbles prayers or psalms.

Lollio (lōl′lyō), **Alberto.** Scholar, writer and orator; b. at Florence at the end of the 15th century; d. at Ferrara, 1568. He spent much of his life at Ferrara. He knew Latin and Greek well and maintained that Italian was their equal. Noted in his day as an orator, he is remembered in literary history as the author of the pastoral play *Aretusa*, produced at the court of Ferrara in 1563.

Lombardi (lôm-bär′dē), **Alfonso.** Sculptor; b. probably at Ferrara, 1497; d. at Bologna, December 2, 1537. He worked chiefly at Bologna, where his principal works are to be found. His *Death of the Virgin* is a monumental work in terra-cotta and shows the influence of Raphael and Michelangelo; it is in the Church of S. Maria della Vita. Works in S. Petronio include a *Resurrection of Christ*, *The Birth of Esau and Jacob*, and *Moses Presented to Pharaoh*, as well as panels with scenes from the life of Rebecca. When Charles V was at Bologna (1530), Lombardi was commissioned to make a portrait bust of him. He also made the marble predella for the tomb of S. Domenico in the saint's church. Other works from his hand are at Bologna, Ferrara, and Faenza. Lombardi worked much in terra-cotta, to which medium he sought to give the dignity and austerity of marble, transforming it from its traditional popular aspects.

Lombardo (lôm-bär′dō), **Antonio.** See **Antonio Lombardo.**

Lombardo, Pietro. See **Pietro Lombardo.**

Lombardo, Tullio. See **Tullio Lombardo.**

Longhi (lōng′gē), **Luca.** Painter; b. at Ravenna, 1507; d. 1580. His *Nativity* is in the Carrara Academy, Bergamo.

Lopes de Castanheda (lô′pẹ̄sh dẹ kush-tạ-nyä′dạ), **Fernão.** See **Castanheda, Fernão Lopes de.**

López de Ayala (lō′peᴛʜ dā ä-yä′lä), **Pedro.** Spanish poet, prose writer, and statesman; b. in Murcia, Spain, 1332; d. 1407. He was taken prisoner at the battle of Nájera (1367) and carried to England. On his return he was made grand chancellor to Henry II. He was again taken prisoner at the battle of Aljubarrota (1385). His principal works are a history, *Cronicas de los reyes de Castillas*, and a poem, *El Rimado de palacio*.

López de Legazpe (dā lā-gäth′pā) (or **Legaspi**), **Miguel.** Spanish conqueror of the Philippine Islands; b. at Zumarraga, Guipúzcoa, Spain, c1510; d. at Manila, Philippine Islands, August 20, 1572. In 1564 he was made general of the forces destined to conquer and settle the Philippine Islands. He founded San Miguel on Cebu, in May, 1565, took possession of various other islands, began the conquest of Luzon in 1571, and founded Manila in May of that year.

López de Villalobos (dā ʙē-lyä-lō′bōs), **Rui.** Spanish navigator; d. at Amboina, East Indies, 1546.

Lorenzetti (lôr-en-zāt′tē), **Ambrogio.** Sienese painter, brother of Pietro Lorenzetti (c1280–1348); b. at Siena, probably between 1290 and 1300; d. there, probably of the Black Death, 1348. A leading painter of the Sienese school, he was at first influenced by Duccio and the Byzantine tradition, especially in his mysticism, but with more breadth of form and a greater preoccupation with space and large areas. His ultimate style, a development from these influences, is his own. Most of his work was done in Siena, Florence (where he joined the Guild of Physicians and Apothecaries, 1327), and Massa Maritima. In his treatment of space and the figure Lorenzetti undertook to deal with problems of perspective and anatomy that were not completely resolved until the time of Masaccio and Piero della Francesca. The Florentine sculptor Ghiberti (c1378–1455) called Ambrogio "the greatest painter of the city of Siena," and "a most noble designer." Notable in his work are his gift for narrative, his treatment of large areas, his interest in landscape, and his typically Sienese sense of color. Among his works are: *Madonna and Child* (c1317), Brera, Milan, another (1319) from Vico l'Abate, Museo Arcivescovile, Florence, and a third (c1340), Palazzo Pubblico, Siena; a fresco *Boniface VIII Receiving St. Louis of Toulouse* (c1326), Church of S. Francesco, Siena, notable for the beautifully conceived composition, the concentrated interest of King Robert of Naples as he watches the pope and his brother, and the features and expressions of the young men who watch the ceremony; the fresco *Martydom of the Franciscans* (c1326), Church of S. Francesco, Siena, in which the drama is heightened by the oriental features and fierce expressions of the Tartar and Mongol spectators to the beheading, and the sense of an alien world by their bizarre headgear; *Maestà* (c1330), Municipio, Massa Maritima; *Consecration of St. Nicholas* and scenes from the life of St. Nicholas (c1332), Uffizi, Florence; *Madonna del Latte* (c1340), Church of S. Francesco, Siena; *Presentation in the Temple,* signed and dated (1342), Uffizi, Florence, in which his increasing mastery of perspective is evident; and *Annunciation,* signed and dated (1344), Pinacoteca, Siena. The earliest landscapes in Italian painting are also attributed to Ambrogio. One is of a castle by a lake, with an empty boat drawn up on shore. No human figure appears. Ambrogio painted the scene as if he were viewing it from the air. The same is true of the other landscape, a castle in a walled town by the sea. Here we look down on all that is inside the walls of the town as well as all that surrounds them. Both are in the Pinacoteca, Siena. His largest work, one full of charm and interest, is the series of frescoes on Good and Bad Government, and the effects thereof, painted (1338–1339) in the Palazzo Pubblico, Siena. On an end wall of the large rectangular room is presented the *Allegory of Good Government*. A personification of the Commune is portrayed on the upper portion of the wall. An imposing figure, he is surrounded by the theological virtues of Faith, Hope and Charity, and the civic virtues Peace, Fortitude, Prudence, Magnanimity, Temperance, and Justice. All of these figures show strong classical influence. Below the allegorical representations is a procession of twenty-four magistrates, in the costume of the time. These are the governors of the Commune. On the adjoining wall is a descriptive painting: the *Effects of Good Government in the Town and in the Country*. A freely rendered portrait of Siena with its houses, palaces, glimpse of the striped tower of the cathedral, and shops forms a background for artisans, traders, dancing girls, and citizens of all classes going about their business in an orderly way. It is an image of a prosperous city. In the country outside the wall appear the hills about Siena, with squares, rectangles and triangles of gardens and vineyards strewn upon them at all angles. Farmers and swineherds do their work in peace and apparent happiness. Huntsmen pursue their quarry. Over all floats an image that represents Security. Besides its interest as a work of art, the fresco is a documentary of life in Siena in the first half of the 14th century. The fresco has been damaged, restored, and repainted. On the other end wall is the *Allegory of Bad Government*. Here Tyranny, with horns, fangs, and crossed eyes (indicating trickery), is personified on the upper portion of the wall. He is surrounded by the vices opposed to the virtues of Good Government: Avarice, Vainglory and Pride, and the civic vices: War, Rage, Fraud, Treason, Cruelty, and Faction. This wall is badly damaged and large parts of the fresco are missing. The same is true of the adjoining wall, on which are shown the effects of bad government: shattered houses, tumbled palaces and empty shops, and in the country a devastated landscape. The figure floating over this scene is Fear. The work was commissioned by the governors of Siena. The lesson it teaches is plain. Many others of his surviving panels and frescoes are at Siena, in the Pinacoteca and churches. At nearby S. Galgano is a series of frescoes in the Oratory of Montesiepi. Other works are at Roccalbegna, Budapest, London, Boston, Cambridge, El Paso, Minneapolis, and New York.

Lorenzetti, Pietro. Sienese painter, brother of Ambrogio Lorenzetti (d. 1348); b. at Siena, c1280; d. there, probably of the Black Death, 1348. Little is known of his early life. By 1305 his reputation as a painter must have been established, for in that year he was paid for a painting for the Council of the Nine at Siena. His early work reveals the influence of Duccio and then of Simone Martini. As he developed, however, the Duccesque mysticism disappeared, his originality of design and execution emerged, an accent on realism and broader forms is more apparent. Characteristic in the later work is the emphasis on line in the drawing of features, virility and monumental character of conception, and the sense expressed in his art of deeply felt religious convictions. In his portrayal of the human body, and in his attempts to show violent movement and expressions of grief or anguish, as in the *Crucifixion* at Assisi, Pietro was probably influenced by Giovanni Pisano, whose famous pulpit, executed with Nicola Pisano and others, was in the cathedral at Siena. The *Crucifixion*, in the left arm of the transept, Lower Church of the basilica of S. Francesco at Assisi, has been called "one of the finest and most harmonious compositions of the Christian drama ever made." The fresco (part of which was destroyed to make room for an altar) has an intensity of feeling and a realism in the expressions of grief on the faces of the spectators that had rarely been depicted in painting up to this time. Other frescoes in the left arm of the transept by Pietro Lorenzetti are a *Deposition*, *Entombment*, and *St. Francis Receiving the Stigmata*. The remaining frescoes were probably done by his assistants. All the work at Assisi was probably carried out between 1325 and 1329, and includes Pietro's *Madonna between St. Francis and St. John*, a poetic and refined expression in glowing color of a profound religious sentiment—a masterpiece. The influence of Pisano can be seen in the sculptural quality of the modeling in the figures of the Assisi frescoes. Other works by Pietro are: a polyptych, *Virgin and Child, with Saints* (1320), over the altar in the Church of S. Maria della Pieve, Arezzo; *Madonna with Child between St. Nicholas of Bari and St. Anthony Abbot, and Angels*, signed and dated (1329), Church of S. Anzano, Dofana; three panels with saints (1332), Pinacoteca, Siena, which have been often repainted but without destroying Pietro's original drawing of the features; a panel from a larger work, representing *St. Catherine of Alexandria*, The Metropolitan Museum of Art, New York; *Virgin with Child*, Diocesan Museum, Cortona, which shows the mystic influence of Duccio and the Byzantine tradition; *Enthroned Madonna with Angels* (1340), Uffizi, Florence; *Birth of the Virgin*, Opera del Duomo, Siena (1342); *St. Peter* and *St. John*, Vatican; a dismembered polyptych, representing Beata Umilità (Saint Humility) and panels with scenes from her life, signed and thought to be of c1341, Uffizi, Florence; *Madonna and Saints*, Poldi Pezzoli, Milan; *Massacre of the Innocents*, Church of S. Maria dei Servi, Siena; and *Christ Before Pilate*, Vatican, in which he captures the drama of the moment as Christ replies to Pilate. Other works are at Castiglion del Bosco (frescoes, S. Michele Arcangelo), Montichiello, S. Angelo in Colle (S. Michele Arcangelo), Altenberg, Berlin, London, Baltimore (Walters Art Gallery), Bridgeport (Connecticut), Cambridge, New Haven, Philadelphia (Johnson Collection), Seattle, Washington (National Gallery), and elsewhere. Lorenzetti was a virile and independent artist, who modified the earlier influence of Duccio and Martini to form his own style. Mysticism, charm and serenity are replaced in his work by realism, power and drama—all endowed with intense religious feeling. In his later work calmness and majesty supersede violent movement and realism.

Lorenzo d'Alessandro da Sanseverino (lō-ren′tsō dä-les-sän′drō dä sän-sā-vā-rē′nō). Painter; b. at Sanseverino, the Marches; d. there, 1503. The first mention of him is of 1468. Absorbed in his work and in public affairs, he passed all his life at Sanseverino, where he painted banners, processional standards, coats of arms, and other minor works, as well as frescoes in churches, and panel pictures. The chief influences on his artistic development were those of Niccolò da Foligno and Carlo Crivelli. The linearity and calligraphic stylization of the drapery in his earlier works are derived from the Gothic. Later his style broadened and achieved an amplitude hitherto unknown among painters of the Marches. The hard, tormented line of Carlo Crivelli appears in many of his works, as *The Marriage of St. Catherine*, National Gallery, London (which even includes that trademark of Crivelli, a cucumber and a piece of fruit on the platform of the Madonna's throne), and the *Nativity* in the Church of S. Lorenzo in Doliolo. The influence of Niccolò da Foligno is more apparent in the types of his Madonnas, as in that in the Church of S. Maria di Piazza at Sarnano. Many examples of his work are extant at Sanseverino; others are at Corridonia, Caldarola, Matelica, the Uffizi, Florence, the Barberini Palace and the Vatican, Rome; at Baltimore, Cleveland, and elsewhere.

Lorenzo di Bicci (dē bēt′chē). Florentine painter; d. 1427. He was enrolled in the Company of St. Luke at Florence in 1400. He worked on some designs for the cathedral at Florence and helped paint the statues, designed by Agnolo Gaddi, for the Loggia dei Lanzi at Florence. Bicci di Lorenzo, his son, worked in his workshop and is often confused with him.

Lorenzo di Credi (dē krā′dē). Painter, goldsmith, and sculptor; b. at Florence, 1456 or 1459/1460; d. there, January 12, 1537. Vasari is the authority that he was a goldsmith, and although no documentary evidence supports the statement, it seems likely enough since Lorenzo's grandfather was a goldsmith. The will of Andrea Verrocchio seems to confirm Vasari's statement that he was a sculptor as it directs Lorenzo to finish the statue Verrocchio had begun of Bartolomeo Colleoni. He received his training as a painter in Verrocchio's workshop, along with Leonardo da Vinci and Perugino, and remained as Verrocchio's assistant at least until 1486. Few dates of his activity as a painter exist: a moody and melancholy self-portrait, National Gallery, Washington, is dated 1488; a *Madonna between SS. Julian and Nicola,* painted not earlier than 1503, is in the Louvre. *St. Bartholomew*, Orsanmichele, a somewhat monotonous *Adoration of the Shepherds*, Uffizi, and *Madonna and Four Saints*, S. Maria delle Grazie, Pistoia, are of 1510; and among the late works is *St. Michael* (c1523) in the Sacristy of the cathedral at Florence. He was highly regarded at Florence, was asked to serve on committees to value other artists' work, his advice was asked on the matter of the façade, and later the dome, of the cathedral, and in 1504 he was among those who decided on the location of Michelangelo's *David*. Vasari writes that he became an ardent follower of Savonarola, and that he destroyed all his secular paintings, except for some portraits and the *Venus* now in the Uffizi, in the Burning of the Vanities (1497). The drama of the spiritual struggle as exemplified by Savonarola does not appear in the religious paintings of Lorenzo. Deeply influenced by Leonardo, he sought spiritual expression in the search for beauty. In the execution of his artistic ideal he produced a number of tranquil, sometimes rather vapid, *Madonnas*. Having achieved a rhythm in his composition that satisfied him he often painted several versions of the same picture, as the *S. Maria Egyptiaca Escorted by Angels* (others have identified it as the *Communion of St. Mary Magdalen*), Johnson Collection, Philadelphia, which is a studio version of a better one at Esztergom, Hungary, and *The Adoration of the Child*, versions of which are at Karlsruhe, Berlin, the National Gallery, London, and the Metropolitan Museum, New York. He left a number of portraits, some of which are notable for the elegiac quality of the background and the general aura of gently melancholy. (One of Verrocchio, Uffizi, is attributed to him by some, to Perugino by others.) Other paintings include *The Annunciation and Three Scenes from Genesis*. Typical of his rather sentimentalized expressions and with a symmetrical, formalized background, it is sensitively realized and is perhaps his masterpiece; it is in the Uffizi. Other works are in the Accademia, Florence, the Carrara Academy, Bergamo, Borghese Gallery and the Vatican, Rome, Turin, the National Gallery, London, Dresden, the Isabella Stewart Gardner Museum, Boston, Fogg Museum, Cambridge, at Cincinnati, Cleveland, Coral Gables (Florida), Kansas City, Muncie (Indiana), Omaha (Nebraska), and elsewhere.

Lorenzo the Magnificent. See **Medici, Lorenzo de'.**

Lorenzo Monaco (mō′nä-kō). [Original name, **Piero di Giovanni.**] Florentine painter; b. at Siena, c1370; d. at Florence, 1425. He entered the Camoldolese monastery (whence his name Monaco) of S. Maria degli Angeli at Florence and was a sub-deacon in 1392. He was not compelled to live at the monastery, and in 1414 rented a house nearby in which he lived until his death. Most of his work was done in and around Florence. In painting he was at first a follower of Agnolo Gaddi, whose forms and plasticity derived from Giotto. To the Giottesque tradition Lorenzo later joined the brilliant color and the linear qualities of Simone Martini, the narrative characteristics of the Lorenzetti, the fluid rhythms and elegance of Ghiberti, and an element of fantasy in his stylized landscapes marked by curving truncated crags that made him an outstanding exponent of the international Gothic style. In the sense that he built on older forms and did not create new ones he was a traditionalist, but his personality is highly individual. His paintings are infused with an austere and religious sentiment. They are elegant, aristocratic, and pervaded by a Gothic mysticism. There are none of the familiar domestic details that, enchanting though they are, impart a worldly spirit to the works of Gentile da Fabriano, a great contemporary painter in the international manner. An early work in the manner of Agnolo Gaddi is a *Madonna of Humility*, at Empoli, that shows the Madonna against an unfigured background; there are no decorative elements. He painted the *Madonna of Humility* (so-called because the Madonna is humbly seated on the ground) a number of times; others are at Brooklyn, Kansas City (Missouri), Milan (formerly Crespi Collection), Moscow (1400), New York, Paris, Philadelphia (Johnson Collection), Pisa (1412), Siena, Toledo, Washington (1413), and one at Berlin that was destroyed in 1945. In his mature work Lorenzo shows all the characteristics of the international style—elongated, gracefully inclined or slightly swaying figures, long thin hands, curlicues of drapery, elaborately patterned fabrics, and backgrounds in which there is an element of the fantastic. About 1409 he began to paint miniatures, and illuminated a book with two full page pictures and fifteen smaller ones, now in the Laurentian Library at Florence. The elaborate capitals of the book are ornamented with stylized curving and pointed leaves and garlands, lines for a purely decorative effect that appear in his later paintings. He also left a number of drawings of fantastic Gothic landscapes. Among his many extant works are: *The Coronation of the Virgin*, his only signed and dated (1413) work, originally painted for the high altar of the Church of S. Maria degli Angeli, and the *Adoration of the Magi* (c1420), both beautiful examples of this master's work and both in the Uffizi, Florence (Gentile da Fabriano's *Adoration of the Magi*, hanging nearby, provides a striking illustration of the different spirit evoked by two masters in the same style); an *Annunciation*, Accademia, Florence; an *Annunciation* and frescoes on the life of the Virgin, in S. Trinità, Florence; a *Crucifixion* and a predella panel, *St. Francis Receiving the Stigmata*, Jarves Collection, Yale University, New Haven. Besides those mentioned above, many more of his works are at Florence (Accademia, Uffizi, Bargello, churches) and in the vicinity. He is also represented at Bergamo, Bologna, Fiesole, Prato, Ravenna, Rome (Vatican), Turin (Museo Civico), Altenberg, Amsterdam, Copenhagen, London, Paris, Prague, Baltimore (Walters Art Gallery), Cleveland, Houston, New York, San Diego, Tulsa, and elsewhere.

Lorenzo di Niccolò Gerini (dē nik-kô-lō′ je-rē′nē). See **Gerini, Lorenzo di Niccolò.**

Lorenzo da Pavia (dä pä-vē′ä). See **Gusnasco, Lorenzo.**

Lorenzo di Pietro (dē pye′trō). See **Vecchietta.**

Lorenzo Veneziano (ve-nā-tsyä′nō). Venetian painter; active between 1356 and 1373. He painted at Bologna on at least two occasions, and a polyptych attributed to him is in the Church of S. Giacomo Maggiore there. His style, though fundamentally Byzantine, shows evidence of the Gothic in its softened outline and freer drapery, and of the Sienese in its bright color. Some critics call him a Venetian primitive in the Byzantine manner; others say he utterly abandoned the Byzantine formulas and revolutionized Venetian painting by introducing into it elements of the Gothic and Sienese. In either case, he was an important influence on contemporary or near contemporary Venetians. His extant works are altarpieces with gold backgrounds painted on wood. Among

Lorenzo Monaco
Group of Saints
Uffizi, Florence Alinari-Art Reference Bureau

his early works are a polyptych (1356) with the *Death of the Virgin, Crucifixion,* panels of saints and a predella, in the cathedral at Vicenza, and an *Annunciation,* part of a polyptych, signed and dated (1357), Accademia, Venice. In the same gallery is a *Mystic Marriage of St. Catherine* (1359), which is a fine example of his grace, elegance, and color. Other examples of these felicities are the central panel of a polyptych, *Giving of the Keys to St. Peter* (1369), Museo Correr, Venice (the central panel of the predella, *St. Peter Walking on the Water,* is at Berlin), and *Virgin Enthroned* (1372), Louvre, Paris. Other examples of his painting are at Bologna, Brescia, Florence (Contini-Bonacossi Collection), London, Prague, Detroit, New York (Lehman Collection), San Diego, and elsewhere.

Lorenzo da Viterbo (dä vē-ter′bō). [**Lorenzo di Jacopo di Pietro Paolo.**] Painter; b. at Viterbo, c1437; d. after 1469. He was a follower of Benozzo Gozzoli. He is noted for a series of frescoes in S. Maria della Verità at Viterbo (some of which were damaged by bombardment in 1944). The frescoes, begun when he was 25 years old, show the influence of Piero della Francesca in the solid composition and the perspective, in the types of the heads and in the clarity of color. This influence is strongest in the last and finest of the series, *The Marriage of the Virgin,* which is also interesting for its many portraits. An altarpiece by Lorenzo is in the Barberini Palace, Rome.

Lorraine (lo̜-rān′), Cardinal of. [Title of **Charles of Guise.**] French prelate, diplomat, and politician; b. February 17, 1524; d. December 26, 1574. He was, with his brother, a leader of the Roman Catholic party against the Huguenots.

Lorraine, Claude de. [Title, 1st Duke of **Guise.**] French general and politician; b. October 20, 1496; d. at Joinville, France, April 12, 1550. Grandfather of Mary, Queen of Scots.

Lorraine, François de. [Surnamed **La Balafre;** title, 2nd Duke of **Guise.**] French general and statesman; b. February 17, 1519; d. February 24, 1563. He captured Calais in 1558, thus finally driving England from the Continent.

Losada (lō-sä′ᵺä), **Diego de.** [Also, **de Lozada.**] Spanish soldier; b. at San Lucar de Barrameda, Spain, c1520; d. at Tocuyo, Venezuela, 1569. He founded Caracas and carried on war with the Indians.

Loschi (lôs′kē), **Antonio.** Humanist, writer, and diplomat; b. at Vicenza, c1365; d. there 1441. He served at the courts of Naples, Verona, and Milan, and as apostolic secretary under several popes. He accompanied John XXIII to the Council of Constance (1415) and when the latter fled returned to Vicenza. He was papal secretary under Martin V and Eugenius IV, and accompanied the latter when he fled to Florence. His best work was done during his stay at Milan, under the Visconti (1388–1420). In this period he wrote letters and speeches, a commentary on some of the *Orations* of Cicero, translated Quintilian into Italian, and was the first to write Latin tragedies based on the *Iliad* and the *Odyssey.* His tragedy drawn from the *Iliad* was *Achilles;* that from the *Odyssey* was *Ulixes.*

Loschi, Jacopo. Painter of the school of Parma; b. at Parma, c1425; d. at Carpi, 1503. Among his works is a signed and dated (1471) *Madonna and Child and Angels,* and *Visitation and SS. Ilarius and Jerome,* National Gallery, Parma.

Lotichius (lo̜-tik′i-us), **Petrus Secundus.** German professor of medicine and neo-Latin poet in the manner of Ovid and Vergil; b. at Niederzell, Germany, 1528; d. 1560. His sincere and lovely elegies and songs were printed in 1551 as *Elegiarum liber et carminum libellus.*

Lotto (lōt′tō), **Lorenzo.** Painter; b. at Venice, c1480; d. at Loreto, 1556. He was probably a pupil of Alvise Vivarini, and was influenced, as were all Venetians of his age, by Giovanni Bellini. Later influences were those of Giorgione, Palma Vecchio, Titian, and possibly Correggio. The influence of Vivarini appears in the earlier work in firm outlines and veiled chiaroscuro, of Bellini in color and form, and of Giorgione in delicate landscapes and play of light. From all these influences he evolved an intensely personal style, one that reflected an individual and emotional concern with the forces that came to ravage Italy: the repressive domination of Spain in Italian affairs and the oppressive role of the Church as the Counter-Reformation took firm hold in the later part of his life. Devoting himself to painting, with apparently few deep personal attachments, he produced a large body of work. Toward the end of his life his preoccupation with religion led him to withdraw to the spiritual center at Loreto (1552), where he became a lay brother (1554) and spent the rest of his life. He painted at Recanati, for the first time when he was still very young, at Treviso, Iesi, Bergamo, Trescore, Ancona, for short periods at Venice, at Loreto, and in smaller places in the Marches. Among his early works, still very much in the 15th-century manner, are *Virgin and Child with St. Peter Martyr* (1503), Naples; the signed and dated (1506) *St. Jerome*, Louvre, notable for his keen observation of landscape and his appreciation of the forms of nature; and *Portrait of Bernardo de' Rossi* (1505), bishop of Treviso, now at Naples, which has so strong a German aura that it is probable he was familiar with the work of northern painters. A cover for the portrait, *Allegory*, is in the National Gallery, Washington. Other works of the early period include an *Assumption* (1506), Asolo, and a polyptych, *Madonna Enthroned between Saints*, Pinacoteca Comunale, Recanati, in which his departure from 15th-century forms begins to be apparent in the greater sensitivity of the expressions and in softened color. In 1509 he went to Rome to paint in the *Stanze* of the Vatican at the invitation of Julius II. It is not known how long he remained there; however, it was long enough for him to be deeply impressed by the work of Raphael. His attempts to fuse Raphael's broad forms, color, and movement with his own style appear in his *Transfiguration* (c1512), Recanati, and *Deposition* (1512), Iesi. The attempt to express his temperament and artistic vision in Raphael's manner was not entirely successful; although he returned to his own manner his contact with Raphael's work left some imprint on his style. Julius II, dazzled by Raphael, turned over the work of decorating the rooms in the Vatican to him; paintings executed there by previous painters were largely replaced; what Lorenzo may have done in Rome has perished. In 1513 he went to Bergamo. The years he spent in and about that city were highly productive. Of 1515 is his double portrait of the Della Torre brothers, National Gallery, London, that shows some traces of the Raphael influence. In succeeding years he painted altarpieces for the churches of S. Bartolomeo (1516), S. Bernardino and S. Spirito (1521) at Bergamo, frescoed the Suardi Chapel at Trescore with scenes from the life of St. Barbara and other saints (1524), and executed frescoes at S. Michele del Pozzo Bianco (1525) near Bergamo. He painted for Celana, Ponteranica, and Spalato, among other places. He was at the full development of his style in the years at Bergamo; the altarpieces, panels, and frescoes are notable for delicacy of feeling, a richer palette, airy and luminous landscapes, and control of light effects. His *Marriage of St. Catherine* (1523), Carrara Academy, Bergamo, is among the great achievements of the period. Other works of about this time are *Madonna between St. Joseph and St. Jerome* (1526), Civica Pinacoteca, Iesi, with its echoes of Correggio, and the passionate and grandiose *Crucifixion* (1531), Monte S. Giusto. Also of the time when he was mainly at Bergamo was a series of designs for the wood inlay of the choir stalls of S. Maria Maggiore. In 1526 he was painting in SS. Giovanni e Paolo at Venice. Hitherto he had worked little in his native city, and it was perhaps from this time that he felt the influence of Titian, an influence that resulted in a loosening of his style and increasingly vibrant color. Leaving Venice, he worked again for patrons at Treviso, Iesi, Ancona, and elsewhere in the area. About 1535 he painted a Madonna for Osimo, in the March of Ancona; the painting was stolen in 1911 and has never been recovered. Of 1539 is the *Madonna del Rosario with Six Saints*, Church of S. Domenico at Cingoli. In the background above the Madonna, who is seated before a rose hedge, are fifteen roundels arched in three groups of five, in each of which appears a complete and finished painting of a scene from the Gospels. In 1545 he was back at Venice, and four years later asked Sansovino to sell certain of his works as he planned to leave Venice. An account book that he kept from 1538 records his works, his assistants, and apprentices, and indicates that he had some difficulty managing money. This may be the reason why such a busy and productive painter found it necessary to raise money at this time. After two abortive attempts to live with friends or relatives he retired to Loreto (1552).

Lotto had little interest in secular subjects and he never painted the nude. Increasingly sensitive and emotional, of a troubled spirit, his work took on elements of 16th-century mannerism; his painting has a strong personal quality, in contrast to the grandiose universality of the great painters of his age, notably Titian. In addition to the large number of religious paintings, he left a number of sensitive portraits, marked by his ability to project the personality of the sitter with a certain intimacy and compassion. Among these are those of *Christopher Columbus*, Chicago, *Cardinal Pompeo Colonna*, Colonna Gallery, Rome, *Portrait of a Youth*, Castello Sforzesco, Milan, and *Gian Giacomo Stuer and His Son Gian Antonio*, Johnson Collection, Philadelphia. In addition to the works in churches mentioned above, and many others, there are examples of Lotto's painting in the Carrara Academy at Bergamo, the Accademia, Venice, Uffizi, Florence, Poldi Pezzoli Museum, Milan, at Rome, Paris, Madrid, London, Berlin, Leningrad, and Vienna; in the Museum of Fine Arts, Boston, Fogg Museum, Cambridge, Johnson Collection, Philadelphia, the Metropolitan Museum, New York, National Gallery, Washington; at Brooklyn, Chicago, Cleveland, Houston, New Orleans, Princeton, Santa Monica, Sarasota (Florida), and elsewhere.

Louis II (lö′i). Duke of Anjou, count of Provence and (titular) king of Naples (1384–1417); b. at Toulon, October 7, 1377; d. at Angers, April 29, 1417. He disputed the claim of Ladislaus to the kingdom of Naples. The basis of Louis' claim was that Joanna I, queen of Naples, had named his father, Louis I, as her heir. Louis I had been unsuccessful in his attempts to take the kingdom. Louis II, supported by the antipope Clement VII, who crowned him king, occupied Naples (1386) and much of the surrounding territory. Ladislaus, who was recognized as king by Pope Boniface IX, drove Louis out of Naples (1399). Although he aided John XXIII to defeat Ladislaus at Roccasecca, the terms of the peace treaty that John signed with Ladislaus granted the latter such concessions that Louis withdrew to France. While Louis was occupied in Italy, his wife Yolande of Aragon governed Anjou. Their son, Louis III, succeeded as duke of Anjou and inherited his father's claims to Naples.

Louis III (of *Anjou*). Duke of Anjou and (titular) king of Naples; b. September 25, 1403; d. at Cosenza, November 15, 1434. He was the son of Louis II of Anjou and Yolande of Aragon. He succeeded his father (1417) as duke of Anjou and king of Naples. At that time, Joanna II was reigning as queen of Naples. Martin V proclaimed (1413) Louis as Joanna's heir and the following year he tried to occupy the kingdom, with the help of Muzio Attendolo Sforza and the secret assistance of the pope. Joanna named (1420) Alfonso V of Aragon as her heir and Louis was unsuccessful against him. By 1423 Joanna feared Alfonso more than Louis, disinherited the former and named the latter duke of Calabria and her heir. Louis was killed (1434) fighting the prince of Taranto, and his claim to the kingdom of Naples passed to his younger brother René.

Louis IX (of *France*). [Known as **Saint Louis.**] King of France (1226–1270); b. at Poissy, April 25, 1214; d. near Tunis, August 25, 1270. He was the son of Louis VIII, whom he succeeded while still a child. His mother kept the royal power intact during his minority. In 1244, Louis declared for a crusade and, after much preparation, left France in 1248. He captured Damietta in 1249, but during an expedition against Cairo was defeated and captured, with the whole of the French army, at Mansura, Egypt, in April 1250. He was liberated later but remained in the East until 1252. He returned to France in 1254. The remainder of his reign was peaceful and Louis' reputation as a just, noble ruler grew with the years. He captured the imagination of his contemporaries as a model Christian king dispensing ready justice and performing touching acts of charity. He was called upon to settle many quarrels, especially with the English. He supported the claim of his brother Charles of Anjou to the throne of Naples, but he did so reluctantly and acted constantly as a brake on the ambitions of that prince. In 1267 Louis declared another crusade which, through the machinations of Charles, sailed against Charles' principal rival, Tunis (1270). Louis died less than two months afterward of plague. He was canonized by Pope Boniface VIII in 1297. He was succeeded by his son, Philip III.

Louis X (of *France*). [Called **Le Hutin**, "the Quarreler."] King of France (1314–1316); b. at Paris, October 4, 1289; d. June 5, 1316. He was the oldest son of Philip IV, and had inherited the kingdom of Navarre through his mother, Joan of Navarre, in 1305. His short reign as king of France was in the shadow of his uncle Charles of Valois, and was marked by a resurgence of the power of the great nobles. He was succeeded by his posthumous son John I, who lived only five days.

Louis XI (of *France*). King of France (1461–1483); b. at Bourges, France, July 3, 1423; d. at Plessis-les-Tours, near Tours, France, August 30, 1483. He was the son and successor of Charles VII. As dauphin, Louis intrigued against his father, and on his accession to the throne (1461) purged his court of adherents of his father and drew his own ministers principally from the middle class. He allied himself with the bourgeoisie in his policy of breaking the power of the nobility and of centralizing authority in the person of the king. He was successful in destroying the power of the great feudatories and laid the foundation of the absolute monarchy that afterward prevailed in France. He firmly established the French border at the Pyrenees, united Burgundy to the French crown, annexed the duchies of Anjou and Bar (1480), Maine and Province (1481), and Picardy, Artois, and Franche Comte (1482). He interfered in the wars of the Yorkists and Lancastrians in England, and had great influence in Italy. The final step in the assertion of claims in Italy was taken when Charles VIII, his son and successor, invaded the peninsula. Louis' last years were spent in fear of murder and in isolation, surrounded by guards and attended by physicians and astrologers.

Louis XII (of *France*). King of France (1498–1515); b. at Blois, France, June 27, 1462; d. January 1, 1515. A son of Charles d'Orléans and a descendant of the younger son of Charles V, he succeeded Charles VIII. He divorced his wife, Jeanne, daughter of Louis XI, and married (1499) Anne of Brittany, widow of Charles VIII, in order to retain the duchy of Brittany for the crown. At his coronation he took the title of duke of Milan (as grandson of Valentina Visconti, although females were expressly excluded from the succession), king of Naples and Jerusalem, as well as king of France. French preoccupation with Italy, initiated by Charles VIII, persisted under Louis. In 1499 he expelled Ludovico Sforza (il Moro) and took possession of Milan. He conquered Naples in 1501 in alliance with Ferdinand V of Castile (Ferdinand the Catholic), but disagreed with his ally over the division of the spoils, with the result that his army was defeated by the Spanish general Gonzalo de Córdoba on the Garigliano in 1503. In 1508 he joined the emperor Maximilian I, Pope Julius II, and Ferdinand the Catholic in the League of Cambrai against Venice. However, the Pope, who feared the presence of the French in Italy, negotiated in 1511 the Holy League with Venice and Ferdinand the Catholic for the expulsion of the French; the league was afterward joined by the emperor and Henry VIII of England. Henry and the emperor defeated the French at Guinegate in the "battle of the spurs" (August 16, 1513), and the French were in the same year expelled from Italy; but Louis succeeded in breaking up the league by diplomacy, and was preparing to reconquer Milan when he died. The year before his death he had married Mary Tudor, sister of Henry VIII of England. He was succeeded by Francis I, a cousin.

Louis IV (of the *Holy Roman Empire*). [Called **Louis the Bavarian.**] Emperor of the Holy Roman Empire (1314–1347); b. c1287; d. near Munich, October 11, 1347. He was the son of Louis II, duke of Bavaria, and was opposed by Frederick, duke of Austria, whom he made prisoner in 1322. He was crowned emperor in 1328, climaxing a struggle with the pope over the right of the secular princes to choose an emperor. He declared John XXII deposed and set up Nicholas V as pope. In 1338 the electoral princes met and adopted resolutions to the effect that the emperor derived his right to the German and imperial crowns by virtue of his election by the electoral princes, independent of any coronation by the pope. He was succeeded by Charles IV.

Louis of Nassau (nas'ô), See **Nassau-Dillenburg,** Count **Louis of.**

Lovati (lō-vä'tē), **Lovato de'.** Jurist and humanist; b. at Padua, 1241; d. 1309. He has been called the first Italian humanist because of his enthusiasm for Livy and Seneca, and for his poems in the classical manner. With Albertino Musatto and others, he belonged to the so-called Cenacolo Padovano, an early humanist circle.

Loveira (lö-vā'rạ), **Vasco de.** See **Lobeira** or **Loveira, Vasco de.**

Lowther (lou'ŦHėr), Sir **Richard.** English

protector of Mary, Queen of Scots; b. 1529; d. at Lowther, Westmorland, England, January 27, 1607.

Luca di Borgo (lö′kä dē bôr′gō), Fra. See **Pacioli, Luca.**

Luca da Perugia (dä pā-rö′jä). Painter of the first quarter of the 15th century. He helped decorate the Church of S. Petronio, Bologna (1417).

Luca di Tommè (dē tôm-mā′). Sienese painter; b. at Siena, c1330; d. there, 1389. He was listed on the register of Sienese painters (1355) and became a close follower, first of Pietro Lorenzetti, whose virile drawing he admired, and then of Simone Martini. He produced many works, including a polyptych, *Madonna and Child Enthroned, with Saints and Angels* (1362), signed by him and Niccolò di Ser Sozzo Tegliacci; another, *St. Anne, Virgin and Child,* signed and dated (1367), both at Siena; a *Crucifixion,* signed and dated (1366), Pisa; *Madonna and Child with Saints,* signed and dated (1370), Rieti; and his masterpiece, *Assumption of the Virgin,* Yale University, New Haven. A number of his works are at Siena and in collections and churches in the vicinity, and he is represented at Perugia, New York, and elsewhere.

Lucantonio de' Uberti (lö-kän-tō′nyō dā ö-ber′tē). Florentine engraver who also worked at Venice, and who became a printer at Verona in 1503.

Luciani (lö-chä′nē), **Sebastiano.** See **Sebastiano del Piombo.**

Lucina (lö-chē′nä). In Lodovico Ariosto's *Orlando Furioso,* the beloved of King Norandino of Damascus. She was captured by the orc, a sea monster, and was freed with the assistance of Gradasso and Mandricardo.

Ludovico d'Angelo Mattioli (lö-dō-vē′kō dän′jā-lō mät-tyō′lē). Perugian painter; active between 1481 and 1525. He was a follower of Perugino. Several panels of saints are in the National Gallery of Umbria at Perugia.

Ludovico il Moro (il mō′rō). See **Sforza, Ludovico.**

Luini (lö-ē′nē), **Bernardino.** Painter; b. c1480; d. at Milan, 1532. Nothing is known concerning his early life and artistic training. He was probably of Lombard origin. His manner shows some contact with the brilliant warm color of Venetian painting but is fundamentally Lombard in style. Early influences on him were those of Bramantino, Andrea Solario, Bergognone, and Foppa. The most important influence then became that of Leonardo da Vinci. From the latter he adopted the half-smile of his *Madonnas,* soft modeling, a light veiling of the atmosphere, and sometimes the composition itself, as a *Holy Family,* Ambrosiana, that follows Leonardo's *Virgin with St. Anne.* Imitating and sentimentalizing Leonardo's manner in many respects, he was enormously popular in his day and produced a large body of work in panel and especially in fresco. Noted for the charm of his female figures in his panel painting, the frescoes are marked by a more exuberant spirit and imagination, and show less dependence on Leonardo than his sweet and gentle *Madonnas.* He passed what is known of his life painting in and about Milan, in Lombardy, and at Lugano. He often painted several versions, or even replicas, of the same subject, as *Salome with the Head of the Baptist,* of which there are versions in the Museum of Fine Arts, Boston, Uffizi, Florence, at Isola Bella, Paris, and Vienna. The earliest work that can certainly be ascribed to him is a fresco, *Madonna and Child* (1512), in the Abbey of Chiaravalle, near Milan. Other fresco series are those in the Chapel of the Sacrament in the Church of S. Giorgio, Milan (c1516); *Madonna and Child between SS. Anthony and Barbara* (1521), originally painted in S. Maria di Brera and now in the Brera Gallery; *The Crowning with Thorns* (1521), Ambrosiana; frescoes on the life of St. Mauritius in the Church of S. Maurizio (1521–1524); a series on the life of the Virgin in the sanctuary of the Madonna dei Miracoli at Saronno (1525–1532); and a great series painted in the Villa Pelucca at Monza. The last series had scenes from mythology, the Bible and Sacred History, and from contemporary life. The frescoes were detached early in the 19th century; most of them are in the Brera, others are at Isolabella (Palazzo Borromeo), Chantilly, London (Wallace Collection), and Paris. Nine scenes on the legend of Procris and Cephalus from the Casa Rabia are in the National Gallery, Washington. Frescoes from a number of churches at Milan are now in the Brera. Other works include a well-known *Crucifixion* and a fresco, *Last Supper,* Church of S. Maria degli Angeli, Lugano, a youthful *Deposition,* S. Maria della Passione, Milan, the altarpiece, *Madonna and Saints,* S. Magno, Legnano, *Madonna del Roseto,* Brera, panels and frescoes in the Certosa di Pavia, and many others. The largest number of his paintings is at Milan, in the Brera especially, and in the Poldi Pezzoli Museum, Castello Sforzesco, and the Ambrosiana. Other examples of his paintings are at Bergamo, Como, Rome, Turin, Brussels, Budapest, Copenhagen, Leningrad, Madrid, Ottawa, Vienna; at Baltimore, Brooklyn, Cambridge, Cincinnati, Cleveland, Detroit, Houston, Los Angeles, Muncie (Indiana), New Orleans, Philadelphia, San Diego, Sarasota, and elsewhere.

Lully (lul'i), **Raymond.** [Latin, **Raimundus Lullus;** Catalan, **Ramón Lull;** Spanish, **Raimundo Lulio;** French, **Raimond Lulle.**] Spanish scholastic, missionary to the Mohammedans; b. at Palma, Balearic Islands, c1235; d. at Bougie, Africa, June 30, 1315. He wrote *Ars Magna,* a treatise on symbolic logic; a novel *Blanquerna,* and such poetry as *El Desconort* and *Lo Cant de Ramon,* all marked by an obscuring mysticism.

Luna (lö'nä), **Álvaro de.** Spanish courtier and poet; b. 1388; d. at Valladolid, Spain, June 2, 1453. He became (1408) a page at the court of John II of Castile, rising quickly to the position of favorite and minister. Twice exiled and reinstated, he lost the favor of the king, fell a victim to a conspiracy of the court nobles, was arrested at Burgos, and shortly after was executed at Valladolid.

Luna, Pedro de. Original name of the antipope **Benedict XIII.**

Luna y Arellano (ē ä-rā-lyä'nō), **Tristán de.** Spanish captain; b. in Aragon, Spain, early in the 16th century; fl. c1530–c1561. He served with Coronado in Mexico in 1539.

Lunette [lū-net']. A crescent-like or semicircular space in a vaulted ceiling, a wall, and so on, as a space at the top of a wall intersected by a vault; a painting or relief filling such a space.

Lusiad (lö'si-ad), **The.** [Portuguese, **Os Lusíadas,** "The Portuguese."] Most famous work in Portuguese literature, an epic poem in ten cantos of *oitavas* (ottava rima) by Luiz de Camões; it celebrates the discovery of the sea route to India by Vasco da Gama, the Portuguese navigator. In treating this epic theme, Camões finds occasion to give much of the history of Portugal, through a variety of lively narrative sections, and to praise the many accomplishments of the Portuguese. Portugal, whose sons are fearless travelers on the sea lanes of the earth, and who bring civilization and Christianity to the unenlightened, is the hero of the epic. The work breathes the new spirit of humanism, in which man, the center of the universe, extends his control over nature. The whole is expressed with a nobility and beauty of language and an artistry of execution that make it one of the great masterpieces of Renaissance literature. First published in 1572, it won for Camões, who desperately needed it, a small royal pension. *The Lusiad* has had scores of editions and has been translated into nearly every European language.

Lusignan (lü-zē-nyäṅ). Noble French family, originating in Poitou, which ruled in Cyprus from 1192 to 1475 and in Jerusalem during the Crusades.

Luteri (lö-te'rē), **Giovanni.** See **Dossi, Dosso.**

Luther (lö'thėr; German, lö'tėr), **Martin.** German religious reformer and translator of the Bible; b. at Eisleben, Germany, November 10, 1483; d. there, February 18, 1546. His father, who was a miner by trade, removed with his family to Mansfeld the year after the birth of his son. His early education was obtained at Magdeburg and at Eisenach (1497). In 1501 he matriculated at Erfurt for the study of jurisprudence. He took his examination in 1505, and subsequently delivered lectures on the physics and ethics of Aristotle. In that same year, against the wishes of his family, he determined to become a monk and entered the Augustinian monastery at Erfurt. In 1507 he was consecrated a priest and in 1508 was called as professor of philosophy to the University of Wittenberg. In 1511 he went to Rome on business connected with his monastic order. It was a traumatic experience for him to be made aware of the corruption, luxury, and licentiousness that prevailed at the capitol of Christendom. In 1512, after his return to Wittenberg, he was made doctor of theology. His first important action in the direction of ecclesiastical reform was his publication (October 31, 1517), on the church door at Wittenberg, of ninety-five theses against the sale of indulgences by the Dominican Johann Tetzel. When he nailed his theses to the church door Luther did not intend to defy the church. He was simply publishing propositions that, as was the custom, he wished to debate, in order to correct abuses. The theses aroused widespread sympathy and support, especially among the German peasantry and among civic authorities. The peasants felt themselves exploited and the civic authorities resented the drain of funds to Rome. The proceeds from the sale of the indulgences provided a rich source of revenue for Rome and, though the sale was condemned by many theologians, it had continued despite strong protests. Luther's propositions were immediately condemned as heretical, and violent attacks were made upon him from various quarters, both before and after a summons to Rome (which he did not obey). He also received powerful support. In 1520 he published three tracts: *Address to the Christian Nobles of the German Nation*, urging the independence of the Germans in ecclesiastical affairs and the supremacy of the civic authorities in temporal matters; *On the Babylonian Captivity of the Church of God*, an affirmation of his belief that no intermediary (priest) is necessary between an individual and his God; and *Christian Liberty*, on the freedom of the individual to be guided by the Bible in his faith, conscience, and religious practice. These tracts are known as his "Primary Works" and contain the first principles of the Reformation. The central theological principle of the Reformation was justification by faith. The ecclesiastical principle was that the Bible is the only rule of faith and practice. Another principle was the priesthood of all believers. In 1520, with his adherents, he was excommunicated by Pope Leo X in the bull *Exsurge Domine*, and his writings were burned at Rome, Cologne, and Louvain. Luther's original aim had been to reform the church from within, not to break it apart. This had now become impossible for him as his views increasingly struck at the foundations of the church, notably in his belief that the priesthood was unnecessary as an intermediary between the individual and his God, and that the sacraments were helpful as an aid to faith but not essential for salvation. He defied the pope by publicly burning, at Wittenberg, the bull of excommunication and the decretals of the pope, to whom he renounced all allegiance. At the Diet of Worms (April, 1521), whither he was summoned by the emperor Charles V, he made the celebrated speech which ended with: "Here, I stand. I cannot do otherwise. God help me. Amen." In spite of his vigorous defense of his doctrines, he was proscribed by the emperor. On his return from Worms through the Thuringian Forest he was, by order of his friend Frederick II, elector of Saxony, ostensibly taken prisoner and conveyed to the Wartburg at Eisenach, where he remained in disguise the following ten months under the name of Junker Georg. Since he considered that the Bible was the ultimate source of faith and conduct, he set about making it available to the Germans in their own language. During his time in disguise he translated the New Testament, and had already completed it when he left the Wartburg in March, 1522. At this time, in spite of a new proscription by the emperor and at great risk to his person, he returned to Wittenberg, and delivered there a series of sermons against the fanaticism of the puritanical image-breakers. Here, too, was published in 1523 the translation of the New Testament. He had already begun the translation of the Old Testament, of which the books of Moses were put into print in 1523 and the Psalms in 1524; and in the latter year appeared also his first hymnbook. In 1524, further, he laid aside his cowl, and in 1525 married Katharina von Bora, a nun who had renounced her vows and left the convent. From 1526 to 1529 he was engaged in the preparation of a new church service. In 1529 he issued two catechisms. In this year also he engaged in the conference at Marburg with Zwingli and other Swiss divines. Differences over the Eucharist and predestination, among others, led to a split in the Protestant movement.

The Lutheran translation of the whole Bible, completed in 1532, was finally published in 1534. It was revised in 1541, and the subsequent editions of 1543 and 1545 also received a few amendments. During the whole of his struggles for the Reformation, he wrote numerous polemical pamphlets which exhibited him as a most powerful and passionate advocate. His *Tischreden* (*Table-Talk*) contains his opinions on a variety of subjects, the principal source of the material being Lauterbach's *Tagebuch* (*Diary*) from 1538. In 1530 he began to make a new version, in prose, of Aesop's and other classical fables. Besides prose, he also wrote a number of sacred hymns, whose prototype in construction and melody he found in the folk songs. The *Hymn-Book* of 1524 contains four hymns written by him; that of 1545 thirty-seven. In the edition of 1528 was published for the first time the most celebrated of his hymns, *Ein feste Burg ist unser Gott* (*A Mighty Fortress Is Our God*), written probably in 1527, the melody of which he is also said to have composed. Luther may also be regarded as the founder of the present literary language of Germany, that is, of so-called New High German. In his *Tischreden* he states his language to be that of the Saxon Chancery, to which in reality his early writings closely conform. It is, however, not the language of the court, but of the people, and much of the vocabulary of the Bible translation was drawn from Low German as well as from High German sources. His own language, contrasted in his early and later writings, shows a distinct progression toward a more consistently normalized and universal form. Books were written afterward, notably in Switzerland, in dialect, but they were an ever decreasing minority, and writers and printers in all parts of German-speaking territory soon accepted the language of Luther as a standard to which they consciously or unconsciously conformed.

Lydgate (lid′gāt), **John.** English poet; b. at Lydgate, near Newmarket, Suffolk, c1370; d. 1451. He entered the church in 1389, and gained a position as poet at the court of Henry IV, which he held during the reign of Henry V and after the accession of Henry VI. After 1390 he made the acquaintance of Geoffrey Chaucer, often calling himself "Chaucer's disciple." His numerous works include *Falls of Princes*, a narrative poem written between 1430 and 1438; *Troy Book*, in heroic couplets, containing a panegyric on Chaucer (1412–1420; first printed in 1513); *The Story of Thebes*, intended as an additional Canterbury tale (1420); *The Life of Our Lady*, a religious narrative poem, printed by Caxton in 1484; *The Dance of Death*, from the French, printed first in 1554 (also, with Holbein's drawings, in 1794); *The Court of Sapience*, a philosophical work printed by Caxton (c1481); *The Temple of Glass*, printed by Caxton (c1479); and a number of lives of saints, allegories, fables, historical and political poems, and satires. *The Complaint of the Black Knight*, which was once attributed to Chaucer, is by Lydgate, as are a number of the minor poems which have been attributed to Chaucer.

Lymodin (lē-mo-dañ), Sieur **de.** Title of **Jodelle, Étienne.**

Lyndsay (lin′zi), Sir **David.** See **Lindsay,** Sir **David.**

M

Mabuse (mȧ-büz). [Original name, **Jan Gossaert** (or **Gessart**).] Flemish painter; b. at Mauberge, in what is now Nord, France, probably c1470; d. at Antwerp, Belgium, 1541. He went to England where he painted the *Marriage of Henry VII and Elizabeth of York*, and portraits of the king's children.

Macaronic or **Maccaronic poetry.** Burlesque verse in an artificial language. The language has the appearance of Latin, but is a mixture of Italian dialect and slang words that have been given Latin endings with classical Latin words, the whole presented with Latin syntax. It is a parody of Latin that only one familiar with that language could employ. The language had been used by students at Padua, and was used by some Renaissance poets, but only with the popular satiric works of Teofilo Folengo did it become an artistic literary medium. He said its name came from a Venetian dish, a coarse country pudding made of flour, cheese, and butter. In general, Maccaronic verse dealt in a light-hearted way with the Bohemian life of poets and students, and was largely concerned with eating, drinking, and wenching.

MacDonnell (mạk-don′ẹl; also, in Scotland, mak-dō-nel′), **Sorley Boy.** Scots-Irish chieftain, b. at Ballycastle, Ireland, c1505; d. there, 1590. He was lord of the Route (northern Antrim), and constable of Dunluce Castle. By overtures to Queen Elizabeth he tried unsuccessfully to secure the Hebridean Scots settlements in Antrim against his rival, Shane

O'Neill. Forced to flee to Scotland, he admitted his lack of legal right to Ulster and submitted to the government.

Machault or **Machaut** (må-shō), **Guillaume de.** See **Guillaume de Machault** (or **Machaut.**)

Machiavelli (mä-kyä-vel′lē), **Niccolò.** Statesman, historian, and man of letters; b. at Florence, May 3, 1469; d. there, June 22, 1527. Machiavelli, whose name has given a word of unpleasant connotation to the English language (first used, 1568), was born of an ancient and noble but not wealthy family. His father was a lawyer and possessed some property that afterward enabled the son to live in comparative comfort in his banishment from political life. Little is known of Machiavelli's early life. From his letters we learn that he was a devoted student and that he possessed a thorough knowledge of the Roman writers. Livy was his favorite. As a young man he held a minor post in the chancery of Florence. Following the death of Savonarola (1498), whose fervor had been instrumental in the downfall of the Medici and the restoration of the republic at Florence (1494), a new government was set up under Piero Soderini. Machiavelli, known to be an able and energetic patriot, became (1498) secretary of the chancery, responsible to the Council of Ten. The Council was the body that dealt with foreign affairs and with war, and in so doing was concerned with nearly all aspects of Florentine political life. Machiavelli held his post from 1498 to the overthrow of Soderini's government in 1512. The post was not highly paid, nor was great honor attached to it, but in it Machiavelli was at the center of affairs and was charged with great responsibility. In 1499 he went on a mission to Caterina Sforza at Forlì; in 1500 to Louis XII of France; in 1502, and again in 1503, to Cesare Borgia in the Romagna and Rome. (In 1502 Cesare Borgia, duke of Valentinois, seemed about to succeed in his attempt to carve out a kingdom in the Romagna; in 1503 it was evident that he had failed to do so.) In 1504 he went again to France, and in 1506 accompanied Pope Julius II on his march through Umbria and Emilia. He went (1508) on a mission to the emperor Maximilian at Bolzano, and (1510) on a third mission to France. To these important diplomatic missions could be added numerous others of less importance. His missions introduced him to all the rulers and tyrants of Italy and to those in lands beyond the Alps. He took careful note of the political institutions in other states. He made shrewd analyses and commentaries on the men with whom he came in contact, and noted well how frequently their publicly expressed policies were at variance with their secret motives and intentions. From all his missions he sent back reports and despatches that are models of clarity and analysis, and practical in their recommendations.

In the war with Pisa, he went often to the camp bivouacked about the besieged city. What he saw there reinforced his conviction that mercenary troops were not only costly but ineffective. They were more interested in their pay than in action and completely unreliable, ready to change sides whenever it suited their interest. From this time, he urged the Florentines to raise a citizen militia, on the ground that only the citizens have the interest and the ardor to protect their state. He succeeded in winning Soderini's approval for a militia and was given the task (1506) of raising, organizing, and training it. Throughout his political writings Machiavelli inveighs against the evils of hired troops, "the bane of all Italy." His advocacy of a citizen militia seemed justified when (June, 1509) with its aid, Pisa finally surrendered and opened its gates to the Florentines, after a 15-year struggle. Machiavelli, who had chosen the time for the successful attack and disposed his militia wisely, was given great credit by the delirious Florentines for the fall of Pisa. This was perhaps, to him, the high point of his career, but it was an ephemeral success. His place in history is secure on other grounds. In 1512 the government of Piero Soderini was overthrown and the Medici were restored. Machiavelli lost his post. He was unjustly accused of complicity in an abortive anti-Medici plot, was imprisoned, put to torture, then freed. With no more part to play in state affairs he left Florence. He retired to his property at San Casciano, there to eat his heart out in longing to return to the theater of Florentine politics. To occupy his time, he resumed his study of the Roman writers. Famous is the letter he sent to his friend Vettori, describing his days in exile: work on his property in the morning; dicing and gaming, to the accompaniment of coarse shouting and accusation, with the villagers at the tavern in the afternoon; then, having attired himself suitably for such company, retiring to his study in the evening for the companionship of learned men of the past. He read, thought, and wrote. In all the time of his banishment he sought by every means, however servile, to secure employment under the Medici, but he had been too ardent a supporter of the republic of Soderini for the Medici to trust him. He was, after a time, allowed to return to visit Florence, and was not persecuted further, but he was not employed. This was a thing he could not understand. As far as he was concerned, it did not matter who was at its head as long as he served Florence. Politics were his life; he was not motivated by personal ambition or a desire for glory as was his contemporary, Francesco Guicciardini. He was quite simply a patriot and burned with the desire to serve his beloved city in the capacity for which he knew he was eminently qualified. When the Medici were overthrown (1527) he hoped for recognition from the restored republic, but he had made no secret of his overtures to the Medici, unrewarded as they had been, and now the republic distrusted him. Soon after the restoration that ended so tragically, he died. Possessed of one of the keenest intellects of the time, fascinated by politics, in his social and family life Machiavelli was a child of his age, a fairly constant husband, an agreeable companion, and a gay and witty spirit.

Machiavelli was driven to set down his thoughts in writing, to analyze and categorize events as he had observed them. He produced an enormous amount of work in a short time. His writings may be roughly classified as literary, historical, and political. In the period of his banishment he wrote what has been called the greatest of Italian comedies, his *Mandragola* (which see), and a second comedy in the same vein, *Clizia* (which see). These are intricately plotted, realistic, racy, Florentine comedies. Though the emphasis is certainly on the cleverness by which, in each case, an old man's folly is exposed, his observation of his Florentine compatriots is shrewd; he knows their habits of mind and portrays their characters with clarity and their own brand of humor. The novella, *Belfagor* (which see), is a satiric tale of an archdevil who comes to Florence and gets a taste of life on earth. In the literary field he also wrote sonnets, canzoni, and other lyrics; *capitoli* on such subjects as Fortune, Opportunity, Ingratitude, and Ambition; carnival songs; two chronicles, *Decennale primo*, in terza rima, covering the period 1494–1504, and the incomplete *Decennale secondo*, covering the period 1504–1509; *Asino d'oro* (*The Golden Ass*) in which he satirized Florentines as various animals; and a dialogue on language, *Dialogo intorno alla lingua*. Much of his poetry, which was not particularly inspired, has been lost. His *Mandragola* is a work of art and is still performed. In the historical field are shrewd reports on France and Germany, *Ritratti delle cose della Francia e dell' Alemagna*, as he had observed the institutions and characteristics of those countries (he admired the Germans for their discipline and sobriety); a description of Cesare Borgia's massacre of his former captains and allies at Senigaglia, *Del modo tenuto dal duca Valentino nell'ammazzare Vitelozzo Vitelli, . . .* ; a summary of the war with Lucca, *Sommario delle cose di Lucca;* a life of Castruccio Castracani, lord of Lucca, that gives an admiring picture of an idealized despot, a forerunner of *The Prince;* and *Storie fiorentine*. The last-named is the most important by far in this group. The work was commissioned for the University of Florence by Cardinal Giulio de' Medici (the future Pope Clement VII) in 1520. The first eight books were dedicated to Clement in 1525. With great economy and clarity, and a thoroughly modern and scientific approach, he presents what happened, why, and the results. The history ends with the death of Lorenzo the Magnificent (1492). Machiavelli, who was given some minor political chores by Pope Clement, died before he could finish his work. In the political field his writings comprised his many lucid reports and despatches from his missions; his dialogues on the art of war, *Arte della guerra;* the *Discorsi sopra le prima deca di Tito Livio* (*Discourses on the First Ten Books of Livy*); and *Il Principe* (*The Prince*). The dialogues on the art of war are detailed and technical, reiterate his conviction that mercenary troops are an evil and that a native militia is essential, and make clear the indissoluble connection between politics and military problems. The *Discorsi* are commentaries on passages from

Livy. In them he seeks by examples from history, his own and contemporary experience, to present various state problems and their solutions for a modern statesman. It was his belief that the experience of the past can provide solutions for the present, since men, he reasoned, are the same in all ages. Of the three books of the *Discorsi,* the first describes the foundation, organization, and internal affairs of the state; the second treats of the expansion and foreign affairs of the state; and the third deals with miscellaneous problems and the effect of various individuals on the state. The *Discorsi* are the distillation of Machiavelli's political thought. Begun in 1513, they were completed in 1517. He read them as they were written to members of a literary group that met in the Rucellai gardens at Florence. In his dedication he states that his object is to set forth all he has learned in the course of long experience and wide reading. Of his conclusions, one is that a government combining a prince, optimates (the best), and the people is the wisest and most satisfactory form. This, he believes is what the government of republican Rome consisted of, and in his own day there was the example of Venice. Among many other political theories, Machiavelli thought religion could be useful to a good statesman, but was wrathfully certain that the Church was the main cause of disunity in the Italy of his day, and was well aware of the corruption that existed at the center of Christendom. He had not missed the lessons provided by the powerful new nations. With these lessons vividly before him he called for unity as the salvation of Italy. In his aims and in his writing he was first and foremost an Italian patriot. In 1513, before he wrote the *Discorsi,* Machiavelli finished his most noted work, *Il Principe* (*The Prince,* which see). The work stirred up a furore, largely because Machiavelli presented facts as he saw them, suggested remedies and methods for their efficiency rather than their ethics, and insisted throughout that the ends justified the means. In his view, the preservation and well-being of the state were paramount. In the conditions of Italy of his day desperate remedies were needed, and he suggested them. Throughout the Middle Ages political writers, theologically inspired, had accepted the state as a divine agency and had concerned themselves with expounding how, in view of its origin, it ought to act. Living in a new and frankly secular age, Machiavelli faced a new kind of state, the absolute monarchy, and with scientific detachment set himself to describe its actual behavior. He had no difficulty in showing that the state which had recently taken over many small principalities in Italy (Cesare Borgia's state) and, far more strikingly, the great monarchies of France, Spain, and England, practiced an unlimited sovereignty, the goal of which was power. Consequently, he deduced that modern states, no longer checked by considerations of religion and morality (if, indeed, they ever had been), dealt with one another on the level of unadulterated power politics. While this contention, commonly called Machiavellianism or Machiavellism, was and has continued to be heatedly rejected by many political scientists, it has so frequently been found to be in accord with the facts that its author has throughout the ages been alternately vilified and praised.

In an age when style and form were supreme, Machiavelli ignored them. His urgent aim was to communicate. His ideas march across the page in unbroken line. There are no detours by way of artistic phrases, no maneuvers for flourishes or elegance. "A state makes war on another either through a desire to become master or through fear of being conquered." "A state may be erected either by natives or by foreigners." "It may be free or not free." "Men act either through necessity or choice." "A ruler may be loved or feared." He states his thesis, develops it, gives examples, and draws his conclusion or makes his recommendations. His style, stripped of embellishment and affected imitation, is vigorous, unvarnished, and virile—a vehicle whose one purpose is to communicate and persuade, to the end that Italy might be saved.

Machiavelli, Zanobi di Jacopo. Florentine painter; b. c1418; d. 1479. He was a follower of Fra Angelico and a pupil and assistant of Benozzo Gozzoli, and was somewhat influenced by Fra Filippo Lippi, with whose work his own was sometimes formerly confused. Of modest gifts, he was uneven in performance, sometimes rather archaic in form and awkward in draftsmanship, as in the predella panel, *St. Nicholas of Tolentino Saving a Man from Hanging,* Amsterdam. A more secure draftsmanship and a stronger decorative sense appear in his symmetrical *Virgin* *and Child with Saints,* Museum of Fine Arts, Boston. Examples of his work are at Lucca, Pisa, Rome, London, Dublin, Baltimore, Minneapolis, New Haven, and elsewhere.

Macinghi Strozzi (mä-chēng′gē strōt′tsē), **Alessandra.** Letter writer; b. at Florence, 1407; d. there, March 11, 1471. Her husband Matteo was exiled with his sons in 1434 on the return of Cosimo de' Medici. He and three of his children died of the plague at Pesaro. The letters, seventy-two of which are extant, were written to her remaining exiled sons between August, 1447, and April, 1470. They advise, console, plan, and tell the news. Spontaneous and sincere, the letters provide a valuable picture and insight into 15th-century Florentine family life.

Maconi (mä-kō′nē), **Stefano di Corrado.** Disciple and secretary of St. Catherine of Siena; d. 1424. Of a noble Sienese family, and a distinguished student, he was perhaps the best-loved of her spiritual sons, and next to her the most important member of her "famiglia." He was one of the secretaries who took down the *Dialogo della Divina Provvidenza,* dictated while she was in ecstasy. On her deathbed she advised him to enter a monastery, and after her death he became a Carthusian monk. He became prior in one monastery after another, including that of the Certosa di Pavia, and was for a time general of the order in Italy. He made copies of the letters she had dictated. His copy was at one time in the Certosa di Pavia, but has been lost, not, however, before others had made copies of his copy. His *Leggenda minore* is an Italian translation and abridgment of Raymond of Capua's life of St. Catherine, *Legenda maior.*

Macrino d'Alba (mä-krē′nō däl′bä). [**Gian Giacomo de Alladio.**] Piedmontese painter; b. at Alba, before 1470; d. before 1525. Nothing is known of his origin or his life. It is only the signature *Macrinus de Alba* or *Macrinus de Alladio* and dates on his work that identify him. The earliest known signed and dated (1494) work, *Madonna and Child Enthroned,* Museo Civico, Turin, indicates an artistic upbringing in the manner of Foppa. Later influences are those of Botticelli, Signorelli, and Ghirlandaio; and the presence of Roman antiquities in some of his work indicates a sojourn in Rome. An exact and careful painter, he left a large number of works of local importance. A favorite subject of his altarpieces and triptychs was *Madonna and Child Enthroned,* usually with some saints. Examples of these are in the Certosa di Pavia (1496); the Sabauda Gallery, Turin (1498); at Tortona (1499); Alba (1501); and a *Nativity* (1505), New York Historical Society, all of which are signed and dated. He also left a few portraits, of which *A Knight of Malta* (1499), Morgan Library, New York, has a look of the northern painters. Other examples of his work are at Rome, Frankfurt, Baltimore, Chicago, El Paso, and elsewhere.

Madruzzo (mä-dröt′tsō), **Cristoforo.** Cardinal; b. in the Madruzzo castle at Trent, July 5, 1512; d. in the Villa d'Este at Tivoli, July 5, 1578. Of an old and noble Tridentine family, he studied at Padua and Bologna. His rise in the Church was rapid. He became canon of Trent (1529), of Salzburg (1536), Bressanone (Brixen, 1537), prince bishop of Trent (1539). He was ordained in 1542, and the following year was named administrator of Bressanone and a cardinal. He was an able politician active in inter-European affairs. Philip II named him governor of Milan (1556), and legate of the Marches (1561). He was on good terms with Charles V and Ferdinand and was able to use his friendship to smooth over difficulties between the Hapsburgs and the Curia at Rome. In 1567 he resigned his see of Trent to his nephew and went to Rome. His outstanding achievement was opening the first Council of Trent (1545–1547), at which he urged discussion of reform of the Church along with theological debates, in the hope of winning over the Protestants. As a churchman interested in reform, he was a friend of the reforming cardinals, Jacopo Sadoleto, Giovanni Morone, Reginald Pole, and Ercole Gonzaga. A fine portrait of Cardinal Madruzzo by Titian is at Trent.

Maffei (mä-fā′ē), **Celso.** Bibliophile and theologian; b. at Verona, c1425; d. there, 1508. A regular canon, he held important offices at Padua, Bologna, and Venice. He was noted as a bibliophile, and enriched the libraries of Verona and Venice with many fine codices and printed books. He left several works of a theological nature.

Maffei, Raffaele. Encyclopedist; b. at Volterra, February 17, 1455; d. there, January 25, 1522. He went to Rome as a young man, and led there a life of austere piety. He studied philosophy, theology, and Greek with George of Trebizond. Some time after a journey to Hungary (1477) with Cardinal Louis of Aragon, he returned to Volterra, where he remained. He compiled an encyclopedia, *Commentariorum rerum urbanarum libri XXXVIII*, published at Rome (1506).

Magellan (mạ-jel′ạn), **Ferdinand.** [Portuguese, **Fernão de Magalhães;** Spanish, **Fernando de Magallanes.**] Portuguese navigator in the Spanish service, discoverer of the Strait of Magellan and of the Philippine Islands, and first to head an expedition that circumnavigated the globe; b. at Saborosa, Traz-os-Montes, Portugal, c1480; d. on the island of Mactan, Philippine Islands, April 27, 1521. Born to the nobility, Magellan grew up at the Portuguese court, and served with the Portuguese forces in the East Indies (1505–1512) and in Morocco (1513–1514). Having fallen from favor with King Manuel I of Portugal, he was unable to secure the latter's backing for a project to find a western passage to the Moluccas. He went therefore to Spain, where he argued that those islands were not in the hemisphere which by treaty had been recognized as the Portuguese zone for conquest, but rather in the Spanish zone. His idea interested Charles I of Spain (later the emperor Charles V), who appointed him and another Portuguese adventurer to joint command (which presently became Magellan's sole command) of a squadron of 5 ships and 265 men which sailed from Sanlúcar de Barrameda, Portugal, on September 20, 1519. The expedition reached the bay of Rio de Janeiro in December, 1519; explored the Rio de la Plata in January and February, 1520; and on March 31 cast anchor in the port of San Julián on the Patagonian coast, where Magellan decided to winter. The captains and crews of three of his ships, and the inspector who accompanied the expedition, mutinied against this order but were subdued. Soon thereafter one of the ships, reconnoitering southward, disappeared. The Spaniards had occasional light encounters with hostile Indians (whom they described as a race of giants). With the return of spring to the Southern Hemisphere the squadron set sail again, and on October 21 came upon the entrance to a westward passage, which Magellan named Todos los Santos, but which has long been known as the Strait of Magellan. Through this they passed, with the loss of another ship, which became separated from the squadron and returned to Spain; and on November 28, 1520, they entered an ocean that Magellan named the Pacific. They sailed northward, then northwestward, and finally westward, suffering from bad food and water, ravaged by scurvy, discovering the Ladrones and other islands, but because of misinformation concerning the location of the Moluccas, persistently missing that group. The voyage was not, however, without notable results, for good and ill. On March 16, 1521, Magellan and his diminished company discovered the Philippines. The king of Cebu, one of these islands, received the voyagers cordially, made a formal act of allegiance to Spain, and was baptized, with several hundred of his people. But when Magellan took sides with one group of natives against another group on the island of Mactan, he was killed in battle on April 27, and seven other Spaniards with him. The king of Cebu, thinking better of the confidence he had at first reposed in these strange and violent visitors, revolted, killing twenty-seven more of them, including two captains. The survivors of these events, after burning one of their ships, resumed their wanderings in the two remaining vessels. Discovering Borneo on the way, they finally reached the Moluccas. There they loaded with spices; one ship, the *Trinidad*, set its course for Panama but was wrecked. The other, appropriately named *Victoria*, rounded the African continent and, with her complement reduced to eighteen men, sailed into harbor at Sanlúcar on September 6, 1522, thus completing the first circumnavigation of the globe. Among the eighteen survivors of the voyage was Antonio Pigafetta, an Italian who had become a good comrade to Magellan and was with him when he died. Pigafetta wrote an account of the voyage, *Primo viaggio intorno al globo terraqueo* . . . , in which he says he tells all the things that happened day by day on the voyage. A copy was presented to Charles V.

Magno (mä′nyō), **Celio.** Venetian poet; b. at Venice, May 12, 1536; d. there, 1602. Of a noble Venetian family, he was trained as a lawyer. He traveled widely on public affairs, as to Syria, Dalmatia, and Spain, and served as secretary to the Council of Ten at Venice. As a man of letters he was a member of the literary groups active at Venice. Some of his poems deal with public events, as one celebrating the victory of Lepanto, but many of his somber lyrics are prevaded with a sense of death. His works were published in 1600.

Maiano (mä-yä′nō), **Benedetto da.** See **Benedetto da Maiano.**

Maid of Norway (nôr′wā). See **Margaret** (of *Scotland*).

Maier (mī′ėr), **Johann.** See **Eck, Johann.**

Mainardi (mī-när′dē), **Sebastiano di Bartolo.** [Also, **Bastiano Mainardi.**] Tuscan painter; b. at S. Gimignano, c1460; d. at Florence, 1513. He was a pupil and assistant of Domenico Ghirlandaio, whose sister he married. Less sophisticated than his master, he was his faithful collaborator and is thought to have had a hand in some of the important works that came from Ghirlandaio's workshop, either assisting in the execution of a work or painting entirely from Ghirlandaio's designs. In about 1475 he was working with Ghirlandaio on the frescoes in the Chapel of St. Fina, cathedral at S. Gimignano, painting the Evangelists, Doctors of the Church, and Prophets. In the same church is a fresco, *Annunciation* (1482). Also at S. Gimignano is a tondo, *Madonna and Child with the Infant Baptist*, other versions of which are at Berlin, Cherbourg, Hamburg, Naples, and Sarasota, and frescoes in the Church of S. Agostino. At his best Mainardi's sunny paintings are bright with gay and luminous color; the features of his graceful figures are serene. After the death of Ghirlandaio (1494), Mainardi's art declined; his color became ruddy and harsh, his figures wooden, and his compositions overcrowded. Among the many works attributed to him is a fine *Portrait of a Cardinal*, the Metropolitan Museum, New York. There are several examples of his work in churches and collections in and about Florence. Others are at Naples, Palermo, Pisa, Rome (Vatican), Siena, Venice; at San Marino; in museums at Berlin, Budapest, Copenhagen, Cracow, Dresden, Hamburg, Leipzig, London, Paris, Lichtenstein, and Vienna; at Birmingham (Alabama), Boston, Brooklyn, Chicago, Denver, Indianapolis, Philadelphia, Sarasota, the Smithsonian Institution, Washington, and elsewhere.

Maineri (mī-ne′rē), **Giovanni Francesco de'.** Painter of Parma; active between 1491 and 1505. He was a pupil of Ercole de' Roberti of Ferrara and an eclectic who borrowed from a number of North Italian painters. His devout *Christ Bearing the Cross*, Uffizi, Florence, is a borrowing from Solario; of the several versions he executed of the painting, others are at Modena, the Doria Pamphili Gallery, Rome, at Copenhagen and Leningrad. *Madonna and Child Enthroned with SS. Thomas and Nicodemus*, the Metropolitan Museum, New York, is attributed to him. Other examples of his work are at Bologna, Ferrara, Milan, Turin; at Berlin, Bucharest, London, Madrid, Paris, and Rotterdam.

Maitland (māt′lạnd), Sir **John.** [Title, 1st Baron **Maitland of Thirlestane.**] Scottish politician; b. c1545; d. at Thirlestane, Scotland, October 3, 1595. He supported the cause of Mary, Queen of Scots, against the Presbyterian party, was raised to the peerage by James VI (afterward James I of England), and by his advice James consented to the act establishing the church on a strictly Presbyterian basis.

Maitland, Sir **Richard.** [Title, Lord **Lethington.**] Scottish lawyer, poet, and collector of early Scottish poetry; b. 1496; d. March 20, 1586. He is remembered for his collection of early Scottish verse, in two volumes, in the Pepysian Library at Magdalene College, Cambridge. His *Satire on Town Ladies* and *The Blind Baron's Comfort* (he was blind from 1560) are his best-known poems.

Maitland of Lethington (leth′ing-tọn), **William.** Scottish politician; b. c1528; d. at Leith, June 9, 1573. He worked for a union of England and Scotland, keeping clear of religious factional disputes, basing his plans on recognition of Mary, Queen of Scots, as heir to the English throne. He was implicated in the murders of Rizzio and Darnley, and because he feared Bothwell, fought against the queen at Langside, but came to her aid later.

Majoragio (mä-yō-rä′jō), **Marcantonio.** [Real name, **Antonmaria Conti.**] Philosopher, humanist, and jurist; b. at Marjoragio (whence his name), near Milan, 1514; d. at Milan, 1555. He had a humanistic and legal education, and held the chair of eloquence at Milan, except for a brief interval at Ferrara, until his death. He was at first an ardent advocate of Cicero as the master stylist and writer, but later changed his views and wrote a commentary criticizing the Ciceronian style and the inconsistency of Ciceronian thought. This provoked an outburst from Mario Nizolio, a supporter of Cicero. The latter suggested that a distinction be made between

Cicero the prose writer and Cicero the thinker. Majoragio answered Nizolio's contentions, and thus began a series of polemics fired off by the two at each other in which they aired their views pro and con Cicero as a model.

Malagigi (mä-lä-jē′jē). In the Italian versions of the Carolingian cycle, an enchanter attached to Charlemagne's court. He is a cousin of Rinaldo, and uses his arts to thwart the enemies of Charlemagne and of Christendom, or to help the paladins. He appears in Luigi Pulci's *Morgante Maggiore*, Matteo Maria Boiardo's *Orlando Innamorato*, and Lodovico Ariosto's *Orlando Furioso*.

Malaspina (mä-lä-spē′nä), **Saba.** Thirteenth century chronicler, who wrote a Latin chronicle, *Rerum Sicularum historia*, that treats the affairs of Naples from the death of Frederick II (1250) to the death of Charles of Anjou (1285), and is of value for the events of this period.

Malatesta (mä-lä-tes′tä). Family of Rimini that ruled that city and parts of the Romagna from 1304 to 1500. Members of the family had become landowners near Rimini by the middle of the 12th century, and became citizens of Rimini in 1216. With their capacity for war and their numerous kinsmen they soon rose to power there. Malatesta da Verucchio became podesta in 1239. As Guelphs, the Malatesta were active in the struggles with the Ghibellines, but deserted the pope whenever it suited their interests. In 1283 or 1284 Gianciotto Malatesta, the hunchback grandson of Malatesta da Verucchio, slew his wife, Francesca da Polenta, and his brother Paolo, on the grounds of adultery. Dante tells their poignant story (*Inferno*, v). By 1304, when Gianciotto died, the Malatesta had won the overlordship of Rimini and of lands in the Romagna and the Marches. Dante (*Inferno*, xxvii) describes them as still "using their teeth" in Rimini. In June, 1324, the pope conferred on Pandolfo Malatesta (d. 1326) and his heirs the title of knight, as a reward for Pandolfo's help in the wars against the emperor Louis IV. In succeeding years they governed Rimini and their territories without regard to the admonitions that came from their overlord, the pope. They switched their support to Louis, and by him were invested (1341) with Fano, Pesaro, and the city they already held, Rimini. In 1392 Boniface IX invested the Malatesta with Rimini, Fano, Mondaino, Cesena, Roncofreddo, Fossombrone, Cervia, Meldola, Borgo San Sepolcro, and some lesser cities, in perpetuity, unless there was a failure of an heir. The warlike members of the family hired their services out to the ruling princes of Italy. Pandolfo III (d. 1427) fought Gian Galeazzo Visconti of Milan, and in the disorder following his death (1402) seized Brescia and Bergamo for himself (1404). Filippo Maria Visconti won them back (1420–1421). Pius II wrote of Pandolfo that "In war he was a coward and a runaway, at home a drunkard and a braggart, and he lived the life of a glutton and the most shameful of seducers." Pandolfo's brother Carlo was a brave but unlucky captain in the armies of the Church. On his death (1429) his lands were divided between the three illegitimate sons of Pandolfo: Galeotto Roberto, Sigismondo Pandolfo, and Domenico (called Malatesta Novello). Galeotto Roberto died soon after; his brothers shared his inheritance. Malatesta Novello, less grasping than Sigismondo, was more interested in the arts of peace than in war, and founded the famous Malatesta library at Cesena, over which he ruled. On his death (1465) Cesena reverted to the Church. Sigismondo waged continual war to enlarge his state. He was defeated by the forces of Pope Pius II (1463), lost his lands, and withdrew to Rimini. His son Roberto seized it after his death, and following his death (1482), it fell to another Pandolfo, who was invested by the pope with a domain reduced to the city itself. His subjects revolted (1497) and besieged him in his castle. He escaped, and "stained as he was with fratricide and every other abomination" was restored by Venice. Cesare Borgia captured Rimini in 1500; it fell to Venice in 1503, and to the Church in 1509. Pandolfo's attempts to regain it were unsuccessful, and the Malatesta became stateless and impoverished wanderers in Italy.

Malatesta, Carlo. Lord of Rimini; b. c1368; d. 1429. He was the son of Galeotto Malatesta, whom he succeeded as lord of Rimini (c1386). Much of his life was spent in arms. As commander of the army of the league against the Visconti, he was unsuccessful; in the pay of Venice in a war against the Hungarians, he was routed; he served as regent for his young nephew, Gianfrancesco Gonzaga of Mantua, until the latter took over the reins of government, defeated him in battle (1426), and took him prisoner. Pope Pius II wrote that he "had the habit of being taken prisoner at least once a year." He was a loyal adherent of Pope Gregory XII in the Great Schism (1378–1417), and acted as the pope's messenger to the Council of Constance when Gregory formally abdicated in the hope of bringing the schism to an end. Pius II described him as a "lover of classical literature, man of letters, friend of such humanists as Bruni, Poggio, and Flavio Biondo." "Except for pride," he added, "it would be hard to find anything in his character to condemn." It was a rare member of a family whose crimes were so readily believed in by the public who could earn such a tribute.

Malatesta, Roberto. Lord of Rimini; b. between September, 1440 and September, 1441; d. September 10, 1482. He was the illegitimate son of Sigismondo Malatesta; Pietro Barbo, the future Pope Paul II, was his godfather; Pope Nicholas V legitimized him (1450). His life was devoted to arms. In 1457 he went, at great peril to himself, on an unsuccessful mission to Alfonso of Aragon, king of Naples, in an attempt to bring his father's war with the king to an end. From 1460 to 1463 he served with great valor in the war waged by Pope Pius II against his father. This war was disastrous for the Malatesta. In 1465 he took possession of Cesena, on the death of his uncle, Malatesta Novello, but could not defend it against the papal armies. On the death of his father he made himself lord of Rimini by treachery, got rid of Isotta, his father's wife, and her son Sallustio, and defended Rimini energetically against Pope Paul II and his allies. In the next years he was a condottiere sought after by the most powerful princes in Italy. Serving Pope Sixtus IV, in his war against Naples, he took Velletri from the duke of Calabria (August, 1482), and died a few days later. It was supposed that he was poisoned. Sixtus honored him with burial in St. Peter's.

Malatesta, Sigismondo. Lord of Rimini, Fano, and Senigallia, soldier, poet, scholar, patron of the arts and letters, and one of the most notorious despots of Renaissance Italy; b. 1414; d. at Rimini, October 9, 1468. He was the natural son of Pandolfo Malatesta (d. 1427), was a highly cultivated man, and was accused by his contemporaries of murder, rape, incest, sodomy, treachery, perfidy, irreligion, unparalleled cruelty, and other crimes. Warlike and grasping, at 18 he was commander of the papal armies in the Romagna and the Marches, but soon turned to wars of self-aggrandizement. He took part in all the wars of Italy from 1433 to 1464, not always with honor and seldom with loyalty to his employers. In 1447 he violated agreements made with Alfonso, king of Naples. Alfonso began a war against him that was ruinous for Sigismondo. It was continued by Alfonso's son Ferrante, recognized by the pope as the successor of Alfonso (d. 1458). In April, 1459, Sigismondo was one of those who helped carry the golden chair of Pius II into Florence (the pope was on his way to the Congress of Mantua). Sigismondo, defeated by Ferrante's captains, turned to the pope to arrange a peace. Pius negotiated one that Sigismondo found too harsh. He soon violated it and set about, by arms and intrigue, to win lands in the Marches for himself. He took Mondavio and Monte Marciano from the pope. Pius II declared him a rebellious vassal who had forfeited his lands, and excommunicated him (December, 1460). The pope vowed war to the death. At a consistory he heard a public denunciation (which he had inspired) of the crimes of Sigismondo. After hearing it, the pope named various saints who had been canonized by his predecessors, and those for whom petitions had been submitted to him (including Catherine of Siena). He declared that no saint had been praised so highly as Sigismondo was cursed. He ordered an investigation, subject to all legal procedures, for the purpose of canonizing Sigismondo to hell. "No mortal heretofore has descended into hell with the ceremony of canonization. Sigismondo shall be the first to be deemed worthy of such honor. By an edict of the pope, he shall be enrolled in the company of hell as a comrade of devils and the damned." The investigation was carried out. Sigismondo was found to be a heretic who denied the immortality of the soul and the resurrection of the dead. He was charged with every crime. In a ceremony unique in church history, in the spring of 1462 a straw effigy was constructed, from its mouth hung an inscription that read, "Sigismondo, son of Pandolfo, king of traitors, hated of God and man, condemned to the flames by vote of the holy senate." The effigy was burned in front of the steps of St. Peter's. The pope's commanders defeated Sigismondo in August, 1462, and prevented him from taking Senigallia. By October, 1463, he had been forced to fall back on Rimini itself. Acknowledging that he was beaten, he sent his representative to the pope to sue for peace. The pope set the terms: Sigismondo was to make a public recantation of his heresy at Rome and at Rimini; he was to pay the pope a yearly tribute; to pay a large indemnity to the Church for the injuries he had inflicted on it; and was required to give up all his lands except Rimini, which was to revert to the Church at his death. Sigismondo could do nothing other than accept the terms. His agents appeared at Rome, and on October 23, 1463, publicly confessed his heresy and abjured it. At Rimini, after three days during which the whole city fasted, Sigismondo himself knelt before the bishop, confessed his sins, asked pardon, and swore his allegiance to Pius. The end of the war marked the end of his power; the Malatesta family ceased to be a power in Italy. In the hope of restoring his fortunes, he took service under Venice and went to fight the Turks in the Morea (1464–1465). Except for the capture of Mistra, his campaign was unsuccessful. Returned to Rimini, he hoped to regain his power under the pontificate of Paul II, but in vain. In his desperation he went to Rome with the intention of stabbing the pope, but when he came into the papal presence found he did not dare do it—it was one of the few things he did not dare do. His first wife was Ginevra, daughter of Leonello d'Este of Ferrara; his second wife was Polissena, daughter of Francesco Sforza of Milan. He was accused of killing both. His third wife was Isotta degli Atti, whom he idolized and to whom he was constantly unfaithful. She, and her son Sallustio, who survived him, were named his heirs in defiance of his agreement with Pius II that Rimini would revert to the Church on his death.

Almost constantly engaged in war and diplomacy, Sigismondo was also a poet (his verses celebrating his love for Isotta express deep feeling), a builder, and a patron of the arts. He welcomed humanists, artists, and men of letters at his court, gave them landed estates or well rewarded offices, and took part in learned discussions on philosophy and poetry with them. In 1446 he built a castle. It is now in ruins but its forbidding fortress-like appearance is known from the reverse of a medal of Sigismondo struck by Matteo de' Pasti, and from a fresco painted by Piero della Francesca in the Tempio Malatestiano. The Tempio is an enlargement and reconstruction of the church of S. Francesco at Rimini that Sigismondo commissioned Leon Battista Alberti to design (1447). The design, which was incompletely carried out by Matteo de' Pasti, incorporated features of classical architecture and is a fine illustration of Alberti's style. The interior was decorated by Agostino di Duccio, and also contains the above-mentioned fresco by Piero della Francesca, *Sigismondo Malatesta Kneeling before S. Sigismondo*. Pius II called it "a splendid church dedicated to Saint Francis, though he filled it so full of pagan works of art that it seemed less a Christian sanctuary than a temple of heathen devils. In it he erected for his mistress a tomb of magnificent marble and exquisite workmanship with an inscription in the pagan style as follows, 'Sacred to the deified Isotta.' " On arches, vaults, friezes, and balustrades were carved the intertwined initials SI, and scattered throughout appeared the arms and emblems of the Malatesta: the elephant (symbolizing strength) and the rose (perhaps symbolizing the arts). Along the outside were placed sarcophagi, patterned after Roman aqueducts, in which he placed the remains of the scholars and artists who had resided at his court. In one of these he entombed (1466) the bones of Georgius Gemistus Plethon, the Greek philosopher who popularized Neoplatonism in Italy. The inscription reads that "induced by the great love with which he burns for men of learning" he brought the bones back from Mistra, where he had campaigned against the Turks. Pius, his enemy and conqueror, wrote of him, "Sigismondo, of the noble family of Malatesta, but illegitimate, was very vigorous in body and mind, eloquent, and gifted with great military ability. He had a thorough knowledge of history (antiquity), and no slight acquaintance with philosophy. Whatever he attempted he seemed born for, but the evil part of his character had the upper hand." According to Pius, and others (chiefly his adversaries), he violated his daughters and his sons-in-law, no marriage was sacred to him, no cruelty revolted him, treachery and perfidy were second nature. He was "the prince of all wickedness," "the poison of all Italy." A notable patron, he came to be regarded as the archtype of the criminal Renaissance despot, whose crimes were paralleled by a sincere passion and respect for learning and the arts.

Malespini (mä-lā-spē′nē), **Celio.** Translator, man of letters, and adventurer; b. at Venice, 1531; d. 1609?. He had been a soldier in Flanders and in Spain; returned to Italy, he earned his living, in various cities, by his wits. He was a forger and cheat when necessary, and a gentleman when possible. He organized entertainments, wrote, translated, and, in 1580, published some cantos of Tasso's *Gerusalemme liberata* without the author's consent. His translations included Brunetto Latini's *Trésor,* from French to Spanish, and Antonio Torquemada's *Jardín de flores curiosas.* His chief work, *Duecento novelle,* was written at Mantua between 1595 and 1605, and published at Venice in 1609. The 202 stories are in the Boccaccesque framework that was almost obligatory. The tales are told by a group who have fled from Venice to escape the plague. Many of them are Malespini's imitations of stories of Boccaccio, Doni, and others. About 90 of them are original, and are of incidents and episodes drawn from Malespini's own life and time—tales of passion and horror.

Malipiero (mä-lē-pye′rō), **Girolamo.** Venetian monk and poet; d. c1547. He was a member of a celebrated and prominent family of Venice, known for its service to the republic. He, however, entered orders and devoted himself to spiritual and literary interests. Among his works are: a treatise on the Holy Scriptures, *Trattato di Sacra Scrittura;* a life of Clement VII and one of St. Francis. He is known also for his curious *Il Petrara spirituale.* This was a collection of Petrarch's sonnets and canzoni "purified" by Malipiero's alterations and substitutions of words, phrases, and entire ideas.

Malpaghini (mäl-pä-gē′nē), **Giovanni di Iacopo.** [Also called, **Giovanni da Ravenna.**] Latin scholar and teacher; b. at Ravenna, c1346; d. at Florence, 1417. He studied at Ravenna and Venice and from 1364 to 1368 was a secretary and copyist in the house of Petrarch. In 1368 he left for Rome, where he was in the service of a member of the curia with whom (1370) he went to Avignon. By 1394 he was in Florence. There he lectured at the university. Among his distinguished pupils were Leonardo Bruni, Carlo Marsuppini, and Poggio Bracciolini.

Manciple's Tale, The. One of Chaucer's *Canterbury Tales.* It is partly from Ovid's *Metamorphoses,* being the story of how the crow, once white, was turned black for telling Phoebus Apollo of the infidelity of Coronis.

Mandorla (man-dôr′lạ). In art, an almond-shaped halo enclosing an entire figure. The space is sometimes outlined by overlapping wings.

Mandragola (män-drä′gō-lä), **La.** Comedy by Niccolò Machiavelli, written some time after 1512 during his enforced retirement from the political scene, and first acted in 1525. Callimaco, a young merchant who has lived most of his life in Paris, returns to his native city, lured thither by tales of the beauty and unassailable virtue of Lucrezia. Dying of love for her, he dares not approach her because of her reputation. She is the young wife of Messer Nicia, a stupid and middle-aged notary. Their hopes of having children have been continually disappointed. To have a son has become an obsession with Nicia. Callimaco, advised by the greedy parasite Ligurio, and aided in carrying out his advice by Lucrezia's amoral mother Sostrata and Lucrezia's venal confessor Frate Timoteo, intrigues to win the charms of Lucrezia for himself by playing on Nicia's desire for a son. He claims to be a noted doctor from Paris who can cure Lucrezia's sterility. The plot revolves around the cure and Callimaco's part in it. (An ingredient of the cure is a draft prepared from the root of the mandrake, whence the title.) Aided by the stupidity of Nicia, the moral indifference of Sostrata, and the greed of Frate Timoteo, to say nothing of the inventiveness of Ligurio, the unwilling Lucrezia is not only thrust into Callimaco's arms, but then willingly sees to it that he becomes an intimate of the household, with Nicia's cordial consent. The comedy has been called one of the greatest, and possibly the greatest, of Italian comedies. Machiavelli takes an unblinking look at the realities of Italian domestic life, in some circles, of his time. The outrageous Sostrata and Frate Timoteo, the foolish Nicia, chaste Lucrezia, and lovelorn Callimaco, provide an amusing situation from which Machiavelli wrings every drop of scandalous humor. The comedy is distinctively Florentine, studded with local proverbs and turns of phrase, and crackling with the mordant Florentine wit.

Mandricardo (män-drē-kär′dō). In Matteo Maria Boiardo's *Orlando Innamorato* and Lodovico Ariosto's *Orlando Furioso*, the son of the Tartar king Agricane. Informed that his father has been slain by Orlando, he seeks out Orlando to avenge his father, and is slain by Ruggiero.

Manetti (mä-nāt′tē), **Antonio di Tuccio.** Florentine biographer; b. at Florence, July 6, 1423; d. there, May 26, 1497. He was a mathematician and astronomer and, as a connoisseur of art and architecture, was a judge in the contest (1490) for the design of the façade of the Cathedral. A pupil of Brunelleschi, he designed the Chapel of the Cardinal of Portugal in S. Miniato al Monte. For his own copy of Dante's *Divina Commedia* he supplied the architectural illustrations for the *Inferno*. He wrote a life of Filippo Brunelleschi that Vasari used as a source for his life of the artist. To him is attributed a fine version of the story, *Novella del grasso legnaiuolo*, that relates the practical joke that Brunelleschi, with the help of Donatello and others who were in on it, played on one Manetto Ammannatini, in 1409. The object of the joke was to convince Manetto that he was not himself at all, but someone else. The poor man was so confused he came to believe it. Manetti also wrote a collection of lives of eminent Florentines and a work on the poet Guido Cavalcanti.

Manetti, Gianozzo. Florentine statesman and humanist; b. at Florence, June 5, 1396; d. at Naples, October 27, 1459. He was one of the most learned scholars of his day and was an outstanding example of the enlightened statesman. Of good birth, he was a bookkeeper in a bank before he decided to devote himself to scholarship and the service of Florence. He was a master of Greek and Latin, knew the *Epistles* of St. Paul, St. Augustine's *City of God* and Aristotle's *Ethics* by heart, and learned Hebrew, in which he became a great scholar, in order to understand the sacred writings and in order to confute the Jews in their own tongue. He was noted for his orations, as that which he gave in Rome, as a representative of Florence, to congratulate Nicholas V on his elevation to the papal chair. After listening to it, says Vespasiano, all the Florentines present shook hands with one another "just as if they had acquired Pisa and all its lands." The orations given in Italian, were then translated into Latin for publication. Manetti wrote the *Life of Nicholas V* and later (1451) became an apostolic secretary. He translated the *Psalms* from the Hebrew and dedicated the work to King Alfonso I of Naples, and began a collection of Hebrew manuscripts that still forms part of the Vatican Library. He was a devout Catholic, yet the purport of his writings was deemed by some to be boldly modern, if not actually heretical. He was criticized for his knowledge of Hebrew by some, and by others for his views on the dignity, value and creative forces of man, as expressed, particularly, in his treatise *De dignitate et excellentia hominus*. In the latter it seemed to his critics that he had ascribed to man powers that belong to God, and he was in fact a trail blazer for many who came after him in his ideas on man's possibilities. Among his many works of history, theology, and moral philosophy were a history of Pistoia, the above-cited life of Nicholas V, and lives of Socrates, Seneca, Dante, Petrarch, and Boccaccio. In addition he made translations from the Greek, as the New Testament and Aristotle's ethical writings, and from the Hebrew. He was a pioneer Biblical scholar, anticipating by many years the better known work of Erasmus and others in the 16th century.

In his service for Florence he acted as governor of Pescia (1440) and Pistoia (1446) and ruled so justly and incorruptly (he stopped the custom of giving presents to the governing vicar or captain), settling disputes and keeping himself aloof from partisan strife, that he won great honor in both places. He represented Florence on missions to Genoa, Rimini, Venice, and Siena, as well as at the courts of Eugenius IV, Alfonso I, and Nicholas V, and was an ornament to Florentine statesmanship. He had enjoyed the confidence of Cosimo de' Medici but found himself at odds with Cosimo when the latter changed the alignment of Florentine allies from Venice to Milan. Manetti, prominent in public as well as literary affairs, was unwilling to shift his allegiance from the old allies, and Cosimo resolved to destroy him. Cosimo could manipulate the capricious system of taxation in Florence, and levied on Manetti a ruinous tax. Manetti went (1453) to Rome, where he was warmly welcomed by Nicholas V and given a pension. His Florentine enemies demanded his return. Nicholas sent him back to Florence as his envoy. Gianozzo was able to reinstate himself in the good graces of the Florentines, many of whom had been saddened and ashamed to have him brought back a virtual prisoner. He served on the Council of Ten, but decided not to stay in Florence and returned to Rome. On the death of Nicholas (1455), his successor invited Manetti to remain, but he preferred to go to the court of Alfonso I of Naples. Alfonso admired him greatly and supported him generously, despite the fact that as a Florentine statesman, Manetti had often represented Alfonso's enemy. He had once persuaded Sigismondo Malatesta to betray his engagement to fight for Alfonso and to fight for Florence against him instead. There was no such thing as enduring enmity or everlasting friendship among the princes and rulers of the Renaissance.

Manfred (man′frẹd). King of Sicily (1258–1266); b. c1232; killed at the battle of Benevento, February 26, 1266. He was an illegitimate son of the emperor Frederick II. He was prince of Tarentum and regent till the accession of his half brother Conrad IV in 1252. On the death of Conrad (1254), he became regent for Conrad's son Conradin, and was crowned king in 1258. The papacy opposed Manfred, as it had opposed his father, and he was excommunicated. Pope Clement IV supported Charles of Anjou as king of Sicily. Charles defeated Manfred at the battle of Benevento, in which Manfred was killed.

Manfredi (män-fre′dē). Ancient noble family, lords of Faenza and other cities of the Romagna, documented from the 11th century. Dante mentions the family in the *Divina Commedia* (*Inferno*, xxxiii), in speaking of Fra Alberigo, who murdered his brother and his nephews at a banquet (1285), and also in his *De vulgari eloquentia*. In the struggles of the communes, the Manfredi were Guelphs. Among the outstanding members of the family were: Francesco (d. 1343) who was named captain of Faenza in 1313, but who was in fact lord of the city, with the right to coin money; Astorre (or Astorgio), who (1378) took Faenza from Niccolò d'Este and, as ecclesiastical vicar and theoretically subject to the Estensi, was officially declared *signore* (lord) in 1379; Astorre I, soldier and poet, friend of Franco Sacchetti, who was named *signore* for ten years in 1390. His term was extended but ended in tragedy: Baldassare Cossa, the papal legate (later John XXIII), had him beheaded (1405) in the square at Faenza for what he called treason. His son Gian Galeazzo returned to Faenza (1412 or 1413), and reformed the laws. He was made count of Valdilamone, an area independent of Faenza, and was succeeded (1417) by his sons. His son Guidantonio, who had become lord of Imola, died in 1448, and his brother Astorre II ruled Faenza alone until his death (1468). With Astorre II's sons the family strife that kept so many of the small Italian states in turmoil broke out again. Carlo was lord of Faenza, but his brother Federico, bishop of the city since 1471, was the effective ruler. Two other brothers, Galeotto and Lancilotto, were exiled. Galeotto returned (1477) and, with the cooperation of the people, drove out his brothers Carlo and Federico. Galeotto (b. 1440), was brave in arms and astute in politics. Of a cultivated mind and a spirit open to and interested in the arts and letters, he continued the building of the cathedral begun by Francesco (d. 1343), was a benefactor of churches and convents, encouraged the manufacture of majolica, for which Faenza was famous, collected a notable library, and was the friend and patron of humanists. He was typical of the Renaissance princelings who passionately participated in the intellectual and artistic movements of the time while at the same time, by arms and intrigue or alliance, they fought for power. Galeotto married (1482) Francesca, daughter of Giovanni II Bentivoglio of Bologna, for strategic reasons. The marriage caused his ruin. He had for long enjoyed a relationship with Cassandra Pavoni, a lady of Ferrara, and continued his relations with her even after she had withdrawn (1480) to a convent (where, under the name Sister Benedetta, she died, 1514). Added to this cause of resentment, the treacherous policies of his father-in-law made the few years of his rule unhappy and full of peril, and his life ended in a tragedy that was as much one of passion as of politics. He was assassinated (May 31, 1488) by a conspiracy in which his twenty-year-old wife, acting as her father's instrument, may have had a hand. His three-year-old son Astorre III became lord under the regency of a group of elders and the protection of Florence, but he was still a youth when the signory of Faenza was brought to an end by Cesare Borgia (1501). A year later Astorre III was slain at Rome, it was said by Cesare himself, and the house of Manfredi came to an end. The Manfredi did much to beautify the city of Faenza, and called upon the most eminent architects, artists, and sculptors, including Giuliano da Maiano, Benedetto da Maiano, and Desiderio da Settignano, for the construction and ornamentation of the cathedral.

Manni (män′nē), **Giannicola.** See **Giannicola di Paolo.**

Mannucci or **Manucci** (mä-nöt′chē), **Aldo.** See **Manutius, Aldus.**

Manny (man′i) or **Mauny,** Sir **Walter de.** [Title, Baron **de Manny.**] Soldier in the English service, founder of the Charterhouse, London; d. at London, January 15, 1372. He was a native of Manny, near Valenciennes, and a fellow-townsman of Froissart. He was one of the ablest of the commanders of Edward III. In 1371 he was licensed to found a house of Carthusian monks. This "Chartreuse" became the London Charterhouse.

Mannyng (man′ing), **Robert.** [Also, **Robert of Brunne.**] English chronicler and poet; active in the latter part of the 13th and the beginning of the 14th century. He wrote *Handlyng Synne* (1303), a translation of the *Manuel des Pechiez* of William of Wadington; *The Chronicle of England* (finished in 1338); and *Medytacyuns of the Soper of our Lorde Ihesus.* His importance is literary rather than historical, but the information about pre-Chaucerian England in his works, as well as his use of the Midland dialect, makes his work a milestone in the development of modern English.

Manoello (mä-nō-el′lō), **Giudeo.** See **Immanuel ben Solomon.**

Man of Law's Tale, The. One of Chaucer's *Canterbury Tales.* It is taken from the Anglo-Norman chronicle of Nicholas Trivet, and tells of the sufferings of the noble Constance, who is comforted in her trials by the prospect of heaven.

Mansfeld (mäns′felt), Count **Peter Ernst von.** German general; b. July 10, 1517; d. May 22, 1604. He served under the emperor Charles V and under Philip II of Spain. He succeeded (1592) the duke of Parma as governor general of the Netherlands.

Mansueti (män-sö-ā′tē), **Giovanni di Niccolò.** Venetian painter; notices of him date from 1485; d. c1527. He called himself a pupil of Gentile Bellini and was influenced by him as well as by Carpaccio and Cima da Conegliano. A productive rather than a gifted painter, he left a number of works. His canvases for the Scuola Grande di S. Marco echo Carpaccio in the attention to minute detail, and he was like Gentile Bellini in filling the spaces with figures that seem to represent actual men. The four works he painted for this series show great interest in Oriental features. Two of them (*Miracle of the True Cross,* 1494, and *Miraculous Cure*) are in the Accademia, Venice, one (*Mark Baptizing Ananias*) is in the Brera, and another (*Mark Led Out of the Synagogue,* 1499) is in the Liechtenstein Gallery, Vaduz. His huge paintings are notable for the crowds of people in them, of whom many are portraits, the rich architecture, and sumptuous furnishings and costumes. Besides those mentioned, other works are in the Accademia and in the Correr Museum, Venice, at Burano, Bergamo, Florence (Uffizi), Modena, Padua, Pavia, Rome (Borghese Gallery), Urbino, Verona, Vicenza, Berlin, London, Omaha (Nebraska), Pittsburgh (Carnegie Museum and Library), and elsewhere.

Mantegazza (män-tā-gät′tsä), **Cristoforo** and **Antonio.** Sculptors who worked on the Certosa di Pavia. The first notice of Cristoforo is of 1466. He helped in executing the plastic decorations of the large cloister, made some reliefs inside the church, and is thought to have worked with his brother on the façade. He died in 1481 or 1482. Antonio is first mentioned in 1473 when the duke of Milan recommended both brothers as accomplished sculptors to the overseers of the Certosa. They began work on the façade in October of the same year but gave it up the following year to Amadeo. Antonio continued to work on the Certosa at intervals until 1495, and died soon after that date. No certainly identifiable work of the brothers on the Certosa is known, but certain groups of statues and reliefs on the façade that are clearly different in style from Amadeo's work are attributed to them. Other works attributed to them are in the Castello Sforzesca at Milan and at London. In 1473 the brothers proposed to cast an equestrian statue of Francesco Sforza in bronze. This task was later assumed by Leonardo da Vinci, who also failed to carry it out.

Mantegna (män-tā′nyä), **Andrea.** Painter; b. at Isola di Carturo, in the territory of Vicenza, 1431; d. at Mantua, September 13, 1506. In the years between 1441 and 1445 he was listed on the rolls of Paduan painters as an apprentice and adopted son of Francesco Squarcione. In exchange for the necessities of life and instruction in painting, some of Squarcione's pupils contracted to work on the commissions of his workshop, and occasionally, perhaps to ensure continuation, he "adopted" a pupil, as in the case of Mantegna. An enthusiastic humanist, he had a collection of antique fragments, casts, and reliefs, as well as drawings and designs which he used to train his pupils. His shop was also a meeting place for Paduan humanists from the university and others who shared his enthusiasm for the classical period. It was here perhaps that Mantegna conceived the interest in the antique, and its revival, that became the passion of his life and profoundly influenced his approach to his art. Donatello was working at Padua in these years. His reliefs, and the work of Paolo Uccello and Filippo Lippi, who also worked at Padua, introduced Tuscan elements to the school founded by Squarcione, elements that the young Mantegna rapidly assimilated to his classical training. About 1446 he went to Venice with Squarcione and saw the painting of Andrea del Castagno in S. Zaccaria. The austerity and forcefulness of the Florentine struck a responsive chord. Marvelously precocious, Mantegna soon far outstripped his master. After six years in the workshop at Padua he sought to free himself from his arrangement with Squarcione, to develop his own style and to reap the rewards of his own work. Through a compromise worked out at Venice he won a measure of freedom in January, 1448, and the lasting enmity of Squarcione. His earliest independent work was an altarpiece, now lost, that he dated (1448) and signed, stating his age as 17. His reputation must already have been high, for on May 16 of the same year he and the painter and sculptor Niccolò Pizzolo won a commission to decorate half of the Ovetari Chapel in the Church of the Eremitani at Padua with frescoes on the life of St. James. The other half of the chapel, with stories from the life of St. Christopher, was to be painted by Giovanni d'Alemagna and Antonio Vivarini. (Because he was still a minor, the contract was signed by Mantegna's brother.) Giovanni d'Alemagna died in 1450, Pizzolo in 1453; Antonio Vivarini withdrew. Mantegna painted the entire cycle on the story of St. James, the *Assumption* in the apse, and figures of SS. Peter, Paul, and Christopher. The first four scenes on the legend of St. Christopher were painted by Bono da Ferrara and others; the last two by Mantegna. The chapel was completely destroyed in a bombardment of March, 1944. Only the *Assumption* and *Martyrdom of St. Christopher*, which had been detached in 1865 and were out of the church at the time, escaped destruction, and Mantegna's first great pictorial cycle, completed about 1458, is now known only from photographs. The period of his work in the Ovetari Chapel was a fruitful one. In 1448 he made a short visit to Ferrara, during which he painted a portrait of Leonello d'Este, now lost, and came into contact with the art of Piero della Francesca which, with its strongly developed and stately forms, had some influence on his own. He frescoed St. Bernardino and St. Anthony, kneeling beside the emblem of Christ, over the main doorway of the Basilica of St. Anthony at Padua (1452), now in the museum of the Basilica; painted the polyptych of St. Luke (1452–1453), now in the Brera, Mialan, and the panel with *St. Euphemia* (1454), National Museum, Naples. He developed close contacts with the Bellini family of painters and by 1454 had married Nicolosia, daughter of Jacopo Bellini. An acknowledged and sought-after master, his Paduan period came to a close with the great altarpiece painted for the Church of S. Zeno at Verona, between 1457 and the end of 1459. In the St. Luke polyptych, mentioned above, the central panel shows the saint reading at a desk, above him is a *Pietà;* on either side of the central panels are four panels: two with full length figures of saints, and two above them with half length figures of saints. The ten panels of the polyptych, separated by divisions of the frame, are treated as separate units with no organic relationship to each other. In a departure from the traditional treatment of multi-paneled works, the panels

ANDREA MANTEGNA
Study for the fresco, *St. James Led to Execution,*
formerly in the Ovetari Chapel, Eremitani, Padua
Louvre, Paris Alinari-Art Reference Bureau

of the S. Zeno triptych, *Virgin and Child Enthroned,* are treated as a unified composition, in which the divisions of the frame serve as columns that are reflected in the painted columns of a rectangular room that contains a single scene: the Virgin and Child in the center, with the groups of saints at either side clearly in the same enclosed space, as the linear perspective makes apparent. The S. Zeno altarpiece, with its predella panels, *Resurrection* and *Agony in the Garden,* now at Tours, and *Crucifixion,* now in the Louvre, is a summation of Mantegna's fully matured style. Later paintings represent the perfecting and refining of that style. His enduring love of the antique appears in architectural backgrounds that portray his romanticized view of Imperial Rome, in medallions with mythological scenes, busts of emperors, in antique vessels, and garlands of fruits and vegetables as decorative motifs. His solidly constructed figures came increasingly to have the visual appearance of marble sculpture. His color is subdued; in later works, as *Tarquinius and the Sibyl* (or is it *Esther and Mordecai?*), Cincinnati Art Museum, and *Judith,* Dublin, he resorted to monochrome for a closer semblance of the antique. Serpentine roads, swirling outcroppings of sharply defined rocks, and elaborate, minutely detailed cities in the backgrounds of the predella panels of the S. Zeno altarpiece appear in many of his paintings: in particular, a fascination with the shaping and definition of rock formations is apparent. Fundamental, however, was the inspiration of the ancient world, for he did not limit himself to the use of antique motifs but sought a re-creation, even in paintings on Christian subjects, of the grandeur, austerity, and purity of the antique world itself as he envisioned it.

About 1460 he accepted the invitation, made as early as 1457, to go to Mantua as court painter to the Marquess Ludovico Gonzaga. At Mantua he found a kindly prince who was a lover of the arts, and who was not put off by Mantegna's brusqueness and prickly temperament (a contemporary wrote that Mantegna could not live at peace with his neighbors; Vasari, on the other hand, made a great point of his kindliness and gentle courtesy). At the cultivated court of Mantua, where elements of Tuscan art were already known, Mantegna became the undisputed master. As was customary at princely courts, he was expected to provide designs for tapestries, vessels, and other objects, and decorations for festivals, as well as to paint pictures. The early years at Mantua were generally happy and productive ones. The paintings executed for the decoration of the chapel of the *Castello*, for which a number were ready by 1464, are not certainly identifiable. Of about this time is the *Agony in the Garden*, National Gallery, London, where there is a painting on the same subject by his brother-in-law Giovanni Bellini, a collocation that points up the flinty, somber, forceful quality of Mantegna's style in contrast to the glow and spirituality of the Bellini painting. In 1464 he made an archeological expedition with friends to the shores of Lake Garda to look for classical inscriptions. The tone of the expedition may be judged from the fact that the friends gave each other classical nicknames and titles, wore garlands on their heads and played the cither as they rowed across the lake; in a church of the Blessed Virgin they said their prayers to "the Divine Thunderer and His Glorious Mother." In 1466 he was at Florence, and the following year was invited to Pisa to advise on the painting in the Camposanto. The influence of Donatello, Andrea del Castagno, and Piero della Francesca is evident in his next great pictorial cycle, the *Camera degli Sposi*, completed in 1474 for Ludovico Gonzaga in the palace at Mantua. The frescoes, damaged, repainted, and restored, in the ducal palace where they were painted, represent on two walls an event in the life of Ludovico's family which is presumed to have been the return of Ludovico's son Francesco to Mantua as a prelate. One scene shows Ludovico and members of his family and entourage in a room or a balcony of the *Castello;* the other shows him meeting the young cardinal at the gates of a city. Intimate yet dignified, the strongly formed figures of the scenes recall the frescoes of Piero della Francesca. The keenly observed figures represent some of the most vivid portraits Mantegna painted; the scenes are among his most Tuscan and least classical, as well as among the most colorful, in the literal sense. A circular balustrade, through which the sky can be seen, is painted on the ceiling. Girls and cherubs lean over the balustrade and look down on the scene below. The ceiling is among the first successful instances of this kind of illusionistic painting. Lunettes and spandrels of the room have busts of emperors and scenes from mythology in monochrome. The elaborate decoration, undoubtedly carried out with or by assistants, bears the imprint of Mantegna's design throughout. Notices concerning his activity following the completion of the *Camera degli Sposi* (which means the Chamber of the Newlyweds, a name that was not given to it until the middle of the 17th century), are scarce. In 1484 he painted a room in the *Castello;* of c1485 is the *Madonna and Child with Cherubim*, Brera, Milan, thought by some to be the one that Francesco Gonzaga (Ludovico's grandson) in 1485 repeatedly asked him to finish for the duchess Leonora of Ferrara; Francesco was betrothed to the duchess' daughter, Isabella d'Este. The period was fraught with financial difficulties, quarrels, and losses. His kindly patron Ludovico died in 1478; Federico, Ludovico's heir, who always defended and protected his irascible painter, died in 1484; and in 1480 Mantegna had suffered a loss from which he never fully recovered in the death of his son Bernardino. To build an elaborate house at Mantua, he sought (1484) financial assistance from Lorenzo de' Medici, who had visited him in his studio (1483), and perhaps even hoped to be called to Florence. His financial situation was uncertain because that of his patrons, drained by war, was difficult. According to custom, the patron paid what he thought just, and seldom on a regular basis (Ludovico gave him money for a house, and land, and in 1492 Francesco gave him more land, partially in payment for the *Camera degli Sposi*—it was all very uncertain, even for such a recognized and respected painter as Mantegna). After the accession of Francesco as marquess of Mantua (1484), Mantegna began, probably 1485, the series of nine canvases on the *Triumph of Caesar*, now at Hampton Court, London, some of which were already completed in 1486. In the design and execution of the nine canvases Mantegna had full scope for the portrayal of his severe vision of the imperial world. The series is conceived as a continuous procession depicted in nine sections. "Here," wrote Vasari, "are seen in most admirable arrangement: the triumphal car, the figure who is cursing the

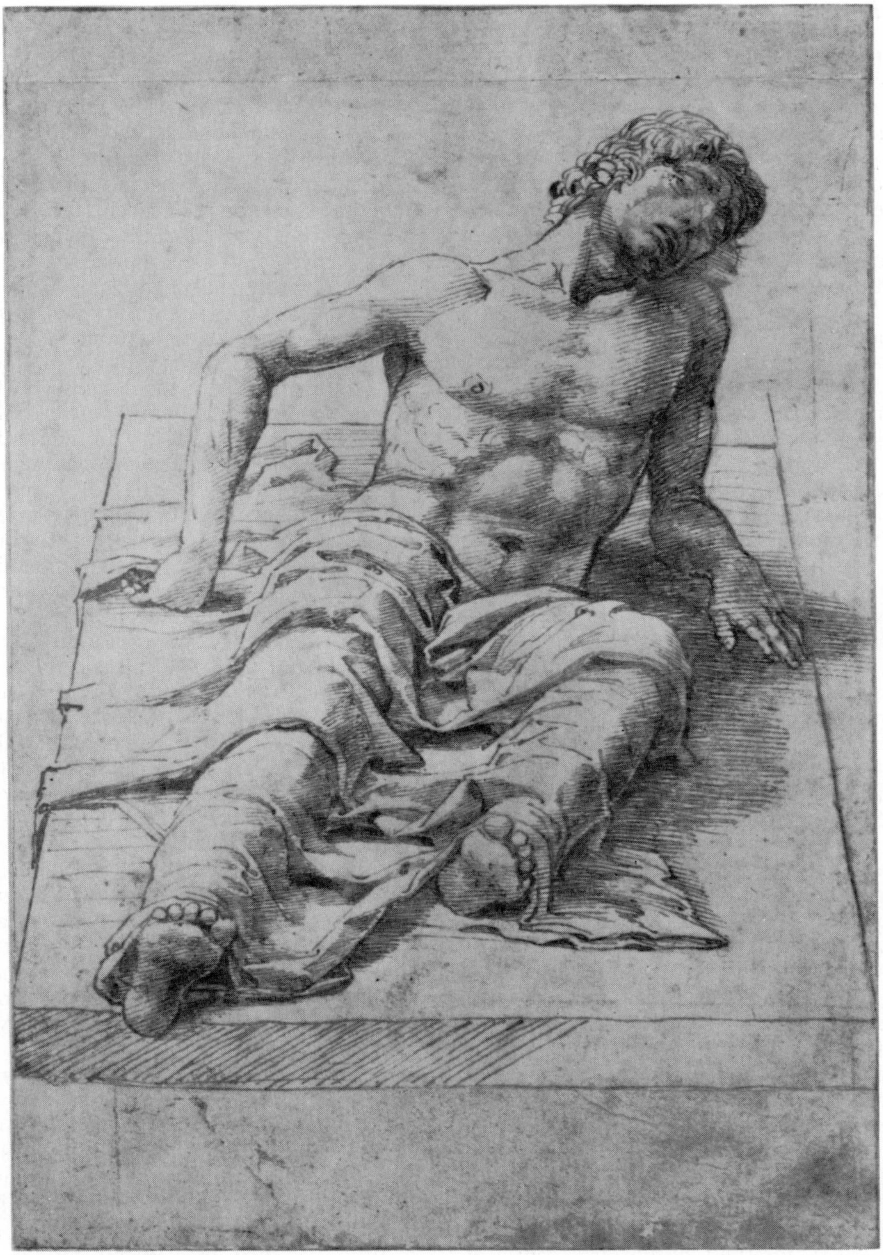

ANDREA MANTEGNA
A Man Lying on a Stone Slab
The British Museum, London

hero, the kindred, the incense bearers, the booty, the spoils, the elephants, the spoils of art, the victories, cities, and fortresses in models borne on huge cars, the trophies carried aloft on spears, an infinite variety of helmets, corselets, and arms of all kinds, with ornaments, vases, and rich vessels innumerable." The single canvases were used from time to time as scenery for entertainments or decorations for ceremonial occasions. In June, 1488, Mantegna left for Rome, called there by Innocent VIII to decorate the pope's private chapel in the Belvedere (destroyed, 1780). Among the sights that intrigued him at Rome was the brother of the Turkish sultan, Prince Djem, a prisoner of the Vatican whose bizarre figure, dress, and chameleonlike personality he described in a letter of 1489 to the marquess Francesco. In the same letter he complained of the meagerness of his reward for the work in the pope's chapel. On his return to Mantua he took up the work on the *Triumph of Caesar* again. In the meantime, Francesco had married (1490) Isabella d'Este, a cultivated but imperious and exacting mistress who did not hesitate to tell the painter exactly how she wanted a picture painted. In 1493 she was displeased with a portrait Mantegna had painted of her, and refused to send it to the friend who had asked for it. She substituted one by Giovanni Santi, whose principal claim to fame is that he was Raphael's father. Old and in poor health, Mantegna continued to work, and produced some of his most important paintings in his last years. Among these is the *Madonna of Victory*, now in the Louvre, painted to commemorate Francesco Gonzaga's victory over the French at the Battle of Fornovo, July 6, 1495. On the first anniversary of the battle the painting was carried in procession from the artist's studio to the Church of Victory, designed by Mantegna, and put in place. In the gleaming painting, Francesco is portrayed receiving the Madonna's blessing as he kneels at her throne. Other works of the last period are the altarpiece, *Madonna and Saints* (1496–1497), for the Church of S. Maria in Organo, Verona, and two canvases for the *studiolo* of Isabella d'Este: *Parnassus* (1497) and *Minerva Chasing the Vices from the Garden of the Muses* (1501–1502), both now in the Louvre. As was her custom, Isabella had probably prescribed the program for both these allegorical paintings. Mantegna was an enthusiastic and knowledgeable collector of antiquities, and had begun a museum-villa in which to show them. His most prized possession was an ancient bust of the empress Faustina. In the last month of his life, ill and in need of money, he appealed to Isabella for aid. She took advantage of his state to buy the beloved statue, which she had always coveted, at a good price.

Vasari wrote that Mantegna made engravings of his work; seven surviving prints are generally accepted as authentic. He is also thought to have supervised the reproduction by others of some of his designs and finished works. Copies of his work were popular, and frequently made without his consent. Zoan Andrea and Simone di Ardizone, engravers of Mantua, complained that he had beaten them for allegedly pirating his designs and left them for dead in the street. By means of the engravings Mantegna's influence was widely diffused; Dürer was among those who reflected his influence. Mantegna left a number of works. Examples are in the Brera, Milan (*Dead Christ*, a tour de force of foreshortening); at Bergamo; Berlin (including a powerful *Portrait of Cardinal Ludovico Mezzarota*, 1459); Copenhagen; Dresden; Dublin; Ferrara; Uffizi, Florence (a triptych with *The Adoration of the Magi*, *Ascension*, and *Circumcision*, and a *Madonna of the Quarries*, a work of lyric intensity); several in the National Gallery, London; Prado, Madrid (*The Death of the Virgin*); the Castello Sforzesco, Milan; Montreal; São Paulo, Brazil; Turin; Venice (Accademia, *St. George*); the Isabella Stewart Gardner Museum, Boston; Cleveland; the Metropolitan Museum, New York; Tulsa; and the National Gallery, Washington.

Mantovano (män-tō-vä′nō), **Battista.** See **Spagnoli, Giovan Battista.**

Manuel II Palaeologus (man′ų̄-ẹl, pā-lẹ̄-ol′-ọ-gus). Byzantine emperor (1391–1425); b. 1350; d. 1425. He was the son and successor of John V. His reign was troubled by constant pressure from the Turks and he was for a time besieged in Constantinople by the sultan, Bajazet I. He twice sought aid from the west. The first time, the army of French, German, and Hungarians that assembled was defeated. The second time he had little success. Bajazet was forced to raise the siege of Constantinople when threatened by the Tartar Tamurlane, and Manuel passed the rest of his reign in comparative peace, but in dependence on Bajazet's successor, Mohammed I. Manuel's successor was his son John VIII Palaeologus.

Manuel (mä-nwel′), Don **Juan**. Spanish statesman and writer; of the royal house of Castile and León; b. 1282; d. 1347. He commanded the army against the Moors. His best known work is *El Conde Lucanor*, a collection of fifty tales in the Oriental style.

Manupello (mä-nö-pel′lō), Count of. Title of various members of the Orsini family.

Manutius (ma̤-nū′shi-us, -shus), **Aldus.** [Italian, **Aldo** (or **Teobaldo**) **Mannucci** or **Manucci** (mä-nöt′chē) or **Manuzio** (mä-nöt′syō).] Renowned publisher, typographer, and humanist; b. at Bassiano, near Velletri, 1449; d. February 6, 1515. He studied Latin at Rome and Greek at Ferrara under Guarino, son of the great humanist teacher Guarino da Verona. In 1482 he went to stay with his friend Pico della Mirandola, continued his Greek studies, and became tutor to Pico's nephews at Carpi. As he continued his studies in Greek language and literature he conceived the idea of establishing a press for the purpose of printing the whole literature of Greece. In furtherance of the ambitious plan, he went (1490) to Venice. Venice was chosen because of the large number of Greeks who had arrived there as a result of the Turkish conquest of the Byzantine Empire and because it was, relatively, free from the wars and disturbances that kept so many of the cities of Italy in constant turmoil. Alberto Pio, one of the nephews of Pico whom he had tutored, gave him substantial financial aid in the establishment of his press. His house in Venice became the home and center of a Greek colony of scholars, teachers, and pressmen. The language spoken in it was Greek and the directions and instructions given to the workers were in Greek. The difficulties of printing and publishing the first Greek editions ever printed were enormous. His Greek friends and scholars assisted in the preparation and examination of texts to secure authoritative ones. He invented and cast his own Greek type, modeled on the handwriting of the Cretan scholar Marcus Musurus. His work was constantly interrupted by the arrival of visitors—scholars, literary men, and others who came to see his press and to discuss scholarly matters with him. Once the books began issuing from the press they were pirated by other publishers. Strikes of the workers and two outbreaks of war interrupted operations for long periods. Nevertheless, Aldus Manutius published thirty-three *first* editions of works by Greek authors in the original language between 1494 and 1515. These included Aristotle, Aristophanes, Thucydides, Sophocles, Herodotus, Euripides, Xenophon, Demosthenes, Plato, Pindar, Hesychius, Athenaeus, the Greek orators, and the *Hero and Leander* attributed to Musaeus. At the same time he was publishing Latin and Italian works by, among others, Dante, Petrarch, Bembo, Poliziano, Pontano, and Erasmus. The last-named visited his shop (1508) and has left a lively picture of the operations and those who took part in them at the press. The books produced were works of art, fine paper from Fabriano and Colle Val d'Elsa was used, the type was brilliant and beautiful (that used for a pocket series is said to have been adapted from Petrarch's handwriting), bindings were rich and sturdy. For the Latin and Italian books he invented a type face, modeled after the Italian manuscript hand, that has since been called "italic."

In the course of an illness, when he feared death, Manutius made a vow to become a priest. The pope later released him from his vow, and in 1505, at the age of 56, he married the daughter (aged 20) of Andrea di Asola, a typographer. Manutius and his father-in-law became associated in the printing operation and the name Asolano was joined to that of Aldus Manutius in their editions. Three of the five children born to Aldus and his wife were boys. His third son, Paolo (1512–1574), continued to publish at Rome and at Venice, and his grandson Aldo (1547–1597) carried on the press at Rome.

Aldus Manutius has been called the greatest publisher that ever lived, for the care in preparation and the authority of his texts, for the beauty of his volumes, for his own profound learning, and for his sincere desire to make available to a wide public at a reasonable price the wealth of Greek, Latin and Italian literature. As it happened, the influx of Greek scholars into the west ceased about 1520. Aldus had made use of them just in time to rescue the literature of Greece from the suffocation that resulted from Turkish rule. The famous colophon of the Aldine Press was a dolphin curled about an anchor: the dolphin signifying swiftness of execution and the anchor signifying firmness. The motto was "Festina lente"—make haste slowly.

Manutius, Aldus. [Italian, **Aldo Manucci** (or **Manuzio**).] Italian printer and classical scholar; b. at Venice, February 13, 1547; d. at Rome, October 28, 1597. He was the grandson of Aldus Manutius and the son of Paulus Manutius, and was the third generation to carry on the work of the Aldine press, which he did at Rome.

Manutius, Paulus. [Italian, **Paolo Manucci** (or **Manuzio**).] Italian classical scholar, author, and printer; b. at Venice, June 12, 1512; d. there, April 6, 1574. He was the third son of Aldus Manutius (1449–1515), whom he succeeded at the famous Aldine Press. An excellent Latin scholar, he concentrated on publishing the Latin classics.

Manuzio (mä-nöt′tsyō), **Aldo.** See **Manutius, Aldus.**

Manzoli (män-dzō′lē), **Pier Angelo.** Poet and philosopher; b. at La Stellata, near Ferrara, between 1500 and 1503; d. c1543. Little is known of his life. He is thought to have been a physician and to have spent some time at Rome. He was suspected of heresy in his lifetime for his connection with the Calvinistic circle of Renée d'Este at Ferrara. After his death he was tried and convicted of heresy; his bones were disenterred and burned. The basis for the charge was largely his poem *Zodiacus vitae*, written between 1520 and 1534. Its twelve independent cantos deal with the question of the *summum bonum*. In the course of discussing it, metaphysical, moral, astronomical and other subjects are covered, with numerous satiric shafts at the clergy. Expressed in fluent and freely treated Latin, and interspersed with passages of great beauty, the material, drawn from many sources, is infused with the spirit of the author. The poem, which began to be talked about only after his death, was condemned by the Church. It was admired and widely read in Protestant countries.

Maranta (mä-rän′tä), **Bartolomeo.** Physician and botanist; b. at Venosa, c1500; d. at Molfetta, March, 1571. He was a pupil of Luca Ghini at Pisa, and then passed the rest of his life at Naples, Rome, and Molfetta, practicing medicine and continuing his botanical studies. His chief work was *Methodi cognoscendorum simplicium* (Venice, 1559), which discusses plants from a medical point of view.

Marbeck (mär′bek), **John.** See **Merbecke** or **Merbeck** or **Marbeck, John.**

March (märch), **Ausías** (or **Auzias**). [Called **the Petrarch of Catalonia.**] Spanish poet of noble rank; b. at Valencia, Spain, toward the end of the 14th century; d. c1460. His verses are said to have been equal to those of Petrarch himself in brilliance of language and perfection of form, and perhaps to have surpassed Petrarch in honesty of emotion.

March and Ulster (ul′stėr), 4th Earl of. See **Mortimer, Roger de** (1374–1398).

Marchesi (mär-kā′zē), **Girolamo.** [Called **Girolamo da Cotignola.**] Painter; b. at Cotignola, c1471; d. at Rome, c1540. In his early years he imitated Francesco Zaganelli, as in his *Annunciation*, Berlin, but he was an eclectic, and borrowed freely from the Ferrarese and Bolognese painters. Among his works is *Madonna in Glory and Saints* (1513), Brera, Milan; *Madonna between SS. Anselm and Augustine*, S. Marino; *Christ* (1520), Louvre; and several portraits, including one of Gaston de Foix, supposed to have been painted as the young French general lay dead on the field following the battle of Ravenna (April 11, 1512), and those of Massimiliano Sforza and Pope Paul III. A *St. Nicholas of Tolentino* is in the Johnson Collection, Philadelphia.

Marchionne di Coppo Stefani (mär-kyō′nā dē kôp′pō stā′fä-nē). See **Stefani, Marchionne di Coppo.**

Marco del Buono (mär′kō del bwō′nō). Florentine painter; active in the middle of the 15th century. He was enrolled in the Physicians' and Apothecaries' Guild at Florence in 1426. After 1446 he was almost exclusively engaged in painting cassoni panels.

Marco d'Oggiono (dôd-jō′nō). Milanese painter; b. at Oggiono in Brianza, c1475; d. c1530. He may have been a pupil of Butinone, and was in the workshop of Leonardo da Vinci about 1490, when one of his fellow-pupils was Boltraffio. To the best of his severely limited ability he assiduously imitated Leonardo. Copies he made of Leonardo's *Last Supper* are in the Louvre, Paris, the National Gallery, London, and in the Church of S. Maria delle Grazie at Milan itself. His *St. Sebastian*, Berlin, is derived from a Leonardo drawing. A number of his works are at Milan, in the Brera, Ambrosiana, Castello Sforzesco, and Poldi Pezzoli museums. His *St. Roch* in the Carrara Academy, Bergamo, is a companion to his *St. Sebastian* in the Poldi Pezzoli Museum; a *Madonna Nursing the Child* at Princeton is a replica of one at Paris. His *St. John* in the sacristy of S. Maria delle Grazie, Milan, has portraits of Ludovico il Moro and his wife. In his mannerist paintings the composition is confused, the color garish; the art historian Kenneth Clark called his style "peculiarly revolting" and labeled his signed altarpiece, *The Three Archangels*, Brera, "monstrous."

Marconi (mär-kō′nē), **Rocco.** Venetian painter; documented 1504; d. at Venice, 1529. He was probably a native of Treviso, and is known from 1504 when he signed an altarpiece, *Redeemer Between SS. Andrew and Peter*, SS. Giovanni e Paolo, Venice. He was a follower of Bellini, and was influenced by Palma Vecchio and Paris Bordone; his work was sometimes confused with or attributed to the latter painter. Among his paintings are *The Redeemer*, Carrara Academy, Bergamo, *Christ Blessing*, Johnson Collection, Philadelphia, and *Christ and the Woman Taken in Adultery*. He must have been enormously pleased with the success of the last, for he made twelve replicas of the painting, four of which are at Venice; others are at Brescia, Berlin, Rome, and elsewhere. It was copied any number of times by other painters.

Marenzio (mä-ren′tsyō), **Luca.** Musician and composer of madrigals; b. at Coccaglio, between Brescia and Bergamo, c1533; d. at Rome, August 22, 1599. He studied singing and counterpoint under Giovanni Contino of the Brescian school, and published a first book of madrigals, for five voices, in 1580, at Venice. The collection, dedicated to Cardinal Luigi d'Este, earned him an invitation to be the cardinal's musician, and from this dated his artistic career. More collections of madrigals were published and showed his mastery of the form. He served King Sigismund III of Poland and Cardinal Aldobrandini at Rome. His fame as a composer of madrigals was great and well-deserved, as under him the form reached a peak of perfection.

Marescalco (mä-räs-käl′kō). Comedy by Aretino.

Marescalco or **Mariscalchi** (mä-rēs-käl′kē), **Pietro.** [Called **Dalla Spado** or **lo Spada.**] Painter; b. at Feltre, c1503; d. 1584. He was a pupil of Titian and was a close follower of Jacopo Bassano. Among his several paintings in the Pinacoteca at Feltre is a portrait, *Doctor Zacharias dal Pozzo at the age of 102* (1561); a *Madonna of Mercy*, with sixteen scenes from the life of the Madonna is in the cathedral at Feltre. Other works are in churches in the neighborhood of Feltre and Belluno, as at Farra, Lamon, Meano, Mel, Mugnai, Pedavena, Sedico, and at Bassanello (Padua), Dresden, Dublin, and in the Johnson Collection, Philadelphia.

Marfisa (mär-fē′zä). In Matteo Maria Boiardo's *Orlando Innamorato* and Lodovico Ariosto's *Orlando Furioso*, an Indian queen, an Amazon who has vowed that she will not put off her armor until she has captured three kings. She is the equal of the knights in strength, courage, and pride. She is engaged in a duel with Rinaldo, at the siege of Albracca, when Galafrone, the king whose city is under siege, comes to her aid. Seeing Rinaldo outnumbered she, in the highest tradition of chivalry, goes to his aid. When she seems about to be bested, Rinaldo returns the compliment by rushing to her aid.

Marganorre (mär-gä-nôr′rā). In Lodovico Ariosto's *Orlando Furioso*, a wicked lord. His two sons died for love, and Marganorre hates women. He will not allow women in his castle, and if any fall into his hands he whips them, then cuts off their clothes. Ruggiero, Bradamante, and Marfisa capture him and turn him over to some of his recent victims. They prick, goad, and stone him to death.

Margaret (mär′ga̤-re̤t) (of *Denmark*, *Norway*, and *Sweden*). Queen of Denmark (1387), Sweden (1388), and Norway (1388); b. 1353; d. aboard ship in Flensburg Harbor, October 28, 1412. The daughter of Waldemar IV of Denmark, she married Haakon VI of Norway, and after the death (1387) of their son became queen of Denmark and Norway. With the aid of disaffected nobles of Sweden, she became queen of that country in 1388. Through her efforts the Union of Kalmar, a union of the three nations, was concluded in 1397.

Margaret (of *England*). Queen of England; b. 1282; d. February 14, 1318. She was the youngest daughter of Philip III of France, and the second wife of Edward I of England to whom she was betrothed at the Peace of Monteuil (1299). She was never crowned queen.

Margaret (of *Scotland*). Queen of Scotland; b. at Windsor, October 5, 1240; d. at Cupar Castle, February 27, 1275. She was the eldest daughter of Henry III of England and Eleanor of Provence. She married Alexander III of Scotland (1251).

Margaret (of *Scotland*). [Called the **Maid of Norway.**] Queen of Scotland; b. in Norway, 1283; d. at sea, 1290. She was the daughter of Eric II of Norway, and granddaughter of Alexander III of Scotland whom she succeeded in 1286. She was betrothed to Edward of England (afterward Edward II) but died while on her way to meet him. Her death was followed by the contests of the Bruce and Baliol families for the throne.

Margaret of Anjou (an′jö). Queen consort of Henry VI of England; b. probably at Pont-à-Mousson or Nancy, France, March 23, 1430; d. at Dampierre, near Saumur, France, August 25, 1482. She was the daughter of René I of Anjou and Isabella of Lorraine. Her marriage (1445), brought about in confirmation of a truce with France, was unpopular in England. The birth of her son Edward (1453) during his father's first attack of insanity resulted in a contest for his regency between Margaret and Richard, duke of York. The king recovered in January 1455, but the birth of the son, and the hostile attitude of Margaret induced the duke of York (until the birth of Edward, the heir presumptive to the throne) to take up arms. This was the start of the Wars of the Roses. Margaret was defeated and captured at Tewksbury in 1471, and her son was killed. Her husband died in the Tower of London in May 1471. Upon renunciation of her claim to the throne, and payment of a ransom by Louis XI of France, Margaret was liberated and returned to the continent.

Margaret of Austria. Regent of the Netherlands (1507–1530); b. at Ghent, Belgium, January 10, 1480; d. at Mechlin, Belgium, December 1, 1530. She was the daughter of the emperor Maximilian I, and married the infante John of Spain (1497), and later (1501), Philibert II of Savoy. She was guardian (1507–1515) of the future emperor Charles V. With Louise of Savoy, mother of Francis I of France, she negotiated the Peace of Cambrai (1529), which in consequence is sometimes called La Paix des Dames (The Ladies' Peace).

Margaret of Burgundy (bėr′gun-di). [Title, Duchess of **Burgundy.**] Wife of Charles the Bold, duke of Burgundy; b. at Fotheringay Castle, Nottinghamshire, May 3, 1446; d. at Mechlin, 1503. Caxton learned the new art of printing in her household.

Margaret of Navarre (nạ-vär). [Also, **Margaret** or **Marguerite of Valois,** or of **Angoulême,** or of **Alençon.**] Queen of Navarre; b. at Angoulême, France, April 11, 1492; d. at Bigorre, France, September 21, 1549. She was the daughter of Charles d'Orléans, duc d'Angoulême, and sister of Francis I of France. She married (1509) Charles d'Orléans, duc d'Alençon, and later (1527) Henri d'Albret (Henry II), king of Navarre. Through the second marriage she was grandmother of Henry IV of France (Henry of Navarre). After the death of the king in 1544, she assumed the direction of the government. For a time she was favorably disposed to Protestantism, but subsequently abandoned it. She is especially famous as a patroness of literature and as the author of the *Heptameron,* a collection of tales modeled on the *Decameron* and believed actually to have been written by members of the literary circle she gathered about her at her courts at Pau and Nerac. A number of her poems were published (1547) by Sylvius de la Haye under the title *Marguerites de la marguerite des princesses.*

Margaret of Parma. [Also, **Margaret of Austria.**] Duchess of Parma; b. 1522; d. at Ortona, 1586. She was an illegitimate daughter of the emperor Charles V. In 1533 she married Alessandro de' Medici, duke of Florence. He was assassinated in 1537, and in 1542 she married Ottavio Farnese, duke of Parma. She was regent of the Netherlands (1559–1567) for Philip II of Spain. At first sympathetic to the disaffected, she turned against them when they resorted to violence. She resigned, however, when the duke of Alva, a harsh administrator, came to the Netherlands to suppress the movement.

Margaret of Scotland (skot′land). Scottish poet; b. c1425; d. at Châlons, France, August 16, 1445. She was the eldest child of James I of Scotland, and wife of the dauphin Louis (Louis XI). She wrote rondeaux and considered herself a pupil of Alain Chartier.

Margaret Tudor (tū′dọr). Queen of Scotland; b. at Westminster, November 29, 1489; d. at Methven Castle, Scotland, October 18, 1541. She was the wife of James IV of Scotland, and daughter of Henry VII of England.

William Dunbar wrote a poem on the occasion of her marriage and was her constant attendant. After the death of James IV she married Archibald Douglas, 6th earl of Angus, by whom she became the mother of Margaret Douglas, the mother of Lord Darnley. She was divorced March 11, 1527, and in March, 1528, acknowledged her marriage with Henry Stewart, created Lord Methven by James V. She shifted continually between the French and English parties, and back again, was in power and in disgrace several times, and to the end of her life continued her intrigues.

Margaritone d'Arezzo (mär-gä-rē-tō′nā dä-ret′tsō). Tuscan painter; mentioned, 1262, and probably active in the second half of the 13th century. His primitive painting is strongly attached to the Byzantine style, formal iconography repeated in much the same design over and over again. A signed retable, *Virgin and Child Enthroned,* with seven incidents from the lives of the saints, is in the National Gallery, London. A *Madonna and Child Enthroned* is in the National Gallery, Washington. His favorite subject was St. Francis. Eight panels of the saint, all signed, are extant. They are at Arezzo, Castiglion Fiorentino, Cortona, Ganghereto, Montepulciano, Rome (Vatican), Siena, and Zurich.

Margutte (mär-göt′tā). In Luigi Pulci's *Morgante Maggiore,* a demi-giant, not twenty feet tall because he had changed his mind about being a giant in mid-growth. He cheerfully accused himself of every sin known to man, and many that were not, except treachery. A glutton, criminal, sinner, and monster of great good humor, in the end he dies of laughter.

Mariana (mä-ryä′nä), **Juan de.** Spanish historian; b. at Talavera, Spain, 1536; d. 1623. His chief work is a *History of Spain* (published in Latin, 1592–1605; in Spanish, 1601).

Mariano d'Antonio Nutoli (mä-ryä′nō dän-tō′nyō nö-tō′lē). Perugian miniaturist and painter; known from 1433; d. 1468. A mediocre painter, he was influenced by Boccati, Benozzo Gozzoli, and Niccolò Alunno. Several examples of his work are in the National Gallery of Umbria at Perugia.

Mariano di Ser Austerio (dē ser aus-tā′ryō). Perugian painter; known from 1493; d. before 1547. He was a follower of Perugino. Predella panels painted by him, for an altarpiece executed by Lo Spagna now in the Louvre, Paris, are in the National Gallery of Umbria at Perugia.

Marignolli (mä-rē-nyōl′lē), **Curzio.** Florentine wit and improviser; b. c1546; d. at Paris, 1606. He was a member of a well-to-do and ancient Florentine family who, by his manner of living, wasted his inheritance and was at times in very reduced circumstances. He was a wit and a scapegrace, with a wonderful facility at improvising mocking and playful verse, and was a leading spirit in the group of gay poets at Florence. In 1600 he went to Paris for the marriage of Maria de' Medici to Henry IV and remained there until his death. He is better known by his appearance in the memoirs of others than by any body of work he left.

Marignolli, Fra **Giovanni de'.** Missionary and traveler; b. at Florence, of a noble family, about the end of the 13th or the beginning of the 14th century; d. 1359. He was a member of the Franciscan convent of Santa Croce at Florence, and for a short time taught at the University of Bologna. In 1338 he was chosen by Pope Benedict XII to head a mission to the Great Khan of China. The mission was sent at the request of the Khan. The party of which Fra Giovanni was the leader set out from Avignon in December, 1338, and reached Peking in the summer of 1342. They had sailed from Naples, passed through the Sea of Azov, crossed the Volga, and traversed Turkestan and the Gobi Desert. They were warmly welcomed by the Chinese emperor and encouraged in their missionary work, but after three years decided to return to Europe. The return journey took them to Java, Sumatra, India, Ceylon, and through the Persian Gulf. Fra Giovanni returned to the papal court at Avignon in 1353. In 1354 he became chaplain to the emperor Charles IV, and was afterward appointed bishop of Bisignano. He incorporated notes of his travels in a chronicle of Bohemia, *Cronaca di Boemia,* which he compiled by order of the emperor.

Marineo (mä-rē-nā′ō), **Luca.** [Latinized, **Lucius Marinus Siculus.**] Humanist and historian; b. at Vizzini, Catania, c1460; d. in Spain, 1533. He studied at Catania and Palermo, spent a year (1478) at Rome, and then returned to Palermo, where he taught grammar (1479–1484). In 1484 he went to Spain, and there taught at the University of Salamanca. With his teaching he continued his own studies, especially of Cicero, Quintilian, and Pliny, and sought to deduce rules of eloquence from the study of their works. He also maintained many contacts with Italian and Spanish humanists. In 1499 he was called to the court of Ferdinand the Catholic and made the king's historian. His *De rebus Hispaniae memorabilibus* (1533), dedicated to Ferdinand and Charles V, is based on documents, seeks causes and motives, and extends beyond a mere recital of events to include material on social and cultural conditions of the period. Marineo also left a large collection of letters, valuable for the information they contain on conditions of his day. Other works include *De parcis*, a medley of mythological, lexicographical, and grammatical items that reveals his wide knowledge of the classical writers.

Mariotto di Nardo (mä-ryōt′tō dē när′dō). Tuscan painter; d. after 1424. He was the son of Nardo, a stonecutter who worked at Siena (1360) and Volterra (1381). In 1394 and 1395 he painted an altarpiece on commission for a church at Villamagna, and in 1394 and 1398 he was painting altarpieces for the cathedral at Florence where (1408), he was listed as one of the artists of the city. He was probably a pupil of Lorenzo di Niccolò Gerini, and was at first a painter in the traditional 14th-century Florentine style. Later he was influenced to some extent by the international style of Lorenzo Monaco, of whom he became a provincial follower. His compositions are simple, symmetrical, and uncluttered; the faces of his figures, just slightly more full than profile, are out of drawing. He left no signed work, but many works are credited to him on the basis of documents, and others are attributed to him on stylistic grounds. These include a number of frescoes (as a *Crucifixion* and others in S. Croce and scenes from the Passion in the Farmacia di S. Maria Novella) and panels in the Accademia (*Annunciation*, *Madonna and Child and Saints*, 1418, and others), churches (*Holy Trinity*, S. Trinità), and other collections at Florence; and works at Arezzo, Bergamo, Empoli, Fiesole, Panzano (Pieve di S. Leonino), Pesaro, Pistoia, Rome (Vatican), Budapest, Cambridge, England, Hampton Court, Kiev, Paris, Vaduz (a twelve-sided marriage plate with *The Garden of Love*, Liechtenstein Collection), Vienna, Baltimore (Walters Art Gallery), Birmingham (Alabama), Detroit (*Madonna of Humility*), Grand Rapids (Michigan), Los Angeles, New Haven (predella panel with a scene from the legend of SS. Cosmas and Damian), Oberlin (Ohio), Princeton, Providence, Sarasota, and elsewhere.

Markos (mär′kōs), Fray. See **Niza, Marcos de.**

Marone (mä-rô′nā), **Andrea.** Poet and improviser; b. at Pordenone, c1474; d. at Rome, 1527. He taught at Venzone, then went to Ferrara. There he was a favorite of Cardinal Ippolito d'Este, whom he accompanied to Hungary. He was later at the court of Pope Leo X at Rome, and won great acclaim there with his Latin improvisations, accompanying himself on the viola as he improvised. When Pope Adrian VI ascended the papal chair, Marone left Rome, but returned when Clement VII succeeded. Overwhelmed by a series of disasters, he planned to retire to a benefice Leo X had given him, but fell ill and died in Rome.

Marot (mȧ-rō), **Clément.** French poet; b. at Cahors, France, 1497; d. at Turin, 1544. His father had been court poet to the queen of France, Anne de Bretagne, and through him the son obtained access to the court circles, where he won the good will of Margaret of Navarre, sister of Francis I. When Francis I came to the throne in 1515, Clément Marot attracted the king's attention by his poem *Le Temple de Cupidon*, and was retained by him at court. The poet followed his royal patron on his expeditions, and led on the whole an eventful life. His tendency was towards humanism and, to some extent, the Reformation, and he was after 1526 always under suspicion of heresy. He was arrested in 1526 but freed the same year, and in 1535 had to flee to Ferrara and later to Rome, where he obtained the aid of Pope Paul III to enable him to return (1539) to France. There he got into a literary quarrel, with the result that he again fled (1543), this time to Geneva and Calvin. But Calvinism was not palatable to the liberal mind of Marot and he left Geneva for Turin, where he died. Besides a great deal of original poetry, light, graceful, satirical, and including *Enfer* (written in prison, 1526), *Adolescence Clémentine* (a collection published 1532), and *Blasons* (c1536), Marot also translated portions of Vergil, Ovid, and Petrarch, and fifty-two

MARIOTTO DI NARDO
Initial Letter A
The British Museum, London

psalms of David. His complete works have been variously edited; the last edition from the author's lifetime is dated 1544.

Marrasio (mär-rä′syō), **Giovanni.** Humanist and poet; b. at Noto (Sicily), c1405; d. there, 1457. Having chosen a career in letters, he went to Siena (1425) to study the humanities, and then to Florence (1430), but fled the plague in that city for Padua, where he studied medicine for three years. He took his doctorate, removed to Ferrara, where he remained ten years, and then returned to Sicily and practiced medicine. His lifelong interest in poetry resulted in a collection of love lyrics that was among the earliest of the humanistic *canzoniere* (1429). It consisted of seven elegies, with a prologue and an epilogue, and was interwoven with many scenes and episodes. The loved lady of the collection was an Angelina Piccolomini (Marrasio was a schoolmate of Enea Silvio Piccolomini, the future Pope Pius II). Also remaining are two elegies, composed for a mythological masque that was produced at Ferrara (1433). Other poems are to be found in several codices.

Marsigli (mär-sē′lyē), **Luigi.** Florentine cleric and humanist; d. August 21, 1394. A member of the Order of Hermits of St. Augustine, he studied at Paris, where he became a master of theology, traveled in France and Italy and returned (c1379) to Florence. Noted for his learning and ability, he several times served as Florentine ambassador to the duke of Anjou (1382, 1385, 1390). Pope Boniface IX was asked to name him bishop of Florence, but the pope was displeased with him because of his writings concerning the corrupt manners and morals of the papal court at Avignon, and also because Marsigli supported the rights of the states in quarrels with the Church, and would not name him bishop. Marsigli's cell, in Santo Spirito across the Arno, became a meeting place for those who wished to discuss theological questions, intellectual matters, and the literature of the ancients, in which he was learned. He defended the study of classical literature and was closely associated with Coluccio Salutati as one of the originators of humanism in Florence. A younger contemporary and correspondent of Petrarch, he left a commentary on two of the poet's sonnets, and some letters and criticisms of the court at Avignon.

Marsili (mär-sē′lē), **Ippolito de'.** Jurisconsult; b. at Bologna, 1450; d. there, 1529. He took his doctorate in civil and canon law at Bologna and then taught there. Later, he gave up teaching and held many positions in his native city, especially in its relations with other states. At length he returned to the practice and teaching of law at Bologna and continued in these two fields until his death. Among his works, his *Practica criminalis* (Venice, 1551) is one of the best known. He also wrote *Singularia* (Bologna, 1501) and *Consilia* and *Commentaria*, on civil and penal matters, as well as other treatises. His works went through many editions.

Marsilio (mär-sē′lyō). [Also, **Marsilius, Marsirio.**] Saracen king in the Carolingian cycle of romance. He appears in the Italian versions of the cycle: Matteo Maria Boiardo's *Orlando Innamorato*, Lodovico Ariosto's *Orlando Furioso*, and Luigi Pulci's *Morgante maggiore*. In the latter, he is slain for his treacherous ambush of Orlando at the Pass of Roncesvalles.

Marsilius of Padua (mär-sil′i-us; pad′ū-ạ). [Italian, **Marsiglio.**] Medieval Italian scholar and political theorist; b. at Padua, 1270; d. c1342. Of his early life nothing is known; he is first noted (c1312) as rector of the University of Paris. When in 1324 Pope John XXII intervened in a dispute over the succession to the imperial crown by excommunicating Louis of Bavaria, Marsilius, probably with the help of the Frenchman John of Jandun, wrote the tract *Defensor Pacis*, one of the crucial political documents of the late Middle Ages. It is a thoroughgoing statement not only of the case for the imperial as against the papal authority, but of the theory of the sovereignty of the people. This theory was a commonplace of scholasticism, but the anti-ecclesiastical turn given it by Marsilius caused even Louis of Bavaria to consider prosecuting him for heresy. Upon second thought, perceiving the tract's utility in his cause, Louis, to whom the work was dedicated, extended his patronage to Marsilius. Marsilius accompanied Louis to Rome, where Louis was crowned emperor not by the Pope, but by adherents who claimed to be delegates of the people (and, for good measure, by two bishops). The coronation occurred in January, 1328, and in April Louis pronounced the deposition of John XXII and caused Pietro Rainalducci, also known as Pietro de Corbara, a mendicant friar, to be proclaimed pope under the title of Nicholas V. Nicholas was stigmatized by the Church as an antipope. Named imperial vicar by Louis, Marsilius persecuted clerics who remained faithful to Pope John. Marsilius contended that the power exercised by the Church over civil affairs was, in fact, usurped power, and that the Church should confine itself to the conduct of worship. He denied to popes and bishops any power of excommunication or interdiction. The Church should be governed by councils, to be summoned only by the emperor; the Bishop of Rome, to whom primacy was conceded, should be only a sort of honorary head of the church, without authority to define dogmas. Moreover, the distribution of benefices should lie with the emperor only. Tithes should be abolished, and church property should be seized, so that the clergy would be constrained to observe the rule of poverty. The *Defensor Pacis*, translated from the Latin into several of the vulgar languages including English, had repercussions for centuries after its publication, and influenced the thought of Wycliffe and of Luther.

Marsuppini (mär-sö-pē′nē), **Carlo.** [Also called, **Carlo d'Arezzo.**] Humanist; b. at Genoa, 1398; d. at Florence, April 24, 1453. Early in life his family, originally from Arezzo, went to Florence. Niccolò Niccoli and Cosimo de' Medici encouraged the promising young man in his studies. He studied Greek under Guarino da Verona and Latin under Giovanni Malphaghini, became a tutor of Lorenzo de' Medici (brother of Cosimo) and (1431) went to the university at Florence to teach. He lectured there until 1444, when he became chancellor of Florence. In this position he was responsible for the foreign correspondence and many state speeches and orations for the republic, and was one of the most distinguished humanists to hold the position. He translated the *Batracomiomachia* of Homer from the Greek, first in prose and then in verse, and began a translation of the *Iliad*, completing two books. Vespasiano, who admired his learning and his remarkable memory, writes, rather severely, that if he had spent more time on his writings and less on other things he "might have produced a rich harvest."

Martano (mär-tä′nō). In Lodovico Ariosto's *Orlando Furioso*, a coward loved by Orrigille.

Martelli (mär-tel′lē), **Ludovico.** Florentine writer, active between 1503 and 1531. He took part in the Battle of Capo d'Orso (1528) and was taken prisoner. While in prison he wrote a poetic description of the battle that is outstanding for the wealth and accuracy of its detail. He also wrote a tragedy, *Tullia*, on the wife of Tarquinius Superbus, and took part in a literary dispute on the authenticity of Dante's *De vulgari eloquentia*. He asserted that Dante did not write it.

Martin IV. [Original name, **Simon de Brie.**] Pope (1281–1285); b. in Touraine, France, c1210; d. at Perugia, March, 1285. He succeeded Nicholas III. He had been chancellor of France under Louis IX. He took the name Martin IV in the belief that two popes named Marinus had been named Martin (Martinus); actually, therefore, he should have been Martin II. Under the influence of Charles of Anjou (Charles I of Naples), who had assured his election, Martin IV excommunicated the emperor Michael Palaeologus, thus terminating the reunion of the Greek and Roman churches effected in 1274 at the Council of Lyons. After the anti-French revolt (1282) known as the Sicilian Vespers, he used the power of his office to foster and protect French interests against those of Aragon and was eventually driven out of Rome by an uprising. He was succeeded by Honorius IV.

Martin V. [Original name, **Oddone Colonna.**] Pope (1417–1431); b. in the Campagna di Roma, 1368; d. at Rome, February 20, 1431. He was a member of a powerful Roman family, was created cardinal by Innocent VII, and was noted for his virtues and his knowledge of canon law. During the Great Schism (1378–1417) he supported the Councils of Pisa and Constance. The latter deposed the antipopes Benedict XIII and John XXIII and accepted the abdication of Pope Gregory XII, ruled for two years and elected Martin (1417) thus ending the Great Schism. (When Martin became pope he denied the authority of councils.) Invited by the French and by Sigismund of Germany to settle in their territories, Martin declined and resolved to return to Rome. He went first to Mantua, then to Florence, where he stayed two years, and entered Rome on September 30, 1420, to great rejoicing. Rome was in a state of ruin and anarchy; brigands roamed the streets; wolves prowled the Vatican gardens at night; the basilicas and shrines were falling into decay. Martin's first concerns were to restore order, to repair and reconstruct the churches, and to rebuild the power and influence of the papacy in the States of the Church. They, and the income they represented, had been lost through usurpation and revolt during the Great Schism. Martin calmed the uproar in the city and set about restoring the churches. In this task he had the help of the cardinals. A new roof was put on St. John Lateran, an inlaid pavement was laid, and Gentile da Fabriano was called to Rome to decorate the walls. Influenced during his stay in Florence by the artistic ferment there, he sent to Florence for artists, among them Lorenzo Ghiberti, to carry out various commissions. His patronage of artists began to have an effect on Rome, which for so many years had been too impoverished to feel a need for art.

His political and diplomatic activities centered about rebuilding his temporal power. When Braccio da Montone, a noted condottiere and enemy, died, Perugia, Assisi, Todi and others submitted to the Church. They were later joined by Imola, Forlì, Fermo, Borgo San Sepolcro and others. He strengthened his own power by a series of advantageous marriages for his relatives, for whom he provided magnificent dowries. He made one brother duke of Amalfi and prince of Salerno, and another count of Alba, with accompanying lands and revenues. Such aggrandizement of the Colonna family increased the antagonism of the Orsini, a rival Roman family, and earned Martin the accusation of nepotism. He attempted to regain papal supremacy abroad and called for a crusade against the Hussites of Bohemia, but it collapsed. Martin showed himself more interested in the restoration of Rome and of the papal power than in reform of the Church. He was reluctant to call a council, as he was urged to do, called one, but it accomplished nothing and he dissolved it. He yielded to further demands and called another which was to meet in 1431. He died before it met, and was buried in the Lateran. He was succeeded by Eugenius IV.

Martin I (of *Aragon*). King of Aragon (1395–1410) and (as Martin II) of Sicily (1409–1410); b. at Gerona, Spain, 1356; d. at Barcelona, May 31, 1410. He was the son of Pedro IV and Pedro's third wife, Leonora of Sicily. When his brother John I died without an heir Martin succeeded him (1395). The early part of his reign was occupied with wars with the count of Foix, and he was not crowned until April 13, 1399. Martin supported the antipope Benedict XIII and sent him ships for his struggle against Boniface IX. Boniface excommunicated Martin and denied his, and his sons', claim to Corsica, Sardinia, and Sicily. Martin the Younger, son of Martin I, married Maria, Aragonese heiress to the throne of Sicily and became king, as Martin I of Sicily. When he was killed, 1409, Martin I of Aragon inherited his throne and became Martin II of Sicily. Martin I of Aragon was succeeded by Ferdinand I.

Martini (mär-tē′nē), **Francesco di Giorgio.** See **Francesco di Giorgio Martini.**

Martini, Simone. See **Simone Martini.**

Martino di Bartolommeo (mär-tē′nō dē bär-tō-lôm-mā′ō). Sienese painter; documented from 1389 to 1434. He was the son of a goldsmith, was a pupil of Giacomo di Mino del Pellicciaio, and was influenced by Andrea Vanni and Taddeo di Bartolo. By 1389 he was enrolled among the Sienese painters. Among his earliest known works is a series of frescoes, partly destroyed, in the Church of S. Giovanni dei Cavalieri Gerosolimitani, Cascina, signed and dated (1398). Several of his works are at Pisa, where he worked at the turn of the century, and more are in the Pinacoteca, Palazzo Pubblico, Spedale di S. Maria della Scala, and churches at Siena. An endearing series of seven scenes from the life of St. Stephen is at Frankfurt, showing, among them, the swaddled infant St. Stephen being stolen by devils and, in another scene, being discovered as he is being nursed by an unlikely looking goat. Other works are at Asciano, Bagnoregio (S. Agostino), Florence (Bargello), Rome (Vatican), Sassari, Berlin, Cambridge (Massachusetts), Columbus (Ohio), El Paso, Los Angeles, New Haven, New York, Philadelphia, Poughkeepsie (Vassar College), and elsewhere.

Martino da Udine (dä ö′dē-nā). See **Pellegrino da San Daniele.**

Martino da Verona (dä vā-rō′nä). Veronese painter; d. 1413. His only extant signed work is a series of frescoes in the Church of S. Fermo Maggiore at Verona. He also worked in other churches in his native city. Martino's painting shows the influence of German painting, introduced by way of the Tyrol, a use of Gothic forms, and an interest in and use of contemporary costume in his work.

Martirano (mär-tē-rä′nō), **Bernardino.** Man of letters; b. at Cosenza, c1490; d. 1548(?). Of a noble family, he was educated at the Cosentine Academy under Parrasio. He was in Rome during the sack (1527), and later became an official in the government of the kingdom of Naples, which he served until his death. At his magnificent villa near Portici he welcomed the poet Luigi Tansillo, who dedicated one of his *capitoli* to him, and the philosopher Bernardino Telesio. Charles V visited him on his way back from Tunis. Among Martirano's works is *Aretusa,* a poem in which he combined the myths of Narcissus and Arethusa and subverted them to a political theme.

Martirano, Coriolano. Ecclesiastic and humanist; b. at Cosenza, 1503; d. at Naples, 1558. He was the brother of Bernardino Martirano (c1490–1548?). His early career was in the law. Clement VII named him bishop of Cosenza, and he played an active part in the Council of Trent. Later he was named secretary to the Council of the Kingdom of Naples. He was an ardent and learned humanist, wrote excellent Latin, including several tragedies mostly on themes taken from the Greek, several comedies, and translated part of the *Odyssey*. He sought in his *Christus* to deal with a religious theme in a classical form derived from Euripides. His Latin tragedies are notable for their style and show some originality of creative interpretation.

Martyr (mär′tėr), **Peter.** See **Anghiera, Pietro Martire d'.**

Marullo (mä′röl-lō), **Michele.** Poet and soldier; b. at Constantinople, 1453; d. at River Cecina, 1500. His family, originally from Achaea in Greece, removed to Italy after the fall of Constantinople (1453). In Italy, Marullo became a soldier. He was in the pay of Caterina Sforza in the defense of Forlì. As a man of letters he was a member of Pontano's circle at Naples, and of literary circles at Florence. In the latter city he met and married the humanist Alessandra Scala. She was the daughter of Bartolomeo Scala, one of Lorenzo the Magnificent's secretaries, and had been wooed by the poet Angelo Poliziano. Marullo's emergence as the successful suitor won Poliziano's enmity. Marullo's poems breathe his melancholy for his fallen country. His love lyrics to Alessandra (*Silvia*) are elegantly reminiscent of Catullus. In his *Hymni naturales* he took Lucretius as a model and, combining his Christian ideas with Neoplatonic themes derived from Gemistus Plethon and Ficino, exalted nature with an almost pagan enthusiasm.

Marulo (mä′rö-lō), **Marco.** Dalmatian humanist; b. at Spalato, 1450; d. there, 1524. He studied at Padua, then returned to Spalato. There he soon gave up his gay and thoughtless life and devoted himself to the study of philosophy. From that time he was a solitary and an ascetic. He is one of the more typical of the Dalmatian humanists who lived and wrote in the spirit of the Christian Renaissance. His Latin moral and religious works, breathing classical culture and a profoundly religious spirit, were highly esteemed in his day and went through several editions and various translations. He also wrote poems and some prose in his native Croation. These are among the earliest examples of Croatian literature.

Mary I or **Mary Tudor** (of *England*). [Called **Bloody Mary.**] Queen of England and Ireland (1553–1558); b. at Greenwich Palace, February 18, 1516; d. November 17, 1558. She was the child of Henry VIII and Catherine of Aragon. Upon the death of her half brother, Edward VI, she was proclaimed queen. She put down an insurrection in favor of Lady Jane Grey early in 1554. She married Philip II of Spain in the same year. In 1555 the papal power in England was restored, and the penal laws against heresy revived. The total number of martyrs during her reign was 300; among them, Ridley, Latimer, and Cranmer. As a result of a war with France, Calais, the last English possession on the continent, was lost.

Mary of Burgundy (bėr′gun-di). [French, **Marie de Bourgogne.**] Duchess of Burgundy; b. at Brussels, February 13, 1457; d. there, March 27, 1482. She was the daughter of Charles the Bold. On her father's death (1477) the duchy was seized by Louis XI of France, who attempted to marry her to the dauphin (later Charles VIII), but she refused and turned to her possessions in the Netherlands. Before the Netherlanders would accept her, she had to sign the Great Privilege, reestablishing local rights and limiting Mary's powers. She married (1477) Maximilian of Austria, who later became (1493) Maximilian I of the Holy Roman Empire.

Mary of France. [Originally called **Mary Tudor.**] Wife of Louis XII of France; b. March, 1496; d. at Westhorpe, December 24, 1533. She was the daughter of Henry VII, who married her to Louis XII after a betrothal to Charles V was withdrawn. She later married Charles Brandon, duke of Suffolk, and was the grandmother of Lady Jane Grey.

Mary of Guise (gēz, gwēz). [Also, **Mary of Lorraine.**] Queen of James V of Scotland, and mother of Mary, Queen of Scots; b. at Bar-le-Duc, November 22, 1515; d. at Edinburgh, June 10, 1560. She became regent of Scotland, James V having died the week his daughter was born. Mary of Guise was pro-French and Catholic, and came into conflict with John Knox and the Reformers, which resulted in her suspension from the regency.

Mary, Queen of Scots. [Also, **Mary Stuart.**] Queen of Scotland (1542–1567); b. in Linlithgow Palace, December 7 or 8, 1542; beheaded at Fotheringay, February 8, 1587. She was the daughter of James V of Scotland and Mary of Guise. As the granddaughter of Margaret Tudor, sister of Henry VIII, she was next in line of succession to Henry VIII and his children. Mary was brought up at the French court in the Roman Catholic faith, and married (1558) the dauphin (later Francis II of France). After the death of Francis, Mary returned to Scotland. She recognized the rights of Protestants, but reserved her own right to her own religion, which brought her into conflict with John Knox and the Reformers. In 1563 Mary pressed her claim to the succession of England by sending an embassy to Elizabeth. In 1565 she married Lord Darnley, her cousin, by whom she had a son who became James VI of Scotland, and James I of England. Her marriage to the Catholic Darnley, the scandals of the murder of her secretary Rizzio, the death of Darnley under suspicious circumstances, and her subsequent marriage (1567) to Bothwell, led to a revolt of the Scottish lords. Mary was compelled to abdicate in favor of her son. The following year her forces were defeated at Langside. She fled to England where she expected asylum, but Elizabeth, recognizing the threat to the throne, kept her confined first at Carlisle and later at Sheffield, where she remained from 1569 to 1583. A long succession of plots, principally by Roman Catholics, disturbed the peace of the country, until, as a result of the Babington plot in 1586, Mary was removed to Fotheringay and was tried on a charge of conspiring against the life of Elizabeth. In spite of a spirited defense in her own behalf Mary was found guilty and beheaded at Fotheringay.

Marziale (mär-tsē-ä′lā), **Marco.** Venetian painter; active between 1492 and 1507. He was a pupil of Gentile Bellini, and a follower of Gentile and Giovanni Bellini, with whom he was working on the great historical paintings in the Ducal Palace at Venice in 1492. Though his painting has elements of the older 15th-century tradition and is marked by heavier forms, the influence of Giovanni Bellini is apparent in his *Circumcision* (1499), now in the Correr Museum, Venice. About 1500 he is thought to have moved to Cremona, where he painted another version of the *Circumcision* (1500) for the Church of S. Silvestro; this version is now in the National Gallery, London. Other works include a signed *Madonna and Child, with a Donor* (1504), Carrara Academy, Bergamo, *Supper at Emmaus* (1506), Accademia, Venice, which shows evidence of the influence of Dürer, and another on the same subject at Berlin (1507). Among his last known signed and dated (1507) works is an altarpiece *The Virgin and Child with Saints*, National Gallery, London, which indicates the influence of Perugino. A number of his paintings are extant, as at Budapest, Dresden, Paris, Verona, Zara, Omaha (Nebraska), and elsewhere.

Marzio (mär′tsyō), **Galeotto.** Humanist, physician, and astronomer; b. at Narni, 1427; d. c1497. He studied medicine at Padua, traveled widely, as to Hungary, France, England, and Spain, then returned to Italy, where he taught Latin literature at Bologna (1464). He was imprisoned by the Venetian inquisition for his work, *De incognitis vulgo*, and was released (1478) only through the efforts of Lorenzo de' Medici and Matthias Corvinus, king of Hungary, to whose court he had made several visits in the years 1465–1473. In the years following his release he visited the court of Hungary several more times, and also that of Charles VIII of France (1492). From his study of the classical literature on astronomy, and his study of Averroist philosophy at Padua, Marzio derived a new approach to the study of astronomy that served as a link between the ancients and Copernicus. He left many writings. In addition to poems and letters, there are extant invectives, as against Francesco Filelfo; his *De homine*, written for a Hungarian humanist; two works, including the above-mentioned *De incognitis vulgo*, for Matthias Corvinus; and other works written for Lorenzo de' Medici and Charles VIII.

Masaccio (mä-zät′chō), Italian painter; b. at Castel San Giovanni (now San Giovanni Valdarno), near Florence, December 21, 1401; d. at Rome, 1428. Vasari, who recognized him as a genius and innovator, said of him that he painted in his native village as a boy, and that, "He was most careless of externals. He had fixed his mind on art and could by no means be induced to care for worldly things, such as his own personal interests and still less for the affairs of others. He gave no thought to his clothing and did not collect debts until he was actually in want. Because of this he was called, not Tommaso (which was his name), but Masaccio (as we would say 'Slovenly Tom'). He was called this without malice, simply because of his negligence, for he was always so friendly and so ready to oblige and do a service to others that a better or kinder man could not be imagined." His father Giovanni was a notary and, with his family, lived with his father, who made chests and boxes. Giovanni died in 1406 and his widow, Monna Iacopa, was soon married again, to a well-to-do and elderly apothecary. Thus it appears that the young Masaccio was brought up in relatively comfortable circumstances.

Little is known of his short life. Some critics believe that, showing an aptitude for painting in early youth, he was apprenticed to Masolino da Panicale, who may have been a fellow-townsman and with whom he later worked in Florence. It is thought he was painting the *Madonna, St. Anne and Angels*, in Florence about 1420. In 1422 he was a member of the Physicians' and Apothecaries' Guild, which despite its name included artists, and in 1424 he was a member of the Company of St. Luke, composed exclusively of artists. In 1426 he was carrying out a commission at Pisa on an altarpiece for the Church of the Carmine there. During the same year, or early in the following year, he was again at Florence, commissioned to paint a fresco of *The Holy Trinity*, in the Church of S. Maria Novella. Late in the summer of 1427 he was working with Masolino on the frescoes for the Brancacci Chapel in the Church of the Carmine at Florence. In the fall of 1428, interrupting his work in the Brancacci Chapel, he went to Rome to help Masolino in decorating the Chapel of Cardinal Branda da Castiglione in the Church of S. Clemente. Just before his twenty-seventh birthday he died suddenly; Vasari writes, "they say of poison." It is not clear whether he painted anything in Rome.

Masaccio has been called the father of modern painting. Giotto, whom he took as his master, had freed painting from the stylization of the Byzantine era, in which, for centuries, painting had proceeded according to strict rules—man was a symbol, portrayed according to a stylized, decorative two-dimensional convention. Giotto broke away from the convention and painted man as a human being. Masaccio went further. He was influenced by the sculptor Donatello to see the human form in the round and to give it, in painting, a sculptural quality. The architect Brunelleschi taught him to observe and portray nature as it is and its relation to man. He was the first to use the newly discovered rules of perspective for placing figures in space. He painted the undraped human figure and was aware of the shape and modeling of that figure when it was clothed. His figures have real arms in the sleeves of their coats and muscles and modeling under their robes. In addition, he used light from one source to provide illumination and shadow from and to a focal point. The play of light from one source falls on one side, casting the other side into shadow. The realization and use of this as a technique gives Masaccio's figures a three-dimensional quality. His techniques were not employed, however, simply as advanced devices—they were informed with his vision of man and the world, and executed with a genius that surpasses mere technique. His vision of man was on a heroic scale, imbued with a more than lifesize dignity and nobility, and set against the reality of nature. Leonardo da Vinci said, "After the time of Giotto the art of painting declined again because everyone imitated the pictures that were already done. Thus it went on from century to century until Tommaso, of Florence, nicknamed Masaccio, showed by his perfect works how those who take for their standard anything but nature–mistress of all masters–weary themselves in vain."

As has been true of the works of many artists, some works known to have been painted by Masaccio have been lost, through the hazards of time, from changing tastes, or in the destruction or reconstruction of buildings in which they were located. One such masterpiece by Masaccio was a fresco painted over the door of the cloister of the Church of the Carmine. It was of a ceremonial procession that took place when the church was consecrated, on April 19, 1422. Masaccio included among the participants many portraits, including those of Brunelleschi "in his wooden shoes," Donatello, Masolino, and Antonio Brancacci. The fresco was destroyed when the old cloister was replaced by a new one at the end of the 16th century.

Masaccio's surviving works include the *Madonna with Child, St. Anne and Angels*. This was painted, with Masolino's help, in the Church of Sant' Ambrogio, about 1420. It is now in the Uffizi. In February, 1426, he was commissioned by a notary of Pisa to paint an altarpiece for the Church of the Carmine there. He worked on it most of the year. This altarpiece, consisting of four main panels and many smaller ones, was disassembled and scattered in the 18th century. Parts of it have been discovered in various museums and private collections. The central panel, *Virgin and Child*, is in the National Gallery, London. The panel originally above this, a *Crucifixion*, is one of the most expressive and dramatic in Italian painting. Aware that this panel would be high above the viewer's head, Masaccio used foreshortening and perspective to compensate. As seen from eye level, the head of Christ seems to rest on the collarbones. Seen from below the illusion is a realistic and dramatic one of a limp head fallen forward. The figures of the Virgin and St. John are lengthened in their upper parts to compensate for the fact that looking up at them they would appear shorter. At the feet of the Savior kneels Mary Magdalen, her arms upflung in an arc of despair. The panel is in the National Gallery, Naples. Other panels of the altarpiece are *St. Paul*, Museo Nazionale, Pisa; *St. Andrew*, Lanckoronski Collection, Vienna; *Adoration of the Magi and Martyrdom of St. Peter and John* from the predella, and *St. Augustine* and *St. Jerome*, Berlin. A fresco was painted in the Church of S. Maria Novella, at Florence, late in 1426 or early 1427. It is the *Holy Trinity*, with the Virgin on one side and St. John on the other; they are contemplating Christ crucified. Contemplating is the true word here, for as compared to the drama of the *Crucifixion* of the Pisa altarpiece this is filled with a calm and realized acceptance of Divine Will. Over the head of Christ is God the Father. Vasari, admiring his mastery of perspective, wrote, "the most beautiful part of the picture is the barrel-vaulted ceiling painted in perspective and divided into square compartments, with a rosette in each, so well done that the surface has all the appearance of being indented." The painting was damaged in the disastrous floods of November, 1966.

The work that made Masaccio's painting a school for future artists is the series of frescoes he painted in the Brancacci Chapel in the Church of the Carmine at Florence. Masolino had originally been commissioned to decorate the chapel by Felice Brancacci. He had finished the vault and the upper walls when he left for Hungary, to fulfill a commission there. On his return, late in the summer of 1427, he resumed the work and Masaccio was called on to help him. For a time they worked together. Then Masolino was called to Rome and Masaccio worked alone. The subject of the frescoes is the life of St. Peter. Masaccio painted the episodes on the left wall, *The Tribute Money*, showing Christ surrounded by his disciples in the central portion, instructing Peter where to find the tribute money. According to Vasari, Masaccio painted a portrait of himself, using a mirror to do so, in the figure of Thomas in this group. On the left side of the panel is St. Peter extracting a coin from the mouth of a fish, and on the right side he appears paying it to the tribute collector. The panel below this one has two scenes, the *Resurrection of the Son of the King of Antioch* and *St. Peter Enthroned*. Some figures in the first scene were painted by Filippino Lippi, fifty years later. The lower panel on the left of the window in the end wall shows *St. Peter Healing the Sick by His Shadow*. The upper panel on the right of the window has the *Baptism of the Neophytes*, in which, to quote Vasari again "there is a very celebrated figure of a naked youth shivering with the cold." Below this is *St. Peter Distributing Alms and the Death of Ananias.* On a pilaster to the left of the entrance to the chapel Masaccio executed the fresco *The Expulsion of Adam and Eve.* The poignancy of their anguish at what they had done and what they were doomed to is familiar to every student of the history of art. The leaves painted around their loins were added in a later and less enlightened age. The other walls of the chapel were painted by Masolino, with some help from Masaccio, the pupil who had become teacher. Neither singly nor together did they complete the decoration of the chapel. Masaccio went to Rome and died there. The decoration was completed about fifty years later by Filippino Lippi. (See also, **Brancacci Chapel.**)

It has been said that Masaccio's frescoes on the walls of the Brancacci Chapel were a school for later artists. Filippo Lippi, Andrea del Castagno, Verrocchio, Ghirlandaio, Botticelli, Leonardo da Vinci, Perugino, Michelangelo, and Raphael were among the distinguished students of these panels. They saw in his knowledge and rendering of anatomy and in his use of perspective to place man in a world where nature held its honored place, an exaltation of the value and dignity of man and a natural world, the whole imbued with moving drama. The frescoes were a demonstration, for later artists, of an ideal marriage of developed technique with a noble vision of man in a realistically portrayed world of nature.

Masci d'Ascoli (mä′shē däs′kō-lē), **Girolamo.** Original name of Pope **Nicholas IV.**

Masegne (mä-sā′nye) or **Massegne** (mäs-sā′-nye), **delle** or **dalle.** See **Dalle Masegne.**

Maso di Banco (mä′sō dē bäng′kō). Florentine painter; active in the first half of the 14th century. He was a pupil and close follower of Giotto and, according to some critics, the greatest 14th-century Florentine painter after Giotto. The vigor of Giotto's form and composition is somewhat diminished in Maso's work, without any loss of mass and solidity in the figures. Perhaps owing to the influence of the Lorenzetti, which he felt strongly in his later career, his color, and the use he made of it, is more subtle than Giotto's. Among his surviving works are a series of frescoes on the life of St. Sylvester and frescoes over the Bardi Tomb, in S. Croce, Florence, and fresco series at Assisi (S. Chiara and S. Francesco, Lower Church) and Pistoia (S. Francesco). Other works include panels at Berlin (two of three were destroyed in 1945) and New York from a polyptych, and works at Budapest, Chantilly, Brooklyn (a portable triptych), and Raleigh (North Carolina). Maso di Banco is also known as Giottino (Little Giotto), a name that for long was thought to apply to a separate artist. It is now believed by many that Giottino and Maso are one and the same.

Masolino da Panicale (mä-zō-lē′nō dä pä-nē-kä′lā). [Original name, **Tommaso di Cristoforo Fini.**] Painter; b. at Panicale, c1383; d. probably at Florence, c1447. Almost nothing is known of his early life and training. He went to Florence early in the 15th century, may have worked with Lorenzo Ghiberti (1403–1407), and was enrolled in the Physicians' and Apothecaries' Guild in 1423. His earliest known work is a *Madonna of Humility,* now at Bremen, dated 1423. The following year he executed frescoes in the Church of S. Agostino at Empoli. Among the surviving fragments of these frescoes is one with the heads of a number of yellow-haired girls. With its soft greens and pinks, composition by patterns of color, and the lyric purity of the faces, the work is typical of Masolino's subtlety and charm. Frescoes that he executed in a chapel of the same church have disappeared, exposing the *sinopie* he drew on the rough plaster underneath as a guide for painting the fresco. The *sinopie* reveal his free and firm line and his developed compositional sense. Not long after painting at Empoli, Masolino was commissioned to decorate the Brancacci Chapel in the Gothic Church of the Carmine at Florence. When he had completed the decoration of the vault and the upper walls he left Florence, in September, 1425, and went to Hungary in the train of the Florentine adventurer Pippo Spano. On his return to Florence (July, 1427) he resumed work in the Brancacci Chapel and called on Masaccio to help him. Working with Masaccio (one of their joint productions was *Madonna and Child with St. Anne,* Uffizi, Florence, of which Masolino painted the angels), Masolino was temporarily affected by that young painter's perspective, use of light to create form, and monumentality. Of the frescoes in the Brancacci Chapel,

Masolino painted *St. Peter Healing the Cripple, Resurrection of Tabitha, St. Peter Preaching,* and *The Temptation of Adam and Eve* (on the pilaster opposite Masaccio's dramatic *Expulsion*). In May, 1428, Masolino abandoned the work in the Brancacci Chapel and went to Rome on the invitation of Cardinal Branda da Castiglione to paint frescoes in the Church of S. Clemente with scenes from the lives of St. Catherine and St. Ambrose. A few years later he went to Castiglione d'Olona, the cardinal's home, where he painted frescoes on the life of the Virgin in the apse of the cathedral and frescoed the scenes from the life of St. John the Baptist in the Baptistery, dated 1435, which some consider to be his masterpiece. Of his frescoes in the Baptistery, that showing *The Delivery of the Head of the Baptist to Salome,* with its two parallel rows of arcades that disappear toward a mountain landscape illustrates his knowledge of the new science of perspective. His Salome, with her shaved forehead and billowing headdress, is in the height of fashion of the period c1435. Also at Castiglione d'Olona, he frescoed landscapes and friezes in the palace. Masolino was a delightful follower of the international style of Lorenzo Monaco. Although he was made aware of new conceptions of light and space by Masaccio, this awareness did not greatly affect his subsequent work. He took some steps in the direction of attaining relief by modeling but fundamentally he remained a charming traditionalist whose purity of color and line and simple masses of color and form in composition endow his painting with poetic delicacy and exquisite charm. Besides those mentioned, among his extant works was a triptych, painted on both sides. It has been sawn apart. The central portion, with the *Assumption of the Virgin* on one side and the *Founding of S. Maria Maggiore* (also called *The Miracle of the Snow*) on the other is in the National Museum, Naples. A side panel, *SS. Peter and Paul,* on one side and *Evangelist and S. Martin* on the other, is in the Johnson Collection, Philadelphia. The third panel had *A Pope and St. Matthias* on one side and *St. John the Baptist and St. Jerome* on the other; the last is attributed by most art historians to Masaccio. The sawn apart paintings of the last panel are in the National Gallery, London. Other works by Masolino are at Berne, Munich, Stockholm, Todi, the National Gallery, Washington, and elsewhere.

Mason (mā′sọn), Sir **John.** English diplomat; b. at Abindgon, Berkshire, England, 1503; d. April 20 or 21, 1566. He served under Henry VIII, Edward VI, Mary, and Elizabeth.

Massimo (mä′sē-mō). Name of an ancient and prominent Roman family that claimed, without much foundation, descent from Fabius Maximus Cunctator, the Roman general of the 2nd century B.C. In the second half of the 15th century, the oldest printing press in Rome was established (1467), in the house of Pietro di Massimo at Rome, by the Germans Pannartz and Sweynheim.

Massone (mäs-sō′nā), **Giovanni.** Ligurian painter; b. c1435; d. before 1512. He was fundamentally a follower of the Lombard school of Foppa, with the influence of that school modified by local Ligurian tradition. Highly esteemed in his day, he was active at Genoa and Savona, and left a number of polyptychs. Among his principal works are a polyptych with the *Annunciation* (c1463), S. Maria di Castello, Genoa; a signed *Nativity* (1490–1495) and *Annunciation* (c1493), Savona; and a signed and dated (1490) *Nativity,* Louvre, Paris, and *Crucifixion,* Savona, which are parts of the so-called Della Rovere polyptych, in which Pope Sixtus IV is presented as being recommended by St. Francis. Other examples of his work are at Liverpool, Taggia, and the Johnson Collection, Philadelphia.

Massys (mä-sīs′) or **Matsys** (mät-sīs′) or **Metsys** (met-sīs′), **Quentin** (or **Quintin**). Flemish painter; b. at Louvain, Belgium, c1466; d. at Antwerp, 1530.

Masuccio Salernitano (mä-zöt′chō sä-ler-nē-tä′nō), **Tommaso.** See, **Guardati, Tommaso.**

Matarazzo (mä-tä-rät′tsō) or **Maturanzio** (mä-tö-rän′tsyō), **Francesco.** Perugian chronicler; b. at Deruta (near Perugia), c1443; d. at Perugia, August 20, 1518. He received a good education and was chosen while still a youth to write the Latin inscriptions under the portraits of famous citizens commissioned by Braccio Baglioni to decorate his palace in the city. He taught at Ferrara (1464) and at Vicenza (1467). In 1472 he sailed for Greece, to be instructed in Greek, and to purchase manuscripts. He stayed some time at Rhodes, where he became proficient in Greek, taught, and sought manuscripts. On his return to Perugia (1473) he was welcomed as a scholar and a traveler and thereafter held high offices in the city. But Perugia was in almost continual uproar, caused largely by the struggles within the turbulent Baglioni family for power. He left his city in 1492, spent some time at Vicenza and Venice, and then returned to Perugia, where he became a professor in the university, wrote funeral orations, and (1503) became chancellor of the state. In his official capacity he served on diplomatic missions to Rome and Florence. His *Chronicles of the City of Perugia* give an animated picture of the life of the city in the period 1492–1503; the *Chronicles* record many of the events that occurred in that stormy period when Cesare Borgia was harrowing the Romagna. The Baglioni family, which Matarazzo so greatly admired for all his acknowledgment of their cruelty and immorality, went into eclipse following this period. The extant manuscript of the *Chronicles* is incomplete, but it is an essential source for events of the times.

Matteo d'Acquasparta (mät-tä′ō däk-kwä-spär′tä). Cardinal and canonist; b. at Acquasparta (Todi), about the middle of the 13th century; d. at Rome, August 28 or 29, 1302. A Franciscan, he studied at Paris and had a brilliant career in his order, of which he became general (1287), and in the Church. He became a cardinal in 1288. An expert in canon law and a skillful politician, he had great influence in the Sacred College. In 1297 and 1298 he served as Pope Boniface VIII's legate in the Romagna, where he reduced Cesena, Forlì, Faenza, and Imola to obedience to the Church. The pope sent him to Florence (1300–1301) to resolve the struggle between the Bianchi and Neri, but he was unable to accomplish this. His life was threatened and he was forced to flee the city, leaving it under an interdict. Dante mentions him disapprovingly (*Paradiso*, XII), accusing him of having relaxed the austere rules prescribed by St. Francis for his order.

Matteo da Bascio (dä bä′shō). Franciscan, founder of the Friars Minor Capuchin, an independent order of the Franciscans; b. at Bascio, c1495; d. at Venice, August 7, 1552. In his convent of Monte Falcone, he was seized with the desire to follow the life of St. Francis exactly. He left the convent at night and went to Rome (early in 1525). There he received (February–March, 1525) from Pope Clement VII the personal right to clothe himself in a coarse tight habit with a pointed hood (whence the name "Capuchin"), to preach wherever he wished, alone or with companions, and to observe the rules prescribed by St. Francis, especially that of poverty, to the letter. He began his apostolate at once, encouraged by the protection of the pope and that of Caterina Cybo, duchess of Camerino. Others soon joined him, and in July, 1528, canonical approval of the Capuchin reform was obtained. Matteo was elected vicar general (1529), but he had not intended to found a new order—his motivation was personal—and after a few months he resigned the vicariate and resumed his preaching. In 1527 he went to Germany and preached to the troops of Charles V, then at war against John Frederick I of Saxony and the landgrave, Philip of Hesse. He was present at the victory of the imperial troops at Mühlberg, and was among the first to cross the Elbe (April 24, 1547). He later returned to Venice, famous as a holy man, and died there.

Matteo di Cione (dē chō′nā). Florentine painter and sculptor; d. c1390. The least known of the four brothers: Andrea Orcagna, Nardo, Jacopo, and Matteo di Cione. He worked with his brother Andrea on the tabernacle for Orsanmichele, and also worked with him at Orvieto.

Matteo di Giovanni (dē jō-vän′nē). [Also called **Matteo da Siena.**] Sienese painter; b. at Borgo San Sepolcro, c1430; d. at Siena, 1495. He is known to have been at Siena by 1453, and may have been a pupil of Domenico di Bartolo. In his first known work, *Madonna and Saints* (1460), Museo dell' Opera del Duomo, Siena, elements of Umbrian painting are combined with the Sienese style of Domenico. Of c1465 are the panels of a polyptych at San Sepolcro; the central panel, *Baptism of Christ*, National Gallery, London, was painted by Piero della Francesca. Matteo was also strongly influenced by Vecchietta, especially in the boniness and elongation of his types, and by the Florentine Pollaiuolo. The influence of the last, and his interest in agitated movements of the body and articulation of limbs, appears in a series Matteo painted on the subject of *The Slaughter of the Innocents*. Examples of these are the intarsia panel in the pavement of the cathedral at Siena (1481); a signed and dated (1482) painting in the Piccolomini Chapel of the

Church of S. Agostino, Siena; one in the Pinacoteca, Naples (1488); and another in the Church of S. Maria dei Servi, Siena (1491). These paintings, as well as a series with the Madonna (Uffizi, Florence; Carrara Academy, Bergamo; Piccolomini Palace and in the cathedral, Pienza; National Gallery, Washington; the Metropolitan Museum, New York; Johnson Collection, Philadelphia; and elsewhere) are characterized by delicate linearity and gemlike, enamel color. His signed and dated (1479) *St. Barbara Enthroned with Angels and SS. Mary Magdalen and Catherine*, S. Domenico, Siena, is typical in its highly decorative effect. A number of Matteo's paintings survive, many of them in the Pinacoteca and churches of Siena. Other examples, besides those mentioned, are at Genoa, Grossetto, Naples, Ravenna, Rome, and Turin; at Berlin, Edinburgh, Esztergom, Hungary, London, and Paris; and at Baltimore, Bloomington (Indiana), Cambridge (Massachusetts), Chicago, Cincinnati, Cleveland, Columbia (South Carolina), Detroit, Providence, San Diego, San Francisco and San Marino (California), Williamstown (Massachusetts), and elsewhere.

Matteo da Gualdo (dä gwäl′dō). [Original name, **Matteo di Pietro,** called **da Gualdo.**] Umbrian painter; b. c1435; d. 1507. He was a pupil of Giovanni Boccati and was influenced by other Umbrians and by the followers of Benozzo Gozzoli in the Marches. From the many influences he forged his own style. Among his early works is a triptych with St. Margaret (1462) at Gualdo Tadino. He painted a number of frescoes, as in the Oratory of the Pilgrims (1468), Assisi, at Nocera Umbra, and in S. Maria della Scirca at Sigillo, including the votive fresco *St. Anne with Madonna and Child in her Lap*, signed and dated 1484. Several detached votive frescoes are in the National Gallery of Umbria at Perugia. Other examples of his work are at Baltimore and in the Museum of Fine Arts, Boston.

Matteo de' Pasti (dā päs′tē). See **De' Pasti, Matteo.**

Matteo di Ser Cambio (dē ser käm′byō). Perugian miniaturist; active in the second half of the 14th century. Also known as a goldsmith, his work as a miniaturist is typical of the fine school of Perugian miniaturists that flourished in the 14th century. Examples of his work are to be found in the library at Perugia, notably a *St. Peter Walking on the Water* (1377) from the registry of the Guild of the Money Changers.

Matthias Corvinus (ma̤-thī′a̤s kôr-vī′nus). [Also, **Matthias I** (of *Hungary*), **Matthias I Hunyadi.**] King of Hungary (1459–1490); b. at Cluj, Transylvania (now in Rumania), probably February 23, 1440; d. at Vienna, April 4, 1490. He was the second son of John Hunyadi, and was elected king on the death of Ladislaus III of Poland, who had ruled in Hungary as Ladislaus V. The opposition of some of the nobles to Matthias' election led to their crowning the Emperor Frederick III king of Hungary in March, 1459, but Matthias forced the emperor to give up his claim and recognize him as king (1462). He had married (1458) the daughter of the king of Bohemia, George of Podiebrad (the first of three marriages), and, after a successful campaign against the Turks (1462–1468) in which he invaded Serbia and won back Bosnia, joined the Catholic League against his father-in-law. In May, 1469, he was elected king of Bohemia by the Czech Catholics. From that time he was engaged in wars with George of Podiebrad (1420–1471) who had been deposed (1466) as king of Bohemia by Pope Paul II, and with Ladislaus of Poland, who claimed the Bohemian throne as successor of George of Podiebrad. By the Treaty of Olomouc (July, 1479), Matthias gave up his claim to the crown of Bohemia and recognized Ladislaus, in return for Moravia, Silesia, and Lusatia. The Bohemian war had brought in its train wars (1477, 1479) against the Emperor Frederick III, and in 1482 Matthias again declared war on the emperor. He captured (1485) Vienna, thenceforth his capital, and took Styria, Carinthia, and Carniola; the holdings he then had, combined with his alliances with Bavaria, Saxony, the Swiss, and the powerful Archbishop of Salzburg, made him the greatest ruler in central Europe. He established a strong central state with a powerful standing army, which was supported by a severe and well-administered tax program. A humane sovereign, his rule was distinguished for mildness and justice. He was a highly cultivated man, interested in all branches of learning, and made his court a center of it. He welcomed poets and men of letters and established one of the great libraries of the time (Bibliotheca Corvina) at Buda. He had no legitimate heir and was succeeded as king of Hungary by Ladislaus II, king of Bohemia.

Mattioli (mä-tyō′lē), **Pierandrea.** Physician and naturalist; b. at Siena, March 23, 1500; d. of the plague at Trento, 1577. He studied medicine and practiced at Siena, Rome, Trento, and Gorizia. When he had gained a sizable competence through the practice of medicine, he gave it up and devoted himself to the study of natural science, especially to the study of botany. He published (1554) a commentary on Dioscorides, a first century Greek physician who wrote a work on *materia medica* that was standard for centuries. Mattioli's work, *Commentarii al Dioscuride*, was an encyclopedia of all the knowledge of medicinal herbs and botany that was available in his time. The work was famous, went through many editions, and was translated into French, German, and Bohemian. Each new edition contained new material, as botanists and collectors sent their finds to him. News of the tulip that was brought back from Turkey by Flemings appeared in the edition of 1581. Of all his writings, the *Commentarii* was most famous.

Maturanzio (mä-tö-rän′tsyō), **Francesco.** See **Matarazzo, Francesco.**

Mauny (mō′ni), Sir **Walter de.** See **Manny** or **Mauny,** Sir **Walter de.**

Maurice (mô′ris, mor′is). [German, **Moritz.**] Duke of Saxony; b. at Freiberg, Saxony, March 21, 1521; d. at Sievershausen, near Hanover, July 11, 1553. He fought with Charles V against the Turks and the French, and against the Schmalkaldic League, and became a Saxon elector. Subsequently he opposed Charles V, was victorious in the battle at Sievershausen, but was mortally wounded.

Maurolico (mou-rō′lē-kō), **Francesco.** Mathematician; b. at Messina, November 19, 1494; d. there, July 21, 1575. He was of Greek parentage, was a scholar of wide learning, was active in the affairs of his community, where he held public office, and was an outstanding teacher of mathematics. He taught at Naples, Rome, and Palermo, before his final return to Messina. His writings included translations of Greek mathematical works into Latin, works on mathematics, astronomy, optics, music, architecture, geography, natural history, civil and religious history, and poetry. Much of his writing was scattered and lost. His work on optics, *Photismi de lumine* (*Light Concerning Light*), completed in 1567, treats shadows, reflection, and refraction.

Maximilian I (of *the Holy Roman Empire*) (mak-si-mil′yạn). Emperor of the Holy Roman Empire (1493–1519); b. at Wiener Neustadt, Austria, March 22, 1459; d. at Wels, Upper Austria, January 12, 1519. He was the son and successor of Frederick III, married Mary, daughter and heiress of Charles the Bold of Burgundy, in 1477, and was elected king of the Romans (that is, of Germany) in 1486. He became emperor in 1493, but was never crowned. In order to suppress the system of private war and restore the imperial authority, he proclaimed a perpetual public peace in 1495, established the imperial chamber (Reichskammergericht) in 1495 and the imperial aulic council (Reichshofrat) in 1501, and divided Germany into six, and afterward (1512) into ten, circles (Landfriedenskreise), over each of which was placed a captain with a force of standing troops for the punishment of disturbers of the peace. In 1499 he carried on an unsuccessful war against the Swiss Confederacy, which resulted in the practical independence of the latter. His second wife was Bianca Maria Sforza, niece of Ludovico Il Moro, whom he married in 1494. In exchange for her huge dowry he invested Ludovico with the duchy of Milan. Through his wife's influence he became involved in a contest with France for the sovereignty of Milan and Naples. In 1508 he joined the League of Cambrai against Venice. In 1513 he joined the Holy League against France, and in the same year assisted Henry VIII of England in gaining the brilliant victory over the French, at Guinegate ("the Battle of the Spurs"). The French, however, defeated him in Italy and he was forced (1516) to cede Milan to them and to permit Venice to take over Verona. During Maximilian's reign the towns and rising merchant classes of Germany assumed increasing influence and importance, at the expense of the barons. He was alive to the developments of the Italian Renaissance, was a patron of artists, including Albrecht Dürer, and encouraged the expansion of the universities of Vienna and Freiburg. Through his son Philip, who married Juana, daughter of Ferdinand and Isabella of Spain, he was the grandfather of his successor as emperor, Charles V.

Maximilian II (of *the Holy Roman Empire*).

Emperor of the Holy Roman Empire (1564–1576); b. at Vienna, August 1, 1527; d. October 12, 1576. He was the son and successor of Ferdinand I, becoming (1564), emperor, archduke of Austria, and king of Hungary and Bohemia. At his accession to the imperial throne he found the empire at war with the Turks. He concluded a truce with Selim II in 1568, each party retaining its possessions and Maximilian continuing the payment of tribute to Turkey for his kingdom of Hungary. He was of a mild and tolerant disposition, and left the Protestants undisturbed in the exercise of their religion. It is probable that, despite his apparent adherence to the Roman Catholic Church, he really was a Protestant. He refused the sacraments on his deathbed.

Maxwell of Terregles (maks′wel, tẹ-reg′lz), Sir **John.** [Titles, Master of **Maxwell,** 4th Baron **Herries.**] Scottish partisan of Mary, Queen of Scots; b. c1512; d. at Edinburgh, January 20, 1583. He fought for Mary at Langside (1568).

Mayr (mīr), **Johann.** See **Eck, Johann.**

Mazarin Bible (maz′ạ-rin). Edition of the Bible printed by Johann Gutenberg at Mainz in 1450–1455, being the first book ever printed with movable types. It is so named because the first known copy was discovered in the Mazarin library at Paris in 1760.

Mazzei (mät-tsā′ē), **Lapo.** Humanist and public official; b. at Prato, 1350; d. at Florence, October 30, 1412. He was a notary, an influential public official, a sincerely pious man who performed and recommended good works, and a cultivated man who admired Dante and the mystic poet Jacopone da Todi. The more than 500 letters, on all kinds of topics, that he wrote to Francesco Datini, a wealthy merchant, are a documentary of 15th-century Tuscan life. Vigorous and lively in style, and rich in Tuscan terms and expressions, they portray the matrix of religious conviction, austerity, curiosity, and vitality in which humanism ripened.

Mazzola (mät-tsō′lä), **Filippo.** Painter; b. at Parma, c1460; d. there, 1505. At first a pupil of Filippo Tacconi of Cremona, he was later at Venice, where he knew the work of Giovanni Bellini and Antonello da Messina. His sacred paintings reflect the influence of Bellini; Antonello had a profound influence on his portraits. Principally of the school of Parma, most of his activity centered in that city. His first work, *Madonna and Child,* is at Padua. After this come *Madonna and Saints* (1491), in the National Gallery of Parma; a seriously damaged *Baptism of Christ* (1493), formerly in the cathedral and now in the National Gallery; a *Resurrection* (1497) after Bellini, at Strasbourg; a polyptych (1499) at Cortemaggiore; and a *Pietà* (1500), at Naples. Other works include *Conversion of St. Paul* (1504) and *Christ Carrying the Cross,* Parma, and a signed *Virgin and Child,* National Gallery, London, and paintings at Cremona, Piacenza, Turin (Galleria Sabauda), Venice (Correr Museum), Berlin, Bonn, Budapest, Zagreb, Baltimore (Walters Art Gallery), Sarasota, Williamstown (Massachusetts), and elsewhere. A rather dry painter, of harsh color, he was successful at painting portraits in which he captured the character of his sitters. Examples of these are at Parma, Modena, Milan (Brera, Poldi Pezzoli, and Borromeo collections), Rome (Doria Gallery), Cracow, Washington, Vaduz, and elsewhere. He was the father of Francesco Mazzola, known as Parmigianino.

Mazzola, Francesco. See **Parmigianino.**

Mazzola Bedoli (be-dō′lē), **Girolamo.** See **Bedoli Mazzola, Gerolamo.**

Mazzolino (mät-tsō-lē′nō), **Ludovico.** Painter; b. at Ferrara, c1480; d. c1530. He was a pupil of Ercole de' Roberti and was influenced by Francesco Cossa, Dosso Dossi, and contemporary northern painters. From these influences he derived a dramatic personal style characterized and heightened by his keen sense of color. Frescoes that he executed (1504–1508) in the Church of S. Maria degli Angeli at Ferrara have been lost. His earliest remaining work is a triptych, *Madonna and Child* (1509), Berlin. Other works are *Adoration* (1512) Borghese Gallery, Rome; an altarpiece, *Jesus in the Temple* (1524), Berlin; *Adoration of the Shepherds* (1524), Bologna; *Slaughter of the Innocents,* one in the Uffizi, Florence, and another in the Doria Gallery, Rome; and *Christ Washing the Feet of the Disciples,* Johnson Collection, Philadelphia. Other works are at Bergamo, Brescia, Cremona, Ferrara, in the Uffizi and Pitti galleries, Florence, Milan, Turin, Budapest, Dresden, Dublin, Lisbon, London, Munich, Paris, New York Historical Society, Sarasota, and elsewhere.

Mazzoni (mät-tsō′nē), **Giulio.** Painter, sculptor, and worker in stucco; b. at Piacenza,

1525; d. there, 1618. He was a pupil of Vasari, with whom he collaborated at Florence (1543) and at Naples (1544) in work on the sacristy of S. Giovanni a Carbonara. His principal interest is as the creator of stucco decoration. About 1550 he made the stucco *Crucifixion with the Virgin* and *St. John and the Magdalen,* in the Piccolomini Chapel of the Church of Monte Oliveto. He went to Rome to study with Daniele da Volterra. At Rome he carried out the stucco decoration in the Palazzo Spada (1555–1559), made a marble bust of Francesco del Nero (1563), in S. Maria sopra Minerva, worked in S. Maria del Popolo, in the Vatican (1563), and elsewhere. In 1576 he was at Piacenza where, among other things, he decorated the vault of S. Maria di Campagna.

Mazzoni, Guido. [Called **il Paganino** and **il Modanino.**] Sculptor; b. at Modena, c1450; d. there, 1518. He began by making masks and by directing public entertainments. Perhaps of 1475 is his *Dead Christ,* Busseto. The group of the *Pietà* (1477–1480), for the Oratory of St. John at Modena, reveals his skill in animating the terra-cotta in which he worked with a powerful realism, as in the passionate expressions and unrestrained gestures of the mourners over the body of Christ. Other works include *Pietà,* S. Maria della Rosa, Ferrara; *Presepe,* cathedral, Modena; a *Pietà* in S. Giovanni at Reggio Emilia and another in S. Lorenzo at Cremona. King Ferrante invited him to Naples (1491), where he made a bust of the king, now in the National Museum at Naples, and a *Deposition* (1494) now at Monte Oliveto. Charles VIII made him a knight and took him off to France, where he worked with Fra Giocondo at Amboise, then at St. Denis on the tomb of the king (destroyed in the 18th century). He returned to Italy (1507), then went back to France to serve King Louis XII, of whom he made an equestrian statue, at Blois. In 1516 he went home to Modena, loaded with honors and riches. His work, lacking Tuscan elegance, is notable for the vigorous sincerity that betrays its provincial Ferrarese origin.

Mazzoni, Iacopo. Humanist and teacher; b. at Cesena, 1548; d. there, 1598. He studied at Bologna and at Padua, and taught philosophy at Macerata, Pisa, and at Rome. Like Marsilio Ficino, he hoped to reconcile classical ideas and Christian doctrine. He took a somewhat superficial interest in reform of the Church. One of his written works is a defense of Dante for not having followed the Aristotelian rules in his great poem.

Mechtilde von Magdeburg (meċh-til′dẹ fon mäg-dẹ-bůrk). German Beguine who wrote in Low German; b. c1212; d. c1280. Sometime after 1270 she wrote the apocalyptic *Das Fliessende Licht der Gottheit.* The original is lost but the work is preserved in a High German translation by Heinrich von Nordlingen (c1344).

Medallion. A circular or oval disk decorated with figures, as a portrait with legends, and cast in metal. Portrait medallions of princes and popes, of fine design and exquisite workmanship, were frequently cast in the period of the Renaissance and given as presents or commemoratives. In architecture the medallion is a tablet—circular, oval, square, or of any other form—bearing on it objects represented in relief, as figures, heads, animals, flowers, coats of arms, and so on, and applied to an exterior or interior wall, a frieze, or other architectural member. Medallions in terra-cotta by Andrea della Robbia ornament the Ospedale degli Innocenti (Foundling Hospital), at Florence.

Medici (me′dē-chē). Eminent Florentine family, members of which officially or unofficially dominated public life, with brief interruptions, from 1434 to 1737. The family is celebrated for the number of statesmen which it produced, and for its patronage of art and letters. The list of artists, sculptors, architects, and men of letters who enjoyed Medici patronage includes most of the men of genius of the times. One of the few outstanding names that is missing is that of Leonardo da Vinci, who at length won recognition at Milan under Ludovico Sforza. The history of the Medici as rulers of an Italian state is unusual for the absence of military men in the family. They did not achieve power in Florence through arms (the only Medici general was Giovanni delle Bande Nere, 1498–1526, and he never fought in the service of Florence), but through their capacity to amass wealth and through their political sagacity. The Medici are thought to have originated in the Mugello, and to have begun entering Florence about 1200. In 1291 an Ardingo de' Medici was prior at Florence, and was gonfaloniere in 1296. In the next century Salvestro de' Medici participated in the revolutionary activities of 1378, although his role is far from clear, and was gonfaloniere in the same year. The direct line of the Medici, as they appear in the political life of Florence, begins with Giovanni di Bicci de' Medici (1360–1429). He amassed a large fortune as a banker and founded the political greatness of the family. His two sons, Cosimo the Elder (1389–1464) and Lorenzo (1394–1440) founded the two principal branches of the family. Cosimo the Elder became the effective, but unofficial, arbiter of public affairs in 1434 and retained his power and influence until his death. He attained his position through his wealth, discretion, and shrewdness in manipulating existing republican institutions. He was succeeded by his son Piero di Cosimo de' Medici (1416–1469), who was invited by the Florentines to assume his father's role. (The Medici arms consisted of six red balls on a gold field. Louis XI granted Piero a patent to add the lily of France to his arms. Piero was tremendously gratified by this gracious act, and derived great satisfaction from adding the lily of France to the ball at the top of the shield. Because the Medici arms carried the balls (*palle*), the rallying cry of the Medici party, heard in Florence when the family was threatened or honored, was *Palle! Palle!*) Piero (Piero I) was succeeded, again on the invitation of the Florentines, by his son Lorenzo (1449–1492), called "the Magnificent." Under him Florence reaped the harvest of Renaissance developments that had begun a century earlier, and enjoyed enormous prestige as the center and soul of Italian intellectual and artistic achievements. The period of his rule is sometimes called the Laurentian Age. Lorenzo's sons were: Piero II (1472–1503), who succeeded his father but was driven out of Florence by an aroused people for yielding to the French in 1494; Giovanni (1475–1521), who became Pope Leo X; and Giuliano (1478–1516), who became duke of Nemours. From 1494 to 1512 the Medici were in exile. They were restored in 1512 with the aid of the imperial troops of Charles V and under the guidance of Giovanni, at this time a cardinal but elevated to the papacy as Leo X in the following year. Leo sent his cousin, Cardinal Giulio de' Medici, the illegitimate son of Giuliano de' Medici, Lorenzo the Magnificent's brother, as his representative to rule Florence. Cardinal Giulio was elevated to the papacy as Pope Clement VII in 1523, and named his nephews, Alessandro and Ippolito, as joint rulers of Florence under the regency of Cardinal Passerini. Rome was sacked (1527) by the troops of Charles V; Clement was imprisoned in Castel Sant' Angelo; Florence drove out the Medici again and restored the republic. It had a brief life (1527–1530). Clement, reconciled with Charles V, sent imperial troops against Florence. After a heroic resistance, the city fell. Alessandro, an illegitimate son of Lorenzo de' Medici (1492–1519), was made hereditary duke of Florence by Charles V (1532), thus ending the tradition of unofficial Medici rulers of a Florence that for long had considered itself a republic. Alessandro, who was murdered by his cousin Lorenzino in 1537, was the last male of the branch of the family descended from Cosimo the Elder. His half sister was Catherine de' Medici, who became queen of France and the mother of three succeeding kings. Alessandro was succeeded by Cosimo I, who represented the younger branch of the family, descended from Lorenzo (1394–1440). Cosimo I obtained possession of Siena and its territories, and in 1569 received the title of grand duke of Tuscany from the pope, although the imperial confirmation was first received by his son and successor Francesco I in 1575. The younger branch ruled as grand dukes of Tuscany until its extinction with the death of Gian Gastone de' Medici in 1737. Anna Maria Luisa de' Medici (b. 1671), the last of her house, was perhaps the greatest contributor to the artistic inheritance of Florence, for she preserved it. She married the Elector Palatine at the age of 24 and lived in Germany for the next twenty-six years. After the death of her husband she returned to Florence and lived in apartments in the Pitti Palace. Her drunken brother Gian Gastone, whom she despised, had separate apartments in the palace. As heiress to the Medici fortune and art collections, she willed the invaluable collections to the state of Tuscany on condition that they never be removed from Florence and that the works in them be available to the public of all nations. Thus it is that the collections formed by the Medici are still to be found in the museums and palaces of Florence, whereas the great collections built up under other ruling houses, as those of the Gonzaga at Mantua, the d'Este at Ferrara, and the Visconti and Sforza at Milan, are scattered in museums and private collections throughout the world. See separate entries below.

Medici, Alessandro de'. First duke of Florence; b. c1510; assassinated January 5, 1537. He was the illegitimate son of Lorenzo de' Medici (1492–1519). In 1523 the head of the Medici at Florence, Cardinal Giulio, became pope under the title of Clement VII. He appointed his nephews Alessandro and Ippolito joint rulers of Florence in his place under the regency of Cardinal Silvio Passerini. In 1527 the populace expelled both Alessandro and Ippolito; but in 1531 the former, who had married Margaret of Parma, natural daughter of the emperor Charles V, was restored by his father-in-law and the following year was made hereditary duke of Florence. Up to this time the Medici had exercised power under the forms of republican institutions. Alessandro's excesses caused bitter feeling in Florence and Ippolito was sent to the emperor to complain. Ippolito died on the way, and the conclusion was that Alessandro had caused him to be poisoned. Alessandro was murdered two years later by one of his cousins and companions in debauchery, Lorenzino de' Medici.

Medici, Caterina de'. See **Catherine de Médicis.**

Medici, Cosimo (or **Cosmo**) **de'.** [Called **Cosimo the Elder.**] Florentine merchant prince, banker, patron of the arts and learning, and statesman; b. at Florence, September 27, 1389; d. at his villa at Careggi, August 1, 1464. He was the son of Giovanni di Bicci de' Medici, one of the richest bankers in Italy, and received a good education based on the medieval curriculum of Latin, logic, and arithmetic. But no son of Florence worthy of the name could remain impervious to the excitement generated by the rediscovery of the ancient writings and ideas, and Cosimo's education was enriched by the addition of the new studies in the classics. One of his teachers was Roberto de' Rossi, a leading humanist, who gave him lessons in Greek and Latin. (Pius II somewhat aristocratically informs us that "he was more cultivated than merchants usually are and had some knowledge of Greek, . . .") Inspired by his studies, he collected books and manuscripts and planned to go to the Holy Land with Niccolò Niccoli and Francesco Barbaro to search for Greek manuscripts. However, his business-minded father, who had already taken Cosimo and his brother Lorenzo into his banking business, put his foot down. Unable to go himself, Cosimo financed the collecting journeys of Ciriaco d'Ancona and Giovanni Aurispa. An inventory of his personal library (1418) showed sixty-three books, including works of Ovid and Livy, among other Latin writers, and Dante, Boccaccio, and Petrarch. By 1430 his collection of classical manuscripts was one of the richest private ones in Europe. Vespasiano says he was well versed in secular and sacred Latin literature, and tells that he often went across the Arno with his brother Lorenzo to the Camoldolese Convent of the Angels (S. Maria degli Angeli), to discuss theology and other subjects with Fra Ambrogio Traversari and his good friends Leonardo Bruni, Niccolò Niccoli, Poggio, and Marsuppini. He accompanied Pope John XXIII to the Council of Constance (1414), and afterward ransomed the rejected and imprisoned pope from the duke of Bavaria. (Later still, he commissioned Donatello to make John XXIII's tomb, in the Baptistery at Florence.) After the Council, Cosimo traveled for two years in Germany and France, attending to business and furthering his education. His interest in the new studies in humanism was one of the constants of his life. He supported and encouraged the humanists and was, except for Filelfo, well-loved by them. In 1439 he met George Gemistus Plethon, the Greek philosopher, who had come to the Council of Ferrara-Florence to reconcile the Greek and Latin Churches. Cosimo was fascinated by Gemistus Plethon's talks on the philosophy of Plato. He conceived the idea of founding an academy of Platonic studies, but could not carry it out in his lifetime. However, he did encourage and endow Marsilio Ficino, the young son of his physician, who later became the center of a circle of men interested in Platonic philosophy: the so-called Platonic Academy. Cosimo employed Michellozzo Michellozzi to rebuild the convent of San Marco. There he had his own cell, decorated as were all the cells, with the luminous frescoes of Fra Angelico, and to it he retired from time to time to meditate and to cultivate his soul. He endowed San Marco with a library (also built by Michellozzo), the nucleus of which consisted of about half the 800 manuscripts and books from the library of Niccoli. The latter died in 1437 and left many debts. Cosimo took his friend's library in exchange for paying his debts, and thus preserved it from being dispersed. The volumes he did not keep he gave to the library, which was open to all and constituted the first great public library in Europe. He also built the Badia of Fiesole and employed Vespasiano to create a library for it. The list of books for the library was prepared and written in his own hand by Pope Nicholas V who, as Tommaso da Sarzana, had known Cosimo well at Florence before he became pope (and after he became pope deposited papal funds in the Medici bank). Cosimo's personal library, to which he continually added, became the foundation of the Laurentian Library in San Lorenzo.

Central to Cosimo's interest, however, was his vast banking business. He never neglected it for any reason, and under his guidance it flourished and brought ever more wealth to the Medici family. Able and shrewd, cautious and at the same time bold in business ventures, modest in his personal life, liberal, and with the reputation of being a friend of the people, he became head of the family on the death of his father (1429) and the possessor, through his own qualities and great fortune, of enormous influence in the affairs of Florence. He served his city as prior (1416) and noted with pride in the diary he always kept that no one was exiled or harmed during his priorate. His many missions for Florence included those to Milan (1420), Lucca (1423), Bologna (1424), and the pope (1426). Rinaldo degli Albizzi, who had succeeded his father as head of the ruling faction at Florence, came to fear Cosimo as a rival. In 1429 Rinaldo led Florence into a war to conquer Lucca. The original enthusiasm with which the Florentines had welcomed the war soon evaporated: Lucca's friends rallied to her cause; Florentine arms were defeated; an ignominious peace was made in 1433. Cosimo, who had not favored the war but had served on the Council of Ten, the committee appointed to carry on the war, was not blamed for the defeats. Rinaldo, who had personally taken the field with disastrous results, was. He felt his hold on the city weakening, and resolved to remove Cosimo by the legal means that previous party leaders had often perverted to secure their power. These means were, first, the *parlamento* and then the *balìa*. The *parlamento* was a gathering of the people in the square before the Palazzo della Signoria at which, by acclamation, they voted for reform of the government. They next delegated all the rights commonly exercised by the Florentine people themselves to a *balìa*, that is, a committee that would effectuate whatever changes they wished. Cosimo, aware of the unrest in the city and the fears of Rinaldo and his party, had withdrawn to his villa in the mountains. Rinaldo sent for him in the name of the priors. Warned that it would be unsafe to answer the call, Cosimo nevertheless came to Florence, in September, 1433. He was immediately arrested (on the false charge of having embezzled funds for the war with Lucca) and was imprisoned high in the clock tower of the Palazzo della Signoria. From his lofty jail he saw the people gather in the square below and understood perfectly what was going on. He feared death, and refused to eat until his friendly jailer proved to him that his food was not poisoned by offering to share it with him. While the priors argued whether Cosimo should be killed or exiled, he was able, through friends, to reach the gonfaloniere sitting in judgment on him, and bribed him. As a result, instead of death, passionately advocated by Rinaldo, the priors decided to exile him and other members of his family to Venice. (Cosimo wrote in his journal that his jailers could have gotten a much higher price out of him than the bribe he actually paid.) In September of 1433 he left Florence. He was received at Venice as a reigning prince. The Albizzi tried to ruin him but in fact his credit and his influence grew while he was in Venice. By the following year, the situation at Florence had changed. A priorate unfriendly to Rinaldo was chosen, and it was decided to recall Cosimo. Rinaldo sought to retain his power by a new *balìa*. Pope Eugenius IV, who was in Florence at the time (having been driven from Rome), attempted to mediate. Rinaldo was abandoned by the moderates and lost his bid to keep power. Cosimo was recalled. He arrived in Florence exactly one year after he had left, and was tumultuously welcomed. In his turn, Rinaldo was exiled (although part of the agreement with the pope was that he should not suffer if he submitted to mediation), and from that time (1434) Cosimo was the effective, and unofficial, political leader for the next 30 years. He maintained a scrupulous regard for the law. In these years he held the office of gonfaloniere only three times (1435, 1439, 1445), for a total of six months as legal head of the state. Otherwise he lived as a simple citizen, one whose power was maintained at the wish of his fellow citizens who could, at any time (and some cost), have deprived him of it. He attained power by his wealth, his connections, and his good sense. He retained it by his ability, skill, popularity, and by manipulating existing devices for his own ends. He did not change the outward appearance of existing forms, but he occasionally added a new one. As much as possible, he kept out of the public eye, never flaunted either his power or his wealth, was readily accessible to humbler citizens, and lived modestly for a man of such great fortune. Splendor and gaiety were alien to his character. Having asked Brunelleschi to design a private palace for him, he rejected Brunelleschi's model on the grounds that the palace was too magnificent. "Envy," he said, "is a plant that should not be watered." His purse was open to all his friends and to many others. He was moderate, humane, and popular. Florence prospered; he encouraged trade and industry, and promoted agriculture, in which he was expert (he is said to have passed hours pruning his own vines at his villa). With great skill and tact, he kept a firm hand on foreign affairs, for the short term of the priors (two months) made the formulation of a consistent foreign policy difficult. He was a friend and supporter of Francesco Sforza against the Visconti, and changed the traditional Florentine-Venetian alignment to one of alliance between Florence and Milan, reasoning that if Milan were weak Venice would be too strong. He kept a sharp eye on the banking business of which he was the head, and used the enormous fortune he gained thereby to beautify the city, to encourage the arts and learning, and as a means of keeping those in official positions friendly to him. Those who idealize the state of Florentine politics before Cosimo revile him as the destroyer of Florentine liberty. In point of fact, he was simply more skillful in operating within the forms of government than those who would dislodge him. He seldom held public office, except in connection with public finances; he had no army. The vitality of governmental institutions was not undermined as a result of his influence. Those who called for the restoration of Florentine liberties were chiefly moved by a burning desire to have their own hands on the helm. He may, perhaps, be likened to a big city "boss," a boss who did not seek power to enrich himself but to protect what he already had. And he seems sincerely to have felt that the best interests of the Medici and of Florence were identical. He was not vindictive or tyrannical, as were so many of the despots of his time, although he did not hesitate to get rid of possible or actual rivals by exile or by using the *catasto* (a tax on income) to ruin them.

Cosimo embraced, and encouraged on a magnificent scale, developments of the Renaissance that had begun to flower long before his time. The palace he caused to be built (1444) to designs by Michellozzo, is a monument to his taste, as well as one of the outstanding examples of Renaissance architecture of the period. The chapel in it was decorated by Benozzo Gozzoli between 1459 and 1463. (The palace, now called the Medici-Riccardi palace, stands on the Via Cavour, formerly the Via Larga.) Cosimo renewed his father's commission to Brunelleschi to rebuild the sacristy of San Lorenzo and added to it the rebuilding of San Lorenzo itself. The church (the façade was never made) and the sacristy are perfect illustrations of 15th-century Florentine architecture. He added to his favorite villa at Careggi and built others at Caffaggiolo, Trebbio, and Fiesole. He extended his generosity to the work of restoration and rebuilding at Assisi and Milan, and rebuilt a monastery at Jerusalem and a college at Paris. He was the friend and patron of the sculptor Donatello, who made ornaments, bronze doors, and vessels for San Lorenzo, marble medallions for the courtyard of the Medici palace, and the *David* now in the Bargello at his command. The rebuilt convent of San Marco was filled with the serene and deeply spiritual frescoes of Fra Angelico; the exasperating and endearing Fra Filippo Lippi worked for Cosimo, whenever the latter could catch him, and was one of his favorites.

Cosimo married Contessina de' Bardi, of a Florentine family formerly distinguished in banking. Their two sons were Piero and Giovanni. The sons, with their wives and children, lived in the family palace. Piero suffered from gout to such an extent that he was sometimes incapacitated. Cosimo himself was greatly afflicted by the disease. In the last years of his life his enemies, among them Luca Pitti, thought he was losing his grip and tried to wrest power from him. Cosimo, remaining quietly in his palace, still held the reins. From contemporary accounts it is known that this highly intelligent and able man shared a widespread belief in astrology. He also was concerned for his soul, and hoped that he would find in Platonism the answers to his questions about the meaning of life and the afterlife. The last year of his life was saddened by his diminishing family. Giovanni, his younger son, died in November, 1463. Crippled by gout, Cosimo had himself carried through the empty rooms of his palace, and murmured that it was "too large a house for so small a family." Vespasiano, and others, cite his prudence, kindness, and patience, and note that he was a man of his word. Pius II, who sought his help for a crusade against the Turks, met him at Mantua in 1459 and wrote, "He was of fine physique and more than average height; his expression and manner of speech were mild; . . . his mind was keen and always alert; his spirit was neither cowardly nor brave; he easily endured toil and hunger and he often passed whole nights without sleep. Nothing went on in Italy that he did not know; indeed it was his advice that guided the policy of many cities and princes. Nor were foreign events a secret to him, for he had correspondents among his business connections all over the world, who kept him informed by frequent letters. . . ." At the end of his long life, a life in which he had consolidated the power of his family, increased its fortune, enriched his city, and given unending patronage to humanists, musicians, artists, sculptors, and builders, he lay in his villa at Careggi. His wife noted that he often kept his eyes closed, and asked him why he did so. "To accustom them to it," was his characteristic reply. Following the death of their most eminent private citizen, the Florentines flocked to his funeral; and afterward gratefully inscribed the words *Pater Patriae* on his simple tomb in San Lorenzo.

Medici, Cosimo I de'. Grand duke of Tuscany; b. June 12, 1519; d. at his villa at Castello, near Florence, April 21, 1574. In him were united the two branches of the Medici family: his mother, Maria Salviati, was a granddaughter of Lorenzo the Magnificent; his father Giovanni de' Medici (Giovanni delle Bande Nere), was the great-grandson of Lorenzo (1394–1440), founder of the younger branch of the family. By his father he was related to the house of Sforza at Milan, his grandmother being Caterina Sforza, "the Amazon of Forlì." The Medici were restored at Florence (1530) through the efforts of Pope Clement VII and imperial troops, and Alessandro de' Medici was proclaimed duke of Florence (1532). He was slain (January, 1537) by his cousin Lorenzino, and Cosimo, a youth not yet 18, was named duke in his place. His title was confirmed by the emperor Charles V in the same year. Young, handsome, seemingly modest and moderate, it was thought by those who favored his accession (including Guicciardini) that he would devote himself to his favorite activities of hunting and athletics and would be easy to manage. The new duke immediately revealed his true colors. Florence seethed with factions. Within was the anti-Medicean party that sought the restoration of the republic; without were the exiles, led by Piero Strozzi and including his father Filippo, ever plotting to overthrow the Medici. Cosimo asked for imperial troops and sent them against the army of the exiles at Montemurlo. The exiles were defeated (July, 1537), their leaders were taken captive and most of them were sent to their deaths: each day for four days four of the prisoners were beheaded. Filippo Strozzi died in prison, a bloodstained sword at his side. Whether his death was by his own hand or at Cosimo's order never became clear. Within the city Cosimo followed a rigorous policy against the dissidents and restored order. To maintain it he had frequent recourse to the headsman or the hangman (over 140 people met their deaths officially in his reign; the number of those stabbed or poisoned by hirelings is unknown). As he reorganized the government, all authority stemmed from him. What was left of the republican constitution vanished. The saving grace of his autocratic rule was that the laws were impartially administered, and were extended to cover, and protect, the country dwellers as well as the city subjects. In his long reign (1537–1574) as duke of Florence and (after 1570) grand duke of Tuscany, he centralized the government not only of Florence but of the cities of Tuscany, under his personal authority; with the consent and assistance of Spain he attacked Siena (January, 1554), subjected it to a siege, and starved it into submission (April, 1555), and Philip II confirmed him in his acquisition in 1557; he also acquired Montalcino, but was unable to take Lucca; he promoted agriculture with financial aid, reclamation, and repopulation of uncultivated lands to the extent that Tuscany became one of the most flourishing areas of Italy; he revived and encouraged commerce and industry; and he united Tuscany politically, judicially, financially, and administratively. Pope Puis V named him grand duke of Tuscany in 1570 over the opposition of Spain and France. His son Francesco was invested with the grand duchy in 1575. He was forceful, ruthless, calculating, given to intrigue and dissimulation, and unscrupulous. Tuscany became one of the most stable states in Italy. His fame as an organizer and ruler was such that Corsica, rebelling against its Genoese overlords, offered him a crown (the opposition of France and Spain compelled him to decline the honor). Generally subordinate to his powerful ally Spain in foreign affairs, he maintained comparative independence in domestic matters. He founded the order of St. Stephen to fight the Turks, took steps to build up a navy, and developed the port of Livorno. In the execution of his clear-cut and firm policy he levied heavy taxes and administered his state as a despot. His rule was unpopular, but he stamped his duchy with an orderly administration and laid the foundations for a dukedom that lasted 200 years. As one historian has written, he "found a chaos; he left to his successors a well-ordered state." (Reumont)

In 1539 Cosimo married Eleonora of Toledo, daughter of the successful Spanish viceroy of Naples. It was a political marriage, to ensure the continuing protection of Spain, and it appears to have been a successful one. But his personal life was saddened by misfortune. Two of his daughters, Maria and Lucrezia, wife of Alfonso II d'Este of Ferrara, died young. His sons Giovanni and Garzia and their mother died within a month of each other (1562). (A third daughter, Isabella, was strangled by her husband, Paolo Giordano Orsini, Duke of Bracciano, on suspicion of infidelity, in 1576.) In 1570 he married Camilla Martelli, who had been his mistress for a number of years and had borne him one child. She neglected him shamefully when, in his very last years, he suffered a paralytic stroke. Cosimo was succeeded by his son Francesco, to whom, about ten years before his death, he had handed over much of the business of the government, without, however, relinquishing all concern in it. Francesco was in his turn succeeded by Cosimo's fourth son, Ferdinando. Not a Maecenas, or even a very generous patron, Cosimo nevertheless left worthy monuments at Florence. Vasari constructed the palace of the Uffizi (intended as offices for the magistrates, hence its name), now known the world over for its collections of paintings. Bartolommeo Ammannati build the bridge of S. Trinità over the Arno (it was destroyed in 1944 but has been rebuilt). Benvenuto Cellini and his rival Baccio Bandinelli worked for Cosimo. Cellini's famous statue, *Perseus with the Head of Medusa*, made for Cosimo, is in the Loggia dei Lenzi; his bronze bust of Cosimo is in the Bargello. Cosimo continued work on the Pitti Palace, begun by Cosimo the Elder's old enemy, Luca Pitti, and lived in it in the last years of his life. Before it was completed he lived in the Palazzo Vecchio, for which Vasari designed and painted many of the decorations. Some of the rooms are still known by the names of members of Cosimo's family, as the Study of Francesco I and the Apartment of Eleonora of Toledo. He could never persuade Michelangelo to return to Florence and work for him but he continued work on the Laurentian Library according to Michelangelo's plan. Bronzino, court painter, has left a number of portraits of Cosimo and members of his family.

Medici, Ferdinando I de'. Grand duke of Tuscany; b. 1551; d. February 7, 1609. He was the son of Cosimo I and Eleonora of Toledo, and was destined for the Church. He was given the red hat by Pius IV at the age of 14, and went to live at Rome at 20. The unexpected death (1587) of his brother Francesco, the reigning duke, opened the path to the throne for him. He resigned the cardinalate (he had never been ordained), assumed the title, and married Cristina of Lorraine, by whom he subsequently had a number of children. After approaches to France yielded no advantage to Tuscany, Ferdinando allied himself to Spain, without, however, becoming dependent on it as his brother had been, and gave the aid of his very respectable navy to the Spanish in the war against the

Turks. He improved and enlarged the port of Livorno, continued draining the marshes around Pisa and the Maremma and thereby reclaiming land for agriculture, promoted commerce and engaged in it himself, and consolidated the grand duchy of Tuscany on the foundations which had been so firmly established by his father. The exposure and repression of intrigues against the government, the establishment of domestic order, and increasing prosperity fastened the Medici dynasty ever more firmly on Tuscany. As a Maecenas he was a worthy successor to earlier members of his family. He built handsome buildings, including the Medici palace at Rome, promoted studies, and especially encouraged studies in science. Giambologna (Giovanni da Bologna), whose patron he was, made an equestrian statue of him now at Florence. Ferdinando was succeeded by his son Cosimo II, who was the patron of Galileo.

Medici, Francesco I de'. Grand duke of Tuscany; b. at Florence, March 25, 1541; d. at Poggio, October 19, 1587. He was the son of Cosimo I and Eleonora of Toledo. His father recognized that his limited intelligence, coupled with an undisciplined arrogance, would make his future role as grand duke of Tuscany difficult. He tried to prepare his son by turning over much of the business of government to him about the time of Francesco's marriage (1565) to Joanna of Austria, sister of the emperor Maximilian II. However, on succeeding as grand duke when his father died (1574), Francesco largely abandoned the government to his ministers, who were able men, and gave himself up to the pursuit of his pleasures, to his experiments in chemistry and alchemy, to creating a luxurious court, and to an insistence on due acknowledgment of himself as its splendid prince. His efforts at economic advancement and the promotion of industry were neither carefully planned nor adequately implemented, and in most matters he put Tuscany in a position of slavish dependence on the Hapsburgs of Austria and Spain. When Bianca Capello, a young Venetian, arrived in Florence with her lover he fell madly in love with her. He gave the lover a high position at his court, whereupon the young man, whom Bianca had in the meantime married, became so insufferable that he was removed by an assassin. Bianca had already become Francesco's mistress, and the open scandal deeply offended his wife's brother, the emperor. Following his wife's death (1578), Francesco married Bianca. The death of Francesco and Bianca on successive days (October 19 and 20, 1587) gave rise to the report that they had been poisoned. The deed was laid at the door of Cardinal Ferdinando de' Medici, Francesco's brother, whose hatred of Francesco was well known and who succeeded him. Similar rumors had been floated following the deaths of Cosimo's other children, but later historians have concluded that Francesco and Bianca died of malaria, and that other deaths in the family came from the same cause or from consumption. Francesco's daughter by Joanna was Marie de' Medici, who became the queen of Henry IV of France.

Medici, Giovanni di Bicci de'. Florentine merchant prince; b. 1360; d. February, 1429. He was a member of a family that originated in the Mugello and always preserved its attachment to that region. Modest and shrewd, a merchant and banker who by his own efforts and ability amassed a great fortune, his main interest was in promoting his business. In 1416 he attended the Council of Constance, called to resolve the schism in the Church, and took advantage of the occasion to improve his business contacts with Germany and Hungary. He was active in public affairs, served several times as prior, was gonfaloniere in 1421, and opposed the policy of the ruling merchant clique of including only their friends in the government. Possibly the richest banker of Italy, he was loved by the Florentines: for his modest ways, for his generosity, and because he had the reputation of being a friend of the people in their contests with the oligarchs. The new developments in art and architecture captured his attention, and he commissioned Brunelleschi to rebuild the sacristy of San Lorenzo. Brunelleschi, at that time completely engaged in raising the great dome of the cathedral, accepted the commission but was unable to carry it out in Giovanni's lifetime. (He finished it under Giovanni's son Cosimo.) Giovanni also endowed the famous Ospedale degli Innocenti (The Foundling Hospital, the first one in Europe). He had two sons: Cosimo, who came to be known as "the Elder," and whose grandson was Lorenzo the Magnificent; and Lorenzo, from whom arose the younger branch of the Medici that, beginning with Cosimo I, grand duke of Tuscany, ruled Florence from 1537 to 1737. Giovanni was, thus, the founder of a powerful family that was unofficial and official ruler of Florence from 1434 to 1737. As much of a democrat as his great wealth and widespread interests permitted, as he lay dying Giovanni advised his sons to accept only such honors from the state as were given in accordance with the laws. A portrait of him by Bronzino (1503–1572) was copied from an earlier portrait by one of Giovanni's contemporaries.

Medici, Giovanni de'. Original name of Pope **Leo X.**

Medici, Giovanni de'. [Called **Giovanni delle Bande Nere,** because he had his troops change their white insignia to black at the death of Pope Leo X.] Warrior; b. at Forlì, April 6, 1498; d. at Mantua, November 30, 1526. He was the son of Caterina Sforza and of Giovanni de' Medici il Popolano of the younger branch of the Medici family (grandson of Lorenzo, Cosimo the Elder's brother). His father died (September 15, 1498) and his mother sent him to Florence, as Forlì was threatened by Cesare Borgia. She lost her states of Imola and Forlì, and after some time as a prisoner of the Borgia, she joined her children in Florence. On her death (1509), her son Giovanni was reared in the house of Iacopo Salviati, whose daughter Maria he married (1517; Maria's mother was a daughter of Lorenzo il Magnifico). A restless and headstrong youth, he entered upon a military career and, as a mercenary, took part in the war of Urbino (1516–1517), when Pope Leo X sought to depose Francesco Maria della Rovere, the rightful duke, and replace him with a Medici. For Leo he was captain of the Marches and Umbria, and in 1521 took part in the war of the pope and Spain against the French. Following the death of Leo, he switched over to the French, and was wounded (February, 1525), just six days before the battle of Pavia, in which the French were defeated. After the collapse of the Morone conspiracy (October, 1525), by which Morone and others hoped to drive the foreigners, especially the Spanish, out of Milan and Italy, it seemed to Machiavelli that Giovanni delle Bande Nere was the only hope Italy had of preventing Florence and the papal states from falling under the Spanish yoke. In the war of the League of Cognac, he was captain of the League's infantry. The Swiss and Germans poured into Italy and neared Mantua. Giovanni prevented them from crossing the Po, and hoped to cut off their retreat. He might have done so. On November 25, 1526, he was hit in the leg by a cannonball and was carried from the field. The shattered leg had to be amputated. Pietro Aretino, his friend and companion in many a rowdy night, was at his bedside and described his death in a letter written from Mantua. He tells of the nobility of the sufferer, and his injunction to his friends, "Love me when I am dead." By his wife Maria, Giovanni delle Bande Nere was the father of Cosimo, who as Cosimo I founded the ducal line of the Medici.

Medici, Giuliano de'. Florentine patron of arts and letters; b. 1453; d. 1478. He was the son of Piero and Lucrezia Tornabuoni and the younger brother of Lorenzo il Magnifico. Handsome, amiable, an able participant in athletics, he was immensely popular with the Florentines. He delighted in the company of artists and scholars, and was an enthusiastic patron, but in all things was content to play second fiddle to his brother. He was slain on April 26, 1478, in the Cathedral of S. Maria del Fiore, in the Pazzi Conspiracy. Immediately after his death it was revealed that he had become the father of a natural son. This was Giulio, the future Pope Clement VII.

Medici, Giuliano de'. Duke of Nemours; b. 1478; d. March, 1516. He was the third son of Lorenzo il Magnifico and Clarice Orsini. Forced to flee Florence when his brother Piero was expelled (1494), he spent many years in exile at the court of Guidobaldo, duke of Urbino. Unlike his brother Piero, he did not exhaust himself or annoy the Florentines by attempts to restore himself at Florence. Gracious in temperament and of a lively and cultivated intelligence, he shared the society of some of the most learned men and women of his day. Castiglione, in his *Il Cortegiano*, mentions him as one of the courtiers who took part in the discussions and entertainments in the evening room of the ducal palace that were presided over by the duchess Elizabetta. This was probably the kind of life he should have continued to lead, but his ambitious brother, Cardinal Giovanni, destined him for a more important role. When the Medici were restored at Florence (1512), Giuliano was named its governor at the instance of Cardinal Giovanni. In June, 1515, the cardinal, now become Pope Leo X, named him gonfaloniere of the Church. The new pope, ever concerned to aggrandize his family, proposed to depose Francesco Maria della Rovere, the new duke of Urbino (Guidobaldo having died), and to name Giuliano duke in his place. To his credit, Giuliano refused to have any part of this plan. He remembered with gratitude the welcome he had received at Urbino when he was forced into exile and the many happy years he had spent there, and would not now betray the court that had offered him such hospitality. Giuliano married Filiberta of Savoy, whose nephew, Francis I, named him duke of Nemours, and he died soon after. He left a natural son, Ippolito, who became a cardinal. Giuliano, a pleasant, cultivated, and ineffectual man, is immortalized in the monument executed by Michelangelo for the New Sacristy of the Church of S. Lorenzo at Florence. In the monument he appears, idealized, as the seated warrior who looks consideringly into the future; it is a representation, not a portrait. A portrait of him by Raphael is in The Metropolitan Museum of Art at New York.

Medici, Giulio de'. Original name of Pope **Clement VII.**

Medici, Ippolito de'. Cardinal; b. at Urbino, 1511; d. at Itri, August 10, 1535. He was the illegitimate son of Giuliano de' Medici, duke of Nemours, and was educated at Rome by his uncle, Pope Leo X. In 1524 his cousin, Pope Clement VII, sent him and his cousin Alessandro to Florence as nominal heads of the government there. Both were expelled from Florence in 1527 when Rome was sacked by imperial troops, Clement was a virtual prisoner in Castel Sant' Angelo, and the Florentines drove out the Medici and restored the republic. Ippolito, who was a churchman against his will, was given many rich benefices, raised to the cardinalate (January, 1529), and became vice-chancellor of the Church (July, 1532). In his magnificent palace at Rome he lived like a prince. Alessandro had gradually assumed control at Florence. After Clement's death Ippolito plotted to dislodge him and assume control himself. He received Florentine exiles in his palace with the aim, he claimed, of restoring Florentine liberty. In August, 1535, he left Rome to meet with the emperor Charles V in order to convey to him the complaints of the Florentine exiles against Alessandro. He died on the way. Many said Alessandro had ordered him to be poisoned, but the cause of his death may have been malaria. He was a cultivated and talented man, wrote lyrics and translated the second book of the *Aeneid* (which he dedicated to Giulia Gonzaga) into blank verse. He surrounded himself with poets, men of letters, artists, and musicians, whose talents he sincerely appreciated. At the same time, he was ruthless, but unsuccessful, in his desire for power and employed a band of cutthroats and thugs to further his aims. His portrait, by Titian, is in the Pitti Palace at Florence.

Medici, Lorenzino de'. Florentine nobleman; b. March 23, 1514; murdered at Venice, February 26, 1548. He was a member of the younger branch of the Medici, descended from Lorenzo (1394–1440). His name was Lorenzo, but because of his slight stature he was always known as Lorenzino. Relations between the older and younger branches of the Medici family were not invariably cordial, and Lorenzino is thought to have envied his more prosperous relatives. His kinsman Pope Clement VII expelled him from Rome for a youthful act of vandalism and he returned to Florence. There he became the intimate of his cousin Alessandro, the natural son of Lorenzo II. Alessandro was named hereditary duke of Florence by Pope Clement VII with the consent of the emperor Charles V, in 1532, and was at first fairly well received by the Florentines. After the death of Clement, however, he abandoned himself to the violent and corrupt elements in his nature and became a tyrant of the most vicious kind. Lorenzino shared in his debauchery and viciousness. The two were inseparable. On the night of January 5, 1537, on the pretext of bringing a woman to him, Lorenzino took Alessandro to his home. On his return, with a hired accomplice, Lorenzino murdered the sleeping Alessandro. Lorenzino was a humanist and a poet. In defense of his murder of Alessandro he wrote an eloquent *Apologia*, in which he justified the slaying on the grounds that it rid Florence of a tyrant and made possible the restoration of liberty. He seems to have acted entirely alone. If he expected the Florentines to rise he was mistaken. He did not attempt to lead a rising himself but fled to Bologna, then to Turkey,

France, and Venice. His younger cousin Cosimo was named duke and put a price on his head. Cosimo ruthlessly hunted him down for, as Lorenzino was the older, his claim to become duke of Florence was somewhat better than Cosimo's. In consideration of Lorenzino's true motives for the murder of Alessandro, opinion was divided as to whether they were patriotic, as so ably claimed in his *Apologia*, or whether they sprang from a personal resentment of his arrogant and brutal cousin. Cosimo's thugs found Lorenzino eleven years later, at Venice, and killed him. As a poet, Lorenzino produced some intensely felt and eloquently expressed lyrics. He also wrote a comedy, *Aridosia*, based on Plautus and Terence, that was produced at Florence in 1536.

Medici, Lorenzo de'. Florentine merchant; b. 1394; d. 1440. He was the son of Giovanni di Bicci de' Medici, and the brother of Cosimo the Elder. Lorenzo was the founder of the younger branch of the Medici family, and the direct ancestor (great-great-grandfather) of Cosimo I (1519–1574) who became duke of Florence and first grand duke of Tuscany (1569). Lorenzo was an ardent collector and patron of the arts and learning, and was content to remain in the shadow of his admired older brother in artistic as well as political affairs.

Medici, Lorenzo di Cosimo de'. [Called **Lorenzo il Magnifico, "the Magnificent."**] Florentine statesman, poet, and patron of the arts and letters; b. January 1, 1449; d. at Careggi, April 8, 1492. He was the son of Piero de' Medici and Lucrezia Tornabuoni. From his mother he received a secure grounding in Catholicism, and ever after remained firmly attached to the faith. Beside the religious instruction that he owed to his mother, he had a thoroughly humanistic education. His teachers included Johannes Argyropoulos, Cristoforo Landino, and Marsilio Ficino. He knew Latin and Greek literature and was at home with the works of Dante, Petrarch, Boccaccio, and early Italian poets. From boyhood he shared his father's confidence and participated in affairs of state. He entertained (1459) Galeazzo Maria Sforza, heir to the duchy of Milan, at Florence; he served (1466) on an embassy to Rome to congratulate Pope Paul II, and went on from there to Naples to win the support of King Ferrante for the Medici party, at that time threatened by the party of Luca Pitti. His father chose Clarice Orsini, of the powerful Roman house, as his bride, in order to strengthen family influence in Italy. This was a departure from the Medici practice of marrying their sons to the daughters of rich Florentine burghers, and led to some grumbling that the Medici considered themselves too good for a Florentine bride. To Clarice, Lorenzo was married in June, 1469, amid spectacular festivities. Clarice, who died in 1488, bore him six children: Piero, who succeeded his father (1492); Giovanni, who became Pope Leo X; Giuliano, who became duke of Nemours; Lucrezia, who married the Florentine Iacopo Salviati and was the grandmother of Giovanni delle Bande Nere and the great-grandmother of Cosimo I, duke of Tuscany; Maddalena, who married Franceschetto Cibo, son of Pope Innocent VIII; and Contessina, who married the Florentine Piero Ridolfi. Lorenzo was an affectionate father, sometimes criticized for playing with his children on their own level. Their letters to him show on what excellent terms he was with them. His constant care was to give them the best education available and to prepare them for the places he expected them to take. Six months after Lorenzo's marriage his father died. Immediately the leading men of Florence came to him to offer their condolences and to invite him to take his father's place in the councils of the republic. Lorenzo, as he afterward wrote in his *Ricordi*, accepted reluctantly because of his youth (just short of 21); he also accepted for the practical reason that "at Florence the rich fare badly without power." His only offices were as a member of various councils that were, theoretically, the governing agencies of the republic but that were, in fact, controlled by a few wealthy and prominent men, all of the Medici party. He was a prince in all but name. The name "il Magnifico," however, was given to him in recognition of his accomplishments and for the splendor in which he bathed his city; it was a tribute to his person, not his power.

Lorenzo's hopes to preside over a peaceful state were soon disappointed. In 1471 a dispute broke out over control of the alum mines that had recently been discovered by the Florentine subject city of Volterra. Lorenzo sent his condottiere, Federico da Montefeltro, to put down what the Florentines considered as a revolt. The city was subjected to siege and fell. The mercenaries, in defiance of orders, plundered it and put it to the sack (June 14, 1472). Lorenzo was horrified. He did what he could to rebuild and repair the damage, but the sack of Volterra ever remained a mark, for his detractors, of his tyranny and cruelty. In 1471 Sixtus IV ascended the papal throne. His plans for reform of the Church evaporated as he turned his full attention to promoting the fortunes of members of his family. He set about winning back lands in the Romagna and Umbria that were, traditionally, lands of the Papal States but that had achieved independence by various means. He bought Imola (1473) and invested his nephew Girolamo Riario with it. His activities in other areas destroyed the cordial relations that had hitherto existed between him and the Medici. Florence was bordered on three sides by territories in which the pope sought dominion. Lorenzo secretly encouraged resistance to his ambitions. He changed the Florentine system of alliances from Florence-Milan-Naples to Florence-Milan-Venice, since the last-named also felt threatened by the pope. Sixtus was enraged when he learned of Lorenzo's assistance to his enemies. He allied himself with Naples. He named Francesco Salviati, an avowed enemy of the Medici, as archbishop of Pisa. Lorenzo had prevented Salviati from being made archbishop of Florence, and now prevented him from occupying his see at Pisa for three years. In December, 1476, Galeazzo Maria Sforza, duke of Milan and ally of Florence, was murdered, leaving an eight-year-old as his heir. Two years later, Francesco Pazzi, member of a rival Florentine banking house (to whose branch in Rome Sixtus had transferred the valuable papal account), and Girolamo Riario (angered because Lorenzo was blocking the territorial expansion to which he aspired), worked out a plot against him. The archbishop Salviati played a part in it, and the pope was privy to it, without, however, specifically sanctioning murder. The plan was to assassinate Lorenzo and his popular younger brother Giuliano and rid Florence once and for all of the Medici. The attack was made on Sunday, April 26, 1478, at which time the brothers were both in the cathedral in honor of young Cardinal Raffaele Riario, who was celebrating the Mass. The signal for the attack was the elevation of the host, the most solemn moment of the Mass. When the bell was sounded for this moment the conspirators set upon Lorenzo and Giuliano. Bernardo Bandini, a young Florentine, and Francesco Pazzi attacked Giuliano. Pazzi's fury was so unbridled that he struck repeatedly and wildly, and wounded himself in the thigh. Giuliano fell, pierced by nineteen wounds. Two inexperienced priests had been substituted at the last moment for the ruffian who was originally charged with the slaying of Lorenzo. They bungled their attack. He drew his sword, drove them back, and leaped over the altar rail to refuge in the sacristy. The huge congregation in the cathedral was in turmoil. Lorenzo's friends rushed to his aid, considerately chose an exit so that he would not see his fallen and bloodstained brother, and escorted him safely to the palace. The Florentines, whom the conspirators had expected to rise up in revolt against the Medici party, were inflamed the more with loyalty to them, and would not rest, in spite of Lorenzo's efforts to calm them, until all who were even remotely connected with the conspiracy were taken. Francesco Pazzi, suffering from his self-inflicted wound, managed to gain his uncle's palace. He was found there, taken to the Palazzo della Signoria and hanged from one of the upper windows. The archbishop was hanged alongside him. (Botticelli was commissioned to paint the scene of the figures swaying from the windows of the Palazzo.) Cardinal Riario, innocent of all knowledge of the plot, was taken into custody to protect him from the mob. Bandini was ultimately brought back from Constantinople, whither he had fled. Sixtus was wild with rage at the failure of what came to be called the Pazzi Conspiracy, and at the humiliation of the Church through the hanging of the archbishop and the detention of the cardinal. He demanded the arrest of Lorenzo, but the Florentines were loyal to a man. Frustrated, the pope excommunicated Lorenzo, "to all appearances," writes Schevill, "for unlawful resistance to murder." He placed Florence under an interdict, and declared for war. Naples, his ally, sent troops against Florence. The war went badly for Florence. Milan could not come to her aid, since it was convulsed by the struggle for power between the brothers of Galeazzo Maria Sforza. Venice was fully occupied in a war with the Turks. The allies of the pope under the duke of Calabria, son of Ferrante of Naples, marched into Tuscany. At Colle Val d'Elsa they met with resistance, and rather than push on, the duke decided to go into winter quarters, as it was now November (1479), and the time when fighting traditionally halted for the winter. Lorenzo took an accurate reading of his situation and realized that it was desperate. He learned from Ludovico il Moro at Milan that he would be received at Naples, and decided to go there himself in an effort to bring the war to an end. In December a thrill of fear and admiration shook the Florentines when they learned that he had taken ship below Pisa and sailed to Naples. King Ferrante was probably the most ruthless, unscrupulous, suspicious, and gratuitously cruel of all of the despots of the age. It would have meant nothing to him to put an end to Lorenzo, as he had done to many others. Lorenzo was thoroughly aware of this. By his act of personal courage, and after months of bargaining, he secured a peace that was not unendurably humiliating. The king demanded a large money indemnity and some concessions in territory. Lorenzo was welcomed as a hero when he returned to Florence in February, 1480; peace was signed the following month. In the same year, the Turks invaded Italy and captured Otranto. The duke of Calabria, who had been lingering on the borders of Tuscany in the hopes of further spoil, hurried back to Naples. The pope was terrified, and suddenly recognized the need for brotherly love in Italy, as well as that for unity against the infidels. Lorenzo was received back into the grace of the Church and the interdict was lifted from Florence. Henceforth, Lorenzo was careful not to underestimate the pope's power. He restored the old alliance of Florence-Milan-Naples, and when (1484) Innocent VIII became pope, Lorenzo was one of the principal props of that weak pontiff. In 1488 his daughter Maddalena was married to the pope's son, Franceschetto Cibo, and in 1489 Lorenzo prevailed upon the pope to create his 14-year-old son Giovanni a cardinal. With the elevation of Giovanni to the Sacred College, Florence had an ambassador at the papal court, and the Medici a member of the family to look out for their interests.

In general, Lorenzo's policy was two-pronged. It comprised, on the one hand, a determination to keep peace in Italy by a balance of power between the leading states, and on the other, a determination to remain on friendly terms with France (an important outlet for Florentine goods), while at the same time keeping the French, who maintained claims on Naples and Milan, out of Italy. Absolute peace did not prevail in the turbulent peninsula. Venice and the pope waged a war for Ferrara, which they intended to partition between them. Florence, Naples, and Milan opposed them. The war lasted from 1482 to 1484, drew in other states and ended inconclusively. But on the whole, Lorenzo, called "Ago della bilancia italiana" (the needle of the Italian balance), prevented, by diplomacy and power, the outbreak of major conflicts that would weaken the Italian states in the face of the growing French menace. He maintained friendly relations with his neighbors: Lucca, Siena, Perugia, and Bologna. Taking the field himself, he won back Sarzana (1487), which had been seized by the Genoese during his war with the pope, and added Pietrasanta (1484) and Piancaldoli (1488) to Florentine dominions. He strengthened his power at home (1480) by means of a new Council of Seventy, whose powers superseded those of all existing councils (although no existing council was abolished). The powers of the new council were delegated to two committees, one of eight, having control over foreign affairs and military matters, and the other of twelve, having control over financial and commercial matters. Lorenzo himself served in the Council of Seventy, and the committees were staffed by his men. By this "reform" the government of Florence was more closely tied to the Medici party, although Florence still thought of itself as a republic. Florence was at peace, prosperity prevailed, Lorenzo provided periodic spectacles and festivities that were more magnificent and interesting than even the Florentines were accustomed to. (Lorenzo's critics claimed the pageants and masques were intended to dull the moral sensibilities of the people, and to make them forget his tyranny; but in fact, there was no people in Italy more entranced by a great show than the Florentines. He added taste and imagination to the traditional spectacles.) In 1492 Florence went delirious in a ceremony of welcome to Giovanni de' Medici, their own cardinal, who in this year reached the age prescribed by the pope for taking the insignia of his office. Lorenzo, ill at his villa at Careggi, could not take part in the festivities. Shortly thereafter, Giovanni set off for Rome. His father wrote him a letter, advising him to remember his youth, to be reticent in discussion, to show proper respect to his elders and betters in the Church, to guard against ostentation, to rise early in the morning, and to get plenty of exercise. He also cautioned his son against the evils he might behold in the Eternal City, "that sink of all iniquity," and against the influence of those who would lead him to corruption and vice through envy of the great honor that had been bestowed on him. A month later Lorenzo died.

While he had been building and bulwarking his power in Florence, Lorenzo, who had little taste for business and lacked the capacity for it possessed by his father and grandfather, had neglected the family banking business, the source of his family's power. Branches in Bruges, London, and Lyon had to be liquidated or reorganized at great cost to the business as a whole. In addition to these losses, he had spent vast sums on splendid festivals, pageants, and ceremonial occasions at Florence; furthermore, other merchants and bankers in Italy and, especially, beyond the Alps, were offering stiff competition. The last years of his life had seen the rise of the Dominican, Fra Girolamo Savonarola. The preacher thundered against the evils he saw at Florence, and prophesied disaster for the iniquitous city, to be followed by purification and absolution. Lorenzo and his circle did not escape Savonarola's wrath. He was prior of San Marco, a foundation endowed and supported by the Medici, yet Lorenzo did not disturb him, nor did he prevent him, as he might easily have done by appealing to Rome, from giving his inflammatory sermons. He may even have been quite interested in Savonarola's mind and motivation, but the latter avoided him. When Lorenzo walked in the gardens, Savonarola withdrew. Two tales are told of Lorenzo's death: one that Savonarola came to him when he was dying and gave him his blessing (this, according to the credible account of the eyewitness Poliziano); the other (which should be discounted) that when, on Lorenzo's invitation, the preacher came to his deathbed, Lorenzo refused to accept the conditions Fra Girolamo laid down for giving his blessing—that Lorenzo restore Florentine liberty—and that Lorenzo died without it. Two years after his death the government of which he was the ruling spirit and partial architect, was overthrown. His son Piero was banished from the city. The balance that had kept Italy relatively peaceful was destroyed. The French had crossed the Alps and French troops under Charles VIII were coursing through the peninsula.

Lorenzo was spontaneously interested in all the artistic and intellectual developments of his age. He expanded the Florentine studio (university), where Landino taught rhetoric and poetry, Ficino, philosophy, Demetrius Chalcondylas, Greek, and Poliziano, Latin and Greek eloquence. He fostered and took part in the sessions of the so-called Platonic Academy, where the philosophy of Plato, as the participants understood it, was discussed with great earnestness. To rehabilitate Pisa, in an economic trough since its conquest (1406) by Florence, he endowed it with a university, and transferred the disciplines of law, medicine, and theology from Florence to the new school. His palace on the Via Larga was a veritable museum with its collections of art objects. During his time Florence bubbled with the intellectual ferment created by men of art, letters, and philosophy. The brilliant period over which he presided came to be called the Laurentian Age: it marked, in most respects, the culmination of the Renaissance in Florence. Of the liveliest intelligence, boundless vitality, and great poetic gifts, Lorenzo gathered about him men of many talents who stimulated each other. The humanists and philosophers Cristoforo Landino, Marsilio Ficino, and Pico della Mirandola formed part of his circle. Poliziano was his devoted friend and the tutor of his children. The poet Luigi Pulci, older than his patron, was a comrade and intimate. Architects, painters, sculptors, and musicians enjoyed his interest and his friendship. (In addition to his own lively interest, there were practical political reasons, largely propagandistic, for promoting the arts.) Among them were Giuliano da Sangallo (architect), Benedetto da Maiano (architect and sculptor), Antonio Pollaiuolo, Andrea Verrocchio (sculptors and painters), Desiderio da Settignano, Andrea della Robbia, the painters Botticelli, Ghirlandaio, Filippino Lippi, and the musicians Squarcialupi and Heinrich

Isaacs, and a host of lesser men. He had notable collections—of gems, cameos, antiques, and other objets d'art. Of these, it was his jewel collection that gave him the greatest pleasure. He placed antique statues and fragments, drawings and models in the garden of San Marco, and opened it (1489) to young students and others as a kind of school. Michelangelo went there when he was about 14 to study the statues and to work on his own. The story is that Lorenzo came upon the young sculptor and watched as he carved a satyr. He remarked that such an old satyr would surely have lost a tooth or two. Michelangelo saw the force of this observation and knocked out one of the teeth. Lorenzo was so impressed by his talent that he took the young sculptor into his own house and gave him a place at his own table. It was the custom for all or any of his friends to drop in at meal time and dine with him, on a first come first served basis. The meals were the occasion for lively discussion, and for readings of works created by members of the company. It was to entertain the diners that Luigi Pulci read the sections of his *Morgante maggiore* as they were written. But what drew all these gifted men to Lorenzo was not his patronage or his place as unofficial prince. It was his personality, his zest for life, his unquestioned taste and judgment in many areas and, above all, perhaps, his own talent that made him an artist among artists. From his youth he had written poetry. He knew and appreciated the classics but preferred the Tuscan poets and the language of Tuscany for his own work. In 1465 he met Federico of Naples at Pisa, and went with him to Milan and Venice. The two young men became good friends, and must have discussed poetry at great length, for Federico asked him for a sampling of Tuscan poetry. Lorenzo compiled (1466) a selection that included about 450 poems by 30 Tuscan poets, from Guittone d'Arezzo and on through Cino da Pistoia. With the collection, one that constituted one of the earliest anthologies of Tuscan poets, he sent a prefatory letter with his own critique of the poets included, a critique that revealed his own complete understanding and judgment. In his youthful poetry he was influenced by Dante and Petrarch, and, especially, by Guido Cavalcanti. The subject and object of many of his early love sonnets and canzoni was Lucrezia Donati, who appears to have been mainly a conventional literary inspiration. His *Selve d'amore* are two "improvisations" on love. Love poetry, however, was not the purest expression of his genius. He was most absorbedly himself when singing his love and appreciation of nature. *Ambra* is a pastoral that celebrates his love for his Tuscan villa at Poggio a Caiano (rebuilt for him by Sangallo between 1480 and 1485). *Caccia col falcone* describes a day spent at hawking, beginning with the bite and freshness of the early morning when the hunters set out, going on through the excitement of the hunt, the physical fatigue at the end of the day, and the revival of spirits over food and wine as the events of the day are recalled. It is a simple record, sparkling with realistic and loving detail, glowing with appreciation of nature and warm with comradeship. *La Nencia da Barberino* is a sophisticated city man's understanding, gay, sincere yet gently mocking version of a rustic love story. (Some critics have ascribed the poem to Giambullari; most agree that it is Lorenzo's). For his deeply religious mother he wrote *laude* (hymns) on various themes. One of these is the cry of a spirit earnestly seeking God, and has been called "the most personal, the most moving, and the greatest, of all the poems of Lorenzo." (Wilkins) A *sacra rappresentazione* (religious drama), *San Giovanni e San Paolo*, in which his children acted in a performance at his home (1489) is an interesting late example of this early form of the drama. *Altercazione* is a youthful dialogue on Neoplatonic ideas. In a completely different vein from any of the above are the poems he wrote for the entertainments given at carnival. Lorenzo organized the traditional disorderly processions given at that time into elaborately prepared and staged spectacles. Masques or pageants, often representing "triumphs," were performed, for which he wrote many of the accompanying songs. These were often deliberately immoral, in the carnival spirit, but gay and full of a youthful urge for enjoyment. A recurrent theme is *carpe diem*. The *Song of Bacchus*, from the masque *The Triumph of Bacchus*, has a refrain that exemplifies the "Gather ye rosebuds" spirit:

"Fair is youth and free of sorrow,
But it quickly flies away;
Youths and maids enjoy today:
You know nothing of tomorrow."

The same theme appears in his *Corinto*, one of the earliest Italian pastoral idylls. *I Beoni* is a hilarious and ribald account of the broaching of a cask of wine. As the songs written for carnival show his thorough understanding of his fellow townsmen and of what appealed to them, so his pastorals and rustic poems reveal his understanding and rapport with the inhabitants of the Tuscan countryside. In a commentary in the manner of Dante's *Vita nuova* and *Convivio*, he writes in prose on forty of his own sonnets, taking the opportunity to discourse on a variety of subjects. The preface to the work is an eloquent defense of Italian as a literary medium. And it is perhaps in this that Lorenzo made his most lasting personal contribution to the arts: the reawakening of Italian as a literary language, and the impulse his use of it gave to the renewal and growth of Italian literature.

Lorenzo was physically strong, loved the hunt and athletics (he won the prize at the tournament given by his brother Giuliano in 1475), was of endless vitality, and he was homely. (The golden youth on horseback in Gozzoli's *Procession of the Three Kings*, in the Medici-Riccardi palace, is an idealized portrait.) His complexion was sallow, his lower jaw protruded, his flattened nose deprived him of a sense of smell and gave him a poor speaking voice. But he won admiration and comradeship by his unfailing courtesy, his accessibility to rich and poor alike, his all-embracing and well-grounded intellectual and artistic interests, and by his radiant personality. He was a tyrant in the sense that he gradually attained almost absolute power in his territory, and had every intention of retaining it and passing it on to his son. However, he was neither cruel nor vindictive. The Albizzi and the Strozzi, forced into exile in his grandfather's time, were restored to Florence. The Pazzi, some of whom had been imprisoned or exiled following the conspiracy, were released and restored. Throughout his short life (from young manhood he suffered increasingly violent attacks of the family malady of gout), he combined his participation in the intellectual life of his age and his patronage of humanists, philosophers, poets, painters, sculptors, and architects with an intelligent statecraft and a domestic policy that, though far from republican, kept Florence at a high level of economic prosperity and in a state of domestic tranquillity unequalled in any other area of Italy except possibly Venice. For more than twenty years he led the Florentines in sports, spectacles, intellectual interests, and patronage of the arts: he was the child and very paradigm of his age.

Medici, Lorenzo II de'. Duke of Urbino; b. 1492; d. 1519. He was the son of Piero II de' Medici and Alfonsina Orsini, and was the grandson of Lorenzo the Magnificent. In 1513, as part of his design to maintain Medici control there and for want of an older and more experienced member of his branch of the family, Pope Leo X made his 20-year-old nephew Lorenzo head of the government of Florence. It was to him that Machiavelli addressed *The Prince*. To add to Lorenzo's prestige and authority, the pope declared Francesco Maria della Rovere deposed as duke of Urbino and named Lorenzo in his place (1516). Francesco Maria resisted. Lorenzo joined the army against him. The campaign was successful but Lorenzo's health was impaired by the rigorous campaign in difficult country. In 1518 Leo saw Lorenzo married to Madeleine, of the royal house of Valois. The following year both Lorenzo and his wife died. Their child was Catherine de' Medici, the last survivor of the older line of the Medici. Lorenzo also had a natural son, Alessandro, who became the first hereditary duke of Florence. Lorenzo's tomb in the New Sacristy of the Church of S. Lorenzo at Florence, with that of his uncle Giuliano across the room, is one of Michelangelo's greatest works.

Medici, Niccolà de'. Florentine banker and humanist; b. 1385; d. 1455. He was a fourth cousin of Cosimo de' Medici (1389–1464). Noted in his time for his learning, he was a member of the circle of Florentine humanists that included Alberti, Poggio, Niccoli, Bruni, Traversari, and others, and was himself the possessor of a rich collection of manuscripts that he freely loaned to his friends. He served the Republic in many official capacities in the course of his life.

Medici, Piero di Cosimo de'. Florentine merchant prince and banker; b. 1416; d. December 2, 1469. He was the son of Cosimo the Elder and Contessina de' Bardi, received a splendid education, and emulated his father as a collector of books and manuscripts, as a benefactor of libraries, and as a patron of the arts and of letters. He continued his father's support of Marsilio Ficino and encouraged the work of the humanists. Early in life he began to suffer from what was called gout (from which he was called "il Gottoso," "the Gouty"), but which was perhaps a form of arthritis. His frequent incapacitating illnesses restricted his activities, but he did serve on embassies for Florence and was once gonfaloniere (1461). By his wife Lucrezia Tornabuoni he had five children: Lorenzo, Giuliano, Maria, Bianca, and Lucrezia. He was the equal of his father in business matters, and under him the family bank and fortunes grew ever greater. On the death of Cosimo (1464) he became the unofficial ruler of Florence. However, because of the unobtrusive manner in which he exercised control, the retired life he led, and the appearance he gave of being utterly absorbed by his famous collections, his enemies thought he was weak. According to Machiavelli, Diotisalvi Neroni, one of Cosimo's righthand men, deliberately gave him bad advice. Neroni looked over the Medici books, at Piero's request, and advised him to call the great number of loans (mostly made by his father) that were owed him. Piero did so, and raised a storm. Neroni, with Luca Pitti and Agnolo Acciaiuoli, observed the anger that was felt toward Piero and thought the moment had come to unseat him. With Niccolò Soderini, the only one who was not motivated by unadulterated self-interest, they succeeded (1465) in abolishing the *accoppiatori* (the more or less permanent committee instituted earlier to choose names to go into the *borse*, the purses of names from which public officials were drawn by lot). Soderini became gonfaloniere, but accomplished little, and Piero's enemies sought help from Venice and Ferrara. Piero, ill at his villa at Careggi, was warned by his friends at Bologna that troops were approaching the borders of the republic. He had himself carried to the Palazzo della Signoria, exposed the danger, and made suitable preparations to meet it. The leaders, who to gain power themselves would have loosed foreign troops on the city, were sent into exile (except for Luca Pitti, who had become reconciled with Piero). The plan had been to have Piero assassinated and to bring Ferrarese soldiers into Florence, but, says Machiavelli, "the citizens, . . . finding Piero fully prepared and his adversaries unarmed, began to consider, not how they might injure him, but how, with least observation, they might glide into the ranks of his friends." The exiles did not give up, but sought help from Venice. Milan and Naples came to Piero's aid. An inconclusive war was fought and inconclusively ended. Acciaiuoli wrote from his exile in Naples, reminding Piero of his past loyalty to the Medici, and claiming that he had acted out of patriotism; he cannot help laughing, he adds, at the quirks of fortune that convert friends into enemies. Piero replied, "Your laughing in your present abode is the cause why I do not weep, for were you to laugh in Florence, I should have to weep at Naples." Piero was now unquestionably the first citizen of Florence, the acknowledged chief of state. He married his daughters to the sons of leading Florentine families, but with Lorenzo, his heir, he sought to strengthen family influence in Italy by alliance with a powerful family of another state. This was a departure from earlier Medici practice, and gave his enemies grounds for asserting that he intended to make himself prince. Nevertheless, Lorenzo was married to Clarice Orsini, of the celebrated Roman family. Piero was too ill to take part in the splendid wedding festivities. Mild, courteous, cultivated, and astute, he died six months later and was buried in S. Lorenzo. His bronze and porphyry sarcophagus was made by Verrocchio. Piero left his son in possession of great wealth, and the Medici name of such repute that on his death Lorenzo was called upon by the leading citizens of Florence to take his father's place in the government.

Medici, Piero II de'. Florentine merchant and politician; b. 1472; d. 1503. He was the son of Lorenzo the Magnificent and Clarice Orsini. He was an intelligent youth, a good student (Poliziano was his tutor), but above all loved active sports. On the death of his father (1492) he inherited the family wealth and the rule of Florence. Unlike his father and grandfather, who had been popular with the Florentines, he offended them by his arrogance and his acceptance of the role of a prince. When Charles VIII entered Italy (1494) to assert the French claim to Naples, Piero first took the side of Naples. But when he saw Charles' armies marching into Tuscany unopposed he was overtaken by panic. He rode out to the French camp, threw himself on Charles' mercy, and surrendered to him powerful fortresses that guarded Florence. When he returned to the city after his shameful capitulation, the democratic party, under the leadership of Savonarola, drove him and his younger brothers, Cardinal Giovanni and Giuliano, out of the city (November 9, 1494). The Medici palace was plundered and a new government was set up. Piero spent some time at Rome, where he was on good terms with the Borgia, and tried many times to rally the Florentine exiles and force an entry into Florence. He was unsuccessful. While serving in the French army, he was drowned in crossing the Garigliano River.

Medici, Salvestro de'. Florentine merchant of the 14th century; he was a member of the Medici family that originated in the Mugello, members of which migrated to Florence about 1200, and was a connection of the Medici family that later rose to power in Florence under Cosimo the Elder. Salvestro, a successful merchant, held public office under the republic: he was gonfaloniere in May–June, 1378, and acted against the city magnates. In the summer of that year the Ciompi Revolt broke out when the woolworkers, popularly called *ciompi,* sought the right to organize into guilds to protect themselves against the oppression of the oligarchs and the greater guilds. Salvestro was knighted. Soon, however, certain popular honors that had been bestowed on him were rescinded. Because of Salvestro's alleged support of the craftsmen and opposition to the magnates, the Medici won the reputation of being the protectors of the people, a circumstance that was of great value to Giovanni di Bicci de' Medici, and especially to his son Cosimo, in winning unofficial control of the republic.

Medoro (mā-dō′rō). In Lodovico Ariosto's *Orlando Furioso,* a faithful follower of the Moorish chief Dardinello. With his comrade Cloridano he makes a night sortie into the French camp to avenge the death of Dardinello. After killing many of the French (in a passage drawn from the Nisus and Euryalus incident in the *Aeneid*), they are surprised by the Scottish chief Zerbino. Cloridano is killed and Medoro left for dead. Angelica comes upon him and, smitten with love for the brave soldier of humble birth, heals his wounds. Medoro returns her love, and the princess and the soldier marry, spend many hours of delight in cottage and bower, and carve their names "Angelica and Medoro," on every available spot. When Orlando sees their names thus linked, he goes mad with jealousy.

Melanchthon (mẹ-langk′thọn; German, mā-längċh′ton), **Philipp.** [Also, **Philipp Melanthon;** original name, **Philip Schwarzerd.**] German reformer; b. at Bretten, Baden, February 16, 1497; d. at Wittenberg, Germany, April 19, 1560. Educated at Tübingen and professor of Greek at Wittenberg (1518), he became a collaborator of Martin Luther. He helped Luther in his translation of the Bible and soon became one of his chief followers in the Reformation. Melanchthon in many ways acted as a balance in the movement; his was the calm moderation that curbed and stated in reasoned terms Luther's more drastic reforms, at the same time recognizing completely Luther's leadership. In his *Loci communes rerum theologicarum* (1521), he set forth in scholarly fashion the first systematic exposition of the theology of the reformers. He served as a disputant in discussions with other reformers and with Roman Catholic theologians, and drew up (1530) the Augsburg Confession, the basic seventeen articles of the evangelical faith. Neither a fanatic nor a rousing preacher, Melanchthon was the articulate spirit of the Lutheran Reformation. He was looked upon as Luther's successor, but Melanchthon's genius lay not in leadership but in scholarly controversy.

Meldolla (mel-dōl′lä), **Andrea.** See **Andrea Schiavone.**

Meliboeus (mel-i-bē′us), **The Tale of.** One of Chaucer's *Canterbury Tales,* represented as being told by Chaucer himself. It is a highly moral tale with which Chaucer follows the tale of Sir Thopas, also supposedly told by himself, which was so lewd that Harry Bailly, the Host, among others, forced him to stop before he had finished the story. The Tale of Meliboeus is a prose translation of the Latin *Liber consolationis et concilii* of Albertano da Brescia (fl. 1225), through a free French version of the latter, the *Livre de Melibée et Dame Prudence.*

Melioli (mā-lyō′lē), **Bartolomeo.** Medalist; b. at Mantua, 1448; d. there, 1514. He was in charge of the mint at Mantua, and made medals of Ludovico III Gonzaga, of his son Ludovico, who was bishop of Mantua, of his grandchildren, and of other members of the family. Among the signed and dated medals is one of King Christian I of Denmark (1474).

Melissa (mā-lēs′sä). In Lodovico Ariosto's *Orlando Furioso*, a friendly enchantress who aids Bradamante and Ruggiero. She prophesies concerning their descendants—members of the Este family.

Melone (mā-lō′nā), **Altobello.** Painter and engraver of Cremona; active between 1497 and 1517. An eclectic, he drew on the Lombard and Ferrarese schools, was a close follower of Girolamo Romanino, and was also influenced by Dosso Dossi and Giorgione. Among his surviving paintings are a *Deposition*, Brera, Milan, that shows the Lombard and Ferrarese influences; *Way to Emmaus*, National Gallery, London, that is reminiscent of Romanino; and frescoes in the cathedral at Cremona (1517). The *Madonna and Child*, University of Missouri, Columbia, Missouri, is the central panel of the Picenardi triptych, painted at Cremona; the side panels are at Oxford, and the predella panels at Algiers and Paris. A number of paintings in the Carrara Academy at Bergamo are attributed to him; these include what is presumed to be a portrait of Cesare Borgia. Other examples of his painting are at Brescia, Rome, Verona, in the Johnson Collection, Philadelphia, and elsewhere.

Melozzo da Forlì (mā-lôt′tsō dä fōr-lē′). Painter; b. at Forlì, 1438; d. there, 1494. He was a pupil of Piero della Francesca and perhaps accompanied him to Rome in 1459. In any case, except for a brief absence, he was at Rome from 1460 to 1475, working with his fellow-pupil Antoniazzo Romano. Probably of this period are his *St. Mark as Pope* and *St. Mark the Evangelist*, in the Church of S. Marco, Rome. Shortly thereafter Giovanni Santi records him at Urbino as a painter unsurpassed at foreshortening. In this city he worked with Justus of Ghent on the palace of Federico da Montefeltro, and designed the allegorical figures *Dialectic* and *Astronomy*. The figures, painted by Berruguete and formerly at Berlin, were destroyed in 1945. Companion figures, *Music* and *Rhetoric*, are in the National Gallery, London. By 1477 he had completed one of his best known works, *Inauguration of the Vatican Library*, Vatican. The fresco, now detached and mounted on canvas, illustrates some of his outstanding qualities. His interest in perspective is revealed in the arched corridor of his architectural setting; his figures, solid and stately in the manner of Piero, have a living intensity that is peculiarly his own. The figures constitute a group of vivid portraits: Pope Sixtus IV and the nephews whose careers he advanced, Girolamo and Raffaele Riario and Giovanni and Giuliano della Rovere (later Pope Julius II), and the humanist and librarian Platina. His great fresco, *Ascension of Christ* (c1480), in the dome of SS. Apostoli, is notable for expressive content, rhythm, and for the skill with which he foreshortened the angels swirling about the figure of Christ to give the illusion that they are floating in space. The fresco was disassembled when the church was reconstructed in the 17th century; the central part, *Christ in Glory among the Angels*, is now in the Quirinal Palace; fragments with music-making angels are in the Vatican. Other works by Melozzo are a portrait of Guidobaldo Montefeltro (c1481), Colonna Gallery, Rome, designs for decoration in the Sanctuary at Loreto (carried out by Palmezzano), for the Feo Chapel in S. Biagio at Forlì, and an apothecary's sign in the Municipal Museum at Forlì. The few works of Melozzo that survive reveal him to have been a painter of powerful individuality, intensity, and remarkable technical skill.

Melville or **Melvill** (mel′vil), **Andrew.** Scottish reformer, scholar, and Presbyterian leader; b. at Baldovie, Forfarshire, Scotland, August 1, 1545; d. at Sedan, France, 1622. He was an active leader in the organization of the Scottish Presbyterian Church, and assisted in drafting the second "book of discipline" in 1581. He reorganized the Scottish universities, particularly St. Andrew's, of which he became rector (1590).

Melville of Hallhill (hôl′hil), Sir **James.** Scottish soldier, diplomat, and historical writer; b. 1535; d. at his estate of Hallhill, Fifeshire, Scotland, November 13, 1617. His autobiography (*Memoirs*) is important historically.

Melzi (mel′tsē), **Francesco.** Milanese painter; b. perhaps at Milan, 1493; d. at Vaprio d'Adda, c1570. A member of a well-to-do Milanese family, he was the pupil and devoted friend of Leonardo da Vinci, and followed him to France in 1516. He remained with Leonardo until the master's death, and was his heir. No work certainly from his hand survives.

Memling (mem'ling), **Hans.** [Also, **Memlinc,** occasionally (wrongly) **Hemling.**] Flemish painter of Bruges; b. c1430; d. 1494. He was one of the leaders of the so-called school of Bruges. He apparently studied under Rogier van der Weyden and came to Bruges c1466. He is noted for the clarity of his line, the warmth of his color, and his smooth style, rich in detail, as in landscape background to his portraits. His works include a *Shrine of Saint Ursula* (Bruges), considered his masterpiece, *Seven Griefs of Mary* (Turin), *Seven Joys of Mary* (Munich), *Last Judgment* (Florence), the *Donne Triptych* (Chatsworth), *Last Judgment* (Danzig), and portraits such as that of *Thomas Portinari and His Wife.*

Memmi (mem'mē), **Lippo.** Sienese painter; active in the first half of the 14th century. He studied under his father, Memmo di Filipuccio, with whom he worked in the decoration of the Palazzo del Popolo at S. Gimignano (1317). The fresco, *Virgin and Saints,* in the Council Chamber of that building, is from his hand. In 1320 he was at Orvieto, where a *Madonna* painted in that year is in the cathedral. With his brother-in-law, Simone Martine, he signed (1333) the *Annunciation,* originally in the cathedral at Siena and now in the Uffizi, Florence. Lippo painted the figures of the saints at each side of the central panel according to Simone's design. His *Virgin with Child* is in the Pinacoteca, Siena. In 1347 he went to Avignon with his brother, and there painted a *Madonna and Child.* He was a close follower of Simone Martini, but without this master's clarity of color and expressiveness. His delicate line and typically Sienese coloring are best revealed in his many small Madonnas. Other works are: *Madonna and Chid,* S. Maria dei Servi, *Madonna Enthroned,* Cloister of S. Domenico, of which only traces remain, and panels from polyptychs, Pinacoteca, Siena; *Crucifixion,* Vatican; *St. Paul* and a portable altarpiece, New York; and works at Pisa (S. Caterina), Altenburg, Berlin, Boston (Isabella Stewart Gardner Museum), Kansas City (Missouri), New Haven, and Washington. Memmi is also credited with the design for the *Mangia,* the belltower on the Palazzo Pubblico, Siena.

Mena (mā'nä), **Juan de.** Spanish poet; b. at Córdoba, Spain, c1411; d. 1456. He was the author of a didactic allegory, *El Laberinto de Fortuna,* sometimes called *Las Trezientas* or *Las Tres Cientas,* published in 1496.

Mendaña de Neyra (men-dä'nyä dā nā'rä), **Álvaro.** [Also, **Álvaro de Mendaña de Neyra.**] Spanish navigator; b. at Saragossa, Spain, 1541; d. in the Solomon Islands, c1596. He discovered and named the Solomon Islands and, on a voyage to colonize them, discovered and named the Marquesas group.

Mendes Pinto (mān'dẹsh pēn'tö), **Fernão.** See **Pinto, Fernão Mendes.**

Mendieta (men-dyā'tä), **Geronimo de.** Spanish Franciscan author; b. at Victoria, Guipúzcoa, Spain, c1530; d. at Mexico City, May 9, 1604. He is best known for his *Historia Eclesiastica Indiana.* It is a work of great historical value.

Mendoza (men-dō'thä), **Ana de.** See **Éboli,** Princesa **de.**

Mendoza, Antonio de. Spanish administrator; b. c1485; d. at Lima, Peru, July 21, 1552. He was the first viceroy of Mexico, and later, viceroy of Peru. In Peru he ordered the preparation of the code of laws called *Libro de Tasas.* He introduced (1535) the printing press into the New World.

Mendoza, Diego Hurtado de. Spanish diplomat, politician, novelist, historian, and poet; b. at Granada, Spain, c1503; d. at Valladolid, Spain, 1575. He held many diplomatic posts under Charles V of Spain. His works include *Guerra de Granada,* and poems.

Mendoza, Juan González de. Spanish prelate and author, a member of the Augustine order; b. at Toledo, Spain, c1540; d. at Popayán, in New Granada (now Colombia), 1617. He was in China from 1580 to 1583, and on his return spent two years in Mexico. His account of China (1586) contains also much of interest concerning America.

Mendoza, Lorenzo Suarez de. [Title, Count of **La Coruña.**] Spanish nobleman, viceroy of New Spain, or Mexico; b. c1510; d. at Mexico City, June 19, 1582.

Mendoza, Pedro de. Spanish captain; b. at Guadix, Granada, Spain, c1487; d. at sea, 1537. Appointed military governor of the territory extending from the Río de la Plata to the Strait of Magellan, he undertook (1534) at his own expense the colonization of the region about the Plata. After suffering from Indian attacks and from famine, he and a few companions left for Spain, but Mendoza died on the voyage. The colony was moved to Asunción, Paraguay, prospered, and led to the settlement of that part of South America.

Menéndez de Avilés (mā-nen′deth dā ä-ʙē-läs′), **Pedro.** Spanish captain; b. at Avilés, Asturias, Spain, 1519; d. at Santander, Spain, September 17, 1574. He founded St. Augustine, Florida (1565), captured a colony of French Protestants on the St. John's River, and after massacring nearly all of them succeeded in establishing Spanish rule in Florida. In later voyages he founded a post on Port Royal Bay, now in South Carolina, and left a mission on Chesapeake Bay, which was destroyed by Indians.

Menno Simons (men′ō sē′mōns) (or **Symons** or **Simonis**) (sē′mō-nis). Friesian preacher and reformer; b. at Witmarsum, Friesland, 1492; d. at Oldesloe, Holstein, January 13, 1559. He was the chief founder of the Mennonites, who take their name from him.

Menochio (mā-nō′kyō), **Giacomo.** Jurist; b. at Pavia, 1532; d. there, 1607. He taught at Pavia, Mondovì, and Padua, and enjoyed a high degree of esteem in his own day. Among his many writings on legal subjects is an important collection of opinions, *Consilia*, published after his death.

Menteith (men-tēth′), Sir **John de.** Scottish knight; d. after 1329. He captured (1305) Sir William Wallace. He was appointed a representative of the Scots barons in the parliament.

Mentel (men′tel) or **Mentelin** (men′te-lin), **Johannes.** German printer of Strasbourg in the 15th century. He was connected in business with Johann Gutenberg after the latter's quarrel with Johann Fust.

Meo da Siena (mā′ō dä sye′nä). Sienese painter; active in Perugia in the first quarter of the 14th century. He moved to Perugia early in the century and later (1319) bought a house there. His work has echoes of Duccio and Pietro Lorenzetti and the characteristic Sienese qualities of careful detail and a highly decorative effect. These elements, adopted by his school, were introduced into Umbrian painting. He painted many altarpieces, featuring a half-length Madonna, usually with saints. A great polyptych, *Madonna and Child with Saints,* his only extant signed work, is in the National Gallery of Umbria at Perugia. The twelve Apostles are depicted on the predella. There are several other *Madonnas* attributed to him in the same gallery, as well as a number of paintings of saints from his workshop.

Meopham or **Mepeham** (mep′am), **Simon.** Archbishop of Canterbury; b. probably at Meopham, near Rochester, Kent, England; d. October 12, 1333. He was involved in constant quarrels with his clergy, which finally resulted in his excommunication in 1333.

Merbecke or **Merbeck** or **Marbeck** (mär′bek), **John.** English scholar and composer; b. 1523; d. at Windsor, England, c1585. In *The Booke of Common Praier noted* (1550) he published the first musical setting to the liturgy sanctioned by the Act of Uniformity (1549). His works show his use of English rather than Latin rhythms. He published (1550) the first concordance to the English Bible.

Mercator (mėr-kā′tor), **Gerardus.** [Original name, **Gerhard Kremer.**] Flemish geographer; b. at Rupelmonde, Belgium, March 5, 1512; d. at Duisburg, Germany, December 2, 1594. He studied philosophy and mathematics at the University of Louvain, and afterward devoted himself to geography. Through the influence of Cardinal Granvella, he received a commission from the emperor Charles V to manufacture a terrestrial globe and a celestial globe, which are said to have been superior to any that had then appeared. He took up his residence at Duisburg in 1559, and eventurally became cosmographer to the duke of Jülich and Cleves. He invented the Mercator system of projection, a projection in which the parallels of latitude and the meridians of longitude intersect at right angles. This, the most famous and widely used of all map projections, is accurate only along the line of the equator, but its greatest distortion occurring in the high and low latitudes makes it less objectionable for ordinary use than projections that distort the areas in the temperate and tropical zones. Mercator is likewise credited with breaking the hold that Ptolemaic maps had on European geographical study by his accurate execution. His chief works are *Tabulae geographicae* (1578–1584) and *Atlas* (1595), the latter being completed after his death by his son.

Merchant's Tale, The. One of Chaucer's *Canterbury Tales*. It is the story of the deception of an old husband (January) by a young wife (May) with the friendly assistance of an enchanted pear tree. The original is Eastern; an account of the Indo-Persian, Turkish, Arabian, Singhalese, and other versions of it is given in the Chaucer Society's *Originals and Analogues*. The Latin versions are Boccaccio's and Caxton's. The immediate source of Chaucer's version, however, is thought to be a Latin fable.

Mercuriale (mer-kö-ryä′lā), **Girolamo.** Physician; b. at Forlì, September 30, 1530; d. there, November 13, 1606. He studied at Bologna and took his doctorate at Pavia. Returned to Forlì, in 1562 he went on a political mission to Rome, where he remained for eight years, under the protection of a Farnese cardinal. In 1569 he was called to the chair of medicine at Padua. The emperor Maximilian II then invited him to Vienna and showered him with benefices and honors while he was in his service. From 1587 to 1593 he taught medicine at Bologna, then at Pisa. He was interested in many branches of medicine, but above all in its history, and sought the best codices of the Greek authors and translated them into Latin. His *De arte gymnastica* (Paris, 1577) is a huge work, dedicated to Maximilian II, in which he describes the uses of gymnastics for the well, the ill, the young, and the old, and in which he displays his wide-ranging erudition.

Merici (mā-rē′chē), Saint **Angela.** See **Angela Merici,** Saint.

Merlin (mėr′lin). Famous enchanter of Arthurian legend. Matteo Maria Boiardo adapts him to the Italian scene in his *Orlando Innamorato,* in which Merlin has a magic well that causes all who drink of its waters to despise the first person they see thereafter. Merlin also appears in Lodovico Ariosto's *Orlando Furioso*.

Merlino Cocai (mer-lē′nō kō-kī′). Pseudonym of Teofilo Folengo, under which he published his *Baldus*.

Merswin (mers′vin), **Rulman.** German wine merchant and mystic of Strasbourg; b. 1307; d. 1382. He was associated with Johannes Tauler. He presented the Knights of Saint John with a cloister and retired to it himself. After his death certain of his writings were found (*Von den vier Jahren seines angefangenen Lebens* and *Von den neun Felsen*).

Merula (mā′rö-lä), **Giorgio.** Humanist and historian; b. at Alessandria, between 1430 and 1431; d. at Milan, March 19, 1491. He studied under Francesco Filelfo at Milan, then went to Rome for the Jubilee Year (1450). There he met Galeotto Marzio, and went with him to Padua for further study. In 1454 he was back at Milan, giving private lessons. He went next to Mantua to hear the lectures of Gregorio Tifernate and remained to teach there until 1465. In that year he went to Venice, where he taught rhetoric for more than fifteen years. While at Venice he worked on the preparation of editions of many Latin writers, as Martial, Cicero, Cato, Varro, Columella, and Plautus. He also wrote commentaries on other texts. In these latter his criticism was sometimes so sharp and arrogant that he became the target of several invectives by his fellow humanists on this account. In 1482 he went to Milan on the invitation of Ludovico Il Moro. He taught at Pavia and Milan and then, again on the invitation of Ludovico, began (1488) a history of the Visconti. He set himself to search, or have searched, the archives and the monasteries of the Visconti state for pertinent documents. In this way his amanuensis, Giorgio Galbiate, discovered (1493) some important ancient codices in a monastery at Bobbio (Merula took credit for the discovery, but a later age has acknowledged its debt to Galbiate as the actual discoverer). Using material he found in his researches, Merula completed the first ten books of his planned history, and outlined the first four of the second ten books. This incomplete history, *Historia Vicecomitum,* is his best work, and is one of the best histories of the 15th century.

Merulo (mā′rö-lō), **Claudio.** [Called **Claudio da Correggio.**] Composer and organist; b. at Correggio, near Parma, April 8, 1533; d. at Parma, May 4, 1604. He probably received his first musical instruction from a French musician then resident at Correggio. At an early age (1556) he was named organist in the cathedral at Brescia. In 1557, as a result of a contest, he was appointed first organist of St. Mark's, at Venice, and remained there until 1584. At Venice he established a press for printing and publishing books of music. Among the early works published was a book of madrigals composed by Merulo. He was commissioned to write the music for many state occasions, such as the music for a tragedy that was to be presented before King Henry III of Poland, the Doge, and the Venetian Senate in honor of Henry's visit to

Venice. In 1591 he went to Parma and in 1594 to Rome. Among his works, besides several books of madrigals, are motets, masses, and organ works.

Metsys (met′sīs), **Quentin** (or **Quintin**). See **Massys** or **Matsys** or **Metsys, Quentin** (or **Quintin**).

Meung or **Meun** (mėṅ), **Jean de.** See **Jean de Meung** (or **Meun**).

Michelangelo (mī-ke̤l-an′je̤-lō; Italian, mē-kel-än′je-lō). [Full name, **Michelangelo Buonarroti.**] Sculptor, painter, architect, and poet; b. at Caprese, March 6, 1475; d. at Rome, February 18, 1564. He was a member of an ancient Florentine family that traced its ancestry back to one Bernardo (d. c1228). (Through Michelangelo's brother Buonarroto, the family survived in direct descent to Cosimo, who in 1858 willed the family house, Casa Buonarroti, to the city of Florence). His father was a magistrate at Caprese, a mountain village under Florentine jurisdiction. A few weeks after Michelangelo's birth his father's term came to an end and the family moved back to Florence. The infant was put to nurse with the wife of a stone-cutter of Settignano and afterwards said that he sucked in the love of the hammers and chisels with which he made his figures with his nurse's milk. His father opposed his desire to become an artist on the ground that to be a craftsman was beneath the family's dignity. However, the boy's impulse towards the arts would not be denied, and on April 1, 1488, he was apprenticed to Domenico Ghirlandaio, one of the busiest artists of Florence at the time. Among his fellow students was Francesco Granacci, who became a close friend. He learned something of the art of fresco and is thought to have assisted Ghirlandaio in the execution of the frescoes in S. Maria Novella. Like many young Florentines he studied Masaccio's frescoes in the Brancacci Chapel in the Church of the Carmine; drawings he made of the frescoes of Giotto and Masaccio are preserved in the Louvre, at Munich, and at Vienna. (Many later drawings, works of art in themselves, are in the Royal Collection at Windsor, the British Museum, the Uffizi, Casa Buonarroti, Louvre, and elsewhere.) In 1489 he was released from his apprenticeship before his three-year term was up and went to work in the sculpture garden arranged by Lorenzo de' Medici at San Marco as a school for young Florentines.

Michelangelo
A Philosopher
The British Museum, London

There he worked under Bertoldo di Giovanni, who had been a pupil of Donatello and who passed on the influence of that master to his young pupil. Copying antique statues and fragments in the garden he made an old laughing satyr. Lorenzo the Magnificent remarked that such an old fellow would surely have lost some teeth. Michelangelo knocked out one and hollowed out the gum so that it would appear to have shrunk as after a tooth has been missing for some time. In 1490 Lorenzo took him into his own house on the Via Larga and gave him a place at his table. Here the young sculptor met the leading poets and thinkers of the day and was introduced to the Neoplatonic theories, there so ardently discussed, that were to become an important factor in his artistic inspiration. Another pupil in Lorenzo's Garden of San Marco was Pietro Torrigiani, who mocked the younger artist's work; in the ensuing fight he broke Michelangelo's nose and disfigured him for life. In April, 1492, Lorenzo the Magnificent died and Michelangelo went home for a while but returned later to the Medici house. Of this period (1492–1494) are the reliefs, *Madonna of the Steps* and *Battle of the Centaurs*, both now in the Casa Buonarroti. The latter subject was suggested to him by the poet Poliziano, who took great interest in his progress, continually encouraged him, and out of his own vast learning contributed to Michelangelo's education. Of the same period is a wooden *Crucifix* in S. Spirito. In return for it, the prior of S. Spirito made available to him a space in the Hospital of S. Spirito where he could pursue his studies in anatomy. As a means to an artistic end (rather than, as with Leonardo da Vinci, as a scientific investigation), he dissected cadavers to study the mechanisms of the body. It was already his passionate conviction that the male nude was the supreme vehicle to convey his artistic vision.

Piero de' Medici, who succeeded Lorenzo, was highly unpopular. His expulsion, as the French marched into Italy (1494) seemed imminent. Michelangelo, perhaps because he feared that his position as a protégé of the Medici put him in danger, fled to Venice and then to Bologna, in October, 1494. Piero was driven from Florence the next month, and the city fell under the domination of Savonarola, who for some time had been preaching woe to the Florentines. His prophecies of doom seemed to have come true with the arrival of the French. The impassioned but gloomy Dominican made a lasting impression on Michelangelo's fundamentally religious spirit. At Bologna he came in contact with the work of Jacopo della Quercia, whose influence was added to that of Donatello and the classical sculpture with which he had become acquainted, and studied Dante. His interest in Dante, with whom he seems to have identified in his love and sorrow for a Florence fallen to tyrants, was lifelong. A noble patron at Bologna took him into his household and secured him commissions to work on the Arca di S. Domenico (Tomb of St. Dominic), in the Church of S. Domenico. Work on the tomb had been proceeding since the 13th century, when it was begun by Nicola Pisano. For it he carved a kneeling angel bearing a candelabrum and figures of *St. Proclus* and *St. Petronius*. When he returned to Florence Savonarola was in the ascendant; the Medici were in exile. Of this time in Florence was a *Sleeping Cupid*, sold by his dealer to Cardinal Riario as an antique. (The figure later came into the possession of Guidobaldo, duke of Urbino; Cesare Borgia stole it from him when he overran Urbino and seized the duke's possessions; Isabella d'Este got it from Cesare Borgia by the simple process of asking for it; it went to England early in the 17th century when Isabella's collections were sold, and was later lost, probably destroyed in a fire.) On the discovery that the statue was not an antique Cardinal Riario wanted to see the sculptor who had made such a remarkable figure. On June 25, 1496, Michelangelo arrived at Rome in the company of a gentleman of Cardinal Riario's suite. The sight of the imperial ruins and statues added a new dimension to his art. Of this first Roman period (1496–1499) are the *Bacchus*, Bargello, and the celebrated *Pietà* in the Vatican. In the highly finished and polished *Pietà*, with its superb solution to the difficult technical and compositional problem of placing a grown man on a woman's lap, Michelangelo expressed a mood of supreme grief and resignation with a tender realism that he later abandoned in his preoccupation with the heroic and the ideal. The *Pietà* is his only signed work. Vasari writes that he was in the chapel where the sculpture stood and overheard some Lombards admiring it. One told the others that the exquisite work was the creation of a fellow Lombard. That night Michelangelo entered the chapel and carved his name on the ribbon across the Virgin's bosom. The statue won him instant recognition. When he returned to Florence he was famous. By 1501 the republic had been restored at Florence. Vasari writes that Piero Soderini, the gonfaloniere, awarded him, on behalf of the republic, the commission for a huge statue of David, but it was the officials of the cathedral who gave him the commission. The statue, carved from a block of marble that had been spoiled by Agostino di Duccio nearly forty years earlier, was begun in 1501 and completed in April, 1504. The youthful *David*, frowning with concentration and tense with the imminence of action, has been interpreted as the young defender who slays the enemy and governs the city wisely—a symbol of the triumph of the

Republic over the (Medici) tyrants. A large committee of artists and others was set up to choose a location for the statue—Leonardo was a member, as were other outstanding painters. At the suggestion of the Herald of Florence it was set up near the entrance door to the Palazzo Vecchio, the seat of the government. (The original is now in the Accademia, Florence; the statue at the Palazzo Vecchio is a copy.) In the same year (1504) he was given the contract to fresco one wall of the Hall of the Great Council in the Palazzo Vecchio. Leonardo da Vinci was to do the fresco on the other wall. Michelangelo began his cartoon (completed 1506) on an incident that occurred at Cascina during a war with Pisa in the 14th century, when a large number of Florentine soldiers were surprised by the enemy while bathing. This subject gave him the opportunity to portray male nudes in a wide variety of poses of violent action, as the soldiers struggled to get dressed, to get out of the water, or to prepare to dash into action. Neither Michelangelo nor Leonardo ever carried out the frescoes, but the cartoons were put on exhibition and became a school for painters. Both cartoons had far-reaching influence, but that of Michelangelo was perhaps the longer lasting in its illumination of the possibilities of the human body as a vehicle of artistic expression. (His later followers and imitators exaggerated his twisted, violent poses, to the distortions that became characteristic of the mannerist style.) The cartoon was ultimately cut up and disappeared. All that remains of *The Bathers* is a copy of a portion of it in the collection of the Earl of Leicester at Holkham Hall, England. Of the same period at Florence is *The Holy Family*, Uffizi, painted for Angelo Doni and known also as the Doni Tondo (a circular painting). In its strong outlines and modeling it reveals Michelangelo's fundamentally sculptural approach to painting. He thought of himself as a sculptor only, and sometimes signed his letters, of which nearly 500 are extant in holograph or documented form, "Michelangelo sculptor in Rome." Also of these fruitful years at Florence are the *Bruges Madonna*, Notre Dame, Bruges, and the circular reliefs of the Madonna of the Taddei and Pitti tondi, the former at Burlington House, London, and the latter in the Bargello, Florence. He began a statue of *St. Matthew* for the cathedral; the unfinished figure is in the Accademia, Florence.

In 1505, while he was still working on the Cascina cartoon, he was called to Rome by Pope Julius II, who had been elected in 1503. Julius was Michelangelo's equal in energy and determination and was in a position to exercise both. He intended to use Michelangelo's great gifts, of which Julius, of his own cultivation and taste, had the highest appreciation, for the glory of God through the beautification of Rome. His commission was for a tomb for himself. All Michelangelo's genius responded enthusiastically to the challenge of the commission, to the opportunity for presenting his philosophical and religious ideas through an ideal realization of his sculptor's art. He made a complex design for a magnificent structure with over forty figures, and went to Carrara to secure the marble. For a time after his return to Rome Julius visited him frequently in his studio. Later, when he called to see the pope he was put off several times and one day was told that the pope refused to see him. He thought that the architect Bramante was jealous of his influence and had perhaps intrigued against him. In a proud rage that Julius would listen to his enemies, he sold all his furniture and rode posthaste to Florence (April, 1506). Later in the same year Julius, at the head of a papal army, marched into Bologna to compel its submission. At the pope's command, Michelangelo was prevailed upon by the gonfaloniere at Florence, who said Florence could not go to war over him, to go to Bologna and seek the pope's forgiveness. Julius rebuked him, but when a prelate who was present thought to excuse Michelangelo on the ground that artists were generally ignorant of other matters, Julius had him driven from the room for daring to say of a great artist what the pope himself would not think of saying. Julius always held Michelangelo in the highest esteem as an artist and as a spirit, but did not hesitate to call on his full authority to force Michelangelo to do his bidding. At Bologna he ordered the sculptor to make a huge bronze statue of the pope. The work, in a medium that was uncongenial to Michelangelo, was carried on under great difficulties and with inadequate funds for the artist. His enemies predicted that it would never be cast. It was raised to its place over the portal of the basilica of S. Petronio in February, 1508, and Michelangelo returned to Florence. (In 1511, the Bolognese drove out the papal forces; the statue was pulled from its place, melted down, and cast into a cannon by Alfonso d'Este, who named it the *Giulia.*) In the same year (1508) Julius called him to Rome and ordered him to paint the ceiling of the Sistine Chapel, built by Julius' uncle, Pope Sixtus IV. Michelangelo, anxious to proceed with the tomb, protested that he was a sculptor, not a painter. Julius would not be deterred and assured him that he was the best judge of that. Michelangelo suspected Bramante and Raphael, also working for Julius in Rome at this time, of putting the idea that he should paint the ceiling into Julius' head in order to discredit him, as painting was not his field. Nevertheless, work on the tomb was abandoned, some said because Julius had decided to rebuild St. Peter's on a scale commensurate with the magnificence of the proposed tomb. In the end, Michelangelo's work and worry over the tomb, on which he later said he had wasted his best years, lasted for forty years (1505–1545). In that span contracts with the heirs of Julius were made and renegotiated a number of times. The original design, through successive alterations, was pitifully reduced. The heirs of Julius, notably Francesco Maria della Rovere, duke of Urbino, made a number of attempts to compel him to finish it and even accused him of embezzlement. The popes succeeding Julius would not release Michelangelo to work on the tomb; none of them was willing to allow his gifts to be employed in the glorification of Julius. Of all the figures he had planned for the tomb, he completed a powerful figure of *Moses* and figures of *Leah* and *Rachel.* These, with figures carved by other sculptors, were set up (1545) in the Church of S. Pietro in Vincoli to constitute a feeble substitute for the splendid tomb originally designed. Other figures planned for the tomb are the two *Captives,* now in the Louvre, and four *Slaves,* brought to the state where they are but just emerging from the stone, in the Accademia, Florence. (Some of the surviving works of Michelangelo are little more than blocked out; others are closer to a finished state; few of his works received the final touches.)

In 1508 he began work on that masterpiece of world painting, the ceiling of the Sistine Chapel in the Vatican. Dissatisfied with the scaffolding that had been erected and with his assistants, he pulled down the scaffolding and erected one to his own design, and decided to carry out the fresco without any appreciable assistance. He overlaid the shallow barrel-vaulted ceiling with a painted architectural framework that has the effect of a trellis, through which the frescoes are seen, and also, as it curves down, divides it into three zones. Michelangelo's subject matter was somewhat conditioned by the presence on one lateral wall of the chapel of scenes from the story of Moses, and on the other of scenes from the life of Christ. These had been painted (1481–1482) by Botticelli, Perugino, Rosselli, and others. The scenes on the story of Moses represented man under the Law; those on the life of Christ represented man under Grace. Michelangelo painted scenes on man before the Law was given to him. In the lunettes and spandrels of the lowest zone are groups of the ancestors of Christ and figures from the Old Testament (*David and Goliath, Judith and Holophernes,* the *Brass Serpent, Esther and Haman*). In the middle zone are prophets and sibyls, each accompanied by two genii. These occupy a higher level in the system because of their capacity to foretell the coming divinity. In the top zone, across the length of the chapel, in rectangular panels, is a series of nine *Histories* from Genesis. At the corners of each panel are naked youths, the "Ignudi," holding monochrome medallions. In series of three, the Histories represent: 1) the creation of the world—*God Separating Light from Darkness; Creation of the Sun, Moon, and Plants; God Separating the Waters from the Earth;* 2) the creation of man—*Creation of Adam; Creation of Eve; Fall of Man;* and 3) the awareness of sin—*Sacrifice of Noah; The Deluge; Drunkenness of Noah.* Groups in some of the panels, as in *The Deluge,* are symbolic of various ideas of the theology and tradition that the entire ceiling represents. It may be noted that, as with all of Michelangelo's painting, there is an almost total absence of landscape in any conventional sense. "Man," to him, was "the measure of all things." Lying on his back on his scaffold, Michelangelo worked the best part of four years on the painting. Julius was wildly impatient, both to see it and to have it finished. From time to time he climbed a ladder up the scaffolding to see what progress had been made and to urge on the artist.

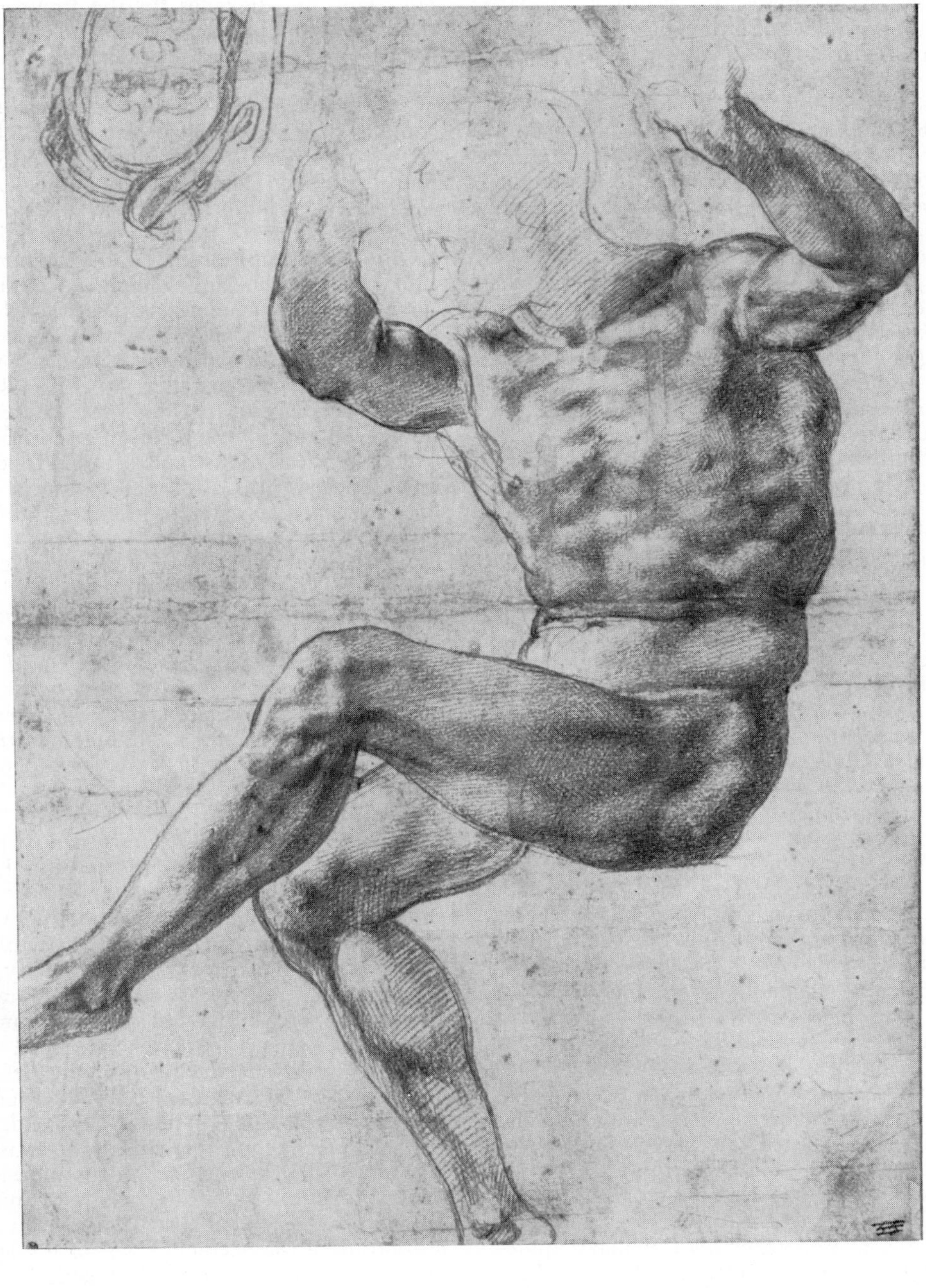

Michelangelo
Study for the nude youth over the Prophet Daniel in the fresco on the ceiling of the Sistine Chapel
The Cleveland Museum of Art, Gift in memory of Henry G. Dalton
by his nephews George S. Kendrick and Harry D. Kendrick

Michelangelo refused to give him a date when he would finish the great work. It is reported that once Julius threatened to have him hurled from the scaffold. When it was about half complete the scaffold was removed and for the first time he himself could see the total effect of his work. After four years the completed work was uncovered to the public, on October 31, 1512. Acclaimed as a supreme work of art from his own day to the present, it is one of the few of his great undertakings that was brought to completion. In the freshness, power and harmony of its scenes, the variety and interest of his inspiration, and the grandeur of its theme, it is one of the great masterpieces of world art.

On August 29, 1512, the town of Prato, on the outskirts of Florence, was sacked by a papal army that was accompanied by Cardinal Giovanni de' Medici. The officials of the Florentine republic, led by Michelangelo's friend, Piero Soderini, panicked and fled, opening the way for the return of the Medici. The following year Julius II died and Cardinal Giovanni succeeded as Leo X. Since the completion of the Sistine ceiling Michelangelo had been working on the tomb of Julius. It was in this period that he completed the statues of *Moses* and the *Captives*. In 1516 Leo ordered him to design a façade for the Medici Church of S. Lorenzo at Florence. He worked on the design and secured the marble, opening up the quarries at Pietra Santa at the pope's command (to benefit Tuscany) at enormous expense of time, energy, and money. He now had a number of enemies in the papal entourage, artists jealous of his genius and his fame, exasperated and frustrated by his refusal to engage in the customary graft, juggling, and granting of favors; some of his fellow artists refused to believe in a man of such instinctive probity and, often thorny, independence. In 1520 the contract for the façade of S. Lorenzo was cancelled; four years of labor on designs and in the quarries were wasted. He was wounded and humiliated by the failure of the project. (Of all the popes Michelangelo served in his long life, Leo, whom he had known as a boy in Lorenzo's house, seems least to have appreciated his genius.) In the same year, Cardinal Giulio de' Medici, Leo's cousin, called on him to design a new sacristy for S. Lorenzo, which was to serve as a memorial chapel and was to house the Medici tombs. His plans and drawings for the tombs went through a number of changes. Of the four tombs originally planned, only those of two of the least effectual and important members of the family were completed, or partially completed. These were the tombs of Giuliano de' Medici, duc de Nemours (d. 1516), brother of Pope Leo, and of Lorenzo de' Medici, duke of Urbino (d. 1519), the pope's nephew. Following the death of Leo (1521), work on the tombs, and on the Laurentian Library that Michelangelo designed adjoining the cloister of S. Lorenzo to house the Medici collection, was suspended. With the election of Giulio (1523) as Clement VII the work was resumed with urgency. In 1527 Rome was sacked; Michelangelo's house there was vandalized and some of the sculptures in his studio were cast down and broken. Clement was besieged in Castel Sant' Angelo and finally escaped to Viterbo. Florence threw off the Medici yoke and reestablished the republic. Of about this time is Michelangelo's strange *Victory*, Palazzo Vecchio, with its echoes of Donatello's *St. George*, especially in the head of the young victor astride his fallen enemy. As with his earlier *David*, the group memorializes the fall of tyrants. Another direct reference to the overthrow of tyrants is his stern and noble bust of *Brutus*, Bargello. Anticipating a siege by the papal and imperial armies (Clement had allied himself with the Emperor Charles V, his erstwhile enemy), the Florentines began preparations to defend the city, and in April, 1529, Michelangelo was put in charge of the fortifications. He drew up (some of his drawings survive) and helped to execute effective plans, and suddenly, in September, fled the city and went to Venice. He was declared a rebel (September 30, 1529) but on his voluntary return (November 20) was pardoned and worked throughout the siege in the defense of Florence. On August 12, 1530, after an epic resistance, the starving city surrendered, not to Clement, but to Charles, whose troops had forced the capitulation, in the hope that some vestiges of republican government might survive. But Clement had insisted on the restoration of the Medici as part of his agreement with the emperor. Michelangelo had every reason to expect to feel the pope's wrath. Clement, however, who had a true appreciation of him as an artist and liked and respected him as a man, soon pardoned his political defiance and urged him to get on with the work in the New Sacristy. By 1534 when, following the death of Clement, he left Florence never to return, he had almost completed the tombs of Giuliano and Lorenzo. Each consists of a huge sarcophagus with a curved lid. In a niche above the sarcophagus is, in the first case, a seated figure of Giuliano dressed in Roman imperial armor. He seems about to rise in command. Although Giuliano was a gentle, cultivated, honorable and peaceful man, the alert warrior over his tomb has traditionally been interpreted as a symbol of the Active Life. The head of the warrior is an idealized portrait; Michelangelo said that in a thousand years no one would know what Giuliano really looked like. The tomb, with its figures, was not intended to represent a man but to express an idea. Lying on each side of the sloping lid are allegorical figures: a highly finished and polished nude female figure, *Night*, and a nude male figure, *Day*, whose masculine strength is clearly carved but whose face is still veiled in stone. Together, *Day* and *Night* equal Time which consumes all things. Over Lorenzo's tomb the seated figure, also in imperial armor (both are in armor as captains of the Church), rests his chin on his hand and, from under the lowered beaver of his helmet, gazes forever at an invisible horizon; this figure symbolizes the Contemplative Life. (Later interpreters, not Michelangelo, termed them Active and Contemplative.) On the lid of Lorenzo's tomb the nude female figure, whose body is much younger and less worn than the figure of *Night*, is *Dawn*, and the nude male figure is *Evening*. The allegory of the tombs is Time and Death. When Michelangelo left for Rome the allegorical figures were lying on the floor of the chapel. Figures representing rivers, in the original design, were never executed. Cosimo I, on his accession (1537) as despot of Florence, urged him to return to finish the tombs. Michelangelo, ever a republican, refused to return to a Florence governed by a tyrant. (In his very last years he softened somewhat towards Cosimo, and may even have planned a visit; if so, he failed to carry it out.) The figures were assembled on the lids of the sarcophagi according to what were presumed to be Michelangelo's plans, and the chapel was opened to the public in 1545. Many admirers wrote epigrams in praise of the noble tombs and their noble significance. Among these was an epigram on *Night*, to the effect that the figure was carved by an "angel" (*angelo*) and that though she seemed to be dead she was alive, "Waken her and talk to her, if you do not believe it." The quatrain Michelangelo wrote in reply reflects his bitterness at the success of the tyrants in Florence, or the parlous state of Italy in general: the statue says she is glad to be asleep, and gladder still to be of stone; as long as shame and ruin endure it is an advantage neither to see nor to feel; "So do not wake me; speak low." About the time that the chapel was opened to the public a statue of the Madonna nursing the Child was added to it. The group by Michelangelo is flanked by statues of SS. Cosmas and Damian, carved by other hands. The Madonna serves as the focal point of the chapel.

Besides his despair over the political situation in Florence an additional reason for Michelangelo's eagerness to get to Rome was that, in 1532, he had met Tommaso de' Cavalieri, and had been captivated by the beauty, charm, and personality of the young Roman nobleman. In spite of his solitary habits and often forbidding manner, Michelangelo had a number of friends who were utterly devoted to him, who found it an honor and a pleasure to serve him, whether in business affairs, household matters, or simply in trying to please him with the few presents he was known to enjoy—trout, *trebbiano* (wine). Among these were Luigi del Riccio, the younger painters Sebastiano del Piombo, Daniele da Volterra, and many others; Vasari and Cellini idolized him. (Michelangelo was the only living artist Vasari included in his *Lives* of 1550.) He had their affectionate understanding and admiration. He gave his whole heart, however, to but two: to young Tommaso de' Cavalieri, who was with him in his last illness, and to Vittoria Colonna. His passion for Tommaso has been viewed as an instance of the ardent Platonic love he used to hear discussed and described by Ficino and others in the house of Lorenzo de' Medici. Platonic love as defined in these circles was fundamentally a love of beauty, beginning with a love of physical beauty, ascending to love of beauty of the soul and, ideally, to divine love. Vittoria was the cultivated, profoundly religious widow of the Marquess de Pescara. Michelangelo met her

Michelangelo
Female Half-length Figure
The British Museum, London
Alinari-Art Reference Bureau

in 1538 and outlived her by nearly twenty years. Their deeply satisfying friendship was strengthened by their mutual concern for reform of the Church and by the fact that she, while admiring his work, admired and valued the man even more. A number of drawings, several Crucifixes, that he made for her survive. For both his dear friends he wrote a number of lyrics. From his early days he had expressed himself in verse. He wrote sonnets as thank-you notes, as tributes to his friends, to express his loyalty, and sometimes his dismay and humiliation (as one to Julius II), to sing of his love of beauty and of God, and, increasingly, of his feeling of unworthiness as he came "So close to death, so far from God." About 250 partial or complete poems survive, most of them sonnets and madrigals. They illuminate his spiritual longings, his loves, and his self-doubt.

When Michelangelo returned to Rome following the death of Clement, he hoped to resume work on the tomb of Julius. This was not to be. Alessandro Farnese was elected as Pope Paul III. By his own account he had waited thirty years to have Michelangelo work for him, and he was not to be thwarted now. He named Michelangelo sculptor, painter, and architect to the Vatican (1535) at a salary of 1,200 scudi a year. Under the appointment Michelangelo was to paint a *Last Judgment*, for which he had earlier prepared designs, on the altar wall of the Sistine Chapel. The existing work by Perugino (who had once crossed swords with him) was destroyed to make place for it. Nothing could be more striking than the contrast between the Olympian freshness and freedom of the Sistine ceiling and the writhing terror of the *Last Judgment*. A nude God raises his arm in anathema. Above Him are the elect, below are the damned. The increasing despair of a devout spirit that had witnessed the sack of Rome and mourned the peril of the Church is immanent. Pope Paul's Master of Ceremonies, one Biagio, with self-righteous piety condemned the painting for the great number of nude bodies. In revenge Michelangelo painted him among the devils. (It is reported that when Biagio complained of this to the pope, Paul answered that if he had been in Purgatory he might have been able to help him, but since he was in Hell there was nothing he could do about it. At a later date Daniele da Volterra was engaged to paint draperies on some of the figures.) The completed work was unveiled on October 31, 1541, and shown to the public on Christmas Day. The acclaim with which it was greeted rivaled that which had been accorded the Sistine ceiling. The figures in violent action and acute foreshortenings had a devastating effect on other artists, who found it easy to imitate the violence and distortions without at all understanding or equaling the spirit that created them. Also for Paul he painted two frescoes in the Pauline Chapel in the Vatican, *The Conversion of St. Paul* (1545) and *The Martyrdom of St. Peter* (1550). In the meantime he had worked on several architectural projects for the pope, and in 1547 succeeded Antonio da Sangallo as architect of St. Peter's. He held this post, in which he served without pay for the glory of God, until his death. His efforts for St. Peter's included bringing it to a point where its essential form could not again be changed, as it had been under the architects who succeeded Bramante, the original architect. Michelangelo said, in tribute to his old enemy, that wherever his successors had departed from Bramante's plan they had been in error. His own contribution, an architectural masterpiece, was the model for the dome, which was completed largely according to his design after his death. In his last days he continued to make drawings and wrote some of his most moving sonnets. His last works of sculpture are the poignant *Deposition*, or *Pietà*, designed for his own tomb and left incomplete in 1556, now in the cathedral at Florence, and the near abstract *Rondanini Pietà*, Castello Sforzesco, Milan, on which he was working a few days before he died. A legend in his own time, his influence on painting and sculpture was inescapable. He maintained that sculpture was the greatest of the arts as it required cutting away to free the shape within. Marble was thus his preferred medium; bronze was uncongenial, as preparation of the model to be cast required adding on, building up. He contended that the closer painting came to sculpture, at least in the appearance of cutting away, the better it was, and that fresco was the only painting medium worthy of a man. He carried out his theories: in his painting there is an emphasis on strong outline and line modeling, and absence of that chiaroscuro, a buildup of light and shade, that obscures boundaries and change of tones; his forms are of notable clarity, his color cool, often near neutral. His exaltation of the human body which, he said, he loved because it was in the image of God, was indiscriminately and exaggeratedly imitated. Without the profound spirit that informed his art, his imitators produced empty distortions. Many influences were active in the formation of his art; his genius shaped them into a creative instrument such as the world has seldom seen, before or since.

Michele di Matteo (mē-kā′lā dē mät-tā′ō). Painter; he is mentioned in documents from 1416 to 1447. A painter in the international Gothic style, there is a work by him in the Accademia at Venice, a *Madonna with St. Helena and Other Saints*. The predella of this polyptych tells the story of the finding of the True Cross. In 1447 he is noted as having been frescoing parts of the Baptistery at Siena.

Michele di Ridolfo (dē rē-dôl′fō). See **Ghirlandaio, Michele di Ridolfo.**

Michele da Verona (dä vā-rō′nä). Veronese painter; b. at Verona, c1470; d. c1540. He was a pupil of Domenico Morone and was somewhat influenced by Bartolomeo Montagna, but on the whole he was rather an old-fashioned painter with few distinguishing marks. To his native Veronese tradition he added elements of Venetian painting as it came to him through Giovanni Mansueti. Among his works is a signed and dated (1501) *Crucifixion*, Brera, Milan; another, signed and dated (1505), is in the Church of S. Maria in Vanzo, Padua. There are frescoes in several churches at Verona and in neighboring places; *Coriolanus Persuaded by his Family to Spare Rome*, is in the National Gallery, London, and *Madonna and Child with the Infant St. John the Baptist*, is in the Metropolitan Museum, New York.

Michelino da Besozzo (mē-kā-lē′nō dä bā-zôt′tsō). Lombard painter, master glazier, and miniaturist; b. at Besozzo (Varese); active from 1388, when he was painting frescoes, now lost, at Pavia; d. after 1450. He worked at Pavia and Milan. For the cathedral at Milan, where his son Leonardo worked with him, he designed glass for the windows and painted frescoes and banners. His *Mystic Marriage of St. Catherine*, signed, is in the Pinacoteca at Siena; *The Marriage of the Virgin* is at New York. Michelino was influenced by the international Gothic style. In his own day he won great praise for his skill in drawing animals.

Michelozzo Michelozzi (mē-ke-lôt′tsō mē-ke-lôt′tsē), **Bartolommeo di Gherardo di.** Sculptor, engraver of gems, and architect; b. at Florence, 1396; d. there, 1472. As a youth he worked cutting dies for the Florentine mint. Later, as sculptor, he worked with the outstanding men of his age: with Lorenzo Ghiberti on his *St. Matthew* for Orsanmichele (1420–1422) and on the second doors of the Baptistery (1420–1424); and with Donatello, on the tabernacle of *St. Louis* for Orsanmichele (1420–1425), on the pulpit for the cathedral at Prato (1425–1438) on the baptismal font at Siena (1425), the funeral monument of John XXIII (c1427), Baptistery, Florence, the Brancacci monument (c1426–1428), Church of S. Angelo Nilo, Naples, and on the Aragazzi monument (c1437), formerly in the cathedral at Montepulciano and now dismembered (two angels from it are in the Victoria and Albert Museum; other parts of it are still in the cathe-

MICHELINO DA BESOZZO
Nativity
Biblioteca Ambrosiana, Milan

dral). The degree to which Michelozzo originated any of these works is not clear. His art reflects the classicism of Donatello but with an individual restraint in works, such as the Aragazzi monument, where he had a larger share of the responsibility. To the order and measure of his classicism he added elements of Donatello's realism, as in his figures of the *Baptist* in S. Romolo di Bivigliano and in SS. Annunziata at Florence, and in several reliefs of the *Madonna,* as those in SS. Annunziata and the Bargello.

Lasting evidence of Michelozzo's art lies in his architecture. In 1433 he followed his patron, Cosimo de' Medici, into exile at Venice. There he made models and drawings of the outstanding buildings, and, at Cosimo's request, constructed a library in the monastery of St. George that Cosimo endowed with many valuable manuscripts (the library was destroyed in 1614). Following his return to Florence (1434), in his architectural work he closely followed Brunelleschi. In the reconstruction of the church and convent of S. Marco, which he undertook for Cosimo (1437–1451) he turned to the rhythmic solemnity and preoccupation with light that characterized his work as an architect. The characteristics appear in the broad round arches with slender columns (adapted from Brunelleschi's loggia on the Foundling Hospital) in the cloister of the convent, and in the alteration of light and shade in the library. The elements of Brunelleschi as adopted by Michelozzo had more grace, less majesty, and since they were adaptations, less originality and less skill in solving architectural problems. Writers since the time of Vasari have criticized the cloister of S. Marco on the grounds that what worked out splendidly as a straight façade on the Foundling Hospital was less successful when Michelozzo bent the straight façade into a rectangle. His failure to increase the size of the columns at the corners produced a weakness there, and he should have avoided bunching the windows at these angles, according to the critics. Nevertheless, it is a lovely cloister. The story is that Cosimo de' Medici asked Brunelleschi to design a palace for him at Florence. Brunelleschi made a model and showed it to Cosimo, who told him it was too grand, that it would arouse the envy of his fellow citizens, and that "Envy is a plant that should not be watered." Cosimo then asked Michelozzo to undertake the design. The result is the famous Medici-Riccardi palace that still stands on the Via Cavour at Florence (built in 1444, it was used by the Medici family until 1540; thereafter it was owned by the Riccardi family, who enlarged it and gave it the present name). In his design for the palace, Michelozzo adopted many elements of Brunelleschi, but he, so to speak, domesticated Brunelleschi's grandeur and his palace design had a durable influence on palace construction at Florence. Symmetry and proportion, simplicity and a certain classical grace, are features of his palace style. Other architectural works of Michelozzo are the Chapel of the Novitiate, S. Croce, Florence (c1445), the Medici *castello* at Caffagiuolo (1451) and the villa at Careggi (1459), and the courtyard of the Palazzo Vecchio (1454) at Florence. Among the gems of Renaissance architecture is the elegant and simple Portinari Chapel, in the Church of S. Eustorgio at Milan. For this Michelozzo designed what amounts to a separate building with a dome and four towers. Inside, the round arches and vault and the decorative architectural elements (and beautiful Foppa frescoes) preserve an atmosphere of classic simplicity and elegance.

Migliorati (mē-lyō-rä'tē), **Cosimo dei.** Original name of Pope **Innocent VII.**

Milano (mē-lä'nō), **Giovanni da.** See **Giovanni da Milano.**

Milič (mē'lich), **Jan.** Bohemian preacher; b. at Kroměříž (Kremsier), in Moravia; d. at Avignon, France, June 29, 1374. He was one of the precursors of the Reformation. He preached not only in Latin, but also in Czech and German, being one of the first to preach in the common tongue.

Miller's Tale, The. One of Chaucer's *Canterbury Tales*. It is a tale of cuckoldry and of deception that finally becomes entangled in its own toils. Nicholas, the Oxford undergraduate, deceives the carpenter and takes his wife, but is in his turn tricked by a parish clerk. Its source is unknown, but the elements of the story were probably in circulation in a number of naughty tales of the time.

Minelli (mē-nel'lē), **Giovanni.** See **De Bardi, Giovanni di Antonio Minelli.**

Mino da Fiesole (mē'nō dä fye'zō-lā). [Also, **Mino di Giovanni.**] Sculptor; b. at Poppi (Casentino), 1429; d. at Florence, 1484. Little is known of his early life and training, but he was influenced above all by Desiderio da Settignano and by Antonio Rossellino. Vasari wrote that he worked with Desiderio and that he followed his master so religiously that he ignored nature, to the loss of his art. Among his earliest surviving works is a bust of Piero de' Medici (1453), Bargello, which is also one of the earliest examples of Renaissance marble portrait busts. It is notable, as were other portrait busts by Mino da Fiesole, for characterization and refined technique. Other portrait busts included those of Niccolò Strozzi (1454), Berlin; Astorgio II Manfredi (1455), National Gallery, Washington; and several others up to that of Diotisalvi Neroni (1464), Louvre, Paris. In 1463 he went to Rome, where he had worked briefly in 1454, to work with other sculptors on a Benediction pulpit for Pope Pius II, but returned to Florence without completing the pulpit. After leaving Rome he worked in the cathedral at Fiesole, where he executed the monument of Bishop Salutati. The realistic portrait bust for the tomb is among his best works, notable as well for the delicate carving of the miter and robe and for the subtle characterization of the bishop. Of this period also are the tomb of Bernardo Giugni (c1468) and the altar of Diotisalvi Neroni (1470), both in the Badia, Florence, both pleasing in their serenity, strongly reminiscent of Desiderio and Antonio Rossellino, and correspondingly lacking in profound personal significance. He began the monument of Count Hugo of Tuscany in the Badia, and worked in the cathedrals at Volterra and Prato. Between 1474 and 1480 he was at Rome again and with other sculptors worked on a number of important sepulchral monuments, as the Forteguerri monument, S. Cecilia in Trastevere (c1473); Riario, SS. Apostoli (c1474); Della Rovere, S. Maria del Popolo (c1479); and that of Francesco Tornabuoni, S. Maria sopra Minerva (c1480). While at Rome he also worked with Giovanni Dalmata (1474–1477) on the tomb of Paul II, fragments of which are now in the crypt of St. Peter's (Giovanni Dalmata is thought to have been the creative spirit of the work); and carved reliefs for a pulpit and altar (now dismembered) for Cardinal d'Estouteville (1475). On his return to Florence he executed a tabernacle for S. Ambrogio (1481) and in the same year finished the monument of Count Hugo in the Badia, which is among his best works. Throughout his career he followed the serene, highly finished manner of Desiderio. His style hardly evolved at all; he remained traditional, pleasing, highly accomplished technically, and somewhat superficial.

Mino del Pelliciaio (del pel-lē-chī′yō). See **Pellicciaio, Giocomo di Mino del.**

Minot (mī′nọt), **Laurence.** English soldier and war poet; b. c1300; d. c1352. He was the author of eleven poems in the Northumbrian dialect, featuring the use of alliteration. These battle songs deal with the period 1333–1352. He was intensely patriotic and loyal to Edward III, whose victories inspired him. Minot's poetry was discovered by Thomas Tyrwhitt, and first published (1795) by Joseph Ritson as *Poems on Interesting Events in the Reign of King Edward III.*

Minturno (mēn-tör′nō), **Antonio.** Humanist; d. at Crotone, 1574. He studied philosophy, and went to Rome (1521), where he pursued his interest in humanistic and vernacular poetry. Later he became involved in the movement for Catholic reform and took part in the opening of the first Jesuit college at Naples. He was made bishop of Uggento (1559), and was a participant in the third group of sessions of the Council of Trent (1562–1563). He wrote verse and prose in Latin and in the vernacular. Many of his letters in the vernacular appeared in collections of his time. Among his Latin works are his *Epistola ad Paulum Iovium,* and a treatise, *De officiis Ecclesiae praestandis* (Venice, 1564). His *De Poëta* (1559) allows great liberty to the poet in his expression of ideas, whereas his *L'Arte Poetica,* published after the Council, emphasizes that the precepts of Aristotle should be interpreted in accordance with the spirit of the Church.

Minuziano (mē-nöt-tsyä′nō), **Alessandro.** Editor and printer; b. at S. Severo (Puglia), 1450; d. at Milan, 1522. He was connected with the first edition of the collected works of Cicero, printed in 1498 and 1499. He prepared for publication many other works, including the statutes of Milan, works of Latin authors, and Corio's *Storia di Milano.* Minuziano was involved in what was perhaps the oldest known case of literary piracy, when he published an edition of Tacitus using the first five books as they had been previously published in an edition by Filippo Beroaldo. He was adjudged guilty but was absolved by the pope.

Miranda (mē-run′dạ), **Francisco de Sá de.** See **Sá de Miranda, Francisco de.**

Mirandola (mē-rän′dō-lä), Count of. See **Pico della Mirandola, Giovanni.**

Miretto (mē-ret′tō), **Giovanni.** Painter of the first half of the 15th century. With assistants, he painted the frescoes in the Palazzo della Ragione at Padua. The Palazzo had originally been frescoed by Giotto or his followers. The early work was destroyed by a fire in 1420. Miretto and his assistants began (c1430) to replace them. The frescoes executed at that time consist of twelve groups of twenty-four frescoes each, the twelve groups forming an illustrated calendar, one for each month of the year. These groups form an upper register. The frescoes of the lower register are in a very dilapidated state. The frescoes in the upper register are being restored.

Mirtillo (mēr-tēl′lō). In Battista Guarini's *Pastor fido,* "the faithful shepherd" who loves Amarilli.

Missaglia (mēs-sä′lyä). Noted Milanese family of armorers, known throughout Europe for their beautiful arms, and active in the 15th and 16th centuries. At the request of Francesco Sforza, duke of Milan, they made armor for King Louis XI of France. Other notable clients were Cardinal Ascanio Sforza (whose armor is now at Turin), and Alfonso I, duke of Ferrara.

Mocenigo (mō-chā-nē′gō). An ancient noble family of Venice, settled there about the year

1000. The family divided into a number of flourishing branches, produced eminent soldiers, diplomats, ecclesiastics, and men of letters, and contributed seven doges to the republic. For the 15th-century doges, Tommaso, Pietro, and Giovanni, see below. The last four doges were all named Alvise, and served between 1570 and 1778. Members of the Mocenigo family had four palaces on the Grand Canal at Venice, still known by their name.

Mocenigo, Andrea. Venetian statesman and humanist; b. at Venice, 1473; d. there, 1542. He was a member of the Great Council at the age of 18, later became a senator, and served the state on many occasions as counsel for the republic. He studied philosophy under Pompanazzi, and earned his laureate at Padua in 1503. His *Pentateuco*, dedicated to Pope Julius II, is a treatise on theology. His *Belli memorabilis Cameracensis adversus Venetos historiae*, is a history of the wars of the League of Cambrai against Venice. First published at Venice, 1525, it was translated into Italian in 1544. The work was dedicated to Andrea Gritti, doge of Venice and valiant defender of the republic, and to the Venetian Senate.

Mocenigo, Giovanni. Venetian doge; b. at Venice, 1408; d. there, November 14, 1485. He held many offices of public trust at Venice, and became doge in 1478. His term of power was darkened by wars. In a war with the Turks, Venice was compelled to cede Scutari (1482). Almost immediately thereafter, the republic was embroiled in a war with the duke of Ferrara and his powerful allies—the king of Naples, Florence, Milan, the duke of Mantua, and others. By the treaty of Bagnolo, 1484, which ended the war, Venice kept possession of Rovigo and the mouth of the Po.

Mocenigo, Pietro. Venetian doge; b. at Venice, 1406; d. there, 1476. He was the brother of Giovanni Mocenigo (1408–1485). He became a member of the Great Council at the age of 18, won glory as a military leader, and held many posts of importance in the republic. His wars against the Turks, waged over the course of years with varying success but with renown for him, caused him to be named doge, 1474. His own experience with the Turks convinced him that the course of wisdom was to seek peace with them.

Mocenigo, Tommaso. Venetian doge; b. at Venice, 1343; d. there, April 4, 1423. Active as a commander, in 1396 he rescued the remains of the Christian army after the defeat by the Turks at Nicopoli. He served as Venetian ambassador to various courts, and was elected doge (1414). His policy was to maintain peace and to develop and expand the prosperity and greatness of Venice. He was on good terms with Sigismund of Hungary and with the Visconti of Milan, and rather than offend the Malatesta of Rimini he refused the surrender of one of their cities. However, when Sigismund declined to take part in agreements with the Turks to end the wars, Mocenigo proposed an alliance of the Italian powers against him, and took up arms. But the basis of his policy was peace and the greatness of Venice. He gave of his own money for the reconstructions of the Ducal Palace and its ornamentation. As he was dying he called several members of the Venetian Senate to his bedside and recited to them the assets of the republic he was leaving in their hands.

Modesti (mō-des′tē), **Publio Francesco.** Poet; b. at Saludecio (Forlì), August 17, 1471; d. there, March 17, 1557. He was a passionate student of Latin literature, and especially of Vergil. His *Veneziade*, on the wars between Austria and Venice (1505–1508) is modeled on Vergil. It contains series of praises for princes, and various imaginary episodes as well as historical data on the wars. Modesti had wandered about Italy in search of a patron, without success. He dedicated his *Veneziade* to the doge Leonardo Loredan in the hope of some reward, but none was forthcoming. In the same volume with the *Veneziade* (published by the aid of his brother in 1521) was a collection of verses, *Selve*, dedicated to Claudia, Queen of France. His *Christiana pietas* (1552) is a collection of religious meditations and epigrams, and was to honor Pope Julius III.

Mohammed I (mọ̄-ham′ẹd) (of *Turkey*). Sultan of the Turks (1413–1421); b. c1387; d. 1421. He was a son of Bajazet I and overcame his brothers to win control. He reunited the empire that had fallen apart as a result of Tamerlane's conquests, and is credited with establishing the Ottoman navy. He was succeeded by his son Murad II.

Mohammed II (mọ̄-ham′ẹd) or **Mahomet** (mạ-hom′ẹt) (of *Turkey*). [Called **Mohammed the Conqueror, Mohammed the Great.**]

Sultan of Turkey (1451–1481); b. c1430; d. 1481. He was the son of Murad II whom he succeeded. In 1444, his father, tired of the continued warfare with the Europeans, abdicated in his favor but soon was forced to resume the throne because of the inroads of the Hungarians. Murad died in 1451 and Mohammed finally became sultan. He prepared a tremendous assault on Constantinople, and on May 29, 1453, after a 53-day siege, carried the city. Constantine XI, the last Byzantine emperor, died in its defense. Constantinople now became the capital of the Ottoman empire and was transformed into a Moslem city. The Cathedral of Hagia Sophia became a mosque and the Levantine inhabitants of the city were given special privileges. Mohammed proceeded with his conquests: he subdued the Morea, Serbia, Bosnia, and Albania, and made (1475) the Crimea a dependency. He was defeated by John Hunyadi and S. Giovanni Capistrano at Belgrade (1456), but won Scutari and other places and a large indemnity from Venice in 1478 after a war of fifteen years. He conquered Trebizond and Karamania in Asia Minor and captured and devastated (1480) Otranto in Italy and threw such terror into the Italians that they ceased, briefly, their murderous internecine wars and made an attempt to unite to repel the Turkish peril. (Otranto was retaken the following year by Alfonso, duke of Calabria, later Alfonso II of Naples, but the city never recovered from the Turkish sack.) Mohammed was a noted patron of the arts. Gentile Bellini went to Constantinople in 1479 to work for him and remained about two years. A portrait of Mohammed in the National Gallery, London, is ascribed to Bellini. Mohammed was also a patron of education, and is credited as well with founding the ulema, the ecclesiastical court of Islam. He is regarded as the real founder of the Ottoman power.

Molay or **Molai** (mo-lā), **Jacques de.** Last grand master of the Templars; b. in Burgundy, France, c1243; burned at Paris, March 18, 1314. In 1306 De Molay was called to France, ostensibly to discuss plans for a new crusade, but on October 13, 1307, all the Templars in France were arrested. De Molay was tortured and admitted certain errors; when he was brought up for sentencing (1314), he recanted his confession and was burned at the stake.

Molyneux (mol′i-nöks, -nūks, -nū) or **Moleyns** or **Molins** (mō′linz), **Adam de.** English bishop and politician; d. at Portsmouth, England, January 9, 1450. Blamed by popular opinion for the surrender of Maine, in France, he was attacked by rioting sailors at Portsmouth and killed.

Molza (mōl′tsä), **Francesco Maria.** Poet and humanist; b. at Modena, June 18, 1489; d. there, February 28, 1544. His parents were wealthy and of noble blood, and gave him a fine education. He studied at Bologna and in 1506, at the age of 16, went to Rome to study Hebrew. He soon came into contact with the leading literary men of the day and won their hearts with his charm, his gentleness, and his wit. Like so many others, he was enchanted by the brooding and beautiful melancholy of the ruins of Rome, and fascinated by the dissolute life that went on in the city. He forgot all about the wife he had married in the course of one of his return visits to Modena, and the children she had borne him, and remained at Rome, except for brief intervals, until 1543. He led a wild and dissolute life. Even the sack of Rome, which he witnessed in 1527, though it saddened him briefly did not cause him to mend his ways. His life was in strange contrast to the sentiments and grace of his poems. He had many loves among the Roman courtesans. For one of them, Faustina Mancina, he wrote his *Ninfa Tiberina,* a pastoral in which he, as a faithful shepherd, sings of his love. (Faustina was famed for her beauty as well as her breeding. When she died the whole city went into mourning. Michelangelo, among others, wrote a sonnet lamenting her death.) Of his lyrics, in Latin and Italian, the Latin love lyrics, infused with sincere feeling, are considered superior to his Italian poems in the Petrarchan manner. His poetry in general is characterized by a deep appreciation for the beauty of the world and by the moral malaise that made it impossible for him to become involved with the ugliness that also existed. His *Ad Sodales,* written when he knew he was dying, is an elegy in which he feelingly invokes the traditional comforts for those departing. Ill with syphilis, and partially paralyzed, he returned to Modena in 1543 and died the following year.

Molza, Tarquinia. Poetess; b. at Modena, November 1, 1542; d. there, August 8, 1617. She was the granddaughter of Francesco

Maria Molza (1489–1544), was learned in the classics, and translated two of Plato's dialogues. Her husband died (1578) and she went to Ferrara. There she was a friend of Torquato Tasso, who addressed several sonnets to her, and who wrote a dialogue on love entitled *La Molza*. She was a member of the court of Ferrara from 1583 to 1595, and was maid of honor to Lucrezia and Leonora d'Este, sisters of Duke Alfonso II. She wrote lyrics in Latin and in Italian. Her fame as a lady, as a poet, and as a learned woman was such that the Senate and people of Rome conferred citizenship upon her.

Mombello (môm-bel′lō), **Luca.** Painter; b. at Orzibecchi (Brescia), 1518; d. c1578. He was a pupil and assistant of Moretto da Brescia. Of indifferent gifts, a number of his paintings are in the churches and art gallery of Brescia; a *Noli me tangere* is in the Carrara Academy at Bergamo.

Mombrizio (môm-brēt′tsyō), **Bonino.** Humanist; b. 1424; d. between 1482 and 1502. He studied at Ferrara and taught at Milan, where he was equally esteemed for his learning and his pure and kindly way of life. He edited a number of ancient writings and is particularly and deservedly remembered for his hagiographic collection, *Sanctuarium*.

Monk's Tale, The. One of Chaucer's *Canterbury Tales*. Dealing with falls of the mighty, it is unfinished, being stopped by the knight. It contains the story of Ugolino, imprisoned and starved to death with his children and grandchildren because of treachery to his native Pisa, taken from Dante (*Inferno*, xxxiii), and follows Boccaccio's *De casibus illustrium virorum* in a general way.

Monstrelet (môṅs-trẹ-le), **Enguerrand de.** French chronicler; d. 1453. He was the author of a chronicle of contemporary French history covering the period 1400–1444.

Montacute (mon′tạ-kūt) or **Montagu** (mon′tạ-gū), **John de.** [Title, 3rd Earl of **Salisbury.**] English soldier; b. c1350; beheaded at Cirencester, England, January 7, 1400. A prominent Lollard, he attended their meetings and kept a Lollard chaplain. He opposed Henry IV, and after his accession to the throne plotted against him, was discovered, and was murdered by a mob.

Montacute or **Montagu, Thomas de.** [Title, 4th Earl of **Salisbury.**] English general; b. 1388; d. at Meung, France, November 3, 1428. He was the father of Alice Neville, mother of Richard Neville, earl of Warwick, known as the "Kingmaker." He was at Harfleur and Agincourt (1415), and continued to fight in France as the most famous and skillful English general until the siege of Orléans (1428) where he received a fatal wound.

Montacute or **Montagu, William de.** [Titles, 3rd Baron **Montacute**, 1st Earl of **Salisbury.**] English soldier; b. 1301; d. January 30, 1344. In 1327 he fought with Edward III in Scotland. During the Parliament of Nottingham (1330) he arrested Roger de Mortimer in the queen mother's apartments. He was appointed marshal of England in 1338.

Montacute or **Montagu, William de.** [Title, 2nd Earl of **Salisbury.**] English soldier; b. June 25, 1328; d. June 3, 1397. He was one of the original knights of the Order of the Garter (1350). He was appointed constable of the king's army in France, served under John of Gaunt in the north of France, and assisted at the coronation of Richard II (1377).

Montagna (mōn-tä′nyä), **Bartolommeo.** Painter; b. at Orzinovi (Brescia), c1450; d. at Vicenza, October 11, 1523. He was probably trained at Venice, where in 1486 he painted canvases (now lost) for the School of St. Mark, but he spent most of his life in and around Vicenza, where he lived almost continually after 1480, and where he was the founder of a school of Vicentine painting. His style was at first influenced by the Paduan school as appears in the plasticity of his figures and the breaking folds of his drapery. At Venice he came into contact with the style of Alvise Vivarini, but was most influenced by Antonello da Messina in the handling of light and relief, and by Giovanni Bellini in composition and arrangement of figures against a background. In drawing on these influences, however, he did not lose his own powerful painting personality; he continued to paint solemn monumental figures. Immune to the chromatic scales, with their warmth and delicacy, of Bellini and Giorgione, he used bright, clear, simple colors that add an elemental strength to his compositions. It was only as he grew older that he softened his forms in softer colors. Among his works is *The Virgin and Child Enthroned and Saints* (1498), painted for the Church of S. Michele at Vicenza and now in the Brera, Milan. It is

BARTOLOMMEO MONTAGNA
Risen Christ
Louvre, Paris   Alinari-Art Reference Bureau

one of his masterpieces. Of 1500 is the *Pietà* in the Sanctuary of Monte Berico, near Vicenza. Between 1504 and 1506 he was at Verona, where he frescoed the Chapel of S. Biagio in the Church of SS. Nazaro e Celso, and painted a polyptych, only partially preserved, and a panel, *Madonna and Child,* in S. Sebastiano that is now in the Accademia at Venice. In 1511 he was working at Padua, painting frescoes in the School of St. Anthony. Of 1520 is an altarpiece in the Pinacoteca, Vicenza, and of 1522 the *Adoration of the Shepherds* in the cathedral of Cologna Veneta, near Verona. Other works include the grandiose altarpiece, a youthful masterpiece, *Madonna with the Baptist, St. Bartholomew, and Other Saints,* with the life of St. Bartholomew in the predella. It was painted for the Church of S. Bartolomeo and is now in the Pinacoteca at Vicenza, and was inspired by a painting by Giovanni Bellini. Many works by Montagna are in the Pinacoteca at Vicenza. A beautiful late work, *St. Mary Magdalen and Saints,* with three scenes from the Magdalen's life in the predella, is in the Church of S. Corona. In addition, there are frescoes in the monastery of Praglia, altarpieces at Pavia, in S. Giovanni Ilarione (near Vicenza), Cartigliano (near Vicenza), Orgiano (near Vicenza), in the Brera and Poldi Pezzoli Museums, Milan, in the Vatican and Borghese Gallery, Rome, at Venice, Belluno, Bergamo, Berlin, Paris, and Turin, at Baltimore, Columbus (Ohio), the Metropolitan Museum, New York, the Johnson Collection, Philadelphia, San Francisco, at Springfield (Massachusetts), the National Gallery, Washington, and at Williamstown and Worcester (Massachusetts).

Montagna, Benedetto. Venetian painter; b. c1481; d. before 1558. He was the son of Bartolommeo Montagna, and was a pupil and weak follower of his father. Examples of his painting are at Lonigo, in the Brera, Milan, at Padua, Vicenza, and in the Johnson Collection, Philadelphia. He was better known as an engraver than as a painter. In the former art he was notable for grace of composition and expressive treatment, as well in sacred themes as in secular. Some of his woodcuts were to designs by his father. Of all his signed woodcuts, the only dated one (1503) is a copy of a Dürer.

Montagnana (mōn-tä-nyä′nä), **Jacopo Parisatti da.** See **Iacopo da Montagnana.**

Montagu (mon′tạ-gū). See **Montacute.**

Montaigne (mon-tān′; French, môṅ-teny′), **Michel Eyquem de.** French essayist and philosopher; b. at the Château Montaigne, Dordogne, France, February 28, 1533; d. there, September 13, 1592. His early education was carried on at home under his father's guidance. After graduating from college at Bordeaux, he studied law. In 1559 he was at the court of Francis II, and in 1571 became attached to the person of Henry III. In this year Montaigne published his friend Étienne La Boétie's translations from the Greek, and in 1572 edited the latter's French verses. In 1580 he traveled in Germany, Switzerland, and Italy. He left Rome in 1581 to become mayor of Bordeaux. Montaigne is chiefly known for his *Essais* (Bordeaux, 1580; the edition of 1588 was the last to be published during the author's lifetime). Mademoiselle de Gournay, a warm admirer of Montaigne who prepared the edition of 1595, did not have access to the copy of his last edition which Montaigne himself had corrected. The famous English translation of 1603, by John Florio, was made from Mademoiselle de Gournay's text. There are many complete modern translations. In his essays, usually considered the best personal essays ever written, Montaigne studies himself as well as the men of the society of his day. He examines everything in a skeptical spirit, is inclined to doubt, and his motto is *Que sais-je?* (What do I know?). Montaigne's ideas and influence are to be traced in many of the best French authors of the 17th and 18th centuries, while outside of France his essays were diligently read by Francis Bacon, Shakespeare, and many succeeding writers.

Montani (mōn-tä′nē), **Cola de'.** [Real name, **Nicola Capponi.**] Humanist teacher who inspired Lampugnani, Olgiati, and Visconti with an ideal of the Roman republic, and with the idea that it was a patriotic duty to get rid of tyrants. His views were suspect and he was banished from Milan. Not long afterward, his pupils assassinated Galeazzo Maria Sforza in the Church of S. Stefano, 1476. He was hanged in 1481.

Montano (mōn-tä′nō), **Giovanni Battista de.** See **Monte, Giovanni Battista de.**

Monte (môn′tā), **Giovanni Battista de.** [Called **Montano.**] Physician, man of letters, and numismatist; b. at Verona, 1498; d. at Padua, 1551. He took his doctorate in medicine at Padua, practiced for a short time at Brescia, then traveled and studied. At Naples he studied Greek under Marcus Musurus. Monte was acclaimed for his revisions and collations of ancient texts. He translated some of the works of Hippocrates and Galen, and wrote commentaries on Rhazes (Arabian physician, c850–c925) and Avicenna (Arabian philosopher and physician, 980–1037). In his day he was famous as a physician, and is known as an early advocate of preventive medicine and for his introduction of clinical teaching at Padua. He left many works on medical subjects, many of which were edited, not always carefully, and published by his students.

Montefeltro (mōn-tā-fel′trō). Ancient family of Montefeltro in the Romagna, members of which were raised to the rank of count by the emperor Frederick Barbarossa (c1160). In the 13th century they were invested as counts of Urbino (1216), and in the 14th century were invited by the people of Cagli (1371) and of Gubbio (1384) to become lords of those cities. The popes recognized them as vassals of the Church in these states. Count Guido da Montefeltro, whose name is recorded in 1268, was a Ghibelline. He subjugated parts of the Romagna (1281), besieged and took Forlì (1282), and was twice excommunicated and twice absolved by the pope. The second time he was forgiven (1295), he decided to withdraw from the world. He entered the Franciscan order and retired to the monastery at Assisi. Pope Boniface VIII, struggling against the Colonna family, bethought him of the old warrior, sought him out at Assisi (1296), and asked his advice on how to deal with the Colonnesi. Count Guido (d. 1298) was reluctant to enter into worldly matters again but the pope assured him of absolution, and in return received some very practical advice. Dante, who tells his story (*Inferno*, xxvii) says he burns in hell for giving fraudulent advice. In the next century the Montefeltri were Ghibellines, held important offices in such cities as Pisa and Siena, and often fought against the Church. By 1376, when Antonio was recalled by the citizens as count of Montefeltro and Urbino, Ghibellinism had died a natural death. Henceforth the Montefeltri were loyal sons of the Church. Antonio, a brave captain who recruited the sturdy men of his state for service abroad, sought peace at home and the expansion of his state. He fought for Florence, Siena, and Milan. Pope Boniface IX (1389–1404) invested him with the lands he acquired, and when he died (April, 1404), his enlarged state devolved to his son Guidantonio. The latter acquired Assisi (1408) and was invested with it by Pope Gregory XII. Guidantonio was favored by Martin V, whose niece Caterina he took as his second wife (1424). When she died (1438), he gave himself up to pious works and the building of the cathedral and the Church of S. Donato (both begun in 1439) at Urbino to assuage his grief. Mild, just, and pious, he attempted to strengthen his state by alliance with other ruling families (marriage alliances as a means of reinforcing a state were never very reliable). His daughter Bianca (b. 1422) married a Manfredi of Faenza and Imola; Violante (b. 1430) married Domenico Malatesta, lord of Cesena; Agnesina (b. 1431) married Alessandro Gonzaga of Mantua; and Brigida Sueva (b. 1428) married (1448) Alessandro Sforza, lord of Pesaro, but left him in 1457 to enter a convent. His son Oddantonio was born either in 1424 or 1426. When Guidantonio died (February 20, 1442), mourned by his well-governed citizens, Oddantonio succeeded him. He had been a good student and of seemingly amenable disposition. He began his rule temperately, but in less than a year had become wild, dissolute, and cruel. Pius II wrote that "Because of his licentious life and his wholesale prostitution of the wives and daughters of the citizens of Urbino Oddantonio was murdered by his citizens together with Manfredo of Carpi, the apostolic notary, who had been his companion in debauchery and counsellor in crime." The citizens, having murdered Oddantonio in his own hall, called on his half brother Federico, a natural son of Guidantonio, to become their new ruler. (Some writers of the period, including Pius II, hint that the murder of Oddantonio was a plot, to which Federico was privy, and that he was standing in the wings waiting for a call that he promptly answered. Others do not question that it was Oddantonio's cruelty and inability to leave other men's wives and daughters alone that led to his murder.) Federico (see **Federico da Montefeltro**), in whose reign Urbino was raised to a duchy, added greatly to his state and left it three times as large as he found it. He was succeeded (1482) by his son Guidobaldo (see **Guidobaldo da Montefeltro**), under whom the duchy included 7 episcopal cities, 300 to 400 castles, and a number of fortified villages. Guidobaldo (d. 1508), being childless, adopted his nephew, Francesco Maria della Rovere (see **Francesco Maria della Rovere**), and was succeeded by him. Through Francesco Maria the della Rovere dynasty was established in the duchy of Urbino.

Montefeltro, Federico da. See **Federico da Montefeltro.**

Montefeltro, Guidobaldo da. See **Guidobaldo da Montefeltro.**

Montelupo (mōn-tā-lö′pō), **Raffaello da.** See **Raffaello da Montelupo.**

Montemayor (mōn-tā-mä-yor′), **Jorge de.** Spanish romancer and poet; b. at Montemayor, Portugal, c1520; d. at Turin, Italy, February 26, 1561. He was the author of the pastoral romance *Diana Enamorada*, which some sources have suggested may have been used in translation by Shakespeare in the preparation of *Two Gentlemen of Verona*.

Montesecco (mōn-tā-sek′kō), **Gian Batista da.** Mercenary captain who was hired by the conspirators of the Pazzi conspiracy to kill Lorenzo and Giuliano de' Medici. He arranged the details of the plot but withdrew at almost the last minute when he learned the assassination was to take place in the cathedral. The original scheme was to kill the brothers at a banquet, which he was willing to do, but he drew the line at murder in church. Giuliano was killed but Lorenzo escaped as the plot was carried into execution on Sunday, April 26, 1478. Montesecco was captured, arrested, tried, and condemned. Before he was executed he wrote a confession detailing the plot and those concerned in it. His confession is an important source for information about the plot.

Montgomerie (mọnt-gum′ẹ-ri), **Hugh.** [Titles, 3rd Baron **Montgomerie**, 1st Earl of **Eglinton.**] Scottish regent; b. c1460; d. 1545. After the death of James IV at Flodden he was nominated one of the guardians of James V. In 1536 he acted as one of the regents during the king's trip to France.

Montgomerie, Hugh. [Title, 3rd Earl of **Eglinton.**] Scottish noble; b. c1531; d. June 3, 1585. He joined Mary, Queen of Scots, in France and returned (1560) with her to Scotland. He was in favor of her Roman Catholic policy, but against her marriage to Bothwell. He fought for the queen at Langside (1568), but later gave his allegiance to the regent (1571).

Montgomerie, Sir **John.** [Title, 9th Lord of **Eaglesham.**] Scottish soldier; d. c1398. He took part in the battle of Otterburn, where he took prisoner Sir Henry Percy, whom he ransomed.

Montgomery (môṅ-gom-rē), **Gabriel de Lorges,** Comte **de.** French commander of the Scots Guards; b. c1530; executed at Paris, May 25, 1574. By accident, he mortally wounded Henry II (of France) in a tournament (June 30, 1559). He became a Protestant and took part in the religious wars of the period. He directed an expedition against France, was captured, and put to death.

Montluc (môṅ-lük), **Blaise de Lasseran-Massencome,** Seigneur **de.** French marshal; b. near Condom, in Guienne, France, c1503; d. in the province of Agénois, France, 1577. He took part in all the campaigns of Francis I against the emperor Charles V, and became celebrated for his exploits in the reign of Henry II. In the later years of his life he dictated from memory his account of the wars from 1521 to 1574. His work is of great value to historians. His *Commentaires* appeared first in 1592 at Bordeaux.

Montmorency (môṅ-mo-räṅ-sē), **Anne,** Duc **de.** French soldier; b. at Chantilly, France, 1493; d. at Paris, March 15, 1567. A boyhood companion of Francis I he accompanied him in his early campaigns, and served him on diplomatic missions. In 1522 he was made marshal of France, and in 1538, constable of France. He became one of Henry II's most valiant captains, suppressing rebellions and fighting against the Spaniards. He sided with the Guises during the wars of religion.

Montmorency, Duchesse **de.** See **Diane de France.**

Montmorency, Henri I, Duc **de.** French marshal, constable of France; b. 1534; d. 1614. He was active on the Catholic side of the French religious wars, but subsequently took part in efforts to restore the country's internal peace. He gave his support to Henry of Navarre as early as 1589, and in 1593 Henry named him constable of France.

Montone (mōn-tō′nā), **Braccio de.** See **Braccio da Montone.**

Montorsoli (mōn-tôr′sō-lē), **Giovanni Angelo.** Sculptor; b. at Montorsoli, near Florence, c1500; d. at Florence, August 31, 1563.

As a very young man he worked with Michelangelo on the Medici tombs in the sacristy of S. Lorenzo at Florence, and thereafter sought, sometimes with unhappy results, to follow faithfully in Michelangelo's footsteps. After a period of wandering, he joined the order of the Servites in the Annunziata at Florence, but continued to practice his art. In 1531 he executed the beautiful statue of St. Cosmas for the new sacristy of S. Lorenzo. Commissions took him about Italy. He worked at Rome on the tomb of Julius II, at Genoa for the Doria family, at Venice, Padua, Verona, Mantua, Bologna, and Naples. Wherever he went he stimulated new interest in his art and left a deep impression. In 1547 he went to Messina, where he became superintendent of the works of the cathedral and designed much sculptural decoration for it. The fountain he designed (completed 1550) for the Piazza in front of the cathedral, the Fountain of Orion, has been called one of the most beautiful in Italy.

Morales (mō-rä′lās), **Luis de.** [Called **el Divino.**] Spanish religious painter; b. at Badajoz, Spain, c1509; d. there 1586. He worked on the decoration of the Escorial.

Morandini (mō-rän-dē′nē), **Francesco.** See **Poppi, il.**

Morando (mō-rän′dō), **Paolo.** See **Cavazzola, Paolo.**

Mordaunt (môr′dạnt), Sir **John.** English politician; d. 1504. He was chosen speaker of the House of Commons in 1487; became (1504) chancellor of the duchy of Lancaster, and served for many years as a privy councilor.

Mordaunt, John. [Title, 1st Baron **Mordaunt of Turvey.**] English courtier; b. c1490; d. 1562. He was a privy councilor and general surveyor of the king's woods. He took part in the trial of Anne Boleyn.

More (mōr), Sir **Anthony.** See **Moro, Attoni** (or **Antonis**).

More, Sir **Thomas.** [Also, Saint **Thomas More.**] English statesman, humanist, and author of *Utopia;* b. at London, February 6, 1477 or 1478; executed there, July 6, 1535. He was the son of Sir John More, a London barrister, and Agnes, daughter of Thomas Graunger. He began his studies at Saint Anthony's School on Threadneedle Street, London, under Nicholas Holt, but at about the age of 12 or 13 was placed in the household of John Morton, archbishop of Canterbury (later cardinal) and chancellor, where he continued his education until 1492, when he entered Canterbury Hall (later merged in Christ Church), Oxford. He entered New Inn, London, in 1494, and Lincoln's Inn in 1496. In 1499 he met Erasmus in England, and corresponded with him throughout the rest of his life. For four years he considered becoming a priest, during which time, although a layman, he lectured on *The City of God* at Saint Lawrence Jewry and lived, without vow, with the monks of the Charterhouse. However, finding himself without a vocation for the life of a priest, he married (c1504) Jane, daughter of John Colt, by whom he had four children. His home was "the old Barge," Bucklesbury, London. He was first elected to Parliament in 1504, where his opposition to Henry VII's extravagant demands for a dowry for his daughter Margaret, lately married to James IV of Scotland, may have necessitated a protective exile. In 1508 he visited the universities of Paris and Louvain. He greeted Henry VIII's coronation in 1509 with exuberant congratulatory Latin. He became under-sheriff of London in 1510. In 1511 his first wife died; in the same year he married Alice Middleton, a widow. In May, 1515, he was sent to Flanders to settle disputes with merchants there, and in August, 1517, to Calais on similar business. Returning in October, he was appointed one of the king's councilors and a judge of the court of requests. In June, 1520, he was with King Henry at the Field of the Cloth of Gold. In 1521 he was knighted and made under-treasurer, in April, 1523, speaker of the House of Commons, in 1524 high steward of Oxford University, and in 1525 high steward of Cambridge University and chancellor of the duchy of Lancaster. In 1524 he was buying property at Chelsea, where he moved his home from London. On October 26, 1529, he succeeded Thomas Wolsey as chancellor. Henry VIII, a monarch educated in the humanistic tradition, appreciated More's scholarship and used his talents. But More could not sympathize with or condone the king's divorce from Catherine of Aragon. Loyal to his faith and to the pope, he refused to support Henry's claim, in order to justify his divorce, to supremacy in ecclesiastical matters. He opened the Parliament of November 3, 1529, to which Henry complained of the divided allegiance of his clergy. The clergy completely surrendered to the king as "Head of the Church" on May 15, 1532, and on the next day More resigned the chancellorship. An act of Parliament in March, 1534, fixed the succession in the issue of Anne Boleyn and demanded oaths of agreement to the act. To this More was willing to swear, but the oath as presented to him contained an illegal rider, introduced by Thomas Audley and Cromwell (made legal by the Act of Supremacy at a later date) which gave the king theological power over the church. To this More refused to swear, but he made no statement against the oath or those who took it. Nevertheless, he was committed to the Tower of London on April 17, 1534, and, though guilty of no word or deed against the king, on July 1, 1535, was charged with silence and convicted of treason for what the court believed he thought. Five days later he was beheaded on Tower Hill. A man of wit and intelligence, supported by a profound religious faith, he had resisted, through the more than a year that he was in the Tower, all efforts by his family and his many friends to persuade him to change his stand and save his life. Somewhat in the manner of Socrates, he refused to deny the attitudes of a lifetime for the sake of a phrase. Secure in his faith and with high courage, he maintained his cheerful humor to the edge of the scaffold. He was beatified by Pope Leo XIII on December 29, 1886, and canonized by Pope Pius XI on May 19, 1935; his feast day is July 6. His literary reputation is based chiefly on the Latin work *Utopia* (published 1516 and first translated into English by Ralph Robinson, 1551), but his English prose style (as evidenced by his *History of Richard III*, a source of Shakespeare's play on the same king) is clear, tough, witty, cadenced, eloquent, and dramatic. Unfortunately his reputation suffers in this respect because much of his writing is concerned with religious controversy, wherein style is not usually looked for, and because many of his pieces have not been reprinted since the collected *English Works* of 1557. The most complete collection of his Latin works is the Frankfort-Leipzig edition of 1689. More's chief writings were: (in Latin) a translation of four dialogues of Lucian, a commentary on the Psalms, a refutation of Luther's charges against Henry VIII, written under the pseudonym of William Ross, 255 epigrams, and *Utopia*; (in both English and Latin) the *History of Richard III* and *Treatise on the Passion*; (in English) some schoolboy poetry, a *Life of John Pico* (Pico della Mirandola) a commentary on *The Four Last Things*, several theological debates, a *Dialogue of Comfort against Tribulation*, and an autobiographical defense of himself, *The Apology of Sir Thomas More* (1533). Besides these, More was in communication with all the important humanists of his day. Of his letters, 218 survive. A portrait by Hans Holbein, in the Frick Collection, New York, is a striking revelation of the qualities of this intelligent, sensitive, and intense personality.

Moretti (mō-ret′tē), **Cristoforo.** Painter of Cremona; documented between 1471 and 1485. Parts of a polyptych, *Madonna and Child with SS. Genesius and Lawrence*, are in the Poldi Pezzoli Museum, Milan.

Moretto da Brescia (mō-ret′tō dä brā′shä). [Original name, **Alessandro Bonvicino.**] Painter; b. at Brescia, c1498; d. there, 1554. His master, Floriano Ferramola, was a follower and imitator of Foppa, and trained Moretto in that tradition. With him, Moretto painted (1516) the inside of the organ shutters for the cathedral at Brescia; they are now in the Church of S. Maria, Lovere. More than from his teacher, Moretto received the tradition of the Lombard school of Foppa as it was passed on by Savoldo and Romanino, and was influenced to a degree by Titian. Of manifest sincerity and dignity, his work is notable for the beauty and nobility of his human forms, for his calm and balanced compositions, and for the gray and silvery harmonies of his palette. Beginning in 1521 he collaborated with Romanino in decorating the Chapel of the Holy Sacrament in the Church of S. Giovanni Evangelista at Brescia. The church constitutes almost a gallery of Moretto's work and covers almost the whole range of his career, beginning with a *Coronation* in the 15th-century manner and going on through his *Elijah Waked by an Angel*, with its figures in a lyrical landscape. The paintings from different periods of his career indicate increasing refinement of a style that did not evolve greatly but that remained firm and fresh to the end. His best paintings are among the most attractive of 16th-century Italy. These include *The Supper of the Pharisee*, S. Maria di Calchera, *Coronation*, SS. Nazaro e Celso, *Madonna with St. Nicholas of Bari*, Pinacoteca Martinengo, all at Brescia, and *St. Justina*, Vienna, which Bernard Berenson called "one of the heroic creations of Italy, with something almost of Antique grandeur and directness." Moretto worked principally at Brescia, with some activity at Bergamo, Milan, and elsewhere in North Italy. His paintings are in many churches of Brescia, including S. Clemente where he is buried, and in the Pinacoteca Martinengo, which has paintings from suppressed churches and orders and from private collections. Notable among the paintings in the Pinacoteca is *Christ Carrying the Cross.* His altarpieces are found in many places near Brescia, as at Maguzzano, Orzinuovi, Prealboino, Comero, Manerbio, Marmantino, Mazzano, Sarezzo, and the lovely *Apparition of the Virgin* (1533) in the Sanctuary of Paitone. One of his most beautiful paintings, *Madonna and Child Enthroned* (1540), is in S. Andrea at Bergamo. Delicate easel paintings and marvellously penetrating portraits, in the silvery tones for which he was noted, are in many public and private collections. Among his few surviving frescoes are those in the Salvadego Palace, formerly the Martinengo Palace, at Brescia, with portraits of noble ladies against a landscape dominated by the castle fortresses of the powerful Martinengo family. Other examples of his painting are at Belluno, Bologna, Genoa, Milan, Naples, Rome, Turin, Venice, Verona, Berlin, Budapest, Escorial, Frankfurt, Leningrad, London, Munich, Paris, Stockholm, Atlanta (Georgia), Bloomington (Indiana), Cambridge (Massachusetts), Chicago, Cleveland, Columbia (South Carolina), the Metropolitan Museum, New York, the Johnson Collection, Philadelphia, the National Gallery, Washington, and elsewhere.

Morgana (môr-gä′nä). In Matteo Maria Boiardo's *Orlando Innamorato* and Lodovico Ariosto's *Orlando Furioso*, a wicked enchantress who rules over a magic lake. Orlando overcomes her. She is the literary descendant of the Arthurian Morgan le Fay and the Fata Morgana of the Carolingian cycle.

Morgante maggiore (môr-gän′tā mäd-jō′rā). Epic by Luigi Pulci, written, between 1460 and 1470, in two sections, and based on the Carolingian legends. The first section consists of twenty-three cantos. To these, five cantos were later added, and the whole poem was published at Florence in 1483. Each canto begins with a mock invocation to the Madonna, a saint or some other figure, and ends with a salute to the listeners. The original listeners were the members of Lorenzo de' Medici's circle, to whom Pulci read each canto as it was completed. (See, **Pulci, Luigi.**) In 1497, copies of the *Morgante* were burned, along with other poems, books, wigs, jewelry, paintings, and so on, in the great bonfires of the "Vanities" called for in the fiery sermons of Savonarola. The tale unfolded in the epic is, briefly, as follows.

Orlando, one of Charlemagne's twelve paladins, overhears the traitor Gan depreciating his deeds and his value to the aged king. Disgusted with Gan, but more because the king listens to him, Orlando leaves Paris and goes off to fight infidels. He wanders about and arrives at a monastery on the border between the land of Christendom and that of Heathendom. As he waits at the portal a stone hurtles down and strikes his horse Rondel. After much clanking and unbolting of bars, the abbot of the monastery opens the portal and hurries Orlando inside. He explains the bolted doors and his unseemly haste by telling of three giants that live on the mountain, whose pleasant pastime it is to hurl boulders on the monastery. The monks dare not go outside. Instead of being fed, as were the ancient fathers, on manna from heaven, rocks and stones rain down on them. The next morning Orlando announces that he must go and return the gift that was made to his horse. The abbot cannot dissuade him from such a dangerous undertaking. He ascends the mountain and, on saluting the first giant he sees, is felled by a huge stone. He rises and slays the giant with his invincible sword Durindana. The second giant to appear is similarly despatched. At sight of the third giant, Morgante, Orlando prepares to slay him, but Morgante calls out in a troubled voice to ask whether Orlando is a Christian. Orlando replies that he is and Morgante informs him that he has decided to renounce the false prophet Mahomet, because of a curious dream he had, and become a Christian too. They return in a comradely spirit to the monastery, Morgante having vowed to be Orlando's friend and helper. After some days in the monastery, during which the terror of the monks at Morgante subsides, Orlando and Morgante set off for Babylon, but not before the abbot has discovered that, by a complicated genealogy, he is related to Orlando. In their travels they come to a castle. The gate is open and they enter. Inside they find a banquet laid out, ready to eat, but the castle is empty. Pleased with their good fortune, they eat and drink to satiety, then go to sleep between the silken sheets with which the beds of the castle are furnished. In the morning the doors, windows, and gates of the castle are closed tight. Orlando and Morgante cannot escape. They hear a voice and follow it to a tomb. The voice says they must let its owner out of the tomb and battle with him before they can leave. Morgante opens the tomb and a devil leaps out. After a struggle, Morgante shuts him back in the tomb. The devil warns that they cannot escape from the castle until Morgante is baptized. Orlando baptizes him, they leave, and, on hearing a frightful noise, look back and see that the entire castle and the devil have vanished. Morgante wishes all devils could be gotten rid of as easily. Morgante and Orlando continue their adventures. Morgante destroys armies of enemies by means of an old bell clapper he has picked up at the monastery. Orlando and Morgante are separated for a time. At a crossroads, Morgante meets Margutte (Pulci's addition to the Carolingian legend, and the first completely developed comic figure in Italian literature). Margutte says he is a demi-giant. He had wanted to be a giant but changed his mind and stopped growing when he was not yet twenty feet tall. Morgante asks him if he is a Christian. Margutte replies that he believes in neither black nor blue, but in a good capon, whether roasted or boiled. He further adds that most men have seven deadly sins but he enjoys seventy-seven, in addition to any number of venial sins. He is a glutton, a drunkard, liar, thief, blasphemer, and so on. On the other hand, he must admit that he is not given to treachery. Morgante is amused by him, and they set off together for Babylon. Morgante continually and delightedly cheats Margutte of his share of the food and drink. This is a form of torture to Margutte but each time he forgives Morgante. On their journey they rescue a Saracen maiden and restore her to her grateful father, engage in prodigious bouts of eating and drinking, and come unscathed through a number of bizarre encounters. On a day when Morgante is absent, Margutte falls asleep. A monkey finds his boots and starts trying them on and taking them off. Margutte wakens, regards the monkey's antics, and is so struck by the absurdity of it all that he is seized with a paroxysm of laughter and dies of it. Morgante runs up too late to save him. He rejoins Orlando and helps him to take Babylon. Together they embark on a sea voyage. On the way a great storm unsteps the masts and hurls them into the sea. Morgante spreads his arms and holds the sails. A whale attacks the vessel. Morgante leaps on its back and kills it. There is no limit to his strength and prowess. A crab bites him on the heel and he dies. Orlando has him embalmed and buries him at Bablyon. (This marks the end of the first twenty-three cantos, which were originally published as *Morgante piccolo*.)

Orlando, returned to Charlemagne's court, finds that the infidel Marsilius has proposed that the king send a mission to the Pass of Roncesvalles on the Spanish border to receive tribute. Orlando and most of the other paladins suspect a trap. Charlemagne, egged on by the traitor Gan, has agreed to send Orlando and a small band as an advance guard to the meeting. Gan has meantime arranged an ambush for Orlando, in which the forces of Marsilius will slay him and his band and get rid of him once and for all. Rinaldo, a fellow-paladin and Orlando's cousin, has gone off to Egypt. Orlando and his band set off for Roncesvalles. There, as arranged by Gan, the forces of Marsilius are arrayed to annihilate him. Meanwhile, the magician Malagigi has called up one of the spirits he controls to go to Egypt and bring back Rinaldo to help Orlando. The spirit, one Astarotte, a fallen angel (Astarotte is another of Pulci's completely invented additions to the cast of characters of his retelling of the *Chanson de Roland*), is sick and tired of serving Malagigi, but goes off as bid. He finds Rinaldo, endows his horse with magical powers and, with Rinaldo mounted on the horse, into which Astarotte has entered to give it the necessary propulsion, they leap the waves for the return to Roncesvalles, preceded by an army of lesser devils and spirits to clear the way. At first Rinaldo is dizzy from the height as they fly through the air. When he gets used to it he and Astarotte engage in friendly and, at times, profound conversation. Astarotte tells him that he was once an angel, and therefore cannot complain of his present state since he brought it on himself, well knowing what he was doing. He assures Rinaldo that there is a certain amount of courtesy among devils, and informs him, as they leap the Pillars of Hercules, that the world is round and there are people living on the other side of it. Rinaldo wants to know whether those people can be saved. Astarotte assures him that Heaven loves all who believe honestly, whatever the belief may be. Just before they arrive at Roncesvalles, Astarotte begs Rinaldo to free him from the service of Malagigi, and vows that in return he will serve Rinaldo. Rinaldo says he will see what he can do, and on this note they touch down. At the pass of Roncesvalles Rinaldo finds a frightful battle in progress. So many Christians have been killed that St. Peter and the angels are worn out from admitting them to heaven. Devils set by Astarotte perch on nearby belfries and snatch the souls of the dead Saracens as they scoot by. Uliviero (Oliver) begs Orlando to sound the horn that will signal Charlemagne that help is needed. Orlando refuses. In epic manner the paladins drive back the infidels, but they are fatally outnumbered. Uliviero is stricken. Orlando, who feels the breath of death, raises the horn to his lips and gives a tremendous blast. It is heard far off in the king's camp. Then a second blast is heard there, and Charlemagne begins to stir. With enormous effort, Orlando sounds the horn a third time, with such force that it bursts in two. He returns to the battle knowing that his end must come soon. His horse Rondel is exhausted and dies. Rinaldo finds Orlando in the midst of a fearful struggle, and Orlando, spent, dies. Charlemagne, whose eyes are at last opened to the treachery of Gan, gallops up with his train, defeats the infidels, captures Marsilius and kills him, and hangs Gan from the very Judas tree under which he and Marsilius had plotted the betrayal.

Mori (mō′rē), **Ascanio de'.** Man of letters; b. at Medole, near Mantua, 1533; d. 1591. Of a noble family, he was for a time in the suite of the marquess Orazio Gonzaga, and later fought against the Turks. On his return to his native city he devoted himself to his studies, and published (1585) a volume of fifteen novelle. His tales, in the comic or adventure vein that he preferred, are of slight literary value, but in one respect are notable: he freed himself from the almost obligatory Boccaccesque framework in presenting them. As did Guardati, he prefaced each of his stories with a dedicatory letter to a highly placed individual. In his dedication he drew moral conclusions as to the tale which was to follow. His conclusions were frequently pessimistic as regards the state of humanity.

Mornay (môr-nā), **Philippe de.** [Title, Seigneur **du Plessis-Marly;** known as **Duplessis-Mornay.**] French diplomat, politician, and Huguenot leader; b. at the Château Buhy, in Normandy, France, November 5, 1549; d. at La Forêt-sur-Sèvre, France, November 11, 1623. His *Mémoires* were published in 1624.

Moro (mō′rō), **Attoni** (or **Antonis**). [Called Sir **Anthony More.**] Dutch portrait painter; b. at Utrecht, Netherlands, c1512; d. at Antwerp, Belgium, c1578.

Moro, Cristoforo. Venetian doge; d. November 2, 1471. He was one of the most celebrated of the ancient and influential Moro family of Venice. After holding positions of trust under the emperor Sigismund, and for the republic of Venice, he was elected doge in 1462. Pope Pius II, who called him "distinguished for his extraordinary piety," recalls that Moro's good friend St. Bernardino of Siena had predicted that he would become doge. When the time came, Moro wished to decline the honor on the grounds of his age, but Pius urged him to accept, and to remain in the post. The pope hoped that Moro would send a fleet to help him in a crusade against the Turks. In fact, Moro did send a fleet to Ancona to meet the pope, in August, 1464, but the pope's death, joined with a great lack of enthusiasm for a crusade, caused the crusade to collapse.

Morone (mō-rō′nā), **Domenico.** Veronese painter; b. at Verona, c1442; d. after 1517. He was a pupil of Benaglio and a vigorous follower of Mantegna, whose manner, as distinct from an older tradition, he propagated at Verona through his pupils and followers: his son Francesco, Girolamo dai Libri, and Paolo Morando. His earliest known work was a fresco (1471) now lost. Of 1481 are his *St. Francis* and *St. Bernardino* on the organ shutters of S. Bernardino at Verona; a signed and dated (1484) *Madonna* is at Berlin. Scenes from the life of St. Thomas Aquinas are in the Metropolitan Museum, New York, at New Haven, San Francisco, Washington, and Paris. Other examples of his work are at Florence, Lovere, Modena, Vicenza, London, Stuttgart, Vienna, Columbia (Missouri), and elsewhere. For Francesco Gonzaga he painted *The Expulsion of the Bonacolsi,* Ducal Palace, Mantua. The large and animated scene presents splendidly clad mounted knights engaged in battle in an ancient square, on one side of which is the Bonacolsi palace at Mantua, and commemorates the event of 1328 by which the Gonzaga family won control of Mantua. It is the last work from Domenico's hand alone. Other works were painted in collaboration with his son Francesco, as a *Virgin and Child Enthroned,* Cannon Collection, Princeton, and frescoes in S. Maria in Organo and in the Library of the Convent of S. Bernardino (1503) at Verona, and in S. Nicola da Tolentino at Valpolicello (1502).

Morone, Francesco. Painter; b. at Verona, c1471; d. 1529. He was the son, pupil and imitator of Domenico Morone (c1442–1517), with whom he collaborated on a number of works, as a *Virgin and Child Enthroned,* Cannon Collection, Princeton, and frescoes in S. Maria in Organo and the Convent of S. Bernardino (1503) at Verona. In general, he carried on, with poetic grace, the tradition of his father, and with it the elements of Mantegna that his father had adopted. A number of his works, frescoes as well as panel paintings, are in the museums, palaces, and churches of Verona and its environs; these include the signed and dated (1498) *Crucifixion,* Church of S. Bernardino, an altarpiece in S. Maria in Organo (1503), and *St. Francis,* in the art museum. There are *Madonnas* by Morone at Verona, Padua, Berlin, London, Venice, and Bergamo, his *Samson and Delilah* is in the Poldi Pezzoli Museum, Milan, and his last dated (1529) work, the altarpiece, *Madonna and Child with SS. Roch and Joachim,* is at Soave, near Verona. Other examples of his work are at Florence, Trent, Berlin, Budapest, London, and Tucson (Arizona).

Morone, Giovanni di. Cardinal and diplomat; b. at Milan, January 25, 1509; d. at Rome, December 1, 1580. He spent his youth at Modena, then completed his law studies at Padua. He decided on an ecclesiastical career at an early age, and at 20 was made bishop of Modena by Clement VII. In the same year (1529) Clement VII sent him as envoy to the king of France to seek peace. Under Pope Paul III, he was charged with important diplomatic missions in Germany, and in 1542 he was raised to the cardinalate. In 1550 he used his influence to help elect Julius III pope, and was a faithful and much employed envoy of that pope, but his successor, Pope Paul IV suspected him of being too much a partisan of the emperor. He was charged with heretical tendencies and imprisoned in Castel Sant' Angelo. He was later released and cleared of all suspicion by the same pope. His own theology, which was not profound, rested on a belief in salvation through faith, and he espoused and expounded on some theories that were later condemned. Nevertheless, Cardinal Morone was a sincere reformer, who sought to woo heretics by gentleness and understanding rather than the threat of punishment. Deeply religious and convinced of his own innocence, while in prison he wrote a *Difesa* that was later printed. After he was freed, Pope Pius IV sent him to preside over the last session of the Council of Trent (1563–1564). One of his last services to the Church was as legate to the Diet of Ratisbon, 1577.

Morone, Girolamo. Politician; b. at Milan, 1470; d. December 15, 1529. He studied law at Pavia and thereafter almost immediately entered into public life. After the flight of Ludovico Il Moro (1499), he prepared the terms of the surrender of Milan to the French. Morone was a devoted supporter of the Sforza, and had a part in the restoration (1552) of Francesco Sforza the younger, son of Ludovico. Morone held offices under the French, and after the restoration of Francesco was virtual ruler of Milan. He was one of a number of intelligent and patriotic Italians who understood that the foreigners who had invaded and taken Milan were a threat to all Italy. On an embassy to Rome (March, 1513) he made an eloquent plea to Pope Leo X to preserve the liberty of Italy, and later worked to promote a league to unite Italy. It was all unavailing. Chafing under the French yoke, he yet advised the Milanese to submit to the French (1524) until a more propitious time. The victory of Charles V over the French at Pavia (1525) was at first a cause for rejoicing at the fall of the hated French, but he and the Milanese soon found the Spanish governors even more intolerable than the French. Morone organized a conspiracy, taking the Marquess of Pescara (Vittoria Colonna's husband) into his confidence, and offering him the crown of Naples in return for his help. Pescara, who had been largely responsible for the defeat of the French at Pavia (February, 1525), concluded that the French would be defeated again, and that the conspiracy would fail. He learned all he could of it and revealed it to Charles V. Morone was taken prisoner (October, 1525), and held for some time but was finally released (1527). From this time he placed himself at the service of Charles V and the French renegade, the Constable of Bourbon. He followed the army of Bourbon and Frundsberg, an army of German and Spanish mercenaries that, in order to sharpen its zest for battle, was not always paid. He was with the army at the sack of Rome (May, 1527), after which he remained at Rome many months to secure the release of Pope Clement VII, and supported the plan of the emperor and the pope to recover control of Florence for the Medici.

Moroni (mō-rō′nē), **Giovanni Battista.** Portrait painter; b. at Albino, near Bergamo, c1525; d. 1578. He was a pupil of Moretto da Brescia. The religious paintings he left in the churches in and about Bergamo are weak and lifeless imitations of his pungent and vital master. Moroni's fame arises from his skill and understanding as a portrait painter, a field of art in which he was unsurpassed and in which he probably influenced Titian and Van Dyck. His faithful representation of the features of his sitters is accompanied by an animating insight into their characters, and is presented in a chromatic scale that is typically Brescian—subdued but sturdy. He was one of the first to paint the whole figure when executing a portrait, thus increasing the problems of positioning and background but creating an entity, as opposed to the portrait busts and half-figures of earlier portrait painters. He worked mostly in and about Bergamo where, in the Carrara Academy, in addition to several paintings on religious subjects, there are sixteen portraits. He painted a vast number of portraits and they are to be found in museums throughout Europe and the United States. Among these is the austere and moving *Prioress Lucrezia Cattanei*, the Metropolitan Museum, New York, *Count Alberghetti and his Son, of Bergamo*, Museum of Fine Arts, Boston, *Ludovico Madruzzo*, Art Institute of Chicago, *The Master of Titian*, National Gallery, Washington, and portraits at Baltimore, the Isabella Stewart Gardner Museum, Boston, the Fogg Museum, Cambridge, at Detroit, Honolulu, Memphis, Minneapolis, the Johnson Collection, Philadelphia, Princeton, Richmond (Virginia), San Francisco, Sarasota, Tucson, Arizona; other works are at Columbus (Ohio) and Worcester. Besides many portraits in the gallery and in private collections at Bergamo, there are a number of works in churches of the city and in the surrounding towns, as well as paintings at Brescia, Florence, Milan, Trent, Amsterdam, Berlin, Budapest, Dublin, Frankfurt, Leningrad, London, Madrid, Paris, Rotterdam, Vienna, and elsewhere.

Morosini (mō-rō-zē′nē), **Antonio.** Venetian historian; b. between 1365 and 1368; d. after 1433. A member of an ancient and prominent family of Venice, he took a more modest part in Venetian political life than his distinguished relatives. He was admitted to the Great Council in 1388, but thereafter devoted himself to a life of commerce and to his passion for observing and recording. A religious man, mild, and pious, he lived a life apart, and satisfied his intense interest in the political life of the age by recording it as he saw it unfold, in his *Diario*. This probably began with the founding of Venice and goes up to 1433. The part of the work that deals with Venice prior to 1202 is fragmentary. The most valuable section is that which concerns the years immediately preceding his own day and the events of his lifetime. He recounts the great events of Venetian history as well as a minute description of the daily events in commerce and in the social and political affairs of his time. In 1418 the Council of Ten condemned it, and he was forced to destroy it. The reasons for the condemnation are unknown. He set to work to rewrite it, suppressing the parts that had offended the Council. With due regret for what was destroyed, what was rewritten forms one of the outstanding documents of Venetian historiography. A codex of the work is at Vienna.

Morte d'Arthur (môrt där′thėr). Compilation of prose romances on the life and death of King Arthur and the knights of the Round Table, compiled (c1470) in prison by Sir Thomas Malory, and printed by William Caxton in 1485. It was originally entitled *The Book of King Arthur and His Knights of* *the Round Table*. There is a metrical English romance with the title *Morte Arthure*, said to have been written at the end of the 14th century by Huchowne (Hutchin), a Scottish ballad writer.

Mortimer (môr′ti-mėr), **Edmund de.** [Title, 3rd Earl of **March.**] English nobleman; b. 1351; d. at Cork, Ireland, 1381. He married Philippa, daughter of Lionel of Antwerp, third son of King Edward III. When Lionel died (1368), he inherited the claim to the throne after the line of Edward the Black Prince and Richard II. This was the basis of the Yorkist claim to the throne prosecuted by them through the Wars of the Roses.

Mortimer, Roger de. [Titles, 8th Baron of **Wigmore,** 1st Earl of **March.**] English nobleman; b. 1287; d. at London, November 29, 1330. As a result of conflict with the Despensers who were favorites of King Edward II, Mortimer was imprisoned in the Tower, but escaped to France where he became the principal adviser to Queen Isabella, Edward II's self-exiled queen, and probably her lover. After the abdication of Edward II, and his subsequent murder, Mortimer became the most powerful man in England, and his arrogance won him many enemies. Following an unsuccessful expedition against the Scots, Mortimer was arrested, imprisoned, and accused before Parliament of causing a breach between Edward II and Isabella, of procuring Edward's death, of usurping royal prerogatives, and of causing the execution of the earl of Kent. He was found guilty, and was hanged, drawn and quartered at Tyburn Hill like a common criminal.

Mortimer, Roger de. [Title, 2nd Earl of **March.**] English nobleman; b. c1329; d. at Rouvray, France, 1360. Under Edward III he gradually regained the estates taken from his family as the result of his grandfather's attempt to usurp the throne and his murder of Edward II.

Mortimer, Roger de. [Title, 4th Earl of **March and Ulster.**] English nobleman; b. 1374; d. at Kells, Ireland, 1398. In 1385 he was declared heir presumptive to the throne by Richard II. His daughter Anne married Richard, earl of Cambridge, a grandson of King Edward III. She was the grandmother of Edward IV.

Morton (môr′to̤n), **John.** English cardinal; b. at Milborne St. Andrew, Dorsetshire, England, c1420; d. October 12, 1500. He was made archbishop of Canterbury and chancellor by Henry VII. Sir Thomas More began his career as a page in Morton's house.

Moscoso (mōs-kō′sō), **Luis de.** [Also, **Luis Muscoço de Alvarado.**] Spanish soldier; b. at Badajoz, Spain, c1505; d. c1560. He was with Hernando de Soto in his expedition to Florida, and after the death of de Soto near the Mississippi River succeeded him in command. He descended (1543) the river and arrived safely in Mexico with over 300 survivors of the expedition.

Mostacci (môs-tät′chē), **Jacopo.** Poet; b. at Pisa, c1190; d. c1250. He studied at Bologna and was later a member of Frederick II's court at Palermo and a poet of the so-called Sicilian school. He was a contemporary of Pier della Vigna and Giacomo da Lentino, and engaged in a poetic exchange with them on the nature of love.

Mowbray (mō′brā), **John.** [Titles, 2nd Duke of **Norfolk,** 4th Earl of **Nottingham.**] English nobleman; b. 1389; d. on the isle of Axholme, Lincolnshire, England, October 19, 1432.

Mowbray, Thomas. [Titles, Earl of **Nottingham,** 12th Baron **Mowbray,** 1st Duke of **Norfolk.**] English nobleman; d. at Venice, 1399. Having been accused of treason by Henry Bolingbroke (afterward Henry IV), he challenged Bolingbroke to single combat. Both combatants were banished by Richard II, Mowbray for life.

Moya y Contreras (mō′yä ē kōn-trā′räs), **Pedro de.** Spanish prelate and administrator; b. in the diocese of Córdoba, Spain, c1520; d. at Madrid, in December, 1591. He established (1571) the Inquisition in New Spain.

Munari (mö-nä′rē), **Pellegrino.** See **Pellegrino da Modena.**

Münster (mün′stēr), **Sebastian.** German geographer; b. at Ingelheim, Germany, 1489; d. at Basel, Switzerland, May 23, 1552. He was also an Orientalist, and mathematician, and professor of Hebrew at Basel. He published, among other works, *Cosmographia universalis* (1544), the first description in detail of the world written in German, a work in which over 100 scholars collaborated.

Münzer (mün′tsėr), **Thomas.** German religious enthusiast; b. at Stolberg in the Harz, Germany, c1490; executed at Mühlhausen, Saxony, Germany, May 30, 1525. On the recommendation of Martin Luther he became an evangelical preacher at Zwickau, where with others he organized the Anabaptist movement. Later he became an opponent of Luther. In 1525 he became a preacher at Mühlhausen, made himself master of the city, and introduced a democratic communistic government. When the peasant insurrection reached Thuringia, he placed himself at the head of 8,000 Anabaptists and insurgent peasants and inaugurated a war of extermination of the nobility and the clergy. He was defeated, captured, tried, and executed.

Murad I (mö-räd′, mū′rad). [Also, **Amurath.**] Sultan of Turkey (1359–1389); b. 1319; killed June 15, 1389. He completed the organization of the Janizaries, begun by his father (Orkhan), and was the first of the Ottoman sultans who made conquests in Europe. In 1361 he occupied Adrianople, which he made the capital of his European dominions. He took Sofia in 1382, and defeated the princes of Serbia and Bosnia in the battle of Kosovo, 1389. He was killed after the engagement by a wounded Serbian who, it is said, stood up from among the dead, and plunged a dagger into his breast as he surveyed the field of battle. He was succeeded by his son Bajazet I.

Murad II. [Also, **Amurath.**] Sultan of Turkey (1421–1451); b. c1403; d. 1451. He was the son and successor of Mohammed I. He unsuccessfully besieged (1423) Constantinople, carried on war against the Hungarians under Hunyadi and the Albanians under Scanderbeg, defeated the Hungarians at Varna in 1444 and Kosova in 1448, and subdued the Morea (Peloponnesus) in 1446. He was succeeded by his son Mohammed II the Great.

Muret (mü-re), **Marc Antoine.** [Latinized, **Muretus.**] French humanist; b. at Muret, France, April 12, 1526; d. at Rome, June 4, 1585. He taught the classics at Poitiers, Bordeaux, Paris, and Toulouse, went to Italy, where he resided at Venice, Padua, and Rome. After his return (1563) to Rome from a visit to France in the train of the legate Cardinal Ippolito d'Este, he taught civil law at Rome until 1584.

Muris (mū′ris), **Johannes** (or **Julianus**) **de.** [Called, **de Francia.**] Music theorist, fl. 14th century. He was probably French, and is mainly noted for the treatise *Speculum musice* (c1321). Other works, including *Summa musice* and *Musica speculativa*, have been attributed to him.

Murner (mür′nėr), **Thomas.** German satirist and opponent of the Reformation; b. at Oberehnheim, near Strasbourg, December 24, 1474; d. there, 1537. He studied at the Franciscan school at Strasbourg, was then a wandering scholar in France, Germany, and Poland, and afterward studied theology at Paris and law at Freiburg im Breisgau, where he lived in 1499. He was subsequently custodian of the Franciscan monastery at Strasbourg. In 1505 he was crowned poet by the emperor Maximilian I, and later was made (c1509) doctor of theology at Verona. His satirical work *Narrenbeschwörung* (*Exorcism of Fools*) was published at Strasbourg in 1512, in which year also appeared his *Schelmenzunft* (*Rogues' Gild*), consisting of sermons originally delivered at Frankfort on the Main. The satire, in rhymed couplets, *Von dem grossen Lutherischen Narren, wie ihn Doktor Murner beschworen hat* (*On the Great Lutheran Fool: how Doctor Murner has Exorcised Him*), published at Strasbourg in 1522, is a virulent and brilliant attack upon the Reformation.

Muscoço de Alvarado (mös-kō′sō dā äl-bä-rä′ᴛʜō), **Luis.** See **Moscoso, Luis de.**

Musi (mö′zē), **Agostino de'.** See **Agostino de' Musi.**

Mussato (mö-zä′tō), **Albertino.** Paduan soldier, politician, historian, and poet; b. at Padua, 1261; d. at Chioggia, May 31, 1329. He held public office at Padua, went on a mission to Pope Boniface VIII, acted as Paduan ambassador at the coronation of Henry VII, and served on many other missions. He was a soldier and patriot who tried to extricate Padua from the ruinous war with Can Grande della Scala over Vicenza. He wrote a Latin tragedy in the style of Seneca, *Ecerinide*, based on the life of the infamous tyrant and vicar of Frederick II, Ezzelino da Romano. He also wrote, in Latin, a history of Henry VII and of Italy from 1313 to 1329. The histories, in the manner of Livy, and the Latin tragedy are among the earliest manifestations of humanism. Mussato was so admired as a poet and writer that he was awarded the poet's crown of laurel by the bishop and the rector of the University at Padua (1310). Every Christmas Day the students and professors of the university marched in procession before his house and brought presents to do him honor. When (1318) he fell from favor with the ruling house of Padua the processions and honors ceased.

Musso (mös′sō), **Cornelio.** Bishop of Forlimpopoli and of Bitonto; b. at Piacenza, 1511; d. at Rome, 1574. He studied at Venice and Padua, taught at Pavia and Bologna, and was theologian to Pope Pius IV. He was known in his day for his sermons, and was for a time regarded as the foremost sacred orator of the time. He left three books of sermons, *Prediche* (Venice, 1576), and several theological works.

Musurus (mö-zö′rus), **Marcus.** Cretan scholar and teacher; b. at Candia, Crete; d. August 9, 1517. He taught Greek literature at the University of Padua and at Venice. In Venice he became associated with the great publisher Aldus Manutius, whom he had known at Carpi, and became one of his most valued assistants. He assisted in the preparation of such Greek texts as Plato and Pindar, among others, translated *Hero and Leander* into Latin, and published a Greek grammar. The Greek type of the Aldine Press was modeled on his handwriting. Leo X called him to Rome and made him bishop of Malvasia, in Greece. Musurus died young, it was said of disappointment that he had not been made a cardinal.

Muziano (mö-tsyä′nō), **Girolamo.** Painter; b. at Acquafredda, near Brescia, 1528; d. at Rome, April 25, 1592. An eclectic, he formed his mannerist style, one that was rather typical of late 16th-century Roman painting, by blending elements of the Brescian school, the first formative influence, with those of the Venetians Campagnola, Paolo Veronese, and Titian. After some time at Padua as a young man, he went to Rome (c1548) and there fell under the influence of Michelangelo and Sebastiano del Piombo, and attempted to add elements from them to his already derivative, mannerist style. Pope Gregory XIII thought highly of him (he was one of the leading Roman mannerists), and made him overseer of the works of the Vatican and put him in charge of the decorating of the Gregorian Chapel in St. Peter's. He worked at Orvieto, Foligno, Loreto, and, for Ippolito II d'Este, at Ferrara. At Rome he had a busy workshop where representatives of various schools of painting were engaged. He was particularly noted for his landscapes, in which he fused Venetian color and Flemish detail. Among his many works is a youthful *St. Jerome*, National Gallery of Parma, showing the influence of Bassano and the school of Brescia; a *Male Portrait* is in the Uffizi, Florence. Other works include *St. Jerome in the Desert*, Carrara Academy, Bergamo, *Holy Family*, Dresden, five scenes on the life of Christ, Orvieto, the signed *Resurrection of Lazarus* and *St. Francis Receiving the Stigmata*, Vatican, and paintings in a number of churches at Rome.

Muzio (mö′tsyō), **Girolamo.** Poet and writer; b. at Padua, 1496; d. at La Paneretta, near Siena, 1576. He became a courtier who wandered from court to court, from that of the emperor Maximilian I to those of the duke of Ferrara and the duke of Urbino. His patrons sent him on various missions which he faithfully carried out. He began his literary career rather late in life, and was influenced by the Counter-Reformation, in support of which he used his talents. His poetical works include *Egloghe* and *Rime diverse*. *Il Duello* and *Il Gentiluomo* are formal treatises in 16th-century style; in *Battaglie per la difesa dell' italica lingua*, he takes up the cudgels in favor of Italian as a literary language. In addition, he wrote a series of polemics on religious subjects, or rather, against those whose religious beliefs or writings ran counter to his own. One such was against Vergerio. He was one of many who longed to see Italy free of foreign domination. In his last years he proposed an Italian league to drive the Spanish from Italy. This was a reversal of his earlier support of Charles V. His proposal included an eventual Italian confederation along Swiss lines.

Muzzarelli (möt-tsä-rel′lē), **Giovanni.** Humanist and poet; b. at Gazzuolo, near Mantua, 1490?; d. at Rocca di Mondarino, in the Romagna, 1518. He was in the service of the bishop of Mantua, the princes of Sabioneta, and then went to Rome, where Pope Leo X appointed him governor of Rocca di Mondarino in the Romagna. He wrote a dialogue in praise of women, *Dialogo in lode di donne*, more or less in imitation of Pietro Bembo's dialogues on Platonic love, *Gli Asolani*. His lyrics, in the style of Petrarch, have his personal stamp. A tale of Narcissus, *Fabula di Narciso*, includes a verse rendering of some of the adventures of his own life.

N

Naddi (näd′dē), **Giorgio.** Dominican; d. December 5, 1398. He entered the Dominican Order as a youth and rose rapidly by his virtue and his intelligence. He taught in the monasteries at Florence and Siena, and was noted as a preacher. In 1378 he was in charge of the *Mantellate* at Siena, as the sisters of the order to which St. Catherine of Siena belonged were called. In the same year he was elected master of theology at the general chapter at Bologna.

Naldini (näl-dē′nē), **Giovanni Battista.** Painter; b. at Florence, c1537; d. there, February 18, 1591. He was a pupil and assistant of Pontormo for eight years (1549–1557), then went to Rome to study. On his return to Florence he assisted Vasari in the decoration of the Palazzo Vecchio. He was one of the painters who worked on the decorations for the funeral of Michelangelo (1564) and on those for the marriage of Francesco de' Medici to Joanna of Austria (1565). The early influence of Pontormo in his painting was replaced by the mannerism of Bronzino and Vasari, and had almost disappeared in a *Pietà* (1572), S. Maria Novella. In a *Nativity* (1573) and *Presentation in the Temple*, in the same church, unabashed mannerism is dominant, as it is in later frescoes and panels. A leading artist of his day, he had a prosperous school and served several times as director of the Academy of Art founded by Cosimo I.

Naldo (näl′dō), **Naldi.** Florentine poet and humanist; b. at Florence, c1435; d. in the reign of Leo X. A friend of Ficino and Poliziano and a member of the so-called Platonic Academy, he was not particularly favored by Lorenzo the Magnificent, and went to Forlì and later to Venice to improve his circumstances. On his return to Florence he held the chair of humanistic studies at the university from 1484 to 1498. Among his writings are three books of amorous, and often adulatory, Latin verses in the manner of Ovid and with overtones of Petrarch; the *Volaterrais*, a poem in hexameters on the war against Volterra in which he lauds Lorenzo and Federico da Montefeltro; a poem describing the tournament given by Giuliano de' Medici, Lorenzo's brother; and four cantos praising the library of Matthias Corvinus. He wrote, in prose, a Latin version of Vespasiano da Bisticci's life of Manetti.

Nanni (nän′nē), **Giovanni.** See **Annio, Giovanni.**

Nanni d'Antonio di Banco (dän-tō′nyō dē bäng′kō). [Also, **Giovanni d'Antonio di Banco.**] Florentine sculptor; b. c1385; d. 1421. He received his first training from his father, a sculptor who was one of a number working on the *Porta della Mandorla* of the cathedral. In 1406 he was enrolled in the Stone- and Woodcarvers' Guild. Shortly thereafter he was commissioned to execute a figure of the prophet *Isaiah* for a buttress of the *Porta della Mandorla*, and in 1408 was commissioned to make a seated figure of *St. Luke* for one of the niches of the west door of the cathedral (Donatello's *St. John the Evangelist* was executed for the niche on the other side of the door). Finished in 1413, the statue shows the classical influence that was appearing in Florentine sculpture as a result of growing interest in the ancient world. His *St. Luke* is seated in a natural pose, swathed in full, soft draperies, and with a dignified and thoughtful expression; the statue fills the niche for which it was intended. Another work, executed for one of the niches of Orsanmichele and commissioned by the Stone- and Woodcarvers' Guild, is his *Four Crowned Martyrs*, unique among the Orsanmichele figures in that the niche is filled by a group rather than by one figure. The figures distinctly reveal their descent from classical models. Also for Orsanmichele is a *St. Philip*. His masterpiece, and a masterpiece of the period, is a relief, *The Assumption of the Virgin* (commissioned 1414), over the door that came to be called the *Porta della Mandorla* from the mandorla of the relief. The arrangement of the composition is traditional, with the Madonna in a mandorla supported by six angels. In this work Nanni employed a more naturalistic and less classical manner in the arrangement of drapery and the modeling of the heads. He apparently spent the last years of his life working on it, for the last payment was made to his heirs in 1422.

Nanni di Bartolo (dē bär′tō-lō). [Called **il Rosso.**] Florentine sculptor; active in the first half of the 15th century. Between 1419 and 1422 he carved a statue (unidentified) for the façade of the cathedral at Florence. He also carved an *Obadiah* and collaborated with Donatello and Ciuffagni on three other figures for the campanile. Thereafter he gave up other commissions for work on the cathedral and went to Venice. Little is known of his activities there. Other works include the marble doorway for S. Niccolò at Tolentino and the signed Brenzoni monument, with a *Resurrection,* in S. Fermo Maggiore at Verona, completed between 1427 and 1439. His early work shows him to have been a vigorous and individual sculptor who had assimilated the elements of naturalism and finish that Donatello added to Florentine sculpture. Later, when he was away from Florence, he reverted to the Gothic tradition, at that time favored by the Venetians, and his work, wavering between the influence of Donatello and the earlier Gothic schools, lost its individuality and is difficult to identify.

Naogeorgus (nā-ǫ-jôr′gus; German, nä-ō-gā-ôr′gůs). [Original name, **Thomas Kirchmaier.**] German writer of plays in Latin, a supporter of Luther, and an implacable foe of the papacy; b. at Hubelschmeiss, Germany, 1511; d. at Wiesloch, Germany, December 29, 1563. His most famous play *Pammachius* (1538), in which the pope is portrayed as the Antichirst, was one of the most powerful polemics of Protestantism. It was performed (1545) at Cambridge by members of Christ's College. His comedy, *Mercator seu judicium* (1540), praises faith rather than good works; in a popular style, it was a favorite for many years. Both plays reveal his command of satire and invective and are marked by the profundity of his feeling. His satirical poem, *Regnum papisticum* (1553) is also an attack on the papacy.

Nardi (när′dē), **Jacopo.** Historian and writer; b. at Florence, 1476; d. at Venice, March, 1563. An ardent lover of liberty, he was active in Florentine affairs, was a supporter of Savonarola, and took part in the popular government. However, on the return of the Medici (1512) he supported the new government. In 1529, when the armies were at the gates of Florence and the city was under siege, he was one of its staunchest defenders, heaving rocks down on the soldiers from the parapets of the fortifications. The short-lived republic again fell and he was forced into exile on the return of the Medici. With other Florentine exiles, he appeared (1535) before Charles V to bring charges against the government of Alessandro de' Medici. The suit of the exiles was fruitless, and Nardi went to Venice. Among his writings are some youthful comedies, based on Boccaccio, carnival songs, and a celebrated and free translation of Livy. He also wrote two political treatises and a *Vita di Antonio Giacomini.* The latter was praised for its natural and lively style. The work that ranks him among the leading Florentine historians is his *Istorie della città di Firenze,* written in his old age. This work reveals his political philosophy as an ardent supporter of liberty. It is notable for the impartiality and balance with which he presents events and treats his enemies. Above all, it is pervaded by a Christian sentiment that was deeply felt by Nardi. Savonarola's influence appears in the work by Nardi, always an admirer of Savonarola. He cherished an unalterable belief in a supreme being that judged and directed the affairs of men, in the state as well as in individual cases. But his religious sentiments did not cloud his vision or his fire, especially in matters concerning Savonarola and the siege of 1530. The work is marked and enlivened by the personality of the author.

Nardo di Cione (när′dō dē chō′nā). Florentine painter; d. 1366. He was the brother of Andrea Orcagna, Jacopo, and Matteo di Cione, and was influenced by the most famous of the brothers, Andrea, but the work of Nardo has a less marked relief and more delicate color than that of his brother. He was also influenced by Giotto's closest follower, Maso di Banco. Nardo joined the Physicians and Apothecaries' Guild in 1343 or 1344. Among a number of surviving works at Florence is a series of frescoes—*Paradise, The Last Judgment,* and a remarkably imagined and fantastic *Inferno*—in the Strozzi Chapel of S. Maria Novella. This series, not signed or documented, was ascribed to Nardo by Lorenzo Ghiberti about 100 years after it was painted and constitutes the standard by which other works are attributed to him. In the execution of the frescoes he was assisted by his brother Jacopo and by Giovanni del Biondo. Nardo reveals his poetic qualities in the delicately hued, graceful, and elongated figures of a series of now fragmentary frescoes in the Badia, comprising *The Mocking of Christ, Flagellation, Way to Calvary, Suicide of Judas, Christ's Farewell to His Mother,* and *Christ Taking Leave of the Three Maries.* Other works at Florence are in the Accademia, Uffizi, S. Croce, Berenson Collection, and elsewhere, and there are paintings at Berne, Dublin, London (National Gallery and Victoria and Albert Museum), Munich, Prague, New Haven, New York (Historical Society), and Washington.

Narni (när′nē), **Erasmo di.** See **Gattamelata.**

Narváez (när-ʙä′eth), **Pánfilo de.** Spanish conquistador; b. at Valladolid, Spain, c1478; drowned somewhere in the Gulf of Mexico, in November, 1528. After Cortés threw off the authority of Diego Velásquez, governor of Cuba, Narváez was appointed captain general of the newly discovered lands in Mexico, and ordered to imprison Cortés (1520). He was defeated, captured, and imprisoned by Cortés. He was released and sent to Spain. In 1526 he obtained a grant to conquer and govern Florida. He took possession of Florida in the name of Spain, and led an unsuccessful search for treasure. On the return he was shipwrecked, and drowned, with nearly all his men.

Nassau (näs′ou), **Elisabeth von.** See **Elisabeth von Lothringen.**

Natta (nät′tä), **Giorgio.** Jurist and man of letters; d. at Casale Monferrato, June 25, 1495. He taught at Pavia and Pisa from 1468 until at least 1478. Later he became a councillor of the marquess of Monferrato, and went on many missions for him. He left a number of Latin treatises on legal subjects and some didactic works.

Natta, Marco Antonio. Latin writer of the first half of the 16th century. He left a number of works, in impeccable Latin, on various matters, as *Consilia seu responsa* (Venice, 1572), *Orationes accademicae* (Venice, 1560 and 1564), and *De doctrina principum* (Frankfurt, 1603).

Navagero (nä-vä-jā′rō), **Andrea.** [Latinized, **Naugerius.**] Venetian poet, orator and diplomat; b. at Venice, 1483; d. at Blois, France, May 8, 1529. Of a patrician Venetian family, he studied under the historian Sabellicus, the Cretan scholar Musurus, and the philosopher Pomponazzi, and was the friend and assistant of Aldus Manutius. For the latter's press at Venice he corrected the texts of Lucretius, Horace, Ovid, Terence, Quintilian, and Vergil. As a master of the Latin style, he became famous for the funeral orations he gave at Venice, and as a man of learning he was made (1516) director of the library Cardinal Bessarion had left to Venice. For the Venetian Republic he went on various diplomatic missions and was one of the negotiators of the treaty that freed (1526) Francis I, following his capture at the Battle of Pavia (1525). In Spain Navagero met the Spanish poet Boscán and, through him, introduced Italian meters into Spain. Navagero wrote Latin lyrics in the manner of Catullus. His *Lusus,* a collection, is in grace, imagination, and sensitivity among the most winning of Renaissance Latin poetry. His Italian poems have less charm, as they show their Petrarchan origins. He also left letters, in Italian, with some interesting notes from his Spanish missions. A letter from Seville (1526) reports on and describes Indians who have arrived in Spain from the New World. In addition to his literary and diplomatic activities, Navagero was known as an ardent botanist. In his garden on the island of Murano, near Venice, he cultivated exotic as well as native plants, and carried out various horticultural experiments.

Navarrete (nä-ʙär-rā′tā) or **Navarete** (nä-ʙä-rā′tā), **Juan Fernández.** [Surnamed **El Mudo,** meaning "the Mute."] Spanish painter of religious subjects; b. at Logroño, Spain, 1526; d. c1579.

Negreti (nā-grā′tē) or **Negretti** (nā-gret′tē), **Jacopo.** See **Palma, Jacopo.**

Negri (nā′grē) or **Negro** (nā′grō), **Gaspare.** Venetian painter; active between 1503 and 1544. He was a follower of Cima da Conegliano and Bartolomeo Montagna and was active in and about Udine. His *Virgin with the Dead Christ and Saints,* Museum of Fine Arts, Boston, is his only known painting.

Negromonte (nā-grō-mōn′tā). Comedy by Ariosto (1520).

Nelli (nel′lē), **Ottaviano.** Umbrian painter; b. at Gubbio; active 1400–1444. He held public office in his native town, worked there and at Urbino, Borgo San Sepolcro, Foligno, and Assisi. He was an important Umbrian painter in the international Gothic style in his time. Possessed of a fine sense of color, his work is ornate, in the international Gothic manner, graceful, and harmonious, and marked with the little genre details, as well as the elegance and elaborateness of costume, that characterized the style. His individual characteristics are an interest in strange faces and exaggerated expressions, and a fondness for the little grotesque figures, in decorative borders and pilasters, that link his work to manuscript decoration. One of his earliest works, and considered by some to be his finest, is a *Madonna del Belvedere*, signed and dated 1403, in the Church of S. Maria Nuova at Gubbio. It is a mural in tempera and is notable for its coloring. Each of the angels in the group of angels, saints, and adorers about the Madonna and Child carries a carefully painted musical instrument—an organ, violin, or lute. Other works at Gubbio are frescoes in the churches of S. Agostino (twenty scenes from the life of St. Augustine, probably painted with assistants to his guiding design), S. Francesco, and S. Domenico. In 1424 he decorated the chapel of the Trinci Palace at Foligno with scenes from the life of the Virgin and the life of Christ. Other frescoes by Nelli are at Assisi (Sacro Convento), Città di Castello (S. Maria delle Grazie), Fano (S. Domenico), Montefalco (S. Francesco), and Urbino (Oratorio di S. Croce, Oratorio di S. Gherardo); there are polyptychs at Perugia and Rome (Vatican), and works at São Paulo, Philadelphia (Johnson Collection), Worcester (Massachusetts), and elsewhere.

Nelli, Pietro. Poet; b. at Siena, 1511?; d. there. What little is known of him must be drawn from his writings. He wrote sonnets and epigrams, and forty-six *capitoli*. The latter were published under the name Andrea da Bergamo. The subjects of his satirical and burlesque verse are those common to his age, and are often expressed in a crudely sarcastic manner, or with a broadness that borders on the popular. His *Satire alla Carlona* condemns Spanish rule in Italy and mourns the sufferings of the peninsula.

Nello (nel′lō), **Bernardo, di Giovanni Falconi.** Pisan painter; active at the end of the 14th century. Vasari called him a pupil of Orcagna. His work shows him to have been a provincial painter who interpreted Florentine painting in his own way. His *Death of the Virgin* is at Pisa.

Nemours (nẹ-mör′), Duc **de.** See **Foix, Gaston de.**

Nencia da Barberino (nen′chä dä bär-bā-rē′nō), **La.** Poem by Lorenzo de' Medici in the dialect of the Tuscan peasants. It celebrates the love of a young peasant, Vallera, for his sweetheart, Nencia, and tells the ways in which he woos her. It presents a vivid, vigorous, and racy description of rural life and its ways. Realistic and simple, the poem is a deeply felt and sympathetic response, in the popular manner, to the charms of rural life. It was much imitated.

Neri (nā′rē). Political faction that arose in Tuscany c1300 and split the Guelph party. The term originated in Pistoia, where the Cancellieri family, having driven out the Ghibellines, then split into two factions, the Bianchi and the Neri (the Whites and the Blacks). The struggle for power between the two parties of the family became so violent that Florence intervened, in the period 1296–1300, and forced the Cancellieri family to leave the city of Pistoia. The controlling party in Florence at this time favored the Bianchi. The Neri entered Florence and were allied with Corso Donati and other violent Guelphs; the Bianchi party in control of Florence was unable to exert its authority and the city was in turmoil. Pope Boniface VIII sent Charles of Valois into the city, theoretically to restore order. He allied himself with the Neri, and the Bianchi, Dante among them, were sent into exile.

Neri (ne′rē), San **Filippo de'.** [Original name, **Filippo Romolo Neri.**] Founder of the Congregation of the Oratory; b. at Florence, July 21, 1515; d. at Rome, May 26, 1595. His father was a Florentine notary who was deeply interested in alchemy. His mother died while he was a child, but he was brought up by a loving stepmother and had a happy childhood. From childhood he was deeply religious. He was also musical, poetic in his outlook, and of an original and nonconforming attitude of mind. At 17 he set out to visit an uncle from whom he had expectations at San Germano. At this place at the foot of Monte Cassino, he fell under the influence of a Benedictine monk and began to devote himself to good works. In 1533 he went to Rome, cutting all ties with his family and arriving penniless. There he acted as tutor to the sons of a Florentine, studied theology with the Augustinians, and visited the churches and the catacombs. He began to visit hospitals and slums, to walk in the public places, and to preach and talk to the passersby. With a joyful spirit he urged them to turn their thoughts to religion. He attracted a group of disciples and in 1548, with the aid of his confessor, he founded the Confraternity of the Most Holy Trinity to aid pilgrims and convalescents. His activities in behalf of the sick and needy earned him the name "Apostle of Rome." In 1551 he finally became a priest and lived at San Girolamo at Rome. At the church he spent his mornings hearing confessions and his afternoons with groups of men and boys, meeting in his rooms for discussion or traveling about Rome urging them to enjoy themselves. His teaching, far from the asceticism of many religious teachers, attracted many people to religion, and Rome was for a time, and due directly to his efforts, pervaded with a religious sense such as it had not known for many years. Some of his followers became priests, and from 1564 they began to live as a community. They ate and prayed together but took no vows. For the afternoon talks on the spiritual life and the exposition of the Scriptures Palestrina composed background music. Since the talks were held in the oratory, the music composed to accompany the talks and readings came to be called oratorio. Palestrina also wrote, in addition to the musical settings, hymns, motets, and other songs of praise for San Filippo, of whom he was a devoted follower. In the same year (1564), Filippo became rector of S. Giovanni dei Fiorentini. In 1575 the group he had gathered about him, and which was called the Congregation of the Oratory, was granted formal approval by Pope Gregory XIII. San Filippo, a lovable and very popular saint, believed and lived a highly personal faith. He was a joyous priest, who felt that God had given too generously to him of His grace, and was often heard to exclaim, "Withdraw Thyself, Lord, I am but a mortal; I cannot bear so much joy." He was canonized in 1622.

Neri di Bicci (dē bēt′chē). Painter; b. at Florence, 1419; d. 1491. He was the son, pupil, assistant, and close follower of Bicci di Lorenzo (1373–1452). Influenced somewhat by Domenico Veneziano and Fra Angelico, he was a craftsman, lacking in a creative spark, who in the main carried on the tradition of his father, which was already that of a previous age, into the full Renaissance. He had a busy workshop with many assistants, among whom were Francesco Botticini, Cosimo Rosselli, and Giusto d'Andrea, and produced, with assistants, an enormous number of paintings. Among these is *St. Nicholas Throwing Balls of Gold to the Daughters of the Poor Nobleman,* Yale University Art Gallery, New Haven, that is notable for its delicacy and intimacy. The greatest concentration of his paintings is in the museums (eight in the Accademia) and churches (in nine churches) at Florence. Many more are in localities in Tuscany; others are at Foligno, Palermo, Parma, Perugia, Pisa, Rome, Siena, Volterra, and other places in Italy, in many of the great museums of Europe, and at Baltimore, Brooklyn, Cambridge (Massachusetts), Claremont (California), Cleveland, Denver, Detroit, Lawrence (Kansas), the New York Historical Society, Oberlin, the Johnson Collection, Philadelphia, San Diego, Worcester, and elsewhere. For a mediocre painter he is abundantly represented.

Neri di Landoccio (dē län-dôt′chō). Disciple and secretary of St. Catherine of Siena; d. March 8, 1406. He was of a noble family of Siena, was a vernacular poet, was sensitive, and often despondent. He was one of St. Catherine's first disciples, one of her dear "spiritual sons." He was one of the secretaries who took down the *Dialogo della Divina Provvidenza,* dictated while she was in ecstasy. Her letters to him were full of tender concern for his spirit and of bracing advice. After her death he lived the life of an anchorite.

Nerli (ner′lē), **Filippo de'.** Florentine historian; b. at Florence, March 9, 1485; d. there, January 17, 1566. He was a member of the literary groups that were active at Florence, and was a good friend of Machiavelli. He held public office in Florence on several occasions, and was a supporter, by political conviction, of the Medici. For this reason he was under suspicion when the republic was restored (1527) and was cast into prison during the siege of Florence. On the fall of the republic and the return of the Medici (1530) he was released, returned to active life, and held many important positions. As with Machiavelli, Nerli's passion was politics. He regarded the history of Florence as a long and tormented struggle toward the principate of the Medici that was achieved in his time. In 1534 he began to write his *Commentari de' fatti civili accorsi dentro la città di Firenze dall' anno 1215 al 1537*. The work, begun in 1534, was laid aside and taken up again and completed at the request of Cosimo I de' Medici. Of the twelve books, the first three are devoted to the history of Florence from 1215 (when, according to Nerli, the city was divided into the factions that kept it in turmoil for the next three centuries), up to the end of the 15th century. As Nerli saw it, this was all a prologue to the historical necessity that brought the Medici to power in Florence near the beginning of the 16th century, to restore peace and bring order to the city.

Neroccio di Landi (nā-rôt′chō dē län′dē). Sienese painter and sculptor; b. at Siena, 1447; d. there, 1500. He was a pupil of Vecchietta. About 1467 he entered into partnership with Francesco di Giorgio Martini, with whom he continued to collaborate to 1475. Among their joint productions was an altarpiece, *Coronation of the Virgin*, for which Neroccio painted the predella, now in the Uffizi, with scenes from the life of St. Benedict. A number of documents concerning his activity are extant. For Bernardino Nini he painted the signed and dated (1476) altarpiece, *Madonna, St. Michael and St. Bernardino*, Pinacoteca, Siena, some cassoni panels and other furniture; another *Madonna, St. Michael and St. Bernardino*, and a *Madonna and Child with SS. Jerome and Mary Magdalen* are in the Metropolitan Museum, New York. In 1483 he designed the marble intarsia of the *Hellespontine Sibyl* for the pavement of the cathedral at Siena; of 1492 is a panel, *Madonna and Six Saints*, Pinacoteca, Siena; and of 1495 the *Vestal Claudia Quinta*, National Gallery, Washington, representing the Vestal Virgin who proved her innocence at Rome in 204 B.C. Also at Washington is his *Portrait of a Lady*. It is one of few Sienese portraits, and is among the earliest in which the painter attempted to reflect the personality of the sitter in the landscape background; the sitter is presumed to have been Alessandra Piccolomini, grandniece of Pope Pius II. A devout and conscientious artist, Neroccio painted many pictures on religious subjects, in which the favorite saints appear to have been Jerome and Bernardino, who was one of the patron saints of Siena. The subjects for his cassoni panels were sometimes drawn from mythology or the classical period, as *The Battle of Actium* and *Cleopatra's Arrival at the Court of Mark Antony*, panels at Raleigh, North Carolina. In the types of his saints and his blonde Madonnas, with round faces, small, pointed chins, and long necks, in the absence of modeling to give relief to features and figures, and in the patterns that he created with line and color, Neroccio remained faithful to the tradition passed to him by Vecchietta, enhancing it by his grace of line and feeling for beauty. The clarity and transparency of his deep color resembles that of the older Sienese, Sassetta. A leader at Siena in painting and sculpture, he had some knowledge of perspective and a good sense of space-composition, as appears in *The Annunciation*, Yale University Art Gallery, New Haven. His paintings are delicate and decorative, still primitive in comparison to the work of his Florentine contemporaries, and of an unstudied purity. His *Madonna and Child with SS. Jerome and Bernardino*, Pinacoteca, Siena, is among his loveliest works in the charm of its delicate tones and for the gentle melancholy of his sacred figures. As delicacy and charm are features of his painting, vigor and naturalism mark his sculpture, which yet retains the gentleness that was a feature of his personality as an artist. One of his earliest sculptural works was a terra-cotta statue of *St. Jerome* (1468); the thoughtful statue of *St. Catherine*, in the saint's house at Siena, is of 1470. Other sculptural works include the tomb of Tommaso Testa Piccolomini, bishop of Siena (d. 1485), above the door to the bell tower in the cathedral, and a statue of *St. Catherine* for the Baptistery, commissioned (1487) by the overseers of the works of the cathedral. Among the paintings of Neroccio at Siena are a number in the Pinacoteca. Other examples of his work are a fresco of the *Madonna*, Montalcino, paintings at Bergamo, Gazzada (Varese), Magliano, Montisi, Berlin, Esztergom, Paris, in the Museum of Fine Arts and the Isabella Stewart Gardner Museum, Boston, at Los Angeles, Notre Dame University, Indiana, the Johnson Collection, Philadelphia, Urbana, Illinois, and elsewhere.

Neville (nev′il), **George.** English archbishop; b. c1433; d. June 8, 1476. He supported both Edward IV and Henry VI, whose chancellor he was during the restoration (1470–1471). He surrendered to Edward, was arrested for treason (1471), and held prisoner in France until 1475.

Neville, John. [Titles, Marquis of **Montagu**, Earl of **Northumberland.**] English soldier in the Wars of the Roses; b. c1430; d. April 14, 1471. He defeated (1464) the Lancastrians at Hexham, but joined the Lancastrians in protest against the restoration to Henry Percy of the estates and earldom of Northumberland, and was killed at Barnet with Warwick while fighting on the Lancastrian side.

Neville (nev′il), **Richard.** See **Warwick,** Earl of.

Neyra (nā′rä), **Álvaro Mendaña** (or **de Mendaña**) **de.** See **Mendaña de Neyra, Álvaro.**

Niccoli (nēk′kō-lē), **Niccolò.** Florentine humanist; b. at Florence, c1364; d. there, February 3, 1437. He was the son of a wealthy merchant and became a merchant himself, but after his father died gave up his business to devote himself to his studies and to his passion for collecting books and manuscripts. With Salutati, Marsigli, Leonardo Bruni and others, he was a member of a circle that met at Santo Spirito, across the Arno, to engage in discussions of classical literature and theology. He became an ardent advocate of classical studies, encouraged promising young men to pursue them by loaning his own books and giving them needed funds, and was instrumental in securing the services of Manuel Chrysoloras, who had taught him Greek, Guarino da Verona, Aurispa, and Filelfo for the university at Florence. In his wanderings to Padua, Venice, and Verona, among other places, he sought ancient manuscripts and codices, bought them if he could or copied them in his own beautiful handwriting. He also commissioned his friends to buy or copy manuscripts for him. Poggio, attending the sessions of the Council of Constance, searched many monastic libraries in the area acting for Niccoli. His house, tastefully ornamented with mementos of the ancient world, many of which had been given him by his admirers, was open to all who wished to consult or borrow any of his large collection of books. When he died he had about 800 manuscripts in his library, many of them copies he had made. Cosimo de' Medici, who had often helped Niccoli when, after spending his personal fortune on his collection, the latter needed funds, paid his debts after his death in return for the library, and erected (1444) a building for it in the monastery of San Marco. The library Niccoli built up was, as he had wished, open to all students. The collection is now part of the Laurentian library at Florence. Vespasiano, who had the highest praise for Niccoli's godly life, describes him as a handsome, smiling, frank, and liberal man, whose house was a meeting place for the distinguished men of his day. He adds that Niccoli "never took a wife so as not to be hindered in his studies."

Niccolò dell' Abate (nēk-kō-lō′ del-lä-bä′tā). See **Dell' Abate, Niccolò.**

Niccolò dall' Arca (däl är′kä). [**Niccolò da Bari.**] Sculptor; d. July 2, 1494. He came from Bari and was called dall'Arca because of his work on the Arca di S. Domenico (Tomb of St. Dominic) at Bologna. He was influenced by works of other sculptors that he saw in his travels but subjected such influences to his own strong personality. A work of furious drama and movement, that recalls the Burgundian sculpture he must have seen on a journey to that region, is the *Pietà* (1462), Church of S. Maria della Vita, Bologna. The unbridled grief and rush of gesture, especially in the figure of the Magdalen, reflect Gothic frenzy rather than Renaissance tranquillity. In 1469 he signed the contract to work on the tomb of St. Dominic in S. Domenico, Bologna. Evidence of Burgundian influence appears in some of the figures of the tomb, but the decorative effects of angels, wreaths, and flowers are in the softer Tuscan manner of the Rossellini, and the figures of St. Francis and St. Dominic are in a simpler, more tranquil mood; the wildness and drama of his earlier work is softened and subdued. Always self-critical, when he was dying he wished that he could smash all his sculpture to bits, having arrived at a new view of his art, in which strength and vigor and a warm sensuality would be expressed with elegance rather than ardor, and with the delicacy of rhythm and fantasy that, in the Arca di S. Domenico, made him the equal of the most tender Tuscan masters.

Niccolò di Buonaccorso (dē bwō-näk-kôr′sō). Sienese painter; known from 1356; d. 1388. A modest Sienese master, his surviving works include a *Crucifixion,* National Gallery of

Umbria, Perugia, that reflects the influence of his great Sienese predecessors, Simone Martini and Ambrogio Lorenzetti; three panels of a triptych, of which one, *The Presentation of the Virgin in the Temple*, is in the Uffizi, Florence, a second, the signed *The Marriage of the Virgin*, is in the National Gallery, London, and the third, *The Coronation of the Virgin*, is in the Lehmann Collection, New York; and *Virgin, Child and Saints*, Museum of Fine Arts, Boston. Other works are at Fiesole, Montecchio, Siena, Cologne, San Diego (California), and elsewhere.

Niccolò da Correggio (dä kôr-red′jō). Poet; b. at Ferrara, 1450; d. there, February 1, 1508. He was the son of a lord of Correggio and the grandson of Niccolò III d'Este. He spent most of his life at the court of the d'Este at Ferrara, serving in many capacities: as emissary to Rome and Naples, as soldier, and as courtier in the suite of Isabella d'Este. In later life he was at the court of Ludovico Il Moro at Milan. In addition to lyrics in the manner of Petrarch, he wrote *Cefalo*, which was presented for the Estense court in January, 1487. The action is all-important in this secular drama modeled on the old *sacre rappresentazioni*.

Niccolò da Foligno (dä fō-lē′nyō). See **Alunno, Niccolò.**

Niccolò di Forzore Spinelli (dē fôr-tsō′rā spē-nel′lē). [Called **il Fiorentino.**] Medalist; b. at Florence, 1430; d. there, 1514. He was a member of the family, many of whom were goldsmiths, that produced Spinello Aretino (c1347–1410). He worked mainly at Florence, but had visited Flanders and had made seals and medals at the court of Burgundy. Five medals signed by him survive. These include those of Alfonso I d'Este and Lorenzo the Magnificent. A great number of other medals are attributed to him. They are notable for the excellence of the portraits and are among the most beautiful of 15th-century Italy. A group of these are of French leaders who were at Florence in the train of Charles VIII in 1494.

Niccolò di Giacomo da Bologna (dē jä′kō-mō dä bō-lō′nyä). Miniaturist; b. at Bologna; d. before 1402. Little is known of his life except that he was extraordinarily productive, as is attested by many codices decorated by him and signed with his name that are scattered about the museums and libraries of Europe. His strong and sturdy forms and naturalistic style influenced the Bolognese school of miniature painting throughout the second half of the 14th century.

Niccolò di Liberatore (dē lē-bā-rä-tō′rā). See **Alunno, Niccolò.**

Niccolò di Pietro (dē pye′trō). Venetian painter; active at the end of the 14th and the beginning of the 15th century. Tuscan, rather than Venetian and Byzantine, influence appears in the solidity of his figures, the realism of his heads, and in his brighter coloring. His signed *Virgin Enthroned* (1394) is in the Accademia at Venice. A *Madonna*, the central panel of a triptych, painted in 1409 in the Church of S. Maria dei Miracoli at Venice, has been entirely repainted. Examples of his work are at Pesaro, Rome (National Gallery), Rovigo, Verucchio, Cambridge (Massachusetts), Detroit, and New York.

Niccolò di Pietro Gerini (dē pye′trō je-rē′nē). See **Gerini, Niccolò di Pietro.**

Niccolò del Priore (del prē-ō′rā). Perugian painter; active between 1480 and 1513. He was influenced by Caporali. Several examples of his work are in the National Gallery of Umbria at Perugia.

Niccolò di Ser Sozzo Tegliacci (dē ser sôt′-tzō tā-lyät′chē). See **Tegliacci, Niccolò di Ser Sozzo.**

Niccolò di Tommaso (dē tôm-mä′sō). Florentine painter; active from 1343 to 1376. The first notice of him is of 1343, when he joined the guild of painters at Florence. A painter in the manner of his contemporaries Nardo and Jacopo di Cione and Giovanni del Biondo, his work has the features of 14th-century Florentine painting as it reached toward the technical and artistic fulfillment of Renaissance painting. The slit eyes, lack of relief, awkward attempt at articulation of limbs, and an overall sense of fantasy in his frescoes of *The Creation* and *Adam Delving and Eve Spinning* at Pistoia exemplify these features. As was customary at the time, the divine figures are many times the size of the human figures in *The Madonna and Child with Four Saints* and the devout *Coronation of the Virgin*, Walters Art Gallery, Baltimore. Among the several portable triptychs he painted is that of *St. Bridget's Vision of the Nativity*, Vatican, with Byzantine echoes in its angular forms and composition. Other paintings on St. Bridget's vision (the saint died in 1373) are at New Haven and in the Johnson Collection, Philadelphia. Examples of Niccolò di Tommaso's work are at Fiesole, in the Uffizi, Accademia, and other collections at Florence, at Naples, Parma, Pisa, Turin, Venice, Prague, Vienna, the Museum of Fine Arts, Boston, Kansas City (Missouri), and elsewhere.

Niccolò da Verona (dä vā-rō'nä). Veronese painter; active in the second half of the 15th century. He perhaps followed Mantegna to Mantua and there signed and dated (1463) a fresco, *Madonna and Child Enthroned and Saints*, in the Church of Ognissanti. Though he was a follower of Mantegna and had undoubtedly seen his altarpiece in the Church of S. Zeno at Verona, his own fresco, with its two kneeling donors on a much smaller scale than the Madonna and saints, looks back to an earlier period in the development of painting. Other works attributed to him are *Madonna of the Angels*, S. Maria degli Angeli, and *St. John the Baptist*, S. Barnaba, both at Mantua.

Niccolò da Voltri (dä vōl'trē). Ligurian painter; active 1385–1417. His work shows the influence of Barnaba da Modena and Taddeo di Bartolo, both of whom worked at Genoa. Of the works attributed to Niccolò, most are also attributed to Barnaba da Modena. A half-length *Madonna*, with four angels and two tiny portraits of donors, in the gallery at Savona, is attributed to Niccolò, and there are works at Genoa (Palazzo Bianco, S. Donato, and S. Rocco), and Baltimore (Walters Art Gallery).

Niccolò Pisano (pē-zä'nō). Ferrarese painter; active at the end of the 15th century and in the first half of the 16th century. A painter of modest endowment, he was influenced by Francia and Garofalo, and to some extent by the Venetians. He worked at Pisa, Pietrasanta, Ferrara (1499–1514), Bologna, and again at Pisa (1537–1538). Among his works are a *Madonna and Saints* (1512), Brera, Milan, *The Punishment of the Sons of Aaron* (1537), cathedral, Pisa, and *Holy Family*, Uffizi, which is typical of his archaicizing manner.

Nicholas III (nik'ō-ląs). [Original name, **Giovanni Gaetani Orsini.**] Pope (1277–1280); b. at Rome, c1216; d. at Soriano, near Viterbo, August 22, 1280. A handsome and energetic member of the powerful Orsini family of Rome, he sought with exceptional intensity to increase the influence of the papacy in Italy and to advance the fortunes of his family. To the former end, he invited Rudolf of Hapsburg to come to Rome to receive the imperial crown, and in return won from Rudolf the cession of the Romagna to the papacy. He also replaced Charles I of Naples as papal vicar with his own nephew, in order to weaken Charles' dominance of Italian affairs, and attempted to reconcile Guelphs and Ghibellines in Tuscany. He possessed superior talents as a diplomat, although his efforts at promoting reunion with Constantinople ultimately failed. He established (July, 1278) a constitution barring foreigners from holding civil offices in Rome in an attempt to eliminate foreign control of the city; and he sent Franciscan missionaries to Persia and China. He was succeeded by Martin IV.

Nicholas IV. [Original name, **Girolamo Masci d'Ascoli.**] Pope (1288–1292); b. at Ascoli; d. at Rome, April 4, 1292. He succeeded Honorius IV, after an interval of ten months during which the papacy was vacant. He had been a Franciscan monk and a cardinal, and was the first of his order to become pope. Without personal or family ambitions, he sought to restore peace to Sicily and crowned (1289) Charles II king of Naples and Sicily. In return, Charles recognized papal suzerainty. In connection with the Sicilian question Nicholas arranged (1291) a treaty by which the Aragonese would ultimately leave Sicily in favor of the Angevins. The treaty was never implemented. He endeavored to launch a crusade for the recovery of the Holy places, and sent missionaries to China. He was succeeded by Celestine V.

Nicholas V. [Original name, **Pietro Rainalducci.**] Antipope; b. in Corvaro; d. October, 1333. He was elected with the support of Louis the Bavarian (the emperor Louis IV) in opposition to John XXII in 1328. He was deposed in 1330.

Nicholas V. [Original name, **Tommaso Parentucelli.**] Pope (1447–1455); b. at Sarzana, Tuscany, November 15, 1397; d. at Rome, March 24, 1455. Of humble background, he early showed great aptitude and enthusiasm for the new learning that came to be called humanism. He began his studies at the University of Bologna, but had to abandon them for lack of money. He went to Florence, the center of humanistic studies, and became a tutor in two prominent families there. After two years, in which the love of learning and the arts that marked his whole life was fostered, he returned to Bologna, took a degree of Master of Theology, and then entered the service of Niccolò Albergati, bishop of Florence. When the latter became a cardinal (1426), Tommaso accompanied him to Rome, then back to Florence when Eugenius IV moved his court there. During this stay in Florence he was on friendly terms with the leading humanists of the time—Gianozzo Manetti, Giovanni Aurispa, Gasparo of Bologna, Poggio, and others—and met with them daily for literary discussions. He was named vice chamberlain (1443), bishop of Bologna (1444), and cardinal (December, 1446). A few months later, Eugenius died and Tommaso Parentucelli was elected, March 6, 1447, to succeed him. In grateful memory of Cardinal Albergati, who had been his benefactor and mentor, and of whom he had been the constant companion for more than twenty years, he took the name Nicholas V. He was noted as a man of peace, learned in theology, the Scriptures, and patristic literature. He was eloquent, modest, amiable and generous; simple and temperate in his habits, and impatient with ceremony.

Nicholas was immediately beset by political and diplomatic, as well as ecclesiastical problems. He cooled republican agitation in Rome by bestowing a measure of self-government. He rebuilt the walls and erected new fortifications to protect it from bands of mercenaries, often in the employ of his own vassals. He restored peace to the States of the Church and won the obedience of Bologna (1447), long a thorny problem for the papacy. Other temporal lords offered their obedience. He reached an agreement (1447) with Alfonso of Naples, whose army had been threateningly encamped at Tivoli, by which he recognized Ferrante, Alfonso's illegitimate son, as heir to Alfonso's throne. He signed the Concordat of Vienna (1448) with Frederick III, which secured recognition of papal rights regarding bishoprics, thus annuling, for Germany, some of the decrees of the Council of Basel. In 1449, the Council, which had moved to Lausanne, acknowledged him as the true pope; the antipope Felix V resigned and the schism and the long struggle between councils and the papacy ended in victory for the papacy. Nicholas later recognized some of the cardinals who had been named by the council and made Feilx a cardinal and papal legate. He proclaimed a jubilee for 1450. During that year thousands of pilgrims from all over Europe came to Rome. Some say as many as 40,000 entered the city daily. The figure is considered high but gives an idea of the throngs that visited the city. In the same year Nicholas canonized St. Bernardino of Siena. In 1452 he crowned Frederick III Holy Roman emperor, at Rome, the last such coronation to take place there. A few days earlier he had united Frederick and Leonora of Portugal in marriage. Both ceremonies were occasions of magnificent pageantry. He sent legates and ambassadors to use the influence of the Holy See to make peace between France and England, to counteract heresy and to preach and make reforms in Germany, Austria, and the Low Countries.

With all this activity, Nicholas set about carrying into execution his aim of making Rome the center of art and learning. "With him," says Pastor (*History of the Popes*), "the Christian Renaissance ascended the Pontifical Throne." A man of profound learning, with a passion for books and translations, he once remarked that if he had money to spend he would spend it on two things—books and buildings. As a student he had collected books and manuscripts to a greater extent than he could well afford. With the vast resources of the papacy at his command he could indulge his appetite for both books and buildings. He instructed his ambassadors to search the libraries, especially monastic libraries, in any area where they might chance to be. He hired translators to translate the Greek authors into Latin, and copyists to copy rare manuscripts. He wrote a beautiful hand himself and demanded the same of the copyists. Translators, whose work was not uniformly good, and copyists were paid fabulous sums. There was no comparison between their rewards and the much lower scale that was paid to artists. Because of Nicholas V's intense interest in the classical writers, many of whose works had been forgotten or neglected for centuries, a greatly increased portion of the treasure of the ancients was rediscovered and preserved. Through his copyists and translators knowledge of these works spread rapidly. His interest in the assembling of libraries was inexhaustible. When Cosimo de' Medici wished to build a library for the Badia at Fiesole, he was advised by Vespasiano, a Florentine bookseller whose customers included the most distinguished men of the time, to have copies made of books and manuscripts, as originals were by then too scarce. Nicholas V wrote out a list of books that should be copied. He did the same for the libraries of Federico da Montefeltro at Urbino and Alessandro Sforza at Pesaro. Of infinite service to future generations, he founded the Vatican Library and stocked it with from 5,000 to 9,000 volumes.

His building program was unlimited. In addition to repairing the aqueducts, bridges, and walls of the city, he sought to repair and restore churches, to rebuild the papal palace and St. Peter's, and to restore and repair the cities of the States of the Church. Architects, artists and craftsmen from all over Europe, but especially from Florence, came to carry out his designs. The roster of these includes the most notable names of the period. Workmen flocked into Rome. His ardent desire was to make Rome a city of splendid buildings and monuments for the glorification of the Church. Enea Silvio (later, Pope Pius II) said of him, "He erected magnificent buildings in his city, though he began more than he finished. . . . He attained success and fame in many great undertakings." Though he did not execute all the many plans he had made, it has been said of him that "single-handed, [he] turned the capital of Christendom into that brilliant center of art and learning that it became."

After a period of comparative peace and great productivity, Nicholas' last years were deeply troubled. From the cheerful, amiable, and impetuous man he had been he became reserved and saddened, and his natural timidity increased. In January, 1453, Stefano Porcari, a Roman nobleman whom he had honored and once magnanimously pardoned, plotted to seize and, if necessary, kill the pope and the cardinals during Mass in St. Peter's, and to make himself Tribune of Rome. The conspiracy was discovered. Porcari was taken, tried, and executed. In June of the same year came the stunning news of the fall of Constantinople (May 29, 1453) to the Turks. Nicholas' attempts to promote a crusade were a failure. He died March 24, 1455, after more than a year's illness. Nicholas, who had healed the schism, restored peace to Rome and the States of the Church, founded the Vatican Library, and generously used the influence and wealth of the Holy See to promote art and learning, was buried in St. Peter's. His epitaph was composed in Latin verse by the future Pope Pius II. Calixtus III was the successor of Nicholas V.

Nicholas of Cusa (kū'zä). [German, **Nikolaus von Cusa**; Latinized, **Nicolaus Cusanus**; Original name, **Nikolas Chrypffs**, or **Cryfts**, or **Krebs.**] German theologian, canon lawyer, and philosopher; b. at Cues (Cusa), near Trier, Germany, 1401; d. at Todi, Italy, August 11, 1464. He was educated by the Brothers of the Common Life at Deventer, then studied at Heidelberg, Padua, and Cologne. He knew Greek and added deep interest in mathematics and philosophy to his theological studies. At the troubled Council of Basel (1431–1449) he worked (1432–1436) earnestly for unity of the Christian church, and promoted reform of the calendar. He broke with the Conciliar party, however, became a supporter of the pope, and took a leading part in the Council of Ferrara-Florence (1438–1439) that sought to unite the Greek and Roman churches. Pope Nicholas V bestowed the red hat of a cardinal upon him in 1448, and in 1450 he was named bishop of Brixen (Bressanone), Italy. Eminently a diplomat, he was appointed a papal legate and traveled widely, correcting abuses in monasteries and sees, convoking synods, laboring to restore discipline and doctrine, trying to compose the Hussite schism, promoting a crusade against the Turks, mediating for peace between England and France, and working to heal the great schism between the Roman and Byzantine churches. He was active in exposing the False or Pseudo-Isidorian Decretals. One of the best and most zealous preachers of the 15th century, his sermons, in Germany, lasting two or three hours, were given in Latin and listened to with rapt attention by huge congregations that did not understand a word he was saying. They were compelled by his ardor and his sincerity. A man of "faith and love," noted alike for his learning and the purity of his life, he was possessed of real tolerance, and believed that all religions were really one, but that they were represented by different prophets according to the needs of different peoples. He had a broad humanistic training and, as did other humanists, collected manuscripts with enthusiasm. In 1429, on a mission to Germany for the Curia, he found some lost plays of Plautus and sent them back to Rome. By the time of his death he had a valuable collection of Hebrew, Greek, and Latin manuscripts, a collection that he left to a hospital he founded at Cues. Before Copernicus, Nicholas of Cusa perceived that the earth moves around the sun. His belief that God and the universe are one, and his pantheistic tendencies are thought to have anticipated Giordano Bruno. However, his ideas, though highly original, were developed on the basis of medieval Platonism, and were completely orthodox. In addition to his theological works he wrote mathematical and philosophical treatises. In his writings he stressed the need for experiment and observation to gain knowledge. His *Idiotae* (*Of Idiots*, or *Of the Unlearned*) deals with experiments and the need for accurate measurements of weight and time. He made many investigations of a physical and physiological nature and devised means to pursue them. His chief work, *De docta ignorantia* (*On Learned Ignorance*), has as its thesis that human knowledge is relative and that perfection in it is unattainable. A devoted and truly pious son of the Church, in some respects a mystic, he was also an important figure in the realm of science at a time when it was about to burst its bonds.

Nicholson (nik′ǫl-sǫn), **John.** Original name of **Lambert, John.**

Nicola da Guardiagrele (nē-kō′lä dä gwär-dyä-grā′lā). Goldsmith and sculptor; b. in the Abruzzi; d. by 1462. His most considerable activity was as a goldsmith, in which art he continued the medieval tradition followed in the Abruzzi. His early works were in the heavily ornamented flowery Gothic style. Later he was influenced by Tuscan goldsmiths and sculptors, and especially by Lorenzo Ghiberti. The influence of the latter is especially apparent in a number of processional crosses, as those at Guardiagrele (1431), Aquila (1434), Monticchio (1436), and St. John Lateran, Rome (1451), and in an altar frontal in the cathedral at Teramo. The last has panels with reliefs, some of which are copies of Ghiberti's reliefs on the Baptistery doors at Florence. Six bas-reliefs at Castel di Sangro and a group of *The Annunciation*, Bargello, Florence, are also attributed to him.

Nicola da Tolentino (dä tō-len-tē′nō), Saint. Ecclesiastic and preacher; b. at S. Angelo in Pontano, 1245; d. at Tolentino, September 10, 1305. He joined the Augustinian hermits at the age of 12, pursued his theological studies at Cingoli, and was ordained priest. He was a fervent and eloquent preacher for thirty years, and soon after his death began to be invoked as a saint. Pope John XXII began the process of canonization (1325) but the proceedings were interrupted, and it was not until 1446, under Pope Eugenius IV, that he was canonized.

Nicola da Verona (dä vā-rō′nä). Poet of the 14th century. In 1343 he dedicated his poem *Pharsale* to Niccolò I d'Este. The poem is written in a composite language, basically French but with many Italian elements. This was a form used traditionally by northern Italian writers of the period. The poem is a retelling of the Carolingian cycle. He also wrote a continuation of the poem *Entrée en Espagne*, on the entry of Charlemagne into Spain, written by an unknown Paduan poet of the 13th century. In his continuation, Nicola da Verona maintained the spirit of the original author. He was one of the early poets to relate the Carolingian legends to the history and legend of Italy. Among the episodes he added to the *Entrée en Espagne* is that of Isoré, the pagan knight who is converted and becomes count of Flanders.

Nicoletto da Modena (nē-kō-let′tō dä mô′-de-nä). North Italian engraver of the 16th century. His prints show a strong influence of Mantegna and Dürer.

Nicot (nē-kō), **Jean.** [Title, Sieur **de Villemain.**] French diplomat and scholar; b. at Nîmes, France, 1530; d. at Paris, May 5, 1600. He introduced (1560) the use of tobacco from Portugal, where he was ambassador, into France. Nicotine and the plant genus *Nicotiana* were named for him.

Nicuesa (nē-kwā′sä), **Diego de.** Spanish conquistador; b. at Baëza, Spain, c1465; d. probably in March, 1511. He went to Hispaniola in 1502, and in 1508 was empowered to conquer and govern the region from the Gulf of Darien to Cape Gracias á Dios. On the voyage from Santo Domingo he was wrecked and endured terrible suffering in Panama; only about 100 men survived. The colonists of Antigua, where his reinforcements stopped, offered to accept him as governor, but he acted in such an overbearing manner that the colonists rebelled, and he was forced to put to sea in an unseaworthy ship. He was never heard from again.

Nifo (nē′fō), **Agostino.** Philosopher; b. at Sessa (or in Calabria), 1473; d. at Salerno, 1538 or 1545. He taught at Padua, Naples, Pisa, Salerno, and Bologna. At Padua he came under the influence of Nicoletto Vernia, an adherent of Paduan Averroism, and adopted the doctrine of the unity of the intellect. He set forth his ideas on this in his *De intellectu et daemonibus* (Padua, 1492), in which he also expressed his views on immortality. His Averroism brought him into some conflict with the Church, although he never abandoned his Catholicism, and he sought reconciliation with Pope Leo X. The pope charged him to write a refutation of Pomponazzi's *De immortalitate animae.* Nifo's refutation was his *Tractatus de immortalitate animae contra Pomponatium* (Venice, 1518), in which he accused Pomponazzi of having misunderstood Aristotle and of having ignored Plato. This drew from Pomponazzi his *Defensorium contra Nyphum,* his defense of his theories. In addition, Nifo wrote many commentaries on the works of Aristotle (collected in fourteen volumes), *De pulchro et amore* (Rome, 1531), *Opuscula moralia et politica* (Paris, 1645), and *De regnandi peritia* (Naples, 1523), which is a free translation into Latin of Machiavelli's *The Prince.*

Nigreti (nē-grā′tē) or **Nigretti** (-gret′tē), **Iacopo.** See **Palma, Jacopo.**

Ninfale fiesolano (nēn-fä′lā fye-zō-lä′nō). Italian idyll by Giovanni Boccaccio (1346–1349). It is the tale of Affrico and the nymph Mensola. The faithless nymph is turned into a stream that flows into the Arno. Affrico kills himself and is also metamorphosed–into a stream that similarly joins the Arno. Lyric descriptions express Boccaccio's love and appreciation of the countryside near Florence.

Niño (nē′nyō), **Pedro Alonso.** [Called "**el Negro.**"] Spanish navigator; b. at Moguer, Spain, c1455; d. c1505. He was connected with several Portuguese expeditions to the West African coast, commanded a fleet which sailed to Santo Domingo, and was with Columbus on his third voyage. In 1499 he was associated with Cristóbal Guerra in a trading expedition to the pearl coast (Venezuela), which was the first financially profitable voyage to the American coast.

Niza (nē′sä), **Marcos de.** [Also **Fray Marcos.**] Franciscan missionary, discoverer of New Mexico; b. at Nice, France; d. at Mexico City, March 25, 1558. By order of the viceroy he went north from Culiacán in 1539 (into what is today New Mexico and Arizona), and in May of that year reached the region called Cibola (the Zuñi pueblos), but turned back. His official report is truthful and judicious, but after his return to Mexico the viceroy caused him to circulate exaggerated reports, in order to influence idlers to go to Cibola in quest of treasure. This led to the expedition of Coronado, which he accompanied, to the valley of the upper Rio Grande. Their failure to find riches cost him his reputation.

Nizolio (nēt-tsō′lyō), **Mario.** Philosopher and man of letters; b. at Brescello, 1498; d. at Sabbioneta, 1576. His great work was in support of the Ciceronian style and language. The issue of imitating Cicero had become a burning one with the rise and increased use of Italian as a literary language. His first great work on the subject was *Observationes in M. T. Ciceronem,* 1536, which was reprinted many times under the title *Thesaurus Ciceronianus.* This established Nizolio as one of the most fervent defenders of the Ciceronian style. However, he did not believe that the ancients should be considered as the source of all wisdom, and distinguished between Cicero the writer and orator and Cicero the thinker. His beliefs and writings led to an exchange of polemics with Marcantonio Majoragio, and also, led to another great work by Nizolio on the true origin of philosophy. The language of the ancients could be used to express thought most lucidly and best, but the language of the ancients should not be confused with the thoughts they themselves expressed in it.

Noailles (no-ȧy′), **Antoine de.** French admiral and diplomat; b. 1504; d. March 11, 1562. He was ambassador to England (1553–1556).

Nogarola (nō-gä-rō′lä), **Isotta.** Humanist; b. at Verona, 1418; d. there, 1466. With her sister Ginevra (b. 1419; d. 1465), she received a solid humanistic education under Martino Rizzoni, himself a pupil of Guarino da Verona. She continued her studies at Venice, but in 1438 was forced by the plague and the war between Venice and Milan to flee from the city with her mother and brothers. She returned to Verona, and there gave up her classical studies and turned to theology. She left some letters and other writings that reveal her knowledge of Latin, the classics, and a certain sincerity. She is more known for the fact that she pursued classical studies at this early date than for any literary attainments.

Nola (nō′lä), Count of. Title of various members of the Orsini family.

Norandino (nō-rän-dē′nō). In Lodovico Ariosto's *Orlando Furioso*, a king of Damascus. He welcomed Grifone and Aquilante to his kingdom. He held splendid tournaments to celebrate the rescue of his wife Lucina from the orc.

Norfolk (nôr′fọk), Duke of. Title held since 1483 by various members of the **Howard** family. The title ranks as the highest in the peerage of England, being preceded only by titles held by members of the royal family. Before the Howards, the title was held by members of the Mowbray family.

North (nôrth), Sir **Thomas.** English translator; b. c1535; d. c1601. He translated *The Diall of Princes* (1557) from an Italian work by Guevara, the *Moral Philosophy* of Doni, and an Italian version of a book of Arabian fables, *Kalilah and Dimnah*. His translation of Plutarch (*Lives of the Noble Grecians and Romans*) was taken from the French of Jacques Amyot and first appeared in 1579. It was from this work that Shakespeare took much of his material for *Antony and Cleopatra, Coriolanus,* and *Julius Caesar*.

Norton (nôr′tọn), **Thomas.** English lawyer, translator, and author; b. at London, 1532; d. at Sharpenhoe, Bedfordshire, England, 1584. He wrote (with Sackville) the first English tragedy, *Gorboduc, or Ferrex and Porrex*. He published a *Translation of Calvin's Institutes* (1561), and translated many of the psalms in the Psalter of Sternhold and Hopkins (1561).

Nostradamus (nos-trạ-dā′mus). [Original name, **Michel de Notredame** (or **Nostredame**).] French astrologer and physician; b. at St.-Rémy, France, December 14, 1503; d. at Salon, near Aix, France, July 2, 1566. He is noted as the author of a book of prophecies entitled *Centuries* (1555) which has been the subject of much controversy.

Nowell (nō′ẹl), **Robert.** English lawyer; b. in Lancashire, England, c1520; d. at Gray's Inn, London, February 6, 1569. He is principally remembered for a fund which he established by his will for benefactions to the poor. A list left by his executors of the persons to whom money was paid contains important facts about Edmund Spenser (who was one of the poor scholars benefited from time to time).

Nucci (nöt′chē), **Benedetto.** Umbrian painter; b. at Gubbio; known from 1515; d. after 1588. After training in a local workshop he became a follower of Dono Doni and Raffaello del Colle. His signed and dated (1588) *Baptism of S. Domitilla* is in the National Gallery of Umbria at Perugia.

Núñez Vela (nö′nyez bā′lä), **Blasco.** First viceroy of Peru; b. at Ávila, Spain, c1490; killed in the battle of Anaquito, near Quito, Ecuador, January 18, 1546. He was appointed viceroy with the special mission of promulgating the "New Laws." Opposition to the New Laws led to a revolt headed by Gonzalo Pizarro. After he killed the factor Suarez de Carbajal, he was arrested by the *audiencia* and put in charge of one of the auditors to be sent back to Spain for trial. Released near the coast, he collected forces against Pizarro but was defeated.

Nun's Priest's Tale, The. One of Chaucer's *Canterbury Tales*. It was suggested by the *Roman du Renart*, and is the story of Chanticleer, who escaped from the jaws of the fox by his cunning in making the latter open his mouth to speak.

Nuzi (nöt′tsē), **Allegretto.** Painter of Fabriano, in the Marches; d. September, 1374. Fabriano was the center of artistic activity in the Marches. Nuzi was the most important painter there in the 14th century, had many followers, and was the founder of the Marchigian school in the international Gothic style. He may have spent some time in Florence. The influence of Bernardo Daddi in his early work disappears with the softer and less rigid drawing of his later paintings. In his frescoes especially, which are in a popular narrative vein, there is a realism that indicates the influence of Giotto and, later, Orcagna. His oldest known works are frescoes (1345–1349) in the Church of S. Lucia (now the sacristy of S. Domenico) at Fabriano. They include a *Crucifixion* with a real feeling of tragedy, a *Death of the Virgin* and a *Coronation of the Virgin*. There are also frescoes on the life of St. Lawrence in the cathedral at Fabriano. A triptych, *Madonna and Child*, signed and dated (1369), is at Macerata. Another triptych, *Madonna and Child with SS. Michael and Ursula*, signed and dated (1365), and his *Mystic Marriage of St. Catherine* are in the Vatican. Other works are at Apiro, San Severino, Urbino, Agen, Berlin, Berne, Strasbourg, Zurich, Birmingham (Alabama), Brunswick (Maine, Bowdoin College), Chicago, Detroit, Philadelphia (Johnson Collection), Portland (Oregon), Raleigh (North Carolina), and Washington.

O

Oberto (ō-ber'tō), **Francesco d'.** Ligurian painter; active at Genoa, 1357–1368. A *Virgin with SS. Dominic and John the Evangelist*, showing Sienese influence, is at Genoa.

Obrecht (ō'brecht) or **Obertus** (ō-bėr'tus), **Jacob.** [Also, **Hobrecht, Hobertus.**] Dutch contrapuntal composer and conductor; b. perhaps at Utrecht, Netherlands, c1430; d. at Ferrara, Italy, 1505. His works include masses, hymns, and motets as well as some secular pieces.

Ocampo (ō-käm'pō), **Sebastian de.** Spanish navigator; b. c1465; d. after 1509. He was one of the early colonists of Hispaniola. In 1508 he was sent by the governor of that island to explore the coasts of Cuba. He circumnavigated it, thus proving that it was an island.

Occleve (ok'lēv), **Thomas.** [Also, **Hoccleve.**] English poet; b. c1370; d. c1450. He was the author of a *Complaint*, a *Dialogue*, and *La Male Règle* (1406), all autobiographical, and *Mother of God*, a religious poem, once ascribed to Geoffrey Chaucer. His principal work is considered to have been *De Regimine Principum* (c1311–1412), a long poem on the responsibilities of a prince or ruler, dedicated to Henry, prince of Wales (later Henry V.)

Ochino (ō-kē'nō) or **Occhino** (ōk-kē'nō), **Bernardino.** Reformer, preacher, and writer; b. at Siena, 1487; d. at Schlackau, in Moravia, c1565. From an early age he showed a strong inclination for an ascetic life, and while still young entered the Franciscan order. He studied medicine at Perugia and followed this with the study of the Scriptures and philosophy. In 1534 he entered the Capuchins and was general of the order in 1538 and 1541. He became noted as a preacher throughout Italy and was in contact with other thinkers, including Vittoria Colonna, Cardinal Pole, Jacopo Sadoleto, Marcantonio Flamminio, who were influenced by the ideas of the Reformation. Because of his friendship with Juan de Valdés, and his interest in the Lutheran idea of justification through faith, and because of some of his utterances reflecting this, he was called (1542) to Rome to answer to the Inquisition newly established there. On his way to answer the charges he talked with other reformers. They advised him to flee. He fled to Geneva, where he became a prize convert of John Calvin. He also married and definitely broke with the Church. He became a minister at Augsburg in 1545, fled to England in 1547 when the forces of the emperor Charles V took the city. Thomas Cranmer welcomed him. He remained in England, in possession of a canonry, until the accession of Mary Tudor ("Bloody Mary") to the English throne. He returned to Switzerland (1555), where he was for a time a pastor at Zurich, but was expelled (1563) by the Swiss Protestants because of the extreme liberality of his views. He had expressed them in his *Thirty Dialogues*, in which he went counter to doctrine on the subjects of polygamy, divorce, and the Trinity. He went to Poland, then, hounded by the papal nuncio, to Moravia. There, having lost three children in the plague, he died. Ochino produced many writings. Of these, *Prediche nove*, a collection of sermons, and *Dialoghi sette* were written before his break with the Church. Works after that event include more sermons, treatises, and many essays on matters of religion and ritual. His writings present his modifications of received theology. His *A Tragedy* or *Dialogue of the unjust usurped Primacy of the Bishop of Rome* (1549) is thought by some to have influenced John Milton's *Paradise Lost*.

Ochis (ō'kēs), **Andreolo de.** Late 14th-century collector of Latin and Greek manuscripts. His passion for collecting was such that he was said to be willing to give up his house, land, and even his wife to add to his library.

Ockeghem (dok′ẹ-gem), **Jean d'**. See **Okeghem, Jean d'** (or **Jan van**).

Ockham or **Occam** (ok′ạm), **William of.** [Known as **Doctor Invincibilis, Venerabilis Inceptor, Princeps Nominalium.**] English scholastic philosopher; b. at Ockham, Surrey, some time between 1270 and 1300; d. at Munich, c1349. A Franciscan, he studied at Oxford and Paris, where he was the pupil of his later great rival Duns Scotus. In 1322 he was present at the Franciscan assembly at Perugia that defended against Pope John XXII the principle of evangelical poverty. He was called to Avignon (1328) and imprisoned there for heresy, but escaped after a few months (along with several other rebels, including Michael of Cesena, the general of the Franciscans) to Pisa, where he was taken under the protection of the emperor Louis IV. The emperor and the pope were engaged in a struggle concerning the temporal power of the papacy and Ockham contributed to the imperial cause with his *Opus nonaginta Dierum* (1330), an answer to John XXII's attack on Michael of Cesena, and with other polemical writings. He became general of the order after Michael of Cesena's death in 1342. His greatest work, the *Dialogus* (c1343), is an attack on the civil authority of the papacy and includes also arguments against even the spiritual powers claimed by the pope. Ockham's philosophy is a revival of the nominalism of such earlier philosophers as Peter Abelard. He distinguishes between the fact and its name: the individual thing is the reality, the universal (its name or noun) is an abstraction and a generalization, and therefore a subjective and conventional tool. Such abstractions have no actual relation to reality; therefore, intellectual knowledge is not valid; the only true approach to such questions of reality as immortality, the nature of the soul, and the existence of God is through intuition. The principle known as Ockham's razor or the law of parsimony is a consequence of this logic: *Entia non sunt multiplicanda praeter necessitatem* (*Entities must not be multiplied beyond what is necessary*), that is, an argument must be shaved down to its absolutely essential and simplest terms.

Oddi (ōd′dē). Ancient and noble family of Perugia, whose members achieved prominent places in the civic life of the city from the 13th century. The family was aristocratic and Guelph and the rival of the Ghibelline Baglioni family. In the civil strife that wracked Perugia in the 14th and 15th centuries, the Oddi were overcome by the Baglioni, partly as the result of two massacres, one in 1455 and the other in 1488, and lost all their holdings. The loss was confirmed in 1489 by Pope Innocent VIII in spite of the previous loyalty and devotion of the Oddi to the papacy.

Oddi, Marco degli. Teacher; b. at Padua, 1526; d. there, July 25, 1591. He was the son of Oddo degli Oddi (1478–1558), was a professor of logic, philosophy, and medicine at Padua, and introduced clinical teaching in a hospital at Padua.

Oddi, Oddo degli. Physician; b. at Padua, 1478; d. there, February 5, 1558. He was learned in Latin and Greek, taught classical studies at Padua, practiced medicine at Venice, then was called to Padua, where he held the chair of medicine. He was such a faithful follower of Galen that he was given the epithet "the soul of Galen."

Oddi, Sforza degli. Writer and jurist; b. at Perugia, 1540; d. at Parma, 1611. In his young manhood he wrote comedies in which he attempted to avoid the buffoonery that was usual in such works by introducing serious meaning and intent with overtones of comedy. Two of his so-called comedies were *I morti vivi* (Perugia, 1572) and *La prigione d'amore* (Florence, 1590). About 1572 he gave up the writing of comedies and devoted himself to his legal studies. He taught at Perugia, Macerata, Pisa, Pavia, Padua, and Parma.

Oderisi (ō-dā-rē′zē), **Roberto.** Neapolitan painter; active in the second half of the 14th century. He worked for King Robert of Naples and for King Charles III, who made him a member of the royal household. An uneven painter, he was yet vigorous and individual, and in his progress from the tradition of Simone Martini to the more robust Florentine forms had a great influence on Neapolitan painting. To him are attributed a series of frescoes, dating from about 1360, on the sacraments and the glorification of the church, in the Church of S. Maria Incoronata at Naples. The frescoes, already in poor condition, were badly damaged in World War II.

Other works at Naples include frescoes in S. Lorenzo Maggiore, and a *Madonna of Humility* in S. Domenico Maggiore. There are also works at Eboli (S. Francesco), Venosa, and Cambridge (Massachusetts).

Oderisi da Gubbio (dä göb′byō). Miniaturist; active in the middle of the 13th century. He was at Bologna in 1268 and several times thereafter, and is thought to have been one of the principal artists of the highly productive Bolognese school of illumination. No authentic work of his survives. Dante cites him in the *Divina Commedia* (*Purgatorio*, xi) as the "Honor of Gubbio" and of the art of illumination. According to Dante, he is in Purgatory because of his pride.

Odorico da Pordenone (ō-dō-rē′kō dä pôr-dā-nō′nā). Missionary and chronicler; b. at Pordenone, c1265; d. at Udine, January 14, 1331. At an early age he determined to enter the monastic life, and did so at the age of 15. He was ordained in 1290. He is particularly remembered for the travels he undertook as a missionary to China. He set out for the East in 1314 (or 1318) and did not return until 1330. On his return he dictated an account of his travels to a fellow ecclesiastic in the Convent of St. Anthony at Padua. His account of his journey, with long stays on the way, from Venice to Peking ranks with the accounts of Marco Polo, Niccolò dei Conti, and one or two others, as one of the oldest and most important sources of information in the west on the lands in the Far East. The lands of which he wrote include Persia, India, China, the islands of Java, Borneo, Sumatra, and Ceylon. On his way home, overland, he passed through Tibet and probably visited Lhasa.

Oertel (ör′tel), **Abraham.** See **Ortelius.**

Oggiono (dôd-jō′nō), **Marco d'.** See **Marco d'Oggiono.**

Okeghem (dō′ke-gem) or **Ockeghem** (dok′e-gem), **Jean d'** (or **Jan van**). [Also, **Johannes Ockenheim.**] Contrapuntal composer of the second Netherlands school; b. in East Flanders, c1430; d. c1495. He was a composer of religious music, such as masses, canons, motets, and chansons.

Oldcastle (ōld′kȧs-l), Sir **John.** [Called Lord **Cobham.**] English nobleman; born in Herefordshire, England; burned at London, December 25, 1417. He was a leader of the Lollards. He became a friend of the prince of Wales (later Henry V). He was called upon to abjure the tenets of Wycliffe, but refused and was imprisoned in the Tower. He escaped and became involved in several plots to overthrow the king. He was captured and burned alive as a heretic. In the *Famous Victories of Henry V* Oldcastle is depicted as a bosom friend of the king, but when Shakespeare adapted it as *Henry IV* the character was changed to Sir John Falstaff, and bears no resemblance to the real Oldcastle.

Olgiati (ōl-jä′tē), **Girolamo.** One of the three conspirators who murdered Galeazzo Maria Sforza in the Church of S. Stefano, on December 26, 1476. He and his companions, Carlo Visconti and Giovanni Lampugnani, had been imbued by their humanist teacher with the ideals of republican Rome and an idealized vision of the liberty that obtained there. In addition, Galezazzo Maria had wounded Olgiati in his honor by outraging Olgiati's sister. The three youths resolved to kill the tyrant. They spent some days practicing dagger thrusts on each other, and agreed that the most certain opportunity to kill the tyrant would arise when he was in church. Once they had vowed to carry out their plan Olgiati invoked the blessing of St. Ambrose, patron saint of Milan, on the undertaking, since it was to free the saint's city. The young men expected that the nobles and plebeians would rise to support them once the death of Galeazzo became known. In the event, each youth stabbed Galeazzo twice and he died almost instantly. Olgiati escaped but his colleagues were captured and put to death. He was captured a few days later. The people had not risen up against the tyranny. While imprisoned, Olgiati wrote or dictated an account of the conspiracy, expressing the highest ideal of republican liberty and deeply religious sentiments, as well as the conviction that he had performed a noble deed. Even under the torture to which he was subjected he did not lose courage, secure in the belief that his glory would be eternal because he had rid the world of a tyrant.

Olid (ō-lēᴛʜ′), **Cristóbal de.** Spanish captain; b. probably at Baëza, Spain, c1487; killed in Honduras near the end of 1524. He was prominent under Hernando Cortés in the conquest of Mexico, and was sent by Cortés in January, 1524, to conquer Honduras. On arrival there he threw off the authority of Cortés, who sent Francisco de las Casas against him.

Olimpia (ō-lēm′pyä). In Lodovico Ariosto's *Orlando Furioso*, a princess of Holland, who is first loved then betrayed by Bireno. He abandons her on a desert island as she sleeps (in a passage reminiscent of Theseus and Ariadne), and she is attacked by the orc, a sea monster. Orlando saves her from the orc and she marries Oberto, who slays Bireno.

Olimpo da Sassoferrato (ō-lēm′pō dä säs-sō-fer-rä′tō), **Baldassarre.** Poet; b. after 1480; d. c1540. A prolific poet, little is known of his life except that he wandered from place to place. He wrote sonnets, madrigals, *capitoli*, eclogues, and lyrics in other forms. Many of his poems are love lyrics. They include *Olimpia* (Perugia, 1518), *Gloria d'Amore* (Perugia, 1520), *Camilla* (Perugia, 1522), and *Pegasea* (Venice, 1524). He also wrote on religious themes, *Parthenia*, and collected some of his lyrics on love and on political subjects in *Nova Phenice* (Venice, 1524). The tone of much of his work is popular.

Olindo (ō-lēn′dō). In Torquato Tasso's *Gerusalemme liberata*, a Christian youth in Jerusalem who has long and silently loved Sofronia. See **Sofronia.**

Oliverio (ō-lē-vā′ryō), **Alessandro.** Bergamasque painter; documented from 1532 to 1544. He employed his modest gifts at Venice and was a follower of Palma Vecchio. Later he was influenced by Girolamo da Santacroce, whose characteristics appear in Oliverio's romantic landscapes. He left a number of portraits; examples of his painting are at Dublin, Florence, Venice, Padua, and elsewhere.

Oliverotto da Fermo (ō-lē-vā-rōt′tō dä fer′mō). Captain; b. at Fermo, c1475; strangled at Senigallia, January 1, 1503. An orphan, he was brought up by his uncle Giovanni Fogliani at Fermo. In 1495 he entered the service of the captain Paolo Vitelli and went through many campaigns with him. He later served under Vitellozzo Vitelli, Paolo's brother, who was one of Cesare Borgia's captains. By his daring and skill he became an outstanding leader of the troops. In a brief visit to Fermo he was chosen prior of the city, and later resolved to seize complete power there. He visited the city and gave a banquet (January, 1502) for the most prominent citizens, including his uncle. At the conclusion of the festivities he brought in his men and had all his guests murdered. Master now of Fermo, he held the power by tyranny and terror. In the same year he entered into a conspiracy with other captains to curb the power of Cesare Borgia. The conspiracy was partly successful, but later Oliverotto was reconciled with Cesare and allowed himself to be deceived by the wily Borgia. Cesare invited the captains who had taken part in the conspiracy to a banquet at Senigallia, without their guards. They accepted and Cesare had them all strangled. Oliverotto da Fermo is cited by Machiavelli in *The Prince* as an example of one who made himself ruler by crime and wickedness and met his end by the same means.

Ondegardo (ōn-dā-gär′ᴛʜō), **Polo de.** Spanish lawyer and antiquarian; b. at Salamanca, Spain, c1500; d. probably at Potosí, in Upper Peru (now Bolivia), c1575. He made a special study of Inca laws and customs, with the object of engrafting the best of them on the Spanish legislation. His two *Relaciones* or reports (1561 and 1571) are still in manuscript, but have been freely used by historians.

Orazia (ō-rä′zyä). Tragedy by Pietro Aretino, based on an incident in Livy concerning the combat between the Horatii and the Curiatii.

Orbecche (ôr-bek′kā). Tragedy by Giambattista Cinzio Giraldi, produced at Ferrara in 1541. A horror story in the Senecan manner, it is more rhetoric than drama.

Orbicciani (ōr-bēt-chä′nē), **Bonaggiunta.** Tuscan poet; b. near Lucca, c1220; d. before 1300. He was one of the so-called Sicilian poets, and a follower of one of the little schools of poets that grew up around Guittone d'Arezzo. His canzoni and sonnets adhere strictly to the conventions of courtly love, but he is somewhat freer and more realistic in his ballate. Dante passes a harsh judgment on him in his *De vulgari eloquentia* and places him in Purgatory in the *Divina Commedia*.

Orcagna (ör-kä′nyä), **Andrea.** [Original name, **Andrea di Cione**; called **Arcagnuolo,** of which name **Orcagna** is a variant.] Florentine painter, sculptor, and architect; b. at Florence, c1308; d. c1368. Called the greatest Florentine painter after Giotto, and the greatest of his day, only one of his paintings now survives in its entirety. It is an altarpiece, *Christ in Majesty*, in the Strozzi Chapel of the Church of S. Maria Novella, Florence. The altarpiece, signed and dated (1357), is a five-paneled polyptych. Christ, in a mandorla formed by cherubs and their folded wings, occupies the central panel, angels kneel at His feet. Christ hands the keys to kneeling St. Peter on His left and doctrine to St. Thomas Aquinas on His right. Behind St. Peter stands St. John the Baptist (the patron saint of Florence). Behind St. Thomas stands the Virgin. The outside panels are occupied by St. Lawrence and St. Paul on one end and St. Catherine of Alexandria and St. Michael. The predella is in three panels. The graceful draperies of the majestic and grave figures have an almost sculptural quality in their modeling and relief. Andrea was the brother of Nardo di Cione, Jacopo di Cione, and Matteo di Cione, also artists, and they often worked with him. Of the many paintings admired and recorded by such early writers as Ghiberti, little survives. An altarpiece of *St. Matthew*, now in the Uffizi, Florence, was designed by him but, except for the central panel, was executed by his brother Jacopo. Fragments of frescoes on *The Triumph of Death*, *The Last Judgment* and *Hell*, in the nave of the Church of S. Croce, Florence, and some figures of prophets in the vault of S. Maria Novella, are also extant. *The Triumph of Death*, probably painted soon after the Black Death, is a masterpiece of mid-14th-century Florentine painting, notable for the power with which Orcagna rendered his profound awareness of the fragility of life and the imminence of death. A polyptych, *Madonna and Child with Saints*, Accademia, Florence, and *Madonna and Child with Angels*, National Gallery, Washington, were executed with his brother Jacopo. From his father he learned the goldsmith's art, and he probably studied sculpture under Andrea Pisano. He was a member of the Guild of Physicians and Apothecaries in 1343, and of the Sculptors' Guild in 1352. As a sculptor his greatest work, and one of the greatest of the century, is the marble tabernacle, or ciborium, he designed and executed, with assistants, for Orsanmichele, completed c1359. The tabernacle, architecturally a modified Gothic, is richly ornamented with twisted columns and statues, carving in relief, mosaic, and painting. (The *Madonna* now in it, however, is by Bernardo Daddi.) The relief of the *Death and Assumption of the Virgin*, which occupies the back of the tabernacle, is a masterpiece and is illustrative of Andrea's style as a sculptor—precise and restrained modeling, and a rhythm of composition that foretells the broader conceptions of the Renaissance. While working on the tabernacle, Andrea was architect in charge at Orsanmichele. In 1359 he went to Orvieto, where he worked on the façade of the Cathedral, for which he designed a mosaic. In his later years he was one of the principal advisers on the work for the cathedral at Florence. Orcagna is an early example of the Renaissance genius who was equally gifted and effective in several fields.

Ordelaffi (ôr-dā-läf′fē). Lords of Forlì and other lands of the Romagna, documented from the end of the 12th century, active in the life of the city from the end of the 13th century. Ghibellines, Dante speaks of them as lords of Forlì in 1300 (*Inferno*, xxvii) and, as a Bianchi exile, was briefly under the protection of Scarpetta Ordelaffi in 1303. Scarpetta clearly established himself as lord by 1307. A conspicuous member of the family, as well as of the Romagna in the 14th century, was Francesco Ordelaffi. From 1333 his state was composed of Forlì, Forlimpopoli, Cesena, and various smaller towns. In 1337, having previously been excommunicated, he was pardoned and named the Church's vicar of his state. Struggles with the Church, which claimed Forlì as a fief, were continual. Cardinal Albornoz, the papal general, was sent to subdue the Ordelaffi and reclaim their state. He found it one of the most stubborn of the states in the Romagna in its resistance. A crusade was launched (1356) and the following year, after a celebrated defense by Francesco's wife, the legendary Cia Ubaldini, Cesena fell. Forlì surrendered after a long siege (1359). Francesco kept only Forlimpopoli and Castrocaro. He tried to regain his city with the aid of the Visconti, but was unsuccessful and ended his days (1374) as a condottiere, first in the pay of the Visconti and then of Venice. His son Sinibaldo regained Forlì with Florentine help in 1376 and was named vicar (1379). Sinibaldo's nephews, Pino (d. 1402) and Cecco succeeded him. Cecco was slain by the people (1405) and for a few years Forlì was a free commune. In 1411 two illegitimate cousins regained power. The first, Giorgio, seized the second, Antonio, kept him imprisoned and ruled alone until his death (1422). Antonio, released on the death of his cousin, seized the city in 1433. He was succeeded (1448) by his sons, of whom Cecco III governed alone until he was imprisoned and put to death (1466), it was said by his brother Pino III. This Pino III was bathed in the sinister atmosphere of family crimes that often typified the princelings of the 15th century in Italy. He was accused of poisoning his first wife (Barbara Manfredi), his second wife, his brother Cecco's wife (Elizabetta Manfredi, Barbara's sister), and other members of the family, and appears to have been poisoned himself by his third wife (1480). Thereafter, rival descendants of Pino III and Cecco III struggled for the lordship. Their strife was summarily ended when Pope Sixtus IV invested his nephew, Girolamo Riario, with the city (1480), although Pino's descendants continued to fight for it. The last of the Ordelaffi was Ludovico, who died at Ravenna in 1504. The Ordelaffi, though violence against kinsmen was commonplace, were patrons of the arts and letters and builders. Among the monuments to their energy is the Palazzo del Podestà.

Orellana (ō-rā-lyä′nä), **Francisco de.** Spanish soldier; b. at Trujillo, Spain, c1490; d. probably in Venezuela, c1546. He was the first explorer of the Amazon, which he followed down from the junction of the Napo and Marañon rivers. In the course of the voyage Indians told him of a tribe of female warriors or Amazons, whom he claimed to have encountered; from this story the river derived its name.

Oresme (*o*-rem), **Nicole.** [Also, **Orem, Oren, Horen, Oremus**; Latinized, **Nicolaus Oresmus.**] French Roman Catholic prelate, one of the greatest mathematicians and economists of the Middle Ages, founder of French scientific terminology; b. near Caen, in Normandy, France, c1323; d. at Lisieux, in Normandy, July 11, 1382. He was Grand Maître of the Collège de Navarre, Paris (1356–1361), and subsequently held several ecclesiastical positions: canon at Rouen (1362), at Paris (1363–1364), dean of the chapter of Rouen (1364–1377), bishop of Lisieux (1377–1382). He served (c1360–1377) as advisor to the dauphin (who became Charles V in 1364) and was one of the scholars employed to translate ancient works into French. His chief work on economics is *De origine, natura, jure et mutationibus monetarum*, the first comprehensive treatise on the theory of money. It contains his discovery (anticipated by others) of the principle known as "Gresham's Law." In his treatises on mathematics he prepared the way for the discovery of analytical geometry, anticipated fractional exponents, and adumbrated the theory of inertia by developing the medieval concept of impetus. He was the first to use symbols for fractional powers in proportions and to give graphical representations of functional relationships. His principal mathematical works are *Tractatus de latitudinibus formarum* (printed 1482), *Tractatus proportionum* (printed 1505), *Algorismus proportionum* (printed 1868), *Tractatus de uniformitate et difformitate intensionum* (partly printed 1914). His chief astronomical works are *De commensurabilitate*, which contains an attack on astrology, *Traicté de l'espère*, a treatise on mathematical geography (printed 1508), *Traité du ciel et du monde*, a translation of Aristotle's *De caelo et mundo* to which Oresme added a commentary which proposed the diurnal rotation of the Earth, although otherwise he favored the Ptolemaic system.

Orfeo (ôr-fā′ō). Pastoral idyll by Poliziano, produced in 1480 at Mantua; adapted in form from the earlier religious pageants or plays called *Sacre rappresentazioni*, it is one of the earliest attempts at a secular play in the Italian language and a forerunner of the drama.

Oriolo (ō-ryō′lō), **Giovanni da.** See **Giovanni da Oriolo.**

Orlandino (ôr-län-dē′nō). A burlesque epic by Teofilo Folengo. It purports to relate the birth and childhood of Orlando (Roland) in Italy, and parodies the high adventure and epic deeds in the youthful Orlando's brawls and scrapes. The court and the knights themselves are ridiculed, as in the tournament of donkeys. Folengo's work was put on the Index because of outspoken criticism of the clergy and hints of Lutheranism.

Orlando (ôr-län′dō). In the Italian versions of the Carolingian cycle Roland, Charlemagne's hero paladin, becomes Orlando. The *Chansons de geste* underwent a transformation when they crossed the Alps to be retold, first by the minstrels and street singers who sang of the heroic deeds of Orlando, and then by the finest poets of Italy. Orlando himself becomes an Italian, born, it is claimed, in Sutri. The characters of the cycle as seen through the Italian prism reflect new qualities. Charlemagne becomes a befuddled old man. Deeds of epic valor in behalf of king and Christendom become deeds of the marvellous, of preposterous dimensions. The Italians loved a story with a bite, a hint of mockery, or even more than a hint, and eye-popping adventures. In Luigi Pulci's *Morgante maggiore,* Orlando performs great feats with the utmost sangfroid, and dies a hero at the Pass of Roncesvalles. In Matteo Maria Boiardo's incomplete romantic epic, *Orlando Innamorato,* which claims to tell a hitherto unpublished chapter in the saga of Orlando, a new element is added: Orlando falls in love with the pagan princess Angelica, notwithstanding his lawful wife, and performs many exploits and carries out dangerous quests for her sake. In Lodovico Ariosto's *Orlando Furioso,* he goes mad with jealousy when Angelica prefers Medoro. His lost wits are at length restored to him through the agency of Astolfo and St. John the Evangelist. Teofilo Folengo's *Orlandino,* is a burlesque that purports to tell the story of Orlando's childhood in Italy. It perverts the knightliness and valor of the peer of Charlemagne into the brawling and trickery of a street urchin.

Orlando Furioso (fö-ryō′sō). ["Roland Maddened."] Romantic epic by Lodovico Ariosto, the first forty cantos of which were published in 1516. A second, heavily revised edition appeared in 1521, and the definitive edition, of forty-six cantos, was published in 1532. In his romantic epic, *Orlando Innamorato,* Matteo Maria Boiardo adds a new dimension to the *Chansons de geste* by telling of Orlando in love. Boiardo's epic was left incomplete at the time of his death. Ariosto took it up in his *Orlando Furioso,* which tells not only of Orlando's love for Angelica, but of his madness, brought on by jealousy when she marries another. Ariosto picks up the story where Boiardo left off, but often reaches back into Boiardo's poem to complete or develop episodes or to expand on characters and clues. In his work he adds hundreds of new characters and episodes and, as did Boiardo, intersperses the main themes with complete and separate stories. All the magic and marvels present in Boiardo's work, and dozens of new ones, appear in *Orlando Furioso,* but the tone is altered. Ariosto, unlike Boiardo, had no illusions at all as to chivalry, courtly love, the sanctity of friendship, or the integrity of princes. His work is pervaded with the irony that his own experience of the world of men and of princes engendered in him. His attitude toward his characters is one of indulgent amusement, and their adventures are painted with just such a tint of humor as to warn that Ariosto himself does not believe in them. They are recounted solely for entertainment; it is only incidentally that they point up the foibles and weaknesses of mankind, and especially of womankind, as observed by Ariosto. Boiardo's poem broke off as Paris was about to undergo attack by the Moors. In Ariosto's poem a principal theme is the recurrent attempts by the Infidels to take Paris. Orlando's madness effectively removes him as a defender of king and country. Instead, he charges about on a rampage of killing—of monsters, enchanters, and evildoers—and in a personal crusade of rescuing beautiful damsels and noble knights in distress. His story is separate from the siege of Paris but linked by common characters and episodes to the general theme of the attacks on the city. A third main strand of the interwoven plot is the love story of Ruggiero and Bradamante. Lesser threads that gleam in Ariosto's jeweled and rich tapestry of plot and subplot involve many of the characters of Boiardo's poem —Mandricardo, Marfisa, Rodomonte, Gradasso, to name a few, as well as the enchanters, wicked lords, faithless lovers, and noble knights of Ariosto's creation.

As the poem opens, Agramante the Saracen is besieging Paris. Angelica, left in Boiardo's poem under the protection of the aged Duke Namo, flees and is pursued by Orlando and Rinaldo, both of whom are besotted with love for her. Orlando forgets his duty to his king to follow her. Rinaldo, recalled to his senses, goes to England to seek aid against the Saracens. There he has many adventures, including the rescue of the Scottish princess Ginevra. Angelica, meanwhile, has decided that with the help of a magic ring that makes her invisible she has no need of men and can do without a champion. Deprived of her ring, she is glad enough to be rescued from the orc, a sea monster, by Ruggiero. Later she comes upon Medoro lying wounded and left for dead. Cupid, to punish her for denying love, shoots an arrow into her heart and she is smitten with love for the humbly born but valiant Medoro. She heals his wounds;

he returns her love; and they spend many a delightful hour in shepherd's cottage or rosy bower, carving their linked names on every available spot. Orlando sees their names, and this is the cause of his jealousy and his madness. Angelica now disappears from the story. Orlando pursues his furious course. Astolfo, son of the king of England, armed with Argalia's invincible lance and a horn whose blast terrifies all who hear it, as well as a book of magic with a very complete index, overcomes Gradasso in single combat and forces him temporarily from the scene. He slays Orrilo, hitherto protected by a magic hair, by shaving every hair from his head with his sword. He rides on a hippogriff to the Infernal regions, which he decides to investigate and gets covered with soot for his pains. He visits St. John the Evangelist and is warmly welcomed. Together he and St. John journey to the moon in Elijah's fiery chariot. On the moon he finds a heap of rubbish, things lost by men on earth. In the heap he finds Orlando's lost wits, as well as his own. He also sees the river of Time destroying the fame of men in forgetfulness. He is permitted to take Orlando's lost wits, and his own. Thus by the agency of Astolfo Orlando is restored to sanity. Among Astolfo's other prodigies is the creation of a fleet by scattering the leaves of various trees upon the water. With this fleet, that of Agramante is overcome. Orlando, his wits restored, joins Oliviero and Brandimarte to duel against the pagans Agramante, Gradasso, and Sobrino. In the triple duel, Brandimarte is slain, and Orlando kills Agramante and Gradasso. Ruggiero and Bradamante suffer many violent partings and dangerous adventures. The development of their story, as the legendary ancestors of the Estensi, is a principal theme of Ariosto's poem. He embroiders it with many flattering references to their supposed descendants. Ruggiero is taken captive by a magician and freed by Bradamante. She suffers strong pangs of jealousy on seeing him embrace Marfisa who, as it turns out, is his sister. Bradamante, separated from Ruggiero, trustingly follows the treacherous Pinabello, who tries to get rid of her by dropping her into Merlin's cave. She escapes and slays him. Ruggiero, shipwrecked in a fearful storm, vows to become a Christian if he survives. He does. Rinaldo has given his consent to the marriage of Ruggiero and Bradamante, but her father has other plans. He wishes for a match between Bradamante and Leone, son of the emperor Constantine. Ruggiero, in despair, resolves to starve himself to death, but Leone, who has admired Ruggiero's courage and courtesy in combat, renounces his own love in Ruggiero's favor. Amone, Bradamante's father, agrees to her marriage to Ruggiero. On the last day of the wedding festivities Rodomonte appears and challenges Ruggiero to single combat. Ruggiero slays him and the poem ends. The wicked enchanters have been overcome; a few faithful ladies have sacrificed their lives for love; less faithful ones have suffered punishment; knights loyal to their loves died in their arms or live with them in triumphant happiness. The most dangerous infidels have been slain or baptized; the Moors are repelled and Christendom is saved. The whole is presented with an airy delicacy, a graceful ease and affectionate mockery, and in phrasing and form of the purest artistry. The poem was immediately acclaimed by cultivated circles in Italy, and its popularity rapidly spread beyond the Alps. It was translated into English, French, and Spanish. The earliest English translation is also one of the most satisfactory. It is that of Sir John Harington, a gay blade at Queen Elizabeth's court who delightedly entered into the spirit of Ariosto's poem. The story is that he first translated the twenty-eighth canto for the entertainment of the ladies of the court. This canto is in general an account of feminine infidelity. The queen ordered him to retire to his estates in Somerset and not to return until he had translated the entire work. His translation was published in 1591. John Addington Symonds wrote of the *Orlando Furioso* that as Dante summarized the Middle Ages as they were passing in the *Divina Commedia*, so Ariosto epitomized the Renaissance as it was about to be eclipsed. His brilliant word painting of manners, men and morals, splendor, gaiety, superficiality, beauty, and cynicism, is a last bright reflection from the mirror of his age.

Orlando Innamorato (ēn-nä-mō-rä′tō). ["Roland in Love."] Romantic epic by Matteo Maria Boiardo. The first two books of the long and incomplete poem were published in 1486. The third book, which breaks off at the time of the invasion of Charles VIII of France (1494) was published in

1495. For the purposes of his story, Boiardo pretends that he has found some lost books of Turpin's Chronicle of the court of Charlemagne. These books, hitherto suppressed says Boiardo, reveal Orlando's love. Thus, to the heroes and epic deeds of the Carolingian cycle, Boiardo adds the element of chivalric and courtly love from the Arthurian legends. The resulting romantic epic is a skillful blending of the two cycles, and successfully introduces into Italian literature the Arthurian cycle. The latter had never been so popular with the Italians as their own versions of the Carolingian legends. The long poem, in sixty-nine cantos, is a series of episodes, loosely linked but dependent upon the theme of Orlando's love for Angelica, a princess of Cathay. She is one of a score or more of new characters that emerged from Boiardo's fertile imagination.

The poem opens with the resolution of Gradasso, a king of Sericania in Africa, to invade France in order to secure Orlando's invincible sword Durindana and Rinaldo's magic horse Baiardo. Hardly has the poem begun, however, when the scene switches to Charlemagne's court at Paris. There, on a feast day, a great tournament is to be held. Before the tournament opens Angelica arrives with her brother. She disguises her aim, which is to take Charlemagne's knights as captives to Cathay. She proposes that her brother Argalia, whom she gives a false name, fight the Christian and Saracen knights assembled for the tournament. Any he unhorses will be his captive, but if any unhorse him, she will be the prize. All the knights instantly fall in love with Angelica, the most beautiful of women, and each is eager to be the first to face Argalia. Astolfo, whom the lots favor, is first, and is unhorsed and taken captive; for in addition to Astolfo's usual rash ineptness, Argalia has a magic lance. Ferraù, a Saracen, is next. He, too, is thrown, but refuses to abide by the knightly code and rushes against Argalia with his sword. Argalia, unprepared for his attack, would willingly give up Angelica to him, but Angelica will have none of the black-a-vised, rough Ferraù. She prefers fair men. Argalia drops his lance, at her suggestion, and flees. Ferraù pursues him and Angelica, who has also fled. Astolfo, whose lance had been broken, picks up Argalia's invincible weapon, unaware of its magic properties. (He never does learn why he has suddenly become invincible.) Orlando and Rinaldo, both of whom are wildly in love with her, pursue Angelica into the forest of Ardennes. In the forest are two fountains: that of Merlin, which causes all who drink of it to despise the first person they see thereafter, and that of Cupid, which inspires the contrary emotion of love. Angelica goes to sleep in the forest. Rinaldo, thirsty from his pursuit of her, drinks of Merlin's fountain, and when he sees Angelica finds all his former love turned to hate. Angelica, who has drunk of the fountain of Cupid, falls in love with him on sight. He flees. Angelica now pursues him, using her magic arts in an effort to win him, but to no avail. Orlando searches for Angelica. From this point, now the adventures of one, now of another are related. Boiardo breaks off in the middle of a titanic struggle to take his story to another character. After relating several other episodes, he returns to the first struggle. He tells of the siege of Albracca, capital of Angelica's father's kingdom, by Agricane, a Tartar king who seeks to win Angelica. She calls on Orlando for help, knowing that his love for her will make him heed her call. Orlando slays Agricane in single combat. Rinaldo, seeking to right a wrong, has many adventures. Boiardo addresses the reader with essays on friendship, riches, love, loyalty: the friendship and loyalty of brave men has his highest admiration; riches are meaningless in comparison to friendship and love; love is admittedly the basis of his poem, but women are capricious, and, in general, false or at best hardly capable of a sustained and pure emotion. He diverts the reader with stories told by his characters to each other, stories that have nothing to do with the main plot. They are spun from his endlessly creative imagination, little complete novelle. He dreams up monsters for his heroes to overcome, creates magical lakes, underwater kingdoms, beautiful bowers, and deep forests. And from time to time he assures the reader that all is according to Turpin.

Rinaldo, about to defend Paris by fighting the Moor Gradasso in single combat, is spirited away by Angelica's magic before the battle can take place. Shamed by his apparent betrayal of king and country he tries to return, but Angelica's magic is too powerful.

He goes to Albracca, surmounting many obstacles and undergoing many adventures on the way, arrives there and fights Orlando. Angelica, a persistent sorceress, interferes in the struggle. She saves Rinaldo by sending Orlando off on a quest to the lake of Morgana the fairy. In the meantime, Agramante, an African king, is preparing an invasion of France. He cannot leave without Ruggiero. Ruggiero being found, the expedition sets out. Ruggiero meets Bradamante, who is dressed as a warrior, and fights her, until Bradamante removes her helmet and reveals herself a beautiful woman. They fall in love. Boiardo obviously intended to develop their story, for Ruggiero and Bradamante are destined in it to become the founders of the house of Este. Rinaldo returns to the forest of Ardennes. He is attacked by the nymphs of Cupid for denying love. They pelt him to a pulp with flowers. Bruised and weary, he drinks of the fountain of Cupid and, when he sees Angelica with Orlando, falls in love with her again. But Angelica has just drunk of the fountain of Merlin and now despises him. Rinaldo fights with Orlando. Angelica rushes to Charlemagne's court. Charlemagne, preparing to meet the onslaught of the Moors without his two most valiant knights, sends to stop the struggle between Rinaldo and Orlando, and has them brought to his court. He sends Angelica off in the care of the aged Duke Namo and promises he will award her to the one of his two heroes who shows the most valor in the coming battle.

The poem breaks off as Boiardo, in one of his many addresses to the reader, laments the invasion of Italy by the barbarian French, and hopes that he will finish the tale on which he had embarked in a happier time. He never took up the work again, and died at the end of the same year, 1494. The poem was enormously popular, pervaded as it is by Boiardo's manly enthusiasm for an idealized age of chivalry, an age that he realized had passed but for which he had a deeply nostalgic yearning; crammed with a series of high adventures swiftly told; richly ornamented with magic rings, glittering armor, invincible swords and shields; marvellously inventive in subsidiary plots and inserted stories; and varied by monsters, magic lakes, enchanted forests, and roseate bowers, to say nothing of its lyricism in the passages describing nature and its glowing descriptions of jeweled cups, rich vestments, and knightly armor. But its popularity was eclipsed on the appearance of Lodovico Ariosto's *Orlando Furioso*, a continuation of Boiardo's poem. For Boiardo, fluent, inventive, original, drawing on his knowledge of classical myth and legend and reshaping these to his ends, wrote swiftly and freshly in a language that, with its inclusion of Lombard regionalisms and unpolished words, seemed crude in comparison with the grace and elegance of Ariosto's language and style. His work appeared in an age that came to value elegance and style almost for themselves alone. Francesco Berni later reworked Boiardo's poem, and created a bland and emasculated shadow with his polished lines. He did not change the episodes but his refinements destroyed Boiardo's vigor and altered the tone of the work. This was the version of the *Orlando Innamorato* that was current until the 19th century.

Orléans (dôr-lā-äṅ), **Charles d'**. [Title, Duc **d'Orléans.**] French poet; b. May 26, 1391; d. at Amboise, January 4, 1465. He was taken prisoner at Agincourt and kept in England until ransomed in 1440. For the rest of his life he kept court at Blois, gathering about him many of the literary figures of the day, including François Villon and Georges Chastelain. His own poetry, consisting of rondels on spring, love, and similar subjects, is considered the best of its kind. By his third marriage, to Mary of Cleves, he was the father of Louis XII of France.

Orléans, Louis, Duc **d'**. French statesman; b. March 13, 1372; killed at Paris, November 23, 1407. He assumed the regency in 1392 when his brother Charles VI became deranged. His assassination by the duke of Burgundy was the signal for the civil war between the Burgundians and the Armagnacs, supporters of Orléans. He married (1389) Valentina Visconti, daughter of the duke of Milan, by whom he was father of Charles d'Orléans (1391–1465). He formed liaisons with several ladies, among them reportedly his sister-in-law Queen Isabella of Bavaria. Among his illegitimate children was Jean Dunois, noted as one of Joan of Arc's lieutenants and known in history as the Bastard of Orléans.

Ormonde (ôr′mo̜nd), 2nd Earl of. [Title of **James Butler**; called **"the Noble Earl."**]

English viceroy (three times) of Ireland; b. at Kilkenny, Ireland, c1331; d. there, 1382. He was a descendant of Edward I, and favorite of Edward III. He served with distinction in the Irish War (1361–1362).

Ormonde, 4th Earl of. [Title of **James Butler**; called **"the White Earl."**] English viceroy of Ireland; d. at Atherdee, Ireland, 1452. After serving with Henry V in the French wars he was appointed lord lieutenant of Ireland. On an accusation of high treason (1447) by John Talbot he was dismissed by the king.

Ormonde, 5th Earl of. [Title of **James Butler**; additional title, Earl of **Wiltshire.**] English soldier; b. 1420; beheaded at Newcastle, England, 1461. He was a leader of the Lancastrians in the War of the Roses. After the battles of Mortimer's Cross and Towton (1461), he was captured and beheaded.

Ormonde, 6th Earl of. [Title of **John Butler**; originally known as Sir **John de Ormonde.**] English knight; d. at Jerusalem, 1478. Edward IV called him ". . . the finest gentleman in Christendom." He died during a pilgrimage to the Holy Land.

Ormonde, 9th Earl of. [Title of **James Butler**; additional title, Viscount **Thurles.**] English nobleman; b. c1490; d. of poison at London, 1546. He was suspected of hostility to the government. He was poisoned while at supper at Ely House.

Ormonde, 10th Earl of. [Title of **Thomas Butler**; called **"the Black Earl."**] English statesman and soldier; b. 1532; d. 1614. He put down several Irish insurrections.

Orrigille (ō-rē-jēl′lā). In Lodovico Ariosto's *Orlando Furioso*, the faithless lover of Grifone, whom she often deceives.

Orrilo (ō-rēl′lō). In Lodovico Ariosto's *Orlando Furioso*, a great fighter who is protected by a single magic hair among all the hairs of his head. As long as this hair remains, a limb, even his head, may be severed by a sword-stroke, and it will instantly rejoin his body. Astolfo, learning why he is invincible, cuts off his head, then, not knowing which one is the magic hair, shaves his head with his sword and Orrilo dies.

Orsi (ôr′sē), **Lelio.** Painter, architect, and designer; b. probably at Novellara; d. there, May 3, 1587. Little is known of his early life and training. His work shows the influence of Correggio, of whom he was believed by some to have been a pupil, and, most strongly, that of Giulio Romano and Michelangelo. In 1536 he was at Reggio Emilia painting decorations for the entry into the city of Ercole II d'Este. Ten years later he was compelled to flee because of his alleged participation in a murder. He returned to Novellara, visited Venice (1553) and Rome (1554–1555), and worked for the counts of Novellara, who became his patrons. Frescoes he executed in the churches of Reggio and Novellara have perished. Among his surviving works are a *Martyrdom of St. Catherine* and a *Pietà*, Estense Gallery, Modena, and paintings in the Pinacoteca, Naples, and the National Gallery, London.

Orsini (ôr-sē′nē). Noble Roman family, noted for its power and wealth, supporters of the popes against the Ghibellines and the empire from the 12th to the 16th century, as famed for having contributed popes, cardinals, and numerous other prelates to the Church as for having contributed statesmen and men of arms to the Church and to Rome. They were traditional enemies of the Colonnesi, another powerful noble family. The power and influence of the Orsini were strengthened by numerous branches in widely held territories. (Members of the family were ultimately counts of Nola, Pitigliano, Soana, and Manopello, dukes of Bracciano and Gravina; there were several branches of the family at Monterotondo, and several in the kingdom of Naples.) The origins of the Orsini are obscure. Some say the name came from a child of a chieftain of the Goths: the infant was nursed by a bear–*orsa*–and hence was called Orsino. In any case, the name was known at Rome as early as 998. Giacinto Orsini was the first of the family to become pope. As Celestine III (1191–1198) he fostered his family's interests. Matteo Rosso Orsini (d. 1246) was a senator of Rome and the founder of family power. He was lord of Mugnano, Marino, Monterotondo, Galeria, S. Angelo, and Licenza. He was a devoted adherent of St. Francis of Assisi. As a supporter of the Church he defended Rome itself against the emperor Frederick II (1241), attacked the Colonnesi supporters of Frederick, and took the mausoleum of Augustus, their stronghold in Rome. In the brief pontificate of Nicholas III (Giovan Gaetano Orsini, pope from 1277 to 1280), the Orsini were highly favored. Following the death of Pope Boniface VIII (1303), a conflict erupted within the family

Lelio Orsi
Flight into Egypt
Courtesy of The Pierpont Morgan Library, New York

itself. Cardinal Matteo Rosso Orsini, grandson of the senator of the same name, supported the partisans of Boniface; Cardinal Napoleone Orsini, a nephew of Nicholas III, favored the French, archenemies of Boniface and his party, and was on the winning side when the French Clement V was elected (1305) in the conclave at Perugia. During the long exile of the popes at Avignon (1305–1376) the Orsini, as Guelphs, waged continual war at Rome with the Ghibelline Colonna family. They surged down from their strongholds on Monte Giordano with the cry "Orsi and Holy Church" and were answered by the war cry of the Colonnesi, "The People, Colonna, and Liberty." Around each of these powerful families were grouped other princely houses; all Rome had a part in the struggle, and the city was often in a state of anarchy. The city was a howling ruin when the pope at last returned. The Orsini prevented Henry VII from being crowned in St. Peter's, and only ceased warfare with the advent of Cola di Rienzi (1347) who was a threat to all nobles. For a time, after the fall of Rienzi (1354), the two families shared power, but with the return of Gregory XI to Rome (1377) the strife erupted anew. In the war with Ladislaus of Naples, Paolo Orsini, Pope John XXIII's captain general, defeated Ladislaus at S. Germano (1411) and at Roccasecca, and won back Rome for the pope. Because of their loyalty, the Orsini were usually favored by the popes, especially by Sixtus IV (1471–1484) of whose wars they were energetic supporters, Innocent VIII (1484–1492), and Leo X (1513–1521). Alexander VI, however, coveted their wealth and feared their power. His son Cesare Borgia besieged their castles of Trevignano and Bracciano, had Gentile Virginio Orsini and Cardinal Giovan Battista Orsini poisoned, and caused Paolo, duke of Gravina and his former captain, to be strangled. When Cesare was overthrown, Fabio, son of Paolo, avenged his father and caused Cesare himself to beg Pope Pius III for asylum in Castel Sant' Angelo. Fabio died at the battle of the Garigliano (1503), while fighting in the Spanish army. The family prospered under Julius II; Giovan Giordano Orsini married Felice, a natural daughter of the pope (1511), and the Orsini made a truce (of brief duration) with the Colonnesi. Lorenzo Orsini, called upon at the last moment by the vacillating Clement VII, tried in vain to defend Rome against the forces of the emperor Charles V, who took and sacked Rome (May, 1527). In the years following, the Orsini often found themselves, as defenders of the Church, pitted against the Colonnesi, as supporters of the empire. A final peace was made between the two families (1562) when Virginio Orsini and Marcantonio II Colonna married nieces of the future pope, Sixtus V.

Orsini, Fulvio. Man of letters, bibliophile, and collector; b. at Rome, December 11, 1529; d. there, May 18, 1600. A passionate collector for himself and others, his name was closely associated with the Farnese collections. For his own account, he collected manuscripts, books, engraved gems, medals, bronzes, and paintings. Part of his collection was left to the Vatican and part to Cardinal Odoardo Farnese. The latter part is now in the National Museum at Naples. Among the important codices of his collection was a Vergil that had belonged to Pontano, a Terence of the 5th century, and a Boethius by Boccaccio. He left a number of Latin treatises and commentaries.

Orsini, Gentile Virginio. Lord of Bracciano and count of Albe and Tagliacozzo; d. at Naples, January 17, 1497. He was the son of Napoleone Orsini, and was a captain and intriguer who regarded war as a financial and diplomatic, rather than a military, operation. He began his career at the Aragonese court at Naples, served King Ferrante in the war to establish his succession, served his son in the war Ferrante and the pope carried on against Lorenzo de' Medici (1478), and then turned against Naples to fight on the pope's side against Ferrara. Ferrante took away the fiefs of Albe and Tagliacozzo, with which he had invested him for his earlier service, but they were later restored. He fought against the French, against the Colonnesi, was taken prisoner by the French, escaped, and tried to restore his kinsmen the Medici at Florence (1495). Next he joined the armies of the French in Naples, was taken prisoner and confined in Castel dell'Ovo at Naples. There, Alexander VI, who wanted to crush the Orsini, caused him to be poisoned.

Orsini, Giovanni Gaetani. Original name of Pope **Nicholas III.**

Orsini, Lorenzo. [Called **Renzo di Ceri.**] Condottiere; d. January 20, 1536. He was a son of Giovanna Orsini, of the Monterotondo branch of the noble Roman family, and of Giovanni, lord of Ceri. He was a brave and knowledgeable captain whose successes were frequently vitiated by lack of support and money. He defended Ceri against Cesare Borgia (1503), and as commander of infantry in the pay of Venice defended Treviso (1511) and Crema (1513–1514) against the Spanish and Germans. He aided Lorenzo de' Medici, duke of Urbino, fought against Florence after the death of Leo X, and vainly opposed Giovanni delle Bande Nere. His most heartbreaking assignment was the last minute charge given to him by Pope Clement VII to defend Rome against the Imperial troops in May, 1527. His task was hopeless, and the sack of Rome followed. After service under France in Naples, and under the Venetians, he died as a result of a hunting accident.

Orsini, Matteo Rosso. Cardinal; b. at Rome, c1230; d. at Perugia, September 4, 1305. Member of the distinguished noble Roman family, a grandson of the senator of the same name (d. 1246), he wholeheartedly embraced the family tradition of support for the papacy. He studied at Paris, and perhaps at Bologna, and was given the red hat, as cardinal deacon of S. Maria in Porticu, by Urban IV (1262). He served as legate in 1264 and the following year shared in the lengthy negotiations to arrange financial support for Charles of Anjou's expedition to Sicily, an expedition sought and sanctioned by Pope Clement IV. By the time his uncle Cardinal Giovan Gaetano Orsini became pope as Nicholas III, Matteo Rosso was one of the most influential members of the Sacred College. However, Martin IV, successor of Nicholas III, was his enemy because the cardinal opposed the French pope's pro-French policy. He continued to oppose Angevin influence under succeeding popes, and supported Benedetto Caetani, who became Pope Boniface VIII in 1294. In the election following the death of Benedict XI, successor of Boniface, Matteo Rosso was outwitted by his kinsman Cardinal Napoleone Orsini in the conclave of Perugia (1305) from which the French candidate emerged as Clement V. He died shortly thereafter, having foretold the exile of the popes at Avignon. One of the most distinguished figures of the Church in the 13th century, he wrote on theology, and was noted for his prudence and piety, as well as for his faithfulness to the Church. In the period of his cardinalate he saw thirteen popes elected.

Orsini, Napoleone. Cardinal; b. at Rome, c1263; d. at Avignon, 1342. A nephew of Pope Nicholas III, he studied at Paris, was created cardinal by Nicholas IV (1288), and was one of those members of the Sacred College who, jealous of the prerogatives of the cardinals, opposed the autocratic Boniface VIII. He was joined in this opposition by members of the rival Colonna family and by Philip the Fair of France. At the conclave of Perugia (1305) he opposed his kinsman, Cardinal Matteo Rosso Orsini, and supported the French candidate, who was elected as Clement V. Clement was the tool of the French king, and moved the papal court to Avignon at his request. Cardinal Napoleone Orsini went to Avignon with him. He was one of the Italian cardinals Dante addressed in a letter denouncing them for having chosen a French pope. As papal legate to Italy, Cardinal Orsini tried to make peace between the warring factions there, and at Bologna (1307) had to flee for his life from the anger of the people. Loyal to the king of France, he yet opposed the permanent removal of the papal seat from Rome and the exploitation of the Church and its wealth by the French. At the conclave of Carpentras (1314–1316), he therefore opposed the election of another French candidate, but was unable to prevent the election of John XXII. He remained faithful to the ideal of papal supremacy in spiritual matters but opposed papal absolutism in temporal matters.

Orsini, Niccolò, Count of Pitigliano. Captain; b. 1442; d. at Lonigo (Vicenza), January 27, 1510. He embarked on a military career at an early age, and in 1459 fought in the papal armies against Viterbo, which had rebelled. In the service of Jacopo Piccinino he perfected his trade, later served Lorenzo the Magnificent, then again entered the service of the popes. At the Battle of Fornovo, 1495, he was taken prisoner but escaped. In 1496 he was named commander of the Venetian forces, and held the post until his death. As a man and a soldier he was one of the better captains of the age.

Orsini, Orso. Soldier; d. at Viterbo, July 5, 1479. He was an illegitimate son of Gentile di Bertoldo, of the Orsini counts of Pitigliano and Soana. He served in the armies of Alfonso of Aragon (later, Alfonso I of Naples), of Francesco Sforza, and of the Venetians. In the war of succession in Naples he first supported Jean of Anjou, then (1461) switched to the support of Ferrante, was rewarded with the countship of Nola, and remained loyal to the Aragonese until his death. He was further rewarded with the duchy of Ascoli Satriano. He fought with the duke of Calabria (Ferrante's son) in behalf of the Florentines (1467), and against Lorenzo de' Medici in 1478. He left a work, which he had presented to Ferrante of Naples, January, 1477, on the art of war, *Governo et exercitio de la militia*. This presents his thorough knowledge of Italian military tactics of the age, and is notable for its recommendation of a standing army of 20,000 men and the proposals it makes for the raising and training of such an army.

Orsini, Paolo. Soldier; strangled at Castello delle Pieve, January 18, 1503. He was the natural son of Cardinal Latino Orsini. He took part in Pope Sixtus IV's war against Ferrara (1482–1484), and in the bloody strife at Rome caused by the pope's desire to crush the Colonnesi. In the service of Florence, he was defeated at Sarzana (1494), a defeat that contributed to the panic that caused Piero II de' Medici to make a humiliating pact with the French. After the expulsion of the Medici from Florence, Paolo continued for a time to support their attempts to return to Florence. He served as a captain for Cesare Borgia, but took part in the conspiracy against him (1502), was tricked by Cesare, and imprisoned at Senigallia. Removed to Castello delle Pieve, he was there strangled, together with his cousin Francesco, duke of Gravina.

Orsini, Paolo Giordano. Duke of Bracciano and marquess of Anguillara; d. at Salò, 1585. He fought against the duke of Alba in the pontifical army, and against the Turks for the Venetians, suffering a wound at the battle of Lepanto (1571). In 1558 he had married Isabella de' Medici, daughter of Duke Cosimo I. Deceived by Troilo Orsini into believing his wife unfaithful, on the night of July 16, 1576, he throttled her in her bed. In Rome he became besotted with love for Vittoria Accoramboni, wife of Francesco Peretti. Peretti was the nephew of a cardinal who later became Pope Sixtus V. The duke caused two of his bravos to murder Vittoria's husband (June 27, 1583). He subsequently had Vittoria released from the prison in which she had been incarcerated following the murder of her husband, and married her. When Francesco Peretti's uncle was elevated to the papal throne, the couple fled to Salò to escape his anger. There the duke died soon after.

Orsua (ôr-sö′ä), **Pedro de.** See **Ursúa, Pedro de.**

Ortelius (ôr-tē′li-us). [Latinized surname of **Abraham Oertel** (or **Ortell**).] Flemish geographer, considered the greatest of his time next to Mercator; b. at Antwerp, Belgium, 1527; d. there, 1598. He published an atlas, *Theatrum orbis terrarum* (1570). He went to England in 1577, and it was his encouragement and solicitation that induced Camden to produce his *Britannia*.

Ortolano (lôr-tō-lä′nō), **l'.** [**Giovanni Battista Benvenuti**, called **l'Ortolano.**] Ferrarese painter; b. before 1487; d. after 1524. Little is known of his life, and his work was for long confused with that of Garofalo (c1481–1559), but in comparison to the mistiness and grace of Garofalo, l'Ortolano often has a certain crude vigor and brilliance. He was a follower of Boccaccio Boccaccino, whom he imitated in his early *Adoration of the Shepherds*, the Metropolitan Museum, New York. A later painting on the same subject, Doria Pamphili Gallery, Rome, has elements of Lorenzo Costa; his *Holy Family*, Pallavicini Collection, Rome, seems, in its monumentality and softened forms, to have been influenced by Raphael's *St. Cecilia*. His style and his technique developed markedly as he drew elements from a number of painters, as from Mazzolino and Ercole de' Roberti. *Woman Taken in Adultery*, Courtauld Institute Gallery, London, *St. Sebastian*, Capitoline Gallery, and *Pietà*, Borghese Gallery, Rome, and *Crucifixion*, Brera, Milan, show the influence of these masters. His rather rigid figures and symmetrical compositions are enlivened by enamel-like color. His masterpiece is the altarpiece, *St. Sebastian with SS. Roch and Demetrius*, National Gallery, London, a work of power and vitality, deeply influenced, as were many of his later works, by Dosso Dossi. Other examples of his work are at Bologna, Ferrara, Naples, Copenhagen (*St. Margaret and the Dragon*, dated 1524, with a rather insipid saint and a dreadful dragon), Paris, Baltimore, the Johnson Collection, Philadelphia, and elsewhere.

Ottocar II (of *Bohemia*) (ot′tọ-kär). King of Bohemia (1253–1278); b. c1230; killed, 1278. By conquest, marriage, diplomacy, and election, he won Austria, Styria, Carinthia, and Carniola over a period of years. In 1273 he contested the election of his enemy Rudolf I of Hapsburg as king of the Germans, and refused to do homage for the fiefs he had won. Rudolf placed him under the ban of the empire. Ottocar gave up (1276) all the lands he held except Bohemia and Moravia, but two years later sought to win back his former conquests. In a war with Rudolf he was defeated and killed on the Marchfeld, 1278. As king of Bohemia he had encouraged the growth and influence of cities and attempted to limit the power of the nobles.

Ovando (ō-bän′dō), **Nicolás de.** Spanish colonial administrator; b. at Valladolid, Spain, c1460; d. at Madrid, c1518. In 1501 he was appointed governor of Hispaniola, his jurisdiction embracing all the Spanish possessions in the New World except those ceded to Ojeda and Pinzón. African slaves were first extensively used in the Spanish colonies under Ovando.

Oviedo y Valdés (ō-byā′ᴛʜō ē bäl-dās′), **Gonzalo Fernández de.** Spanish historian; b.

at Madrid, 1478; d. at Valladolid, Spain, 1557. He held a number of colonial offices, and for some years was official chronicler of the Indies. His principal work, and one of the first and best of the early histories of America, is *Historia natural y general de las Indias,* in fifty books. Of these nineteen were published at Seville in 1535, and the twentieth, finishing the first part, at Valladolid soon after.

P

Pacchiarotti (päk-kyä-rōt′tē) or **Pacchiarotto** (-rôt′tō), **Iacopo** or **Giacomo.** Painter; b. at Siena, 1474; d. at Viterbo, probably 1540. He was an eclectic who drew freely on the styles of a great number of painters in turn, and on the whole looked back to 15th-century Sienese and Florentine traditions. A pupil of Matteo di Giovanni, he was influenced by Fungai, Cozzarelli, Francesco di Giorgio, Perugino, and others, and succeeded in blending elements of numerous styles to suit and express his modest artistic vision. A number of his works are in the Pincacoteca and other collections at Siena, and in localities near Siena. Others are at Dublin, London (*Nativity with Saints*), Stockholm, Zagreb, Baltimore (*Sulpicia,* a companion of Neroccio di Landi's *Vestal Claudia Quinta,* National Gallery, Washington), the Fogg Museum, Cambridge, El Paso, Nashville (Tennessee), San Diego (California), and elsewhere. Many of these are parts or panels from what was originally an integral painting.

Paccioli (pät-chō′lē), **Luca.** See **Pacioli, Luca.**

Pace (pās), **Richard.** English diplomat; b. near Winchester, England, c1482; d. 1536. He was sent to Switzerland (1515) by Cardinal Wolsey to stir up the Swiss against Francis I and the growing power of France, and to Germany (1519) to promote (without success) Henry VIII's election as successor to Emperor Maximilian. He was also employed to support Wolsey's candidacy for the papacy.

Pacheco (pä-chā′kō), **María.** Spanish leader (after the death of her husband, Juan de Padilla) in the defense of Toledo by the insurrectionists (1521–1522); fl. in the first part of the 16th century; d. in Portugal, 1531.

Pacini (pä-chē′nē), **Piero.** Publisher; b. at Pescia, c1440; d. after 1513. Among the earliest publishers, his name is linked to a series of works of Italian literature published at Florence at the end of the 15th and the beginning of the 16th centuries. He used a variety of type faces and adorned the books, often of a popular nature, with wood engravings that are among the best examples of the art of the time. His colophon was a crowned dolphin or a raven with the name *Piscia.* Among the more precious of the books printed by Pacini are *Epistole et Evangeli* (1495), *Favole d'Esopo* (1496), Petrarch's *Trionfi* (1499), and Frezzi's *Quadriregio* (1500), all published at Florence. Pacini's son Bernardo was also a publisher.

Pacino di Buonaguida (pä-chē′nō dē bwō-nä-gwē′dä). Florentine painter; active in the first half of the 14th century. He joined the Guild of Physicians and Apothecaries in 1320, and was a follower of Giotto, especially in the monumental quality of his figures. A signed work, *Crucifixion with Saints,* is in the Accademia, Florence. It was painted between 1320 and 1325.

Pacioli (pä-chō′lē), **Luca.** [Also called, **Luca di Borgo** and **Fra Luca di Borgo.**] Mathematician; b. at Borgo San Sepolcro, c1445; d. after 1509. One of his fellow-townsmen was his older contemporary, Piero della Francesca. They became great friends through their common interest in proportion, perspective, and mathematics. Luca went to Venice as a young man and studied arithmetic and algebra. He later took advantage of the journeys he made for a Venetian merchant to add to his mathematical knowledge. When he became tutor to his patron's sons, he compiled (1470) a mathematical treatise for their edification. Between 1470 and 1476 he left Venice and entered the Franciscan order. Thereafter he devoted himself to the teaching of mathematics in such scattered cities as Perugia, Zara, Rome, Naples, Milan (where he was a pensioner with Leonardo da Vinci of Ludovico Il Moro), and Bologna. He completed (1476) a treatise on algebra for his students, and published (1494) his *Summa de arithmetica, geometria proportioni et proportionalità.* This great work was a compendium, including his own earlier works, of the great writings of the past on the subject. A summary of mathematical knowledge up to the discovery of the solution of the cubic equation, it is the first general treatise on mathematics ever printed. In addition to presenting practical arithmetic and algebra, it contains the earliest examples of the calculation of probabilities. His *De viribus quantitatis* (c1498), is a collection, in three books, of mathematical games, puzzles, and problems, collected from all periods and all areas, and including the magic square. Under the influence of his artist friends Piero della Francesca, Leon Battista Alberti, and Leonardo da Vinci, all of whom were absorbed in mathematical speculation either in furtherance of their art or for its own sake, he wrote *De divina proportione,* in which he sought to deduce principles of proportion for architecture and for the human figure. The book, published at Venice (1503), contained drawings of solids in perspective by Leonardo da Vinci. Luca also translated (1509) Euclid into Latin. He was one of the most influential mathematicians of the early modern period.

Padilla (pä-ᴛʜē′lyä), **Juan López de.** Spanish revolutionist; b. at Toledo, Spain; executed in April, 1521. He was a leader of the insurrection of the communes against absolutism in 1520.

Pagani (pä-gä′nē), **Vincenzo.** Painter; b. at Monterubbiano, in the Marches, c1490; d. there, 1568. He was a pupil of his father, who was a follower of Crivelli, and was strongly influenced by the contemporary Umbrian school, by other followers of Crivelli, and by Raphael, but remained a provincial painter. Among his works are *Coronation of the Virgin,* Brera, Milan, the signed and dated (1539) *Assumption of the Virgin,* Appignano del Tronto, *Angel of the Annunciation* and two predella panels, *The Flagellation* and *The Purification,* Johnson Collection, Philadelphia. Many examples of his work survive in the Marches, as at Ascoli Piceno, Altidona, Carassai, Cossignano, Moresco, Porchia, Ripatransone, and elsewhere.

Paget (paj′ẹt), **William.** [Title, 1st Baron Paget of Beaudesert.] English statesman; b. at Wednesbury, England, 1505; d. in Middlesex, England, 1563. A chief councilor of Henry VIII, he was sent to France to explain Henry's repudiation of Catherine Howard. He was prominent in the plot to set aside Henry's will on the accession of Edward VI and was stricken from the rolls of the Order of the Garter. For sanctioning the proclamation of Mary's accession he was restored to the Order of the Garter. He relinquished all offices on Elizabeth's accession.

Painter (pān′tėr), **William.** English translator; b. in Middlesex, England, c1540; d. at London, 1594. In 1566 he published the first volume of *The Palace of Pleasure,* containing 60 tales. He originally intended it to contain only translations from Livy and the older writers, but altered his plan and added tales taken from Boccaccio, Bandello, Straparola, and other Italian and French novelists. The second volume was published in 1567, containing 34 tales; a third volume, although announced, did not appear. In later editions 6 more tales were added, so that there were 100 stories in all. It is the largest prose work between *Morte d'Arthur* and North's *Plutarch,* and is the source from which the Elizabethan dramatists took many of their plots.

Painting. In the history of human endeavor few periods of creative activity have ever achieved so legendary a fame as that of Italian Renaissance painting. The names of its protagonists may be encountered in almost every field of the world's literature, past and present. Nevertheless, the character of Renaissance painting is so complex that it eludes definition, even by scholars. This is not an unreasonable situation when one considers that it unfolded over a span of 300 years and did not take place in one unified nation, but in several small city-states, each championing its own individuality and culture. To gain an understanding of Renaissance painting it would be necessary to experience as many of its examples as possible. This is not easy. The practice of painting of the time fell, generally, into two main categories: altarpieces, usually done in tempera before 1475 and in oil afterward, and frescoes. By now most of the altarpieces have been removed from their original settings and dispersed into museums and private collections. Here they are not only seen out of context, but cutting, fading, over-cleaning or drastic repainting have frequently made detrimental alterations in their appearance. The frescoes, though many of them are still in place, have suffered, and do suffer, from water-seepage, mildew, candle smoke, and man-made damage, such as war, vibrations, and air pollution. In certain instances they, too, must be detached from their original settings, remounted and relocated. Sometimes very few works by great masters remain, whereas there may be an abundance of those by lesser artists on display in museums. Though these have definite historical and esthetic value, they cannot match the significance of the fewer works available by more creative personalities. In fact, if the history of Renaissance painting is to be surveyed at all, it must be by traveling from one great artist to the next.

Toward the end of the Dugento, in central Italy where art had been largely dominated by the Italo-Byzantine style, there emerged a new concept that broke with the past, and laid the foundation for all of Renaissance painting. Starting with Cavallini in Rome, artists began to explore the possibilities of three-dimensional representation. Before Cavallini the prevailing convention had been to paint only two-dimensional works that manifested little to no space or depth. Actually, not since the art of antiquity had painters shown any interest in creating physiological experiences of this kind. Fortunately for the new style, which might have died with Cavallini and the Roman school when the Papacy moved to Avignon (1305), the great Florentine painter, Giotto, adopted it as his own and spread it throughout Italy. Giotto was mainly preoccupied with the recording of natural observations as a vivid means of telling a story. In his scenes, though they are built upon the principles of order and harmony, he successfully communicates a human appeal that evokes the sympathy of the observer. This is most evident in his thirty-eight small frescoes of the Arena Chapel cycle at Padua, where, in each fresco, the composition is arranged in simple, understandable terms, and the main elements of the narrative are gently emphasized by Giotto's empirical ideas of space and perspective. In his *Adoration of the Magi*, for instance, the foremost corner of the shed not only creates a projection, but also leads the observer's eye down to the Madonna and Child. The camel at the left is cut off by the frame, which, in all the frescoes, is like a window, giving the impression that the picture scene continues beyond its boundaries.

In his art Giotto purposely created a permanent, ideal world with no setting or building that could be identified with anything actually in existence. Furthermore, his people are universal types. It remained for the school of Siena, in the first half of the Trecento, to guide the art of painting toward the depiction of contemporary life. The founder of this school, Duccio di Buoninsegna, began, in some of his outdoor scenes, such as his *Entry into Jerusalem*, to give a semblance of actual Italian cityscapes. His follower, Simone Martini, enriched his stories, especially his frescoes at Assisi, with a variety of characterized individuals: a rugged commoner, an aristocratic knight, an amusingly absurd musician, and so on. This narrative and naturalistic approach to art in Tuscany culminated with the Ambrogio Lorenzetti fresco cycle in the Palazzo Pubblico, Siena's town hall. In an allegory of Good and Bad Government, Ambrogio portrayed his native Siena and its surrounding countryside in an immense, continuous panoramic view that is an encyclopedic display of the many aspects of Trecento life. Ambrogio's explorative attitude toward perspective in his altarpieces was equally daring. His *Presentation in the Temple* is an achievement in the construction of coherent interior spaces that climaxed the experimentation begun by Giotto and Duccio. In the middle of the Trecento, however, Florence and Siena witnessed the rise of quite a different style that dominated the rest of the century. The traditions discussed above were submerged (though they spread strongly northward, especially in Padua and in France) as supernatural values replaced experimental naturalism; and ritualistic and dogmatic symbolism triumphed over warm, human narrative. Examples of this style are foreboding, bleak, and emotionally disturbing. To appreciate its expressiveness, the historical context in which it grew must be understood. Following several political and economic reverses, the bubonic plague of 1348, known as the Black Death, destroyed over half the populations of both cities. In the resulting pessimism, themes dealing with death, such as the Last Judgment, Hell, the Triumph of Death, received the majority of commissions. The leading painter of this age, Andrea Orcagna, used all three subjects in a gigantic fresco in the Church of S. Croce at Florence. These works, now moved, exist only in fragments, but they are sufficient to illustrate the emotional intensity of this style.

The first two decades of the Quattrocento brought a renewed interest in the human figure, the rationalization of optical experience, and dramatic narrative. It was confined, however, mostly to sculpture. Painters resisted the new ideas that so fascinated the sculptor, Donatello, and the architect, Brunelleschi. This is evident in the paintings of the *Adoration of the Magi* by Lorenzo Monaco and Gentile da Fabriano, both done in the early 1420's. Lorenzo's weightless shapes, opalescent light from no natural source, and allover delicate elegance, create an unrealistic, visionary effect most expressive of his mystic religiosity. This same theme in the hands of the worldly Gentile is equally ornate and Gothic in character, but its rich, secular narrative could only be found on earth and in a courtly milieu. The fact that Gentile's masterpiece was commissioned by Palla Strozzi, the wealthiest man at Florence at the time, should have guaranteed his style a wide following. However, at that very moment, a young Florentine painter, Masaccio, revolutionized the field by at last bringing to painting the stylistic principles of Donatello and Brunelleschi. Masaccio, in his works, used a constant scale to give his composition a proportional, mathematical unity. His perspective, as seen in his *Trinity* fresco, is created by the convergence of all lines perpendicular to the picture plane into a single vanishing point. This point corresponds to the height of the observer. In his frescoes in the Brancacci Chapel he recreated the world of nature in extremely convincing terms. All of his devices, such as light emanating from one source, depth of landscapes, shadows on the ground, gave intense reality to the solemn, grandiose actions of his figures. For Masaccio, painting should contain the demonstration of optical experience, whether it entailed architectural settings or open air scenes. In the decades after Masaccio's early death a handful of artists in Florence continued his idea of rendering religious symbols in terms of credible reality. Only one artist, however, Andrea del Castagno, followed Masaccio in making this visual presentation a dramatic experience. Fra Angelico and Domenico Veneziano, on the contrary, gave gentle poetry and emotional control to their sacred themes recreated as terrestrial events. Their *Sacra Conversazione* (a group picture in which the Holy Family is shown in intimate, psychological contact with various saints), a type of altarpiece of which both artists left the earliest examples, indelibly stamped the development of Quattrocento painting. These artists, and many others, benefited from the writings of the humanist, Leon Battista Alberti, who in his treatise *On Painting* (1435) explained how to draw one point, linear perspective construction in terms of a foreshortened checkerboard pavement, and how to incorporate, through the depth of this pavement, proportionally related figures. With Alberti's treatise painting began to be acknowledged as an intellectual pursuit, related to the science of optics through perspective. In consequence, a painter, Piero della Francesca, wrote his own treatise on the subject. Piero, in painting, took up where Domenico Veneziano and Fra Angelico left off. His main aim, throughout his career, was to impose absolute order upon the multifarious elements of life. Whatever specific component is represented, he has transmuted it into a symbol of eternal reality, impervious to change. His psychological expression is at a minimum and his architectural spaces have the astringent logic of a geometrical theorem. Piero's art had a great impact upon that of central and northern Italy, providing the principal model for such artists as Melozzo da Forlì, Perugino, and, partially, the ubiquitous Antonello da Messina.

While Piero's style was spreading throughout Italy, other currents developed along less abstract principles. One of these involved the representation of contemporary personages. Just as the individual portrait, in the Quattrocento, became an increasingly common type of painting, so did the depiction of group scenes composed of actual people become a convention of style. In Mantua, ruled by Ludovico Gonzaga, Andrea Mantegna created a series of illusionistically forceful frescoes showing episodes of life at court. In Florence the alternate convention, started by Masaccio and continued by Filippo Lippi, of employing important persons as actors in religious scenes, was further utilized in Botticelli's *Adoration of the Magi*. Here tradition has always held the eldest Magus to be Cosimo de' Medici, while other characters have been tentatively considered as members of his family. Art, obviously, was a means to do homage or show allegiance. A Florentine contemporary of Botticelli, Ghirlandaio, became the leading specialist in this aspect of painting. Later Botticelli grew dissatisfied with this style and went on to create mythological and religious paintings that no longer resembled any external reality. They were the products of pure, imaginative fancy. The most famous of these, the dreamlike *Birth of Venus*, is a milestone in the revival of classical antiquity through its full-sized representation, for the first time, of a nude, pagan goddess.

Despite the success enjoyed by Botticelli in the sophisticated circles of Lorenzo de' Medici, it was not his style that shaped the course of European painting, but that of his contemporary, Leonardo da Vinci. To Leonardo science, technology and art were one, indivisible study, and his entire life was spent in an empirical research based upon observation and experience. He was trained in the large workshop of Verrocchio, and was probably a visitor in that of Pollaiuolo, where craftsmanship and technological experimentation were almost synonymous. Stylistically, both Verrocchio and Pollaiuolo presented the human body in correct, anatomical detail, with vigorous, tensed motion, thus expressing their belief that art should recreate life in dynamic terms, as opposed to Piero della Francesca's ideal of abstract order. Leonardo's style evolved from a combination of these two divergent schools of thought. After 1478 Leonardo conceived of compositional structure as being analogous to that of an organism whose components function responsively to one another, each indispensable to the rhythmic life of the whole. To achieve this, in his paintings, he invented psychological and physical situations which would trigger his figures into a chain reaction of motion. In the creation of this illusion of mobility, he showed his indebtedness to Verrocchio and Pollaiuolo. At the same time, he imposed Pieresque order on this mobility by compounding his figures into geometrical shapes. All this is seen in his *Adoration of the Magi*, whose unfinished state also reveals that he gave immediate three-dimensionality to his form without the use of color. This revolutionary technique (previously painters had always used color to model form) was necessary for Leonardo's sfumato, i.e., his elusive gradations of dark into light, where shapes emerge softly, as if veiled in atmosphere, and color is used only for emphasis. Even more important was his wish to paint whatever intrigued his imagination, whether or not it corresponded literally to anything in existence. This concept freed his Cinquecento followers from representational copying and brought about the Florentine High Renaissance. His reach for an ideal in painting also had a deep and lasting influence on the Lombard school of painting that had developed under such a master as Vincenzo Foppa.

Florence was not alone during these latter years of the Quattrocento in opening new horizons for painting. In Venice, Giovanni Bellini was considered by his contemporaries as the only artist equal to Leonardo da Vinci. Bellini shared Leonardo's deep feeling for nature, but this was manifested entirely in an instinctive worship of its visual existence rather than in an intellectual pursuit of its laws. Bellini had the ability to portray scenes, especially landscapes, of deep poetic beauty, through a phenomenal use of color. To understand this ability it is necessary to turn to Antonello da Messina, a Sicilian who intruded upon Venice and Venetian art in 1475. At some time in his early youth, Antonello had learned the Flemish masters' oil techniques, plus their style of diffused yet controlled luminosity, which he combined with his own warmth and gradation of color. By adopting Antonello's devices, pantheistic Bellini subsequently created his landscapes with richer, more intense colors that seem to glow in a mellow sunlight. His figures have lost their primary importance, and blend into a representation of nature as a whole.

Meanwhile, in Florence, under the influence of Leonardo, a new style began to develop known as the High Renaissance. Artists of this style strove to communicate, through their works, only lofty, noble feelings and ideas. They dismissed from their repertory anything that might appear insignificant, prosaic, or defective. Though the style began in Florence, Rome soon became its official home, thanks to Pope Julius II, who brought its two great protagonists, Michelangelo and

Raphael, into his court. Michelangelo, though primarily a sculptor, was eventually, in 1508, commissioned to paint the ceiling of the Sistine Chapel, while in 1509 Raphael started the walls of the *Stanza della Segnatura* in the Vatican. Raphael created his first frescoes with his characteristic untroubled serenity perfect balance, and calm control of tensions. Michelangelo, however, moved steadily toward the most dramatic moment of the Renaissance as he explored all the possibilities of his style so as to carry it to its most dynamic potential. His figures, begun as medium-scaled, smooth-surfaced, carefully delineated objects, explode into enormous forms with great complexity of movement and deep foreshortening. Their physical action demonstrates the power of a state of mind upon the body. Michelangelo's imagination had been stimulated by studying examples of Hellenistic art such as the *Laocoön* and the *Belvedere Torso*, and this brought about his new perception of the human figure. When, in 1511, Raphael at last experienced Michelangelo's new style, the impact reverberated throughout his work. Though still graceful and controlled, he also became dramatic in both style and subject matter. The departure of its greatest masters (Leonardo had gone for a second time to Milan) had not left Florence static. Fra Bartolommeo returned home here after a sojourn in Venice filled with impressions of Bellini's vivid paintings. His subsequent works, still following the precepts of the Florentine High Renaissance, show a new richness of tone and a fluctuating vibrancy of color. It was natural that his contemporaries, such as Albertinelli and Andrea del Sarto, the great colorist known as "the faultless painter," were influenced by this new approach. For the first two decades of the Cinquecento the High Renaissance style dominated Florentine and Roman art. Because of the instant fame that resulted from their tremendous achievements, its major exponents were considered classic and their works shared the status held, at this time, by those of the ancients. However, around 1518, a new generation of artists emerged who seemed to challenge the very foundations of this style. Rosso and Pontormo in Florence and Beccafumi in Siena produced works of a strident, violent, and emotionally irrational nature, distorting almost to the point of awkwardness their shapes and forms, and employing a minute, tight handling of their painted surfaces. This phase of their style suffered a metamorphosis when they, and also the strange, young Emilian, Parmigianino, ventured to Rome and were exposed to the grandiose art of Michelangelo, Raphael and the surviving heirs of Raphael's workshop, Giulio Romano and others. From this encounter evolved a new artistic language and a new ideal of beauty known to later generations as mannerism. Mannerist artists transposed from the Roman High Renaissance style only ideas of gracefulness, ornamentalism, and monumentality. They were no longer interested in experiencing nature, but wished to create, capriciously, a personal, intellectual game. Their paintings, still tending toward proportional distortion, are ambiguous in meaning and extravagantly pagan in character. This Roman period of mannerism was terminated in 1527 with the sack of Rome by mercenaries of Charles V. Its artists were dispersed, Parmigianino going to the north, Rosso eventually to France, where they continued to popularize their style. In the years that followed, the painters who came into prominence in Rome and Florence supported and developed this passion for enigmatic erudition, ornamental grace and calculated restraint of natural emotion. The works of Salviati, Giorgio Vasari, author of the famous *Lives*, and especially of Bronzino, the student of Pontormo and court painter to Florentine Cosimo I, emphasize this. The hard perfection of Bronzino's decorative form, the frigid brilliance of his color and light, his lack of spontaneity, were well suited to the sophisticated world of manners ruled by the second duke of Florence. During this period Michelangelo, whose long life carried him through many phases of art, returned to painting after an absence from it of twenty-five years. His *Last Judgment*, a fresco occupying the whole end wall of the Sistine Chapel, is difficult to categorize in terms of the art being created around him. His style has definitely changed from the classic one seen in his adjacent ceiling. It is no longer an embodiment of the exalted, orderly grandeur of the human spirit, but rather of the confusion, guilt, and oppression of human existence. Whether or not this resulted from his age, his republican despair at the restoration of the Medici to power, or the atmosphere of reform abroad in Italy, it is impossible to say.

Northern Italy, although affected at several moments throughout the Cinquecento by mannerist currents, managed to produce a whole trend of art which, sustained by poetical naturalism, sensuous pleasure, candid enjoyment of pagan mythology, actually increased its spontaneity of expression and warmth of communication. In Parma, Correggio, unlike his compatriot, Parmigianino, approached erotic themes with no self-consciousness. In his mature works, whether pagan or religious, his painted surfaces glow with rich, velvety color whose whole texture appears to palpitate and flow. His *Adoration of the Shepherds*, built, as most of his paintings are, upon a diagonally uncentered composition, shows, in its warm, reflected light, its casual momentary action, and the foreshortening of its figures, Correggio's desire to give to his paintings the feeling of an intimate, transitory moment of life in nature. In Venice, the tradition of Bellini's naturalism continued to provide inspiration for a new generation of artists. One of Bellini's pupils, Giorgione, is intricately connected with the history of landscape painting. His *Tempest* is believed by many to have no specific subject other than what is seen: a landscape in a thunderstorm, with a soldier and a nude woman nursing a child. If this is true, the painting was revolutionary, since previous representation always involved a religious, historical, or mythological theme. Giorgione painted his landscapes as momentary moods of nature. His figures, who seem to exert no energy for their existence, are only part of the natural whole, and are immersed in its atmosphere. Later, Giorgione broke with this poetic, pastoral style in his Fondaco dei Tedeschi frescoes, long since destroyed, where he, reportedly, gave torsion and exaggerated animation to his figures. Titian, supposedly Giorgione's assistant on the lost Fondaco frescoes, had an artistic career that extended for almost seventy years and, throughout its many phases, Titian never ceased to affirm his passionate enjoyment of life. He viewed human existence in epic terms, always sensuous and lavish, and saw the world as being in a constantly exciting state of flux. In his earlier, highly pagan period he demonstrated this in outdoor scenes where his form, asymmetrically placed geometrical shapes, seems to burst into the surrounding space. In his late years he carried this sensation of explosion into the whole composition, charging it with fervent emotion. In his superb portraiture he always gave a sense of noble dignity to his sitters, whether he presented them as majestically timeless creations or painted them in a momentary, journalistic style. Titian's luxurious, sumptuous female form became the symbol of the Venetian High Renaissance, as Michelangelo's male had been for that of Florence and Rome. More than any previous artist Titian released his brush from the bondage of precision and gave it free rein in the creation of light. His famous color is a combination of these vibrant brush strokes and the many warm glazes he applied over a finished work of art.

Painting in Venice during the later Cinquecento was not entirely dominated by Titian. Tintoretto and Veronese were also towering, creative personalities whose contributions insured the leadership of the Venetian school as a whole over the rest of Europe. The outlook of these two artists could not have been more different, and their styles developed in opposite directions. Tintoretto's paintings, from the 1560's on, are expressive of an urgent sense of crisis. The effect of a physical struggle between disparate forces in tension, seen in some of his paintings, comes from his sensational compositional method of creating of the whole painting a tunnel-like diagonal recession of space toward a lateral focal point with the main figures, in Michelangelesque foreshortening, placed in the corner of the foreground. Another of his compositional devices, used in his *Adoration of the Magi*, could be equated to a whirling movement in which the masses of figures are made the subjects of a prodigious phenomenon. Tintoretto made speed of execution one of the essential components of his creative process. Although it is known that some of his compositional effects were the result of calculated preparatory studies, Tintoretto's canvases always give the impression that the finished work was the product of a spontaneous, creative act. His velocity of execution could not have been for the financial remuneration to be gained through expediency and innumerable commissions, since the artist's willingness to work for moderate compensation is well documented.

Painting themes from the Old and New Testaments on a monumental scale was, for the artist, an intrinsic part of his religious experience. Ultimately, his main aim was to show in painting how the supernatural could be experienced through a transfiguration of objects of reality and this aim could be best fulfilled when the artist worked on large canvases where he could exploit to the maximum his visionary effects of light and color. To step from the world of Tintoretto into that of Veronese is to go from high nervous tension and oppression into a state of joyful exuberance. Veronese, too, turned out enormous canvases with representations from the New Testament, but his are endowed with a festive air and a devotion to luxurious existence. His famous *Marriage at Cana* and the *Feast in the House of Levi* are sumptuous spectacles where urban architecture on a grandiose scale, wide airy skies, provide an exhilarating stage effect for these lavish banqueting scenes.

The closing decades of the Cinquecento saw painting divided into two main schools of thought. One school believed that art should communicate overt feelings to the viewer, be openly expressive, and continue to investigate nature along the lines of Renaissance naturalism. The other school, mannerism, based itself upon an esthetic, intellectual pursuit, divorced from nature, that was intended above all to display the virtuosity of the artist. This latter style, though perhaps the more triumphant throughout Europe at the time, was subsequently discarded by the masters of the 17th century. The former style, however, which was warmly received in Venice and its territories, even in Lombardy, can be considered as the catalyst for the formation of the Baroque style, and as an important influence on European painting for generations thereafter. L.B.

Palazzolo (pä-lät-tsō′lō), **Lauro.** Jurisconsult, from Fano, who lived in the 15th century. He studied law at Padua, and wrote a treatise on the statutes excluding women from the succession (Pavia, 1490), and other legal works.

Paleario (pä-lā-ä′ryō), **Aonio.** [Also, **Antonio della Paglia** (or **degli Pagliaricci**); Latinized, **Aonius Palearius.**] Reformer and humanist; b. at Veroli, c1503; hanged at Rome, July 3, 1570. He passed his youth at Rome and then went to Perugia, Padua, and Siena, where he was the friend of learned men, pursued his studies in literature, philosophy, and theology, and tutored the children of prominent families to earn his living. From 1546 to 1555 he held the chair of eloquence at Lucca. He went next to Milan, where he held the same position. He was twice, 1542 at Siena and 1559 at Milan, denounced to the Inquisition on suspicion of following Protestant doctrines but both times was cleared of the charges. In 1567, however, a new charge was lodged against him. He was taken to Rome and imprisoned. After two years he signed a retraction of any heretical views. Since he refused to recant publicly in church, he was sentenced to death. He was hanged and his body was burned. Paleario's opinions and ideas appear in his writings. His *Actio in pontifices romanos et eorum asseclas* is a youthful work in which, besides condemning the popes and their sycophantic followers, he expresses the longing for the unity of all Christians. His *De immortalitate animorum,* in three books, is a poem written to contrast with, or in antithesis to, Lucretius' *De rerum natura.* It is a religious treatise that deals with important spiritual questions. It combines, along with echoes of Lucretius, traces of Vergil, Ovid, and the Scriptures, and is orthodox in its ideas as to the soul and what becomes of it after death. Works written in Italian include four books of letters and fourteen excellent humanistic orations.

Paleotti (pä-lā-ōt′tē), **Gabriele.** Cardinal; b. at Bologna, October 4, 1522; d. at Rome, July 23, 1597. He took his doctorate in law at Bologna, taught in the university, and then became canon of the cathedral (1549). He went to Rome in the suite of a cardinal, took part in the Council of Trent (1561), and was named a cardinal in 1565. He held many high ecclesiastical positions. He left a juridical treatise, *De nothis et spuriis* (1550), many pastoral letters and sermons, and a moral treatise, *De bono senectutis* (Rome, 1595), an Italian translation of which was published at Rome two years later.

Palestrina (pä-lās-trē′nä), **Giovanni Pierluigi da.** [Called **Princeps Musicae,** "Prince of Music."] Composer; b. at Palestrina, near Rome, c1524; d. at Rome, February 2, 1594. He went to Rome as a boy to study singing, and was a pupil (at least in 1539) of the Frenchman Robin Mallapert, who was choirmaster of S. Maria Maggiore. Later, he may have been a pupil of Jacob Arcadelt. In 1544 he was organist in the cathedral at Palestrina, of which the future Pope Julius III was then bishop. Soon after the elevation of Julius to the papacy Palestrina was invited (1551) to Rome to become choirmaster of the Cappella Giulia in the Vatican. He dedicated his *First Book of Masses* (1554) to Julius, and was made (January, 1555) a singer in the Pontifical Choir as a reward. Julius died in March of the same year. He was succeeded by Marcellus II, who died after a reign of three weeks and was succeeded by Paul IV. Marcellus had expressed his concern that the music was obscuring the meaning of the sacred texts which were being sung to it. Paul, a reformer, maintained that clarity of the text should be paramount in church music. He also rectified what he considered abuses in the musical organization of the church, and issued an edict declaring that membership in the Pontifical Choir was restricted to unmarried men. Palestrina, who had married (1547) when he was organist at Palestrina, and two others were dismissed, with pensions, as a result of this edict. He gave up his post as choirmaster in the Cappella Giulia, and then incurred the pope's displeasure by publishing (1555) a collection of secular compositions, his *First Book of Madrigals*. He became choirmaster in St. John Lateran in the same year, and held the post until 1560 when he gave it up for financial reasons. Other posts he held in the course of a busy life were as master of musical events (in 1564 and again in 1567) for Cardinal Ippolito d'Este at Tivoli, first master of music in the Roman Seminary, and again as choirmaster in the Cappella Giulia from 1571 to his death. About 1568 he completed a Mass for Duke Guglielmo Gonzaga of Mantua, and began an association with the duke that lasted until the duke's death (1586). Between 1572 and 1580 he lost two of his sons. They had been his pupils and he had high hopes for their musical futures. In the same period his wife died (1580) and for a time he entertained, briefly, the idea of taking orders. Instead, within less than a year he married a wealthy widow and for a time even took an active part in her deceased husband's business as a furrier. In the period (1572–1580) he published little, but between 1581 and his death in 1594 he published 17 volumes with 320 compositions, including Masses, madrigals, Motets, hymns, Lamentations, Magnificats, Psalms, Litanies, and other works.

The Council of Trent (1545–1563), convoked to combat Protestantism, consider reform and strengthening of the Church, took up, among other things, the question of church music. A Commission of Cardinals to study the subject was established and sat (1564–1565) at Rome. The conclusion of the commission was that music in the church should be an extension of the liturgy; that its purpose was not to serve as a vehicle to give pleasure, but that it should clarify and enhance the sacred text. Secular tunes were forbidden. The question of polyphony was discussed. Some felt that polyphonic music, with its overlapping voices, tended to obscure the text, and the possibility of restricting church music to monody was discussed. Palestrina, a master of counterpoint, was able to convince the pope with three of his Masses that the sacred words could be clear and comprehensible in contrapuntal compositions. He set the texts to music that deepened and adorned the spirit and intent of the words. In the Preface to his *Second Book of Masses* (1567), he wrote that he had "endeavored to adorn the Mass with music of a new order in accordance with the most serious and religious-minded persons in high places." Of his 105 surviving Masses, the *Missa Papae Marcelli*, written after the death of Pope Marcellus II and published in the *Second Book of Masses*, is called by some his greatest work, notable for its architectonic structure, dignity, and restraint. In 1569 he published his *First Book of Motets* which, in the novelty and freshness of his phrasing and the variety of his rhythms, added to his already considerable fame. He composed at an astonishing rate (and published as he could afford to). His compositions had enormous influence on ecclesiastical music, and enormous importance for the artistry, now intense and moving, now balanced and serene, with which his music illuminated the texts.

Palingenio (pä-lēn-jen'yō). See **Manzoli, Pier Angelo de la Stellata.**

Palissy (pȧ-lē-sē), **Bernard.** French potter and enameler; b. at Chapelle Biron, near Agen, France, probably c1510; d. in the Bastille, Paris, 1589. In 1539 he established himself at Saintes, where he married and practiced the business of surveying. In 1553 he chanced to see a glazed cup which suggested experiments with enamels. He at first sought only a white enamel, and for some time failed in his attempts, but at length succeeded. He then tried to produce the various colors of nature. For sixteen years he labored in extreme destitution before he succeeded in making the ware in high relief and rustic figurines associated with his name. He embraced the Reformed religion, and was one of the principal founders of the Calvinistic Church at Saintes. In 1562 his atelier was raided and devastated as a place of politico-religious meetings. He was arrested and imprisoned at Bordeaux, but was saved from the lot of his co-religionists by Anne de Montmorency (then high constable of France), who interceded with the queen, Catherine de Médicis. Set at liberty, Palissy attached himself to the king, the queen mother Catherine, and Montmorency. The latter brought Palissy to Paris, where he set up his furnaces in the tileyards (*tuileries*), where the palace known as the Tuileries was built (in the 19th century, four of his furnaces were discovered under the palace). In 1566 he was commissioned by Catherine with the construction of grottoes and other works in the Tuileries gardens. He was engaged in this work in 1572 when the massacre of Saint Bartholomew occurred. His life was saved by the protection of Queen Catherine herself. In 1573 he opened a course of lectures in natural history, and continued this until 1584. He was among the very first to substitute positive experiment for the explanations of the schoolmen. He also investigated the geology of the Paris basin, and formed the first cabinet of natural history in France. In 1588 he was arrested because of his religion and thrown into the Bastille, and died there. His writings were published between 1557 and 1580.

Palla degli Strozzi (päl′lä dā′lyē strōt′tsē). Florentine humanist and merchant prince; b. at Florence, c1373; d. at Padua, 1462. A wealthy and cultivated man, he was active in civic and political affairs at Florence. He was above all interested in humanistic studies, and especially in Greek. He was instrumental in bringing Manuel Chrysoloras to Florence as the first teacher of Greek in the university there, and was one of his pupils. He had tried to remain neutral in the struggle between the Albizzi and Medici families for control of Florence. However, when Cosimo returned from exile, 1434, and the Albizzi were banished, Palla, as an outstanding and wealthy man, conspicuous in the republic and a potential rival, was banished to Padua and never allowed to return to Florence. In Padua he continued his literary studies and lent his encouragement and patronage to others who wished to do the same. His house became a center for Hellenic studies. Such Greek scholars as Argyropoulos and Andronicos Callistus, whom Palla provided with Greek codices and befriended in other ways, read Aristotle in Greek and expounded on the text to the assembled listeners. Palla gathered an important collection of Greek codices, which he made available to students and which he willed to the Convent of Santa Giustina (the collection has since been scattered). Vespasiano tells how Palla determined to bring Greek studies to a par with Latin studies in Florence, and of how he succeeded in raising them to a position that they had not hitherto enjoyed. He also tells of Palla's system of educating his children (he early engaged Tommaso Parentucelli, the future Pope Nicholas V, as tutor for his children and befriended the future pope in many ways), his virtuous wife, and of how he turned to matters of the spirit when, one by one, death took his sons from him. Palla was the first to plan a public library, but was prevented from carrying out his plans by his political misfortunes. His great contributions were as a cultivated and upright man who began the revival of Greek studies in Florence and the preservation of Greek literature for Italy and the West.

Palladio (päl-lä′dyō), **Andrea.** [Original name, **Andrea di Pietro.**] Architect; b. at Padua, November 30, 1508; d. at Vicenza, August 19, 1580. The son of a carpenter, he became the protégé of the wealthy humanist Gian Giorgio Trissino. Trissino fostered his talents, encouraged and aided his classical studies, gave him the name Palladio (from Pallas), and took him to Rome several times. At Rome, following the accepted method of training architects in the Renaissance, Palladio enthusiastically set to work drawing the ancient monuments and, in some cases, drawing reconstructions of those that had fallen into ruin. Some drawings are preserved in the Royal Institute of British Architects and in the Uffizi, and are the more precious as they show more of the monuments than survives today. The drawings of the monuments at Rome and of those in other parts of Italy are reproduced in his *Quattro libri dell' architettura*. In the four books (published first in 1570, in a number of editions thereafter, and in several translations) are illustrations of the classical orders, drawings of certain ancient buildings, and many of Palladio's own plans and elevations. The treatise had great influence, especially on English architecture through the work of the 17th century English architect Inigo Jones, who traveled in Italy, studied Palladio's buildings, and introduced his style to England. One of the finest of late 16th-century architects, Palladio's style was based on his enthusiasm for the classical and his study of Vitruvius (for the Barbaro edition of which (1556) he made the illustrations), and was influenced by that of Bramante and, especially in mannerist ornamentation, by that of Michelangelo. He spent most of his life and carried out most of his constructions in and about the city of Vicenza where, in his time, a period of prosperity led to great building activity. The number of private palaces and houses built to his designs in the city gave it the name "the city of Palladio."

When he was about 40 he was commissioned to construct a reinforcement for the medieval Sala della Ragione (the Town Hall) at Vicenza. The existing building, a basilica, recalled the great Roman monuments and his design for its reconstruction was in the monumental classical style. He designed a double portico or loggia of two tiers of superposed arches that runs around three sides of the building. Round arches rest on columns that in turn rest, in the upper story, on a balustrade. The arches, with their smaller supporting columns, are separated by massive, engaged, superposed columns which form the supporting piers of the portico. These run the height of the story, are double at the ends to weight the corners, and are Doric in the lower story and Ionic in the upper. Above the cornice is a balustrade ornamented with statues. The double portico presents a series of framed arches, grandiose and rhythmical, and beautifully proportioned. In his design for it Palladio employed the classical orders, round arches, balustrades, and ornamental statues that became features of many of his designs, whether for public buildings, palaces, houses, or villas. The work of construction of the portico proceeded very slowly, as by 1580 only a few of the arches were finished, but it was carried out in faithful adherence to his design, which was published in the third of his *Quattro libri* and had great influence on contemporary architects. Among the palaces remaining at Vicenza that illustrate Palladio's style are the Palazzo Valmarana, Palazzo Porto Barbaran, Palazzo Chiericati, and Palazzo Porto Breganze ("Casa del Diavolo"). In the Chiericati Palace (now the Museo Civico) Palladio achieved elegance and grace through the strict horizontals and harmoniously spaced verticals of a double portico, the columns of which are Doric in the lower story and Ionic in the upper. Public buildings either wholly or partly designed by Palladio are the Loggia del Capitano at Vicenza, never finished, and the Teatro Olimpico, completed after his death. The latter is his interesting attempt to adapt the plan of an antique Roman theater to a covered hall. The auditorium is a semi-ellipse with rows of seats that rise steeply to the back away from the stage. Behind the proscenium he designed a permanent stage setting. Sloping upward from front to back, the stage was constructed to give the appearance of one side of a piazza, from which several streets disappear into the background, the buildings along the side streets being constructed in perspective to give the illusion of depth and distance. As the ancient theaters were open, the ceiling of Palladio's theater was painted with clouds to resemble the sky. The building is the outstanding example of this type of construction, of which a number were erected in the 16th century. Other buildings designed by Palladio are the churches of S. Giorgio Maggiore and Il Redentore at Venice, in both of which he employed the classical orders and pediments on the façades and made use of columns in the interior to control the flow of light and compose the space. But Palladio's principal and most important activity, and the one that had such influence in the design of English country houses was in the design of villas in the countryside around Vicenza. We have the best accounts of such work from Palladio himself, who gives precise plans in his *Quattro libri* (although the buildings were not always built precisely according to the design). In the country houses the constant characteristics were harmonious proportion and perfect symmetry about one or two axes, and mathematically exact proportions in the progression of the rooms, that is, the rooms opening from what was often a large central hall decreased in size proportionately as they were farther away from the center. Proportion and symmetry are maintained in the architectural elements themselves—doors, windows, intercolumniation, arches, staircases, on the façade and in the interior. Typically, a Palladian villa consisted of a central block, with a portico, and symmetrical blocks on each side, sometimes attached and sometimes connected to the main block by passages. Frequently the central block, or its portico, was crowned by a pediment supported by columns and adorned with statues at the apex and the side angles, or by a balustrade ornamented with statues. His designs for the Villa Godi at Lonedo and the Villa Malcontenta on the Brenta exemplify these features. One of the most famous of Palladio's villas is the Villa Rotonda, about two miles from Vicenza. It is atypical in that it is a square central block surmounted by a dome over a circular hall. At the center of each side of the square block is an attached portico, with Ionic columns and a pediment.

After Brunelleschi and Bramante, Palladio was perhaps the leading Renaissance architect. Although he never conceived designs of such originality and monumentality as Brunelleschi's dome at Florence or Bramante's plan for a new St. Peter's, he was unsurpassed in his time in his feeling for the antique and in his generally successful attempts to apply antique motifs and ideas to the architectural needs of his day. He was also extremely fortunate in his clients who, in the main, left him free to make plans according to his own esthetic judgment and taste.

Palladio, Blosio. [Real name, **Biagio Pallai.**] Humanist; b. at Colleveteri; d. at Rome, August 13, 1550. He was secretary to popes Clement VII and Paul III, and was named bishop of Foligno by the latter. He wrote elegant Latin prose and verse. An example of his poetry is his description of the villa of Agostino Chigi outside Rome. His *Coryciana* (Rome, 1524) is a selection of the poems written in a contest to honor Hans Goritz, a German Maecenas living at Rome. The poems were contributed by the many poets at Rome who had enjoyed his favor.

Palma (päl′mä), **Jacopo.** [Original name, **Iacopo d'Antonio Negreti** (or **Nigreti** or **Nigretti**), called **Palma il Vecchio,** "the Elder."] Painter; b. at Serinalta (Bergamo), c1480; d. at Venice, July 30, 1528. He probably went to Venice as a very young man and formed his style under the influence of Giovanni Bellini, whose art was probably passed to him through a group of provincial Bergamasque imitators of Bellini. The Bergamasque influence remained a constant in his work in his brilliant color, of which the later *Judith*, Uffizi, is a characteristic example. Also Bergamasque and provincial was the simplicity of his compositions and his practice of painting each panel of a triptych as if it were a separate painting long after the Venetians had abandoned that custom and had adopted the idea of a triptych as a unity. In other respects Palma departed from the provincialism of the Bergamasque painters to follow the developments of Venetian art, and was among the first to follow Giorgione. The influence of the latter is already apparent in some of his youthful *Madonnas*. From early in the 16th century date a group of mythological paintings, of excellent color and execution, with romantic landscape backgrounds. One of these, *Halberdier Watching a Woman Seated in a Meadow with Two Infants*, Museum of Art, Philadelphia, is a variation on Giorgione's *Tempest* (according to some, the subjects are Rhea Silvia, Mars, and Romulus and Remus). Later Palma gave a broader form to his compositions and made much more use of the nude, as in his *Adam and Eve*, Brunswick, *Two Nymphs*, Frankfurt, and *Venus*, Dresden. He was for a time strongly attracted to the dreamlike, Arcadian world of Giorgione, and for some years after the latter's death followed this manner. Later he was influenced by Titian and veered off in a new direction. Palma's Giorgionesque lyricism gave way to an art that, failing to achieve the dramatic grandeur of Titian, seemed to anticipate the Baroque. About this time (after 1518) he began that series of portraits of women in which he exalted a grave, blonde, sensual beauty, as in the portraits at Berlin, the Poldi Pezzoli, Milan, and the Lichtenstein collection. Perhaps because of his predilection for painting opulent blonde beauties, one of his favorite subjects became the *Sacra Conversazione* (*Holy Conversation*) with groups of female saints gathered, often in a pleasant landscape. His *St. Barbara*, in the triptych of S. Maria Formosa at Venice, is the embodiment of the new Venetian ideal of feminine beauty, and was painted in the period 1522–1523. Another very beautiful work of the same period is the *Holy Conversation with the Baptist, Magdalen and Joseph*, Accademia, Venice (finished by Titian). In this late masterpiece, as in earlier works, Palma remains placid and harmonious, brilliant in color, and without the high drama of the art of Titian. In his will of 1528 Palma left a list of sixty-two paintings, many of which were unfinished. His friends and pupils completed a number of them. Lotto, who had also influenced his work, finished *Assassination of Peter Martyr*, Church of S. Martino, Alzano Lombardo (Bergamo), Cariani finished two paintings on *The Holy Family with St. Francis*, one at Brescia and another at Budapest. *Concert*, National Gallery, London, and most of *Holy Family and Saints*, San Francisco, were finished by Bonifazio; *Christ Among the Doctors*, Accademia, Venice, by Girolamo da Santacroce; and *Storm at Sea*, Ścuola Grande di S. Marco, Venice, by Paris Bordone. Many of his paintings are at Venice, in churches, the Accademia, and other collections. Other examples of his work are at Bergamo, Florence (Uffizi), Genoa, Milan (Brera, Poldi Pezzoli), Naples, Rome (Borghese, Colonna, Capitoline), Rovigo, Serina, Turin, Vicenza, in the principal museums of Europe, and at Brooklyn, Fogg Museum, Cambridge, Chicago, Minneapolis, San Diego (California), Sarasota (Florida), Worcester, and elsewhere.

Palma, Jacopo. [**Iacopo Nigretti,** called **Palmail Giovane,** "the Younger."] Painter; b. at Venice, 1544; d. there, 1628. He was the son of Antonio Nigretti, a painter, and the grand-nephew of Palma il Vecchio (c1480–1528), was a pupil of his father and probably of Titian, whose last masterpiece, *Pietà*, he finished. In 1559 he was at Rome and in 1568 at Urbino and in these places came in contact with the art of Michelangelo and mannerism. Returned to Venice after 1568, he formed his definitive style under the influence of Tintoretto, of whom, in a somewhat superficial and theatrical manner, he became the faithful imitator. He was very active at Venice, where many of his paintings

Jacopo Palma il Giovane
Virgin and Child in the Clouds Adored by Five Saints
Courtesy of The Pierpont Morgan Library, New York

survive, and was among the more important painters who, after the great fire of 1577, collaborated in redecorating the Ducal Palace. He also made cartoons for mosaics for S. Marco. Distinguished for his fresh coloring, in his earlier works he was compared not unfavorably with Tintoretto and Paolo Veronese, who also influenced him. Later he became careless and was therefore categorized by the scholar Luigi Lanzi as the last painter of the good and the first of the bad epoch in the Venetian school. Among his paintings is *The Crucifixion of St. Peter*, Accademia, Venice,

St. Margaret, Uffizi, one of his finest works, and *The Annunciation: God the Father*, Museum of Fine Arts, Boston. Other works are in the Brera, Milan, at Naples, National Gallery, London, Madrid, Munich, and elsewhere.

Palmerucci (päl-mā-röt′chē), **Guido** or **Guiduccio.** Painter of Gubbio; b. 1280; d. after 1349. His name is mentioned in documents from 1315 to 1342, when he was commissioned to paint an *Assumption* in the Palazzo dei Consoli at Gubbio. Most of his surviving work is at Gubbio (Pinacoteca, Palazzo dei Consoli, frescoes in S. Maria dei Laici and S. Maria Nuova), and reveals the influence of Sienese painting, especially in the types. He may have been a pupil of Meo da Siena, who was active at Perugia, and was a follower of the Lorenzetti brothers. Other examples of his work are at Forlì, Nancy, and Cambridge (Massachusetts).

Palmezzano (päl-med-dzä′nō), **Marco.** Painter; b. at Forlì, 1456 (according to a dubious inscription on a self-portrait at Forlì) or 1459; d. 1539. Some confusion exists about his life and work, as many signatures and dates on his paintings seem to be false. He was the pupil and assistant of Melozzo da Forlì, who had the greatest influence on him. To the influence of Melozzo was grafted, in later years, traces of the influence of Mantegna, the Ferrarese Lorenzo Costa, and finally, as a result of frequent contacts with Venice, that of the Venetians Cima da Conegliano, Bellini, and Rondinelli. He was probably with Melozzo at Loreto between 1485 and 1492, and there executed the fresco *The Entry of Christ into Jerusalem*, in the Chapel of the Treasury, to designs by Melozzo. Among the works in which the influence of Melozzo is evident are *Crucifixion* (1492) and *Annunciation*, in the Pinacoteca, Forlì, and a *Crucifixion* in the Uffizi. From the time of his signed and dated (1493) *Madonna between Four Saints*, Brera, Milan, other influences become apparent, as those mentioned above. After 1500 he produced a great number of paintings, often making several versions, or even copies, of the same one, as his *Christ Carrying the Cross*, versions of which are in the Johnson Collection, Philadelphia (1532), Bob Jones University, Greenville (South Carolina), at Bonn (1503), Brescia, Cracow (1536), Faenza, Forlì (1535), Lovere (1537), Prague (1534), the Vatican, Weimar, and Zagreb. Among the notable works of this minor provincial painter are the *Communion of the Apostles*, Forlì, *Coronation of the Virgin*, Brera, *Christ Supported by Angels*, Louvre, each of which is reminiscent of a different painter. Among the portraits he left is one presumed to be Cesare Borgia, Forlì, and self-portraits at Forlì and in the Carrara Academy Bergamo. The most consistent period of his painting career was in his young days when the influence of Melozzo was dominant. Thereafter his eclecticism led to confusion and loss of identity as an artist. He left a great number of paintings, especially in and about Forlì, in many other cities of Italy, and examples of his work are to be found in many of the great museums of Europe, as well as at Baltimore, Brooklyn, Cambridge, Phoenix (Arizona), and Sarasota (Florida).

Palmieri (päl-mye′rē), **Matteo.** Florentine humanist and public official; b. at Florence, January 13, 1406; d. there, April 13, 1475. He became proficient in Latin, wrote in that language and in Italian as well. He held many official positions at Florence and served on several diplomatic missions. His masters had been among the famous humanists of the day. His Latin writings included an historical chronicle, *De temporibus*, in which he continued the work of an ancient chronicler and brought his history from 449 to 1449, thus being among the first to attempt a history of the Middle Ages. He also wrote a history of Florence and a chronicle of the Pisan war. His Italian works were *Della vita civile*, a dialogue in four books in which he discussed the qualities needed for proper management of the family and for the guidance of a state and a good citizen. His *La città di vita* is a long poem, in 100 cantos in imitation of Dante. He told his friend Leonardo Dati that he was ordered to write the poem in a dream. In it the poet is guided by the Cumaean Sibyl through the Elysian Fields. Among other things, he sees the souls of those angels who had refused to make a choice either for God or for Satan. These angels are about to be reborn as men to compel them to choose. As, in human form, they choose good or evil they will enjoy eternal glory or suffer damnation. The work is divided into three parts, also in imitation of Dante. In the first the angels who are to be reborn appear. In the second, the houses of evil of earth are traversed under the guidance of a malign spirit. In the third the houses of good of earth are traversed under the guidance of a good spirit. Matteo did not publish his work in his lifetime. He sent it, under seal, to the Guild of the Notaries at Florence, with instructions that it should not be opened until after his death. At the public funeral that was decreed for this public servant, the sealed manuscript was placed on his breast. When it was later opened the work was condemned as heretical by the Church.

Palsgrave (palz′grāv, pôlz′-), **John.** English scholar; b. at London, c1480; d. there, 1554. He was appointed teacher of French to the Princess Mary, sister of Henry VIII, before her marriage (1514) to Louis XII of France. He remained in her service, returning to England with her when she married (1515) Charles Brandon, 1st duke of Suffolk. He became tutor to the king's bastard son, Henry Fitzroy, duke of Richmond (1525), went to Oxford in 1531, and was presented with the living of Saint Dunstan's in the East, London, by Thomas, Archbishop Cranmer, in 1533. He wrote a book containing his method of instruction, a grammar and dictionary combined, entitled, *Lesclaircissement de la Langue Francoyse, composé par Maistre Jehan Palsgrave, Angloys, Natif de Londres, et Gradué de Paris,* in 1530. It is a valuable record of the exact state of the French and English languages at the time.

Pancirolli (pän-chē-rōl′lē), **Guido.** Jurisconsult; b. at Reggio Emilia, April 17, 1523; d. at Padua or Venice, March 5, 1599. He studied at Ferrara, Bologna, and Padua, and taught at Padua and Turin. Among his learned and elegant Latin works is his *De claris legum interpretibus,* a history of Roman and Medieval jurisconsults as well as of jurists of the Church.

Pandolfini (pän-dôl-fē′nē), **Agnolo.** Florentine public official and humanist; b. 1360; d. 1446. He was a member of a wealthy and prominent Florentine family, and was highly respected for both his learning and his integrity. He served Florence as a member of the Signory, gonfaloniere of justice, ambassador to King Ladislaus of Naples (from whom he secured the city of Cortona for Florence), Pope Martin V, and to the Emperor Sigismund when the latter was at Siena and extremely annoyed with the Florentines because they refused him passage through their territory. According to Vespasiano, he was a man of peace and a moderating influence on turbulent Florentine affairs of state. Although he favored the return of Cosimo de' Medici (he had protested against his exile) in 1434, he was grieved by the exile of his relative Palla degli Strozzi that resulted from Cosimo's return, and withdrew from public life. He retired to his villa and devoted himself to letters. All men of note who came to Florence visited him at his villa which, again according to Vespasiano, was sumptuously appointed, and sought his advice on literary as well as on political matters. Formerly a work entitled *Governo della famiglia* was attributed to him. Later research has established that it was part of Book III of Leon Battista Alberti's *Della Famiglia.* Vespasiano records that on his wedding night Pandolfini told his bride what he expected of her in her management of the household, and advised her to take it to heart as he did not intend to repeat it. She bore him three sons and died at an early age. He remained a widower until his death, about fifty years.

Pandone (pän-dô′nā), **Porcelio.** Humanist; b. at Naples, c1405; d. January, 1485. In 1434 he was sent on a mission to the Council of Basel, but on his return was imprisoned for having taken part against Pope Eugenius IV. After about ten years he was released, and wandered from court to court in Italy, composing adulatory poems (in return for rewards) for Martin V, Alfonso of Naples, Sigismondo Malatesta (*De amore Iovis in Isottam, Jove's love for Isotta;* Isotta was Sigismondo's mistress), Federico da Montefeltro, and others. He also wrote *Commentaria,* a report in two books of hexameters on the campaign of the Milano-Venetian War. Alfonso of Naples commissioned the work; Pandone spent the years 1452 and 1453 at Piccinino's camp to gather material for it; and in writing it compared Piccinino to Scipio Aemilianus and his adversary, Francesco Sforza, to Hannibal. Pandone's Latin verse is fluent (although his hexameters in the *Commentaria* were severely criticized). He owned a famous codex of Terence that later became part of Pietro Bembo's library.

Panigarola (pä-nē-gä-rō′lä), **Francesco.** Orator, preacher, and writer; b. at Milan, January 6, 1548; d. at Asti, May 31, 1594. He entered orders at an early age, studied at Padua, Pisa, and Paris, and, returned to Italy, spent thirteen years preaching in all parts of the peninsula. In 1587 he was named bishop of Asti. The following year Sixtus V sent him to Paris to plead the cause of the Holy League against Henry IV. Panigarola left many works on theology, some commentaries, a manual of eloquence, and collections of sermons. He was one of the foremost preachers of his day, notable as well for the literary structure of his sermons as for the cogency of his arguments. In his literary ornamentation he was a forerunner of 16th-century mannerism in rhetoric.

Panormita (pä-nōr′mē-tä), **Antonio.** [Original name, **Antonio Beccadelli.**] Humanist; b. at Palermo, 1394; d. at Naples, January 19, 1471. His name Panormita comes from Panormus, the Latin name of Palermo. Of good family, he left Palermo (1419) to pursue his studies. In Siena, where Enea Silvio (later Pius II) was a fellow pupil, he studied law and took enthusiastic part in the disorderly and sensual student life that was typical in Siena at the time. From this period is derived much of the material of his celebrated work *Hermaphroditus*. This came out at Bologna (1425) where he passed the years 1425–1427. It was greeted with scandalized cries and shouts of applause. The work, in two books, is a collection of erotic, obscene, and satirical epigrams, all expressed in elegant and ringing Latin verse. Panormita was an ardent student of the classics and a celebrated humanist. It is said he once sold a farm in order to buy a manuscript of Livy. His *Hermaphroditus* derives from the works of Martial, a 1st century Latin poet who graphically described the degenerate life of his time in fourteen books of epigrams. Panormita's book was forbidden by the Church. He also studied at Florence, Rome, and Pavia and finished his law course, but he decided that the law was not for him and sought a patron under whom he could pursue his literary interests. He obtained a post at Milan as professor of history, was named (1429) court poet by Filippo Maria Visconti and crowned (1432) with the laurel by the emperor Sigismund. In 1434 he joined Alfonso I at Palermo, and later accompanied him to Naples when Alfonso was victorious in establishing his claim to that tormented kingdom. Panormita served as his secretary, and read and discoursed on Livy to the king and his court daily. He was tutor to Alfonso's son Ferrante and served on several diplomatic missions for the king. He enjoyed the friendship of a number of the outstanding men of his time and had a wide correspondence with them. Two collections of his letters are in the Vatican. He wrote a life of Alfonso I of Naples, with the object of establishing that monarch's fame in history. His verse, of which he wrote a great deal, is of interest for the skill and grace with which he followed Latin forms.

Pantagruel (pän′-tȧ-grü-el). King of the Dipsodes and son of Gargantua, in François Rabelais' *History of Gargantua and Pantagruel*.

Pantaléon (päṅ-tȧ-lā-ôṅ), **Jacques.** Original name of Pope **Urban IV.**

Panurge (pȧ-nürzh). Character in François Rabelais' *History of Gargantua and Pantagruel*. He is a companion whom Pantagruel picks up at Paris, much as Morgante picked up Margutte in Pulci's *Morgante maggiore*, and like Margutte, a completely developed comic character. A roguish libertine, he cannot decide whether to marry, and the investigation of the entire problem of marriage occupies entertainingly the latter part of Rabelais' work.

Panvinio (pän-vē′nyō), **Onufrio.** [Real name, **Giacomo Panvinio.**] Historian and humanist; b. at Verona, February 23, 1530; d. at Palermo, April 7, 1568. He took the Augustinian habit at the age of 11. Thereafter he studied at Verona, Padua, and Naples. Called to Rome in 1549, he remained there and enjoyed the patronage of cardinals and popes. Pope Pius IV named him to a post at the Vatican Library. His great interest was in the study and interpretation of ancient Rome, and to this he devoted himself with great energy. Among his many works is *Comizi imperiali*, histories of such Roman families as the Savelli, Mattei, Massimi, and Frangipani. He was noted in his own day for his learning and industry. Titian painted his portrait.

Paolino da Pistoia (pä-ō-lē′nō dä pēs-tō′yä), Fra. Painter and sculptor; b. at Pistoia, 1490; d. there, 1547. About 1503 he went to Florence and in 1516 was at Siena. He had become a Dominican monk and was a close follower of Fra Bartolommeo, also a Dominican, whose drawings Fra Paolino inherited on Fra Bartolommeo's death. He worked chiefly in Florence and Pistoia; a number of his works are in the museum (*Annunciation*)

Fra Paolino da Pistoia
Crucifixion
Study for a fresco in the Cloister of S. Spirito, Siena
Gabinetto Disegni e Stampe degli Uffizi
Foto Soprintendenza

and churches of Pistoia. Other examples of his work are at Empoli, Florence, Modena, Rome, S. Gimignano, Siena, Vinci, Viterbo, Notre Dame University (Indiana), and elsewhere.

Paolo da Castro (pä′ō-lō dä käs′trō). Jurist; active at the end of the 14th century and the beginning of the 15th century. He was a pupil of Baldo degli Ubaldi, took his doctorate at Avignon, and taught law there with great success. He then taught at Siena, returned to Avignon (1394–1412), taught at Padua (1429–1441), and next went to Florence, where he had earlier (1415) helped to reform the statutes. He was a keen student of both the theory and the practice of law, and his comments and opinions rank next in importance after those of Bartolo and Baldo.

Paolo di Dono (dē dō′nō). See **Paolo Uccello.**

Paolo di Giovanni Fei (dē jō-vän′nē fā). See **Fei, Paolo di Giovanni.**

Paolo da Perugia (dä pā-rö′jä). Man of letters; b. at Perugia; d. at Naples, 1348. Boccaccio, who knew him, spoke of him as the "librarian of King Robert." He was a minor clerk, with numerous offspring, and died poor. His *Collectiones,* his most important work, mentioned by Boccaccio, who mourned the fact that it had been lost, was a genealogy of God. He also wrote commentaries on Horace and Aulus Persius Flaccus (Latin poet of the 1st century), and was a forerunner of Neapolitan humanism.

Paolo di Stefano (dē stā′fä-nō). [Called **Paolo Schiavo.**] Florentine painter; d. at Pisa, 1478. Listed among the Florentine painters (1428), he was a pupil and follower of Bicci di Lorenzo. A *Crucifixion and Adorers,* signed and dated (1440), was painted for S. Apollonia at Florence. One of his most important works was a fresco cycle with scenes from the lives of St. Stephen and St. Lawrence in the Collegiata in Castiglione d'Olona, where he was influenced by Masolino di Panicale. A fresco of *The Madonna and Child Enthroned,* was recently detached from the façade of SS. Apostoli, Florence, and revealed a lovely *sinopia* with the fluid line reminiscent of Masolino. Many of his works survive; among them are a signed and dated (1436) fresco, *Madonna and Child and Saints,* S. Miniato al Monte, Florence; a signed and dated (1460) *Assumption* and frescoes at Monticelli (S. Maria della Querce), near Florence; and works at Arezzo (S. Francesco), Pisa, San Piero a Sieve (Tabernacolo delle Mozzete), Vespignano (S. Martino), Berlin, Minneapolis, and elsewhere.

Paolo Uccello (öt-chel′lō). [Real name, **Paolo di Dono.**] Painter; b. at Pratovecchio, Casentino, 1397; d. at Florence, 1475. It is reported that his name "Uccello" was given to him for his delight in painting birds (*uccelli*). He appears to have had his early training, perhaps under Starnina, in the late International Gothic style, which eminently appealed to his love of fantasy and nostalgia for the romance of the past. To this style he added the plasticity of Masaccio in some degree and the strict perspective of Brunelleschi, developing perspective in a scientific manner as no earlier artist had done. Vasari writes that he spent long hours over his studies, and when his wife urged him to come to bed he sighed instead, "How delightful is this perspective." Vasari rather sharply criticized him for this preoccupation, and remarked that if he had spent less time on it he might have become one of the best and most original artists of his time. The critic would have preferred him to concentrate on creating his exact and wondrous drawings of birds and animals (some of which were in

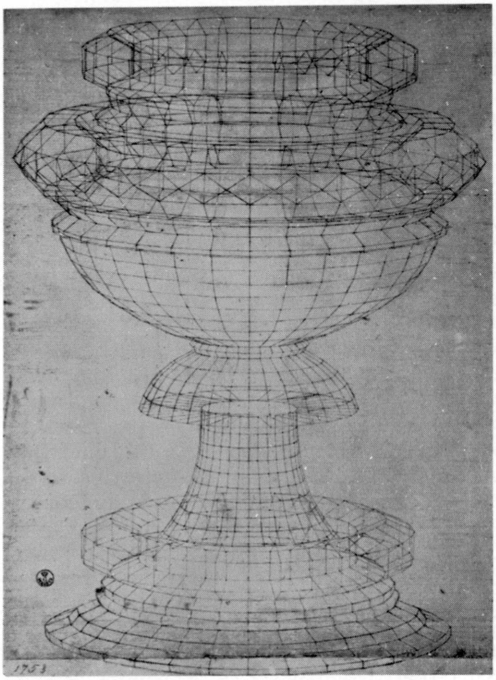

PAOLO UCCELLO
Study in perspective for a chalice
Gabinetto Disegni e Stampe degli Uffizi
Foto Soprintendenza

Vasari's possession), rather than wasting his time in working out problems in perspective. Uccello's studies, however, made of perspective a science, and provided a tool that marked a great step forward in the ability of artists to represent the space and depth of reality, a representation that was no longer a matter of chance and a particular artist's eye but that became the result of operative rules. Uccello's work had great influence on subsequent painters, as Piero della Francesca, Signorelli, and others. In his highly decorative works he filled his sharply outlined forms with pure, vibrant, almost shadowless color; his relief was obtained principally by line and perspective. (Another complaint of Vasari's was that Uccello painted pink and green horses and buildings as he chose and in defiance of nature, but he gave Uccello credit for painting realistic landscapes when he wished.) Intrigued as he was by his romantic notions of medieval chivalry, and fascinated as he was by the science of perspective, he produced works that in their clear statement of his principal interests and temperament bear his unique mark.

As a boy Uccello was apprenticed to Lorenzo Ghiberti and worked (1407) on the first set of bronze doors that Ghiberti made for the Baptistery. In 1414, when he perhaps left Ghiberti's shop, he joined the Company of St. Luke (Painters' Guild). The influence of Ghiberti's late Gothic style was a dominant factor in his development; he was also influenced by Pisanello and other North Italians in his meticulous studies of animals, birds, and plants. From 1425 to 1430 he was at Venice, but a mosaic of *St. Peter* for the façade of S. Marco has been lost. In Florence again (1432), he worked for some time in the cathedral. Among his works there is the fresco of *Giovanni Acuto* (Sir John Hawkwood), the English captain who had often put his company of mercenaries at the service of Florence. In an unwonted surge of gratitude, the Florentines had proposed to erect a monument to the captain. In a more prudent moment, the proposed monument was transformed into a fresco in the cathedral. This was unsatisfactory, and in 1436 Uccello was commissioned to replace it. His own first work failed to please and he did another, that now in the cathedral, in which he carried to their limits the possibilities of perspective. In monochrome *terra verde* (literally, "green earth"), with masterly use of chiaroscuro, he executed an equestrian portrait of Giovanni Acuto that gives the impression of being a standing sculpture. The fresco is a masterpiece of illusionism. Of 1443 were four heads of *Prophets* for the clockface of the cathedral. Since they would be seen from below, and also to make them appear as sculptured heads such as those of high relief on the doors of the Baptistery, he painted them in bold perspective. Of the same year were cartoons for windows in the cupola of the cathedral. Of the four cartoons he made, three were made into stained glass windows, and of these the *Nativity* and *Resurrection* survive. In 1445 he was at Padua, where he visited Donatello. The *Giants* in *terra verde*, now lost, he painted for the Casa Vitaliani at Padua are said to have influenced Mantegna. According to Vasari, Donatello, with whom Uccello had friendly contact at Florence, chided him for his absorption in perspective studies, on the ground that he was "losing the substance for the shadow" and that this work of "circles, spirals, squares, and all" was more suited to intarsia workers than to painters. He returned to Florence the same year. A masterpiece of this period, and earlier, is the series of frescoes in the Chiostro Verde (so-called because the decoration was executed in terra verde, with touches of color), S. Maria Novella, on stories from the Old Testament. The series included the *Creation of the Animals*, in which some of the animals are faithful to nature and others, that Uccello had never seen, are the fantastic creations of his imagination; the *Creation of Man and the Fall*; *The Deluge* (c1445) which compels admiration for the skillfully foreshortened figures of terrified and struggling men and animals, and is notable for a rather horrid realism, as in the bloated body of one who has already drowned; *The Drunkenness of Noah*; and the *Sacrifice of Noah*. In the latter, God the Father is shown above the Ark, heading inward, and so foreshortened that the figure, according to Vasari, seems to be "flying toward the wall with such force as to press through and divide it." The frescoes, badly damaged, have been detached and remounted. Underneath were found the remarkable *sinopie* that Uccello had made as a guide. Of about the same period is a series, now in poor condition, of frescoes on monastic legends in S. Miniato al Monte, and three panels, originally in the Medici Palace, *The Rout of San Romano* (c1456), depicting three incidents of a battle of June 1, 1432, in which Niccolò da Tolentino, serving as a captain for the Florentines, defeated the Sienese. The battle scenes, nostalgic and fanciful portrayals of medieval chivalry, bristle with lances and swords that form patterns against the background. Mounted men in all sorts of positions reveal his virtuosity at foreshortening. The panels are in the Uffizi, Louvre, and National Gallery, London. Two panels on *St. George and the Dragon*, one in the Musée Jacquemart-André, Paris, the other at London, feature a marvellous storybook dragon in center stage, flanked by a demure princess with a delicate profile and a youthful St. George. The panels epitomize the storybook and decorative charm of Uccello's work. At Urbino (1465–1469) he was commissioned to paint an altarpiece, of which six predella panels he executed on *The Miracle of the Host* remain (the altarpiece was completed (1473) by Justus of Ghent). The panels are fine examples of Uccello's use of flat patterns of color, his bizarre narrative sense, and his decorative qualities. A *Nocturnal Hunt*, Ashmolean Museum, Oxford, characteristically shows the huntsmen heading into the forest, rather than toward the spectator or in the picture plane, as this provided a more difficult problem in perspective; deeper in the forest greyhounds of slim grace leap after the quarry.

Vasari writes that Uccello was so much more interested in his studies than in painting pictures that he never made much money and could not afford living models of the animals and birds he drew and painted. Toward the end of his life he wrote on his tax return that he was old and feeble, that he was poor, and that his wife was ill. His reward was in the satisfaction that his scientific studies in perspective and foreshortening afforded him. Called by some a "learned workman," he was not the least among those who turned the stream of Florentine art from the tradition of the followers of Giotto into a vigorous realism, and his mastery of the problems of perspective was influential throughout the High Renaissance. Some critics note, however, that while he was spectacularly successful in projecting depth by his perspective and in showing figures in various positions and from numerous angles with expert foreshortening, his rigid observance of the rules tended to freeze his scenes into immobility. Thus, even the battle and hunt scenes, as well as the tumultuous *Deluge*, portray moments of action crystallized, rather than action itself. At the same time, it is quite possible that this is exactly what Uccello intended to do.

Paolo Veneto (ve-nā′tō). Servite theologian and preacher; b. at Venice, c1430; d. there, 1475. He entered the Servites (1446), and studied at Padua and Bologna. He preached in the most important cities of Italy. His native city often made use of his talents, and sent him on many missions, including one to the Turks. He was celebrated in his own day as learned in philosophy, theology, and astrology, and as a commentator on Dante.

Paolo Veneziano (ve-nā-tsyä′nō). [Also called **Maestro Paolo.**] Venetian painter; d. before 1362. His work is strongly in the Byzantine manner, with hints of the Gothic in the less rigid structure of the bodies and in the drapery. His earliest known works include *Coronation of the Virgin* (1324), National Gallery, Washington, where there is also a *Crucifixion* (c1340) notable for its enamel-like colors; *Death of the Virgin* (1333), Vicenza; and an altarpiece (1339), S. Maria dei Frari, Venice. Other works at Venice include a polyptych, *Coronation of the Virgin*, and *Virgin Enthroned*, Accademia. In 1345 he and his sons signed the painted cover of the Pala d'Oro in S. Marco, Venice. Other works are: *Madonna Enthroned* (1347), Parish Church, Carpineta; another (1349), Oratorio di S. Martino, Chioggia; a *Coronation*, Frick Collection, New York, signed (1358) with his son Giovanni; and works at Bologna (S. Giacomo Maggiore), Parma, Turin (Sabauda Gallery), the island of Rab (cathedral), Pirano (cathedral), Cambridge (Massachusetts), Chicago, Hartford, Los Angeles, New Haven, Worcester, and elsewhere.

Paolo Veronese (vā-rō-nā′zā). [Real name, **Paolo Caliari.**] Painter; b. at Verona, 1528; d. at Venice, April 9, 1588. When he was ten years old he was set to learn painting under his uncle, Giovanni Antonio Badile (c1516–1560), who directed his education beyond the range of Veronese painting. Paintings in churches at Verona by such Brescians as Girolamo Romanino, Moretto, and Gian Girolamo Savoldo also contributed to his early formation and made him aware of the new sense of color of which Venice was the source. To some degree his art was also influenced by the mannerist elegance of Parmigianino and the monumental scale of Giulio Romano, and ultimately it was further enriched through contact with the color and light of Titian. He adapted various influences to his own temperament and evolved a serene and limpid art notable for its clear color, harmonious tones, understanding and control of space, and for the simplicity, candor, and cheerfully materialistic attitude of the painter toward life. He painted huge canvases and frescoes on allegorical, mythological, and religious subjects, and filled them with beautiful, blonde, richly dressed, and bejeweled women and handsome, luxuriously clad men in splendid settings with gorgeous appointments.

His first dated work is the Bevilacqua altarpiece (1548), Museo Civico, Verona. In 1551 he was commissioned to decorate the Soranza villa, near Castelfranco (the villa was demolished in the 19th century). The youthful Bernardino Zelotti assisted him in this, and also in the decoration of other villas and churches. Of 1553 is the altarpiece, *The Temptation of Anthony Abbott*, now at Caen. About the same year he went to Venice and began a series of paintings that reveal his fully developed style, with its marvellous chromatic harmonies and superb decorative sense. Among the early, large paintings at Venice were the ceilings of the halls of the Council of Ten and of the Three Chiefs of the Council in the Ducal Palace. In these he represented *Juno Pouring her Treasures on Venice, Youth and Age, Virtue Rewarded, Victory Pursuing Vice*, and others, painting a number of nude mannerist figures in complicated poses that show his skill at foreshortening. In 1555 he finished a *Coronation* and other paintings on the ceiling of the sacristy, S. Sebastiano and, after painting a number of other works, painted the ceiling of the nave with a series of magnificent scenes from the story of Esther. Continuing to work in S. Sebastiano intermittently until 1570, he painted the entire interior decoration, and made of that church one of the principal treasuries of his works. It is thought that about 1560 he made a visit to Rome and came into contact with the Roman school, but most of the time from about 1553 to 1566 was spent at Venice, where he executed a number of fresco cycles in Venetian palaces, most of which are now lost. Traces of those in the house of the Trevisani remain at Murano, but the best examples are those in the Palladian Villa Barbaro, at Maser, one

PAOLO VERONESE
Studies for a *Finding of Moses*
Courtesy of The Pierpont Morgan Library, New York

of the most complex fresco cycles in the history of painting, notable for sophisticated illusionism and beauty of landscape in which gods, goddesses, nymphs, and other figures surge in a riotous display of the painter's wealth of invention. In 1561 Titian selected him as one of the younger painters to decorate the great hall of the Library designed by Sansovino. When the work was completed Veronese was awarded a gold chain as the best of the painters who worked on it. At Verona he painted the altarpiece, *Martyrdom of St. George*, S. Giorgio in Braida, and in 1563 he painted at Venice one of the most famous of his several banquet scenes, *The Marriage at Cana*, now in the Louvre. Typically, the painting portrays wealth and luxury in the rich dress of the blooming, bountiful women and virile men, in the opulent appointments of the table and the elegance of the setting; many of the figures, including the bride and groom, are portraits of Paolo's notable contemporaries. If it were not for the title one would never guess that the painting, with its lovely colors, sense of movement and atmosphere of wealth, has a Biblical subject. In 1566 he went back to Verona to marry Elena, the daughter of his old teacher, then returned to Venice and remained there the rest of his life. Of the early 1570's is his *Supper in the House of Levi*, Accademia, Venice, notable for the pictorial sense and freshness and novelty of its color. Nevertheless, it brought down on him the wrath of the Inquisition, on the grounds that many of the decorative details—dwarfs, dogs, Germans—were irrelevant. Veronese made one of the earliest defences of the independence of the artist in affirming that he must paint according to his inspiration, but was compelled to paint out or over the features to which the Inquisition objected. Other memorable works are such banquet scenes as *The Marriage at Cana*, Dresden, *The Feast in the House of Levi*, Brera, Milan, and *The Feast of Gregory*, Monte Berico, near Vicenza; *The Family of Darius at the Feet of Alexander*, National Gallery, London; portraits, or groups of portraits at Florence, Dresden, and Amsterdam; and paintings on sacred subjects. For the restoration of the Ducal Palace, after the fire of 1577, he executed some magnificent canvases on allegorical subjects, *The Victory of Lepanto*, and the decoration of the Hall of the Great Council. In the history of Venetian painting of the 16th century, Paolo is outstanding for his frank enjoyment in portraying the material pleasures of life, for the harmony of his brilliant, limpid, gay color, and for the transparency of his atmospheres, which so peculiarly and happily expressed the serene genius of a great decorative artist. Venice is a treasury of Paolo's work; the Church of S. Sebastiano glows with his gorgeous paintings; there are many other examples of his painting in the city, including a number in the Accademia, in the several halls of the Ducal Palace, as previously mentioned, and in a great number of churches. Many other works survive outside Venice. He is represented at Florence (Pitti, Uffizi, Contini-Bonacossi Collection), Modena, Naples (Certosa di S. Martino), Padua, Rome (Borghese, Colonna, Doria Pamphili and Capitoline galleries and the Vatican), Turin, Verona, Vicenza, Amsterdam, Berlin (where several were destroyed in 1945), Budapest, Dublin, Edinburgh, Grenoble, Hampton Court, Leningrad, London, Madrid, Munich, Paris, Vienna, Baltimore (Walters Art Gallery), Boston (Museum of Fine Arts, Isabella Stewart Gardner Museum), Chicago, Cleveland, Detroit, Greenville (South Carolina), Houston, Kansas City (Missouri), Los Angeles, Minneapolis, New Orleans, New York (the Metropolitan Museum, Frick Collection), Philadelphia (Johnson Collection), Princeton, St. Louis, San Diego, San Francisco, Santa Monica (Getty Museum), Sarasota, Seattle, Washington, and elsewhere.

Papacello (pä-pä-chel′lō), **il.** [Real name, **Tommaso di Arcangelo di Bernabeo.**] Umbrian painter; b. at Cortona; d. there, May 10, 1559. He was a pupil of Signorelli, whom he followed closely in his early work. About 1525 he worked with Giovanni Battista Caporali and through him was introduced to the style of Raphael, which thereafter influenced his own. His best work is a series of frescoes, executed with assistants, on the life of Braccio da Montone and Perugian heroes, in the National Gallery of Umbria at Perugia. An *Annunciation* of 1527 is in the Church of S. Maria del Calcinaio at Cortona.

Papal States. See **Patrimony of St. Peter.**

Parabosco (pä-rä-bōs′kō), **Girolamo.** Writer and musician; b. at Piacenza, c1524; d. at Venice, 1557. As a writer he produced much in his short life: lyrics, comedies, a tragedy, and other works. Most of these are of little literary merit. His best work is *I Diporti*, a collection of novelle. The Boccaccesque framework of the collection consists of a group of young men who have gathered on an island in the lagoons of Venice for a fishing and hunting party and are prevented from enjoying their sport by bad weather. To while away the time they tell stories. The seventeen stories of the collection are lively, sometimes comic, and knowledgeable as to human psychology. As a musician, Parabosco was organist at St. Mark's in Venice from 1551, and composed a number of vocal works and some motets.

Pardoner's Tale, The. One of Chaucer's *Canterbury Tales*. An old man sends three revelers to a tree, where they find a heap of gold. Because of their avarice they come to grief. The plot of the story is found in ancient Eastern tales but the figure of the old man who sends the revelers to the gold and their doom is Chaucer's creation.

Paré (pȧ-rā), **Ambroise.** French surgeon, the founder of scientific surgery in France; b. at Laval, Mayenne, France, c1517; d. at Paris, December 22, 1590. He was an army surgeon and royal physician. He introduced improvements in the treatment of gunshot wounds and the use of ligatures, thus eliminating the wholesale use of cauterization to seal off blood vessels. His works were published in 1561.

Parentucelli (pä-ren-tö-chel′lē), **Tommaso.** Original name of Pope **Nicholas V.**

Parenzano (pä-ren-tsä′nō) or **Parentino** (-tē′nō), **Bernardo.** Painter; b. at Parenzo, c1434; d. at Vicenza, October 28, 1531. A gifted draftsman but an indifferent painter his inclination for the detail of miniature painting appears in a signed work, *The Redeemer between SS. Augustine and Jerome,* Estense Gallery, Modena, *Adoration of the Magi,* Louvre, *Conversion of St. Paul,* Municipal Museum, Verona, and *Betrayal of Christ,* Borromeo Collection, Milan. The broader forms and relief of Mantegna, of whom he was early a follower, are often negated in the profusion of his meticulous detail. His *Temptation of St. Anthony,* Doria Pamphili Gallery, Rome, notable for the intensity of its color, and *Jugglers,* Berlin, indicate that he was most comfortable as a genre painter. He became a Benedictine monk and spent his last years at Vicenza. An active painter, there are a number of examples of his work extant, including fragments of frescoes in the Cloister of S. Giustina at Padua, paintings at Lucca, Mantua, Pavia (detached fresco from Padua), Venice, Hampton Court, Baltimore, Boston (Isabella Stewart Gardner Museum), Brooklyn, Cleveland, Denver, and elsewhere.

Parker (pär′kėr), **Matthew.** Archbishop of Canterbury; b. at Norwich, England, August 6, 1504; d. at London, May 17, 1575. He devoted himself to the organization and discipline of the English Church. The revision of the Thirty-nine Articles (1562) was carried out under his direction, as was the publication of the Bishop's Bible (1572). He did considerable historical research and published editions of early chroniclers.

Parlamento (pär-lä-men′tō). An organ of government at Florence that was, in theory, thoroughly democratic. The great bell of the city was tolled, calling the people to the square in front of the Palazzo della Signoria (Palazzo Vecchio), to consider changes or "reforms" in the government. Such gatherings, in which voting was by acclamation, were regarded as expressing the sovereign will of the people. However, by stationing guards at the narrow streets that debouched into the square, those who called the *parlamento* could bar any who might oppose change. Then, with the square filled with supporters, the demand for reform was voted. Since the *parlamento* was too large and unwieldy to function, the people sometimes delegated all the rights they commonly exercised themselves to a *balìa,* or a *balìa* could be created in a number of other ways. It was a committee, appointed for a definite period and varying as to size, which was to consider and effectuate reforms. In effect, the *parlamento* and the *balìa* constituted a suspension of the regular government of Florence, supposedly because the city was threatened in some way, by either internal or external enemies. Any number of Florentine leaders used the devices of the *parlamento* and the *balìa* to weaken or dispose of their opponents and to secure their own power.

Parliament of Fowls. [Also, **Assembly of Fowls.**] Poem by Geoffrey Chaucer, mostly taken from Italian sources. Sixteen of the ninety-eight stanzas are from Giovanni Boccaccio's *Teseide.* It is a poetical abstract of Cicero's *Dream of Scipio.*

Parmigianino (pär-mē-jä-nē′nō). [Original name, **Girolamo Francesco Maria Mazzola,** called **il Parmigianino** from his birthplace.] Painter and etcher; b. at Parma, January 11, 1503; d. at Casalmaggiore, August 24, 1540. His father, Filippo Mazzola, also a painter, died in 1505 and the child was brought up by two of his father's brothers. According to Vasari, they were indifferent painters but excellent uncles. Observing the child's gift for drawing they put him under the best local masters. In 1521 they sent him to Viadana with another young painter, Girolamo Bedoli (who later married Parmigianino's cousin and added the name Mazzola to his own), to escape the war then threatening Parma. Thanks to the energy and resolution of Francesco Guicciardini, at that time governor of Parma, the city was spared. Of this period is one of his certainly known early paintings, *Mystic Marriage of St. Catherine,* Church of S. Maria, at Bardi (near Parma). He returned to Parma in the spring of 1522 and had commissions to paint in the south transept of the cathedral and in the nave and chapels of S. Giovanni Evangelista there. Towards the end of 1524, armed with samples of his work, he went to Rome. There he was presented to the newly elected pope, Clement VII. Clement was so pleased with his work that he promised him employment in the Vatican, a promise that was not fulfilled. On May 5, 1527, the troops of the Constable de Bourbon entered Rome and began their barbaric sack of the city. Vasari writes that Parmigianino was at his easel when they burst into his studio. He was working on his *Vision of St. Jerome,* now

PARMIGIANINO
Study for a *Nativity*
Pinacoteca Nazionale, Parma Alinari-Art Reference Bureau

in the National Gallery, London, and the invaders were so charmed by the beauty of the painting that for a time they did not disturb him. Some days later when he went out into the streets he was captured and imprisoned, and earned his ransom by making sketches for his captors. He escaped and fled to Bologna. He remained at Bologna until the spring of 1530, and made a journey, in March of that year, to Verona and Venice to buy marbles and colors for a proposed chapel of S. Maurizio in S. Petronio, Bologna (the projected chapel was not constructed). In May of the following year he signed a contract to decorate the apse and vaulting of S. Maria della Steccata at Parma. The contract stipulated that the work be completed within a specified time. Parmigianino failed to fulfill its terms and the contract was renewed. Again he was dilatory. In frustration, his patrons had him arrested (late in the summer of 1539) for breach of contract. He was imprisoned briefly, released, and fled to Casalmaggiore. In December, 1539, he was dismissed from the work in the Steccata and the contract was awarded to Giulio Romano, a friend from his Roman days. Parmigianino wrote him, reproaching him for accepting it. In 1540 he was at Casalmaggiore painting *Madonna with SS. Stephen and John the Baptist*, now at Dresden. He died in the same year. Vasari tells that at his own request he was buried naked, with a cross standing upright on his breast.

Parmigianino was one of the foremost of the earlier mannerist painters. In the course of his short career he developed an elegant and refined personal style. He does not seem to have been a pupil of Correggio, but was deeply influenced by him. The Correggio influence, strong but not overwhelming, is apparent in frescoes Parmigianino painted in the Church of S. Giovanni Evangelista in 1522 and 1523 (where Correggio was painting between 1520 and 1525), and in other youthful works and drawings. Of his frescoes there, that of *St. Isidore Martyr* illustrates the drama and movement that Parmigianino added to the pure pleasure in form and light of Correggio's painting. An eruptive energy and dynamism unknown to Correggio are evident in the saint's rearing horse, in the nervous line that gives life and movement to the group. At Rome Parmigianino came in contact with the works of Raphael and Michelangelo, and was somewhat influenced by the classicism and broader forms of the former and the intensity of the latter. His *Holy Family with the Magdalen*, also known as the *Madonna with St. Zacchariah*, Uffizi, although of his Bolognese period has some of the monumental quality of Raphael. More conspicuous is

PARMIGIANINO
Study for the *Madonna dal collo lungo*, Uffizi, Florence
Courtesy of The Pierpont Morgan Library, New York

the Raphael influence in his *Vision of St. Jerome,* with its near classical and monumental figure of John the Baptist. Parmigianino's own imprint is in the energy of the saint's gesture as he points to the vision of the Madonna in the clouds above the sleeping St. Jerome, but the play of light recalls Correggio. However, Parmigianino's style, influenced in its development to some degree by Correggio, Raphael, and Michelangelo, was eminently personal and individual. A refined, disciplined abstraction took the place of Cor-

Parmigianino
Nymphs Bathing
Gabinetto Disegni e Stampe degli Uffizi   Foto Soprintendenza

reggio's sensuality and exuberance; his sensitive, suggestive line supports an intellectual and formalized elegance; an intensification of the drama is achieved by the excitement of ancillary figures, as in the *Adoration of the Shepherds*, Doria Pamphili Gallery, Rome. The epitome of his style is perhaps to be found in his *Madonna dal collo lungo* (*Madonna of the long neck*), Uffizi. (He received payment for the work in December, 1534, but this must have been a payment in advance, as the work was not completed at the time of his death.) The Madonna's long, slender, curving neck, her elongated torso and limbs and those of the Child on her knees, the delicacy of her features and the elegance of her tapering fingers are deliberate and free expressions of a new artistic vision that floats beyond naturalism and realism. Elegance and refinement, a harmony of complementing curves, axes that tilt away from the vertical (with, in *Madonna dal collo lungo*, a single upright column to accentuate the variations), a nervous, flexible line, and flickering chiaroscuro, are features of his style.

Vasari complains that Parmigianino was so taken up by his experiments in alchemy that he neglected his painting and accomplished far less than he might have. Nevertheless he left a number of notable paintings that confirmed his style. Of his years at Bologna are a *Madonna with St. Margaret and other Saints*, Pinacoteca, and an allegorical portrait of Charles V, who was at Bologna in 1530 to be crowned emperor by his erstwhile enemy, Clement VII. The painting shows the emperor seated; at his right an angel supports a globe of the world over which hovers the angel of victory–a fitting expression of Charles V's power at this moment in the history of Italy. A copy of the painting is in the Cook Collection, Richmond, England. Shortly after leaving Bologna, perhaps in 1531, he decorated a room in the Castello Sanvitale at Fontanellato (near Parma) with frescoes on the myth of Diana and Actaeon. The background for the scenes is a painted trellis, ornamented with fruits, flowers, and putti in a charming fantasy that recalls Correggio's frescoes in the Convent of S. Paolo at Parma. Among the figures he completed in the Steccata at Parma are those of *St. Cecilia, David*, on the organ shutters, and a number of frescoed maidens bearing amphorae (a decorative motif he often employed, delighted as he was by the purity of its line and shape), and monochrome frescoes of *Moses, Aaron*, and others. The quality and atmosphere of his mannerist style is apparent in the slight elongations and shifting chiaroscuro of a number of distinguished portraits, as in that of Gian Galeazzo Sanvitale, Naples, and the self-portrait, Vienna, that he painted with a mirror. The distortions created in the convex mirror he used are effectively recreated in this mannerist portrait. Other portraits at Naples are the full-length portrait, called *Antea*, and a half-length *Portrait of Girolamo de Vincenti*. There are also portraits in the Uffizi, Borghese Gallery, Rome, National Gallery at Parma (*La schiava turca*), the Prado, Madrid, Copenhagen, Hampton Court, and elsewhere. Over 500 drawings by Parmigianino survive, and show his delight in the possibilities of line, the shape and modeling and pattern available through shading, his preoccupation with drawing for its own sake rather than as a preliminary to painting. He had some of his drawings engraved and through them the influence of his style was diffused through

PARMIGIANINO
Study of Figures
Biblioteca Nazionale, Parma
Alinari-Art Reference Bureau

thin; ᴛʜ, then; y, you; (variable) ḍ as d or j, ṣ as s or sh, ṭ as t or ch, ẓ as z or zh; *o*, F. cloche; ü, F. menu; ċh, Sc. loch; ṅ, F. bonbon; ʙ, Sp. Córdoba (sounded almost like v).

north Italy, in Tuscany, and beyond. In addition, he prepared designs specifically intended to be reproduced and made etchings of them himself, for which reason he came to be known as "the father of Italian etching." Important collections of his drawings, many of them preparatory studies that he often changed when he began to paint, are in the Louvre and École des Beaux Arts at Paris, in the Uffizi, the National Gallery at Parma, the British Museum, and elsewhere. Besides those mentioned above, other examples of Parmigianino's painting are at Rome, Madrid, Dresden, Vienna, and elsewhere.

Parr (pär), **Catherine.** Sixth and last wife of Henry VIII; b. at Kendal Castle, Westmorland, England, c1512; d. at Sudeley Castle, Gloucestershire, England, September 7, 1548. She had been married twice before her marriage to the king in 1543, and after his death married Thomas Seymour in 1547.

Parrasio (pär-rä′syō), **Aulo Giano.** [Original name, **Giovan Paolo Parisio.**] Humanist; b. at Cosenza, December 28, 1480; d. there, 1522. He learned Greek at Lecce and Corfu and opened (1491) a school at Cosenza that was later moved to Naples. At Naples he became a member of the academy founded by Pontano, and became a beneficiary of the king's patronage. He went to Rome, having fallen from favor at Naples, and later to Milan, where he was professor of eloquence and was on warm terms with the leading humanists. Political conditions compelled him to leave Milan (1506), but in the eight years he had spent there he had begun his critical study and teaching of law that led to a new approach to legal studies. The years following his departure from Milan were spent in wandering from place to place as a teacher–to Vicenza, Padua, Venice, and Rome. In 1521 he returned to Cosenza. Parrasio, who lectured on the principal Latin authors at Rome (1514–1517), wrote learned commentaries on Caesar, Cicero, Horace, Ovid, and other Latin writers, and left a valuable collection of letters. In his interest in philology and criticism he was in the tradition of Poliziano and Lorenzo Valla.

Parri Spinelli (pär′rē spē-nel′lē). [Real name, **Gaspare di Spinello.**] Painter; b. at Arezzo, 1387; d. there 1453. He was the son and pupil of Spinello Aretino, and worked with his father in executing the fresco decoration in the Palazzo Pubblico at Siena (1407). Influenced by the Florentine followers of Lorenzo Monaco, he was a painter in the late international Gothic style. His surviving works are at Arezzo and include a *Madonna of Mercy* and fragments of frescoes in the museum. A second *Madonna of Mercy* is in the Church of S. Maria delle Grazie. A fresco, *Christ on the Cross with the Virgin and St. John the Evangelist,* is in the Palazzo Comunale. The fresco was detached in 1958, revealing a lively and beautiful *sinopia* underneath. The pure, flexible, and swift strokes of the drawing show Parri Spinelli to have been a draftsman whose pencil breathed life. In the fresco that covered the *sinopia* the figures are elongated, conventional, and Gothic, in contrast to the proportion, movement, and modern rendering of the figures in the drawing. In the Church of S. Domenico there is a fresco of *St. Catherine* and a *Crucifixion with Saints.* A lunette above the latter is in two panels with scenes from the legend of St. Nicholas (painted c1440) typical of Parri's style in the elongated figures, vigor of movement, and strong, lively colors.

Parsons (pär′sọnz) or **Persons, Robert.** English Jesuit; b. at Nether Stowey, Somersetshire, England, 1546; d. at Rome, April 15, 1610. He intrigued actively against Elizabeth and the Protestants until his death. He founded several English seminaries in Spain while urging Spanish invasion of England. He published many polemical works.

Parson's Tale, The. One of Chaucer's *Canterbury Tales.* It is a long prose sermon on the theme of penitence, derived from the works of a 13th-century Dominican.

Partenio (pär-te′nyō), **Bernardino.** [Real name, **Bernardino Franceschini.**] Humanist; b. at Spilimbergo (Friuli); d. at Venice, 1589. He founded an academy at Spilimbergo for the teaching of Latin, Greek, and Hebrew, and later taught classical languages at Ancona, Vicenza, and Venice. He wrote Latin verse, an oration in defense of the Latin language, and a treatise, in Italian, *Dell' imitazione poetica* (Venice, 1560), which he later translated into Latin (Venice, 1565).

Paruta (pä-rö′tä), **Paolo.** Venetian historian and statesman; b. at Venice, May 14, 1540; d. there, December 6, 1598. He was

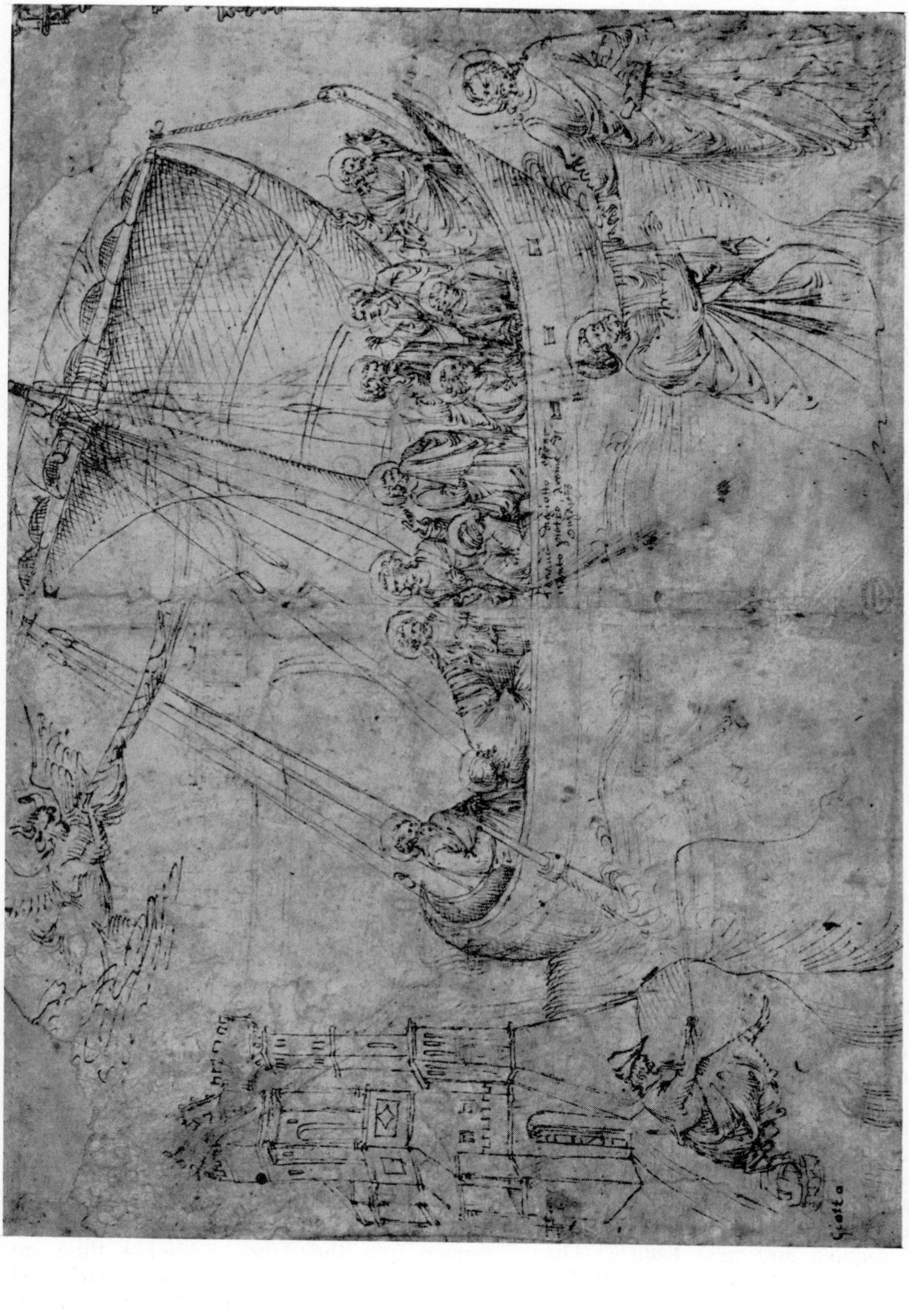

Parri Spinelli
St. Peter Walking on the Water
Sketch of Giotto's mosaic, *Navicella*, in St. Peter's
Courtesy of The Metropolitan Museum of Art, New York, Hewitt Fund, 1917

thin; ᴛʜ, then; y, you; (variable) ḑ as d or j, ş as s or sh, ţ as t or ch, z̧ as z or zh; *o*, F. cloche; ü, F. menu; ċh, Sc. loch; ṅ, F. bonbon; ʙ, Sp. Córdoba (sounded almost like v).

of a noble family that originally came from Lucca, pursued his studies in eloquence and philosophy at Padua, and returned to Venice (1561) where he opened an academy for the study of political science. Almost at once he entered upon a public career, and served the republic of Venice in many capacities, in local affairs as well as in diplomatic affairs. In addition to his public life he continued an intense intellectual life, his special interest being political matters and history. In his Ciceronian dialogue, *Della perfezione della vita politica,* published at Venice in 1579, he discusses the ideal city and the ideal statesman, reviving, in the course of the dialogue, the old question of the contemplative life versus the active life. His own preference, an intellectual one, seems to have been in favor of the contemplative life but, as in his own life, he recognizes the responsibility of the citizen to the state of which he is a member. His *Discorsi politici* considers the greatness and decline of Rome, discusses the character of other European states, and is particularly detailed in its consideration of Venice. In 1579 the Venetian Council of Ten commissioned him to complete *Rerum Venetarum Historiae,* the history of Venice begun by Pietro Bembo. Paruta's history, *Istoria veniziana,* in Italian, covers the period 1513 to 1552. A separate work, *Storia della guerra di Cipro,* tells the history of the war with Cyprus and attempts a justification of the Venetian cession of Cyprus to the Turks. In his major work, *Istoria veniziana,* Paruta's approach has been likened to that of Guicciardini, without Guicciardini's dispassionate analysis but with a more ardent patriotism for his native state than Guicciardini permitted himself. His interest lies more in diplomatic and political affairs than in the economic and social life of the city. Influenced by Machiavelli in his work and like him an ardent patriot, pervading his work is his love and admiration for the institutions of Venice. Tintoretto's portrait of him is in the Ducal Palace, Venice.

Pasolini (pä-zō-lē′nē). Family of Cotignola, said to have resided in Bologna in the first half of the 13th century. Ghibellines, they were expelled from Bologna in 1274 and took refuge at Cotignola and near Faenza. The Pasolini were the traditional rivals of the family of Muzio Attendolo Sforza at Cotignola, and being defeated by the Sforza, the Pasolini scattered through the Romagna and gave rise to branches of the family at Cesena, Faenza, and at Ravenna where they still exist.

Pasquali (päs-kwä′lē) or **Pascale** (päs-kä′lā), **Lodovico.** 16th-century lyric poet; b. in Dalmatia, early in the 16th century; d. c1551. He was a member of a prominent Venetian family, and completed his studies at Padua. In the course of a voyage on the Adriatic he was captured by corsairs. Freed, he was a soldier for Venice in Crete, and leavened his military duties with ardent humanistic study of the ruins of Crete. He was a friend of Lodovico Dolce, who published his Latin verses at Venice (1551). Pasquali also wrote, in Italian, *Rime volgari.* The love lyrics of the first part of the collection are marked with the literary mannerisms of the mid-16th century. They are characterized by an essential elegance and musicality. The second section of the collection contains lyrics addressed to his friends and to men of letters. These are less conventional and more sincere in spirit, especially when the theme is his love for Venice and Italy.

Pasquier (pä-kyā), **Étienne.** French jurist and author; b. at Paris, 1529; d. there, 1615. His chief work is *Recherches sur la France* (c1560 *et seq.*).

Pasquino (päs-kwē′nō). In 1501 a mutilated statue of the Hellenistic period was set up on a pedestal on a square in Rome by Cardinal Oliviero Carafa. To the statue was given the name Pasquino, commemorating, as tradition had it, a tailor of that name (or a schoolteacher, or a cobbler, or a barber) who lived at Rome about the end of the 15th century, was noted for his caustic wit, and was supposed to have had his shop on the site where the statue was excavated. Very shortly it became the custom to post anonymous lampoons (pasquinades) on the statue itself, the pedestal, and the walls behind it. They were in Latin and in the vernacular, in prose and in verse. Their arrows were directed against the popes and their courts, against the cardinals and the Curia, against anyone who for one reason or another drew unfavorable attention. (Pope Adrian VI, in his short reign, drew so many pasquinades that it was rumored he threatened to have the statue thrown into the Tiber.) After a time, an annual festival to Pasquino was celebrated on St. Mark's day (April 25). The verses, by the thousands, that were attached to and about the statue on that day were collected and printed. A series of these collections, with some gaps, exists for the years from 1509 to 1525. At the opposite end of the city from Pasquino was an ancient statue of Marforio, a gigantic reclining figure of the 1st century (now in the Capitoline Museum). Gibes and jeers pasted upon Pasquino were answered by similar effusions affixed to Marforio. By this effectively anonymous system of thrust and parry the most serious matters were disclosed, and the most distinguished persons attacked and defended.

Passavanti (päs-sä-vän′tē), **Jacopo.** Dominican preacher; b. at Florence, c1300; d. there, 1357. After studying and teaching at Paris, Rome, and Siena, he returned to Florence and began (1340) to preach at the Church of S. Maria Novella. He was placed in charge of maintenance and construction of the great Dominican Church (begun 1279), and from 1354 until his death was prior of the convent. Among his writings is *Lo Specchio di Vera Penitenza,* a treatise on the necessity for penitence, in which he states, in sober, measured language, the belief that man is a sinner whose only hope of salvation lies in true penitence. The work is studded with citations from earlier writers and little anecdotal examples to illustrate his points. It is a close reflection of the religious spirit of the 14th century.

Pastene (päs′tā-nā), **Giovanni Battista.** Navigator and explorer; b. at Genoa, 1507; d. at Santiago, Chile, 1582. As a young man he went to Spain in his own ship, attracted thither by news of the New World. In 1534 he joined an expedition that left from Seville for the New World, and in succeeding years made many expeditions. Francisco Pizarro sought his help in the conquest of Peru. He afterwards went to Chile, where he founded several cities and became governor of Santiago. His discoveries and reports provided valuable information as to Chilean waters. Unusual in the cutthroat competition between the conquistadors and explorers of the time, he remained faithful to his several commanders. He was named Captain-general of the Southern Seas and was rewarded with great possessions in the New World.

Pasti (päs′tē), **Matteo de'.** See **De' Pasti, Matteo.**

Pastor fido (päs-tōr′ fē′dō), **il.** [English, "The Faithful Shepherd."] A pastoral drama by Battista Guarini, composed to celebrate the marriage of a duke of Savoy. Modeled on Tasso's *Aminta* (1573), equally elegant and sensuous but less spontaneous, it was even more successful than *Aminta.* It won great popularity with its seductive presentation of life and love in Arcadia, an idealized world of nature where love and its pleasures are the rule of life. Mirtillo is the faithful shepherd of the title. The obstacles in the way of his love for Amarilli, who loves him, are overcome through the good offices of a blind seer. The play, in five acts with choruses of shepherds and nymphs, was translated into many languages, widely adapted, and often imitated. The Englishman John Fletcher's *The Faithful Shepherdess* (c1609) is an instance of the wide appeal this form of Arcadian drama had for other writers.

Pastura (päs-tö′rä), **il.** See **Antonio da Viterbo.**

Pasture (pä-tür), **Roger de la.** See **Weyden, Roger** (or **Rogier**) **van der.**

Patrimony of St. Peter. Lands over which the Church claimed temporal authority. These consisted of lands that had been donated to the Church from the 4th century onward, and included Rome and its surroundings, other enclaves on the Italian mainland, Sicily, and Sardinia. In the 8th century the popes, who had gradually been breaking away from the Eastern emperor, declared themselves temporal rulers of the duchy of Rome and the lands conquered from the Lombards. Pepin the Short recognized (754) their sovereignty over these areas, in return for papal support against the Lombards, and added to them the Exarchate of Ravenna and the Pentapolis (Rimini, Ancona, Fano, Pesaro, and Senigallia). Charlemagne confirmed his father's donation (774). From time to time other areas were added to the papal dominions, notably the duchy of Spoleto and the lands bequeathed to the Church by Countess Matilda of Canossa (1115). Pope Innocent III (1161–1216) received confirmation from the emperor Otto IV of the right of the Church to all the lands claimed up to that time (1201). From the time of Innocent dates the first general recognition of the territory of the Church and the description of it as an administrative unit. On the confirmation received in his time rested all the future history of the States of the Church, as they came to be called. Besides those mentioned above, these included also the March of Ancona. Over these lands the popes claimed temporal authority. However, the popes were almost never able to exercise the authority they claimed in all or even in large parts of the areas. In some, independent rulers had arisen who refused to recognize the pope's authority. Others, for their own interest, gave their allegiance to the emperor. Others bought their independence, and still others were seized by states more powerful than the papacy. Even in Rome itself the pope was unable at times to exercise authority. This was especially true in the long period of the Babylonian Captivity (1305–1376) and the Great Schism (1378–1417). During these periods Rome was in chaos, a prey of the powerful Roman nobles who struggled continuously among themselves for control of the city. The efforts of the popes to establish their domination over their fiefs or to influence those whose independence was unwillingly recognized, kept the papacy in an almost continual state of war, and led to a series of rapidly shifting alliances with now one, now another powerful Italian state. Native princes, republics, or tyrants were not the only enemies of papal dominion. The Holy Roman Emperors for a long period tried to reestablish their authority in temporal matters in Italy, and were frequently marching down from the Alps to do so, but after Henry VII (1269–1313) the marches were either exercises in futility or ceremonial, and sometimes ludicrous, parades. In the 16th century Cesare Borgia, son of Pope Alexander VI, conquered the Romagna and the Marches, and after his death (1503) these passed to the Church. Pope Julius II (1443–1513), the warrior pope, consolidated papal power at the price of continual warfare. In the century preceding the coronation of Charles V at Bologna (1530), the Papal States formed one of the five most powerful states of Italy, the others being Milan, Venice, Florence, and Naples. The Papal States, expanding and contracting through wars and invasions, continued to exist as a political unit until 1870, when the unification of Italy was accomplished. At that time the pope, refusing to recognize the loss of his temporal power, became a "prisoner" in the Vatican. His successors remained so until 1929, when a treaty was signed by which the pope retained temporal authority over Vatican City, but gave up all other claims, and the long struggle to hold the Patrimony of St. Peter came to an end.

Patrizzi (pä-trēt′tsē), **Francesco.** Ecclesiastic, Latin poet, and political theorist; b. at Siena, February 20, 1413; d. at Gaeta, 1492. He completed his studies at Siena and then took part in public life. A conspiracy in which he was implicated led to his banishment from Siena and he went into exile at Verona (1457). Through the instrumentality of his fellow-student and good friend, Pope Pius II, the exile was revoked. Shortly afterward (1461), Patrizzi having in the meantime been ordained, he was named bishop of Gaeta and governor of Foligno by Pope Pius. An uprising at Foligno with which he could not cope caused him to retire from that city. He retired to his diocese of Gaeta and gave himself over to his humanistic studies. He wrote Latin poetry and some Latin orations, but is best known for his two treatises, *De institutione reipublicae* and *De regno*. The first exalts the free institutions of a republic; the second presents the advantages of a monarchy. Both forms of government were widely discussed at this stage of humanism, when the works of Plato were beginning to be known and to challenge the long-standing predominance of Aristotle. The two works were immensely popular, went through many editions, and were translated into several languages, but after the publication of Machiavelli's works, those of Patrizzi were forgotten.

Patrizzi, Francesco. Philosopher and man of letters; b. at Cherso, 1529; d. at Rome, February, 1597. He studied at Padua; published some minor works in 1553; and published his poem in praise of the Estensi, *Eridano*, at Ferrara in 1558. His *Della Historia,* ten dialogues published at Venice in 1560, presents his conception of history as of value as a science, rather than as a literary or artistic undertaking. He also wrote *Della Poetica,* in seven volumes, only two of which were published (1586). Each volume was to contain ten books, and hence was known as *Deca*. The work is a comprehensive history of ancient poetry, a review of ancient poetic theories, and an exposition of his own ideas, all from a Platonic point of view. He made many journeys, including trips to Spain and Cyprus, and then went (1578) to Ferrara to teach philosophy. In 1592 he went to Rome to teach and remained there until his death. Patrizzi was an exponent of Platonic philosophy. He was one of the last defenders of the Platonic as opposed to the Aristotelian system. His main work is *Nova de universis philosophia,* . . . in which he asserts that light, not motion, is the first principle. Metaphysically, he opposed the spiritual to the physical.

Patyn (pat′in), **William.** Original name of **Wayneflete, William of.**

Paul II. [Original name, **Pietro Barbo.**] Pope (1464–1471); b. at Venice, February 23, 1417; d. at Rome, July 26, 1471. Of a noble Venetian family, his mother was the sister of Pope Eugenius IV, a circumstance that considerably advanced his own career. At the age of 23 he was named cardinal by his uncle. Wealthy in his own right, he received a princely income from numerous benefices. Handsome, affable, and generous, as a young man he was immensely popular with the Romans, and under Nicholas V and Calixtus III had great influence in the Curia. Because he had "shamelessly cast aside all decency" and sought the papacy for himself in the conclave of 1458 (according to Pope Pius II, the successful candidate), his influence under Pius II, whom he succeeded, had not been great. He owed his election in 1464 to cardinals who had been elevated before the pontificate of Pius. Before the election of 1464, the cardinals signed certain Capitulations. These included promises to limit the College of Cardinals to twenty-four, to reform the Curia, to call a general council within three years, and to resume the war against the Turks. Once elected, as he was on the first ballot, Paul refused to confirm the Capitulations. Vain, jealous, addicted to pomp and luxury, he lived like a Renaissance prince, meant to rule as a monarch, and would accept no limits on his power. His relations with the Curia became strained; business was slowed as he refused to hold audiences; he became suspicious, inaccessible, and moody. In the war against the Turks he supported Scanderbeg, the valiant and effective Albanian commander, but he lacked the support of Louis XI of France, with whom he was at odds over the Pragmatic Sanctions (to appease the king, he gave him the title, "Most Christian King"). A conflict with George Podiebrad and the Hussites in Bohemia diverted his energies. He excommunicated and deposed him, denouncing him as the "son of perdition," and named his own ally, King Matthias of Hungary, as king of Bohemia in place of George. Unsuccessful skirmishes with Naples and Venice dissipated his strength in Italy; he was forced to recognize the overlordship of Roberto Malatesta at Rimini (1470); and Negroponte fell to the Turks (1470). Not a humanist himself (his Latin was not fluent, he held audiences in Italian, and advised the Romans that it was enough to teach their children reading and writing), he clashed with the humanists, distrusted their paganizing influence, dismissed them from their posts, and dissolved (1468) the Roman Academy of Pomponius Laetus, accusing the latter of conspiring against him. He detested Platina, who returned the compliment and took his revenge by writing a malicious biography. However, Paul was not insensitive to the developments of his age. He had rich collections of antiquities, gems, and other art treasures. He encouraged scholars, the arts, and the new invention of printing. The first printing press in Italy was opened at Subiaco during his pontificate (1465). He enthusiastically embraced Renaissance principles in architecture, beautified Rome, rebuilt his church of S. Marco, and began (1455) his Palazzo S. Marco (now the Palazzo Venezia), which after 1466 became his principal residence. His tomb in the Vatican, a magnificent example of Renaissance sculpture, was by Mino da Fiesole and Giovanni Dalmata. Paul died suddenly, on July 26, 1471. He was succeeded by Sixtus IV.

Paul III. [Original name, **Alessandro Farnese.**] Pope (1534–1549); b. at Canino, in February, 1468; d. at Rome, November 10, 1549. He was the son of Pier Luigi Farnese and the cultivated Giovanella Caetani, and was educated at Rome under Julius Pomponius Laetus. Destined for a diplomatic career, he went to the court of Lorenzo the Magnificent and there became a good friend of Giovanni de' Medici (later Pope Leo X). At his mother's urging, he abandoned a career in diplomacy for one in the Church. His rise was rapid. Through the influence of his sister Giulia, who was the mistress of Alexander VI, he was given the red hat in 1493, whence his sobriquet "the petticoat cardinal." He held several bishoprics, served Alexander and Julius II, under Leo X had great influence in political matters, and under Clement VII (with whom he took refuge in Castel Sant' Angelo during the sack of Rome) enjoyed great authority. By the time he succeeded Clement as Pope Paul III (October 13, 1534), he had gained wide experience and skill in diplomacy. He has been called the last Renaissance pope, for his nepotism, his own broad and worldly culture, and for his patronage of the arts and letters. He was the father of at least four children whose interests he assiduously promoted. Of these, his favorite was Pier Luigi, whom he made duke of Parma, Piacenza, and Castro, and who was murdered in 1547. He gave the red hat to his grandsons Alessandro Farnese and Ascanio Sforza. He loved pomp and magnificent ceremonies, was an ardent follower of the hunt, and a patron of the arts and letters. He commissioned Sangallo the Younger to build the Farnese Palace, one of the most beautiful Renaissance buildings in Rome. It was begun in 1514, continued by Michelangelo after Sangallo's death (1546), and completed (1580) by Michelangelo's pupil Giacomo della Porta. For him, Michelangelo continued work on the building of St. Peter's and painted *The Last Judgment* in the Sistine Chapel. He also commissioned decorations in the Vatican and in the apartments in Castel Sant' Angelo.

Paul III has also been called the first reform pope. From 1509, when he was bishop of Parma, he administered his diocese with care and resolution. He was ordained in 1519, and by the time he was elected pope his reputation as a prelate and as an administrator raised great hopes for his future conduct of affairs of the Church. As with his predecessors, the problems that faced him were political as well as spiritual. First of all he wished to secure peace between the rival political powers: the king of France and the emperor. Once peace was restored steps could be taken to halt the spread of Protestantism, and thereafter a united Europe could march against the Turk. He adopted a policy of neutrality in the struggle between France and the emperor, in the hope that he might mediate between them. He sent any number of missions to each of them to discuss peace, and in 1538 succeeded in negotiating a ten-year truce at Nice, which he hoped to transform into a permanent peace. In the same year, he excommunicated Henry VIII of England. From the beginning of his pontificate he worked for reform. He urged the French king and the German princes to suppress Protestantism, and joined (1546) the war on the Schmalkaldic League (supporters of the Protestant cause) but withdrew when he became suspicious of the political motives of Charles V. He admonished the cardinals to live modestly and worked for an ecumenical council. Many of those he raised to the cardinalate were sincere reformers, as Giovanni Pietro Caraffa (who became Paul IV), Reginald Pole, John Fisher, and Giovanni Morone, or enlightened humanists, as Girolamo Aleandro, Gasparo Contarini, Jacopo Sadoleto, and Pietro Bembo. As early as November 20, 1534, he appointed commissions to investigate conditions in the Church and suggest reforms. Their reports, embodied in the *Concilium de emendanda Ecclesia*, the *Consilium super reformatione*, and other studies, constituted an agenda for sessions of a future council. Paul's attempts to call a council were several times frustrated, especially by the refusal of the German and Spanish prelates to meet in an Italian city. There was also some thought that he was not as resolute in summoning the council as he wished the emperor to believe. At last, in a compromise, the Council of Trent opened on December 13, 1545. The three principal purposes were: the reconciliation of the Protestants, reform of abuses, and preparation for a crusade against the Turks. Paul allowed the council as much independence as he thought was consonant with the authority and dignity of the Holy See. Such matters as the role of the Scriptures, justification, the sacraments, and the doctrine of original sin were considered, and decisions were taken, but on the crucial question of Protestantism and reform little was accomplished. In 1540 Paul recognized the Society of Jesus, founded by Ignatius Loyola. He recognized the Ursulines (1544), and encouraged the work of the Theatines (Oratory of Divine Love), and the Barnabites. He organized the Inquisition at Rome (1542), and established censorship and the Index (1543). In the governing of the Papal States he took advantage of a rebellion that broke out in Perugia against a salt tax (the Salt War) to send his son Pier Luigi against the city, crush the rebellion, and to restore papal control over that turbulent city. (To maintain control, he razed a number of buildings, palaces of the Baglioni, and constructed the Rocca Paolina, a forbidding fortress that dominated the city until the 19th century, when it was enthusiastically demolished by the people of Perugia.) By education and inclination a Renaissance prince, Paul responded to the needs of the Church with able diplomacy, considerable resolution, and the first steps in the direction of long-demanded reform.

Paulet (pôʹlẹt), Sir **Amias.** English statesman; b. c1536; d. at London, 1588. He was keeper of Mary, Queen of Scots, during her imprisonment, and acted as commissioner at her trial. Although he urged her execution, he refused the suggestion that he murder her secretly.

Paulet, Sir **William.** [Titles, 1st Marquis of **Winchester,** 1st Earl of **Wiltshire,** 1st Baron **St. John.**] English statesman; b. near Basingstoke, England, c1485; d. there, 1572. He held important posts under five English rulers.

Paulet, Sir **William.** [Title, 3rd Marquis of **Winchester.**] English nobleman; b. c1535; d. 1598. He is chiefly remembered for a curious little work entitled *The Lord Marques Idlenes* (1586). He was one of the commissioners for the trial of Mary, Queen of Scots, and steward of her funeral.

Pazzi (pätʹtsē). Distinguished Florentine merchant and banking family of ancient lineage. According to legend, a Pazzo di Rinieri brought back three stones from the Holy Sepulchre in Jerusalem when he returned from the first crusade. It is in commemoration of this event that the ceremony (still observed at Florence at Easter) of the Explosion of the Cart was instituted. However this may be, there was a Pazzi captain of the Florentines at the battle of Montaperti (1260). The family, with its many branches, rose to prominence at Florence as successful merchants and bankers, and became rivals of the Medici. They had full political rights, Cosimo having exempted them from disabilities placed on the nobility. After the Pazzi Conspiracy of 1478, in which Giuliano de' Medici was killed and his brother Lorenzo escaped, many of the Pazzi were killed or exiled. Two years later Lorenzo de' Medici allowed the exiles to return to Florence, but the influence of the family never reached its former height. The lovely Renaissance Pazzi Chapel in the cloister of the Church of S. Croce at Florence was begun by Brunelleschi (c1430) at the order of Andrea Pazzi (d. 1445). Andrea was the father of that Jacopo Pazzi who played such a despicable and miserable role in the conspiracy of 1478. The Pazzi Chapel is one of Brunelleschi's masterpieces.

Pazzi, Alessandro de'. Poet and translator; b. 1483; d. 1530. He was a cousin of Pope Clement VII, under whom he held public office, and was one of the pope's most faithful friends. He made metrical translations of Euripides and Sophocles, and drew his inspiration for his tragedy, *Dido in Cartagine,* from the *Aeneid* of Vergil.

Pazzi, Alfonso. [Called, **l'Etruso.**] Florentine poet; b. October 19, 1509; d. November 3, 1555. Nearly 500 of his sonnets, epigrams, madrigals, carnival songs, and *capitoli* on various subjects are extant. He also left a number of burlesque verses satirizing the Florentine Academy.

Pazzi Conspiracy. A conspiracy hatched by Girolamo Riario, the nephew of Pope Sixtus IV, and Francesco Pazzi, of a prominent Florentine family, to murder Lorenzo de' Medici and his brother Giuliano. Girolamo, who had been invested with Imola (1473) by the pope, wished, with the pope's full support, to carve out a larger dominion in the Romagna, and possibly to control Florence. Lorenzo was putting obstacles in his path. The cause of Pazzi's enmity to Lorenzo is less certain. The banking family of which he was a member had supplied the pope with money to buy Imola, and had persuaded the pope to transfer papal funds from the Medici branch in Rome to the Pazzi branch there. Resentment was heightened when Lorenzo hurriedly caused a law to be passed at Florence that prevented the Pazzi from receiving an inheritance to which they thought they were entitled. Francesco Salviati, an enemy of Lorenzo's, was also in the plot, with the pope privy to it although he was probably unaware of (or preferred not to know) the exact details. Lorenzo had resisted Salviati's appointment as archbishop of Florence and refused to allow him to occupy the See of Pisa when the pope nominated him. The conspirators hired a mercenary captain, Gian Battista da Montesecco, who had served Girolamo, to arrange the details of the plot and to carry it out. Essential to the plan was an occasion on which Lorenzo and his popular younger brother Giuliano would be in the same place at the same time. They arranged to have a young kinsman of Girolamo's, Cardinal Raffaele Riario, make a visit to Florence from the University of Pisa, where he was studying. In the course of his visit some festivity would surely take place at which both the brothers would be present. The occasion on which they fixed was a banquet, but at the last minute Giuliano was prevented from attending. A number of people were by this time involved, and delay was hazardous lest existence of the plot become known. Hurriedly, the plotters decided on a Mass to be celebrated in the cathedral by the 17-year-old Cardinal Riario on April 26, 1478. At this point a new hitch developed. Montesecco, a bloodstained condottiere, was perfectly willing to commit murder on men as they sat at dinner, but he balked at killing them as they knelt in prayer. Thus at the last minute some substitutions were necessary. The signal for the attack was the elevation of the host, the most solemn moment in the Mass. As the bell sounded for this moment Bernardo Bandini, a young Florentine, and Francesco Pazzi assaulted Giuliano. He fell at once, and when his body was later examined it was found to have been pierced by nineteen wounds. Two inexperienced priests were substituted for Montesecco, charged with the slaying of Lorenzo. Their attack was clumsy; he drew his sword, and while friends rushed to his aid, leaped over the altar rail and retreated into the sacristy. The heavy bronze doors clanged to behind him. Tumult broke out in the huge congregation. In the confusion few were sure of exactly what had happened. Lorenzo's friends escorted him safely to the palace. In the meantime, as part of the plot, Archbishop Salviati had gone to the Palazzo della Signoria to seize it and take over the government. Instead he was seized by the priors and hanged from one of the upper windows. Those who had come with him to seize the palace were hurled out of the windows to the crowd in the piazza below. Jacopo Pazzi, uncle of Francesco and the head of the family, had long refused to take part in the plot, but had finally consented. An old man, his role was to ride through the streets of Florence and exhort the Florentines to rise up against the Medici. He undertook to play his part, but when he rode into Florence crying *Popolo e Libertà*, the people responded with shouts of *Palle, Palle*, the Medici rallying cry. Frightened at this evidence of loyalty, Jacopo galloped out of the city. He was seized by peasants in the countryside, returned to Florence, tortured, and hanged. (After the burial of Jacopo in hallowed ground, Florence was drenched by rain for days. The people decided it was because the wicked old man was buried in sacred ground. They dug up his body and finally hurled it into the Arno. The rain stopped.) Francesco Pazzi had struck so furiously at Giuliano that he wounded himself, and with difficulty escaped to his uncle's palace. He was found there and taken to the Palazzo della Signoria, where he was hanged beside the archbishop. The people were enraged at the murder of Giuliano and the attempt on Lorenzo, and called for blood. Lorenzo himself, now stronger than ever, could not calm them. Bandini was ultimately brought back from Constantinople, whither he had fled. Renato Pazzi, who had nothing to do with the conspiracy, was executed. Other members of the family were exiled or imprisoned. Cardinal Riario, the innocent decoy of the conspirators, was taken into custody to protect him from the mob. Montesecco, who had not left the city when he balked at murder in Church, was arrested. Before his execution he wrote out a full confession detailing the development of the plot. Guglielmo Pazzi, who was married to Lorenzo's sister Bianca, and who had been loyal throughout, was not only protected but rewarded. Two years later, Lorenzo freed those who had been imprisoned in the fortress at Volterra, and restored the Pazzi family to Florence, but they never regained their former power and influence. Girolamo Riario, the chief cause and one of the principal architects of the conspiracy, prudently took no part in its actual execution, and was safely in Rome when his tools, the Pazzi, played their parts and met the consequences.

Pecock (pē'kok), **Reginald.** English prelate; b. probably in Wales, c1395; d. c1460. He was the author of *Repressor of Overmuch Weeting* (Blaming) *of the Clergy* (c1455), an anti-Lollard work, important as a fine example of 15th-century English.

Pecora (pe'kō-rä), **Iacopo del.** See **Del Pecora, Iacopo.**

Pecorone (pe-kō-rô′nā), **Il.** [*The Dunce.*] Collection of fifty tales by Ser Giovanni Fiorentino. He began to write them in 1376, but the book was not published until 1558 at Milan. The stories were mostly drawn from the chronicles of Giovanni Villani. William Painter, in his *Palace of Pleasure*, and subsequent writers are indebted to it.

Pedersen (pā′dėr-sen), **Christiern.** Danish writer; b. c1480; d. 1554. His most important work was the translation, after Martin Luther's German version, of the Bible into Danish. Known as the Christian III Bible, it is considered the first step in the growth of the Danish literary language. His work includes an edition of Saxo Grammaticus's *Danish History*, Danish versions of the Ogier and Charlemagne legends, and a number of Lutheran tracts.

Pedrarias (pā-ᴛʜrä′ryäs). [Also, **Pedrarias Dávila;** usual form of the name of **Pedro Arias de Ávila.**] Spanish soldier and colonial administrator; b. in Segovia, Spain, c1440; d. at León, Nicaragua, c1531. Sent to replace Balboa as governor of Darien, his quarrels with the latter led to the trial and execution of Balboa. He founded the city of Panama. He sent (1522) Francisco Fernández de Córdoba to take power in Nicaragua, but killed him when he sought autonomy. He alternately aided and hindered Pizarro and de Almagro in the Peruvian quests.

Pedrini (pā-drē′nē), **Giovanni.** See **Giampetrino.**

Pedro IV (of *Aragon*) (pā′ᴛʜrō). King of Aragon (1336–1387); b. 1319?; d. 1387. He succeeded his father, Alfonso IV. He won back Majorca (1344), and fought an indecisive naval war with Genoa. He was succeeded by his son John I.

Pelacani (pā-lä-kä′nē), **Biagio.** Mathematician and astrologer; b. at Parma; d. there, 1416. He studied at Pavia, where he took his doctorate and where he taught (1377). At some time he went to Paris. He taught logic, philosophy, and astrology at Bologna, Padua, Pavia, and again at Padua. As an astrologer he made predictions, one of which, made in June, 1386, was that the Carrarese of Padua would defeat the Scaligeri of Verona and take them prisoners. After a false start, this turned out to be the case. He wrote on mathematics, physics, logic, theology, astronomy, and astrology, and wrote commentaries on Aristotle and others. In the *Il paradiso degli Alberti* of Giovanni Gherardi, he is called "the most universal philosopher and mathematician of his time."

Pellegrino da Modena (pel-lā-grē′nō dä mō′de-nä). [Real name, **Pellegrino Aretusi;** also called **Pellegrino Munari.**] Painter; b. at Modena, 1463–1465; assassinated there, 1523. About 1510 he went to Rome where, between 1513 and 1515 he was in the service of Pope Leo X. He was a faithful follower of Raphael and was one of the painters who frescoed scenes in Raphael's Loggia in the Vatican. A beautiful drawing, *The Madonna Enthroned between St. Joseph and St. Dominic*, is in the Accademia, Venice. Other works are attributed to him on doubtful grounds.

Pellegrino da Montichiari (dä mōn-tē-kyä′rē). Lute-maker; b. at Montichiari, c1520. He is credited by some with having been the inventor of the violin.

Pellegrino da San Daniele (dä sän dänye′lā). [Also known as **Martino da Udine.**] Painter; b. at Udine, 1467; d. there, 1547. His father was a Dalmatian painter and was probably his first teacher. Later he was influenced by Giovanni Bellini, by Giorgione and Palma Vecchio. At various times he worked at S. Daniele (a small town northeast of Venice), and left a number of frescoes, dating from 1498 to 1522, in the Church of S. Antonio there. A number of his works are to be found in and about Udine and in the Friuli, as at Aquileia, Belluno, Cividale, Feltre, Gemona, Osoppo, Treviso, and at Strasbourg, Trieste, and Vienna.

Pellicciaio (pel-lēt-chī′yō), **Giacomo di Mino del.** Sienese painter; mentioned from 1344 to 1389. He was a follower of Lippo Memmi and the Lorenzetti, was enrolled in the register of Sienese painters (1355), and several times held municipal office. He is known to have worked with Bartolo di Fredi in decorating the Chapel of S. Ansano, in the cathedral at Siena. Of the works known to be his, one is a *Madonna* (1342), SS. Martino e Vittoria, Sarteano (near Chiusi), where there is also (S. Francesco), a fragment of a polyptych; a triptych, *Coronation of St. Catherine and Saints*, signed and dated (1362), Siena; and a *Madonna* (1364), S. Maria dei Servi, Siena. The last is more refined and more enriched with decorative detail than the earlier ones.

Pennacchi (pen-näk′kē), **Girolamo.** [Called

Girolamo da Treviso il Vecchio, "the Elder."] Painter; b. at Treviso, c1450; d. 1496? His early work, as a *Pietà* in the Brera, Milan, shows the influence of Squarcione, Mantegna's teacher. His *Death of the Virgin,* Treviso, signed and dated (1478), reflects the influence of Antonello da Messina and Mantegna. In the cathedral at Treviso is his *Virgin Enthroned* (1487), a solid and vigorous work that is Antonellesque in its composition. Other works include a *Pietà,* Lovere; *Nativity,* Padua; a signed *Madonna,* Portland, Oregon; an altarpiece, *Madonna Enthroned with Four Saints* (1494) and a *Transfiguration,* Accademia, Venice; *St. Martin and the Beggar,* Parish Church, Paese, near Treviso; and *Madonna and Four Saints,* cathedral, Treviso. The last works are somewhat less vigorous than the earlier ones.

Pennacchi, Pier Maria. Painter; b. at Treviso, 1464; d. between July, 1514, and March, 1515. His early work shows him to have been influenced by his slightly older contemporary, Girolamo da Treviso il Vecchio, and by Antonello da Messina, especially in the simplicity and solidity of his composition; later he was influenced by Bellini. Among his works are: *Madonna and Saints* and *Dead Christ Supported by Angels* (derived from Bellini), both of which were destroyed at Berlin in 1945; *Holy Family,* Bassano, that bears eloquent witness to the influence of Antonello; *Dormition of the Virgin,* Accademia, Venice; and works at Padua, Basel, and Baltimore (Walters Art Gallery). His last and finest work is in the vault of S. Maria dei Miracoli, Venice; it was finished by his followers in 1528.

Penni (pen′nē), **Gianfrancesco.** [Called **il Fattore,** "the Journeyman."] Painter; b. at Florence, c1488; d. at Naples, 1528. He was the most faithful pupil of Raphael, and perhaps followed him to Rome. In any case, he assisted Raphael at Rome: in the *Loggie* in the Vatican, the Farnesina (Chigi Palace), with the cartoons for tapestry, and in the *Stanza dell' Incendio di Borgo* in the Vatican. His work on these important projects is difficult to isolate, and was in any case in execution of Raphael's designs. After the death of Raphael (1520) he worked with Giulio Romano, Raphael's artistic heir. In 1526 he went to Mantua and assisted Giulio Romano there, but returned soon to Rome, and then went to Naples where he remained until his death. According to Vasari, his principal gifts were in landscape backgrounds and in perspective, and he seems to have employed them generally in the service of other painters.

Percy (pėr′si), Sir **Henry.** [Title, 1st Earl of **Northumberland.**] English military commander; b. 1342; killed at Bramham Moor, England, 1408. Although appointed marshal of England, he was instrumental in dethroning Richard II, and engaged in conspiracies against Henry IV. He was killed invading England.

Percy, Sir **Henry.** [Called **Hotspur.**] English soldier; b. 1364; killed in the battle of Shrewsbury, England, 1403. In 1402 he fought at Homildon Hill and captured the earl of Douglas. Angered because Henry IV refused to accept Douglas as ransom for Edmund Mortimer, Percy's brother-in-law, whom the king was holding, Percy associated himself with Owen Glendower, a Welsh rebel who had proclaimed himself prince of Wales in 1402, and was killed at the battle of Shrewsbury. Shakespeare introduces him in *Henry IV,* first part.

Percy, Sir **Henry.** [Title, 2nd Earl of **Northumberland.**] English nobleman; b. 1394; d. at St. Albans, England, 1455. Son and heir of Sir Henry (Hotspur) Percy. Restored to his grandfather's dignities and estates, he became a member of the council of regency for Henry VI. He was killed fighting Richard, duke of York, in the first battle of St. Albans.

Percy, Sir **Henry.** [Title, 8th Earl of **Northumberland.**] English nobleman; b. at Newburn Manor, England, c1532; d. in the Tower of London, 1585. Three times imprisoned for supporting the cause of Mary, Queen of Scots, following the third arrest he was found shot through the heart. The jury's verdict of suicide was upheld by a Star Chamber inquiry.

Pereira (pẹ-rā′rä), **Duarte Coelho.** See **Coelho Pereira, Duarte.**

Perinetto da Benevento (pā-rē-net′tō dä bā-nā-ven′tō). 15th-century painter who assisted Leonardo da Besozzo in frescoing the chapel of the Caracciolo in the Church of S. Giovanni a Carbonara at Naples (c1442).

Perino del Vaga (pā-rē′nō del vä′gä). See **Pierin del Vaga.**

Perotto (pā-rōt′tō), **Niccolò.** Humanist; b. at Fano, 1429; d. at Sassoferrato, December 14, 1480. He studied under Vittorino da Feltre at Mantua and Guarino da Verona at

Ferrara. In the latter place he was a protégé of William Grey, bishop of Ely, a noted English humanist who was in Italy as Henry VI's representative to the Roman Curia. In 1447 Perotto went to Rome and entered the service of Cardinal Bessarion, whom he accompanied to Bologna. In 1455 he became an apostolic secretary, in 1458 an archbishop, and in the following years fulfilled several administrative posts for the Church. He was an ardent humanist, knew Greek and Latin, and made several translations from the Greek into Latin, as of Plutarch, Epictetus, and Polybius. Pope Nicholas V paid him 500 ducats for his translation of Polybius. His *Rudimenta grammatices* is one of the best of the Latin grammars produced by the humanists. His chief work, *Cornucopia*, is a commentary on the Roman poet Martial, and the exposition of the Latin language in it is an awesome display of erudition. His *Epitome* contains transcriptions of the fables of the Latin fabulist Phaedrus, originally a Greek who was brought to Rome as a young slave in the time of Augustus. These transcriptions are of great value in the study of classical philology. Like so many of the humanists of his day, Perotto took up his pen when he disagreed with his fellow humanists. He waged brisk literary warfare on Poggio Bracciolini in defense of Lorenzo Valla, and on George of Trebizond in defense of Plato.

Perrers (per′ėrz), **Alice.** [Also **de Windsor.**] Mistress of Edward III, d. 1400. She was notorious for her influence in English affairs, and had great influence in the law courts in her friends' favor. Twice banished, she nevertheless retained influence at court under Richard II.

Persons (pär′sọnz), **Robert.** See **Parsons** or **Persons, Robert.**

Perspective. In its most general sense, the term perspective refers to the various techniques used by artists for representing the third dimension on a flat surface. In the context of art after 1420, however, it is employed widely, but not exclusively, to refer to a representation of space achieved by means of a single mathematical, proportional system. Brunelleschi is credited by historians with the discovery of one such system. According to his biographer, Antonio Manetti, Brunelleschi, near 1420, evolved a procedure for reproducing actual buildings on a constant scale with the effect of distance mathematically controlled so that the diminution in size of the more recessed buildings is proportional to their distance from the picture plane. Masaccio's *Trinity* in Florence is the first painting designed in terms of Brunelleschi's mathematical perspective.

Leon Battista Alberti, in his treatise *On Painting* (1435), published a simplified formula for the construction of a mathematically correct perspective scheme that would provide artists with an easy procedure for incorporating figures into the projection of space. Alberti's procedure consisted in the representation of a foreshortened pavement divided into proportionally diminishing squares. Each figure to be represented would be given a size-ratio of three to one in relation to the square upon which it stood. Thus the scale preexistent in the squared floor would regulate the dimensions of all the figures represented. This type of perspective, which always entailed the depiction of architecture, is called linear or one point perspective.

Aerial or atmospheric perspective, on the other hand, refers to a creation of depth in which the effect of distance is achieved not only through a diminution of size, but also through the gradual fading of color in objects the farther away they are depicted from the picture plane.

Empirical perspective is the general term employed by historians to refer to the methods by which painters from the end of the Dugento down to Brunelleschi's time recorded in their works the physiological experience of the third dimension. L.B.

Perugino (pā-rö-jē′nō). [Original name, **Pietro di Cristoforo Vannucci.**] Painter; b. at Città della Pieve, Umbria, c1448; d. at Fontignano, in February, 1523. Little is surely known of his early life and artistic training. He appears to have worked under local Perugian masters and perhaps at Arezzo with Piero della Francesca. About 1470 he went to Florence, according to Vasari because his Perugian masters told him that was the place where he could perfect himself in his art. Also according to Vasari, he was in Verrocchio's studio at Florence, where a fellow pupil was Leonardo da Vinci. In 1472 he was enrolled in the Corporation of St. Luke, the Painters' Guild at Florence. At Rome (1478–1479) he painted in the old St. Peter's Basilica, work that is lost. In 1481, with Botticelli, Ghirlandaio, Cosimo Rosselli, and others, he was summoned to Rome by Sixtus IV to fresco the Sistine Chapel. There he executed the stately and beautiful *Christ Delivering the Keys to St. Peter*. Other frescoes he executed in the Sistine Chapel were effaced to make place for Michelangelo's *Last Judgment*. By the end of 1482 he was back at Florence. The following year he was at Perugia, and thereafter traveled frequently to fulfill his many commissions. He was at Rome in 1484 and 1492, helping to prepare the decorations for the coronations of Pope Innocent VIII and Pope Alexander VI, respectively. In 1507 and 1508 he was again at Rome, painting in the *Stanze* in the Vatican for Julius II, for whom he had earlier (1491) painted the polyptych with a *Nativity*, *Crucifixion*, and *Annunciation*, now in the Villa Albani-Torlonia, Rome. He owned property at Florence, had a busy workshop there, and appeared to have planned to make it his home, as he bought a tomb for himself in the Church of SS. Annunziata. (He was not buried there. He died of the plague at Fontignano where he was working on a *Nativity*, now at London, and was buried in an open field to inhibit the spread of the infection.) In 1485 he became a citizen of Perugia. In 1489 he was invited by the overseers of the cathedral at Orvieto to finish the decoration, begun by Fra Angelico, of the Chapel of S. Brizio. He agreed to do it and went to Orvieto, but despite pleas, reproaches, and threats never began the work. In 1491 such was his reputation that he was one of a committee to decide on the decoration of the façade of the cathedral at Florence. In 1493 he married Chiara Fancelli, the daughter of Luca Fancelli, the architect and friend of Leon Battista Alberti. Vasari writes that Perugino was so enamored of her beauty that he delighted to arrange her headdresses himself. She bore him six children. For more than a decade (until c1505) he was among the most sought-after painters in Italy, and has remained, after Raphael, the most important of the Umbrian masters. To carry out his numerous commissions he employed a number of assistants. Vasari writes that, out of greed for money, he greatly overextended himself in accepting commissions which were then executed in part, or even entirely, by his assistants. By about 1505 repetitions of figures or groups became noticeable in his paintings. His art began to seem old-fashioned at Florence, and in 1506 he returned to Perugia and made that city his headquarters, at the same time maintaining a workshop at Florence for a number of years thereafter. His reputation declined, and in his last years his commissions were often from rather obscure towns in Umbria. Vasari writes that he was an atheist and that the religious paintings that constitute the bulk of his work were not a reflection of spirituality but were painted to make money. A certain violence of disposition is revealed in his plot with a fellow painter to ambush and attack a personal enemy at Florence (December, 1486), for which he was fined twenty florins. He crossed swords with Michelangelo, whose work he criticized and who called him a blockhead in art, and came out of the encounter with little honor. A great number of surviving documents record his business activities and lawsuits.

The earliest documented work of Perugino is a fresco of *St. Sebastian* (1478) in the parish church at Cerqueto, near Perugia. Other figures of the fresco have been destroyed or gravely damaged. The body of the saint is strongly and beautifully modeled, but it is slightly out of true, anatomically off. This characteristic appears in much of Perugino's work. Besides the fresco at Cerqueto there are paintings of St. Sebastian at Paris (two in the Louvre), at Stockholm, Leningrad (a bust), São Paolo (which even to the decoration of the pilasters of the portico in which the saint is bound is practically a copy of one in the Louvre), the Church of S. Sebastiano at Panicale, and in the National Gallery of Umbria at Perugia. The *Adoration of the Magi*, National Gallery, Perugia, once thought to be by Fiorenzo di Lorenzo, who may have influenced Perugino and who was certainly influenced by him, is thought to be of an earlier date (c1475). It shows some influence of Piero della Francesca and Verrocchio. It is one of the more animated and forceful of Perugino's on the whole placid and often sentimentalized paintings. The Madonna of the *Adoration* has a pure, chiseled profile, a certain austerity of expression and pose quite different from the bland expressions and drooping poses of later paintings; the expressions and gestures of the spectators have considerable vitality. After his *Vision of St. Bernard* (1490–1494), Munich, beautiful in its sense of space, almost all his

Madonnas and female figures have the same roundish face with regular features. With all the beauty of color and lovely misty Umbrian landscapes with their soft hills and feathery trees, there is an undeniable lack of force and drama in Perugino's painting which, with his addiction to perfectly symmetrical compositions, results in a certain monotony. His draftsmanship, his skill in the use of perspective, his landscapes, and his limpid color are outstanding qualities of his art. He was the first of the Umbrians to paint in oil and introduced the technique to the region. His landscape backgrounds, derived from Flemish painting, influenced a number of other painters, and his genius for creating space by perspective and tone have been continuously admired. As master of a busy workshop at Florence and later at Perugia, he produced a great quantity of paintings. Among these is the signed and dated (1493) *Madonna between St. John the Baptist and St. Sebastian,* Uffizi, typical of his rather superficial religiosity; the upturned eyes and the willowy reverse curve of St. Sebastian's long body is also typical. His *Dead Christ* (1495), National Gallery, Perugia, is a masterwork of his finest period. Once attributed to Raphael, it is a part of the Decemviri altarpiece now in the Vatican. In 1496 the members of the Collegio del Cambio at Perugia invited him to decorate the Hall of Justice in the Collegio. Francesco Matarazzo, humanist and chronicler of Perugia, drew up the program for the decoration, which was to show the cardinal virtues with the six ancient sages and six ancient heroes who best exemplified them. Of the same year is another fine work, the fresco, *Crucifixion,* Church of S. Maria Maddalena de' Pazzi, Florence, in which a broad landscape forms the background. When his reputation was at its height Isabella d'Este, marchioness of Mantua and a noted collector, wished to have a Perugino painting for her *studiolo.* As was her imperious custom, she gave detailed instructions as to the subject and the manner of its presentation. The painting, *Struggle between Love and Chastity,* now in the Louvre, was finally delivered to her in June, 1505, years after she had ordered it. Though she was pleased with the draftsmanship and coloring, she was connoisseur enough to realize it was not carefully finished and did not hesitate to say so. In the years between 1512 and 1523 he painted, with the help of assistants, a great altarpiece for the Church of S. Agostino at Perugia. The thirty panels of the altarpiece, which was painted on both sides, were split apart in 1654. Some of the panels were lost; others went abroad; a number are in the National Gallery, Perugia. In contrast to the facility and formula of many of the religious paintings are several powerful, firmly characterized portraits. According to some, his individuality and personality are best and most freely expressed in these forceful portraits. Among them is the uncompromisingly realistic self-portrait and the *Portrait of Francesco delle Opere* (1494), Uffizi.

Perugino had many pupils. Most famous of them was Raphael, who was in his shop from about 1500 to about 1504, and who in his short life far surpassed his master. In his early works he was deeply influenced by Perugino, as his *Marriage of the Virgin,* Brera, Milan, derived from Perugino's painting on the same subject at Caen. In 1505 Raphael began a fresco of *Six Saints* in the Church of S. Severo, Perugia. He left the work unfinished. In his last years Perugino was called upon to finish it, thus combining in one painting the early work of the pupil still under the influence of his master with the last work of the master, whose manner had not greatly changed in the meantime. (When Raphael was ordered by Julius II to replace the decorations Perugino and others had begun in the *Stanze* in the Vatican, he left undisturbed his master's painting on the vault of the *Stanza dell' Incendio.*) Other pupils were Benedetto Caporali, Bacchiacca, Lo Spagna, L'Ingegno, and Eusebio di S. Giorgio; Pinturicchio, his fellow-townsman, was an active assistant at various times. With a flawless sense of color, Perugino expresses the softness and glow of Umbria. His work was highly popular in the region. The churches in and about Perugia were formerly rich in paintings by Perugino. In 1797 Napoleon had many of them gathered up and carried off to France; of these, some were placed in the Louvre, others in smaller cities, as at Caen, Grenoble, Lyons, Nancy, Nantes, and elsewhere in France. A number of paintings are in Perugia, in the National Gallery, in the Collegio del Cambio, and in neighboring towns. Others are at Bologna, in the Certosa di Pavia, in his native Città della Pieve, at Rome, Cremona, Florence, Foligno, Siena,

Berlin, Dublin, Edinburgh, London, Frankfurt, Vienna, Birmingham (Alabama), Chicago, Detroit, the Metropolitan Museum and the Morgan Library, New York, in the National Gallery, Washington, Williamstown (Massachusetts), and elsewhere.

Peruzzi (pā-röt′tsē). Ancient and distinguished Florentine family that played an active part in Florentine civic life for generations, and an important economic role as merchants and bankers from the middle of the 13th to the middle of the 14th century. In civic affairs the Peruzzi contributed fifty-four priors and nine gonfalonieri, as well as numerous ambassadors, governors, and other officials. As bankers they loaned money to Philip the Fair for the plot by which Pope Boniface VIII was taken at Anagni, and to the princes of France, England, and Naples for the prosecution of their various wars. As leading citizens of their own commune they entertained visiting dignitaries on a lavish scale in their numerous palaces. As merchants their business was farflung; the house of Peruzzi was one of the strongest in Europe, with branches in Italy and beyond the Alps, and their interests in so many places involved them in the political events taking place in many areas. In 1343 Edward III of England defaulted on the enormous loan that had been made to him to carry on his war with France. The banking house failed, and never again recovered its vast economic power and political influence. The family chapel in the Church of S. Croce at Florence was decorated by Giotto with scenes from the lives of St. John the Baptist and St. John the Evangelist.

Peruzzi, Baldassarre. Architect and painter; b. at Siena, 1481; d. at Rome, January 6, 1536. As a painter he may have been a pupil of Pacchiarotti at Siena. By the time he was 20 he was working as an assistant of Pinturicchio, painting in the Chapel of S. Giovanni in the cathedral at Siena. Shortly thereafter he went to Rome, where he came in contact with the works of Raphael and Michelangelo, and where he became an enthusiastic student of the antique. In 1503 he was executing frescoes on the life of the Virgin in the Church of S. Onofrio with Pinturicchio. His development as a painter is evident in the Farnesina, a villa that, as architect, he built (1508–1511) at Rome for the enormously wealthy Sienese banker Agostino Chigi. (The villa derives its present name from the Farnese, who came into possession of it in 1580.) The theme of the decorations of the villa, in which Raphael, Giulio Romano, Sodoma, and Sebastiano del Piombo collaborated with Peruzzi, is taken from Ovid's *Metamorphoses*. Peruzzi's frieze in a ground floor room has a number of small figures in the Pinturicchio manner, with signs of the Zodiac and illustrations of the myths of the constellations. By the time he came to the decoration for the first floor salon his style had broadened and developed, influenced by Raphael. The decorations of the salon are illustrations of the fables of Ovid. Notable in the painting of the room, called *Salone della Prospettive*, is the illusion of space and the out-of-doors he created by painting columns in relief and in perspective which recede toward splendid views of Rome to give the illusion that the room ends in a columned portico. About 1515 Sodoma arrived at Rome and thereafter Peruzzi's painting reflected his influence in some degree. Among his paintings the frescoes in S. Maria della Pace constitute his pictorial masterpiece. These, *Presentation in the Temple*, *Madonna*, and scenes from the Old and New Testaments, show his love of the antique and his preoccupation with architectonic and perspective elements. The frescoes were painted in 1516–1517. When Rome was sacked (1527) he was captured, but escaped and fled to Siena. There he painted *Augustus and the Sibyl*, Church of Fontegiusta, with its overtones of Sodoma. He frescoed a *Judgment of Paris* in the vestibule of the Castello di Belcaro (near Siena) and ornamented the chapel of the *castello* with religious paintings (1534). Peruzzi passed most of his career at Rome where, besides the works already mentioned, there are examples of his painting in the Borghese Gallery, Cancelleria, Villa Albani, Villa Madama, and in several churches. He was also noted in his day as a designer of stage sets and prepared the scenery for a presentation in the Vatican of Dovizi's (Cardinal Bibbiena's) *Calandria*. A gifted artist, he is better known as an architect. He appears to have begun his architectural studies under Francesco Giorgio di Martini, and to have pursued them enthusiastically after his arrival at Rome, where he became an assistant to Bramante. His first great architectural achievement is the above-mentioned Villa Farnesina,

BALDASSARRE PERUZZI
The Holy Family with Saints
Courtesy of The Pierpont Morgan Library, New York

in which the simple elegance and restraint of 15th-century Sienese style are evident. Essentially, the building is a central block with a loggia of five bays (now glassed in), and two projecting wings. The villa, on the outskirts of Rome when it was built, was intended as a pleasant place to spend a summer's day. The decoration was planned to enhance the atmosphere of delightful relaxation as the villa provided spacious rooms and a splendid garden in which to enjoy it. According to Peruzzi's plan, the façade was originally decorated with frescoes but these, exposed to the weather, have long since disappeared. As he had earlier assisted Bramante on St. Peter's, he also assisted Raphael, who was in charge after Bramante's death, and succeeded as master of the works on Raphael's death (1520). His aim was to carry on in the spirit of Bramante, but he had little impact. In 1522 he made designs for the façade and other parts of the Basilica of S. Petronio at Bologna. On his return to Siena after the sack of Rome he was named architect of the city and was in charge of fortifications of the city and of other territories of Siena and of projects for public buildings. In 1530 he was again named chief of the works of St. Peter's but he was mainly at Siena, from which he did not return permanently to Rome until about a year before his death, and his influence on St. Peter's, on which construction had been halted for some time following the sack of Rome, was limited. His contacts with Rome continued however, and he made frequent trips to the city. In 1532 he began, for two members of the Massimo family, the construction of the Palazzo Massimo alle Colonne on the site of a palace that had been destroyed in the sack. It is, according to some, his architectural masterpiece. An innovation is the curved façade, so designed to fit the site. In essence the palace (which was not finished until after his death) consists of two adjoining buildings, one for each Massimo brother, whose central axes are at an angle. Each has its own façade but the palace as a whole is called "alle Colonne" because of the columned portico of the curved façade. The portico is richly decorated with stuccos of statues and classical motifs designed by Peruzzi. From the portico a corridor leads to a central court patterned after a Roman atrium, with a double loggia of superposed orders at each end. The atrium is abundantly ornamented with friezes and medallions. The opulence and magnificence of 16th-century style is typified in the Palazzo Massimo and is a measure of Peruzzi's departure from the simple elegance of the Farnesina. He left a great number of drawings illustrating architectural problems, important collections of which are in the Uffizi and at Siena. He appears to have planned an architectural treatise but never wrote it. Peruzzi's two careers overlapped. His greatest influence was as an architect, notably on his older contemporary, Sebastiano Serlio, and as an important exponent of High Renaissance architectural style.

Peruzzi, Giovanni Salustio (or **Salverio** or **Salvestro**). Architect; b. at Siena. He was the son of Baldassarre Peruzzi (1481–1536) and followed in his father's footsteps as an architect. In the reign of Pope Paul IV he was working on the fortifications of Rome and particularly on the portal of Castel Sant' Angelo, which he designed in the form of a great triumphal arch with five niches for statues. He designed the façade of S. Maria in Transpontina at Rome, and in 1567 left the city to enter the service of the emperor Maximilian II at Vienna, where he remained until his death.

Pescara (pās-kä′rä), Marquis of. [Title of **Fernando Francesco d'Ávalos.**] General in the service of Charles V; b. at Naples, 1489; d. at Milan, November 25, 1525. Of Spanish descent, he had nothing but contempt for the Italians. Betrothed to Vittoria Colonna at the age of 4 and married at 19, he succeeded to his father's title in boyhood, and was destined to a brilliant military career. In 1511 he left his young bride for the wars. In 1512 he was wounded and made prisoner at the battle of Ravenna; in 1515 he served in the war in Lombardy. He contributed largely to the victory at Pavia, where King Francis I was captured. In the struggle of the Spanish for Milan he played a treacherous role, acting for both sides, and finally betrayed to Charles V a plot formed by Girolamo Morone and others for driving the Spaniards and Germans out of Italy. He died soon afterwards of illness and his wounds.

Pesellino (pā-sel-lē′nō). [**Francesco di Stefano,** called **il Pesellino.**] Painter; b. at Florence, c1422; d. there, July 29, 1457. He was the grandson of Pesello (1367–1446), from whom his name Pesellino is derived. He was a pupil of Fra Filippo Lippi and was influenced by Fra Angelico, Masaccio, and Domenico Veneziano. He painted the predella panels for the polyptych, *Madonna Enthroned with Saints*, Uffizi, that Lippi executed (c1445) for the Medici chapel in S. Croce. Of the five panels of the predella, those of *St. Anthony and the Miser's Heart*, *Nativity*, and *Martyrdom of SS. Cosmas and Damian* are in the Uffizi with the polyptych. The two others, *The Dream of the Deacon Justinian* and *St. Francis Receiving the Stigmata* (copies of which are also with the

PESELLINO (?)
Court Lady Walking in Profile toward the Right
Fogg Art Museum, Harvard University.
Bequest of Charles A. Loeser

polyptych in the Uffizi), are in the Louvre at Paris. The last-mentioned panel, with its rocky crags, desolate landscape, and atmosphere of divine intervention recalls the austerity and spirituality of Lorenzo Monaco, while the acute plastic sense with which the figures of all the panels are rendered reflects the influence and advances of Masaccio as they may have been passed to the young painter by Lippi. The panels are also distinguished for their brilliant color. The religious pictures produced in the short career of Pesellino are notable for depth of feeling and absence of ornamentation; no genre details distract from the spiritual intention of the painting. His only documented work, the *Trinity with Saints*, National Gallery, London, was begun in 1455. In it Pesellino's distinctive qualities—plasticity, concentration, color, and freshness—are intensified. The painting was completed, following Pesellino's early death, in Lippi's studio, a small part of the central panel by Lippi himself and the predella with assistants. Other religious paintings by Pesellino include *Construction of the Temple*, Fogg Museum, Cambridge, and companion panels, *David Dancing before the Ark*, Kansas City, Missouri, *Penitence of King David* and *Death of Absalom*, LeMans, France; *Madonna and Child*, Isabella Stewart Gardner Museum, Boston, and a similar painting at Esztergom, Hungary; and paintings at Milan (Poldi Pezzoli), Rome (Doria Pamphili), Berlin, Dresden, the Metropolitan Museum, New York, the Johnson collection, Philadelphia, Toledo (Ohio), the National Gallery, Washington, Worcester (Massachusetts), and elsewhere. In his cassoni panels Pesellino reflects the enthusiasm for humanism that absorbed the Florentines of his time. With youthful freshness, energy, and fantasy, he painted *The Triumphs of Love, Chastity and Death* and *The Triumphs of Fame, Time and Eternity*, Isabella Stewart Gardner Museum, Boston, based on Petrarch's *Trionfi*. Each panel presents three scenes in series, with the allegorical figures riding their triumphal cars, surrounded by figures in contemporary Florentine dress. Another cassone panel, *Story of Griselda*, is in the Carrara Academy, Bergamo, a delightful illustration, again in contemporary dress, of a popular story.

PESELLO (pā-sel′lō). [**GIULIANO D'ARRIGO**, called **IL PESELLO.**] Painter; b. at Florence, 1367; d. there, 1446. He was the grandfather of Pesellino (c1422–1457). He was enrolled in the Physicians' and Apothecaries' Guild at Florence in 1385, is said to have worked on designs for two tombs in the cathedral, on the cupola, and with Ghiberti (1419). No certain work of his is identifiable.

PETER MARTYR. See **ANGHIERA, PIETRO MARTIRE D'.**

PETER THOMAS, Saint. Carmelite monk and preacher; d. at Famagusta, Cyprus, 1366. As bishop, archbishop, patriarch, and papal legate, he worked for the unification of the Greek and Latin churches.

PETRARCH (pē′trärk). [Italian, **FRANCESCO PETRARCA**; original name, **PETRACCO.**] Poet, moral philosopher, and humanist; b. at

Arezzo, July 20, 1304; d. at Arquà, near Padua, July 19, 1374. His father, a notary, belonged to the party of the Bianchi (Whites: Guelphs of the wealthy commercial class) in Florence and was banished at the same time as Dante and, like him, went into exile at Arezzo. In 1350, when at the height of his fame, Petrarch (who had changed his name from Petracco to Petrarca) visited Arezzo and was shown the house where he was born. He was moved to learn that the ruling fathers had decreed that it should never be changed. Reconstructed in 1948, it stands on a quiet street on the hilltop near the cathedral. Ser Petracco, having moved his family from Arezzo to Incisa and then to Pisa, where Petrarch remembered seeing Dante, at length decided to take his family to France. He expected to find more opportunities to practice his profession at the papal court, which had moved to Avignon in 1309. Thus it was that in 1312 the family went to Carpentras, about fifteen miles from Avignon. There the boy Petrarch became acquainted with Guido Sette, who was to become his lifelong friend, and began his studies. Ser Petracco was an enthusiast for classical literature and inculcated that enthusiasm in his son. In 1316 Petrarch went to Montpellier to study civil law. From this period dates his intense interest in and acquisition of copies of classical writers. His father thought he was spending too much time and money on books and, though he himself had commissioned a copy of Vergil, threw some of the books into the fire, but seeing his son's great distress he snatched the Vergil and Cicero from the flames. (This copy of Vergil was later stolen and its whereabouts remained unknown for a number of years. It was at length mysteriously restored and became Petrarch's greatest treasure. On the flyleaf he noted, after her death, that he had first seen Laura on Easter Sunday in 1327. He wrote the information there because he so often read his precious Vergil and would thus be continually reminded of the important dates in his personal life. Simone Martini painted a frontispiece for the volume, and this copy is now in the Ambrosian Library at Milan.) When he was 14 or 15, Petrarch's mother died. The Latin elegy he wrote then is his earliest surviving work. In 1320, with his beloved brother Gherardo and his friend Guido, he went to Bologna to complete his law studies. Except for several long visits to Avignon, he remained there until 1326. In that year his father died and he returned to Avignon. In the meantime he had realized that though the theory of civil law interested him, what he had observed of it in practice repelled him. His interests, from an early age, lay in study, in writing, and in books, which he said delight us, converse with us, give us good advice, and provide living and lively companionship. Therefore, since he was free of parental guidance, he gave up the law.

On April 6, 1327, he first saw Laura in church, at Avignon. As was Beatrice for Dante, Laura became the object of Petrarch's love. The sonnets he wrote, in Italian, expressing his longing love for her, his dreams, his innermost passion, have become his greatest legacy. He did not expect this to be the case, and toyed with the idea of destroying them as trifles. Nevertheless, he later chose those he considered to be the best among them and collected them under the title *Canzoniere*. In his sonnets Petrarch perfected the sonnet form, which was not new with him, and fixed it for all time. In them also he gave expression to the hope and hopelessness, the romantic yearning, realization of futility, melancholy, and grief of a man whose love is unrequited. There have been many theories as to Laura's identity. That generally received is that she was the daughter of Audibert de Noves, married Hugues de Sade in 1326, and became the mother of eleven children. Petrarch was faithful, in his inspiration and works, to her until her death in the Black Death, 1348. This date marks a dividing line in his Italian lyrics. His love for her, idealized and spiritualized, persisted, and he continued writing poems about her, but the lyrics now took on religious overtones. Laura's identity has been disputed, but her real identity is unimportant: what is important is the effect she had on Petrarch's lyric poems of unrequited love and consequent melancholy, together with his inner conflict between desire and religious duty. These reactions were distilled into verse of remarkable elegance, clarity of expression, and formal perfection. Petrarch's homage was conventional, and personal relations are not supposed to have existed between the wife of De Sade and the poet. (His love for Laura, deep, real, and lasting as it was, did not prevent him from becoming the father of two children by a woman whose name is unknown. A son Giovanni was born in 1337, and a daughter Francesca in 1343. He had both legitimized by papal bull and did what he thought best for them. Giovanni, a disappointment to his father, died at the age of 25. Francesca lived to comfort her father in his old age.)

For a number of years Petrarch lived near Avignon. He was appalled and disgusted by the frivolity and corruption of the papal court, felt strongly that the pope should return to Rome as the center of Christendom, and wrote several letters to that effect. In later years he declined an offer of a papal secretaryship, and other offers as well, lest such positions interfere with his work, destroy his leisure, and interrupt his studies. In 1337 he bought a little house at Vaucluse, not far from Avignon, in a secluded valley watered by the Sorgue, "the prince of streams." There he enjoyed the solitude, worked in his garden, and did much of his best work. There too, he entertained his friends, who were many and devoted, and carried on his vast correspondence. In these years he frequently left Vaucluse: to travel, as to Paris, the Low Countries, and Germany; to go on missions; and to visit in Italy. Wherever he went he searched for books and manuscripts, buying them when he could but more often copying them in his own hand. In 1330 (he had earlier taken minor ecclesiastical orders) he became household chaplain to Cardinal Giovanni Colonna, and later (1335) received a canonry under Bishop Giacomo Colonna. It was the first of several benefices that provided him with a living, for his inheritance had been small. In the service of the Colonnas he performed various missions. In 1337 he began a series of biographies, *De viris illustribus*, and in 1338 or 1339 he began an epic poem, *Africa*, on Scipio the Elder and the Second Punic War. Neither was ever completed, although he worked on both from time to time throughout his life. He expected his *Africa* to be his magnum opus, that his fame in future years would rest on it, and refined and polished it continually, but was never satisfied that it was ready for circulation. The reputation of the *Africa* that developed from the early sections spread, and Petrarch won great renown for it and his Italian lyrics. As a result, he received from the University of Paris (where the rector was a Florentine) and from King Robert of Naples, invitations on the same day (September 1, 1340) to be crowned with the laurel. He preferred to receive the crown in his native Italy, went to Naples to confer with King Robert, who offered to award the crown himself, but decided he wished to receive it from the Roman Senate and departed for that city, which he had first visited in 1336. The splendid ceremony of his coronation on the Capitoline took place on April 8, 1341. Later in his life, in his *Letter to Posterity* (written probably in 1373), he spoke modestly of his unworthiness for the crown at the time when it was awarded to him. In point of fact, Petrarch longed for fame and was intensely gratified at the recognition. Some have even thought that he had, by means of his many contacts, engineered the coincidence that brought him the two invitations on the same day. Be that as it may, with his coronation Petrarch became one of the most famous men of his day. He was famous for his learning, for his championship of the ancient writers, for his collection of books and manuscripts (he was one of the earliest to attempt such a collection), for his connections and friendships and, above all, for his works. His discovery (1345) of sixteen books of Cicero's letters to his friend Atticus, *Ad Atticum*, in a cathedral library gave him the idea of collecting his own letters. In addition to the letters to his friends he began to write letters to eminent men of old—Cicero, Seneca, Livy, Horace, Vergil, Homer, and others—letters in which he addressed them with such familiarity as to their times, circumstances, and activities that it was as if he knew them. From his many letters he ultimately selected about 600 that he, at various times, included in his several collections—*Epistolae familiares*, *Epistolae seniles*, *Epistolae sine nomine* and *Epistolae metricae*. These, in careful and polished Latin, were written to be read not by the addressee only but by all who might profit by their erudition, style, and language. The subject matter varied. Some were of everyday events, descriptions of work in his garden or trees that he had planted. The letters were often in the nature of essays on great themes, sometimes pleas, and frequently exhortations to rulers or clerics to act on some matter as Petrarch directed. Even after they had been delivered, he continued to revise and polish the copies of those that he wished to include in his collections. He approached the problems of his day in writing rather than in action. He urged the popes to return to Rome but stayed in or near Avignon himself, always professing to despise the life of the court there. He loved Italy, was glad that he was born an Italian, agonized over the plight of his land and condemned the "foreign swords" (mercenaries) that tormented it and, intellectually, yearned for the return of an emperor who might bring it peace. To this end he wrote (1351) Charles of Bohemia, urging him to assert himself as emperor in Italy. (Later, when he met Charles, he was less enthusiastic about him, but not about his idea of an emperor.) He had met Cola di Rienzi in Avignon (1343), and was impressed by his ideals for democratic government in Rome. When (1347) Rienzi came to power there briefly, Petrarch was enthusiastic, deserted his former patrons, the Colonna family, to support, in writing, Rienzi's ideals, but did not go to Rome. He often expressed a love of liberty, yet was a friend and guest of many of the despots of northern Italy, as in Verona, Mantua, Ferrara, Parma, and especially in Milan, whither the archbishop Giovanni Visconti, virtual tyrant there, had invited him, simply "for the honor of his presence." He remained in Milan from 1353 to 1361, the longest stay he made in any Italian city, and performed several diplomatic missions for the Visconti. His acceptance of the Visconti invitation dismayed his Florentine friends. Milan was the enemy of Florence. Milan was a despotism. Florence was a republic. Petrarch's expressions in favor of liberty and democracy were not taken seriously by his various hosts, and the dichotomy between his expressed ideals and the circumstances in which he chose to live did not seem to concern Petrarch. His own freedom was never in doubt. Throughout his life he moved restlessly about Europe and Italy. After the death of Laura and of many of his friends he had proposed to some of those remaining that they retire to Vaucluse with him and establish a community of ideas and ideals. The proposal came to naught, but reflected Petrarch's increasing preoccupation with matters of the spirit. He knew himself to be torn between a love of worldly glory and a desire for spiritual peace and purity of soul. He could not tear himself from the world, in spite of his comment that, "The more I go about the world the less I like it." In 1362 he moved to Padua, where he had held a canonry since 1347. In the same year he went to Venice, where he was given a palace, and presented that republic with his personal library. In 1370, with his daughter and son-in-law, he moved to a house in Arquà, a village in the Euganean Hills near Padua. There he continued to work and study. He had often expressed a wish to die with his books. He was found dead among them on the eve of his seventieth birthday, July 19, 1374.

Petrarch has been called the father of humanism, for his deep interest and knowledge of the Latin classics, for his activity in copying and collecting examples of them, for his constant exhortations to read them in their original purity, free of medieval emendations and interpretations, and for the ease and grace of his own Latin works. In all respects he was the prototype of 15th-century humanists. Unlike some of his followers, he felt no conflict between his love for the ancient writers, his profound understanding and knowledge of the classical world, and his Catholic training and unquestioning faith. In 1354 he was given a manuscript of Homer. He regarded it with reverence but, as he did not know Greek, confessed to his donor that "Your Homer is dumb with me, or rather I am deaf to him. Yet I delight in the mere sight of him." His love for antiquity was profound and, as he says, if it had not been for friends dear to him, "I should have preferred to have been born in any other period than our own." He sincerely anticipated that he would be remembered for his Latin writings. (He had begun to write in Latin, it is said, because of his irritation and distress at the mispronunciations suffered by his Italian lyrics.) For him, the Latin authors, language, and style came to represent the height of literary endeavor. As it turned out, it is the odes and sonnets of the *Canzoniere*, of which there are nearly 400, that have conferred immortality on him. His only other Italian writings, *I Trionfi*, were not very successful. His Latin works, however, had a powerful influence in his own day and in succeeding generations on the development of humanism. They include his beloved and incomplete *Africa*; *Secretum*, begun 1342, a dialogue in which he analyzed his soul; *Rerum memoran-*

darum libri, an unfinished work that he began at Parma in 1344, in which he intended to discuss the cardinal virtues; *De vita solitaria* (1346), on the life of solitude (dedicated to one of his oldest friends, but not presented until twenty years of polishing and refining had brought it to the desired perfection); *Bucolicum carmen* (1346), twelve eclogues in the manner of Vergil; *De otio religioso* (after 1347), a treatise on the freedom from worldly cares in the monastic life; *De remediis utriusque fortunae* (1354) on the remedies and perils of good and bad fortune; and *De sui ipsius et multorum ignorantia* (1367), a treatise which is concerned, chiefly, with the ignorance of doctors, whom he distrusted as a class. In most cases, he worked on these titles over a period of years revising, editing, refining, and polishing. Of Petrarch, Pius II's comment was that "His equal would be hard to find if his Latin works were comparable to those he wrote in Italian." He was the outstanding literary figure of his day. His reputation was not confined to Italy but was great throughout Europe. He was the friend and guest of princes and clerics. He says, truthfully, "The greatest kings of this age have loved and courted me." His gift for friendship and the value he set on it were great. Many of his friends were lifelong, but he continued to make new ones as he grew older. Boccaccio, who had written him an admiring letter in 1350, became a devoted friend and disciple to the end of Petrarch's life. He had traveled widely, under conditions that would be unimaginable today, lived in many cities, was an ardent gardener, loved solitude and his leisure but needed the intellectual stimulus of other minds. He made friends, but he also made enemies through the controversies he engaged in in writing. His love and knowledge of antiquity led to a revived interest in the ancient writers, and his Latin works spurred others to interest in a pure Latin style and vocabulary. His Latin works initiated and gave shape to almost every important idea and attitude of Renaissance humanism. However, it is for his lyrics in Italian that he is today remembered, honored, and imitated. Some elements of his poetic form were traditional, but his attitude, in its subjectivity and introspection, in its instability and many-sidedness, anticipates later developments. He carried the prestige of Italian literature to the rest of Europe, and he still serves as a model for formal perfection and for harmony of verse and content in poetical expression.

Petrucci (pe-tröt′chē), **Alfonso.** Cardinal; b. at Siena, 1492; d. at Rome, July 4, 1517. He was the son of Pandolfo Petrucci, lord of Siena (1452–1512). Julius II made him bishop of Massa Maritima and created him cardinal (1511). In the conclave of 1513 he was a supporter of Giovanni de' Medici, who became Pope Leo X. Later, disappointed in his hopes of special favors from Pope Leo, he withdrew from Rome and was said to have taken part in an attempt to kill the pope by means of his doctor. Ultimately, Cardinal Petrucci concluded an agreement with the pope by which he was permitted to remain at Siena. With a promise of safety from the pope he returned to Rome on June 18, 1517. The next day he was arrested for his earlier conspiracy. He confessed his error, was deprived of his cardinalate, and then was secretly killed in prison, probably without the pope's knowledge.

Petrucci, Antonello. Neapolitan official; b. at Teano; d. May 11, 1487. He came from an obscure family but, by his own talent, won a place of confidence and responsibility at the courts of Alfonso I of Naples and of his son and successor Ferrante. For both monarchs he filled many confidential and important posts. Even the suspicious Ferrante trusted him, and rewarded him with a title, lands, and fiefs. To bring his social position to the level of his court position, Petrucci sought to link himself through the marriages he arranged for his children to the Neapolitan barons. He intrigued with them against the king. Ferrante learned of his betrayal, seized him, cast him into prison and, after wringing a confession from him by torture, had him killed.

Petrucci, Ottaviano. Printer of music; b. at Fossombrone, July 14, 1466; d. there, May 7, 1539. In Venice he conceived the idea of printing musical notation with movable type. The Republic of Venice granted him a patent (1498) and with two friends and two wealthy patrons who supported him, he succeeded in perfecting his invention. In 1501 he printed *Harmonice Musices Odhecaton*, a collection of 100 songs. This was the first book of musical notation printed with movable type. Later he brought out books of French, religious and Italian songs. He left

Venice (1511) and returned to Fossombrone where, under a patent granted by the pope, he continued to print books of music.

Petrucci, Pandolfo. Lord of Siena; b. at Siena, 1452; d. there, May 21, 1512. In 1487 he returned to Siena after a long exile and with his brother Giacoppo became master of the city. Giacoppo died in 1497 and Pandolfo ruled alone. Although he had no official title, by 1500 he exercised great authority in Siena. He maintained himself in power with the aid of foreign mercenaries and by ruthless suppression of his rivals. In foreign affairs he played one enemy against another. At one time he was allied with Louis XII of France; at another with Cesare Borgia. Florence sent Machiavelli to Siena on several occasions to attempt to fathom his policies. Machiavelli said of him that he "governed his state with the help of those he held suspect rather than the others." (*The Prince*, xx) Petrucci was one of the masterminds of the conspiracy against Cesare Borgia in October, 1502. Cesare overcame him and he was compelled to give up Siena but was restored a few months later with the help of the French. He was saved from Cesare's wrath by the untimely death of the latter. He made secret agreements against the French and Florence, aided Julius II against the French, and finally (1511) was forced to cede Montepulciano to Florence. After this he retired to private life. Petrucci was typical of the political leaders who kept Italy in turmoil in his time, and who sought foreign aid to maintain their power. His treachery and betrayal of his allies, and his ruthlessness to his rivals were also typical. On the other hand, he maintained order in turbulent, restless Siena, promoted trade, reformed the currency, and protected the arts and literature. He was just and kind when it did not cost him anything.

Petruccioli (pā-tröt-chō′lē), **Cola.** Umbrian painter; d. at Perugia, 1401. In 1372 he assisted Ugolino di Prete Ilario in painting the choir of the cathedral at Orvieto, and remained in Orvieto, working on the cathedral, until 1380. He lived at Perugia for the last twenty years of his life, working from there in nearby Assisi in 1394. Not a great painter, he was a spirited provincial artist who, through Ugolino, was somewhat influenced in his care for detail by Sienese painting, and by his presence and the work he carried out had an important influence on the Umbrian school of his time. A fresco of the *Crucifixion*, signed and dated 1380, is in the cathedral at Orvieto. A number of examples from his workshop are in the Pinacoteca at Perugia.

Petrus Platensis (pē′trus pla-ten′sis). Latinized name of **Rue, Pierre** (or **Pierchon**) **de la.**

Pettie (pet′i), **George.** English writer of prose romances; b. 1548; d. at Plymouth, Devonshire, England, July, 1589. He was the author of a work important for the part it played in developing Elizabethan prose fiction, *A Petite Pallace of Pettie his Pleasure, contayning many pretie Hystories by him, set foorth in Comely Colours, and most Delightfully Discoursed* (1576), an imitation of William Painter's *Palace of Pleasure* (1567), and written in the ornate style later further developed by John Lyly.

Peucer (poi′tsėr), **Kaspar.** German physician and Protestant theologian; b. at Bautzen, Saxony, Germany, January 6, 1525; d. at Dessau, Germany, September 25, 1602. He was imprisoned as one of the leaders of the crypto-Calvinist movement.

Peutinger (poi′ting-ėr), **Konrad.** German humanist; b. at Augsburg, Germany, October 14, 1465; d. there, December 24, 1547. He was a lawyer, historian, antiquarian, classicist, and, as a German patriot, an adviser to Emperor Maximilian. He is best known for his publication of an ancient map of the military roads in the Roman Empire, called for him *Tabula Peutingeriana.*

Phaer or **Phayer** (fār, fā′ėr), **Thomas.** English translator; b. c1510; d. at Kilgerran, Pembrokeshire, Wales, 1560. He was the first Englishman to attempt to translate all of Vergil's *Aeneid* into English. In 1558 he published his translation of the *Seven First Books of the Eneidos of Virgil*. He had begun the tenth book when he died (the translation was completed by Thomas Twyne, 1573). Nine books were published in 1562. He also wrote on various subjects, including law and medicine.

Philargos (fē′lär-gôs), **Petros.** Original name of the antipope **Alexander V.**

Philip (of *Burgundy*). [Called **le Hardi,** "the Bold."] Duke of Burgundy (1363–1404); b. January 15, 1342; d. April 27, 1404. He was the younger son of John II (John the Good) of France. He earned his epithet for his bravery at the battle of Poitiers (1356). After the battle he accompanied his father into captivity in England. The death of the last Capetian duke of Burgundy in 1361 united Burgundy to the French reigning family and in 1363 Philip became duke. In 1369 he married Margaret, widow of the preceding duke of Burgundy and heiress of Flanders, which latter he ruled after his father-in-law's death in 1384. He was appointed by his brother Charles V one of the regents during the minority of Charles VI, who acceded (1380) to the throne of France. Philip now found himself virtual ruler of France and fought in campaigns in the Netherlands (1382 *et seq.*) and against the English. When the insanity of Charles VI incapacitated him in 1392, Philip again became paramount in the kingdom. His diplomacy succeeded, among other things, in securing a truce with England and appeared about to succeed in healing the schism in the Roman Catholic Church when the rivalry of Louis d'Orléans, brother of the king, forced him to turn his attention to internal politics. He was succeeded by his son John the Fearless.

Philip (of *Burgundy*). [Called **le Bon,** "the Good."] Duke of Burgundy (1419–1467); b. at Dijon, June 13, 1396; d. at Bruges, June 15, 1467. He was the son of John the Fearless, whom he succeeded. He signed the treaty of Troyes in 1420, as the result of which he was allied with England against Charles VII of France until 1435. According to the treaty he recognized Henry V of England as heir to the French throne, but gradually he became reconciled to Charles, although he sided with the rebellious nobles of the Praguerie and gave asylum to the dauphin (later Louis XI) when he fled from the king. Thus when Louis XI ascended the throne in 1461, Philip supported him against any claim the English might have. He often had to suppress revolts in the Netherlands, the most notable being that of Ghent (1448–1453). In April, 1465, he turned over the government of his duchy to his son Charles, known as "the Bold." During Philip's reign Burgundy rose to its greatest eminence and prosperity and was probably the first state in Europe at the time. His court was famous for its brilliance. He was a noted patron of men of letters, founded a valuable collection of manuscripts (the *Bibliothèque de Bourgogne*), and a university at Dôle (1421). He sent representatives to the Congress at Mantua called (1459) by Pope Pius II to organize a crusade against the Turks. Later, overcome by a severe illness, he promised to send troops for the crusade, and to lead them himself if his health permitted. However, he recovered from his illness, and when Pius was ready to launch the crusade (1464), Philip forgot his promise. His first two wives were Michelle (d. 1422), daughter of Charles VI of France, whom he married in 1409; and Bonne of Artois (d. 1425) whom he married in 1424. In 1429, in honor of his third marriage, to Isabella of Portugal, he instituted the Order of the Golden Fleece.

Philip I (of *Castile*). [Called **Felipe el Hermoso,** "Philip the Handsome"; sometimes called **Philip I** of *Spain*.] King of Castile; b. at Bruges, 1478; d. in Spain, September 25, 1506. He was the son of the emperor Maximilian I and Mary of Burgundy, and grandson of Charles the Bold. On the death (1482) of his mother, he became titular duke of Burgundy and thus ruler of the Netherlands as well as of the other possessions of Burgundy. He married (1496) Joanna, daughter of Ferdinand and Isabella of Spain. When Isabella died in 1504, Joanna became queen of Castile and Philip and his father-in-law contested the actual rule of the kingdom. Philip, who had been in the Netherlands, returned to Spain in 1506 to press his claims but shortly thereafter died, apparently from typhoid, but according to rumor from poison. Philip's long absence in the Netherlands and his open infidelities had aroused a possessive jealousy in the unstable Joanna (his treatment of her was one of the arguments advanced by Ferdinand for keeping him from ruling Castile) and his sudden death made her completely insane. She refused to permit his body to be buried for a long time, and after his entombment lived out her life near his tomb at Tordesillas. The emperors Charles V and Ferdinand I were their sons.

Philip III (of *France*). [Called **le Hardi,** "the Hardy."] King of France (1270–1285); b. April 3, 1245; d. at Perpignan, France, 1285. He was the son and successor of Louis IX. In a struggle between the parties of the queen and the queen mother, Philip's uncle Charles of Anjou emerged as a dominant factor. Philip supported Charles, who had become Charles I of Naples, in Italy. Philip died during a futile expedition to secure the crown of Aragon for his son, and was succeeded by his son Philip IV.

Philip IV (of *France*). [Called **Philip the Fair.**] King of France (1285–1314); b. at Fontainebleau, France, 1268; d. November 29, 1314. He was the son of Philip III. In 1284 he married Jeanne, heiress of Navarre, whereby he united that kingdom with France. In 1292 or 1293 he summoned Edward I of England, as the holder of French fiefs, to his court to answer for depredations committed by Edward's subjects on the Norman coast. Edward sent his brother, Edmund, earl of Lancaster, who surrendered Guienne to Philip as security for a satisfactory settlement. Philip thereupon declared Edward's fiefs forfeited on account of his nonappearance. War broke out in consequence in 1294; peace was restored in 1299, Guienne being restored to Edward. In 1296 he became involved in a quarrel with Pope Boniface VIII, as the growing expenditures occasioned by the centralization of the government led him to tax ecclesiastical property. Boniface issued (1296) the bull *Clericis laicos* opposing this, whereupon Philip cut off the export of coin, cutting the papal revenue and forcing the pope to back down (1297). When Philip arrested (1301) the bishop of Pamiers, Boniface issued (1302) the bull *Unam Sanctam*, asserting strongly his right to intervene. The quarrel culminated in 1303 in the seizure of the pope, who, although released by the Roman populace, died shortly after. Boniface's successor, Benedict XI, dying in 1304, Philip procured the election of a Frenchman, Clement V, who removed (1309) the papal residence to Avignon. He suppressed (1307–1313) the Order of the Templars, whose lands he confiscated. Three of his sons by Jeanne of Navarre, Louis X, Philip V, and Charles IV, succeeded him as kings of France; their daughter Isabella married Edward II of England.

Philip V (of *France*). [Called **le Long,** "the Tall."] King of France (1316–1322); b. c1293; d. January 2, 1322. He was the second son of Philip IV and succeeded (November 19, 1316) his brother, Louis X, who died on July 5, 1316, leaving his widow pregnant. Philip served as regent until the birth of the child, John I, who died within a week of his birth. Philip seized the throne and obtained (1317) confirmation of his tenure by the States General, which invoked the Salic Law, barring women from succession, Philip's rival to the throne being a daughter of Louis X. His reign was marked by frequent meetings of the States General and by attempts at reform in such matters as coinage. Popular persecutions of the Jews were suppressed by Philip (who exacted heavy donations from the Jews in return). He was succeeded by his younger brother Charles IV.

Philip VI (of *France*). King of France (1328–1350); b. 1293; d. August, 1350. Charles IV, his predecessor, left only a daughter. The Salic law (barring women from the succession) was invoked and Philip VI, son of Charles of Valois (brother of Philip IV), became king. He was the first king of the House of Valois. In his reign began (1338) the Hundred Years' War with England. He was defeated by Edward III at Crécy in 1346, lost Calais in 1347, and acquired Dauphiné in 1349. He was succeeded by his son John II.

Philip I (of *Spain*). See **Philip I** (of *Castile*).

Philip II (of *Spain*). King of Spain, Naples, and Sicily (1556–1598), and of Portugal (1580–1598); b. at Valladolid, Spain, May 21, 1527; d. in the Escorial Palace, near Madrid, Spain, September 13, 1598. He was the son of Charles I of Spain (the Holy Roman emperor Charles V) and Isabella of Portugal. Already invested by his father with the rule of Milan, Naples, Sicily, Franche-Comté, and the Netherlands, he succeeded to the crown of Spain upon Charles' abdication in 1556. In that year France and the pope (Paul IV) made war against Spain. The pope was defeated by Philip's forces, and in 1559 France, by the Treaty of Cateau-Cambrésis, acknowledged Spanish suzerainty in Franche-Comté and in the Italian states. It was at the time of his victory over the French in the battle of St.-Quentin in 1557 that Philip made the vow which he fulfilled by building the vast aggregation of the monastery, church, college, library, and palace of San Lorenzo del Escorial. In 1543 he had married Maria, daughter of John III of Portugal, who died in 1545. With Philip, marriage was strictly a political matter. His second wife (1554–1558) was Mary of England, whom he assisted in returning that country officially to the fold of the Roman Catholic Church, but to whom he gave no progeny; and by the marriage treaty he had renounced any claim to the English crown upon her death. His offer of marriage to Mary's sister Elizabeth was rejected, and in 1559 he married another Elizabeth, daughter of Henry II of France; she died in 1568. His last consort (1570–1580) was Anne, daughter of Emperor Maximilian II. The great objectives of Philip II's polity were to prevent the diffusion of Protestantism, to restore the Roman Catholic religion in countries where Protestantism had taken root, and to impose a uniform government throughout his diversified dominions. The second and third of these aims did not sit well with the provinces of the Netherlands, where revolt broke out in 1567. Resistance began among the nobles and wealthy bourgeoisie, but was taken over by the common people. The duke of Alva, appointed by Philip regent of the Netherlands, shed much blood but was unable to cow the Dutch, and in 1573 gave up the task. His successors, including Don John of Austria, had no better success in the northern provinces, which declared their independence in 1581 and maintained it until it was internationally recognized in 1648. The southern Netherlands provinces, however, were reconciled to Spanish rule during the regency of the duke of Parma (1578–1592). In 1571 Spain, in the person of Philip's half brother John of Austria, took the lead of Christendom in breaking the Turkish naval power at Lepanto. In that year also, Philip completed the ruthless suppression of the Moors in Spain. Claiming inheritance from his mother, Isabella of Portugal, Philip in 1580 seized that country, with the aid of the clergy and some of the nobility, against the opposition of the Portuguese people in general. As Philip I of Portugal he kept his promise to respect that nation's rights and to rule there only through Portuguese officials. In 1585 he formed an alliance with the Holy League in France, but was unable to prevent the accession of Henry IV (Henry of Navarre) to the French throne. Mary, Queen of Scots, claimant to the throne of England, in her last will named Philip as her heir in that respect. On this ground Philip prepared the invasion of England, creating for this purpose the "Invincible Armada," the defeat of which in 1588 marked the passing of the rule of the seas from Spain to England.

Philip Neri (ne′rē), Saint. See **Neri,** San **Filippo de'.**

Philodoxeos (fil-ǫ-dok′sę-us). Latin comedy written by Leon Battista Alberti when he was 20 years old. An original comedy, he pretended, so that it would be more readily accepted, that he had transcribed it from an ancient codex.

Philogenia (fil-ǫ-ję-nī′ạ). Latin drama by Ugolino Pisani (1430).

Physician's Tale, The. One of Chaucer's *Canterbury Tales,* told by the Doctor of Physic. It is the Roman story of Virginia, killed by her father to save her from the wicked Apius, but was expanded from the same story in the *Roman de la Rose,* though the account purports to be direct from Livy.

Pia (pē′ä), **Emilia.** Court lady; d. 1528. She was a member of the Pio family of Carpi, in Lombardy, and married Antonio, the natural son of Federico da Montefeltro. Her husband died at an early age (1500) and she remained at the court at Urbino, where she was the inseparable companion of the Duchess Elizabetta. A highly accomplished woman, of great charm, wit, winning manners, and tact, she was one of the principal ornaments of the cultivated court at Urbino. In Castiglione's *Il Cortegiano,* which memorializes that court, Emilia Pia appears as the mistress of ceremonies who directs the discussions on the perfect courtier.

Piazza (pyät′tsä), **Albertino.** [Original name, **Albertino de' Toccagni.**] Painter; b. at Lodi, c1475; d. 1529. He and his brother Martino (d. 1527) were active at Lodi and were influenced by a number of their Milanese contemporaries. In the softened line and tone of some of Albertino's painting, critics detect the influence of Leonardo and Perugino. The brothers almost always worked in collaboration. Their masterpiece is a polyptych (1514) in the Church of the Incoronata at Lodi, in which Albertino seems to have had the dominant role. In another polyptych, in the Church of the Incoronata at Castiglione d'Adda, Martino's seems to have been the principal hand. A number of works by the brothers in collaboration are in the museum and churches at Lodi, and at Brescia, Denver, and elsewhere. Works attributed to Albertino alone include a triptych with *The Ascension* *of the Virgin*, cathedral, Lodi, *St. Rosa*, Carrara Academy, Bergamo, and works at Turin, Verona, Vienna, and elsewhere.

Piazza, Calisto. [Also called **Calisto Piazza da Lodi.**] Painter; b. c1500; d. 1562. He was the son of Martino Piazza (d. 1527), and was active at Brescia, Lodi, and Milan. Among the many painters who influenced him he was especially influenced by the Venetians and Pordenone. He was a highly productive painter of modest gifts and was assisted by his brothers Scipione and Cesare and by his son Fulvio. A number of his works are in the museum and churches of Lodi; others are in collections and churches at Milan, in and about Lodi, Milan, and Brescia, in the Johnson Collection, Philadelphia, Sarasota (Florida), and elsewhere.

Piazza, Martino. Painter; b. at Lodi; d. 1527. He worked mostly with his brother Albertino (see above). *St. John in the Wilderness*, National Gallery, London, and *Madonna and Child with the Young St. John*, Carrara Academy, are among the works attributed to Martino alone.

Piccinino (pēt-chē-nē′nō), **Jacopo.** Mercenary captain; d. at Naples, 1465. He was the son of Niccolò Piccinino (1386–1444). After the death of his father, he and his brother took command of Niccolò's forces. His brother died shortly thereafter and Jacopo assumed sole command. Pope Pius II, in his *Commentaries*, called him a "general who could not endure peace." On the fall of the Milanese republic (1450) to Francesco Sforza as duke of Milan, Piccinino went into the pay of the Venetians. Later, in the service of Alfonso of Naples, he took up arms against Siena, but fled before the troops sent by Francesco Sforza, the Venetians, and Pope Calixtus III. He shut himself up in Castiglione and lived for several days on wild plums. Escaping from Castiglione through treachery, he entered Orbetello by bribing Luca Sclavo, who was supposed to be holding that place for Siena. There he was besieged but the town "was difficult to take by storm, especially for those who did not desire to succeed." Piccinino had marvellous success in persuading others to betrayal for his sake. The Sienese sued for peace with Alfonso of Naples. Enea Silvio, the future Pope Pius II, was one of the negotiators for the Church. In 1457 Piccinino, now in the pay of the Church, fought with Federico da Montefeltro against Sigismondo Malatesta, lord of Rimini, and the hated enemy of the Church. He then deserted the Church and went into the service of Jean of Anjou, who claimed the kingdom of Naples from Ferrante, son and heir of Alfonso I of Naples and recognized by the Church as the rightful heir to the throne. In August, 1462, he was decisively beaten by the combined forces of Ferrante and Alessandro Sforza, at the battle of Troia. This was a turning point in the war between the Aragonese, represented by Ferrante, and the Angevins, represented by Jean of Anjou, for control of Naples. According to the *Commentaries* of Pope Pius II, when talk of peace arose, Piccinino made a speech to the enemy troops exalting war and saying that it was through him that troops on both sides were rich and famous, that peace was advantageous to none but merchants and priests, and that Italy would not be at peace even after his own death. He urged the troops on both sides to continue the war, for without it they would have no pay. Nevertheless, in August, 1463, he began to make peace overtures. Alessandro Sforza accused him of treachery; he had been in the pay of Alfonso of Naples but waged war upon his son; he had been in the pay of the Church and had attacked it. Alessandro persuaded him to change sides again: to enter the service of Ferrante and fight against the Angevins. Piccinino agreed, after wringing many concessions from Ferrante and the pope, and peace was concluded (1463). Ferrante was dissatisfied with the treaty and never trusted Piccinino. The latter went to Milan, where he married Drusiana, the natural daughter of Francesco Sforza (1464). In 1465 he went back to Naples and received a splendid welcome. But Ferrante was determined to destroy him. Before Piccinino left for his fief of Sulmona, granted to him under the peace terms of 1463, Ferrante gave him a farewell banquet. At the close of the banquet Piccinino was arrested, June 24, 1465, accused of threatening the kingdom of Naples and the peace of Italy, cast into prison, and strangled in the Castelnuovo.

Piccinino, Niccolò. Mercenary captain; b. at Callisciana (Perugia), 1386; d. at Cusago (Milan), October, 1444. Orphaned at the age of ten, he became a woolworker but gave that up at an early age to go to Rome as a soldier in the armies of Bartolomeo Sestio. He won his master's respect, rose in his army, and married Bartolomeo's daughter, but killed her within the year on suspicion of infidelity. This cooled relations with Bartolomeo. He passed to the pay of another captain, and from him went to Braccio da Montone, a noted captain whose army was a school for military leaders. The death of Braccio at the battle of Aquila (1424) left Niccolò in command of his forces. Pope Pius II, in his *Commentaries,* says that Niccolò was renowned for his skill in arms and speaks with emotion of the great harm he inflicted on the Church during the pontificate of Pope Eugenius IV. As leader of Braccio da Montone's forces he served the Florentines for a year and a half and then became the loyal captain of Filippo Maria Visconti, duke of Milan. For the Visconti he fought, usually successfully, many times against the Venetians, and took Bologna for his duke. His opponents were Francesco Carmagnola, Gattemalata, and Francesco Sforza. The last-named had earlier been his companion in arms. By his operations in Lombardy in 1441 he came close to becoming master of Italy. Filippo Maria, always suspicious, feared he might become too powerful. He gave his natural daughter to Francesco Sforza in marriage, thus eliminating a powerful foe, one who had formerly been his own captain, and after this Niccolò's star was somewhat in eclipse. He was on the point of overcoming Sforza in the Marches, 1442–1443, when Filippo, fearing his success, called him away from his army. During his absence his troops were overcome by Sforza at Montolano, August 19, 1444. Niccolò was heartbroken; he fell sick and died on the 15th of October. He was buried in Milan Cathedral.

Piccolomini (pēk-kō-lō′mē-nē), **Alessandro.** Philosopher, poet, and humanist; b. at Siena, June 13, 1508; d. there, March 12, 1578. He taught philosophy at Padua and Rome, and returned to Siena towards the end of his life. In 1574 he was made archbishop of Patrasso. Learned in Latin and Greek, a man of broad culture, he translated Vergil and Ovid from the Latin and Xenophon and Aristotle from the Greek. He left a notable collection of sonnets, three Italian comedies, a dialogue, and many philosophical and scientific works.

Piccolomini, Alfonso. Captain and public official. He was a member of the noble Piccolomini family of Siena and a nephew of Antonio Piccolomini (d. 1493). In 1494 he fought against Charles VIII of France. The emperor Charles V named him to a high post in the kingdom of Naples, and in 1529 the commune of Siena elected him captain of the people. Charles V caused him to be dismissed in 1530 but he was recalled in 1531. After holding several public offices he was suspected by Charles V of dealing with France on behalf of Siena and, although again chosen captain by the Sienese, was compelled by the emperor to decline. After this he retired from public life.

Piccolomini, Antonio. Papal captain; b. at Siena; d. at Naples, January, 1493. He was the son of Pope Pius II's sister Laudomia. The pope, as was his custom for members of his family, promoted his interest. He was named governor of Castel Sant' Angelo at Rome, and had a command in the wars of the pope and Ferrante, king of Naples, against the Angevins. To strengthen relations between pope and Ferrante, Antonio was betrothed to Ferrante's natural daughter, and was married to her in 1461. At the same time he was made duke of Amalfi and count of Celano and given other fiefs. Ferrante had been recognized by Pope Pius II as the legitimate heir of Alfonso I, king of Naples, but spent most of his first years on the throne defending his claims against the Angevins. Antonio Piccolomini was one of his faithful captains, and one of the few who remained loyal to him in his continuous wars with his own barons.

Piccolomini, Arcangelo. Physician; b. at Ferrara, 1525; d. at Rome, October 19, 1586. He completed his studies at Ferrara, held the chair of philosophy at Bordeaux (where he translated Galen's *De humoribus*), and then was called to Rome by Pope Pius IV. At Rome he taught practical medicine and anatomy. His treatise on anatomy, *Anatomicae praelectiones explicantes . . . ,* dedicated to Pope Sixtus V, was published in 1586. In it he sets forth his observations and findings resulting from his study of human anatomy. He was the first to describe the orifice of the heart of the embryo, and also described the diaphragm, abdominal muscles, and the cerebral nerves.

Piccolomini, Enea Silvio or **Aeneas Sylvius.** Original name of Pope **Pius II.**

Piccolomini, Francesco di Niccolò. Philosopher; b. at Siena, 1520; d. there, 1604. He studied at Padua and then taught philosophy at the Universities of Siena, Macerata, Perugia, and, lastly, Padua. He remained at Padua for forty years, then returned to Siena. His interest was centered about the works of Aristotle, on which he wrote many commentaries.

Piccolomini, Francesco Todeschini. See **Pius III.**

Pico della Mirandola (pē′kō del′lä mē-rän′dō-lä), Count **Giovanni.** Philosopher and humanist; b. February 24, 1463; d. at Florence, November 17, 1494. He was one of the foremost scholars of the Renaissance. In addition he had, according to his friend and older contemporary Angelo Poliziano, every gift that nature could bestow: good looks, a powerful memory, mental brilliance, eloquence, and charm. His mother, a niece of the great lyric poet Boiardo, encouraged him in his studies. At the age of 14 he went to Bologna, and thereafter continued his studies at Ferrara, Padua, and Pavia. He became a master of Greek, Latin, Hebrew, and Arabic. When he was about 20 he arrived at Florence, where he was an immediate and brilliant social success. His acknowledged scholarly accomplishments opened a place for him in the circle of scholars and literary men surrounding Lorenzo de' Medici. After a brief youthful fling he abandoned the pleasures of youth and society and devoted himself to his philosophical and religious interests. He was an active member of the so-called Platonic Academy. At some point he purchased a manuscript of the Cabala, a mystic Hebrew interpretation of the Scriptures, and became fascinated by it. From his studies of Aristotle and Averroës at Pavia, his discussions and studies of Plato at Florence, and his absorption in the Cabala, he conceived the idea of harmonizing philosophy, Christianity, and Hebrew and Arabic mysticism. In 1486 he published at Rome 900 theses, in theology, philosophy, mathematics, and other subjects, which he was prepared to defend in public debate. As an introduction to the anticipated debate he published an oration, famous as an expression of an attitude toward man and a view of his possibilities that had been maturing for a century. This was his *Oratio de hominis dignitate*, on the dignity of man, in which he declared that there are no upper limits on man's capabilities. The debate, however, for which this was the introduction, never took place. Pope Innocent VIII declared 13 of Pico's theses heretical and condemned him. He fled to France and was imprisoned there briefly. In 1488 he issued an *Apologia* and returned to Florence. (Pope Alexander VI cleared him of the charges of heresy in 1493.) In Florence he heard the fiery preacher and reformer Savonarola, and was so impressed by him that he appears to have planned to become a missionary preacher. In the event, he is thought to have joined the Dominican order on his deathbed, though this is not certain.

Pico's great preoccupation was with the unity of knowledge—Aristotelian, Platonic, Arabic, Christian, and Hebrew. He seems to have thought that if he could fuse them he could present a synthesis with which no one could quarrel, that the knowledge of all systems, not just classical thought, could be properly evaluated, and that thereby the Hebrews and Moslems might be converted. He died, at the age of 31, before he could commit his intentions to writing. Among the works he left are the *Heptaplus* (1489), which is a mystical account of the creation, and *In astrologiam*. In this attack on astrology (although he accepted some forms of magic) he emphasized the impiety and immorality of astrology: impiety because astrology assigns to planets the powers of God, therefore astrologers must worship planets and not God; immorality because of the belief that man's actions, including evil ones, arise from the planets and thus man is relieved of all responsibility. Finally, Pico reaffirmed his profound belief in free will and man's responsibility for his fate. The *De ente et uno* is an attempt to reconcile the Aristotelian and Platonic systems. Brilliant, of great promise, and an important influence on the thought of his own and later times, Pico died (though probably not, as was charged, of poison) before he had time to crystallize his ideas in writing.

Pienza (pyen′tsä). Small cathedral city in Tuscany, about thirty-two miles from Siena; it was created at the order of and named for Pope Pius II. On February 21, 1459, he was traveling from Rome to Mantua and stopped to visit his native village, Corsignano, much of the land around which had once belonged to the Piccolomini family. (Pius II's original name was Enea Silvio Piccolomini.) It made him sad to see the acquaintances of his youth grown old, as he had done. He realized that he was an old man, "ready to drop," and wished to honor this town "of little repute but possessed of a healthful climate, excellent wine, and everything that goes to sustain life." He dreamed of erecting a new city to serve as the summer seat of the papal court, and implemented his dream by entrusting the work to the Florentine architect Bernardo Rossellino (Bernardo Gambarelli detto il Rossellino). The work went forward with speed and was brought to completion between the years 1459–1462. On August 29, 1462, the cathedral was consecrated. Pius, who had heard much murmuring and gossip against his architect, remarked, "You did well, Bernardo, to conceal the true cost from us (about 50,000 gold florins), for if we had known it in the beginning we would neither have had the courage to undertake the charge, nor would the world have had this miracle of art." In his *Commentaries*, Pius gives an enthusiastic description of the buildings and records his delight that they were brought into being so speedily.

The principal buildings of Pienza surround a square (Piazza Pio II) on the crest of a hill overlooking the valley of the Orcia River. It is one of the loveliest squares in Italy. The Cathedral (dedicated to the Assumption of the Virgin) is a felicitous combination of a Renaissance façade and a Gothicized interior. The façade has three doors. Over the central one the armorial bearings of Pius II appear in a medallion. The interior has three naves of equal height. In describing it, Pius wrote, "At the ends of the naves were four similar windows, which when the sun shines admit so much light that worshipers in the church think they are not in a house of stone but of glass." Among the decorations of the church are works by Sienese artists. By a bull issued September 16, 1462, Pius forbade the making of any changes in the church in the future.

On the right of the cathedral rises the Piccolomini Palace, inspired by the Rucellai Palace in Florence. It is one of Rossellino's masterpieces. It was presented to Pius on July 19, 1463. The exterior is simple, elegant and pure. The main doorway is on the north, with another doorway on the east. Outside the east door, in the square, is a lovely Renaissance fountain. The palace is square, with matching rows of twin windows in the two upper stories. It encloses a very fine arcaded courtyard. "On the fourth side, which has a most delightful view of Mt. Amiata to the south, were three porticoes raised above one another on stone columns. The first, with its high and splendid vaulting, providing a most delightful promenade near the garden; the second which had an elaborately painted wooden ceiling, made a very pleasant place to sit in winter. It had a balustrade which with its cornice was as high as a man's waist. The third was similar to the second but less elaborate in its coffering." Great cellars were quarried out of the rock on which the palace stands, to serve as vaults for the storage of wine, oil and other provisions, "Certainly a noble larder and one it would be hard to fill." There were no kitchens in the palace. These were located in an adjoining building, one on each of three floors to match the three floors of the palace and connected to it by covered passages. This made service to each of the floors of the palace most convenient.

On the left of the square is the Bishop's Palace, adapted to the Renaissance style from an earlier building. Facing the cathedral is the City Hall (Palazzo Comunale), a severe building of an earlier period, with a portico of Ionic columns. Nearby are the palaces of the cardinals Gonzaga, Ammannati, and Atrebatense, and the one-time residence of Rodrigo Borgia, vice-chancellor under Pius and for many years thereafter, and later Pope Alexander VI.

The name Corsignano was changed to Pienza in 1462 and, at Pius' request, the town was raised to the rank of city-state. As Pienza it has been called "The Pearl of the Renaissance." Its principal buildings have been preserved in their pure form as if crystallized for all time from the moment of their creation. The little city has been spared the ravages of warfare (except in World War II, when a bomb fell through the roof of the cathedral) as well as the destructive attention of those who would "improve" it.

Pier. In architecture or building, the solid support from which an arch springs. The solid part, or parts, between such openings in a wall as windows or doors, may also be described as a pier.

Pier Francesco Fiorentino (pyer frän-chās′kō fyō-ren-tē′nō). Florentine painter; active between 1474 and 1497. He was a follower of Benozzo Gozzoli and was influenced by such other Florentines as Neri di Bicci,

thin; ᴛʜ, then; y, you; (variable) d̦ as d or j, ș as s or sh, ț as t or ch, z̦ as z or zh; o, F. cloche; ü, F. menu; ċh, Sc. loch; ṅ, F. bonbon; ʙ, Sp. Córdoba (sounded almost like v).

Pier Francesco Fiorentino
St. Michael Between SS. Francis and Jerome and Catherine of Alexandria and Clare
Gabinetto Disegni e Stampe degli Uffizi Foto Soprintendenza

Andrea del Castagno, and Baldovinetti. A pleasing, old-fashioned, and unpretentious painter, he worked mainly at S. Gimignano and in Val d'Elsa. His signed and dated (1494) *Madonna and Child with Eight Saints and a Donor*, S. Agostino, S. Gimignano, is a good example of his style. In the large central panel the Madonna and eight saints, against an austerely bare background, are all about the same size. The donor, as befits his mortal state, is painted to a much smaller scale in the manner of the 14th and early 15th centuries. There are four saints in each of two framing pilasters and a predella of seven panels. Many works by Pier Francesco are in the museum and churches of S. Gimignano; others are in the Val d'Elsa, as in S. Barbara at Castelnuovo, the Palazzo dei Priori at Certaldo, in the museum, Church of S. Maria in Canonica, and frescoed tabernacles in the streets of Colle Val d'Elsa, and the Pieve at Ulignano. Still others are at Empoli, the Castagno Museum, Florence, at Siena, Volterra, the Victoria and Albert Museum, London, and elsewhere.

Pier della Vigna (del'lä vē'nyä). Minister of Frederick II and poet of the Sicilian school; b. at Capua, c1190; d. April, 1249. Of an obscure and not wealthy family, he studied, enduring great hardship to do so, at Bologna. In 1221 the archbishop of Palermo introduced him to the Holy Roman emperor Frederick II. He was welcomed at Frederick's court at Naples and became, in the course of time, his trusted friend and adviser. Among other positions, he served as a judge, as Frederick's ambassador to the pope (1232–1233), as negotiator for the agreement with the Lombard League (1237), as Frederick's envoy to England (1234) to conclude arrangements for the marriage of Frederick to Isabella, sister of Henry III, and as negotiator of a peace between Frederick and the Venetians when Frederick was excommunicated by Pope Innocent IV. In short, no matter of moment arose but what he played an im-

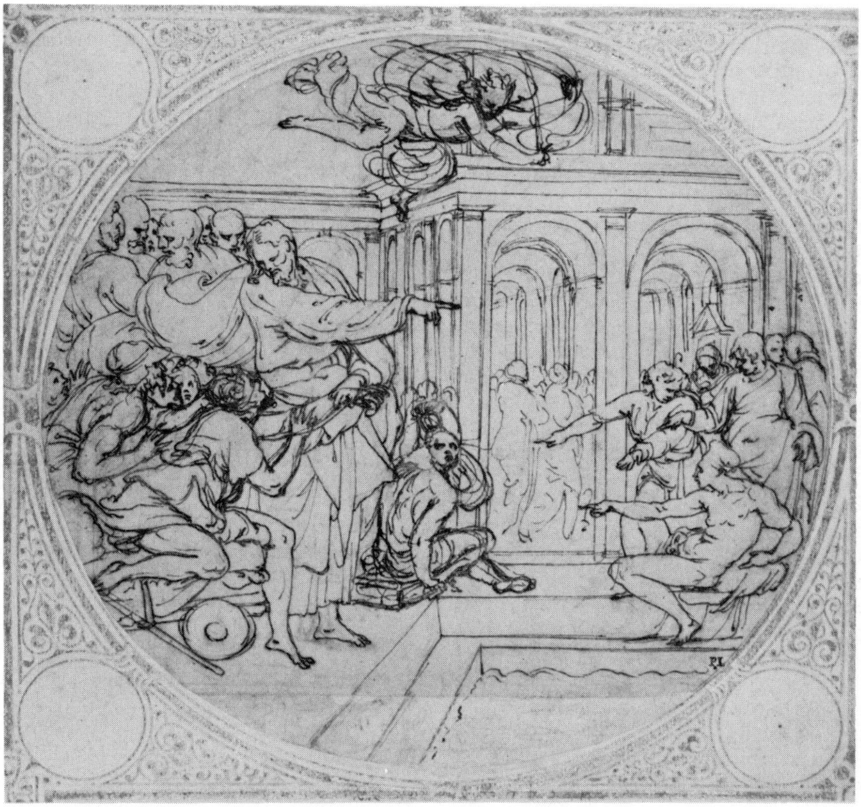

PIERIN DEL VAGA
The Pool of Bethesda
Courtesy of The Pierpont Morgan Library, New York

portant part. The emperor's confidence in him was such that he was at times the emperor's alter ego. His power and influence aroused the jealousy of the nobles, who besides resenting his power despised his humble origin. A conspiracy of 1246 caused Frederick to look with suspicion on his trusted adviser. Pier was implicated in a plot to poison the emperor. Whether he was actually involved is not certain. Frederick arrested him (1249), had him carried in chains from city to city as an example, and accused him of *lèse majesté*. At San Miniato he was blinded with a red-hot iron. Some say that he died as a result of the tortures he suffered. Others say he killed himself by cracking his head against a wall or by flinging himself from a mule, committing suicide in his despair that he should have been accused of betraying his lord. This was Dante's view. In the *Divina Commedia* he meets Pier (in the Inferno because he had committed suicide), and hears his story. The emperor's minister, who called himself the

> "*soul of one who guarded well/The keys that opened the great Frederick's heart/ Or locked it, as occasion might compel.,*" swore to Dante that "*. . . never to my noble Sire,/So well deserving of my fealty,/Did I play false.*" (*Inferno*, xiii)

He begged Dante to clear his name. Other contemporaries, knowing his great power and sudden loss of it, defended his innocence. Pier's letters are an important contemporary source for the era of Frederick. He also wrote a verse satire against the Dominicans and the Franciscans, one against Pope Innocent IV, and some poems in the vernacular. As a poet he was a member of the so-called Sicilian school, that is, the poets about Frederick II's court who followed the tradition of the lyric love poetry of the troubadors.

Pierin (or **Perin** or **Pierino**) **del Vaga** (pye-rēn′; pā-rēn′; pye-rē′nō del vä′gä). [Original name, **Pietro Buonaccorsi.**] Painter; b. at Florence, 1501; d. at Rome, 1547. At Florence he was at first a pupil of a Master Andrea, then of Ridolfo Ghirlandaio, and finally was an assistant of a painter called "il Vaga," from whom he took his name. He went to Rome as a youth, studied the works of Michelangelo and Raphael, and became an assistant to Raphael, for whom he executed some of the Biblical episodes in the *Loggie* of the Vatican. A charming and industrious youth, honored as a painter in his young manhood, he approached Raphael in the refinement of his drawing. He is said to have become lazy and greedy in his later years. In 1523 he was at Florence. He prepared to take up a challenge to add a figure to Masaccio's frescoes in the Brancacci Chapel but an outbreak of plague caused him to flee Florence and Masaccio's masterpiece was spared. Returned to Rome, he married (1525) a sister of Gianfrancesco Penni, another of Raphael's assistants. He was taken prisoner in the sack of Rome (1527) and the following year went to Genoa, where he frescoed a number of rooms in the Doria Palace with mythological and historical scenes. He worked at Genoa until 1534, then at Pisa (1534–1538), after which he returned to Rome, where he remained until his death. He left a great many frescoes at Rome, as those in the Palazzo Massimo alle Colonne on incidents from the *Aeneid*, which show some influence of Michelangelo, those in the Church of S. Marcello, decorative bits in the Borgia Apartments and in the *Stanze* in the Vatican, in Castel Sant' Angelo, and elsewhere. Other works are in the Borghese and Doria Pamphili galleries, Rome, at Florence, Milan, Rimini, Chantilly, France, the Victoria and Albert Museum, London, Vaduz, and a *Nativity* (1534), National Gallery, Washington.

Pierino da Vinci (pye-rē′nō dä vēn′chē). Sculptor; b. at Vinci, c1530; d. at Pisa, 1553. He was the nephew of Leonardo da Vinci. He received his early training under Bandinelli at Florence, then worked with Tribolo. The latter's influence is apparent in the models (cast by others) of putti for the basin of the fountain at Castello (c1546). A group he executed of two putti holding a coat of arms is in the Victoria and Albert Museum, London. At Rome he was somewhat influenced by classical sculpture and by Michelangelo, and his compositions became more sophisticated, his figures more vigorous. For his Florentine patron, Luca Martini, he carved the nude figure of a young male to represent a *River God*, Louvre, which his patron had commissioned as a gift for Eleanora of Toledo, wife of Cosimo I de' Medici. The statue, with putti holding an urn, was to serve as a fountain. For the same patron he carved the group, *Samson and the Philistine*, Palazzo Vecchio, Florence, which shows the influence of Michelangelo in the energetic, muscular figures. Pierino was important for the vigor, understanding of anatomy, and technique of his mannerist style of reliefs, as that of *The Death of Count Ugolino and his Sons*, Ashmolean Museum, Oxford, and the allegory, *Cosimo I and Pisa*, Victoria and Albert Museum, London.

Piermatteo da Amelia (pyer-mät-tā′ō dä ä-mā′lyä). [Original name, **Pier Matteo Lauro de' Manfredi.**] Painter; b. at Amelia, c1450; d. between 1503 and 1508. He was an assistant of Fra Filippo Lippi at Spoleto (1467–1469), and worked at Rome in the Sistine Chapel, the Belvedere, where he frescoed decorative elements in the lunettes, and the Borgia apartments, where he contributed to the frescoed decoration. Other examples of his work are in the Municipal Museum, Amelia, monochrome frescoes in the Papal Palace at Civita Castellana, at Narni and at Terni.

Piero di Cosimo (pye′rō dē kō′zē-mō). [Original name, **Piero di Lorenzo di Chimenti.**] Painter; b. at Florence, c1462; d. there, 1521. He was the pupil and assistant of Cosimo Rosselli, and from this circumstance derived the name by which he is now generally known. More important in his development than the influence of his master, whom he far surpassed in creativity and technique, were the influences of Verrocchio, Leonardo, Signorelli, and Filippo Lippi. Sensitive to so many influences, he is yet among the most outstandingly original painters of his time, fascinating and unusual in his profound feeling for nature, for the force that energizes his paintings on mythological subjects, for the wealth of vaguely suggested allegorical interpretations, for his fervid imagination and romantic inspiration. In several series of mythological paintings his sometimes macabre and sometimes melancholy poetic vein is presented with the greatest pictorial subtlety. Poetic melancholy and fantasy also appear in his religious paintings, and the culmination of his bizarreries is reached in his *Portrait of Simonetta Vespucci*, Musée Condé, Chantilly. In other portraits, however, as those of *Giuliano da Sangallo* and *Francesco Giamberti*, Amsterdam, his vigorous rendering is accompanied by deep psychological insight.

When Botticelli, Ghirlandaio, Perugino, Cosimo Rosselli, and others went to Rome (1481) to paint in the Sistine Chapel, Piero accompanied his master and worked as his assistant; the landscape background in Rosselli's *Preaching of Christ*, is attributed to him. By 1486 he was working as an independent painter at Florence where, despite increasing peculiarities, he was highly regarded. In 1503 he was one of a committee to decide on the location of Michelangelo's *David;* in the same year he was enrolled in the Physicians' and Apothecaries' Guild. Vasari devotes considerable space to a description of his personality and, perhaps more than most painters, his personality is reflected in his work. Vasari writes that he was "an odd and thoughtful person"; that "He loved solitude and knew no greater pleasure than building castles in the air, alone and uninterrupted." After Cosimo Rosselli died (1507) Piero became more or less of a recluse. He neglected his person and his house, his garden and his orchards, on the grounds that it was "better to leave all to nature." He limited his nourishment to hard boiled eggs, which he cooked fifty at a time when he boiled his glue and ate when he felt hungry. His imagination transformed the stains on walls and the clouds in the sky into fantastic cities and fabulous creatures and combats. He put his imagination to work in the service of the young Florentine nobles, devising spectacles for their entertainment. He is supposed to have been one of the first to design an allegorical Triumph, with triumphal car and a train of costumed and masked marchers in a great procession. Vasari says he composed words and music for these shows. The most celebrated was the *Triumph of Death* (1511) in which a colossal figure of Death rode a funereal car; Death was surrounded by tombs from which skeletons rose whenever the procession stopped. The terrifying spectacle sent shivers of fear through the crowds of spectators who, however, thoroughly enjoyed it. Vasari writes that years afterward people, including Piero's pupil Andrea del Sarto, remembered and spoke of this *Triumph*. Piero's interest in nature and in landscape backgrounds appears especially in his mythological paintings, in which he also gave vent to his zest for painting animal forms, either in close fidelity to nature or with imaginative fantasy. One set of these is on man before civilizing influences have been at work. *Primitive Hunt* and *Return from the Hunt*, the Metropolitan Museum, New York, show men and satyrs hunting animals with clubs and each other with their bare hands in a wild setting and with primitive frenzy. In *Fire in the Forest*, Oxford, a fire in the forest set by natural causes, perhaps lightning, leads to the discovery of its blessings; it also gives Piero a splendid opportunity to paint the animals fleeing the fire. Another series shows *The Fall of Vulcan*, Athenaeum, Hartford, the god of fire coming to earth to bring the arts of civilization to man; and *Vulcan and Aeolus*, Ottawa, in which Vulcan, in amicable collaboration with Aeolus whose bellows keep the fire going, shows man how to forge tools and build shelter. The atmosphere of these two panels, both of which can be referred to myths of Vulcan (Hephaestus), is of gentle domestication, in contrast to the violence and terror of the previous series. (A feature of *Vulcan and Aeolus* is a giraffe obviously painted from nature, and her foal, an imagined creature. A giraffe was added to Lorenzo de' Medici's menagerie in 1491, to the delight of the Florentines, but died soon after.) In the *Discovery of Honey*, Worcester, Massachusetts, men and satyrs celebrate with riotous exuberance against a background that contains an unmistakable church, an indication of the forward march of civilization. The subject of a companion panel, *The Misfortunes of Silenus*, may be imagined from its alternate title, *Bacchanal*. Other works on mythological subjects include the poignant *Death of Procris* and a *Battle of Lapiths and*

PIERO DI COSIMO
St. Jerome at the Mouth of a Cave
Gabinetto Disegni e Stampe degli Uffizi   Foto Soprintendenza

Centaurs, National Gallery, London, panels on the story of Prometheus at Munich and Strasbourg, and others. A touch of terror sometimes accompanies the poetic melancholy and exemplary piety of his religious paintings. *The Visitation,* National Gallery, Washington, has echoes of Verrocchio in the strongly sculptural lines of the figures and faces of the Virgin and St. Elizabeth in the center and of SS. Nicholas and Anthony in the foreground. Vasari admired the animation of the figures, Piero's rendering of an ancient and worn parchment book, and the lights reflected from the golden balls that were attributes of St. Nicholas. Even in this affecting painting, with its soft, olive greens and warm golden tans, Piero's fancies and symbolic episodes are apparent. Heads are thrust from the upper windows of a building in impeccable perspective on the right of the picture to observe an agitated group of women and children in the square below; they are watching a *Slaughter of the Innocents.* On a gentle hillock behind the desperate women is a tabernacle with an *Annunciation.* His *St. John the Evangelist,* Honolulu, a painting that has been almost destroyed by restoration and repainting, shows the saint with his right hand raised in blessing over a chalice that holds a completely unintimidated serpent. In the *Portrait of Simonetta Vespucci,* called *La Bella Simonetta,* mentioned above, against a simple landscape background is painted the pure, wide-eyed profile of a lovely young woman. Her elaborate hair arrangement gleams with pearls; her breasts are bare; a wicked, glinting viper encircles her neck. (Vasari says the picture represents Cleopatra.) As noted earlier, Piero was subject to a number of influences, but he was never overwhelmed by any of them. Nor did he adapt any one or several to form a consistent style. Vasari lamented that he weakened his genius by painting in so many different manners. What is consistent in the work of Piero di Cosimo is the plasticity of his figures, his shimmering color, the endless resources of his imagination, his absorption in nature, and his search for significance. Besides those mentioned, there are examples of his work at Borgo S. Lorenzo (Florence), paintings in the Uffizi, Pitti Palace, Foundling Hospital, and other collections at Florence, at Perugia, Rome (Barberini Palace), Berlin, Dresden, Leningrad (*Madonna and Child,* another version of which is in the Borghese Gallery, Rome), Louvre, Paris, São Paulo, Stockholm, Vaduz, the Johnson Collection, Philadelphia, St. Louis (Missouri), San Diego (California), Sarasota (Florida), Toledo (Ohio), and elsewhere.

Piero della Francesca (del'lä frän-chās'kä). Italian painter; b. c1416 at Borgo San Sepolcro; d. and was buried in the Church of the Badia there, October 12, 1492. He was the son of Benedetto de' Franceschi and Romana di Perino da Monterchi. The unusual feminine form of his name, *della Francesca* rather than *dei Franceschi,* is thought to derive from the fact that his father died when he was a child and he was brought up by his mother. Little is known of his life. Documents show that he assisted Domenico Veneziano in painting a series of frescoes in Sant' Egidio (S. Maria Nuova), at Florence. While there, he saw the Procession of the Council (1439) that took place when John VIII Palaeologus of the Byzantine Empire met with leaders of the Western church to discuss the unification of the Eastern and Western churches. The exotic costumes he saw then impressed him and later appeared in the frescoes he painted in the Church of San Francesco at Arezzo. He probably saw and studied Masaccio's series of great frescoes in the Brancacci Chapel, Church of the Carmine at Florence, a series that became a school for later artists, including Michelangelo. As far as is known, this was his only stay in Florence. Except for commissions that took him to various ducal courts and to Rome, as well as to Ancona and Pesaro, most of his life was spent in and around his native Borgo San Sepolcro, where he owned land, and where he was elected (1442) Town Councillor. He was a friend of Raphael's father, taught perspective to the eminent architect Bramante, and numbered Luca Signorelli among his pupils. According to Vasari, he was blind at the end of his life and was led around by a little boy.

Piero's sense and use of clear color was influenced by the Sienese and by Domenico Veneziano. He knew the work of Pietro Lorenzetti in Arezzo and of Sassetta in Borgo San Sepolcro. The formality and rhythm of his composition derive from his interest and studies in perspective and geometry. From his early years he had been an absorbed student of mathematics, and his later works, with

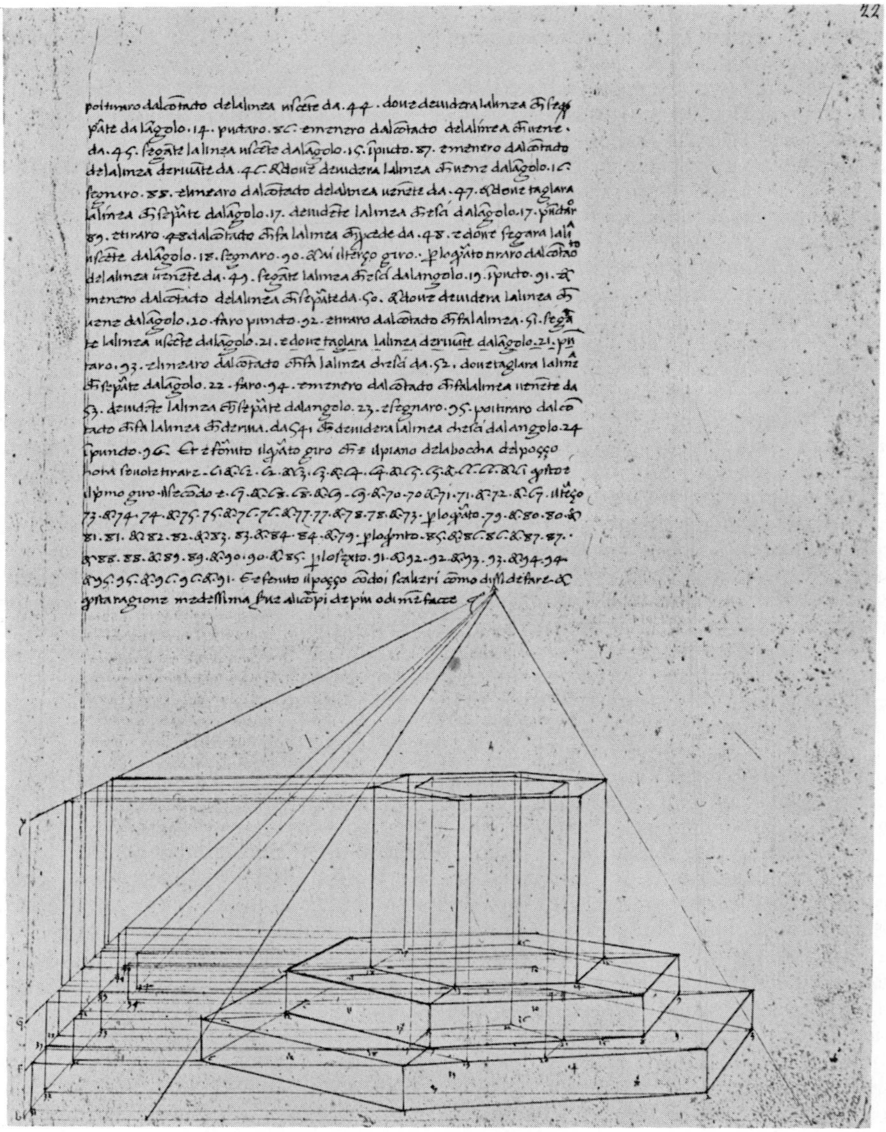

PIERO DELLA FRANCESCA
Perspective study from *De perspectiva pingendi*
Biblioteca Palatina, Parma

their concern for geometric harmonies and architectural features in perspective, are demonstrations of his application of mathematics to painting. In later life he wrote *De perspectiva pingendi*, a treatise on perspective, and *De quinque corporibus regularibus*, a treatise on the five regular solids. The manuscript of the former, in his own hand and with his illustrations, is in the Biblioteca Palatina at Parma. Both works won great respect. His great contributions to his art were in his use of perspective and of light and shade to

fat, fāte, fär, fâll, ȧsk, fãre; net, mē, hėr; pin, pīne; not, nōte, möve, nôr; up, lūte, pùll; oi, oil; ou, out; (lightened) ẹlect, agọny, ụnite; (obscured) errạnt, ardẹnt, actọr; ch, chip; g, go; th, provide three-dimensional space for figures and objects. He was highly regarded in his lifetime, as can be seen from the fact that Federico da Montefeltro, the cultivated duke of Urbino, was his lifelong friend and patron, and that he numbered among his other patrons Sigismondo Malatesta of Rimini (at whose court he perhaps met the influential architect and scholar, Leon Battista Alberti), the d'Este family of Ferrara, and the outstanding humanist pope, Pius II. He was a deliberate and meditative worker, and of the paintings he finished some have been lost or destroyed. Even when Vasari wrote, less than seventy-five years after his death, he noted that some of Piero's work had been lost; the frescoes he painted at Ferrara had disappeared; the rooms he painted for Pope Pius II in the Vatican were later repainted by Raphael, the noted *Stanze*. Following his death, Piero's great works were neglected for centuries. Appreciation for his mastery of form and color revived toward the end of the 19th century, and he is now numbered among the great innovators and masters of Renaissance painting.

His earliest known surviving work is a polyptych, an altarpiece commissioned by the Company of the Misericordia at San Sepolcro on January 11, 1445. By the terms of the commission, the background was to be gold and the work was to be finished in three years; apparently, it took nearer seventeen years to complete it, but in that time he was working on other paintings in various places, and also went to Rome. The polyptych, in four principal panels, was broken up in 1807 but was reassembled in 1892 for the 400th anniversary of Piero's death. It is in poor condition. It was damaged by fire and partially restored, and the flesh tones, particularly, are discolored. The center, and largest, panel has the *Madonna of Mercy* (*Madonna della Misericordia*) sheltering beset, erring, and humble humanity under her all-encompassing robe. Above this is a *Crucifixion*, with the Virgin and St. John, which is the most intense and emotional of all Piero's paintings, and is thought to reflect the influence of Masaccio's great *Crucifixion*. To the left of the *Madonna of Mercy* panel are Saints Sebastian and John the Baptist, with St. Francis and the Angel of the Annunciation in smaller panels above them; and to the right are Saints Andrew and Bernardino, with the Virgin Annunciate and St. Benedict in smaller panels above them. Most critics think that at least the small figures of saints were painted by assistants, although the commission specified that Piero was to do the whole painting himself. The polyptych is now in the Palazzo Comunale (Town Hall) at San Sepolcro. Another painting there is a powerful *Resurrection*, with a vibrant and militant Christ rising from the tomb while the soldiers sprawl in sleep about it. Critics date this painting as of about 1463. Outside the village of Monterchi, where Piero's mother was born and not far from San Sepolcro, is an ancient cemetery with a chapel. Here there is a much revered fresco, *Madonna del Parto* (*Madonna in Childbirth*), an extremely rare subject in Italian painting. It is the only decoration in the present tiny chapel and shows the Madonna, her robe slightly opened, standing between two identical, but reversed, angels. The Madonna is an imposing, almost disdainful, figure. Pregnant women still pray to Her for an easy delivery. She is so highly regarded that when (1954) it was proposed to lend the fresco to an exhibition in Florence, the Mayor of Monterchi refused to let it go. He could not answer for the consequences if any accident should befall a pregnant woman while the Madonna was absent.

Other works in Italy are *St. Jerome and a Donor*, Accademia, Venice, signed, thought to have been painted between 1450 and 1455; *Sigismondo Malatesta Kneeling before St. Sigismund*, a fresco that has been transferred to canvas, dated 1451, in a chapel of the Tempio Malatestiano at Rimini for which it was painted. The work is in poor condition, some of the fresco having crumbled away. In the National Gallery at Urbino, housed in what was once Federico da Montefeltro's ducal palace, are a *Flagellation of Christ* (the significance of which continues to be a puzzle) and *The Senigaglia Madonna*. A diptych with portraits of Federico and his wife Battista Sforza, with allegorical scenes on the back of each, is in the Uffizi at Florence. The *Montefeltro Altarpiece*, Brera, Milan, centers about a seated Madonna holding a sleeping Child. She is surrounded by saints and angels. Federico da Montefeltro, an unmistakable portrait, kneels in the right foreground. The upper half of the painting is an exercise in perspective showing an arched alcove behind the Madonna. The lunette at the rear, formed

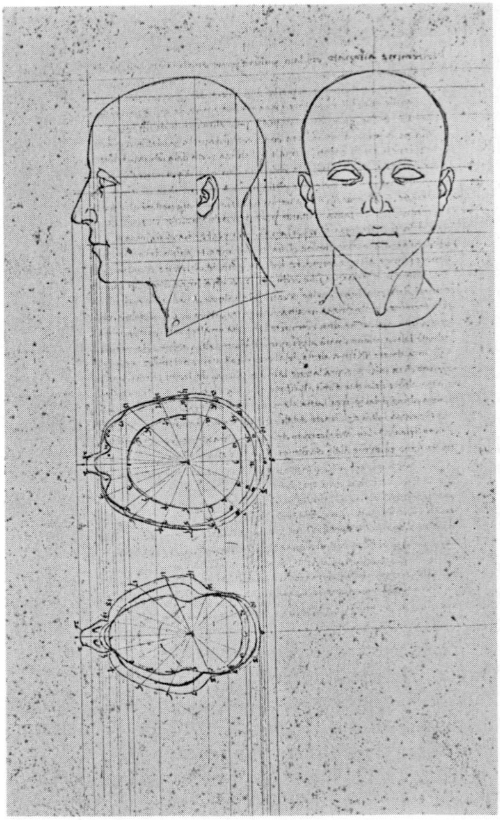

PIERO DELLA FRANCESCA
Perspective study from *De perspectiva pingendi*
Biblioteca Palatina, Parma

by the barrel vaulting of the alcove, is filled by a scallop shell, from whose cusp is suspended an ostrich egg, perhaps a symbol of the Immaculate Conception. The painting dates from about 1472. In Perugia, National Gallery, is a polyptych consisting in general of three main sections: 1) a central panel, with a gold background, has the *Virgin and Child Enthroned*, flanked by Saints Anthony of Padua and John the Baptist on the left, and Saints Francis and Elizabeth of Hungary on the right; 2) above this is an *Annunciation*, with the Angel and the Virgin placed before a series of arches that is a demonstration in perspective; 3) below the central panel is a predella, one section of which is missing. It is thought that the different panels were painted at different times, and that it was completed with the help of assistants.

Piero's masterpiece and most ambitious work is a series of frescoes in the choir of the Church of San Francesco at Arezzo. He worked on them at intervals from 1452 to 1466. The frescoes were, in many areas, in poor condition, the plaster having crumbled away or fallen out in patches. Work on them completed in 1965 has done much to restore their beauty, especially as regards the clarity and brilliance of the color. The frescoes constitute a symposium of Piero's qualities at the height of his powers. They cover three walls and depict *The Story of the True Cross*. The incidents portrayed are drawn from *The Golden Legend*, a collection of lives of the saints compiled by Jacobus de Voragine in the 13th century. (See **Story of the True Cross, The.**) Also in Arezzo is a fresco of a not very repentant appearing *St. Mary Magdalen*, in the cathedral.

Works of Piero della Francesca now outside Italy include: *Baptism of Christ* and *Nativity*, National Gallery, London; *Madonna and Child with Four Angels*, Clark Art Institute, Williamstown, Massachusetts; and *Hercules*, Isabella Stewart Gardner Museum, Boston. A polyptych painted for the high altar of the Church of St. Augustine in San Sepolcro, and finished in 1469, was broken up in 1555. Parts of it are to be found in the Poldi Pezzoli Museum, Milan (*St. Nicholas of Tolentino*); Lisbon (*St. Augustine*); National Gallery, London (*St. Michael*); Frick Collection, New York (*St. John the Evangelist*); John D. Rockefeller Collection, New York (*Crucifixion*); and the National Gallery, Washington, D.C. (*St. Apollonia*).

Piero di Puccio (dē pöt′chō). Painter and mosaicist; active in the second half of the 14th century. In 1364 he began assisting Ugolino di Prete Ilario in painting in the cathedral at Orvieto. He remained there, painting, designing, and working at the mosaics of the façade, until 1388, and was again in Orvieto in 1392 and 1394. In 1376 he signed the mosaics on the façade of the cathedral; in 1381 he was made master of the works for one year; and in 1399 he designed a silver cross for the cathedral and painted a fresco in S. Giovenale. Thus, most of his life was spent at Orvieto, but his most important surviving painting is at Pisa. He went to that city in 1389 to paint frescoes on events from the Book of Genesis in the Camposanto. He began the frescoes in October, 1389, and had completed as much as he was ever to complete by January, 1391. The frescoes include such scenes as *The Creation of Eve, Cain and Abel, The Building of the Ark,* and *The Sacrifice of Noah after the Flood.* Benozzo Gozzoli (1420–1497) finished the series on the Old Testament. Piero's frescoes, somewhat hard in outline, reveal his taste for landscape, his interest in animals and plants, and the narrative character of his painting. In movement and realism Florentine influence is evident. Some of the scenes, faded and in poor condition, were restored in 1665. In July, 1944, a bomb fell on the Camposanto and shattered the frescoes, Piero's as well as those of others. The plaster fell, revealing the artist's *sinopia* sketches underneath. The fragments have been carefully reassembled and bonded to canvas. The *sinopia* drawings, whose existence was unknown, are free and animated sketches for the painter to follow; they have also in many cases been detached and bonded to canvas.

Piers Plowman (pirz' plou'mạ̈n). [Full title, **The Vision Concerning Piers Plowman.**] Allegorical and satirical poem in 14th-century English, generally attributed to William Langland (c1330–c1400), though other authors may have been involved in the original composition of 2,567 lines, as first circulated in 1362, and even more in the elaboration of the later texts, which by c1393 had grown to 7,357 lines. The forty-seven manuscripts of the poem still preserved are evidence that it was widely circulated in that form before printing came to England. The great interest and historical value of the poem lie in the vivid, crowded, sharply characterized pictures of life in 13th-century England when, as feudalism began to break down, swarming evils and injustices evoked determination to bring about better times, and in the spirit of the deeply pious Catholic Christian social ideals which the poet shared with the plain people of the land.

Pietro d'Abano (pye'trō dä'bä-nō). [Also, **Pietro di Apono;** Anglicized, **Peter of Abano;** Latinized, **Petrus Aponensis, Petrus Aponus.**] Physician, philosopher, and translator from Greek and French into Latin; b. at Abano, 1257; d. at Padua, c1315. He traveled widely and spent a long period at Constantinople and at Paris, where he studied and taught. Returned to Padua, where he taught medicine and natural philosophy in the university, he spent the rest of his life there. He talked with Marco Polo (c1295–1310) and spoke of him in his *Conciliator,* this being the only reference to Marco Polo in a contemporary scientific work. He was primarily an astrologer and defended the doctrine that man's fate is controlled by planetary and stellar events, but his interest in man and nature was wide-ranging. The main purpose of his most famous work, *Conciliator differentiarum philosophorum et praecipue medicorum* (completed 1310), was to reconcile conflicting opinions (Greek, Arabic, Jewish, Latin) on more than 200 questions (*differentiae*). These questions concern science in general, medical philosophy, medical art, astrology, and similar subjects. The central interests are medical and astrological. The Florentine humanist Coluccio Salutati (1331–1406), in a debate on which is most valuable, law or medicine, puts Pietro at the head of the list of physicians for his *Conciliator,* and calls him a "universal man." His *Lucidator astronomiae* (1310) is the most important astronomical treatise written during the first part of the 14th century in Italy. Pietro made the first Latin translation of the Problems of Aristotle from a copy of the work he found in Constantinople and thus introduced these writings to the west. Perhaps because of his astrology, or because he was suspected of practicing black magic, or because of his unorthodox explanations of the miracles of Christ, the Inquisition instituted proceedings against him twice, first in 1306 (or before 1303), when he was acquitted, and then in 1315, when he died during the trial. Thomas of Strasbourg, general of the Augustinian order from 1345 to his death in 1357, stated that he witnessed the burning of Pietro's bones in Padua as a posthumous punishment for heresy.

Pietro d'Ancarano (dän-kä-rä'nō). Jurist; b. at Ancarano, 1333; d. at Bologna, May 13, 1416. He was a pupil of Baldo degli Uberti, and taught at Bologna, Siena, Padua, Ferrara, and again at Bologna. He wrote commentaries, as on the Decretals and on Sextus, and a collection of highly valuable opinions. His fame as a jurist was great in his day and he was usually consulted when matters of great importance were under argument.

Pietro da Barsegapé (dä bär-sā-gä-pā′). Religious poet; b. near Milan, c1240; d. c1300. He wrote a rhymed *Sermone* on the creation of the world, the Passion, and the Last Judgment, in 1274, which is of interest for the Milanese dialect in which it is written.

Pietro dei Cerniti (dā cher′nē-tē). Jurisconsult; d. at Bologna, 1338. He taught at Bologna, where his name appears frequently in public records. His writings include a commentary on the Roman code. He was one of the earliest to apply critical methods to the study of ancient legal sources.

Pietro di Giovanni d'Ambrogio (dē jō-vän′nē däm-brôd′jō). Painter; b. at Siena, 1409; d. there, 1449. He was an assistant and close follower in the late Gothic manner of Sassetta, with whose work his own has sometimes been confused. Among the works certainly known to be from his hand are a signed and dated (1444) *St. Bernardino*, Church of the Osservanza, Siena, a signed and dated (1444) banner with a *Crucifixion and Flagellants*, Musée Jacquemart-André, Paris, and a signed and dated (1448) *St. Bernardino*, Lucignano. With these as a standard, other works have been attributed to him, as predella panels in the Vatican, at Basel and Berlin, and a triptych with the *Nativity*, *St. Augustine*, and *St. Galganus*, in the cathedral at Asciano. Other examples of his paintings include a fresco of *St. Bernardino* at Assisi, and works in the Acton Collection and the Horne Museum, Florence, at Paganico, Parma, Terni, the Cini Collection, Venice, and at Brooklyn (*Madonna and Child*, central panel of a triptych), Johnson Collection, Philadelphia, San Diego (California), and elsewhere.

Pietro da Montepulciano (dä mōn-tā-pöl-chä′nō). Marchigian painter; active in the first half of the 15th century. Like Gentile da Fabriano, of whom he was a follower, he delighted to portray the intricate and rich patterns of fabrics, curves of drapery for decorative effects, and numerous delicate details. In his panel, *Madonna and Child in the Midst of Angels*, in The Metropolitan Museum of Art, New York, signed and dated (1420), there is not one vertical line; all the figures lean away from the vertical in graceful curves. A polyptych with a *Madonna of Humility* is in the Palazzo Comunale, at Recanati. Other works are in the parish church at Altidona, at Osimo (Baptistery), Perugia, Washington (Howard University), and elsewhere.

Pietro di Ser Mino (dē ser mē′no). See **Sermini, Pietro di.**

Pietro Lombardo (lôm-bär′dō). Sculptor and architect; b. at Carona, on Lake Lugano, Lombardy, c1435; d. at Venice, in June, 1515. A native of Lombardy, as his name indicates, he may have worked at Florence under Desiderio da Settignano. The first notice concerning him refers to the Roselli monument, in the Basilica at Padua (1464–1467), which appears to have been inspired to some extent by the Marsuppini monument that Desiderio executed in S. Croce at Florence. Soon after 1467 he left Padua for Venice, where he remained the rest of his life and carried out many important works, ultimately assisted by his sons Tullio (c1455–1532) and Antonio (c1458–1516?). One of his first works at Venice was the sepulchral monument of Doge Pasquale Malipiero (d. 1462). Other monuments were those of Doge Niccolò Marcello (d. 1474), SS. Giovanni e Paolo, and of Doge Pietro Mocenigo (d. 1476), Church of the Frari. The Mocenigo monument, with its numerous figures and reliefs with scenes of pagan, Christian, and historical events, and its form of a great triumphal arch, marked a turning point in Venetian Renaissance sculptural decoration. Other monuments were the Zanetti and Onigo monuments at Treviso and the tomb of Dante at Ravenna (1482). His first major architectural work at Venice was the design and decoration of the Cappella Maggiore in the Church of S. Giobbe. He and his studio furnished some of the sculptural decoration for the church itself as well as for the chapel. He also served as architect for the elegant and simple Church of S. Maria dei Miracoli (1481–1489), one of the gems of Venetian Renaissance architecture, and from 1498 until his death was overseer of public works at Venice. After about 1490 his role was increasingly that of planner and designer of work that was carried out by his sons and his studio, products of which were to be found at Ferrara and in cities up and down the Adriatic. In both sculpture and architecture Pietro's ornate Lombard style, modified by classical elements as they were revived by the Tuscans, influenced Venetian Renaissance style.

Pigafetta (pē-gä-fät′tä), **Antonio.** Explorer; b. at Vicenza, between 1480 and 1491; d. there, c1535. Little is known of his life before he voyaged with Magellan. He was a Knight of Rhodes in 1519, which indicates that he had sailed and fought in the galleys of the Order. He went to Spain in the suite of the papal nuncio in 1510, was at Barcelona in 1519, and there learned of the proposed expedition of Magellan to the Moluccas. On September 20, 1519, he sailed on the *Victoria* with Magellan, attached, as a kind of marine, to the explorer's person. Relations between him and his captain were harmonious; Magellan respected him, and he admired Magellan. He enjoyed a special relationship, took part in the engagements with the Indians when such engagements occurred, and accompanied Magellan to the ceremonies at which friendly relations with the Indians were sought. Pigafetta, though wounded, was at the side of Magellan when the latter was killed in the Philippines, April 27, 1521. Pigafetta was one of the 18 members of the original complement of the expedition (265 men and 5 ships) to return to Spain, September 6, 1522. He reported to Charles V at Valladolid, then went to Portugal and France. In 1523, at the court of the Gonzaga at Mantua, he was asked to write a detailed description of the voyage. The Grand Master of the Knights of Rhodes, whom he met at Monterosi in 1525, urged him to carry his description of the voyage to completion. He did so and dedicated it to the Grand Master (1525). His description, in a strange Venetian dialect sprinkled with Spanish words, is by far the most important account of this great first circumnavigation of the globe. It is the only complete description of the voyage from start to finish, and is notable for its careful and complete descriptions of such places as Patagonia, the Philippines, and the Moluccas, where extended stops were made. He noted the flora and fauna of the regions visited, the customs and manner of living of the inhabitants, and made lists of the words in common use. As he said in presenting a copy of his work to Charles V, his account tells all the things that happened day by day on the voyage. He wrote out two copies of his work, later entitled by his editors, *Primo viaggio intorno al globo terraqueo*, . . . , and the account was quickly published in several languages. An early Italian manuscript, not by the hand of Pigafetta, is in the Ambrosian Library at Milan. The house where Pigafetta was born at Vicenza still stands at No. 7 Via Pigafetta.

Pigna (pē′nyä), **Giovan Battista.** Man of letters; b. at Ferrara, 1530; d. there, November 4, 1575. He received a splendid education at Ferrara, and by the time he was 20 was a professor in the university there. Attached to the court of the cultivated Ercole II, duke of Ferrara, he became the intimate friend and confidant of Ercole's successor, Alfonso II. He was Alfonso's secretary, trusted chancellor, and official historian. His works include: *Istoria de' Principi d'Este* (1570), a history of the d'Este family to 1476 that was soon translated; his *I Romanzi* (1554), in which he set forth his ideas about poetry and treated the life and work of Ariosto; and *Gorgoferusa, il Monte Feronia e il Castello d'Amore* (1561), describing the festivities and performances that took place at Ferrara at the carnival of 1561 and on the occasion of the marriage of Alfonso II to Barbara of Austria. His many other writings reveal the wide range of his interests, his lively curiosity, and the acuteness of his perception. His literary colleagues at the court (Tasso, Giraldi, Bartolomeo Ricci, and others) respected his talent and the influence he had with the duke.

Pilaster. In architecture, an ornamental rather than a structural element, consisting of a square pillar, with its capital and base, projecting from a pier or from a wall (usually), to the extent of from one quarter to one third of its breadth; an engaged pillar. This type of ornamentation was much used by Leon Battista Alberti in his adaptations of classical elements to buildings designed to fit the circumstances of his own time.

Pilgrimage of Grace. Insurrection in Yorkshire and Lincolnshire (1536–1537), headed by Robert Aske. It was precipitated by the ecclesiastical and political reforms of Henry VIII, especially the dissolution of the monasteries.

Pimenta (pē-män′tạ), **Diogo Bernardes.** See **Bernardes, Diogo.**

Pinabello (pē-nä-bel′lō). In Lodovico Ariosto's *Orlando Furioso*, a treacherous son of Anselmo. He tries to kill Bradamante, who trusts him, by dropping her into Merlin's cave. She escapes and later slays him.

Pinelli (pē-nel′lē), **Gian Vincenzo.** Bibliophile; b. at Naples of a noble Genoese family, 1535; d. at Padua, 1601. He went to Padua (1558) and studied science and letters there. A learned man, he knew Greek, Latin, Hebrew, and some modern languages. At Padua he amassed a library that constitutes his chief memorial. Most of this magnificent library was acquired for the Ambrosian Library at Milan (1609).

Pino (pē′nō), **Paolo.** Painter and writer on art; active between 1534 and 1565. He was a follower of Girolamo da Brescia and of Gian Girolamo Savoldo. His modest talents are exhibited in a signed and dated (1534) *Male Portrait*, Chambéry, France, which is the earliest date known in connection with him, and in a *Portrait of Doctor Coignati*, Uffizi. He is better known as the author of *Dialogo di Pittura* (Venice, 1548), which is one of the earliest examples of Venetian art criticism and which, predictably, extols Venetian painting.

Pinto (pēn′tö), **Fernão Mendes.** Portuguese adventurer and traveler in the East; b. near Coimbra, Portugal, c1509; d. near Lisbon, Portugal, July 8, 1583. He wrote an account of his travels entitled *Peregrinação*, a work then considered to be made up of fabrications but since shown to be extremely accurate. It is now recognized as one of the great travel books of all time.

Pinturicchio (pēn-tö-rēk′kyō) or **Pintoricchio** (-tō-). [Real name, **Bernardino di Betto.**] Painter; b. at Perugia, 1454; d. at Siena, September 11, 1513. He was called "Pinturicchio" because of his small stature; because of his deafness he was sometimes also called "Sordicchio" (*Deaf*). The influence of Benozzo Gozzoli, along with that of Umbrian painters working in the second half of the 15th century, especially Fiorenzo di Lorenzo and Bartolomeo Caporali, appears in his youthful works. Caporali, a miniaturist as well as a painter, may have passed on to Pinturicchio the love for precise detail that characterized his youthful works especially and that was never entirely absent in his later work. Examples of Pinturicchio's own miniatures are in the Vatican and at Vienna. Two panels on the legend of St. Bernardino (painted perhaps in collaboration with Perugino), *St. Bernardino Curing a Wounded Man* and *Liberation of a Prisoner*, National Gallery of Umbria, Perugia, show his love of detail and predilection for elegant costume. He worked with Perugino at Perugia and was greatly influenced by him in certain respects, as in his preference for symmetrical architectural backgrounds and his capacity to represent space in landscape, but his artistic temperament was distinct from Perugino's. There is a sprightliness in Pinturicchio's detailed, gaily colored, and humanistic approach that is absent from Perugino's tranquil, glowing, and beautifully wrought apparent religiosity. He joined the Painters' Guild at Perugia in 1481 and the same year went to Rome as Perugino's assistant and collaborator in the Sistine Chapel in the Vatican. The frescoes there, *Baptism of Christ* and *Circumcision of the Sons of Moses*, were executed largely by Pinturicchio, to designs by Perugino and under Perugino's supervision. Decorations he executed in the Della Rovere and Colonna palaces and in the apartments of the Belvedere at the Vatican have largely perished. His pleasing, detailed narrative style appears in his frescoes on *St. Bernardino* in the Bufalini Chapel in S. Maria in Aracoeli and in a *Nativity* in S. Maria del Popolo. In the latter church there are also scenes from the life of St. Jerome and of the Virgin, and figures of Evangelists, Fathers of the Church, Sibyls, and a *Coronation of the Virgin*. His Roman paintings express his love of splendor and romantic landscapes, his predilection for lovely faces and his ability to paint them. Between 1492 and 1495 he worked on the decoration of the Borgia apartments in the Vatican, intended to glorify the pontificate of Alexander VI, his patron, through historical and allegorical representations. In this work he employed his talent as an expert, if superficial, decorator to the full. He made lavish use of glimmering gold and glowing ultramarine, to the dismay of the papal secretary, who said he drank too much wine and used too much gold and ultramarine (that the patron had to pay for). The work of decorating the five rooms of the apartment was carried on with a number of assistants and shows Pinturicchio's power of invention at its best. Stories of saints, allegorical representations of the liberal arts, figures of prophets, apostles, and sibyls animate the walls. He planned and supervised the decoration, and mixed his humanist program with Christian scenes, but painted only portions of the decoration himself. In the Room of the Saints, along with myths of Isis and

PINTURICCHIO
Warriors
Louvre, Paris   Alinari-Art Reference Bureau

Osiris and of Io and Apis (the bull was a feature of the Borgia coat of arms), is a fresco of *St. Catherine Disputing with the Emperor,* much of which is by Pinturicchio's own hand. The model for the gentle saint was supposedly Lucrezia Borgia, Alexander's daughter. The winsome saint is surrounded by philosophers robed in the rich apparel that Pinturicchio loved to paint, which may, in fact, be the excuse for the appearance of so many of them. In the Room of the Mysteries of the Faith the fresco with its portrait of Alexander VI kneeling in adoration, *Resurrection,* is also his work. On the completion of the decoration he returned to Umbria where he painted (1495–1498) a beautiful polyptych for the Church of S. Maria dei Fossi, the central panel of which, *Madonna and Child Enthroned with the Young St. John,* with other panels and parts of the predella, is now in the National Gallery of Umbria, Perugia. Frescoes he executed (1497) in the cathedral at Spoleto are now in ruinous condition. Frescoes he executed in the Baglioni Chapel in S. Maria Maggiore, Spello (1500–1501) depict with persuasive sincerity an *Adoration, Christ Among the Doctors,* and an *Annunciation* in which he has placed his own portrait (a picture hanging on the wall of the Virgin's room). From 1502 until his death he made frequent and long stays at Siena. He frescoed a chapel in the cathedral and completed a cartoon for a marble intarsia for the pavement of the cathedral. Between 1503 and 1508 he worked on the fresco decoration of the Piccolomini Library in the cathedral, executing there ten scenes from the life of Pius II (Enea Silvio Piccolomini). The frescoes, along with those in the Borgia apartments, constitute his most important works. Lacking perhaps in profundity of feeling and the grandeur of genius, the panels have a lively charm as decoration and are in an excellent state of preservation. In the scenes are a number of groups of richly clad courtiers and ecclesiastics, and often a turbaned Turk as a symbol of the desire of Pius to wage a crusade. One scene shows Enea Silvio being received at the Scottish court of King James I, whither he had been sent in 1435 on a mission for the Council. The king, represented as a white-bearded old man (though he died at the age of 43), receives him in what appears to be the loggia of an Italian villa set in a typical and lush Italian landscape. One of his great patrons was Pandolfo Petrucci, despot of Siena, for whom he frescoed some of the decorations in his palace, the Palazzo del Magnifico. A detached fresco from the palace, *The Return of Odysseus,* is in the National Gallery, London. Twenty-two panels with mythological scenes, formerly on the ceiling of a hall in the palace, have been detached and are in the Metropolitan Museum, New York. The two last works known by him are the *Madonna in Glory with Saints* (1512), S. Gimignano, and the signed and dated (1513) *Christ Carrying the Cross,* Borromeo Collection, Isolabella. In 1512 his protector, Pandolfo il Magnifico, died. Pinturicchio's wife, who had betrayed him repeatedly and ill-treated him consistently, abandoned him. Friendless and in need, he died in 1513. In his lifetime he was recognized as the leading Umbrian painter after Perugino and, though to a lesser degree than the latter, was an important influence on the Umbrian character that marked the youthful works of Raphael. Vasari writes that he knew how to please princes "because he worked fast and delivered the pictures promptly," and comments that speed prejudiced excellence. But Vasari took a severe tone with Pinturicchio, being proof against the seductions of charm. Besides those mentioned, examples of Pinturicchio's work are at Assisi (S. Maria degli Angeli, Oratorio dei Pellegrini), Città del Castello, Massa Carrara, Perugia (National Gallery, Sala di Consiglio, Opera del Duomo), San Severino in the Marches, Berlin, Dresden, Glasgow, Leningrad, Oxford, Valencia, Warsaw, Baltimore, Isabella Stewart Gardner Museum, Boston, Brooklyn, Fogg Museum (Cambridge), Cleveland, Denver, Oberlin (Ohio), the Johnson Collection, Philadelphia, Raleigh (North Carolina), San Marino (California), the National Gallery, Washington, and elsewhere.

Pinzón (pēn-thōn′), **Martín Alonso.** Spanish navigator; b. at Palos de la Frontera, Spain, c1441; d. there, 1493. He was the head of a family of shipbuilders at Palos, and had made many voyages. He joined Columbus in 1492, probably because he was part owner of the smaller vessels and had aided Columbus' preparations for the voyage. He commanded the *Pinta,* of which his brother Francisco Martín (c1440–c1493) was the pilot. In November, 1492, he parted company with Columbus on the coast of Cuba. He was the first to discover Hispaniola, and rejoined the admiral on the coast of that island on January 6, 1493. Columbus afterward asserted that he had deserted with the intention of returning to Spain. During the return voyage the *Pinta* was separated from the *Niña* in a storm and eventually reached Bayona, a port of Galicia. Thence Pinzón sent a letter to the sovereigns with an account of the discovery, and sailed on to Palos de la Frontera, reaching it on the same day as Columbus (March 15). His death, shortly after, is said to have been hastened by chagrin because Columbus received the honor of the discovery.

Pinzón, Vicente Yáñez. Spanish navigator; b. at Palos de la Frontera, Spain, c.1460; d. c1524. He commanded the *Niña* in the first voyage of Columbus. In December 1499 he was in command of four exploring ships, crossed the Equator, the first Spanish commander to do so, sailed along the coast of Brazil, discovering the mouth of the Amazon, and sailed as far as Costa Rica. He was associated with Juan Diaz de Solís in exploration of the Gulf of Honduras, and a portion of Southeast Yucatán, and later in an exploration of the East coast of South America.

Piombo (pyôm′bō), **Sebastiano del.** See **Sebastiano del Piombo.**

Pippi (pēp′pē), **Giulio.** See **Giulio Romano.**

Pisa, Council of. Ecclesiastical council called at Pisa, 1409, to end the Great Schism in the Church that had begun in 1378. The Council was called by a group of Roman Cardinals who had deserted Gregory XII. They were joined by the French cardinals from the court of Benedict XIII at Avignon. The Council deposed both Gregory and Benedict, and elected Petros Philargos, the cardinal archbishop of Milan, as Alexander V. The Council, attended by representatives from all over Europe, was uncanonical, and neither Gregory nor Benedict recognized its authority. There were thus three who claimed to be pope, and the schism was deepened. Nevertheless, the meeting of the Council strengthened the conciliar movement and led, at a later date, to the calling of other councils that attempted to dominate the papacy. As a result of the Council of Pisa, Gregory, the canonical pope, lost many of his supporters.

Pisanello (pē-zä-nel′lō), **Antonio.** [Original name, **Antonio Pisano;** formerly known as **Vittore Pisano.**] Painter, medalist, and draftsman; b. near Verona, between 1380 and 1397; d. at Rome, 1455. Little is known of his antecedents, his training, or indeed of his life, other than that as one of the most imaginative, creative, and competent of early Italian Renaissance painters and the greatest of Italian medalists, he was patronized by several of the chief rulers and nobles of his time, especially by Leonello d'Este, lord of Ferrara. In 1431 and 1432 he was at Rome, working on the frescoes Gentile da Fabriano had begun in St. John Lateran; these have perished. By 1435 he was at Ferrara and was on good terms with Leonello d'Este. He is known to have worked at Venice, Mantua, Milan, Pavia, and Naples as well. Wherever he went he was associated with the court, and delighted to portray, as court painter, in a purely secular spirit the wealth and luxury of the courts of his patrons in works on religious subjects. For his patrons, including Alfonso I of Naples who gave him a salary of 400 ducats a year as a member of his household, Leonello, and the Gonzaga of Mantua, he also designed jewelry, rich fabrics, and costumes. Among the most fascinating of his extant works are his careful and correct drawings and studies in water color of animals, especially those of the chase, birds, fashions, and the studies he made of heads for his medals. The animals and birds, especially, are executed with scientific accuracy and in exquisite detail. A valuable collection of his drawings is in the Louvre. His paintings have a touch of the macabre; they are Gothic in a literary sense. Of them there is a *St. George and the Princess,* a fresco which survives from a series in the Pellegrini Chapel of the Church of Sant' Anastasia at Verona. St. George, having slain the dragon and saved the princess, has an almost grotesque expression on his face as he stares away from the princess. He is about to mount his beautifully foreshortened horse. The princess, erect and expressionless, stands nearby. In the background, on a hill, two men hang from a gibbet. The area about the two principals is filled with figures and animals. Another painting that exhibits his love of painting animals and birds (in utter disregard of the demands of composition), is the *Vision of St. Eustace,* in the National Gallery, London. St. Eustace, mounted on his horse, is brought up short by the vision of

Pisanello
Eleven Gentlemen in Contemporary Costume
Biblioteca Ambrosiana, Milan

PISANELLO
Copy of a sarcophagus with an *Indian Triumph of Bacchus*
Biblioteca Ambrosiana, Milan

a stag bearing a crucifix between its antlers. All about are animals and birds. Also in the National Gallery at London are his *St. Anthony and St. George,* which has been heavily repainted, and his *St. Jerome.* A portrait thought to be of the youthful Ginevra d'Este of Ferrara is in the Louvre. Many of his paintings, especially his frescoes at Venice, Rome, Pavia, Florence, and Verona, have perished. Besides the fresco in Sant' Anastasia, there remains another, in poor condition, of the *Annunciation* in the Church of S. Fermo at Verona, and a panel, *Madonna della Quaglia* (*The Madonna of the Quail,* so called because of the carefully painted quail in the corner at the Madonna's feet), in the museum of the same city. In the earlier phase of his career there is some evidence that he was influenced by Stefano da Verona. The later phase of his career shows some influence of Gentile da Fabriano in his forms, his interest in details, his love of animals and birds and splendid costumes, and in the enchanted world he depicts, but with Pisanello the enchantment is sometimes sinister. In the later phase of his life he began casting medals. These, considered the finest struck since ancient times, have fared better than his paintings. In 1438 he saw John VIII Palaeologus, the Byzantine emperor who had come to Ferrara for the council called by Pope Eugenius IV, which it was hoped would unite the Eastern and Western churches. Pisanello cast and signed (1438) a medal of the emperor wearing his odd, pointed hat. He also made medals of Filippo Maria Visconti (c1441), Alfonso of Naples (1449), and seven of Leonello d'Este. One of these latter, commemorating his patron's marriage, shows Love conquering the lion on its reverse. Pisanello was celebrated in his own time, was eagerly sought after by princely patrons, and was praised by contemporary poets and writers. He was an expert draftsman who excelled at spirited, minutely observed renditions of animals and birds, a gifted medalist who consulted the classical age for the symbols on the reverses of his medals, and a painter who combined realism in detail with a Gothic imagination. The only panel painting from his hand remaining in Italy is a portrait of Leonello d'Este in the Carrara Academy at Bergamo, a magnificent profile portrait of the refined features of that cultivated prince.

Pisani (pē-zä'nē), **Ugolino.** Adventurer, soldier, jurist, poet, musician, and writer of comedies; b. at Parma at the beginning of the 15th century. In the forty years of his life he dabbled in many fields. He traveled through the Balkan peninsula in search of adventure; studied law at Pavia (1435), and took his doctorate at Bologna (1437); fought for Alfonso of Aragon, at whose court he met Lorenzo Valla and studied Greek; went to the Council of Basel (1441) and joined the party that elected the antipope Amadeus VIII of Savoy as Felix V; and wrote a comedy, *Repetitio Zanini* (1435) and gave a copy of it to Leonello d'Este of Ferrara (1437). Two of his letters, and numerous notes on a Latin manuscript of the works of Aristotle remain.

Pisano (pē-zä'nō), **Andrea.** [Original name, **Andrea da Pontaderra.**] Sculptor and architect; b. c1290; d. at Florence, c1349. Not of the same family as Nicola and Giovanni, he was called Pisano because he came from Pisa. There he had the benefit of studying the remains of classical sculpture in the Camposanto. Otherwise, nothing is known of his early training. By 1330 he must have been a recognized sculptor, for in that year he was commissioned to make the bronze doors for the Baptistery. He completed (1336) one pair, that now on the south side. The doors have twenty-eight quatrefoil panels, with twenty scenes from the life of St. John the Baptist (patron saint of Florence) and eight allegories of the theological and cardinal virtues. Andrea Pisano also executed (some from the designs of Giotto) some of the figures in low relief in the first two rows of Giotto's Campanile next to the Duomo. The figures, in oval compartments, represent the mechanical and practical arts, the planets, virtues, liberal arts, and the sacraments. As architect, Pisano carried on the building of the Campanile after Giotto's death (1337) Also as architect, he had raised the fortification walls of Florence when (1312) the city was threatened by the presence of Henry VII. He enlarged and strengthened the Palazzo Vecchio (begun by Arnolfo di Cambio) with great walls and fortifications to render it a safe residence for Walter de Brienne, titular duke of Athens, whom the Florentines had made governor of their city. After the expulsion (1343) of Walter, the arms that Andrea had carved for him over the door were destroyed. Among his other sculptural works are *Christ Blessing*, *St. Reparata*, and other statues, in the Museo dell' Opera del Duomo, Florence. In the last years of his life he went to Orvieto to work on the façade of the cathedral there (1347). Andrea was most influenced in his style and sense of design by Giotto, his contemporary and colleague, and introduced to Florentine sculpture the new elements that Giotto had brought to Florentine painting. Vasari says of him, "Andrea's work so far surpassed the rude work of the masters in sculpture who had preceded him that it seemed a miracle."

Pisano, Giovanni. Sculptor and architect; b. at Pisa, c1245; d. c1320. He was the son of Nicola Pisano (c1220–1278?), with whom he worked on the pulpit for the cathedral at Siena (1265–1266) and on the Fontana Maggiore at Perugia (1278). The three bronze caryatids surmounting the fountain are attributed to Giovanni by many, and the group is the first in Italian casting to have been cast in the round. Giovanni lived a number of years (1284–1299) at Siena and became a citizen of the commune. In his role as architect he designed the façade of the cathedral, and as sculptor he carved many of the decorations for it. Some of his figures, including some from the Old and New Testaments, are now in the Opera del Duomo at Siena. These have been replaced on the façade with copies. From 1299 to 1308 he was in charge of the work for the cathedral at Pisa. Earlier, he had been in charge of decorating the Baptistery there. In this period he also carved the pulpit for the Church of Sant' Andrea at Pistoia. The hexagonal platform is supported by six columns of red porphyry. The five panels with decorations carry reliefs: *Annunciation, Nativity,* and *Annunciation to the Shepherds; Adoration of the Magi, Dream of the Magi, The Angel's Warning to the Holy Family to Flee; Massacre of the Innocents; Crucifixion;* and *Last Judgment.* The work, completed in 1301, is typical of the drama, realism, and movement with which Giovanni Pisano invested his work. Between 1302 and 1310 he worked on the pulpit for the Cathedral of Pisa, another expressive example of his Gothic style. The pulpit was dismantled in 1602 and reconstructed in 1926. A few parts, such as those now in the Metropolitan Museum, New York, have been replaced by copies. Fragments of the tomb he carved for Margaret, wife of the Emperor Henry VII, are in the Palazzo Bianco, Genoa. Other works include a *Virgin with Child,* on the altar of the cathedral at Prato; and a *Madonna with Two Angels,* on the altar of the Scrovegni Chapel at Padua. Giovanni did not continue the serene classical tradition in sculpture that his father had revived. His style and that of his many followers, to the time of Donatello (c1386–1466), reflects the fervor and spiritual agitation of the late Middle Ages, to which is added a strong flavor of realism in expression and movement.

Pisano, Nicola. [Also called, **Nicola d'Apulia.**] Sculptor; b. c1220; d. between 1278 and 1287. He may have been born at Pisa, or he may have come from Apulia and received some of his early training there. His name Pisano derives from his residence and work at Pisa. Nicola studied the many fragments of antique sculpture to be found at Pisa, and made the serenity and grace of the ancient statuary his own. The more intense, less proportioned, and more emotional style of the late Middle Ages was also known to him. His own work is a combination of the classical and the late medieval, with more of the antique proportion, moderation and ease of line, and was stamped with his own personality and style. As Giotto was the father of Italian Renaissance painting, Nicola was the father of Renaissance sculpture. His earliest identifiable work is the pulpit of the Baptistery at Pisa, finished between 1259 and 1260. As it is the masterpiece of a mature artist other works must have preceded it, but cannot be identified. The hexagonal pulpit of the Baptistery rests on seven marble columns, three of which are supported by marble lions. It is adorned with beasts, allegorical figures, saints, prophets, and evangelists. In the panels that surround the platform are carved scenes from the life of Christ and a *Last Judgment.* Every inch of the six panels is carved, filled with figures. In the *Adoration of the Magi,* several of the figures, especially the Virgin, Joseph, and the horses' heads, are notably classical in feeling and plasticity. Nicola also carved the pulpit of the cathedral at Siena, similar to that at Pisa but larger, showing greater movement, greater narrative power in the panels and a less contemplative spirit than the pulpit at Pisa. In completing the pulpit at Siena, Nicola was assisted by his son Giovanni, Arnolfo di Cambio, and others. The Siena pulpit has more of the tension and fervor of the late Middle Ages than the pulpit at Pisa. A third great work is the Fontana Maggiore (Great Fountain) in the piazza of the cathedral at Perugia. It is composed of a bronze bowl, with three bronze caryatids, surmounting an upper and a lower basin. The upper basin has twenty-four panels separated by twenty-four statuettes, each of which is placed against a column with a capital. The lower basin is surrounded by bas-reliefs. As at Siena, Nicola was assisted by his son Giovanni, who perhaps finished the work, and Arnolfo di Cambio. To Giovanni is credited the group of bronze caryatids. The fountain was completed c1278. Other works by Nicola and his pupils are the *Deposition,* in the tympanum of the left door of the cathedral at Lucca, and the tomb of St. Dominic in the Church of San Domenico at Bologna. The tomb is decorated with bas-reliefs showing scenes from the life of the Saint. Other sculptors, including Michelangelo, worked on enlarging and embellishing it in later times. Vasari writes of Nicola that he "liberated sculpture from the rude manner of the Greeks" (meaning Byzantine Greeks), and that he had worked under them in the construction of the cathedral at Pisa. He also calls Nicola the architect of several important buildings. Confirmation of his work as an architect, however, is lacking. Giovanni did not continue his father's exploration of classical forms nor share his serene and contemplative interest in matters of this world. Giovanni and others reverted to the tense, mystic, emotional, and abstract vision of another world as it was revealed in late medieval sculpture.

Pitati (pē-tä'tē), **Bonifacio de'**. See **Bonifazio Veronese.**

Pitigliano (pē-tē-lyä'nō), Count of. See **Orsini, Niccolò.**

Pitti (pēt'tē), **Buonaccorso.** Writer and adventurer; b. at Florence, April 25, 1354; d. c1431. In 1374 he left Florence and began a roving and adventurous life that, except for a few intervals, he continued until his death. He traveled to Avignon, Paris, Croatia, Hungary, the Low Countries, and Savoy, making and losing great sums at gambling, acting as a banker and merchant, and generally enriching himself. In 1391 he returned to Florence and married, but did not tarry long in his native city. Isabella of France sent him back to Florence (1396) to persuade the Florentines to ally themselves with France against the Visconti of Milan. In this he was successful. From 1398 he was in Florence and carried out diplomatic missions for the republic, as ambassador to Robert of Bavaria, to the pope, and to his friend the duke of Orléans. After 1419 he took up his travels again, and went to Hungary, France, England, the Low Countries, and Switzerland. He left a *Cronaca*, a kind of diary that he began to write in 1412 and continued to 1430. In this are to be found accounts of the political events of his time, along with much entertaining biographical material.

Pitti, Jacopo. Florentine historian and public official; b. 1519; d. 1589. He was a member of an ancient Florentine family, one that was for long a rival of the Medici. Because of this rivalry, perhaps, Jacopo became a fervent democrat. The fragments of his *Istorie fiorentine* show him to have been an ardent supporter of the popular party. His other works include a *Vita di A. Giocomini Tebalducci*, and his *Apologia de' Cappucci*, a defense of his party against the accusations of his older contemporary, Francesco Guicciardini.

Pitti, Luca. Florentine official; b. at Florence, 1395. He was of an old and wealthy family and, after the death of Neri Capponi, who had been influential in Florentine affairs, was second only to Cosimo de' Medici as a citizen of Florence. In 1454 he joined with two other prominent men in an attempt to wrest control of the city from Cosimo. The old method of choosing the members of the Signoria by lot was restored. (It was charged that under Cosimo's influence many office holders had been handpicked.) Unfortunately for Luca, an independent Signoria proposed to raise taxes. As he was a very rich man and had heretofore managed to avoid many burdensome levies, he was opposed to this proposal and had to seek Cosimo's help. He was Gonfaloniere of Justice at the time and had to suffer the humiliation of restoring Cosimo's method of choosing a Signoria that could be counted on to do as Cosimo bid. After Cosimo's death he again conspired (1466) against Medici influence, and sought the help of Venetian arms to overthrow Cosimo's son Piero. Piero learned of the conspiracy, went to the Signoria and informed them of it, and the affair collapsed. Luca was the only one of the four principal conspirators who was not banished; he had, in private, made his peace with Piero. Thereafter he had little political influence. By this time he was an old man, and anxious to finish the magnificent palace he was having constructed as his monument on the other side of the Arno. It is the Pitti Palace, now the home of the Pitti Gallery. The Medici grand dukes of Tuscany and their successors occupied it from 1550 to 1859.

Pitti Palace. Palace on the left bank of the Arno. It was begun by Luca Pitti, a rich Florentine merchant and politician, according to a tradition that has been questioned, to designs by Brunelleschi. The building was incomplete at the time of Luca's death (shortly after 1466), and work on it was abandoned for a time. When work was resumed the simple magnificence thought to have been planned by Brunelleschi was changed in a number of important respects. Additions made by Ammannati in the 16th century and by other architects transformed the building into massive, fortresslike regality. The building did not arrive at its present state until 1839. From 1550 it was the residence of the court of Cosimo I de' Medici, later grand duke of Tuscany (and descendant of Luca's old enemy Cosimo de' Medici the Elder), of his descendants and of the successors of the House of Medici until 1859. The palace houses the Gallery of Modern Art on the top floor, the Silver Museum with precious objects that came in great part from Medici collections, and, most famous of all, the Pitti or Palatine Gallery with paintings partly from the Medici collections, from the 15th to the 18th century, including examples of the work of the most important Italian masters of the period. Behind the Pitti Palace are the Boboli Gardens, designed by Tribolo in 1549 for Cosimo I de' Medici and continued to designs by Ammannati (1560) and Buontalenti (1583), magnificent example of Italian landscape architecture.

Pius II (pī'us). [Original name, **Enea Silvio Bartolomeo Piccolomini;** in literature, called **Aeneas Sylvius.**] Humanist, poet, historian, diplomat, and pope (1458–1464); b. at Corsignano, near Siena, October 18, 1405; d. near Ancona, August 15, 1464. The Piccolomini were an old and noble family of Siena. In the perennial upheavals of government at Siena they had been excluded from holding office. They retired to Corsignano and there, impoverished, lived on what remained to them of their estates. Enea Silvio, the son of Silvio Piccolomini and Vittoria Forteguerri, was the eldest of eighteen children, though, as he says in his *Commentaries,* "there were never more than ten living at once," and plagues finally carried off all but Enea and his sisters Laudamia and Caterina. After a childhood and youth spent at Corsignano, he went to Siena to study civil law. The law did not appeal to him. He became fascinated by the classical writers; Cicero, Livy, and Vergil were his favorite authors. He was, for a time, a pupil of the noted humanist Francesco Filelfo, at Florence. Twice he heard St. Bernardino preach in Siena, and listened to him as "to another St. Paul." Moved by his preaching, Enea had fleeting thoughts of a religious life but easily gave them up, followed a life of pleasure, and for long declined to join the priesthood. He became secretary to Domenico Capranica, bishop (later cardinal) of Fermo, and went (1432) with him to Basel, to the Council meeting there for the purpose of effecting a union of the Greek and Latin churches, reconciling the Bohemians, and proposing certain reforms within the Church. His wit, genial personality, and eloquence won him many friends on the Council. He served it as Scriptor, Abbreviator, and Chief Abbreviator in the course of several meetings. In 1438 he was sent on a secret mission to Scotland. The English refused him a safe-conduct to Scotland; he returned to Holland and sought passage from there. The passage was stormy, the ship was driven to Norway; seas were so high and dangerous that Enea made a vow: to make a pilgrimage to a holy shrine if they reached land safely. In fulfillment of his vow he walked barefoot through snow and ice to the shrine of Whitekirk in Scotland. Some thought that this was the cause of the so-called gout that plagued him throughout his life.

In 1439 the Council of Basel, which had been called by Pope Eugenius IV, deposed the pope because he refused to acknowledge its authority. The Council elected Amadeus, duke of Savoy, in his place, although Eugenius IV continued to be recognized as the true pope by the majority. The antipope Amadeus took the name Felix V. Enea Silvio, who had served under several ecclesiastics, on diplomatic missions, and on several embassies to the Council, now became secretary to Felix V and wielded his polished and eloquent pen on behalf of Felix and against Eugenius. It seems doubtful that he did this from compelling religious conviction. In the course of time he came to the conclusion that the position of the Council vis-à-vis the pope was untenable. Thus he welcomed the opportunity afforded while he was on an embassy to Frankfurt-am-Main (1442), to enter the service of Frederick III, king of Germany. This was a change of sides and Enea was severely criticized as a turncoat and opportunist. He went to Austria with Frederick, was named poet laureate at his court, and became a secretary in his chancery and his eventual historian. In 1445 he wrote a letter to Eugenius in which he apologized for his actions against him at Basel. The letter, noted by Pastor (*History of the Popes*) as "a masterpiece of style . . ." that "has been described as the address of a vanquished king to his captor," won Eugenius' forgiveness. He recognized Enea's qualities and made him his secretary. (When, later, Enea became Pope Pius II, he issued a bull in which it was pronounced heretical for any council to hold itself superior to the pope. He thus reversed his earlier stand at Basel.) The year after his reconciliation with Eugenius he resolved to reform his way of life and was ordained at Vienna. Subsequently, he was named bishop of Trieste (1447) and bishop of Siena (1450), by

Nicholas V, and was made a cardinal (1456) by Calixtus III. In the service of the popes he was engaged on many missions and diplomatic errands. In 1450 he arranged a marriage between Frederick III and Leonora, daughter of the king of Portugal. At the same time he arranged for the coronation of Frederick III as Holy Roman emperor at Rome; marriage and coronation (the last such to take place at Rome) took place within a few days of each other (March, 1452).

Cardinal Capranica, whom Enea had served as secretary, was a leading candidate for the papal chair when Calixtus III died, August 5, 1458. He died suddenly, August 14, 1458, just before the conclave to elect a new pope opened. In his *Commentaries*, Enea candidly describes the persuasions and pressures he and his friends used to get himself elected. A decisive argument was that if he were not chosen either a French or a Spanish cardinal might become pope (the leading contender was a Frenchman, Cardinal d'Estouteville), and no one in Italy wanted another foreign pope. At his election "all the Italian powers, with the exception of Florence and Venice, were delighted at the elevation of the pacific and statesmanlike Piccolomini" (Pastor). When asked what name he would be known by he immediately said "Pius," in allusion to "pius Aeneas" of his beloved Vergil. A full description of the processions and ceremonies that took place at his coronation, September 3, 1458, appears in his *Commentaries*.

Pius was 53 when he became pope, and already seemed old and worn. His health was poor; he suffered grievously from what was called gout. Immediately, he was confronted by urgent problems. The States of the Church were in turmoil. His Italian policy was to restore peace and to strengthen them; to enhance the power of the Church with a united band of states across Italy under the pope's control. He sought to subdue the rebellious barons, drive out marauding mercenaries, and win back the principates, duchies, and cities that had rebelled or been seized by temporal lords. His chief enemy in the latter connection was Sigismondo Malatesta, lord of Rimini, whom he characterized as "the poison of all Italy," and whom, in a ceremony unique in Church history, he canonized to hell. In addition, to whatever degree was possible, he sought to keep foreign powers out of Italy. He recognized Ferrante, illegitimate son of Alfonso I, king of Sicily, Sardinia, and Naples (who as Alfonso V was also king of Aragon), as heir of Alfonso and king of Sicily and Naples. In this he confirmed a decree of Nicholas V and contravened the decision of Calixtus III, who had held that the kingdom reverted to the Church when Alfonso died, earlier in 1458. The struggle between the French, who claimed the kingdom through Louis of Anjou, and Ferrante for control went on during most of Pius II's pontificate. Pius feared the French, of whom he had a low opinion, more than the Spanish in Italy. His *Commentaries* are full of descriptions of campaigns and sieges to win back or to hold cities and principalities for the Church and to support Ferrante. All Italy was in commotion. Pius used his great diplomatic skill in attempts to settle one quarrel after another, always with the interests of the Church in mind. Germany erupted over the question of the Bohemian heresy. George Podiebrad, king of Bohemia, sought to oppose Frederick III. There was a portentous struggle with Diether of Mainz over his right to be archbishop of Mainz. The French, under Louis XI, attempted to bribe Pius into recognizing their claim to Sicily and Naples by a promise to abrogate the Pragmatic Sanction of Bourges (a system of limitations set by the French on the spiritual powers of the pope). Failure to win this recognition caused endless friction between Pius and Louis. The spiritual head of Christendom was beset on all sides by temporal struggles.

Outside Italy, his policy centered about one cherished wish: to drive the Turks out of Constantinople, which they had taken in 1453. To this end he summoned all the princes of Europe to a Congress at Mantua, for the purpose of organizing a crusade. He left Rome in January, 1459, and made a slow and triumphal journey across Italy on his way to Mantua. In the course of it he stopped at his native Corsignano, and resolved to build a church and palace there as a memorial to himself and his birthplace. This he ordered to be done and entrusted the work to Bernardo Rossellino. In a few years the cathedral and palace were completed, to his immense satisfaction, and the name Corsignano was changed to Pienza in his honor (see **Pienza**). The Congress was less successful. Some of the princes refused to attend or to send embassies, either they were under pressure at home or had little interest in a crusade that would not enhance their own powers; others showed by the quality of the embassies they did send that they were not serious about the crusade; others sent embassies whose primary concern was to win concessions from the pope. Many criticized him for leaving Rome at so critical a time (he was away about a year, during which time there were serious disorders in the city); others objected to the location of the Congress in Mantua. They complained about the flat wine, the heat and unhealthy climate, and the noise of the frogs. Pius, disappointed with the results of the Congress of Mantua, did not abandon his plan for a crusade, though other grave demands on his attention caused him to put it off. The discovery at Tolfa of alum (1462), an important ingredient in dyeing, brought revenue to the Church and funds for a crusade. In the fall of 1463 Jacopo Piccinino, a condottiere in the pay of the French, came to terms with the papacy and Ferrante and switched sides. The prince of Taranto, who had threatened to aid France against Ferrante, died, to the great joy of his subjects. Sigismondo Malatesta acknowledged that he was defeated, asked for peace and publicly recanted his heresies. The turmoil in Germany lessened. Philip of Burgundy expressed enthusiasm for a crusade, remembered the promises made in his name at Mantua, and said he would send men whom, if his health permitted, he would lead himself. The Venetians, for their own always suspect reasons, had equipped a fleet that was even then attacking the Turks in Greece, and promised to send a fleet to Ancona, the meeting place for the start of the crusade. Envoys were sent throughout Europe to proclaim the crusade and to seek help. At the end of the year 1463, all signs seemed favorable. This state did not last long. Philip was persuaded to seek a delay in departure; other princes began to make excuses for defaulting. Pius, in the knowledge that many lesser men were already converging on Ancona, resolved to go ahead and to lead the crusade himself. With the words, "Farewell, Rome! Never will you see me again alive," he set out for Ancona, June 18, 1464. He arrived there to find that the Venetians had not come and that many soldiers had returned to their homes. Broken in health and weary at heart, he withdrew to a place overlooking the harbor. The Venetian fleet finally put in an appearance, but it was too late. Pius died soon after it arrived. Plans for the crusade collapsed.

As pope, Pius II strengthened the temporal power of the Church by curbing the barons, defeating Sigismondo Malatesta and supporting Ferrante of Naples. This was accomplished by the use of mercenaries, an astute application of influence and supple diplomacy. He secured the abrogation of the Pragmatic Sanction of Bourges and proclaimed the supremacy of the papacy over councils. For the canonization of St. Catherine of Siena (1461) he wrote the Bull himself, as well as an epitaph and several Latin hymns. He was a generous patron and protector of his family and appointed several of his nephews or adopted nephews to rich and important posts. It was said that those who surrounded the pope were almost all Sienese, "and of the Sienese the majority were Piccolomini." Some criticize him for his nepotism. Others take the view that this was a way of securing loyal aides. As a great humanist and outstanding Renaissance figure, he was a thorough and enthusiastic student of the classics, a diplomat, and a man of unlimited interest in and wide knowledge of the world of his day. His was one of the foremost intellects of his time. He had traveled in Germany, Austria, France, England, and Scotland. He knew the princes and lords of every important state or principality of Europe. Alfonso of Sicily and Naples had been his friend; Federico da Montefeltro and Francesco Sforza were his friends and allies. He was an eloquent speaker and a brilliant writer. His works give a vivid picture of the ideas, personalities and events of 15th-century Europe. In his youth he wrote a love story that was widely translated. (When he became pope he preferred to forget that he was the author of this charming novel in the style of Boccaccio.) He wrote poems, a bawdy play, *Chrisis*, and orations; he compiled a geography that is thought to have influenced Columbus, and wrote histories of Bohemia and of Frederick III. In his *Commentaries* Pius tells how he came to write part of his geography. He and Federico da Montefeltro were riding to Tivoli together and enjoying a pleasant and learned conversation and, "Since they mentioned Asia Minor also and did not agree about its boundaries, the Pope later, when he got a little leisure at Tivoli, wrote a description of Asia itself, quoting from Ptolemy, Strabo, Pliny, Q. Curtius, Julius Solinus, Pomponius Mela and other ancient authors passages that seemed to him relevant to an understanding of the subject." Of greatest importance, as a memoir of his pontificate, a record of his times, and as a literary work are his *Commentaries (Pio II Comentarii rerum memorabilium quae temporibus suis contigerunt)*. These reveal his genial personality, his wide learning, his love of nature, and his shrewd observations on men and events (see **Commentaries of Pius II**). Compared to his successors, he was not a great builder or patron of the arts. He repaired and restored, appreciated art and employed architects, sculptors, artists, and craftsmen, but did not undertake great projects as Nicholas V had done. However, he did try to preserve the relics of antiquity and the buildings he did cause to be erected have remained, as at Pienza, as pure specimens of Renaissance architecture. He lives in art in the delightful, highly decorative, and freely imagined paintings, by Pinturicchio, of some of the events in his life. These are in the Piccolomini Library, in the cathedral at Siena, given to it by Pius II's nephew and the future Pope Pius III, Francesco Todeschini Piccolomini. Pius II was succeeded by Paul II.

Pius III. Pope (September 22, 1503–October 8, 1503); b. c1440; d. at Rome, October 8, 1503. He was the son of Pope Pius II's sister Laudomia. To his own name, Francesco Todeschini, he added the name of his famous and beloved uncle and was known as Francesco Todeschini Piccolomini. Pope Pius II made him archbishop of Siena, and raised him to the purple (1460). The young cardinal was noted for his piety, for his zeal for a crusade against the Turks, and for his absolute freedom from the taint of simony. He served as papal legate in Germany (1471) and in Perugia (1488–1489), and prevented the loss of that city to the Church. He deplored the worldliness of the Curia, refused to be bribed in the conclave of 1492 that elected Alexander VI, and opposed Alexander's flagrant nepotism. He was a gentle, honest, pious, cultivated man. In 1492 he laid the foundation for the Piccolomini Library in the cathedral at Siena, and in 1502 entrusted to Pinturicchio the task of decorating it. The Library was to contain the books and manuscripts of his uncle Pius II. Not many of them arrived there. In the conclave of 1502 he was elected, September 22, as Pope Pius III. His first aim was to reform the Church. But weakened by gout, the family malady, and prematurely aged, he succumbed to illness and died within a month of his election. His great memorial is the abovementioned Piccolomini Library at Siena, a Renaissance gem. Pius III was succeeded by Julius II.

Pizarro (pi-zär′ō; Castilian Spanish, pē-thär′rō; American Spanish, pē-sär′rō), **Francisco.** Spanish conquistador, remembered as the conqueror of Peru; b. at Trujillo, Estremadura, Spain, c1471; d. at Lima, Peru, June 26, 1541. He first appears in American history at Darien where he was left in charge of the colony (1510). He was with Balboa in the discovery of the Pacific, and settled at Panama in 1519. Following two abortive attempts to sail south where there was rumored to be a rich empire, his expedition finally reached Tumbes and other rich Inca towns, and saw evidence of great wealth. He went to Spain where he received a concession to conquer and govern Peru, and on November 15, 1532 entered Cajamarco. He seized the Inca Atahualpa, and although he demanded and received a huge ransom for his release, murdered the Inca. The Spanish marched to Cusco where Manco Inca surrendered. In January 1535 he founded Lima, and soon afterward was made a marquis, with territory extending from the Santiago River southward for 270 leagues. He was killed by followers of Diego de Almagro, after a war between him and Pizarro over disputed territory.

Pizarro, Hernando. Spanish conquistador; half brother of Francisco Pizarro; b. at Trujillo, Estremadura, Spain; d. there, 1578. He accompanied his brother to Peru, returning in 1534 with the royal fifth of the ransom of Atahualpa. He returned to Peru; commanded the defense of Cusco; was captured by Almagro, and released on his promise to leave the country. Instead he took command of his brother's army and defeated and killed Almagro. For this he was kept in mild confinement in Spain for twenty years (1540–1560).

Plantin (plän-tañ), **Christophe.** French printer at Antwerp; b. near Tours, France, 1514; d. at Antwerp, Belgium, 1589. He published a polyglot Bible (1569–1572).

Platina (plä'tē-nä), **il.** [Original name, **Bartolommeo Sacchi.**] Humanist; b. at Piadena (or Platina) near Cremona, 1421; d. at Rome, 1481. He gave up the military career on which he had embarked to study at Mantua, and there became tutor to Ludovico Gonzaga's children. In furtherance of his humanistic studies, especially Greek language and literature, he went (1457) to Florence, where he became friendly with Cosimo and Piero de' Medici. Cardinal Francesco Gonzaga, who became his protector and patron, employed him as a secretary and took him to Rome, and Pius II made him an apostolic abbreviator. In Rome he was a member of the so-called Roman Academy. The group gave banquets, celebrated festivals, produced Latin plays and promoted Latin studies, under the leadership of Julius Pomponius Laetus. Pope Paul II, who succeeded the great humanist pope, Pius II, had no use for the humanists, distrusted their learning, and considered them pagans. He dissolved the College of Abbreviators thus eliminating Platina's employment. Platina wrote him a letter in which he threatened him with a council to curb his powers. Paul II imprisoned him, but he was released through the activity of his patron Cardinal Gonzaga. In 1468 a supposed conspiracy by the humanists against Paul II was discovered. Platina, with other members of the Roman Academy, was imprisoned. He was charged, among other things, with Paganism, and was not released from prison until May, 1469. Under Sixtus IV, his fortunes and posts were restored, and he passed his remaining years peacefully at Rome. From 1475 until his death he was director of the Vatican Library. His portrait appears, with those of Pope Sixtus IV and four of the pope's nephews, in a fresco by Melozzo da Forlì in the Vatican, *The Inauguration of the Vatican Library*. His work *Liber de vita Christi ac omnium pontificum*, completed 1474, is a history of the popes. From the time of Calixtus III through to his own day, the work is interesting for his personal knowledge and reminiscences. The material before that contains little of historical value. Not unnaturally, in this work Platina took gleeful vengeance on Paul II for his cavalier treatment of the humanists. He also wrote such Latin treatises as *De principe, De optimum cive, De falso et vero bono*, and *De vera nobilitate* (*On True Nobility*), one of the favorite themes of Renaissance writers.

Pléiade (plā-yåd). Name given in literature to several groups of seven poets living at the same time. In the 16th century, it was applied in a metaphorical way (it was never an official name) to the group formed by Ronsard with Joachim du Bellay, Antoine de Baïf, Jodelle, Pontus de Tyard, Dorat, and Rémi Belleau. These united in a close league to impose a classical form on French language and literature. Basing their work on Greek and Latin poetry, and adding to that Petrarchan poetry, they established the sonnet, the ode and the alexandrine in France.

Plethon (plē'thon), **Georgius Gemistus.** See **Gemistus Plethon, Georgius.**

Poggio (pôd'jō), **Giovanni.** Cardinal; b. at Bologna, January 21, 1493; d. there, February 12, 1556. He traveled in Spain, then returned to Italy and married. Following the death of his wife he entered upon an ecclesiastical career (1528). He went to Rome, where he won the favor of Pope Clement VII and a high office in the Church. He served Pope Paul III as nuncio to Spain, was attached to the suite of Charles V, and later took part in the religious conferences at Worms (1540) and Ratisbon (1541). Continuing in the service of the pope, he was treasurer of the Camera and again went as nuncio to Spain. Named bishop of Tropea in Calabria, he never visited his see. Pope Julius III gave him the red hat (1551).

Poggio Bracciolini (brät-chō-lē'nē), **Gian Francesco.** Scholar and author; b. at Terranuova, in Tuscany, February 11, 1380; d. at Florence, October 30, 1459. In Florence, where he studied Latin and Greek, he became a protégé of the noted humanist Coluccio Salutati, and a friend of Niccolò Niccoli. In 1403 he left Florence for Rome, and became an apostolic secretary to Boniface IX, continuing in this post under John XXIII, with whom he went to the Council of Constance (1414) in an official capacity. Theological and canonical questions held no interest for Poggio however, who had never pretended to an inclination for the life of a religious, and, bored with the sessions, he began to investigate the nearby monastic libraries for manuscripts and books. He said he heard the voices of the ancients imploring him to free them from their prisons. Such searches became a passion with him. In the course of several in various places he discovered many ancient manuscripts or complete copies of works that had hitherto been available only in corrupt or incomplete form. His finds included a complete copy of the *Institutio oratorica* of Quintilian, which he copied in his own beautiful hand in thirty-two days since he could not get possession of the manuscript, *De re rustica* (an agricultural treatise) of Columella, *De rerum natura* of Lucretius, nearly a dozen orations of Cicero, and he was instrumental in finding the last twelve comedies of Plautus. In the same period he studied Hebrew, for which he was criticized by some on the ground that it was an injurious language. Discontented with his treatment at the court of Martin V, he accepted the invitation of Cardinal Henry Beaufort to go to England (1418). He spent four unhappy years there, but collected many witty stories about the English and their way of life with which he regaled his friends in after years. He found it astonishing that the most important men in England lived on large estates in the country rather than in cities. In 1423 he returned to Rome, resumed his post as apostolic secretary and took up his researches with increased fervor. He walked about Rome, studying the ruins—the temples, theaters, arches, and aqueducts—and longing for the grandeur of the past, for he considered his own age one of decline and barbarism. He made a collection of ancient inscriptions that is still extant. His *De varietate fortunae* (1431–1448), in four books, describes the ruins of Rome. Viewing them he discourses on man who, by a strong spirit, can meet the blows of adverse fortune and become great, yet who can be brought low again, even as Rome. His many works are written in a sparkling, easy style, studded with anecdotes, often hurling shafts of ridicule, free from the larding of citations from the classics that was so characteristic of many humanistic writers and from cant and pedantry. They include the dialogues *De avaritia* (1428–1429) in which he cites not only the evils of this vice but gives some advantages for it as well; *De nobilitate* (1440), with the Renaissance idea that true nobility arises from the spirit and not from birth; *De infelicitate principum* (1440), and *Contra hypocrita* (1447–1448), a bitter condemnation of hypocrisy. In many of his works he hurled his bitterest blows at the clergy. His *Liber facetiarum* (1438–1452) is a collection of anecdotes and tales, witty, satirical, often indecent, widely read and condemned by many for the spirit of irreligion and ridicule that was an outstanding feature. He also wrote a history of Florence from 1350 to the Peace of Lodi, and translated Xenophon's *Cyropaedia* from the Greek for Alfonso I, who paid him 500 pieces of gold for it. Most of Poggio's life was spent in Rome where, in spite of his pungent and frank writings and his disorderly personal life, he was attached to the papal court for about fifty years. For along with his true gift for writing, his mordant tongue and apt and vivid expression, he took great delight in the sensual pleasures of life, and was regarded by many as a pagan. He was about 56 when he at last married a virtuous and beautiful young girl of 18 who was devoted to him. He had engaged in many tilts with his fellow humanists, and his bite and irony, along with libels that he invented, were unrestricted in his attacks on his rivals and enemies, as when he took up the cudgels to defend his friend Niccolò Niccoli against the attacks of Filelfo. For in rivalry for place and popularity the humanists were unsurpassed. In 1453 he returned to Florence as chancellor and remained there to the end of his days.

Poldi Pezzoli Museum (pōl′dē pet-tsō′lē). An extremely rich collection of paintings and objets d'art given, with the building containing it, to the city of Milan under the will of Gian Giacomo Poldi Pezzoli di Albertone (1822–1879). To the original collections of paintings, tapestries, porcelain, armor, jewelry, sculpture, and so on, many additions have been made. The building suffered great damage in a bombardment of August 15, 1943. Frescoes and other immovables were destroyed, including much priceless paneling. Thanks to the heroic efforts and generosity of a number of people, the building was reconstructed, and was reopened in 1951.

Pole (pōl), **Reginald.** English Roman Catholic prelate, archbishop of Canterbury (1556–1558); b. at Stourton Castle, Staffordshire, England, March 3, 1500; d. at London, November 17, 1558. He was the son of Sir Richard Pole and Margaret, countess of Salisbury, niece of Edward IV. Brought up by his mother, he was educated at the Charterhouse school at Sheen and at Oxford, where he took his degree in 1515. Destined for the Church, he held many benefices. In 1521, at his request, Henry VIII, his kinsman, sent him to Italy to complete his education. At Padua he made friends with Bembo and other humanists, and in 1525 began to correspond with Erasmus. He visited Rome, and returned to England (1527) and continued his studies at the Carthusian monastery at Sheen. Henry, having begun divorce proceedings against Catherine of Aragon, sought the influence and support of Pole. To avoid having any role in the proceedings, Pole asked the king's permission to go to Paris to study theology. In 1529 he left England but was back in 1530. He refused to accept the archbishopric of York or the bishopric of Winchester as he would not deny his deep conviction that Henry was in the wrong. In January, 1532, he went back to Padua, where he remained some time, visited Venice, and studied theology. He wrote a treatise, *Pro Ecclesiasticae Unitatis Defensione,* as an answer to Henry's questions: whether marriage with a deceased brother's wife was permissible; and whether papal supremacy was of divine origin. In it he upheld the Church and criticized Henry's divorce proceedings. Pope Paul III called him to Rome (1536) and, against Pole's will and his judgment (for he knew it would enrage Henry, deprive him of all influence with Henry, and possibly endanger his family), the pope created him cardinal (December 22, 1536), though he was not a priest. The king was enraged. He caused a bill of attainder to be passed against Pole and set a price on his head. His mother was thrown into the Tower and beheaded; his brother, Henry, also lost his head for the implied treason of discussing the matter with Reginald. Reginald made several attempts to obtain the intervention of Francis I of France and Charles V of the Holy Roman Empire, but was not successful. His own life was in danger. As he traveled through Europe in an effort to return to England, he was made aware that his presence was not welcome, especially in France, which did not wish to become involved in Henry's quarrel with him. At Rome he had been one of a group, including Cardinal Gasparo Contarini, Vittoria Colonna, Juan de Valdés, and others, who sought reform in the Church, and in 1545 he was a legate-president of the Council of Trent. Henry died (1547) and Pole hoped that England could be reclaimed for the Church, but it was not until the accession of Mary Tudor that he could safely start back to England. On the death of Edward VI (1553) he was sent to England as papal legate to assist the Queen. Pole, who was only in deacon's orders, desired to marry her, and she for a time favored the project, but it was finally abandoned and she married Philip II of Spain. After the burning of Thomas Cranmer (archbishop of Canterbury who had supported Henry VIII in his divorce), Pole was ordained priest, and on March 22, 1556, was consecrated archbishop of Canterbury. His legation as papal ambassador to England was canceled by Pope Paul IV, largely because of his refusal to burn heretics indiscriminately, although he had been tireless in his attempts to reestablish the Church in England and was the queen's chief adviser in that field. His death occurred on the same day as that of the queen.

Pole, William de la. [Titles, 4th Earl and 1st Duke of **Suffolk.**] English politician; executed 1450. He was a prominent soldier under Henry V, and in 1428 commanded the English armies in France. Because of his position as a leading adviser to the king, his enemies sought constantly for a way to depose him. He was accused of crimes against the state, and sentenced by the House of Commons to five years' exile; the ship carrying him into banishment was stopped by his enemies and he was beheaded.

Polenta (pō-len′tä), **Guido della.** Member of a powerful family of Ravenna, whose members ruled the city for a century and a half. He became lord of Ravenna in 1316, and is famous in literary history for having given asylum to Dante.

Polenton (po-len-tôn′), **Sicco.** Writer; b. at Levico in Valsugana, c1376; d. at Padua, 1447. He studied at the University of Padua and became a notary. He was in the chancellery of the Carrara, lords of Padua, until the city fell to the Venetians, after which (1411–1430) he worked for the republic of Venice. His writings include commentaries on Cicero, a comedy called *Catinia,* some moral and didactic works, saints' lives, a *Dialogue on Christian Confession,* and a collection, *Exemplorum,* on the model of the 1st century Roman rhetorician and historian Valerius Maximus. His great works are eighteen books of *Scriptores illustres latinae linguae,* an early attempt at a literary history of Latin. He also

Polidoro da Caravaggio
Studies for a figure of the Baptist
The British Museum, London

left some letters that are useful for the information they contain of the leading humanists of his time.

Polidoro Caldara da Caravaggio (pō-lē-dō'rō käl-dä'rä dä kä-rä-väd'jō). Painter; b. at Caravaggio (Bergamo), between 1495 and 1500; d. at Messina, 1546. He was a follower of Raphael and was noted for his imitation, in chiaroscuro and graffiti, of antique bas-reliefs. When he was 18 he worked as an assistant of Giovanni da Udine frescoing Raphael's *Loggie* in the Vatican. In association with a contemporary, Maturino da Firenze, he decorated the façades of a number of houses and palaces at Rome, ornamenting them with friezes of mythological and historical scenes, trophies, and allegories. Most of these decorations have weathered away but some of the legends of ancient Rome that he painted on the Palazzo Ricci remain. The collaborators also worked in the Church of S. Silvestro al Quirinale. After the sack of Rome (1527) he went to Messina where, away from the great examples of Rome, his art declined. Of his years in Messina is a *Way to Calvary*, National Museum, Naples.

Polidoro da Lanciano (dä län-chä'nō). Painter; d. at Venice, 1565. Originally from the Abruzzi, he worked at Venice from 1514 until his death. A signed and dated (1545) *Descent of the Holy Spirit*, Accademia, Venice, indicates some influence of Titian and the school of Bonifacio Veronese. He was also influenced by Pordenone and Paolo Veronese. A great number of works are attributed to him, some on questionable grounds. Favorite subjects were the *Holy Family* and the *Madonna*, often in a landscape. Examples of these are at Bergamo, Florence (Pitti Palace), Lucca, Turin (Albertina), Venice (Accademia, S. Maria della Salute), Bonn, Budapest, Cambridge (England), Cassel, Dresden, Edinburgh, Glasgow, Nantes, Paris, Baltimore (Walters Art Gallery), and Cambridge, Massachusetts. Among a number of works in other collections is a *Portrait of Isabella d'Este*, Isabella Stewart Gardner Museum, Boston.

Politian (pọ-lish'ạn). See **Poliziano, Angelo.**

Poliziano (pō-lēt-syä'nō), **Angelo.** [Original name, **Angiolo Ambrogini;** Latin, **Angelus Politianus;** English, **Politian.**] Florentine poet and humanist; b. at Montepulciano, July 14, 1454; d. at Florence, September 24, 1494. The Italian name by which he is known, with its Latin and English variants, comes from the Latin name of his birthplace, Mons Politianus. (The house where it is supposed that he was born still stands at Montepulciano, at No. 1, Via Poliziano.) The son of an impoverished family, he went to Florence at the age of ten and began his studies in Latin, Greek, and philosophy under Cristoforo Landino, Argyropoulos, Callistus Andronicus and Marsilio Ficino. He mastered Latin and Greek, and from youth composed Latin poems and Greek epigrams. Before he was 20 he had published Latin letters, edited Catullus, and translated the second, third, fourth, and fifth books of the *Iliad* into Latin verse. (The first book had been translated into verse earlier. For reasons now unknown he never finished his contemplated complete translation.) This last achievement won him great renown and the epithet *Homericus juvenis*. Lorenzo de' Medici, to whom it was dedicated, began to encourage him and took him (1473) into his own household as a tutor to his sons. After some years, Lorenzo's wife Clarice, apparently disapproving of the influence he had on her sons, caused his removal from the household (1479). He went to Mantua and there, in the suite of Cardinal Gonzaga, composed an early Italian secular play, his *Orfeo* (1480). This work, which he wrote in two days, was modeled on the religious dramas known as *sacre rappresentazioni*, but with a classical rather than a religious subject. Like the earlier plays, it has no dramatic unity, but contains passages of great lyric beauty. The same year he was restored at least to Lorenzo's favor, and resumed his duties as teacher to his sons, although he never again became an intimate member of the household. In the year of his return to Florence he began his lectures on Latin and Greek literature at the University, work that he continued until 1490.

Poliziano was a prodigious worker. He complained that anyone and everyone who wanted a verse, a nosegay of rhyme, an epigram, greeting, or memorial, applied to him. In addition to his lectures he translated Epictetus, Herodian, Hippocrates, Galen, some of Plutarch, Plato's *Charmides*, and the *Pandects* of Justinian, first correcting the texts, wrote philosophical studies, and published notes on his courses on Ovid, Suetonius, Statius, Quintilian, and others. His lectures and commentaries on ancient literature made him the outstanding literary critic of the Quattrocento in the judgment of contemporary scholars. Above all he was a poet of great productivity and talent. He wrote Latin prose and poetry as if it were a living language. His work was not, as that of many of the earlier humanists had been, a mere imitation of form. It was imbued with his own spirit and genius. For his lectures on Vergil and Homer he wrote four Latin poetic introductions, which he later grouped together under the name *Sylvae*. *Manto*, the first of these, is named for the mythological seeress of Mantua, and is a long prophesy on her part and an analysis on Poliziano's of Vergil's career. *Rusticus* introduces Vergil's *Georgics*. As the *Georgics* constitute a kind of horticultural treatise, so the *Rusticus* is a calendar of the Tuscan peasant's year—the rounds he follows to win nature's harvest and the festivities with which he celebrates its reaping. *Ambra* is the introduction to Homer, and *Nutricia* (on Poetry, the foster mother), also an introduction to Homer, is a history of poetry, with accounts of legendary and historical poets (up to Lorenzo de' Medici), and an analysis and exhaltation of the blessings poetry bestows on mankind. United in these four works are Poliziano's great scholarship, classical learning, and poetic genius. He was the author of a number of sparkling epigrams in Latin and Greek addressed to various people and on a number of topics. His poems in Latin and Greek breathe his own spirit, but it is in his Italian lyrics that his poetic genius and inspiration are forever crystallized. Many of these were written for his patron Lorenzo. They abound in classical allusion but are free of pedantry; they simply and skillfully sing. The poems include odes, a few elegies, *rispetti*, and ballate. The ode on the death of Lorenzo, evidencing in moving accents his anguish at the loss, was set to music by Lorenzo's organist and composer, Heinrich Isaac. An incomplete epic, *Stanze per la giostra*, was written to commemorate the tournament given in 1475 by Giuliano de' Medici in honor of Simonetta Cattaneo. It begins with Cupid's capture of Giuliano by giving him a glimpse of the fair Simonetta. Giuliano is immediately lost in love. Cupid returns to Cyprus to report on his success to his mother. Here Poliziano permits himself to describe the palace of Venus, with further descriptions of the bas-reliefs that adorn it and the stories they tell, as well as the gardens and woodlands of the goddess of love. In the course of so doing Poliziano fuses classical learning and allusion with the Renaissance worship of beauty, and at the same time presents a model of Tuscan style. It has been suggested that the description of the realm of Venus in Poliziano furnished the subject matter of two of Botticelli's best known paintings, *Spring* and the *Birth of Venus*. (Giuliano was killed in the Pazzi conspiracy, 1478, and Poliziano never finished the epic.)

Poliziano was a rare success as a teacher. He has been described as unusually unimpressive in appearance, but once he began to speak his audiences were spellbound by his melodious voice, his enthusiasm, and his wide learning and brilliant control of it. Scholars came from all over Italy and Europe to attend his lectures. Among them were the German Reuchlin and the Englishmen Grocyn and Linacre, who became ambassadors and exponents of Florentine culture in their homelands. His fame spread throughout Europe. He corresponded on terms of familiarity with the great and near great of his age. His letters are masterpieces of style and brilliant examples of the art of letter writing. His *Miscellanea* (1489), a collection on literary and philological matters, is supposedly a record of conversations he had with Lorenzo and other members of his circle. His love lyrics have won a place for him in world literature as a poet, but it should not be forgotten that his great scholarship and his ability to communicate it were of vast influence in the spread of classical learning throughout Europe in his own day and in the days following him. With Poliziano Renaissance poetry, scholarship and spirit are expressed with exquisite taste and style. His life, which was devoted to a worship and expression of beauty and the tranquil joys of nature, and was colored by reflections on the glory and grace of the ancient Golden Age, ended in the clamor of Savonarola's denunciations of all that he stood for—as a scholar, a poet, and a man.

Pollaiuolo (pōl-lä-ywō'lō), **Antonio.** [**Antonio di Jacopo Benci**, called **Antonio del Pollaiuolo.**] Goldsmith, painter, and sculptor; b. at Florence between 1426 and 1433; d. at Rome, 1498. Son of a prominent Florentine goldsmith, he was trained in that art, practiced all its techniques, and with his brother Piero and others had one of the most flourishing workshops at Florence. In 1473 he was listed as a goldsmith and painter in the Company of St. Luke at Florence. The earliest example of his work that has survived is the silver base of a cross, begun in 1457, now in the Cathedral Museum, Florence. The decoration of the base consists of reliefs with scenes from the life of John the Baptist. (Vasari writes that many of his goldsmith's works were melted down when the city needed money in times of war.) Throughout his life, Antonio's closest collaborator was his brother Piero (b. at Florence, 1443; d. at Rome, 1496). Bound by ties of affection and interest they worked so closely together that it is difficult to separate and assign their works, since no signed painting by Antonio exists. However, in consideration of certain known works of Piero and of a number of drawings by Antonio, the best undifferentiated Pollaiuolo paintings are unhesitatingly assigned to Antonio, often with the proviso that Piero may have made some contribution to the finished work. One of the greatest of the 15th-century Florentine masters in the development of the figure arts, Antonio's special quality, displayed in his signed engraving, *Battle of the Ten Nudes*, Uffizi, is a marked preoccupation with violent movement and an ability to express it in vibrant, forceful line. Like Andrea del Castagno, of whom he was a follower, he employed a vigorous and powerful line rather than relief as an abstraction of form, and accentuated his line to the point of making it his principal means of expressing energy and the structure of forms. In the *Battle of the Ten Nudes* every muscle of the figures bulges and strains as the five pairs of combatants wage their desperate duels. The impression of violent effort and movement is almost tangible and is achieved almost entirely by a powerful line. His masterpiece, *Martyrdom of St. Sebastian*, National Gallery, London, with its six archers tensed in readying their bows, reveals his mastery of anatomy, the art of foreshortening, and of rendering motion and tension. His scientific interest in movement and how it is achieved made him one of the first to study anatomy by dissection. The work is also notable for its landscape with the Arno river and a tiny city on its banks representing Florence. The two works cited place Antonio between Donatello and Castagno, on the one hand, both of whom were influences on his development and forerunners in their concern with naturalism and motion, and Botticelli, who employed a sensitive, flexible line as an abstraction of form in the service of an artistic vision of a fundamentally symbolic character, on the other. For Antonio action was superbly exalted for its own sake. Spiritual expression and subtlety had small place in his scientific approach to his art. Other works by Antonio include *David*, Berlin, and *Hercules and Antaeus* and *Hercules and the Hydra* (c1460), Uffizi, both of the two last eminently suited to his love of portraying fierce struggle. The two last are small versions of larger works, now lost, painted for the Medici; the small paintings disappeared in 1944 and were recovered about twenty years later at San Francisco. A fresco of *Dancing Nudes*, Torre del Gallo, Florence, in the wild abandon of the figures provides a touch of humor otherwise absent in his work. Other works are the wind-driven *Apollo and Daphne*, National Gallery, London, and *Hercules and Nessus* (*Rape of Deianeira*), Yale University, New Haven. The subjects by themselves indicate his preoccupation with violent action. In addition to painting he made designs for gold and silver embroideries, as those in the Cathedral Museum at Florence on scenes from the life of John the Baptist, and designs for the engraver, Maso Finiguerra. As a sculptor he executed a bronze group of *Hercules and Antaeus*, with the same fluid, animated rhythms as the small painting in the Uffizi, a terra-cotta *Bust of a Young Warrior*, and a marble *Bust of a Man*, all in the Bargello, Florence. His last great works, executed with his brother to his designs, were the bronze tombs of Sixtus IV, signed and dated 1493, with its realistic portrait of the aged pope and ornamental reliefs, and the tomb of Innocent VIII (1492–1498), both in the Vatican. Works executed by the brothers in collaboration include SS. *Eustace, James and Vincent* (1467), Uffizi, on Antonio's design, a fresco of *St. Jerome* in the Church of S. Domenico, Pistoia, and *Tobias and the Archangel*, Turin. A revealing *Portrait of Gian Galeazzo Sforza* (c1471) is attributed to Antonio by some critics, to Piero by others. *Providence* (1470), Uffizi, one of six Virtues intended to ornament chair backs, was painted by Piero on a design by Antonio.

ANTONIO POLLAIUOLO
Battle of the Ten Nudes
Courtesy of the Pennsylvania Academy of the Fine Arts, Philadelphia

fat, fāte, fär, fâll, ȧsk, fãre; net, mē, hėr; pin, pīne; not, nōte, möve, nôr; up, lūte, pu̇ll; oi, oil; ou, out; (lightened) ẹ̄lect, agọ̄ny, ụ̄nite; (obscured) errạnt, ardẹnt, actọr; ch, chip; g, go; th,

(Botticelli painted one of these, *Fortitude*, Uffizi; and others were painted in Antonio's workshop.) An altarpiece, *Coronation of the Virgin with Saints*, Church of S. Agostino, S. Gimignano, is signed and dated (1483) by Piero alone. An *Annunciation*, Berlin, with a view of Florence showing the dome and campanile of the cathedral, is perhaps Piero's most genuinely original work, the one least dependent on his far greater brother. A superb draftsman, whose control of line is especially evident in a group of his drawings in the Uffizi, in his scientific study of anatomy and movement Antonio was the forerunner of, and of deep influence on, such great masters of the High Renaissance as Leonardo and Michelangelo.

Pollaiuolo, Piero. See **Pollaiuolo, Antonio.**

Pollaiuolo, Simone. See **Cronaca, il.**

Polo (pō′lō), **Marco.** Venetian traveler; b. at Venice, c1254; d. there, c1324. His father and uncle left Constantinople for the Crimea on a commercial enterprise in 1260. Their business eventually brought them to Bukhara, where they fell in with some envoys of Kublai Khan. They were persuaded to accompany the envoys to Kublai, whom they found either at Cambaluc (Peiping) or at Shangtu, north of the Great Wall. Kublai received them well, and sent them as his envoys to the pope with a request for 100 educated men to instruct his subjects in Christianity and in the liberal arts. The brothers arrived at Acre in 1269. They obtained from Gregory X, who had just been elected, two Dominicans who turned back at an early stage of the return journey. The brothers left Acre on the journey in 1271, accompanied by Marco, then 17 years of age. They traveled through Khurasan, up the Oxus to the Pamir, by Kashgar, Yarkand, and Khotan, to Lob Nor, and across the great desert of Gobi to Tangut, thence to Shangtu, where they found Khublai Khan in 1275. They were kindly received, and retained in the public service. Marco rose rapidly in the emperor's favor, and was employed in important missions in various parts of the empire. With his father and uncle, Marco left China in 1292, as escorts of a Mongol bride for the Khan of Persia, and after many adventures reached Venice by way of Sumatra, India, and Persia in 1295. In 1298 Marco was taken prisoner in the battle of Curzola between the Venetians and the Genoese. He was detained for a year at Genoa. Here he dictated, in French, to a fellow captive, Rusticiano of Pisa, an account of his adventures, which ultimately obtained a wide popularity, inasmuch as his report was virtually the only source of material in Europe on central Asia. Much that is apparently fantastic traveler's tales appears in the account, but basically the book is factual.

Polyptych (pol′ip-tik). A combination of more than three panels or frames bearing pictures, carvings, or the like.

Pompeo di Anselmo (pōm-pā′ō dē än-sel′mō). Perugian painter; active in the second half of the 15th century and the beginning of the 16th century. He was a follower of Perugino. A *Holy Family* (1511), National Gallery of Umbria, Perugia, was executed in collaboration with Domenico Alfani to a cartoon supplied by Raphael.

Pomponazzi (pôm-pō-nät′tsē), **Pietro.** Philosopher; b. at Mantua, September 16, 1462; d. at Bologna, May 18, 1525. He studied at Padua and earned his doctorate in medicine (1487). He was professor of philosophy at Padua, went to Ferrara when the university at Padua was closed by war (1509), and from Ferrara went to Bologna (1512), where he remained the rest of his life. At this time, philosophy was considered as a branch of the physical sciences, which is the reason so many philosophers were physicians. The separation of philosophy and theology dates back to the founding of the medieval universities in the 12th and 13th centuries. Natural philosophy and dialectic were taught under the Arts Faculty, theology under the Theology Faculty. In the Italian universities of the Renaissance, natural philosophy continued to be central to the Arts Faculties, which also granted the medical degree. Theology was taught for the most part in special schools of the religious orders, or students went to Paris. Therefore the tradition of philosophy in Italy was strongly secular, and this was true also of Pomponazzi. In his chief work, *De immortalitate animae*, published in 1516, he states that there are no rational proofs of the immortality of the soul, that the basis for the belief in immortality rests on faith in the Bible and the teachings of the Church. For Pomponazzi, as for other philosophers of his age, man is the center of the universe. For him the fulfillment of man's ultimate aim is in this life, not in an afterworld. Thus, in his thinking, the reward of virtue is virtue itself, and the punishment of vice is vice itself. The genesis of his thoughts on immortality lies in Aristotle. His own work is an attempt to set right and to expound Aristotle's work, and to correct what he conceives to be misinterpretations of Aristotle by earlier commentators. As the Church, in the Lateran Council of 1513, had proclaimed the immortality of the soul (as distinct from resurrection of the body) as official dogma and condemned those who challenged it, Pomponazzi's work caused an immediate and violent reaction. His book was burned in Venice, and Pope Leo X commissioned a refutation. Pomponazzi defended himself by maintaining that he was a loyal son of the Church in all matters of faith, but held to his independence in matters of philosophical speculation. He endured fierce attacks for his independence. It was probably thanks to the influence of his former pupil, Pietro Bembo, that his daring was not punished by ecclesiastical prosecution. In his work *De incantatione*, as a scientific thinker he rejects magic, miracles, and demons, as being contrary to the immutable order of nature, yet recognizes, as a Christian, the power of the supernatural. His *De fato, libero arbitrio, . . .* , on fate, free will, and predestination, supports the Stoic concept of fate and predestination as divine forethought. This presents some difficulties for freedom of the will, difficulties that he could not satisfactorily resolve. Pomponazzi did not question Church doctrines as such, but in a philosophical and scientific spirit reexamined the bases on which some of the doctrines rested. A principal source of the doctrines was the work of Aristotle. This had been assimilated to Church doctrine, notably by St. Thomas Aquinas, and had achieved the force and weight of dogma. Aristotle was also the source of many of Pomponazzi's ideas, although Stoic influence on his thought is also evident. His importance rests in the independence he maintained as a thinker and in conclusions that preserved the traditional separation of science and theology of the universities. He opposed the Averroist interpretation of Aristotle that denied the importance of the individual mind. His restudying of Aristotle and the conclusions he drew made possible an approach to nature and the world that led to the development of modern science.

Ponce de León (pōn′thā dā lā-ôn′), **Juan.** Spanish explorer, noted for his discovery of Florida while supposedly searching for the legendary fountain of youth; b. at San Servos, Campos, Spain, c1460; d. in Cuba, 1521. He is thought to have accompanied Columbus on his second voyage; took part in the conquest of Higuay (eastern Hispaniola); led an expedition to Puerto Rico where he found gold, and later an expedition for the conquest of Puerto Rico of which he was made governor. Ferdinand II of Aragon sent him on an expedition to discover the island of Bimini where there was supposed to be a spring whose waters held the power of rejuvenation. In the course of this expedition he discovered Florida and sailed round the peninsula from the Indian River Inlet to approximately Charlotte Harbor. Again he was sent to find the magic fountain, but was wounded in battle against the Indians in Florida, and taken to Cuba where he died.

Ponce de León, Luis. Spanish scholar, theologian, and poet; b. at Belmonte, Spain, 1528; d. 1591. A professor of theology and sacred literature at the University of Salamanca, he was examined by the Inquisition and imprisoned, but finally set free.

Ponsonby (pun′sọn-bi), **William.** English publisher; b. c1546; d. before September, 1604. He is remembered for his connection with Edmund Spenser. He published John Alday's *Praise and Dispraise of Women* (1579). In 1590 he published Spenser's *Faerie Queen* (books I–III; books IV–VI, 1596), and also his *Complaints* (1591), *Amoretti* (1595), and *Colin Clout's Come Home Again* (1595), and several other volumes of Spenser's poetry.

Pontano (pōn-tä′nō), **Giovanni.** [Latin, **Jovianus Pontanus.**] Humanist, poet and diplomat; b. at Cerreto, May 7, probably in 1426; d. at Naples, 1503. He was educated at Perugia. He lost his father and most of his inheritance in the civil strife that wracked Umbria, turned over what remained of his legacy to his sisters, and set out to make his own fortune. In this he was eminently successful. He met Alfonso I and went with him to Naples (1447). There Panormita, the celebrated humanist and one of Alfonso's secretaries, became his friend and patron. He studied Greek under George of Trebizond and soon became part of the group of poets, writers, historians, and other humanists at the court. The members called themselves the Neapolitan Academy (although it was not a formal organization), Latinized their names, and devoted themselves to the study and discussion of Latin literature. Pontano ultimately became its acknowledged leader. Under him a flourishing school of Neapolitan poets was established. As secretary, tutor to the royal children, and ambassador, he served three kings of Naples. (His capacity as a public official was recognized at Perugia, where he was offered the chancellorship, 1461, but he declined the office.) His duties as secretary and ambassador involved the preparation of documents on public matters. These reflect his mastery of the Latin style, as well as his keen political sense, his decision and swiftness in action, and his awareness of the advantage of surprise in dealing with the enemies of his sovereign. Ferrante, illegitimate son and acknowledged heir of Alfonso, was compelled to fight the Angevins and subdue rebellious barons to keep his throne following the death of Alfonso. Pontano was loyal to him throughout, and described the wars in his *De bello neapolitano*. He became a trusted adviser of Ferrante, a cruel and suspicious king, and became his chancellor. In this exalted and dangerous post (his predecessor had fallen a victim to the king's suspicious nature), he maintained his independence and integrity. Ferrante was succeeded by his son the duke of Calabria, who had been Pontano's pupil. Before the oncoming French he abdicated in favor of his son Ferdinand II. The latter went into exile as Charles VIII of France entered Naples (1495), and Pontano swore allegiance to the French conqueror. Charles could not maintain himself in Naples and withdrew. Pontano spent his last years in political obscurity.

In spite of his preoccupation with public affairs, Pontano produced a large body of writing in Latin prose and verse. He was perhaps along with Poliziano one of the few humanists who wrote Latin poetry as if Latin were his native language. In his verse appears his enchantment with the brilliant Neapolitan landscape and its rich endowment of classical allusion. A typical example is an eclogue, *Lepidina*, in which he describes a wedding procession with its attendant nymphs, dryads, oreads and so on, adapted from classical literature and bathed with the beauty of the Neapolitan atmosphere. Among his best poems are those in *De amore coniugali*, a collection on the joys, and sometimes sorrows, of an affectionate family life. A moving elegy mourns the death of his 13-year-old daughter Lucia. Other poems celebrate his mother and his wife, among the many that deal with the charms of an unusually happy personal life. On the other hand, he did not hesitate to make ribald fun of his own family in his dialogue, *Antonius*, which also included wittily unkind remarks on a number of Italian figures, beliefs, and customs. He wrote an astrological work, *De rebus caelestibus*, in which he described the power of the stars and planets over human life. He later repented of his belief in astrology in the dialogue *Aegidius*, and in its place exalted free will. Other prose dialogues and treatises on a variety of topics, as *De fortitudine*, *De fortuna*, and so on, show him to have been an original and vigorous thinker, and a leading humanist moral philosopher. He recognized the defects of his own age, and uses the events and instances (as the list of superstitions prevalent among the Neapolitans) of his own time to illustrate his theses.

Pontano, Lodovico. Jurisconsult; b. at Spoleto, 1409; d. at Basel, 1439. He studied at Bologna and taught civil law at Siena. Made protonotary by Pope Eugenius IV, he was a delegate of Alfonso of Aragon to the Council of Basel, and died of the plague while there. He left commentaries on the Pandects of Justinian and on the Justinian Code.

Pontormo (pōn-tôr′mō), **Jacopo.** [Original name, **Jacopo Carucci da Pontormo.**] Painter; b. at Pontorme (Empoli), 1494; d. at Florence, 1556. His father is known to have been a Florentine painter but no works of his are identifiable. His parents died while he was still young, and in 1506 he went to Florence and worked briefly under Leonardo da Vinci. Subsequently he worked with Piero di Cosimo, Mariotto Albertinelli, and Andrea del Sarto. He fused the influences of his masters into a restless, tormented, personal style. It was a style marked at times by exaggerations of size, symmetry, or composition, by unexplained or unlikely figures or motifs. In the *Visitation* (1516), SS. Annunziata, Florence, a naked child sits on a step of the porch where St. Elizabeth and the Virgin

JACOPO PONTORMO
Head of a Youth
Study for the head of the youth who supports the legs of Christ in the *Entombment*,
Capponi Chapel, S. Felicita, Florence
Gabinetto Disegni e Stampe degli Uffizi   Foto Soprintendenza

Jacopo Pontormo
Virgin
Study for the Virgin in the fresco, *Annunciation,* in the Capponi Chapel,
S. Felicita, Florence
Gabinetto Disegni e Stampe degli Uffizi Foto Soprintendenza

are meeting, nonchalantly scratching his outstretched leg; willowy statues on unsteady pedestals ornament his *Joseph in Egypt*, a scene painted (c1518) as decoration for the marriage chamber of Pier Francesco Borgherini in the Palazzo Borgherini at Florence, and now in the National Gallery, London. (Granacci, Andrea del Sarto, and Bacchiacca also painted decorations for this celebrated room.) Frequently absent in Pontormo is a sense of depth achieved by the perspectives that painters of the 15th century worked so hard to perfect; rather than penetrating toward a horizon, the impression in Pontormo's works is of rising toward an unknown sphere. His first independent work was the painting of *Faith* and *Charity* and the coat of arms of Leo X in the portico of SS. Annunziata (c1513). The story is that he made preparatory drawings in secret. When he showed them to Andrea del Sarto the latter barred him from his studio thereafter out of jealousy. Although he did not remain long with Andrea (he did not remain with anyone long), it was perhaps under him that he perfected his ability to create solid forms and natural gestures. In 1514 he worked on the decoration of the papal apartments in S. Maria Novella. Of 1518 is the Pucci altarpiece in S. Michele Visdomini, *Holy Family with SS. John the Evangelist, James, Francis and Infant St. John*, that Vasari called his most beautiful work. The unquiet atmosphere of this early mannerist painting is heightened by restless rhythms and the intense expressions of the figures. For the Medici villa at Poggio a Caiano he painted (1520–1521) a masterpiece of lyrical fancy, a delicate, gay, and abandoned pastoral scene, known since the time of Vasari as part of the myth of Vertumnus and Pomona. In the subtly painted fresco Pontormo displayed a relaxed charm rare in his surviving works. (Frescoes he painted for the Medici villas at Careggi and Castello have perished.) Ever restless and searching, he found a satisfying means of expressing profound religious feeling in the angularity and harsh realism of Dürer. The series of frescoes on the Passion (1522–1527) in the cloister of the Certosa del Galluzzo reflect the Dürer influence. The *Supper at Emmaus*, Uffizi, was painted at the same time and is closest to Dürer in its strongly individualized figures and dramatic tension. About this same period he worked (1526–1528) in the Capponi Chapel in S. Felicita at Florence and created one of his masterpieces, *Entombment*. The painting is suffused with a rosy haze and has an extra-terrestrial quality that makes it a stunning example of his developed mannerist style; it also exemplifies the sense of ascension rather than penetration mentioned earlier. Another lovely work in the same chapel is an *Annunciation*. Both are notable for their vibrant and delicate colors, and for the degree to which the painter ignores the laws of perspective and gravity, and the demands of naturalism, and recreates an intense spiritual experience. After 1530 Pontormo was deeply influenced by Michelangelo, as appears in his *St. Anthony Abbott*, Uffizi, and other works. *Venus and Cupid*, Accademia, Florence, is on a cartoon by Michelangelo. In the last years of his life (1546–1556) he painted a series of frescoes in the choir of S. Lorenzo which have since perished. In addition to his paintings on religious subjects, Pontormo left a number of sensitive portraits. Among these is an idealized portrait of Cosimo de' Medici the Elder (d. 1464), and other Medici portraits, as of Duke Alessandro, Johnson Collection, Philadelphia, Cosimo I as a youth, Medici-Riccardi Palace, Florence, and one of Cosimo I's mother, Maria Salviati, Uffizi. A number of other portraits are in museums and private collections in Europe and at Baltimore, Dayton, Ohio, and the National Gallery, Washington.

The support of Pontormo's intense, often tormented artistic vision was always the reality of his superb draftsmanship. In a period that knew a number of great draftsmen, his skill was unsurpassed. A fine collection of his drawings and preparatory studies is in the Uffizi. He was a solitary, secretive person (he walled up the chapel where he was painting the *Entombment* so that none could intrude as he developed his spiritual revelation), one who was ever seeking new solutions, and who frequently destroyed his work and redid it, convinced that he had found a better way. He had a morbid fear of madness and death, great need of solitude, and finally lived alone in near squalor in a house that he entered by means of a ladder, pulling it up after him. Besides his work, his great preoccupation in his later years was with his health. His bizarre temperament is most clearly revealed in a *Diario* he kept (1555–1556) that records his concern with his art, health, food, the weather and occasional reference to friends. Bronzino was his pupil and friend but there were times when he did not even see him. Another pupil was Giovanni Battista Naldini, who assisted him from 1549 until Pontormo's death. Pontormo's quality as an artist of deep religious feeling and searching temperament is preserved in a number of subtle, flickering, unquiet, highly personal paintings and frescoes. The greatest number of his surviving works is in and about Florence, in the Uffizi, Pitti, in palaces and churches; others are at Dublin, Leningrad, Munich, Louvre, Paris, San Francisco, National Gallery, Washington, and elsewhere.

Popham (pop'ạm), Sir **John.** English jurist, lord chief justice of England; b. in Somerset, 1531; d. June 10, 1607. He was presiding justice at the trials of Sir Walter Raleigh for conspiracy (1603) and of Guy Fawkes for attempted assassination of the king (1606).

Poppi (pôp'pē), **il.** [**Francesco Morandini,** known as **il Poppi.**] Painter; b. at Poppi, 1544; d. at Florence, 1597. A mannerist, he was a pupil of Vasari and became painter to the Medici court and to the noble families of Florence. His better works, less exaggeratedly mannerist, are characterized by harmonious rhythms and a delicate chiaroscuro derived to some extent from Andrea del Sarto. Among them is the vault of the *studiolo* of Francesco I in the Palazzo Vecchio at Florence. Other works include *The Three Graces*, Uffizi, *Crucifixion* (1575), Church of S. Salvi, Florence, and *Christ Driving the Money-changers from the Temple*, Vienna.

Porcari (pôr-kä'rē), **Stefano.** Revolutionary; hanged at Rome, January 9, 1453. He was of an ancient Roman family, was well-read in classical literature, an eloquent orator, and in love with the idea of the ancient Roman republic. In 1427 and 1428 he was captain of the people of Florence, and on good terms with such scholars as Gianozzo Manetti and Poggio Bracciolini. He idealized Florence as a republic. An able administrator, he served Eugenius IV as captain of Bologna (1433), of Siena (1434) and of Orvieto (1435). He performed any public duties he undertook ably. Nicholas V, aware that Porcari had become the center of a restless group that wanted to restore the republic in Rome, thought to win him over by generosity and granted him many benefits. His generosity failed to win Porcari from his schemes. Nicholas exiled him to Bologna, but granted him a pension. Porcari escaped (1452) in disguise from Bologna, returned to Rome and gathered his conspirators together. Cardinal Bessarion, at that time papal legate in Bologna, warned the pope of Porcari's absence. Porcari's plan was to set fire to the papal palace, seize and, if necessary, kill the pope and the cardinals during High Mass, proclaim freedom in Rome and himself tribune of the people. The plot, haphazardly worked out, was discovered. Porcari tried to flee, was captured, confessed, and was hanged. The Roman populace made no move to aid their self-styled liberator. Perhaps Porcari thought of himself as a second Brutus. Like Brutus, he has had his admirers who regarded him as a republican and a patriot. To others he has seemed a visionary steeped in classical literature, with no well-formed plan of action, and driven by the *ignis fatuus* of regaining a republic that in reality had never existed.

Porcia (pôr-chē'ä), **Iacopo di.** Humanist; b. 1462; d. 1538. Descendant of a noble family of Friuli, he was the author of several historical works and of works on the art of war.

Pordenone (pôr-dā-nō'nā), **Giovanni Antonio de'.** [Original name, **Giovanni Antonio de' Sacchis.**] Painter; b. at Pordenone, c1484; d. at Ferrara, 1539. He was trained in the Friuli in the atmosphere of such provincial painters as Domenico and Gianfrancesco da Tolmezzo, and later became a follower of Giovanni Bellini and Giorgione, without, according to some critics, ever losing traces of his provincial origins. Works before 1520, as *Madonna Enthroned* (1511), Accademia, Venice, are in the 15th-century manner of Bellini. In 1516 he probably made his first trip to Rome and soon afterwards the influence of Michelangelo and Raphael begins to appear in his work. His natural tendency was toward the grandiose and dramatic. His dramatic treatment of light, portrayal of movement, and rich color are evident in a number of frescoes in and about Pordenone and Udine. These include his earliest signed work, a fresco of *St. Michael between Valerian and St. John the Baptist* (1506), Church of S. Stefano, and a *Nativity* (1527) Church of S. Maria dei Battuti, Valeriano (Udine), frescoes in the Church of S. Odorico (1514), Villanova, and *St. Thomas Receiving the Virgin's Girdle* (1516) on the ceiling of the

GIOVANNI ANTONIO DE' PORDENONE
Death of St. Peter Martyr
Gabinetto Disegni e Stampe degli Uffizi Foto Soprintendenza

Church of S. Lorenzo at Rorai Grande (Udine). In 1520 he executed fresco decorations in the Malchiostro Chapel in the cathedral at Treviso. The painting in the cupola, *Eternal Father Blessing*, was destroyed in 1944. (Frescoes at Collalto were destroyed in the First World War.) In the same year he began the fresco decoration in the cathedral at Cremona with scenes of the Passion. In these grandiose and dramatic scenes he explored to the full the possibilities of foreshortening and the portrayal of motion. In the scene *Nailing to the Cross* (1521) the illusion is heightened: an arm of one of the figures as well as part of the Cross extend beyond the edge of the frame enclosing the scene. Between 1530 and 1535 he was painting in the Church of S. Maria di Campagna, Piacenza. His painting, *God the Father*, in the dome, shows the influence of Correggio's *Christ in Glory* in the Church of S. Giovanni Evangelista, Parma. The illusion of looking at a scene that opens out of the dome, such as he painted on several occasions, derives also from Mantegna's painting in the Ducal Palace at Mantua. His masterpiece in panel painting is the altarpiece, *S. Lorenzo Giustiniani and Other Saints* (1532), Accademia, Venice. According to Vasari he was at Genoa briefly in 1532 at the request of Andrea Doria, and was also at Venice in the same year. From 1535 to 1538 he was active at Venice where the frescoes he then executed have largely disappeared. His last work *Annunciation* (1537), is in the Church of S. Maria degli Angioli, Murano. In 1508 he had been at Ferrara with Pellegrino da S. Daniele. In his later years he was repeatedly invited to return. Early in 1539 he went there to work for Ercole II, but died almost at once. Rich color, strong contrasts of light and shade, illusionism, and sweeping, dramatic movement are among the qualities of his painting. Many of his surviving works are in churches of the Friuli; others are at Bergamo, Florence (Uffizi and Pitti), Milan (Brera), Naples, Rome (Borghese), Amsterdam, Budapest, Dresden, Hampton Court and the National Gallery, London, Vienna, the Johnson Collection, Philadelphia, San Francisco, and Sarasota, Florida.

Porta (pōr′tä), **Antonio della.** See **Della Porta, Antonio.**

Porta, Costanzo. Musician; b. at Cremona, c1530; d. at Padua, May 26, 1601. He studied at Venice, where he may have been a fellow pupil of Claudio Merulo. He entered a Franciscan conventual order and served as choirmaster in a number of churches, including the Basilica of St. Anthony at Padua and the cathedral at Ravenna. His compositions included several books of madrigals, so popular in his day, but the majority of his work was sacred music. He was regarded as a master of counterpoint in his own time as well as by later musicians.

Porta, Giambattista della. Natural philosopher and writer of comedies; b. at Naples, c1540; d. there, 1615. He had traveled widely as a young man, and was an ardent student. Natural history and magic became his chief interests. For his estate at Naples he collected so many specimens that it became a kind of museum. As an amateur scientist he wrote Latin works on astronomy, refraction, distillation, mnemonics, and other subjects. He founded an academy at Naples devoted to unraveling the secrets of nature, and was a member of a similar academy at Rome. His physical experiments contributed to optics and the knowledge of light. His book on optics, *De refractione optices* . . . , deals with refraction, lenses, the anatomy of the eye, the nature of light, and the rainbow. He had some good ideas, but did not develop them as he was more interested in magic and alchemy than in scientific investigation. His best known work was *Magia naturalis* (*Natural Magic*), which is a mixture of magic and physics. It became very popular but was placed on the Index for its emphasis on magic. In addition to his scientific interests he was also a prolific writer of comedies, more than thirty, of which about half are extant, being known to have come from his pen. He adapted plots from Plautus, from the novelle, and from earlier comedies, fleshed them out with lively dialogue, and drew the plot lines firmly together.

Porta, Giovanni Giacomo della. See **Della Porta, Giovanni Giacomo.**

Porta, Guglielmo della. See **Della Porta, Guglielmo.**

Porta, Simone. See **Porzio, Simone.**

Portinari (pōr-tē-nä′rē), **Beatrice.** See **Beatrice Portinari.**

Porto (pōr′tō), **Luigi da.** Prose writer and gentleman; b. at Vicenza, 1486; d. 1529. He wrote novelle. In one of these he took Tommaso Guardati's tale of Mariotto and Gianozza, two lovers of Siena, as a basis and converted it into his one masterpiece. He changed the locale of his tale from Siena to Verona, changed the names of his unfortunate lovers to Romeo and Giulietta, and produced the novella from which, after further renderings, came Shakespeare's *Romeo and Juliet*.

Porzio (pōr′tsyō), **Camillo.** Historian; b. at Naples, 1526; d. 1580. He was the son of the philosopher Simone Porzio (1496–1554). He studied at Bologna and Pisa, then returned to his native city where he practiced law and managed his family's property. He was successful in both and acquired, in addition to the family estates, the fief of Centola. With his legal practice and his administrative duties he combined an active interest in literary studies, and was especially interested in history. His historical writings include *Congiura dei Baroni*, a lively and sometimes inaccurate account of the conspiracy of the barons against King Ferrante, modeled on Sallust; *Storia d'Italia*, a continuation of Giovio's history; and *Sommario delle più notabile cose, . . . di Napoli*, a short and unaffected account of some features of Naples.

Porzio, Simone. Philosopher and physician; b. at Naples, December, 1496; d. there, August 27, 1554. He spent much of his youth at Pisa and, between 1520 and 1525, taught logic and physics at the university there. He later taught at Naples and, after 1545, again at Pisa. He was a disciple of Pomponazzi, knew Greek, could read the philosophers in the original language, and came to doubt the authenticity of some manuscripts that purported to be Aristotelian. His chief work is *De humana mente disputatio* (Florence, 1551). Among other things, in this work he states his belief that the human soul is no different from the souls of animals or plants.

Possevino (pōs-sä-vē′nō), **Antonio.** Jesuit missionary and diplomat; b. at Mantua, July 12, 1533 or 1534; d. at Ferrara, February 26, 1611. He was for a number of years in the service of the Gonzaga at Mantua and then (1559) joined the Society of Jesus. His talent as a diplomat and a writer won for him many important missions for the Society. He worked against the Valdensians and Calvinists in the Piedmont (1560), against the Huguenots in France (1563–1572), and founded colleges and upheld the proceedings of the Council of Trent. In 1573, while at Rome, he was named secretary of the Society. Continuing his activities for his order, he secretly converted John III of Sweden (1579–1580), to Catholicism, without, however, winning over Protestant Sweden. In 1580 he went on a mission to Ivan the Terrible at Moscow and attempted to secure peace between Russia and Poland with an ambitious program that involved the support of both nations against the Turks, increased trade with Venice and Russia, and the unification of the Russian and Latin churches. The program could not be carried out, but a peace was secured (1582). Thereafter he spent a great deal of time in Poland supporting the policy of King Stephen Bathory and persuaded him to introduce the Society of Jesus into Poland. At length recalled to Italy, he lived most of the rest of his life at Padua, where he taught in the Jesuit college. An ardent and independent spirit, and an enthusiastic missionary, in 1595 he defended his order, which had been driven from France. His activities on behalf of the Counter-Reformation were especially important in keeping Poland Catholic. He left a number of works, including *Moscovia* (1586), a vivid description of his mission to Russia and interesting and valuable for its account of the Russia of that time; *Il Soldato Cristiano* (1569); *Atheismi Lutheri, Calvini,* and so on (1594); and a *Iudicium*, a treatise against the writings of Machiavelli and others.

Poynings (poi′ningz), Sir **Edward.** English soldier and administrator; b. 1459; d. 1521. He became a supporter of the Earl of Richmond and accompanied him to England when he returned (1485) to become Henry VII. He went to Ireland as deputy of the viceroy, and convened the parliament of Drogheda which passed Poynings' Law, the most important provisions of which were that all English laws "lately made" (which was construed to include all prior English laws) should be in force in Ireland, and that thereafter no parliament should sit in Ireland without the license of the king and his council, and that no act passed by such parliament should be effective unless affirmed by them. These acts are sometimes called the Statute of Drogheda. They were repealed in 1782.

Pragmatic Sanction of Bourges. Term applied to a system of limitations set, under Charles VII, to the spiritual power of the pope in France, in 1438. These laid the foundations of the so-called Gallican Church.

The limitations removed almost all papal influence in ecclesiastical appointments in France and, more damaging still, deprived the papal court of the revenues formerly drawn from France. Pope Pius II strove earnestly to remove this threat to papal power. He persuaded Louis XI, who was anxious at that point to improve relations with the Holy See, to abrogate the Pragmatic Sanction (1461). Louis later claimed he had done so only on condition that Pius II recognize the French claim to the kingdom of Naples. Since Pius II feared the French in Italy more than the Spanish, he refused to do this and supported Ferrante, illegitimate son of Alfonso V, in his struggle for the throne of Naples. The question of the Pragmatic Sanction was finally settled in 1516, when Francis I and Pope Leo X signed a Concordat abolishing it. By their Concordat, the king had the right to name certain ecclesiastics (bishops, abbots, priors), and the pope had the right to confirm these nominations and to name others.

Predella (prā-del′lä). In painting, a band projecting at the base of an altarpiece and serving as an ornamental step below the painting. It is often composed of three or five small rectangular panels, on each of which is depicted an episode or scene from the life of the subject of the painting.

Predis (prā′dēs), **Giovanni Ambrogio de′.** Milanese painter; b. at Milan, c1455; d. after 1508. With his brother Cristoforo, he worked at first as a miniaturist, but by 1482 was numbered among the painters working at the court of Ludovico il Moro. To this number Leonardo da Vinci was added, about 1482, and he joined Ambrogio, who at first helped him to find commissions and then learned from the great Florentine. It has long been thought that some of Ambrogio's better works had the best touches added to them by Leonardo. In 1483 Ambrogio, his brother Evangelista, and Leonardo had a contract from the Confraternity of the Conception to paint an altarpiece, the details of which were carefully prescribed in the contract. The contract was not carried out according to the specifications and resulted in a long suit, but the central panel of the altarpiece was painted by Leonardo; it is the *Virgin of the Rocks*, now in the National Gallery, London. Ambrogio furnished the angels that were to be at the sides. He perfected a technique of portrait painting and was commercially successful at it, producing careful, profile portraits with a hard outline. At Innsbruck, where he worked (1493) at the court of the emperor, he made portraits of the most important people at the court. A signed and dated (1502) portrait of Maximilian is at Vienna. Most of the portraits, however, were not signed, and many have been attributed to him on stylistic grounds. These include one thought to be of Beatrice d'Este, now in the Ambrosiana, Milan, once attributed to Leonardo himself. Other works are a portrait of Bianca Maria Sforza, who became the wife of Maximilian, National Gallery, Washington, a portrait, traditionally of Francesco Brivio, Brera, one of a young girl, at Amsterdam, two portraits in the National Gallery, London, a *Profile of an Elderly Man*, Johnson Collection, Philadelphia, and *Girl with Cherries*, the Metropolitan Museum, New York. Other portraits attributed to Ambrogio are at Bergamo, Florence (Uffizi), Modena, Bristol, Hannover, Paris (Musée Jacquemart-André), and Cambridge (Massachusetts).

Previtali (prā-vē-tä′lē), **Andrea.** Painter; b. at Berbenno (Bergamo), 1480; d. 1528. He was influenced by Giovanni Bellini, Carpaccio, and later, by Palma Vecchio and Lorenzo Lotto. His earliest known work (1502) is a *Madonna*, at Padua. Other works include a number of *Madonnas* and other paintings in the Carrara Academy, Bergamo; *Christ*, Brera, and *Portrait of a Man*, Poldi Pezzoli, Milan; *Nativity* and *Christ on the Cross*, Accademia, Venice, *Virgin and Child*, Pittsburgh; and paintings in the Church of S. Sigismundo, Bergamo, the National Gallery, London, and elsewhere.

Prignani (prē-nyä′nē), **Bartolommeo.** Original name of Pope **Urban VI.**

Primaticcio (prē-mä-tēt′chō), **Francesco.** Painter, sculptor, and architect; b. at Bologna, 1504; d. at Paris, 1570. He was a pupil of Innocenzo da Imola and then of Bagnacavallo, and studied the works of Michelangelo, Correggio, and Giulio Romano. With the latter he went to Mantua (c1526) and worked with him on the decoration of the Palazzo del Tè until 1532. This association had undoubted influence on shaping and developing his talent for interior decoration, a talent he employed to the full when, called to France (1532) by Francis I, he worked on the decoration of the palace at Fontainebleau. Rosso Fiorentino, one of the founders of

Italian mannerism, had already been working there a year when he arrived. Of the work Primaticcio carried out for the king at Fontainebleau in a number of halls and rooms, almost nothing remains. The quality and character of his art is known from a number of drawings preserved in the Louvre, including designs for stories of Hercules. In 1540 Francis sent him to Italy to collect antiques and casts. (Six years later he went on another such mission). While he was in Italy Rosso Fiorentino died (Vasari says he was a suicide), and on his return Primaticcio became overseer of the works at Fontainebleau and began a period of intense activity. His duties included landscaping the gardens and designing tapestries, as well as painting and modeling stucco decorations. He is known with Rosso as the founder of "the School of Fontainebleau" which refers to the French art influenced by contact, through them, with Italian mannerism. His refined and subtle mannerism appears in the elongated proportions of his figures (in the stuccos as well as in his exquisitely shaded paintings), strongly marked outlines, and a vigor softened by grace. He found scope for his poetic imagination in recreating, in fresco and stucco, scenes from mythology. The greatest undertaking of this character was the *Gallery of Ulysses* at Fontainebleau. The walls and ceiling of the Gallery were painted with fifty-eight episodes from the *Odyssey*. The Gallery was demolished in 1736 and the work is now known only from drawings and engravings. One of his foremost collaborators at Fontainebleau was Niccolò dell' Abate. Primaticcio remained in France until his death, decorating royal chateaux and other buildings and carrying out architectural works under four kings. Some of his painted, high relief stucco decorations are preserved at Fontainebleau. Other works include *The Continence of Scipio*, Louvre, and *The Return of Ulysses*, Castle Howard, England.

Prince, The. [Italian, **il Principe.**] A treatise by Niccolò Machiavelli, written in 1513 (published, 1532). At the time when Machiavelli wrote Italy was in disarray, "Leaderless, beaten, despoiled, lacerated, overrun and crushed under every kind of misfortune" (Chap. XXVI). He was a true patriot and longed to see Florence, and all of Italy, restored and strong, equal to the states of France, England, and Spain, and able to decide its own destiny. He believed that a strong prince made a strong state. *The Prince* presents his views on how a prince, or other ruler, can fulfill his first and overriding duty —to preserve and enhance his own power and his state.

In presenting his guide on how to be a successful ruler, Machiavelli takes as his model Cesare Borgia, the thoroughly immoral, ruthless, perfidious, and brilliant son of Pope Alexander VI. Cesare had, with his father's influence and aid, carved out a principality for himself in the Romagna in a very short time. By intrigue, murder, betrayal, shifting, and secret alliances, he had won a state and imposed his will on it. To his state he brought order. In 1502 his success seemed assured. In 1503 his father died, Cesare's state was crumbling, and he himself died a few years later (1507). It was the fact that he had created a state that stirred Machiavelli's admiration. In *The Prince* he adapts Cesare's methods, adding examples from the equally ruthless and perfidious methods of other successful rulers, and recommends them in urgent terms to Lorenzo de' Medici as the only means of uniting and saving Italy. Lorenzo, to whom the work is dedicated, was the grandson of Lorenzo the Magnificent and became head of the republic of Florence on the elevation of his uncle to the papal chair as Leo X (1513). Machiavelli is completely realistic. He does not pretend to be outlining a philosophy of good government. He cites examples, from ancient times and from contemporary history, to illustrate his points. He says he writes of things as they are, and not as they should be. Thus, although it would be ideal for a ruler to be loved and feared, since this is not possible under human conditions it is better to be feared. As between being generous and miserly, it is better to be miserly, for that way the prince will not waste either his own or his subjects' substance. "Pope Julius made use of his reputation for generosity to make himself Pope but later, in order to carry on his war against the king of France, he made no effort to maintain it; and he has waged a great number of wars without having had recourse to heavy taxation because his persistent parsimony has made up for the extra expenses" (Chap. XVI). Often it is good to be cruel, for the prince's cruelty to a few will benefit the many by keeping order in the state. He recommends the prince to break his word whenever it is necessary to do so to preserve his state and his power. "A certain prince of our times (Ferdinand, king of Spain), . . . preaches nothing but peace and faith and yet is the enemy of both, and if he had observed either he would already on numerous occasions have lost both his state and his renown" (Chap. XVIII). He strongly advises the prince to dispense with mercenaries and to have his own troops, for mercenaries, he says, have been "the bane of Italy." Furthermore, the prince should reward those few who make contributions to the state in any way, as in the arts or commerce, and he should make certain that the rewards are spectacular. In addition, the prince should undertake great enterprises, for these add to his renown and keep the minds of his subjects occupied.

The reaction against the treatise was almost immediate. In the atmosphere of the Counter-Reformation its complete political amorality was abhorrent, and the book was placed on the Index. Machiavelli's descriptions were exact and his prescriptions were intended to be effective for the situation as it existed. Utterly lacking was any trace of ethics and any hint that conditions might be improved in some other way. But this did not mean that Machiavelli scorned morality. He was not talking about the ideal, realized that systems might be better, but urged a strong prince as the only practical means of uniting Italy, or large parts of it, and rescuing it from the invaders who he foresaw would gobble it up. Because of the cold detachment with which he set down the above-mentioned precepts, and more like them, Machiavelli came to be regarded as an amoral, cunning, and unscrupulous man, from whose name we have the word *Machiavellian*, "placing expediency above political morality, and countenancing the use of craft and deceit in order to maintain the authority and effect the purposes of the ruler; hence, characterized by subtle or unscrupulous cunning; . . ." But Machiavelli drew his conclusions from the world as he observed it in his own day, a world in which power was the deciding factor, not political morality or justice; a world in which authority derived from the power to exercise it, not, as had traditionally been piously maintained, from divine will.

Prior. A magistrate at Florence; eight priors and a gonfaloniere were the magistrates to whom the government of Florence was entrusted. (The office of prior had existed since 1282, at which time there were six priors.) The gonfaloniere was the chief of the priors, but had no extra powers. The priors lived and took their meals in the Palazzo della Signoria during their terms, which were of two months. Since the list of those eligible for the office was limited, many prominent Florentines served at least once, and some several times, but there was a prohibition against members of the same family serving in too rapid succession.

Prioress's Tale, The. One of Chaucer's *Canterbury Tales*. It is told by Madame Eglantine, and is a retelling of the medieval legend of the child of a Christian widow killed in Asia by the Jews.

Pseudo-Isidorian Decretals (sō′dọ̄-iz-i-dō′-ri-ạn). See **False Decretals.**

Pucci (pöt′chē), **Antonio.** Florentine lyric poet; b. at Florence, c1309; d. there, 1388. By profession he was a bell founder and bell ringer and, as town crier, went about the streets of Florence announcing his presence by blasts on a silver trumpet. He wrote *cantari*, popular poems on themes of chivalry to be sung for the entertainment of the public; set Villani's *Chronicle* to verse; wrote a descriptive poem on the beauty of the *Mercato vecchio* at Florence; wrote on such public events as the war with Pisa (1362–1364); and wrote humorous verse.

Puccinelli (pöt-chē-nel′lē), **Angelo.** Lucchese painter; active 1350–1399. The linear, decorative qualities of his early work show the influence of Simone Martini. In his later work, his attempts at adapting the more solid forms of the Florentine style to his own talents were not always successful. His *Mystical Marriage of St. Catherine*, signed and thought to be dated 1350, is in the Museo di Villa Guinigi, Lucca, and a signed and dated (1386) *Death and Assumption of the Virgin*, the central panel of a triptych, is in S. Maria Fuorisportam, Lucca. A signed and dated (1394) polyptych, *Madonna and Child*, is in the parish church at Varano. Other works are at Siena, Altenburg, and Bonn.

Puccio di Simone (pöt′chō dē sē-mō′nā). Florentine painter of the 14th century. He was influenced by Bernardo Daddi. A signed polyptych, *Madonna of Humility with Saints*, is in the Accademia, Florence. Two panels of saints, laterals from a triptych, are in the National Gallery, Parma, and show Daddi inspiration.

Pulci (pöl′chē), **Bernardo.** Florentine humanist; b. at Florence, October 8, 1438; d. there, February 9, 1488. He was the brother of Luigi and Luca Pulci. A follower of the Medici, he wrote a sonnet mourning the death (1464) of Cosimo de' Medici, wrote verse for Piero and Lorenzo de' Medici, and dedicated his translation of Vergil's *Bucolics* to Lorenzo. His ancient and noble family had fallen on evil days and suffered further with the collapse of his brother Luca's business, but Bernardo showed his spirit by taking Luca's daughter into his own household and bringing her up. In 1471 he entered the service of Borso d'Este at Ferrara. He later taught at the Universities of Florence and Pisa.

Pulci, Luca. Florentine poet and banker; b. in the Mugello, December 3, 1431; d. at Florence, April, 1470. He was the brother of Bernardo and Luigi Pulci. In 1458 he went to Rome and engaged in the banking business. The business failed some time after 1465 and his brothers shared his reverses. He was imprisoned at Florence and died there. Luca wrote many verses, with the principal aim of giving pleasure. He dedicated his *Driadeo d'amore*, a pastoral modeled after Boccaccio's *Ninfale fiesolano*, to Lorenzo de' Medici. The poem, on the mythical origins of rivers and streams, involves many metamorphoses in the Ovidian manner. His *Ciriffo Cavalaneo*, also dedicated to Lorenzo, has to do with marvelous deeds in the days of chivalry.

Pulci, Luigi. Florentine poet; b. at Florence, August 15, 1432; d. at Padua, November, 1484. He was a member of an ancient and noble family that had fallen on evil days, and suffered further in the failure of his brother Luca's business. Lucrezia Tornabuoni, wife of Piero de' Medici, became his friend and benefactress. Of her son Lorenzo, although Pulci was considerably older, he became the dear and trusted friend, partner in his gaiety, and agent for his delicate missions (Naples, 1471; Milan, 1473). Other friends at Florence included the fellow-poet Poliziano, Michelangelo, the philosopher Ficino, and the scholar Cristoforo Landino, all members of the brilliant circle with which Lorenzo de' Medici surrounded himself. In 1477 Pulci went into the service of Roberto Sanseverino, a noted condottiere, but remained on terms of affectionate friendship with his Medici patrons.

Pulci was the poet of laughter. He was continually tickled by the ripe absurdities of life and could not resist celebrating them in his poetry. The gaiety of his spirit bubbles through his work. Extravagant notions and preposterous adventures are presented with a perfectly straight face that, by contrast, heightens the humor. He wrote of the ridiculous as if it were the most natural thing in the world. At the same time, his mockery and levity frequently served as vehicles for the expression of serious thought and criticism of existing customs and beliefs. His masterpiece, *Morgante maggiore,* written in pure, swift, and racy Italian, is an epic that he wrote for Lucrezia Tornabuoni. It is a retelling, transformed by Pulci's comic spirit and grace, of the tales of chivalry in the *Chanson de Roland.* The episodes of these tales were known through the length and breadth of Italy, where they had been recited and sung to the public by storytellers and streetsingers for generations. In the Italian atmosphere, the *Song of Roland* was translated from an epic of heroic deeds and chivalry to a parody. Charlemagne, for example, appears as a befuddled old man, too easily duped by the traitor Ganelon. It pleased the Italians to cut Charlemagne down. (Even Pope Pius II, in his *Commentaries,* shares the general Italian irritation with the idea of Charlemagne as a great man. In speaking of an herb, supposed miraculously to have sprung up to restore Charlemagne's plague-stricken army, he says the whole story of the herb is a tale made up by Charlemagne's admirers, of whom he was evidently not one.) Pulci presented the Italian attitude to the Carolingian legends in his transformation of epic deeds into bizarre and marvelous adventures. His work is not simply a retelling of the familiar legends. He invented new characters and episodes, enveloped his tale in a shower of light mockery and deadpan humor, and inserted theological discussions and scientific theories, seemingly in passing, as an expression of his own views (see **Morgante maggiore**). He wrote many verses in the vernacular for the entertainment of his patrons and friends. His *La giostra* is a description of a glorious tournament given by Lorenzo de'

Medici, and his *La Beca da Dicomano* is a parody of Lorenzo's *La Nencia da Barberino*. He left many delightful and indiscreet letters, especially those written to Lorenzo. They are full of witty comment and acute observation and analysis of men. Suspected of heresy, on the basis of charges by Ficino whom he had mocked, he published a *Confessione*. This was considered insincere, and he was buried in unhallowed ground when he died at Padua.

Puligo (pö-lē′gō), **Domenico.** Florentine painter; b. at Florence, 1492; d. there, 1527. He was a pupil of Ridolfo Ghirlandaio and a follower of Fra Bartolommeo and, especially, of Andrea del Sarto. Of modest gifts and great industry, a large number of his works survive. Among the most beautiful of these is his *Portrait of Pietro Carnesecchi*, Uffizi. Many of his works are at Florence: in the Pitti Palace, Uffizi, S. Maria Maddalena dei Pazzi, Foundling Hospital, and outdoor tabernacles. There are others in the neighborhood of Florence, at Bari, Modena, Pisa, Rome (Borghese, Colonna, Venezia, and Capitoline galleries), Berlin, Brussels, Leningrad, Ottawa, Paris, Baltimore, Columbus (Ohio), Coral Gables (Florida), Muncie (Indiana), New Haven, the Johnson Collection, Philadelphia, Sarasota (Florida), and elsewhere.

Puttenham (put′ẹn-ạm), **Richard.** English author; b. c1520; d. c1601. The *Arte of English Poesie* (1589) has been attributed both to him and to his brother George (d. 1590).

Q

Quercia (kwer′chä), **Jacopo della.** See **Della Quercia, Jacopo.**

Quirini (kwē-rē′nē), **Giovanni.** Fourteenth-century poet; b. at Venice. He was a great admirer of Dante, with whom he corresponded in verse, whose death he lamented, and whose work he defended. About thirty of his lyrics remain. These include some rather mannered sonnets and pleasing ballate. He wrote in the *dolce stil nuovo*.

R

Rabelais (rab′ẹ-lā, rab-ẹ-lā′; French, ràb-le), **François.** [Pseudonym, **Alcofribas Nasier** (an anagram of his name).] French satirist and humorist; b. at or near Chinon, in Touraine, France, c1494; d. probably at Paris, in April, 1553. Little is known of his life before 1520, although tradition has it that he lived at Angers from 1515 to 1518 and studied at the Franciscan monastery of La Baumette near that town. Late in 1520 he became a monk in the Franciscan monastery of Puy-Saint-Martin, at Fontenay-le-Comte, in Poitou, where, thanks to the encouragement of a group of erudite lawyers with whom he became associated, and the eminent scholar Guillaume Budé with whom he corresponded, he began the study of Greek. Greek being then in disrepute among the Franciscans, Rabelais moved to a nearby Benedictine convent, the better to pursue his humanistic studies. As secretary to the bishop, Geoffroy d'Estissac, he traveled widely in Poitou, gaining that detailed knowledge of the local terrain, speech, customs, amusements, and legends which was to lend his writings their special popular and realistic flavor. He probably lived at Paris in the period 1528–1530 and attended the university there. At the University of Montpellier, where he matriculated and received the degree of bachelor of medicine in 1530, he distinguished himself by his learned commentaries on Greek medical texts. By 1532 he was a practicing physician at Lyons, though he did not receive the doctor's degree until 1537. In 1534 he became physician to Jean du Bellay, bishop of Paris, in whose company he did considerable traveling, including several sojourns at Rome. In 1539 he was engaged as physician to Guillaume du Bellay-Langey, governor of Piedmont. From 1543, when the latter died, to 1546, Rabelais is lost to view. In 1546, his *Tiers Livre* having been condemned by the Sorbonne theologians, he took refuge at Metz. From 1548 to 1550 he was at Rome with Jean du Bellay, now a cardinal.

Rabelais is best known as the author of *Gargantua and Pantagruel*, one of the world's literary masterpieces, the five books of which appeared from 1532 to 1564, the last posthumously and of debatable authenticity. Each book has a character and emphasis of its own. This epic of men and giants presents a juxtaposition on a vast scale of erudition and popular lore, of serious philosophy and obscene buffoonery, of crass realism and esoteric allegory. His extended discussions of contemporary life and thought, although placed in a framework of unrestrained fantasy, provide a faithful mirror of Renaissance social customs and intellectual interests. In his opposition to war Rabelais assumed, for the most part, the enlightened humanist position represented by Erasmus. His satire of legal practices and his attack on monasticism are applications of his expansive spirit. In the quarrel on the worth of women, which raged in the 1540's, Rabelais took an anti-feminist stand. In his detailed treatments of navigation and of mechanical inventions he is to be associated with the forward-looking thinkers who, by about 1600, brought about a fusion of scholarship and the skilled crafts to produce modern science. Readers of Rabelais have usually been impressed by his exuberance, his optimism, and his generally expansive view of the world and man. The best known English translation is that of Thomas Urquhart and Pierre Motteux (1653–1708).

Rada (rä′ᴛʜä), **Juan de.** [Also, **Juan de Herrada.**] Spanish cavalier; b. c1490; d. at Jauja, Peru, 1542. He followed Pedro de Alvarado to Guatemala and Peru; was with the elder Diego de Almagro in Chile, and later headed the conspiracy against Francisco Pizarro, killing him, it is said, with his own hand.

Raffaellino (räf-fä-el-lē′nō). See **Del Colle, Raffaello.**

Raffaellino de' Carli (dā kär′lē). See **Raffaellino del Garbo.**

Raffaellino del Garbo (del gär′bō). Florentine painter; b. c1470; d. after 1525. Surviving paintings are variously attributed to Raffaellino del Garbo (so named from the Via Garbo where he had his workshop), Raffaellino de' Carli, Raffaellino Capponi (a name possibly derived from that of a benefactor), and Raffaellino da Firenze. Vasari attributed a large number of works to Raffaellino del Garbo, and a large number of works survive. The style and quality of the paintings differ markedly; some are in the manner of Botticelli and Filippino Lippi; others are influenced by Verrocchio, Ghirlandaio, and the Umbrians. Because of the variations in style some critics have considered that the surviving paintings are those of two contemporary Florentine painters, whom they name Raffaellino del Garbo and Raffaellino de' Carli. Others, however, assign all the works to the same painter, in the belief that this painter, Raffaellino del Garbo, signed his work in various ways (but never Raffaellino del Garbo), and that his art, which was never of very high quality, declined in the second half of his career. Works assigned to this single painter (but variously signed Raffaellino de' Carli, Raffaellino Capponi, Raffaellino da Firenze, or simply Raffaelle), are in several churches at Florence, as the Annunziata, S. Maria Maddalena dei Pazzi, S. Spirito and others. Other works include a *Resurrection*, Uffizi, *Madonna between Saints* (1500), Uffizi, a panel, *Madonna and Child in Glory with Saints* (1502), Church of S. Maria dei Angeli, near Siena, a *Pietà*, Munich, paintings in the National Gallery, London, at Sarasota, Florida, and in a number of other European and American collections.

Raffaello da Montelupo (räf-fä-el′lō dä mōn-tā-lö′pō). [Original name, **Raffaele Sinibaldi.**] Sculptor and architect; b. c1505; d. at Orvieto, 1566. He was the son and pupil of Baccio da Montelupo (1469–1535). After working at Carrara (c1520) on some figures that were to be sent to Spain for the tomb of Cardinal Ximenes, from 1521 to 1523 he assisted his father on the Gigli tomb in S. Michele at Lucca. His relief, *Virgin and Child*, is all that remains of the tomb in the church. In 1524 he went to Rome, where he was one of those who collaborated on the tomb of Raphael in the Pantheon; he carved the *Madonna del Sasso*, on a model of Raphael's. He left Rome after the sack (1527), of which he left a vivid description in memoirs now in the National Library at Florence, and returned to Florence, but fled in 1530 and took refuge at Loreto. He remained there until 1533, carving some mar-

Raffaellino del Garbo
Martyrdom of St. Lucy
Cabinet des Dessins Musée du Louvre Cliché Musées Nationaux

ble reliefs, *Visitation* (1530), *Adoration of the Magi* (1532), and *Birth of Mary,* for the Santa Casa. In 1538, again at Florence, he carved his masterpiece, the statue of *St. Damian* for the New Sacristy in S. Lorenzo. It was modeled to a design by Michelangelo, and never again did Raffaello achieve the same drama and immediacy, even when he followed designs of Michelangelo, as in the *Madonna, Prophet,* and *Sibyl* that he carved from Michelangelo's designs for the tomb of Julius II.

Beginning in 1543 Raffaello worked as architect of Castel Sant' Angelo, completing, among other things, stucco decorations in a number of rooms, corridors, windows, and doors, and a statue of the archangel Michael. From 1552 to his death he was at Orvieto as architect-in-chief of the cathedral. Among other things he designed mosaics and carved sculptures for the façade, statues (now lost) for the interior, and stucco decorations. Among his works at Orvieto is the relief *The Adoration of the Magi.* Other works by Raffaello include the statue of the pope on the tomb of Leo X in S. Maria sopra Minerva, Rome, and the sepulchral stone of Andrea del Sarto in SS. Annunziata, Florence. An uneven artist, he was principally influenced by Michelangelo and was one of that master's most faithful and able assistants. He left a number of drawings that so closely resemble Michelangelo's that for long they were thought to be his, but Raffaello was left-handed.

Raffaello Sanzio (sän′tsyō). See **Raphael.**

Raibolini (rī-bō-lē′nē), **Francesco.** Original name of **Francia, Francesco.**

Raimondi (rī-môn′dē), **Marcantonio.** One of the chief Italian engravers of the Renaissance; b. at Bologna, c1480; d. there, 1534. He served his apprenticeship under his fellow-townsman, the noted painter, goldsmith, and niellist, Francesco Francia. The earliest print known to be from his hand is his *Pyramus and Thisbe* (1505), in which he borrowed elements of the landscape from Dürer. He was, in fact, the most prolific of the many copiers of Dürer, and went so far as to copy a woodcut set of Dürer's *Life of Mary,* and signed his copies with Dürer's name (1506). Dürer, who was visiting in Italy in that year, complained to the Venetians of Marcantonio's plagiarism. Marcantonio worked at Venice between 1505 and 1509, and the following year set out for Rome. On his way he visited Florence and made a drawing, which he subsequently engraved, of Michelangelo's cartoon, later lost, *The Bathers*. At Rome, as elsewhere, he willingly gave himself to the work of carrying out the ideas of others. He came to work almost exclusively at copying the designs of Raphael, for whose line and intent in painting he had a wonderful understanding and sympathy, and whose line he reproduced to perfection. He also made prints to designs by Giulio Romano and others. The prints he made to designs by Romano for Aretino's *Sonetti* were so lewd that he was banished for a time from Rome. After the sack of Rome (1527) he returned to Bologna, where he died. His work on Raphael's designs was a partnership of understanding by which Raphael's work was extended and popularized, to the satisfaction of the painter. In his chosen field of expression, engraving, he reached a high degree of technical skill. No work in any other field of art is known to have been executed by him. With his technical skill, and his artistic understanding of the work of others, he had many followers, and founded what was practically a school of 16th-century Italian engravers, who devoted themselves, on the whole, to engraving to the designs of others rather than to perfecting the art as an original means of expression.

Rainalducci (rī-näl-döt′chē), **Pietro.** Original name of antipope **Nicholas V.**

Rais (res), Baron **de.** See **Retz,** Baron **de.**

Ralph Roister Doister (ralf rois′tėr dois′tėr). Comedy by Nicholas Udall, probably written between 1534 and 1541. It was licensed and printed in 1566, and is considered to be the first English comedy. The *Miles Gloriosus* of Plautus appears to be its direct forerunner.

Rambaldoni (räm-bäl-dô′nē), **Vittore dai.** Original name of **Vittorino da Feltre.**

Ramenghi (rä-māng′gē), **Bartolomeo.** See **Bagnacavallo.**

Ramenghi, Giovan Battista. Painter; he was the son of Bagnacavallo (1484–1542), from whom he had his first lessons in painting. He was one of Vasari's assistants in the decorating of the *Cancelleria* at Rome, and assisted Primaticcio in France.

Ramusio (rä-mö′zyō), **Giovanni Battista.** Humanist, historian, and geographer; b. at Treviso, July 20, 1485; d. at Padua, July 10, 1557. He studied at Padua under Pomponazzi, knew Latin, Greek, and some Near Eastern languages, and was passionately interested in cosmography and geography. He became a public servant of the Venetian Republic, valued for his integrity and discretion, and held the positions, among others, of secretary of the Senate and of the Council of Ten. In an official capacity he traveled to foreign lands on important and confidential missions. They carried him to France, Switzerland, Rome, Egypt, and Africa. He was on friendly terms with men of his time who shared his interest in the expanding world. The physician Fracastoro was one of his correspondents, and he was in constant touch with Navagero when the latter was in Spain, and received from him accounts that were brought back from the New World. Ramusio's great contribution was as editor and commentator of *Delle navigationi et viaggi*. This work is a collection of accounts by travelers and their descriptions of foreign lands. It includes a fine edition of the travels of Marco Polo, and an account of Magellan's circumnavigation of the globe. The accounts (some of which Ramusio translated himself), are accompanied by discourses by the editor that treat of a variety of geographical questions, such as the annual flooding of the Nile. The collection is in three volumes; the first is on Africa (published, 1550), the second on Asia (1557), and the third on the New World (1553). A classic in the history of geography, the volumes have gone through many editions, and have served as models for similar collections in other countries.

Ramusio, Girolamo. Physician and humanist; b. at Rimini, 1450; d. at Damascus, 1486. He was a friend of Pico della Mirandola, knew Arabic, and translated part of the works of the Arabic physician and philosopher Avicenna.

Raphael (raf′ạ-ẹl, rā′fạ-ẹl). [Original name, **Raffaello Sanzio** or **Santi.**] Painter and architect; b. at Urbino, March 28, 1483; d. at Rome, April 6, 1520. His father, Giovanni Santi (d. 1494), a competent painter who became better known as the author of a rhymed chronicle, was his first teacher. He may have trained as well under Timoteo Viti at Urbino. The house where Raphael lived still stands on a steep street at Urbino, surrounded by high, narrow houses of the same period. On one wall of his house is a fresco, called *Madonna and Child*, which is supposed by some to have been painted by

RAPHAEL
St. George Killing the Dragon
Uffizi, Florence Alinari-Art Reference Bureau

Raphael when he was 11 years old. Others attribute the fresco, which is in poor condition and has been largely repainted, to his father. About 1499 the young artist was at Perugia in the workshop of Perugino. A fundamental factor of Raphael's development was his capacity to grow by assimilating lessons learned from other painters. The list of painters who thus contributed to his development is long. Before he was 30 his fame equaled that of his older contemporaries, Leonardo and Michelangelo. His work was never suffused with the mystery of Leonardo nor stirred with the passion of Michelangelo. Raphael's was notable for balanced rhythms, harmony of space and composition, order and tranquillity in the classic manner, an unerring sense of beauty, and a glowing palette. With Leonardo and Michelangelo he formed the great triad of High Renaissance painting.

At Perugia, young as he was, he was more than a mere apprentice, since he carried out some commissions on his own. The earliest work attributed to him, aside from the fresco in the house at Urbino, is a Standard, on one side of which is a *Crucifixion* and on the other a *Madonna of Mercy*, painted at the end of the 15th century. The Standard, now in poor condition, in the Misericordia Hospital, Città di Castello, indicates the influence of Piero della Francesca as well as that of Perugino, and has echoes of Flemish painting in the landscape. Piero della Francesca had worked at Urbino, and Raphael would have seen his work, as well as the works of Flemish painters, in the collections of the cultivated dukes of Urbino. Thus from the very beginning he began to assimilate. The character of his art, notable for tranquillity and harmony rather than for dramatic accents, is clear in what are thought to be parts of a dismembered diptych, *The Knight's Dream*, National Gallery, London, and *The Three Graces*, Musée Condé, Chantilly, variously dated from 1498 to 1504. In *The Three Graces* the movements of the figures and the presentation of what is almost an antique statuary group foretell the classical spirit and inspiration of Raphael the mature painter. Here, as in two almost contemporary paintings of *St. Michael and the Demon* and *St. George and the Dragon*, Louvre, Raphael attains to the increasingly evident harmony in his art between the circumambient atmosphere and composition. (Another *St. George and the Dragon*, National Gallery, Washington, was originally commissioned (c1506) by Guidobaldo, duke of Urbino, to be sent as a gift to Henry VII of England when Guidobaldo was decorated with the Order of the Garter.) His early work shows Raphael closely following Perugino. Some of his first paintings are almost indistinguishable from his master's. In this group is *The Coronation of the Virgin* (c1503), Vatican, derived from Perugino but with Raphael's facility at locating figures in a composition and with a luminous intensity of color that was unknown to Perugino. Also close to Perugino are the *Mond Crucifixion*, National Gallery, London, *Madonna and Saints*, Berlin, formerly attributed to Perugino and with some indications of the influence of Pinturicchio, with whom, according to Vasari, Raphael worked at Siena, and *Christ Blessing*, Pinacoteca Tosio Martinengo, Brescia; all have a freshness and innocence of vision that mark them as Raphael's own. His first signed and dated (1504) work, *The Marriage of the Virgin*, Brera, Milan, shows its derivation from Perugino's painting on the same subject now at Caen, but with rhythms of composition and a luster of color quite beyond Perugino's reach. In this work, in which the figures from daily life are exalted to a spiritual level, with its nobly resolved architectonic forms, and formal harmonies, Raphael was established as a painter of the High Renaissance. A fresco, *Trinity and Saints*, Church of the Monastery of S. Severo, Perugia, was left incomplete by Raphael. It was finished (1521) by Perugino, one of his old master's last works. Between 1504 and 1508 Raphael was at Florence, where he became aware of an approach to painting that, in its science and emphasis on form, differed widely from the sober, lovely, often sentimental, manner of Perugino and the Umbrians. The mystery imparted by Leonardo's sfumato and his acute perception of the natural world, the dramatic intensity and powerful structures of Michelangelo, were revelations that he absorbed and made his own. The cartoons the older masters had made for frescoes in the Palazzo Vecchio were on exhibition at Florence, and provided a vivid demonstration of the tension and drama evoked by nude bodies in violent action. He undoubtedly studied the frescoes of Masaccio in the Brancacci Chapel and was impressed by the nobility and dignity of man on a larger-than-life scale as presented there by Masaccio. At Florence he became the friend of Fra Bartolommeo, an older contemporary; each influenced the other. Among the works of the Florentine period especially illustrative of his absorption of Florentine forms and technique are the *Colonna Altarpiece*, the Metropolitan Museum, New York, the *Ansidei Altarpiece*, National Gallery, London, and *St. George*, National Gallery, Washington. In his signed and dated (1507) *Deposition*, Borghese Gallery, Rome, he experimented with the broad forms and dramatic movement that he had observed especially in the work of Michelangelo. It is one of the few paintings by Raphael expressive of profound grief. It was commissioned by Atalanta Baglioni of Perugia, and reflects her anguish over the death of her son Grifonetto at the hands of a kinsman in an interfamilial struggle for control of the city. In the *Grand Duke Madonna*, Pitti Palace, Florence, is reflected the influence of Leonardo in its soft modeling and the dark background from which the Madonna emerges. (The painting is so-called from the fact that the Grand Duke Frederick III of Hapsburg-Lorraine, who acquired it in 1799, was so devoted to it that he carried it about with him when he traveled.) The *Madonna of the Meadows*, Vienna, is constructed on a pyramid, a compositional form perhaps derived from Leonardo's *Virgin with St. Anne*, Louvre. Other paintings that followed a pyramidal composition include the *Belvedere Madonna*, Vienna, *Madonna of the Goldfinch*, Uffizi, *La Belle Jardinière*,

RAPHAEL
Study for St. John at the foot of the Cross
Accademia, Venice Alinari-Art Reference Bureau

Louvre, and others. Numerous exquisite pen and ink studies, for the Madonnas and other paintings, survive, and show Raphael's characteristic upward swirls for locating position and establishing form—spiral motion that was translated to the painted work. With his series of Madonnas in the open air Raphael established a presentation of the subject that was easy to imitate and became standard among his many followers. The Madonnas are notable for the plasticity of the groups of figures, for their air of calm contemplation, their fresh and lovely landscapes and for the classic beauty of the individual faces. Other works of this period include the portraits of Agnolo and Maddalena Doni, Pitti Palace *The Pregnant Woman,* Pitti, *Orléans Madonna,* Chantilly, *St. Catherine,* National Gallery, London, and the *Canigiani Madonna,* Munich. The *Madonna of the Canopy,* Pitti, which he left incomplete, is a forerunner of the monumental Roman works. Nearly fifty surviving paintings attributed to Raphael were executed by the time he was 25 years old. These include a number of his finest altarpieces and Madonnas. There are also a number of portraits, including those of Elizabetta Gonzaga, of her husband, Guidobaldo, duke of Urbino, both in the Uffizi, and of her companion and the leader of the discussions in Castiglione's *Il Cortegiano,* Emilia Pia, Epstein Collection, Baltimore.

Toward the end of 1508 Raphael went to Rome, possibly called there by Julius II and perhaps at the suggestion of Raphael's fellow-townsman Bramante. In the middle of the 15th century Nicholas V had renovated the 13th-century palace of Nicholas III and built four rooms there. Piero della Francesca, Luca Signorelli, and Bartolomeo della Gatta had executed some decorations in them. When Julius II became pope he refused to live in the apartment inhabited by his detested predecessor, Alexander VI, and took over the four rooms built under Nicholas. He commissioned Perugino, Sodoma, Bramantino, Peruzzi, and others to decorate them, and these artists were there when Raphael arived. By January, 1509, he was at work, and shortly afterward Julius ordered the decorations already on the walls removed and placed Raphael in charge of the entire project. No work that he had done up to this time was on the scale of the area he was now called upon to decorate. The four rooms, the famous *Stanze,* in order, have come to be called *Stanza dello Incendio, Stanza della Segnatura, Stanza di Eliodoro,* and *Sala di Costantino,* the last opening onto what is called *Raphael's Loggie,* facing the courtyard of S. Damaso. Raphael worked at intervals on the *Stanze* from 1509 until his death. In this period Michelangelo was painting the ceiling of the Sistine Chapel. Leonardo was also at Rome, but accomplished little. Of the four rooms, Raphael painted the *Stanza della Segnatura* and the *Stanza di Eliodoro.* Some of the decoration of the *Stanza dello Incendio* may have been carried out by assistants according to his designs and the *Sala di Costantino* was painted after his death and has little of Raphael. Taken together, the rooms in which he played a major role are a record of the continuing development of his art as he came in contact with other painters, and comprise the most complete representation of his artistic expression. On the death of Julius (1513), his successor, Leo X, had the work in the *Stanze* continued. The program of the decoration changed from a series that exalted Julius, as in the *Stanza della Segnatura,* painted first and completed about 1511, and the *Stanza di Eliodoro,* painted next and completed in 1514, to a series that exalted Leo (see **Stanze**).

The most sought after painter of Italy, his work at Rome was by no means confined to the decoration of the *Stanze.* He frescoed (c1513) the myth of Galatea in the Farnesina, a villa belonging to the wealthy banker Agostino Chigi. Other painters engaged in decorating the villa (which was called the Farnesina after the Farnese family acquired it) were Peruzzi, Sodoma, and Sebastiano del Piombo. From the last-named he was inspired to the richness of Venetian color. Of about the same time as the Galatea fresco are the *Madonna di Foligno,* Vatican, notable for its luminous contrasts and spirituality, and the *Alba Madonna,* National Gallery, Washington. Probably the most famous of all Raphael's paintings is the *Sistine Madonna,* now at Dresden. The painting, for the monks of S. Sisto at Piacenza, is the first he executed on canvas; it appears to be almost entirely by his hand. The features of St. Sixtus in the painting are thought to be those of Julius II; the model for the dark-eyed Madonna floating above St. Sixtus and St. Barbara is the same as that in his *La Velata* (*Lady with Veil*), Pitti Palace. For sheer beauty—of color, lightness of composition, and sensitive spirituality—the *Sistine Madonna* with its characteristic upward spiraling movement is unrivaled among his paintings on this subject. Other famous paintings of the Roman period, to name only a few of many, were the *Madonna of the Chair,* Pitti, *St. Cecilia,* Pinacoteca, Bologna, that had great influence on Emilian painting, and his last work, *The Transfiguration.* At the time of his death he was working on *The Transfiguration,* of unusual dramatic impact in a Raphael. It was finished by Giulio Romano. There are also a great number of striking portraits of the Roman period, including that of *Fedra Inghirami,* Isabella Stewart Gardner Museum, Boston, the portrait of *Baldassare Castiglione,* Louvre, regarded as the summation in Renaissance portraiture of a Renaissance figure, the portrait of *Leo X and Two Cardinals,* Uffizi, and *La Fornarina,* Borghese Gallery, Rome, supposedly a portrait of an inamorata of Raphael's, and considered by many to be largely the work of Giulio Romano. Other works included the painting (1517), with assistants, of the fable of Cupid and Psyche in the Villa Farnesina, the design of mosaics for the Chigi Chapel in S. Maria del Popolo, and the colored cartoons for ten tapestries (1515–1516). The tapestries, on stories from the New Testament, were commissioned by Leo and were intended to be hung below the 15th-century frescoes on the walls of the Sistine Chapel. In their monumentality and dignity, their sweep and drama, the cartoons recall the Masaccio frescoes in the Brancacci Chapel. The finished tapestries, woven at Brussels, were hung in place and exhibited at Christmas time, in 1519. The tapestries, still in the Vatican, were woven with great amounts of silk and gold, and aroused great acclaim for their beauty. Seven of the cartoons survive, Victoria and Albert Museum, London. They represent *Christ's Charge to Peter; The Miraculous Draught of Fishes; The Death of Ananias; The Healing of the Lame Man; The Blinding of Elymas; The Sacrifice at Lystra;* and *St. Paul Preaching at Athens.* The lost cartoons represented *The Conversion of St. Paul; St. Paul in Prison;* and *The Stoning of St. Stephen.* The huge cartoons (the largest is seventeen feet, nine and one-half inches wide and eleven feet, four and one-half inches high, and the smallest is thirteen feet, one inch wide and ten feet, five and one-half inches high) were cut apart for the convenience of the weavers. It was not until the beginning of the 18th century that they were pasted together and shown as works of art rather than used as patterns for tapestry making. Tapestries were made from some of the cartoons for Francis I, Henry VIII, Ercole Gonzaga of Mantua, and Philip II of Spain. Other tapestry manufactories at Brussels besides the original one, and at Paris, made tapestries from them for various clients in the course of the next century. The tapestries constituted an important additional means by which Raphael's art and influence were diffused throughout Europe. Beginning about 1517 he designed the decoration of the *Loggie* in the Courtyard of S. Damaso in the Vatican (originally designed by Bramante and remodeled and enlarged by Raphael), and supervised its execution by assistants. Because fifty-two frescoes of the

Raphael
Studies of heads
Accademia, Venice Alinari-Art Reference Bureau

thin; ᴛʜ, then; y, you; (variable) ḏ as d or j, s̶ as s or sh, ṯ as t or ch, z̶ as z or zh; o, F. cloche; ü, F. menu; ċh, Sc. loch; ṅ, F. bonbon; ʙ, Sp. Córdoba (sounded almost like v).

decoration represent scenes from the Old and New Testaments, the *Loggie* came to be called *Raphael's Bible*.

After the death of Bramante (1514) Raphael was named overseer of the works of St. Peter's. As an architect he was influenced by the work of Laurana that he had seen at Urbino and by that of Bramante. His inclination toward the elegant austerity of Bramante's classicism and the harmony of rhythm that marked his painting in his architecture was modified by a richer variation of texture and ornamentation. Among the buildings he designed at Rome were the above-mentioned Chigi Chapel, the Palazzo Vidoni-Caffarelli (since greatly enlarged by additions), and, just outside Rome, the Villa Madama, with decoration, executed by Raphael and his pupils, in imitation of Nero's Golden House. In his last years his enthusiasm and study of archaeology that had developed at Rome were intensified. Leo X named him Prefect of Antiquities, and he planned to make a great map of the monuments of Imperial Rome but died before he could carry out the project.

Some critics have noted a decline in the painting of Raphael's later years, a lack of serenity, a thickening of the forms, and an almost formula-like scheme of composition. In the last years of his short life, as in the earlier ones, he produced an enormous amount of work. He was the friend of popes and princes and was continually in demand to execute commissions. There were so many that a kind of assembly line procedure was required to carry them all to completion. Many were in fact largely completed by pupils, to his designs, and usually with his hand in some areas. Industrious, intelligent, and of great tact and charm, he had swarms of pupils and assistants who accompanied him about Rome (a fact that provoked some scornful remarks from Michelangelo, who was notorious for his solitary habits). In a letter to his friend Baldassare Castiglione, Raphael wrote what is taken as his artistic credo—that he began with the idea of beauty. His representation of beauty, through harmonious forms, masterly composition, glowing color, complete control of technique, and uninterrupted growth made him the painter *par excellence* of the High Renaissance at its apogee. His death was mourned as a universal disaster. At his own request he was buried in the Pantheon, his great *Transfiguration*, the forerunner of what might have been a new phase in his art, was hung over his bier. The largest group of the many surviving paintings attributed to Raphael is at Florence, in the Pitti and Uffizi galleries. In addition to works named, and others, in the museums already mentioned, there are Raphaels in the Carrara Academy, Bergamo, at Naples, Urbino, Berlin, Budapest, Cracow, Hampton Court, Hanover, the Hermitage, Leningrad, Lisbon, the Prado, Madrid, Liechtenstein, São Paulo (Brazil), the Walters Art Gallery, Baltimore, Museum of Fine Arts, Boston, and elsewhere.

Ravizza (rä-vēt′tsä), **Giovita.** [Latinized, **Jovita Rapicius.**] Grammarian and Latin stylist; b. at Chiari (Brescia), February 15, 1476; d. at Venice, August 16, 1553. He taught at Caravaggio, Bergamo, Vicenza (where he was made an honorary citizen), and at Venice. From 1544 to 1548 he was a private tutor in the family of Giovanni Battista Ramusio. He wrote innumerable orations and funeral eulogies, but was most highly thought of as a teacher and as a writer of polished Latin by the outstanding stylists of his day, including Pietro Bembo. Other extant works include letters, treatises on a number of topics, a poetic paraphrase in Italian of the Psalms of David, and a Latin treatise on pedagogy, *De instaurazione scholarum* (Venice, 1551). His chief work is on his favorite subject and the one for which, as a stylist, he was most honored. It was *De numero oratorio* (Venice, 1554), in five books.

Raymond of Capua. (rā′mọnd, kap′ū-ạ-). Dominican, confessor and biographer of St. Catherine of Siena; b. at Capua, c1330; d. at Nuremberg, 1399. He was a descendant of a brother of the poet and official, Pier della Vigna. He studied at Bologna, and then entered the Dominican Order. From 1363 he was at Montepulciano, where he was abbot of the Convent of St. Agnes, whose *Life* he wrote. In 1367 he was prior of the Convent of the Minerva at Rome, then went to Siena, where he was chapter general of the Dominican Order, and where, from 1374 to 1378, he was confessor and spiritual adviser to St. Catherine of Siena. He went with her to Avignon (1376) and served as her interpreter to Pope Gregory XI. In 1378 Pope Urban VI sent him and his friars to France to preach a crusade against the schismatics who supported the antipope Clement VII, but he was not permitted into France. After St. Catherine's death he ardently defended, as she had done, the canonicity of the election of Urban, and supported Urban's successor, Pope Boniface IX. As a result of his missions in Italy, Hungary, and Germany, and his visits to the convents of his order, he resolved to make sweeping reforms of the order, of which he had become general in 1388. He also worked unceasingly for the canonization of St. Catherine, but did not live to see it. In 1384 he began his life of St. Catherine, in Latin, *Legenda maior*, which is the primary source for events of her life. He used notes made by her earlier confessor, Fra Tommaso della Fonte, as the basis of some of his material, noted what had been his own experience, and brought witnesses to events when possible; many of the witnesses were still living when he wrote. He admitted with regret that through laziness or from some other cause he had not recorded during her lifetime many of the events that took place, and confesses that he sometimes dozed when she talked to him about doctrine, and that she sometimes took him to task for it also. He finished the work in 1395, and very soon Italian translations of it were made. Seventeen of the letters of St. Catherine to Fra Raimundo survive.

Recorde (rek′ọrd), **Robert.** British mathematician and physician; b. at Tenby, Wales, c1510; d. at London, 1558. He wrote *The Grounde of Artes, teachinge the Perfect Worke and Practice of Arithmeticke* (1540), *The Pathway to Knowledge, containing the First Principles of Geometry* (1551), *The Castle of Knowledge* (1551), and the first English book on algebra (1557).

Reeve's Tale, The. One of Chaucer's *Canterbury Tales*. He probably took it from a French fabliau, but it forms the sixth novel of the ninth day of Giovanni Boccaccio's *Decameron*.

Reformation. Great religious revolution in the 16th century, which led to the establishment of the Protestant churches. It assumed different aspects, and resulted in alterations of discipline or doctrine more or less fundamental in different countries, and at different stages of its progress. John Wycliffe, John Hus, and other great reformers had appeared before the 16th century, but the Reformation proper appeared nearly simultaneously in Germany under Martin Luther and in Switzerland under Huldreich Zwingli. The chief points urged by the Reformation were the need of justification by faith, the use and authority of the Scriptures and the right of private interpretation, the abandonment of the doctrine of transubstantiation, the adoration of the Virgin Mary, the supremacy of the Pope, and various other rites and doctrines. In the German Reformation the leading incidents were the publication at Wittenberg of Luther's ninety-five theses, the excommunication of Luther, his testimony before the Diet of Worms, the Diet of Augsburg, and the prolonged struggle between Protestants and Roman Catholics which ended in the Peace of Augsburg (1555). The Reformation spread to Switzerland under Zwingli and John Calvin, and elsewhere in Europe. In Scotland it was introduced by John Knox. In England it led to the abolition of the papal supremacy and the liberation of the Church of England from papal control. In many countries the Reformation led to an increased strength and zeal in the Roman Catholic Church, sometimes called the Counter-Reformation.

Regiomontanus (rē-ji-ọ̄-mon-tā′nus; German, rā-gẹ̄-ō-mon-tä′nủs). [Pseudonym (translation into Latin of the German Königsberg, his birthplace) of **Johann Müller.**] German mathematician and astronomer, bishop of Regensburg; b. at Königsberg, Franconia, June 6, 1436; d. at Rome, July 6, 1476. In an effort to correct errors in the Alfonsine Tables, a revision of the Ptolemaic planetary tables, he traveled (1462) to Rome to search for better manuscripts and to learn Greek. He wrote a work on trigonometry, the study of which he was later to foster in Germany, but was forced to leave Rome after a quarrel with the papal secretary and translator, George of Trebizond, over the latter's translation of the *Almagest*. He went to Vienna, then to Buda, and then settled at Nuremberg (1471). There with the financial help of Bernhard Walther, he built an observatory and established a printing press. He made observations of the comet of January, 1472 (later known as Halley's comet), and published a series of calendars as well as an *Ephemeris* covering the years 1474–1506 (said to have been used by Columbus). He was called to Rome in 1472 by Pope Sixtus IV to help in the work of reforming the calendar and died there.

Rej (rā), **Mikolaj.** Polish Protestant moralist and writer; b. at Żórawno, near Halicz (now in the Ukraine), February 4, 1505; d. 1569. Generally considered the father of Polish literature because of his pioneer use of the vernacular, he was a country squire whose education was acquired through his wide reading. Included in one of his collections in prose and verse is an account of his idea of what the life of a country squire should be. In 1546 he became a Calvinist, and some of his works indicate a wide knowledge of theology. He wrote verse (of no great quality), energetic and vivid prose, plays, and satirical verse dialogues.

Relief. A piece of sculpture on a background; the projection of a figure or feature from the ground or plane on which it is formed. Any material suitable for carving or casting may be employed as the ground. In general, there are three forms of relief: low relief or bas-relief (*bassorilievo*), half or middle relief (*mezzorilievo*), and high relief (*altorilievo*). The distinction between them lies in the degree of projection. In low relief the figures project but slightly from the ground, in such a manner that no part of them is entirely detached from it, as in coins, medals, medallions, and so on, the chief effect being produced by the treatment of light and shade. Representations of Giotto and Brunelleschi in low relief are on the interior walls of S. Maria del Fiore (the Duomo) at Florence. In high relief the figures project at least one half of their natural circumference from the background and sometimes entire elements or extremities are in the round. Half relief is intermediate between the other two. For the bronze panels of the doors of the Baptistery at Florence, Ghiberti modeled in low, high, and half relief, often all three in the same panel, and produced the effect of perspective. The series of portrait heads representing artists, including Ghiberti's own, that forms a frame around the panels of each door is in high relief. Relief was lavishly used in the Renaissance for decoration.

Reliquary (rel′i-kwā-ri). A vessel, coffer, or box designed to hold a relic. Some reliquaries are as large as small chapels, others are small enough to hold in the hand. Sometimes the shape of the reliquary indicates the relic within, as an arm or a hand. The reliquary in the Cathedral of Florence that contains part of the skull of St. Zenobius is in the form of a bust. Reliquaries are often of precious metals, or of rock crystal and metal, and are richly ornamented and often studded with precious stones.

René I (of *Anjou*) (rė-nā). [Called **le Bon**, "the Good."] Duke of Anjou, count of Provence, and (titular) king of Naples; b. at Angers, France, January 16, 1409; d. at Aix, July 10, 1480. He was the son of Louis II of Anjou and Yolande of Aragon. His claim (through his wife) to the duchy of Lorraine was disputed and he was taken prisoner (1431) but released the following year. On the death (1434) of his brother, Louis III, he claimed the kingdom of Naples. Alfonso V of Aragon (who became Alfonso I of Naples) won the long struggle for control of Naples and René returned (1442) to France. More a scholar than a warrior, he rejected the crown of Aragon when it was offered to him (1467) and passed it to his son John. After John's death (1470), René moved his court, which was renowned for its brilliance, from Anjou to Provence. He was a patron of art and literature and was a noted writer himself. He left a moral treatise, *Mortifiement de vaine plaisance,* as well as romances and poetry.

Resende (rẹ-zen′dẹ), **Garcia de.** Portuguese poet; b. at Évora, Portugal, c1470; d. 1536. He compiled the *Cancioneiro Geral* (1516), a collection of nearly 1,000 poems by almost 300 authors, including himself. This collection, in addition to its philological and literary interest, is a major source of information about Portuguese society of the 15th century.

Ressaut (res-ȧt′). In architecture, a projection of any member or element, as a molding, entablature or pilaster, or any part, as a story, from or before another.

Retz (rets), Baron **de.** [Also, **Rais, Raiz;** title of **Gilles de Laval.**] French marshal; b. c1401; executed at Nantes, France, October, 1440. A contemporary and ally of Joan of Arc in the wars against the English, he was notorious for his cruelties to children, and was executed after confessing to the mistreatment of some 100 boys.

Reuchlin (roiċh′lin), **Johann.** [Grecized, **Capnio.**] German humanist; b. at Pforzheim, Baden, December 28 (or February 22), 1455; d. at Liebenzell, Bavaria, June 30, 1522. He studied and traveled in Germany, Switzerland, France, and Italy. He settled at Tübingen in 1481 as a teacher of jurisprudence and the liberal arts, and was a judge in the Swabian League from 1500 or 1502 to 1512. He opposed, in a formal opinion to the emperor in 1510, the suppression of Jewish books hostile to Christianity, advocated by the converted Jew Johann Pfefferkorn, which involved him in a controversy (1510–1516) with the Dominicans and the obscurantists generally. In 1514 he published *Epistolae Clarorum Virorum* (*Letters of Illustrious Men*), which led to the publication of the anonymous satire, *Epistolae Obscurorum Virorum* (*Letters of Obscure Men*) in 1515. These, by way of a satirical and exaggerated defense of the Dominican cause, attacked its hypocrisy and narrow-mindedness, and defended humanism as against Medieval Scholasticism. Instead of suppressing Jewish books, Reuchlin proposed that the Jewish communities be required to supply books to support two chairs of Hebrew at every German university. The controversy ended in his victory when an accusation against him at Rome was dropped. He promoted education in Germany by publishing Greek textbooks, and wrote various works on Latin, Greek, and Hebrew, including a Hebrew grammar, *Rudimenta Hebraica* (1506). He also published the cabbalistic works *De verbo mirifico* (1494) and *De arte cabbalistica* (1517), and two Latin plays, *Henno* and *Sergius*.

Riario (ryä′ryō), **Girolamo.** Lord of Imola and Forlì; murdered, April 14, 1488. He was the son of Bianca della Rovere, sister of that Francesco della Rovere who became Pope Sixtus IV (1414–1484). On the elevation of the latter to the papacy the fortunes of the Riario, an obscure family, shot up. When the Church bought Imola from Galeazzo Maria Sforza, Sixtus IV invested his nephew Girolamo with the territory (1473) and betrothed him to Caterina Sforza, the young, illegitimate daughter of Galeazzo Maria. The marriage took place in 1477. Frustrated by Lorenzo de' Medici in his efforts to enlarge his territories, in 1478 Girolamo was one of the chief architects of the Pazzi Conspiracy against Lorenzo, in which his brother Giuliano de' Medici was killed. Girolamo, however, though a principal instigator and planner, prudently took no active part in the execution of the plot. In 1480 Pino III Ordelaffi, lord of Forlì, died. Sixtus added Forlì to Girolamo's dominions. The partisans of the Ordelaffi, with the help of Lorenzo de' Medici, sought to wrest it from him. Having escaped the consequences of the Pazzi conspiracy, Girolamo suffered from a conspiracy against himself: members of the Ordelaffi party murdered him, April 14, 1488. His wife Caterina seized the castle, drove off her enemies, and held the city and the state for her son Ottaviano.

Riario, Pietro. Cardinal; b. c1445; d. January, 1474. He was the son of Bianca della Rovere, sister of Francesco della Rovere who became Pope Sixtus IV, and the brother of Girolamo Riario (d. 1488). On his elevation to the papacy Sixtus IV immediately began to repair the fortunes of his beloved and indulged nephews. At the age of 26 Pietro was made cardinal, archbishop of Florence, and patriarch of Constantinople. He had enormous influence with his uncle and was active in the intrigues of the Curia and of Italian politics. His life was utterly dissolute and his profligacy knew no bounds. The historian Corio devotes several pages to the magnificent and costly entertainment he offered Leonora of Aragon when she passed through Rome on her way to Ferrara for her marriage to Ercole d'Este. Machiavelli reports the rumor that Pietro bargained with Galeazzo Maria Sforza to establish the latter as king of Lombardy. Galeazzo Maria in his turn agreed to supply men and money to secure the papacy for Pietro, Sixtus, as it was rumored, being willing to abdicate in his favor. Machiavelli says that the Venetians were suspected of poisoning Pietro to prevent the implementation of the bargain.

Riario, Raffaele. Cardinal of S. Giorgio; b. c1461; d. at Naples, 1521. He was a nephew of Sixtus IV, who gave him the red hat of a cardinal while Raffaele was still in his teens. In 1478 the young cardinal was the innocent decoy around whom the Pazzi Conspiracy was carried into execution at Florence. The cardinal was saved from the wrath of the Florentine mob by the officials at Florence, but was held in protective custody, to the anger of the pope. He became one of the wealthiest cardinals and was even considered as a candidate for the tiara. In May, 1517, he was arrested, with Cardinals Alfonso Petrucci, Adriano Castellesi, Francesco Soderini, and Bandinello Sauli on charges of conspiring to kill Pope Leo X. Cardinal Petrucci was executed. The other cardinals were imprisoned, and then freed on payment of a fine. Cardinal Riario was compelled to give up his magnificent palace, one of the finest in Rome. It became the residence of the vice-chancellor of the Church, and has since been known as the *Cancelleria*, a Roman landmark to Renaissance taste.

Ribault or **Ribaut** (rē-bō), **Jean.** French navigator; b. at Dieppe, France, 1520; d. in Florida, September 23, 1565. He established a colony of French Protestants near Port Royal, in what is now South Carolina, which was abandoned. In 1565 he went with reinforcements for the colony at Fort Carolina on the St. John's River in Florida. While he was exploring the coast the colony was destroyed by the Spanish under Pedro Menendez de Avilés. On his return Ribault was shipwrecked and captured by the Spanish, who killed him.

Ribeiro (rē-bā′rö), **Bernardim.** Portuguese writer and poet; b. at Torrao, Portugal, 1482; d. insane at Lisbon, Portugal, 1552. He introduced bucolicism into Portuguese literature with his eclogues and his novel *Menina e moca* (1554).

Riccardo da San Germano (rēk-kär′dō dä sän jer-mä′nō). Notary and chronicler; fl. 1250. Little is known of his life aside from the place of his birth and the fact that he was a notary in the time of the Emperor Frederick II. His *Chronica,* written out of his own experience of the political life of the time and his acquaintance with some of the leading political figures, is an important source of information on this region in the time of the German (Swabian) rulers. It covers the period from 1189 to 1254. His careful and impartial account gives the most complete extant picture of southern Italy under Frederick II.

Riccardo da Venosa (ve-nō′sä). Jurist and writer; b. at Venosa, c1200; fl. 1230. His poem *Liber de Paulino et Polla,* composed between 1230 and 1244, was written to entertain Frederick II. It is the tale of a lively adventure, presented with some realism and understanding of psychology, as well as with many indications of the poet's classical culture.

Ricciardetto (rē-chär-dāt′tō). In the *Orlando* romances of Matteo Maria Boiardo and Lodovico Ariosto, the brother of Bradamante. He loves Fiordispina, daughter of Marsilio, and is condemned to death by Marsilio. Saved by Ruggiero, he is overthrown by Mandricardo, but is again rescued, this time by Malagigi's magic.

Ricciarelli (rēt-chä-rel′lē), **Daniele.** See **Daniele da Volterra.**

Riccio (rēt′chō), **David.** See **Rizzio** or **Riccio, David.**

Riccio, Domenico. See **Brusasorci, Domenico.**

Riccio, il. See **Briosco, Andrea.**

Riccobaldo da Ferrara (rēk-kō-bäl′dō dä fer-rä′rä). Thirteenth-century chronicler, of whom little is known; d. after 1312. He is said to have been present at a miracle in Padua (1243) and to have heard Pope Innocent IV (d. 1254) preach at Ferrara. He lived at some time at Ravenna, where he was a canon. He wrote a universal history covering the period 700 to 1297. The first part of this three-part work covered the history of the Holy Roman Empire from Charlemagne to 1298 and was translated by Matteo Maria Boiardo (1440–1494) under the title *Istoria imperiale.*

Rich (rich), **Barnabe.** English pamphleteer and writer of romances; b. c1540; d. at Dublin, November 10, 1617. The best known of his many works are *Riche his Farewell to the Militarie Profession* (1581), *A Looking Glass for Ireland* (1599), *The Excellency of Good Women* (1613), *The Honestie of this Age, proving that the World was never Honest Till Now* (1614), and *The Irish Hubbub* (1617). The chief interest of the *Farewell* is its second tale, "The History of Apolonius and Silla," which Shakespeare used as the source for the main plot of *Twelfth Night.*

Richard II (of *England*). King of England (1377–1399); b. at Bordeaux, France, January 6, 1367; probably murdered at Pontefract, England, February 14, 1400. He was the son of Edward, the Black Prince, and grandson of Edward III, whom he succeeded. During his minority the government was conducted by his uncles John of Gaunt, duke of Lancaster, and Thomas of Woodstock, duke of Gloucester. A rebellion of the peasants under Wat Tyler was put down in 1381. Richard assumed the government personally in 1389. He was overthrown (1399) by the duke of Hereford, whom he had banished (1398), was deposed by Parliament, and Hereford became king as Henry IV. Richard was captured and probably murdered in prison.

Richard III (of *England*). [Nicknamed "Crouchback."] King of England (1483–1485); b. at Fotheringay, England, October 2, 1452; killed at the battle of Bosworth,

August 22, 1485. He was the third son of Richard, 3rd duke of York, and the younger brother of Edward IV. He was known as the duke of Gloucester before his accession. He served in the battles of Barnet and Tewkesbury in 1471, and invaded Scotland in 1483. On the death of Edward IV, in April, 1483, he was proclaimed protector of the young Edward V whom he had confined in the Tower of London along with the heir apparent's younger brother, Richard, duke of York. In 1483 the young princes were declared illegitimate and Richard assumed the crown in June of that year. (The deaths of the Tower princes were laid at Richard's door, but responsibility for their deaths has never been satisfactorily resolved. Apologists for Richard assert that the young princes outlived Richard and that Henry VII, who succeeded him, destroyed all evidence that would have either cleared Richard or involved another as the instigator of their deaths.) Having attained the throne Richard suppressed the powerful rebellion of Henry Stafford, 2nd duke of Buckingham, in 1483, and was defeated and slain in the battle of Bosworth Field by Henry Tudor, earl of Richmond, who became king of England as Henry VII. Richard's nickname "Crouchback" was given to him on account of a (probably slight) bodily deformity. Richard, last of the Yorkist kings in the period of the Wars of the Roses, has had a generally bad reputation, but some historians now support the thesis that he was an able ruler whose often ruthless means were typical of his age, and at that, not so many men prominent in public life lost their heads in his reign as did later in the reign of Henry VIII. The latter had much more time however in a reign of thirty-eight years.

Richard Coeur de Lion (rich′ąrd kėr dẹ lē′on; French, kėr dẹ lyôṅ). Old romance, printed by Wynkyn de Worde in 1509. It appears to have been written in French in the time of Edward I, and afterward translated into English.

Richard the Redeless (rēd′lẹs). Poem probably by William Langland, written in 1399. The title was given by W. W. Skeat, and refers to the "redeless" Richard II, or Richard "without counsel."

Richier (rē-shyā), **Légier.** French sculptor; b. at Dagonville, near Ligny, France, c1500; d. c1572. He is said to have come under the personal influence of Michelangelo at Rome. He executed *The Sepulcher of Saint-Mihiel* (1532), one of the most beautiful creations of the Renaissance; and the mausoleum of René, prince of Orange, with its extraordinary "Squelette" (a carved skeleton holding in its right hand a small casket containing the heart of the deceased prince).

Ridley (rid′li), **Nicholas.** English bishop and Protestant martyr; b. in Northumberland, England, c1500; burned at Oxford, England, October 16, 1555. He was closely associated with Cranmer in outlining the Thirty-Nine Articles, and in preparing the English prayer book. He denied the legitimacy of both Elizabeth and Mary, insisting that only Lady Jane Grey could be considered a lawful child of Henry VIII. He refused to compromise this position, and on Mary's accession (1553) was arrested; two years later he was tried as a heretic, and burned at the stake with Latimer.

Rienzi (ryen′tsē) or **Rienzo** (ryen′tsō), **Cola di.** Roman revolutionary; b. at Rome, 1313 or 1314; killed there, October 8, 1354. After being brought up at Anagni, he returned to Rome (1333 or 1334) and began to read the classics. From his study he was imbued with the glory of ancient Rome and, since Rome was in a state of anarchy and Italy in turmoil, dreamed of restoring not only the ancient splendor of the city but the power and unity of the old Roman empire. He was employed (1343) on a mission to the pope at Avignon, by whom he was made a notary of the apostolic chamber. While in Avignon he met Petrarch, who ardently shared his aspirations of restoring Rome and the empire. As a papal notary, Rienzi held several public offices at Rome, in which he was able to make himself and his ideas known. Of obscure birth, but handsome and well-traveled, he stirred the enthusiasm of the beset Roman populace by his defense of their interest and by reminders of past glory. In May, 1347, before a multitude gathered in the Campidoglio, he offered his life for the salvation of the people. The next day he was given dictatorial powers to bring order to the city which meant, chiefly, to curb the warring factions of the nobles. He declared himself "tribune" of the people and was recognized by Pope Clement VI, who in his seat at Avignon had been taken unaware by events. He energetically set about carrying out the acts which a hastily convened parliament passed. The nobles were subdued, a militia was formed, fortified places were seized, and speedy and severe justice was rendered. In his delusion, Rienzi called on all the Italian states to send ambassadors to discuss the union of Italy in an empire under Roman leadership. Such an empire had no appeal for the Italian states and cities, some of which had won and zealously guarded independence from the Holy Roman emperor. The pope could not view an empire under the leadership of Rome with equanimity, and turned against Rienzi. The Roman nobles sought to regain their power. Rienzi invited them to a banquet with the intention of putting them to death once they were assembled. He changed his mind and spared them, but they were not grateful and fought against him. In a bloody battle at the San Lorenzo gate the Colonnesi were massacred (November 20, 1347) and the nobles routed. The victory did not improve Rienzi's position. He saw that he was losing the confidence of the people and sought to restore it by depositing the crown and sceptre, earlier awarded to him in a spectacular ceremony, on the altar of the Church of S. Maria in Aracoeli. He revoked the harshest decrees. Nothing did any good. The nobles rose against him again. He called the people to arms. They did not answer. Rienzi abdicated (1348), took sanctuary with the monks in the Apennines, and finally went to Prague (1350) to seek the aid of Charles IV. The archbishop of Prague imprisoned him on a charge of heresy. While in prison, Rienzi wrote many letters, his thoughts turning to the afterlife, to his wife and children, and to his innocence of the charge of heresy. Thanks partly to the influence of Charles IV and Petrarch, but mostly to the new pope, Innocent VI, who wanted to offset the power of the Roman nobles, he was absolved of the charge at Avignon, whither he had been permitted to go (1352) to defend himself. In 1354 he triumphantly returned to Rome. But the moment, if it had ever existed, was past. He needed money desperately. He caused Moriale, who had befriended him, to be beheaded and seized his wealth. He raised the price of salt and levied extortionate taxes. His tyranny was as oppressive as that of any other despot. The people revolted against him and killed him in a riot, October 8, 1354. Rienzi is an example of those, often looked upon as patriots, whose studies of ancient Rome gave rise to dreams of the restoration of ancient glory. He was an eloquent speaker and a personable man. He was also a visionary who lacked a policy and the experience to put into execution his ideals—noble as they undoubtedly originally were.

Rinaldo (rē-näl′dō). In the Italian versions of the Carolingian cycle, Orlando's brave and turbulent cousin. In Luigi Pulci's *Morgante maggiore* he is swiftly brought back from Egypt by the fallen angel Astarotte to help Orlando at the Pass of Roncesvalles. In Matteo Maria Boiardo's *Orlando Innamorato* he is smitten on sight with love for Angelica, beautiful princess of Cathay, as are all the other paladins. He then drinks of the spring of Merlin, in the forest of Ardennes where he is searching for Angelica. This spring has the property of causing all who drink of it to take a violent dislike to the first person they see, and now beholding Angelica he comes to despise her. She, however, having drunk of the spring of Cupid, fails desperately in love with him and uses all her magic to win him, to no avail. Having been thrashed nearly to a pulp by flowers wielded by Cupid's nymphs (after first undergoing prodigious adventures), Rinaldo drinks at Cupid's spring and falls deeply in love with Angelica again, thus becoming Orlando's rival. Angelica meanwhile has drunk of Merlin's fountain, with predictable results. In Lodovico Ariosto's *Orlando Furioso*, a continuation of Boiardo's work, he is sent to England to seek aid against the Moors who are besieging Charlemagne. In Scotland he saves Ginevra, unjustly accused. In company with the Archangel Michael and Silence (which he had a hard time finding in the monasteries where he looked first), he goes to the relief of Paris. Discord, meanwhile has entered the Moorish camp, and Paris is saved. Rinaldo is cured of his love for Angelica by a draft offered him from the jeweled Fountain of Disdain.

Rinaldo. In Torquato Tasso's *Gerusalemme liberata*, one of the Crusaders who goes to liberate Jerusalem with Godfrey of Bouillon in the first Crusade. He represents an ancestor of the Estensi of Ferrara, Tasso's patrons, and through him Tasso exalts the House of Este. In the poem, Rinaldo becomes enthralled by the enchantress Armida and is absent from the struggle for Jerusalem for a time. By means of a Christian talisman he is freed from Armida's wonderful garden, overcomes the terrors of an enchanted forest, and takes a valiant part in freeing Jerusalem from the Saracens.

Rinaldo d'Aquino (dä-kwē′nō). Poet of the so-called Sicilian school; b. c1200 or 1210; d. c1280. He was attached to the court of Frederick II. Twelve canzoni have been attributed to him. One of these, in the manner of the Provençal poets, is *Farewell*, expressing the sorrow of a girl whose lover is leaving on a crusade.

Rinuccini (rē-nöt-chē′nē), **Cino.** Poet; b. at Florence, c1350; d. there, 1417. He was a wool merchant who wrote sonnets, canzoni, ballate, and madrigals. He defended the glory of Florence and her three great poets: Dante, Petrarch, and Boccaccio, in invectives against humanist detractors. He was, above all, an ardent admirer of Dante, and placed him before all poets, ancient or modern.

Rinuccio d'Arezzo (rē-nöt′chō dä-ret′tsō). [Latinized, **Rinucius Aretinus.**] Humanist; b. at Castiglione, c1395; d. after 1450. About 1415 he was in the island of Candia, where he learned Greek, sought codices, and occupied himself with translating them. After a period at Constantinople, in which he established friendly relations with the emperor Manuel II, he returned to Italy (1423). There he entered the service of the cardinal legate of Bologna, Gabriele Condolmieri (later Pope Eugenius IV), went with him to Rome, and remained there the rest of his life. In the pontificate of Nicholas V he was a secretary and a colleague of Poggio Bracciolini. Rinuccio's chief work was in translation. Among others, he translated Diogenes, Hippocrates, Euripides, Aesop, Aristophanes, Plato, Demosthenes, Plutarch, and Lucian.

Rishanger (rish′ąng-ėr), **William.** English chronicler; active about the beginning of the 14th century. He compiled a chronicle covering the period from 1259 to 1307, which is looked upon as a continuation of that of Matthew Paris.

Rispetto (rē-spet′tō). Italian verse form that is a Tuscan adaptation of the *strambotto*. It varies from the latter in that the last two lines of the eight-line stanza introduce a new rhyme, thus: ABABABCC. Most poets of the Golden Age of Renaissance poetry included a number of *rispetti* among their lyrics.

Ristoro d'Arezzo (rē-stō′rō dä-ret′tsō). Thirteenth century cosmographer, of whom little is known. He compiled an astronomical and geographical work, *Della composizione del mondo* (1282), in eight books, in the dialect of Arezzo. Making use of the works of Aristotle and the Arab scientists, he added to these sources information resulting from his own keen observation of nature and natural phenomena, as eclipses, fossils, mineral springs, and so on. He also showed an interest in and artistic evaluation of the fragments of Etruscan vases that he found. These he kept, at a time when others discarded them as of no value.

Rivalto (rē-väl′tō), **Giordano.** See **Giordano da Pisa.**

Rizzi (rēt′tzē), **Gian Pietro.** See **Giampetrino.**

Rizzio (rēt′tsē-ō) or **Riccio** (rēt′chō), **David.** Secretary to Mary, Queen of Scots; b. c1533; killed at Edinburgh, March 9, 1566. A native of Piedmont, he entered the Scottish queen's service as a musician in 1564, and afterward became her French secretary and confidential adviser. He promoted Mary's marriage to Darnley, who, however, did not supplant him in her confidence. Convinced that Rizzio was Mary's lover, Darnley organized a conspiracy of Protestant lords against him and at their head burst into the Queen's supper chamber, wounded Rizzio in her presence and killed him outside the chamber.

Rizzo (rēt′tzō), **Antonio.** Veronese sculptor, working in the second half of the 15th century. He was confused, by Francesco Sansovino and Giovio, with Antonio Briosco of Como, who was also called il Rizzo or il Riccio, and with whose art his showed certain similarities. He went to Venice some time before 1464 and became an outstanding representative of Venetian sculpture in the developed 15th-century manner. Soon after his arrival at Venice he carved the monument of Orsato Giustiniani in S. Andrea della Certosa, now destroyed. The marked Renaissance flavor of the monument is known from a drawing. In 1465 he worked at the Certosa di Pavia. The full development of his art and style is indicated in the figures of *Adam* and *Eve* executed for niches of the Arco Foscari in the Ducal Palace. Other works include the monument to the Doge Tron (d. 1473) in the Church of the Frari, Venice, and the monument of Giovanni Emo (d. 1483), lost, but known from a water color and indicating that in the work the architecture rather overwhelmed the sculpture. From 1483 he was chief of the works of the Ducal Palace, of which he designed the Renaissance façade facing the prisons, to which they are connected by the Bridge of Sighs, and designed the famous *Scala dei Giganti*.

Robbia (rôb′byä), **Luca della.** See **Della Robbia, Luca.**

Robert (of *Naples*). King of Naples (1309–1343); b. 1278; d. at Naples, January 19, 1343. He was the third son of Charles II, duke of Anjou and king of Naples. With his elder brothers he was sent to Provence, in 1282, on the outbreak of the Sicilian Vespers. Next (1288), given as a hostage to the king of Aragon, he remained a prisoner until 1295, when a treaty was signed between James of Aragon and Charles II. Robert, who was unjustly accused of clearing his path to the throne by bringing about the murder of one brother and persuading the second to enter a monastery, was recognized, 1297, by Boniface VIII as the heir to Charles II. In 1297 he married Yolande of Aragon, and when she died (1303) he married again. His marriages and those he arranged for others had the one aim of securing or enhancing his power. In 1305 he gave his aid to the election of Clement V as pope, and in the same year, in the pay of Florence, he besieged Pistoia. In 1309, at Avignon, he assumed the crown of Naples on the death of his father. His was a war-ravaged kingdom and his external difficulties were many. He sought to improve his situation by negotiation. When his attempts to win Henry VII, who was descending into Italy with the pope's blessing, failed, be became a Guelph for good. The pope regretted his endorsement of Henry VII and betrayed him. Robert sent (1312) his younger brother to occupy Rome, when Henry was on his way to that city, and Neapolitan troops won control of the Vatican. Thus Henry was compelled to accept the imperial crown in St. John Lateran rather than, according to tradition, in St. Peter's. In 1313 Florence, fearing for her independence, asked Robert to become *signore* (lord) for five years, with the right to name the *podestà* (captain) of the city, and renewed the agreement with him for another four years. At the end of that time (1322) the Florentines were glad to see the last of the Neapolitans. John XXII, who made him papal vicar of Italy, was his ally and supporter, but when he died Robert, having lost his northern Italian power and the friendship of Florence, concentrated on securing the succession to his throne, although he had no direct heirs. From 1325 to 1341 he was almost continuously at war in an attempt to win Sicily from the Aragonese. In 1340 he invited Petrarch to Naples to receive the poet's crown. Petrarch had an invitation from Paris on the same day, and decided to go to Naples. There King Robert questioned him, and Petrarch speaks in glowing terms of the days he spent with the king. Robert offered to crown Petrarch himself but the latter wanted to receive the crown from the Roman Senate. Perhaps because of his flattering reception by Robert, Petrarch called him, "the only monarch of our age who was the friend of both learning and virtue." Robert, in the time he could spare for it, patronized and protected poets, writers, and jurists, and gathered a library that was unusual for its time. He was a friend and patron of Giotto and Simone Martini. Robert was succeeded by his granddaughter, Joanna I.

Robert I (of *Scotland*). [Also, **Robert Bruce,** the **Bruce;** the surname is also spelled **de Brus, de Bruis, Braose, Breaux.**] King of Scotland (1306–1329); b. probably at Turnberry, Ayrshire, Scotland, July 11, 1274; d. at Cardross, Scotland, June 7, 1329. A leader in the struggle against Edward I for Scottish independence, he was crowned king of Scotland in 1306. Outlawed by Edward I and excommunicated by the pope, he took refuge on Rathlin Island, where the legendary incident of the spider is supposed to have occurred. He returned to Scotland in 1307, where, Edward I having died, he won successive victories over Edward culminating in the decisive battle of Bannockburn (June 24, 1314). The Scottish parliament convened and settled the crown of the kingdom on the house of Bruce. In 1328, by the Treaty of Northampton, the English recognized Scottish independence.

Robert II (of *Scotland*). [Called "the Steward."] King of Scotland (1371–1390); b. March 2, 1316; d. at Dundonald, May 13, 1390. He was a grandson of Robert Bruce, and the first of the Stuart (Stewart) dynasty. A regent under his uncle, David II, when David threatened to permit the crown of Scotland to pass to Edward III of England,

Robert rebelled and was imprisoned. He took no direct part in the struggle with England.

Robert III (of *Scotland*). [Originally known as **John Stewart,** Lord of **Kyle.**] King of Scotland (1390–1406); b. c1340; d. April 4, 1406. He was the son of Robert II. Having been incapacitated by an injury received before he became king, the government was administered by his brother Robert Stewart, and by his son David. After the death of David, and the capture of his remaining son (afterward James I) by the English, Robert III died of grief.

Robert of Brunne (brůn′e̤). See **Mannyng, Robert.**

Robert of Geneva (je̤-nē′va̤), Count. Original name of the antipope **Clement VII.**

Robert the Steward. See **Robert II** (of *Scotland*).

Roberti (rō-ber′tē), **Ercole de'.** [Also called **Ercole da Ferrara.**] Painter; b. at Ferrara, c1450; d. there, 1496. He was a pupil of Cosmè Tura and a collaborator of Francesco Cossa. From 1482 to 1486 he was active at Bologna and was later court painter at Ferrara, where he performed the variety of tasks expected of the court painter in his day. His earliest work is thought to be on the panel *September*, in the Hall of the Months in the palace of Schifanoia at Ferrara. Cossa was in general charge of the decoration of the Hall until his departure for Bologna (c1470). Another early work of Roberti was an altarpiece at Berlin (destroyed in 1945) that was begun by Tura and completed by Roberti. Roberti followed Cossa to Bologna soon after, where he painted the predella panels of Cossa's Griffoni polyptych of *St. Vincent Ferrer* for S. Petronio, the central panel of which is now in the National Gallery, London. Roberti's predella panels with *Miracles of St. Vincent Ferrer*, are in the Vatican. Even in this early group of works, Roberti's individual style, with its differences from the older Ferrarese masters, Tura and Cossa, is apparent. His style is characterized by a subtle and sensitive linearity and economy still somewhat limited by stylization. Under the influence of Jacopo and Giovanni Bellini he breathed new life into the somewhat harsh Ferrarese style by replacing the metallic coldness typical of the Ferrarese palette with richer, warmer colors. His characteristics are fully evident in the altarpiece *Madonna and Child Enthroned with Saints* (1480) for S. Maria in Porto, Ravenna, and now in the Brera, Milan. A quality of his manner is to present strongly outlined figures in intense tones against a misty background in which the light is diffused in broad planes of color. An example is the predella panel *Pietà*, Liverpool. The Madonna's dark garment in angular outline is stark against a dim and distant landscape, and presents the strongest contrast to the pallor of her dead Son's body on her lap. In the shifting and uncertain light of the background flickers the scene of Calvary. Other panels of this predella from an altarpiece for the Church of S. Giovanni in Monte, Bologna, are at Dresden. Illustrative of his dramatic power is his *St. John the Baptist*, Berlin. Behind the gaunt and tragic figure of the Baptist is a strip of silent and desolate landscape; the light flickers from the sea to a reddish haze; most of the saint's emaciated and elongated form is silhouetted against the sky. In the frieze-like *Gathering of the Manna*, National Gallery, London, the figures are strongly outlined, almost as if superimposed on the dim background. His last work was perhaps the *Deposition*, Pinacoteca, Bologna, in which the figures of some of the saints and the landscape were finished by another hand. Other works include two outstanding examples of Ferrarese portraiture, *Giovanni di Bentivoglio*, despot of Bologna, and his wife, *Ginevra Bentivoglio*, daughter of Alessandro Sforza, lord of Pesaro, in the National Gallery, Washington. There are other paintings at Berlin, the National Gallery, London; panels from the pilasters of the Griffoni polyptych at Paris, Ferrara, Rotterdam, and Venice, and works at Chicago, Philadelphia, Turin, and elsewhere.

Roberto da Lecce (rō-ber′tō dä let′chā), Fra. See **Caracciolo,** Fra **Roberto.**

Roberto di Oderisio (dē ō-dā-rē′syō). See **Oderisi, Roberto.**

Robetta (rō-bāt′tä), **Cristofano.** Florentine goldsmith and engraver; b. at Florence, 1462; d. after 1522. In general, his prints were based on the work of others, as a set on the Creation and on the history of mankind to designs by Filippino Lippi. He made other prints on designs by Lippi, as well as on the work of Antonio Pollaiuolo and Luca Signorelli, and used elements of background and landscape that he borrowed from Dürer. Yet he was not a mere copyist. It might be said, from one point of view, that he took liberties with the originals or, from another point of view, that he impressed his own style on the work of others.

Robin of Redesdale (rob′in, rēdz′dāl). Assumed name of Sir William Conyers (d. 1495), leader of a peasants' revolt in Yorkshire against Edward IV in 1469.

Robortello (rō-bôr-tel′lō), **Francesco.** Humanist; b. at Udine, September 9, 1516; d. at Padua, March 18, 1567. He studied at Bologna, and was professor of eloquence at Lucca, Pisa, Venice, and Padua where, except for an interlude at Bologna (1557–1560), he remained the rest of his life. He published annotated editions of Latin and Greek works, and wrote treatises on ancient Rome. His chief work was his *In librum Aristotelis de arte poetica explicationes, . . .* (Florence, 1548). This was a fully annotated, emended text of the Latin version of Aristotle's work, to which Robortello added discussions of the rules of ancient poetry.

Robusti (rō-bös′tē), **Jacopo.** See **Tintoretto.**

Roch (rok), Saint. French Franciscan; b. at Montpellier, France, c1295; d. there, 1327. He was noted for his ministrations to the plague-stricken. The dog that appears with him in art symbolizes the dog that is said to have sustained him by bringing him bread when, ill with plague, he was cast out of Piacenza.

Rodomonte (rō-dō-môn′tā). In Matteo Maria Boiardo's *Orlando Innamorato*, a boastful, defiant, brave African, who decides to invade France alone while Agramante, his king, is gathering his forces. In Lodovico Ariosto's *Orlando Furioso*, a continuation of Boiardo's romantic epic, Rodomonte is killed by Ruggiero in single combat, but not before he has raised havoc inside Paris.

Roger (ro-zhā), **Pierre.** Original name of Pope **Clement VI.**

Rolandino de' Passeggeri (rō-län-dē′nō dā päs-sed-jā′rē). Notary; b. at Bologna at the beginning of the 13th century; d. there, 1300. He practiced his profession with great success, and taught it at the University of Bologna. He was also active in civic life, as one of the leaders of the Guelph faction against their rivals. Among his writings was his *Summa artis notariae* (1255), a work honored and known in his own times and later, and in his own city and beyond, for the clarity, exactness, and simplicity with which he described the notarial profession. The work is in four parts: on contracts, wills, judicial acts, and copies and revisions of the laws. Known as the *Rolandino*, or *Orlandino*, it became an indispensable text, in and out of Italy, and went through many editions.

Rolando da Piazzola (rō-län-dō dä pyät-tsō′lä). Paduan jurist; d. between 1324 and 1333. He took an active part in the political life of his native city. In the struggle that erupted between Guelphs and Ghibellines when the emperors Henry VII and Louis IV descended into Italy in their turn, he was on the side of the Ghibellines. He wrote *De regibus*.

Roldán (rôl-dän′), **Francisco.** Spanish adventurer; b. c1450; drowned in July, 1502. He went to Hispaniola with Columbus. He headed a rebellion against Bartholomew Columbus who was governor of the island. Roldán was arrested by Nicolás de Ovando and ordered to Spain, but he was drowned in a storm.

Rollenhagen (rol′e̤n-hä-ge̤n), **Georg.** German Protestant clergyman and schoolmaster; b. at Bernau, Germany, April 22, 1542; d. at Magdeburg, Germany, May 18, 1609. He was the author of the animal epic *Froschmeuseler* (1595) modeled after the Greek *Batrachomyomachia,* the war of frogs and mice, which belongs in the tradition of the didactic Reynard stories. There are no humans in it, but neither is there any attempt to draw animals as animals. Their vices and virtues are human, and the epic as a whole turns out to be an allegory.

Rolle of Hampole (rōl; ham′pōl), **Richard.** [Known as the **Hermit of Hampole.**] English hermit and religious writer; b. at Thornton, Yorkshire, England, c1290; d. at Hampole, England, 1349. The nature of his many prose treatises marked him as the first English mystic. His works include *Melum Contemplativorum, Incendium Amoris, Emendatio Vitae*, and several works in English. *The Prick of Conscience*, the most popular poem of the 14th century, was formerly ascribed to him.

Roma Triumphans. [Full title, **Romae Triumphantis Libri Decem.**] Written by Flavio Biondo, it was the first great attempt at a complete exposition of the institutions and customs of Roman antiquity. It was dedicated to Pope Pius II. Its first dated edition was at Brixen (1482).

Romanino (rō-mä-nē′nō), **Girolamo.** [Real name, **Girolamo di Romano.**] Painter; b. at Brescia, between 1484 and 1487; d. after 1562. He was trained under local painters and his early works are in the local tradition. Among these are *Madonna and Child Enthroned* (c1502), Church of S. Francesco, Brescia, in which the silvery, moonlike tone of Moretto prevails, and the signed and dated (1510) *Pietà*, Accademia, Venice. A fresh and imaginative painter who delighted in a fanciful recreation of the everyday world, he was strongly influenced by the Venetians. The poetic approach of Giorgione is apparent in a number of portraits; the ardent color of Titian is reflected in the altarpiece, *Madonna and Child Enthroned* (1513), painted for S. Giustina at Padua and now in the Museo Civico. Other influences on his style were those of Lotto and Pordenone. As a result of contact with the work of the latter intensified color, vigorous modeling and an atmosphere of drama that often approached the turbulent replaced the fairytale richness of his earlier painting. Many of his works are to be found in the Pinacoteca and churches of Brescia, as the *Mass of St. Apollonius*, Church of S. Maria in Calchera, with its subtle delineation of daily life, and the dramatic paintings in S. Francesco. Other works are frescoes in a monumental style at Cremona, in S. Maria della Neve, Pisogne, and a series of delightful frescoes in magnificent color in the Castello del Buonconsiglio at Trent. Among the portraits are the lively *Portrait of a Boy* and the strikingly modern *Portrait of a Gentleman*, Pinacoteca, Brescia, and others. There are examples of his work in the cathedral, Salò, in the Brera and Castello Sforzesco, Milan, at London, Bergamo, Asola, Allentown (Pennsylvania), Atlanta (Georgia), Brooklyn, Memphis, New Orleans, Savannah, Seattle, and elsewhere. One of the most important of the Brescian painters, he influenced other Brescians and painters in the surrounding areas as well.

Romano (rō-mä′nō), **Antoniazzo.** See **Antoniazzo Romano.**

Romano, Gian Cristoforo. Roman sculptor, architect, medalist and gem-engraver; b. at Rome, c1470; d. at Loreto, 1512. He was the son of the sculptor Isaia da Pisa and was a pupil of Giovanni Antonio Amadeo. In 1491 he was working with Amadeo and Benedetto Briosco on the façade of the Certosa di Pavia. Of about this time is his *Bust of Beatrice d'Este*, now in the Louvre, Paris. In his stay at Pavia and Milan he also executed (1493–1497) the tomb of Gian Galeazzo Visconti, Certosa di Pavia. After the death of Beatrice d'Este (1497) he went to Mantua, where he was one of the artists and courtiers surrounding Isabella d'Este. He advised and assisted her with her collections, made a medal of her, carved the doorway to her private rooms, *Il Paradiso*, and executed a bust of her husband, Francesco Gonzaga. In 1505 he went to Urbino as a member of that cultivated court. Castiglione includes him as one of the participants in the conversations that constitute *Il Cortegiano*. He was at Rome when the *Laocoön* was discovered (1506) and was one of the group, which included Michelangelo, delegated by Julius II to examine it.

Romano, Giulio. See **Giulio Romano.**

Rondel (rôn′del). In Luigi Pulci's *Morgante maggiore*, a reworking of the *Chanson de Roland*, Orlando's faithful horse. During the battle at the Pass of Roncesvalles, the horse kneels in homage to Orlando, begs his forgiveness, and dies of exhaustion.

Rondinelli (rôn-dē-nel′lē), **Niccolò.** Painter; b. at Ravenna, c1450; d. c1510. He was a pupil of Giovanni Bellini, whom he at times imitated closely, borrowing elements directly from the master's work. His attempts to free himself from too great dependence on Bellini reveal the essential provinciality of his work. A facile painter, given to lively color, in the course of his career he succeeded to a limited extent in overcoming the defects of his cylindrical figures with vacant expressions. His chief works include *St. John the Evangelist Appearing to Galla Placida*, Brera, Milan; several paintings of the *Madonna and Saints*, in the art gallery, Ravenna; and a *St. Sebastian*, cathedral, Forlì. Other examples of his work are at Rome (Barberini Palace, Doria Pamphili Gallery), Venice (Accademia, Correr Museum), Baltimore, Indianapolis, the Johnson Collection, Philadelphia, Washington (Smithsonian), Worcester, and elsewhere.

Ronsard (rôṅ-sȧr), **Pierre de.** French poet,

chief of the Pléiade; b. at the Chateau de La Poissonnière, in Vendômois, France, September 11, 1524; d. at the priory of St.-Côme, in Touraine, France, in December, 1585. After a brief stay at the Collège de Navarre at Paris, at the age of ten he became page to Charles, duke of Orléans, second son of Francis I of France. He spent a couple of years in the service of James V of Scotland, and then returned to his former post, and was attached to various diplomatic embassies that took him to the Netherlands and Alsace, among other places. On his final return to France in 1542, he lost his sense of hearing in consequence of a severe illness. This infirmity compelled him to give up the life at court at the age of 18, and led him to turn all his attention to literary labors. Together with his friend Jean Antoine Baïf, he took up a course of study that extended over seven years (1542–1549) and made of him an excellent Greek scholar. The ultimate end he had in view was to regenerate his native tongue, and demonstrate in his own works that the French language was capable of as much power and nobility of expression as it had of acknowledged grace and refinement. Between 1550 and 1552 he began to publish his *Odes*. These reflect the thorough knowledge of Greek and Latin literature he possessed, the influence of Pindar and Horace and, later, of Anacreon. Of Petrarchan inspiration are his *Sonnets à Cassandre*, love poems written for Cassandre de Salviati, whom he met at a ball and whom he is supposed to have continued to love after her marriage. This love was without prejudice to others, however, and later sonnets in his series of *Amours* (1555–1556), less Petrarchan, are addressed to a Marie, whose further identity is uncertain. He attained great success in his own day with his *Hymnes* (1555–1556) on great men or addressed to his friends, and became a great favorite with King Charles IX, who gave him rich ecclesiastical benefices (he had received the tonsure but had never been ordained). His *Les Discours* (1560–1570) are poems in alexandrines that treat the religious wars in France from a Roman Catholic and patriotic viewpoint. On the death of his royal patron (1574), Ronsard was gradually relegated to the background. He finally left the court in utter discouragement. The last years of his life (1574–1585) were spent in quiet and sad retirement. Ronsard brought to French poetry the new conceptions of humanism; more than that, he was the father of lyric poetry in France. Perhaps his best-known work is the *Sonnets pour Hélène*, written to Hélenè de Surgères, a primarily literary love of the poet's. His great ambition, however, had been to rank as the Homer or Vergil of his country, and in this spirit he undertook to write a long poem, *La Françiade;* he labored on it for twenty-five years, and finally left it unfinished. His other works include *Les Bocages* (1550, 1554), *Les Folastries* (1553) and *Elégies, Mascarades et Bergerie* (1565). Neglected for 250 years, Ronsard is now considered one of the outstanding figures of French Renaissance poetry.

Rore (rō′rẹ), **Cipriano de.** Flemish composer of the Venetian school; b. at Antwerp or at Mechelen, Belgium, 1516; d. at Parma, Italy, 1565. He composed motets, psalms, Masses, a passion, and, notably, madrigals.

Rosa (rō′zä), **Loise de.** See **De Rosa, Loise.**

Rosate (rō-sä′tā), **Ambrogio da.** See **Ambrogio da Rosate.**

Roselli (rō-zel′lē), **Antonio.** Jurisconsult; b. at Arezzo, 1380; d. at Padua, December 16, 1466. He lectured on canon law at Bologna (1406–1407), and later served on important embassies for the emperor Sigismund and the king of Naples, and as legate of Pope Eugenius IV. He then went to Padua to teach, and remained there the rest of his life. He left a number of treatises on legal subjects, as on marriage contracts, succession, the powers of the emperor and the pope, the succession when there is no will, and one on usury.

Roses, Wars of the. Series of armed contests (1455–1485) for the throne of England, between the houses of Lancaster and York; so-called because the Yorkists took as their symbol the white rose, whereupon the Lancastrians adopted the red rose. It began during the minority of Henry VI of the house of Lancaster, and ended with the death of Richard III of the house of York at Bosworth, and the accession of Henry Tudor, earl of Richmond, and a Lancastrian, to the throne as Henry VII. No issue of importance to the English people was at stake, and they remained for the most part unaffected by the mutual slaughter of the nobles and their retainers, which prepared the way for the near-absolutism of the Tudor and Stuart dynasties.

Rosinante (roz-i-nan′tē̦). [Spanish, **Rocinante.**] In Cervantes' *Don Quixote*, Don Quixote's charger, all skin and bone.

Rosmunda (rōz-mön′dä). Tragedy by Giovanni Rucellai, presented in the Rucellai gardens on the occasion of a visit to Florence by Pope Leo X. It is an adaptation, with Lombard characters, of the *Antigone* of Sophocles.

Rosselli (rōs-sel′lē), **Bernardo di Girolamo.** Florentine painter; active at Perugia between 1532 and 1569. To his native Tuscan style he added elements of Umbrian painting. His *Presentation in the Temple* is in the National Gallery of Umbria, at Perugia.

Rosselli, Cosimo. Painter; b. at Florence, 1439; d. there, 1507. Member of a distinguished Florentine family, he was a pupil of Neri di Bicci. In his development he was somewhat influenced by the work of Baldovinetti, Domenico Veneziano, and Antonio Pollaiuolo. Not a painter of a high order, his figures are stiff, his composition and sense of space shaky, his work lacking in dramatic focus. These deficiencies are illustrated from his first work. His earliest dated work (1471), *St. Anne, Madonna and Child Enthroned, and Four Saints*, Berlin, shows the diluted influences of the painters noted above in its stiff, symmetrical figures, all of whom have the same stare. Another early work is an *Annunciation* (1473), Louvre. A decorator who achieved his effects by his use of color, he was one of the painters invited by Sixtus IV to decorate the walls of the Sistine Chapel (1481–1482). His pupil, Piero di Cosimo, assisted him. The other painters working in the Sistine Chapel—Botticelli, Ghirlandaio, Perugino—were rather scornful of Cosimo for the lavish use he made of ultramarine and gold to cover up his lack of skill in composition and draftsmanship. They were discomfitted when Sixtus declared Cosimo's work the best and urged the others to copy it. The subjects of his frecoes, by common consent the weakest paintings in the Chapel, are *Moses Destroying the Tables of the Law, Sermon on the Mount and Healing of the Leper*, and *Last Supper*. Cosimo had a flourishing workshop at Florence and left a large number of rather pedestrian paintings and frescoes. There are examples of his work in a number of churches at Florence, as the frescoes in a chapel (1486) and an altarpiece, *Madonna in Glory* (1501), in the Church of S. Ambrogio, and in the Accademia, Uffizi, Palazzo Vecchio, and other collections. He is also represented in galleries in Italy and other countries of Europe, and in the Walters Art Gallery, Baltimore, at Birmingham (Alabama), Boston (Museum of Fine Arts), Cleveland, Columbia (South Carolina), Houston, Minneapolis, New York (the Metropolitan Museum), Notre Dame (Indiana), Philadelphia (Johnson Collection), Tulsa, Winter Park (Florida), and elsewhere.

Rossellino (rōs-sel-lē′nō), **Antonio.** Sculptor; b. at Settignano, 1427; d. at Florence, 1479. He was the son of Matteo Gamberelli and was the brother of Bernardo Rossellino (1409–1464). Other sculptor brothers were Domenico (b. 1407), Giovanni (b. 1417), and Tommaso (b. 1422). The brothers had an active workshop in which Giovanni, Domenico, and Tommaso often assisted Antonio and Bernardo in the execution of commissions. Antonio was trained under Bernardo and developed his own style, in which were combined the delicacy and refinement of design of Ghiberti and the pictorial sense of Donatello. His work tends to a virile classical elegance and is notable for its dynamism, such as the figures of the flying and half-kneeling angels that animate his masterpiece, the monument of the Cardinal of Portugal in S. Miniato al Monte. By 1452 his reputation was established; in that year he was one of those chosen to evaluate Buggiano's pulpit in S. Maria Novella. His earliest signed and dated (1456) work is the strongly modeled marble *Bust of Giovanni Chellini*, Victoria and Albert Museum, London, whose tomb at S. Miniato al Tedesco Bernardo designed. The bust, thought to have been modeled from a life mask, is notable for its powerful projection of an austere and intelligent personality and the skill with which Antonio handled the shifting planes of the sunken cheeks, folds of skin, thin lips and domed head of his subject. A later bust, that of *Matteo Palmieri* (1468), reflects the wit and animation of the noted humanist. Antonio's first recorded commission was for the monument of the Cardinal of Portugal. In his will the young cardinal (1413–1439) directed that a chapel be erected in S. Miniato al Monte for daily Mass. (His own estate was insufficient to bear the expense, and most of it was carried by the duchess of Burgundy.) The chapel that contains his monument was created expressly for the purpose and presents a rare unity of architectural, sculptural, and painting elements. Antonio Manetti, pupil of Brunelleschi designed it, Luca della Robbia made the enameled terra-cotta ceiling, Antonio Pollaiuolo and Alessio Baldovinetti executed frescoes, Antonio and Piero Pollaiuolo painted an altarpiece, and Antonio Rossellino designed and executed the monument. The monument is one of the most beautiful in Italy. Rossellino designed a niche (as his brother Bernardo had done for the monument of Leonardo Bruni in S. Croce) to hold the sarcophagus and effigy. In carving the head of the cardinal (taken, as were the hands, from a death cast), Rossellino achieved a sublime youthful serenity. On each end of the sarcophagus sits a sweetly animated cherub; angels that seem to have just alighted rest, half-kneeling, on pedestals at the head and foot of the effigy. Above is a deeply carved relief of the *Madonna and Child*. The wreath in which it is framed is supported in the air by flying angels. The total effect is of exquisite sensitivity and grace. The monument was completed probably by 1466, when the chapel was dedicated; the other decoration was completed later. Several reliefs of the Madonna, in marble and in terra-cotta, are attributed to Antonio on the basis of the relief in the Chapel of the Cardinal of Portugal and others he is known to have carved for other monuments. Among those in marble is one in the Metropolitan Museum, New York. Others are in the Morgan Library, New York, the National Gallery, Washington, in the Hermitage, Leningrad, and at Vienna. Other works by Antonio include an altar with St. Sebastian and two angels for the cathedral at Empoli, now in the Museum of Sacred Art there, and reliefs, *Assumption of the Virgin, Stoning of St. Stephen, Funeral of St. Stephen*, for the inside pulpit, designed in the Rossellino studio, of the cathedral at Prato. In his reliefs, as the monumental *Nativity*, for an altar in the Piccolomini Chapel, Church of S. Anna dei Lombardi, Naples, his emphasis is pictorial, with great use of perspective and foreshortening. The relief was completed, as was the tomb of Mary of Aragon in the same chapel (on which he worked 1470–1475), by his pupil Benedetto da Maiano. He assisted his brother Bernardo on the shrine of Beato Marcolino at Forlì (1458) and the tomb of Neri Capponi, S. Spirito (after 1457), and contracted to finish the monument of Filippo Lazzari in the cathedral at Pistoia after Bernardo's death.

Rossellino, Bernardo. Sculptor and architect; b. at Settignano, 1409; d. at Florence, September 23, 1464. He was the son of Matteo Gamberelli, was the brother of Antonio Rossellino (1427–1479), the noted sculptor, and had three other sculptor brothers. Nothing is known of his early training or masters. His earliest surviving work, on the façade of the Misericordia at Arezzo, is a relief of the *Madonna of Mercy* in an irregular lunette above the portal, and shows that he had made his own the architectural and sculptural forces at work in Florence in his day. Notable among these are the austerity and elegance of Brunelleschi and the dynamic plasticity of Donatello. After other work at Arezzo and Florence he began (1444) work on the tomb of Leonardo Bruni, the noted scholar and historian. He designed a triumphal arch to frame a niche containing the sarcophagus and effigy of the scholar, and designed and carved the sculptural decoration. Bruni was buried at Florence in a splendid civic ceremony. He was dressed in a long silk robe, such as he wore in life; a copy of his *History of Florence* was placed in his hands. As the oration was pronounced over his corpse a wreath of laurel was placed on his head. This is how he is shown in Rossellino's effigy. The effigy rests on two pedestals decorated with imperial eagles, which in turn rest on the sarcophagus. In the lunette above, a medallion with a relief of the *Madonna and Child* is supported by two angels. The tomb in S. Croce, completed in 1446 or 1445, is notable for rhythmic harmony of architectural and sculptural elements and influenced all subsequent monuments of the 15th century at Florence. Other monuments executed by Rossellino are those of Beata Villana (1451), S. Maria Novella; Orlando de' Medici (1456–1457), SS. Annunziata; Neri Capponi (1458), S. Spirito, all at Florence, and of Beato Marcolino da Forlì (1458), Forlì; Giovanni Chellini (1462–1464), S. Miniato al Tedesco; and Filippo Lazzari (begun 1462), cathedral, Pistoia. In the execution of that of Beato Marcolino he was assisted by his brother Antonio, who largely carried out that of Filippo Lazzari at Pistoia. Other sculptural works of Bernardo include two figures, *The Angel of the Annunciation* and the *Virgin Annunciate* (1447) at Empoli, and a tabernacle (1449) in S. Egidio, Florence.

As an architect, Bernardo was influenced chiefly by Leon Battista Alberti, for whom he worked on the Rucellai Palace at Florence between 1446 and 1451. Toward the end of the latter year he went to Rome as architect of Pope Nicholas V, and assisted in the restoration and rebuilding that Nicholas so eagerly encouraged. His greatest work as an architect, however, was carried out for Pope Pius II in the creation of one of the loveliest Renaissance squares in Italy. Pius, wishing to exalt his native village of Corsignano, whose name he changed to Pienza, commissioned Bernardo to erect a papal palace, a cathedral, and a bishop's palace at Pienza. According to the pope's wishes, the cathedral on the south side of the Piazza Pio II is in the Gothic manner in the interior; Bernardo brought it into his own age by designing a Renaissance façade. On the right of the cathedral rises the Piccolomini Palace, inspired by the Rucellai Palace at Florence. It is one of Rossellino's masterpieces. The exterior is simple, elegant, and pure. Three superposed porticoes on the south side of the palace take advantage of the exposure and provide a beautiful view of Mt. Amiata. On the left of the cathedral is the Bishop's Palace, an existing building that Rossellino modernized with the addition of Renaissance elements. The constructions were carried out with dispatch, beginning late in 1459 or early in 1460. In 1462 the cathedral was dedicated. Pius was delighted with it, and issued a bull that the church should never be changed. To his architect he said, "You did well, Bernardo, to conceal the true cost from us, for if we had known it in the beginning we would neither have had the courage to undertake the charge, nor would the world have had this miracle of art" (See **Pienza**). While principally occupied at Pienza from 1460 to 1463, Bernardo also took a few other commissions, and served as superintendent of the works of the cathedral at Florence until his death.

Rossello di Jacopo Franchi
Young Saint in a Tabernacle
Gabinetto Disegni e Stampe degli Uffizi
Foto Soprintendenza

Rossello di Jacopo Franchi (rōs-sel′lō dē jä-kō-pō fräng′kē). Florentine painter; b. c1376; d. at Florence, 1457. In 1429 he was painting miniatures, and in 1435 he was working with Bicci di Lorenzo. He was a traditional painter of charm, whose early works closely follow the 14th-century Florentine forms derived from Giotto and carried on, with varying degrees of success and understanding, by his many followers. He was also influenced by Lorenzo Monaco and, later, by Gentile da Fabriano. His later works reveal some skill at achieving plastic effects and solidity of form, as well as in portraying features. Many of his works are at Florence, as *The Coronation of the Virgin and Saints*

(1420), Accademia, frescoes on the façade of the Bigallo, and works in the Bargello, Palazzo Davanzati, Palazzo Vecchio, Cathedral (*St. Blaise Enthroned with Two Angels,* 1408), frescoes of *St. Lucy* and *A Male Saint,* S. Miniato al Monte, and *Madonna of Humility,* Spedale degli Innocenti. Other works are at Borgo San Lorenzo (S. Lorenzo), Empoli, Ortimino (S. Vito), Pisa, Siena (a signed and dated, 1439, *Coronation of the Virgin*), Pistoia (*St. Nicholas* and *St. Julian,* wings of a triptych, the central panel of which was painted by Mariotto di Nardo, who is thought by some to have been Rossello's teacher), Barcelona, Berlin, Moscow, Paris (Musée de Cluny), Zagreb, Baltimore (Walters Art Gallery), Cleveland, Madison (Wisconsin), New Haven, New York, and elsewhere.

Rossi (rôs′sē), **Francesco de'.** See **Salviati, Cecchino.**

Rossi, Niccolò de'. Poet; b. at Treviso, c1290; d. after 1348. He took his doctorate in law at Bologna (1317), and taught in his native city the year following. A Guelph, he also served his city in official posts and embassies. As a poet, he adopted the style and subject matter of the early realists, and produced rather lifeless verses. Sonnets he wrote on political matters give evidence of more feeling.

Rossi, Roberto de'. Florentine humanist; b. 1355; d. 1417. He was a member of an ancient family of Florence and, since his family was considered of the nobility, he was barred from holding the highest offices of the republic. (The nobles had been barred from holding office shortly after the *Ciompi* rebellion of 1378. They were barred partly in order to prevent the constant strife between rival factions, and partly to assure that the lesser magnates and representatives of the guilds would have a place in the government.) Rossi had the reputation of being a learned and prudent man. He held some lesser offices of the republic up to the year 1393, and was sometimes called on by the *Signoria* to give advice. A highly educated man, he was a pupil of Chrysoloras and was one of the first Florentines to read classical Greek. His family was not wealthy and he gave private lessons in Latin and Greek. Cosimo de' Medici was one of his pupils.

Rossi, Vincenzo de. See **De Rossi, Vincenzo.**

Rosso (rôs′sō), **Antonio.** Painter; b. at Tai di Cadore, c1440; d. at Belluno, 1509 or 1510. A provincial painter, his *Madonna Enthroned,* Accademia, Venice, is in the early manner that depicted the divine figures on a much larger scale than the human figures. In the linearity and woody slenderness of his figures he appears as a follower of the Vivarini, but without their gifts. Most of his figures have doll-like faces, thin, long figures, and stand in stiff poses. He painted several panels on the *Madonna and Saints,* Musée Jacquemart-André, Paris, São Paulo, Brazil (1494) and Selva di Cadore. Fragments of *St. Roch* and *St. Sebastian* are at Treviso.

Rosso, Fra **Paolo del.** See **Del Rosso,** Fra **Paolo.**

Rosso Fiorentino (fyō-ren-tē′nō). [Original name, **Giovanni Battista di Jacopo.**] Painter, architect, and designer; b. at Florence, March 8, 1494; d. at Paris, November 14, 1540. He was a pupil of Andrea del Sarto. He was among those who painted decorations for the entry into Florence of Leo X in 1515, and entered the Painters' Guild at Florence in 1516. About 1523 he went to Rome, where he remained until the sack (1527). After brief stays at Borgo San Sepolcro, Arezzo, and Venice, he went (1530) to France at the invitation of Francis I. Little in his work reflects his training under Andrea del Sarto. Possessed of an original, if not perverse, imagination, he was influenced by Pontormo and Michelangelo and became one of the earliest and one of the more bizarre of the mannerists. He created a world of fantasy with a persistent emphasis on linear angularity, sombre, menacing, but rich color, and flashing highlights. Among the works of his Italian period are the *Deposition* (1521), Volterra, *The Marriage of the Virgin* (1523), S. Lorenzo, Florence, *Moses Defending the Daughters of Jethro,* Uffizi, frescoes (1524) on *The Creation of Eve* and *The Fall of Man,* S. Maria della Pace, Rome, and a signed and dated (1521) *Madonna and Child with SS. John the Baptist and John the Evangelist,* Pieve, Villamagna. In his *Madonna and Child with St. Anne and the Infant St. John,* Los Angeles, the face of St. Anne is almost an abstraction of gaunt old age. He also left several strong, thrusting portraits. His most important work is at Fontainebleau, where he was joined (1532) by Primaticcio, and where he was the founder

Rosso Fiorentino
Study for the St. John in the *Deposition,* Volterra; ink drawing of a squirrel
Gabinetto Disegni e Stampe degli Uffizi Foto Soprintendenza

thin; ᴛʜ, then; y, you; (variable) d̤ as d or j, s̤ as s or sh, t̤ as t or ch, z̤ as z or zh; o, F. cloche; ü, F. menu; ċh, Sc. loch; ṅ, F. bonbon; ʙ, Sp. Córdoba (sounded almost like v).

of the so-called School of Fontainebleau—given this name because of the influence the Italians at Fontainebleau had on French painting. His work there in the Gallery of Francis I included thirteen historical, mythological, and allegorical scenes in fresco, surrounded by stucco decoration that he designed. Other examples of his work are at Borgo San Sepolcro, Città di Castello, in the Pitti, Uffizi, and churches at Florence, at Naples, Frankfurt, Leningrad, Liverpool, Paris, Boston, and elsewhere.

Rota (rō'tä), **Bernardino.** Poet; b. at Naples, 1508; d. there, 1575. He was of an ancient family that had come to Naples from Asti in the train of Charles of Anjou, and had flourished in succeeding centuries. Devoted to literature, he married a young relative of Scipione Capece, who had become the leader of the Academy founded by Pontano, and won for himself some reputation as the center of a literary circle. In his poetry Rota was a disciple and imitator of Sannazzaro. He wrote (1533) fourteen piscatorial eclogues in the vernacular after the manner of Sannazzaro's *Piscatoriae*. In these, the evidence of imitation is stronger than that of talent. He also wrote on subjects that others of the Neapolitan circle had treated, among them, the joys and sorrows of conjugal life. These won him fame as a poet of conjugal life but again, cold, elegant, and restrained, were better as imitations than as art. His Latin elegies and epigrams have the same qualities, and his chief interest for a later day lies in the many warm contacts he had with the leading literary men of his time.

Rovere (rō'vä-rā), **della.** See **Della Rovere.**

Rucellai (rö-chel-lä'ē), **Bernardo.** Florentine humanist; b. 1448; d. 1514. He was the son of Giovanni Rucellai (1403–1481) for whom Leon Battista Alberti designed the Rucellai palace, one of the outstanding examples of Renaissance architecture at Florence. He was a noted humanist, who founded the Orti Oricellari, the Florentine Academy where Machiavelli read his discourses on Livy, and who opened the Rucellai gardens for the meetings of the Academy. Bernardo was the author of *Historia de bello pisano* and *De bello gallico*, the latter on the invasion of Charles VIII into Italy in 1494.

Rucellai, Giovanni. Humanist and poet; b. at Florence, October 20, 1475; d. at Rome, April 3, 1525. His mother was Nannina de' Medici, sister of Lorenzo the Magnificent (1449–1492); his father was the humanist and historian, Bernardo Rucellai (1448–1514). Giovanni studied the classics and put the final polish to his education with travels to Venice and Provence. A Medicean partisan, he entered upon an ecclesiastical career and received many benefits from his cousin, Pope Leo X. A close friend of the poet Giangiorgio Trissino, he wrote his tragedy, *Rosmunda*, in friendly rivalry with Trissino's *Sophonisba*. A contemporary account describes how the two poets would break into recitation of their lines and ask the company about them to decide who was the better writer. Rucellai's *Rosmunda*, an early attempt at a classical tragedy, borrows from Sophocles' *Antigone*, but lacks the forward movement that makes the tragedy inevitable. It is, rather, a horror story of the time of the barbarian Lombards. His *Oreste*, based on Euripides' *Iphigenia in Tauris*, is marked with the same ease of verse as the *Rosmunda*, and the same lack of motivation. His poem on bees, *Api*, on Vergil's theme, is characterized by grace and melody rather than true poetic inspiration.

Rudolf I (of the *Holy Roman Empire*) (rö'dolf). [Also, **Rudolph, Rudolf of Hapsburg.**] German king and Holy Roman emperor (1273–1291); b. at Limburg, May 1, 1218; d. at Germersheim, Germany, July 15, 1291. He was the son of Albert IV, count of Hapsburg and landgrave of Alsace, and succeeded his father in Hapsburg and Alsace in 1239. Following the death of Conrad IV (1254), the Hohenstaufen king, the attempt to unite Germany under one king was constantly frustrated. The period 1254–1273, known as the Great Interregnum, during which the throne of Germany was vacant, was marked by struggle and intrigue. The papacy, fearing a resurgence of Hohenstaufen power in Italy, encouraged and abetted Charles of Anjou, who became Charles I of Naples, as a counterweight to Hohenstaufen claims in Italy. Charles then became so powerful that in his turn he caused alarm to the papacy. It was on this account that Pope Gregory X used his influence in securing the election of Rudolf, a relatively obscure German count, as king of the Germans, and invited him to Rome to receive the imperial crown. Rudolf, for one reason or another, never made the journey to Rome and was never crowned by the pope. Rudolf was the first monarch of the Hapsburg line. In exchange for papal support (also very large papal loans), and in order to restore peace between papacy and empire, Rudolf gave up all claim to the States of the Church and southern Italy. To balance these losses, he warred against Ottocar II of Bohemia, who was slain on the Marchfeld in 1278. Rudolf obtained Austria, Styria, and Carniola for his house. He established his sons as rulers of these regions, thus founding a dynasty that endured, with intervals, for over 700 years (1916). Rudolf failed in his attempt to have his son Albert made king of the Germans, and was succeeded by Adolf of Nassau.

Rue (rü), **Pierre** (or **Pierchon**) **de la.** [Latinized, **Petrus Platensis.**] Netherlands contrapuntal composer; b. c1450; d. 1518. He was a follower of Ockeghem, and served at the Burgundian court.

Rueda (rö-ā′ᴛʜä), **Lope de.** Spanish dramatist and actor; b. in Seville, Spain, c1510; d. 1565. He occupies an important place in the history of Spanish drama as the founder of the popular national theater.

Ruggeri (röd-je′rē), **Ugo.** Printer and founder; b. at Reggio Emilia, c1450; d. there, c1508. He went to Bologna (c1471) to study, but became so interested in the art of printing that he gave up his studies to devote himself to it. At Bologna (1473–1476) he produced some fine editions. The next three years were occupied by political and university obligations, and by family and business cares. He spent them at Reggio, where the first printed book was an *Algorismo* (1478). In 1481 he took up printing at Bologna again, and remained there until the end of the century, when he returned to Reggio. About 1490 he became a founder and cast munitions for Giovanni Bentivoglio, lord of Bologna. A highly cultivated man, he wrote prefaces to his editions and wrote Latin verse. One of the most accomplished printers of the last quarter of the 15th century, his editions are noted for the choice of text, the design and elegance of the type faces, and the ornamentation and brilliance of the page. Among his rare and beautiful editions is an *Itinerario* Bologna, 1488), a version of John Mandeville's *Travels*.

Ruggiero (röd-je′rō). In Matteo Maria Boiardo's *Orlando Innamorato*, a youthful Saracen knight. His king, Agramante, decides to invade France, but learns from a seer that he will be unsuccessful unless he takes Ruggiero with him. Thus is Ruggiero, destined to be a founder of the house of Este of Ferrara, introduced into Boiardo's romantic epic. He left the work incomplete. Lodovico Ariosto, continuing Boiardo's story in his *Orlando Furioso*, carries on the tale of Ruggiero, a very Galahad. Among his deeds is that of saving Angelica, princess of Cathay, from a sea monster. This episode is reminiscent of the myth of Perseus and Andromeda. Ruggiero, having been baptized, marries Bradamante, and they, in the epics, are the ancestors of the Estensi, in whose honor the poems were written.

Ruiz (rö-ēth′), **Juan.** [Called **the Archpriest of Hita.**] Spanish poet; fl. c1350. He has been compared to Geoffrey Chaucer, in tribute to the skill of his verse and the earthy flavor of his themes. His major work is the *Libro de buen amor*, a collection which draws a picture of Spanish life in his time.

Rupert (of *Germany*) (rö′pėrt). [German, **Ruprecht.**] King of Germany (1400–1410); b. at Amberg, May 5, 1352; d. near Oppenheim, May 18, 1410. He became elector of the Palatinate in 1398, and was chosen king in 1400. He failed in an expedition to Italy to overthrow the Visconti at Milan, and was forced to return to Germany.

Ruscelli (rös-chel′lē), **Girolamo.** Writer; b. at Viterbo; d. at Venice, 1566. A man of broad culture, he was especially interested in grammatical studies. He spent some time at Rome, where he founded an academy, and then went to Venice (1548). He wrote on many subjects, translated Claudio Tolomeo's *Geografia* into the vernacular (Venice, 1574), compiled an anthology of literature and poetry, and edited and annotated such Italian classics as Petrarch and Ariosto. His writings on language include a commentary on the Italian language (1581), a vocabulary of Latin words with Italian words chosen from the best writers (1588), a work on composing Italian poetry, with a rhyming dictionary that had lasting fame (1559), and a treatise on prose (1572).

Rusconi (rös-kô′nē), **Benedetto.** See **Diana, Benedetto.**

Russi (rös′sē), **Franco di Giovanni de.** See **De Russi, Franco di Giovanni.**

Rustication (rus-ti-kā′shun). Masonry in which the courses and separate blocks are marked by deep chamfered or rectangular grooves. Rustication enhances the appearance of strength and solidity. The Medici Palace at Florence, designed by Michelozzo and erected in the middle of the 15th century, has graduated rustication in its three stories. The heavier rustication of the first story forms a solid base; the lesser degrees of rustication in the two upper stories provide variety and interest by the difference in texture.

Rustici (rös′tē-chē), **Giovan Francesco.** Sculptor; b. at Florence, November 13, 1474; d. at Tours, 1554. A wealthy man, he was not dependent on commissions; his sculpture was an expression of his own taste and skill, and was influenced in its development by Verrocchio, in whose workshop he was for a time a member, by Leonardo, whose friend he was, and by Michelangelo. His first dated work, a marble bust of *Boccaccio* (1503), Collegiata, Certaldo, is in the classical manner. Later work showed an inclination toward pictorial expression. His most important work is the bronze *Preaching of John the Baptist* (1506–1511), over the north entrance to the Baptistery at Florence. Leonardo da Vinci was living in the same house with him during the period of his work on the group (John the Baptist flanked by a Levite and a Pharisee), and the strength and power of the figures reflect his influence. Other works that indicate strong Leonardo influence are four groups of *Fighting Horsemen,* in terracotta (Louvre, Bargello, and Palazzo Vecchio). The *Horsemen* appear to derive from the Leonardo cartoon for the *Battle of Anghiari* and from sketches for the Sforza monument. In 1514 he was working on Verrocchio's Forteguerri monument for the cathedral at Pistoia, and in 1515 was among the artists who prepared decorations for Leo X's entry into Florence. Cardinal Giulio de' Medici was impressed by his share in the latter work and commissioned him to execute a bronze *Mercury* as a fountain for the Medici Palace. The boldly modeled musculature of the figure is reminiscent of Pollaiuolo. Aside from its artistic merits, the *Mercury* aroused interest for its ingenious mechanical aspects —a stream of water from the figure's mouth hit a whirligig once held in the statue's right hand and caused it to turn. When the Medici were driven from Florence, Rustici went (1528) to France to work for Francis I, but no work he did there is certainly identifiable. Vasari called him a painter as well as a sculptor; of his work in the field of painting nothing is known.

Rusticiano da Pisa (rös-tē-chä′nō dä pē′sä). Tuscan writer; b. c1250; d. c1300. He compiled, in French, versions of the Arthurian legends. He first published, in French, the account of Marco Polo's travels, which may have been dictated to him, in the Venetian dialect, by the traveler himself.

Rustico di Filippo (rös′tē-kō dē fē-lē′pō). Florentine lyric poet of the 13th century. Of his nearly sixty extant poems about half are conventional lyrics in the manner of Guittone d'Arezzo. The rest, including some of the first satirical sonnets in Italian verse, have themes pertinent to his time. Many of these are so allusive that they are meaningless today, but a few of them are gems. Rustico's mockery was a wide departure from the sentiment of the Provençal poets.

Ruysbruck (rois′brůk), Blessed **John.** [Also, **Ruysbroeck;** called the **Divine Doctor, Admirable Doctor.**] Flemish mystic and writer; b. at Ruisbroek, near Brussels, Belgium, 1293; d. at Groenendael, Belgium, December 2, 1381. He wrote, in the vernacular, against certain heresies of the day, and produced work on mystical and ascetical subjects which influenced Gerhard Groote, Johannes Tauler, Thomas a Kempis, and others of the German school of mystics. His cult was confirmed by Rome, December 1, 1908.

Ruzzante (röd-dzän′tā), **il.** [Real name, **Angelo Beolco.**] Playwright and comic actor; b. at Padua, 1502; d. there, March 17, 1542. He spent his youth on farms around Padua, and in his manhood managed many of them. His neighbor Luigi Cornaro was his friend and patron. In his comedies, almost entirely in the rustic dialect of Paduan peasants, he made full use of his knowledge of peasant speech and humor. A chief character in his comedies is Ruzzante, a boastful, quarrelsome, witty, vulgar, often cowardly, and usually tricky peasant. From this character, which he enacted, he gets his name. His *Moschetta* and *Fiorina,* probably written in 1520 and 1521, are the most original and witty of his plays. *Anconitania, Pivoana,* and *Vaccaria* show their Plautine derivation more clearly, though the scene is transferred to the Paduan countryside and the characters have become peasants. For his writing and his acting he was likened to Plautus and Roscius. Ruzzante, who portrayed the rough humor and shrewdness of the peasants in his plays, was well aware of the hardships of their lives, and often sought to alleviate them and to secure for the peasants the justice that was normally available only to the rich.

Rymer (rī′mėr), **Thomas.** See **Thomas the Rhymer.**

S

Sá (sä), **Estacio de.** Portuguese captain; b. in Portugal, c1520; d. at São Sebastião (now Rio de Janeiro), February 20, 1567. In 1564 he was sent against the French Protestant colony in Brazil. Aided by his uncle, Mem de Sá, he founded what is now Rio de Janeiro, in March, 1566, but was closely besieged by the French and Indians, who were defeated only on the arrival of Mem de Sá, with reinforcements. Estacio de Sá died of a wound received in the engagement.

Sá, Mem (or **Men**) **de.** Portuguese governor general of Brazil from 1558; b. at Coimbra, Portugal, c1500; d. at Bahia, Brazil, March 2, 1572. In March, 1560, he took the French fort of Villegagnon in the harbor of Rio de Janeiro, but was unable to dislodge the French from the interior, and they returned after he had left. In 1566 the city of São Sebastião (now Rio de Janeiro) was founded, and in January, 1567, Mem de Sá completely defeated the French and their Indian allies.

Sabellico (sä-bel′lē-kō), **Marcantonio.** [Real name, **Marcantonio Coccio.**] Humanist and historian; b. at Vicovaro, c1436; d. at Venice, 1506. He studied at Rome and there was a member of the Roman Academy of Julius Pomponius Laetus. Under the classicizing influence of the academy he changed his name to Sabellicus, since Italianized to Sabellico. He taught rhetoric, first at Udine and then at Venice. At the latter place he was one of many scholars who worked on the texts for the press of Aldus Manutius. Sabellico's reputation rests on his two histories. The first is a history of Venice from its founding, *Rerum venetarum ab urbe condita* . . . (1486), and the other a universal history in ninety-two books, *Enneades sive Rapsodiae historiarum,* from ancient times to 1504. His works, following the model of Flavio Biondo, are pervaded by his humanism, marked by his interest in literary style, and marred by his uncritical use of his sources.

Sabinus (sạ-bī′nus), **Georg.** [Real name, **Georg Schuler.**] German humanist, philologist, and Neo-Latin poet; b. at Brandenburg, April 23, 1508; d. at Frankfort on the Oder, December 2, 1560. He began his university studies at Wittenberg (1523 or 1524). There he met Melancthon, with whom he became friendly and whom he accompanied to the Diet of Augsburg (1530). (He later married Melancthon's 14-year-old daughter Anna, 1536.) In 1533 he made a journey to Italy, where he came into contact with many of the leading humanists and men of letters, including Pietro Bembo, who became his friend. In 1538 he went to Frankfort on the Oder at the request of its prince, and served as a professor of eloquence. From there he went (1544) to Königsberg, as rector of a school there, but following theological differences with the duke, he left Königsberg and returned to Frankfort (1555). Among his works as a philologist was an edition of Cicero's *De oratore,* and an interpretation of Ovid's *Metamorphosis.* A description (1544) of the election and coronation of Charles V and biographies of two margraves of Brandenburg have historical interest. However, the chief importance of Sabinus is as a poet. His six books of elegies, in graceful style and with a fresh viewpoint, present such subjects as his love for Anna, the reactions he had to the great events of his day, and his laments for the harshness of his times. These elegies represent his finest work. He also wrote a book of epigrams, in which he turned his pen against the evils of his age.

Sacchetti (sä-kāt′tē), **Franco.** Florentine poet and writer; b. probably at Ragusa, in Dalmatia, c1330; d. c1400. He was a member of an ancient and noble Florentine Guelph family. As a young man, business caused him to travel widely and broadened his knowledge of the world and of men, a knowledge that he used to advantage in his writing. About 1362 he returned to Florence, where he was active in public affairs and held important offices on several occasions. Self-taught, he wrote on the evils of ignorance and the wickedness of injustice. He was more interested in ethical questions than in dogma. Of profound and simple faith, he had nothing but scorn for hypocrisy and phariseeism, especially in the clerical ranks. A democrat, as the word was understood in his day, he distrusted and feared the Signory that threatened the liberties of Florence, as well as the tyrants who kept all Italy in turmoil for their own selfish ends. His preoccupation with religious, moral, and civic questions appears in his writings. His lyrics—sonnets, canzoni, ballate, madrigals, and so on—were intended to be sung, and at least two which he composed were set to music. Among his prose writings, in Italian, is *Il libro delle trecento-novelle*, which was planned to contain 300 short stories (over 200 of them are extant). The stories are simply told for an ordinary audience. They are intended to entertain and amuse, and only incidentally to instruct. Some of them are a retelling of traditional tales. Many are Sacchetti's own, drawn from his wide experience of human nature, and marked by his own good common sense, tolerance, and humor. They are about ordinary men and women, in general, "characters" who by their ready wit extricate themselves from predicaments or turn the tables on their tormentors. Some of the heroes are animals, some are from life, including Boccaccio, Dante, Sacchetti himself, and others whose names are otherwise unknown to history. The stories gave, and still give, great delight.

Sacchetti, Giannozzo. Poet and revolutionary; b. at Florence, c1340; executed there, 1379. He was the brother of Franco Sacchetti (c1330–c1400), was a follower of St. Catherine of Siena, and took part in the revolt of the *Ciompi* (1378). It was for his part in the revolt that he was hanged in 1379. Sacchetti's sonnets, canzoni, and *laude* reflect in moving terms his desire for religious peace and his spirituality.

Sachs (zäks), **Hans.** German poet, the most celebrated of the Meistersingers; b. at Nuremberg, Germany, November 5, 1494; d. there, January 19, 1576. His father, a tailor, sent him to the Latin school, which he left in his 15th year to become a shoemaker. Two years later, as a journeyman of his trade, he wandered through Germany, studying when the opportunity presented itself in the larger cities, the art of Meistersong. Four years afterward, in 1515, he returned to Nuremberg, where he married in 1519. A prolific writer, he composed well over 6,000 works—Meistersongs, dramas, narratives, fables, and the like. He supported Luther in the Reformation, and wrote in his praise, in 1523, *Wittenbergisch Nachtigall*. He was a real poet, as Goethe pointed out, and his influence upon German literature has been lasting.

Sackville (sak′vil), **Thomas.** [Titles, Baron **Buckhurst**, 1st Earl of **Dorset.**] English poet and statesman; b. at Buckhurst, Sussex, England, 1536; d. at London, April 19, 1608. He was one of Elizabeth's most trusted councillors, and it was he who formally informed (1586) Mary, Queen of Scots, that she had been condemned to death. His poems were the models for some of Spenser's best work, and his "Induction" to the *Mirror for Magistrates* (2nd ed., 1563) is now considered the best part of that book. He wrote, with Thomas Norton, the blank verse tragedy *Gorboduc* (1563) generally classified as the earliest English tragedy.

Sacripante (säk-rē-pän′tā). In Matteo Maria Boiardo's *Orlando Innamorato*, a gentle and fearless suitor of Angelica, princess of Cathay.

Sá de Miranda (sä′ dẹ mē-run′dạ), **Francisco de.** Portuguese poet; b. at Coimbra, Portugal, c1485; d. at Quinta da Tapada, Amares, Portugal, 1558. He traveled to Italy, and under the influence of Italian masters introduced into Portuguese literature the classical comedy in prose, the sonnet, and other literary forms of the Renaissance. His two comedies were *Os Estrangeiros* (c1527) and *Vilhalpandos* (c1537). The first edition of his poems appeared posthumously (1595).

Sadoleto (sä-dō-lā′tō), Cardinal **Jacopo.** Humanist and ecclesiastic; b. at Modena, July 12, 1477; d. at Rome, October 18, 1547. Originally intended for the law, he abandoned his legal studies and went to Ferrara to study literature and philosophy. There he met the Latin and Italian stylist Pietro Bembo, with whom he was later associated in the so-called Roman Academy. He went to Rome (c1502), studied Greek, and won renown for his Latin prose. Leo X named him a secretary (1513) and he became, with Bembo, one of the two most accomplished papal secretaries. In 1517 he was named bishop of Carpentras, in France, and lived in his See for many years. Paul III called him to Rome and made him cardinal in 1536. Sadoleto was one of the humanists of his age who maintained a profound religious belief and an interest in humanistic studies at one and the same time. His studies and learning had no adverse effect on the piety and purity of his own life. Serious and sincere, he was aware of the perils that threatened the Church. He wrote to Clement VII from Carpentras, after the sack of Rome (1527), expressing the hope that the evils the Church had suffered might lead to its reformation. His literary fame had begun in 1506 with the poem *De Laocoontis statua,* a rather rigid effort commemorating the finding of the *Laocoön,* in that year. He wrote moral treatises, a book on pedagogy, annotated the Psalms, and left a large correspondence (widely published and republished) that is a valuable contribution to the literary history of the time. He was one of a group of humanists and ecclesiastics known as "Irenists" who sought a peaceful solution of the Lutheran revolt.

Sadoleto, Paolo. Bishop; b. at Modena, 1508; d. 1572. He was related to Cardinal Jacopo Sadoleto, who instructed him and assisted him in his ecclesiastical career. Of his writings, famed in his day for skill, elegance, and the knowledge with which they were informed, some Latin and Italian letters remain.

Sahagún (sä-ä-gön′), **Bernardino de.** Spanish Franciscan missionary and historian; b. at Sahagún, Spain, c1499; d. either at Mexico City or at the Convent of Tlatelolco, February 5, 1590. He lived in Mexico from 1529, and held various offices in his order. His historical works were freely used in manuscript by the old historians. They include accounts of the Aztecs and of the conquest of Mexico. He also published works in the Aztec language.

Saint-Gelais (saṅ-zhẹ-le), **Mellin** (or **Merlin** or **Melusin**) **de.** French poet; b. at Angoulême, 1487; d. at Paris, October, 1558. Court poet of Francis I, he was the most important poet of the school of Clement Marot. He translated Trissino's tragedy *Sofonisba,* but is known above all as the poet who introduced the sonnet from Italy into France.

Salernitano (sä-ler-nē-tä′nō), **Masuccio.** See, **Guardati, Tommaso.**

Salerno (sä-ler′nō), Prince of. Title of various members of the Orsini family.

Saliba (sä-lē′bä), **Antonello da.** Painter; b. 1466/67; d. c1535. He was a nephew of Antonello da Messina, and got his training in a workshop at Naples, after which he traveled to Venice. On the whole he was a painter in the Sicilian tradition, to which were added influences of his uncle and, in his later work, of the Venetians Giovanni Bellini and Cima da Conegliano. Although he was influenced by his uncle he never approached him in power or technique. A number of his works are in Sicily, southern Italy, and museums of Europe. His *Veronica's Handkerchief* is in the Johnson Collection, Philadelphia; *Madonna Adoring the Child* is in the Metropolitan Museum, New York. Other paintings are at Cambridge (Massachusetts), and Detroit.

Saliba, Pietro de. Painter of Messina, active in the second half of the 15th century. He was a follower and imitator of Antonello da Messina and Giovanni Bellini. Examples of his Madonnas are at Padua and Venice, and of his *Christ at the Column* at Budapest and Venice.

Saliceto (sä-lē-chā′tō), **Bartolomeo.** Jurist; b. at Bologna; d. December 28, 1411. He was educated at Bologna and taught at Padua, Bologna, and Ferrara. Most of his writing consisted of commentaries on the Justinian Code. He wrote a commentary also on the *Digestum vetus,* and published many of his opinions.

Salimbene da Parma (säl-ēm-be′nā dä pär′mä). Chronicler; b. at Parma, October 9, 1221; d. c1288. He was a member of a deeply religious family of the lesser nobility, and himself entered the Franciscan order in 1238. He traveled over much of Italy and into France on business or missions for his order, and took acute notice of all that he observed. His *Cronica,* which covers the years 1167–1287, is one of the great Medieval chronicles. An ardent believer in established religion, he was nevertheless a sharp and sincere critic of men and religious institutions. His chronicle, which is badly mutilated, is personal, witty, and all-embracing; it is a picture of his own life and an important source for the life of his times.

Salimbeni (sä-lēm-be′nē), **Lorenzo.** Marchigian painter; b. at Sanseverino, 1374; d. by 1420. He and his brother Jacopo (d. after

1427), with whom he often worked, were followers of the international Gothic style of Gentile Fabriano, with traces in some of their earlier works of the art of the north—Germany, France, and North Italy. The influence of the north appears in an increased use of homely detail and an emphasis on realism and activity. Their best works, in the manner of Gentile (with the addition of some Gothic grotesqueries), are a series of frescoes, signed and dated (1416), in the Oratory of S. Giovanni Battista at Urbino. The series on the life of the saint is characterized by graceful, elongated figures and individualized faces, architectural backgrounds, and such genre details as children fighting, a dog scratching itself, and horses rearing. A triptych by Lorenzo, *Mystic Marriage of St. Catherine,* is in the Palazzo Comunale at Sanseverino; panels from a polyptych are in the Walters Art Gallery, Baltimore. At Sanseverino there are remains of frescoes executed by the brothers in the churches of S. Lorenzo in Doliolo, where there are many, S. Maria del Mercato, S. Maria della Misericordia, S. Maria della Pieve, and S. Severino. Other frescoes are at Cingoli (S. Domenico), Foligno (Palazzo Trinci), Perugia, and Pesaro. The influence of the Salimbeni, though they were no more than competent craftsmen, was wide. Works by their many followers are to be found throughout the Marches.

Salinas (sä-lē′näs), Marquis of. Title of **Velasco, Luis de.**

Salutati (sä-lö-tä′tē), **Lino Coluccio di Piero.** Celebrated Florentine humanist; b. at Stignano in Valdinievole, February 16, 1331; d. at Florence, May 4, 1406. His name di Piero comes from the Pierides and indicates his lifelong devotion to the Muses. He was a notary who became an outstanding public official and a celebrated humanist. Having been chancellor of Todi (1367) and of Lucca (1371), he was appointed (1375) chancellor of Florence, a center of stability in turbulent Florentine public life, and held the position to the end of his life. As the official in charge of foreign correspondence he elevated the style and language of chancellery letters by producing them in a fluent and dignified Latin. Salutati, in his admiration for the ancient language and literature, dreamed of making eloquence a substitute for arms in settling disputes. His state papers won great respect and Gian Galeazzo Visconti, ruler of Milan, remarked that one of them was equal to a thousand horsemen. Salutati also dreamed of restoring the greatness of Italy, united under the leadership of Rome. As a student of classical literature, he was the first to apply critical methods to ancient texts, such as the comparison of manuscripts to note differences and omissions, and to seek to derive from such comparisons the original of the text. His official letters reveal his love for liberty and his scorn of despots. Typical are those he wrote in 1375 and 1376 when Florence was at war with the papacy. The element of propaganda in these, since their purpose was to win allies and sympathizers for Florence, does not distort his true sentiments. His private letters, collected in fourteen books, show him to have developed a private and personal philosophy, according to which he felt that the first aim should be in accordance with the Socratic injunction, "Know thyself." The good life could then be attained by the power of the will. Such belief in the power of the will, rather than the whim of Fortune, to shape one's life became a foundation stone for Renaissance individualism. Salutati set forth his ideas in a number of important treatises. *De seculo et religione* compares secular and monastic life to the advantage of the latter. Yet he defended the active life and the role of will in his *De nobilitate legum et medicinae* and *De fato et fortuna.* His *De laboribus Herculis* presents his views of poetry and interprets the legends of Hercules allegorically as symbolizing the active civic life that he favored.

Salviati (säl-vyä′tē). Distinguished Florentine family, securely documented from the first half of the 14th century, when Cambio di Salvi was gonfaloniere (1335). Members of the family held the highest offices, contributing sixty-two priors and twenty gonfalonieri to the government of Florence. Iacopo di Francesco Salviati was commissioner in the war against Pisa (1405) and was ambassador to the pope and to the king of France. The notorious Francesco Salviati was archbishop of Pisa and was hanged for his part in the Pazzi Conspiracy (1478). Another Iacopo was a patriot who fought for Florentine liberty in 1530 and 1532, and died in 1533. He married Lucrezia, daughter of Lorenzo de' Medici, and was the grandfather of Cosimo I de' Medici. Two of

Iacopo's sons became cardinals: Giovanni (d. 1553) and Bernardo (d. 1568). Alamanno (d. 1509), of a collateral branch of the family, was prominent in the days of the Savonarola republic. His daughter Maria was the wife of the statesman and historian Francesco Guicciardini.

Salviati, Cecchino. [Real name, **Francesco de' Rossi.**] Painter; b. at Florence, 1510; d. at Rome, November 11, 1563. He was a pupil of Andrea del Sarto. At Rome, where he went as a young man, he studied the works of Michelangelo, Parmigianino, and Polidoro da Caravaggio. He worked at Rome and Venice, returned several times to Florence, and in 1554 was in France under the patronage of the king. About 1540 he painted a *Psyche* at Venice for Cardinal Grimani which was admired by Venetian artists for its foreshortening. For Cosimo I he frescoed (1544–1548) the Audience Chamber of the Palazzo Vecchio at Florence with stories of the *Peace between the Gauls and Romans* and *The Triumph of Camillus,* notable examples of his mannerist style. Also at Florence he made cartoons for tapestries and paintings for many churches and private patrons. He left many examples of his great productivity at Rome. Among his works there are *Visitation* and *Birth of the Baptist,* among others, in the Oratory of S. Giovanni Decollato, notable for warm, intense colors glowing from a darkened background; frescoes on the life of the Virgin, S. Marcello; a *Deposition,* S. Maria dell' Anima; frescoes of the *Creation* and the *Fall of Adam,* Chigi Chapel, S. Maria del Popolo; *Marriage of Cana,* S. Salvatore; frescoes in the Chapel of the Pallio, Palazzo della Cancelleria, which was entirely decorated by Salviati (1548–1550), and which include an *Adoration of the Child* showing Cardinal Farnese as one of the adorers; and decorations in the Farnese and Sacchetti palaces. His *Incredulity of Thomas,* Louvre, was painted at Florence for a church in France; *Charity,* Uffizi, is typical of his work and shows the extent to which he was influenced by Michelangelo.

Salviati, Iacopo. Florentine statesman and patriot; d. 1533. Of an old and prominent Florentine family, he married Lucrezia, daughter of Lorenzo de' Medici, and served Florence on many embassies. He fought to defend Florentine liberty in 1530. He was a kinsman of that archbishop, Francesco Salviati, who had a leading role in the Pazzi Conspiracy (1478), and was the father-in-law of Giovanni delle Bande Nere.

Salviati, Leonardo. Writer; b. at Florence, 1540; d. there, September, 1589. He had a solid education and was prominent in literary circles from young manhood. Early in his life he had worked with the historian Benedetto Varchi, and he was a member of the Accademia della Crusca from its founding (1582). (This was an academy founded for the purpose of purifying the Italian language and literature.) His many writings include *Orazioni* (Florence, 1573), a collection of orations prepared for ceremonial occasions, the eloquence of which was greatly admired; critical essays on the sonnet of Petrarch and the language of the *Decameron;* verses; two comedies, *Il Granchio* (presented at Florence with elaborate scenic arrangements in 1566), and *La Spina;* a polemic against Tasso's *Gerusalemme Liberata,* which led to answering polemics (he reversed his criticism of Tasso when he entered the service of Tasso's patron, Duke Alfonso of Ferrara, and called him a distinguished poet). For the grand duke of Tuscany he worked on a revision or rearrangement of the *Decameron,* an effort that was criticized by all men of learning and taste. His most important work was *Avvertimenti della lingua sopra il Decamerone* (Florence, 1584–1586), a sound treatise on the use of Italian and the right of the writer to choose his own vocabulary.

Salviati, Maria. Wife of Giovanni de' Medici (Giovanni delle Bande Nere, 1498–1526), and mother of Cosimo I (1519–1574).

Salviati, Veri di Giovanni. Florentine humanist; b. 1411; d. 1474. Member of an old Florentine family, he studied under Carlo Marsuppini and Francesco Filelfo, and had a good knowledge of Greek and Latin. He left some letters and translations that, according to Vespasiano, show him to have had a good Latin style.

Sambuco (säm-bö'kō), **Giovanni.** [Real name, **János Zsámbok;** Latinized, **Johannes Sambucus.**] Hungarian physician and humanist; b. at Trnava (Slovakia), 1531; d. there, 1584. He was among the most celebrated of the Hungarian humanists who studied at the Italian universities. After study at Wittenberg, Ingolstadt, Strasbourg, and Paris, he went to Padua (1553) to study medicine. He remained there until 1557, when he received his degree. After that, he went to Vienna where he was court physician and librarian to the emperors Ferdinand and Maximilian II. He published a book of poems at Padua (1555), and wrote *Dioscoridis Libri VIII, graece et latine*.

Sancho Panza (san′chō pan′zạ; Spanish, sän′-chō pän′thä). The "round, selfish, and self-important" squire of Don Quixote, in Cervantes' romance of that name. He is humanly materialistic, skeptical, and loyal.

San Concordio (sän kōn-kôr′dyō), **Bartolomeo da.** See **Bartolomeo da San Concordio.**

Sandeo (sän-de′ō), **Felino Maria.** Jurist and historian; b. at Felino (Emilia), 1444; d. at Lucca, October, 1503. He taught canon law at Ferrara (1465) and Pisa (1474), held many positions in the Church, and was named bishop of Atri (1495) and of Lucca (1499). He defended the rights of the papacy against Ferrante of Naples and Charles VIII of France. Among his writings are: *De regibus Siciliae et Apuliae* (Milan, 1485), that gives the history of these regions from 537 to 1494; a three-volume commentary on the Decretals (Venice, 1497–1499); a collection of his opinions; and diplomatic dispatches.

Sandoval (sän-dō-bäl′), **Gonzalo de.** Spanish soldier; b. at Medellín, Estremadura, Spain, 1496; d. at Palos de la Frontera, Spain, probably in December, 1528. He was one of Hernando Cortés' principal lieutenants in the conquest of Mexico (1519–1521).

Sandys (sandz), **Edwin.** English prelate; b. probably at Hawkshead, Lancashire, England, 1516; d. at Southwell, Nottinghamshire, England, July 10, 1588. A staunch anti-Catholic, he refused to proclaim Mary as the lawful sovereign of England, and was imprisoned in the Tower. After the accession of Elizabeth he became archbishop of York (1576–1588). He was one of the translators of the *Bishops' Bible* (1565).

Sangallo (säng-gäl′lō), **Antonio da.** [Called **Sangallo the Elder;** real name, **Antonio Giamberti.**] Architect and military engineer; b. at Florence, c1455; d. there, 1534. He was the younger brother of Giuliano da Sangallo (c1445–1516) and was greatly influenced by him. However, the strong, masculine style of his civil and religious architecture is in contrast to the delicate grace of Giuliano's style. His masterpiece is the Church of S. Biagio at Montepulciano, on which he worked between 1518 and 1529 (completed 1545). It is built, in the manner of Giuliano's S. Maria in Carceri (1485), at Prato, on the plan of a Greek cross with a dome at the crossing, and is reminiscent of Bramante's model for St. Peter's. S. Biagio is unusual in that the beautiful church stands alone below the hilltop town of Montepulciano and is not hemmed in by other buildings that would lessen the impact of its style. Several palaces at Montepulciano are attributed to him, including the Palazzo Nobili Tarugi opposite the cathedral. He was one of the architects associated with Raphael in beginning the Villa Madama at Rome and was active as a military architect and engineer; the octagonal dungeons of Castel Sant' Angelo, the fortress of Civita Castellana, and the old fortress at Livorno (1515) are among his works in this field.

Sangallo, Antonio da. [Called **Sangallo the Younger;** real name, **Antonio di Bartolomeo Cordiani.**] Architect; b. at Florence, 1483; d. at Terni, 1546. He was the nephew of Antonio da Sangallo the Elder (c1455–1534) and Giuliano da Sangallo (c1445–1516), and like his maternal uncles was a joiner and woodcarver. While still very young he went to Rome (1503), where he studied the antique and where he enjoyed the good will of Bramante, whose assistant he became. His earliest work is thought to be the Church of S. Maria di Loreto at Rome, which he began about 1507 and which was completed in 1582 by Giacomo del Duca. As planned by Sangallo the church is linked in style to that of his uncle Giuliano, but with Antonio's own taste revealed in his emphasis on structural elements rather than on ornamentation. His predilection for massive masonry and his rationale of harmony and balance found their best expression in the reconstruction of the Church of S. Spirito in Sassia which, with its façade in two planes, became a model for numerous 16th- and 17th-century churches, and above all, in the Farnese Palace at Rome. Sangallo had entered the service of Cardinal Alessandro Farnese early and began the great palace for the Farnese family about 1513. When Cardinal Farnese became Pope Paul III (1534) the design of the building was changed; it was greatly enlarged and is the largest and most magnificent of the princely palaces at Rome. The building, in the form of a block with a central courtyard, is distinguished for its subtly proportioned façade of three stories and elegantly simple, symmetrical, and somewhat severe rows of superposed windows framed by slender columns; the windows of the first row all have the same squared tops, those of the next row are finished in classic Renaissance style, with alternating triangular and shallow curved pediments, and those of the top row are all alike with shallow triangular pediments. The massive simplicity of the façade is relieved by a great central arched doorway surrounded by rustication and surmounted by a window over which are the Farnese arms. (When Sangallo died the façade was completed to the base of the third story. Michelangelo, who took over, raised the height of the third story. He designed a massive cornice to cap the building, and designed the arms and window over the central doorway as well.) The entrance tunnel to the courtyard is lined with granite columns, its classicism possibly derived from the Theater of Marcellus; the courtyard itself incorporates elements derived from the same theater and from the Colosseum. When Raphael died (1520), Antonio Sangallo succeeded him as chief of the works of St. Peter's. Not much was done on the building for some time after the sack of Rome (1527). Sangallo made a model of St. Peter's that incorporated a revision of Bramante's original plan and of the changes Raphael had made in it, and provided for a small dome. Since his model nowhere near approached Bramante's heroic scale it was fortunate that he was prevented by death from putting his plan into effect, and that his successor was Michelangelo, whose soaring imagination was on the same scale as Bramante's. Sangallo was active as an architect in the military, civil, and religious fields; a number of palaces and churches at Rome are attributed to him. Other works included the fortifications of Civitavecchia, the Paoline Fortress at Perugia (built at the command of Paul III to subdue and control the turbulent Perugians, and torn down in the 19th century), fortifications at Rome, and others.

Sangallo, Francesco da. Sculptor and architect; b. at Florence, 1494; d. February 17, 1576. He was the son of Giuliano da Sangallo (c1445–1516), went to Rome with his father (1504) and was present (1506) with him and Michelangelo when the great recently discovered statuary group was identified as the *Laocoön* group described by Pliny. As a sculptor, his predilection for realistic detail was exercised with powerful effect in his monument (1546) of Angelo Marzi, bishop of Assisi and a friend and secretary of the Medici family for thirty-four years. The monument is in SS. Annunziata, Florence. The same characteristic interest in realistic detail appears in the sepulchral monument of Leonardo Bonafede (1550), Certosa, Florence. His masterpiece is a bust of Giovanni delle Bande Nere (c1552), Bargello, Florence; with its firm and balanced volumes and planes, it is a sober and powerful portrait of the youthful captain. His earliest dated work is *Madonna and Child with St. Anne* (1522–1526), Orsanmichele. The sculptural composition, with the Madonna seated on St. Anne's knee, is derived from the painting by Leonardo, but whereas Leonardo's composition rises to a pyramid, Sangallo's is an uncompromising and awkward rectangle in which the figures pull the composition apart rather than unite it. Sangallo collaborated with Tribolo and Raffaello da Montelupo (1533) in the sculptural decoration of the S. Casa at Loreto, carving for it, among others, *The Presentation in the Temple.* In 1543 he succeeded Baccio d'Agnolo as chief architect and overseer of the works of the cathedral at Florence but his contributions are not identifiable. He left a number of striking portrait medals.

Sangallo, Giuliano da. [Real name, **Giuliano Giamberti.**] Architect, sculptor, and military engineer; b. at Florence, c1445; d. there, 1516. He was the older brother of Antonio da Sangallo the Elder (c1455–1534) and the father of Francesco da Sangallo (1494–1576). He began his activity at Florence as a woodcarver. His first architectural creations seem to have been the Atrium of S. Maria Maddalena dei Pazzi, the beginning of an Augustinian convent near the San Gallo Gate (whence his adopted name), and the Medici Villa at Poggio a Caiano (1483–1485). From Brunelleschi and Michelozzo he derived the rhythms that characterize a number of his civil buildings, as the Gondi (c1490) and Strozzi (begun after 1489) palaces at Florence. Benedetto da Maino and il Cronaca collaborated with him on the latter. A follower and interpreter of Brunelleschi, his religious architecture is character-

GIULIANO DA SANGALLO
Judith with the Head of Holophernes
Biblioteca Comunale, Siena
Alinari-Art Reference Bureau

ized by a complex and grandiose sense of movement, as in the Church of S. Maria in Carceri, Prato (c1485), which is on the plan of a pure Greek cross and follows Brunelleschi's ideas of centrally planned churches. Also in the Brunelleschi tradition is the octagonal sacristy Giuliano designed for S. Spirito at Florence. In both, his style is characterized by a symmetry of structural and ornamental elements that lends it great distinction and elegance. He was a friend of Cardinal Giuliano della Rovere and is thought to have been in France with him in 1494 and for a year or two thereafter. When the cardinal became pope as Julius II (1503), Giuliano was given a number of commissions by him, and he was one of those sent by the pope to identify a great statuary group found (1506) in a vineyard at Rome; this was the *Laocoön* group described by Pliny. Bramante's daring and grandiose ideas immediately appealed to Pope Julius II, and soon after his arrival at Rome Sangallo's influence with the pope waned. Other works carried out by Giuliano included the completion of the dome of the basilica at Loreto (which later cracked and was repaired by Francesco di Giorgio Martini). As a military architect he constructed the fortifications of Poggio Imperiale, near Poggibonsi. Two sketchbooks of architectural and other studies and drawings of ancient Roman buildings are attributed to Sangallo. One of these is in the Vatican Library; the other is in the Biblioteca Comunale at Siena.

SANMICHELI (sän-mē-ke'lē), **MICHELE.** Architect; b. at Verona, 1484; d. there, 1559. His father, Giovanni, also an architect, was from the region around Como, but the son was educated (from 1500) at Rome. There he may have been a pupil or assistant of Antonio da Sangallo, but he was especially influenced by Peruzzi and Sansovino. About 1509 he went to work at Orvieto. He worked there on and off for about twenty years, building a number of structures in the city itself, and, in 1519, began the cathedral at Montefiascone, about twenty miles from Orvieto. After the sack of Rome (1527) building activity in and about the city came to a halt. Sanmicheli went back to Verona and worked as a military architect in the Veneto. As military architect for Venice he fortified Verona, which was at that time under Venetian dominion, Padua, and some cities of Dalmatia that were also under Venetian control. His activity as a military architect constructing fortified gates (as the Porta Palio and Porta Nuova at Verona) that not only had to be strong but also to give the impression of impregnability, affected his work as a civil architect, and perhaps accounts for the air of massive strength in his civil buildings. Among the latter are three palaces at Verona, all probably constructed in the 1530's. They are the Palazzo Canossa, Palazzo Pompei, and Palazzo Bevilacqua. Each of these, in two stories, has marked rustication, with its impression of strength, on the ground floor. The upper stories are divided into bays separated by columns or pilasters with rich capitals. The Palazzo Bevilacqua is the most complicated and richly ornamented of the three. The rhythmic curves of the upper story are achieved by a series of alternating large and small arches resting on proportionately longer and shorter pilasters in large and small bays that are separated by great columns, each of which is different. The spandrels of the large arches are filled with sculptural decoration. The vertical space above the smaller arches is treated with shallow triangular and segmental pediments, and other elements. The entire façade is richly ornamented and incorporates a number of mannerist ideas and complications that derive from Giulio Romano, utilizing and imitating elements from antique architecture. In this building, as in the Pellegrini Chapel that he built at Verona (and which is modeled on the Pantheon at Rome) Sanmicheli shows himself as attached as were Bramante and his followers to the elements and rich ornamentation of later Roman architecture, and he was one who contributed greatly to the spread of Roman classicism in architecture in northern Italy. Sanmicheli's pictorial sense was accentuated after coming into contact with the architecture of Venice itself, and was given free rein in his design for the Grimani Palace, built on the Grand Canal (1556–1572).

Sannazzaro (sän-näd-dzä′rō), **Iacopo.** [Latin name, **Actius Syncerus.**] Neapolitan man of letters; b. at Naples, July 28, 1456; d. there, April 24, 1530. Of an ancient and noble but impoverished family, he entered the service of Alfonso, duke of Calabria (and future king of Naples) in 1481, and remained loyal to the Aragonese throughout his life. When Naples was taken by Charles VIII, Sannazzaro followed King Federico into exile in France. He returned to Naples in 1504. As a member of the court circle and also of the so-called Neapolitan Academy, he was on friendly terms with Pontano, whom he succeeded as leader of the Academy. Sannazzaro took Naples, its beautiful bay, brilliant landscape, and the life lived therein as subjects for his Latin elegies, epigrams, and eclogues. The five eclogues of the *Piscatoriae* are on the fishermen of Mergellina, and the Tritons and Nereids that inhabit their waters. His epigrams were highly valued. The republic of Venice paid him 600 ducats for one of six lines. The familiar themes of love and loss, joy and sorrow, are treated in other lyrics. All are overlaid with a faintly melancholic shadow. His *De partu Virginis,* on the birth of Christ, is a religious poem in which the Christian event is presented with a mingling of Christian and pagan elements (passages from Vergil are inserted) that now seem incongruous. Although he could appropriate pagan elements and sentiments to satisfy the demands of his humanistic and artistic muse, the poem, written in fluent Latin verse, is fundamentally an expression of religious inspiration. Sannazzaro also wrote idyllic sonnets and canzoni in Italian. His *Arcadia,* in pure Tuscan, written between 1480 and 1485, is a pastoral romance in twelve prose chapters alternating with twelve poems, and relates the story of a Neapolitan shepherd who goes to Arcadia in Greece and his life among the shepherds there. The subject and the locale give abundant occasion for idyllic descriptions and classical allusion. As was almost a literary necessity in his day, the work shows the influence of Vergil, Theocritus, and Ovid. The work made him famous. He was honored throughout Italy and bombarded with invitations to various courts. He preferred to remain at his villa at Mergellina and work quietly on his poetry. His last years were darkened by poor health and his unhappiness and concern for Cassandra Marchese, a young noblewoman whose husband had repudiated her. He went each day to visit her. On one such visit he was stricken, and died in her arms.

Sano di Pietro (sä′nō dē pye′trō). Painter; b. at Siena, 1406; d. 1481. He was a pupil of Sassetta and was greatly influenced by that master, but lacked his lyricism and childlike sincerity. Sano's painting was pretty rather then poetic, pious rather than spiritual. He was a highly productive painter and of considerable importance in his town, and was in great demand in the outlying districts as a painter of polyptychs, panels, miniatures, and *biccherne* covers (covers of the annual registers of the Sienese public offices called *Biccherna*). A *Coronation of the Virgin,* Yale University Art Gallery, New Haven, is characteristic in its gay and decorative colors. Other pious hymns to the Virgin on this theme are in the Accademia, Florence and the Palazzo Pubblico, Siena. For its naive naturalism *The Adoration of the Magi,* also at New Haven, is one of his more attractive works. His *St. Bernardino Preaching in the Piazza del Campo,* in the cathedral, Siena, is interesting for its background of the Palazzo Pubblico, and for portraying the contemporary custom of separating the women from the men in the congregation listening to the saint. A great many of his surviving works are at Siena, in the Pinacoteca, Palazzo Pubblico, churches, and other collections, and in churches in neighboring towns. There are examples of his painting in many other galleries of Italy and in European museums outside Italy, and at Amherst (Massachusetts), Birmingham (Alabama), Boston, Cambridge, Cleveland, Coral Gables (Florida), Detroit, El Paso, Houston, Louisville, New York, Northampton (Massachusetts), Philadelphia (Johnson Collection), San Diego (California), Tucson (Arizona), and Washington. Many examples of his miniatures survive, as in the Piccolomini Library, Siena, and the Municipal Library at Bologna.

Sanseverino (sän-sā-vā-rē′nō). Ancient Neapolitan family, one of the oldest and most distinguished houses of the kingdom of Naples, and one of the noblest of Italy. The family held the castle at Sanseverino from the 11th century. The founder of the family was Turgisio, who came into the area with Robert Guiscard (middle of the 11th century) and obtained the countship of Sanseverino, from which the family took its name. Ruggiero was one of the barons who called Charles I of Anjou into Naples to fight Manfred, Frederick II's son, and fought bravely at the battle of Benevento, in which Manfred was defeated (1266). The Sanseverini were from that time supporters of the Angevin claim to the throne of Naples. When Louis II of Anjou was definitively defeated by Ladislaus and left the kingdom (1399), Ladislaus, under the pretext of making peace with the valiant defenders of the Angevins, tricked several members of the Sanseverino family into meeting with him, imprisoned them, and had them killed. The family regained its influential role under the Aragonese kings of Naples, whom they supported. In the early centuries, the Sanseverini had become linked with the Norman kings, the kings of the house of Durazzo, and with the Aragonese kings. As the years passed they solidified relationships with the leading houses of Italy: the Sforza, the Montefeltri, and the most eminent families of southern Italy. They held the principal offices in the kingdom of Naples, were cardinals, vicars, marshals, and captains. They belonged to all the knightly orders (Knights of Malta, Golden Fleece, orders of the Church and of princes). Their vast holdings constituted a state within a state, and included 300 fiefs, 40 countships, 9 marquessates, 21 duchies, and 10 principates. Galeazzo Sanseverino married a daughter of Ludovico il Moro, was named an equerry of Francis I, and died fighting bravely at the battle of Pavia (1525). Roberto, grand admiral of Naples, was made prince of Salerno (1463), and was a noted captain, in the service of Lorenzo de' Medici and Venice, among others. After supporting the Aragonese and receiving many honors, titles and lands from King Ferrante, the Sanseverini quarreled with the Aragonese, and were among the Neapolitan barons who invited Charles VIII of France into the kingdom (1494). They later supported the emperor Charles V, who was welcomed to Naples with great splendor by Pierantonio, a captain in the pay of Charles.

Sanseverino, Ferrante. Prince of Salerno; b. at Naples, January 18, 1507; d. in France. He was taken prisoner at the battle of Capo d'Orso, was released, and represented the Neapolitan nobles at the coronation of Charles V at Bologna (1530). He served Charles V as a captain in Tunis, Algiers, and Spain. As captain general of Italian troops in the wars between France and Spain, he was a brilliant soldier. He was the patron and employer of Bernardo Tasso, who accompanied him on his campaigns. On the declared intention of the Spanish to set up the Inquisition in Naples as it existed in Spain, Bernardo, reflecting Neapolitan sentiment, strongly advised Ferrante to protest. Ferrante was sent as ambassador from Naples to the emperor to see if he could prevent this thoroughly detested Spanish form of the institution from being established at Naples. For his efforts, he was given a magnificent welcome when he returned to Naples, so splendid and enthusiastic, in fact, that it aroused the jealousy of the imperial vicar. Ferrante came into conflict with him and with the imperial court because of his opposition to the Inquisition. He was obliged to flee to France, where he was warmly welcomed by King Henry II. The Spanish declared him a rebel, as an excuse for confiscating his estates, and he died in France, the last of his line of the Sanseverino family.

Sanseverino, Roberto da. Captain; d. 1487.

He was a member of an ancient and powerful house of the kingdom of Naples, whose power and possessions almost constituted a state within the kingdom. Roberto, a highly able and valiant captain, was a strong supporter of Ferrante, heir of Alfonso I, in the early years of his reign. He was later in the service of Venice and is referred to somewhat slightingly by Machiavelli in *The Prince*, as an example of a hired captain who cost his employers more than money.

Sansovino (sän-sō-vē′nō), **Andrea.** [Full name, **Andrea Contucci da Monte Sansovino.**] Sculptor and architect; b. at Monte Sansovino, in Tuscany, c1460; d. there, 1529. According to Vasari, he was a pupil of Antonio Pollaiuolo; he was also influenced by Giuliano da Sangallo, Benedetto da Maiano, and Leonardo. Inscribed in the Woodcarvers' and Stonemasons' Guild in 1491, in the following year he executed the altar in the Corbinelli Chapel in S. Spirito at Florence. Again according to Vasari, from 1492 to 1501 he worked as sculptor and architect for King John of Portugal. Works attributed to him are preserved at Lisbon and Coimbra, but some critics question whether he was ever in Portugal at all and doubt that these are from his hand. In 1502 he made the Baptismal font at Volterra, and in the same year was commissioned to execute a marble *Baptism of Christ* (completed a number of years later) to be placed over the east door of the Baptistery at Florence. A signed *Virgin and Child* and *St. John the Baptist* were executed for the cathedral at Genoa in 1503. In 1505 he moved to Rome where he executed the monuments to Cardinal Ascanio Sforza and Cardinal Girolamo Basso della Rovere on either side of the choir in S. Maria del Populo. The monuments, considered by some his masterpieces, were both completed by June, 1509. They are similar in that each has a central triumphal arch that encloses the reclining effigy of the cardinal. In the lunette above the effigy is a *Virgin and Child*, and above, on a cornice over the central arch, is a figure of God the Father, flanked by angels. In niches at the sides of the central arch are figures of Virtues. Inscriptions on the monuments indicate that they were commissioned by Julius II, who was having his favorite church restored and decorated, and included the funeral monument to his old enemy, Cardinal Ascanio Sforza, as part of his embellishment of the church. Also at Rome he carved the group *Madonna and Child with St. Anne* (1512) in S. Agostino. The group was commissioned by the German prelate and humanist, Johann Goritz, who was the patron of artists and men of letters, and was the object of a number of laudatory sonnets and epigrams that were put together in the collection known as the *Coryciana*, from his Latinized name, Corycius. After 1512 Sansovino was at Loreto, where he was named master of the works after the accession of Leo X. For the marble temple designed by Bramante to enclose the S. Casa there, he was for some time in charge of the sculptural decoration. He designed some reliefs, worked on others, and himself carved an *Annunciation*, on the west face, and *Annunciation to the Shepherds* and *Adoration of the Shepherds*, on the south face. His reliefs, distinguished for pictorial refinement, reflect the ideal calm of Raphael's rhythms, especially the *Annunciation*, completed in 1522. By temperament inclined to order and measure in the classical manner, and untouched by Michelangelo's turbulence, Andrea fused a composure derived from classicism with personal sincerity and immediacy, and was the foremost classicizing sculptor of his time.

Sansovino, Francesco. Writer; b. at Rome, 1521; d. at Venice, 1586. He was the son of the architect and sculptor Jacopo Sansovino (1486–1570), who took him to Venice after the sack of Rome (1527). A productive writer, he was the author of poetry, prose writings on literature, history, and rhetoric, and a translator and editor. Among his more important works are *Venetia* (1581), a description of Venice in fourteen books, in which he gives generous space to his father's buildings, *Origini e fatti delle famiglie illustri d'Italia* (*Origin and Deeds of Famous Italian Families*), which, according to some critics, may be a mere reworking of an earlier work by Giuseppe Betussi, *Secretario*, a treatise in seven books on the art of writing letters, and *Del Governo dei regni e delle repubbliche . . .* (1561) (*On the Government of Kingdoms and Republics*) that is valuable for its observations of contemporary customs and for statistical data.

Sansovino, Jacopo. [Original name, **Jacopo Tatti.**] Sculptor and architect; b. at Florence, 1486; d. at Venice, November 27,

1570. He was a pupil of Andrea Sansovino, from whom he took his name, perhaps helped him on the *John the Baptist* for Genoa, and followed him to Rome (1505). There he may have been present with Michelangelo and Giuliano and Francesco da Sangallo when the recently found statuary group was identified (1506) as the *Laocoön* described by Pliny. In any case, he made a wax model of it in a competition and was judged the winner by Raphael. His model brought him to the attention of that painter and Bramante and through them to that of the pope. About 1510 he was living in the Della Rovere palace, where Perugino was also living. At that time he made a wax model for a *Deposition* Perugino proposed to paint. The painting has been lost but the model exists, Victoria and Albert Museum, London, as Sansovino's earliest surviving work. He is known sometimes to have made small models for his own works and sometimes for his friend Andrea del Sarto, with whom he set up a workshop after his return (1511) to Florence. At Florence he was commissioned to carve a *St. James the Apostle* for the cathedral. Michelangelo had originally had the commission to carve the twelve Apostles. He had begun the *St. Matthew* (the uncompleted figure is now in the Accademia, Florence), then returned to Rome to work on the Sistine ceiling. Commissions for the other eleven Apostles were given to various sculptors, including Sansovino. He had felt the influence of Michelangelo somewhat in Rome, but his *St. James the Apostle* reflects rather the gentle pictorial quality of Andrea Sansovino and is in strong contrast to the tortured planes and angles of Michelangelo's *St. Matthew*. At Florence he was considered a rival of Michelangelo and, in a competitive spirit, began work on a marble *Bacchus*, now in the Bargello, in which he sought to recreate the poetry of the antique, in contrast to the realism and distinctive spiraling of Michelangelo's *Bacchus*. Also at Florence he and Andrea del Sarto supervised the preparation of the decorations for the entry of Leo X into the city (1515). He hoped to be commissioned to execute some of the sculptural decoration for the façade of S. Lorenzo, but Michelangelo objected and his hopes in this respect were not realized (nor was the façade ever constructed). On his return (1517) to Rome he carved the somewhat grandiose and monumental *Madonna del Parto*, S. Agostino, which was completed by 1519. Of about the same time is his *St. James of Campostella*, originally in S. Giacomo degli Spagnuoli and now in S. Maria di Monserrato, Rome. Also at Rome he executed (c1519) the double tomb of Antonio Orso, Bishop of Agen (d. 1511) and Cardinal Giovanni Michiel (d. 1503) (a kinsman of Pope Paul II who was poisoned in the reign of Alexander VI), in S. Marcello. When Rome was sacked (1527) he fled to Venice, where he settled permanently, became a close friend of Titian and Aretino, and where he became (1529) Chief Architect of the City. The atmosphere of Venice was conducive to the exploitation of his pictorial tendencies. He developed his ability to secure light and shade and vibrancy by shifting planes, as in his *Madonna and Child* (1534), Arsenal, and his relief, *Miraculous Cure of a Youth of the Caprilla Family* (1535), Basilica of St. Anthony, Padua. His most grandiose and perhaps best known sculptural works, carved toward the end of his life (1554), are the two gigantic statues of *Mars* and *Neptune*, symbolic of Venetian dominion over land and sea, at the head of the *Stairway of the Giants* in the Doges' Palace. Also of his later years are the bronze doors (cast 1562–1563) of the Sacristy of St. Mark's. The doors, with echoes of Donatello and Ghiberti, have, among other decorative elements, portrait heads of Sansovino and his friends Aretino and Titian.

Architecturally, several of Sansovino's buildings are among the most notable at Venice. His masterpiece is the Library of St. Mark's, on the Piazzetta of St. Mark's, across from the Doges' Palace. Cardinal Bessarion had left his priceless collection of manuscripts to the Venetian Republic (1468), and in 1537 Sansovino began a building to house it. The building he designed and began (it was completed after his death by Vincenzo Scamozzi) was called by Palladio "the richest and most ornate building that has been put up, perhaps since the time of the ancients." Basic to the design are classical columns and arches, manipulated to provide light and shade and sparkle to a building that had to compete with the Basilica of St. Mark's and the Doges' Palace across the Piazzetta. The building is richly ornamented with sculptural decoration, some of it carved by Sansovino himself. Complementing and complemented by the splendor of the buildings around it, the Library, sometimes called the Sansoviniana after its architect, is one of the landmarks of Venice. It has been greatly admired since his own time (but when, in 1545, as the result of an unusually heavy frost, part of the vaulting collapsed, Sansovino was thrown into prison, from which he was at length released through the agency of Aretino, Titian, and the emperor Charles V). Among his other buildings at Venice are the Mint, next to the Library on the waterfront, notable for the impression it gives of impregnability proper for a place where bullion is stored; the Loggia at the base of the Campanile of St. Mark's, decorated with statues and low reliefs on the outside and with a terra-cotta group of the *Madonna and Child and the Young St. John* within; and the Palazzo Corner della Ca' Grande, commissioned by the Cornaro family and the model for some 17th-century Venetian palaces. In his architectural work Sansovino combined and recombined classical elements, creating richly decorated, imposing structures largely free from the exaggeration and fantasy of mannerism as it was developing under his rival, Michelangelo. In architecture as well as in sculpture, Sansovino's energy and imagination found outlet in the classic Roman manner, which he brought with him to Venice.

Santacroce (sän-tä-krô′chā), **Girolamo da.** Painter; active in Venice from 1503; d. 1556. He was a member of a family of painters that originated in Bergamo, was perhaps a pupil and assistant of Gentile Bellini, and was a close follower of Giovanni Bellini. Of little inspiration, in his work he was largely influenced by and dependent on other painters, as Lorenzo Lotto, Palma Vecchio, Giorgione, Bonifazio de' Pitati, Cima da Conegliano, and others. He left a number of paintings, many of which are slight rearrangements of the works of the most famous painters of his time. Among them is a signed and dated (1516) *Madonna and Child*, Art Institute of Chicago, for which he borrowed a motif from the Giovanni Bellini altarpiece in S. Zaccaria, Venice, a *Madonna with SS. Sebastian, Jerome, Francis, John the Baptist and Two Donors*, Bergamo, after a Bellini *Holy Conversation* in S. Francesco della Vigna, Venice, and a *Virgin and Child*, also after Bellini, Johnson Collection, Philadelphia. Other paintings derived from other painters include *Madonna Crowned by Angels*, Correr Museum, Venice, from Lotto, an altarpiece in S. Martino, Burano, from Palma Vecchio, *Last Supper*, S. Martino, Venice, from Bonifazio de' Pitati, a number of pastoral scenes at Bergamo from Giorgione, and others. Besides those mentioned, other examples of his work are at Milan (Brera, Castello Sforzesco, Poldi Pezzoli), Padua, Verona, Vicenza, in a number of other European museums, and at Columbus (Ohio), Kansas City, Minneapolis, New Haven, New York, Princeton, San Diego, and Worcester (Massachusetts).

Santi (sän′tē), **Giovanni.** Painter; b. at Urbino, c1430; d. 1494. He was a pupil of Melozzo da Forlì, and was influenced by Perugino and by Justus of Ghent, who painted at the court of Federico da Montefeltro at Urbino. Best known as the father of Raphael, he is also noted for a rhymed chronicle that mentions a number of 15th-century artists and others. Several of his not very important paintings are in the National Gallery of the Marches at Urbino, and a fresco, in poor condition, *Madonna and Child*, on the wall of his house at Urbino is attributed to him by some, to his son Raphael by others. Other paintings are at Milan (Brera), Rome (Vatican), Berlin, Budapest, London, and elsewhere.

Santillana (sän-tē-lyä′nä), Marqués **de.** [Title of **Íñigo López de Mendoza.**] Spanish poet; b. at Carrion de los Condes, Spain, August 19, 1398; d. at Guadalajara, March 25, 1458. He was distinguished in the military and political service of Castile, captured Huelma from the Moors, and intrigued against John II's favorite. At the same time, he actively pursued his humanistic and poetic interests. He imitated the style of Petrarch, Dante, and Boccaccio, was the first to use the sonnet form in Spanish, and may justly be called the first Spanish Renaissance poet. Among his works are the didactic dialogue poem *Bias contra fortuna; Los Proverbis*, a collection of rhymed proverbs made at the request of John II, printed in 1496 (he made another collection, first printed in 1508, which were not rhymed); the *Comedieta de Ponza*, in praise of Alfonso I of Naples; and shorter poems, in his native tradition rather than the Italian model, on his encounters with mountain girls.

Sanudo (sä-nö′dō), **Marino.** [Called **il Vecchio,** "the Elder."] Traveler and writer; b. at Venice, c1270; d. after 1343. Of an illustrious Venetian family, he traveled widely in the Near East as a young man, on family and political business. In these years he acquired a good knowledge of the classical languages, and visited many cities of the eastern Mediterranean. Wherever he went he inquired into and observed the conditions and topography of the area visited. He spent some time at the court of Palermo, and then at Rome. In 1304 he was at Venice and took part in the war against Padua. In between times, he continued his travels in the Near East. After the fall of the Knights of St. John at Acre (1291), he longed for a crusade to recover the Holy Land. His book, *Conditiones Terrae sanctae,* presented to Pope Clement V (1309), suggests an economic blockade of the Turks as a means of weakening them and winning back the Holy Land. The work was rewritten and enlarged, and under its new title, *Opus Terrae sanctae,* was presented to Pope John XXII in Avignon by Sanudo himself, in September, 1321. In it he outlined definite proposals for the organization of a crusade. In his zeal for a crusade, he did not neglect the commercial interests of his native Venice. The pope was favorably impressed with his proposals but was too occupied with his struggles in Europe to initiate any activity. Sanudo never gave up his attempts to organize a crusade. He made a third presentation to the pope at Avignon between 1321 and 1323 with his further enlarged work, *Liber secretorum fidelium Crucis.* He wrote cardinals, prelates, and princes, urging a crusade, not only to overcome the Turks but to unite Italy which, he grieved, the popes themselves divided. He was at Constantinople in 1334 when an expedition was organized, and continued to fight for a crusade until the end of his life. His works on the Holy Land contained maps, charts, and geographical descriptions far superior to any contemporary, or even later, accounts. The maps, made by a Genoese who lived at Venice, included one of the Mediterranean, one of the western world, one of the Holy Land, and one of Egypt.

Sanudo, Marino. [Called **il Giovane,** "the Younger."] Historian; b. at Venice, June 22, 1466; d. there, April 4, 1536. Of a noble Venetian family, from his youth he studied the classics and gave evidence of his great abilities. He searched out and collected a library, entered into correspondence with learned men, and at the age of 15 published a little work on mythology. This was followed by further collections: of epigraphs, epigrams, poems of chivalry, translations, and other epitomes. He was one of many scholars who worked on texts for the press of Aldus Manutius. He owned a large library of manuscripts and rare books, collections of paintings, drawings, maps, and charts. His intellectual curiosity was insatiable. Added to the literary interest was his profound and unalterable love for his native city and for Italy. In 1498 he entered public life and served the republic as chamberlain of Verona, as member of the Great Council, and in furtherance of the war against Padua, among others. In all his public positions he sought to sustain the well-being and honor of Venice, satisfied, as he thought, that the gratitude of the republic would reward him. He was one of few who dared to decry what he considered weaknesses in the government and to censure those who intrigued for favors from the state. His integrity and strict observance of the law, as well as his public service, were highly esteemed by his contemporaries, but he was not rewarded as he had expected. He was at last reduced to such circumstances that he was compelled to sell part of his library. It was not until he was old and sick that the Council of Ten awarded him a pension. With all his activity as a public official, Sanudo turned out a prodigious body of writing. His histories and chronicles in his native dialect are among the most valuable sources for information on the daily life, economics, commerce, and public acts of Venice. An honest and tireless researcher and writer, his collection of facts is astounding. As a historian, however, he was not always critical of his sources and could not always manage the enormous mass of material he had accumulated. Among his works are: *Itinerario per la terraferma veneta,* an account of a trip he had taken in 1483 through the mainland possessions of Venice; *Commentarj della guerra di Ferrara,* on the war between Venice and Ferrara; and *De origine situ et magistratibus urbis Venetae,* a short chronicle of Venice that is rich in early history. His *Vite dei dogi* is an account of the lives of the doges that begins with the legendary doge Paoluccio and covers the doges up to December, 1494. His *La spedizione di Carlo VIII*, dedicated in 1495, is a valuable collection of exact information. Most important and valuable of all his works are the sixty large volumes of his *Diarî*. He began to keep his daily diary in January 1, 1496, and continued it until almost the end of his life. In it he not only noted what was said and done in the Council, he inserted documents, letters, items from all parts of Venice, Italy, and Europe. He reports on artistic and literary matters, on commerce, customs, costumes, festivals, and public works. He lists the salaries of professors and quotes his correspondents on the scandals of Rome and the rumors attaching to the popes and prelates. In fact, he covers every phase of Venetian life. He himself was well aware of the richness, detail, and value of his meticulous recording of the life of the age, and asserted that no historian would ever write a good modern history without consulting his Diaries.

Sardi (sär′dē), **Tommaso.** Dominican preacher and writer; b. at Florence, c1460; d. there, October 17, 1517. He taught theology at the *Studio* (University) at Florence, and through his eloquent preaching acquired great fame. Crowds flocked to hear him. He became disgusted because his congregations were more impressed by his eloquence than by the sense of his sermons, and gave up preaching. He wrote a poem in terza rima, in three books, that was inspired by Dante and imitative of the great poet. The poem, *L'Anima Peregrina*, dedicated to Cardinal Giovanni de' Medici (later, Pope Leo X), describes the long pilgrimage of the soul of the writer in his search for God. It was noted in its time, and interesting for the theological discussions contained in it, as the soul pursued its pilgrimage. Several manuscripts of the work are extant at Rome and Florence.

Sarmiento de Gamboa (sär-myen′tō dā gäm-bō′ä), **Pedro.** Spanish navigator; b. in Galicia, Spain, c1530; d. after 1589. Long prominent on the Peruvian coast, he was sent in 1579 to intercept Sir Francis Drake at the Straits of Magellan, who, it was thought, would return that way after his ravages of the Pacific coast. He was associated with Flores Valdez in an effort to plant a colony on the strait. The commanders quarreled, and Sarmiento was left with four vessels. He left a colony on the strait (1583) which perished of hunger, while he was a prisoner, having been captured by Sir Walter Raleigh on the voyage to Spain. His report was published in 1708.

Sarno (sär′nō). Small town northwest of Salerno, in southern Italy. Here (1460) the Angevins won a victory over the papal armies and their Milanese allies in the struggle of the Aragonese heir, Ferrante, to succeed to his father's throne as king of Naples. In this battle, muskets were used for the first time in Italy. Pope Pius II, whose armies suffered defeat in the battle, describes the new weapon in his *Commentaries* as a weapon invented in Germany in his own time. "It is of iron or copper as long as a man, as thick as the fist, almost entirely hollow. Powder made of charcoal from the fig or willow mixed with sulphur and nitre is poured into it; then a small ball of lead the size of a filbert is inserted in the front end. The fire is applied through a small hole in the back part and this explodes the powder with such force that it shoots out the ball like lightning with a report like a clap of thunder." Significantly, he adds that the ball thus ejected can penetrate armor or wood.

Sarto (sär′tō), **Andrea del.** See **Andrea del Sarto.**

Sassetta (säs-sāt′tä). [Original name, **Stefano di Giovanni.**] Sienese painter; b. 1392; d. at Siena, 1450. The place of his birth is unknown, but his father was from Cortona, and he may have been born there. His artistic training, however, was fundamentally Sienese. (He was never called Sassetta in his own time; the name was given to him in the middle of the 18th century as the result of an erroneous reading of an inscription.) One of the most delightful representatives of the Sienese pictorial tradition of the 15th century, he was perhaps a pupil of Paolo di Giovanni Fei, who transmitted to him, especially in his early works, the style of Simone Martini and the Lorenzetti. To the linear, narrative manner of the earlier Sienese were added, in Sassetta, some elements of the International Gothic, as in calligraphic curves of drapery and elongated figures, and his own mysticism and winning simplicity. By 1428 he was enrolled in the Painters' Guild at Siena. His earliest known work (1423–1426) was an altarpiece for the Wool Guild of Siena. The altarpiece, long ago dismembered and scattered, was described by writers who had seen it, and had an unusual theme—*The Adoration of the Sacrament*. The central panel, side panels, and a small *Coronation of the Virgin* above the central panel have disappeared. Figures of the patron saints of Siena and Doctors of the Church from the pilasters, and two panels from the predella—*Last Supper* and *Flagellation of St. Anthony by Demons*—are in the Pinacoteca, Siena. The latter is rather typical of Sassetta's painting style in its stark, tawny landscape dotted with tufted trees, and of his imagination in the hairy bodies, claws, and lively gestures of the demons attacking the prostrate saint. Other panels from the predella are at Budapest, in the Vatican, and at London. In March, 1430, he began work on the altarpiece *Madonna of the Snow* for the Cathedral of Siena, now in the Contini Bonacossi Collection at Florence. An *Angel of the Annunciation,* one of the cusps of the polyptych, is in the Municipal Museum, Massa Marittima; *The Virgin Annunciate,* a matching cusp, is at New Haven. The altarpiece commemorates a miracle of 352 when the Madonna appeared in a vision to a certain Giovanni at Rome and commanded him to found a church in her name where fresh snow had fallen. At the same time, the Madonna appeared to Pope Liberius and gave him similar instructions. Giovanni located the newly fallen snow and found the plan of a church traced in it. There Pope Liberius founded and dedicated the Church of S. Maria Maggiore. The contract for the altarpiece was explicit: there were to be figures of the Virgin and Child, SS. Francis, Peter, Paul, and John the Baptist, and a predella with five scenes of the story of the Miracle of the Snow. Except that he made a predella of seven panels, Sassetta carried it out faithfully. Especially in the predella panels, with views in perspective showing the construction of the Church and an un-Gothic solidity of form, Sassetta reveals an awareness of the formal developments that were taking place in Florentine art, in particular, an awareness of the work of Masaccio in the Carmine at Florence. Another masterpiece is his great polyptych for the high altar of S. Francesco at Borgo San Sepolcro (commissioned 1437, begun perhaps in 1440, and completed in 1444). The altarpiece was painted on both sides, and has since been dismembered. The central panel of the front, *Madonna and Child with Angels,* was flanked by figures of *St. John the Evangelist* and *St. Anthony of Padua* on the right, all in the Louvre, and by *The Blessed Ranieri* and *John the Baptist* on the left, now in the Berenson Collection, Florence. The central panel of the back, *St. Francis in Ecstasy,* Berenson Collection, Florence, was flanked by two superposed rows of two panels each. These panels are among the most charming of Sassetta's paintings. Especially winning is *The Mystic Marriage of St. Francis with Poverty,* Musée Condé, Chantilly, showing St. Francis, accompanied by a monk, placing a ring on the finger of the middle one of three willowy girls standing before him. They represent Chastity, Poverty, and Obedience. In the upper right of the picture the three girls are shown being wafted heavenward in an airy swoop, Chastity carrying a lily, Obedience with a yoke over her shoulders, and Poverty looking back at her bridegroom. Others of the panels, all of which are in the National Gallery, London, in their narrative grace, delicacy, and exquisite detail, show the influence of Franco-Flemish painters as well as knowledge of Florentine painting. Among them are the delightful *St. Francis and the Wolf of Gubbio,* a mystic *Stigmatization of St. Francis,* and *The Funeral of St. Francis.* Sassetta's work is notable for its refined technique, clarity and decorative harmony of color, freedom from cluttering detail (he had no objection to an empty space), poetic imaginativeness, and lyrical line. A lovely example is the *Journey of the Magi,* the Metropolitan Museum, New York, with its file of mounted knights descending a snow-covered hill. The clear pinks and blues of their raiment are reflected in a pink castle or fortified town in the background under a sky of a blue that deepens almost to purple. At the foot of the hill, heading the procession, is a mule with a monkey riding on its back, a gift for the Christ Child. In the background, on another hill, are two large birds that look like ostriches, and overhead a single row of cranes flies in a straight line in the direction of Bethlehem. The Star that leads the way is in the foreground. A companion to this panel, possibly from the same altarpiece, is the *Adoration of the Magi,* Chigi Saracini Collection, Siena, that shows the same nobles, in almost the same costumes, worshipping at the Manger. In the same collection are a dramatic *Mourning Madonna, St. John,* and a panel of *St. Martin and the Beggar* (1433), fragments of a *Crucifix* originally painted for S. Martino, Siena. Other examples of the work of this sincere and delicious painter are at Basciano, Corridonia, Cortona (S. Domenico), Grosseto, Porta Romana, Siena (a fresco, *Coronation of the Virgin*), Musée Fabre, Montpellier, Bordeaux, Cleveland, Detroit, El Paso, and elsewhere. A number of paintings similar in narrative skill and poetical conception have been attributed to Sassetta. These include the *Birth of the Virgin*, at Asciano, a triptych, *Madonna and Child with SS. Jerome and Ambrose*, Osservanza, Siena, a number of panels with scenes from the legend of St. Anthony Abbot in various museums, and others. The more observable elements of the International Gothic style in these paintings have led some modern critics to assign them to another painter whom they call "Master of the Osservanza," because of qualities in that triptych which appear to be common to the other paintings.

Sassetti (säs-sāt′tē), **Filippo.** Merchant and writer; b. at Florence, September 26, 1540; d. at Goa, India, September 3, 1588. After a period as a merchant, he abandoned commerce and gave himself up to literary studies, studies that he pursued at Pisa and Florence. In 1578 he was compelled by family necessity to return to business, but never gave up his literary interests. In that year he left Italy and went to Seville, Madrid, and Lisbon, as agent for the commercial house of Capponi. In 1582 he took ship from Lisbon for India, where he was engaged to run the pepper trade for a Portuguese merchant. He landed at Coccino on the coast of Malabar on November 8, 1583, and went from there to Goa, where he remained until his death. Everything about India interested him and he observed and investigated his surroundings, and reported on them. He had always written, as a defense of Dante, an attack on Ariosto, a work on Florentine prose, and others. In India he intensified his interest in philology. His letters are notable, and valuable, for the reports he gives of all phases of Indian life and geography. He was impressed by the number of languages spoken in India, and his description, in one of his letters, of the phonetics of Sanscrit is unique. Remarkable as well was his intuitive realization that elements of Sanscrit appear in European languages, a discovery that was not confirmed by linguistic means until the end of the 18th century. Sassetti is an outstanding example of the cultivated man who combined his interest in letters with commerce.

Sassi (säs′sē), **Panfilo.** [Real name, **Sasso de' Sassi.**] Latin and Italian poet; b. at Modena, c1455; d. at Lonzano, Romagna, September, 1527. He left his home after the loss of his family's property and went to Verona. After a brief stay there and at Brescia he returned to Modena, where he had a private school for the teaching of literature and poetry. Here he became involved in theological controversy and was charged with heresy (1523). For this reason he accepted the post of governor of Lonzano in the Romagna and removed there. He was gifted with a remarkable memory and was noted as a facile and versatile improviser, a talent much admired in his day. He was a prolific writer of the verses fashionable in his age, verses which were sometimes contorted by efforts at style and elegance, and were often bare of poetic inspiration. His sonnets and *strambotti* in the popular vein have more real sentiment. His Latin elegies indicate technical facility. His most poignant works are the patriotic sonnets, epigrams, and *capitoli* in which he laments the ruin of Italy.

Saulx (sō), **Gaspard de.** See **Tavannes,** Seigneur **de.**

Saunders (sôn′dėrz, sän′-), **Nicholas.** English polemical writer; b. near Reigate, England, 1527; d. in Ireland, between 1580 and 1583.

Savelli (sä-vel′lē). Noble family, powerful at Rome and in its environs from the 13th century. The wealth and power of the family stemmed from the time of Pope Honorius III (d. 1227), one of its early outstanding members. Another Savelli was Pope Honorius IV (c1210–1287). The territories possessed by the family at the height of its power included Albano, Castel Savello, Castel Gandolfo, and a number of fortified castles with their clustering towns, as well as Scrofano, Turrita, Palombara, Castelleone, and Monteverde in Sabina. In addition they owned palaces in Rome. The Savelli, with the Colonna, Orsini, Annibaldi, and Caetani, was among the most powerful families of Rome, one of the noble families that kept the city in turmoil for generations. Inimical to Pope Boniface VIII (c1228–1303), it was, in general, a supporter of the papacy. Its members held important posts in the Church and contributed a number of cardinals to the Sacred College.

Savelli, Giacomo. Original name of Pope **Honorius IV.**

Savile (sav′il), Sir **Henry.** English classical scholar and mathematician; b. near Halifax, England, November 30, 1549; d. at Eton, England, February 19, 1622. Besides mathematical works, he published *Rerum Anglicarum scriptores post Bedam* (1596), an edition of Chrysostom, and others. He was one of the translators of the King James Version of the Bible. In 1619 he endowed professorships at Oxford in geometry and astronomy.

Savoldo (sä-vōl′dō), **Gian Girolamo.** Painter; b. at Brescia, c1480; d. after 1548. He was influenced in his art by Giovanni Bellini, Giorgione, and Titian, and also borrowed from the Lombards. One of the best examples of his lyricism and breadth of treatment is *The Transfiguration*, Uffizi. The painting is also illustrative of his preoccupation with luminous effects and the use of light as part of the composition; the light emanating from the halo about Christ reflects in a pattern from the garments of the spectators. Again, in a *Magdalen*, National Gallery, London, light shimmers from the silky material of the Magdalen's hooded cape. One of his most poetic works is *Tobias and the Archangel Raphael*, Borghese Gallery, Rome, where there is also a *Portrait of a Youth*, notable for its twilit luminosity. Among his dated works are *Nativity* (1527), Hampton Court, and *Madonna in Glory* (1533), S. Maria in Organo, Verona. Other examples of his painting are at Brescia, Florence (Uffizi, Contini Bonacossi), Genoa, Milan (Brera), Rome (Borghese, Capitoline, Castel Sant' Angelo, Albertini Collection), Treviso, Turin (Sabauda Gallery), Venice, Verona, Amsterdam, Berlin, Budapest, Dublin, Moscow, Paris, Vienna, Cleveland, New York, Washington, and elsewhere.

Savonarola (sä-vō-nä-rō′lä), **Girolamo.** Dominican reformer; b. at Ferrara, September 21, 1452; executed at Florence, May 23, 1498. He received a good education, studied scholastic theology, particularly Thomas Aquinas, and knew the Bible, especially the Old Testament, thoroughly. His grandfather, Michele Savonarola, had been a noted physician and professor at Padua before removing to Ferrara, and Girolamo was destined to follow that profession. However, as a youth he became more and more oppressed by the wickedness and corruption he saw in the world. In April, 1475, he secretly left home and went to Bologna, where he entered the Dominican monastery. In 1479 he was back at Ferrara for study. His early sermons at Ferrara made no great impact, nor did those he first gave at Florence, where (1482) he was assigned to San Marco. In the next years he preached at San Gimignano and at Brescia and found his vocation. His reputation grew from the eloquence that passion and conviction lent to his speaking, rather than from style, and from the element of prophecy that soon entered into his sermons. In 1490 he was recalled to Florence at the request of Lorenzo de' Medici, and the following year was made prior of San Marco. In that year he gave his first sermons in the cathedral, sermons characterized by denunciations of vice and corruption. Cosimo de' Medici had rebuilt the convent of San Marco, and Lorenzo was its great patron, but Savonarola refused to pay the customary courtesy call on the latter when he was named prior, as he maintained that his election came from God and not from a prince. Although Lorenzo had great power at Rome, and could have silenced him, he did not interfere with Savonarola, allowing himself only to send messages urging the friar to preach less about the future. Savonarola paid no attention to this, but he played no role in politics until after the overthrow of Lorenzo's son Piero. And even then, it was his moral influence that drew him into the political arena. The burden of his message was that simplicity must be restored to religious life and practice, and that morality on the part of the people as well as the clergy must be revived; otherwise, the punishment of God would be swift. In an age when the clergy was believed to be corrupt and depraved, and when political confidence had waned, his eloquent forebodings fitted the times. He took his texts in general from the Old Testament, and around them created invectives against corruption and prophecies of doom. He says that from 1491 to 1494 he preached every Advent and every Lent on the book of Genesis, "taking it up at each time where I had left off before; I could not, however, reach the chapter on the Deluge until the tribulations had come." The coming of the tribulations was the arrival of Charles VIII in Italy. In Lent, 1494, he began on the chapter of the Deluge. He spoke of the construction of an Ark, one of Christian virtues. In each sermon he added a new virtue as a plank of his symbolic Ark, which was completed at Easter. He urged all to enter the Ark of the Lord while it was still open, for soon it would be too late. His sermons were so popular that people went to the cathedral in the middle of the night to be sure of a place in the morning. The congregations came to number anywhere from 13,000 to 15,000 rapt and weeping listeners. He preached at Prato and Bologna, and on his return to Florence was deliriously received. With some difficulty, he secured the separation of San Marco from control of the Lombard Dominicans, which gave him a free hand in affairs of the convent and assured his remaining at Florence.

Savonarola's entrance into politics was facilitated by his ready assimilation of the Florentine civic tradition. For two centuries Florence had been on terms of friendship with France, to no small extent for economic reasons. With the invasion of Italy by the French (1494) Savonarola, who had predicted his coming, called Charles VIII *gladius Domini* (*the sword of God*), who would chastise the wicked, reform the Church, and purify Florence. This was the wrath of God of which he had prophesied. A contemporary chronicler wrote, "He preached in the Church of Santa Reparata (the cathedral); and when, at the moment the king of France entered the city, he announced that the ark was closed, the whole assembly amid terror and dismay and outcries went out into the streets, and wandered up and down, silent and half-dead." Piero de' Medici was expelled, with others of his party, after his abject surrender of Florentine fortresses—Sarzana, Pietrasanta, and others—to Charles without a struggle. The departure of the Medici left a vacuum in Florentine affairs. Savonarola had become immensely influential. He was chosen as one of the envoys to the French king (November 5, 1494) because of the known respect the king had for him, and after the French moved out of Florence (November 30, 1494) he began to preach on the kind of government that should be established. Luca Landucci, a contemporary diarist, relates that for the sermon of December 14, he requested that no women be present, and that he "did his utmost in the pulpit to persuade Florence to adopt a good form of government." In succeeding sermons he "preached much about state matters, and that we ought to love and fear God, and love the commonweal; and no one must set himself up proudly above the rest." He "favored the people and he insisted that no one ought to be put to death." As early as January, 1495, Landucci notes that he "exculpated himself from certain accusations." For though he had tremendous influence, such a strong personality roused strong reactions, and there were always, even when he was at the top of his powers, groups who distrusted or feared him not only for his preaching on moral matters but more for his influence on the life of the state. To secure what was thought to be a truly popular government, a Grand Council was proposed that would embrace all those who could show that at least one of their ancestors of the last three generations had served as a magistrate. (This automatically excluded the vast majority of the Florentines but was considered dangerously democratic by opponents.) The function of the Grand Council was to choose the chief magistrates and a senate of eighty that would sit for six months. In its turn, the senate would advise the Signory (eight priors and a gonfaloniere, as of old), and choose ambassadors and commissioners with the army. The new government was based on the Venetian system, adapted to existing Florentine institutions. Savonarola created "an over-powering public feeling" in favor of the proposed government. He advised the Council in his sermons. To restore tranquility, he proposed a political amnesty. He advocated a lifting of taxes and the reopening of shops to revive commercial life. He favored the abolition of the *parlamento*. He suggested methods of taxation, penalties for gambling and unnatural vice, the regulation of dress, and the establishment of *monti di pietà* (state pawnshops where the poor could borrow money at low interest). He began to regard the opposition that soon arose to his political views as a sin. Under Lorenzo de' Medici, the season of carnival at Florence had reached a peak of gaiety considered by some to be licentious. Savonarola proposed to change this. He encouraged bands of boys to go through the streets singing hymns, and stopping at each house to collect whatever "vanity" of this world had become too dear to the householder. Such vanities were cosmetics, hair pieces, masks, cards, dice, lewd pictures and books. They were heaped (1497) on a great pyre and burned in the Piazza della Signoria, to the singing of hymns. (It was true that in the second burning of vanities some threw dead cats on the pyre, and that others, in the traditional sardonic Florentine manner, ridiculed the wild dances performed by aged monks in honor of God.) So great was the enthusiasm for reform and repentance that prominent men flocked to join the Dominicans. The stronger Savonarola grew, the stronger became his opposition. It was roughly divided into parties: the *Arrabbiati* (Enraged Ones) were the anti-Medicean aristocrats who looked to the pope and Milan for the salvation of Florence, and longed to break with France. The *Compagnacci* were young men who objected to Savonarola's strict measures and interference in private life. The *Bigi* (Greys) were the remnants of the Medici party. The great masses, ardent followers, were called the *Piagnoni* (Snivellers or Weepers), and accepted Savonarola as a prophet. None of the parties had clear lines of demarcation; each of them included members on the borderline. Savonarola soon found that Charles VIII did not keep his promises. The fortresses Piero had turned over to him were not restored. Pisa, the lodestar of Florentine policy, was released not to Florence, as promised, but to its citizens, who immediately rebelled against Florence. Sarzana was sold to Genoa; Pietrasanta went to Lucca. Other territories of Florence rebelled or were lost. Florence turned its energies to regaining Pisa, which Savonarola, a true Florentine, intensely imperialistic and with no interest at all in liberty for Pisans, promised would be regained. The emperor Maximilian made a quick sortie from over the Alps in defense of Pisa but, unprepared for the undertaking, was forced to retire. Savonarola's reputation soared. Francesco Valori, an ardent disciple, was chosen gonfaloniere (January, 1497) and was said to go to San Marco frequently to consult with the prior on political matters. The year 1497 was a bad one; Florence was battered by poor crops, by famine, poverty, and plague.

Alexander VI had not paid much attention to the fiery denunciations of the friar, but he could not ignore his political influence. The pope feared a return of the French. A league between the pope and other Italian states was formed, but Florence clung to the French and would not join. As early as July, 1495, Savonarola had been summoned to Rome, but made his excuses. The pope attacked his alleged gift of prophecy, his invectives against Rome, and his separation of the Tuscan congregations of the Dominicans from the Lombards, which he had originally authorized. To combat the separation and Savonarola's influence, in November, 1496, the pope ordered the union of all Tuscan Dominican convents in a new Tuscan-Roman Congregation. This was to destroy Savonarola's position as an independent prelate. He resisted. On June 18, 1497 a bull of excommunication came from Rome and was read in the main churches of Florence. The accusation was disobedience and doctrinal heterodoxy. Savonarola's *Compendium Revelationum* was his defense of prophecy. His *Triumphus Crucis* (*Triumph of the Cross*) defended his doctrine. He ceased preaching, as the Florentines, for all their scepticism, or their devotion to Savonarola, feared an interdict, and fell away from him. His friends besieged the pope. Conspiracies seeking the return of the Medici were discovered and further agitated the city. Five of the most prominent, and in some cases, respected, citizens were accused and denied the right of appeal to the Grand Council—a signal right established by the new government of 1494. They were executed and moderates recoiled in horror. On Christmas day, 1497, in open defiance of the pope, he celebrated mass at San Marco. On February 11, 1498, he preached on the excommunication, and Alexander was forced to act. He demanded either that Savonarola be sent to Rome or be silenced at Florence. Bowing to the request of the state, Savonarola preached a farewell sermon that contained a fierce diatribe against Rome. No longer in the pulpit, he wrote letters, and secretly appealed to the princes of Europe to depose a pope who had been elected by simony and was therefore not a true pope. Feeling was high at Florence; faction and civil strife were rampant. On March 25, 1498, a Franciscan took up an offer that Domenico da Pescia, one of Savonarola's most devoted disciples, had previously made: to pass through fire to justify his master. The Franciscan, who perhaps took up the challenge as part of a plot to destroy Savonarola, said he knew he would be burned, but he would do this to banish the delusion of the people that Savonarola was a prophet of God. Savonarola was opposed to the test, scrupling to demand a miracle of heaven. Rome also opposed the ordeal. But the government at Florence, in the hope of satisfying the city, yielded to the clamor of the people and arranged the ordeal. Domenico da Pescia was to undergo the test on Savonarola's behalf and Fra Rondinelli represented the Franciscans. The spectacle was prepared in the piazza—two great tiers of faggots were erected, with a narrow path between them. On the appointed day, citizens roosted like crows on the roofs, every window facing the square was black with semi-hysterical spectators. Then the Franciscans began to raise obstacles. They demanded that Domenico be deprived of the Host as he entered the flames; other wrangles caused delay; a torrent of rain fell; the government called off the ordeal. The thirst for blood and pain had reached such a height that the spectators were enraged to be deprived of it. Their wrath turned on Savonarola, although it was the Franciscans who caused the cancellation by their objections. The next day, Palm Sunday, there were riots. Valori, considered Savonarola's creature, was seized and killed. San Marco was attacked. Savonarola called the brothers to the library of the convent and make his farewells. He and Domenico surrendered. They were taken to the Palazzo through a howling mob that attacked and cursed them. The city was in turmoil. Alexander asked that Savonarola be sent to Rome for trial. Florence refused and brought him to trial herself. The questions of his examiners were heavily weighted on his claim to prophecy; the aim was to destroy his credit as a prophet, to expose him as an impostor, as only in this way would he lose his vast influence. From April 9 to May 20 he was questioned by his civil examiners. Under torture he confessed but retracted immediately when the torture ceased. The record of his answers was later falsified. The popular democratic government, which had such explicit measures for the protection of accused persons, collapsed. Cowardice and fear gave Savonarola to the flames. He and his companions were declared heretics and schismatics; they had sinned against the state and the Church. (Commissioners from the pope had followed the Florentine examiners with three more days of torture and questions.) Florence was awarded three-tenths of Church revenues, "thirty pieces of silver" according to Savonarola's followers, none of whom "dared to say a word for the Frate." A great pyre was erected in the piazza. From it rose a gibbet from which swung three halters. Fra Domenico and Fra Silvestro, his closest disciples, preceded Savonarola along a raised path to the pyre. He said nothing as the halter was placed around his neck, thus disappointing his partisans, some of whom still expected a miracle. The three men were hanged and their bodies burned as the great pyre was set alight. Their ashes were gathered and thrown into the Arno. (A disk set into the pavement marks the spot where the executions took place.) In a few years Savonarola had won such influence that for a time he held Florence in the hollow of his hand. At first he made little of his prophetic powers. Then he began to believe in them himself. He had prophesied the death of Innocent VIII, Lorenzo de' Medici, and the king of Naples, and the coming of the French. Luca Landucci writes that on April 1, 1495 "Fra Girolamo preached, and said and testified that the Virgin Mary had revealed to him, that after going through much trouble, the city of Florence was to be the most glorious, the richest, and the most powerful that ever existed; and he promised this absolutely. All these things he spoke as a prophet, and the greater part of the people believed him." In his ecstasy he had proclaimed Christ King of Florence. Politically his choice was disastrous and he never saw that it was so. His reliance on the French persisted long after it was obvious that they had betrayed every promise and trust. His attacks on the clergy were well merited and highly popular. Alexander was willing to endure attacks on his personal life, and did not hasten to reply, but he could not ignore disobedience, and above all, could not allow the friar to interfere with policy. However, the day before the execution Alexander sent Savonarola absolution. A sincere and passionate spirit, Savonarola was an echo of the Middle Ages. He was not the first to rouse the people to hysterical repentance by his prophetic sermons. His undoing was that his eloquence and influence brought him into opposition to the papacy, with dire results for himself and the city that he had envisioned as a watchtower that would diffuse light over all Italy. His influence on morals and politics was ephemeral (though his followers persisted at least until 1530, and many lived out their lives under his spell), yet his name is forever linked to that of Florence. His doctrine could never seriously be called into question. He left collections of sermons and letters, the theological writings mentioned above, essays on devotional and moral themes, a few poems, and a treatise on the government of Florence, none of which provide any evidence of heresy. Fra Bartolommeo, a devoted follower who became a Dominican, has left the portrait of Savonarola that seems definitively to reveal the passionate, ascetic, and doomed personality. It is in the convent of San Marco, in Savonarola's cell.

Savonarola, Michele. Physician; b. at Padua, c1384; d. at Ferrara, 1468. He studied medicine at Padua, where he became a professor (1434), and then went to Ferrara (1440). There, in the service of Niccolò III, Leonello, and Borso d'Este, he won fame as a physician and as a teacher. His *Opus medicinae seu Practica de aegritudinibus de capite usque ad pedes* (printed at Colle Val d'Elsa, 1479), is a work of six treatises on the various ills that attack the body. It is historically interesting and valuable for its descriptions of medical instruments and practices, for his observations on special therapy and on pathology, and for its treatment of various malfunctions and malformations. His *De balneis et thermis* (Ferrara, 1485), a description of the baths and mineral springs of Italy, was very successful and was translated into Greek by Theodore Gaza. He also left didactic works and a description of Padua and its famous men. He was the grandfather of Girolamo Savonarola (1452–1498).

Scala (skä'lä), **della.** [Plural, **Scaligeri.**] Veronese family that had the lordship of Verona from 1277 to 1387. The coat of arms of the family carries a ladder (*scala*). In 1350 Regina della Scala married Bernabò Visconti of Milan. In gratitude for the birth of her first son she caused the Church of S. Maria della Scala to be raised on the site now occupied by the famous opera house at Milan that perpetuates the Scala name.

Scala, Alessandra. One of the earliest humanists of her sex; b. 1475; d. 1506. She was the daughter of Bartolommeo Scala (1428–1497). She studied Greek under Lascaris and Chalcondylas and attended the lectures of Poliziano. A great beauty as well as a scholar, she was courted by both Lascaris and Poliziano, but married (1494) the Greek poet Marullo, to the anger and dismay of her suitors. When he died (1500) she entered a convent, where she died a few years later. She played the part of Electra in a representation of Sophocles' tragedy, presented in Greek. Of her writing, a Greek epigram for Poliziano remains.

Scala, Bartolommeo. Humanist; b. at Colle Val d'Elsa, 1428; d. at Florence, 1497. He went to Florence as a youth and attended the lectures of Carlo Marsuppini. He later became friendly with the Medici and was a member of the circle of literary men that gathered about Lorenzo de' Medici. In Florence, of which he became a citizen in 1471, he held public office, including the chancellorship, and pursued his studies. Among his writings are verse, prose, histories, and speeches. He was the father of Alessandra Scala (1475–1506).

Scala, Can Grande della. Lord of Verona (1311–1329); b. at Verona, March 9, 1291; d. at Treviso, July 22, 1329. He was the son of Alberto della Scala; was a Ghibelline, and was named imperial vicar of Verona by Henry VII during the latter's Italian expedition (1311). As captain of the Ghibelline League and active in its wars against the Guelphs, he was excommunicated by Pope John XXII. Most of his reign was filled with wars, his own and other peoples'. He won Vicenza from Padua but was compelled to fight Padua for most of the rest of his reign in order to hold it. He at last won the ascendancy over Padua. He also acquired Feltre, Belluno, and Treviso and had dominion over one of the strongest states in the north of Italy. He maintained a brilliant court at Verona, and was the patron of artists and writers. Dante, who fled to his court after his exile from Florence, was warmly received by Can Grande. Dante dedicated his *Paradiso* to him, and memorialized him thus (*Paradiso*, xvii):

> ". . . one who at his birth
> Was stamped so deeply by this stalwart star
> That his deeds shall deserve a wide acclaim."

Able, energetic, daring, quick to make decisions and to take action, Can Grande was an eminent example of the 14th-century despots who won lordship over states; an example too, of the interest of such despots in assembling at their courts and encouraging the finest artistic and literary talents of their day. The Scaligeri ruled Verona from 1277 until 1387. Can Grande was the most illustrious of his line.

Scaliger (skal'i-jėr), **Joseph Justus.** Protestant scholar; b. at Agen, France, August 5, 1540; d. at Leiden, January 21, 1609. He was the tenth child of Julius Caesar Scaliger (1484–1558). He studied at Bordeaux, Paris, and Valence, and was learned in Latin, Greek, Arabic, Hebrew, and Roman law. His life was disrupted by war and religious controversy. He spent four years in Italy, and traveled in England and Scotland. Having become a Calvinist, he fled to Geneva after the St. Bartholomew Massacre, August 24, 1572, and taught there in the university. In 1593 he became professor at Leiden, where he produced many of his critical works. In his *De emendatione temporum* (1583), a survey of all known means of measuring time, for the purpose of correcting chronology, and his *Thesaurus temporum* (1606), a lexicon of dates, he became the founder of modern chronology. He edited Catullus, Propertius, Tibullus, and others, doing pioneer work in modern textual criticism of the classics. For the breadth and depth of his learning he was known as "the bottomless pit of erudition."

Scaliger, Julius Caesar. Humanist, naturalist, critic, and physician; b. at Riva del Garda, 1484; d. at Agen on the Garonne, France, October 21, 1558. From young manhood he followed the profession of arms, and distinguished himself at the Battle of Ravenna (1512). The military life did not hinder his pursuit of literary and scientific studies. From 1514 to 1519 he studied medicine at Bologna, and it was in the capacity of physician that he accompanied Bishop Angelo della Rovere to Agen (1525). He began his career as a writer with a sharp attack on the *Ciceronianus* of Erasmus. When Erasmus made no reply he fired off an even harsher invective. Cardano was another who was the object of his literary attacks. His interest in language caused him to write *De causis linguae latinae*, the first scientific approach to a Latin grammar. In it he analyzed Cicero's style, and pointed out more than 600 errors made by the humanists. He wrote commentaries on the botanical works of Theophrastus and those supposed to be by Aristotle, and on the medical works of Hippocrates. His *Poetica* is an interpretation of Aristotle's *Poetics*. Scaliger found the ideal of perfection in the classical Latin models. His conviction that Latin was superior to Greek, Vergil and Ovid superior to Homer, and Romans superior to Greeks held the field for generations.

Scaligeri (skä-lē'jā-rē). Plural of Scala; see **Scala, della.**

Scanderbeg or **Skanderbeg** (skan'dėr-beg). [Original name, **George Castriota.**] Albanian national hero; b. 1403; d. at Alessio (Lesh), January 17, 1468. He was the son of Ivan (John) Castriota, lord of a hereditary principality in Albania, and in his youth was sent as a hostage to the Ottoman court. There he became a Moslem and was given the name *Iskander* (Alexander), to which was later added the title *Bey* (Lord or Prince); the two names were subsequently combined and shortened to Scanderbeg. He rose rapidly in the administrative ranks and was a successful fighter for the Turks against the Serbs and the Venetians. On the death of his father in 1443, the Porte decided to annex this principality, which had hitherto enjoyed a semi-independent status. The Albanians rose up against the Turkish garrison. Scanderbeg learned of the unrest in his fatherland and returned to Albania in 1444. He declared himself a Christian, proclaimed his independence, and gathered the Albanian and Montenegrin chieftains about his standard. From then, with the aid of Venice and of the papacy, he organized a brilliant resistance against Murad II and Mohammed II. The Turks signed (1461) a truce, but Scanderbeg was induced by Pope Pius II to break it (1463) in order to join the pope on a crusade against the Turks. Pius died (1464) and the crusade never took place. Scanderbeg was deserted by his allies, and fought alone against Mohammed II, who besieged the Albanian fortress of Kroja in 1466. Scanderbeg went to Rome to seek help from Pope Paul, who did what he could for him. He returned to Albania and held out, with his small, valiant army, until his death. Following this, the chiefs split ranks, beset as they were by inter-clan jealousies, and Scanderbeg's son, faced with insurmountable difficulties, sold his rights to the areas of Albania not conquered by the Turks to the Venetians. In turn (1478) they were sold back to the Turks.

Scannabecchi (skän-nä-bāk'kē), **Dalmasio.**

[Also known as **Lippo Dalmasio.**] Bolognese painter; b. at Bologna, c1352; d. there, before 1421. He was the nephew and pupil of Simone dei Crocifissi; his work reflects the influence of his master in its earlier stages, but that of Vitale da Bologna and the Sienese in the greater delicacy of his later works. He was also called Lippo delle Madonne from his preference for painting Madonnas. These include *Madonna of Humility,* Collegio di Spagna, Bologna, and another at London; *Madonna Suckling the Child,* Pinacoteca, and a signed and dated (1397) fresco on the same subject, S. Maria della Misericordia; and other *Madonnas* at Pistoia. Other works include the signed and dated (1394) *Coronation of the Virgin,* Pinacoteca, and frescoes in S. Isaia, S. Petronio, and S. Procolo, Bologna.

Scarampo (skä-räm′pō), **Lodovico.** Papal admiral and cardinal; active in the middle of the 15th century; d. after 1459. In 1440 he was named captain general of the papal armies, having previously served under Giovanni Vitelleschi. He won back some lands for the papacy and was rewarded by being named, successively, bishop of Traù, in Dalmatia, archbishop of Florence, cardinal, patriarch of Aquileia, and papal chamberlain. In 1445 he was made papal captain general and admiral, with broad powers to deal with foreign states and to govern the places he occupied in the name of the Holy See. In 1456 he led a large and well-armed fleet into the eastern Mediterranean, captured new islands and defended Rhodes and Cyprus. The following year he defeated a strong Turkish fleet. After a royal welcome at Rome, in April, 1459, he drops from sight. Some of his letters are preserved at Vatican City and at Brescia.

Scarpazza (skär-pät′tsä), **Vittore.** Original name of **Vittore Carpaccio.** The name Carpaccio, applied since the 17th century, is derived from the Latin *Carpathius.*

Scarperia (skär-pe-rē′ä), **Jacopo da.** Florentine humanist and papal secretary; b. c1360; d. 1411. In 1395 he went to Constantinople to study Greek. He returned to Florence (1397) with Chrysoloras, to whom he had conveyed the offer of a post at the university at Florence. With other humanists, he became an ardent student of Greek under Chrysoloras. He also studied under Giovanni Malpaghini, and was on friendly terms with such a prominent humanist as Coluccio Salutati. Scarperia was an early (perhaps the earliest) collector of Greek manuscripts, translated Ptolemy's *Geography,* some of Plutarch's *Lives* and parts of Plutarch's *Moralia,* into Latin, and found a complete set of Cicero's *Philippics.*

Schiavo (skyä′vō), **Paolo.** See **Paolo di Stefano.**

Schiavone (skyä-vō′nā), **Andrea.** See **Andrea Schiavone.**

Schiavone, Giorgio. [Original surname **Čulinović, Chulinovich** or **Chiulinovich,** called **Schiavone** from the fact that he was a Slav.] Painter; b. at Scardona (Skradin), Dalmatia, c1436; d. at Sebenico, December 6, 1504. His early training was in Dalmatia. In 1456, after meeting Squarcione at Venice, he went to Padua where he signed a contract by which he agreed to work for Squarcione for three years in return for the necessities of life and instruction in painting. The influence of Squarcione's training and his attempts to imitate Mantegna are evident in his rather awkward paintings, as in the versions of the *Madonna and Child* at Baltimore, Turin, London, and Berlin, with their garlands of fruit, over-ornamentation, and decorative motifs from the antique. Schiavone renewed his contract with Squarcione in 1458, but by 1461 he had fled and returned to Dalmatia, carrying with him a series of important drawings from Squarcione's workshop. After a stay at Zara he settled at Sebenico, where he married and took a pupil (1464), and where (1489) he signed a contract for a polyptych for the cathedral. Painting was not his main occupation after his return and any work he may have done then has disappeared. Other examples of his work are at Berlin, Bergamo, Florence, London, Padua, Paris, and Venice.

Schöffer or **Schoeffer** (shė′ėr), **Peter.** Early German printer; b. at Germersheim, Bavaria; d. c1502. He was an associate of Gutenberg and Fust (whose son-in-law he was), and won an unwarranted reputation as inventor of matrices and the type-mold, probably through his own false claims.

Schöner (shė′nėr), **Johann.** German mathematician and geographer; b. at Karlstadt, Germany, 1477; d. at Nuremberg, January 16, 1547. He was a friend of Melanchthon, and was professor of mathematics at Nuremberg. He made at least two globes (1515 and

1520; the former known only in copies), which are among the earliest showing the name America. They also indicate a strait (probably conjectural, so far as Schöner was concerned, because Magellan did not discover the strait which now bears his name until October, 1520, and news of the discovery did not reach Europe until 1522) at the southern end of South America.

Schongauer (shōn′gou-ėr), **Martin.** [Called **Bel Martino, Hipsch (Hübsch) Martin,** and **Martin Schön.**] German historical painter and engraver, said to be the greatest of the 15th century; b. at Kolmar, in Alsace, c1446; d. there February 2, 1488. He founded a school of painting at Kolmar. His chief painting is a Virgin and Child, called *The Madonna of the Rosehedge* (1473), at Kolmar.

Schwarz (shvärts), **Berthold.** [Original name, **Konstantin Ancklitzen** (or **Anklitzen** or **Ancklitzer** or **Angelisen.**] German Franciscan monk and alchemist; b. at Freiburg, Germany; active in the first half of the 14th century. He was long credited with the invention (c1330) of gunpowder. Modern authorities now generally agree that gunpowder was already known by the early 14th century, and that Schwarz's contribution (like that of Roger Bacon) was actually to introduce into Europe an understanding of its possible uses. It has been suggested, however, that he may have been the first European to cast a bronze cannon.

Scipione del Ferro (skē-pē-ō′nā del fer′rō). Mathematician; d. 1526. He was a professor of mathematics at Bologna for thirty years. His work on the cubic equation foreshadowed Niccolò Tartaglia's solution.

Scogan (skō′gạn), **Henry.** English poet; fl. at the end of the 14th and beginning of the 15th century. He was a contemporary of Chaucer to whom he refers frequently as "my maistre." He inserted in one of his poems (called *Scogan unto the Lords and Gentilmen of the King's house*) Chaucer's ballade *Gentilesse*. He is probably the man to whom Chaucer's *Lenvoy to Scogan* was written.

Scola (skō′lä), **Ognibene della.** Humanist; b. at Padua, c1370; d. at Pinerolo, June, 1429. A pupil of Giovanni da Ravenna, he later studied law at the university at Padua and then (1406) held a chair there. His life was soon occupied by political affairs. Under the Carrara, lords of Padua for a time, he served on many missions. On the fall of his lords he joined the parties of the successive rulers, served the emperor Sigismund and the duke of Savoy, but always longed for the patronage of a prince that would provide him with the peace and quiet for study. He left two moral treatises and several letters that are interesting for their comments on the events of his time.

Scot (skot), **Reginald.** English author; d. 1599. He wrote a book against the persecution of witches, entitled *Discoverie of Witchcraft* (1584) which was burned by order of James I.

Scott (skot), **Alexander.** Scottish author of satirical and amatory verse; b. c1525; d. 1584. Of his thirty-six poems, critics regard as his best *The Lament of the Maister of Erskyn* (1547), *A New Year Gift to Quene Mary* (1562), and *The Justing at the Drum*, a satire on tournament conventions.

Scrovegni (skrō-vā′nyē) **Chapel.** Chapel at Padua, commissioned by Enrico Scrovegni, a wealthy Paduan, to atone for his father's sin of usury. The chapel was dedicated (1304 or 1305) to Our Lady of Charity, as charity is the virtue opposed to the vice of usury. The interior of the chapel is entirely decorated with frescoes, executed by Giotto and assistants probably between 1304 and 1306. It is also called Arena Chapel, Giotto's Chapel, and the Annunziata, because the chapel was dedicated to the Virgin of the Annunciation. See **Giotto.**

Sculpture. Italian Renaissance sculpture is customarily thought of in terms of the single, freestanding statue created to be a self-sufficient entity. Actually, only a few statues done in the Renaissance were conceived initially as independent units. The majority of lifesize or monumental statues which the modern public now encounters in museums were originally planned as incorporate parts of large programs, such as the decoration of cathedrals, tombs, civic buildings, or fountains. Moreover, Renaissance sculpture has a much greater repertory than figures in the round. It includes many varieties of reliefs, medals, statuettes, and bust portraits.

The origins of Renaissance sculpture can be traced to the second half of the Dugento. During this period three greatly influential personalities—Nicola Pisano, Giovanni, his son, and Arnolfo di Cambio, his pupil—brought to life a new style, adopting freely the conventions of French Gothic sculpture then spreading throughout Europe but capitalizing on a local tradition that resisted the close association of sculpture to architecture. In France, teams of sculptors and architects worked together blending statues and architectural features to create their great cathedral façades. In Italy, the emergence of the new style can be seen in pulpits, tombs, or fountains, comparatively small structures under the direction of one master. This factor helped in the formation of self-aware artistic personalities who, as in the case of Nicola and Giovanni Pisano, even signed their works with self-laudatory inscriptions. In the beginning Nicola Pisano had been a classicist, and to some extent he relied on ancient Roman sarcophagi in order to create figures that would at once approximate natural appearance and possess monumental qualities, regardless of their actual size. In his pulpit in the Baptistery of Pisa the six small figures placed over the column capitals were carved in such high relief that they appear to be almost statuettes in the round, and autonomous from any architectural role. Nicola's first pulpit was a manifestation of an attitude that spread throughout Tuscany. Thereafter, sculpture evolved along two main lines: it became increasingly independent of architecture, and it absorbed the naturalistic elements of style emanating from northern Europe. Figures were given greater freedom of movement and were made to register a wider range of human feelings. Giovanni Pisano was the most daring of the three artists. His figures are always charged with dramatic spontaneity, as if their action were the expression of an excited psychic state. His monumental contribution to the emancipation of sculpture from architecture was made when, as chief architect of the Siena Cathedral during the 1290's, he designed the lower half of the façade and planned its decoration so that the statues are not subject to the architectural systems. The accomplishments of the Pisanos and Arnolfo di Cambio contain several indications of the development of Italian sculpture in the Quattrocento. However, in the first half of the Trecento, the art of painting forged ahead and sculpture could only trail in its influential wake. Sculptors, such as those who, under the direction of Lorenzo Maitani, carved the reliefs for the cathedral façade at Orvieto, approached marble swayed by the ideal of delicacy and gentleness created by the painters. Tino di Camaino's tombs were charming, serene translations of those of Arnolfo di Cambio. Historically, the most important monument of this period is the pair of bronze doors for the Baptistery at Florence. Andrea Pisano's ornamental clarity and simplicity of composition, as well as the directness of his narrative, were considered such a perfect solution to the designing of such doors that their basic scheme was chosen as the model for the next set in 1401.

In the second half of the Trecento Italian sculpture, as a whole, created works of comparatively little significance. Possibly the most consequential workshop of the period was that of the Dalle Masegne brothers. Their style, specifically their energetic handling of the figure in space, and an overall austere naturalism, assist us, if only partially, to comprehend the formation of those of Brunelleschi and Jacopo della Quercia, who, together with Ghiberti and their younger contemporaries, Donatello and Nanni di Banco, were the founders of the Renaissance in sculpture. With the exception of Jacopo della Quercia all of these artists were Florentines. Therefore, Florence well deserves to be regarded as the birthplace of the new style.

The new chapter in the history of sculpture begins with Brunelleschi's and Ghiberti's trial reliefs (the only ones surviving) for the 1401 competition for the Baptistery's second set of bronze doors. Brunelleschi presented the prescribed subject, *The Sacrifice of Isaac*, with vivid realism, making the viewer conscious of the physical as well as of the psychological reality of the dramatic event. Ghiberti, who won the competition, handled the theme in a lyrical and poetical manner, showing the nude Isaac in a heroic, triumphant pose. Although the two artists offered rather opposing views of a moment of high drama, they shared, at this point, a similar interest in the revival of antiquity, both of them borrowing motifs from ancient statues for some of the figures in their reliefs. Eventually this reliance upon ancient art gave character to the whole period. However, during the years immediately following the competition, the antique and realism were temporarily forgotten in favor of a sophisticated style fostered by Ghiberti in his first reliefs for the doors—a style based partially on the linear rhythms and disregard of plausibility of the elegant Gothic International Style then sweeping throughout Europe.

During the first two decades of the Quattrocento, Florentine civic and religious institutions sponsored large sculptural programs, offering young sculptors the opportunity of creating public works of art. Donatello and Nanni di Banco received commissions in 1408 for statues of two seated Evangelists to be placed in the niches of the Florentine cathedral several feet above the heads of the passersby. The two artists designed these statues so that their serious, noble presences would be coherently impressive only when seen from a low point of view. Here, the sculptors no longer thought of their works in terms of artistic decoration, but as a means of conveying specifically to the public ideals of human dignity. Later, at Orsanmichele, a shrine and a grain hall situated in the heart of Florence, they were commissioned to fill lower exterior niches with statues of patron saints of the city's guilds. The two artists created these statues as examples of moral strength and individual freedom. Both of them relied on ancient Roman sculpture and eliminated from their repertories any Gothic mannerisms. Donatello was unique and superior to Nanni di Banco in that he had a capacity to blend classical motifs with vivid naturalism, and possessed a penetrating insight into human psychology. His statues appear as living counterparts of human beings endowed with highly characterized personalities. *St. Mark*, his first statue for Orsanmichele, demonstrates this. His *St. George*, destined for a very shallow niche, projects forward dynamically, displaying physical readiness, and showing on his face an apprehensive anticipation of adversity. The figure presents not only a frontal but two equally valid profile views. This new approach was later expanded when Donatello created isolated statues such as his *David* (1430's), the first freestanding, bronze nude of the Renaissance, so designed as to make every aspect of the figure a functional part of a coherently expressive whole. Evocative of the antique, and studied in naturalism, the *David* also reveals Donatello's highly unusual and colorful imagination. His relief of *St. George and the Dragon*, done in 1417 for the base of his *St. George*, is an epoch-making achievement. It is carved in a very flat relief, known as *rilievo schiacciato*, a technique invented by the artist so as to realize an impression of landscape receding in depth with effects of fluctuating air in space. Also included is an arcaded building that comes very close to being organized into one point perspective. Donatello's first experiment with linear perspective and atmosphere was more or less contemporary with Brunelleschi's discovery of how to reproduce actual buildings according to a constant scale and with the effect of distance in space regulated by mathematical diminution. After these innovations and discoveries sculptors had at their disposal the means for unifying narrative compositions in a relief according to principles consistent with visual perception. They reacted to this concept in very individual ways. Ghiberti, especially in his second doors for the Baptistery, modulated the height of the relief so that it would vary gradually from the more pronounced forms in the foreground to the extremely shallow ones in the far distance. He also gilded the entire surface of his panels to achieve atmospheric as well as spatial unity. The world is presented not only in accordance with the newly formulated laws of perception, but also in terms of an ideal of harmony and resplendent beauty. Jacopo della Quercia remained untouched by the new influence. Primarily a marble carver, he developed a dramatic style centered on the representation of the human figure. In his relief for San Petronio in Bologna the nude was brought to a height of epic power that remained unique throughout the Quattrocento and made a lasting impression on Michelangelo. The period was also characterized by technical experimentation focused, above all, on finding new media for the decoration of architectural interiors. This need arose, in part, from the fact that architectural concepts had been so revolutionized by Brunelleschi that marble or bronze were often not considered suitable. Luca della Robbia came forth with a unanimously accepted solution when he developed the technique of glazing terra-cotta reliefs, relying on the simple and harmonious coloristic contrast of white figures against a blue background.

In Florence, after the 1430's, commissions for public statuary began to wane. One of the chief remaining opportunities for sculpture lay in church appointments such as tombs, doors, choir lofts, small reliefs, and so forth. Sculptors, conscious of living in a new period, rejected Gothic formulae and sought steadily for innovations. Furthermore, with the emergence of new personalities, styles became polarized. Luca della Robbia and Donatello, when commissioned to execute two choir lofts for the cathedral of Florence, produced works almost antithetical in expressiveness.

The glorification of actual individuals in accordance with humanistic culture became one of the main themes of the Quattrocento. Bernardo Rossellino's wall tomb for Leonardo Bruni (1445–1450) is the prototype for Quattrocento tomb sculpture. Framed with a motif reminiscent of the ancient triumphal arch, the contained, limited sculpture is almost entirely dedicated to the ennoblement of the deceased. This scheme spread throughout Italy, acquiring further statuary and architectonic features as local tradition dictated, especially in Venice, where, from 1475 on, Pietro Lombardo established a full understanding of Florentine art. The equestrian statue also preserved the fame of public figures for posterity. Donatello's *Gattamelata* in Padua was the first grandiose bronze outdoor monument commemorating a common military leader. Later, the Venetian general, Bartolommeo Colleoni, bequeathed to Venice funds for an equestrian statue in his memory. This statue, by Verrocchio, is an even more monumental and dramatic representation than Donatello's *Gattamelata*. An antique type of glorification that regained stature in the Quattrocento was the gold, bronze, or lead medal (or medallion) bearing the portrait of the honored personage on the obverse and a symbolic scene or emblem on the reverse. Antonio Pisanello was foremost in the production of these medals. His first, of Emperor John Palaeologus (1439), was influenced by gold Trecento medallions originating in Paris. Later his style became more brilliantly his own. The Roman marble bust portrait was also re-adopted by persons of wealth and distinction. The first known dated example, Mino da Fiesole's *Piero de' Medici*, though cut horizontally and planned about a central axis, is strongly influenced by the antique. Antonio Rossellino, in his *Giovanni Chellini* (1456), employed a life mask model to incorporate in the finished marble bust every realistic detail, as his brother, Bernardo, used death masks for his tomb effigies. Now realism, physical and psychological, became the prime requirement. The most dramatic development of this trend was Verrocchio's *Bust of a Young Woman* (1480's). The bust is lengthened and, for the first time, the subject's hands are included so that she is presented more as a living individual.

The reawakening of interest in the antique Roman statuette (as can be seen in catalogues of Quattrocento collectors), the extensive use of metal statuettes on reliquaries, and the change from public to private commission all contributed to the return of the freestanding bronze statuette, almost forgotten in the Middle Ages. Made on a small scale, usually of a religious or classical personage, the statuette was meant to be closely viewed and touched. The earliest dated Quattrocento bronze statuette is the *St. Christopher* in the Boston Museum of Fine Arts. The first signed example, a *Marcus Aurelius* by Filarete, given to Piero de' Medici in 1465, is in Dresden. Donatello's pupil, Giovanni di Bertoldo, Antonio Pollaiuolo, and Andrea Briosco in Padua, among others, aided in the development of the statuette's style and expanding success.

The sculptors of the Quattrocento brought a new concept to art. Their protagonist was a type of man who was culturally, psychologically, and physically understandable and significant. Also, they discovered logical means by which the nature of reality could be opened to interpretation. Michelangelo, the founder of the High Renaissance in sculpture, came to believe that a work of art should go beyond this objective reality and recreate life in terms of the artist's personal vision of beauty. Concentrating his creative forces on the human figure, he saw the function of the body as a realization of a psychological state, its every aspect an outward manifestation of the inner world of feeling. Each of his statues is a statement of universal human experience. Throughout his long life he abhorred the depiction of any specific resemblance, he disregarded mathematical rules of proportion, and he preferred to work only in marble. The nude was, for him, the most challenging form of artistic communication. His style, however, underwent dramatic changes. His early works, such as the Rome *Pietà*, manifest the noble, stoic, unsentimental ideals of human existence. They are relief-like in their shallow depth and rhythmic linear design. Later, after his exposure to Hellenistic statuary, especially the *Belvedere Torso* and the *Laocoön*, Michelangelo took greater license with nature, expanding his scale and creating a moving whole from juxtaposed masses that seem to be resisting unseen pressures and forces. Finally, at the end of his career, becoming totally preoccupied with mystic religious feelings, he rejected physical beauty and sought to reveal the spirit within. The *Rondanini Pieta*, left unfinished at his death, has been carved away to the point it appears as a bodiless flame.

During his lifetime Michelangelo was acclaimed by his contemporaries as the greatest sculptor of all ages, and for the majority of Cinquecento artists he became the model to emulate. One of the few sculptors who successfully resisted his influence was Jacopo Sansovino. After the sack of Rome (1527), Sansovino transplanted to Venice an energetic and graceful classicism. More moderate in his recreation of natural forms than Michelangelo, he found Venice a sympathetic environment where his style could develop in a naturalistic vein.

After 1540, Cosimo I de' Medici established a stable, absolutistic regime in Florence, making the city again, as it had been at the beginning of the Quattrocento, the most attractive center of patronage for sculpture in Italy. With Michelangelo in more or less voluntary exile at Rome, sculptors vied with one another for the prestigious commissions issued by Cosimo I. Baccio Bandinelli was placed in charge of extensive programs in the cathedral and in the Palazzo Vecchio. Niccolò Tribolo was entrusted with the garden decoration of the Villa of Castello, and Benvenuto Cellini, who had achieved international fame as a goldsmith, turned to monumental sculpture when asked personally by Cosimo I to prepare the *Perseus* for the main square at Florence. Ammannati won the competition for the *Fountain of Neptune* for the same square, another project sponsored by Cosimo I, that entailed the carving of a colossal marble Neptune and the casting of sixteen bronze statues. Giambologna also participated in this competition and gained the attention of Cosimo I. He eventually became the major sculptor at Florence, and a favorite of Cosimo's successor, Francesco I, who continued his father's liberal patronage of sculpture.

All of these artists were highly gifted individuals, clearly distinguishable from one another in their personal styles. Yet it is possible to find in their works traits that reveal a common attitude toward art. Artistic invention is no longer guided by nature, but is a calculated, intellectual game that entails a degree of academic erudition about art. Some of the sculptors, such as Ammannati and Giambologna, freely adopted Michelangelo's motifs, copying the complexities of his sculptural designs, but making no attempts to communicate any human values other than elegant refinement and sophistication. Cellini's *Perseus* may reveal the artist's study of Donatello's compositional principles for isolated statues, such as the *Judith and Holofernes*, but ultimately his statue engenders admiration purely as an esthetic object, a visual delight, and a display of virtuosity. The work of art is no longer a means to convey overt feelings or an insight into human experience, but has become completely self-inclusive. It is its own cause and effect, its own purpose, its own reason for existence. L.B.

Scuola (skö-ō′lä). An institution peculiar to Venice, the scuola was an organization with a religious basis, with a particular patron saint who was honored by the members in annual procession, but the *scuola* was not attached to a particular church. The *scuole* were, in some respects, fraternal clubs. They engaged in charitable works, helped fellow members in times of difficulty and in arranging doweries for their daughters, and supported the state. Membership in any particular scuola cut across all classes. There were six major scuole at Venice: Scuola Grande di S. Teodoro (1258), Scuola Grande di S. Maria di Caritas (1260), Scuola Grande di S. Marco (1261), Scuola Grande di S. Giovanni Evangelista (1261), Scuola Grande di S. Maria della Misericordia (1308), and the Scuola Grande di S. Rocco (1478). In addition, there were innumerable lesser scuole. On the Feast of the Ascension all the Scuole of Venice joined in a great procession. Some of these organizations had splendid buildings which, as a matter of fraternal pride, they had decorated by the most famous artists of the day. Many of the paintings commissioned by the confraternities remain, scattered in galleries throughout Europe. The paintings in the Scuola di S. Rocco by Tintoretto and those by Carpaccio in the Scuola di S. Giorgio degli Schiavoni remain intact in the locations for which they were originally intended.

Sebastiano del Piombo (sā-bäs-tyä′nō del pyôm′bō). [Real name, **Sebastiano Luciani.**] Painter; b. at Venice, 1485; d. at Rome, June 21, 1547. He was commonly called del Piombo from his office of keeper of the leaden papal seals, which he held (from 1531) under Clement VII and Paul III. He was a pupil of Giovanni Bellini and was strongly influenced by Giorgione. The Giorgionesque tonalism of his early painting at Venice was modified by a tendency toward the monumental and by a certain firmness and assurance in positioning figures in space, as appears in such early works as the organ shutters with *Saints*, S. Bartolomeo di Rialto and the altarpiece, *St. John Chrysostom Enthroned and Saints*, S. Giovanni Crisostomo, Venice. In 1511 he was called to Rome to assist in the decoration of the Farnesina, the villa built by the banker Agostino Chigi (and called the Farnesina after it passed into the hands of the Farnese family). Raphael was in charge of the decoration of the Farnesina, and Giulio Romano, Baldassarre Peruzzi and Sodoma were working there. As a result of this contact with Roman art, especially with the work of Raphael, Sebastiano's natural tendencies toward broad treatment and monumentality were enhanced. His work in the Farnesina included the fresco of *Polyphemus* and eight scenes from Ovid's *Metamorphoses* frescoed in the lunettes of the Loggia. After 1515 he added to the elements adapted from Raphael the heroic quality of Michelangelo, whose friend he became. Influenced as he was by the most famous painters of his day, in his own reflective and poetic approach he fused the glowing, sensuous color of Venetian painting with the disciplined forms of Florentine and Roman styles as he had come in contact with them through Michelangelo and Raphael, and created a coherent, magnetic style of his own. Evidence of the influence of Raphael's rhythms and harmonies appears in his *Death of Adonis*, Uffizi, with its full-bodied nude ladies under the trees mourning the dead Adonis, against a background of a Venetian palazzo on a canal. The influence of Raphael is also apparent in some magnificent portraits. Among these is the so-called *La Fornarina*, Uffizi, long attributed to Raphael himself, *Dorotea*, Berlin, the intensely poetic *The Sick Man* (1514), Uffizi, a signed *Christopher Columbus* (1519), the Metropolitan Museum, New York, *Andria Doria*, Doria Collection, Rome, and others. In his turn Sebastiano probably influenced Raphael who, then the most famous and sought-after painter in all Italy, was impressed by the Venetian's rich color and willingly learned from him, as appears in the *Stanza di Eliodoro*, and especially in *The Mass of Bolsena* in that room that Raphael painted in the Vatican. The heroic quality of such paintings as a *Pietà*, Museo Civico, Viterbo, derives from his contact with Michelangelo, as does the dark drama and movement of *The Raising of Lazarus*, National Gallery, London. Michelangelo supplied drawings for the former, as well as for the vigorous and dramatic fresco, *Flagellation*, in the Borgherini Chapel, S. Pietro in Montorio, Rome, and others. After the sack of Rome (1527), Sebastiano worked at Orvieto, Mantua, and Venice, and some evidence of mannerism cropped up in his work. He painted less, but continued to produce fine portraits. In addition to the paintings already mentioned, there are works by Sebastiano at Florence (Pitti, Contini Bonacossi), Rome (Vatican, Chigi Chapel in S. Maria del Popolo), Barcelona, Budapest, Burgos (cathedral), Cambridge, Dublin, Leningrad, Madrid, Paris, Vienna, Columbus (Ohio), Detroit, Philadelphia (Johnson Collection), Sarasota, Washington, and elsewhere.

Second Nun's Tale, The. One of Chaucer's *Canterbury Tales*. It is a tale of the life and passion of Saint Cecilia, and was probably taken from the *Legenda Aurea* of Jacobus de Voragine. There was a French version of this by Jehan de Vignay, c1300. The preamble to Chaucer's poem contains 14 or 15 lines translated from the 33rd canto of Dante's *Paradiso*, or perhaps from their original in some Latin prayer or hymn.

Segna di Buonaventura (sān′yä dē bwōn-ä-ven-tö′rä. [Also, **Segna di Tura.**] Sienese painter; active in the first quarter of the 14th century. He was a pupil of Duccio, and worked in and around Siena, at Arezzo and Massa Marittima. Many painted *Crucifixes* and *Madonnas* are attributed to him. Among the *Crucifixes* attributed to him or in his manner

SEBASTIANO DEL PIOMBO
St. Agatha
Gabinetto Nazionale delle Stampe, Rome Alinari-Art Reference Bureau

are those at Arezzo (Badia), Bibbiena (S. Lorenzo), London, Massa Marittima (cathedral), Moscow (Pushkin Museum), and Pienza (S. Francesco). A *Madonna with Angels, Saints and Donors* is at Castiglione Fiorentino; *St. John the Evangelist* is in the Metropolitan Museum, New York. Among the number of other works ascribed to him are those at Asciano, Assisi (Sacro Convento), Grosseto (Museo di Arte Sacra), Lucignano, Monatalcino (Museo Diocesano), Boston, Honolulu, New Haven, New York, and Raleigh (North Carolina).

Segni (sā′nyē), **Bernardo.** Florentine historian; b. at Florence, 1504; d. there, April 13, 1558. He studied literature and law at Padua, then returned to Florence to go into business. He was not particularly successful and gave up a commercial career to enter the service of the Medici. Cosimo I sent him as ambassador to the emperor Ferdinand (1541), and thereafter he held many offices of trust under the Medici. Segni was learned in Latin and Greek; he translated the *Oedipus Rex* of Sophocles, and the *Politics, Poetics,* and *Nicomachean Ethics* of Aristotle, among others, but he was primarily a historian. His two chief works are *Istorie fiorentine*, covering the period 1527 to 1555, and not published until 1723, and his *Vita di Niccolò Capponi*. Capponi was Segni's uncle, favored an accommodation with Pope Clement VII in 1527, and was gonfaloniere at the time of the siege of Florence (1530). Like Guicciardini and Machiavelli, Segni was a witness of the events that he records, but his part in them was not nearly so decisive as Guicciardini's had been. The period he covers marked the end of the Florentine revolution and the restoration of the Medici. He records the events accurately and without passion, moved more as an analyst and searcher for the truth as he saw it than as an activist. His narrative is lucid and succinct, and enlivened with his admirations and prejudices as to men. Most importantly, he describes the institutions of Florence and how they were manipulated. Politically, he was a neutral with leanings toward the Medici, for while he cherished the liberty of Florence he understood that the republic could not withstand both the pope (Clement VII) and the emperor (Charles V). He favored the restoration of the Medici as a leading, but not absolute, authority in Florentine affairs. His middle way politics had little chance of being adopted.

Segni, Rinaldo, Conti **di.** Original name of Pope **Alexander IV.**

Selim II (sē′lim, se-lēm′). [Called **Selim the Sot.**] Sultan of Turkey; b. c1524; d. December 12, 1574. He was the son of Suleiman I whom he succeeded. The conquest of Cyprus in 1570–1571, and the defeat at Lepanto in 1571 were the principal events in a reign marked by the king's personal debauchery.

Sellaio (sel-lä′yō), **Iacopo** (or **Jacopo**) **del.** See **Iacopo del Sellaio.**

Semitecolo (sā-mē-te-kō′lō), **Nicoletto.** Painter of the Paduan school; active in the second half of the 14th century. His narrative form of painting, in which Venetian influence is almost totally lacking, is executed with vigor and realism, and indicates his special interest in architectural backgrounds and perspective. The influence of Giotto is marked. Six panels in the chapter house at Padua, signed and dated 1367, include a *Trinity, Madonna,* and four scenes from the life of St. Sebastian. A *St. Augustine* in the Church of the Eremitani at Padua has been restored after being badly damaged by bombs in 1944.

Sempill (sem′pil), **Robert.** [Also, **Semple.**] Scottish soldier, balladist, and humorous and satirical poet; b. c1530; d. 1595. He was violently opposed to Mary, Queen of Scots, and the Roman Catholics. He was the author of *Ane Complaint upon Fortoun* (1581), *The Legend of the Bischop of St. Androis Lyfe* (1584), *Sege of the Castel of Edinburgh* (1573) and others.

Semple (sem′pl), **Robert.** See **Sempill, Robert.**

Sepúlveda (sā-pöl′bā-ᵺä), **Juan Ginés de.** Spanish theologian and historian; b. near Córdoba, Spain, c1490; d. at Mariano, near Córdoba, c1573. He was one of the most noted opponents of Bartolomé de Las Casas, holding in his treatise *Democrates Secundus* that war on the Indians, and Indian Slavery were justified. His works were all in Latin, and referring to the elegance of the Latin, Erasmus called him "the Spanish Livy."

Serafini (sā-rä-fē′nē), **Paolo.** Modenese painter; active early in the 15th century. He was the son of Serafino Serafini. His *Virgin of the Disfida* is in the cathedral at Barletta.

Serafini, Serafino. Modenese painter; b. at

Modena, between 1320 and 1324; d. after 1393. He was an original and independent artist, and a subtle draftsman. His only extant work is a polyptych, *Coronation of the Virgin*, signed and dated (1384), in the cathedral at Modena.

Serafino dell'Aquila (sā-rä-fē'nō del-lä'kwē-lä). [Original name, **Serafino de' Ciminelli;** also called **Serafino Aquilano.**] Court poet, musician, and improviser; b. at Aquila, 1466; d. at Rome, August 10, 1500. He spent most of his life in the service of various princes and lords, as at the courts at Rome, Milan, Urbino, and Mantua. He composed sonnets and ballate for his princely patrons, and accompanied himself on the lute as he sang them. The combination of a sound musical foundation and his facile and graceful poetic talent, plus his ardent manner of rendering his songs, made him an ideal improviser at court functions and festivities. He enjoyed great success in his art. Of his vast production of sonnets, eclogues, and stage pieces (in which he acted), only a sonnet here and there speaks with the simplicity of the heart. However, his polished and somewhat precious form of entertainment eminently satisfied the demands made on a court poet in his day.

Sercambi (ser-käm'bē), **Giovanni.** Writer and public official; b. at Lucca, February 18, 1347; d. May 27, 1424. He was a supporter of the Guinigi, the ruling family of Lucca, held public office under them, and aided Paolo Guinigi to gain power after the assassination of the regent. Sercambi wrote *Croniche delle cose di Lucca*, a record of events in that city-state from 1164 to 1424. It is especially valuable for events of the later years, in which Sercambi himself played a role. He wrote many novelle (short stories). These, modeled after Boccaccio's *Decameron*, are supposedly stories told by the author to a group of companions as they wandered about Italy fleeing the plague of 1374.

Serdini (ser-dē'nē), **Simone.** [Called **il Saviozzo.**] Poet; b. at Siena, c1360; committed suicide, at Toscanella, c1420. His life was unhappily passed in wandering from one princely court to another and in the service of various captains. He committed suicide in prison. Serdini's lyrics, in Tuscan, combine all the elements of courtly poetry that were to be found at the end of the 14th and the beginning of the 15th century. His poems contain classical and mythological allusions and are frequently imitative of Dante. Very often they rail at Fortune, which he felt had deserted him.

Serdonati (ser-dō-nä'tē), **Francesco.** Writer and compiler; b. at Lemole, in Tuscany, January 7, 1540; d. at Rome, after 1602. He compiled a work on Rome, in three books, wrote a life of Pope Innocent VIII, a collection of lives of famous women, treatises on war and on the customs of the Turks, and translated from the Latin. Parts of a collection of proverbs that he left in manuscript were published at Padua in 1870.

Seripando (sā-rē-pän'dō), **Gerolamo.** [Original name, **Troiano Seripando.**] Ecclesiastic; b. at Naples, May 6, 1493; d. at Trent, March 17, 1563. At the age of 12 he fled to the convent of San Domenico Maggiore, from which he entered (1507) the Augustinian order and took the name Gerolamo. He studied grammar, jurisprudence, theology, and philosophy, was ordained (1513), and became secretary to the general of the order, Egidio da Viterbo. Continuing his study of philosophy and theology, he was named *magister studii*, and taught at Bologna. In 1523 he was at Rome, then went to Naples, where he had many contacts with the followers of the reformer, Juan de Valdés, and especially with Giulia Gonzaga, with whom he corresponded until his death. However, although he ardently desired reform of the Church he took no part in separatist movements. In 1538 he was made prior general of his order and began to put his ideas for reform into effect, first of all by making visits of rigorous inspection to the Augustinian monasteries of Italy, France, and Spain. At the first sessions of the Council of Trent he supported the efficacy of preaching, as well as views that came close to those of the Lutherans on justification by faith. He returned to Naples (1550), declined various ecclesiastical honors, gave himself up to study, and founded the library of S. Giovanni a Carbonara. In 1551 he had a stroke, and resigned as general of the Augustinians (he had been elected in 1539). Having recovered, he was sent by Pope Pius IV as his legate to the Council of Trent, but fell into disgrace with the pope because of his ideas, that the bishop should live in his see, among other things. He left many works, most of which are now in the National Library at Naples, including commentaries on Paul's *Epistle to the Galatians* and *Epistle to the Romans,* sermons, a diary of his life, and commentaries on the Council of Trent.

Serlio (ser′lyō), **Sebastiano.** Architect and architectural theorist, painter, and engraver; b. at Bologna, September 6, 1475; d. at Fontainebleau, France, 1554. As a painter he was early considered an expert in perspective and worked as such at Pesaro (1509–1514). In 1514 he went to Rome, where he remained until 1527, working with Baldassarre Peruzzi, whose pupil he may have been, and studying the antique. After the sack of Rome (1527) he fled to Venice and there published (1537) the fourth book of his great *Trattato di architettura,* for which he planned seven books. Book IV came out under the title *Regole generali di architettura . . .* (*General Rules of Architecture*). Book III, dealing with the antiquities of Rome, was published in 1540, Books I and II, on geometry and perspective, in 1545, and Book V, on churches, in 1547. The seventh book was published posthumously (1575), while the manuscript of the sixth and of the beginning of an eighth were unpublished. The *Trattato* is of great importance in the development of Italian, and later of French and English architecture, as it was a practical handbook with illustrations of architectural forms and ornamentation that, in theory at least, a master mason could execute. In Book IV, for example, there were diagrams of the classical orders and instructions for their construction. For this reason it was enormously popular and was widely translated. In 1541 he went to France and worked for a time at Fontainebleau with Primaticcio, but his work there is unidentifiable. After the death of Francis I the supremacy of the Italians passed away, and Serlio left for Lyons. There he published (1551) his *Libro extra-ordinario delle porte,* a treatise on doorways and gates. Serlio's activity as an architectural theorist constitutes his great and deserved importance in the history of architecture. As a theorist, his *Trattato* resulted from his study of antique buildings and of the architectural works of the 16th century. Especially after becoming acquainted with Venetian architecture, he tried to free Italian mannerist architecture from its great dependence on classic theory, and to bring to it the variations of light and shade and a sense of movement as these had been developed by Sansovino, Sanmicheli, and Palladio. A three-part architectural unit for a window or opening, called the *serliana* from the many beautiful illustrations of it in his works, consists of a central arch flanked by trabeated lateral openings. The form is derived from such ancient buildings as the propylaea at Baalbek, in Syria, and Diocletian's Palace at Spalato (Split) on the Dalmatian coast.

Sermini (ser-mē′nē), **Gentile.** Sienese writer of novelle, of whose life nothing is known. After 1424 he collected forty of his novelle and some didactic and moralizing works. His tales, which owe little to other writers, are licentious and, because of the few favorite themes, rather monotonous. His *Il Giuoco della pugna* is a lively description of the Sienese boxing matches, with crisp and colorful dialogue. The Sienese language he used is now the chief interest in his work.

Sermini, Pietro di. Florentine humanist; active between 1390 and 1424. He studied rhetoric at the university at Florence under Giovanni Malpaghini, and became a notary, as were his father and grandfather before him. Against his father's wishes he pursued his humanistic studies, and was on friendly terms with the leading humanists of his day, as Coluccio Salutati, who loaned him books and encouraged his studies. In 1406 he was named chancellor of Florence, a powerful position that gave him considerable influence, but in 1410 he withdrew from public life and retired to a monastery. He later became famous as a preacher.

Servetus (sėr-vē′tus), **Michael.** [Latinized name of **Miguel Serveto.**] Spanish controversialist and physician; b. probably at Tudela, Spain, 1511; burned at Geneva, Switzerland, October 27, 1553. He published (1531), an essay against the doctrine of the Trinity, *De trinitatis erroribus,* which attracted considerable attention. It was revised and reprinted (1532) under the title of *Dialogorum de trinitate, libri duo.* He practiced medicine in various cities in France, and is credited with the discovery of the pulmonary circulation of the blood. In 1553 he published *Christianismi restitutio,* for which he was arrested in Lyons; he escaped, but was apprehended at the instigation of John Calvin at Geneva on his way to Naples. He was burned after a trial for heresy which lasted for two and a half months.

Servier (ser-vyā), **Jean Grolier de.** See **Grolier de Servier, Jean,** Vicomte **d'Aguisy.**

Settignano (set-tē-nyä′nō), **Desiderio da.** See **Desiderio da Settignano.**

Seven Cities, Island of the. Fabled island which, in the 14th and 15th centuries, was supposed to exist in the Atlantic. The geographers of the period frequently called it Antilla or Antillia.

Seymour (sē′mōr), **Edward.** [Titles, 1st Earl of **Hertford,** Duke of **Somerset;** called **the Protector.**] English politician; b. c1506; beheaded at London, January 22, 1552. He was the brother of Jane Seymour and uncle of Edward VI. He was a favorite of Henry VIII. He broke the power of the Howards, and on the death of Henry was named protector of the realm, and soon established himself as absolute ruler of the kingdom, paying nominal allegiance to Edward VI. The Scots never accepted him, and an attack by them combined with the French led to his deposition and imprisonment. Although released, in 1551 he was arrested on a charge of treasonable conspiracy, was tried on and found guilty of another charge, and was beheaded by means of a forged order.

Seymour, Jane. Third queen of Henry VIII; b. in England, c1510; d. October 24, 1537. She was a sister of Edward Seymour, and the mother of Edward VI of England.

Sforza (sfōr′tsä). Eminent family of Milan, members of which ruled as dukes of Milan, with interruptions, from 1450 to 1535. The founder of the family was Muzio Attendolo Sforza (1369–1424), son of a thriving peasant family of Cotignola who became a noted condottiere. Of his illegitimate sons, Francesco became the first Sforza duke of Milan and Alessandro became lord of Pesaro. His legitimate sons lived out their lives in comparative obscurity. Francesco (1401–1466) was a famous condottiere who served various princes and states. As an inducement to fight for Filippo Maria Visconti of Milan he was offered Filippo Maria's natural daughter Bianca in marriage. Ultimately the marriage took place. After the death of Filippo Maria (1447) without a male heir, the Milanese established the Ambrosian republic. Beset by enemies, notably Venice, and then besieged by Francesco Sforza in his own behalf, the republic yielded to Francesco as its conqueror and savior and named him duke of Milan (1450). Under his prudent and beneficent rule Milan enjoyed relative peace and great prosperity. Francesco, who had even more illegitimate children than his father, was succeeded by his legitimate son Galeazzo Maria (1444–1476). Galeazzo Maria was able and cultivated. He did much to promote agriculture, industry, and commerce, was a builder, and a patron of art and letters. Perhaps from his Visconti ancestors he inherited a streak of ferocious cruelty and was psychotically compelled to bloodthirsty tortures. Self-indulgent and sensual, he was detested by members of his court, whose ladies he had dishonored, feared for his cruel reprisals, and regarded with awe and disgust for his extravagance and love of display. He was assassinated (December 26, 1476). His heir was eight-year-old Gian Galeazzo. (Among his illegitimate children was Caterina, "the Amazon of Forlì.") Galeazzo Maria's brothers struggled among themselves to wrest the duchy from Gian Galeazzo. Ludovico il Moro was the victor and was named duke of Milan after the legal heir's death (October, 1494); he had in fact been ruler of Milan since 1480. It was Ludovico who encouraged the French invasion of Charles VIII into Italy (September, 1494). This led to Ludovico's undoing. Charles VIII came and went. He was followed by his successor, Louis XII, who claimed Milan as the grandson of Valentina Visconti. Louis seized Milan in 1499, captured Ludovico in April, 1500, and carried him off to France a prisoner. Gian Galeazzo's son was also sent to France, where he died at an early age. Ludovico's elder son, Massimiliano (1493–1530), was restored as duke of Milan in 1512. With the victory of the French under Francis I at Marignano (1515), Massimiliano resigned his claims to the duchy and went to live in France. His brother, Francesco II (1495–1535), ruled (1521–1525 and 1529–1535) as a puppet of the emperor Charles V. After his death the duchy of Milan was incorporated into the imperial dominions of Charles V. The numerous progeny of Muzio Attendolo and his descendants established branches of the Sforza family in various cities of Italy. See separate entries below.

Sforza, Alessandro. Lord of Pesaro; b. at Cotignola, 1409; d. near Ferrara, April 3, 1473. He was the natural son of Muzio Attendolo and the brother of Francesco Sforza, who became duke of Milan. Alessandro followed his brother in his military career, and helped him to win a principality in the Marches. He also, at one time, intrigued with the French against his brother. He was a valiant and able captain who took part in many campaigns and won honors from the pope and from the kingdom of Naples. He fell in love with Costanza Varano, who had been brought up at her grandfather's court at Pesaro. Federico da Montefeltro noted the condition of his heart and told him he might marry Costanza if he had a state of his own. Francesco helped him to buy Pesaro. He married Costanza (1444), but she died a few years later. Sigismondo Malatesta wrested Pesaro from him and held it briefly. The pope restored it to him (July, 1477) and made it hereditary, thus establishing the Sforza branch at Pesaro. After the death of Costanza Alessandro married again (1448). His second wife entered a convent (1457) and he passed the rest of his life in arms. He was a mild ruler, a cultivated man, and a patron of letters and the arts. The walls of Pesaro, the ducal palace, and the Villa Imperiale just outside the city were begun at his order. Alessandro was succeeded by his son Costanzo (1447–1483), a brave captain who took part in most of the campaigns of his time. He too was a mild ruler and a patron of letters, especially of poetry. The Rocca Costanza, the fortress of Pesaro, was built to designs by Laurana at his order. Alessandro's daughter Battista (1446–1472) married her father's champion, Federico da Montefeltro. A natural daughter, Ginevra (c1440–1507), allied his house to the Bentivoglio family of Bologna.

Sforza, Ascanio Maria. Cardinal; b. at Milan, March 3, 1455; d. of the plague at Rome, May 28, 1505. He was the son of Francesco, duke of Milan, and Bianca Maria, and was early destined for an ecclesiastical career, a career that turned out to involve more of politics than of religion. In 1477 he took part in the intrigues of his brothers against Bona of Savoy, the widow of his brother Duke Galeazzo Maria, and against her adviser, Cicco Simonetta. The intrigues failed and Ascanio was banished to Perugia. When his brother Ludovico il Moro took over the reins of government at Milan, Ascanio was named administrator of Pavia (1479), but he quarreled with Ludovico and was again forced to flee, this time to Venice for aid against Ludovico. Reconciled (1483), through the favor of Ludovico and the king of Naples, he was raised to the purple (March, 1484) and held several bishoprics, as well as the abbeys of Chiaravalle and S. Ambrogio at Milan, and he was, at the same time, papal legate at Bologna. Ultimately, he became the devoted supporter of Ludovico in the Roman Curia. He led the party in favor of Rodrigo Borgia at the conclave of 1492, from which Rodrigo emerged as Pope Alexander VI. His rewards for his support and his influence with the pope were great. But he broke with Alexander over the pope's French policy (1494), left Rome, was imprisoned on his return, but was freed by the French king, Charles VIII. Ascanio tried to persuade Charles to depose Alexander and call a council to reform the Church. The council was never called, and Ascanio was again reconciled to the pope, cooled toward him, and fled to Milan (1499). From Milan he also fled when the French overthrew Ludovico. In April, 1500, he was captured by the Venetians, who released him to the French. They shut him up in a tower at Bourges, from which he was freed by the Cardinal d'Amboise (1502). He returned to Rome with the French cardinal, following the death of Alexander, and favored the election of Pius III, who lived only a short time, and then of Julius II. A worldly and corrupt prelate, he lived in a luxurious palace at Rome. He was a lover of the arts and letters, wrote Latin and Italian verses and orations himself, and indulged his taste for feasting and the chase. The people held him in affection for his generosity. He was responsible for the beginning of the great cathedral at Pavia and the Portico of the Canonica of S. Ambrogio at Milan.

Sforza, Battista. Countess of Urbino; b. 1446; d. at Urbino, July 6, 1472. She was the daughter of Alessandro Sforza of Pesaro and of Costanza da Varano. At the age of 11 she was betrothed to Federico, count of Montefeltro and Urbino. She married him at Urbino on February 10, 1460, and had her first child the next year. After eleven years of marriage and eight daughters, she went to Gubbio to pray to its patron saint, Ubaldo, for a son. While there, according to tradition, she had a prophetic dream of a phoenix. Late in the year 1471, when she was carrying her ninth child, she went to Gubbio, that the child might be born there where her dream had occurred. On January 24, 1472, she was delivered of a son. She named him Guido Paolo Ubaldo (thereafter shortened to Guidobaldo) in honor of the saint. She had vowed her life in exchange for a son. She died on July 6 of the same year. A gentle, cultivated girl, she shared in the learned pleasures of her husband's court, and ruled his state with wisdom and firmness in his frequent absences. Federico, and his subjects as well, mourned her deeply. She was "the delight alike of my public and my private hours," "the ornament of my house and the devoted sharer of my fortunes." Her portrait by Piero della Francesca forms one half of a diptych, of which the other half is a portrait of Federico. The diptych is in the Uffizi at Florence.

Sforza, Bosio. Soldier; b. 1411; d. 1476. He was one of the many illegitimate sons of Muzio Attendolo Sforza, and was the brother of Francesco, duke of Milan, and of Alessandro, lord of Pesaro. He was governor of Orvieto for the pope as early as 1430, took a prominent part in his brother Francesco's wars, and passed his entire life in arms. He won numerous cities for himself, and was count of Cotignola. In 1439 he married Cecilia, daughter of Guido Aldobrandeschi, count of Santa Fiora, gained some of her fiefs, including Santa Fiora, and founded the Santa Fiora branch of the Sforza family. His son Francesco (d. 1523) succeeded him as count of Cotignola, and his son Guido (1445–1508?) became count of Santa Fiora.

Sforza, Caterina. Countess of Forlì; b. c1463; d. at Florence, May 28, 1509. She was the natural daughter of Galeazzo Maria Sforza, and was brought up by his good-natured wife, Bona of Savoy, with her own children. In 1473 she was betrothed to Girolamo Riario, nephew of Pope Sixtus IV, and married him in 1477. Beautiful (noted for her fair hair), cultivated, and energetic, she soon dominated a husband whose most conspicuous attribute was his doting uncle Sixtus. The pope invested Girolamo (1480) with Forlì and Imola, which he had bought, and the couple lived at Forlì a number of years, improving their time by strengthening the fortress of Ravaldino, a few miles south of Forlì. As usurping rulers they were subject to the conspiracies of those they had replaced. In one such conspiracy Girolamo was slain (April 14, 1488). Caterina escaped and succeeded in withdrawing to the Ravaldino. She held out against her enemies, supporters of the Ordelaffi, the former ruling family, even when the lives of her children, who had been taken as hostages, were threatened. Soldiers from Milan and Bologna came to beat off her enemies and she returned to Forlì, which she governed as regent for her son Ottaviano. She prevented a sack of the city by the troops who had come to her aid, and then wreaked a merciless vengeance on the slayers of Girolamo. With Jacopo Feo, governor of the fortress of Ravaldino (and either her lover or her secret husband), she played a prominent role in Italian politics. Milan, Florence, Naples, and the pope sought the friendship of "the Amazon of Forlì." She had maintained her state, and her friendship was the more important in view of the French invasion of Italy (1494). After some maneuvering, and a few French victories, she elected to side with the French and Florence. In August, 1495, Jacopo Feo was slain before her eyes. She crushed the authors, or supposed authors, of the crime with a vengeance of unparalleled bloodthirstiness. Soon after (1496 or 1497) she secretly married Giovanni de' Medici, a second cousin of Lorenzo the Magnificent. A quiet and peaceable man, he died a year later, leaving a son by Caterina who came to be known as Giovanni delle Bande Nere, the founder of the line of Medici dukes at Florence. In 1499 Cesare Borgia, Alexander VI's son, set out with the support of his father to carve out a principality for himself in the Romagna. Caterina was his first target. In March, 1499, Alexander declared her deprived of her states. In the fall Cesare marched against her. Imola fell in November. Forlì fell the next month. Caterina sent her children and her treasure to Florence and withdrew to the fortress of Ravaldino, one of the strongest in the Romagna. Every house, barn, and shed outside the walls was leveled; every tree was felled. The marshes were flooded. Nothing was left that would afford protection to an attacking enemy. Rain fell as Cesare attacked. The water of the marshes froze, snow buried the ice. Cesare had heavy artillery with which, day after day, he bombarded the massive towers of the fortress. The defenders, under Caterina's personal command, returned shot for shot. Cesare twice asked to parley under a flag of truce. Twice, citing her distinguished ancestry (her great grandfather was a peasant), she refused the terms offered by the bastard son of the pope. When one of the enormous towers crumbled under the pounding of Cesare's guns, she ordered withdrawal to the citadel within the fortress. Some of Cesare's men, having entered through the breach in the walls, succeeded in entering the citadel as the Forlivese defenders withdrew. Seeing that her case was hopeless, Caterina ordered her people to fire the magazines. The fortress did not surrender; in the turmoil of hand to hand fighting, fire and explosion, Caterina was captured (January 12, 1500), and carried off a prisoner to Rome. All Italy had watched Caterina's struggle; she was called a *virago*, a term of admiration for her beauty, her culture, and for "the man's heart that beat in her woman's breast." After more than a year in prison, Caterina was released through French intervention (a French officer had actually taken her prisoner) in June, 1501. Force and intrigue failed in her subsequent attempts to regain her state, and she withdrew to Florence. There she gave herself up to good works and prayer, and imposed upon herself, with the same vigor she had manifested in defending Forlì, a regime of the most rigorous austerity. Although possessed of a warrior's heart, Caterina was fully aware of her feminine charms and never neglected her looks. She left a collection of prescriptions, recipes for the enhancement or achievement of personal beauty. One of these described a means of attaining golden or, if preferable, auburn hair. She bore her first husband eight children, two or three to Jacopo Feo, and one to her last husband. A portrait of her by Lorenzo di Credi is at Forlì.

Sforza, Costanzo. Lord of Pesaro; b. 1447; d. 1483. He was the son of Alessandro Sforza and Costanza da Varano, and succeeded his father as lord of Pesaro in 1473. A brave warrior, he fought in most of the wars of his time. He was a mild and just ruler, encouraged and protected letters, was especially fond of poetry, and built the fortress of Pesaro that bears his name. He was succeeded by his natural son Giovanni. A second natural son, Galeazzo (d. 1519) ruled as lord of Pesaro (1510–1519), first as regent for his nephew Costanzo II, Giovanni's son, and when, at two years of age, Costanzo II died (1512), as lord of Pesaro in his own right.

Sforza, Francesco. Duke of Milan; b. at San Miniato, July 23, 1401; d. March 8, 1466. He was the natural son of Muzio Attendolo by his mistress Lucia Tregani. He was educated with the princes of the court of Niccolò d'Este at Ferrara until he was 11 years old, at which time he was given by his father as a hostage to Ladislaus of Naples. He remained at Naples a year and then began his military career. In the struggle between Alfonso of Aragon and Louis of Anjou for control of Naples, Braccio da Montone supported Alfonso and Muzio Attendolo fought for Louis, Queen Joanna II, and the pope. Francesco was with his father's troops. On the death of his father at the Pescara River (January 4, 1424), he won the confidence of the troops and succeeded as commander, although still a very young man. In the campaign that followed he defeated Braccio at Aquila (June, 1424) and, in his own right, became one of the leading captains of his time. Like all the mercenary captains, he fought now on one side, now on the other. He left the service of Queen Joanna to enter the pay of Filippo Maria Visconti, duke of Milan, against the Venetians. Filippo Maria became suspicious of him, and when, with the other Milanese captain, Niccolò Piccinino, he was defeated and captured by the Venetian captain Carmagnola at Maclodio (1427), Filippo Maria dismissed him. Francesco went over to Filippo's enemies, and soon Filippo Maria required his services. To woo him back, he offered Francesco the hand of his natural daughter Bianca Maria in marriage. She was his only child and his heir, and probably from this time Francesco nourished the ambition to become duke of Milan, an ambition that caused him to modify his tactics when he was, in the future, in the pay of Milan's enemies. The betrothal took place in the presence of the emperor Sigismund, in 1432, when Francesco was 31 and Bianca Maria was 8. But relations with Filippo Maria were always uncertain, and the path to the altar and the duchy was strewn with mistrust and delays. Francesco decided to erect his own principality. He won cities of the March of Ancona for his own account. Although these cities formed part of the papal domain Pope Eugenius IV, reluctant but realistic, recognized him as count of his newly won territories, and named him papal vicar and gonfaloniere of the Church. Filippo Maria used one pretext after another to put off the marriage of his daughter. Francesco joined a league against Milan. He visited Florence in 1435 and met Cosimo de' Medici there. The two conceived great respect for each other. In the future Cosimo became Francesco's chief supporter, and after the latter became duke of Milan Cosimo altered the traditional policy of Florentine alliance with Venice to one of alliance and friendship with Milan. (Another good friend to Francesco was Federico da Montefeltro, the Renaissance prince *par excellence*.) Filippo Maria see-sawed between need for Francesco's services and fear of his success. In 1441, threatened anew by Venice and Francesco, he was compelled to let the marriage take place. The ceremony was performed in the Church of S. Sigismondo at Cremona. (Cremona was one of the cities included in Bianca Maria's dowry. The altarpiece by Giulio Campi showing the couple kneeling, was put in place in the church in 1540.) The marriage of his general and his daughter rather increased than lessened Filippo Maria's fears. He turned against his new son-in-law and sought to take the cities of the Marches from him. The pope revoked Francesco's office as gonfaloniere of the Church and declared him a rebel. (Bianca Maria remained loyal to her husband and was a great help to him; he is said to have sought her advice on many occasions.) In November, 1443, Sforza and the Venetians defeated the armies of the pope and of Jacopo Piccinino, the duke of Milan's captain. Peace was made (October, 1444) and the March of Ancona was restored to Francesco. Like most, it was an ephemeral peace. Filippo Maria sent troops to assault Cremona. Bianca Maria herself led in the defense of her city. Alfonso of Aragon feared Francesco would descend into Naples in behalf of the Angevins. The Venetians resumed the war against Milan. Again Filippo Maria sent for Francesco. He was on his way when he received news of Filippo Maria's death (1447). Before he could reach Milan and claim it as his duchy the enraptured Milanese had set up the Ambrosian Republic. The new republic hired Sforza to carry on the war against Venice, and offered him the countship of Pavia. Piacenza appealed to Venice. Francesco captured it and leveled it, and overcame the Venetians at the battle of Caravaggio (1448). Now it was the turn of the republic to fear him. The Venetians persuaded him that it was more to his interest to fight on their side and indicated that his reward would be Milan. He went over to them. They betrayed him, as he had betrayed the Milanese. Cosimo de' Medici advised him to fight on his own account, and to win Milan himself. He besieged the city and cut off the food supply. At length the city yielded. Envoys rode out from the starving city, February 26, 1450, and proclaimed him duke of Milan. He entered the city at the head of a train of wagons loaded with bread and was wildly acclaimed by the populace which had so lately detested him. On March 22, 1450, accompanied by Bianca Maria, his six-year-old son Galeazzo Maria, and his brother Alessandro, he made his official entrance into the city and was formally invested with the ducal insignia in the piazza before the cathedral. A few years later the wars with Venice were ended by the peace of Lodi (1454). The alliance between Milan, Florence, and Naples kept Italy in a state of relative equilibrium, and Milan enjoyed a period of peace and prosperity until Francesco's death. By his wise administration he consolidated the duchy of Milan, and by his friendship with Louis XI of France, whom he had aided, he won Genoa (1464).

Francesco Sforza was among the last and most successful of the great captains of Italy. A brave warrior (his horse was killed under him at the assault on Piacenza) and a skillful general, he won his duchy by arms and marriage, and maintained his power there by tact, moderation, and diplomacy. He said he did not wish to be a despot but a father to his people. He encouraged its prosperity by promoting the silk industry and by maintaining order. Bianca Maria kept the affection and respect of the Milanese as their own duchess, and Francesco gradually won their loyalty. Their decorous court was free from the luxury and ostentation that ruined other princes. A patron of art and letters, Francesco welcomed some of the leading humanists, as Francesco Filelfo, to his court. He beautified the city, began the rebuilding of the *Castello*, and built the Ospedale Maggiore (now the seat of the university) to designs by Filarete. Unlike the Visconti dukes and many other princes of that age, he had nothing but contempt for astrology, and scoffed at the portents of his future greatness that were said to have occurred at his birth. Unlike the Visconti also, he was not gratuitously cruel. Machiavelli, in *The Prince*, writes "Francesco by the proper means and through his own ability rose from private station to be Duke of Milan and preserved with little effort the duchy which had cost him many pains to acquire." Pope Pius II, who met him at the Congress of Mantua (1459), said, "He sat his horse like a young man; he was very tall and bore himself with great dignity; his expression was serious, his way of speaking quiet, his manner gracious, his character in general such as became a prince. He had great physical and intellectual gifts. Unconquered in war, he came from a humble family to a throne. He married a lady of great beauty, rank, and virtue, by whom he had a family of very handsome children. He was rarely ill." Nevertheless, Pius goes on, his life was tempered by some misfortune: his mistress was murdered at the command of his wife; some ancient comrades betrayed him; his brother intrigued against him; and his son plotted against him and was imprisoned. He had married his first wife, Polissena Ruffo, countess of Montalto, in 1418. She and her infant daughter were poisoned by her aunt within a year. Altogether, Francesco had about thirty children, twenty-one of whom were illegitimate. Among his children were: Galeazzo Maria, his first legitimate son and his heir; Ludovico Il Moro, the favorite of Bianca Maria; Ascanio, who became a cardinal and helped elect Pope Alexander VI; Polissena, the unfortunate wife of Sigismondo Malatesta; Ippolita, who married Alfonso, duke of Calabria and heir to the kingdom of Naples; and Drusiana (1437–1474) who married (1464) Jacopo Piccinino, famed condottiere and ancient enemy of Francesco. Duke Francesco was never formally invested with the duchy of Milan, although it was said that he could have had the investiture quite cheaply from the emperor Frederick III, "but," says Guicciardini, "he scorned it, being sure that he could retain the Duchy with the same arts by which he first acquired it."

Sforza, Francesco II. Duke of Milan; b. February 4, 1495; d. November, 1535. He was the second son of Ludovico il Moro, and fled with his father into Germany when Milan fell to the French (1499). He returned to Milan when his elder brother Massimiliano was restored as duke, fled again when the French deprived Massimiliano of his duchy (1515), and returned again when the French were defeated by the forces of the pope and the emperor Charles V at Bicocca (1521). Massimiliano having retired to France, Francesco was named duke. Milan was a football in the struggle between France and the emperor Charles V. Francesco was a victim of the secret maneuverings of the popes in the struggle. Clement VII's intrigues were revealed to Charles. Despite protestations of loyalty, Francesco was regarded as a traitor, and an imperial army occupied Milan (1525). Francesco shut himself up in the *Castello*, but was forced to yield after eight months. Charles promised him Como and a pension, but did not keep his promise. However, Francesco was at length restored as duke (1529) on condition that if he died without issue the duchy would pass to the emperor. Restored, he set about reorganizing the duchy. He was brave, cultivated, intelligent, and mild; his subjects held him in deep affection. He wished to reorganize the duchy, but all circumstances were against him. A virtual puppet of the emperor, he was unable to protect his people from the harshness of the Spanish. In 1534 Charles gave him his own niece, Christina, daughter of the king of Denmark, in marriage. Francesco died the following year without issue and the duchy of Milan became part of the imperial dominions.

Sforza, Galeazzo Maria. Duke of Milan; b. at Fermo, January 24, 1444; d. at Milan, December 26, 1476. He was the son of Francesco Sforza, duke of Milan, and Bianca Maria Visconti. A winning and precocious child, he was well-educated and, as heir to the duchy, early began his career in diplomatic life. When Frederick III came into Italy to be crowned as emperor (1452), Galeazzo Maria was sent to him as ambassador extraordinary. His appearance, manner, and intelligence won him great admiration, as they did also when he went before Pope Pius II at the Congress of Mantua (1459). His father at first sought an alliance with Mantua by betrothing him to Dorotea Gonzaga, but when a link to the French throne became possible because of Francesco's friendship with Louis XI, Dorotea was jettisoned and Bona of Savoy, sister of the French queen, became Galeazzo Maria's wife. Louis became involved in a war with the "league of the public weal," and Francesco sent Galeazzo Maria with troops to aid him. Galeazzo Maria proved a valiant captain. He was in France when his father died (1466). His mother kept firm hold of his duchy for him. On his return, he soon quarreled with her, and sent her to her city of Cremona. On the way, she died, and it was whispered that he had caused her to be poisoned. Under Galeazzo Maria, Milan reached a peak of prosperity and splendor. He introduced the growing of rice, promoted the silk industry by planting mulberry trees, and encouraged trade. He was handsome, affable, easy of access, quick to respond with generosity, and intelligent. At the same time, he held a court of fantastic magnificence and luxury, and was obsessed with a desire for lavish display. His hounds and horses were without equal. He was a patron of arts and letters, employed painters and architects, called Bramante to Milan, and continued the building of the *Castello*, begun by his father Francesco. He was perversely demanding and is said to have required that an entire hall be decorated in one twenty-four hour period—the painters were locked in at night. Many humanists were welcomed at his court. Francesco Filelfo was tutor to his children. He was fond of music and a musician himself. In 1471 he and his wife made a visit to Florence with a splendid suite that deeply impressed, even shocked, the decorous Florentines. (It was at this time, it is thought, that the portrait of him by Pollaiuolo was painted. The portrait, from the collection of Lorenzo de' Medici, and now in the Uffizi at Florence, reveals the cruelty and arrogance of which he was readily capable.) To his great wealth, intelligence, and ability, Galeazzo Maria joined cruelty and lust. His wife Bona, a placid and rather stupid woman, brought up his illegitimate daughter Caterina as her own child, and made nothing of his many mistresses. Others were not so complacent. Galeazzo Maria dishonored the ladies of his court and took pleasure in advertising his conquests. He was hated for his dissolute life by many. On December 26, 1476, he went to the Church of S. Stefano despite many dire portents. There he was assassinated by three conspirators. The conspirators, Carlo Visconti, Giovanni Lampugnani, and Girolamo Olgiati expected the populace to rise up and throw off the yoke of the Sforzas and restore the republic on news of his death. The people turned on the conspirators instead. Galeazzo Maria had ten children, six of whom were illegitimate. Gian Galeazzo, the heir, was eight years old when his father was slain. Of his other children, Caterina, mentioned above, first married Girolamo Riario, nephew of Pope Sixtus IV, and became one of the most famous and forceful women of her age. His daughter Bianca Maria (1472–1510) married (1493) the emperor Maximilian; and his daughter Anna Maria (1476–1497) was the first wife of Alfonso I d'Este of Ferrara.

Sforza, Gian Galeazzo. Duke of Milan; b. at Castello de Abbiategrasso, June 10, 1469; d. at Pavia, October 24, 1494. He was the son of Galeazzo Maria Sforza and Bona of Savoy. At the time of Duke Galeazzo Maria's death, Gian Galeazzo, his heir, was in his eighth year. His mother acted as his guardian and tried to rule his duchy with the help of Cicco Simonetta, a trusted secretary of Francesco Sforza. Galeazzo Maria's brothers hurried to Milan on news of Galeazzo Maria's assassination, to look out for their own interests. After various intrigues, Ludovico il Moro won the upper hand. Gian Galeazzo, a youth of weak and biddable character, trusted his uncle Ludovico, and was willing to do as he was told. He was crowned duke (1480) and Ludovico, having got rid of Cicco Simonetta, served as his guardian. Gian Galeazzo was married (1489) to Isabella, daughter of Duke Alfonso of Naples. She was an intelligent young woman and deeply resented the place of prominence in the court assumed by Beatrice d'Este, wife of Ludovico. She clearly understood that Ludovico had usurped her young husband's place, and wrote to her father of her unhappiness at Milan. Alfonso, failing in his attempts to secure for his son-in-law the power to which he was legally entitled, cooled in his friendship for Milan. It was partly because of the worsening relations between Naples and Milan caused by Ludovico's usurpation that the latter intrigued with the French. The result of the intrigues was the invasion of Italy by the French in 1494. Gian Galeazzo, a virtual prisoner at Pavia, died there in the same year. He left two legitimate children: Francesco (1491–1512) and Bona (1493?–1557), who married (1517) Sigismund I, king of Poland.

Sforza, Giovanni. Lord of Pesaro, b. 1466; d. 1510. He was the natural son of Costanzo Sforza. At his father's death (1473) Pesaro was threatened by the armies of Pope Sixtus IV, who was promoting the ambitions of his nephew Girolamo Riario. Costanzo's widow protected and held the state for Giovanni, and his investiture of it was confirmed by Sixtus (1483) and again by Innocent VIII (1490). Pope Alexander VI, desirous of a political and military alliance with the Sforza family, gave his daughter, Lucrezia Borgia, to Giovanni in marriage (1493). Later (1497), an alliance with the Sforza seemed less necessary to Alexander. He wished instead to strengthen his ties with the kingdom of Naples. Blandly charging that the marriage of Lucrezia and Giovanni had never been consummated, he had it annulled, while Italy rocked with laughter. Giovanni's protests concerning his manhood did nothing to dampen the hilarity. Two years later (1499) Cesare Borgia, Alexander's son, threatened Pesaro as he began his conquest of a principality for himself. As Giovanni had no allies willing to come to his aid (a situation that was not unique with him as Cesare proceeded on his march), he was forced to flee. On the collapse of Cesare's principality, following the death of Pope Alexander (1503), Giovanni was restored and invested anew by Pope Julius II. He was known as a just and able administrator and a patron of letters. His natural daughter Isabella (1503–1561) married Cipriano del Nero, of a noble Florentine family. His son, Costanzo II, died (1512) at the age of two years.

Sforza, Ippolita Maria. Duchess of Calabria; b. 1445; d. 1488. She was the daughter of Francesco Sforza, duke of Milan, and Bianca Maria Visconti. She was betrothed to Alfonso, duke of Calabria (1455), and married him in 1465. A cultivated young woman, she had been a pupil of Guiniforte Barzizza and of Constantine Lascaris. She was a student of classical literature and philosophy, was a friend and patron of men of letters, and collected a rich library in the Castel Capuano in Naples where she lived.

Sforza, Isabella. Natural daughter of Giovanni Sforza, lord of Pesaro; b. 1503; d. 1561. She lived at Milan, Florence, and Rome, and was married to Cipriano del Nero, of a noble Florentine family. She was noted for her wide learning and as a writer. Among her works are the treatises *Della vera tranquillita dell' animo* (Venice, 1544), *Dello stato feminile,* and many letters.

Sforza, Ludovico. [Called **il Moro,** "the Moor."] Duke of Bari and of Milan; b. at Vigevano, July 27, 1452; d. in the castle of Loches, in France, May 27, 1508. He was the fourth legitimate son of Francesco Sforza and Bianca Maria Visconti. His name was originally Ludovico Maurus. His mother changed the Maurus to Maria, but the nickname Moro stuck, and Ludovico encouraged it. In later life a Moor's (*moro*) head and a mulberry tree (*mora*) were two of his many personal devices. A responsive, studious child, he was his mother's favorite, and remained closely attached to her as long as she lived. She supervised his early education, and later engaged the humanist Francesco Filelfo as his tutor. A willing pupil, he achieved familiarity with the ancient languages and literature and an interest in the intellectual and artistic developments of his day without, however, attaining to any security in his own taste or encouraging new directions as a patron of art and literature. He was in France with his brother Sforza Maria when word reached him that his brother Galeazzo Maria, the reigning duke of Milan, had been assassinated (December 26, 1476). The heir to the duchy was Galeazzo Maria's young son Gian Galeazzo. The child's mother, Bona of Savoy, assumed the rule of Milan as regent for her son. Her adviser was Cicco Simonetta, a trusted councillor of Francesco Sforza, the first Sforza duke of Milan. Several of the brothers of Galeazzo Maria intrigued against his widow and his son for the throne. A plot to make Sforza Maria duke was exposed. He was exiled with his brothers Ludovico and Ascanio. Ludovico was exiled to Pisa, from where he made frequent trips to Florence to savor its famed intellectual and artistic atmosphere, and where he was impressed by the rewards to a prince of patronage of the arts and the construction of great buildings as monuments to his memory. After various intrigues he contrived to ingratiate himself with Bona of Savoy (who was besotted with love for her carver, one Tassino), and returned to Milan. Cicco Simonetta, when he learned that Ludovico was restored to Bona's favor, warned her, "I shall lose my head, and before long Your

Serene Highness will lose your state." Simonetta was a true prophet. Roberto Sanseverino, a noted condottiere and a confederate in Ludovico's plots, was also restored at Milan. Ludovico, who for all his many failings was not gratuitously cruel, allowed Sanseverino to wreak vengeance on Simonetta. The latter's influence was removed by his decapitation (1480). Ludovico also managed to get rid of Tassino, who had achieved unlimited influence. And he obtained a statement from the young duke (crowned in 1480) that he preferred the advice of his uncle Ludovico to that of his mother. Bona was banished from the court, and from this time (November, 1480) Ludovico was the ruler of Milan in all but name. In the meantime, his brother Sforza Maria had died (1479) and King Ferrante of Naples had named Ludovico duke of Bari in his place. For a time he continued his friendship with Naples, supported Ferrante in the war of Ferrara (1482–1484) and in the conspiracy of the barons (1485), and confirmed the marriage contract of Isabella of Aragona, Ferrante's granddaughter, and the young Gian Galeazzo. But he had quarreled with his brother Ascanio, and had declared Sanseverino a rebel. He did not turn over the rule of the duchy to Gian Galeazzo after the latter's marriage (1489) to Isabella. She was a spirited young woman who immediately realized the secondary place to which her docile husband had been relegated, complained bitterly in letters to her father at Naples, and urged his help in securing her husband's rights. Her resentment was deepened after the marriage (January, 1491) of Ludovico and Beatrice d'Este, a lively girl (she was just over 15) who soon became the center of the Milanese court. Isabella's humiliation was ultimately one cause of Ludovico's ruin. His former allies, the Aragonese of Naples, turned against him. He felt himself isolated in Italy and began to treat with the French king. He armed his castles and fortresses with men whom he thought were loyal to him, and in January, 1492, formed a defensive alliance with Charles VIII. Later in the year, Alexander VI was elected pope with great assistance from Cardinal Ascanio, and Ludovico congratulated himself that now a man favorable to his interests was pope. His diplomacy thereafter consisted in seeking alliances, and then building up counter-alliances to them. In his twistings and turnings he at length outwitted himself. Charles VIII, who claimed Naples as the heir of Louis XI and who envisioned its conquest as a stepping stone to a crusade against the Turks, led a powerful army into Italy. In the meantime, Ludovico had secretly been negotiating with the emperor Maximilian I. The terms of their agreement were that Ludovico's niece, Bianca Maria, would marry Maximilian with a dowry of 400,000 ducats (Maximilian always needed money), and in return Maximilian promised to invest Ludovico with the duchy of Milan. Gian Galeazzo died (October, 1494) at Pavia, a day or two after Charles VIII, having entered Lombardy with his army, had visited him. Rumor had it that the young duke's convenient death was the result of poison administered at Ludovico's order. He called the councillors of Milan together and proposed that Gian Galeazzo's infant son be named duke. He did this with the more assurance since he had packed the meeting, and yielded gracefully when, as previously arranged, the councillors protested that this was no time for children to govern Milan and insisted that Ludovico, who had been its actual ruler for so many years, be named duke. Charles marched triumphantly down the peninsula and easily took Naples. His rapid success frightened the Italian powers. Ludovico's understanding with him was of brief duration. He recalled his troops and made overtures to Venice. His fear of France and Charles, whom he had thought he could easily outwit, was intensified because with Charles on his Italian march was the Duc d'Orléans, who claimed Milan through his grandmother, Valentina Visconti. The Italian powers, too late, formed a league to prevent Charles from escaping from Italy with his army. Although the Italians claimed a victory at Fornovo (July, 1495), the French in fact escaped. Charles recrossed the Alps (October, 1495); Novara, which the French had taken in June, was recaptured. Ludovico flattered himself that it was thanks to him that the French had left Italy (glossing over the fact that it was thanks to him that they had entered it), and that he was now the arbiter of the affairs of Italy. He boasted that "the pope was his chaplain, the emperor his condottiere, Venice his chamberlain and the king of France his courier, going and coming at his pleasure." Maximilian came to visit him at Vigevano. They had a lovely time, but no profit accrued to Ludovico from the visit. Maximilian was too poor, too capricious, and too inconsistent in his policy to be of service to Ludovico, as events proved. Ludovico's delusions of grandeur were of short duration. Papal policy shifted; Venice continued as protector of Pisa to the detriment of Milan; the Aragonese were restored at Naples; Charles VIII died (April, 1498) and was succeeded by Ludovico's enemy, the Duc d'Orléans, who now became Louis XII and had himself crowned duke of Milan and king of Naples as well as king of France. Once again Ludovico was surrounded by enemies. Maximilian abandoned him and made a treaty with Louis. Venice joined France and the pope, as Ludovico secretly plotted with the Turks to wage war on Venice. Louis sent his armies into Italy and Ludovico's strongest fortresses fell before them. He left his fortified castle at Milan in charge of Bernardino de Corte, supposedly his most trusted lieutenant, with instructions to hold it, and fled (September, 1499) with his treasure to the emperor at Innsbruck. Maximilian was glad of the treasure and relieved him of a large part of it. In the meantime, Bernardino da Corte had given up the castle at Milan to the French in return for a payment of 150,000 ducats. Ludovico gathered an army of Swiss and Burgundians and returned to Milan (February, 1500). He was enthusiastically welcomed, as the French had made themselves hated almost immediately. But Ludovico's Swiss mercenaries betrayed him, and he fell into the hands of the French (April 8, 1500). He was sent to France a prisoner and remained a prisoner in the castle of Loches until his death. Although Louis XI had schemed and planned an invasion of Italy, it was Ludovico's express encouragement of Charles VIII that led to the actual invasion and showed the rest of Europe how easily Italy, with its rich culture and prosperous cities, could be conquered.

Under Ludovico, the court at Milan was the most brilliant and gayest in Italy. He had come to power in a rich and prosperous duchy, and did his utmost to preserve and promote its prosperity. He had a model farm, La Sforzesca, where the soil was irrigated with an ingenious system of canals. He rebuilt and improved his favorite city of Vigevano, his birthplace, and stimulated art, literature, science, and trade. He was an able administrator, but the military requirements of his policy and the extravagance of his court put a great strain on his treasury. He was forced to impose heavy taxes and imposts and became intensely unpopular as a result. He is known as the patron of Leonardo da Vinci and of Bramante. In fact, he was not a generous patron of these two giants. Bramante was so poorly treated that he left Milan. Leonardo, who had come to Milan in 1482 or 1483, was considered as any other workman and paid accordingly, until his model for the great equestrian statue of Francesco Sforza was completed (1489) and won him fame. As Ludovico's military preparations advanced, the bronze for casting the huge statue was sent to Ferrara to be cast into cannon; Leonardo's model, standing in the courtyard of the castle at Milan, was destroyed by French archers, who shot at it to improve their marksmanship. In his first years at Milan, Leonardo was largely employed, and frequently not paid, for designing decorations for festivals and ceremonial occasions. But it must be remembered that it was Ludovico who commissioned Leonardo to paint *The Last Supper*, in the refectory of the convent of S. Maria delle Grazie. This was Ludovico's favorite church, and one which he almost completely rebuilt. Its famous dome was designed by Bramante at Ludovico's order. He continued work on the cathedral and on the Certosa di Pavia; had a real respect for learning, improved the university, and did much for the library at Pavia (which Louis XII carried off to France). He was a lover of good music (according to some accounts, Lorenzo de' Medici sent Leonardo da Vinci to Ludovico with a silver lyre that Leonardo had made in the shape of a horse's skull, because Lorenzo wanted to gain Ludovico's good will and knew that he was a music lover), and maintained a fine, and well-paid, choir of Flemish and German singers. He invited the Tuscan poet Bellincioni to Milan that the Milanese might be influenced by the admired Tuscan language. In his patronage of art and literature he was a child of his age, but his approach was to encourage talent that others had already recognized. In his personal life he was fairly discreet. He had proposed to marry Isabella d'Este, but she was promised to Francesco Gonzaga of Mantua, and he became betrothed to her younger sister Beatrice. The marriage was delayed because of his attachment to his mistress, Cecilia Gallerani. Cecilia bore him a son, Cesare, and he had other children by other mistresses. However, for most of the few years he was married to Beatrice he was constant, became enchanted by her liveliness and reckless courage, and sincerely mourned her early death. Through Beatrice he became greatly attached to her sister Isabella; correspondence between Milan and Mantua was so frequent that he sent a courier to Mantua weekly. Beatrice bore him two sons, Massimiliano and Francesco, who each reigned briefly as duke of Milan. In addition to his natural ability as an administrator, his sound education and interest in the cultural and scientific developments of his day, Ludovico's main characteristics were a passion for intrigue and a mask of impassivity to conceal his designs, a strong dependence on astrology, and an exalted notion of his own cleverness. His niece Caterina, the Amazon of Forlì, bluntly told him that words do not defend states. He learned to his cost, and that of Italy, that she was right.

Sforza, Massimiliano. Duke of Milan; b. at Milan, January, 1493; d. at Paris, 1530. He was the elder son of Ludovico il Moro and Beatrice d'Este. His name, originally Ercole, was changed to Massimiliano at the request of the emperor Maximilian I. His mother died while he was still a very young child. His father was driven out of Milan and then imprisoned by the French. Massimiliano and his brother Francesco went to Innsbruck, where they were brought up by Bianca Maria Sforza, their cousin, who was the wife of the emperor Maximilian I. As a result of their upbringing they were more German than Italian. Massimiliano was restored to the duchy of Milan with the aid of the Swiss (1512). He was enthusiastically welcomed at Milan by the people, who had had their fill of the French, and with Swiss backing defeated the French at Ariotta, June, 1513, and sent them back across the Alps. After the death of Louis XII the French returned to Lombardy under Francis I and won a great victory at Marignano (September, 1515). Massimiliano surrendered to the French, resigned his claims to the duchy, and agreed to go and live in France.

Sforza, Muzio Attendolo. Condottiere and count of Cotignola; b. at Cotignola, in the Romagna, May 8, 1369; d. at the Pescara River, January 4, 1424. He was one of the twenty-one children of a peasant family of Cotignola. His original name was Muzio Attendolo. His mother, a strong-willed and energetic woman, brought up her sons to work in the fields and to fight, and took up arms herself whenever she thought it necessary. According to one story, when he was 15 Muzio was working in the fields. The condottiere Boldrino da Panicale passed by and invited him to join his band. Muzio hesitated. He had an axe in his hand and said he would hurl it at a tree trunk. If the axe stuck it would be a sign that he should go and seek his fortune. It stuck. Another account says he left home at the age of 12 to join a mercenary band. In either case, he began his military career at an early age. After a few years he joined the well-known captain Alberico da Barbiano, and remained with him twelve to fifteen years. One of his comrades in arms under Alberico was Braccio da Montone. Muzio and Braccio became the leading condottieri of their time, and met their deaths in battle against each other's forces. The followers of Muzio were called the Sforzeschi; those of Braccio were the Bracceschi. During their time, when one served a prince or state the other was almost invariably his adversary. In the course of his career Muzio fought in the pay of Gian Galeazzo Visconti of Milan, and against him. He fought for Florence, for Pope John XXIII (the pope could not pay him, and made him lord of his native land of Cotignola instead, an honor that gave Muzio endless pleasure), and then for Ladislaus, king of Naples and the pope's enemy. On the death of Ladislaus (1414), he was in and out of the service of Queen Joanna II, successor of Ladislaus, depending on whether her lovers, in their turn, feared him more or needed him more. Twice he was arrested and imprisoned in fear of his power. Each time he was released (once through the agency of his sister). He was made Grand Constable of Naples and was given castles and lands. In the struggle for control of Naples between Alfonso of Aragon and Louis of Anjou, each at one time or another named her heir by the vacillating Joanna, Braccio da Montone invaded the Abruzzi as the ally of Alfonso of Aragon. Muzio opposed him as the ally of the pope and of Naples. Braccio besieged Aquila. Muzio led his men to its relief. As he was about to cross the Pescara River his page, who was carrying his helmet, slipped.

Muzio, in full armor, reached out to rescue him. His horse reared and he was thrown into the river. Weighted down by his armor he sank beneath the water. His body was never found. Pius II in his *Commentaries* describes Muzio as a man of splendid physique, quick to act, and of great presence of mind. He was noted for his strength, which won him the nickname *Sforza*. After his death, Queen Joanna commanded his son Francesco, who succeeded as commander of his army, to take the name *Sforza* in his honor. Francesco, who became duke of Milan, was his natural son by Lucia Tregani, who bore him six other children, including Alessandro, who became lord of Pesaro, and several who achieved eminence in the Church. When an advantageous marriage to Antonia, the sister of the lord of Cortona, was arranged for him, Muzio gave his mistress Lucia to one of his officers in marriage. Antonia died, and Muzio had two more wives. The children by his three wives never attained the prominence of Lucia's children. Known for his honesty and general (but not invariable) fair dealing, Muzio took his religion seriously, heard mass every day, went to confession at least once a year, paid his debts, maintained discipline, and by his powerful example and common sense won a great reputation for himself and his army. He is said to have given his son Francesco three simple rules: leave other men's wives alone; never strike a servant or a companion, but if you must do so, send him far away at once; and never ride a hard-mouthed horse.

Sforza, Polissena. Natural daughter of Francesco Sforza, duke of Milan; b. 1428; d. 1449. She married (1442) Sigismondo Malatesta of Rimini. He is said to have caused her early death.

Sfumato (sfö-mä′tō). An Italian word, meaning "smoked" or "smoky," or "vanished, cleared." In painting it is applied to a misty atmosphere that is created in producing form by such delicate gradations of light and shade that line and outline vanish. Leonardo da Vinci, who noted that lines do not separate tones in nature, was the earliest and greatest exponent of painting in this manner; many succeeding painters imitated him.

Shipman's Tale, The. One of Chaucer's *Canterbury Tales*. Similar in some respects to the first stories of the eighth day of Boccaccio's *Decameron*, it is a tale of a wife's clever deception of her miserly husband, aided by the monk with whom she shares her favors.

Ship of Fools, The [*The Shyp of Folys.*] Translation and adaptation by Alexander Barclay of the *Narrenschiff*, a long poem in rhymed couplets by the German satiric poet Sebastian Brant (1457–1521). It was composed in 1508 and published in 1509, and is believed to be the first English book in which mention is made of the New World.

Shipton (ship′tọn), **Mother.** [Maiden name, **Ursula Southiel.**] Semi-legendary English prophetess; b. near Knaresborough, Yorkshire, England, July, 1488; d. c1559. She is said to have married Toby Shipton, a builder. According to tradition, she was the child of Agatha Shipton and the devil, and author of *Mother Shipton's Prophecies*. No evidence actually exists of her really having lived.

Shirley (shėr′li), **John.** English traveler and collector of manuscripts, especially those of Geoffrey Chaucer and John Lydgate; b. c1366; d. at London, October 21, 1456.

Shore (shōr), **Jane.** Mistress of King Edward IV; b. at London, c1445; d. 1527. While still a girl she married William Shore, a citizen of London. After her intrigue with the king began (c1470) she lived in the greatest luxury, and after his death she became the mistress of William, Baron Hastings, who was beheaded by Richard III, June 13, 1483. Richard imprisoned Jane Shore (largely out of malice, but with a great show of virtuous indignation), robbed her house, accused her of witchcraft, and obliged her to do penance for unchastity at Saint Paul's Cross. She afterward became the mistress of Thomas Grey, 1st marquis of Dorset. The agonizing details of her death in a ditch from starvation are without authority, though an old ballad cites them with great precision.

Sicilian Vespers. Uprising of March, 1282, at Palermo in Sicily. It was occasioned by the resentment and outrage caused in his subjects by the harsh rule of Charles I. He had won, with the pope's consent, the throne of Sicily from the Hohenstaufen heirs, replaced Sicilian officials with Frenchmen, and levied crushing taxes. The Sicilians hated the French and dreamed of a return of the Hohenstaufen. On Easter Monday, March 31, 1282, a Frenchman abused a young Sicilian matron on her way to Vespers with her family. The Frenchman was slain immediately. The cry, "Death to the French," arose. The French were massacred. Revolt spread rapidly throughout the island, and the French withdrew to Naples, whither Charles had moved his capital. The Sicilians invited Pedro III of Aragon, husband of the Hohenstaufen Constance (Manfred's daughter) to become their ruler. Thus were the French driven out of Naples, not, however, relinquishing the claim of the counts of Anjou to the island, and thus was the claim of the Aragonese begun.

Sickingen (zik′ing-ẹn), **Franz von.** German knight; b. near Kreuznach, Germany, March 2, 1481; d. May 8, 1523. Influential in the reigns of Maximilian I and Charles V, he aided in the election of Charles as emperor. He favored the Reformation, and became head of a league for the forcible introduction of the Reformation.

Sigismund I (of the *Holy Roman Empire*) (sij′is-mund, sig-). Holy Roman emperor (1411–1437); b. February 15, 1368; d. December 9, 1437. He was the son of Charles IV, Holy Roman emperor and king of Bohemia, and the half brother of Wenceslaus III, who succeeded Charles. In the course of time, Sigismund acquired great dominions through inheritance and marriage, lost some of them, and gave some of them away. The margravate of Brandenburg, received (1378) from Wenceslaus, he transferred (1415) to Frederick Hohenzollern (Frederick I, Elector of Brandenburg). Through his wife Maria, daughter of Louis I, he won the right of succession to the throne of Hungary, and was crowned king (1387). When Rupert, king of the Germans (and uncrowned Holy Roman emperor), died (1410) the electors could not agree on a successor. One group chose Sigismund and a second chose Jobst of Moravia, Sigismund's cousin. Wenceslaus III, who had been deposed in 1400, had never renounced his rights and constituted a third claimant. Jobst died (1411) and Wenceslaus yielded to Sigismund, whom the electors unanimously named king of the Germans (1411). At the same time, he was king of Hungary and heir apparent, through Wenceslaus, of Bohemia. He sold or transferred Neumarkt to the Teutonic Knights and Saxony (1423) to Frederick the Warlike (Frederick I of Saxony). The latter was in payment for Frederick's services in the Hussite wars. Sigismund's reign was turbulent. The Turks were pushing westward and his kingdom of Hungary was a target of their attack. In 1396 they defeated Sigismund at Nicopolis. After he became king of Germany he called again for a European coalition and crusade against the Turks, but to no avail. Within his realm, as in all Europe, the Great Schism in the Church that had brought forth two who claimed to be pope gave rise to heretical agitation. Sigismund, in Italy to wage war against the Venetians over Dalmatia (which he lost) persuaded Pope John XXIII to take part in a Council to end the Schism. (He later handed over John to his enemies, who imprisoned him.) For his part in the success that the Council of Constance temporarily enjoyed, Sigismund was acclaimed throughout Europe. But the Council only made matters worse in Bohemia, for John Hus, who had been persuaded to attend the Council under the emperor's safe-conduct, was tried for heresy and burned at the stake (July 6, 1415) at Constance. Bohemia was inflamed, and when Wenceslaus died (1419) the crown of Bohemia, which was Sigismund's by hereditary right, was denied him. It was not until 1436 that he received it. Sigismund made several sorties into Italy. When he was there in 1414 he and John XXIII were taken up the tower of Cremona (the highest in Italy) by their host, the tyrant Gabino Fondolo, to look at the view. Fondolo later confessed that he was seized with an almost overwhelming desire to hurl them both over and rid the world of two troublemakers, a desire that he resisted to his subsequent regret. In 1431 Sigismund was again in Italy, and received the Iron Crown of Lombardy at Milan. But he was not so welcome as he had expected to be, so shut himself up in the safety of Siena for six months before recrossing the Alps. At a later date (May 31, 1433) he was crowned in Rome by Pope Eugenius IV. Sigismund, the last of the Luxemburg emperors, made some attempts to correct weaknesses in the empire, but the constant wars of the German barons and the religious uprisings in Bohemia brought his attempts to nothing. He designated the husband of his daughter Elizabeth, Albert V of the Hapsburg house of Austria, as his successor. Albert reigned as Albert II of Germany.

Signorelli (sē-nyō-rel′lē), **Luca di Egidio.** Painter; b. at Cortona, between 1445 and 1450; d. there, October 16, 1523. Nothing is known of his early life and training. Luca Pacioli, the mathematician and friend of Piero della Francesca, and Vasari wrote that

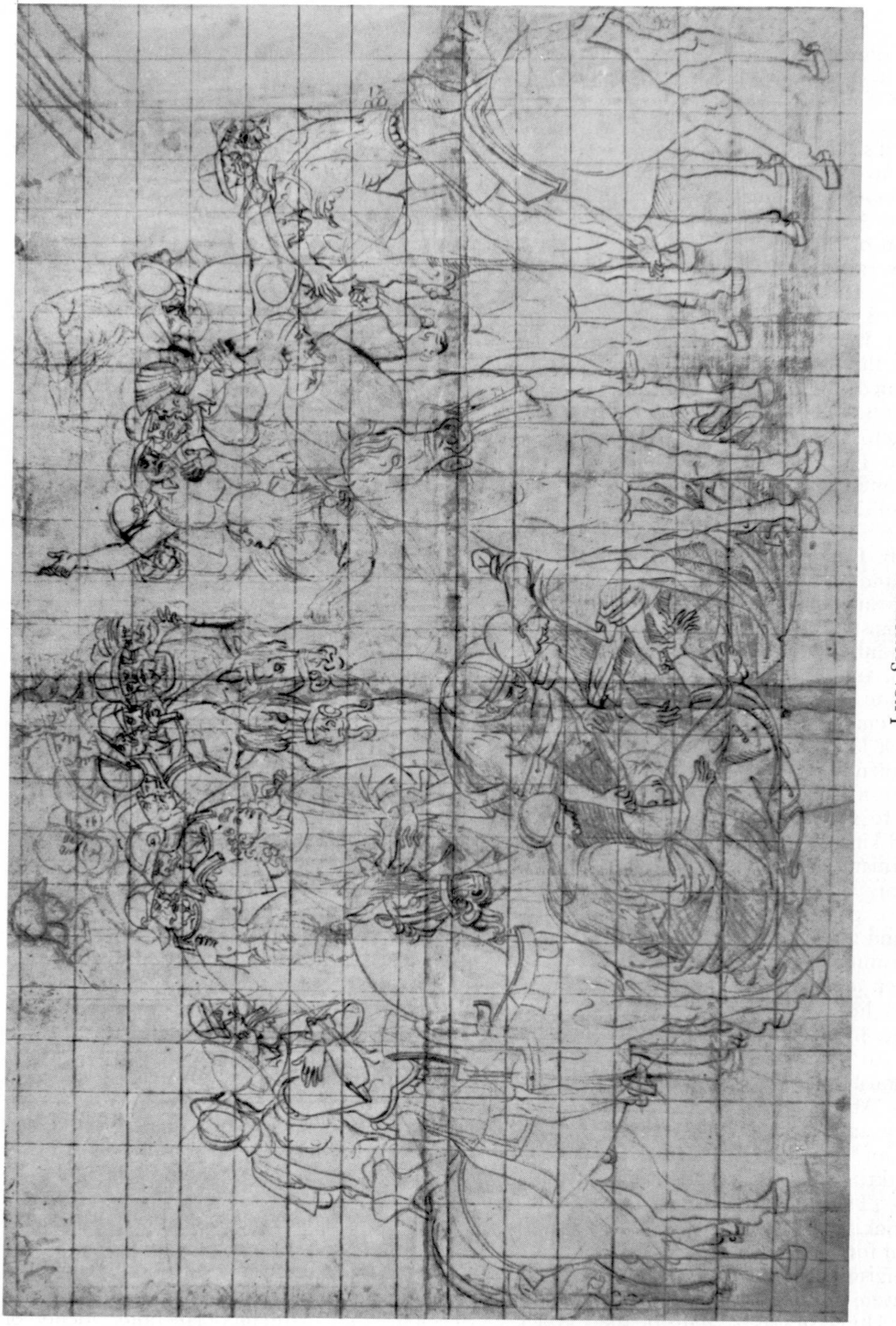

Luca Signorelli

Study for a fresco, with a group of mounted knights about the Cross, the stem of which is embraced by the Magdalen. In the center three women attend the Virgin.

Cabinet des Dessins Musée du Louvre Cliché Musées Nationaux

he was a pupil of Piero. Their statements seem confirmed by fragments of an early fresco, *Madonna and Child between SS. Jerome and Paul* (1474), Municipal Museum, Città di Castello, that has elements of the style of Piero. Perhaps it was study with Piero that brought out his breadth of conception and treatment, his tendency toward grandeur and solemnity. He learned to be a superb draftsman, skilled in modeling, and was the possessor of a dynamic and functional line that he delighted to use in the portrayal of the male nude in action. His study of the nude became a passion. Vasari writes that when his beautiful and beloved son was killed in the city and brought to him, Signorelli took the youth's body into a separate room, stripped it, and there, dry-eyed, painted the handsome corpse. The restless energy of Signorelli's temperament was in contrast to the serene dignity of Piero's spirit. Signorelli's earliest painting, recorded 1470, has been lost, but other early work, perhaps before 1480, already shows his interest in the nude and indicates contact with developments that were taking place in Florence and, especially, the influence of Antonio Pollaiuolo. One such is a *Flagellation*, Brera, Milan, originally one side of a processional standard. The curved backs and twisting trunks, straining legs and muscular arms of the soldiers lashing Christ recall the pulsing energy of Pollaiuolo. A later (1498) *Martyrdom of St. Sebastian*, Città di Castello, repeats with Olympian assurance the effort and energy expended as the soldiers bend and stretch to fit their bolts to the cross bows. In 1480 he went to Loreto to fresco the octagonal sacristy of the basilica. The winding, floating draperies of the angel musicians in the vault accentuate a sense of movement that reflects Verrocchio, and the pairs of Apostles on the walls below are linked, two to a panel, in the manner of Donatello's Apostles on the doors of the sacristy of S. Lorenzo, Florence. Other influences of Donatello appear in Signorelli's strong realism, his preference for painting mature and older men without idealizing them. A *Conversion of Saul* on one wall of the sacristy at Loreto, in the dramatic use of light to give volume and in the violent reaction of the soldiers to the vision, is in startling contrast to the dignity of the Apostles figured on the other walls. In 1481 he was one of the painters (others were Perugino, Ghirlandaio, Botticelli and Cosimo Rosselli) called to Rome to help decorate the Sistine Chapel. There, with assistants, he frescoed *The Last Days and Death of Moses*. In succeeding years he painted a number of religious pictures, including a tondo, *Holy Family* (c1487), Uffizi, in which the heroic forms are beautifully adapted, following the example of Botticelli, to the circular form. The powerful work is a forerunner of the *Doni Tondo* of Michelangelo. Another painting of about this period was the poetic and celebrated *Realm of Pan* (c1490), with its heroic nude figures of deities and ancient shepherds set in a shadowy Arcadia under a crescent moon. This work, his only one on a classical theme, expressed the humanism of the circle of Lorenzo de' Medici, to whom the painter gave it; it was destroyed at Berlin in 1945. In addition to a number of religious paintings of this period (*Annunciation*, 1491, Municipal Gallery, Volterra, *Circumcision*, National Gallery, London, *Visitation*, Berlin, *Standard*, Urbino, *Madonna*, Munich, altarpiece, New York, and others), he frescoed (1497–1498) ten of the many scenes (others were painted by Sodoma) on the life of St. Benedict in the Abbey of Monteoliveto Maggiore. Some of these are notable for the swift narrative power that marks many of his predella panels.

Signorelli anticipated Michelangelo in his devotion to the nude in violent and rapid action as the highest expression of his artistic aim and vision. More interested in the possibilities of the human body than in decorative effect, his color, often of a bronzed tone, is sometimes harsh and melancholic; on occasion, as in most of the S. Brizio frescoes, he dispensed with landscape as an element of composition entirely. A superb draftsman, he portrayed his powerful nudes in the widest variety of pose and activity, with magnificent foreshortening and with the emphasis of his living line and massing of shadows. His masterpiece is the well-preserved fresco decoration of the Chapel of S. Brizio in the cathedral at Orvieto. Fra Angelico had begun the decoration of the chapel. In 1447, when he was called to Rome, he had finished painting two segments of the vault. Thereafter the overseers of the cathedral had sought in vain an artist of what they considered equal stature to complete the work. Long negotiations carried on with Perugino came to nothing. At length, in April, 1499, a cautious contract

LUCA SIGNORELLI
Dante and Vergil with Count Ugolino
The British Museum, London

was signed with Signorelli, by which he agreed to decorate the six remaining segments of the vault. In spirit and temperament it would have been difficult to find two painters more opposed. Signorelli painted choirs of angels and apostles, martyrs and virgins, doctors and patriarchs in the six segments of the vault. The following year, well satisfied, the overseers extended his contract and he undertook the decoration of the four walls. Theologians drew up the program he was to follow. It was to be a colossal and awesome rendering of the Apocalypse. Over the entrance doorway is *The Last Judgment*. On the left wall is *The Preaching of Antichrist*, an unusual subject, in which Antichrist, with the features of Christ distorted, stands on a small podium in the foreground and listens to the evil words whispered into his ear by a devil and which he is to repeat to the multitude. In the right background is a splendid Renaissance Temple that some of the soldiers are despoiling while others slay the bystanders. In the center the Antichrist raises a dead person, while against a landscape background in the upper left avenging angels assault the Antichrist. In the lower left corner Signorelli painted himself, in contemporary dress, accompanied by Fra Angelico (another self-portrait is in the cathedral museum). A separate portion of the same wall shows *The Arrival of the Blessed in Paradise*. The terror of *The Separation of the Damned and the Elect* is on the back wall; *The Resurrection of the Flesh* occupies the larger part of the right wall, with *The Arrival of the Damned in Hell* filling the remainder. Completing the decoration are monochrome illustrations of the ancient poets and of Dante's *Divine Comedy*, and medallions of poets and philosophers. The walls of the Chapel swarm with bodies in every conceivable position, with an infinite variety of gesture and expression, and with enormous invention in the creation of the demons and devils attacking the damned. The figures are disposed in interlocking groups; doom and awe emanate from the monumental, dramatic conception; green-tinged brazen tones enhance the ominous atmosphere. The scenes prefigure Michelangelo's *Last Judgment* in the Sistine Chapel.

A highly regarded and busy painter, with the completion (1502) of the Chapel of S. Brizio Signorelli had more commissions than he could handle, and many of them were carried out to some extent by assistants in his prosperous workshop. He went to Rome (c1504 or 1505)) but the work he did in the Vatican was removed to make way for Raphael's decoration in the *Stanze*. To the end of his life he continued to produce paintings, some not of the highest quality, and many critics find that his work declined after the decoration of the S. Brizio chapel. Throughout his life he had been active in civic affairs, serving his native town many times as prior and councillor, and once as ambassador to Florence. Vasari, who claimed kinship with him, wrote that the aged Luca visited the Vasari family at Arezzo when young Giorgio was a lad of eight, and advised his father to have the boy taught to draw. Vasari describes him as good and gracious, a man who dressed splendidly and lived as a noble, not as a painter. Active and admired in his own day, a dedicated artist and a patient teacher, he lived to see the full flowering of his vigorous exaltation of the human body in Michelangelo, and the fulfillment of the ideals of Renaissance painting in that master and Leonardo and Raphael. Many beautiful drawings, studies for his S. Brizio frescoes and others, are preserved in the Uffizi, the Louvre, and elsewhere. Besides those mentioned, examples of his paintings are to be found at Arezzo, Bergamo, Cortona (Diocesan Museum, S. Domenico, S. Niccolò), Florence (Uffizi, Pitti), Montepulciano, Naples, Perugia, Rome (Castel Sant' Angelo, Vatican, Pallavicini Collection), San Sepolcro, Turin (Sabauda Gallery), Umbertide (S. Croce), Venice (Ca' d'Oro), Amsterdam, Berlin, Dublin, London, Oxford, Paris, Atlanta (Georgia), Baltimore (Walters Art Gallery), Boston, Detroit, Greenville (South Carolina), Kansas City (Missouri), New Haven, Philadelphia (Johnson Collection), Richmond (Virginia), Toledo, Washington, Williamstown (Massachusetts), and elsewhere.

Signoria (sē-nyō-rē'ä) or **Signory** (sē'nyô-rē). A governing body in many Italian communes whose constitution and powers varied widely from city to city and even, from time to time, within the same city. In Florence the Signoria was for some time composed of the Gonfaloniere of Justice and eight priors. In the time of Dante (1265–1321) their term of office was limited to two months. By a reform of 1502 the Gonfaloniere was appointed for life. At times the Signoria was effectively the chief governing body. At other times its powers were limited or annulled by the creation of other committees or bodies, although the Signoria continued to exist in form. Government by commission (*balìa*) and augmented bureaucracy were more in evidence in the 15th century as fiscal and military problems came to dominate.

Sigoli (sē′gō-lē), **Simone.** Fourteenth-century prose writer; b. at Florence. He accompanied Leonardo Frescobaldi and four others on a journey to the Holy Land, in which they passed through Egypt on the way to Sinai. He left an account of the journey, *Viaggio al Monte Sinai*, that is worthy for his accurate and factual observations of the places visited and is revealing of the religious zeal that moved him.

Sigonio (sē-gō′nyō), **Carlo.** Historian and humanist; b. at Modena, c1520; d. at his villa at Ponte Basso, near Modena, August 28, 1584. He was learned in Latin and Greek, studied at Bologna and Pavia, and then entered the service of Cardinal Grimani. He remained in the cardinal's service until he was called to Modena to succeed his old master, Francesco Porto (1546). He later taught at Venice and Padua, and (1563) accepted an invitation to the university at Bologna, where he remained until his death. Sigonio left many writings. He is best known for his learned and carefully researched histories. In these he relied on documents, and critically examined his sources. An outstanding characteristic of his approach is his realization of the development of institutions. Unlike so many humanists of his day, who looked with scorn on the Middle Ages and preferred to leap all the way back to classical times, Sigonio studied the Middle Ages with a view to tracing the origins of contemporary institutions in that era. His *De regno italiae*, which covers the period from 570 to 1200, is his most important work. Among his other works, all in a Latin of precision and beauty, are those on Roman institutions, Roman names, Roman law, and a collection of fragments of Cicero. He wrote a history of Bologna that was later placed on the Index.

Silvestri (sil-ves′trē), **Francesco.** [Called **Francesco da Ferrara.**] Dominican; b. at Ferrara, 1474; d. at Rennes, France, September 19, 1528. He entered the Dominican order at the age of 14, and quickly distinguished himself for his wisdom and piety. He taught at Mantua, Milan, and Bologna, was vicar general of the Lombard congregation (1519), vicar of the order (1524), and, finally, general of the order (1525). He was one of the outstanding representatives of the Thomist school in the 16th century. His most important work was a commentary on the *Summa contra Gentiles* of St. Thomas Aquinas.

Silvestri, Guido Postumo. Soldier, poet, and physician; b. at Pesaro, 1479; d. at Capranica, 1521. He studied medicine at Padua. On his return to Pesaro he was caught up in the political intrigues and wars that kept Italy in a turmoil. He had married at Padua, and mourned the death of his young wife in delicate Latin lyrics. His collection of elegies, with their gently Ovidian flavor, was printed at Bologna in 1524 and ranks high among the Latin poets.

Silvia (sēl′vyä). In Torquato Tasso's pastoral play *Aminta*, a disdainful nymph. She is dedicated to Diana and the pleasures of the hunt and spurns the love of the shepherd Aminta. He rescues her from a satyr but she returns no thanks. He hears from a messenger that she has been devoured by wolves. In despair he hurls himself from a precipice. But Silvia had escaped the wolves. Remorseful, she seeks his body. When she finds it she bathes his face with her tears. He revives as love unites them.

Simone di Ardizone (sē-mô′nā dē är-dēt-tsō′nā). Engraver who worked at Mantua about 1475, and was accused by Mantegna of pirating his work.

Simone dei Crocifissi (dā krō-chē-fēs′sē). Bolognese painter; b. c1330; d. 1399. Somewhat influenced by Vitale and the Sienese in his earlier years, his drawing later became coarser and his detail cruder. His tendencies are narrative, popular, and realistic, the Sienese influence being replaced by animation of expression and sturdier forms. Among his extant works are: an elaborate polyptych in three tiers, *Coronation of the Virgin;* a second signed *Coronation;* a realistic portrait of *Pope Urban* V, and others, in the Pinacoteca at Bologna. In the Church of S. Giacomo Maggiore in the same city is a *Crucifix*, signed and dated 1370; a *Nativity* is in the Uffizi at Florence; *The Crucifixion and the Coronation of the Virgin* is at New Haven. His name comes from the number of *Crucifixes* he painted, but judging by the number he left, the *Coronation of the Virgin* seems to have been his favorite subject. He was a gifted painter, but undertook to do too much, which perhaps accounts for the coarsening of his technique in the later works.

Simone Martini (mär-tē′nē). Sienese painter; b. at Siena, 1284?; d. at Avignon, 1344. He is one of the most glowing and delicate masters of the Sienese school that followed Duccio, of whom he was a pupil. He was the most important painter of the Sienese school of the 14th century, for his art is all his own—ethereal, serene, and of the most wondrous clarity and delicacy of color. Simone Martini worked at Siena, perhaps with Memmo di Filipuccio, whose daughter Giovanna he married and whose son, Lippo Memmi, was sometimes associated with him in his work. It is owing to these connections with the family that he was formerly erroneously called Simone Memmi. His earliest datable work is the *Maestà* in the Palazzo Pubblico, Siena, painted 1315 and signed by him. In it the Virgin, holding the Child, is enthroned and is surrounded by saints and angels who offer gifts and homage. The painting, a marvel of color, reveals a purity of line in the drawing of the many figures in this large fresco that was unequaled up to this time. Salt stored nearby kept the atmosphere of the Palazzo Pubblico humid and injured the color. Simone repainted the central figures in 1321 and they are in better condition than the others. He must have produced many fine works before he painted the *Maestà* to have been selected by the Sienese officials to decorate their Town Hall, but nothing is known of his earlier work except for a half-length panel, *Christ*, in the Vatican, of unknown date but, according to experts, before 1315. About 1317 he went to Naples, to the court of King Robert. He was warmly welcomed and much admired there; the Neapolitan school of painters felt his influence and Robert was so delighted with him he gave him an annual salary. His *St. Louis of Toulouse Crowning Robert of Anjou*, is in the National Gallery, Naples. St. Louis and King Robert were brothers, and the figures representing them are portraits. The painting is memorable for composition, concentration, and expressiveness, as well as for the keen attention to the ritual details of the ceremony it portrays. In 1320, Simone was back in Siena, and in the same year went to Pisa, where he painted the polyptych, *The Virgin, St. Catherine and other Saints*, for the Church of S. Caterina. The polyptych was dismembered, as so often happened. The main parts of it are in the National Museum at Pisa. Also in 1320, he went to Orvieto, where, with Lippo Memmi, he painted a polyptych for the Church of San Domenico, *Virgin with Child and Saints*, now in the Opera del Duomo, Orvieto. Another polyptych painted by him in Orvieto (for S. Francesco) is in the Isabella Stewart Gardner Museum, Boston. According to some, the work he did in Orvieto marks a transition from the influence of Duccio that appeared slightly in his early work to Gothic, that is, to an approach to painting that did not reflect the humanizing influence of Giotto, whose work Simone must have known, but rather tended, at least with Simone, toward an ethereal, decorative end, full of grace and serene beauty, yet lacking the impact of a moment of drama caught forever. This is not to say that his work lacks drama, as is evidenced by his fresco of *Guidoriccio da Foligniano* (1328), also in the Palazzo Pubblico, Siena. Guidoriccio, a famous captain, fully armed, sits his horse, caparisoned like its rider in medieval panoply, alone in the center of the wide panel. Before him is the castle he intends to take, behind him an armed camp, and off center in the background is a fortified castle. A midnight blue sky arches over all. The fresco is the epitome of the medieval military scene. The drama springs from the lone figure in the bristling landscape. Between 1322 and 1326 he worked with assistants at Assisi, painting ten scenes from the life of the saint in St. Martin's Chapel in the Lower Church of the basilica of San Francesco at Assisi. These frescoes, badly damaged by dampness, are among the most important artistic treasures of the basilica. It would be difficult to choose which of his paintings was his masterwork, but the St. Martin frescoes must rank high, notable as they are for their rhythmical composition as well as for the loving and knowledgeable rendering of the knightly and noble world from which St. Martin came. The stained glass windows in the Chapel of St. Stephen, also in the Lower Church, are among the loveliest there and were executed from designs by Simone.

With the *Annunciation* (1333), originally painted for the Chapel of Sant' Ansano

(Siena's patron saint) in the Cathedral of Siena and now in the Uffizi, Florence, Simone returns to the ethereal, highly decorative aspects of his work. To many, this beautiful painting has an almost oriental splendor, owing perhaps to the almond-shaped eyes of the Angel and the Virgin, and the almost Chinese exquisiteness in the patterning of leaves and flowers against the golden background. The saints on either side of the main panel were painted, according to Simone's design, by Lippo Memmi. This painting too is marked by his eloquent fluid line and unerring sense of design. In 1339, Simone packed up his family and went to Avignon to work on the new palace of the popes there. Only a few of the works he executed at Avignon remain. Among these is *Christ Returning from the Temple* (1342), Liverpool, notable for animation and its subtle Gothic arabesques. A polyptych of the Passion, now scattered among museums at Antwerp, Berlin, and Paris, may also have been painted at Avignon; scholarly opinion has not yet resolved its chronology. The frescoes he painted in the porch of the cathedral, exposed to the weather for centuries, are in a ruined state. In 1961–1962 they were detached, restored as much as possible, and cleaned. The removal of the frescoes—*Virgin and Child Enthroned* in a lunette surmounted by a triangular tympanum with *Christ the Redeemer and Angels*—revealed a series of delicate, rhythmic, highly finished *sinopie*, which have now also been detached and preserved. At Avignon Simone made the acquaintance of Petrarch, whose warm friend he became. For the poet he painted a portrait of Laura (now lost) that gave great satisfaction and won him two Petrarchan sonnets (Nos. 49 and 50 of the *Canzoniere*). He also painted a frontispiece for Petrarch's beloved copy of Vergil, now in the Ambrosiana, Milan. This last, a bucolic scene with a poet reclining under a tree, is considered more a tribute to friendship than a work of art, as Simone was not a miniaturist. Through the work of Simone, the Sienese style was spread in Naples, Orvieto, Assisi, Pisa, and even in France. Besides those mentioned, other examples of his work are at Altomonte (S. Maria della Consolazione), Massa Marittima (cathedral), and a triptych of the Blessed Agostino Novello and four of his miracles in the Piccolomini Chapel, S. Agostino, Siena; at Birmingham and Cambridge, England, Cologne, London (Courtauld Institute), Ottawa, Boston, Cambridge (Massachusetts), New York, and Washington, where an *Angel of the Annunciation* is one half of a diptych; the other half, with *The Virgin Annunciate*, is in the Hermitage, Leningrad.

Simonetta (sē-mō-nāt′tä), **Cicco.** [Real name, **Francesco Simonetta.**] Statesman; b. at Caccuri (Catanzaro), 1410; d. at Pavia, October 30, 1480. He was a man of culture, who had a good knowledge of law, of classical, Hebrew, and modern languages, and had a notable library in his castle at Sartirana. In the days of his power he was a patron and friend of learning. His fortunes had begun to rise when he entered the service of Francesco Sforza, later duke of Milan. He distinguished himself in the wars in Lombardy, was governor of Lodi (1449), lord of Sartirana (1451), and held other lands and castles. He became the faithful secretary of Francesco Sforza, and after him of his successor Galeazzo Maria. When the latter was assassinated (1476), Simonetta was able to hold the duchy together. In theory, he was the councillor of Galeazzo Maria's widow, Bona of Savoy, who was the guardian of the youthful heir Gian Galeazzo. In fact, Simonetta was effective ruler of the duchy. However, the uncles of the young duke intrigued to gain power. Simonetta could not prevent the loss of Genoa and other cities to Ludovico il Moro, Gian Galeazzo's uncle. Ludovico emerged as the most powerful and shrewdest of the brothers. Bona of Savoy, besotted with love for a member of her household, resented Simonetta's power. Ludovico had him arrested and confined in the castle at Pavia. There, after an infamous trial on a number of manifestly false charges, and after torture, Simonetta was condemned and beheaded. He left *Constitutiones et ordines*, that he had drawn up for the chancellery of the Sforza, a diary, and letters.

Simonetta, Giovanni. Historian, brother of Cicco (1410–1480). With his brother he was in the service of Francesco Sforza, and like him became a secretary and friend. He too was rewarded with fiefs and castles. However, on the accession to power (through intrigue and force) of Ludovico il Moro, when Cicco was arrested and accused, Giovanni was also. There were no visible grounds against the modest Giovanni. He was exiled to

Vercelli. His *Rerum gestarum Francisci Sfortiae*, is a vivid description of the events of Italian history from 1421 to 1466. In its objectivity (despite the evident hero worship of Francesco Sforza) and its attention to detail and breadth of scope, it foreshadows Francesco Guicciardini.

Simonis (sē′mô-nis) **Menno.** See **Menno Simons** (or **Symons** or **Simonis**).

Sinibaldi (sē-nē-bäl′dē), **Antonio.** Celebrated 15th-century Florentine copyist and calligrapher; in the years between 1461 and 1491 he made copies for Federico da Montefeltro, for the king of Naples, for Matthias Corvinus, king of Hungary, and for Lorenzo de' Medici, among others. He worked at Naples and at Florence, where he was an adherent of the Medici party. About twenty codices prepared by him are known. They are to be found at the Vatican, the Laurentian Library at Florence, at Naples, Ferrara, Berlin, Monaco, Paris, and the Escorial in Spain.

Sinibaldi, Bartolomeo. See **Baccio da Montelupo.**

Sinibaldi, Raffaele. See **Raffaello da Montelupo.**

Sinibaldo di Ibo (sē-nē-bäl′dō dē ē′bō). Perugian painter; b. c1475; d. after 1548. He was a weak follower of Perugino and Raphael, and executed several works in collaboration with Berto di Giovanni, examples of which are in the National Gallery of Umbria at Perugia.

Sinopia (si-nō′pi-ạ). A red pigment named for the town of Sinope on the Black Sea, from which it was originally obtained. Artists, especially in the 14th and 15th centuries, preparing to execute a large fresco on a wall made a sketch, more or less complete and detailed, to lay out the composition. The sketches were made with sinopia, and came to be called *sinopie*. They were made on the rough plaster surface (*arriccio*) over which the smooth plaster (*intonaco*) was to be laid. The fresco was then painted on the *intonaco*. The color (earth pigments mixed with lime water) applied to the wet intonaco chemically united with it. Thus the color was not on the surface but in it. The painter laid as much *intonaco* over the *arriccio* as he could paint in one day, since the intonaco must be wet when it was painted, following the outlines or other divisions of his sinopia. (Sometimes, as an example, all the gold haloes were done at once or, if they were in the same course, all robes of the same color.) In the course of following centuries it has sometimes happened that the *intonaco*, either from natural or manmade causes, has fallen away to reveal the sinopia underneath. (A bombardment in July, 1944, shattered and caused to fall the *intonaco* of many of the frescoes in the Camposanto at Pisa and revealed the immense *sinopie*.) At other times it has become necessary to detach the frescoes from the walls on which they are painted in order to protect them from damage or destruction caused by dampness seeping into the wall from behind. This was widely true of frescoes in certain areas of Tuscany after the terrible flood of November, 1966. The fact that the *intonaco* and the *arriccio* are separate layers makes possible the separation of the finished fresco and the *sinopie*. The separation, in turn, of the thin layer of the *intonaco* in which the color has penetrated and with which it is united is accomplished by an extremely delicate and highly refined process. In many cases the *sinopie*, preparatory sketches, are executed with a freedom, verve, and grace, since they were not expected to be seen again, that does not appear in the covering fresco, where established rules for the presentation of certain elements had to be followed. A process for detaching and mounting *sinopie* has also been perfected, and in many cases these superb drawings are the only examples in existence of the drawings of the earlier masters.

Sistine Chapel (sis′tēn). Papal private chapel in the Vatican, constructed by Pope Sixtus IV, for whom it was named. It was built in 1473, and is in plan a rectangle 157½ by 52½ feet, and 59 feet high. Architecturally it is not particularly notable, but it has long been world famous for the paintings which cover its walls and vault, including works by Perugino, Botticelli, Luca Signorelli, Ghirlandaio, and above all the ceiling decorated by Michelangelo and his *Last Judgment* on an end wall. The singing of the papal choir of the chapel (the Pontifical Choir) has also long been celebrated, and its archives contain a remarkable collection of illuminated manuscript works of the composers of the 15th and 16th centuries.

Sixtus IV (siks′tus). [Original name, **Francesco della Rovere.**] Pope (1471–1484); b. at Celle, near Savona, July 21, 1414; d. at Rome, August 12, 1484. Son of a humble family of Liguria, he was educated by the Franciscans and joined the order. He studied at Padua and Bologna, taught at a number of universities, and won renown as a student of philosophy and theology, as a teacher, and as a preacher. He became general of his order in 1464, was raised to the purple in 1471, and, through the intrigues of Cardinals Orsini, Borgia, and Gonzaga, was elected to succeed Pope Paul II in 1471. Prior to his election he had been active as a reformer, and it seemed that his aims were to keep peace in Italy and to unite Europe against the Turks. He sent out letters of appeal and exhortation to the rulers of Europe for a war against the Turks. In the first enthusiasm a fleet was assembled that, under the command of the Venetians and Neapolitans, retook Smyrna (1472). But the allies fell to quarreling, the enthusiasm waned, and interest in the war slackened. Sixtus had high hopes that the marriage (1472) of Zoë (or Sophia) Palaeologus, a Catholic, to Ivan III (the Great) of Russia would bring Russia to obedience to the Holy See. These hopes were without result. Thereafter, though plans for the war continued, Sixtus gave his whole attention to furthering the fortunes of members of his family. Other popes had practiced nepotism; Sixtus indulged in it wholesale. He doted on his nephews and stopped at nothing to advance their interests. Pietro Riario (his sister's son) and Giuliano della Rovere (later Julius II) were made cardinals. Leonardo della Rovere was named prefect of Rome, duke of Sora, and was married to an illegitimate daughter of King Ferrante of Naples. Giovanni della Rovere became vicar of Senigallia and Mondavio, succeeded his cousin Leonardo as prefect of Rome, and was married to a daughter of Federico da Montefeltro. Other kinsmen, fellow townsmen, and friends were rewarded with benefices, offices, and wealth. Justification for nepotism on such an unprecedented scale was fear of the king of Naples. When Pietro Riario died at an early age as a result of his excesses, Sixtus devoted his affection and efforts to promoting his brother Girolamo. With the aid of Pazzi money he bought Imola (1473) and invested Girolamo with it. Girolamo aspired to a larger dominion in the Romagna and Sixtus set out to satisfy his aspirations. He sought to win back control of lands in the Romagna and Umbria that traditionally belonged to the papacy but that had won their independence, though some of the princelings in them gave nominal obedience to the pope. Lorenzo de' Medici, who felt that Florence was threatened by the activities of the pope in states on its borders, secretly encouraged resistance to his ambitions. Girolamo, intriguing in the Romagna, plotted with Francesco Pazzi to assassinate Lorenzo, and his brother Giuliano as well. Giuliano was murdered (April 26, 1478), but Lorenzo escaped. Sixtus excommunicated Lorenzo and laid Florence under an interdict, ostensibly because an archbishop, implicated in the Pazzi Conspiracy, had been hanged and a young kinsman, Cardinal Raffaele Riario, had been taken into custody. He called upon his ally, Naples, to make war on Florence. The war ended (1480) after Lorenzo, taking his life in his hands, made a visit to Naples to put his case before King Ferrante. In the same year, the Turks invaded Italy and took Otranto. Sixtus was rapidly recalled to his duties as head of Christendom, called on the Italian states to unite in the face of the Turkish menace, received Lorenzo back into the Church, and lifted the interdict from Florence. He continued, however, to promote Girolamo, and made him count of Forlì and a captain general of the Church. In 1481 Otranto was retaken and Sixtus resumed his quarrels. At odds with Naples, he offered Ferrara, an independent state, to Venice in exchange for support against Naples. The two went to war against Ferrara, having agreed to partition it between them. But when, Venetian arms having prevailed, Venice refused to give up Ferrara to suit the pope's new strategy, Sixtus laid Venice under an interdict. At length, a peace was signed, a few days before Sixtus died, in which the interests of the pope and his Riario kinsmen were ignored. It was Sixtus who, by a bull of November 1, 1478, established the Inquisition in Spain, gave Ferdinand and Isabella the right to name the Inquisitors, and later proved powerless to curb their savagery against converted Jews and other excesses. By his nepotism Sixtus brought the papacy to the edge of disaster. The enormous amounts of money he spent on his wars, his relatives, on his building program, and as a patron of artists and humanists left the papal treasury in a condition of near-ruin. The practice of simony, to refill the papal coffers, increased at a rapid pace. His extravagance and nepotism were so flagrant that an attempt, unsuccessful, was made to call him before a council to give an accounting of his acts.

In his favor, it must be said that, except for the sack of the Colonna palace by the Orsini and Riario forces, Sixtus kept order in Rome. He was a generous patron of artists and humanists, and began to rebuild Rome on a vast scale. He built the churches of S. Maria della Pace (c1479) and S. Maria dell' Popolo (built between 1472 and 1477, and a museum of works of art). He built the Sistine Chapel in the Vatican (between 1473 and 1481) and called Botticelli, Perugino, Pinturicchio, Ghirlandaio, and other painters and sculptors to Rome to decorate it. He enlarged and rearranged the Vatican Library and opened it to scholars. (A painting in the Vatican by Melozzo da Forlì, *Inauguration of the Vatican Library*, shows Sixtus, his nephews, and the humanist and librarian, Platina.) Once noted as a scholar himself, he left a number of theological works. His tomb in the Basilica of St. Peter, by Antonio Pollaiuolo, is one of the great monuments of Renaissance art. He was succeeded by Innocent VIII.

Skanderbeg (skan′dėr-beg). See **Scanderbeg.**

Skelton (skel′tọn), **John.** English scholar and poet; b. c1460; d. at Westminster, London, June 21, 1529. He was a noted scholar, and tutor of Henry VIII. He was the author of *The Bowge of Court*, *Colin Clout*, a satire on the clergy, and others.

Sobrino (sō-brē′nō). In Lodovico Ariosto's *Orlando Furioso*, a Moorish king, ally of Agramante. After the first repulse of the Moors before the paladins of Charlemagne, he tries to persuade Agramante to make peace, or to decide the war by single combat. Eventually Agramante agrees to meet with Orlando in a duel to end the war. Sobrino wishes to be included in any such struggle, as does Gradasso. In the end the three pagans, Agramante, Gradasso, and Sobrino, meet the three Christian knights, Orlando, Oliviero, and Brandimarte. Sobrino is sorely wounded and is tended by Orlando. He is baptized and, the only one of the three pagans to survive the knightly duel, goes with the Christian knights to France.

Socini (sō-chē′nē), **Mariano.** Jurist; b. at Siena, 1401; d. there, 1467. He studied at Siena and Padua, and taught in the universities of both cities. In addition to canon law, in which he was most interested, he studied civil law and became outstanding in that field. He was also interested in the study of history, poetry, music, painting, and sculpture. His principal legal works are: *Consilia*, a four-volume work in which he was aided by his son Bartolomeo; *Tractatus de iudiciis*; *Tractatus de testibus*; and *Tractatus de oblationibus*, all published at Venice over 100 years after his death.

Socini, Mariano the Younger. Jurist; b. c1482; d. at Bologna, August 20, 1556. He was the grandson of Mariano Socini (1401–1467), and taught law at Pisa, Siena, Padua, and Bologna. A great practitioner as well as a theorist, he was highly regarded in his own time. He left commentaries on the *Digestum vetus* and on the Decretals.

Socinians (sọ-sin′i-ạnz). Followers of the doctrines of the Italian theologians Laelius Socinus and Faustus Socinus and their followers. The term Socinianism is in theological usage a general one, and includes a considerable variety of opinion. The Socinians believed that Christ was a man miraculously conceived and divinely endowed, and therefore entitled to honor and reverence, but not to divine worship; that the object of His death was to perfect and complete His example and to prepare the way for His resurrection, the necessary historical basis of Christianity; that baptism is a declarative rite merely, and the Lord's Supper merely commemorative; that divine grace is general and exerted through the means of grace, not special and personally efficacious; that the Holy Spirit is not a distinct person, but the divine energy; that the authority of Scripture is subordinate to that of the reason; that the soul is pure by nature, though contaminated by evil example and teaching from a very early age; and that salvation consists in accepting Christ's teaching and following His example. The Socinians thus occupy theologically a position midway between the Arians, who maintained the divinity of Jesus Christ, but denied that He is coequal with the Father, and the Humanitarians, who denied His supernatural character altogether.

Socinus (sọ-sī′nus), **Faustus.** [Latinized name of **Fausto Sozzini.**] Theologian; b. at Siena, December 5, 1539; d. near Krakow, Poland, March 4, 1604. He was the nephew of Laelius Socinus (1525–1562). He developed the anti-Trinitarian doctrine originated by his uncle into the system known as Socinianism. Socinus lived in Italy and Basel, visited (1578–1579) Transylvania, and resided in Poland after 1579. He developed his ideas on the Trinity and the place and interpretation of the Scriptures in *De Jesu Christo servatore* and *De auctoritate s. scripturae*.

Socinus, Laelius. [Latinized name of **Lelio Sozzini.**] Theologian; b. at Siena, January 29, 1525; d. at Zurich, Switzerland, May 14, 1562. He fled to Switzerland in 1544 to escape the Inquisition in Italy. Having been influenced by the writings of Luther, he was attracted to Calvin, at Geneva, and to still the latter's doubts concerning any differences of doctrine he might harbor, signed a confession of faith (1555). Socinus did not himself deny the Trinity, but the thoughts he expressed on it gave rise to the anti-Trinitarianism of his nephew, Faustus Socinus, and led to the development of Socinianism.

Soderini (sō-dā-rē′nē). Distinguished Florentine family, of which the founder seems to have been Soderino di Bonsignore, who was already dead by 1268. Members of the family played a prominent role in Florentine affairs, serving thirty-four times as prior and sixteen as gonfaloniere. Ruggero Soderini, son of Soderino di Bonsignore, fought in the battle of Montaperti (1260) and died in 1294. Soderino's grandson Stefano had several children. Of these, Ruggero and Guccio became the founders of two principal branches of the family. Ruggero's son Niccolò (d. 1382) was a follower and friend of St. Catherine of Siena. Luigi (b. 1476), a descendant of Niccolò, was a supporter of Francesco Carducci, and was a member of an embassy sent from Florence in 1529 to Pope Clement VII to plead for Florentine liberty; he was beheaded (November 23, 1530) when the city, after a glorious defense, fell to the papal and imperial forces. In the other branch, Guccio's son Niccolò (1401–1474), at first a Medici supporter, later conspired with Luca Pitti and was banished. A second son of Guccio was Tommaso (1403–1485), the friend and confidant of Lorenzo de' Medici. Tommaso's son Francesco (1453–1524), a cardinal and bishop, was an enemy of Pope Leo X but became reconciled with Clement VII. A second son, Paolantonio (1448–1449) was a follower of Savonarola; he died fighting at Pisa. A third son was Piero, who in 1502 became, in the newly formed popular government, gonfaloniere for life. Of his two other sons, Giovanvettorio (1460–1527) was a professor of civil law. Giovanvettorio's grandson of the same name (1526–1597), though a republican at heart, served the Medici dukes. He left an important work on agriculture, and also wrote on Duke Francesco I de' Medici and his mistress (later wife) Bianca Capello. For this he was sentenced to death, a sentence commuted to exile.

Soderini, Francesco. Bishop and cardinal; b. 1453; d. 1524. He was a member of an ancient and eminent Florentine family, and was the brother of Piero di Tommaso Soderini (1452–1522). Unfriendly to the Medici party, he was prominent in Florentine affairs and served on missions to Charles VIII for the republic when that monarch descended into Italy in 1495.

Soderini, Paolantonio. Florentine statesman and democrat; b. 1448; d. 1499. Member of an ancient and prominent Florentine family, he was the brother of Piero di Tommaso Soderini (1452–1522) and of Francesco Soderini (1453–1524). He had been somewhat critical of what he considered tyrannical acts of Lorenzo the Magnificent, and on the succession to power of the latter's son Piero the Younger, had tried to persuade Piero to modify the government in favor of more liberty to the people. The results of his effort were easily predictable: Piero kept him at a distance thereafter. It was perhaps for this reason that Paolantonio turned to Savonarola. Guicciardini, who called him a "wise and highly respected statesman," records (in his *History of Italy*) a speech he is supposed to have made in support of a popular government after the exile of the Medici (1494). In the government he advocated the distribution of offices and the voting of new laws would depend on universal consent. He served in the popular government that was established and was killed in the war to regain control of Pisa.

Soderini, Piero di Tommaso. Florentine statesman; b. at Florence, May 18, 1452; d. at Rome, June 13, 1522. He had served as prior under Lorenzo the Magnificent, and served his successor, Piero the Younger, as ambassador to Charles VIII of France (1493). (Guicciardini writes, in his *History of Florence*, that Piero favored Piero di Tommaso in order to annoy the latter's elder brother Paolantonio.) On the fall of the Medici (1494), Piero di Tommaso helped to reform the government, and was named gonfaloniere for life in 1502. An honest man and a good administrator, he reorganized the public finances, reformed the judiciary, suppressed the magistracies of podesta and captain of the people, and supported the plan of the secretary of the chancellery, Niccolò Machiavelli, to organize a citizen militia. But events moved too fast for his rather weak character. Louis XII of France persuaded him to a course that offended Pope Julius II. As a result the warrior pope was reconciled with the Medici and sent his vicar against Florence. Prato fell, and Soderini fled, ultimately to Rome, where he died.

Sodoma (sō′dō-mä). [Original name, **Giovanni Antonio Bazzi.**] Painter; b. at Vercelli, 1477; d. at Siena, 1549. He was a pupil (1490–1497) of Giovanni Spanzotti (c1450–1526/28) and was trained in the Lombard-Piedmontese tradition, but was most strongly influenced by Leonardo da Vinci. The influences of such other painters as Bergognone and Fra Bartolommeo may also be observed in his work. From 1501 he was at Siena, where he worked most of his life, painting for churches and public buildings in the city and its environs. Of 1503 is a series of frescoes in S. Anna in Camprena, near Pienza, and between 1505 and 1508 he worked in the monastery of Monteoliveto Maggiore, completing the frescoes on the life of St. Benedict begun there by Signorelli. The influence of Signorelli led to a broadened treatment of form and composition. In 1508 and again in 1513 he journeyed to Rome, where he fell under the influence of Raphael. Of his work at Rome some ceiling paintings in the *Stanza della Segnatura* in the Vatican remain (other frescoes he painted there were destroyed to make way for Raphael's painting), as well as decorations on the life of Alexander the Great in the Farnesina, painted in 1513. Of these, *The Marriage of Roxana and Alexander* is notable. Other notable works include the frescoes in the Oratorio of S. Bernardino and in S. Domenico, Siena. In the latter church his paintings on the life of St. Catherine show his characteristic type of languid feminine beauty. *The Swooning of St. Catherine* there has been much praised for its affecting portrayal of the event. The fact that the event took place in this very church and that the whole area is pervaded by the strong and winning personality of the saint lends great poignancy to the painting. In his best work, Sodoma attained freshness, delicacy of tone, and breadth of treatment, and seems to have been inspired by a spirituality that in lesser works verges on sentimentality. His characteristic bluish shadows are his interpretation of Leonardo da Vinci's sfumato. He left a large number of works of varying quality. Among them are an early tondo, *Love and Chastity*, Louvre, *Judith* and *Deposition from the Cross*, Pinacoteca, Siena (where there are a large number of his paintings), *Adoration of the Magi*, S. Agostino, Siena, *Lucrezia*, Hannover, *Madonna and Saints*, Sabauda Gallery, Turin, and a standard with *St. Sebastian*, Pitti Palace, Florence. Most of his works are at Siena: in the Pinacoteca, Palazzo Pubblico, several churches besides those mentioned, and in public buildings. Other paintings are at Bergamo, Florence (Uffizi, Pitti), Grosseto, Lucca, Milan (Brera, Ambrosiana, Castello Sforzesco, Poldi Pezzoli), Montalcino, Montepulciano, Naples, Pisa, Rome (National and Borghese galleries, S. Maria Maggiore and S. Maria dell' Orto), S. Gimignano, Vercelli, Hamburg, London, Munich, Strasbourg, Vienna, Baltimore (Walters Art Gallery), Detroit, Philadelphia (Johnson Collection), Portland (Oregon), Princeton, Sarasota (Florida), Washington, Worcester (Massachusetts), and elsewhere.

Sofonisba (sō-fō-nēz′bä). Tragedy by Trissino, presented in 1556. It is based on an episode in the Punic Wars and, perhaps because Trissino tried to hew too closely to what he thought were Aristotle's rules but more probably because he had no poetic or dramatic genius, it is a lifeless, rhetorical exercise. Nevertheless, it is among the first regular Italian tragedies.

Sofronia (sō-frō′nyä). In Torquato Tasso's *Gerusalemme liberata*, a beautiful Christian maiden in Jerusalem. The pagan tyrant of Jerusalem, advised by his sorcerer Ismeno, steals the image of the Virgin from the Christian temple, because it is supposed to be a source of strength to the Crusaders who are approaching Jerusalem. He places it in the mosque. The next day the image has disappeared without trace. Aladine, the pagan king, having failed to find the Christian who had taken the image from the mosque, resolves to massacre all the Christians. Sofronia, to save her fellow worshipers, goes to the king and asserts that she alone stole the image, which she burned, and she alone must have the honor of the punishment. She is tied to the stake awaiting her fate when Olindo, who has long silently loved her, arrives. He claims that it was he who stole the image, not this foolish girl. Since both have confessed the king decrees that both shall burn. They are tied back to back and the fire is lighted. Olindo mourns that they are to be united only in death. As the flames crackle nearer, the Amazon warrior Clorinda rides up. She learns why the young couple are being burned and orders the fire put out. Mohamet himself, she states, has removed the image that was defiling his mosque. She offers her services to Aladine, which she assures him will be of far more value than a Christian image. Sofronia, moved at last to love for Olindo by his willingness to die for or with her, unites her love to his.

Sogliani (sō-lyä′nē), **Giovannantonio.** Painter; b. at Florence, 1492; d. there, c1544. He was a pupil of Lorenzo di Credi, and was also strongly influenced by Fra Bartolommeo, Albertinelli, and Andrea del Sarto. He painted at Florence and Pisa, sometimes collaborated with or finished pictures begun by Lorenzo di Credi, or used his, and others', designs. Of somewhat indifferent endowment, he left a number of paintings in pleasing color in collections and churches at Florence, as *St. Arcadius and Saints* (1511), S. Lorenzo, *Annunciation*, Ospedale degli Innocenti, and a fresco, *St. Dominic Fed by Angels*, San Marco Museum. Perhaps from Andrea del Sarto he learned to fuse tones to achieve modeling. In one of his best works, *Christ Washing the Feet of the Apostles*, S. Maria, Anghiari, he achieved a certain amount of drama in his use of light playing about the elongated, emaciated head of Christ. Other examples of his work are at Modena, Palermo, Pisa (where there are several paintings in the cathedral), Prato, Rome (Capitoline), Turin, Volterra, Berlin, Brussels, Chantilly, London, Nancy, Baltimore (Walters Art Gallery), New Haven, and elsewhere.

Solario (sō-lä′ryō), **Andrea.** Milanese painter; b. c1460; d. 1524. He was the brother of the sculptor Cristoforo Solario (active 1489–1520), whose pupil he may have been. In any case he received his early training in Milan in an artistic atmosphere that had been transformed by the presence of Leonardo da Vinci. As the result of a prolonged sojourn in Venice he was influenced by such Venetians as Alvise Vivarini, Antonello da Messina, and Giovanni Bellini. He spent some time in Normandy (1508–1510) and perhaps from this, or from some other contact, was somewhat influenced by Flemish painters. He frequently made several versions of the same painting, as the signed *Salome with the Head of John the Baptist*, the Met-

Giovannantonio Sogliani
Madonna and Child
Gabinetto Disegni e Stampe degli Uffizi
Foto Soprintendenza

ropolitan Museum, New York, other versions of which are at Turin and in the collection of the duke of Northumberland, Syon House, Middlesex, England, and *Ecce Homo*, Johnson Collection, Philadelphia, other versions of which are at Dijon and Leipzig. His earliest signed and dated (1495) painting is *Madonna and Child between Two Saints*, Brera. Other works include a signed and dated (1515) *Flight into Egypt*, Poldi Pezzoli Museum, *Portrait of Chancellor Morone*, Gallerati Scotti Collection, Milan, *Madonna of the Green Cushion*, Louvre, and paintings at Bergamo, Brescia, Pavia, Rome (National Gallery, Borghese), Dublin, London, Nantes, Paris, Vienna, Boston, Columbia (South Carolina), Greenville (South Carolina), Washington, Worcester (Massachusetts), and elsewhere.

Solario, Antonio. [Called **lo Zingaro**, "the Gipsy."] Venetian painter; active c1495–c1515. He was influenced by his Venetian contemporaries Alvise Vivarini, the Bellini (the types of his Madonnas are strongly reminiscent of Giovanni Bellini), and Carpaccio, and was influenced as well by the Lombards and Umbrians. He worked in Naples, in the Marches (1502–1514) and at Milan. Among his works are frescoes (1495) on the life of St. Benedict in the Cloister of SS. Severino e Sosio at Naples, and paintings, many signed, at Fermo (S. Maria del Carmine), Macerata (SS. Trinità), Milan (Ambrosiana, Castello Sforzesco), Osimo (S. Giuseppe da Copertino), Rome (Doria Pamphili Gallery), Vicenza, Berlin, Bristol, Budapest, Copenhagen, London, Baltimore (Walters Art Gallary), Omaha, Princeton, and elsewhere.

Solario, Cristoforo. Lombard sculptor; active between 1489 and 1520. In 1489 he was working on an altar (since destroyed) at Venice. Soon afterward he was in Lombardy and became official sculptor of Ludovico il Moro (1495). Following the sudden death (1497) of Beatrice d'Este, Ludovico's wife, he was commissioned to make her tomb. Of the tomb, originally in S. Maria delle Grazie at Milan, the effigies of Beatrice and Ludovico are now in the Certosa di Pavia. He worked on the Cathedral of Milan (1501–1503) and became overseer of the works (1506). Among his works for the cathedral are figures of *Adam* and *Eve* and a *Christ at the Column*. As an architect he worked on S. Maria presso S. Celso at Milan and designed (1513) the apse of the cathedral at Como. He achieved a considerable reputation and was employed by the duke of Ferrara and by Isabella d'Este. Vasari writes that when Michelangelo's *Pietà* was first exhibited at Rome, a group of Lombards who were admiring it credited the work to their fellow countryman Cristoforo Solari. Michelangelo overheard them, and that night went into the chapel and carved his name on the ribbon across the Virgin's bosom. This is his only signed work.

Soliman (sol'i-ma̤n). See **Suleiman.**

Solís (sō-lēs'), **Juan Diaz de.** Spanish navigator; b. at Lebrija, Andalusia, Spain, c1470; killed on the bank of the Río de la Plata, Argentina, 1516. He was associated with Yanez Pinzón in exploring the coasts of Honduras and Yucatan. On a later expedition he sailed along the coast of South America. On a voyage to seek a southwestern route to the Pacific he entered the Río de la Plata and explored it for a distance.

Solyman (sol'i-ma̤n). See **Suleiman.**

Sommariva (sōm-mä-rē'vä), **Giorgio.** Man of letters, versifier, and public official; d. after 1497. Of an ancient Veronese family, he studied law, practiced for a time, then held various civic positions at Verona and served Venice (1488) as governor of Gradisca. He is remembered for the poetic correspondence he carried on with other humanists, for his love poems, including some Petrarchan sonnets to various ladies who won his love in his youth, and for his poetic renderings in the vernacular of some of the ancient writings. The last include translations of Homer's *Batracomyomachia* and Juvenal's *Satires* in terza rima. He also published *Sonetti villaneschi*, sonnets in the dialects of Verona and Bergamo, which are early examples of a cultivated writer who chose the cruder speech for poetic expression. He also wrote the lives of some saints; a series against Charles VIII; on events in the kingdom of Naples from 537 to 1495; a work on Latin and vernacular poetry; a work on the Gallic Sickness (syphilis), in which he describes the symptoms and suggests mercury as a cure; and a little chronicle in verse covering the period of Veronese history from 1260 to 1478, an autograph copy of which is at Verona.

Soranzo (sō-ränt′tsō). Ancient patrician family of Venice, known in Venice from the 12th century, and by the 14th century already named among the twenty-four ancient families of the Venetian nobility. From earliest times they engaged in commerce, and from 1400 also engaged in banking. Members of the family served the republic of Venice as procurators, magistrates, ambassadors, and captains. The family produced one doge, Giovanni (1312–1328), and a number of prelates.

Sordello (sôr-del′lō). Provençal troubadour; b. at Goito, near Mantua, c1200?; d. c1270? A varied, lively, and virile lyricist, who practiced his art at various courts of Italy and Provence, excelled in the poetry of love, bringing to it traces of real sentiment as opposed to the conventional courtly love poetry, and died in the service of Charles of Anjou. His *planh*, a lament for his patron and a criticism of other princes is an outstanding poem. He was the most famous of the Italian troubadours. Dante, who thought of him as a patriot and reformer, immortalized him in the *Divina Commedia*. He calls him a "noble spirit," "proud and self-contained." About forty of his lyrics are extant.

Sorel (so-rel), **Agnès.** Favorite mistress of Charles VII of France; b. at Fromenteau, in Touraine, France, c1409; d. near Jumigny, France, February 9, 1450. She was the first officially acknowledged king's mistress in France. Her position won her many enemies, including the dauphin who later became Louis XI. She was brought up with Isabelle, the wife of René d'Anjou, and remained her friend through life. According to the usual story, Charles, who first saw her when she was about 20 years old, was captivated by her beauty and wit and remained faithful to her till her death. Unlike some of the mistresses of later kings, whose influence can only be characterized as vicious, she utilized her power in a fashion that was generally beneficial to the realm.

Soriano (sō-ryä′nō), **Francesco.** [Also, **Suriano, Surianus, Suriani.**] Composer and singer; b. at Rome, 1549; d. there, January, 1620. Among his works are motets, madrigals, masses, psalms, and canons.

Sousa (sō′zạ), **Martim Affonso de.** Portuguese captain; b. at Bragança, Portugal, c1500; d. at Lisbon, July 21, 1564. He commanded the first colonizing expedition sent to Brazil (1530–1533), and founded the first Portuguese settlement at São Vicente. He was admiral of the seas of India, and governor of the Portuguese East Indies. He was a brother of Pero Lopes de Sousa.

Sousa, Pero Lopes de. Portuguese captain; b. c1503; d. on the coast of Madagascar, about December, 1539. He received in hereditary right three portions of Brazil, in which he attempted settlements through two lieutenants. He wrote an account of his travels.

Sousa, Thomé de. Portuguese administrator; b. c1510; d. after 1563. He was first governor general of Brazil, and founder of São Salvador (1549).

Spada (spä′dä), **lo** or **Spado** (spä′dō), **Dalla.** See **Marescalco, Pietro.**

Spagna (spä′nyä), **lo.** [Real name, **Giovanni di Pietro.**] Painter; b. c1450, probably in Spain (whence his name); d. at Spoleto, 1528. He was at Perugia for a number of years (1470–1504), where he was a pupil of Perugino, whose style he adapted to his own. The influence of Perugino appears in such works as a *Nativity*, Berlin, and another in the Vatican. Later he was influenced by Raphael, as appears in frescoes at Trevi (1512) and Spoleto (1513–1516). Surviving paintings by Lo Spagna are at Assisi (S. Francesco Museum), Florence (Pitti), Gavelli, Milan (Poldi Pezzoli), Narni, Perugia, Spoleto (Pinacoteca, S. Ansano), Terni, Trevi, Caen (*Marriage of the Virgin*, with Perugino), London, Paris, Vienna, Baltimore (Walters Art Gallery), Berkeley (California), Chicago, Detroit, Indianapolis, Philadelphia (Johnson Collection), San Diego (California), Tucson (Arizona), and elsewhere.

Spagnoli (spä-nyō′lē), **Giovan Battista.** [Called **Battista Mantovano.**] Poet and cleric; b. at Mantua, 1448; d. 1516. He studied at Padua and other cities and then entered the order of the Discalced Carmelites. Noted for his piety, he rose through the ranks of the order and became its general (1513). He left many works, in prose and verse, and nearly all in Latin. Notable among these are ten eclogues, in the Vergilian manner but stamped with the poet's own personality and talent. They treat of the injuries love deals to men, religious and moral topics, and the corruption of the Church. He also wrote courtly poetry. His *Parthenicae* is a collection of songs dedicated to the Virgin and saints. In his *De calamitatibus temporum* he treats of the seven monsters (the seven deadly sins) of his time and roundly censures the humanists by classing them with the monster Pride. His *Opus aureum in Thomistas* criticizes the theology of St. Thomas Aquinas. Spagnoli was beatified in 1885.

Spandrel (span′drel). In architecture, the space, roughly triangular, formed by the outer curve of half an arch, and the right triangle that encloses it. Also, the roughly triangular space formed by the outer curves of two adjoining arches and the horizontal line or string course above them. Such spaces were often adorned with sculpture or painting. The spandrels in the loggia of the Ospedale dei Innocenti at Florence are decorated with the famous terra-cotta *bambini* of Andrea della Robbia.

Spencer (spen′sėr), **Henry le.** See **Despenser, Henry le.**

Sperandio (spā-rän′dyō). Medalist and sculptor; b. at Mantua, c1425; d. c1495. He worked at Ferrara and Mantua. At Ferrara he was the chief medalist for the Estensi, and designed medals of the princes of the family, poets, humanists, courtiers, men of letters, and others. He also executed sculptures in low relief, as a marble bust of Leonora of Aragon and a bust of Ercole I d'Este (now in the Louvre). From 1460 to 1477 he was mostly at Mantua, with stays at Faenza, as in 1476 and 1477, where he made a terracotta *Annunciation* in low relief in the cathedral, and visits to Ferrara. At Bologna he made the tomb of Alexander V and a *Madonna* (now at Berlin). Among the medals of the princes of his day are those of Federico da Montefeltro of Urbino, Niccolò da Correggio, Giovanni Bentivoglio II of Bologna and his wife, Francesco Sforza of Milan, and a noble portrait of Cardinal Francesco Gonzaga.

Speroni (spā-rō′nē), **Sperone.** Humanist and critic; b. at Padua, 1500; d. 1588. He studied under Pomponazzi at Bologna and later held the chair of logic in that city. Noted for his learning, he was famous in Italy and beyond the Alps, the friend of princes and prelates, honored alike by men of letters and rulers. He wrote lyrics that betray the utmost care for style and literary language but no particular poetic inspiration, and discourses on the *Divina Commedia*, *Orlando Furioso*, and the *Aeneid*. His dialogues were on such subjects as love, women, language, and rhetoric. In the last he goes into great detail in analyzing the perfection of his own style, which he claimed to have achieved by an almost microscopic study of Petrarch and Boccaccio and a meticulous compilation of the vocabularies used by those men of genius. His tragedy, *Canace*, is on the mythological subject of the incestuous love of the children of Aeolus. The work is rigidly modeled on Seneca but instead of encompassing the "pity and terror" recommended by Aristotle it mounts to meaningless horror.

Spinelli (spē-nel′lē), **Parri.** See **Parri Spinelli.**

Spinello Aretino (spē-nel′lō ä-rā-tē′nō). [**Spinello di Luca Spinelli,** called **Spinello Aretino.**] Tuscan painter; b. at Arezzo, c1347; d. there, March, 1410. Vasari, a fellow-townsman, praises him highly; Spinelli's Virgins, he says, "breathe a kind of divinity that invites mankind to veneration." Later critics have been less fulsome in their praise: they decry the hardness of outline in some of his frescoes, the tendency he indulged of running several events together in one large scene thereby betraying a lack of narrative sense, his archaic renderings of backgrounds and architectural details, and his lack of a feeling for composition. He was, however, a gifted artist of the Giottesque tradition, deeply influenced by Andrea Orcagna in the vigor and solidity of his forms, in his effective rendering of mass, and in the strength and movement that infuse his paintings. His work, characterized in his later years by softer, warm colors, has purpose and spirit; decorative details for their own sake, arabesques, and Gothic landscapes are absent in the work of this purely Tuscan painter. Again according to Vasari, he was a prodigious, and much sought after worker, and possessed of great speed in execution. The many works known to be from his hand corroborate this view. Most of his frescoes have suffered damage with the passage of time, some are lost. Of his remaining works there is an altarpiece, made (1385) for Monte Oliveto. The polyptych has been broken up. Parts of it are in the Fogg Art Museum, Cambridge, Massachusetts, others are at Budapest and Siena. About 1387 he frescoed a series of fourteen scenes from the life of St. Benedict in the sacristy of the Church of S. Miniato al Monte at Florence; these have been repainted. About the same year he decorated the Oratory of S. Caterina at Antella with scenes from the saint's legend. The design, modeling, and spirit of these frescoes place them among his finest works. In 1391 he went to Pisa to fresco the walls of the Camposanto. He executed scenes from the legends of S. Efiso and S. Potito. Of these, the three lower scenes on S. Potito had long since been lost, and the rest were in poor condition. A bomb that fell on the Camposanto in July, 1944, caused a great fire and the remaining frescoes fell in fragments. These have been collected and bonded to canvas. The best preserved of his frescoes are those he executed in the Palazzo Pubblico at Siena (begun 1408) with the assistance of his son Parri. There are sixteen scenes on the war of the Sienese Pope Alexander III against Frederick Barbarossa. Completed in great haste, the scenes are of uneven quality. Many of them are handsome, well-designed, of lovely color, and full of vigor and movement expressed with poetic feeling and dignity. They are purely Tuscan in inspiration, with the Sienese influence appearing in the soft colors. For those who enjoy the touching archaism in Florentine painting before it burst from Giotto's chrysalis into the finished product of the Renaissance, Spinello Aretino has great charm. There are remains of many frescoes in Arezzo, the native town to which he returned often, as in the churches of S. Agostino, SS. Annunziata, S. Bernardo, S. Domenico, S. Maria Maddalena, and S. Maria della Pieve, and in the museum. Other frescoes are at Cortona (S. Francesco) and Florence (S. Croce, S. Maria Novella). After the terrible flood of November, 1966, the frescoes painted by Lorenzo Monaco in S. Trinità at Florence were covered with a green mold as the result of dampness seeping in from the back. The frescoes were removed for cleaning. Under them was discovered a series of frescoes by Spinello Aretino, and under those the *sinopie* that he had sketched for guidance in painting the frescoes. The frescoes and *sinopie* of Spinello Aretino are now to be seen in the adjoining chapel in S. Trinità, Lorenzo Monaco's frescoes having been cleaned and restored to their original place. Other paintings by Spinello are at Città di Castello, Florence (Accademia), Montepulciano, Parma, Rome (Vatican), Altenburg, Copenhagen, Enschede, Oxford (Christ Church Library), Chicago, New York (the Metropolitan Museum, Morgan Library), St. Louis, Missouri, and elsewhere.

Spiritata (spē-rē-tä′tä). Comedy by Anton Francesco Grazzini, who was among the first to attempt a modern Italian comedy.

Squarcione (skwär-chô′nā), **Francesco.** Painting contractor; b. at Padua, 1397; d. there, after May 21, 1468. He is mentioned as a painter for the first time in 1429; earlier (1423) he had been referred to as a tailor. A mediocre painter himself, he had a workshop at Padua in which, employing pupils and assistants, he undertook to fill commissions. Pupils and apprentices signed contracts to work for him for specified periods; on occasion he adopted the more promising of them as his sons and exploited their talents; the most distinguished of such adopted sons was Andrea Mantegna. Padua in Squarcione's day was a center of humanistic ferment. He was himself an enthusiast for the antique and was a collector, and perhaps dealer, in coins, medals, antique fragments, and reliefs. He had as well a collection of drawings and designs, and instilled an interest in the antique in his pupils by compelling them to copy objects from his collection and his designs. Over 130 works have been ascribed to his workshop but only 2 are with certainty ascribed to Squarcione himself, 1 in the Museo Civico at Padua and the other at Berlin. He was highly thought of at Padua and was frequently asked to give his opinion as an expert in disputes or in estimating the value of paintings. He has been regarded on the one hand as a shrewd entrepreneur who derived great financial advantage from his "adopted sons," and on the other as the founder of a school of painting that produced such masters as Mantegna, Zoppo, and a number of lesser painters. Although his best pupils, notably Mantegna and Zoppo, took to the courts to free themselves from him, the fact remains that they were trained in his workshop and that the influence of it was lasting for a generation of Paduan painters and their followers.

Squire's Tale, The. One of Chaucer's *Canterbury Tales*. Unfinished, it is the story of Canace and her magic ring, and is told by the squire "who left half told the story of Cambuscan bold." Cambuscan, the king of Tartary, was the father of Canace.

Stabili (stä′bē-lē), **Francesco.** See **Cecco d'Ascoli.**

Stampa (stäm′pä), **Gaspara.** Poetess; b. at Padua, between 1520 and 1525; d. at Venice, April 23, 1554. Her father, a jewel merchant, died when she was young. Gaspara and her brother and sister left Padua and went to Venice. There, through their gifts as singers and poets, they were launched on the swift current of highly cultivated, luxurious, and utterly dissolute Venetian society. Gaspara, poetess and singer, endowed with intellectual capacity and an ardent temperament, was sought after, courted, and lauded as one of the stars of the brilliant group of men of letters and artists assembled at Venice in her day. She fell deeply in love with Count Collaltino di Collalto, a nobleman of learning, a poet, and a warrior, and of a considerably higher social station than her own. This great love of her life brought her intense joy and, ultimately, pain and humiliation, for he abandoned her after three years. Her *Canzoniere* trace the course of her life at Venice and her love affair with a frankness that was startling. They indicate that she realized it was an unbridgeable chasm between their temperaments, and not the difference in social position, that made her union with Collalto impossible. She had other lovers, both before and after Collalto, and dedicated lyrics to them, but the depth of feeling and the anguish of her verses concerning Collalto are missing from these others. With her passion for life, it may be that, abandoned by Collalto, she sought from others a rekindling of the spark that to her was life. The passion and tragedy of her short life blazes through her poems. Her last poems, imploring Heaven to help her, are expressed with moving simplicity. Her lyrics are true cries from a tormented heart, and give her a place among the more remarkable women poets.

Stanze (stän′zā). In the middle of the 15th century Pope Nicholas V tore down part of the 13th-century palace of Nicholas III in the Vatican and had a new section constructed. Some of the new rooms were partially decorated by Piero della Francesca, Luca Signorelli, Bartolomeo della Gatta, Bramantino, and others. When Julius II became pope he decided to take the rooms on the top floor of the new section for his own apartment, since he could not bear to live in the apartment that had been inhabited by his predecessor, Alexander VI, and called on Perugino, Sodoma, Bramantino, and others to redecorate them. Soon after the arrival of Raphael at Rome Julius, with his gift for recognizing genius, ordered the decorations made up to that time removed and put Raphael in charge of the entire project. The four rooms, the *Stanze*, located consecutively, are the *Stanza dello Incendio*, named for one of the frescoes in it, the *Stanza della Segnatura*, so called because it was the seat of a Tribunal whose decrees were signed by the pope, and intended as Julius II's library, *Stanza di Eliodoro*, named for one of the frescoes, and the *Sala di Costantino*, celebrating events of the life of Constantine. Raphael began working (1509) in the *Stanza della Segnatura*. The program for the decoration, derived from theological and Neoplatonic principles, was drawn up, some say, by humanists at the papal court. Giovio said Julius himself devised it. The frescoes on the four walls represent Theology, Philosophy, Law, and the Arts (but not the figural arts). The shapes of the areas to be painted presented technical problems, since each of the large lunette-shaped areas is cut by an opening, small in the case of the larger panels and large in the case of the smaller ones. Raphael filled the space of the first great area he undertook with *The Dispute of the Sacrament* (properly, *The Exaltation of the Eucharist*). On a terraced dais in the lower center is an altar with a monstrance, the exact center of perspective of the entire wall. On either side of the altar are saints, theologians, and Doctors of the Church engaged in animated discussion. Raphael painted his contemporaries to represent some of these, including Julius as Gregory the Great, and represented figures from the more recent past, as Dante and Savonarola. Directly above the monstrance is the Dove of the Holy Spirit, and above that Christ sits between Mary and John the Baptist. On either side, resting on upcurving films of cloud, are the patriarchs and prophets of the Old Testament and the Apostles of the New. Rising from a semicircle of cherubs' heads that encloses the figures of Christ, Mary and St. John, is a half-figure of God and Father, with the incurving figures of three angels on each side. From the top of the lunette descend rays of dimly seen smaller angels. The entire surface is horizontally divided into a series of slight concave curves that ascend to the convex curve of the lunette. Above the fresco is the allegory of *Theology*. Opposite the *Disputa* is the famous *School of Athens*, with its figures of the thinkers of the ancient world represented against the architectural background of the interior of a great basilica, thought to have been patterned after Bramante's design for St. Peter's, but also showing elements from classical buildings at Rome, and decorated with painted medallions and statues. Among the philosophers represented are Plato and Aristotle, the central figures of the composition, and Zeno, Epicurus, Pythagoras, Diogenes, Euclid, Zoroaster, and others. Contemporaries whose features were given to the ancients included Leonardo (according to some) as Plato, Bramante as Euclid, and a self-portrait of Raphael. In tribute to Michelangelo, Raphael has represented him, in the costume of a contemporary mason, as Heraclitus, isolated in his greatness, in the foreground. The figure does not appear in the famous cartoon of the frescoe in the Ambrosiana, Milan, and was added later in graceful recognition and homage to the great artist, whose incomplete Sistine Ceiling had been exhibited in August, 1511, and had a profound influence on Raphael's work, as is clear from subsequent paintings. The fresco, completed in 1511, is by Raphael's own hand. Above it is the allegory of *Philosophy*. One of the two smaller walls, with a window cutting into the lower center, is devoted to the *Parnassus*, with the allegory of *Poetry* above it. Included among the poets represented are Homer, Vergil, Dante, Alcaeus, Sappho, and Petrarch, and others, some with the features of living poets. The last wall, cut by a large opening, is devoted to the *Cardinal and Theological Virtues* in a lunette above the opening. Of the Virtues, the head of *Prudence*, in the traditional manner, has two faces in back-to-back profile. That of a beautiful young woman looks to the left, that of a bearded old man, made wise by age and experience, looks to the right. Raphael has so painted the bearded man's face that one must look carefully to realize it is not the elaborate coiffure of the young woman's head. Panels on either side of the opening represent civil and theological law in *Tribonian Handing the Code to Justinian* and *Gregory IX Approving the Decretals*, in which the features of Gregory are those of Julius. Above is the allegory of *Justice*. The fresco was executed not earlier than 1511, as is indicated by the fact that Julius as Gregory is shown with a beard; it was late in 1510 that he vowed not to shave again until Italy was liberated from the foreigners. An additional interpretation of the decoration is that the four walls represent Truth, in its theological and philosophical aspects (*Dispute of the Sacrament* and *School of Athens*); Good, as exemplified in the virtues (*Cardinal and Theological Virtues*) and as promoted and protected by canonical and civil law (*Gregory IX Approving the Decretals* and *Tribonian Handing the Code to Justinian*); and Beauty, as expressed by Poetry (*Parnassus*). Of the four chambers of the apartment the *Stanza della Segnatura* is most completely by Raphael himself.

Perhaps in June, 1511, he began the decoration of the *Stanza di Eliodoro*. The theme of this chamber is an exaltation of the temporal and spiritual power of the papacy, and was undoubtedly chosen by Julius himself; his policy was to restore and exalt the power of the Church, to destroy those who attempted to weaken it, and to drive out "the barbarians." The subjects of the frescoes illustrate divine protection of the Church, as *The Expulsion of Heliodorus from the Temple*. According to the account in the Apochrypha, Heliodorus was sent by King Seleucus to rob and violate the temple of Jerusalem. The high priest's prayers were answered and Heliodorus was scourged by a celestial messenger on horseback and two angels. On the left of the painting, the pope, with the features of Julius, dressed in contemporary costume and borne in his gestatorial chair, watches the rout of Heliodorus, thrown to the ground by the rearing horse of the divine avenger. The reference is to traitors in the papal curia and to Julius' success against his enemies. The scene is one of power and upward spiraling movement, in strong contrast to the lyrical serenity of the scenes in the *Stanza della Segnatura*, and reflects the force and energy that he had seen in Michelangelo's Sistine Ceiling and the intensity and richness of color that he had observed in the painting of the Venetian Sebastiano del Piombo. Some of the fresco may have been executed by Raphael's assistants to his design, but the figure of the pope and his bearers and attendants is by Raphael himself. The fresco was severely damaged in the sack of Rome (1527) by the fires of Spanish troops who were billeted in the room. The space on the right of *The Expulsion of Heliodorus* is interrupted by an off-center opening that rises almost halfway up the painting area. In this space is *The Mass of Bolsena*, commemorating a miracle of 1263 when a priest, about to celebrate the Mass, was shaken by doubt as to the Presence in the host. Miraculously, the host shed drops of blood that formed a cross on the Corporal (Cloth). (The cathedral at Orvieto was built in honor of the miracle, the Corporal is preserved in a chapel there and is exhibited to the faithful once a year.) Raphael solved the problem of the opening by using the top of it as the floor of a dais on which rests an altar. On one side of the altar is the celebrant; kneeling on the other side is a prelate with the features of Julius—a marvelously intent portrait. Steps lead down from where Julius kneels, to fill the space at the side of the opening. Ecclesiastics kneel on them, and on the lowest level Raphael shows members of the Swiss Guard that Julius inaugurated. In the space on the other, narrower side of the opening, observers of the miracle register their astonishment, fear, or awe in agitated gestures. On the side of the doubting priest all is drama and movement; on the opposite side, where even the flames of the candles are still, is the calm of faith vindicated. The allusion is to the protection of the Faith. A third fresco, *The Deliverance of St. Peter*, is an illustration of St. Luke's narrative in the Acts of the Apostles. The titular church of Julius as a cardinal was S. Pietro in Vincoli, and he ever remained warmly attached to it. The fresco is remarkable for the assured treatment of light itself as a major artistic element. By the time of the fourth fresco, *The Meeting of Attila with St. Leo the Great*, Julius was dead and Leo X had succeeded him. The subject represents a meeting between Leo and Attila that took place near Mantua, but that Raphael transferred to Rome with views of its monuments. In the course of the meeting the Apostles Peter and Paul appeared in the sky over the unarmed pope and so terrified Attila that he turned back from his planned invasion of Rome. In reference to the Battle of Ravenna (1512) in which he had been present, the face of Leo the Great is a portrait of Leo X. Much of the fresco, completed after 1514, was executed by Raphael's pupil and assistant Giulio Romano. The episodes in the *Stanza dello Incendio* concern events connected with the lives of Pope Leo III and Pope Leo IV, in obvious celebration of Leo X. *The Fire in the Borgo* (the Vatican quarter) memorializes a dangerous fire that Leo IV extinguished (847) with the sign of the Cross. The fresco was executed, to Raphael's design, largely by assistants. The same is true of all the decoration in this room. *The Battle of Ostia* commemorates a victory of Leo IV's troops over the Saracens in 849. On the shore of the port where the battle is being won Leo IV (a portrait of Leo X) sits on his throne to receive prisoners. Behind him are Cardinal Bibbiena, Leo's intimate, and Cardinal Giulio de' Medici, his cousin and the future pope Clement VII. With the remaining frescoes in the room, *The Coronation of Charlemagne* and *The Oath of Leo III*, Raphael had little or no connection. He is thought to have provided some of the designs for the second but to have contributed nothing to the first. The *Sala di Costantino* was completed several years after his death and at most has one or two figures and a few sketches of details from his hand. The differences in artistic merit of the rooms painted by Raphael and those painted by his assistants are obvious.

Stanze per la Giostra (per lä jôs′trä). Incomplete poem in Italian by Poliziano, written to celebrate Guiliano de' Medici and the tournament he gave (1475) in honor of his love, Simonetta Vespucci. Some of Poliziano's loveliest lyrics appear in this work, left incomplete following the assassination (1478) of Giuliano in the Pazzi conspiracy.

Starnina (stär-nē′nä), **Gherardo.** Florentine painter; b. (according to Vasari) 1354; d. 1413. He was a pupil of Antonio Veneziano and a follower and fellow worker of Agnolo Gaddi. His name was inscribed on the rolls of the Company of St. Luke in 1387. About 1398 he fled to Spain, where he worked at Valencia and Toledo until 1402, after which he returned to Florence. Vasari asserted that his paintings, most of which have been lost, showed the influence of his Spanish travels in a tinge of exoticism. Of the works that remain, and which indicate that his work was still in the Gothic tradition, there is a triptych, *Madonna and Child, with Saints,* Perugia; *The Thebaid,* Uffizi, Florence; fragments of frescoes on events in the life of St. Jerome, Church of the Carmine, Florence; and a series of frescoes in the Castellani Chapel, Church of Santa Croce, Florence, on events in the lives of St. John the Baptist, St. Nicholas of Bari, and St. Anthony, among others. Concerning the last-named frescoes, Starnina was an assistant of Agnolo Gaddi.

States of the Church. See **Patrimony of St. Peter.**

Stefani (stā′fä-nē), **Marchionne di Coppo.** Florentine statesman, diplomat, and chronicler; b. at Florence, 1336; d. there, August, 1385. He wrote a chronicle of Florence, *Cronaca fiorentina,* from the dawn of time to 1385. He drew on earlier chroniclers, notably Villani, for the early periods. His work is most valuable for the period of his own time (1348–1385), as he held office in Florence (among others, prior, 1379) and wrote of events as he observed them from his central position. Of particular interest is his account of the revolt of the *Ciompi* (1378).

Stefano Fiorentino (stā′fä-nō fyō-ren-tē′nō). Florentine painter; supposed to have been a younger contemporary and perhaps pupil of Giotto, he was called one of the most important painters of Florence of the generation after Giotto by the poet and writer Franco Sacchetti, and was praised by Villani and Ghiberti. Works surviving of the period of about 1330 to the mid-century have never so far been definitively assigned, and the painting personalities of Maso di Banco, Giottino, and Stefano Fiorentino as three individual painters who may have executed them have not yet been reconstructed. Some modern scholars attribute a *Madonna Enthroned Between Two Angels,* Vatican, formerly attributed to Pietro Lorenzetti, a *Crucifixion,* New York, frescoes at Assisi, and others, to Stefano.

Stefano da San Genesio (dä sän je-nā′syō). See **Folchetti, Stefano.**

Stefano da Venezia (dä vā-nā′tsyä). Venetian painter; active 1369–1385. His earlier work is characterized by the Byzantine stylization of Paolo Veneziano. Later he was influenced, especially in his coloring, by Lorenzo Veneziano, and his style was close to Jacobello di Bonomo and Giovanni da Bologna. The more delicate and subtle coloring of Lorenzo Veneziano is evident in his *Coronation of the Virgin* (1381), Accademia, Venice. Other works include *Virgin with Two Saints* (1385), S. Zaccaria, Venice, with the vibrant color of the Gothic manner, and *Madonna Enthroned* (1369), Correr Museum, Venice.

Stefano da Verona (dä vā-rō′nä). [Also called **Stefano da Zevio.**] Veronese painter; b. before 1375. Vasari, who praised him especially for his work in fresco, mentions many examples from his hand, many of which are now lost. Vasari also calls attention to the representations of peacocks that Stefano loved to paint and that serve as a kind of hallmark. The grace and elegance, and the meticulous detail required in portraying that bird, must have satisfied some artistic need. Several of his backgrounds may be thought of as adaptations of the peacock's tail. His most important extant work is an *Adoration of the Magi,* signed and dated (1435), now in the Brera at Milan. It is notable for its advance towards realism and for the highly decorative detail that characterizes this primitive Veronese painter. Another fine example is a *Madonna of the Rose Garden,* in the Colonna Gallery at Rome. There is another on the same subject at Verona and another in the Worcester Art Museum; all are notable for their exquisite delicacy and elegance. Stefano is the most characteristic painter of the North Italian school in the international Gothic style, and had wide influence in the area. His graceful, slightly elongated figures, his love for genre detail, his gay colors, and his tendency towards realistic touches mark his work with his own artistic personality. A number of detached frescoes are at Verona (S. Eufemia, S. Fermo Maggiore, museum); others are at Illasi (Parish Church) and Mantua (S. Francesco).

Steinhöwel (shtīn′hė-vel), **Heinrich.** German humanist; b. at Weil, Germany, 1412; d. at Ulm, 1482. He studied at Vienna and Padua. He was a practicing physician at Ulm, and translator of Latin works that played an important part in the development of High German prose literature. His translations include the novel *Apollonius von Tyrus* (1461); *Griseldis* (1471), after Petrarch's Latin version of Boccaccio's story; and a collection of fables published (1477) in Latin and German under the title of *Esop.* He also translated Boccaccio's *De mulieribus claris* and Rodríguez de Zamora's *Speculum vitae hu-*

Stefano da Verona
A Seated Prophet in Profile
The British Museum, London

manae. His original treatise *Regimen sanitatis* (1472) is a handbook of plague hygiene.

Sternhold (stėrn′hōld), **Thomas.** English writer; b. near Blakeney, Gloucestershire, England, c1500; d. August, 1549. He was joint author with John Hopkins of a metrical version of the Psalms (c1547).

Steuco (stā-ö′kō), **Agostino.** [Latinized **Steuchus Eugubinus.**] Ecclesiastic and man of letters; b. at Gubbio, 1497 or 1498; d. at

Venice, March, 1548. In 1513 he entered the regular canons, at which time he changed his original name of Guido to Agostino. A noted student, he was called to Venice to preside over the rich library given by Cardinal Domenico Grimani. He was also at Reggio, again at Gubbio, and finally at Rome where (1538) Pope Paul III made him titular bishop of a see in Crete, and put him in charge of the Vatican Library. He was on his way to the Council of Trent when he died. He had a good knowledge of Hebrew, and left many works on religious and Biblical subjects. His *De perenni philosophia libri X* (Lyons, 1540), traces the steady growth of philosophical thought from the ancients to the Scholastics. His collected works were published at Paris, 1577–1578.

Stewart or **Stuart** (stū′ạrt), Lord **James.** [Title, Earl of **Moray;** called **the Good Regent.**] Regent of Scotland; b. c1531; killed, January 21, 1570. Although an adherent of John Knox he became a chief adviser to his half sister, Mary, Queen of Scots, on her accession. He opposed the Darnley marriage, and was implicated in Darnley's murder, but became, after Mary's abdication, regent for her son.

Stewart or **Stuart, James.** [Title, 2nd Earl of **Moray;** called **the Bonny Earl.**] Scottish nobleman; slain in Fifeshire, Scotland, 1592. After assisting the laird of Grant against George Gordon, 1st marquis of Huntly, he was induced to come south for the king's pardon, but was killed by Huntly's men.

Stewart, John. See **Robert III** (of *Scotland*).

Stewart, Matthew. [Title, 4th Earl of **Lennox.**] Scottish nobleman and soldier; b. in Scotland, 1516; d. at Stirling, September 4, 1571. He was the male claimant to the rights and titles of the Stuarts at the death of James V. He tried to marry Mary of Guise, and did marry Lady Margaret Douglas, daughter of the earl of Angus and the queen dowager, Margaret. He was imprisoned for planning the marriage of his son, Lord Darnley to Mary, Queen of Scots, but the marriage took place, and he returned to Scotland. After the death of the earl of Moray he became regent.

Stewart, Robert. [Title, 1st Duke of **Albany.**] Younger son of Robert II of Scotland, and brother of Robert III; b. c1340; d. 1420. He was regent of Scotland during the reigns of Robert II, Robert III, and James I.

Stewart of Bothwellmuir (boᴛʜ′wẹl-mür; both′), **James.** [Title, Earl of **Arran.**] Scottish nobleman, murdered at Symington, Scotland, 1596. A soldier of fortune, by careful plotting he gained recognition as chief of the Hamiltons, and the confidence of James VI, but his arrogance in power soon led to his banishment.

Stifel (shtē′fẹl), **Michael.** [Latinized, **Stifelius.**] German mathematician and Protestant theologian; b. at Esslingen, Germany, April 19, 1487 (or 1486); d. at Jena, Germany, April 19, 1567. He wrote numerous works on arithmetic, astrology, and algebra, of which the greatest is his *Arithmetica integra* (1544).

Stow (stō), **John.** English historian and antiquary; b. at London, c1525; d. there, April 6, 1605. He published *A Summarie of Englysche Chronicles* (1565), and *Annales, or Generale Chronicle of England from Brute until the Present Yeare of Christ 1580*, but is best known for his *Survey of London* (1598), long the standard authority on old London.

Strambotto (sträm-bōt′tō). Italian verse form adapted from the rhyme scheme and meter of folk song or folk verse. It consists of an eight-line stanza, each line having eleven syllables, and a rhyme scheme of alternating rhymes, thus ABABABAB. Many of the *strambotti* are love lyrics, but some are humorous, religious, or have overtones of other subjects. The form was used with eminent success by such lights of the Golden Age of Renaissance poetry as Poliziano.

Straparola (strä-pä-rō′lä), **Gianfrancesco.** Writer of novelle and poet; b. at Caravaggio; d. after 1557. Almost nothing is known of his life. He published *Sonetti, strambotti, epistole e capitole* (1508), but is best remembered by his collection of stories called *Le piacevoli notti*, published at Venice in two series in 1550 and 1553. The stories are told on thirteen separate nights by a party of ladies and gentlemen enjoying the cool air on the island of Murano, near Venice. The seventy-five stories of the collection are interspersed with riddles. The collection is notable for its inclusion of fables of animals, for its fairy tales of adventure and of the supernatural, for its mixture of the marvelous with the ordinary, and for its folk stories. Straparola preceded Charles Perrault, writer of *Les Contes de ma mère l'oye* (*"Tales of my mother, the goose"*) by more than a century. Many editions of Straparola's collection were published, it was translated into French and German, and it has been a storehouse from which succeeding writers have obtained plots and other material. Shakespeare and Moliére are indebted to it.

Strega (strā'gä). Comedy by Anton Francesco Grazzini.

Strozzi (strōt'tsē). Florentine family, known from the second half of the 13th century, that played an active part in the civic affairs of the city. They were merchants and bankers whose economic importance rose from the establishment of their house after the financial disasters of the mid-14th century. Members of the family were men of letters, soldiers, scientists, and statesmen, and served as priori ninety-three times and as gonfalonieri sixteen times. The family expanded through a number of flourishing branches, beginning with the four sons of Strozza di Ubaldino, the 13th-century founder of the family. At the beginning of the 14th century, Bardo degli Strozzi moved from Florence to Ferrara and established the family there of which Tito Vespasiano and Ercole were distinguished members. Palla degli Strozzi was an outstanding member of the Florentine family; he was exiled (1434) on the return to Florence of Cosimo de' Medici the Elder. Filippo (1426–1491), an extremely wealthy merchant and banker, was in his turn banished from Florence by the Medici, but the banishment was finally annulled, and he returned to Florence (1466). The Strozzi palace on the Via Tornabuoni, one of the finest Renaissance buildings in Florence, was begun for him (1489) on designs by Benedetto da Maiano. Il Cronaca completed it. His son, Giovan Battista, called Filippo the Younger (1488–1538) was also extremely rich. He married Clarice, daughter of Piero II de' Medici, but turned against the Medici when they tried to regain power in 1527. Disdaining Duke Alessandro's attempts to win his favor, he went to Venice and later (1533) accompanied Catherine de Médicis to France, where he remained some time. When Alessandro was assassinated (1537), Filippo again took up arms for the freedom of Florence. With a band of exiles he had collected at Bologna he marched against the new Medici duke, Cosimo I. Filippo and his band were defeated at Montemurlo (1538); the leaders of the exiles were captured and Filippo was taken to Florence, where he was killed (September 18, 1538), despite the pleas and protests of the king of France and other princes. His son Piero was an implacable enemy of the Medici and of the imperial rule of Florence and Italy. A rash and courageous soldier, he was the last of the Florentine exiles to resist Medicean control. He long fought for the king of France in Italy, was given a marshal's baton, and was finally recalled to France. There he was killed in the siege of Thionville, June 21, 1558. A second son of Filippo the Younger was Leone (1515–1554), who was an admiral in the service of France. He fought the Medici and the Turks, and was killed in battle.

Strozzi, Barbara Torelli. Poet; b. 1475; d. at Bologna, November 17, 1533. She was the wife of Ercole Strozzi, who was murdered shortly after the marriage. The moving sonnet in which she lamented his death is extant.

Strozzi, Ercole. Poet; b. at Ferrara, 1473?; d. there, June 5/6, 1508. He was the son of Tito Vespasiano Strozzi (1424–1505). Inspired by the example and training of his illustrious father, he was even more apt and elegant in Latin. He entered public life at an early age and held posts of great trust. His elegies and sonnets, delicate and elegant but rather impersonal, were published with those of his father by Aldus Manutius (1513) as a memorial of his former pupil, Ercole. Among other works, Ercole wrote a lament in the form of an epic on Cesare Borgia that mixes mythology itself and mythological allusions with the facts of Cesare's life. Ercole was married to the beautiful but ill-fated Barbara Torelli. In the morning of June 6, 1508, his body, pierced by twenty-two wounds, was found. The reasons for the crime are obscure. Some said Alfonso d'Este had arranged it, either because Ercole was suspected of interest in Alfonso's wife Lucrezia Borgia, or because Alfonso was interested in Ercole's wife. Others said the crime was perpetrated by relatives of Barbara's first husband.

Strozzi, Filippo. Captain and sailor; b. at Venice, 1541; d. at sea near the Azores, July

26, 1582. As a child he was taken to France by his father and became a page of the dauphin (later King Francis II). At an early age he left his father's house and entered upon a military career. After a brief period fighting in the Piedmont, he returned to France and spent the rest of his life in the service of the French, always proving himself a brilliant and brave soldier. He took part in the religious wars that wracked France, and was the first to attack at the siege of La Rochelle (1573). In 1582 he put to sea for the purpose of seizing the Azores and of preventing a Spanish fleet from coming to the assistance of the Spanish governor. In an action at sea he was wounded, taken prisoner, stabbed, and thrown into the sea.

Strozzi, Giovan Battista. [Known as **the Elder**, to distinguish him from another poet of the same name who lived 1551–1634.] Florentine poet; b. 1505; d. 1571. He wrote madrigals, and sonnets that were free from a narrow dependence on Petrarch.

Strozzi, Lorenzo di Palla. Florentine humanist; b. 1404; d. 1451. He was the son of Palla di Noferi degli Strozzi (c1373–1462), and was educated by three leading humanists, including Tommaso Parentucelli (later Pope Nicholas V), who was a tutor in the Strozzi household. He was left at Florence to manage family affairs when his father was banished (1434) but was himself banished four years later. According to Vespasiano, he was murdered at Gubbio by a Florentine.

Strozzi, Matteo di Simone degli. Florentine humanist; b. 1397; d. 1436. A friend of Francesco Filelfo and Leonardo Bruni, he studied Aristotle's *Ethics* under Giannozzo Manetti, and was reputed to be learned in Latin and philosophy. He was an ardent collector of manuscripts. As a man with a reputation for wisdom and judgment he held many of the highest offices in Florence, from which he was banished (1434) on the return of Cosimo de' Medici from exile.

Strozzi, Palla degli. See **Palla degli Strozzi.**

Strozzi, Tito Vespasiano. Statesman and poet; b. at Ferrara, 1424; d. there, August 30, 1505. He was the father of Ercole Strozzi (1473?–1508). As a court official at Ferrara, he served three princes of the House of Este —Borso, Ercole, and Alfonso I. His duties and position caused him to lay heavy burdens on the people, which earned their hatred for himself and his son. In his lifetime he owed his fame to his high position at court. A later age remembers him for his exquisite Latin verse, including some eclogues and elegies of truly poetic inspiration.

Sturm (shtůrm), **Johannes.** German pedagogue; b. at Schlieden, Germany, October 1, 1507; d. at Strasbourg, March 3, 1589. He received a humanistic education at Liége and Louvain, and then went to Paris. There he met Martin Bucer and was converted to Protestantism. He became a professor of rhetoric and dialectic at Strasbourg (1537), and, charged with reorganizing the educational system, founded a Gymnasium (1538), which was one of the first to combine Protestant and humanistic principles. He left a number of pedagogical works.

Suarez de Mendoza (swä′reth dā men-dō′thä), **Lorenzo.** See **Mendoza, Lorenzo Suarez de.**

Suleiman I (sö-lā-män′). [Also, **Soliman I, Solyman I;** sometimes called **Solyman** (or **Soliman**) **II;** called **the Magnificent.**] Sultan of Turkey (1520–1566); b. c1490; d. at Szigetvar, Hungary, September 5, 1566. He raised the Turkish empire to its highest point of power. He was noted both as a ruler and as a patron and encourager of the fine arts and learning.

Summoner's Tale, The. One of Chaucer's *Canterbury Tales;* it follows *The Friar's Tale*, in which a summoner is borne off by the devil. The Summoner in his tale retorts to the friar by telling, in salty terms, of a bequest made by a peasant to a hypocritical and avaricious friar.

Summonte (söm-môn′tā), **Pietro.** [Latinized, **Petrus Summontius.**] Humanist; b. at Naples, 1453; d. there, August 14, 1526. He lectured at the *Studio* (University). He left some Latin letters, dedications, and epigrams, and some letters in the vernacular. Among the last was a long one that embodies an early critique of Neapolitan Renaissance art. He was a close friend of Pontano, il Cariteo, and Sannazzaro, and saved the autograph copy of the latter's *Arcadia* from almost certain loss, preserved many of the works of his other two friends, and made publication of correct editions of their works possible.

Suppositi (söp-pō′sē-tē). Comedy in five acts by Ariosto; it is an adaptation from the Latin forms and treats the old topic of the lost heir. It was produced at Ferrara in 1509.

Surville (sür-vēl), **Clotilde de.** French poet; said to have lived in the 15th century. She is the reputed author of *Poésies de Clotilde*.

Swynford (swin′fo̩rd), **Catherine.** [Title, Duchess of **Lancaster.**] Third wife of John of Gaunt; b. c1350; d. 1403. She was the mistress of John of Gaunt, and bore him four children who were legitimized after she was married to John. The children were known as the Beauforts, and one of them, John, was the great-grandfather of Henry VII who traced his claim to the throne through him.

Sylvius (sil′vi-us), **Aeneas.** See **Pius II.**

Syncerus (sin-sēr′us), **Actius.** Latin name taken by Iacopo Sannazzaro in the Neapolitan Academy.

T

Taddeo di Bartolo (tä-de′ō dē bär′tō-lō). Sienese painter; b. at Siena, 1362 or 1363; d. there, 1422. He was enrolled in the register of Sienese painters in 1389, and was a follower of Simone Martini in his delicacy and richness of ornamental detail, but without his inspiration. Echoes of Bartolo di Fredi and of the realism of the Lorenzetti brothers are strong in his work. He worked in many places: at Genoa, San Gimignano, Pisa, Montepulciano, Perugia, Volterra, and Siena. Through his workshop, in which he had many assistants who helped him to produce the great body of work he left, and through his wanderings he propagated the Sienese school of painting. A fine draftsman, his drawings are free of the heaviness that characterized much of his painting. Among his works are the frescoes, *Dormition of the Virgin* and *Assumption*, Palazzo Pubblico, Siena; a polyptych, *Virgin and Saints*, Pinacoteca, and frescoes in S. Maria Assunta, S. Gimignano; frescoes (1397) in S. Francesco at Pisa; a polyptych, *Assumption of the Virgin* (1401), cathedral, Montepulciano; pinnacle of an altarpiece, *Descent of the Holy Ghost* (1403) and fragments of a polyptych, *Madonna and Child with Saints* (1403), Perugia; a triptych, *Virgin with Child* (1411), Volterra; and a signed and dated (1418) *Madonna and Child in Glory*, Cambridge, Massachusetts. Many of his works are at Siena; other examples are to be found in numerous collections, museums, and churches of Italy, including Naples, Palermo, Ravenna, Rome (Vatican), and Savona, as well as in other European museums, and at Chicago, Hartford, Memphis, Minneapolis, New Haven, New Orleans, Northampton (Massachusetts), Notre Dame (Indiana), Philadelphia, San Antonio, San Francisco, Tucson, and Tulsa (Oklahoma).

Talbot (tôl′bo̩t, tal′-), **John.** [Titles, 1st Earl of **Shrewsbury,** Earl of **Waterford.**] English general; b. c1388; killed at the battle of Castillon, France, July, 1453. He fought with distinction in the wars in France.

Talbot, John. [Title, 2nd Earl of **Shrewsbury.**] English politician; b. c1413; d. in the battle of Northampton, England, July 10, 1460. He was the son of the 1st earl of Shrewsbury, and died fighting in the forces of Henry VI.

Tallis or **Tallys** or **Talys** (tal′is), **Thomas.** [Called the **Father of English Cathedral Music.**] English composer; b. c1505; d. November 23, 1585. His works, some of them written with his pupil, William Byrd, are among the monuments of English church music, and include *First Service in the Dorian Mode* and *Litany*.

Talpa (täl′pä), **Bartolomeo.** Medalist and decorator, who worked at Mantua in the last decades of the 15th century. He decorated the palaces and villas of the Gonzaga family of his day, and made medals. Two medals signed by him are extant: one of Federigo I Gonzaga and the other of Francesco II commemorating his victory over Charles VIII at Fornovo (1495). Both are correct but somewhat lifeless portraits.

Tamagnino (tä-mä-nyē′nō), **il.** See **Della Porta, Antonio.**

Tanagli (tä-nä′lyē), **Guglielmo di Francesco.** Florentine humanist and public official; b. 1391; d. 1460. He studied canon and civil law at Padua, where he took his doctorate. He was a protégé and friend of Niccolò Niccoli, and was known for his skill and artistry in writing the new script. He was prominent in public affairs, served on many embassies and councils, and was knighted in 1451.

Tancred (tang′krẹd). In Torquato Tasso's *Gerusalemme liberata,* one of the Crusaders who goes to deliver Jerusalem from the Saracens. His name and prowess are based on the Norman soldier who was one of the chief heroes of the first Crusade (1096–1099). In Tasso's poem, as in history, he was at the siege of Antioch. When the city fell, according to Tasso, Tancred became the guard of Erminia, daughter of the slain king of Antioch. She fell in love with her guard, but was parted from him when the Crusaders turned her over to the pagan king of Jerusalem. At the battle for Jerusalem, Tancred refused to fight Clorinda, with whom he had fallen in love. He later pursues the pagan knight who has entered the Crusaders' camp and set fire to their siege tower, engages him in single combat, and mortally wounds him. The dying pagan begs for baptism. Tancred raises his helmet and discovers that the pagan warrior is his beloved Clorinda. In the final battle for Jerusalem, Tancred is first to leap on the walls. After the victory he is discovered sorely wounded. Erminia rushes off to cure him by her magic arts.

Tansillo (tän-sēl′lō), **Luigi.** Poet, sailor, and soldier; b. at Venosa, 1510; d. at Teano, December 1, 1568. As a sailor with the son of the vicar of Naples, he fought against the Turks and pirates in the Mediterranean. In his last years he was captain of justice at Naples and Gaeta. His full and restless life enlarged his view of man and the world, and left him untouched by the pedantry that marred the work of many men of letters of his time. Spiritually, he enjoyed the wonders of nature and the commonplaces of domestic life, and related them with good humor and sound sense in his poetry. His *Vendemmia* celebrates the unbridled gaiety of the southern peasants during the harvest of the grapes. *Clorida* is a mythological, narrative poem, hymning life on the Bay of Naples. In his *Stanze a B. Martirano* he tells of the hardships of his life at sea and expresses his attraction to the bleak landscapes and harsh crags of some coasts. His twenty-four *Capitoli,* in the manner of Horace and Ariosto, are on personal matters, handled in a pleasing manner and lacking any trace of irony. Sonnets best suited his lyric temperament and these, in which he put his personal stamp on well-worn themes, are among his best works. In all his works Tansillo gives evidence of his love of nature and expresses with graceful simplicity the joys of love and of domestic life. His lyrics are on the Petrarchan model and free from the rigidity and affectation of Pietro Bembo, who was regarded as the paragon of style of the age. Tansillo's *Le lagrime di S. Pietro,* in which he sought to produce a Christian epic, was rewritten after some of his works were placed on the Index.

Tapia (tä′pyä), **Andrés de.** Spanish soldier; b. in Spain, c1495; d. in Mexico, after 1539. He joined Cortés in 1519, took a prominent part in the conquest of Mexico, and settled at Mexico city. He wrote an incomplete but valuable account of the conquest.

Tarantasia (tä-rän-tä′zyä), **Pietro di.** Original name of Pope **Innocent V.**

Taranto (tä′rän-tō), Prince of. Title of various members of the Orsini family.

Tarlatti (tär-lät′tē), **Bernardo di.** See **Dovizi, Bernardo.**

Tarsia (tär′syä), **Galeazzo di.** Soldier and poet; b. at Naples, c1520; d. 1553. Of an eminent family, he was lord of Belmonte, and was, after Tansillo, one of the most original of the southern lyric poets. He wrote verses on the Petrarchan model, one of these, celebrating his return to Italy after a period of exile, is, in its poetic fervor, worthy of Petrarch himself. His verses were for Vittoria Colonna, among others. He wrote many for his young wife, Camilla Carafa. Three sonnets lamenting her early death are especially lyrical and moving.

Tartaglia (tär-tä′lyä), **Niccolò.** Mathematician and engineer; b. at Brescia, probably 1499; d. at Venice, December 3, 1557. He did not know his father's name, and said the name Tartaglia, meaning "stutter" or "stammer" was given to him because of a speech impediment he suffered as a result of a wound by a French soldier at the siege of Brescia (February 19, 1512). He says he went to school at about the age of 14 for a few weeks, and learned the first letters of the alphabet. He was then forced to withdraw because of his mother's poverty. From that time he educated himself. He taught at Verona, Brescia, and Venice. He became one of the greatest mathematicians of the 16th century, studied fortifications and projectiles, and discovered a solution of the cubic equation. His solution, known as the "formula of Tartaglia," was confided to Girolamo Cardano under a strict pledge of secrecy, but Cardano broke his pledge and completed and published the method in his *Ars magna* of 1545. Although he gave credit to Tartaglia as the discoverer, Cardano's publication gave rise to a bitter dispute, and Tartaglia published his own work on the solution in 1546. His books include one on gunnery, *Della nuova scienza* (1537) in which he applied the principles of mathematics to artillery, and an Italian translation (based upon one of William of Moerbeke) of part of the work of Archimedes (1543), but his most important book was his *General trattato di numeri et misure* (2 vols., 1556–1560), a treatise on pure and applied mathematics.

Tartagna (tär-tä′nyä), **Alessandro.** Jurist; b. at Imola, 1424; d. at Bologna, 1477. He studied civil and canon law at Bologna, and taught civil law at Pavia, Bologna, Ferrara, Padua, and again at Bologna. A productive writer, he won deserved renown in his time for his opinions, and above all, for his Latin commentaries on the *Justinian Code*, the *Digestum vetus*, and on the *Decretals*.

Tasso (täs′sō), **Bernardo.** Poet and courtier; b. at Venice, of a noble Bergamesque family, November 11, 1493; d. at Ostiglia, September 5, 1569. Orphaned as a child, he was brought up by an uncle who was assassinated when Bernardo was 17. He studied at Padua, where Bembo was his patron, and then entered the service of Count Guido Rangoni of Modena as secretary. For his patron he went to Paris to assist in the arrangements for the marriage of Renée of France and Ercole d'Este of Ferrara, and on his return entered the service of Renée at Ferrara. He left this post (1532), perhaps because of Renée's Protestant sympathies, and became secretary to Ferrante Sanseverino, prince of Salerno. Ferrante treated him as a friend and paid him well, and while in his service Bernardo married, and for a few years lived a tranquil and happy life with his wife and family at Sorrento. But he was often away from home on his patron's business. In 1547 the Spanish vicar of Naples proposed to introduce the Inquisition there. Bernardo, aware of the fear that the prospect inspired in the inhabitants, advised his patron to intercede with Charles V on their behalf. Ferrante did so and was disgraced and forced into exile. Bernardo and his young son Torquato were included in the ban when Ferrante, who openly went over to the French, was declared a rebel. Bernardo accompanied Ferrante into exile, but when his patron could no longer pay him he returned to Italy. His wife, whom he had not seen since he went into exile, died (1556) and a long struggle with her relatives began over her dowry and the settlement he had made on her. Not only was his suit to recover a failure, but his wife's relatives refused to send his daughter to him. His search for a post at court and a livelihood took him to Urbino, Ravenna, Pesaro, and Venice, where, with his son Torquato, he published his *Amadigi* (1559). This work, in 100 cantos, is based on the Spanish romance *Amadis of Gaul*, reworked in Bernardo's style and with his embellishments, in an attempt to create a heroic epic based on the Aristotelian unities. To the original story he added episodes of his own invention and sought by his treatment to satisfy the spiritual requirements of the Counter-Reformation. The poem was highly regarded in its time, but did not bring Bernardo the rewards he had expected. His life continued to be wretched and painful in its poverty. In 1569 he was made podesta of Ostiglia. His duties were light, but the climate was bad, and he died in the same year. In addition to his *Amadigi*, Bernardo produced many other poetic works. His sonnets, on the Petrarchan model, celebrate the joys of conjugal love, joys largely denied to him. His odes, modeled after Horace, are more concerned with classic content than with poetic inspiration. He was greatly influenced by Bembo in style, and also shows the influence of Ovid in his *Favola di Piramo e Tisbe*. On the whole, his work is indistinguishable from that of many other poets of his time who were fascinated by elegance of style and a passion for classicism rather than moved by poetic feeling. His importance to literature lies in the effect that his pride in his noble blood, his literary example, and the wretched life he led as a courtier had on his gifted son Torquato.

Tasso, Torquato. Poet; b. at Sorrento, March 11, 1544; d. at Rome, April 25, 1595.

He was educated at the Jesuit schools at Naples, Rome, and Bergamo. His father, Bernardo Tasso (1493–1569), was involved in the political troubles of the prince of Salerno, his patron, and joined the prince in Rome. When that city became unsafe for him he left Rome, and went ultimately to the court of the duke of Urbino at Pesaro, where his son Torquato was taught with the son of the duke. In 1557 Bernardo sent his son to study law at Padua, with the aim and hope of giving him a profession that would make him independent of patrons. Torquato, a loving and admiring son, was more influenced by his father's writings than by his worthy aims. While still at Padua he published his romantic epic *Rinaldo* (1562). When it was successful his father ceased his opposition to a literary career, and Torquato went to Bologna to study philosophy and literature. In 1565 he entered the service of Cardinal Luigi d'Este at Ferrara. He was well received at court, was soon on friendly terms with the members of the House of Este, especially with the ladies, and was encouraged to finish the epic *Il Goffredo* (later named *Gerusalemme liberata*), which he had begun at Bologna. Between 1567 and 1570 he wrote his *Discorsi dell'arte poetica* . . . , three discourses on poetry with particular emphasis on the heroic epic. The first treats the theme of the heroic epic. Tasso concludes that the theme should be Christian and historical; the event to be celebrated should have occurred in the not too distant past, but long ago enough to be separate from contemporary times. The second discusses the character of the poem and stresses unity of action. The third treats matters of style. The ideas and ideals outlined in the *Discorsi* were to be exemplified in his *Gerusalemme liberata*. In 1570 he accompanied the cardinal to Paris, where he met Ronsard and other distinguished men. He left the cardinal's service after his return on account of a difference of opinion on religious matters, but was received (1572) by Duke Alfonso d'Este. The duke loaded his court poet with favors. Tasso's *Aminta*, called "a perfect pastoral play," was produced under his own direction for the delight of the court at Ferrara in 1573. In 1574, when he had nearly completed his *Goffredo*, he was seized with fever. The happy and honored years were over. He became suspicious, quarrelsome, deeply resentful of the criticism he humbly and fearfully sought, and wounded in his sensitive pride because he felt he was not properly honored by his patron. He worried about the orthodoxy of his poem and became subject to delusions. He came to fear he would be accused of heresy and dreaded death by assassination or poison. At length he was placed in a convent at Ferrara for medical treatment. He escaped and fled in the disguise of a shepherd. Dodging across Italy through lanes and byways he arrived at Sorrento, at the house of his sister. She had not seen him for years and did not recognize him. To test her, he pretended to be a messenger but when assured of her good will revealed himself to her. She welcomed him and cared for him, but the condition of his mind was not stable. After some time when he enjoyed his return to his native heath he was again seized with restlessness and decided to return to Ferrara. The duke received him again (1578) but his delusions continued. He resumed his wandering, to Mantua, Turin, and elsewhere, finally returning to Ferrara. There he became so violent in accusing the duke that he was placed in Sant' Anna, a hospital for the insane (1579). He remained in seclusion for seven years, during which time he wrote feverishly, including many letters in which he begged piteously for release and mercy. In 1586, on the personal promise of the lord of Mantua that Alfonso should not again be exposed to his insane attacks, he was released. He went to Mantua, where he remained a year, during which he wrote an unsuccessful drama, *Torrismondo*, and again resumed his wanderings. He had many friends eager to help him, but he was broken in health and spirit. While Tasso was in seclusion at the hospital of Sant' Anna, an unauthorized and incorrect edition of his *Goffredo* was published at Venice (1580). Tasso was unreasonably concerned lest the style of his poem fall below the current literary standard. He had submitted his manuscript to various friends, seeking their suggestions for improvement. Many had criticized it according to the artificial criteria of the time. On seeing the unauthorized version that was printed, however, they realized how unjust it was to Tasso and caused a new and complete, but still unauthorized edition to be printed at Parma

(1581). The title they gave to the new edition was *Gerusalemme liberata,* and by this title the poem has been known ever since. In 1593 Tasso published *Gerusalemme conquistata,* a revision of his great poem in which he sought to remove any trace of unorthodoxy and to attain to the literary style that was current at the time. It was a lifeless reflection of his masterpiece. Two years later he died at Rome, whither he had been summoned by Pope Clement VIII to be crowned poet laureate. The ceremony was not performed owing to his illness. Tasso's other writings included many lyrics, even more musical than the verses of his *Aminta,* discourses, orations, dialogues, and many letters, those from the period of his confinement being especially moving. He was difficult to befriend, too suspicious to be guided; a man whose fragile pride could not support the give and take of life even in a highly cultivated and friendly court. His mind was clouded by the fears of his own inadequacy and those inspired by the Counter-Reformation. He was a tormented soul who produced the culminating literary work of the Italian Renaissance. See **Aminta** and **Gerusalemme liberata.**

Tasso, Del. See **Del Tasso.**

Tauler (tou'lėr), **Johann.** German mystic and preacher; b. at Strasbourg, in Alsace, c1300; d. there, June 16, 1361. He entered (c1318) the Dominican order, was driven from Strasbourg with other Dominicans who disregarded the interdict of Pope John XXII in 1339, and established himself at Basel. Here he became intimately associated with the "Friends of God." In 1352 he returned to Strasbourg. His *Sermons* were published in 1498. Other works (*Book of Spiritual Poverty,* and others) also have been ascribed to him.

Tavannes (tȧ-vȧn), Seigneur **de.** [Title of **Gaspard de Saulx.**] Marshal of France; b. at Dijon, France, March, 1509; d. near Autun, France, 1573. He took a leading part in the wars against the Huguenots, and in the Massacre of Saint Bartholomew's Day in 1572.

Taverner (tav'ėr-nėr), **John.** English composer and organist; b. c1495; d. October 25, 1545. He composed Masses, magnificats, and motets.

Taverner, Richard. English religious reformer; b. at Brisley, Norfolk, England, c1505; d. at Wood Eaton, Oxfordshire, England, July 14, 1575. He is remembered for his writings, which helped spread the Reformation in England. He published an English version of the Bible (1539) which was a revised edition of Matthews' Bible.

Taylor (tā'lọr), **Rowland.** English Protestant martyr; b. at Rothburg, Northumberland, England; burned at the stake at Aldham Common, near Hadleigh, Suffolk, England, February 9, 1555. He was one of the most famous martyrs to be executed under Queen Mary Tudor. After being converted to Protestantism he became domestic chaplain to and a close associate (1540–1543) of Archbishop Thomas Cranmer. He must have been particularly obnoxious to Mary, who, on the sixth day after her proclamation as queen (1553), ordered his arrest. Subsequently released, he objected (1553–1554) strenuously to the performance of Mass at his church, and was arrested, examined, tried, and condemned in January, 1555.

Tebaldeo (tā-bäl-de'ō), **Antonio.** [Real name, **Antonio Tebaldi.**] Poet; b. at Ferrara, November 4, 1463; d. at Rome, 1537. He spent a long time at the courts of Ferrara and Mantua, was the tutor and friend of Isabella d'Este, and the secretary of Lucrezia Borgia. On the elevation of Leo X to the papacy (1513) he went to Rome, where he enjoyed the pope's patronage. In the sack of Rome (1527) he lost his books and his property, and thereafter lived in straitened circumstances. His letters to friends gave a vivid and pitiful account of the sack and his own sufferings. His lyrics, including pastoral eclogues, sonnets, and letters in terza rima, are characterized by elegance and artifice, a mannered imitation of Petrarch that emphasizes literary effects at the expense of content and inspiration. Some lyrics on the state of Italy show sincere sentiment.

Tedaldi (tā-däl'dē), **Pieraccio.** Poet; b. at Florence, c1285; d. c1353. Little is known of his life. He was in the Battle of Montecatini (1315) and was taken prisoner by the Pisans. He lived at Lucca, Faenza, and other cities of the Romagna, and probably never returned to Florence. His forty-three extant sonnets reveal the facets of his temperament and the vagaries of his life in such subjects as love, fate, politics, money, lament for the death of Dante, curses on his second wife, despair, penitence, and hope. He expressed the joys, demands, and travails of youth, and as he grew older turned his thoughts to penitence and salvation. His lyrics are realistic, sometimes crude as to language and style, and sincere in their feeling.

Tedesco (tā-dās′kō), **Arrigo.** See **Isaac, Heinrich.**

Tegheler (tī′lėr), **Wat** (or **Walter**). See **Tyler, Wat** (or **Walter**).

Tegliacci (tā-lyät′chē), **Niccolò di Ser Sozzo.** Sienese miniaturist and painter; d. June, 1363. He worked chiefly at Siena, where he was a pupil of the Lorenzetti, and where he held municipal office on several occasions. Among his works are a polyptych, dated 1362, Pinacoteca, and a miniature of the *Assumption,* signed by him and Luca di Tommè (1362), State Archives, Siena; *Madonna and Child,* Uffizi, Florence; *Madonna Enthroned,* National Gallery, Washington; *Death and Assumption of the Virgin,* Boston; and *Madonna and Child,* Kansas City, Missouri. A number of miniatures from his hand are in the Museo di Arte Sacro, S. Gimignano.

Tegrimi (tā-grē′mē), **Niccolò.** Statesman and writer; b. at Lucca, c1448; d. 1527. Of an ancient noble family of Lucca, he served in many important public positions, as ambassador to Naples, to Milan to make a truce between Charles VIII of France and the king of Spain (1497), and to the emperor Maximilian to make peace among the emperor, the pope, and Ferrara. He served under Ludovico Il Moro and under Pope Julius II. In 1514 he withdrew from public life and entered the Church. Tegrimi was the author of a life of Castruccio Castracani that is not only the first biography of that lord of Lucca, but is notable as typical of the humanist approach to biography: long on classical reference and sources and short on information, of the lofty and laudatory tone that would glorify his subject. Although documents, since lost, were available to Tegrimi, he made little critical use of them. The biography, which precedes Machiavelli's, is more interesting as a typical humanistic exercise than as an analytical and definitive biography.

Telesforo di Cosenza (tā-les′fō-rō dē kō-zen′tsä). [Latinized, **Telesphorus Cosentinus.**] Franciscan hermit of the 14th century. Between 1356 and 1365 he wrote a prophecy that is practically an anthology of the authentic writings, and of many attributed to him, of Gioacchino de Fiore (Calabrian prophet, d. 1201).

Telesio (tā-le′zyō), **Antonio.** Humanist and poet; b. at Cosenza, 1482; d. there, 1534. He was in Milan in 1518, and from there went to teach at Rome, taking his nephew Bernardino with him. He wrote Latin poems in praise of natural objects, as the glowworm, spider, and pomegranate tree.

Telesio, Bernardino. Philosopher; b. at Cosenza, 1509; d. there, October 2, 1588. He was the nephew of the learned humanist Antonio Telesio (1482–1534), with whom he lived from his childhood and from whom he learned Latin and Greek. He accompanied his uncle to Rome when the latter went there to teach Latin at the university, and in the sack of Rome (1527) was taken prisoner but was released after two months. Antonio went to Venice to teach after the sack and Bernardino went to Padua where he studied mathematics, optics, and philosophy. He remained at Padua about ten years, then retired to a Benedictine convent for a period of meditation and research. After leaving the convent he went to Naples. There he lectured and founded his Accademia Cosentina for the study of philosophy, and there he began his great work, *De rerum natura juxta propria principia* (published at Naples, 1587). He continued with the writing and publication of his main work until almost the end of his life. Even before he had published any of it, the fame of his work was widespread. It represented a new and anti-Aristotelian approach to philosophy. A later philosopher and ardent admirer sang the praises of Telesio in verse for having freed Truth from Aristotle, "tyrant of intellects." Fundamental to Telesio's approach was the thesis that knowledge, hitherto sought in faith or from the ancients, derives from the senses and can be obtained only through the observation of nature and through experiment; matter is its own source of knowledge. This is the foundation of the modern scientific method. The ideas expressed by Telesio collided with Church doctrine and his work was placed on the Index.

Tempera (tem′pe-rạ). A painting medium consisting of ground solid pigments mixed with egg yolk and water. Applied to a prepared panel, tempera dries quickly and produces a brilliant, glazed, durable surface. It was the medium used for panel painting before the introduction of the technique of painting in oil in the 15th century.

Temperelli (tem-pe′rel-lē), **Cristoforo de'.** See **Caselli, Cristoforo.**

Tempio Malatestiano (tem′pyō mä-lä-tes-tyä′nō). Name by which the Church of S. Francesco at Rimini has come to be known. About 1450 Sigismondo Malatesta, lord of Rimini, commissioned Leon Battista Alberti to redesign the outside of the 13th-century church, and to provide for six new chapels, three on a side, in its Gothic interior. Alberti's design for the façade called for three great arches, modeled after the triumphal arch of Augustus that still stands at Rimini, and a shallow pediment. On the flank are deep niches, patterned after Roman aqueducts. These were intended to hold sarcophagi with the bones of illustrious men. Matteo de Pasti was the architect who carried out Alberti's designs. Inside, the church and the new chapels were richly decorated with sculptures, reliefs, and carvings. Agostino di Duccio, perhaps under the supervision of Matteo de' Pasti, was in charge of the sculptural decoration. Almost every inch of surface is carved and ornamented. There are ninety-six reliefs in the chapels alone, to say nothing of the sculptural monuments, wall decorations, figures on the balustrades, piers, and in the spandrels. The chapel of the Relics has a fresco by Piero della Francesca, *Sigismondo Malatesta Kneeling before St. Sigismund*. Another chapel contains the monument of Isotta degli Atti, Sigismondo's mistress, carved by Agostino di Duccio. Pius II wrote of his "splendid church dedicated to Saint Francis, though he filled it so full of pagan works of art that it seemed less a Christian sanctuary than a temple of heathen devils. In it he erected for his mistress a tomb of magnificent marble and exquisite workmanship with an inscription in the pagan style as follows, 'Sacred to the deified Isotta.' " On arches, vaults, friezes, and balustrades are carved the intertwined initials $, and scattered throughout appear the arms and emblems of the Malatesta: the elephant (symbolizing strength), and the rose (perhaps symbolizing the arts). Agostino di Duccio, whose name has been found inscribed in the church as the sculptor, has been credited with much of the decoration. Some of the finest reliefs, as those in the chapel of Isotta (but not her monument), the chapel of the Planets, and the reliefs of the Liberal Arts, are ascribed to Matteo de' Pasti.

Tenda (ten′dä), **Beatrice di.** Wife of Filippo Maria Visconti; d. at Milan, September 14, 1418. Her first husband was Facino Cane, one of the most important of the mercenary captains of Giovanni Maria Visconti. Giovanni Maria was killed in a conspiracy and Facino, dying, urged his wife to take as her second husband, Filippo Maria, Giovanni Maria's brother. She was twenty years older than Filippo Maria, but he was glad to have her, as she brought with her the soldiers who had followed her husband, the cities he had conquered, and vast treasure. Once he had all this dowry, Filippo Maria accused her, on no grounds at all, of adultery and had her beheaded.

Terracina (ter-rä-chē′nä), **Laura.** Poetess; b. at Naples, 1519; d. there, c1577. She was the daughter of one of the great families of Naples, was known at an early age for her lyrics, and was admired and praised by the most eminent men of letters of her time. The first edition of her poems was published at Venice in 1548. Many more collections followed, as she was one of the most productive of 16th-century poetesses. She was more noted, in after years at any rate, for her productivity than for the artistry of her work. Her lyrics have too often a moralizing and didactic tone, and a dullness that vitiates the sincerity of her sentiments.

Terrail (te-rȧy′), **Pierre.** Original name of **Bayard,** Chevalier **de.**

Teseida (te-ze′ē-dä). Italian epic by Giovanni Boccaccio (1340–1342). It is modeled on the *Aeneid*, comprises twelve books, and tells the romantic tale of two friends, prisoners in Athens, who fall in love with the same lady, with all the complications that situation creates.

Testagrossa (tes-tä-grōs′sä), **Angelo.** Singer at the court of Ludovico il Moro. After the death of Ludovico's duchess, Beatrice d'Este, Testagrossa went to Mantua where he composed songs for Isabella d'Este and gave her lessons on the lute.

Tetzel (tet′sel), **Johann.** German Dominican monk and inquisitor; b. at Leipzig, Germany, c1465; d. there, July 4, 1519. He was famous as a preacher whose picture of punishment avoidable by the purchase of indulgence brought much money into the coffers. In

1517 he embarked on a mission to sell indulgences that aroused the anger of Martin Luther, who published his 95 theses at Wittenberg. Tetzel answered in 106 theses, but found lack of support among more solid Roman Catholics and retired in disgrace to a Leipzig convent. His career has been the subject of much partisan writing from both Protestants and Roman Catholics but it is perhaps not too much to say that his flagrant sale of indulgences was a spark that set alight the smoldering desire for reform in the Church.

Theresa or **Teresa** (tẹ-rē′sạ, -zạ, tā-rā′sä), Saint. [Spanish, **Teresa de Ávila.**] Spanish saint and author; b. at Ávila, Spain, March 28, 1515; d. at Alba de Tormes, Spain, 1582. She entered the Carmelite order in 1534, began the Carmelite reform (Discalced Carmelites) in 1562, and became famous for her mystical experiences. Her works, including *El Camino de la perfección* (*Way of Perfection*) and *El Castillo interior* (*Castle of the Soul*), were published in 1587.

Thomas of Brotherton (broᴛʜ′ėr-tọn). [Title, Earl of **Norfolk.**] English nobleman and marshal of England; b. 1300; d. 1338. A son of Edward I, he acted as warden of England during the absence of Edward II. When Queen Isabella invaded England with Mortimer he joined their forces. He later welcomed Edward III to the throne.

Thomas of Erceldoune (ėr′sẹl-dön). See **Thomas the Rhymer.**

Thomas of Woodstock (wu̇d′stok). [Titles, Earl of **Buckingham,** Duke of **Gloucester.**] English politician; b. at Woodstock, England, January 7, 1355; murdered at Calais, France, September 1397. The youngest son of Edward III and Philippa of Hainaut, after the accession of Richard II he tried to gain control of the political situation, eventually joining John of Gaunt in opposition to the king. In 1397 he was found to be involved in a plot to overthrow Richard, was arrested and transported to Calais where he was murdered.

Thomas the Rhymer. [Also, **Thomas of Erceldoune, Thomas of Earlston, Thomas Rymer, Thomas Rimor, Thomas Learmont;** called **True Thomas.**] Scottish poet; fl. c1220–1297. He was noted in folklore and Arthurian legend as a prophet and guide to the mysterious halls beneath the Eildon Hills. According to the popular story, the queen of the elves came to him as he sat under the Eildon tree, and carried him to elfland, where they lived in happiness for seven years, at the end of which time she brought him back to the Eildon tree and told him of many things that were to happen in the wars between England and Scotland. He was called "True Thomas" from the truth of these prophecies. He finally disappeared in a forest, following a hart and a hind, and was seen no more. There are five versions of the Scottish popular ballad *Thomas Rymer,* which tell the story of Thomas and the queen of Elfland. This same story is told also of Ogier the Dane and Morgan le Fay.

Thopas (thō′pạs), **The Tale of Sir.** One of the *Canterbury Tales* Chaucer is supposed to have told himself. Sly and lewd, it was so raw even Harry Bailly, the Host, could not stomach it and it was shouted down.

Throckmorton (throk-môr′tọn) or **Throgmorton** (throg-môr′tọn), Sir **Nicholas.** English politician; b. in 1515; d. 1571. He supported Lady Jane Grey's party; he was forgiven by Mary Tudor, but was implicated in Wyatt's rebellion and imprisoned. As Elizabeth's ambassador to France he became friendly with Mary, Queen of Scots. After Darnley's death he intrigued for Mary's marriage to Thomas Howard, duke of Norfolk; he was arrested for alleged participation in a Roman Catholic plot against Elizabeth but was released. Sir Walter Raleigh was his son-in-law.

Tibaldi (tē-bäl′dē), **Pellegrino.** [Also called **Pellegrino de' Pellegrini.**] Painter, sculptor and architect; b. at Bologna (or at Puria di Valsolda), 1527; d. at Milan, May 27, 1596. He was a pupil of Bagnacavallo but was also influenced by the grandeur and monumentality of Michelangelo. A *Marriage of St. Catherine,* Pinacoteca, Bologna (where there are several other paintings by him), and an *Adoration of the Shepherds,* Municipal Museum, Cento nell' Emilia, reveal the influence of his training under Bagnacavallo. One of his best works, *Adoration of the Shepherds,* Borghese Gallery, Rome, indicates his transformation of the heroic forms of Michelangelo by his deep modeling and use of light. A subtle mannerist of the late period, he sought pictorial illusion by means of bold foreshortening, deep shadows, and the addition of depth by architectural perspective. For a time he worked at Rome (1547–1550), where he executed frescoes in S.

Luigi dei Francesi and in Trinità dei Monti. In 1550 he returned to Bologna and began his most ambitious undertaking in Italy, the completion and decoration, with scenes from the *Odyssey*, of a palace for Cardinal Poggi (now the University). Other works at Bologna include *Miracle of St. Mark* and *The Fall of Simon Magus*, in S. Giacomo Maggiore. At Ancona (1561) he decorated the Palazzo Ferretti, construction of which he had begun earlier (it is now a National Museum), and in the same city is an altarpiece in the Church of the Gesù. He was in Ferrara in 1562 and in the same year went to Milan where, thanks to the patronage of Cardinal Carlo Borromeo, he was named architect of the city. He built (1564–1568) the Borromeo College at Pavia, the churches of S. Fedele and S. Sebastiano (1576) at Milan, rebuilt (1566) S. Gaudenzio at Novaro, and built palaces, villas, gates, façades, fortifications, and other structures in a number of cities. In 1587 he went to Spain to work for Philip II and expressed his original personality in the decoration of the ceiling of the Library of the Escorial. His sojourn in Spain was eminently successful; he was given a title, honors, and returned (1596) to Italy greatly enriched. At Milan he took up work on the cathedral and continued there until his death. As a sculptor Tibaldi seems to have confined himself to creating designs for stuccos and other ornamental works that others carried out. A number of works by Tibaldi in Lombardy reveal the new style of late mannerism as he developed it.

Tifernate (tē-fer-nä′tā), **Gregorio.** Humanist; b. at Città di Castello (whose ancient name was Tifernum, whence his name), 1414; d. at Venice, after 1462. He studied medicine, Latin, and Greek, and to perfect himself in Greek made a journey to Greece. On his return to Italy he was an enthusiast for Greek studies, taught Greek, and made translations. In 1447 he was at Naples, where one of his pupils was Pontano, and in 1449 he was at Rome, where he made a translation of the *Nicomachean Ethics* of Aristotle for Pope Nicholas V. Going next to Milan, he translated the remaining two parts (*Africa* and *Asia*) of Strabo's *Geography*. (Guarino da Verona had translated *Europe*.) He went to France, taught Greek at Paris, returned to Italy, and at Mantua transcribed codices for the Gonzaga and gave lessons in Greek. His last move was to Venice, where he died. In addition to his translations he wrote Latin verse. His brother Lelio, whose work is sometimes confused with his, was his pupil. Lelio spent a long time at Constantinople to perfect his Greek, and made translations of the works of Philo Judaeus (Hellenistic Jewish philosopher of Alexandria, c20 B.C.–after 40 A.D.).

Tiger Earl. Epithet of **Lindsay, Alexander** (d. 1454).

Timone (tē-mô′nā). Comedy in terza rima by Boiardo, produced before 1494. It represents one of the earliest attempts at a play in Italian. The subject comes from Lucian (Greek satirist of the 3rd century), and concerns the misanthrope Timon of Athens. Many of the characters are allegories.

Tindal or **Tindale** (tin′dạl), **William.** See **Tyndale, William.**

Tino di Camaino (tē′nō dē kä-mä-ē′nō). Sculptor and architect; b. at Siena, c1285; d. at Naples, 1337. Son of the sculptor and architect Camaino di Crescentino, his name appears (1312) for the first time at Pisa, where he helped carve a baptismal font, fragments of which are now in the Camposanto and in the museum, Pisa. In 1315 he worked on the tomb of Henry VII for the cathedral at Pisa, only fragments of which remain, and in the same year is mentioned as Overseer of the Works of the cathedral. On his return to Siena he worked (1317–1318) with his father on the tomb of Cardinal Petroni; the parts of the tomb were reassembled in 1951 and it is one of his best preserved works in Tuscany. In 1320 he became Overseer of the Works of the cathedral at Siena. Subsequently he built the monument of Bishop Antonio d'Orso (d. 1321) in the cathedral at Florence. In its tranquil, almost abstract presentation of the dead bishop, seated on his throne, it is an outstanding example of 14th-century sculpture. In 1323 he was called to Naples by King Robert and remained there the rest of his life, working as architect and engineer for the Angevin court. Other artists at the court were Giotto, Simone Martini, and Pietro Lorenzetti, and some critics think Tino's grace of line was derived rather from the Sienese painters than from the sculptors. His relations with Pietro Lorenzetti appear to have been particularly close, as the latter became guardian of his children after Tino's death. Among his works at Naples are the tomb (1325–1326) of Queen Mary of Hungary, S. Maria Donnaregina, the tomb (1333) of Charles, duke of Calabria, and that (1332–1337) of his daughter, Mary of Valois, both in S. Chiara. Other works are at Turin, Berlin, London (Victoria and Albert Museum), Paris, Detroit, and elsewhere. One of the most notable of the immediate followers of Giovanni Pisano, whose pupil he may have been, Tino depended for his effects on solid construction, an elegant, sinuous line, and serene forms, all in sharp contrast to the tormented compositions of Pisano. The harmony and balance of his Neapolitan tombs, which were increasingly architectural rather than sculptural, had great influence on Gothic sculpture in southern Italy.

Tintoretto (tēn-tō-rāt′tō). [Real name, **Jacopo Robusti.**] Painter; b. at Venice, September or October, 1518; d. there, May 31, 1594. His father was a dyer (*tintore*) of silks, whence the name, "Little Dyer," by which he is known. Few details of the life of this purely Venetian painter are known. A precocious child, he was encouraged to draw and to use his father's colors, and at an early age was placed under Titian. Titian dismissed him after ten days because, according to Tintoretto's early biographer, he was jealous of his pupil's talent. Such stories of jealousy of the master for a pupil are fairly common and relatively meaningless. It has been suggested that it may have been Tintoretto's exuberant and free style of drawing that caused Titian's impatience. Without the benefit of workshop training and the contact with possible future clients, Tintoretto worked on his own and developed his genius independently. All about him were the works of the great Venetians–Bellini, Cima da Conegliano, Carpaccio, and Titian himself, whom Tintoretto never ceased to admire. He made charcoal drawings of casts, of the models he had of the figures of *Night*, *Day*, *Dawn*, and *Evening* that Michelangelo had carved for the New Sacristy in S. Lorenzo at Florence, of the statues of Sansovino, and sometimes worked by lamplight for heightened contrast of light and shadow. He drew from living models, dissected corpses to study muscle action, and made numerous rapid sketches to catch articulation and movement. He is said to have made small models in wax or clay that he placed in wood or paper houses with windows and doors cut in them, to see the effect of light falling upon his figures from various openings. He sometimes suspended his models from wires to study them from below, and thus learned to show figures that seem to float. He became a master in the treatment of light; his use of it as a compositional element to impart drama and movement, to enhance atmosphere and create space, and to produce a gleam and glow as of a living substance is one of the most notable elements and achievements of his art, and is a peculiarly personal attribute of it. Forever learning, to improve his skill he worked with Andrea Schiavone, painting cassoni and furniture panels, and frescoed decorations (now lost) on the outsides of buildings. Other influences on his development were Bonifazio Veronese, Lorenzo Lotto, and Michelangelo. It is reported that tacked to the wall of his

Tintoretto
Study of a male nude
Accademia, Venice
Alinari-Art Reference Bureau

studio was the motto, "the drawing of Michelangelo and the color of Titian." Influenced in his natural tendency to the heroic by Michelangelo, he was never a mere imitator. His own temperament caused him to see man as somewhat larger than life, great and glorying in action but not godlike. His heroic figures are bursting with vitality or furious energy, in constant impetuous motion or, sometimes, luminous with a profound spirituality.

By May, 1539, Tintoretto was listed as an independent painter. Works of his early period include an *Apollo and Marsyas* (1545), Atheneum, Hartford, that he painted for Aretino's house. The picture reflects the pastoral mythology of his cassoni panels for Schiavone. The early period culminates in a *Last Supper* (1547), S. Marcuola, Venice, which dates back to earlier Venetian painting but already shows his skill at grouping and his tendency to add figures from the workaday world that seem extraneous to the meaning of the painting yet which bind it in a unit and maintain the realism with which he ever flavored his art. Of 1548 is his *Miracle of the Slave,* painted for the Scuola di S. Marco and now in the Accademia, Venice. It was one of four paintings commissioned for the Scuola di S. Marco. Two others, *St. Mark's Body Brought to Venice* and *St. Mark Rescues a Saracen at Sea,* are also in the Accademia, and *The Finding of St. Mark's Body in Alexandria* is in the Brera, Milan. The three latter were painted later. With *The Miracle of the Slave* his reputation was established. Even Aretino wrote in praise of it. The characteristics of Tintoretto's independent genius are all present in the painting. It has the sense of depth and atmosphere, the realism of subsidiary figures, the daring contrasts of light and deep shade in the figure of the saint hovering over the tormented slave, and the drama of light and concentration of focus that Tintoretto increasingly developed in his work.

Of the vast number of paintings produced by Tintoretto and his shop, the greatest record of his artistic development, and a magnificent treasury of his art, is in the Scuola di S. Rocco, of which he became a member in 1565. The figure of St. Roch the Healer was one to which he intuitively and fervently responded. The legends of the saint's life were especially susceptible to his dramatic, turbulent treatment. He painted (1549) *St. Roch Heals the Sick of the Plague* and, on a cupboard, painted (1559) *The Pool of Bethesda and The Miracle of the Paralytic,* with its restless, muscular figures, for the Church of S. Rocco. In May, 1564, the members of the Scuola di S. Rocco (a brotherhood dedicated to the saint and engaged in charitable and humanitarian works) voted to decorate their building, which had been completed in 1545. They invited Paolo Veronese, Giuseppe Salviati, Taddeo Zuccaro, and Tintoretto to submit sketches for a *St. Roch in Glory.* The winner of the competition, to be decided by the members, was to paint a picture on the subject for the ceiling of the Hall of the Albergo (Hostelry), a room opening from the large Upper Hall. Tintoretto, ever eager for commissions, executed a finished painting and smuggled it into the building. On the appointed day the other competitors appeared with their sketches, but he pointed to the ceiling where his completed painting was already in place. Over the objections of his fellow artists he offered his painting as a gift. It was not difficult, thereafter, for him to secure the commission to complete the paintings for the ceiling and the walls. In the course of the next twenty years or so he painted the decoration of the entire building; the decoration of the Hall of the Albergo was carried out first (1564–1567), that of the great Upper Hall next (1576–1581), and that of the Lower Hall last (1583–1587). Contracts were renewed from time to time and Tintoretto eventually asked for, and received, an annual stipend rather than a fixed price for each painting. The program for the huge paintings (some as high as sixteen feet) was devised by theologians, but Tintoretto was free to execute it as his spirit demanded. In the Upper Hall there are thirteen scenes from the Old Testament on the ceiling and ten scenes from the Life of Christ on the walls. The latter include an *Adoration of the Magi* (1587) in which the Holy Family is shown in a loft on an upper level, while the animals and worshippers look up from below. The two-level composition gave the painter the opportunity to present remarkable interactions of light. In the Lower Hall are scenes from the Life of the Virgin, a self-portrait (1573), and two singularly moving panels, *The Magdalen in the Wilderness* and *St. Mary of Egypt,* in which the solitary figures

TINTORETTO
Study for a figure in *The Worship of the Golden Calf*, Church of the Madonna dell' Orto, Venice
Uffizi, Florence Alinari-Art Reference Bureau

of the saints maintain their integrity and power against a remote and poetic landscape. In the Hall of the Albergo the paintings include a tremendous *Crucifixion* in which the drama and grief of the central theme are the more poignant for the furious activity that surrounds it, *Christ before Pilate*, with its flickering, focusing light, and others. The many paintings (over fifty) of the Scuola di S. Rocco epitomize the genius of this highly original, impetuous painter. Remarkable for the plasticity of the figures, fitful and luminous color that often has an almost phosphorescent glow, for their dramatic power, and an unequaled mastery of light, as well as for sublime contrasts of action and sentiment, they constitute an artistic monument on the scale of Michelangelo's Sistine Ceiling and Raphael's *Stanze* in the Vatican.

While he was painting in the Scuola di S. Rocco Tintoretto also fulfilled a great number of other commissions, as in the Ducal Palace. Many of these were destroyed in the fires of 1574 and 1577. Thereafter, he, with Paolo Veronese, was commissioned to replace the lost decorations. Among those then painted were a number of allegories and glorifications of Venice, *The Forge of Vulcan* and other mythological paintings, still in the Ducal Palace, *The Origin of the Milky Way*, National Gallery, London, and, in the Hall of the Great Council, the enormous *Paradise* (begun 1588). The latter, supposedly the largest oil painting ever executed, is famous, for its movement and sweep, and possibly also for its great size and the over 500 figures represented in it; it has been largely repainted. He painted for the Library of St. Mark's, designed mosaics (1568–1592) for S. Marco, and executed paintings for numerous churches. Among the latter is a series of *Last Suppers*, beginning with that in S. Marcuola (1547), and continuing with others in S. Trovaso, S. Stefano, S. Polo (1565–1570), S. Simeone Grande, and S. Giorgio Maggiore (1594) (there is another in St. François Xavier, Paris, and those in the Scuola di S. Rocco). The series shows his development of the subject from the frieze-like early painting to the swirling movement and gleaming light of the last. Other paintings in churches at Venice include *The Worship of the Golden Calf*, *The Presentation of the Virgin*, and others, Madonna dell' Orto, *Marriage at Cana* (1561), S. Maria della Salute, *Crucifixion* and *Descent into Limbo* (1568), S. Cassiano, and paintings in a great number of other churches, in the Accademia, Ca' d'Oro, and the Correr Museum. The vast corpus of his work also includes a large number of splendid portraits. Those representing vigorous old Venetians, as that of Jacopo Sansovino, painted when the subject was 80, Pitti Palace, Florence, are especially fine.

In his own day Tintoretto was noted for his great speed. With swift, impetuous strokes of his brush he translated the passion and spontaneity of his inspiration in a technique totally his own—a technique that lent an urgent sense of life and movement to the enormous number of paintings he produced in a lifetime devoted to work. Unlike Titian, with whose thoughtful methods Tintoretto's hasty execution was unfavorably compared by some, he had few contacts with the great of the world. His personal life was uneventful. He married (1550) and subsequently became the father of six children, three of whom became painters in his flourishing workshop. In his studio his pupils and assistants worked from models and casts, and executed paintings from designs that were frequently versions of works he had himself painted. His adored daughter Marietta (b. 1552) was known for her portraits, and Domenico (b. 1560) was his father's most able assistant in that line. Tintoretto, except for a brief visit to Mantua (1580) to deliver and install eight battle scenes painted for the Gonzaga family, hardly left Venice. He passed his life painting portraits for Venetian clients and works on religious, mythological, and allegorical subjects for the churches, great Venetian confraternities, the Ducal Palace, and other public buildings at Venice. From what has gone before it is evident that his best works are at Venice, and there the record of his art unfolds to its fullest extent. He is also represented in all the great museums of Europe, and at Baltimore (Walters Art Gallery), Birmingham (Alabama), Boston (Museum of Fine Arts, Isabella Stewart Gardner Museum), Brooklyn, Cambridge, Chicago, Cleveland, Columbia (South Carolina), Detroit, Glens Falls (New York, Hyde Collection), Greenville (South Carolina), Indianapolis, Lawrence (Kansas), Manchester (New Hampshire), Minneapolis, New Haven, New Orleans, New York (Metropolitan Museum, Morgan Library), Philadelphia (Johnson Collection), Poughkeepsie, Princeton, Providence, Richmond (Virginia), Rochester (New York), St. Louis, San Francisco, Santa Monica (California), Sarasota, Seattle (Washington), and Worcester (Massachusetts). Many of the examples are portraits, and many of the paintings in museums were executed to varying degrees by assistants.

Tinucci (tē-nöt′chē), **Niccolò.** Writer and notary; b. at Florence, 1390; d. August 20, 1444. He practiced his profession as a notary from 1409 to 1422, and played a part in public affairs, opportunistically supporting now the Medici and now their rivals, the Albizzi. He wrote vigorous and realistic love poems, and exchanged sonnets with Burchiello. With some fellow spirits he convinced (contrary to fact) a fellow townsman that the latter had been elected podesta of Norcia. The joke formed the basis of a tale of the 15th century.

Tiptoft (tip′toft), **John.** [Title, Earl of Worcester.] English scholar and politician; b. at Everton, Bedforshire, England, c1427; beheaded on Tower Hill, London, October 18, 1470. He was the son of John, Baron Tiptoft, inherited his father's estates in 1443, was educated at Oxford, and was created earl of Worcester in 1449. Always a Yorkist, he held high office under the Yorkist king and was treasurer of the exchequer in 1452. Noted in his own day for his scholarship, he went to Italy, in 1457 or 1458, and from Venice took ship to the Holy Land. On his return to Italy he went to Padua to study Latin, "though," as Vespasiano says, "he was well versed in the same." At Ferrara he became acquainted with the famous teacher Guarino da Verona, and at Florence he heard the lectures of Argyropolous and bought books and had copies transcribed by Vespasiano's copyists. His knowledge of Latin was such that it was said Pope Pius II wept at the eloquence and purity of his Latin in an oration Worcester made to him and the cardinals at Rome. On his return to England he held high office under Edward IV (1442–1483). As constable of England (1462–1467) he tried and sentenced to death John de Vere, earl of Oxford, his eldest son, and other Lancastrians. In the summer of 1464 he sentenced Sir Ralph Grey and others to death, and as deputy of Ireland he executed his predecessor and members of his family, including two young children. In 1470 a revolt in Lincolnshire brought more executions. Some of the victims, having been hanged, were drawn and quartered and their heads were then impaled. For his tyrannical acts and his cruelty, Worcester was hated by the people. They said he followed "Paduan law," and called him "the butcher of England." When Edward IV was forced to flee, Worcester fled also. He was discovered in his hiding place among a group of herdsmen in the forest of Weybridge, and was taken to London. He was condemned to be beheaded on Tower Hill. Before he went to his death, which he met with great dignity, he asked the headsman to give three strokes of the axe in honor of the Holy Trinity. Many of the books of his rich collection, of which it was said that he despoiled the libraries of Italy to enrich those of England, were given to Oxford.

Tirsi (tēr′sē). In Torquato Tasso's pastoral play *Aminta,* a shepherd and friend of

Aminta. Into his mouth Tasso is thought to have put his own ideas of the joys of the idealized Arcadia as opposed to the envy, bitterness, and struggle of court life.

Tisi (tē′zē), **Benvenuto.** See **Garafolo.**

Titian (tish′a̤n). [Real name, **Tiziano Vecelli** or **Vecellio.**] Painter; b. at Pieve di Cadore, in the Friuli, c1488–1490; d. of the plague, at Venice, August 27, 1576. He was a member of an ancient family of the region. When he was about nine years old he was sent to an uncle at Venice, who placed him in the workshop of a mosaicist. His stay with the mosaicists was brief, as he moved on to the workshop of Gentile Bellini, and then to that of Giovanni Bellini. The influence of the Bellini on his development was not great, however; it was Giorgione who was his real teacher. He worked (1508) with Giorgione in the execution of the fresco decoration (now lost) on the exterior of the Fondaco dei Tedeschi at Venice. According to tradition, his success in this work led to a coolness between him and Giorgione. However that may be, the lyricism, poetic vision, and sense of color that he developed was so close to that of Giorgione in Titian's early work that some paintings are variously attributed to both painters. It was perhaps also from Giorgione that his marked predilection for landscapes derived, a preference more noticeable in his early years, but one that was not absent in his later career. Vasari writes that "he owed the excellence of the landscapes in his pictures to his studies with some German painters whom he had entertained in his house for several months," and he surely was familiar with the work of Dürer, who visited in Venice (1505, 1506). Examples of the lyrical landscapes, which won him great praise, are *Orpheus and Eurydice* (before 1510), Carrara Academy, Bergamo (formerly attributed to Giorgione), and the cassoni panels, *Birth of Adonis* and *Forest of Polydorus* (before 1511), Civic Museum, Padua. Other works formerly attributed to the mature Giorgione and ascribed to the youthful Titian by some critics, include *Fête Champêtre,* Louvre, Paris, with the ripe, sensual nudes that Titian painted to perfection, against a poetic landscape, *Noli me tangere,* National Gallery, London, *Madonna with SS. Roch and Anthony,* Prado, Madrid, *Gypsy Woman,* Vienna, and the intuitive yet realistic *Concert,* Pitti Palace, Florence, in which the painter has crystallized an instant of spiritual and emotional accord between musicians. In 1510 (the year of Giorgione's early death), he was commissioned to paint frescoes in the Scuola del Santo at Padua. The work he carried out there shows him to have passed beyond the Bellini and Giorgione to a new means of pictorial expression, one marked by vivid movement, realism, and a powerful expressivity. In these paintings he used color as an integral painting element and to create form, rather than as an extension or embellishment of draftsmanship. He originated a technique of applying color in patches, so that at close range the forms are somewhat indistinct, but from a distance, as they were intended to be seen, the shape and movement is clear and living. In the Scuola the highly expressive *The Child Affirms its Mother's Honesty* is notable for its warm, rich color; *The Saint Heals a Woman Wounded by her Husband* concentrates the drama on the instant of the wounding, while the miracle of the healing by St. Anthony takes place in a vignette to one side of the painting. By this time he was also painting portraits pulsing with energy and vitality, as *Man in a Red Cap,* Frick Collection, New York, and *La Schiavona,* National Gallery, London. His *Sacred and Profane Love* (c1515), Borghese Gallery, Rome, the meaning of which is obscure, is derived from a literary subject. It embodies his ideal of feminine beauty in the richly dressed lady seated at one end of a rectangular fountain and the opulent nude at the other. Between them a child dabbles in the water, as the pellucid rays of the setting sun bathe a castle in the background with a vibrant light. Many find this a sublime example of the poetic enchantment of which Titian was capable. In 1513, at Venice, he agreed to execute a battlepiece for the Hall of the Great Council in the Ducal Palace, and applied for the first vacancy as broker at the Fondaco, a lucrative patent already accorded to Bellini and Carpaccio. (The promised battlepiece was still undelivered in 1537; the authorities revoked his patent and demanded he repay the money he had received under it. He finished the painting the next year; it hung in the Library of the Ducal Palace until it was destroyed in the great fire of 1577.) In the same year he was invited by Cardinal Bembo to visit the court of Leo X at Rome, but declined the honor. On the

Titian
Landscape with a Castle
Musée Bonnat, Bayonne

thin; ᴛʜ, then; y, you; (variable) ḏ as d or j, ş as s or sh, ţ as t or ch, ẓ as z or zh; o, F. cloche; ü, F. menu; ċh, Sc. loch; ṅ, F. bonbon; ʙ, Sp. Córdoba (sounded almost like v).

death (1516) of Bellini he became his successor as broker at the Fondaco and as portrait painter to the doges.

Opposed to the earthly sensuality of some of his mythological and allegorical pictures is the sincerely religious spirit of such paintings as *Baptism of Christ* (c1512–1515), Capitoline Gallery, Rome, *Tribute Money*, Dresden, and *Madonna with the Cherries*, Vienna. Of 1518 is his lovely *Assumption*, Church of the Frari, Venice, with a dynamism in its soaring movement and sparkling color hitherto unknown. He painted religious pictures, mythological subjects, and portraits concurrently. After the death of Bellini he completed that master's *Feast of the Gods* for Alfonso d'Este of Ferrara. The duke commissioned him to paint several pictures for his Alabaster Chamber at Ferrara. The paintings, based on passages from the *Immagini* of Philostratus and works of Ovid and Catullus, are delightful for the spontaneity of the painter's invention, for a gay and airy spirit, and for complete mastery of design and clear, bright color. Of these, the *Worship of Venus* (1519), Prado, Madrid, shows scores of cupids gamboling before the goddess in a pastoral landscape; the *Bacchanal* (c1519) depicts Bacchus arriving on the island of Andros to find the natives perpetually intoxicated from the stream of pure wine that flowed through their island; and *Bacchus and Ariadne* (1523), National Gallery, London, recreates the landing of Bacchus with his car on the island of Naxos to rescue Ariadne, as told in Ovid and Catullus. In his frequent visits to Ferrara in the course of painting for Alfonso, Titian came into contact with Raphael's art through cartoons Raphael had sent his regal patron in lieu of the finished paintings he had promised. Titian's connection with the ruling Gonzaga of Mantua began about 1523, and a *Deposition* (c1525), Louvre, may have been painted for Isabella d'Este, or for her son, the Marquess Federigo, whose portrait, painted in 1531, is now in the Prado. By this time Titian was enormously celebrated and had many commissions. He also had a number of irate clients because of his dilatoriness in delivering works he had promised. His aristocratic patrons did not like to be kept waiting and sometimes resorted to threats. After the sack of Rome (1527), Aretino arrived at Venice and soon became a close friend of Titian. He used his notable talents as a writer (often employed for his own sinister ends) in the service of Titian, acting as a publicity agent to bring to the attention of the great the merits of the painter, or to soothe them for delays in the delivery of paintings, or to suggest paintings that Titian might offer as gifts in order to bring himself to the notice of a particularly important person. In the same year Jacopo Sansovino came to Venice and the three became great friends. Titian painted revealing portraits of Aretino, among them one now in the Frick Collection, New York, in which the writer's vulgarity is redeemed by a virile arrogance that scorns apologies (another portrait is in the Pitti Palace, Florence). In 1529–1530 he contrived to have Titian at Bologna, where Charles V was to be crowned by Clement VII. Through the influence of the marquess of Mantua, who had managed to come out on the winning side in the struggles in Italy between Spain and France, Titian painted the emperor's portrait (now lost) and began the relationship with Charles that was to prove so fruitful for him. In time he became what was even then rare as between artists and the aristocracy, a friend and intimate of the imperial family. At this time, however, his most important patron was the marquess of Mantua, and for him he painted the charming and poetic *Madonna with the Rabbit*, Louvre. The model for the Madonna was Titian's young wife Cecilia (d. 1530) whom he had married five years earlier, thus legitimizing their three children: Lavinia, Orazio, who became a painter, and Pomponio, who was unsuccessful in an ecclesiastical career and ever a worry to his father. In 1531 he left his old studio at Venice and took a house out on the lagoon, in a spot notable for views of the distant mountains and of the nearer island of Murano. In 1532 Charles V visited Federigo Gonzaga at Mantua. There he saw a number of paintings Titian had painted for the young ruler, admired Titian's portrait of Federigo, and decided to sit for his own portrait. Titian came from Venice and between December, 1532, and February, 1533, painted him a second time. The standing emperor is dressed in full state regalia and holds a dog by the collar. The formal and stately portrait, now in the Prado, so pleased the emperor that, according to tradition, he declared that henceforth no one but Titian should paint his portrait. He rewarded the painter by naming him Count Palatine and a Knight of the Golden Spur. Also at Bologna he painted a striking *Portrait of Cardinal Ippolito de' Medici*, Pitti Palace. The cardinal was a man irresistibly drawn to the military life, despite the ecclesiastical career on which he had embarked in accordance with his father's wishes. He is shown in Hungarian dress, in commemoration of his recent return from the wars in Hungary, with a sword in his left hand and the baton of a commander, or a mace, in his right. Isabella d'Este, then (1534) a woman of about 60, asked Titian to paint her as a young woman, and sent him a portrait Francia had painted of her over forty years earlier. Titian painted the portrait of a radiant, lively girl that is now at Vienna. Other masterly portraits of the period include *La Bella* (1536), Pitti Palace, painted for the duke of Urbino, *Young Woman in a Fur*, Vienna, and *Young Woman in a Feather Hat*, Hermitage, Leningrad (the model is the same in all three), and one of Francis I, Louvre, the old enemy of Titian's patron Charles V, supposed to have been painted from a medallion by Benvenuto Cellini. Other noble patrons included Francesco Maria della Rovere, duke of Urbino (the duke did not actually sit for his portrait, but sent his armor to the artist's studio), and his successor Guidobaldo, for whom he painted the *Venus of Urbino*, Uffizi. Between 1536 and 1538 he painted portrait busts of eleven (out of twelve commissioned) Roman emperors for Federigo Gonzaga. The paintings, now lost, of the emperors in their ancient armor were immensely popular and widely imitated. In this period he was especially occupied in painting portraits; anybody of any consequence who passed through Venice sat for Titian. Among the portraits are two of Cardinal Bembo, one in the National Gallery, Washington, and another at Naples, and two especially winning portraits of children, that of Clarice Strozzi (1542), Berlin, and of Ranuccio Farnese as a boy (1542), National Gallery, Washington. Pope Paul III went into Emilia, in April, 1543, and sat for him in the course of his stay. The portrait, now at Naples, pleased the old pope, who offered Titian the office of Keeper of the Seal, but as Sebastiano del Piombo, Titian's friend, held the post at the time Titian declined it. Finally (1545), on the invitation of the Farnese family he went to Rome. There he was welcomed by Pietro Bembo, Cardinal Farnese, and Pope Paul himself. He stayed in the Belvedere in the Vatican; Michelangelo, whom he had met at Venice in 1529, visited him; Vasari and Sebastiano del Piombo showed him the sights of Rome. His knowledge of the Roman school, to which he had been introduced by the cartoons of Raphael at Ferrara, was broadened by contact with the great works of Raphael, Michelangelo, Sebastiano del Piombo, and others, and his knowledge of the classical age through his observation of Roman monuments and statuary. He painted the shatteringly realistic *Paul III and his Nephews;* caught in a moment of family tension, the hunched old pope with his sharp, monkey-like face clearly dominates the scene. The nephews back away before the lightning of his piercing eyes. The swift, sketchy portrait with its bald illumination of personalities was a new departure in portraiture. Also at Rome he painted *Danaë*, Naples, the first of several of this type of nude. Others are at Vienna, Madrid (Prado), and Leningrad (Hermitage). In March, 1546, he was granted Roman citizenship, and three months later he was back at Venice. In January, 1548, Charles V, at Augsburg for the Diet, requested his presence in that city. There he painted the magnificent equestrian portrait, *Charles V on Horseback*, Prado, and the simpler, more human portrait of Charles seated in a loggia, now at Munich. Late in 1550 he made another trip to Augsburg, and gave the emperor the *Mater Dolorosa*, Prado, that Charles took with him to the monastery after his abdication. On the occasion of his second visit to Augsburg he painted Prince Philip (as well as many other notables), and ever after remained on warm terms with him. He painted a number of pictures for Philip when he succeeded his father as emperor. (Being on friendly terms with the emperor was no assurance of being paid for his work; a number of letters are extant in which the painter reminds the emperor that he owes him money.) By August, 1551, Titian was back at Venice and never left it again.

His painting continued to develop as he grew older. His style became freer, and took on a flavor of universality, especially in a great series of portraits of dignified, richly clad, patently accomplished and able men, and executed with a richness of color and depth that was unsurpassed. He also painted on biblical and mythological subjects and executed, for Philip II, a series of paintings on what he called "poetic subjects." Among these are *Venus and Adonis* (1554), Prado, *Diana and Actaeon* (c1559) and *Diana and Callisto*, Edinburgh. According to Vasari, his later works, "executed in bold strokes and patches of color, are unintelligible at close range but appear perfect when seen at a dis-

TITIAN
Angel of the Annunciation
Gabinetto Disegni e Stampe degli Uffizi
Foto Soprintendenza

tance." Many drawings are extant that indicate the manner in which Titian prepared himself before applying paint to canvas. It was a merit, according to Vasari, that his draftsmanship, even though not applied to the canvas, was the basis of his technique with color, for "He who can draw need not rely on color alone to hide the lack of design as many of the Venetians do." Michelangelo, observing the patches of color by which Titian obtained his effects of form and depth, criticized his draftsmanship. A contemporary wrote of his technique "he weighed down his canvases with masses of color sufficient to form a ground or foundation for his forms; he then superposed on and modelled through them. The ground thus provided, he turned the paintings to the wall without looking at them sometimes for months; when he finally took to the brush again, he scrutinized them with the careful attention he would give a formidable enemy, to see what faults he could find . . ." He made any revisions required and, in completing them, "he used his fingers rather than his brush." A celebrated painting in this technique is *Rape of Europa*, Isabella Stewart Gardner Museum, Boston. As vigorous as ever, in his old age he produced some of his most significant work. Among these are the dramatic *Entombment* (1559), Prado, sent to Philip II, for whom he painted some of the most important works of his last period. Other versions of the painting are at Vienna and in the Ambrosiana, Milan. Of the same year is *Adoration of the Magi*, Escorial. Other paintings for Philip included *Last Supper* (1564), Escorial, marred by repainting, *Crucifixion*, Escorial, and *Adam and Eve*, Prado. Other paintings of his last years are *Annunciation* (before 1566), S. Salvatore, Venice, *Education of Cupid* (c1566), Borghese Gallery, Rome; the emotional *Martyrdom of St. Lawrence*, Escorial, with its moving nocturnal effects, *Religion Defended by Spain*, Prado, *Madonna with St. Andrew, St. Tiziano and the Artist* (c1565), that he gave to the archbishop's church in his birthplace, and others. He repeated many paintings, some very closely, others with broadened treatment and swifter brushwork, as *Venus with an Organist*, Madrid (2), Berlin, Uffizi, *Venus with a Lute Player*, the Metropolitan, New York, and Cambridge, England, *Venus and Adonis*, London, and Madrid, and others. To the end of his days he was fully engaged with commissions for churches and palaces, and continued to produce masterpieces. His last paintings have a drama and violence, a sense of agitated motion and play of light that in impetuosity and energy excel his earlier works. Examples are the two paintings of *Tarquin and Lucretia*, Cambridge, England, and Vienna, in which the violence of the attack is incomparably more realistic, the dynamic impulse much greater, than in the early *The Saint Heals a Woman Wounded by her Husband*, Padua, which has the same central action.

Celebrated in his own day, court painter to Charles V and Philip II, Titian was the greatest of the Venetian painters and is ranked with Raphael, Michelangelo, and Leonardo among the painters of the High Renaissance. Noted for his rich, vibrant color, sense of movement and energy, whatever subject he undertook seemed to possess him so that he breathed its spirit into the painting. He developed a technique of painting, as noted above, that is fundamental to modern painting. Uninterested in teaching, he had few pupils, but his influence on such European painters as Velazquez, Rubens, Rembrandt, and Van Dyck, perhaps especially in portraiture, was incalculable. The greatest single collection of his paintings is in the Prado, Madrid. Other large collections are at Vienna, Venice (Accademia, Ducal Palace, and a number of churches), Paris (Louvre), Florence (Pitti Palace, Uffizi), London, and Washington (National Gallery). He is represented in many other European museums and at Baltimore (Walters Art Gallery), Boston, Chicago, Cincinnati, Cleveland, Detroit, Indianapolis (portrait, supposed to be of the poet Ariosto), Kansas City (Missouri), Los Angeles, Minneapolis, Omaha, Philadelphia (Museum of Art, Johnson Collection), St. Louis, San Diego, San Francisco, and Santa Monica (California), in addition to the museums previously cited.

Todeschini (tō-des-kē′nē), **Francesco de′.** Cardinal; b. c1440; d. at Rome, October 8, 1503. He was the nephew of Pius II, was adopted by the pope, and added the name Piccolomini to his own. Pius II made him archbishop of Siena, in January, 1460, and raised him to the purple in March of the same year. See **Pius III.**

Toledo (tō-lā′ᴛʜō), **Francisco de.** Spanish colonial administrator; b. c1515; d. at Seville, Spain, in September, 1584. While he was viceroy of Peru (1569–1581) the young Inca Tupac Amaru was executed, the Inquisition was introduced, and the code of laws called Libro de Tases was promulgated.

Tolomei (tō-lō-me′ē), **Claudio.** Sienese writer, diplomat, and public official; b. at Siena, 1492; d. at Rome, 1555 or 1557. At Rome he was in the service of Ippolito de' Medici, and at Piacenza in the service of Pier Luigi Farnese. When the latter was killed (1547), he went to Padua, and in 1549 he was named bishop. Returned to Siena, from which he had been exiled (1526) because of his support of the Medici, he held public office and served as ambassador to France. Among the many writings he left were critical, historical, and philological works, as well as many lyrics. As a poet he shared the nostalgia and idealistic vision of peasant and rural life of Navagero and other lyricists. In his technical writings he discoursed on metrics, supported Tuscan as a literary language in opposition to Castiglione, Trissino, and others, and advocated a reform of the alphabet. His *Versi, et regole de la nuova poesia toscana* (1539) gives rules by which the length or shortness of Italian syllables can be determined. He proposed that Italian meter, which depends upon natural verbal accents, be modified by classical meter, which depends upon long and short syllables.

Tomacelli (tō-mä-chel′lē), **Pietro.** Original name of Pope **Boniface IX.**

Tomitano (tō-mē-tä′nō), **Martino.** See **Bernardino da Feltre.**

Tommaso della Fonte (tōm-mä′zō del′lä fōn′tā), Fra. Dominican professor and spiritual adviser of St. Catherine of Siena. He made a collection of her sayings and deeds on which Raymond of Capua, her biographer, drew largely. Fra Tommaso's work is now lost.

Tommaso da Modena (dä mō′dā-nä). Modenese painter; b. at Modena, 1325 or 1326; d. 1379. He worked at Modena and Treviso, and went to Bohemia to decorate Karlstein castle there. The work he did at Karlstein includes a *Madonna and Child with SS. Wenceslas and Dalmasius*, and is more refined and spiritual, less crude and vigorous than some of his other work. He was a virile and imaginative artist, of marked originality. His *Virgin and Child with Saints* is in the Estense Gallery (Palazzo dei Musei), Modena. Of many works at Treviso, the series of forty Dominican monks he painted in the Chapter Room of S. Niccolò is outstanding. The series, dated 1352, includes representations of such noted Dominicans as St. Thomas Aquinas, St. Dominic, and Albertus Magnus. All the figures are shown in a studious or meditative aspect, and the great variety of pose, gesture, and facial expression of these forty figures is indicative of Tommaso's ingenuity and imaginativeness. The outlines are hard and rigid, and the perspective is weak, but each figure forms a lively and appealing panel. Other works at Treviso include a number of detached frescoes in the museum, and frescoes in S. Francesco and S. Lucia. Other examples of his work are at Bologna and Baltimore (Walters Art Gallery).

Tommasuccio da Foligno (tōm-mä-söt′chō dä fō-lē′nyō). [Original name, **Tommaso Unzio.**] Franciscan; b. near Nocera Umbra, 1319; d. at Foligno, September 15, 1377. He was a Franciscan tertiary who wrote verses and prophecies. His crude verses against vice and discord glowed with sincerity. His prophecies dealt with the misfortunes of Italy and the schism that was splitting the Church.

Tonstall (tun′stal), **Cuthbert.** See **Tunstall, Cuthbert.**

Torbido (tôr′bē-dō), **Francesco.** [Called **il Moro,** "the Moor."] Painter; b. c1482; d. at Verona, 1562. He may have been a pupil of Giorgione at Venice, and was in any event strongly influenced by him, an influence that appears in, for example, his signed and dated (1516) *Portrait of a Youth,* Munich. While still young he went to Verona and there became an assistant and perhaps a pupil of Liberale da Verona. He worked at Verona, Venice, and in the Friuli, was an uneven painter, and was subject to a number of influences. A *Holy Family and Saints,* an altarpiece in S. Zeno, Verona, reflects the Liberale Influence. He was also influenced by the mannerists, as appears in one of his best works, *Mystic Marriage of St. Catherine,* Neues Palais, Potsdam, and frescoes he painted (1534) in the apse of the cathedral at Verona on designs of Giulio Romano. In his portraits, for which he was perhaps best known, the influence of Lotto and of Titian (*Portrait of Fracastoro,* National Gallery, London) appears. Other works include a *Virgin and Child with Angels, St. Anthony and Donor,* Cannon Collection, Princeton, *Lady in a Turban,* Isabella Stewart Gardner Museum, Boston, and paintings at Mantua (S. Andrea), Messina, Milan (Brera), Naples, Rome (Doria Pamphili), Verona (museum and churches), Amsterdam, Berlin, Brussels, and elsewhere.

Tordesillas (tôr-ŧнā-sē′lyäs) or **Tordesilhas** (tôr-dẹ-sē′lyạsh), **Convention of.** Treaty between Spain and Portugal, signed at Tordesillas, near Valladolid, Spain, June 7, 1494, regulating their rights of discovery and conquest. The pope, by his celebrated bull of May 3, 1493, had drawn a meridian "100 leagues west of the Azores and Cape Verde Islands," giving to Spain the right of conquest to the west of it, and to Portugal the same right on the east. The Convention of Tordesillas removed this line to a meridian 370 leagues west of the Cape Verde Islands. At that time the continental character of America was unknown, and the powers supposed that they were dividing "the Indies," or Asia; but apparently it never occurred to them that, in pushing their conquests, they would eventually meet on the same meridian, but on the opposite side of the world. Unfortunately the meridian was not definitely fixed: first, because it was reckoned from an archipelago, and not from one island or point; and second, because the term "league" admitted of several different meanings. The Brazilian coast, discovered soon after, was clearly to the east of the Tordesillas line, and it was accordingly settled by the Portuguese; but the line passed near the mouths of the two great rivers Plata and Amazon, and in the uncertainty as to its position disputes arose in those regions. Eventually, and partly because of the uncertainty, the Portuguese pushed their conquests far westward. In the course of time the two powers met in the East Indies, and here the field of dispute was broader, owing to the defective methods of determining longitude that were then in vogue. The Philippine Islands, discovered by Ferdinand Magellan, were claimed and held by Spain as lying within her hemisphere (although, in fact, they were in the hemisphere which had been assigned to Portugal).

Torelli (tō-rel′le), **Lelio.** Jurisconsult; b. at Fano, October 28, 1489; d. March 28, 1576. He was a member of an old family, originally of Ferrara, that had scattered and had various branches around Ferrara. He studied the humanities at Ferrara and law at Perugia, and served his native Fano on embassies to various princes and to the pope. Later he established himself at Florence, where he was podesta (1543) and filled other official positions under the Medicean Signory. He left a number of writings on legal subjects, but is above all noted for his careful editing of the Florentine manuscript of the Pandects, *Digestorum seu*

Pandectarum libri L ex Florentinis Pandectis repraesentati (three volumes, Florence, 1553).

Torelli-Strozzi (strôt'tsē), **Barbara.** See **Strozzi, Barbara Torelli.**

Torgau (tôr'gou), **Alliance of.** [German, **Torgauer Bund.**] League formed at Torgau, 1526, by Saxony and Hesse and other Protestant states against the Roman Catholic states.

Tornabuoni (tôr-nä-bwō'nē). Distinguished Florentine family, whose name dates from 1393 when Simone, the son of Tieri di Ruggero Tornaquinci, took the name of Tornabuoni. Members of the family were among the early partisans of the Medici family. Francesco, son of Simone, fought against the Visconti (1424) and supported the return from exile of Cosimo de' Medici the Elder in 1434. His daughter Lucrezia married Piero de' Medici, Cosimo's son, and was the mother of Lorenzo il Magnifico. A son Giovanni lived mostly at Rome, where he attended to the financial and political interests of the Medici. His grandson of the same name was an intimate of Clement VII. A second Simone (1472–1543) was named a senator of Rome by Clement, was gonfaloniere at Florence after 1530, and was a member of the Council of Forty-eight, the new governing body at Florence. Donato (1505–1587), son of Simone, served Cosimo I de' Medici; his brother, Giuliano (1532–1605), served Ferdinando I de' Medici. In another branch of the family, Ludovico (d. 1519), a knight of Jerusalem, fought against the Turks at Rhodes (1480), returned to Florence, and was banished (1497) for his part in a plot to restore Piero II de' Medici. His brother Pietro (d. 1527) was also banished (1497), but was later reinstated and regained his influence after the Medici were restored (1512). Other members of the family served Florence and the Medici dukes as ambassadors and captains, and many were prelates. Simone, a knight of St. Stephen, was killed in the battle of Lepanto (1571); Niccolò (d. 1598), a bishop and ambassador to the court of France, introduced the cultivation of tobacco into Tuscany; Alfonso (d. 1577) had been a friend of Clement VII and was one of few trusted by Duke Cosimo I.

Tornabuoni, Lucrezia. Wife of Piero de' Medici, mother of Lorenzo the Magnificent, and poet; b. at Florence, 1425; d. March 25, 1482. A gifted and spiritual woman, she was the center and support of her family, the adviser of her husband and of her son Lorenzo, yet without mixing or intriguing in politics. A poet herself, she was the friend and patron of poets and men of letters. Among them, by whom she was revered, were Poliziano, Bellincioni, and Luigi Pulci. The last-named wrote his epic *Morgante maggiore* to please her. A remarkable woman of virtue and talent in an age when the former, at least, could not be taken for granted, she brought up her children (three daughters, Lorenzo, and his brother Giuliano, whose death in a conspiracy she bore with fortitude) in strict accordance with the teachings of the Church. They never abandoned the Church, and remained devoted to their mother. Her Italian *Laude* (hymns) and writings of the lives of the saints reveal her profound religious conviction, and are moving in their sincerity, without being manifestations of a great poetic gift. But it must be remembered that poetry was the favored form of expression in that age, an accomplishment rather than an art.

Torquemada (tōr-kā-mä'ᴛʜa), **Juan de.** [**Johannes de Turrecremata.**] Theologian and cardinal; b. at Valladolid, Spain, 1388; d. at Rome, September 26, 1468. He entered the Dominican order as a youth, and by his profound study of theology and canon law came to be ranked as the most distinguished theologian of the 15th century. He studied at Paris and taught in Spain, and attended the Council of Constance (1417–1418). From 1432 to 1437 he was at the Council of Basel, as theologian for Pope Eugenius IV and as representative of King John II of Castile. He was a vigorous defender of papal power, as opposed to the limitations on it that the Council proposed, and expressed his views on the powers of the pope vis-à-vis councils in his *Summa de ecclesia* (1433). In 1438 he was with the pope at the Council of Ferrara, called to unite the Greek and Roman churches, and took part in the discussions. The following year he helped to prepare the decree of union signed at Florence (whither the Council had moved to escape the plague). Eugenius, who suffered grievously at the hands of the Council of Basel, named him "Defender of the Faith," and raised him to the cardinalate (1439). Eugenius, Calixtus III, and Pius II employed him on embassies of the highest importance. He wrote on nearly all the questions that were causing agitation in the Church of his day. Because of his interest in the new art of printing, he invited Ulrich Hahn, a printer from Ingolstadt, to come to Rome and establish a press there, the first at Rome. By 1465 the press had printed the Latin grammar of Donatus (4th-century Roman grammarian and rhetorician) and Cicero's work on orators. Throughout his life, and regardless of his exalted positions, Cardinal Torquemada lived simply and followed the rule of his order. His nephew, Tomás de Torquemada (1420–1498) earned a black reputation, as chief inquisitor of the Spanish Inquisition, for the cruelty with which he carried out his duties, and for his expulsion of the Jews from Spain in 1492; their confiscated property went to the crown.

Torquemada, Juan de. Spanish historian; b. at Valladolid, Spain, c1545; d. in Mexico, after 1617. His principal work is the *Monarquía indiana* (3 vol., folio, 1615). It is the most voluminous and one of the best of the early histories of Mexico.

Torquemada, Tomás de. Dominican prior; b. c1420; d. 1498. Ferdinand and Isabella made him first inquisitor general for Castile. He organized the Inquisition in Spain and became infamous for the severity with which he administered his office. He forwarded the plan for the expulsion of the Jews from Spain in 1492.

Torrigiani (tôr-rē-jä′nē), **Pietro.** Sculptor; b. at Florence, 1472; d. at Seville, Spain, 1528. He was among the Florentine youths who studied and drew the casts and marbles set up in the garden of S. Marco by Lorenzo de' Medici as a school for young artists. A fellow student there was Michelangelo, with whom he quarreled. In the ensuing fight Torrigiani won enduring notoriety by breaking Michelangelo's nose and disfiguring him for life. About 1492 he worked at Bologna, then at Siena and Rome. About 1510 he was invited to England by Henry VII. Benvenuto Cellini recounts, in his *Autobiography*, that Torrigiani, on his way to England a second time, invited him to go with him, and that he was tempted, but when he learned that Torrigiani had assaulted Michelangelo he was so angry that he could hardly restrain himself, and refused to go. In England Torrigiani executed the tombs of Henry VII, his masterpiece, and of Elizabeth of York, Henry's wife, in Westminster Abbey. After 1519 he went to Spain, where he fell into the hands of the Inquisition and subsequently starved himself to death.

Tortelli (tôr-tel′lē) or **Tortello** (-lō), **Giovanni.** Humanist and first librarian of the Vatican Library; b. near Arezzo, c1400; d. April 26, 1466. He studied medicine, went (1435) to Constantinople to perfect his Greek, earned (1445) his doctorate in theology, and was, as Pius II said, "as well versed in theology as in classics." At Florence he was on friendly terms with Leonardo Bruni, and at Rome, where he became attached to the papal court (1449), he became one of Nicholas V's most intimate friends. Nicholas chose him to become the first head of the Vatican Library and to make a catalogue of the books. According to his catalogue there were 9,000 volumes in the Library. In his position at Rome he occupied a central place in Italian humanism, under one of the most enthusiastic of humanist popes. He was in touch with and admired by the outstanding humanists of his day. Lorenzo Valla dedicated his work *Elegantiarum latinae linguae*, a work to restore the purity of the ancient Latin language, to him. Apparently Tortelli did not find it necessary to engage in the wars of words against other humanists which were often so violent and abusive between rivals. He wrote (1449) *Orthographia*, on the spelling of Latin words derived from the Greek. He also wrote one of the first histories of medicine.

Toscanelli (tôs-kä-nel′lē), **Paolo dal Pozzo.** Florentine scientist; b. at Florence, 1397; d. there, May 10, 1492. Toscanelli, whose life spanned almost the entire 15th century, was an astronomer, astrologer, mathematician, and geographer. His work, with that of a few others, made Italy preeminent in mathematics and the natural sciences in 15th-century Europe. He was ahead of his time, as the consuming interest of potential patrons and princes was in the humanistic studies and the arts. After study at Padua, where he was a friend of Nicholas of Cusa, and receiving his doctorate, he returned to Florence and enrolled in the Physicians' and Apothecaries' Guild (1425). At Florence he became acquainted with the outstanding men of his day. To his friend Brunelleschi he gave lessons in geometry and advice on the completion of the great dome of S. Maria del Fiore (the cathedral). The Florentine Signory consulted him as an astrologer concerning an earthquake (1453). He wrote extensively. Most of his mathematical and astronomical works have been lost. There remains, however, a manuscript containing accurate celestial maps with the paths of comets as they appeared on certain dates. In his scientific studies he abandoned complete reliance on ancient Greek and Arabic texts to make his original observations and deductions. His curiosity concerning the unknown areas of the world and the universe was insatiable. In 1468 he constructed a gnomon in the cathedral at Florence by which he determined the obliquity of the ecliptic. He sought out travelers to learn their accounts of foreign lands and set great value on the account of Marco Polo's travels. In 1474 he wrote a letter to a Portuguese ecclesiastic expressing his conviction that the shortest way to the Orient was not, as the Portuguese thought, by way of rounding Africa, but by going straight out across the Atlantic. His theories and charts influenced the plans of Columbus, but Toscanelli died before he saw his theory vindicated.

Tosini (tō-zē′nē), **Michele.** See **Ghirlandaio, Michele di Ridolfo.**

Traini (trä-ē′nē), **Francesco.** Pisan painter; active in the middle of the 14th century. His name is mentioned in documents between 1321 and 1347. Two panels on the life of St. Dominic, 1344 and 1345, now in the National Museum, remain of a series he painted for the Church of St. Catherine at Pisa. Also at Pisa, painted for the same Church, is a large panel, *Triumph of St. Thomas,* 1363. A remarkable series of frescoes in the Camposanto, Pisa, painted c1350, is attributed to him by many. Others attribute them to an unknown artist whom they call Master of the Triumph of Death. One scene in the series is the *Triumph of Death.* It shows a group of mounted hunters, men and women, who have been brought to a halt before three open coffins. The horses draw down their heads in terror; Death threatens a nearby mounted youth with his scythe; in one area the poor, old, and crippled plead with Death to release them from their misery, but he ignores them and attacks the young and noble. In another area are the anchorites whose saintly lives have freed them from the fear of death. The series, which also includes a *Last Judgment,* presents a minutely detailed picture of the rewards of penitence and virtue and the punishments for those who disregard them. The frescoes, and others like them, are thought to reflect the view that the Black Death of 1348 was sent to punish mankind for his sins, and to urge on him the necessity for penitence and a return to a spiritual life. The frescoes were heavily damaged in a bombardment of July, 1944. In his realism and violent movement Traini was strongly influenced by his fellow-townsman Giovanni Pisano, and by the Lorenzetti.

Traversari (trä-ver-sä′rē), **Ambrogio.** [Also, **Ambrogio Camaldolese;** Saint **Ambrose of Camaldoli.**] Ecclesiastic and humanist; b. at Portico, near Florence, September 16, 1386; d. at Florence, October 21, 1439. He entered the Camaldolensian order at the age of 14. A man of great piety, he was a theologian who knew Greek, had studied the Greek Fathers in the original, and translated many of them into Latin. His cell at the Convent of the Angels at Florence became a meeting place for some of the most distinguished humanists of the time. Leonardo Bruni, Carlo Marsuppini, Niccolò Niccoli, Poggio, and others went there to discuss theology with him. Gianozzo Manetti was his pupil and protégé. Cosimo de' Medici and his brother Lorenzo were occasional interested participants. Eugenius IV, who spent many years at Florence, named him general of his order (1431) and entrusted him with diplomatic missions for the Church. He took part in the Council for the reunification of the Greek and Latin Churches, in the Council of Basel, where he upheld the primacy of Rome, and in a mission to Emperor Sigismund. He was a better scholar than a diplomat. He made the first Latin translation of Diogenes Laertes' *Lives of the Philosophers,* and also translated a number of Greek Church Fathers. In addition to his translations, he left his own collection of *Lives* of the saints, a chronicle of Montecassino, and accounts of his order and of his diplomatic missions.

Trevisa (trẹ-vē′sạ), **John de.** English translator; b. in Cornwall, England c1326; d. c1412. He translated (1387) Ranulph Hidgen's *Polychronicon* into English and the *De Proprietatibus Rerum* of Bartholomew Anglicus (1398), and other Latin works.

Trevisan (trä-vē-zän′), **Zaccaria.** Venetian

humanist; d. 1414. He was a member of an old Venetian family that had been ennobled in 1381, and served Venice as an ambassador. His son Zaccaria (d. 1466) was also a humanist and ambassador for Venice.

Tribolo (trē′bō-lō). [Real name, **Niccolò Pericoli.**] Sculptor; b. at Florence, 1500; d. there, 1550. He carried out a number of works, at Florence (where he began the Boboli Gardens), Rome, Bologna, and Loreto. In his reliefs at Loreto on the *Translation of the Holy House,* and in his *Annunciation,* S. Petronio, Bologna, there is evidence of the influence of Michelangelo. His graceful art is shown to best advantage in a number of fountains he designed for villas at Castello and Petraia, in the neighborhood of Florence.

Tribraco (trē-brä′kō), **Gaspare.** [Original name, **Gaspare de' Tirimbocchi.**] Humanist and poet; b. at Reggio nell' Emilia, February 23, 1439; d. at Mantua, c1493. His father was from Modena, and Gaspare spent his youth in that city, devoting himself to humanistic studies, in which he soon became proficient. He taught grammar at Modena (1464) and went from there to Ferrara (1466), where he lectured on poetry at the university. He next went to Mantua and was tutor to Francesco Gonzaga. A facile versifier, his Latin verse included elegies, epigrams, eclogues, and satires, and reveal him more as one gifted in choosing from the best classical poetry than as a poet in himself. A narrative poem, *Triumphus in Borsium Atestinum carmen,* honors Borso d'Este of Ferrara.

Trippenmeker (trip′ẹn-mā-kėr), **Heinrich.** Original name of **Heinrich Aldegrever.**

Trissino (trēs′sē-nō), **Giangiorgio.** Man of letters; b. at Vicenza, July 8, 1478; d. at Rome, December 8, 1550. Of a noble and wealthy family, he did not begin his serious education until 1506, by which time he was married and had two children. He went to Milan, where Demetrius Chalcondylas was one of his teachers, and devoted himself to the study of Greek philosophy, the collection of manuscripts, and to his literary studies. In 1509 he was exiled from Vicenza for his earlier adherence to the emperor Maximilian, and deprived of his property. He went to Germany for a time, then returned to Italy and journeyed from court to court. At Rome he became a favorite of Pope Leo X, who sent him as ambassador to Germany, had the decree of exile revoked, and his property restored. Trissino also served Clement VII on various diplomatic missions, and accompanied him when the pope went to Bologna for the coronation of Charles V (1530). Charles made Trissino a count. He served the popes, including Paul III, and princes without pay, his own wealth having made him independent. He lived like a great noble, had a train of servants preceding and accompanying him when he traveled, and built a sumptuous villa at Cricoli. As the patron of the youthful Palladio, to whom he gave the name (from Pallas), and whose studies he encouraged and supported, he promoted the development of one of the greatest architects of the age. His wealth could have freed him from the necessity of flattering his patrons, but he was as extravagant in his praises of them as any who depended on the good will of a patron for a livelihood. He spent the last years of his life at his villa at Cricoli, at Padua, Milan, and Rome, ever hungry for the recognition that only princes could give. These years were embittered by ugly quarrels with his son Giulio, whom he attacked in his epic, *Italia liberata dai Goti,* disinherited, and accused of heresy. (Giulio was excommunicated and died in prison.)

Trissino's literary interests were varied. He wished to interpret the classics, to deduce rules and principles from them that could be applied to Italian poetry. In his *Arte poetica* he discussed literary and philological problems, as the language and meter of Bembo. He sought to define mimesis, catharsis, poetry, and tragedy, and to lay down principles for their treatment. These were all widely discussed questions in his time, the work was well received, and had a lasting influence. He emphasized structure and technique, and seemed unaware of the need for poetic genius. Furthermore, in his search for form and principles he went beyond the Latin writers to the Greeks. His tragedy, *Sofonisba,* written between 1514 and 1515 at Rome and first produced in 1556, is based on a story from Livy. The Carthaginian Sofonisba drinks the poison sent to her by her second husband, Masinissa, who has defeated her first husband, Syphax. In elaborating his tragedy Trissino held rigidly to the Greek rules of unity of action and time. He introduced a chorus that marked off the main divisions of the action, and kept it on stage throughout.

It is the first work of any importance to be written in blank verse. Faithful to the rules he had worked out, the tragedy is devoid of inspiration and is a lifeless demonstration of rules rather than a work of art. The story is told, not enacted. Nevertheless, it was highly praised in its time, gave him a place among the leading poets, and is regarded as the first neoclassical tragedy of modern literature. He devoted twenty years to the composition of his epic *Italia liberata dai Goti* in an attempt to create a Homeric epic based on history. The subject is the struggle between the Goths and Byzantium for Italy. The work, in hendecasyllabic blank verse, is a mixture of mythology and Christianity, allegory and history, and is an arid exhibition of his vast learning. His comedy, *I Simillimi* (1548), is an attempt to combine the Latin comedy of Plautus with Greek technique. Trissino was also a contributor to the discussion of the time on language. He proposed such changes as the introduction of certain Greek letters into the Italian alphabet, and changes in pronunciation. His proposals raised a hornet's nest of outraged comment. In his *Castellano* (1529) he discusses Dante's *De vulgari eloquentia*, the manuscript of which he had discovered and which he in this way introduced to the literary world. He referred to this treatise in support of his own view, which was to eliminate the special local elements of the various Italian dialects, select the words common to all, and create an Italian rather than a Tuscan or other regional language. This work also produced controversy; many doubted the authenticity of the Dante manuscript. A scholar, critic, and man of great learning untouched by any trace of poetic genius, Trissino's contributions lay in philology, form, and technique, and in his influence on his own and later ages. His literary interests were the preoccupation of many men of letters of his day. He is interesting also for his manner of life as a courtier, and for his quarrels—all typical of his age.

Trivet (triv′e̤t), **Nicholas.** [Also **Trevet.**] English chronicler; b. c1258; d. c1328. He was the author of *Annales sex Regum Angliae qui a Comitibus Andegavensibus originem traerunt*, a history covering the years 1136–1307. He also wrote many theological and philosophical works.

Trivulzio (trē-völ′tsyō), **Gian Giacomo.** [Called **the Great.**] Milanese general; b. at Milan, 1441; d. at Chartres, France, 1518. Son of an ancient and noble Milanese family, he became its most outstanding member for the fame he won in arms. He began his military career under Francesco Sforza and fought with his troops in France (1465), when Sforza sent aid to Louis XI. From that time, except for a pilgrimage to the Holy Land, his life was devoted to warfare. He fought valiantly for many years for Ludovico il Moro but when the latter felt threatened by the French (whom he had himself called into Italy, 1494), he named his favorite, Galeazzo Sanseverino, as commander of his forces. On being replaced, Trivulzio entered the service of the Aragonese of Naples, now the enemies of Milan. In the course of the invasion of Charles VIII into the kingdom of Naples, Trivulzio suddenly went over to the side of the French, and thereafter served them. He entered Milan (1499) in the army of Louis XII, was made a marshal of France, and was named governor of Milan by Louis. Following the brief return of Ludovico il Moro to Milan (1500), Trivulzio reentered the city. His harsh government aroused the hatred of the Milanese and he was relieved of his position, and returned to France. He was in Italy again in 1508–1509, and as a general of the League of Cambrai defeated the Venetians at Agnadello (1509). The last and greatest battle of his life, one that he called "a battle of giants," was the defeat of the Swiss and Massimiliano Sforza by the French forces at Marignano (1515). Nevertheless, in spite of his successes, the French general Lautrec intrigued against him out of jealousy and caused him to fall from favor at the French court. He returned to France to clear himself of charges that he was a rebel, but was coldly received. He died soon afterward.

Troilus and Criseyde (troi′lus or trō′i-lus; kri-sā′de̤). Long romance in rime royal by Geoffrey Chaucer, written c1385 and based on the plot of Giovanni Boccaccio's *Il Filostrato*. There are additions which show his reading of Boccaccio's *Il Filocolo*, Benoît de Sainte Maure's *Roman de Troie*, Guido delle Colonne's *Historia Troiana* (a Latin prose paraphrase of Benoît), Joseph of Exeter's *Frigii Daretis Ilias*, Boethius' *De consolatione philosophiae*, and other writings. Benoît and Guido had told of Briseida's faithlessness to Troilus. Boccaccio invented Troilo's falling in love with Criseida (as the names are spelled in Italian), and his wooing and winning of her with the aid of Pandaro. In *Troilus and Criseyde* Chaucer reveals his power especially in the atmosphere, the poetry, and the subtle characterization. The Lollius to whom, for his artistic purposes, he credits the story, probably originated in a scribal mistake in the first line of Horace's *Epistolae* (I, ii).

Troyes (trwä), **Treaty of.** Treaty between England and France, 1420, by which Henry V of England was to marry Catherine of Valois, daughter of Charles VI, to become regent of France, and to succeed Charles at his death. The resistance of the dauphin, Charles VII, aided by Joan of Arc, prevented Henry from realizing his claim to the French throne.

True Cross, The Story of the. 1. A legend recounted by Jacobus de Voragine, the 13th-century compiler, in *The Golden Legend,* a collection of the lives of the saints. The legend tells the story of the disappearance and subsequent rediscovery of the cross on which Christ was crucified.

2. A series of frescoes in the choir of the Church of San Francesco at Arezzo, painted by Piero della Francesca between the years 1452 and 1466. Bicci di Lorenzo, a Florentine artist, had been commissioned to paint the choir and the subject had been fixed. He had completed decorating the vaulting when he died (1452), and Piero della Francesca took over the work. The story told by the series is as follows. When Adam was dying, he sent his son Seth to the Archangel Michael for the Oil of Mercy that had been promised him. Instead, Seth was given a seed of the Tree of Life and told to plant it in Adam's mouth when he died. Adam died and was lamented. The seed was planted in his mouth, and from his tomb grew a tree that proved to have miraculous powers. Moses transplanted the tree, and later King David took it to Jerusalem. Wood from the tree was found to be unfit for the temple at Jerusalem; it was rejected, and was used to build a little bridge across the rill of Siloam. When the Queen of Sheba was on her way to visit King Solomon she came to the bridge. She recognized the sacred character of its wood and knelt down and worshiped it. Received by Solomon, she prophesied that because of the wood the earth would tremble, the sun and moon grow dark, and the veil in the temple be rent from top to bottom. She accused Solomon of neglecting and abusing the Holy Wood. This prophesy links the death of Adam with the Crucifixion. When Solomon learned that the end of the kingdom of Judah would come with the death of One who should be crucified on a cross made from this wood, he ordered the bridge taken up and the wood buried deep in the ground. In the time of Constantine (4th century A.D.), the tyrant Maxentius threatened Rome. Constantine dreamed that an angel appeared to him, and that he saw a cross in the sky and the words "In signo hoc confide et vinces" ("Trust in this sign and conquer"). He caused a small cross, similar to the one he had seen in his dream, to be made. Carrying it in his hand, he rode out at the head of his troops against Maxentius. The hand of God caused Maxentius to flee without giving battle, and he and his army were drowned in the Tiber. After this, Constantine was converted to Christianity and sent his mother, St. Helena, to look for the True Cross. She went to Jerusalem and at last heard of a Jew, Judas, who knew where the True Cross was hidden. He refused to tell. St. Helena had him placed at the bottom of a dry well and tortured. At the end of six days he agreed to lead her to the place, on Mount Calvary, where the True Cross was buried. Workmen, and Judas himself, began to dig, and brought up three crosses. No one knew which of them was the True Cross. They waited for a sign. The funeral procession of a young man came by and the three crosses were passed over him in turn. Under the shadow of the True Cross, the body of the young man rose up, drawn to life by its miraculous power. Years later, in 615, Chosroes the Persian set out on a wave of conquest of Christendom. He captured Jerusalem and carried off the True Cross to his palace, where he inserted it in his throne. The emperor Heraclius marched against him and defeated him on the banks of the Danube. Chosroes and his sons were slain. Heraclius took the True Cross back to Jerusalem, but as he was about to enter the city by the same gate through which Christ had carried His cross to Calvary the stones of the gate fell down and blocked his way. This reminded him that Christ had entered Jerusalem, on Palm Sunday, on the back of an ass. Heraclius took off his royal robes and, barefooted, entered Jerusalem and restored the Cross.

Piero della Francesca did not paint the incidents narrated above in chronological order, but changed the order as his artistic needs and vision demanded. The three walls of the choir are divided into three rows of about equal depth, with an incident from the legend, or related incidents, occupying each row. The end wall is pierced by a pointed window, leaving two narrow panels, divided into three rows, on each side. The lunette at the top of the right wall shows Adam dying, the Tree of Life, and lamentation for Adam, all with an over-arching sky. This is balanced by the scene in the lunette on the opposite wall, of Heraclius restoring the True Cross to Jerusalem, again a landscape with figures and an over-arching sky. The middle row of each wall has two incidents, each including architectural features. On the right wall is the Queen of Sheba worshiping the Holy Wood of the bridge. This scene is divided from the next by a column that marks King Solomon's court, where he is receiving the queen and her retinue. Opposite this row is St. Helena and the finding of the crosses, in one half of the row. In the background is a walled city, a picture of Arezzo that represents Jerusalem. The second scene in this row represents the finding of the True Cross by the resurrection of the dead youth whose funeral procession was passing before the gate of the city. The bottom row of each wall is filled by a battle scene, on the right wall the victory of Constantine over Maxentius, and on the left wall the victory of Heraclius over Chosroes. These are filled with color and movement and provide a solid base for the rows above them. The scenes of the burying of the wood and the torturing of Judas appear in the middle row of the small panels to the right and left, respectively, of the pointed window. The dream of Constantine, the first nocturne in Italian painting, appears in the bottom row of the small panel to the right of the window. Opposite this, in the same plane, is an *Annunciation,* that seems to have no connection with the legend. Various interpretations have been put forward regarding its significance. Although parts of the work, notably that showing the victory of Heraclius and the burying of the wood were executed by assistants, the entire series is based on Piero's own cartoons.

3. Variations of the legend were painted by Agnolo Gaddi in the choir of S. Croce at Florence, at the end of the 14th century, and by Cenni di Francesco in the Church of S. Francesco at Volterra, at the beginning of the 15th century. It was a popular theme outside Italy.

Tschudi (chö′dē), **Aegidius.** [Also, **Gilg Tschudi.**] Swiss historian and Roman Catholic theologian; b. at Glarus, Switzerland, 1505; d. February 28, 1572. He is considered "the father of Swiss history," the first Swiss historian to use and incorporate original documents and manuscripts in his chief work, *Chronicon Helveticum.* This covered Swiss history in the period 1000–1470. Tschudi also incorporated legends, such as that of William Tell, into his history, and thus preserved them. His work, published after his death (1734–1736), is marred by a number of inaccuracies.

Tudor (tū′dọr), **Elizabeth.** See **Elizabeth** (of *England*) (1533–1603).

Tudor, Jasper. [Called **Jasper of Hatfield;** titles, Earl of **Pembroke,** Duke of **Bedford.**] English soldier; d. in December, 1495. He was a son of Owen Tudor and Catherine of Valois, and uncle of Henry VII. A Lancastrian partisan, he fought in many battles of the Wars of the Roses, but fled to France after the Battle of Tewksbury (1470). After the accession of Henry VII he became earl marshal.

Tudor, Mary. See **Mary I** or **Mary Tudor** (of *England*); see also **Mary of France.**

Tullio Lombardo (töl′lyō lôm-bär′dō). Sculptor and architect; b. c1455; d. at Venice, November 17, 1532. He was the son of Pietro Lombardo (c1435–1515), and with his brother Antonio (c1458–1516?) was trained in his father's studio and worked on many of its commissions, as on the monument of Giovanni Zanetti for the cathedral at Treviso. The new chapel built to house the monument (which was being carved at Venice for assembly at Treviso) collapsed in 1486. Two years later Tullio went to Treviso to supervise its reconstruction. Among the works he is presumed to have designed are the monuments of Giovanni Mocenigo and of Andrea Vendramin, SS. Giovanni e Paolo, Venice. Other works include a marble altarpiece with a relief, *Coronation of the Virgin*, S. Giovanni Crisostomo, Venice, and a relief, *Bacchus and Ariadne*, now at Vienna. Tullio's taste and style were greatly influenced by the enthusiasm for the revival of everything pertaining to the classical age that was going on in his formative years. His classical approach is apparent in his *Adam*, the Metropolitan Museum, New York, and in the warriors and the draped figures of the Vendramin monument. Between 1500 and 1502 he was commissioned to furnish reliefs for the chapel of the saint in the Basilica of St. Anthony at Padua. These were *The Miracle of the Miser's Heart* (completed 1525), and *The Miracle of the Repentant Youth* (completed after 1520). He was highly esteemed in his day, and worked, sometimes with his brother and sometimes alone, on the sculptural decoration for the Ducal Palace at Venice, at Belluno, at Mantua, where he carved a doorway for Isabella d'Este, and at Feltre. One of his most noted works is the effigy of Guidarelli, in the Academy of Fine Arts, Ravenna. The sculpture has an atmosphere of gentle melancholy and tender emotion rare in the work of this usually rather cool humanist sculptor who took the classical as the model for his exquisitely worked sculptures.

Tunstall or **Tonstall** (tun'stạl), **Cuthbert.** English prelate; b. at Hatchford, Yorkshire, England, 1474; d. at Lambeth Palace, 1559. He advanced rapidly in the Church, became bishop of London, 1522, and succeeded Thomas Wolsey as bishop of Durham, 1530. When Henry VIII broke with the Catholic Church he maintained a passive role. Under Edward VI he reluctantly participated in the Reformation in England. Implicated in the events leading to the fall of Edward Seymour, the Protector, he was accused (1551) of treason. The charge was dropped but he was kept in custody and deprived of his offices. Under Mary he again assumed the bishopric of Durham, but took no part in the persecution of the Protestants. He refused in 1559 to take the oath of supremacy of Elizabeth or to assist at the consecration of Matthew Parker as archbishop of Canterbury, and was again deprived of his offices and placed in custody.

Tura (tö'rä), **Cosmè** or **Cosimo.** Ferrarese painter; b. 1430; d. at Ferrara, in April, 1495. His early life and training are obscure, but the Gothic elements that survive in his work were probably derived from local Ferrarese painters. Roger van der Weyden was at Ferrara in 1449, and it may have been from observation of his work that such Flemish elements as the careful attention to the most minute detail are derived. In addition, there were a number of northern craftsmen working at Ferrara. Tura frequently worked with them, making designs for tapestries, bench covers, chairbacks, and textiles, and was affected by their needs and manner of work. From 1453 to 1455 he was at Padua, and was impressed by Squarcione's classicism and by the frescoes Pizzolo was painting in the Church of the Eremitani (frescoes that Squarcione's pupil, Andrea Mantegna, completed). There is also evidence of Sienese decorativeness in his painting. Much of Tura's work is preeminently decorative but in comparison with the brilliance, lyricism, and spirituality of Sienese painting, Tura's, though frequently brilliant, is possessed of a sorcery that is often harsh and worldly. For any influences that may be detected in his work, he was above all an individualist, with a style that was thoroughly his own. It was an austere, eminently virile and original style, in which naturalism, possibly derived from the works of Donatello at Padua, and Squarcione's classicism were fused into an entirely new manner of pictorial expression. For thirty years he was one of the foremost painters at Ferrara, ranked with his great contemporaries Piero della Francesca (who visited and worked in the city) and Andrea Mantegna. Borso d'Este, lord of Ferrara, was his chief patron, and from 1452 gave him a regular salary. For the restless and highly cultivated court he performed many artistic chores. He made designs for the decorations of furniture, and for textiles, designed (1472) the canopy and cover for the bridal bed of Duke Ercole I and Leonora of Aragon, painted flags, banners, and horse cloths on wool and leather, and designed costumes for the numerous festivities that delighted the Ferrarese; he made models for goldsmiths and designs for silver servies; he painted allegories, religious paintings and a number of portraits of the Estense family. A *Portrait of a Member of the Este Family* (c1451), the Metropolitan Museum, New York, is one of his earliest known paintings; the clear-cut profile of the youth is reminiscent of the Pisanello portrait of Leonello d'Este. From 1459 to 1463 he worked on the decoration (destroyed in a fire, 1483) of the Estense villa Belfiore. He is thought by some to have been the leading master in the decoration of the Hall of the Months in the Schifanoia palace; what remains of the panel *September*, with its grotesque figures and heads of Vulcan and workers in his forge, and Mars and Venus betraying Vulcan under a sheet, is attributed to him by some critics. Between 1465 and 1467 he was at Mirandola, decorating the library of Count Francesco I Pico with a series of allegorical panels on the theme of literature (all lost). From 1469 to 1472 he was decorating the chapel near the Villa Belriguardo for the Estensi; these decorations too, have perished. In the meantime, he was executing panels, polyptychs, and altarpieces for various ecclesiastical and princely patrons. After 1480 his great popularity, which had earned him so many commissions and so much money that he left generous legacies, declined. He withdrew to a tower on the city walls and lived there with a fellow artist. Soon after his death, Tura, who was a founder and one of the greatest representatives of the old Ferrarese school, was almost forgotten.

An intense and highly individual painter, Tura applied his great gifts as a draftsman to decoration rather than to naturalism. Folds of drapery, sometimes with the edges sharpened with white as in the *St. John the Baptist* and *St. Peter* of the Johnson Collection, Philadelphia, run and fall in angular geometric shapes. (The panels at Philadelphia are thought to be part of a polyptych, other parts of which, in the shape of roundels, are in the Isabella Stewart Gardner Museum, Boston, the Fogg Museum, Cambridge, and the Metropolitan Museum, New York.) The drapery of *The Madonna of the Garden*, National Gallery, Washington, is an extreme example of this treatment. In the allegorical figure, *Spring*, National Gallery, London, the drapery is again exaggeratedly angular and such calligraphic treatment of drapery is a characteristic of Tura's painting. The *Spring*, with a throne decorated with dolphins whose open jaws reveal terribly menacing teeth, indicates his delight in fantastic details. His tendency to fantasy is also apparent in the skull-like head of the princess and the swirling movement of the mounted saint of the *St. George*, painted (1469) on the outside wings of the organ door in the cathedral at Ferrara, and now in the Cathedral Museum. On the inside of the door wings is an *Annunciation* with an elaborate architectural background ornamented with nude statues. The harmony and tranquillity of the painting are in sharp contrast to the demonic energy of the *St. George*. There is an impression of distortion in many of Tura's paintings, of a mannerism deliberately employed for effect—drapery falls in angles; figures sometimes seem out of drawing; sinuous curves mark the outlines of eyelids and the shapes of mouths; cheekbones, especially in the female faces (as also in the *Portrait of an Unknown Man*, National Gallery, Washington) are prominent; hands, and sometimes heads, are exaggeratedly bony. There is also an impression of force and flintiness in figures as well as in landscape (in the *St. John in Patmos*, Genoa, the saint is set against a petrified landscape). Often his color is sharp and clashing, as in the *Madonna* at Bergamo (part of a polyptych of which other panels are in the Uffizi, the Louvre, Nantes, and New York), or it may be rich and heavy, as in the *Spring*, or frankly sumptuous, as in the *Virgin and Child Enthroned* (1474), National Gallery, London. The last, the central panel of the Roverella Altarpiece, is a vigorous composition in which the element of distortion is subdued. Other panels from the Roverella Altarpiece are the *Lamentation*, Louvre, Paris, a side panel with saints, Colonna Gallery, Rome, and a fragment with the head of *St. George*, San Diego, California. His peculiarly personal style, with its exaggerations, brittle forms, fascination with line, and touch of fantasy, makes him one of the most interesting painters of his age. Other works by Tura are in the Pinacoteca, Ferrara, the Accademia and the Correr Museum, Venice, the Brera and the Poldi Pezzoli Museum, Milan, the Estense Gallery, Modena (his monumental *St. Anthony of Padua*, his last dated work, 1484), at Ajaccio, Corsica, and elsewhere.

Turberville or **Turbervile** (tėr′bėr-vil), **George.** English poet, translator, and writer on hunting; b. in Dorsetshire, England, c1540; d. c1610. Among his works are *Epitaphs, Epigrams, Songs and Sonets* (1567) and *The Booke of Faulconrie* (1575). He is of some importance for his early use of blank verse in translating Ovid (1567).

Turone (tö-rô′nā). Veronese painter; active

in the middle of the 14th century. A spirited and realistic painter, but lacking any great gift, he was influenced by Giotto and by the Sienese. A polyptych with the *Trinity*, signed and dated 1360, is in the museum at Verona. He also painted a *Crucifixion* in the Church of S. Fermo Maggiore at Verona.

Turpin (tėr′pin). At the beginning of the 12th century there appeared a Latin chronicle, supposed to have been compiled by the 8th-century Turpin, archbishop of Rheims. It claimed to be an account of some years of Charlemagne's reign. This was a written account of a cycle of legends that had long been known among the people. As the legends were recited and then written down, with infinite variations of incident, Turpin became one of the cast of characters. Matteo Maria Boiardo, in his *Orlando Innamorato*, for the purposes of his story and the new element of love (drawn from the Arthurian romances) that he wished to add, says that Turpin suppressed the books of the Chronicle of Charlemagne's court that told of Orlando's love for Angelica. Boiardo having found them, he will recount the events that occurred because of Orlando's love.

Tusser (tus′ėr), **Thomas.** English poet; b. at Rivenhall, Essex, England, c1524; d. at London about April, 1580. After ten years at court, he settled on a farm in Suffolk. He wrote *A Hundred Good Points of Good Husbandry* (1557) and *Five Hundred Points of Good Husbandry United to as Many of Good Wiferie* (1573).

Tye (tī), **Christopher.** English composer and organist; b. c1500; d. before March 15, 1573. He was noted for *The Actes of the Apostles, translated into Englyshe Metre . . . to synge and also to play upon the Lute . . .* (1553).

Tyler (tī′lėr), **Wat** (or **Walter**). [Also, **Tegheler, Helier.**] Leader of a revolt of peasants in England in 1381; killed at Smithfield, London, June 15, 1381. With Jack Straw he led the men of Kent and Essex to London. He was killed by Lord Mayor Walworth while meeting with Richard II at Smithfield.

Tyndale or **Tindal** or **Tindale** (tin′da̤l), **William.** English reformer and translator of the Bible; b. in Gloucestershire, England, c1484; executed at Vilvorde, near Brussels, Belgium, October 6, 1536. His expressions of sympathy with the new learning having exposed him to persecution he went to the Continent in 1524. He visited Luther at Wittenberg, and settled at Worms where he published his octavo edition of the New Testament (1525). His translation of the Pentateuch appeared at Marburg (1530). At the insistence of Henry VIII he was arrested, imprisoned in the castle of Vilvorde, and after a trial for heresy was strangled, his body being burned at the stake. Among his works are *Parable of the Wicked Mammon* (1528), *Obedience of a Christian Man* (1528), and *Practice of Prelates* (1530).

Tyrrell or **Tyrell** (tir′e̤l), Sir **James.** English nobleman; executed at Tower Hill, London, May 6, 1502. He is remembered as the confessed murderer of Edward V and his brother Richard, duke of York.

U

Uberti (ö-ber′tē), **Farinata degli.** See **Farinata degli Uberti.**

Uberti, Fazio degli. See **Fazio degli Uberti.**

Uberti, Lucantonio de'. See **Lucantonio de' Uberti.**

Ubertini (ö-ber-tē′nē), **Francesco.** See **Bacchiacca.**

Uccello (öt-chel′lō), **Paolo.** See **Paolo Uccello.**

Udall (ū′da̤l), **Nicholas.** [Also, **Uvedale.**] English dramatist and Latin scholar; b. in Hampshire, England, 1505; d. 1556. He was the author of the first extant English comedy, *Ralph Roister Doister*. His translation of Erasmus' *Apothegms* was published in 1542. He also translated Erasmus' paraphrase on Luke.

Uffizi (öf-fē′tsē). One of the chief art galleries in the world, situated at Florence near the Arno River. The building was begun (1560) in the reign of Cosimo I de' Medici (1519–1574), later grand duke of Tuscany, and was intended to house the public offices (*uffizi*). The building is the masterpiece of its architect, Giorgio Vasari, who also designed the gallery over the Ponte Vecchio by which the Uffizi is joined to the Pitti Palace across the Arno where Cosimo lived. Cosimo de' Medici the Elder (1389–1464) collected paintings and sculptures to decorate his own palaces and villas. Other members of the family did the same. Grand Duke Francesco I (1541–1587) was the first to begin to arrange the Medici collections in the Uffizi. Subsequently, other members of the family added their collections. Anna Maria Ludovica de' Medici (b. 1671), heiress of the last grand duke of Tuscany, Gian Gastone (d. 1737), left the Medici art collections she inherited to the state of Tuscany on condition that they never be removed from Florence and that the works be available to the public of all nations. Of this rich patrimony many objects and paintings are in other collections and museums at Florence, but many paintings are in the Uffizi, making of it probably the richest collection of Italian Renaissance painting in the world. Other collections have been added to it by private collectors and by the government of Italy, and the collections include important examples of other European schools. The building has been enlarged from time to time, and by a reorganization undertaken in the 19th-century, collections of sculpture, gems, armor, tapestries, coins and other objects were removed to other institutions, but the rich collections of drawings remain in the Gabinetto Disegni e Stampe on the first floor of the building. The considerable damage inflicted on the building in World War II has been repaired.

Ufford (uf′ọrd), **Robert de.** [Title, 1st Earl of **Suffolk.**] English politician and soldier; b. August 10, 1298; d. November 4, 1369. He was a chief counselor of Edward III, and distinguished himself at Crécy (1346) and at Poitiers (1356).

Ugolino della Gherardesca (ö-gō-lē′nō del′lä ger-är-dās′kä). Pisan Ghibelline leader; d. 1289. He conspired to obtain the supreme power, and was imprisoned in 1274, but escaped and joined the Florentines who were then at war with Pisa. He returned to power in Pisa by force of arms. He subsequently led the Pisans against the Genoese and the Florentines and was unsuccessful. The Ghibellines turned against him and he sought aid from the Guelphs. He was finally overthrown, and with his two sons and two grandsons was starved to death in prison. His story forms a celebrated episode in the *Inferno* of Dante (Canto xxxiii). His tomb is in the Church of San Francesco at Pisa.

Ugolino da Montecatini (dä mōn-tā-kä-tē′nē). Physician and professor; b. at Montecatini Alto, 1345; d. at Florence, October 10, 1425. He studied medicine at Bologna, and practiced at Montecatini, Pistoia, and Pescia. In 1371 he was professor of medicine at Pisa, and later taught at Florence and at Perugia. Montecatini, a few miles from his birthplace, has been famous from antiquity to the present day for its sulphur and other springs. Ugolino wrote a book, *De balneorum Italiae proprietatibus ac virtutibus*, on the properties and curative powers of the waters that is one of the earliest treatises on the subject of balneotherapy.

Ugolino di Prete Ilario (dē prā′tā ē-lä′ryō). Painter of Orvieto; d. before 1408. He was influenced by his older contemporary Luca di Tommè, and seems to have passed a great part of his life working on the decoration of the great cathedral at Orvieto. With assistants, he executed extensive series of frescoes, as in the Chapel of the Corporal Cloth (1364), the choir and the vault, for which he did a series on the life of the Virgin and the Virgin in Glory (1370–1384). He is also credited with the design of some of the mosaics of the façade of the cathedral.

Ugolino da Siena (dä sye′nä). [Also called **Ugolino di Nerio.**] Sienese painter; active between 1317 and 1327. He was a follower and one of the most important pupils of Duccio, although without his master's grace of line. The only surviving work that can be securely ascribed to him consists of fragments of a polyptych (c1325) that once graced the High Altar of S. Croce at Florence. Among the fragments are those at Berlin, London, Los Angeles, New York (Lehman Collection), Philadelphia (Johnson Collection), and Richmond, England (Cook Collection). Other works attributed to him or to his studio are to be found in European museums and in the United States, as at Cleveland, Princeton, St. Louis, San Francisco, Urbana (Illinois), and Williamstown (Massachusetts), among others.

Ugolino di Vieri (dē vye′rē). Sienese goldsmith; active in the 14th century. He is thought to have died at an advanced age between 1380 and 1385. With an assistant, Viva di Lando, he created one of the masterpieces of the Italian goldsmiths' art. It is a reliquary, made between 1337 and 1338, to hold the Corporal Cloth, in the Chapel of the Corporal Cloth in the cathedral at Orvieto. In silver, it is encrusted with enamel paintings of thirty scenes having to do with the life of Christ and the Eucharist, and is ornamented with statuettes of the Apostles and Prophets, angels, and a Crucifixion. The reliquary is exposed only on Corpus Domini, a feast day established by Pope Urban IV (1264) to celebrate the Miracle of Bolsena, of which the Corporal Cloth is a relic. Another reliquary by Ugolino is in the cathedral museum at Orvieto. Others that he made, as for the churches of Siena, have been lost.

Uguccione della Faggiuola (ö-gö-chô′nā del′lä fä-jwō′lä). Ghibelline captain; b. at Massa Trabaria, c1250; d. at Vicenza, November 1, 1319. Captain of the Ghibelline League (1295), he also served as podesta (captain) of several cities, and was named imperial vicar of Genoa in 1312 by Henry VII. The hopes of many Ghibellines were dashed on the death of Henry, but Pisa remained firmly Ghibelline and named Uguccione its podesta for a term of ten years. His armies defeated the Guelphs at Montecatini, 1315, and he made himself tyrant of Lucca, but his political policy failed to wring advantage from his military successes. His tyrannous rule, ruination of trade, and his own luxurious style of living caused his people to revolt. He was betrayed by Castruccio Castracani, a Lucchese who had helped him win control of Lucca, and fled. He died in Vicenza where, because of his fame as a military man, he had been named podesta.

Uguccione da Lodi (dä lō′dē). Religious poet; b. c1200; d. c1260. Little is known of his life. He is thought to have been of Lombard origin, but his only extant work is in the Venetian dialect. His *Libro* is a moral treatise on the Creation of the world and pangs of Hell, written in verse of varying meter and rhyme. As was customary in much religious poetry of the time, it treats in a hortatory manner of the corruption, avarice, and wickedness of man. Written with conviction but without art, the work is of interest for its language.

Ulloa (ö-lyō′ä), **Francesco de.** Spanish captain; d. c1540. He was with Hernando Cortés in the conquest of Mexico. In 1539 he was sent to explore the Gulf of California. He sailed to the head of the gulf and subsequently explored the western coast of the peninsula, proving that Lower California is a peninsula.

Ulrich (ůl′rich). Duke of Württemberg; son of Henry IV; b. 1487; d. 1550. He succeeded to the duchy in 1498, and was expelled by the Swabian League in 1519. He was restored with the aid of Philip of Hesse in 1534 and joined the Schmalkaldic League against Charles V.

Universities. Universities constitute one of the unique contributions of western medieval Europe to the modern world. During the epoch of the so-called Renaissance in Italy they retained for the most part the features that had characterized them in the preceding centuries of their origin. They had been established both in the Italian peninsula and in Europe north of the Alps at the close of the 12th and the beginning of the 13th century as corporate associations either of foreign students, as at Bologna, or of teaching masters, as at Paris. These universities, unlike those of our own day, always referred to the corporate group of which they were comprised, rather than to the place (*studium*) where the teaching was done. The medieval as well as Renaissance university was comparable to our modern corporation, a legal entity, made up of scholars, who had come from various parts of Europe, as indicated in the several "Nations" in the university associations. At Bologna it was the foreign students studying law who first formed themselves into two universities, the Transalpine University, made up of students from across the Alps, and the Cisalpine University, made up of students from the Italian peninsula, with the exception of Bolognese students and professors. The latter were excluded from the universities. The Bologna universities of foreign students became the model, with some slight deviations, for most of the Italian universities. In Paris, on the other hand, and in most northern European countries, it was the teaching masters who organized themselves into a university. It should be noted that the emergence of the universities coincided not only with the expansion of the intellectual horizon through the introduction of Greek and Arabic works in Latin translations, but also with the appearance of other corporate associations, such as the guilds of foreign merchants and the guilds of local artisans in urban centers. In each instance the major objective was the protection and safeguarding of the members of the association. In the case of the foreign students' universities of Bologna it was the need to protect themselves from the discriminatory practices of the local townspeople toward non-citizens as well as to ensure observance of their rights and privileges as scholars, that led the students to form the university associations headed by their own elected rector. On the other hand, in Paris where the university was established by the teaching masters, particularly in arts, the principal purpose was to achieve independence from the Chancellor of Notre Dame as well as from the jurisdiction of the local magistrates. As corporate and autonomous associations which could use the weapons of cessation of lectures and of departure from the city, since the university had no buildings or special equipment of its own to tie it to a given locality, the universities were able to protect their members against injustices such as rent gouging, as well as from any violations of their traditional scholarly privileges. These comprised, among others, the right to be exempt from military service and the payment of local taxes, dues, or imposts. At Bologna, moreover, since the foreign students in the law universities paid the professors' stipends, they were also able to supervise both the curriculum and the professors. However, after the second half of the 14th century, the communal authorities in Bologna, as well as in the other Italian cities, took over the payment of professors' salaries, and in so doing assumed the power to choose and to control the professors and the curriculum. In Bologna the communal magistrates shared this power with the colleges of professors as well as with the universities. The close association of the Italian universities with the municipalities has in fact led to their characterization as municipal institutions. In the late 14th and 15th centuries they were looked upon as a source of civic pride. Individual ruling families, as the Medici in Florence, the Este in Ferrara, and the Bentivoglio in Bologna, vied with each other in their endeavors to attract the leading humanists or other scholars to the university in their particular municipality. Their zeal in this respect was further exemplified by their efforts to prohibit the inhabitants of the municipality from going elsewhere to study. In the course of the 15th century, too, the municipalities not only brought famous professors to the universities but also began the building of handsome edifices to house them. In so doing, of course, they reduced the earlier autonomy and independence of the universities.

The traditional curriculum of the universities, that is, of arts, medicine, law, and theology, was still in use during the so-called Renaissance. The basic arts courses, to which the Aristotelian works in natural and moral philosophy had been added in the 13th and 14th centuries, served as preparatory studies for the other divisions, that is, of medicine, law, and theology. At Bologna, where arts and medicine were in the same university, particular emphasis was placed on the subjects of logic and astrology, as well as on Aristotle's works in natural philosophy. Humanistic studies in language and literature came in slowly. In the late 14th century, through the efforts of the humanist Salutati who held the post of chancellor in Florence, a chair in poetry was established in the University of Florence. To it, in 1373–1374, Boccaccio was appointed to give lectures on Dante; and in 1376, the Calabrian Greek, Leonitus Pilatus, was presumably given a post to teach Greek. He in turn was followed by Manuel Chrysoloras, who was appointed professor of Greek in 1396. At Pavia, in the first half of the 15th century (1434–1435), the Visconti dukes of Milan, who controlled both Milan and Pavia, appointed professors to lecture on oratory, poetry, and rhetoric. The University of Ferrara, under the aegis of the Estensi, from 1430 on, with the arrival of the noted Guarino da Verona, became the center of humanist teaching. Similarly in Bologna, the Bentivoglio, and in Padua, the Venetian Doges, were able to provide the stipends for attracting famous scholars to their universities. In general, however, while the universities reflected to some extent the humanists' interests in language and literature, they remained throughout the Renaissance more largely centers for professional training in medicine, law, and theology. P.K.

Urban IV (ėr′bn̤). [Original name, **Jacques Pantaléon.**] Pope (1261–1264); b. at Troyes, France, in late 12th century; d. at

Perugia, October 2, 1264. He succeeded Alexander IV, and opposed Manfred of Sicily by offering the throne of Sicily to Charles of Anjou, brother of Louis IX of France. He died before terms satisfactory to Charles were worked out. Urban IV also sought to reunite the Eastern and Western Churches. He was succeeded by Clement IV.

Urban V. [Original name, **Guillaume de Grimoard.**] Pope (1362–1370); b. at Grisac, in Languedoc, France, 1310; d. at Avignon, December 19, 1370. He held many ecclesiastical offices, and was in Italy on a mission for the pope when he learned that he had been elected by the cardinals at Avignon to succeed Innocent VI (1362). A pious and just man, who lived an ascetic life himself, he made reforms of the clergy and bent his efforts toward promoting peace in Europe. Cardinal Albornoz, who had earlier (1354) gone to Italy with Cola di Rienzi, acted for Urban V in pacifying the Papal States (the results, however, were not enduring). Urban proclaimed a crusade to win back the Holy Land, with fleeting results. Petrarch, among others, urged him to restore the papal seat to Rome. He left Avignon and entered Rome, to great rejoicing, late in 1367. There, in 1368, he received Charles IV (one of those who had urged his return), and the next year he met John V Palaeologus, Byzantine emperor. In 1370, because of unrest in Rome and the outbreak of war between France and England, he returned to Avignon and died a short time later. Urban recognized the lay order of the Gesuati, founded by Giovanni Colombini, founded the Medical School at Montpellier, helped other universities, and aided many students. He was succeeded by Gregory XI.

Urban VI. [Original name, **Bartolommeo Prignani.**] Pope (1378–1389); b. at Naples, c1318; d. at Rome, October 15, 1389. On the death of Gregory XI (March 26, 1378), who had ended the Babylonian Captivity at Avignon, the Italians demanded the election of an Italian as pope, fearful that if a Frenchman were elected the popes would again leave Rome. The Conclave chose Urban VI (April 8, 1378). He at once aroused the resentment of the cardinals, most of whom were French, by his obstinate and undiplomatic measures to curb their powers and reform the Church. They revolted against him and in August, 1378, a group of them met at Anagni and (September 20, 1378) elected a new pope, Clement VII. The dissidents claimed the election of Urban had been illegal as they had been compelled by force to choose him. Clement established his court at Avignon and began to sell Church lands to gain revenue. Thus began the Great Schism (1378–1417) that divided the Church into two parties, each of which supported a different pope. St. Catherine of Siena, ardent pleader for peace and Church reform, wrote Urban, "I have learned that those devils in human form (the cardinals) have made an election. They have not chosen a Vicar of Christ, but an Anti-Christ; never will I cease to acknowledge you, my dear Father, as the Representative of Christ upon earth. Now forward, Holy Father! Go without fear into this battle, . . ." Urban had the fighting spirit but not the ability to persuade. He created a new college of cardinals at Rome, and proceeded with his attempts at reform, but, lacking prudence and diplomacy, he made more enemies than friends and accomplished little. Affairs of the Church were in a sorry state when he died. The Roman cardinals elected Boniface IX as his successor.

Urbino (ör-bē′nō), Dukes of. See **Federico da Montefeltro; Guidobaldo da Montefeltro; Francesco Maria della Rovere.**

Urceus (ör′sẹ-ůs), **Antonius Codrus.** See **Codrus Urceus, Antonius.**

Ursúa (ör-sö′ä), **Pedro de.** [Also, **Orsua.**] Spanish soldier; b. at Ursua, near Pamplona, in Navarre, Spain, c1510; killed at Machiparo, on the upper Amazon, January 1, 1561. He was governor of New Granada (1545–1546); led expeditions from Bogota in search of El Dorado; founded Pamplona (in Colombia); and subdued the Cimarrones of Panama.

Urswick (ėrz′wik), **Christopher.** English cleric and diplomat; b. at Furness, England, 1448; d. March 25, 1522. He was an adviser to Henry VII.

Utopia (ụ̄-tō′pi-ạ). Political romance by Sir Thomas More, published in Latin in 1516; so called from an imaginary island, the seat of an ideal commonwealth. The name itself means "no place." The original title was *De Optimo Reipublicae Statu, deque Nova Insula Utopia*. It was translated in 1551 by Ralph Robinson, and by Bishop Gilbert Burnet in 1683. The name Utopia has given rise to the adjective "utopian" with the meaning of "impracticable" or "ideal," especially as applied to schemes for the advancement of social conditions. Utopian literature, a genre widely used for the expression of social criticism, occurs in the literatures of many peoples throughout the ages.

Utraquists (ū′tra̤-kwists). See **Calixtines.**

Uvedale (ūv′dāl), **Nicholas.** See **Udall, Nicholas.**

Uzzano (öt-tsä′nō), **Niccolò da.** Florentine statesman; b. at Florence, 1359; d. there, April 20, 1431. Of an ancient Florentine family, he was one of the most loyal colleagues of Maso degli Albizzi, and was one of those oligarchs who tried to limit the growing power of the Medici. He held public office on many occasions, membership in the Council of Ten (1391, 1405, 1423) and gonfaloniere (1393, 1407, 1421) being among the most important of these offices. He was a patron of higher learning at Florence, and left money by his will to promote it.

V

Vaca de Castro (vä′kä dā käs′trō; Spanish, bä-); **Cristóbal.** Spanish lawyer and colonial administrator; b. 1492; d. c1562. He was sent by Charles V, in 1540, to Peru to inquire into certain alleged abuses, and to act as governor in case of Francisco Pizarro's death. After landing on the coast of New Granada in the spring of 1541, he crossed to Popayán, where he heard of the assassination of Pizarro and the rebellion of the younger Diego de Almagro. Aided by loyal Spaniards he advanced into Peru, defeated Almagro, and held the government until the arrival of the viceroy Blasco Núñez Vela. The viceroy imprisoned him on suspicion of conspiring against the new laws; he escaped and reached Spain where he was arrested, but was exonerated after eleven years' imprisonment.

Vaga (vä′gä), **Perino** or **Pierino del.** See **Pierin del Vaga.**

Valdés (väl-dās′; Spanish, bäl-), **Juan de.** Spanish theologian; b. at Cuenca, Spain, c1500; d. at Naples, 1541. He went to Naples about 1530, and became the center of a group interested in Church reform. He held several views which were at variance with Roman Catholic doctrines, had attacked ecclesiastical abuses, and seems to have adopted Luther's doctrine of justification by faith alone. However, he continued to be a son of the Church, although he was a strong influence on several who broke away from it, including the reformers Ochino and Vermigli. He wrote *Diálogo de Mercurio y Caron* (c1528), *Diálogo de la lengua* (1533; a philological treatise), and others.

Valdivia (bäl-dē′bya), **Pedro de.** Spanish soldier, conqueror of Chile; b. near La Serena, Estremadura, Spain, 1498 or 1500; executed near the fort of Tucapel, southern Chile, about January 1, 1554. He served with Francisco Pizarro's forces at the battle of Las Salinas (1538). Associated with Pedro Sanchez de Hoz, an incompetent who had been sent from Spain to complete the conquest of Chile, he became effective leader of the expedition. He founded Santiago (1541), defeated the Indians, founded Valparaíso (1544), and pushed into the Araucanian country (1546), founding Concepción (1550), Imperial, and Valdivia (1552). In 1553 during a great uprising of the Indians, Valdivia went to the relief of Tucapel, was attacked, defeated, and put to death.

Valentine and Orson (val′e̤n-tīn, ôr′so̤n). Romance of the Charlemagne cycle, written during the reign of Charles VIII, and first printed in 1495 at Lyons.

Valentino (vä-len-tē′nō), **Il.** Italian title of **Cesare Borgia.**

Valeriano (vä-lā-ryä′nō), **Pierio.** [Real name, **Giovanni Pietro dalle Fosse.**] Humanist and poet; b. at Belluno, February 3, 1477; d. at Padua, June, 1560. He studied at Belluno and Venice, and at the age of 15 was writing Latin poetry. He also became learned in Greek and was in contact with such leading humanists of his day as Sabellicus (and like him, latinized his name). In 1509 he went to Rome, where popes Julius II and Leo X became his patrons. He was a special favorite of Pope Leo X, and under his patronage spent his time writing Latin verse and studying the antiquities of Rome. Among his writings is a dissertation on the hieroglyphics of the Roman obelisks. His *De literatorum infelicitate* describes Rome in the time of Leo and recalls the fortunate state of men of letters, artists, and philosophers during his pontificate. The work was written after the sack of Rome (1527), during which Valeriano was absent from the city, and goes on to lament the terrible changes he found in Rome when he returned there after the sack, and the miserable condition of those men of letters who had survived. Valeriano calls the roll of his former friends and records their sad fates. In the controversy over the proper source and structure of an Italian language, Valeriano sided with Trissino, who advocated an Italian purified of regional dialectical elements that should be the common literary language of all. Among his other works, he left *Amorum libri,* five books of Latin elegies.

Valier (vä'lyer) or **Valerio** (vä-le'ryō), **Agostino.** Cardinal; b. at Legnano, April 7, 1530; d. at Rome, May 23, 1606. He taught philosophy at Venice, then joined his uncle, bishop of Verona, whom he succeeded as bishop in 1565. He was made cardinal by Pope Gregory XIII (1583) and went to Rome. Noted for his piety and charity (especially in the plague of 1576), he was also noted for his erudition.

Valla (väl'lä), **Lorenzo.** Humanist and philologist; b. at Rome, 1407; d. there, August 1, 1457. He studied at Rome and there wrote a lost work, *De comparatione Ciceronis Quintilianique,* a comparison of Cicero and Quintilian as stylists, in which he favored Quintilian, though by this time in the history of humanism Cicero was greatly admired. In 1429 he went to Pavia, where he held the chair of rhetoric, but his *De voluptate,* or *De vero bono* as he later called it (1431), an outspoken philosophical dialogue, created a furor; and his criticism, *Epistola de insigniis et armis,* of judicial methods, including criticism of the work of the famed jurist Bartolus (Bartolo da Sassoferrato), raised such a storm that he was compelled to leave Pavia. He spent some time at Milan and Florence and then (1437) went to Naples and became a secretary to Alfonso I. In the ten years he spent at Naples he produced his most important work. In 1448 Pope Nicholas V invited him to Rome as a papal secretary. In this post he translated the works of Thucydides and Herodotus, among others, into Latin. Under Calixtus III, successor of Nicholas, he continued as papal secretary. Valla's career as a student, humanist, and philologist was spent in continual and violent controversy with other humanists and, at times, with the religious establishment. His approach to the study and understanding of the ancient literature, which his fellow humanists accepted with unbounded and uncritical enthusiasm, was to examine it and apply scientific methods to it. His approach to philosophical problems was equally level-eyed. In his *De voluptate,* he examined the pagan philosophies of Epicureanism and Stoicism, and concluded that, since pleasure is a natural desire of the human condition, only the more powerful Christian desire for beatitude could replace a pagan Epicureanism. A Christian Epicureanism, therefore, is the best philosophy. Under his system, the pleasures of this life would be abandoned for those in the world to come. In his treatise on free will, *De libero arbitrio,* he concluded that faith and not reason explains and supports free will. In neither case was he attacking established religion, for he remained loyal to the Church. But his conclusions were provocative, as was his work on the Apostles Creed and his commentary on the Greek New Testament. While in Naples the Inquisition sought to try him for heresy, but Alfonso I protected him. Valla was essentially a philologist, who sought to purge Latin of the crudities it had acquired in the Middle Ages, to understand its structure and its grammar, and to restore it to its original purity. In his study of vocabulary and orthography he discovered (1440) that the famous Donation of Constantine (supposed to have been issued in 324 and conferring spiritual and temporal authority over the West and Italy on the Holy See), was a forgery; that it could not have been written earlier than the 8th century because some of the language of it was not in use at the earlier date. The discovery was of great philological importance and a vindication of Valla's methods. It was not an attack on the authority of the papacy, as the Donation was of little significance by that time except as a matter of historical interest. His *Elegantiarum latinae linguae* (1435–1444) is one of the earliest treatises on grammatical and stylistic Latin. In it he sought, by examples from Quintilian and Cicero, to rid the language of the impurities that had accrued to it in the Middle

Ages. Valla himself did not advocate a slavish imitation of the ancient writers. His interest was in a true understanding and proper use of Latin. Other works included a history of Ferdinand of Aragon, a collection of notices on the monarch's life lacking in the critical spirit with which he approached the ancient texts, and *Disputationes Dialecticae*, in which he attacked scholastic philosophy and Aristotelianism. With his revolutionary ideas and scientific methods, which were far in advance of his time, Valla was in constant conflict with his fellow humanists who had set themselves up as the authorities on the classical literature and who resented having the special positions they had taken regarding it, and the privileges they had won because of their knowledge, attacked, even indirectly. While he was at the court of Alfonso I there was bitter rivalry with other humanists there. In Rome under the popes his quarrels with Poggio, literary in nature, were titanic. He carried on a wide correspondence in which he defended his ideas and methods, and was in the midst of a great battle when he died. Time vindicated him.

Valle (väl'lā) **della.** See **Della Valle.**

Valvason (väl-vä'sōn), **Erasmo da.** Poet and translator; b. in the ancestral fief of Valvason al Tagliamento (in Friuli), 1523; d. at Mantua, 1593. He spent most of his life in his fief, prudently attending to its administration, and pursuing his studies, literary work, and translations. He was in touch by correspondence with many of the leading literary men of his day, including Bernardo Tasso and his son Torquato. Valvason was the most distinguished writer of Friuli of his time, a valued minor poet, and an exponent, in some of his works, of the spirit of the Counter-Reformation. Artistic influences were chiefly Ariosto and then Tasso. Most of his original work is didactic in tone and narrative in form. His works include the narrative poems, *Le lagrime di S. Maria Maddalena* (Ferrara, 1586), and *Angeleida* (Venice, 1590). The latter has as its subject the struggle between the good angels and the faithless angels and the fall of Lucifer, and antedates by some years Milton's *Paradise Lost,* on the same theme. *La Caccia*, a youthful work, is one of his best, and is distinguished for its freshness, simplicity, variety, skill at rendering a sense of place, and for the love of nature it feelingly portrays. Valvason also translated the *Electra* of Sophocles and the *Thebais* of Statius.

Van der Does (vän dėr dös), **Jan.** See **Dousa, Janus.**

Van der Weyden (vän dėr wī'dẹn), **Roger.** See **Weyden, Roger van der.**

Vanni (vän'nē), **Andrea.** Sienese painter; b. at Siena, c1330; d. there, c1414. He may have been a pupil of Lippo Memmi, was influenced by Barna da Siena, Simone Martini, and the Lorenzetti brothers, and between 1353 and 1355 he shared a workshop at Siena with Bartolo di Fredi. Like his fellow painter, he was active in civic affairs and went on many missions for Siena, as several times to Naples and once each to Avignon and Florence. Except for a signed triptych now in the National Gallery, Washington, most of the work he did at Naples, as well as in Sicily, has been lost. For the most part he worked at Siena. A follower of Simone Martini, his work lacks the grace, delicacy, and ethereal qualities of that master, and is rather marked by a hardness of line. A number of his surviving works are at Siena, as a triptych, *Crucifixion* (1396), Pinacoteca, *Madonna and Child Enthroned* (1398), S. Francesco, a polyptych, *Madonna and Child*, surmounted by an *Annunciation*, and with fourteen saints in side panels, pilasters, and pinnacles, and with a seven-part predella, S. Stefano, *Madonna and Child Enthroned*, S. Spirito, as well as frescoes in the Palazzo Pubblico. Other works are at Florence (Berenson Collection), Perugia (Museo dell' Opera del Duomo), Altenburg (panel of a polyptych, *St. Francis;* another panel from the same polyptych, *St. James*, is at Naples), Berlin, Cambridge, England, Frankfurt, Leningrad, Oxford (Ashmolean), Boston (a portable altarpiece with *Crucifixion*, Isabella Stewart Gardner Museum; panels from a polyptych, Museum of Fine Arts), Cambridge, Massachusetts, New Orleans, Washington (Corcoran Gallery), and elsewhere. Vanni was a follower of his famous contemporary, St. Catherine of Siena. Probably his best known work, now dilapidated from frequent repainting, is what is said to be an authentic portrait, *St. Catherine with a Disciple*, in S. Domenico, Siena. In the crypt of the same church are traces of frescoes from his hand.

Vanni, Lippo. Sienese painter and miniaturist; active between 1341 and 1373. He was listed on the register of Sienese painters in

1355, and several times held municipal office. Early influenced by the Lorenzetti brothers, he later became a close follower of Simone Martini. Many works have been attributed to him, but few have been authenticated. The latter include a number of miniatures, Opera del Duomo, Siena; *Madonna and Child* (c1355), Perugia; traces of a fresco (1372) in the Cloister of S. Domenico, Siena; *Battle of the Val di Chiana* (1373), Palazzo Pubblico, Siena. Other works attributed to him are a number of frescoes in and near Siena, miniatures at Amsterdam, Bayonne (Musée Bonnat), Cracow, Detroit, and Paris, and paintings at Naples, Rome (Vatican, SS. Domenico e Sisto), Altenburg, East Berlin, Frankfurt, Göttingen, Baltimore (Walters Art Gallery), Cambridge (Massachusetts), Coral Gables (Florida), and New York.

Vanni, Turino. Pisan painter; active at the end of the 14th and the beginning of the 15th century. A provincial painter who blended the Sienese and Florentine traditions in his own manner, he was the most important Pisan artist at the end of the 14th century. Several of his works are to be found at Pisa, among them a *Baptism of Christ* (c1395) and a polyptych, *Madonna and Child Enthroned*, National Museum, and three paintings on the same subject in S. Donnino in S. Giusto (1402), S. Paolo a Ripa d'Arno (1397), and Pieve di S. Marco (c1410). Other paintings include a triptych (1415), S. Bartolomeo, Genoa, an altarpiece, Palermo, and works at Randazzo, Sicily, Altenburg, Bayonne, Paris, and Birmingham (Alabama).

Vannozza Cattanei (vän-nōt′tsä kät-tä-nā′ē). See **Cattanei, Vannozza.**

Vannucci (vän-nöt′chē), **Pietro.** Original name of **Perugino.**

Vanozzo (vä-nôt′tsō), **Francesco di.** Poet; b. at Padua, c1340. His lyrics reflect his adventurous life at the courts of Padua, Verona, and Milan. Notable among his works is a group of sonnets written for Gian Galeazzo Visconti and his *Cantilena pro comite virtutum*, in which Italy and some of her leading cities are represented as pleading with him to redeem Italy and bring it peace. He was a friend of Petrarch and his love lyrics are in the Petrarchan manner. He also composed songs for the lute and was noted as a lutanist.

Varano (vä-rä′nō). Eminent family of Camerino, of which they were lords from 1259 until 1545, with some interruptions. In 1259 Camerino had been virtually destroyed by Percivalle Doria, acting for Manfred. Gentile I da Varano gathered the scattered citizens together and led them in the reconstruction of the city. From this he was called the founder of the city and was recognized as its lord by the popes. When Gentile I died (1284), his sons Berardo (d. 1325) and Rodolfo (d. 1316) succeeded him. The Varani were loyal allies of the Church; Berardo was captain general of the pontifical forces of John XXII; Giovanni, a very young captain, distinguished himself by conquering Spoleto; Gentile II, son of Berardo, was papal vicar, having declined to accept the imperial vicariate from Emperor Louis IV. Rodolfo II (d. 1384) was a celebrated captain. For the pope's general Cardinal Albornoz, he reconquered the papal lands and himself became absolute ruler of Rimini, Fano, Pesaro, and Fossombrone in the name of the Church. Thirty cities recognized him as their lord. Giovanni II, a son of Rodolfo III, was a distinguished soldier and ruled Camerino with his brothers Gentile Pandolfo, Berardo, and Pier Gentile. The brothers fell to intriguing against each other for complete control. Between 1433 and 1434 the family was almost wiped out. Pier Gentile was captured and put to death (September 6, 1433) by the pope's general, Cardinal Vitelleschi, probably through the intrigues of his brothers; Giovanni was killed by his brothers' hirelings; Berardo was killed at Tolentino, and the next year a rebellion, fomented by Francesco Sforza, broke out in the city against what remained of the family. Two children survived the fratricidal strife and the rebellion: Rodolfo, son of Pier Gentile, and Giulio Cesare, son of Giovanni II. The latter, two years old, was rescued by an aunt, who fled with him first to Foligno, then to Fabriano, and lastly to a nunnery, in which he was hidden. Alessandro Sforza, having become lord of Pesaro (1439), and having married (1444) Costanza da Varano, Pier Gentile's daughter, wished to restore her family at Camerino. He proclaimed Rodolfo and Giulio Cesare (now 12 years old) lords of Camerino. From this time (1444) until the advent of Cesare Borgia, Camerino enjoyed relative peace and prosperity. In 1502 Borgia, by one of his customary deceptions, trapped Giulio Cesare, and strangled him and three of his sons. One son, Giovanni

Maria, escaped the slaughter. After the death of Alexander VI and the collapse of Cesare's power, Giovanni Maria returned to Camerino, of which he was named duke by Julius II. He died (1527) leaving an only daughter, Giulia, as his heir. Strife broke out at once, as Rodolfo, a natural son of Giovanni Maria, and Ercole, of the Ferrarese branch of the family, sought power. The city was devastated. Paul III excommunicated Giulia and her mother, Caterina Cybo, because Caterina had married Giulia to Guidobaldo della Rovere, and the pope had wanted her to marry his nephew Ottavio Farnese. In 1542 Guidobaldo surrendered his rights to Camerino. It was given to Ottavio, who in his turn renounced his rights to it (1545) and the state reverted to the Church. The Varani, who had contributed distinguished soldiers to the service of the princes of Italy and to the Church, also produced many men of letters and statesman. The ducal palace, which they caused to be raised in the 15th century, was later enlarged and is now the seat of a university.

Varano, Costanza da. Writer of Latin letters and orations; b. at Camerino, 1426; d. at Pesaro, July 13, 1447. Her father was slain by his brothers (1433) and the following year her mother fled, with her children, to her father's house in Pesaro. Costanza received her education there. On December 8, 1444, she married Alessandro Sforza, lord of Pesaro, and a few years later died after giving birth to a son. She was typical of the cultivated ladies of her time, and was known for her Latin letters and state orations.

Varchi (vär'kē), **Benedetto.** Historian and humanist; b. at Florence, March 9, 1503; d. there, December 18, 1565. He studied law at Pisa and became a notary. On the death of his father he inherited a substantial property, abandoned the law, and devoted himself to letters. He became proficient in Greek and was a student of Provençal. In the turbulent period when the emperor Charles V was fastening his hold on Italy, Varchi was compelled to move from place to place. An ardent supporter of Florentine liberty, he had been among those responsible for the expulsion of the Medici from Florence (1527). He was absent from the city during the siege (1530) by Pope Clement VII and his new ally Charles V, was in Bologna for the coronation of Charles (1530), went to Padua, and then back to Bologna. His estate was dissipated and his property lost. When, therefore, he returned to Florence (1543) at the call of Cosimo I to become a courtier, he was grateful for a patron. Varchi wrote a great deal, in prose and poetry, and was known to and respected by the leading men of letters of his day. He was a facile versifier and left sonnets, *capitoli, canti carnascialeschi,* eclogues, and Latin verse, none of which was of great artistic merit. He wrote funeral and commemorative orations, and lectured, especially on Dante and Petrarch, for the Florentine Academy. He took part in the heated discussions of the time on what should constitute a literary Italian language. He favored Tuscan. He was one of those who doubted that the manuscript discovered by Trissino, *De vulgari eloquentia,* was in fact by Dante. As a critic, he realized that the headlong style and colloquial language of Benevenuto Cellini's *Autobiography* exactly suited the material and the personality of the author and should not be "improved." Varchi also tried his hand at comedy and other literary forms. To list his works is to indicate the extent to which he engaged in the varied interests and activities of the humanists of his day, but he is remembered for his *Storia fiorentina,* a history of Florence covering the period 1527–1538, and commissioned (1547) by Cosimo I de' Medici. Varchi, a former opponent of the Medici and now a dependent, manfully presents the facts of those violent years, beginning with the reestablishment of the republic (1527), dealing with the three years of its existence, and going on to the reinstatement of the Medici (1530) and the establishment of the duchy under Alessandro and then Cosimo I. His review of these years and events is realistic and honest. He consulted documents with care, did not hesitate to condemn Pope Clement VII, or to level censure at other members of the Medici family, even though it was Cosimo I who commissioned the work. At the same time, however, he included many adulatory references to the duke himself. His judgment on events is sober and careful, and the record formed by his *Storia fiorentina* is among the more precious sources for the events of those years.

Varchi was typical of the humanists of his time in many ways: he engaged in various literary occupations, was concerned with style and technique, often at the expense of content and feeling, and was deeply involved in literary controversies. His culture was broad but not profound; he was a man of many but not original ideas. Politically a supporter of liberty, he was not blind to the realities of political life and accommodated himself to them. Throughout his studies of the ancients he held fast to the faith, and turned more and more to an ascetic life as he grew older.

Vargas (bär′gạs), **Luis de.** Spanish painter of religious subjects; b. at Seville, Spain, 1502; d. there, c1568. Many of his works are at Seville.

Varignana (vä-rē-nyä′nä). [Real name, **Domenico Aimo;** called **il Varignana** or **il Bologna.**] Sculptor; d. at Bologna, 1534. In 1506 he took part in a contest for the best reproduction of the recently found *Laocoön.* Jacopo Sansovino was adjudged the winner. He worked in S. Petronio at Bologna, among other things possibly finishing some small part of the statue of Sant' Ambrogio begun by Jacopo della Quercia. From 1512 to 1529 he was carving sculptural decoration for the Santa Casa at Loreto. According to Vasari, after the death of Andrea Sansovino he finished (1524) the *Death of the Virgin,* in collaboration with other sculptors, including Francesco da Sangallo. In 1514 he was commissioned to carve the statue of Leo X now in S. Maria d'Aracoeli at Rome. This clumsy representation of the gross and flabby Leo is typical of the modest talents of Varignana.

Varoli (vä-rō′lē; vä′rō-lē), **Costanzo.** Italian anatomist; b. c1543; d. 1575. The pons Varolii, the group of nerve fibers connecting the several parts of the brain, was first described by him.

Vasari (vä-zä′rē), **Giorgio.** Painter, architect, and art historian; b. at Arezzo, July 30, 1511; d. at Florence, 1574. He studied drawing under Guglielmo de Marcillat, a glass painter, then at the age of 13 went to Florence. According to his own account, at Florence he studied under Michelangelo, who became his hero, Andrea del Sarto, Baccio Bandinelli, and others. On the expulsion of the Medici from Florence (1527), Vasari returned to Arezzo, fled to the country to escape the plague, returned briefly to Florence where he worked as a goldsmith, and again returned to his native city. In 1531 Cardinal Ippolito de' Medici passed through Arezzo and invited Vasari to enter his service. Vasari accepted and accompanied the cardinal to Rome. During his stay there he worked hard, studying the works of Michelangelo, Raphael, and others. This period left a lasting influence on his work as a painter and, perhaps because of the eminence of his teachers and models, caused him to set a higher value on his own work than posterity has done. He returned to Florence (1536) and began a life of great productivity and many journeys. He worked as painter, architect, or sculptor at Florence, Rome, Bologna, Venice, Arezzo, Naples, and Ravenna; his works are found all over Italy. An important man, he knew everybody, including the leading men of letters and artists, and was sought by princes and popes. He worked for Cardinal Ippolito de' Medici, popes Julius III and Pius V, and Cosimo I, among others. He was often at Rome (where he painted some chapels in the Vatican, among other things), and often at Florence, and always fully engaged in his numerous projects. In 1543 he was at Rome, where his friend and idol Michelangelo advised him to concentrate on architecture, as being most suited to his gifts. It was in this field that he became most finished and was most creative, but he did not give up painting. It was also at Rome (1546) that Giovio, the historian, discussed with him the idea of a history of the artists. Vasari's reaction was so perceptive and enthusiastic that Cardinal Alessandro Farnese, generous patron of Giovio and other men of letters, advised Vasari to write the work himself. He undertook to do so, while continuing with his painting commissions, and in March, 1550, published the first edition of his *Vite de' più eccelenti architetti, pittori e scultori italiani.* (A second, enlarged edition, was published in 1568.) For his *Lives of the Most Excellent Architects, Painters and Sculptors,* Vasari stated as one of his aims the revival and preservation of the names of those painters, sculptors and architects "who do not merit that their names and works should remain the prey of death and oblivion." He wished to honor the arts and those who had worked in them, and set out to distinguish the relative excellence of the artists and works under discussion, as well as to describe methods, processes, and modes of treatment of the various artists. In an introduction to his work, Vasari separated the arts of design into painting, architecture, and sculpture, and gave a treatise on each. He presented his view that the arts pass through natural stages of development, from childhood (Cimabue to the end of the 14th century), through youth (Jacopo della Quercia to the end of the 15th century), to maturity (culminating in Michelangelo), and stated his conviction that maturity had been achieved in his own age with his glorious Michelangelo. Henceforth, since perfection had been attained, could art only decline? Altogether, his *Vite* comprise about 200 biographies, beginning with the earliest times of Cimabue and Giotto and coming down to artists who were living at the time he wrote (in the second edition). He consulted early sources, traveled tirelessly about Italy looking at pictures and consulting artists and friends, and drew on his own vast experience and knowledge for the material of the work. He describes paintings in detail, listing many that were lost even in his own time and many that have been lost since. The biographies are studded with illustrative stories and anecdotes (some of which are apochryphal) that illuminate the personality, character, manner of work, or special peculiarities of the artist under discussion. He describes the engines that Leonardo da Vinci contrived for entertainments at Milan, the floats designed by Piero di Cosimo for the carnival parade at Florence, the scientific works of Piero della Francesco and Paolo Uccello. Nothing escapes his notice. The style is at times informal and conversational and at others formal and expository. There are the inevitable errors of fact, but in the ages following his when questions have arisen on the attribution of various paintings, Vasari has often, after being doubted, had the last word. In the first edition his tendency was to exalt the artists of Florence, his adopted city, over all others. By the time of the second edition his critical view and judgment had broadened. He was a sound critic and was among the first to appreciate the accomplishments and value of the early painters and sculptors. His view that with Cimabue and Giotto the arts, long dead, underwent a rebirth was the first application of the term "rinascimento" (renaissance) to the arts, although the concept of a rebirth had been earlier formulated by Petrarch, Boccaccio, and Alberti. Vasari's *Vite* constitutes a landmark in the history of art, an indispensable source for serious students of Italian art. His fame in after ages as an art historian has eclipsed his accomplishments as a practitioner of the arts, the area in which he considered himself to be preeminent. He painted a prodigious amount. Among the best works in painting are those he executed in 1541 in his house at No. 59 Via XX Settembre, at Arezzo, and the historical and allegorical paintings commissioned by Cosimo I (1554) in the Palazzo Vecchio at Florence (finished 1565). Also in the Palazzo Vecchio, he decorated the Apartments of the Elements and the Apartment of Eleanor of Toledo, Cosimo's wife, and designed the barrel-vaulted study of Francesco I de' Medici. In architecture his masterpiece is the Uffizi, so-named because it was originally intended for offices of the magistrates, and commissioned (1560) by Cosimo I. This structure on the banks of the Arno now houses a world-famous collection of paintings. He was also the architect of the passageway (begun 1565) over the Ponte Vecchio that connects the Palazzo Vecchio to the Pitti Palace across the Arno. In sculpture he designed (1550) the tomb of Cardinal dal Monte, at Rome, for Pope Julius III, and designed (1564) Michelangelo's tomb in S. Croce at Florence (he also designed the decorations for the latter's funeral). As was the case with many prominent artists who had more commissions than they could possibly execute, Vasari was often aided by assistants or had others carry out his designs.

A man of prodigious activity and uneven accomplishments, Vasari left a number of letters, to such men as Michelangelo, Bembo, Giovio, Aretino, Caro, Varchi, and others; his memoirs; a description of the festivals that took place at the marriage of Francesco I de' Medici (1566); and dialogues supposedly between Francesco and himself on the paintings he executed in the Palazzo Vecchio. Although his work as a painter must rank far below the true and great artists of his age, in the range of his activities and the variety of his interests, in his own broad culture and sound judgment (except where his own work was concerned), in his conspicuous place among the outstanding men of his time, and in his enormous vitality, Vasari was an outstanding example of the energetic and gifted men of the High Renaissance.

Vaux (vôks, vōks, vôz), **Thomas.** [Title, 2nd Baron **Vaux of Harrowden.**] English lyric poet and courtier; b. 1510; d. October, 1556. Some of his poems appear in *Tottel's Miscel-*

lany (1557) and the *Paradise of Dainty Devices* (1576).

Vecchietta (vek-kyet′tä). [Real name, **Lorenzo di Pietro.**] Painter and sculptor; b. at Castiglione d'Orcia, c1412; d. at Siena, 1480. To the Sienese tradition in which he was brought up, and from which he never completely detached himself, he added Florentine elements derived from his teacher Sassetta and, particularly in sculpture, accentuated plasticity and naturalism to a degree approaching the art of Donatello. His earliest dated painting, *The Virgin Receiving the Souls of Foundlings* (1441), Spedale di S. Maria della Scala, Siena, is a complicated composition based on architectural forms derived from the antique, with a central corridor of arches (resting on square pilasters with ornate capitals) shown in perspective. In the center at the far end of the archway, naked foundlings ascend a ladder to the Virgin. Unsigned and undated frescoes on scenes from the lives of St. Stephen and St. Lawrence, in the cathedral at Castiglione d'Olona, are thought to be earlier. Many of his works, in fresco or on panel, are at Siena: in the Spedale di S. Maria della Scala (where, in addition to that named above, there are a number of frescoes from his hand), the Baptistery (frescoes), Palazzo Pubblico (frescoes), State Archives (book covers), and the Pinacoteca. A panel, *Madonna and Child and Saints* (1457), is in the Uffizi, and there are works at Pienza, including a triptych, *Assumption* (1461–1462), in the cathedral there, S. Maria Maddalena, Castiglione d'Orcia (*Madonna and Child with Four Angels*), the Vatican, Liverpool, and Munich (three companion predella panels). His earliest known sculptures are the gaunt and human *Risen Christ* (1442), in wood, Parish Church, Vico Alto, and the marble *St. Peter and St. Paul* (1460–1462), Loggia dei Mercanti, Siena. Among his important works in bronze are the tomb figures of Mariano Socino (or Sozzini) (1467) for a tomb in S. Domenico, now in the Bargello, Florence, and that of Bishop Girolamo Foscari, S. Maria del Popolo, Rome, and his moving, naturalistic, Donatellian *Risen Christ* (1476), Church of the Spedale, Siena. Other works include the bronze ciborium (1472) now in the cathedral at Siena, a bronze relief, *Resurrection of Christ*, Frick Collection, New York, and a number of figures in polychrome wood: *St. Bernardino* (c1475), Bargello; *Madonna and Child*, Istia d'Ombrome; relief, *Assumption* (finished by Neroccio di Landi), Pinacoteca, Lucca; *St. Paul* and relief, *Assumption*, Montemerano; and *St. Anthony Abbott* (1475), cathedral, Narni.

Vegio (ved′jō), **Maffeo.** Humanist; b. at Lodi, 1407; d. at Rome, 1458. An enthusiastic student and scholar, he studied at Milan and Pavia and then (1435) went to Rome to seek his fortune. There he held various posts at the courts of Eugenius IV and Martin V. He was a great admirer of St. Augustine and of his mother St. Monica, wrote a life of the latter and caused a chapel to be built for her tomb in the Church of San Agostino in Rome. In 1455 he joined the Canons of St. Augustine, substituting a life of religious zeal for the worldly one he had led, but did not give up his interest in classical studies. Interest in classical literature was the hallmark of the humanists. Many of them wrote extensions of ancient works and myths. Vegio's hero was Vergil and he wrote (1427) a 13th book continuing the *Aeneid*, which was highly thought of in his time. Vespasiano says he lived by his pen. Among his other writings, very well received by his contemporaries, were *Convivium deorum* (c1430) in praise of the Visconti, *De verborum significatione*, on the origin and meaning of many words, *De rebus memorabilibus basilicae S. Petri*, in which he applied archaeological methods in a description of St. Peter's, and *De educatione liberorum . . .*, a humanistic treatise on education that is permeated with his vast knowledge of classical and patristic literature. Vegio, in many of his writings, attempted to harmonize the classical and Christian ideals, as many of the humanists, who loved the classical literature and ideas and were at the same time devoted Christians, tried to do.

Vela (bā′lä), **Blasco Núñez.** See **Núñez Vela, Blasco.**

Velasco (bā-läs′kō), **Luis de.** [Title, Count of **Santiago.**] Spanish administrator, second viceroy of Mexico; b. at Toledo, Spain, c1500; d. at Mexico City, July 31, 1564. He enforced the "New Laws" (emancipating, it is said, 150,000 Indians), put down the revolt of the Chichimecs, and fitted out Miguel López de Legazpe's expedition to the Philippine Islands.

Velasco, Luis de. [Titles, Count of **Santi-**

ago, Marquis of **Salinas.**] Spanish administrator; b. at Madrid, 1539; d. at Seville, Spain, c1617. He was the son of Luis de Velasco (c1500–1564). He was viceroy of Mexico (1590–1595), (1607–1611); viceroy of Peru (1596–1604), and president of the Council of the Indies.

Velásquez (bā-läs′keth), **Diego.** Spanish soldier and administrator; b. at Cuéllar, Segovia, Spain, c1465; d. at Havana, Cuba, c1523. He went to Hispaniola with Christopher Columbus in 1493 and was prominent in the affairs of the island until 1511, when he was sent by Diego Columbus to conquer Cuba. He founded Santiago (1514), and Havana (1515); furnished a vessel for the expedition of Francisco de Córdoba which discovered Yucatán; and in 1519 sent Hernando Cortés to conquer Mexico.

Velluti (vel-lö′tē), **Donato.** Chronicler and public official; b. at Florence, July 6, 1313; d. there, July 1, 1370. He was the son of a substantial merchant family, studied law at Bologna, and remained in that city from 1329 to 1338. He was at first a supporter of the duke of Athens at Florence, but when he saw the duke's popularity dissipated he gradually separated himself from the duke's party. He held the highest offices in Florence, and served the republic as ambassador to Bologna and Siena. In December, 1367, he began to write his *Cronica domestica,* and continued working on it until just before his death. It is notable for the intimate picture of family life it presents, for the sincerity and vigor of its language and style, for the many portraits included of Florentine men and women of the time, and is especially valuable as a contemporary source for the years 1342–1370.

Veneto (ve-nā′tö), **Bartolomeo.** Venetian painter; active between 1502 and 1530. Nothing is known of his life, and all that is known of his work is derived from the dating of his paintings. These, as a *Madonna and Child* which he repeated a number of times, show him to have been a close follower of the Bellini. A *Madonna and Child* at Venice is almost exactly the same as a signed and dated (1505) one at Bergamo. On another, signed and dated (1509), he calls himself a pupil of Gentile Bellini. He left a number of portraits, several in collections in Italy and a number in other museums (Brooklyn, Culver, Indiana, Houston, South Bend, Indiana, Washington, and elsewhere), that reveal him to have been strongly influenced by Lombard and northern painters, especially Dürer, and that lead to the conclusion he must have spent considerable time in Lombardy. This conclusion is confirmed to some extent by the number of his works that are to be found in that region. Among the portraits, which are more individual and interesting than his Madonnas is a *Portrait of a Youth,* Cleveland, and *Lady Lutanist* (1520), Isabella Stewart Gardner Museum, Boston (another on the same subject is in the Brera, Milan). In his many drawings, collections of which are in the Albertina at Vienna and the Ambrosiana, Milan, northern influences, again Dürer, are also apparent.

Veneziano (ve-nā-tsyä′nō), **Antonio.** Florentine painter; b. probably at Venice, c1340; d. in Tuscany, after 1388. He received his early instruction in Venice, where he probably knew the work of Altichieri, Avanzo, and Giotto, and later went to Florence. He is known to have been painting the ceiling of the cathedral at Siena with Andrea Vanni in 1370, to have joined the Physicians' and Apothecaries' Guild at Florence (1374), and to have worked at Pisa (1386). Like Giotto in his interest in realism in form and feature, he was not equal to him in catching the drama of a moment; his work is more decorative, less dramatic and not illustrative. Many works have been attributed to him. Among his known works is a series of frescoes in the Camposanto, Pisa, on the St. Ranieri story. These are typical of his interest in decoration, his fine draftsmanship, and his keen sense of color. Other examples of his work are at Figline (fresco, *Crucifixion,* Convento di S. Francesco), Torre degli Agli (frescoed tabernacle), Palermo (Diocesan Museum), Rome (Vatican), Siena, Göttingen, Hannover, Toledo, Spain (cathedral), Boston, San Francisco, and elsewhere.

Veneziano, Antonio. Sicilian poet; b. at Monreale, January 7, 1543; d. at Palermo, August 2, 1593. He had a stormy and adventurous life. Captured (1578) by Algerian pirates, he was released and went to Spain. He was a friend of Cervantes, to whom he dedicated some of his octaves. He was exiled, was in and out of prison, and died in prison. His life became a legend and his poetry was fervently admired in his native Sicily, especially the 290 *strambotti,* in the Sicilian dialect, of his *Celia*. He produced a mass of poetry, Latin epigrams, Italian prose, and was most famous in his own day as an improviser and for his use of the Sicilian dialect, which he raised to the dignity of a literary form. He left canzoni on various themes, proverbs, burlesque poems, and four *Trionfi*, one of which was in Spanish. His poetry lacked the verve and originality of his life, and was too often imitative of Petrarch, more interested in stylistic considerations than in inspiration, but with sometimes a popular appeal and charm.

Veneziano, Caterino. See **Caterino.**

Veneziano, Domenico. See **Domenico Veneziano.**

Veneziano, Lorenzo. See **Lorenzo Veneziano.**

Veneziano, Paolo. See **Paolo Veneziano.**

Venier (vā′nyer), **Antonio.** Doge of Venice (1382–1400); he distinguished himself in the wars between Venice and Genoa, and was captain at Candia when he was elected doge. Thereafter, he devoted himself to the many problems that remained after the war of Chioggia (1378–1380) with Genoa. During his dogate Venice won back Corfu, enlarged its dominions in the Aegean, and carried on a series of shifting alliances with the main city states of north Italy in an attempt to prevent any one of them from becoming powerful and a threat to Venice. Venier was implacable toward his son Alvise, who had been convicted of an offense and was imprisoned in the dungeons of the Ducal Palace, where he sickened and died.

Venier, Domenico. Venetian poet; b. 1517. He was a member of an ancient Venetian family, and was noted in his day for the gatherings of artists, musicians, poets, and literary men in his sumptuous house at Venice. The entertainment on such occasions was often musical. He was a facile versifier and was highly praised in his own time.

Venier, Sebastiano. Doge of Venice (June, 1577–March, 1578); b. c1496; d. 1578. He was a member of an ancient Venetian family, was elected duke of Candia (1548), served as captain of Brescia (1561–1562), podesta of Verona (1566–1568), and held many other offices of responsibility, including important posts during the wars with the Turks. At the age of 75 he was named captain general of the sea, besieged Durazzo, and organized the campaign of the Holy League against the Turks. He was at the side of Don John of Austria, and was one of the heroes of the battle of Lepanto (1571). His dogate was saddened by the great fire of 1577 that gutted the Ducal Palace and destroyed the masterworks that generations of artists had painted in it. A portrait of Sebastiano by Tintoretto is in the Uffizi at Florence.

Venusti (ve-nös′tē), **Marcello.** Painter; b. at Como, 1512 or 1515; d. at Rome, 1579. The first influences on his development were those of the Lombard painters, as appears in his *Apparition of the Virgin to Two Saints*, S. Antonio dei Portoghesi, Rome. From 1548 until his death he lived at Rome. He was deeply influenced by Michelangelo, whose friend and follower he became, and for whom he named one of his sons. An *Annunciation* in St. John Lateran was painted on a design by Michelangelo, and the Michelangelo influence is apparent in a *Pietà*, Borghese Gallery, Rome, and *Holy Family*, Vienna. Other works at Rome include frescoes in S. Maria sopra Minerva, *Madonna and Saints*, S. Maria della Pace, and paintings in S. Caterina dei Funari and in the National Gallery of Ancient Art.

Vergerio (ver-jā′ryō), **Pietro Paolo.** Humanist; b. at Capodistria, July 23, 1370; d. at Budapest, July 8, 1444. At the age of 15 he was at Padua studying Grammar. The following year (1386) he went to Florence and became a friend of the distinguished humanist Coluccio Salutati and the canonist, Francesco Zabarella. He studied and worked at Bologna and Padua, and withdrew from Florence to Pavia when plague struck Florence, and Chrysoloras, who was teaching Greek there, fled to Pavia. He passed the years 1400–1405 in Padua and earned his doctorate in the Arts, Medicine, and Law. In 1405 he went to Rome and was attached to the papal court. Having become involved in ecclesiastical affairs, and ardently desirous of ending the Great Schism, he attended the sessions of the Council of Constance (1414–1418). There he met the emperor Sigismund, who crowned him poet laureate, invited him to his court and gave him a pension. Vergerio went to Germany with Sigismund and never returned to Italy. His many writings include a Latin comedy in the manner of Terence, a treatise, *De arte metrica*, in collaboration with Zabarella, an invective against Carlo

Malatesta for removing a statue of Vergil from Mantua (it was put back), and a pedagogical treatise that prescribed a program of liberal and fine arts, combined with physical exercises and moral philosophy, for the education of young noblemen.

Vergerio, Pietro Paolo. [Called "the Younger."] Jurist and religious reformer; b. at Capodistria, 1498; d. at Tübingen, Germany, October 4, 1565. A judge, university professor, and lawyer, when his wife died (1527) he devoted himself to the service of the Church, although remaining a layman. In 1533 he was papal nuncio to Germany, and in 1536 he was ordained and, the same day, made bishop. He became bishop of Capodistria the same year. At the meeting at Worms (1540) he opposed, on instructions from Rome, the conciliatory moves of Charles V, but he was in fact more closely allied personally to the moderate policy of Cardinal Gasparo Contarini. And from his days as nuncio to Germany he had established friendly contacts with the German reformers, with whom he tended more and more to agree. His deviations from the Catholic faith became so pronounced that he was summoned to Rome, and forced into exile at Switzerland, where he matriculated at the University of Basel and then became a pastor. He served in Tübingen and Poland, evangelized in several cities of Switzerland, returned again to Poland, and resisted efforts of the Church to win him back to the fold. He left numerous politico-religious writings, as well as translations of the works of other religious reformers. According to Vergerio, Francesco Berni's reworking of Boiardo's *Orlando* included Lutheran opinions that he had come to hold and that he wished to propagate by this means. But the stanzas expressing these ideas were reworked and reduced to eliminate them when the work was published, after Berni's sudden death.

Vergil or **Virgil** (vėr′jil), **Polydore.** Italian-English ecclesiastic and historian; b. at Urbino, c1470; d. there, c1555. He studied at Bologna and Padua and served as secretary to the duke of Urbino. He was sent to England as deputy collector of Peter's pence by the pope in 1501. Henry VII became his patron and he secured many benefices. In 1510 he became a naturalized subject. He was imprisoned for a short time (c1515) on the charge of slandering Thomas Wolsey; thereafter he took little part in the religious controversies of the time. He returned (c1550) to Italy. Among his works the chief is his history of England, *Historiae Anglicae libri xxvi* (1534; a 27th book was added in the 3rd edition, 1555). The work, especially valuable for the reign of Henry VII, was translated into English and influenced Shakespeare.

Verino (vā-rē′nō), **Ugolino.** Humanist and poet; b. at Florence, January, 1438; d. there, May 10, 1516. He was a pupil and follower of Cristoforo Landino, and was like him in harmonizing his interest in the classics with his strong Christian faith, which is especially apparent in his *Paradisus.* His *Flametta* (1463) is a collection of eighty-two elegies on love. Eventually, he became a religious poet, and his *Carliade* (1480; 1493) exalts Charlemagne as a defender of the faith. Verino, spiritually oriented as he was, was deeply influenced by Savonarola, but turned against him when Savonarola was disgraced. Among other writings, he left *De illustratione urbis Florentinae,* a history of Florence.

Vermigli (ver-mē′lyē), **Pietro Martire.** [Called **Peter Martyr.**] Protestant reformer; b. at Florence, September 8, 1500; d. at Zurich, November 12, 1562. One of the most learned of the reformers, he was also a systematic theorist of the doctrines of Zwingli and Calvin. Of a good and wealthy family, at 16 he entered an Augustinian convent at Fiesole. He studied at Padua, traveled about preaching and teaching, and studied Hebrew at Bologna. After three years at Spoleto he was named (1528) prior of a convent at Naples. It was at Naples that he came into contact with Juan Valdés and others who held his reforming views, and especially with Bernardo Ochino, who had a great influence on him. In 1542 he was named prior of the convent of San Frediano at Lucca. He was greatly occupied with the education of the novices, and brought some outstanding teachers to the convent. He had also begun, in his sermons, to outline some of his ideas for reform of the Church, and had published (anonymously) his first work urging reform. When he was called to Rome to give an account of himself, he fled. He left Italy (1542) and went to Zurich and then to Strasbourg, where he remained several years as a teacher of Hebrew. At the invitation of Thomas Cranmer, archbishop of Canterbury, he went to England (1547), became a professor at Oxford, and collaborated on the reform of English ecclesiastical life. When Mary ascended the throne of England (1553) the Catholic reaction set in, and Vermigli left England. He returned to Strasbourg and Zurich, having refused professorships at Heidelberg and Geneva. In two great disputes among the reformers, Vermigli took an active part. His view was that the Eucharist was a ceremony of remembrance and that the dogma of transubstantiation should be eliminated; and he supported the Calvinist concept of predestination. He left many writings expounding his theology, as well as commentaries on various books of the Bible.

Vernia (ver′nyä), **Nicoletto** (or **Nicolò**, or **Paolo Nicola**). Philosopher; b. at Chieti, c1420; d. at Padua, October, 1499. He taught at Padua from 1465 until his death. As a philosopher, he departed somewhat from the Thomistic interpretation of Aristotle, and emphasized the distinction between natural philosophy and metaphysics. Questions concerning the human soul were of great interest to him. His works were, in general, treatises on particular questions, rather than extended theoretical theses.

Verona (vā-rō′nä), **Guarino da.** See **Guarino da Verona.**

Veronese (vā-rō-nā′zā), **Paolo.** See **Paolo Veronese.**

Veronica of Binasco (ve-rôn′i-kä, bē-näs′kō), Saint. Augustinian nun; b. 1455; d. 1497. From childhood she was given to contemplation, and after she joined the Augustinian nuns at Milan enjoyed many visions. She left a collection of *Revelations*.

Verrazano (ver-rä-tsä′nō) or **Verrazzano** (ver-rät-tsä′nō), **Giovanni da.** Italian navigator; b. in Italy, c1480; d. c1527. In command of a French expedition in 1523, he explored the coast of North America from North Carolina to Newfoundland (1524) discovering New York and Narragansett bays.

Verrocchio (ver-rôk′kyō), **Andrea.** [Real name, **Andrea di Michele di Cione.**] Goldsmith, painter, and sculptor; b. at Florence, 1435; d. at Venice, 1488. He took his name from his first master, the Florentine goldsmith Giuliano Verrocchi. His sculpture derived from Donatello, whose pupil he may have been, from Desiderio da Settignano, whom he may have assisted on the Marsuppini monument in S. Croce, and from whom he perhaps derived the delicacy and subtlety of some of his works, and from Antonio Pollaiuolo. He fused the elements he took from these masters into a distinctively personal art, and was, after the death of Donatello, the leading Florentine sculptor. As a painter he was influenced by Pesellino and by Alessio Baldovinetti. He had a busy workshop at Florence, with many pupils and assistants, including Leonardo da Vinci, Perugino, and Lorenzo di Credi. Of the celebrated *Baptism of Christ* (c1470), Uffizi, Verrocchio is thought to have painted but little. Leonardo painted the angel in profile in the lower left and much of the landscape background. According to Vasari, when he saw Leonardo's angel Verrocchio put aside his brush forever, chagrined that a mere youth in his studio so far surpassed him as a painter. Whatever the merits of this story, it is true that Verrocchio left few paintings that can be securely ascribed to him. The altarpiece, *Madonna Enthroned with John the Baptist and St. Donato* (c1478), in the cathedral at Pistoia, was largely the work of Lorenzo di Credi to Verrocchio's cartoon. Other paintings attributed to him are Madonnas at New York and Washington. He is known to have executed a number of works as a goldsmith, but the only one surviving is a silver relief, *Beheading of John the Baptist* (1480), notable for its plasticity and a Pollaiuolo-like linearity. A panel of the altar of the Baptistery, it is now in the Opera del Duomo at Florence. If questions surround Verrocchio's work as a painter, his work as a sculptor is secure. In this art his style is notable for the sense of movement and for the lightness and grace of his forms. The tomb (1472), decorated with bronze leaves and cords, of Piero and Giovanni de' Medici, S. Lorenzo, Florence, is a masterpiece of the purely decorative art. (Earlier, perhaps between 1465 and 1467, he had designed the simple tomb of Cosimo de' Medici in the same church.) His bronze *David* (before 1476), Bargello, is marked by an elegance and lithe grace in strong contrast to the searing naturalism of Donatello. In the same museum is his marble *Bust of a Woman*, supposed by some to be a portrait of Lucrezia Donati, Lorenzo de' Medici's inamorata. His bronze *Christ and St. Thomas* (1483), on the exterior of Orsanmichele, on which he worked for fifteen years, is one of his finest works. It is on a monumental scale, as is his masterpiece, the heroic equestrian statue

ANDREA VERROCCHIO
Head of a Woman with an Elaborate Coiffure
The British Museum, London

(1479–1488) of Bartolomeo Colleoni at Venice. Colleoni, captain general of the Venetian forces, died at Bergamo, leaving his silver, furniture, arms, horses, and the sum of 216,000 florins to the republic of Venice, on condition that his statue should be set up in St. Mark's Square (Piazza di S. Marco). (In fact, the statue was set up in the Campo di SS. Giovanni e Paolo, as the Venetians refused to give anyone the great honor of a statue in their splendid square, regardless of his service or his bequests.) Verrocchio had completed the clay model and nearly finished the horse when he died; the statue was later finished, and cast, by Alessandro Leopardi, who put his name on it. In contrast to the severe and monumental effects he sought in the Colleoni monument is the earlier *Putto with a Fish*, or *Boy with a Dolphin*, Palazzo Vecchio, Florence, with its appealing grace and mercurial fluidity. Other sculptural works include a terra-cotta bas-relief of the *Resurrection* (c1465) and a terra-cotta relief, *Virgin and Child*, Bargello, the marble Forteguerri monument (begun 1473), in the cathedral at Pistoia, terra-cotta busts of Giuliano and Lorenzo de' Medici, National Gallery, Washington, and works at Amsterdam, Berlin, and Paris.

Vesalius (vę-sā'li-us), **Andreas.** Belgian anatomist; b. at Brussels, December 21, 1514; d. in a shipwreck on the island of Zante, October 15, 1564. He was physician to Charles V, and after Charles' death, to Philip II. His chief work is *De corporis humani fabrica libri septem.*

Vesica piscis (vę-sī'ką pi'sis). A design of almond shape, formed of two intersecting arcs and enclosing a sacred figure, most frequently Christ. The shape derives from the form of a fish bladder and is symbolic.

Vespasiano da Bisticci (ves-pä-syä'nō dä bē-stēt'chē). Florentine bookseller and biographer; b. at Bisticci, 1421; d. at Antella, July 27, 1498. Vespasiano's *Vite d'uomini illustri del secolo* XV, a collection of lives of eminent prelates, princes, writers, and statesmen, is a treasury of information and kindly comment on over 100 figures, most of whom were Florentines. He was personally acquainted with many of the men of whom he wrote. His acquaintanceship and often warm friendship with them arose from his occupation as a bookseller. In his day this meant a seller of manuscripts or copies. He lived in an era when the collection of manuscript libraries amounted almost to a mania. Without a profound education, he loved books, and learned from them and from his clients. He was an ardent searcher for the eagerly sought Latin and Greek manuscripts, and as near expert as could be at judging them. Manuscripts acquired were copied, in a beautiful hand, with great fidelity to the texts, and richly bound, sometimes with crimson velvet and silver clasps. He helped build the three foremost libraries of 15th-century Italy: those of Pope Nicholas V, Federico da Montefeltro, and Cosimo de' Medici. For the latter he hired 45 copyists and produced 200 volumes in less than two years. He supplied books to the Estensi of Ferrara, the Aragonese of Naples, Matthias Corvinus, king of Hungary, and the Englishmen, John Tiptoft and the bishop of Ely. The invention of printing destroyed the need and the market for his handsome manuscript copies—works he revered as objects of beauty as well as learning. He scorned the products of the printing press, retired to his property at Antella and wrote his *Vite*. Included among them are biographies of Pope Nicholas V, the statesmen and rulers, Cosimo de' Medici, Federico da Montefeltro, and Alfonso I of Naples, numerous writers and prelates, and a few women. He wrote in unadorned and often ungrammatical Italian, modestly stating that his object was to preserve certain facts for the biographies he felt sure more learned men would produce in Latin. The material is poorly organized and usually lacking in dates. Nevertheless, the biographies represent Vespasiano's attachment to men whom he knew through a common interest and, studded as they are with bits of odd detail, remembered conversation, incidents of local politics, and a generally charitable and sincerely pious attitude, they are immensely winning in their immediacy.

Vespucci (vās-pöt'chē), **Amerigo.** [Latinized, **Americus Vespucius.**] Navigator; b. at Florence, c1451; d. at Seville, Spain, February 22, 1512. He was the son of Nastugio Vespucci, a notary of Florence, received his education from his uncle, a Dominican friar, and became a clerk in the commercial house of the Medici family. He was sent to Spain by his employers about 1490 and some years after appears to have entered the service of the commercial house of Juonato Berardi at Seville, of which he became a member in 1495. This house fitted out Columbus' second expedition (1493), and it has been suggested that Vespucci may have accompanied Columbus' first or second expedition, although the supposition is unsupported by any proof. Vespucci himself claims to have accompanied at least four expeditions to the New World. Two of these sailed from Spain by order of King Ferdinand in May, 1497, and May, 1499, respectively; the other two were dispatched from Portugal by King Manoel in May, 1501, and June, 1503. The first expedition, in which he would appear to have held the post of astronomer, left Cádiz May 10 or 20, 1497, and after touching at the Canaries came "at the end of twenty-seven days upon a coast which we thought to be that of a continent." If this expedition is authentic, Vespucci reached the continent of America a week or two earlier than the

Cabots and about fourteen months earlier than Columbus. His account of these expeditions was contained in a diary said to have been written after his fourth voyage, and entitled *Le Quattro Giornate*, no portion of which is extant. He also wrote several letters to his former schoolfellow Soderini, gonfaloniere of Florence, one of which remains in a Latin translation printed at St.-Dié in 1507. The German geographer Martin Waldseemüller (Hylacomylus), who made use of this letter in his *Cosmographiae Introductio*, published at St.-Dié in the same year, was the first to suggest the name America for the new continent, in honor of Amerigo Vespucci. His portrait appears, along with those of other members of his family and prominent Florentines, in the *Madonna of Mercy*, a fresco executed by Domenico Ghirlandaio in the Vespucci Chapel in the Church of Ognissanti, Florence.

Vettori (vet-tō′rē), **Francesco.** Florentine public official and historian; b. at Florence, 1474; d. 1539. He was a contemporary and good friend of Machiavelli. He held the most important offices in Florence, was instrumental in securing the collapse of the republic of Piero Soderini (1512), and thereafter linked his fortunes with those of the Medici. Through his friendship with Pope Leo X he secured the release of his friend Machiavelli (imprisoned and exiled on suspicion of complicity in an anti-Medicean plot). Vettori served Pope Leo X, Lorenzo, duke of Urbino, and Pope Clement VII. He was supple enough to serve the republic when it was briefly restored (1527) and to maintain his good relations with the Medici. After the fall of Florence (1530) he supported Alessandro de' Medici, and when he was assassinated, Vettori supported Cosimo I. He wrote *Sommario della storia d'Italia*, a summary history of Italy covering the complicated and violent period from 1511 to 1527. The work is outstanding for its keen observation, and interesting in its parallels with Machiavelli's political thought.

Vicentino (vē-chen-tē′nō), **Nicola.** Composer and music theorist; b. at Vicenza, c1511; d. 1572. In his madrigals he sought to recapture Greek modes, and invented the archiorgano, an instrument with six keyboards, to further his system.

Victoria (bēk-tō′ryä), **Tomás Luis de.** [Italian, **Tommaso Lodovico da Vittoria.**] Spanish church composer; b. at Ávila, Spain, c1540; d. at Madrid, August 27, 1611. He was successor to Palestrina at the Collegium Romanum; among his works are madrigals, the *Officium Defunctorum* for the empress Maria, motets, hymns, Masses, and psalms.

Vida (vē′dä), **Marco Girolamo.** Latin poet; b. at Cremona, 1485; d. at Alba, September 27, 1566. A sincerely religious man, he had studied theology and law and had spent much of his youth at Mantua, where he was exposed to Renaissance literary developments. These, strongly classical, if not actually pagan, directed his attempts to reconcile a lively moral conscience with Latin culture. He went to Rome and was immersed in the highly cultivated but not very spiritual atmosphere of the court of Leo X. The latter gave him a benefice at Frascati so that he could devote himself to Latin poetry. Clement VII named him bishop of Alba, an office he piously fulfilled for over thirty years. He was active at the Council of Trent, where he was noted for his integrity and sound theology, and expressed his proposals for reform of the Church in his *Constitutiones Synodales*. His chief work, *Christiad*, is of profound religious inspiration. It celebrates the Redemption in an epic modeled on Vergil's *Aeneid*. Although the expression of the Christian event in humanistic, classically derived terms creates a jarring dichotomy, the work was popular in its own time and influenced later writers, notably Tasso. Vida also wrote, in Latin, on the cultivation of the silkworm and on the game of chess. His *Ars poetica*, one of the first to be influenced by Aristotle's *Poetics*, proposes Vergil as the perfect poetic model and states his criteria for poetry.

Viète (vyet), **François.** [Latinized, **Franciscus Vieta.**] French mathematician, the greatest of the 16th century; b. at Fontenay-le-Comte, in Vendée, France, 1540; d. at Paris, December 13, 1603. His most important contributions were to trigonometry and the application of algebra to geometry. By some he is regarded as the inventor of analytic geometry. His interest in cryptoanalysis enabled him to decipher Spanish secret messages for Henry IV of France. His *Opera mathematica* appeared at Leiden in 1646.

Vigna (vē′nyä), **Pier della.** See **Pier della Vigna.**

Vignola (vē-nyō′lä). [Original name, **Iacopo**

Barozzi or **Barozio.**] Architect; b. at Vignola, near Modena, 1507; d. at Rome, 1573. He began his career as a painter, then devoted himself to perspective drawings, and was influenced in his development as an architect by Sebastiano Serlio. At Rome, after 1530, he studied the antique and made drawings of ancient buildings, and was influenced in his classic approach to architecture by Peruzzi (in his turn influenced by Bramante) with whom he worked as architect in the Vatican (1534–1536). Later (1541–1543) he was in the service of Francis I in France. On his return to Italy he worked for a time (1543–1550) at Bologna, and then returned to Rome, where he entered upon a period of great activity. The villa (now the Museum of Etruscan Antiquities) of Pope Julius III is his principal palace at Rome. The rather austere façade has a linear simplicity in its two stories, with pairs of windows on each end and a great central portal, in the form of a triumphal arch, flanked by niches on the ground floor; the elements of the ground floor are repeated in the upper story. The back of the very shallow building has a court consisting of a semicircular colonnade and is derived from the classical villas described by Pliny. The villa was built as a place to which one could withdraw from the city for a day of rest and relaxation. It was not intended as a residence. Its charm and beauty rest in its exterior design and ornamentation, and in the gardens and building at the back which were designed by Ammannati. Of 1554 is the little Church of S. Andrea on the Via Flaminia at Rome. It is an early example of a variation of a central plan, for instead of being based on a circle in a square it is based on an ellipse within a rectangle and is the first example of a church with an oval dome. Vignola derived the design from Roman tombs, especially, that of Cecilia Metella which may still be seen at Rome. In 1559 Cardinal Alessandro Farnese commissioned him to work on his castle at Caprarola, which had been begun in the 1520's by Antonio da Sangallo the Younger and Peruzzi. Its pentagonal plan was established by Sangallo. The plan was for a massive, fortresslike building suitable for the seat of the owner of vast possessions. The exterior architectural and ornamental elements that transform it into a less forbidding structure are Vignola's. The same cardinal commissioned him to build the Church of the Gesù at Rome, begun in 1568 and not completed until after Vignola's death. The church was to be the mother church of the Society of Jesus, founded by Ignatius Loyola in 1540, and was to be designed for large audiences who were expected to listen to the sermons that were a feature of Jesuit practice. Its short single nave with side chapels and shallow transepts, patterned after Alberti's S. Andrea at Mantua, were so designed for acoustical reasons. The façade, designed by Giacomo della Porta after Vignola's death, is based on Alberti's design for S. Maria Novella at Florence. The church became the model for Jesuit churches wherever the Jesuits went, throughout the world (but great departures were made from Vignola's original severe design for the interior when it was revised in later centuries). After the death of Michelangelo (1564), Vignola was in charge of the construction of the Basilica of St. Peter's, at first with Pirro Ligorio and then alone, and carried on Michelangelo's work.

A central figure in the late Renaissance phase of architecture, Vignola was also a writer whose treatises were widely distributed and had great influence on 17th- and 18th-century architecture. The treatise *Due regole della prospettiva pratica* (1583) was a manual on perspective. More influential was his *Regola delli cinque ordini d'architettura* (1562), on the five orders. The precise and easily applicable rules he laid down came to be followed strictly by many later architects. In his own work, however, Vignola employed wide variation in decorative elements. He intended his rules for guidance, not ossification.

Vignoles (vē-nyol), **Étienne de.** See **La Hire.**

Vigo (vē′gō), **Giovanni da.** Surgeon; b. at Rapallo, 1450?; d. 1525. He practiced at Saluzzo and Savona, and became (1503) surgeon to Pope Julius II and lived at Rome as a member of his court. After the death of Julius, he became physician of Cardinal Sisto della Rovere. At this time surgery was not a profession. Physicians were required to have a degree, but almost any skilled person could be a surgeon. Vigo was the first to assert that surgeons also should be learned men and receive training in their art. Most manuals of surgery were written in the vernacular, since surgeons were assumed to be ignorant of Latin. Vigo wrote on the art of surgery, *Practica in arte chirurgica* (Rome, 1514). His

Latin work was often reprinted and was translated into French, English, Italian, German, Dutch, Spanish, and Portuguese. Vigo was among the first to describe the wounds caused by the new weapons—firearms—and to prescribe treatment for this new kind of wound. He also devised surgical instruments.

Villagrá (bē-lyä-grä′) or **Villagran** (bē-lyä-grän′), **Francisco de.** Spanish soldier; b. at Astorga, in León, Spain, 1507; d. at Concepción, Chile, July 15, 1563. He was prominent in the conquest of Chile (1540–1546). As acting governor, and governor *ad interim*, he carried on numerous campaigns against the Indians.

Villalobos (ʙe-la-lō′bōs), **Rui López de.** See **López de Villalobos, Rui.**

Villani (vēl-lä′nē), **Filippo.** Chronicler and public official; b. 1345; d. 1407. He was the son of Matteo Villani (1295?–1363) and the nephew of Giovanni Villani (d. 1348). He served as chancellor of Perugia, and lectured on Dante at the University of Florence. He added one book to his father's continuation of his uncle's *Cronica*, and brought the record to 1364.

Villani, Giovanni. Florentine chronicler; b. at Florence; d. there, in the Black Death, 1348. He was a merchant who, in the course of business, traveled in France and Spain between the years 1302 and 1308; thus he was out of Florence during the bitter struggle between the Black and the White Guelphs that ended in the triumph of the former. He had gone to Rome for the Jubilee of 1300, and later recorded that it was the sight of the ancient monuments and the ruins, and the overwhelming sense of the history and glory of ancient Rome that prompted him to write his chronicle of Florence, that the history of his beloved city, the "daughter of Rome," might be preserved. However, he did not begin his *Nuova Cronica* until some years after 1300. In addition to his business enterprises he served his city in many positions: as prior (1316, 1317, 1321), and in other posts. In 1331 he was in charge of building the new circuit of the city walls, and was filled with pride that his growing city needed a larger circumvallation. In his public positions as in his commercial undertakings he was notable for his integrity and his patriotism. In 1345 two great banking houses failed. He was involved and was imprisoned briefly for debt. He died of the Black Death in 1348, having left in his *Cronica* a blank space for recording the number of lives that the plague took in Florence.

Villani's *Nuova Cronica*, in twelve books and in his native tongue, is thought to have been begun some time after 1308. It covers Florentine history from the mists of antiquity to 1346. The early history is drawn from legend and early chronicles, and is of interest principally for the recording of legends and the incorporation of other chroniclers. Books VII to XII, however, from 1266 to 1346, form an invaluable record of events as he had observed them, or learned of them from persons still living, from documents, and from statistics that he compiled himself. He was enormously proud of his city, which was the banker and manufactory for Europe when Rome itself was in decline. He observed and recorded everything that struck his alert interest. He gives statistics on the population, number of schools and their students, new buildings, and businesses. He describes the standards of the various guilds (the standard of the Physicians and Apothecaries, who later included artists, was a red field charged with the Virgin holding the Christ Child in Her arms; that of the bankers was a red field sewn with golden florins). He tells of the creation of the office of prior, records the outbreaks of fire and the number of buildings destroyed (that of June, 1304, destroyed 1,700 palaces, towers, and houses, to say nothing of stores and treasure), floods and their toll in lives (that of November, 1333, was the worst, equaled again in its fury by that of November, 1966). In recording the disasters he reveals himself as susceptible to the superstitions of the time: strange occurrences are told as portents (a lion given to Florence by Pope Boniface VIII was attacked and killed by an ass); the position of the planets is soberly described as having been ominous; above all, disaster is sent by God to punish the sins of the city. But in recounting economic disasters his shrewdness overcomes superstition. With monotonous regularity he records the outbreak of fire (Florence was a wooden city in his time) and famine, the upward spiraling of prices as grain became scarce, and the plagues that followed famine. For details of economic, social, and political life at the end of the 13th century and the first half of the 14th century, Villani's *Cronica* is a treasure house. It has been mined by scholars and historians of his city ever since.

Villani, Matteo. Florentine chronicler; b. at Florence, 1295?; d. there, 1363. He was the brother of Giovanni Villani (d. 1348), and added ten books to Giovanni's *Nuova Cronica*, bringing the record to 1363. In that year Matteo fell a victim to a new outbreak of the plague.

Villegaignon (vēl-ge-nyôṅ), Chevalier **de.** [Title of **Nicolas Durand;** also **Villegagnon.**] French soldier; b. 1510; d. near Nemours, France, January 9, 1571. In 1555 he was given command of an expedition sent by Coligny to found a colony in Brazil. He entered the harbor of Rio de Janeiro, establishing friendly relations with the Indians. (The colony was destroyed by the Portuguese in 1597). Villegaignon published (in Latin) works on the wars in which he had been engaged.

Villiers de L'Isle-Adam (vē-yā de lēl-å-däṅ), **Philippe de.** Grand master of the order of Saint John of Jerusalem; b. at Beauvais, France, 1464; d. in Malta, 1534. In 1522, after six months' siege, he was compelled to surrender the island of Rhodes to Suleiman. In 1530 he secured from Charles V the islands of Malta and Gozo, which became the new seat of the order.

Villon (vē-yôṅ), **François.** [Original name perhaps **François de Montcorbier** (or **Corbier** or **Corbeuil** or **des Loges**); also known as **Michel Mouton.**] French poet; b. at Paris, 1431; d. after 1463. Law court records and his writings are the chief sources of information concerning his life. Because of the protection afforded him by certain Bourbons, it is surmised that he may have been distant kin to that royal house. But he was born in humble circumstances, and after his father's death he was reared by Guillaume de Villon, canon of the Church of Saint-Benoît-le-Bestourné, whom he called "more than father" and whose name he took. His patron saw him through the Sorbonne, where he took the degrees of B.A. in 1449 and M.A. in 1452. At that time degrees were easily granted and Villon, by his own account, spent little time studying but much time roistering with the notoriously unruly students, drinking, wenching, brawling, engaging in petty thievery, and fighting the police. He seems to have taken clerical orders but never to have held a benefice. In 1455 he fatally stabbed a priest; his punishment was banishment from France. He left Paris but not France, and roamed the countryside with a gang of ruffians, amusing them and celebrating their deeds and ways in numerous ballads in their special slang, known as *le jargon.* Villon at this time was already famous and had friends in high places, who presently managed to have his banishment revoked. Returning to Paris, he also returned to his former company and old ways, and presently was involved in an affray, for which he blamed Catherine de Vaucelles, following which he thought it discreet to flee his beloved city again. During this second period of exile the authorities, rounding up a criminal gang, came upon facts connecting Villon with a recent large-scale robbery. At this time he wrote a poem, *Le Dit de la naissance Marie,* dedicated apparently to a daughter of Charles, Duc d'Orléans. Charles d'Orléans himself was a poet, and seems to have become Villon's protector at this time. In or about 1457 Villon is known to have taken part in a contest of poets held by his Bourbon patron at Blois. In 1461 a church in the archdiocese of Orléans was burglarized. The archbishop of Orléans accused Villon, secured his conviction, and had him imprisoned all summer. Fortunately for the poet, 1461 also saw the accession to the French throne of Louis XI, and Villon was liberated in the course of a general amnesty proclaimed by the new monarch. He returned to Paris in 1462; with no great delay he was again convicted of theft and imprisoned. With the help apparently of influential personages, he was released, only to be convicted the following year of attempted murder, a charge of which for once he was innocent. He was sentenced to be hanged, but successfully appealed the case and was let off with a decree of ten years' banishment from Paris. Rabelais wrote that Villon thereafter found refuge at London, and there are other stories, but actually nothing is known of his movements after 1463 and it is generally supposed that he died shortly after his last escape from the gallows. Villon's principal poetical works can be dated by his misadventures with the law. We have seen that after his first arrest and banishment he wrote his ballads for thieves and ruffians in *le jargon.* After his second arrest he composed his poem to the Orleanist princess, and after his release through her or her father's good offices he wrote the *Little* (or *Lesser*) *Testament*. It was in the archbishop of Orléans' dungeon that he composed the *Dialogue Between the Heart and Body of François Villon;* it was after his rescue from that harrowing experience that he put together his *Grand* (or *Great*) *Testament;* and the *Epitaph of Villon,* also known as *Ballad of the Hanged,* was the fruit of his meditations when the noose threatened his neck at Paris. During the reign of classical ideals in the French literature of the 17th and 18th centuries, he was little regarded in his native land and almost unknown beyond its borders. He has since come to be regarded as the fountainhead of modern French poetry and acknowledged moreover as one of the great poets of all times. Villon seems preeminently to deserve the appellation "a genius." In the eyes of the law a criminal; in the view of the world a failure; socially, by the most generous estimate, an irresponsible wastrel, in him a great passion for life and a clear-eyed, searing honesty that did not spare himself were wedded to a spontaneous gift for lyrical utterance hardly ever surpassed. Boisterously humorous and mercilessly satiric, he could also be compassionate, as in the poem commiserating the lot of the chimney sweeps, and tenderly pious, as in the lines to the Blessed Virgin, written at his mother's request. The *Little* and the *Grand Testaments* are alike compositions in eight-line stanzas, interspersed with ballades and rondeaus, all alive with passion, ribaldry, piety, patriotism, pity, rebellion, contrition, and a pervading concern with death. Many leading English poets have translated Villon, and Rossetti's version of the most famous of all Villon's poems, the *Ballade of Dead Ladies,* is especially effective, with its rendering of the haunting last line of each stanza, *Mais où sont les neiges d'antan?,* as "But where are the snows of yesteryear?"

Vincent Ferrer (vin′sent fer-rer′), Saint. Spanish Dominican friar; b. at Valencia, Spain, January 23, 1350; d. at Vannes, France, April 5, 1419. He entered the Dominican order at Valencia, and made his vows in 1368. He studied at Tarragona, taught at Lerida, and wrote the treatises *De suppositionibus dialecticis* and *De natura universalis.* In 1373 he began his studies in theology at Barcelona, and completed them at Toulouse in 1379, in which year he was ordained at Barcelona by Cardinal Pedro de Luna who later (1394) was elected as Pope Benedict XIII in the Great Schism. At the beginning of the Schism, Vincent Ferrer supported Clement VII while St. Catherine of Siena was supporting Urban VI, and he later supported Benedict XIII. Commanded in a vision to go forth and preach, he left Avignon in November, 1399, and spent the next twenty years in preaching. "Like an angel flying in the midst of the sky," he preached repentance in Spain, France, Lombardy, Switzerland, and the Low Countries. He made numerous conversions in Spain among the Moors and Jews, and among the Waldenses and Cathari in other parts of Europe. At first a supporter of the Avignon popes, whom he defended in his writings, he worked ardently to heal the schism in the Church. To this end, he urged Benedict XIII to resign, as he had agreed to do if Gregory XII would also resign, and when Benedict refused he became disillusioned with his former preceptor. Vincent Ferrer was canonized in 1455 by Calixtus III.

Vinci (vēn′chē), **Leonardo da.** See **Leonardo da Vinci.**

Vinciguerra (vēn-chē-gwer′rä), **Antonio.** Poet; b. at Venice, between 1440 and 1446; d. at Zovon, Padua, December 9, 1503. He held public offices at Venice, among them, secretary of the republic. Among his works are ten satires in terza rima. He was one of the first to write satires in that form.

Virgilio (vēr-jē′lyō), **Giovanni del.** See **Del Virgilio, Giovanni.**

Vischer (fish′ėr), **Peter.** [Called **Peter Vischer the Elder.**] German sculptor and bronze founder; b. at Nuremberg, Germany, c1455; d. there, January 7, 1529. He was an architectural sculptor. His best known works are the tomb of Saint Sebaldus at Nuremberg, the tombs of Archbishop Ernst in the Cathedral of Magdeburg, and of Eitel-Friedrich I and his wife at Hechingen; the figures of Theodoris and of King Arthur at Innsbruck, and the *Crowning of the Virgin* in the Cathedral of Erfurt.

Vischer, Peter. [Called **Peter Vischer the Younger.**] German sculptor; b. in Germany, 1487; d. there, 1528. He was the ablest and most renowned of the five sons who worked with the father, Peter Vischer the Elder. He may have been one of the two of those sons who are known to have visited Italy, to whom are traced the Renaissance influences which mingled with the Gothic tradition in the later products of the Vischer workshop.

Visconti (vēs-kōn′tē). An ancient family of Milan that was in effective control of the city and much of north Italy from 1287 until 1447. The family's rise to power began when the archbishop Otto, or Ottone (1207–1295), overcame the powerful Torriani family at Milan and established his nephew Matteo I as captain of the people (1287). Matteo I (1250–1322) was named imperial vicar by Henry VII (1311) and brought many important cities of north Italy under his control. Matteo I was succeeded by his son Galeazzo I (c1277–1328), who carried on war against the Guelphs and the popes and built up his wealth and his power. His son Azzo (1302–1339) succeeded him. His rule, though marked by the usual wars, was notable for his attempt to treat Guelph and Ghibelline with equal justice, for his moderation, and for his beautification of the city of Milan. Azzo left no son and the lordship of the Milanese dominions reverted to his uncles Luchino (1292–1349) and Giovanni (1290–1354). Giovanni, the archbishop of Milan, defied the pope, extended his control over Bologna and Genoa, and was the admiring host of Petrarch. On Giovanni's death, the rule passed to his nephews Matteo II (c1319–1355), Bernabò (1323–1385), and Galeazzo II (c1320–1378). Gian Galeazzo (1351–1402), son of Galeazzo II, seized his uncle Bernabò (1385) and had him put to death, established himself as lord of Milan, bought the title duke of Milan from the emperor Wenceslaus III, and was the first duke. He was ahead of his time in what appeared to be an ambition to unite much of Italy under a single prince. Gian Galeazzo's son Giovanni Maria (1389–1412) succeeded him as duke of Milan but was murdered for his excesses. Giovanni Maria's younger brother, Filippo Maria (1392–1447), became duke and, after a nine-year struggle, effective ruler of the Milanese dominions. Filippo's only child was a natural daughter. The long domination of the Visconti family over north Italy and much of Italian politics came to an end with him. The duchy of Milan, after a brief period as a republic, came into the hands of Francesco Sforza, who had married Filippo Maria's daughter Bianca Maria. The Visconti, like the Sforza who succeeded them, produced powerful rulers but were unable to establish a dynasty. See separate entries below.

Visconti, Azzo or **Azzone.** Ruler of Milan; b. at Ferrara, 1302; d. August 16, 1339. He was the son of Galeazzo I and Beatrice d'Este, and the grandson of Matteo I Il Grande. A loyal and energetic son of Galeazzo, he shared in his father's wars against the Guelphs and took part in the defeat of the Florentines by Castruccio Castracani at Altopascio (1325). He was imprisoned with his father and uncles at Monza by the perfidious Emperor Louis IV, but all were released after some months, and by the beginning of 1329 Azzo had reached agreement with the emperor and was named imperial vicar. When he also attempted to secure reconciliation with the pope, Louis was enraged, and sent his forces into Italy again. Azzo was able to buy off the greedy Louis for 25,000 florins. Azzo's policy was to govern Guelph and Ghibelline with equal justice. A mild and prudent man, a wise ruler, he restored order and enlarged his domain. When John of Bohemia, son of Emperor Henry VII, descended into Italy (1331), the hopes of the Ghibellines for a strong prince around whom they could rally against the Church were revived. Many of the cities under Azzo's sway offered allegiance to John. Azzo himself offered submission, more from discretion than desire, and was named John's vicar, so that after the departure of John the state of affairs was much the same as it had been before his arrival. Azzo kept order, ruled with moderation, and cultivated the arts. He invited Giotto to Milan to decorate the royal palace he built. (Of the work Giotto carried out at Milan in 1335 and 1336 and of the palace itself, nothing remains.) Azzo's tomb is in the Church of S. Gottardo at Milan. The beautiful campanile that adjoins the church was built at his order in 1330. He left no sons and was succeeded by his uncle Luchino.

Visconti, Bernabò. Ruler of Milan; b. 1323; d. at Trezzo, December 19, 1385. He was the son of Stefano Visconti and the grandson of Matteo I Il Grande. With his brothers Matteo II and Galeazzo II he had been exiled from Milan (1346) by Luchino, his uncle, who feared a plot by the brothers against him. He was allowed to return when Luchino's brother, Archbishop Giovanni, succeeded Luchino in 1349, and the three brothers were recognized as heirs. When the archbishop died (1354) the brothers divided the inheritance. Bernabò's share included Cremona, Crema, Brescia, and Bergamo. Milan and Genoa were to be ruled jointly. In 1355 Bernabò and Galeazzo II assassinated Matteo and divided his share between them. Galeazzo moved his court to Pavia. Bernabò kept his at Milan and from there, for the next thirty years, intrigued and warred unceasingly to implement his policy of aggrandizement and consolidation of his dominions. The states (republics, dukedoms, lordships) of Italy entered upon a period of shifting alliances and leagues in an effort to resist and prevent him from fulfilling his policy at their expense. Genoa revolted and broke away. His war to regain control of Bologna, which had revolted, caused the pope to excommunicate him (1362) and to preach a crusade against him. (Bernabò forced the legates who brought him the bull of excommunication to eat it "together with the leaden seals and silken strings.") At length he sold his interest in Bologna to the pope for 500,000 florins. Pope Urban V, who had returned to Italy from Avignon (1367), organized a new league against him in an effort to contain him, but gave up and went back to Avignon (1370). Bernabò sent his condottiere Sir John Hawkwood to aid the Perugians in their struggle against the pope. The Florentines, formerly in terror of Visconti ambitions on their own account, now feared the encroachment of the papacy and allied themselves with the Visconti, although they took little part in the fighting. By intrigue and money he won the dependence of Pisa. In 1350 Bernabò had married Regina della Scala of Verona. (Her memory is perpetuated in the famous opera house at Milan; it was built, late in the 18th century, on the site of the Church of Santa Maria della Scala that she had caused to be erected in gratitude for the birth of her first son.) In 1378 he waged war on Verona to secure the rights of his wife and children, threatened by the claims of illegitimate sons of the Scaligeri in Verona. This war ended in a payment to him of 440,000 florins. He made an alliance with his old enemies the Venetians in an attempt to win back Genoa and intrigued in the struggles of Joanna I in the kingdom of Naples. Italy was seething with leagues and counter-alliances. And meanwhile, though victory was often canceled by subsequent failure to hold its effects, Bernabò was expanding his domains and consolidating his power. He had seventeen legitimate children (and any number of illegitimate ones) and married them off, with fabulous dowries for the daughters, to the sons and daughters of lords of Italy and Germany. One of his illegitimate daughters was married to his condottiere, the Englishman Sir John Hawkwood. Visitors came from all Europe on business to the magnificent city of Milan; Chaucer, on an embassy from England, was one of them. A tough and capable warrior, Bernabò also had the will to consolidate his power. Order of a sort was imposed. His government was repressive and the taxes heavy. He was possessed of an extraordinarily perverse cruelty. Historians of the period write of the 5,000 hounds he kept for the chase. These were farmed out on the peasants. If, on inspection by his agents, any hound was found to be in less than perfect condition, the peasant responsible for its care was punished, often by mutilation of one kind or another. Bernabò also instituted a program of tortures extending over forty days, which was to be applied to those who had offended or had been accused of offending the state. His brother Galeazzo died in 1378 and left one son as his heir, Gian Galeazzo, a quiet-seeming youth who devoted himself to his studies and who was notoriously timid. Bernabò regarded him with contempt and planned to seize his inheritance. Gian Galeazzo was as ruthless as he was timid. He informed his uncle that he was going on a pilgrimage and would like to meet him on his way. Bernabò, with some of his sons, rode out to meet him (May 6, 1385). Gian Galeazzo, surrounded by an enormous bodyguard, gave a signal in German to his men. They seized Bernabò and his sons, and shut them up in a castle at Trezzo. Bernabò died December 19th of the same year, probably of poison. Gian Galeazzo rode in triumph into Milan.

Visconti, Bianca Maria. Duchess of Milan; b. March 31, 1425; d. at Melegnano, October 23, 1468. She was the natural daughter of Filippo Maria Visconti and Agnese del Maino. His only child, Filippo Maria sought without success to have her legitimized by the emperor Sigismund; Filippo was unwilling to grant Sigismund's conditions. He gave his daughter the affection of which he was capable, and interested himself in her education. At the age of seven she was betrothed to her father's thirty-one-year-old general Francesco Sforza. The marriage did not take place until October, 1441, and in the meantime Bianca was the bait that held Sforza for Filippo. On her marriage she received Cremona and Pontremorli as dowry. An intelligent, well-educated, and astute woman, she remained loyal to her husband even when he went over to the side of her father's enemies and in spite of his many infidelities. (She succeeded in having one of his mistresses, to whom he was passionately devoted, murdered.) When, in 1450, Francesco rode into Milan in triumph as its new lord, Bianca was at his side. She was the patron of the humanists and was beloved by the people. Francesco died in 1466 and she took the reins of government firmly into her own hands, maintaining her son's inheritance until such time as he should return from France. Galeazzo Maria, the heir, returned in 1468. He soon quarreled with his mother and forced her to flee from Milan. On her way to her city of Cremona she died, rather suddenly, at Melegnano. Pope Pius II, who had met her at Mantua, spoke highly of her ability and her piety—she supported his call for a crusade. The humanists she had encouraged in her lifetime took part in her funeral ceremonies. Francesco Filelfo pronounced the funeral oration.

Visconti, Filippo Maria. Duke of Milan; b. at Milan, September 3, 1392; d. there, August 13, 1447. He was the second son of Gian Galeazzo and Caterina Visconti, and was ten years old when his father died and left him the countship of Pavia. But on the death of Gian Galeazzo the duchy he had constructed with such skill fell apart. The captains he had held in loyalty and check, and on whom he depended to preserve his realm for his children, seized what areas they could. Other lordships revolted and proclaimed their independence under their own lords. The duchess Caterina attempted to rule Milan herself and was poisoned (1404). Milan itself was in the power of Facino Cane, a noted general in the service of Gian Galeazzo. Filippo Maria, although nominally the lord of Pavia, was a virtual prisoner during his brother's reign. On May 16, 1412, Giovanni Maria, Filippo Maria's brother and the duke of Milan, was assassinated. Two sons of Bernabò Visconti (Filippo Maria's grandfather) were acclaimed as lords in his place. On the same day, Facino Cane also died, but as he lay dying he had urged his wife Beatrice di Tenda to marry Filippo. She did so, and brought to the latter an invaluable dowry consisting of money, cities her husband had seized and, above all, his troops. With these immense advantages Filippo Maria entered Milan (June 16, 1412), seized the sons of Bernabò and shut them up in the dungeons of Monza. (These dungeons, in which it was impossible to either stand or lie at full length, had been constructed by the Visconti themselves and had at one time held, on the order of Louis of Bavaria, Galeazzo I, his son Azzo, and his brothers Luchino and Giovanni.). Filippo Maria's efforts to regain control were not unresisted but, physically timid to the edge of madness, superstitious, and suspicious of everyone, he was yet ambitious, treacherous, a bold strategist, and a skillful diplomat. He was as able as his father in choosing men of ability and employing the best captains, but he never trusted them. He won the neutrality of Venice by relinquishing his claim to Verona and Vicenza; made a treaty with Genoa; and became reconciled with Amadeus VIII of Savoy. His general Carmagnola succeeded in winning back the petty lordships, and he regained Como, Lodi, Trezzo, Piacenza, Cremona, Bergamo, and Brescia. By arms, bribery, treachery, and diplomacy, by 1421 he had practically reconstituted his father's duchy. This was not the limit of his ambition, however, and, although he made a league with Florence and Venice by which all agreed to respect the others' territory, the peace was transient. In fulfillment of his ambitions he kept north and central Italy in turmoil for the next twenty-five years. His generals defeated the Florentines on several occasions, as at Zagonara where, says Machiavelli, although this was regarded as a famous victory throughout Italy, "no death occurred except those of Lodovico degli Obizzi and two of his people, who having fallen from their horses were drowned in the morass." This was an example of the careful warfare of mercenaries, who spared themselves in battle and preyed on the peasantry, plundered helpless towns, and switched sides as it became their interest. Filippo Maria intervened in Forlì in a dispute over control of the young heir and took the city. Florence and

Venice sought to restrain him, but their generals were repeatedly defeated. Another coalition of Florence, Venice, and Savoy was formed (1426). (Florence persuaded Venice to join with the threat to make Filippo Maria king of Italy if she was forced to submit to him.) Carmagnola, distrusted by Filippo Maria for his very success and betrayed by his master, now in the tradition of the time went over to the enemy. He won a decisive victory at Maclodio (October, 1427) but frittered it away by subsequent inaction. Filippo wooed Amadeus VIII of Savoy from the coalition by offering him Vercelli and by marrying his daughter Maria. (In 1418 he had had his wife Beatrice executed on trumped-up charges of unfaithfulness.) He then (April, 1428) made peace with Venice and Florence and gave up Brescia and Bergamo to Venice. His policy changed direction and he took advantage of the struggle between Pope Eugenius and the Council of Basel to go into the Romagna. He also played a shifting role in the war between the Angevins and the Aragonese for the kingdom of Naples. Alfonso of Naples, the Aragonese claimant, was captured by a Genoese fleet and brought to him as a captive, but was able to persuade Filippo Maria that the French were more dangerous to Italy than the Spanish, and in another switch, Filippo Maria released his royal captive. (After his death a will of doubtful authenticity was found that named Alfonso as his heir. Needless to say, only Alfonso took this will seriously.) In his wars, Francesco Sforza, the Milanese general, had won many victories, and expected as his reward the hand of Filippo Maria's only child Bianca Maria. In 1432, under pressure of his need for Sforza's skill, Filippo had announced the betrothal of his seven-year-old daughter to his thirty-one-year-old general, but he kept delaying the marriage. Sforza became impatient and went over to the enemy. He so successfully resisted the Milanese advance that Filippo Maria tried to make into Tuscany that the duke found it prudent to make peace (1441). To win back his general, he now permitted the marriage of his daughter. Henceforth, he devoted his energies, in the face of multiplying enemies, to preserving his dominions. This was the more essential as his new son-in-law, with the loyal support of his wife, had again gone over to the enemy. The duke found himself isolated. The Venetians defeated his attempt to regain Cremona and Pontremoli; Milan itself was threatened. Sforza, whose wife was the presumptive heir, feared the growing power of Venice and switched sides again. His troops were in Lombardy to aid his father-in-law when Filippo Maria, the last lord of the Visconti, died leaving only his illegitimate daughter as heir. Under the terms by which Gian Galeazzo had bought the title, the duchy could not pass through the female line.

Filippo was not a great soldier, a man of learning, or a patron of the arts. He was neurotically superstitious and kept his astrologer at his side almost constantly. He thought himself to be so physically ugly and repulsive that he would never have his portrait done. (Yet a medal of his head in profile by the master medalist Pisanello, an example of which is in the Isabella Stewart Gardner Museum at Boston, does not give the impression of extraordinary ugliness.) He was a despot who obstructed the implementation of his policy by his perpetual fear for his own safety and his complete distrust of those upon whom he most depended. Yet for all his weaknesses and timidity, he was in many respects an able administrator who knew how to choose men and how to take advantage of the fluid political situation in Italy to build up his own duchy. He put the finances of his realm in order, protected the peasantry, and promoted industry. He made no arrangements for his successor, possibly because his illegitimate daughter was married to Francesco Sforza. On his death the enraptured people of Milan threw off the yoke of the Visconti and established a short-lived republic. However, it would be an exaggeration to view him, or the other Visconti, as purely tyrannical rulers of centralized states, since magistrates and councils in Milan and the subject cities continued to function, and many traditional privileges and immunities persisted.

Visconti, Galeazzo I. Ruler of Milan; b. c1277; d. at Pescia, August 6, 1328. He was the son of Matteo I Il Grande, whose fortunes he shared and to whom he was an able and energetic lieutenant. In 1302 he followed his father into exile at Ferrara. There his wife, Beatrice d'Este, bore his son Azzo. From Ferrara he went to Treviso as podesta. In 1311 he returned to Milan with his father and took part in the successful plot by which the rival Torriani were discredited in the eyes of Emperor Henry VII. As he fought with his father against the Church and the Guelphs, repelling a French army under Philip of Valois in this cause, he was included in the ban of excommunication on charges of heresy and witchcraft that Pope John XXII laid on Matteo. But Galeazzo was not so oppressed by it as his father and succeeded to the control of Milan on the abdication of his father in May, 1322. Later in the same year he was forced by the returned Torriani to flee Milan. The Pope had preached a crusade against Milan. The crusading army was encamped under the very walls. Galeazzo drove it off (June, 1323). Having repelled his enemies and nullified the Guelph threat, he governed Milan and the cities under his control peacefully until 1327. In that year the Holy Roman emperor Louis of Bavaria descended into Italy. His greed was aroused by the wealth of his host Galeazzo and by his well-trained German mercenaries. To satisfy that greed, he arrested his imperial vicar, with his sons and brothers, and imprisoned them in the castle at Monza. Louis then proceeded to seduce the Germans and seize the treasure. Thanks to Castruccio Castracani, lord of Lucca, on whom Louis was dependent for his very safety, Galeazzo was released and restored to favor in the emperor's eyes. He died the following year and was succeeded by his son Azzo.

Visconti, Galeazzo II. Ruler of Milan; b. c1320; d. at Pavia, August 4, 1378. He was the son of Stefano Visconti and the grandson of Matteo I Il Grande. After the death of Stefano, who was probably poisoned, Galeazzo remained at Milan for a time with his mother, then went to Palestine. Later, with his brothers Matteo II and Bernabò, he was exiled from Milan (1346) by his uncle Luchino. The brothers returned to Milan on the death of Luchino (1349) and were recognized as heirs of Luchino's brother, the archbishop Giovanni, who had succeeded Luchino. When Giovanni died (1354) the three brothers divided up the inheritance. Galeazzo's share included Como, Novara, Vercelli, Asti, Alba, Tortona, and Alessandria. The brothers agreed to rule Milan and Genoa jointly. In 1355 Galeazzo and Bernabò assassinated Matteo II and divided his lands between them. When the emperor Charles IV descended into Italy he appointed Galeazzo and Bernabò imperial vicars (1355) but later distrusted their ambitions and organized a league against them. Galeazzo lost some of his cities to members of the league but later regained most of them, and in addition got Pavia (1360). He built the great rectangular castle that still stands at Pavia in 1365, moved his court there, and lived in unparalleled splendor. An able man, he organized a bureaucracy, brought the heterogeneous collection of lordships that constituted his domain into a unified state, ruled firmly, and did not indulge in the cruelties that scarred Bernabò's rule. He was a lover of books, and surrounded himself with men of letters and artists; Petrarch was one of his honored guests. He founded a famous library at Pavia, and a university (1361) that became famous for the quality of its instruction. Peace was not repugnant to him. He married his daughter Violante to Lionel, son of Edward III of England (who died three months later), and his son Gian Galeazzo to Isabella, daughter of the king of France. The marriages indicate that the Visconti had raised themselves to the level of a powerful ruling house. The festivities and the gifts he made to the guests at the weddings of his children reveal a taste for display, lavishness and, except that he could afford it, extravagance that was unequaled in his time. Gifts made to the guests, included horses with trappings of silk and silver, suits of armor, jeweled belts and surcoats, and bolts of cloth of gold. Gilded fruits were part of the repast. A cool and skillful diplomat, he brought order and peace to the lands under his control, which, with those of brother Bernabò's, included all Lombardy and much of north Italy. He was succeeded by his son Gian Galeazzo.

Visconti, Gian Galeazzo. Ruler of Milan; b. October 16, 1351; d. at Melegnano, September 3, 1402. He was the son of Galeazzo II Visconti and Blanche of Savoy, and was a quiet, timid, and studious youth whose intellectual accomplishments won the praises of Petrarch. In 1360 his father arranged a marriage for him with Isabella of Valois, daughter of King John II of France. Galeazzo gave the French king over 400,000 scudi on the occasion of the marriage of his son. Nevertheless, this alliance with a ruling house of Europe was an acknowledgment of the power and importance of the Visconti. As part of her dowry, Isabella brought Gian Galeazzo the countship of Vertus, a county in Champagne, hence his title count of Vertus, or Virtù, as it was more scornfully rendered. Blanche bore him Valentina (1366), Azzo (1369) and Carlo (1372), of whom only Valentina survived. Under his father's guidance, Gian Galeazzo took some part in political affairs, and on occasion shared in the almost constant wars, but he was not a warrior. He preferred his studies, letters, and meditation. In 1375 his father gave him some territory in order to prepare him to rule the inheritance that would be his. In 1378 Galeazzo II died, and Gian Galeazzo became, in theory, joint ruler with his uncle Bernabò over the Visconti dominions of Lombardy. For a number of years he remained quietly in his castle at Pavia, pursuing his studies and apparently absorbed in religious contemplation. He was notoriously timid. Bernabò looked upon him with contempt and laid plans to seize his inheritance for his own sons. Gian Galeazzo had discovered and foiled several plots, but said nothing and applied himself to his devotions. Isabella died (1372) and he married Bernabò's daughter Caterina (1380). The marriage neither enhanced nor protected Bernabò's interests. Gian Galeazzo was as ruthless and fearless in spirit as he was cowardly in the face of physical action. Under the pretext of going on a pilgrimage to a shrine above Milan he invited Bernabò to meet him on the way. Bernabò and some of his sons rode out to do so (May 6, 1385). They were astonished at the size of fearful Gian Galeazzo's guard, and showed their scorn of his terror. Gian Galeazzo leapt from his horse to salute his uncle, then uttered a signal in German to his men. They seized Bernabò and his sons and carried them off to Trezzo where they imprisoned them. Bernabò died later in the year, probably of poison, unmourned by the oppressed people, who sacked and razed his palaces. Gian Galeazzo established order with his troops and made himself master of all the Visconti dominions.

The emblem of the Visconti family was a serpent from whose mouth a child was issuing. From this they were called, by their enemies who said the child was being swallowed, "the Vipers of Milan." Gian Galeazzo was the viper *par excellence*. He was an able, ambitious, wily, and utterly ruthless man who envisioned the union of all north and central Italy, by whatever means were necessary, under the leadership of Milan and the house of Visconti. By its position, Milan was strategic: whoever controlled it could control Italy. Gian Galeazzo set about expanding his lordship and centralizing its control. He knew how to pick lieutenants and keep them loyal to him. The best captains in Italy were in his pay or ready to become so at a moment's notice, for he paid promptly and pensioned off the old soldiers and captains (whose names he could recall long after they had left his service). He kept accurate records of the expenditures of his household and his government, and established a bureaucracy under his tight control. His territories, unified under his firm hand, constituted a first rate political and military power. He set out to increase them. For the next seventeen years he combatted, successfully on the whole, the numerous leagues of shifting allies that rose and fell in Italy in an effort to contain him. In 1387 he took the part of the lords of Padua in their quarrel with Verona, and then seized Verona and Vicenza for himself. He then, with the acquiescence of Venice, turned on Padua and drove out its lord (1388). Not long afterward he won Treviso also. By intrigue and slander he made the Estensi of Ferrara and the Gonzaga of Mantua dependent on him. Florence sought to rally the other Italians against him; Venice saw the mistake she had made in encouraging him to take areas on her borders; and he was unable to prevent the loss of Padua (1390). To counteract the anti-Viscontean league organized by the Florentines he sought powerful allies for himself. He married his daughter Valentina to Louis d'Orléans, brother of the French king (1386), and bought the titles of duke of Milan (1395) and count of Pavia (1396) from the emperor Wenceslaus III. The area included in the investiture, and which was to be hereditary, included north Italy almost to Venice. He was the first to have the title, duke of Milan, and his coronation, which took place in the Piazza di Sant' Ambrogio at Milan on September 5, 1395, was spectacular. In 1396 he was made count of Anghiera and in 1397, duke of Lombardy. Siena gave him the sovereignty (1399) and he governed it with circumspection, strictly limiting the powers of his representatives there, and seeing to it that the limitations were scrupulously observed. He bought the sovereignty of Pisa, after having with unparalleled treachery secured the murder of its lord. He exercised considerable authority over most of the north, including Genoa and Lucca, and was ahead of his time in his plan to conquer and unite Italy. Florence, however, still resisted him, and the new king of Germany, Rupert of Bavaria, was hostile, but Rupert's forays into Italy turned into routs before the well-trained Italians. Alberico da Barbiano, the founder of the Italian Company of St. George and one of Gian Galeazzo's most able captains, brought Bologna to its knees (1400), and Perugia was occupied. Florence was surrounded by the Viscontean ring and in despair, when it was miraculously saved. Plague broke out in Milan. Gian Galeazzo fled to escape infection but was overtaken by the infection at Melagnano and died there, September 3, 1402.

Gian Galeazzo was an able organizer, constructed a rudimentary territorial state, and might have united Italy. (But by the marriage of his daughter Valentina he gave France a claim that led to disaster at the end of the century.) He was not himself a warrior. Indeed, he went to ludicrous lengths to protect himself, jumped at the least noise, was unnerved by any unexpected movement near him, and in terror of assassination, as well he might have been. Even so, he had a will and spirit of iron. He had attempted to consolidate the unruly lordships that made up his dominions by imposing on them the discipline and systematization of a single prince. He held a splendid court, beautified the castle at Pavia, added to the rich library there, was a great benefactor of the university, gave his patronage to artists and men of letters, and undertook the construction of magnificent buildings. In 1386 he began the construction of the cathedral at Milan, and dedicated it to "Mary the Babe" in gratitude for the birth of a male heir: Giovanni Maria, son of Caterina. Henceforth the name Maria was part of the name of all Visconti children. The famous Certosa di Pavia (the Carthusian monastery) was begun in 1396 and carried to completion in the next two centuries. Gian Galeazzo's mausoleum is in it. His accomplishments, political and intellectual, made him feared and admired in his own time. Caterina had borne him two sons and by his will, in the tradition of his family, he fragmented the state he had built: Giovanni Maria inherited the duchy of Milan, Filippo Maria inherited Pavia, and Gabriele Maria (an illegitimate son) was given Pisa (which he soon lost). His sons were children when Gian Galeazzo died, and the duchy he had constructed with such skill and ruthlessness at once fell apart: a prey to revolt in the absence of his strong hand and to his former captains, supposedly protecting the interests of his sons, who enthusiastically seized the cities they had helped him to win.

Visconti, Giovanni. Archbishop and lord of Milan; b. 1290; d. October 5, 1354. As a youth he had wanted to follow a military career, but was persuaded by his father, Matteo I Il Grande, to enter upon an ecclesiastical one instead. He had held several ecclesiastical offices, including that of cardinal under the antipope Nicholas V, when he was made (1339) archbishop of Milan. By the time Clement VI had confirmed him in this office (1342), he had used it and his influence to become a leading political figure in Milan. After the death of his brother Luchino (1349), with whom he was the heir of his nephew Azzo, he was increasingly active in the affairs of the state. His policy was to make peace with his neighbors and to aggrandize Milan by control of areas and cities at a distance. In 1350 he brought Bologna under his control. This brought him into conflict with the pope. Clement ordered him to come to Avignon, where the papal court was then fixed. Giovanni replied that he would arrive at Avignon at the head of 12,000 cavalry and 6,000 infantry. He marched up to his throne in the cathedral at Milan bearing the cross in his left hand and a drawn sword in his right. As the cross was the symbol of his spiritual power, so the sword would be used to defend his temporal power—this was the announcement he made to the assembled congregation. The pope excommunicated him. But Giovanni's agile diplomacy, money, and threats won him absolution. The pope gave up Bologna to him (1352) for 12,000 florins. He made war on Florence (1351–1352) and ended it with a treaty. In 1353 the Genoese, after a disastrous war from which the Visconti rescued them, submitted to Milan. It was about this time that Giovanni invited Petrarch to Milan as his guest, with no conditions, saying he wanted only "your presence here, which would honor us." He promised Petrarch a house and peace. Petrarch accepted the invitation, in spite of his announced convictions concerning liberty, and remained in Milan long after the death of Giovanni. The treaty between Milan and Florence that resulted in the formation of the Tuscan League roused alarm at Venice, and a counter league was formed. Giovanni sent Petrarch on a mission to Venice which, though Petrarch impressed the Venetians with his Latin speech, was inconclusive. For all his political activity, and the often ruthless execution of his power, Giovanni did not neglect ecclesiastical duties. He made attempts to reform clerical life and was engaged in promoting religious foundations and furthering pious works. By the time of his death he had established Visconti rule over all north Italy except Piedmont, Verona, Mantua, Ferrara, and Venice, and had established the Visconti as independent of both pope and emperor, as despots whose worst enemies became members of their own family. On his death his lands were divided among his nephews Matteo, Bernabò, and Galeazzo.

Visconti, Giovanni Maria. Duke of Milan; b. 1389; d. at Milan, May 16, 1412. He was the elder son of Gian Galeazzo and Caterina Visconti, and at the age of 14 succeeded his father as duke of Milan. His mother, the daughter of that tough warrior Bernabò, acted as regent for him and his brother Filippo Maria, but in point of fact the duchy created by Gian Galeazzo was rapidly disintegrating under the raids of his former captains. Each of them seized whatever he could; Bologna, Perugia, and Assisi were lost to the pope (1403). Giovanni Maria quarreled with his mother and she was forced to flee the city. (She died at Monza, where she was a virtual prisoner, on October 17, 1404, perhaps of poison.) Facino Cane, his father's captain, entered the young duke's service and did what he could to preserve his inheritance. Giovanni Maria, however, was perverted in character and psychotically cruel (the inbreeding of which he was a product may have been significant). His grandfather Bernabò had kept 5,000 hounds for the chase; Giovanni Maria kept his hounds to feed on human flesh and derived insane satisfaction from seeing them do so. He was incapable of ruling and was assassinated by some Ghibelline nobles while he was at Mass.

Visconti, Luchino. Ruler of Milan; b. 1292; d. January 24, 1349. He was the fourth son of Matteo I Il Grande, shared his father's exile, and returned with his father to Milan in 1310. Thereafter, for a number of years he was active as a leader of Milanese troops. He was wounded at the battle of Montecatini (1315); fought the Guelphs and the Angevins in Piedmont; and commanded at the bloody battle of Parabiagio (1339) in the struggle against the Company of St. George, a band of mercenaries that sought to seize and plunder Milan. When his nephew Azzo died (1322) without sons, he and his brother Giovanni, the archbishop, were named lords of Milan. Giovanni remained in the background, establishing his power as an ecclesiastic, and Luchino held the reins of government. He governed the ten cities left by Azzo with a firm hand, and to them added others by conquest, purchase (as in the case of Parma), or cession. He intervened in Tuscany to help Pisa prevent Florence from taking Lucca, and made Pisa a dependency of Milan; his troops were besieging Genoa when he died. He brought organization to the government of the Milanese dominions, cleared the roads of bandits; and abolished some of the worst feudal obligations. The excommunication of his family and the interdict on Milan were lifted during his rule. His administration was repressive, but not in terms of the times, and orderly; and he permitted all the exiles except the Torriani to return. He increased the power and influence of his house and initiated a policy of Visconti dominion over Italy. These accomplishments, and the manner in which they were obtained, left Luchino in fear of his life. He had not, after all, obliterated all his rivals. Fearing a plot by his nephews Galeazzo II and Bernabò, he drove them out of Milan (1346) but did not, in spite of a cruel nature, kill them or have them killed, as might have been expected. Moody, fearful, and jealous, he was an able general and had some idea of administration. His personal affairs were in great disorder. His third wife created a scandal with her love affairs. He was planning to kill her but she, suspecting his intentions, poisoned him. His one supposedly legitimate son, Luchino Novello, was declared illegitimate with the consent of his mother and the archbishop Giovanni succeeded Luchino as ruler of the Milanese dominions.

Visconti, Marco. Son of Matteo I Il Grande;

d. at Milan, in September, 1329. He was the brother of Stefano, Galeazzo, Giovanni, and Luchino Visconti. A distinguished soldier who carried out many military missions for his father, he took part in the struggles against Pope John XXII, the siege of Genoa, the wars in Piedmont, and in the defense of Milan against the pope's crusading armies in 1322 and 1324. He intrigued against his brother Galeazzo I with Emperor Louis IV of Bavaria, and later entered into negotiations with the Florentines. When these collapsed he returned to Milan. Galeazzo gave him a hostile reception and he died soon after, flung out of a window, according to some chroniclers.

Visconti, Matteo I. [Called **Il Grande**, "the Great."] Ruler of Milan; b. at Invorio (Novara), August 15, 1250; d. at Milan, June 24, 1322. He was the great-nephew of Archbishop Ottone, by whose help he was named Captain of the People in 1287. However, the Torriani, a powerful family of Milan that had been defeated by Archbishop Ottone (1277) returned to Milan and forced Matteo into exile (1302). He rallied the Ghibelline nobles and exiles about him and when the emperor, Henry VII, descended into Italy, succeeded in discrediting the Torriani in the emperor's eyes (Machiavelli tells how he stirred up strife, which the Torriani tried to quell, whereupon Matteo and his sons assaulted the Torriani and blamed the uproar on them). Henry named him imperial vicar (1311), encouraged to do so by the fact that Matteo could supply him with badly needed funds. His support from the emperor brought Matteo into conflict with the papacy and the Guelphs, and much of the rest of his life was engaged in fending off their attacks. By 1315 he and his sons controlled Piacenza, Bergamo, Lodi, Como, Cremona, Alessandria, Tortona, Pavia, Vercelli, and Novara. In 1317 a violent struggle with Pope John XXII erupted. To placate the pope, Matteo renounced his title of imperial vicar, remaining, however, lord of Milan and many cities. The pope, the Guelphs, Robert of Naples, and the interested Torriani feared the growing power of the Visconti in north Italy and combined against him—to no avail. He shut King Robert up in Genoa, drove out the French, defeated the general of the crusading army the pope had launched against him, and arrived at an accommodation with the Germans, who had come into Italy, by which their troops were withdrawn. The pope excommunicated Matteo and his sons (1320) and laid an interdict on Milan (1321). Matteo, a mild and prudent ruler, an able general, and a diplomat who understood the power of money to soothe his rivals, unstained by tyrannical crimes and considerate of the people, was beloved by the Milanese. He was also a religious man. The fears for his soul aroused by the excommunication so worked on him that his alarmed sons convinced him that he should abdicate. He handed over the reins to his son Galeazzo (May, 1323), vowed thenceforth to devote himself to good works but died a month later. He left five sons: Galeazzo, Marco, Giovanni, Luchino, and Stefano, as well as a number of daughters. Galeazzo, Giovanni, Luchino, and the sons of Stefano, became rulers of the Milanese dominion in succeeding years. Marco was murdered.

Visconti, Matteo II. Ruler of Milan; b. c1319; d. in September, 1355. He was the son of Stefano Visconti, and the grandson of Matteo I Il Grande. With his brothers Bernabò and Galeazzo II he was an heir of his uncle, Archbishop Giovanni (d. 1354), to the Visconti rule of the Milanese dominions. Matteo's share included the cities of Bologna, Lodi, Piacenza, Parma, and Monza. The brothers agreed to share the rule of Milan and Genoa. Matteo neglected his responsibilities in favor of his personal pleasures. When Bologna flamed into rebellion he did nothing to secure the city. His brothers, lest he lose the heritage of the Visconti by his neglect and his excesses, assassinated him. They divided his share between them.

Visconti, Otto or **Ottone.** Archbishop of Milan, and founder of the Visconti family fortunes; b. 1207; d. August 8, 1295. He held many important ecclesiastical positions. In 1257 the throne of the archbishopric of Milan fell vacant and the canons could not agree on a candidate. Pope Urban IV named Ottone as archbishop. The most powerful family in Milan at that time was the Torriani family. Members of it had been captains of the people over a number of years, and they were also acknowledged as lords by several neighboring cities, as Lodi, Novara, Como, Vercelli, and Bergamo. It was to curb their power that Urban named Ottone archbishop. The Torriani contested the nomination, strife erupted, and the pope laid an interdict on the city. Ottone was forced into exile when the new pope, Clement IV, failed to support him. He gathered many exiled Ghibelline nobles about him and continued his struggle against the Torriani. In 1287 he captured Napo della Torre and five of his relatives and shut them up in three iron cages. He entered Milan, where he was enthusiastically welcomed by the oppressed people, and was acknowledged as *signore* and virtual ruler of the city. Cremona and Lodi also received him. He recalled the exiled Ghibellines in several cities that now acknowledged his leadership and effectively, and with moderation, established his control. In the same year (1287) he caused his great-nephew Matteo I to be named Captain of the People. Having established his relative (and definitively made Milan into a principality), Ottone retired from the political struggle and devoted himself to his ecclesiastical duties. He died at the Abbey at Chiaravalle, a few miles outside Milan, to which he had retired in his last years.

Visconti, Teobaldo. Original name of Pope **Gregory X.**

Visconti, Valentina. Daughter of Gian Galeazzo Visconti and Isabella of France; b. 1366; d. at Blois, December 4, 1408. Her father married her to Louis d'Orléans, brother of the king of France, amid festivities of awesome splendor and display. Her dowry was 400,000 florins in addition to the countships of Asti in Piedmont and of Vertus in France. In addition, her children were to have the right of succession to Milan, since she was married in 1386 and there was not at that time a male heir. She left Milan in June, 1387, and arrived in Paris at the end of August. By 1393 she had two children, one of whom was Charles d'Orléans, father of King Louis XII, who in his time put forth a claim to Milan. Valentina was accused of witchcraft because of her treatment of King Charles VI, her husband's brother, and had to retire to Blois. Her husband was murdered by assassins, November 23, 1407, and although the king promised her justice, he never delivered, and she died the following year.

Visconti da Oleggio (dä ō-led′jō), **Giovanni.** Visconti captain; d. at Fermo, 1366. He was an offspring of a branch of the Visconti family of Milan that had settled in Oleggio. Archbishop Giovanni Visconti took an interest in him and persuaded him to turn from an ecclesiastical to a military career. In 1351 he was sent to Bologna as captain of the people and agent of the Visconti, and in the same year led a Viscontean raid into Tuscany. After the death of the archbishop, Giovanni da Oleggio took advantage of the discontent of the Bolognese to make himself lord of the city (1355). Since he could not withstand the attacks of Bernabò Visconti he ceded Bologna to the papacy (1360) and received the lordship of Fermo in return.

Vitale da Bologna (vē-tä′lā dä bō-lō′nyä). Bolognese painter; active between 1330 and 1359. His early works show Sienese influence; later works show a somewhat coarsened technique, and marked contrasts of light and shade that was passed on to the many disciples of the school of Bolognese painting of which he is considered the founder. He was one of several artists who frescoed the Abbey Church at Pomposa (1351). Among other subjects, these represented scenes from the life of St. Eustace. He painted so many Madonnas he was called "Vitale delle Madonne." Among these are a *Coronation of the Virgin* and detached frescoes, Pinacoteca; part of a dismembered polyptych (1345), Davia Bargellini Gallery; *Madonna of Victory* and a polyptych, *Madonna Kneeling, Being Crowned by Her Son* (1353), S. Salvatore; and a *Madonna*, S. Michele dei Leproseti, all at Bologna, and Madonnas at Forlì (Chiesa dell' Addolorata), Milan (Poldi Pezzoli), Rome (Vatican), and Viterbo. Other works are in the Pinacoteca (*St. George Killing the Dragon, Last Supper and Four Saints, Resurrection*, and others), Bologna, and at Pesaro, Udine (cathedral, frescoes, 1348–1349), Edinburgh, and elsewhere.

Vita Nuova (vē′tä nwô′vä). ["*New Life.*"] A work of Dante's youth, finished probably c1292. It is composed of thirty-one sonnets and canzoni (songs) that the poet had written over a period of nine years in praise of his love and inspiration, Beatrice Portinari. The poems, written after the death (1290) of Beatrice, are strung on a thread of Italian prose that explains the circumstances in which each poem was written, interprets, and connects them all. The whole is an account of the development of Dante's love for Beatrice, with all its joys, pangs, and final grief. In this work he relates that he first saw Beatrice when he (and she, too) was 9 years old, and that when he was a youth of 18 he realized what his love for her was. Many of the poems are a departure from the conventionally expressed idealized love of the troubadors for their ladies, popularized by the Provençal troubadors. Dante presents the pains and joys of his own experience. The work is filled also with the activities of his daily life and accounts of his associations with his friends. In its deeper and more general sense it is a lyrical, philosophical, and theological analysis of the "new" or "marvelous" life of love in all its forms from romantic passion through Platonic, "courtly," and artistic love to the divine infusion of supernatural charity. In the last chapter Dante expresses the desire to write more worthily of Beatrice in the future, to write of her, in fact, as no woman has ever been written of before. He more than fulfilled this wish in the *Divina Commedia*.

Vitelleschi (vē-tel-les′kē), **Giovanni.** Churchman and condottiere; b. at Corneto, 1390–1400; killed at Rome, April 2, 1440. He was of a worthy family, began life as a soldier, and continued it much more as a condottiere than as a man of God, though he held high offices in the Church. He entered the service of the popes, was made (1431) bishop of Recanati and was sent by Pope Eugenius IV to restore order in Rome in 1434, after rebellion had broken out there and caused Eugenius to flee. Vitelleschi, as leader of the papal forces, put down the rebellion and restored order by his energetic attacks on the rebellious factions. He became prefect of Rome (1435), subdued the barons, and took Palestrina, the stronghold of the Colonnas. Because he restored order to tormented Rome he was named Third Father of Rome, and a statue of him bearing this inscription was erected on the Campidoglio. Eugenius made him patriarch of Alexandria (1435), archbishop of Florence (1435) and cardinal (1437) for his services. Vitelleschi continued to rule Rome, in the pope's name to be sure, but in his own manner, which was a ruthless suppression of possible adversaries, and a reign without law or justice. His armies fought everywhere. His enemies increased and he was betrayed by the castellan of Sant' Angelo, seized on the bridge and imprisoned. The pope allowed his life to be taken.

Vitelli (vē-tel′lē), **Vitellozzo.** Mercenary captain; he was a partner of Oliverotto da Fermo in the conspiracy by which the latter seized power in Fermo. At a banquet given by Cesare Borgia at Senigallia, both were strangled (1502).

Viti (vē′tē), **Timoteo.** Umbrian painter; b. at Urbino, 1467; d. there, 1525. He was a pupil of Francia at Bologna and was influenced by Lorenzo Costa and Perugino. Among his principal works are *SS. Thomas of Canterbury and Martin Worshipped by Guidobaldo and Archbishop Arrivabene* (1504), National Gallery of the Marches, Urbino, where there is also his *SS. Roch and Joseph; Magdalen* (1508), Pinacoteca, Bologna; and *Noli me tangere*, Cagli. He acquired a collection of Italian drawings, including many by Raphael, some of which ultimately became possessions of Vasari. Other paintings are at Bergamo (Carrara Academy), Florence (Corsini Gallery), Gubbio (cathedral), Milan (Brera), Cleveland, and elsewhere.

Vittoria (vēt-tô′ryä), **Tommaso Lodovico da.** Italian name of **Victoria, Tomás Luis de.**

Vittorino da Feltre (vē-tō-rē′nō dä fel′trā). [Original name, **Vittore dai Rambaldoni.**] Teacher and humanist; b. at Feltre, near Venice, c1378; d. at Mantua, February 2, 1446. He studied literature and the sciences at Padua (c1396), and Greek at Venice, where he became the intimate friend of another celebrated teacher, Guarino da Verona. After resigning the chair of Rhetoric at Padua, and serving as director of a school for young noblemen at Venice, he went to Mantua at the invitation of Gian Francesco Gonzaga and founded (1423) a school to educate the sons and daughters of that prince. With this school, in which he had unlimited opportunity to carry out his theories and philosophy of education, he won fame throughout Europe. His thesis was that the ideal education prepared the young for whatever station or profession in life their individual talents and situation might demand. The school day alternated between occupations of the mind—that is the disciplines of the trivium (grammar, rhetoric, and logic) and the quadrivium (arithmetic, music, geometry, and astronomy)—and exercises in gymnastics and warlike games for the body. The courses of study were varied from time to time to prevent dullness. Equally important in his educational program were a thorough knowledge of the sacred writings,

TIMOTEO VITI
Standing Male Nude
The British Museum, London

knowledge and control of self, and obedience to the Church. He sought to harmonize the new humanistic learning with devotion to Christian religion. Teachers and pupils lived on terms of close association in all phases of school and daily life. His school attracted pupils from other princely courts, from all regions of Italy, and even from outside Italy. In the service of God and a democratic spirit Vittorino also offered, not only his program of education, but housing, clothing, and other necessities to promising boys of poor families. All his pupils, of whom those attending the school at his expense numbered up to seventy, were subject to the same discipline and the same opportunities. Vittorino ran his school on the basis of equality for all and respect for the individuality of each one of his pupils. He imbued the teachers, whose numbers increased as the school grew, with his own enthusiasm and spirit. The Gonzaga family, proud of the renown the school brought to Mantua, underwrote it. When he needed money, as was often the case, Vittorino did not hesitate to apply for it either to the Gonzaga or to other wealthy patrons. His school lasted twenty years after his death and produced some of the most eminent men of 15th-century Italy—statesmen (Federico da Montefeltro was one of his great pupils), prelates, educators, humanists, and condottieri. His theories and approach were the basis of modern higher education.

VIVARINI (vē-vä-rē′nē), **ALVISE.** Painter; b. at Murano, c1446; d. at Venice, between 1503 and 1506. He was the son of Antonio Vivarini and received his first training from his father and his uncle Bartolomeo. Other influences on his development were those of Antonello da Messina and Giovanni Bellini. The influence of Mantegna may also be noted in the linearity that is characteristic of some of his work, as in the rocks and generally arid atmosphere of his *St. Jerome in the Wilderness*, National Gallery, Washington. The Madonna of his *Madonna and Six Saints* (signed and dated 1480), Accademia, Venice, is reminiscent of Bellini but the linearity of the elongated, slightly archaic saints with their faces and features in a rather Flemish style, derive from other sources. His first dated work is the polyptych, *Madonna Enthroned between Saints* (1476), National Gallery of the Marches, Urbino. Among his last works is an altarpiece with *St. Anthony*, Church of S. Maria dei Frari, Venice, which was begun in 1503 and was finished by Marco Basaiti. A number of his paintings are at Venice (Accademia, Ca' d'Oro, Correr Museum,

S. Giovanni in Bragora, Redentore); others are at Milan (Brera), Naples, Padua, Verona, Berlin, Budapest, Hampton Court, Leningrad, London, Paris, Vienna, Baltimore (Walters Art Gallery), Brooklyn, Denver, and elsewhere.

Vivarini, Antonio. Painter; b. at Murano, c1415; d. at Venice, 1476–1484. A follower of Iacobello del Fiore and of Gentile da Fabriano, he was to some extent the founder of the school of Murano, and injected new life into the Byzantinized painting that had hitherto flourished at Venice. An *Adoration of the Magi*, Berlin, painted with his brother-in-law Giovanni d'Alemagna, has some of the glitter of Gentile de Fabriano's work on the same theme in the Uffizi, but fewer genre details and a more sober atmosphere. He worked at Venice and at Padua and for a period (1440–1450) with Giovanni d'Alemagna, and later (after 1450) with his younger brother Bartolomeo (c1432– after 1491). His own part in a number of works in collaboration with these two is difficult to distinguish. By Antonio alone is a polyptych, *Madonna and Saints* (c1440), in the cathedral, Parenzo, another, surrounding a statue carved in wood, of *St. Anthony Abbott* (1464), Vatican, and another *St. Anthony of Padua* (1467), Bari. Many examples of his work in collaboration survive, as well as some that he executed by himself, as at Bergamo (Carrara Academy), Ravenna, Venice (Accademia, Ca' d'Oro, and churches), Verona, Berlin, Esztergom, Paris, Prague, Vienna, Houston New York, Philadelphia (Johnson Collection), Poughkeepsie, Princeton, Washington, and elsewhere.

Vivarini, Bartolomeo. Painter; b. at Murano, c1432; d. after 1491. He was the brother and pupil of Antonio Vivarini (c1415–1476/1484), and was also somewhat influenced by Mantegna, an influence that in his work is adapted to his own conservative style. After 1450 he worked with his brother Antonio. Together they produced a great number of works in which it is difficult to distinguish their individual contributions. The paintings by Bartolomeo alone are marked by a rather harsh color and linearity that recall Crivelli, and seem old-fashioned rather than archaic. But he was not entirely conservative, for he is thought to have been one of the first of the Venetians to experiment and paint in the new methods of oil and varnish, although he never abandoned painting in tempera. As he grew older and won renown and many commissions, more and more he left the execution of them to his assistants. A number of his paintings are in the Accademia and churches of Venice; others are at Bari (S. Nicola), Bergamo, Florence (Uffizi, Contini Bonacossi), Naples, Padua, Taranto, Turin, Amsterdam, Barcelona, London, Paris, Baltimore (Walters Art Gallery) Boston, (Museum of Fine Arts), New Haven, New Orleans, New York, Philadelphia (Johnson Collection), Poughkeepsie, San Francisco, Seattle, Washington, and elsewhere.

Volterra (vōl-ter′rä), **Daniele.** See **Daniele da Volterra.**

W

Wainfleet (wān′flēt), **William of.** See **Waynflete, William of.**

Walch (välċh), **Jacob.** See **De Barbari, Iacopo.**

Waldis (väl′dis), **Burkard.** German poet; b. at Allendorf, in Hesse, Germany, c1495; d. at Abterode, in Hesse, probably in 1557. The greater part of his early life was spent in Livonia. A Franciscan, in 1523 he was sent by his archbishop to the pope to solicit aid against the inroads of Protestantism. On his return from Rome he was taken prisoner by the Protestants at Riga, where he himself went over to Protestantism whole-heartedly. He wrote fables in verse. His *Verlorener Sohn* (1527) is a Shrovetide play; his *Esopus*, containing 100 fables in verse, was written in 1548 and was enormously popular.

Waldseemüller (vält′zā-mül-ėr), **Martin.** [Called by himself **Ilacomilus** or **Hylacomylus.**] German humanist and geographer; b. probably at Radolfszell, on Lake Constance, Germany, between 1450 and 1475; d. c1522. In 1507 he was, with his friend Philesius

Ringmann, in the printing establishment of Walter Ludd at St.-Dié. In this year he published a little treatise in Latin, the *Cosmographiae Introductio*. . . . In this book he says, ". . . and a fourth part (of the earth) has been discovered by Amerigo Vespucci . . . . Inasmuch as both Europe and Asia received their names from women, I see no reason why anyone should justly object to calling this part Amerige, i.e. the land of Amerigo, or America, after Amerigo, its discoverer." The publication met with success and soon ran through several editions. Waldseemüller made a "mappemonde" for which the volume was explanatory, entitled *Universalis Cosmographia* (1507), eight feet long and four and one-half feet high, on which the name America was used (on South America, shown as an island) for the first time. No copy was known to exist until 1900, when one was discovered in the library of Castle Wolfegg in Württemberg.

Wallace (wol′ạs), Sir **William.** [Also, **Walays, Wallensis.**] Scottish patriot and national hero; b. c1272; executed at London, August 23, 1305. Outlawed early in life he became a leader of a party of insurgents against the rule of Edward I of England, and totally defeated the English at the battle of Stirling Bridge in 1297. He was made guardian of Scotland, and was defeated by Edward I at Falkirk (1298). He was betrayed to the English in August, 1305. Taken to London and condemned for treason, he was hanged, drawn, and quartered.

Walsingham (wôl′sing-ạm), Sir **Francis.** English statesman in the service of Queen Elizabeth; b. at Chislehurst, Kent, England, c1530; d. at London, April 6, 1590. He built up an efficient spy system and uncovered the Babington plot which led to the trial of Mary, Queen of Scots. He gave advance warning of the preparations for the Spanish Armada, but his warnings were unheeded. He was the father-in-law of Sir Philip Sidney and was a patron of learning.

Walsingham, Thomas. English historian and monk; d. c1422. He was the author of a history of England (*Brevis Historia*) from Edward I to Henry V, and a history of Normandy.

Walworth (wôl′wėrth, wol′-), Sir **William.** English politician; d. 1385. He is remembered chiefly for the killing (1381) of Wat Tyler, leader of the peasants' revolt, whom he stabbed when Tyler tried to speak to the king during a chance encounter at Smithfield.

Warbeck (wôr′bek), **Perkin.** Pretender to the English crown; b. c1474; executed at London, November 23, 1499. He claimed to be Richard, duke of York, son of Edward IV, actually murdered in the Tower in 1483.

Warham (wôr′ạm), **William.** English prelate, Archbishop of Canterbury; b. in Hampshire, c1450; d. August 22, 1532. He married Henry VIII and Catherine of Aragon, but took little active part in the divorce proceedings, and gave passive acquiescence to Henry's assumption of ecclesiastical power.

Warwick (wor′ik), Earl of. [Title of **Richard Neville;** also, Earl of **Salisbury:** called **the Kingmaker.**] English politician and military commander; b. November 22, 1428; killed at the battle of Barnet, April 14, 1471. Related to both the Yorkist and Lancastrian families, at first he sided with the Yorkists and after the defeat of the Lancastrians at Northampton took Henry VI prisoner. He opposed Edward IV's marriage to Elizabeth Woodville, and an alliance with Burgundy. He conspired with the duke of Clarence against Edward IV, fled to France and turned to the Lancastrians. He landed in England in 1470, drove out Edward IV and restored Henry VI. He was finally defeated and overthrown by Edward IV at Barnet in 1471.

Waynflete or **Wainfleet** (wān′flēt), **William of.** [Original surname, **Patyn.**] English prelate; b. c1395; d. 1486. He was the founder (1458) of Magdalen College, Oxford. He was lord high chancellor under Henry VI and remained loyal to him during the Wars of the Roses.

Wedderburn (wed′ėr-bėrn), **James.** Scottish poet and dramatist; b. at Dundee, Scotland, c1495; d. in France, 1553. Brother of John Wedderburn (c1550–1546) and Robert Wedderburn (c1510–c1557), he was the author of anti-Roman Catholic ballads, of *The Beheading of John the Baptist* (1539–1540), a tragedy, *Dionysus the Tyrant*, a comedy (1539–1540), and satires on practices in the Roman Catholic Church. With his brothers he wrote several satirical ballads later published in book form as *Ane Compendious Booke of Godly and Spirituall Songs* (1567). Charged with heresy, he escaped to France.

Wedderburn, John. Scottish poet, author of anti-Catholic ballads; b. at Dundee, Scotland, c1500; d. in England, 1546. As was his brother James, he was charged with heresy for writing ballads attacking the Roman Catholic Church, and fled to Wittenberg. He returned (1542) to Scotland, and continued to publish his so-called Dundee Psalms. He fled to England in 1546.

Wedderburn, Robert. Scottish poet, author of anti-Roman Catholic ballads; b. at Dundee, Scotland, c1510; d. there, c1557. As were his brothers, James and John, he was charged with heresy and fled, but later returned to Scotland, and was made vicar of Dundee.

Welser (vel′zėr), **Bartholomeus.** German banker; d. at Augsburg, Germany, c1559. Head of one of the richest banking and commercial firms of his time, he lent large sums to Charles V, and in 1527 was granted the right to colonize Venezuela. Great numbers of the Indians were enslaved, and far more were killed. The charter was revoked in 1546, after the Welsers were reputed to have lost three million florins.

Wenceslaus III (of *Bohemia*) (wen′ses-lôs). King of Bohemia (1378–1419) and of the Germans (1389–1400); b. at Nuremberg, February 26, 1361; d. at Prague, August 16, 1419. He was the son of the emperor Charles IV, had been named his father's heir in 1363, and was elected king of the Germans (thus Holy Roman emperor) in 1376. He succeeded to the thrones of Bohemia and Germany in 1378 on his father's death. Germany was in a state of near-anarchy because of the struggles between rival princes. Wenceslaus gave Brandenburg, which he had received in 1373, to his half brother Sigismund, and later gave up his attempts to bring peace to Germany. He gave most of his attention to Bohemia. There for a time he was successful, but his attempts to curb the nobles and his championship of the cities roused the wrath of the nobles, and his insensate murder of St. John of Nepomuk, a patron saint of Bohemia, made him more enemies. In 1394 he was imprisoned by the Bohemians but was released under pressure from the Germans. He soon stirred up another hornets' nest when, in conjunction with Charles VI of France, he attempted to end the Great Schism in the church by urging the rival popes, Benedict XIII and Boniface IX, to resign. The Germans supported Boniface as the true pope, distrusted anything French, and considered this action a betrayal. In any case, the action was ineffective. Wenceslaus further angered the Germans by selling (1395) the duchy of Milan to Gian Galeazzo Visconti. He was deposed as German king in 1400. His half brother Sigismund, who had become a more or less overt rival, took him prisoner and kept him in custody for nearly two years, after which Wenceslaus resumed the Bohemian throne. In the meantime the Hussites were becoming active in Bohemia. Wenceslaus supported Hus against the archbishop of Prague, and the city was laid under an interdict (1412). When Hus was burned by the Council of Constance (in spite of a safe-conduct) Wenceslaus did little to quell the outbursts that took place in Bohemia. When the riots began to assume the aspect of civil war he sought to restore order. Wenceslaus had no children by either of his marriages and was succeeded by Sigismund, who also had become king of the Germans (1411) following the death of Rupert, the latter having been elected when Wenceslaus was deposed.

Weyden (wī′dẹn), **Roger** (or **Rogier**) **van der.** [Also known as **Roger de la Pasture.**] Painter of the Flemish school; b. at Tournai, c1400; d. 1464. He is thought to have been a goldsmith before turning to painting. It was formerly accepted, on the word of Vasari and others, that he studied under Jan van Eyck, but this is now very much doubted, and it is supposed rather that he was apprenticed to his fellow townsman Robert Campin, whose realistic style was transmuted by Van der Weyden's warmth and sensitivity to one of emotion, drama, and mysticism. He was admitted as a member of the Guild of Saint Luke in 1432, and when he moved to Brussels (1435) his competence was sufficiently established for him to be appointed painter to the municipality. He is known to have embellished the town hall of Brussels with four compositions, namely *The Emperor Trajan Punishing a Murderer, Saint Gregory at Prayer, Herkenbald Beheading his Own Son, Guilty of Violating a Maiden,* and *Miraculous Communion,* but these have perished. In 1449 he visited Rome, Florence, Milan, and other Italian cities, lingering especially at Ferrara. He was much honored by Italian artists, and executed works for Italian patrons. Piero della Francesca, working at Ferrara at the time of his visit, was one who took advantage of it to study Flemish painting at first hand. Some think that the Flemish pianter's panel, *The Deposition in the Tomb*, once in the Medici villa at Careggi and now in the Uffizi, Florence, was painted, about 1449, for Leonello d'Este for his villa at Belfiore; another opinion is that it was painted at Florence, as it shows strong compositional affinity with Fra Angelico's *Deposition* in a predella panel now at Munich. The Metropolitan Museum, New York, has a souvenir of the Ferrara stay in his superb portrait, *Francesco d'Este*. His entire career was prosperous, marked by many commissions from churches, public bodies, and individual patrons. Roger van der Weyden has been called the only mystic among the religious painters of the Flemish school. His religious emotion was seconded by a strong sense of drama. In contrast with the serene, somewhat static beauty observed in the works of the Van Eycks, his pictures are alive with grief and tragedy, seen in bowed figures, agonized faces marked by tears, clenched hands or arms outstretched in appeal to heaven, all drawn together in compositions of tortuous and broken lines. In these characteristics of his art some influence of his Italian journey can be seen. In turn he influenced Italian painters and still more the German artists of the Cologne and Swabian schools, and somewhat paradoxically prepared the way for the later Flemish school which dropped religious subjects and turned to the celebration of frankly human passions. Roger van der Weyden's masterpiece is by general consent his *Descent from the Cross*, now in the Escorial, Spain. There are numerous authenticated examples of his work, together with disputed ascriptions, at Antwerp, Brussels, Berlin, London, Paris; at Boston, Chicago, Detroit, Johnson Collection, Philadelphia, the National Gallery, Washington, and elsewhere. His *Last Judgment* is in the hospital at Beaune in Burgundy. The Metropolitan Museum of Art in New York, in addition to that mentioned above and others, possesses an impressive and typical Van der Weyden, *Christ Appearing to His Mother*, which was originally one wing of a triptych, the other two panels of which are in the cathedral of Granada, Spain. The National Gallery, London, has recently acquired a Roger van der Weyden painting of St. Ivo Helory that had been privately owned for generations. The discovery of the painting, whose authorship seems to have been unknown, has been called "a milestone in art history."

Whitchurch (hwit′chėrch), **Edward.** [Also, **Whytchurch.**] English publisher; d. at Camberwell, South London, November 1561. He was associated with Richard Grafton in publishing *Thomas Matthews' Bible* (1537; printed at Antwerp), the first complete version of the Bible in English, Miles Coverdale's version of the New Testament (1538; printed at Paris), the *Great Bible* (1539), Erasmus's text of the New Testament (1540) in English, and the first edition of the *Book of Common Prayer* (1549). He also published secular works.

Wife of Bath's Tale, The. One of Chaucer's *Canterbury Tales*. It is that of the Loathly Lady who cannot return to her original beautiful form until a knight is found courageous enough to marry her. Variants and analogues of this tale are known in Sanskrit, Turkish, Kaffir, Old Irish, and Icelandic, in the Gawain stories of the Arthurian cycle, the English and Scottish traditional ballads, and in Gower's *Confessio Amantis*.

Willaert (wil′ärt), **Adrian.** Flemish founder of the Venetian school of composition; b. in Flanders, c1480; d. at Venice, December 7, 1562. He was named (1527) choirmaster at Saint Mark's, Venice, and is notable for first employing the double chorus. His many compositions include motets, madrigals, and Masses.

William IV (of *Hesse-Cassel*). [Called **William the Wise.**] Landgrave of Hesse-Cassel; b. 1532; d. August 25, 1592. He distinguished himself as an astronomer and as a patron of astronomy.

William of Shoreham (shōr′ạm). English monk of Leeds priory; b. at Shoreham, Kent, England; active in the first part of the 14th century. He translated (c1327) the Psalms of David into English prose, and wrote a number of poems.

Windsor (win′zọr), **Alice de.** See **Perrers, Alice.**

Wishart (wish′ạrt), **George.** Scottish reformer and martyr; b. early in the 16th century; burned at the stake at St. Andrews, Scotland, March 1, 1546. He began and diligently continued to preach the doctrines of the Reformation. At the instigation of Cardinal David Beaton he was burned at St. Andrews. He had great influence on John Knox.

Wolsey (wůl′zi), **Thomas.** English statesman and cardinal; b. at Ipswich, England, probably in 1475; d. at Leicester, England, November 29, 1530. He was educated at Magdalen College, Oxford, studied divinity, and rose rapidly in the Church and in affairs of state. Under Henry VIII he planned the invasion of France (1513) and accompanied the king on the expedition. In 1515 he rose to the cardinalate, and in the same year became lord chancellor, having become by this time the most influential person in the kingdom. Wolsey actively carried out the king's policy of the centering of power in the monarchy and was his principal instrument in foreign affairs. In the struggle between the French and the Holy Roman Empire, Wolsey used English power in an atempt to maintain a balance between the two, supporting France at first, and then Charles V, nephew of Henry's queen, Catherine of Aragon. However, Charles, who had agreed to military alliances with England in 1521 and 1522, avoided the earlier decision to marry Mary Tudor, Henry's eldest daughter, failed to support Wolsey's candidacy for the papacy in 1521 and 1524, and, using England as a tool, secured supremacy on the Continent by defeating Francis I of France at Pavia (1525). The failure of Wolsey's costly foreign policy, combined with his arrogance and his actually regal style of living, made him many enemies at home. He at length supported Henry's decision to divorce Catherine of Aragon, but was superseded in trying the case by a cardinal sent from Rome. The suit dragged on, and the long delay (caused by the politics of Spain and the pope) brought Wolsey the enmity of Anne Boleyn, whose influence over the king told against the cardinal, and in 1529 he was stripped of all his offices, excepting the archbishopric of York. Accused of treason, Wolsey was arrested in November, 1530, but died on his way to London.

Woodville (wůd′vil), **Anthony.** [Also, **Wydville**; titles, Baron **Scales**, 2nd Earl **Rivers**.] English politician; b. c1442, beheaded at Pontefract, England, June 25, 1483. He was put to death by Richard III. He was a patron of William Caxton, whose first book printed in England was a translation from the French by him, the *Dictes and Sayings of the Philosophers* (1477).

Woodville, Elizabeth. See **Elizabeth Woodville.**

Worde (wôrd), **Wynkyn de.** [Original name, **Jan van Wynkyn.**] English printer; b. in Alsace; d. c1535. He went to England (1476) as an assistant to William Caxton, and in 1491 became his successor.

Wyatt or **Wyat** (wī′ạt), Sir **Thomas.** English poet and diplomat; b. in Kent, England, 1503; d. at Sherborne, Dorsetshire, England, October 11, 1542. He wrote the first English sonnets, and his poems were printed with Surrey's in 1557.

Wyatt, Sir **Thomas.** English soldier; son of Sir Thomas Wyatt (1503–1542); b. c1520; executed at London, April 11, 1554. He commanded at Boulogne; joined with the duke of Suffolk in favor of Lady Jane Grey; and led the men of Kent against London in February, 1554, but was captured and executed.

Wycliffe or **Wyclif** (wik′lif), **John.** English religious reformer, called "the Morning Star of the Reformation"; b. at Spreswel, near Richmond, Yorkshire, c1320; d. at Lutterworth, Leicestershire, December 31, 1384. A superb teacher, he was a fellow, and later (1360) master, of Balliol College, Oxford, and became rector of Fillingham, Lincolnshire, in the same year, and in 1368 of Ludgershall, Buckinghamshire, and in 1374 of Lutterworth. (The warden of Canterbury Hall, 1365–1367, was probably another John Wyclif, of Merton, Oxford, vicar of Mayfield; there is much confusion between the early lives of these two.) He went with John of Gaunt as royal ambassador to confer with papal nuncios at Bruges (1374) on the payment of tribute to the Holy See. He was a popular preacher at London, and was summoned before the Convocation in 1377 as an enemy to Rome on account of his attacks on the inordinate arrogance and wealth and power of the higher clergy (this blow was really aimed at John of Gaunt). The pope signed five bulls against him, authorizing his imprisonment. The schism in the papacy, due to the election of Clement VII, in place of Urban VI, induced Wycliffe to throw off his allegiance to the papacy. He argued against the doctrine of transubstantiation at Oxford in 1380, espousing a position that was a variant of "realism," and was condemned by the university. His party was opposed and persecuted by the archbishop of Canterbury and others in 1382. He went back to Lutterworth, where he wrote ceaselessly and fearlessly against papal claims, and in opposition to mere formalism. On December 28, 1384, he was seized with paralysis while hearing Mass, and died in a few days. In 1428 his bones were exhumed, burned, and their ashes cast into the Swift, by order of the Synod of Constance. Wycliffe's fundamentalism led him to believe that the authority of the Scriptures was supreme. In furtherance of his belief, he wished to make them available to all, and he inspired two translations of the Bible into English (c1382). The first was a literal translation; the second, made by his secretary, was more idiomatic and soon became quite popular. He wrote many tracts and sermons: *De Juramento Arnaldi, Trialogus, De officio pastorali, De ecclesia, De benedicta incarnatione, De Dominio divino,* and others.

Wydville (wid′vil), **Anthony.** See **Woodville, Anthony.**

Wykeham (wik′ạm), **William of.** English statesman and prelate; b. at Wykeham, Hampshire, England, 1324; d. 1404. He founded Winchester School and New College at Oxford. In 1404 he finished rebuilding the nave of Winchester cathedral. He is buried in the chantry.

Wynkyn de Worde (wing′kin dẹ wôrd). See **Worde, Wynkyn de.**

Wyntoun (win′tun), **Andrew of.** Scottish chronicler; b. about the middle of the 14th century. His *Oryginale Cronykil of Scotland,* in rhymed eight-syllabled verse, was finished between 1420 and 1424.

X

Xeres (hā′res), **Francisco de.** [Also, **Jeres.**] Spanish historian; b. c1504; d. after 1547. From 1530 to 1534 he was secretary to Francisco Pizarro, taking part in the conquest of Peru. By order of Pizarro he wrote a history of the conquest down to Atahualpa's death; it was published at Seville, 1534 and 1547.

Ximenes de Cisneros (hē-mā′nes dā thēs-nā′rōs), **Francisco.** See **Jiménez de Cisneros, Francisco.**

Ximenes de Quesada (kā-sä′ᴛʜä), **Gonzalo.** See **Jiménez de Quesada, Gonzalo.**

Y

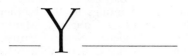

Yeomen of the Guard. Military corps established by Henry VII of England in 1485 as a personal bodyguard for the sovereigns of England. After kings ceased to accompany their troops to battle, and when violence as a means of securing succession to the throne went out of fashion, real need for such a body ceased, but the corps has been continued for its symbolic interest and ceremonial usefulness.

Yepes y Álvarez (yā′pās ē äl′ʙä-reth), or **Yepis y Álvarez** (yā′pēs), **Juan de.** See Saint **John of the Cross.**

York (yôrk), 3rd Duke of. [Title of **Richard Plantagenet.**] English statesman; b. 1411; killed at the battle of Wakefield, England, 1460. He was a descendant of Edward III; was constable of England and regent of France under Henry VI; and was protector during the incompetency of Henry VI. After the birth of Henry's son, York laid claim to the heirship of the throne, and precipitated the Wars of the Roses. He was defeated and killed at Wakefield. He was the father of Edward IV.

York, Duke of. [Title of **Richard Plantagenet.**] Second son of Edward IV; b. 1472; murdered in the Tower of London, 1483.

Z

Zabarella (dzä-bä-rel′lä), **Francesco.** Cardinal and canon lawyer; b. at Piove di Sacco (Padua), August 10, 1360; d. at Costanza, September 26, 1417. He studied letters and law at Padua, then at Bologna, where he received his degree (1383). The same year he went to Florence as the bishop's vicar. At Florence he received the rank of doctor, ecclesiastical benefices, and taught canon law for five years. Pietro Paolo Vergerio the Elder was one of his pupils and remained on terms of warm friendship with him throughout his life. In 1390 he went to Rome to take part in attempts to end the schism in the Church. Next, he returned to Padua, where he taught for twenty years. In addition to his ecclesiastical duties (he was archpriest of the cathedral), he carried out many diplomatic missions for the lords of the city. In 1410 he was named bishop of Florence, and the following year was raised to the Sacred College. He was tireless in his efforts to resolve the conflict in the Church, and was most active at the Council of Constance (1414–1417). His efforts were directed toward reconciliation. His doctrine concerning the conciliar movement, arising as it did from a judicial basis, was condemned by the Holy Office. His writings included legal opinions and treatises on the law, and literary works in dialogue form on poetry and other subjects.

Zabarella, Giacomo. Philosopher; b. at Padua, September 5, 1533; d. there, October 15, 1589. He was an exponent of Aristotelianism. His solution to the problem of the immortality of the soul was close to Pomponazzi's, but was so expressed that it was not offensive to the Church, of which he was a loyal son. In his writings on nature and natural phenomena, he treated the questions that absorbed his mind with complete independence, following the Aristotelian command to observe and to deduce from observation. His *De rebus naturalibus libri* XXX (Padua, 1589) is a compendium of treatises on separate questions, each of which may be treated independently of the others. In his own time he received much publicity for his writings on logic and for a literary quarrel he carried on with Francesco Piccolomini.

Zaganelli (dzä-gä-nel′lē), **Francesco.** Painter; b. at Cotignola, between 1470 and 1480; d. at Ravenna, 1531. He had a workshop at Cotignola with his brother Bernardino (b. at Cotignola, between 1460 and 1470; d. there, between 1510 and 1512), with whom he executed a number of works in collaboration. The brothers were influenced in the development of their art by Marco Palmezzano and by the Ferrarese, Lorenzo Costa and Ercole de' Roberti. The earliest work signed by the two brothers is *Madonna and Saints* (1499), Brera, Milan; the last signed by both is a *Holy Family* (1509), Carrara Academy, Bergamo. A *Madonna and Child* (1505), Brera, is by Francesco alone, as are paintings at Bologna, Ferrara, Forlì, Naples, Ravenna, and Viadana (SS. Martino e Nicola), near Cremona. The work of Bernardino is somewhat differentiated from that of his brother by delicacy of detail, as in his *St. Sebastian* (1506), National Gallery, London. After the death of Francesco, Bernardino's style was modified by Tuscan-Emilian influences and by Lotto. Other works by him alone are at Amsterdam, Baltimore, Brussels, Chambéry, and Paris. Paintings by the brothers in collaboration are at Cotignola, Mantua, Milan (Brera), Modena, Naples, Parma, Pesaro, Rome (Colonna Gallery, Villa Albani), Berlin, Budapest, Dublin, Baltimore (Walters Art Gallery), Boston (Museum of Fine Arts), Cambridge (Massachusetts), and elsewhere.

Zamberti (dzäm-ber′tē), **Bartolomeo.** Venetian mathematician and humanist; active in the 15th and 16th centuries. He made the first translation from the Greek to Latin of the *Elements* of Euclid.

Zancariis (dzäng-kä-rē′ës), **Alberto de.** Physician; b. at Bologna, 1280; d. 1348. He took his doctorate in 1310, and in 1314 became physician of the city of Ravenna for a year. Returned to Bologna, he became professor of anatomy at the university. In 1319 he was accused of stealing a cadaver in order to dissect it. He wrote *De cautelis medi-*

corum habendis; a commentary on Avicenna; and left some minor works. Well-known in his day, he is mentioned in the tenth story of the first day of Boccaccio's *Decameron.*

Zanchi (dzäng'kē), **Basilio.** Humanist; b. at Bergamo, 1501; d. at Rome, 1558. He completed his studies at Bergamo, compiled a dictionary of Latin epithets at age 17, went to Rome, and won the favor of Pope Leo X for his Latin verses. After the death of Leo, he entered a monastic order, to study theology. Pope Paul IV issued a decree (1558) ordering the monks to return to their monasteries. Zanchi, who led a wandering life, disobeyed and was arrested. It is thought that he died in prison. His writings include a religious poem, *De horto Sophiae* (1540), three books of verses, *Poemata* (1550), and a work of religious commentary. His verses were highly praised in his day.

Zanchi, Girolamo. Protestant reformer; b. at Brescia, 1516; d. at Neustadt, Germany, 1590. He entered the Augustinian order at Brescia (1531) after completing his studies. He became converted to the ideas of the reformers under the leadership of Pietro Martire Vermigli at Lucca. A profoundly learned man, he tried to coordinate in some definitive manner the theories and doctrines of the various reforming groups. The works of Calvin, the Swiss theologian Heinrich Bullinger, and the German Martin Bucer were, for him, fundamental to the reform doctrines. Like his master Vermigli, Zanchi carried the Calvinist doctrine of predestination to its ultimate point. He left Italy (1551) and after a brief stay in Switzerland went to Strasbourg. There he came into conflict with Lutheran theologians because he did not fully accept the Augsburg Confession. His conflict with the Lutherans placed him at the head of the Calvinists. He went to Grisons as a preacher and from there to Heidelberg, where he was eminent as a teacher. He left Heidelberg (1576) when the Lutherans became dominant there and, at the invitation of its prince, went to Neustadt. He remained there until his death. Zanchi's hope was to unite the various reforming groups, apart from the Lutherans. Although his theology was rigid, he was himself a man of broad tolerance and was among the more moderate and liberal of the Italian Calvinists, and was highly esteemed throughout Germany and Protestant Switzerland for his doctrinal judgment and his pious life. He argued against the anti-Trinitarians, and his most important work, *De tribus Elohim . . . ,* is a treatise against their doctrines.

Zannino (dzän-nē'nō). [Also called **Giovannino di Pietro.**] Venetian painter; active in the last part of the 14th and the early part of the 15th century. There is little evidence of Byzantine influence in his work, which shows him to have been familiar with the Tuscan school, especially in his soft coloring. Two *Crucifixions* are attributed to him, one at Rieti, Palazzo Comunale, and the other at Paris (Musées Nationaux, Campana Collection).

Zarlino (dzär-lē'nō), **Gioseffe** (or **Giuseppe**). Musician; b. at Chioggia, March 22, 1517; d. at Venice, February 14, 1590. He is best known for his theoretical works on music, including *Istituzioni armoniche* (1558), *Dimostrazioni armoniche* (1571), and *Sopplimenti musicali* (1588).

Zavattari (dzä-vät-tä'rē). A family of painters who worked in and around Milan in the 15th century. The names of those who are known are: Cristoforo, active in 1404, Franceschino, active in 1414 and 1417, Ambrogio, active in 1456 and 1459, and Gregorio, active in 1475. Members of the family, perhaps all of them, decorated the Chapel of Queen Theodolinda in the cathedral at Monza, near Milan. The work is notable for the elegant gatherings of richly dressed people, for its banquet scenes, and for the trappings, horses, and dogs of courtly life. Ornamented with a wealth of decorative detail, the backgrounds, crowns, ladies' girdles, and parts of the horses' harness are in gold and worked in relief. The series, signed and dated 1444, has been called by the art historian Raimond van Marle, "one of the finest ensembles of mural decoration in Italy and of great importance also on account of the number and extent of the paintings." The same historian calls these painters the last of the Gothic Lombard painters of the 15th century.

Zelotti (dzā-lôt'tē), **Giambattista.** (Also called **Battista Farinato** and **Battista de Verona.**] Painter; b. at Verona, c1526; d. at Mantua, 1578. He was a pupil of Badile and of his uncle, Paolo Farinato, and was subject to other influences, notably Domenico Brusasorci and Paolo Veronese, with the latter of whom he worked on the decoration of the Villa Soranza, at Thiene, and in the

Ducal Palace (1553–1554) and Library at Venice. After 1575 he was chief of the ducal works at Mantua. A number of frescoes from his hand survive, as at the Castello del Catajo (1571) at Battaglia, near Padua; in the Villa dei Carli, at Costozza, near Vicenza; frescoes on allegorical and mythological subjects executed as Paolo Veronese's assistant in the Villa Emo at Fanzolo; others on mythological subjects in the Villa Foscari at Malcontenta; also surviving are paintings in the Badia and in the Church of S. Maria Assunta, Praglia, at Verona, Vicenza, Dresden, Leningrad, Lille, London, and elsewhere.

Zenale (dzā-nä′lā), **Bernardino.** Painter and architect; b. at Treviglio, c1436; d. at Milan, 1526. He is thought to have been a pupil of Foppa, and was influenced by Bramante and Leonardo. As a painter he was associated with Bernardino Butinone in the execution of two important works. These were the decoration of the Grifi Chapel (1489–1493), S. Pietro in Gessate, Milan, where scenes from the legend of St. Ambrose were painted on the vault and walls, and a polyptych, commissioned in 1485, in S. Martino, Treviglio. The influence of Bramante appears in Zenale's monumental forms in the latter. Other paintings attributed to him are in the Ambrosiana, Brera, Castello Sforzesco, Poldi Pezzoli, S. Ambrogio, and S. Maria delle Grazie, Milan, and works at Florence (Contini Bonacossi Collection), Venice (Cini Collection), and Lawrence, Kansas (University). As an architect he worked (1514) on the construction of S. Maria sopra S. Celso, and a few years later (1522) succeeded Amadeo as chief architect of the cathedral at Milan.

Zeno (dzā′nō), **Niccolò.** Venetian explorer; b. c1340; d. c1395. He is said to have visited Greenland, Newfoundland, and the coast of North America. A narrative of his discoveries, with map, was published by Carlo Zeno in 1558.

Zerbino (dzer-bē′nō). In Lodovico Ariosto's *Orlando Furioso*, a Scottish prince who surprises Cloridano and Medoro in their attack on the Christian camp. Later, accused of killing Pinabello by Gabrina, whom he had befriended, he is condemned to death but is saved by Orlando. He and his beloved, Issabella, find Orlando's armor (it once belonged to Trojan Hector) and hang it on a tree with a warning that no one is to touch it. Mandricardo takes it, and he and Zerbino fight. Zerbino is outmatched because Mandricardo is fighting with Orlando's armor. Issabella pleads with Doralice to stop the fight. The fight is stopped, but Zerbino has been mortally wounded. He dies in Issabella's arms. It was to describe the gallant, loyal, noble Zerbino that Ariosto wrote the line, "Nature fashioned him and then broke the mold."

Zimara (dzē-mä′rä), **Marco Antonio.** Physician and philosopher of the Paduan school; b. at San Pietro in Galatina (Lecce), 1460; d. at Padua, 1523. He was a faithful follower of the Averroistic interpretation of Aristotle. He did not develop his own system but wrote commentaries on the Arab commentators. His chief work, *Antrum magico-medicum . . .*, is on magic, astrology, alchemy, and other topics. He also edited the works of several medieval philosophers, including Albertus Magnus.

Zoan Andrea (dzwän än-drā′ä). Engraver who was working at Mantua about 1475. He copied the works of Mantegna and Dürer without permission, agreement, or acknowledgment. Mantegna attacked him and his fellow-engraver, Simone di Ardizone, for pirating his designs and left the two on the street, thinking they were dead. Zoan Andrea probably went to Milan after leaving Mantua, and there he copied some designs of Leonardo da Vinci.

Zoppo (dzôp′pō), **Marco.** [Original name, **Marco di Antonio di Ruggero.**] Painter; b. at Cento, 1433; d. at Bologna, 1478. From Bologna, where he had his early training, he went to Padua, and in May, 1452, entered the workshop of Francesco Squarcione and became one of Squarcione's "adopted sons." This meant, largely, that Squarcione availed himself of Zoppo's servies and reaped the financial reward of his work. As Mantegna had done before him, Zoppo sought to free himself. He fled to Venice in October, 1455. There, as the result of a suit brought against him by Squarcione, the latter was compelled to pay him twenty ducats for his previous work at Padua. In his stay at Padua Zoppo was deeply influenced by Mantegna, who was at that time working in the Ovetari Chapel of the Church of the Eremitani. His subsequent sojourn at Venice was of undetermined length and by 1461 he was at Bologna. Of this Bolognese period is his masterpiece, a polyptych in the Collegio di Spagna at Bologna. The work indicates the influence of

Marco Zoppo
Three Men
The British Museum, London

Mantegna, as well as that of Squarcione's school and its elements of Donatello, Andrea del Castagno, Filippo Lippi, and Piero della Francesca. Zoppo individualized these influences with his sensitive, flexible line and his intense color softened by a pearly light. In 1468 he returned to Venice and in that year signed an altarpiece, panels of which are at Baltimore (*St. Jerome*), National Gallery, Washington (*St. Peter*), National Gallery, London (*St. Augustine*), and at Oxford (*St. Paul*). His painting *Dead Christ Supported by Angels*, Museo Civico, Pesaro, painted at Venice (1471), may have been inspired by a composition of Giovanni Bellini, but the type of the head of Christ, thin and elongated, and the incised lines of the torso, are in Zoppo's own manner. Of the same year was an altarpiece for the Zoccolanti fathers at Pesaro, now at East Berlin. In the altarpiece, *Madonna and Child Enthroned*, as in several of his other paintings, Zoppo combined elements—antique urns on the Madonna's throne, garlands of fruit, and curving, sharply defined rocks in the background—derived from Squarcione's workshop and Mantegna. Other examples of his work are at Bucharest, Rome, and Vienna.

Zuccaro (zö′kä-rō), **Federico.** Painter; b. at S. Angelo in Vado, c1540; d. at Ancona, 1609. He was the son of Ottaviano Zuccaro (b. c1505), also a painter, and the brother of Taddeo Zuccaro (1529–1566), who gave him his early training. Like his brother, he was one of the last of the Roman eclectic mannerists. He finished (1578–1579) the fresco Vasari had begun of *The Last Judgment* in the cupola of the cathedral at Florence, and worked in Rome on frescoes in the Casino of Pius IV, the Sala Regia, and the Pauline Chapel in the Vatican. In his lifetime he traveled widely, to France, the Netherlands, England (1574–1575), Spain (1585–1589), where his work did not satisfy Philip II, Titian's patron, and all over Italy, leaving examples of his work wherever he went. Though he left drawings of Queen Elizabeth in England (British Museum), the portraits he is supposed to have painted of her are of dubious authenticity. At Rome he founded (1593) the Academy of St. Luke, became its first head (1598), and built and decorated the bizarre palace (now the Hertzian Library) on the Via Gregoriana; bizarre because of its fantastic architectural decorative elements—for example, a window is the square, open mouth of a monster. He wrote on painting, sculpture, and architecture, and a book on his travels in Italy.

Zuccaro, Taddeo. Painter; b. in S. Angelo in Vado, 1529; d. at Rome, 1566. He was the son of Ottaviano Zuccaro (b. c1505), an indifferent painter who gave him his first instruction, and the brother of Federico Zuccaro (c1540–1609). A mannerist and an eclectic, he adapted elements from Correggio, Raphael, and Michelangelo, and enhanced his facility at invention with delicate, sometimes rather monotonous color. He worked at Vito (or Alvito), in the Abruzzi, painted the façade of the palace of Jacopo Mattei at Rome with decorations in grisaille, and worked at Pesaro. Again at Rome, he frescoed (1551) two ceilings of Pope Julius III's villa at Rome, finished the frescoes Salviati had begun in the Farnese Palace at Rome, and began the cycle on events in the Farnese family in the Farnese Palace at Caprarola. Other works at Rome are in the Trinità dei Monti and the Sala Regia (completed by his brother) in the Vatican.

Zumárraga (thö-mär′rä-gä), **Juan de.** Spanish churchman; first bishop of Mexico; b. near Durango, Vizcaya, Spain, 1486; d. at Mexico City, June 3, 1548. Soon after his arrival in Mexico he had a careful search made for Aztec manuscripts and had them burned as heretical books. He championed the rights of the Indians, and extended misson work to all parts of the Spanish conquests in Mexico and Central America.

Zúñiga y Azevedo (thö′nyē-gä ē ä-thā-bä′ᴛʜō), **Gaspar de.** [Title, Count of **Monterrey.**] Spanish administrator; b. c1540; d. at Lima, Peru, February 10, 1606. While viceroy of Mexico (1595–1603) he organized many expeditions for colonization and exploration in New Mexico, California, and elsewhere. The city of Monterrey, and the Bay of Monterrey were named in his honor. He was a zealous protector of the Indians.

Zurita (thō-rē′tä), **Alonzo.** Spanish lawyer and author; b. c1500; d. after 1564. He wrote a treatise on the Indians of New Spain, which has been published in modern times. It relates principally to their customs and laws, and is a standard authority.

Zwingli (tsving′lē), **Huldreich** or **Ulrich.** Swiss reformer; b. at Wildhaus, St. Gallen, Switzerland, January 1, 1484; killed at the

Federico Zuccaro
The Vision of St. Eustace
Courtesy of The Metropolitan Museum of Art, New York, Rogers Fund, 1962

battle of Kappel, Zurich, October 11, 1531. He received a strong classical education, with humanist overtones, at Bern, Vienna, and Basel, and became (1506) pastor in the canton of Glarus. Like John Calvin who came after him, Zwingli believed that the Bible is the source of God's law and thus of all law. He was also an advocate of independence for the Swiss cantons, and promoted political as well as religious reform. By his preaching, he inaugurated the Reformation at Zurich in 1519 (the Reformation was legalized by the Council of Zurich in 1523). He met (1529) the Saxon Reformers in the great conference called at Marburg to restore harmony among the reformers, but could reach no basic agreement with Luther and Melanchthon on doctrine. He accompanied (1531) the Zurichers against the Roman Catholic Forest Cantons and was killed in an ensuing battle. Zwingli laid the foundations, to some extent, for Calvin's doctrines, and his movement was later submerged in and superseded by Calvinism. Among Zwingli's works is his *De vera et falsa religione* (*Of True and False Religion*).

fat, fāte, fär, fâll, ȧsk, fãre; net, mē, hėr; pin, pīne; not, nōte, möve, nôr; up, lūte, pu̇ll; oi, oil; ou, out; (lightened) ẹ̄lect, agọ̄ny, ụ̄nite; (obscured) errạnt, ardẹnt, actọr; ch, chip; g, go; th, thin; ᴛʜ, then; y, you; (variable) ḓ as d or j, ş as s or sh, ţ as t or ch, ẓ as z or zh; *o*, F. cloche; ü, F. menu; ċh, Sc. loch; ṅ, F. bonbon; ʙ, Sp. Córdoba (sounded almost like v).

above: Pietro Cavallini
Saints (detail from *The Last Judgment*)
S. Cecilia in Trastevere, Rome

Nicola Pisano
Adoration of the Magi (relief)
Baptistery, Pisa

Giovanni Pisano
Massacre of the Innocents (relief)
Sant' Andrea, Pistoia

above: View of Florence with (from the left) the Palazzo Vecchio S. Maria del Fiore (with Brunelleschi's Dome and Giotto's Campanile) and S. Croce

above: Arnolfo di Cambio
Nave of S. Croce
Florence

Arnolfo di Cambio
Palazzo Vecchio (*Palazzo della Signoria*)
Florence

below: Giotto
Raising of Lazarus
Scrovegni Chapel, Padua

above: Cimabue
Madonna Enthroned
Uffizi, Florence

below: Arnolfo di Cambio
Censing Angel
Fogg Art Museum, Harvard University, Cambridge

Giotto
Ascension of St. John
Peruzzi Chapel, S. Croce, Florence

left: Tino di Camaino
Monument of Bishop Antonio d'Orso
Cathedral, Florence

right: Andrea Pisano
Baptism (panel)
South Door of the Baptistery, Florence

below: Andrea Orcagna
Triumph of Death (detail)
S. Croce, Florence

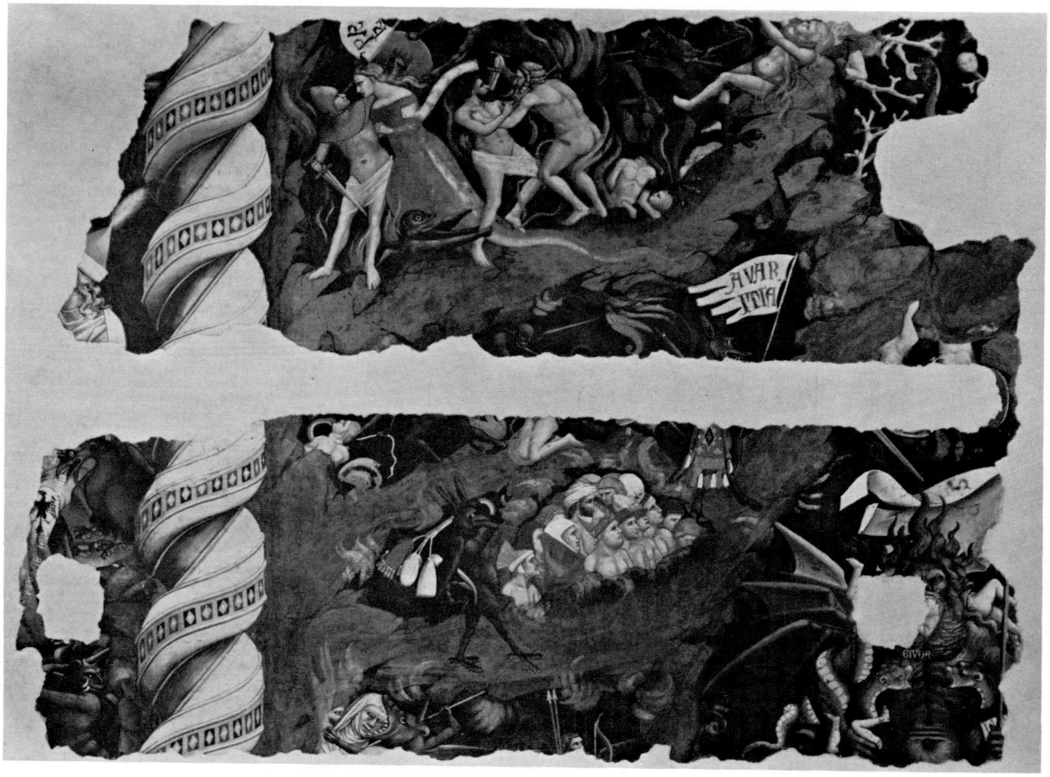

right: Andrea Orcagna
Death and Assumption of the Virgin (relief)
Orsanmichele, Florence

Duccio di Buoninsegna
Entry into Jerusalem
Museo dell' Opera del Duomo, Siena

Duccio di Buoninsegna
Calling of the Apostles Peter and Andrew
National Gallery of Art, Washington, D.C.

Simone Martini
Guidoriccio da Foligniano
Palazzo Pubblico, Siena

Simone Martini
Annunciation
Uffizi, Florence

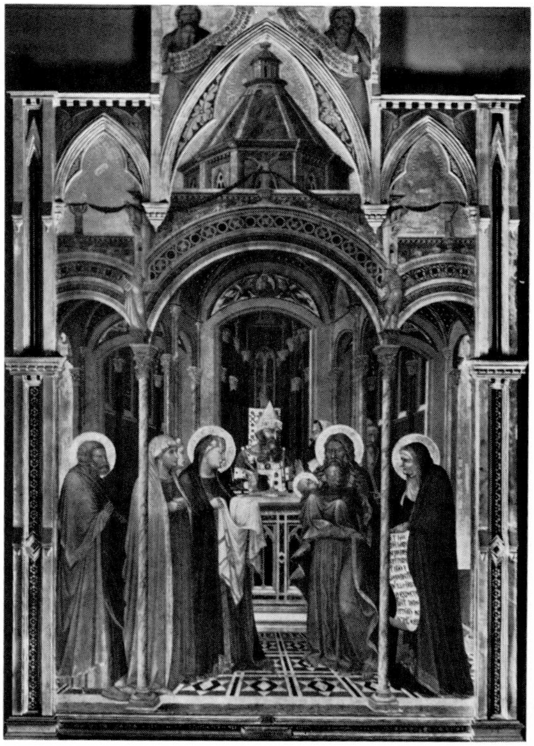

Ambrogio Lorenzetti
Presentation in the Temple
Uffizi, Florence

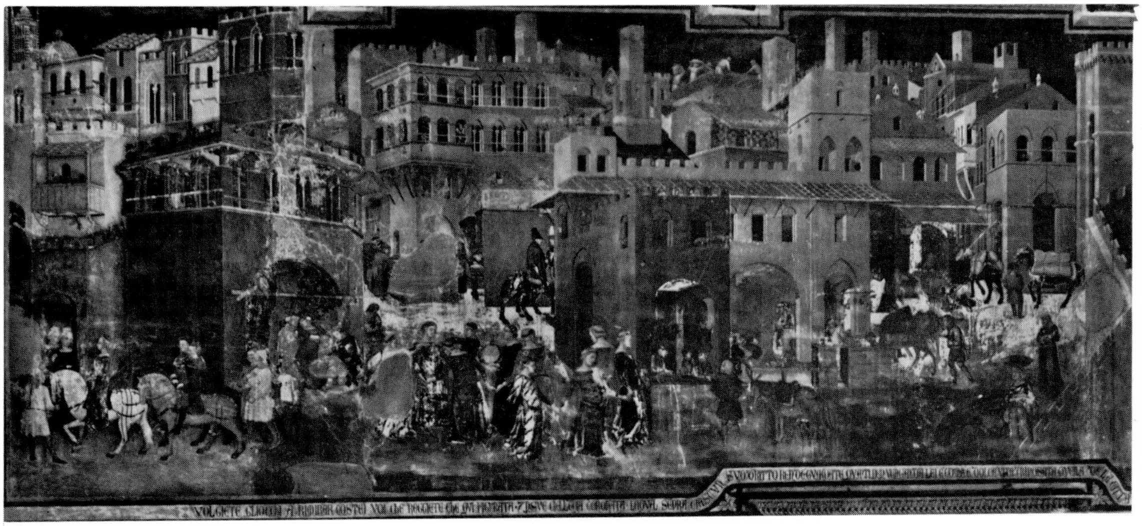

AMBROGIO LORENZETTI
Effects of Good Government in the Town
Palazzo Pubblico, Siena

PIETRO LORENZETTI
Crucifixion
Lower Church, S. Francesco, Assisi

PIETRO LORENZETTI
Christ Before Pilate
Vatican

Sassetta
Journey of the Magi
The Metropolitan Museum of Art, New York

below: Sassetta
The Mystic Marriage of St. Francis with Poverty
Musée Condé, Chantilly

Gentile da Fabriano
Madonna and Child
National Gallery of Art, Washington, D.C.

Lorenzo Monaco
Coronation of the Virgin
Uffizi, Florence

JACOPO DELLA QUERCIA
Tomb of Maria del Carretto
Cathedral, Lucca

left: PISANELLO
Sigismondo Malatesta
National Gallery of Art, Washington, D.C.

right: PISANELLO
Leonello d'Este
National Gallery of Art, Washington, D.C.

PISANELLO
Vision of St. Eustace
National Gallery, London

Paolo Uccello
Rout of San Romano
National Gallery, London

Filippo Brunelleschi
Ospedale degli Innocenti
Florence

Filippo Brunelleschi
S. Lorenzo (view of the nave)
Florence

Filippo Brunelleschi
Pazzi Chapel
Florence

Filippo Brunelleschi
Brunelleschi's Dome and Giotto's Campanile
Cathedral, Florence

Filippo Brunelleschi
The Sacrifice of Isaac (contest panel)
Bargello, Florence

Lorenzo Ghiberti
The Sacrifice of Isaac (contest panel)
Bargello, Florence

LORENZO GHIBERTI
Jacob and Esau (panel)
East Door of the Baptistery, Florence

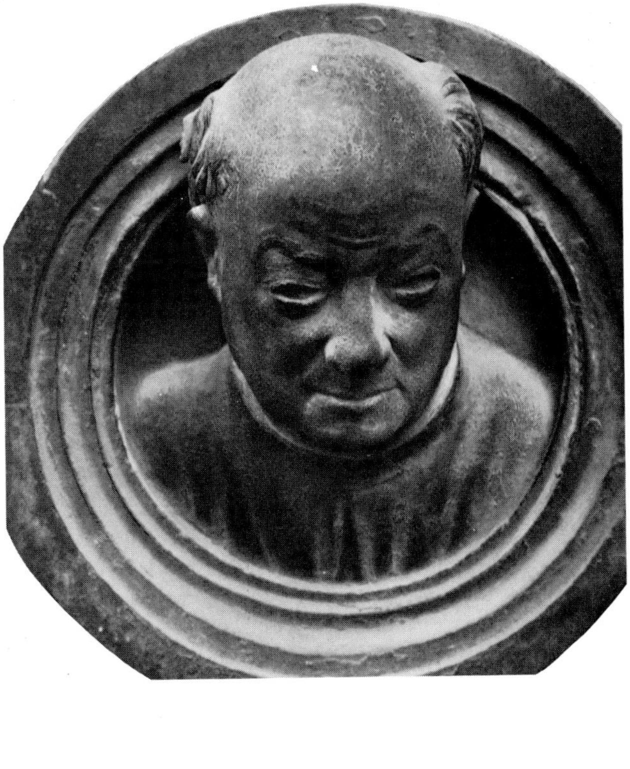

LORENZO GHIBERTI
Self-Portrait
East Door of the Baptistery, Florence

Fra Angelico
Crucifixion
San Marco, Florence

Masaccio
Trinity
S. Maria Novella, Florence

Masaccio
Crucifixion
National Gallery, Naples

Masaccio
Baptism of the Neophytes
Brancacci Chapel, Church of the Carmine
Florence

Iacobello and Pier Paolo Dalle Masegne
Iconostasis with the Virgin, St. John and Twelve Apostles
St. Mark's, Venice

left: NANNI D'ANTONIO DI BANCO
The Assumption of the Virgin (relief)
Porta della Mandorla, Cathedral, Florence

DONATELLO
David
Bargello, Florence

DONATELLO
Gattamelata
Padua

DONATELLO
Annunciation
S. Croce, Florence

DONATELLO
A *Miracle of St. Anthony* (relief)
Basilica of St. Anthony, Padua

DONATELLO
St. Mary Magdalen (detail)
Baptistery, Florence

MICHELOZZO MICHELOZZI
Riccardi-Medici Palace
Florence

MICHELOZZO MICHELOZZI
Courtyard of the Riccardi-Medici Palace
Florence

Luca della Robbia
Cantoria
Museo dell' Opera del Duomo, Florence

Luca della Robbia
Resurrection (terra-cotta relief)
Cathedral, Florence

Leon Battista Alberti
S. Andrea
Mantua

above: Leon Battista Alberti
Rucellai Palace
Florence

below: Leon Battista Alberti
Tempio Malatestiano
Rimini

Filippo Lippi
Annunciation
S. Lorenzo, Florence

Bernardo Rossellino
Tomb of Leonardo Bruni
S. Croce, Florence

Bernardo Rossellino
Piccolomini Palace
Pienza

Luciano Laurana
Courtyard of the Ducal Palace
Urbino

Luciano Laurana
Turret façade of the Ducal Palace
Urbino

Piero della Francesca
Resurrection
Town Hall, San Sepolcro

Piero della Francesca
Baptism of Christ
National Gallery, London

Clemente da Urbino
Federico da Montefeltro
National Gallery of Art, Washington, D.C.

below: Piero della Francesca
The Queen of Sheba Worshiping the Holy Wood
S. Francesco, Arezzo

above: MELOZZO DA FORLÌ
The Inauguration of the Vatican Library
Vatican

ANTONIO POLLAIUOLO
Hercules and Antaeus
Bargello, Florence

BENOZZO GOZZOLI
The Dance of Salome
National Gallery of Art, Washington, D.C.

ANTONIO POLLAIUOLO
Martyrdom of St. Sebastian
National Gallery, London

ANTONIO ROSSELLINO
Bust of Matteo Palmieri
Bargello, Florence

ANTONIO ROSSELLINO
Monument of the Cardinal of Portugal
San Miniato al Monte, Florence

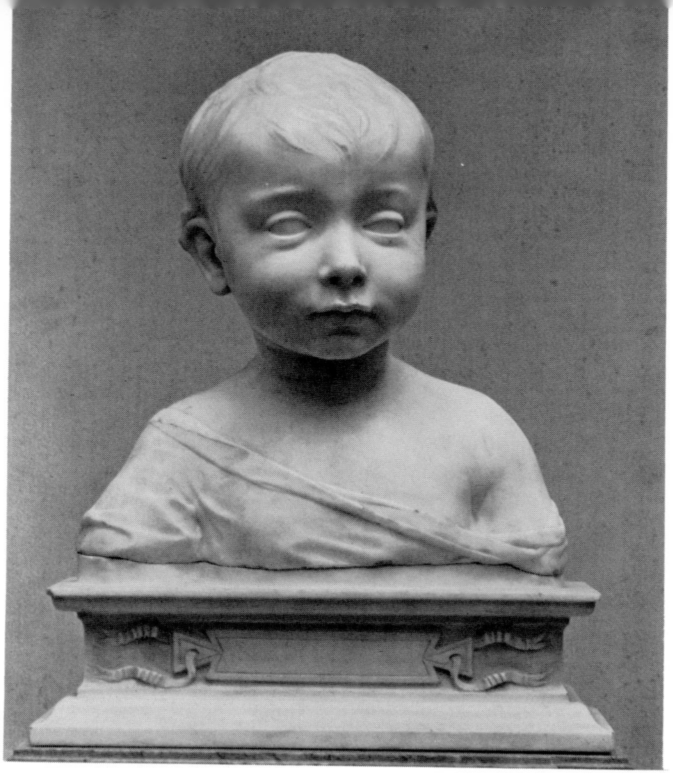

Desiderio da Settignano
Bust of a Little Boy
National Gallery of Art, Washington, D.C.

Desiderio da Settignano
St. Jerome in the Desert (relief)
National Gallery of Art, Washington, D.C.

above: Pietro Lombardo
Tomb of Dante
Ravenna

below: Desiderio da Settignano
Marsuppini Monument
S. Croce, Florence

ANTONELLO DA MESSINA
St. Sebastian
Dresden

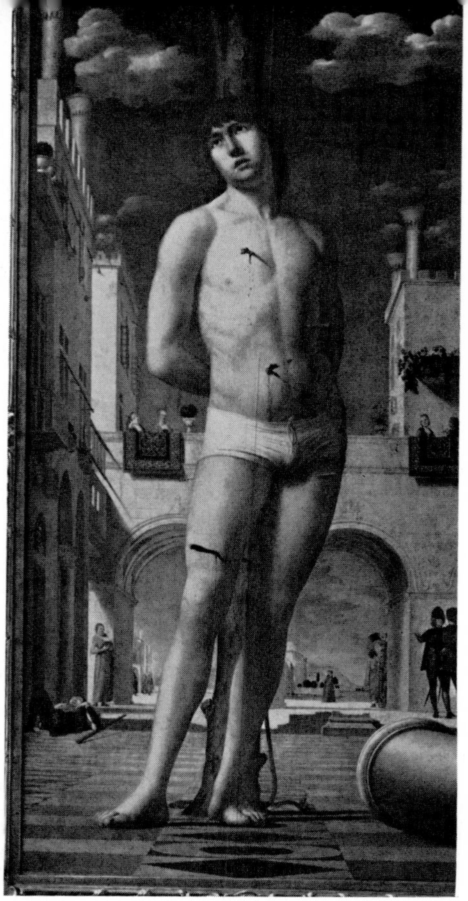

ANTONELLO DA MESSINA
Crucifixion
Antwerp

ANTONELLO DA MESSINA
St. Jerome in His Study
National Gallery, London

GENTILE BELLINI
Mohammed II
National Gallery, London

CARLO CRIVELLI
Annunciation
National Gallery, London

GIOVANNI BELLINI. *Agony in the Garden*. National Gallery, London

GIOVANNI BELLINI. *St. Francis in Ecstasy*. The Frick Collection, New York

ANDREA MANTEGNA. *Agony in the Garden*. National Gallery, London

ANDREA MANTEGNA. *Family of Ludovico III*. Camera degli Sposi, Ducal Palace, Mantua

Andrea Mantegna
Dead Christ
Brera, Milan

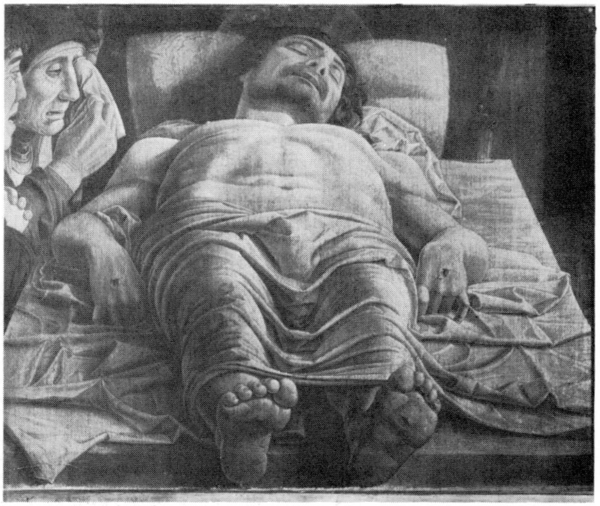

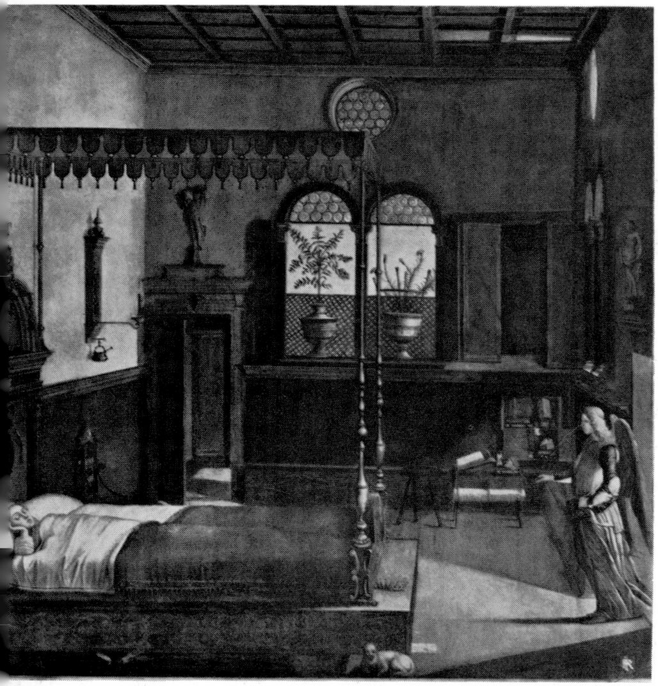

Vittore Carpaccio
The Dream of St. Ursula
Accademia, Venice

Vittore Carpaccio
Meditation on the Passion
The Metropolitan Museum of Art, New York

Cima da Conegliano
St. Jerome in the Wilderness
National Gallery of Art, Washington, D.C.

Andrea Verrocchio
Putto with a Fish
Palazzo Vecchio, Florence

Andrea Verrocchio
Christ and St. Thomas
Orsanmichele, Florence

DOMENICO VENEZIANO
St. John in the Desert
National Gallery of Art, Washington, D.C.

SANDRO BOTTICELLI
Madonna of the Eucharist
Isabella Stewart Gardner Museum, Boston

SANDRO BOTTICELLI
The Birth of Venus
Uffizi, Florence

GIULIANO DA SANGALLO
S. Maria della Carceri
Prato

ANDREA BRIOSCO
Pascal Candlestick
Basilica of St. Anthony, Padua

GIOVANNI ANTONIO AMADEO
Colleoni Chapel
Bergamo

above: DOMENICO GHIRLANDAIO
Pope Honorius III Giving the Rule to St. Francis
Sassetti Chapel, S. Trinita, Florence

PERUGINO
The Crucifixion with the Virgin, SS. John, Jerome, and Mary Magdalen
National Gallery of Art, Washington, D.C.

LEONARDO DA VINCI
Baptism of Christ (with Verrocchio)
Uffizi, Florence

LEONARDO DA VINCI
Ginevra de' Benci
National Gallery of Art, Washington, D.C.

LEONARDO DA VINCI
The Virgin of the Rocks
Louvre, Paris

below: LEONARDO DA VINCI
The Virgin and St. Anne (cartoon)
National Gallery, London

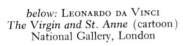

Giovanni Boltraffio
Casio Madonna
Louvre, Paris

Filippino Lippi
Apparition of the Virgin to St. Bernard
Badia, Florence

Andrea del Castagno
The Youthful David
National Gallery of Art, Washington, D.C.

Piero di Cosimo
The Visitation with St. Nicholas and St. Anthony Abbot
National Gallery of Art, Washington, D.C.

Piero di Cosimo. *Death of Procris*. National Gallery, London

above: Donato Bramante
Tribune
S. Maria delle Grazie, Milan

below: Donato Bramante
Tempietto
Rome

left: Donato Bramante
Courtyard of S. Damaso
Vatican

Mariotto Albertinelli
The Visitation
Uffizi, Florence

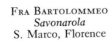

Fra Bartolommeo
Savonarola
S. Marco, Florence

MICHELANGELO
Pietà
Basilica of St. Peter's, Rome

MICHELANGELO
David
Accademia, Florence

MICHELANGELO
Moses
S. Pietro in Vincoli, Rome

above: MICHELANGELO
Day
Tomb of Giuliano de' Medici
S. Lorenzo, Florence

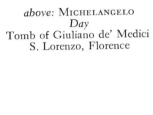

below: MICHELANGELO
Rondanini Pietà
Castello Sforzesco, Milan

below: MICHELANGELO
The Last Judgment (detail)
Sistine Chapel, Vatican

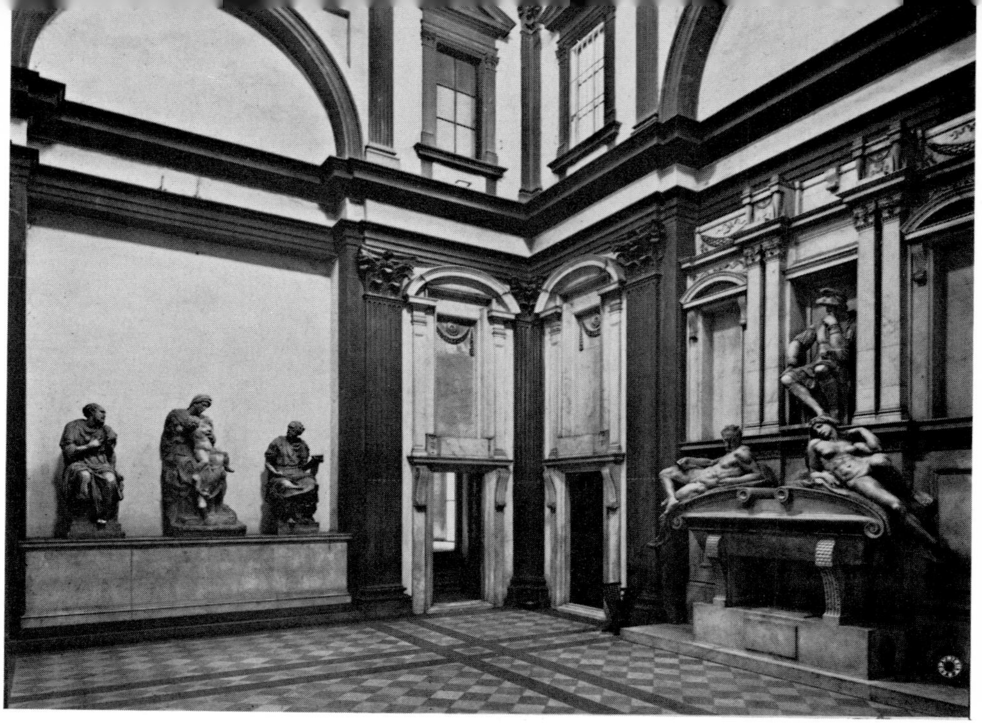

Michelangelo
Medici Chapel
S. Lorenzo, Florence

Michelangelo
Stairway to the Laurentian Library
Florence

Michelangelo
Dome of St. Peter's
Rome

Michelangelo
The Conversion of St. Paul
Pauline Chapel, Vatican

Baldassare Peruzzi
Farnesina
Rome

Baldassare Peruzzi
Palazzo Massimo
Rome

Raphael
Deposition
Borghese Gallery, Rome

Raphael
St. George and the Dragon
National Gallery of Art, Washington, D.C.

Raphael
Baldassare Castiglione
Louvre, Paris

above: Raphael
Alba Madonna
National Gallery of Art, Washington, D.C.

below: Raphael
Sistine Madonna
Dresden

left: Raphael
Julius II
National Gallery, London

Raphael
Transfiguration
Vatican

Raphael
Palazzo Vidoni-Caffarelli
Rome

Lorenzo Lotto
Marriage of St. Catherine
Accademia Carrara, Bergamo

Domenico Beccafumi
St. Michael Casting down the Rebellious Angels
S. Maria del Carmine, Siena

Michele Sanmicheli
Palazzo Grimani
Venice

above: Jacopo Sansovino
Bacchus
Bargello, Florence

below: Jacopo Sansovino
Mars, Stairway of the Giants
Doge's Palace, Venice

below: Jacopo Sansovino
Library of San Marco
Venice

right: Giulio Romano
The Martyrdom of St. Stephen
S. Stefano, Genoa

below: Giulio Romano
Palazzo del Tè
Mantua

Giulio Romano
Giulio Romano's House
Mantua

GIORGIONE
The Tempest
Accademia, Venice

below: ANDREA DEL SARTO
The Sacrifice of Isaac
The Cleveland Museum of Art

BACCIO BANDINELLI
Bust of Cosimo I
Bargello, Florence

Andrea del Sarto
Madonna of the Sack
Chiostro della SS. Annunziata, Florence

Benvenuto Cellini
Perseus with the Head of Medusa
Loggia dei Lanzi, Florence

Andrea del Sarto
The Baptism of the Multitude
S. Giovanni Battista allo Scalzo, Florence

right: Titian
Pietro Aretino
The Frick Collection, New York

above: Titian
Assumption
Frari, Venice

right: Titian
Cardinal Bembo
National Museum, Naples

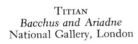

Titian
Entombment
Prado, Madrid

Titian
Bacchus and Ariadne
National Gallery, London

CORREGGIO
Danaë
Borghese Gallery, Rome

below: CORREGGIO
The Assumption of the Virgin (detail)
Cupola, Cathedral, Parma

CORREGGIO
Madonna with St. Jerome (*Day*)
National Gallery, Parma

Correggio
Madonna and Child (*La Zingarella*)
National Museum, Naples

Rosso Fiorentino
Deposition
Volterra

Jacopo Pontormo
Annunciation
Capponi Chapel, S. Felicita, Florence

Jacopo Pontormo
Entombment
Capponi Chapel, S. Felicita, Florence

Parmigianino
Madonna dal collo lungo
Uffizi, Florence

Parmigianino
Vision of St. Jerome
National Gallery, London

Agnolo Bronzino
Maria de' Medici
Uffizi, Florence

Agnolo Bronzino
Venus, Cupid, Folly, and Time
National Gallery, London

Andrea Palladio
Villa Rotonda
Vicenza

Andrea Palladio
S. Giorgio Maggiore
Venice

Bartolomeo Ammannati
Naiad, Fountain of Neptune
Piazza della Signoria, Florence

TINTORETTO
Miracle of the Slave
Accademia, Venice

TINTORETTO
St. Mary of Egypt
Scuola di S. Rocco, Venice

PAOLO VERONESE. *Supper in the House of Levi*. Accademia, Venice

PAOLO VERONESE. *The Marriage at Cana*. Louvre, Paris

right: GIAMBOLOGNA
Neptune Fountain
Bologna

GIAMBOLOGNA
Rape of the Sabines
Loggia dei Lanzi, Florence

GIAMBOLOGNA
Mercury
Bargello, Florence

ITALY IN 1492
Bormio
Como
DUCHY
OF
MILAN
Milan
Pavia
Bergamo
Brescia
REPUBLIC
OF
VENICE
Vicenza
Treviso
Verona
Padua
Venice
DUCHY
OF
MONT-
FERRAT
Casale
Tortona
Cremona
Mantua
SAVOY
REP. OF GENOA
Genoa
Parma
Fornovo
Modena
PO
Ferrara
DUCHY
OF FERRARA
Sarzana
Bologna
Ravenna
Pietrasanta
Lucca
Imola
Cesena
Pisa
Pistoia
Fiesole
Rimini
Prato
ARNO
Florence
Leghorn
REP.
OF FLORENCE
Urbino
Pesaro
Volterra
Arezzo
Cortona
Siena
Ancona